Plain
English
DICTIONARY

Collins

Plain
English
DICTIONARY

Plain
English
DICTIONARY

Collins
An Imprint of HarperCollinsPublishers

HarperCollins Publishers
Westerhill Road, Bishopbriggs, Glasgow G64 2QT

The HarperCollins website address is
www.**fire**and**water**.com

First Edition 1996
Second Edition 2001

10 9 8 7 6 5 4 3 2 1

© HarperCollins Publishers 1996, 2001

ISBN 0-00-710918-0

Collins® is a registered trademark
of HarperCollins Publishers Limited

A catalogue record of this book is
available from the British Library.

Corpus Acknowledgements
We would like to thank those authors and publishers
who kindly gave permission for copyright material to
be used in the Bank of English. We would also like to
thank Times Newspapers Ltd for providing valuable data.

Typeset by Morton Word Processing Ltd,
Scarborough, England

www.**fire**and**water**.com
Visit the book lover's website

Printed and bound by William Clowes Ltd.,
Beccles and London.

This dictionary has been written using the Bank of English. This is a unique database of the English language with examples of over 400 million words which allows Collins lexicographers to analyse how English is actually used today and how it is changing. This is the evidence on which the changes in this dictionary are based.

The Bank of English was set up by HarperCollins Publishers and Birmingham University as a resource for language research and lexicography. It contains a very wide range of material from books, newspapers, radio, TV, magazines, letters, and talks reflecting the whole range of English today. Its size and range make it an unequalled resource and the purpose-built software for its analysis is unique to Collins Dictionaries.

This ensures that Collins Dictionaries accurately reflect English as it is used today in a way that is most helpful to the dictionary user.

Introduction
by Sir Trevor McDonald, OBE

I feel I should begin by declaring an interest in the subject of plain English. Although it may not always appear to be the case, it is one of the principal requirements of my profession. All journalists and prospective journalists have it constantly drummed into them that only plain, accessible, easy to understand English will do. Its alternatives confuse, frustrate and irritate.

Secondly, I was asked some years ago to be the Chairman of the Better English Campaign, the aim of which was to impress upon young people the great benefits and the power of the language plainly and properly used. I remember making several speeches about the subject and I always found the occasion to remind my audiences about John Kennedy's famous quotation about Winston Churchill. At a ceremony in the White House honouring the memory of the great man Kennedy said: When the dark clouds of war threatened England and Europe, Churchill mobilised the language and sent it into battle. The late President could easily have mentioned the brave Spitfire pilots, the heroism of the little boats of Dunkirk or any of the few who did so much for so many. Instead Kennedy praised the brilliance of Churchill's use of plain English to stiffen the sinews of a nation in the grip of a battle for its very survival.

There's been the tendency in the past to invest even in some dictionaries, encyclopedias and other texts, which after all are intended as aids to comprehension, a kind of obscure intellectualism which ends up as more baffling than illuminating. This **Plain English Dictionary** published by HarperCollins attempts to change that dramatically and to my mind succeeds wonderfully in doing so. It dispenses with the gobbledygook, and helps to present the language in a way in which it could be understood by all. This is the essence of how language should be used. It should never be the preserve of the few, but should cast its net to be as inclusive as possible and accessible to all seekers of true meaning. I commend any publication in praise of clear and straightforward sentences in plain understandable English free of annoyingly confusing jargon. May its message be spread far and wide across our land.

A a

a (an) A and **an** are called the 'indefinite article'. You use them when you are mentioning someone or something for the first time. *A motorist escaped injury when her car overturned on the M25.* ■ You use **a** or **an** when you are making a general statement about a kind of person or thing. *It is virtually impossible to force an aircraft to change course.* ■ **A** and **an** are sometimes used instead of the number one. *The meeting was all over in less than an hour.* ■ **A** and **an** are used to talk about rates, prices, and measurements. For example, if someone charges £10 an hour for their work, they charge £10 for each hour.

AA The **AA** is a British organization which helps members when their cars break down. AA stands for 'Automobile Association'. ■ **AA** is an organization which helps people suffering from alcoholism. AA stands for 'Alcoholics Anonymous'.

aback See **take.**

abacus (*pron:* ab-a-cuss) (**abacuses**) An **abacus** is a device for counting. It consists of horizontal metal rods mounted on a frame; on the rods are coloured beads, which you slide to left or right.

abandon (**abandoning, abandoned; abandonment**) If people **abandon** a place or vehicle, they leave it empty with nobody to look after it. *...an abandoned Catholic church.* ■ If someone **abandons** a member of their family, they leave them for good, because they do not love them or cannot look after them. ■ If you **abandon** something you are doing, you stop doing it without finishing it. *He abandoned his studies after two years.* ■ If you **abandon** a theory or belief, you reject it because you no longer believe in it. *I will not abandon hope.* ■ If you do something **with abandon,** you do it in an unrestrained way.

abate (**abating, abated; abatement**) If something unpleasant **abates,** it becomes less severe. *The violence seems unlikely to abate in the near future. ...the Noise Abatement Society.*

abattoir (*pron:* ab-a-twahr) An **abattoir** is a place where animals are taken to be killed for their meat.

abbess (**abbesses**) An **abbess** is a nun in charge of other nuns, especially in an abbey.

abbey An **abbey** is a church with buildings attached where monks or nuns live or used to live.

abbot An **abbot** is a monk in charge of other monks in a monastery or abbey.

abbreviate (**abbreviating, abbreviated; abbreviation**) If something is **abbreviated,** it is made shorter. *...an abbreviated schedule.* ■ If a word or phrase is **abbreviated,** it is made shorter by leaving out some of the letters, or by using only the first letters of each word. The shortened form is called an **abbreviation.**

ABC When children learn their **ABC,** they learn the alphabet. ■ **ABC** often appears in the titles of books which claim to tell you the most important things about a subject. *'The ABC of Communism'*

abdicate (**abdicating, abdicated; abdication**) When a monarch **abdicates** or **abdicates** the throne, they formally give up their position of monarch. ■ If you **abdicate** a right, you give it up. ■ If you **abdicate** responsibility for something, you say you will not be responsible for it any more.

abdomen (**abdominal**) The **abdomen** is the part of the body below the chest where the stomach and intestines are. *...abdominal pain.*

abduct (**abduction, abductor**) If someone **abducts** another person, they take them away illegally, usually by force; you say they are the person's **abductor.**

aberrant (*pron:* ab-ber-ant) (**aberration**) If you say something is **aberrant** or an **aberration,** you mean it is not normal or natural. *Violations of human rights were not aberrations but part of official policy.*

abet (**abetting, abetted**) If you **abet** someone, you help or encourage them to do something wrong or illegal. *He was charged with aiding and abetting the bombing.*

abeyance If something is **in abeyance,** it will not be carried out for the time being. *The threat is likely to remain in abeyance.*

abhor (*pron:* ab-hor *or* ab-bor) (**abhorring, abhorred; abhorrent, abhorrence**) If you **abhor** something or find it **abhorrent,** you feel it is extremely unpleasant or evil. *The world community has marked its abhorrence of what happened last year.*

abide (**abiding, abided**) If you say you cannot **abide** someone or something, you mean you dislike them intensely. ■ If you **abide by** a law or decision, you do what it says. See also **law-abiding.** ■ An **abiding** feeling or impression lasts for a long time. *His abiding passion was ocean racing. ...my abiding memory of the Games.*

ability (**abilities**) If you have the **ability** to do something, you have the skills or qualities needed for it.

abject (**abjectly**) Abject is used to emphasize how shameful or depressing something is. *...abject poverty. ...a policy that ended in abject failure.* ■ If someone's behaviour is **abject,** they show no courage or self-respect.

ablaze If something is **ablaze,** it is on fire. ■ You can say something is **ablaze** with colours or lights when you want to emphasize how bright they are. *The churchyard is ablaze with crimson lobelia.*

able (**abler, ablest; ably**) If you are **able** to do something, you have the skill, qualities, knowledge, means, or opportunity to do it. ■ An **able** person can be relied on to do something well. If you do something **ably,** you do it well.

able-bodied people are fit and healthy.

ablutions If you perform your **ablutions,** you wash yourself.

ably See **able.**

abnegate (**abnegating, abnegated**) If you **abnegate** a duty or responsibility, you do not do what you are supposed to.

abnormal (**abnormally; abnormality, abnormalities**) You say something is **abnormal** when it is unusual or unnatural. ...*abnormal behaviour.* You call something like this an **abnormality.** ...*bone abnormalities.*

aboard If you are **aboard** a ship or plane, you are on it or in it.

abode Your **abode** is the place where you live. ■ If you have the **right of abode** in a country, you are legally entitled to live there.

abolish (**abolishes, abolishing, abolished**) If something like a system is **abolished,** it is officially ended.

abolition (**abolitionist**) The ending of something like a system is called its **abolition.** *He argued for the abolition of the monarchy.* **Abolitionists** are people who want something to be ended.

abominable (**abominably**) If you say something is **abominable,** you mean it is extremely unpleasant or evil. ...*an abominable crime.* ■ **Abominable Snowman:** see **yeti.**

abominate (**abominating, abominated; abomination**) If you **abominate** something or regard it as an **abomination,** you find it completely unacceptable, because you think it is wrong or evil.

aboriginal An **Aboriginal** is a descendant of the people already living in Australia when Europeans arrived. ■ The **aboriginal** people of a place are the ones who lived there first, before others arrived. ...*India's aboriginal tribes.*

Aborigine (*pron:* ab-or-**rij**-in-ee) An **Aborigine** is the same as an Aboriginal.

abort (**abortion**) If a woman has an **abortion,** her pregnancy is deliberately ended and the foetus dies. When this happens, you can say the foetus is **aborted.** ■ In medical terms, if a pregnant woman **aborts,** she has a miscarriage. ■ If something which had been planned is **aborted,** it is stopped before it is completed. ...*an aborted attack.*

abortive If an attempt to do something is **abortive,** it fails. ...*an abortive coup.*

abound If things **abound** in a place, there are a lot of them there. *Such problems abound.*

about is used to mention the subject of something like a book or speech. ...*a book about the monarchy.* **About** is also used to mention the subject of someone's thoughts or feelings. ...*public concern about unemployment.* ■ **About** is used when mentioning characteristics. For example, if you say there is something strange **about** someone, you mean they are strange in some way. ■ If you **do** something **about** an unsatisfactory situation, you do something to change it. ■ **About** is used to say an amount is not exact. ...*a population of about ten million.* ■ If you are **about** to do something, you are just going to do it. Similarly, something can be **about** to happen. *His wait is about to end.*

about-turn When someone completely changes their opinions or plans, you call this an **about-turn** or **about-face.** ...*a dramatic about-turn in policy.*

above If something is **above** something else, it is in a higher position, or directly over it. ■ **Above** is used to say something is more than a particular amount or level. *The inflation rate has risen above 15% a year.* ■ If someone is **above** another person, they are more important than the other person. If someone is **above** something, they are too important or too good to do it or be affected by it. *They think they're above the law.* ■ In a piece of writing, **above** is used to refer to something which has appeared earlier in the text. *I hope the above will reassure the reader.* ■ If you hear something **above** other noise, you hear it in spite of it.

abrasion An **abrasion** is an area of something, especially a person's skin, which has been damaged by scraping. *They were treated for cuts and abrasions.*

abrasive (**abrasiveness**) An **abrasive** person is rude and unkind. ■ An **abrasive** substance is rough and can be used to clean hard surfaces.

abreast When a group of people or vehicles are moving along in rows, you use **abreast** to say how many there are in each row. *Thousands of cars, seven abreast, queued at the frontier.* ■ If you **keep abreast of** something, you make sure you have all the latest information about it.

abridged An **abridged** version of a book or article has had parts removed, to make it shorter. **Abridged** is also used to describe other things which have been reduced in this way. ...*an abridged education.*

abroad If you are **abroad,** you are in a country which is not the one you usually live in.

abrogate (**abrogating, abrogated; abrogation**) If something like a law or agreement is **abrogated,** it is cancelled or withdrawn.

abrupt (**abruptly, abruptness**) **Abrupt** is used to talk about things ending suddenly, and perhaps unpleasantly. *The happy family life came to an abrupt end with Nikola's sudden death.*

ABS brakes are designed to prevent skidding and increase control in road vehicles to which they are fitted by sensing and compensating for overbraking.

abscess (*pron:* ab-sess) (**abscesses**) An **abscess** is a painful pus-filled swelling on the skin or in the body.

abscond If someone **absconds,** (a) they escape from somewhere like a prison. (b) they walk out on someone who depends on them. *He got his girlfriend pregnant and absconded to London.*

abseil (*pron:* ab-sale) (**abseiling, abseiled**) When people **abseil** down a cliff or rock face, they walk or slide down backwards using a rope which is attached to the top.

absent (**absently, absence**) If someone is **absent** from a place, they are not there. Their **absence** is the fact that they are not there. ■ If people **absent themselves** (*pron:* ab-**sent**), they are not in the place where they should be. *He pleaded guilty to absenting himself without leave.* ■ You say someone is **absent** when they are not paying attention, because they are thinking about something else. *Rob was staring absently at the cigarette machine.*

absentee An **absentee** is someone who is not in the place where they should be.

absenteeism is regularly being away from work or school without good reason.

absentia See **in absentia.**

absent-minded (absent-mindedly, absent-mindedness) **Absent-minded** people are forgetful and often make mistakes. ■ You say someone is **absent-minded** when they are not paying attention to what they are doing, because they are thinking about something else. *He munched absent-mindedly on a sausage sandwich.*

absolute (absolutely) **Absolute** is used to say something is total and complete. *...absolute adherence to principle... He's absolutely right.* ■ **Absolute** rulers have complete authority over their people. ■ **Absolute** principles are believed to be true or appropriate in all situations. Principles like these are sometimes called **absolutes.** ■ **Absolute** is used to talk about amounts when they are considered independently of other amounts. For example, if defence spending this year has risen in **absolute** terms, the actual amount has gone up, although as a proportion of government expenditure it may have gone down. ■ People sometimes use **absolute** and **absolutely** to emphasize what they are saying. *...an absolute disgrace... It's absolutely amazing.*

absolute majority If a political party wins an **absolute majority,** they win more seats or votes than all the other parties put together.

absolute zero is the coldest possible temperature (about -273° Centigrade).

absolution In some Christian Churches, if someone is given **absolution,** their sins are forgiven, because they have repented.

absolutism is a political system in which one person has all the political power in a country.

absolve (absolving, absolved) If someone is **absolved** of blame or responsibility for something, they are declared or shown not to be responsible for it.

absorb (absorption) If a substance or force is **absorbed,** it is soaked up or taken in by something. This process is called **absorption.** ■ If something **absorbs** time, money, or effort, it uses it up. *Income taxes absorb 32% of the pay of a British executive.* ■ If a group is **absorbed** by a larger group, it becomes part of it. ■ If you **absorb** something you read or hear, you remember it well. ■ If something **absorbs** you or you find it **absorbing,** you are greatly interested by it and give it all your attention. *It was an absorbing contest.*

absorbent materials soak up liquid easily.

absorption See absorb.

abstain (abstaining, abstained; abstention) If you **abstain** from something, you do without it, or do not involve yourself with it. You can also talk about someone's **abstention** from something. *Patients were supposed to abstain from alcohol... The armed forces would in future abstain from politics. ...his abstention from sexual relations.* ■ If you **abstain** in a vote, you do not vote. The **abstentions** are the people who choose not to vote.

abstemious people avoid doing too much of something enjoyable like eating or drinking.

abstinence is denying yourself pleasures like alcohol or sex.

abstract (abstraction) **Abstract** is used to describe very general ideas and theories, which can seem a long way from people's everyday concerns. Ideas and theories like these can be called **abstractions.** *...abstract disputes about European unity.* ■ If you talk **in the abstract** about something, you talk about it generally, without mentioning specific examples. ■ **Abstract** paintings and sculptures use shapes and bold colours, rather than showing people or things as they actually look. You can call a painting or sculpture like this an **abstract.** ■ An **abstract** of an article or speech is a summary of its main points.

abstracted If a person is **abstracted,** they are deep in thought and do not notice things going on around them.

abstruse ideas are complicated and difficult to understand.

absurd (absurdly; absurdity, absurdities) If you say something is **absurd,** you mean it does not make sense. You can talk about the **absurdity** of something. *...life's absurdities.*

absurdum See reductio ad absurdum.

abundant (abundantly, abundance) If something is **abundant,** there is a lot of it. *Mongolia has abundant wildlife... The pages are abundantly illustrated with photographs.* You can also say there is an **abundance** of it or it is present **in abundance.** ■ If something is **abundantly clear,** it is very clear and obvious.

abuse (abusing, abused) If someone is **abused** (*pron:* ab-**yoozd**) or suffers **abuse** (*pron:* ab-**yoos**), they are ill-treated in some way, often by someone who should be taking care of them. *...a victim of child abuse.* ■ You say someone is **abused** when people say rude insulting things to them. You call what they say **abuse.** *He was kicked and verbally abused... The word 'Communist' has become a term of abuse.* ■ If people's rights are **abused** or subjected to **abuse,** they are ignored, and the people are treated badly. *They accused the government of abusing civil liberties.* ■ If someone **abuses** something, they use it in a wrong way or for a bad purpose. Such wrong use is called **abuse.** *He had abused his position of trust. ...abuse of power. ...drug abuse.*

abuser People who abuse things or other people are sometimes called **abusers.** *...drug and alcohol abusers.*

abusive (abusively) If someone is **abusive,** they say rude insulting things. *...abusive letters.*

abut (abutting, abutted) If land or a building **abuts** something, it is next to it. *The Duke's estates abut the Mar Forest.*

abuzz If a place or group of people is **abuzz,** there is an atmosphere of excitement. *The place was abuzz with reporters.*

abysmal (abysmally) If you say something is **abysmal,** you mean it is extremely bad or of extremely poor quality. *...an abysmal performance.*

abyss (abysses) An **abyss** is a very deep hole in the ground. ■ If someone is heading for an **abyss,** they are heading for a disastrous situation. *The world trading community is on the edge of an abyss.*

AC is used to describe an electric current which continually changes direction as it flows. AC stands for 'alternating current'. See also **DC.**

acacia (*pron:* a-**kay**-sha) (*plural:* **acacia** *or* **acacias**) The **acacia** is a tree with small, usually yellow flowers, which grows in warm countries. This tree is also called 'mimosa'.

academia (*pron:* **aka**-dee-mia) *or* **academe** (*pron:* **aka**-deem) is used to talk about universities and the people who work and study in them. *Many of these students now occupy senior positions in academia.*

academic (**academically**) An **academic** is a person who teaches or does research at a university or college. ■ **Academic** is used to talk about study or research in schools or colleges, as opposed to work in places like factories or offices. *...his academic background.* ■ If a young person is **academic,** they are good at studying and passing exams. *...an academically gifted girl.* ■ If you say something like the solution to a problem is **academic,** you mean it is hardly worth bothering with because it is of no practical use. *My judgment on compensation is purely academic. Bellcorp has refused to pay a penny.*

academy (**academies; academician**) Schools and colleges, especially those specializing in particular subjects or skills, sometimes have **Academy** as part of their name. *...the Royal Scottish Academy of Music and Drama.* ■ **Academy** appears in the names of some societies formed to promote and maintain standards in a particular field. *...the British Academy of Film and Television Arts.* Members of some academies are called **academicians.**

accede (*pron:* ak-**seed**) (**acceding, acceded**) If you **accede** to someone's request, you agree to what they want. ■ If a country **accedes** to a treaty, it signs it. ■ If someone **accedes** to a position of importance, especially the position of a ruler, they take it up. *King Ludwig III acceded to the throne of Bavaria in 1913.* ■ If one country **accedes** to another, it becomes part of it.

accelerate (**accelerating, accelerated; acceleration**) When a vehicle or other moving thing **accelerates,** its speed increases. Its **acceleration** is the rate at which its speed increases. ■ If something which is growing or developing **accelerates,** it does it at an increasing rate. *Job losses were expected to accelerate to 9,000 a month. ...an acceleration in sales.* ■ When people **accelerate** something, they make it happen more quickly. *The two leaders considered how to accelerate European integration.*

accelerator A vehicle's **accelerator** is the pedal you press to make it go faster. ■ Some devices used to speed up the movement of things are called **accelerators.** *...the electron accelerator.*

accent (**accented**) A person's **accent** is the way they pronounce the words of a language, especially when this shows where they come from or their social class. **Accented** is used to describe someone's accent. *...the heavily accented Brazilian voice.* ■ An **accent** is a mark written above or below certain letters in some languages, to indicate a change in pronunciation. See **acute, grave, circumflex, cedilla, tilde, umlaut.** ■ If you say the **accent** is on a particular feature, you mean that is what is regard-ed as most important. *The accent is on youth in this new government.*

accentuate (**accentuating, accentuated**) If an aspect of something is **accentuated,** it is emphasized or made more noticeable. *His shaven head accentuates his large round face.*

accept (**acceptance**) If you **accept** something someone offers you, you take it. ■ If you **accept** an idea, plan, or decision, you go along with it or agree to it. **Accepted** ideas are generally thought to be correct. ■ If you **accept** the blame or responsibility for something, you admit it is your fault. ■ If you **accept** a difficult situation, you recognize it cannot be changed and put up with it. ■ When an organization or group **accepts** someone, they let them join, or give them a job.

acceptable (**acceptably, acceptability**) If something is **acceptable** to people, they do not object to it. *...the social acceptability of divorce.* ■ **Acceptable** is used to say something is good enough for a particular purpose. *...an acceptable substitute.*

access (**accesses, accessing, accessed**) If you have **access** to a building or other place, you are able or allowed to go into it. ■ If you have **access** to something like information or equipment, you have the right or opportunity to use it or see it. *Lawyers were denied access to official documents.* ■ If you have **access** to a person, you have the right or opportunity to see them or meet them. *They can have access to a lawyer.* ■ If you **access** information stored on a computer, you succeed in finding it.

accessible (**accessibility**) If a place is **accessible,** it is easy to reach or get into. ■ If something is **accessible** to people, they can easily use it or obtain it. *All the main components are easily accessible.* ■ An **accessible** person is approachable and friendly. ■ If something like a piece of writing is **accessible,** it is not difficult for people to understand and appreciate.

accession Someone's **accession** to ruler of a country is the act of taking up that position. ■ A country's **accession** to a treaty is their formal acceptance of it. ■ A country's **accession** to a group of countries or an association is the act of joining that group or association.

accessory (**accessories**) Accessories are extra parts added to a machine, tool, or vehicle to make it more useful, efficient, or decorative. ■ **Accessories** are things like shoes, belts, or handbags which you wear or carry in addition to your main outfit. ■ An **accessory** to a crime is someone who helped the person who committed it or who knew it was being committed but did not tell the police.

accident (**accidental, accidentally**) If something happens **by accident,** it happens by chance, rather than because of someone's intention. *...an accidental meeting.* ■ An **accident** is an unintended happening which causes damage, injury, or death. If you say someone is **accident-prone,** you mean they have a lot of accidents.

acclaim (**acclaiming, acclaimed**) If someone or something is **acclaimed** or wins **acclaim,** they are praised enthusiastically.

acclamation is loud or enthusiastic praise or applause. ■ If someone is elected by **acclamation**, they are elected by people showing support for them at a meeting, rather than by a ballot.

acclimatize (or **acclimatise**) (**acclimatizing, acclimatized; acclimatization**) If you **acclimatize** to something, you get used to it. ...*a period of acclimatising themselves to the heat of the desert.*

accolade You say someone receives an **accolade** when they receive public recognition or admiration for something they have done. ...*the great accolade of a Nobel Prize.* If you say something is the ultimate **accolade**, you mean it is the highest honour someone can receive. *To ride for one's country is the ultimate accolade.*

accommodate (**accommodating, accommodated; accommodation**) If someone is **accommodated**, they are provided with a place to stay or live. **Accommodation** is places where people can stay or live. ■ If a place can **accommodate** someone or something, it has enough space for them. ...*a conference centre able to accommodate 500 delegates.* ■ If you **accommodate** something in a schedule, you find time for it. ■ If you **accommodate** someone when planning something, you arrange things to fit in with what they want. ■ If you say someone is **accommodating**, you mean they are helpful and considerate.

accompanist An **accompanist** is a musician who plays one part of a piece of music while someone else sings or plays the main part.

accompany (**accompanies, accompanying, accompanied; accompaniment**) If you **accompany** someone, you go somewhere with them. ■ If one thing **accompanies** another, it happens at the same time and as a result of it. *The blaze was accompanied by a series of explosions.* ■ You say something **accompanies** something else when it appears with it. *The article is accompanied by a photograph.* ■ If one food **accompanies** another or is an **accompaniment** to it, it is served with it. *The food is accompanied with a very hot mango pickle.* ■ If you **accompany** a singer or musician, you play one part of a piece of music while they sing or play the main part. Your part is called the **accompaniment.**

accomplice An **accomplice** is a person who helps someone commit a crime.

accomplish (**accomplishes, accomplishing, accomplished**) If you **accomplish** something, you succeed in doing it. ■ **Accomplished** is used to describe (a) someone who is very good at something. *Townsend is a most accomplished writer.* (b) something which is done well. *It was Lewis's most accomplished performance.*

accomplishment An **accomplishment** is something difficult that has been done or achieved. ■ Your **accomplishments** are the things you do well or the important things you have done. ...*his accomplishments in his previous two Olympics.*

accord An **accord** is an agreement between countries or organizations. ■ If people are **in accord**, they agree. ■ If something is done **in accord with** a requirement, it is done the way the requirement says. ...*in accord with the orders given by the head of*

the military district. ■ The treatment that someone or something is **accorded** is the treatment they get. *Actors are accorded more respect than singers.* ■ If you do something **of your own accord**, you do it without being asked or forced to do it.

accordance If something is done **in accordance with** a law, it is done in the way the law says it should be done. You can say something is done **in accordance with** someone's wishes.

according — **According to** is used to say where some information is obtained from. *According to eye-witnesses, there was a demonstration of about ten thousand people.* ■ If something is done **according to** a principle or plan, it follows that principle or plan. *Children are grouped according to age.*

accordingly is used to say something is done in a way which fits in with what you have just described. *Any soldier failing to report would be considered absent without leave and punished accordingly.*

accordion The **accordion** is a box-shaped musical instrument which you hold between your hands. You play it by pressing keys on one side and buttons on the other, and moving the two sides together and apart.

accost If a stranger **accosts** you, they stop and insist on speaking to you.

account An **account** is a written or spoken record of something which has happened. ■ **Accounts** are detailed records of the money a person or organization receives and spends. ■ If you have a **bank account,** you keep an amount of money in a bank. ■ If you have an **account** with a shop or other business, you buy goods or services there and pay later. ■ If you **take account of** something or **take it into account,** you consider it when you are working something out or deciding what to do. *The latest figures did not take into account the recent fall in interest rates.* ■ If you do something **on account of** something else, you do it because of it. *I did get a bit cross, on account of my health.* ■ If you say something should **on no account** be done, you are emphasizing that it should not be done under any circumstances. ■ To **account for** something means to explain it, or explain what has happened to it. ■ See also **current account, deposit account.**

accountable (**accountability**) If you are **accountable** for things you do, you can be held responsible if they go wrong. ■ If you are **accountable** to someone else, they have authority over you and you must explain and justify to them the things you do. *There was a lack of government accountability to the governed.*

accountant (**accountancy**) **Accountants** are people whose job it is to keep financial accounts. The work they do is called **accountancy.**

accounting is the same as accountancy. ■ **creative accounting:** see **creative.**

accoutrements (*pron:* ak-koo-tra-ments) are all the things you have with you when you travel or when you take part in a certain activity. ...*the complex accoutrements of modern photography.*

accredit (**accrediting, accredited; accreditation**) If an educational qualification or institution is **accredited**, it is officially declared to be of an approved standard. This declaration is called **accreditation**. ■ If diplomats or journalists are **accredited** somewhere, they are officially accepted in that place as representatives of their country or organization. *About half a dozen Hungarian journalists are now accredited to the State Department... Dobbs checked the press accreditation list.*

accretion (*pron:* ak-**kree**-shun) An **accretion** is a layer of material which gradually forms on top of something. *...an accretion of sand.* The process by which layers like this are formed is also called **accretion**. *Soon ice accretion would cause the engine to stop.* ■ **Accretion** is used to talk about things building up gradually. *...the accretion of more presidential powers.*

accrue (**accruing, accrued**) If a sum of money **accrues**, it gradually increases. *...profits accruing from overseas sales.* ■ You can say things **accrue** when they build up over a period of time. *...the benefits which may accrue from a single currency.*

accumulate (**accumulating, accumulated; accumulation**) When things **accumulate**, they build up over a period of time. An **accumulation** of something is a large amount of it which has built up over a period of time. *...the accumulation of carbon dioxide in the atmosphere.* ■ If you **accumulate** things, you gradually add to the number or amount you have.

accurate (**accurately, accuracy**) An **accurate** description gives a true idea of what someone or something is like. You talk about the **accuracy** of a description like this. ■ An **accurate** prediction or forecast turns out to be correct. ■ An **accurate** machine or instrument performs a task without making mistakes. You can also say the work a person does or a method of doing something is **accurate**. *...the accurate analysis of minerals.* ■ If a weapon is **accurate**, it will hit its intended target. Similarly, you say someone's aim is **accurate** when they throw, kick, or hit a ball to exactly the right place. *He bowled with accuracy and pace.*

accusatory If someone's behaviour or something they say or write is **accusatory**, it gives the impression they are blaming or criticizing someone. *...an accusatory glance.*

accuse (**accusing, accused; accusation, accuser**) If you **accuse** someone of doing something wrong, you say they did it. An **accusation** is a statement in which someone is accused of doing something wrong. A person's **accusers** are people who accuse them of something. ■ If someone is **accused** of a crime, they have been charged with it. In court, they are called the **accused.**

accustom (**accustoming, accustomed**) If you **accustom** yourself to something or become **accustomed** to it, you get used to it and become familiar with it. *Both sides have become accustomed to a state of permanent hostility.* ■ **Accustomed** is used to talk about people behaving in their usual way. *...their accustomed brutality.*

ace An **ace** is a playing card with a single symbol on it. It is usually the highest ranking card. ■ **Ace** is used to describe things which are extremely good, or people who are extremely good at something.

...Fulham's ace stricker. ■ In tennis, an **ace** is a serve which is so fast that the other player fails to hit it. ■ If you come **within an ace** of doing something, you very nearly do it.

acerbic (*pron:* ass-**sir**-bik) (**acerbity**) If something someone says is **acerbic,** it is clever and witty, but in a bitter or cruel way.

acetate (*pron:* **ass**-it-tate) is a man-made fabric used for making clothes.

acetic acid (*pron:* ass-**see**-tik) is a colourless acid which is the main ingredient of vinegar.

acetylene (*pron:* ass-**set**-ill-een) is a colourless gas. When mixed with oxygen, it produces a very powerful flame, which is used in cutting and welding metal.

ache (**aching, ached; achingly**) If your body **aches,** you feel a constant dull pain. An **ache** is a pain like this. ■ **Aching** is used to describe strong feelings, especially of sadness. *...achingly beautiful ballads.* ■ If you **ache** for something, you want it very much.

achieve (**achieving, achieved; achievement**) If you **achieve** an aim or effect, you succeed in getting it or bringing it about. An **achievement** is a success of this kind.

achiever is used to talk about how successful people are. For example, you can talk about **high-achievers** or **low-achievers.**

Achilles heel (*pron:* ak-**kill**-eez) If a powerful person has an **Achilles heel,** they have a weak point which their opponents can use to attack them. *Colleagues say that his Achilles heel is that he is far too nice.*

Achilles tendon (*pron:* ak-**kill**-eez) Your **Achilles tendon** is the cord of tissue which connects your heel bone to your calf muscle.

acid (**acidic, acidity; acidly**) **Acids** are a group of liquids with certain chemical characteristics such as the ability to dissolve metals to form salts. If something is **acidic,** it has acid in it. This property is called **acidity.** ■ If someone suffers from stomach **acidity,** they feel uncomfortable, because they have too much acid in their stomach. ■ An **acid** taste is sour or sharp. ■ **Acid** is used to describe things people say or write which are harsh or unkind. *He acidly remarked that subsidised farming was not unique to the EU.* ■ The drug LSD is sometimes called **acid.** ■ An **acid test** is a sure way of proving whether something works properly or is of good quality. *The acid test will come next Friday with the retail sales figures.*

acid house is the same as house music.

acid rain is rain which has been made acidic by fumes and gases. Acid rain damages the environment.

acknowledge (**acknowledging, acknowledged; acknowledgement**) If you **acknowledge** that something is true, you accept or admit it is true. *He acknowledged that three-thousand people have been arrested.* ■ If someone or something is **acknowledged** as a certain thing, they are recognized as being that thing. *Scottish beef is acknowledged as the best in the world.* ■ If you **acknowledge** applause, you show your gratitude or appreciation in some way.

He acknowledged his ovation with a wave. ■ In a book, the **acknowledgements** are the author's notes, thanking people for their help while the book was being written, or for permission to include copyright material.

acne (*pron:* **ak**-nee) is a skin disease which causes spots and blackheads on the face, neck, and upper body.

acolyte (*pron:* **ak**-o-lite) An **acolyte** is a person who assists a priest at certain church ceremonies. ■ An important person's **acolytes** are people who support them uncritically and agree with everything they say.

acorn — **Acorns** are brown or green oval nuts which are the fruit of the oak tree.

acoustic (**acoustically**) **Acoustic** is used to talk about things to do with sound or hearing. *The torpedo transmits acoustic pulses into the water.* ■ An **acoustic** guitar is not amplified or electrified. ■ When people talk about the **acoustic** or **acoustics** of a building, they mean the physical features which determine how well an audience can hear music or speech. *The church is acoustically perfect.*

acquaint If you are **acquainted** with someone, you know them. If you are **acquainted** with something, you are familiar with it. ■ If you **acquaint** yourself with something, you get to know it. *He recently returned to Snowdonia to acquaint himself with the terrain.* ■ If you **acquaint** someone with something, you tell them about it. *He always seemed to feel the need to acquaint us with his sexual exploits.*

acquaintance An **acquaintance** is someone you have met but do not know well. ■ If you **make** someone's **acquaintance,** you meet them for the first time. ■ Your **acquaintance** with a subject is your knowledge or experience of it. *My first acquaintance with the A-level system came through my children.* ■ If you have a **nodding** or **passing acquaintance** with someone, you know them, but not well. Similarly, you can have a **passing acquaintance** with a subject.

acquiesce (*pron:* ak-wee-**ess**) (**acquiescing, acquiesced; acquiescent, acquiescence**) If you **acquiesce** in something, you agree to accept it. When someone agrees to accept something, you can say they are **acquiescent** or talk about their **acquiescence.**

acquire (**acquiring, acquired; acquisition**) If you **acquire** something, you get it, for example by buying it. When you acquire something, you can talk about your **acquisition** of it; your **acquisitions** are things you have acquired. ■ If you **acquire** a certain reputation, you get it as a result of your behaviour. *He has acquired a reputation for being temperamental.* ■ If you **acquire** a skill, you obtain it through experience. ■ If you say something is an **acquired taste,** you mean it has to be experienced several times before it can be enjoyed.

acquisitive people like to keep getting new possessions.

acquit (**acquitting, acquitted; acquittal**) If someone is **acquitted** of a crime, they are found not guilty. You call this their **acquittal.** ■ If you say someone **acquits** themselves well on a particular

occasion, you mean they do something well, or deal with a situation well.

acre Area is sometimes expressed in **acres.** An acre is 4840 square yards (about 4047 square metres). ■ **Acres** of something means a lot of it. *...acres of newsprint.*

acreage The **acreage** of a piece of land is its area, expressed in acres.

acrid An **acrid** smell or taste is strong, sharp, and unpleasant.

acrimonious (*pron:* ak-ri-**moan**-ee-uss) (**acrimoniously**) You say discussions are **acrimonious** when the people taking part say angry and bitter things.

acrimony (*pron:* **ak**-ri-mon-ee) is bitterness and anger. *The meeting ended in acrimony.*

acrobat An **acrobat** is an entertainer who performs difficult jumps, somersaults, and balancing acts.

acrobatic (**acrobatically**) **Acrobatic** movements involve fitness and skill and include things like jumps or somersaults. *...acrobatic dance routines.*

acronym (*pron:* **ak**-ro-nim) An **acronym** is a series of letters which stand for the name of an organization and which can be pronounced as though they were a single word. For example, NATO (*pron:* **nay**-toe) is an acronym for 'North Atlantic Treaty Organization'.

across something means from one side of it to the other. *They walked across the lawn ...the bridge across the River Jordan... He lay across the bed.* ■ **Across** something means on the other side of it. *Just across the Thames is the Department of Education.* ■ **Across** is used when giving the width of something. *Each satellite will measure one metre across and two metres high.* ■ **Across** means involving a wide area or range of something. *...a wave of protests across the political spectrum.*

acrylic fibres are man-made fibres resembling wool. ■ **Acrylic** paints are durable quick-drying paints.

act When you **act,** you do something. **Acts** are things people do. *The government wants the police to act quickly in cases of violence. ...acts of terrorism.* ■ If you **act** as a particular thing, that is your role. *He acted as a go-between.* ■ **Acting** in front of a title means someone is holding a post temporarily. *...the acting President.* ■ If an object or substance **acts** in a particular way, it has a particular effect. *Cocaine acts on the central nervous system.* ■ If you say someone's behaviour is an **act,** you mean it does not show their true feelings. You can also say they are **acting** in a particular way. *Chris acted astonished as he examined the note.* ■ If someone **acts** in a play or film, they have a part in it. **Acting** is doing this for a living. ■ An **act** in a play, opera, or ballet is one of the sections it is divided into. ■ The **acts** in a cabaret or circus are the separate performances in it. An **act** is also a person or group specializing in a type of performance. ■ An **Act** or **Act of Parliament** is a law passed by Parliament. *...the Financial Services Act.*

action is doing something, especially something with a definite purpose. *Urgent action was needed.* An **action** is something someone does. See also **direct action.** ■ A legal **action** is a process in which someone tries to get a court to force some-

actionable   8   adaptor

one else to do something, for example pay compensation. ...*a libel action.* ■ The **action** of a chemical is the way it works, or the effects it has. *This drug will inhibit the action of an enzyme.* ■ **Action** is used to talk about important or exciting things happening, for example in a film. ...*two hours of non-stop action.* ■ Military **action** is fighting between armed forces. If soldiers **go into action,** they start fighting. If they are killed **in action,** they are killed during fighting. ■ If someone or something is **out of action,** they cannot do what they are supposed to because there is something wrong with them.

actionable If what someone says or does is **actionable,** it is a valid reason for bringing a legal case against them.

action replay On TV, if viewers are shown an **action replay** of something, they are shown it again in slow motion.

activate (activating, activated; activation) If a device or system is **activated,** something makes it start working. ...*the sudden activation of the radar system.*

active (actively) An **active** person is energetic and always busy or moving about. ■ If someone is **active** in an organization or cause, they do a lot to help it. ■ **Active** is used to say someone does something in a positive or determined way. *His mother actively discouraged him.* ■ If something is **active,** it is moving, working, or having an effect. *The virus is still active.* ■ An **active** volcano has erupted recently or may erupt soon.

active service People on **active service** or **active duty** are fighting as members of the armed forces.

activist (activism) An **activist** is someone who tries to bring about political or social change by doing things like organizing campaigns and taking part in demonstrations. ...*the growing activism of native peoples in Australia.*

activity (activities) An **activity** is something someone does. ...*leisure activities.* ■ If you say there is **activity** in a place, you mean things are happening or being done there. *There were few signs of activity.*

act of God (acts of God) If people say something serious such as an accident is an **act of God,** they mean it was beyond human control and nobody is to blame.

Act of Parliament See **act.**

actor An **actor** is a person whose job is acting in films or plays.

actress (actresses) An **actress** is a woman whose job is acting in films or plays.

actual (actually) Actual is used to emphasize that you are talking about something real or genuine. ...*the actual working platform where the tunnelling is taking place... More than 500 executions have been reported and the actual number is probably higher.* ■ **Actual** and **actually** are used with words like 'no' and 'not' to say something is not a particular thing, although it may be like it. *Nobody is actually rioting... He was charged with attempted rather than actual murder.* ■ You use **actually** when you are saying what you claim is the truth about something, as distinct from what has just been said or mentioned. *They*

claim they work to promote the family, but actually they are involved in separating families.

actual bodily harm If someone is charged with causing **actual bodily harm,** they are charged with injuring someone deliberately.

actuality is things which really exist, rather than imaginary things. ...*the actuality of Chinese boy actresses.*

actually See **actual.**

actuary (actuaries; actuarial) An **actuary** is a person whose job is to calculate insurance risks and work out how much insurance companies should charge their clients. **Actuarial** is used to talk about things to do with actuaries and their work. ...*actuarial calculations.*

acuity (pron: ak-kew-it-ee) is (a) sharpness of vision or hearing. (b) quickness and clarity of thought.

acumen (pron: ak-yew-men) is the ability to make good decisions and judgments. ...*business acumen.*

acupuncture is a traditional Chinese treatment of illness or pain, now used to some extent in the West. It involves putting fine needles into the skin in different parts of the body.

acute (acutely, acuteness) Acute is used to emphasize how bad a situation or illness is. ...*the country's acute economic crisis.* ■ **Acute** is used to describe strong feelings about something unpleasant. ...*acute concern... The situation is acutely embarrassing.* ■ If a faculty such as someone's sight or memory is **acute,** it is very sensitive and powerful. ■ The **acute** accent is a symbol written over a letter, indicating a change in its pronunciation, as in 'café'. ■ An **acute angle** is any angle of less than 90 degrees. See also **obtuse, reflex.**

AD is used in dates to say something happened a certain number of years or centuries after Christ is believed to have been born. AD stands for 'anno Domini', which is Latin for 'in the year of our Lord'.

ad An **ad** is an advertisement.

adage (pron: ad-ij) An **adage** is a saying. ...*the old adage that one player does not make a team.*

adamant (adamantly) If you are **adamant** about something, you are determined not to change your mind about it.

Adam's apple A man's **Adam's apple** is the lump sticking out at the front of his throat.

adapt (adaptation) If you **adapt** to a new situation, you change your ideas or behaviour, to be able to deal with it. ■ If you **adapt** something, you alter it to make it suitable for a new purpose or situation. ■ If someone **adapts** a story or novel, they write a version which can be performed as a play or made into a film. This new version is called an **adaptation** of the story.

adaptable (adaptability) If someone or something is **adaptable,** they can change or be changed to deal with different situations. *The flu virus is amazingly adaptable.*

adaptation See **adapt.**

adaptive is used to talk about ways of adapting to new situations. ...*the adaptive capacity of all living systems.*

adaptor An **adaptor** is (a) a device which two or more plugs can be fitted into, so they can be used from the same wall socket. (b) a device for connecting a plug into a socket in which it would not normally fit. ■ A mains **adaptor** is an electrical lead with a plug which allows you to power a device from the mains rather than by battery. ■ Various devices which link things together or allow them to be used in different ways are called **adaptors**. ...*a fine-spray hose-pipe adaptor.*

add If you **add** one thing to another, you attach the first thing to the second, or include the first thing with the second. ■ If something **adds** to a feeling, it increases it. *This can only have added to his frustration.* ■ If you **add** numbers or **add** them **up,** you calculate their total. You can say numbers **add up** to a certain total. ■ **Add up** is used to talk about the result of putting several things together. *It all adds up to a very disturbing picture.* ■ If you say something like a statement **adds up,** you mean it is believable or makes sense. ■ If you **add** something when you are speaking, you say something more. *He added that he had refused the offer.*

addendum (*plural:* **addenda**) An **addendum** is a section at the end of a book or document, containing extra information.

adder The **adder** is a small poisonous snake.

addict (**addicted, addiction**) If someone is **addicted** to a drug, they cannot stop taking it. You call someone like this an **addict;** you talk about their **addiction** to the drug. ■ You say someone is **addicted** to something when they enjoy it very much and spend as much time on it as they can. *She is addicted to golf.* ...*sci-fi addicts.*

addictive If a drug is **addictive,** people find they need to keep taking it. ■ You can say activities are **addictive** when people like them so much they spend all their time doing them.

addition (**additional, additionally**) Addition is calculating totals. ■ When something is added to something which already exists, you can talk about the **addition** of this extra thing. *The final five wickets fell for the addition of just 25 runs.* Something added like this can be called an **addition.** *An airlift would be a welcome addition to our contribution.* ■ **Additional** is used to describe things which are extra to something which already exists. *An additional 400 job losses have been announced.* ■ People say **in addition** or **additionally** when they are giving extra information. *In addition, other companies organise excursions from riverside towns.*

additive — **Additives** are substances added to products by manufacturers, especially chemicals added to food to preserve, colour, or flavour it.

addled is used to describe people who are unable to think properly, for example because they are on drugs.

add-on is used to describe things which are not essential but can be added to something to make it more useful or effective. ...*a home computer with add-on memory.*

address (**addresses, addressing, addressed**) Your **address** is the number of your house, the street, the town, and the postcode where you live or work. If a letter is **addressed** to you, it has your name and address on it. ■ If you **address** a group of people,

you make a speech to them. A speech can be called an **address.** ...*a televised address to the nation.* ■ If you are **addressing** someone, you are speaking to them. ■ If you **address** a problem or **address yourself** to it, (a) you start dealing with it. *Callwell addressed himself to the problem of reprisals.* (b) you talk about it when you are making a speech.

addressee The **addressee** of a letter or parcel is the person it is addressed to.

adduce (**adducing, adduced**) If you **adduce** a fact or piece of evidence, you bring it forward to support a claim or argument. *The plaintiff could not adduce evidence of actual loss.*

adenoids A child's **adenoids** are two soft lumps of flesh at the back of its nose, just above its tonsils.

adept (**adeptly**) If someone is **adept** at something, they are very good at it. ...*an adept public speaker.*

adequate (**adequately, adequacy**) If something is **adequate,** it is good enough, or there is enough of it.

adhere (**adhering, adhered; adherence**) If something **adheres** to a surface or object, it sticks to it. ■ If you **adhere** to a rule, agreement, or principle, you keep to it. You can talk about someone's **adherence** to one of these things.

adherent The followers of a religion or other set of beliefs can be called its **adherents.**

adhesion is used to talk about things sticking together. ...*the adhesion of the fibre to its matrix.* ■ A car's **adhesion** is its ability to grip the road.

adhesive An **adhesive** is a substance used to stick things together. ■ If something is **adhesive,** it sticks firmly to something else. ...*adhesive tape.*

ad hoc is used to say something is not done as part of a regular arrangement or system. *Large projects are put out to agencies on an ad-hoc basis.*

adieu (*pron:* a-**dew**) means goodbye.

adjacent If two things are **adjacent,** they are next to each other.

adjective — **Adjectives** are words used to describe things. For example, in 'The night was dark', 'dark' is an adjective.

adjoin (**adjoining, adjoined**) If one thing **adjoins** another or if two things are **adjoining,** they are next to each other.

adjourn (**adjournment**) If a meeting or trial is **adjourned,** it is stopped temporarily. A stoppage like this is called an **adjournment.**

adjudge (**adjudging, adjudged**) If you are **adjudged** to be something, it is officially decided that you are that thing. *He was adjudged bankrupt.* You can also be **adjudged** to have done something. *The ref adjudged him to have committed a professional foul.*

adjudicate (**adjudicating, adjudicated; adjudication, adjudicator**) If someone **adjudicates** on a dispute, they make an official decision about it.

adjunct If something is an **adjunct** to something larger or more important, it is part of it, or helps to perform the same task. *Physical therapy is an important adjunct to drug treatments.*

adjust (**adjustment**) If you **adjust** to a new situation, you get used to it by changing your behaviour or ideas. ■ If someone is well **adjusted,** they get on well with other people and are good at coping with everyday problems. ■ If you **adjust** something, you make slight changes, to make it more effective or appropriate. ■ If you **adjust** a TV or radio, you change its setting to get a clearer picture or sound. ■ If you **adjust** something you are wearing, you change its position to get it looking the way you want it to.

adjustable If something is **adjustable,** you can change its position or setting. ...*an adjustable spanner.*

adjutant (*pron:* aj-oo-tant) An **adjutant** is an army officer who deals with administrative work.

ad-lib (**ad-libbing, ad-libbed**) If someone **ad-libs** in a play or speech, they say something which has not been prepared beforehand, often because they have forgotten what they were supposed to say.

adman (**admen**) An **adman** is someone who works in advertising.

administer (**administering, administered**) The people who **administer** a country, organization, or event are the ones who control and supervise it. ■ If you **administer** a medicine or drug, you give it to someone, for example by injecting it or giving it to them to swallow.

administrate (**administrating, administrated**) To **administrate** a country or organization means the same as to administer it.

administration (**administrative, administratively; administrator**) The **administration** of a country or area is its government. ■ **Administration** is the work of organizing and controlling something. ...*the administration of justice.* **Administrative** is used to talk about things connected with this work. ...*administrative costs.* People responsible for administration are called **administrators.** ■ If a company with financial problems is **in administration,** a representative of creditors or shareholders has been chosen to take over its management. This person is called an **administrator;** it is their job to try to improve the company or sell it, so people get their money back.

admirable (**admirably**) If you say something is **admirable,** you mean it deserves to be praised and admired. ...*an admirable aim.*

admiral An **admiral** is a high-ranking naval officer.

Admiralty – The Admiralty is the former name of the Navy Department of the Ministry of Defence.

admire (**admiring, admired; admiringly, admiration, admirer**) If you **admire** someone, you like and respect them, because you think they have special qualities or talents. ■ If you **admire** something like a view, you look at it with pleasure.

admissible If evidence is **admissible,** it can be considered in court.

admit (**admitting, admitted; admission; admittance**) If you **admit** something is true, you reluctantly say it is true. What you say is called an **admission.** ■ If you **admit** responsibility for something, you say you are responsible for it. *Hospital authorities admitted liability for mistakes during her birth.* ■ If you **admit** defeat, you accept you have lost, or cannot achieve what you wanted to. ■ If you are **admitted** to a place or gain **admission** or **admittance,** you are allowed in. Similarly, if someone is **admitted** to a group or organization, they are allowed to join. ■ If you are **admitted** to hospital, you are taken in as a patient. People admitted to a hospital are called **admissions.** ■ **Admissions** is the process of deciding which students will go to which university. ...*admissions interviews.*

admittedly You say **admittedly** when you are mentioning something which weakens the main point you are making. *The risk is admittedly small.*

admonish (**admonishes, admonishing, admonished; admonishment**) If you **admonish** someone, you tell them off or warn them not to do something.

admonition An **admonition** is something you say or do to warn someone not to do something.

ad nauseum (*pron:* ad naw-zee-am) If someone does something **ad nauseum,** they keep doing it and it gets boring or annoying.

ado (*pron:* a-**doo**) If something is done **without further ado,** it is done immediately. *He ordered the men to be released without further ado.*

adolescent (**adolescence**) An **adolescent** is a young person at an age between childhood and adulthood. This stage of your life is called **adolescence. Adolescent** is used to talk about things connected with people of this age, especially behaviour which shows they are not yet fully grown up. ...*a typically adolescent joke.*

adopt (**adoption, adoptive**) If you **adopt** an attitude or way of doing things, you start thinking or behaving like that. *Britain and the United States have adopted a more cautious approach.* ■ If people **adopt** something like a plan, they decide to put it into action. *The Security Council has adopted a resolution to relax the sanctions.* ■ If a child is **adopted,** a couple take it into their own family and make it legally their own. This process is called **adoption.** The couple are called the child's **adoptive** parents. ■ If you **adopt** a country you have gone to live in, you regard it as your home; you can call a country your **adopted** home or **adoptive** home. ■ If you **adopt** a name, you start using it as your own name.

adorable Some people use **adorable** to describe people or animals they find delightful, lovable, and attractive.

adore (**adoring, adored; adoringly, adoration**) If you **adore** someone, you love and admire them, and tend to ignore their faults. ■ If you **adore** something, you enjoy it very much. *He adores music.*

adorn If something is **adorned** with things, it is decorated with them.

adornments are things worn for decoration, such as jewellery.

adrenal glands The **adrenal glands** are glands on top of your kidneys which secrete adrenalin and other hormones.

adrenaline (*or* **adrenalin**) is a hormone produced by your body when you are angry, frightened, or excited. It makes your heart beat faster and gives you more energy.

adrift If a boat is **adrift,** it is not tied up or under control and is being carried along by the wind or tide. ■ In sport, if a competitor is a number of points **adrift,** they are that number of points behind.

adroit (**adroitly**) If someone is **adroit,** they act or think quickly and skilfully.

adulation (**adulatory**) Adulation is enthusiastic admiration and praise. You use **adulatory** to describe a reaction like this. ...*adulatory reviews.*

adult An **adult** is a mature fully-developed person or animal. ■ **Adult** is used to describe things intended or suitable for adults. ...*adult prisons.* ...*adult entertainment.*

adulterate (**adulterating, adulterated**) If food, drink, or a drug is **adulterated,** something is added which weakens or contaminates it.

adultery (**adulterer, adulteress; adulterous**) If a married person commits **adultery,** they have sex with someone they are not married to. An **adulterer** is someone who commits adultery; a woman who commits adultery can also be called an **adulteress. Adulterous** is used to describe people who commit adultery, and relationships involving adultery. ...*an adulterous affair.*

adulthood is the part of your life when you are an adult.

advance (**advancing, advanced; advancement**) When people or things **advance,** they move forward. ■ If someone or something **advances,** they make progress or become more successful. *There have been enormous advances in computer technology.* ...*economic advancement.* ■ **Advanced** is used to describe someone or something that has reached a high level of skill or development. ...*advanced students... Britain's most advanced fighter plane.* ■ **Advance** is used to talk about something being done a certain length of time before an event takes place. *The bill requires unions to give advance notice of strikes... I plan the work in advance.* ■ If something like a meeting is **advanced,** it is brought forward to an earlier time. ■ If you **advance** a theory or point of view, you suggest it and argue in favour of it. ■ If you are given an **advance,** you are given some money before it is due. ■ If someone makes **advances** to you, they try to (a) start a friendly relationship with you. *The President had shunned any advances from Libya.* (b) start a sexual relationship with you.

Advanced Level See **A-Level.**

advantage (**advantaged**) An **advantage** is something which puts you in a better position than others. ■ The **advantages** of something are the good things about it, which make it more desirable than other things. ■ If you **take advantage of** an opportunity, you make use of it while you can. ■ If someone **takes advantage** of you, they treat you unfairly for their own benefit. ■ In tennis, **advantage** is the first point scored after deuce. If the same player wins the next point, he or she wins the game.

advantageous If something is **advantageous** to you, it benefits you or puts you in a better position than others.

advent When something new is introduced which brings significant changes to people's lives, you can talk about its **advent.** ...*the advent of the personal computer.* ...*the advent of democracy in eastern Europe.* ■ **Advent** is the period just before Christmas, including the four Sundays before Christmas Day, when Christian worship concentrates on the coming of Jesus.

adventure (**adventurer**) Adventure is doing unusual exciting things. *He always had a taste for adventure.* An **adventurer** is someone who likes doing things like this. ■ An **adventure** is a series of exciting things someone is involved in.

adventure playground An **adventure playground** is an area of land with special equipment for children to play on, such as climbing frames.

adventurism (**adventurist**) Adventurism is behaving in a reckless way, to try and get some advantage for yourself. *He warned against military adventurism.* When someone behaves like this, you say their behaviour is **adventurist** or you call them an **adventurist.**

adventurous (**adventurousness**) An **adventurous** person is willing to take risks and eager to have new experiences.

adverb An **adverb** is a word which says where, when, or how something is done. In 'They went outside', 'She arrived late', and 'He stood up quickly', 'outside', 'late', and 'quickly' are adverbs.

adversarial (pron: ad-ver-**sair**-ree-al) An **adversarial** system is based on the idea of two people or groups being opposed to each other, with one of them eventually beating the other. ...*the adversarial nature of criminal trials.*

adversary (pron: **ad**-ver-ser-ree) (**adversaries**) Your **adversary** is someone you are competing or fighting against.

adverse (**adversely**) Adverse is used to describe things which make it difficult for you to achieve what you want. ...*adverse weather conditions.* ...*adverse publicity.* You can also talk about the **adverse** effects of something. *The team has not been too adversely affected by the news.*

adversity is used to talk about times when you experience misfortune and hardship. *He showed courage in adversity.* ...*the will to triumph against adversity.*

advert An **advert** is an advertisement.

advertise (**advertising, advertised; advertiser**) When a product is **advertised,** people are told it is available and encouraged to buy it. Jobs and events can also be **advertised.** ■ **Advertising** is the job of designing and producing advertisements. Companies who advertise products are called **advertisers.** ■ An **advertising feature** is the same as an advertorial. ■ If you do not want to **advertise** something about yourself, you want to avoid making people aware of it. *He did not want to advertise his presence.*

advertisement An **advertisement** is an announcement in a newspaper, on television, or on a poster about something like a product, event, or vacancy. ■ If you say one thing is a good **advertisement** for another, you mean the first thing gives a good impression of the second. *My parents aren't a good advertisement for marriage.*

advertorial An **advertorial** is an item in a magazine or newspaper which is made to look like a real article, but is actually an advertisement.

advice If you give someone **advice,** you tell them what you think they should do.

advisable If you say something is **advisable,** you mean it is a good idea to do it or have it. *It is advisable to avoid mountain roads... A packed lunch is advisable.*

advise (**advising, advised; adviser**) If you **advise** someone, you tell them what you think they should do. An **adviser** is someone whose job is to help people in this way. *...financial advisers.* ■ If you say someone would be **well advised** to do something, you mean they ought to do it, for their own sake. See also **ill-advised.** ■ If you are **advised** that something is the case, you are told about it. *He was advised that he was likely to be arrested.*

advisedly If you say you use a word or phrase **advisedly,** you mean you have chosen it deliberately, because it is the right word or phrase for what you want to say. *I say 'boys' advisedly because we are talking almost entirely about male behaviour.*

adviser See **advise.**

advisory An **advisory** group gives suggestions, help, or information. *...the Government's advisory committee on social security.*

advocate (**advocating, advocated; advocacy**) If you **advocate** something or are an **advocate** (*pron:* **ad**-vo-kut) of it, you say publicly you think it should be done, used, or introduced. *...the constitutional changes advocated by the Labour Party... I am not an advocate of the death penalty. ...his advocacy of the use of 'necessary' violence.* ■ An **advocate** is a lawyer who puts someone's case in court. Putting a case in court is called **advocacy.**

aegis (*pron:* **ee**-jiss) If something is done **under the aegis** of an organization, it is done with their support and backing. *...the joint international response under the aegis of the United Nations.*

aeon (*or* **eon**) (*both pron:* **ee**-on) An **aeon** is an extremely long period of time. *Aeons ago, there were deserts where there is now fertile land.*

aerate (**aerating, aerated; aeration**) If something is **aerated,** air is introduced into it.

aerial is used to describe things happening in or from the air. *...aerial combat ...aerial photographs.* ■ An **aerial** is a long thin piece of metal for sending or picking up TV or radio signals.

aerobatics are skilful and spectacular movements made by planes, usually to entertain people on the ground.

aerobics is a type of vigorous exercise, often to music, which increases the amount of oxygen in your blood and strengthens your heart and lungs.

aerodrome is an old word for an airfield.

aerodynamic (**aerodynamics**) Aerodynamic is used to talk about the movement of objects through air. If something is **aerodynamic,** its shape is designed to stop it being slowed down by air resistance. *...the aerodynamic Lotus Sport bike.* ■ **Aerodynamics** is the study of movement through air. The **aerodynamics** of an object are the things about it which affect the ease with which it moves through the air. *Modifications have resulted in improved aerodynamics.*

aeronautics (**aeronautical**) Aeronautics is the design and construction of aircraft. *...aeronautical engineering.*

aeroplane An **aeroplane** is a powered aircraft with wings.

aerosol An **aerosol** is a pressurized container with liquid inside. The liquid is forced out as a fine spray when a button is pressed on the top.

aerospace industries are involved in developing and making rockets, missiles, and spacecraft.

aesthete (*Am:* **esthete**) (*pron:* **eess**-theet) An **aesthete** is a person who loves and appreciates beautiful things, especially works of art.

aesthetic (*Am:* **esthetic**) (*pron:* iss-**thet**-ik) (**aesthetically**) Aesthetic is used to talk about things involving beauty or art, and people's appreciation of these things. *...aesthetic responses. ...work that is aesthetically attractive.* ■ **Aesthetics** is the study of beauty in art, literature, and music.

afar If something is seen or done from **afar,** it is seen or done from a long way off.

affable (**affably**) An **affable** person is good-natured and friendly.

affair An **affair** is a series of happenings which attracts a lot of attention, especially one which involves dishonest or careless behaviour. *The government has mishandled the whole affair.* ■ You can describe something by saying it is an **affair** of a particular kind. *The European conquest of the Americas was a brutal affair... The train was quite an elaborate affair.* ■ If you say something is someone's **affair,** you mean it is their business and nobody else's. ■ An **affair** is a sexual relationship between two people who are not married to each other when one or both of them is married to someone else. ■ Things which people are concerned with or responsible for can be called **affairs** of different kinds. *...the minister for economic affairs.* ■ Your **affairs** are the things you are involved in, especially things to do with money and business. *He resigned because of the police investigation into his affairs.* ■ See also **state of affairs, current affairs.**

affect (**affectation**) If something **affects** something else, it influences it or causes it to change. *He was asked if today's failure would affect his future chances. ...people affected by cystic fibrosis... The storms are now easing in the worst-affected areas.* ■ If someone **affects** a characteristic or style of behaviour, they adopt it and pretend it is natural to them. *She affected a lisp.* You call a pretence like this an **affectation.** ■ If you say someone's behaviour is **affected** or **affectation,** you mean they are acting in a false unnatural way to impress other people.

affection is a feeling of fondness for someone. *She thought of him with affection... She saw me as a rival for my father's affections.*

affectionate (**affectionately**) If your behaviour is **affectionate,** you show fondness for someone.

affidavit (*pron:* af-fid-**dave**-it) An **affidavit** is a written statement which you swear is true and which may be used as evidence in court.

affiliate (**affiliating, affiliated; affiliation**) If an organization **affiliates** itself to another organization, it becomes a part of it or forms a close official link with it; this makes it an **affiliate** of the other organization. ...*the affiliation of unions to the Congress of Trade Unions.* ■ Your political **affiliation** is the party you regularly support. Your religious **affiliation** is the church you belong to.

affinity (**affinities**) If you have an **affinity** with someone or something, you feel you understand them, belong with them, or are like them in some way. ...*the cultural affinity of black people with Africa.*

affirm (**affirmation**) If you **affirm** something like an intention, you say you definitely have it. ... *a very public affirmation of NATO's resolve.*

affirmative If you give an **affirmative** response, you say 'yes', or something which means yes.

affix (**affixes, affixing, affixed**) If you **affix** something somewhere, you stick, fasten, or attach it there.

afflict (**affliction**) If someone is **afflicted** by a serious illness, they have it. An illness can be called an **affliction.** ...*one of the most tragic afflictions facing modern medicine.* People can also be **afflicted** by other things, such as war or famine. ...*Ethiopia's drought-afflicted highlands.*

affluent (**affluence**) **Affluent** people have a lot of money and a high standard of living. You talk about the **affluence** of people like these.

afford If you can **afford** something, you have enough money to buy it or pay for it. ■ If you say someone cannot **afford** or can **ill afford** to do something or let something happen, you mean they must avoid it, because of the trouble it would bring. *The president cannot afford to upset his farmers any further.* ■ If you are **afforded** something, you are provided with it. *His business interests afforded him the chance for extensive travel.*

affordable You say something is **affordable** when people can afford to buy it or pay for it. ...*affordable housing.*

afforestation is the planting of large numbers of trees on bare land.

affray An **affray** is a noisy and violent fight, especially in a public place. **Affray** is the criminal offence of using or threatening to use violence in a public place.

affront If you are **affronted** by something or regard it as an **affront,** you feel insulted by it.

aficianado (*pron:* af-fish-yo-**nah**-do) (**aficianados**) An **aficianado** of something is an enthusiastic and knowledgeable fan of it. ...*whisky aficionados.*

afield – Far **afield** is used to emphasize how far away something is. ...*20 competitors, from as far afield as Russia and Canada.* ■ **Further afield** is used to say something is further away than the place just mentioned. *It became necessary to look further afield.*

afloat If a boat is **afloat,** it is floating rather than resting on something solid. ■ If a business or a country's economy is kept **afloat,** there is just enough money to keep it going.

afoot If you say something is **afoot,** you mean people are planning something. *Moves are afoot to establish a new company.*

aforementioned is used to talk about someone or something that has already been mentioned.

afraid If you are **afraid** of someone or something, you are frightened because of them. ■ If you are **afraid** for someone, you are worried something bad will happen to them. ■ If you are **afraid** something unpleasant will happen, you are worried it will happen. ■ You say **'I'm afraid'** when you are mentioning something which might upset people. *I'm afraid England were out for 194.*

afresh If you do something **afresh,** you start doing it again, as if doing it for the first time. *The government says it will look afresh at the legislation.*

African-American An **African-American** is a black American whose ancestors came from Africa.

afro An **afro** is a hairstyle in which a black person's hair is allowed to grow in a frizzy mass.

Afro-Caribbean An **Afro-Caribbean** is a black person from the Caribbean.

aft See **fore.**

after If something happens **after** an event or time, it happens later than that event or time. *We met after lunch... The fight ended after 51 seconds of the third round.* ■ If one person or thing comes **after** another, they follow it or are behind it. ■ If something happens **day after day** or **time after time,** it happens repeatedly. ■ **After** is used when giving a reason for a statement. *You deserve better after what you've done for us.* ■ If you are **after** someone or something, you are trying to catch, find, or obtain them. ■ If a person or thing is named **after** someone, they have been given that person's name. *The Walpole Committee is named after Sir Robert Walpole.*

afterbirth The **afterbirth** is the material which comes out of a woman's or female animal's womb after she has given birth.

after-effects The **after-effects** of something are the bad or harmful effects which continue after it is over. *He is still suffering the after-effects of a bout of glandular fever.*

afterglow The **afterglow** of an enjoyable experience is a pleasant feeling which remains after it is over. ...*the afterglow of victory.*

afterlife The **afterlife** is used to talk about a life some people believe begins after you die, for example a life in heaven.

aftermath The **aftermath** of a major event is the period just after it. ...*the aftermath of the Gulf War.*

afternoon The **afternoon** is the part of each day between lunchtime and about 5 o'clock.

aftershave is men's perfume.

aftershocks The **aftershocks** of an earthquake are a series of lesser tremors which come after it. ■ The **aftershocks** of an important and dramatic event are a series of smaller events which follow it and are a result of it. ...*the aftershocks of last week's failed coup.*

aftertaste An **aftertaste** is a taste, especially an unpleasant one, which remains in your mouth after you have finished eating or drinking something.

afterthought If you say or do something as an **afterthought,** you say or do an extra thing which you had not planned beforehand.

afterwards (**afterward**) **Afterwards** or **afterward** is used to say something happens at a later stage, after something else has finished. *Afterwards, the con-*

gregation staged a torch-light procession through the streets.

afterword An **afterword** is a brief extra chapter or section at the end of a book.

again is used to talk about things being repeated. *Stockton won the PGA championship in 1970 and again six years later.* If something happens **again and again,** it keeps happening. ■ **Again** is used to talk about things going back to the way they were. *The laundry was working again.* ■ If for instance, an amount is **half as much again** as another amount, it is 50 per cent larger.

against is used to talk about something being in contact with something else. *She leant against the wall.* ■ If you are **against** something or someone, you disapprove of them or oppose them. *...the tendency of children to rebel against their parents' ideas. ...Norwich City's glorious efforts against Liverpool.* ■ If something is **against** the law or the rules, it is not allowed. Similarly, you can say something is **against** someone's principles or orders. ■ If you decide **against** doing something, you decide not to do it. ■ If something goes **against** a current or wind, or **against** a trend, it is moving or changing in the opposite direction. ■ **Against** is used to mention the circumstances or context in which something happens or is measured. *The congress comes against a background of new fighting between the rebels and government forces... The pound has risen against the franc.* ■ The odds **against** something happening are the odds that it will not happen. ■ Evidence **against** an idea or claim is evidence which suggests it is wrong. Evidence **against** a person suggests they have done something wrong or committed a crime.

agape If someone's mouth is **agape,** it is wide open with suprise. ■ If you say people are **agape,** you mean they are amazed at something which is happening. *...a bitter feud that has left New York agape.*

agar is a jelly-like substance made from seaweed. It is used for growing cultures in biological experiments.

agate is a type of striped quartz which is used in jewellery.

age (ageing *or* aging, aged) Your **age** is how old you are. **Aged** is used to say how old someone is. *...youngsters aged 11 to 13.* ■ **Age** is being old. *Age has begun to leave its mark.* When someone or something **ages,** they get older, or seem to get older. *She aged about 20 years in 2 weeks. ...London's ageing transport system.* ■ An **aged** (*pron:* **age**-id) person is very old. Old people in general are sometimes called the **aged.** ■ You say something or someone **comes of age** when they reach the stage where they are fully developed. *By the turn of the century the bicycle had come of age.* ■ An **age** is a period in history. *...the beginning of a new age of friendship between the two countries.* ■ If something takes **ages** or an **age,** it takes a long time.

aged See **age.**

ageism (ageist) **Ageism** is discriminating against people because they are middle-aged or old.

ageless If you say someone is **ageless,** you mean (a) they never seem to get any older. (b) it is im-

possible to tell how old they are. ■ If you say something is **ageless,** you mean it does not seem to belong to any particular period in history. *...ageless ceremonies.*

age limit The **age limit** for something is the oldest or youngest age at which you are allowed to do it or be it.

agency (agencies) An **agency** is a business which provides a particular service. *...an advertising agency.* ■ In the US, an **agency** is a government organization. *...the Central Intelligence Agency.*

agenda An **agenda** is a list of subjects for discussion at a meeting. ■ An **agenda** is a list of things to be done. *He set out a bold agenda for reform in Europe.* ■ If you say something is **high on the agenda,** you mean it is one of the first things you intend to deal with. ■ **hidden agenda:** see **hidden.**

agent An **agent** is someone who arranges work for other people, especially people like actors and musicians. ■ An **agent** is someone who works for a country's secret service. ■ An **agent** of something is a cause of it. *A leader is one who inspires, an agent of change.*

agent provocateur (agents provocateurs) (*pron:* **azh**-on prov-vok-at-**tur;** *the 'zh' sounds like 's' in 'pleasure'*) An **agent provocateur** is a person employed by a police force or government to encourage people to cause trouble or break the law, so they can then be arrested or public opinion can be turned against them.

age of consent The **age of consent** is the age at which a person can legally marry or have a sexual relationship.

age-old If something is **age-old,** it has been around for a very long time. *...the age-old conflict between fathers and sons.*

agglomeration An **agglomeration** is a group of different things gathered together in no particular order. *The album is a bizarre agglomeration of styles.*

aggrandizement (*or* aggrandisement) (aggrandizing) If someone does something for their own **aggrandizement,** they do it so people will think they are powerful and important. *...self-aggrandizing propaganda.*

aggravate (aggravating, aggravated; aggravation) If something **aggravates** a problem, it makes it worse. ■ If something **aggravates** people, it upsets and angers them.

aggregate (aggregating, aggregated; aggregation) An **aggregate** is a total of several amounts added together. *MISYS is buying SCSS and SCPM for an aggregate £2.87 million.* You can say several amounts **aggregate** a total. *RWC's commercial director anticipated eight prime sponsorships aggregating around £16m.* ■ In football, if one team beats another **on aggregate,** it wins by scoring more goals over two matches between the teams. ■ If things are **aggregated,** they are grouped together, although they may have no connection with each other. *Society is more than an aggregation of individuals.*

aggressive (aggressively, aggressiveness, aggression) If people are **aggressive,** they behave in an angry threatening way. You call behaviour like this

aggressiveness. If actual violence is used, you call it **aggression.** ■ When one country attacks another, this is called **aggression.** *...military aggression.* ■ You say people are **aggressive** when they behave in a forceful and determined way because they are eager to succeed.

aggressor When there is a fight or battle, the **aggressor** is the person or country that started it.

aggrieved If you feel **aggrieved,** you feel upset and angry because of the way you have been treated.

aggro is aggressive and violent behaviour.

aghast If you are **aghast** at something, you are surprised and horrified.

agile (agility) An **agile** person moves with ease and speed. ■ If someone can think quickly and cleverly, you can say they have an **agile** brain or talk about their mental **agility.**

aging See **age.**

agitate (agitating, agitated; agitation) If you **agitate** for political change, you get involved in campaigns and protests. ■ If you are **agitated,** you are worried and cannot relax.

agitator You call someone an **agitator** when they get involved in political campaigns and protests, especially if you see them as a trouble-maker.

agitprop is stories, plays, and art which promote political views, especially left-wing ones, in a crude and obvious way.

AGM An **AGM** is a meeting held once a year by a company or other organization to discuss business such as the accounts for the previous year. AGM stands for 'Annual General Meeting'.

agnostic (agnosticism) An **agnostic** is someone who is unsure whether God exists or not. Some agnostics also say that nobody can ever know whether God exists. ■ You can say someone is **agnostic** or an **agnostic** when they are unsure about something. *He is agnostic about the European single currency.*

ago is used to talk about the past. For example, you say something happened five years ago.

agog If you are **agog,** you are excited by something, and eager to know more about it.

agonize (or agonise) (agonizing, agonized; agonizingly) If you **agonize** over something, you spend a lot of time worrying about it. ■ If something is **agonizing,** it causes great pain, worry, or frustration. *...slow, agonizing deaths. ...the agonizingly slow rate of progress.* ■ You can call someone's expression **agonized** when it shows they are suffering great pain or misery.

agony (agonies) Agony is severe physical or mental pain. *...the agonies that writing caused him.*

agony aunt (agony uncle) An **agony aunt** or **agony uncle** is someone who writes a newspaper or magazine column, or has a slot on TV or radio in which they reply to people who have written to them for advice on their personal problems.

agoraphobia (agoraphobic) Agoraphobia is a fear of open spaces, public places, or of going outside your own home. An **agoraphobic** is someone who has this fear.

agrarian means to do with the ownership and use of land, especially farmland. *...agrarian reforms.*

agree (agreeing, agreed; agreement) If you **agree** with someone or are **in agreement** with them, you have the same opinion about something. ■ If you **agree** with something, you approve of it. ■ If something like food does not **agree** with you, it makes you feel ill. *Booze just doesn't agree with me.* ■ If you **agree** to do something, you say you will do it. ■ If something like a deal is **agreed,** the people involved reach a joint decision on it. What they decide is called an **agreement;** the document setting out their decision, which they sign, is also called an **agreement.** ■ If two accounts of an event **agree,** they are the same, and so are probably both correct. Similarly, you can say two sets of figures **agree.**

agreeable (agreeably) If something is **agreeable,** it is pleasant. ■ If someone is **agreeable,** they are pleasant and friendly. ■ If you are **agreeable** to something, you are willing to do it or allow it.

agribusiness is the commercial side of farming, involving the production, processing, distribution, and selling of farm products.

agriculturalist An **agriculturalist** or **agriculturist** is an expert on agriculture.

agriculture (agricultural, agriculturally) Agriculture is farming. *...Europe's common agricultural policy.*

agriculturist See **agriculturalist.**

agro-chemicals (or agrochemicals) are chemicals used in farming, for example fertilizers.

agronomy (pron: ag-ron-om-mee) (agronomist) Agronomy is the study of the scientific and economic issues involved in the cultivation of land and crop production.

aground If a ship runs **aground,** it becomes stuck on rocks or a sandbank, or the bottom of a shallow river or lake.

ahead If something is **ahead,** it is in front of you. ■ If something happens or someone arrives **ahead** of something else, they happen or arrive first. ■ If you are **ahead** of someone, you are making better progress than them or beating them. *His inventiveness keeps him ahead of the field.* ■ **Ahead** is used to talk about the future. *There are difficult times ahead.* ■ **go ahead:** see **go.**

AI See **artificial insemination.**

aid (aiding, aided) Aid is money, food, equipment, or services provided for people in need. If an event is **in aid of** something like a charity, it is organized to raise money to provide things like this. ■ If you say what something is **in aid of,** you are saying what its purpose is. *This is all in aid of widening the audience for classical music.* ■ If you **aid** someone, you help them. ■ **Aid** is help or assistance. An **aid** is a device which helps you do something. *With the aid of the binoculars he could see into the room. ...children's swimming aids.* ■ If one thing **aids** another, it makes it easier or more likely to happen. *Creatine aids recovery after exertion.*

aide An **aide** is an assistant to someone with an important job, especially in the government or armed forces.

aide-de-camp (pron: aid-de-kom) (plural: aides-de-camp) An **aide-de-camp** is an officer in the armed forces who serves as a personal assistant to a senior officer.

AIDS (*or* **Aids** *or* **aids**) is a disease which destroys the body's natural system of protection against other diseases. AIDS stands for 'acquired immune deficiency syndrome'.

ail (**ailing, ailed**) An **ailing** person is ill. If you ask what **ails** someone, you are asking what their illness is. ■ If something is **ailing,** it is having serious problems. *...an ailing marriage.*

ailment An **ailment** is an illness.

aim (**aiming, aimed**) If you **aim** a gun at someone, you point it towards them, intending to fire it. Your **aim** is your skill at hitting a target with a gun. ■ If you **aim** an object or a punch at someone, you try to hit them by throwing the object or punching them. ■ If an action or remark is **aimed** at particular people, they are the ones it is intended to affect. *The army operation is not aimed against the civilian population... Some of the cruel comments aimed at me.* ■ If you **aim** at something, you try to achieve it. *He is aiming at a compromise.* You can also say an action or policy is **aimed** at achieving something. Your **aim** is what you are trying to achieve.

aimless (**aimlessly**) You say a person or activity is **aimless** when they have no clear purpose or plan. *These meetings seem an aimless shambles.*

air (**airing, aired**) **Air** is the mixture of gases which forms the earth's atmosphere and which we breathe. ■ Things that happen in the **air** happen in the space above the ground. *...an air crash.* ■ If you **air** something, you let fresh air get into it or around it. ■ If someone **airs** their feelings or a subject, they discuss them publicly. ■ When a TV or radio programme is **aired** or goes **on air,** it is broadcast. ■ If you say someone or something has a particular **air,** you are describing the general impression they give. *The capital has taken on the air of a city at war.* ■ If you do something to **clear the air,** you try to sort out misunderstandings and get rid of resentment. ■ If someone puts on **airs,** they behave in an exaggerated unnatural way, intended to impress people. ■ An **air** is a simple tune.

airbag An **airbag** is a safety device in a car which inflates automatically in a crash to protect the driver or passenger when they are thrown forward.

air base (*or* **airbase**) An **air base** is a place where military aircraft are stationed.

airborne is used to describe (a) people or things being transported by plane. *...airborne troops.* (b) things carried by the wind. *...airborne bacteria.*

air brakes are brakes operated by compressed air, typically used on larger vehicles like buses.

airbrick An **airbrick** is a brick with holes in it, put into the wall of a building for ventilation.

airbrush (**airbrushes, airbrushing, airbrushed**) An **airbrush** is a tool which uses compressed air to spray paint onto a surface. If a photograph is **airbrushed,** it is altered using an airbrush. Alterations made in this way are difficult to detect.

air commodore An **air commodore** is a high-ranking officer in the RAF.

air-conditioned (**air-conditioner, air-conditioning**) If a building or vehicle is **air-conditioned,** it has a machine in it called an **air-conditioner** which keeps the air inside cool and dry. This method of regulating temperature is called **air-conditioning.**

aircraft (*plural:* **aircraft**) An **aircraft** is any vehicle which can fly, for example a plane or helicopter.

aircraft carrier An **aircraft carrier** is a warship which can carry several planes and has a deck for them to land and take off.

aircraftsman (**aircraftswoman**) **Aircraftsman** or **aircraftswoman** is the lowest rank in the RAF.

aircrew The **aircrew** on a plane are the pilot and the other people on board who help to fly it or look after passengers.

airfield An **airfield** is an area of land where aircraft land and take off.

airflow The **airflow** in something like a wind tunnel is the movement of air in it.

air force (*or* **airforce**) A country's **air force** is the part of its armed forces which is involved in making attacks from the air and fighting air battles.

airframe A plane's **airframe** is its body and wings, not including the engines.

airgun (*or* **air gun**) An **airgun** is a pistol or rifle which fires pellets or darts by means of compressed air.

air hostess The women who look after the passengers on a plane used to be called **air hostesses.** They are now called in-flight attendants.

airily See **airy.**

airing cupboard An **airing cupboard** is a warm cupboard, especially one with a water heater in it, where you put things like clothes, sheets, and towels after they have been washed and partly dried, to get them completely dry.

airless If a place is **airless,** no fresh air gets into it.

airlift If people or goods are **airlifted,** they are moved by air, especially during wartime or when land routes are closed. An operation like this is called an **airlift.**

airline An **airline** is an organization which provides regular plane services carrying people or goods.

airliner An **airliner** is a large passenger plane.

airlock An **airlock** is a compartment between places which do not have the same air pressure, for example in a spacecraft. Airlocks are used to prevent the air pressure in one place changing when someone enters from the other place. ■ An **airlock** is a blockage in a pipe caused by a bubble of air.

airmail is the system of sending mail by air.

airman (**airmen**) An **airman** is a man who serves in his country's air force.

airplane In the US, aeroplanes are sometimes called **airplanes.**

airport An **airport** is a place where aircraft land and take off, and which has facilities for passengers.

airpower is the military power exerted by a country's air force. *The no-fly zone is being enforced by Nato airpower.*

air raid An **air raid** is an attack by military aircraft on a ground target using bombs.

air rifle An **air rifle** is a rifle which fires pellets by means of compressed air.

air-sea rescue is the use of aircraft and boats to rescue people in danger of drowning in the sea.

airship An **airship** is a powered aircraft which is held up in the air by a large gas-filled balloon. Passengers sit in a compartment underneath the balloon.

air show (or **airshow**) An **air show** is an event in which aircraft perform stunts to entertain spectators.

airspace A country's **airspace** is the sky above it, which is considered to belong to it.

airstream An **airstream** is a current of moving air.

air strike An **air strike** is the same as an air raid.

airstrip An **airstrip** is a stretch of land which has been cleared so planes can land and take off.

air terminal An **air terminal** is a building in a city from which passengers are taken by road or rail to an airport.

airtight If a container is **airtight,** no air can get into it or out of it.

air time is broadcasting time on TV or radio.

air-to-air missiles are fired by one aircraft at another.

air traffic control (air traffic controller) Air traffic **control** is the activity of organizing air flights from the ground. It includes constantly checking the position of aircraft, and giving instructions to pilots. The people who do this work are called **air traffic controllers.**

airwaves If something is sent out over the **airwaves,** it is broadcast on TV or radio.

airway An **airway** is a route for aircraft between major cities, mapped out to prevent collisions. ■ Your **airway** is the passage which connects your mouth and nose to your lungs, through which air enters and leaves your body.

airworthy If an aircraft is **airworthy,** it is safe to fly.

airy (airily) An **airy** room is large and has plenty of fresh air. ■ **Airy** is used to describe a light-hearted or casual response to something which ought to be taken seriously. *The Government is airily dismissing the complaints.*

airy-fairy ideas are vague and inappropriate in the real world.

aisle (rhymes with 'mile') An **aisle** is a narrow gap separating blocks of seats or rows of shelves.

ajar If a door is **ajar,** it is slightly open.

aka (pronounce each letter separately) is used when mentioning someone's false or alternative name. It stands for 'also known as'. *...Muhammad Ali (aka Cassius Clay).*

akimbo If you stand **arms akimbo,** you stand with you hands on your hips.

akin If something is **akin** to something else, it is similar to it. *English club sides tend to regard playing Australia as somewhat akin to being attacked by an angry boar.*

à la in front of a name means 'in the style of'. *...the wind rustling her dress à la Marilyn Monroe.*

alabaster is a white stone used to make statues, vases, and other ornaments.

à la carte If you eat **à la carte** in a restaurant, you choose individual dishes from the menu, rather than paying a fixed price for a complete meal.

alacrity If you do something with **alacrity,** you do it quickly and eagerly. *He made and spent money with alacrity.*

alarm (alarming, alarmingly) If something **alarms** people, it makes them worried or anxious. You say something like this is **alarming;** the feeling it gives people is called **alarm.** *...the alarming increase in crime. ...the alarmingly high rate of heart disease... Israel has watched these developments with alarm.* ■ An **alarm** is an automatic device which warns you of something, usually by making a loud noise. ■ If you **sound the alarm** or **raise the alarm,** you warn people about something. ■ If something **sets the alarm bells ringing,** people recognize it as a sign of trouble.

alarm clock An **alarm clock** is a clock you can set to wake you up at a particular time by making a noise.

alarmist If you accuse someone of being **alarmist** or an **alarmist,** you mean they are causing unnecessary worry. *...alarmist talk of a slump.*

alas is used to express regret or sadness. *Belize is beautiful but, alas, also extremely expensive.*

albatross (albatrosses) The **albatross** is a very large sea bird with a hooked beak and long narrow wings. ■ You can say something is an **albatross** when it is a burden and causes serious problems. *...an albatross round the government's neck.*

albeit You use **albeit** when you are adding a comment which takes something away from what you have just said. *Their dream turned into a success story, albeit on a smaller scale than they expected.*

albino (albinos) An **albino** is a person or animal with very white skin, white hair, and pink eyes, caused by lack of pigment.

album An **album** is (a) a book for putting photographs or stamps in. (b) a record with approximately 25 minutes of music on each side.

albumen is (a) another name for egg white. (b) another name for albumin.

albumin is a protein in substances like blood plasma and egg white.

alchemy (pron: al-kem-ee) (alchemist) In the Middle Ages, **alchemy** was a combination of chemistry and magic by which people called **alchemists** tried to discover how to change ordinary metals into gold. ■ Nowadays, people use **alchemy** to talk about things being achieved by secret and mysterious means.

alcohol is drinks like beer, wine, and whisky which can make people drunk. ■ **Alcohol** is the chemical made by fermenting sugars which can make people drunk.

alcoholic (alcoholism) An **alcoholic** is someone who is addicted to alcohol. This addiction is called **alcoholism.** ■ **Alcoholic** drinks such as beer, wine, and whisky can make people drunk.

alcopop An **alcopop** is an alcoholic drink that tastes like a soft drink.

alcove An **alcove** is a small area of a room where part of a wall has been built farther back than the rest.

alder The **alder** is a small tree with toothed rounded leaves, woody cones, and catkins.

ale is an alcoholic drink similar to beer except that it is not flavoured with hops. ■ **Ale** is another word for beer.

alert (**alertness**) If you are **alert,** you are paying full attention to what is happening and are ready to deal with it. *A doctor's alertness saved her son.* ■ If you are **alert** to something, you are fully aware of it or quick to notice it. *The public is alert to environmental abuse.* ■ If something **alerts** you to something, it draws your attention to it. *Users are alerted to an incoming message by a flashing light.* ■ If you **alert** someone, you warn them of danger or trouble. ■ If people are **on the alert,** they have been warned of a danger and are ready to deal with it. *Coastal districts are on the alert in case the oil comes ashore.* If people are **on red alert,** they are ready to deal with a serious situation which is likely to happen at any moment. *The government has put security forces on red alert, fearing sabotage by militants.*

A-Level — **A-levels** are educational qualifications. English, Welsh, and Northern Irish teenagers usually sit **A-level** exams when they are 18. 'A-level' stands for 'Advanced Level'.

alfalfa or **lucerne** is a green plant grown to feed farm animals.

alfresco meals or other activities take place in the open air.

algae are plants, such as seaweed, without stems or leaves which grow in water or on damp surfaces.

algebra (**algebraic**) **Algebra** is a branch of maths in which letters are used to represent unknown amounts. **Algebraic** means to do with algebra. *...an algebraic formula.*

algorithm An **algorithm** is a series of mathematical procedures which lead to the solution of a problem.

alia See **inter alia.**

alias (**aliases**) An **alias** is a false or alternative name. *...funds held by an individual with several aliases.* **Alias** is used when mentioning someone's false or alternative name. *...David Taylor, alias the Silver Fox.*

alibi (*pron:* **al**-i-bye) (**alibis**) If you have an **alibi,** you can prove you were somewhere else when a crime was committed.

alien If something is **alien** to you, you have never experienced it before and are not familiar with it. *A stock market was an alien concept in the Soviet Union.* ■ An **alien** is someone who is not a legal citizen of the country in which they are living. ■ In science fiction, an **alien** is a creature from another planet.

alienate (**alienating, alienated; alienation**) If you **alienate** someone, you make them unfriendly or unsympathetic towards you. *Potential supporters may be alienated by headline-grabbing tactics.* ■ If you are **alienated** from something, it seems strange or hostile and you feel emotionally separated from it. *Young people in Britain feel alienated from adult society.*

alight If something is **alight,** it is on fire. ■ When you **alight** from a bus, train, or plane, you get out of it at the end of a journey.

align (**alignment**) If you are **aligned** with a group of people, you support them and have similar aims. *He firmly aligned himself with the government of Lebanon... India continued to profess non-alignment.* ■ If you **align** one thing with something else, you make it agree with it or conform to it. *We must aim to keep managers' behaviour aligned with shareholders' interests.* ■ If countries **align** their economies or currencies, they try to keep the value of their currencies as stable as possible in relation to each others'. ■ You say two objects are **aligned** when they are in the position you want in relation to each other. *They will cease drilling to allow for any readjustment in the alignment of the two tunnel-boring machines.*

alike If people or things are **alike** in some way, they are similar. ■ If people are treated **alike,** they are treated the same way. ■ **Alike** is used to emphasize that something applies equally to two people, things, or groups. *...a world trade war affecting rich and poor countries alike.*

alimentary canal Your **alimentary canal** is the passage in your body through which food travels from your mouth to your anus.

alimony is an American term for maintenance, the money a court decides someone must pay to their former wife or husband after they have been separated or divorced.

alive If a person or animal is **alive,** they are not dead. ■ If you say something is still **alive,** you mean it is still functioning or existing. *The big companies are trying to stay alive by cutting cost... Tribal politics is still alive.* If you say something is **alive and kicking** or **alive and well,** you are emphasizing that it still exists and is thriving. ■ If you say a place is **alive** with people or animals, you are emphasizing that it is full of them and they are very active. *The reef is alive with fish.* You can also say a place is **alive** with activity or noise. *Budapest was alive with demonstrations.* ■ You can say a place is **alive** with stories, when you are emphasizing that a lot of them are being passed. *Westminster was alive with rumours.* ■ If an event or performance **comes alive,** it suddenly gets lively and interesting. You can also say a subject **comes alive** when something makes it more interesting for you. ■ If you are **alive** to something, you are aware of it. *The Bank of England should have been alive to the legal risks.*

alkali (**alkaline**) **Alkalis** are a group of substances with a pH value of more than 7. When they are combined with acids, they form chemical salts. An **alkaline** substance either is an alkali or contains one.

all and **all of** are used to show you are talking about the whole of something or every one of a group of people or things. *They are calling on all their staff to ignore the strike call... All of the building is above ground level.* ■ **All** is used to mean 'the only thing'. *All that is missing from the show is a self-portrait.* ■ In some sports, **all** is used to say two competitors have an equal score. *The overall score is tied at six games all.* ■ **All** is used to emphasize that something is completely true or applies in every case. *I ran and left her all alone... I forgot all about it... It's the same all over India.* ■ If you say that something is, for example, **all** the better for something, you mean it is better because of it. ■ **After all** means 'in spite of what was expected.' *I came out here on the chance of finding you at home after all.* ■ **After all** is used to mention a well-known fact which supports what you have been saying. *Animal physiology is after all significantly different from our own.* ■ **At all** is used in sentences with 'not' in them, for emphasis. *A lot of the girls didn't play tennis at all before they came.* ■ If you say that something is **not all that** good or bad, you mean it is not as good or bad as might be expected. *It wasn't all that wonderful living in a thatched house.* ■ You say **all in all** when you are summarizing a situation. *All in all, this was a surprisingly mild response.* ■ If something is done **once and for all,** it is done in such a way that it will not need to be done again.

Allah is the Muslim name for God.

allay If you **allay** someone's fears or doubts, you do or say something to stop them worrying.

all-clear The **all-clear** is a signal that some danger is over. ■ If you are given the **all-clear** to do something, you are given official permission to do it.

all-comers If someone competes against **all-comers,** they compete against anyone who is willing to face them.

allege (**alleging, alleged; allegedly, allegation**) If you **allege** that someone has done something wrong, you claim they have done it, although you cannot prove it. *...officers removed from power because of alleged corruption. ...allegations of brutality.*

allegiance If you swear **allegiance** to someone or something, you swear to be loyal to them and support them. ■ If you talk about a person's political **allegiance,** you mean the political group they support.

allegory (**allegories; allegorical**) An **allegory** is a story or painting in which characters and events are symbols of something else. You say a story or painting like this is **allegorical.**

allergic (**allergy, allergies; allergen**) If you are **allergic** (*pron:* al-**ler**-jik) to something or have an **allergy** (*pron:* **al**-ler-jee) to it, you become ill or get a rash when you eat it, touch it, or breathe it in. A substance people can be allergic to is called an **allergen** (*pron:* **al**-ler-jen).

alleviate (**alleviating, alleviated; alleviation**) If you **alleviate** an unpleasant situation, you make it less severe. *...the alleviation of poverty.*

alley An **alley** or **alleyway** is a narrow street between two groups of buildings. See also **blind alley.**

alliance An **alliance** is a group of countries or organizations which have formally agreed to work together to achieve the same aims. Countries or organizations like these are **in alliance.**

alligator – **Alligators** are large meat-eating reptiles with long bodies and tails. They live in rivers in China and the south-eastern US.

all-in is used to say a price covers everything. *Weekend courses start from £56 all-in.*

alliteration (**alliterative**) **Alliteration** or **alliterative** speech or writing uses several words together

which begin with the same sound, as in 'Full fathom five thy father lies'.

allocate (**allocating, allocated; allocation**) If something is **allocated** to you, it is decided you shall have it. Similarly, something can be **allocated** for a particular purpose. *...the allocation of tickets.*

allot (**allotting, allotted**) If something is **allotted** to you, it is decided you shall have it as your share.

allotment – **Allotments** are small areas of land which people rent to grow vegetables on. ■ An **allotment** of something is an amount given to someone as their share.

all-out is used to say people use all their efforts to achieve something. *...an all-out attack.*

allow If you are **allowed** to do something, you are given permission to do it, or are not prevented from doing it. *They were allowed to smoke.* Similarly, if you are **allowed** something, you are not prevented from having it. *They were demanding that the public be allowed unlimited access to personal files.* ■ If you **allow** something to happen, you do not prevent it. ■ If circumstances **allow** something to happen, they make it possible. *The lull in the fighting has allowed residents to leave their shelters.* ■ If you **allow for** certain problems or expenses, you take them into consideration in your plans. *Allow ten hours for the drive from Calais.*

allowable If something is **allowable,** you can have it or do it without breaking a law. ■ If something is **allowable** for tax purposes, its cost can be deducted from your income before calculating how much tax you must pay.

allowance An **allowance** is an amount of money given regularly to someone to pay for their needs. ■ Your tax **allowance** is the amount of money which is deducted from your income before calculating how much tax you must pay. ■ If you **make allowances** for something, you take it into consideration when making plans.

alloy An **alloy** is a metal made by mixing two or more metals together.

all right (*or* **alright**) If you say something is **all right,** you mean it is satisfactory or acceptable. ■ **All right** is used to emphasize that something is true. *They gave the Angolans a hard time all right.*

all-round is used to say someone or something is able to do many different things. *...an all-round family entertainer.*

all-rounder In cricket, an **all-rounder** is a player who is good at both batting and bowling.

all-time If you say something is at an **all-time** high or low, you mean it is higher or lower than it has ever been. ■ **All-time** is used to say someone is one of the best people ever at something. *...one of golf's all-time great players.*

allude (**alluding, alluded; allusion**) If you **allude** to something or make an **allusion** to it, you mention it indirectly.

allure (**alluring**) The **allure** of something is the pleasing or exciting qualities it has, which attract people to it. If something is **alluring,** it has qualities like these.

allusion See **allude.**

allusive writing or art makes indirect references to, for example, myths.

ally (**allies, allying, allied**) If you **ally** yourself with someone, you agree to help each other. When this happens, you can say you become **allies.** Similarly, countries or organizations can become **allies.** ■ If two qualities are **allied,** they are combined effectively. *He had a childlike simplicity allied to a determination to go his own way.* ■ If something is **allied** to something else, it is similar to it or related to it. *...an eating disorder allied to anorexia.*

alma mater (*usual pron:* **al**-ma **mah**-ter) Your **alma mater** is the school or university you attended.

almanac An **almanac** is a book published every year containing facts, figures, and other information about a subject. *...Wisden Cricketers' Almanac.*

almighty – **The Almighty** is another name for God. ■ **Almighty** is used in a sarcastic way to talk about very powerful things or people. *...the almighty dollar.* ■ **Almighty** is used with some words to say something is very extreme. *...an almighty row.*

almond – **Almonds** are edible, flattish oval nuts. Almond trees grow mainly in Asia and Africa.

almost means the same as 'nearly', but is not used after 'not', 'very', or 'so'.

alms are charitable gifts to poor people.

almshouse – **Almshouses** are groups of small, usually old, houses built and run by charities for local poor or old people to live in.

aloe – **Aloes** are plants used in some medicines and cosmetics.

aloft means up in the air. *He was raised aloft by his supporters.*

alone If you are **alone,** there is nobody with you. If you are **alone** with someone else, there are just the two of you. ■ You can say someone is **alone** when they live on their own and have no close relatives. ■ If you do something **alone,** you do it without help from anyone else. *She has brought up her two children alone.* When someone deals with a difficult situation without help, you can say they **go it alone.** ■ If you **leave** someone **alone,** you let them do what they want, without interfering. ■ **Alone** is used to talk about something being true of only one person or thing, or being restricted to just one person or thing. *Financial criteria alone must not be allowed to dictate policy.* ■ If you say there are a certain number of things in one place **alone,** you mean there are a lot of them just in that one place, so the total number must be very great indeed. *A million copies have been sold in the UK alone.*

along If you travel **along** something like a road, you move forward on it. *He was just walking along on his own.* ■ If things are situated **along** something like a road, they are at various places on its edges. *...the population living along the coast.* ■ **Along** is used to talk about going to a place or event with other people. *She invited everyone to come along.* ■ **Along** is used to talk about things advancing or progressing. *Trade officials see no good reason to hurry things along.* ■ **Along with** means 'together with' or 'as well as'. *ICI, along with the rest of the drugs industry, is trying to find ways to cut costs.* ■ **All along** is used to say something has been going on throughout a period of time. *I think she had been planning all along to leave Hungary.* ■ **go along with:** See **go.**

alongside If something is **alongside** something else, it is next to it. ■ If you work **alongside** other people, you work in the same place and co-operate with them. ■ **Alongside** is used to talk about things existing together. *Vocational qualifications should be introduced alongside A-levels.*

aloof (**aloofness**) If you say someone is **aloof** or talk about their **aloofness,** you mean they are not friendly or open with people. ■ If you remain **aloof** from something, you do not get involved with it.

aloud If you read or think **aloud,** you say the words so people can hear them. *Frustrated negotiators have wondered aloud whether it is worth carrying on.*

alpaca The **alpaca** is a South American animal related to the llama. **Alpaca** is the wool from this animal.

alpha is α, the first letter of the Greek alphabet.

alphabet (**alphabetical**) The **alphabet** is the letters of a language in a fixed order. Words arranged so their first letters are in this order are in **alphabetical** order.

alpine means connected with high mountains, especially the Alps. *...alpine villages. ...Alpine weather.* **Alpines** are plants from areas like these.

already is used to say something has happened earlier than expected. *He had already left.* ■ **Already** is used to emphasize that a situation has existed since before the present time. *The institute already has a chief executive.*

alright See **all right.**

Alsatian – **Alsatians** are large, usually fierce dogs which are often used as guard dogs. They are also called 'German Shepherds'.

also You use **also** when adding an extra piece of information. *We've got a table and also some stools and benches.* ■ You use **also** to say something applies to other people or things, besides the ones you have just mentioned. *The appointment will also be welcomed by the Government.*

also-ran In horse-racing, an **also-ran** is a horse not listed among the winners. ■ You call a person or thing an **also-ran** when they are far less successful than others of their kind. *Orange, once dismissed as an also-ran, is powering ahead.*

altar An **altar** is a table or raised platform used for religious purposes, especially in a Christian church. ■ If you say something has been **sacrificed on the altar of** something else, you mean it has suffered because of efforts to make the other thing succeed.

altarpiece An **altarpiece** is a painting, tapestry, or carving mounted above and behind the altar in a church.

alter (**altering, altered; alteration**) If something **alters** or is **altered,** it changes; the change is called an **alteration.**

altercation (*pron:* ol-ter-**kay**-shun) An **altercation** is a noisy argument.

alter ego Your **alter ego** is the other side of your personality from the one people usually see. ■ An actor's **alter ego** is the character he or she usually plays.

alternate (alternating, alternated; alternately, alternation) If you **alternate** (pron: **all**-ter-nate) between two things, you repeatedly use or do each in turn. *He alternated between pink and blue jackets.* You say things **alternate** when they happen in turn. *...the alternation of civilian and military governments.* **Alternate** (pron: alt-**ter**-nat) things keep happening one after another in turn. *He was pulled in alternate directions... Muscles are alternately tensed and relaxed.* ■ If something happens on **alternate** days, it happens every other day.

alternating current See **AC.**

alternative (alternatively) If something is an **alternative** to something else, it can be used or done instead of it. *Blinds are a cheap alternative to curtains... He has to sign the declaration or alternatively register a protest.* ■ **Alternative** is used to describe things which are different from what is traditional or established. *...alternative medicine.*

alternator An **alternator** is an electric generator which produces alternating current, especially in a car.

although You use **although** to mention something which contrasts with the rest of what you are saying. *He didn't complain, although he must have been in a lot of pain.*

altimeter An **altimeter** is an instrument which measures height above sea level, or above the ground.

altitude The **altitude** of something is its height above sea level.

alto (altos) An **alto** is a woman with a low singing voice. ■ An **alto** or **male alto** is a man with the highest male singing voice. ■ An **alto** musical instrument has a range of notes of medium pitch.

altogether means 'completely'. For example, if something has stopped **altogether,** it has stopped completely. ■ **Altogether** is used to emphasize that something is better or more impressive than something else. *He faces a new and altogether more daunting opponent.* ■ **Altogether** is used to show an amount is a total. *Altogether £187m is to be spent on improving old jails.*

altruism (altruistic) **Altruism** is helping other people without having any selfish motive. When someone behaves like this, you say they are being **altruistic.**

aluminium is a light silvery-white rust-resistant metal. In the US, aluminium is called **aluminum** (pron: al-**loom**-in-um).

alumnus (plural: **alumni**) An **alumnus** of a college or university is a person who has studied at it or graduated from it. A woman graduate is sometimes called an **alumna** (plural: **alumnae**).

always is used to say something is constantly happening or is true all the time. *It was always a delight to visit him.* ■ If you say someone can **always** do something, you mean that option will continue to be open to them. *If I didn't like it, I could always put it back.*

am See **be.**

AM In Wales, an **AM** is a person who has been elected to represent people in the National Assembly for Wales. AM stands for 'Assembly Member'.

a.m. is used when stating a time between midnight and noon. For example, 7 a.m. means 7 o'clock in the morning. **a.m.** stands for 'ante meridiem', which is Latin for 'before noon'.

amalgam An **amalgam** of two or more things is a mixture of them. ■ **Amalgam** is an alloy of mercury and other metals, sometimes used by dentists to make fillings.

amalgamate (amalgamating, amalgamated; amalgamation) When two or more organizations **amalgamate,** they join together as a single organization.

amanuensis (plural: **amanuenses**) (pron: am-man-yew-**en**-siss, am-man-yew-**en**-seez) An **amanuensis** is a person employed to take dictation or copy manuscripts.

amass (amasses, amassing, amassed) If you **amass** something, you gradually get more of it.

amateur (amateurism, amateurish) An **amateur** is someone who does something like acting or playing sport for pleasure and is not paid for it. Taking part in sport for pleasure rather than money is called **amateurism.** ■ **Amateur** and **amateurish** are used to describe things which are not done skilfully. *...amateurish musicianship.*

amaze (amazing, amazed; amazingly, amazement) If something **amazes** you or you are **amazed** by it, you are extremely surprised by it. ■ If you say something is **amazing,** you mean it is remarkable or impressive. *The flu virus is amazingly adaptable.*

ambassador (ambassadorial) An **ambassador** is someone who is the official representative of their own country in a foreign country. **Ambassadorial** means to do with ambassadors. *Diplomatic ties have been restored to the ambassadorial level.* ■ You can say someone is an **ambassador** for something like a sport or a cause when they act as a representative of it, or behave in a way which is good for its public image.

amber is a yellowish-brown fossilized resin. ■ **Amber** is a gold or yellowish-brown colour.

ambiance See **ambience.**

ambidextrous An **ambidextrous** person can do things equally well with either their right or left hand.

ambience (or ambiance) The **ambience** of a place is its character and atmosphere. *....a hotel with a 1940s ambience.*

ambient music is produced by computer and intended to create background atmosphere rather than be danced or listened to. ■ The **ambient** temperature of an object is the temperature of the air surrounding it.

ambiguous (ambiguously; ambiguity, ambiguities) If something is **ambiguous,** it can be understood in different ways, or could have more than one meaning. You talk about the **ambiguity** of something like this. The aspects of something which are unclear because they can be understood in different ways are called **ambiguities.** *...an ambiguously-worded statement. ...the ambiguities of contemporary Italian history.*

ambit The **ambit** of something like a law is the range of people or things it applies to.

ambition (**ambitious, ambitiously**) An **ambition** is something you want to achieve. *He fulfilled a lifelong ambition by becoming a fully qualified football referee.* ■ **Ambition** is a strong desire to be successful or powerful. You say people who have this desire are **ambitious.** ■ An **ambitious** plan is on a large scale.

ambivalent (*pron:* am-**biv**-a-lent) (**ambivalence**) If you are **ambivalent** about something, you are not sure what you think about it. This feeling of uncertainty is called **ambivalence.**

amble (**ambling, ambled**) If you **amble** somewhere, you walk there slowly, in a relaxed manner.

ambulance An **ambulance** is a vehicle for taking people to and from hospital.

ambulanceman (**ambulancewoman**) Ambulancemen and **ambulancewomen** are people who drive ambulances and take care of patients on their way to hospital.

ambush (**ambushes, ambushing, ambushed**) If you are **ambushed,** people hide and wait for you, then attack you when you come past. An attack like this is called an **ambush.**

ameba See **amoeba.**

ameliorate (*pron:* a-**meal**-yor-ate) (**ameliorating, ameliorated**) If you **ameliorate** a bad situation, you improve it.

amen is said or sung at the end of a prayer. 'Amen' is a Hebrew word meaning 'certainly'.

amenable (*pron:* a-**mean**-a-bl) If you are **amenable** to something, you are willing to do it or accept it.

amend (**amendment**) If you **amend** or make an **amendment** to something which has been written or said, you alter it. ■ If you **make amends** for harm you have caused, you do something to make up for it.

amenity (*pron:* a-**mean**-i-tee) (**amenities**) Amenities are facilities provided for people's convenience or enjoyment.

American is used to talk about (a) people and things in or from the US. (b) things to do with the continent of America. ■ An **American** is someone who comes from the US.

Americana is used to describe objects which come from or relate to America.

American Indian − American Indians are people descended from the tribes who lived in North America before Europeans arrived.

Americanise See **Americanize.**

Americanism An **Americanism** is an expression first used by Americans. 'Kick-ass' is an Americanism. *We have even ceased to call them chips, accepting the Americanism 'fries'.*

Americanize (*or* **Americanise**) (**Americanizing, Americanized; Americanization**) If a country is **Americanized,** its way of life becomes similar to that of the US.

Amerindian An **Amerindian** is the same as an American Indian.

amethyst (*pron:* **am**-myth-ist) is a purple semiprecious stone.

amiable (**amiably, amiability**) If someone is **amiable,** they are friendly and likeable. This quality is

called **amiability.** *We chatted amiably about old friends.*

amicable (**amicably**) An **amicable** agreement or relationship is free of disagreement or unpleasantness.

amid (**amidst**) If something happens **amid** or **amidst** other things, it happens while those things are happening. *This statement comes amidst growing disarray among the forces.* ■ If something is **amid** or **amidst** other things, it is surrounded by them. *The body was found amid a mass of wreckage.*

amidships is used to talk about the middle part of a ship.

amidst See **amid.**

amino acid (*pron:* am-**mean**-oh) Amino acids are molecules used by the body to make proteins. Some amino acids are produced by the body while others are obtained from food.

amir See **emir.**

amiss If you say there is something **amiss,** you mean something is wrong. ■ If you say something would **not go amiss,** you mean it would be welcome.

amity You say there is **amity** between people or countries when they have a friendly peaceful relationship.

ammeter An **ammeter** is a device for measuring electric current.

ammonia is a colourless liquid or gas with a strong sharp smell.

ammunition is bullets and missiles which can be fired from a gun. ■ You can describe information which can be used against someone as **ammunition.** *He used the better-than-expected inflation figures as ammunition against his critics.*

amnesia is loss of memory.

amnesty (**amnesties**) An **amnesty** is (a) a period during which people can confess to a crime or give themselves or their weapons up without being punished. (b) an official pardon granted to prisoners by the state.

amniocentesis is the process of extracting fluid from a woman's womb to check on the health of her baby.

amniotic fluid is the liquid surrounding a foetus in the womb.

amoeba (*Am:* ameba) (*pron:* am-**mee**-ba) (*plural:* **amoebas** *or* **amoebae**) Amoebas are microscopic animals, each consisting of a single cell. They keep changing shape, and reproduce by dividing themselves in two.

amok (*pron:* a-**muck**) If people or animals **run amok,** they behave in a violent uncontrolled way.

among (*or* **amongst**) is used to say something is one of several things. *Temporary buildings are amongst the most urgent needs for the people made homeless by the earthquake.* ■ **Among** is used to talk about several people having the same experience. *The news has caused considerable alarm amongst finance ministers.* ■ If something is divided **among** a group of people, they all get some of it. ■ If people talk or fight **among themselves,** they do it without involving anyone else.

amoral (pron: aim-**mor**-ral) (**amorality**) If you say someone is **amoral** or talk about their **amorality**, you mean they have no sense of right and wrong.

amorous is used to talk about things to do with sexual love.

amorphous If something is **amorphous,** it has no clear shape or structure.

amount An **amount** of something is a quantity of it. ■ You say numbers **amount to** a total when they add up to it. ■ **Amount to** is used to say what something really means, or what its significance is. *Such a change amounts to a social revolution.*

amour is the French word for love.

amp Electric current is measured in **amps.** 'amp' is short for 'ampère'.

ampersand An **ampersand** is the symbol **&** which means 'and'.

amphetamine (pron: am-**fet**-am-mean) **Amphetamines** are illegal drugs which make people energetic and excited. Amphetamines are sometimes called 'speed'.

amphibian – **Amphibians** are a group of animals such as frogs which breathe air as adults, but lay their eggs in water and have gills for the first part of their lives.

amphibious creatures live both in water and on land. ■ An **amphibious** vehicle can operate both in water and on land. ■ In war, an **amphibious** attack is made from the sea.

amphitheatre An **amphitheatre** is a large bowl-shaped area, used for theatrical performances. The performances take place in the centre and the audience look down from the sides.

amphora (plural: **amphoras** or **amphorae**) An **amphora** was an ancient Greek or Roman jar with a narrow neck and two handles.

ample (**amply**) **Ample** is used to say there is plenty of something. *The two Presidents will have ample time to talk to each other... The chapters are amply illustrated with superb photographs.* ■ **Ample** is used to say someone's figure is large in an attractive way. *...her ample bosom.*

amplifier An **amplifier** is an electronic device for increasing power in such things as stereo systems.

amplify (**amplifies, amplifying, amplified; amplification**) If you **amplify** a sound, you make it louder, usually by using electronic equipment. ■ You say something is **amplified** when its strength or intensity is increased. ■ If you **amplify** an idea, you explain it more fully.

amplitude The width of a radio or sound wave is called its **amplitude.**

ampoule (**Am: ampule**) An **ampoule** is a small glass container, in which a liquid for use in an injection is kept sealed so no air can get in or out.

amputate (**amputating, amputated; amputation, amputee**) If a surgeon **amputates** someone's arm or leg, he or she cuts it off in an operation, because it is diseased or badly injured. Someone who has had a limb amputated is called an **amputee.**

amulet An **amulet** is a small object worn or carried by someone who believes it will protect them from harm.

amuse (**amusing, amused; amusingly, amusement**) If something **amuses** you, it makes you want to laugh or smile. *I find this amusingly apt.* Being amused is called **amusement.** ■ If you **amuse** yourself, you find things to do which stop you getting bored. **Amusements** are things which keep people amused. ■ **Amusements** are slot machines like video games and fruit machines.

amusement arcade An **amusement arcade** is a covered area full of slot machine games for people to play on.

amusement park An **amusement park** is a large outdoor area with fairground rides, amusement arcades, and other forms of entertainment.

an See **a.**

anabolic steroid – **Anabolic steroids** are substances which speed up muscle growth and which are sometimes secretly used by sports people to improve performance.

anachronistic (pron: an-nak-kron-**niss**-tik) (**anachronism**) If you say someone or something is **anachronistic** or an **anachronism,** you mean they belong to an earlier period in history and do not fit in with the modern world. *...anachronistic theories about class struggle.*

anaemia (or **anemia**) (**anaemic**) If you have **anaemia** or are **anaemic,** you do not have enough red cells in your blood, so you look pale and feel tired. ■ If you describe something as **anaemic,** you mean it is not as strong or effective as it should be. *America's recovery from the recession was anaemic.*

anaerobic (or **anerobic**) things do not contain or use oxygen. *...anaerobic organisms.* ■ **Anaerobic** exercise can only be performed for a short period because it makes you short of breath.

anaesthesia (or **anesthesia**) (pron: an-niss-**theez**-ee-a) is the use of anaesthetics in surgery.

anaesthetic (or **anesthetic**) (pron: an-niss-**thet**-ik) An **anaesthetic** is a drug which doctors use to stop you feeling pain during an operation. See also **general anaesthetic, local anaesthetic.**

anaesthetise See **anaesthetize.**

anaesthetist (or **anesthetist**) (pron: an-**neess**-thet-ist) An **anaesthetist** is a doctor who specializes in giving anaesthetics.

anaesthetize (also **anesthetize, anaesthetise**) (pron: an-**neess**-thet-ize) (**anaesthetizing, anaesthetized**) If someone is **anaesthetized,** they are given an anaesthetic.

anagram An **anagram** is a word or phrase formed by rearranging the letters of another word or phrase. For example, 'integral' is an anagram of 'triangle'.

anal See **anus.**

analgesic (pron: an-nal-**jeez**-ik) An **analgesic** is a drug which reduces pain.

analog See **analogue.**

analogous (pron: an-**nal**-o-guss) If one thing is **analogous** to another, the two things are similar in some way.

analogue (or **analog**) If one thing is an **analogue** of another, it is similar in some way. *They see the Antarctic base as the terrestrial analogue of a space station.* ■ An **analogue** device stores, records, or reproduces electronic signals in a continuously varying form, similar to the pattern of a sound wave.

analogy (*pron:* an-**nal**-lo-jee) (**analogies**) If you make an **analogy** between two things, you show they are alike in some way.

analyse (*Am:* **analyze**) (**analysing, analysed**) If you **analyse** something, you (a) consider it carefully to understand it fully. *...analysing the causes of crime.* (b) examine it using scientific methods to find out what it consists of. *The test analyses blood samples.* ■ See also **psychoanalyse.**

analysis is (a) the process of considering something carefully to understand it or explain it. *...an analysis of the way that government money has been spent.* (b) the scientific process of examining something to find out what it consists of. *They collect blood samples for analysis.* ■ You use **in the final analysis** to emphasize a basic truth about a situation. *In the final analysis he did not have quite enough money.* ■ See also **psychoanalysis.**

analyst An **analyst** is a person whose job is to analyse a subject and give opinions about it. *...political analysts. ...City analysts.* ■ **Analyst** means the same as 'psychoanalyst'.

analytic means the same as 'analytical'.

analytical (**analytically**) **Analytical** is used to talk about people's ability to reason logically. *I learned to think analytically.* ■ **Analytical** is used to describe people and procedures involved in analyzing things. *...an analytical chemist.*

analyze See **analyse.**

anarchic (*pron:* a-**nar**-kik) behaviour shows no respect for laws, rules, or customs. *...anarchic humour.*

anarchism (*pron:* an-ar-kizm) (**anarchist, anarchistic**) **Anarchism** is the theory or belief that people should not be controlled by laws or governments, but should work together freely. *...anarchist groups. ...an anarchistic bomb plot.* **Anarchists** are people who support this view. ■ If you describe someone as **anarchistic,** you mean they pay no attention to rules or laws that everyone else obeys. *...anarchistic bike gangs.*

anarchy (*pron:* an-ark-ee) is a situation where nobody is in control, and there is general disorder and violence.

anathema (*pron:* an-**nath**-im-a) If something is **anathema** to you, you dislike it strongly.

anatomy (**anatomies; anatomical, anatomically; anatomist**) **Anatomy** is the study of the structure of human or animal bodies. *...anatomical features.* An **anatomist** is an expert on anatomy. ■ A person's body can be referred to as their **anatomy.** *...the more sensitive portion of his anatomy.* ■ The **anatomy** of something is a detailed analysis of it. *...the anatomy of the English class system.*

ancestor Your **ancestors** are the people you are descended from. ■ An **ancestor** of something modern is an earlier thing which it has developed from. *The immediate ancestor of rock 'n' roll is rhythm-and-blues.*

ancestral is used to describe things which have belonged to or have been associated with a family for many generations. *...the Duke's ancestral home.*

ancestry A person's **ancestry** is the people they are descended from. *Northrop traced his ancestry back to 1638. ...Americans of Japanese ancestry.*

anchor (**anchoring, anchored; anchorman, anchorwoman**) An **anchor** is a heavy hooked object attached to a long chain, which is dropped from a ship to stop it moving. You say the ship is **anchored** or has **dropped anchor.** When the anchor is pulled out of the water, you say the ship **weighs anchor.** ■ Anything used to keep something stable can be called an **anchor.** You say one thing is **anchored** to another. *Italy saw the Community as an anchor in democracy... The tendon is no longer anchored to the bone.* ■ If one thing is **anchored** in another, it is firmly linked with it. *His basic outlook remains anchored in the liberal tradition.* ■ When someone **anchors** a TV or radio programme, especially a news programme, they present the programme and act as a link between interviews and reports from other places or studios. The person who does this is called an **anchorman** or **anchorwoman.** ■ In a relay race, the person who **anchors** a team is the one who runs the final leg.

anchorage An **anchorage** is a place where ships can anchor.

anchovy (*pron:* an-chov-ee) (**anchovies**) Anchovies are very small fish with a strong salty taste.

ancien régime (*pron:* ons-yan ray-**zheem;** *the 'zh' sounds like 's' in 'pleasure'*) The **ancien régime** was the political and social system in France before the Revolution. Nowadays, people use this term to talk about other systems which are old and outdated.

ancient things existed a long time ago, or have been around for a very long time. ■ People who lived a long time ago, for example the Greeks and the Celts, are sometimes called **the ancients.** ■ **Ancient history** is the study of civilizations which existed from earliest times until the collapse of the Western Roman Empire in A.D. 476. ■ If you call something **ancient history,** you mean it is outdated and no longer relevant.

ancillary (**ancillaries**) The **ancillary** workers in an institution are people such as cleaners and cooks whose work supports the main work of the institution. ■ **Ancillaries** or **ancillary** items are additional things not used for something's main purpose.

and is used to link words or groups of words. *...fish and chips... He asked me out for a drink and I went. ...and so on and so forth.*

androgynous (*pron:* an-**droj**-in-us) (**androgyny**) **Androgynous** is used to describe people, animals, and plants with characteristics of both sexes. ■ If you say someone or something is **androgynous** or talk about their **androgyny,** you mean they are not distinctly masculine or feminine. *...androgynous clothes.*

android In science fiction, an **android** is a man-made creature which is part robot, part human.

anecdote (**anecdotal**) An **anecdote** is a short amusing account of something which has happened. **Anecdotal** speech or writing is full of anecdotes. ■ **Anecdotal** evidence is based on individual accounts, rather than on reliable research or statistics, and so may not be valid.

anemia (anemic) See **anaemia.**

anemone (*pron:* an-**nem**-on-ee) **Anemones** are garden plants with red, purple, or white flowers.

anerobic See **anaerobic.**

anesthesia See **anaesthesia.**

anesthetic See **anaesthetic.**

aneurysm (*pron:* **an**-yer-iz-um) An **aneurysm** is a blood-filled sac caused by the swelling of a weakened blood-vessel wall.

anew If something happens **anew,** it happens again. *The war has flared up anew.*

angel (angelic) **Angels** are spiritual beings some people believe are God's messengers and servants in heaven. **Angelic** means like angels or connected with angels. *...angelic messengers.* ■ If you say someone is an **angel,** you mean they have been kind or helpful. ■ You describe someone as **angelic** when they are, or pretend to be, morally good. *As always when evading a question, he treats me to his most angelic smile.*

angelica is a sweet-scented herb, used in crystallized form for decorating cakes.

anger (angering, angered) **Anger** is the strong emotion you feel when you think someone has behaved badly or stupidly, and you feel like expressing your feelings forcefully or violently. When someone or something **angers** you, they make you feel like this.

angina (*pron:* an-**jine**-a) is pain in the chest and left arm, usually caused by heart disease.

angle (angling, angled; angler) An **angle** is the difference in direction between two lines. ■ If something is **angled** or **at an angle,** it is not straight, horizontal, or vertical. ■ If you look at something from an **angle,** you are not directly in front of it when you look at it. Similarly you can aim at something from an **angle.** ■ If you consider something from a particular **angle,** you look at it from that point of view. ■ **Angling** is fishing with a rod as a hobby. A person who does this is called an **angler.** ■ If someone is **angling** for something, they are trying to get people to offer it to them without having to ask for it.

Anglican (Anglicanism) An **Anglican** is a member of one of the churches belonging to the Anglican Communion, a group of Protestant churches which includes the Church of England, the Church of Ireland, the Scottish Episcopal Church, and the Church in Wales.

anglicize (*or* anglicise) (anglicizing, anglicized) If something is **anglicized,** it is adapted to make it seem English or to fit in with English custom and practice.

angling See **angle.**

Anglo- is added to other nationality words to describe something which involves England or Britain and another country. *...Anglo-Iranian relations.*

Anglophile (*pron:* ang-glo-file) (Anglophilia) An **Anglophile** is someone from another country who admires England or the English. This admiration is called **Anglophilia** (*pron:* ang-glo-**fill**-ee-a).

Anglophobe An **Anglophobe** is someone from another country who dislikes England or the English.

Anglophone communities are English-speaking communities in areas where more than one language is commonly spoken.

Anglo-Saxon The **Anglo-Saxons** were the people from Germanic tribes who settled in Britain from the 5th century A.D. ■ **Anglo-Saxon** is used to describe English-speaking people descended from white British people.

angora An **angora** is a breed of rabbit with long silky hair. **Angora** is soft yarn made from this hair. Some long-haired breeds of goats and cats are also called **angoras.**

angry (angrier, angriest; angrily) If you are **angry,** you think someone has behaved in a bad or stupid way, and you feel like expressing your feelings about it forcefully or violently.

angst is a feeling of anxiety, especially one about the general state of things rather than anything specific.

angstrom An **angstrom** is a very small measurement, equal to one ten-millionth of a millimetre. The wavelengths of electromagnetic radiation are measured in angstroms. 'Angstroms' is usually written 'A' or 'Å'.

anguish (anguished) **Anguish** is being extremely upset about something. **Anguished** is used to describe people who are in this state, and their behaviour. *...anguished protests.*

angular If something is **angular,** its shape has a lot of straight lines or sharp points. ■ An **angular** person is thin and bony.

animal In science, an **animal** is any living creature which is not a plant. However, when people talk about **animals,** they usually mean non-human mammals like dogs, horses, and mice, rather than people, insects, or birds. ■ **Animal** is used to describe people's behaviour when it is related to their physical needs, rather than to rational thought. *...man's animal instincts.* ■ You can describe a person's interests by calling them a particular kind of **animal.** *I've always been a political animal.*

animate (animating, animated; animatedly, animation, animator) **Animate** is used to describe things which are alive, in contrast to things like stones or machines which are not. ■ If something **animates** people, it gets them to show interest or excitement. *My companion was talking animatedly to his girlfriend.* ■ An **animated** film is one in which puppets or drawings appear to move. Making films like this is called **animation;** a person who does it is called an **animator.**

animism (animist, animistic) **Animism** is any religion based on the idea that things, especially animals, trees, or rivers, have spirits. **Animist** and **animistic** are used to describe people who believe in animism, and beliefs and practices which conform to the ideas of animism. *...animist tribesmen. ...the old animistic world view.*

animosity (animosities) **Animosity** is a strong feeling of dislike and hostility. *...ethnic animosities.*

animus An **animus** is a feeling of strong dislike. *Francis had something of an animus against Veronica.*

aniseed is a flavouring made from the seeds of the anise plant. It tastes of liquorice, and is used in sweets, drinks, and medicines.

ankle Your **ankle** is the joint where your foot meets your leg.

anklet An **anklet** is an ornamental chain worn around the ankle.

annals If you say something will be written in the **annals** of a subject or activity, you mean it will always be remembered by people interested in that subject or activity. ...*an occasion writ large in the annals of world rugby.*

annex (annexes, annexing, annexed; annexation) If a country **annexes** another country or area of land, it takes control of it. ■ See annexe.

annexe (*Am:* annex) An **annexe** is a building joined to or next to a larger main building.

annihilate (*pron:* an-nye-ill-ate) (annihilating, annihilated; annihilation) If a group of people are **annihilated,** they are all killed. ■ In a contest, if one person or group **annihilates** another, they beat them easily.

anniversary (anniversaries) An **anniversary** is a date which is remembered or celebrated because something special happened on that date in a previous year.

annotate (annotating, annotated; annotation) If a piece of writing is **annotated,** it has explanatory notes called **annotations** added to it.

announce (announcing, announced; announcement) If you **announce** something, you tell people about it publicly or officially.

announcer An **announcer** is a person on TV or radio who announces the programmes or gives information about them.

annoy (annoying, annoyed; annoyingly, annoyance) If someone or something **annoys** you, they make you angry and impatient. This feeling is called **annoyance.** *Alex looked annoyingly cheerful.* ■ **Annoyances** are minor things which annoy you.

annual (annually) **Annual** is used to describe things which happen every year. *The prize is awarded annually.* ■ **Annual** is used to talk about amounts received or spent each year. *Thirty billion dollars are spent annually on health research.* ■ An **annual** is (a) a book or magazine published every year. (b) a plant with a life cycle of one year.

annuity (annuities) An **annuity** is a sum of money paid to someone every year from an investment or insurance policy.

annul (annulling, annulled; annulment) If a marriage or contract is **annulled,** it is declared invalid, so that legally it never existed.

annum See per annum.

anode In an electric cell, the **anode** is the positive electrode. See also **cathode.**

anodyne is used to describe things which are neutral or bland. ...*anodyne love songs.*

anoint If someone is **anointed** in a religious ceremony, they have holy oils poured on them. ■ You can describe someone as **anointed** when they have been chosen to do an important job. *Anthony Eden was Churchill's anointed successor as prime minister.*

anomalous (anomaly, anomalies) If you say something is **anomalous** you mean it does not fit in, or does not conform to what is usual. ...*to reduce anomalies in the tax systems.*

anomie (*pron:* an-oh-mee) is a lack of conviction, purpose, or moral standards.

anon. means 'anonymous'.

anonymous (anonymously, anonymity) When doing something, if you remain **anonymous,** you do not let people know you are the person doing it. *Total anonymity and confidentiality is assured.* ■ If a way of doing things is **anonymous,** it does not involve people meeting each other. ...*the anonymity of the phone.* ■ If you say someone or something is **anonymous,** you mean there is nothing distinctive about them. ...*anonymous men in business suits...* ■ **Anonymous** is used in the names of organizations which help people with personal problems without asking about their identities. ...*Alcoholics Anonymous.*

anorak An **anorak** is a waterproof jacket, usually with a hood. ■ If you call someone an **anorak** you mean they are very interested in a hobby that other people find boring, and usually they are not very good at making friends.

anorexia (anorexic) **Anorexia** or anorexia nervosa is an illness in which a person dreads getting fat, so refuses to eat, making themselves thin and ill. You say someone suffering from this illness is **anorexic** or an **anorexic.** See also **bulimia.**

another means (a) in addition to the people or things you have just mentioned. *The prison has room for another 820 prisoners.* (b) different to the person or thing you have just mentioned. *He referred her to another therapist.* ■ You use **one another** to indicate that each member of a group does something to or for the other. *Charities have to compete with one another for donations.* ■ **One after another** is used to say that several things are repeated in a sequence. *One country after another ditched Communism.*

answer (answering, answered) If you **answer** someone, or **answer** a question or appeal, you respond to it in the appropriate way. ■ An **answer** to a problem is a possible solution to it. ■ When you **answer** the phone, you pick it up when it rings. When you **answer** the door, you open it when someone knocks or rings the bell. ■ If you **answer** a criticism or accusation against you, you say or write something in your defence. ■ If someone has to **answer for** something, they have to explain it or accept punishment for it, because they are responsible for it.

answerable If you are **answerable** to someone, you have to report to them and explain the things you do. ■ If you are **answerable** for certain actions, you are held responsible for them.

answering machine An **answering machine** or **answerphone** is a device you connect to your telephone to record messages from people who phone when you are out.

ant – **Ants** are small insects which live in large colonies.

antacid An **antacid** is a substance used to treat stomach acidity.

antagonise See antagonize.

antagonism See antagonistic.

antagonist In a fight or game, your **antagonist** is your opponent. ■ An **antagonist** is a drug which counteracts the effects of other drugs or of substances produced in excess by the body.

antagonistic (antagonism) If people are **antagonistic,** they are hostile and suspicious. ■ If you are **antagonistic** to something, you are hostile to it.

antagonize (or **antagonise**) (antagonizing, antagonized) If you **antagonize** someone, you make them angry.

anteater The anteater is a South American animal with a long snout and a long sticky tongue which it uses to catch ants and termites.

antecedent Your antecedents are your ancestors. ■ An **antecedent** of something is a similar thing which happened or existed previously, and from which it developed. *The Scottish law system traces its antecedents back to the judicial codes of ancient Rome.*

antechamber An antechamber is the same as an ante-room.

antediluvian (pron: an-ti-dil-**loo**-vee-ann) is used to describe things which are extremely old or old-fashioned. *...the country's antediluvian attitude to women.*

antelope (plural: antelopes or antelope) The ante-lope is a deer-like animal with long legs and horns. Antelopes live in Africa and Asia.

antenatal (or ante-natal) care is given to pregnant women and their unborn children.

antenna (plural: antennae or antennas) The antennae of an insect are the two long thin parts attached to its head which it feels things with. ■ An antenna is an aerial.

anterior is a medical term used to describe the front parts of things. *...the anterior margin of the limb.*

ante-room (or anteroom) An ante-room is a small waiting room adjoining a larger room.

anthem An anthem is (a) a song written or chosen to represent a country or organization. (b) a sacred choral work, sung as part of a church service. ■ A powerful and popular piece of rock music is sometimes called a **rock anthem.** *...'Smoke on the water' by Deep Purple – a classic hard rock anthem.*

anthology (anthologies; anthologist) An anthology is a collection of writings by different authors, published in one book. A person who compiles an anthology is called an **anthologist.**

anthracite is a type of high-quality coal which burns slowly, giving off a lot of heat.

anthrax is a serious, highly infectious disease which is most common in cattle, but can be caught by humans.

anthropology (anthropologist, anthropological) Anthropology is the study of the human race, its social systems and cultures. *...anthropological research.*

anthropomorphism (anthropomorphic) Anthropomorphism is the idea that animals or non-living objects have human thoughts and feelings.

anti- is added to words to form words used to talk about (a) people's opposition to something. *...anti-abortion protesters.* (b) things intended to

prevent other things. *...anti-theft devices.* See also **Antichrist, anticlockwise, antifreeze, antihistamine, antimatter, antisemitism, antisocial.**

anti-aircraft weapons are designed to destroy enemy aircraft.

antibiotic – Antibiotics are medicines that kill bacteria and fight infections.

antibody (antibodies) Antibodies are proteins produced in the blood, which destroy harmful bacteria.

Antichrist (or anti-Christ) The Antichrist is the enemy of Christ, who some Christians believe will rule the world before being overthrown when Christ returns.

anticipate (anticipating, anticipated; anticipation) If you anticipate something, you foresee it happening. *We do not anticipate too much trouble.* ■ You say someone **anticipates** something when they produce something of a similar kind before it. *His organisation anticipated the Charter by several years.* ■ You say you **anticipate** something when you look forward to it with pleasure and excitement. Looking forward to something is called **anticipation.**

anticlimax (anticlimaxes) If something is an **anticlimax,** it is disappointing because it is not as exciting as you had expected.

anticlockwise (or anti-clockwise) If something moves in an **anticlockwise** direction, it moves in the opposite direction to the hands of a clock.

antics Someone's antics are the funny, silly, or unusual things they do.

anticyclone An anticyclone is an area of high atmospheric pressure, bringing fine, settled weather conditions.

antidote An antidote is a chemical substance which counteracts the effect of a poison. ■ An **antidote** to a problem is something which solves it or makes it less severe. ■ An **antidote** to something such as an activity, is a different thing, which makes a pleasant change. *For me, television is the perfect antidote to writing.*

antifreeze (or anti-freeze) is a liquid you put in the radiator of a car to stop it freezing in winter.

antigen (pron: an-tee-jen) An antigen is anything harmful which causes your body to produce antibodies when it enters your body.

anti-hero The main male character of a play or novel is called its **anti-hero** when he is the opposite of what is traditionally expected of a hero.

antihistamine (or anti-histamine) Antihistamines are medicines used to treat allergies such as hay fever.

antimacassar An antimacassar is a decorative cloth for protecting the back of a chair.

antimatter (or anti-matter) is a form of matter which has properties opposite to those of ordinary matter.

antipathy (pron: an-**tip**-a-thee) (antipathetic) Antipathy is a feeling of strong dislike towards a person or thing.

antiperspirant (pron: an-tee-**pers**-per-ant) An antiperspirant is a substance you put on your skin to reduce sweating.

Antipodes (*pron:* an-**tip**-oh-deez) Australia and New Zealand are sometimes called the **Antipodes.**

antiquarian is used to talk about old and rare things. *...antiquarian books.*

antiquary (**antiquaries**) An **antiquary** is a person who collects, deals in, or is an expert on antiquities.

antiquated things are old and out-of-date.

antique — Antiques are old objects which are valuable because of their beauty or rarity.

antiquity (**antiquities**) **Antiquity** is used to talk about the distant past, especially the ancient Egyptian, Greek, and Roman periods. ■ **Antiquities** are objects from earlier times, for example statues or coins.

anti-Semitism (*or* **antisemitism**) (anti-Semitic, anti-Semite) **Anti-Semitism** is racism directed against Jewish people. People with racist beliefs of this kind are called **anti-Semites.** You say their beliefs and behaviour are **anti-Semitic.**

antiseptic An **antiseptic** is a substance which kills harmful bacteria.

antisocial (*or* **anti-social**) behaviour is behaviour which is annoying or upsetting to others. ■ You say a person is being **antisocial** when they are unwilling to meet other people.

anti-tank weapons are designed to destroy enemy tanks.

antithesis (*pron:* an-**tith**-iss-iss) The **antithesis** of something is its exact opposite.

antler A deer's **antlers** are its horns.

antonym The **antonym** of a word is a word which means the opposite. For example, the antonym of 'good' is 'bad'.

anus (*pron:* **ain**-uss) (**anuses; anal**) A person's or animal's **anus** is the hole through which they get rid of faeces from their body. **Anal** is used to talk about things which involve the anus.

anvil An **anvil** is a heavy iron block on which hot metals are beaten into shape.

anxious (**anxiously; anxiety, anxieties**) If you are **anxious,** you feel nervous or worried about something. This feeling is called **anxiety.** *Candidates are anxiously awaiting the results of today's voting.* ■ If you are **anxious** to do something, you are very eager to do it, in order to avoid or bring to an end an unpleasant situation. Similarly, you can be **anxious** for something to happen. *India is very anxious for the fighting to end.*

any You use **any** to say something is true about every person, group, or thing of a certain kind. *The Lensman can be mounted onto any 35mm camera.* ■ You use **any** in questions to ask if something exists. *Does it have any basis in fact?* ■ You use **any** with words like 'not' and 'never' to say something of a particular kind does not exist. *There has never been any doubt about his keenness.*

anybody See **anyone.**

anyhow means the same as 'anyway'.

anymore means the same as 'any more'. See **more.**

anyone (*or* **anybody**) You use **anyone** to say something is true about every person, or each person of a certain kind. *Anyone can make a mistake.* ■ You use **anyone** in questions to ask if there are people

about whom something is true. *Can anyone keep a secret?* ■ You use **anyone** with words like 'not' and 'never' to say there is nobody about whom something is true. *I've never met anyone with a good word to say about him.*

anything You use **anything** to say something is true about every thing of a certain kind. *Seaside audiences will laugh at almost anything.* ■ You use **anything** in questions to ask if something of a certain kind exists. *Can you see anything?* ■ You use **anything** with words like 'not' to say there is nothing of a certain kind. *The student had not stolen anything.* ■ You use **anything like** with words like 'not' to emphasize that there is not enough of something. *The city does not have anything like the funds needed for such large-scale redevelopment.*

anyway You say **anyway** when adding something extra to support the point you are making. *She isn't interested and anyway they wouldn't fit her.* ■ You say **anyway** when making a slight correction to what you have just said. *Parents can breath a sigh of relief. Most of them, anyway.* ■ **Anyway** is used to say something is true or will happen despite other things. *I don't care, I'll do it anyway.*

anywhere You use **anywhere** to say something is true about every place, or every part of a place. *He can work anywhere.* ■ You use **anywhere** in questions to ask if there is a place where something exists or is true. *Is there anywhere people can get this information?* ■ You use **anywhere** with words like 'not' to say there is no place where something exists or is true. *Motorists cannot find anywhere to fill up.*

aorta The **aorta** is the body's main artery. It conveys oxygen-rich blood from the heart to other parts of the body.

apace is used to say something happens at a steady rate. *The military build-up continues apace.*

apart If people or things are **apart,** they are not together. ■ If things happen a certain length of time **apart,** there is that amount of time between them. *...two photographs taken 80 years apart.* ■ If you **take** something **apart,** you separate it into its parts. If it **falls apart,** it breaks into pieces. ■ If an organization or arrangement **falls apart,** it comes to an end, because of problems. ■ If you cannot **tell** two people or things **apart,** they seem the same to you. ■ You say **apart from** when mentioning an exception. *Apart from a shower at noon, the day passed in bright sunshine.*

apartheid was a system in South Africa in which people of different races were kept apart by law.

apartment is the usual American word for a flat. ■ **Apartments** are a set of large rooms used by an important person like a queen or president.

apathetic (**apathy**) You say people are **apathetic** when they are not interested in something important that is going on and do not care what happens. You call this feeling **apathy.**

ape (**aping, aped**) **Apes** are animals like chimpanzees which look similar to monkeys but do not have tails. ■ If you **ape** someone's speech or behaviour, you imitate it.

apéritif (*pron:* ap-per-rit-**teef**) An **apéritif** is any alcoholic drink you have just before a meal.

aperture An **aperture** is a hole, gap, or other opening.

apex (**apexes**) The **apex** of a triangle or pyramid is the point at the top. ■ The **apex** of an organization is its highest managerial level. *At the apex of the party was its central committee.* ■ An **Apex** ticket is a plane or rail ticket which costs less than the standard fare, but which must be booked a specified time in advance.

aphasia is a mental condition in which people are unable to remember or recognize simple words.

aphid (*pron:* eh-fid) **Aphids** are small insects which suck sap from plants. Greenflies and blackflies are aphids.

aphorism An **aphorism** is a short saying which expresses something people think is generally true.

aphrodisiac (*pron:* af-roh-**diz**-zee-ak) An **aphrodisiac** is a food, drink, or drug which is said to increase sexual desire.

apiary (*pron:* **ape**-yar-ee) (**apiaries; apiarist**) An **apiary** is a place where bees are kept, usually in hives. An **apiarist** is someone who keeps or studies bees.

apiece If people have a number of things **apiece,** they each have that number. ■ If things cost a certain amount **apiece,** they cost that much each.

aplenty is used to say there is a lot of something. *There were chances aplenty to win the game.*

aplomb (*pron:* ap-**plom**) If you do something with **aplomb,** you do it calmly and confidently.

apocalypse (*pron:* a-**pok**-ka-lips) (**apocalyptic**) When people talk about the **apocalypse,** they mean the end of the world. **Apocalyptic** is used to describe things involving the end of the world. *...apocalyptic horrors.* ■ People sometimes call a serious disaster an **apocalypse.** *He believes humanity faces an environmental apocalypse.*

apocryphal (*pron:* ap-**pok**-rif-fal) An **apocryphal** story is probably not true.

apogee (*pron:* **ap**-oh-jee) The **apogee** of something is its most successful time.

apolitical If someone is **apolitical,** they do not have any political interests or allegiances.

apologetic (**apologetically**) If you are **apologetic,** you say or show you are sorry.

apologia (*pron:* a-pol-**loje**-ee-a) An **apologia** is a statement or piece of writing in which someone defends something they believe in.

apologise See **apologize.**

apologist An **apologist** for a belief or cause is someone who writes or speaks in its defence.

apologize (*or* **apologise**) (**apologizing, apologized; apology, apologies**) If you **apologize,** you say you are sorry. What you say is called an **apology.**

apoplexy (*pron:* **ap**-pop-plex-ee) (**apoplectic**) If someone has **apoplexy** or an **apoplectic** attack (*pron:* ap-pop-**plek**-tik), they suffer a stroke. ■ You say someone is **apoplectic** when they are very angry.

apostate (*pron:* ap-**poss**-tate) (**apostasy, apostasies**) An **apostate** is someone who has abandoned

their religious faith or some other strongly-held belief. Abandoning your faith is called **apostasy.**

apostle (*pron:* ap-**poss**-l) The **Apostles** were the twelve disciples chosen by Christ to preach the gospel. ■ An **apostle** of an idea or cause is a strong supporter and promoter of it.

apostolic (*pron:* ap-poss-**toll**-ik) means connected with or appointed by the Pope. *...an apostolic administrator.* ■ **Apostolic** is used to talk about traditions believed to date back to the Apostles. *...apostolic faith.*

apostrophe (*pron:* ap-**poss**-trof-fee) An **apostrophe** is the punctuation mark ' used to show a letter has been missed out, for example when 'do not' is shortened to 'don't'. It is also used to show something belongs to someone or something. *...Japan's aircraft makers.*

apothecary (*pron:* ap-**poth**-ik-ar-ee) (**apothecaries**) People who prepared medicines and drugs used to be called **apothecaries.**

apotheosis (*pron:* ap-poth-ee-**oh**-siss) The **apotheosis** of something is the best example of it, or the time when it is at its best. *The Oriental in Bangkok is the apotheosis of the grand hotel.*

appal (*Am:* **appall**) (**appalling, appalled; appallingly**) If you are **appalled** by something, it shocks and disgusts you.

apparatus (**apparatuses**) The **apparatus** for a task or activity is the equipment needed for it. *...weight-lifting apparatus.* ■ The **apparatus** of an organization is its structure, methods, and other things which enable it to operate.

apparel (*pron:* ap-**par**-rel) Someone's clothing can be referred to humorously as their **apparel.**

apparent (**apparently**) **Apparent** is used to describe something which seems to be a particular thing, or seems to be true. *...an apparent attempt to end the siege.* ■ If something is **apparent,** it is clear or obvious. *It became apparent that it was going to be a good year for rainfall.*

apparition An **apparition** is a supernatural figure which someone claims to have seen, for example a ghost.

appeal (**appealing, appealed; appealingly**) If you **appeal** or make an **appeal** for something, you make an urgent request for it. ■ If you **appeal** or make an **appeal** to someone in authority against a decision, you make a formal request for it to be changed. ■ If something **appeals** to you, you find it attractive or interesting. You can say something like this is **appealing** or has **appeal.** *He is appealingly witty.*

appear (**appearing, appeared**) If something **appears,** it becomes visible. *The sun appeared from behind the clouds.* ■ When a person **appears,** they turn up somewhere unexpectedly. ■ When something like a new product **appears,** it becomes available. ■ If you **appear** in something such as a play, you have a part in it. ■ If you **appear** in court, you go there to answer charges or give evidence. ■ If something **appears** to be true, it seems to be true.

appearance When someone turns up at a place, you can call this their **appearance.** *...the appearance of riot police.* ■ If someone makes an **appearance** in a film, play, or show, they have a part in it. ■ If someone makes an **appearance** in court, they go there to answer charges or give evidence. ■ When something new comes into existence or becomes available, you call this its **appearance.** ■ Your **appearance** is what you look like. ■ **Appearance** is used to talk about the impression created by someone's behaviour. *At least they give the appearance of trying to do something.*

appease (appeasing, appeased; appeasement, appeaser) If you **appease** someone who is making demands, you give in to some of their demands.

appellant An **appellant** is someone who has lodged an appeal against an official decision.

appellation An **appellation** is a name or title.

append If you **append** one thing to another, especially a note to a document, you add the first thing to the second.

appendage If you say something is an **appendage** of something else, you mean it is joined to that thing or controlled by it, and is regarded as an unimportant extra part of it. *The central bank was little more than an administrative appendage of the government.*

appendectomy (appendectomies) An **appendectomy** is a surgical operation to remove a person's appendix.

appendices See **appendix.**

appendicitis is a painful illness caused by an infected appendix.

appendix Your **appendix** (*plural:* **appendixes**) is a small closed tube inside your body which is attached to your digestive system. It has no particular function. ■ In a book, an **appendix** (*plural:* **appendices,** *pron* ap-**pend**-iss-eez) is extra information added at the end of it.

appetiser See **appetizer.**

appetising See **appetizing.**

appetite Your **appetite** is your desire to eat. ■ If you have an **appetite** for something, you enjoy it a lot. *...his appetite for gossip.*

appetizer (*or* appetiser) An **appetizer** is a small amount of food you eat before a meal, which is intended to give you an appetite.

appetizing (*or* appetising) (appetizingly) Appetizing food looks and smells good and makes you want to eat it. *The fish was appetizingly cooked and served.*

applaud (applauding, applauded; applause) When people **applaud,** they clap their hands to show approval. This clapping is called **applause.** ■ You say people **applaud** an action or attitude when they praise it. *He should be applauded for his courage.*

apple – Apples are round fruit with smooth green, red, or yellow skins and firm white flesh.

applecart If you **upset the applecart,** you do something which causes a plan or system to go wrong.

appliance An **appliance** or **domestic appliance** is a machine for doing a job in the home, for example a washing machine.

applicable (applicability) If something is **applicable** to a person, thing, or situation, it concerns or affects them. You talk about the **applicability** of something to a person, thing, or situation.

applicant See **apply.**

application See **apply.**

applicator An **applicator** is a device for applying a substance to a surface.

applied See **apply.**

appliqué (*pron:* ap-**plee**-kay) is a type of decoration in which pieces of one fabric are sewn onto another.

apply (applies, applying, applied; application; applicant) If you **apply** for something like a job or a loan, you formally ask to be given it, usually in writing. An **application** is a request like this; a person making it is called an **applicant.** ■ If something **applies** to certain people or things, it concerns or affects them. *The sanctions do not apply to food or medicine.* ■ If a term is **applied** to someone or something, it is used to describe them. *'Liberal' is a term I don't think we can apply to the present government.* ■ If you **apply** yourself to something, you work hard at it. ■ If you **apply** a technique or theory to something, you use it or put it into practice. *...the application of genetic engineering to brewing. ...applied economics.* ■ If you **apply** a substance to a surface, you paint it on or spread it on.

appoint (appointment, appointee) If someone is **appointed** to a job, they are officially chosen to do it. The person chosen is sometimes called the **appointee;** the job itself is called an **appointment.** ■ The **appointed** time for something is the time chosen for it to take place. Similarly, there can be an **appointed** place for something. ■ If you have an **appointment** with someone, you have arranged to meet them.

apportion (apportioning, apportioned; apportionment) If something is **apportioned** among a group, it is decided how much each of them will get. *...the apportionment of resources.*

apposite If you say something like a comment is **apposite,** you mean it fits a situation or sums it up nicely.

appraise (appraising, appraised; appraisal) If you **appraise** something or make an **appraisal** of it, you consider it carefully and make a judgment about it.

appreciable (appreciably) An **appreciable** amount of something is quite a large amount. *His authority has grown appreciably.* Similarly, you can say something has an **appreciable** effect.

appreciate (appreciating, appreciated; appreciation) If you **appreciate** a situation or problem, you are aware of it. *We appreciate how tough it is in business.* ■ If you **appreciate** something like music, you enjoy it because you recognize its good qualities. ■ An **appreciation** of someone like a writer is a discussion and evaluation of their work. ■ If you say you **appreciate** what someone has done, you mean you are grateful for it. ■ If something **appreciates** in value, its value increases.

appreciative An **appreciative** reaction shows pleasure or gratitude.

apprehend (apprehension, apprehensive, apprehensively) If the police **apprehend** someone who is suspected of a crime, they catch them and arrest them; this is called the **apprehension** of the person. ■ **Apprehension** is a feeling of fear or anxiety. If you are **apprehensive** about something, you feel like this about it. *People listened apprehensively to the thud of artillery.*

apprentice (apprenticed, apprenticeship) An **apprentice** is a young person who works with a skilled worker for a number of years in order to learn that skill. You say they are **apprenticed** to that person; the learning period is called their **apprenticeship.** ■ Any period spent gaining useful experience can be called an **apprenticeship.**

approach (approaches, approaching, approached) When someone or something **approaches** you, they get nearer; you call this their **approach.** ■ An **approach** to a place is a road or path leading to it. ■ If you **approach** someone or make an **approach** to them about something, you mention it to them. ■ If a time or situation is **approaching,** it will happen soon. You talk about the **approach** of a time or situation. ■ If something is **approaching** a level or state, it has almost reached it. *Inflation is approaching 30%.* ■ Your **approach** to a situation or problem or the way you **approach** it, is the way you deal with it.

approachable If someone is **approachable,** they are friendly and understanding.

approbation is approval of something or agreement to it.

appropriate (appropriating, appropriated; appropriately, appropriateness, appropriation) If something is **appropriate** to a situation, it is suitable. *In cold conditions, dress appropriately. ...doubts about the appropriateness of government policy.* ■ If you **appropriate** (pron: a-pro-pree-ate) something belonging to someone else, you take it without getting permission. *...the appropriation of property.* ■ If words or ideas are **appropriated** by someone, they begin using them in a new way for their own purposes. *...the appropriation of reggae by mainstream culture in Jamaica.*

approve (approving, approved; approvingly, approval) If someone in authority **approves** an idea or gives it their **approval,** they officially agree to it. ■ If you **approve** of what someone says or does or it has your **approval,** you have a good opinion of it. *He has spoken approvingly of China's contribution... She will do anything to win the approval of total strangers.*

approx means 'approximately'.

approximate (approximating, approximated; approximately, approximation) **Approximate** is used to show that a figure or number is not exact. *...approximately three hours later.* ■ If something **approximates** (pron: ap-prox-i-mates) to something else or is an **approximation** of it, it is similar to it but not quite the same.

après ski (pron: **ap**-ray **skee**) is evening entertainment and social activities in skiing resorts.

apricot – Apricots are small soft round fruit with yellowish-orange flesh and a stone in the middle.

a priori (pron: eh pry-**or**-rye) An **a priori** reason or idea is based on an assumed principle that a certain thing is true, rather than finding out facts about it. *We can only argue here on a priori grounds because we don't have the numbers to be able to calculate gains and losses.*

apron An **apron** is a piece of protective clothing worn over the front of other clothes. ■ The **apron** at an airport is the area where aircraft are parked.

apropos (pron: ap-prop-**poh**) **Apropos of** something means 'with regard to' it. *Apropos your obituary of Viscount Muirshiel, allow me to add a small footnote.*

apt (aptly, aptness) An **apt** description of something sums it up nicely. *She gave one last tour, aptly named 'Farewell'. ...the aptness of those words.* ■ If someone is **apt** to do something, they often do it or tend to do it.

aptitude If you have an **aptitude** for something, you are able to learn it quickly and do it well.

aquaculture is fish farming and underwater plant farming.

aqualung An **aqualung** is a piece of equipment which enables divers to breathe underwater.

aquamarine is a greenish-blue colour.

aquarium (plural: **aquariums** or **aquaria**) An **aquarium** is (a) a water-filled glass tank for keeping fish in. (b) a building, often in a zoo, where fish and other underwater animals are kept.

aquatic is used to describe (a) animals and plants which live in water. (b) things which take place in water. *...aquatic exercise.*

aqueduct An **aqueduct** is a bridge carrying water across a valley or river.

aquifer (pron: **ak**-wiff-er) An **aquifer** is a layer of rock that has absorbed water which can be used to supply wells.

Arab – **Arabs** are people whose first language is Arabic, especially people from North Africa and the Middle East.

arabesque (pron: ar-ab-**esk**) An **arabesque** is a design made up of complex patterns of intertwining lines and shapes, sometimes including pictures of plants and animals.

Arabia (Arabian) **Arabia** is the area of land between the Red Sea and the Persian Gulf. **Arabian** is used to talk about things to do with Arabia. *...the Arabian peninsula.*

Arabic is a language spoken mainly in the Middle East and north Africa.

arable land is used for growing crops.

arbiter An **arbiter** is someone appointed to judge a dispute. ■ If someone or something is regarded as an **arbiter,** people always accept what they say as right. *The umpires are sole arbiters of when play should start.*

arbitrary (arbitrarily, arbitrariness) You say something is **arbitrary** when it does not seem to be based on fairness or reason. *...the arbitrariness of fate.*

arbitrate (arbitrating, arbitrated; arbitration, arbitrator) If someone **arbitrates** in a dispute, they try to settle it fairly. A person who does this is called an **arbitrator;** settling disputes in this way is called **arbitration.**

arbor See **arbour.**

arboreal (pron: ahr-**bore**-ee-al) is used to describe things to do with trees. **Arboreal** animals live in trees.

arboretum (*pron:* ahr-bore-**ree**-tum) An **arboretum** is a place where trees are grown, especially for their scientific interest.

arbour (*Am:* **arbor**) An **arbour** is a shelter in a garden formed by plants growing over a light framework.

arc An **arc** is a smoothly curving line. If something **arcs,** it moves in a line like this. ■ In maths, an **arc** is part of the circumference of a circle.

arcade An **arcade** is a covered passageway with shops on each side. ■ An **arcade game** is a computer game of the type often played in amusement arcades.

arcane things are mysterious or difficult to understand. *...the arcane world of international law.*

arch (**arches, arching, arched; archly, arch-**) An **arch** is a structure that has a curved top supported on either side by a pillar or wall. ■ When something **arches,** it forms a curved shape. ■ You say someone is being **arch** when they say things in a clever knowing way, to make fun of someone. *'My favours are at your disposal',* she told him archly. ■ **Arch-** is added to words like 'rivals' and 'enemies' to emphasize that people are bitter, longstanding rivals or enemies. ■ **Arch-** is used to describe people who have extreme and inflexible views. *...an arch-traditionalist.*

archaeology (*or* **archeology**) (**archaeological, archaeologist**) **Archaeology** is the study of the past by examining the remains of buildings and other things found buried in the ground. An **archaeologist** is an expert on this. *...archaeological sites.*

archaic (*pron:* ark-**kay**-ik) (**archaism**) If something is **archaic,** it is old-fashioned. You call something like this an **archaism** (*pron:* **ark**-kay-iz-zum).

archangel (*pron:* **ark**-ain-jel) An **archangel** is a high-ranking angel.

archbishop An **archbishop** is a bishop of the highest rank.

archdeacon An **archdeacon** is an Anglican clergyman ranking just below a bishop.

archdiocese (*pron:* arch-**die**-a-siss) (**archdioceses**) An **archdiocese** is the area under an archbishop's control.

archeology See **archaeology.**

archer (**archery**) An **archer** is someone who shoots arrows from a bow. **Archery** is the sport of shooting arrows at a target.

archetypal (*pron:* ark-ee-**type**-al) (**archetype**) You say something is **archetypal** or an **archetype** when it is a perfect example of its kind.

archipelago (*pron:* ark-ee-**pel**-a-go) (**archipelagos**) An **archipelago** is a group of small islands.

architect An **architect** is someone whose job is designing buildings. ■ The **architect** of a plan or policy is its inventor.

architectural (**architecturally**) **Architectural** is used to talk about things to do with the design and construction of buildings. *...architectural drawings.*

architecture is the art of designing and constructing buildings. ■ The **architecture** of a building is the style it is constructed in.

archive (*pron:* **ark**-ive) (**archivist**) **Archives** are collections of documents relating to past events. An

archivist (*pron:* **ark**-iv-ist) is someone whose job is to collect, sort, and preserve archives.

archway An **archway** is a passage or entrance with a curved roof.

arctic weather is extremely cold.

ardent (**ardently**) **Ardent** is used to describe people who strongly support or oppose something. *...ardent opponents of abortion.*

ardour (*Am:* **ardor**) is passion or great enthusiasm.

arduous If something you do is **arduous,** it is very hard work.

are See **be.**

area An **area** of a city or region is a part of it. ■ The **area** of a surface is the amount of flat space it covers, expressed in square units. ■ An **area** is a field of interest. *...a prominent US researcher in the area of breastfeeding.*

arena An **arena** is a place where sports or other public events take place. It has seats for spectators around the edge. ■ The field of competition or public life in which someone operates can be called an **arena.** *Colleagues urged him not to withdraw from the political arena.*

argot (*pron:* **ahr**-go) An **argot** is the slang used by a group of people. *...prison argot.*

arguable (**arguably**) If a claim is **arguable,** you can make a good case for it. *The battle was arguably a tactical defeat for the Americans.* ■ You can describe an idea as **arguable** when it is rather doubtful whether it is true. *It is arguable whether he ever had much control over the army.*

argue (**arguing, argued; argument**) When people **argue,** they say things which show they disagree, and sometimes speak angrily or shout. ■ If you **argue** for something, you say it is a good idea and give reasons why. Similarly, if you **argue** that something is true, you say it is true and give reasons why.

argumentative people argue a lot.

aria (*pron:* **ah**-ree-a) An **aria** is an elaborate song for a solo singer, especially in an opera.

arid (**aridity**) If a place is **arid,** it is extremely dry. ■ If you call what someone says or writes **arid,** you mean it is uninteresting, and lacks relevance to people's everyday lives.

arise (**arising, arose, have arisen**) When something like a problem or opportunity **arises,** it comes into existence.

aristocracy (**aristocrat, aristocratic**) The **aristocracy** are people of high social rank, such as dukes and earls. **Aristocratic** means relating to or typical of the aristocracy. *...his aristocratic manner.*

arithmetic (**arithmetical**) **Arithmetic** is the part of maths to do with addition, subtraction, multiplication, and division.

arm Your **arms** are the parts of your body between your hands and your shoulders. ■ The **arms** of a chair are the raised parts on each side where you rest your arms. ■ An **arm** of an organization is a section of it. ■ **Arms** are weapons of war like guns, tanks, and missiles. If someone is **armed,** they have a weapon or weapons like this. *The crisis may escalate into armed conflict.* ■ If someone is **up in arms** about something, they are angry about it and are strongly voicing their objections. ■ If you go somewhere **armed** with equipment or information, you have it with you ready for use.

armada An **armada** is a large fleet of warships. ■ Any large group of boats can be called an **armada.**

armadillo (**armadillos**) The **armadillo** is a Central and South American animal which is covered with hard protective plates.

Armageddon When people refer to **Armageddon** they mean the final battle between good and evil which some Christians believe will come at the end of the world.

armament A country's or army's **armaments** are its weapons.

armband An **armband** is a band of fabric someone wears around their arm, usually to indicate their official position. A black armband shows that someone is in mourning.

armchair An **armchair** is a comfortable chair with armrests.

armhole The **armholes** of a piece of clothing are the openings you put your arms through.

armistice An **armistice** is an agreement between countries at war to stop fighting for a time.

armlock If you have someone in an **armlock**, you have twisted their arm behind their back so they are under your control.

armory See **armoury.**

armour (*Am:* **armor**) (**armoured**) An **armoured** vehicle has a hard metal covering to protect it from attack. This covering is called its **armour.** ■ **Armour** is groups of armoured vehicles, especially tanks. ■ When battles were fought with swords and arrows, the metal suits worn by soldiers were called **armour.** In modern times, people like the police sometimes wear clothing called **body armour,** as protection from gunfire.

armour-plated An **armour-plated** vehicle has a hard metal covering to protect it from attack.

armoury (*Am:* **armory**) (**armouries**) An **armoury** is a place where weapons are stored. ■ A country's **armoury** is its total collection of weapons and other military equipment. ■ Any large collection of useful things with something can be called an **armoury.** *Modern medicine has a large armoury of drugs for the treatment of mental illness.*

armpit A person's **armpits** are the areas under their arms where their arms join their shoulders.

armrest The **armrests** on a chair are the arms.

army (**armies**) An **army** is a large organized group of people who are armed and trained to fight, especially one controlled by a government. ■ An **army** of people or things is a large number of them together. *...an army of reporters.*

A-road An **A-road** is a major road, narrower than a motorway but wider than a B-road.

aroma An **aroma** is a pleasant smell.

aromatherapy (**aromatherapist**) Aromatherapy is a treatment which involves massaging the body with special fragrant plant oils.

aromatic plants or food have a strong pleasant smell.

arose See **arise.**

around can be used instead of 'round' for some of its meanings. See **round.** ■ You use **around** to say someone or something is present or nearby. *He's around somewhere.* ■ If you say something has been **around** for a certain length of time, you mean it has existed for that time. ■ **Around** is used to say a number is not exact. *...around 30%.*

arouse (**arousing, aroused; arousal**) If something **arouses** certain feelings, it makes people have them. You talk about the **arousal** of feelings. *...sexual arousal.*

arraign (*pron:* ar-**rain**) (**arraignment**) If someone is **arraigned,** they are brought before a court to answer charges. *On arraignment, he pleaded not guilty.*

arrange (**arranging, arranged; arrangement, arranger**) If you **arrange** something or make **arrangements** for it, you make the necessary preparations for it to take place. ■ If people **arrange** to do something at a certain time, they agree to do it at that time. ■ In an **arranged marriage,** the parents choose the person their son or daughter will marry. ■ If things are **arranged** in a certain way, they are positioned or ordered that way. The way they are positioned or ordered is called an **arrangement.** *...arranged in alphabetical order. ...an arrangement of flowers.* ■ If someone **arranges** a piece of music, they adapt it to be performed in a different way, usually on different instruments. An adaptation like this is called an **arrangement.** A person who arranges music is called an **arranger.**

arrant is used to mean 'utter' or 'total' when you are criticizing something strongly. *They dismissed the claims as arrant nonsense.*

array (**arrayed**) An **array** of things is an impressive display or collection of them. *...a dazzling array of colours.* ■ If something like a military force is **arrayed against** someone, it is ready to be used against them.

arrears If you are **in arrears,** you are behind with your payments for something. ■ If you are paid **in arrears,** your wages are paid at the end of each period in which you earn them.

arrest (**arresting, arrestingly**) If the police **arrest** someone or make an **arrest,** they take them into custody and question them, because they are suspected of committing a crime. You say people in this situation are **under arrest.** ■ If something or someone **arrests** a process, they stop it continuing. *A sudden jolt arrested our progress.* ■ If something is **arresting,** it attracts your attention, because it is surprising, interesting, or beautiful. *His storytelling is arrestingly honest.*

arrhythmia (*pron:* a-**rith**-mee-a) is any variation in the normal rhythm of a person's heartbeat.

arrive (**arriving, arrived; arrival**) When you **arrive** at a place, you get there. You talk about your **arrival** there. People who have just arrived somewhere can be called **arrivals.** ■ If something like a letter **arrives,** it is delivered. ■ When something new is introduced to a place, you can say it **arrives** there. *...the arrival of multichannel television.* ■ When an expected event **arrives,** it happens. ■ When a new baby **arrives,** it is born. ■ When people **arrive** at a decision or conclusion, they reach it.

arriviste (*pron:* a-**reeve**-ist) An **arriviste** is a ruthlessly ambitious person.

arrogant (**arrogantly, arrogance**) If someone is **arrogant,** they behave in an unpleasantly proud way. Behaviour like this is called **arrogance.**

arrow An **arrow** is (a) a pointed weapon fired from a bow. (b) a pointed symbol showing which direction something is.

arrowhead An **arrowhead** is the sharp pointed end of an arrow.

arrowroot is starch from a West Indian plant, used in cooking.

arsenal A country's **arsenal** is all its military weapons and equipment. ■ An **arsenal** is a building where weapons and ammunition are made and stored. ■ An **arsenal** of things is a large collection of them ready for use. *Swiss-born director Carl Schenkel lets loose an arsenal of flashy effects.*

arsenic is a strong poison.

arson (**arsonist**) **Arson** is the crime of deliberately setting fire to a building. An **arsonist** is someone who does this.

art is painting, drawing, and sculpture. ■ When people talk about the **arts,** they mean things like drama, music, and poetry, as well as painting and sculpture. ■ At a school or college, **arts** subjects are literature, languages, and history, rather than science or engineering. ■ If you have learned the **art** of doing something, you have learned how to do it. *...the art of dealing with the press.*

Art Deco was a style of art, decoration, and architecture popular in the 1920s and 1930s. It involved the use of simple, bold, and often geometrical designs and man-made materials.

artefact (*or* **artifact**) An **artefact** is a man-made object, especially an old one which is of historical interest.

arteriosclerosis is a serious condition in which the walls of a person's arteries thicken and lose their elasticity.

artery (**arteries; arterial**) Your **arteries** are tubes which carry blood from your heart to the rest of your body. **Arterial** means to do with the arteries. *...the arterial wall.* ■ An important road or railway can be called an **artery.** Main roads are sometimes called **arterial** roads.

artesian well (*pron:* art-**teez**-yan) In an **artesian well** the water is continually forced up out of the ground by pressure from water flowing in from a higher level.

artful (**artfully**) **Artful** people are cunning. ■ If something has been made in an **artful** way, it has been made with great skill.

arthritis (**arthritic**) **Arthritis** is a condition in which the joints become painfully swollen. If someone is **arthritic,** they suffer from arthritis.

artichoke The **artichoke** or **globe artichoke** is a round green vegetable with fleshy leaves. ■ The **artichoke** or **Jerusalem artichoke** is a small yellowish-white vegetable which grows underground and looks like a knobbly potato.

article (**articled**) An **article** is a piece of writing in a newspaper or magazine. ■ A section of something like a treaty or Act of Parliament is called an **article.** ■ If you say something is an **article of faith** with someone, you mean they believe in it strongly. ■ An **article** is any object, especially a small man-made one. ■ A person who is **articled** to a firm of solicitors is employed by the firm and training to become qualified. **Articles** is the two-year period of training which all solicitors must complete before qualifying. ■ 'A', 'an', and 'the' are called **articles.** ■ See also **definite article, indefinite article.**

articulate (**articulating, articulated; articulacy, articulation**) If you are **articulate** (*pron:* ar-**tik**-yoo-let), you are able to express yourself well. This ability is called **articulacy.** ■ When you **articulate** (*pron:* ar-**tik**-yoo-late) your ideas or feelings, you say what you think or feel. ■ If you talk about someone's **articulation,** you are talking about how clearly they pronounce their words. ■ An **articulated** vehicle is made in two sections, so it can bend in the middle.

artifact See **artefact.**

artifice is deceiving people in a clever way.

artificial (**artificially, artificiality**) **Artificial** things are made by man, rather than produced by nature. ■ An **artificial** situation is one which has been created, rather than arising of its own accord. *Financial regulation kept interest rates artificially low.* ■ If someone's behaviour is **artificial,** they pretend to have certain attitudes and feelings. ■ You can say things are **artificial** when they seem unnatural, contrived, or false. This characteristic is called **artificiality.**

artificial insemination or **AI** is the placing of sperm into a woman or female animal, to make her pregnant without direct contact with a male.

artificial intelligence is a type of computer technology concerned with making machines work in an intelligent way, similar to the way the human mind works.

artificial respiration When someone who has stopped breathing is given **artificial respiration,** air is forced into their lungs, to keep them alive and help them start breathing again.

artillery consists of large powerful guns like cannons, howitzers, and missile launchers.

artisan Skilled workmen such as carpenters used to be called **artisans.**

artist An **artist** is someone who draws, paints, or produces other works of art. ■ Musicians, actors, or other performers can be called **artists.**

artiste (*pron:* ar-**teest**) An **artiste** is a professional entertainer, for example a singer.

artistic (**artistically**) **Artistic** means involving art or artists. ■ If someone is **artistic,** they are good at drawing, painting, or creating attractive things. ■ artistic licence: see **licence.**

artistry is the creative skill of an artist, writer or musician.

artless You say someone is **artless** when they are simple, honest, and do not try to deceive people.

Art Nouveau was a style of decoration and design common at the end of the 19th century. Its typical features were flowing lines and many leaves and flowers.

artwork is the drawings or photographs in a book or advertisement.

arty people are artistic or seem preoccupied with fashionable intellectual ideas.

Aryan (*pron:* **air**-ree-an) people have the racial characteristics associated with Northern Europeans, especially fair skin and hair and blue eyes.

as is used to say one thing happens while something else is happening. *The play started as he got there.* ■ **As** is used to talk about the job, role, or function that someone or something has. *He was forced to step down as prime minister... The composted material was then used as fertiliser... Soldiers are expected to shoot in the air as a warning.* ■ **As** is used when making comparisons. *The problem is not nearly as bad as Labour claims.* ■ To leave something **as** it is means to leave it in the way that it is. To act **as** someone tells you means to act in the way that they tell you. *This gave them carte blanche to behave as they liked.* ■ **As** is used when mentioning someone's description or opinion of something. *Current-affairs programmes are dismissed as being soft on terrorists.* ■ **As** is used to mean 'because'. *I am livid, particularly as they have details of my income.* ■ **As** is used in expressions such as 'as a result' and 'as a consequence' to indicate how two situations or events are related. ■ **As if** and **as though** are used to say how something appears. *He looked as if his mind was elsewhere.* ■ **As to** is used to say what something like a statement or question is about. *The packaging doesn't give any indication as to what the products contain.* ■ You say **as for...** when you are going on to a different aspect of a subject.

asbestos is a heat-resistant mineral used in the past to make fireproof materials. It is now known to cause lung problems.

asbestosis is a lung disease caused by breathing in asbestos dust.

ascend If something **ascends,** it moves upwards. ■ If you **ascend** something like a staircase, you go up it. ■ If a group of things is arranged in **ascending** order, the smallest is put first, followed by the next smallest, and so on. ■ You can use **ascend** to talk about someone progressing to a position of power or success. *He ascended to the world number 1 spot.* ■ When a monarch **ascends** the throne, they are crowned.

ascendancy (*or* **ascendency**) (**ascendant**) If one group is gaining **ascendancy** or is **in the ascendant,** it is becoming more powerful or successful than other groups. *Democratic trends are now in the ascendant in many African countries.*

ascent (**ascension**) An **ascent** is a movement from a lower to a higher level. *...a balloon ascent.* ■ When someone reaches a position of power or success, you can talk about their **ascent** or **ascension** to that position.

ascertain (**ascertaining, ascertained**) If you **ascertain** something, you find it out, by questioning or investigation.

ascetic (*pron:* ass-**set**-tik) (**asceticism**) If someone is **ascetic** or an **ascetic,** they have a simple and strict lifestyle, for example because of their religious beliefs.

ascribe (**ascribing, ascribed**) If you **ascribe** something to a particular thing, you say that thing caused it. *An autopsy eventually ascribed the baby's death to sudden infant death syndrome.* ■ If you **ascribe** a quality or characteristic to someone, you say they have it. *Ethiopian ancestry was ascribed to Pushkin.*

asexual (*pron:* eh-**sex**-yew-al) (**asexually**) If an animal or plant is **asexual,** it has no sex organs. **Asexual** reproduction takes place without sexual activity. *These parasites reproduce asexually.* ■ You say someone is **asexual** when (a) their appearance is not particularly masculine or feminine. (b) they are not interested in sex.

ash (**ashes**) **Ash** or **ashes** is the black or grey powdery substance left after something has burned. ■ If something **rises from the ashes** of something which has ended or been destroyed, it appears in its place. ■ The **ash** is a tree which produces black buds and winged seeds.

ashamed If you feel **ashamed,** you feel embarrassed and guilty about something you have done. ■ If you are **ashamed** to do something, you are reluctant to do it because you would feel embarrassed and guilty about it. ■ If you are **ashamed** of someone, you disapprove of them or of something they have done, and feel embarrassed to be connected with them.

ashen If someone is **ashen** or **ashen-faced,** they are pale with shock or fear.

ashore If you come **ashore,** you come onto the land from a boat.

ashtray An **ashtray** is a small dish for ash and stubs from cigarettes and cigars.

Asian is used to talk about people and things in or from the continent of Asia. ■ An **Asian** is someone who comes from Asia. ■ An **Asian** is someone who comes from the Indian subcontinent or whose ancestors came from there. **Asian** means connected with these people.

aside If you **move aside,** (a) you get out of someone's way. (b) you give up a post so someone else can take your place. ■ You use **aside** to say you are ignoring one aspect of something for the moment. *Politics aside, unemployment insurance deserves another look.* ■ If money is set **aside** for a certain purpose, it is saved for that purpose. ■ If you **take** someone **aside,** you lead them away from people, so you can talk to them privately. ■ An **aside** is a brief comment you make in the middle of saying something else.

ask If you **ask** someone something, you put a question to them. ■ If you **ask** someone to do something, you say you would like them to do it. ■ If you **ask** for something, you say you would like it to be given to you. ■ If you **ask** someone to something like a party, you invite them to it. ■ If you say someone is **asking for trouble,** you mean they are doing something which will probably get them into trouble. ■ The **asking price** for something is the price the person selling it says they want for it.

askance (*pron:* ass-**kanss**) If you say someone **looks askance** at something, you mean they disapprove of it.

askew If something is **askew,** it is not straight or level.

asleep If someone is **asleep,** they are sleeping.

asp – Asps are small poisonous southern European snakes.

asparagus is a vegetable which consists of long thin green shoots with pointed ends.

aspect An **aspect** of something is a part of its character or nature. *...the radical change which is affecting every aspect of Algerian life... Perhaps the most interesting aspect of the proposals is the language employed by the Khmer Rouge.*

aspen The **aspen** is a type of poplar. Its leaves are attached by long flat stalks, and quiver in the breeze.

aspersions If you **cast aspersions** on someone or something, you make critical remarks about them.

asphalt is a mixture of bitumen, oil, and small stones, used to make surfaces for roads.

asphyxiate (pron: ass-**fix**-ee-ate) (**asphyxiating, asphyxiated; asphyxia, asphyxiation**) If someone is **asphyxiated,** they become unconscious through lack of oxygen, and may die. You can say someone dies of **asphyxia** or **asphyxiation.**

aspic is a clear jelly made from meat or fish juices. ■ If you say a place or way of life is preserved **in aspic,** you mean it has remained unchanged for a long time.

aspirant An **aspirant** to something is a person who wants to achieve it. *...gold medal aspirants.* ■ **Aspirant** is used to describe someone who wants to be a particular thing. For example, an **aspirant** writer is someone who wants to be a writer.

aspiration People's **aspirations** are the things they hope to achieve.

aspire (**aspiring, aspired**) If you **aspire** to something like an important job, you have an ambition to have it.

aspirin is a drug which reduces pain and fever. It is often sold as tablets called **aspirins.**

ass (**asses**) The **ass** is an animal like a horse but smaller and with longer ears. A wild ass is always called an ass; a domesticated ass is usually called a donkey. ■ If you call someone an **ass,** you mean that they are stupid.

assail (**assailing, assailed; assailant**) If you are **assailed** by doubts, fears, or problems, you are greatly troubled by them. ■ If you are **assailed** by someone, you are threatened or attacked by them. You call this person your **assailant.** ■ You say someone is **assailed** when they are strongly criticized.

assassinate (**assassinating, assassinated; assassination, assassin**) If an important person is **assassinated,** they are murdered, usually for political reasons. A murder like this is called an **assassination.** The murderer is called an **assassin.**

assault An **assault** by an army is a strong attack on an enemy. ■ **Assault** weapons are intended for use in battle rather than for things like hunting. *...an AK-47 assault rifle.* ■ If someone is **assaulted,** they are physically attacked. An attack like this is called an **assault.** ■ An **assault** on something is a strong criticism of it, or an attempt to weaken it. *His book is a radical assault on feminism.*

assault course An **assault course** is an area of land covered with obstacles such as rope nets and water-filled ditches. People like soldiers make their way round it to improve their fitness.

assay An **assay** is an analysis to see how much metal there is in an ore, or to what extent a precious metal consists of impurities.

assemblage An **assemblage** is a collection of different kinds of people or things.

assemble (**assembling, assembled; assembly, assemblies**) When people **assemble,** they gather together. **Assembly** is the gathering together of people, especially for political meetings. ■ An **assembly** is a group of people gathered together, especially a group who meet regularly to take important decisions. ■ If you **assemble** a number of people, objects, or facts, you get them together. ■ When something like a machine is **assembled,** its parts are fitted together.

assembler An **assembler** is a person who works on an assembly line. ■ An **assembler** is a firm which assembles products from components supplied by other firms.

assembly line An **assembly line** is an arrangement of workers and machines in a factory where each product passes from one worker to another until it is finished.

assent If someone in authority **assents** to something or gives their **assent** to it, they agree to it.

assert (**assertion**) If you **assert** something or make an **assertion,** you make a firm statement. ■ If you **assert** yourself, you speak and act in a forceful way, so people take notice of you. Similarly, if you **assert** your authority, you speak or act forcefully, so people see you are in control.

assertive (**assertively, assertiveness**) You say someone is being **assertive** when they speak and act in a forceful way, so people take notice of them.

assess (**assesses, assessing, assessed; assessment**) When you **assess** someone or something, you consider them carefully and make a judgment about them. This judgment is called an **assessment.**

assessable Your **assessable** income is the part of your income you pay tax on.

assessor An **assessor** is an expert whose job is to assess something, usually the cost of something.

asset An **asset** is a useful quality or skill. *My greatest asset is my pace.* ■ The **assets** of a person or company are all the things they own.

asset-stripping (**asset-stripper**) **Asset-stripping** is buying a company in difficulties, then selling off its assets at a profit. The company is then often closed down. An **asset-stripper** is someone who makes money this way.

assiduous (**assiduously**) An **assiduous** person works hard, and with care and dedication.

assign (**assignment**) If you are **assigned** a task, you are given it. The task is called an **assignment.** ■ If you are **assigned** to a place, you are sent to work there.

assignation (pron: ass-sig-**nay**-shun) An **assignation** is a secret meeting.

assimilate (assimilating, assimilated; assimilation) If something is **assimilated** by something else, it is absorbed by it and becomes a part of it. ■ If immigrants or ethnic groups are **assimilated** into the population of a country, they adopt the way of life and become accepted there. ■ If you **assimilate** facts or ideas, you learn them and make use of them.

assist (assistance) If you **assist** someone or give them **assistance,** you help them. If something **assists** something else, it helps it. *Good ventilation assists in preventing stem-rot.*

assistant Someone's **assistant** is a person who helps them in their work. ■ **Assistant** is used in front of job titles to indicate a slightly lower rank. For example, an assistant director is one rank lower than a director. ■ A **shop assistant** helps customers in a shop, or sells things to them.

assizes were regular court sessions held by an important travelling judge in county towns in England and Wales until 1971.

associate (associating, associated; association) If you **associate** something with something else, you connect the two things in your mind. *Revolutions have unhappy associations for most Afghans.* ■ If one thing is **associated** with another, the two things usually happen together, often one as a result of the other. *...the problems associated with inner-city housing.* ■ If someone is **associated** with an organization or cause, they are involved with it, or publicly support it. ■ If you **associate** with a group of people, you spend time with them. If you do something **in association with** someone else, you do it together. ■ Your **associates** are your work colleagues. ■ An **association** is a group formed by people with the same occupation, aim, or interest. *...the British Medical Association.* ■ **Associated** appears in the name of some organizations made up of smaller organizations. *...Associated British Ports.* ■ **Associate** in front of a word like 'member' means someone does not have full membership of an organization, or is of slightly lower rank than others with the same title.

assorted (assortment) A collection of things in a variety of sizes, colours, or types can be called an **assortment** or an **assorted** collection. *...assorted chocolates. ...an assortment of motorbikes.* Similarly, you can talk about an **assorted** group of people. *...the usual crowd of assorted hangers-on.*

assuage (pron: ass-**wage**) (assuaging, assuaged) If you **assuage** someone's fear, anger, or guilt, you calm it.

assume (assuming, assumed; assumption) If you **assume** something is true, you behave as if it were true, although you cannot be sure. This is called making an **assumption.** ■ You say **assuming...** when you are mentioning something which might happen or might be true; you then go on to talk about the possible consequences. *But assuming that the talks make progress, won't they do too little, too late?* ■ When someone **assumes** power, they become the new ruler of a country. Similarly, you can talk about someone **assuming** control or **assuming** responsibility for something. ■ If something **assumes** a particular characteristic, it begins to have it. *The dispute has assumed an increasingly bitter and personal character.*

assurance If you give someone an **assurance** about something, you tell them it is definitely true. ■ If you do something with **assurance,** you do it with confidence and certainty. ■ **Assurance** or **life assurance** is the same as life insurance.

assure (assuring, assured) If you **assure** someone that something is true, you tell them it is definitely true. ■ If you are **assured** of something, you will definitely get it. ■ If someone is **assured,** they are confident and at ease.

assuredly If you say something is **assuredly** true, you mean it is definitely true.

asterisk An **asterisk** is the symbol * which is used in a piece of writing to indicate that there is more information at the bottom of the page.

astern If something is **astern** of a ship, it is behind it.

asteroid — **Asteroids** are large lumps of rock, between one and several hundred miles across, which orbit the sun, especially between Mars and Jupiter.

asthma (pron: **ass**-ma) (asthmatic) Asthma is an illness, often brought on by allergies. People who suffer from asthma are called **asthmatics**; they have sudden sharp attacks when they cough and gasp for breath. **Asthmatic** is used to talk about things relating to asthma.

astonish (astonishes, astonishing, astonished; astonishingly, astonishment) If something **astonishes** you, you are extremely surprised by it.

astound (astounding, astoundingly) If something **astounds** you, you are absolutely amazed by it.

astray If someone is **led astray,** they do things which are foolish or wrong, as a result of the bad influence of other people. ■ If something **goes astray,** it goes missing.

astride If you are **astride** something, you are sitting or standing with one leg on each side of it. ■ If a place is **astride** something, it is situated on both sides of it.

astringent An **astringent** is a substance for drying greasy skin. ■ **Astringent** comments are sharp and sarcastic.

astrology (astrologer, astrological) Astrology is the study of the movements of the planets, sun, moon, and stars in the belief that they influence people's lives. **Astrological** is used to talk about things to do with astrology. *...astrological predictions.*

astronaut An **astronaut** is a person who travels in a spacecraft.

astronomy (astronomical, astronomer; astronomic, astronomically) Astronomy is the scientific study of the planets, stars, and other natural objects in space. **Astronomical** means to do with astronomy. *...an astronomical telescope.* ■ If an amount is **astronomical** or **astronomic,** it is extremely high.

astrophysics (astrophysicist) Astrophysics is the study of the physical and chemical structure of the planets, stars, and other natural objects in space.

AstroTurf is artificial grass used as a playing surface for sports. 'AstroTurf' is a trademark.

astute (astutely, astuteness) If someone is **astute,** they are good at interpreting situations and at making the right judgments and decisions.

asunder If something is torn **asunder,** it is forcefully separated into two parts.

asylum See **political asylum, lunatic asylum.**

asymmetric (asymmetrical, asymmetry) If something is **asymmetric** or **asymmetrical,** its two halves are a different size or shape. You talk about the **asymmetry** of something like this.

asymptomatic If someone who has an illness is **asymptomatic,** they are not yet showing any of its usual symptoms.

at is used to say where something happens, or where it is. *...a meeting held at the Central Science Laboratory.* ■ **At** is used to say where an action is directed. *I glanced at my watch... Someone threw an egg at him.* ■ **At** is used to say when something happens. *...at eight o'clock this evening.* ■ **At** is used to talk about the speed, amount, or level of something. *He was driving at over 100 miles per hour. ...glossy cookery books published at £25... The television was left on at full volume.* ■ **At** is used to mention what causes an action or reaction. *She was surprised at the news.* ■ **At** is used to describe the state, condition, or manner of something or someone. *Their countries had been at war for nearly six weeks... We are not at liberty to disclose that information. ...shots fired at random.* ■ If you are good or poor at something, you do it well or badly.

atavistic is used to describe instinctive feelings and behaviour which are inherited from our primitive ancestors. *...an atavistic fear of spiders.*

ate See **eat.**

atelier (*pron:* at-**tell**-yay) An **atelier** is an artist's studio.

atheism (*pron:* aith-ee-iz-zum) **(atheistic, atheist)** **Atheism** is the belief that there is no god. An **atheist** is someone who believes this. **Atheist** and **atheistic** are used to describe things connected with this belief.

athlete An **athlete** is a person who takes part in athletics competitions.

athletic (athletics, athletically, athleticism) **Athletics** consists of sports like running, the high jump, and the javelin. **Athletic** is used to talk about things to do with athletics and athletes. *...my athletic career.* ■ If you say someone is **athletic** or talk about their **athleticism,** you mean they are fit, active, and agile. *...an athletically executed cartwheel.*

atlas (atlases) An **atlas** is a book of maps.

atmosphere (atmospheric) An **atmosphere** is a layer of gases round a planet. The **atmosphere** is the layer of air round the earth. **Atmospheric** means to do with the atmosphere. *...atmospheric pollution.* ■ The **atmosphere** of a place is (a) the air you breathe there. *...the smoky atmosphere of the gaming room.* (b) its special character. *Durrell had lived in Alexandria and had absorbed its unique atmosphere.* ■ The **atmosphere** in a place is the mood of the people there. *There is a tense atmosphere.*

atoll An **atoll** is a ring-shaped coral island enclosing a lagoon.

atom An **atom** is the smallest amount of a substance which can take part in a chemical reaction. It consists of a central nucleus, containing protons and neutrons, with electrons orbiting around it.

atom bomb See **atomic bomb.**

atomic is used to talk about (a) things to do with atoms. *...atomic physics.* (b) things to do with the power produced by splitting atoms. *...atomic energy.*

atomic bomb The **atomic bomb** or **atom bomb** was the earliest nuclear bomb. It used nuclear fission to produce a powerful explosion.

atomizer An **atomizer** is a device which turns a liquid into a fine spray.

atone (atoning, atoned; atonement) If you **atone** for something wrong you have done, you do something to show you are sorry.

atop If one thing is **atop** another, it is on top of it. *...the stone statue atop the mountain.*

atrium (*pron:* ate-ree-um) An **atrium** is a cavity or chamber in the body, especially the two upper chambers of the heart. ■ In a building like a shopping mall, an **atrium** is a central hall which often has a glass roof and extends through several storeys.

atrocious (atrociously) If you say something is **atrocious,** you mean it is extremely bad. *The place stank atrociously.* ■ An **atrocious** act is shocking and cruel. *...atrocious crimes.*

atrocity (atrocities) An **atrocity** is a shocking cruel act.

atrophy (*pron:* **at**-trof-fee) is the wasting away of an organ or some other part of the body, as a result of disease or a poor diet. *...spinal muscular atrophy.* ■ **Atrophy** is the reduction in size or importance of something, because it is no longer needed or used. When this happens to something, you say it **atrophies.**

attach (attaches, attaching, attached; attachment) If you **attach** something to something else, you join or fix it to it. ■ An **attachment** is a device fixed to something like a machine to enable it to do different jobs. ■ If conditions are **attached** to an agreement, they are included as part of it. ■ If someone is **attached** to an organization, they are working for it on a temporary basis. A period of time spent working with an organization is sometimes called an **attachment.** ■ If you **attach** importance to something, you consider it to be important. ■ If you are **attached** to someone or something, you are fond of them and would not like to be without them; you can talk about your **attachment** to them.

attaché (*pron:* at-**tash**-shay) An **attaché** is a member of an embassy's staff or a representative of an organization, especially one with a particular area of responsibility. *...the cultural attaché of the ANC.* ■ An **attaché case** is a reinforced briefcase.

attack (attacker) If a person is **attacked** or is the victim of an **attack,** someone tries to hurt or kill them. The person who attacks them is called their **attacker.** ■ If soldiers are **attacked** or they come

under attack, enemy forces open fire on them. ■ You say someone **attacks** a person or thing when they criticize them strongly. *China has bitterly attacked the proposal.* ■ If you **attack** a problem, you start dealing with it in a determined way. ■ When a sports team **attacks,** the players make an effort to score, rather than just trying to stop the other side scoring. ■ An **attack** of an illness is a short period in which you suffer badly from it. *...an asthma attack.*

attain (**attaining, attained; attainment**) If you **attain** something you are aiming for, you achieve it. Your **attainments** are things you have achieved.

attainable If something is **attainable,** it can be achieved, although it may be difficult.

attempt If you **attempt** something or make an **attempt** at it, you try to do it. ■ **Attempted** is used to describe an unsuccessful attempt to do something, especially something criminal. *...attempted robbery. ...an attempted coup.* ■ An **attempt on** someone's life is an attempt to kill them.

attend (**attendance**) If you **attend** something like a meeting, you are present at it. ■ The **attendance** at a meeting is the total number of people present. ■ If someone is present when something is happening, you can say they are **in attendance.** ■ If you **attend** a school or college, you are taught there regularly. ■ If you **attend** to something, you deal with it.

attendant An **attendant** is a person whose job is to serve or help people. ■ If something is **attendant** on something else, you get the first thing as a result of the second. *...inequality and its attendant misery.*

attender An **attender** at some kind of event or meeting is someone who goes to it regularly. *She was a regular attender at opera first nights.*

attention is the notice that someone takes of something, or the interest that they show in it. If something or someone has your **attention,** you are looking at them, listening to them, or dealing with them. ■ If someone needs medical **attention,** they need medical treatment. ■ Sexual advances are sometimes called **attentions.** *She seemed both flustered and flattered by his attentions.*

attentive (**attentively**) If you are **attentive,** you are paying close attention to what is being said or done. ■ You say someone is **attentive** when they are helpful and polite.

attenuate (**attenuating, attenuated**) If something is **attenuated,** it is reduced or weakened.

attest If someone **attests** to something, they say it is true or exists. ■ If something **attests** to something else, it shows it exists. *Such popularity attests to the club's success.*

attic An **attic** is a room at the top of a house, just below the roof.

attire (**attired**) A person's **attire** is the clothes they are wearing, especially clothes worn for a special occasion or activity. *...people in funeral attire.* The way you are **attired** is the way you are dressed. *Her Majesty was attired in black satin.*

attitude Your **attitude** to someone or something is the way you think and feel about them, which shows in your behaviour.

attitudinizing (*or* **attitudinising**) is pretending to have certain attitudes or opinions, for the sake of effect.

attorney is the usual American word for a lawyer.

Attorney General A country's **Attorney General** is its chief law officer, who advises its government or monarch.

attract If something **attracts** people, it has features which make them come to it. *The show is expected to attract 50,000 visitors.* ■ If someone or something **attracts** you, you find them interesting or desirable. *The structure of the detective story is what has always attracted me.* ■ If something magnetic **attracts** an object, its magnetic force pulls the object towards it.

attraction If you have a feeling of **attraction** for someone, you enjoy their company or you desire them sexually. ■ The **attractions** of something are the things which make it interesting or desirable. ■ The **attractions** in an area are the buildings and other things which people visit for interest or enjoyment.

attractive (**attractively, attractiveness**) An **attractive** person is good looking. ■ If you call an object or place **attractive,** you mean it has a pleasant appearance. ■ You say something is **attractive** when it seems desirable. *...an attractive proposition.*

attributable If something is **attributable** to an event, situation, or person, it was caused by that event, situation, or person. *...personal injury directly attributable to a crime of violence.*

attribute (**attributing, attributed; attribution**) If you **attribute** (*pron:* at-**trib**-byoot) something to an event or situation, you decide it was caused by that event or situation. *...diseases directly attributed to smoking.* ■ If a piece of writing, work of art, or remark is **attributed** to someone, people say they wrote, created, or said it. *He is questioning the attribution of two items due to be sold at Sotheby's.* ■ If you **attribute** a quality or feature to someone or something, you think or say they have it. *It would be unwise to attribute too much importance to the photographs.* ■ An **attribute** (*pron:* **at**-trib-byoot) is a quality or feature.

attrition is a process in which people or things are gradually weakened or worn out. *There is likely to be further attrition of older industries.* A **war of attrition** is a war or some other kind of activity in which people gradually weaken their opponents by continual attack.

attuned If you are **attuned** to something like people's wishes, you understand them and can respond appropriately to them.

atypical (*pron:* eh-**tip**-ik-al) If something is **atypical,** it does not have the usual features of other things of its kind.

aubergine – Aubergines are pear-shaped vegetables with smooth purple skins. In the US, they are called 'eggplants'.

auburn hair is reddish-brown.

auction (**auctioning, auctioned**) An **auction** is a public sale at which goods are sold to the person who offers the highest price. When goods are sold like this, you say they are **auctioned** or **auctioned off.**

auctioneer An **auctioneer** is a person who is in charge of an auction.

audacious (**audacity**) If something you do is **audacious,** it is daring and risky. **Audacity** is doing daring or risky things. ■ **Audacity** is cheeky behaviour.

audible (**audibly, audibility**) If a sound is **audible,** it can be heard. Something's **audibility** is how well it can be heard.

audience The **audience** is the people watching or listening to a programme or performance. ■ The **audience** for someone's ideas, is the people who hear or read them. *The Dalai Lama's words are now reaching a wider audience.* ■ An **audience** with an important person is a formal meeting with them.

audio means to do with recording and reproducing sound. *...video and audio equipment.*

audio book An **audio book** is a book recorded on cassettes or CD.

audio-typist An **audio-typist** types letters and reports which have been dictated into a recording machine.

audio-visual equipment and materials involve both recorded sound and pictures.

audit (**auditing, audited**) When accountants **audit** an organization's accounts or do an **audit,** they check the accounts to make sure they are accurate. The job of carrying out audits is called **auditing.** ■ An **audit** can be a check on any aspect of an organization. For example, a **safety audit** checks that safety regulations are being observed.

audition (**auditioning, auditioned**) If you **audition** for a part in a play or film or are **auditioned** for it, you do a short performance so people can see if you are suitable for it. This performance is called an **audition.**

auditor An **auditor** is an accountant who officially checks the accuracy of an organization's accounts.

auditorium (*plural:* **auditoriums** *or* **auditoria**) In a building like a theatre or concert hall, the **auditorium** is the place where the audience sits.

auditory means to do with hearing. *...auditory information. ...the human auditory range.*

au fait (*pron:* oh **fay**) If you are **au fait** with a subject, you know quite a lot about it.

augment If you **augment** something, you make it larger by adding something else to it. *His wife augmented the family income by growing food crops for sale.*

augur (**auguring, augured**) If something **augurs** well, it suggests things will go well. If it **augurs** badly, it suggests things will go badly.

augury (**auguries**) An **augury** is a sign of what is likely to happen in the future.

august (*pron:* aw-**gust**) An **august** person is dignified and impressive.

auk – **Auks** are a group of sea-birds including razorbills and puffins. They have black and white feathers, a heavy body, and a short tail.

aunt Your **aunt** is the sister of your mother or father, or the wife of your uncle.

auntie (*or* **aunty**) (**aunties**) A person's **auntie** is their aunt. ■ **Auntie** is a jokey name for the BBC.

au pair An **au pair** is a young person who lives for a time with a family in a foreign country to learn the language. Au pairs help with housework and the care of small children and receive a small wage.

aura If you say someone or something has a certain **aura,** you mean the general impression created by their reputation or behaviour. *She had an aura of authority.*

aural (**aurally**) **Aural** means to do with the hearing process and things people hear. *...the aural nerves... The film is visually and aurally audacious.*

aurora borealis (*pron:* aw-**raw**-ra bor-ee-**ay**-liss) The **aurora borealis** or **Northern Lights** is a natural phenomenon consisting of moving bands of coloured lights seen in the sky in Arctic regions. A similar phenomenon in Antarctic regions is called the **aurora australis.**

auspices (*pron:* **aw**-spiss-siz) If something is done **under the auspices** of a person or organization, it is done with their approval and support. *...arms control negotiations under United Nations auspices.*

auspicious If something is **auspicious,** it gives hope of future success. *His career had an auspicious start.*

Aussie means 'Australian'. An **Aussie** is an Australian.

austere (**austerity**) If you describe something like a room as **austere,** you think it is plain and not very cheerful. ■ An **austere** way of life is simple and has no luxuries. **Austerity** is a situation in which people have to live like this. ■ If you describe someone as **austere,** you mean they are serious, strict, and severe.

Australasia (**Australasian**) **Australasia** is a name given to the south-west Pacific area, including Australia, New Zealand, New Guinea, and sometimes other islands.

authentic (**authentically, authenticity**) If something is **authentic,** it is genuine rather than an imitation or forgery. *Nobody doubts the authenticity of the diaries.* ■ An **authentic** account of something is reliable and accurate. *They should examine the authenticity of the players' claims.*

authenticate (**authenticating, authenticated; authentication**) If something is **authenticated,** it is shown or officially stated to be genuine. *It was accompanied for authentication purposes by a photograph.*

author (**authorial**) The **author** of a piece of writing is the person who wrote it. *In Barchester Towers, the authorial voice breaks into a description of the bishop's throne.* ■ The person responsible for bringing any situation into existence can be called its **author.** *Britain is the author of its own misfortunes.*

authorise See **authorize.**

authoritarian (**authoritarianism**) An **authoritarian** person or government keeps strict control of the people under them. You can also say behaviour or policies are **authoritarian.** *...authoritarian rule. ...an* increasingly *authoritarian approach.* An authoritarian style of government is called **authoritarianism.**

authoritative (**authoritatively**) You can describe a person as **authoritative** when they display a great deal of knowledge about a subject. *The magazine has established itself as the sport's most authoritative voice.*

authority (**authorities**) An **authority** is an official organization with the power to make decisions. *...the National Rivers Authority.* ■ The **authorities** in a place are the people officially in control there. ■ The **local authority** in an area is the local council. ■ If someone has **authority** over a group of people, they have the legal right or power to tell them what to do. ■ **Authority** is official permission. *The bank changed my current account to a business account without my authority.* ■ If someone is an **authority** on a subject, they know a great deal about it.

authorize (*or* **authorise**) (**authorizing, authorized; authorization**) If someone **authorizes** something or **authorizes** someone to do something, they give official permission for it. This permission is called **authorization.**

authorship The **authorship** of a piece of writing is the identity of the person who wrote it. *This is not proof of authorship.* ■ **Authorship** is writing books or articles for a living. *In due course his job led to acting, though not before he had considered authorship.*

autistic (**autism**) If someone is **autistic,** they have a serious mental disorder called **autism** which makes them unable to relate to the world around them. Autism usually begins in childhood.

auto is an American word for car.

autobahn (*plural:* **autobahns** *or* **autobahnen**) In places where German is spoken, motorways are called **autobahns.**

autobiography (**autobiographies; autobiographical**) If someone writes their **autobiography,** they write their life story. If a book or film is **autobiographical,** it is based on things which really happened to the author or director.

autocracy (**autocracies; autocrat**) **Autocracy** is government or management by one person who has complete power. An **autocracy** is a country or organization controlled like this. The person who controls it is called an **autocrat.**

autocratic (**autocratically**) If someone is **autocratic,** they have complete power and make decisions without consulting other people.

autocue (*or* **Autocue**) An **autocue** is a device used by people speaking on TV. It displays words for them to read in such a way that they can also look straight at the camera. 'Autocue' is a trademark.

autograph If you ask a famous person for their **autograph,** you ask them to sign their name on something for you. If they **autograph** something like a book or record, they sign it.

auto-immune diseases involve antibodies attacking normal tissues in the body rather than the harmful bacteria they are meant to attack.

automate (**automating, automated; automation**) If something like an industrial process is **automated,** machines do the jobs previously done by people.

automatic (**automatically**) **Automatic** is used to describe machines which do things without needing someone to control them. *...automatic gearboxes.* ■ An **automatic** or **automatic** weapon is a weapon which continues to fire shells until you stop pressing the trigger. ■ An **automatic** right or punishment is one which always applies in particular circumstances. *...automatic promotion to the First Division. He was given an automatic one-match suspension.* ■ If something you do is **automatic,** you do it without thinking about it.

automatic pilot (*or* autopilot *or* auto-pilot) An **automatic pilot** is a device in an aircraft which controls its speed and direction automatically. ■ If you say you are **on automatic pilot,** you mean you are doing something without thinking about it, usually because you have done it so many times before.

automaton (*pron:* aw-**tom**-mat-ton) (*plural:* **automatons** *or* **automata**) An **automaton** is a robot. ■ If you say someone is an **automaton,** you mean they do things without thinking about them, like a machine.

automobile An **automobile** is a car.

automotive is used to talk about things to do with motor vehicles.

autonomous (*pron:* aw-**tonn**-nom-muss) (**autonomously, autonomy.**) An **autonomous** region has a large degree of self-government but does not have the full status of a country. Having this degree of self-government is called **autonomy.** ■ When part of an organization has a large degree of independence, you can talk about it being **autonomous.** *The latest venture proposed by Delta would operate autonomously with its own management.*

autopilot See **automatic pilot.**

autopsy (**autopsies**) An **autopsy** is an examination of a dead body by a pathologist to try to discover the cause of death. This examination is also called a 'post-mortem'.

autumn is the season between summer and winter. In the US and Canada, autumn is called the **fall.**

autumnal is used to describe things which are characteristic of autumn. *...a chilly autumnal evening.*

auxiliary (**auxiliaries**) **Auxiliary** is used to describe people employed to provide assistance and backup. *...auxiliary staff.* People like these are sometimes called **auxiliaries.** ■ **Auxiliary** equipment is extra equipment which is there for use in emergencies or when the usual equipment fails. *...an auxiliary generator.*

auxiliary verb An auxiliary verb is a verb which is used with another verb. 'Do' is called an **auxiliary verb** when it is used in questions, as in 'Do you want an apple?' or in negative sentences like 'I do not want to go out'. 'Have' and 'be' are auxiliary verbs when they are used to form tenses, as in 'I have eaten my lunch' or 'I am eating my lunch'. Verbs such as 'can' and 'will' are also called auxiliary verbs.

avail (**availing, availed**) If something you do is to **no avail,** it does not achieve what you want. ■ If you **avail** yourself of something, you make use of it.

available (**availability**) If something is **available**, it is there for you to use, or you can obtain it. ■ You say a person is **available** when they are free to talk to you, or free to take part in something.

avalanche An **avalanche** is a large mass of snow or rock falling down the side of a mountain. ■ An **avalanche** of things is a large amount of them happening at the same time. ...*an avalanche of applications.*

avant-garde (*pron:* av-ong-**gard**) art, music, and theatre are concerned with trying out new ideas and techniques.

avarice (*pron:* **av**-a-riss) (**avaricious**) Avarice is a greedy desire for money.

avenge (**avenging, avenged; avenger**) If you **avenge** something wrong which has been done to you, you make the person who did it suffer in return.

avenue An **avenue** is a wide road with trees on either side. ■ An **avenue** is a way of getting something done. *China wanted every avenue for a peaceful solution explored.*

aver (*pron:* av-**vur**) (**averring, averred**) If you **aver** that something is the case, you state it as a definite fact.

average (**averaging, averaged; averagely**) An **average** is the result you get when you add several amounts together and divide the total by the number of amounts. You say something **averages** a certain amount when the amount is calculated in this way. *Production averaged 14,412 barrels a day.* You can also say something is a certain amount **on average.** *Every tonne of coal contains on average 30 kilograms of nitrogen.* ■ **Average** is used to say someone or something is standard or normal, rather than extreme or exceptional. ...*an averagely fit person.*

averse If you say someone is not **averse** to doing something, you mean they see nothing wrong in it and do it fairly often. ■ If you say someone would not be **averse** to doing something, you mean they would be quite happy to do it.

aversion If you have an **aversion** to someone or something, you dislike them.

avert If something undesirable is **averted**, it is prevented from happening. ■ If you **avert your eyes**, you avoid looking at something, because you find it embarrassing or unpleasant.

aviary (**aviaries**) An **aviary** is a large cage in which birds are kept.

aviation is used to talk about the operation and manufacture of aircraft.

aviator In the early days of flying, pilots were called **aviators.**

avid (**avidly**) Avid is used to say someone is keen and enthusiastic about something. ...*an avid fisherman.*

avionics is electronics technology applied to aircraft, missiles, and spacecraft.

avocado (**avocados**) The **avocado** or **avocado pear** is a dark green tropical fruit with a large stone and smooth oily flesh.

avoid (**avoiding, avoided; avoidance**) If you **avoid** something bad which looks like happening, you succeed in preventing it. ■ If you **avoid** doing something, you deliberately do not do it. ■ If you **avoid** someone or something, you deliberately keep away from them. ■ If you **avoid** a subject, you deliberately do not talk about it. ■ **Tax avoidance:** see tax.

avoidable If you say something bad which has happened was **avoidable**, you mean it could have been prevented.

avoidance See avoid.

avow (**avowal; avowed, avowedly**) If you **avow** something, you admit it or declare it. What you say is called an **avowal.** ■ **Avowed** is used to describe intentions and beliefs which people openly admit they have. ...*Kennedy's avowed aim to seek re-election.* ...*South Yemen, the only avowedly Marxist state in the Arab world.*

avuncular You say an older man is **avuncular** when he is kind and helpful to younger people.

await (**awaiting, awaited**) If you are **awaiting** someone or something, you are waiting for them. ■ If something **awaits** you, it is going to happen to you in the future. *Jail awaits anybody who publishes a classified document.*

awake (**awaking, awoke, have awoken**) If someone is **awake**, they are not asleep. ■ When you **awake**, you wake up. If something **awakes** you, it wakes you up. *Mr Didier was awoken by a bang on his front door.* ■ If people **awake to** a danger, they become aware of it.

awaken (**awakening, awakened**) If feelings are **awakened**, people start having them. ...*the fears and anxieties awakened by unification.* The beginning of certain kinds of feelings and beliefs can be called an **awakening.** ...*sexual awakening.* ...*the story of a young boy's moral awakening.* ■ If you **awaken** to problems or facts, you become aware of them. ■ If you have a **rude awakening,** you are suddenly made aware of an unpleasant fact. ■ When you **awaken,** you wake up.

award If you are **awarded** something like a prize, you are given it for doing something well. What you are given is called an **award.** ...*an award-winning film.* ■ If someone is **awarded** a pay rise or bonus, they are given it. ■ If you are **awarded** money by a court, you are given it as compensation. The money is called an **award.** ■ If the government or some other organization **awards** money, it gives it to people for a special purpose. *The museum has been awarded a £25,000 grant by the heritage department.*

aware (**awareness**) If you are **aware** of a fact, you know about it. ■ If you say someone is **aware,** you mean they are alert to what is going on around them. ■ You say someone is **aware** when they are knowledgeable about a subject and notice new developments quickly. *They are becoming more politically aware every day.*

awash If a place is **awash,** there is water all over it. ■ If you say a place is **awash** with certain people or things, you mean there are a lot of them there. ...*a nation awash with guns.*

away If you move **away** from a person, place, or object, you move so you are no longer near to them. You can say that people, places, or objects are a certain distance **away** from each other. *The nearest town is 40 miles away.* ■ You say someone is **away** when they are not in their usual place, for example at work or at home. ■ If something is a certain length of time **away,** that time will pass before it happens. ■ In sport, an **away** game is played at the opposing team's ground. ■ **Away** is used to say an action or sound goes on continuously. *...with the engine humming away.*

awe (awed) Awe is a feeling of great admiration and respect. If you are **in awe** of something or someone, you feel like that about them. If someone is **awed** by something, they are overcome with admiration for it, and may feel inferior because of it. *Di Falco is clearly awed by the magnificent medieval architecture.*

awe-inspiring You say something is **awe-inspiring** when it makes a great impression on you, because of its beauty or other outstanding qualities. *...an awe-inspiring canyon.*

awesome (awesomely) If you say something is **awesome,** you mean it is extremely impressive. *Their strength is awesome.* ■ If you call a problem or task **awesome,** you mean it will be very difficult to deal with.

awestruck If you are **awestruck** by something, it fills you with amazement and admiration.

awful (awfully, awfulness) Awful is used to describe things which are very bad or unpleasant. *...awful conditions... They've been treated so awfully.* ■ People use **awful** to express their dislike of someone or something. *...awful jokes.* ■ People use **awful** and **awfully** in front of other words to emphasize them. *An awful lot of people have no insurance... It's an awfully simple thing to do.*

awhile means for a short time. *They must wait awhile.*

awkward (awkwardly; awkwardness, awkwardnesses) Awkward situations and problems are difficult to deal with. ■ If someone is **awkward,** they are unreasonably difficult to deal with. ■ You say someone is **awkward** when they do not behave in a confident way, because they are shy. ■ If someone's movements are **awkward,** they are clumsy and inelegant.

awning An **awning** is a piece of canvas or other material attached to something like a caravan or the front of a shop to provide shelter from the rain or sun.

awoke (awoken) See **awake.**

awry (*pron:* a-**rye**) If something **goes awry,** it goes wrong. ■ If something is **awry,** it is not in its proper position. *...men with shirts open to the waist and ties awry.*

axe (*Am:* **ax**) (**axes, axing** *or* **axeing, axed**) An **axe** is a tool for cutting wood. It has a heavy metal blade and a long handle. ■ If a project is **axed,** it is scrapped. You can also talk about people's jobs being **axed.** ■ If the **axe falls** on something, it is brought to an end. ■ If you say someone **has an axe to grind,** you mean they have personal motives for doing something. *...a journalist with an axe to grind against her newspaper.* ■ **Axes** is the plural of 'axis'.

axiom An **axiom** is a saying or idea which people accept as true. *It's an axiom of mountaineering that the good climber knows when to turn back.*

axiomatic If you say something is **axiomatic,** you mean it is a basic truth which cannot be questioned.

axis (*plural:* **axes** *pron:* **ak**-seez) An **axis** is an imaginary line through the centre of something, around which it seems to turn. *...a shift in the earth's axis.* ■ An **axis** is one of the lines on a graph on which the scales of measurement are marked. Most graphs have two axes: one horizontal and one vertical. ■ An **axis** is a friendly relationship between two countries. *...the Franco-German axis.*

axle An **axle** is a bar or shaft on which a wheel or wheels rotate.

ayatollah An **ayatollah** is a Shi-ite Muslim religious leader.

aye (*rhymes with 'lie'*) is an old word for 'yes'. It is still used in some parts of Britain, especially Northern England and Scotland. ■ In Parliament, the **ayes** are the people who vote in favour of a motion. The people who vote against it are called the 'noes'.

azalea (*pron:* a-**zayl**-ya) The **azalea** is a garden shrub with brightly coloured sweet-smelling flowers.

AZT is a medicine which has been tried as a treatment for people who are HIV positive and for AIDS sufferers. AZT is short for 'azidothymidine'.

azure is a bright blue colour.

B b

b & b See **bed and breakfast.**

B.A. A **B.A.** is a university degree in a subject such as languages, literature, history, or social science. B.A. stands for 'Bachelor of Arts'.

babble (**babbling, babbled**) If someone is **babbling,** they are talking in a confused or excited way. ■ You can call the sound of a lot of people talking at once a **babble.** ...*the babble of the crowd.*

babe A **babe** is a baby. ■ Some men refer to a very attractive woman as a **babe.**

baboon − **Baboons** are a type of African monkey with pointed faces, large teeth, and long tails.

baby (**babies**) A **baby** is a very young child who cannot walk or talk. ■ **Baby** is used to talk about young animals and plants. ...*baby carrots.* ■ If someone tries to get rid of the bad parts of a system, and in doing so also gets rid of something important, you can say they have **thrown the baby out with the bathwater.**

baby-boom A **baby-boom** is a period of time when a lot of babies are born in a particular place.

baby-boomer A **baby-boomer** is someone born in the period just after the Second World War.

baby buggy A **baby buggy** is a lightweight folding pushchair.

baby-sit (**baby-sitter**) If you **baby-sit,** you look after someone's children while they go out.

baccarat (*pron:* **back**-a-rah) is a card game in which players bet against the dealer.

bachelor A **bachelor** is a man who has never married. ■ A **bachelor's** degree is a first university degree, for example Bachelor of Arts (B.A.).

Bachelor of Arts See **B.A.**

Bachelor of Science See **B.Sc.**

back (**backing**) If you move **back,** you move away from something, or in the opposite direction to the one you are facing. ■ If a vehicle **backs** or is **backed,** it moves backwards. ■ **Back** is used to say someone returns to where they were before, or to what they were doing before. *I went back to sleep.* ■ If you get something **back,** you get it again after having been without it for a while. ■ If you do something **back** to someone, you do what they have done to you. *She smiled back at me.* ■ You use **back** when you are talking about the past. *The house dates back to 1756.* ...*a back issue of New Scientist.* ■ A person's or animal's **back** is the part of their body between their neck and their buttocks. ■ The **back** of something is the part furthest from the front. You add **-backed** to say what kind of back something has. ...*straight-backed chairs.* See also **backing.** ■ The area a building **backs onto** is the area just behind it. ■ A **back** road is small and narrow with very little traffic. ■ In games like football and hockey, a **back** is a player whose main job is to stop the other team from scoring. ■ If you **back** someone or something or give them **backing,** you support them, often by giving them money. A **backer** is someone who does this. ...*an American-*

backed film. ■ If musicians or singers **back** a singer or provide the **backing** for them, they accompany them. ■ If you **back** a horse in a race, you bet on it. ■ To **back** someone or something up means to support them. ■ **Back** is used in some verbs, for example **back down** and **back out,** to talk about someone deciding not to go ahead with something, usually something they have threatened or promised to do.

backache is a pain in your back.

back bench (**backbencher**) The **back benches** are MPs who are not leading members of the government or opposition. These MPs are also called **backbenchers.**

backbiting is saying unpleasant things about someone when they are not there.

backbone A person's or animal's **backbone** is the column of small linked bones down the middle of their back. ■ If you say something is the **backbone** of an organization or system, you mean it makes it work, or holds it together. *The regimental system is the backbone of the British army.*

back-breaking work is very hard physical work.

backcloth See **backdrop.**

backcomb (*or* **back-comb**) If you **backcomb** your hair, you move a comb through your hair towards the scalp rather than away from it, so that your hair looks fuller.

backdate (**backdating, backdated**) If something like an agreement or law is **backdated,** it is made to operate from an earlier date than when it is settled or approved.

back door (*or* **backdoor**) If something is done through the **back door,** it is done secretly and avoiding the usual procedures.

backdrop (**backcloth**) A **backdrop** or **backcloth** is a large piece of cloth, often with scenery painted on it, hung at the back of a stage when a play is being performed. ■ If you say something happens against a particular **backdrop,** you are talking about the general situation at the time it happened, or about other things happening then. ...*a love story, played out against a backdrop of revolution.*

backer See **back.**

backfire (**backfiring, backfired**) If a plan **backfires,** it has the opposite effect from what is intended. ■ If a motor vehicle **backfires,** unburnt exhaust gases explode in the exhaust pipe, making a loud bang.

backgammon is a game for two people, played on a board marked with long triangles.

background Someone's **background** is the kind of family they come from and the education and experience they have had. ...*her middle-class background.* ■ The **background** to a situation is what has led up to it. ■ **Background** is used to talk about things you can hear or see at the same time as the thing you are paying attention to. ...*the constant background noise.*

backhand In games like tennis, a **backhand** is a stroke made with the back of the player's hand facing the direction they are hitting the ball. See also **forehand.**

backhanded (or **back-handed**) A **backhanded** compliment contains a criticism as well as praise.

backhander A **backhander** is a bribe.

backing is a layer of material put on the back of something, to protect it or make it stronger.

backlash You say there is a **backlash** when people react strongly against something.

backlog A **backlog** is a build-up of things waiting to be dealt with.

backpack (or **back-pack**) (**backpacker, backpacking**) A **backpack** is a rucksack. People who travel around with their belongings in a backpack are called **backpackers.** You say people like this are **backpacking.**

back-pedal If someone **back-pedals,** they go back on something they have said. ■ You can say someone **back-pedals** when they do something more slowly than before.

backroom People who do important work but are never seen by the public are sometimes called **backroom boys.** ■ **Backroom** is used to talk about things which are arranged or decided in secret. ...*a backroom deal.*

back-seat driver A **back-seat driver** is a car passenger who keeps telling the driver what to do. ■ You say someone is a **back-seat driver** when they give unwanted advice.

backside A person's **backside** is their bottom.

back-slapping behaviour is friendly in a rather hearty way.

backsliding is going back on something which has been agreed or promised. ■ **Backsliding** is a return to something bad after a period of reform. *They resent any backsliding towards the old Soviet model.*

backstage is the part of a theatre behind the stage.

back street (or **backstreet**) The **back streets** of a town or city are the parts with smaller and poorer houses, away from the main streets. ■ **Back-street** activities are carried out unofficially, secretly, and often illegally. ...*a back-street abortion.*

backstroke is a swimming stroke in which you lie on your back, kick your legs, and move your arms back over your head.

backtrack (or **back-track**) If someone **backtracks** on something they have said, they change their mind and no longer stand by it.

back-up A **back-up** is something like an extra plan, which is there in case the main one goes wrong. ■ **Backup** is used to talk about extra support which is available if it is needed. *There is a demand for better back-up facilities.* ■ See also **back.**

backward (**backwards; backwardness**) If you move **backwards** or make a **backward** movement, you move in the direction your back is facing. ■ If you do something **backwards,** you do it the opposite way to the way it is usually done. *He is telling the story backwards.* ■ **Backward** is sometimes used to describe someone or something that is considered to be less developed than other people or things of the same kind. ...*the country's ability to overcome its economic backwardness.* ■ If you say someone **knows** something **backwards,** you mean they know it very well. ■ If you **bend** or **fall over backwards** to do what someone wants, you do everything you can to achieve it. ■ People who are **backward-looking** are not interested in new ideas and prefer things not to change.

backwash The **backwash** of a moving boat is the wave spreading out behind it. ■ **Backwash** is used to talk about the effects one thing has on other things. *The Treasury has been blaming the pound's weakness on the backwash from the falling dollar.*

backwater You call a place a **backwater** when it is cut off from new ideas or influences, and from important events happening elsewhere in the world.

backwoods When people talk about the **backwoods,** they mean the parts of a region which are a long way from large towns and are cut off from modern ideas.

backwoodsman (**backwoodsmen**) People described as **backwoodsmen** are satisfied with old-fashioned ways of doing things.

backyard (or **back-yard**) A **backyard** is a small paved area behind a house. ■ In America, a **backyard** is a small garden behind a house. ■ When people talk about things happening in **their own backyard,** they mean things happening close to their country, rather than in distant parts of the world.

bacon is salted meat from the sides or back of a pig.

bacteria See **bacterium.**

bacteriology (**bacteriologist; bacteriological**) **Bacteriology** is the study of bacteria. **Bacteriological** means connected with bacteriology.

bacterium (plural: **bacteria**) **Bacteria** are very small organisms, many of which cause disease.

bad (**badly, badness**) **Bad** is used to describe something unpleasant, undesirable, or of poor quality. ...*bad weather.* ...*bad news... The whole project was badly managed.* ■ A **bad** person is wicked or evil. ...*a just world order, where goodness is rewarded and badness punished.* ■ If someone uses **bad** language, they use swear words. ■ If you feel **bad** about something, you feel guilty or uncomfortable. ■ If someone has, for example, a **bad** leg, there is something wrong with it. ■ When food has gone **bad,** it is no longer fit to eat, because it has decayed. ■ A **bad** debt is unlikely to be repaid. ■ When people say something is **not bad,** they mean they are impressed by it. ■ See also **badly.**

baddy (or **baddie**) (**baddies**) The bad characters in a story or film are sometimes humorously called the **baddies.**

bade See **bid.**

badge A **badge** is a small piece of metal, plastic, or cloth worn on someone's clothes to show their rank, to show they belong to an organization, or for decoration. ■ When something is regarded as standing for a particular quality, you can say it is a **badge** of that quality. *What better badge of culture than a scarf from the British Museum?*

badger (**badgering, badgered**) The **badger** is a wild animal which lives underground and is active mainly at night. It has a white head with two broad black stripes along the sides. ■ If someone **badgers** you, they keep trying to get you to do something, or asking you questions.

badinage (*pron:* **bad**-in-nazh; *the 'zh' sounds like 's' in 'pleasure'*) **Badinage** is humorous or light-hearted conversation that often involves teasing someone. ...*the Bishop's light-hearted badinage.*

badly is used to emphasize the harmful effects of something. *Some people have suffered badly.* ■ If someone is **badly** off, they are poor. ■ If you say something reflects **badly** on someone, you mean it gives a bad impression of them. You can also say they come out of it **badly.** ■ If you think **badly** of someone, you have a poor opinion of them. ■ If someone wants or needs something **badly,** they want or need it very much. ■ See also **bad.**

badminton is a game in which players with racquets hit a small feathered object called a shuttlecock over a high net.

bad-mouth If you **bad-mouth** someone, you say unpleasant things about them.

baffle (**baffling, baffled; bafflement**) If something **baffles** you, you cannot understand it or solve it. You say something like this is **baffling.** *The general response was one of bafflement.*

bag (**bagging, bagged**) A **bag** is a container made of something like leather or paper and used for carrying things. ■ When something is **bagged,** it is put into a bag or bags. *Compost was bagged and sold.* ■ A person's **bags** are their luggage. ■ If you **bag** something, you get it for yourself before anyone else has a chance to. *I arrived early enough to bag the corner table.* ■ **Bags of** something means a lot of it. *The house has bags of character.* ■ If you say something is **in the bag,** you mean you are certain to get it or achieve it.

bagel (*pron:* **bay**-gl) **Bagels** are hard ring-shaped bread rolls traditional in Jewish baking.

baggage Your **baggage** is the suitcases and bags you have packed for a journey. ■ You can use **baggage** to refer to someone's emotional problems, fixed ideas, or prejudices. *They cannot escape their emotional baggage.*

baggy clothing hangs loosely on your body.

bagpipes are a musical instrument consisting of reed pipes supplied with air from a bag.

baguette (*pron:* bag-**get**) A **baguette** is a small narrow loaf.

bail (**bailing, bailed**) In Britain, someone awaiting trial can be **bailed** or released on **bail,** which means they are set free until they are due to appear in court, usually provided someone agrees to pay a sum of money if they fail to do so. ■ If you **bail** (or **bale**) someone **out,** you help them out of a difficult situation, often by providing money. ■ When someone **bails out** (or **bales out**) a boat, they scoop or pump water out of it. ■ In cricket, the **bails** are the two wooden bars across the stumps. ■ See also **bale.**

bailiff A **bailiff** is an officer of the law courts who enforces decisions of the court, often by taking someone's property as payment for money which is owed.

bairn is a Scottish word for 'child'.

bait (**baiting, baited**) **Bait** is food put on a hook or in a trap for catching fish or animals. When you **bait** a hook or trap, you put food on it or in it. ■ If someone or something is used as **bait,** they are used to tempt or encourage someone to do something. ■ If someone **rises to the bait** or **takes the bait,** they react to something in the way they are meant to. ■ If someone **baits** a person, they deliberately try to make them angry by teasing them. ■ You use **-baiting** to form another word which shows a certain person or group of people is being ridiculed or persecuted. ...*audience-baiting taunts.* ■ Badger-**baiting** and bear-**baiting** involve letting dogs attack these animals, while ensuring they cannot defend themselves.

baize is a smooth thick woollen cloth, usually green, used for covering things such as snooker and card tables.

bake (**baking, baked**) If you **bake** something, you cook it in an oven without extra fat or liquid. ■ You can use **baking** to describe hot, dry weather or places. ...*the baking Jordanian desert.* ■ You can describe the ground as **baked** when the sun has made it very dry and hard. ...*sun-baked countryside.*

baker (**bakery, bakeries**) A **baker** is a person or firm that makes bread, cakes, and pastry. A **bakery** is a place where these things are made. ■ A **bakery** or **baker's** is a shop where bread and cakes are sold.

balaclava A **balaclava** is a close-fitting woollen hood which covers all your head and neck except your face.

balalaika A **balalaika** is a guitar-like instrument from Russia. It has a triangular body and three strings.

balance (**balancing, balanced**) If someone or something **balances** on something, they remain there without falling. *I balanced on the ledge.* ■ If someone or something is **off balance,** they are unsteady and likely to fall. If they do fall, you can say they **lose their balance.** ■ **Balance** is used to talk about situations in which everything is in the right proportion to everything else. If you **balance** one thing with another, you get them in the right proportion to each other. ...*a balance between work and play.* ...*a balanced diet.* ■ If a small political party holds the **balance of power** in a parliament, it is able to give a larger party a majority by supporting this larger party. ■ When someone **balances** their finances, they make sure the amount spent is not more than the amount received. You say the two amounts **balance** or the books **balance.** ■ The **balance** in a bank account is the amount of money in it. ■ The **balance** of an amount of money is what remains to be paid for something or what remains when part of the amount has been spent. ■ A country's **balance of payments** is the difference between the amount paid for its imports and the amount paid for its exports. Its **balance of trade** or **trade balance** is the difference in value between its imports and exports. ■ If a situation is finely **balanced** or **in the balance,** it is uncertain what the outcome will be. ■ If something like a report is **balanced** or **well-balanced,** it is fair and reasonable. ■ If you say a person is **well-balanced,** you mean they are calm and reasonable. ■ You say **on balance** to show you are stating an opinion after considering all the relevant details. *The deal was not very good but, on balance, preferable to no deal at all.* ■ A **balance** is a pair of scales.

balcony (**balconies**) A **balcony** is a platform on the outside wall of a building, with a wall or railing along its outer edge, usually reached from a door or window inside the building. ■ In a theatre or cinema, the **balcony** is an upstairs seating area.

bald (**balding; baldly; baldness**) If someone is **bald,** they have little or no hair on top of their head. When they are beginning to lose their hair, you say they are **balding.** ...*the cause of baldness.* ■ When tyres are **bald** or **balding,** they have worn smooth. ■ A **bald** statement is made plainly and often bluntly. *'They didn't want me,' he said baldly.*

bald eagle The **bald eagle** is a large North American eagle. It is the US national bird.

balderdash When people say something is **balderdash,** they mean it is silly or untrue.

bale (**baling, baled; baler**) A **bale** is a large amount of something like hay, paper, or cloth tied into a bundle. When something is tied up into bundles like this, you say it is **baled.** ■ When someone **bales out** of an aircraft, they make an emergency parachute jump. ■ See also **bail.**

baleful (**balefully**) Baleful people are full of hatred. A person's expression can also be **baleful.** ...*staring balefully.* ■ If something has a **baleful** effect, it causes harm.

balk (*or* **baulk**) If someone **balks** at something, they are unwilling to do it.

ball A **ball** is a round object used in games like tennis, cricket, and football. Games like these are called **ball** games. See also **ball game.** ■ Anything with a round shape can be called a **ball.** *Roll the dough into a ball.* ■ If someone **keeps their eye on the ball,** they pay careful attention to what is going on. If they **take their eye off the ball,** they lose concentration for a time. ■ If someone **sets** or **starts the ball rolling,** they start something happening. ■ If someone **plays ball,** they co-operate. ■ A **ball** is a formal event where people dance.

ballad A **ballad** is (a) a long song or poem which tells a story. (b) a slow romantic popular song.

ballast is a material carried by ships when they have no cargo, to make them more stable. Some balloons carry ballast; it is released to make the balloon go upwards. ■ **Ballast** is the small stones used as a foundation for railways or roads.

ball bearing – Ball bearings are small metal balls used to make the moving parts of a machine run smoothly.

ballcock A **ballcock** is a device which controls the flow of water into a tank or cistern.

ballerina A **ballerina** is a female ballet dancer.

ballet (**balletic**) Ballet is a style of graceful and athletic dancing, with set steps and movements. ■ A **ballet** is a work for the theatre in which ballet and mime are used to tell a story. ■ Groups of ballet dancers often have **Ballet** as part of their name. ...*the New York City Ballet.* ■ **Balletic** (*pron:* bal-

let-tik) is used (a) to talk about things to do with ballet. ...*a balletic entertainment.* (b) to describe movements which remind you of ballet. *The penguin is at its balletic best underwater.*

ball game When Americans talk about the **ball game,** they mean a baseball match. ■ If you say something is **a different ball game** or **a whole new ball game,** you mean a new situation has arisen and things have to be looked at differently.

ballgown (*or* **ball gown**) A **ballgown** is a long dress worn at formal evening occasions.

ballistic – Ballistics is the study of the movement of things shot or thrown through the air, for example bullets fired from a gun. **Ballistic** is used to talk about things to do with ballistics. ...*ballistic tests.* ■ A **ballistic missile** is guided automatically in the first part of its flight, then falls freely near the target.

balloon (**ballooning, ballooned; balloonist**) A **balloon** is a small bag made of thin rubber which expands when you blow air into it. ■ A **balloon** or **hot-air balloon** is a large strong bag filled with gas or hot air, which can carry passengers underneath. Travelling in a balloon like this is called **ballooning.** ■ If an object **balloons,** it gets bigger and rounder. *My knee ballooned again with fluid.* ■ If an amount **balloons,** it suddenly gets bigger. *The cost of health has ballooned.*

ballot (**balloting, balloted**) A **ballot** is a system of secret voting. Each voter has a **ballot paper,** which they mark their vote on. ■ When **balloting** takes place, a ballot is held. ■ When people are **balloted,** a ballot is used to find out their views.

ballot box A **ballot box** is a strong box which people put their ballot papers in when they vote. ■ When people talk about the **ballot box,** they mean the system of democratic elections. ...*trying to win power through the ballot box.*

ballot-rigging is the act of interfering with a vote, to make the result go in favour of a particular party or person.

ballpoint A **ballpoint** or **ballpoint pen** is a pen with a small metal ball at the end which transfers the ink from the pen onto the paper.

ballroom A **ballroom** is a large room, often in a hotel, used for dancing. ■ **Ballroom dancing** is a style of dancing in which a man and woman dance together following a set routine of steps.

ballyhoo The publicity surrounding a planned event is sometimes called **ballyhoo.**

balm is sweet-smelling soothing ointment.

balmy (**balmier, balmiest**) Balmy weather is mild and pleasant.

balsa or **balsa wood** is a very light wood used for making things like model aeroplanes.

balsam is (a) a sweet-smelling resin used in medicines and ointments. (b) a type of flowering plant.

balti is a type of cooking which came originally from Baltistan in north Pakistan. Balti dishes are cooked and served in wok-like pans.

Baltic The **Baltic States** are Lithuania, Latvia, and Estonia.

balustrade A **balustrade** is a rail or wall along a balcony or staircase.

bamboo is a tall fast-growing tropical grass. The stems are woody and are used to make things like furniture. The young shoots can be eaten.

bamboozle (**bamboozling, bamboozled**) If someone **bamboozles** you, they deliberately trick or confuse you.

ban (**banning, banned**) If someone in authority **bans** something, they forbid it to be done, shown, or used. ■ If someone is **banned** from something, they are officially forbidden to go somewhere or do certain things. ■ An order forbidding something is called a **ban.** ...*a trade ban.*

banal (**banality, banalities**) If something is **banal** (*pron:* ban-**nahl**), it is very ordinary and not interesting. You can talk about the **banality** (*pron:* ban-**nal**-i-ty) of something like this. **Banalities** are uninteresting remarks and happenings.

banana — Bananas are long curved fruit with yellow skins. ■ A **banana skin** is something which causes someone to make a mistake and look silly. *The government was slithering from one banana skin to another.* ■ Poor countries with unstable governments are sometimes called **banana republics.** This is an offensive use. ■ You can say someone has **gone bananas** when (a) they behave in a silly or excitable way. (b) they become very angry.

band A **band** is a group of musicians who play together. Musicians who play brass instruments together are called a **brass band.** A **military band** is a group of wind and percussion musicians in the armed forces. ■ A group of people who share the same interests or beliefs can be called a **band.** ...*a band of enthusiastic supporters.* ■ When people **band together,** they join together to try and get something done. ■ A **band** is a flat narrow strip of cloth, worn around a person's head or wrist. ■ A **band** is a strip of colour or light. *A band of light glowed in the space between floor and door.* ■ A **band** is a range of numbers or values in a system of measurement. When something is divided into bands, this is called **banding.** ...*a basic-rate tax band of up to £20,000.* ...*the banding system for valuing houses.*

bandage (**bandaging, bandaged**) A **bandage** is a strip of cloth wrapped round an injured part of the body. When someone wraps a bandage round a part of someone's body, you say they **bandage** it.

Band-Aid A **Band-Aid** is a sticking plaster for covering small cuts. 'Band-Aid' is a trademark.

bandanna (*or* **bandana**) A **bandanna** is a large brightly-coloured handkerchief worn around the neck or head.

bandit (**banditry**) A **bandit** is an armed robber, usually belonging to a gang. **Banditry** is armed robbery.

bandolier (*pron:* ban-dol-**leer**) A **bandolier** is a shoulder belt with small loops for holding things like gun cartridges.

bandsman (**bandsmen**) Musicians who play in brass or military bands are called **bandsmen.**

bandstand A **bandstand** is a platform with a roof and open sides where a brass band can play in the open air.

bandwagon If you talk about someone jumping on the **bandwagon,** you mean they are supporting a movement because they think it will succeed, or because it has become popular. ■ If someone starts a **bandwagon** rolling, they start a movement which they hope will attract a lot of support.

bandwidth A **bandwidth** is the range of frequencies within a particular waveband used for a radio transmission.

bandy (**bandies, bandying, bandied**) When people **bandy** ideas, they discuss them in a casual way. You can also say ideas are **bandied about** or **bandied around.** ■ When words are **bandied around,** people use them a lot without paying much attention to their meaning. *The catch phrase bandied about by the company's chairman is 'global localization'.* ■ If someone has **bandy** legs or is **bandy-legged,** their legs curve outwards at the knees.

bane If something or someone is the **bane** of a person or organization, they cause them a lot of annoyance.

bang A **bang** is a short loud noise. ■ If you **bang** something, you hit it noisily. ■ If you **bang** a door or window, you shut it quickly and noisily. ■ If you **bang** into something, you collide with it. ■ **Bang** is used to emphasize that something is exactly in a particular place, or happens at exactly a particular time. ...*bang in the middle of Whitehaven town centre... He arrived bang on time.* ■ If you say someone is **banging on** about something, you mean they keep talking about it. ■ People use the **big bang** to refer to the enormous explosion which, according to many scientists, caused the beginning of the universe.

banger A **banger** is (a) an old car in bad condition. (b) a type of small firework which goes off with a loud bang. (c) a sausage.

bangle A **bangle** is a decorative band of something such as silver worn round a person's wrist or ankle.

banish (**banishes, banishing, banished; banishment**) If someone is **banished** from a place or area of activity, they are sent away from it and not allowed to return. You call this their **banishment.** ■ If someone is **banished** from an activity, they are prevented from doing it. ■ If you **banish** something unpleasant, you get rid of it.

banister (*or* **bannister**) A **banister** is a rail supported by posts along the side of a staircase.

banjo (**banjos** *or* **banjoes**) The **banjo** is a guitar-like instrument with a long fingerboard, a flat circular body, and usually five strings.

bank A **bank** is an institution where people or businesses can keep their money. Banks also offer services such as lending, exchanging, or transferring money. When people pay money into a bank, you say they **bank** it. ■ A store of something can be called a **bank.** For example, blood is stored in a **blood bank.** ■ The **bank** of a river or lake is the ground along its edge. ■ A **bank** is an area of raised ground, usually with sloping sides and a flat top. ■ Rows of things can be called **banks.** ...*banks of empty seats.* ■ When an aircraft **banks,** one of its wings rises higher than the other, usually when it turns. ■ If you **bank on** something, you depend on it. *He should not bank on their support.*

banker A **banker** is someone who works in banking at a senior level.

bank holiday A **bank holiday** is a public holiday.

bank note (*or* **banknote**) A **bank note** is a piece of paper money.

bankrupt (**bankruptcy, bankruptcies**) If someone is **bankrupt,** they do not have enough money to pay their debts. If they are declared **bankrupt** in a court of law, they have to hand over the running of their affairs to a trustee or the Official Receiver, and their property can be sold to repay their debts. Someone in this situation is called a **bankrupt;** their situation is called **bankruptcy.** ■ If something **bankrupts** someone, it makes them go bankrupt or lose a lot of money. ■ **Bankrupt** is used to say someone is completely without a particular quality. ...*a morally bankrupt leadership.*

banner A **banner** is a long strip of material with a message on it. ■ If you say something is done **under the banner of** a particular belief, that belief is the reason given for doing it. ...*under the banner of economic efficiency.* ■ A **banner** headline in a newspaper is a large one extending across the front page.

bannister See **banister.**

banns The **banns** are a spoken or printed declaration of an intended marriage in church.

banquet (**banqueting**) A **banquet** is a grand formal dinner. A **banqueting** hall or room is a place where banquets are held.

bantam A **bantam** is a small-sized breed of chicken.

banter (**bantering, bantered**) **Banter** is friendly joking or teasing.

bap A **bap** is a soft bread roll.

baptise See **baptize.**

baptism is a Christian religious ceremony in which a person is baptized. ■ If you say someone has had a **baptism of fire,** you mean they have had a particularly difficult first experience of something.

Baptist A **Baptist** is a Christian who believes that baptism is necessary for a Christian, and that it should happen only to someone who is old enough to understand what they are doing.

baptize (*or* **baptise**) (**baptizing, baptized**) When someone **is baptized,** water is sprinkled on them or they are immersed in water, as a sign they have become a member of a Christian Church.

bar (**barring, barred**) A **bar** is a place where you can buy and drink alcoholic drinks. The counter where the drinks are served is also called a **bar.** ■ Some stalls and small shops offering a limited range of items or services are called **bars.** ...*a burger bar.* ...*a heel bar.* ■ A **bar** is a strong straight narrow piece of wood or metal. ■ A **barred** window has bars across it. ■ Some small rectangular objects are called **bars.** ...*a bar of soap.* ...*a chocolate bar.* ■ In Britain, when a lawyer is accepted as a barrister, you say he or she is called to **the Bar. The Bar** is also used to talk about barristers as a group. ■ If someone is **barred** from doing something, they are officially prevented from doing it. An order or rule preventing them is called a **bar.** ■ A **bar** is one of several short equal parts which a piece of music is divided into. ■ **Bar** is sometimes used to mean 'ex-

cept for'. *He won every match, bar one... Barring illness or accident, he will win the race.*

barb (**barbed**) A **barb** is a sharp curved point on the end of something like an arrow or fish-hook. ■ A **barb** is an unkind or unpleasant remark.

barbarian The **barbarians** were warlike tribes who lived in Europe in earlier times. ■ People sometimes get called **barbarians** when they behave roughly or violently.

barbaric If you describe something as **barbaric,** you mean it is cruel or uncivilized. *This barbaric slaughter of whales is inhuman.*

barbarism is cruel or uncivilized behaviour.

barbarity (**barbarities**) **Barbarity** is extremely cruel behaviour. **Barbarities** are cruel and shocking acts.

barbarous (**barbarously**) People use **barbarous** to express their disgust at behaviour they think is cruel or uncivilized.

barbecue (**barbecuing, barbecued**) If you **barbecue** food, you cook it on a grill over hot charcoal, usually out of doors. A **barbecue** is an outdoor occasion when food is cooked like this; the grill the food is cooked on is also called a **barbecue.**

barbed wire is twisted strands of strong fencing wire with sharp points sticking out.

barbell A **barbell** is a metal bar to which disc-shaped weights can be added at each end. It is used in weightlifting.

barber A **barber** is a man who cuts men's hair. The place where a barber works can be called a **barber's** or **barber's shop.**

barbershop is a type of close harmony singing usually performed by four men and especially popular in the US.

barbiturate – **Barbiturates** are drugs which people take to calm them or help them sleep.

bar chart A **bar chart** is a type of graph which uses parallel rectangular shapes to represent variations in amounts or rates.

bar code (**bar-coded**) A **bar code** is a small rectangle of thick and thin vertical lines printed on something. When it is electronically scanned, a computer 'reads' the information in the code.

Bar Council The **Bar Council** is the professional organization responsible for the training, appointment, and professional conduct of barristers.

bard is an old-fashioned word for a poet.

bare (**baring, bared; barer, barest, barely**) If someone is **bare,** they are not wearing any clothes. ■ If someone **bares** part of their body, they uncover it. You say the uncovered part is **bare.** ...*bare feet.* ■ If a place is **bare,** it is empty. ...*a patch of bare earth... Their room was bare of furniture.* ■ If facts or feelings are **laid bare,** people are told about them. ■ **Bare** and **barely** are used to mean 'only just'. ...*a bare 15 seconds of applause. ...barely 30 miles across... They can barely look after themselves.* ■ **Bare** is used to describe something that is the very least that is necessary. *Reduce your luggage to the barest minimum... There is only room here to outline the bare facts.* ■ **bare bones:** see **bone.**

bare-faced (*or* **barefaced**) You use **bare-faced** to describe someone's behaviour when they show they are not ashamed of behaving wrongly. ...*bare-faced lying.*

barefoot (barefooted) If someone is **barefoot**, they are not wearing anything on their feet.

bargain (bargaining, bargained) A **bargain** is an agreement in which two people or groups agree what each of them will do, pay, or receive. When people or groups try to reach an agreement like this, you say they **bargain** with each other. ■ A **bargain** is something sold at a lower price than usual, which is good value for money. ■ If something unexpected happens which interferes with your plans, you can say you had not **bargained for** it. ■ You say **into the bargain** when you are mentioning something extra about the person or thing you have just been talking about. *Wood flooring not only looks smart, it's environmentally friendly into the bargain.*

barge (barging, barged) A **barge** is (a) a large flat-bottomed boat carrying goods or people, usually on a canal or river. (b) a large motorboat used by a high ranking naval officer. ■ If you **barge into** someone, you bump into them roughly and rudely. ■ If you **barge** into a place, you rush in without taking any notice of what might be in the way. ■ If you say you **would not touch** someone or something **with a barge pole**, you mean you do not want to have anything to do with them.

baritone A **baritone** is a man with a fairly deep singing voice. ■ The **baritone** saxophone is a large saxophone with a range of notes lower than a tenor saxophone.

barium is a soft silvery-white metal. ■ A **barium meal** consists of the chemical barium sulphate. It is swallowed by people having an X-ray of their alimentary canal.

bark A **bark** is the short loud noise made by dogs and some other animals, for example foxes. When an animal makes this noise, you say it **barks**. ■ If someone **barks** an order, they shout it at someone. ■ If you say someone is **barking up the wrong tree,** you mean they have got the wrong idea about something. ■ The **bark** of a tree is its tough outer skin.

barley is a cereal grown for food, which is also used in the making of beer and whisky.

barley water is a soft drink made from barley and water, often flavoured with lemon or orange.

barmaid A **barmaid** is a woman who serves drinks in a bar.

barman (barmen) A **barman** is a man who serves drinks in a bar.

bar mitzvah A Jewish boy's **bar mitzvah** is a ceremony marking his 13th birthday, after which he takes on the status, religious duties, and responsibilities of an adult. See also **bat mitzvah.**

barmy (barmier, barmiest) If you say an idea is **barmy,** you think it is nonsensical. ■ If someone goes **barmy,** (a) they go mad. (b) they get very angry.

barn A **barn** is a large building on a farm for storing grain, other crops, or equipment.

barnacle – **Barnacles** are small shellfish which fix themselves to rocks and the bottoms of boats.

barn dance A **barn dance** is a social event at which people take part in country dancing.

barn owl The **barn owl** is a type of owl with pale brown and white feathers and a heart-shaped face, which often nest in old barns.

barnstorming is used to describe a politician's campaign tour when he or she travels round a country making speeches. *He delivered a barnstorming speech about the reform of the welfare state.* ■ **Barnstorming** is used to describe things done in an energetic or forceful way. ...*a barnstorming performance.*

barometer (barometric) A **barometer** is an instrument which measures air pressure and shows when the weather is changing. The pressure measured by a barometer is called **barometric** pressure. ■ Something which gives a hint of how a situation is likely to develop can be called a **barometer.** *The housing market is regarded as a barometer of the economy.*

baron (barony, baronies) A **baron** is a man who is a member of the lowest rank of the nobility. A **barony** is the position of being a baron. Some barons inherit an area of land called a **barony.** ■ Powerful people at the head of large organizations are sometimes called **barons.** ...*drug barons.*

baroness (baronesses) A **baroness** is either the wife or widow of a baron, or a woman holding the rank of baron.

baronet (baronetcy, baronetcies) A **baronet** is a commoner who holds a hereditary title of honour ranking below that of a baron. A baronet puts 'Bart.' or 'Bt.' after his name. ■ A **baronetcy** is the position of being a baronet.

baronial is used to describe castle-like houses. ...*baronial halls.*

baroque (pron: bar-rock) was a European style of architecture and art from the late 16th to the early 18th century. **Baroque** buildings, paintings, and other objects are elaborately decorated. ■ **Baroque** music was a style of music from about 1600 to 1750. Bach, Handel, and Vivaldi wrote music in this style.

barrack A **barracks** (*plural:* **barracks**) is a building or group of buildings where members of the armed forces live. **Barrack** is used to talk about things connected with a barracks. ...*a barrack room.* ■ If people **barrack** someone who is making a speech, they interrupt what the speaker is saying, by shouting comments disagreeing with what is said.

barracuda (pron: ba-rak-kew-da) The **barracuda** is a large tropical fish with sharp teeth and an extended lower jaw.

barrage (pron: bar-rahzh; the 'zh' sounds like 's' in 'pleasure') A **barrage** of questions or complaints is a lot of them coming one after another. ■ A **barrage** is a rapid series of missiles such as rockets or stones being directed at someone. ■ A **barrage** is a barrier built across a river to control the water level.

barrage balloon – **Barrage balloons** are large balloons which float above the ground at the end of long steel cables. They were used especially in the

2nd World War, when the cables were intended to destroy low-flying enemy aircraft.

barred See **bar.**

barrel (**barrels; -barrelled**) (*Am: -barreled*) A **barrel** is a round container, which is wider in the middle than at the top and bottom. ■ The volume of large quantities of oil is expressed in **barrels.** A barrel is usually taken as 35 gallons (about 159 litres). ■ If someone's situation forces them to agree to someone else's demands, you can say they are **over a barrel.** ■ You can say someone is **scraping the barrel** when they produce something of very low quality. ■ The **barrel** of a gun is the tube which the bullets come out of. **-barrelled** is added to words to describe a gun's barrel or to say how many barrels it has. *...double-barrelled shotguns.*

barrel organ A **barrel organ** is a machine on wheels which plays music when you turn a handle on the side.

barren (**barrenness**) If a place is **barren,** trees and plants do not grow there. ■ A **barren** woman or female animal cannot have babies. ■ When trees or plants fail to produce fruit, you say they are **barren.** ■ A **barren** period for someone is one when they fail to achieve anything.

barricade (**barricading, barricaded**) When people **barricade** a road or put up a **barricade,** they set up a line of vehicles or other objects across it to stop people getting past. ■ If you **barricade** yourself inside a building, you block up the doors and windows so no one can get in.

barrier A **barrier** is something like a wall which stops people or things moving from one place to another. ■ You can call something a **barrier** when it stops people doing something. *The lack of cheap child care is the main barrier to women having choice.* ■ In sport, a particular level of achievement is sometimes called a **barrier.** *The European champion shattered the ten-second barrier.*

barrier cream is a cream used to protect the skin, especially the hands, against things like dirt or water.

barrier reef A **barrier reef** is a long narrow coral reef running parallel to the shore.

barring See **bar.**

barrio A **barrio** is a mainly Spanish-speaking neighbourhood in an American city.

barrister A **barrister** is a lawyer in England, Wales, or Northern Ireland who speaks in court for the defence or prosecution. Unlike solicitors, barristers can speak in the higher courts, such as the crown courts.

barrow A **barrow** is (a) a wheelbarrow. (b) a cart from which fruit or other goods are sold in the street. ■ A **barrow** is a mound of earth built over a burial site by prehistoric people.

bartender In the US, a **bartender** is a person who serves drinks in a bar.

barter (**bartering, bartered**) **Barter** is a system of trading by exchanging goods for other goods, instead of selling them for money. When people trade like this, you say they **barter.**

basalt is a dark, fine-grained volcanic rock.

base (**basing, based; baser, basest**) The place an organization or part of an army, air force, or navy operates from can be called its **base;** you say the organization is **based** there. *The Australian Chamber Orchestra is based at the Sydney Opera House.* ■ In rounders and baseball, the **bases** are the corners of the square or diamond round which players must run to score points. ■ The **base** of an object is its lowest part. *...the base of a small tree.* ■ A **base** is something which is already established and from which it is possible to develop other things. *One of his main aims now is to expand his political base.* ■ You say a statement is **based** on something when you are mentioning where the information came from. *He said he was basing his remarks on a conversation with an official of ministerial rank.* You can also say a decision is **based** on some information. *The ban was not based on any scientific evidence.* ■ If one story, play, or film is **based** on another, it is developed from it, keeping the main characters but changing many details. *...a play based on Henry James's novel The Turn of the Screw.* ■ **Base** is used to describe feelings and behaviour which are not honourable or moral. *Love has the power to overcome the baser emotions.* ■ **Base** metals are metals like copper and tin, as distinct from precious metals like gold. ■ You can add **-based** to a word to talk about the main ingredient of something. *...oil-based products.*

baseball is a bat and ball game played by two teams of nine players. Players hit the ball, also called a **baseball,** and try to score runs by running round four points called 'bases'.

baseless If you say a rumour or accusation is **baseless,** you mean it is untrue and there is no evidence to back it up.

baseline The **baselines** of a tennis or badminton court are the lines at each end marking the limits of play. ■ A **baseline** is a standard by which things can be measured. *The organization wants to establish baselines for monitoring their future progress.*

basement The **basement** of a building is a floor partly or completely below ground level.

base rate The **base rate** is the rate of interest banks use when calculating the rates they charge on loans.

bases See **base** or **basis.**

bash (**bashes, bashing, bashed**) If you **bash** someone or give them a **bash,** you hit them. ■ If you **bash** into something, you bump into it accidentally. ■ You can say someone **bashes** a person or group when they constantly criticize them or make things difficult for them. *...a decade of remorseless teacher-bashing in the press.* ■ A **bash** is a party.

bashful (**bashfully**) **Bashful** people are shy and easily embarrassed.

basic is used to describe the simplest and most essential things of a particular kind. *...the basic needs of day-to-day living.* You call things like these the **basics.** ■ The **basic** rate of something like a tax is the standard level of payment before any extra allowances or payments are calculated. ■ If something is very plain, with only the essential features and no luxuries, you can say it is **basic.** *The accom-*

modation at the camp was basic but clean. ■ See also **basically**.

basically is used to mention the most important feature of something, or to explain something in a simple or general way. *This was basically a political row... Basically they want to make politicians accountable.* ■ **Basically** is used to say something is generally true, though not entirely so. *He is basically healthy.*

basil is a sweet-scented herb used to flavour food.

basilica A **basilica** is a rectangular-shaped church with a rounded end, a central nave, and two or four side aisles. ■ In the Roman Catholic church, a **basilica** is a church or cathedral which has special ceremonial rights.

basin A **basin** is a deep bowl for mixing, cooking, or storing food. ■ A **basin** is the same as a washbasin. ■ The **basin** of a large river or lake is the area around it, from which streams run into it. ■ A **basin** is a sheltered area of water where boats can be moored.

basis (*plural:* **bases,** *pron:* **bay**-seez) The **basis** of something is the essential part of it, from which the rest is developed. *...a document which would become the basis of a treaty.* ■ If you say you are acting on the **basis** of something, you are giving that as the reason for your action. *We were all selected on the basis of outstanding ability in maths and science.* ■ If something is done on a particular **basis**, it is done according to that system or principle. *We have been able to send out help on an emergency basis. ...the chance to save on a regular basis.*

bask If you **bask** in sunshine, you lie in it and enjoy the warmth. ■ If someone has become very famous or successful, you can say they are **basking** in fame or glory.

basket A **basket** is a container traditionally made of thin strips of wood or cane woven together. Baskets can also be made of wire or plastic. ■ **Basket** is used to describe things which look as if they have been woven like a basket. *...a basket chair.* ■ A **basket** of goods or currencies is a group of them, especially one used to measure changes in prices. *The survey is based on a basket of 151 products ranging from food to transportation.* ■ **put all your eggs in one basket:** see **egg.**

basketball is a game played on a court between two teams of five players. At opposite ends of the court are two circular nets called 'baskets' hanging from metal rings. Each team tries to score points by throwing a large ball called a **basketball** so it drops through their opponents' basket. A point scored like this is also called a 'basket'.

basket-case If people call someone or something a **basket-case,** they mean they are mad or useless.

basque A **basque** is a tight-fitting women's corset, usually worn as underwear.

bas-relief (*pron:* **bah**-relief *or* **bass**-relief) is a method of sculpture in which shapes are carved so they stand out from a flat surface. A sculpture done in this way is called a **bas-relief.**

bass (**basses**) A **bass** (*pron:* **base**) is a man with a deep singing voice, who can sing a slightly lower range of notes than a baritone. ■ Several musical instruments have **bass** as part of their name. They usually have the lowest range of notes. *...a bass trombone.* ■ In popular music, a bass guitar or a double bass is often called a **bass.** ■ On a hi-fi or radio, the **bass** is the reproduction of low musical notes. ■ The **bass** (*rhymes with 'gas'; usual plural:* **bass**) is a fish which people catch in rivers or the sea.

basset hound The **basset hound** is a smooth-haired dog with a long body, short legs, and long ears.

bassoon (**bassoonist**) The **bassoon** is a large woodwind instrument which can produce very low notes.

bastard A **bastard** is someone who was born to parents who were not married at the time. 'Bastard' is an offensive word.

bastardized (*or* **bastardised**) A **bastardized** version of something has another thing mixed with it, and so is not as good as the pure form. *Scots is a separate language, not a bastardized or inferior version of something else.*

baste (**basting, basted**) If you **baste** food, you spoon hot fat or other liquids over it while it is cooking. ■ If you **baste** pieces of material together, you sew them with large temporary stitches. See also **tack.**

bastion A **bastion** is part of the wall of something like a castle. It sticks out from the main part of the wall. ■ Something is called a **bastion** when it is seen as important in defending a way of life. *...one of the last remaining male bastions – the pavilion at Lords.*

bat (**batting, batted; batsman**) A **bat** is a specially shaped piece of wood used to hit the ball in games like cricket. In games, when a team is **batting,** they try to hit the ball with the bat. In cricket, a player whose turn it is to bat, or who specializes in batting, is called a **batsman.** ■ If someone does something **off their own bat,** they do it without anyone else suggesting it. ■ **Bats** are small mouse-like flying animals with leathery wings. They usually fly at night. ■ If someone does something **off their own bat,** they do it without anyone else suggesting it. ■ **bat an eyelid:** see **eyelid.**

batch (**batches**) A **batch** of things or people is a group of them of the same kind. *...the latest batch of EU statistics.*

bated If you say someone is waiting **with bated breath,** you mean they are waiting very anxiously to see what happens.

bath A **bath** is a large container which you fill with water and sit in to wash your body. ■ A public swimming pool is often called the **baths** (plural: **baths**).

bathe (**bathing, bathed**) When you **bathe** or go for a **bathe,** you swim in the sea or in some other natural area of water. ■ If you **bathe** something like a wound, you wash it gently. ■ If something is **bathed** in light, light is shining all over it. ■ If someone is enjoying having a lot of attention, you can say they are **bathing** in it.

bathmat A **bathmat** is (a) a mat you stand on while you dry yourself after a bath. (b) a rubber mat placed on the bottom of a bath to stop you slipping.

bath oil is a perfumed liquid put in the bath water to make it smell nice and soften the skin.

bathos (pron: **bay**-thoss) In drama and literature, **bathos** is a sudden change in speech or writing from a serious or important subject to a silly or very ordinary one.

bathrobe A **bathrobe** is a dressing-gown, usually made of towelling.

bathroom The **bathroom** in a house is a room with a bath or shower, washbasin, and often a toilet.

bath salts are mineral salts which are dissolved in bath water to soften it and make it smell nice.

bathtub A **bathtub** is a bath.

batik (pron: bat-**teek**) is a method of printing designs on cloth using wax to protect areas that are not meant to be dyed. A **batik** is a cloth printed in this way.

batman A serviceman who acted as a personal servant to an army officer used to be called a **batman.**

bat mitzvah A Jewish girl's **bat mitzvah** is a ceremony and celebration marking her 12th birthday, after which she takes on the status, religious duties, and responsibilities of an adult. See also **bar mitzvah.**

baton A **baton** is (a) a thin stick used by a conductor to direct an orchestra or choir. (b) a short metal or wooden stick passed from one runner to another in a relay race. (c) a short heavy stick used as a weapon by a policeman.

batsman See bat.

battalion A **battalion** is a large group of soldiers, made up of three or more companies and forming part of a brigade.

batten (**battening, battened**) A **batten** is a long strip of wood fixed to something to strengthen it or hold it firm. ■ If you **batten** something **down,** you make it secure, either by fixing battens to it or by closing it firmly. ■ When people **batten down the hatches,** they make preparations to deal with a coming crisis or difficulty. ■ If someone **battens on** something, they make use of it for their own purposes. ...extremist parties, battening on fears about mass immigration.

batter (**battering, battered**) If someone **batters** a person or thing, they repeatedly hit them hard. You use **battered** to describe someone who has been hit like this; you also say they have taken a **battering.** ■ If something like a storm **batters** something, it keeps beating against it. ■ If someone **batters down** something like a door, they hit it so hard and often that it breaks and falls down. ■ A **battering ram** was a long heavy piece of wood which was used in the past to batter down the doors of a fortified building. ■ **Battered** is used to describe something which is old, worn, and damaged. ...a battered old suitcase. ■ You say something like an organization has been **battered** or has taken a **battering** when it has suffered a lot of problems. ■ **Batter** is a liquid mixture, usually of milk, eggs, and flour, used to make food such as pancakes, or to coat other foods before cooking them.

battery (**batteries**) A **battery** is a device which produces electricity to provide the power for something. ■ A **battery** of equipment like computers is a large group of them operating in one place. ■ A lot of things which have to be dealt with together can be called a **battery.** This battery of tests covers literally hundreds of drug types. ■ A **battery** farm is one where a lot of hens are kept in rows of small cages to produce large amounts of eggs as cheaply as possible. The hens are called **battery** hens and their eggs are called **battery** eggs.

battle (**battling, battled**) A **battle** is a fight between armies, ships or planes. ■ When people fight, you can say they **battle.** Police and demonstrators battled for several hours. ■ A **battle** is a struggle between people competing for power or to achieve opposite things. ...a takeover battle. ■ An attempt to achieve something difficult can be called a **battle.** His company is battling for survival. ■ When people **battle it out,** they compete very hard with each other. ■ If you say something is **half the battle,** you mean it is the most important step towards achieving something.

battle cry A **battle cry** is a phrase or speech used to encourage people to support a cause or campaign.

battledress is the ordinary uniform worn by a soldier, rather than a uniform used for ceremonial occasions.

battlefield A **battlefield** is a place where a battle is fought. ...lack of battlefield experience.

battleground A **battleground** is the same as a battlefield. ■ Something which people disagree or compete over is called a **battleground.** ...the battleground of education.

battlements The **battlements** of a fortress consist of a wall built round the top, with gaps through which guns or arrows could be fired.

battleship A **battleship** is a large, heavily armoured warship.

batty (**battier, battiest**) If you say someone is **batty,** you mean they are slightly mad or eccentric.

bauble A **bauble** is a small, cheap, shiny ornament. ■ If you call a piece of jewellery a **bauble,** you mean it is not worth much, although it looks expensive.

baulk See balk.

bauxite is an ore from which aluminium is obtained.

bawdy stories or songs contain humorous references to sex.

bawl If someone **bawls,** they shout, sing, or cry very loudly.

bay A **bay** is a part of a coastline where the land curves inwards. ■ A **bay** is a space used for a particular purpose, for example a parking bay. ■ In a room, a **bay** is a recess formed where part of the room is set back from the rest. ■ When a dog **bays,** it howls loudly. ■ When people call loudly and angrily for something, you can say they **bay** for it. ■ The **bay** is a type of laurel tree. Its leaves can be dried and used as a herb. ■ A **bay** horse is reddish-brown horse. ■ If you **keep** someone or something **at bay,** you stop them reaching you.

bayonet (bayonetting, bayonetted) (*Am:* bayoneting, bayoneted) A **bayonet** is a long sharp blade fixed to the end of a rifle. If someone is **bayonetted,** they are stabbed with a bayonet.

bay window A **bay window** is a window which sticks out from the main wall of a building, forming a bay inside it.

bazaar A **bazaar** is an area with a lot of small shops and stalls, especially in the Middle East. ■ A **bazaar** is a sale held to raise funds for something like a charity.

bazooka A **bazooka** is a long tube-shaped gun, held on the shoulder, which fires rockets.

BBC The **BBC** is an organization which broadcasts television and radio programmes. BBC stands for 'British Broadcasting Corporation'.

BC is used to say something happened a certain number of years before Christ is believed to have been born. BC stands for 'before Christ'. ...*the Peloponnesian War in 431 BC.*

BCG is a tuberculosis vaccine. BCG stands for 'Bacillus Calmette-Guérin'.

be The words **be, being, been, am, are, is, was,** and **were** are used (a) in front of words ending in '-ing' to talk about something continuing to happen. *The government is considering the introduction of student loans.* (b) in front of 'to' to talk about something which is going to happen. *She is to appeal against the decision.* (c) after mentioning a person or thing to talk about something happening to that person or thing. *Mr Harris was elected by the Council last month.* (d) to describe someone or something, or give information about them. *The head of the Corporation is Paul Simpson.* ■ **Be** is used when telling someone to behave in a particular way. *Be quiet!* ■ See also **been, being.**

beach (beaches, beaching, beached) A **beach** is an area of sand or pebbles beside the sea. ■ If you **beach** a boat, you pull it onto the land. ■ If a whale is **beached,** it has been washed up on land and is stranded and helpless.

beachhead (*or* beach-head) A **beachhead** is a beach where an attacking army has taken control and is preparing to advance.

beacon A **beacon** is a light or fire on top of a hill or tower, which acts as a signal or warning. ■ A **beacon** is a transmitter which sends out signals to guide or warn ships or aircraft. ■ Someone or something that acts as an inspiration to other people can be called a **beacon.**

bead (beaded) Beads are small pieces of a hard material like glass or wood, each with a hole through the middle. They can be threaded to make a necklace or bracelet, or sewn onto a dress or cushion as a decoration. ■ A **bead** of moisture is a small drop of it. If something is **beaded** with moisture, it is covered with small drops.

beading is a narrow strip of wood used for decoration or edging furniture.

beady eyes are small, round, and bright. ■ If you say someone has a **beady eye** on something, you mean they are paying close attention to it.

beagle The **beagle** is a short-haired black and brown dog with long droopy ears and short legs.

beak A bird's **beak** is the hard curved or pointed part of its mouth.

beaker A **beaker** is (a) a large drinking cup without a handle. (b) a glass or plastic jar with a lip, used in chemistry.

be-all and end-all If you regard something as **the be-all and end-all** of doing something, you think it is the only good reason for doing it.

beam (beaming, beamed) If someone **beams,** they smile broadly. ■ A **beam** of light is a ray of it shining from something like a torch or the sun. You can also talk about a **beam** of something like electric waves or particles. ■ If you **beam** information somewhere, you send it by radio waves. ■ A **beam** is a long thick bar of wood, metal, or concrete, especially one used to support the roof of a building. **Beamed** is used to describe the parts of a building where wooden beams can be seen. ...*beamed ceilings.*

bean – Beans are the pods of certain tall climbing plants, or the seeds inside the pods, which are eaten as vegetables. Some other seeds are also called **beans,** for example the seeds which coffee, cocoa, and some kinds of oil are made from.

beansprout – Beansprouts are small edible bean shoots, which are often used in Chinese food.

bear (bearing, bore, have borne) Bears are large wild animals with thick fur, sharp claws, and a short tail. ■ If you **bear** something, you carry it. ...*a country where every man has the right to bear arms.* ■ If something **bears** someone **out,** it supports what they are saying. ■ **Bear** can be used instead of 'have', for example when you are talking about a feature or mark that something or someone has. *In profile he bears a resemblance to Pele.* ■ If something **bears** a heavy weight, it supports it. ■ If you **bear** pain or difficulty, you put up with it without complaining. You can say someone who is doing this is **bearing up.** ■ If you **bear up** when you are having problems or suffering pain, you stay cheerful and brave. ■ If you have to **bear** the cost or responsibility for something, you have to pay or take responsibility for it. ■ When a woman **bears** a baby, she gives birth to it. ■ When a tree or plant **bears** flowers, fruit, or leaves, it produces them. ■ If someone **brings** pressure **to bear** on you, they try and persuade you to do something. ■ If you are driving somewhere and you **bear** left or **bear** right, you turn slightly in that direction. ■ If someone or something is **bearing down** on you, they are moving towards you in a threatening way. ■ A **bear market** on the stock exchange is when people are selling shares in expectation of a drop in price, in order to make a profit buying them back at a lower price. See also **bull.** ■ **bear witness: see witness.** See also **bearing.**

bearable If something is **bearable,** you can put up with it, although it is unpleasant.

beard (bearded) A man's **beard** is the hair on his chin and cheeks. If a man has a beard, you can describe him as **bearded.**

bearer People who carry certain types of things are called **bearers.** ...*a stretcher bearer.* ■ The **bearer** of news is the person bringing it. ■ The **bearer** of something like a passport is the person entitled to possess it. ■ The **bearer** of a name or title is the person who has it.

bearing If something **has a bearing on** a situation, it is relevant to it. *My private friendship has no bearing on my ministerial duties.* ■ A person's **bearing** is the way they move or stand. *...an imposing military bearing.* ■ **Bearings** are small metal balls that are placed between moving parts of a machine in order to reduce friction by making them move more smoothly over each other. ■ If you **get** or **find your bearings,** you find out where you are or what to do next. If you **lose your bearings,** you are not sure where you are or what you should be doing. ■ **-bearing** is used to form words which describe what something supports or produces. *...load-bearing branches. ...a seed-bearing plant.*

bear market You can describe a stock market situation as a **bear market** when dealers sell large quantities of shares expecting them to drop sharply in price, enabling them to repurchase the shares at a profit.

bearskin A **bearskin** is a tall fur hat worn by soldiers of some British regiments on ceremonial occasions.

beast You can refer to an animal as a **beast.** ■ A man whose behaviour is violent and uncontrolled is sometimes called a **beast.** *...a mean, vicious sex beast.* ■ You can use **beast** to talk about someone or something in a light-hearted way, usually because of a particular quality they have. *...that rare beast, a sports movie that isn't boring.*

beastly behaviour is very unpleasant.

beat (beating, beat *not 'beated',* **have beaten)** If you **beat** someone or something that you are fighting or competing against, you defeat them. ■ If you **beat** a record, you improve on it. ■ If you say one thing **beats** another, you mean the first thing is better than the second. ■ If someone **beats** another person or **beats** them **up,** they hit them hard and repeatedly. When this happens to someone, you say they have been **beaten** or have suffered a **beating.** ■ **Beat** is used with 'against', 'at', or 'on' to say someone or something repeatedly hits something with force. *I beat against the door.* ■ If you **beat** a drum, you hit it repeatedly. You can talk about the **beat** or **beating** of a drum, or say someone **beats out** a rhythm on it. ■ In cooking, if you **beat** something, you mix it vigorously. ■ When a bird **beats** its wings, it moves them up and down. ■ The **beating** or the **beat** of a person's heart or pulse is its regular rhythm. ■ The **beat** of a piece of music is its regular rhythm. You can describe the rhythm of a piece of music by saying it has a certain number of **beats** to the bar. ■ The **beat** of someone like a police officer is the area they are responsible for. When they patrol their area, you say they are **on the beat.** ■ If you **beat off** an attack, you manage to stop it. ■ If you **beat** someone **down** or **beat** their price **down,** you persuade them to accept a lower price for something they are selling. ■ When the sun **beats down,** it is very bright and hot. When the rain **beats down,** it rains very

hard. ■ **beat about the bush:** see **bush. beat a retreat:** see **retreat.**

beater A **beater** is a person employed to drive birds or animals out into the open so they can be shot. ■ **Beater** is used to talk about (a) someone who hits another person. *...a wife beater.* (b) a device for beating something. *...a carpet beater.* (c) someone or something that defeats a problem. *...an inflation beater.*

beatific (*pron:* bee-at-**tif**-ic) is used to describe someone's expression when it shows great calm and happiness.

beatify (*pron:* bee-**at**-if-fie) (**beatifies, beatifying, beatified; beatification**) In the Roman Catholic church, when a dead person is **beatified,** the Pope formally declares them to be a blessed person, usually as a first step towards making them a saint. You talk about their **beatification.**

beatitude (*pron:* bee-**at**-it-tude) is extreme blessedness or happiness.

beatnik — Beatniks were young people in the late 1950s and early 1960s who rejected conventional ways of dressing and behaving.

beau (*pron:* boh) (*plural:* beaus or beaux, *pron:* boze) A woman's **beau** is her boyfriend or admirer.

beautician A **beautician** is a person whose job is giving people beauty treatments.

beautiful (**beautifully**) **Beautiful** is used to describe (a) someone or something that is extremely attractive. (b) something which is done in a skilful way. *...a beautifully taken goal.*

beautify (**beautifies, beautifying, beautified**) If you **beautify** something, you make it look attractive.

beauty (**beauties**) If you think something or someone is beautiful, you can talk about their **beauty.** *...the beauty of the music.* ■ A beautiful woman is sometimes called a **beauty.** ■ The **beauties** of something are its beautiful features. *...the beauties of the countryside.* ■ **Beauty** is used to talk about things to do with make-up and treatments intended to make women look beautiful. ■ You can show admiration for something by calling it a **beauty.** *His second goal was a beauty.* ■ The **beauty** of something is what makes it good or special. *The beauty of this job is that you are constantly learning.*

beauty spot A **beauty spot** is a place famous for its beautiful scenery.

beaver The **beaver** is a furry animal like a large rat with a big flat tail. ■ If someone **beavers** or **beavers away** at something, they work hard at it.

becalmed If a sailing ship is **becalmed,** it cannot move because there is no wind. ■ You say something like a process or system is **becalmed** when it has stopped making progress. *...Britain's becalmed manufacturing industry.*

became See **become.**

because is used to show the reason for something. *There's been no play because of rain.*

beck and call If you are at someone's **beck and call,** you have to be constantly available and ready to do what they ask.

beckon (**beckoning, beckoned**) If you **beckon** to someone, you signal them to come to you, using your hand. ■ If something **beckons** you, it appears so attractive that you want to become involved with it. *...mountains where the dramatic slopes beckon walkers and horse riders.* ■ You say something **beckons** when it seems likely to happen. *...disaster beckoned.*

become (becoming, became, have become) If someone or something **becomes** a particular thing, they start to be that thing, or develop into it. *The crowd became angry.* ■ If you wonder **what has become of** someone or something, you wonder what has happened to them. You can also wonder **what will become of** someone or something. ■ If something **becomes** you or is **becoming,** it looks attractive on you. *...the uniform is most becoming.*

becquerel (*pron:* be-ke-**rel**) Radioactive activity is measured in **becquerels.** 'Becquerels' is usually written 'Bq'.

B.Ed. A **B.Ed.** is a university degree qualifying someone to teach in state schools. B.Ed. stands for 'Bachelor of Education'.

bed (bedding, bedded) A **bed** is a piece of furniture for sleeping on. ■ If you **bed down** somewhere, you sleep there for the night. ■ When a system or organization is **bedded down,** it becomes established and starts working. ■ **Bed** is used to talk about something which something else rests on. For example, you can say food is served on a bed of rice. ■ A flower **bed** is a part of a garden or park where flowers are grown. ■ The **bed** of the sea, a river, or a lake is its bottom.

bed and breakfast Is a system in which you pay for a room for the night with breakfast the following morning. A **bed and breakfast** (or **b & b**) is a house providing accommodation like this.

bedclothes are the sheets and covers on a bed.

bedding is sheets, blankets, and other covers used on beds. ■ **Bedding plants** are ornamental plants grown indoors from seed and planted outside when they are big enough. They only last one season.

bedeck (*pron:* bid-**dek**) If something is **bedecked** with flags or flowers, it is decorated with them.

bedevil (*pron:* bid-**dev**-ill) **(bedevilling, bedevilled)** If you are **bedevilled** by someone or something, they keep causing ycu problems.

bedlam If you say a place or situation is **bedlam,** you mean it is very noisy and confused.

bed linen is sheets and pillowcases.

bedpan A **bedpan** is a shallow bowl used by people as a toilet when they are too ill to get out of bed.

bedraggled is used to describe someone or something that is untidy, wet, or dirty.

bedridden is used to describe someone who is so ill or disabled they cannot get out of bed.

bedrock is the solid rock underneath soil or loose rocks. ■ The **bedrock** of something like a belief is the principles, ideas, or facts it is based on. *Education is the bedrock of civilized society.*

bedroom A **bedroom** is a room for sleeping in.

bedside If you are at a sick person's **bedside,** you are next to their bed. ■ A doctor's **bedside manner** is their behaviour towards their patients.

bedsit (bedsitter) A **bedsit** or **bedsitter** is a rented room, furnished as a combined living-room and bedroom.

bedspread A **bedspread** is a decorative cover put over a bed.

bedstead A **bedstead** is the metal or wooden frame of an old-fashioned bed.

bedtime A person's **bedtime** is the time they usually go to bed.

bee – Bees are insects which make a loud buzzing noise when they fly. They make honey and wax.

Beeb People sometimes call the BBC the **Beeb.**

beech (beeches) The **beech** is a large tree with a smooth grey trunk.

beef (beefing, beefed) Beef is the meat of a cow, bull, or ox. ■ If you **beef** something **up,** you make it stronger, more effective, or more interesting. *...beefing up security at airports.*

beefburger – Beefburgers are flat round cakes of minced beef, mixed with flavourings which are grilled or fried.

Beefeater – Beefeaters are the guards at the Tower of London, who wear a 16th century style uniform. They are also called **Yeoman Warders.**

beefy (beefier, beefiest) Beefy is used to describe a person, usually a man, who is strong and muscular. ■ **Beefy** is used to describe things which are strong and forceful. *...a beefy speech from the top table.*

beehive A **beehive** is a structure in which bees are kept so their honey can be collected easily.

bee-keeper A **bee-keeper** is a person who keeps bees and collects their honey.

been See be. ■ If you have **been** to a place, you have visited it.

beep (beeping, beeped) If a device **beeps** or makes a **beep,** it makes a short high-pitched sound.

beer (beery) Beer is an alcoholic drink brewed from hops and malt. ■ **Beery** people have drunk a lot of beer. ■ If you say something is **small beer,** you mean it is relatively unimportant.

beeswax is wax produced by bees. It is used to make candles.

beet is a root vegetable used for cattle food. ■ In the US, **beet** is the usual word for beetroot. ■ See also **sugar beet.**

beetle – Beetles are insects whose front wings form a hard covering over their rear wings when they are not flying.

beetroot is a dark red root vegetable often eaten in salads.

befall (befalling, befell, have befallen) If something bad **befalls** someone, it happens to them.

befit (befitting, befitted) If you say something **befits** a person or thing, you mean it is suitable for them. *She never offered him a post befitting his seniority.*

before If something happens **before** a certain time or event, it happens at an earlier time. ■ If something has happened **before,** it has happened on an earlier occasion. *Many had never set foot on a yacht before.* ■ If something is **before** you, it is in front of you. ■ When a person comes **before** a court or a committee, they appear in front of it to give evidence or information.

beforehand is used to say something has been prepared or arranged in advance, or someone has been told about something in advance. *The pieces they performed had been thoroughly learned beforehand... He had been warned beforehand.*

befriend If you **befriend** someone who is lonely, you make friends with them.

befuddle (befuddling, befuddled) If something **befuddles** someone, it makes them confused and muddled.

beg (begging, begged) If you **beg** someone to do something, you ask them anxiously or eagerly to do it. ■ When poor people **beg**, they ask other people to give them money or food. ■ A **begging bowl** is a container people collect money in when they are begging. If you say a country or organization is holding out a **begging bowl**, you mean they are asking other people or countries for money or aid. ■ If you say something is **going begging**, you mean it is available for anyone who wants it. ■ **beg the question:** see **question**.

began See **begin**.

beggar (beggaring, beggared) A person who begs is called a **beggar**. ■ If you say something **beggars** belief or **beggars** description, you mean it is impossible to believe it or describe it.

begin (beginning, began, have begun) Begin is used to say you start something or start doing it. If you **begin with** a particular thing, it is the first thing you say, do, or deal with. *We begin with this announcement by the Home Secretary.* ■ When something **begins**, it starts to happen. The **beginning** of something is the time it starts, or its earliest part. *...the beginning of the 17th century.* ■ If something **begins** as a particular thing, it is like that at first, before it changes to something else. *What began as a pastime quickly became an obsession.* ■ You use **to begin with** to talk about the earliest part of something, before it changes. *He will be employed on a part-time basis to begin with.* ■ You say **to begin with** when you are mentioning the first of a series of things. *To begin with, I know nothing about sailing.*

beginner A **beginner** is someone who is learning to do something, and is not yet very good at it.

begonia – Begonias are garden or pot plants with bright flowers and leaves.

begrudge (begrudging, begrudged) If someone **begrudges** you something you have, they are resentful because of it. *Nobody could begrudge the Sussex girl her victory.* ■ If you do not **begrudge** something such as time or money, you do not mind giving it up.

beguile (*pron:*** big-ile) (beguiling, beguiled; beguilingly)** If you are **beguiled** by something or find it **beguiling,** you are delighted by it. ■ You can say someone is **beguiled** by something when they are misled by it, because it seems pleasing or attractive.

begum (*pron:*** bay-gum)** is a title used by a Muslim woman of high rank.

begun See **begin**.

behalf If you do something on someone's **behalf,** you do it for them.

behave (behaving, behaved) Behave is used to describe the way someone acts on a particular occasion. *She behaved oddly.* ■ If you **behave** or **behave yourself,** you act in a way people think is correct. If someone acts like this you say they are **well-behaved.** ■ If you say an object **behaves** in a particular way, you mean it acts or functions that way.

behaviour (*Am:*** behavior)** A person's **behaviour** is the way they behave. ■ The **behaviour** of an object is the way it acts or functions.

behead (beheading, beheaded) If someone is **beheaded,** their head is cut off.

beheld See **behold.**

behemoth (*pron:*** bi-hee-moth)** In the Old Testament, the **behemoth** was a huge beast, probably a hippopotamus. ■ Extremely large things can be called **behemoths.** *...IBM, another behemoth.*

behest If you do something at someone's **behest,** you do it because they order or request you to.

behind If one thing is **behind** another, it is at the back of it, or on the other side of it. ■ If you are **behind** someone, you are facing their back, or following them. ■ If you are **behind** with something, you are failing to keep up with it. ■ If a person or team is **behind** in a sport or competition, they are losing. ■ If you leave someone or something **behind,** you do not take them with you. ■ The person or reason **behind** an action is the real cause of it. ■ If you say you are **behind** a person or idea, you mean you support them. ■ If a part of someone's life or an experience is **behind** them, it is over. ■ Your **behind** is the part of your body you sit on.

behold (beholding, beheld; beholder) If you **behold** something, you see it or look at it.

beholden If you are **beholden** to someone, you are under an obligation to them.

behoves If it **behoves** you to do something, it is necessary or fitting for you to do it.

beige (*pron:*** bayzh;*** the 'zh' sounds like 's' in 'pleasure')** is a pale creamy-brown colour.

being See **be.** ■ A **being** is a living person or creature. ■ When something comes **into being,** it starts to exist.

bejewelled (*Am:*** bejeweled)** A **bejewelled** person or object is wearing a lot of jewellery or is decorated with jewels.

belabour (*Am:*** belabor) (belabouring, belaboured)** If you **belabour** someone, you (a) hit them repeatedly. (b) criticize them severely.

belated (belatedly) Belated is used to talk about things happening later than they should. *...a belated Christmas present.*

belch (belches, belching, belched) When someone **belches** or lets out a **belch,** wind from their stomach comes out noisily through their mouth. ■ If something **belches** smoke, it sends out large amounts of it.

beleaguered (*pron:*** bil-leeg-ed)** A **beleaguered** person or organization is having a lot of difficulties or being criticized by a lot of people. ■ A **beleaguered** place is surrounded by enemies.

belfry (**belfries**) The **belfry** of a church is the tower where the bells are.

Belgian is used to talk about people and things in or from Belgium. ...*Belgian beers.* ■ A **Belgian** is someone who comes from Belgium.

belie (**belying, belied**) You say something **belies** something else (a)when it makes it seem surprising. *Her looks belie her age.* (b)when it shows it is not true or correct. *The economy has taken a turn for the worse, belying government forecasts.*

belief (**beliefs**) If you have a particular **belief**, you think something is true. *Contrary to popular belief, the police have almost no powers over noise.* ■ A person's **belief** or **beliefs** are their religious faith, or the principles they try to live by.

believable If what someone says is **believable**, you can accept that it might be true. ■ If you say something in a book or film is **believable**, you mean something like that could happen or exist in real life.

believe (**believing, believed; believer**) If you **believe** something, you think it is true. ■ If you **believe** something, you are sure they are telling the truth. ■ If you **believe in** God, or are a **believer** in God, you are sure God exists. ■ If you **believe in** ghosts or miracles, you are sure they exist or can happen. ■ If you **believe in** a principle, or are a **believer** in it, you think it is right. ...*believers in human rights.* ■ If you **believe in** a person, you think they will be successful.

Belisha beacon (*pron:* bel-**lee**-sha) A **Belisha beacon** is a post with a round flashing orange light, used as a warning to motorists at zebra crossings.

belittle (**belittling, belittled**) If you **belittle** something, you make it out to be of little value or importance.

bell A **bell** is a small device which makes a ringing sound to attract people's attention, such as a doorbell. ■ A **bell** is a cup-shaped metal object with a loose piece inside which hits the sides and makes a loud sound.

belladonna or **deadly nightshade** is a bushy plant with poisonous leaves, from which several important drugs are obtained.

bell-bottomed (**bell-bottoms**) **Bell-bottomed** trousers or **bell-bottoms** are trousers which flare out from below the knee and become very wide round the ankles.

belle A **belle** is a beautiful woman.

bellicose (**bellicosity**) **Bellicose** behaviour is aggressive and threatening. You can call someone who behaves in this way **bellicose** or talk about their **bellicosity.**

belligerent (**belligerently; belligerence**) A **belligerent** person is hostile and aggressive.

bellow If someone **bellows** or lets out a **bellow**, they call out in a deep loud voice. ■ When a large animal like a bull **bellows**, it makes a deep loud sound. ■ A **bellows** (plural: **bellows**) is (a) a device for blowing air into a fire to make it burn more fiercely. (b) part of an instrument like an accordion or organ, which blows air into the pipes to produce the sound.

belly (**bellies, bellied**) Your **belly** is your stomach or abdomen. ■ You can call the underside of something like a plane its **belly.** ...*a wide-bellied US cargo plane.*

belly dance (**belly dancing, belly dancer**) A **belly dance** is a Middle Eastern dance performed by a woman making movements of her belly and hips.

belong If something **belongs** to you, it is yours. ■ If you **belong** to an organization, you are a member of it. Similarly, you can say someone or something **belongs** to a group of people or things. *He belongs to a new generation of politicians.* ■ If something **belongs** in a place, that is where it is usually kept. ■ You say someone or something **belongs** somewhere when you are expressing an opinion about where they should be. *The Queen Mary should come back to Southampton where she belongs.* ■ If you say you **belong** somewhere, you mean you feel happy and comfortable there. ■ If something **belongs** to a period in the past, it is typical of that period, or originates from that period.

belongings Your **belongings** are your personal possessions.

beloved (*pron:* bi-**luv**-id) is used to describe someone or something a person loves. ...*his beloved wife.* ■ Someone's **beloved** is the person they are in love with. *I was standing next to my beloved at the altar.* ■ If someone or something is loved by a group of people, you can say they are **beloved** (*pron:* bi-**luvd**) by them. *These books are still beloved by me and my son.*

below If something is **below** something else, it is in a lower position, or underneath it. ■ **Below** is used to say something is under a certain amount or level. *The temperature dropped below freezing point.* ■ In a piece of writing, **below** is used to say something will come later in the text. *Most good libraries will have some of the books listed below.*

belt A **belt** is a strip of leather or other material you fasten round your waist. ■ If you say remarks or actions are **below the belt,** you mean they are unkind or unfair. ■ If you say someone has something like knowledge **under their belt,** you mean they have acquired it. ...*with a decade of experience under our belts.* ■ You can say you have to **tighten your belt** when you have to manage with less money than you used to. ■ A **belt** is a circular strip of rubber used to drive a moving part in a machine. ■ A **belt** of something such as land is a long narrow strip of it. ■ If you **belt** somewhere, you move or travel very fast. If someone **belts** through something, they deal with it very quickly. ■ If you **belt** someone or something, you hit them hard. ■ If someone **belts out** a song, they sing it loudly.

bemoan (**bemoaning, bemoaned**) If you **bemoan** something, you grumble about it. *She was bemoaning the shortage of qualified staff.*

bemused (**bemusement**) If you are **bemused** by something, you are puzzled by it.

bench (**benches**) A **bench** is a long seat for two or more people, usually made of wood or metal. ■ In Parliament, the seats used by MPs are called **benches.** You talk, for example, about the government benches or opposition benches. See also back bench, front bench. ■ In court, the judge or magistrates are sometimes called the **bench.** *The chairman of the bench imposed a fine.* ■ A **bench** is a long narrow table in a laboratory or workshop.

benchmark A **benchmark** is a mark on something like a stone post, showing the height above sea level. ■ You say something is a **benchmark** when its quality, quantity, or capability is used as a standard by which to judge other things. *Their pay deals are regarded as a benchmark for the rest of the industry.*

bend (**bending, bent**) When you **bend** or **bend down,** you lean forwards and downwards. ■ If you **bend** your knee or elbow, you move it so the joint forms an angle; you then say the knee or elbow is **bent.** See also **bended.** ■ If you **bend** something, you force it into a curved or angled shape. ■ When a road or river changes direction, you say it **bends.** The place where it does this is called a **bend.** ■ You can use **bend** to talk about someone or something becoming more flexible. *Do you think she's likely to bend on her attitude to Europe?... Surely you can bend the rules.* ■ **bend over backwards:** see **backward. the bends:** see **decompression.** See also **bent.**

bended If someone asks for something **on bended knee,** they do it in a very humble way.

beneath If something is **beneath** something else, it is in a lower position, or underneath it. ■ If you say something is **beneath** someone, you mean they would object to doing it, because they would regard it as undignified, or think they were too important or intelligent for it.

benediction A **benediction** is a prayer asking for God's blessing, especially at the end of a religious service. ■ A **benediction** is a gesture in which you ask God to bless someone, using your arm and hand. *He lifted a hand in benediction.*

benefactor A person's **benefactor** is someone who helps them out by giving them money.

beneficial is used to describe things which do good. *The treatment has had beneficial results.*

beneficiary (**beneficiaries**) A **beneficiary** of something is someone who benefits from it. ■ A person who is left money or property in someone's will is called a **beneficiary.**

benefit (**benefiting, benefited**) If something **benefits** you or you **benefit** from it, you are better off as a result of it. You call something like this a **benefit.** *...the benefits of fresh air.* ■ If you do something **for** someone's **benefit,** you do it especially for them. ■ **Benefit** is money paid out by the DSS, for example child benefit or housing benefit. ■ If you **give** someone the **benefit of the doubt,** you assume they have told the truth or behaved properly, although you cannot be sure this is the case.

Benelux The **Benelux** countries are Holland, Belgium, and Luxembourg.

benevolent (**benevolence**) **Benevolent** people are kind and helpful.

benevolent fund A **benevolent fund** is money kept to help members of a group of people when they are in need.

benighted is sometimes used to describe people who are thought to be unfortunate or ignorant.

benign (*pron:* bin-**nine**) (**benignly**) **Benign** people are kind, gentle, and harmless. *She smiled benignly.* ■ A **benign** tumour or disease is one which will not cause death or serious harm.

bent See **bend.** ■ If something is **bent,** it is not straight. ■ If you are **bent** on doing something, you are determined to do it. ■ If you have a **bent** for something, you like doing it or are naturally good at it.

benzene is a colourless flammable liquid obtained from petroleum.

benzine (*pron:* **benz**-een) is a liquid obtained by distilling petroleum, used for example as a cleaning fluid and an insecticide.

bequeath If someone **bequeaths** money or property to you, they leave it to you in their will. You can also say a dead person **bequeaths** other things, for example their ideas. *His aunt had bequeathed him a deep interest in medicine.* ■ If someone leaves a situation for someone else to deal with, you can say they **bequeath** them the situation.

bequest A **bequest** is money or property which someone leaves you in their will.

berate (**berating, berated**) If you **berate** someone, you tell them off angrily.

bereaved (**bereavement**) A **bereaved** person has recently had a relative or close friend die. You say someone like this has suffered a **bereavement.** Bereaved people are sometimes called **the bereaved.**

bereft If you say a person or thing is **bereft** of something, you mean they are completely without it. *The novel is bereft of vitality.*

beret (*pron:* **ber**-ray) A **beret** is a soft round flat hat with no brim.

berry (**berries**) **Berries** are small round fruit.

berserk If people go **berserk,** they lose control of themselves and become angry and violent.

berth A **berth** is a space for a ship to stay in a port. When a ship moves into a space like this, you say it **berths.** ■ A **berth** is a bed in a boat, train, or caravan. ■ If you **give** someone or something **a wide berth,** you avoid them.

beseech (**beseeches, beseeching, beseeched** *or* **besought; beseechingly**) If you **beseech** someone to do something, you insistently and urgently appeal to them to do it.

beset (**besetting, beset** *not* '**besetted**') If you are **beset** by problems, you are faced with a lot of them.

beside (**besides**) If someone or something is **beside** another person or thing, they are next to them. ■ You use **beside** when saying how something seems when compared to something else. *By the 1970s, zoos seemed drab beside theme parks and other new entertainments.* ■ You say people are **beside themselves** with anger or joy when they are extremely angry or happy. ■ You use **beside** or **besides** (a) when saying an additional thing about someone or something. *Beside being the guardians of our frontiers, they will be the guardians of our Amazon rainforest.* (b) when mentioning an additional person or thing something applies to. *He did, however, blame others beside himself... There are other risks be-*

sides. ■ **Besides** is used to introduce an additional point. *Besides, breast-milk is naturally clean and wholesome.*

besiege (**besieging, besieged**) If armed forces **besiege** a place, they surround it and try to capture it. ■ You say people **besiege** a place when a lot of them try to get in to get something or see someone. *He agreed to make a statement to the local press, who were besieging his hotel.*

besmirch (**besmirches, besmirching, besmirched**) If something **besmirches** a person's reputation, it damages it.

besotted If you are **besotted** with someone, you are in love with them and constantly thinking about them. If someone is **besotted** with something like an idea, they are excessively excited and enthusiastic about it.

besought See **beseech.**

bespectacled A **bespectacled** person is wearing glasses.

bespoke is used to describe clothes made specially to suit someone's requirements. A **bespoke** tailor makes or sells clothes like these. ■ **Bespoke** is used to describe things arranged to suit a particular person's needs. *...a bespoke holiday service.*

best You use **best** to describe things which are of the highest quality or level, or which are the most successful. *He scored the best try of the match. ...the best form of treatment available.* ■ Your **best** friends are your closest friends. The things that you like **best** are your favourite things. ■ If someone or something does something **best,** they do it to the highest standard or with the highest level of skill. *Performing is what I do best.* ■ The thing someone is **best** known for is the one people usually associate them with. ■ A person's **best** is the highest standard they are capable of. If you **do your best** at something or do it **as best you can,** you try as hard as you can to do it successfully. ■ If you **make the best** of an unfavourable situation, you accept it and try to manage as well as you can. ■ If you say something is **for the best,** you mean it will eventually have good results, and is therefore worthwhile. ■ You use **at best** to show you are putting the most favourable interpretation on something which is not good. *The outlook for the economy was gloomy at best.* ■ If you are **bested** by someone, they do something more successfully than you, or beat you in a competition.

bestial behaviour is revolting or animal-like.

bestiality is (a) revolting or animal-like behaviour. (b) sexual activity in which a person has sex with an animal.

bestiary (**bestiaries**) A **bestiary** is a medieval book containing pictures of real and imaginary animals.

best man At a wedding, the **best man** is the bridegroom's attendant and helper.

bestow If someone **bestows** a gift or honour on you, they give it to you.

bestride (**bestriding, bestrode**) If someone **bestrides** something, they stand with one leg on each side of it. ■ When someone was the outstanding figure in an activity over a period of time, you can

say they **bestrode** it. *Frank Sinatra bestrode 20th-century popular music.*

best-seller (*or* **bestseller**) (**best-selling**) A **best-seller** is a book which sells a very large number of copies. A **best-selling** author writes books like these.

bet (**betting, bet** *or* **betted**) If you **bet** or put a **bet** on something, you gamble money on what will happen in the future. ■ If you are **betting** on something happening, you are expecting it to happen, and relying on it. *Most economists are betting on output starting to rise this year.* ■ If you say **the betting is** something will happen or it is a good **bet** it will happen, you mean it is likely to happen. *It is a fair bet there will be another cut in interest rates.* ■ If someone is about to make a choice, you use **bet** to comment on what they might choose. For example, you say something would be 'a good bet' or 'a safe bet'. *These companies were always going to be a safe bet for investors.*

beta (*pron:* **bee**-ta) **Beta** is β, the second letter of the Greek alphabet. ■ **Beta** is used to describe things involving or relating to electrons. For example, a **beta particle** is an electron sent out from a radioactive nucleus.

beta blocker A **beta blocker** is a drug which slows down the action of the heart by blocking the action of nerve endings. Beta blockers are used in the treatment of angina and high blood pressure.

bête noire (*plural:* **bêtes noires**) (*both pron:* **bet nwahr**) If you say a person or thing is your **bête noire,** you mean you especially dislike them. *...our bête noire is the car-boot sale.*

betide If you say **woe betide** the person who does something, you mean something nasty will happen to them if they do it. *Woe betide them if they vote against the government.*

betoken (**betokening, betokened**) If something **betokens** something else, it is a sign of it. *His expression betokened embarrassment.*

betray (**betrayal**) If someone you trust **betrays** you, they do something disloyal. You call their behaviour a **betrayal.** ■ If someone **betrays** a secret, they tell it to other people. ■ If someone **betrays** something like an ideal, they go back on it. *...the fastest betrayal of election promises in history.* ■ If someone **betrays** their feelings, they show them without meaning to. *She studied his face, but it betrayed nothing.*

betrothed (**betrothal**) If you are **betrothed,** you are engaged to be married. Your **betrothed** is the person you are engaged to. A **betrothal** is an engagement.

better (**bettering, bettered; betterment**) **Better** is used to compare things when you want to say that one thing is of a higher quality or standard than another, or has been improved in some way. *Their produce tastes better than anything bought in the shops... He speaks English better than I do.* When something has been improved, you can talk about its **betterment.** ■ If you say a sick or injured person is **better,** you mean (a) they are less ill. (b) they are completely recovered. ■ If you are **better off** than you were before, you have more money or are in a more pleasant situation. ■ If you **get the**

better of someone in a contest, you defeat them. ■ If you **better** what someone else has done, you improve on it. ■ If something changes **for the better,** it improves. ■ If you say someone will **be the better for** something, you mean they will benefit from it. ■ If you say something has happened **for better or worse,** you mean you are not sure whether it is a good thing or a bad thing. ■ If you say someone **had better** do something, you mean they ought to do it. *Investors who want to secure the best buys had better act fast.* ■ You say **the sooner the better** to emphasize that you want something to happen as soon as possible.

between If someone or something is **between** two people or things, they are in the middle of them. ■ If something is **between** or **in between** two numbers, it is higher than one and lower than the other. ■ **Between** is used to say that someone or something moves or travels regularly from one place to another. *These meetings alternated between Paris and New York.* ■ The distance **between** two places is the distance from one to the other. ■ If something happens **between** two times, (a) it begins at one and ends at the other. *He was Prime Minister between 1970 and 1974.* (b) it happens after the first one but before the second one. *...sometime between May and October next year.* ■ **Between** is used to talk about two people or groups being involved in some way with each other. *Fighting has continued between government troops and rebels.* ■ If people have an amount of something **between** them, that is the total amount they have. If something is divided **between** them, they each have a share of it. ■ You talk about a gap **between** two things. *...the widening rift between the poor and the prosperous.* ■ If something stands **between** you and something you want, it stops you having it.

bevelled (*Am:* **beveled**) If a piece of wood, metal, or glass has **bevelled** edges, its edges are cut sloping.

beverage A **beverage** is a drink.

bevy (**bevies**) A **bevy** of people or things is a large number of them altogether. *...a bevy of little girls.*

bewail (**bewailing, bewailed**) If you **bewail** something, you express sorrow or regret about it. *Scientists bewail cuts in the money the government pays for their work.*

beware If you tell someone to **beware** of something, you are warning them to be on their guard against danger or deception. *Beware of schemes promising lots of money without much effort.*

bewilder (**bewildering, bewildered; bewilderment**) If someone is **bewildered** or in a state of **bewilderment,** they are confused and unable to understand what is going on.

bewitch (**bewitches, bewitching, bewitched**) If you are **bewitched** by someone or something, it has a strong effect on you, as if you were under a spell. *North Sligo is bewitching country.*

beyond If something is **beyond** a wall or river, it is on the far side of it. ■ If something extends **beyond** a place, it extends to other places. *The conflict has shown signs of spreading beyond the area.* Similarly, you can talk about something extending **beyond** a time, level, or limit. ■ If a task is **beyond** you, it is

too difficult for you. ■ If you cannot understand something, you can say it is **beyond** you. *Why these books have not been banned is beyond me.* ■ If something is, for example, **beyond** belief, it is so extreme that it cannot be believed. *In the last few years their world has changed beyond recognition.*

bi- Some words beginning with **bi-** can be spelled with a hyphen after the 'i'. For example, 'bicentenary' can be spelled 'bi-centenary'. See entries at **biannual, bicentenary, bifocals, bilateral, bilingual, bipartisan.**

biannual (*or* **bi-annual**) (**biannually**) **Biannual** is used to describe things which happen twice a year. *...their biannual conference.* See also **biennial.**

bias (**biases; biased**) If someone is **biased,** or shows a **bias,** towards something or someone, they prefer them to other things or people, often unfairly. ■ A **bias** is a tendency for things to happen in one way rather than another. *Female chimpanzees show the same left side bias for cradling as human mothers.* ■ If a piece of cloth is cut on the **bias,** it is cut at an angle to the weave of the cloth.

bib A **bib** is a piece of cloth or plastic fastened under the chin of young children to protect their clothes while they are eating.

bible (**biblical**) The **Bible** is the sacred book of the Christian religion. The first part of it, the Old Testament, is also a sacred book for Jews. ■ **Biblical** describes things that are in, or relate to, the Bible. *...the biblical account of the creation of man.* ■ The best or most important book on a subject can be called the **bible** of that subject. *His 50 hand-drawn guide books are the walker's bible.*

bibliography (**bibliographies; bibliographical**) A **bibliography** is a list of books on a subject or by a particular author. ■ The **bibliography** at the end of a book or article is a list of the books and articles used by the author when writing it, or suggested for study. ■ **Bibliography** is the study of different editions of books. ■ **Bibliographical** information is information about a book, such as the publisher and date of publication.

bibliophile A **bibliophile** is (a) a person who loves books. (b) a book collector.

bibulous If someone is **bibulous,** they are very fond of alcohol.

bicarbonate of soda or **bicarb** is a white powder used to make cakes rise or as a medicine to relieve indigestion.

bicentenary (*or* **bi-centenary**) (**bicentenaries**) A **bicentenary** is a year when you celebrate something important which happened exactly 200 years earlier.

bicentennial is the usual American word for a bicentenary.

biceps (*plural:* **biceps**) Your **biceps** are the large muscles at the front of your upper arms.

bicker (**bickering, bickered**) When people **bicker,** they quarrel about unimportant things.

bicycle (**bicycling, bicycled**) A **bicycle** is a two-wheeled vehicle propelled by pedals. If you **bicycle** somewhere, you go there on a bicycle.

bid (**bidding, bid** *or* **bade, have bid** *or* **have bidden;** *if you are talking about the past, you say someone bid* for something, but that they **bade** someone good morning or **bade** someone to do something) If someone **bids** for something or makes a **bid** for it, they try to get it or do it. *Wigan are bidding to win the trophy for a third successive year.* ■ If you **bid** for something which is being sold or make a **bid** for it, you offer an amount of money for it. ■ **Bid** is used to talk about greetings. For example, if you **bid** someone good morning, you say good morning to them. ■ If you **bid** someone to do something, you ask, order, or invite them to do it. If you do someone's **bidding**, you do what they ask, order, or invite you to do. You can also be **bidden** to do something.

biddable A **biddable** person is willing to do what they are told. *...a most biddable child.*

bidder Someone who makes a bid for something which is being sold is called a **bidder.**

bide (**biding, bided**) If you **bide** your **time,** you wait for a good opportunity before doing something.

bidet (*pron:* **bee**-day) A **bidet** is a low basin, for washing your bottom.

biennial things happen once every two years. See also **biannual.** ■ **Biennial** plants or **biennials** live for two years.

bier (*pron:* **beer**) A **bier** is a movable frame on which a corpse or coffin is placed.

bifocals (*or* **bi-focals**) are spectacles in which the top part of each lens is for looking at distant things, and the bottom part is for looking at things nearby.

big (**bigger, biggest; biggish**) **Big** is used to describe things which are of a greater size than normal. *...big crowds.* ■ **Big** is used to describe things which are very significant, and people who are powerful and important. *There could soon be a big increase in unemployment.* ■ If you say someone is **big** in something, you mean they are important in it. *The company is big in insurance.* ■ If someone is a **big name,** they are successful and famous. ■ The **big time** is the highest level of success, fame, or importance in an activity or career. *One way for a young performer to break into the big time is as an 11th-hour substitute.* ■ **Big business** involves large companies and large sums of money. If you say something is **big business,** you mean it has become an important commercial activity. *The trade in illegal immigrants has become big business.* ■ A person's **big** brother or sister is their older brother or sister.

bigamy (**bigamist; bigamous**) If a person who is already married gets married to someone else, this is called **bigamy;** you say their second marriage is **bigamous.**

big game is large wild animals like lions which used to be hunted for sport.

big-hearted people are kind and generous.

bigot (**bigoted; bigotry**) If you describe someone as a **bigot,** you mean they have strongly held prejudices which they refuse to change. **Bigoted** is used to describe someone like this; their behaviour and attitudes are called **bigotry.**

big top The **big top** is the large round tent which a circus uses for its performances.

bigwig Important people are sometimes humorously called **bigwigs.**

bijou (*pron:* **bee**-zhoo; the 'zh' sounds like 's' in 'pleasure') is used to describe buildings which are small but very fashionable or elegant.

bike A **bike** is a bicycle or motorcycle.

bikini A **bikini** is a woman's two-piece swimming costume.

bilateral (*or* **bi-lateral**) is used to describe things which involve two people, groups, or countries. *...bilateral negotiations.*

bilberry (**bilberries**) **Bilberries** are bluish-black berries which grow on small bushes.

bile is a bitter liquid produced by the liver which helps the digestion of fat in the bowels. ■ **Bile** is anger or bitterness towards someone. *He has reserved his bile for investigative journalists.*

bilingual (*or* **bi-lingual**) If someone is **bilingual,** they can speak two languages fluently. A **bilingual** document is written in two languages.

bilious If you feel **bilious,** you feel sick and have a headache. ■ A **bilious** colour looks revolting. ■ **Bilious** comments show extreme irritation and dislike.

bill A **bill** is a written statement of how much money needs to be paid for something. If someone **bills** you for something, they send you the bill. ■ In the US, banknotes are called **bills.** ■ A bird's **bill** is its beak. ■ A **bill** is a poster advertising an event. ■ In a concert, the **bill** is the performers taking part in it. You say someone is **billed** to appear in a show. ■ If a person or event is **billed** as a particular thing, they are advertised as being that thing. *The film is billed as a political comedy.* ■ When it has been announced that an event is going to happen, you can say it is **billed** to happen. ■ In parliament, a **bill** is a proposed law which is discussed and then voted on. ■ If someone or something **fits** or **fills the bill,** they are just what is needed.

billboard A **billboard** is a large board for displaying posters.

billet (**billeting, billeted**) When servicemen or women are **billeted** somewhere, they live in non-military accommodation; this accommodation is called their **billets.** ■ You can say groups of people are **billeted** somewhere when accommodation is found for them at short notice.

billiards is a game for two people, played on a large table with three balls. Players use a cue to hit one ball against another; the aim is to hit balls into pockets at the edges of the table.

billion (**billionth**) A **billion** is the number 1,000,000,000.

billionaire A **billionaire** is a person whose wealth is equal to at least a billion pounds or dollars.

billow When something like a sail **billows,** it swells out and flaps slowly in the wind. ■ When smoke or cloud **billows,** large amounts of it roll slowly along and upwards.

billy goat A **billy goat** is a male goat.

bimbo (**bimbos**) Young women who are thought to be empty-headed but sexually attractive are sometimes called **bimbos.**

bi-monthly (or **bimonthly**) is used to say (a) something happens every two months. (b) something happens twice a month.

bin (**binning, binned**) A **bin** is a container for putting rubbish in. If you **bin** something, you throw it away. ■ A **bin** is a container for keeping things in.

binary (pron: bine-a-ree) The **binary** system is a way of writing down numbers using only two digits, 0 and 1, in various combinations. It is used especially in computing. ■ **Binary** is used to describe things which are made up of two different parts. *Pluto and its moon together orbit the sun as a binary planet.*

bind (**binding, bound** not 'binded') If you **bind** something, you tie rope or string round it so it is held firmly. ■ If you **bind** something like a carpet, you cover the edges with stitching or a strip of material, to stop it fraying or to decorate it. Material used for this purpose is called **binding.** ■ When a book is **bound**, the pages are joined together and the covers put on. The **binding** of a book is its cover. ■ If something **binds** people together, it unites them because they have the same feelings about it. ■ If two or more things are **bound** together, they are closely linked so that each affects the other. *Economic and political reform are inextricably bound together.* ■ If you **bind** a mixture of food, you mix it with a liquid so all the ingredients stick together. Other things can be **bound** in a similar way. *The plastic melts and, on cooling, binds the aluminium together as a thin, light fabric.* ■ If something like a legal order **binds** you to do something, it forces you to do it. A **binding** agreement must be carried out. ■ If you say something you have to do is a **bind,** you mean it is unpleasant and boring.

binder A **binder** is a hard cover with metal rings inside, used to hold loose papers.

bindweed is a climbing plant with pink or white trumpet-shaped flowers.

binge (**binging** or **bingeing, binged**) If someone goes on a **binge,** they drink a lot of alcohol. ■ When people do something intensively for a short time you can call this a **binge.** *...a consumer spending binge.* ■ If someone **binges** on something, they over-indulge in it. *I binged on pizzas or milkshakes.*

Bingo is a game in which each player has a card with numbers on. Someone calls out numbers and if you are the first person to have all your numbers called out, you win the game.

binoculars are a device like two small telescopes joined side by side, for seeing things at a distance.

biochemistry (**biochemist; biochemical**) Biochemistry is the study of the chemical processes in living things. *...the biochemical basis of the disease.*

biodegradable If something is **biodegradable,** it decomposes naturally without any special scientific treatment, and so does not cause pollution.

biodiversity is the existence of a wide variety of plant and animal species living in their natural environment. *...marine biodiversity.*

biography (**biographies; biographer, biographical**) A **biography** is an account of a person's life

written by someone else. Someone who writes a biography is called a **biographer.** *...a biographical film.*

biological (**biologically**) Biological means connected with the natural processes in living things. *...using biological methods to control pests.* ■ **Biological** sciences are concerned with the study of living things. ■ **Biological** weapons and warfare involve the use of chemicals or living organisms which harm people, animals, and plants. ■ Your **biological clock** is your body's way of telling you it is time, for example, to wake up or have a meal. ■ A person's **biological** parent is their real father or mother, rather than someone who has adopted them.

biology (**biologist**) Biology is the study of living things. The **biology** of a living thing is the way it works. *The biology of many of these diseases is terribly complicated.*

bionic In science fiction, a **bionic** person has superhuman powers, such as exceptional strength or eyesight, because parts of their body have been replaced by electronic machinery.

biophysics (**biophysicist**) Biophysics is a science which tries to explain how living things work using the laws of physics.

biopic (pron: bi-oh-pick) A **biopic** is a film based on the life of a real person.

biopsy (**biopsies**) If someone has a **biopsy,** a small sample is taken from part of their body and examined medically to find out the cause of a disease or see how far it has spread.

biosphere The **biosphere** is the part of the earth's surface and atmosphere which is inhabited by living things.

biotechnology (**biotechnologist**) Biotechnology is the use of living organisms to improve medical, agricultural, and industrial processes.

bipartisan (or **bi-partisan**) If something is **bipartisan,** it involves two different political groups. *The policy has bipartisan support.*

biped (pron: bye-ped) A **biped** is any creature with two feet.

biplane A **biplane** is an old-fashioned plane with two sets of wings, one above the other.

birch (**birches, birching, birched**) The **birch** is a tree which has thin peeling bark and long catkins. ■ The **birch** was a cane or bunch of twigs, used in the past to flog people. If someone was **birched,** they were flogged with a birch.

bird – Birds are two-legged creatures with feathers and wings. ■ If you have a **bird's eye view** of a place, you see it from a great height.

birdie In golf, a **birdie** is a score of one below par on any hole. See also **bogey, eagle.**

bird of prey (**birds of prey**) Birds of prey are birds like hawks and owls which kill and eat other birds and animals.

bird-watcher (or **birdwatcher**) Bird-watchers are people whose hobby is observing wild birds in their natural surroundings.

Biro (**Biros**) A **Biro** is a ballpoint pen. 'Biro' is a trademark.

birth The **birth** of a person or animal is the time when they are born. ■ When a woman **gives birth,** she has a baby. ■ The place of someone's **birth** is the place where they were born. If someone has a particular nationality **by birth,** they have that nationality because they or their parents were born in that country. ■ The **birth** of something like an organization is its beginning. ■ If something like a type of music started in a place, you can say the place **gave birth** to it.

birth control is the same as contraception.

birthday Your **birthday** is the anniversary of the date you were born.

birthday suit If you are in your **birthday suit,** you are not wearing any clothes.

birthmark A **birthmark** is a mark on the skin formed before birth. Birthmarks are usually brown or dark red.

birthplace Your **birthplace** is the place where you were born.

birth rate The **birth rate** in a place is the number of babies born live for every 1000 people during a certain period of time.

birthright A person's **birthright** is something they are entitled to because of the place where they were born or the family they were born into.

biscuit A **biscuit** is a small flat crisp cake, usually sweet.

bisect In maths, if you **bisect** something like a line or angle, you draw a line exactly through the middle of it. ■ If a road cuts across an area dividing it in two, you say it **bisects** the area.

bisexual (**bisexuality**) If someone is **bisexual** or a **bisexual,** they are sexually attracted to both men and women.

bishop In many Christian churches, a **bishop** is the head of a diocese or group of parishes. ■ The **bishop** is a piece in chess.

bison (*plural:* **bison**) The **bison** is a large hairy animal that is a member of the cattle family. Bison used to be very common in North America and Europe.

bistro (**bistros**) A **bistro** is a small restaurant or bar.

bit A **bit** of something is a small piece or amount of it. ■ **A bit** means to a small extent. *Lower the flame a bit.* ■ **For a bit** means for a short time or distance. *I was sad for a bit.* ■ **Quite a bit** means rather a lot. *They made quite a bit of money.* ■ The **bit** on a tool is the drilling part. ■ A horse's **bit** is the piece of metal held in its mouth by the bridle and reins. ■ In computing, a **bit** is the smallest unit of information held in a computer's memory. 'Bit' is short for 'binary digit'. See also **byte.** ■ See also **bite.**

bitch (**bitches, bitching, bitched; bitchy, bitchiness**) A **bitch** is a female dog. ■ If someone calls a woman a **bitch,** they mean she behaves in an unpleasant way and causes trouble. ■ If someone is **bitchy,** they say nasty things about people. *...petty-minded bitchiness.* ■ If someone **bitches** about something, they complain about it.

bite (**biting, bit, have bitten**) When a person or animal **bites** something, they use their teeth to cut through it or into it. ■ If an insect or snake **bites** you, it pierces your skin and leaves a poisonous substance there. ■ A **bite** is the injury you get if a person, animal, or insect bites you. ■ If you have a **bite** to eat, you have a snack. ■ If a policy **bites,** it has a noticeable effect. ■ If you say **once bitten twice shy,** you mean someone will not do something again, because they had a bad experience the first time. ■ If someone **bites the bullet,** they do something unpleasant but necessary. ■ If someone **bites off more than they can chew,** they try to do something which is too difficult for them.

biting cold or a **biting** wind is extremely cold and piercing. ■ **Biting** remarks are cruel or sarcastic. ■ See also **bite.**

bit part A **bit part** is a small unimportant part for an actor in a film or play.

bitten See **bite.**

bitter (**bitterly, bitterness**) If someone is **bitter,** they are angry and resentful because they feel they have been unfairly treated. *He made no attempt to hide his bitterness.* ■ If someone has had a **bitter** disappointment, they are very unhappy and disappointed about something. *He was bitterly disappointed.* ■ If you know something **from bitter experience,** you know it because of unpleasant things which have happened to you. ■ In a **bitter** war, struggle, or argument, people fight or argue fiercely and angrily. ■ **Bitter** is used to describe very cold weather. *...a bitterly cold night.* ■ If something tastes **bitter,** it has a sour unpleasant flavour. ■ **Bitter** is a type of beer made with more hops than other beers. ■ **bitter pill:** see **pill.**

bittern The **bittern** is a long-legged wading bird related to the heron.

bitter-sweet (*or* **bittersweet**) If something tastes **bitter-sweet,** it tastes both bitter and sweet. ■ A **bitter-sweet** memory is both sad and happy.

bitumen (*pron:* **bit**-yoo-min) is a black sticky substance obtained from petroleum, used for surfacing roads and waterproofing roofs.

bivouac (*pron:* **biv**-oo-ak) (**bivouacking, bivouacked**) A **bivouac** is a temporary camp made by soldiers or mountaineers. When they **bivouac,** they set up a camp like this.

bizarre people or things are very strange.

black (**blackness**) **Black** is the colour of coal. ■ A **black** person belongs to a race of people with dark skins. ■ If someone has a **black eye,** they have a bruise around their eye. ■ **Black** coffee or tea is drunk without milk or cream. ■ **Black** humour involves jokes about death or suffering. ■ If someone **blacks out** or has a **blackout,** they lose consciousness for a short time. ■ If a place is **blacked out** or there is a **blackout,** there are no lights, because the power supply has been cut off. ■ If there is a news **blackout,** no news is allowed to be broadcast or published. ■ If a bank account is **in the black,** it is not overdrawn. ■ If you describe a situation as **black,** you mean that it is bad and not likely to improve.

black and white A **black and white** film, television, or photograph shows things in shades of black, white, and grey. ■ If you say you have something **in black and white,** you mean you have it written down, so there can be no doubt about it.

blackball If someone is **blackballed,** they are excluded from a club, because its members vote against them.

black belt If someone is a **black belt** in judo or karate, they have achieved a particular high standard. The black sash they are entitled to wear is also called a **black belt.**

blackberry (blackberries) Blackberries are small soft black fruit which grow on prickly bushes.

blackbird – Blackbirds are common European birds belonging to the thrush family. Males have black feathers and a bright yellow beak; females have brown feathers.

blackboard A **blackboard** is a board with a hard dark surface suitable for writing on with chalk.

black box See **flight recorder.**

blackcurrant – Blackcurrants are very small dark purple fruit which grow in bunches on a bush.

black economy A country's **black economy** is money earned without the government being informed, so no income tax is paid on it.

blacken (blackening, blackened) If something is **blackened,** its colour changes to black. ■ If someone **blackens** your name or reputation, they make people believe bad things about you.

blackhead – Blackheads are small black spots on a person's skin, caused by a pore in the skin being blocked by grease.

black hole – Black holes are areas which scientists believe exist in space and where gravity is so strong that nothing, not even light, can escape from them. Black holes are thought to be formed by collapsed stars.

black ice is a thin transparent layer of ice on a road.

blackjack is another name for the card game pontoon or vingt-et-un.

blackleg is an insulting word used to describe (a) a person who keeps working when other people are on strike. (b) someone brought in from outside to do the work of a person who is on strike.

blacklist (blacklisted) A **blacklist** is a list of people or organizations that it is thought cannot be trusted, or that have done something wrong.

black magic is magic used for evil.

blackmail (blackmailing, blackmailed; blackmailer) If someone **blackmails** you, they threaten to do something like revealing a secret unless you give them money or do what they want. This is called **blackmail.**

black market (black marketeer; black marketeering) Illegal trade in goods or currency is called the **black market** or **black marketeering.** A person who trades in this way is called a **black marketeer.**

blackout See **black.**

black pudding is a thick sausage with black skin. It is made from pork fat and pig's blood.

blacksmith A **blacksmith** is someone who makes and mends metal items.

black spot A **black spot** is (a) a place where road accidents often happen. (b) a part of the country where a problem is especially bad.

black tie At a **black tie** event, the men wear formal clothes including dinner jackets and black bow ties.

bladder A person's **bladder** is the bag-like organ in their body which holds urine.

blade The **blade** of a knife or other tool is the part with a sharp edge. ■ The **blades** of a propeller, fan, or engine are the parts which turn. ■ The **blade** of an oar is the thin flat part which is pushed against the water to propel the boat. ■ A **blade** of grass is a single leaf of it.

blag (blagging, blagged) If someone **blags** something such as a concert ticket, they get it free, usually by persuading someone to give it to them. *She'd heard he was a musician and blagged a tape off a friend of his.*

blame (blaming, blamed) If you **blame** a person or thing for something bad which has happened, you hold them responsible for it. *The police blamed the explosion on terrorists.* ■ If you say you do not **blame** someone for doing something, you mean their action was reasonable in the circumstances.

blameless If you say someone is **blameless,** you mean they have done nothing wrong.

blanch (blanches, blanching, blanched) If someone **blanches,** they turn pale. ■ If you say someone **blanches** at something, you mean they are shocked by it.

blancmange (*pron:* blam-**monj**) is a flavoured milk pudding similar to custard, which you eat cold.

bland (blandly, blandness) Bland things are dull and unremarkable. *...a bland performance.* ■ If someone makes a **bland** statement, they deliberately avoid saying anything controversial.

blandishments are attempts to persuade someone to do something by flattering or coaxing them.

blank (blankly) If something like a piece of paper is **blank,** there is nothing on it. ■ If someone looks **blank,** their face shows no feeling or interest. ■ If your mind goes **blank,** you cannot think of anything. ■ If you **draw a blank,** you fail to find what you are looking for. *The search has so far drawn a blank.* ■ If you **blank out** something which has happened to you, you avoid thinking about it. ■ If you give someone a **blank cheque,** you sign it but leave the amount for them to fill in. ■ If someone is given a **blank cheque,** they are given the freedom to do what they want, or spend as much money as they want. ■ **Blank** cartridges or **blanks** contain explosive but no bullet, so when the gun is fired there is a loud bang, but nothing else happens.

blanket (blanketing, blanketed) A **blanket** is a large bed cover, often made of wool. ■ If something like snow **blankets** an area or forms a **blanket** over it, it covers it. ■ **Blanket** is used to describe something which includes every person or thing in a group. *...a blanket ban on all supporters travelling to away matches.*

blank verse If a poem is written in **blank verse,** the lines do not rhyme.

blare (blaring, blared) When something like a radio or siren **blares,** it makes a loud harsh noise. *...the continual blare of pop music.*

blarney is saying flattering and amusing things to please someone or persuade them to do something.

blasé (*pron:* **blah**-zay) You say someone is **blasé** when they behave or talk in a calm and casual manner about something other people regard as important or exciting.

blaspheme (**blaspheming, blasphemed; blasphemy, blasphemous**) If someone **blasphemes,** they say or write something disrespectful about God, or use God's name as a swear word. You can describe someone or what they say as **blasphemous.**

blast A **blast** is a big explosion. You can say a place is **blasted** by an explosion or gunfire. ■ When people **blast** through rock, they force a way through using explosives. ■ A **blast** is a short loud noise on a whistle or horn. ■ When music or noise **blasts** from something like a radio, it is very loud. If it is **at full blast,** it is at full volume. ■ A **blast** is a sudden strong rush of something like liquid or gas. ■ When a space rocket **blasts off,** it is launched into the air. **Blast-off** is the moment it leaves the ground. ■ You can say someone **blasts** a person or thing when they severely criticize them.

blast-furnace A **blast-furnace** is a large furnace used to extract pure iron from iron ore.

blatant (*pron:* **blay**-tant) (**blatantly**) You say someone's actions are **blatant** when they do something bad in an obvious way. *...blatant disregard for international law.*

blather (**blathering, blathered**) You say someone is **blathering** when they are saying silly pointless things.

blaze (**blazing, blazed**) When a fire **blazes,** it burns fiercely and brightly. ■ A **blaze** is a large destructive fire. ■ **Blazing** is used to talk about very hot weather. *...a blazing Saturday afternoon.* ■ You can talk about a **blaze** of colour or light when it is very bright. ■ A **blaze** is a broad light-coloured mark down the front of a horse's face. ■ When something attracts a lot of media attention, you can say there is a **blaze** of publicity. *She went out in a spectacular blaze of scandal.* ■ **Blazing** is used to describe extremely strong feelings of anger or excitement. *...a blazing row.* ■ If someone **blazes a trail,** they lead the way to something new and exciting.

blazer A **blazer** is a kind of jacket, especially one worn by schoolchildren or members of a sports team.

bleach (**bleaches, bleaching, bleached**) Bleach is a chemical used as a disinfectant, or to whiten things like clothes or sheets. ■ If something is **bleached,** it is made white or paler in colour, either by bleach or by something like strong sunlight. *...bleached blond hair.*

bleak (**bleaker, bleakest; bleakly, bleakness**) A **bleak** situation is bad, and seems unlikely to improve. ■ If a person looks or sounds **bleak,** they seem depressed or hopeless. ■ A **bleak** place is cold and bare. ■ **Bleak** weather is cold and miserable.

bleary If someone is **bleary-eyed,** their eyes are red and watery from tiredness.

bleat (**bleating, bleated**) When a sheep or goat **bleats,** it makes a high-pitched quavery sound. ■ If a person **bleats,** they complain in a weak ineffective way.

bleed (**bleeding, bled**) When you **bleed,** you lose blood from your body as a result of injury or illness. ■ You say a coloured piece of cloth **bleeds** if the colour runs when it is washed. ■ If you **bleed** something like a radiator or brake system, you release the seal for a while, to let out liquid or gas. ■ If someone **bleeds** you **dry,** they gradually take all your money.

bleep (**bleeping, bleeped; bleeper**) When an electronic device **bleeps,** it makes a short high-pitched sound. A **bleeper** is a small device carried by someone like a doctor which bleeps when someone wants to contact them. When this happens, you say someone **bleeps** them.

blemish (**blemishes, blemished**) If something is **blemished** or has a **blemish,** it has a small mark or stain on it. ■ A **blemish** is a failing or shortcoming. *Another blemish on British justice was revealed this week.*

blend (**blender**) If you **blend** two or more substances together, you mix them together to make one substance. A **blender** is a kitchen appliance which mixes liquids and soft foods together. ■ A **blend** of something like tea or whisky is a combination of different types, with its own special flavour. You say a product like this is **blended.** ■ When things are **blended,** they are combined in a pleasant or satisfactory way. You can talk about a **blend** of things like these. *...a blend of youth and experience.* ■ If something **blends in** with its surroundings, it fits in with them and does not stand out.

bless (**blesses, blessing, blessed**) When a priest **blesses** someone or something, he asks for God's favour and protection for them. ■ If you say something like a plan is **blessed** by someone or it has their **blessing,** you mean it has their support. *The deal has been blessed by the Monopolies and Mergers Commission.* ■ If you say someone is **blessed with** a quality or skill, you mean they have it. ■ If you call something a **blessing,** you mean it is a good thing. *The new system has been a blessing.* ■ If you say something is a **blessing in disguise,** you mean it seemed to be a problem but has turned out to be an advantage. ■ If something is a **mixed blessing,** it has advantages and disadvantages.

blessed (*pron:* **bless**-id) (**blessedly**) People use **blessed** to describe things they feel especially thankful for. *...blessedly comfortable.* ■ **Blessed** is used to describe holy people or things.

blew See **blow.**

blight A **blight** is the harmful effect of something over a period of time. If one thing **blights** another, it spoils it. *...companies blighted by recession.* ■ **Blight** is a disease which makes plants wither.

blind (**blindly, blindingly, blindness**) If someone is **blind,** they cannot see. **Blindness** is being unable to see. If something **blinds** you, it makes you unable to see. ■ **Blinding** is used to describe light or colour which is dazzling. ■ If something is **blind-**

ingly obvious, it is very obvious. ■ If someone is **blind** to something, they do not notice it. If one thing **blinds** them to another, the first thing prevents them from noticing the second. *Their political dogma has blinded them to the real needs of the country.* ■ If you **turn a blind eye** to something, you pretend not to notice it. ■ You describe people's behaviour as **blind** when they do something without thinking. *We blindly follow their lead.* ■ A **blind** corner curves sharply, so you cannot see what is coming. ■ A **blind** is a roll of cloth which can be pulled down to cover a window. See also **Venetian blind.**

blind alley If you describe a situation as a **blind alley,** you mean no further progress is possible.

blind date A **blind date** is an arrangement made for you to spend a romantic evening with someone you have never met before.

blindfold A **blindfold** is a strip of cloth tied round someone's eyes so they cannot see. When someone is prevented from seeing like this, you say they are **blindfold** or **blindfolded.**

blind man's buff is a party game in which a blindfold person tries to catch one of the other players.

blind spot A **blind spot** is a part of an area which you cannot see, because it is hidden behind something. ■ You say someone has a **blind spot** about something when they seem unable to understand it. *Computers are a blind spot with me.*

blink When you **blink,** you close and open your eyes quickly. A movement like this is called a **blink.** ■ If you say something happens **in the blink of an eye,** you mean it happens very quickly. ■ You can say people **blink** when they are surprised at something. *...blinking in astonishment.* ■ When a light **blinks,** it flashes on and off. ■ If something is **on the blink,** it is not working.

blinkers (**blinkered**) **Blinkers** are two flaps fixed to the sides of a horse's bridle, so it can only see straight ahead. ■ If you say a person is wearing **blinkers** or has **blinkered** views, you mean they have a fixed narrow point of view.

blip A **blip** is a small spot of light flashing on and off regularly. ■ A **blip** is a sudden brief change in something which is proceeding in a regular way. *Last year's problems were just a temporary blip.*

bliss (**blissful, blissfully**) **Bliss** is a state of extreme happiness. A **blissful** time or state is a very happy one.

blister (**blistering, blistered**) If you get a **blister** or your skin **blisters,** you get a bubble-like swelling on the surface of your skin. ■ If paint **blisters,** small bumps appear on its surface. ■ **Blistering** heat is extreme heat. ■ If someone makes a **blistering** attack on a person or thing, they make extremely savage remarks about them. ■ **Blistering** can be used to emphasize that a sporting action is done with great speed or force. *...a burst of blistering pace.*

blithe (**blithely**) **Blithe** is used to say something is done in a carefree way.

blitz (**blitzes, blitzing, blitzed**) When a town is **blitzed,** it is heavily bombed by enemy aircraft. A **blitz** is an attack like this. ■ A **blitz** is (a) a deter-

mined effort to get something done. *...a blitz on illegal parking.* (b) a concentrated series of events. *...a blitz of television interviews.*

blizzard A **blizzard** is a heavy snowstorm with strong winds.

bloated If someone's body or a part of their body is **bloated,** it is uncomfortably swollen. *...a bloated stomach.* ■ If you say an organization is **bloated,** you mean it is larger and less efficient than it should be. *...a bloated bureaucracy.*

bloater A **bloater** is a salted, smoked herring.

blob A **blob** is a small amount of thick or sticky liquid. ■ Something which appears unclear or shapeless can be called a **blob.**

bloc A **bloc** is a group of people or countries with similar interests acting together. See also **en bloc.**

block A large building containing flats or offices is called a **block.** ■ In a town, an area bounded on four sides by streets can be called a **block.** *Mrs Hewings lives two blocks away.* ■ A **block** of a substance is a large rectangular piece of it. *...a block of marble.* ■ A **block** of something like tickets or shares is a large number of them, grouped together or numbered consecutively. ■ If something **blocks** other things, it prevents them from getting past, or prevents them from happening. ■ If something **blocks** your view, it gets in your way and prevents you from seeing something.

blockade (**blockading, blockaded**) When a place is **blockaded** or there is a **blockade,** no people or goods are allowed in.

blockage If there is a **blockage** in a pipe or tube, something is blocking it.

block and tackle A **block and tackle** is a device for lifting heavy objects. It consists of a rope or chain passed round blocks containing pulleys.

block-book (**block-booking**) If someone makes a large number of reservations in a theatre or hotel, you say they **block-book** the reservations or they make a **block-booking.**

blockbuster A **blockbuster** is a film or book which is very popular and makes a lot of money.

block capitals or **block letters** are capital letters.

block vote A **block vote** is a large number of votes all cast in the same way by one person on behalf of a group of people.

blonde (**blond**) **Blonde** hair is pale yellow. The spelling **blond** is used when referring men and boys. ■ A **blonde** is a woman with blonde hair.

blood is the red fluid which the heart pumps around the body. ■ You can use **blood** to talk about the race or social class of someone's parents or ancestors. *...a woman of royal blood.* ■ If someone is a **blood relation,** they are part of your family by birth, rather than by marriage. ■ If something is **in your blood,** it is part of your nature, and other members of your family may have it too. ■ If there is **bad blood** between people, they dislike each other. ■ If something cruel is done **in cold blood,** it is done deliberately and without emotion. ■ New people taken into an organization to improve it can be called **new blood.**

blood bank See **bank.**

bloodbath You say there is a **bloodbath** when a lot of people are violently killed.

blood cell – **Blood cells** are the red and white cells in the blood.

blood count A **blood count** is a check on the number of red and white blood cells in a blood sample. It shows how healthy a person is.

bloodcurdling A **bloodcurdling** cry is horrible and terrifying.

blood donor A **blood donor** is someone who gives a quantity of their blood for use in transfusions or operations.

blood group A person's **blood group** or **blood type** is the type of blood they have. The commonest blood groups are O and A.

bloodhound The **bloodhound** is a large dog with a smooth coat, droopy ears, sagging jowls, and a good sense of smell.

bloodless In a **bloodless** coup, nobody is killed. ■ If someone's face is **bloodless,** they look very pale.

blood-letting (*or* **bloodletting**) is killing and injuring during an outbreak of violence. ■ You say there is **blood-letting** when there is anger and quarrelling among a group of people.

blood poisoning is a serious illness caused by a blood infection.

blood pressure A person's **blood pressure** is the force with which their blood is pumped round their body.

bloodshed You say there is **bloodshed** when quarrelling turns to violence, and people get killed or injured.

bloodshot If someone's eyes are **bloodshot,** the white parts have turned red.

blood sport A **blood sport** is a sport which involves killing animals.

bloodstain (**bloodstained**) **Bloodstains** are marks left by blood. When something is marked or covered with blood, you say it is **bloodstained.**

bloodstock Thoroughbred racehorses are called **bloodstock.**

bloodstream A person's **bloodstream** is the flow of blood round their body.

bloodthirsty people are cruel and violent. ■ You say people are **bloodthirsty** when they enjoy watching or hearing about violence.

blood transfusion See **transfuse.**

blood type See **blood group.**

blood vessel – **Blood vessels** are the tubes in the body which blood flows through. Arteries, veins, and capillaries are all blood vessels.

bloody (**bloodier, bloodiest**) A **bloody** conflict involves a lot of killing and injury. ■ A **bloody** object has blood on it. ■ If someone gets a **bloody nose,** they come off worse in a fight which they started.

bloody-minded (**bloody-mindedness**) **Bloody-minded** people are deliberately unhelpful.

bloom (**blooming, bloomed**) A **bloom** is a flower on a plant. When flowers **bloom,** their buds open and the petals appear. ■ If someone is **blooming,** they are healthy and full of energy.

bloomers are large baggy knickers.

blossom (**blossoming, blossomed**) **Blossom** is the flowers on fruit trees before the fruit grows. When a fruit tree **blossoms,** blossom appears on it. ■ If a person **blossoms,** they develop new qualities or abilities and become more interesting or attractive. ■ You can say things **blossom** when they develop successfully.

blot (**blotting, blotted**) A **blot** is a drop of liquid, especially ink, which has been spilled and has left a mark on a surface. ■ If you **blot** something which is wet, you soak up the liquid on it with soft paper. ■ If something damages someone's reputation, you can say it is a **blot** on it. **blot your copybook:** see **copybook.** ■ If something is ugly and spoils the look of a place, you can say it is a **blot** on the landscape. ■ If one thing **blots out** another, it prevents it being seen. ■ If you **blot out** a thought, you avoid thinking about it.

blotch (**blotches; blotched, blotchy**) A **blotch** is a discoloured area, for example on a person's skin. When something has marks like this, you can say it is **blotched** or **blotchy.**

blotting paper is absorbent paper for soaking up ink.

blouse A **blouse** is a kind of shirt worn by a woman.

blow (**blowing, blew, have blown**) You say a wind **blows.** If something is carried somewhere by a wind, you say it is **blown** there. ■ When you **blow,** you send out a stream of air from your mouth. ■ If you **blow** something or **blow** it **up,** you force air through it or into it. ■ When you **blow** your nose, you force air out through your nostrils, to clear it. ■ A **blow** is (a) something which causes harm or damage. *...yet another blow to the reputation of British justice.* (b) something which saddens or disappoints you. ■ If you get a **blow** on the head, something hits you there. ■ If you strike a **blow** for a cause, you do something to help it succeed. ■ If you **blow** your money, you spend a lot of it quickly on things you do not really need. ■ If you get a chance to do something and then do it badly, you can say you **blew** the chance. ■ When a fuse **blows,** it burns out. ■ When trouble **blows over,** it comes to an end. ■ If something is **blown up,** it is destroyed by an explosion. ■ If a photograph is **blown up,** it is made larger; an enlarged photograph is called a **blow-up.**

blow-by-blow accounts of events describe every stage in detail.

blow-dry If someone has their hair **blow-dried,** they have it styled with a hand-held hairdryer.

blowlamp See **blowtorch.**

blown See **blow.**

blow-out If there is a **blow-out** on a vehicle, a tyre bursts suddenly. ■ A **blow-out** is a very large meal.

blowpipe A **blowpipe** is a long tube which arrows are blown from.

blowtorch (**blowtorches**) A **blowtorch** or **blowlamp** is a hand-held device which uses gas to produce a hot flame.

blow-up See **blow.**

blubber is the thick layer of fat beneath the skin of animals like whales and seals.

bludgeon (*pron:* **bluj**-jon) (**bludgeoning, bludgeoned**) A **bludgeon** is a thick heavy stick used as a weapon. ■ If someone is **bludgeoned,** they are badly beaten with a heavy object. ■ If someone is **bludgeoned** into doing something, they are threatened or bullied into doing it.

blue is the colour of the sky on a sunny day. ■ If you feel **blue** or have **the blues,** you feel depressed. ■ **Blues** or **the blues** is a type of music developed by black American musicians. It has a slow tempo, strong rhythm, and often sad lyrics. ■ **Blue** movies and jokes are about sex. ■ If something happens **out of the blue,** it happens suddenly and unexpectedly. ■ If you say someone can do something until they are **blue in the face,** you mean they can keep doing it but it will have no effect.

bluebell – **Bluebells** are woodland plants with thin stems and blue flowers.

blueberry (blueberries) In the US, bilberries are called **blueberries.**

blue blood (blue-blooded) If you say someone has **blue blood** or describe them as **blue-blooded,** you mean they belong to a royal or noble family.

bluebottle The **bluebottle** is a large fly with a shiny dark-blue body.

blue-chip companies and shares are considered safe to invest in while also being profitable.

blue-collar workers do manual work in industry. See also **white-collar.**

blueprint A **blueprint** is a photographic print of an architect's or engineer's plan. It consists of white lines on a blue background. ■ A **blueprint** for something is a plan of how it is expected to work. *...a detailed blueprint for agricultural reform.*

blue tit The **blue tit** is a small European bird with a blue head, wings, and tail, and a yellow breast.

bluff A **bluff** is an attempt to make someone believe you will do something you do not really intend to do. If you think someone is behaving like this, you can say they are **bluffing.** If you **call someone's bluff,** you tell them to do what they are threatening to do, because you think they will not really do it. See also **double bluff.** ■ If you **bluff** your way through a difficult situation, you get through it by pretending to know more than you really do. ■ A **bluff** person is frank and down-to-earth, and does not try to be polite.

blunder (blundering, blundered) If you **blunder** or make a **blunder,** you make a silly mistake. ■ If someone **blunders** about, they move about in a clumsy way.

blunderbuss (blunderbusses) A **blunderbuss** is an old-fashioned gun with a short wide barrel which scatters shot at close range. ■ **Blunderbuss** is used to describe things done in a clumsy or forceful way. *Your blunderbuss question about shutter speeds involves too many variables.*

blunt (bluntly, bluntness) If someone is **blunt,** they say what they think. ■ A **blunt** object has a rounded or flat end, rather than a pointed one. ■ A **blunt** knife has lost its sharpness. ■ If something **blunts** an emotion or desire, it weakens it.

blur (blurring, blurred; blurry) A **blur** is a shape whose outline you cannot see clearly because it is far away or moving fast. ■ If something is **blurred** or **blurry,** you cannot see it clearly because it is indistinct. ■ If you cannot remember something

well, you can say it is a **blur.** ■ If the difference between two things becomes **blurred,** there are no longer distinct differences between them.

blurb The **blurb** on a book is information on the cover about the book and encouraging people to buy it. ■ A **blurb** is a leaflet or advertisement promoting goods or services for sale.

blurt If you **blurt** something **out,** you say it suddenly, without thinking about the consequences.

blush (blushes, blushing, blushed) If you **blush,** your face goes red, because you are embarrassed.

blusher is a cosmetic women use to add colour to their cheeks.

bluster (blustering, blustered) If someone **blusters,** they talk angrily or boastfully, to hide their fear or embarrassment.

blustery weather is rough and windy.

boa – **Boas** are large non-poisonous snakes such as pythons, which coil around their prey and squeeze it to death. ■ A **boa** is a long fluffy scarf often made of feathers.

boar (*plural:* **boar** *or* **boars**) A **boar** is an uncastrated male pig. ■ The **boar** or **wild boar** is a wild pig with tusks.

board (boarder) A **board** is a long flat piece of wood. ■ A **board** is a flat piece of wood or other material used for a special purpose. *...a notice board.* ■ If a door or window is **boarded up,** pieces of wood are fixed over it, for security reasons. ■ The **board** of an organization is the group of people who control it. ■ When you **board** a boat, train, or plane, you get on it; you then say you are **on board.** ■ Your **board** is the food you pay for when you stay somewhere. See also **board and lodging, full board, half board.** ■ You say a pupil who lives at school during the term **boards** there or is a **boarder.** ■ If you say something is **above board,** you mean it is open, fair, and honest. ■ If something like a policy applies **across the board,** it affects everyone. ■ If someone **sweeps the board** in a competition, they win everything, or nearly everything.

board and lodging is food and a place to sleep, usually provided in a boarding house or sometimes offered as part of the conditions of a job.

board game – **Board games** are games like chess or Monopoly, in which people move pieces around on a board.

boarding card A **boarding card** is a card which permits a passenger to board a plane or boat for a journey.

boarding house A **boarding house** is a private house which provides meals and accommodation for paying guests.

boarding party A **boarding party** is a group of people sent on board a ship to carry out an investigation or to take over the ship.

boarding pass A **boarding pass** is the same as a boarding card.

boarding school A **boarding school** is one where pupils live during the term. See also **day school.**

boardroom The **boardroom** of a company is the room where board meetings are held. **Boardroom** is also used to talk about people at the highest level of management in a company. ...*a boardroom reshuffle.*

boardwalk In the US, a **boardwalk** is a raised footpath made of boards.

boast (boastful) If someone **boasts** or is **boastful,** they talk too proudly about something they own or have done. ■ If someone or something **boasts** a feature, they have it. *The town boasts a 12th-century domed church.*

boat (boating) A **boat** is a vessel for travelling across water, especially a small one. If you go **boating,** you go on a lake or river in a boat for pleasure. ■ If you say someone has **missed the boat,** you mean they have missed an opportunity, because they did not act quickly enough. ■ If you say people are **in the same boat,** you mean they are in the same bad situation.

boater A **boater** is a hard straw hat with a flat top and a brim.

boat-hook A **boat-hook** is a long pole with a hook at the end, used to pull a boat to the bank or push it away from other boats.

boathouse A **boathouse** is a building near a lake or river where boats are stored.

boat people are refugees who have escaped from their country in small boats, especially refugees who left Vietnam in the 1970s and 1980s.

boatswain See **bosun.**

boat train A **boat train** is a train which takes you to or from a port.

bob (bobbing, bobbed) When something **bobs,** it moves up and down repeatedly. *Yachts bobbed up and down in the bay.* ■ If a woman's hair is **bobbed** or she has a **bob,** her hair is cut to about chin length all round. ■ In the past **bob** was often used to mean 'shillings'. For example, people would say something cost 'five bob' (25p).

bobbin A **bobbin** is a reel for holding thread.

bobble – Bobbles are small fluffy balls, used to decorate clothes or furnishings.

bobby (bobbies) A **bobby** is a policeman.

bobsleigh (*pron:* **bob**-slay) A **bobsleigh** is a large metal sledge, used for racing.

bode (boding, boded) If something **bodes well,** it shows something good is likely to happen. If it **bodes ill,** it shows you can expect something bad.

bodice The **bodice** of a dress is the part above the waist.

bodice-ripper A **bodice-ripper** is a sensational romantic novel or film, often with a historical setting.

bodily means relating to a person's body. ...*bodily pain.* ■ **Bodily** is used to say something happens to the whole of someone's body. ...*lifting him bodily into the air.*

bodkin A **bodkin** is a blunt large-eyed needle used to thread cord through the waistband of a garment.

body (bodies) Your **body** is (a) the whole of your physical shape, including your head, arms, and legs. (b) the main part of this shape, not including your head, arms, or legs. ■ A dead person can be referred to as a **body.** ■ A **body** of people is an organized group. ...*the governing body of football.* ■ The main **body** of something is its largest or most important part. *They had broken away from the*

main body of the crowd. ■ A **body** of something like information or opinion is a large amount of it. ■ The **body** of a car is the main part, not including the engine. ■ If you receive a **body blow,** something happens which causes you great disappointment and difficulty. ■ **heavenly body:** see **heavenly.**

body-builder (body-building) A **body-builder** is a person who regularly does special exercises to develop their muscles.

bodyguard Someone's **bodyguard** is the person or people employed to protect them.

body language is the way your feelings are revealed by the movements of your body.

body politic The **body politic** in a country is the people who operate its political system.

bodywork The **bodywork** of a vehicle is its outside part.

boffin is a humorous word for a scientist or technical expert.

bog (bogged) A **bog** is an area of wet spongy ground. ■ If a vehicle is **bogged down,** it is stuck in something like mud. ■ If you get **bogged down** by something, it prevents you from making progress.

bogey (*or* **bogy**) **(bogeys, bogies)** A **bogey** is something which causes problems. ...*the twin bogeys of soaring budget deficits and hyper-inflation.* ■ In golf, a **bogey** is a score of one above par on any hole. See also **birdie, eagle.**

bogeyman (bogeymen) A **bogeyman** or **bogey** is a frightening evil spirit. ■ Someone who is thought to be evil can be called a **bogeyman.** ...*that bogeyman of the communists known as a capitalist.*

boggle (boggling, boggled) If your mind **boggles** at something, you find it difficult to grasp.

bogus (*pron:* **boh**-guss) is used to describe (a) people who pretend to be something they are not. ...*bogus health visitors.* (b) things which are not genuine. ...*bogus receipts.*

bogy See **bogey.**

bohemian A **bohemian** is an artistic person with an unconventional lifestyle. ...*her bohemian life in north London.*

boil (boiling, boiled) When a heated liquid **boils** or comes to the **boil,** it bubbles and starts to change into steam or vapour. If a liquid **boils over,** it rises and spills out of a container. ■ When you **boil** a kettle, you heat the water in it until it boils. ■ When you **boil** food, you cook it in boiling water. ■ If someone is **boiling** with anger, they are extremely angry. ■ If people's anger **boils over,** they become uncontrollably angry. ■ If you say something **boils down** to a particular thing, you mean that is its most important or most basic aspect. ■ A **boil** is a painful red swelling on a person's skin.

boiler A **boiler** is a piece of equipment which burns fuel to provide hot water. Steam-driven vehicles and machinery are powered by steam from boilers.

boiler suit A **boiler suit** is a piece of protective clothing consisting of trousers and a top joined together in one piece.

boiling point The **boiling point** of a liquid is the temperature at which it starts to change into steam or vapour. ■ If a situation has reached **boiling point,** the people involved can no longer remain calm and in control of themselves.

boisterous people are rough, noisy, and lively.

bold (**boldly; boldness**) Bold people behave in a confident fearless way. ■ **Bold** writing stands out clearly and distinctly.

bolero (**boleros**) A **bolero** (pron: bol-er-o) is a very short jacket, often sleeveless. ■ The **bolero** (pron: bol-**air**-o) is a traditional Spanish dance.

bollard – Bollards are (a) short thick concrete posts, used to mark off an area and stop vehicles getting past. (b) fixed or movable posts, often with a light inside, used to mark road junctions.

bolster (**bolstering, bolstered**) If you **bolster** someone's confidence, you increase it. ■ If someone **bolsters** their position in a situation, they strengthen it. ...*cash aid to help bolster the reform process.* ■ A **bolster** is a long firm pillow or cushion.

bolt A **bolt** is a long metal pin which screws into a nut to fasten two things together. When you **bolt** things together, you fasten them with nuts and bolts. ■ If you **bolt** a door or window, you fasten it with a sliding metal device called a **bolt.** ■ If a person or animal **bolts,** they suddenly run away, often because they are frightened. When a prisoner or captured animal **bolts,** they escape. ■ A **bolt** of lightning is a flash of it, especially one which hits the ground. ■ If a piece of news comes as **a bolt from the blue,** it comes as a complete surprise.

bolt hole A **bolt hole** is a place where you can go to get away from people.

bomb (**bombing**) A **bomb** is a weapon which explodes and damages or destroys a large area. ■ If a place is **bombed**, it is attacked by bombs. A **bombing** is a bomb attack. If you say people have been **bombed out,** you mean the place they live in has been destroyed by bombs. ■ If there is a **bomb scare** or a **bomb threat,** a warning is received claiming a bomb has been placed somewhere. ■ A **bomb factory** is a place where bombs are made illegally. ■ **Bomb disposal** is the job of removing unexploded bombs safely. ■ When people talk about **the bomb,** they mean nuclear weapons.

bombard (**bombardment**) If a place is **bombarded,** it is attacked with continuous heavy gunfire or bombing. ■ You say people are **bombarded** when a lot of things are thrown at them. ■ You say an object is **bombarded** when it is hit by many smaller objects. *Objects in orbit are constantly bombarded by space dust.* ■ If you are **bombarded** with something, you have to face a lot of it. ...*bombarded with advertising.*

bombardier A **bombardier** is an NCO in an artillery regiment.

bombast (**bombastic**) Bombast is the use of long, important-sounding words with little meaning in an attempt to impress other people. You say a person is **bombastic** when they talk like this.

bomber A **bomber** is (a) an aircraft which drops bombs. (b) a person who places a bomb somewhere.

bomber jacket A **bomber jacket** is a short jacket gathered into a band at the waist or hips.

bombshell A **bombshell** is an unwelcome surprise.

bona fide (pron: **bone**-a **fide**-ee) (**bona fides**) Bona **fide** means genuine or real. *It was a bona fide mistake.* A **bona fide** action is done in good faith. ...*acting bona fide in the interests of another person.* ■ Someone's **bona fides** are their good intentions.

bonanza A **bonanza** is something which makes people suddenly rich.

bond A **bond** is a strong feeling of love or friendship which unites people. ■ When someone develops a close relationship with another person, you can say they **bond** with them. For example you can talk about a mother **bonding** with her baby. ■ **Male bonding** is the development of close friendships between men, often based on their shared experience of all-male activities. ■ When someone is tied up, you can call the rope they are tied up with their **bonds.** ■ When two things are **bonded** together, they are closely joined, for example with an adhesive substance. You say the substance acts as a **bond.** ■ A **bond** is a certificate of debt issued by a government or company to raise funds. It carries a fixed rate of interest and is repayable at a specified future date. ■ A **bond** is an agreement, especially a promise. If someone says **their word is their bond,** they mean they will definitely do what they have promised. ■ A **bonded** travel company belongs to an association of travel agents which provide a guarantee that a person will not forfeit their holiday if the company they book it with goes out of business.

bondage is slavery. ■ **Bondage** is sexual activity which involves a person being tied up.

bonded labour is a system in which people are forced to repay a debt by working for the person who lent them the money.

bone (**boning, boned; bony**) The **bones** of a person or animal are the hard parts which form their skeleton. **Bony** people or animals are thin, with not much flesh covering their bones. ■ If you **bone** a piece of meat or fish, you take out the bones before cooking it. ■ The **bare bones** of something are the most important parts, which the other parts are constructed around. *The bare bones of representative democracy are there.* ■ A **bone of contention** is something people argue over. ■ If you say someone **makes no bones about** something, you mean they talk openly about it, rather than trying to keep it a secret. ■ If something is **bone dry,** it is very dry indeed. ■ If you cut spending **to the bone,** you reduce it to the lowest possible amount. ■ If you **bone up** on a subject, you learn as much as you can as quickly as possible.

bone china is fine porcelain containing the ash of burned animal bones.

bone marrow See **marrow.**

bone meal (*or* **bonemeal**) is dried ground animal bones, used as fertilizer or animal feed.

bonfire A **bonfire** is a large outdoor fire, usually burning garden rubbish. ■ **Bonfire Night** is the night of November 5, when people have bonfire parties and let off fireworks.

bongo (**bongos**) Bongo drums or **bongos** are small drums, usually in pairs, played by tapping with the fingers.

bonhomie (*pron:* **bon**-om-ee) is happy jolly friendliness.

bonkers If you say someone is **bonkers,** you mean they are mad.

bonnet The **bonnet** of a car is the metal cover over the engine. ■ A **bonnet** is a woman's or baby's hat which ties under the chin.

bonny (**bonnier, bonniest**) A **bonny** person or thing is attractive or beautiful.

bonsai (*pron:* **bon**-sigh) A **bonsai** (*plural:* **bonsai** *or* **bonsais**) is a dwarf tree which is kept small by growing it in a little pot and trimming it in a special way. The art of growing trees in this way, which originated in Japan, is called **bonsai.**

bonus (**bonuses**) A **bonus** is an amount of money you get on top of your usual pay. ■ A **bonus** is something good you get in addition to what is expected. *Any sunshine we get is a bonus.*

boo (**booing, booed**) When people **boo,** they shout 'boo' to show their disapproval.

boob (**boobing, boobed**) If you **boob** or make a **boob,** you make a silly mistake. ■ A woman's **boobs** are her breasts.

booby trap (**booby-trapped**) A **booby trap** is something like a bomb which is hidden or disguised and explodes when it is touched or moved. If something is **booby-trapped,** it has a booby trap in it.

boogie (**boogying, boogied**) If you **boogie,** you dance to pop music.

book (**booking, booked**) A **book** consists of sheets of paper bound together inside a cover. ■ A **book** is one of the large sections which a long work like the Bible is divided into. ■ The **books** of an organization are its written records of money paid and received. ■ If you say someone is **on the books** of a organization, you mean they work for it or are a member of it. ■ When you **book** something like a hotel room or make a **booking,** you arrange to use it. When all rooms have been booked, you say the hotel is **booked up** or **fully booked.** ■ When you **book into** a hotel, you inform the receptionist you have arrived and sign your name in the register. ■ When a police officer **books** someone, he or she officially records their name and the offence they may be charged with. Similarly, when a football referee **books** someone who has broken a rule, he officially records the player's name. ■ If someone is **brought to book,** they are punished for an offence or made to explain their actions. ■ If you say something is a **closed book** to you, you mean you know nothing about it.

bookable If something is **bookable,** it can be booked in advance. ■ In football, a **bookable** offence is one a player can be booked for.

bookbinding is the work of fastening the pages of a book together and putting the covers on.

bookcase A **bookcase** is a piece of furniture with shelves for books.

bookends are a pair of supports for keeping a row of books upright.

bookie A **bookie** is the same as a bookmaker.

booking office A **booking office** is a place where tickets are booked and sold, especially in a railway station.

bookish If you say someone is **bookish,** you mean they are quiet and serious, and enjoy studying and reading.

book-keeping (**book-keeper**) Book-keeping is the work of keeping a record of money paid and received by a business.

booklet A **booklet** is a book with a small number of pages and often a paper cover.

bookmaker A **bookmaker** is someone who takes your money when you bet on something like a horse race, and pays you if you win. A betting shop is sometimes called a **bookmaker's.**

bookmark A **bookmark** is a strip of material that you put between the pages of a book to mark your place. If you mark a website on your computer so you can find it again, this is also called a **bookmark**.

bookseller A **bookseller** is (a) a person who runs an independent bookshop. (b) a bookshop, or a company which controls a chain of bookshops.

bookshelf (**bookshelves**) A **bookshelf** is a shelf for books.

bookshop A **bookshop** is a shop which specializes in selling books.

bookstall A **bookstall** is (a) a stall where books are sold, for example at a jumble sale. (b) a small shop with an open front where books, magazines, and papers are sold, for example at a railway station.

bookstore is the usual American word for a bookshop.

bookworm If you call a person a **bookworm,** you mean they read a lot.

boom (**booming, boomed**) If there is a **boom** in something, it increases rapidly. *...a boom in tourism... The economy was booming.* A **boom** time is one when there is a boom. *...the boom years of yuppie extravagance.* A **boom** town is one which grows rapidly as a result of a boom. ■ When something like a drum **booms,** it makes a loud deep echoing sound. ■ A **boom** is a floating barrier used to stop oil spills from spreading. ■ On a sailing boat, the **boom** is the horizontal pole which the bottom of the main sail is attached to. ■ A **boom** is a long pole with a microphone on the end, used in a film studio.

boomerang A **boomerang** is a curved piece of wood, originally thrown by native Australians as a weapon. Some boomerangs are designed to come back to the person who throws them.

boon If something is a **boon,** it makes life better.

boor (**boorish**) If you say someone is a **boor,** you mean they behave in a rude and uneducated way.

boost (**booster**) If one thing **boosts** or gives a **boost** to another, it improves or increases it. *...a boost to inflation.* Something which has this effect can be called a **booster.** ■ A **booster** injection is an additional injection given some time after the original one, to make sure the immunization remains effective. ■ A **booster** is a rocket used to give extra power to a missile or spacecraft.

boot (**booting, booted**) Boots are strong shoes which cover the ankle and sometimes the lower leg. ■ If you **boot** a ball, you kick it hard. ■ You say someone **puts the boot in** when they behave in a cruel way towards a person who is already upset. ■ If someone is **booted out** of a job or place, they are forced to leave. ■ The **boot** of a car is a covered space for carrying things like luggage or shopping. ■ The phrase **to boot** means 'as well' or 'in addition to'. ...*more mature than most other rock 'n' rollers and a father to boot.*

boot camp In the United States, a **boot camp** is a military establishment for training recruits to the armed forces. A prison institution which imposes a strict military regime on young criminals can be called a **boot camp.**

booth A **booth** is (a) a small compartment screened off from a larger area. (b) a small tent or stall where you can buy something or watch an entertainment.

bootleg (**bootlegging, bootlegged; bootlegger**) **Bootleg** or **bootlegged** things have been illegally produced or transported. ...*bootleg liquor.* ...*bootlegged tapes.* Producing or transporting something in this way is called **bootlegging.**

bootstraps If you **pull yourself up by your bootstraps,** you achieve success by your own efforts.

booty is valuable things taken from a place, especially by troops after a battle.

booze (**boozing, boozed; boozy, boozer**) **Booze** is alcoholic drink. When someone **boozes,** they drink alcohol. If they drink a lot, you say they are **boozy** or a **boozer.** A **boozy** occasion is one when a lot of alcohol is drunk.

bop (**bopping, bopped**) When you **bop** or have a **bop,** you dance to pop music. ■ **Bop** or **bebop** is a style of jazz.

bordello (**bordellos**) A **bordello** is a brothel.

border (**bordering, bordered**) The **border** between two countries or regions is the dividing line between them, or land close to this line. ■ A country that **borders** or **borders on** another country, a sea, or a river is next to it. ■ A **border** is a long narrow flowerbed. ■ A **border** is a strip or band around the edge of something, often added for decoration. ■ If you say someone's behaviour **borders on** a certain state or condition, you mean it is almost in that state or condition. *His confidence borders on arrogance.*

borderline is used to talk about situations which are not clear-cut. *They would be borderline cases for getting housing benefit.*

bore (**boring, bored**) If you say someone or something is **boring,** you mean they are uninteresting. You can say you are **bored** by them or with them. You can call something uninteresting a **bore.** ■ If you call a person a **bore,** you mean they talk a lot about things nobody is interested in. ■ If you are **bored,** you have lost interest in something, or you have nothing interesting to do. ■ If you **bore** a hole in something, you make a hole in it using something like a drill. ■ The **bore** of a gun is the inside diameter of its barrel. ■ See also **bear.**

boredom is the feeling you have when you are bored.

borehole A **borehole** is a deep hole drilled in the ground, especially when searching for water or oil.

born When a baby is **born,** it comes out of its mother's womb. ■ **-born** is added to words to show where someone was born. ...*Jamaican-born poet James Berry.* ■ If you say who someone is **born of,** you are saying who their parents are. ■ You use **born** to say someone has a natural ability to do something well. ...*a born storyteller.* If you say someone was **born to** do something, you mean they seem destined to do it. *He was born to be a soldier.* ■ You use **born** to say when or where something was created. *The movement was born 12 years ago.* ■ If you say one thing was **born of** another, you mean it happened because of it. ...*fear born of ignorance.*

born-again A **born-again** Christian is a person who has experienced a spiritual conversion and become an evangelical Christian. ■ **Born-again** is used to describe someone who is an enthusiastic convert to something new, or who has renewed an interest in something. ...*a born-again rock fan.*

borne See **bear.**

borough (*pron:* bur-ruh) A **borough** is a small town, or a district within a large town, which has its own council.

borrow (**borrower**) If you **borrow** something which belongs to someone else, you take it, intending to return it. ■ If you **borrow** money from a person or organization, they give it to you and you agree to pay it back at some future time, usually with interest. A person who borrows money is called a **borrower.** ■ If you **borrow** something like an idea from someone, you make use of it for your own purposes.

borscht (*or* borsch) is a Russian or Polish soup which has beetroot as its main ingredient.

borstal Prisons for young criminals used to be called **borstals,** but are now known as 'young offenders' institutions'.

bosom (*pron:* buz-um) A woman's **bosom** is her breasts. ■ A **bosom** friend is a very close friend. ■ If someone is living in the **bosom** of their family or community, they are among people who love and protect them.

boss (**bosses, bossing, bossed**) Someone's **boss** is the person in charge of the organization where they work. ■ If someone **bosses** you **about,** they keep telling you what to do.

bossy (**bossiness**) A **bossy** person enjoys telling other people what to do. You can talk about the **bossiness** of someone like this.

bosun A ship's **bosun** or **boatswain** (*pron:* boh-sn) is the person on board who is officially responsible for the ship's maintenance and equipment.

botany (**botanic, botanical; botanist**) **Botany** is the scientific study of plants. **Botanic** and **botanical** mean to do with botany. ■ **Botanic** or **botanical gardens** grow plants for public display and scientific study.

botch (**botches, botching, botched**) If you **botch** something or make a **botch** of it, you do it badly.

both When you mention two people or things, you use **both** to make it clear you are including each of them in what you say. *My sister and I both chose spaghetti bolognese.*

bother (**bothering, bothered; bothersome**) **Bother** is trouble or fuss. ■ If you do not **bother** to do something or cannot be **bothered** to do it, you do not do it because you think it is too much trouble. ■ If you think it is pointless to do something, you can say **why bother** to do it? ■ If you are not **bothered** about something or it does not **bother** you, you do not mind it. ■ If someone or something **bothers** you, they worry or irritate you. You can say they are **bothersome**.

bottle (**bottling, bottled**) A **bottle** is a glass or plastic container, especially one for liquids. ■ A baby's **bottle** is a drinking container with a rubber teat on the end through which the baby sucks. You say a baby is **bottle-fed** when it drinks milk from a bottle rather than its mother's breast. ■ If you **bottle** something like alcohol or fruit, you put it into bottles to store it. ■ **Bottled** gas is kept under pressure in special metal cylinders. ■ If you **bottle up** strong feelings, you do not express them.

bottle bank A **bottle bank** is a large container in a public place for people to dispose of glass bottles so the glass can be recycled.

bottleneck A **bottleneck** is a narrow part of a road where traffic has to slow down or stop, often causing a jam. ■ Something which slows progress can be called a **bottleneck.**

bottom (**bottoming, bottomed**) Your **bottom** is the part of your body you sit on. ■ The **bottom** of something is its lowest part. ■ The **bottom** thing in a series is the lowest one, the last to be added, or the least important. *...the bottom shelf... They put their health at the bottom of their list of priorities.* ■ The **bottom** of a street or garden is its furthest end. ■ If someone comes **bottom** in a test or a league, their performance is worse than everyone else's. ■ If you say someone is **at the bottom of the pile,** you mean they are lower in status than everyone else. ■ If you **get to the bottom of** something, you discover the truth about it or its real cause. ■ When something **bottoms out,** it stops falling or getting any worse.

bottomless If you talk about someone's purse being **bottomless,** you mean they have an unlimited supply of money. ■ If you talk about resources disappearing into a **bottomless** pit, you mean someone's requirements are never satisfied, no matter how much help they receive.

bottom line The **bottom line** is the thing which counts most in a situation. *The bottom line is value for money.* ■ In business, the last line of a financial statement summarizing the net profit or loss of a company is called the **bottom line.** When you talk about a company's **bottom line,** you mean its profit or loss.

botulism is a serious form of food poisoning.

boudoir (*pron:* boo-dwahr) A **boudoir** is a woman's bedroom or private sitting room.

bouffant (*pron:* boof-fon) A **bouffant** hairstyle is one where the hair is backcombed to achieve a higher and fuller appearance.

bougainvillea (*pron:* boo-gan-**vill**-ee-a) is a colourful tropical climbing plant.

bough (*rhymes with 'now'*) A **bough** is a large tree branch.

bought See **buy.**

boulder – **Boulders** are large rocks.

boulevard (*pron:* boo-le-vard) A **boulevard** is a wide city street, often with trees on either side.

bounce (**bouncing, bounced; bouncy**) When an object **bounces,** it springs back from something after hitting it. If you **bounce** an object, such as a ball, you throw it against a surface to make it do this. ■ If you **bounce,** you jump up and down. If an object **bounces,** it moves up and down. ■ If a person is **bouncy** or full of **bounce,** they have a lot of energy and confidence. ■ When someone or something **bounces back** after a setback, they quickly return to their previous state. ■ If a cheque **bounces,** a bank refuses to pay out the money. ■ A **bouncing** baby is fit and healthy.

bouncer A **bouncer** is a person whose job is to stop undesirable people getting into a place like a pub or nightclub, and to throw people out if they cause trouble. ■ In cricket, a **bouncer** is a ball which bounces very high after it has been bowled.

bound (**bounding, bounded; -bound**) If you say something is **bound** to happen, you mean it is certain to happen. ■ If you are **bound** by something like an agreement or law, you have a responsibility to obey it. ■ If one thing is **bound up** with another, the two things are closely linked. See also **bind.** ■ If you are **bound** for a place, you are on your way there. *...homeward-bound commuters.* ■ The **bounds** of something are its limits. You add **-bound** to a word to show what someone or something is restricted to. *...his wheelchair-bound mother.* ■ If an area is **out of bounds,** you are forbidden to go there. ■ If an area is **bounded** by something, it is bordered by it. ■ When someone **bounds** somewhere, they move there quickly with large strides or leaps.

boundary (**boundaries**) The **boundary** of an area of land is its outer edge, which separates it from other areas. ■ In cricket, the **boundary** is the line marking the edge of the pitch. When a batsman hits the ball beyond this line, he scores a **boundary.** ■ The **boundary** between two similar kinds of thing is the point at which something ceases to be one thing and becomes the other. *...the boundary between public and private health care.*

bounty (**bountiful**) If someone is very generous, you can talk about their **bounty** or say they are **bountiful.** ■ If there is a **bountiful** supply of something, there is a lot of it. ■ **Bounty** is a reward or payment for something. In the past, a person could be paid **bounty** for capturing or killing a dangerous criminal; someone who made a living from this was called a **bounty hunter.**

bouquet (*pron:* boo-**kay**) A **bouquet** is an attractively arranged bunch of flowers, especially one given as a present. ■ A wine's smell is called its **bouquet.**

bouquet garni (*plural:* bouquets garni) (*both pron:* boo-kay gah-**nee**) A **bouquet garni** is a small bunch of herbs tied together and used for flavouring soups and stews.

bourbon (*pron:* **bur**-bon) is a type of American whisky made from maize.

bourgeois (**bourgeoisie**) (*pron:* **boorzh**-wah, boorzh-wah-**zee**; *the 'zh' sounds like 's' in 'pleasure'*) **Bourgeois** means middle-class. The **bourgeoisie** are middle-class people. If you say someone has **bourgeois** attitudes, you mean they are materialistic and narrow-minded.

bout If you have a **bout** of an illness, you have it badly for a short time. ■ A concentrated burst of activity can be called a **bout**. *Shops remained open for a final bout of trading.* ■ A **bout** is a boxing or wrestling match.

boutique (*pron:* boo-**teek**) A **boutique** is a small shop which sells fashionable clothes, shoes, or jewellery.

bouzouki (*pron:* boo-**zoo**-kee) The **bouzouki** is a Greek stringed instrument, which sounds similar to a mandolin.

bovine is used to talk about things to do with cattle. *...bovine growth hormone.*

bow (*rhymes with 'now'*) (**bowing, bowed**) If you **bow** or make a **bow**, you briefly bend forward as a formal greeting, or to show respect. ■ If you **take a bow**, you acknowledge applause or praise, often by actually bowing. ■ If you **bow** your head, you bend it downwards as a mark of respect, or because you are ashamed. ■ If you **bow** to someone's wishes, you give in to them. ■ If you **bow out** of something, you stop taking part in it. ■ The front part of a ship is called the **bow** or **bows**.

bow (*rhymes with 'low'*) A **bow** is a knot with two loops and two loose ends, for tying things such as shoelaces or ribbons. ■ A **bow** is a weapon for shooting arrows. It consists of a long piece of wood or other material bent into a curve by a string attached to both ends. ■ The **bow** of a violin or other stringed instrument is a long thin piece of wood with horsehair stretched along it, which you move across the strings to play the instrument.

bowdlerized (*or* **bowdlerised**) (**bowdlerization**) A **bowdlerized** version of a book has had words or sections removed or changed, because they are thought to be offensive.

bowel A person's **bowels** are the tubes in the lower part of their body through which waste matter passes on its way to their anus. ■ You can call the parts deep inside something its **bowels**. *...the bowels of the earth.*

bowl A **bowl** is a circular container with a wide uncovered top, used especially for serving food. ■ A **bowl** is the hollow rounded part of something. *... a lavatory bowl.* ■ **Bowls** is a game in which players roll heavy wooden balls called **bowls** as near as possible to a small white ball. ■ In cricket, when the bowler **bowls** he or she sends the ball down the pitch towards a batsman. If the batsman's wicket is hit, you say he is **bowled** or **bowled out**. ■ If you are **bowled over** by something, you are greatly impressed by it.

bowler In a cricket match, the **bowler** is the person who is bowling. ■ A **bowler** or **bowler hat** is a stiff round black hat with a narrow curved brim, worn by some British businessmen.

bowling is a game in which you roll a heavy ball down a long narrow track called a **bowling alley** to try to knock down ten objects called pins. A **bowling alley** is also a building containing several tracks.

bowling green A **bowling green** is an area of smooth short grass on which the game of bowls is played.

bowls See bowl.

bow window A **bow window** is a curved window sticking out from a wall.

box (**boxes, boxing, boxed; boxer**) A **box** is a container with a firm base, sides, and usually a lid. **Boxed** things are packed in boxes. ■ On a form, a **box** is a rectangular space to write something in. ■ At a theatre or sports ground, a **box** is a separate area like a little room where a small number of people can sit to watch the performance. ■ If you are **boxed in,** you are unable to move from a particular place because you are surrounded by other people or cars. ■ **Boxing** is a sport in which two people called **boxers** punch each other wearing large padded gloves. ■ **Boxers** are smooth-haired dogs with flat faces. ■ **Box** is a slow-growing evergreen shrub with shiny leaves, often used for hedges.

boxer shorts are loose-fitting men's underpants shaped like shorts.

Boxing Day is the first weekday after Christmas, observed as a public holiday.

box office The **box office** in a theatre, cinema, or concert hall is the place where the tickets are sold. **Box office** is often used to say how successful a production is in terms of tickets sold. *...one of the greatest box-office hits of all time.*

boy A **boy** is a male child.

boycott If people **boycott** a product or event, or take part in a **boycott** of it, they express their disapproval by refusing to buy it or go to it.

boyfriend A person's **boyfriend** is the man they are having a romantic relationship with.

boyhood A man's **boyhood** is the period of his life when he is a boy.

boyish If you say someone is **boyish,** you mean they look or behave like a boy.

Boy Scout See scout.

bra A **bra** is a piece of underwear worn by a woman to support her breasts.

brace (**bracing, braced; braces**) If you **brace** yourself for something unpleasant, you prepare to face it. ■ A **brace** is an object fastened to something to straighten or support it. *...a knee brace.* ■ **Braces** are elasticated straps worn over the shoulders to hold up a pair of trousers. ■ A **brace** (*plural:* **brace**) of things is a pair of them. *...a few brace of grouse.* ■ If something is **bracing,** it is refreshing and stimulating. *...a bracing walk.*

bracelet A **bracelet** is a chain or band worn around the wrist.

bracken is a large fern which grows on hills and in woods.

bracket (bracketing, bracketed) A **bracket** is a piece of metal or wood fastened to a wall to support something like a shelf. ■ **Brackets** are a pair of written marks, such as ( ), placed round a word or several words, to separate them from the surrounding words. ■ A **bracket** is a range of things, for example ages or prices. ...*the 35-54 age bracket.* ■ If you **bracket** two or more things together, you treat them as if they belong together. *She objected to pregnant women being bracketed with the sick.*

brackish water is slightly salty.

brag (bragging, bragged) If someone **brags** about something, they boast about it.

Brahmin (*or* Brahman) A **Brahmin** is a Hindu of the highest caste.

braid (braiding, braided) **Braid** is a strip of contrasting cloth or twisted threads used to decorate clothes or soft furnishings. ■ If you **braid** hair or thread, you plait it. A **braid** is a plaited length of hair.

Braille is a system of printing for the blind, in which letters are represented by raised dots which can be felt with the fingers.

brain Your **brain** is the mass of nerve tissue inside your skull which controls your body and enables you to think and feel. ■ If you say someone has **brains** or a good **brain,** you mean they are intelligent. ■ The **brains** behind something is the person organizing it. ■ When people talk about the **brain drain,** they mean the movement of large numbers of highly qualified people away from their own country to countries where they can earn more money.

brainchild Someone's **brainchild** is their clever idea or invention.

brain death (brain dead) **Brain death** is a condition in which someone's brain has permanently stopped working, though their heart and lungs may be kept going by a machine.

brainstorm (brainstorming) If someone has a **brainstorm,** they suddenly become unable to think sensibly, and do things they would not normally do. ■ **Brainstorming** is intensive discussion to solve problems or develop ideas.

brainwash (brainwashes, brainwashing, brainwashed) If someone is **brainwashed,** they are made to believe something by continually telling them it is true while they are kept in isolation or deprived of sleep.

brainwave If you have a **brainwave,** you suddenly have a good idea.

brainy A **brainy** person is intelligent.

braise (braising, braised) When you **braise** food, you brown it lightly by frying, then cook it slowly in a small amount of liquid.

brake (braking, braked) A **brake** is a device for slowing or stopping a vehicle. When you **brake,** you apply the brakes on a vehicle. A road vehicle's **brake lights** are lights at the back which light up when the brakes are applied. ■ A **brake** is something which has the effect of slowing something down. *The skills shortage in Britain is still a brake on economic recovery.*

bramble – Brambles are thorny bushes which produce blackberries.

bran is the brown flakes left over when wheat grains are made into white flour.

branch (branches, branching, branched) The **branches** of a tree are the parts growing out of its trunk. ■ A **branch** of an organization is one of its offices, shops, or local groups. ■ A **branch** of a subject is one of its areas of study. ■ If you **branch out,** you start doing a greater variety of things. ■ If a road **branches off,** it goes off at an angle from another one. ■ A **branch line** is a railway built to serve small towns, as distinct from a main line between cities.

brand (branded) A **brand** of something is a variety of it. ...*his own brand of socialism.* ■ A **brand** of a product is the version made by one manufacturer. The **brand name** of a product is the name of the company which makes it, or its trademark. ■ A **branded** product is made by a well-known manufacturer and has the manufacturer's name on it. ■ **Own-brand** products are made and sold by a supermarket or chain store, and have the store's name on them. ■ When an animal is **branded,** a permanent mark is made on its skin, either by burning or freezing, to show who owns it. A **branding iron** is a long-handled metal tool used for this purpose. ■ If someone is **branded** as something bad, they are given a reputation for being that thing. ■ If something is **brand new,** it is completely new and unused.

brandish (brandishes, brandishing, brandished) If you **brandish** something like a weapon, you wave it in a threatening way. You can also **brandish** an object to draw people's attention to it. *Demonstrators brandished placards.*

brandy is a strong alcoholic spirit distilled from wine or fermented fruit juice.

brash (brashness) If you say someone is **brash,** you mean they are loud and over-confident.

brass is an alloy of copper and zinc. ■ In an orchestra, the **brass section** consists of the brass wind instruments, such as the trumpets and tubas. ■ The **top brass** of an organization are its most senior members.

brasserie A **brasserie** is (a) a bar where food is sold. (b) a small restaurant.

brassiere (*pron:* bra-zee-er) A **brassiere** is the same as a bra.

brassy A **brassy** woman is showy and rather tasteless. ■ **Brassy** music is played on brass instruments and is harsh and loud.

brat People sometimes call a badly-behaved child a **brat.** ■ A group of successful young people is sometimes called a **brat pack.**

bravado (*pron:* bra-vah-doh) is an appearance of courage or self-confidence, put on to impress people.

brave (braver, bravest; braving, braved; bravely, bravery) You say people are **brave** or talk about their **bravery** when they put themselves in danger to achieve something. ■ If you **brave** an uncomfortable or dangerous situation, you put up with it to do something. *About 150,000 people braved the downpour to listen to the concert.*

bravura (*pron:* brav-**yoor**-a) When someone puts on a **bravura** performance, they show off their skill at something.

brawl A **brawl** is a rough violent fist fight. When people fight like this, you say they are **brawling.**

brawn (**brawny**) If you talk about someone's **brawn** or describe them as **brawny,** you mean they are strong and muscular. ■ **Brawn** is meat taken from a cooked pig's head, set in jelly and eaten cold.

bray When a donkey **brays,** it makes a loud 'hee-haw' sound. ■ If a person **brays,** they speak or laugh with a loud harsh sound.

brazen (**brazenly**) You say someone is **brazen** when they do something shocking without caring what people think. *...her brazen admission that she was cheating.* ■ If someone who has done something wrong **brazens it out,** they show no shame.

brazier A **brazier** is a metal container in which coal or charcoal is burned to keep people warm out of doors.

brazil nut – Brazil **nuts** are large three-sided nuts from a South American tree.

breach (**breaches, breaching, breached**) If a law or promise is **breached** or there is a **breach** of it, it is broken. ■ If someone is charged with a **breach of the peace,** they are charged with behaving threateningly in a public place, in a way which frightens other people. ■ A **breach** in a relationship is a serious disagreement. ■ When someone **breaches** a barrier, they make a gap in it. *...the Mexicans who breached and scaled the walls.* You can also say a river **breaches** its banks. ■ If someone **steps into the breach,** they help out in a difficult situation by taking over someone else's duties.

bread is a food made from flour, water, and often yeast, which is made into a soft dough and baked in an oven. ■ The work which provides someone's main income can be called their **bread and butter.** ■ The basic or routine parts of a job or subject are sometimes called its **bread and butter.** *It's the bread and butter of police work, checking if anybody has seen anything suspicious.*

bread-bin A **bread-bin** is a container for bread.

breadboard A **breadboard** is a board for cutting bread on.

breadcrumbs are tiny pieces of bread, often used in cooking.

breadline If you say someone is living on the **breadline,** you mean they are very poor.

breadth The **breadth** of something is the distance between its sides. ■ If you talk about the **breadth** of something like a person's knowledge, you mean it covers a wide range of things.

breadwinner The **breadwinner** of a family is the person who earns the money to pay for its needs.

break (**breaking, broke, have broken**) When an object **breaks,** it splits or is split into pieces. ■ If a system **breaks down,** it no longer works. *...the temporary breakdown in law and order.* ■ If a machine is **broken** or **broken down,** it is damaged and does not work. ■ You use **break** to say a situation which has existed for some time is brought to an end.

Graham broke the silence... If you smoke, keep trying to break the habit. ■ If someone **breaks** a promise or rule, they fail to keep it ■ If someone **breaks** a record, they improve on the previous best performance. ■ When something like a meeting or demonstration **breaks up** or is **broken up,** it finishes. ■ If you **break off** in the middle of doing something, you suddenly stop doing it. ■ If people **break with** tradition, they no longer observe it. ■ When someone **breaks** a piece of news, they tell it to other people. ■ When something like a crisis **breaks,** it suddenly happens. ■ When something like a fight or a disease **breaks out,** it begins suddenly. ■ When a boy's voice **breaks,** it becomes permanently deeper. ■ If people **break away** from a group, they leave, often to form a new group. A group formed like this is called a **breakaway** group. ■ If you **break free** from someone or a situation, you get away from them. ■ If someone **breaks into** a car or building, they get into it illegally, using force. When this happens, you say there is a **break-in.** ■ If someone **breaks out** of jail, they escape. A **breakout** is an escape. ■ If a person **breaks down,** they start crying uncontrollably. ■ A **break** is a pause in something. When people take a **break,** they stop work for a short time. ■ **Break into** is used to say someone starts to do something. *She broke into a run.* ■ If someone gets a **break,** they have an unexpected lucky opportunity. ■ If a business **breaks even,** it makes enough money to cover its costs, but does not make a profit. ■ If you **break off** a relationship, you end it. ■ If people in a relationship **break up,** they separate, and the relationship ends. ■ **break the ice:** see **ice. break ranks:** see **rank.**

breakage When something is broken, you say there is a **breakage.** *...breakage of plate glass.*

breakaway See **break.**

breakdown If there is a **breakdown** of a system, it does not work. ■ A **breakdown** is a psychological condition in which a person becomes extremely depressed. ■ If a driver has a **breakdown,** his or her car stops working.

breaker – **Breakers** are large waves in the sea.

breakfast is the first meal of the day.

break-in See **break.**

breaking point If something is at **breaking point,** it has reached the limits of what it can cope with. *The city's public services are at breaking point.*

breakneck If something is happening at **breakneck** speed, it is happening very fast.

breakout See **break.**

breakthrough A **breakthrough** is an important development or achievement.

breakwater A **breakwater** is a wall extending from the shore into the sea. It is built to protect a harbour or beach from the force of the waves.

breast A woman's **breasts** are the two soft rounded fleshy parts on her chest which can produce milk to feed a baby. When a woman **breast-feeds** her baby she feeds the baby with milk from her breasts. ■ A person's chest can be called their **breast.** ■ A bird's **breast** is the front of its body. ■ If you say someone is **beating their breast,** you mean they are making a show of feeling upset about something. ■ If someone **makes a clean breast of** something they have done wrong, they admit they have done it.

breastbone See **sternum.**

breastplate A **breastplate** was the part of a suit of armour which covered a soldier's chest.

breaststroke is a swimming stroke in which you lie on your front, moving your arms horizontally through the water and kicking both legs in a frog-like way.

breath Your **breath** is the air you take in and let out when you breathe. If you take a **breath,** you breathe in. ■ If you are **out of breath, short of breath,** or **gasping for breath** you are breathing quickly and with difficulty. ■ If you **hold your breath,** you stop breathing for a short time. ■ You say someone is **holding their breath** when they are anxiously waiting for something. ■ If you **catch your breath,** you have a short rest in the middle of doing something. ■ If you say something **takes your breath away,** you are emphasizing that it makes a strong impression on you ■ If you say something **under your breath,** you say it very quietly so few people can hear. ■ You use **in the next breath** to show someone seems to be contradicting what they have just said. *He opposed over-the-top salaries for executives. But in the next breath, he admitted there was nothing he could do to halt their multimillion pound pay rises.*

breathalyze (*or* **breathalyse**) (**breathalyzing, breathalyzed; breathalyzer**) If the driver of a vehicle is **breathalyzed,** they are asked by the police to breathe into a machine called a **breathalyzer,** which measures the amount of alcohol they have drunk. 'Breathalyzer' is a trademark.

breathe (**breathing, breathed**) When a person or animal **breathes,** they take air into their lungs and let it out again. ■ You say you **breathe a sigh of relief** or **breathe more easily** when you feel relieved about something. ■ If you are given a **breathing space,** you have a short time in which to recover from one thing and prepare for something else. ■ If you **breathe new life** into something, you revive interest in it, or improve it.

breather If you take a **breather,** you stop what you are doing and have a short rest.

breathless (**breathlessly; breathlessness**) If you are **breathless,** you are having difficulty breathing properly. ■ **Breathless** is used to describe someone's behaviour when they are very excited. *...a breathless phone call.*

breathtaking If you say something is **breathtaking,** you are emphasizing that it is amazingly beautiful.

breath test If someone is given a **breath test,** they are breathalysed by the police.

bred See **breed.**

breech In a **breech** birth, the baby is born with its feet or buttocks appearing first. ■ The **breech** of a firearm is the part behind the barrel.

breeches (*pron:* **brit**-chiz) are trousers which come down to the knees.

breed (**breeding, bred; breeder**) A **breed** of an animal is one particular kind of it. For example, terri-

ers are a breed of dog. ■ **Breed** can be used to talk about a kind of person. *...that increasingly rare breed, the true British eccentric.* ■ A new version of something can be called a **new breed** of it. *...a new breed of portable computers.* ■ When animals **breed,** they mate and produce offspring. ■ When people **breed** animals, they select pairs for mating to produce the types they want. When people **breed** plants, they use special cultivating methods to produce the types they want. People who breed animals or plants are called **breeders.** *...pig breeders.* ■ If one thing **breeds** another, it causes it. *Success has bred complacency and self-satisfaction.* ■ If you say someone was **born and bred** somewhere, you mean they were born and spent their childhood there. ■ If you say someone has **breeding,** you mean they belong to the upper classes and are very well-mannered. See also **well-bred.**

breeding ground An animal's **breeding ground** is the place where it goes to breed. ■ You say something is a **breeding ground** when a certain thing is likely to develop there. *Slums may well be breeding-grounds of crime.*

breeze (**breezing, breezed; breezy**) A **breeze** is a gentle wind. ■ If the weather is **breezy,** there is a light wind. ■ You say someone **breezes into** a place when they stride confidently in there. ■ If someone's behaviour is **breezy,** it is bright and lively. ■ If you **breeze through** something, you get it done quickly.

breeze block — **Breeze blocks** are lightweight building blocks made from the ashes of coal or coke mixed with cement.

brethren is an old word for brothers. People who belong to the same religion are sometimes called **brethren. Brethren** is also used to talk about other people with something in common. *...their academic brethren.*

brevity When you talk about the **brevity** of something, you mean it does not last long.

brew When you **brew** tea or coffee, you make it by pouring hot water over tea leaves or coffee grounds, then letting it stand while the water absorbs the flavour. A pot of tea or coffee can be called a **brew.** ■ **Brewing** is the process by which beer is made. It involves boiling malt and other ingredients, then allowing the mixture to ferment. ■ A mixture of things can be called a **brew.** *...a curious brew of African and Latin rhythms.* ■ If something unpleasant is **brewing,** it is developing. *There's trouble brewing.*

brewer A **brewer** is a person or company that makes beer.

brewery (**breweries**) A **brewery** is (a) a company which makes beer. (b) a place where beer is made.

briar — **Briars** are wild roses with long thorny stems.

bribe (**bribing, bribed; bribery**) If someone offers you a **bribe** or tries to **bribe** you, they offer you money or something else, to try to get you to do something wrong or illegal. Bribing people is called **bribery.**

bric-a-brac is assorted small ornamental objects.

brick — **Bricks** are rectangular building blocks made from clay mixed with water and baked hard. ■ If a doorway or window is **bricked up,** it is filled in with bricks.

brickbats are blunt criticisms.

bricklayer A **bricklayer** is a person trained in building with bricks.

brickwork The **brickwork** of a building is the parts made from bricks.

bride (bridal) A **bride** is a woman who is getting married or has just got married. **Bridal** is used to talk about things to do with a bride or wedding. ...*bridal gowns.*

bridegroom A **bridegroom** is a man who is getting married or has just got married.

bridesmaid At a wedding, a **bridesmaid** is the bride's attendant.

bridge (bridging, bridged) A **bridge** is a structure built over a river, road, or railway so people or vehicles can cross from one side to the other. ■ If you act as a **bridge** between two groups of people, you make it possible for them to communicate with each other. Establishing links between people who are not communicating is often called **bridge building.** ■ If someone or something **bridges the gap** between two people or things, they overcome the differences or disagreements between them. ■ A ship's **bridge** is the platform or area above the main deck from which it is controlled. ■ **Bridge** is a card game for four players.

bridgehead A **bridgehead** is (a) an area of captured ground, from which an army can advance or attack. (b) a secure position from which someone can advance or improve their prospects.

bridging loan A **bridging loan** is a loan from a bank or other institution to provide money for a short period between two transactions, for example when you are buying a new house before the sale of the old one is completed.

bridle (bridling, bridled) A **bridle** is a harness fitted round a horse's head to enable its rider to control it. ■ If someone **bridles** at something, they take offence at it.

bridleway A **bridleway** is a public path which can be used by horse riders.

brief (briefing, briefed; briefly) Brief is used to describe something which lasts only a short time. ...*a brief visit... He paused briefly.* ■ If you **brief** someone, you give them information or instructions. See also **briefing.** ■ A person's **brief** is what they have officially been instructed to do. ■ A **brief** is a set of documents containing all the facts about a legal case. ■ **Briefs** are pants or knickers.

briefcase A **briefcase** is a small case for carrying things like documents and books.

briefing A **briefing** is a meeting at which people are given information or instructions. ...*a press briefing.*

brigade A **brigade** is an army unit consisting of three battalions. ■ Some groups of people organized for a particular task are called **brigades,** for example the fire brigade. ■ People use **brigade** to talk about groups of people they dislike. ...*the anti-zoo brigade.*

brigadier A **brigadier** is a high-ranking army officer.

brigand A **brigand** is a highway robber, especially a member of a gang operating in remote or mountainous country.

bright (brightly, brightness) A **bright** colour is strong and noticeable, and not dark. ■ A **bright** day is very sunny. ■ A **bright** light shines strongly. ■ A **bright** idea is clever and original. ■ **Bright** people are clever and quick at learning things. ■ If someone looks or sounds **bright,** they seem cheerful. ■ A **bright spot** is a good feature in an otherwise bad situation.

brighten (brightening, brightened) When something **brightens** or is **brightened,** it becomes brighter. ■ When a place is **brightened up,** it is made more attractive and colourful. ■ When a person **brightens,** they become more cheerful.

brilliant (brilliantly; brilliance) If you call a person, plan, or idea **brilliant,** or talk about their **brilliance,** you mean they are extremely clever. ■ **Brilliant** is used to say someone does something extremely well. *She's a brilliant cook... He writes brilliantly.* ■ You say something is **brilliant** when you are very pleased about it, or think it is very good. *This is brilliant news.* ■ If someone has a **brilliant** career, they are very successful. ■ A **brilliant** light or colour is extremely bright.

brim (brimming, brimmed; brimful) The **brim** of a hat is the wide sticking-out part round the bottom. ■ If a container is filled **to the brim,** it is filled right to the top. ■ If something is **brimming** with things or **brimful** of them, it is very full of them. ■ If someone is **brimming** with a feeling or **brimming over** with it, they are full of it.

brimstone is an old word for sulphur. ■ When evangelical preachers talk about **fire and brimstone,** they mean hell and the punishment awaiting people there. ■ **Fire and brimstone** is used to talk about fierce threatening behaviour. *The editor is breathing fire and brimstone down the phone.*

brine is salt water.

bring (bringing, brought) If you **bring** someone or something somewhere, you take them there with you. ■ If something has a certain effect, you can say it **brings** that effect. ...*as the recession brings prices down. ...a heart attack brought on by overwork.* ■ If something **brings** a certain price, that is how much it is sold for. ■ If something from the past is **brought back,** it is re-introduced. *The government has refused to bring back free eye tests.* ■ If something **brings back** memories, it reminds you of them. ■ If you cannot **bring** yourself to do something, you cannot make yourself do it, because it is so unpleasant. ■ If a legal action is **brought** against someone, they are officially accused of doing something unlawful. ■ If you **bring forward** an event, you arrange for it to take place earlier than planned. ■ If you **bring up** a subject, you introduce it into a discussion. ■ When a person or system is **brought in** to deal with a task, they are employed specially for it. ■ If someone succeeds in doing something difficult, you can say they **bring** it **off.** ■ When a new product is **brought out,** it is made available for people to buy. ■ If something **brings out** a type of behaviour in someone, it makes them behave like that. ■ When someone **brings up** a child, they care for it while it is growing up.

brink If you are on the **brink** of something, it could happen to you at any moment. *He was on the brink of bankruptcy.*

brinkmanship is the tactic of deliberately taking a risky situation to the limit, to try to get an advantage.

brisk (**briskly**) People say business is **brisk** when things are being sold quickly and a lot of money is being made. ■ If something happens at a **brisk** pace, it happens quite quickly. ■ You call someone's behaviour **brisk** when they deal with things in a quick efficient way. ■ A **brisk** action is quick and energetic. *...a brisk walk.* ■ If the weather is **brisk**, it is cold but pleasant.

brisket is a cut of beef from the breast.

bristle (**bristling, bristled**) **Bristles** are short stiff animal hairs, often used to make brushes. Short tufts of man-made fibres like nylon or plastic are also called **bristles.** ■ A **bristling** moustache has thick rough hairs. ■ When an animal **bristles,** the hair or fur on its back stands up, because it is afraid or angry. ■ You say a person **bristles** when something angers them. ■ If a place or thing **bristles** with people or with other things, it contains a great number of them. *...a team bristling with star names.*

Brit British people are sometimes called **Brits.**

British people and things are in or from the United Kingdom. The **British** are the British people.

British Summer Time See **BST.**

Briton A **Briton** is someone from the United Kingdom.

brittle (**brittleness**) **Brittle** things are hard but easily broken. ■ **Brittle** is used to describe things like relationships when they are unstable and could easily break down. ■ If you call a person **brittle,** you mean they behave in a hard unfeeling way.

broach (**broaches, broaching, broached**) If you **broach** a subject, you introduce it into a conversation.

broad (**broader, broadest; broadly**) If something is **broad,** it is wide. ■ You use **broad** to describe things which involve a wide variety of things. *...a broad and balanced education.* ■ **Broad** and **broadly** are used to talk about the general idea of something, rather than its details. *Party officials say the report is broadly accurate.* ■ A **broad** accent is strong and noticeable. ■ If you give a **broad** hint, you reveal information in an indirect but obvious way. ■ If you say a crime took place **in broad daylight,** you are expressing your surprise that it took place during the day, rather than at night when nobody would see it.

B-road A **B-road** is a minor road.

broad bean – **Broad beans** are light-green beans with thick flat edible seeds.

broadcast (**broadcasting, broadcast** *not 'broadcasted';* **broadcaster**) When a TV or radio programme is **broadcast,** it is transmitted. A person who presents TV or radio programmes can be called a **broadcaster.** A programme can be called a **broadcast.** ■ You

can say an announcement is **broadcast** over something like a loudspeaker system.

broaden (**broadening, broadened**) When something **broadens,** it becomes wider. ■ You say something is **broadened** when it is extended to include a wider variety of things. *She has broadened the scope of her research.*

broad-minded If you say someone is **broad-minded,** you mean they are tolerant of different kinds of behaviour and opinions.

broadsheet A **broadsheet** is a newspaper printed on large sheets of paper. Broadsheets are usually more serious than other newspapers. See also **tabloid.**

broadside If one person launches a **broadside** against another, they criticize them severely. ■ If a vehicle is moving **broadside on,** it is moving with its side to the front.

brocade is a thick expensive fabric, woven with a raised pattern, often using gold and silver threads.

broccoli is a vegetable with green stalks and green or purple flower heads.

brochure (*pron:* broh-sher) A **brochure** is a booklet containing information about a product or service.

brogue (*pron:* broag) **Brogues** are sturdy shoes with a pattern punched into the leather. ■ A **brogue** is a broad accent, especially an Irish one.

broil (**broiling, broiled**) When Americans grill food, they say they **broil** it.

broiler – **Broilers** are young tender chickens reared in large sheds called **broiler houses.**

broke See **break.** ■ If you are **broke,** you have no money. You say a company goes **broke** when it is unable to pay its debts and goes out of business. ■ If you **go for broke,** you take a risky course of action in the hope of achieving a great success.

broken See **break.**

broker (**brokering, brokered**) A **broker** is a person or firm that is paid commission to buy and sell shares, currency, or goods on behalf of other people. *...an insurance broker.* See also **stockbroker.** ■ A **broker** is someone who acts as a negotiator between people or organizations. ■ If someone **brokers** a deal or agreement, they negotiate something which is acceptable to everyone involved.

brokerage A **brokerage** is a broker's business or office. ■ **Brokerage** is the commission charged by a broker.

brolly (**brollies**) A **brolly** is an umbrella.

bromide is a chemical (a) used to make **bromide paper,** which is used in photographic processes. (b) used as a sedative. ■ Bland remarks can be called **bromides.**

bronchial (*pron:* bronk-ee-al) A person's **bronchial tubes** connect their windpipe to their lungs. **Bronchial** is used to talk about things to do with these tubes. *...a bronchial infection.*

bronchitis (*pron:* bronk-**eye**-tiss) is an illness in which the bronchial tubes become inflamed.

brontosaurus (**brontosauruses**) The **brontosaurus** was a type of large four-legged plant-eating dinosaur, with a long neck and a long tail.

bronze (**bronzed**) **Bronze** is a hard yellowish-brown alloy made mainly of copper and small amounts of tin. It is used to make sculptures. ■ Bronze sculptures are often called **bronzes.** ■ A **bronze medal** is awarded as third place in a competition. ■ **Bronze** is a yellowish-brown colour. ■ **Bronzed** people are attractively sun-tanned.

Bronze Age The **Bronze Age** was the phase of human cultural development between the Stone Age and the Iron Age. It began in the Middle East about 4000BC, lasting in Britain from about 2000BC to 500BC.

brooch (*rhymes with 'coach'*) (**brooches**) A **brooch** is a piece of jewellery with a pin at the back for attaching to clothing.

brood (**brooding, brooded; broody**) A **brood** is a group of baby birds hatched from the same batch of eggs. ■ A **broody** hen is ready to lay or sit on eggs. ■ You can refer to someone's young children as their **brood** when you want to emphasize that there are a lot of them. ■ If someone **broods** about something, they think about it a lot, seriously and often unhappily. ■ **Brooding** is used to describe something disturbing and threatening. ...*a dark, brooding sky.*

brook (**brooking, brooked**) A **brook** is a small stream. ■ If you say someone will **brook** no interference or opposition, you mean they will not tolerate any interference or opposition.

broom A **broom** is a long-handled brush. ■ When someone who has just started a new job intends to make a lot of changes, you can call them a **new broom.** ■ **Broom** is a thorny shrub with yellow flowers.

broomstick A **broomstick** is (a) the long handle of a broom. (b) a broom which has a bundle of twigs at the end instead of bristles.

broth is soup, usually with meat or vegetables in it.

brothel A **brothel** is a house where men pay to have sex with prostitutes.

brother Your **brother** is a boy or man who has the same parents as you. ■ You can use **brother** to describe a man who belongs to the same group or organization as yourself. ...*brother architects.* ■ **Brother** is a title given to a man who belongs to a religious community like a monastery.

brotherhood is affection and loyalty between groups of people who have something in common. ■ An organization of men can be called a **brotherhood.**

brother-in-law (**brothers-in-law**) Your **brother-in-law** is the brother of your husband or wife, or your sister's husband.

brotherly A man's **brotherly** feelings are feelings of love and loyalty like those of a brother. ...*brotherly affection.*

brought See **bring.**

brouhaha (*pron:* **brew-hah-hah**) is a lot of fuss.

brow Your **brow** is your forehead. ■ Your **brows** are your eyebrows. ■ The **brow** of a hill is its top.

browbeat (*or* **brow-beat**) (**browbeating, browbeat** *not* '**browbeated**', **have browbeaten**) If someone **browbeats** you, they bully you.

brown is the colour of earth or wood. ■ If you **brown** food, you cook it till it turns brown.

brownie A **Brownie Guide** or **Brownie** is a girl aged 7 to 10 who belongs to the junior branch of the Girl Guides. ■ **Brownies** are small square nutty chocolate cakes. ■ You say someone earns **brownie points** when they do something because they think it will impress people. *They're just trying to score brownie points with politicians.*

brownish If something is **brownish,** it is slightly brown.

browse (**browsing, browsed; browser**) If you **browse** or have a **browse** through a book or magazine, you look through it in a casual way. ■ If you **browse** in a shop, you look at things in a casual unhurried way. ■ If you **browse** on your computer you are looking on the World Wide Web for a particular text to read. ■ A **browser** is the software package that helps you to do this. ■ When animals **browse,** they continually nibble at grass or leaves.

bruise (**bruising, bruised**) A **bruise** is a purple mark on your skin caused by an injury. Marks like this are called **bruising.** ■ If fruit or grain is **bruised,** it has been damaged. ■ You can say a person's feelings are **bruised** when they are upset. ■ You can say things are **bruised** when they are affected badly by something. ...*their bruised reputation.* ■ In a **bruising** encounter, people behave aggressively towards each other. ... *a bruising political row.*

bruiser A **bruiser** is a tough person who enjoys fighting.

brunch is a meal combining breakfast and lunch.

brunette A **brunette** is a girl or woman with dark brown hair.

brunt If someone **bears the brunt** of something unpleasant, they suffer most of its effects.

brush (**brushes, brushing, brushed**) A **brush** is an object consisting of bristles fixed into a firm back or handle. If you **brush** something, you clean or tidy it with a brush. ■ You say you **brush** something when you touch against it lightly in passing. ■ If you have a **brush** with someone, you have a disagreement with them. ■ **Brush** is used to talk about unpleasant experiences. ...*a brush with death.* ■ If you **brush** something **aside** or **brush** it **off,** you refuse to consider it, because you think it is unimportant. ■ If someone gives you the **brush-off,** they ignore you completely. ■ If you **brush up** on a subject, you renew or improve your knowledge of it. ■ **Brush** is shrubs and small trees growing thickly together.

brushwood is (a) cut or broken-off branches or twigs. (b) shrubs and small trees growing thickly together.

brushwork An artist's **brushwork** is their technique in applying paint with a brush.

brusque (*pron:* **broosk**) (**brusquely**) If someone is **brusque,** their manner is blunt. *He brusquely demanded that they get to business.*

Brussels sprouts See **sprout.**

brutal (**brutally; brutality, brutalities**) **Brutal** behaviour is cruel and vicious. Behaviour like this is also called **brutality;** cruel acts can be called **brutalities.** ■ If you say something like the truth is **brutal,** you mean it is unpleasant or hurtful. Similarly, you can say someone is **brutally** honest.

brutalize (*or* **brutalise**) (**brutalizing, brutalized**) If people are **brutalized** by their experiences, they become cruel and heartless.

brute (**brutish**) You call a man a **brute** when he is rough and insensitive. ■ If you use **brute** force to do something, you use physical strength rather than reason.

B.Sc. A **B.Sc.** is a university degree in a science subject. B.Sc. stands for 'Bachelor of Science'.

BSE See **mad cow disease.**

BST or **British Summer Time** is the system of telling the time used in Britain from late March to late October, when clocks are set one hour ahead of Greenwich Mean Time. See also **GMT.**

BTEC courses are work-related courses available to people aged 16 and over, usually at a college of further education.

bubble (**bubbling, bubbled**) A **bubble** is a ball of air in a liquid, or on its surface. When a liquid **bubbles**, bubbles form in it. ■ When something like a feeling **bubbles up**, it gradually increases. ...*a bubbling up of enthusiasm.* ■ If someone is **bubbling** with a feeling, they are full of it. ■ When something which has been going well suddenly collapses, you can say the **bubble has burst.**

bubble-bath is scented liquid soap which you pour into running bathwater to make foam.

bubble gum is chewing gum which you can blow into bubbles.

bubbly people are lively and cheerful. ■ Champagne is sometimes called **bubbly.**

buccaneer (**buccaneering**) **Buccaneers** were pirates, especially the ones who attacked ships in the Caribbean during the 17th and 18th centuries. ■ People who are adventurous, especially in their business dealings, are sometimes called **buccaneers** or described as **buccaneering.** ...*buccaneering capitalists.*

buck The males of various animals, including the goat, hare, kangaroo, rabbit, and reindeer, are called **bucks.** ■ A US or Australian dollar is often called a **buck.** If someone **makes a fast buck,** they make a lot of money quickly, usually by doing something dishonest. ■ If you **pass the buck,** you pass responsibility for something to someone else. If you say **the buck stops here,** you mean there is nobody to pass things on to, and you have to deal with them yourself. ■ If a business **bucks the trend,** it is successful when other businesses are in difficulty. ■ When a horse **bucks,** it jumps about wildly, to try and unseat its rider.

bucket A **bucket** is an open-topped metal or plastic container with a handle.

bucket shop A **bucket shop** is a travel agency which sells airline tickets at a discount to fill seats which would otherwise be empty.

buckle (**buckling, buckled**) A **buckle** is a device attached to one end of a belt, which is used to fasten it. When you **buckle** a belt, you fasten it using its buckle. ■ When something **buckles,** it bends as a result of severe heat or force. ■ If your legs **buckle,** they suddenly bend because you are weak. ■ If someone **buckles** under pressure, they are overcome by it. ■ If you **buckle down** to something, you start working hard at it.

buckwheat is a type of black grain used for feeding animals and making flour.

bucolic (*pron:* bew-**kol**-ik) means to do with the countryside or country people. ...*bucolic peace.*

bud (**budding, budded**) A **bud** is a small pointed lump which appears on a plant and develops into a leaf or flower. When this happens, you say the plant **buds.** ■ **Budding** is used to describe someone who is just starting to be a success at something. ...*a budding writer.* ■ If you **nip** something **in the bud,** you put a stop to it before it has a chance to develop.

Buddha or **the Buddha** is the title given to Siddhartha Gautama, a religious teacher and the founder of Buddhism. A **Buddha** is a statue or picture of the Buddha.

Buddhism (**Buddhist**) **Buddhism** is an Eastern religion which teaches that the way to end suffering is by overcoming your desires.

buddleia (*pron:* bud-**lee**-a) The **buddleia** is a bush with spikes of scented mauve or white flowers.

buddy (**buddies**) Your **buddy** is a close friend, usually someone of the same sex as yourself.

budge (**budging, budged**) If someone will not **budge** on a matter, they refuse to change their mind. ■ If someone will not **budge** from a place, they will not move from it. ■ If you cannot **budge** something, you cannot get it to move.

budgerigar — **Budgerigars** are small brightly-coloured birds belonging to the parakeet family. They are wild birds in Australia, and are kept as pets in other countries.

budget (**budgeting, budgeted; budgetary**) A **budget** is a plan showing how much money an organization has available for a certain period, and how it will be spent. ■ The **Budget** is the financial plan announced by the government, showing how much money it intends to raise through taxation and how it is going to spend it. ■ **Budgetary** means to do with a budget. ...*budgetary policies.* ■ If you **budget,** you plan carefully how you will spend your money. If you **budget for** something, you allow money for it in your plan. ■ **Budgeted** is used to talk about the amount of money allocated for something. ...*a modestly budgeted courtroom comedy.* **-budget** is used in a similar way after 'high' and 'low'. ...*low-budget films.*

budgie A **budgie** is the same as a budgerigar.

buff You call a person a **buff** when they know a lot about a subject. For example, a film buff is a person who knows a lot about films. ■ If you **buff** something, you polish it with a soft cloth or brush. ■ **Buff** is a pale yellow or yellowish-brown colour.

buffalo (*plural:* **buffaloes** *or* **buffalo**) **Buffaloes** are a type of cattle found in southern and eastern Africa with large upward-curving horns. ■ American bison are sometimes called **buffaloes.** ■ See also **water buffalo.**

buffer The **buffers** on a train are two metal discs on springs at the ends of each carriage. They lessen the impact when carriages bump against each other. ■ If something acts as a **buffer,** it is placed between two groups of people, to prevent fighting. *The federal army has been called in to act as a buffer in areas of high tension.* A **buffer zone** is an area of land between two rival areas, which is meant to keep them apart. ■ A **buffer state** is a small, usually neutral, country between two rival countries.

buffet (**buffeting, buffeted**) A **buffet** (*pron:* **buff**-ay) is a meal of cold food at a party or public occasion. Guests usually help themselves to the food. ■ On a railway station, a **buffet** is a cafe. On a train, the **buffet car** is a carriage where snacks and drinks are sold. ■ If the wind or sea **buffets** something (*pron:* buff-its), it keeps beating against it. ■ If you say someone is **buffeted** by an experience, you mean they are shaken or upset by it.

buffoon (**buffoonery**) If you say someone is a **buffoon,** you mean they are extremely silly.

bug (**bugging, bugged**) A **bug** is a tiny insect, especially one which causes damage. ■ When someone has a minor illness, you can say they have a **bug.** ...*a stomach bug.* ■ A **bug** in a computer program is a small error which stops the program working properly. ■ If a place is **bugged,** tiny microphones called **bugs** are hidden there to pick up what people are saying. ■ When someone suddenly becomes very enthusiastic about something like a hobby, you can say they have been **bitten by** a **bug.** *We got bitten by the sight-seeing bug in Italy.* ■ If something **bugs** you, it annoys you.

bugbear A **bugbear** is something which worries or annoys people.

buggery is anal intercourse.

buggy (**buggies**) A **buggy** is (a) a small cart or truck. (b) a pushchair.

bugle (**bugler**) A **bugle** is a brass instrument like a cornet but usually without valves.

build (**building, built**) When something like a house is **built,** it is constructed from separate parts. ■ When someone **builds** something or **builds** it **up,** they establish it and develop it. *He has built a name as a solo performer.* ■ If something is **built into** a product or system, it is included as part of it. *A tiny loudspeaker is built in to the unit.* ■ If something **builds up,** it gradually increases. ...*a military build-up.* ■ The **build-up** to an event is everything connected with it which happens just before it, especially the preparations and publicity. ■ If you **build on** a previous achievement, you make further progress. ■ A person's **build** is the shape their bones and muscles give to their body. *The man was built like an ox.*

builder A **builder** is a person whose job is building and altering buildings. ■ Some other people and firms who construct things are called **builders.** ...*aircraft builders.*

building A **building** is a structure with walls and a roof.

building block The **building blocks** of a structure are the basic parts it is made up of. *Transistors are the building-blocks of computers.*

building site A **building site** is an area of land where building is taking place.

building society A **building society** is an organization which lends money to people to buy houses, and pays interest to people who invest money in it. Since 1986, building societies have also been able to offer banking services.

built See **build.**

built-in cupboards and wardrobes are constructed against a wall in the room where they are to be used. They cannot usually be moved. ■ A **built-in** feature of something is included as an essential part of it. *The device is powered by a built-in battery.*

built-up A **built-up** area is one where there are a lot of buildings.

bulb A **bulb** is an onion-shaped root which a plant grows out of. Flowers grown from bulbs, for example daffodils, are sometimes called **bulbs.** ■ A **light bulb** is an object consisting of a filament surrounded by glass, which lights up when electricity is passed through it.

bulbous things look unattractively fat or swollen.

bulge (**bulging, bulged**) A **bulge** is a swelling or outward curve. When something swells outwards, you say it **bulges.** ...*a creature with bulging black eyes.* ■ If a container is **bulging** with things, it is full of them. ■ A **bulge** is a sudden increase. ...*a big bulge in debt repayments.*

bulimia (**bulimic**) Bulimia or **bulimia nervosa** is an eating disorder in which people eat compulsively and then make themselves vomit. A **bulimic** is someone who suffers from bulimia. See also **anorexia.**

bulk (**bulky, bulkier, bulkiest**) If an object is very large, you can talk about its **bulk.** A **bulky** object is large and heavy. ■ If goods are bought or sold **in bulk,** they are dealt with in large quantities. ...*bulk orders.* ■ When you talk about the **bulk of** something, you mean most of it. *The great bulk of India's poor live in the countryside.*

bulk carrier – **Bulk carriers** are large ships designed to carry cargoes like timber or oil.

bulkhead On a ship or aircraft, the **bulkheads** are strong partition walls which divide the inside into separate compartments.

bull – **Bulls** are adult male cattle. ■ The males of some other species are called **bulls,** for example elephants, seals, and whales. ■ A **bull market** on the stock exchange is when people are buying a lot of shares in expectation of a price increase, in order to sell them later at a profit.

bull bar (*or* **bullbar**) A **bull bar** is a metal guard made of tubular steel that is fitted to the front of some trucks and 4-wheel drive vehicles to protect them from damage.

bulldog The **bulldog** is a stocky short-haired dog with a broad head and strong square jaws.

bulldog clip A **bulldog clip** is a spring-operated clip for holding papers together.

bulldoze (**bulldozing, bulldozed; bulldozer**) A **bulldozer** is a large powerful tractor with a broad blade in front, used for moving earth or knocking things down. If something is **bulldozed,** a bulldozer is used to demolish it. ■ If someone gets something done in an unpleasantly forceful way, you can say they **bulldoze** it through. *The government bulldozed the amendment through parliament.*

bullet A **bullet** is a small piece of metal fired from a gun. ■ **bite the bullet:** see **bite**.

bulletin A **bulletin** is (a) a short news report on TV or radio. (b) a short official report about something, saying what the latest situation is. *A medical bulletin on his health is expected soon.* (c) a regular newspaper or leaflet produced by an organization. *...The Bank of England Quarterly Bulletin.*

bulletin board A **bulletin board** is a facility which people can access by computer to send or receive information on topics which interest them. ■ Americans call a notice board a **bulletin board**.

bullfight (**bullfighting; bullfighter**) A **bullfight** is a traditional Spanish, Portuguese, or Latin American entertainment in which a man called a **bullfighter** taunts, and usually kills, a fierce bull.

bullfinch (**bullfinches**) The **bullfinch** is a small bird with a short thick bill.

bullfrog – Bullfrogs are large frogs which make a loud deep croaking noise.

bullion is gold or silver in the form of bars.

bullish If someone is in a **bullish** mood, they are confident and optimistic.

bullock A **bullock** is a castrated bull.

bullring A **bullring** is a circular arena where bullfights are held.

bull's-eye The **bull's-eye** is the small circular area at the centre of a target.

bull terrier The **bull terrier** is a dog with a muscular body, a thick neck, and a short smooth whitish-coloured coat.

bully (**bullies, bullying, bullied**) Bullies are people who use their strength to hurt or frighten people weaker than themselves. When they do this, you say they **bully** people. ■ A **bully-boy** is a tough aggressive man, especially one hired to hurt or frighten people. ■ If someone **bullies** you into doing something, they make you do it, using force or threats.

bulrush (**bulrushes**) Bulrushes are tall stiff reeds.

bulwark A **bulwark** against an unpleasant situation is something which protects you from it. *...a bulwark against tyranny.*

bum A person's **bum** is their bottom. ■ Bum is the usual American word for a tramp.

bum-bag A **bum-bag** is a small zip-top bag attached to a belt worn around the waist. You use it to carry things like money and keys.

bumble (**bumbling, bumbled**) When someone speaks or behaves in a confused or disorganized way, you can say they **bumble**. *...a clumsy, bumbling, inarticulate figure.*

bumblebee – Bumblebees are large fuzzy bees.

bumf (**or bumph**) Things like pamphlets and forms can be called **bumf**.

bump (**bumpy**) If you **bump** into someone or something, you accidentally knock against them. A **bump** is a collision like this. ■ A **bump** on a surface is a raised part. A **bumpy** surface has a lot of bumps. ■ When a vehicle **bumps** over a surface or has a **bumpy** journey, it travels in a rough bouncing way, because the surface is uneven. ■ **Bumpy**

is used to describe things which do not go smoothly. *The talks got off to a bumpy start.* ■ If you **bump into** someone, you meet them by chance. ■ If something is suddenly increased by a large amount, you can say it is **bumped up**.

bumper – Bumpers are the bars at the front and back of a vehicle which protect it if it bumps into something. ■ **Bumper** is used to talk about things being much larger than usual. *...bumper harvests.*

bumph See **bumf**.

bumpkin A **bumpkin** is a simple country person.

bumptious A **bumptious** person is unpleasantly full of their own importance.

bun A **bun** is a small round cake. ■ If a woman has her hair in a **bun**, it is fastened in a round shape at the back of her head.

bunch (**bunches, bunching, bunched**) A **bunch** of flowers is a number of them held or tied together. ■ A **bunch** of fruit is several of them growing on the same stem. *...a bunch of grapes.* ■ A **bunch** of keys is several of them on one ring. ■ A **bunch** of people is a group of them. ■ When people or things are **bunched** together, they are grouped closely together.

bundle (**bundling, bundled**) A **bundle** is a number of things tied together or wrapped in a cloth, so they can be carried or stored. ■ If you are **bundled** somewhere, you are pushed there in a rough hurried way.

bung A **bung** is a round piece of wood, cork, or rubber for closing the hole in a barrel or flask. ■ If you **bung** something somewhere, you put it there quickly and carelessly.

bungalow A **bungalow** is a single-storey house.

bungee-jumping or **bungy-jumping** is jumping off a high place, usually a bridge or crane, with an elastic rope attached to you, the other end of which is secured to the thing you jump off.

bungle (**bungling, bungled; bungler**) If someone **bungles** something, they do not do it properly because they make mistakes. You say someone like this is **bungling** or a **bungler**.

bungy-jumping See **bungee-jumping**.

bunion A **bunion** is a large painful lump at the base of the big toe.

bunk A **bunk** is a narrow bed fixed to a wall. ■ **Bunk beds** are beds constructed one above the other. ■ If someone **does a bunk**, they suddenly leave a place without telling anyone. ■ If you say something is **bunk**, you mean it is nonsense.

bunker A **bunker** is an underground shelter. ■ A **bunker** is a container for storing coal or some other fuel. ■ On a golf course, a **bunker** is a large hollow filled with sand, placed there as an obstacle.

bunkum If you say a theory is **bunkum**, you mean it is nonsense.

bunny (**bunnies**) A **bunny** is a rabbit.

bunsen burner A **bunsen burner** is a small gas burner used in laboratories.

bunting is rows of small decorative flags.

buoy (*pron: boy*) A **buoy** is a floating object anchored to the seabed, marking the route a ship should take, or warning of dangers like rocks. ■ If someone or something in a difficult situation is

buoyed or **buoyed up** by something, it makes them stronger or more optimistic. *Domestic consumption buoyed the German economy.*

buoyant (*pron:* **boy**-ant) (**buoyancy**) If something is **buoyant,** it floats easily. **Buoyancy** is the ability to float. ■ If you feel **buoyant,** you feel lively and cheerful. ■ **Buoyant** is used to describe something like the economy when it is doing well and seems unlikely to be affected by any crisis. *...buoyant sales growth.*

burble (**burbling, burbled**) You say someone is **burbling** when they are talking continuously and not making much sense. ■ If water **burbles,** it makes a continuous low bubbling sound; you can call this sound a **burble.**

burden (**burdening, burdened; burdensome**) A **burden** is a heavy load which is difficult to carry. ■ If you are **burdened** with something, you are unable to be happy or make progress because of it. You say something like this is **burdensome** or a **burden.** ■ If the **burden of proof** is on someone, it is up to them to prove what they say is true.

bureau (*pron:* **byoo**-roh) (*plural:* **bureaux** or **bureaus,** both *pron:* **byoo**-rose) A **bureau** is a writing desk with drawers and pigeonholes. ■ A **bureau** is an office, organization, or government department which collects and distributes information.

bureaucracy (*pron:* byoo-**rok**-rass-ee) (**bureaucracies**) A **bureaucracy** is an administrative system run by a large number of officials. ■ The civil servants who run the administration of a country are often called the **bureaucracy.** ■ **Bureaucracy** is all the rules and procedures followed by government departments and similar organizations.

bureaucrat (*pron:* byoo-roh-crat) (**bureaucratic**) A **bureaucrat** is an official who works in a large administrative system, especially one who seems to follow rules and procedures too strictly. ■ **Bureaucratic** is used to describe rules and procedures which seem unnecessarily complicated and slow things up.

burgeon (**burgeoning, burgeoned**) When something **burgeons,** it grows quickly.

burger A **burger** is a flat round cake of minced food, which is grilled or fried.

burgh (*pron:* **bur**-ruh) A **burgh** is a Scottish borough.

burgher (*pron:* **burg**-er) In the past, the important citizens of a city were called its **burghers.**

burglary (**burglaries; burglar**) **Burglary** is the crime of breaking into a building and stealing things. A **burglar** is someone who does this.

burgle (**burgling, burgled**) If a house is **burgled,** someone breaks in and steals things.

burgundy is (a) any wine from the Burgundy region of France. (b) any heavy red table wine. ■ **Burgundy** is a dark purplish-red colour.

burial or a **burial** is the burying of a dead body.

burlesque (*pron:* burl-**lesk**) was a type of comedy show popular in the US in the late 19th and early 20th centuries. ■ **Burlesque** is used to describe something which makes fun of a type of thing by imitating it in an exaggerated way. *...a burlesque gothic melodrama.*

burly A **burly** man has a broad body and strong muscles.

burn (**burning, burnt** *or* **burned**) You say a fire **burns.** If you **burn** something, you destroy it by setting fire to it. If something is **burning,** it is on fire. ■ **Burnt-out** buildings or vehicles have been badly damaged by fire. If a building is **burnt down,** it is completely destroyed by fire. ■ If you **burn** yourself, you are injured by fire or something hot. You can also be **burnt** by chemicals, electricity, radiation, or the sun. Injuries caused in any of these ways are called **burns.** ■ When something stings or feels hot, you can say it **burns.** ■ **Burning** is used to describe things which are extremely hot. *...the burning sun.* ■ If a light is **burning,** it is on. ■ If you **burn up** energy, you use a lot of it. ■ If you **burn yourself out,** you make yourself exhausted or ill by working too hard. Someone who does this is said to suffer **burn-out.** ■ **Burning** is used to describe strong feelings. *...his burning desire for revenge.*

burner A **burner** is a device which produces heat or a flame, especially as part of a cooker or heater. ■ If something is put **on the back burner,** it is left to be dealt with later, because it is not urgent.

burnish (**burnishes, burnishing, burnished**) If you **burnish** something like metal, you polish it until it shines.

burp When someone **burps,** they make a noise because gas from their stomach has been forced up through their throat. A noise like this is called a **burp.**

burr – **Burrs** are seed pods covered in tiny hooks which stick to people's clothes and animals' fur. ■ You say someone has a **burr** when they pronounce their 'r's strongly.

burrow A **burrow** is a hole in the ground, dug by a rabbit or other small animal. When the animal digs a burrow, you say it **burrows.**

bursar The **bursar** of a college is the person in charge of its finances or administration.

bursary (**bursaries**) A **bursary** is a sum of money awarded to someone to enable them to study at a university.

burst (**bursting, burst** *not* 'bursted') When something **bursts,** it splits open and air or some other substance comes out. *...a burst pipe.* ■ If a river **bursts** its banks, the water rises over them, causing a flood. ■ If you say a place is **bursting** with people or things, you are emphasizing how full it is. ■ You say someone is **bursting** with a feeling to emphasize how strong the feeling is. *They're all bursting with pride.* ■ If you **burst** into tears or song, you suddenly start crying or singing. ■ If you **burst** into a place, you suddenly enter it. If you **burst through** something, you force your way through it. ■ If someone **bursts onto the scene,** they suddenly come to people's notice. ■ A **burst** of something is a sudden short period of it. *...bursts of gunfire.* ■ **burst into flames: see flame.**

bury (**buries, burying, buried**) If you **bury** an object, you put it in a hole in the ground and cover it with earth. ■ If something is **buried** under other things, it is covered by them. ■ If you **bury** feelings of dislike or suspicion, you try not to feel or show them. ■ If you **bury** yourself in your work, you concentrate hard on it and do not think about anything else.

bus (**bussing, bussed**) (*usual American spelling:* **busing, bused**) A **bus** (*plural:* **buses**) is a large motor vehicle used for public transport. ■ You say people are **bussed** to a place when arrangements are made for them to travel there by bus.

busby (**busbies**) A **busby** is the same as a bearskin.

bush (**bushes**) A **bush** is a woody plant similar to a small tree. ■ The **bush** is large areas of land, especially in Africa and Australia, where nothing grows but trees or shrubs, and few people live. ■ If you tell someone to stop **beating about the bush,** you mean they should get to the point of what they are saying.

bushel The volume of a quantity of grain can be expressed in **bushels.** A British bushel is 8 gallons (about 0.036 cubic metres). A US bushel is slightly smaller (about 0.035 cubic metres). ■ If you say someone is **hiding their light under a bushel,** you mean they are being modest or not revealing their good qualities.

bushy hair grows thickly.

busily If you do something **busily,** you do it in an energetic way.

business (**businesses**) A **business** is an organization which operates for profit. ■ **Business** is buying and selling goods and services. ■ If a company goes **out of business,** it stops trading because it is not making enough money. ■ **Business as usual** means things are carrying on as normal, despite a crisis. ■ Any activity or series of events can be called a **business.** *Divorce can be a dreadful business.* ■ If you **get down to business,** you start dealing with something in a serious way. If you say someone **means business,** you mean they are serious and determined about what they are doing. ■ If you are **minding your own business,** you are paying attention to your own concerns and not involving yourself in what other people are doing. ■ If you say someone **has no business** doing something, you mean they have no right to do it.

businesslike If someone is **businesslike,** they deal with things in an efficient way, without wasting time.

businessman (**businesswoman**) A **businessman** or **businesswoman** is a person who works in a business, especially as an owner or executive.

busker (**busking**) A **busker** is a person who plays music in public places, hoping to get money from passers-by.

busman's holiday When someone spends their holiday doing something similar to their usual work, you call this a **busman's holiday.**

bus stop A **bus stop** is a place where buses stop to let people on and off.

bust (**busting, busted**) If something is **bust,** it is broken. ■ If a business **goes bust,** it loses so much money it is forced to close down. ■ **Busting** is used to talk about ways of overcoming rules. *...sanctions-busting.* ■ If someone is **busted,** they are arrested by the police. *He was busted on a drugs charge.* You say a place is **busted** when the police

raid it to arrest people. A raid or arrest can be called a **bust.** ■ A **bust** is a statue of someone's head and shoulders. ■ A woman's **bust** is her breasts.

bustle (**bustling, bustled**) If someone **bustles** somewhere, they move in a busy hurried way. ■ **Bustle** is busy noisy activity. You say a place is **bustling** when there is a lot of noise and activity there.

busy (**busier, busiest; busies, busying, busied**) If you are **busy,** you are working hard at something, and do not have much time for other things. ■ A **busy** place is full of people or traffic. ■ If you **busy** yourself with something, you occupy yourself by doing it. ■ See also **busily.**

busybody (**busybodies**) If you call someone a **busybody,** you mean they are always interfering in other people's affairs.

but is used to contrast two things. *The rooms are small but spacious.* ■ **But** is used after words like 'everything' or 'nobody' to mean 'except'. *They refused to eat anything but steak.* ■ **But for** is used to say what prevents something happening. *Seven players would be in contention for places but for injuries.* ■ **All but** means 'almost'. *The town is all but deserted.*

butane is a gas used as fuel.

butch is used to describe a man or woman with a strong masculine appearance. Many people find this word offensive.

butcher (**butchering, butchered; butchery**) A **butcher** is a shopkeeper who sells meat. A shop where meat is sold is called a **butcher** or **butcher's.** ■ When people are killed in a particularly brutal way, you can say they are **butchered.** Someone who kills people like this can be called a **butcher. Butchery** is the brutal killing of a lot of people.

butler A **butler** is the chief male servant in a rich household.

butt The **butt** of a handgun is the thick end of its handle. ■ The **butt** of a cigar or cigarette is the small part left when someone has finished smoking it. ■ A **butt** is a large barrel for collecting or storing liquid. ■ If people are making fun of someone, you can say that person is the **butt** of their jokes. ■ If someone **butts** you, they hit you with the top of their head. ■ If someone **butts in,** they interrupt when someone else is speaking.

butter (**buttering, buttered**) **Butter** is a yellow substance made from cream, which you spread on bread or use in cooking. If you **butter** bread, you spread butter on it.

buttercup — **Buttercups** are small wild plants with yellow flowers.

butterfly (**butterflies**) **Butterflies** are insects with large colourful wings. ■ **Butterfly** is a swimming stroke which you do on your front, kicking your legs and bringing your arms over your head together.

butterscotch is a hard sticky sweet made by boiling sugar, butter, and water.

buttery (**butteries**) **Buttery** things taste of butter or contain a lot of butter. ■ A **buttery** is a room where you can buy meals and drinks, especially at a university.

buttocks A person's **buttocks** are the part of their body they sit on.

button (**buttoning, buttoned**) **Buttons** are small objects used as fastenings on clothes. If you **button** a piece of clothing, you fasten it with its buttons. ■ A **button** is a small knob you press to operate something.

buttonhole (**buttonholing, buttonholed**) **Buttonholes** are the holes buttons fit through. ■ If you **buttonhole** someone, you stop them and get them to listen to you.

buttress (**buttresses, buttressing, buttressed**) **Buttresses** are stone supports built against a wall. ■ If something **buttresses** something else, it strengthens it. *He has opted to buttress his position through an alliance with the army.*

buxom A **buxom** woman is attractively plump and full-bosomed.

buy (**buying, bought**) When you **buy** something, you pay money to obtain it. ■ If you say something is a **good buy,** you mean it is good value for money. ■ If someone **buys up** something, they buy large amounts of it, or all that is available. ■ If someone **buys into** a business, they buy part of it, often to gain some control of it. If they **buy it out,** they buy enough shares to get complete control; this is called a **buyout.** ■ When the senior staff of a company buy it to run it themselves, this is called a **management buyout.** ■ If you **buy** someone **off,** you offer them money or something else so they will stop opposing you or give up a claim against you. ■ If you do something to **buy** time, you do it to gain time in which to think what to do next.

buyer A **buyer** is (a) someone who buys something. *He found a buyer for his town house.* (b) someone who works for a large store or organization, and whose job is to decide what to buy for sale in the store or for use by the organization.

buyout See **buy.**

buzz (**buzzes, buzzing, buzzed**) A **buzz** is a low humming sound, like the sound a bee makes when it is flying. When something makes this sound, you say it **buzzes.** ■ If you say a place is **buzzing,** you mean there is a lot of excitement or activity there. *The city has been buzzing with rumours.* ■ If you get a **buzz** from something, you enjoy it.

buzzard The **buzzard** is a large brown and white bird of prey.

buzzer A **buzzer** is a device which makes a buzzing sound, for example on an alarm clock.

buzz word (*or* **buzzword**) A **buzz word** is a word which has become fashionable. *...'transparency' being a big buzz word in government these days.*

by is used to say who or what does something. *...a painting by Van Gogh.* ■ **By** is used to talk about the means used to do something. *He travelled south by train.* ■ If you are **by** someone or something, you are beside them. ■ If someone or something goes **by,** they go past without stopping. ■ If something happens **by** a certain time, it happens before that time. ■ If something is true **by** law or **by** certain standards, it is true according to the law or to those standards. *The gift is generous by any standards.* ■ In calculations, you multiply or divide one figure **by** another. ■ **By** is used when giving the length and width of a shape. *The painting measures 20 inches by 18.* ■ **By** is used to talk about amounts or quantities. *Exports rose by 5%... You can buy sheeting by the metre.* ■ **By** is used when mentioning an increase, decrease or difference. *Exports of cars rose by 5.5 per cent... Middlesex beat Leicestershire by 103 runs.* ■ **By** can be used when describing someone's job or character. *He was a carpenter by trade... By temperament I'm always dissatisfied.* ■ **By** is used to say what time of day something happens. *The owl hunts by night.* ■ **by accident:** see **accident. by and large:** see **large.**

bye In sport, you say there is a **bye** when a competitor automatically goes through to the next round because they do not have an opponent.

bye-law See **by-law.**

by-election A **by-election** is an election to choose a new MP for a constituency whose previous MP has resigned or died during a parliamentary term.

bygone is used to talk about things in the distant past. *The streets still retain much of the flavour of a bygone Elizabethan England.* ■ If you say people should **let bygones be bygones,** you mean they should agree to forget their quarrels.

by-law (*or* **bye-law**) A **by-law** is a law made by a local authority which applies only in that authority's area.

byline A **byline** is a note at the top of a newspaper article giving the author's name.

bypass (*or* **by-pass**) (**bypasses, bypassing, bypassed**) A **bypass** is a main road which takes traffic round the edge of a town. ■ If you **bypass** a place, you avoid going through it. ■ If you **bypass** a person or part of a system, you miss them out, usually to save time. ■ In a **bypass** operation, doctors redirect the flow of blood to avoid the heart.

by-product A **by-product** is something produced during manufacture or processing, which is not as important as the main product. ■ The **by-product** of an event or situation is an unexpected result of it.

bystander A **bystander** is a person who is present when something happens, but is not involved in it.

byte In computing, a **byte** is a unit of storage equal to eight bits. See also **bit.**

byway – **Byways** are quiet roads which do not get much traffic. ■ The **byways** of a subject are the less well-known areas of it.

byword If you say someone is a **byword** for a certain quality, you mean they are well known for having it. *...a region that was once a byword for stability.*

byzantine methods and systems are extremely complicated. *...byzantine negotiations.*

C c

C stands for 'Centigrade' or 'Celsius'. ■ **C** is the name of a computer programming language.

c. See circa.

cab A **cab** is a taxi. ■ The **cab** of a lorry is the part where the driver sits.

cabal (*pron:* kab-**bal**) You can refer to a group of people as a **cabal** when you think they are secretly plotting to influence a situation. *...a cabal of managers, bankers and lawyers.*

cabaret (*pron:* **kab**-a-ray) A **cabaret** is live entertainment at a nightclub or restaurant.

cabbage — Cabbages are large green leafy vegetables.

cabbie (*or* cabby) A **cabbie** is a taxi-driver.

caber A **caber** is a long heavy pole which contestants try to throw end over end in the traditional Scottish Highland sport of tossing the caber.

cabin A **cabin** is a small room in a ship or boat. ■ A **cabin** is one of the areas inside a plane. ■ A **cabin** is a small wooden house.

cabin crew The **cabin crew** on a plane are the people who look after the passengers.

cabin cruiser A **cabin cruiser** is a motorboat with a cabin for people to live or sleep in.

cabinet The **cabinet** is a group of the most senior ministers in a government. ■ A **cabinet** is a small cupboard.

cabinet maker A **cabinet maker** is a person who makes high-quality wooden furniture.

cable (**cabling, cabled**) A **cable** is a thick strong rope. ■ A **cable** is one or more electrical wires in a rubber or plastic covering. ■ **Cable television** is a television system in which signals are sent along wires, rather than by radio waves. ■ A **cable** is a telegram. If you **cable** someone, you send them a telegram.

cable car A **cable car** is a cabin suspended from a moving cable which takes people up a mountain.

cacao (*pron:* kak-**kah**-oh) The **cacao** is a tropical tree whose seeds are used to produce cocoa and chocolate.

cache (*pron:* **kash**) A **cache** is a hidden store of things.

cachet (*pron:* **kash**-shay) If someone or something has **cachet**, they have a quality of prestige or distinction. *...the social cachet of joining the rich man's club.*

cackle (**cackling, cackled**) If someone **cackles** or gives a **cackle,** they laugh in a loud unpleasant way.

cacophony (*pron:* kak-**koff**-on-nee) (**cacophonous**) A **cacophony** is a mixture of loud unpleasant noises. *...cacophonous outbursts.*

cactus (*plural:* **cactuses** *or* **cacti**) Cactuses are thick fleshy plants which grow in deserts and are often covered in sharp spines.

CAD is the use of computer technology in the design of products. **CAD** stands for 'computer-aided design'.

cad In the past, a man who behaved badly was sometimes called a **cad.**

cadaver (*pron:* kad-**dav**-ver) A **cadaver** is a corpse.

caddie (*or* caddy) (**caddies, caddying, caddied**) If you **caddie** for a golfer or act as their **caddie,** you carry their clubs and equipment.

cadence (*pron:* **kade**-enss) The **cadences** of someone's voice is the way their voice gets higher and lower as they speak. ■ In music, a **cadence** is the end of a phrase.

cadet A **cadet** is a young person training for the police force, or to be an officer in one of the armed forces.

cadge (**cadging, cadged**) If someone **cadges** something from you, they get you to give it to them. *I can probably cadge a lift.*

cadmium is a bluish-white metal used in making alloys and in electroplating.

cadre (*pron:* **kah**-der) A **cadre** is a person or small group of people specially chosen and trained for a particular purpose within an organization.

Caesarean (*pron:* see-**zair**-ee-an) A **Caesarean** or **Caesarean section** is an operation in which a woman's body is cut open and her baby is lifted out.

cafe (*or* café) A **cafe** is a small restaurant.

cafeteria A **cafeteria** is a self-service restaurant.

caffeine (*or* caffein) is a substance in coffee and tea which makes you feel more alert.

caftan (*or* kaftan) A **caftan** is (a) a long loose robe with long sleeves, worn in Arab countries. (b) a similar garment worn by Western women.

cage (**caging, caged**) A **cage** is a container with bars to keep animals or birds in. If you **cage** something, you put it in a cage.

cagey You say someone is being **cagey** when you think they are deliberately not telling you what they know or think about something.

cagoule (*pron:* kag-**gool**) A **cagoule** is a lightweight waterproof jacket with a hood.

cahoots If you say someone is **in cahoots** with someone else, you mean they are plotting something together.

cairn A **cairn** is a pile of stones built as a memorial or to help people find their way across wild country.

cajole (*pron:* ka-**jole**) (**cajoling, cajoled**) If you **cajole** someone into doing something, you persuade them to do it.

cake (**caked**) A **cake** is a sweet food, usually made by baking a mixture of flour, sugar, eggs, and fat. ■ Food formed into flat round shapes before cooking can be called **cakes.** *...potato cakes.* ■ A **cake** of soap is a small block of it. ■ If you say something is a **piece of cake,** you mean it is easy to do. ■ If someone says you cannot **have your cake and eat it,** they mean you have a choice of two things but you cannot have both. ■ **Cake** can be used to refer to the whole of something which is divided up or shared. *They should get a larger slice of the cake when* *all the pension fund surplus is carved up.* ■ If something is **caked** with dirt or blood, it is covered with a thick dry layer of it.

calamity (**calamities; calamitous**) A **calamity** is an event which causes a lot of destruction or distress. *...the country's calamitous economic decline.*

calcium is a soft silvery-white chemical element found in teeth and bones, and in rocks such as chalk.

calculate (**calculating, calculated; calculation**) If you **calculate** an amount, you work it out. *...mathematical calculations.* ■ If you **calculate** the effects of something, you think carefully about it before reaching a conclusion. *We calculated that Matt would play.* ■ A **calculating** person carefully plans situations to get what they want. ■ If someone does something in a **calculated** way, they do it deliberately. *...a brutal calculated killing.* ■ If something is **calculated** to have an effect, it is intended to have that effect. *...calculated to shock.* ■ A **calculated** risk is one you decide to take after carefully weighing up your chances of success.

calculator A **calculator** is an electronic device for doing calculations.

calculus is a branch of mathematics concerned with variable quantities.

calendar A **calendar** is a system of dividing time into fixed periods. *...the Chinese calendar.* ■ A **calendar** is a chart showing the days, weeks, and months of a year. ■ A **calendar** is a list of important dates. *...a big event in the city's calendar.* ■ A **calendar month** is one of the twelve months in a year known by a particular name, for example March. ■ A **calendar year** begins on January 1st and ends on December 31st. See also **financial year.**

calf (**calves**) A **calf** is a young cow or bull. ■ Some other young animals, including elephants and whales, are called **calves.** ■ A person's **calves** are the backs of their legs between their knees and their ankles. ■ **Calf-length** clothes reach to your calves.

caliber See **calibre.**

calibrate (**calibrating, calibrated; calibration**) If a tool or instrument is **calibrated,** marks are put on it so it can be used to measure things accurately.

calibre (*Am:* **caliber**) The **calibre** of a person is the standard of their ability or intelligence, especially when it is high. *A player of his calibre cannot be ignored forever.* ■ The **calibre** of something is its quality, especially when it is good. *Few people get the chance to taste wines of this calibre.* ■ The **calibre** of a gun is the width of the inside of its barrel.

calico is a plain white cotton fabric.

caliper See **calliper.**

call (**called**) You use **called** when mentioning the name of a person, place, or thing. *She called him Fred.* ■ If you **call** a person something, you use a word or phrase to describe them. *I wouldn't call myself a feminist.* ■ If you **call** someone or give them a **call,** you phone them. ■ If someone like a doctor is **on call,** they are available to be called out if needed. ■ If someone is **called up,** or gets their **call-up,** they are ordered to join one of the armed forces. ■ If you **call** something like a meeting, you an-

nounce that it will take place. ■ If something is **called off,** it is cancelled. ■ If you can **call on** something, it is there to be used if you need it. *They can call on my experience if they have a problem.* ■ If you **call** or make a **call** somewhere, you make a short visit there. ■ When a ship, bus, or train **calls** at a place, it stops there for a short time. ■ If you **call** something or **call** it **out,** you shout it. ■ Some sounds made by birds or animals are known as **calls.** *...a whale distress call.* ■ **call** someone's **bluff:** see **bluff. call it a day:** see **day.**

call box A **call box** is a telephone box.

call centre A **call centre** is an office where the staff carry out the organization's business by telephone.

caller A **caller** is someone who phones you, or who comes to see you for a short visit.

call girl A **call girl** is a prostitute who makes appointments by phone.

calligraphy (*pron:* kal-**lig**-ra-fee) (**calligrapher**) **Calligraphy** is the art of doing beautiful handwriting. A **calligrapher** is someone who does beautiful handwriting.

calliper (*Am:* **caliper**) **Callipers** are measuring instruments made of two long pieces of metal joined at one end by a hinge. ■ **Callipers** are devices for supporting a person's leg if they cannot walk properly. They are made of metal rods held together by straps.

callous (**callously; callousness**) **Callous** behaviour is cruel.

callow If you say a young person is **callow,** you mean they are immature and inexperienced.

call sign Someone's **call sign** is a series of letters and numbers used to identify them when radio messages are sent or received.

callus (**callused**) A **callus** is an area of thick hard skin caused by rubbing, usually on someone's palms or feet. You can say someone's hands or feet are **callused.**

calm (**calmly; calmness**) You say someone is **calm** when they do not panic or get excited in a difficult or dangerous situation. ■ If you **calm** someone's worries or fears, you do something to make them less worried or upset. ■ If someone **calms down,** they become less upset, excited, or angry. ■ If a place or situation is **calm,** there is no fighting or trouble. When things are like this, you say there is **calm.** ■ When fighting or an argument gets less intense, you can say things **calm down.** ■ **Calm** weather is very still. ■ If the sea is **calm,** there are no big waves.

Calor Gas is gas sold in portable metal containers. 'Calor Gas' is a trademark.

calorie The **calorie** is a unit of measurement for the energy value of food. 'Calorie' is often written as 'cal'.

calorific means to do with calories.

calumny (**calumnies**) If you say something is **calumny** or a **calumny,** you mean it is untrue and is meant to get people to lose respect for someone.

Calvinism (**Calvinist**) **Calvinism** is a type of strict Protestantism based on the religious theories of John Calvin. A **Calvinist** is a follower of Calvinism.

calypso

calypso (**calypsos**) A **calypso** is a type of West Indian song with improvised words which comment on topical subjects.

cam A **cam** is a device which changes circular motion into up-and-down or side-to-side motion.

camaraderie (*pron:* kam-mer-**rard**-er-ree) is a feeling of trust and friendship among a group.

camber The **camber** of a road is the slight downward slope towards each side, which allows water to flow off.

camcorder A **camcorder** is a combined video camera and recorder which is small enough to be held in one hand.

came See **come.**

camel The **camel** is a large desert animal with one or two humps and a long neck.

camellia The **camellia** is a tall evergreen shrub with shiny leaves and large rose-like white, pink, or red flowers.

cameo (**cameos**) A **cameo** or **cameo role** is a small part in a film or play performed by a well-known actor or actress. ■ A **cameo** is a piece of jewellery, usually oval, with a raised stone design on a different coloured flat stone.

camera A **camera** is a device for taking photos or making films. ■ A television **camera** is a piece of equipment for changing images into electrical signals, so live pictures can be shown on television. ■ If something is done **on camera,** it is televised. ■ If a hearing is held **in camera,** the public and the press are not allowed in.

cameraman (**cameramen**) A **cameraman** is a person who operates a television or film camera.

camisole A **camisole** is a woman's sleeveless top.

camomile (*or* **chamomile**) is a scented plant with daisy-like flowers. It is used to make herbal tea.

camouflage (*pron:* **kam**-moo-flahj) (**camouflaging, camouflaged**) **Camouflage** is things like leaves, paint, and special clothes worn by soldiers to make them blend in with their surroundings. Camouflage is also used on ships, planes, lorries, and buildings. ■ If a soldier **camouflages** himself or his equipment, he uses camouflage. ■ When an animal's skin markings or shape help it blend with its surroundings, this is called **camouflage.** ■ If a fact or feeling is **camouflaged,** it is disguised.

camp (**camping**) A **camp** is (a) a group of buildings specially built for people like prisoners or refugees to live in. (b) a group of huts and other buildings built for members of the armed forces to live in temporarily. (c) a group of tents, caravans, or buildings which people like travellers or gypsies live in. (d) a group of tents for people on holiday to live in. ■ When people **set up camp** somewhere, they make a camp there. ■ If you **camp** somewhere, you stay there in a tent. ■ If you go **camping,** you go somewhere on holiday and stay in a tent. ■ If you **camp out** somewhere, you sleep outdoors or in an uncomfortable place. ■ A **camp** is a group of people who support a person or belief. ...*the Brown camp.* ■ People say something like a show is **camp** when it is done in an exaggerated way which makes it absurd and funny. ■ If someone **camps it up,** they deliberately behave in an ex-

aggerated and artificial way. ■ If you say a man is **camp,** you mean he behaves in a way usually associated with homosexuals.

campaign (**campaigner**) A **campaign** is a series of planned activities aimed at achieving a particular result. A person who organizes something like this is called a **campaigner;** you say they **campaign** for something. ■ In a war, a **campaign** is a series of planned movements or actions aimed at achieving a particular result.

campanile (*pron:* camp-an-**nee**-lee) A **campanile** is a bell tower, especially one which stands on its own and is not attached to another building.

camp bed A **camp bed** is a small portable folding bed.

camper A **camper** is (a) someone who goes camping. (b) a van with beds and cooking equipment.

camp fire A **camp fire** is a fire you make outdoors when you are camping.

camp follower A **camp follower** is someone who does not officially belong to a group, but supports it. Originally, a **camp follower** was someone who travelled with an army and earned money by doing jobs for them.

camphor is a strong-smelling whitish substance, usually in the form of crystals, which is used in medicines and mothballs.

campion – Campions are a kind of red, pink, or white wild flower.

camp site A **camp site** is a place where holidaymakers can put their tents or caravans.

campus (**campuses**) A university or college **campus** is the area where its main buildings are.

camshaft A **camshaft** is a part of an engine consisting of a rod with one or more cams attached to it.

can (**canned**) If you **can** do something, it is possible for you to do it. You write **cannot** or **can't** instead of 'can not'. ■ **Can** is used to talk about people being allowed to do things. *You can apply to as many schools as you like.* ■ **Cannot** is used (a) to express a strong belief that something is not true or will not happen. *I cannot believe he was not informed of what was going on.* (b) to say someone should not do something, or something should not happen. *The current situation cannot be allowed to continue indefinitely.* ■ A **can** is a sealed metal container for food, drink, or paint. When food or drink is **canned,** it is put in a can. **Canned** food or drink comes in a can. ■ **Canned** music, laughter, or applause is prerecorded rather than live. ■ If you **carry the can** for something, you take the blame for it.

Canada goose The **Canada goose** is a common wild goose with a black head and neck and a white face-patch.

canal A **canal** is a long man-made strip of water, built for boats to travel along or to bring water to an area. ■ Some tubes inside the body are called **canals.** ...*the alimentary canal.*

canapé (*pron:* **kan**-nap-pay) A **canapé** is a small piece of biscuit or bread with meat, cheese, or other savoury food on top. Canapés are often served with drinks at parties.

canard (*pron:* kan-**nahd**) A **canard** is a piece of false information which circulates among people, and is sometimes spread deliberately.

canary (**canaries**) **Canaries** are small yellow birds with a pleasant song, often kept as pets.

canasta is a card game similar to rummy, played with two packs of cards.

cancan The **cancan** is a dance in which women kick up their legs and shake their skirts to fast music.

cancel (**cancelling, cancelled; cancellation**) (*Am:* **canceling, canceled, cancellation**) If you **cancel** something which has been arranged, you stop the arrangement and it does not take place. ■ If you **cancel** a cheque you have written, you instruct your bank not to pay it. ■ If two things **cancel** each other **out**, they have opposite effects, producing no real effect at all.

cancer (**cancerous**) **Cancer** is a serious disease caused by cells in part of the body dividing quickly in an uncontrolled way. This produces a growth or tumour called a **cancer.** You call a growth of this kind **cancerous.**

candelabra (*pron:* kan-del-**lah**-bra) (*plural:* **candelabra** *or* **candelabras**) A **candelabra** is a large ornamental candle holder with several arms.

candid (**candidly**) If you are **candid** with someone, you speak to them openly and honestly, especially about something difficult or painful. ■ A **candid** photo of someone is one that they did not know was being taken.

candidate (**candidacy, candidacies; candidature**) A **candidate** is someone being considered for a position, for example one of the people standing in an election or applying for a job. You can talk about the **candidacy** or **candidature** of a person who is standing in an election.. *There were calls for him to withdraw his candidature.* ■ A **candidate** is a person taking an exam. ■ You say a person or thing is a **candidate** for something when it is likely to happen to them. *He seemed an unlikely candidate for success in Hollywood.*

candied fruit or other food has a covering of sugar, or has been cooked in sugar syrup to preserve it.

candle A **candle** is a stick of wax with a wick through the middle which is burnt to provide light.

candlelight (**candlelit**) **Candlelight** is the light from a candle. A **candlelit** room or table is lit by candles.

candlestick A **candlestick** is a holder for a candle.

candour (*Am:* **candor**) If you speak with **candour,** you are honest and open.

candy (**candies**) **Candy** is the usual American word for sweets. A **candy** is a sweet.

candy floss (*or* **candyfloss**) is a large fluffy mass of sugar threads eaten from a stick.

cane (**caning, caned**) **Cane** is the long hollow stems of plants like bamboo. ■ A **cane** is a walking stick, particularly an ornamental one. ■ A **cane** is a long thin flexible stick for hitting people as a punishment, especially at school. If someone is **caned** or given the **cane,** they are hit with a cane.

canine (*pron:* **kay**-nine) is used to talk about dogs. *...the canine star, Lassie.* ■ A **canine** is (a) a dog. (b) any member of the dog family, which includes wolves, foxes, and jackals. ■ Your **canines** or **canine teeth** are the two pointed teeth towards the front of your mouth. They are sometimes called **eye teeth.**

canister A **canister** is a metal container, often used for storing gas under pressure.

canker You can call something evil which is growing and spreading a **canker.** *...the canker of anti-Semitism.*

cannabis is an illegal drug made from the hemp plant.

canned See **can.**

cannery (**canneries**) A **cannery** is a factory where food is canned.

cannibal (**cannibalism**) A **cannibal** is a person who eats human flesh, or an animal which eats its own species.

cannibalize (*or* **cannibalise**) (**cannibalizing, cannibalized**) If you **cannibalize** something like a machine, you take parts from it to repair another one.

cannon (*plural:* **cannons** *or* **cannon**) (**cannoning, cannoned**) A **cannon** is a large gun, usually on wheels, which used to be used in battles. ■ A **cannon** is a heavy automatic gun, especially one fired from an aircraft. See also **water cannon.** ■ If a moving object **cannons** off something, it hits it and rebounds with great force.

cannonball (*or* **cannon ball**) **Cannonballs** are heavy metal balls which used to be fired from a cannon.

cannon fodder You can call soldiers **cannon fodder** when their leaders regard them as unimportant and they are killed in large numbers.

cannot See **can.**

canny (**cannier, canniest; cannily, canniness**) You say someone is **canny** when they are clever and make the right decisions, especially where money is concerned.

canoe (*pron:* kan-**noo**) (**canoeist; canoeing**) A **canoe** is a small narrow boat which you propel through the water using a paddle.

canon A **canon** is a priest on the staff of a cathedral. ■ A **canon** is a rule or principle. ■ A **canon** is an entire range of literary or musical compositions of a particular kind.

canonize (*or* **canonise**) (**canonizing, canonized; canonization**) If a dead person is **canonized,** they are officially recognized as a saint by the Catholic Church.

canon law is a set of rules for running the affairs of a Christian church, for example the Roman Catholic Church or the Anglican Church.

canoodle (**canoodling, canoodled**) If a couple are **canoodling,** they are kissing and cuddling.

can-opener A **can-opener** is the same as a tin opener.

canopy (**canopies**) A **canopy** is a cover suspended above something, for decoration or shelter. ■ The branches and leaves of trees can be called a **canopy** when they spread out, covering a wide area. ■ The **canopy** of a parachute is the large circle of nylon or silk connected to the harness.

cant When someone talks in an insincere and pompous way about religious or moral matters, you can call what they say **cant.**

cantankerous A **cantankerous** person tends to argue and complain a lot.

cantata (*pron:* kan-**tah**-ta) A **cantata** is a musical work for singers and instruments, usually based on a religious text.

canteen A **canteen** is part of a place like a factory where the workers go to eat.

canter (**cantering, cantered**) When a horse **canters** or moves at a **canter**, it moves at a speed slower than a gallop, but faster than a trot.

cantilever A **cantilever** is a long horizontal structure fixed in only one place with the rest overhanging. A **cantilever** bridge is made of two or more connecting cantilevers.

canton A **canton** is a political or administrative region in some countries, for example Switzerland.

cantor A **cantor** is a singer employed to lead the services in a synagogue.

canvas (**canvases**) **Canvas** is strong heavy cloth used for making tents, sails, and bags. ■ If you sleep **under canvas,** you sleep in a tent. ■ A **canvas** is a piece of canvas on which an oil painting is done.

canvass (**canvasses, canvassing, canvassed; canvasser**) If you **canvass** for a person or a party, you go round an area trying to persuade people to vote for them. ■ If you **canvass** people's opinions, you find out how they feel about something by asking them.

canyon A **canyon** is a long narrow steep-sided valley, often with a river at the bottom.

CAP The **CAP** or **Common Agricultural Policy** is the system used by the European Union to protect the incomes of farmers by keeping agricultural prices at agreed levels.

cap (**caps, capping, capped**) Several kinds of hats are called **caps,** including hats worn as part of a uniform. You use **-capped** to say what kind of cap someone is wearing. *...white-capped policemen.* ■ If you go to someone **cap in hand,** you go to them humbly, to ask for something. ■ If someone is **capped** or awarded a **cap,** they are chosen to represent their country in a game like rugby or cricket. ■ The **cap** of a bottle is its lid. ■ A **cap** is a protective covering. *...a lens cap.* See also **diaphragm.** ■ **Caps** are very small explosives used in toy guns. ■ You use **capped** to say something is on top of something else. *...snow-capped mountains.* ■ If the government **caps** a local authority, it limits the amount of money the authority can spend. ■ You can say something good or bad **caps** a series of events when it forms an appropriate or satisfying end. *Wright's late goal capped a dramatic finale.*

capability (**capabilities**) A country's military **capability** is the number of weapons and armed forces they have. *...nuclear capability.* ■ If you have the **capability** or **capabilities** to do something, you have the ability or qualities to do it.

capable (**capably**) If someone or something is **capable** of doing something, they have the ability to do it. ■ If you say someone is **capable** of a kind of behaviour, you mean they could easily behave like that. *Someone who'd killed twice would be capable of killing a third time.* ■ A **capable** person can be relied on to do something well. *They are capably led by Mark Benson.*

capacious If something is **capacious,** there is a lot of room in it.

capacitor A **capacitor** is a device for storing electric charge.

capacity (**capacities**) The **capacity** of something is the largest amount it can hold or produce. ■ If something is filled **to capacity,** it is completely filled. ■ In a place like a stadium, if there is a **capacity** crowd, the place is completely full. ■ If a factory or industry is working to **capacity,** it is producing as much as it is able. ■ If you have the **capacity** to do something, you are able to do it. *...the capacity to handle the business.* ■ If someone does something **in** a particular **capacity,** they do it as part of that job. *...acting in his capacity as chairman of the Super League.*

cape A **cape** is a short cloak. ■ A **cape** is a large piece of land that sticks out into the sea.

caper (**capering, capered**) **Capers** are the flower buds of a Mediterranean bush which are pickled and used to season food. ■ A **caper** is (a) a practical joke. (b) an illegal activity. ■ If someone **capers** around, they leap around energetically.

capillary (**capillaries**) **Capillaries** are tiny blood vessels.

capital The **capital** of a country or region is its main city or town, usually where its government is based. ■ A town which is famous for something can be called the **capital** of that thing. *...Nashville, the capital of country music.* ■ **Capital** is a sum of money used to start or expand a business, or invested to make money. ■ **Capital** is money you invest or save in order to obtain interest. ■ In industry, **capital** investment or expenditure is money spent on things like buildings and machinery. ■ You can refer to any useful resource as **capital.** *Money spent on education is investment in human capital.* ■ If you **make capital** out of a situation, you use it to your advantage. *...an attempt to make political capital out of the riot.* ■ A **capital** or **capital** letter is the large form of a letter used at the beginning of a name or sentence. ■ A **capital** offence is one which, according to the law, can be punished by death.

capital gains are the profits made when you buy something then sell it again at a higher price.

capitalise See **capitalize.**

capitalism is an economic and political system where property, business, and industry are owned by individuals and not by the state.

capitalist A **capitalist** country or system supports or is based on capitalism. ■ People who own capital or businesses are sometimes called **capitalists.** *...a life of capitalist luxury.*

capitalize (*or* **capitalise**) (**capitalizing, capitalized; capitalization**) If you **capitalize** on a situation, you use it to your own advantage. ■ **Capitalized** is used to say how much capital an organization has. *...an under-capitalized tourist trade.* ■ If you **capitalize** something you own, you sell it to make money.

capital punishment is the legal killing of someone convicted of a serious crime.

capitation fees or charges are set at a fixed amount per person.

Capitol In the US, the **Capitol** is the main building in Washington where Congress meets. The media often talk about things happening on **Capitol Hill,** the hill where the Capitol is.

capitulate (capitulating, capitulated; capitulation) If an army **capitulates,** it surrenders. ■ If you **capitulate,** you give in to other people and agree to what they want. *...the government's capitulation on the poll tax.*

cappuccino (*pron:* kap-poo-**cheen**-oh) (**cappuccinos**) Cappuccino is coffee which has hot frothy milk and often powdered chocolate on top.

caprice (*pron:* kap-**reess**) A **caprice** is an unexpected action which has no real purpose.

capricious (capriciousness) A **capricious** person often changes their mind unexpectedly. ■ **Capricious** is used to describe things which change unexpectedly and cannot be relied on. *...the capriciousness of the English weather.*

capsicum – Capsicums are large mild-tasting peppers.

capsize (capsizing, capsized) If a ship or boat **capsizes,** it tips upside-down or on its side. You can talk about its **capsize.**

capstan A **capstan** is a machine with a rotating drum that pulls in a heavy rope or something, such as an anchor, attached to a rope.

capsule A **capsule** is a small edible tube containing powdered or liquid medicine. ■ A **time capsule** is a container with items in it representing various aspects of present-day life. The capsule is buried so it can be recovered at some future time. ■ The **capsule** on a manned spacecraft is the part where the crew are.

captain (captaining, captained; captaincy, captaincies) The **captain** of a plane or ship is the officer in charge. ■ A **captain** is (a) a middle-ranking officer in the army. (b) a high-ranking officer in the navy. ■ The **captain** of a sports team is its leader. You can say someone **captains** a sports team, or talk about their **captaincy** of it. ■ You can refer to the person in charge of a large industrial company as a **captain of industry.**

caption (captioning, captioned) A **caption** is the words next to a picture, explaining what it is about. When a picture is **captioned,** a caption is put next to it or underneath it.

captivate (captivating, captivated) If you are **captivated** by someone or something, you find them charming. *...his captivating smile.*

captive (captivity) A **captive** is a prisoner. When someone is **taken** or **held captive,** they are taken or held prisoner. ■ A **captive** person or animal is imprisoned somewhere. ■ If you have a **captive audience,** a group of people have to watch or listen to you because they are unable to leave. ■ A **captive market** is a group of consumers who have to buy a particular product or buy from a particular seller because no-one else produces or provides that thing.

captor Someone's **captor** is the person who has captured them.

capture (capturing, captured) If someone is **captured,** they are taken prisoner. You can talk about their **capture.** ■ If an animal is **captured,** it is caught. ■ If military forces **capture** something, they take control of it by force. ■ If you **capture** something in a competitive situation, you win it. ■ If someone **captures** the atmosphere or quality of something, they represent it successfully in pictures, music, or words. *...poems that captured the mood of his times.* ■ If something **captures** your imagination, you find it very exciting or interesting.

car A car is a motor vehicle which can carry a small number of people. ■ **Car** is the usual American word for a railway carriage. ■ In Britain, railway carriages used for a particular purpose used to be called **cars.** *...a dining car.*

carafe (*pron:* kar-**raff**) A **carafe** is a glass container for water or wine.

caramel A **caramel** is a kind of toffee. ■ **Caramel** is burnt sugar used for colouring and flavouring food.

caramelize (*or* caramelise) (**caramelizing, caramelized**) When sugar **caramelizes,** it turns into caramel.

carapace The **carapace** of a creature like a tortoise or crab is its thick hard upper shell.

carat (*Am:* karat) The weight of diamonds and other precious stones is expressed in **carats.** A carat is 0.2 grams (about 0.007 of an ounce). ■ The purity of gold is measured in **carats.** The purest gold is 24-carat.

caravan (caravanning) A **caravan** is a vehicle without an engine where people live or spend their holidays. Caravans can be towed by cars. Having a holiday in a caravan is called **caravanning.** ■ A **caravan site** is a place where caravans are parked. ■ A **caravan** is a group of people and animals travelling together in places like the desert.

caraway is a plant with seeds which are often used to flavour cakes and bread.

carbine A **carbine** is a light automatic rifle.

carbohydrate is a substance in foods like sugar and bread which gives you energy. Foods with a lot of carbohydrate in them are called **carbohydrates.**

carbolic acid is a liquid used as a disinfectant and antiseptic.

carbon is a chemical element which diamonds, graphite, and coal are made of. ■ A **carbon** is the same as a carbon copy.

carbonate (carbonating, carbonated) A **carbonate** is a chemical compound of carbon, oxygen, and another chemical element. *...calcium carbonate.* ■ **Carbonated** drinks have carbon dioxide added to them, to make them fizzy.

carbon copy A **carbon copy** is a copy made using carbon paper. ■ If you say something is a **carbon copy** of an earlier thing, you mean they are identical.

carbon dating or **radiocarbon dating** is a method of calculating the age of something very old by measuring the amount of radioactive carbon in it.

carbon dioxide is an odourless gas breathed out by people and animals. It is also produced by certain chemical reactions.

carbon monoxide is an odourless poisonous gas produced when carbon is burnt in a very small amount of air.

carbon paper is thin paper with a dark waxy substance on one side, used for making copies.

car boot sale A **car boot sale** is a sale where people sell things from their car boots on a car park or field.

carbuncle A **carbuncle** is a large swelling under the skin like a group of boils.

carburettor (*Am: carburetor*) The **carburettor** is the part of an engine where air and petrol are mixed together.

carcass (*or* **carcase**) (**carcasses, carcases**) An animal's **carcass** is its dead body.

carcinogen (**carcinogenic**) A **carcinogen** is a substance which causes cancer. If something is **carcinogenic**, it causes cancer.

carcinoma A **carcinoma** is a cancerous growth.

card is strong stiff paper or thin cardboard. ■ A **card** is a piece of card or plastic with information on it. ...*a business card*. ...*credit cards*. ■ A person's business **card** is a small piece of card with their name, address, phone number, and occupation on it. ■ Greetings cards and postcards are often called **cards.** ■ **Cards** or **playing cards** are pieces of card with numbers or pictures on them, for playing games. If you play **cards,** you play a game using cards like these. ■ If something is **on the cards,** it is very likely to happen. ■ See also **smart card, wild card.**

cardboard is thick stiff paper used to make boxes. ■ People call an area where homeless people are living in boxes **cardboard city.**

card-carrying members of a political organization are official fully-committed members of it.

cardiac means to do with the heart. ...*cardiac surgery*. ■ A **cardiac arrest** is a heart attack.

cardigan A **cardigan** is a knitted sweater-like garment but with buttons or a zip down the front.

cardinal A **cardinal** is a senior archbishop of the Roman Catholic church. ■ A **cardinal** rule is one which is extremely important because other things are based on it or depend on it. ■ The **cardinal sins** are the seven deadly sins. People also jokingly call something a **cardinal sin** when it breaks a rule which other people think is very important.

cardinal number The **cardinal numbers** are the numbers used for counting, like 1, 7, or 23, as distinct from numbers like 1st, 7th, and 23rd. See also **ordinal number.**

card index A **card index** is a set of cards with information on them, usually arranged alphabetically.

cardio- is used in front of other words to talk about things to do with the heart.

cardiogram A **cardiogram** is an electrocardiogram.

cardiology (**cardiologist**) **Cardiology** is the study of the heart and heart disease. A **cardiologist** is an expert on these things.

cardiomyopathy is a disease of the heart muscle.

cardiovascular means to do with the heart and the blood vessels. ...*cardiovascular treatments*.

card vote A **card vote** is a way of voting at trade union conferences, where one delegate votes on behalf of all their union's members.

care (**caring, cared**) If you **care** about something, you are concerned about it or interested in it. ■ If you **care for** someone or **take care of** them, you look after them. ■ **Care** is providing what people need to make or keep them healthy. Children who are **in care** are being looked after by the state. ■ A **caring** person is affectionate, sympathetic, and helpful. ■ If you do not **care** for something, you do not like it. ■ If someone asks you if you would **care** to do something, they are suggesting politely that you do it. ■ If you do something with **care,** you make sure you do not make any mistakes or damage anything. ■ If you **take care** of a problem, you deal with it. ■ Someone's **cares** are their worries.

career (**careering, careered**) A **career** is a job or profession that you train to do, usually one offering the opportunity for advancement. ■ **Career** politicians or soldiers are people who work in the same type of work for all or most of their lives. ■ A **career** woman is one with a career who concentrates on her job, rather than being a housewife. ■ **Careers** advisers or offices give advice and information about jobs. ■ The time you spend doing a particular type of work is called a **career.** *My career as a music teacher was over.* ■ You say a vehicle **careers** somewhere when it is moving fast and out of control.

careerist A **careerist** is someone who thinks their career is more important than anything else and will do anything to succeed in it.

carefree A **carefree** time is one when you do not have any worries or responsibilities.

careful (**carefully**) If you are **careful,** you try to avoid having an accident, making a mistake, or upsetting someone.

careless (**carelessly; carelessness**) If you are **careless,** you do not pay enough attention to what you are doing, so that you make mistakes or have an accident. *The major cause of car theft is carelessness.* ■ If someone is **careless** with something like money, they do not use it sensibly.

carer A **carer** is someone who looks after an ill, disabled, or elderly person, usually a relative living with them.

caress (*pron:* ka-**ress**) (**caresses, caressing, caressed**) If you **caress** a person or give them a **caress,** you stroke them gently and affectionately.

caretaker A **caretaker** is someone who looks after a large building like a school or block of flats. ■ **Caretaker** is used to talk about someone who is doing an important job temporarily. ...*a caretaker administration*.

careworn If someone looks **careworn,** they look worried, tired, and unhappy.

cargo (**cargoes**) A plane's or ship's **cargo** is the goods it is carrying.

caribou (*plural:* **caribou** *or* **caribous**) The **caribou** is a North American deer.

caricature (**caricaturing, caricatured; caricaturist**) A **caricature** is a comical drawing or description of someone, which exaggerates their appearance or personality. You can say someone is **caricatured** in a drawing or piece of writing. A person who draws or writes caricatures is called a **caricaturist.** ■ If information is presented in a distorted way, you can call it a **caricature** of the truth.

caries (pron: care-reez) is tooth decay.

carjack (**carjacker**) If your car is **carjacked,** a thief steals it from you by force while you are in it. **Carjacking** is stealing a car in this way.

carmine is a deep bright red colour.

carnage You say there is **carnage** when many people are killed, especially in a war.

carnal is used to talk about bodily feelings and activities, especially sexual ones. ...carnal activity.

carnation – Carnations are many-petalled red, pink, white, or yellow scented flowers.

carnival A **carnival** is a public festival with music, processions, and dancing. ■ If there is a **carnival** atmosphere or mood, everyone is happy and light-hearted.

carnivorous (**carnivore**) A **carnivorous** animal eats meat. Meat-eating animals are also called **carnivores.** ■ A **carnivorous** plant eats insects.

carob is the powdered pods of a Mediterranean tree. It is used instead of cocoa or chocolate in some health foods.

carol A **carol** is a religious song, sung at Christmas.

carotid The **carotid** arteries are the two arteries in the neck which supply blood to the head.

carouse (pron: ka-**rowz**) (**carousing, caroused**) When people **carouse,** they enjoy themselves by drinking lots of alcohol and making lots of noise.

carousel At an airport, a **carousel** is a rotating conveyor belt where luggage is collected. ■ In the US, a **carousel** is a merry-go-round.

carp (plural: carp) The **carp** is a large freshwater fish. ■ If someone is **carping,** they keep complaining, especially about things which are not important.

car park (or carpark) A **car park** is a place where people can leave their cars.

carpenter (**carpentry**) A **carpenter** is a person who makes, repairs, and installs wooden objects. A carpenter's work is called **carpentry.** See also **joiner.**

carpet (**carpeting, carpeted**) A **carpet** is a thick covering for a floor, made of wool or a similar material. ■ **Carpeting** is (a) the carpets fitted in a building. ...wall-to-wall carpeting. (b) material used for carpets. ...woven carpeting. ■ If you **carpet** a room, you lay a carpet in it. ■ If you sweep a problem **under the carpet,** you try to hide it, rather than dealing with it. ■ A **carpet** of something is a layer of it covering the ground or another surface. ...a carpet of volcanic ash.

carpet bombing is heavy bombing from aircraft, with the intention of hitting as many places as possible in a particular area.

car port (or carport) A **car port** is a shelter for one or two cars, consisting of a flat roof supported on pillars.

carriage A **carriage** is (a) one of the sections of a passenger train. (b) a four-wheeled horse-drawn vehicle for carrying passengers. ■ **Carriage** is the act of transporting things or the cost of transporting them.

carriageway A **dual carriageway** is a road with a strip of grass or concrete down the middle separating traffic going in opposite directions. Each half of the road can be called a **carriageway.**

carrier A **carrier** is a vehicle for transporting people and things, especially soldiers and their equipment. ■ Carrier bags are sometimes called **carriers.** ■ A **carrier** is (a) an airline. (b) a person employed to carry things. He became a hod carrier on a building site. ■ A **carrier** of a disease is a person or animal infected with it and capable of spreading it.

carrier bag A **carrier bag** is a plastic or paper bag with handles for carrying shopping.

carrier pigeon – Carrier pigeons are pigeons trained to fly back to a place, carrying messages attached to their leg.

carrion is the decaying flesh of dead animals. Crows circled overhead, looking for carrion.

carrot – Carrots are thin orange root vegetables. ■ You can call something a **carrot** when it is something offered to someone to persuade them to do something. The WMF is dangling the carrot of a major British project before potential sponsors. ■ A **carrot and stick** approach involves persuading someone to do something by both offering them a reward and threatening them.

carry (**carries, carrying, carried**) If you **carry** something, you move it somewhere, holding it off the ground. Things can also be carried in vehicles, or by water or wind. ■ If you **carry** something like an identity card, you have it with you wherever you go. ■ If a woman is **carrying** a child, she is pregnant. ■ If a person, animal, or thing is **carrying** a disease, they are infected with it and can infect someone else. ■ The person who **carries** the cost of something is the one who pays for it. ■ If something **carries weight,** they are influential. ■ If you **carry out** a task or order, you do what is required. ■ If you **carry on** doing something, you continue doing it. ■ In a meeting, if a proposal is **carried,** it is agreed by a vote. ■ If someone does something successfully, you can say they **carry it off.** ...anyone who dresses unusually and carries it off. ■ If something **carries** a risk, there is a risk involved in it. ■ If an action like breaking the law **carries** a punishment, anyone caught doing it gets that punishment. ...an offence which carries the death penalty. ■ If something **carries over** from one situation to another, it continues in the new situation. The effect of the privatization campaign has not carried over to other companies. ■ If a sound **carries,** it can be heard a long way away. ■ If you get **carried away** by something, you are so enthusiastic that you behave in a silly way.

carrycot A **carrycot** is a light portable cot for a baby.

cart A **cart** is (a) a wooden vehicle pulled by an animal. (b) a two-wheeled wooden vehicle pulled or pushed by hand. ■ If you **cart** things or people somewhere, you transport them, using whatever means are available. ■ If someone is **carted off,** they are removed from a place, often against their will. ■ If you say someone is **putting the cart be-**

fore the horse, you mean they are doing things in the wrong order.

carte blanche (*pron:* **kart blahnsh**) If someone gives you **carte blanche,** they give you the authority to do whatever you want.

cartel (**cartelize, cartelizing, cartelized; cartelization**) (*or* **cartelise,** *etc*) If a group of companies operate as a **cartel** (*pron:* kar-**tell**), they work together to stop other companies competing with them, and to keep prices high. ■ If an industry is **cartelized** (*pron:* **kar**-tell-ized), it is turned into a cartel.

carthorse A **carthorse** is a big powerful horse used to pull heavy loads.

cartilage (*pron:* **kar**-till-ij) is a strong flexible substance in the body, for example round the joints.

cartography (**cartographer, cartographic**) Cartography is the art of drawing maps.

carton A **carton** is (a) a plastic or cardboard container in which food or drink is sold. (b) a large, strong cardboard box.

cartoon (**cartoonist**) A **cartoon** is a humorous drawing or series of drawings in a magazine or newspaper. ■ A **cartoonist** is a person who draws cartoons. ■ A **cartoon** is a film in which the characters and scenery are drawings.

cartridge A **cartridge** is a tube containing a bullet and an explosive substance which is inserted into a gun. ■ A **cartridge** is a removable part of a device, which you replace when it is empty or worn out.

cartridge pen A **cartridge pen** is a type of fountain pen. It has an ink-filled tube which can be replaced.

cartwheel (**cartwheeling, cartwheeled**) If you do a **cartwheel,** you do a circular movement, throwing yourself sideways on to one hand and then on to the other, ending up back on your feet. ■ If a vehicle **cartwheels** out of control, it turns over several times. ■ **Cartwheels** are large wheels with wooden spokes and metal rims fitted to horse-drawn carts.

carve (**carving, carved; carver**) If you **carve** an object, you make it out of a piece of wood, stone, or some other substance, by cutting pieces away. An object like this is called a **carving.** ■ If you **carve** a design on something, you cut it into the surface. ■ If you **carve** meat, you cut slices from it. ■ If something is **carved up,** it is divided into smaller pieces and shared out among two or more people. ■ If you **carve out** something for yourself, you establish it. *He carved out a career in music.*

carving knife A **carving knife** is a large knife for cutting cooked meat.

Casanova (*pron:* kass-a-**noh**-va) A man who has a lot of love affairs is sometimes called a **Casanova.**

casbah See kasbah.

cascade (**cascading, cascaded**) A **cascade** is a waterfall or series of waterfalls. ■ When water **cascades** over something, a large quantity pours down over it. ■ A **cascade** of things is a lot of them coming one after the other. *...a cascade of laughter.*

case A **case** is a container specially designed to hold or protect something. Suitcases are often called **cases.** ■ A **case** of wine or beer is a box containing twelve bottles or cans. ■ A **case** is an instance of something. *In cases like this you have to move fast.* ■ If you say something **is the case,** you mean it is true. ■ You say **in case** to show something is done because a certain thing might happen. *A plane stood by in case evacuation was needed.* ■ You use **in any case** to mean 'anyway'. *I don't know yet, but in any case, I shouldn't say.* ■ In law, a **case** is (a) a trial or other legal inquiry to settle a lawsuit or decide if a person is guilty or not. (b) the evidence presented for or against a person or issue. ■ A **case** is a crime being investigated by the police. ■ A **case** is a person or problem being dealt with by someone like a doctor or a social worker. ■ If there is a **case** for something, there are good reasons for it. *There is a case for higher taxes.*

casebook The **casebook** of someone like a social worker, is the cases they have dealt with.

case history Someone's **case history** is a record of their background and the problems affecting them, especially their medical history.

case law is law established by decisions made by judges in earlier cases.

caseload (*or* **case load**) A doctor's or social worker's **caseload** is the number of cases they have to deal with.

casement A **casement** is a window hinged on one side.

case study A **case study** is an account giving detailed information about a person, group, or thing and their development over a period of time.

casework is social work which involves dealing directly with people who need help rather than doing administrative duties.

cash (**cashes, cashing, cashed**) **Cash** is money in the form of notes and coins, rather than cheques. **Cash** is also used to talk about money in general. ■ If you **cash** a cheque, you exchange it at a bank for the amount it is worth. Similarly, you can **cash in** something like an insurance policy. ■ If someone **cashes in** on a situation, they use it to their advantage, especially by doing something unfair or dishonest.

cash-and-carry (**cash-and-carries**) A **cash-and-carry** is a shop or warehouse where goods are sold at wholesale prices.

cashback If you are paying for goods in a shop with your debit card and ask for **cashback,** it means that the shop will give you some money that they can deduct from your bank account.

cash book A **cash book** is a book kept as a record of payments made and money received by an organization or person.

cash card A **cash card** is a plastic card for withdrawing money from a cash dispenser.

cash crop A **cash crop** is a crop grown to be sold. See also **subsistence.**

cash desk A **cash desk** is the place in a large shop where you pay.

cash dispenser A **cash dispenser** is a machine at a bank or building society where you can withdraw money from your account.

cashew – **Cashews** or **cashew nuts** are edible curve-shaped nuts.

cash flow

cash flow is the amount of cash a firm has readily available to pay its expenses and keep it going.

cashier (cashiering, cashiered) A **cashier** is a person that customers pay money to or get money from in a shop, garage, or bank. ■ If a member of the armed forces is **cashiered,** they are forced to leave, because they have done something wrong.

cashmere is a kind of very fine soft wool.

Cashpoint A **Cashpoint** is the same as a cash dispenser. 'Cashpoint' is a trademark.

cash register A **cash register** is a machine in a shop for adding up how much people have to pay and for keeping the money in.

casing A **casing** is something surrounding or covering something else, usually to protect it.

casino (casinos) A **casino** is a place where people play gambling games like roulette.

cask A **cask** is a wooden barrel for storing alcoholic drink.

casket A **casket** is a small box for keeping valuable things such as jewellery in. ■ In the US and Canada, a **casket** is a coffin.

cassava (*pron:* ka-**sah**-va) is a plant grown in some tropical countries from which a kind of flour is made, also called **cassava.**

casserole A **casserole** is a dish made by slowly cooking meat or fish with vegetables in liquid in an oven. ■ A **casserole** is a large deep container with a lid, for cooking food in an oven.

cassette A **cassette** or **cassette tape** is a rectangular plastic container with a reel of magnetic tape inside. Cassettes are used for recording and playing sound. ■ A **cassette player** is a machine for playing cassettes. A cassette player which can also record sound is called a **cassette recorder.** ■ A **cassette deck** is part of a hi-fi system for playing cassettes.

cassock A **cassock** is a long robe worn by some priests, church officials and choir members.

cast (casting, cast *not* **'casted')** The **cast** of a play or film is all the people acting in it. When an actor is given a part, you say they are **cast** in that part. ■ If you say someone is **cast** in a particular way, you mean they are represented in that way *She claims the article cast her as a 'social outcast and leper'.* ■ The **cast** of someone's mind is the sort of mind they have. *...an authoritarian cast of mind.* ■ If you **cast** a vote, you vote. ■ At a meeting, when there are an equal number of votes for and against a proposal, the chairperson is sometimes allowed a **casting vote.** This vote allows a decision to be reached. ■ If you **cast** doubt on something, you make people less sure about it. ■ If you **cast around** for something, you look for it. ■ If you **cast your mind back** to a time in the past, you think about it. ■ If you **cast** your eyes in a particular direction, you look in that direction. ■ If you **cast** something like a stone, you throw it. ■ If you **cast** a fishing line, you flick the rod and send the line out into the water. ■ If something **casts** a light or shadow onto a place or thing, it makes it appear there. ■ In children's stories, when someone **casts** a spell, they use magic to put someone or something into a particular state. ■ If an object is **cast** in plaster,

metal, or glass, that material is poured into a mould called a **cast.** The object is called a **cast;** if it is metal, it is called a **casting.** ■ If you are in a boat and you **cast off,** you untie the rope fastening it to its mooring.

castanets are a Spanish musical instrument made of two small round pieces of wood which you click together in your hand.

castaway A **castaway** is a person who has survived a shipwreck and has managed to reach an isolated coast.

caste (*pron:* **kahst**) A Hindu's **caste** is the social class they are born into. In other cultures where social class is regarded as important, you can talk about someone belonging to a particular **caste.**

castellated A **castellated** wall or building has turrets and battlements like a castle.

caster See **castor.**

caster sugar is finely ground white sugar.

castigate (castigating, castigated; castigation) If you **castigate** someone or something, you scold them or criticize them severely. *Helen's merciless castigation of Michelle was prompted by jealousy.*

cast iron is iron with a small amount of carbon in it. ■ A **cast-iron** guarantee, assurance, or excuse is certain to be effective, real, or true.

castle A **castle** is a large building with thick high walls for protection against attack. ■ A **castle** is a piece in chess. It is sometimes called a **rook.**

castor (*or* **caster**) Castors are the small wheels on furniture.

castor oil is an oil which comes from the seeds of the castor oil plant. In the past, it was used as a laxative.

castrate (castrating, castrated; castration) If a man, boy, or male animal is **castrated,** their testicles are removed. This is called **castration.**

casual (casually; casualness) If someone is **casual,** they are calm and do not seem worried about what is happening or what they are doing. ■ **Casual** is used (a) to talk about things being done carelessly through lack of attention. *...a certain casualness with details.* (b) to describe something said or done which was not planned beforehand. ■ **Casual** work is done occasionally for short periods of time, and not on a permanent or regular basis. ■ **Casual** clothes are for wearing at home or on holiday, rather than on formal occasions.

casualty (casualties) A **casualty** is a person who has been killed or injured in a war or accident. ■ The **casualty department** in a hospital is the place where you are taken if you have had an accident or need emergency treatment. Officially, these departments are usually called 'Accident and Emergency Departments'. ■ A **casualty** of something which has happened is a person or thing that has suffered badly because of it. *Fiat has been one of the greatest casualties of the recession.*

casuistry is the use of clever arguments to persuade people that something is true or right, often when it is not.

cat The **cat** family includes lions, tigers, and leopards, as well as the ordinary domestic **cat.** ■ If you play **cat and mouse** with someone, you provoke them by letting them think they have an advantage, then taking it away from them.

cataclysm (*pron:* **kat**-a-kliz-zum) (**cataclysmic**) A **cataclysm** is an event which causes great change or harm. **Cataclysmic** (*pron:* kat-a-**kliz**-mik) is used to describe an event like this, or its effects. ...*a cataclysmic climate change that killed off the dinosaurs.*

catacomb (*pron:* **kat**-a-koom) **Catacombs** are underground passages and rooms where bodies used to be buried.

catalogue (*Am:* **catalog**) (**cataloguing, catalogued**) A **catalogue** is a book showing goods you can buy from a company. ■ A **catalogue** is (a) a list of objects in an exhibition, museum, or art gallery. (b) a list of books and documents in a library. ■ If someone **catalogues** a collection of things, they make a list of them. You can also say someone **catalogues** a series of events. ...*cataloguing the failures resulting from administrative problems.* ■ A **catalogue** of unpleasant things is a series of them. ...*a catalogue of disasters.*

catalyse (*Am:* **catalyze**) (**catalysing, catalysed**) If one thing **catalyses** another, it causes it to happen. *Any unexpected circumstance that arises may catalyze a sudden escalation of violence.* ■ If a chemical reaction is **catalysed**, it is speeded up by a catalyst.

catalyst (**catalysis**) A person or thing that causes an event or change to happen can be called a **catalyst**. *He's willing to act as a catalyst for peace* ■ In chemistry, a **catalyst** is a substance which speeds up a chemical reaction, without changing itself. This process is called **catalysis**.

catalytic converter A **catalytic converter** is a device fitted to a car's exhaust system to reduce the amount of pollution from its engine.

catalyze See **catalyse**.

catamaran A **catamaran** is a boat with two parallel hulls held in place by a single deck.

catapult A **catapult** is a device for shooting small objects like stones at something. It is Y-shaped with a piece of elastic tied to the two top parts. ■ A **catapult** is a device for launching aircraft from an aircraft carrier. ■ If something is **catapulted** somewhere, it is suddenly hurled through the air. ■ If something **catapults** you into a situation, you find yourself suddenly and unexpectedly in it.

cataract If you have a **cataract**, part of the lens of your eye has become cloudy, causing partial blindness. ■ A **cataract** is a large waterfall.

catarrh (*pron:* kat-**tar**) If you have **catarrh**, you have a lot of mucus in your nose and throat.

catastrophe (*pron:* kat-**tass**-trof-fee) (**catastrophic**) A **catastrophe** is a sudden terrible disaster. You say an event like this is **catastrophic** (*pron:* kat-ass-**strof**-ik).

catcall – **Catcalls** are loud shouting noises which people make to show disapproval.

catch (**catches, catching, caught**) If you **catch** a person or animal, you capture them. ■ In fishing, the **catch** is the number of fish caught on a single trip. ■ If you **catch** a ball moving through the air, you get hold of it. This is called a **catch**. ■ If you **catch** a bus or train, you get on it to travel somewhere. ■ If you **catch** something like a TV programme or

an event, you manage to see it or go to it. ■ If you **catch** an illness you become ill with it. If an illness is **catching**, it is infectious. ■ If you **catch** someone doing something wrong, you see them doing it. ■ If you **catch** someone **out,** you trap them into doing something which shows them to be mistaken or dishonest. ■ If you are **caught out** by something unpleasant, it takes you by surprise. *Firms have been caught out by the fall in sales.* ■ If you are **caught** in something which is happening, you become involved in it, without meaning to. *They have been caught up in the fighting.* ■ If a moving object **catches** something, it hits it. ■ If a moving object **catches on** something, it becomes attached to it. *Their nets apparently caught on a submarine.* ■ If something **catches the light,** it shines because it is reflecting the light. ■ If someone or something **catches** a mood or atmosphere, they successfully represent it in pictures, words, or music. ■ If a feeling is **catching,** it spreads quickly among people. ■ If something **catches on,** it becomes popular. ■ If something **catches** your imagination, you find it interesting or exciting. ■ If you **catch sight** of someone or something, you suddenly see them or notice them. If you **catch a glimpse** of them, you see them briefly. ■ If you **catch up** with someone, you reach them by moving faster than they do. ■ You say someone **catches up** with someone else when they reach the same standard. ■ If something unpleasant **catches up with** you, you can no longer avoid dealing with it. ■ If someone **catches on** to something, they understand it. ■ A **catch** is a device for fastening something. ■ A **catch** is a draw-back which makes something less attractive. ■ **catch your breath:** see **breath.**

Catch-22 If you describe something as a **Catch-22** situation, you mean it is an impossible one because you cannot do one thing until you do another thing, but you cannot do the second thing until you have done the first.

catch-all is used to describe things designed to cover all types of situations or possibilities. ...*catch-all regulations.*

catcher In baseball, the **catcher** is the player who stands behind the batter. ■ You can refer to someone who catches something as a **catcher.** ...*the city's rat-catcher.*

catchment area The **catchment area** of something like a school or hospital is the area it serves.

catch-phrase A **catch-phrase** is a saying which becomes well-known for a time.

catchy (**catchier, catchiest**) A **catchy** tune is easy to remember.

catechism (*pron:* kat-ti-kiz-zum) A **catechism** is a set of questions and answers which sums up the main beliefs of a religion.

categoric means the same as 'categorical'.

categorical (**categorically**) A **categorical** statement is firm and definite. *They categorically denied any involvement in illegal acts.*

categorize (*or* **categorise**) (**categorizing, categorized; categorization**) If you **categorize** someone or something, you decide what group they belong to. *Her first novel defies easy categorisation.*

category (**categories**) If people or things are divided into **categories,** they are divided into groups according to their qualities and characteristics.

cater (**caterer; catering**) If you **cater** for someone's requirements, you provide the things they need or want. ■ When someone **caters** for a social event or does the **catering** for it, they provide the food and drink. A person or firm that does this is called a **caterer.**

caterpillar – Caterpillars are small grubs which feed on plants and develop into butterflies or moths. ■ The **caterpillar tracks** on a tank or bulldozer are the ridged belts round its wheels which allow it to travel over different terrain.

catfish (*plural:* **catfish**) The **catfish** is a freshwater fish which has spines round its mouth which look like a cat's whiskers.

catgut is strong cord made from animal intestines. The strings of some musical instruments are made from it, and surgeons use it for sewing cuts.

catharsis (*pron:* kath-**thar**-siss) (**cathartic**) If you experience a feeling of **catharsis,** you feel psychologically or spiritually refreshed through releasing strong emotions or unhappy memories by expressing or reliving them in some way. You say something which allows you to do this is **cathartic** or has a **cathartic** effect.

cathedral A **cathedral** is the main church in a diocese.

catheter (*pron:* kath-it-er) A **catheter** is a tube put into a person's body to drain fluid, especially urine, or to insert fluid.

cathode In an electric cell, the **cathode** is the negative electrode. See also **anode.**

cathode ray tube A **cathode ray tube** is the device in a television or VDU which sends an image on to the screen.

Catholic (**Catholicism**) A **Catholic** is someone who belongs to the Roman Catholic Church. **Catholicism** (*pron:* ka-**tholl**-iss-izz-um) is the set of beliefs held by Catholics. ■ If a person has **catholic** tastes, they have a wide range of interests.

catkin – Catkins are long, thin, soft flowers hanging from trees like the birch and hazel.

cat litter is absorbent material put in a box for a cat to urinate and defecate on indoors.

cat's eyes are small pieces of glass or plastic set into a road to reflect light so motorists can see the road at night.

catsuit A **catsuit** is a tight-fitting female garment made in one piece and covering the body, arms, and legs.

catsup See ketchup.

cattery (**catteries**) A **cattery** is a place where cats are bred, or where they are cared for while their owners are away.

cattle are cows and bulls.

cattle-grid A **cattle-grid** is a metal grid in a road, allowing vehicles to pass across it, while stopping animals from doing so.

catty (**cattily**) A **catty** remark is spiteful.

catwalk In a fashion show, the **catwalk** is the long platform the models walk along. ■ A **catwalk** is a

narrow bridge or platform, often one high above the ground.

Caucasian A **Caucasian** is a white person.

caucus (**caucuses**) A **caucus** is a small group of influential people within an organization who meet to discuss important things. A **caucus** is also a meeting of a group like this.

caught See **catch.**

cauldron (*or* **caldron**) A **cauldron** is a large round metal pot for cooking over a fire. ■ If you call a situation a **cauldron,** you mean it is unstable. *...a cauldron of ethnic unrest.*

cauliflower – Cauliflowers are cabbage-like vegetables which have green leaves around a large white ball of flower buds.

causal (**causation, causality**) If there is a **causal** relationship between two things, one thing makes the other happen. The relationship is called **causation** or **causality.** *...the causal link between smoking and ill health.*

cause (**causing, caused**) If a person or thing **causes** a situation or is the **cause** of it, they make it happen. ■ If you have **cause** for a particular feeling or action, there are reasons which justify you feeling it or doing it. *There is no cause for alarm.* ■ A **cause** is an aim or principle which some people support or fight for.

cause célèbre (*plural:* **causes célèbres**) (*both pron:* **kaws** sill-**leb**-ra) A **cause célèbre** is a controversial issue or criminal trial which attracts a lot of public attention.

causeway A **causeway** is a raised path or road crossing water or marshland.

caustic (**caustically**) **Caustic** chemicals can dissolve other substances. ■ A **caustic** comment is extremely critical, cruel, or bitter.

caustic soda is a powerful chemical substance used to make cleaning materials.

cauterize (*or* **cauterise**) (**cauterizing, cauterized**) If a wound is **cauterized,** it is burnt using heat or a chemical to close it up and prevent infection.

caution (**cautioning, cautioned; cautionary**) Caution is care taken to avoid danger or mistakes. ■ If someone **cautions** you, they warn you of possible problems or danger. ■ If someone **cautions** you **against** doing something, they advise you not to do it. ■ A **cautionary** tale is intended to warn people about something. ■ If you are **cautioned** or get a **caution** when you have broken a rule, you are warned you will be punished if you do it again. ■ When the police **caution** someone, they warn them that anything they say may be used as evidence in court.

cautious (**cautiously; cautiousness**) A **cautious** person does things very carefully to avoid possible danger or mistakes.

cavalcade A **cavalcade** is a procession of people on horses or in cars or carriages.

cavalier If someone has a **cavalier** attitude, they are careless and insensitive.

cavalry In the past, the **cavalry** was the part of an army which consisted of soldiers on horses. Nowadays, the **cavalry** is the part of an army which uses armoured vehicles.

cave (**caving, caved**) A **cave** is a large hole in the side of a cliff or hill, or under the ground. ■ If a roof **caves in**, it collapses. ■ If a person **caves in** to someone who is putting pressure on them, they give in to them. *Labour's agriculture spokesman called the settlement a cave-in.*

caveat (*pron:* **kav**-vee-at) If someone adds a **caveat** to what they have just said, they mention something like a disadvantage or an exception. ■ A **caveat** is a legal clause restricting what someone is allowed to do.

caveman (**cavemen**) **Cavemen** were people in prehistoric times who lived in caves.

cavern A **cavern** is a large deep cave.

cavernous A **cavernous** room is extremely large.

caviar (*or* **caviare**) is a food consisting of the salted eggs of a fish called the sturgeon.

cavil (**cavilling, cavilled**) (*Am:* **caviling, caviled**) If someone **cavils**, they complain about a minor aspect of something. A complaint like this is called a **cavil**.

cavity (**cavities**) A **cavity** is a hollow area in something solid. Some parts of the body are called **cavities**. *...the nasal cavity.* ■ A **cavity** is a small hole or soft area in a tooth, caused by decay.

cavity wall A **cavity wall** consists of two parallel walls with a narrow space between them. Cavity walls help keep in warmth and keep out damp and noise.

cavort (**cavorting**) If people **cavort**, they dance and leap around. ■ Sexual activities are sometimes called **cavorting**.

cawing is the noise made by crows.

cay A **cay** is a low island or bank made of fragments of sand and coral.

cayenne or **cayenne pepper** is a hot-tasting red powder made from dried chillies.

CB is the range of radio waves which the general public is allowed to use to send messages to one another. CB stands for 'citizens' band'.

CBE The **CBE** is an honour given by the British monarch for an outstanding service or achievement. CBE stands for 'Commander of the Order of the British Empire'.

CD A **CD** is a compact disc.

CD-ROM A **CD-ROM** is a compact disc containing large amounts of information for use with a computer system that has a CD-ROM drive. CD-ROM stands for 'compact disc read-only memory'.

cease (**ceasing, ceased**) If something **ceases**, it stops. ■ If you **cease** something, you stop doing it.

ceasefire (*or* **cease-fire**) A **ceasefire** is an agreement to stop fighting between countries or groups at war.

ceaseless (**ceaselessly**) If something is **ceaseless**, it never stops.

cedar The **cedar** is a large evergreen tree.

cede (**ceding, ceded**) If one country **cedes** territory to another, it gives it away, usually because it is forced to.

cedilla The **cedilla** is a symbol written under 'c' in French and Portuguese to show you pronounce it like 's' rather than 'k', as in 'Françoise Sagan'.

ceilidh (*pron:* **kay**-lee) A **ceilidh** is an organized entertainment in Scotland or Ireland with folk music, singing, and dancing. Originally, ceilidhs were informal events in people's houses.

ceiling In a room, the **ceiling** is the surface above your head. ■ A **ceiling** on something like wages is an official upper limit.

celeb (*pron:* sil-**leb**) Celebrities are sometimes called **celebs**.

celebrant A **celebrant** is a person who performs or takes part in a religious ceremony.

celebrate (**celebrating, celebrated; celebration, celebratory**) If you **celebrate** something or have a **celebration**, you do something enjoyable like having a party, to show it is a special occasion. A **celebratory** drink or meal takes place to celebrate something. ■ A **celebration** of something is an expression of praise and appreciation for it. *He sees the poem as a celebration of human love.* ■ A **celebrated** person or thing is famous. ■ When a priest **celebrates** Mass, he performs the actions and ceremonies involved in it.

celebrity (**celebrities**) A **celebrity** is someone famous, especially in show business.

celery is a vegetable with long, pale green stalks.

celeste A **celeste** is a keyboard instrument which looks like a miniature piano.

celestial is used to describe things connected with heaven or the sky.

celibate (**celibacy**) Someone who is **celibate** does not marry or have sex. **Celibacy** is not marrying or having sex.

cell (**celled**) **Cells** are the tiny basic units which living things are made of. ■ A **cell** is a small room where prisoners are locked up, or a similar room where a monk or nun lives. ■ A **cell** is a small group of people specially trained to work together as part of a larger organization. ■ A **cell** is a device which uses energy from chemicals, heat, or light to produce electricity.

cellar A **cellar** is a room underneath a building, often used for storing things like wine. ■ A person's **cellar** is the wines stored in their cellar. *He keeps a modest cellar.*

cellist See **cello**.

cellmate (*or* **cell-mate**) People sharing the same prison cell can be called **cellmates**.

cello (*pron:* **chell**-oh) (**cellos; cellist**) A **cello** is a low-pitched instrument from the violin family. It is played in an upright position between the player's knees.

Cellophane is a thin transparent material for wrapping things like food. 'Cellophane' is a trademark.

cell-phone (*or* **cellphone**) A **cell-phone** is a cordless telephone which operates using radio signals.

cellular means to do with animal and plant cells. *...cellular protein.* ■ **Cellular** means to do with cellphones. *...the cellular market.* A **cellular** telephone is a cell-phone.

cellulite is a layer of fat in places like the thighs, which is hard to get rid of.

celluloid is a plastic material which is used to make children's toys and photographic film. 'Celluloid' is a trademark. ■ **Celluloid** is used to talk about films and the cinema. *...a celluloid fantasy... He decided that the tour should be captured on celluloid for posterity.*

cellulose is a substance found in the cell walls of plants. It is used to make paper, plastic, and various textiles.

Celsius or **Centigrade** is a scale for measuring temperature, in which water freezes at 0° and boils at 100°. 'Celsius' is usually written 'C'.

Celt (*pron:* **kelt**) (**Celtic**) The **Celts** were a race of people who lived in Britain, Ireland, and other parts of Europe, but were driven to remoter areas by other invaders. If you call someone a **Celt**, you mean they come from somewhere like Scotland, Wales, Cornwall, or Ireland. **Celtic** means to do with the Celts. *...the Celtic languages.*

cement is a grey powder made from clay and limestone or chalk. It is mixed with sand and water to make concrete. This mixture can also be used to fix something firmly in place; you say something is **cemented** in a particular place. ■ Some types of glue are called **cement.** If you **cement** things together, you stick them together using glue or something similar. ■ If something **cements** a relationship, it makes it stronger.

cemetery (**cemeteries**) A **cemetery** is a place where the dead are buried, especially one which is not next to a church.

cenotaph A **cenotaph** is a monument built in honour of soldiers killed in a war.

censor (**censoring, censored; censorship**) If someone **censors** material which is intended to be published or broadcast, they officially examine it and cut out any parts they think are unacceptable. A person who does this is called a **censor;** making cuts like this is called **censorship.**

censorious If someone is **censorious,** they strongly criticize someone's behaviour.

censure (**censuring, censured**) If you are **censured** for something you have done, someone in authority tells you that they strongly disapprove of it. What they say is called **censure.**

census (**censuses**) A **census** is an official survey of a country's population.

cent In many countries, a **cent** is a small coin or unit of money worth one hundredth of the country's main currency unit. For example, there are 100 cents in a US dollar or a Dutch guilder.

centaur In Greek myths, a **centaur** was a creature with the head, arms, and upper body of a man, and the body, legs, and tail of a horse.

centenarian A **centenarian** is a person who is over a hundred years old.

centenary (*pron:* sen-**teen**-a-ree) (**centenaries**) A **centenary** is a year when people celebrate something which happened a hundred years earlier.

centennial is the American word for a centenary.

center See **centre.**

centi- at the beginning of a word indicates that a unit of measurement is one-hundredth of a larger unit. For example, a centigram is one-hundredth of a gram.

Centigrade see **Celsius.**

centime (*pron:* **son**-teem) In France and many other countries, a **centime** is a hundredth of a franc.

centimetre (*Am:* **centimeter**) A **centimetre** is a hundredth of a metre, or about 0.3937 inches. 'Centimetres' is usually written 'cm'.

centipede A **centipede** is a creature with a long thin body divided into many segments, each with a pair of legs.

central (**centrally, centrality**) The **central** part of something is the part in the middle. ■ If something is in a **central** position, it is in the middle of something. ■ **Central** is used to distinguish the main government of a country from regional governments or local authorities. *...central government.* ■ **Central** is used to say something is very important to a process. You can talk about the **centrality** of something to a process. *...the centrality of education to economic performance.*

central heating (**centrally heated**) Central heating is a system in which water or air is heated and passed round a building through pipes. When a building has this system, you say it is **centrally heated.**

centralise See **centralize.**

centralism (**centralist**) Centralism is the idea that the affairs of a country or group of countries should be controlled by one central government. **Centralist** is used to talk about people and things connected with this idea.

centrality See **central.**

centralize (*or* **centralise**) (**centralizing, centralized; centralization**) When power in a country or organization is **centralized,** it is concentrated in one place, or in the hands of one person or group.

central processing unit The **central processing unit** or **central processor** of a computer is the part which interprets and carries out the instructions of a program. 'Central processing unit' is often shortened to CPU.

centre (*Am:* **center**) (**centring, centred; -centred**) The **centre** of something is the part furthest from its edges or outer surface. ■ The **centre** of a town is the part where the largest number of shops, cinemas, etc are. ■ If something **centres** on a place, it is positioned around it, or happening there. ■ If a discussion **centres** on something, that is what it is mainly about. ■ If someone is the **centre** of attention, people are particularly interested in them. ■ **-centred** is added to words to describe a system in which one group of people is given special importance. *...a child-centred approach to education.* ■ If a place is a **centre** for an activity, that activity is particularly important there. ■ A building used for a particular purpose can be called a centre. *...a leisure centre.* ■ In politics, groups who are neither left-wing nor right-wing can be called the **centre.**

centrefold (*Am:* **centerfold**) A **centrefold** is a picture that covers the two central pages of a magazine, especially a photograph of a naked or semi-naked woman.

centre of gravity (**centres of gravity**) An object's **centre of gravity** is the one point on it where it would balance perfectly.

centrepiece The **centrepiece** of an organized event is the most important part of it. ■ The **centrepiece** in a display of objects is the most important one.

centre stage You say someone takes **centre stage** when a lot of attention is paid to them.

centrifugal A **centrifugal** force is one which makes objects tend to move outwards when they are spinning around or moving in a curve.

centripetal (pron: **sen**-tri-**peet**-al) A **centripetal** force is one which acts against a centrifugal force and prevents an object from moving outwards when it is spinning or moving in a curve.

centrist In politics, a **centrist** is someone with moderate political views.

centurion A **centurion** was an officer in the Roman army, in charge of 100 men.

century (**centuries**) A **century** is (a) a 100-year period beginning with a year ending in '00'. (b) any period of 100 years. ■ In cricket, a **century** is a total of 100 runs scored by a batsman in one innings.

ceramic (pron: si-**ram**-ik) (**ceramicist**) **Ceramics** or **ceramic** objects are made of clay which has been heated to a very high temperature. A person who makes ceramics is called a **ceramicist** (pron: si-**ram**-iss-ist).

cereal A **cereal** is a plant like wheat or rice which produces grain. ■ **Cereal** is a breakfast food made from grain.

cerebellum (pron: serr-rib-**bell**-um) (plural: **cerebellums** or **cerebella**) The **cerebellum** is a part of the brain, situated towards the back. It is responsible for co-ordinating muscle movements and for the sense of balance.

cerebral (pron: **ser**-rib-ral) is used to talk about (a) things to do with thinking and reasoning. ...cerebral work. (b) things to do with the brain. ...cerebral arteries.

cerebral palsy If someone has **cerebral palsy,** their limbs and muscles are permanently weak and uncontrollable, usually because their brain was damaged during or before birth.

cerebrum (plural: **cerebrums** or **cerebra**) The **cerebrum** is the front part of the brain. It is concerned with thought and perception.

ceremonial (**ceremonially**) **Ceremonial** is used to talk about things to do with ceremonies. ...a ceremonial drinking cup. ■ The **ceremonial** at something like a royal occasion is all the formal and traditional aspects of it.

ceremony (**ceremonies**) A **ceremony** is the formal part of an event such as a wedding, when certain traditional things are done and said. ■ **Ceremony** is used to talk about all the special things said and done on formal occasions. The ship was launched with much ceremony. ■ **Ceremony** is very formal and polite behaviour. If you say someone **does not stand on ceremony,** you mean they behave in a natural, rather than formal, way.

cerise (pron: ser-**reess**) is a cherry-red colour.

certain (**certainly**) If you are **certain** about something or know it **for certain,** you have no doubt about it. ■ If you say something is **certain** to happen, you mean it will definitely happen. ■ If you **make certain** something is done, you take action to make sure of it. ■ **Certain** is used to say something will definitely have a particular effect. ...a certain cure. ■ You use **certainly** to emphasize that you feel strongly about something. It is certainly disappointing. ■ **Certain** is used to talk about a particular person, group, or thing, without naming them. ...certain ambitious cabinet members. ■ **Certain** is used to talk about a special quality which something has. The city has a certain magic. ■ If something is true **to a certain extent,** it is only partly true.

certainty (**certainties**) If there is **certainty** about something or it is a **certainty,** there is no doubt about it. ■ **Certainty** is used to talk about things being certain to happen. The best deterrent is the certainty of detection. ■ If you call a contender in a competition a **certainty,** you mean they will definitely win.

certifiable If you call a kind of behaviour **certifiable,** you mean it is extremely foolish.

certificate A **certificate** is an official document stating particular facts. ■ The qualification someone receives after a course of study or training can be called a **certificate.** ...the General Certificate of Secondary Education. ■ A film's **certificate** is one of five categories it is put into by the censors, depending on who they think it is suitable for.

certify (**certifies, certifying, certified; certification**) If something is **certified** as being a particular thing, it is officially declared to be that thing. ■ **Certified** is used to say someone has gained a professional qualification. ...a certified accountant. ■ If someone is **certified,** they are officially declared insane.

certitude is the same as certainty.

cervical means relating to (a) the cervix. ...a cervical smear test. (b) the neck. ...cervical vertebrae.

cervix (pron: **ser**-viks) (plural: **cervixes** or **cervices**) The **cervix** is the entrance to the womb.

cessation When something stops, you can talk about its **cessation.**

cesspit A **cesspit** is a hole or tank in the ground which waste water and sewage flow into.

cetacean (pron: sit-**tay**-shun) **Cetaceans** are members of the whale family, for example dolphins and porpoises.

cf. In a piece of writing, **cf.** is used to mention something which can give further information about the thing being discussed. For more remarks on the matter, cf. Isis Unveiled, Vol.I.

CFC – **CFCs** are chemicals used in aerosols, fridges, and air-cooling systems. They harm the ozone layer. CFC stands for 'chlorofluorocarbon'.

CFS See **chronic fatigue syndrome**.

chafe (**chafing, chafed**) If you **chafe** at something like a restriction, you feel annoyed about it. ■ If your skin is **chafed,** it becomes sore as a result of being rubbed.

chaff is the outer parts of grain, which are removed before the grain is used to make food. ■ If you **separate the wheat from the chaff,** you decide which things or people in a group are good, so they can be given special treatment.

chaffinch (**chaffinches**) The **chaffinch** is a small European songbird. The male has an orange chest and face; the top of its head is grey.

chagrin (*pron:* **shag**-grin) (**chagrined**) Chagrin is a feeling of annoyance and disappointment.

chain (**chaining, chained**) A **chain** is a set of metal rings linked together. If you **chain** one thing to another, you fasten the first thing to the second with a chain. ■ A **chain** of things is a group of them arranged in a line. *...the small chain of islands.* ■ A **chain** of shops or hotels is several of them owned by the same company. ■ A **chain** is a series of things in which each one is affected by the one before it. *...the first event in the chain of destruction.* ■ Things which restrict people's freedom can be called **chains.** *...the chains of Communist oppression.*

chain gang In the US, a **chain gang** is a group of prisoners chained together.

chain letter A **chain letter** is a letter, often with a promise of money, that is sent to several people who then send copies on to several other people.

chain mail is flexible armour made from small metal rings joined together.

chain reaction A **chain reaction** is (a) a series of chemical changes, each of which causes the next. (b) a series of events, each of which causes the next. *The first company to cut prices could start a chain reaction.*

chain saw A **chain saw** is a large motorized saw.

chain-smoke (**chain-smoker**) If someone **chain-smokes,** they keep smoking one cigarette straight after another.

chain store A **chain store** is one of many similar shops owned by the same company.

chair (**chairing, chaired**) A **chair** is a piece of furniture for one person to sit on. ■ At a university, a **chair** is the post of professor. *...the chair of Medieval History at Birmingham.* ■ If you **chair** a meeting or are the **chair,** you are the chairperson; you can also say you are **in the chair** or **take the chair.**

chairlift A **chairlift** is a line of chairs attached to a moving cable for carrying people up a mountain.

chairman (**chairmen; chairmanship**) The **chairman** of a meeting is the person in charge. A chairman can be a man or a woman, but some people prefer the title 'chairperson' or 'chair'. ■ The **chairman** of an organization or committee is its head. ■ **Chairmanship** is used to talk about the position of being chairman, or the period when a particular person is chairman.

chairperson The **chairperson** of a meeting is the person in charge.

chairwoman (**chairwomen**) The **chairwoman** of a meeting is the woman in charge.

chaise longue (**chaises longues**) (*pron:* **shaze long**) A **chaise longue** is a couch with only one arm and usually a back along half its length.

chalet (*pron:* **shal**-lay) A **chalet** is a small wooden house.

chalice (*pron:* **chal**-liss) A **chalice** is a large metal cup with a thin stem.

chalk (**chalky**) Chalk is a kind of soft white rock. If something is **chalky,** it contains chalk or is covered with chalk. ■ **Chalks** are small sticks of white or coloured chalk for writing with. ■ If you say two people or things are as different as **chalk and cheese,** you mean they are complete opposites. ■ If you **chalk up** a success, you achieve it. If you **chalk up** a number of points in a game, you win them.

challenge (**challenging, challenged; challengingly, challenger**) If you say something you are doing is **challenging** or a **challenge,** you mean it is new and exciting and will need great effort and determination. *...a challengingly inventive show.* ■ If you **challenge** someone to do something, you invite them to do it, believing that they will not be able to. *They challenged him to prove his claim.* An invitation like this is called a **challenge.** ■ If one person **challenges** another for the leadership of a party, they try to become leader instead of them. You call this a leadership **challenge.** ■ If you **challenge** a statement or belief, you question whether it is true or valid. You can also **challenge** someone's authority or do or say something which is a **challenge** to it. ■ If a sentry **challenges** you, they order you to stop, and ask you who you are.

chamber A **chamber** is a large room for formal meetings. The room where a parliament meets is often called a **chamber,** and **chamber** is often used to talk about the parliament itself. *The President himself will address the chamber.* ■ A **chamber** is a room designed and equipped for a particular purpose. *...a burial chamber.* ■ The **chambers** of a group of barristers are the set of offices where they are based. ■ Some hollow places inside the body are called **chambers.** *...the chambers of the heart.*

chambermaid A **chambermaid** is a woman who cleans the bedrooms in a hotel.

chamber music is classical music written for a small number of instruments.

Chamber of Commerce A **Chamber of Commerce** is a group of business people who work together to improve business and industry in their area.

chamber orchestra A **chamber orchestra** is a small orchestra which plays classical music.

chamber pot A **chamber pot** is a round china bowl for urinating in during the night.

chameleon (*pron:* kam-**meal**-yon) A **chameleon** is a small lizard which changes colour according to its surroundings.

chamois (*plural:* **chamois**) The **chamois** (*pron:* **sham**-wah) is a small antelope which lives in the mountains of Europe and South West Asia. ■ A **chamois** (*pron:* **sham**-ee) or **chamois leather** is a soft leather cloth used for cleaning and polishing.

chamomile See **camomile.**

champ People sometimes call a champion the **champ.**

champagne is an expensive sparkling white French wine.

champion (**championing, championed; championship**) A **champion** is someone who has won first prize in a competition, or who has beaten everyone else in a contest. ■ A **championship** is a competition to find the best player or team of a particular sport. ■ If you **champion** something like a cause or principle or you are its **champion,** you actively support it.

chance (**chancing, chanced; chancy**) If there is a **chance** of something happening or being true, it could possibly happen or be true. ■ If you talk about someone **standing a chance** of doing something, you are talking about the possibility that they will be able to do it. If you say someone does not **stand a chance** of doing something, you mean there is no possibility they will be able to do it. ■ A **chance** is an opportunity for someone or something to do something. ■ If you **take a chance,** you do something even though there is a risk of danger or failure. You can also say you **chance** something. ■ Something which is **chancy** is risky. ■ If you are in a risky situation and **take your chances,** you make the most of opportunities which come along and hope things will work out. ■ **Chance** is used to talk about things which happen for no special reason and in a way which cannot be predicted. ...*a chance discovery.* You say things like these happen **by chance.** ■ If someone **leaves nothing to chance,** they take all possible precautions to make sure something is a success. ■ If you **chance to do** something, or **chance on** it, you do it or find it without planning or trying to.

chancel The **chancel** is the part of a church where the altar is and the priest and choir usually sit.

chancellery (**chancelleries**) A **chancellery** is (a) the residence or office of a chancellor. (b) an office in an embassy or consulate.

chancellor (**chancellorship**) The **Chancellor** is the head of government in Germany and Austria. ■ In Britain, the **Chancellor** is the Chancellor of the Exchequer. ■ The **Chancellor** of a British university is its official head. ■ **Chancellorship** is the position of chancellor.

Chancellor of the Exchequer In Britain, the **Chancellor of the Exchequer** is the minister who makes decisions about finance and taxes.

chancer If you say someone is a **chancer,** you mean they exploit situations to their own advantage, often in a dishonest way.

Chancery The **Chancery Division** is a department of the British High Court of Justice which deals with problems which cannot be solved by applying the law in the normal way.

chancy See **chance.**

chandelier (*pron:* shan-dill-**eer**) A **chandelier** is an ornamental light fitting decorated with lots of hanging pieces of glass.

chandler A **chandler** is someone who sells ships' supplies.

change (**changing, changed**) If there is a **change** in something or if it **changes,** it becomes different in some way. ■ If you **change** something, you replace it with a different thing of the same kind. *I changed the tyre on my car once.* ■ When you **change,** you change your clothes. A **change** of clothes is a spare set to change into. ■ When you **change** trains, you get off one train and get on another one. ■ **Change** is (a) the money you get back when you pay for something with more money than it costs. (b)

coins rather than notes. ■ **change hands:** see **hand.**

changeable If something is **changeable,** it is likely to change.

changeling In stories, a **changeling** is a baby who has been substituted for another baby by fairies.

change of life The **change of life** is the same as the menopause.

changeover A **changeover** is a change from one system to another.

channel (**channelling, channelled**) (*Am:* **channelling, channeled**) A **channel** is (a) a wavelength on which TV programmes are broadcast. (b) a wavelength for sending and receiving radio messages. ■ A **channel** is (a) a passage along which water or some other liquid flows. (b) a route used by boats to cross an area of water. ■ The **Channel** is the English Channel. ■ If you **channel** something like money, you control and direct it so it is used in a particular way or for a particular purpose. ■ If you talk about something being done through particular **channels,** you mean the people who arrange it. *He dispensed with the usual channels that arrange official press conferences.*

channel-hopping means switching quickly between different television channels because you are looking for something interesting to watch.

chant If you **chant,** you repeat a word or group of words over and over again. A **chant** is a word or group of words repeated like this. ■ A **chant** is a religious song or prayer sung or spoken on only a few notes. ...*Gregorian chant.*

chaos (**chaotic, chaotically**) **Chaos** is complete disorder and confusion. If a situation is **chaotic,** it is disordered and confused.

chap (**chapping, chapped**) You can use **chap** to talk about a man or boy. ■ If your skin **chaps,** it becomes raw and cracked by exposure to the cold.

chapati (*or* **chapatti**) In Indian cookery, a **chapati** is a flat piece of unleavened bread.

chapel A **chapel** is (a) a building used for worship by some Protestant churches. (b) part of a church with its own altar for private prayer. (c) a small church in a school, hospital, or prison.

chaperone (*or* **chaperon**) (*pron:* **shap**-per-rone) (**chaperoning, chaperoned**) If you **chaperone** someone or are their **chaperone,** you go with them to make sure they do not come to any harm.

chaplain (**chaplaincy, chaplaincies**) A **chaplain** is a member of the clergy who works in the armed forces, a hospital, school, prison, or for an important person like a monarch. **Chaplaincy** is used to talk about things relating to the work of a chaplain. ...*his industrial chaplaincy work.*

chapter A **chapter** is one of the parts of a book. ■ If someone gives you **chapter and verse,** they tell you every single detail about something. ■ A **chapter** is a period in history, or in someone's life. ■ The **chapter** of a cathedral is the clergy who work in it or are connected with it. ■ In the US, a **chapter** is a local branch of an organization.

char (**charring, charred**) If something **chars,** it turns black after being burned.

charabanc (*pron:* **shar**-rab-bang) A **charabanc** was a large old-fashioned coach for taking people on holiday.

character A person's **character** is all the qualities they have which make up their personality. Similarly, the **character** of a place is the qualities which make up its atmosphere. ■ **Character assassination** is trying to destroy someone's reputation by criticizing them unfairly. ■ If you say someone has **character,** you mean they are courageous and determined. ■ If you talk about the **character** of something, you mean the special features which make it what it is, or make it work the way it does. ■ If you say something has **character,** you mean it has interesting or unusual qualities. ■ The **characters** in a film, book, or play are the people in it. ■ If you call someone a **character,** you mean they are interesting, unusual, or amusing. ■ A **character actor** is an actor who specializes in playing unusual or eccentric people. ■ A **character** is a letter, number, or other symbol that is written or displayed on a VDU.

characterise See **characterize.**

characteristic (**characteristically**) The **characteristic** of a person or thing is a quality or feature which is typical of them. ■ If something is **characteristic** of a person, thing, or place, it is typical of them. *His defence of the deal has been characteristically negative.*

characterize (*or* **characterise**) (**characterizing, characterized; characterization**) If you say something **characterizes** a thing, you mean it is a typical feature of it. ■ If you **characterize** someone in a particular way, you describe them by saying they have particular characteristics. ■ If you talk about the **characterization** in a story or film, you mean the extent to which the characters are made interesting or believable.

characterless things are uninteresting.

charade (*pron:* shar-**rahd**) If you call something that is happening a **charade,** you mean it is not what it is supposed to be and nobody is really deceived by it. ■ **Charades** is a party game in which two teams act a word or phrase for the other team to guess.

charcoal is a black substance used as fuel, which is made by burning wood without much air. ■ **Charcoals** are small sticks of charcoal used for drawing with.

charge (**charging, charged**) The money you are **charged** for something is the amount you have to pay for it; this money is called a **charge.** ■ If goods or services are **charged** to someone, the bill is sent to them. ■ When the police **charge** someone, they formally accuse them of having committed a crime. An accusation like this is called a **charge.** ■ If you are **in charge** of someone or something, or **have charge** of them, they are under your control and you are responsible for them. You can also say they are **in your charge.** If you **take charge** of someone or something, you become responsible for them. ■ If someone is your **charge,** they have been given to you to look after and you are responsible for them. ■ If you **charge** somewhere, you dash there in a clumsy way. If police or soldiers **charge,** they move forward quickly, to attack or dis-

perse people. ■ An electrical **charge** is an amount of electricity stored in something. If you **charge** something, you give it an electrical charge by passing electricity through it. ■ **Charged** is used to describe situations in which there is a lot of tension. *...a highly-charged debate.* ■ If someone is **charged** with doing something, it is their responsibility.

chargeable If something is **chargeable,** (a) you have to pay money for it. (b) you have to pay tax on it.

charge card A **charge card** is a card allowing you to buy goods on credit.

chargé d'affaires (**chargés d'affaires**) (*both pron:* **shar**-zhay daf-**fair;** *the 'zh' sounds like 's' in 'pleasure'*) A **chargé d'affaires** is (a) the acting head of a diplomatic mission in a foreign country while the ambassador is away. (b) the head of a small diplomatic mission.

charge hand A **charge hand** is a worker of slightly less importance than a foreman.

charge nurse A **charge nurse** is a senior male nurse in a hospital, equivalent to a sister.

charger A **charger** is a device for charging or recharging batteries. ■ In the Middle Ages, a **charger** was a horse ridden by a knight in battle.

charge sheet A **charge sheet** is the official form on which the police write down charges against a person.

chariot A **chariot** was a horse-drawn vehicle with two wheels used in ancient times for racing and fighting.

charisma (*pron:* kar-**rizz**-ma) (**charismatic**) If someone has **charisma,** they can attract, influence, and inspire people by their personal qualities. You say someone like this is **charismatic** (*pron:* kar-rizz-**mat**-ik). ■ The **charismatic** church is part of the Christian Church which believes people can receive supernatural gifts from God such as speaking in tongues.

charitable (**charitably**) A **charitable** person is kind and tolerant. ■ If you say you are being **charitable,** you mean you are describing someone or something in a more favourable way than they deserve. *Still, he reflected charitably, it was hardly her fault.* ■ A **charitable** organization or activity helps people or animals in need.

charity (**charities**) A **charity** is an organization which raises money for a particular cause. ■ If you give money to **charity,** you give it to a charitable organization. ■ **Charity** is a kind and sympathetic attitude towards other people.

charlady (**charladies**) A **charlady** is the same as a **charwoman.**

charlatan (*pron:* **shar**-lat-tan) A **charlatan** is someone who pretends to have skills or knowledge they do not really have.

charleston The **charleston** was a lively dance popular in the 1920s.

charm (**charming, charmed; charmingly**) **Charm** is the quality of being attractive and pleasant. If you are **charmed** by someone, you are delighted by them. *...this charming man.* ■ If someone **charms** you, they use their charm to please you, often to get you to do something. ■ A **charm** is an action, saying, or object believed to bring luck. ■ A **charm** is a small ornament fixed to a bracelet or necklace. ■ If you say someone leads a **charmed life**, you mean they keep narrowly escaping danger.

charmer If you call someone a **charmer**, you mean they are charming but insincere.

charnel house A **charnel house** is a place for the bones of the dead.

chart A **chart** is something like a graph which is intended to make information easier to understand. ■ A **chart** is a map of part of the sea, or of the stars. ■ When an area of land or water is **charted**, it is surveyed and a map is made of it. ■ When something like progress is **charted**, it is studied and recorded carefully. ■ If you **chart** a course of action, you plan it. ■ The **charts** are weekly lists of the top selling pop records.

charter (**chartering, chartered; charterer**) A **charter** is (a) a document showing the rights of a group of people, or demanding rights for them. ...*a customers' charter.* (b) a list of the aims and principles of an organization. ...*the United Nations Charter.* (c) a document issued by the government or ruler of a country allowing an organization to be founded and listing its rights and functions. ...*the BBC's royal charter.* ■ **Chartered** is used in front of words like 'accountant' to show someone is fully qualified in their profession. ■ If you **charter** a plane or ship, you hire it for your private use. The **charterer** is the person or firm hiring it. ■ A **charter** plane or boat is hired by a person or organization and is not part of a regular service.

charwoman (**charwomen**) A **charwoman** is a woman employed as a cleaner.

chary (*pron:* **chair**-ee) If you are **chary** of doing something, you are not keen to do it.

chase (**chasing, chased**) If you **chase** someone or **give chase**, you follow them quickly, to try to catch them. Following someone like this is called a **chase.** ■ If you **chase** something you want, you spend a lot of time and effort trying to get it. ...*the chase for memorabilia.* ■ If you **chase** someone **up**, you try to find them because you want them to do something. ■ If you **chase up** something that is needed, you try to find it. *When I didn't hear from the suppliers, I chased the matter up.* ■ If you **chase** someone from a place, you force them to leave.

chaser A **chaser** is an alcoholic drink drunk straight after a different kind of alcoholic drink.

chasm (*pron:* **kaz**-zum) A **chasm** is a very deep crack in rock or ice. ■ A **chasm** is a great difference between two things or groups of people. ...*the chasm between rich and poor.*

chassis (*pron:* **shass**-ee) (*plural:* **chassis**) A vehicle's **chassis** is the framework it is built on.

chaste (**chastity**) A **chaste** person does not have sex, or only has sex with their husband or wife. You call their behaviour **chastity**. ■ **Chaste** things are very simple in style. ...*a chaste diamond.*

chasten (**chastening, chastened**) If you are **chastened** by something, it makes you regret your behaviour. ...*chastened by his ten days in detention.*

chastise (**chastising, chastised; chastisement**) If someone is **chastised**, they are told off or punished; you call this their **chastisement.**

chastity See **chaste.**

chat (**chatting, chatted**) When people **chat** or have a **chat**, they talk in an informal friendly way. A **chat show** is a TV or radio programme in which people talk like this. ■ If you **chat up** someone you are attracted to, you talk to them in a friendly way to try and get them interested in you.

chateau (*plural:* **chateaux**) (*both pron:* **shat**-toe) A **chateau** is a large country house or castle in France.

chatline A **chatline** is a commercial telephone service allowing you to have a conversation with other people who have rung in.

chatroom A **chatroom** is a site on the Internet where you can use e-mail to talk to other people about a common interest.

chattel Your **chattels** are the things you own.

chatter (**chattering, chattered; chatterer, chatterbox, chatterboxes**) If someone **chatters**, they talk quickly and continuously, often about unimportant things. This kind of talk is called **chatter**; someone who does it a lot is called a **chatterer** or a **chatterbox.** ■ The media often refer to trendy professional people who talk a lot about things like politics as the **chattering classes.** ■ If a small animal or bird **chatters**, it makes quick short high-pitched noises. ■ If your teeth **chatter**, they rattle together because you are cold.

chatty A **chatty** person is friendly and informal.

chauffeur (**chauffeuring, chauffeured**) A **chauffeur** is someone employed to drive and look after a rich or important person's car. ■ If you **chauffeur** someone somewhere, you drive them there.

chauvinism (*pron:* **show**-vin-iz-zum) (**chauvinist; chauvinistic**) **Chauvinism** is a strong unreasonable belief that your own country, race, or sex is the best. Someone who has this belief is called **chauvinistic** or a **chauvinist.**

cheap (**cheaper, cheapest; cheaply, cheapness, cheapish**) **Cheap** goods or services do not cost much. ■ You say things are **cheap** when they are of poor quality. ■ If something is done **on the cheap**, not enough money is spent on it, and it is not done properly as a result. ■ If you say **life is cheap**, you mean a situation such as a war has stopped people caring about large numbers of people dying unnecessarily. ■ **Cheap** behaviour and remarks are unkind and unnecessary.

cheapen (**cheapening, cheapened**) If something **cheapens** you, it lowers your reputation or dignity.

cheapskate A **cheapskate** is someone who does not like spending money. ■ **Cheapskate** things are produced as cheaply as possible.

cheat (**cheating, cheated**) If someone **cheats**, they behave dishonestly to get what they want. You call someone who does this a **cheat.** ■ If someone **cheats** you out of something, they get it from you dishonestly. ■ If you feel **cheated**, you feel bitter, because you have not got something you were expecting. ■ If someone **cheats on** their sexual partner, they have a secret sexual relationship with someone else.

check (**checker**) If you **check** something or **check on** it, you make sure it is satisfactory, safe, or correct. An inspection like this is called a **check**. ■ If something harmful is **checked**, it is prevented from continuing or spreading. ■ If you keep or hold something **in check**, you keep it under control. ■ If you **check into** a hotel, you arrive and fill in the necessary forms. ■ When you **check in** at an airport, you arrive at a place called the **check-in** and show your ticket before going on a flight. ■ **Check** or **checked** fabric has a pattern made up of squares. ■ In a restaurant in the US, the **check** is the bill. ■ **Check** is the American spelling of 'cheque'. ■ In chess, **check** is a position in which a player's king is threatened with capture.

checkered See **chequered**.

checkers is the usual American word for draughts.

check-in See **check**.

checklist A **checklist** is a list of things you must remember to do or bring.

checkmate In chess, **checkmate** is a situation in which you cannot stop your king being captured and so you lose the game.

checkout In a supermarket, a **checkout** is a counter where you pay for your goods.

checkpoint A **checkpoint** is a place where traffic is stopped and checked.

check-up A **check-up** is a routine examination by a doctor or dentist.

cheek (**-cheeked**) A person's **cheeks** are the soft parts of their face on either side of their nose. You can add **-cheeked** to a word to describe someone's cheeks. ...*a rosy-cheeked woman.* ■ If you **turn the other cheek,** you decide not to get angry when someone has treated you badly. ■ If things are **cheek by jowl,** they are very close together. ■ If you say someone has a **cheek,** you mean they are doing something they have no real right to do.

cheekbone A person's **cheekbones** are the two bones in their face just below their eyes.

cheeky (**cheekier, cheekiest; cheekily**) A **cheeky** person or action is rude or disrespectful.

cheer (**cheering, cheered**) When people **cheer,** they shout loudly to show approval or encouragement. A shout like this is called a **cheer**. ■ If you **cheer** someone **on,** you cheer loudly to encourage them. ■ If a piece of news brings people **cheer** or they are **cheered** by it, it makes them pleased or relieved. ■ If you **cheer up** or someone **cheers** you **up,** you stop feeling depressed and become more cheerful.

cheerful (**cheerfully; cheerfulness**) A **cheerful** person is happy and joyful. ■ **Cheerful** things make you feel cheerful. ...*cheerful music.*

cheerleader In the US, **cheerleaders** are people who lead the crowd in cheering at a large public event like a football match. ■ If you say someone is a **cheerleader** for a particular cause, you mean they actively support it. *He is among the cheerleaders for constitutional change.*

cheerless things are gloomy and depressing.

cheery (**cheerier, cheeriest; cheerily**) **Cheery** behaviour is bright and cheerful. ■ **Cheery** things make you feel cheerful. ...*cheery news.*

cheese (**cheesy**) **Cheese** is a solid food made from milk. ■ A **cheese** is (a) a kind of cheese. *We use only British cheeses.* (b) a block of cheese before it is cut up. ■ **Cheesy** things contain cheese or look, taste, or smell like cheese. ...*cheesy sauce.*

cheeseboard A **cheeseboard** is a tray on which a selection of cheeses is served, usually as the last course of a meal. This course can itself be called the **cheeseboard**.

cheeseburger A **cheeseburger** is a burger with a slice of cheese served in a bread roll.

cheesecake A **cheesecake** is a cake with a soft sweet topping made of cream cheese on a biscuit or pastry base.

cheesecloth is a thin, light cotton material.

cheetah The **cheetah** is a large African wild cat with spots. Cheetahs can run extremely fast.

chef (*pron:* **sheff**) A **chef** is a cook in a restaurant or hotel.

chef-d'oeuvre (*plural:* **chefs-d'oeuvre**) (*both pron:* shay-**durv**) A writer's, artist's, or composer's **chef-d'oeuvre** is the best piece of work they have produced.

chemical (**chemically**) **Chemical** is used to talk about things to do with chemistry or made by a process in chemistry. ...*a chemical reaction.* ■ A **chemical** is a substance used in or made by a chemical process. ■ **Chemical** weapons have dangerous chemicals in them.

chemist A **chemist** or **chemist's** is a shop selling medicine, cosmetics, and some household goods. ■ A **chemist** is a person qualified to sell medicines prescribed by a doctor. ■ A **chemist** is a scientist who does research in chemistry.

chemistry is the scientific study of the characteristics and composition of substances. ■ The **chemistry** of a substance is its characteristics and composition, and the way it reacts with other substances. ■ **Chemistry** is used to talk about how two people react to each other. *The personal chemistry between the two leaders has improved a lot.*

chemotherapy (*pron:* kee-mo-**theh**-rap-ee) is the treatment of diseases, especially cancer, using drugs.

cheque (*Am:* **check**) A **cheque** is a printed form on which you write an amount of money and who it is to be paid to. Your bank then pays them the money from your account. *I'd like to pay by cheque.* ■ **blank cheque:** see **blank.**

chequebook (*Am:* **checkbook**) A **chequebook** is a book of cheques.

cheque card A **cheque card** is a small plastic card given to you by your bank, which you show when paying for something by cheque.

chequered (*Am:* **checkered**) If a person or organization has had a **chequered** career, they have had a varied past with good and bad parts. ■ **Chequered** fabric has a pattern of squares of two or more colours. ■ In motor racing, the **chequered flag** is the black and white checked flag waved at the finishing line.

cherish (**cherishes, cherishing, cherished**) If you **cherish** a hope or memory, you keep it in your mind so that it continues to give you happy feelings. ■ If you **cherish** someone, you care for them in a loving way. ■ If people **cherish** a right or privilege, they believe it is important and try hard to keep it.

cheroot A **cheroot** is a cigar with both ends cut flat.

cherry (**cherries**) **Cherries** are small round fruit with red or black skins and a hard stone in the middle. ■ **Cherry red** is a deep red colour.

cherub (plural: **cherubs** or **cherubim**) (**cherubic**) A **cherub** is an angel represented in art as a plump naked child with wings. ■ If you say someone looks **cherubic** (pron: cher-**rew**-bic), you mean they look sweet and innocent like a cherub.

chess is a game for two people, played on a chessboard. Each player has sixteen pieces of various kinds. You try to move your pieces so your opponent's king cannot escape being taken.

chessboard A **chessboard** is a square board for playing chess. It is divided into sixty-four squares of two colours, usually black and white.

chessman (**chessmen**) A **chessman** is a playing piece used in chess, usually coloured black or white.

chest (**-chested**) A person's **chest** is the front of their body between the neck and the waist. You can add **-chested** to a word to describe someone's chest. ...hairy-chested men. ■ If you **get** something **off your chest,** you tell people what you have been worrying about. ■ If you **keep** or **hold your cards close to your chest,** you do not tell people your plans. ■ A **chest** is a large heavy box for storing things.

chestnut – **Chestnuts** are shiny reddish-brown nuts with a prickly green outer casing. See also **horse chestnut.** ■ **Chestnut** is a reddish-brown colour. ■ An **old chestnut** is a joke or story which is so well-known it is no longer funny.

chest of drawers (**chests of drawers**) A **chest of drawers** is a piece of furniture with drawers.

chesty If you have a **chesty** cough, you have a lot of catarrh in your lungs.

chevron (pron: **shev**-ron) A **chevron** is a V shape. ■ A **chevron** is one of the V shapes on the sleeve of a person in the armed forces or the police force, which shows their rank.

chew (**chewy**) When you **chew** food, you break it up with your teeth to make it easier to swallow. **Chewy** food needs to be chewed a lot before you can swallow it. ■ If you **chew** something like gum, you keep biting it without eating it. ■ If an animal **chews** a hole in something, it makes a hole by biting. ■ If you **chew over** something like a problem, you think carefully about it. ■ If you say someone has **bitten off more than they can chew,** you mean they are trying to do something too difficult for them.

chewing gum is a kind of sweet you chew but do not swallow.

chic (pron: **sheek**) people or things are fashionable and sophisticated.

chicanery (pron: shi-**kane**-er-ee) is deceitful and dishonest behaviour.

chick A **chick** is a baby bird.

chicken A **chicken** is a bird kept for its meat or eggs. **Chicken** is the meat from a chicken. ■ If you

say someone is **counting their chickens,** you mean they are making plans based on the idea that something will happen, when it may not happen at all. ■ If you talk about a **chicken-and-egg** situation, you mean it is impossible to decide which of two things caused the other.

chickenpox is a disease which gives you a high temperature and itchy red spots.

chickpea – **Chickpeas** are hard round edible seeds that look like pale brown peas.

chickweed is a common garden weed with small white flowers.

chicory is a plant with crunchy sharp-tasting leaves which people put in salads. The root of this plant is also called **chicory;** it is roasted and used in some types of coffee.

chide (**chiding, chided**) If you **chide** someone, you tell them off.

chief (**chiefs; chiefly**) The **chief** of an organization is the person in charge. ■ The main person in an organization, or the head of a department, often has **chief** in the name of their job. ...the chief fire officer. ■ The **chief** of a tribe is its leader. ■ The **chief** person, thing, or item in a group is the most important one. ...the chief guest of honour. You can say one person or thing is **chief** among others. Chief among their demands was the establishment of an independent television station. ■ If something is done **chiefly** in a particular way, it is done mainly that way. You can also say something is done **chiefly** in a particular place.

Chief Constable The **Chief Constable** of an area is the officer in charge of the police force.

Chief of Staff (**Chiefs of Staff**) The **Chiefs of Staff** are the highest-ranking officers of each service of the armed forces.

chieftain A **chieftain** is a tribal leader.

chiffon (pron: **shif**-fon) is a very thin silk or man-made fabric which you can see through.

chignon (pron: **sheen**-yon) A **chignon** is a knot of hair worn at the back of the head.

chihuahua (pron: chee-**wah**-wah) The **chihuahua** is a tiny short-haired dog with large pointed ears.

chilblain – **Chilblains** are painful or itchy red swellings on the fingers or toes caused by cold weather.

child (**children**) A **child** is (a) a human being who is not yet an adult. (b) a newborn or unborn baby. ■ If you say something is **child's play,** you mean it is very easy to do. ■ Your **children** are your sons and daughters. ■ If you say someone is the **child** of a particular time, you mean they were strongly influenced by what was going on then. ...a child of the Sixties.

childbearing is the process of giving birth.

childbirth is the act of giving birth.

childcare (or **child-care**) is the care provided by people like child-minders who look after children while their parents are at work.

childhood A person's **childhood** is the time when they were a child.

childish (**childishly; childishness**) A **childish** person behaves immaturely.

childminder (or **child-minder**) (**childminding**) A **childminder** is someone who is paid to use their own home to look after children. **Childminding** is the supervision and care given by a childminder.

childproof If something is **childproof,** it is designed so children cannot be harmed by it.

children's home A **children's home** is a place where children live if their parents cannot look after them properly.

chili See **chilli.**

chill (**chilling, chillingly; chilly, chillier, chilliest**) If you **chill** something, you lower its temperature without freezing it. ...*a chilled beer.* ■ If a room or the weather is **chill** or **chilly,** it is cold and unpleasant. When it is cold in a place, you can talk about the **chill** there. ■ If something **chills** you or gives you a **chill,** it makes you frightened or anxious. ...*a chillingly cold-blooded plan.* ■ If the relationship between two people **chills** or becomes **chilly,** it becomes less friendly. You can talk about a **chill** developing in a relationship. ■ If the response to something you do is **chilly,** it is not friendly or enthusiastic. ■ A **chill** is a mild illness which can give you a slight fever and headache.

chilli (*or* **chili**) (**chillies**) **Chillies** are the small hot-tasting red or green seed pods of a pepper plant, used to flavour food.

chill out If you **chill out,** you relax after doing something tiring or stressful. *When the pressure of being nice to everyone becomes too much, he'll run away to Australia and chill out for a while... After raves, we used to chill out in each others' bedrooms.*

chime (**chiming, chimed**) When bells or clocks **chime,** they make a series of deep ringing sounds. You can talk about the **chime** of a bell or clock. ■ If something new **chimes with** something which already exists, it fits in well with it.

chimera (*pron:* kime-**meer**-a) A **chimera** is an unrealistic hope. ■ In Greek mythology, a **chimera** was a fire-breathing monster with a lion's head, a goat's body, and a serpent's tail.

chimney A **chimney** is a hollow structure above a fireplace or furnace, for letting the smoke out.

chimney breast In a room, a **chimney breast** is a projecting part of a wall, built round a chimney.

chimney pot A **chimney pot** is a short pipe on top of a chimney stack.

chimney stack A **chimney stack** is the brick or stone part of a chimney on the roof of a building.

chimney sweep A **chimney sweep** is someone whose job is cleaning chimneys.

chimp A **chimp** is a chimpanzee.

chimpanzee – **Chimpanzees** are intelligent African apes with black or brown fur and large ears.

chin A person's **chin** is the part of their face below their mouth and above their neck. ■ If something unpleasant happens to you and you **take it on the chin,** you accept it bravely.

china is crockery made from a soft white clay called **china clay.**

chinchilla The **chinchilla** is a South American rodent with soft grey fur.

Chinese is used to talk about things to do with China or its people. ...*the Chinese authorities.* ■ **Chinese** is any of the main languages spoken in China, for example Mandarin or Cantonese. ■ The **Chinese** are the people who live in or come from China.

chink A **chink** is a very narrow opening. ■ A **chink** of light is a thin ray of light. ■ If someone has a **chink in their armour,** they have a small weakness which makes it easy for people to attack them.

chinless If you call someone **chinless,** you mean they are weak and cowardly.

chinos are trousers made out of a hardwearing cotton twill fabric.

chintz (**chintzy**) **Chintz** is a shiny cotton fabric with bright patterns on it. It is used for making curtains or covering chairs and cushions. **Chintzy** things are covered in chintz, or look like chintz.

chip (**chipping, chipped**) **Chips** are thin pieces of deep-fried potato. ■ In the US and Canada, **chips** are potato crisps. ■ A **chip** or **silicone chip** is a very small piece of silicone with electric circuits on it. ■ If something **chips** or is **chipped,** a small piece of it is broken off. **Chips** or **chippings** are small pieces broken off something. ■ If someone **chips away at** something, they gradually weaken it by removing small parts of it. ■ **Chips** are counters used in gambling to represent money. ■ You say **when the chips are down** when you are discussing how people will behave in a serious situation when there is a lot at stake. ■ When people **chip in,** they contribute money towards something. ■ In sports like golf or football, if a player **chips** the ball, they make it go high in the air and land a short distance away. A shot like this is called a **chip.** ■ If someone has a **chip on their shoulder,** they behave aggressively, because they feel they have been treated unfairly.

chipboard is a hard material made out of wood chips pressed together.

chipmunk The **chipmunk** is a small North American animal like a squirrel with a striped back.

chipolata A **chipolata** is a small sausage.

chiropody (**chiropodist**) **Chiropody** (*pron:* kir-**rop**-pod-y) is the professional care and treatment of people's feet by a person called a **chiropodist.**

chiropractic (*pron:* kire-oh-**prak**-tik) (**chiropractor**) **Chiropractic** is a system of treating things like back injuries by manipulating the spine. A person who does this is called a **chiropractor.**

chirp When a bird **chirps** or **chirrups,** it makes short high-pitched sounds.

chirpy people are cheerful and lively.

chirrup See **chirp.**

chisel (**chiselling, chiselled**) (**Am: chiseling, chiseled**) A **chisel** is a tool for cutting and shaping wood or stone. It has a long metal blade with a sharp straight edge at the tip. ■ If you **chisel** wood or stone, you cut and shape it with a chisel. ■ If someone has **chiselled** features, their features are sharply defined.

chit A **chit** is a short official note such as a receipt.

chit-chat is informal talk.

chitty (**chitties**) A **chitty** is a chit.

chivalrous (*pron:* shiv-val-russ) (**chivalry**) **Chivalrous** people are polite, kind, and unselfish. You call behaviour like this **chivalry.**

chives is a herb with long thin hollow leaves tasting of onions.

chivvy (chivvies, chivvying, chivvied) If you **chivvy** someone, you keep urging them to do something they do not want to do.

chloride A **chloride** is a compound of chlorine and another chemical element. *...potassium chloride.*

chlorine (chlorinated) Chlorine is a strong-smelling gas used to disinfect water and make cleaning products. ■ **Chlorinated** water has had chlorine added to it, to disinfect it.

chloroform is a colourless liquid with a strong sweet smell. You become unconscious if you breathe its vapour.

chlorophyll is a green substance in plants which enables them to use the energy from sunlight to grow. See also **photosynthesize.**

choc-ice A **choc-ice** is a small block of ice cream covered in chocolate.

chock A **chock** is a block or wedge used to stop a heavy object moving. ■ If a place is **chock-a-block,** it is very full. ■ If something is **chock-full** of things, it is very full.

chocolate is a sweet food made from cocoa beans. ■ **Chocolates** are sweets or nuts covered with chocolate. ■ **Hot chocolate** is a hot drink made from a powder containing chocolate. ■ **Chocolate** is a dark brown colour.

chocolate-box is used to describe scenery or pictures which are pretty in a rather conventional way. *...chocolate-box timbered houses.*

choice (choicest) You say there is a **choice** when there are at least two people or things you can choose from. Your **choice** is the one you choose. ■ **Choice** things are high quality. *...the choicest pubs.*

choir A **choir** is a group of people who sing together. ■ In a church or cathedral, the **choir** is the area in front of the altar where the choir sits.

choirboy (choirgirl) A **choirboy** is a boy who sings in a church choir.

choirmaster A **choirmaster** is a person whose job is to train a choir.

choirstall In a church, the **choirstalls** are the benches where the choir sits.

choke (choking, choked) If you **choke** or something **chokes** you, you cannot breathe properly because something is blocking your windpipe. ■ If someone **chokes** someone else, they squeeze their neck until they die. ■ If something **chokes** something else **off,** it stops it happening. ■ If a place is **choked** with people or things, it is full of them and nothing can move. ■ If you are **choked** about something, you are angry, upset, or disappointed. ■ The **choke** in a car is a device which reduces the amount of air going into the engine, making it easier to start.

choker A **choker** is a close-fitting necklace.

cholera (*pron:* **kol**-ler-a) is a serious and often fatal disease affecting the small intestine, usually caught by drinking infected water.

choleric (*pron:* **kol**-ler-rik) A **choleric** person is angry or bad-tempered.

cholesterol (*pron:* kol-**lest**-er-oll) is a substance in the tissues and blood of all animals. Too much cholesterol in your blood can cause heart disease.

chomp If someone **chomps** their food, they chew it noisily.

choose (choosing, chose, have chosen) If you **choose** a person or thing, you decide which one you want from a range of people or things. ■ If there is **not much to choose between** things, it is difficult to decide which is best. ■ If you talk about the **chosen few,** you mean a group of people who are special or important in some way. ■ If you **choose** to do something, you do it because you want to or feel it is right.

choosy A **choosy** person will only accept something if it is exactly right or of very high quality.

chop (chopping, chopped) If you **chop** something, you cut it by hitting it with a sharp tool like an axe. ■ If you **chop** food, you cut it into small pieces. ■ If something is **for the chop,** it is going to be stopped or closed down. ■ If people **chop and change,** they keep changing their minds about what to do or how to act. ■ A **chop** is a small piece of meat cut from the ribs of a sheep or pig.

chopper A **chopper** is (a) an axe. (b) a helicopter.

choppy When water is **choppy,** there are a lot of small waves on it.

chopsticks are a pair of thin sticks used for eating food by people in the Far East.

choral music is sung by a choir.

chorale (*pron:* kor-**rahl**) A **chorale** is a slow stately hymn tune.

chord (*pron:* **kord**) A **chord** is three or more different musical notes played or sung at the same time with a pleasing effect. ■ If something **strikes a chord** with you, you respond to it with feelings of sympathy and understanding.

chore A **chore** is a tedious or unpleasant task.

choreograph (choreography, choreographer, choreographic) If someone **choreographs** (*pron:* **kor**-ee-o-grafs) a ballet or other dance, they invent the steps and movements and tell the dancers how to perform them. *...her choreographic work.* ■ When something looks spontaneous but has actually been carefully planned, you can say it is **choreographed.**

chorister (*rhymes with 'forester'*) A **chorister** is a singer in a church choir.

chortle (chortling, chortled) If you **chortle,** you laugh with pleasure or amusement.

chorus (choruses, chorusing, chorused) A **chorus** is a large group of people who sing together. *...the City of Birmingham Symphony Orchestra and Chorus.* ■ In a show, the **chorus** are the people who sing or dance in a group, rather than the soloists. ■ A **chorus** is a piece of music written to be sung by a large group of people. ■ The **chorus** of a song is the part repeated after each verse. ■ When there is a **chorus** of disapproval or praise, that attitude is expressed by a lot of people at the same time. ■ If a group of people **chorus** something, they all say it at the same time.

chorus girl A **chorus girl** is a young woman who sings and dances in the chorus of a show.

chose (chosen) See **choose.**

chow The **chow** is a thick-coated dog with a curled tail, originally from China.

Christ See **Jesus.**

christen (christening, christened) When a baby is **christened,** it is given Christian names during the Christian ceremony of baptism. ■ If you **christen** a place or thing, you choose a name for it. ■ You say you **christen** something new when you use it for the first time, especially if you do something special to mark the occasion.

Christendom is all the Christian people and countries in the world.

Christian (Christianity) A **Christian** is someone who believes in Jesus Christ and follows his teachings. The religion based on Jesus and his teachings is called **Christianity.** ■ **Christian** is used to describe things connected with Christianity.

Christian name Some people call their first names **Christian names.**

Christian Science (Christian Scientist) **Christian Science** is a type of Christianity which emphasizes the use of prayer to cure illness.

Christmas (Christmases) **Christmas** is the Christian festival celebrating the birth of Jesus Christ.

Christmas Day is December 25th, when Christmas is celebrated.

Christmas Eve is December 24th.

Christmas pudding A **Christmas pudding** is a special round pudding eaten at Christmas, made of dried fruit, spices, and suet.

Christmas tree A **Christmas tree** is a fir tree, or an artificial tree which looks like a fir tree. People have decorated Christmas trees in their houses during Christmas.

chrome is metal plated with chromium.

chromium is a hard shiny metallic element used to make steel alloys and to coat other metals.

chromosome The **chromosomes** are the parts in an animal or plant cell which contain the genes.

chronic (chronically) A **chronic** illness lasts for a very long time. ■ You call someone's bad habits or behaviour **chronic** when they have behaved like that for a long time and do not seem able to stop. ■ A **chronic** situation is severe and unpleasant.

chronic fatigue syndrome (or **CFS**) is a serious condition that can occur after a viral illness. It makes your muscles very sore and you feel exceptionally tired.

chronicle (chronicling, chronicled; chronicler) A **chronicle** is a formal record of a series of happenings. ■ If you **chronicle** things, you write about them in the order in which they happen.

chronological (chronologically; chronology) If you describe a series of events in **chronological** order, you describe them in the order in which they happen. A **chronology** of past events is a list of them in the order in which they happened, giving their times or dates.

chrysalis (chrysalises) A **chrysalis** is a butterfly or moth in the stage between a larva and a fully grown adult. A chrysalis has a hard protective covering, and does not move.

chrysanthemum – **Chrysanthemums** are flo with a lot of long thin petals.

chub The **chub** is a fish of the carp family.

chubby (chubbier, chubbiest) A **chubby** person is rather fat.

chuck If you **chuck** something somewhere, you throw it there. ■ If you **chuck** something **away** or **chuck** it **out,** you throw it away. ■ If you **chuck** a person **out** of a job or place, you force them to leave. ■ If you **chuck in** your job or some other activity, you stop doing it.

chuckle (chuckling, chuckled) If you **chuckle** or give a **chuckle,** you laugh quietly.

chuffed If you feel **chuffed,** you feel pleased about something.

chug (chugging, chugged) If a vehicle **chugs** somewhere, it moves along slowly, making short thudding sounds. ■ If an activity **chugs along,** it continues steadily and uneventfully.

chum (chummy) Someone's **chums** are their friends. If someone is **chummy,** they are friendly.

chunk (chunky) A **chunk** of something solid is a large piece of it. ■ A **chunk** is a large part of something. *...a big chunk of my mortgage.* ■ A **chunky** person or thing is large and heavy.

chunter (chuntering, chuntered) You say someone **chunters on** about something when they keep grumbling or muttering about it.

church (churches) A **church** is a building where Christians worship. **Church** is used to talk about the services held in a church. *We always went to church.* ■ A **Church** is one of the groups of people within the Christian religion, for example Methodists, who have their own particular beliefs. ■ The **Church** is the people who have authority in a Church and who decide what its doctrines are.

churchgoer A **churchgoer** is someone who goes to church regularly.

churchman (churchmen) A **churchman** is the same as a clergyman.

Church of England The **Church of England** is the Anglican church in England. Its head is the Queen. 'Church of England' is often shortened to 'C of E'.

churchwarden In the Anglican church, a **churchwarden** is someone chosen by the congregation to help the vicar with administration.

churchyard A **churchyard** is an area of land around a church, often used as a graveyard.

churlish people are unfriendly and bad-tempered.

churn A **churn** is a container for milk, or one in which milk is made into butter. ■ If something **churns** mud or water it stirs it up violently. *The recent rain had churned up the waterfall into a muddy whirlpool.* ■ If your stomach **churns,** you feel sick, because something has upset you. *...stomach-churning atrocities.* ■ If a person or factory **churns out,** they produce large numbers of them.

chute A **chute** is a steep narrow slope for people or things to slide down. ■ A **chute** is a parachute.

chutney is a relish made from fruit, vinegar, sugar, and spices.

chutzpah (pron: hoots-pa, to rhyme with foot-spa) If someone behaves with **chutzpah,** they do things boldly and impudently.

CIA The **CIA** is the US government agency responsible for espionage and intelligence activities. CIA is short for 'Central Intelligence Agency'.

cicada (pron: sik-**kah**-da) **Cicadas** are large insects which live in hot countries. They make a loud high-pitched noise.

CID The **CID** is the detective branch of the British police force. CID is short for 'Criminal Investigation Department'.

cider is an alcoholic drink which is made from fermented apples.

cigar – **Cigars** are rolls of dried tobacco leaves which people smoke.

cigarette – **Cigarettes** are small tubes of paper with tobacco inside which people smoke.

cigarette holder A **cigarette holder** is a narrow tube for smoking a cigarette through.

cigarette paper A **cigarette paper** is a thin piece of paper which you put tobacco on and roll into a tube to make a cigarette.

cinch (pron: **sinch**) If you say something **is a cinch,** you mean it is easy to do.

cinder – **Cinders** are the small pieces of blackened material left after coal has burned.

Cinderella If you say someone or something is a **Cinderella,** you mean they are neglected. *Cycling is the cinderella sport in this country.*

cine camera (pron: **sin**-ee) A **cine camera** is a camera which takes moving film rather than still photographs.

cinema (**cinematic**) A **cinema** is a place where people go to watch films. ■ **Cinema** is the business and art of making films. **Cinematic** means to do with films.

cinemagoer A **cinemagoer** is someone who goes to the cinema regularly.

cinematography (**cinematographer**) **Cinematography** is the technique of photographing films for the cinema. A **cinematographer** is a person who is skilled in this technique.

cinnamon is a sweet spice used for flavouring food.

cipher (or **cypher**) A **cipher** is a secret system of writing. ■ If you say a person is a **cipher,** you mean they have no real power or importance.

circa is used to show you are giving an approximate date. 'Circa' can be shortened to 'c.' *...circa 1910.*

circle (**circling, circled**) A **circle** is a flat, perfectly symmetrical round shape. Every part of its edge is the same distance from its centre. ■ A **circle** of people or things is a group of them arranged in the shape of a circle. ■ If one thing is **circled** by another, the second thing is arranged in a circle around the first. ■ If a bird or aircraft **circles,** it flies in a circle. ■ If you **circle** something on a piece of paper, you draw a circle round it. ■ If you are **going around in circles,** you are not achieving anything because you keep coming back to the same point. ■ A **circle** of people is a group of them with the same interest or profession. ■ In a theatre, the **circle** is an area of seats on an upper floor. ■ **full circle:** see **full.**

circuit (**circuitry**) An electrical **circuit** is a complete route which an electric current can flow around. **Circuitry** is a system of electronic circuits. ■ A **cir-**cuit is a series of places visited regularly by a person or group for a particular purpose, for example to play a sport. *...the most promising young players on the international circuit.* ■ A **circuit** is a journey all the way around a place or area. *...a 500-mile circuit of the Ulster Way.* ■ A racing **circuit** is a track on which cars or motorbikes race.

circuit breaker A **circuit breaker** is a safety device which stops the flow of electricity around a circuit if anything goes wrong.

circuitous (pron: sir-**kew**-it-uss) If you go somewhere by a **circuitous** route, you go there by a long indirect route.

circular (**circularity**) **Circular** is used to describe (a) things shaped like a circle. (b) things which go round in a circle. ■ A **circular** argument or process gets nowhere because it keeps returning to the same point. *There is a dreary circularity about the campaign.* ■ If you make a **circular** journey, you go somewhere then return by a different route. ■ A **circular** is a letter or advertisement sent to a large number of people at the same time.

circulate (**circulating, circulated; circulation, circulatory**) When you **circulate** something among people, you pass it round or tell it to all the people. ■ The **circulation** of a newspaper or magazine is the number of copies sold each time it is produced. ■ If a substance **circulates,** it moves around within a closed place or system. *...immune cells circulating in the blood.* ■ A person's **circulation** is the movement of blood around their body. **Circulatory** (pron: sir-kew-**late**-tor-ree) means to do with the circulation of the blood. ■ When money **circulates** or is in **circulation,** it is in use by the public.

circumcise (**circumcising, circumcised; circumcision**) If a man is **circumcised,** the loose skin is cut off the end of his penis. If a woman is **circumcised,** part or all of her clitoris is removed; the entrance to her vagina may also be sewn together. **Circumcision** is an operation in which someone's genitals are cut in one of these ways.

circumference The **circumference** of a circle, place, or round object is its outer edge, or the distance around this edge.

circumflex The **circumflex** is a symbol sometimes written over 'a', 'e', 'i', 'o', or 'u' in French and some other languages, usually to show the letter should be pronounced with a longer sound than usual, as in 'château'.

circumlocution A **circumlocution** is a way of saying or writing something using more words than necessary, instead of being clear and direct.

circumnavigate (**circumnavigating, circumnavigated; circumnavigation**) If you **circumnavigate** something, you sail right round it.

circumscribe (**circumscribing, circumscribed**) If something like a person's power is **circumscribed,** it is limited.

circumspect (**circumspection**) If someone is **circumspect,** they are cautious. **Circumspection** is cautious behaviour.

circumstance – **Circumstances** are the conditions in which something happens or is done. *The referee* *did a reasonable job in difficult circumstances.* ■ The **circumstances** of an event are the way it happened or the causes of it. *...the circumstances of the accident.* ■ You say **in the circumstances** or **under the circumstances** to show you have considered everything affecting a situation. ■ You can use **under any circumstances** to emphasize that something will not or must not happen. *Don't under any circumstances buy it.* ■ A person's **circumstances** are the conditions they live in. ■ **Circumstance** is things which happen which have not been planned and cannot be controlled. *...victims of circumstance.*

circumstantial evidence makes it seem likely that something happened, but does not prove it.

circumvent (**circumvention**) If someone **circumvents** a rule or restriction, they get round it.

circus (**circuses**) A **circus** is a travelling show performed in a large tent, with acts like clowns and acrobats. ■ If you call an event like a meeting a **circus,** you mean it is put on to attract attention or impress people, rather than to achieve anything.

cirrhosis (*pron:* sir-**roh**-siss) is a serious liver disease, often caused by drinking too much alcohol.

cirrus is a type of thin cloud very high in the sky.

cissy (**cissies**) See **sissy.**

cistern A **cistern** is a container which holds water, for example to flush a toilet.

citadel A **citadel** is a strongly fortified building in a city.

cite (**citing, cited; citation**) If you **cite** something, you quote or mention it as an example or proof of what you are saying. *Most families can cite a tragedy caused by drink.* ■ A **citation** from a book is a quotation from it. ■ If someone is **cited** in a legal case, they are officially named or requested to appear in court. ■ A **citation** is an official document praising a person for something they have done.

citizen (**citizenship; citizenry**) If someone is a **citizen** of a country or has **citizenship** of it, they are legally accepted as belonging to it. ■ The **citizens** of a town are the people who live there; they can also be called its **citizenry.** ■ **Citizenship** is belonging to a community and being prepared to take on the responsibilities of being part of it.

Citizens' Band See **CB.**

citric acid is a weak acid found in many kinds of fruit, especially citrus fruits.

citrus fruits are juicy sharp-tasting fruit like oranges and lemons.

city (**cities**) A **city** is a large town. ■ **The City** is the part of London where many financial institutions have their main offices. People often call this group of institutions **the City.**

civic (**civics**) **Civic** is used to talk about people or things with an official or important status in a town or city. *...civic and business leaders.* ■ **Civic** is used to describe people's duties, rights, or feelings as members of a community. *...civic pride.* ■ **Civics** is the study of central and local government, and the rights and duties of citizens.

civil (**civility**) **Civil** is used to describe (a) people or things in a country which are not connected with its armed forces. *...civil aviation.* (b) things connected with the state rather than a religion.

They were married in a civil ceremony by the mayor. ■ If someone is **civil,** they are polite, but not very friendly; you call their behaviour **civility.**

civil defence is the organization and training of ordinary people so they can help the armed forces and emergency services if their country is attacked.

civil disobedience A campaign of **civil disobedience** involves ordinary people protesting against a law they consider unjust by refusing to obey it.

civil engineering (**civil engineer**) **Civil engineering** is the planning, design, and construction of roads, bridges, harbours, and public buildings.

civilian A **civilian** is anyone who is not a member of the armed forces.

civilize (*Am:* **civilise**) (**civilizing, civilized; civilization**) A **civilized** society is one with a highly developed culture and social system. Societies which have these things are called **civilizations.** ■ **Civilized** behaviour is polite and reasonable. ■ You say a way of doing things is **civilized** when it is well-arranged for people's comfort or convenience. *...after a very civilized dinner.*

civil law is the part of a country's set of laws concerned with the private affairs of citizens. It deals with things like marriage and property ownership. See also **criminal law.**

civil liberties are the rights people have in many countries to do and say what they like, provided they respect other people's rights.

civil list The **civil list** is the money paid by the state each year to members of the Royal Family to cover their living expenses.

civil rights are rights to such things as equal treatment and equal opportunities, regardless of race, sex, or religion.

Civil Service (**civil servant**) A country's **Civil Service** is its government departments and the people who work in them. **Civil servants** are people who work in the Civil Service.

civil war A **civil war** is fought between groups of people living in the same country.

civvies People like soldiers often call clothes which are not part of their uniform **civvies.**

CJD is a fatal disease that affects the central nervous system, leading to a loss of mental capacity and coordination of the limbs. CJD stands for 'Creutzfeldt-Jakob Disease'.

clack If something **clacks**, it makes a short loud sound, like the sound of two flat pieces of wood being struck together.

clad (**-clad, cladding**) If you are **clad** in particular clothes, you are wearing them. *...leather-clad cowboys.* ■ You use **-clad** to say an area is covered with things like trees. *...birch-clad mountains.* ■ If a building is **clad** with stone, wooden boards, or other materials, its exterior is covered with them to protect it against bad weather or to improve its appearance. This covering is called **cladding.**

claim (**claiming, claimed; claimant**) You say someone **claims** something is true when they say it is true but you cannot be certain they are correct. ■ If someone **claims** responsibility for something, they say they were responsible for it. ■ If you **claim** something like property or money, or **lay claim to**

it, you say it legally belongs to you. ■ If you **claim** money from someone like the government or an insurance company, you officially apply for it, because you think you are entitled to it. ■ A **claimant** is a person who asks to be given something they think they are entitled to. ■ If you have a **claim** on someone, you have the right to demand things from them. ■ If something like a war **claims** someone's life, they are killed in it.

clairvoyance (**clairvoyant**) **Clairvoyance** is the ability some people claim to have to see into the future or communicate with dead people. A **clairvoyant** is someone who claims to have this ability.

clam (**clamming, clammed**) **Clams** are edible shellfish with a shell in two parts which can close very tightly. ■ If someone **clams up,** they refuse to talk about something.

clamber (**clambering, clambered**) If you **clamber** somewhere, you climb there with difficulty.

clammy things are unpleasantly damp and sticky.

clamour (*Am:* **clamor**) (**clamouring, clamoured; clamorous**) If people **clamour** for something, they demand it noisily or angrily. You can talk about the **clamour** for something. ■ If people are talking or shouting together loudly, you can say they are making a **clamour. Clamorous** sounds are very noisy.

clamp A **clamp** is a device for holding two things together firmly. If you **clamp** one thing to another, you fasten them together. ■ If your car is **clamped,** a wheel clamp is fitted to one of its wheels to stop you driving away until you have paid a fee. ■ If you **clamp** something somewhere, you put or hold it there firmly. *The animal clamped its jaws on his left hand.* ■ When people in power **clamp down** on something, they stop it or restrict it. You call their action a **clampdown.** ■ If a restriction is **clamped** on a place, it is imposed on it.

clampdown (*or* **clamp down**) See **clamp.**

clan A **clan** is a group of families all descended from the same person, especially in Scotland.

clandestine (**clandestinely**) **Clandestine** things are hidden or secret.

clang When large metal objects **clang** or make a **clang,** they make a long loud noise by banging together or against something hard.

clanger If you **drop a clanger,** you do or say something embarrassing.

clank When metal objects **clank,** they make a loud noise by banging together or against something hard.

clap (**clapping, clapped**) When you **clap,** you hit your hands together to show your appreciation. ■ If you **clap** someone on the back, you hit them with the palm of your hand in a friendly way. ■ If you **clap** an object somewhere, you put it there quickly and firmly. ■ A **clap** of thunder is a sudden loud burst of it.

clapboard consists of long narrow pieces of wood fixed onto the roof or outside walls of a house to protect it from the weather.

clapped-out If you say a person or machine is **clapped-out,** you mean they are old and worn out.

clapperboard A **clapperboard** is a device used by film makers to match the pictures and sound. It is made of two pieces of wood connected by a hinge with the scene number written on it and is banged together just before a scene.

claptrap If you call what someone says **claptrap,** you mean it is stupid or silly.

claque A **claque** is a group of people who all admire, support, and flatter someone in a position of power.

claret is a type of French red wine.

clarify (**clarifies, clarifying, clarified; clarification**) If you **clarify** something, you make it easier to understand. ■ **Clarified** butter has been heated to remove impurities from it.

clarinet (**clarinettist**) A **clarinet** is a woodwind instrument with a single reed in its mouthpiece.

clarion A **clarion call** is a strong emotional appeal to people to do something.

clarity If you talk about the **clarity** of something like a statement, you mean it is easy to understand. ■ **Clarity** of thought is the ability to think clearly. ■ You can talk about the **clarity** of things which you can see or hear clearly.

clash (**clashes, clashing, clashed**) If people **clash** or there is a **clash** between them, they fight or argue. ■ In sport, when people compete against each other, you can say they **clash.** ■ If there is a **clash** of beliefs or systems, they contradict each other. *...clashing legal systems.* ■ If two events **clash,** they happen at the same time, so you cannot go to both. ■ If colours or styles **clash,** they do not look good together. ■ A **clash** is a loud noise made by metal objects being hit together.

clasp If you **clasp** someone or something, you hold them tightly. ■ A **clasp** is a small device for fastening something or holding it shut.

class (**classes, classing, classed**) A **class** is a group of pupils being taught together. If something is done **in class,** it is done during lessons. ■ A **class** is a short period of regular teaching given in a subject. *...an aerobics class.* ■ **Class** is used to talk about the division of people according to their social status. ■ A **class** of things is a group of them with similar characteristics. *I would class my garden as medium in size.* ■ **-class** is added to words like 'first' and 'second' to talk about things of a particular standard. *...business-class fares.* ■ In Britain, university degrees are graded into **classes.** *...a first class honours degree.*

classic (**classicist**) A **classic** example of something has all the features you expect that kind of thing to have. *It was a classic case of turning a hobby into a business.* ■ A **classic** is a well-known book of a high literary standard. ■ A **classic** film, piece of music, or piece of writing is of high quality and has become a standard against which similar things are judged. *...his classic book on economic management. ...one of the classics of modern popular music.* ■ **Classic** clothes are simple but elegant, and never go out of fashion. ■ **Classic** cars are cars which are no longer made, but are still admired and collected. ■ **Classics** is the study of ancient Greek and

Roman civilization. Someone who studies these things is called a **classicist** (*pron:* **klass**-iss-sist).

classical (**classically**) **Classical** is used to describe things which are well established in form, style, or content. ...*classical ballet.* ■ **Classical** music is music written by composers like Bach and Sibelius. ■ **Classical** is used to talk about (a) things connected with ancient Greek and Roman civilization. ...*classical Greek sculptures.* (b) architecture which imitates Greek or Roman buildings.

classicism (*pron:* **klass**-iss-iz-um) is a style of art and architecture which has simple regular forms and in which the artist does not try to express strong emotions. It is associated especially with the 18th century in Europe.

classify (**classifies, classifying, classified; classification**) If you **classify** people and things, you group them so that those with similar characteristics are together. A **classification** is a system of this kind. ■ **Classified** advertisements are small advertisements placed in newspapers and magazines by people wanting to buy or sell things. ■ **Classified** information is kept secret by a government.

classless (**classlessness**) When people talk about a **classless** society, they mean one where everyone has the same social and economic status. ...*a move towards classlessness.* ■ A **classless** person is one who does not belong to any particular social class.

classmate A schoolchild's **classmates** are the other students in the same class.

classroom A **classroom** is a room in a school where lessons take place. **In the classroom** is used to talk about things to do with teaching and lessons. ...*the increase of pupil violence in the classroom.* ■ A **classroom teacher** is one who spends most of his or her time teaching, rather than doing administrative duties like a head teacher.

classy (**classier, classiest**) You can say people or things are **classy** when you think they are stylish and sophisticated.

clatter (**clattering, clattered**) If something **clatters** or makes a **clatter,** it makes a series of short loud noises.

clause A **clause** is a section of a legal document. ■ A **clause** is a group of words containing a verb.

claustrophobia (**claustrophobic**) **Claustrophobia** is a fear of being in enclosed places. Someone who has this fear is called a **claustrophobic.** ■ If you call a place or situation **claustrophobic,** you mean it makes you feel restricted or anxious.

clavichord (*pron:* **klav**-vi-kord) A **clavichord** is an instrument similar to a small piano, in which wires are hit by pieces of metal when the keys are pressed. Clavichords were especially popular before the piano was invented.

clavicle The **clavicle** is the same as the collarbone.

claw The **claws** of a bird or animal are the thin curved nails on its feet. ■ The **claws** of a lobster, crab, or scorpion are the two pointed parts at the end of its legs, which it uses for grasping things. ■ If an animal **claws** something, it scratches or damages it with its claws. ■ If you **claw back** money or power you had lost, you get it back using

whatever methods are available. Getting back money like this is called a **clawback.**

clay is a substance found in the ground which is soft when wet and hard when dry. It is used to make things like pots. ■ **feet of clay:** see **foot.**

clay pigeon A **clay pigeon** is a baked clay disc used as a shooting target. It is launched into the air by a machine.

clean (**cleaner, cleanest; cleaning, cleaned; cleanly**) If something is **clean,** it is free from dirt, mess, or contamination. If you **clean** something, you make it clean. ■ You say people or animals are **clean** when they keep themselves or their surroundings clean. ■ If a game or contest is played fairly. ■ If someone has a **clean** record, they have never been convicted of committing a crime. ■ If the police or other authorities **clean up** a place or activity, they make it free from crime. ■ If you **come clean** about something you have been keeping secret, you admit to it. ■ If you are **cleaned out,** all your money or possessions are taken. ■ A **clean** movement is skilful and accurate. *He jumped neatly and cleanly.*

clean-cut A **clean-cut** man looks neat and tidy.

cleaner A **cleaner** is someone paid to clean the inside of a building. Other people who clean things for a living have **cleaner** as part of the name of their job. ...*street cleaners.* ■ A **cleaner** is (a) a substance for cleaning things. ...*household cleaners.* (b) a device for cleaning. ■ If someone **takes** you **to the cleaners,** they take all your money or possessions away from you unfairly.

cleanliness (*pron:* **klen**-lee-ness) is the degree to which you keep yourself and your surroundings clean. *Many beaches fail to meet minimum standards of cleanliness.*

cleanse (**cleansing, cleansed; cleanser**) If you **cleanse** your skin or a wound, you clean it, often using a liquid called a **cleanser.** ■ If someone **cleanses** something like an organization, they get rid of the bad elements in it.

clean-shaven A **clean-shaven** man has no beard or moustache.

clear (**clearing, cleared; clearly**) If something is **clear,** it is easy to see, hear, or understand. ■ If you are **clear** about something, you understand it properly. ■ If you **clear up** a problem or disagreement, you settle it. ■ If it is **clear** that something is true, it is obviously true. ■ If the weather is **clear,** there is no rain, mist, or cloud. ■ A **clear** substance is one you can see through. ■ If a place is **clear,** it is free from obstructions or unwanted things. If you **clear** a place, you remove things like these from it. You also say you **clear up** a place, **clear** things **away,** or have a **clear-out.** ■ If a person or animal **clears** a fence, wall, or hedge, they jump over it without touching it. ■ If two or more things are **clear** of each other, they are not touching. *The tractor towed a truck clear of the highway.* ■ If someone in authority **clears** something like a plan, they say it can go ahead. ■ If someone is **cleared** of a crime or mistake, they are proved to be not guilty of it. ■ **clear the air:** see **air. clear the way:** see **way. clear the decks:** see **deck.**

clearance is used to talk about the removal of unwanted buildings or other things from an area. *The job of mine detection and clearance is a massive one.* ■ If a shop holds a **clearance sale,** its goods are sold off cheaply to make room for new stock. ■ If you are given **clearance** to do something, you get official permission.

clear-cut things are straightforward.

clear-headed people are sensible and think clearly in difficult situations.

clearing See **clear.** ■ A **clearing** is a small area of bare ground in a wood.

clearing bank In Britain, a **clearing bank** is one which handles the finances of companies and individuals and is a member of the London Bankers' Clearing House.

clearing house A **clearing house** is (a) an organization which collects, sorts, and distributes specialized information. (b) a central bank which deals with all the transactions between the banks which use its services, for example exchanging cheques.

clear-out See **clear.**

clear-sighted A **clear-sighted** person is good at weighing up people and situations.

cleavage A woman's **cleavage** is the space between her breasts.

cleave (**cleaving, cleaved**) (*'clove' can be used instead of 'cleaved' and 'have cleft' instead of 'have cleaved'*) If you **cleave** something, you split it in two.

cleaver A **cleaver** is a knife with a large square blade for chopping meat or vegetables.

clef A **clef** is a symbol at the beginning of a line of music showing the range of notes. There are several clefs, the most common being the treble clef for high notes, and the bass clef for low notes.

cleft See **cleave.** ■ A **cleft palate** is a narrow opening along the roof of the mouth which makes it difficult to speak properly. ■ A **cleft lip** is a harelip.

clematis (*pron:* **klem**-mat-tiss *or* klem-**mate**-iss) is a climbing plant with purple, pink, or white flowers.

clemency If someone is shown **clemency,** they receive merciful treatment from those with the authority to punish them.

clementine A **clementine** is a small citrus fruit similar to a tangerine.

clench (**clenches, clenching, clenched**) If you **clench** your fist, you curl your fingers up tightly. ■ If you **clench** your teeth, you squeeze them firmly together.

clergy The **clergy** are the religious leaders of a Christian church. Leaders of other churches are sometimes called **clergy.** *...Buddhist clergy.*

clergyman (**clergymen**) A **clergyman** is a male member of the clergy.

cleric A **cleric** is a member of the clergy.

clerical means to do with the clergy. *...anti-clerical slogans.* ■ **Clerical** is used to talk about routine office jobs and the people who do them.

clerk A **clerk** is someone who works in an office, bank, or law court and looks after things like records or accounts. ■ In the US, a **clerk** is a sales assistant or hotel receptionist.

clever (**cleverer, cleverest; cleverly, cleverness**) A **clever** person is intelligent, and can learn and understand things easily. ■ If someone is **clever** at something which requires expertise, they are good at it. ■ You say someone is **clever** when they are good at handling people and situations, especially to their own advantage. ■ If you say something is **clever,** you mean it is skilfully done or made, and very effective. *...a clever compromise.*

cliché (*pron:* **klee**-shay) (**clichéd**) A **cliché** is a phrase or idea which has been used so much it no longer has any real effect. You can say something which is full of clichés is **clichéd.**

click If something **clicks,** it makes a short sharp sound. This sound is called a **click.** ■ If you **click** on your mouse when you are using your computer, you are pressing and releasing its button so you can select a particular function on your machine. ■ When you suddenly understand something, you can say it **clicks.**

client A **client** of a professional person or organization is someone they are providing a service for.

clientele (*pron:* klee-on-**tell**) The **clientele** of a business are its customers or clients.

cliff A **cliff** is a place where the land falls away suddenly and very steeply, often down to the sea.

cliff-hanger (*or* **cliffhanger**) (**cliff-hanging**) If you call a situation a **cliffhanger,** you mean it is very exciting, because you are left for a long time not knowing what is going to happen next. A **cliff-hanging** situation is like this.

climactic is used to describe a very exciting or important moment in something like an event, story, or piece of music. *...the climactic ballroom scene.*

climate (**climatic**) The **climate** of a place is the typical weather conditions there. **Climatic** is used to talk about things to do with a place's climate. *...climatic changes.* ■ **Climate** is used to talk about some aspect of the general situation in a place. *...changes in the political climate.*

climatologist A **climatologist** is someone who studies climates.

climax (**climaxes**) The **climax** of something like an experience, series of events, or story is the most exciting or important part, usually near the end. You can say something **climaxes** with a particular happening. ■ A **climax** is an orgasm.

climb (**climber**) If you **climb** something, you move towards the top, often with some effort or difficulty. Climbing something can be called a **climb.** ■ **Climbing** is the sport of climbing mountains; a person who does it is called a **climber.** A **climb** is a route up a mountain. ■ If you **climb** over or through something, you get over or through it with difficulty. ■ If a road **climbs,** it moves gradually towards a higher position. ■ A **climber** or **climbing** plant is one which grows upwards, attaching itself to other plants or objects. ■ If something like inflation **climbs** it rises. This rise is called a **climb.** ■ In a dispute, if you **climb down,** you admit you are wrong, or agree to accept less than you were insisting on. Doing this is called a **climbdown.**

climbing frame A **climbing frame** is a structure of metal or wooden bars for children to play on.

clime is used to talk about a place with a particular type of climate. *...the sunnier climes of Antigua.*

clinch (clinches, clinching; clincher) If you **clinch** something like a victory or business deal, you succeed in getting it. ■ If something uncertain is **clinched**, it is settled in a definite way. ...*the clinching argument.* ■ A **clincher** is something which decides something which had been uncertain. *DNA fingerprinting has proved the clincher in many criminal and other forensic identifications.*

cling (clinging, clung, have clung) If you **cling** to someone or something, you hold onto them tightly. ■ If a village is built on the side of a mountain, you can say it **clings** to it. ■ **Clinging** clothes fit tightly around the body. ■ If you **cling** to something such as a belief, you are unwilling to give it up. ■ If someone **clings on** to a lead in a contest, they just succeed in maintaining it.

clingfilm (or **cling film**) is a thin transparent plastic material for wrapping food in to keep it fresh.

clinic A **clinic** is a place where people get medical treatment.

clinical (clinically, clinician) Clinical is used to talk about the medical treatment of patients, as opposed to research done in a laboratory. ...*clinical trials... The next stage is to test it clinically.* ■ **Clinical** is used to describe a doctor, psychologist, or psychiatrist who deals with patients, as opposed to doing theoretical research. ...*a clinical neurologist.* A person like this can also be called a **clinician.** ■ **Clinical** behaviour is very logical and unemotional. ■ If you call a room **clinical,** you mean it is very plain, or so neat and clean that people do not enjoy being in it.

clink If glass or metal objects **clink,** they touch each other and make a short light sound. ■ If you **clink** glasses with someone, you touch their glass with yours before drinking.

clip (clipping, clipped) A **clip** of film is a short piece shown by itself. ■ If you **clip** something like hair, you cut small pieces from it. **Clipped** things such as a hedge are neatly trimmed. ■ **Clippings** are small pieces of something that have been cut from something larger. ...*grass clippings. ...newspaper clippings.* ■ If you **clip** a small amount off something, you reduce it by that amount. ■ If you **clip** someone's **wings,** you restrict their freedom to do what they want. ■ A **clip** is a small metal or plastic device for holding things together. If you **clip** one thing to another, you fasten it with a clip. ■ If you **clip** someone or give them a **clip,** you hit them lightly with your hand. You can also **clip** an object with part of your body, especially accidentally. ■ If someone has a **clipped** way of speaking, their speech comes out as a series of short quick sounds.

clipboard A **clipboard** is a board with a clip at the top for holding together pieces of paper and providing a firm base to write on.

clipper – **Clippers** are a tool for cutting small amounts from something, for example someone's nails. ■ A **clipper** was a fast sailing ship.

clique (pron: **kleek**) A **clique** is a small group of people who spend a lot of time together and seem unfriendly towards other people.

clitoris (clitoral) A woman's **clitoris** is the small sensitive sexual organ above her vagina. **Clitoral** means relating to the clitoris. ...*clitoral stimulation.*

Cllr. in front of a person's name means 'Councillor'.

cloak (cloaking, cloaked) A **cloak** is a wide loose sleeveless coat which fastens at the throat. ■ If one thing **cloaks** another, it hides it. Something which is intended to hide the truth can be called a **cloak.** ■ If something is **cloaked** in something, it is covered with it. *The coastline was cloaked in mist.*

cloak-and-dagger situations involve a lot of mystery and secrecy.

cloakroom The **cloakroom** is a place where you can leave your coat. ■ Toilets are sometimes called **cloakrooms.**

clobber (clobbering, clobbered) You can refer to someone's belongings, especially their clothes, as their **clobber.** ■ If you are **clobbered** by something, you come off badly as a result of it. *Trading has been clobbered by the recession.* ■ If you **clobber** someone, you hit them.

cloche (pron: **klosh**) A **cloche** is a long low plastic or glass cover, put over young plants to protect them from the cold. ■ A **cloche** was a close-fitting woman's hat worn in the 1920s and 1930s.

clock A **clock** is an instrument which tells you the time. ■ In a car, the **clock** is the instrument which shows the speed of the car and its mileage. ■ A **clock** or **time clock** is (a) a device which makes things happen automatically at preset times. (b) a device in a workplace which is used to record the hours that people work. ■ When workers **clock in** or **clock on** at their workplace, they record the time they arrive, by putting a special card into a time clock. When they finish work, they **clock off** or **clock out.** ■ If someone or something **clocks** a particular time or speed, they are recorded as having reached that time or speed, for example in a race. ■ If you **clock up** an amount, you reach it. *Japanese motorists clock up an average of 8,000 kilometres a year.* ■ If something is done **round the clock,** it goes on continuously all day and night. ■ If you do something **against the clock,** you do it hurriedly, to meet a deadline. ■ If you want to **turn the clock back,** you want to return to the way things used to be, usually because the present situation is unpleasant.

clockwise If something moves in a **clockwise** direction, it moves round in the same direction as the hands on a clock.

clockwork A **clockwork** toy or device has machinery inside it which makes it move or operate when it is wound up with a key. ■ If something happens **like clockwork,** it happens without problems, or happens regularly.

clod A **clod** of earth is large lump of it.

clog (clogging, clogged) If something **clogs** a hole or a place or **clogs** it **up,** it blocks it up. ■ **Clogs** are leather or wooden shoes with thick wooden soles.

cloister (cloistered) A **cloister** is a paved area around a square in a monastery or a cathedral. ■ If someone leads a **cloistered** life, they have little contact with the outside world.

clone (cloning, cloned) If an animal, plant, or substance has been **cloned**, it has been produced from the cells of another identical animal, plant, or substance. Something produced like this is called a **clone**. ■ If you say someone is a **clone** of another person, you mean they look or behave like that person, and have no individuality of their own. *I am not a Paxman clone.*

close (*pron:* **kloze**) **(closing, closed)** If you **close** a door, window, or lid, you move it so it covers an opening. ■ When a shop or other public place **closes**, work or business stops for a short time, or until the next working day. ■ If a factory, business, or public building **closes** or **closes down**, all work stops there permanently. ■ If the authorities **close** a road, border, or airport, or **close** it **off**, they block it off so nobody can use it. ■ If you **close** a bank account, you take all the money out and inform the bank you will no longer be using the account. ■ A **closed** group of people does not welcome new people or ideas from outside. ■ If you **close** something or bring it to a **close**, you end it or complete it. *The prosecution closed its case. ...the closing ceremony.* ■ When a share **closes** at a particular value, it has that value at the end of the day's trading. ■ If you **close** a deal with someone, you complete it. ■ If people **close in** on someone or something, they come towards them and surround them.

close (*pron:* **klohss**) If something is **close** it is only a short distance away. ■ If you look at something **close up**, you get near to it to look at it. ■ You say people are **close** to each other when they are fond of each other. ■ Your **close** relatives are the members of your family most directly related to you, for example your mother or sister. ■ **Close** is used to emphasize the extent to which people are involved in something together. *...close co-operation... The two men had worked together closely.* ■ If there is a **close** connection or resemblance between two things, they are strongly connected or look very similar. ■ **Close** is used to say something is done carefully and thoroughly *The patient is now under close observation. ...a closely guarded secret.* ■ A **close** contest is won by only a small margin. ■ If something is **close**, it is likely to happen or come soon. *We are very close to peace.* ■ If the weather is **close**, it is uncomfortably warm.

close-cropped hair or grass has been cut very short.

closed circuit A **closed circuit** is a complete electrical circuit, which electricity can flow right round. ■ A **closed circuit** television or video system is one which operates within a limited area such as a building.

closed-door See **close**.

closed shop If you say a place of employment is a **closed shop**, you mean the employees have to belong to a particular trade union.

close-fitting clothes fit tightly and show the shape of the body.

close-knit (*or* **closely-knit**) A **close-knit** group of people are closely linked and share similar beliefs or interests.

close season (*pron:* **klohss**) In hunting and fishing, the **close season** is the time of the year when you are not allowed to kill certain birds, animals, or fish. ■ In certain sports, the **close season** is the time of the year when the sport is not played professionally.

closet (closeted) Closet is the usual American word for a cupboard. ■ **Closet** is used to describe people who have beliefs, habits, or feelings which they keep private and secret. *...closet homosexuals.* If someone decides to tell people about their beliefs, habits, or feelings, you can say they **come out of the closet**. ■ If you are **closeted** somewhere, you hide yourself away, because you want to be alone or to talk privately to someone.

close-up A **close-up** is a photograph or film taken very near to a subject and showing a lot of detail.

closing time is the time when places such as pubs or shops shut.

closure When a business is permanently shut down, this is called a **closure**. *...large-scale pit closures.* ■ If something causes the **closure** of something like a road or airport, it causes it to be closed, usually temporarily.

clot (clotting, clotted) When blood or another liquid **clots**, it dries and becomes thick, forming a lump. The lump is called a **clot**.

cloth is fabric made by a process such as weaving or knitting. A **cloth** is a piece of cloth used for a particular purpose, like cleaning. ■ People sometimes use **the cloth** to refer to the Christian clergy. *...a man of the cloth.*

clothe (clothing, clothed; -clothed) If you are **clothed** in something, you are dressed in it. You can add **-clothed** to a word to say what sort of clothes someone is wearing. *...poorly-clothed guards.* ■ If you **clothe** someone, you provide them with clothes.

clothes are the things people wear except shoes and jewellery.

clothes horse If you call someone a **clothes horse**, you mean they are fashionably dressed but have no other positive qualities. ■ A **clothes horse** is a folding framework for hanging wet washing on inside a house.

clothing is the clothes people wear.

clotted cream is very thick cream.

cloud (clouding, clouded; cloudy, cloudier) A **cloud** is a mass of water vapour floating in the sky. ■ If the sky **clouds over**, it becomes covered with clouds. If there are a lot of clouds, you say it is **cloudy**. ■ A **cloud** of smoke or dust is a mass of it floating in the air. ■ A **cloudy** liquid is not as clear as it should be. ■ If one thing **clouds** another, it makes it difficult to understand. ■ **Cloudy** is used to describe things which are confused or uncertain. *... a cloudy political debate.* ■ If something **clouds** a situation or event, it makes it unpleasant. *Poor job prospects have clouded the outlook for the economy.* ■ You can say someone is **under a cloud** when they are in disgrace. *Some politicians left government under a cloud.*

cloudburst A **cloudburst** is a sudden heavy fall of rain.

cloud-cuckoo-land If you say someone is living in **cloud-cuckoo-land,** you mean they mistakenly think that there are no problems and that everything will happen as they want.

clout (**clouting, clouted**) If someone has **clout,** they have influence and power. ■ If you **clout** someone or something, you hit them.

clove – **Cloves** are small strong-smelling dried flower buds from a tropical tree. They are used as a spice. ■ A **clove** of garlic is one of the small sections of a garlic bulb. ■ See also **cleave.**

clover is a small plant with three leaves at the end of each stem. ■ If you say someone is **in clover,** you mean they are living a luxurious comfortable life.

clown (**clowning**) A **clown** is a performer who wears funny clothes and bright make-up, and does silly things to make people laugh. ■ If you **clown around,** you do silly things. This sort of behaviour is called **clowning.** ■ If you call someone a **clown,** you mean they behave in a silly way and you cannot take them seriously.

cloying (**cloyingly**) If something is **cloying,** it is unpleasant because it is too sweet and sickly, or too sentimental.

club (**clubbing, clubbed; clubber**) A **club** is (a) an organization for people with the same interest. ...*a vintage car club.* (b) an organization with its own premises where members go to drink, eat, or read. ■ A sports **club** is an organization of people, including players and coaches, who form teams to compete against other clubs. ■ Nightclubs are often called **clubs. Clubbing** is going to nightclubs; someone who does this regularly is called a **clubber.** ■ If people **club together,** they all give money to share the cost of something. ■ A **club** is a thick heavy stick used as a weapon. ■ If you **club** someone, you hit them with something blunt and heavy. ■ A **club** or **golf club** is a long thin stick with a curved end for hitting a golf ball. ■ **Clubs** is one of the four suits in a pack of playing cards. All cards in this suit have the symbol ♣ on them.

clubhouse A **clubhouse** is the place where members of a sports club meet.

clubland is used to talk about the nightclubs in an area, and the people who go to them. ...*the latest music style to hit clubland.*

cluck When a hen **clucks,** it makes a short repeated sound in its throat. ■ If someone **clucks,** they make disapproving noises.

clue A **clue** is a piece of information which helps you solve a problem. ■ If someone **hasn't got a clue,** they have no idea what the answer to a question is, or no idea how to do something.

clued-up If you say someone is **clued-up,** you mean they have a lot of detailed knowledge about something.

clueless If you say someone is **clueless,** you mean they are stupid and incapable of doing something properly.

clump A **clump** of things like plants is a small group of them. ...*clumps of white tulips.* ■ If someone **clumps** about, they walk with heavy clumsy footsteps.

clumsy (**clumsier, clumsiest; clumsily, clumsiness**) A **clumsy** person moves or handles things awkwardly. ■ **Clumsy** things are badly designed or made, and awkward to use. ■ If something is done in a **clumsy** way, it is done carelessly or tactlessly.

clung See **cling.**

clunk A **clunk** is the sound made when two heavy objects hit against each other.

cluster (**clustering, clustered**) A **cluster** of people or things is a small group of them close together. ■ If people or things **cluster** somewhere, they gather together or are found together in small groups.

cluster bomb A **cluster bomb** is a bomb dropped from an aircraft which scatters a lot of smaller bombs as it falls.

clutch (**clutches, clutching, clutched**) If you **clutch** something, you hold it tightly. If you **clutch at** something, you move your hand quickly to take hold of it. ■ If you are in someone's **clutches,** they have power or control over you. ■ A **clutch** of people or things is a small group of them. ■ The **clutch** in a car is the mechanism which disconnects the power from the engine when you change gear. The pedal you press to control the mechanism is also called the **clutch.** ■ **clutch at straws:** see **straw.**

clutch bag A **clutch bag** is a handbag without a handle.

clutter (**cluttering, cluttered**) If things **clutter** a place or **clutter** it **up,** they fill it in an untidy way. ■ **Clutter** is a lot of things arranged untidily, especially useless or unnecessary things.

cm See **centimetre.**

Co is short for 'company' in the names of companies. ...*European Credit Co Ltd.*

co- is used to form words which say someone does something jointly with someone else, rather than on their own. ...*the co-chairman of the Geneva conference.*

coach (**coaches, coaching, coached**) A **coach** is a bus which carries passengers on long journeys. ■ A **coach** is an enclosed four-wheeled vehicle pulled by horses. ■ A **coach** on a train is one of the separate sections for passengers. ■ If you **coach** someone, you help them to improve their skills at a sport or subject. Someone who does this is called a **coach.**

coachman (**coachmen**) In the past, a **coachman** was a man who drove a horse-drawn coach.

coachwork The **coachwork** of a car is its exterior.

coagulate (*pron:* koh-**ag**-yew-late) (**coagulating, coagulated; coagulation**) When a liquid like blood **coagulates,** it becomes thick.

coal is a hard black substance mined and burned as fuel. Pieces of coal for burning on a fire are sometimes called **coals.**

coalesce (*pron:* koh-a-**less**) (**coalescing, coalesced**) If things or people **coalesce,** they join together to form a larger group.

coalfield A **coalfield** is a region where there is coal under the ground.

coalition (*pron:* koh-a-**lish**-un) A **coalition** is a government made up of people from two or more political parties. ■ A **coalition** is a temporary alliance between two or more groups of people.

coalmining (**coalmine, coalminer**) **Coalmining** is the mining of coal.

coal scuttle A coal scuttle is a bucket for keeping coal in.

coal tar is a thick black liquid made from coal. It is used to make drugs and chemical products.

coarse (**coarser; coarsely, coarseness**) You say something is **coarse** when it has a rough texture. ■ A **coarse** person is rude and offensive.

coarse fishing is the sport of catching freshwater fish other than trout or salmon. See also **fly-fishing.**

coarsen (**coarsening, coarsened**) If something **coarsens,** it becomes rougher in texture.

coast (**coastal**) A **coast** is a place where an area of land meets the sea. ■ **Coastal** is used to describe things which are on, next to, or involve a coast. *...coastal erosion.* ■ If something happens **from coast to coast,** it happens in every part of a large country bordered by sea. ■ If a vehicle is **coasting,** it is moving without being driven by its motor, or without being pushed or pedalled. ■ If you are **coasting,** you are doing something without effort or worry.

coaster A **coaster** is a mat you put underneath a glass to protect the table. ■ A **coaster** is a ship which sails along a coast, taking goods to the ports there.

coastguard The **coastguard** is an organization which provides sea rescue services and prevents smuggling. The members of the coastguard are called **coastguards.**

coastline The **coastline** is the outline of a coast, especially as seen from the sea or the air.

coat (**coating, coated**) A **coat** is a piece of clothing with long sleeves worn over other clothes to keep you warm or protect you from bad weather. ■ An animal's **coat** is its fur or hair. ■ If you **coat** something with a substance, you cover it with a thin layer of it; the layer is called a **coat** or **coating.**

coat of arms (**coats of arms**) A **coat of arms** is a design in the form of a shield used as an emblem by a family, town, or organization.

coat-tails are the two long parts at the back of a man's formal dress coat. ■ You can say someone **rides on your coat-tails** when they take advantage of something you have done, without making any real effort of their own.

coax (**coaxes, coaxing, coaxed**) If you **coax** someone, you gently try to persuade them to do something.

cob A **cob** is a small round loaf of bread.

cobalt is a hard silvery-white metal. ■ **Cobalt** is a deep greenish-blue colour.

cobble (**cobbling, cobbled**) **Cobbles** are cobble-stones. A **cobbled** street has a surface made of cobblestones. ■ If you **cobble** something **together,** you put it together in a hurry.

cobbler A **cobbler** is a person who mends or makes shoes for a living.

cobblestone – **Cobblestones** are stones with a rounded upper surface. They used to be used for making roads.

cobra (*pron:* **koh**-bra) The **cobra** is a large poisonous hooded snake from Africa and Asia.

cobweb (**cobwebbed**) A **cobweb** is a spider's web. ■ If something **blows away the cobwebs,** it makes you feel alert and lively when you had been feeling tired. ■ If something has been left unchanged for a long time, you can talk about the **cobwebs** on it.

cocaine is an addictive drug which some people take for pleasure. In most countries, it is illegal to take cocaine.

coccyx (*pron:* **kok**-six) The **coccyx** is the small triangular bone at the base of the spine in humans and some apes.

cochineal is a red food colouring obtained from a Mexican insect.

cochlea (*pron:* **kok**-lee-a) (*plural:* **cochleae**) The **cochlea** is a spiral tube in the inner ear, shaped like a snail's shell. It converts sound vibrations into nerve impulses.

cock A **cock** is (a) an adult male chicken. (b) a male bird of any species. *...a cock pheasant.* ■ If you **cock** an eyebrow, you raise it. ■ If you **cock** your head, you lean it to one side. ■ If you say someone's ear is **cocked,** you mean they are listening for something. ■ If you **cock** a gun, you set the hammer so it is ready to fire. ■ **cock a snook:** see **snook.**

cock-a-hoop If you are **cock-a-hoop,** you are very pleased about something.

cock-and-bull A **cock-and-bull** story is an improbable one, especially one given as an excuse.

cockatoo (**cockatoos**) The **cockatoo** is a crested parrot from Australia and New Guinea.

cockerel A **cockerel** is a young male chicken.

cock-eyed A **cock-eyed** idea is stupid and unlikely to succeed.

cockle – **Cockles** are small edible shellfish.

cockney (**cockneys**) A **cockney** is a person born in the East End of London. **Cockney** is the dialect and accent of this area.

cockpit The **cockpit** of a racing car or small plane is the part where the driver or pilot sits.

cockroach (**cockroaches**) **Cockroaches** are large brown beetle-like insects found especially in dirty rooms and in places where food is kept.

cocksure If you say someone is **cocksure,** you mean they are too confident of their own abilities.

cocktail A **cocktail** is an alcoholic drink containing several ingredients. ■ An unusual mixture of substances is sometimes called a **cocktail.** *...a cocktail of chemicals.* ■ Some kinds of food eaten as the first course of a meal are called **cocktails,** for example a prawn cocktail.

cocktail dress A **cocktail dress** is a short dress suitable for formal occasions.

cock-up A **cock-up** is something which has been done very badly because of mistakes or stupidity.

cocky (**cockily, cockiness**) A **cocky** person is conceited and very self-confident. You can talk about the **cockiness** of someone like this. *He was tired but confident to the point of cockiness.*

cocoa is (a) a brown powder made from the seeds of the cacao tree, used to make chocolate. (b) a hot drink made with cocoa powder and milk.

coconut A **coconut** is a very large nut with white flesh, milky juice, and a hard hairy shell. **Coconut** is the white flesh of a coconut.

cocoon (**cocooning, cocooned**) A **cocoon** is a covering of silky threads made by the larvae of moths and other insects before they grow into adults. ■ If someone is **cocooned,** they are protected from everyday life, or from something unpleasant. Something which protects someone like this can be called a **cocoon.**

cod (*plural:* **cod**) are large edible sea fish found especially in the North Atlantic.

coda (*pron:* kode-a) A **coda** is a small extra section added at the end of a book, speech, or piece of music.

coddle (**coddling, coddled**) If you **coddle** someone, you treat them too kindly and over-protect them. ■ If you **coddle** eggs, you cook them in near-boiling water.

code (**coding, coded**) A **code** is a set of rules about how people should behave. ■ If you **code** a message, you change it by replacing the letters and symbols with different ones, so people who do not know the code cannot understand it. A system like this is called a **code.** ■ A **code** is a group of numbers or letters which enable you to identify something. If you **code** something, you identify it using numbers or letters like these. ■ **Coded** is used to talk about things said in a rather indirect way, often because it would be dangerous or embarrassing to express them more plainly.

codebreaker A **codebreaker** is someone who works out what codes mean, so that coded information can be understood.

co-defendant A **co-defendant** in a court case is one of two or more people accused of the same crime.

codeine (*pron:* kode-een) is a pain-killing drug.

codename (*or* **code name**) (**codenamed**) A **codename** is a name given to someone or something to keep their identity secret. If a police or military operation is **codenamed** in a particular way, it is known by a special name to the people involved in it.

code of practice (**codes of practice**) A **code of practice** is a set of written rules which explain how people in a particular profession should behave.

code word A **code word** is a word or phrase which has a special meaning for people who have agreed to use it that way.

codger Old men are sometimes called **old codgers.**

codicil (*pron:* kode-iss-ill) A **codicil** is an instruction added to a will after the main part has been written.

codify (**codifies, codifying, codified; codification**) If something like a group of laws is **codified,** it is organized into a proper system.

cod-liver oil is a thick yellow oil full of vitamins A and D.

co-ed A **co-ed** school is a co-educational one.

co-education (**co-educational**) **Co-education** is teaching girls and boys together in the same school. **Co-educational** is used to talk about things to do with this type of education.

coerce (*pron:* koh-**urss**) (**coercing, coerced; coercion, coercive**) If people are **coerced** into doing something, they are made to do it. Forcing people to do something like this is called **coercion. Coercive** powers are used to force people to do things they do not want to.

coeval (*pron:* koh-**eev**-al) Someone who is your **coeval** is the same age as you.

co-exist (*or* **coexist**) (**co-existence**) If two or more things **co-exist,** they exist at the same time or in the same place. *...the principle of peaceful coexistence between states.*

C of E See **Church of England.**

coffee is (a) a substance made by roasting and grinding the beans of a tropical shrub. (b) a hot drink made by pouring boiling water onto ground coffee beans or instant coffee powder.

coffee morning A **coffee morning** is a social event which takes place in the morning at someone's house, usually held to raise money for a charity.

coffee shop A **coffee shop** is (a) a restaurant which sells tea, coffee, and light meals and snacks. (b) a shop which sells different kinds of ground coffee and coffee beans.

coffee table A **coffee table** is a small low table. ■ A **coffee-table book** is a large expensive book with a lot of pictures which is designed to be looked at rather than read.

coffer A **coffer** is a large strong chest for storing valuable objects. ■ When people talk about an organization's **coffers,** they mean the money it has to spend.

coffin A **coffin** is a box in which a dead person's body is buried or cremated. ■ If you say that one thing is a **nail in** another thing's **coffin,** you mean it will help bring about its end or failure.

cog A **cog** is a small wheel with teeth around the edge, which connects with other wheels in a machine. ■ If you say someone is a **cog in the machine,** you mean they have no importance or power, and are just a small part of a large organization.

cogent (*pron:* koh-jent) (**cogently, cogency**) A **cogent** reason or argument is strong and convincing. You can talk about the **cogency** of something like this.

cognac (*pron:* kon-yak) is a kind of brandy made in south-western France.

cognisance See **cognizance.**

cognitive means to do with the process of learning. *...cognitive skills.*

cognizance (*or* **cognisance**) If you **take cognizance** of something, you take account of it when you are making decisions about what to do.

cognoscenti (*pron:* kon-yo-**shen**-ti) The **cognoscenti** are people who know a lot about a subject. *...the football cognoscenti.*

cohabit (*or* **co-habit**) (**cohabiting, cohabited; cohabitation**) If a man and woman are **cohabiting,** they are living together and have a sexual relationship, but are not married. ■ When politicians from different parties **cohabit,** they share power. ■ When groups of people from different backgrounds **cohabit,** they live in the same area.

coherence You talk about the **coherence** of something like an idea when its parts fit together well and form a united whole.

coherent (coherently) If something is **coherent,** it is clear and easy to understand.

cohesion (cohesive) If something has **cohesion,** its parts fit together well and form a united whole. You say something like this is **cohesive.** ...*a cohesive leadership.*

cohort A person's **cohorts** are their friends or supporters. ■ A **cohort** is a group of people with something in common. *He faces a growing cohort of doubters at home.*

coiffed (coiffure) If someone has carefully **coiffed** hair (*pron:* **kwaft**), their hair has been carefully styled. Someone's **coiffure** (*pron:* kwa-**fyoor**) is their hairstyle.

coil (coiling, coiled) A **coil** of rope is a length of it wound into a series of loops. ■ If you **coil** something or **coil** it **up,** you wind it into a series of loops. ■ A **coil** is a thick spiral of wire through which an electric current is passed, for example to make a magnetic field. ■ In a petrol engine, the **coil** is the part which sends electricity to the spark plugs. ■ See **IUD.**

coin (coining, coined) A **coin** is a flat piece of metal used as money. ■ If you say things are **two sides of the same coin,** you mean they are two different aspects of the same thing. ■ You can call an aspect of a situation which contrasts with other aspects **the other side of the coin.** *It's short, but the other side of the coin is that it's very light.* ■ If you **coin** a word or phrase, you invent it, or use it for the first time.

coinage The **coinage** in a country is the coins used there.

coincide (coinciding, coincided) When things happen at the same time by chance, you can say they **coincide.** *The kick-off coincided with a cloudburst.* ■ If things like people's opinions **coincide,** they are the same.

coincidence (coincidental, coincidentally) You say there is a **coincidence** when by chance two things happen at the same time or appear to be connected. You say things like these are **coincidental.** *The similarities are entirely coincidental.*

coir is a rough material made from the hairy outer shell of coconuts. It is used to make ropes and mats.

coitus (*pron:* koh-it-uss) **(coital)** Coitus is sexual intercourse. **Coital** means to do with sexual intercourse. ...*the post-coital pill.*

coke (coking) Coke is a grey-black substance produced from coal and burned as a fuel. **Coking** means to do with making coke. ...*a coking plant.* ■ Cocaine is sometimes called **coke.** ■ **Coke** or **Coca-Cola** is a brand of cola. 'Coke' and 'Coca-Cola' are trademarks.

cola is a sweet brown non-alcoholic fizzy drink.

colander A **colander** is a bowl-shaped container with holes in it for draining food.

cold (coldly, coldness) If something is **cold,** it has a very low temperature. ■ If you say it is **cold** or talk about the **cold,** you mean the air temperature is very low. If you feel **cold,** your body feels at an unpleasantly low temperature. ■ A **cold** is a common mild illness which makes you sneeze and gives you a sore throat or cough. ■ A **cold** person does not show much emotion, especially affection. ■ If you get **cold feet** about doing something, you become very nervous about doing it. ■ If someone is **out cold,** they are unconscious or sleeping very heavily. ■ **cold comfort:** see **comfort. in cold blood:** see **blood.**

cold-blooded (cold-bloodedly) You say someone is **cold-blooded** when they do something cruel without any emotion. ■ **Cold-blooded** animals have a body temperature which changes according to the surrounding temperature. Reptiles, fish, frogs, and toads are cold-blooded. See also **warm-blooded.**

cold frame A **cold frame** is a box-like structure with a glass or plastic top for protecting small plants in cold weather.

cold-shoulder (cold-shouldering, cold-shouldered) If you **cold-shoulder** someone, you behave in an unfriendly way towards them.

cold sore — **Cold sores** are small sore spots which can appear on or near someone's lips and nose when they are unwell.

cold storage If food is put in **cold storage,** it is kept in an artificially cooled place to preserve it. ■ If you put a plan into **cold storage,** you postpone doing anything about it.

cold store A **cold store** is an artificially cooled building or room where chilled food is kept.

cold sweat If someone is in a **cold sweat,** they are cold and sweating at the same time, because they are afraid.

cold turkey is the unpleasant physical reaction someone gets when they suddenly stop taking a drug they are addicted to.

Cold War The **Cold War** was the situation of hostility and tension which existed until recently between the US and its allies and the former Soviet bloc.

coleslaw is a salad of chopped cabbage, carrots, and onions, mixed together in mayonnaise.

colic is a sudden pain in the stomach and bowels. It mainly affects babies.

colitis (*pron:* ko-**lie**-tiss) is an illness in which a person's colon becomes inflamed.

collaborate (collaborating, collaborated; collaboration, collaborator, collaborative, collaborationist) When people **collaborate,** they work together to achieve something. You can call them **collaborators.** You can also say people do something in **collaboration,** or call their work **collaborative.** ■ If someone **collaborates** with an enemy which has taken control of their country, they help them or co-operate with them. You call a person who does this a **collaborator** or describe them as **collaborationist.**

collage (*pron:* kol-**lahzh**; *the 'zh' sounds like 's' in 'pleasure'*) is a method of making pictures by glueing things like newspaper cuttings, cloth, and photographs onto a flat backing. A picture like this is called a **collage.** ■ A **collage** of things is a number of them brought together to create a special effect. *The film includes a collage of recent events.*

collagen is a natural protein often used as an ingredient in cosmetics or injected into the face in cosmetic surgery, in order to make the skin look younger.

collapse (**collapsing, collapsed; collapsible**) If something like a building **collapses,** it falls down. ■ If a person **collapses,** they fall down, because they are ill or exhausted. ■ If something like a system **collapses,** it suddenly fails completely. ■ A **collapsible** object is designed to fold flat when not in use.

collar (**collared**) The **collar** of a shirt or coat is the part which fits round the neck and is usually folded over. *...a stiff-collared black shirt.* ■ A **collar** is a leather band or chain put around the neck of an animal like a cat or dog.

collarbone The **collarbone** is one of two long bones which run from the base of your neck to your shoulder. It is also called the **clavicle.**

collate (**collating, collated; collation**) If you **collate** pieces of information, you gather them together and examine them.

collateral is money or property used as a guarantee that someone will repay a loan. ■ **Collateral damage** is accidental injury to civilians, or damage to non-military buildings during a military operation.

colleague A professional person's **colleagues** are the people they work with.

collect (**collection, collector, collectable**) If you **collect** things you need, you obtain them from several places. ■ If you **collect** things like stamps, you acquire different kinds, because you are interested in them. A person who does this is called a **collector;** the things they have obtained are called their **collection.** If you say a type of thing is **collectable,** you mean it is worth collecting, because it is interesting or valuable. If something is a **collector's item,** it is highly valued by collectors, because it is rare or beautiful. ■ Any group of similar things gathered together can be called a **collection.** *...a collection of short stories.* ■ Someone's **collected** works are all their writings published together. ■ If you **collect** someone or something, you get them from somewhere. *Motorists will start collecting their ration cards tomorrow.* ■ If you **collect** for something like a charity, you ask people to give you money for it. ■ If you **collect** money from someone who owes it, you get it from them. ■ If a sportsperson **collects** a title or prize, they win it.

collected If someone is **collected,** they are calm and self-controlled.

collective (**collectively**) **Collective** decisions, actions, or feelings are shared among all members of a group. ■ A **collective** is a group of people who share the running of something like a farm. ■ **Collective bargaining** is the talks a trade union has with an employer to settle workers' pay or conditions. ■ If a word is used as a name for a group of people or things, you can say they are known **collectively** by that name.

collectivise See **collectivize.**

collectivism (**collectivist**) **Collectivism** is the belief that the needs of the state are more important than the needs of the individual. **Collectivist** systems are systems like communism and fascism, based on this belief.

collectivize (*or* **collectivise**) (**collectivizing, collectivized; collectivization**) In the former USSR, when farms or factories were **collectivized,** they were brought under state ownership and control, usually by combining a number of small farms or factories into one large one.

college A **college** is a place where people study after they have left school. ■ Some universities are divided into separate institutions called **Colleges.** ■ See also **electoral college.**

collegiate (*pron:* col-**leej**-yit) means to do with colleges. *...collegiate rivalries.*

collide (**colliding, collided**) If you **collide** with something, you bump into it. ■ You can say people **collide** when they have different ideas about how something should be done.

collie A **collie** is a type of sheepdog with long hair and a long muzzle.

colliery (**collieries; collier**) A **colliery** is the same as a coalmine. A **collier** is a coalminer.

collision You say there is a **collision** when a moving object hits something. ■ You say there is a **collision** of cultures or ideas when people with different cultures or ideas come into contact and this leads to problems. ■ If people are on a **collision course,** there is likely to be a violent disagreement between them.

colloquial (**colloquially, colloquialism**) **Colloquial** language is the kind of language people use in ordinary conversation, rather than in formal writing. A word or phrase which is only used in conversation is called a **colloquialism.**

collude (**colluding, colluded; collusion**) If you **collude** with someone, you co-operate with them secretly or illegally. This is called **collusion.**

cologne (*pron:* kol-**lone**) is a kind of weak perfume.

colon The **colon** is the part of the intestine above the rectum. ■ A **colon** is the mark **:** often used in front of a list.

colonel (*pron:* **ker**-nel) A **colonel** is a high-ranking officer in the army.

colonialism (**colonial, colonialist**) **Colonialism** is a system in which a powerful country controls less powerful countries and uses their resources to increase its own power and wealth. *...colonial rule. ...colonialist oppression.* ■ A **colonial** is someone who comes from a colony.

colonize (*or* **colonise**) (**colonizing, colonized; colonization**) If a place is **colonized,** it is made into a colony. *...the European colonization of America.* ■ If animals **colonize** a place, they move there and make it their home.

colonnade (**colonnaded**) A **colonnade** is a row of evenly spaced columns. If something is **colonnaded,** it has a colonnade.

colony (**colonies; colonist**) A **colony** is a country controlled by a more powerful country, which uses the colony's resources to increase its own power and wealth. A **colonist** is someone who founds a colony, or one of the first people to live in a colony. ■ A **colony** is a place where a particular group of people lives. ...*a leper colony.* ■ A **colony** of animals or insects is a group of them living together. ...*North sea seal colonies.*

color See **colour.**

coloration The **coloration** of something is its colours.

coloratura is ornamental and complicated music for an operatic singer.

colossal is used to describe things which are very large in size, amount, or degree.

colossus (colossuses) A **colossus** is an enormous statue. ■ An extremely large or important and significant person or institution can be called a **colossus.**

colour (*Am:* color) **(colouring, coloured)** The **colour** of something is the way it appears as a result of reflecting light. ■ A **colour** or **colouring** is a substance used to give things a particular colour. ...*a range of nail colours.* ■ A person's **colour** is the colour of their skin. Their **colouring** is the colour of their hair, facial skin, and eyes. ■ A **coloured** person belongs to a race of people who do not have pale skins. ■ A **colour** TV, film, or photograph shows things in all their colours. ■ If you pass a test with **flying colours,** you do very well in it. ■ If someone reveals **their true colours,** they show they are not as nice as people thought. ■ **Colour** is a quality which makes something enjoyable and exciting. *The audiences liked the romance and colour of 'The Lady's Not for Burning'.* ■ If something **colours** your opinion, it affects the way you think about something. ■ **nail your colours to the mast:** see **nail.**

colour bar A **colour bar** is a system which does not allow non-white people to take part in the same activities or go to the same places as white people.

colour-blind people cannot distinguish clearly between certain colours.

colour-coded things have different colours on them to show, for example, what group they belong to.

colour fast If a fabric is **colour fast,** its colours do not fade when it is washed.

colourful (*Am:* colorful) **(colourfully)** Colourful things are brightly coloured. ■ **Colourful** is used to describe things which are interesting and exciting. *They have a colourful and rather romantic history.* ■ If you call a person **colourful,** you mean they behave in an interesting and amusing way. ■ If you say someone's language is **colourful,** you mean they use a lot of rude words.

colourless (*Am:* colorless) things have no colour. ■ If you say a person or place is **colourless,** you mean they are unexciting.

colour scheme (*Am:* color scheme) A **colour scheme** is the colours chosen for a group of things which will be seen together, such as the curtains and carpet in a room.

colour supplement A **colour supplement** is a magazine you get free with a newspaper.

colt A **colt** is a young male horse.

column (columnist) A **column** is a stone or wooden cylinder standing on its end, especially one supporting part of a building. ■ A **column** is something that has a tall narrow shape. ...*columns of smoke.* ■ A **column** of people or vehicles is a group of them moving in a line. ■ In a newspaper, magazine, or dictionary, a **column** is a vertical section of writing. ■ A **column** is a regular section or article in a newspaper or magazine. ...*a gardening column.* A journalist who writes a section or article like this is called a **columnist.**

coma (comatose) If someone is in a **coma** or is **comatose,** they are deeply unconscious.

comb A **comb** is a metal or plastic object with a row of narrow teeth for tidying your hair. When you **comb** your hair, you tidy it with a comb. ■ If you **comb** a place for something, you search that place for it thoroughly.

combat (combating, combated) Combat is fighting in a war. ■ If people in authority **combat** something, they try to stop it happening.

combatant (*pron:* kom-bat-ant) The **combatants** in a war are the people taking part.

combative (*pron:* kom-bat-tiv) **(combatively, combativeness)** A **combative** person is aggressive and eager to fight or argue. *The Swiss people are not renowned for their combativeness.*

combination A **combination** of things is two or more of them together. ■ The **combination** of a lock is the series of letters or numbers used to open it. A **combination lock** is one which can only be opened this way.

combine (combining, combined) If you **combine** two or more things, you get them to exist or operate together. *The issue is how to combine low inflation and sustainable growth.* ■ If something **combines** several features, it has all of them. Similarly, a person can **combine** qualities or abilities. ■ If people **combine** or make a **combined** effort, they join together to achieve something. ■ A **combine** (*pron:* kom-bine) is a group of people or organizations working together. ■ A **combine** or **combine harvester** is a large machine used on a farm to cut, sort, and clean grain.

combo (combos) A **combo** is a small group of musicians.

combustible If something is **combustible,** it catches fire and burns easily. ■ If you call a situation **combustible,** you mean trouble or fighting is likely.

combustion is the burning of something ...*the combustion of fuel for energy.*

come (coming, came, have come) If a person or thing **comes** to a place, they move there or arrive there. ■ **Come** is used to say someone or something enters or reaches a particular state. *His self-built bike came apart... His government came to power last December.* ■ When a particular event or time **comes,** it happens. *Most of the action came late in the day.* ■ **Come** is used to say where a person or thing originates from. *She came from Stourport... The word 'idea' comes from Greek.* ■ If one thing **comes** from another, it is the result of the other thing. *There is a feeling of power that comes from driving fast.* ■ If you

come across something, you find it by chance. ■ If particular things are hard to **come by,** there are not many around. ■ If something **comes off,** it succeeds. ■ If something is **coming on,** it is making progress. ■ If someone **comes round** or **comes to,** they recover consciousness. ■ If you **come round** to an idea or situation, you eventually accept it. ■ When a regular event **comes round,** it happens. ■ If a subject **comes up,** it is mentioned or discussed. ■ If you **come up against** a problem, you are faced with it. ■ If you **come up with** an idea, you think of it.

comeback (or **come-back**) If someone or something makes a **comeback,** they become successful again.

comedian A **comedian** is an entertainer whose job is to make people laugh by telling jokes and funny stories.

comedienne A **comedienne** is a female comedian.

comedown If you say something is a **comedown,** you mean it is not as good as a similar thing you had before.

comedy (**comedies**) **Comedy** is entertainment which makes people laugh. ■ A **comedy** is an amusing play or film.

comely (pron: kum-ly) If you describe someone as **comely,** you think they are attractive.

come-on A **come-on** is a gesture or remark which someone makes to encourage another person to make sexual advances towards them. He ignores come-ons from the many women who seem to find him attractive.

comet A **comet** is an object which orbits the sun and has a long bright tail of gas and dust.

come-uppance (or comeuppance) If you say a person gets their **come-uppance,** you mean something unpleasant happens to them and they deserve it.

comfort (**comforting, comfortingly**) **Comfort** is a feeling of being physically relaxed, because of such things as the clothes you wear. ■ If someone lives in **comfort,** they have a pleasant lifestyle free of financial worries. ■ **Comforts** are things which are not necessary but make your life more pleasant. ■ If you **comfort** someone, you make them less distressed. Something which has this effect can be called **comforting.** You can also say something gives you **comfort.** ■ If you say something is **cold comfort,** you mean it is no real comfort at all. ■ If you say something is, for example, **too close for comfort,** you mean it is very close, and you are worried about it. The levels of crime were still too high for comfort.

comfortable (**comfortably**) If you are **comfortable,** you have a feeling of being physically relaxed, because of things like the clothes you are wearing. My room was comfortably furnished. ■ You say you are **comfortable** when you feel confident and are not worried, afraid, or embarrassed. ■ You say someone is **comfortable** when they are able to live pleasantly without any major worries. ■ If a sick or injured person is **comfortable,** their condition is stable. ■ **Comfortable** is used to say something is done or achieved easily. He appeared to be heading for a comfortable victory.

comfy (**comfier, comfiest**) **Comfy** means comfortable.

comic people and things make you want to laugh, often as part of a comedy performance. ■ A **comic** is a comedian. ■ A **comic** or **comic book** is a magazine which tells stories in pictures.

comical (**comically**) **Comical** people or things are oddly amusing.

comic strip A **comic strip** is a series of pictures which tell a story.

comma A **comma** is the punctuation mark , used to separate parts of a sentence or items on a list.

command (**commanding**) If someone in authority **commands** you to do something, they order you to do it. An order like this is called a **command.** ■ A **command** is an instruction given to a computer. ■ An officer who **commands** part of one of the armed forces is in charge of it. You talk about someone being **in command** of forces, or the forces being **under their command.** ■ In the armed forces, a **command** is (a) a group of officers in charge of part of an army. (b) a part of an army or air force with a particular function. ...Strike Command. ■ If you are **in command** of a situation, you have control of it. ■ If someone is in a **commanding** position, they are well ahead of their competitors. ■ If someone has a **commanding** presence, they seem powerful or confident. ■ If someone **commands** respect, they get it because of their personal qualities. ■ A person's **command** of a language is their knowledge of it. ■ If there is a good view from a place, you can say it has a **commanding** view.

commandant (pron: kom-man-dant) A senior army officer in charge of a place or group of people is sometimes called the **commandant.**

commandeer (**commandeering, commandeered**) If the armed forces or police **commandeer** something, they officially take it for their own use.

commander A **commander** is an officer in charge of a military operation. ■ A **commander** is a middle-ranking naval officer. See also **wing commander.**

commander-in-chief (**commanders-in-chief**) The **commander-in-chief** is the officer in charge of all the armed forces fighting on one side in an area or military operation.

commanding officer A **commanding officer** is an officer in charge of a military unit.

commandment The ten **Commandments** are the rules of behaviour which, according to the Old Testament, everyone should obey.

commando (**commandos**) A **commando** is a soldier or small group of soldiers specially trained to attack targets which are difficult to reach.

command post A **command post** is a place from which an army commander controls and organizes his forces.

commemorate (**commemorating, commemorated; commemoration, commemorative**) If an object **commemorates** a person or event, it is intended to remind people of them. ...commemorative mugs. ■ If people **commemorate** something, they do something special to show they remember it. What they do can be called **commemorative** or a **commemoration.** ...a commemorative service.

commence (**commencing, commenced; commencement**) When something **commences,** it begins. The **commencement** of something is its beginning. ■ If you **commence** doing something, you start doing it. ■ In the US, **Commencement** is a ceremony in which graduates formally receive their degrees or diplomas.

commend (**commendation; commendable, commendably**) If you **commend** someone or **commend** what they do, you praise them to other people. *The Lithuanians deserve commendation for courage.* **Commendable** behaviour is behaviour you think should be praised. ■ A **commendation** is official recognition of something someone has done. ■ If you **commend** something to someone, you tell them it is very good. ■ If a course of action **commends** itself to you, you think it is a good idea.

commensurate (*pron:* kom-**men**-sur-ret) (**commensurately**) If one thing is **commensurate** with another, it is in proportion to it. *Japanese real wages have not yet increased commensurately with the wealth of Japan.*

comment If you **comment** on something or make a **comment** about it, you say something about it. ■ **Comment** is criticism or discussion. *Much media comment has been critical of this unexpected step.*

commentary (**commentaries**) On TV or radio, a **commentary** is a description of an event while it is taking place. ■ A **commentary** is a book or article explaining or discussing something.

commentate (**commentating, commentated; commentator**) When a broadcaster **commentates,** they give a TV or radio commentary. A broadcaster who does this is called a **commentator.**

commerce is the buying and selling of things on a large scale.

commercial (**commercially**) **Commercial** is used to talk about things to do with commerce and business. *...the country's commercial and political leaders.* ■ A **commercial** activity involves producing goods to make a profit. **Commercial** can also be used to say something makes a profit. *...a huge commercial success.* ■ **Commercial** products or services are available to the public. *Of the three cars, only the Fiat is available commercially.* ■ **Commercial** TV and radio are paid for by broadcasting advertisements. A **commercial** is an advertisement broadcast on TV or radio.

commercial art (**commercial artist**) **Commercial art** is designing and drawing advertisements and designing the way products look. A person who does this is called a **commercial artist.**

commercial bank – **Commercial banks** are ones which operate current and deposit accounts and make short-term loans.

commercialise See **commercialize.**

commercialism is emphasis on making a profit, rather than on things like 'quality'.

commercialize (*or* **commercialise**) (**commercializing, commercialized; commercialization**) If something is **commercialized,** it is used or changed in such a way that it makes money.

commercial traveller (*Am:* **commercial traveler**) A **commercial traveller** is a travelling salesperson.

commercial vehicle – **Commercial vehicles** such as lorries and vans are used for carrying goods by road.

commie Some people call communists or people with left-wing views **commies.**

commis chef A **commis chef** is a trainee chef.

commiserate (**commiserating, commiserated**) If you **commiserate** with someone, you show sympathy for them when something unpleasant has happened to them.

commissar A **commissar** was an official responsible for political education in the former USSR.

commission (**commissioning, commissioned**) If someone **commissions** a piece of work, they arrange to pay someone to make or do it; you can also say they **commission** the person. A **commission** is a piece of work that someone, usually an artist, is asked to do and is paid for. ■ A **commission** is a group of people appointed to do something. ■ **Commission** is money paid to a salesperson for each sale they make. ■ A **commission** is a sum of money paid to an organization for carrying out a service. ■ If a member of the armed forces is **commissioned,** he or she is made an officer. You can say that they have been given a **commission.**

commissionaire A **commissionaire** is a uniformed doorman employed somewhere like a hotel.

commissioner A **commissioner** is an important official in a government department or some other organization.

commit (**committing, committed; committal**) If someone **commits** a crime, they do it. ■ If someone **commits** suicide, they take their own life. ■ If an organization **commits** money or resources to something, it makes them available for that purpose. ■ If you **commit** yourself to something, you say you will definitely do it. ■ If you are **committed** to a cause or belief, you believe in it strongly. ■ If someone is **committed** to prison, they are sent there. You can talk about a person's **committal** to prison.

commitment is a strong belief in something such as an ideal, shown in a person's behaviour. ■ A **commitment** is a regular task which takes up some of your time. ■ If you give a **commitment** to something, you make a firm promise to do it.

committal See **commit.**

committee A **committee** is a group of people who make decisions or plans on behalf of a larger organization.

commode A **commode** is a chair or stool containing a large pot, which is used as a toilet.

commodity (**commodities**) A **commodity** is anything sold commercially on a large scale, such as foodstuffs or raw materials.

commodore A **commodore** is a high-ranking naval officer.

common (**commoner, commonest; commonly**) If something is **common,** it is found in large numbers, or it happens often. ■ **Common** is used to talk about things possessed, done, or used by two or more people or groups. *...our common interests.* ■ You say people or things have something **in**

common when they share the same characteristics or interests. ■ When people who are in disagreement find **common ground,** they find something they can agree about. ■ If something is done for the **common good,** it is done for everyone's benefit. ■ You can refer to ordinary people as the **common people.** ■ If you say someone is **common,** you mean they show a lack of taste, education, or good manners. ■ If something is **common knowledge,** it is known generally. ■ A **common** is an area of grassy land near a village. ■ The **Commons** is the House of Commons.

Common Agricultural Policy See **CAP.**

common denominator A **common denominator** is a characteristic shared by all the members of a group. See also **lowest common denominator.**

commoner A **commoner** is anyone who is not a member of the peerage.

common land is land everyone is allowed to go on.

common law is the system of law, especially in England, which is based on judges' decisions and custom, rather than Acts of Parliament. ■ When an unmarried couple have lived together a long time, their relationship is sometimes called a **common-law** marriage.

Common Market The **Common Market** is a former name for the European Union.

commonplace If something is **commonplace** it is not worth commenting on as it happens so often.

common room A **common room** is a sitting room in a place like a university or school.

common sense is the natural ability to make good judgments.

Commonwealth The **Commonwealth** or **British Commonwealth** is an association of countries which are or were ruled by Britain.

commotion is a lot of noise and confusion.

communal (**communally; communalism**) **Communal** things are used by a group of people, rather than by one person or family. ■ **Communal** is used to describe a way of life in which a group live and do things together. *They eat communally.* ■ **Communal** is used to talk about things taking place between the different racial or religious groups in a place. *...communal violence.* **Communalism** is loyalty to the interests of your own racial or religious group, rather than to the social system as a whole.

commune (**communing, communed**) A **commune** (*pron:* **kom**-mune) is a group of people who live together and share everything. ■ If you **commune** (*pron:* kom-**mune**) with nature or some other power, you spend time thinking about it, feeling you are in close contact with it in some way.

communicable diseases can be passed on easily.

communicant A **communicant** is a person who receives Communion.

communicate (**communicating, communicated; communication**) If you **communicate** with someone, you exchange information with them, by speaking, writing, or radio signals. ■ **Communications** are the systems and processes used to communicate or broadcast information. ■ A **communication** is a letter or phone call. ■ If you

communicate a feeling or idea, you make people aware of it. ■ If people who live or work together can **communicate,** they can understand each other's feelings. ■ **Communicating** doors link one room directly with another.

communicative A **communicative** person is willing to talk to other people.

communicator If you say someone is a good **communicator,** you mean they are good at getting ideas across.

communion or **Holy Communion** is the Christian ceremony in which the priest and congregation eat bread and drink wine in remembrance of Christ's death and resurrection. Communion is also called the Eucharist.

communiqué (*pron:* kom-**mune**-ik-kay) A **communiqué** is an official statement or announcement. *The NATO communiqué included a commitment to modernise nuclear weapons.*

communism (**communist**) **Communism** is the doctrine that the state should control all means of producing things, and that there should be no private property.

community (**communities**) The **community** is all the people living in an area. A sense of **community** is a feeling of having something in common with people living in your area and a sense of responsibility towards them. ■ A **community** is a group of people with something in common, living among other people. *...the black community.* ■ A **community** is a group of countries who have agreed to work together. *...the West African Economic Community.*

community centre A **community centre** is a place where local people can hold meetings and run courses or other social activities.

community charge In Britain, the **community charge,** popularly known as the Poll Tax, was a tax paid to the local authority and used to pay for local services.

community policing is a system in which policemen and women work only in one area, so people get to know them.

community service is unpaid work that criminals sometimes do as a punishment instead of being sent to prison.

commute (**commuting, commuted; commuter**) If you **commute,** you travel a fairly long distance regularly between your home and your workplace. A person who does this is called a **commuter.** ■ If a death sentence or prison sentence is **commuted** to a less serious punishment, it is changed to that punishment.

compact If something is **compact** (*pron:* kom-**pakt**), it takes up little space. ■ If you **compact** something, you press it to make it more dense. ■ A **compact** person is small and muscular. ■ A **compact** (*pron:* **kom**-pakt) is a small flat round case containing a mirror and face powder. ■ A **compact** is an official agreement.

compact disc A **compact disc** or **CD** is a small circular piece of hard plastic on which recorded sound or information can be stored.

companion (**companionship**) A **companion** is someone you spend time with. **Companionship** is having a friend or companion, rather than being on your own.

companionable A **companionable** person is friendly and pleasant to be with.

companionway A **companionway** is a stairway or ladder between the decks of a ship.

company (**companies**) A **company** is a business organization owned by shareholders. ■ A theatre or dance **company** is a group of performers who work together. ■ A **company** is a group of soldiers, usually part of a battalion or regiment. ■ **Company** is having someone with you, rather than being on your own. *While he was working, he avoided company.* ■ If you **keep** someone **company**, you spend time with them and stop them feeling lonely or bored. If you **keep company with** someone, you spend a lot of time with them. ■ If you **part company** with someone, you end a friendship or association, often as a result of an argument. ■ If you talk about someone's behaviour **in company**, you mean the way they behave when they are with a group of people, for example on a social occasion. ■ If someone is good **company**, they are pleasant to be with. ■ **In company with** means 'as well as'. *In company with Ford and his contemporaries, Taylor deified efficiency.*

comparable (*pron:* **kom**-pra-bl) (**comparably; comparability**) If two things are **comparable**, they are similar or correspond to each other in some way.

comparative (**comparatively**) You use **comparative** or **comparatively** to show you are judging something against another thing or against what would be expected. *The city remained comparatively calm.* ■ A **comparative** study involves the comparison of similar things.

compare (**comparing, compared; comparison**) If you **compare** things or make a **comparison**, you consider them together and note their differences or similarities. ■ If you **compare** one person or thing to another or make a **comparison**, you say they are similar. *I can only compare the experience to falling in love.* ■ If you say something can **stand comparison** with something else, you mean it is good enough to be judged against it. If one thing **compares favourably** with another, it is better.

compartment A **compartment** is (a) one of the separate sections of an old-fashioned railway carriage. (b) one of the separate parts of a container. (c) a small cupboard in a boat, plane, or road vehicle.

compartmentalize (*or* **compartmentalise**) (**compartmentalizing, compartmentalized**) If something is **compartmentalized**, it is divided into separate sections.

compass (**compasses**) A **compass** is an instrument for finding directions. It has a magnetic needle which always points north. ■ **Compasses** are a hinged V-shaped instrument for drawing circles. ■ The **compass** of something is its range. *It is a subject beyond the compass of my feeble brain.*

compassion (**compassionate, compassionately**) **Compassion** is a strong feeling of pity and sympathy for someone who is suffering. A **compassionate** person has feelings of this kind. If they do something to help someone who is suffering, you say they act **compassionately** or for **compassionate** reasons. ■ If you are granted **compassionate leave,** you are allowed time away from work for personal reasons, usually because a member of your family is seriously ill or has died.

compatible (**compatibility**) If things or ideas are **compatible,** they can exist together, or be used together. ■ If people are **compatible,** they are suited to each other, and can live or work together successfully.

compatriot Your **compatriots** are people from your own country.

compel (**compelling, compelled**) If something **compels** you to do something, it forces you to do it. ■ If you say something **compels** an attitude or feeling, you mean you cannot help responding to it like that. ■ A **compelling** reason for doing something is very strong. ■ A **compelling** book or film is so exciting you have to keep reading or watching it.

compendium (*plural:* **compendiums** *or* **compendia**) A **compendium** is a short but detailed collection of information, usually in a book.

compensate (**compensating, compensated; compensation, compensatory**) If someone is **compensated** for something unpleasant which has happened to them, they are given money to make up for it. The money is called **compensation.** *...a package of compensatory measures for farmers hit by the cuts.* ■ If something **compensates** for an unpleasant experience or is a **compensation** for it, it helps to make up for it.

compere (*pron:* **kom**-pare) (**compering, compered**) A **compere** is a person who introduces a TV, radio, or stage show. You can also say they **compere** the show.

compete (**competing, competed; competition, competitor**) If one firm **competes** with another, it tries to get people to buy its goods in preference to the other firm's. When this happens, you say there is **competition** between the firms. Firms which sell the same kind of goods are called **competitors.** ■ If you **compete** with someone for something, you both try to get it. ■ If a person or team **competes** in a contest, they take part in it. ■ A **competition** is an event held to find out who is best at something. The people taking part are called **competitors.** ■ **Competing** accounts of something which has happened are different, and cannot both be right. Similarly, **competing** proposals conflict with each other, and cannot both be carried out.

competent (**competently, competence, competency, competencies**) You say someone is **competent** or talk about their **competence** when they can do something efficiently and effectively.

competitive (**competitively, competitiveness**) A **competitive** situation is one where people or firms are competing with each other. ■ A **competitive** person is eager to be more successful than other people. ■ You say goods or prices are **competitive**

when they are cheaper than similar ones elsewhere.

compile (compiling, compiled; compiler, compilation) If you **compile** something like a report, you
produce it by collecting and putting together different pieces of information. ■ A **compilation** is
something like a book or record containing different items gathered together, usually ones which
have already appeared elsewhere.

complacent (pron: kom-**play**-sent) (**complacently,
complacency**) You say someone is **complacent**
about a problem or talk about their **complacency**
when they behave as if they have nothing to worry
about.

complain (complaining, complained; complaint,
complainer) If you **complain** or make a **complaint,**
you say you are not satisfied with something. People who make complaints are sometimes called
complainers. ■ If you **complain** of a pain or illness,
you say you have it. A **complaint** is an illness.

complainant A **complainant** is a person who starts
a court case.

complaisant If you are **complaisant,** you are willing
to accept what other people want without complaining.

complement (complementary) If two people or
things **complement** each other, they make a good
combination, because their qualities go well together. You say people or things like these are
complementary. ■ A **complement** or **full complement** of things is a complete set of them.

complementary medicine is the same as alternative medicine.

complete (completing, completed; completely,
completeness, completion) If something is **complete,** it contains all the parts it should have. ■ If
something **completes** a group, it is the last item
needed to make it complete. ■ If you **complete**
something, you finish doing or making it. You then
say it is **complete.** ■ **Complete** and **completely** are
used to say something is true to its fullest extent.
He was completely bald. ■ If something comes **complete with** something else, it has that thing as one
of its parts. ■ **Completion** is the finishing of the legal and financial formalities involved in buying or
selling a house or land.

complex (complexes; complexity, complexities)
Complex things are made up of many different
parts and are often difficult to understand. You can
talk about the **complexity** of things like this; its different parts or details can be called **complexities.**
■ A **complex** is a group of things connected with
each other in a complicated way. *...the whole complex of issues to do with birth control.* ■ A **complex** is
a group of buildings used for a particular purpose.
■ If someone has a **complex** about something,
they are worried or obsessed about it.

complexion Your **complexion** is the natural colour
and appearance of your facial skin. ■ The **complexion** of something is its general nature or character.

compliance See **comply.**

compliant You say people or organizations are
compliant when they do what they are asked to.

complicate (complicating, complicated; complication) If something **complicates** a situation, it
makes it more difficult to understand or deal with.
*An added complication is the growing concern for the
environment.* ■ If something is **complicated,** it has
many parts or details. ■ In medicine, a **complication** is an additional problem which makes the
treatment of an illness more difficult.

complicity (complicit) **Complicity** in something
wrong is being involved in it. *He is himself complicit
in mass murder.*

compliment (complimentary) If you **compliment**
someone or pay them a **compliment,** you praise
them or say you admire something they own. If you
are **complimentary** about something, you express
admiration for it. ■ If you send your **compliments**
to someone, you express good wishes for them.
■ If something is **complimentary,** you get it free.

comply (complies, complying, complied; compliance) If you **comply** with a request or order you do
what you are required to. *The document calls for full
compliance with the ceasefire.*

component The **components** of a machine are its
parts. You can also talk about the **components** of
something like a policy.

comport The way you **comport** yourself is the way
you behave.

compose (composing, composed; composer) If
something is **composed** of certain people or things,
they are what it consists of. You can also say people or things **compose** something, or **compose** a
part of it. *Before long, Scots will compose little more
than 8% of the population of the United Kingdom.* ■ If
someone **composes** a piece of music, they write it.
A person who writes music is called a **composer.**
■ If you **compose** a letter, poem, or speech, you
write it, taking some trouble over it. ■ A **composed**
person is calm and able to control their feelings.

composite (pron: kom-poz-it) things or a **composite**
is made up of several different things or parts.

composition (compositional) The **composition** of
something is the things it consists of and the way
they are arranged. ■ **Composition** is composing
music. *...a study of Olivier Messiaen's compositional
style.* A **composition** is a piece of music. ■ A **composition** is a piece of writing produced as part of
school work.

compositor A **compositor** is a person who arranges
the text and illustrations for a book, magazine, or
newspaper before it is printed.

compost is decayed leaves, grass, and kitchen
waste which is used to enrich the soil. If you **compost** things, you make them into compost.

composure is the ability to stay calm and unwor-
ried.

compound A **compound** is an enclosed area of land.
■ In chemistry, a **compound** is a substance consisting of two or more elements. ■ If something is
a **compound** of different things or is **compounded**
of them, it consists of them. ■ If something **compounds** a problem, it makes it worse.

compound fracture A **compound fracture** is a broken bone which has cut through the flesh near it.

compound interest is calculated both on the original amount of money invested and on any interest previously added to the amount. See also **simple interest.**

comprehend If you cannot **comprehend** something, you cannot fully understand or appreciate it.

comprehensible (**comprehension**) If something is **comprehensible,** it can be understood. Someone's **comprehension** is their ability to understand or appreciate something. ■ **Comprehension** is an exercise to find out how well schoolchildren understand a piece of text.

comprehensive (**comprehensively**) If something is **comprehensive,** it includes everything. *...a comprehensive training programme.* ■ In sport, if someone has a **comprehensive** win or defeat, they win or lose by a large margin. ■ In a **comprehensive** system of education, children of different abilities are taught in the same school.

compress (**compresses, compressing, compressed; compression, compressor**) If you **compress** something, you squeeze it so it takes up less space. *...the compression of molecules.* Similarly, you can talk about a lot of information being **compressed** into a short book or a talk being **compressed** into a short period of time. ■ A **compressor** is a machine which compresses gas or air.

comprise (**comprising, comprised**) If a group **comprises** a number of people or things or is **comprised** of them, it has them as its members or parts. *The delegation will comprise 40 people from the United States and other countries.* You can also say people or things **comprise** a group or organization. *...the many nationalities that comprise Ethiopia.*

compromise (**compromising, compromised**) When people **compromise** or reach a **compromise,** they agree to accept less than they originally wanted. ■ If someone **compromises** themselves or their beliefs, they do something which makes people doubt their sincerity or honesty.

comptroller A **comptroller** is a person responsible for financial planning and control in an organization.

compulsion A **compulsion** is a strong desire to do something, which is difficult to control. ■ **Compulsion** is the use of threats or violence to make people do something.

compulsive (**compulsively**) **Compulsive** is used to describe people's behaviour when they keep doing something, and seem unable to stop themselves. ■ If a book or TV programme is **compulsive,** it is so interesting you do not want to stop reading it or watching it.

compulsory (**compulsorily**) If something is **compulsory,** people have to do it because a law or someone in authority insists on it.

compunction If you do something without **compunction,** you do not feel guilty about doing it.

computation (**computational**) **Computation** is mathematical calculation, especially using a computer. A **computation** is a calculation. **Computational** means things to do with calculations, or with computers.

compute (**computing, computed**) If you **compute** a quantity or number, you calculate it. ■ **Computing** is using a computer and writing programs for it.

computer A **computer** is an electronic machine which can rapidly make calculations, store, rearrange, and retrieve information, or control another machine.

computerize (*or* **computerise**) (**computerizing, computerized; computerization**) If a system or type of work is **computerized,** the work is transferred to computers. *...the benefits of computerization.* ■ **Computerized** equipment uses a computer or is controlled by one. ■ If information is **computerized,** it is stored or processed in a computer.

computer-literate If someone is **computer-literate,** they have the necessary skills to be able to use a computer.

comrade (**comradely, comradeship**) Communists and socialists sometimes call each other **comrade.** ■ Someone's **comrades** are their friends or companions. ■ **Comradely** behaviour or **comradeship** is friendly behaviour, especially between people working closely together.

comrade-in-arms (**comrades-in-arms**) You say people are **comrades-in-arms** when they are working for the same cause, and sharing the same difficulties.

con (**conning, conned**) If someone **cons** you, they trick you into believing something, by telling you things which are not true. You call this a **con** or a **con trick.** ■ A **con man** or **con artist** makes a living by persuading people to give him money or property in return for something which turns out to be worthless. ■ A **con** is a convict.

concave A **concave** lens or mirror curves inwards towards its centre. See also **convex.**

conceal (**concealing, concealed; concealment**) If you **conceal** an object, you put it somewhere where it cannot be seen or found. *The policy was introduced to prevent the concealment of weapons.* ■ If you **conceal** information or a feeling, you do not let other people know about it.

concede (**conceding, conceded**) If you **concede** something, you unwillingly admit it is correct. ■ If a country **concedes** something like territory, it gives it to another country which has been trying to get it. ■ In a contest, if someone **concedes** defeat, they accept that they have lost. ■ When a sports team **concedes** goals or points, it fails to stop the other side scoring them.

conceit (**conceited**) **Conceited** people have an absurdly high opinion of themselves or their achievements. You can talk about the **conceit** of people like these. ■ A **conceit** is an clever or unusual metaphor or comparison. *The conceit that the whole play is set in a music hall does become rather tiresome.*

conceivable (**conceivably**) If something is **conceivable,** you can imagine it or believe it. *The world could conceivably divide into three giant trading blocs.*

conceive (**conceiving, conceived**) If a woman or female animal **conceives,** she becomes pregnant. ■ If you **conceive** something like a plan, you think of it and work out how it can be put into practice. ■ If you **conceive** something in a particular way, that is how you see it. *These things are conceived as beneficial to the nation.* ■ If you cannot **conceive** of something, you cannot imagine it or believe it.

concentrate (**concentrating, concentrated; concentration**) If you **concentrate**, you give something all your attention. *Neal kept interrupting, breaking my concentration.* ■ If a serious situation **concentrates your mind**, it forces you to think more clearly and carefully than usual. ■ If you **concentrate** on something, you give it more attention than other things. ■ If something is **concentrated** in one place, it is nearly all there, rather than being spread over a wider area. *There has been too much concentration of power in the hands of central authorities.* ■ A **concentrated** activity involves a lot of things being done in a short time. *...a week of concentrated political activity.* ■ A **concentrated** liquid or a **concentrate** has had substances like water removed from it, to increase its strength. ■ The **concentration** of a substance in a liquid is the proportion of the substance in it. *...water with aluminium concentrations above the authorised level.*

concentration camp A **concentration camp** is a prison where non-military prisoners are kept in poor conditions, especially during a war.

concentric circles have the same centre.

concept A **concept** is an idea or abstract principle.

conception is the forming of an idea in someone's mind. Your **conception** of something is your idea of what it is. ■ **Conception** is the process in which an egg in a woman's or female animal's womb is fertilized, and she becomes pregnant.

conceptual (**conceptually**) **Conceptual** means to do with ideas and the mind.

conceptual art attempts to convey an idea without necessarily using conventional art forms such as painting or sculpture.

concern If something **concerns** you or causes you **concern**, it worries you. ■ If you are **concerned** with something, you give attention to it, because you think it is important. Your **concerns** are things which are important to you. ■ If you feel **concern** for someone, you want them to be happy, safe, and well. ■ **Concern** is used to say what something is about. *The plot concerns missing treasure.* ■ You use 'as far as' or 'where' with **concerned** to say what aspect of something you are talking about. *They have tried to improve their image where human rights are concerned.* ■ If you talk about the people **concerned,** you mean the people involved in something. ■ A **concern** is a company or business.

concert (**concerted**) A **concert** is a performance by one or more musicians. **In concert** is used to say someone is giving a live performance. *...José Carreras in concert.* ■ If people do something **in concert** or take part in a **concerted** action, they do it together.

concertina (**concertinaing, concertinaed**) A **concertina** is a musical instrument like a small accordion, but with buttons instead of a keyboard. ■ If something is **concertinaed**, it is squeezed into a smaller shape or area.

concerto (*pron:* kon-**cher**-toe) (*plural:* **concertos** or **concerti**) A **concerto** is a piece of music for one or more solo instruments and an orchestra.

concession (**concessionary, concessional; concessionaire**) If you make a **concession,** you agree to let someone do or have something, often in order to end a conflict or argument. ■ A **concession** is something given to someone as a special privilege. **Concessionary** and **concessional** are used to describe things given like this. *...concessional loans.* ■ A **concession** is a business run on another business's property, for example within a department store. A person who owns or runs a concession is called a **concessionaire.**

concierge (*pron:* kon-see-**airzh;** *the 'zh' sounds like 's' in 'pleasure'*) A **concierge** is a person, especially in France, who looks after a block of flats and checks people entering and leaving the building.

conciliate (**conciliating, conciliated; conciliatory, conciliator, conciliation**) If you do something to **conciliate** someone, you do it to try to end a disagreement with them. When someone behaves like this, you say they are being **conciliatory.** ■ If someone **conciliates,** they try to end a disagreement between other people; a person who does this is called a **conciliator.**

concise (*pron:* kon-**sice**) (**concisely**) If something you say or write is **concise,** it is brief and to the point.

conclave A **conclave** is a meeting whose proceedings are kept secret, especially the meeting of cardinals which elects a new Pope.

conclude (**concluding, concluded**) If you **conclude** something is true, you decide it is true on the basis of other things you know. ■ When something **concludes,** it finishes. The **concluding** part of something is the last part. ■ If you **conclude** something, you finish it. ■ If you **conclude,** you say the last thing you are going to say. ■ When people **conclude** a treaty or a deal, they agree on the final version of it.

conclusion If you come to a **conclusion,** you decide something is true, after considering all the facts. ■ If you **jump to conclusions,** you decide too quickly that something is true, without knowing all the facts. ■ The **conclusion** of something is its end. ■ People say **in conclusion...** when they are beginning the last part of a report or speech. ■ The final settling of a treaty or deal can be called its **conclusion.** ■ **foregone conclusion:** see **foregone.**

conclusive (**conclusively**) If evidence is **conclusive,** it shows with certainty something is true.

concoct (**concoction**) If you **concoct** an excuse or explanation, you invent one. ■ If you **concoct** something like an unusual drink, you make it by mixing several things together. The thing you make is called a **concoction.**

concomitant If one thing is **concomitant** with another thing, you always get the first thing when you get the second. You can say it is the other thing's **concomitant.** *Low wages are the inevitable concomitant of low skills.*

concord is widespread peaceful agreement.

concordance A **concordance** is an alphabetical list of the words in a book or set of books. It says where each word can be found and how often it is used.

concourse A **concourse** is a wide hall in a public building.

concrete is a building material made from cement, sand, small stones, and water. ■ **Concrete** means specific and definite, rather than vague. *So far there is little concrete evidence to back up their words.*

concubine (*pron:* **kon**-kew-bine) In the past, a **concubine** was a woman who lived in the house of a man she was not married to and was kept by him for his sexual pleasure.

concur (**concurring, concurred; concurrence**) If you **concur** with someone, you agree with them. ■ If something is done with someone's **concurrence**, they have agreed to it.

concurrent (**concurrently**) If two things are **concurrent,** they happen at the same time.

concussed (**concussion**) If someone is **concussed,** they lose consciousness or feel sick or confused after being hit hard on the head.

condemn (**condemnation, condemnatory**) If you **condemn** something or you are **condemnatory** of it, you say it is bad or wrong. ■ If someone is **condemned** to death, they are sentenced to death. *...condemned prisoners.* ■ If you are **condemned** to something unpleasant, you have to suffer it. ■ If a building has been **condemned,** the authorities have decided it is not safe and must be pulled down.

condensation consists of tiny drops of water on a cool surface, formed when steam or moist air touches the surface.

condense (**condensing, condensed**) If a piece of writing is **condensed,** it is shortened by taking parts out. ■ When a gas or vapour **condenses,** it changes into a liquid.

condensed milk is milk thickened by having some of the water removed from it, and sugar added.

condenser A **condenser** is (a) a device for changing vapour into liquid. (b) a device for storing electric charge.

condescend (**condescending; condescension**) You say someone is **condescending** when they behave as if they think they are superior to other people. You call this sort of behaviour **condescension.** ■ If you say someone **condescends** to do something, you mean they do it, although they consider it beneath them.

condiment – **Condiments** are things like salt, pepper, and mustard, which you add to food which has already been served.

condition (**conditioning, conditioned**) The **condition** of someone or something is the state they are in. ■ A **condition** is an illness or other medical problem. ■ The **conditions** in which you live or work are the things around you which affect your comfort, health, and safety. ■ The **conditions** in which something is done are all the factors affecting it. *They tried to simulate the conditions of an Olympic final.* ■ A **condition** is something which must happen for something else to be possible. *Sanc-tions could not be dropped until five conditions had been met.* If you agree to do something **on condition that** something else happens, you say you will do it only if that thing happens. ■ If you are **conditioned** to do something, you do it as a result of your upbringing or training. ■ If you **condition** your hair, you put conditioner on it to keep it healthy.

conditional (**conditionally**) If something is **conditional** on something else happening, it will happen only if the other thing happens. ■ If someone who has committed a minor crime is given a **conditional discharge,** they are not punished, provided they do not re-offend within a certain period.

conditioner is (a) a cosmetic put on hair, usually when washing it, to make it smoother and more manageable. (b) a thick liquid used when washing clothes to make them softer. (c) a substance designed to improve the condition of something. *...a soil conditioner.*

condo (**condos**) A **condo** is the same as a condominium.

condolence If you express your **condolences,** you tell someone in a formal way that you are sorry a relative or friend of theirs has died.

condom A **condom** is a thin rubber covering which a man wears on his penis during sex as a contraceptive or as protection against disease. A similar device called a **female condom** can be worn inside a woman's vagina.

condominium In the US, a **condominium** is a block of flats in which each flat is owned by the occupier. The individual flats are also sometimes called **condominiums.**

condone (**condoning, condoned**) When people **condone** wrong behaviour, they accept it and allow it to happen.

conducive If something is **conducive** to something else, it has qualities which make the other thing likely to happen. *...a business climate conducive to foreign investment.*

conduct (**conductivity, conduction**) If someone **conducts** an inquiry or survey, they carry it out. The **conduct** (*pron:* **kon**-dukt) of something like this is the way it is carried out. ■ Your **conduct** or the way you **conduct** yourself is the way you behave. ■ If you **conduct** someone somewhere, you go with them, to show them the way. ■ A **conducted tour** is a tour of a building or area led by a guide. ■ When someone **conducts** an orchestra or choir, they stand in front of it and direct its performance. ■ If heat or electricity can pass through a substance, you say the substance **conducts** heat or electricity. The extent to which it is allowed through is called the substance's **conductivity.**

conductor The **conductor** of an orchestra or choir is the person who conducts it. ■ On trains and some buses, the **conductor** is the official who checks people's tickets and sometimes issues them. ■ A **conductor** of heat or electricity allows heat or electricity to pass through it. See also **lightning conductor.**

conduit A **conduit** is a small tunnel, pipe, or channel which water or electricity cables pass through. ■ You say a person or organization is a **conduit**

when they are used as a means of communication between other people or organizations. ■ You say a place is a **conduit** when things are allowed to pass through it, often illegally.

cone A **cone** is a three-dimensional shape with a circular base and a pointed top. ■ **Cones** are cone-shaped objects made of plastic, used for temporary traffic control. ■ Ice-cream cornets are sometimes called **cones**. ■ The **cones** on a conifer tree are its fruit. Each cone consists of a cluster of woody scales containing seeds.

confection A **confection** is a sweet food such as a cake. ■ Things which are elaborately put together can be called **confections**. ...*an extraordinary architectural confection.*

confectionery (**confectioner**) **Confectionery** is sweets, chocolates, and fancy cakes. A **confectioner** is a person or company that makes or sells confectionery.

confederacy (**confederacies**) A **confederacy** is an alliance of states or people trying to achieve the same thing.

confederate A person's **confederates** are other people involved with them in an activity.

confederation (**confederated, confederative**) A **confederation** is a group of allied states, often considered as a single country. A **confederated** group of states operates as a confederation. **Confederative** is used to talk about things to do with a confederation. ...*a new confederative system.* ■ Some organizations representing a group of people's interests have **Confederation** as part of their name.

confer (**conferring, conferred; conferment**) If an honour is **conferred** on someone, it is given to them. ■ If you **confer** with someone, you discuss an issue with them, before deciding what to do.

conference A **conference** is a meeting, often lasting several days, where people discuss a subject. ■ If people are **in conference,** they are having a formal meeting.

confess (**confesses, confessing, confessed; confession**) If you **confess** something or make a **confession,** you admit you have done something wrong. ■ When Christians **confess** their sins, they tell God or a priest about their sins so they will be forgiven. **Confession** is the act of doing this.

confessional In a Catholic church, a **confessional** is a small room in which a priest hears confessions.

confessor A **confessor** is (a) a priest who hears confessions. (b) someone who confesses to something.

confetti is small pieces of coloured paper.

confidant (**confidante**) (*both pron:* kon-fid-ant) A **confidant** is a male friend you discuss your private problems with. If the friend is a woman, you call her your **confidante.**

confide (**confiding, confided**) If you **confide in** someone, you tell them about a private matter. ■ If you **confide** a secret to someone, you tell it to them and trust them not to tell it to anyone else.

confidence If you have **confidence** in someone or something, you feel you can trust them to do what they are supposed to. ■ Someone who has confi-

dence is sure of their own abilities. ■ If you tell someone something **in confidence,** you do not want them to repeat it to anyone else. This is called **taking** someone **into your confidence.** A **confidence** is something you tell someone which you do not want repeated.

confidence trick A **confidence trick** is a trick in which someone persuades you to give them money or property in return for something which turns out to be worthless.

confident (**confidently**) If you are **confident** about something, you are certain things will happen in a particular way. *He confidently expects his firm's sales to grow to $6 billion a year.* ■ Someone who is **confident** is sure of their own abilities.

confidential (**confidentially, confidentiality**) If something is **confidential,** it is meant to be kept secret. You can talk about the **confidentiality** of something like this.

configuration A **configuration** is a group of things arranged in a particular way. ...*an ancient configuration of giant stones.*

confine (**confining, confined; confinement**) If something is **confined** to one place, it exists there and nowhere else. Similarly, if something is **confined** to one group of people, they are the only ones involved in it or affected by it. ■ If you **confine** yourself to something, you do not deal with anything except that thing. ■ The **confines** (*pron:* kon-fines) of a subject or system are the limits of what it can deal with. ■ If someone is **confined** to a place, they cannot leave it. ...*his years of confinement.* ■ If people **confine** something to a place, they stop it spreading beyond it. ■ The **confines** of an area are its boundaries. ■ A **confined** space is enclosed and very small, so movement inside it is difficult.

confirm (**confirmed; confirmation**) If someone **confirms** something like a report, they say it is true. ■ If something **confirms** your fears or beliefs, it shows you were right. ■ If you **confirm** an appointment or arrangement, you say it is definite. ■ If someone **confirms** their position, they do something to make it stronger. ■ If someone is **confirmed,** they are formally accepted as a member of a Christian church at a ceremony called **confirmation** in which they say they believe in the church's teachings. ■ **Confirmed** is used to describe someone who has a habit or belief which they are unlikely to change. ...*a confirmed atheist.*

confiscate (**confiscating, confiscated; confiscation**) If someone in authority **confiscates** something, they take it away from someone.

conflagration A **conflagration** is (a) a sudden outburst of violence involving a large number of people. (b) a large fire.

conflate (**conflating, conflated; conflation**) If you **conflate** two accounts or issues, you combine them into one. A combination of things like this is called a **conflation.**

conflict (**conflicting**) **Conflict** (*pron:* kon-flikt) is serious disagreement and argument. When people are disagreeing or arguing, you say they are **in conflict.** ■ **Conflict** is war. A **conflict** is a war or battle.

■ If ideas **conflict** (*pron:* kon-**flikt**), they are different in a way which would make it impossible for them to be held by the same person at the same time. You can talk about a **conflict** of ideas. Similarly, if laws **conflict,** they say opposite things and cannot all be observed. ■ If people's interests **conflict,** some people want things to happen which others do not want. You can talk about a **conflict** of interests. ■ **Conflicting** accounts of an event are different and cannot all be correct.

confluence The **confluence** of two rivers is the place where they join. ■ When things mingle together to form one thing, you can call this a **confluence.**

conform (**conformist, conformity, conformism**) If you **conform,** you behave the way you are expected to behave. You can say a person like this is a **conformist,** or talk about their **conformity** or **conformism.** ■ If something **conforms** to a law or regulation or is **in conformity** with it, it meets its requirements. Similarly, something can **conform** to someone's wishes or be **in conformity** with them.

confound If someone **confounds** their critics, they prove them wrong, by succeeding when they were expected to fail. ■ If something **confounds** you, you are unable to explain it.

confront If a problem or task **confronts** you, you have to deal with it. You can also say someone **confronts** a task or problem, especially when they make a determined effort to deal with it. ■ If you are **confronted** by an object or a group of people, they are there in front of you. ■ If you **confront** a person, you meet them face to face, to fight or argue with them.

confrontation (**confrontational**) A **confrontation** is (a) a fight, battle, or war. (b) a serious dispute between two groups of people with opposing ideas or policies. ■ If someone's behaviour is **confrontational,** they are ready to fight or argue, rather than solve things peacefully.

confuse (**confusing, confused; confusion**) If you **confuse** two things, you get them mixed up. ■ If something **confuses** you, it makes it difficult for you to understand something. You say something like this is **confusing.** In a situation like this, you talk about your **confusion** or say you are **confused.** ■ If something **confuses** a situation or **throws it into confusion,** it makes it complicated and difficult to resolve. ■ A **confused** person does not really understand what is happening around them.

conga The **conga** is a Latin American dance performed by a number of people in single file, each holding onto the back of the person in front.

congeal (**congealing, congealed**) If a liquid **congeals,** it becomes thick and sticky.

congenial (*pron:* kon-**jeen**-ee-al) If you call your surroundings **congenial,** you mean you find them pleasant. Similarly, you can call people **congenial** when you like them and get on well with them.

congenital (**congenitally**) Congenital disorders are ones which people have from birth. ■ **Congenital** faults seem to be part of a person's character.

conger The **conger** or **conger eel** is a large seawater eel.

congestion (**congested**) If there is **congestion** in a place or it is **congested,** it is so crowded with traffic or people that normal movement is impossible.

conglomerate A **conglomerate** is a large business made up of several companies.

conglomeration A **conglomeration** is a group of many things.

congratulate (**congratulating, congratulated; congratulation, congratulatory**) If you **congratulate** someone or offer them your **congratulations,** you express pleasure for something good which has happened to them, or praise them for something they have achieved. **Congratulatory** is used to describe things which express congratulations. ...*a congratulatory speech.*

congregate (**congregating, congregated**) When people **congregate,** they gather together in groups.

congregation The **congregation** are the people attending a church service.

congress (**congresses; congressional**) A **congress** is a large meeting held by a national or international organization to discuss ideas and policies. ■ **Congress** is the elected group of politicians responsible for making the law in the US. It is made up of two parts: the House of Representatives and the Senate. **Congressional** is used to talk about things to do with Congress. ...*a congressional committee.*

congressman (**congresswoman**) A **congressman** is a member of the US Congress, especially in the House of Representatives.

congruence If there is **congruence** between things, they correspond closely to each other.

conical objects are cone-shaped.

conifer (**coniferous**) A **conifer** is a tree which produces cones, for example the pine. **Coniferous** woodland is made up of conifers.

conjecture (**conjecturing, conjectured**) If you **conjecture** or make a **conjecture,** you make a guess, basing it on incomplete or doubtful information.

conjugal (*pron:* **kon**-jew-gal) means to do with the relationship between a husband and wife, especially their sexual relationship. ...*conjugal bliss.*

conjunction A **conjunction** of things is (a) a combination of them. (b) two or more of them happening at the same time. ■ If someone does something **in conjunction with** someone else, they do it together.

conjunctivitis (*pron:* kon-junk-tiv-**vie**-tiss) is a painful inflammation of the membrane covering the eyeball.

conjure (**conjuring, conjured**) If you **conjure** something into existence or **conjure** it **up,** you make it appear, as if by magic. *Under its restructuring plan, the bank is seeking to conjure up some $4 billion of capital.* ■ If you **conjure up** a memory or idea, you create it in your mind.

conjurer See **conjuror.**

conjuring trick A **conjuring trick** is a trick in which an object is made to appear or disappear, as if by magic.

conjuror (*or* **conjurer**) A **conjuror** is an entertainer who does magic tricks.

conker – **Conkers** are large brown nuts from the horse chestnut tree. ■ **Conkers** is a children's game. You tie your conker to a piece of string and try to break your opponent's conker by hitting it with your own.

conk out If a machine **conks out,** it stops working.

connect (**connection**) If you **connect** one thing to another, you join the two things. A **connection** is something put between two things to join them. ■ When a building or piece of equipment is **connected** to the electricity, gas, or water supply, wires or pipes are put in so the supply can reach the building or equipment. ■ If a road or railway **connects** two places, it runs between them. You can also say a ferry, bus, or air service **connects** two places. ■ If one train, plane, or boat **connects** with another one, it arrives in time to allow passengers to change to the other one. When this happens, you say the passengers make a **connection.** ■ If one thing is **connected** with another or if there is a **connection** between them, they are linked in some way. If you realize this link exists, you say you **connect** the two things or make a **connection** between them ■ If one thing is done **in connection with** another, the purpose for doing it comes from the other thing. *The equipment was purchased for use in connection with the study of body tissues... Four men have been arrested in connection with the robbery.* ■ **In this connection** is used to say something relates to the thing you have just mentioned. *It was for his work in this connection that he was awarded the OBE.* ■ A person's **connections** are the influential people they know in the business or social world, especially people who can help them.

connecting rod In a machine, a **connecting rod** is part of a system for converting the back-and-forward motion of a piston into circular motion.

connection See **connect.**

conning tower A submarine's **conning tower** is the raised part containing the periscope.

connive (**conniving, connived; connivance**) If someone **connives** at something, they allow it to happen, although they know it is wrong and they ought to prevent it; you can also say it is done with their **connivance.** ■ When people **connive,** they secretly plan to do something together, especially something bad.

connoisseur (*pron:* kon-noss-**sir**) A **connoisseur** is someone who knows a lot about the arts, food, or drink.

connotation The **connotations** of a word are the ideas or qualities it suggests to you.

conquer (**conquering, conquered; conquest, conqueror**) If one country or group of people **conquers** another, they defeat them in battle and take control of them and their land. You call this the **conquest** of the defeated people or their land. The people who win the battle are called **conquerors;** the territories they capture are called their **conquests.** ■ If a sports team **conquers** another team, especially a higher-placed one, they beat them. ■ If someone **conquers** something which is causing unhappiness or hardship, they succeed in getting rid of it. *They dream of conquering poverty.* ■ If

people **conquer** a mountain, they are the first ones to climb it. You talk about the **conquest** of a mountain. ■ A person's **conquests** are the people who have fallen in love with them, or the people they have succeeded in seducing.

conscience Your **conscience** is the part of your mind which tells you whether what you are doing is right or wrong. ■ If you have a **guilty conscience,** you feel guilty. If you say your **conscience is clear,** you mean you have done nothing wrong. ■ If you say you cannot **in conscience** do something, you mean you cannot do it because you believe it is wrong. ■ See also **prisoner of conscience.**

conscientious (**conscientiously**) If someone is **conscientious,** they always do their work thoroughly.

conscientious objector A **conscientious objector** is someone who refuses to join the armed forces, because they think it is morally wrong.

conscious (**consciously**) If you are **conscious** of something, you notice it or are aware of it. ■ **Conscious** and **-conscious** are used after words like 'fashion' and 'socially' to describe people who are very concerned about a certain aspect of life. *...fashion-conscious kids. ...environmentally conscious drivers.* ■ A **conscious** action is deliberate. ■ If someone is **conscious,** they are awake rather than asleep or unconscious.

consciousness Your **consciousness** is your mind and thoughts. ■ If someone loses **consciousness,** they become unconscious.

conscript (**conscription**) If someone is **conscripted** (*pron:* kon-**skrip**-tid), they are officially made to join the armed forces. People who have been made to do this are called **conscripts** (*pron:* **kon**-skripts).

consecrate (**consecrating, consecrated; consecration**) If a building, place, or object is **consecrated,** it is officially declared to be holy, and can therefore be used for religious purposes. When a person is **consecrated,** they are officially declared to be a bishop.

consecutive (**consecutively**) **Consecutive** things happen one after the other, without interruption. *...his third consecutive victory.*

consensual A **consensual** approach or decision is one that is based on general agreement amongst all the members of a group. *What I did argue for was a less abrasive, more consensual approach to policy.*

consensus (**consensuses**) If there is a **consensus** about something, there is general agreement about it.

consent (**consenting**) If someone **consents** to something or gives their **consent,** they allow it or agree to it. ■ When there is **consent,** people agree about something. ■ **Consenting** is used to say someone takes part in sexual activities willingly, rather than being made to. *...homosexual acts between consenting males.* See also **age of consent.**

consequence A **consequence** of something is a result or effect of it. ■ If something happens **in consequence** of something else, it happens as a result of it. ■ A thing **of consequence** is a significant or valuable thing.

consequent (**consequently**) **Consequent** and **consequently** are used to say something happens as a result of something you have just mentioned. ...*the Gulf crisis and the consequent rise in oil prices.*

consequential things are important or significant. ■ **Consequential** is sometimes used to mean 'consequent'.

conservation (**conservationist**) **Conservation** is the preservation and protection of the environment. ■ The **conservation** of old buildings or works of art is the preservation and protection of them. ■ The **conservation** of a supply of something is careful use of it, to make it last as long as possible.

conservatism is unwillingness to accept changes and new ideas. ■ **Conservatism** is the political philosophy of the Conservative Party.

conservative (**conservatively**) **Conservative** is used to talk about a country's Conservative Party. ...*Conservative policies.* ■ People with right-wing views are sometimes called **conservatives.** ■ You say people are **conservative** when they are unwilling to accept change. ■ A **conservative** estimate is cautious and puts a figure at a lower level than it is likely to be.

Conservative Party The **Conservative Party** is the main right-of-centre party in the United Kingdom.

conservatoire (pron: kon-**serv**-a-twahr) A **conservatoire** is a school where musicians are trained.

conservator A **conservator** is someone whose job is to maintain and restore historical objects or works of art.

conservatory (**conservatories**) A **conservatory** is a glass room attached to a house. ■ A conservatoire is sometimes called a **conservatory.**

conserve (**conserving, conserved**) If you **conserve** a supply of something, you use it carefully, so it lasts as long as possible. ■ When people try to **conserve** something like their environment, they try to keep it in its original form, protecting it from harm or change.

consider (**considering, considered**) If you **consider** a person or thing to be a particular thing, that is your opinion of them. *Nick considers his life a success.* ■ If you **consider** something, you think about it carefully. A **considered** opinion or action is the result of careful thought. ■ If a group of people **consider** a report or case, they discuss it before coming to a decision about it. ■ If you **consider** a person's needs, wishes, or feelings, you pay attention to them. ■ You use **considering** to say you are taking something into account in what you are saying. *The casualty figures appear to be small, considering the size of the earthquake.*

considerable (**considerably**) A **considerable** amount is a large amount.

considerate A **considerate** person pays attention to other people's needs and feelings.

consideration is careful thought. ■ If something is **under consideration**, it is being discussed or thought about. ■ If you **take** something **into consideration**, you think about it when you are planning or deciding something. Things which affect plans and decisions are called **considerations.** ...*commercial considerations.* ■ If someone shows **consideration**, they pay attention to the needs and feelings of other people.

consign If someone or something is **consigned** to an undesirable situation, they are put in it. *The Communist Party was consigned to the political dustbin.*

consignment A **consignment** of goods is a load of them being delivered somewhere.

consist If something **consists of** certain things, it is made up of them. ■ If something **consists in** a particular thing, it has that thing as its main or only part. *Labour's primary task consisted in restoring some degree of social peace.*

consistent (**consistently; consistency, consistencies**) You say something is **consistent** or talk about its **consistency** when it stays the same and is reliable. ... *a consistent supply of food.* ■ If reports or ideas are **consistent,** they do not contradict each other. ■ If something is **consistent** with a type of thing, it has many of its features and could therefore be that thing. *The injuries were consistent with injuries sustained from missiles.* ■ The **consistency** of a substance is its thickness and texture.

consolation prize A **consolation prize** is something given to someone who has failed to get what they really wanted.

console (**consoling, consoled; consolation, consolatory**) If something **consoles** you (pron: kon-**soles**) or provides **consolation** when you have had a loss or disappointment, it makes you feel less sad. You use **consolatory** to talk about things which console someone. ...*consolatory words.* ■ A **console** (pron: **kon**-sole) is a panel with switches or knobs for operating a machine.

consolidate (**consolidating, consolidated; consolidation**) If you **consolidate** something, you strengthen it, to make it more effective or secure. *Women are consolidating their place in the workforce.* ■ When small organizations are **consolidated,** they are formed into one large one.

consommé (pron: kon-**som**-may) is a thin clear soup, usually made from meat juices.

consonant A **consonant** is a sound like 'p', 'f', 'n', or 't', which you pronounce by stopping the air flowing freely through your mouth. See also **vowel.** ■ If one thing is **consonant** with another, it fits in with it or agrees with it.

consort If someone is spending time with someone you do not like, you can say they are **consorting** (pron: kon-**sort**-ing) with them. ■ The **consort** (pron: **kon**-sort) of a reigning monarch is their husband or wife. ■ A **consort** is a small group of musicians who perform old music on old-fashioned instruments like viols.

consortium (plural: **consortiums** or **consortia**) A **consortium** is a group of firms who have agreed to work together on a project.

conspicuous (**conspicuously**) If something is **conspicuous**, it is easily seen or noticed.

conspiracy (**conspiracies; conspirator, conspiratorial**) A **conspiracy** is a secret plan between a group of people to do something wrong or illegal. The people involved in a conspiracy are called **conspirators. Conspiratorial** is used to describe things connected with a conspiracy. ■ If you say someone is being **conspiratorial,** you mean they are behaving as if they are sharing a secret with you. ■ A

conspiracy of silence is an agreement by a group of people not to talk publicly about something.

conspire (**conspiring, conspired**) If people **conspire,** they secretly plan to do something wrong or illegal. ■ When everything that happens seems to make a particular result more likely, you can say things **conspire** to produce this result.

constable A **constable** is a police officer of the lowest rank.

constabulary (**constabularies**) The **constabulary** is the local police force in an area.

constant (**constantly, constancy**) If something is **constant,** it happens all the time or is always there. ■ A **constant** level or amount stays the same. ■ When something does not change, you can call it a **constant** or talk about its **constancy.** ■ **Constancy** is faithfulness and loyalty.

constellation A **constellation** is a group of stars which has been given a name.

consternation is alarm and anxiety.

constipated (**constipation**) If someone is **constipated** or suffering from **constipation,** they are having difficulty emptying their bowels.

constituency (**constituencies, constituent**) An MP's **constituency** is the area he or she represents. The people who live there are called the MP's **constituents.** ■ A **constituent** assembly is a group of people who have the power to frame a country's constitution or to decide who will be its government. ■ The **constituents** or **constituent** parts of something are the parts it is made up of.

constitute (**constituting, constituted**) If something **constitutes** a particular thing, it can be regarded as being that thing. *26% of the vote hardly constitutes a victory.* ■ If something consists of a number of parts, you can say the parts **constitute** the whole. *...the four companies constituting the Aramco partnership.* ■ When a committee or government is **constituted,** it is formally established and given authority to operate.

constitution (**constitutional, constitutionally**) A country's **constitution** is usually a written statement of the way its government is organized and the rights and duties of its citizens. The British constitution, however, consists of various traditions and customs which have never been written down in a single document. *...a constitutional amendment.* ■ A country with a **constitutional monarchy** has a king or queen but is governed by a democratically elected government. ■ Your **constitution** is your general health, especially your ability to resist illness or recover from it quickly.

constrain (**constraining, constrained; constraint**) If something **constrains** something else or acts as a **constraint** on it, it prevents it developing freely. ■ If something **constrains** you, it limits your freedom to do what you want. ■ If you feel **constrained** to do something, you feel forced to do it, although you might prefer not to.

constrict (**constricted; constriction**) If something **constricts** an object, it squeezes it tightly. ■ If something **constricts** you, it limits your freedom to do what you want; you call something like this a **constriction.**

construct (**construction, constructor**) When something is **constructed,** it is built or put together. Some firms which build or assemble things are called **constructors.** If something is **under construction,** it is being built or made. ■ If someone **constructs** an idea, story, or system, they create it. ■ A **construct** (*pron:* **kon**-struct) is a complex idea. ■ The **construction** you place on something is the way you interpret it. *He rejected the construction put on his remarks.*

constructive (**constructively**) If what someone says or does is **constructive,** it is helpful.

construe (**construing, construed**) If something is **construed** as a particular thing, people see it as being that thing. *Such actions may be construed as significant by foreign observers.*

consul (**consular, consulate**) A **consul** is a government official who lives in a foreign city and looks after the interests of people there from his or her own country. **Consular** means to do with a consul. A **consulate** is the place where a consul works.

consult (**consulting; consultation**) If you **consult** someone, you ask their opinion or advice. ■ **Consulting** is used to describe some people who give professional advice. *...a firm of consulting actuaries.* ■ A **consultation** document is produced for people to read and make comments on. ■ When people **consult,** they exchange ideas and opinions. ■ If you **consult** a book or map, you refer to it for information.

consultancy (**consultancies**) A **consultancy** is a group of people who give professional advice. *...a management consultancy.*

consultant A **consultant** is (a) a senior doctor specializing in one area of medicine. *...a consultant anaesthetist.* (b) someone who gives expert advice. *...a design consultant.*

consultation See **consult.**

consultative A **consultative** committee is set up to give advice or make suggestions. ■ A **consultative** document is the same as a consultation document. See **consult.**

consulting room A **consulting room** is a room where a doctor sees patients.

consumables are goods which are quickly used up and replaced.

consume (**consuming, consumed**) If something **consumes** fuel, energy, or time, it uses it up. ■ If you **consume** something, you eat or drink it. ■ If something is **consumed** by fire, it is destroyed by it. ■ If someone is **consumed** with a feeling, it affects them so strongly they cannot think of anything else. *...a consuming passion for the theatre.*

consumer A **consumer** is anyone who buys goods or pays for a service. ■ **Consumer goods** are items bought by people for their own use, rather than by businesses. ■ **Consumer durables** are things like cars and TV sets which last a long time and so are not bought very often, in contrast to things like clothes and food.

consumerism (**consumerist**) **Consumerism** is the belief that it is good to buy and use a lot of goods. **Consumerist** means connected with this belief.

consummate (**consummating, consummated; consummation**) **Consummate** (*pron:* **kon**-syoo-mat) is used to describe someone who is very skilful. ...*a consummate politician.* ■ If two people **consummate** (*pron:* **kon**-syoo-mate) their relationship, they make it complete by having sex. ■ If an agreement is **consummated,** it is completed.

consumption The **consumption** of fuel or food is the using of it or the amount used. ...*high water consumption.* ■ If something is for a particular person's or group's **consumption,** it is meant to be seen or heard by them. *The film should be available for public consumption.*

contact involves meeting or communicating with someone regularly. *We do keep in contact.* ■ If you **contact** someone, you get in touch with them. ■ If you **make contact** with someone, you find out where they are and talk or write to them. ■ If you **come into contact with** someone or something, you meet them in the course of your work or other activities. ■ If something comes into **contact** with something else, it touches it. ■ A **contact** is someone you know who is in a position to give you help.

contact lens – **Contact lenses** are small plastic lenses which you wear directly on the surface of your eyes, instead of glasses.

contagion is the spreading of a particular disease by touch. ■ You use **contagion** to describe the spreading of ideas that you do not like. ...*the contagion of foreign ideas.*

contagious A **contagious** disease can be caught by touching people that have it. ■ A **contagious** feeling or attitude spreads quickly.

contain (**containing, contained; containable**) If something like a box **contains** certain things, those things are inside it. You can also say a book or document **contains** information or ideas. ■ If a substance **contains** something, that thing is part of it. *Turkey contains even less fat than chicken.* ■ If something **contains** a quality or feature, it has it. *Not one of these reports contained any truth.* ■ If you **contain** something, you control it and stop it spreading or increasing. If a problem is **containable,** it can be prevented from getting worse. ■ If you cannot **contain** a feeling, you cannot help showing it.

container A **container** is a very large sealed metal box for transporting goods. A **container** vehicle is designed to carry containers. ■ Anything which is used to hold or store things can be called a **container.**

containment is used to talk about actions taken to keep a country's influence within limits. ■ The **containment** of something dangerous is keeping it under control within a particular area.

contaminate (**contaminating, contaminated; contamination, contaminant**) If something is **contaminated** by dirt or other substances, it becomes polluted by them. Substances which contaminate are called **contaminants.**

contemplate (**contemplating, contemplated; contemplation**) If you **contemplate** doing something, you think about whether to do it or not. ■ If someone will not **contemplate** something, they will not

consider it as a possibility. *He refuses to contemplate failure.* ■ If something which might happen would be extremely unpleasant, you can say it is too unpleasant **to contemplate.** ■ If you **contemplate,** you spend a long time thinking deeply about something. ...*prayer and contemplation.* ■ If you **contemplate** someone or something, you look at them for a long time.

contemplative Someone who is **contemplative** thinks deeply, or is thinking in a serious and calm way. *I went for long contemplative walks.*

contemporaneous (**contemporaneously**) If two things are **contemporaneous,** they happen or exist at the same time.

contemporary (**contemporaries**) **Contemporary** things are modern and relate to the present time. ...*one of Australia's finest contemporary writers.* ■ You can use **contemporary** to describe things which existed or happened at the same time as something else you are talking about. ...*the Elizabethan house was roughly contemporary with the original college.* ■ Someone's **contemporaries** are people who are or were alive at the same time as them. ...*Columbus and his contemporaries.*

contempt If someone feels **contempt** for a person or **holds** them **in contempt,** they have no respect for them. ■ **Contempt of court** is the criminal offence of disobeying an instruction from a judge or court, or behaving disrespectfully in court. Someone who commits this offence is said to be **in contempt.**

contemptible If you call someone **contemptible,** you are emphasizing your strong dislike and disrespect for them. ...*a contemptible moral coward.*

contemptuous (**contemptuously**) If you are **contemptuous** of someone, you have no respect for them.

contend (**contender**) If you have to **contend** with a difficulty, you have to deal with it. ■ When people **contend** for something, they compete with each other for it. The people competing for something are called the **contenders.** ■ If you **contend** that something is true, you state or argue that it is true.

content (**contents; contented, contentedly, contentment**) The **contents** (*pron:* **kon**-tents) of something are the things inside it. ■ The **content** or **contents** of a piece of writing, speech, or TV programme are the subject matter and the ideas expressed in it. ■ **Content** is used to talk about the amount of something that a substance contains. ...*the carbon content of fossil fuels.* ■ If you are **content** (*pron:* kon-**tent**) with something, you are satisfied with it. You can also be **content** to do something. ■ If you **content** yourself with something, you make do with it. *Having missed a tour, I contented myself with a visit to nearby Mount Diablo.* ■ If you are **content** or **contented,** you are happy with your way of life. This feeling is called **contentment.**

contention (**contentious**) If someone keeps saying something is true, you can say it is their **contention** that it is true. ■ If something is **contentious** or a source of **contention,** there is disagreement about it. ■ If you are **in contention** in a competition, you have a chance of winning. If you are **out**

of contention, you have no chance. ■ **bone of contention:** see **bone.**

contentment See **content.**

contest (contestant) A **contest** is a competition or game. The people taking part are called the **contestants.** ■ When people compete for power, this is called a **contest.** ■ If someone **contests** (pron: kon-**tests**) an election or competition, they enter it and try to win it. ■ If someone **contests** a statement or decision, they make a formal objection to it.

context The **context** in which something happens is the circumstances which surround it and help to explain it. *This conflict needs to be placed in its historical context.* ■ The **context** of a word or sentence is the words or sentences before it and after it. ■ If part of a statement is taken or quoted **out of context,** the rest of what is said is left out, giving a misleading impression. ■ If something is **put in context,** it is considered together with all the factors that relate to it. *Statistics of this kind need to be put into context.*

contiguous If things are **contiguous,** they are next to each other, or touching each other.

continent (continental) A **continent** is a large land mass, for example Europe or Africa. **Continental** means to do with a continent. ■ In Britain and Ireland, the mainland of Europe is sometimes called the **Continent,** especially central and southern Europe. **Continental** means to do with this area; the people who live in this area are sometimes called **continentals.**

continental breakfast A **continental breakfast** is a light breakfast, usually consisting of bread, butter, jam, and a hot drink.

continental quilt A **continental quilt** is the same as a duvet.

continental shelf The **continental shelf** is the shallow sea bed surrounding a continent, as distinct from the deep ocean.

contingency (pron: kon-**tin**-jen-see) **(contingencies)** A **contingency** is something which might happen in the future. ■ A **contingency plan** is one intended to be used if a possible future situation arises.

contingent A **contingent** is a group of people representing a country or organization. ■ A **contingent** of police or soldiers is a group of them. ■ If one thing is **contingent** on another, it can only happen if the other thing happens or exists.

continual (continually) Continual is used to describe (a) something which goes on without stopping. (b) something which is repeated again and again.

continuance The **continuance** of something is the same as its continuation.

continuation The **continuation** of something is the fact that it continues to happen or exist. ■ If one thing is a **continuation** of another, it follows on from it and forms an extra part of it.

continue (continuing, continued) If someone or something **continues** to do something, they keep doing it. ■ If you **continue** with something, you keep doing it or using it. ■ If something **continues,** it does not stop. ■ You say something **continues** when it starts again after stopping for a period of time. ■ You say someone **continues** when they begin speaking again after stopping. ■ If someone or something **continues** in a particular direction, they keep going in that direction.

continuing education consists of courses for adults in subjects which interest them or further their existing skills.

continuity (continuities) You say there is **continuity** when something stays the same although other things are being changed. *...continuity between the old government and the new.* ■ In film-making, **continuity** is the smooth arrangement of the scenes so there are no gaps between them.

continuous (continuously) If something is **continuous,** it goes on without stopping or being interrupted. ■ A **continuous** line or surface has no gaps or holes in it.

continuum (pron: kon-**tin**-yu-um) A **continuum** is a series or progression of things in which each thing is slightly different from the next one to it in the series.

contorted (contortion) If something is **contorted,** it is twisted into an unnatural and unattractive shape. *...the contortions of gymnasts* ■ You can describe people's actions as **contortions** when they are forced to do something difficult or complicated to achieve what they want. *Governor Casey went through public contortions appointing an interim successor.*

contortionist – **Contortionists** are entertainers who twist their bodies into strange and unnatural positions.

contour If you talk about the **contours** of something, you mean its shape. ■ On a map, a **contour** is a line joining points of equal height.

contraband is goods taken into or out of a country illegally, to avoid taxation.

contraception (contraceptive) Contraception is preventing pregnancy, especially by using a device or pill. ■ A **contraceptive** is a device or pill for preventing pregnancy.

contract (contraction) A **contract** (pron: **kon**-trakt) is a legal agreement, usually to do with the sale of something or with work done for a set amount of money. If you **contract** (pron: kon-**trakt**) with someone to do something, you legally promise to do it. ■ If you are **under contract** to someone, you have signed a contract agreeing to work for them and nobody else during a fixed period of time. ■ If something **contracts,** it gets smaller. *...the contraction and expansion of blood vessels.* ■ A **contraction** is a shortened form of a word or words. ■ **Contractions** are the painful tightenings of the muscles of a woman's uterus during childbirth. ■ If you **contract** an illness, you get it.

contractor A **contractor** is a company that does work for other people.

contractual (contractually) Contractual means to do with a legal contract.

contradict (contradiction, contradictory) If you **contradict** someone, you say the opposite of what they have said. ■ If two statements **contradict** each other or are **contradictory,** they cannot both be correct. When you get statements like these, you say there is a **contradiction.**

contraflow During repairs on major roads, a **contraflow** is a line of traffic using a lane normally used by traffic going in the opposite direction.

contralto A **contralto** is a female singer with a low singing voice.

contraption People sometimes call a strange-looking machine a **contraption.**

contrary opinions are opposing ones which cannot be held by the same person at the same time. ■ If something is **contrary** to accepted practices, it goes against them. ■ You say **contrary to...** when mentioning an incorrect statement or mistaken belief, before going on to say what the truth is. *Contrary to reports, no one had been executed.* ■ You say **on the contrary** when you are contradicting what has just been said. ■ If you talk about a statement **to the contrary,** you mean a statement which says the opposite of what has just been said. *He denounced statements to the contrary as slanderous and untrue.*

contrast (**contrasting, contrastingly**) If one thing **contrasts** (*pron:* kon-**trasts**) with another or there is a **contrast** (*pron:* **kon**-trast) between them, they appear very different when you compare them. ■ If you **contrast** two or more things, you compare them to show the differences between them. ■ You say **by contrast** or **in contrast** when you are mentioning something which has very different features from the thing you have just described.

contravene (**contravening, contravened; contravention**) If someone **contravenes** a law, they do something which is forbidden by it. You call this a **contravention** of the law.

contretemps (*pron:* **kon**-tra-ton) (*plural:* **contretemps**) A **contretemps** is a small but embarrassing disagreement.

contribute (**contributing, contributed; contribution; contributor, contributory**) When people make a **contribution** or **contribute** to something, they do something to help it succeed. ■ When people **contribute** money to a cause or make a **contribution,** they give money. You say each person is a **contributor.** ■ If something **contributes** to a situation, it is one of the factors responsible for it. You call something like this a **contributor** to a situation or a **contributory** factor. *High blood pressure is known to be a major contributory factor in heart attacks.* ■ If you **contribute** to a book or magazine, you write a piece which is printed in it. Each piece like this is called a **contribution;** the people who write the pieces are called **contributors.**

contrite (**contrition**) If you are **contrite,** you are sorry about something you have done wrong. This feeling is called **contrition.**

contrivance A **contrivance** is an unorthodox or dishonest way of achieving something. ■ People sometimes call an unusual machine a **contrivance.**

contrive (**contriving, contrived**) If you **contrive** to do something difficult, you succeed in doing it. ■ If you **contrive** a situation, you arrange for it to happen, often by dishonest means. ■ If you say the

plot of a novel or film is **contrived,** you mean it is unlikely and unconvincing.

control (**controlling, controlled**) The people who **control** or have **control** of a country or organization are those who decide how it is run. ■ If something is **controlled** by an automatic system, the system makes it do whatever is required. ■ A machine's **controls** are the devices used to operate it. ■ **Controls** are methods a government uses to restrict certain things, like wage increases. ■ If you **control** yourself or **keep control** of yourself, you act calmly and do not give way to your feelings. ■ If you **lose control** of yourself, you give way to your feelings. ■ If people **control** something unpleasant or dangerous, they stop it getting worse; when they succeed, you say it is **under control.** ■ If something has got **out of control,** nobody has the power to stop it causing damage. ■ If something is **outside your control** or **beyond your control,** you have no power to do anything about it.

controllable If something is **controllable,** it can be managed or limited.

controller A **controller** in an organization is someone with responsibility for a part of its work. *...the BBC's controller of editorial policy.*

control tower A **control tower** is an airport building from which take off and landing instructions are given to aircraft.

controversial (**controversially; controversy, controversies**) If something is **controversial** or causes **controversy,** it causes a lot of discussion, disagreement, or disapproval.

contusion A **contusion** is a bruise.

conundrum A **conundrum** is a puzzling problem.

conurbation A **conurbation** is a large urban area formed when several towns have grown and joined together.

convalesce (**convalescing, convalesced; convalescent, convalescence**) If you are **convalescing,** you are resting and getting your health back after an illness or operation. **Convalescence** is the period during which you do this. *...a convalescent home.*

convection is the process by which heat travels through gases and liquids.

convector A **convector** or **convector heater** is a heater which heats a room by circulating hot air.

convene (**convening, convened**) When a meeting or conference is **convened,** someone arranges for it to take place, according to an established procedure. ■ When a group of people **convene,** they come together for a meeting.

convener (*or* **convenor**) A **convener** is (a) someone who arranges for a meeting to take place. (b) a trade union official responsible for organizing shop stewards.

convenience If something is done for your **convenience,** it is done to make things easy for you. **Conveniences** are things which are there to make things easy for you. *...luxury tents containing every convenience.* See also **public convenience, flag of convenience, marriage of convenience.**

convenience food – **Convenience foods** are frozen, dried, or tinned foods which require no preparation except heating.

convenience store – Convenience stores are shops which stay open long hours.

convenient (conveniently) You say something is **convenient** when it fits in well with what you want. ■ If something like a shop is **convenient,** it is nearby.

convenor See **convener.**

convent A **convent** is (a) a building where nuns live. (b) a school run by nuns.

convention – Conventions are accepted ways of behaving or doing things. ■ A **convention** is (a) a large meeting of an organization. (b) an international agreement, especially one concerned with people's rights.

conventional (conventionally) Conventional opinions and behaviour are accepted by most people as normal and right. ■ If you say a person is **conventional,** you mean there is nothing unusual about them. ■ The **conventional** way of doing something is the way it is normally done. ...*conventionally produced British wines.* ■ Conventional forces, weapons, or wars are non-nuclear.

converge (converging, converged; convergence, convergent) When people **converge** on a place, they reach it from different directions. ■ When roads or rivers **converge,** they meet or join together. ■ If there is a **convergence** of things like ideas or systems or they **converge,** they become more and more alike until there is no difference between them. If different people's ideas are **convergent,** they are the same.

conversant If you are **conversant** with something, you are familiar with it.

conversation (conversational, conversationally; conversationalist) When people have a **conversation,** they talk to each other informally. If you **make conversation,** you talk to someone to be polite, rather than because you want to. **Conversational** means to do with conversations. If someone is a good **conversationalist,** they are good at keeping a conversation going.

converse (conversing, conversed; conversely) When people **converse** (*pron:* kon-**verse**), they talk to each other. ■ **Converse** (*pron:* **kon**-verse) is used to talk about something working or applying in opposite ways. For example, if John admires Rita, the **converse** would be that Rita admires John.

convert (conversion) If something is **converted** into something else, it is turned into it. You talk about the **conversion** of one thing to another. ■ If you **convert** to a different set of beliefs or are **converted** to them, you adopt them in place of the ones you had before. A **convert** (*pron:* **kon**-vert) is someone who has changed their beliefs. ...*his conversion to Christianity.* ■ In rugby, if a player **converts** a try, he scores extra points by kicking the ball over the crossbar. This is called a **conversion.**

converter See **catalytic converter.**

convertible If something is **convertible,** it can be changed from one thing into another. ■ A **convertible** currency is one which can easily be exchanged for another currency. ■ A **convertible** is a car with a soft roof which can be folded down or taken off.

convex A **convex** lens or mirror curves outwards towards its centre. See also **concave.**

convey If you **convey** a piece of information, you succeed in making it understood. ■ If a vehicle **conveys** you somewhere, it takes you there.

conveyance A **conveyance** is a vehicle. ■ The **conveyance** of something is the process of carrying or transporting it from one place to another. ...*piles of luggage waiting conveyance.*

conveyancing is the process of transferring legal ownership of property.

conveyor belt A **conveyor belt** is a moving strip or series of rollers used to move items from one place to another.

convict (conviction) If someone is **convicted** (*pron:* kon-**vikt**-id) of a crime, they are found guilty of it. *Her conviction for murder was upheld.* ■ A **convict** (*pron:* **kon**-vikt) is a person serving a prison sentence. ■ A person's **convictions** are their strongly held beliefs. **Conviction** is believing strongly in something. ■ If something **carries conviction,** it is likely to be believed.

convince (convincing, convinced; convincingly) If you **convince** someone of something, you persuade them it is true. ■ If something is **convincing,** it makes you believe something is true. *He has demonstrated convincingly that stammering is not simply a psychological problem.*

convivial (conviviality) A **convivial** person or occasion is friendly and cheerful.

convocation A **convocation** is a large meeting, especially of clergy.

convoluted If something is **convoluted,** it is complicated and difficult to follow.

convoy A **convoy** is a group of ships or other vehicles travelling together.

convulse (convulsing, convulsed; convulsion) If a violent or dramatic event **convulses** an area, it stops it functioning in its normal way. ■ If someone **convulses** or has **convulsions,** their body muscles jerk violently and uncontrollably.

convulsive (convulsively) Convulsive body movements are violent and uncontrollable. *His arms and legs jerked convulsively.*

coo When doves **coo,** they make soft low sounds. ■ If a person **coos,** they say something in a soft low voice.

cook (cooking, cooked) If you **cook** food, you heat it, to make it ready to eat. **Cooking** is preparing food like this. **Cooking** is also used to talk about a particular style of preparing and cooking food. ...*French cooking.* A **cook** is someone who prepares food, especially as their job. ■ If you say someone is **cooking the books,** you mean they are changing figures, to deceive people. ■ If someone **cooks up** a dishonest scheme, they plan it.

cookbook See **cookery.**

cooker A **cooker** is a piece of equipment for heating food using gas or electricity.

cookery is preparing and cooking food. ■ A **cookery book** or **cookbook** is a book which tells you how to prepare different dishes.

cookie is the usual American word for biscuit.

cool (cooler, coolest; coolness; cooling, cooled; coolly) If something is **cool**, it has a low temperature but is not cold. ■ When something **cools** or you **cool** it, its temperature lowers. ■ If you **cool off**, you make yourself cooler after being too hot. ■ If you are **cool** towards another person, you are unfriendly to them. ■ If someone is **cool** towards an idea or suggestion, they are unenthusiastic about it. ■ If you stay **cool** in a situation, you remain calm. If you **cool down**, you gradually become less angry. ■ If you say that someone or something is **cool**, you mean they are fashionable and attractive. ...*a really cool dress.*

coolant A **coolant** is a liquid or gas used for cooling machinery.

cooler A **cooler** is a container for keeping something cool.

coolie Unskilled workers in China, India, and other parts of Asia used to be called **coolies.**

cooling-off A **cooling-off period** is time taken by both sides during a dispute to rethink their position before taking further action.

cooling tower A **cooling tower** is a large round high building for cooling water from factories or power stations.

coop (cooped) A **coop** is a cage for a small number of hens. ■ You say someone is **cooped up** in a place when the place is too small for them, or they are unable to leave it.

co-op A **co-op** is (a) a co-operative. (b) a co-operative society.

co-operate (or **cooperate**) (**co-operating, co-operated; co-operation**) When people **co-operate**, they work together to try to achieve something. ■ If you **co-operate** with someone, you help them and do not make difficulties for them.

co-operative (or **cooperative**) (**co-operatively**) A **co-operative** is a business or organization owned by the people who run it. ■ **Co-operative** activities involve people working together. *They were used to working co-operatively.* ■ If someone is being **co-operative,** they are being helpful.

co-operative society A **co-operative society** is a commercial organization with several shops in a particular district. Customers can join the organization and get a share of its profits.

co-opt If the members of an organization **co-opt** you, they vote to make you a member. ■ If you **co-opt** someone, you persuade them to help or support you.

co-ordinate (or **coordinate**) (**co-ordinating, co-ordinated; co-ordination, co-ordinator**) If you **co-ordinate** a project or activity, you organize the people taking part and make sure they work together properly. A person who does this is called a **co-ordinator.** ■ If you cannot **co-ordinate** your body's movements, you cannot get them to work together properly. ■ A **co-ordinate** is one of a pair of numbers or letters which give the location of a point on a map or graph. ■ **Co-ordinates** are clothes or soft furnishings which are similar, and which are intended to be worn or used together. If you **co-ordinate** clothes or furnishings, or if they **co-ordinate,** they are similar in some way, and look nice together.

coot – Coots are small water birds with black feathers and a white patch above their beaks.

cop (copping, copped) A **cop** is a police officer. ■ If you say someone is **copping out** of something, you mean they are avoiding doing something you think they ought to do. A **cop-out** is a way of avoiding doing something.

cope (coping, coped) If you **cope** with a problem, you manage to deal with it.

copier A **copier** is a machine which can make an exact copy of a piece of writing or a picture.

co-pilot The **co-pilot** of a plane helps the chief pilot and sometimes flies the plane.

copious (copiously) A **copious** amount of something is very large. *They drink copiously.*

copper is (a) a soft reddish-brown metal. (b) a reddish-brown colour. ■ **Coppers** are brown coins of low value. ■ A **copper** is a police officer.

copper beech The **copper beech** is a type of beech tree with purple or copper-coloured leaves.

copper-bottomed is used to describe things which are financially reliable. ...*a copper-bottomed business plan.*

copperplate is a style of very neat and regular handwriting.

coppice When trees are **coppiced,** they are cut very low, so they will grow shoots which can be used to make poles. ■ A **coppice** is the same as a copse.

copse A **copse** is a small dense wood.

copulate (copulating, copulated; copulation) When people or animals **copulate,** they have sex. **Copulation** is having sex.

copy (copies, copying, copied) A **copy** is something made to look exactly like something else. ■ If you **copy** a document, you make a copy of it on a machine such as a photocopier. ■ If you **copy** what someone has written, **copy** it **down,** or **copy** it **out,** you write it down. ■ If you **copy** another person's behaviour or clothes, you act like that person or dress like them. ■ A **copy** of a book, newspaper, or record is one of many identical ones produced at the same time.

copybook If someone **blots their copybook,** they spoil their record of good behaviour or success by doing something wrong.

copycat A **copycat** crime imitates one that has been committed earlier. ■ A **copycat** is someone who copies your behaviour, dress, or ideas.

copyright If someone has the **copyright** on something like a piece of writing or music, it is illegal to print it or perform it without their permission.

copywriter A **copywriter** is someone who writes the words for advertisements.

coquettish If you say that a woman is being **coquettish,** you mean she behaves in a playful way, to make herself attractive to men.

coracle A **coracle** is a simple rounded rowing boat made of woven sticks covered with skins or canvas.

coral is a hard substance made up of the skeletons of very small sea animals.

cor anglais (*plural:* **cors anglais**) The **cor anglais** is a double-reed woodwind instrument with a slightly lower pitch than the oboe.

corbel A **corbel** is a piece of stone or wood sticking out of a wall and supporting an arch, pillar, or beam.

cord is a type of strong string or thin rope. ■ **Cords** are corduroy trousers.

cordial (**cordially, cordiality**) If relationships are **cordial,** they are friendly and polite. ■ **Cordial** is a sweet non-alcoholic fruit drink. ■ In the US, **cordial** is a sweet liqueur.

cordite is an explosive substance used in guns and bombs.

cordon (**cordoning, cordoned**) If police or soldiers form a **cordon** round an area or **cordon** it **off,** they form a line round it to stop people entering or leaving.

cordon bleu (*pron:* **bluh**) is cookery of the highest standard.

corduroy is a thick velvety ridged cotton fabric.

core (**coring, cored**) The **core** of a fruit is the hard part through its centre where the seeds are. If you **core** an apple or pear, you remove its core. The **core** of some other object is its central part. *...the sun's core.* ■ The **core** of something like a problem or proposal is its most important part. ■ If you say someone is a certain type of person **to the core,** you mean they are like that and are never likely to change. *The villagers are royalist to the core.* ■ In a school or college, **core** subjects are ones a group of subjects which have to be studied. ■ The **core** businesses or **core** activities of a company are their most important ones.

corgi – Corgis are a type of dog with short legs, a sturdy body, and a pointed nose.

coriander is a plant with parsley-like leaves. Its seeds are used as a spice and its leaves as a herb.

cork is the soft light spongy bark of a Mediterranean tree. A **cork** is a stopper made from cork.

corkscrew A **corkscrew** is a device for removing the corks from bottles.

cormorant – Cormorants are large dark-coloured sea birds.

corn Various cereal crops are called **corn,** for example wheat or barley in England and maize in the US. ■ **Corn on the cob** is the long round part of the maize plant with sweetcorn on it. ■ A **corn** is a small painful area of hard skin which can form on your foot, usually caused by ill-fitting shoes.

cornea (*pron:* **korn**-ee-a *or* korn-**ee**-a) (**corneal**) The **cornea** is the curved transparent layer of skin covering the front of your eyeball. **Corneal** means to do with the cornea. *...corneal grafts.*

corned beef is beef which has been cooked, preserved in salt water, then tinned.

corner (**cornering, cornered**) A **corner** is a place where two sides or edges of something meet. ■ A **corner** is a place where a road bends sharply. ■ If you say something happens **in every corner** of a place, you mean it happens in all parts of it. ■ If you **corner** someone, you trap them in a place or situation. ■ If you are **in a corner,** you are in a difficult situation from which there seems to be no escape. ■ If someone **corners the market** in a commodity, they gain complete control of the trade in it. ■ If you **cut corners,** you do a task quickly by being less thorough than you should. ■ In games like football, a **corner** is a free kick taken from the corner of the pitch.

corner shop A **corner shop** is a small shop, usually on a street corner, which sells food and household goods.

cornerstone The **cornerstone** of something is the basis of its existence or success. *The family doctor is the cornerstone of the health service.*

cornet The **cornet** is a brass band instrument like a small trumpet. ■ A **cornet** is a cone-shaped wafer filled with ice cream.

cornfield A **cornfield** is a field where corn is being grown.

cornflakes are a breakfast cereal of flakes made from maize.

cornflour is a fine white flour made from maize, used to thicken sauces.

cornflower – Cornflowers are small flowers with deep blue petals.

cornice (*pron:* **korn**-iss) A **cornice** is a decorative strip of plaster, wood, or stone along the top of a wall.

Cornish pasty A **Cornish pasty** is a flat meat and vegetable pie with pointed ends.

cornucopia (*pron:* korn-yew-**kope**-ee-a) A **cornucopia** of good things is a large number of them.

corny (**cornier, corniest**) **Corny** jokes and stories are simple, obvious, and unoriginal.

corollary (*pron:* kor-**roll**-a-ree) (**corollaries**) A **corollary** of something is an idea or fact which results directly from it.

corona (*pron:* kor-**rone**-a) (*plural:* **coronas** *or* **coronae**) The moon's **corona** is a circle of light surrounding it. ■ The sun's **corona** is the outermost part of its atmosphere, visible as a faint halo during an eclipse.

coronary (**coronaries**) **Coronary** means relating to the arteries around the heart. *...coronary disease.* ■ A **coronary** or **coronary thrombosis** is a heart attack caused by a clot in one of the arteries around the heart.

coronation A king's or queen's **coronation** is the ceremony during which they are crowned.

coroner A **coroner** is an official responsible for investigating sudden, violent, or suspicious deaths.

coronet A **coronet** is a small crown.

corpora See **corpus.**

corporal A **corporal** is a junior NCO in the army and the RAF.

corporal punishment is punishing people by hitting them.

corporate means relating to large companies. *...corporate affairs.*

corporation A **corporation** is a large company. ■ The **corporation** of a town or city is the local authority responsible for running it.

corporation tax is a tax companies pay on their profits.

corporatism is a system in which large self-interest groups such as employers' associations and trade unions co-operate with the government in return for a large say in how the country is governed.

corporeal (*pron:* kor-**pore**-ee-al) means relating to the human body, rather than the mind or spirit. *...corporeal desires.*

corps (*pron:* **kore**) (*plural:* **corps**) A **corps** is a part of the army which has special duties. *...the catering corps.* ■ A **corps** is a small group of people who do a special job. *...the New Zealand press corps.*

corpse A **corpse** is a dead body.

corpulent (**corpulence**) If someone is **corpulent,** they are fat. **Corpulence** is being fat.

corpus (*plural:* **corpora**) The **corpus** of an author's work is all his or her writings which have been collected or identified. Similarly, you can talk about the **corpus** of writing on a subject.

corpuscle – **Corpuscles** are red or white blood cells.

corral (*pron:* kor-**rahl**) (**corralling, corralled**) In the US and Canada, a **corral** is a fenced-off area where cattle or horses are kept. When horses or cattle are **corralled,** they are driven into a corral. ■ You say people are **corralled** when a lot of them are forced into a confined place.

correct (**correctly, correctness, correction**) If something is **correct,** there are no mistakes in it. ■ If you **correct** a fault, you put it right. ■ If you **correct** a piece of writing or make **corrections** to it, you indicate the mistakes, or alter them to put them right. ■ If you say someone is **correct,** you mean what they have said is true. ■ If you **correct** a person, you point out that what they have said is wrong, and tell them what they should have said. ■ The **correct** thing is the right or most suitable one. ■ **Correct** behaviour is doing what is thought to be the right thing in a particular situation. ■ **political correctness:** see **politically correct.**

corrective actions are intended to put something right. An action or piece of writing which puts something right can be called a **corrective.** ■ **Corrective** treatment of offenders is intended to stop them offending again.

correlate (**correlating, correlated; correlation**) If one thing **correlates** with another or there is a **correlation** between them, there is a definite connection or similarity between them, so that a change in the second thing tends to produce a change in the first.

correspond (**corresponding, correspondingly; correspondence**) If one thing **corresponds** to another or there is a **correspondence** between them, the two things are similar or closely related. ■ If people **correspond** or carry on a **correspondence,** they write letters to each other. ■ A person's **correspondence** is the letters they receive.

correspondence course A **correspondence course** is one where you study at home and your work is sent to you by post.

correspondent A **correspondent** is a reporter who covers a special subject or a particular country.

corridor A **corridor** is a passage between rooms in a building. ■ When people talk about the **corridors of power,** they mean the places where the most important government decisions are made. ■ A **corridor** is a strip of land or air space across a country along which vehicles or planes from another country are allowed to travel.

corroborate (**corroborating, corroborated; corroboration, corroborative**) If you **corroborate** what someone says, you provide facts which suggest it is true. You call these facts **corroboration** or describe them as **corroborative.**

corrode (**corroding, corroded; corrosive, corrosion**) When a metal **corrodes** or is **corroded,** it is eaten away by chemical action. A **corrosive** substance is one which has this effect. Damage caused in this way is called **corrosion.**

corrugated (**corrugation**) **Corrugated** cardboard or metal has parallel grooves and ridges in it to strengthen it. These folds are called **corrugations.**

corrupt (**corrupting, corrupted; corruptly, corruption**) A **corrupt** person behaves dishonestly in exchange for money or power. ■ If there is **corruption** in a system or if a system is **corrupt,** it is run dishonestly. ■ If someone is **corrupted** by another person, they are made dishonest or immoral.

corruptible If someone is **corruptible,** they are easily corrupted.

corsage (*pron:* kor-**sazh**; *the 'zh' sounds like 's' in 'pleasure'*) A **corsage** is a small bunch of flowers that is fastened to a woman's dress below the shoulder.

corsair A **corsair** was a pirate, or a pirate ship.

corset A **corset** is a stiff tight piece of underwear worn by some women to make them look slimmer.

cortege (*pron:* kor-**tayzh**; *the 'zh' sounds like 's' in 'pleasure'*) A **cortege** is a funeral procession.

cortex (**cortices**) The **cortex** of the brain, or of another organ, is its outer layer.

cortisone is a hormone used to treat arthritis, allergies, and some skin diseases.

coruscating A **coruscating** speech or performance is lively, intelligent, and impressive. *...an unstoppable flow of coruscating humour.*

corvette A **corvette** is a lightly armed warship.

cosh (**coshes, coshing, coshed**) A **cosh** is a heavy blunt weapon. If someone **coshes** you, they hit you on the head with a cosh.

cosily (**cosiness**) See **cosy.**

cosmetic – **Cosmetics** are things like lipstick which people use on their face, to make it look better. ■ **Cosmetic surgery** is an operation carried out to improve someone's appearance. ■ **Cosmetic** changes alter the appearance of something without actually improving its basic nature.

cosmic means occurring in, or coming from, outer space. *...cosmic dust.* ■ **Cosmic** means things belonging to or connected with the universe. ■ **Cosmic** means to do with everyone, rather than just a few people. *...themes of cosmic significance.*

cosmology (**cosmological, cosmologist**) **Cosmology** is the study of the origin and nature of the universe. *...cosmological theories.*

cosmonaut is a Russian name for an astronaut.

cosmopolitan (**cosmopolitanism**) You say a place is **cosmopolitan** when the people there come from many different countries or cultures. ■ You can say someone is **cosmopolitan** if they have lived in many different countries and as a result are open to different ideas.

cosmos The **cosmos** is the universe.

cosset (cosseting, cosseted) If you **cosset** someone, you do everything for them and protect them from anything unpleasant.

cost The **cost** of something or what it **costs** is how much you need to spend to buy it, make it, or do it. ■ If you **cost** something, you work out how much it will cost to do or make it. ■ If something is sold at **cost price**, it is sold for what it cost the manufacturer to make it or the seller to buy it. ■ The **cost of living** is the average amount people need to pay for things like food, clothing, and housing. ■ The **cost** of achieving something is the loss, damage, or injury involved in achieving it. ...*profits made at the cost of much misery to thousands of people.* ■ If a mistake **costs** you something, you fail to get it as a result of the mistake. *It was his error that cost the team its first victory.* ■ If you say something must be done **at all costs**, you mean it must be done even if it means making sacrifices.

co-star (co-starring, co-starred) If an actor **co-stars** or is a **co-star** in a film or play, they star in it with someone else.

cost-effective If something is **cost-effective**, it saves or makes more money than it costs to do or make.

costly (costlier, costliest) If something is **costly**, it is expensive. ■ You can say something people do is **costly** when it causes great loss or damage.

costume is used to talk about the style of clothing traditional to a place or worn during a certain time in history. ...*medieval costume.* ■ An actor's **costume** is the set of clothes they wear on stage. ■ A **costume drama** is a play or film set in the past, with the actors wearing the style of clothing from that period.

costume jewellery is jewellery made from cheap materials.

costumier A **costumier** is a person or firm that makes or supplies theatrical or fancy dress costumes.

cosy (*Am:* cozy) (**cosier, cosiest; cosily, cosiness**) **Cosy** places are small, warm, and comfortable. ■ If people are on friendly terms, you can call their relationship **cosy.**

cot A **cot** is a bed with high sides for a very young child. ■ Americans call a camp bed a **cot.** ■ A **cot death** is the sudden unexplained death of a young baby in its sleep. This phenomenon is also known as **SIDS** or 'sudden infant death syndrome'.

coterie (*pron:* kote-er-ee) A **coterie** is a small group of people who work together or are close friends and do not want other people to join them.

cottage A **cottage** is a small house in the country.

cottage cheese is a soft mild white cheese made from sour milk.

cottage industry A **cottage industry** is a small business run from someone's home.

cottage pie is a dish of minced beef, with a layer of mashed potato on top.

cotton (cottoning, cottoned) **Cotton** is cloth made from the soft white fibres of a plant called the **cot-**ton plant. ■ **Cotton** is thread used for sewing. ■ If you **cotton on** to something, you realize it or understand it.

cotton wool is a white fluffy substance made from the fibres of the cotton plant. It is used for things like cleaning the skin.

couch (couches, couching, couched) A **couch** is a long cushioned piece of furniture for sitting or lying on. ■ If something like a statement is **couched** in a certain style, it is expressed in that way. *The government's radical objectives are often couched in moderate terms.*

couchette (*pron:* koo-**shet**) A **couchette** is a bed in a railway carriage or ferry boat, which is either folded against the wall or used as an ordinary seat during the day.

couch potato A **couch potato** is a lazy person who spends all their spare time watching TV.

cougar (*pron:* koo-gar) A **cougar** is the same as a puma.

cough When you **cough,** you force air out of your throat with a sudden harsh noise. ■ If you have a **cough,** you have an illness which makes you cough a lot. ■ If you **cough** blood or phlegm or **cough** it **up,** it comes out of your throat when you cough. ■ If you have to **cough up** money, you have to give it to someone when you do not want to.

could is the past tense of 'can'. You use it when you are talking about the past, or reporting what someone said or thought. *He could speak the language fluently... I was thankful I could walk again... She said that she could not get the time off work.* ■ If you are talking about the present, you use **could** to say someone is able to do something, but is not actually doing it. *A fifth of Europe's chemical producers could easily do such deals.* You use **could have** in a similar way when you are talking about the past. *The soldiers could have used tear gas or rubber bullets; instead they had mown people down with live ammunition.* ■ You use **could** to talk about a possibility in the present or the future. *Don't eat it. It could be a toadstool.* ■ You use **could** when you are asking for something politely. *Could I take the car to meet him, please?*

council (councillor) A **council** is the organization responsible for local government in an area. **Councillors** are elected members of a council. ■ A **council** is a panel of people who give advice or run an organization. ...*the Arts Council.* ■ A **council** is a specially organized meeting. *The union hopes that a successor will be appointed at its December council.*

Council of Europe The **Council of Europe** is an organization which promotes unity between European countries.

Council Tax The **Council Tax** is a local government tax based on the value of people's houses.

counsel (counselling, counselled; counsellor) (*Am:* **counseling,** *etc*) **Counsel** is advice or guidance. *I value her counsel.* If you **counsel** a course of action, you advise someone to take it. ■ If you **counsel** someone, you give them advice on how to deal with their problems. Giving advice like this is called **counselling;** a person who does it is called a

counsellor. ■ Someone's **counsel** is a lawyer who advises them and represents them in court.

count When you **count**, you say all the numbers in order, up to a certain number. ■ If you **count** a number of things, you add them up, to see how many there are. A figure worked out like this is called a **count**. *No wholly reliable count has yet been given.* ■ If you **keep count** of a number of things, you keep a record of how many there have been. ■ If something **counts**, it matters. *It's the small victories that count.* ■ If something **counts against** you, it puts you at a disadvantage. ■ If you **count** someone or something when you are making a statement, you include them in what you are saying. *Fishing is still the single most popular sport unless you count rambling.* ■ If you **count** someone or something as a particular thing, you regard them as that thing. *This will count as a victory.* ■ If you say you can **count on** someone or something, you mean you can rely on them. ■ A **count** is a legal charge brought against someone. *He was convicted on three counts of fraud.* ■ A **count** is a European nobleman with the same rank as a British earl.

countdown A **countdown** is the counting aloud of numbers in reverse order before something happens, especially before a spacecraft is launched. ■ The period of time leading up to any keenly awaited event can be called a **countdown.**

countenance (**countenancing, countenanced**) If someone will not **countenance** something, they will never agree to it. ■ A person's **countenance** is their face.

counter (**countering, countered**) In a place like a shop or café, a **counter** is a long narrow table or flat surface at which customers are served. ■ If you buy something **under the counter,** you buy it secretly and illegally. ■ A **counter** is a small flat disc used in board games. ■ If you **counter** something that someone does, you take action to limit its effects. ■ If you **counter** what someone says, you put forward a different point of view. ■ If one thing **runs counter to** another, the first thing is the opposite of the second, or conflicts with it. *...sale of its US holdings runs counter to the national trend.*

counter- is added to words to talk about actions or activities (a) intended to prevent other actions or activities. *...counter-corruption measures.* (b) which respond to other actions or activities. *...accusations and counter-accusations.*

counteract If you **counteract** something, you do something which reduces its effects.

counter-attack When someone **counter-attacks** or launches a **counter-attack,** they hit back at someone who has attacked them.

counterbalance (**counterbalancing, counterbalanced**) If one thing **counterbalances** another, it makes up for it with something which has an equal but opposite effect.

counterclockwise is the usual American word for 'anti-clockwise'.

counter-culture (*or* **counterculture**) A **counter-culture** is a set of values or a lifestyle which is completely different from the rest of society. *...the hippy counter-culture.*

counter-espionage is the actions a country takes to limit the effects of another country spying on it.

counterfeit (**counterfeiting, counterfeited; counterfeiter**) If someone **counterfeits** money or a document, they illegally make something which looks like the real thing. You say the thing they make is **counterfeit** or a **counterfeit.**

counterfoil A **counterfoil** is part of a cheque or ticket which you keep as proof of payment.

countermand If you **countermand** an order, you cancel it, usually by giving a different order.

counter-measure A **counter-measure** is an action taken to reduce the effects of something else, especially something harmful.

counterpane A **counterpane** is a decorative bed cover.

counterpart Someone's or something's **counterpart** is a person or thing with a similar role in a different place. *London Zoo now has fewer visitors than its counterpart in Chester.*

counterpoint If one thing **counterpoints** another or acts as a **counterpoint** to it, it contrasts with it in a satisfying way. ■ In music, **counterpoint** is a technique in which two or more different tunes are played together.

counter-productive If something is **counter-productive,** it has the opposite effect from what is intended.

counter-revolution (**counter-revolutionary, counter-revolutionaries**) A **counter-revolution** is a revolution aimed at undoing the effects of a previous revolution. ■ A **counter-revolutionary** is a person who is trying to undo the effects of a previous revolution. You can describe their activities as **counter-revolutionary.**

countersign If you **countersign** a document, you sign it after someone else has signed it.

countertenor A **countertenor** is a man who sings with a high voice that is similar to a low female singing voice.

counterweight If something acts as a **counterweight** to something else, it acts in an opposite way, and prevents its extreme effects. *...how to produce an effective counterweight to his growing influence.*

countess (**countesses**) In Britain, a **countess** is the wife or widow of an earl, or a peeress in her own right. ■ In some countries, a **countess** is the wife or widow of a count, or a woman with the same rank as a count.

countless means a great many, too many to be counted.

country (**countries**) A **country** is one of the political units the world is divided into, covering a particular area of land. ■ The people who live in a country are sometimes referred to as the **country.** ■ When a prime minister **goes to the country,** he or she holds a general election. ■ The **country** is all land which is away from towns and cities. ■ **Country** music is the same as country-and-western music.

country-and-western is popular music in the style of white people's folk music in the southern and western US.

country club A **country club** is a club in the country where members can play sports or attend social events.

country dancing is traditional folk dancing which people dance in rows, circles, or squares.

country house A **country house** is a large house in the country owned by a rich or titled family.

countryman (**countrywoman**) Your **countrymen** are people who belong to the same country as you. ■ A **countryman** is a person who lives in the country rather than in the town.

country seat The **country seat** of a rich or titled person is their large house in the country, as distinct from their house in town.

countryside The **countryside** is land away from towns and cities.

countrywide means happening or existing across an entire country.

county (**counties**) A **county** is a region of England, Wales, or Ireland which has its own local government.

county council A **county council** is the organization responsible for local government in a county.

county town A **county town** is the most important town in a county, from which the county is run.

coup (*pron:* **koo**) A **coup** is the same as a coup d'état. ■ A **coup** is a brilliant achievement which someone manages to pull off.

coup de grâce (*pron:* **koo** de **grahss**) If you give something the **coup de grâce**, you destroy its last chance of success.

coup d'état (**coups d'état**) (*pron:* **koo** day-**tah**) When there is a **coup d'état**, a group of people seize power in a country.

coupé (*pron:* **koo**-pay) A **coupé** is a car with a sloping back, two doors, and seats for two or four people.

couple (**coupling, coupled**) A **couple** is two people who are having a relationship. ■ You can refer to a small number of people or things as a **couple** of them when you are not sure how many there are. ■ If you say one thing **coupled with** another produces a particular effect, you mean the two things combined produce that effect. *A brilliant script coupled with Pacino's superb acting made this film a delight.* ■ If one piece of equipment is **coupled** to another, the two pieces are joined together.

couplet A **couplet** is two lines of poetry which come next to each other, especially lines which rhyme and have the same rhythm.

coupon A **coupon** is a slip of paper issued by the maker or supplier of a product which allows you to pay less money for it. ■ A **coupon** is a small form you send off to request information, to order something, or to enter a competition. ■ A football **coupon** is an entry form for the football pools.

courage (**courageous, courageously**) You talk about a person's **courage** or say they are **courageous** when they do something difficult or dangerous in spite of being afraid.

courgette (*pron:* koo-er-**zhet**; *the 'zh' sounds like 's' in 'pleasure'*) **Courgettes** are a type of small thin green marrow.

courier A **courier** is (a) someone paid to take letters or parcels direct from one place to another. (b) someone employed by a travel company to look after people on holiday.

course (**coursing, coursed**) You add **of course** to a statement to suggest that what you are saying is obviously true. ■ A **course of action** is a way of dealing with a problem. ■ A **course** is a series of lessons or lectures on a subject. ■ A **course** of medical treatment is a series of treatments given by a doctor. ■ A **course** is one part of a meal. ■ A racecourse or golf course is often called a **course**. ■ The **course** taken by a ship or plane is the direction it goes in. ■ If something happens **in the course of** a period of time, it happens during that period of time. ■ When something **runs** its **course**, it progresses naturally and comes to a natural end. ■ If something is done **as a matter of course**, it is done as part of your normal work or way of life. ■ If water or some other liquid **courses** somewhere, it flows there quickly.

court A **court** or **court of law** is a place where legal matters are decided by a judge and jury or by a magistrate. The judge and jury are sometimes called **the court**. ■ A **court** is an area marked out for playing a game like tennis, badminton, or squash. ■ If you say the **ball is in** someone's **court**, you mean it is now up to them to take some action. ■ The **court** of a king or queen is the household where they live and work, and the people who work for them. ■ If someone **courts** popularity, they do things which they hope will make them popular. ■ If you say someone is **courting** danger, you mean they are doing something very risky. ■ If a man and woman are **courting**, they are spending a lot of time together.

courteous (**courteously**) A **courteous** person is well-mannered and considerate.

courtesan (*pron:* kor-tiz-**zan**) In the past, a **courtesan** was a woman who was looked after financially by a wealthy man she had sex with.

courtesy (**courtesies**) **Courtesy** is polite behaviour. **Courtesies** are polite words or actions. ■ If you say something happens **courtesy of** someone or something, you mean they made it possible. ■ If something is done **courtesy of** someone, they have given their permission for it.

courthouse is the name given in the US to a building containing one or more law courts.

courtier In the past, **courtiers** were people who spent a lot of time at the court of a king or queen.

courtly behaviour is dignified and polite.

court martial (**martialling, martialled**) (*Am:* **martialing, martialed**) If someone in the armed forces is **court martialled,** they are tried by a military court called a **court martial**. The plural of 'court martial' is **court martials** or **courts martial.**

court of appeal (**courts of appeal**) A **court of appeal** deals with appeals against legal decisions.

court of inquiry (**courts of inquiry**) In the armed forces, a **court of inquiry** is an official investigation into a serious incident. The people who carry out the investigation are also called a **court of inquiry.**

court of law (**courts of law**) See **court.**

courtroom A **courtroom** is a room where a law court meets.

courtship A couple's **courtship** is the time they spend getting to know each other, before deciding to get married. ■ Displays by birds and animals to attract a mate are called **courtship.**

courtyard A **courtyard** is a small area surrounded by buildings or walls.

cousin Your **cousins** or **first cousins** are the children of your aunts and uncles. See also **second cousin.** ■ Groups of people or things that have something in common are sometimes called **cousins.** *The average European kitchen is smaller than its American cousin.*

couture (*pron:* koo-**tyoor**) (**couturier**) **Couture** is high fashion designing and dressmaking. A **couturier** is someone who designs, makes, and sells high fashion clothes for women. See also **haute couture.**

cove A **cove** is a small bay.

coven (*pron:* **kuv**-ven) A **coven** is a meeting of witches.

covenant (*pron:* **kuv**-ven-ant) A **covenant** is a legal written agreement between two people or groups. ■ If you **covenant** money to a charity or a trust, you make a formal written promise to pay that sum each year for a fixed period. The promise is called a **covenant** or **deed of covenant.**

cover (**covering, covered**) If you **cover** something or **cover** it **up,** you put something over it to protect it. ■ A **cover** is something put over an object to protect it. ■ The **cover** of a book or magazine is its outside part. ■ You say something **covers** something else when it forms a layer over it. ■ If you **take cover,** you shelter from something like the weather or gunfire. ■ If you **cover** a certain distance, for example when you are driving, that is how far you go. ■ If something **covers** a certain area, it extends over that area. ■ If someone or something **covers** a certain topic, they deal with it or discuss it. ■ If a sum of money **covers** something, it is enough to pay for it. ■ A **cover charge** is a set sum you have to pay in some clubs and restaurants, in addition to the money you spend on food and drinks. ■ If an insurance policy **covers** someone or something, it guarantees that money will be paid if they come to some harm. ■ A **cover** is something used to hide or disguise what is really going on. *He accused the government of using the relationship as a cover for drug activities.* ■ If someone **covers up** something they do not want other people to know about, they hide it from them. Hiding something like this is called a **cover-up.** ■ A **cover** of a song is another version made by a different performer from the original one.

coverage The **coverage** of something in the news is the reporting of it.

cover girl A **cover girl** is a model whose photograph appears on the front of a magazine.

covering A **covering** of something is a layer of it on top of something else.

covering letter A **covering letter** is a letter sent with another document or a parcel, to give more information.

coverlet A **coverlet** is a fancy cover for a bed.

covert (**covertly**) **Covert** is used to describe things which are done secretly.

cover-up See **cover.**

covet (**coveting, coveted; covetous, covetousness**) If you **covet** something belonging to someone else, you want it very much. Behaviour like this is called **covetous.**

cow (**cowed**) **Cows** are adult female cattle. ■ The females of some animal species are called **cows.** *...a cow elephant.* ■ If someone is **cowed,** they are frightened into behaving a certain way.

coward (**cowardly, cowardice**) A **coward** is someone who lacks courage and is unable to face difficult situations. You say someone like this is **cowardly** or talk about their **cowardice.** ■ People call a violent act **cowardly** when it involves little risk to the person who commits it.

cowboy In the US, a **cowboy** is a man whose job is to look after cattle. ■ A **cowboy** is a male character in a Western. ■ If you call contractors or tradesmen **cowboys,** you mean they do their job badly or sell shoddy goods.

cower (**cowering, cowered**) If you **cower,** you bend forward and downwards because you are very frightened.

cowhide is leather made from the skin of a cow.

cowl A **cowl** is a large loose hood, especially one worn by a monk.

cowpat A **cowpat** is a pile of cow's dung.

co-write (**co-writer**) If two or more people **co-write** or are the **co-writers** of something like a book, they create it together.

cowshed A **cowshed** is a building where cows are kept or milked.

cowslip — **Cowslips** are small wild plants with sweet-smelling yellow flowers.

cox (**coxes**) The **cox** of a rowing boat is its coxswain.

coxswain (*pron:* **kok**-sn) The **coxswain** of a rowing boat or lifeboat is the person who steers it.

coy (**coyly, coyness**) If a woman is being **coy,** she is pretending to be shy and modest. *There was no need for this coyness.* ■ If someone is **coy** about something, they are unwilling to give information about it.

coyote (*pron:* koy-**ote**-ee) **Coyotes** are wolf-like wild dogs in North America.

cozy See **cosy.**

CPU In a computer, the **CPU** is the part that processes all the data and makes the computer work. CPU is short for 'central processing unit'.

crab — **Crabs** are edible sea creatures. They have a flat oval body covered by a shell, and claws on their front legs.

crab apple A **crab apple** is a kind of small sour apple.

crabbed handwriting is squashed up and difficult to read. ■ **Crabbed** means the same as 'crabby'.

crabby A **crabby** person is bad-tempered and unpleasant to other people.

crack If something **cracks,** it gets damaged and lines called **cracks** appear in it. ■ **Cracks** are narrow gaps in something. ■ A **crack** is a loud sharp sound, as if something is breaking. ■ If a person cracks or cracks up, they become mentally ill, because of stress. ■ If you have a **crack** at something, you make an attempt at it. ■ If you **crack** a problem or code, you succeed in working it out. ■ If you **crack** a joke, you make a witty remark. ■ A **crack** is a slightly rude or cruel joke. ■ **Crack** is a crystalline form of the drug cocaine. ■ **Crack** is used to describe someone who is excellent at what they do. ...*crack troops.* ■ If people in authority **crack down** or if there is a **crackdown** on someone or something, strong official action is taken against them. ■ If something is done at a **cracking pace,** it is done very briskly.

crackdown See **crack.**

cracker A **cracker** is a thin crisp savoury biscuit. ■ A **cracker** is a cardboard tube wrapped in fancy paper, which is pulled apart with a bang to get the small gift inside. ■ You can praise something highly by saying it is a **cracker.** *It is a cracker of a book.* ■ If you say someone is **crackers,** you mean they are crazy.

crackle (**crackling, crackled**) If something **crackles,** it makes a series of short harsh noises. ...*the crackle of flames.* ■ If a performance **crackles with** excitement, it is lively and exciting. ■ **Crackling** is the crunchy brown skin of roast pork.

crackpot ideas are strange or crazy. You say someone who has ideas like these is a **crackpot.**

cradle (**cradling, cradled**) A **cradle** is a small bed for a baby which can be rocked from side to side. ■ If you **cradle** something, you hold it very carefully in your arms. ■ The **cradle** of something is the place where it began. *Egypt is the cradle of civilization.*

craft A boat or spacecraft can be called a **craft** (*plural:* **craft**). ■ A **craft** (*plural:* **crafts**) is an activity like weaving or pottery which involves making things skilfully by hand. **Craft** is used to talk about things connected with crafts. ...*craft fairs.* Other skilful activities can be called **crafts.** *He learned his craft in provincial theatre.* ■ If someone makes something in a skilful way, you can say they **craft** it. ...*a well-crafted script.*

craftsman (**craftsmen; craftsmanship**) Craftsmen are people who make things skilfully with their hands. Their skill is called **craftsmanship.** You also talk about the **craftsmanship** of something which is skilfully made.

crafty (**craftily**) A **crafty** person gets what they want by using clever and often deceitful methods. You can also call their ideas or methods **crafty.** ...*a craftily designed referendum.*

crag (**craggy**) A **crag** is the rocky top of a mountain, or a steep rocky cliff. A **craggy** mountain or cliff is steep and rocky. ■ A **craggy** face has strong features and deep lines.

cram (**cramming, crammed**) If people or things **cram** a place or are **crammed** into it, it is very full of them. *The place was crammed with people.*

cramp If you have **cramp** or **cramps,** you feel a severe pain caused by a muscle suddenly contracting. ■ If you say a person or a thing **cramps** something, you mean they limit or restrict it. *The system*

cramps productivity gains. ■ If a place is **cramped,** there is not enough room there.

crampon — Crampons are metal plates covered with spikes which climbers attach to their boots so they can climb ice-covered rocks.

cranberry (**cranberries**) Cranberries are sour-tasting red berries.

crane (**craning, craned**) A **crane** is a large machine which moves heavy things by lifting them in the air. ■ **Cranes** are long-legged wading birds with long necks and long bills. ■ If you **crane** your neck, you stretch it so you can see better.

crane fly See **daddy-long-legs.**

cranial means to do with the cranium. ...*a cranial haemorrhage.*

cranium (*plural:* **craniums** or **crania**) The **cranium** is the part of the skull containing the brain.

crank (**cranky**) If you call someone a **crank,** you mean they have odd ideas or behave oddly. *Vegetarians were once dismissed as cranky nuisances.* ■ If you **crank** a machine, you turn a handle called a **crank** to make it work. ■ If you **crank up** an engine, you start it. ■ If you **crank up** the volume of something, you increase it. ■ If a person **cranks** something **out,** they produce it in large numbers.

crankshaft In an internal combustion engine, the **crankshaft** is the main shaft, which the connecting rods are attached to.

cranny (**crannies**) Crannies are very narrow openings or spaces in something. ■ **nook and cranny:** see **nook.**

crap is used to say that someone or something is useless or no good. ...*a crap actor.* ...*crap jokes.* ■ If you say someone is talking **crap,** you mean they are talking nonsense.

crash (**crashes, crashing, crashed**) If a vehicle **crashes,** it runs into something and gets damaged. An accident like this is called a **crash.** ■ If someone or something **crashes** to the ground, they fall noisily. ■ A **crash** is a sudden loud noise. ■ If a business **crashes,** it fails suddenly, due to money problems. ■ If a computer or computer program **crashes,** it fails suddenly.

crash barrier A **crash barrier** is a safety fence along a road or racetrack.

crash course A **crash course** is a very short course in a subject.

crash helmet A **crash helmet** is a protective helmet worn by cyclists and motor cyclists.

crash-land (**crash-landing**) If a plane **crash-lands** or makes a **crash-landing,** it makes an emergency landing and is damaged.

crass If something is **crass,** it is stupid and insensitive.

crate A **crate** is a large wooden box for storing or transporting things.

crater A **crater** is a very large hole in the ground, caused by an explosion or something crashing into it. ■ The **crater** of a volcano is the bowl-shaped area surrounding its mouth.

cravat (*pron:* cra-**vat**) A **cravat** is a scarf which a man wears tucked inside his open shirt-collar.

crave (**craving, craved**) If you **crave** something or have a **craving** for it, you desperately want it.

craven If you say someone is **craven,** you mean they are cowardly. *...a craven anxiety to please.*

crawl (crawler; crawling) If you **crawl,** you move forward on your hands and knees. When insects, worms, or snakes **crawl,** they creep along with their bodies close to the ground. ■ If something **crawls** or moves at a **crawl,** it moves very slowly. ■ The **crawl** is a swimming stroke in which you lie on your front and kick your feet like paddles, while bringing your arms over your head one after the other. ■ If someone **crawls** to someone else, they try to win their favour by flattering them. You call someone like this a **crawler.** ■ If a place is **crawling** with people or things, it seems full of them.

crayfish (*plural:* **crayfish** *or* **crayfishes**) are freshwater shellfish like small lobsters.

crayon A **crayon** is a coloured pencil, or a stick of coloured wax or clay.

craze A **craze** is something which is very popular for a short time.

crazed A **crazed** person is wild and out of control.

crazy (crazier, craziest; crazily, craziness) If you say someone is **crazy,** you mean they behave oddly, because they are mentally ill. ■ You say someone is **crazy** when they do or say something very silly. An action or idea can also be called **crazy.** ■ **Crazy** is used to describe things which seem very strange or extreme. *The ball ricocheted crazily. ...the craziness of the situation.* ■ If someone is **crazy** about something, they are very keen on it.

crazy paving is a ground covering made up of differently sized and shaped pieces of stone.

creak (creaking, creaked; creaky) If something **creaks,** it makes a harsh squeaking sound. *...creaky shutters.* ■ You say something is **creaking** if it is likely to break down or collapse. *...a creaking bureaucracy.*

cream (creaming, creamed) **Cream** is a fatty substance made from milk which can be used in cooking or added to desserts. ■ Substances which have a similar texture to cream are called **cream.** *...moisturizing cream.* ■ If you **cream** two or more substances, you mix them together until they are smooth. ■ You can call the best people or things in a group the **cream.** *...the cream of British athletes.* ■ If a person or organization **creams off** the best part of something, they take it for themselves. ■ **Cream** is a yellowish-white colour.

cream cheese is a rich soft white cheese.

cream cracker A **cream cracker** is a crisp unsweetened biscuit often eaten with cheese.

cream tea A **cream tea** is an afternoon snack of tea and scones with jam and clotted cream.

creamy food has cream in it. ■ **Creamy** things are a yellowish-white colour.

crease (creasing, creased) If you **crease** a material, you crush it and cause lines or folds called **creases** to appear in it. ■ If your face **creases** or is **creased,** lines appear there, because you are laughing or frowning. ■ The **creases** in someone's trousers are the folds at the front and back. ■ In cricket, the **crease** is a line near the wicket where the batsman stands.

create (creating, created; creator, creation) If someone **creates** something, they make it happen or exist. When this happens, you say they are the thing's **creator.** *The fireplace mirror is also his creation.* ■ In the Bible, the making of the universe by God is called the **Creation.** God is often called **the Creator.**

creative (creativity) If someone is **creative,** they are able to think up and develop original ideas. You call this ability **creativity. Creative** is used to describe activities in which people are encouraged to develop original ideas. *...a creative writing course.* ■ **Creative accounting** is the practice of setting out accounts in such a way that they give a misleading impression.

creature A **creature** is any living thing which can move about. ■ You can call someone a particular type of **creature** to emphasize a particular quality they have. *She's a fastidious creature.* ■ **Creature comforts** are the things you need to live comfortably.

crèche (*pron:* **kresh**) A **crèche** is a place where parents can leave their children while they are at work.

credence (*pron:* **creed**-dens) If something gives **credence** to an idea, it makes it easier to believe.

credentials If you talk about someone's **credentials,** you mean their experience and qualifications, which make them suitable for a particular task or job. You can use **credentials** to talk about a document which proves they have these things.

credible (credibly, credibility) If something is **credible,** you can believe it might be true. ■ You use **credible** to say someone or something could be successful in the future. *...the lack of a credible alternative candidates... He was the only figure who could credibly run the country.* ■ You say there is a **credibility gap** when there is a difference between what someone says and what they actually do.

credit (crediting, credited) **Credit** is a system by which goods or services can be obtained before they have been paid for. You say goods and services like these are bought **on credit.** ■ If a bank account is **in credit,** it has money in it and is not overdrawn. ■ If you get the **credit** for something or are **credited** with it, people believe you are responsible for it and praise you. ■ The list of people who helped make a film, record, or TV programme is called the **credits.** ■ If you say you cannot **credit** something, you mean you cannot believe it.

creditable (creditably) If you say something is **creditable,** you mean it deserves credit or praise.

credit card A **credit card** is a plastic card with which you can buy goods on credit.

credit note A **credit note** is a slip of paper given to someone who returns goods to a shop; it allows them to buy other goods of the same value without paying for them.

creditor Someone's **creditors** are the people they owe money to.

creditworthy (creditworthiness) A **creditworthy** person is one who can safely be lent money or allowed goods on credit, for example because in the past they have always paid back what they owe.

credo (*pron:* **kree**-doh *or* **kray**-doh) (**credos**) A person's **credo** is a set of beliefs or principles which strongly influences their behaviour.

credulous (**credulity**) You say someone is **credulous** or talk about their **credulity** (*pron:* cred-**yool**-it-y) when they are too ready to believe what they are told.

creed A **creed** is a set of beliefs or principles which strongly influences the way people live. ■ You can call a religion a **creed.**

creek A **creek** is an arm of the sea which stretches a long way into the land. ■ In America and Australia, a **creek** is a small river.

creep (**creeping, crept** *not 'creeped'*) If you **creep** somewhere, you move there slowly and quietly. ■ If someone **creeps up on** you, they approach you slowly, without you noticing. ■ If an amount **creeps up,** it gradually gets higher. ■ If something **creeps in,** it gradually begins to appear. *You can't allow complacency to creep in.*

creeper – **Creepers** are plants with long stems which wrap themselves around things.

creepy If something is **creepy,** it makes you uneasy or frightened.

creepy-crawly (**creepy-crawlies**) People sometimes call small creatures like insects **creepy-crawlies.**

cremate (**cremating, cremated; cremation**) When someone is **cremated,** their dead body is burned.

crematorium (*plural:* **crematoria** *or* **crematoriums**) A **crematorium** is a building where cremations take place.

crème de la crème (*pron:* **crem** de la **crem**) If you talk about the **crème de la crème,** you mean the very best people or things.

creole A **creole** is a language developed from a mixture of different languages, which has become the main language in a place. See also **pidgin.** ■ A **Creole** is a person descended from the Europeans who first colonized the West Indies or the southern US. You can also call someone a **Creole** if they are of mixed African and European race and live in the West Indies.

creosote is a thick dark liquid made from coal tar which is used to protect wood from the weather.

crepe is a fabric with a wrinkled surface.

crepe paper is stretchy paper with a ridged surface, often used for making decorations.

crept See **creep.**

crescendo (*pron:* kre-**shen**-doh) (*plural:* **crescendos** *or* **crescendi**) A **crescendo** is a gradual increase in loudness, particularly in music. ■ You can call an increase in intensity of behaviour or feelings a **crescendo.** *...a crescendo of discontent.*

crescent A **crescent** is a curved shape which is wide in the centre with narrow pointed ends, like the moon in its first and last quarters. ■ A **crescent** is a curved row of buildings, or a curved street.

cress is a plant with small strong-tasting green leaves.

crest (**crested**) The **crest** of a hill or wave is the highest part. If you **crest** a hill, you reach its highest point. ■ You say someone is **on the crest of a wave** when things are going very well for them. ■ A

crest is a design used as a symbol by a family or organization. If something has a crest on it, you can say it is **crested.** ■ Some birds have a tuft of feathers on their head called a **crest.** Birds with a crest sometimes have **crested** as part of their name. *...the crested tit.*

crestfallen If someone looks **crestfallen,** they look sad and disappointed.

cretin If you call someone a **cretin,** you mean they are very stupid.

crevasse (*pron:* kriv-**vass**) A **crevasse** is a deep crack in thick ice.

crevice (*pron:* **krev**-iss) A **crevice** is a narrow crack in rock.

crew (**crewed**) The **crew** of a ship, plane, or spacecraft are the people on it who operate it. You can say a ship, plane, or spacecraft is **crewed** by particular people. ■ A **crew** is a group of people with special technical skills who work together. *...the camera crew.*

crew cut A **crew cut** is a short cropped hairstyle for men.

crewman (**crewmen**) A **crewman** is a member of a ship's or boat's crew.

crib (**cribbing, cribbed**) If you **crib,** you copy something written by someone else. ■ A **crib** is a translation or list of answers used by students, often to cheat. ■ Americans call a baby's cot a **crib.**

cribbage is a card game in which you keep the score by putting pegs in a wooden board.

crick If you have a **crick** in your neck, you have a pain there caused by a sore muscle.

cricket (**cricketer**) Cricket is an outdoor game played between two teams who try to score points, called runs, by hitting a ball with a wooden bat. ■ **Crickets** are small jumping insects which produce a chirping sound by rubbing their wings together.

crime A **crime** is an illegal action for which someone can be punished by law. ■ You can call an action a **crime** when you think it is morally wrong or a serious mistake.

criminal (**criminally**) A **criminal** is someone who has committed a crime, especially someone who has done so on a regular basis. ■ You use **criminal** to talk about things connected with crime. *These people are criminally insane.*

criminal law is the part of country's set of laws concerned with what counts as a crime, and with the punishment of people who commit one. See also **civil law.**

criminology (**criminologist**) Criminology is the scientific study of crime and criminals.

crimp If you **crimp** a piece of pastry or fabric, you make small folds along its edges. ■ If you **crimp** your hair, you make tight waves in it, usually with heated tongs.

crimson is a dark purplish-red colour.

cringe (**cringing, cringed**) If something makes you **cringe,** it makes you feel very embarrassed. ■ If you **cringe** from someone or something, you back away because you are afraid.

crinkle (**crinkling, crinkled; crinkly**) If something **crinkles** or is **crinkled,** it gets small creases in it.

Crinkles are small creases or folds. ■ If something has a lot of crinkles, you can say it is **crinkly.**

crinoline (pron: **krin**-o-lin) **Crinolines** were metal frames worn by mid-Victorian women to make their skirts stick out.

cripple (**crippling, crippled**) If someone is **crippled** or a **cripple,** they cannot move their body properly because of illness or injury. Using 'cripple' like this can be offensive. ■ You can say something **cripples** an organization or system if it stops it working properly.

crisis (plural: **crises,** pron: **cry**-seez) A **crisis** is a situation in which there are very serious problems.

crisp (**crisply, crispness**) If something is **crisp,** it feels pleasantly stiff and fresh. ...*crisp new banknotes.* ■ If the weather is **crisp,** it is pleasantly fresh, cold, and dry. ■ If a speech or piece of writing is **crisp,** it does not go into unnecessary details. ■ **Crisps** are thin slices of potato fried until they are hard and crunchy.

crispbread is a thin dry biscuit made from rye or wheat.

crispy You say food is **crispy** when it has been cooked until it is pleasantly hard and crunchy.

criss-cross A **criss-cross** pattern is one with lots of lines crossing each other. If things **criss-cross** an area, they create a pattern like this.

criterion (plural: **criteria**) A **criterion** is a standard by which you judge or decide something.

critic A **critic** is someone who is paid to give their opinions on books, films, music, or art. ■ A **critic** of a person or system is someone who condemns them in public.

critical (**critically**) You say a situation or time is **critical** when what happens is extremely important, because it will determine which way things go in the future. ■ If someone is **critically** ill, they are very seriously ill. ■ If you are **critical** of someone or something, you show you disapprove of them or are dissatisfied with them. ■ A **critical** approach involves examining and judging something carefully.

criticise See **criticize.**

criticism is the action of showing disapproval of someone or something. A **criticism** is a statement of disapproval. ■ **Criticism** is the serious examination and judgment of things such as books, films, music, or art.

criticize (or **criticise**) (**criticizing, criticized**) If you **criticize** someone or something, you say what you think is wrong with them.

critique (pron: krit-**teek**) A **critique** is a written study and judgment of something.

croak (**croaking, croaked**) If a frog or bird **croaks,** it makes a low hoarse cry. ■ If a person **croaks** something, or speaks in a **croak,** they speak in a rough hoarse voice.

crochet (pron: **kroh**-shay) (**crocheting, crocheted**) **Crochet** is a craft similar to knitting but using only one needle, with a hook at the end. When someone **crochets,** they do this kind of work.

crock is an old word for an earthenware pot.

crockery is plates, cups, and saucers.

crocodile – **Crocodiles** are large scaly reptiles with long bodies and short legs. They eat meat and live in tropical rivers. ■ If you say someone sheds **crocodile tears,** you mean their display of grief is not genuine.

crocus (**crocuses**) **Crocuses** are small yellow, white, or purple flowers which bloom in early spring.

croft (**crofter**) In Scotland, a **croft** is a small piece of land attached to a house and farmed by one family. The owner or tenant of a croft is called a **crofter.**

croissant (pron: krwah-son) A **croissant** is a light flaky crescent-shaped sweet bread roll.

crone In stories, a **crone** is an unpleasant old woman.

crony (**cronies**) You can call a person's friends or companions their **cronies.**

crook (**crooking, crooked**) A **crook** is a criminal. ■ A **crook** is a long pole with a large hook at the end. ■ The **crook** of someone's elbow is the inside of their arm at the point where it bends. If you **crook** your arm or finger, you bend it.

crooked (pron: **kruk**-id) A **crooked** person is a criminal. ■ If something is **crooked,** it is twisted or bent.

croon (**crooning, crooned; crooner**) If you **croon** something, you sing or say it softly.

crop (**cropping, cropped**) **Crops** are food plants grown in large quantities. ■ The plants gathered at a particular time are called a **crop.** ■ A lot of people, things, or events appearing together can be called a **crop.** ...*a crop of manic crimes.* ■ If you **crop** someone's hair, you cut it very short; you say their hair is **cropped.** ■ If something **crops up,** it happens without warning.

cropper You say someone **comes a cropper** when their attempt to do something fails completely.

croquet (pron: **kroh**-kay) is a game in which the players use long-handled wooden hammers to hit balls through small metal arches stuck in a lawn.

croquette (pron: kroh-**kett**) A **croquette** is a savoury cake of minced food coated in breadcrumbs.

cross (**crosses, crossing, crossed; crossly**) If you **cross** something such as an area of land or water, you go over to the other side. ■ If lines or roads **cross,** they meet and go across each other. ■ If you **cross** your legs, arms, or fingers, you put one on top of the other. ■ If an expression **crosses** your face, it appears there briefly. ■ If a thought **crosses** your mind, it suddenly occurs to you. ■ A **cross** is a written mark in the shape of an X. ■ A **cross** is an upright post with a horizontal bar across it. When Christians talk about the **Cross,** they mean a cross like this on which Jesus Christ died. ■ If someone is **cross,** they are angry. *She spoke to me crossly.* ■ If you **cross** someone, you make them angry by opposing them. ■ If something is a **cross** between two things, it is neither one thing nor the other but a mixture of both. ■ If you **cross off** items on a list, you draw a line through them, one by one. ■ If you **cross out** words on a page, you put a line through them.

crossbar In games like football, the **crossbar** is the horizontal piece of wood across the top of the goal.

crossbones See **skull.**

crossbow The **crossbow** is a weapon consisting of a small bow fixed across a piece of wood, which releases an arrow with great force when the trigger is pressed.

cross-check If you **cross-check** something, you make sure it is correct by checking it in different ways or against different sources.

cross-country is a long race across open countryside. ■ If you go somewhere **cross-country,** you go there across land rather than following roads.

cross-cultural is used to talk about anything involving two or more cultures.

cross-dress (**cross-dresser**) If someone **cross-dresses,** they wear the clothes of the opposite sex, especially for sexual pleasure.

cross-examine (**cross-examination**) If someone is **cross-examined** in court, they are questioned about evidence they have given. ■ You can say someone is **cross-examined** when they are questioned very thoroughly.

cross-eyed If someone is **cross-eyed,** their eyes seem to look towards each other.

crossfire is gunfire from different directions which meets and crosses at the same point. ■ If you get **caught in the crossfire,** you get involved in a conflict against your will.

crossing A **crossing** is a boat journey across a stretch of water. ■ A **crossing** is a place where you cross a street.

crossing point A **crossing point** is a point on the border between two countries where people and vehicles are allowed through.

cross-legged If someone sits **cross-legged,** they sit with their feet pulled up to their body, their calves crossing, and their knees pointing outwards.

cross-purposes If people are **at cross-purposes,** they cannot understand each other, because they are talking about different subjects without realizing it.

cross-question If someone is **cross-questioned,** they are questioned very thoroughly.

cross-reference (**cross-referencing**) A **cross-reference** is a note in a book which tells you there is more information in another part of the book.

crossroads A **crossroads** is a place where roads meet and cross. ■ If you say someone is **at a crossroads,** you mean they are at a stage when they need to make an important decision.

cross-section A **cross-section** of a group of people is a representative sample of them. ■ A **cross-section** of an object is what you would see if you cut through the middle of it.

crosswind A **crosswind** is a strong wind blowing across the direction a plane or boat is travelling in.

crossword A **crossword** or **crossword puzzle** is a printed word game where you work out answers to clues, then write them in the white squares of a black and white grid.

crotch (**crotches**) A person's **crotch** is the area of their body between the tops of their legs.

crotchet A **crotchet** is a musical note with the same time value as two quavers or half a minim.

crouch (**crouches, crouching, crouched**) If you **crouch,** you bend your legs under you so you are near the ground and leaning forward slightly.

croup (*pron:* **kroop**) is a disease in which the throat swells, making breathing difficult and causing a hoarse cough. It particularly affects children.

croupier (*pron:* **kroop**-ee-ay) A **croupier** is someone who works at a gambling table in a casino.

crouton (*pron:* **kroot**-on) **Croutons** are small pieces of toasted or fried bread which are added to soup.

crow – Crows are large black birds with a loud harsh cry. ■ When a cock **crows,** it makes a loud squawking sound. ■ If someone **crows** about their achievements, they boastfully tell people about them. ■ If you say something is a certain distance away **as the crow flies,** you mean it is that distance measured in a straight line.

crowbar A **crowbar** is a heavy iron bar for levering things open.

crowd A **crowd** is a large number of people gathered together in one place. ■ If people **crowd** a place or **crowd** into it, they gather in large numbers and completely fill it. You say the place is **crowded.** ■ If people **crowd** round someone or something, they gather closely around them. ■ You can say problems are **crowding in on** someone if they have to deal with a lot of them at once.

crown A **crown** is an ornamental gold headdress with jewels, worn by a king or queen on ceremonial occasions. The **Crown** is whoever happens to be king or queen at the time. ■ When someone is **crowned,** a crown is put on their head at a ceremony to show they have become king or queen. Kings and queens are sometimes called **crowned heads.** ■ If one thing **crowns** another, it is on the top of it. ■ If you say something **crowns** an event or achievement, you mean it completes it perfectly. ■ A **crown** is a championship in sport. ■ A **crown** is an artificial top piece fixed over a broken or decayed tooth.

crown court In England and Wales, a **crown court** is a court where crimes are tried by a judge and jury, rather than a magistrate.

crown jewels A country's **crown jewels** are the crown and other jewels used by the king or queen on state occasions.

Crown Prince A **Crown Prince** is a prince who will be king of his country when the present king or queen dies.

Crown Princess A **Crown Princess** is (a) the wife of a Crown Prince. (b) a princess who will be queen of her country when the present king or queen dies.

crow's feet are the wrinkles which some people have at the outside corners of their eyes.

crucial (**crucially**) If something is **crucial** it is vitally important.

crucible A **crucible** is a pot in which metals can be melted or heated to high temperatures. ■ You say a situation or place is a **crucible** when a lot of different people, things, or ideas are brought together and something worthwhile comes out of it. *Perugia was to become the crucible of painting in Umbria.*

crucifix (**crucifixes**) A **crucifix** is a model of Christ on the Cross.

crucifixion was a method of execution in the ancient world. The victim was tied or nailed to a cross and left to die. When people talk about the **Crucifixion,** they mean the death of Christ on the Cross.

crucify (crucifies, crucifying, crucified) If someone is **crucified,** they are killed by being tied or nailed to a cross and left to die. ■ You can say someone is **crucified** when they are humiliated or they are severely criticized.

crude (cruder, crudest; crudely, crudity) You say a system or idea is **crude** or talk about its **crudity** when it is very basic and unsophisticated. ■ You can say an object is **crude** or **crudely** made when it has been roughly made and is very basic in style. ■ If someone's behaviour or language is **crude,** it is vulgar and offensive.

crude oil is oil in its natural state before it has been processed.

crudity See **crude.**

cruel (crueller, cruellest; cruelly) (Am: crueler, cruelest) If someone is **cruel,** they deliberately cause pain or distress.

cruelty (cruelties) Cruelty is cruel behaviour. **Cruelties** are cruel acts.

cruet A **cruet** is a frame for holding small pots of salt, pepper, and mustard.

cruise (cruising, cruised) If you **cruise** or go on a **cruise,** you spend a holiday on a large ship which visits a number of different places. ■ If a car, ship, or plane **cruises,** it travels at a steady speed. ■ If you **cruise** through a competition, you win without any effort.

cruise missile A **cruise missile** is a missile which carries a nuclear warhead.

cruiser A **cruiser** is (a) a motor boat with a cabin for people to sleep in. (b) a large fast warship.

crumb – Crumbs are tiny pieces which have broken off bread, cakes, or biscuits. ■ A **crumb** is a very small amount of something. *There is one small crumb of comfort.*

crumble (crumbling, crumbled; crumbly) If something **crumbles,** it breaks into small pieces. If this happens to something easily, you say it is **crumbly.** ■ If you say a system or organization is **crumbling,** you mean it is beginning to break down.

crummy If you say something is **crummy,** you mean it is poor and unsatisfactory.

crumpet – Crumpets are round, flat bread-like cakes which are toasted and eaten with butter.

crumple (crumpling, crumpled) If you **crumple** paper or material, you crush it until it is creased and out of shape. ■ If something **crumples,** it collapses suddenly. *Profits have crumpled by more than a third.*

crunch (crunches, crunching, crunched) If you **crunch** something between your teeth or under your feet, you crush it noisily. ■ **The crunch** is used to talk about a critical situation when a decision must be made. *If it came to the crunch, I would have to stay.* ■ If you **crunch numbers,** you do a lot of calculations using a calculator or computer.

crunchy (crunchier, crunchiest) If food is **crunchy,** it is crisp or brittle and makes a noise when you eat it.

crusade (crusading; crusader) A **crusade** is a long determined attempt to win support for a cause, or to put an end to something unjust. A **crusading** person is someone who tries to do this; you also call them a **crusader.**

crush (crushes, crushing, crushed) If something is **crushed,** it is squeezed until it loses its shape or is broken into pieces. ■ **Crushed** material is deliberately made with creases in it. *...crushed velvet.* ■ If people are **crushed** or caught in a **crush,** they are pressed against something or against each other, as a result of the movement of a large crowd. ■ **Crush barriers** are safety fences used to split up large crowds and prevent people being crushed. ■ If something like a revolt is **crushed,** it is defeated completely, often by force. If someone suffers a **crushing** defeat, they are overwhelmingly defeated.

crust (crusted) The **crust** on a loaf is the crisp dark outer edge. ■ If things have a **crust** or are **crusted** with something, they have a hard layer surrounding them or on top of them. *The water was crusted over with ice.* ■ The earth's **crust** is its hard outer layer.

crustacean (pron: cruss-**taysh**-an) **Crustaceans** are creatures with hard outer shells and several pairs of legs. Crabs, lobsters, and shrimps are crustaceans.

crusty (crustier, crustiest) If something is **crusty,** it has a hard outer layer. *...crusty bread.* ■ **Crusty** people are impatient and short-tempered.

crutch (crutches) A **crutch** is a stick which fits under your armpit to support you if you have an injured leg. ■ You can call a person or thing a **crutch** when someone depends on them for help or support. ■ A person's **crutch** is the same as their crotch.

crux The **crux** of a problem is the central, most important aspect of it.

cry (cries, crying, cried) If you **cry** or have a **cry,** tears come from your eyes, because you are upset. ■ If you **cry** something or **cry** it **out,** you shout it. ■ A **cry** is (a) a loud call made by a person. (b) a call made by a large bird. ■ If you **cry off,** you decide not to do something you had arranged to do. ■ If you say something is **crying out for** a particular thing, you mean it needs it badly. You can also say there is a **crying** need for something. ■ If you say something is a **crying shame,** you mean it is very regrettable. ■ If you say something is a **far cry** from something else, you mean the two things are very different. ■ **cry wolf:** see **wolf.**

cryogenic (cryogenically; cryogenics) Cryogenic means concerned with freezing things to extremely low temperatures. *Crew members begin to die as a cryogenic experiment goes wrong.* **Cryogenics** is the branch of physics that studies what happens to things at extremely low temperatures.

crypt The **crypt** of a church is an underground room, often used as a burial place.

cryptic (cryptically) A **cryptic** remark or message has a hidden meaning.

crypto- If you describe someone as **crypto-**communist or a **crypto-**facist, you mean they have hidden or secret beliefs.

crystal A **crystal** is a piece of a substance which has formed naturally into a regular shape. ■ **Crystal** is high quality glassware with patterns cut into its surface. ■ If you say something is **crystal clear,** you mean it is very easy to understand.

crystal ball A **crystal ball** is a clear glass globe in which fortune-tellers claim they can see the future.

crystalline If something is **crystalline,** it is made up of crystals. ■ **Crystalline** means clear or bright. ...*crystalline lakes.*

crystallize (*or* **crystallise**) (**crystallizing, crystallized**) If a substance **crystallizes,** it turns into crystals. ■ If a thought **crystallizes,** it becomes clear.

CS gas is a gas used by riot police. It makes breathing difficult and causes crying.

cub – **Cubs** are the young of certain animals, for example lions, bears, and seals. ■ A **cub** is a boy who belongs to the Cub Scouts, a junior branch of the Scout Association.

cubby-hole A **cubby-hole** is a small closed-in storage space.

cube (**cubing, cubed**) A **cube** is a three-dimensional shape, with six square surfaces of equal size. ■ If you **cube** food, you cut it into cubes. ■ The **cube** of a number is another number obtained by multiplying the first number by itself twice. For example, the cube of 2 is 8. In maths, this is expressed as $2^3 = 8$.

cube root The **cube root** of a number is another number which when multiplied by itself twice produces the first number. For example the cube root of 27 is 3. In maths, this is expressed as $\sqrt[3]{27} = 3$.

cubic is used in front of units of length to change them to units of volume. ...*cubic metres.*

cubicle A **cubicle** is a small enclosed area, for example one where you have a shower or change your clothes.

cubism (**cubist**) **Cubism** was an early 20th century style of art, in which objects were represented as if seen from several positions at once.

cub reporter A **cub reporter** is a young newspaper reporter who is still being trained.

cuckold In the past, a man whose wife was unfaithful to him was called a **cuckold.** The wife and her lover were said to have **cuckolded** the husband.

cuckoo The **cuckoo** is a bird that has a call of two quick notes. Cuckoos lay their eggs in other birds' nests.

cuckoo clock A **cuckoo clock** is a wooden clock in the shape of a small house. When the hour strikes, a toy bird springs out of a small door and makes a sound like a cuckoo.

cucumber – **Cucumbers** are long salad vegetables with dark green skin and white flesh.

cud is the partly digested food which a cow brings back up to chew again.

cuddle (**cuddling, cuddled**) If you **cuddle** someone or give them a **cuddle,** you put your arms round them and hold them close. ■ If you **cuddle up** to someone, you press your body against theirs.

cuddly If you say a person, animal, or toy is **cuddly,** you mean they appeal to you and you would like to cuddle them.

cudgel A **cudgel** is a short thick stick used as a weapon. ■ If you **take up the cudgels** for someone, you speak or fight on their behalf.

cue A **cue** is a word or action from one performer which is a signal for another performer to say or do something. ■ In other situations, a **cue** is a signal for something to begin. ■ If you **take** your **cue** from someone, you use their behaviour as an indication of what you should do. ■ If something happens **on cue,** it happens just at the time it is expected to. ■ A **cue** is a long narrow stick used to hit the ball in snooker, billiards, or pool.

cuff – **Cuffs** are the ends of the sleeves on a piece of clothing. ■ If you speak **off the cuff,** you have not prepared what you are saying. ■ If you **cuff** someone, you hit them lightly with your hand.

cufflinks are small decorative objects for fastening shirt cuffs.

cuisine (*pron:* quiz-**zeen**) is used to talk about styles of cooking. ...*traditional French cuisine.*

cul-de-sac A **cul-de-sac** is a road which does not lead to other roads.

culinary means to do with meals and cooking. ...*culinary skills.*

cull When a group of animals is **culled,** the weaker ones are killed, to reduce the numbers. You call an action like this a **cull.** ■ If you **cull** things from a large number of things, you take the ones you want from them. *The selection has been culled from over 100,000 photographs.*

culminate (**culminating, culminated; culmination**) When something **culminates** in something else, it finally develops into it.

culottes are women's wide trousers or shorts, cut to look like a skirt.

culpable (**culpability**) If someone is **culpable,** they are to blame for what has happened; you can also talk about their **culpability.**

culprit The **culprit** is the person or thing responsible for something bad.

cult A **cult** is a religious group with its own special rituals, especially one which is seen as dangerous. ■ A **cult** is something which is popular or fashionable among a small group of people. ...*the cult TV space series Dr Who.*

cultivate (**cultivating, cultivated; cultivation**) If land is **cultivated,** crops are grown on it. ■ If you **cultivate** an appearance, attitude, or friendship, you try to develop it.

cultivated A **cultivated** person is well-educated and interested in the arts. ■ **Cultivated** plants have been developed specially to be grown in gardens or on farms.

cultural (**culturally**) **Cultural** is used to talk about (a) things to do with the arts. ...*the biggest cultural event of the year.* (b) things to do with social systems and ways of life. ...*cultural differences.*

culture A **culture** consists of the ideas, customs, and art created and shared by the people of a country, region, or ethnic group. ...*western culture.* ■ **Culture shock** is the feeling of confusion and anxiety people sometimes experience when they first arrive in a country with very different traditions from their own. ■ **Culture** is used to talk about a way of life shared by many people which seems to be based on a particular idea or represented by a particular thing. ...*contemporary dance culture.* ■ **Culture** is used to talk about the arts generally. ...*France's Minister of Culture.* ■ A **culture** is a group of bacteria or cells grown in a laboratory.

cultured A **cultured** person is well-educated and interested in the arts. ■ A **cultured** pearl is created by putting sand or grit in an oyster's shell.

culvert A **culvert** is a water pipe or sewer which crosses under a road or railway.

-cum- is placed between two words to talk about something which is a mixture of two different things. ...*a kitchen-cum-dining room.*

cumbersome If something is **cumbersome**, it is heavy and awkward to carry. ■ A **cumbersome** system is complicated and inefficient.

cummerbund A **cummerbund** is a wide sash worn round the waist, as part of a man's evening dress.

cumulative (**cumulatively**) The **cumulative** effect of several things happening is the effect they produce together.

cumulus (*pron:* **kyoo**-myoo-luss) is a type of thick fluffy white cloud formed when hot air rises quickly.

cunning (**cunningly**) A **cunning** person is clever and deceitful. You can talk about the **cunning** of someone like this.

cup (**cupping, cupped**) A **cup** is a small drinks container with a handle. ■ Some round hollow things are called **cups.** ...*egg cups.* ■ A **cup** is a metal container, often with two handles, given as a prize. ■ If you **cup** something in your hands, you wrap your hands around it in a cup-like shape, to support or hold it gently.

cupboard A **cupboard** is a piece of furniture or a recess with a door, often with shelves inside it, which is used for storage.

cupidity is a greedy desire for money and possessions.

cupola (*pron:* **kyoo**-po-la) A **cupola** is a domed roof.

cuppa A **cuppa** is a cup of tea.

curate (**curacy, curacies**) A **curate** is a clergyman who helps a vicar or priest. A **curacy** is the position held by a curate, or the work they do.

curative If something is **curative,** it can cure illnesses.

curator A **curator** is someone in charge of a museum's or gallery's contents.

curb If you **curb** something or put a **curb** on it, you keep it within certain limits. ■ See **kerb.**

curd is the thick white substance formed when milk goes sour.

curdle (**curdling, curdled**) When something **curdles,** it turns sour.

cure (**curing, cured**) If an illness is **cured,** it is ended by treatment or medicine; you also say the person who has been ill is **cured.** A successful treatment or medicine is called a **cure.** ■ If you **cure** a habit, you successfully break it. ■ If you **cure** a problem or find a **cure** for it, you manage to solve it. ■ If food is **cured,** it is salted or smoked, to preserve it.

cure-all A **cure-all** is something people believe will solve all their problems.

curfew A **curfew** is a law requiring people to stay indoors between certain hours.

curio (**curios**) A **curio** is a small unusual ornament.

curiosity (**curiosities**) **Curiosity** is a desire to find out about things. ■ A **curiosity** is an unusual and interesting thing.

curious (**curiously**) If something is **curious,** it is strange or unusual. ...*a curiously shaped washbasin.* ■ If you are **curious** about something, you want to find out more about it.

curl (**curly**) **Curls** are strands of hair shaped in curves and circles. When hair grows like this, you say it is **curly** or **curls.** ■ If something **curls,** it moves in a curve or spiral. ■ When you **curl up,** you sit or lie with your arms, legs, and head pulled in towards your stomach.

curler — **Curlers** are plastic or metal tubes which strands of hair are rolled around to make curls.

curlew — **Curlews** are brownish wading birds with long downwards-curving bills.

curling is a game like bowls, played on ice with large stones.

curly See **curl.**

curmudgeon (**curmudgeonly**) If you say someone is **curmudgeonly** or a **curmudgeon,** you mean they are bad-tempered or mean.

currant — **Currants** are small dried grapes.

currency (**currencies**) A country's **currency** is (a) its money system. (b) the coins and notes used there. ■ If an idea or story gains **currency,** people get to hear about it and accept it.

current (**currently**) **Current** is used to talk about (a) things which are taking place now, or are being done or used now. *He is currently touring America.* (b) the people who have a particular position now. ...*the current leadership.* ■ A **current** of air or water is a continuous flow of it. ■ An electric **current** is a flow of electricity through a circuit.

current account A **current account** is a bank account which you can take money out of at any time, using your cheque book or cheque card.

current affairs are political and social events happening at the present time.

curriculum (*plural:* **curricula** *or* **curriculums**) The **curriculum** at a school or university is the choice of courses there. ■ The **National Curriculum** is a feature introduced into the educational system in England and Wales in 1988. It established that children aged 5 to 16 in state schools should all study the same group of subjects. ■ **Curriculum** is used to talk about a particular course of study. ...*the history curriculum.* ■ **curriculum vitae:** see **CV.**

curry (**curries, currying, curried**) A **curry** is a hot spicy Asian dish. If you **curry** food, you make it into a curry. ■ If you **curry favour** with someone, you try to win their goodwill or co-operation by doing things to please them.

curse If someone **curses,** they swear angrily. If you **curse** someone or something, you swear at them. ■ If people say there is a **curse** on someone, they mean something supernatural is causing unpleasant things to happen to them. ■ When something causes a lot of trouble or distress, you can say people are **cursed** by it or call it a **curse.** ...*the curse of unemployment.*

cursor A **cursor** is a moving mark on a computer screen which shows you where anything you type will appear.

cursory is used to describe things done in a hasty and superficial way. ...*a cursory inspection.*

curt (curtly) If someone is **curt** or speaks **curtly,** what they say is very brief and abrupt.

curtail (curtailing, curtailed; curtailment) If you **curtail** something, you restrict it.

curtain (curtained) Curtains are large pieces of material hung at a window or other opening as a screen. A **curtained** window has curtains. ■ In a theatre, the **curtain** is a hanging which conceals the stage until the performance starts. You say there is a **curtain call** when the artists come on stage at the end of a performance to receive applause.

curtain-raiser A **curtain-raiser** is a small event which takes place before a larger one.

curtsy (or curtsey) (curtsies, curtsying, curtsied) If a woman **curtsies** or makes a **curtsy,** she puts one foot in front of the other and briefly lowers her body by bending her knees.

curvaceous A woman is sometimes described as **curvaceous** when she has attractively large breasts and hips.

curvature The **curvature** of something is the extent to which it curves.

curve (curving, curved; curvy) A **curve** is a line which bends gradually and smoothly. ■ If something **curves** or is **curved,** it moves in a curve, or has the shape of a curve. ...*the sidespin causes the ball to curve.* ...*a curved blade.* If something is **curvy,** it has several curves.

cushion (cushioning, cushioned) A **cushion** is a soft object put on a seat to make it more comfortable. ■ If something is **cushioned** from something harmful, it is prevented from receiving its full effects.

cushy (cushier, cushiest) A **cushy** job is very easy.

cusp If someone or something is on the **cusp** of another thing, they are at the point where they cease to be one thing, and become the other.

cussed (*pron:* **kuss**-id) people are very stubborn.

custard is a sweet yellow sauce made from milk and eggs or milk and a powder.

custodial A **custodial** sentence is one in which someone is sentenced to prison.

custodian The **custodian** of a building is the person in charge. ■ If someone has the responsibility of looking after something important, you can say they are its **custodian.** ...*custodians of the national interest.*

custody If someone has **custody** of a child, they have the legal right to look after it. ■ If someone is **in custody,** they are being kept in prison.

custom A **custom** is an activity which has been taking place on special occasions for a very long time. ■ If it is the **custom** to do something in a particular situation, that is what is usually done. ■ **Customs** is the place where people arriving from

another country must declare goods they have brought with them from that country. ■ If a business has your **custom,** you regularly buy things from it, or use its services.

customary (customarily) You use **customary** to describe what normally happens in particular circumstances.

customer A business's **customers** are the people who buy things from it, or use its services.

customize (or customise) (customizing, customized) If something is **customized,** it has been specially made to someone's requirements.

custom-made (custom-built) If something is **custom-made** or **custom-built,** it is made or built to someone's special requirements.

cut (cutting) If you **cut** something, you use a knife or other sharp tool to mark it, damage it, or remove part of it. Each action is called a **cut.** ■ If you **cut** yourself or get a **cut,** you suffer an injury which makes you bleed. ■ If money or a service is **cut,** it is reduced; the reduction is called a **cut** or a **cutback.** ...*the cutback in consumer spending.* ■ If a supply of something is **cut off,** you no longer get it. ■ If you **cut down** on something you do or use, you do or use less of it. If you **cut** it **out,** you stop it altogether. ■ If a piece of writing is **cut,** parts of it are not printed or broadcast. ■ If an engine **cuts out,** it suddenly stops working. ■ If someone is not **cut out** for a particular task, they do not have the right qualities to do it. ■ If you talk about the **cut** of someone's clothes, you are describing the way the clothes have been made or designed. ■ A **cut** of meat is a joint of it that you buy to cook. ■ If something is a **cut above** other things of the same kind, it is better than them. ■ If you **cut** through or across a place, you go that way because it is shorter. ■ If a place or person becomes **cut off,** they become isolated from other places or people.

cut-and-dried If you say something is **cut-and-dried,** you mean its outcome is obvious.

cutback See **cut.**

cute If something is **cute,** it is pretty and attractive. ...*a cute smile.*

cut glass is glass with patterns cut into its surface.

cuticle – Cuticles are the strips of skin at the base of fingernails and toenails.

cutlass (cutlasses) A **cutlass** is a curved sword with one sharp edge.

cutlery is knives, forks, and spoons.

cutlet A **cutlet** is (a) a small chop. (b) a mixture of nuts and vegetables, pressed into a flat shape.

cut-off The **cut-off** or **cut-off point** is the level or limit at which something will be stopped.

cut-price items are on sale at a reduced price.

cutter A **cutter** is (a) a person whose job involves cutting something. ...*a glass cutter.* (b) a tool or machine for cutting something. ...*wire cutters.* ■ A **cutter** is a small fast boat.

cut-throat is used to describe situations where people ruthlessly compete for something. ...*the cut-throat world of US politics.*

cutting A **cutting** is a piece cut from a plant, used to grow a new plant. ■ A **cutting** is a piece of writing or a photograph cut from a newspaper or magazine. ■ A railway **cutting** is a narrow valley cut through a hill for a railway line to pass through. ■ A **cutting** remark is hurtful. ■ If you are **at the cutting edge** of something, you are involved in its most recent developments.

cuttlefish (*plural:* **cuttlefish** *or* **cuttlefishes**) are squid-like animals with hard internal shells, which live on the seabed.

CV Your **CV** is a short written account of your education, work experience, and personal details, which you send when you apply for a job. CV stands for 'curriculum vitae'.

cwt See **hundredweight.**

cyanide is an extremely poisonous chemical.

cybercafe A **cybercafe** is a cafe where you can pay to use a computer so you can look at the Internet.

cybernetics is a branch of science which involves studying the way electronic machines and human brains work, and developing machines which do things or think rather like people.

cyberspace In computer technology, **cyberspace** is used to talk about data banks and networks, considered as a space.

cyborg In science fiction, a **cyborg** is a being who is part human and part robot, or a robot that looks like a human being.

cyclamen (*pron:* **sik**-lam-men) **Cyclamens** are plants with white, pink, or red flowers whose petals turn back.

cycle (**cycling, cycled**) If you **cycle**, you ride a bicycle. You call this activity **cycling.** ■ A **cycle** is another name for a bicycle. ■ A **cycle** is a series of events repeated over and over in the same order. *...the cycle of famine and disease.* ■ A **cycle** in an electrical, electronic, mechanical, or organic process is one complete series of movements or events.

cyclic (**cyclical**) If something is **cyclic** or **cyclical,** it happens again and again in cycles.

cyclist A **cyclist** is someone who rides a bicycle.

cyclone A **cyclone** is a violent storm, in which the wind moves in a circular direction.

cygnet A **cygnet** is a young swan.

cylinder (**cylindrical**) A **cylinder** is a three-dimensional shape with straight sides and circular ends. You say something with this shape is **cylindrical.** ■ An **engine's** cylinder is the part in which the piston moves backwards and forwards.

cymbal A **cymbal** is a brass plate used as a musical instrument. You hit it with a stick or another cymbal to produce a crashing or hissing sound.

cynic (**cynical, cynically**) A **cynic** is someone who always believes the worst of people or their actions. *The postman eyed him cynically.*

cynicism is the belief that people always behave selfishly.

cypher See **cipher.**

cypress (*pron:* **sigh**-pruss) (**cypresses**) **Cypresses** are evergreen trees with dark green leaves and rounded cones.

cyst (*pron:* **sist**) A **cyst** is a lump containing liquid which grows inside your body or on your skin.

cystic fibrosis is a hereditary disease which causes poor digestion, difficulty in breathing, and excessive mucus.

cystitis (*pron:* siss-**tite**-iss) is an inflammation of the bladder.

czar See **tsar.**

czarist See **tsarist.**

D d

D.A. See **district attorney.**

dab (**dabbing, dabbed**) If you **dab** something, you touch it quickly and lightly several times, for example with a tissue. ■ A **dab** of something is a small amount of it. ■ If you are a **dab hand** at something, you are very good at it.

dabble (**dabbling, dabbled**) If you **dabble** in something, you take part in it, but not very seriously.

dacha (*pron:* **datch**-a) A **dacha** is a country house in Russia.

dachshund (*pron:* **daks**-und) The **dachshund** is a small dog with short legs, a long body, and long ears.

dad (**daddy**) Your **dad** or **daddy** is your father.

daddy-long-legs (*plural:* **daddy-long-legs**) The **daddy-long-legs** is a flying insect with long legs. It is also called the 'crane fly'.

dado (**dadoes**) A **dado** is the lower part of the wall of a room decorated differently from the upper part. A **dado rail** is a decorative strip fixed around the middle of a wall decorated in this way.

daffodil – **Daffodils** are yellow bell-shaped flowers which bloom in early spring.

daft If you say someone is **daft,** you mean they are silly.

dagger A **dagger** is a weapon like a knife with two sharp edges.

dahlia (*pron:* **day**-lya) **Dahlias** are brightly-coloured garden flowers with many petals.

Dáil (*pron:* **doil**) The **Dáil** is the lower house of parliament in the Irish Republic.

daily (**dailies**) If something happens **daily,** it happens every day. ■ **Daily** is used to say how much of something is used or received each day. *Daily wage rates were around two dollars.* ■ A **daily** is a newspaper published every day except Sunday.

dainty (**daintier, daintiest; daintily**) You call a woman or girl **dainty** when she is small, delicate, and pretty. ■ **Dainty** movements are small and delicate. ■ A **dainty** object is pretty and delicate.

dairy (**dairies**) **Dairy products** are foods like butter and cheese. ■ A **dairy** is a company which sells milk and dairy products. ■ A **dairy** is a building where milk is processed or kept, or dairy products are made. ■ **Dairy cattle** are cows kept for their milk. ■ A **dairy farm** is one where dairy cattle are kept.

dais (*pron:* **day**-iss) (*plural:* **dais**) A **dais** is a raised platform used by a person when speaking to a group of people.

daisy (**daisies**) **Daisies** are small wild flowers with yellow centres and white petals.

daisywheel A **daisywheel** is a small flat disc on an electric typewriter or word processor with letters round the edge which prints what you type. Type-writers and printers with a daisywheel can be called **daisywheels.**

dale A **dale** is a valley in Scotland or Northern Eng-land.

dally (**dallies, dallying, dallied**) If someone **dallies,** they waste a lot of time before deciding to do something. ■ If you **dally** with the idea of doing something, you consider doing it, but not very seri-ously. ■ If someone **dallies** with you, they flirt with you.

dalmatian – **Dalmatians** are large white short-haired dogs with black or brown spots.

dam (**damming, dammed**) A **dam** is a wall built across a river to hold back the water and make a lake. When a wall like this is built, you say the river is **dammed** or **dammed up.** ■ The **dam** of a farm animal, for example a horse or sheep, is its moth-er.

damage (**damages, damaging, damaged**) If you **damage** something or do **damage** to it, you break it or spoil its appearance. ■ When a law court awards **damages** to someone, it orders a person who has harmed them to pay them money.

damask is a heavy cloth, usually silk or linen, used to make tablecloths and curtains.

Dame is an official title given to a woman in recog-nition of something she has achieved.

damn (**damnation**) According to some religions, if someone is **damned** or condemned to **damnation,** they are sent to Hell. ■ If you call something like a report **damning,** you mean it suggests strongly that someone is guilty of a crime or serious error.

damp (**dampness**) If something is **damp,** it is slight-ly wet. ■ **Damp** is moisture on the inside walls of houses or in the air. ■ A **damp course** or **damp-proof course** is a layer of waterproof material put into the bottom of a wall to prevent damp from ris-ing. ■ If you **damp down** a situation where people are angry, you calm them.

dampen (**dampening, dampened; dampener**) If something **dampens** a feeling like hope, it makes people feel it less strongly. Something which has this effect can be called a **dampener.** ■ If you **dampen** a surface, you wet it slightly.

damper If something **puts a damper** on things, it spoils people's enjoyment of them. ■ A **damper** is a metal plate on a fire, boiler, or furnace which you move to control the amount of air getting in.

damsel A young unmarried woman used to be called a **damsel.**

damson – **Damsons** are small sour purple plums.

dance (**dancing, danced**) When you **dance,** you move your body in time to music. The steps and other movements you make are called a **dance.**

■ A **dance** is a social event where people dance with each other. ■ A **dance-floor** is the part of a restaurant or nightclub where people can dance. ■ **Dance** is the art of performing dances in front of an audience. ■ If a person **dances** about, they move lightly and quickly, because they are happy.

dancer A **dancer** is a person who earns money by dancing. ■ A **dancer** is anyone who dances.

dandelion – **Dandelions** are bright yellow wild flow-ers with many thin petals. When the petals drop off, they leave fluffy balls of seeds.

dandruff is tiny flakes of dry skin from a person's scalp, which are sometimes seen in their hair or on their shoulders.

dandy (**dandies**) A **dandy** is a man who thinks a lot about his appearance and wears smart clothes.

Dane A **Dane** is a person from Denmark.

danger is a risk of someone being hurt. A **danger** is something which can hurt people. ■ If you say there is a **danger** of something unpleasant happen-ing, you mean there is a risk it will happen. ■ A **danger sign** or **danger signal** is something which warns you of possible trouble. ■ **Danger money** is extra money paid to someone for doing a danger-ous job.

dangerous (**dangerously**) If something is **danger-ous,** it could lead to people being hurt or killed. ■ A **dangerous** person or animal is capable of kill-ing or injuring people.

dangle (**dangling, dangled**) If something **dangles** or is **dangled,** it hangs or swings loosely. ■ If you **dangle** something attractive in front of someone, you suggest they might get it if they do what you want.

Danish is used to talk about people and things in or from Denmark. ...*the Danish national anthem.* ■ **Danish** is the main language spoken in Denmark.

Danish pastry A **Danish pastry** is a cake made of rich pastry with a sweet filling like apple or almond paste.

dank A **dank** place is damp and cold.

dapper A **dapper** man is slim and neatly dressed.

dappled If something is **dappled,** it has light and dark patches, often caused by patterns of light and shade.

dare (**daring, dared**) If you **dare** to do something, you are brave enough to do it. ■ If you **dare** some-one else to do something, you challenge them to prove they are not frightened of doing it. A chal-lenge like this is called a **dare.** ■ **Daring** is used to describe (a) actions which involve danger. ...*a dar-ing helicopter rescue.* (b) things which are likely to shock people. ...*daring new ideas.* ■ You say some-one is **daring** when they do dangerous things or behave in a way likely to shock people. ...*a daring reformer.* **Daring** is the courage shown by someone like this. ■ You say **'I dare say...'** to show you think something is probably true. *We are all going to be uncomfortable for the next few days but I dare say we will survive.* ■ People say **'dare I say it'** when they are going to say something which might be regard-ed as shocking or indiscreet. *I can see he's got, dare I say it, baggier eyes.*

daredevil people enjoy doing dangerous things.

dark (**darkly, darkness**) When it is **dark,** there is not enough light to see clearly. You can talk about the **dark** or **darkness** in a place. ■ When **darkness** falls, it gets dark because the sun is setting. ■ If you do something **after dark,** you do it at night. ■ If you are kept **in the dark** about something, you are not told anything about it. ■ **Dark** colours are like the colours things seem to have when they are seen in shadow. ■ **Dark** is used to talk about things to do with evil. *...the dark side of human nature.* ■ When someone suggests that something unpleasant is going to happen, you can say they say it **darkly.** *One man hinted darkly that there would be violence.* ■ A **dark** period is one when there is great suffering or danger. *...the dark days of July 1940.* ■ You say someone is a **dark horse** when they have been involved in something unusual or exciting and have not told anyone about it.

dark age – **The Dark Ages** were the period of European history between about 500 and 1000 A.D.

darken (**darkening, darkened**) If something **darkens** or is **darkened,** it becomes darker. ■ If something **darkens** a situation, it makes it less hopeful or enjoyable.

darkroom A **darkroom** is a room without daylight where photographs are developed.

darling People who are very fond of each other sometimes call each other **darling.** ■ **Darling** is used to talk about a person someone is very fond of. *...her darling baby brother.* ■ The **darling** of a group of people is their favourite. *...the darling of the art world.*

darn If you **darn** something made of wool, you mend a hole in it by weaving stitches across the hole. A repair like this is called a **darn.**

dart If a person or animal **darts** somewhere, they move there suddenly and quickly. ■ If you **dart** a glance at something, you look at it quickly, then look away. ■ **Darts** are small pointed objects which you throw at a numbered board in a game called **darts.** ■ **Darts** are pointed objects fired from something like a blowpipe.

Darwinism (**Darwinian**) **Darwinism** is Charles Darwin's theory of the development of plants and animals by natural selection. **Darwinian** is used to talk about things connected with this theory.

dash (**dashes, dashing, dashed**) If you **dash** somewhere or make a **dash** for a place, you go there quickly. ■ If you **dash off** something you are writing, you write it quickly, without thinking much about it. ■ If your hopes are **dashed,** something spoils your chances of getting what you want. ■ A **dash** of something is a small amount of it. *...a much-needed dash of glamour.* ■ A **dashing** person is stylish and attractive. You can say someone like this **cuts a dash.** ■ A **dash** is the punctuation mark – .

dashboard A car's **dashboard** is the panel facing the driver, where most of the instruments and switches are.

dastardly people are cunning and evil.

DAT is the same as 'digital audio tape'.

data is information, usually in the form of facts or statistics. ■ **Data processing** is a series of operations carried out on a computer to obtain, interpret, or present information from data.

database A **database** is an easily accessible collection of data stored on computer.

date (**dating, dated**) A **date** is a particular year or day. ■ When you **date** a letter or a cheque, you write the day's date on it. ■ If something **dates back to** a particular time or **dates from** it, it started or was made then. ■ You use **to date** when you are saying what has happened so far, although the situation may change. *200 vampire movies have been made to date.* ■ If something is **out of date,** it no longer applies, or is no longer useful. ■ **Dated** things seem old-fashioned, although they were once fashionable. ■ A **date** is an appointment to go out with someone. You call the person you meet your **date.** ■ If you are **dating** someone, they are your girlfriend or boyfriend. ■ **Dates** are small sticky brown fruit. The trees they grow on are called **date palms.**

daub (**daubing, daubed**) If you **daub** something like paint onto a surface, you put it on with a brush in a quick careless way. *They had daubed slogans on the walls.*

daughter A person's **daughter** is their female child.

daughter-in-law (**daughters-in-law**) A person's **daughter-in-law** is their son's wife.

daunt If you are **daunted** by something, you are worried at having to deal with it. *...a daunting task.*

dawdle (**dawdling, dawdled**) If you **dawdle,** you spend more time than necessary doing something or going somewhere.

dawn When a day **dawns,** the sky grows light after the night. *Nancy woke at dawn.* ■ The **dawn chorus** is the singing of birds at dawn. ■ When a period of time **dawns,** it begins. *...the dawn of the 20th century.* ■ If the truth about something **dawns on** you, you realize it.

day A **day** is one of the seven 24-hour periods in a week. ■ **Day** is the part of a day when it is light. ■ **Day-to-day** things happen as part of ordinary life. ■ **Day** is used to talk about a particular time in history. *...in Shakespeare's day.* ■ If you talk about the **day** of a person or thing, you mean the time when they were successful or important. *The day of the yuppie is gone.* ■ If you decide to **call it a day,** you give up what you are doing altogether, or leave it until another day. ■ If something **wins the day,** it is the strongest force in a situation, and determines what happens. *The views of the moderates seem to have won the day.*

daybreak is the beginning of the day, when light first appears.

day care is care that is provided during the day for people who cannot look after themselves such as children or the sick.

day centre – **Day centres** are places where people like the old or the homeless can spend time during the day.

daydream (**daydreaming, daydreamed**) If you **daydream,** your attention wanders and you think about pleasant things; these thoughts are called **daydreams.** ■ A **daydream** is a hope or ambition you are unlikely to achieve.

Day-glo (or **Dayglo**) colours are shades of orange, pink, green, and yellow which are so bright that they seem to glow. 'Day-glo' is a trademark.

daylight – Daylight is (a) the light during the day. (b) the part of the day when it is light. ■ **in broad daylight:** see **broad.**

day return A **day return** is a ticket which allows you to go somewhere and come back the same day for a lower price than an ordinary return ticket.

day school A **day school** is one which pupils go to each day from their own homes. It is usually a fee-paying school.

daytime is the part of the day when it is light. ■ **Daytime** things are used or operate during the day, when most people are at work. ...your daytime telephone number.

day trip A **day trip** is a journey to a place and back the same day, made for pleasure.

dazed (**daze**) If someone is **dazed** or **in a daze** after an accident or an unpleasant experience, they are shocked and unable to think clearly.

dazzle (**dazzling, dazzled**) If you are **dazzled** by something, you are amazed and impressed by its quality or beauty. ...a dazzling smile. ■ If you are **dazzled** by a bright light, you cannot see properly because of it. You talk about the **dazzle** of a light like this.

dB See **decibel.**

DC is used to describe an electric current which always flows in the same direction. DC stands for 'direct current'. See also **AC.**

DDT is a poisonous chemical used to kill insects. DDT stands for 'dichlorodiphenyltrichloroethane'.

deacon (**deaconess, deaconesses**) In some churches, including the Church of England, a **deacon** or **deaconess** is a member of the clergy who is lower in rank than a priest. In other churches, they are non-ordained people who assist the minister.

deactivate (**deactivating, deactivated**) When someone **deactivates** something like a bomb, they make it incapable of exploding.

dead A **dead** person, animal, or plant is no longer living. People gathered in the city centre to mourn the dead. ■ If a phone or radio **goes dead,** it seems to have stopped working. ■ A **dead** language, such as Latin, is one which is no longer generally used. ■ If you say an idea, plan, or belief is **dead,** you mean most people no longer think it is appropriate or important. Socialism is dead. ■ **Dead** is used to mean complete or absolute. ...a dead stop. ...dead silence. ■ The **dead of night** is the middle of the night, when it is darkest. Similarly, you can talk about the **dead of winter.**

deaden (**deadening, deadened**) If something **deadens** a feeling, it weakens it. ■ If something **deadens** a sound, it makes it less loud.

dead end If a street is a **dead end,** there is no way out at one end. ■ A **dead end job** is one in which you are unlikely to progress or achieve fulfilment.

dead heat If a competition ends in a **dead heat,** two or more competitors finish in first place.

deadline A **deadline** is a time by which something must be finished.

deadlock (**deadlocked**) If a dispute reaches **deadlock** or is **deadlocked,** neither side is willing to give in, so no agreement can be reached.

deadly (**deadlier, deadliest**) If something is **deadly,** it is capable of killing people. ■ **Deadly** is used to mean 'extreme' or 'extremely'. ...a deadly accurate shot from close range. They were deadly serious.

deadpan If someone's behaviour or expression is **deadpan,** they hide the fact that they are joking and pretend to be serious.

dead weight You say a person or thing is a **dead weight** when they are heavy and difficult to lift. ■ You can call something a **dead weight** when it makes progress difficult.

deaf A **deaf** person cannot hear very well, or cannot hear at all. The **deaf** are people who are deaf. ■ If you are **deaf** to what someone says or **turn a deaf ear** to it, you ignore it.

deafen (**deafening, deafened**) If a person is **deafened,** they are temporarily made deaf. ■ If you are **deafened** by a noise, it is so loud you cannot hear anything else. You say a noise like this is **deafening.**

deaf-mute A **deaf-mute** is a person who cannot hear or speak.

deal (**dealing, dealt**) A **deal** is an agreement, especially a business one. ■ If a person **deals in** a type of goods, they buy and sell them. ■ When you **deal with** a situation, you do what needs to be done to get the result you want. ■ A **great deal** or **good deal of** something is a lot of it. ■ If you **deal** someone a blow, you hit them. ■ If something **deals** you a blow, it harms you in some way. The reforms could deal a serious blow to their living standards. ■ In a game of cards, when someone **deals** the cards, they give them out to the players. If it is your **deal,** it is your turn to deal. ■ If you say someone has had a **bad deal,** you mean they have been unlucky or treated unfairly.

dealer A **dealer** is a person who makes money by buying and selling things for a profit. ...an antiques dealer. ■ In a game of cards, the **dealer** is the person who gives out cards to the other players.

dealership A **dealership** is a company which sells cars, usually for one car manufacturer.

dealings If you have **dealings** with someone, you are involved with them in some way, for example you do business with them.

dean A **dean** at a university or college is the chief administrator of a faculty. ■ In the Church of England, a **dean** is a high-ranking priest who is the administrator of a cathedral.

deanery (**deaneries**) A **deanery** is an area for which a rural dean has responsibility. It consists of several parishes.

dear (**dearer, dearest**) If a person or thing is **dear** to you, you care deeply about them. ■ If something is **dear,** it costs a lot of money.

dearly If you love someone **dearly,** you love them very much. ■ If you would **dearly** like to do something, you want to do it very much. ■ If you **pay dearly** for something you have done, you suffer a lot because of it.

dearth

decency

dearth If there is a **dearth** of something, there is not enough of it.

death is the end of a person's or animal's life. ■ If someone has a **death wish,** they are attracted by the idea of dying and are likely to do dangerous things. ■ The **death toll** of a disaster or war is the number of people killed. ■ A **death warrant** is an official document ordering someone to be killed. ■ If someone faces the **death penalty** or is given a **death sentence,** they are going to be executed as punishment for a crime. **Death row** is the part of a prison where they are kept until execution. ■ The **death** of an organization or way of life is its end. ■ You say a place or vehicle is a **death trap** when it is in such a dangerous condition that it could cause someone's death.

deathbed If someone is on their **deathbed,** they are in bed and about to die.

death certificate A **death certificate** is an official statement signed by a doctor which gives the cause of a person's death.

deathly is used to describe things which remind you of a dead person. *Her feet were deathly cold.*

debacle (*pron:* day-**bah**-kl) A **debacle** is a complete and embarrassing failure.

debar (**debarring, debarred**) If you are **debarred** from something, you are legally prevented from doing it.

debase (**debasing, debased**) If something has been **debased,** its standard has been lowered.

debate (**debating, debated; debater, debatable**) When people **debate** something, they discuss it formally, putting forward different opinions. A **debate** is a discussion like this. ■ If you say something is **debatable** or **open to debate,** you mean there is no certainty about it. ■ If you **debate** what to do, you think about possible alternatives before making up your mind.

debauched (*pron:* dib-**bawcht**) (**debauchery**) If you call someone **debauched,** you mean they indulge too much in physical pleasures like alcohol or sex. Behaviour like this is called **debauchery.**

debenture – **Debentures** are portions of a long-term loan made to a company by investors who receive a fixed rate of interest.

debilitated (**debilitating, debility**) If a person is **debilitated** or suffers **debility,** they are made weak. *The humidity is debilitating.* ■ **Debilitated** and **debilitating** are used to talk about other things being weakened, such as a country's economy. *...debilitating subsidies.*

debit (**debiting, debited**) If your bank account is **debited,** money is taken from it by your bank and paid to someone else. ■ A **debit card** is a card which acts like a cheque. When you use it to pay someone, the money is transferred automatically from your bank account to theirs. ■ If you pay bills by **direct debit,** you arrange for regular payments to be made from your bank account.

debonair (*pron:* de-bon-**air**) A **debonair** man is handsome, well-dressed, and confident.

debrief (**debriefing, debriefed**) If someone is **debriefed,** they are interrogated about something they have just done or experienced. An interroga-tion like this is called a **debriefing** or a **debriefing session.**

debris (*pron:* **deb**-ree) is broken pieces of something which has been destroyed, such as a plane or a building.

debt (**debtor**) A **debt** is an amount of money you owe someone. If you are **in debt,** you owe someone money. Your **debtors** are the people who owe you money. ■ If you say you are **in** someone's **debt,** you mean you are grateful for something they have done for you. ■ **bad debt:** see **bad.**

debug (**debugging, debugged**) If someone **debugs** a computer program, they find the faults and put them right, so the program will work properly.

debunk If you **debunk** a belief, you show it is false.

debut (*pron:* **day**-byoo) The **debut** of an actor or musician is their first public performance. ■ A sportsperson's **debut** with a team is their first game as a member of that team.

debutante (*pron:* **day**-byoo-tont) A **debutante** is a young upper-class woman who has just started going to dances and parties.

decade A **decade** is a period of ten years, especially one beginning with a year ending in 0.

decadent (*pron:* **dek**-a-dent) (**decadence**) People are sometimes described as **decadent** when their behaviour shows low moral standards.

decaffeinated coffee has had most of the caffeine removed from it.

decamp If someone suddenly leaves a place and goes to live somewhere else, you can say they **decamp** there.

decant If you **decant** wine, you pour some of it carefully from one container to another, making sure any sediment is left behind.

decanter A **decanter** is a glass bottle or jug used for serving drinks like sherry or whisky.

decapitate (**decapitating, decapitated; decapitation**) If a person is **decapitated,** their head is cut off. *...the decapitation of Louis XVI.*

decathlon (**decathlete**) The **decathlon** is a competition in which athletes called **decathletes** take part in ten different sporting events.

decay If something **decays,** it rots. This process is called **decay.** ■ If buildings or parts of a town **decay,** they become run down. *...decaying inner city areas.* ■ If something like an organization or country **decays,** it gradually becomes weak or corrupt.

deceased A **deceased** person is one who has recently died. People sometimes call someone who has just died **the deceased.**

deceit (**deceitful**) **Deceit** is behaviour intended to make people believe things which are not true.

deceive (**deceiving, deceived**) If you **deceive** someone, you deliberately make them believe something untrue.

decelerate (**decelerating, decelerated; deceleration**) If something **decelerates,** it slows down.

decency (**decencies**) **Decency** is behaviour which is respectable and follows accepted moral standards. ■ **Decencies** are accepted standards of behaviour. *They cling to the old decencies.*

decent (**decently**) **Decent** is used to say something is of an acceptable standard or quality. ■ **Decent** behaviour is honest and respectable.

decentralize (or **decentralise**) (**decentralizing, decentralized; decentralization**) If a large organization **decentralizes,** it transfers some of its functions from its main office to smaller offices in other areas.

deception is deceiving people. A **deception** is something you say or do to deceive someone.

deceptive (**deceptively**) If you say something is **deceptive,** you mean it might make people believe something which is not true.

decibel The intensity of sound is measured in **decibels.** 'Decibels' is often written 'dB'.

decide (**deciding, decided; decidedly, decider**) If you **decide** to do something, you make up your mind to do it. ■ If you **decide on** a plan or course of action, you choose it from two or more possibilities. ■ When something like a court case is **decided,** the evidence is considered and a verdict is reached. ■ If what happens is **decided** by a particular thing, it is determined by that thing. *The team's World Cup fate was decided by a penalty shoot-out.* ■ If something is a **deciding factor,** it is one of the things which affect what happens. ■ In a competition, a **decider** is the game or part of a game which determines who wins the competition. ■ If you **decide** something is true, you form that opinion on the basis of what you know. ■ **Decided** and **decidedly** are used in front of some words and expressions to emphasize something is definitely a particular thing. *His views became decidedly more hardline.*

deciduous trees shed their leaves in the autumn.

decimal A **decimal** system involves counting in units of ten. ■ A **decimal** is a fraction written as a dot followed by one or more numbers. For example, three-eighths can be written .375. The dot in a fraction like this is called the **decimal point.**

decimalization (or **decimalisation**) was the change made to the money system in February 1971 when the old system of pounds, shillings, and pence was replaced by the present decimal system.

decimate (**decimating, decimated; decimation**) If a group of people or things is **decimated,** most of them are killed or destroyed. ■ People talk about things being **decimated** when they are reduced to a fraction of their former strength or importance. ■ Originally, to **decimate** something meant to reduce it by a tenth.

decipher (**deciphering, deciphered**) If you **decipher** a piece of writing, speech, or coded information, you work out what it says.

decision When you make a **decision,** you make up your mind about something.

decisive (**decisively, decisiveness**) If something is **decisive,** it determines which way things will go in the future. ■ In sport, if a person or team gets a **decisive** victory, they win by a large margin. You can also say they suffer a **decisive** defeat. ■ A **decisive** person makes quick firm decisions. *...lack of decisiveness.* ■ If you do something **decisively,** you do it in a firm deliberate way.

deck The **deck** of a ship is the level part you stand on. ■ A **deck hand** is a person who does the cleaning and other work on a ship's deck. ■ If you **clear the decks,** you finish off the things you are dealing with at present, so you can concentrate on something else. ■ The **decks** of a bus are its upper and lower floors. ■ In the US, a patio is called a **deck.** ■ A pack of playing cards can be called a **deck.** ■ If something is **decked** with attractive things, it is decorated with them. ■ If someone is **decked out** in something bright and attractive, they are wearing it.

deckchair – **Deckchairs** are adjustable folding chairs.

declaim (**declaiming, declaimed; declamatory; declamation**) If you **declaim** something, you say it dramatically, as if you were on a stage. Speaking like this can be called **declamation.** Anything which reminds you of a dramatic speech can be called **declamatory** (*pron:* dik-**klam**-a-tor-y).

declaration A **declaration** is an official announcement. ■ A **declaration** is a firm, emphatic statement which shows you have no doubts about what you are saying.

declare (**declaring, declared**) If you **declare** something, you say it in a firm clear way. You can also **declare** an attitude or intention. ■ When a country or government **declares** something, it announces it officially. ■ If you **declare** goods you have bought overseas or money you have earned, you say how much you have bought or earned so you can pay tax on it. ■ If a cricket team **declares,** they decide to stop batting and let the other team in, though some of their own players are not yet out.

declassify (**declassifies, declassifying, declassified**) If secret documents or records are **declassified,** it is officially stated they are no longer secret.

decline (**declining, declined**) If something **declines,** it becomes poorer or weaker. *Living standards are declining.* You can talk about a **decline** in something like this; you can also say it is **in decline** or **on the decline.** ■ If you **decline** something or **decline** to do something, you politely refuse to accept it or do it.

decode (**decoding, decoded**) When information is **decoded,** it is changed into a form which can be easily understood.

decoder A **decoder** is something used to decode information. ■ A **decoder** is a device you need to attach to your TV set to watch some satellite and cable TV programmes.

décolleté (**décolletage**) If a woman is **décolleté** (*pron:* day-**kol**-tay), she is wearing a low-cut or strapless dress or blouse. You can also say her dress or blouse is **décolleté.** The neckline of a dress or blouse like this is called its **décolletage** (*pron:* day-**kol**-tazh; *the 'zh' sounds like 's' in 'pleasure'*).

decolonization (or **decolonisation**) means giving political independence to a country that was formerly a colony.

decommission (**decommissioning, decommissioned**) If something like an industrial plant or military equipment is **decommissioned,** it is dismantled and taken out of use. *...the difficulties of decommissioning old power stations.*

decompose (**decomposing, decomposed; decomposition**) When something **decomposes,** it begins to rot.

decompression If something undergoes **decompression,** the air pressure on it is reduced. ■ **Decompression** is the process by which deep-sea divers are brought back to normal air pressure after they have been at great pressure underwater. This usually takes place in a **decompression chamber.** ■ **Decompression sickness** is a serious condition which affects divers who rise to the surface of the water too quickly. Decompression sickness is sometimes called the 'bends'.

decongestant A decongestant is a medicine which helps someone with a cold to breathe more easily.

decontaminate (**decontaminating, decontaminated; decontamination**) If something is **decontaminated,** radioactivity, germs, or other dangerous substances are removed from it.

decontrol (**decontrolling, decontrolled**) If prices or rents are **decontrolled,** they are no longer set by the government.

decor The **decor** of a house or room is the style it is furnished and decorated in.

decorate (**decorating, decorated; decoration**) If you **decorate** something, you add something attractive to it to brighten it up. Things added like this are called **decorations.** ■ If you **decorate** a building or room, you paint or wallpaper it. The **decoration** of a building is its paintwork, wallpaper, and ornaments. ■ If a person is **decorated,** they are given a medal as an official honour. Medals like these are called **decorations.**

decorative things are intended to look attractive rather than be useful. ■ The **decorative arts,** are arts and crafts like pottery and cabinet-making, which involve making things to be used for decoration or furnishing.

decorator A decorator is a person who paints and wallpapers houses and other buildings for a living.

decorous (**decorously; decorum**) Someone's behaviour is called **decorous** (*pron:* dek-a-russ) when it is polite, dignified, and correct. People like this are also said to behave with **decorum** (*pron:* dik-core-um).

decoy A **decoy** is something intended to attract someone's attention, either to catch them or to stop them noticing something.

decrease (**decreasing, decreased; decreasingly**) If something **decreases,** it gets smaller in quantity, size, or intensity. ■ A **decrease** is a reduction in size, number, or intensity. ■ You use **decreasingly** to say something has less and less of a quality.

decree (**decreeing, decreed**) If someone in authority **decrees** something or issues a **decree,** they officially order that it shall be done.

decree absolute A **decree absolute** is the final order which ends a marriage, made by a court in a divorce case.

decree nisi (*pron:* nice-sigh) A **decree nisi** is an order issued by a court saying a divorce will take

place at a certain time unless a good reason is produced to prevent it.

decrepit (**decrepitude**) You say something is **decrepit** or talk about its **decrepitude** when it is old and in bad condition.

decriminalize (*or* **decriminalise**) (**decriminalizing, decriminalized; decriminalization**) If something is **decriminalized,** it is no longer a crime to have it or do it.

decry (**decries, decrying, decried**) If you **decry** someone or something, you publicly criticize them.

dedicate (**dedicating, dedicated; dedication, dedicatee**) If you **dedicate** yourself to something, you make it the most important thing in your life. ■ If a writer or composer **dedicates** a book or piece of music to someone, they say they want them to be associated with it, to show fondness or respect for them. They announce this at the beginning of the book or piece of music in a statement called a **dedication.** The **dedicatee** of a book or piece of music is the person it is dedicated to. ■ When a monument, building, or church is **dedicated** to someone, a formal ceremony is held to show it will always be associated with that person.

deduce (**deducing, deduced**) If you **deduce** something, you work it out from what you already know.

deduct When you **deduct** an amount from a total, you reduce it by that amount.

deductible If something is **deductible** or **tax-deductible,** the cost of it can be deducted from your income before your income tax is calculated.

deduction A **deduction** is an amount taken off a total. ■ A **deduction** is something you work out from what you already know. *What scientific deductions can you make from an observation of this eclipse?*

deed A **deed** is something which is done, especially something good or bad. *...a dirty deed.* ■ A **deed** is a legal document, especially concerning the ownership of land or a building.

deed poll If you change your name by **deed poll,** you do it officially.

deem (**deeming, deemed**) If something is **deemed** to be a particular thing, it is believed or declared to be that thing.

deep (**deeper, deepest; deeply**) If something is **deep,** it extends a long way down from its surface. ■ **Deep** is used to talk about measurements. For example, if something is two metres deep, it measures two metres from top to bottom or from front to back. ■ You talk about things being **deep** into a period of time or place when you mean they happen a long way inside that time or place. *...a goal scored deep into injury time. ...boat trips upstream, deep into the jungle.* ■ **Deep** is used to emphasize that something is serious, strong, or intense. *...in deep trouble. ...deep feelings of grief and loss... When he thought deeply about it, he wished Livy would stay at university.* ■ You say someone is **deep** when they spend a lot of time thinking about serious subjects. ■ **Deep breathing** is taking in long slow breaths which fill your lungs. ■ If you say you **took a deep breath** before doing something, you mean you tried to prepare yourself, knowing it was going to be difficult or dangerous. ■ **Deep** colours are

deepen · 165 · defer

strong and rather dark. ■ A **deep** sound is low in pitch.

deepen (**deepening, deepened**) If a river or the sea **deepens** somewhere, it gets deeper. ■ If you **deepen** something, you make it deeper. ■ If a situation or feeling **deepens** or is **deepened**, it becomes more serious or intense. ...*the deepening crisis.* ■ If your knowledge of something is **deepened**, you learn more about it. ■ When a sound **deepens**, it becomes lower in pitch.

deep freeze A **deep freeze** is the same as a freezer. ■ If something is kept **in deep freeze**, it is stored at an extremely low temperature.

deep-fried food has been fried by being submerged in deep fat or oil.

deep-rooted feelings or ideas are firmly fixed and difficult to change.

deep-seated A **deep-seated** problem, feeling, or belief is difficult to change, often because has been around for a long time.

deer (*plural:* **deer**) Deer are large wild animals which eat grass and leaves. In most species, the male deer has branching horns called antlers.

deface (**defacing, defaced**) If someone **defaces** something like a wall or a notice, they spoil it by writing or drawing on it.

de facto (*pron:* day **fac**-to) is used to say something exists in practice, although it is not officially or legally recognized. ...*thirty years of de facto single party rule.* See also **de jure.**

defame (**defaming, defamed; defamatory, defamation**) If you say you have been **defamed**, you mean someone has said or written untrue things about you which may damage your reputation; you call what they have said or written **defamatory** (*pron:* dif-**fam**-a-tree). You can take legal action against someone for this; this is called an action for **defamation** (*pron:* def-fam-**may**-shun).

default (**defaulter**) If you **default** on something you are legally supposed to do, such as make a payment, you do not do it. You are then said to be **in default.** An individual case of someone doing this is called a **default;** the person doing it is called a **defaulter.** ■ If something happens **by default,** it happens only because something else has not happened. *He kept the title by default because no one else wanted to compete for it.*

defeat (**defeating, defeated**) If you **defeat** someone in a battle or contest, you beat them. If you suffer a **defeat,** you lose. ■ If a proposal is **defeated,** more people vote against it than for it. ■ If you **defeat** a problem, you solve it. ■ If someone's efforts are **defeated,** they fail to achieve what they want.

defeatist (**defeatism**) A **defeatist** is someone who thinks and talks in a way which shows they expect to be unsuccessful. ...*a defeatist attitude... This is spineless defeatism.*

defecate (*pron:* def-fe-cate) (**defecating, defecated**) When animals or people **defecate,** they get rid of solid waste through their anus.

defect (**defection, defector**) A **defect** (*pron:* **dee**-fect) is a fault. ■ If someone **defects** (*pron:* dif-**fects**), they secretly leave their country, political party, or other group and join an opposing one. Someone doing this is called a **defector.** ...*the defection of sixteen Parliamentary deputies.*

defective If something is **defective,** it does not work properly.

defector See **defect.**

defence (*Am:* **defense**) is action taken to protect someone or something from attack. *He said the new missiles were purely for defence.* ■ A **defence** is something people or animals use or do to protect themselves. ...*the body's defences against disease.* ■ A **defence mechanism** is an instinctive reaction to something, which may protect you from a possible danger. ■ **Defence** is used to talk about a country's armed forces and weapons. ...*the Ministry of Defence.* ■ The **defences** of a place are its armed forces, weapons, and other things used to protect it, such as fortifications. ■ If someone puts up a **defence** of something which is being criticized, they say things in support of it. ■ In court, an accused person's **defence** is the evidence produced in their favour. The accused person and lawyers representing them are also called the **defence.** ■ The **defence** in a game like football is the group of players whose main job is to stop the opposing team scoring. ■ In games and sports, when someone makes a **defence** of their title, they compete with other people to decide whether or not they remain champion.

defenceless If someone is **defenceless,** they are unable to protect themselves.

defend If you **defend** someone or something when they are being attacked, you try to protect them. ■ When a lawyer **defends** an accused person in court, he or she represents them. ■ In games or sports, when a champion **defends** their title, they compete with other people to decide whether or not they remain champion.

defendant The defendant in a court case is the person who is accused of a crime or has had an action brought against them.

defender When someone supports people, ideas, or values which are being criticized or threatened, you say they are a **defender** of those people, ideas, or values. ...*a defender of law and order.* ■ A **defender** in a game like football is a player whose main job is to stop the other side scoring.

defense See **defence.**

defensible If you say a point of view is **defensible,** you mean there are good reasons for having it, though you may may not agree with it. ■ If you say someone's behaviour is **defensible,** you mean they can be excused for what they have done. ■ A **defensible** place can be defended against attack.

defensive (**defensively**) You use **defensive** to describe things intended to protect someone or something from attack. ...*a defensive strategy.* ■ If people are **on the defensive,** they are ready to protect themselves or their interests because they feel threatened. ■ If someone is **defensive,** they talk as if they think they are being accused of something.

defer (**deferring, deferred; deferment, deferral**) If you **defer** something, you arrange for it to take place at a later date than planned. An arrangement like this is called a **deferment** or a **deferral.** ■ If you **defer** to someone, you accept their opinion or do what they want, because you respect them.

deference (**deferential**) If you treat someone with **deference** or you are **deferential** towards them, you have a polite and respectful attitude towards them, for example because they hold an important position. ■ If you do something **in deference** or **out of deference** to someone, you do it to show politeness and respect for them, though you may not want to do it.

defiant (**defiantly, defiance**) If someone is **defiant** or behaves with **defiance,** they show they are not willing to obey someone or are not worried about someone's disapproval.

deficiency (**deficiencies**) A **deficiency** in something, especially something your body needs, is a shortage of it. ■ A **deficiency** is a weakness or a fault. *They have complained of deficiencies in the electoral system.*

deficient If someone or something is **deficient** in something, they do not have as much of it as they need. ■ **Deficient** is used to say something is not good enough. *...deficient standards of hygiene.*

deficit (*pron:* **def**-fiss-it) A **deficit** is the amount by which the money received by a country or organization falls short of the amount it has spent. ■ In sport, a **deficit** is the amount by which the number of goals or points scored by one side is less than those scored by the other. *Germany retrieved a two-goal deficit to win 3-2.*

defile (**defiling, defiled**) If someone **defiles** something that people think is holy or important, they treat it disrespectfully or damage it.

definable If something is **definable,** it can be described clearly and distinguished from other similar things.

define (**defining, defined**) If you **define** something like a policy, you say what it is. *...a new treaty to define the relationship between Moscow and the republics.* ■ If you **define** a word or expression, you say what it means. ■ If you talk about the way an area is **defined,** you ate talking about its extent and its boundaries. *...a wide scorched area defined by a perimeter of burning grass.*

definite (**definitely**) If something is **definite,** it is fixed and unlikely to be changed. ■ If you are **definite** about something, you are sure about it. ■ **Definite** is used to emphasize the strength of your opinion or belief. *This kid is definitely a future champion.*

definite article The **definite article** is the word 'the'.

definition A **definition** of a word or expression is a statement giving its meaning. ■ If you say something has a quality **by definition,** you mean it has that quality simply by being what it is. ■ If something has **definition,** it is clear and distinct. *...high definition television.*

definitive (**definitively**) If something is the **definitive** thing of its kind, it is the best example of it. *Transplants can be considered as a definitive solution to kidney disease.* ■ **Definitive** is used to say some-

thing is established clearly and without any doubt. *The Constitution did not definitively rule out divorce.*

deflate (**deflating, deflated**) If something **deflates** your hopes or feelings, it suddenly weakens them. ■ When a tyre or balloon **deflates** or is **deflated,** the air is let out of it.

deflation (**deflationary**) **Deflation** is a reduction in the rate of inflation. When there is deflation, prices stop rising or go down and wages do not rise so quickly. A **deflationary** measure is meant to cause deflation. See also **disinflation.**

deflect (**deflection**) If you **deflect** something like criticism from something, you get people to turn their attention to something else. ■ If a moving object is **deflected** or takes a **deflection,** it hits something and changes direction slightly.

defoliate (**defoliating, defoliated; defoliation, defoliant**) If something **defoliates** trees or plants, it makes their leaves fall off. ■ A **defoliant** is a chemical which makes trees lose their leaves. It is used in wartime to prevent an enemy using forest as cover.

deforest (**deforestation**) If a tree-covered area is **deforested,** all the trees are cut down or destroyed.

deform (**deformity, deformities**) If someone is **deformed** or they have a **deformity,** part of their body has an unnatural shape. You can also talk about things such as trees being **deformed.**

deformation in something like rock is a change in its shape caused by powerful forces such as an earthquake.

defraud (**defrauding, defrauded**) If someone **defrauds** you of something which belongs to you, they use tricks and lies to take it away from you or stop you getting it.

defray If someone **defrays** your costs, they give you money to make up for an amount you have spent, for example when you have done something for them.

defrost When you **defrost** a fridge or freezer, you switch it off so the ice inside can melt. ■ If you **defrost** frozen food, you allow its temperature to increase until it is no longer frozen and is ready to be cooked or eaten.

deft (**deftly, deftness**) A **deft** action is quick, neat, and skilful.

defunct If something is **defunct,** it no longer exists or is no longer used.

defuse (**defusing, defused**) If someone **defuses** a tense situation, they calm it down. ■ If someone **defuses** a bomb, they make it incapable of exploding.

defy (**defies, defying, defied**) If you **defy** a law or restriction, you break it in order to do something you believe is morally right. Similarly, you can **defy** a person who is trying to stop you doing something. ■ If you **defy** someone to do something difficult, you challenge them to do it. *I defy anyone to look at the evidence for ghosts and say there are no such things.* ■ If you say something **defies** belief, you mean it is almost too strange to believe.

degenerate (**degenerating, degenerated; degeneration, degeneracy**) If things or people **degenerate** (*pron:* di-**jen**-er-ait), they get worse in some way. ■ If you say someone is **degenerate** (*pron:* di-**jen**-er-et) or a **degenerate**, you mean they behave in an immoral or disgusting way. Behaviour like this is called **degeneracy**.

degenerative A **degenerative** illness is one which slowly gets worse.

degrade (**degrading, degraded; degradation**) If someone is **degraded** by an experience, they feel less human and less respectable as a result of it. *Criminals are kept in degrading circumstances.* ■ If a substance is **degraded**, it is broken down into its simplest chemical elements, usually by a natural process like the action of bacteria. ■ If rock is **degraded**, it is worn down by something such as the action of water or wind. ■ If soil is **degraded**, it is made poorer as a result of substances being washed out of it.

degree If there is a high **degree** of something, there is a lot of it. *There were varying degrees of enthusiasm for military action.* ■ If you say there is **a degree** of something, you mean there is some of it, but not a lot. *Most pension policies provide a degree of choice.* ■ If something happens **by degrees**, it happens gradually. ■ Measurements such as temperature and angles are expressed in **degrees**. See **Celsius** and **Fahrenheit**. 'Degrees' is usually represented by the symbol °; for example 30 degrees is written 30°. ■ A **degree** is a qualification you get after completing a university course.

degustation is wine tasting.

dehumanize (*or* **dehumanise**) (**dehumanizing, dehumanized**) If something **dehumanizes** people, it takes away from them the qualities thought to be most typically human, such as kindness and individuality.

dehydrate (**dehydrating, dehydrated; dehydration, dehydrator**) **Dehydrated** food has had all the water removed from it to preserve it. A **dehydrator** is a machine which does this. ■ If someone is **dehydrated** or suffering from **dehydration**, they are ill because of a lack of water in their body.

deify (*pron:* **day**-if-fie) (**deifies, deifying, deified; deification**) You say someone or something is **deified** when they are treated as if they were a god. *...the deification of science.*

deign (*pron:* **dane**) If you talk about someone **deigning** to do something, you are suggesting they might think it is beneath their dignity to do it.

deity (*pron:* **dee**-it-ee) (**deities**) A **deity** is a god or goddess.

déjà vu (*pron:* **day**-zhah **voo**; the 'zh' sounds like 's' in 'pleasure') is the feeling that something you are experiencing has happened to you before.

dejected (**dejection**) If you are **dejected**, you are unhappy and disappointed.

de jure (*pron:* day **jew**-ray) is used to talk about things which are recognized by law, as distinct from things which operate without being recognized by law. *Full de jure independence was accorded to the new state on 4 October 1932.* See also **de facto**.

delay (**delaying, delayed**) If you **delay** doing something, you put it off until a later date. ■ If someone or something is **delayed**, they are slowed down or made late. *His flight to London was delayed.* ■ If there

is **delay** or a **delay**, something does not happen until later than expected.

delectable is used to describe things, especially foods, which are extremely pleasant.

delectation If something is done for your **delectation**, it is done for your pleasure.

delegate (**delegating, delegated; delegation**) A **delegate** (*pron:* **del**-i-get) is someone chosen to make decisions on behalf of other people, especially at a meeting. A **delegation** is a group of people chosen to represent a larger group. ■ If you **delegate** (*pron:* **del**-i-gait) someone to do something, you formally ask them to do it on your behalf. ■ If you **delegate** duties or responsibilities, you give them to someone else so they can act on your behalf.

delete (**deleting, deleted; deletion**) If you **delete** information which is written down or stored on a computer, you remove it.

deleterious (*pron:* del-lit-**eer**-ee-uss) If something is **deleterious**, it is harmful or damaging.

deli A **deli** is a delicatessen.

deliberate (**deliberating, deliberated; deliberately, deliberation**) If something you do is **deliberate**, you intend to do it. ■ **Deliberate** is used to describe things being done or said in a slow careful way. *...precise, deliberate speech.* ■ If you **deliberate** (*pron:* di-**lib**-er-ait), you think about something carefully before making a decision. ■ **Deliberations** are formal discussions to decide something.

delicacy (**delicacies**) **Delicacy** is gracefulness and attractiveness. ■ **Delicacy** is careful behaviour in a situation where people might easily be offended. If you talk about the **delicacy** of a situation, you mean it requires this sort of behaviour. ■ A **delicacy** is a rare and expensive food which is considered to be particularly good.

delicate (**delicately**) **Delicate** things are small, graceful, and attractive. *...delicately embroidered tablecloths.* ■ **Delicate** things are easily broken or damaged. *...a delicate china vase.* ■ A **delicate** colour, taste, or smell is pleasant and not strong or intense. ■ A **delicate** movement is gentle and controlled. ■ A **delicate** situation or problem needs to be handled carefully. You can talk about someone's **delicate** handling of a situation like this. ■ If a situation is **delicately** poised or **delicately** balanced, it is unstable, and a small change in circumstances may have a large effect.

delicatessen A **delicatessen** is a shop which sells high quality foods such as cheeses and cold meats imported from other countries.

delicious (**deliciously**) **Delicious** food tastes extremely good. ■ If you describe something as **delicious**, you mean it is extremely pleasant.

delight is a feeling of great pleasure. If someone or something **delights** you, they give you this feeling. ■ If you say something is a **delight**, you mean it gives you great pleasure. ■ The **delights** of a place or event are the things about it you like. ■ If you **delight** in something, you enjoy it. If you **take delight** in doing something, you enjoy doing it.

delighted (delightedly) If you are **delighted**, you are very pleased.

delightful (delightfully) If you say something is **delightful**, you mean it is very pleasant and enjoyable.

delimit (delimiting, delimited; delimitation) If the borders of a country or region are **delimited**, their exact positions are established.

delineate (*pron:* dill-lin-ee-ate) **(delineating, delineating; delineation)** If an idea or theory is **delineated**, it is defined or described in detail. ■ If the borders of a country or region are **delineated**, their exact positions are established.

delinquent (delinquency) A **delinquent** is someone, especially a young person, who behaves in a criminal or antisocial way. Behaviour like this is called **delinquency**. ...*delinquent teenagers.*

delirious (deliriously; delirium) If someone is **delirious** or in a **delirium**, they are unable to speak or think in a rational way, usually because they have a fever. ■ You can say someone is **delirious** when they are extremely excited and happy.

delirium tremens See **DTs.**

delist If a stock exchange **delists** a company, the company's shares can no longer be bought and sold there.

deliver (delivering, delivered; deliverance) If you **deliver** something somewhere, you take it there. ■ When someone **delivers** something like a speech, they give it in public. ■ When someone **delivers** a baby, they help the woman who is giving birth. ■ If you **deliver** something you have promised to do or something which is expected of you, you do it. You can also say you **deliver the goods.** ■ If someone is **delivered** from something unpleasant, they are saved from it. You can talk about someone's **deliverance** from something unpleasant; you can also say the thing which saves them is a **deliverance.**

delivery (deliveries) Delivery is the bringing of things like letters, parcels, or goods to somewhere like a house or office. When someone **makes a delivery,** they deliver something; the person who receives it **takes delivery** of it. ■ A **delivery** of something is the goods which are delivered. ■ **Delivery** is used to describe the way someone gives a speech or sings a song. *His delivery of lyrics is perfect.* ■ **Delivery** is the process of giving birth to a baby.

dell A **dell** is a small wooded valley.

Delphic A **Delphic** statement is one whose meaning is unclear.

delphinium – Delphiniums are large garden plants which have tall stems with blue flowers growing up them.

delta is Δ or δ, the fourth letter of the Greek alphabet. ■ A **delta** is a triangular-shaped area of flat land where a river has split into several small branches before it enters the sea.

delude (deluding, deluded) If you are **deluding yourself,** you are letting yourself believe something which is not true. ■ If you **delude** someone, you deceive them into believing something which is not true.

deluge (*pron:* del-lyooj) **(deluging, deluged)** A **deluge** is a sudden heavy fall of rain. You can say rain **deluges** a place. ■ A **deluge** of things is a very large number of them arriving at the same time. You can say someone is **deluged** by something. ...*deluged by messages of goodwill.*

delusion A **delusion** is a false belief. ■ **delusions of grandeur:** see **grandeur.**

de luxe things are better and more expensive than other things of the same kind.

delve (delving, delved) If you **delve** into a subject, you try to find out more about it. ■ If you **delve** inside something like a bag, you put your hand inside it, to try to find something.

demagogue (*pron:* dem-a-gog) **(demagogic, demagogy, demagoguery)** A **demagogue** is a political leader who tries to win people's support by appealing to their emotions rather than using reasoned arguments. You use **demagogic** to describe a person who behaves like this, or the things they say. ...*demagogic claims.* The behaviour of a demagogue is called **demagogy** or **demagoguery.**

demand If you **demand** something or make a **demand,** you ask for something forcefully. ■ If someone asks a question in a forceful way, you can say they **demand** it. *'Where is your luggage?' he demanded.* ■ If a job or a situation **demands** something, it needs that thing so it can be performed or resolved successfully. *Skilled political leadership demands balanced judgement.* ■ The **demands** of something are the things which have to be done or provided for it. ...*the demands of family life.* ■ If someone or something is **in demand,** or there is a **demand** for them, they are very popular and a lot of people want them. ■ If something is available **on demand,** people can get it whenever they want.

demanding A **demanding** job requires a lot of time, energy, or attention. ■ A **demanding** person is not easily satisfied.

demarcate (demarcating, demarcated; demarcation) If something is **demarcated,** its limits are clearly established, to distinguish it from other similar things. ■ If the border between two countries or regions is **demarcated,** its position is established.

demarche (*or* **démarche**) (*pron:* dem-**marsh**) A **demarche** is a formal statement made to a government. *A quiet approach will probably have a better chance of success than any public demarche.* ■ A **demarche** is a move made by a country in its dealings with other countries.

demean (demeaning, demeaned) If something **demeans** someone, it makes people lose respect for them. You say something like this is **demeaning.**

demeanour A person's **demeanour** is the way they behave, which gives an impression of their character and feelings.

demented If you say someone is **demented,** you mean their behaviour is irrational, foolish, or uncontrolled.

dementia (*pron:* dim-**men**-sha) is an illness in which a person's mind deteriorates.

demerara sugar is a type of light brown, unrefined sugar from the West Indies.

demerge (demerging, demerged; demerger) If a company is **demerged** from another company or group of companies, it separates from them. When this happens, you say there is a **demerger.**

demijohn A **demijohn** is a very large wine bottle, often in a wicker case.

demilitarize (or **demilitarise**) (demilitarizing, demilitarized; demilitarization) When an area is **demilitarized,** all armed forces are taken out of it.

demise (pron: di-**mize**) A person's **demise** is their death. ■ The **demise** of something like a system is its end.

demister The **demister** on a car is a mechanism which removes condensation from the windscreen.

demo (demos) A **demo** is a demonstration.

demob (demobbing, demobbed) When someone is **demobbed,** they are demobilized.

demobilize (or **demobilise**) (demobilizing, demobilized; demobilization) When a member of the armed forces is **demobilized,** he or she is released from military service.

democracy (democracies) **Democracy** is a system in which people choose their leaders or make other important decisions by voting. A **democracy** is a country where the people choose their government in this way.

democrat A **democrat** is a person who believes in democracy. ■ A **Democrat** is a supporter of a political party which has 'Democrat' or 'Democratic' in its name.

democratic (democratically) In a **democratic** system, leaders are chosen or decisions are made by voting. ■ **Democratic** is used in the titles of some political parties. ...*the Christian Democratic party.*

democratize (or **democratise**) (democratizing, democratized; democratization) If a country, organization, or system is **democratized,** it is made democratic.

demography (demographics, demographic, demographer) The **demography** or **demographics** of a group of people are statistics about them, including things like numbers of births and deaths and numbers in different income groups. ...*demographic changes.* A **demographer** is a person who studies and analyzes these statistics.

demolish (demolishes, demolishing, demolished; demolition) When a building is **demolished,** it is knocked down. When this happens, you talk about the **demolition** of the building. ■ If you **demolish** an argument or belief, you prove it is completely wrong.

demon A **demon** is an evil spirit.

demonic (pron: di-**mon**-ik) If something is **demonic,** it is evil.

demonize (or **demonise**) (demonizing, demonized) If someone is **demonized,** they are made to seem evil.

demonology (demonologies) The **demonology** of a group of people is the people or things it considers to be evil or its enemies. *The snipers have secured a special place in the demonology of the city's population.*

demonstrable (demonstrably) If something is **demonstrable,** it is obvious, or it can be shown to exist.

demonstrate (demonstrating, demonstrated; demonstration, demonstrator) If something is **demonstrated,** people are made aware of it. *It was an unforgettable demonstration of the power of reason.* ■ If you **demonstrate** something to someone, you show them how to do it, or how it works. ■ If you **demonstrate** a skill, quality, or feeling, you show you have it. ■ When people **demonstrate,** they take part in a march or a meeting to show they oppose or support something. A march or meeting like this is called a **demonstration;** the people taking part are called **demonstrators.**

demonstrative A **demonstrative** person shows their feelings freely and openly.

demonstrator See **demonstrate.**

demoralize (or **demoralise**) (demoralizing, demoralized; demoralization) If something **demoralizes** people, it causes them to lose confidence and feel depressed.

demote (demoting, demoted; demotion) If someone is **demoted,** their rank or status is reduced, often as a punishment.

demotic (pron: di-**mot**-tik) is used to describe things which are typical of or used by ordinary people.

demotivate (demotivating, demotivated) If you are **demotivated,** you lose your determination to do something.

demur (demurring, demurred) If you **demur,** you say you do not agree with something, or do not want to do something.

demure (demurely) A **demure** woman is quiet, modest, and rather shy.

demystify (demystifies, demystifying, demystified; demystification) If something which seems complicated or strange is **demystified,** it is made easier to understand or made to seem more ordinary.

den A Lion's **den** is its home. Foxes and some other wild animals also have dens. ■ A **den** is a secret place where people meet, usually to do something illegal or immoral. ...*a gambling den.*

denationalize (or **denationalise**) (denationalizing, denationalized; denationalization) If a government-owned industry is **denationalized,** its ownership is transferred to private hands.

dengue (pron: deng-ee) is a dangerous tropical illness spread by mosquitos.

denial A **denial** of something you have been accused of is a claim that it is not true. ■ If there is **denial** of something, people are not allowed to have it. ...*denials of human rights.*

denier (pron: den-yer) The thickness of nylon or silk thread is often measured in **denier.** ...*a pair of 15 denier stockings.*

denigrate (denigrating, denigrated; denigration) If you **denigrate** someone, you say things about them which damage their reputation.

denim is a thick, hard-wearing cotton cloth used to make clothes. **Denims** are clothes made of denim, such as jeans.

denizen The **denizens** of a place are people or animals who live there or spend most of their time there.

denominate (**denominating, denominated**) When an amount of money is **denominated** in a currency, it is expressed in that currency. *...claims and liabilities denominated in Canadian dollars.*

denomination (**denominational**) The **denomination** of a bank note is what it is worth. ■ A **denomination** is a division of Christianity, such as the Church of England or the Baptist Church. If something like a school is **denominational**, it is connected with a particular denomination.

denominator The **denominator** is the number under the line in a fraction. For example, in the fraction $\frac{1}{5}$, the denominator is 5. See also **common denominator** and **lowest common denominator.**

denote (**denoting, denoted**) If you say something **denotes** something else, you mean it is a sign or indication of it. *The agreement seems to denote a virtual surrender.* ■ If a word or expression **denotes** something, that is what it means or refers to.

denouement (*or* **dénouement**) (*pron:* day-**noo**-mon) The **denouement** of a story is the final sorting-out of the plot, which brings the story to an end.

denounce (**denouncing, denounced; denunciation**) If you **denounce** a person or their actions, you publicly accuse them of being bad or doing something wrong. A **denunciation** is an accusation like this. *Today's court hearing was denounced by the protesters as anti-democratic.*

dense (**denser, densest; densely**) If something is **dense**, it contains a lot of people or things in proportion to its size. ■ **Dense** fog or smoke is thick and difficult to see through. ■ A **dense** substance is very heavy. ■ If you say someone is **dense**, you mean they are unintelligent.

density (**densities**) **Density** is the extent to which something is filled with people or things. *...high population density.* ■ The **density** of a substance is how heavy it is. Densities are usually given as **relative densities;** the relative density of a solid or liquid is how much heavier it is than water. For example, copper has a relative density of 8.96, which means it is 8.96 times heavier than water.

dent If you **dent** something, you damage its surface by hitting it and making a hollow in it. The hollow is called a **dent.** ■ If your confidence or pride is **dented,** it is weakened. ■ If something makes a **dent** in an amount, it reduces it. *Price cutting does not make too big a dent in their profit margins.*

dental means to do with teeth or dentists.

dental floss See **floss.**

dental surgeon A **dental surgeon** is the same as a dentist.

dentist A **dentist** is a person qualified to treat people's teeth.

dentistry is the treatment of teeth.

dentures are false teeth.

denude (**denuding, denuded**) If something is **denuded** of things which cover it or belong to it, they are taken away from it. *The Embassy is now denuded of all foreign and local staff.*

denunciation See **denounce.**

deny (**denies, denying, denied**) If you **deny** something, you say it is not true. ■ If you are **denied**

something, you are prevented from having it. *The system denied them the chance of a fair trial.*

deodorant is a substance people spray or wipe on their bodies to reduce the smell of sweat.

depart (**departure**) If someone **departs** from a place, they leave. You call this their **departure.** ■ **Departed** friends or relatives are people who have died. ■ If you **depart** from the normal way of doing something, you do it a different way.

department (**departmental**) A **department** is one of the sections of a large shop or organization. **Departmental** means connected with a department. *...a departmental committee.*

department store A **department store** is a large shop divided into sections, each selling a particular type of goods.

departure See **depart.**

departure lounge The **departure lounge** at an airport is the area where passengers spend time waiting to board an aircraft.

depend If you **depend** on someone or something, you need them. ■ If you say you can **depend** on someone or something, you mean you can rely on them. ■ If one thing **depends** on another, the first thing will be decided by the second. *Observers believe that the outcome may depend on a handful of votes.*

dependable (**dependability**) If you say someone or something is **dependable,** you mean they can be relied on to do what is needed. *He had a reputation for toughness and dependability.*

dependant (*or* **dependent**) A person's **dependants** are their children or other members of their family who they support financially.

dependence See **dependent.**

dependency (**dependencies**) A **dependency** is a country controlled by another country. ■ If you have a **dependency** on something, you rely on it. *...drug dependency.* ■ When people talk about a **dependency culture,** they mean a situation where many people do not work, because they know they can rely on the government to provide everything.

dependent (**dependence**) If you are **dependent** on someone or something, you need them. *...the city's traditional dependence on tourism.* ■ If one thing is **dependent** on another, the first thing will be decided by the second. *The company's future is dependent on its aerospace division.* ■ See also **dependant.**

depict (**depiction**) If an artist **depicts** someone in a particular way, they show them in that way in a picture. Similarly, you can say a writer **depicts** someone or something in a particular way. *...a lovely depiction of the complications of family life.*

depilatory (**depilatories**) **Depilatory cream** or a **depilatory** is a substance which removes unwanted hair from your body.

deplete (**depleting, depleted; depletion**) If something is **depleted,** the amount of it is reduced. *...the depletion of Brazil's forests.*

deplore (**deploring, deplored; deplorable, deplorably**) If you **deplore** something, you think it is extremely bad. You say something like this is **deplorable.**

deploy (**deployment**) When troops or resources are **deployed,** they are organized and moved into position, ready for immediate action. *...America's rapid military deployment.*

depoliticize (*or* **depoliticise**) (**depoliticizing, depoliticized; depoliticization**) If an organization is **depoliticized,** it no longer serves the interests of a particular political group.

depopulate (**depopulating, depopulated; depopulation**) If an area is **depopulated,** the number of people living there is greatly reduced. **Depopulation** is a reduction in the population of an area.

deport (**deportation, deportee**) If someone is **deported,** they are officially forced to leave a country. A person who is being deported is called a **deportee.**

deportment A person's **deportment** is the way they behave, especially the way they walk and move.

depose (**deposing, deposed**) If a leader is **deposed,** they are removed from their position by force.

deposit (**depositing, deposited**) If you **deposit** something somewhere, you put it there. ■ A **deposit** is (a) an amount of money you put in a bank account or other savings account. (b) money given in part payment for something, or as security. ■ If a substance is **deposited** somewhere, it is left there as a result of a chemical or geological process. A **deposit** is an amount of a substance left like this. *...oil deposits.*

deposit account A **deposit account** is a bank account in which money earns interest.

depositary (**depositaries**) A **depositary** is a person or organization you can leave money or valuables with for safekeeping. See also **depository.**

deposition A **deposition** is a sworn statement by a witness to a crime, used in court if the witness cannot be present. ■ **Deposition** is the depositing of a substance. *...excess fat deposition.*

depositor – **Depositors** are people with a bank or building society account.

depository (**depositories**) A **depository** is a place where things are stored. See also **depositary.**

depot A **depot** is a place where goods or vehicles are kept when they are not being used. ■ In the US and Canada, a railway station is sometimes called a **depot.**

deprave (**depraving, depraved; depravity**) If you say a book or film is likely to **deprave** people, you mean it is likely to make them behave immorally. ■ A **depraved** person is morally bad. **Depravity** (*pron:* dip-**prav**-i-ty) is immoral behaviour.

deprecate (*pron:* dep-re-kate) (**deprecating, deprecated**) If you **deprecate** something, you say you strongly disapprove of it. See also **self-deprecating.**

depreciate (**depreciating, depreciated; depreciation**) If something **depreciates,** it loses some of its value. *...currency depreciation.*

depredations are attacks aimed at destroying something.

depress (**depresses, depressing, depressed; depressingly**) If something **depresses** you or makes you **depressed,** it makes you sad and disappointed. You say something like this is **depressing.** ■ If

something **depresses** things like wages or prices, it causes them to fall in value. ■ If an industry or place is **depressed,** business is bad, unemployment is high, and not much money is being made. ■ When something is **depressed,** it is lowered or pushed down. *Keep the steam button constantly depressed.*

depression A **depression** is a time when economic activity is very low and unemployment is high. ■ **Depression** is a form of mental illness in which someone feels miserable all the time, and has no energy. ■ A **depression** in a surface is a part which is lower than the rest. *...a depression in the ground.*

depressive A **depressive** is someone who often suffers from depression. ■ A **depressive** illness includes periods of depression.

depressurize (*or* **depressurise**) (**depressurizing, depressurized; depressurization**) When divers are **depressurized** or undergo **depressurization,** the air pressure inside them is reduced artificially as they come to the surface, to stop them suffering illness caused by a sudden change from high to low pressure. See also **decompression.** ■ If an aircraft or spacecraft **depressurizes,** the air pressure inside is reduced by escaping air.

deprive (**depriving, deprived; deprivation**) If someone is **deprived** of something they need or are entitled to, they do not get it or are not allowed to have it. ■ **Deprived** people lack things such as adequate housing or education.

dept is short for 'department'.

depth The **depth** of something like a river is the distance between its surface and its bottom. If something happens at a particular **depth,** it happens at that distance below the surface. ■ The **depths** of an ocean are the parts a long way down. ■ If you say someone is **out of their depth,** you mean they are trying to do something which is too difficult for them. ■ The **depth** of something like a cupboard is the distance from its front to its back. ■ If you deal with a subject **in depth,** you deal with it very thoroughly. ■ If someone has strong feelings of anger or unhappiness, you can talk about the **depth** of their feelings. ■ The **depths** of winter is the time in the middle when it is coldest.

depth charge A **depth charge** is a bomb which explodes underwater.

deputation A **deputation** is a small group of people sent to represent a larger group.

depute (**deputing, deputed**) If someone is **deputed** to do something, they are chosen to do it as the representative of a group.

deputize (*or* **deputise**) (**deputizing, deputized**) If you **deputize** for someone, you do something on their behalf.

deputy (**deputies**) A **deputy** is the second most important person in an organization. *...the deputy president.* Someone's **deputy** often stands in for them when they are absent.

derail (**derailing, derailed; derailment**) If a train is **derailed,** it comes off the track. ■ If discussions are **derailed,** something stops them from progressing.

deranged people behave wildly or strangely, often because they are mentally ill.

derby (pron: **dar**-bee) (**derbies**) The **Derby** is a famous English horse race which takes place at Epsom. Some other countries also have horse races with 'Derby' in their names. ...the Irish Derby. ■ A **derby** or **local derby** is a sporting event between teams from the same city or area.

deregulate (**deregulating, deregulated; deregulation, deregulatory**) If something like an industry is **deregulated,** it is no longer required to conform to government controls. You call this the **deregulation** of the industry. A **deregulatory** measure is one which brings about deregulation.

derelict (**dereliction**) A **derelict** building or area of land has not been used for a long time and is in a bad state. You can also say it is in a state of **dereliction.** ■ **Derelicts** are people with no home or money, who live on the streets. ■ If someone is guilty of a **dereliction of duty,** they have deliberately or accidentally failed to do something they should have done as part of their job.

deride (**deriding, derided; derision**) If you **deride** someone or treat them with **derision,** you make fun of them.

de rigueur (pron: de rig-**gur**) If something is **de rigueur,** you must have it or do it if you do not want to seem old-fashioned or out-of-place.

derisive (**derisively**) A **derisive** expression or remark shows contempt.

derisory If you say an amount of money is **derisory,** you mean it insults you and is not worth considering, because it is very small.

derivation The **derivation** of something, especially a word, is its origin.

derivative A **derivative** is something which has been developed from something else. ...the cocaine derivative, crack. ■ If you say something is **derivative,** you mean it is not original but has been copied or developed from something else.

derive (**deriving, derived**) If one thing is **derived** from another, it comes from it. ■ If you **derive** pleasure or benefit from someone or something, you get it from them.

dermatitis is a medical condition affecting the skin.

dermatology (**dermatologist**) **Dermatology** is the study of the skin and the treatment of its diseases.

derogatory A **derogatory** remark is one which shows your low opinion of someone or something.

derrick A **derrick** is a tower over an oil well where the drill is operated from. ■ A **derrick** is a crane used to move cargo on a ship.

derring-do is a humorous word for heroic deeds.

derv See **diesel.**

dervish (**dervishes**) **Dervishes** are a Muslim religious group whose worship includes a lively dance in which they spin round and round.

desalinate (**desalinating, desalinated; desalination**) When sea water is **desalinated,** the salt is taken out of it.

descend When someone or something **descends,** they move downwards. ■ If people **descend on** a place, a lot of them suddenly arrive there. ■ If

someone **descends** into a bad condition or situation, they suffer from that condition or have to cope with that situation. The region was descending into anarchy... They descended into alcoholism. ■ If someone does something which they would normally consider to be beneath them, you can say they **descend to** it. ■ If a mood or atmosphere **descends** on a group of people, it affects them all. ...silence descended on the room. ■ The people you are **descended** from are your relatives who lived a long time ago. ■ If a group of things is arranged in **descending** order, each thing is smaller or less important than the one before it.

descendant A person's **descendants** are the people of later generations who are related to them.

descent A person's **descent** is their family origins. ...of African descent. ■ When someone or something moves to a lower level, you can talk about their **descent.** ■ When you are emphasizing that a situation or a person's behaviour becomes very bad, you can talk about their **descent into** that condition. ...his descent into madness.

describe (**describing, described**) If you **describe** someone or something, you say what they are like. If you **describe** a series of events, you say what happened. ■ If you **describe** someone or something **as** a certain thing, you say they are that thing. She described him as a cheerful lively man.

description If you give a **description** of someone or something, you say what they are like. ■ **Description** is used to mean 'type' in phrases like 'of every description' and 'of any description'. Events of this description occurred daily.

descriptive writing shows what someone or something is like.

desecrate (**desecrating, desecrated; desecration**) If someone **desecrates** something which people regard as sacred, they deliberately damage or insult it. ...the desecration of Muslim shrines.

desegregate (**desegregating, desegregated; desegregation**) If a place, organization, or public service is **desegregated,** the people using it are no longer kept in separate racial groups. ...the desegregation of schools.

deselect (or **de-select**) (**deselecting, deselected; deselection**) If an MP is **deselected,** their local constituency party decides not to select them for re-election.

desert (**desertion**) A **desert** (pron: **dez**-ert) is an area of land with very low rainfall and few trees or plants. ■ If a place is **deserted** (pron: diz-**zert**-id), there is nobody there. ■ If someone **deserts** a person or an organization, they abandon them. ■ If someone **deserts** from the armed forces, they leave without permission. Leaving the armed forces in this way is called **desertion.**

deserter A **deserter** is a member of the armed forces who leaves without permission and has no intention of returning.

desertification (pron: dez-ert-if-i-**kay**-shun) is the gradual transformation of fertile land into desert.

desert island A **desert island** is a small tropical island where nobody lives.

deserve (deserving, deserved; deservedly) If you say someone **deserves** something, you mean they ought to have it. ■ If you say something someone has is **deserved,** you mean it is right they should have it. ...*this deservedly popular hotel.* ■ If you describe a person, organization, or cause as **deserving,** you think they should be helped. ■ If someone or something is **deserving of** a certain thing, they are worthy of it. *She was deserving of her place in the final.*

desiccated food has been dried, in order to preserve it. ■ If you call a person **dessicated,** you mean they have no enthusiasm or vitality.

design When someone **designs** something, they plan how it will be made or built, usually by preparing detailed drawings. **Design** is the process of doing this. A **design** is a drawing of something which is going to be made. ■ When someone **designs** a system or a policy, they plan all its details. ■ The **design** of something is the form in which it is made. ■ A **design** is a decorative pattern. ■ If something is **designed** for a purpose, it is intended for that purpose. ■ If someone has **designs on** something, they want it and are planning to get it.

designate (designating, designated; designation) If someone or something is **designated** a particular thing, they are officially declared to be that thing. ■ A **designation** is a description or title given to someone or something. ...*the designation 'Chartered Chemist'.* ■ If something is **designated** for a particular purpose, it is officially chosen for that purpose. ■ If someone is **designated** to do a job, they are officially chosen to do it. ■ **Designate** is used to describe someone who has been officially chosen to do a job but has not yet started doing it. ...*editor designate of Country Life.*

designer A **designer** is someone whose job involves planning the forms or styles of new things. ■ **Designer** clothes are expensive and fashionable and made by a famous designer rather than mass-produced in a factory. ■ **Designer** drugs are made in a laboratory and are intended to have a similar effect to drugs like heroin or mescaline.

desirable (desirability) If something is **desirable,** it is worth having or doing.

desire (desiring, desired) If you **desire** something, you want it. You can talk about someone's **desire for** something. ■ **Desire** or **sexual desire** for someone is a feeling of wanting to have sex with them. ■ If you say something **leaves a lot to be desired,** you mean that it is not as good as you think it should be.

desist If you **desist** from doing something, you stop doing it.

desk A **desk** is a table where you write or work. ■ A department of a newspaper or broadcasting company can be referred to as a **desk.** ...*our foreign news desk.* ■ A **desk** is part of a shop, station, or airport where you go for a particular service. ...*the information desk.*

desktop (or desk-top) computers are the right size for using on a desk but are not designed to be portable. ■ **Desktop publishing** is the production of printed materials such as magazines using a desktop computer and a laser printer, rather than using conventional printing methods.

desolate (desolation) A **desolate** area is wild and empty of people. ■ If someone feels **desolate,** they feel lonely and depressed.

despair (despairing, despaired; despairingly) Despair is a feeling of hopelessness. If you **despair,** you lose hope. ■ If you **despair of** something, you feel it will never happen or improve. If you **despair of** someone, you feel they will never improve. *He often despaired of finding work... I despair of some journalists.*

despatch (or dispatch) (despatches, despatching, despatched) If you **despatch** someone or something somewhere, you send them there. ■ A **despatch** is a report sent to a person or organization from one of their representatives in another place.

desperate (desperately, desperation) If you are **desperate,** you are in a very bad situation and will do anything to get out of it. **Desperation** is the feeling you have in a situation like this. ■ A **desperate** situation is very difficult. If you do something **desperate** in a situation like this, you take an extreme action because it seems the only thing left to do. ■ If you are **desperate** for something, you want it or need it urgently. ■ **Desperately** is used to add emphasis to a remark. *Environmentalists are desperately concerned.*

despicable If you say someone or something is **despicable,** you mean they are extremely nasty or evil.

despise (despising, despised) If you **despise** someone or something, you have a very low opinion of them.

despite If one thing happened **despite** another thing, it happened though the second thing might have prevented it. *Despite the force of the wind, he was keeping the boat on a straight course.*

despoil (despoiling, despoiled) If countryside is **despoiled,** it is ruined, for example by pollution.

despondent (despondently, despondency) If you are **despondent,** you are unhappy because of difficulties which seem hard to overcome. This feeling is called **despondency.**

despot (despotic, despotism) A **despot** is a powerful person, often a political ruler, who acts cruelly or unfairly. *The country was ruled by a despotic tyrant.* **Despotism** is rule by a despot.

dessert (pron: diz-**zert**) is a pudding or fruit eaten at the end of a meal.

dessertspoon A **dessertspoon** is a spoon which is in between a teaspoon and a tablespoon in size.

destabilize (or destabilise) (destabilizing, destabilized; destabilization) If something **destabilizes** a government or economy, it makes it unable to function properly and makes a sudden change likely. *This could lead to a serious destabilization in the Balkans.*

destination Your **destination** is the place you are going to.

destined If someone or something is **destined** for a place, they are going there, or will be sent there. ■ If something is **destined** to happen, it is going to happen and nothing can prevent it.

destiny (destinies) A **person's** destiny is the major events in their life, especially events they consider to be outside their control. ■ **Destiny** is the force some people believe controls the things which happen to us. ...*the cruel and fickle hand of destiny.*

destitute (destitution) If someone is **destitute,** they have no money or possessions. *They slipped into unemployment and destitution.*

destroy If something is **destroyed,** it is damaged so badly it is completely ruined.

destroyer A **destroyer** is a small fast heavily armed warship. ■ The **destroyer** of something is the person or thing that destroys it.

destruction When something is destroyed, you can talk about its **destruction.**

destructive (destructively, destructiveness) If something is **destructive,** it causes a lot of damage. ...*the destructiveness of modern weapons.*

desultory is used to describe things which are done in a half-hearted way. *His speech ended with only desultory applause.*

detach (detaches, detaching, detached; detachment) If you **detach** something, you remove it from the thing it is attached to. ■ A **detached** house is not joined to any other house. ■ If you **detach** yourself from something, you drop your involvement or concern with it. ...*the pressures upon the US to detach themselves from PLO contacts.* ■ If you stay **detached** from something you are dealing with, you do not get personally or emotionally involved in it. *He views events with a certain cynical detachment.* ■ A **detachment** of soldiers is a group of them sent away from the main group to do a particular task.

detachable If something is **detachable,** it can be removed from the larger thing it is attached to.

detachment See **detach.**

detail (detailing, detailed) The **details** of something are the individual elements it is made up of. If you are concerned with **detail,** you are concerned with these elements. ■ If you examine, explain, or discuss something **in detail,** you do it thoroughly. ...*a detailed account of the decisions.* ■ **Details** about someone or something are items of information about them. ■ If you **detail** things, you list them or give full information about them.

detain (detaining, detained) When people like the police **detain** someone, they keep them in a place under their control. ■ If something **detains** you, it delays you.

detainee – Detainees are people who are being held prisoner by a government because of their political beliefs or activities.

detect (detection) If you **detect** something, you notice it or discover it. ...*an advertising campaign to promote early detection of the disease.*

detectable If something is **detectable,** it can be noticed or discovered.

detective A **detective** is someone, usually a police officer, whose job is to discover the facts about something like a crime.

detector A **detector** is a machine for discovering whether something exists or is taking place. ...*a metal detector. ...a lie-detector.*

detente (*or* **détente**) (*pron:* day-**tont**) **Dentente** is a friendly relationship between countries where there had been disagreement and mistrust.

detention is the arrest or imprisonment of someone, especially for political reasons. ■ A **detention centre** or **detention camp** is a place where prisoners or refugees are kept on a temporary basis.

deter (deterring, deterred) If something **deters** you from doing something, it stops you wanting to do it.

detergent – Detergents are chemicals for washing things like clothes and dishes.

deteriorate (deteriorating, deteriorated; deterioration) If something like a situation or a person's health **deteriorates,** it gets worse. ...*a sharp deterioration in Anglo-Irish relations.*

determinant A **determinant** of something is one of the things which decides what form it will take. *Inflation is the main determinant of people's sense of economic well-being.*

determinate A **determinate** period is fixed at a particular length. ...*the possession of land for some determinate period.*

determine (determining, determined; determinedly, determination) If you are **determined** to do something, you have made a firm decision to do it and will not let anything stop you. ■ If you **determine** the cause of something or the truth about something, you find it out. ...*experiments to determine the cause of cancer.* ■ If what happens depends on a particular thing, you can say that thing **determines** what happens. *Community rules will determine who needs a visa to get into the EU.* ■ When something is **determined,** it is decided or settled. *The amount of government money has yet to be determined.*

determinism (deterministic, determinist) **Determinism** is the belief that everything that happens is the result of other things which have already happened, and so people's choices are already made for them. **Determinist** or **deterministic** ideas are based on determinism.

deterrence (deterrent) **Deterrence** is preventing people from doing something by making them afraid of the consequences for themselves. ...*its strategy of nuclear deterrence.* Something which stops people doing something is called a **deterrent.**

detest (detestable) If you **detest** someone or something or find them **detestable,** you hate them.

dethrone (dethroning, dethroned) If someone in a powerful position is **dethroned,** they are removed from power.

detonate (detonating, detonated; detonation) If something like a bomb **detonates** or is **detonated,** it explodes. ...*the accidental detonation of a shell.*

detonator A **detonator** is a device which causes something like a bomb to explode.

detour If you make a **detour** on a journey, you take a longer route than necessary, because the usual way is blocked or because you want to call somewhere on the way.

detoxify (detoxifies, detoxifying, detoxified; detoxification) If something is **detoxified,** poisonous

detract   175   devotional

substances are removed from it. ■ You say a person is **detoxified** when they are gradually cured of alcohol or drug addiction, usually at a place called a **detoxification centre.**

detract If one thing **detracts** from another, it makes it seem less good or impressive.

detractor A person's or thing's **detractors** are people who criticize them.

detriment (**detrimental**) If one thing is to the **detriment** of another or is **detrimental** to it, it has a harmful effect on it.

detritus (*pron:* dit-**trite**-uss) is damaged things left as a result of something happening. *...burnt out buildings, littered with the detritus of war.*

deuce (*pron:* **dyewss**) is the score in tennis where each player has a score of forty.

Deutschmark (*pron:* **doytch**-mark) The **Deutschmark** is the unit of currency in Germany.

devalue (**devaluing, devalued; devaluation**) If a country's **currency** is devalued, its value is reduced in relation to other currencies. *...a devaluation of 11.5%.* ■ When you talk about things being **devalued**, you mean they are made to seem less important or less worthy of respect.

devastate (**devastating, devastated; devastatingly, devastation**) If something **devastates** a place or thing, it damages it very badly or destroys it completely. *...a devastating blow to the Prime Minister's hopes. ...the devastation caused by the earthquake.* ■ If you are **devastated** by something, you are very shocked and upset by it. *The diagnosis was devastating. She had cancer.* ■ **Devastating** is used to say something or someone is very effective or very funny. *Its advertising was devastatingly successful.*

develop (**developing, developed**) When something **develops**, it grows or changes over a period of time into a better, more advanced, or more complete form. ■ When people **develop** something like a new product, they design and produce it. ■ If you **develop** a skill, you acquire it or improve it by working hard at it. ■ If an area of land is **developed**, houses or other buildings are built there. ■ The **developed** countries are the rich industrialized countries. ■ The **developing** countries are the poorer, less industrialized countries. ■ When a photographic film is **developed**, the pictures on it are made visible by treating it with chemicals.

developer A **developer** is a person or company that buys land in order to build on it for profit. ■ The **developer** of a product is a person or company responsible for producing it, especially by improving on earlier ideas. ■ If you call someone a **late developer**, you mean they were older than usual when they acquired a skill or started doing something. ■ **Developer** is a chemical used for developing films.

development (**developmental**) The **development** of something is its growth or progress into a more advanced form. ■ **Development** is the process of improving a basic design. **Developmental** means connected with this process. *...developmental engineering.* ■ A **development** is an estate of houses, offices, or other buildings built by a developer. **Development** is the process of preparing land for this

purpose and building on it. ■ **Development** projects and aid are intended to help poorer, less industrialized countries produce more of the things their people need. ■ If you say there have been **developments** in a situation, you mean further things have happened which may affect its outcome.

deviant (**deviance**) People are called **deviants** when they behave in ways not considered socially or politically acceptable. **Deviance** is behaviour like this.

deviate (**deviating, deviated; deviation**) If you **deviate** from a belief or an accepted way of doing something, you do something which does not fit in with it. *...the Communist Party's deviations from strict Marxism.*

device A **device** is a thing made for a particular purpose, for example for recording or measuring something. ■ A **device** is a way of getting a result you want. *...a device for bringing down inflation.* ■ If you say someone is **left to their own devices**, you mean they are allowed to do what they want.

devil In Christianity, the **Devil** is the most powerful evil spirit. He is also called 'Satan' and 'Lucifer'. ■ A **devil** is an evil spirit. ■ If you say someone has a **devil-may-care** attitude, you mean they are relaxed and unconcerned about the consequences of their actions. ■ If you play **devil's advocate** in a discussion, you argue in favour of an alternative or unpopular point of view, to make the argument more interesting.

devilish is used to describe things which are cruel or wicked. *...a devilish dictatorship.* ■ If someone behaves in a mischievous but rather likeable way, you can describe their behaviour as **devilish**. *...a devilish laugh.*

devious (**deviousness**) A **devious** person uses dishonest and complicated strategies in a secretive way to get what they want.

devise (**devising, devised**) If you **devise** something like a system, you think of it and design it.

devoid If someone or something is **devoid** of a certain thing, they are completely without it. *...an area devoid of wildlife.*

devolve (**devolving, devolved; devolution**) If power is **devolved**, it is transferred from a central government or other organization to regional governments or organizations. This process is called **devolution.**

devote (**devoting, devoted; devotion**) If you **devote** yourself to something, you spend most of your time and energy on it. ■ If you are **devoted** to someone or something, you love them and do all you can for them. ■ If you **devote** money, time, or space to something, you use it on that thing. ■ If something is **devoted** to a subject, it deals only with that subject. *...magazines devoted to interior design.* ■ **Devotion** is strong religious feeling. ■ **Devotions** are prayers or acts of worship.

devotee (*pron:* dev-vote-**tee**) A **devotee** of a subject is someone who is very interested and enthusiastic about it.

devotion See **devote.**

devotional activities and objects are dedicated to a religious faith. *...devotional music.*

devour (**devouring, devoured**) If you **devour** food, you eat it quickly and eagerly. ■ If you **devour** a book, you read it enthusiastically.

devout (**devoutly**) **Devout** people have strong religious beliefs. People like these are sometimes called the **devout.** ■ You can call strongly held beliefs **devout.** *He was devoutly committed to a devolved United Kingdom.*

dew is small drops of water which form on the ground during the night.

dewlap A **dewlap** is a loose fold of skin which hangs under the throat of an animal like a dog or cow.

dewy-eyed If you say someone is **dewy-eyed,** you mean they are innocent and inexperienced.

dexterity (**dextrous**) **Dexterity** is the ability to do things quickly and skilfully, especially with your body or hands. If someone is **dextrous,** they have this ability.

DI is a way of trying to make a woman pregnant by artificially putting sperm in her womb from an anonymous man. DI stands for 'donor insemination'.

diabetes (*pron:* die-a-**beet**-eez) (**diabetic**) **Diabetes** is a name given to several illnesses, all of which make the sufferer thirsty and want to pass urine. The most common kind, **diabetes mellitus** ('sugar diabetes'), results in too much sugar in the blood. Sufferers from this kind of diabetes are called **diabetics** (*pron:* die-a-**bet**-iks).

diabolic means relating to the devil. ...*diabolic powers.*

diabolical (**diabolically**) Very wicked acts are sometimes described as **diabolical.** ...*diabolical crimes.* ■ **Diabolical** is used to say something is done very badly. *Their forecasting record has been diabolical.*

diadem A **diadem** is a crown, especially a small jewelled one.

diagnose (**diagnosing, diagnosed**) When a doctor **diagnoses** an illness in someone, he or she identifies what is wrong.

diagnosis (*plural:* **diagnoses**) A **diagnosis** is the opinion a doctor forms about what is wrong with a patient. The process of forming this opinion is called **diagnosis.**

diagnostic (**diagnostics**) **Diagnostic** equipment, drugs, and methods are used to discover what is wrong with people who are ill. ■ **Diagnostics** is the study of the making of diagnoses.

diagonal (**diagonally**) A **diagonal** is a line which joins opposite corners of a four-sided shape. **Diagonal** is used to say something moves or is placed along this line. *Screens are placed diagonally across the table.*

diagram A **diagram** is a drawing used to explain something.

dial (**dialling, dialled**) (*Am:* **dialing, dialed**) The **dial** of a clock is the part which shows the time. The **dial** of a meter or other measuring device is the part where you read a measurement. ■ On a radio, the **dial** is the part you move to tune in to a station. ■ The **dial** on an old-fashioned telephone is a circle with holes in it which you turn to dial a number. If you **dial** a number, you turn the dial or press the buttons on a telephone to phone someone.

dialect A **dialect** is a form of a language spoken in a particular area. It includes words and expressions not used in the standard form of the language.

dialling code A **dialling code** is a number you dial before someone's personal telephone number to connect you with the right area.

dialogue You say there is a **dialogue** when discussions are taking place between groups of people, especially governments or political groups. ■ **Dialogue** is the things people say in a play, film, or book.

dialysis (*pron:* die-**al**-iss-iss) is a process in which particles are separated from liquids. It is used in purifying the blood of people whose kidneys do not work properly.

diamanté (*pron:* die-a-**man**-tee) **Diamanté** jewellery is made from small pieces of cut glass which look like diamonds.

diameter The **diameter** of a circle or sphere is its width measured by a straight line passing through its centre.

diametrically If things like opinions are **diametrically** opposed, they are exactly opposite to each other.

diamond A **diamond** is a hard bright colourless precious stone. ■ The shape ♦ is called a **diamond.** ■ **Diamonds** is one of the four suits in a pack of playing cards. All cards in this suit have the symbol ♦ on them. ■ The **diamond** anniversary of something is its 60th anniversary.

diaper is the usual American word for 'nappy'.

diaphanous (*pron:* die-**af**-fan-ous) material is thin and transparent.

diaphragm (*pron:* **die**-a-fram) Your **diaphragm** is a muscle between your lungs and your stomach. ■ A **diaphragm** is a circular contraceptive device, which a woman puts inside her vagina. The diaphragm is also known as the 'cap'.

diarist A **diarist** is a person who records things in a diary.

diarrhoea (*or* **diarrhea**) (*pron:* die-a-**ree**-a) When someone who is ill has **diarrhoea,** they produce frequent and watery excrement.

diary (**diaries**) A **diary** is a book with a separate space for each day of the year. You use it to write down things you plan to do or to record what happens in your life.

diaspora (*pron:* die-**ass**-spor-a) A **diaspora** is a spreading of people from their country of origin to other countries. The spreading of Jewish people from ancient Palestine to other places is often called **the Diaspora.**

diatribe (*pron:* **die**-a-tribe) A **diatribe** is an angry speech or piece of writing attacking someone or something.

dice (*plural:* **dice**) (**dicing, diced**) A **dice** is a small cube with dots or numbers from 1 to 6 on each side, used in games to provide random numbers. A single dice is sometimes called a 'die'. ■ When you **dice** food, you cut it into small square pieces.

dichotomy (*pron:* die-**kot**-a-mee) You say there is a **dichotomy** between things when they are very different or contradict each other. ...*the dichotomy between town and countryside.*

Dickensian is used to describe people or things like those described in the novels of Charles Dickens. **Dickensian** is especially used to describe dirty or cramped working and living conditions.

dictaphone A **dictaphone** is a machine into which you dictate something like a letter. The dictation can be played back later for someone to type. 'Dictaphone' is a trademark.

dictate (**dictation**) If you **dictate** something like a letter, you speak it into a machine or say it aloud for someone else to write down. ...*secretaries taking dictation.* ■ If someone in power **dictates** something, they say it shall be done. **Dictates** (*pron:* dik-tates) are orders issued by someone in power. ■ If one thing is **dictated** by another, it is caused by or influenced by the other. *The president's approach was partly dictated by election considerations.*

dictator (**dictatorial, dictatorially**) A **dictator** is a ruler who has complete power, which they have often taken by force. You call people or governments like this **dictatorial** (*pron:* dik-ta-**tor**-i-al). You also say someone is a **dictator,** or being **dictatorial,** when they behave like a dictator. *The government is acting dictatorially.*

dictatorship is government by a dictator. A **dictatorship** is a country ruled by a dictator.

diction A person's **diction** is how clearly they pronounce words.

dictionary (**dictionaries**) A **dictionary** is a book which lists words alphabetically and gives their meanings.

dictum (*plural:* **dictums** or **dicta**) A **dictum** is a wise saying.

did see **do.**

didactic (*usual pron:* die-**dak**-tik) If something like a novel is **didactic,** it is intended to teach people something. Similarly, if a person is being **didactic,** they are talking to you like a teacher talking to a class.

didgeridoo A **didgeridoo** is a musical instrument used by Australian Aborigines. It is a long wooden tube which you blow down to produce a deep wavering note.

die (**dying, died**) When a living thing **dies,** it stops living. ■ When people **die off,** they die one by one, until there are none left. ■ If a type of animal **dies out,** it becomes extinct. ■ If something **dies out,** it becomes less and less common and finally comes to an end. ■ If a sound **dies away,** it fades until it can no longer be heard. ■ If something like an emotion **dies down,** it loses its intensity. ■ **Dying** is used to say something happens very close to the end of an event or period of time. *A 60-yard penalty broke the deadlock in the dying minutes of the game.* ■ If something like a habit **dies hard,** it is difficult to change. ■ If you are **dying** to do something, you are very eager to do it. ■ A **die** is a specially shaped tool, used to form metal or other material into a particular shape. ■ See also **dice.**

diehard A **diehard** is someone who has fixed ideas or beliefs which are unlikely to change.

diesel or **diesel oil** is the oil used in a diesel engine. Diesel is also called 'derv'. ■ A **diesel** is a vehicle with a diesel engine.

diet (**dieting, dieted; dieter**) Your **diet** is the kind of food you eat. ...*a low-fat diet.* ■ If you are **dieting** or on a **diet,** you eat less fattening foods to lose weight. People doing this are called **dieters.**

dietary means connected with the kinds of foods people eat. ...*dietary habits.*

dietician A **dietician** is someone whose job is advising people what they should eat to be healthy.

differ (**differing, differed**) If two things **differ,** they are unlike in some way. ■ If people **differ** about something, they disagree about it.

difference A **difference** between things is a way in which they are unlike each other. ■ **With a difference** is used to say something has a feature which makes it different to, and better than, other things of the same kind. ...*a holiday with a difference.* ■ If you say something **makes a difference,** you mean it changes a situation. *He fitted a new pump but it made no difference.* ■ The **difference** between two amounts is the amount by which one is greater than the other. For example, the difference between 8 and 5 is 3. ■ People's **differences** are the things they disagree over.

different (**differently**) If two things are **different,** they do not have the same set of features or characteristics. If two people do something **differently,** they do not do it the same way. ■ You use **different** to emphasize that the things you are talking about are distinct from each other. *He was treated in three different hospitals.*

differential A **differential** is a difference between two rates.

differentiate (**differentiating, differentiated; differentiation**) If you **differentiate** between things, you recognize or show the differences between them. ...*the lack of a clear differentiation between 'urban' and 'rural' land-use.* ■ If two things are the same except for one feature, you can say the feature **differentiates** one from the other.

difficult If something is **difficult,** it is hard to do, solve, or understand. ■ If someone is being **difficult,** they are behaving unreasonably.

difficulty (**difficulties**) Difficulties are problems. If you are **in difficulty,** you are having problems. ■ If you have **difficulty** doing something, you find it hard to do.

diffident (**diffidently, diffidence**) If you say someone is **diffident** or talk about their **diffidence,** you mean they are rather shy and modest. *I approached Clyde diffidently and he agreed to explain the system to me.*

diffuse (**diffusing, diffused; diffusion**) If something like light is **diffuse** (*pron:* dif-**fyooss**), it is spread over a large area. ■ If you say something written or spoken is **diffuse,** you mean it is vague and difficult to follow. ■ If a liquid or a gas **diffuses** (*pron:* dif-**fyooz**-iz), it spreads over a wider area. This process is called **diffusion.**

dig (**digging, dug**) If you **dig,** you make a hole in the ground or move the earth, with something like a spade. ■ If you **dig** something **up,** you get it out of the ground by digging. ■ A **dig** is an archaeological excavation. ■ If you **dig** one thing into another, you press the first thing forcefully into the second. *I dug my nails into her hand.* ■ If you **dig** someone **out** when they are trapped, you get them out by removing the things trapping them. ■ If you **dig up** information, you discover it through careful searching. ■ If someone has to **dig deep,** they are forced to spend a lot of money on something. ■ If you have a **dig** at someone, you make an unkind remark about them.

digest (digestion, digestible) When you **digest** food, your body breaks it down, absorbs all it can, and gets rid of what is left. This process is called **digestion. Digestible** food is easy to digest. ■ If you **digest** something you have heard or read, you think about it carefully. If something like this is easily **digestible,** it is easy to understand.

digestive means connected with the digestion of food. *...digestive juices.*

digger A **digger** is a vehicle with an arm for scooping up large amounts of earth.

digit — **Digits** are numbers between 0 and 9. ■ Your **digits** are your fingers, thumbs, and toes.

digital (digitally) Digital systems record or transmit information in the form of many very small electrical pulses. *...digitally recorded music.* ■ **Digital** devices display information as numbers rather than with a dial. *...digital watches.*

digital audio tape is a type of magnetic tape used to make high quality sound recordings in digital form.

digitalize (or digitalise) means the same as 'digitise'.

digitize (or digitise) (digitizing, digitized; digitization) If information is **digitized,** it is turned into a form that can be read easily by a computer. *The picture is digitised by a scanner.*

dignify (dignifies, dignifying, dignified) Dignified behaviour is calm and impressive. A **dignified** occasion is one when people behave like this. ■ If you **dignify** something, you make it seem more respectable than it really is.

dignitary (dignitaries) Dignitaries are high-ranking officials.

dignity If someone behaves with **dignity,** their behaviour is calm and impressive. ■ If you talk about human **dignity,** you mean people's right to be treated with respect. ■ A person's **dignity** is their sense of self-respect. ■ If you regard something as **beneath your dignity,** you consider yourself too important to do it.

digress (pron: die-gress) (digresses, digressing, digressed; digression) If you **digress,** you stop talking about your main subject and talk about something else for a while; what you say is called a **digression.**

dike See **dyke.**

diktat A **diktat** is an order made without considering the opinions of the people expected to obey it.

dilapidated (dilapidation) A **dilapidated** building or vehicle is old and in bad condition. *...churches in advanced stages of dilapidation.*

dilate (dilating, dilated; dilation) When your pupils, blood vessels, or other parts of your body **dilate,** they become wider. *...the full dilation of the uterus.*

dilatory (pron: dill-a-tree) (dilatoriness) If someone is being **dilatory,** they are taking too long over something. *They are often accused of dilatoriness.*

dilemma A **dilemma** is a difficult situation where you have to choose between two or more unsatisfactory alternatives.

dilettante (pron: dill-it-**tan**-tee) A **dilettante** is someone who is involved in something like politics or the arts, but not in a serious way.

diligent (diligently, diligence) A **diligent** person works hard and carefully and does everything which is expected of them. You talk about the **diligence** of someone like this. *We worked diligently on our final assignments.*

dill is a sweet-smelling herb with yellow flowers.

dilute (diluting, diluted; dilution) If someone's power is **diluted,** it is weakened. You call this a **dilution** of power. Similarly, if something is **diluted,** it is made less effective. ■ If you **dilute** a liquid, you make it weaker by adding water or another liquid.

dim (dimmer, dimmest; dimming, dimmed; dimly, dimness) A **dim** light is not bright. If a light **dims** or is **dimmed,** it becomes less bright. If a place is **dimly lit,** there are few lights on, or they are not very bright. If something is **dimly visible,** you can only just see it. ■ If your memory of something is **dim,** you can hardly remember it. ■ If you **dimly** understand something, or are **dimly** aware of it, you have a vague idea or awareness of it. ■ If you say someone is **dim** or **dim-witted,** you mean they are of low intelligence. ■ If your prospects are **dim,** they are not very good. ■ If you take a **dim view** of something, you disapprove of it.

dime A **dime** is a US coin worth ten cents.

dimension A **dimension** of a subject is an aspect of it. *This adds a new dimension to our work.* ■ When people talk about the **dimensions** of something that is happening, they mean its seriousness or importance. *The affair is beginning to take on national dimensions.* ■ The **dimensions** of an object are its length, width, and other measurements.

diminish (diminishes, diminishing, diminished) If something **diminishes** or is **diminished,** it becomes smaller or less significant. ■ If a court accepts **diminished responsibility** as a defence for an accused person, it agrees that the person was mentally ill when they committed a crime and so their punishment should be less severe.

diminution A **diminution** of something is a reduction in its size or importance.

diminutive A **diminutive** person or thing is very small.

dimmer A **dimmer** is a controller which allows you to alter the brightness of an electric light.

dimple (dimpled) Dimples are small hollows, for example in a person's cheeks.

din A **din** is a loud unpleasant noise.

dinar (pron: dee-nahr) The **dinar** is the unit of currency in some north African and Middle Eastern countries, and also in the republics which were parts of Yugoslavia.

dine (**dining, dined**) When you **dine,** you eat your dinner.

diner People eating dinner, especially in a restaurant, can be called **diners.** ■ In the US, a **diner** is a small cheap restaurant.

ding-dong A **ding-dong** is an argument or fight.

dinghy (**dinghies**) A **dinghy** is a small boat which you can sail, row, or power by outboard motor.

dingo (**dingoes**) Dingoes are Australian wild dogs.

dingy A **dingy** place is dark and gloomy or dirty.

dining car The **dining car** on a train is a carriage where passengers are served meals.

dinner is the main meal of the day. ■ A **dinner** is a formal evening meal.

dinner dance A **dinner dance** is a social occasion, usually at a hotel or large restaurant, where guests have a formal meal after which they dance.

dinner jacket A **dinner jacket** is a black jacket a man wears with a bow tie on formal social occasions in the evening.

dinner lady A **dinner lady** is a woman employed in a school, especially a state primary school, to serve dinners or look after children during their lunch break.

dinner party If you have a **dinner party,** you invite a small group of people to your house to spend the evening with you and have dinner.

dinner service A **dinner service** is a set of matching plates and dishes.

dinosaur – Dinosaurs were large reptiles which lived millions of years ago. ■ If you call a large organization a **dinosaur,** you mean it is old-fashioned, clumsy, and inefficient.

dint If you achieve a result **by dint** of something, you achieve it by means of that thing.

diocese (*pron:* die-a-siss) (**dioceses, diocesan**) A **diocese** is the area over which a bishop has control. **Diocesan** means to do with a diocese.

diode A **diode** is an electrical device with two terminals which allows electrical current to flow in only one direction. It is used in circuits for converting alternating current to direct current.

dioxide appears in the names of chemical compounds which have two oxygen atoms in each molecule. See **carbon dioxide** and **sulphur dioxide.**

dioxin is a highly poisonous substance produced during the manufacture of certain herbicides.

dip (**dipping, dipped**) If you **dip** something into a liquid, you put it in the liquid then take it out again straight away. ■ A **dip** is a thick creamy mixture which you eat by dipping things like biscuits or raw vegetables in it. ■ When farmers **dip** sheep, they herd them through a trough filled with liquid disinfectant which kills parasites. ■ If you take a **dip,** you have a quick swim. ■ If something **dips,** it makes a sudden downward movement. ■ If something like a road **dips,** it suddenly goes down steeply. ■ A **dip** in a surface is a part which is lower than the rest. ■ If there is a **dip** in an amount of something, it decreases briefly before returning to its original level. *Holiday companies must expect a dip in profits.* ■ If you **dip into** an amount of money,

you use some of it. ■ If you **dip into** a book, you have a quick look at it.

diphtheria (*pron:* dif-**theer**-ya) is a dangerous infectious disease which causes fever, weakness, and difficulty in breathing.

diphthong (*pron:* **dif**-thong) A **diphthong** is a combination of two vowel sounds. For example, the sound 'ow' in 'cow' is a diphthong.

diploma A **diploma** is a college or university qualification which has a lower status than a degree.

diplomacy is the management of relations between countries. ■ **Diplomacy** is saying or doing the right thing in difficult or dangerous situations to avoid offending people.

diplomat A **diplomat** is a government official, usually in an embassy in a foreign country, who helps manage relations between that country and his own.

diplomatic (**diplomatically**) Diplomatic means connected with diplomacy and diplomats. *He did not want to see China diplomatically isolated.* ■ The **Diplomatic Service** is the part of the Civil Service which provides diplomats to work abroad. ■ The **diplomatic corps** is the group of all the diplomats from different countries working in one city or country. ■ **Diplomatic immunity** is a legal privilege which exempts diplomats from paying taxes and being taken to court in the foreign country they are working in. ■ Someone who is **diplomatic** is tactful and can do things without offending people.

dipsomania (**dipsomaniac**) Dipsomania is an uncontrollable craving for alcohol. A **dipsomaniac** is someone who suffers from dipsomania.

dipstick A **dipstick** is a notched metal rod which you dip into a container to measure how much liquid is in it.

dire (**direr, direst**) Dire is used to emphasize how serious or terrible something is. *...dire consequences.* If someone or something is **in dire straits,** they are in serious trouble. ■ Dire is used to say something is of very poor quality. *Hospital food was dire.*

direct (**directness**) Direct involvement, experience, or contact includes only the people, things, or actions actually concerned, with nobody or nothing coming between them. ■ If a person or action is **direct,** their meaning is clear and straightforward. *The move is seen as a direct challenge to the King's power.* ■ **Direct** is used to say you do not have to change planes or trains on a journey. *...direct flights from Glasgow to Florida.* ■ If something like gunfire is **directed** at a place, it is aimed at it. ■ If something you say is **directed** at a person, it is intended for them to take notice of. ■ If you **direct** someone somewhere, you tell them how to get there. ■ If you **direct** something like a project, you are in charge of it. ■ When someone **directs** a film, play, or TV programme, they control the making or performance of it.

direct action involves doing things like going on strike or demonstrating to put pressure on a government or employer, instead of relying on persuasion.

direct current See **DC.**

direct debit See **debit.**

direct hit If something suffers a **direct hit,** a bomb or missile lands exactly on it.

direction You can describe the way something is progressing by saying it is moving in a particular **direction.** *Health authorities are moving in the right direction.* ■ If you say what **direction** something is in, you are saying, for example, that it is to the north. Similarly, you can say something is moving or pointing in a particular **direction.** ■ **Directions** are instructions which tell you how to get to a place, or how to do something. ■ The person responsible for the **direction** of a film, play, or piece of music is the one who controls the way it is made or performed. ■ If you do something under someone's **direction,** they tell you what to do.

directional is used to talk about transmitting sound in one direction only, or receiving it from just one direction. *...highly directional transmitting aerials.*

directionless You say an activity is **directionless** when it is not operating to any real plan.

directive A **directive** is an official instruction.

directly If you do something **directly,** you do it in a clear and open way. *He denied bidding directly for the leadership.* ■ If one person, thing, or action is **directly** involved with another, they are actually involved, with nobody or nothing coming between them. *They are directly accountable to the Minister.* ■ If something points **directly** at something else, it points straight towards it. ■ If one thing is **directly** above, below, or in front of another thing, it is exactly in that position.

direct mail is advertising material sent to people's homes without them asking for it. It is sometimes called 'junk mail'.

director (directorial) A **director** is a person who controls the way something like a film, play, or piece of music is made or performed. **Directorial** means to do with directors and their work. ■ A **director** is someone on the board of a company or in charge of a group, institution, or project.

directorate A company's **directorate** is its board of directors. ■ A **directorate** is a branch of government with a particular responsibility. *...the Food Safety Directorate.*

director general The person in charge of a large organization is sometimes called the **director general.**

Director of Public Prosecutions The **Director of Public Prosecutions** or **DPP** is the person in charge of the Crown Prosecution Service, who takes responsibility for all prosecutions made by the police.

directorship A **directorship** is the job or position of a company director.

directory (directories) A **directory** is a book which lists things like names, addresses, and phone numbers, usually in alphabetical order.

directory enquiries is a service you can phone to find out someone's phone number.

direct rule is a system in which a central government rules a province which previously had its own government or law-making organization.

dirge A **dirge** is a slow sad song or piece of music, for performing at a funeral. Any piece of music which sounds like this can also be called a **dirge.**

dirt If there is **dirt** on something, there is dust, mud, or a stain on it. ■ **Dirt** is earth. ■ If someone has **dirt** on another person, they have damaging or embarrassing information about their private life. ■ If something is **dirt cheap,** it costs very little, often because it is of poor quality.

dirty (dirtier, dirtiest; dirties, dirtying, dirtied) If something is **dirty,** it has dust, mud, or stains on it. If you **dirty** something, you make it dirty. ■ **Dirty** is used to talk about unfair ways of gaining an advantage. *...the dirtiest leadership contest the party has seen.* ■ **Dirty** jokes, books, and language deal with sex in a way many people find vulgar or offensive. ■ A person whose sexual behaviour offends people can be called **dirty.** *...a dirty old man.*

disability (disabilities) A person with a **disability** has a serious permanent problem with their body or mind which restricts their way of life.

disable (disabling, disabled) If something **disables** you, it affects you physically or mentally and restricts your way of life. *...a disabling illness.* People whose lives are affected in this way are sometimes called the **disabled.** ■ If a machine is **disabled,** it is damaged so badly it no longer works.

disabuse (*pron:* dis-a-**byooz**) **(disabusing, disabused)** If you **disabuse** someone of a belief they hold, you show them it is not true.

disadvantage (disadvantaged) A **disadvantage** is a factor which makes something less desirable. ■ If you are **at a disadvantage,** you have a problem which other people do not have. ■ **Disadvantaged** people live in bad conditions and do not have the means to improve their situation.

disadvantageous If something is **disadvantageous** to you, it puts you in a bad position compared to other people.

disaffected (disaffection) You say people are **disaffected** when they no longer believe in something and have stopped supporting it.

disagree (disagreeing, disagreed; disagreement) If you **disagree** with someone about something, you have a different opinion from them about it. You say there is a **disagreement** between the two of you. ■ If you **disagree** with what someone does, you disapprove of it.

disagreeable (disagreeably) If something is **disagreeable,** it is unpleasant or annoying. ■ A **disagreeable** person is unpleasant or unfriendly.

disallow If something is **disallowed,** it is not officially allowed or accepted because it has not been done properly.

disappear (disappearing, disappeared; disappearance) If someone or something **disappears,** they are not where they should be, and cannot be found. When this happens, you talk about their **disappearance.** ■ You say someone **disappears** when they go somewhere where they cannot be seen. *He disappeared into the trees.* ■ If something like a feeling **disappears,** it ceases to exist.

disappoint (disappointing, disappointed; disappointingly, disappointment) If you are **disap-**

pointed by something, it is not as good as you expected, or does not do what you wanted it to.

disapprove (**disapproving, disapproved; disapprovingly, disapproval**) If you **disapprove** of something, you do not like it, or you think it is morally wrong. When people express **disapproval,** they show they disapprove of something.

disarm (**disarmament**) If someone is **disarmed,** they have their weapons taken away. ■ If a country or organization **disarms,** it gets rid of some or all of its weapons. This process is called **disarmament.** ■ If a bomb is **disarmed,** its detonator is removed so it cannot explode.

disarming (**disarmingly**) If someone is **disarming,** they are so pleasant it is difficult to have any hostile feelings towards them.

disarray If people are in **disarray,** they are confused and disorganized. ■ If something is in **disarray,** it is in an untidy state.

disassociate (**disassociating, disassociated**) If you **disassociate** yourself from someone or something, you say you are not involved with them or their activities or opinions.

disaster (**disastrous, disastrously**) A **disaster** is something like an earthquake which happens unexpectedly and causes a lot of damage or suffering. You say something like this is **disastrous.** ■ If you say something someone does is **disastrous** or a **disaster,** you mean it is very unsuccessful.

disavow (**disavowal**) If you **disavow** something, you say you are not responsible for it or do not agree with it. ...*his disavowal of territorial claims on the Baltic states.*

disband (**disbandment**) If an organized group **disbands,** it breaks up.

disbelieve (**disbelieving, disbelieved; disbelief**) If you **disbelieve** what someone tells you, you do not believe it. **Disbelief** is unwillingness to accept that something is true.

disburse (**disbursing, disbursed; disbursement**) When an amount of money is **disbursed,** it is paid out, usually from a special fund. ...*monthly disbursements.*

disc (*Am:* **disk**) A **disc** is a flat circular object. ■ **Discs** are pieces of cartilage between the bones in your spine. If a piece gets displaced, you say you have **slipped a disc.** ■ See also **disk.**

discard If you **discard** something, you get rid of it.

disc drive See **disk drive.**

discern (**discernible**) If you can **discern** something, you can see it, or see that it exists. ...*a discernible shift in public opinion.*

discerning (**discernment**) A **discerning** person is good at judging the quality of something; this ability is called **discernment.**

discharge (**discharging, discharged**) When someone is **discharged** from hospital, prison, or the armed forces, they are allowed to leave. ■ When a substance is **discharged,** it is released somewhere. ...*the discharge of effluent into the sea.* A quantity of a substance released like this is called a **discharge.** ■ If someone **discharges** their duties, they carry them out.

disciple The **disciples** of a teacher or leader are his or her followers. Christ's **disciples** were his twelve closest male followers during his life on Earth.

disciplinarian If you call someone in authority a **disciplinarian,** you mean they insist on people obeying rules and punish them if they do not.

discipline (**disciplining, disciplined; disciplinary**) **Discipline** is insisting on people obeying rules and punishing them when they do not. **Disciplinary** is used to talk about enforcing discipline. *Two players face disciplinary action.* ■ If someone is **disciplined,** they are punished for breaking rules or behaving badly. ■ **Discipline** or **self-discipline** is the ability to control your behaviour and finish the things you set out to do. A **disciplined** or **self-disciplined** person has this ability. ■ In some sports competitions, each competitor does several different events called **disciplines.** For example, the three disciplines of world cup skiing are downhill, slalom, and giant slalom. ■ A **discipline** is a subject which people study.

disc jockey A **disc jockey** or **DJ** is someone who introduces or mixes records on radio programmes or at nightclubs.

disclaim (**disclaiming, disclaimed; disclaimer**) If you **disclaim** a feeling, you say you do not have it. ■ If you **disclaim** knowledge of something, you say you know nothing about it. ■ If you **disclaim** responsibility for something, you say you are not responsible for it. A statement in which someone disclaims responsibility for something is called a **disclaimer.**

disclose (**disclosing, disclosed; disclosure**) If someone **discloses** new or secret information, they tell people about it. ...*recent disclosures about a military plot.*

disco (**discos**) A **disco** is a place or event at which people dance to pop records. ■ A **disco** is equipment for putting on a disco. ■ **Disco** is a type of dance music with a regular beat.

discolour (*Am:* **discolor**) (**discolouring, discoloured; discolouration**) If something **discolours** or is **discoloured,** its original colour changes in an unattractive way.

discomfit (**discomfiting, discomfited; discomfiture**) If something **discomfits** you, it makes you embarrassed or confused. This feeling of embarrassment or confusion is called **discomfiture.**

discomfort is an unpleasant or slightly painful feeling in part of your body. ■ **Discomforts** are conditions which make you physically uncomfortable. ...*the discomforts of camping.* ■ **Discomfort** is a feeling of worry or embarrassment. If something **discomforts** you or is **discomforting,** it makes you feel like this.

disconcert (**disconcertingly**) If something **disconcerts** you, it makes you feel worried or uneasy. *Ruth has a disconcertingly unblinking stare.*

disconnect If you **disconnect** things which are joined together, you separate them. ■ If you **disconnect** a piece of equipment, you detach it from its power source. ■ If a gas, electricity, water, or telephone company **disconnects** someone, they turn off the supply to their house.

disconsolate (**disconsolately**) If someone is **disconsolate**, they are deeply unhappy or disappointed. *I walked disconsolately back to the hotel.*

discontent (**discontented, discontentedly**) If you are **discontented**, you are unhappy with your situation. This feeling is called **discontent.** You can also be **discontented** with a particular thing. *...public discontent over rising prices.* People's **discontents** are the things they are dissatisfied with.

discontinue (**discontinuing, discontinued**) If you **discontinue** something, you stop doing it.

discontinuous (**discontinuity, discontinuities**) A **discontinuous** process happens in stages, with breaks in between. A **discontinuity** is a break in something.

discord is disagreement between people.

discordant sounds are harsh and unpleasant. *...discordant music.* ■ If something is **discordant**, it clashes with other things. *...the one discordant note.*

discotheque A **discotheque** is a disco.

discount A **discount** is a reduction in something's price. If a product is **discounted**, it is sold at a cheaper price. ■ **Discount** things are cheap and usually of poor quality. *...discount clothing.* ■ If you **discount** something, you reject or ignore it.

discourage (**discouraging, discouraged; discouragement**) If something **discourages** you, it makes you lose hope. ■ If someone **discourages** you from doing something, they try to persuade you not to do it. Their attempts at persuading you are called **discouragement.** ■ If something **discourages** you from doing something, it makes you less keen to do it.

discourse A **discourse** is a talk or piece of writing which is intended to teach or explain something. ■ **Discourse** is spoken or written communication between people.

discourtesy (**discourteous**) **Discourtesy** is impolite and bad-mannered behaviour. People who behave like this are **discourteous.**

discover (**discovering, discovered; discovery, discoveries**) If you **discover** something, you find it or find out about it. A **discovery** is something which has been discovered. *...scientific discoveries.* ■ If you **discover** that something is the case, you find it or find out about it for the first time. *Halfway through filming Amanda discovered she was pregnant.* ■ When a talented person is **discovered**, someone realizes how talented they are and helps them to become famous.

discoverer The **discoverer** of something is the first person to find it or find out about it.

discredit (**discrediting, discredited**) If someone is **discredited,** people stop trusting or respecting them. ■ If something like a belief is **discredited,** it is shown to be false. ■ **Discredit** is shame and disapproval. *This will serve only to bring discredit on him.*

discreditable behaviour is considered shameful and wrong.

discreet (**discreetly**) If you are **discreet,** you avoid causing embarrassment when dealing with private matters. ■ You say things are **discreet** when they have been designed not to draw attention to themselves. *...discreet lighting.*

discrepancy (**discrepancies**) A **discrepancy** is a small difference between two things which ought to be the same.

discrete things are separate and distinct from each other.

discretion (**discretionary**) If you behave with **discretion,** you avoid causing embarrassment when dealing with private matters. ■ **Discretion** is the ability to judge a situation and make the right sort of decisions. ■ If a decision is at the **discretion** of someone in authority, it depends on what they think is best. When someone uses this power, you say they are **exercising their discretion. Discretionary** is used to describe things connected with decisions like this. *...the president's discretionary powers.*

discriminate (**discriminating, discriminated; discrimination, discriminatory**) If someone **discriminates** against you, they do not treat you as well as they treat others. *...discriminatory laws.* Unfair treatment like this is called **discrimination.** ■ If you can **discriminate** between two things, you can recognize the difference between them. ■ A **discriminating** person recognizes and appreciates fine things.

discursive speech or writing expresses things in a roundabout way.

discus (**discuses**) The **discus** is a field event in athletics. Competitors throw a heavy disc-shaped object called a **discus** as far as they can.

discuss (**discusses, discussing, discussed; discussion**) When people **discuss** things, they talk about them seriously. Talking seriously about things is called **discussion;** a **discussion** is a serious conversation. If something is **under discussion,** it is being talked about and no decision has yet been made.

disdain (**disdaining, disdained; disdainful, disdainfully**) If someone behaves with **disdain,** they show they dislike someone and treat them contemptuously. You call behaviour like this **disdainful.** *The idea was dismissed disdainfully.* ■ If you **disdain** to do something, you refuse to do it, because you think it is beneath you.

disease (**diseased**) A **disease** is an illness caused by something like an infection. ■ A common bad habit or attitude can be called a **disease.** *...the disease of racism.*

disembark (**disembarkation**) When you **disembark** from a ship or plane, you get off it at the end of a journey.

disembodied A **disembodied** head has been separated from its body. ■ A **disembodied** voice seems to come from a place where you cannot see anyone.

disembowel (**disembowelling, disembowelled**) If a person is **disembowelled,** their intestines are removed.

disenchanted (**disenchantment**) If you are **disenchanted** with something, you are disappointed by it and no longer think it is good or worthwhile. *...his disenchantment with American society.*

disenfranchize (or **disenfranchise**) (**disenfranchizing, disenfranchized**) If someone is **disenfranchized,** they lose their right to vote.

disengage (**disengaging, disengaged; disengagement**) If an army **disengages** from an area, it withdraws. ■ If you **disengage** something, you separate it from the thing it is attached to. *...the throttle disengaged itself.* ■ If someone is **disengaged** from something, they are not as involved in it as you would expect.

disentangle (**disentangling, disentangled; disentanglement**) If you **disentangle** something, you separate it from other things it has become attached to. ■ If you **disentangle** a complicated issue, you sort out the different things involved, so it can be better understood.

disequilibrium If something is in **disequilibrium**, it is uncertain, unstable, and likely to change.

disestablish (**disestablishes, disestablishing, disestablished; disestablishment**) When people talk about the Church of England being **disestablished**, they mean a change which would no longer make it the United Kingdom's official religion.

disfavour is dislike or disapproval. If someone is **in disfavour**, they are disliked by someone in authority.

disfigure (**disfiguring, disfigured; disfigurement**) If something is **disfigured**, its appearance is spoiled. ■ If a person is **disfigured**, they have a scar or mark on their face or some other part of their body which spoils their appearance. Something like this is called a **disfigurement.**

disgorge (**disgorging, disgorged**) When a lot of people get out of a vehicle, you can say it **disgorges** them. ■ If a substance is **disgorged** into the atmosphere or the sea, it is released into it. ■ If someone **disgorges** information, they release it.

disgrace (**disgracing, disgraced; disgraceful, disgracefully**) If someone is **disgraced** or **in disgrace**, they have done something which has made people lose respect for them. ■ If someone **disgraces** an organization they belong to, or is a **disgrace** to it, they do something which harms its reputation. ■ If you **disgrace yourself,** you behave badly in public. ■ If you say something is a **disgrace** or **disgraceful,** you mean it is shocking and unacceptable.

disgruntled people are cross and dissatisfied about something.

disguise (**disguising, disguised**) If someone is **disguised** or **in disguise,** they have changed their appearance to prevent people recognizing them. A **disguise** is something like a set of clothes which someone uses to change their appearance. ■ If something **disguises** what is happening, it prevents people noticing it.

disgust (**disgusting**) Disgust is a strong feeling of dislike or disapproval. If something **disgusts** you or you are **disgusted** by it, it makes you feel like this. *Chewing gum is a disgusting habit.*

dish (**dishes, dishing, dished**) A **dish** is a round shallow container for cooking or serving food in. ■ A **dish** is food prepared in a particular style. *...fish dishes.* ■ When food is **dished up,** it is served. ■ A **dish** is a dish-shaped TV aerial for picking up satellite signals. ■ If money or a punishment is **dished out** to people, it is given to them.

disharmony You say there is **disharmony** when a group of people fail to get on together.

dishcloth A **dishcloth** is a cloth for washing up.

dishearten (**disheartening, disheartened**) If something **disheartens** you, it makes you less hopeful.

dishevelled (*Am:* **disheveled**) **Dishevelled** people look very untidy.

dishonest (**dishonestly, dishonesty**) You say someone is **dishonest** when they lie, cheat, or break the law. *She accused the government of dishonesty.*

dishonour (**dishonouring, dishonoured**) If you **dishonour** someone or something such as your country or bring **dishonour** on them, your behaviour damages their reputation.

dishonourable behaviour is dishonest or morally unacceptable.

dishwasher A **dishwasher** is a machine for washing crockery and cutlery.

dishwater is water which has been used for washing up.

disillusion (**disillusioning, disillusioned; disillusionment**) If you are **disillusioned,** you are disappointed because someone or something is not as good as you thought they were. This feeling is called **disillusion** or **disillusionment.** A **disillusioning** experience makes you feel like this.

disincentive A **disincentive** is something which discourages people from doing something.

disinclined (**disinclination**) If you are **disinclined** to do something, you are unwilling to do it.

disinfect (**disinfectant**) If you **disinfect** something, you clean it using a liquid called a **disinfectant** which kills germs.

disinflation (**disinflationary**) Disinflation is a reduction in the rate of inflation. When there is **disinflation,** prices stop rising or go down, but without the usual problems associated with price decreases like unemployment and lack of investment. A **disinflationary** policy or measure is meant to cause disinflation. See also **deflation.**

disinformation is false or misleading information, spread to deliberately deceive people.

disingenuous (**disingenuously**) If someone is being **disingenuous,** they are being insincere and slightly dishonest.

disintegrate (**disintegrating, disintegrated; disintegration**) If an object **disintegrates,** it breaks into many small pieces. ■ If something like a relationship or organization **disintegrates,** it breaks up, or the people involved separate into smaller groups.

disinter (*pron:* diss-in-**ter**) (**disinterring, disinterred**) If you **disinter** something, you start using it again after it has not been used for a long time. *The government plans to disinter an anti-subversive law dating from 1952.* ■ When a dead body is **disinterred,** it is dug up.

disinterested (**disinterest**) If people are **disinterested** in something, they are not interested in it, or not enthusiastic about it. This feeling is called **disinterest.** *Registration figures indicate a general disinterest towards the elections.* Some people think this use is wrong. Instead of 'disinterested', they say you should say 'uninterested' and instead of 'disinterest', you should say 'lack of interest'. ■ You say someone is **disinterested** when they are not personally involved in something and so can make unbiased judgments about it.

disinvestment If there is **disinvestment** in a country, other countries withdraw money they have invested there.

disjointed If something is **disjointed**, it has sudden gaps or changes, and does not proceed in a flowing way. ...*a scrappy, disjointed game.*

disk A **disk** is a part of a computer which stores information. See also **hard disk, floppy disk.** ■ **Disk** is the usual American spelling of 'disc'.

disk drive (*or* **disc drive**) A **disk drive** is a device attached to a small computer which allows you to store and retrieve information on disk.

dislike (**disliking, disliked**) If you **dislike** someone or something or feel **dislike** towards them, you find them unpleasant. Your **dislikes** are things you do not like.

dislocate (**dislocating, dislocated; dislocation**) If you **dislocate** a part of your body, a bone is forced away from another bone it is normally connected to. ■ If something like a system is **dislocated**, other things interfere with it and it cannot function normally.

dislodge (**dislodging, dislodged**) If you **dislodge** someone or something, you cause them to move from the place where they are.

disloyal (**disloyalty**) If someone is **disloyal** to their friends, family, colleagues, employer, or country, they do things which harm them, or they fail to support them. Behaviour like this is called **disloyalty.**

dismal (**dismally**) If you call a person's attempt at doing something **dismal,** you mean it is very unsuccessful. ■ **Dismal** is used to say something is unattractive and depressing.

dismantle (**dismantling, dismantled; dismantlement**) If you **dismantle** something like a machine, you take it apart. ■ If an organization or political system is **dismantled**, it is brought to an end by taking away its parts or functions, one at a time. ...*the virtual dismantlement of the country's armed forces.*

dismay If something **dismays** you, it makes you sad or alarmed. This feeling is called **dismay.**

dismember (**dismembering, dismembered; dismemberment**) If a body is **dismembered,** its arms and legs are removed. ■ If a country is **dismembered,** it is split into separate parts. *The country was plunged into a civil war that led to its dismemberment.*

dismiss (**dismisses, dismissing, dismissed; dismissal**) If you **dismiss** something like a person's ideas, you say they are incorrect or unimportant, and therefore not worth bothering about. You call this a **dismissal** of a person's ideas. ■ When a judge **dismisses** an action in court, he or she says it cannot proceed. ■ If an appeal is **dismissed,** it is turned down. ■ If someone is **dismissed** by their employer, they lose their job. *The authorities threatened mass dismissals.* ■ If the people in a room are **dismissed,** they are given permission to leave. ■ In

cricket, when a batsman is **dismissed,** the opposing team gets him or her out.

dismissive (**dismissively**) If you are **dismissive** of something, you show you are unwilling to accept it or take it seriously.

dismount If you **dismount** from a horse or bicycle, you get off it.

disobedient (**disobedience**) If someone is **disobedient,** they do not do what someone in authority tells them to.

disobey If you **disobey** a person or an order, you do not do what you are told to do.

disorder (**disordered; disorderly**) **Disorder** is violence and rioting in public. You say people who behave like this are **disorderly.** ■ If something is **disordered, disorderly,** or **in disorder,** it is very untidy or disorganized. ■ A **disorder** is an illness of the mind or body.

disorganized (*or* **disorganised**) (**disorganization**) If something is **disorganized,** it is in a confused and badly prepared state. *The army is suffering from low morale, disorganization and indiscipline.* ■ A **disorganized** person is no good at planning things.

disorientate (**disorientating, disorientated**) If something **disorientates** you, it makes you confused or unsure of where you are; if you are in this state, you say you are **disorientated** or **disoriented.** Something which has this effect can be called **disorientating** or **disorienting.**

disown If you **disown** something or someone, you claim you have no connection with them, or say you no longer wish to be connected with them.

disparage (**disparaging, disparaged; disparagingly, disparagement**) If you **disparage** someone or something, you talk about them in a way which shows you have a low opinion of them. ...*his disparaging comments about the European Union... Reviewers have been unanimous in their disparagement of this book.*

disparate (*pron:* diss-par-et) If things are **disparate,** they are very different from each other.

disparity (**disparities**) A **disparity** between things is a difference between them.

dispassionate (**dispassionately**) A **dispassionate** account or judgment is calm and reasonable and not affected by emotions.

dispatch See **despatch.**

dispel (**dispelling, dispelled**) If something **dispels** an idea or feeling, it stops people having it.

dispensable If someone or something is **dispensable,** you can do without them.

dispensary (**dispensaries**) A **dispensary** is a place, for example in a hospital, where medicines are stored and given out.

dispensation If someone is given a **dispensation,** they are given official permission to do something which is not normally allowed.

dispense (**dispensing, dispensed**) If you **dispense** something, you hand it out. *He dispensed advice on how to sterilize needles.* ■ A machine which **dispenses** something provides it when you put money in it or a card. ■ When pharmacists **dispense** medicine, they give it to people, making sure the doctor's instructions are understood. ■ If you **dis-**

pense with something, you get rid of it, or do without it.

dispenser A **dispenser** is a machine or container you can obtain things from. ...*a cash dispenser.* ...*a drinks dispenser.*

dispensing optician See **optician.**

dispersant – **Dispersants** are chemicals sprayed on oil slicks to break them up so they do not pollute the coastline.

disperse (**dispersing, dispersed; dispersal, dispersion**) When a group of people **disperse** or are **dispersed,** they move away in different directions. *Police ordered the dispersal of the crowds.* ■ When things **disperse,** they spread out over a larger area. ...*the dispersal of radioactive material.* ...*the dispersion of immigrants throughout the Paris region.*

dispirit (**dispiriting, dispirited; dispiritingly**) If you are **dispirited,** you are disappointed and have lost your enthusiasm or determination. If something is **dispiriting,** it has this effect on you.

displace (**displacing, displaced; displacement**) If one thing **displaces** another, it forces it out and takes its place. ■ If people are **displaced,** they are forced to move away from the area where they live, usually because of a war. ...*the displacement of two million people.* ■ The **displacement** of a boat is the weight of water it displaces when it is afloat.

display If you **display** something, you put it somewhere where people can see it; you then say it is **on display.** ■ A **display** is an attractive arrangement of things. ■ A **display** is a public performance or show, especially an outdoor one. ...*a firework display.* ■ The **display** of a computer is the electronic representation of information on the screen. ■ If you **display** a quality, skill, or emotion, you show you have it.

displease (**displeasing, displeased; displeasure**) If something **displeases** you, it makes you dissatisfied or annoyed. When this happens, you say you are **displeased;** you call this feeling **displeasure.**

disposable things are designed to be thrown away after they have been used once. ...*disposable nappies.* ■ Your **disposable income** is the money you have left to spend after you have paid your taxes. **Disposable income** is sometimes used to mean the amount of money someone has left to spend on luxuries, after paying for essentials like rent and food.

disposal If something is **at your disposal,** you can use it whenever you want. ■ **Disposal** is getting rid of something. ...*the disposal of hazardous waste.*

dispose (**disposing, disposed**) If you **dispose** of something, you get rid of it. ■ If a business **disposes** of some of its property, it sells it off. ■ If you say someone is **disposed** to do something, you mean they want to do it, or are willing to do it. ■ If you are **well disposed** towards someone or something, you have a favourable attitude towards them.

disposition A person's **disposition** is the way they tend to behave and respond to things. ...*not recommended for those of a nervous disposition.* ■ A **disposition** to do something is a willingness to do it.

dispossess (**dispossesses, dispossessing; dispossession**) If you are **dispossessed** of something you own, especially your home, it is taken away from you. People who have lost their homes are often called the **dispossessed.**

disproportionate (**disproportionately**) If something is **disproportionate,** there is an unusually large amount of it compared to other things. *Australia had a disproportionately large share of the market.*

disprove (**disproving, disproved**) If you **disprove** something, you show it is not true.

disputable If you say something is **disputable,** you mean it is not necessarily true.

disputatious people tend to argue about things.

dispute (**disputing, disputed**) A **dispute** is a disagreement or quarrel. ■ If people are **in dispute,** they are having a serious disagreement about something. ■ If something is **in dispute,** people disagree about it. ■ If you **dispute** something, you say it is not true.

disqualify (**disqualifies, disqualifying, disqualified; disqualification**) If someone is **disqualified** from a competition, they are no longer allowed to compete, because they have broken a rule. ■ If someone is **disqualified** from doing something, they are not allowed to do it, usually because they have broken the law. ...*disqualification from driving.*

disquiet (**disquieting, disquieted**) If you are **disquieted** by something or it causes you **disquiet,** it makes you anxious or worried.

disregard If you **disregard** something, you ignore it, or do not take it seriously. ...*the regime's total disregard for human rights.*

disrepair If something like a building is **in disrepair,** it is in bad condition because it has not been maintained properly.

disreputable A **disreputable** person is not respectable or trustworthy.

disrepute If something is brought into **disrepute,** it loses its good reputation.

disrespect (**disrespectful**) If you show **disrespect** for someone or you are **disrespectful** towards them, you behave in a way which shows a lack of respect for them.

disrobe (**disrobing, disrobed**) When someone **disrobes,** they take their clothes off.

disrupt (**disruption**) If you **disrupt** something, you interfere with it and stop it proceeding smoothly. ...*widespread disruption caused by transport strikes.*

disruptive A **disruptive** person causes problems and prevents things proceeding smoothly.

dissatisfied (**dissatisfaction**) If you are **dissatisfied,** you are not content.

dissect (**dissection**) If someone **dissects** a dead animal or person, they cut up their body so they can examine it. This is called a **dissection.** ■ If someone examines something carefully and in great detail, you can say they **dissect** it. ...*the dissection of the mind under psychoanalysis.*

dissemble (**dissembling, dissembled**) If someone **dissembles,** they hide their real motives or feelings by pretending to have different ones.

disseminate (disseminating, disseminated; dissemination) If information is **disseminated,** it is distributed to many people.

dissent (dissenter, dissension) When people **dissent,** they express disagreement with established ideas. People who do this are called **dissenters;** their disagreement is called **dissent** or **dissension.**

dissertation A **dissertation** is a long essay, especially one written for a university degree.

disservice If you do someone a **disservice,** you do something which harms them when they do not deserve it.

dissident (dissidence) A **dissident** is someone who criticizes their government or the organization they belong to, especially when such behaviour is not normal or not allowed. **Dissidence** is behaviour like this.

dissimilar (dissimilarity, dissimilarities) If two things are **dissimilar,** they are not alike. **Dissimilarities** are differences between things.

dissipate (dissipating, dissipated; dissipation) If something **dissipates** or is **dissipated,** it gradually gets less and disappears.

dissociate (dissociating, dissociated; dissociation) If you **dissociate** yourself from someone or something, you say you are not involved with them, or you refuse to have anything to do with them. ■ If you **dissociate** one thing from another, you regard them as two separate things.

dissolute A **dissolute** person lives in a way considered to be immoral.

dissolve (dissolving, dissolved; dissolution) If something solid **dissolves** in a liquid, it becomes absorbed in it. ■ If an organization is **dissolved,** it is officially ended. You call this its **dissolution.** ■ When parliament is **dissolved,** it breaks up just before a general election. You call this the **dissolution** of parliament. ■ If someone **dissolves into** tears, they begin to cry. If something **dissolves into** chaos, it becomes chaotic. *The two of them dissolved into laughter.*

dissonant (dissonance) If music is **dissonant,** groups of notes are played together which do not harmonize. The effect produced is called **dissonance.**

dissuade (dissuading, dissuaded) If you **dissuade** someone from doing something, you persuade them not to do it.

distaff The **distaff side** means women generally, or the female members of a particular group.

distance (distancing, distanced) The **distance** between two places is how far it is between them. ■ If something is **in the distance** or **at a distance,** it is a long way away. If you do something **from a distance,** you do it from a long way away. ■ You can talk about the **distance** between two things when you mean how different they are. ■ If you **distance** yourself from a person or situation, you become less friendly or less involved with them. ■ If a boxing match **goes the distance,** it lasts its full number of rounds, and is not stopped because of an injury or knockout.

distant (distantly) **Distant** is used to describe things which are a long way away. *...the rumble of distant artillery.* ■ **Distant** is sometimes used to say how far away something is. *Wimereux is four-and-a-half miles distant.* ■ If you talk about the **distant past,** you mean a very long time ago. ■ **Distant** memories are of things which happened a long time ago. ■ **Distant** is sometimes used to say how long it will be before something happens. *A general election is four years distant.* ■ A **distant** relative is one you are not closely related to. ■ **Distant** people are cold and unemotional. ■ Someone who is **distant** is not paying attention, because they are thinking about something else. *His eyes took on a glazed, distant look.*

distaste (distasteful) **Distaste** is a strong feeling of dislike. If you find something **distasteful,** you strongly dislike it.

distemper is a dangerous infectious disease which affects animals, especially dogs. ■ **Distemper** is a type of paint which used to be used for decorating.

distended If a part of someone's body is **distended,** it is swollen.

distil (distilling, distilled; distillation) When a liquid is **distilled,** it is heated into a vapour, then cooled until it is a liquid again, usually to remove impurities. ■ You say something is **distilled** when it is condensed into a smaller form. *Reid distilled her work on these themes into a book.*

distiller A **distiller** is a person or company that makes whisky or other spirits by distillation.

distillery (distilleries) A **distillery** is a place where whisky or other spirits are made.

distinct (distinctly) If one thing is **distinct** from another, it has features the other thing does not have, and is therefore not the same thing. You say several things are **distinct** when each has features the others do not have. *The survey identifies three distinct stages.* ■ You use **as distinct from** to show you are talking about one thing rather than another. *...the benefits paid to the disabled as distinct from the long-term sick.* ■ **Distinct** and **distinctly** are used to say something is noticeable or significant. *...a distinctly cool response.*

distinction A **distinction** is a difference between two similar things. ■ If you do something with **distinction,** you do it extremely well. ■ A **distinction** is (a) an honour. *The Order of Merit was created in 1902 as a special distinction for eminent men and women.* (b) something which makes someone special or unique. *The goal gave him the distinction of being Northern Ireland's all-time leading scorer.*

distinctive (distinctively, distinctiveness) If something is **distinctive,** there is something about it which distinguishes it from other similar things.

distinguish (distinguishes, distinguishing, distinguished) If you can **distinguish** one thing from another, you can see or understand the difference between them. ■ If a feature **distinguishes** one thing from another, it makes them recognizable as different things. ■ If you can **distinguish** something, you can just see it, hear it, or taste it. ■ If you **distinguish** yourself, you do something which makes you famous, important, or admired. *...one of Australia's most distinguished artists.*

distinguishable If something is **distinguishable** from other things, it can be recognized as different from them. ■ You say something is **distinguishable** when it can just be seen or heard.

distort (**distortion**) If a fact or idea is **distorted**, it is represented wrongly. *Jana said the charges were a distortion of what had actually happened.* ■ If an object is **distorted**, it is changed in an unusual way or forced into a strange shape.

distract (**distraction**) If something **distracts** you or your attention from something, it takes your attention away from it. You say something like this is **distracting** or a **distraction.** ■ If someone is **distracted,** they are not concentrating on what they are doing, because they have something on their mind. ■ **Distractions** are activities which are intended to entertain and amuse you.

distraught If someone is **distraught,** they are extremely worried or upset.

distress (**distresses, distressing, distressed; distressingly**) **Distress** is extreme anxiety, sorrow, or pain. *She wrote with obvious distress about being betrayed.* If you are **distressed** or something **distresses** you, it gives you these feelings. *He had a distressingly sad start in life.* ■ **Distress** is used to talk about dangerous situations in which people urgently need help. *The vessel sent out a distress call.*

distribute (**distributing, distributed; distribution**) If you **distribute** things like leaflets, you post or hand them out to people. ■ When goods are **distributed,** they are supplied to the businesses which sell them or use them. ■ If you talk about the way things are **distributed,** you are talking about the numbers of them in different places. *...changes in the distribution of animals and plants.*

distributor A **distributor** is a person or organization that supplies goods to businesses. ■ Shops are sometimes called **distributors.** ■ In a petrol engine, the **distributor** is a device which sends electric current to the spark plugs.

district A **district** is a particular area of a town or country. *I drove around the business district.* ■ A **District** is an area which has official boundaries for administration purposes. *...North Cornwall District.*

district attorney (*pron:* a-**ter**-nee) In the US, a **district attorney** or **D.A.** is a lawyer who prosecutes criminal cases on behalf of the State or Federal government.

district nurse A **district nurse** is a nurse who visits and treats people in their own homes.

distrust (**distrustful**) If you **distrust** someone or something or are **distrustful** of them, you do not think they are honest or reliable. *...a profound distrust of all authority.*

disturb (**disturbingly**) If you **disturb** someone, you interrupt them while they are doing something. ■ If someone or something **disturbs** a situation, they make it less peaceful, organized, or stable. ■ If something **disturbs** people or if they are **disturbed** by it, it makes them upset or worried. You say something which has this effect is **disturbing.** ■ A **disturbed** person has serious psychological problems. ■ If you **disturb** something, you move it away from its usual position.

disturbance If there is a **disturbance** somewhere, people behave violently. ■ If there is a **disturbance** of something, it is made less peaceful or stable. *...a disturbance of the heart's rhythm.* ■ **Disturbance** is extreme unhappiness or mental illness.

disunity (**disunited**) **Disunity** is a lack of agreement between people, which prevents them working together effectively. You say people like these are **disunited.**

disuse (**disused**) If something falls into **disuse** (*pron:* dis-**yooss**) or is **disused** (*pron:* dis-**yoozd**), it is no longer used.

ditch (**ditches, ditching, ditched**) A **ditch** is a long narrow channel cut into the ground at the side of a road or field, usually for water to drain into. ■ If you **ditch** something, you get rid of it. ■ If you make a **last ditch** attempt to achieve something, you make a final attempt to achieve it.

dither (**dithering, dithered; ditherer**) If someone **dithers,** they hesitate because they cannot decide what to do.

ditto You use **ditto** to represent a word or phrase you have just used, to avoid repeating it. *Lister's dead. Ditto three Miami drug dealers.* In written lists, 'ditto' can be represented by the symbol " underneath the word or phrase which you want to avoid repeating.

ditty (**ditties**) A **ditty** is a short simple song or poem.

diuretic (*pron:* die-yoo-**ret**-ik) **Diuretics** are medicines or drinks which increase the amount of urine produced by the body.

diurnal (*pron:* die-**urn**-al) **Diurnal** means happening or active during the day. *...diurnal birds of prey.*

diva (*pron:* **dee**-va) A **diva** is a famous female opera singer.

Divali See **Diwali.**

divan (*pron:* di-**van**) A **divan** or **divan bed** is a bed with a thick padded base.

dive (**diving, dived; diver**) If you **dive** or do a **dive** into water, you enter it head-first. The sport or activity of doing this is called **diving;** the people who do it are called **divers.** ■ You say someone **dives** when they fling their body in a particular direction. ■ If an aircraft **dives** or goes into a **dive,** it falls rapidly with its nose towards the ground. ■ **Diving** is used to talk about people going underwater for long periods. A person who does this is called a **diver.** ■ When things like prices **dive** or **take a dive,** they drop suddenly by a large amount.

diverge (**diverging, diverged**) If things **diverge,** they are different, or become different. *...diverging interests.* ■ When someone **diverges** from something like a rule, they do not follow it. ■ If a road **diverges,** it splits into two or more roads.

divergent (**divergence**) If things are **divergent,** they are opposing or different. *...the wide divergence between opinion polls.*

diverse (**diversity**) **Diverse** people or things are different and distinct from each other. *The world of politics relies on persuasion to reconcile diverse interests.* ■ If something is **diverse,** it is made up of a wide variety of things. *...the diversity of British broadcasting.*

diversify (diversifies, diversifying, diversified; diversification) When a business **diversifies,** it increases the variety of things is does or makes.

diversion A **diversion** is something which distracts your attention and makes you think about something else. ■ A **diversion** is an activity that is done for fun. ■ A **diversion** is a special route for traffic when the usual route cannot be used. ■ The **diversion** of something is the changing of its route or destination. ...the illegal diversion of profits from secret arms sales.

diversionary activities are intended to draw people's attention away from something.

diversity See **diverse.**

divert If something is **diverted,** its route or destination is changed. ■ If something like money is **diverted,** it is used for a purpose it was not intended for. ■ If you **divert** someone's attention, you stop them thinking about one thing by making them think about another.

divest If you **divest** yourself of something, you get rid of it. If you **divest** someone else of something, you take it away from them.

divide (dividing, divided) If something **divides** or is **divided,** it separates into two or more parts. ■ If you **divide** something among a group of people or **divide** it **up,** you give some of it to each of them. ■ If something **divides** two areas, it forms a barrier or boundary between them. ■ If you **divide** one number by another, you work out how many times the second one will go into the first. ■ If people are **divided** about something or it **divides** them, they disagree about it. ■ If someone has **divided loyalties,** they feel they have a duty towards two or more people and cannot choose between them. ■ A **divide** is a significant difference between people or things. ...the divide between classical music and jazz. ■ A **dividing line** is something which distinguishes one type of people or things from another. The 80-metre mark is the dividing line between throwers of true class and the rest.

dividend A **dividend** is a part of a company's profits which is paid to its shareholders.

dividers are an instrument for measuring and marking points along lines. They are made of two pointed arms joined together with a hinge.

divination is the supernatural ability some people claim to have to predict the future or find out other unknown information.

divine (divining, divined; divinely) **Divine** is used to talk about things connected with God, or with some other god or goddess. If people say something has happened as a result of **divine intervention,** they mean God made it happen. ■ If someone claims to have a **divine right** to something, they mean their right to it is decreed by God. ■ If you **divine** something, you sense it or find it out intuitively.

diving bell A **diving bell** is a chamber where people can work deep underwater. It is open underneath and is supplied with pressurized air by tube.

diving board A **diving board** is a board above a swimming pool which people can dive from.

divinity (divinities) **Divinity** is the study of the Christian religion. ■ **Divinity** is the quality of being divine. ■ A **divinity** is a god or goddess.

division When the **division** of something takes place, it is separated into two or more parts. ■ The **division** of something is its sharing among people or groups. ...the division of authority between federal and republican governments. ■ **Division** is disagreement within a group of people, or between groups. ■ A **division** is one of the groups of teams of a similar standard which make up a ieague. ■ A **division** is (a) a group of military units fighting as a single unit. (b) a section of a large organization dealing with one part of its business. ■ **Division** is the mathematical process of dividing one number by another.

divisional is used to talk about (a) things connected with a military division. ...a divisional commander. (b) things connected with one of the divisions of a business. ...the store's divisional manager for fashion.

divisive (divisiveness) If something is **divisive,** it makes people split into groups with opposite points of view. ...the divisiveness of party politics.

divorce (divorcing, divorced; divorcee) When someone **divorces** their husband or wife or gets a **divorce,** their marriage is legally ended. A **divorced** person or **divorcee** is someone whose marriage has ended in this way. ■ If one thing is **divorced** from another, it is separated from it.

divot A **divot** is a small piece of grass and earth which is dug out accidentally, especially by a golf club.

divulge (divulging, divulged) If you **divulge** secret or private information, you tell it to people.

Diwali (or Divali) **Diwali** (pron: di-wah-lee) is the major Hindu festival honouring Lakshmi, the goddess of wealth. It takes place in the Autumn. People give each other presents, and there is feasting and the lighting of lamps.

DIY or **do-it-yourself** is making or repairing things in your home. **DIY** and **do-it-yourself** are also used to talk about unqualified people doing things usually done by experts. ...a little legal DIY. ...do-it-yourself cholesterol tests.

dizzy (dizzying, dizziness) If you feel **dizzy,** you have a feeling of loss of balance. You say something is **dizzying** when it makes you feel like this. ■ If someone rises to **dizzy heights,** they become very successful and famous.

DJ See **disc jockey.**

DNA is an acid in the cells of living things. It contains a biological code which determines the characteristics of a person or other living thing. DNA stands for 'deoxyribonucleic acid'.

do (does, doing, did, have done) **Do** is used to form questions, negative statments, and short answers. 'Do not', 'does not', and 'did not' are often shortened to 'don't', 'doesn't', and 'didn't'. When did it happen?... You don't believe me, do you?... Don't worry... 'Does that surprise you?'—'Yes it does.' ■ **Do** is used instead of repeating a word. She knew more about Dorothy than I did. ■ **Do** is used to give emphasis. You really do deserve the award. ■ When you **do** something, you perform an action, activity, or task. ■ **Do** is used to say something has a particular result or effect. *Sulphur does far less damage to forests than car exhausts.* ■ **To do with** is used to say what something is related to or concerned with. *The attacks had nothing to do with drugs-related terrorism.* ■ If you say you **could do with** something, you mean you need it or it would be helpful. ■ If you **do without** something, you manage or survive in spite of not having it. ■ If you say something will **do,** you mean it is satisfactory. ■ If you have **done** with something, you have finished with it. ■ If you **do away** with something, you get rid of it. *...the proposal to do away with nuclear weapons.* ■ If someone **does away** with someone else, they kill them. ■ If you ask how someone or something is **doing,** you are asking how they are getting on. ■ If someone **does you out** of something you are entitled to, they cheat you out of it. ■ If you say something is **the done thing,** you mean it is respectable, fashionable, or usual to do it. ■ If food, especially meat, is **well done,** it has been cooked very thoroughly. ■ **make do with:** see **make.**

docile A **docile** person or animal is quiet and easily controlled.

dock A **dock** is an enclosed area of water where ships are loaded, unloaded, and repaired. When a ship **docks,** it comes into a dock. ■ When spaceships **dock,** they move together and connect. ■ In court, the **dock** is the place where the accused person stands or sits. ■ If your pay is **docked,** some of it is kept by your employer, for example because you have been absent from work. ■ If an animal's tail is **docked,** it is cut off.

docker – **Dockers** or **dock workers** are people who work at the docks, loading and unloading ships.

dockland The **dockland** of a large port is the area around its docks.

dockside The **dockside** area of a large port is the area next to its docks.

dockyard A **dockyard** is a place where ships are built, maintained, and repaired.

doctor (**doctorate, doctoral; doctoring, doctored**) A **doctor** is a person qualified in medicine who treats sick or injured people. In front of a person's name, 'Doctor' is usually shortened to 'Dr'. ■ **Doctor** is a title given to someone who has been awarded the highest kind of academic degree. This degree is called a **doctorate. Doctoral** work is completed to achieve this degree. ■ If something is **doctored,** it is deliberately changed, to deceive people. *...a doctored photograph.*

doctrinaire If someone is **doctrinaire,** they have fixed principles which they try to impose on other people.

doctrine (**doctrinal**) A **doctrine** is a principle or belief, or a set of principles or beliefs. **Doctrinal** means to do with doctrines. *...doctrinal disputes.*

docudrama A **docudrama** is a film based on actual events, with actors playing the parts of real people.

document A **document** is an official piece of paper containing written information. ■ If you **document** something, you make a detailed record of it.

documentary (**documentaries**) A **documentary** is a TV or radio programme or film which shows real events or gives information. ■ **Documentary** evidence is written evidence.

documentation is written permission or evidence.

docu-soap A **docu-soap** is a television documentary series which presents the lives of the people filmed as entertainment or drama.

doddering Old people are sometimes called **doddering** or **doddery,** especially when they are weak or unsteady.

doddle If you say something is a **doddle,** you mean it is extremely easy.

dodge (**dodging, dodged; dodger**) If you **dodge** something, you avoid doing it, dealing with it, or paying it. *Mr Baker dodged the question.* A **dodge** is a way of avoiding something. *...a tax dodge.* People who try to avoid doing things or paying for things are called **dodgers.** *...fare dodgers.* ■ If you **dodge** a moving object, you get out of its way quickly.

dodgem – **Dodgems** are small electric cars driven for fun in special enclosures at fairgrounds.

dodgy If you call something someone does **dodgy,** you mean it seems dishonest or not respectable. ■ You can call something **dodgy** when it is unreliable or of poor quality.

dodo (**dodos**) **Dodos** were large flightless birds which lived on the island of Mauritius. They became extinct in the 17th century.

doe The females of various animals, including deer, rabbits, and hares, are called **does.**

doer If you call someone a **doer,** you mean they do things, rather than just talking about them.

dog (**dogging, dogged**) **Dogs** are four-legged animals, kept as pets or for guarding or hunting. There are many different breeds. ■ The **dog** family includes wild animals like foxes, wolves, and hyenas, besides the dog kept by man. The male of any of these species is called a **dog,** to distinguish it from the female. ■ If you are **dogged** by something, it continually causes you trouble. *Her career has been dogged by ill health.* ■ See also **dogged.**

dog-collar A **dog-collar** is a stiff white collar which fastens at the back, worn by Christian priests and ministers.

dog-eared A **dog-eared** book has been used so much the corners of the pages are folded.

dogfight (**dogfighting**) A **dogfight** is a mid-air battle between two fighter aircraft. ■ When there is fierce competition for something, you can call this a **dogfight.** ■ **Dogfighting** is an illegal blood sport in which two specially trained dogs are allowed to fight to the death.

dogged (*pron:* **dog**-gid) (**doggedly**) If someone is **dogged,** they are persistent and do not give up easily.

doggerel You call poetry **doggerel** when it is of very poor quality.

dogma A **dogma** is a rigid belief or system of beliefs, especially one held by a religious or political group.

dogmatic (**dogmatically, dogmatist, dogmatism**) If someone is being **dogmatic,** they are following a set of principles rigidly, regardless of other people's opinions. Someone who behaves like this is called a **dogmatist;** their behaviour is called **dogmatism.**

do-gooder If you call someone a **do-gooder,** you mean they think they are helping people, but in fact they are just interfering.

doily (doilies) A **doily** is a decorative mat for a plate made of paper or cloth patterned with small holes.

doings Someone's **doings** are their activities. *...her business doings.*

do-it-yourself See **DIY.**

Dolby is a system which reduces the amount of background noise on a sound recording. 'Dolby' is a trademark.

doldrums If something is **in the doldrums,** it is in a depressed state.

dole (doling, doled) The **dole** is another name for unemployment benefit. ■ If you **dole** something **out,** you give amounts of it to several people or groups.

doleful (dolefully) If someone is **doleful,** they are depressed. *He shook his head dolefully.*

doll (dolled) A **doll** is a small model of a person or baby used as a child's toy. ■ A **doll's house** is a model house used as a toy. ■ If someone is **dolled up,** he or she is wearing eye-catching clothes.

dollar The **dollar** is the unit of currency in the US, Canada, Australia, New Zealand, and many other countries.

dollop A **dollop** of something is a large scoop of it.

dolphin – Dolphins are small whales with long snouts.

dolphinarium A **dolphinarium** is a large pool where trained dolphins and killer whales perform.

domain Someone's **domain** is the area they control. ■ If an activity or interest is the **domain** of a group of people, it is regarded as something they deal with, rather than anyone else.

dome (domed) A **dome** is a round roof shaped like half a ball. A **domed** building has a roof like this.

domestic (domestically) Domestic means happening within a country, rather than between that country and others. *...Canada's domestic air traffic.* ■ **Domestic** is used to talk about (a) things to do with the home and the family. *...domestic bliss.* (b) objects for use in the home. *...domestic appliances.* ■ A **domestic** is a person employed to cook and clean in someone's home. ■ **Domestic** animals are kept in people's homes or on farms as pets or to do work or provide food.

domesticate (domesticating, domesticated) When wild animals are **domesticated,** they are brought under human control and kept as pets or to do work or provide food. ■ If you say someone, especially a man, is **domesticated,** you mean they do household tasks like cooking and cleaning willingly.

domesticity is being at home with your family.

domestic science is the old-fashioned name for home economics.

domicile (domiciled) Your **domicile** or the place you are **domiciled,** is the place where you live. *...the Surrey-domiciled New Zealander.* ■ An organization's **domicile** or the place it is **domiciled,** is its location for tax and legal purposes.

dominant (dominance) You say someone is **dominant** or talk about their **dominance** (a) when they have a lot of power over others. *...a dominant figure in US politics.* (b) when they are more successful at something than other people. *...Wigan's dominance of the game.* ■ The **dominant** feature of something is its most noticeable feature.

dominate (dominating, dominated; domination) If an organization is **dominated** by a group of people, they are the most powerful ones in it. ■ If one country **dominates** another, it has control over it. ■ If someone **dominates** something like a sport, they are better at it than anyone else. ■ If a feature **dominates** a place or view, it is so large it draws your attention more than anything else. *His statue dominated the main square.*

domineering people like telling others what to do.

dominion If someone has **dominion** over people, they have control or authority over them.

domino (dominoes) A **domino** is a small flat rectangular block divided in two, with a number of spots in each half. A set of these blocks is used to play **dominoes,** a game in which players try to get rid of all their dominoes by matching up their halves. ■ When people talk about the **domino** effect, they mean a series of events in which each thing sets off the next one like a row of toppling dominoes.

don (donning, donned) A **don** is a lecturer at Oxford or Cambridge University. ■ If you **don** a piece of clothing, you put it on.

donate (donating, donated; donation) If you **donate** something, you give it for free; your gift is called a **donation.**

done See **do.**

doner kebab See **kebab.**

donkey The **donkey** is an animal related to the horse but smaller and with longer ears. ■ The **donkey work** is the boring part of a job which does not require much intelligence or imagination.

donkey jacket A **donkey jacket** is a workman's jacket with a waterproof panel across the shoulders.

donnish A **donnish** person is clever and rather serious.

donor A **donor** is someone who gives money or something else to a charity. ■ A **donor** is someone who allows organs to be removed from their body, either before or after their death, for use in transplants. ■ See also **blood donor.**

doodle (doodling, doodled) If you **doodle,** you draw a pattern or picture on the paper in front of you, often because you are bored. Drawings like these are called **doodles** or **doodlings.**

doom (dooming, doomed) Doom is used to talk about death or some other terrible situation which cannot be avoided. *The fish are lured to their doom.* *...forecasts of environmental doom.* You can say someone or something is **doomed** to something like this. *The species seems doomed to extinction.* ■ If you say something like a project was **doomed,** you mean it was certain to fail.

doomsayers are people who expect the worst to happen.

doomsday is the end of the world.

door A **door** is a swinging or sliding piece of wood, glass, or metal which is used to open and close the entrance to a building, room, cupboard, or vehicle. ■ If you **lay** something **at** someone's **door,** you blame them for it.

doorbell A **doorbell** is a bell on or near an outside door.

doorknob A **doorknob** is a round handle on a door, for opening it.

doorman (**doormen**) A **doorman** is a man whose job is to stand at the entrance of a place like a hotel or club, maintain security and help visitors.

doormat A **doormat** is a mat by a door for wiping your feet on. ■ If you say a person is a **doormat,** you mean they let others treat them badly.

doorstep (**doorstepping, doorstepped**) A **doorstep** is a step on the outside of a building, in front of a door. ■ When reporters **doorstep** someone, they wait outside their house or workplace, asking them questions when they go in or out. ■ If something is **on the doorstep** of a place, it is very near to it.

doorstop A **doorstop** is an object used to hold a door open.

door-to-door activities involve people calling at one house after another along a street, to sell things or get information.

doorway A **doorway** is the space left in a wall when a door is open.

dopamine (*pron:* **dop**-a-min) is a chemical in the brain which helps nerve impulses to travel from one nerve to another, or from a nerve to a muscle.

dope (**doping, doped**) **Dope** is any drugs taken illegally by sportspeople to improve their performance, or given to racehorses, to make them go faster or slow them down. All these practices are called **doping.** When a horse is given drugs, you say it is **doped.** ■ If someone **dopes** a person or animal, they put a drug in their food or drink to make them drowsy or unconscious. ■ **Dope** is another name for cannabis.

dopey means (a) half-asleep. (b) slow and rather stupid.

doppelgänger In myth and fairytale, a person's **doppelgänger** is a ghostly double. If someone looks exactly like someone else, you can say they are their **doppelgänger.**

dorm A **dorm** is a dormitory at a boarding school.

dormant If something is **dormant,** it is not active at present but might become so in the future. ...*a dormant volcano.*

dormer window A **dormer window** or **dormer** is an upright construction with a window projecting from a sloping roof.

dormitory (**dormitories**) A **dormitory** is a large room where a number of people sleep.

dormouse (**dormice**) The **dormouse** is a small animal similar to a mouse.

dorsal fin A fish's **dorsal fin** is the fin sticking up on top of its back.

dosage A **dosage** of a medicine is an amount taken at one time.

dose (**dosing, dosed**) A **dose** of a medicine or drug is an amount taken at one time. ■ If you **dose** a person or animal with drugs or medicine, you administer an amount to them.

dosh is money.

doss (**dosses, dossing, dossed**) If you **doss down** somewhere, especially in an uncomfortable place, you settle down to sleep there.

dosser A **dosser** is a person in the city who has no job or home.

doss-house A **doss-house** is a cheap unpleasant city hotel for homeless people.

dossier A **dossier** is a collection of papers containing information on a subject.

dot (**dotting, dotted**) A **dot** is a small round mark. ■ If things are **dotted** around an area, they are scattered around that place. ...*refugee camps dotted around Italy... The shoreline was dotted with lights.*

dotage If someone is **in their dotage,** they are very old and have lost some of their mental powers.

dotcom (*or* **dot.com**) A **dotcom** is a company that does most of its business on the Internet.

dote (**doting, doted**) If someone **dotes on** you, they are obsessively fond and affectionate towards you. ...*a doting father.*

doth is an old word for 'does'.

dot matrix printer A **dot matrix printer** is a computer printer using a device with a series of dots stamped onto it to produce words and numbers.

dotty If you say someone is **dotty,** you mean they are slightly mad.

double (**doubling, doubled**) **Double** is used to talk about pairs of similar things. ...*double yellow lines.* ■ **Double** is used to talk about things intended for two people. ...*a double bed.* ■ **Doubles** is a game of tennis or badminton played by two people against two other people. ■ If something is **double** the size of something else, it is twice as big. ■ If something **doubles** or is **doubled,** it becomes twice as large. ■ A **double** portion of food or drink is twice as big as a normal portion. ■ A person's **double** is someone who looks just like them. ■ If something **doubles** as something else, it is used as that thing, in addition to its main use. ■ If someone is **bent double,** they are bending right over.

double-act A **double-act** is a team of two people, especially comedians, who work together.

double agent A **double agent** is a spy who works for two opposing countries at the same time.

double-barrelled (*Am:* **double-barreled**) A **double-barrelled** shotgun has two barrels. Only one can be fired at a time. ■ A **double-barrelled** surname has two parts joined by a hyphen, for example 'Miss J. Hunter-Dunne'.

double bass The **double bass** is a large stringed musical instrument shaped like a violin.

double bill A **double bill** is a theatre or cinema performance or a sporting event in which there are two main items.

double bluff A **double bluff** is an attempt to deceive people by telling them the truth, knowing they will assume you are lying.

double-book If theatre seats or hotel rooms are **double-booked,** the theatre or hotel accidentally books the same seats or rooms to two sets of people.

double-breasted A **double-breasted** suit has buttons on each of the overlapping sections of the jacket.

double-check If you **double-check** something, you check it twice, in case you missed something the first time.

double chin If someone has a **double chin,** they have a fold of loose skin under their chin.

double-cross If someone **double-crosses** you, they betray you instead of doing what they had promised.

double-dealing is deceitful or treacherous behaviour.

double-decker A **double-decker** is a bus with two floors. ■ **Double-decker** is used to describe things with two levels. ...*a double-decker conservatory.* ...*double-decker sandwiches.*

double-edged If you say a remark is **double-edged,** you mean it could be taken two ways, one of which is not very pleasant. ■ If you say something is **double-edged** or a **double-edged sword,** you mean it has disadvantages as well as advantages.

double entendre (*pron:* **doob**-bl on-**tond**-ra) You call something someone says a **double entendre** when it has two meanings, one of which is rude and often sexual.

double-glaze (**double-glazing, double-glazed**) If you **double-glaze** windows or fit them with **double-glazing,** you fit them with a second layer of glass to keep the house warm or quiet.

double header In sport, a **double header** is (a) two separate contests one after the other on the same occasion. (b) two consecutive matches between the same two teams.

double life If you say someone is leading a **double life,** you mean they have a secret private life which is very different from their public one.

double-quick If something happens in **double-quick** time, it happens very quickly indeed.

double standards If you say someone is applying **double standards,** you mean they are unfairly treating one group of people differently from another.

doublet A **doublet** was a short tight-fitting jacket worn by men in the 15th, 16th, and 17th centuries. See also **hose.**

double-take If you do a **double-take,** you are very surprised at something, and have to think twice about it or look at it again.

double talk If you accuse someone of **double talk,** you mean they are deliberately trying to deceive or confuse people, by saying things which can be taken two ways.

double-think is the ability to hold contradictory beliefs, and to ignore the fact that they cannot both be true.

double vision If you have **double vision,** you see two images of everything you look at, for example because of a blow to the head.

double whammy (**double whammies**) A **double whammy** is two problems or mistakes, one coming straight after the other.

doubly means 'twice as', and usually indicates that there are two reasons for something. *Trying to block them now would be doubly difficult.*

doubt is a feeling of uncertainty. If you have **doubts** about something or are **in doubt** about it, you are unsure about it. ■ If you **doubt** something, you think it is probably not true. ■ If you say something is **in doubt** or **open to doubt,** you mean it is uncertain. ■ If you say something is **beyond doubt,** you mean it is definitely true. ■ **benefit of the doubt:** see **benefit.**

doubter You call people **doubters** when they are unwilling to believe something.

doubtful (**doubtfully**) If something is **doubtful,** it seems unlikely or uncertain. ■ If you are **doubtful** about something, you are unsure about it.

doubtless (**doubtlessly**) You say **doubtless** or **doubtlessly** when you are assuming something is true. *She is doubtlessly a strong and worthy, if prickly, contender.*

douche (*pron:* **doosh**) (**douches, douching**) A **douche** is a method of washing in which a jet of water is directed into the vagina. Washing like this is called **douching.**

dough is a mixture, mainly of flour and water, which is cooked to make bread, pastry, or biscuits.

doughnut A **doughnut** is a lump or ring of sweet dough cooked in hot fat.

doughty (*pron:* **dowt**-ee) is used to describe people who are brave and determined.

dour (*pron:* **doo**-er *or* **dow**-er) (**dourly, dourness**) **Dour** people are stern and unfriendly.

douse (**dousing, doused**) If you **douse** something with liquid, you throw the liquid over it. ■ If you **douse** a fire, you stop it burning.

dove – **Doves** are birds of the pigeon family. They are smaller than most pigeons and are often white. ■ In politics, a **dove** is someone who believes a problem should be solved by peaceful means, rather than by war or threats. See also **hawk.**

dovecote (*or* dovecot) A **dovecote** is a shelter or part of a house built for doves or pigeons to live in.

dovetail (**dovetailing, dovetailed**) If you **dovetail** things, you get them to work together. *It is important that we dovetail our respective interests.* ■ In carpentry, a **dovetail joint** is a wedge-shaped joint for fitting pieces of wood tightly together.

dowager When a duke or other nobleman dies and his title is passed on, his widow keeps her own title but adds **Dowager** to it. ...*the Dowager Viscountess Hambleden.*

dowdy If you call someone **dowdy,** you mean they are wearing dull and unfashionable clothes. ■ A **dowdy** place is shabbily decorated or badly lit.

Dow Jones The **Dow-Jones index** or the **Dow-Jones average** is an index of share prices based on the average price of shares in 30 American companies on the New York Stock Exchange. It is used to check general changes in share prices.

down is used to talk about movement towards a lower place. *John came briskly down the steps.* ■ If you **down** an alcoholic drink, you drink it. ■ If workers **down tools,** they stop working and go on strike. ■ If an aircraft is **downed,** it is shot down. ■ If an amount goes **down,** it gets lower. ■ **Down to** a particular detail means including everything, even that detail. *The suite was lavishly furnished down* *to the last ash-tray.* ■ If a computer is **down,** it is not working. ■ If you are feeling **down,** you are depressed. ■ **Down** is the small soft feathers on young birds, often used as stuffing in pillows and quilts.

down-and-out A **down-and-out** is a poor and homeless person.

down-at-heel people wear old shabby clothes, because they cannot afford new ones. Similarly, a **down-at-heel** place has a shabby look, because no money has been spent on it.

downbeat behaviour is deliberately casual and restrained. *He was in a curiously downbeat mood.*

downcast If someone is **downcast,** they are sad, disappointed, and pessimistic.

downer – Downers are drugs which make you feel sleepy or calm, for example barbiturates. ■ If you say you are **on a downer,** you mean you feel depressed.

downfall The **downfall** of a person or institution is their loss of success or power. The thing which causes this loss can also be called their **downfall.** *His pride may be his downfall.*

downgrade (**downgrading, downgraded**) If someone or something is **downgraded,** their importance or value is reduced.

downhearted If you are **downhearted,** you feel sad and discouraged.

downhill If something is moving **downhill,** it is moving down a slope. ■ If you say something is going **downhill,** you mean it is getting worse. *Since he's been manager the team's gone downhill.*

Downing Street is the London street where the Prime Minister and the Chancellor of the Exchequer live. **Downing Street** can be used to mean the Prime Minister and his or her officials.

download (**downloading, downloaded**) In computing, if you **download** data or a program from a central source, you transfer it to your own computer.

down-market If you describe a product or service as **downmarket,** you mean it is cheap and of poor quality.

down payment A **down payment** is a sum of money paid as a deposit when you buy something. The remaining amount is paid later.

downplay If you **downplay** something, you try to make it seem less important.

downpour A **downpour** is a heavy fall of rain.

downright is used to emphasize that something is extremely bad. *...downright dangerous.*

downs are low rounded grassy hills.

downside The **downside** of something is its bad side.

Down's syndrome is a medical condition caused by an additional chromosome being present in a baby. Sufferers typically have sloping eyes, a flat forehead, and short stocky build, together with limited mental ability.

downstairs If something is **downstairs,** it is on the ground floor of a building, or on a lower floor than you. ■ **Downstairs** rooms are situated on the ground floor of a building.

downstream If something is moving **downstream,** it is moving towards the mouth of a river from a point further up.

downswing If there is a **downswing** in a country's economy, there is a sudden decline in its success.

downtime In industry, **downtime** is the time when equipment is not operating. *On the production line, downtime has been reduced from 55% to 26%.*

down-to-earth people are concerned with sensible practical things.

downtown places are in or towards the centre of a city.

downtrodden is used to describe people who have been so badly treated by those with power that they do not have the will to fight back.

downturn A **downturn** is a decline in the success of an economy or a business.

down under You can use **down under** to refer to Australia and New Zealand.

downward (**downwards**) If you move or look **downwards,** you move or look towards the ground or a lower level. You can also talk about a **downward** look or movement. ■ If an amount or rate moves **downwards,** it decreases. You can also talk about a **downward** movement or trend.

downwind If someone or something is moving **downwind,** they are moving in the same direction as the wind. If someone or something is **downwind,** the wind is blowing towards them.

dowry (**dowries**) A woman's **dowry** is money or property which, in some cultures, her family gives to the man she marries.

dowsing (**dowsers**) **Dowsing** is a procedure by which people search for underground water or mineral deposits by holding a special stick or pendulum over a place. A person who does this is called a **dowser.**

doyen (**doyenne**) The **doyen** of a group or profession is the most senior and respected man in it. A woman with this status is called the **doyenne.**

doze (**dozing, dozed**) If you **doze** or have a **doze,** you sleep lightly, or for short periods. ■ If you **doze off,** you fall asleep.

dozen A **dozen** is twelve. ■ You can talk about **dozens** of people or things when you want to emphasize that there are a great many.

dozy If someone is **dozy,** they are not alert.

DPP See **Director of Public Prosecutions.**

Dr See **doctor.**

drab (**drabness**) If you say something is **drab,** you mean it is dull and unattractive.

drachma The **drachma** is the unit of currency in Greece.

draconian laws or measures are extremely harsh.

draft (**drafter**) If you **draft** a piece of writing or a speech, you prepare an early version of it. This version is called a **draft.** ■ When people **draft** a plan or agreement, they draw it up. The people who do this are called the **drafters** of the plan or agreement. ■ In the US, if someone is **drafted** or selected for the **draft,** they are conscripted into the armed forces. ■ If people are **drafted in** to a place, they are moved there to do a particular job. ■ See also **draught.**

draftsman See **draughtsman.**

drag (**dragging, dragged**) If you **drag** something somewhere, you pull it there along the ground. ■ You can say you are **dragged** somewhere when you are made to go there unwillingly. You can also say you are **dragged into** an unpleasant situation. ■ If you say something is a **drag,** you mean it is a nuisance. ■ If something **drags,** it seems to last a long time, because it is boring. ■ If you **drag** something **out,** you make it last longer than necessary. ■ If you say someone is **dragging their feet,** you mean they are deliberately taking a long time over something. ■ If something is **a drag on** something else, it slows it down. ■ If a man is **in drag,** he is dressed up as a woman.

dragnet A police **dragnet** is a concentrated search of an area using extra forces in order to try to capture a suspect.

dragon A **dragon** is a mythical monster like a big lizard. It has wings and breathes out fire.

dragonfly (**dragonflies**) **Dragonflies** are large brightly-coloured insects with long bodies and two pairs of wings.

dragoon (**dragooning, dragooned**) In the past, certain kinds of soldiers were called **dragoons.** ■ If you are **dragooned** into doing something, you are made to do it.

drag racing is a sport in which people try to achieve fast times driving specially built cars or motor bikes over very short distances.

drain (**draining, drained**) When a wet place or object is **drained,** liquid is drawn from it. ■ A **drain** is a pipe which carries water or sewage away. ■ If you **drain** a glass, you drink all the liquid in it. ■ If you are **drained,** you feel tired and weak. ■ If something is a **drain** on resources, it uses them up. ■ If something like a feeling **drains away,** it decreases until there is none left.

drainage is the system or process by which liquids are drained away from a place.

draining board A **draining board** is the part of a sink unit where you put the clean dishes to drain.

drainpipe A **drainpipe** is a pipe down the outside of a building, through which water flows into a drain.

drake A **drake** is a male duck.

dram A **dram** is a small measure of whisky or some other spirit.

drama A **drama** is a serious play for the theatre, TV, or radio. **Drama** is used to refer to plays in general. *...studying drama at Bristol University.* ■ **Drama** is used to talk about exciting aspects of real situations. *...the drama of the budget crisis.*

dramatic (**dramatically**) A **dramatic** change is sudden and striking. ■ **Dramatic** events are exciting or alarming. ■ **Dramatic** means to do with theatre, drama, or plays. *...the American Musical and Dramatic Academy.*

dramatise See **dramatize.**

dramatis personae (*pron:* drah-mat-tiss per-**soh**-nigh) The **dramatis personae** of a play is the list of characters in that play.

dramatist A **dramatist** is someone who writes plays.

dramatize (*or* **dramatise**) (**dramatizing, dramatized; dramatization**) If a book is **dramatized,** it is rewritten as a play or film. ■ If someone **dramatizes** a situation, they try to make it seem more serious or exciting than it is.

drank See **drink.**

drape (**draping, draped**) If a piece of cloth is **draped** over something, the cloth is placed over it so that it hangs down gracefully. ■ In the US, curtains are called **drapes.**

draper A **draper** or **draper's** is a shop which sells cloth and household linen.

drapery (**draperies**) is used to talk about cloth or clothing hanging in folds.

drastic (**drastically**) If you take **drastic** action, you do something extreme, usually because you have to. ■ If something **drastic** happens to you, you suffer badly because of it. ■ A **drastic** change is sudden, striking, and usually for the worse.

draught (*Am:* **draft**) (**draughty**) If there are **draughts** or a place is **draughty,** cold currents of air are coming in. ■ **Draught** beer and cider are served from barrels. Drinks served like this are **on draught.** ■ **Draught** animals, are large animals like horses, which pull heavy loads. ■ **Draughts** is a game for two played on a chequered board. To win the game, you have to capture all your opponent's pieces.

draughtboard A **draughtboard** is a square chequered board for playing draughts on.

draughtsman (*Am:* **draftsman**) (**draughtsmen; draughtsmanship**) A **draughtsman** is a person whose job involves the preparation of technical drawings. ■ **Draughtsmanship** is the ability to draw well.

draw (**drawing, drew, have drawn**) If you **draw** a picture, pattern, or diagram, you create it using a pencil, pen, or crayon. A **drawing** is a picture created like this. ■ **Draw** is used to say someone or something slowly comes nearer or moves away. *Her train drew away.* ■ If something like a cart is **drawn** by an animal, the animal is pulling it. ■ If you **draw** a curtain or blind, you pull it across a window to cover or uncover it. ■ If someone **draws** a gun, sword, or knife, they pull it out, ready for use. ■ If you **draw** a breath, you take air into your lungs. ■ If you **draw on** a cigarette, you suck it and breathe in the smoke. ■ If something like a blow **draws blood,** it causes bleeding. ■ If something such as money, water, or energy is **drawn** from a source, it is taken from it. ■ If you **draw** a conclusion, you come to it after considering the facts. ■ If you **draw** a comparison, parallel, or distinction between two things, you compare or contrast them. ■ If someone **draws** something to your attention, they point it out to you. ■ If people are **drawn** by something, they are attracted by it. ■ If you are **drawn into** something, you become involved in it. ■ If you **draw up** a document, list, or plan, you prepare it and write it out. ■ In a competition, if two people or teams **draw,** they get the same number of points, runs, or goals. You can also say the competition ends in a **draw.** ■ If someone looks **drawn,**

drawback they look tired and worried. ■ **draw a blank:** see **blank.**

drawback A **drawback** is a snag or difficulty which makes something less than ideal. *The main drawback is its weight.*

drawbridge A **drawbridge** is a bridge which can be pulled up or lowered.

drawer A **drawer** is a box-shaped part of a piece of furniture which slides in and out.

drawing board A **drawing board** is a large flat board, often on a metal frame. You fix paper on it when you are drawing or designing something. ■ If you say you have to go **back to the drawing board,** something you have done has not succeeded and you have to start again.

drawing pin A **drawing pin** is a small pin with a broad circular top, used for such things as pinning notices to walls.

drawing room A **drawing room** is a room in a large house where people relax or entertain guests.

drawl If someone **drawls** or speaks with a **drawl,** they speak slowly, making each word longer than usual.

drawn-out If something is **drawn-out,** it lasts a long time.

drawstring A **drawstring** is a cord which goes through a seam round an opening, for example at the top of a bag. When the cord is pulled tighter, the opening gets smaller.

dray A **dray** is a low cart for carrying heavy loads, pulled by horses also called **drays.**

dread (**dreading, dreaded**) If you **dread** something which is going to happen or likely to happen, you are anxious or frightened about it. This feeling is called **dread. Dread** and **dreaded** are used to describe things which make people feel like this. *...dread diseases.*

dreadful (**dreadfully, dreadfulness**) If you say something is **dreadful,** you mean it is extremely unpleasant or evil. ■ You say something is **dreadful** when it is of very poor quality. ■ **Dreadfully** is used to emphasize a bad quality. *It seems dreadfully expensive.*

dreadlocks If someone has **dreadlocks,** they have their hair in long matted or tightly curled strands.

dream (**dreaming, dreamed** *or* **dreamt**) If you **dream** or have a **dream,** you have experiences in your mind while you are asleep. ■ A **dream** is something you often think about and would love to happen. *As a schoolgirl she had dreamed of becoming an actress.* ■ If you call a place a **dream world,** you mean it seems very strange and unreal, like a dream. ■ You say you **would not dream** of doing something to emphasize that you would never consider doing it. ■ If you think a new invention or idea is strange or silly, you can say someone has **dreamed** it **up.**

dreamer You say someone is a **dreamer** when they are always looking forward to pleasant things which might never happen.

dreamily See **dreamy.**

dreamlike See **dreamy.**

dreamt See **dream.**

dreamy (**dreamily, dreamlike**) If someone's expression is **dreamy,** they look as though they are thinking about something pleasant. ■ If something is **dreamy** or **dreamlike,** it seems strange and unreal, like a dream.

dreary (**dreariest; drearily, dreariness**) You say something is **dreary** when it is dull and makes you feel bored or depressed.

dredge (**dredging, dredged; dredger**) When a river, harbour, or other water is **dredged,** mud and other unwanted material is removed from the bottom. A **dredger** is a boat fitted with machinery for doing this. ■ When police divers **dredge** an area of water, they search it thoroughly for a body or for evidence. ■ If you **dredge up** an old memory, you manage to recall it.

dregs The **dregs** are what is left at the bottom of a container when all the liquid has been poured out. ■ If you call someone or something the **dregs,** you mean they are the worst examples of their kind. *...the dregs of society.*

drench (**drenches, drenching, drenched**) If you are **drenched** by something like rain, you get very wet. ■ A **sun-drenched** place has a lot of sunshine.

dress (**dresses, dressing, dressed**) When you **dress,** you put on your clothes. ■ If you are **dressed,** you are wearing clothes. You can also be **dressed** in a particular way. *He is always elegantly dressed. ...a man dressed as a police officer.* ■ If you **dress** up, you put on different clothes, to look like someone else or to look smarter. ■ A **dress** is a piece of clothing worn by a woman or girl which covers her body and extends down over her legs. ■ If you **dress** something **up,** you add something superficial to it, to make it more acceptable. ■ If you **dress** someone's wounds, you clean them and put protective coverings called **dressings** on them. ■ A salad **dressing** is a mixture of oil, vinegar, and herbs or flavourings, which you pour over a salad.

dressage (*pron:* **dress**-ahzh; *the 'zh' sounds like 's' in 'pleasure'*) In horse-riding, **dressage** is the performance of controlled movements by the horse in response to signals from the rider.

dress circle The **dress circle** is the first level of seats above the ground floor in a theatre.

dresser A **dresser** is a piece of furniture with cupboards or drawers in the lower part and shelves in the top part. ■ You can use **dresser** to talk about the kind of clothes someone wears. For example, you can say someone is a 'neat dresser'. ■ A **dresser** is someone who works in a theatre, helping actors to dress.

dressing-down If you give someone a **dressing-down,** you tell them off.

dressing gown A **dressing gown** is a long loose-fitting coat worn over nightclothes when you are not in bed.

dressing room A **dressing room** is a room in a theatre in which actors can get themselves ready for a performance.

dressing table A **dressing table** is a small bedroom table with drawers and a mirror.

dressmaker (**dressmaking**) A **dressmaker** is a person who makes women's and children's clothes for a living.

dress rehearsal A **dress rehearsal** of a play, opera, or show is the final rehearsal. The performers wear their costumes and lights and scenery are used. ■ You can say something is a **dress rehearsal** for a later event when it has similar features but is less important.

dress shirt A **dress shirt** is a smart shirt worn by a man with a dinner jacket and a bow tie on special occasions.

drew See **draw.**

dribble (**dribbling, dribbled**) When a liquid **dribbles** down a surface, it moves down it in a thin stream. A **dribble** of liquid is a thin stream of it. ■ When a person or animal **dribbles,** saliva trickles from their mouth. ■ When footballers **dribble,** they move with the ball, keeping it under close control.

dribs and drabs If people or things arrive in **dribs and drabs,** they arrive in small numbers over a period of time.

dried See **dry.**

drier (**driest**) See **dry.**

drift When something **drifts** somewhere, it is carried there by the movement of wind or water. ■ A **drift** is a snowdrift, or a pile of other material created by the wind. ...*great drifts of leaves.* ■ When people **drift** somewhere, they move there slowly and without a sense of purpose. ■ If people are **drifting** towards a bad situation, they are slowly getting into it. ...*a drift towards political instability.* ■ If something **drifts away** from you, you gradually lose it. *There is a danger that control will drift away from shareholders.* ■ If you **drift off** to sleep, you gradually fall asleep.

drifter A **drifter** is a person who does not stay in one place or job for long. ■ A **drifter** is a fishing boat that catches herring. It uses a very long net called a **drift net.**

driftwood is wood floating on the sea or a river, or washed up on the shore.

drill When you **drill** something, you make a hole in it using a tool called a **drill.** ■ When people **drill** for oil or water, they search for it by drilling deep holes in the ground or the sea bed. ■ When people carry out a **drill,** they practise doing the things they are supposed to do in an emergency. ...*a fire drill.* ■ If people are **well-drilled,** they have practised and know exactly what to do in a certain situation. ■ When people in the armed forces **drill,** they march and move together in response to commands.

drily See **dry.**

drink (**drinking, drank, have drunk**) When you **drink** a liquid, you take it into your mouth and swallow it. ■ A **drink** is an amount of liquid in a cup or glass for someone to drink. ■ **Drinking** is used to talk about drinking alcohol. *She smokes and drinks too much.* ■ **Drink** is any alcoholic drink like whisky, wine, or beer. ■ See also **drunk.**

drinkable water is clean and safe to drink. ■ If you say some other drink is **drinkable,** you mean it is not especially good, but at least it is not too unpleasant to drink.

drink-driving is breaking the law by driving a vehicle with more than a certain level of alcohol in your bloodstream.

drinker A **drinker** is someone who drinks alcohol, especially a lot of it. ■ The **drinkers** in a place are the people having a drink there. ■ **Drinker** is used to talk about people who regularly drink particular drinks. ...*coffee drinkers.*

drinking fountain A **drinking fountain** is a device, usually in a public place, which supplies drinking water.

drinking water is water which is safe to drink.

drip (**dripping, dripped**) When something **drips** or liquid **drips** from it, drops of liquid fall from it. ■ If something is **dripping** wet, it is very wet indeed. ■ A **drip** is a piece of medical equipment by which a liquid is slowly passed through a tube into a patient's bloodstream. ■ **Dripping** is the fat which comes out of meat when it is fried or roasted.

drive (**driving, drove, have driven**) If you **drive** a vehicle, you control its movement. ■ A **drive** is a journey by car. ■ A **drive** is the same as a driveway. ■ You say something **drives** a machine when it supplies the power to make it work. ■ You say something **drives** a system when it keeps it going. *It is conflict that drives the arms trade.* ■ If something **drives** you to do something, it makes you do it. ■ If people or animals are **driven** somewhere, they are gathered together and forced to go there. ■ If you **drive** a post or nail into something, you hammer it in forcefully. ■ If you **drive** a ball in a game like cricket or golf, you hit it straight and hard. A shot like this is called a **drive.** ■ **Drive** is energy and determination. ■ A **drive** is a special effort by a group of people to achieve something. ...*recruiting drives.* ■ **drive home:** see **home.**

drive-in places offer a service which people can use without getting out of their cars. ...*a drive-in cinema.*

drivel If you call what someone says **drivel,** you mean it is silly and tedious.

driven See **drive.**

driver A **driver** is someone who drives a vehicle.

drive shaft In a motor vehicle, the **drive shaft** is a rotating rod which turns the wheels and is connected to the gearbox.

driveway A **driveway** is a private road, usually a short one, leading from a public road to someone's house or garage.

driving seat The **driving seat** in a car is the seat where the driver sits. ■ You can talk about the person **in the driving seat** when you mean the person in charge.

drizzle (**drizzling, drizzled; drizzly**) Drizzle is light rain. When it is raining like this, you say it is **drizzling** or **drizzly.**

droll (*pron:* **drole**) is used to describe humour which is witty but calm and restrained.

dromedary (*usual pron:* **drom**-mid-er-ee) A **dromedary** is a one-humped camel.

drone (**droning, droned**) If something **drones,** it makes a low continuous humming noise. ...*the continual drone of aircraft.* ■ If someone **drones on**

about something, they talk about it at length in a boring way. ■ A **drone** is a male bee. ■ People who work hard at dull routine jobs are sometimes called **drones.**

drool (**drooling, drooled**) If someone **drools,** saliva falls from their lips. ■ You say someone is **drooling** when they show their eagerness for something in a ridiculously obvious way. *Politicians began drooling with expectation.*

droop (**drooping, drooped; droopy**) If something **droops** or is **droopy,** it hangs or leans downwards with no strength or firmness.

drop (**dropping, dropped**) A **drop** of liquid is a very small amount, shaped like a tiny ball. ■ If something **drops** or is **dropped,** it falls straight down. ■ A **drop** is a vertical distance between the top and bottom of something like a cliff. ■ If an amount **drops** or there is a **drop** in it, it suddenly gets lower. ■ If you **drop** your voice, you start speaking more quietly. ■ If you **drop** what you are doing, you stop doing it. ■ If you **drop out** of something, you give it up before completing it. ■ If someone is **dropped** from a team, they are left out of it. ■ In a competition, if you **drop** a game or point, you lose it. ■ If you **drop** a hint, you give it in a casual way. ■ If you **drop** someone **a line,** you write to them. ■ If a vehicle **drops** you somewhere or **drops** you **off,** it takes you there. ■ If someone **drops by** or **drops in,** they call on you, usually unannounced. ■ If you **drop off,** you fall asleep.

drop-dead If you describe someone as, for example, **drop-dead** gorgeous, you think they are so gorgeous that people cannot fail to notice them. You can also use **drop-dead** to emphasize an attractive quality of someone or something. *...the drop-dead glamour of the designer decade.*

droplet A **droplet** is a very small drop of liquid.

drop-out (*or* **dropout**) **Drop-outs** are people who reject the accepted ways of society, especially by choosing not to do a regular job. ■ **Drop-outs** are people who have left school or university without completing their studies.

dropper A **dropper** is a small tube with a rubber bulb on one end. It is used to suck up and release small amounts of liquid.

droppings are the faeces of birds and small animals.

dropsy is a medical problem in which parts of the body become swollen with fluid. It can be caused by various illnesses.

dross If you call something **dross,** you mean it is of very poor quality. ■ **Dross** is the waste material left floating on the surface when a metal like gold has been melted.

drought or a **drought** is a long period when there is no rain.

drove See **drive.** ■ If you say people are doing something **in droves,** you mean very large numbers of them are doing it.

drown When someone **drowns,** they die underwater because they cannot breathe. ■ If one sound **drowns out** another, the one sound is so much louder that you cannot hear the other.

drowsy If you feel **drowsy,** you feel sleepy.

drubbing If someone is given a **drubbing** in a contest, they are humiliatingly beaten.

drudgery (**drudge**) **Drudgery** is boring repetitive work. A **drudge** is someone who does work like this.

drug (**drugging, drugged**) A **drug** is a chemical given to people to treat or prevent illness or disease. ■ **Drugs** are substances, especially illegal ones, which people take to enjoy their effects. ■ If someone is **drugged,** they are given a drug which makes them sleepy or unconscious.

drugstore In the US, a **drugstore** is a shop where you can buy things like medicine, cosmetics, newspapers, and snacks.

druid – **Druids** were priests of a pre-Christian religion in Britain, Ireland, and France. Modern followers of this religion also call themselves **druids.**

drum (**drumming, drummed**) A **drum** is a musical instrument consisting of a skin stretched tightly over a round frame. ■ If you **drum** on a surface, you hit it regularly, making a continuous beating sound. ■ If you **drum** something **into** someone, you keep saying it, to make them remember it. ■ If you **drum up** support for something, you go round getting people to support it. Similarly, you can **drum up** business.

drumbeat A **drumbeat** is the sound of a beat on a drum.

drum majorette See **majorette.**

drummer A **drummer** is someone who plays a drum.

drum roll A **drum roll** is a series of drumbeats following each other rapidly.

drumstick A **drumstick** is (a) a thin rod for beating a drum. (b) the lower part of the leg of a cooked bird like a chicken.

drunk See **drink.** ■ If someone is **drunk,** they cannot behave sensibly as they have drunk too much alcohol. A **drunk** is someone who is drunk or often gets drunk.

drunkard A **drunkard** is someone who gets drunk too often.

drunken (**drunkenly, drunkenness**) **Drunken** is used to describe drunks and their behaviour.

dry (**dryer** *or* **drier, driest; dryly** *or* **drily; dryness; dries, drying, dried**) If something is **dry,** it has no liquid in or on it. ■ When you **dry** something or when it **dries** or **dries out,** it becomes dry. ■ If the weather is **dry,** there is no rain. A **dryer** is a machine which dries things. ■ When a supply of things **dries up,** it stops. ■ **Dry** is used to describe less sweet varieties of some alcoholic drinks. *...dry gin.* ■ **Dry** humour is subtle and sarcastic.

dry-clean (**dry cleaner**) When clothes are **dry-cleaned,** they are cleaned using a liquid chemical rather than water. A **dry cleaner** or **dry cleaner's** is a shop where clothes are dry-cleaned.

dry dock A **dry dock** is one from which water can be removed so a ship can be repaired.

dry ice is solid carbon dioxide used to keep food cold and create smoke effects.

dry rot is a rapid-spreading disease caused by a fungus which turns timber brittle and powdery.

dry-run A **dry-run** is a trial to see if something works properly.

dry-stone wall A **dry-stone wall** is built by fitting loose stones together without using mortar.

D.Sc. A **D.Sc.** is the highest degree awarded by a university in the sciences. D.Sc. stands for 'Doctor of Science'.

DSS The **DSS** or **Department of Social Security** is the government department responsible for benefit payments.

DTs If alcoholics get the **DTs**, they shake uncontrollably and may see hallucinations. DT stands for 'delirium tremens'.

dual is used to talk about things which have two parts, functions, or aspects. *The irrigation canals served a dual purpose.*

dual carriageway A **dual carriageway** is a road with a grass or concrete strip down the middle.

dualism and **duality** are used to talk about something having two parts or aspects. *...the traditional Christian dualism between body and soul.*

dub (**dubbing, dubbed**) If you **dub** someone something, you give them that name. ■ If a film is **dubbed**, the actors voices are replaced with the voices of actors speaking a different language. ■ **Dub** is a style of music originally associated with reggae. It is mainly characterized by a lot of echo and bass.

dubious (**dubiously**) If you say something is **dubious**, you do not think it is completely honest, respectable, or reliable. *Some of their wins have been dubiously gained.* ■ If you say something is a **dubious** pleasure, you mean you are not sure it is really a pleasure at all. Similarly, you can talk about something being a **dubious** distinction or honour. ■ If you are **dubious** about a proposal, you are not sure it is a good idea.

ducal (*pron:* **duke**-al) means belonging to or connected with a duke. *...the old ducal palace.*

duchess (**duchesses**) A **duchess** is a duke's wife, or a woman with an equivalent title in her own right.

duchy (**duchies**) A **duchy** is an area of land owned or ruled by a duke or duchess.

duck A **duck** is a water bird with short legs, webbed feet, and a large flat beak. **Duck** is the meat of a duck. ■ When you **duck**, you suddenly move your head downwards in order to avoid being hit or seen. ■ If someone **ducks** someone else, they force them under water for a short time. ■ If someone **ducks** a responsibility, they avoid it. If they **duck** an issue, they avoid thinking about it. ■ In cricket, if a batsman is out for a **duck**, he or she is out without scoring any runs. ■ **lame duck: see lame.**

duckling A **duckling** is a young duck.

duct (**ducting**) A **duct** is (a) a tube or channel for a liquid or gas to pass through. (b) a tube in your body which a liquid passes through.

ducting is a system of ducts.

dud If something is a **dud**, it does not work properly.

dude A **dude** is a man, especially a man who is considered cool.

dudgeon If someone is **in high dudgeon**, they are angry or resentful.

due If something is **due** to something else, it exists or happens as a result of it. ■ If something is **due** at a certain time, it is expected to happen or arrive then. ■ **Dues** are sums of money you pay regularly to an organization you belong to. ■ If some money is **due** to you, you have a right to it. ■ **Due** is used with words like 'respect' and 'consideration' to mean 'an appropriate amount of'. *Governors have to give such advice due consideration.* ■ **Due** is used to talk about exact compass directions. For example, 'due north' means exactly to the north. ■ See also **due process.**

duel (**duelling, duelled**) (*Am:* **dueling, dueled**) A **duel** is a fight in which two people use guns or swords to settle a quarrel. When people **duel**, they fight like this. ■ You can call any contest between two people or groups a **duel.**

due process In the US, **due process** or **due process of law** means the procedures set out in the Constitution to protect an individual's rights and freedom. ■ **Due process** means done in accordance with rules and regulations. *He was removed from office by due process and without bloodshed.*

duet A **duet** is a piece of music for two people.

duff things are no good.

duffel bag A **duffel bag** is a tube-shaped shoulder bag with a drawstring around the top which is also attached to the bottom.

duffel coat A **duffel coat** is a hooded coat with toggles down the front.

duffer If you call someone a **duffer**, you mean they are a very slow learner, or not very bright generally.

dug See **dig.**

dug-out (*or* **dugout**) The **dug-out** at a football ground is a shelter at the side of the pitch where managers and substitutes sit during games. ■ A **dug-out** is a shelter made by digging a hole in the ground and covering it with a roof. ■ A **dug-out** canoe is made by hollowing out a log.

duke A **duke** is a male aristocrat ranking just below a prince.

dull (**dullness**) If someone or something is **dull**, they are not interesting or exciting. ■ You can say someone is **dull** when they are slow to learn or understand. ■ If something is **dull**, it is not bright, sharp, or clear. *...dull weather. ...dull pain. ...a dull thud.* ■ If something **dulls** a feeling or sensation, it makes it less intense. *Drugs dulled the pain.*

duly is used to say something is done according to the correct procedure, or at the appropriate time. *...the duly elected government.*

dumb If someone is **dumb**, they are unable to speak. ■ You say someone is **dumb** when they cannot say anything on a particular occasion, for example because they are shocked. ■ If you call a person or something like a question **dumb**, you mean they are stupid.

dumbbell A **dumbbell** is a short bar with weights at each end.

dumb down If something, such as a television programme, is **dumbed down**, it is made less serious and intellectual.

dumbfound (**dumbfounded**) If you are **dumbfounded** by something, you are so shocked and surprised by it you cannot speak.

dumb waiter A **dumb waiter** is a lift for carrying things like food from one floor of a building to another.

dummy (**dummies, dummying, dummied**) A **dummy** is a rubber or plastic object given to a baby to suck, to comfort it. ■ A **dummy** is a model of a person, used to display clothes. ■ **Dummy** is used to describe things made to look like a particular object, often in order to deceive someone. *...a dummy hand grenade.* ■ When a footballer **dummies,** he pretends to play the ball but allows it to run past him or stay where it is.

dump When something is **dumped,** it is put somewhere and left there, because it is not wanted. A **dump** is a place where unwanted material is dumped. ■ An ammunition or arms **dump** is a place where weapons are stored. ■ If you **dump** something somewhere, you put it there quickly and carelessly. ■ If you **dump** someone, you end your relationship with them. ■ If you **dump** computer data or memory, you copy it from one storage system onto another, such as from disk to magnetic tape. ■ If you call a place a **dump,** you mean it is ugly and unpleasant.

dumping ground A **dumping ground** is a place where waste material is left. ■ You can call a place a **dumping ground** for unwanted people or things when large numbers of them are sent there. *Such schools would increasingly become dumping grounds for no-hopers.*

dumpling – **Dumplings** are small balls of suet dough, usually cooked in a stew.

dump truck A **dump truck** or **dumper truck** is a truck with a carrying part which can tip backwards so the load falls out.

dumpy If you call someone **dumpy,** you mean they are short and fat.

dunce If you call someone a **dunce,** you mean they are a very slow learner.

dune – **Dunes** are hills of sand in a desert or near the sea.

dung is the faeces of large animals.

dungarees are a one-piece garment consisting of trousers and a front part covering your chest which is held up by straps over your shoulders.

dungeon A **dungeon** is a dark underground prison, especially in a castle.

dunk If you **dunk** something in a liquid, you hold it there briefly, then take it out again.

duo A **duo** is two people who do something together. *...a comedy duo.*

duodenum (**duodenal**) Your **duodenum** is the part of your intestine just below your stomach. **Duodenal** means to do with the duodenum. *...duodenal ulcers.*

duopoly (**duopolies**) If there is a **duopoly** in an area of business, two companies share complete control over it.

dupe (**duping, duped**) If someone **dupes** you, they trick you. A **dupe** is someone who has been tricked.

duplex (**duplexes**) In the US, a **duplex** is a building divided into two living units. It can be either a pair of semi-detached houses or two flats, one above the other.

duplicate (**duplicating, duplicated; duplication**) If you **duplicate** something (*pron:* **dyoo**-pli-kate), you make an exact copy of it. The copy is called a **duplicate** (*pron:* **dyoo**-pli-ket). ■ If work is being **duplicated,** two people or groups are doing the same task.

duplicity (**duplicitous**) If you accuse someone of **duplicity** or say they are being **duplicitous,** you mean they are being deceitful.

durable (**durability**) If a product is **durable,** it is strongly made and should last a long time. ■ A **durable** arrangement is likely to last. ■ **consumer durables:** See **consumer.**

duration The **duration** of something is the length of time it lasts for.

duress If you do something **under duress,** you are threatened or forced into doing it.

Durex (*plural:* **Durex**) A **Durex** is a condom. 'Durex' is a trademark.

during is used to say something happens (a) continuously or repeatedly over a period. *Our unity will be tested during the months ahead.* (b) at some point in a period. *Six prison staff were injured during the protest.*

dusk is the time just after sunset when the light is dim but it is not completely dark.

dusky If something is **dusky,** it is dark or dark-coloured.

dust (**dusty**) Dust is a powder-like substance made up of fragments of things such as earth, dirt, and pollen. If something is **dusty,** it is covered in dust. ■ When you **dust** or do the **dusting,** you wipe dust from things like furniture using a duster. ■ If you **dust** a surface with a powder, you cover it lightly with it. A **dusting** is a light covering like this. ■ If you say something is being **dusted down** or **dusted off,** you mean it is being prepared for use again, after it has not been used for a long time. ■ If something **bites the dust,** it fails. ■ If you say you are waiting for **the dust to settle,** you mean you are waiting for things to calm down after a period of excitement or change.

dustbin A **dustbin** is a large round container which people put their rubbish in ready for collection.

dustcart A **dustcart** is a lorry for collecting rubbish from people's dustbins.

duster A **duster** is a cloth for dusting.

dust jacket A book's **dust jacket** is a loose paper cover put on to protect it. It often contains information about the book and its author.

dustman (**dustmen**) A **dustman** is a person whose job is to collect rubbish from dustbins.

dustpan A **dustpan** is a small flat container with an opening at the front. You hold it flat on the floor and sweep dirt and dust into it.

dustsheet A **dustsheet** is a large piece of cloth put over furniture to protect it from dust, especially when it is not in use.

Dutch is used to talk about people and things in or from Holland (the Netherlands). *...Dutch beer.* ■ The **Dutch** are the Dutch people. ■ **Dutch** is the main language spoken in Holland.

Dutchman (Dutchwoman) A **Dutchman** or **Dutchwoman** is a person from Holland (the Netherlands).

dutiful (dutifully) A **dutiful** person does everything they are expected to do.

duty (duties) A person's **duties** are the things they have to do as part of their job. ■ When people like doctors and police are **on duty,** they are working. ■ If something is your **duty** or you are **duty bound** to do it, you have a moral or legal responsibility to do it. ■ **Duties** are taxes you pay on things you buy.

duty-free goods cost less than usual, because no tax is paid on them. You can buy them at places such as airports.

duvet (pron: **doo**-vay or **dyoo**-vay) A **duvet** is a bed cover filled with feathers or similar material.

DVD A **DVD** is a type of compact disc that can store large amounts of video and audio information. DVD stands for 'Digital Versatile Disk'.

dwarf (dwarfs, dwarfing, dwarfed) If one thing **dwarfs** another, it is so large it makes the other thing look small. ■ **Dwarf** plants and animals are much smaller than other plants and animals of the same kind. ■ A **dwarf** (plural: dwarfs or dwarves) is a person who is much shorter than normal. This use of 'dwarf' is offensive. ■ In children's stories, a **dwarf** is a very small ugly man with magical powers.

dwell (dwelling, dwelt not 'dwelled'; dweller) If you **dwell** somewhere, you live there. **Dweller** is used after words like 'town' to say where someone lives. ...slum dwellers. ■ If you **dwell on** something unpleasant, you keep thinking or talking about it.

dwelling A **dwelling** is a place where someone lives.

dwelt See **dwell.**

dwindle (dwindling, dwindled) If something **dwindles,** it becomes smaller or weaker.

dye (dyeing, dyed) If you **dye** hair or cloth, you change its colour by soaking it in a coloured liquid called a **dye.**

dyed-in-the-wool is used to describe people with strongly held beliefs which they refuse to change.

dying See **die.**

dyke (or **dike**) A **dyke** is a wall which stops water flooding onto land from a river or the sea.

dynamic (dynamically, dynamism) A **dynamic** person is full of energy and purpose. This quality is called **dynamism.** ■ If something is **dynamic,** it is energetic and exciting. ...a dynamic performance. ■ The **dynamics** of a situation are the forces which cause it to change.

dynamite (dynamiting, dynamited) **Dynamite** is an explosive containing nitroglycerin. If you **dynamite** something, you blow it up with dynamite. ■ You can say a person or thing is **dynamite** when you find them extremely exciting and stimulating.

dynamo (dynamos) A **dynamo** is a device for converting mechanical energy into electrical energy. ■ If you describe someone as a **dynamo,** you mean they are very energetic and always busy and active.

dynasty (dynasties; dynastic) A **dynasty** is a series of rulers of a country who all belong to the same family. ...China's dynastic history. ■ Families are called **dynasties** when they have been successful in politics, business, or entertainment over several generations.

dysentery is an infection of the lower intestine which causes pain, fever, and severe diarrhoea.

dysfunction If there is a **dysfunction** in a part of your body, the part is not working properly.

dysfunctional families and relationships are abnormal and problematic.

dyslexic (dyslexia) **Dyslexic** people or **dyslexics** are people of normal intelligence who have difficulty with reading. This problem is called **dyslexia.**

dyspeptic (dyspepsia) If someone is **dyspeptic** or has **dyspepsia,** they have indigestion.

dystrophy See **muscular dystrophy.**

E e

E is the drug ecstasy.

each is used to talk about all the people or things in a group, considered as individuals. Each country can enter two swimmers per event... The guests paid two hundred pounds each. ■ **Each other** is used to say two people or groups do the same thing. They glared at each other. ■ If you bet on a horse **each way,** you bet on it to come first, second, or third.

eager (eagerly, eagerness) If you are **eager** for something, you want it very much. If you are **eager** to do something, you are very keen to do it.

eagle — Eagles are large birds of prey with hooked bills, long broad wings, and exceptionally good eyesight. ■ If someone is **eagle-eyed,** they are quick to spot small details or irregularities. ■ In golf, an **eagle** is a score of two below par on any hole. See also **birdie, bogey.**

ear Your **ears** are the organs you hear with. ■ An **ear-splitting** noise is extremely loud. An **ear-piercing** noise is very loud and shrill. ■ If you have an **ear** for music, you are able to listen to it and reproduce it accurately. ■ An **ear** of a cereal plant like wheat or barley is the part at the top of the stalk which contains the seeds, grains, or kernels.

ear-bashing If someone is given an **ear-bashing,** they are given a telling-off.

eardrum Your **eardrums** are the thin pieces of skin stretched across the inside of your ears, which help you to hear sounds.

earful If you give someone an **earful,** you speak angrily to them for quite a long time.

earl An **earl** is a British nobleman, ranking between a marquess and viscount.

earlobe Your **earlobes** are the soft fleshy parts at the bottom of your ears.

early (**earlier, earliest**) **Early** means soon after the beginning of something. *...early in the morning. ...the early 1980's.* ■ **Early** is used to talk about something happening soon. *Hopes of an early end to the war have received another setback.* ■ If something happens **early,** it happens before the usual or expected time. *Most shops will close early.*

early warning An **early-warning** system is a system designed to give advance warning of something bad that is about to happen. It is usually used to talk about a network of radar stations and satellites, designed to give advance warning of an air or missile attack.

earmark If something is **earmarked** for a particular purpose, it is set aside for that purpose.

earn (**earning, earned** *or* **earnt; earnings**) The amount of money you **earn** is the amount you are paid for the work you do; you call this money your **earnings.** ■ The amount a business or investment **earns** is the profit it makes or returns; this profit is called its **earnings.** ■ If something you do **earns** you something, you get it as a result of doing it. *His next foul earned him a booking.* ■ If you say something is **well-earned** or **hard-earned,** you mean it is thoroughly deserved.

earner An **earner** is (a) a person who earns money. (b) something which makes money for someone. *Shipping is the country's greatest earner.*

earnest (**earnestly, earnestness**) **Earnest** people are very serious and sincere. *They talked earnestly to each other. ...speaking with great earnestness.* ■ If someone is **in earnest,** they mean what they say. ■ If something starts **in earnest,** it gets going properly. ■ An **earnest** is an indication of what will happen. *They took it as an earnest of even bigger changes to come.*

earnings See **earn.**

earphone An **earphone** is a small receiver which fits inside your ear, so you can listen to a radio, tape, or CD player, without anyone else hearing. See also **headphones.**

earpiece The **earpiece** is the part of a telephone receiver you hold next to your ear. ■ An **earpiece** is a small receiver, which TV presenters wear in their ear, so they can receive instructions without anyone else hearing. ■ The **earpieces** of a pair of glasses are the parts which fit over your ears.

earplug (*or* **ear-plug**) **Earplugs** are small pieces of soft material which fit inside the ears and keep out noise or water.

earring – **Earrings** are items of jewellery which people attach to their ears.

earshot If you are **within earshot** of something, you are close enough to hear it. If you are **out of earshot,** you are too far away to hear something.

earth The **Earth** is the planet we live on. ■ The ground can be called the **earth.** ■ **Earth** is another name for soil. ■ An **earth** is a wire fitted to a plug or electrical appliance, through which electricity can pass into the ground, making the appliance safe to use. If you **earth** a plug or electrical appliance, you fit it with an earth. ■ People use **on earth** after words like 'how', 'why', 'what', and 'who' to make a point more strongly. *What on earth are you doing?* ■ If a person or group of people is brought **down to earth,** they are forced to be more realistic about what they can achieve. See also **down-to-earth.**

earthbound means (a) heading towards the Earth. (b) confined or attached to the Earth. *...earthbound telescopes.*

earthen structures are made of compacted earth.

earthenware pottery is made of baked clay.

earthly things exist on Earth, as opposed to Heaven. *...earthly pleasures.* ■ **Earthly** is often used to mean 'possible'. *What earthly reason would they have for lying to us?*

earthquake An **earthquake** is a series of vibrations along the Earth's surface, which make the ground shake. Earthquakes are caused by movements along cracks in the Earth's surface.

earthwork – **Earthworks** are large banks of earth put up at an early time in history, usually for defensive purposes. ■ You can call excavations where earth has been piled up in banks **earthworks.**

earthworm See **worm.**

earthy (**earthier, earthiest; earthiness**) If you call a person or their behaviour **earthy,** you mean they are coarse or slightly vulgar. *...earthy language.* ■ You can use **earthy** to describe something which reminds you of soil. *...earthy colours.*

earwig – **Earwigs** are small brown insects, with pincers at the rear end of their bodies.

ease (**easing, eased**) If you do something **with ease,** you do it without difficulty. ■ If you are **at ease,** you are comfortable and relaxed. If you are **ill at ease,** you are anxious or awkward. ■ When something **eases,** or when you **ease** it, its intensity decreases. *I'm taking tablets to ease the pain.* ■ If you **ease** something somewhere, you move it slowly and gently. *He eased the door open.*

easel An **easel** is a wooden stand on which a blackboard or artist's canvas is placed.

easily See **easy.**

east (**eastern**) **East** is one of the four main points of the compass. ■ The **east** is the direction where the sun rises. If you go in that direction, you go **east;** a place in that direction is **east of** the place where you are now. ■ The **east** or **eastern** part of a place is the part east of its centre. *...Iraq's eastern neighbour, Iran.* ■ **East** winds blow from the east. ■ The **East** is used to talk about (a) Russia and the other former Communist countries in Eastern Europe. (b) China, Japan, and other Asian countries, taken as a whole.

eastbound traffic is heading towards the east.

Easter is (a) a religious festival held on a Sunday in March or April, in which Christians celebrate Jesus Christ's resurrection. (b) the period of time around Easter.

Easter egg – **Easter eggs** are large chocolate eggs, given as gifts at Easter.

easterly winds blow from the east. ■ If you travel or face in an **easterly** direction, you travel or face towards the east. ■ The most **easterly** part of a place is the part furthest to the east. Similarly, the most **easterly** place of a group of places is the one furthest to the east.

eastern See **east.** ■ **Eastern** is used to talk about things which come from Asia. ...*Eastern religions.*

easterner An **easterner** is a person who was born or lives in the eastern part of a country or region.

easternmost The **easternmost** part of a place is the part furthest to the east.

eastward (eastwards) If you go **eastward** or **eastwards,** you go towards the east.

easy (easier, easiest; easily) If something is **easy** to do, it can be done without much effort or difficulty. ■ **Easy** is used to say things are relaxed and comfortable. ...*an easy life.* ■ You use **easily** after 'could', 'can', or 'might' to say something is quite likely to happen. *The events of 1987 could easily be repeated.* ■ You use **easily** to emphasize that something is beyond a doubt. *It is easily the fastest boat in the regatta.*

easy chair An **easy chair** is a large comfortable chair.

easy-going An **easy-going** person is relaxed and tolerant.

easy listening is gentle, uncomplicated music.

eat (eating, ate, have eaten) When you **eat** something, you chew it and swallow it. ■ If you **eat** at a certain time, that is when you normally have a meal. If you **eat** at a particular place, you have meals there regularly. ■ If you **eat in,** you have a meal at home, rather than in a restaurant. If you **eat out,** you do the opposite. ■ If something **eats up** resources, it uses them in large amounts. ■ If one thing **eats away** at another, it gradually destroys it. *The sea had eaten away at the headland.*

eater is used to describe how a person eats, or what they eat. ...*a fast eater.* ...*a meat eater.*

eatery (eateries) Restaurants are sometimes called **eateries.**

eau de cologne (*pron:* **oh** de kol-**lone**) is a lightly scented perfume, originally made in Cologne.

eaves are the overhanging edges of a roof.

eavesdrop (eavesdropping, eavesdropped: eavesdropper) If you **eavesdrop** on someone, you secretly listen to what they are saying. This is called **eavesdropping;** someone doing it is called an **eavesdropper.**

ebb (ebbing, ebbed) When something like a feeling or a person's strength **ebbs** or **ebbs away,** it gets weaker. ■ If something is **at a low ebb,** it has become very weak or unsuccessful. *Confidence is at a very low ebb.* ■ When the tide **ebbs,** it goes out. When it is going out, you can talk about its **ebb** or call it an **ebb tide.** ■ The **ebb and flow** of something is the way its pace picks up then slows down again. ...*the ebb and flow of the match.*

ebony is (a) a dark black colour. (b) a hard black wood.

ebullient (ebullience) An **ebullient** person is overflowing with enthusiasm and excitement. You can talk about the **ebullience** of someone like this. ...*his characteristic ebullience.*

EC See **European Commission.**

eccentric (eccentricity, eccentricities: eccentrically) **Eccentric** behaviour or **eccentricity** is odd or unconventional. A person who behaves like this is called an **eccentric.** You can also talk about a person's **eccentricities.**

ecclesiastical (ecclesiastic) **Ecclesiastical** means to do with the Church. ...*ecclesiastical history.* ■ An **ecclesiastic** is a member of the clergy.

ECG See **electrocardiograph.**

echelon (*pron:* **esh**-e-lon) An **echelon** is a level or rank within an organization or group of people. ...*the lower echelons of the police.* ■ An **echelon** is a military formation in which each of the vehicles, ships, or soldiers in a group is behind and slightly to the left or right of the one in front.

echo (echoes, echoing, echoed) An **echo** is a repetition of a sound, caused by the sound bouncing off a surface such as a wall. If a sound **echoes,** it creates an echo. If a place **echoes,** it is filled with echoes. ■ The signal reflected by a radar target is called an **echo.** ■ If you **echo** someone's views, you repeat them, or say something very similar. ■ If something like an attitude or opinion finds an **echo** in another place or situation, people there have it too. *The mutiny is the first sign that the unrest has found an echo in the army.* ■ If you say something **echoes** something else, you mean it resembles it in some way.

éclair An **éclair** is a finger-shaped cake made of choux pastry filled with cream and covered with chocolate.

eclectic (eclecticism) An **eclectic** mixture of people, ideas, or things comes from a wide range of sources, rather than just one. Mixing people, ideas, or things in this way is called **eclecticism.** ■ If you have **eclectic** tastes, you enjoy a wide range of things.

eclipse (eclipsing, eclipsed) When there is an **eclipse** of the sun or a **solar eclipse,** the moon passes between it and the Earth, hiding the sun partly or completely from view and briefly blocking out the sunlight. When there is an **eclipse** of the moon or a **lunar eclipse,** the earth passes between the sun and the moon, casting a shadow on the moon. ■ If something suffers an **eclipse** or is **eclipsed,** it goes into decline or is overshadowed or surpassed by something else. ...*the eclipse of the influence of the Republican party.*

eco- (*pron:* **eek**-oh) is short for 'ecology' or 'ecological'. It is added to words to create new words describing things connected with the environment. ...*eco-friendly packaging.*

ecology (ecologies; ecological, ecologically; ecologist) **Ecology** is the study of the relationship between living things and their environment. An expert on this is called an **ecologist.** ■ When people talk about the **ecology** of an area, they mean the balance between living things and their environment. ■ **Ecological** means to do with ecology. ■ **Ecological** groups or movements campaign to protect the environment.

e-commerce (*or* **ecommerce**) is business transactions that take place on the Internet.

economic (economics; economically, economist) **Economic** means to do with a country's or region's economy. ...*the economically important Firestone rubber plantation.* ■ If a business is **economic,** it has reasonable running costs, and makes a profit.

■ **Economics** is the study of the way in which money, industry, and trade are organised in a society. An expert in economics is called an **economist**.
■ When people talk about the **economics** of a business, they mean the cost of setting it up and running it, and the profit it makes.

economical (**economically**) If something is **economical**, it does not cost much to run. ■ If a person is **economical**, they are careful with their money. ■ You use **economical** to talk about something being done with the minimum of effort or waste. *His gestures were economical.* ■ If you say someone has been **economical with the truth**, you mean they have not told the whole truth about something.

economic refugee An **economic refugee** is a person who moves from a poor country to a rich one, in the hope of finding a higher standard of living.

economize (*or* **economise**) (**economizing, economized**) If you **economize**, you cut down on your spending, to save money.

economy (**economies**) The **economy** of a country or region is the system it uses to organize and manage its money, industry, and trade, or the wealth it obtains from business and industry. *The monarchy pulls in millions of pounds in tourism for the British economy.* ■ **Economy** is careful spending, or the careful use of things to avoid waste or save money. *The corporation is already making economies.* ■ **Economy** is used to talk about using no more of something than is necessary. *...economy of movement. ...economy of language.* ■ **Economy class** travel is cheaper than first or business class, with no luxuries or extras.

ecosystem The **ecosystem** of a place is all the plants and animals living there considered as one large system, in which any change to one affects them all.

ecstasy (**ecstasies; ecstatic, ecstatically**) Ecstasy is a feeling of overwhelming happiness. If someone has this feeling, you say they are **ecstatic**. ■ You say people are **ecstatic** when they are thoroughly delighted with something. ■ **Ecstasy** is an illegal drug which acts as a stimulant and can cause a trance-like state.

ecu (*or* **Ecu** *or* **ECU**) (*pron:* **ay**-kew) (*plural:* **ecu** *or* **ecus**) The **ecu** was a unit of money used for accounting purposes by the European Union's financial institutions, though it was not a currency in its own right. The ecu was replaced by the euro in the late 1990s. 'ecu' stands for 'European Currency Unit'.

ecumenical (*pron:* ee- *or* ek-kew-**men**-ik-al) (**ecumenism, ecumenist**) Ecumenical activities, ideas, or movements try to unite different Christian Churches, or Christians and people of other religions. *...ecumenical prayer meetings.* The movement is also called **ecumenism;** the people involved are called **ecumenists.**

eczema (*pron:* **ek**-sim-a) is a skin condition which causes parts of the skin to become red and itchy.

eddy (**eddies, eddying, eddied**) If water, wind, fog, or snow **eddies**, it swirls round and round. The swirling patches it forms are called **eddies.**

edema See **oedema**.

edge (**edging, edged**) The **edge** of something is the part around its outside or the line where it ends. ■ If an area or object is **edged** with something, it has it around its edges. An **edging** is a decorative border round something. ■ The **edge** of a blade is the sharp part. ■ If you **edge** towards something, you move towards it slowly and cautiously. ■ If you have an **edge** over someone, you have an advantage over them. ■ If you are **on the edge** of something unpleasant, it is likely to happen to you soon. *The country is hovering on the edge of civil war.* ■ If you are **on edge,** you are tense and irritable. ■ If a person's voice has an **edge** to it, it shows feelings of anger or strain. ■ If something **takes the edge off** an achievement or enjoyable experience, it makes it less impressive or enjoyable.

edgy (**edginess**) You say someone is **edgy** when they are tense, nervous, and likely to lose control of their feelings.

edible If something is **edible**, it is safe to eat.

edict (*pron:* ee-dict) An **edict** is an order issued by a ruler or some other high authority.

edifice People sometimes call a large impressive building an **edifice**. ■ A very large institution can be called an **edifice**. *...the whole edifice of free trade.*

edifying If something is **edifying,** it benefits you, especially by broadening your knowledge.

edit (**editing, edited**) When someone **edits** written material, they correct it and adapt it for publication. ■ When someone **edits** a collection of essays, letters, stories, or poems, they choose which ones to include, and often write an introduction or notes. ■ When someone **edits** a film or a TV or radio programme, they choose which material to use, and arrange it in a particular order. ■ If someone **edits** a newspaper or magazine, they are its editor.

edition An **edition** of a book or newspaper is a particular version of it. ■ An **edition** of a TV or radio programme is a single programme which is part of a series.

editor (**editorship**) The **editor** of a newspaper or magazine is the person in charge, who decides which news stories or articles go into it. The position of editor is called the **editorship.** ■ The person in charge of a section of a newspaper or magazine is called an **editor.** *...the fashion editor of Vogue.* ■ An **editor** is a person whose job is to edit written material or film. ■ An **editor** is a senior TV or radio journalist who reports on a particular type of news. *...the BBC's Foreign Affairs editor.*

editorial (**editorially**) An **editorial** is a newspaper article which gives the opinions of the editor or publisher on a topic. **Editorial** comments appear in an editorial. ■ The people who plan the contents of a newspaper, magazine, or book are called the **editorial** staff. ■ **Editorial** is used to talk about things like the opinions and choice of contents of a newspaper or TV programme. *...editorial policy.*

educate (**educating, educated**) When someone is **educated,** they are taught a variety of subjects at a school or college. ■ If you say someone is **educat-**

ed or **well-educated,** you mean they have had a good education. ■ If people are **educated** in something like health care or protecting the environment, they are given information about it and made aware of its importance. ■ An **educated** guess is based on previous experience, and therefore more likely to be correct.

education (**educational, educationally**) Education is the process by which a person gains knowledge and understanding through study or experience. ■ A country's **education** system is the system it uses for teaching people in schools and colleges. If someone is **in education,** they are attending a school or college. **Educational** means to do with education. ...*educational reforms.* ■ If you say something is an **education,** you mean you can learn a lot from it. ■ An **educational** toy helps a child learn.

educationalist (**educationist**) An **educationalist** or **educationist** is a specialist in the theories and methods of education.

educative is used to talk about things which increase people's knowledge. *The exhibition is an educative and moving experience.*

educator An **educator** is a person who contributes something to education, for example by teaching at a school or university, or by writing educational books.

edutainment You can refer to things such as computer games which are designed to be entertaining and educational at the same time as **edutainment.**

Edwardian The **Edwardian** period was from 1901 to 1910, the reign of King Edward VII. **Edwardian** is used to describe people or things from that time. ...*an Edwardian country house.* People associated with the Edwardian period are sometimes called **Edwardians.**

eel – Eels are long thin snake-like fish.

eerie (**eerily**) If something is **eerie,** it is strange and unsettling. ...*an eerie silence.*

efface (**effacing, effaced**) If something **effaces** a bad memory or impression, it creates a new one and the old one is forgotten. ■ See also **self-effacing.**

effect The **effect** of one thing on another is the change the first thing causes in the second. ■ The **effect** something creates is the impression it gives. *The effect was of an indoor garden.* ■ If someone does something **for effect,** they do it to impress people. ■ If you **effect** a change, you bring it about. ■ If something **takes effect,** it starts to happen or produce results. ■ **In effect** is used to say something is true for all practical purposes, though it is not officially true. *He has in effect declared martial law.* ■ A person's belongings are sometimes called their **effects.** ■ The **effects** in a film are the sounds or scenery. **Special effects:** see **special.**

effective (**effectively, effectiveness**) If something is **effective,** it produces the desired result. ■ If a law or treaty becomes **effective** from a particular date, it starts to apply then. ■ **Effective** is used to say something is true in practice, though not officially. *He has been the effective leader of the party*

since the revolution... *The area is effectively closed to foreigners.*

effectual If something is **effectual,** it produces the result you want.

effeminate If you say a man is **effeminate,** you mean he looks, sounds, or behaves like a woman.

effervescent (**effervescence**) An **effervescent** liquid is fizzy. ■ An **effervescent** person is enthusiastic, lively, and energetic.

effete is used to describe people who are weak and powerless, especially people who have grown soft or lazy as a result of too much good living.

efficacious (*pron:* eff-i-**kay**-shus) (**efficacy**) If something, particularly a treatment or remedy, is **efficacious,** it is very good at producing the result you want. You can talk about the **efficacy** (*pron:* **ef**-ik-ass-ee) of something like this.

efficient (**efficiently; efficiency**) If someone is **efficient,** they do things well, without wasting time or energy. You can also say that their methods are **efficient.** ■ If something like a machine is **efficient,** it does its work using a minimum amount of power.

effigy (**effigies**) An **effigy** is a roughly made figure, made to look like a well-known person. Effigies are sometimes publicly burned as a demonstration of hatred for the person they represent. ■ An **effigy** is a statue or carving of someone, especially one from an earlier period of history.

effluent is liquid waste, especially from factories and sewage works.

effort is hard work. ■ An **effort** is an attempt to do something. ...*an effort to combat drug trafficking.*

effortless (**effortlessly**) If something is **effortless,** it is achieved without effort. ...*an effortless victory.*

effrontery is bold, rude, or cheeky behaviour.

effusion When someone expresses a strong feeling by talking or writing a lot, you can call what they say an **effusion** of the feeling. *His employer greeted him with an effusion of relief.*

effusive (**effusively**) If someone is **effusive,** they are full of praise or enthusiasm for a person or thing.

e.g. means 'for example'.

egalitarian (**egalitarianism**) In an **egalitarian** system, everyone is treated equally. The principle of treating people equally is called **egalitarianism;** someone who supports or follows it is called an **egalitarian.**

egg – Eggs are round or oval objects, laid by female birds, reptiles, fish, and insects, in which their young develop before they hatch. ■ An **egg** is a hen's egg, eaten as food. ■ An **egg** or **egg cell** is a cell produced in a woman's or female animal's body, which can develop into a baby if it is fertilized by sperm. ■ If someone is **egged on** into doing something foolish or aggressive, they are encouraged to do it. ■ If something leaves you **with egg on your face,** it leaves you looking foolish. ■ If you **put all your eggs in one basket,** you pin all your hopes on the success of one person or thing, without giving yourself someone or something else to fall back on.

egg cup An **egg cup** is a small cup-shaped container for putting a boiled egg in while you eat it.

egghead is a humorous word for a very intelligent person.

eggplant See **aubergine**.

eggshell An **eggshell** is the hard outer part of an egg.

egg timer An **egg timer** is a device for telling you when an egg has boiled.

egg white is the transparent liquid surrounding the yolk of a hen's egg. It is also called 'albumen'.

ego (*pron*: **ee**-go *or* **egg**-go) A person's **ego** is their own high opinion of their abilities and importance. *He had a massive ego.* ■ If you say someone is on an **ego trip**, you mean they are doing something just to satisfy their feeling of being cleverer or more important than other people. ■ In psychoanalysis, a person's **ego** is their conscious mind. ■ See **alter ego**.

egocentric people only think of themselves.

egoism is the same as egotism.

egoist (**egoistic, egoistical**) An **egoist** is the same as an egotist.

egomaniac (**egomania**) An **egomaniac** thinks only of their own personal interests and does not worry about harming others. This sort of behaviour is called **egomania.**

egotist (**egotism; egotistical, egotistic**) An **egotist** is someone who acts selfishly and believes they are more important than other people. You can talk about a person's **egotism** or say they are **egotistical** or **egotistic.**

egregious (*pron*: ig-**greej**-uss) (**egregiously**) People use **egregious** to express their extremely low opinion of someone or something. *...the most egregious abuses of human rights.*

Egyptology (**Egyptologist**) **Egyptology** is the study of ancient Egypt. An expert on this subject is called an **Egyptologist.**

eiderdown An **eiderdown** is a quilt filled with feathers or some other warm material.

eight (**eighth**) **Eight** is the number 8.

eighteen (**eighteenth**) **Eighteen** is the number 18.

eighty (**eightieth, eighties**) **Eighty** is the number 80. ■ The **eighties** was the period from 1980 to 1989. ■ If someone is in their **eighties**, they are aged 80 to 89.

Eire is another name for the Republic of Ireland.

eisteddfod (*pron*: ice-**sted**-fod) An **eisteddfod** is a Welsh festival in which competitions are held in music, poetry, dance, or drama.

either means one or the other. *If either side deserved a goal, United did... The government no longer listens to either of them.* ■ If something is on **either** side of something, it is on each of its sides. *...giant video screens on either side of the stage.* ■ **Either** is used with 'or' to show there are two or more possibilities or alternatives. *You'll either love it or loathe it... China must either go along or be isolated.* An **either/or** situation is one where someone only has two alternatives. ■ You use **either** when you make a statement with 'no' or 'not' in it and you want to show it applies to another person or thing. *It would not be in the interests of France, or of Israel either.*

ejaculate (**ejaculating, ejaculated; ejaculation**) When a man **ejaculates,** he expels semen from his penis.

eject (**ejecting, ejected; ejection**) When something is **ejected** by or from something else, it is pushed or sent out with considerable force. ■ If someone is **ejected** from a place, they are forced to leave. ■ If someone is **ejected** from a position of power, they are sacked or forced to resign. ■ When a pilot **ejects** from a plane, he or she escapes using the ejector seat.

ejector seat An **ejector seat** is a special seat fitted in some aircraft. It is used in an emergency to eject the person sitting in it out of the plane, so they can parachute to safety.

eke (**eking, eked**) If someone **ekes out** a living, they earn just enough to buy the things they need. ■ If you **eke out** a supply of something, you make it last by using it sparingly.

elaborate (**elaborating, elaborated; elaborately, elaboration**) If something is **elaborate**, it is complicated or has many parts. ■ If something decorative is **elaborate**, it is full of small details. *...elaborately carved thrones.* ■ If you **elaborate** (*pron*: i-**lab**-er-ate) something, or **elaborate** on it, you develop it, or give more details about it.

élan (*pron*: ale-**an**) is style and flair.

elapse (**elapsing, elapsed**) When a period of time **elapses,** it passes.

elastic (**elasticated, elasticity**) **Elastic** is a kind of flexible tape, usually made of rubber. If part of a piece of clothing is **elasticated,** it has elastic threaded through it, to make it fit more closely. ■ An **elastic band** is a thin loop of elastic which you put around things to hold them together. ■ If a material is **elastic,** it stretches and returns to its original shape, like elastic. You can talk about the **elasticity** of a material.

elated (**elation**) If you are **elated,** you are extremely happy. This feeling is called **elation.**

elbow Your **elbow** is the joint between your upper arm and forearm, which allows your arm to bend. ■ If you **elbow** someone, you give them a sharp dig with your elbow. If you **elbow** them **aside,** you push them aside with your elbow. You also say someone **elbows** someone **aside** when they force them out of a position of power or advantage, and take their place. ■ **Elbow grease** is physical effort. ■ **Elbow room** is space to move in, or freedom to do what you want.

elder The **elder** of two people is the one who was born first. You can call people who are older than you your **elders.** ■ An **elder** is (a) a senior member of a tribe or community, with influence or authority in it. (b) a lay member of the Presbyterian church, who plays a part in all its courts and assemblies. ■ An **elder** or **elderberry** is a small tree or shrub, with clusters of tiny white flowers and red, purple, or black berries called **elderberries.**

elderberry (**elderberries**) See **elder.**

elderly people are old. **The elderly** are old people in general.

elder statesman An **elder statesman** is an experienced and respected member of an organization or profession, especially a politician.

eldest The **eldest** of a group of people is the one born first.

elect When people **elect** someone, they choose them to lead or represent them, by voting for them. ■ If someone is **elected** to a prestigious body, they are voted in by its members. ■ **-elect** is used after a person's title, to show that they have not yet formally taken office. ...*the president-elect of Peru.* ■ If you **elect** to do something, you choose to do it.

electable politicians or political parties stand a chance of being elected.

election An **election** is a process in which people vote to choose a person or group to lead or represent them. ■ The **election** of a person or political party is their success in winning an election.

electioneering is the things politicians and their supporters do to persuade people to vote for them in an election, such as making speeches and visiting voters in their homes. Governments are sometimes accused of **electioneering** when they do something just to win votes in a forthcoming election.

elective An **elective** system of government is one in which people elect their leaders. ■ An **elective** post is one someone is elected to. ■ **Elective** surgery is planned in advance.

elector (**electorate**) An **elector** is someone who has the right to vote in an election. All the electors in a place are called the **electorate.**

electoral (**electorally**) **Electoral** means to do with elections or being elected.

electoral college In the US, the **Electoral College** is a body of electors chosen by voters in each State, who formally elect the country's President and Vice-President. Any similar body of electors can be called an **electoral college.**

electoral register The **electoral register** or **electoral roll** is an official list of all the people in an area who have a right to vote in an election.

electorate See **elector.**

electric (**electrics**) **Electric** things produce or carry electricity, or are powered by electricity. ...*electric cables.* ■ The electrical wiring in a house or vehicle is sometimes called the **electrics.** ■ If you say the atmosphere in a place is **electric,** you mean the people there are very excited about something.

electrical (**electrically**) **Electrical** things produce or carry electricity, or are powered by electricity. ...*electrically powered cars.* ■ **Electrical** is used to describe people or companies involved in developing, maintaining, manufacturing, or selling electrical goods or equipment. ...*the German electrical group Siemens.*

electrical engineering (**electrical engineer**) **Electrical engineering** is concerned with the practical applications of electricity and electronics.

electric blanket An **electric blanket** is a blanket with wires inside which can be heated electrically to warm up a bed.

electric-blue is a very bright blue colour.

electric chair An **electric chair** is a special chair used in some states in the US to execute criminals. The condemned person is killed by a powerful electric current.

electrician An **electrician** is a person whose job is to install, service, and repair electrical equipment.

electricity is a form of energy used for heating and lighting, and to power machines. An **electricity company** produces electricity and supplies it to homes and businesses.

electric shock An **electric shock** is a shock caused by electricity passing through a person's body.

electrify (**electrifies, electrifying, electrified; electrification**) If a system is **electrified,** it is converted to run on electricity. ...*the electrification of the East Coast main line.* ■ An **electrified** fence has an electric charge running through it, which gives a shock to any person or animal touching it. ■ If something **electrifies** you, you find it very exciting.

electrocardiograph An **electrocardiograph** is a machine used to measure the electrical activity of a person's heart, which it records on a tracing called an **electrocardiogram** or **ECG.**

electrocute (**electrocuting, electrocuted; electrocution**) If someone is **electrocuted,** they are killed or injured by electricity.

electrode An **electrode** is a piece of metal which carries an electric current to or from a source of power such as a battery.

electrolysis (*pron:* ill-lek-**troll**-iss-iss) is (a) a process in which an electric current is passed through a substance or solution to break it down into its chemical elements. (b) a process for removing unwanted facial or body hair, by destroying the roots with an electric current.

electrolyte An **electrolyte** is a liquid which conducts electricity.

electromagnet An **electromagnet** is a magnet consisting of an iron or steel core with a coil of wire around it. An electric current is passed through the coil, and this magnetizes the core.

electromagnetic (*or* **electro-magnetic**) is used to describe magnetic forces and effects produced by an electric current.

electron An **electron** is a tiny particle of matter with a negative electrical charge, which orbits round the nucleus of an atom. ■ An **electron microscope** uses a beam of electrons, rather than light, to magnify objects.

electronic (**electronically; electronics**) An **electronic** device, such as a computer, contains transistors, silicon chips, or valves which control the electric current flowing through it. The electronic parts of something are often called its **electronics.** ■ **Electronic** processes involve or are controlled by electronic equipment. ...*electronic tagging of offenders.* ...*electronically operated doors.* ■ An **electronics** company manufactures electronic equipment or components. ■ **Electronics** is the study and development of electronic equipment and components. ■ **Electronic** is used to talk about things connected with electrons. ...*a stream of electronic pulses.*

electrostatic is used to talk about things connected with static electricity.

elegant (**elegantly; elegance**) If you say someone or something is **elegant,** you mean they are graceful and stylish. *The furniture combined practicality with elegance.* ■ An **elegant** idea or plan is clever and simple.

elegy (**elegies; elegiac**) An **elegy** is a sad poem, written in memory of someone who has died. ■ An **elegy** is a story or piece of music which expresses regret at the loss of someone or something. You say a story or piece of music like this is **elegiac** (*pron:* el-li-**jie**-ik).

element An **element** of something is one of the parts which make up the whole thing. ■ The **elements** of a subject are its basic points. ■ If you are **in your element,** you are doing something you are good at and enjoy doing. ■ An **element** of something is a certain degree of it. *His victory had an element of luck about it.* ■ When people talk about **the elements,** they mean the weather, especially when it is severe. *...weeks of futile struggle against the elements.* ■ The **element** in something like an electric fire is the part which gets hot when electricity passes through it. ■ The chemical **elements** are the basic substances, for example oxygen or carbon, which all matter consists of.

elemental is used to describe the basic forces of nature, and things which remind you of those forces. *He has always appeared more like an elemental force than an earthbound being.*

elementary is used to describe the simplest or most basic things of a particular kind. *...elementary human rights.* ■ **Elementary** things are very easy to do or understand. *...an elementary duet.*

elementary school Primary schools in Britain used to be called **elementary schools.** In the US, an **elementary school** is a school for children aged between about 5 and 13.

elephant – Elephants are very large animals with trunks and large ears. They live in Africa and India. ■ If you say something, for example a new building, is a **white elephant,** you mean it is a waste of money because it is completely useless.

elephantiasis (*pron:* el-lee-fan-**tie**-a-siss) is a disease which causes a person's legs or other parts to swell to an enormous size.

elephantine is used to describe something which is very large or slow-moving.

elevate (**elevating, elevated; elevation**) If a person is **elevated,** they are raised to a higher rank or status. Similarly, something like an activity can be **elevated** when its status is raised. *John Ford elevated the western into an art form.* ■ If someone **elevates** a discussion, they raise it to a higher intellectual or moral level. ■ **Elevated** is used to describe things which are higher than their surroundings. *...an elevated expressway.* ■ The **elevation** of a place is its height above sea level. *The city of Bogota sits at an elevation of nearly 8,700 feet.* ■ An **elevation** is a plan or drawing showing one side of a building or other structure.

elevator In the US, a lift is called an **elevator.** ■ Some machines which raise and lower things are called **elevators.**

eleven (**eleventh**) Eleven is the number 11. ■ If something is done at the **eleventh hour,** it is done at the last possible moment.

elf (**elves**) In folklore, an **elf** is a small mischievous fairy.

elfin If someone has an **elfin** face, their features are small and delicate.

elicit (**eliciting, elicited**) If something **elicits** a certain reaction, that is how people react to it. *The mere mention of her name elicits scorn.* ■ If you **elicit** something you want from someone, for example information, you succeed in getting it.

elide (**eliding, elided**) In a description or account, if something unpleasant or embarrassing is **elided,** it is glossed over or missed out.

eligible (**eligibility**) If you are **eligible** for something, you are entitled to have it. You can also be **eligible** to join or do something. *The rules covering eligibility for benefits changed in the 1980s.* ■ An **eligible** bachelor is an unmarried man who people think would make a good husband.

eliminate (**eliminating, eliminated; elimination**) If you **eliminate** something, you get rid of it completely. *It should be possible to eliminate all these diseases.* ■ If someone **eliminates** a rival or enemy or has them **eliminated,** they murder them or have them murdered. ■ When a person or team is **eliminated** from a contest, they can take no further part in it, because another person or team has beaten them. ■ When someone is **eliminated** from a police inquiry into a crime, they are no longer considered to be a suspect.

elite (or **élite**) An **elite** is a group of rich, talented, or powerful people who have special rights or privileges. ■ **Elite** is used to describe people or things which are the best of their kind. *...a force of more than 1000 elite troops.*

elitism (**elitist**) Elitism is treating one group of people better than others, for example because of their social background. Something which discriminates in this way can be called **elitist.**

elixir (*pron:* ill-**ix**-ir) An **elixir** is a magic potion.

Elizabethan The **Elizabethan** period was from 1558-1603, the reign of Queen Elizabeth I. **Elizabethan** people and things are from that time. People who lived during that period are called **Elizabethans.**

elk (*plural:* **elk** or **elks**) Elk are large deer with broad flat antlers. They live in parts of northern Europe and Asia, and in North America, where they are called moose.

ellipse An **ellipse** is an oval shape, like a flattened circle.

elliptical If something is **elliptical,** it is shaped like an ellipse. *...an elliptical orbit.* ■ **Elliptical** references to something are indirect, rather than clear and straightforward.

elm – Elms are tall trees with broad leaves, which they shed in winter.

elocution is the art of speaking clearly in public.

elongated If a shape or object is **elongated,** it is long and thin, and looks as if it has been unnaturally stretched out. ■ You can say something is

elongated when it goes on longer than usual. ...*an elongated lunch hour.*

elope (**eloping, eloped; elopement**) When a couple **elope,** they run away to get married. This is called an **elopement.**

eloquent (**eloquently; eloquence**) If people are **eloquent,** they express themselves clearly and persuasively. You can talk about the **eloquence** of such people, or describe what they say as **eloquent.** ...*an eloquent plea for leniency.*

else is used (a) after words like 'someone', 'somewhere', and 'anything' to talk about another person, place, or thing, without saying which. *Get someone else to do it.* (b) after words like 'everyone' and 'everything' to talk about all the other people, places, or things except the one you have just mentioned. *Everyone else was wearing jeans.* ■ **Else** is used after words like 'nobody', 'nowhere', and 'anything' to mean 'besides' or 'in addition'. *There's nowhere else to go... There was little else he could say.* **Else** is also used like this after words like 'who' and 'what'. *Who else was there?... What else do I need to do?* ■ You say **if nothing else** when you are mentioning the one good thing about someone or something. *If nothing else, he is decisive.* ■ **Or else** means 'otherwise'. *Junk mail must work, or else the advertisers wouldn't keep sending it.* ■ **Or else** is used as a warning or threat. *Pay up or else.* ■ You say **above all else** to emphasize that one thing is more important than other things. *She prizes friends above all else.*

elsewhere You use **elsewhere** to say something happens in another place, or is in another place, without saying exactly where. *Demonstrations took place elsewhere throughout Europe... The majority would prefer to go elsewhere.*

elucidate (**elucidating, elucidated; elucidation**) If you **elucidate** something, you explain it.

elude (**eluding, eluded**) If something you want **eludes** you, you fail to get or achieve it. ■ If something like an idea **eludes** you, you fail to understand it. ■ If you **elude** someone, they fail to capture you.

elusive (**elusiveness**) If a person or animal is **elusive,** they are difficult to find or catch. ■ You say something is **elusive** when it is difficult to obtain. *Peace remains elusive.*

elves See **elf.**

emaciated people or animals are extremely thin, usually through illness or lack of food.

e-mail (*or* **email**) **E-mail** is a system of sending written messages electronically from one computer to another. E-mail is an abbreviation of 'electronic mail'. If you **e-mail** someone, you send them a message in this way.

emanate (**emanating, emanated**) You use **emanate** to say where something comes from. *A series of penetrating blasts emanated from the tower.* ■ If someone **emanates** a quality, they show it in the way they behave. *Field was one of nature's gentlemen, emanating kindness, courtesy and humour.*

emancipate (**emancipating, emancipated; emancipation**) If something **emancipates** people, it frees them from oppression of some kind or from

slavery. ...*female emancipation.* ■ **Emancipated** is used to describe people who reject restrictive social conventions. ...*an emancipated woman.*

emasculate (**emasculating, emasculated**) If someone or something is **emasculated,** they are deprived of their power.

embalm When a dead person is **embalmed,** their body is treated with chemicals to stop it decaying.

embankment An **embankment** is a mound of earth or stone which carries a road or railway over an area of low ground, or holds back water.

embargo (**embargoes, embargoing, embargoed**) An **embargo** is a ban on trade with a country, or a ban on supplying certain goods to it. If something is not allowed to be sold because of a ban, you say it is **embargoed.** ■ An **embargo** is an order prohibiting the release of information before a certain time. When this happens, you say the information is **embargoed.**

embark (**embarkation**) When you **embark** on a ship or plane, you board it. ...*the embarkation point for the islands.* ■ If you **embark on** or **upon** something, you begin it.

embarrass (**embarrasses, embarrassing; embarrassingly, embarrassment**) If something **embarrasses** you, it makes you feel self-conscious, awkward, or ashamed. This feeling is called **embarrassment.** Someone or something which embarrasses people can be called an **embarrassment.** *Her name had been an embarrassment to her since her early school days.* ■ You say something is **embarrassing** when people do not know what to do or say about it, because it is so rude or of such poor quality. ...*embarrassingly awful versions of the latest hits.* ■ If you have a wide range of attractive things to choose from, and do not know which to go for, you can say there is an **embarrassment of riches.**

embassy (**embassies**) An **embassy** is (a) a group of officials, headed by an ambassador, who represent their government in a foreign country. (b) the building they work in.

embattled An **embattled** person or organization is facing lots of difficulties. ■ An **embattled** area or country is one that is fighting a war, or under siege.

embed (**embedding, embedded**) If an object is **embedded** somewhere, it is fixed there, firmly and deeply. You can also talk about something like a firmly held attitude or feeling being **embedded** among a group of people.

embellish (**embellishes, embellishing, embellished; embellishment**) If you **embellish** something, you add things to it for decoration. You call this process **embellishment;** the things you add are called **embellishments.** ■ If you **embellish** a story, you add things to it for effect, sometimes things which are not true. This is called **embellishment.**

ember – **Embers** are the glowing pieces of wood or coal in a dying fire. ■ The **dying embers** of something are its last remains.

embezzle (**embezzling, embezzled; embezzlement, embezzler**) If someone **embezzles** money which has been entrusted to them, they steal it, usually over a period of time.

embitter (**embittering, embittered**) An **embittered** person is very bitter.

emblazon (**emblazoning, emblazoned**) If something is **emblazoned** with a design of some kind, that design is displayed very noticeably on it.

emblem (**emblematic**) An **emblem** is a design representing a country or organization. ■ Something which seems to sum up an event, situation, or period in history can be called an **emblem.** You say something like this is **emblematic.** *Blazing oil wells and a huge oil slick are emblems of the destruction that is a part of war.*

embody (**embodies, embodying, embodied; embodiment**) If you **embody** a quality, or are an **embodiment** of it, you are a perfect example of it. *He was the embodiment of excellence.* ■ If something **embodies** certain features, it has them. *The new draft constitution embodies reforms first called for several weeks ago.*

embolden (**emboldening, emboldened**) If something **emboldens** you, it encourages you to do something.

embolism An **embolism** is a blockage in a vein or artery, caused by a blood clot or air bubble.

embossed If something is **embossed** with a design or letters, the design or letters stand up slightly from its surface.

embrace (**embracing, embraced**) If you **embrace** someone or give them an **embrace,** you hug them. ■ If you **embrace** something which other people are doing, you start doing it yourself. ■ If something **embraces** certain things, they are covered by it or included in it. *The championship embraces 35 events and 16 countries.*

embroider (**embroidering, embroidered; embroidery**) If you **embroider** fabric, you sew a design on it. Doing work like this is called **embroidery;** the work produced is also called **embroidery.** ■ If someone **embroiders** a story, they add things to it for effect.

embroil (**embroiling, embroiled**) If you are **embroiled** in a fight or argument, you become involved in it.

embryo (*pron:* em-bree-oh) (**embryos; embryonic, embryology**) An **embryo** is an unborn human being or animal at an early stage of development. **Embryonic** means to do with embryos. *...embryonic development.* **Embryology** is the scientific study of embryos. ■ If something exists in **embryo,** it exists, but has not yet developed into its full form. You say something like this is **embryonic.** *The idea was at an embryonic stage.*

emerald is a bright green colour. ■ An **emerald** is a bright green precious stone.

emerge (**emerging, emerged; emergence**) If you **emerge** from something, you come out of it. *They emerged from their meeting describing their talks as constructive.* ■ You say someone **emerges** when they suddenly become well-known, because of something they have achieved. *The 1992 Games saw the emergence of African women runners.* ■ If you **emerge** from an experience in a particular state,

that is what you are like at the end of it. *He emerged from that traumatic year a stronger and wiser man.* ■ When information **emerges,** it becomes known. ■ When something like a new country **emerges,** it comes into existence. *...imports from struggling emerging countries.*

emergency (**emergencies**) An **emergency** is a sudden serious situation which must be dealt with quickly. **Emergency** is used to describe things which are available for use in a situation like this. *...an emergency exit.* ■ **Emergency** is used to describe things done quickly in response to an emergency. *...emergency repairs.* ■ The **emergency services** are the police, fire brigade, and ambulance service.

emergent An **emergent** country, political group, or movement is just coming into existence or becoming powerful. *...the emergent field of sports psychology.*

emeritus (*pron:* im-**mer**-rit-uss) is used before or after a person's title to show they have retired, but have kept their title as an honour. *...Professor Emeritus L.C. Green.*

emery is a hard grey mineral, which is ground into a powder and used to make various articles for smoothing or polishing things. An **emery board** is a strip of wood or card coated with this powder; people use it to file their nails.

emetic (*pron:* im-**met**-ik) An **emetic** is a medicine which causes vomiting. If something is **emetic,** it makes people vomit.

emigrate (**emigrating, emigrated; emigration, emigrant**) If you **emigrate,** you leave your own country, to live in another country. Someone who does this is called an **emigrant.** See also **immigrant.**

émigré (*pron:* em-mig-gray) An **émigré** is someone living in a country which is not their own, especially someone who has had to leave their own country for political reasons.

éminence grise (*plural:* **éminences grises**) (*both pron:* em-mi-nons **greez**) An **éminence grise** is a person who wields power behind the scenes, using their influence over someone in power.

eminent (**eminently, eminence**) **Eminent** people are well-known and respected. *...an eminent scientist.* ■ **Eminent** is used to emphasize that someone obviously has a particular quality. *Michael is an eminently likeable man.* ■ Roman Catholic cardinals are called **His Eminence** and addressed as **Your Eminence.**

emir (*pron:* em-**meer**) (*or* **amir**) (**emirate**) An **emir** is a Muslim ruler. Some countries ruled by emirs or other Muslim rulers are called **emirates.**

emissary (**emissaries**) An **emissary** is a representative or messenger sent by one government or leader to another.

emit (**emitting, emitted; emission**) If something **emits** a gas, it gives it off. *...car exhaust emissions.* You can also say something **emits** sounds or light.

Emmy (**Emmys** *or* **Emmies**) An **Emmy** is an American TV industry award.

emollient An **emollient** is a cream or oil which soothes or softens the skin. ■ If someone is being **emollient,** they are trying to calm things down.

emolument (*pron:* im-**moll**-yoo-ment) **Emoluments** are money or other forms of payment received for doing work.

emotion is strong feeling, such as joy, anger, or sorrow. Feelings like these are called **emotions.**

emotional (**emotionally**) **Emotional** means connected with a person's feelings. ...*emotional turmoil.* ■ **Emotional** means involving or causing strong feelings. ...*an emotional homecoming.* ...*an emotional issue.* ■ If you call someone **emotional,** you mean they give way to their emotions very easily. ■ If you say someone is **emotional** on a particular occasion, you mean they are overcome by emotion, and close to tears.

emotionalism is a display of emotion, or an attempt to rouse people's emotions.

emotive An **emotive** issue arouses strong feelings.

empathize (*or* **empathise**) (**empathizing, empathized; empathy**) If you **empathize** with someone, you understand their feelings because you can imagine what it would be like to be in their position. This ability to put yourself in someone else's position is called **empathy.**

emperor An **emperor** is the male ruler of an empire.

emphasis (**emphases**) **Emphasis** is special importance given to one aspect of something. *There should be less emphasis in schools on academic results.* ■ If you put **emphasis** on a word or syllable, you say it with extra force.

emphasize (*or* **emphasise**) (**emphasizing, emphasized**) If a speaker or writer **emphasizes** something, they give particular importance to it. *His campaign for the leadership emphasized his own humble origins.* ■ If someone **emphasizes** a point, they make it forcefully. *They emphasized that there was no quick solution in sight.* ■ If you **emphasize** a word or syllable, you say it with extra force.

emphatic (**emphatically**) An **emphatic** statement is firm and forceful. *He was emphatic that he wanted to stay.* ■ An **emphatic** victory is complete and decisive. ■ You say **emphatically** to emphasize that something is not the case. *It is emphatically not a wine to be gulped.*

emphysema (*pron:* em-fiss-**see**-ma) is a lung disease which makes breathing difficult.

empire An **empire** is (a) a group of countries under the control of one powerful country or ruler. (b) a large group of companies controlled by one person.

empirical (**empirically**) **Empirical** knowledge is based on experiment and observation, rather than theory.

emplacement An **emplacement** is a prepared position for a large gun.

employ (**employment**) If someone **employs** you, they pay you to work for them. *He found employment as a window dresser.* ■ If you **employ** a method or device, you use it.

employable If someone is **employable,** they have skills, abilities, or experience likely to get them a job.

employee An **employee** is a person who works for another person or an organization, in return for a wage.

employer Your **employer** is the person or organization you work for.

employment See **employ.**

employment agency An **employment agency** is an agency which places people in work.

emporium (*plural:* **emporiums** *or* **emporia**) In the past, a large store selling a variety of things was sometimes called an **emporium.**

empower (**empowering, empowered; empowerment**) If someone is **empowered** to do something, they have the authority to do it. ■ If a group of people are **empowered,** they are given some control over what happens to them.

empress (**empresses**) An **empress** is (a) the female ruler of an empire. (b) the wife of an emperor.

empty (**emptier, emptiest; emptiness; empties, emptying, emptied**) If a container is **empty,** there is nothing in it. If you **empty** a container, you remove its contents or tip them out. You can also say that you **empty** the contents. ■ Empty bottles are often called **empties.** ■ If something like a room is **empty,** there is nobody in it. If it **empties,** everyone leaves. ■ If a seat is **empty,** nobody is sitting there. ■ If you call a threat or promise **empty,** you mean it will not be carried out. ■ If your life is **empty,** it lacks meaning or purpose.

empty-handed If you come away from a place **empty-handed,** you have failed to get something you wanted.

empty-headed If you say someone is **empty-headed,** you mean they are silly and unintelligent.

emu — **Emus** are large flightless Australian birds with long legs.

emulate (**emulating, emulated; emulation**) If you **emulate** someone you admire, you imitate them, or try to do as well as them.

emulsifier An **emulsifier** is a substance which binds molecules together. In the manufacture of food and other products, emulsifiers bind oil and water molecules together, and keep them from separating.

emulsify (**emulsifies, emulsifying, emulsified**) When oil or fat and another liquid **emulsify,** they combine to form an emulsion.

emulsion (**emulsioning, emulsioned**) An **emulsion** is a milky liquid, in which particles of oil or fat are evenly distributed. ■ **Emulsion** or **emulsion paint** is a water-based paint. If you **emulsion** something, you paint it with emulsion. ■ **Emulsion** is a substance used to coat photographic film, to make it sensitive to light.

enable (**enabling, enabled**) If someone or something **enables** you to do something, they make it possible for you to do it.

enact (**enactment**) When a government **enacts** a piece of legislation, they make it law. ■ When people **enact** a story or play, they perform it.

enamel (**enamelled**) (*Am:* **enameled**) **Enamel** is a glass-like substance, used as a protective or decorative coating, especially on metal. An **enamel** or **enamelled** object is coated with enamel. ...*enam-*

elled cast-iron pans. ■ **Enamel** is the hard white substance which coats and protects the surface of teeth.

enamoured (*Am:* **enamored**) If someone is **enamoured** of an idea or system, they are very keen on it, and want to see it implemented or used. ■ If someone is **enamoured** of another person, they are in love with them.

en bloc (*pron:* on **block**) is used talk about something happening to, or being done by, a whole group of people or things together. *The radicals may leave the Party en bloc.*

encamp When people **encamp** somewhere, they establish themselves there and show no signs of leaving. *The press were encamped outside his home.*

encampment An encampment is a place where a camp has been set up, especially a soldiers' camp.

encapsulate (**encapsulating, encapsulated**) If a remark, piece of writing, or photograph, **encapsulates** something, it sums it up concisely.

encase (**encasing, encased**) If something is **encased** in a container or material, it is completely enclosed within it. *His leg was encased in plaster.*

encash (**encashes, encashing, encashed; encashment**) If you **encash** something like shares, you cash them in. *The company charges investors for early encashment.*

encephalitis (*pron:* en-sef-a-**lite**-iss) is an inflammation of the brain, usually caused by an infection.

enchant (**enchanting, enchanted; enchantingly, enchantment**) If something **enchants** you, it charms and delights you. You can talk about the **enchantment** of something like this or say it is **enchanting.** ■ In fairy tales, when someone with magical powers **enchants** someone or something, they place them under a spell.

enchantress (**enchantresses**) In fairy tales and legends, an **enchantress** is a woman with magical powers, which she uses to cast spells. ■ A woman whose beauty captivates men is sometimes called an **enchantress.**

encircle (**encircling, encircled; encirclement**) If one thing **encircles** another, it forms a circle round it. *The M25 motorway encircles London.* ■ If people **encircle** something, they surround it. *The Red Army completed its encirclement of Berlin.*

enclave An **enclave** is (a) a small territory belonging to one country but lying within another country's borders. (b) an area where an ethnic or religious group lives surrounded by a much larger group. *...the Christian enclave in Beirut.*

enclose (**enclosing, enclosed; enclosure**) If an object or area is **enclosed** by something, it is completely surrounded by it or sealed within it. *...an enclosed courtyard.* ■ An **enclosure** is an area of land surrounded by a wall or fence, and used for a special purpose. *...the unsaddling enclosure.* ■ An **enclosed** community is self-contained, and has little to do with the outside world. ■ If you **enclose** something with a letter, you put it in the same envelope.

encode (**encoding, encoded**) When information is **encoded,** it is put into code. *The signal contains en-*

coded information which indicates the type of message being transmitted.

encompass (**encompasses, encompassing, encompassed**) If something **encompasses** a wide range of things, it includes them all. *...a remarkable display, encompassing architecture, painting, and furniture.*

encore An **encore** is a short extra item added by a performer at the end of a show, because the audience asks for more.

encounter (**encountering, encountered**) If you **encounter** someone, you meet them unexpectedly. A meeting like this is called an **encounter.** ■ If you **encounter** something, you experience it. *It was his first encounter with sophisticated food.* People often talk about **encountering** problems, difficulties, or setbacks. ■ An **encounter** is a battle or contest. *He was killed in an encounter with the security forces.*

encourage (**encouraging, encouraged; encouragingly**) If you **encourage** someone to do something, you urge them to do it, because you think they will benefit from it. ■ If you **encourage** an activity, you give it your backing and support. *...allegations that the CIA encouraged a wave of terrorist attacks.* ■ If something **encourages** you to do something, it gives you the courage or confidence to do it. *Her success encouraged her to leave the shop and become a professional film actress.* ■ If news or a development **encourages** you, it gives you hope or confidence for the future. *He said that he had been encouraged by their discussions.* ■ If something **encourages** an attitude or kind of behaviour, it makes it more likely to happen. *Paying ransoms encourages further criminal acts.*

encouragement If someone or something gives you **encouragement,** they give you courage, confidence, or hope.

encroach (**encroaches, encroaching, encroached; encroachment**) If a country **encroaches** on another country's territory, it moves onto part of it and takes it over. An action like this is called an **encroachment.** ■ If something **encroaches** on your time, it takes up more of it than you would like. ■ If something **encroaches** on people's rights, it takes some of them away. ■ If something **encroaches** on an area of land or water, it gradually eats away at it. *Sand dunes began encroaching on agricultural land.*

encrusted If a surface is **encrusted** with something, it is thickly covered with it. *...boxes encrusted with mother of pearl. ...snow-encrusted pavements.*

encrypt (**encryption**) When a TV signal is **encrypted,** it is deliberately distorted so that it cannot be picked up without special equipment.

encumber (**encumbering, encumbered; encumbrance**) If you are **encumbered** by something you are wearing or carrying, it makes movement difficult. Similarly, you can say you are **encumbered** by something when it makes it difficult for you to do what you want. *She considered the past an irrelevant encumbrance.* ■ In law, an **encumbrance** is a charge upon land, such as a mortgage.

encyclical (*pron:* en-**sik**-lik-kl) An **encyclical** is a letter written by the Pope, stating the Roman Catholic Church's official teaching about something.

encyclopaedia (or **encyclopedia**) (**encyclopaedic**) An **encyclopaedia** is a reference book, set of books, or a CD-ROM, giving information on a single subject or a range of subjects. ■ If something is **encyclopaedic,** the information contained in it is very full and complete. *He had an encyclopaedic knowledge of medals.*

end (**ending**) The **end** of something is its furthest or last part. ■ When something **ends** or you **end** it, it finishes. ■ The **ending** of a story is the way it finishes. *...a happy ending.* ■ If something goes on for a long time, you can say it goes on for hours, days, months, or years **on end.** ■ If you **end up** in a place or situation, that is where you are at the end of a series of events. ■ Someone's **end** is their death. ■ An **end** is an aim or purpose. *Terrorists often resort to violence to accomplish their ends.* ■ If you manage to **make ends meet,** you make just enough money to live on. ■ **No end** means a lot. *This has caused no end of trouble.* ■ **loose end:** see **loose.** See also **dead end.**

endanger (**endangering, endangered**) If something **endangers** something else, it puts it at risk. *Some people are so overweight that they endanger their health.* ■ An **endangered** group of people or things is in danger of becoming extinct or of being destroyed.

endear (**endearing, endeared; endearingly**) If a person or animal **endears** themselves to you, they make you fond of them. *His antics endeared him to those he worked with.* You say their attractive characteristics are **endearing.**

endearment – **Endearments** are words like 'darling' which people use to show affection.

endeavour (*Am:* **endeavor**) (**endeavouring, endeavoured**) If you **endeavour** to do something, you try hard to do it. An **endeavour** is an attempt at something. *The Guinness Book of Records refuses to accept endeavours which might put people in danger.*

endemic If something bad is **endemic** in a country or region, it occurs everywhere there. *Yellow fever is endemic in South America.*

ending See **end.**

endless (**endlessly**) You say something is **endless** when it seems to go on forever.

endocrine The **endocrine** system is the system of glands that produce hormones which go directly into the blood stream, such as the pituitary and thyroid glands.

endorphin – **Endorphins** are chemical substances produced in the brain and other parts of the body, which relieve pain.

endorse (**endorsing, endorsed; endorsement, endorser**) If an important person **endorses** you or **endorses** what you are doing, they publicly support you. ■ When a celebrity **endorses** a product, they allow their name to be associated with it, in return for a fee. Fees received this way are called **endorsements.** ■ When someone's driving licence is **endorsed,** details are recorded on it of a motoring offence they have committed. Each entry on their licence is called an **endorsement.**

endow (**endowment**) If someone is **endowed** with a desirable quality or ability, they have it. *He was endowed with good looks.* A person's qualities or abilities can be called their **endowments.** ■ If you **endow** someone with a quality or ability, you talk about them as if they have it. *She endows babies with more complicated emotions than evidence can support.* ■ When people say a woman is **well-endowed,** they mean she has large breasts. When people say a man is **well-endowed,** they mean he has a large penis. ■ When someone **endows** an organization, they provide it with land, property, or a large sum of money for its use. A gift like this is called an **endowment.** ■ In finance, an **endowment** policy is an insurance policy in which you make regular payments which are invested to provide you with a large sum of money at the end of a fixed period. An **endowment** mortgage is a mortgage which uses this sum to pay off the loan.

endure (**enduring, endured; enduringly, endurance**) If you **endure** something unpleasant, you suffer it or put up with it. ■ If you say someone can **endure** something, you mean they can survive it without breaking down physically or mentally. Their ability to do this is called their **endurance.** ■ If something has **endured,** it has lasted. *...an enduring problem.*

enema (*pron:* **en**-im-a) If someone is given an **enema,** their bowels are cleared by an injection of liquid into their rectum.

enemy (**enemies**) Your **enemies** are people you are fighting against in a war, or who oppose you or want to harm you. *...enemy aircraft.* Often a country or army you are fighting against is just called **the enemy.** ■ Something which does harm can be called an **enemy.** *Inflation was the real enemy.*

energetic (**energetically**) An **energetic** person is full of energy.

energize (or **energise**) (**energizing, energized**) If something **energizes** you, it fills you with energy, enthusiasm, and determination.

energy (**energies**) **Energy** is the ability and strength a person has to do active physical things. ■ If you put all your **energy** or **energies** into something, you give it all your time, effort, and attention. ■ **Energy** is power from things like oil and electricity, which makes machines work or provides heat and light.

enervated (**enervating**) If you feel **enervated,** you feel tired and weak. *...a hot and enervating climate.*

enfant terrible (**enfants terribles**) (*both pron:* on-fon ter-**reeb**-la) People sometimes call someone an **enfant terrible** when they are very talented but their behaviour is often upsetting or shocking.

enfeeble (**enfeebling, enfeebled**) If something **enfeebles** you, it makes you very weak.

enfold If you say something **enfolds** a place or person, you mean it is all around them. *Silence enfolded the couple.*

enforce (**enforcing, enforced; enforcement, enforcer, enforceable**) If people in authority **enforce** a law, they make sure it is obeyed. People employed to enforce the law are sometimes called law **enforcers.** If a law is **enforceable,** it is possible to enforce it. ■ **Enforced** is used to describe a situation which has been forced on someone who did not want it. *...enforced retirement.*

enfranchise (enfranchising, enfranchised; enfranchisement) When people are **enfranchised**, they are given the right to vote in elections.

engage (engaging, engaged; engagement) If you **engage** in an activity, you take part in it. ■ If something **engages** you, it occupies your attention or interest. ■ When a military force **engages** an enemy, it attacks it. A battle can be called an **engagement**. ■ An **engagement** is an arrangement made to meet someone or attend something. ■ If someone's telephone is **engaged**, you cannot get through to them because there is someone else on the line. ■ If a public toilet is **engaged**, it is already in use. ■ If two people are **engaged**, they have formally agreed to marry each other. ■ If you **engage** someone, you employ them to do something for you.

engaging (engagingly) An **engaging** person is pleasant and charming.

engender (engendering, engendered) If something **engenders** a feeling, it gives it to people. *The vote has engendered disappointment as well as joy.*

engine (-engined) An **engine** is a machine which converts heat or other energy into power, especially the power to make a vehicle move. **-engined** is used to describe the type of engine or number of engines a vehicle has. *...petrol-engined boats.* ■ An **engine** is a railway locomotive. ■ If you say something is the **engine** of something like progress, you mean it is the means of achieving it.

engineer (engineering, engineered) An **engineer** is a person who designs and supervises the construction of machinery, engines, or electrical devices, or things like roads and bridges. The construction of these things is called **engineering**. ■ An **engineer** is a person who repairs and services mechanical or electrical devices. *...a television engineer.* ■ In the US, the driver of a railway engine is called the **engineer**. ■ If you **engineer** something, you plan it and bring it about. *He engineered the overthrow of the country's hard-line Communists.*

English people and things are in or from England. *...English villages.* ■ The **English** are the English people. ■ **English** is the main language spoken in the British Isles, the US, Canada, Australia, and many other countries.

Englishman (Englishwoman) An **Englishman** is a man from England.

engorged If an organ is **engorged**, it is swollen with blood.

engrained See **ingrained**.

engrave (engraving, engraved; engraver) If you **engrave** a design or inscription onto a surface, you cut it into the surface. An **engraving** is an engraved picture or design, or a print made from an engraved metal sheet. An **engraver** is a person who produces engravings.

engross (engrossing, engrossed) If you are **engrossed** in something, it completely absorbs your attention. *...an engrossing novel.*

engulf If war or fire **engulfs** a place, it quickly spreads over every part of it. ■ If a feeling **engulfs** you, it overwhelms you.

enhance (enhancing, enhanced; enhancement) If something **enhances** something else, it improves it or makes it more attractive.

enigma (enigmatic, enigmatically) You can call a person or thing an **enigma** when they are puzzling and you cannot explain them. You can say someone like this is **enigmatic**. *She smiled at him enigmatically.*

enjoin (enjoining, enjoined) If someone is **enjoined** to do something, they are urged to do it.

enjoy (enjoyment) If you **enjoy** something or get **enjoyment** from it, it gives you satisfaction and pleasure. ■ If you **enjoy** yourself, you have a good time. ■ If someone **enjoys** an advantage, right, or privilege, they have it.

enjoyable (enjoyably) If something is **enjoyable**, it gives you pleasure.

enlarge (enlarging, enlarged; enlargement) If you **enlarge** something, you make it bigger. If something **enlarges**, it gets bigger. *...an enlarged liver. ...the enlargement of the European Union.* ■ An **enlargement** is a photograph that has been made bigger. ■ If you **enlarge on** a particular subject, you give more details about it.

enlighten (enlightening, enlightened) If someone **enlightens** you, they make something clearer to you by giving you more information. *She gave an enlightening talk... The book provides some enlightenment.* ■ If you call people **enlightened** you think they have sensible modern attitudes. ■ In Buddhism, **enlightenment** is a final blessed state in which there is no desire or suffering.

enlist (enlistment) If someone **enlists**, they join one of the armed forces. *...the enlistment of new recruits.* ■ If you **enlist** someone or **enlist** their help, you get them to help you with something.

enliven (enlivening, enlivened) If someone or something **enlivens** an event, they make it more lively or cheerful.

en masse (pron: on **mass**) If a group of people do something **en masse**, they do it all together at the same time.

enmeshed If you become **enmeshed** in a complicated process, you become involved in it.

enmity (enmities) **Enmity** is a long-lasting feeling of hatred towards someone.

ennoble (ennobling, ennobled) If someone is **ennobled**, they are made a member of the nobility. ■ If something **ennobles** you, it makes you more noble or dignified.

ennui (pron: on-**nwee**) is a feeling of listlessness, boredom, and dissatisfaction.

enormity (enormities) The **enormity** of something is its sheer size or scale.

enormous (enormously) **Enormous** things are very large in size or scale.

enough of something is as much as is needed. *She hasn't secured enough votes to win.* ■ **Enough** is used to say someone or something is able to do something, because they have reached a certain age or standard. *She is legally old enough to refuse medical treatment.* ■ If you say you have had **enough**, you mean you are unhappy with a situation and want it to stop. ■ If you say **enough is enough**, you mean you are not prepared to put up with a situation any longer. ■ **Enough** is used after words like 'pleasant' to indicate that something is true to a fairly large degree. *Tottenham were happy enough with their evening's work.* ■ You use **enough** with words like 'curiously' when you are saying something which might seem strange or surprising. *Oddly enough, I found them quite tasty.*

en passant (*pron:* on pass-on) If you say something **en passant**, you say it in the middle of saying something else.

enquire (**enquiry, enquirer**) See **inquire.**

enrage (**enraging, enraged**) If something **enrages** you, it makes you very angry.

enrapture (**enrapturing, enraptured**) If something **enraptures** you, it fills you with delight.

enrich (**enriches, enriching, enriched; enrichment**) If something is **enriched**, something else is added to it which improves its quality. *...job enrichment.* ■ If you feel **enriched** by something, you feel it has made your life better in some way. *...an enriching experience.* ■ If you **enrich** yourself, you take advantage of a situation to make yourself richer. *They are accused of corruption and self-enrichment.* ■ If uranium is **enriched,** it is processed to produce more energy or a more powerful explosion.

enrol (*Am:* **enroll**) (**enrolling, enrolled; enrolment**) If someone **enrols** at a school or college, they sign on to be a student there. Similarly, you can **enrol** for a particular course. *...applications for enrolment.*

en route (*pron:* on **root**) If you are **en route** somewhere, you are on your way there.

ensconce (**ensconcing, ensconced**) If you are **ensconced** somewhere, you are comfortably settled there.

ensemble (*pron:* on-**som**-bl) An **ensemble** is a group of musicians, actors, or dancers who perform together. ■ **Ensemble** is used to say how well musicians or dancers keep together during a performance. *Some acute problems of ensemble marred the performance.* ■ An **ensemble** is a woman's matching set of clothes.

enshrine (**enshrining, enshrined**) If a right or principle is **enshrined** in something like a country's constitution, it is specifically mentioned in it, and therefore cannot be disregarded.

ensign An **ensign** is a flag flown on a ship to show what country it belongs to. ■ An **ensign** is an officer of the lowest rank in the US Navy.

enslave (**enslaving, enslaved; enslavement**) If people are **enslaved,** they are made into slaves. *...the enslavement of up to thirty million Africans.*

ensnare (**ensnaring, ensnared**) If you become **ensnared** in something bad, you become involved in it and have great difficulty escaping from it. *...a poverty trap that ensnares women.*

ensue (**ensuing, ensued**) If something **ensues,** it happens immediately after another event, usually as a result of it. *The police were met with gunfire and a battle ensued.*

en suite (*pron:* on **sweet**) If a bedroom has a bathroom **en suite**, it has its own bathroom leading directly off it.

ensure (**ensuring, ensured**) If you **ensure** that something happens, you make sure of it.

entail (**entailing, entailed**) If one thing **entails** another, it necessarily involves or causes it. *This will certainly entail a sharp rise in unemployment.*

entangle (**entangling, entangled; entanglement**) If something becomes **entangled** in a rope or net, it gets caught up in it and cannot easily be freed. *...measures to avoid entanglement in drift nets.* ■ If issues or problems become **entangled,** they get mixed up, and it becomes difficult to deal with them separately. ■ If you become **entangled** in a process or relationship, you become involved in it and cannot easily escape. *She was entangled in a bitter court case.*

entente (*pron:* on-**tont**) An **entente** or **entente cordiale** (*pron:* cor-dee-**al**) is a friendly agreement between two or more countries.

enter (**entering, entered**) When you **enter** a place, you go into it. ■ If you **enter** a profession or institution, you become a member of it. *She entered Parliament in 1959.* ■ When something **enters** a new period in its development or history, this period begins. ■ If you **enter** for a competition, you apply to take part in it and are accepted. ■ When people **enter** into something like discussions, they take part in them. ■ If something **enters into** a decision, it is one of the factors influencing it. *The fact that she is a woman did not even enter into it.* ■ If you **enter** something in a book such as a log book, you write it in. Similarly, if you **enter** something into a computer, you type it in.

enterprise (**enterprising**) An **enterprise** is a business or company. ■ See **free enterprise.** ■ If someone is **enterprising,** they show boldness and initiative. You can talk about the **enterprise** of someone like this. ■ An **enterprise** is an undertaking or venture, especially one involving a certain amount of risk.

entertain (**entertaining, entertained; entertainingly**) When comedians, singers, or dancers **entertain** people, they perform for them. ■ If you say someone or something is **entertaining,** you mean they are interesting and amusing. ■ If you **entertain** guests, you receive them in your house and offer them food and hospitality; this is called **entertaining.** ■ When a sports team **entertains** another team, they play at home against them. ■ If you say someone will not **entertain** something, you mean they will not consider it.

entertainer An **entertainer** is someone whose job is to entertain audiences, for example by telling jokes, singing, or dancing.

entertainment consists of films, plays, and activities such as reading and TV, that give people pleasure.

enthral (*Am:* **enthrall**) (**enthralling, enthralled**) If something **enthrals** you, you find it so interesting and enjoyable that it holds your attention completely. *...an enthralling biography.*

enthrone (**enthroning, enthroned; enthronement**) When a new king, queen, or religious leader is **enthroned,** they officially take up their position in a ceremony during which they sit on a throne. ...*the emperor's enthronement in November.*

enthuse (**enthusing, enthused**) If you **enthuse** over something, you speak excitedly about it, saying how wonderful or pleasing it is. ■ If something **enthuses** you, it fills you with enthusiasm.

enthusiasm is eagerness to do or to be involved in something. ■ **Enthusiasm** is a passionate interest in something. An **enthusiasm** is something you are passionately interested in. ...*his great enthusiasm for motor sport... Racing was one of his many enthusiasms.*

enthusiast An **enthusiast** is someone with a special interest or hobby. ...*wine enthusiasts.* ■ An **enthusiast** for something is someone who is very keen on it. *He is an enthusiast for closer European integration.*

enthusiastic (**enthusiastically**) If you are **enthusiastic** about something, you are very keen on it. *The plan has been enthusiastically received.*

entice (**enticing, enticed; enticement, enticingly**) If someone **entices** you, they try to get you to do something or go somewhere, by offering you something. The thing they offer is called an **enticement.** ■ If something is **enticing,** it is extremely tempting. *Estimates are enticingly low.*

entire is used to talk about the whole of something. ...*the entire population.*

entirely means 'wholly' or 'completely'.

entirety If something is done **in its entirety,** all of it is done. *He has not yet met any of those conditions in their entirety.*

entitle (**entitling, entitled; entitlement**) When you are **entitled** to receive or do something, you have a right to it. Your **entitlement** to something is your right to receive or do it. ...*his entitlement to unemployment benefit.* **Entitlements** are things you are entitled to. ...*holiday entitlements.* ■ If a book or record is **entitled** something, that is its name. ...*a new album entitled 'Love Hurts'.*

entity (**entities**) An **entity** is something which exists separately from other things and has its own distinct identity. *France and Germany will never become one political entity.*

entomb When a body is **entombed,** it is placed in a grave or tomb. ■ If an object is **entombed,** it is encased in something, or buried underground.

entomology (**entomologist**) **Entomology** is the study of insects. An **entomologist** is an expert on insects.

entourage (*pron:* on-toor-**ahzh***; the 'zh' sounds like 's' in 'pleasure'*) An important person's **entourage** is the group of people travelling with them.

entrails A person's or animal's **entrails** are their intestines.

entrance (**entrancing, entranced**) **Entrance** is (a) getting into a place. *They had been refused entrance.* (b) the money you pay to get in ...*entrance: £6 adults, £4 children.* ■ The **entrance** to a place is the way in. ■ When someone comes into a room, you can say they **make their entrance,** especially if they do it in a noticeable way. ■ In the theatre, an actor's arrival on stage is called his or her **entrance.** ■ If you gain **entrance** to a school or university, you get accepted as a student. ■ If someone or

something **entrances** you (*pron:* en-**tran**-siz), they fill you with delight and wonder.

entrant An **entrant** is (a) someone who has entered a competition. (b) someone who has just started working for a firm or other organization.

entrap (**entrapping, entrapped; entrapment**) If the police **entrap** someone, they trick them into committing an offence, in order to arrest them. ...*an entrapment operation.* ■ If someone or something becomes **entrapped** in something, they become trapped in it.

entreat (**entreating, entreated; entreaty, entreaties**) If you **entreat** someone to do something, you beg them to do it. The things you say are called your **entreaties.**

entrée (*pron:* on-tray) An **entrée** is (a) a dish served before the main course of a meal. (b) the main course itself. ■ When someone is first accepted as belonging to a group of people, you can call this their **entrée** into the group. *He gave her her entrée into the New York literary establishment.*

entrench (**entrenches, entrenching, entrenched; entrenchment**) If something such as a belief is **entrenched,** it is firmly established, and difficult to change. ■ If an army is **entrenched,** it is firmly established in a well-defended position.

entrepôt (*pron:* **on**-tr-poh) An **entrepôt** is a warehouse at a port or airport, where goods are stored temporarily.

entrepreneur (*pron:* on-tr-pren-**ur**) (**entrepreneurial**) An **entrepreneur** is someone who arranges business deals in order to make a profit. **Entrepreneurial** is used to talk about things to do with entrepreneurs and their deals. ...*entrepreneurial skills.*

entropy has various meanings in science. In one meaning, it is a measure of the efficiency of a system, in another it is the amount of disorder in a system. It is also a measure in thermodynamics.

entrust (**entrusting, entrusted**) If you **entrust** something important to someone or **entrust** them with it, you place it in their care.

entry (**entries**) If you gain **entry** into a place, you get in. ■ An **entry** is a way into a place. ■ When a country joins an existing organization, you call this their **entry** into it. Similarly, you can talk about a country's **entry** into a war. ■ The **entries** for a competition are the items entered for it. ■ The **entry** for a competition is the total number of items or people entered. ■ The separate items in a diary, ledger, dictionary, or encyclopaedia are called **entries.**

entwine (**entwining, entwined**) If two objects are **entwined,** they are threaded through or wrapped round each other. ■ You say things are **entwined** when there are strong connections between them. *Britain's fortunes are inextricably entwined with Europe's.*

E number – E numbers are (a) numbers with the letter 'E' in front of them, which appear on food labels, to indicate which additives the product contains. (b) additives themselves.

enumerate (**enumerating, enumerated**) If you **enumerate** a list of things, you name each one in turn.

enunciate (enunciating, enunciated; enunciation) If you **enunciate** a word, you pronounce it clearly. If someone has good **enunciation,** they pronounce words clearly. ■ If something like a policy is **enunciated,** it is set out clearly in a speech or document.

envelop (*pron:* in-**vel**-up) (enveloping, enveloped) If something **envelops** a person or place, it completely covers or surrounds them.

envelope An **envelope** is a flat rectangular paper container with a gummed flap, for sending letters in.

enviable (enviably) If you describe something someone has as **enviable,** you mean a lot of people would be glad to have it. *...an enviably slender waist.*

envious (enviously) If you are **envious** of someone, you wish you had something they have.

environment (environmental, environmentally) A person's **environment** is their surroundings, especially the conditions in which they grow up, live, or work. *They have seen their working environment decline sharply.* Similarly, an animal's or plant's **environment** is its living conditions. ■ The **environment** is the natural world: the land, the sea, the air, and all creatures and plants. **Environmental** means to do with the environment. *...environmental issues. ...environmentally friendly cars.*

environmentalism (environmentalist) **Environmentalism** is a concern to protect and preserve the environment. People who have this concern are called **environmentalists.**

environs A place's **environs** are the areas surrounding it.

envisage (envisaging, envisaged) If you **envisage** something, (a) you form a mental picture of it. *Mention the word 'pump' and most people envisage a bicycle pump.* (b) you foresee it as likely to happen in the future. *He envisages peace talks within the next few weeks.*

envision (envisioning, envisioned) To **envision** something means the same as to envisage it.

envoy An **envoy** is (a) a representative sent by one government to another country to deliver a message, or to represent them at talks. (b) a diplomat in an embassy, ranked just below the ambassador.

envy (envies, envying, envied) If you **envy** someone, you wish you had something they have. This feeling is called **envy.** ■ If something you have is **the envy** of other people, they wish they had it too.

enzyme – Enzymes are proteins produced by animal and plant cells, which speed up natural chemical processes such as the digestion of food. They can be extracted from animal and plant materials, or they can be manufactured.

eon See **aeon.**

EP An **EP** is a record with four tracks.

epaulette (*or* epaulet) (*both pron:* ep-pol-et) **Epaulettes** are pieces of decorative material worn on the shoulders of certain uniforms.

épée (*pron:* ep-pay) An **épée** is a thin light sword, used in fencing.

ephedrine (*pron:* **eff**-fid-dreen) is a drug used to treat asthma and other allergies.

ephemeral (*pron:* if-**fem**-er-al) (ephemera) If something is **ephemeral,** it lasts only a short time. *The ephemeral nature of pop music.* You can call things like this **ephemera.**

epic Originally, an **epic** was a long poem about the deeds of a legendary hero. **Epic** is now used to describe real-life happenings which are like those in an epic. *...an epic battle.* ■ Any book or film which is very long or involves a great number of events or people can be called an **epic.**

epicene (*pron:* ep-i-seen) If you describe a man as **epicene,** you mean he looks or behaves rather like a woman.

epicentre (*Am:* epicenter) The **epicentre** of an earthquake is the point on the ground immediately above the place where it starts.

epicure (epicurean) An **epicure** is a person who enjoys good food and drink. You say someone like this is **epicurean.**

epidemic An **epidemic** is a widespread occurrence of a disease. ■ If something else unpleasant becomes widespread, you can call it an **epidemic.** *...the crime epidemic.*

epidemiology (epidemiological, epidemiologist) **Epidemiology** is the study of disease as it affects groups of people rather than individuals. *...epidemiological research.*

epidermis (epidermises, epidermal) The **epidermis** is the thin protective outer layer of your skin. **Epidermal** means relating to the epidermis. *...epidermal cells.*

epidural (*pron:* ep-pid-**dure**-al) An **epidural** is an injection of anaesthetic into a patient's spine to relieve pain.

epiglottis (epiglottises) Your **epiglottis** is a thin flap at the back of your tongue, which closes when you swallow food, to stop the food going down your windpipe.

epigram An **epigram** is a short poem or remark which expresses an idea in a clever and amusing way.

epigraph An **epigraph** is a quotation at the start of a book or chapter.

epilepsy (epileptic) **Epilepsy** is a brain disorder which can cause people to have convulsions and lose consciousness. **Epileptic** means connected with this disorder. *...an epileptic fit.* People who suffer from epilepsy are called **epileptics.**

epilogue An **epilogue** is a short poem or passage at the end of a play or book.

epiphany (epiphanies) **Epiphany** is a Christian festival held on the 6th of January. It commemorates the visit of the Three Wise Men to Bethlehem. ■ An **epiphany** is a moment when you suddenly understand something which has been puzzling you.

episcopal (*pron:* ip-**piss**-kop-al) means relating to bishops. *...episcopal duties.*

Episcopal Church In Scotland, the US, and several other countries, the **Episcopal Church** is a Protestant church which has bishops and is similar to the Church of England.

Episcopalian An **Episcopalian** is a member of an Episcopal Church.

episode An **episode** is an incident, usually one in a series of incidents. *She hoped to put that terrible episode in her life behind her.* ■ An **episode** of a TV serial is one of its separately broadcast parts.

episodic If the plot of a novel or film is **episodic**, it consists of a series of separate incidents, rather than a continuous sequence of events. You say other things are **episodic** when they happen at irregular and infrequent intervals.

epistle The **Epistles** are the letters written by the Apostles to early Christians, collected in the New Testament. ■ Any letter can jokingly be called an **epistle.**

epistolary An **epistolary** novel is written in the form of a series of letters from the characters.

epitaph An **epitaph** is an inscription on a gravestone, or a short poem or passage commemorating a dead person. ■ If you say something will be someone's **epitaph**, you mean it is what they will be remembered for.

epithet An **epithet** is a word or phrase used to describe someone or something. *He attracted epithets such as 'scruffy', 'ugly' and 'dirty'.*

epitome (*pron:* ip-**pit**-a-mee) If someone or something is the **epitome** of a quality, they are a perfect example of it. *He was the epitome of calm.*

epitomize (*or* epitomise) (epitomizing, epitomized) If someone or something **epitomizes** a particular thing, they are a perfect example of it. *The house epitomizes the classic country farmhouse.*

epoch (*pron:* ee-pok) (epochal) An **epoch** is a period of history. An important change or development can be called **epochal** or **epoch-making.**

eponymous (*pron:* ip-**pon**-im-uss) An **eponymous** character in a novel, play, or film has the same name as the title of the book, play, or film. For example, the eponymous hero of the film 'Rocky' is Rocky.

epoxy (epoxies) An **epoxy** or **epoxy resin** is a tough synthetic resin used in plastics, paints, and adhesives.

equable (equably) **Equable** behaviour is fair and reasonable.

equal (equalling, equalled; equally) (*Am:* equaling, equaled) **Equal** is used to talk about things being the same in some way, for example having the same size, effect, or importance. *EU legislation guarantees equal pay for men and women... Equally important, solar energy can be significantly cheaper than other forms of power.* ■ If something **equals** an amount, it comes to that amount. *2 plus 2 equals 4.* ■ If someone is your **equal,** they are as good as you at something. ■ If you **equal** something someone else has done, you do as well as them. ■ If you are **equal** to something, you have the ability, strength, or courage to deal with it.

equalise See **equalize.**

equality If there is **equality** in a place or organization, everyone has the same rights and opportunities as everyone else.

equalize (*or* equalise) (equalizing, equalized; equalization, equalizer) If two things are **equalized,** they are made equal. ■ If a football team

equalizes, they score a goal which levels the score. The goal is called an **equalizer.**

equanimity is a calm state of mind.

equate (equating, equated) If you **equate** one thing with another, you regard them as being the same. *They equate money with power.* ■ If one thing **equates** to another, it is equivalent to it. *The level of stocks equated to 67 days' forward consumption.*

equation In mathematics, an **equation** is a statement that two amounts or values are equal, for example $x^2 - y^2=(x+y)(x-y)$. ■ In chemistry, an **equation** is a representation of a chemical reaction using symbols. ■ All the factors which have to be taken account of in a situation can be called an **equation.** *The variability of rainfall is a crucial element in the whole equation.* ■ You can talk about the **equation** of two things when one is linked to the other. *...the equation of salaries with responsibility.*

equatorial is used to describe places and conditions on or near the Equator. *...equatorial Africa.*

equerry (*pron:* **ek**-kwer-ee) (equerries) An **equerry** is an officer of the royal household who acts as a personal assistant to a member of the royal family.

equestrian means connected with horse-riding. *...equestrian magazines.*

equestrianism is the art of horse riding.

equidistant If something is **equidistant** from two or more places, it is the same distance from each.

equilateral An **equilateral** triangle has all its sides the same length.

equilibrium is a balance between several different influences or aspects of a situation. *A flood of new goods may threaten the equilibrium of the market.* ■ A person's **equilibrium** is their calm state of mind, which can be upset when things go wrong.

equine means to do with horses. *...an equine vet.*

equinox (equinoxes) An **equinox** is one of the two days each year when the hours of daylight and darkness are of equal length. The spring equinox is in March and the autumn equinox in September.

equip (equipping, equipped) If you **equip** yourself with something you need for an activity, you obtain it. ■ If something is **equipped** with a particular feature, it has it. *...a helicopter equipped with powerful searchlights.* ■ If something **equips** you for a task or experience, it prepares you for that task or experience. *...the skills that equipped him so well for international diplomacy.*

equipment is the things needed for a particular activity. *...medical equipment.*

equitable (equitably) If a system or arrangement is **equitable,** it is fair to all people concerned.

equity (equities) **Equity** is fairness. ■ In law, **equity** is the principle which allows a fair judgment to be made where the existing law does not provide a reasonable answer to a problem. ■ **Equities** are shares which do not have a fixed rate of interest. They are also called 'ordinary shares'. ■ Your **equity** is the sum of your assets, for example the value of your house once your debts have been subtracted from it.

equivalent (equivalence) If one thing is **equivalent** to another, it is the same in size, amount, or function. If there is an **equivalence** between two things, they are equivalent.

equivocal (**equivocally**) If something someone says is **equivocal**, it is open to different interpretations. ...*an equivocal statement.*

equivocate (**equivocating, equivocated; equivocation**) If someone **equivocates**, they deliberately say things which can be interpreted in different ways.

era An **era** is a period of time, especially one dominated by a particular person or feature. ...*the jazz era.*

eradicate (**eradicating, eradicated; eradication**) If you **eradicate** something, you destroy it, or remove all traces of it.

erase (**erasing, erased**) If you **erase** a piece of writing, you rub it out. Similarly, you can **erase** a recording on tape. ■ You say a bad memory is **erased** when something good happens which makes you forget about it.

eraser An **eraser** is a rubber.

ere (*pron:* air) is an old word meaning 'before'.

erect (**erection**) When a building is **erected**, it is put up. ■ When a tent or flagpole is **erected**, it is raised to an upright position. ■ If you say someone is **erect**, you mean they are straight and upright. ■ When a system is **erected**, it is set up. ■ If a man has an **erection** or his penis becomes **erect**, his penis becomes firm and rises, because he is sexually aroused.

ergo is sometimes used to mean 'therefore' when the conclusion of an argument is being presented. *Neither side would have an incentive to start a war. Ergo, peace would reign.*

ergonomics (**ergonomic**) **Ergonomics** is the study of how working environments can be designed to ensure maximum comfort and convenience. **Ergonomic** is used to describe things which have been devised with this in mind. ...*ergonomic designs.*

ERM See **Exchange Rate Mechanism.**

ermine (*plural:* ermine *or* ermines) The **ermine** is a stoat which has its white winter coat. **Ermine** is the white fur taken from the dead animal.

erode (**eroding, eroded; erosion**) If rock is **eroded**, it is gradually worn away. This process is called **erosion**. ■ You can talk about other things being **eroded** when they are gradually reduced or taken away. ...*the erosion of educational standards.*

erogenous (*pron:* ir-**roj**-i-nuss) Your **erogenous** zones are the parts of your body which respond to sexual stimulation.

erosion See **erode.**

erotic (**erotically, eroticism**) If something is **erotic**, it is sexually stimulating. You can talk about the **eroticism** (*pron:* i-**rot**-iss-iz-um) of something like this.

erotica is sexually stimulating art or literature.

err If you **err**, you make a mistake. ■ If you **err on the side of** something, you decide to act in that way rather than in any other way. *The plan appears to err on the side of caution.*

errand If you go on an **errand**, you go somewhere to do something for someone.

errant is used to describe people who behave badly. For example, an **errant** husband is unfaithful to his wife.

errata An **errata** slip is a slip of paper inserted into a book after printing, listing errors and corrections.

erratic (**erratically**) If something is **erratic**, it is irregular and unpredictable. ...*erratic weather... He had been driving erratically.*

erroneous (*pron:* ir-**rone**-ee-uss) (**erroneously**) If information is **erroneous**, it is incorrect. ■ If something someone does is **erroneous**, it is a mistake and they should not have done it.

error An **error** is a mistake. **Error** is making mistakes. *There is no room for error.* If something is done **in error**, it is done by mistake.

ersatz (*pron:* **air**-zats) is used to describe things which are an imitation, especially a poor imitation. ...*ersatz soul music.*

erstwhile means 'former'. *He was critical of his erstwhile friend.*

erudite (*pron:* **air**-rude-ite) (**erudition**) If you say someone is **erudite** or talk about their **erudition**, you mean they are well-read and show great academic knowledge.

erupt (**eruption**) When a volcano **erupts**, it throws out lava and ash. When this happens, you say there is an **eruption**. ■ If something suddenly begins to burn fiercely, you can say it **erupts** in flames. ■ When fighting **erupts**, it suddenly breaks out or becomes more widespread. ■ If someone **erupts**, they suddenly lose their temper.

escalate (**escalating, escalated; escalation**) When costs **escalate** or there is an **escalation** in costs, they increase considerably. ■ When fighting or a dispute **escalates**, it becomes more fierce and widespread.

escalator An **escalator** is a moving staircase.

escalope (*pron:* ess-kal-lop) An **escalope** is a thin boneless slice of meat or fish.

escapade (*pron:* **ess**-kap-paid) An **escapade** is a reckless adventure.

escape (**escaping, escaped; escaper, escapee**) If someone **escapes** from a place, they get away. Someone who has escaped from prison can be called an **escaper** or **escapee**. ■ If you **escape** something unpleasant which seems likely to happen to you, you manage to avoid it. *They narrowly escaped arrest.* ■ If something **escapes** you, you fail to understand it or you cannot remember it. ■ If something **escapes** your notice, you fail to notice it. ■ Something which provides a temporary relief or distraction can be called an **escape**. *For many, alcohol is an escape from pain, grief or sheer boredom.* ■ If a gas or liquid **escapes**, it leaks out.

escapist (**escapism**) You say a book or film is **escapist** when it deals with things far removed from everyday life and problems, and can therefore take your mind off them. Finding relief in things like this is called **escapism**.

escapologist (**escapology**) An **escapologist** is an entertainer whose gets free of chains and handcuffs, often while in a confined space. Performing acts like this is called **escapology**.

escarpment An **escarpment** is a steep slope on one side of a hill which has a much gentler slope on the other side.

eschew If you **eschew** something, you avoid using it or associating with it. *He eschewed alcohol and tobacco products.*

escort If someone **escorts** you somewhere, they go with you to make sure you get there all right. ■ An **escort** is a person or group of people who travel with someone to protect or guard them. ■ An **escort** is a person who accompanies another person of the opposite sex to a social event. Sometimes people are paid to be escorts.

Eskimo (**Eskimos**) Eskimos are a group of people who live in various parts of the Arctic. Although the name 'Eskimo' is very common, the people themselves prefer to be called 'Inuits'.

esophagus See **oesophagus.**

esoteric (*pron:* ee-so-**ter**-rik) is used to describe things which can only be understood by a small number of people with special knowledge of a subject.

ESP is the ability some people believe they have to send or receive telepathic messages. ESP stands for 'extra-sensory perception'.

espadrille – **Espadrilles** are light canvas shoes with braided cord soles.

especial means exceptional or special in some way. *Friday's press conference was of especial interest.*

especially is used to say something applies more to one situation, person, or thing than others. *This year's negotiations will be especially difficult.*

Esperanto is an invented language based on words common to several European languages. It was designed to help people from different countries communicate with each other.

espionage (*pron:* ess-pyon-ahzh; *the 'zh' sounds like 's' in 'pleasure'*) **Espionage** is spying.

esplanade The **esplanade,** usually in a seaside town, is a wide open road where people walk for pleasure.

espouse (**espousing, espoused; espousal**) If you **espouse** a cause, you support it. *...his espousal of free-market principles.*

espresso is strong black coffee made by forcing steam or boiling water through ground coffee beans.

esprit de corps (*pron:* ess-pree de **kore**) is a feeling of loyalty and pride in belonging to a particular group.

espy (**espies, espying, espied**) If you **espy** something, you catch sight of it.

Esq. (*or* **Esquire**) is sometimes written after a man's name, especially when addressing an envelope. *...Chris Green Esq.*

essay (**essayist**) An **essay** is a piece of writing on a subject, either written by a student as part of a course, or by a writer for publication. A writer whose essays are well-known is called an **essayist.** ■ If you **essay** something, you attempt it. An **essay** is an attempt at something.

essence The **essence** of something is the most important thing about it. *The essence of a good government is that it is prepared to take difficult decisions.*

■ When people say time or speed is **of the essence,** they mean it is very important. ■ **In essence** means 'basically' or 'fundamentally'. *In essence, all computers are the same.* ■ **Essences** are highly concentrated liquids used for flavouring food or for their smell.

essential (**essentials**) If something is **essential,** you must have it, do it, or show it. *Caution is essential.* ■ Things people must have are called **essentials.** ■ The **essential** aspects of something are its most basic or important aspects. *Amendments are possible if they do not alter the essentials of the plan.* ■ **Essential oils** are concentrated aromatic oils extracted from plants and used in aromatherapy.

essentially You use **essentially** (a) when you are mentioning the main characteristic that someone or something has. *Her nature is essentially cheerful.* (b) to say something is generally true. *The rules remain essentially unchanged.* ■ You use **essentially** when you are saying what a situation really amounts to. *Essentially, the opposition groups want to curb the President's powers.*

establish (**establishes, establishing, established; establishment**) If something is **established,** it is created or set up in a permanent way. *...the establishment of a multi-party system.* ■ If you **establish** that something is the case, you find out that it is true. ■ People in positions of power in a country or organization are sometimes called **the establishment.** *...the cricketing establishment.* ■ A shop, restaurant, or other business premises is called an **establishment.**

estate An **estate** is a large area of land in the country, owned by one person or organization. ■ A housing or factory development is called an **estate.** ■ Someone's **estate** is the money and property they leave when they die. ■ An **estate** or **estate car** is a car with a long body, a rear door, and luggage space behind the back seats.

estate agent An **estate agent** is a person or company that arranges the sale of property.

esteem (**esteemed**) **Esteem** is admiration and respect. *He was esteemed by his neighbours.*

ester – **Esters** are a class of chemical compounds produced by the reaction between an alcohol and an acid.

esthete See **aesthete.**

esthetic See **aesthetic.**

estimable You use **estimable** to describe people who you think deserve to be praised and admired.

estimate (**estimating, estimated; estimation**) If you **estimate** a quantity or value, you calculate it approximately. *Sotheby's were left with 13 paintings, worth on their own estimation $23.5m.* An approximate calculation is called an **estimate.** ■ An **estimate** is a statement from someone like a builder of how much a job is likely to cost. ■ Your **estimation** of someone or something is your opinion of them.

estrange (**estranging, estranged; estrangement**) An **estranged** wife or husband is not living or communicating with their partner. ■ If you are **estranged** from your family, friends, or people who have been supporting you, you have quarrelled with them and are no longer in touch with them.

The trip will bring to an end more than twenty years of estrangement.

estrogen See **oestrogen.**

estuary (estuaries) An **estuary** is the wide part of a river where it joins the sea.

e-tail is retail that takes place on the Internet.

et al means 'and others'. It is used after a name to show there are others that you have not mentioned.

etc (*or* **etcetera**) (*both pron:* it-**set**-ra) **etc** means 'and so on' or 'and other things'.

etch (etches, etching, etched) If you **etch** a design or pattern on a surface, you cut it into the surface with acid, a sharp tool, or a laser. This process is called **etching.** ■ An **etching** is a picture printed from a metal plate which has had a design cut into it. ■ If something is **etched** on your mind, it has made such a deep impression on you that you are unlikely ever to forget it.

eternal (eternally) If something is **eternal,** it will never end. ■ **Eternal** truths and values never change, and are thought to be true in all situations. ■ You can talk about a personal relationship involving three people as the **eternal triangle,** when one person has to choose between their regular partner and their lover.

eternity is time without end, or a state of existence outside time, especially the state some people believe they will pass into when they die.

eternity ring An **eternity ring** is a ring given to someone as a token of lasting affection. It usually has tiny stones in a row all the way round it.

ether is a colourless sweet-smelling liquid, used in industry as a solvent. In the past, it was also used as an anaesthetic. ■ The air or sky is sometimes called the **ether.**

ethereal (*pron:* ith-**eer**-ee-al) is used to describe things which are very light and delicate, and seem to have a magical quality. *...her ethereal voice.*

ethic (ethics) Ethics are moral beliefs about right and wrong. ■ The **ethics** of a decision or course of action are the rights and wrongs of it. ■ **Ethics** is a branch of philosophy which deals with moral questions.

ethical (ethically) Ethical means to do with questions of right and wrong. *...ethical issues.* ■ If what you do is **ethical,** it conforms to accepted principles of correct behaviour.

ethnic (ethnically) Ethnic is used to describe (a) things based on racial or cultural differences. *...an ethnic conflict.* (b) things relating to minority racial or cultural groups. *...ethnic Chinese Cambodians.*

ethnic cleansing is the forcible removal of an ethnic group from an area where they live, so that another ethnic group dominates the area.

ethnicity Someone's **ethnicity** is their racial or cultural origins.

ethnography (ethnographic, ethnographer) Ethnography is the detailed study of ethnic groups, mainly through interviews and observation.

ethnology (ethnologist, ethnological) Ethnology is the comparative study of different cultures. ■ **Ethnology** is another name for ethnography.

ethos (*pron:* **eeth**-oss) The **ethos** of a group of people or an activity is the distinctive attitude, spirit, or values associated with them.

ethylene is a colourless gas. It has many industrial uses, for example in the manufacture of polythene.

etiolated (*pron:* ee-tee-oh-late-id) If a plant becomes **etiolated,** it turns pale through lack of sunlight. ■ If someone or something is **etiolated,** they lack colour, strength, or vigour.

etiquette (*pron:* et-ik-ket) is the polite behaviour expected on a particular occasion, or among members of a group or profession. *...business etiquette.*

etymology (*pron:* et-tim-**ol**-loj-ee) **(etymologies; etymological, etymologist) Etymology** is the study of the origins and historical development of words. **Etymological** is used to talk about things connected with etymology. ■ The **etymology** of a word is a description of how it is derived from other words.

EU See **European Union.**

eucalyptus trees are evergreen trees found mainly in Australia. They are grown for their timber, and for the strong-smelling medicinal oil produced by their leaves.

Eucharist (*pron:* **yew**-kar-ist) See **communion.**

eugenics (*pron:* yew-**jen**-iks) is selective breeding, especially a policy of only allowing certain people to have children.

eulogize (*or* **eulogise**) **(eulogizing, eulogized)** If you **eulogize** someone, you praise them highly.

eulogy (eulogies) A **eulogy** is a speech or piece of writing praising someone or something, especially someone who has recently died.

eunuch (*pron:* **yoo**-nuk) A **eunuch** is a man who has had his testicles removed.

euphemism (euphemistic, euphemistically) A **euphemism** is an inoffensive word or phrase people use to talk about subjects which people find embarrassing such as sex or death. **Euphemistic** is used to describe expressions like these. *...mobile brothels, euphemistically named 'comfort stations'.*

euphonious means pleasant to listen to. *...euphonious verse.*

euphonium A **euphonium** is a large brass instrument similar to a tuba.

euphoria (euphoric) Euphoria is a feeling of great happiness. If you are **euphoric,** you are extremely happy.

Eurasian people are of mixed European and Asian descent.

euro The **euro** is the unit of currency used by most of the members of the European Union.

Euro- at the beginning of a word shows it has something to do with Europe or the European Union. *...the Lisbon Euro-summit.*

Eurocentric (Eurocentrism) You say people or things are **Eurocentric** when you think they are biased towards Western Europe.

Eurocrat Civil servants who work for the European Commission are sometimes called **Eurocrats.**

Euroland (*or* **Eurozone**) **Euroland** is the geographical area containing the countries that have joined the European single currency.

European means in or from Europe. ■ A **European** comes from Europe.

European Commission The **European Commission** or **EC** is the executive body of the European Union, based in Brussels. It can propose legislation, and implements it when it is passed.

European Community The European Union was formerly called the **European Community** or **EC.**

Europeanise See **Europeanize.**

Europeanism is support for closer European integration.

Europeanize (or **Europeanise**) (**Europeanizing, Europeanized; Europeanization**) If a country is **Europeanized,** its way of life becomes like that of Europe.

European Monetary System The **European Monetary System** or **EMS** is a system which seeks to regulate the currencies of EU member states that have not adopted the euro.

European Parliament The **European Parliament** is the assembly of the European Union, based in Luxembourg.

European Union The **European Union** or **EU** is an association of European countries, founded by the Treaty of Rome in 1957. The current members are Austria, Belgium, Finland, France, Denmark, Germany, Greece, Italy, Luxembourg, the Netherlands, Portugal, the Republic of Ireland, Spain, Sweden, and the United Kingdom.

Europhile – **Europhiles** support closer European integration.

Europhobe – **Europhobes** are hostile to the European Union.

Eurosceptic – **Eurosceptics** are against closer European integration.

Eurozone See **Euroland.**

euthanasia is painlessly killing people who have illnesses or injuries which are going to be fatal, to end their suffering.

evacuate (**evacuating, evacuated; evacuation, evacuee**) If you are **evacuated** from a place, you leave it, because it has become dangerous. People who have been evacuated are called **evacuees.**

evade (**evading, evaded; evader**) If you **evade** doing something, you find ways of not doing it. ■ If you **evade** someone, you avoid meeting them. ■ If you **evade** someone or something, you avoid being caught by them. ■ If you **evade** a question, you avoid answering it. ■ People who avoid paying tax are called tax **evaders.**

evaluate (**evaluating, evaluated; evaluation**) If you **evaluate** something, you decide how good it is, or how much it is worth.

evanescent is used to describe things which fade away and disappear. *...an evanescent fragrance.*

evangelical is used to describe Protestant Christian beliefs which stress the importance of the Bible and of a personal conversion to Jesus Christ. Christians with these beliefs are called **evangelicals.**

evangelise See **evangelize.**

evangelism (**evangelist, evangelistic**) Evangelism is the preaching and spreading of the gospel, especially to non-Christians. A person who travels around doing this is called an **evangelist. Evangelistic** means to do with evangelism. ■ The **Evangelists** were Matthew, Mark, Luke, and John, the writers of the four New Testament Gospels.

evangelize (or **evangelise**) (**evangelizing, evangelized; evangelization**) If the people in a place are **evangelized,** attempts are made to convert them to Christianity.

evaporate (**evaporating, evaporated; evaporation**) When a liquid **evaporates,** it changes to a vapour. ■ You say things **evaporate** when they disappear. *Suddenly the joy evaporated and tenousness enveloped us.*

evaporated milk is tinned creamy milk with over half the water removed.

evasion (**evasive, evasiveness**) If someone deliberately avoids doing something, you can talk about their **evasion** of it. *...tax evasion.* ■ **Evasion** is deliberately not telling someone what they want to know. When someone does this, you say they are being **evasive,** or talk about their **evasiveness.** The things they say to avoid telling you what you want to know are called **evasions.** ■ If the driver of a vehicle takes **evasive action,** he or she does something to avoid a collision.

eve The **eve** of an event is the period just before it.

even (**evening, evened; evenly, evenness**) You use **even** (a) when you are mentioning something surprising. *Even the experts make mistakes.* (b) to say something is better, larger, etc than something else which is itself very good or very large. *This year the prize is even bigger.* ■ **Even as** is used to say something happens at exactly the same time as something else. *Even as he was speaking, shots were being fired less than two kilometres away.* ■ **Even** surfaces are flat and level. ■ If a measurement or rate is **even,** it stays at about the same level. *...an even pulse.* ■ If something **evens out,** it levels. ■ If there is an **even** distribution of something, it is shared out equally. *Ability is not evenly distributed.* ■ If there is an **even chance** of something happening, it is equally likely to happen or not happen. ■ An **even** number can be divided exactly by two.

even-handed (**even-handedly, even-handedness**) You say someone is **even-handed** when they treat all sides equally fairly.

evening The **evening** is the part of the day between the end of the afternoon and bedtime.

evening class An **evening class** is a course of study for adults, taught in the evening.

evening dress is the kind of clothing people wear on formal occasions in the evening. An **evening dress** is a woman's long dress worn on these occasions.

evensong is a Church of England service held in the late afternoon or early evening.

event An **event** is something which happens, especially something important. *The news has been dominated by events in Russia.* ■ An **event** is an organized social occasion. *The event is in aid of Cancer Research.* ■ In sport, an **event** is one of the competitions in a sporting programme. ■ You say **in the event** when you are describing what actually happened, as distinct from what people expected to happen or were afraid might happen. *In the event, both candidates gained a similar share of the votes.* ■ You say **in any**

event when you are mentioning something which is true regardless of what you have just said. *In any event, there will be political repercussions.*

even-tempered people are not easily provoked.

eventful An **eventful** time is full of exciting or important happenings.

eventing is taking part in a horse-riding competition which includes dressage, cross-country, and show jumping.

eventual The **eventual** result of a process or series of events is what happens at the end of it.

eventuality (**eventualities**) An **eventuality** is a possible future event.

eventually is used to say (a) something happens after a lot of delays. *Eventually, she told me what had happened.* (b) something happens at the end of a series of events, or as a final result of it. *He was a director and eventually became company chairman and chief executive.*

ever means at any time. *I am playing better than ever before.* ■ **Ever** is used to say someone or something is showing a characteristic which is typical of them. *Ever optimistic, airlines betted on a recovery and piled on extra flights.* ■ **Ever-** is used to say something continues to get larger or smaller, or to have more or less of a quality. *...the ever-swelling numbers of the homeless. ...ever-more sophisticated missiles.* ■ If something has been the case **ever since** a particular time, it has been the case all the time from then until now. *He's been there ever since you left.* ■ You use **ever** after words like 'how' and 'where' to express surprise. *How ever did you find me?*

evergreen An **evergreen** tree or shrub has green leaves all the year round. Trees and shrubs like these are also called **evergreens.**

everlasting (**everlastingly**) **Everlasting** is used to say something will never end, or seems as if it will never end. *...everlasting life.*

evermore (*or* **ever more**) For **evermore** means the same as 'forever'. *The hurt will be with us both for ever more.*

every is used to say something about all people or things of a particular kind. *Every child has a right to education.* ■ **Every** is used to say what proportion of a group something applies to. For example, if you say 'Every third applicant was a graduate', you mean one-third of the applicants were graduates. ■ **Every** is used to say things are positioned at regular intervals or happen at regular intervals. *Cleaning takes place once every five months.* ■ **Every** is used in phrases like 'every now and then' and 'every so often' to say something happens occasionally or fairly often. *Every so often the telephone rang.* ■ **Every** is used with words like 'chance', 'intention', and 'reason' to emphasize a point. For example, if you say there is every chance something will happen, you mean there is a very good chance it will happen.

everybody means the same as 'everyone'.

everyday things are happening all the time and are not unusual. *...the everyday problems of living in the city.*

everyone means all the people in a group, or people in general. *Everyone in the room was listening by this time... Everyone loves a wedding.*

everything means all the things in a group or place, or things in general. *Everything in the museum has to be cleaned... He said everything was under control.*

everywhere means all parts of a place or area, or all places in general. *Everywhere else in Hanoi, the cooking was even better... Carlos is accompanied everywhere by his bodyguard.*

evict (**eviction**) If people are **evicted,** they are forced to move out of the house they are living in, usually by a court order. This is called an **eviction.**

evidence (**evidencing, evidenced**) **Evidence** is anything you see, hear, or experience which suggests something is true or something exists. *The report found no evidence of fraud.* If something is **evidenced** by something else, the second thing shows the first thing is true or exists. ■ If you **give evidence,** you appear in court to say what you know about something. ■ If you say people or things are **in evidence,** you mean they are present and can be clearly seen.

evident If something is **evident,** it can easily be seen to exist or be a fact. *Deep discontent has been evident for some time.*

evidently You use **evidently** when you are mentioning something which seems to be true. *He had evidently made up his mind to attack Poland whatever happened.*

evil is a wicked power which some people believe exists and which is supposed to be opposed to God and all that is good. ■ If you call someone or something **evil,** you mean they are totally wicked. ■ The **evils** of something are all the bad or harmful things about it. *...the evils of drugs.* ■ If you have two choices, but think they are both bad, you can call the one which is less bad the **lesser of two evils.**

evince (**evincing, evinced**) If someone **evinces** a quality, feeling, or ability, they show they have it. *He evinced no surprise.*

eviscerate (**eviscerating, eviscerated; evisceration**) When a dead bird, animal, or fish is **eviscerated,** its intestines are removed.

evocation If you describe something as an **evocation** of a place or time, you mean it gives a vivid impression of it. *The film is a wonderful, gritty evocation of the style and music of the Weimar era.*

evocative (**evocatively**) If something like a description is **evocative,** it gives a vivid impression of a place or time. *The story is sharply evocative of Italian provincial life.*

evoke (**evoking, evoked**) If something **evokes** a sensation or impression, it causes you to have that sensation or impression. *...songs that evoke images of bright summer mornings.*

evolution (**evolutionary**) **Evolution** is a process of gradual change, often over millions of years, by which scientists believe living things adapt to their environments and sometimes form new species. **Evolutionary** means to do with this process. *...evolutionary change.* ■ The **evolution** of something is the process by which it gradually develops and changes. ...*the evolution of musical tastes.*

evolve (**evolving, evolved**) When animals or plants **evolve**, they gradually change by evolution. ■ If something like an organization or system **evolves**, it gradually develops or changes.

ewe A **ewe** is an adult female sheep.

ewer A **ewer** is a large wide-mouthed pitcher or jug.

ex- is used with words like 'president' and 'husband' to say someone is no longer the thing described by the word. ...*ex-servicemen.*

exacerbate (*pron:* ig-**zass**-er-bate) (**exacerbating, exacerbated; exacerbation**) If something **exacerbates** a bad situation, it makes it worse.

exact (**exactly, exactness; exacting**) Exact means accurate or precise. ...*an exact copy... Its screams were exactly like a baby's... Cook writes with a stomach-churning exactness about murder and mutilation.* ■ If you **exact** something such as an apology from someone, you make them give it to you. ■ If you **exact** your revenge on someone, you get it. ■ **Exacting** standards are very high and difficult to achieve. An **exacting** job or employer demands high standards.

exactitude If something is done with **exactitude**, it is done with great accuracy and care.

exactly See **exact.**

exaggerate (**exaggerating, exaggerated; exaggeratedly, exaggeration**) If you **exaggerate**, you make what you are talking about seem larger, better, worse, or more important than it really is. *It would not be an exaggeration to call it a national scandal.* ■ **Exaggerated** behaviour is extreme, and is usually put on to create an impression. ...*an exaggeratedly casual gesture.*

exalt (**exalted, exaltation**) If people **exalt** something, they praise it very highly. ■ **Exalted** is used, usually humorously, to talk about people who have a very important position. ...*the more exalted members of the British government.* ■ **Exaltation** is a powerful feeling of joy and happiness.

exam See **examine.**

examine (**examining, examined; examination**) If you **examine** something, you look at it closely and carefully. ■ When people **examine** something like a plan or problem, they investigate it and consider it in detail. ...*a wide ranging examination of adolescents' rights.* ■ When students are **examined**, they are set questions, usually on paper, to test their knowledge of a subject. This test is called an **exam** or an **examination.** ■ If you are **examined** by a doctor, he or she checks your body to find out whether there is anything wrong with you. This check is called an **examination.**

examinee An **examinee** is a person who is taking an examination. 'Candidate' is the more usual word.

examiner An **examiner** is a person who sets or marks an examination.

example If you give an **example** of something, you mention one thing which is typical of that kind of thing. ■ You say **for example** when you are giving an example of something. *Other historians, for example Charles Maier, have advanced similar arguments.* ■ If

you say someone is an **example** to other people, you mean they behave in a way which other people would do well to copy. You can also say someone **sets an example.** ■ If you **follow** someone's **example**, you do what they have done. ■ If people in authority **make an example** of someone who has done something wrong, they punish them severely, to discourage other people from behaving the same way.

exasperate (**exasperating, exasperated; exasperatingly, exasperation**) If something **exasperates** you, it makes you annoyed or frustrated. ...*an exasperatingly inconsistent genius.*

excavate (**excavating, excavated; excavation**) When archaeologists **excavate** a piece of land, they remove earth from it, to search for things buried there and find out more about the past. A search like this is called an **excavation.** ■ You say people **excavate** when they remove earth while digging a hole or tunnel.

excavator An **excavator** is a large machine with a mechanical arm used for digging, for example on a building site.

exceed (**exceeding, exceeded**) If something **exceeds** an amount, it is more than that amount. *Debts are believed to exceed £500,000.* ■ If you **exceed** a limit, you go beyond it. *Exceeding the stated dose can be harmful.*

exceedingly means the same as 'extremely'. *Progress is exceedingly slow.*

excel (**excelling, excelled**) If you **excel** at something, you are extremely good at it.

excellence See **excellent.**

Excellency (**Excellencies**) Some high-ranking officials, for example ambassadors, are given the title **His Excellency** or **Her Excellency.**

excellent (**excellently, excellence**) If something is **excellent**, it is extremely good. *The tournament was excellently organized.* ...*academic excellence.*

except (**excepting, excepted**) You use **except, except for, excepting,** or **excepted** when you are mentioning the only person or thing the statement does not apply to. ...*a bare room with nothing in it except a mirror... We are self-supporting for every kind of food excepting sugar and salt. Most knitwear (rayon excepted) can be handwashed.* ■ If someone or something is **excepted** from a requirement or restriction, it does not apply to them.

exception An **exception** to what you are saying is someone or something it does not apply to. ■ If you **make an exception**, you do something which goes against a general rule. ■ If you **take exception** to something, it annoys or offends you.

exceptional (**exceptionally**) Exceptional is used to describe situations which are very unusual. ...*quite exceptional circumstances.* ■ **Exceptional** and **exceptionally** are used to say someone or something has a quality to an unusual degree. *He's an exceptional athlete... ...exceptionally warm weather.*

excerpt An **excerpt** is a short piece of writing, film, or music taken from a longer piece.

excess (**excesses**) If there is an **excess** of something, there is more than is necessary or appropriate. ■ **In excess of** an amount means more than that amount. *He is estimated to be worth in excess of $5 billion.* ■ **Excesses** are examples of extreme or immoral behaviour, for example extreme cruelty or wastefulness. *...the excesses of the 1980s.*

excessive (**excessively**) If something is **excessive**, it goes beyond what is appropriate or reasonable. *...excessively high salaries.*

exchange (**exchanging, exchanged**) When people **exchange** things, they give them to each other at the same time. You can talk about an **exchange** of things. ■ If you **exchange** one thing for another, you replace the first thing with the second. ■ If you agree to do something **in exchange for** something else, you agree to do it if the other thing is done. ■ An **exchange** is a brief conversation, especially an angry one. ■ If there is an **exchange** of fire between two groups of soldiers, they fire at each other for a short time. ■ **Exchange** is used to talk about things connected with trading one currency for another. *...the exchange rate.*

exchangeable If something is **exchangeable** for something else, it can be given up in return for the other thing.

exchange rate An **exchange rate** is the number of units of one country's currency you get for each unit of another country's currency.

Exchange Rate Mechanism The **Exchange Rate Mechanism** or **ERM** is an agreement involving the EU countries that have not adopted the euro, under which governments must take action to stop the exchange rate values of their currencies going above or below certain limits. This is to keep exchange rates stable, making trade easier.

Exchequer The **Exchequer** is the government department responsible for collecting taxes and paying out public money.

excise (**excising, excised; excision**) **Excise** is a tax on certain goods such as tobacco and alcohol which are sold in the country where they are produced. ■ If something is **excised** from a piece of writing, it is removed, because someone disapproves of it.

excitable (**excitability**) An **excitable** person is easily excited.

excite (**exciting, excited; excitement, excitedly, excitingly**) If something **excites** you, it makes you feel very enthusiastic or eager. *He was trembling with excitement.* You say something which has an effect like this is **exciting.**

exclaim (**exclaiming, exclaimed; exclamation**) If a character in a book **exclaims** something, they say it in a way which shows they are surprised, angry, or excited. You call what they say an **exclamation.**

exclamation mark An **exclamation mark** is the punctuation mark **!** written after an exclamation, as in 'Oh no!'

exclude (**excluding, excluded; exclusion**) If you are **excluded** from an activity or place, you are prevented from taking part in that activity or entering that place. You can talk about someone's **exclusion** from an activity or place. ■ If you **exclude** something, you leave it out.

exclusion zone An **exclusion zone** is an area where specified people, planes, or ships are forbidden to go.

exclusive (**exclusiveness, exclusivity**) You call something **exclusive** when it is only available to a certain type of people, for example rich people. You talk about the **exclusiveness** or **exclusivity** of something like this. ■ If someone has **exclusive** ownership of something, they own it completely. Similarly, you can say someone has **exclusive** use of something. ■ When a newspaper calls one of its stories an **exclusive,** it means no other paper has it. ■ If two things are **mutually exclusive,** they contradict each other, so you can choose one or the other, but not both. ■ **Exclusive of** is used to say something is not included in what you are talking about. *They earn up to £100 a week, exclusive of board.*

exclusively If something is **exclusively** a particular thing, it is nothing but that thing. *The congregation is almost exclusively white and middle-class.* You can also say something is done **exclusively** in a particular way. *...making judgments exclusively on the basis of cost.*

excommunicate (**excommunicating, excommunicated; excommunication**) If a Roman Catholic or a member of the Orthodox church is **excommunicated,** they are proclaimed no longer a member of their Church, as a punishment.

excoriate (**excoriating, excoriated**) If someone is **excoriated,** they are strongly criticized for something they have done.

excrement (*pron:* eks-krim-ment) is the solid waste matter which passes out of the body through the bowels.

excrescence (*pron:* iks-**kress**-ens) An **excrescence** is a lump or growth on a plant or an animal's body. ■ You can call something such as a building an **excrescence** when you think it is ugly or unnecessary.

excreta (*pron:* iks-**kree**-ta) is human or animal waste matter, for example faeces, urine, or sweat.

excrete (**excreting, excreted; excretion**) When you **excrete** waste matter from your body, you get rid of it through faeces, urine, or sweat.

excruciating (**excruciatingly**) An **excruciating** pain is extremely severe and difficult to bear. ■ **Excruciating** is used to describe things which are frustrating or embarrassing.

exculpate (**exculpating, exculpated; exculpatory**) If someone is **exculpated,** they are shown to be free from guilt or blame. **Exculpatory** is used to describe things which have this effect. *...exculpatory evidence.*

excursion An **excursion** is a short journey, especially one taken for pleasure. ■ If you make an **excursion** into a subject or new activity, you try it out.

excusable If you say something is **excusable,** you mean it is understandable in the circumstances.

excuse (**excusing, excused**) An **excuse** is a reason why someone should not be blamed or punished for doing something wrong. ■ If you **excuse** (*pron:* ex-**kyooz**) someone's behaviour, you give reasons to justify it. ■ If you **excuse** someone for something they have done, you forgive them. ■ If someone **excuses** you from a duty, they let you off it. ■ You say someone is **excused** when they are given permission to leave.

ex-directory If you are **ex-directory**, you have arranged for your phone number not to be in the phone book.

exec An **exec** is an executive.

execrable If you say something is **execrable**, you mean it is of extremely poor quality.

execrate (**execrated; execration**) If you **execrate** someone or something, you dislike them intensely.

execute (**executing, executed; execution**) If someone is **executed**, they are put to death for committing a crime. Killing someone like this is called an **execution**. ■ The way you **execute** something is the way you carry it out.

executioner An **executioner** is someone whose job is executing criminals.

executive An **executive** is someone employed by a company at a senior level. ■ **Executive** is used to describe luxurious things intended for rich or important people. *...his plush executive suite.* ■ The **executive** or **executive committee** of an organization is a group of people who make important decisions on its behalf.

executor (*pron:* ik-**zek**-yoo-tor) Your **executor** is the person you appoint in your will to deal with your affairs after your death. ■ The **executor** of an order, wish, or policy is the person who carries it out.

exegesis (*pron:* eks-sij-**jee**-siss) (*plural* **exegeses**) (*pron:* eks-sij-**jee**-seez) An **exegesis** is an explanation and interpretation of a piece of writing, especially the Bible, based upon very careful study.

exemplar An **exemplar** of something is a perfect example of it.

exemplary is used to describe things which are done extremely well, and people who do something extremely well. *...an exemplary host.* ■ An **exemplary** punishment is intended to discourage others from committing the same crime.

exemplify (**exemplifies, exemplifying, exemplified**) If something **exemplifies** the situation you are talking about, it is a typical example of it. Similarly, a person can **exemplify** a quality. ■ If you **exemplify** something, you provide an example of it.

exempt (**exemption**) If you are **exempt** or **exempted** from something like a rule, it does not apply to you.

exercise (**exercising, exercised**) When you **exercise**, you do something energetic to keep yourself fit. **Exercises** are activities which keep you fit, usually involving repeated body movements. ■ If something like a problem **exercises** your mind, it requires a lot of thought. ■ An **exercise** is a short activity or piece of work you do which is designed to help you learn a particular skill, especially at school. ■ You can explain the purpose of something by saying it is an **exercise** of a particular kind. *...a public relations exercise.* ■ When people **exercise** their authority or rights, they use them. ■ If you **exercise** something like restraint, you show it in the way you behave.

exercise bike An **exercise bike** is a stationary machine which you pedal like a bicycle to get fit.

exercise book An **exercise book** is a book for doing school work in.

exert (**exertion**) If you **exert** something like influence or pressure, you use it to get what you want. ■ If you **exert** yourself, you make a physical or mental effort to achieve something. Efforts made to achieve something are called **exertions**.

ex gratia (*pron:* eks **gray**-sha) If someone is given an **ex gratia** payment, they are given money as a favour or a gift, rather than because it is legally owed to them.

exhale (**exhaling, exhaled; exhalation**) When you **exhale**, you breathe out.

exhaust (**exhausted, exhaustion**) If an activity **exhausts** you or leaves you **exhausted**, it uses up all your energy and makes you extremely tired. ■ If you **exhaust** something, you use it all up. *...the need to exhaust all peaceful ways of solving the crisis.* ■ **Exhaust** is waste gases produced by the engine of a motor vehicle. It is released through a pipe called the **exhaust** or **exhaust pipe.**

exhaustive (**exhaustively**) If something like a search or investigation is **exhaustive**, it is complete and thorough.

exhibit (**exhibiting, exhibited**) If something is **exhibited**, it is put on public display, for example in a museum. Items displayed like this are called **exhibits**. ■ An **exhibit** is an object shown in court as evidence. ■ In the US, an exhibition is sometimes called an **exhibit**. ■ If you **exhibit** something like a skill or characteristic, you show you have it.

exhibition An **exhibition** is a collection of things such as pictures which are put on display somewhere. ■ If a sportsperson's skills are very obvious during a game, you can say they give an **exhibition** of their skills.

exhibitionist (**exhibitionism**) You say someone is an **exhibitionist** when they keep doing things to make people notice them. You call this type of behaviour **exhibitionism.**

exhibitor An **exhibitor** is someone who has provided things for display at an exhibition.

exhilarate (**exhilarating, exhilarated; exhilaration**) If you are **exhilarated** by something, it gives you a feeling of pleasure and excitement. *I miss the physical exhilaration of singing.*

exhort (**exhortation**) If you **exhort** someone to do something, you urge them to do it as persuasively as you can.

exhume (**exhuming, exhumed; exhumation**) When a dead body is **exhumed**, it is taken out of its grave. This is called an **exhumation** of the body.

exigencies The **exigencies** of a situation or a job are the difficulties you have to deal with as part of it.

exile (**exiling, exiled**) If someone is **exiled** or sent into **exile**, they are sent away from their home country and not allowed to return. When this has happened to someone, you call them an **exile** or describe them as **exiled.** ■ People who have left their own country voluntarily to live somewhere else can be called **exiles.**

exist (**existence**) If something **exists,** it is really there, and not just something in someone's imagination. *No one doubts the existence of a lucrative market.* If something **exists** for a particular purpose, that is why it is there. *The arch exists to commemorate a victory.* ■ **Existing** is used to describe things which are there now, as distinct from things which may replace them in the future. ■ You call someone's way of life an **existence** when you think they get very little enjoyment from it, for example because they are very poor or very lonely.

existentialism (**existentialist, existential**) Existentialism is a philosophical belief which stresses the importance of human experience and the responsibility of each person for their own actions. **Existential** behaviour and feelings are those caused by thinking about human existence.

exit An **exit** is a way out of a building or other place. ■ An **exit** is a place where traffic can leave a motorway. ■ When someone leaves a place, an organization, or an activity, you can call their leaving an **exit**. *She made a dignified exit. ...their early exit from the World Cup.* ■ **Exit** is used to describe official documents which give people permission to leave their country. *...exit visas.* ■ An **exit** or **exit route** is a way out of an undesirable situation. *He is desperately trying to find an exit from the crisis.*

exit poll In an election, an **exit poll** is a survey carried out as people leave the polling stations, in which they are asked who they voted for.

exodus In the Bible, the **Exodus** was the journey of the Jews, led by Moses, out of their slavery in Egypt. **Exodus** is now used to talk about any large group of people leaving a place or organization.

ex officio (*pron:* eks off-**fish**-ee-oh) is used to describe something such as a rank or privilege that someone is entitled to because of their job or position.

exonerate (**exonerating, exonerated; exoneration**) If someone is **exonerated,** it is shown that they are not to blame for something.

exorbitant (**exorbitantly**) If you say the price of something is **exorbitant,** you mean it is much higher than it should be.

exorcize (*or* **exorcise**) (**exorcizing, exorcized; exorcism, exorcist**) People who believe a place or person can be possessed by evil spirits often think these spirits can be **exorcized;** this means driving them out in a special ceremony called an **exorcism.** The person who conducts the ceremony is called an **exorcist.** ■ If you **exorcize** something like a bad memory or a run of bad luck, you succeed in getting rid of it or putting an end to it.

exotic (**exotically; exoticism, exotica**) If something is **exotic,** it is unusual and interesting, because it is connected with a faraway country. You can talk about the **exoticism** of something like this. Exotic things generally can be called **exotica.**

expand (**expansion**) If something **expands** or is **expanded,** it gets larger. When this happens, you talk about its **expansion.** *...a rapidly expanding market.* ■ If you **expand on** something you have already mentioned, you talk about it in greater detail.

expanse An **expanse** of something is a very large area of it.

expansionary is used to describe policies and conditions which lead to an increase in a country's economic activity.

expansionism (**expansionist**) If a country has a policy of **expansionism,** it aims to increase its size by taking land from other countries.

expansive (**expansively, expansiveness**) If an area is **expansive,** it is unusually large. ■ If someone is **expansive** or in an **expansive** mood, they are relaxed, happy, and able to express their feelings freely.

expat (*or* **ex-pat**) means the same as expatriate.

expatriate (*or* **ex-patriate**) (*pron:* eks-**pat**-ree-it) An **expatriate** is someone who lives in a country which is not their own.

expect If you **expect** something to happen, you think it will happen. ■ If you are **expecting** something like a letter, you believe it will arrive soon. ■ If you say someone can **expect** a certain kind of treatment, you mean that is the way they are likely to be treated. *A member of the royal family can never expect the privacy of a commoner.* ■ If you say you **expect** someone to do something, you mean they ought to do it, as their duty. *We expect our governments and employers to protect us.* ■ People say **I expect...** when they are saying something which they think is probably true. *I expect you're right.* ■ If a woman is **expecting** a baby, she is pregnant.

expectant (**expectantly, expectancy**) If people are **expectant,** they are excited, because they think something interesting is going to happen. This feeling is called **expectancy.** *The media gathered expectantly outside the Treasury building.* ■ An **expectant** mother or father is someone whose baby is going to be born soon. ■ See also **life expectancy.**

expectation Your **expectations** are your beliefs about what is going to happen. *Contrary to our expectations, he did not try to take over the running of the home.* ■ People's **expectations** are their beliefs about what should happen or what other people should do. *...to live up to her family's expectations.*

expedient (**expediency**) If you do something because it is **expedient,** you do it because it is easy and convenient, rather than because it is morally right or the best thing to do. Behaviour like this is called **expediency.** ■ An **expedient** is something you do which gets you out of an immediate problem, though it may not be the best thing to do in the long run.

expedite (**expediting, expedited**) If you **expedite** something like a plan, you hurry it up.

expedition An **expedition** is an organized journey made for a special purpose, for example exploration. A group of people who make a journey like this can also be called an **expedition.**

expeditionary An **expeditionary** force is a group of soldiers sent to fight in a foreign country.

expeditious (**expeditiously**) Expeditious is used to describe things which are carried out quickly and efficiently. *Arbitration is a fair and expeditious decision-making process.*

expel (**expelling, expelled; expulsion**) If someone is **expelled** from a school or other organization, they are made to leave because of bad behaviour. This is called **expulsion.** ■ When people are **expelled** from a place, they are forced to leave. ...*the forcible expulsion of civilians.* ■ If something like a liquid or gas is **expelled** from a place, it is forced out of it.

expend If you **expend** time, energy, or money on something, you spend or use it that way. *Little effort has been expended on finding an alternative.*

expendable If you say someone or something is **expendable,** you mean they are not important and can be sacrificed if necessary.

expenditure is the amount of time, energy, or money spent on something. *They should cut their expenditure on defence.*

expense The **expense** of doing something is what it costs. An **expense** is something you have to spend money on. ■ **Expenses** are amounts of money you spend in connection with your job, which you can claim back from your employer. ■ If someone provides the money for something, you can say it is done **at** their **expense.** ...*a government that bailed out banks at local taxpayers' expense.* ■ You can say something is done at someone's **expense** when they are worse off as a result of it. *Costs may be trimmed at the expense of the patient.* ■ If you make a joke at someone's **expense,** they are the subject of it and it can make them seem foolish.

expense account An **expense account** is an arrangement by which a company allows an employee to spend its money on things which are part of the job, for example travelling or entertaining clients.

expensive (**expensively**) If something is **expensive,** it costs a lot of money.

experience (**experiencing, experienced**) If you have had **experience** of something, you have seen it, done it, or felt it. ■ An **experience** is something which happens to you or something you do. ■ If you **experience** a situation or feeling, it happens to you or you are affected by it. ■ Your **experience** is all the things which have happened to you, especially things which have increased your knowledge or understanding. ■ If someone is **experienced** at something, they have been doing it for a long time and know a lot about it.

experiment (**experimentation, experimenter, experimentalist**) An **experiment** is a scientific test to prove or discover something. When a scientist **experiments** with something, he or she does a test like this. This method of gaining knowledge is called **experimentation.** ■ If you do something new to see how it works out, you can say you are **experimenting** or call it an **experiment.** People who try out new things can be called **experimenters** or **experimentalists.** Trying out new things is called **experimentation.**

experimental (**experimentally**) If something is **experimental,** it involves new ideas being tried out to see if they work. *The scheme was run experimentally in Scotland.* ■ You call something like a novel or play **experimental** when it involves new ways of telling

a story or new ways of presenting drama, music, or dance. ■ **Experimental** means involving scientific experiments. ...*experimental evidence.*

experimentalist See **experiment.**

expert (**expertly**) An **expert** on a subject is someone who is extremely knowledgeable about it. ■ If someone is an **expert** at something, they are extremely good at it. ...*three expertly-taken goals.*

expertise (*pron:* eks-per-**teez**) is special skill or knowledge.

expiate (**expiating, expiated; expiation**) If you **expiate** some wrong you have done, you do something which makes up for it.

expire (**expiring, expired; expiration, expiry**) When something **expires,** it comes to an end, or the period for which it is valid comes to an end. ■ When a person **expires,** they die.

explain (**explaining, explained; explanation**) If you **explain** something or give an **explanation** of it, you go into details about it, to help people understand it. ■ If you **explain** something you have done, you give reasons for it. ■ If someone asks you to **explain yourself,** they want to know why you seem to have behaved badly. ■ If you **explain away** a problem or a mistake, you try to show it is not really your fault or it is not important.

explanatory is used to describe something like a diagram or piece of writing which is provided to help people understand something. ...*an explanatory video.*

expletive (*pron:* iks-**plee**-tiv) An **expletive** is a swear word.

explicable If something is **explicable,** it can be explained.

explicate (**explicating, explicated**) If you **explicate** something, you explain it.

explicit (**explicitly, explicitness**) If you are **explicit** about something, you say clearly and openly what you mean. ■ If a book or film is sexually **explicit,** it deals with sex in a frank and open way, which some people might find shocking.

explode (**exploding, exploded**) When a bomb **explodes,** it goes off. ■ You say something **explodes** when it increases suddenly and rapidly. *The sports market has exploded in the past twenty years.* ■ If someone **explodes,** they lose their temper. ■ If a situation **explodes,** violence suddenly breaks out. ■ If you **explode** a belief, you prove it is wrong.

exploit (**exploiting, exploited; exploitation, exploiter**) If someone **exploits** you, they treat you unfairly by using your work or ideas and giving you little in return. Behaviour like this is called **exploitation;** a person who exploits people is called an **exploiter.** ■ If you **exploit** something, you make use of it, to make money or get some other advantage. ...*the commercial exploitation of fast-growing trees.* ■ When you talk about a person's **exploits** (*pron:* **ex**-ploits), you mean the exciting or interesting things they have done.

exploitable If someone or something is **exploitable,** you can use them to make money or get something else you want. *Slaves were exploitable cheap labour.*

exploitative If a person or organization is **exploitative,** they treat people unfairly by using their work or ideas and giving them little in return.

exploratory is used to describe something like a preliminary meeting which takes place to assess the situation before going ahead with the main meeting. ...*exploratory talks.*

explore (**exploring, explored; exploration**) If you **explore** a place, you travel around it to find out what it is like. ■ Oil or gas **exploration** is searching for oil or gas. ■ If you **explore** an idea, you consider it carefully and in detail.

explorer An **explorer** is a person who travels to places about which little is known, to discover what is there. ■ An oil or gas **explorer** is a person or organization whose business involves searching for oil or gas.

explosion An **explosion** is a sudden violent release of energy, for example one caused by a bomb. ■ An **explosion** of something is a sudden rapid increase in it. ...*an explosion of new magazines.* ■ When people suddenly become very angry, you can say there is an **explosion** of anger.

explosive (**explosively**) An **explosive** substance is one which can cause an explosion. ■ An **explosive** is a substance manufactured for the purpose of causing explosions. ■ An **explosive** issue could cause a lot of controversy. ■ An **explosive** situation could easily lead to violence. ■ An **explosive** increase is sudden and rapid.

exponent An **exponent** of an idea is someone who argues in favour of it or explains it to people. ...*an exponent of free enterprise.* ■ An **exponent** of a skill is someone who is good at it. ...*the greatest serve-and-volley exponent we have seen.*

exponential (**exponentially**) If there is **exponential** growth in something, it grows at an increasing rate.

export If materials or goods are **exported,** they are sent out of the country and sold to people or firms in other countries. You talk about the **export** of goods or materials; the goods and materials are called **exports.** ■ If a country's ideas or values are **exported,** they are introduced to other countries and adopted by the people there. ■ In computing, if you **export** files or information from one type of software into another, you change their format so that they can be used in the new software.

exportable If a product is **exportable,** you mean people in other countries are willing to buy it.

exporter An **exporter** is a country, firm, or person that sells goods to people or organizations in other countries. *The Ivory Coast became the world's fourth-largest coffee exporter.*

expose (**exposing, exposed**) If you **expose** something which is normally covered, you uncover it and make it visible. ■ If a well-known person is **exposed,** they are shown to have been behaving in a shocking or dishonest way. You can also say someone's wrongdoings are **exposed.** ■ If you are **exposed** to something dangerous or unpleasant, you are in a situation where you can be affected by it. *Redecorating had exposed him to high levels of asbestos.* ■ An **exposed** place is one where you get little

protection from bad weather. ■ If a man **exposes** himself, he deliberately shows his genitals in a public place.

exposé (*pron:* iks-**pose**-ay) An **exposé** is a newspaper article or TV programme which reveals the truth about something shocking or dishonest.

exposition (**expository**) An **exposition** of an idea is a detailed explanation of it. **Expository** is used to talk about explaining things. ...*expository writings.*

expostulate (**expostulating, expostulated**) If you **expostulate,** you protest at something someone has just said. *'I didn't say that,' he expostulated.*

exposure to something harmful is being in a situation where you can be affected by it. ...*a possible link between aluminium exposure and brain damage.* ■ If someone is suffering from **exposure,** their body temperature has become dangerously low as a result of being out in very cold weather. ■ **Exposure** is publicity. ...*the instant success that national television exposure can offer.* ■ If you talk about the **exposure** of some wrongdoing, you mean it is discovered and made public. You can also talk about the **exposure** of the people responsible. ■ In photography, an **exposure** is a single photograph.

expound If you **expound** an idea, you go into details about it.

express (**expresses, expressing, expressed; expressly**) The way you **express** yourself is the way you use language to say what you mean. ■ If you **express** an idea, you put it into words. ■ If you **express** your feelings, you do something which shows how you feel. *Truck drivers expressed their anger by blocking major roads.* ■ If an amount is **expressed** as a fraction or percentage of another amount, it is given in that form. ■ An **express** order is stated clearly, without any possibility of misunderstanding. *We were expressly forbidden to join in any singing.* ■ The **express** purpose of something is the whole reason for doing it. ■ An **express** service gets things done quicker than usual. ...*express mail.* ■ An **express** is a fast train or coach which makes fewer stops than other trains or coaches.

expression When ideas or feelings are put into words, you call this the **expression** of those ideas or feelings. ■ An action can be described as an **expression** of someone's feelings, or of their intentions. *The 1976 Constitution was an expression of the state's attempts to acquire complete control over its citizens' lives.* ■ Your **expression** is the look on your face, which shows what you are thinking or feeling. ■ An **expression** is a word or phrase. *Alfred Sauvy coined the expression 'the Third World'.*

expressionism (**expressionist, expressionistic**) **Expressionism** is a style of art, literature, and film which uses symbolism and exaggeration to represent emotions rather than representing physical reality. ...*expressionistic imagery.*

expressionless If someone is **expressionless,** their face shows no emotion.

expressive (**expressively, expressiveness**) If something is **expressive,** it clearly shows someone's feelings. ...*her wonderfully expressive face.* ■ If a musical performance is **expressive,** it succeeds in bringing out the emotional qualities in the music.

expressway An **expressway** is a road with several lanes designed for a lot of traffic to move along quickly, especially in a city.

expropriate (expropriating, expropriated; expropriation) If something is **expropriated,** it is taken away from its owner, especially by a government.

expulsion See **expel.**

expunge (expunging, expunged) If something unpleasant is **expunged** from your memory, you succeed in forgetting about it. ■ If something is **expunged** from written records, it is removed from them.

expurgate (pron: eks-per-gate) (expurgating, expurgated) If something like a film or article is **expurgated,** parts of it are cut to avoid shocking or offending people.

exquisite (exquisitely) Exquisite is used to describe things which are extremely beautiful, especially things done or made with great skill and artistry. ...*exquisitely crafted dolls' houses.* ■ **Exquisite** is sometimes used to emphasize the intensity of a feeling. ...*exquisite embarrassment.*

extant is used to describe things from the past which have survived, rather than being lost or destroyed. ...*the one extant Holbein portrait of Henry.*

extempore (pron: eks-**tem**-por-ree) An **extempore** talk or speech has not been prepared in advance.

extend If you **extend** something, you make it bigger or last longer. ■ If something **extends** over a certain area, it covers that area. ■ If something **extends** over a period of time, it continues for that period. ■ If you **extend** your arm or leg, you straighten it or stretch it out. ■ If you **extend** an invitation to someone, you offer it to them. ■ If you say something **extends** to certain things or people, you mean it includes or applies to them. ■ Your **extended** family includes people like your aunts, uncles, and cousins, as well as your father, mother, sisters, and brothers.

extension An **extension** is something added to something else, making it larger. ■ An **extension** is an added amount of time, making something last longer. ...*a six-month extension to his visa.* ■ An **extension** of a law is an alteration which makes it apply to more people or things. ■ A telephone **extension** is one of several phones in a building or group of buildings connected to a central phone or switchboard.

extensive (extensively) If something is **extensive,** there is a lot of it or it covers a large area.

extent The **extent** of something is its size or scale. *The full extent of the damage is not yet known.* ■ The **extent** to which something is the case is the degree to which it is the case. *To a certain extent it is easier for men to get work.*

extenuating If you say there are **extenuating circumstances,** you mean someone's mistake or crime can be considered less serious because of the situation they were in at the time.

exterior The **exterior** of something is its outside. ...*exterior warning lights.* ■ When you talk about a person's **exterior,** you mean their appearance and the kind of impression they create, which may be different from their real character.

exterminate (exterminating, exterminated; extermination) When a group of people are **exterminated,** they are all killed. You can also talk about animals or plants being **exterminated.**

exterminator An **exterminator** is a person or substance that destroys animals or plants which are considered to be a nuisance or danger. ...*a pest exterminator.*

external (externally) External is used to talk about the dealings a country or an organization has with other countries or organizations. ...*Argentina's minister of external affairs.* ■ **External** is used to talk about things on the outside of a building or other object. ...*an external staircase.*

extinct (extinction) If a species of animal becomes **extinct,** the whole species dies out. ■ If a volcano is **extinct,** it is not expected to erupt again. ■ You can say beliefs or types of people are **extinct** when they no longer exist. ...*an ethical principle that now looks threatened with extinction.*

extinguish (extinguishes, extinguishing, extinguished) If you **extinguish** a fire or a light, you put it out. ■ If someone's hopes or fears are **extinguished,** something puts an end to them.

extirpate (pron: eks-tir-pate) (extirpating, extirpated; extirpation) If you **extirpate** something, you get rid of it completely.

extol (extolling, extolled) If you **extol** something, you praise it highly and talk about it enthusiastically.

extort (extortion) If someone **extorts** money from you, they use force or threats to get it. **Extortion** is the crime of obtaining money in this way. ■ If someone **extorts** a confession from you, they use force or threats to make you confess to something.

extortionate If you say the price of something is **extortionate,** you mean it costs far more than is fair.

extra is used to talk about something being added to other things of the same kind. *Hospitals will receive extra money.* ■ **Extras** are things which are not standard or essential but which make something more comfortable, useful, or enjoyable. ■ **Extras** are additional amounts of money added to the basic price of something. ■ An **extra** is someone who plays an unimportant part in a film, especially a non-speaking part. ■ **Extra** is used to mean 'greater or larger than usual'. ...*an extra special weekend... Take extra care.* ...*extra-long sleeves.*

extract If something is **extracted,** it is taken out or pulled out. ■ When coal or other raw materials are **extracted,** they are taken from the ground. ■ You say a substance is **extracted** when it is obtained by separating it from other substances. An **extract** is a substance obtained in this way. ...*vegetable extract.* ■ If you **extract** something from someone, you get it from them although they do not want to give it to you. *Moscow seemed to be using the occasion to extract every possible concession from Bonn.* ■ An **extract** from a piece of writing or music is a small part printed or played separately.

extraction If you say someone is of a particular **extraction,** you mean their family originally came from a different country. *...an American of German extraction.* ■ **Extraction** is the removal of something, especially the removal of things like minerals from the ground.

extractor An **extractor** or **extractor fan** is a device in a window or wall which draws steam, air, or smoke out of a room.

extra-curricular activities are activities for students, like sports, which are not part of the regular timetable.

extradite (**extraditing, extradited; extradition**) If someone is **extradited,** they are officially sent back to their own country to stand trial for a crime. An **extradition warrant** is a legal document issued by one country and sent to another country, asking them to hand over someone they want to put on trial. An **extradition treaty** is an official arrangement between two countries under which each agrees to send back any of the other's citizens if they are wanted for trial in their home country.

extra-judicial (**extra-judicially**) **Extra-judicial** killings are carried out on behalf of a government but without a trial or any other legal procedure.

extra-marital (*or* extramarital) An **extra-marital** relationship is between a married person and someone who is not their husband or wife.

extraneous is used to describe matters which are brought into something like a discussion and which are not relevant to it.

extraordinaire (*pron:* eks-tra-ord-in-**air**) is used to say someone is outstandingly successful at something. *Billie Holiday, jazz singer extraordinaire.*

extraordinary (**extraordinarily**) **Extraordinary** is used to say someone or something has a quality or characteristic to a very high degree. *...the extraordinary beauty of the setting.* ■ If you say someone or something is **extraordinary,** you mean they are remarkable or unusual. *...extraordinary events.* ■ An **extraordinary meeting** is one specially arranged to deal with a particular problem.

extra-parliamentary political activity is aimed at producing changes to society without involving parliament.

extrapolate (*pron:* eks-**trap**-a-late) (**extrapolating, extrapolated; extrapolation**) In maths or statistics, if you **extrapolate** a result which cannot be calculated exactly or measured directly, you estimate it from figures which you know are correct. A result obtained like this is called an **extrapolation.**

extra-sensory perception (*or* extrasensory perception) See **ESP.**

extraterrestrial (*or* extra-terrestrial) is used to describe things which happen, exist, or come from somewhere beyond the planet Earth. ■ In science fiction, an **extraterrestrial** is a creature from another planet.

extra time In knock-out competitions, **extra time** is an additional period of playing time which is added on if the result is still a draw after normal playing time.

extravagant (**extravagantly, extravagance**) If someone is **extravagant,** they keep spending money on things which are not really necessary. You talk about the **extravagance** of someone like this. You say the things they buy are **extravagances.** ■ **Extravagant** is used to describe things people say or do which are exaggerated. *...extravagantly dramatic gestures.* ■ **Extravagant** ideas or claims are unrealistic and impractical. ■ **Extravagant** entertainments or designs are colourful or spectacular.

extravaganza An **extravaganza** is an elaborate and impressive performance or public event.

extreme (**extremely**) **Extreme, extremely,** and **in the extreme** are all used to say something has a characteristic to a very great degree. *It is proving controversial in the extreme.* ■ **Extremes** are the highest and lowest points on a scale. *...extremes of weather.* ■ The **extreme** points or edges of something are the ones furthest from its centre. *...the extreme north-east of the country.* ■ **Extreme** opinions or methods go beyond what most people believe is sensible or reasonable. *...extreme nationalists.* ■ If you say someone is going to **extremes,** you mean they are behaving in a foolish way by taking something too far.

extremis See **in extremis.**

extremist (**extremism**) An **extremist** is a person who wants to bring about social or political change using extreme methods which most people find unacceptable. You talk about the **extremism** of someone like this.

extremity (**extremities**) The **extremities** of something are its farthest points or edges. *...the north-west extremity of Europe.* ■ A person's **extremities** are the outermost parts of their body such as their hands and feet. ■ When people do things which are unacceptable, you can talk about the **extremity** of their actions. ■ An **extremity** is a very serious situation. *Never has the public been reduced to such an extremity of helplessness as by this recent strike.*

extricate (**extricating, extricated**) If you **extricate** someone from a difficult situation, you get them out of it.

extrovert An **extrovert** is an outgoing person who enjoys being the centre of attention.

extrude (**extruding, extruded**) If a substance is **extruded,** it is squeezed out through a small opening.

exuberant (**exuberantly, exuberance**) **Exuberant** behaviour is energetic and high-spirited.

exude (**exuding, exuded**) If you say someone **exudes** a characteristic or feeling, you mean they seem to have a lot of it. *The chief minister exudes confidence.* ■ If something **exudes** a substance, the substance comes out through its surface. *...fatty acids exuded from the human skin.* ■ If something **exudes** a smell, it gives it off.

exult (**exultant, exultation**) If you **exult** at something or **exult** in it, you feel or show triumphant pleasure about it. You say someone who feels or behaves like this is **exultant;** you call their feelings or behaviour **exultation.**

eye (**eyeing, eyed; -eyed**) Your **eyes** are the organs you use for seeing. ■ You can add **-eyed** to a word to say what someone's eyes look like or to indicate their facial expression. *...a blue-eyed blonde.*

...*starry-eyed teenagers.* ■ If you **eye** someone or something in a particular way, you look at them in that way. *He eyed the scene with distaste.* ■ A person's **eye** for something is their ability to spot it or make good judgments about it. *Honda has a keen eye for market opportunities.* ■ **With an eye to** is used to say why something is done. *They have travelled around Europe with an eye to expansion.* ■ You say **in the eyes of...** when you are describing someone's interpretation of events. *It is still, in the eyes of thousands, the best car ever made.* ■ If you do not **see eye to eye** with someone, you disagree with them. ■ The **eye** of a needle is the hole at the blunt end which you pass the thread through. ■ On a potato, the **eyes** are the tiny buds on its surface from which shoots grow if it is left for long enough. ■ The **eye** of a storm is the small area of calm at its centre.

eyeball A person's **eyeballs** are the whole of their eyes. ■ If people are **eyeball to eyeball,** they are facing each other in a confrontational way.

eyebrow A person's **eyebrows** are the lines of hair on the ridges above their eye-sockets. ■ If you say **eyebrows are raised,** you mean people are rather surprised at something.

eye-catching things are very noticeable.

eyelash (**eyelashes**) A person's **eyelashes** are the hairs on the edges of their eyelids.

eyelet An **eyelet** is a small hole with a metal or leather ring round it, for example in a sail, through which cord or rope is threaded.

eyelid A person's **eyelids** are the flaps of skin which cover their eyes when they are shut. ■ If you say nobody **bats an eyelid** when something happens, you mean nobody is shocked or surprised.

eyeliner is make-up used to draw an outline round the eyes.

eye-opener If something is an **eye-opener,** it makes you unexpectedly aware of things you knew nothing about before.

eyepiece The **eyepiece** of a telescope or microscope is the glass at the end you look through.

eye-shadow is make-up put on the eyelids to colour them.

eyesight Your **eyesight** is your ability to see.

eye socket A person's **eye sockets** are the two bony holes on either side of their face which hold their eyeballs.

eyesore If you call something like a building or area an **eyesore,** you mean it is ugly.

eye tooth See **canine.**

eyewitness (or **eye-witness**) (**eyewitnesses**) If someone is an **eyewitness** to something like a crime or accident, they saw it happen.

eyrie (*pron:* ear-ree) An **eyrie** is the nest of an eagle or similar bird, usually built high up on the side of a cliff or mountain. Any high room or place can be called an eyrie.

F f

fable A **fable** is a story with a moral.

fabled people, things, and places are well-known because of the stories told about them.

fabric is a type of cloth. ■ The **fabric** of a building is its basic structure, for example its walls and roof. ■ When people talk about the **fabric** of a social system, they mean the way it holds together. *Racism is destroying the fabric of the community.*

fabricate (**fabricating, fabricated; fabrication**) If someone **fabricates** a statement, they make it up.

fabulous (**fabulously**) If you say someone or something is **fabulous,** you are emphasizing how pleasing or impressive you find them. *Wendy looked fabulous. ...fabulously wealthy.*

facade (or **façade**) (*pron:* fas-**sahd**) The **facade** of a large building is the part of its front wall facing the street. ■ You call people's behaviour a **facade** when it hides their real feelings. *...the grim facts behind the facade of gaiety.*

face (**facing, faced; -faced**) Your **face** is the front of your head from your chin to your forehead. **-faced** can be added to a word to describe someone's face or expression. *...a chubby-faced teenager.* See also **two-faced.** ■ A clock's **face** is the part which shows the time. ■ The **face** of a mountain or cliff is a very steep side of it. ■ You can talk about the **face** of a particular organization, place, or activity when you mean the image people have of it. *...changing the face of rugby in Wales. ...the transformation of the face of London.* ■ If you are **facing** someone or **facing** a particular direction, you are looking at that person or in that direction. ■ If you **face** a difficulty or challenge, you have to deal with it. ■ If someone **faces up to** a difficult situation, they reluctantly accept it and deal with it. ■ If you do something to avoid **losing face** or to **save face,** you do it to stop people losing respect for you. ■ **In the face of** is used to say how someone behaves or feels in a difficult situation. *...a feeling of helplessness in the face of insurmountable odds.* ■ **face value:** see **value. fly in the face of:** see **fly.**

faceless If you describe people or things as **faceless,** you think they lack personality or individuality. **Faceless** people are people you deal with from an organization but never get to meet or get to know. *...faceless bureaucrats.*

facelift A **facelift** is an operation to tighten the skin on someone's face, to make them look younger. ■ When a building or district is given a **facelift,** work is done to improve its appearance.

face-saving (**face-saver**) A **face-saving** arrangement is intended to prevent someone losing other people's respect.

facet (*pron:* **fas**-it) A **facet** of something is an aspect of it. *...an interesting facet of his character.* ■ The **facets** of a jewel are its flat regularly-shaped sides.

facetious (*pron:* fas-**see**-shuss) If someone makes a humorous remark during a serious discussion, you can say they are being **facetious.**

facia See **fascia.**

facial (*pron:* **fay**-shal) means to do with the face. *...facial hair.* ■ A **facial** is a type of beauty treatment for the face.

facile (*pron:* **fas**-sile) is used to say that something such as an explanation is too simple and obvious. *...the temptation to make facile judgements.*

facilitate (**facilitating, facilitated**) If something **facilitates** a process, it makes it easier.

facility (**facilities**) **Facilities** are buildings or equipment which are provided for a particular purpose. *...play facilities for young children.* ■ You can call a useful feature a **facility.** *...a computer with a message-swapping facility.*

facsimile (*pron:* fak-**sim**-ill-lee) A **facsimile** of something is an exact copy of it. See also **fax.**

fact – **Facts** are correct pieces of information. You can call the truth about something **the facts.** *The facts of the case will be brought to the public's attention.* If something is **a fact,** it can be proved to be true. ■ If you say something is **a fact of life,** you mean people have to put up with it, because it cannot be changed. *Hunger is already a fact of life in some areas.* ■ If you tell a child **the facts of life,** you tell him or her about sex.

fact-finding If someone goes somewhere on a **fact-finding** mission, they visit that place to find out what is happening there, usually on behalf of an official organization.

faction (**factional, factionalism**) A **faction** is an organized group of people inside a larger group, with their own ideas and beliefs. When there is **factionalism,** a group splits up into factions.

factor A **factor** is one of the things affecting a decision or something that happens. *There are other important factors to be considered.*

factory (**factories**) A **factory** is a building or group of buildings where goods are made using machinery.

factory farming is a method of farming in which animals are kept indoors in a confined space and given special food to speed up their growth.

factory floor is used to talk about the activities or opinions of the workers in a factory, as distinct from those of the management. *Concern has also come from the factory floor.*

factory ship A **factory ship** is a large fishing boat which processes its catch at sea.

factual (**factually**) If something like a report is **factual,** it consists of facts, rather than theories or opinions. ■ If information is **factually** correct, the facts it contains are accurate. *This was not factually accurate.*

faculty (**faculties**) A person's **faculties** are their physical and mental abilities. *He is in full control of his faculties.* ■ In a university or college, a **faculty** is a group of departments.

fad A **fad** is something which is popular for a short time. *...the spicy food fad sweeping Britain.*

fade (**fading, faded**) If something **fades,** it becomes less colourful, bright, loud, or strong. *...a faded blue suit... The afternoon light was fading... Interest in the story will fade.* ■ If something **fades away,** it gradually gets weaker until it stops altogether. *Your enthusiasm for running will soon fade away.*

faecal (*Am:* **fecal**) (*pron:* **fee**-kal) is used to talk about things connected with faeces. *...faecal bacteria.*

faeces (*Am:* **feces**) (*pron:* **fee**-seez) is the solid waste matter excreted from a person's or animal's body.

fag A **fag** is a cigarette. ■ In the US, some people refer to homosexual men as **fags.**

faggot – **Faggots** are balls of minced pork mixed with herbs and breadcrumbs. ■ In the US, some people refer to homosexual men as **faggots.**

Fahrenheit (*pron:* **fa**-ren-hite) is a scale for measuring temperature, in which water freezes at 32° and boils at 212°.

fail (**failing, failed**) If you **fail** to do something, your attempts to do it are unsuccessful. ■ If something you do **fails,** it does not have the effect you want. *Should military force be used if sanctions fail?* ■ If you **fail** a test, you do not pass. ■ You use **failed** to describe (a) an attempt which has not succeeded. *...a failed coup attempt.* (b) a person who has not been a success at something. *...a failed novelist.* ■ If you **fail** to do something you are supposed to do, you do not do it. *The driver failed to stop at a barrier.* ■ If something mechanical **fails,** it stops working. ■ If someone **fails** you, they let you down. ■ If something happens **without fail,** it always happens.

failing A person's **failings** are small faults in their character. ■ The **failings** of a system or organization are the ways in which it does not work. ■ You use **failing that, failing this,** or **failing which** (a) to suggest an alternative, in case the thing you have just mentioned is not possible. *Wear your national dress, or, failing that, a suit.* (b) to say what will happen if something is not done. *It gave them a year to resolve their differences, failing which they would go to the International Court.*

fail-safe A **fail-safe** mechanism stops dangerous things happening if a machine or system goes wrong.

failure is lack of success. If something is a **failure,** it does not produce the results you want. ■ If someone is a **failure,** they have not succeeded in the things they set out to do. ■ If someone has not done something they were supposed to, you can talk about their **failure** to do it. *...his failure to appear at the party.* ■ You use **failure** to talk about something that stops working properly. *...kidney failure.*

faint (**faintly**) If something is **faint,** it can only just be seen, heard, smelled, or tasted. *...a faint smell of gas.* ■ If there is a **faint** hope or chance of something happening, it might possibly happen. ■ **Faintly** is used to say someone or something has a quality, but only a small amount of it. *They were faintly amused.* ■ If you **faint,** you lose consciousness for a short time.

faint-hearted people are timid and lack courage.

fair (**fairer, fairest; fairly, fairness**) If something is **fair,** it is just and reasonable. *...a fair trial... You haven't played the game fairly... There is no such thing as fairness in business.* ■ If people think someone is **fair game,** they think it is all right to criticize them. ■ A **fair** number or size is reasonably large. *...a fair-sized bedroom.* ■ If you have a **fair** idea of something, you know reasonably well what it is like. ■ If there is a **fair** chance of something happening, it is quite likely to happen. ■ If the weather is **fair,** it is not raining. ■ Someone who is **fair** has light coloured hair or skin. ■ A **fair** is an event where businesses display or sell goods. *...the Leipzig Trade Fair.* ■ A **fair** is the same as a funfair.

fairground A **fairground** is the piece of ground where a funfair is held.

fairly means to quite a large degree. *The information was fairly accurate.* ■ See also **fair.**

fairway On a golf course, the **fairways** are the areas of short grass between the tees and the greens.

fairy (**fairies**) In children's stories, **fairies** are tiny people with wings and magical powers.

fairy tale (**fairy story**) A **fairy tale** is a children's story about magical happenings and imaginary creatures. ■ **Fairy-tale** is used to describe events which have a happy ending. **Fairy-tale** places seem like pictures in a child's storybook. *...a fairy-tale castle.*

fait accompli (*pron:* fate ak-**kom**-plee) You say an action is a **fait accompli** when it has been done and cannot be changed.

faith If you have **faith** in something or someone, you believe you can trust or rely on them. ■ If you **keep faith** with someone or something, you continue to support them, even in difficult circumstances. ■ If you do something **in good faith,** you believe at the time it is right or honest. ■ A **faith** is a religion, such as Christianity. ■ **Faith** is strong religious belief. *...their faith in God.*

faithful (**faithfully**) If you stay **faithful** to a person or organization, or if you are one of the **faithful,** you go on supporting them. *...the Tory faithful.* ■ Someone who is **faithful** to their partner does not have sex with anyone else. ■ A **faithful** translation or adaptation of a book sticks closely to the original version.

faith healer (**faith healing**) A **faith healer** is someone who tries to cure sick people through the power of prayer and religious faith.

fake (**faking, faked**) A **fake** is a copy made to look like the original, in order to deceive people. ■ If you **fake** something, you make or do something which looks like the real thing. *They faked antiques of all kinds... Fourteen years ago he faked suicide.*

falcon – **Falcons** are birds of prey which are sometimes trained to hunt other birds and animals.

fall (**falling, fell, have fallen**) If something **falls,** it drops towards the ground. ■ If someone **falls** or has a **fall,** they lose their balance and end up on the ground. ■ If a person's hair or teeth **fall out,** they come away at the roots. ■ If something **falls apart,** it breaks into pieces. ■ If you say someone **falls apart,** you mean they suffer an emotional or mental breakdown. ■ If you talk about the **fall** of a person or organization, you mean their sudden loss of power or status. ■ In a war, if a place **falls,** an opposing force captures it. *...the fall of Saigon.* ■ If an amount **falls,** it decreases. *...a sharp fall in the price of oil.* ■ When night or darkness **falls,** it gets dark. ■ **Fall** can be used to say someone or something changes to a different state. *They both fell silent... I fell asleep.* ■ When you are classifying people or things, you can say they **fall** into a number of categories. *30% of men fell into this age group.* ■ If something **falls** on a particular day, that is when it happens. *The first of May fell on a Sunday.* ■ If you **fall back on** something, you use it when other things fail. *...emergency cash to fall back on if an unexpected bill comes up.* ■ If an arrangement **falls through,** it does not go ahead. ■ If you **fall for** a lie or trick, you are taken in by it. ■ If you **fall for** a person, you suddenly realise you are in love with them. ■ If you **fall out** with someone, you quarrel with them. ■ You can call a waterfall the **falls.** ■ Americans call autumn the **fall.** ■ **fall flat:** see **flat. fall short:** see **short.**

fallacious (*pron:* fal-**lay**-shus) If you say an argument or idea is **fallacious,** you mean it is based on false information or poor reasoning. *The notion that by becoming Christian you become infallible is fallacious and dangerous.*

fallacy (*pron:* **fal**-lass-ee) (**fallacies**) A **fallacy** is an idea or argument which is incorrect because it is not based on sound reasoning or accurate information. *It is one of the fallacies of the left to think that the police are stupid.*

fall-back is used to describe something like a plan which is kept in reserve in case something else fails. *As a fall-back position, Pena is proposing a deal with another airline.*

fallen is used to describe (a) an object lying on the ground which has dropped from a high place. *...fallen leaves.* (b) a tall object which has collapsed onto the ground. *...a fallen tree.* ■ See also **fall.**

fall guy (**fall guys**) If someone is the **fall guy,** they are blamed for something which is not their fault. *They branded him as the fall guy for the real thief.*

fallible (**fallibility**) If you say someone is **fallible,** you mean they are capable of making mistakes. *Errors may have been made due to human fallibility.*

fallopian tube A woman's **fallopian tubes** are the two tubes which eggs pass along from the ovaries to the womb.

fallout The **fallout** from a nuclear explosion is the radioactive material which spreads and settles over a large area. ■ If you talk about the **fallout** from an event, you mean its unpleasant side-effects. *...the political fallout from the riots.*

fallow land has been ploughed but no crops are planted there, so the soil can rest and improve. A **fallow** period in someone's life is a fairly uneventful time.

false (**falsely**) **False** information is not true. ■ A **false** impression of something is a wrong idea about it. ■ If someone is the victim of **false** imprisonment, they are imprisoned for something they did not do. ■ You use **false** to describe something which is not real or genuine. ...*a false beard.* ...*false modesty.*

false alarm If there seems to be a danger but nothing happens, you can say there was a **false alarm.**

falsehood is telling lies. A **falsehood** is a lie.

false start A **false start** is an unsuccessful attempt to start something. ■ At the beginning of a race, if there is a **false start,** one competitor moved before the starting signal was given.

falsetto If a man sings in a **falsetto,** his voice is a higher pitch than normal, sounding more like a woman's.

falsify (**falsifies, falsifying, falsified; falsification**) If someone **falsifies** a written record, they include false information in it.

falter (**faltering, faltered**) If something **falters,** it loses momentum and is likely to stop altogether. *The economy is faltering.* ■ If someone **falters,** they hesitate, because they lack confidence or purpose. ...*her first faltering steps in her quest to read and write.* ■ If your voice **falters,** you hesitate because you are nervous or upset.

fame If someone finds **fame,** they become famous.

famed If someone or something is **famed** for something, they are well-known because of it.

familial (*pron:* fam-**mil**-ee-al) is used to talk about something to do with families or a particular family. ...*familial activities.*

familiar (**familiarity**) If you are **familiar** with something, you know it well. ...*the familiarity of the surroundings.* ■ If someone or something is **familiar** to you, you recognize them or know them well. ■ You say someone is being **familiar** when they speak or behave in an intimate way to someone they do not know well.

familiarize (*or* **familiarise**) (**familiarizing, familiarized**) If you **familiarize** yourself with something, you get to know about it.

family (**families**) A **family** is a group of people who are related to each other. ■ **Family** entertainment is suitable for parents and children to enjoy together. ...*a family film.* ■ You can talk about a particular related group of animals or plants as a **family.** *The weaver bird is a member of the sparrow family.*

family credit is an allowance paid to families in Britain on low earnings with at least one child.

family name Your **family name** is your surname.

family planning is the use of contraception to control the number of children in a family.

family tree A **family tree** is a chart showing a family over several generations and how they are related.

famine is a serious shortage of food, leading to many deaths.

famished If someone is **famished,** they are starving.

famous If someone or something is **famous,** they are very well-known.

famously If you get on **famously** with someone, you get on very well with them.

fan (**fanning, fanned**) If you are a **fan** of someone or something, you like them and support them. ■ A **fan** is a flat object which you wave in front of you to cool yourself down. If you **fan** yourself, you cool yourself by waving a fan in front of your body. ■ A **fan** is a piece of electrical equipment with revolving blades which keeps a room or machine cool, or gets rid of smells. ■ If wind **fans** a fire, it creates a current of air which makes it burn more fiercely. ■ If people **fan out,** they move forward, getting gradually further apart from each other.

fanatic (**fanaticism; fanatical, fanatically**) A **fanatic** is someone with strong political or religious views who behaves in an extreme or violent way. Behaviour like this is called **fanaticism** (*pron:*fa-**nat**-is-iz-um). *They are fanatically devoted to their cause.* ■ If you call someone a **fanatic,** you think their interest in something is too excessive. ...*a fitness fanatic.*

fanbelt (*or* **fan belt**) A car's **fanbelt** is the belt that drives the fan which keeps the engine cool.

fancier A bird **fancier** is someone who breeds certain types of birds, for example pigeons, as a hobby. ■ See also **fancy.**

fanciful (**fancifully**) **Fanciful** stories or ideas are based on imagination rather than reality.

fan club A **fan club** is an organized group for fans of a particular person or activity.

fancy (**fancies, fancying, fancied; fancier, fanciest**) If you **fancy** something such as an object or activity, or it **takes your fancy,** you want to have it or do it. ■ If you **fancy** someone, you are sexually attracted to them. ■ If you say that someone **fancies** themselves as having a particular skill, you mean they act as if they have that skill. *He fancies himself as a wine buff.* ■ If you **fancy** that something is the case, you believe it is the case. *I fancy that Scott would have enjoyed that.* ■ **Fancy** things are elaborate rather than simple or plain. ■ **Fancy** means to do with the imagination. ■ **flight of fancy:** see **flight.**

fancy dress When people wear **fancy dress,** they dress up in costumes.

fanfare A **fanfare** is a short loud tune played on trumpets at a public ceremony, to announce a special event. ■ You can talk about the **fanfare** surrounding an event when you mean the excitement or publicity it generates. *The restaurant opened amid great fanfare in January.*

fang The **fangs** of an animal such as a wolf are its long sharp teeth.

fan heater A **fan heater** is an electric heater with revolving blades for spreading warm air round a room.

fanlight A **fanlight** is a small window above a door.

fantasize (*or* **fantasise**) (**fantasizing, fantasized**) If someone **fantasizes,** they get pleasure thinking about something they would like to happen.

fantastic (**fantastically**) If you say something is **fantastic,** you like or admire it a lot. ■ **Fantastic** is used to emphasize how big something is. *The divorce rate is fantastically high here.* ■ You can say something is **fantastic** when it is strange or improbable. *The truth behind the fantasy is even more fantastic.*

fantasy (**fantasies**) Fantasy is what goes on in someone's imagination. *She can't distinguish between fantasy and reality.* ■ A **fantasy** is something that someone enjoys imagining. *...sexual fantasies.*

fanzine (*pron:* **fan**-zeen) A **fanzine** is a magazine produced by and for fans of the same type of music or the same football team.

FAQ In computing, an **FAQ** is a text file containing basic information on a particular subject. FAQ stands for 'frequently asked questions'.

far (**farther** *or* **further**, **farthest** *or* **furthest**) Far is used to talk about distance. *How far is York from here?* ■ If something is **far** away, it is a long way from where you are, or in an isolated place. *...the Borkuta coal field in the far north of Russia.* ■ The **far** end or side of something is the one which is the greatest distance from you. ■ If something happens **far and wide**, it happens over a large area. *The town attracts visitors from far and wide.* ■ **Far** is used to talk about a period of time in the past or in the future. *The fourth of July isn't far off. ...as far back as the twelfth century... No details have emerged so far.* ■ **Far** is used to talk about extent or degree. *How far have things changed? ...a far greater problem.* ■ You use **by far** or **far and away** to emphasize that someone or something has much more of an ability or quality than any other person or thing. *She was by far the best swimmer.* ■ If you say that something is **far from** the case, you are emphasizing that it is not the case at all. *It was far from easy.* ■ See also **further.**

faraway places are a long way away from where you are. ■ If someone has a **faraway** look in their eyes, they appear to be thinking about other things rather than paying attention.

farce A **farce** is a comic play in which the characters get involved in very unlikely situations. ■ If you say a situation is a **farce,** you do not take it seriously.

farcical If you say a situation is **farcical,** you think it is ridiculous or very badly organized.

fare (**faring, fared**) The **fare** is the money you pay to travel on transport such as a bus or taxi. ■ If someone **fares** badly, they are unsuccessful. If they **fare** well, they are successful. ■ **Fare** is used to talk about a particular kind of food. *...vegetarian fare.*

Far East The countries of eastern Asia, including China, Japan, Korea, and Indochina are sometimes called the **Far East.**

farewell – 'Farewell' is an old-fashioned way of saying goodbye. ■ **Farewell** is used to talk about something done for someone who is leaving their job or moving to another place. *...a farewell dinner.*

far-fetched If you say an idea or claim sounds **far-fetched,** you mean it is difficult to believe.

far-flung places are a great distance from where you are, or from other important places.

farm A **farm** is an area of land where crops are grown or animals are raised. If someone **farms** an area of land, they grow crops or raise animals there.

farmer A **farmer** is someone who owns or manages a farm.

farmhouse On a farm, the **farmhouse** is the house where the farmer lives.

farmland is land used for farming.

farmyard On a farm, a **farmyard** is a small area with buildings or fences around it.

far-off A **far-off** place is a long way away from where you are. ■ A **far-off** time was a long time ago.

farrago (*pron:* far-**rah**-go) (*plural* **farragos** *or* **farragoes**) A **farrago** of things such as lies or fantasies is a confused mixture of them. *...a farrago of deceit.*

far-reaching decisions or actions affect many things, in many ways.

farrier A **farrier** is someone who makes and fits horseshoes.

far-sighted people are good at judging what is likely to happen in the future.

farther (**farthest**) See **far.**

farthing The **farthing** was a British coin worth a quarter of an old penny.

fascia (*or* **facia**) (*pron:* **fay**-shya) In a car, the **fascia** is the dashboard.

fascinate (**fascinating, fascinated**) If something **fascinates** you, you find it very interesting.

fascination If someone is very interested in something, you can talk about their **fascination** with it. ■ The **fascination** of something is a feature which makes that thing very interesting.

fascism (*pron:* **fash**-iz-zum) (**fascist**) Fascism is a right-wing political philosophy which stands for centralized government under one ruler, with no political opposition or individual freedom. **Fascist** is used to talk about things connected with fascism. *...fascist regimes.* A **fascist** is someone who supports fascism or a fascist regime. ■ People in authority who behave in a bullying way sometimes get called **fascists.**

fashion (**fashioning, fashioned**) Fashion is used to talk about things like styles of clothing, which keep changing. ■ A **fashion** is a style of clothing or hairstyle which is popular for a time. ■ If you do something in a particular **fashion,** that is how you do it. *He greeted us in his usual friendly fashion.* ■ If you say something is done **after a fashion,** you mean it is done, but not very well. ■ If you **fashion** something, you make it, using whatever materials and tools are available. *...tools fashioned from flint.*

fashionable (**fashionably**) If something is **fashionable,** a lot of people do it, have it, or wear it.

fast is used in questions and statements saying how quickly someone or something moves or the speed that something happens. *How fast will it go?... It'll only take an hour if you move fast. ...a fast car.* ■ **Fast** is used to say something is done without delay. *They hoped to sort it out as fast as possible.* ■ If a clock is **fast,** it is showing a time later than the real time. ■ If something is stuck **fast,** it is stuck firmly. ■ When people **fast** or go on a **fast,** they go without food for a time, usually for religious reasons. ■ If you **hold fast** to a belief, you refuse to accept it can be wrong.

fast breeder reactor A **fast breeder reactor** is a type of nuclear reactor which produces more plutonium than it uses.

fasten (**fastening, fastened**) If you **fasten** something, you fix it in a closed position with something like a button or strap. ■ If you **fasten** one thing to another, you attach the first thing to the second. ■ If you **fasten on** something, you focus your attention on it.

fastener A **fastener** is a device like a button, zip, or safety pin.

fastening A **fastening** is a device which keeps something fixed or closed.

fast food is food you buy such as hamburgers which can be prepared and served very quickly.

fastidious (**fastidiously**) A **fastidious** person is very particular about details, and insists on things being done properly.

fast track is used to talk about methods for getting something done as quickly as possible. ...*the fast track to career success.* ...*a fast-track divorce.*

fat (**fatter, fattest; fatness**) A **fat** person has a lot of flesh on their body. ■ The **fat** in your body is the layer of flesh which stores energy and keeps you warm. ■ **Fat** is (a) a substance in food which gives you energy. (b) a substance used in cooking which comes from vegetables or meat. ■ A **fat** object is very thick. ...*a fat file of applications.* ■ **Fat** is used to talk about large sums of money. ...*fat salaries.*

fatal (**fatally**) A **fatal** accident, injury, or illness causes someone's death. ■ A **fatal** mistake is one which has terrible results. ■ If something like a system is **fatally flawed**, it is wrong and cannot be put right without being completely changed.

fatalism (**fatalist; fatalistic**) **Fatalism** is the belief that people have no control over what happens.

fatality (**fatalities**) A **fatality** is a death resulting from an accident or violent incident.

fate is a power which some people believe controls everything that happens. ■ Someone's **fate** is what happens to them. *The fate of thousands of prisoners is still unclear.*

fated If you say someone is **fated** to do something, you mean they will end up doing it, whatever happens. See also **ill-fated.**

fateful You use **fateful** when you are mentioning something which has had serious consequences. ...*Vorster's fateful decision.* ...*that fateful Thursday.*

father (**fathering, fathered**) Your **father** is your male parent. If a man **fathers** a child, he is its father. ■ If a man is a **father figure**, he gives you the support and advice a father might give. ■ Christians often call God **Father** in their prayers. ■ In some Christian churches, priests are called **Father.** ■ If you say a man is the **father** of something, you mean he invented it or had a strong influence on its development. ...*the father of English poetry.*

fatherhood is the state of being a father.

father-in-law (**fathers-in-law**) Your **father-in-law** is the father of your husband or wife.

fatherland When people talk about their **fatherland,** they mean the country where they or their ancestors were born.

fatherless Children are described as **fatherless** when their father has died or has left them.

fatherly If someone behaves in a **fatherly** way, they behave like a kind father.

fathom (**fathoming, fathomed**) If you cannot **fathom** something or **fathom** it **out,** you cannot understand it, however hard you try. ■ A **fathom** is 6 feet or about 1.8 metres. The depth of the sea used to be measured in **fathoms.**

fatigue (**fatiguing, fatigued**) If you are **fatigued** or suffering from **fatigue,** you are exhausted. See also **metal fatigue.** ■ **Fatigues** are clothes worn by the armed forces, especially in combat.

fatten (**fattening, fattened**) If you **fatten** an animal or **fatten** it **up,** you feed it a lot to increase its weight. ■ **Fattening** foods tend to make you fat.

fatty foods contain a lot of fat.

fatuous If you say someone's remarks or actions are **fatuous,** you mean they are pointless and silly.

fatwa (*or* **fatwah**) A **fatwa** is an order issued by a Muslim leader.

faucet is the usual American word for a water tap.

fault If something bad is your **fault** or you are **at fault,** you are to blame for doing it. ■ If you **find fault** with someone or something, you criticize them. ■ A person's **faults** are weaknesses in their character. ■ If you say something **cannot be faulted,** you mean there is absolutely nothing wrong with it. ■ If you say, for example, someone is generous **to a fault,** you mean they are almost too generous. ■ If a machine has a **fault,** there is something wrong with it. ■ In tennis, a **fault** is a serve which breaks the rules. ■ A **fault** is a large crack in rock caused by movement in the Earth's crust.

faultless (**faultlessly**) You say something is **faultless** when there is absolutely nothing wrong with it.

faulty equipment does not work properly.

fauna The **fauna** of an area is the animal life there. See also **flora.**

faux pas (*plural:* **faux pas**) (*pron:* foe pah) A **faux pas** is an embarrassing social blunder.

favour (*Am:* **favor**) (**favouring, favoured**) If you regard someone or something with **favour,** you like or support them. ■ If you are **in favour** of something, you think it is a good thing. ■ If you **favour** something, you prefer it to the alternatives. ■ If you **favour** someone, you treat them better than other people. ■ If you do someone a **favour,** you do something to help them out. ■ If something is **in favour,** people like it. ■ If something is **in your favour,** it gives you an advantage. *The system is biased in favour of young people.* ■ If something is rejected **in favour of** something else, the second thing is chosen instead of the first. ■ See also **most-favoured-nation.**

favourable (*Am:* **favorable**) (**favourably**) If there is a **favourable** reaction to something or it makes a **favourable** impression, people approve of it. *Many reacted favourably to the plan.* ■ If someone gives a **favourable** account of something or presents it in **a favourable light,** they emphasize its good points. ■ If one thing compares **favourably** with another, it is at least as good as it. ■ **Favourable** conditions make something more likely to succeed.

favourite (*Am:* **favorite**) Your **favourite** thing of a particular type is the one you like best. ■ The **fa-**

vourite in a contest is the person or animal most people expect to win.

favouritism (*Am:* **favoritism**) If you accuse someone of **favouritism,** you think they are treating one person or group better than the others.

fawn is a pale yellowish-brown colour. ■ A **fawn** is a young deer. ■ If you say someone is **fawning** over a powerful person, you dislike the way they are flattering them to get something out of them.

fax (**faxes, faxing, faxed**) A **fax** is a machine used to copy documents by sending information electronically along a telephone line, and to receive copies sent in this way. The copy is also called a **fax.** If you **fax** a document to someone, you send it from one fax machine to another.

faze (**fazing, fazed**) If something **fazes** you, it puts you off what you are doing, because it is confusing, surprising, or upsetting.

FBI The **FBI** is a US government organization that investigates crimes in which a national law is broken or the country's security is threatened. FBI stands for 'Federal Bureau of Investigation'.

fear (**fearing, feared**) **Fear** is the feeling you get when you are afraid. ■ If you **fear** someone or something, you are afraid of them. ■ If you **fear** something unpleasant will happen, you are worried it might happen. A **fear** is a worry that something unpleasant might happen. ■ If you **fear for** someone or something, you are worried they might be in danger.

fearful If someone is **fearful** of something or **fearful** it will happen, they think it might happen, and are worried about it. *Japan is particularly fearful of instability in China.* ■ If someone is **fearful** of doing something, they are afraid to do it. ■ **Fearful** is used to say something is particularly severe and unpleasant. *...a fearful attack... The leg was fearfully gashed.*

fearless (**fearlessly**) You say someone is **fearless** when they show no fear in a dangerous situation.

fearsome is used to describe something terrible or frightening. *The dog had a fearsome set of teeth.*

feasible (**feasibility**) If something like a plan is **feasible,** it could work and is worth considering. *...a feasibility study into a new power station.*

feast When there is **feasting** or a **feast,** people eat a very large meal, usually as part of a celebration or festival. ■ When people **feast** on something, they eat or enjoy a lot of it. *We feasted on the contents of the gourmet menu... Our eyes feasted on the natural beauty of our environment.* ■ A **feast** of enjoyable things is a lot of them at once. *...a feast of goals.*

feat A **feat** is an impressive act or achievement.

feather (**feathering, feathered**) A bird's **feathers** are the soft light things covering its body. ■ A **feathered** object is covered with feathers. *...feathered head-dresses.*

feather boa A **feather boa** is a long thin scarf made of soft feathers.

feathery objects remind you of feathers, because of their shape or softness. *...feathery palm trees.*

feature (**featuring, featured**) A **feature** of something is a significant part or aspect of it. *Every car*

will have built-in safety **features.** ■ Your facial **features** are your eyes, nose, mouth, etc. ■ If someone or something **features** in something such as a book, they play an important part in it. *This isn't the first time he has featured in allegations of violence.* ■ A **feature** is (a) a special programme on TV or radio. (b) a special article in a newspaper or magazine. ■ A **feature film** is a full-length film in the cinema.

featureless If something is **featureless,** it has no interesting features.

febrile (*pron:* **fee**-brile) behaviour is nervous and agitated. *...febrile chatter.* ■ A **febrile** illness is one in which you get a fever.

fecal See **faecal.**

feces See **faeces.**

feckless You say someone is **feckless** when you think they are irresponsible, and cannot run their life properly.

fecund (*pron:* **fek**-und *or* **feek**-und) If something is **fecund,** it is fertile.

fed See **feed.** ■ If you are **fed up** with someone or something, you are annoyed with them and you do not want to put up with them any longer.

federal In a **federal** country or system, a group of states have a central government as well as governments of their own. ■ **Federal** means connected with the central government in a federal country, rather than one of the state governments.

federalism (**federalist**) **Federalism** is belief in or support for a federal system. *Holland tried to stamp its own federalist views on political union.*

federated A **federated** country is formed by countries or territories joining together to form a federation. *...the Federated States of Micronesia.*

federation A **federation** consists of territories which have been formed into a federal country. ■ A **federation** is an organization formed by several smaller organizations. Federations usually deal with general matters of policy. *...the International Judo Federation.*

fee A **fee** is (a) a fixed sum you pay to have something, belong to something, or do something. *...the £10 membership fee.* (b) a fixed sum charged by someone for a job or service.

feeble (**feebly, feebleness**) **Feeble** people or things lack power, strength, or energy. *He waved feebly.* ■ If you call what someone says **feeble,** you mean it is unconvincing or ineffective. *...a feeble joke.*

feed (**feeding, fed**) When you **feed** a person, animal, or plant, you give them food. ■ You call each occasion when a baby is given food a **feed.** *What time is his next feed?* ■ When an animal **feeds** on something, it eats it. ■ **Feed** is food given to farm animals. ■ If you **feed** something into a container or other object, you gradually put it in. ■ If something **feeds on** something else or is **fed** by it, it gets stronger because of it. *Anger feeds on disappointment.*

feedback When you get **feedback** on something you have done, you get comments on how good or bad it is.

feeder A **feeder** road, railway, or air service is a minor one which connects up with a major network. ■ A **feeder** is a device for feeding animals.

feel (**feeling, felt**) If you **feel** a sensation or emotion, you experience it. *Mrs Oliver felt a sudden desire to burst out crying... What does it feel like to watch yourself on TV?* ■ If you **feel like** doing something, you want to do it. ■ If you **feel** like a type of person or thing, you think you have some of their characteristics. *I felt like a murderer.* ■ If you **feel** something is true, you believe it is true. ■ If you **feel** something should be done, you think it should be done. ■ If you ask someone how they **feel** about something, you want to know their opinion of it. ■ If you can **feel** something, you are aware of it touching your body. ■ If you **feel** something, you touch it, to find out what it is like. Its **feel** is the way it seems when you touch it. ■ If you **feel for** an object, you try to find it using your hands. ■ If you have a **feel** for something, you understand it well and know how to deal with it. *He has a good feel for grassroots opinion.* ■ If you **feel for** someone, you have a lot of sympathy for them.

feeler An insect's **feelers** are the two thin stalks on its head which it touches and senses things with. ■ You can say you are **putting out feelers** when you are making discreet enquiries to find out how people would react to something you are thinking of doing.

feeling A **feeling** is an emotion, such as anger. ■ If you **hurt** someone's **feelings,** you upset them. ■ Your **feelings** about something are your opinions about it. ■ If you have a **feeling** something is true or will happen, you think it is probably true or will probably happen. ■ If you have a **feeling** of something such as tiredness or hunger, you experience it. ■ **Feeling** is the ability to experience the sense of touch. *After the accident I had no feeling in my legs.*

feet See **foot.**

feign (*pron:* **fane**) If you **feign** an emotion or condition, you pretend that you are experiencing it. *The prisoners feigned illness to attract the guards' attention.*

feint (*pron:* **faint**) If someone **feints** in a sport like boxing, they make a movement intended to mislead someone. A movement like this is called a **feint.**

feisty (*pron:* **fice-ty**) people are lively and energetic.

felicitous If you describe a remark or an action as **felicitous,** you mean it is well-chosen or apt. ■ You use **felicitous** to describe a state of happiness or good fortune. *The company's expansion into the estate agency business has not been felicitous.*

feline (*pron:* **fee-**line) means to do with cats. *Cases of feline distemper in zoos were documented in the 1980s.* ■ You can use **feline** to describe someone whose movements or behaviour are cat-like. *The women scowled with feline fury.*

fell See **fall.** ■ If someone **fells** a tree, they cut it down. ■ If someone is **felled,** they are tripped or hit, and fall to the ground. ■ In the north of England, a **fell** is a mountain, hill, or moor.

fellow A **fellow** is a man. ■ You use **fellow** to describe someone who has something in common with you. *...fellow Muslims.* ■ **Fellow feeling** is understanding between people who have had simi-

lar experiences. ■ A **fellow** of a society or academic institution is a senior member.

fellowship A **fellowship** is a university post involving research and sometimes teaching. ■ **Fellowship** is a feeling of friendship between people involved in something together. ■ **Fellowship** appears in the names of some organizations for people who have a shared aim or interest. *...the Christian Fellowship.*

felony (**felonies; felon**) A **felony** is a serious crime. A **felon** is someone who has committed a felony.

felt See **feel.** ■ **Felt** is a type of thick smooth cloth made by pressing fibres together.

felt-tip A **felt-tip** pen has a felt nib.

female A **female** is a person or animal belonging to the sex which can have babies or lay eggs. ■ **Female** is used to talk about things connected with women. *...female emancipation. ...female members of parliament.* ■ A **female** plant or flower contains the part which will produce seeds when it is fertilized.

feminine (**femininity**) **Feminine** is used to talk about (a) characteristics thought to be typical of women. *...feminine handwriting.* (b) a woman thought to have attractive features which are typical of women. *Despite her femininity, she is considered to be independent and realistic.*

feminism (**feminist**) **Feminism** is the belief that women should have the same rights, power, and opportunities as men. A **feminist** is someone who believes this, and tries to bring it about. **Feminist** is used to talk about things produced or done by feminists. *...feminist literature.*

femme fatale (*pron:* **fam** fat-**tahl**) If a woman has a reputation as a **femme fatale,** she is thought to be very attractive sexually, and likely to lead men into danger.

femur (**femoral**) The **femur** (*pron:* **fee-**mer) is the thigh bone. **Femoral** (*pron:* **fem**-er-al) means to do with the femur. *...the femoral artery.*

fen (**fenland**) **Fens** are areas of low-lying flat land which are marshy or have been artificially drained. They are also called **fenland** or **fenlands.**

fence (**fencing, fenced; fencer**) **Fencing** or a **fence** is a wood, metal, or wire barrier, supported by posts. ■ If an area is **fenced** or **fenced off**, it has a fence round it. ■ In horseracing, the jumps are usually called the **fences.** ■ If you say someone is **sitting on the fence,** you mean they are avoiding taking sides in a discussion or argument. ■ **Fencing** is a sport in which two people called **fencers** fight each other with thin swords.

fend If you **fend off** something difficult or embarrassing, you avoid having to deal with it. ■ If you **fend off** something which is aimed at you, you hold up your arms or something else to stop it hitting you. *He raised his hand to fend off the blow.* ■ If you have to **fend for yourself,** you have to look after yourself without help from anyone else.

fender A **fender** is (a) a low metal wall round a fireplace. (b) a fireguard. ■ On a boat, a **fender** is an object hanging over the side to protect the boat if it bumps against something. ■ **Fender** is the American word for the wing of a car.

feng shui (*pron:* fung shway) **Feng shui** is the Chinese art of deciding the best design or position of something, such as furniture, to bring good luck.

fenland See **fen.**

fennel is a herb with a strong aniseed-like smell and taste.

feral is used to describe animals born in the wild whose ancestors were at one time kept by people as pets or as a food supply. ...*a feral cat.*

ferment (**fermentation**) When wine, beer, or fruit **ferments** (*pron:* fer-**ments**) or is **fermented,** a chemical change takes place in it, producing alcohol. ■ **Ferment** (*pron:* **fer**-ment) is unrest caused by change or uncertainty.

fern – **Ferns** are plants with long stems, feathery leaves, and no flowers.

ferocious (**ferociously, ferocity**) **Ferocious** behaviour or a **ferocious** conflict involves a great deal of aggression and determination. *They tackled ferociously.* ...*a ferocious battle to select a new candidate.* You can talk about the **ferocity** of an action. *They were shocked by the ferocity of the attack.*

ferret (**ferreting, ferreted**) **Ferrets** are small fierce animals used for hunting rabbits and rats. ■ If you **ferret around** for something, you make a thorough search for it. If you **ferret** it **out,** you find it.

ferrous metals contain iron.

ferry (**ferries, ferrying, ferried**) A **ferry** is a boat which takes people or vehicles across a river or stretch of sea. ■ You say a vehicle **ferries** goods or people somewhere when it makes several journeys to take them all there.

fertile (**fertility**) If land is **fertile,** plants grow well in it. *Soil fertility is declining.* ■ If people or animals are **fertile,** they are able to have babies or young. *Women have only a short period of fertility each month.* ■ If someone has a **fertile** imagination, they keep having clever or unusual ideas. ■ You say a situation is a **fertile ground** for an activity or feeling when it encourages that activity or feeling.

fertilize (*or* **fertilise**) (**fertilizing, fertilized; fertilization**) When an egg or plant is **fertilized,** sperm joins with the egg, or pollen gets to the reproductive part of the plant, and reproduction begins. This process is called **fertilization.** ■ When land is **fertilized,** manure or chemicals are spread on it to help plants grow. This process is called **fertilization.**

fertilizer (*or* **fertiliser**) is a substance used to help plants grow.

fervent (**fervently**) **Fervent** is used to describe very strong and enthusiastic beliefs. *The vast majority of North Africans fervently supported Iraq.*

fervour (*Am:* **fervor**) is a very strong feeling in favour of something. ...*revolutionary fervour.*

fester (**festering, festered**) If a bad situation or feeling **festers,** it gets worse. ...*festering resentment.* ■ If a wound **festers,** it becomes infected.

festival A **festival** is (a) an organized series of events and performances. ...*the London Film Festival.* (b) an annual religious holiday. ...*a 3 day holiday marking the Muslim festival of Eid-ul-Adha.*

festive If people are in a **festive** mood, they are ready to celebrate and enjoy themselves. When this happens, you can say there is a **festive** air or atmosphere. ■ Christmas is often called the **festive season.**

festivity (**festivities**) **Festivity** is the celebrating of something in a happy way. **Festivities** are events celebrating something.

festoon (**festooning, festooned**) If something is **festooned** with objects, there are a lot of them draped over it or hanging above it.

fetal See **foetal.**

fetch (**fetches, fetching, fetched**) If you **fetch** something, you go and get it. ■ If something **fetches** a particular price, that is what someone pays for it.

fetching is used to say someone or something is pretty or attractive. ...*a fetching outfit in purple and green.*

fete (*or* **fête**) (**feting, feted**) A **fete** is an outdoor event, usually to raise money for charity, with entertainments, competitions, and home-made goods for sale. ■ If someone is **feted,** they are given an enthusiastic public welcome.

fetid (*or* **foetid**) (*pron:* **fet**-id *or* **feet**-id) **Fetid** water or air has a foul smell.

fetish (**fetishes; fetishism, fetishist**) If someone has a **fetish** for something, they need to have it or do it to become sexually aroused. You call someone like this a **fetishist.** ...*a shoe fetishist.* ■ You can say someone has a **fetish** for something when they have a strong irrational desire to have it or do it. ...*our fetish for pomp and pageantry.*

fetlock A horse's **fetlock** is the back part of its leg, just above the hoof.

fetter (**fettering, fettered**) If something **fetters** your powers or rights, or is a **fetter** on them, it stops you exercising them. ...*the fetters of social morality.*

fettle If someone or something is **in fine fettle,** they are healthy or performing well.

fetus See **foetus.**

feud (**feuding**) A **feud** is a long-lasting series of fights or arguments between two people or groups. When people carry on a feud, you say they are **feuding.**

feudal (**feudalism**) The **feudal** system was a social system in which people were given land or protection by people of higher rank; in return, they worked or fought for them.

fever is excitement in a place caused by something happening there. ...*election fever.* When people are extremely excited about something, you can say their feelings are at **fever pitch.** ■ If someone has a **fever,** their temperature is higher than usual, because they are ill. **Fever** appears in the names of several illnesses. ...*glandular fever.*

feverish (**feverishly**) **Feverish** activity is busy and agitated. ...*a long day of feverish trading in the City.* ■ If someone is **feverish,** they have a fever.

few – **A few** is a small amount. ...*a few inches... A few were smoking.* ■ **Quite a few** or **a good few** is a fairly large amount. *We had quite a few arguments.* ■ **Few** means not many. *Very few people survived.*

fey behaviour is strange, unpredictable, and rather unnatural.

fez (**fezzes**) A **fez** is a round flat-topped hat without a brim.

fiancé (**fiancée**) If a man and a woman are engaged, you say he is her **fiancé** and she is his **fiancée.**

fiasco (**fiascos**) You say something is a **fiasco** when it fails completely and makes the people involved look silly.

fiat (pron: **fee**-at) When someone in power issues an official order which must be carried out, you can call this order a **fiat.**

fib (**fibbing, fibbed; fibber**) If you say someone is **fibbing** or telling a **fib,** you mean they are not telling the truth.

fibre (Am: **fiber**) A **fibre** is a thin thread of a natural or artificial substance. ■ You use **fibre** to talk about a type of cloth or other material made from fibres. ...coconut fibre. ...synthetic fibres. ■ **Fibre** is the parts of fruit and vegetables which the body cannot digest, but which help food to pass through the body. ■ **Moral fibre** is courage and determination to do what is right.

fibreglass (Am: **fiberglass**) is (a) a plastic strengthened with glass fibres. (b) an insulating material made from glass fibres.

fibre optics is a way of sending information in the form of light, using long thin threads of glass.

fibrillate (**fibrillating, fibrillated; fibrillation**) If a person's heart **fibrillates,** the heart muscles twitch in an irregular way, and the working of the heart may be affected.

fibrosis See **cystic fibrosis.**

fibrous (pron: **fie**-brus) things contain a lot of fibres or fibre.

fibula (pron: **fib**-yew-la) (plural: **fibulas** or **fibulae**) The **fibula** is the outer and thinner of the two bones in your lower leg.

fickle (**fickleness**) If someone is **fickle,** they keep changing their mind.

fiction is stories about imaginary people and events. ■ If you call something someone says a **fiction,** you mean they have made it up.

fictional people, places, and things exist only in books, plays, or films. ■ **Fictional** means connected with the writing of fiction. ...fictional technique.

fictionalize (or **fictionalise**) (**fictionalizing, fictionalized**) If someone **fictionalizes** something which really happened, they write a story or play based on it.

fictitious people or things do not exist and have been invented to deceive someone. They acted as buyers for a fictitious businessman.

fiddle (**fiddling, fiddled; fiddler**) If you **fiddle** with something, you keep moving or touching it with your fingers. ■ If someone **fiddles** something or gets involved in a **fiddle,** they do something to get money dishonestly. He was sacked for fiddling expenses. ■ A violin is sometimes called a **fiddle.** ■ If you talk about someone **playing second fiddle** to someone else, you mean they are less important than them and have to accept their decisions and do what they say.

fidelity to a promise or belief means sticking to it. ■ **Fidelity** to your partner means not having a sexual relationship with anyone else.

fidget (**fidgeting, fidgeted; fidgety**) If you **fidget,** you keep moving your hands or changing position slightly, because you are nervous or bored.

fiefdom (pron: **feef**-dom) If someone has complete control over a place or organization, you can call it their **fiefdom.**

field A **field** is an enclosed area of land, for example where crops are grown or animals are kept. ■ A sports **field** is an area of grass where sports are played. ■ A **field** is an area of land or sea under which large amounts of a mineral are found. ...the Victor gas field in the North Sea ■ In athletics, a **field** event is one which is not a race. The javelin and high jump are field events. ■ **Field sports** are activities like hunting. ■ The people or horses in a race are called the **field.** ■ The players **fielded** by a sports club are the ones chosen to play in a particular game. ■ In cricket or baseball, the team which is **fielding** is the one which is not batting. ■ A **field** is a subject or area of interest. ...specialists in the field of Italian art. ■ **Field** studies or tests are performed in a natural environment, rather than, for example, in a laboratory. See also **fieldwork.** ■ **Field** is used to talk about things used in a battlefield. ...a field hospital. ■ Your **field of vision** is the area you can see without turning your head.

fielder In cricket and baseball, the **fielders** are the players who stand in the field trying to get the batting team out.

field marshal A **field marshal** is an officer of the highest rank in the army.

fieldwork (or **field work**) is the part of a course or job which involves going to a place to gather information or to do some kind of practical work.

fiend (pron: **feend**) Newspapers often call someone who behaves in a very cruel way a **fiend.** Sex fiend strangles boy.

fiendish (**fiendishly**) Fiendish is used to describe (a) very cruel people, their behaviour, or their weapons. (b) things which are very difficult to deal with. ...fiendish obstacles.

fierce (**fiercely**) A **fierce** battle or argument is carried on in an intense and determined way. ■ **Fierce** feelings are very strong. ...fierce loyalty. ■ A **fierce** kick or blow is very powerful. ■ A **fierce** wind blows very strongly. ■ **Fierce** people and animals easily become aggressive.

fiery A **fiery** person gets angry easily. ■ **Fiery** is used to describe things which are burning, or very hot. Hysen looked flustered in the fiery heat. ■ **Fiery** colours are bright and flame-coloured. The leaves turn fiery red.

fiesta A **fiesta** is a carnival or religious holiday, especially in Spain and Latin America.

fife A **fife** is a kind of small flute.

fifteen (**fifteenth**) Fifteen is the number 15.

fifty (**fiftieth, fifties**) Fifty is the number 50. ■ The **fifties** was the period from 1950 to 1959. ■ If someone is in their **fifties,** they are aged 50 to 59. ■ When something is divided **fifty-fifty** between two people, each gets half. ■ If there is a **fifty-fifty**

fig　　241　　**film noir**

chance of something happening, it is equally likely to happen or not happen.

fig – Figs are soft sweet tropical fruit.

fig. is short for 'figure'. ...*see fig. 3.*

fight (fighting, fought) If you **fight** something, you try hard to stop it. You can talk about a **fight** against something. ...*the fight against drugs.* ■ If you **fight** for something, you try hard to get it or keep it. You can talk about a **fight** for something. ...*the fight for equality.* ■ When two countries or armies **fight,** they have a war or battle. When a battle is taking place, you can call it the **fighting.** *We were only metres away from the fighting.* ■ When people **fight** or have a **fight,** they try to hurt each other physically. You can also say people **fight** when they quarrel. ■ When a political leader **fights** an election, he or she tries to win it. ■ When you **fight** an emotion, you try not to feel it, show it, or act upon it. ■ If you **fight back** against someone who is harming you, you defend yourself by attacking them. ■ **fight shy: see shy.**

fighter A **fighter** is a fast military aircraft used for destroying other aircraft. ■ People who do not belong to an official army but who are fighting an enemy are often called **fighters.** ...*a resistance fighter.* ■ Boxers are sometimes called **fighters.** ■ You say someone is a **fighter** when they keep trying and are not put off by difficulties or opposition.

fig leaf A **fig leaf** is a large leaf from a fig tree. In paintings and sculpture, you sometimes see a fig leaf covering the genitals of a nude figure.

figment If you say something is a **figment** of someone's imagination, you mean they are imagining something which does not exist.

figurative (figuratively) Figurative art attempts to show people or things realistically, as they actually look. ■ You use **figurative** to show you are not using a word or expression with its most obvious meaning. ...*his attempts to offer a figurative olive branch to the gay community.*

figure (figuring, figured) A **figure** is an amount expressed as a number. ...*unemployment figures.* ■ A **figure** is a symbol representing a number, like 3 or 8. ■ Your **figure** is the shape of your body. ■ You can call an unknown person a **figure** when you cannot see them clearly. *I could see a small female figure advancing towards us.* ■ You can call a well-known or important person a **figure.** ...*a key figure in the independence struggle.* ■ In a book, a **figure** is a drawing or diagram. ■ If someone or something **figures** in a discussion, report, or story, they are mentioned in it. ■ If you **figure** something **out,** you work it out.

figurehead The **figurehead** of a group or organization is the person thought of as its leader. People sometimes call a leader a **figurehead** when they do not have any real power. *He is now simply a figurehead president.* ■ Originally, a **figurehead** was a large wooden model of a person under the prow of a sailing ship.

figure skating is skating in an attractive pattern, often with spins and jumps.

figurine (*pron:* fig-yoo-**reen**) A **figurine** is a small ornamental model of a person.

filament – Filaments are very thin pieces or threads of something. ...*multitufted nylon filaments.*

filch (filches, filching, filched) If someone **filches** something, they steal it.

file (filing, filed) A **file** on someone or something is a collection of information about them. ■ A **file** is a box or folder for keeping documents in. If you **file** a document, you put it in the file where it belongs. ■ A computer **file** is a set of data with its own name. ■ If you **file** a lawsuit, complaint, or request, you make it officially. *She has filed for divorce.* ■ When a reporter **files** a news story, he or she hands it in. ■ When people **file** somewhere or move **in single file,** they go in a line, one behind the other. ■ A **file** is a tool with rough surfaces, used for smoothing and shaping. If you **file** an object, you smooth or shape it with a file.

filial is used to talk about some aspect of a person's relationship with their parents. For example, 'filial respect' means respect for your parents.

filibuster A **filibuster** is a way of stopping a law being passed. A long speech or series of speeches is made, so that time runs out before a vote can be taken.

filigree is delicate ornamental designs made with gold or silver wire.

fill If you **fill** an object or **fill** it **up,** you keep putting something into it until it is full. You can also say an object or area **fills** or **fills up** with something. *Their boat filled with water... His office began to fill up with people.* ■ If you **fill in** a form or **fill** it **out,** you write down the information it asks you for in the spaces provided. ■ If someone **fills in** for someone, they take their place. ■ If someone is appointed to a vacant post, you say they **fill** it. ■ If something **fills** people with an emotion, they feel it strongly. ■ If you have **had your fill** of something, you do not want any more. ■ See also **filling.**

filler is a substance used for filling cracks or holes.

fillet (filleting, filleted) When fish or meat is **filleted,** the bones are taken out. A **fillet** is a filleted piece of fish or meat.

filling A **filling** is a small amount of metal or plastic a dentist puts in a hole in a tooth. ■ The **filling** in a pie, sandwich, or cake is the mixture inside. ■ If food is **filling,** it makes you feel full.

filling station A **filling station** is the same as a petrol station.

fillip If something gives you a **fillip,** it encourages you in what you are doing.

filly (fillies) A **filly** is a young female horse.

film A **film** is a motion picture shown in the cinema or on TV. If someone is **filming,** they are making a film. ■ If you **film** something which is happening, you record it using a cine camera or video camera. ■ A **film** is a roll of thin plastic used in a camera to take photographs. ■ A **film** of powder or liquid is a very thin layer of it.

film noir is a cinematic style which was especially popular in the 1930s and 1940s. Films made in this style tend to be dimly lit and have plots involving crime and corruption.

Filofax (Filofaxes) A **Filofax** is a personal filing system in the form of a small ring-bound book. 'Filofax' is a trademark.

filter (filtering, filtered; filtration) If you **filter** a substance, you pass it through a device called a **filter,** which removes particles from it. The process is called **filtration.** ■ When help or information **filters** through to people, it gradually reaches them.

filthy (filthier, filthiest; filth) If something is **filthy,** it is very dirty. **Filth** is a lot of dirt. ■ When people call a book, picture, or film **filth** or say it is **filthy,** they think its sexual content is shocking and disgusting.

filtration See **filter.**

fin A fish's **fins** are the flat parts sticking out of its body which it uses for swimming and balance.

final The **final** one of a series of events, things, or people is the last one. ■ The **final** of a competition is the last game or contest, which decides the winner. Sometimes the last few games or contests are called the **finals.** ■ **Finals** are the last and most important exams in a university degree course. ■ If a decision is **final,** it cannot be changed.

finale (pron: fin-**nah**-lee) The **finale** of a show or piece of music is the last part.

finalise See **finalize.**

finalist A **finalist** is one of the people taking part in the final of a competition.

finality If you say something with **finality,** you make it clear you are not prepared to discuss things any further.

finalize (or **finalise**) (**finalizing, finalized; finalization**) When something like a deal or plan is **finalized,** it is completed.

finally If you say something **finally** happened, you mean (a) it happened after a long time. *House prices have finally started to fall.* (b) it was the last of a series of things to happen. *He finally chose music for his career.* ■ People say **finally** to introduce a final point or question. *Finally, I would add that we have invested heavily in the area.*

finance (financing, financed; financier) When someone **finances** something, they put up the money for it. Someone who does this is called a **financier.** The money is called **finance.** ■ **Finance** is the management of money. *...local government finance.* ■ If you talk about someone's **finances,** you mean their money, and how they organize it.

financial (financially) **Financial** is used to talk about things connected with money. *...financial advisers.*

financial year The **financial year** is a twelve-month period which businesses and other organizations operate by. For most businesses, the financial year begins on 1st April, but for income tax purposes it starts on 6th April.

financier See **finance.**

finch (finches) **Finches** are small seed-eating birds.

find (finding, found) If you **find** something you are looking for, you discover where it is. ■ If you **find** something, you come across it. If it turns out to be interesting or useful, you call it a **find.** ■ If you **find** something you need or want, you succeed in getting it. *He cannot find work.* ■ If you **find your way**

somewhere, you manage to get there. ■ If you **find** time or money to do something, you do it in spite of being busy or not having any money to spare. ■ If you find something is the case, you realize it. *I found that the reading lamp would not work.* ■ You use **find out** to say someone gets to know the truth about something. *We found out that she was wrong.* ■ You use **find** to describe impressions and experiences. *I don't find that funny at all... He found it hard to make friends.* ■ If you **find** yourself in a situation, you are in it without intending to be. *He found himself out of work.* ■ When someone is discovered doing something dishonest, you can say they are **found out.** ■ When a court or jury reaches a verdict, you say they **find** someone innocent or guilty. ■ If you say particular things are **found** somewhere, you mean that is where they are. *Four different species of lungfish are found in Africa.* ■ **find fault:** see **fault.**

findings You can call the results of someone's research or investigations their **findings.**

fine (finer, finest; fining, fined; finely) **Fine** is used to say something is very good, or someone is very good at something. *...fine walking country... Wilson is a fine rugby player.* ■ In conversation, if you say something is **fine,** you mean it is satisfactory. ■ When the weather is **fine,** it is fairly bright and dry. ■ **Fine** is used to say something is very narrow, or consists of very small or narrow parts. *...fine hair.* ■ **Fine** is used to say something is very small, and therefore hard to see or distinguish. *...fine detail.* ■ If you say a situation is **finely** balanced, you mean things could go one way or the other. ■ If you are **fined,** you are punished by being ordered to pay a sum of money called a **fine.**

fine art When people talk about **fine art** or the **fine arts,** they mean painting, sculpture, or the making of any objects meant to be beautiful rather than useful.

finesse (pron: fin-**ness**) If something is done with **finesse,** it is done with skill and elegance.

fine tune If you **fine tune** something which is already operating, you make small adjustments to it, to make it work better.

finger (fingering, fingered) Your **fingers** are the four long jointed parts at the end of each hand. Sometimes thumbs are also counted as fingers. ■ If you **finger** something, you touch it with your fingers. ■ If you **point the finger** at someone, say they are to blame for something. ■ If you **put your finger** on something like a problem, you identify it. ■ If you have **had your fingers burned,** you have had a bad experience and so are likely to be cautious in future. ■ **green fingers:** see **green.**

fingernail Your **fingernails** are the hard flat parts at the end of your fingers.

fingerprint A **fingerprint** is a mark made by the tip of someone's finger, showing the pattern of lines there. When the police **fingerprint** someone, they make a record of their fingerprints. See also **genetic fingerprinting.**

fingertip Your **fingertips** are the ends of your fingers. ■ If you have information **at your fingertips,**

you know it, or know where you can get it immediately.

finish (**finishes, finishing, finished; finisher**) When you **finish** something, you complete it. ■ If you have **finished** with something, you no longer want it. ■ When something **finishes**, it ends. ■ The **finish** of something like a race is the last part. You call the people or horses that finish a race the **finishers.** ■ You use **finish up** to say what happens to someone or something at the end of a series of events. *He finished up as a doctor in Berlin.* ■ If someone **finishes off** an injured person or animal, they kill them. ■ The **finish** on a product is the treatment given to its outside or surface, which gives it its appearance or texture.

finishing school A **finishing school** is a private school where upper-class young women are taught manners and other social skills.

finite If something is **finite,** there is only a limited amount of it. ■ A **finite** period of time is fixed at a particular length.

Finn A **Finn** is someone who comes from Finland.

Finnish is used to talk about people and things in or from Finland. *...a Finnish farmhouse.* ■ **Finnish** is the main language spoken in Finland.

fiord See **fjord.**

fir – **Firs** or **fir trees** are tall pointed evergreen trees.

fire (**firing, fired**) **Fire** is the flames produced by something burning. When something is burning, you say there is a **fire.** ■ If you **set fire** to something, you start it burning. ■ A **fire** is a burning pile of coal or logs. ■ Gas and electric **fires** are heating appliances. ■ When a gun is **fired,** it sends out a bullet or shell. Shots fired from guns are called **fire.** *We climbed up the hill under fire.* ■ In a battle, if you are **in the firing line,** you are in a place where you might be killed. ■ If someone **fires** questions at you, they ask them quickly, one after the other. ■ If someone is **fired,** they are dismissed from their job. ■ When a piece of pottery is **fired,** it is heated in a special oven called a kiln, as part of the manufacturing process.

firearm A **firearm** is a gun, especially one you can carry.

fireball A **fireball** is a ball of fire, like the one at the centre of a nuclear explosion.

firebomb A **firebomb** is a bomb designed to start a fire. When a place is **firebombed,** firebombs are dropped or thrown into it.

firebrand You call someone involved in politics a **firebrand** when they are always calling for strong action.

fire brigade The **fire brigade** is the organization responsible for putting out fires.

firecracker A **firecracker** is a firework which makes a series of loud bangs.

fire door A **fire door** is a door made from fire resistant materials, which is kept closed when not in use, to stop fire spreading.

fire engine A **fire engine** is a large vehicle which carries firemen and their equipment.

fire escape A **fire escape** is a staircase on the outside of a building, to help people escape if there is a fire.

fire extinguisher A **fire extinguisher** is a metal cylinder with water or a chemical inside, used to put out a fire.

firefighter (**firefighting**) A **firefighter** is a member of a fire brigade, or someone helping to put out a fire.

firefly (**fireflies**) **Fireflies** are beetles which glow in the dark.

fireguard A **fireguard** is a wire mesh screen put in front of a fire to stop people burning themselves.

fire hydrant A **fire hydrant** is a pipe in the street which firemen can get water from.

fireman (**firemen**) A **fireman** is a male member of a fire brigade.

fireplace A **fireplace** is a space in a chimney for a fire.

firepower An army's **firepower** is the number and effectiveness of its weapons.

fireproof materials do not melt or catch fire and are used to stop fire getting to something.

fire sale A **fire sale** is a sale of goods damaged in a fire. ■ If a company has to sell some of its assets for less than they are worth, this is called a **fire sale.**

fire service The **fire service** is the organization responsible for fighting fires.

fireside If you sit by the **fireside,** you are close to the fire in a room.

fire station A **fire station** is a building where fire engines are kept.

firewood is wood for burning on a fire.

firework – **Fireworks** are small objects with chemicals inside, which explode or burn colourfully when lit. ■ You can say there are **fireworks** when there is an angry argument.

firing line See **fire.**

firing squad A **firing squad** is a group of soldiers chosen to execute someone by shooting them.

firm (**firmly, firmness**) A **firm** is a business. ■ A **firm** object keeps its shape when you press something against it. ■ If the ground is **firm,** it is not soft or muddy. ■ If you give something a **firm** hit, you hit it hard but in a controlled way. ■ If you have a **firm** grip on an object, you are holding it tightly. ■ **Firm** is used to say something is clear and definite. *He has no firm plans to run for the presidency.* ■ **Firm** opinions and beliefs are strongly held, and unlikely to change. ■ If people **stand firm,** they do not give in to threats or attacks. ■ You use **firmly** to say someone strongly supports or opposes something. *He is firmly opposed to the death penalty.* If someone **firmly** denies something, they say emphatically it is not true. ■ If you are **firm** with someone, you do not let them do something they are not supposed to.

firmament The **firmament** is the sky. ■ If you talk about the **firmament** in an organization or area of activity, you mean the top of it. *...a rising star in the political firmament.*

first (**firstly**) The **first** thing of a particular kind happens or exists before all the others. The **first** person to do something does it before anyone else. You can talk about the **first** time something happened, or say it **first** happened at a particular time.

■ If you do something **first,** you do it before you do anything else. *First I went to see the editor.* ■ You use **at first** when you are talking about the early stages of an event or experience, compared to what happened later. *At first I was reluctant.* ■ If you do something **first thing,** you do it at the beginning of the day. ■ You say **first** or **firstly** when you are mentioning the first in a series of items. *They agreed to a three-point plan. Firstly, there would be a ceasefire in Slovenia.* ■ **First** is used to talk about the best or most important thing of a particular kind. *She won first prize.*

first aid is medical treatment given immediately to someone who has had an accident or suddenly become ill.

first-class is used to describe people or things of the highest quality or standard. *...a first-class administrator.* ■ If you travel **first class,** you do it in greater comfort and pay more for it. ■ If you send a letter **first class,** you pay more and the letter gets there more quickly.

first cousin Your **first cousins** are the children of your aunts and uncles.

first-degree burns are the least serious kind, in which only the surface of the skin is burned.

first floor In Britain, the **first floor** of a building is the one above the ground floor. In the US, the **first floor** is the ground floor.

first-hand You get **first-hand** knowledge when you experience something directly. Afterwards, you can give a **first-hand** account of it.

First Lady The **First Lady** in a country is the wife of the president or head of state. ■ If you refer to a woman as the **first lady** of something, you think she is better at the thing mentioned than any other woman. *...America's first lady of modern art.*

firstly See **first.**

first name A person's **first name** is the first of the names before their surname. Sometimes all the names before someone's surname are called their **first names.**

first officer The **first officer** of a plane or merchant ship is second-in-command to the captain.

first-past-the-post A **first-past-the-post** electoral system is one in which the political candidate who gets the most votes wins. See also **proportional representation.**

first person (**first-person**) If you make a statement in the **first person,** you make it about yourself, or about yourself and someone else, using 'I' or 'we'.

first-rate is used to describe people or things of the highest quality. *...a first-rate golfer.*

first refusal See **refuse.**

first school A **first school** is a school for young children, usually aged 5 to 9.

First Secretary The **First Secretary** of a communist party is its leader. ■ The **First Secretary** at an embassy is second-in-command to the ambassador.

first-time (**first-timer**) **First-time** is used to talk about someone doing something for the first time. *In 1983 the average price paid for a house by first-time buyers was £21,839.* A **first-timer** is someone doing something for the first time.

firth In Scotland, a **firth** is a long strip of water stretching inland from the sea.

fiscal is used to talk about things connected with government-controlled finances. *...fiscal policy.* ■ In the US, the **fiscal year** is similar to the British financial year.

fish (**fishes, fishing, fished**) (*usual plural:* **fish**) **Fish** are creatures with fins which live in water and breathe using gills. ■ When people **fish,** they try to catch fish. ■ If you **fish** something out of a liquid or container, you take it out. ■ You say someone is **fishing** for something when they are trying to get you to say something they would like to hear. *...fishing for compliments.*

fish cake A **fish cake** is a mixture of fish and mashed potato pressed into a flat round shape and coated in breadcrumbs.

fisherman (**fishermen**) A **fisherman** is a man who catches fish as his job, or for pleasure.

fishery (**fisheries**) **Fisheries** are areas of sea where fish are caught.

fish farm (**fish farming**) A **fish farm** is an enclosed area of water where fish are bred for food. Breeding fish like this is called **fish farming.**

fishing grounds are the same as fisheries.

fishing net A **fishing net** is (a) a large net for fishing from a boat. (b) a small net on a pole used by children for fishing.

fishing rod A **fishing rod** is a pole with a line and hook, used for fishing.

fishmonger A **fishmonger** is a shopkeeper who sells fish.

fishnet is a net-like material used for making stockings and tights.

fishy (**fishier, fishiest**) If something has a **fishy** smell, it smells like fish. ■ You say something is **fishy** when it makes you suspicious.

fissile material contains atoms which can be split by nuclear fission. See **nuclear.**

fission See **nuclear.**

fissure A **fissure** is a deep crack in rock or in the ground.

fist Your **fist** is your hand when it is tightly closed.

fistful A **fistful** of things is several of them held in someone's fist.

fisticuffs If people are involved in **fisticuffs,** they are hitting each other.

fit (**fitting, fitted; fitter, fittest; fitness**) You say something **fits** or is a good **fit** when it is the right size or shape. ■ If you **fit** something, you attach it somewhere. *When we tried to fit the door, it was too large.* ■ **Fitted** cupboards, wardrobes, or carpets have been made to fit into a particular space. ■ **Fitted** clothes follow the line of a person's body. ■ If someone or something **fits** a particular description, they could be the person or thing described. ■ If someone is **fit,** they are strong and healthy as a result of taking exercise. *They were trained to a peak of physical fitness.* ■ If something is **fit** for a particular purpose, it is good enough for that purpose. *...houses fit for human habitation.* ■ If someone is **fitted** to do something, they have the right qualities for it. ■ If you deal with something **as you see fit,** you deal with it in whatever way you think is best. ■ If you say someone has **seen fit** to do something, you mean they have done it and you do not approve of it. ■ If someone has a **fit**, they lose consciousness and their body makes violent movements. ■ If someone does something in a **fit** of anger, they do it because they are very angry. You can also say that someone does something in a **fit** of enthusiasm or panic. ■ If something happens **in fits and starts**, it keeps starting and stopping. ■ See also **fitter, fitting.**

fitful (**fitfully**) Fitful is used to describe things which keep starting and stopping. ...*fitful sunshine.*

fitment – Fitments are things fixed to the wall of a room or the inside of a car, which can be removed fairly easily. ...*bathroom fitments.*

fitted See **fit.**

fitter A fitter is a person whose job is to assemble or install machinery or other equipment.

fitting (**fittingly**) If you say something is **fitting**, you mean it is right or suitable. ...*a fittingly exciting finish to a magnificent sixth-round replay.* ■ A **fitting** is a small object or device fitted to the outside of something. Taps and handles are fittings. ■ The **fittings** in a house are things like cookers and gas fires, which are fixed but can be taken away when you move. See also **fixture.**

five (**fifth**) Five is the number 5.

fiver A fiver is (a) five pounds. (b) a five-pound note.

fix (**fixes, fixing, fixed**) If you **fix** something somewhere, you attach it there securely. ■ If you **fix** something which is not working, you mend it. ■ If you **fix** something **up**, you arrange it. *I fixed up an appointment to see her.* If you **fix** someone **up** with something, you arrange for them to have it. ■ When an amount is **fixed,** someone decides what it will be. When a date is **fixed** for something, someone decides when it will happen. ■ If someone's eyes are **fixed** on something or someone, they are looking at them attentively. ■ If someone **fixes** a competition, they arrange the result unfairly or illegally. ■ If you **fix** a drink or food for someone, you prepare it. ■ A **fix** is an injection of a drug like heroin. ■ See also **fixed, fixer, fixing.**

fixated (**fixation**) If someone is **fixated** on something or they have a **fixation** with it, they are obsessed with it.

fixative is (a) a substance for preserving the surface of something like a drawing. (b) a substance for preserving scientific or medical specimens. (c) a glue-like substance for holding something in place.

fixed is used to talk about (a) things which do not change. ...*fixed interest rates.* (b) things which have a definite form, length, or position. ...*a fixed agenda.* ...*a fixed period.*

fixed-wing aircraft have rigid wings rather than folding wings or helicopter blades.

fixer You can call someone a **fixer** when they are good at arranging for things to happen, often by knowing the right people.

fixing – Fixings are small objects for holding something in place.

fixture A fixture is a sporting event arranged for a particular date. ■ The **fixtures** in a house are things like power points and fitted cupboards which cannot be taken away when you move. See also **fitting.** ■ You say someone or something has become a **fixture** somewhere when they are often there. ...*the Checker Board Lounge where Dave was a fixture for years.*

fizz (**fizzes, fizzing, fizzed**) If a drink **fizzes,** it produces gas bubbles. ■ **Fizz** is champagne, or some other fizzy white wine. ■ You can say something **fizzes** or talk about its **fizz** when it is exciting. *Politics has lost its fizz.*

fizzle (**fizzling, fizzled**) If something **fizzles out,** it ends in a weak or disappointing way.

fizzy drinks are full of gas bubbles.

fjord (or **fiord**) (pron: fee-**ord**) A fjord is a long narrow sea inlet entering the land between high cliffs, especially in Norway.

flab See **flabby.**

flabbergasted If you are **flabbergasted,** you are extremely surprised.

flabby (**flab**) Flabby people are fat, and have loose flesh called **flab** on their bodies.

flaccid (pron: **flas**-sid or **flak**-sid) If part of your body is **flaccid,** it is soft or limp, rather than firm. ■ If you call a performance or piece of writing **flaccid,** you mean it is weak or ineffective.

flag (**flagging, flagged**) A flag is a piece of coloured cloth used as a symbol of a country or organization. Flags are also used as signals or markers. ■ If you call someone the **flag bearer** of a group, you mean they are helping its reputation by doing something extremely well. ■ If you **flag down** a vehicle, you wave at it as a signal for it to stop. ■ If you are **flagging,** you are getting tired, and losing your ability to do something. ■ You say something is **flagging** when it is becoming weaker and is no longer successful. ...*her flagging career.* ■ **Flags** or **flagstones** are large flat square pieces of stone used for paving. A **flagged** path, area, or floor is paved with flags.

flagellate (pron: **flaj**-i-late) (**flagellating, flagellated; flagellation**) When people **flagellate** themselves, they beat themselves, as a religious penance. ■ If one person **flagellates** another, they beat them for sexual pleasure.

flag of convenience (**flags of convenience**) If a ship sails under a **flag of convenience,** it has been registered in a country with lower safety standards and lower taxation than its country of origin.

flagon A flagon is a large wide bottle or jug.

flagpole A flagpole or **flagstaff** is a tall pole for displaying a flag.

flagrant (**flagrantly**) Flagrant is used to describe wrong or harmful actions carried out in an open and unashamed way. ...*a flagrant violation of the law.*

flagrante See **in flagrante delicto.**

flagship The flagship of a fleet is its most important ship. ■ **Flagship** is used to talk about the most important thing owned or produced by an organization. *DW Homes is building its flagship development at Kenilworth.*

flagstaff See **flagpole.**

flagstone See **flag.**

flail (**flailing, flailed**) If you **flail** your arms or legs, you wave them about. ■ You use **flailing** to describe a clumsy and not very successful attempt to do something.

flair If you have **flair,** you do things in an original and stylish way. ■ If you have a **flair** for something, you are naturally good at it.

flak If you get **flak** from someone, they criticize you a lot. ■ **Flak** is explosive shells or missiles fired in large numbers at aircraft from the ground. ■ A **flak jacket** is a thick sleeveless jacket worn for protection against bullets.

flake (**flaking, flaked**) A **flake** of something is a small thin piece, broken off a larger piece. ■ When something like paint **flakes,** pieces of it come loose.

flambé (**flambéing, flambéed**) When food is **flambéed,** it is served in flaming brandy or some other spirit.

flamboyant (**flamboyantly, flamboyance**) **Flamboyant** people behave in a confident, unconventional, and very noticeable way.

flame (**flaming, flamed**) A **flame** is a pointed stream of burning gas coming from something which is on fire. ■ If something **bursts into flames,** it suddenly starts burning. If it is **in flames,** it is burning. ■ If someone **flames** you, they send you a rude or insulting message by e-mail. A **flame** is a rude or insulting e-mail message. ■ **Flaming** is used to describe things which are burning and sending out flames. *...flaming torches.* ■ An **old flame** is someone you once had a romantic relationship with.

flamenco is a Spanish dance.

flameproof (*or* **flame-proof**) is the same as fireproof.

flame-thrower A **flame-thrower** is a weapon which sends out a stream of burning liquid.

flamingo (**flamingos** *or* **flamingoes**) Flamingos are large pink wading birds.

flammable materials catch fire easily.

flan A **flan** is a tart filled with something like fruit or cheese.

flank A **flank** of something is one side of it. When an army is fighting a battle, you talk, for example, about its western **flank.** ■ If you are **flanked** by people or things, you have them on each side of you. ■ An animal's **flanks** are its sides.

flannel is a lightweight cloth used for making clothes. ■ A **flannel** is a small cloth you wash yourself with. ■ If someone talks a lot but does not tell you what you want to know, you call what they say **flannel.**

flap (**flapping, flapped**) When a bird **flaps** its wings, it moves them quickly up and down. ■ A **flap** is a piece of material or a flat object attached loosely to something by one edge. ■ If someone is **in a flap,** they are anxious and excited about something.

flare (**flaring, flared**) A **flare** is a signalling device which produces a bright flame. ■ If violence **flares** or **flares up,** it starts suddenly. You can say there is a **flare-up** of violence. ■ If tempers **flare,** people become angry. ■ **Flared** skirts or trousers widen towards the hem or the bottom of the legs. Trousers like these are called **flares.**

flare-up See **flare.**

flash (**flashes, flashing, flashed**) When a light **flashes,** it shines brightly, once or several times. You can talk about a **flash** of light. ■ If something **flashes** past, it passes very quickly. ■ If news **flashes** somewhere, it gets there very quickly. ■ If you have a **flash** of something such as inspiration or anger, that idea or emotion comes over you very suddenly and lasts for a short time. ■ If you flash something such as an identity card, you show it to someone very quickly, then put it away again. ■ If you call an achievement a **flash in the pan,** you mean it is not likely to be repeated.

flashback A **flashback** is a scene in a film or book where the story suddenly goes back to the past.

flashbulb A **flashbulb** is a small bulb which you fix to a camera. It makes a flash so you can take photos indoors.

flashlight A **flashlight** is a portable lamp powered by batteries.

flashpoint The **flashpoint** in a situation of resentment is the moment when something causes violence to break out. You call a place a **flashpoint** when fighting breaks out there and spreads to other places.

flashy (**flashier, flashiest; flashily, flashiness**) If you say something is **flashy,** you think it is too bold, bright, and expensive-looking.

flask A **flask** is the same as a Thermos flask.

flat (**flatter, flattest; flatly, flatness**) A **flat** is a set of rooms for living in, on one floor of a building. ■ A **flat** surface is level and smooth. ■ **Flat racing** is horseracing without jumps. ■ A **flat** fee is the same for everyone. ■ **Flat** is used to say an amount is not increasing or decreasing. *Underlying profits are expected to be flat.* ■ If you do something **flat out,** you do it as fast as you can. ■ If something is done in a number of seconds or minutes **flat,** it is done in exactly that time. ■ A **flat** denial or refusal is firm and absolute. You can also say someone turns something down **flat.** ■ In music, **flat** is used to talk about a note a semitone lower than another note. For example, E flat is a semitone lower than E. 'Flat' is usually written ♭. ■ If a note is played or sung **flat,** it is slightly lower than it should be. ■ If a plan **falls flat,** it fails badly. ■ If you call something like a performance or piece of writing **flat,** you mean it is not exciting or interesting. ■ A **flat** battery has lost its power. ■ A **flat** tyre does not have enough air in it. ■ If a drink is **flat,** it is no longer fizzy.

flat cap A **flat cap** is a man's cloth cap with a stiff peak.

flatfish (*usual plural:* **flatfish**) Flatfish are sea fish with wide flat bodies, like plaice or sole.

flat-footed A **flat-footed** person has feet whose arches are too low. ■ If someone is caught **flat-footed,** they are made to seem slow or clumsy because of someone else's speed or skill.

flatly See **flat.**

flatmate Someone's **flatmate** is the person they share a flat with.

flat screen computer consoles and TV sets use a liquid crystal display instead of a cathode ray tube, giving a sharper image.

flatten (**flattening, flattened**) If you **flatten** something, you make it flat. A **flattened** object has been made flat, or has a flatter shape than usual. ■ If you **flatten** someone, you hit them hard, knocking them down. ■ If something which has been rising **flattens out,** it stops rising and stays at the same level. *Consumerism has flattened out.*

flatter (**flattering, flattered; flattery**) If someone **flatters** you, they praise you in an exaggerated way. You call their praise **flattery.** ■ If something **flatters** someone, it makes them seem more attractive or better at something than they really are. *...a slightly flattering 4-1 win.* ■ If someone is **flattered** by something, they are pleased because it makes them feel important.

flatulent (**flatulence**) If someone is **flatulent** or suffers from **flatulence,** they have too much gas in their stomach or bowels, and feel uncomfortable.

flaunt If someone **flaunts** something they have, they display it in an obvious way. *They drove around in Rolls Royces, openly flaunting their wealth.*

flautist A **flautist** is someone who plays the flute.

flavour (*Am:* flavor) (**flavouring, flavoured; flavourless**) The **flavour** of food or drink is its taste. If food has no taste, you say it is **flavourless.** ■ If you **flavour** food or drink, you add something to it to give it a special taste. What you add is called **flavouring.** ■ You call a special quality something has its **flavour.** *The race had an international flavour to it.*

flaw (**flawed, flawless, flawlessly**) If something is **flawed** or has a **flaw,** it has a fault or mistake which spoils it. ■ If you say something is **flawless,** you mean it is perfect. ■ **fatally flawed:** see **fatal.**

flax is a plant used for making rope and linen.

flaxen hair is pale yellow.

flay If someone **flays** a dead animal, they cut off its skin. ■ If you **flay** someone, you criticize them severely for their beliefs or actions.

flea A **flea** is a small wingless blood-sucking insect.

flea market A **flea market** is an outdoor market selling cheap second-hand goods.

fleapit You can call a shabby old cinema or theatre a **fleapit.**

fleck (**flecked**) **Flecks** are small spots of something on a surface. If there are a lot of them, you say the surface is **flecked** with them.

fled See **flee.**

fledgling (*or* fledgeling) A **fledgling** is a young bird. ■ You use **fledgling** to describe a person, organization, or system which is new or without experience. *...a fledgling career as a model.*

flee (**fleeing, fled**) If someone **flees,** they run away.

fleece (**fleecing, fleeced; fleecy**) A sheep's **fleece** is its wool. When this wool is cut off in one piece, it is called a **fleece.** ■ A **fleece** is a warm outdoor jacket or top made from polyester. ■ You use **fleecy** to describe something which looks or feels like a fleece. *...fleecy clouds.* ■ If you are **fleeced** by someone, they get a lot of money out of you dishonestly.

fleet A **fleet** is a large group of ships operating together. You can also talk about a **fleet** of aircraft or road vehicles.

fleet-footed If you call someone **fleet-footed,** you mean they can run very quickly.

fleeting (**fleetingly**) **Fleeting** is used to describe things which last only a short time. *...fleeting glimpses... He smiled fleetingly.*

Fleet Street is used to talk about British national newspapers and the people who write for them.

Flemish is one of the two main languages spoken in Belgium.

flesh (**fleshes, fleshing, fleshed**) Your **flesh** is the soft part of your body between your bones and your skin. ■ When a part of someone's body is exposed, you can say you see their **flesh.** ■ **Flesh** is used to talk about the human body, as distinct from the mind or spirit. *...the pleasures of the flesh.* ■ The **flesh** of a fruit or vegetable is the soft inner part. ■ If you **flesh** something **out,** you add details to it. ■ If someone demands their **pound of flesh,** they insist on having something they are entitled to, though it may hurt other people. ■ You use **flesh and blood** to emphasize that you are talking about something real and alive, rather than something imaginary or artificial. ■ If you are in the same place as someone famous and you see them, you can say you saw them **in the flesh.**

fleshy (**fleshier, fleshiest**) **Fleshy** people have a lot of fat on their bodies. ■ The **fleshy** part of something like fruit is the soft part inside.

fleur-de-lis (*or* fleur-de-lys) (*pron:* flur-de-**lee**) A **fleur-de-lis** is a design of a lily with three petals, often on something like a flag or coat of arms.

flew See **fly.**

flex (**flexes, flexing, flexed**) A **flex** is a length of plastic tube with electric wires inside. ■ If you **flex** part of your body, you bend or stretch it. ■ If a group or country **flexes its muscles,** it behaves in a threatening way.

flexible (**flexibly; flexibility**) **Flexible** objects bend easily without breaking. ■ **Flexible** is used to describe things which can be varied to suit different circumstances. *...flexible working hours.* ■ If you are **flexible** about something, you are willing to change it if necessary.

flexitime is a system which allows employees to vary the time they start or finish work, provided they work an agreed number of hours.

flick If something **flicks** in a particular direction or is **flicked** there, it is sent there in a sudden sharp movement. A movement like this is called a **flick.** *Fried scored with a brilliant flick into the net.* ■ If you **flick through** a book or magazine, you turn the pages quickly, without reading carefully.

flicker (**flickering, flickered**) When a flame or light **flickers,** it shines unsteadily. ■ A **flicker** of feeling lasts only a short time. *...a flicker of hope.*

flick knife A **flick knife** has a hidden blade which springs out when a button is pressed.

flier see **flyer.**

flight A **flight** is (a) a journey made by flying. *The flight will take 17 hours.* (b) a scheduled plane journey. *...Flight DA 1392 from Gatwick.* ■ **Flight** is used to talk about the action of flying. *...space flight.* ■ Running away from something is called **flight.** *...the flight of refugees.* ■ A **flight** of steps or stairs is a row of them leading to another level. ■ You can call an idea which is imaginative but not at all practical a **flight of fancy.**

flight deck On a plane, the **flight deck** is the area where the controls are and where the pilot and crew are. ■ On an aircraft carrier, the **flight deck** is the long flat deck where aircraft take off and land.

flightless birds cannot fly.

flight lieutenant A **flight lieutenant** is a middle-ranking officer in the RAF.

flight recorder A plane's **flight recorder** or **black box** is an instrument on the plane which records information about a flight. If there is a crash, the information can show what went wrong.

flighty (flightier, flightiest) If you describe someone, especially a woman, as **flighty,** you think that person is not serious or reliable.

flimsy (flimsier, flimsiest) **Flimsy** things are badly made, or not very strong. ■ **Flimsy** clothing is very thin. ■ You say something like evidence or an excuse is **flimsy** when it is poor and unconvincing.

flinch (flinches, flinching, flinched) If you **flinch** when you are startled or hurt, you make a small sudden movement without meaning to. You can call the movement of **flinch.** ■ If you say someone does not **flinch** from doing something, you mean they are not afraid to do it.

fling (flinging, flung) If you **fling** something somewhere, you throw it. ■ If you **fling** up an arm, you move it upwards suddenly. ■ If you **fling** open a door, you open it violently. ■ If you **fling** yourself somewhere, you move suddenly and quickly. *He flung himself to the floor.* ■ If someone **has a fling,** they have a brief sexual or romantic relationship. ■ A final **fling** is a final opportunity to do something.

flint is a type of hard grey stone. In prehistoric times pieces of it were made into tools. When these tools are found now, they are called **flints.** ■ The **flint** in a cigarette lighter is a small piece of an iron alloy, used to produce a spark.

flip (flipping, flipped) If you **flip** a small object, you turn or spin it with a sudden rapid movement. ■ If you **flip through** a book, you turn the pages quickly, without reading them properly. ■ If someone **flips,** they suddenly become angry. ■ When people talk about the **flip side** of something, they mean the unpleasant or less familiar aspects of it. *...the flip side of their country's brand of socialism.*

flip-flops are plastic sandals held on by a strap across the toes.

flippant (flippantly, flippancy) You say someone is being **flippant** when their remarks show they are not taking something seriously.

flipper The **flippers** of an animal like a seal are the flat limbs it uses for swimming. ■ **Flippers** are flat pieces of rubber which swimmers wear on their feet to help them swim faster.

flirt (flirtation, flirtatious) If you **flirt** with someone or have a **flirtation** with them, you behave as if you are sexually attracted to them, in a not very se-rious way. ■ If someone flirts a lot, you say they are **flirtatious** or a **flirt.** ■ If you **flirt** with an idea, or have a **flirtation** with it, you consider it, but do not actually do anything.

flit (flitting, flitted) If someone **flits** around or from one place to another, they move quickly to lots of places, without staying long in any. *She flits athletically about the stage... She flits from one exotic location to another.* ■ If an idea **flits** across your mind, it is only there for a moment. Similarly, you can talk about a look **flitting** across someone's face.

float (floating, floated) If something is **floating,** it is lying on the surface of a liquid. ■ A **float** is a light buoyant object which helps keep someone or something afloat. ■ If an idea is **floated,** it is suggested as a possible course of action. ■ If a company is **floated,** shares in it are offered to the public. See also **flotation.** ■ If a government **floats** its country's currency, it lets it find its own value. ■ A **float** is a decorated lorry in a procession or carnival. ■ A **milk float** is an electric vehicle used to deliver milk. ■ A **float** is a small amount of money kept by shopkeepers for buying small items, or for use as change. ■ If you say a place has a **floating population,** you mean people keep arriving and leaving. ■ Someone who votes in elections but is not a firm supporter of any party is called a **floating voter.**

flock A **flock** of birds, sheep, or goats is a group of them. ■ A clergyman's **flock** are the people attending his church. ■ When a lot of people go to a place or event, you can say they **flock** there.

flog (flogging, flogged) If someone **flogs** a person or animal, they whip them. ■ If you **flog** something, you sell it.

flood (flooding, flooded) If a river or lake **floods,** the water flows onto areas which are usually dry. When this happens, you say there is a **flood.** ■ You can use **flood** to talk about the arrival of a large number of people or things. *...a flood of refugees. ...a flood of applications.*

floodgates If events **open the floodgates** to something, they make it possible for that thing to happen much more often or to a much greater degree.

floodlight (floodlighting; floodlit) **Floodlights** are powerful lamps used to light sports grounds or the outside of large buildings.

floodwater is the water covering flooded land.

floor (flooring, floored) The **floor** of a room is the flat part you walk on. ■ A **floor** of a building is all the rooms on one level. ■ The **floor** of the stock exchange is the area where trading takes place. ■ People talk about official debates taking place on a **floor.** *Labour's allegations prompted furious exchanges on the floor of the Commons.* ■ The seabed is sometimes called the sea **floor** or the ocean **floor.** ■ If someone **floors** you, they knock you down.

flooring is hard material used to cover a floor.

flop (flopping, flopped) If something such as a business venture **flops** or is a **flop,** it fails. ■ If you **flop** somewhere, you sit down heavily, because you are tired.

floppy (floppier, floppiest; floppies) If something is **floppy,** it hangs down loosely. ...*a floppy brimmed hat.* ■ A **floppy** is a floppy disk.

floppy disk A **floppy disk** is a flexible magnetic disk used for storing computer data.

flora The **flora** in a place are all the plants there. See also **fauna.**

floral is used (a) to describe something consisting of flowers. ...*floral tributes.* (b) to describe something with a flower pattern on it. ...*a floral carpet.*

floret – Florets are small flowers which form part of a large flower head. The head of a cauliflower is made up of white florets.

florid If you describe someone's language as **florid,** you mean it is unnecessarily elaborate. ■ If someone has a **florid** complexion, their face is red.

florin The **florin** was a British coin which was worth two shillings.

florist A **florist** or **florist's** is a shop which sells flowers and house plants. Someone who runs a shop like this is called a **florist.**

floss (flosses, flossing, flossed) When you **floss** your teeth, you clean between them using a thread called **dental floss.**

flotation If there is a **flotation** of a company or its shares, shares in the company are offered to the public.

flotilla A **flotilla** is (a) a small fleet of naval ships. (b) a group of small ships of any kind.

flotsam is bits of rubbish floating in the sea or washed up on the shore. See also **jetsam.**

flounce (flouncing, flounced) If someone **flounces** somewhere, or **flounces around,** they walk with exaggerated movements, usually to show they are angry. ■ A **flounce** is a frill or ruffle, for instance on a dress.

flounder (floundering, floundered) You talk about people **floundering** through mud or water when they are getting through it with great difficulty. ■ You say someone is **floundering** when they are struggling to cope with something. ■ **Flounders** are a type of flatfish.

flour (floury) Flour is the powder made by grinding grain. It is used to make bread, cakes, and pastry.

flourish (flourishes, flourishing, flourished) If something like a business is **flourishing,** it is doing well. ■ When plants or animals **flourish,** they thrive, because they are in conditions which suit them. ■ If you do something with a **flourish,** you do it with a bold movement intended to attract attention.

flout (flouting, flouted) If someone **flouts** a law or rule, they deliberately disobey it.

flow You say liquid, gas, or electricity **flows** when it moves in a continuous stream. You talk about the **flow** of liquid, gas, or electricity. You also say a river **flows.** ■ When people or things are **flowing** from one place to another, large numbers of them are moving there steadily and continuously. You talk about the **flow** of people or things. ■ Cash **flow** is the movement of money in and out of a business. ■ **Flowing** hair or clothing hangs freely and loosely. ■ If one thing **flows** from another, it

results from it. *They dispute other medical benefits claimed to flow from such research.*

flow chart A **flow chart** is a diagram which shows a sequence of operations, and how they follow from each other.

flower (flowering, flowered) Flowers are small plants, often with brightly-coloured petals. ■ The **flowers** on a plant or tree are the parts which produce seeds. When a plant or tree **flowers,** it produces flowers or blossom. ■ **Flowered** fabric or paper has a pattern of flowers on it. ■ If something **flowers,** it develops fully and is successful. *A planned career as a film actor had flowered, briefly, in 1954.*

flowerbed A **flowerbed** is an area where flowers are grown.

flowery things have a pattern of flowers. ...*flowery wallpaper.* ■ **Flowery** speech or writing is unnecessarily elaborate.

flown See **fly.**

fl.oz. See **fluid ounce.**

flu is an illness which makes you weak and your muscles ache. 'Flu' is short for 'influenza'.

fluctuate (fluctuating, fluctuated; fluctuation) If something **fluctuates,** its level keeps going up and down. ...*fluctuations in the exchange rate.*

flue A **flue** is a chimney, or a pipe which is acting as a chimney.

fluent (fluently, fluency) If someone is **fluent** in a foreign language, they can speak it easily and correctly. ■ If someone's speech, reading, or writing is **fluent,** they speak, read, or write easily and clearly. ■ **Fluent** movements are graceful and flowing.

fluff is bits of wool-like material on clothes. ■ If you **fluff** something, you mess it up. *The full back fluffed his clearance.*

fluffy (fluffier, fluffiest) You say a small animal is **fluffy** when its fur is thick and soft. ■ You say things are **fluffy** when they are soft and woolly. ...*fluffy white towels.* ■ You say food is **fluffy** when it has been whipped up to make it light.

fluid (fluidity) A **fluid** is a substance which can flow and change shape. ■ If a situation is **fluid,** things are likely to change. ■ **Fluid** movements are smooth and efficient.

fluid ounce The volume of an amount of liquid can be expressed in **fluid ounces.** There are 20 fluid ounces in an imperial pint and 16 in an American pint. 'Fluid ounces' is usually shortened to 'fl.oz'.

fluke If you say something fortunate was a **fluke,** you mean it happened by accident. ■ **Flukes** are a type of parasitic worm.

flummox (flummoxes, flummoxing, flummoxed) If you are **flummoxed** by something, it catches you by surprise, and you do not know what to do or say.

flung See **fling.**

flunk If someone **flunks** an exam or course, they fail to reach the required standard.

fluorescent materials shine brightly when light falls on them in the dark. ■ A **fluorescent** light consists of a tube which shines with a strong bright light. ■ **Fluorescent** colours are very bright.

fluoridate (fluoridating, fluoridated; fluoridation) When drinking water is **fluoridated,** fluoride is added to it. *Most UK regions have resisted fluoridation of the water supply.*

fluoride is a mixture of chemicals sometimes added to drinking water or toothpaste, because it is good for people's teeth.

fluorine is a pale yellow poisonous gas.

flurry (flurries) A **flurry** of things is several of them, happening one after the other. *...a flurry of meetings.* ■ When lots of things are happening at the same time, you can say there is a **flurry of activity.** ■ A **flurry** of snow is a sudden shower of it.

flush (flushes, flushing, flushed) If someone's face **flushes,** it turns red. ■ If someone is **flushed** with success, they are excited because something they are involved in has turned out well. ■ If you talk about the **first flush** of something, you mean the start of it, when it seems exciting and new. ■ When a toilet is **flushed,** water is released which washes it out. ■ When people in hiding are **flushed out,** they are forced to come out. ■ If you are **flush** with money, you have plenty of it. ■ If one thing is **flush** with another, it is level with it, forming a smooth surface. ■ In card games, a **flush** is a hand consisting of all the same suit.

flustered If someone is **flustered,** they are confused or nervous, because they are having difficulty coping with something.

flute The **flute** is a musical wind instrument consisting of a long metal tube with holes and keys. You hold it sideways and blow over a hole near one end. In Britain, a flute player is called a 'flautist'. In the US, he or she is called a 'flutist'.

fluted If something is **fluted,** it has long grooves cut or shaped into it.

flutist See **flute.**

flutter (fluttering, fluttered) When something like a flag **flutters,** it makes rapid movements in the wind. ■ When a butterfly **flutters** somewhere, it flies there with rapid movements of its wings. ■ If someone's heart **flutters,** it beats faster than usual, often because of fear or excitement. ■ If there is a **flutter** of excitement, people become mildly excited about something. ■ If you have a **flutter,** you bet a small amount of money on something.

flux If a situation is in a state of **flux,** it keeps changing.

fly (flies, flying, flew, have flown) When a bird, insect, or aircraft **flies,** it moves through the air. ■ If you **fly,** you travel by aircraft. You say the pilot **flies** the aircraft. ■ **Flies** are small two-winged insects. ■ The front fastening on a pair of trousers is called the **fly** or **flies.** ■ When a flag is **flying,** it is displayed on a pole. ■ If you want to emphasize how fast something moves, you can say it **flies.** *A stunning volley flew past the goalkeeper.* ■ A **flying visit** lasts a very short time. ■ If something gets off to a **flying start,** it begins very well. ■ If someone **lets fly** at someone or something, they start criticizing them severely. ■ If someone **flies at** another person, they suddenly attack them. ■ If someone **flies into** a rage, they suddenly become very angry.

■ If someone is hurled through the air by the force of something, you can say they are sent **flying.** ■ If something **flies in the face of** what has previously been believed or agreed, it contradicts it. ■ **flying colours:** see **colour.**

flyer (or flier) A **flyer** is a leaflet or pamphlet advertising something. ■ A **flyer** is (a) an aircraft pilot. (b) a passenger on an aircraft.

fly-fishing is a kind of fishing using an imitation fly as bait. See also **coarse fishing.**

flying boat — **Flying boats** were large aeroplanes fitted with floats so they could operate from water.

flying doctor A **flying doctor** is a doctor who travels by air to visit patients.

flying fish are fish which can jump out of the water and move through the air using their large fins.

flying officer A **flying officer** is a junior officer in the RAF.

flying saucer — **Flying saucers** are saucer-shaped flying objects which people claim to have seen and which some people think come from outer space.

flyleaf (flyleaves) The **flyleaf** of a book is the blank page at the beginning or end.

flyover A **flyover** is a road or railway line which crosses another road or railway line by a bridge.

flypast At a ceremony or air display, when there is a **flypast,** a group of aircraft fly over in formation.

flywheel A **flywheel** is a wheel which regulates the speed of a machine.

FM is a broadcasting system in which a signal is transmitted by varying the frequency of the radio wave. FM is short for 'frequency modulation'.

foal (foaling, foaled) A **foal** is a very young animal of the horse family. When a mare **foals,** she has a foal.

foam (foaming, foamed) Foam is a mass of small bubbles. When a liquid **foams,** it has small bubbles on its surface. *...foaming waterfalls.* ■ Some substances made up of small bubbles are called **foam,** for example shaving foam. ■ **Foam** or **foam rubber** is a light sponge-like material used for packing and insulating.

fob (fobbing, fobbed) If you are **fobbed off** when you want to talk to someone, you are prevented from doing so by being told lies or excuses. If you are **fobbed off** with something, you are persuaded to have it instead of what you really want.

focal point The **focal point** of something is its central feature. ■ The **focal point** of an event is where most of it takes place. *The war memorial became a focal point of the protests.* ■ The **focal point** of a lens is the point on its axis where parallel rays of light passing through it meet.

focus (focuses, focusing, focused) (or focusses, *etc*) If you **focus** on one part of something, you pay particular attention to it. ■ If people are paying a lot of attention to something, you can say it is the **focus** of attention. ■ If you **focus** your eyes or the lens of an instrument, you adjust your eyes or the lens so you can see an object more clearly.

focus group A **focus group** is a group of people gathered by a market research company to discuss and rate a product or service.

fodder is food given to animals like cows and horses. ■ If you say someone is being used as **fodder,** you mean they are being exploited for a particular purpose. *Migrants were factory fodder.* See also **cannon fodder.**

foe Your **foe** is your enemy or opponent.

foetal (*or* **fetal**) (*both pron:* **fee**-tal) **Foetal** means to do with the foetus. *...foetal research.* ■ If someone is in the **foetal** position, they are curled up like a human foetus in the womb.

foetid See **fetid.**

foetus (*or* **fetus**) (*both pron:* **fee**-tuss) (**foetuses, fetuses**) A **foetus** is an unborn human being or animal in the womb.

fog (**fogging, fogged**) When there is **fog,** tiny drops of water in the air form a thick cloud and make it difficult to see. ■ If a photograph is **fogged,** it is blurred or cloudy.

fog-bound If a place such as an airport is **fog-bound,** thick fog makes it dangerous to make a journey.

fogey (*or* **fogy**) (**fogeys, fogies**) If you call someone a **fogey** or an **old fogey,** you mean they are boring and old-fashioned.

foggy (**foggier, foggiest**) When there is fog, you say it is **foggy.** ■ If you do not have the **foggiest** idea about something, you do not understand it or know anything about it.

foghorn A **foghorn** is a loud horn sounded by a ship or on land as a warning in fog.

fogy See **fogey.**

foible Someone's **foibles** are their odd habits, or strange ways of doing things.

foil (**foiling, foiled**) **Foil** is metal in the form of a thin sheet. ■ A **foil** is a thin flexible sword, used in fencing. ■ If a plan or attempt is **foiled,** it is prevented from succeeding. ■ If one thing acts as a **foil** for another, they contrast, the one showing off the other's good qualities.

foist If something is **foisted** on people, they are forced to accept it.

fold (**-fold**) If you **fold** something like paper or cloth, or **fold** it **up,** you bend it, so one part covers another. A **fold** is a crease made in paper or cloth when it is bent. ■ **Folding** objects are designed to fold up. *...folding chairs.* ■ If you **fold** your arms, you link them across your chest. ■ If you **fold** your hands, you put them together with the fingers intertwined. ■ In cooking, if you **fold** something into a mixture, you mix it in gently. ■ If a business **folds,** it closes down. ■ A **fold** is a small fenced-off area where sheep are kept. ■ **-fold** is used to talk about rates of increase. For example, if something is four times as big as it was, you say there has been a **four-fold** increase. ■ **-fold** is used to say how many parts something has. *The US was faced with a two-fold dilemma.*

folder A **folder** is a thin piece of cardboard, plastic, or leather folded to make a container for papers.

foliage is the leaves of plants and trees.

folio A **folio** is a book made from large-size paper folded in two.

folk is used to talk about traditional music, art, and customs. *...English folk tales.* ■ A **folk hero** is a well-known and popular figure, often one from a nation's history, who is admired for something they have done. ■ **Folk** means the same as 'people'. *...the good folk of Lanark.* ■ Some people call their close relatives their **folks.**

folklore A nation's traditional stories are called its **folklore.** You can also refer to stories told about a particular sport or profession as its **folklore.** *His celebratory jig across the Maine Road pitch is part of football folklore.*

folksy things are intended to appeal to people because they are simple and ordinary in a traditional way. *...his folksy manner.*

follicle – Follicles are the small hollows in the skin which hairs grow out of.

follow If something **follows** something else, it happens after it. *...the firework display that followed the dance.* **Follow** is often used to say something happens as a result of something else. *The decision follows negotiations with the trades unions.* ■ If you **follow** someone into a profession, you do the same thing. *He followed his father into acting.* You can also talk about **following** someone's lead or example. ■ If something **follows** from something else, it is true because the other thing is true. ■ You say **as follows** before giving a list of things. *Fares are as follows.* ■ If you **follow** someone somewhere, (a) you go behind them. (b) you go to the same place at a later time. ■ If you **follow** something like a path or river, you keep on it or beside it. ■ If you **follow** instructions or advice, you do what you are told or advised to do. ■ If you **follow** a plan or policy, you carry it out. ■ People who **follow** a religion accept its teachings. ■ If you **follow** something, you take a keen interest in it. ■ If you can **follow** what someone or something says, you can understand it. ■ If you **follow up** something you hear, you try to get more information about it.

follower The **followers** of a religion are people who accept its teachings and base their way of life on it. ■ The **followers** of a political party or leader are the people who support them. ■ The **followers** of a particular sport or team are its fans.

following You use **following** to talk about the next period of time of a particular kind. *My intention had been to retire the following year.* ■ You use **following** when you are introducing some information. *The following companies offer a men's wear hire service.* ■ A person's or organization's **following** are the people who support them. ■ A **following wind** is one which is behind you and can help you move faster.

folly (**follies**) **Folly** is foolish behaviour. A person's **follies** are foolish things they have done. ■ A **folly** is a building put up in the 18th or early 19th century and made to look like something like a castle or ruin, to create a picturesque effect.

foment (*pron:* foam-**ment**) If someone **foments** trouble, they stir it up.

fond (**fondly, fondness**) If you are **fond** of someone, you feel affection for them. ■ If you have **fond** memories of someone or something, you remember them with affection. ■ If you are **fond** of an activity like music or a sport, you enjoy it.

fondant is a soft sugary paste used to make sweets and icing.

fondle (**fondling, fondled**) If someone **fondles** you, they touch or stroke you gently, in a sexual way.

fondue is a pot of hot sauce, often made with melted cheese, into which you dip pieces of bread, meat, or vegetables.

font In a church, the **font** is the bowl which holds the water for baptisms. ■ In printing, a **font** is a typeface.

fontanelle The **fontanelles** are the gaps in a baby's skull which are covered with a tough flexible membrane.

food is what people and animals eat. ■ If you give someone **food for thought,** you cause them to think carefully about something.

food chain A **food chain** is a series of living things. Each thing feeds off the one below it in the series.

food poisoning is an illness caused by eating contaminated food. It results in sickness and diarrhoea.

food processor A **food processor** is an electrical device for mixing, chopping, or mincing food.

foodstuff A **foodstuff** is any substance which people eat.

fool (**fooling, fooled**) If you call someone a **fool,** you mean they have done something silly. ■ If someone **fools** you, they trick you. ■ When people **fool about, fool around,** or **play the fool,** they behave in a playful or silly way.

foolhardy If someone is **foolhardy,** they behave recklessly or take unnecessary risks.

foolish (**foolishly, foolishness**) **Foolish** means silly or unwise. *It would be foolish to put too much trust in opinion polls.* ■ If someone is made to look **foolish,** they are put in an embarrassing position.

foolproof If something like a machine or plan is **foolproof,** it cannot go wrong or be used wrongly.

foolscap is a size of writing or printing paper, measuring about 34 by 43 centimetres (13.5 by 17 inches).

foot (**feet; foots, footing, footed**) Your **feet** are the parts of your body you stand on. ■ The **foot** of something is the bottom or lower end of it. *...the foot of the cliff. ...the foot of the bed.* ■ Length can be expressed in **feet.** A foot is 12 inches or 30.48 centimetres. 'Feet' is usually written 'ft'. ■ If you go somewhere **on foot,** you walk. ■ When someone visits a place, especially for the first time, you can say they **set foot** there. ■ If you **put your foot in it,** you say something which causes embarrassment. ■ If someone in authority **puts their foot down,** they stop something happening. ■ If someone you admire turns out to have **feet of clay,** you discover they have a serious fault which spoils your good opinion of them. ■ If you **foot the bill** for something, you pay for it.

footage of something is a piece of film which shows it happening.

foot-and-mouth disease is a serious and highly infectious disease of cattle, sheep, pigs, and goats.

football (**footballer; footballing**) **Football** is a game played by two teams of eleven players. You score by kicking or heading a round ball called a football into the other team's goal. In some countries, football is called 'soccer'. ■ **Footballing** is used to talk about things to do with football. *...his great footballing achievements.* ■ **football pools:** see **pool.**

footbridge A **footbridge** is a bridge for people to walk across.

foothills are low hills at the base of mountains.

foothold — **Footholds** are small ledges or hollows where climbers can put their feet. ■ If someone gains a **foothold** in an organization, they get established in a position from which they can make further progress.

footing When you are walking or climbing, your **footing** is the grip your feet have on the ground. If you lose your **footing,** you slip or stumble. ■ **Footing** is used to talk about the basis on which something is able to proceed. *The company still needs a breakthrough to put it on a firm financial footing.*

footlights In a theatre, the **footlights** are the row of lights along the front of the stage.

footloose If you say someone is **footloose,** you mean they have no responsibilities or commitments and can do what they like.

footman (**footmen**) A **footman** is a male servant who does things like opening doors and serving food.

footnote A **footnote** is a note at the bottom of a page giving more information about something on it. ■ If you say something will become a **footnote in history,** you mean it will be remembered, but not thought of as important.

footpath A **footpath** is a path for people to walk on.

footprint A person's or animal's **footprints** are the marks their feet leave on the ground.

Footsie means the same as 'FTSE Index'.

footstep — **Footsteps** are the sound of someone walking or running. ■ If you **follow in** someone's **footsteps,** you do what they did earlier.

footstool A **footstool** is a low stool for someone to rest their feet on while sitting down.

footwear is things like shoes, boots, and sandals.

footwork In sport or dancing, someone's **footwork** is the way they move their feet. ■ **Footwork** is used to talk about clever ways of dealing with difficult situations. *...his mastery of political footwork.*

fop (**foppish**) In the 17th, 18th, and 19th centuries, a **fop** was a vain man who wore fancy clothes. Men like this were called **foppish.**

for is used to say who or what a statement applies to. *For the Baltic governments this was a final hurdle before complete statehood... It's a good life for a young man... The process released valuable floor space for production.* ■ **For** is used to say who will benefit from something. *Special arrangements will be made for blind people.* ■ If you work **for** a person or organization, they employ you. ■ **For** is used to talk about time. *The whole area remained cordoned off for five hours... The meeting was scheduled for eleven o'clock.* ■ **For** is used to talk about distances *...a traffic jam that stretched for several miles.* ■ **For** is used to talk about quantities. *You can take one bonus share for every ten* *shares allocated.* ■ **For** is used to say where someone is going. *...fifteen trucks bound for Phnom Penh.* ■ **For** is used to talk about someone's feelings about someone or something. *I'm very happy for Peter ...their hopes for the UN.* ■ If you are **for** something, you are in favour of it. ■ **For** is sometimes used to mean 'because'. *This is where he spent most of his time, for he had nowhere else to go.*

forage (rhymes with 'porridge') (**foraging, foraged**) **Forage** is food for horses or cattle, especially hay or straw. ■ When animals **forage,** they look for food. ■ When people **forage** for something, they search about for it.

foray If someone makes a **foray** into a new activity, they try doing something new. ■ If someone makes a **foray** somewhere, they make a short trip there.

forbade See **forbid.**

forbearance is patience and self-control.

forbears See **forebears.**

forbid (**forbidding, forbade, have forbidden**) If someone is **forbidden** to do something, they are not allowed to do it. ■ A **forbidden** place is one people are not allowed to visit.

forbidding people, places, or things look grim and unfriendly.

force (**forcing, forced**) A **force** is a group of people trained and organized for a special purpose. *...an international peace-keeping force.* ■ The **forces** are the army, navy, and air force. ■ If people or circumstances **force** you to do something, they make you do it. You can also say people or circumstances **force** someone into a state or situation. *By dumping food the EU depresses prices and forces poorer farmers out of business.* See also **market forces.** ■ If people use **force** to achieve something, they use physical strength or violence. ■ If you **force** something open, you use your physical strength or something like a lever to open it. ■ If you **force** your **way** into a place, you gain entry despite someone trying to stop you. ■ You talk about a person or group being a **force** when they exert a strong influence in a particular field. *The party is now the leading political force in the country.* ■ When people **join forces,** they work together to achieve something. ■ If people do something **in force,** they do it in large numbers. *Police were out in force.* ■ When a law or system **comes into force,** it starts to apply. ■ **Force** is used to talk about the power exerted by things like gravity and magnetism. ■ **Force** is used to show the speed and strength of a wind. *...a force nine gale.*

forceful (**forcefully**) You use **forceful** to say someone expresses their views or wishes in a strong and effective way. *...his most forceful speech yet.* ■ **Forceful** actions (a) are strong and effective. *...the forceful programme now being implemented by the government.* (b) involve the use of force. *The Governor rejected the calls for more forceful tactics.*

forceps are a medical instrument with two pincer-like arms for holding things.

forcible (**forcibly**) **Forcible** actions involve physical force or violence. *The Community would not accept any forcible change of borders.* ■ If you express yourself in a **forcible** way, you make it clear how strongly you feel.

ford If you **ford** a river or stream, you cross it at a shallow place. A place where people regularly do this is called a **ford.**

fore If something comes **to the fore,** it is given more attention than other things. ■ **Fore** and **aft** are the front and back parts of a ship.

forearm Your **forearm** is the part of your arm between your wrist and elbow.

forebears (or **forbears**) Your **forebears** are your ancestors.

foreboding is a feeling that something bad is going to happen.

forecast (**forecaster**) If you **forecast** something or make a **forecast,** you say what is going to happen.

foreclose (**foreclosing, foreclosed; foreclosure**) If a financial institution **forecloses** on someone they have lent money to, they take possession of property bought with the loan, because repayments have not been made.

forecourt The **forecourt** of a large building or petrol station is an open area at the front.

forefather Your **forefathers** are your ancestors.

forefinger Your **forefinger** is the one next to your thumb.

forefront If someone is at the **forefront** of something, they are playing an important part in it. *She has been at the forefront of British fashion for 20 years.* ■ If something is at the **forefront** of your mind, you are continually thinking about it.

forego See **forgo.**

foregoing (or **forgoing**) is used to talk about something which has just been mentioned. *No order shall be made under any of the foregoing rules.*

foregone (or **forgone**) If you say something is a **foregone conclusion,** you mean there can be no doubt about what will happen.

foreground The **foreground** of a picture is the part which seems nearest to you.

forehand In games like tennis, a **forehand** is a stroke made with the palm of the player's hand facing the direction they are hitting the ball. See also **backhand.**

forehead Your **forehead** is the front of your face above your eyebrows.

foreign is used to talk about things connected with other countries. *...foreign languages.* ■ **Foreign** is used to describe jobs and activities related to other countries. *...the Foreign Secretary. ...Britain's foreign affairs.* ■ A **foreign national** is a person staying in a country they are not a citizen of. ■ **Foreign exchange** is (a) the foreign currency held in a country. (b) the system by which one country's currency can be converted to another's. ■ A **foreign** object is one that has got into something, usually by accident, and should not be there. An object like this is sometimes called a **foreign body.** ■ If you say something is **foreign** to you, you mean it is unknown or unfamiliar to you.

foreigner A **foreigner** is someone from another country.

foreknowledge If you have **foreknowledge** of something, you know about it in advance.

foreleg An animal's **forelegs** are its front legs.

forelock A **forelock** is a lock of hair which falls over the forehead.

foreman (**foremen**) A **foreman** is the person in charge of a group of workers. ■ The **foreman** of a jury is the person chosen as its leader.

foremost People say **first and foremost** when mentioning the most important thing about someone or something. *He is first and foremost a great storyteller.* ■ The **foremost** of a group of things or people is the best or most important one. *...some of the foremost British artists of this century.*

forename Your **forenames** are the names in front of your surname.

forensic means connected with the scientific examination of evidence when a crime is being investigated. *...forensic tests.*

foreplay is kissing and caressing before sex.

forerunner The **forerunner** of something like a machine is something similar which existed at an earlier period in history.

foresee (**foreseeing, foresaw, have foreseen**) If you **foresee** something, you say it is going to happen.

foreseeable If you say something will happen **for the foreseeable future,** you mean it will continue to happen for a long time. If you say something will happen **in the foreseeable future,** you think it is likely to happen soon. ■ **Foreseeable** is used to talk about things which could reasonably be predicted. *Industry has enough excess capacity to meet any foreseeable upturn in demand.*

foreshadow If something **foreshadows** something else, it suggests it is going to happen. *The change was foreshadowed in the Chancellor's March Budget.*

foreshortened You say something is **foreshortened** when it is drawn or photographed from an angle that makes its two ends appear closer to each other than they really are.

foresight You say someone has **foresight** when they see what is likely to happen and take the right sort of action.

foreskin A man's **foreskin** is the loose skin covering the end of his penis.

forest (**forestry, forester, forested**) A **forest** is a very large area of woodland. Someone who manages an area like this is called a **forester.** The work they do is called **forestry.** ■ A **forested** area is covered in trees. ■ A **forest** of objects is a large group of them clustered together. *...a forest of chairs and tables.*

forestall If something is **forestalled,** it is prevented from happening.

forester (**forestry**) See **forest.**

foretaste A **foretaste** of something is a small part or early stage, which gives people some idea what the rest might be like.

foretell (**foretelling, foretold**) If someone **foretells** things in the future, they say what will happen.

forethought is thinking carefully about something before doing it. *A little forethought can avoid a lot of problems.*

foretold See **foretell.**

forever (*or* **for ever**) If you say something will go on **forever,** you mean it will never come to an end.

■ If, for instance, you say something has gone **forever,** you mean it has gone and will not come back. ■ If you say someone is **forever** doing something, you mean they keep doing it.

forewarn (**forewarning**) If you are **forewarned** of something or receive **forewarning** of it, you are told in advance it is going to happen.

foreword The **forward** of a book is an introduction.

forfeit (**forfeiting, forfeited; forfeiture**) If someone **forfeits** something they own, they have to give it up, because of something they have done. People can also **forfeit** things like rights and privileges.

forgave See **forgive.**

forge (**forging, forged; forgery, forgeries**) When people **forge** an agreement, they succeed in creating it. ■ If someone **forges** a signature, document, banknote, or painting, they produce an illegal copy called a **forgery.** This activity is called **forgery.** ■ **Forged** metal objects are made by shaping heated metal, usually in a place called a **forge.** ■ If someone **forges ahead,** they make a lot of progress with something.

forger A **forger** is someone who forges things like signatures, documents, banknotes, or paintings.

forget (**forgetting, forgot, have forgotten**) If you **forget** something you used to know, you cannot remember it. ■ If you **forget** something like an appointment, or **forget** to do something, you do not remember it at the right time. ■ If you **forget** something you meant to bring, you do not remember to bring it. ■ **Forgotten** is used to describe places and people that are ignored by the rest of the world. *...this forgotten corner of Ethiopia.*

forgetful (**forgetfulness**) People who are **forgetful** often forget things.

forget-me-not — **Forget-me-nots** are small plants with tiny blue flowers.

forgettable If you say something is **forgettable,** you mean it has nothing special or memorable about it.

forgivable If something someone has done is **forgivable,** they should be forgiven because circumstances forced them to do it.

forgive (**forgiving, forgave, have forgiven**) If you **forgive** someone for something they have done, you stop blaming them or being angry with them. ■ If an organization **forgives** a debt, they no longer expect it to be repaid. ■ If you say people **could be forgiven for** thinking something, you mean they could easily get that impression, however wrong it is. *Looking at its present sorry state, you could be forgiven for thinking that Somalia is a poor country.*

forgiveness If you ask someone for **forgiveness,** you ask them to forgive you for something wrong you have done.

forgo (*or* **forego**) (**forgoes, forgoing, have forgone**) If you **forgo** something, you go without it or give it up. See also **foregoing, foregone.**

forgot (**forgotten**) See **forget.**

fork (**forked**) A **fork** is an object with prongs, used for eating. ■ A **fork** is a large tool with prongs, used in gardening. ■ If a road or river **forks,** it divides into two. You call the place where it divides a

fork. You also use **fork** to say which direction someone takes when they reach a fork. ...*fork right.* ■ A **forked** object divides into two at one end. ■ If you **fork out** for something, you spend a lot of money on it.

fork-lift truck A **fork-lift truck** is a small vehicle with two movable arms at the front, for lifting heavy loads.

forlorn (forlornly) A **forlorn** person, place, or thing looks sad and lonely. ■ A **forlorn** hope or attempt has little or no chance of success.

form When something is **formed**, it is created or started. *Another possibility is that the planet formed after the supernova explosion.* ■ If one thing is changed so that it becomes similar to something else, you say it **forms** that thing. *The two pieces of metal together form a complete tube.* ■ A **form** of something is a type or kind of it. ...*cheaper forms of energy.* ■ The **form** of something is its shape or structure. *They placed candles in the form of a cross... The book is in the form of a travel diary.* ■ If a group of things together **form** a shape, they have that shape. *Queues formed outside many stores.* ■ **Form** is used to talk about the shape of the human body. ...*the female form.* ■ A **form** is a sheet of paper with questions on and space for people to write the answers. ■ At a school, a **form** is a class, or all the classes for children of a similar age. ■ In sport, someone's **form** is their level of fitness and ability. ■ You use **true to form** to say someone is behaving in their normal way. *True to form she kept her guests waiting for 90 minutes.*

formal (formally; formality, formalities) Formal is used to talk about the official aspect of something. *The formal opening of the conference is due in a few hours time.* ■ **Formal** education is your official education, for example at school or college, as distinct from things you may learn at other times. ■ **Formalities** are things which have to be done for official or legal reasons on a particular occasion. *They would be free to leave as soon as passport formalities had been completed.* ■ If you say something is a **formality,** you mean it has to be done, but will not make much difference to a situation. *A survey was arranged which we thought would be a mere formality.* ■ People's behaviour is described as **formal** when they are being very correct, rather than relaxed or casual. *May I call you Archie? I hate formality.* ■ On **formal** occasions, people wear smart clothes and behave according to accepted rules. *He was less formally dressed than usual.*

formaldehyde (*pron:* for-**mal**-de-hide) is a strong smelling gas used as a preservative.

formalise See **formalize.**

formality See **formal.**

formalize (*or* **formalise**) **(formalizing, formalized; formalization)** When a plan or agreement is **formalized,** it is made official.

format The **format** of something is the way it is arranged or presented. ...*a large format book.* ■ The **format** of a piece of computer software or a musical recording is the type of equipment it is designed for. ...*available on cassette and CD formats.* ■ If

you **format** a computer disk, you run a program which prepares the disk to be written on.

formation When something is brought into existence, you call this its **formation.** ...*the formation of a special commission.* ■ You can say people or things are in a particular **formation** when they are arranged in a pattern. *The troops had regrouped into a battle formation.* ■ A rock or cloud **formation** is the shape of a group or mass of rocks or clouds.

formative A **formative** period in someone's life is a time when their character and attitudes are being shaped by things happening around them. You can also talk about **formative** influences on someone or on their life. ■ The **formative** stage of something is the period during which it is beginning to take shape or develop.

former (formerly) Former and formerly are used to say what someone or something used to be. ...*the former world champion... The territory was formerly used as a training site.* ■ When people talk about **former** times, they mean the past. ■ When you have mentioned two things or people, you can call the first one the **former.**

Formica is a stiff hard plastic used for covering surfaces like kitchen worktops. 'Formica' is a trademark.

formidable (formidably) Formidable is used to say someone or something is very impressive and slightly frightening. ...*a formidable opponent.*

formula (*plural:* **formulae** *or* **formulas**) A **formula** is a group of symbols which stand for a scientific or mathematical rule. ■ The chemical **formula** of a substance is a group of symbols representing the proportion of elements in each molecule of the substance. ■ The **formula** for a substance is the set of instructions for making it from other substances. ■ A plan for dealing with a problem can be called a **formula.** ■ In motor racing, **formula** is used to talk about particular categories of car. ...*Formula One cars.* ■ Baby or infant **formula** is specially prepared milk powder which you mix with water to make baby food.

formulate (formulating, formulated; formulation) When people **formulate** something like a plan, they draw it up. ...*the formulation of national economic programmes.* ■ If you **formulate** an opinion or thought, you put it into words. ■ When something like a cream or drug is **formulated,** it is prepared according to a formula. This kind of formula is sometimes called a **formulation.**

fornicate (fornicating, fornicated; fornication, fornicator) Religious people who do not approve of sex outside marriage sometimes call it **fornication.**

forsake (forsaking, forsook, have forsaken) If you **forsake** something, you give it up. *The government is not willing to forsake its status as a nuclear power.* ■ If you **forsake** a person, you stop helping them or looking after them. ■ **Forsaken** is used to describe someone or something that is forgotten or neglected. ...*a forsaken church.*

forsythia is a bush with yellow flowers which appear in the early spring before its leaves.

fort A **fort** is a strong building used as a base for soldiers defending a place.

forte (*pron:* **for**-tay) Someone's **forte** is the thing they are particularly good at.

forth When someone leaves a place, you can say that they set or go **forth.** ■ **Forth** is used to talk about sounds coming out of a place. *Loud music blared forth.* ■ If someone sets **forth** a proposal or plan, they give details of it. ■ If something is brought **forth,** it is made to appear or happen. *One giggle can bring forth uncontrollable laughter from others.* ■ **hold forth:** see **hold. and so forth:** see **so.**

forthcoming A **forthcoming** event will happen soon. *...the forthcoming elections.* ■ If help or information is **forthcoming,** it is provided or made available. *Financial help has not yet been forthcoming.* ■ If someone is **forthcoming,** they are willing to talk freely about something.

forthright If you are **forthright,** you say what you think clearly and directly. *She condemned the move in forthright language.*

forthwith If you do something **forthwith,** you do it straight away.

fortify (**fortifies, fortifying, fortified; fortification**) When people **fortify** a place, they strengthen it against attack, for example by putting up walls or ditches. This process is called **fortification;** the walls, ditches, etc are called **fortifications.** ■ If you are **fortified** by something, it makes you feel stronger, or better able to deal with something. *Fortified by a large breakfast we set off.* ■ **Fortified** food and drink has had something added to it to make it healthier or stronger. *...fortified breakfast cereals.*

fortitude You say someone shows **fortitude** when they cope bravely with pain or difficulty.

fortnight (**fortnightly**) A **fortnight** is a period of two weeks.

fortress (**fortresses**) A **fortress** is a large fort or a fortified town. ■ **Fortress** is sometimes used in front of the name of a geographical area when talking about laws which would make it difficult for people outside to come to live in it or trade with it. *...Fortress Europe.*

fortuitous (**fortuitously**) You say something is **fortuitous** when it is lucky for someone. *...a fortuitous discovery.*

fortunate (**fortunately**) You say people are **fortunate** when they have some special advantage in life, or when things turn out well for them on a particular occasion. ■ You can express relief at something by saying it is **fortunate,** or by adding **fortunately** to what you are saying. *It was fortunate that there were no other casualties... Fortunately, he was not hurt.*

fortune A **fortune** is (a) a very large amount of money. *That dress must have cost a fortune.* (b) all the money and valuables belonging to a very rich person. *...a personal fortune of $13 billion.* ■ **Fortune** or **good fortune** is good luck. **Ill fortune** is bad luck. ■ The **fortunes** of a person or organization are the good or bad things that happen to them. *The fortunes of the party have gone from bad to worse.* ■ If someone **tells your fortune,** they claim to tell you

what will happen to you in the future. A **fortune teller** is someone who does this.

forty (**fortieth, forties**) **Forty** is the number 40. ■ The **forties** was the period from 1940 to 1949. ■ If someone is in their **forties,** they are aged 40 to 49.

forum A **forum** is a meeting where people exchange ideas and discuss issues.

forward (**forwards**) If someone or something moves **forward** or **forwards,** they move in the direction they are facing. ■ **Forward** and **forwards** are used to talk about things making progress or becoming more modern. *Reform is the only way forward.* ■ **Forward-looking** people are interested in modern ideas and new ways of doing things. ■ If you are **looking forward to** something, you are pleased it is going to happen and are expecting to enjoy it. ■ If a document or letter is **forwarded** to someone, it is sent on to them. ■ In football and hockey, a **forward** is a player who tries to score goals rather than defend. In rugby, a **forward** is a player who takes part in the scrum.

fossil A **fossil** is the hardened remains or impression of a prehistoric plant or animal preserved inside rock.

fossil fuel — Fossil fuels are fuels like coal, oil, and natural gas, formed from the decayed remains of plants and animals.

fossilize (*or* **fossilise**) (**fossilizing, fossilized**) When the remains of a plant or animal become **fossilized,** they become hard and form a fossil. ■ If you say an organization or its methods have become **fossilized,** you mean they have not changed at all for a long time. *...fossilised banking attitudes.*

foster (**fostering, fostered**) If a couple **foster** a child, they officially look after it for a time as part of their family, without becoming its legal parents. ■ If something **fosters** a feeling, activity, or idea, it helps it develop.

fought See **fight.**

foul (**fouler, foulest; fouling, fouled**) You use **foul** to describe things which taste or smell nasty. ■ You can describe things such as very bad weather as **foul.** ■ **Foul** language is swear words or other rude words. **Foul-mouthed** people use a lot of foul language. ■ If someone is in a **foul** mood, they are very bad tempered. ■ In a game or sport, a **foul** is an action which is against the rules. If someone **fouls** someone else, they do something to them which breaks a rule. ■ If you **fall foul** of a law or of someone in authority, you are in trouble because of something you have done. ■ **Foul play** is (a) a violent crime which causes someone's death. (b) unfair or dishonest behaviour. ■ If an animal **fouls** a place, it drops faeces there. ■ If you **foul** something **up,** you spoil it by doing something wrong or stupid. You can call what you have done a **foul-up.**

found See **find.** ■ When something like a business or institution is **founded** by someone, they are responsible for starting it. ■ If something is **founded** on a particular thing, it is based on it. *His success was founded on his ability to counter-attack.* ■ If an idea, opinion, or feeling is **well-founded,** there are good reasons for having it. If it is **ill-founded**, there is no good reason for having it.

foundation The **foundation** for a belief or way of life is the thing it is based on. *Good communication is the foundation for a strong marriage.* ■ An organization's **foundation** is the time when it was first started. *...the ANC's biggest rally since its foundation.* ■ A **foundation** is an organization which provides money for a special purpose. *...the National Foundation for Educational Research.* ■ The **foundations** of a building are the parts below the ground which support the main structure.

foundation course A **foundation course** is a university or college course which prepares students for more advanced studies.

foundation stone A **foundation stone** is a block of stone built into a public building, with details of the building's official opening carved on it.

founder (foundering, foundered) The **founder** of an organization or town is the person who created it. A **founder member** of a group or organization is one of the members who started it. ■ If something **founders** on a particular thing, it fails because of that thing. *His negotiations have foundered on economic grounds.*

foundry (foundries) A **foundry** is an industrial works where metal is melted down and cast into moulds to form a variety of objects.

fount If you call a person or place the **fount** of something, you mean they are its source. *...London's days as the fount of all things fashionable.*

fountain A **fountain** is an ornamental structure consisting of a jet of water forced up into the air by a pump.

fountain pen A **fountain pen** is a pen with a nib which is supplied with ink from a container inside the pen.

four is the number 4. ■ If someone is **on all fours**, they are on their hands and knees.

four-letter word – **Four-letter words** are short words which people think are rude or offensive, because they refer to sex or bodily functions.

foursome A **foursome** is a group of four people.

fourteen (fourteenth) Fourteen is the number 14.

fourth The **fourth** item in a series is the one counted as number 4.

four-wheel drive On a **four-wheel drive** vehicle, power from the engine is transmitted to all four wheels, rather than to either the front or back wheels.

fowl (*plural:* **fowls or fowl**) Birds which people eat can be called **fowl.**

fox (foxes, foxing, foxed) Foxes are dog-like animals with reddish-brown fur and bushy tails. ■ If someone or something **foxes** you, they baffle you.

foxhole A **foxhole** is a small hole which soldiers dig to shelter in and shoot from.

foxhound The **foxhound** is a type of dog bred and trained for fox-hunting.

foyer (*pron:* foy-ay *or* foy-er) The **foyer** of a large building is the area just inside the main doors.

Fr. – Fr. is short for 'franc'. ■ **Fr.** in front of a priest's name means 'Father'.

fracas (*pron:* frak-ah) (*plural:* **fracas**) A **fracas** is a noisy quarrel or fight.

fractal A **fractal** is a mathematical code which can be used in computing to express the basic similarities of irregularly-shaped natural objects, for example clouds. **Fractal** images are irregular shapes made up of a large number of smaller shapes which are all identical to each other.

fraction (fractional, fractionally) In maths, a **fraction** is an exact part of a number. $\frac{1}{4}$ and $\frac{2}{3}$ are fractions. ■ A **fraction** of something is a very small part of it. *...this tiny fraction of Sarajevo's population.* A **fractional** amount is very small.

fractious You say someone is being **fractious** when they are irritable.

fracture (fracturing, fractured) If something **fractures**, it cracks or breaks. A **fracture** is a crack or break in something. ■ You say something like a system or relationship **fractures** when it breaks down. You can talk about a **fracture** in something like this. *This could widen the ethnic fractures in the republic.*

fragile (fragility) Fragile things are easily broken, damaged, or destroyed.

fragment (fragmentation) A **fragment** of something is a small part of it. ■ If something **fragments**, it breaks up into smaller less unified parts. *...the bloody fragmentation of the country.*

fragmentary You say something is **fragmentary** when it is incomplete and the parts you have do not fit together. *...fragmentary evidence.*

fragrant (fragrance) You say something is **fragrant** when it has a sweet or pleasant smell. You call this smell its **fragrance.** ■ Perfumes are sometimes called **fragrances**.

frail people are weak and unhealthy.

frailty (frailties) People's **frailties** are their small weaknesses. ■ **Frailty** is used to talk about physical weakness brought on by age or ill health. *...as frailty and age set in.*

frame (framing, framed) A **frame** is a structure that something fits into, for example a door frame or a picture frame. ■ If you **frame** a picture, you put it in a frame. ■ A **frame** is a structure which gives an object its shape and strength. ■ The **frames** of a pair of glasses are the parts which hold the lenses in place. ■ You can refer to a person's body as their **frame.** *...his skinny frame.* ■ A **frame** is (a) one of the many photographs a cinema film consists of. (b) one still photograph on a reel of film. ■ If someone **frames** an innocent person, they make it look as though he or she has committed a crime. ■ In snooker, a **frame** is one game. ■ Your **frame of mind** is the mood you are in at a particular time. ■ If you say someone is **in the frame** for something, you mean they have a good chance of achieving or getting it. *I hope I'm in the frame for the top job.*

framework The **framework** of a system is the set of rules or guidelines within which it works. *...an internationally accepted framework for peace.* ■ A **framework** is a structure which forms or supports something. *A mesh-covered wooden framework should be hung around the area.*

franc The **franc** is the unit of currency in France, Switzerland and Belgium.

franchise A **franchise** is an authority which a company grants to someone, allowing them to sell its products. If a company **franchises** someone, they grant them this authority. ■ The **franchise** is the right of each person to vote in his or her country's parliamentary elections.

frank (**frankly, frankness**) If you are **frank**, you talk in an open and honest way. *He asked me to tell him frankly what I wished to do. ...speaking with complete frankness.* ■ If a letter or parcel is **franked**, it is marked with a symbol which shows the postage has been paid.

frankfurter A **frankfurter** is a type of smoked sausage.

frantic (**frantically**) You say someone is **frantic** when they behave in a wild and desperate way, because they are frightened or worried. ■ If there is **frantic** activity, people are very busy doing a lot of things.

fraternal is used to describe friendly actions and feelings between countries or groups of people. *The talks are continuing in a fraternal atmosphere.* ■ **Fraternal** twins are twins born from two eggs, so they are not identical. They may be different sexes and may look different from each other.

fraternity (**fraternities**) People belonging to the same profession or having the same interest are sometimes called a particular **fraternity.** *...the banking fraternity.* ■ **Fraternity** is friendship between groups of people. ■ In the US, a **fraternity** is a society of male college students.

fratricide If someone commits **fratricide,** they kill their brother. ■ When people from the same country or community kill each other, for example during a civil war, this can be called **fratricide.**

fraud is the crime of obtaining money by deceit. ■ If you say someone is a **fraud,** you mean they are pretending to be something they are not.

fraudulent statements are deliberately deceitful or untrue.

fraught If something is **fraught** with problems, it is full of them. ■ If people are **fraught,** they are worried and anxious.

fray If your nerves or temper **fray,** you become irritable because of stress. ■ When a material **frays,** its threads or strands become unravelled or worn. ■ If you say someone enters **the fray,** you mean they get involved in something like a conflict.

freak (**freakish**) People or things that seem strange or unusual sometimes get called **freaks.** ■ If you say someone is, for example, a health **freak,** you mean they are obsessed with keeping healthy. *...a fitness freak.* ■ If you call something that has happened a **freak,** you mean it was the result of unusual circumstances, and is not likely to be repeated. *...a freakish gust of wind.* ■ If someone **freaks out,** they become extremely excited, and lose control of their feelings.

freckles are light-brown spots on a person's skin.

free (**freer, freest; freeing, freed; -free**) You say someone or something is **free** when they are not restricted, limited, or controlled by rules, customs, or other people. When they get rid of a restriction, you can say they **free** themselves from it. ■ When prisoners are **freed** or **set free,** they are released. You can say a released prisoner is **free.** ■ If a person or place is **free** from something unpleasant, they are not affected by it. *...a life free from terror.* ■ If you **free** something which is fixed or trapped, you release it. You can also pull something **free.** ■ Something is **free** when people do not have to pay for it. ■ If something like a seat is **free,** it is not occupied or not being used. ■ If you are **free** at a particular time, you are not busy then. ■ If you say someone is **free** with something, you mean they give it away or use it a lot. *He is not known for being free with his money.* ■ **-free** can be added to another word to show that something is not affected by, or does not have or involve, the thing described. *...tax-free savings schemes. ...a frost-free greenhouse.* ■ If you believe in **free will,** you believe people choose what they do, rather than having their actions controlled by God or fate. ■ **a free hand:** see **hand.** See also **freely.**

freedom If you have the **freedom** to do something, you are allowed to do it without being restricted or limited by someone or something. *...the freedom to do the job his way. ...freedom of speech.* ■ If there is **freedom** from something unpleasant, people do not have it or are not affected by it. *...freedom from hunger.* ■ When prisoners gain their **freedom,** they escape or are released.

freedom fighter If you support a group of people who are fighting to overthrow the government of their country, you can call them **freedom fighters.**

free enterprise is an economic system in which businesses compete for profit with little government control or interference.

free fall In parachuting, **free fall** is the part of the jump before the parachute opens. ■ If things like prices go into **free fall,** they begin to drop rapidly and uncontrollably.

free-for-all A **free-for-all** is a fight or argument which everyone gets involved in. ■ You call a situation a **free-for-all** when several people or groups are trying to get something and there are no controls on how they do it.

freehand drawing is done without using any implements such as a ruler or compasses.

freehold (**freeholder**) If you own the **freehold** of a building or piece of land, you own it for life, rather than leasing it from someone else. See also **leasehold.**

free kick When there is a **free kick** in football, a player is allowed to kick the ball once without interference, because a member of the other side has broken a rule.

freelance A **freelance** occupation is one in which someone is self-employed and is paid for each job he or she does.

freeloader If you call a group of people **freeloaders,** you mean they are using people because they accept things such as food or accommodation without paying their share.

freely If you can do something **freely,** you can do it without being restricted in any way. ■ If something is **freely** available, you can get hold of it easily. ■ **Freely** is used to say something is done, used, or produced in large quantities. *During a recession consumers do not spend so freely.*

free market In a **free market** economy, people decide what prices to sell their goods at, rather than having them determined by the government.

Freemason (**Freemasonry**) A **Freemason** is a man who belongs to a secret society whose members promise to help each other. Their beliefs and practices are called **Freemasonry.**

free-range poultry and pigs are allowed to move freely on an area of open ground.

freesia — **Freesias** are white, yellow, pink, or mauve tube-shaped flowers with a pleasant smell.

free-standing A **free-standing** building or other object stands on its own and is not joined or attached to anything else. ■ You can say an organization is **free-standing** when it is independent of other organizations.

freestyle is used to talk about sports competitions, especially swimming and wrestling, in which competitors can use any style or method they want.

free trade is trade between countries without restrictions or taxes on what is bought or sold.

freeway In the US, a **freeway** is similar to a motorway.

freewheeling is used to describe events or arrangements which are not limited by rules or fixed ideas about the way things should be done. *He said he thought the meetings should be informal to allow freewheeling discussions.*

freeze (**freezing, froze, have frozen**) When a liquid **freezes,** it becomes solid because the temperature has dropped below a certain level. ■ If an area of water **freezes over,** it becomes completely covered by a layer of ice. ■ If something like a pipe **freezes,** it becomes completely blocked with ice. ■ If it is **freezing,** the temperature is below freezing point. ■ If you **freeze** food, you store it at a temperature below freezing point, so it will keep longer. ■ You say someone **freezes** when they suddenly become completely still. ■ If things such as prices are **frozen,** they are prevented from rising. ■ If money held somewhere is **frozen,** a legal order is made preventing anyone, including the owner, from using it.

freeze-dried food has been frozen then dried very quickly, to make it keep longer.

freezer A **freezer** is a metal container with an inside temperature kept below freezing point, used for storing food for long periods.

freezing point — Freezing point or freezing is 0°Celsius, the temperature at which water freezes. ■ The **freezing point** of any liquid is the temperature at which it becomes solid.

freight is goods that are transported in large quantities by lorries, trains, ships, or planes.

freighter A **freighter** is a ship or plane designed to carry goods rather than people.

freight train A **freight train** carries goods rather than passengers.

French is used to talk about people and things in or from France. *...the French coast.* ■ The **French** are the French people. ■ **French** is the main language spoken in France.

French beans are long thin green beans.

French doors are the same as French windows.

French dressing is a thin sauce for putting on salads. It is made of oil, vinegar, and spices.

French fries See **fry.**

French horn See **horn.**

Frenchman (**Frenchwoman**) A **Frenchman** or **Frenchwoman** is a person who comes from France.

French polish is a type of varnish painted onto wood to give it a hard shiny surface.

French windows are a pair of doors made mostly of glass, which lead onto a garden or balcony.

frenetic (*pron:* frin-**net**-ik) (**frenetically**) **Frenetic** behaviour is fast, energetic, and uncontrolled.

frenzy (**frenzied**) **Frenzy** is violent, excited, or uncontrolled behaviour. *...a frenzy of shopping. ...a frenzied mob.*

frequency (**frequencies**) The **frequency** of something is how often it happens. *The frequency of guerrilla attacks has increased.* ■ The **frequency** of a sound or radio wave is the rate at which it vibrates.

frequent (**frequently**) **Frequent** is used to describe things which happen often. *She frequently accompanied him to concerts.* ■ If you **frequent** a place, you go there often.

fresco (**frescoes**) A **fresco** is a picture painted onto a plastered wall while the plaster is still wet.

fresh (**freshness**) A **fresh** thing is something new which replaces another thing, or is added to it. *Rose had given him fresh instructions.* ■ You use **fresh** to describe things done in a new way which you find interesting or attractive. *This gives the novel freshness and charm.* ■ If something is **fresh in your mind,** you remember it clearly, because it is recent or because it made a strong impression on you. ■ If you are **fresh from** a place or experience, you have just been to that place or had that experience. ■ **Fresh** food has been produced or picked recently, and so has not been preserved in any way. ■ **Fresh** air is the air you get outside, compared to the air inside a building. ■ **Fresh** water is water which is not polluted or salty. See also **freshwater.** ■ You use **fresh** to describe things which feel, taste, or smell pleasant and refreshing. *Grated lemon peel gives a fresh flavour to almost anything.* ■ If you describe someone or something as **fresh,** you mean they look pleasant, bright, and clean.

freshen (**freshening, freshened**) If you **freshen** something, or **freshen** it **up,** you make it look, taste, or smell cleaner and fresher. *A thorough brushing helps freshen up your mouth.* ■ If a wind **freshens,** it gets stronger.

fresher A **fresher** is a student who has just started at university or college.

fresh-faced people are young and innocent-looking.

freshly is used to say something has been made or done recently. *...freshly ground coffee.*

freshman (**freshmen**) In America, a **freshman** is a first-year student at a university or college.

freshwater A **freshwater** river, lake, or pool is one where the water is not salty.

fret (**fretting, fretted**) If you **fret** about something, you worry about it.

fretful people behave in a way which shows they are worried or uncomfortable.

fretwork is thin wood or metal with bits cut out to make a pattern.

Freudian (*pron:* **froy**-dee-an) is used to talk about the ideas and methods of the psychiatrist Freud, especially his ideas about people's hidden sexual feelings.

Freudian slip If someone accidentally says something which reveals their subconscious feelings, this is referred to as a **Freudian slip.**

friar A **friar** is a member of a Catholic religious order.

friction (**frictional**) You say there is **friction** when one thing rubs against another. *...any type of frictional contact results in wear and damage.* ■ In science, **friction** is the force that stops things moving freely when they are touching each other. ■ **Friction** is quarrelling and disagreement. *The issue has caused friction within the governing coalition.*

fridge A **fridge** is a large metal container for storing food at low temperatures, to keep it fresh. 'Fridge' is short for 'refrigerator'.

friend A **friend** is someone you like and know well. ■ People who help and support a country, cause, or institution are sometimes called its **friends.**

friendless A **friendless** person has no friends.

friendly (**friendlier, friendliest; friendliness, friendlies, -friendly**) **Friendly** people are pleasant, helpful, and kind. *He had been received with friendliness and warmth.* ■ If you are **friendly** with someone, you like each other and enjoy spending time together. ■ In a war, a **friendly** country or armed force is one fighting on the same side as your own. When people are hit by **friendly fire,** they are hit by bombs or missiles fired from their own side. ■ A **friendly** is a sports match which is not part of a competition. *...pre-season friendlies.* ■ **Friendly** places or objects make you feel comfortable and safe. *...a small room lit by friendly lamps.* ■ **-friendly** is often added to words to say something is designed to suit a particular group of people or to fit in with a particular policy. *...an environment-friendly weedkiller.*

friendly society A **friendly society** is an organization people regularly pay small amounts of money to, and which then pays them money if they are ill or when they retire.

friendship is the relationship between people who are friends. ■ **Friendship** is used to talk about the relationship between countries who help and support each other.

frieze A **frieze** is a decorative strip or border along a wall of a building.

frigate A **frigate** is a small fast ship used by the navy to protect other ships.

fright is a feeling of fear. ■ If someone **takes fright** at something, they become alarmed and often change their mind about something they were intending to do.

frighten (**frightening, frightened; frighteningly**) If something **frightens** you, it makes you afraid, nervous, or worried. ■ If someone is **frightened off** or **frightened away,** something makes them decide not to become involved with a certain person or activity. *Building society repossessions have frightened buyers off.*

frightful (**frightfully**) **Frightful** is used to describe something very bad or unpleasant. *...the frightful nature of modern weapons.*

frigid Women who are not easily sexually aroused are sometimes described as **frigid.** This word can be offensive.

frill (**frilly**) A **frill** is a strip of cloth with many folds, attached to something as a decoration.

fringe (**fringed**) If someone has a **fringe,** the front of their hair has been cut so it hangs down over their forehead. ■ A **fringe** is a row of hanging threads attached to something as a decoration. *...a suede fringed jacket.* ■ If a place is **fringed** with things, it has them along its edges. *...blue water fringed by palm trees.* ■ The **fringes** of a place are the parts furthest from its centre. ■ **Fringe** is used to talk about the unofficial or unconventional parts of an activity or organization. *...fringe theatre. ...the radical fringe of the Labour party.* ■ **Fringe benefits** are extra things which you get with some jobs.

frippery (**fripperies**) If you refer to something as **frippery,** you mean it is unimportant or extravagant and is only done or worn to impress people. *A sombre display, with no frills or frippery, in dark greys and browns.*

frisk If someone **frisks** you, they search you quickly with their hands, to see if you are hiding something. ■ When animals **frisk,** they run around in a lively way.

frisky (**friskier**) A **frisky** animal or person is energetic and high-spirited.

frisson (*pron:* **frees**-sonn) If something gives you a **frisson,** you get a feeling of excitement because of it.

fritter (**frittering, frittered**) **Fritters** are fruit or vegetables dipped in batter and fried. ■ If you **fritter** time or money **away,** you waste it. *The country's oil wealth is being frittered away on unnecessary schemes.*

frivolity (**frivolities**) **Frivolity** is silly, light-hearted behaviour. **Frivolities** are amusing and silly activities, rather than serious and sensible ones.

frivolous (**frivolously**) If you say someone is being **frivolous,** you mean they are being silly and not taking things seriously. ■ If you do something **frivolous,** you do it for fun, rather than for any practical reason.

frizzy hair has stiff wiry curls.

fro If someone or something moves **to and fro,** they move repeatedly from one place to another. Behaviour like this is called **to-ing and fro-ing.**

frock A **frock** is the same as a dress.

frock coat – **Frock coats** were long jackets worn by men in the 19th century.

frog – **Frogs** are small smooth-skinned creatures with long back legs which they use for jumping.

frogman (**frogmen**) A **frogman** is a person whose job involves diving and working underwater.

frog-march If you are **frog-marched** somewhere, you are forced to walk there by two people, each holding one of your arms.

frolic (**frolicking, frolicked**) When animals or people **frolic**, they enjoy themselves in a lively way.

from is used to talk about the source or origin of something, or to say where or when something starts. *...water from the canal... She was deaf from birth.* ■ **From** is used to say where someone lives or was born. *She came from Ilford.* ■ **From** is used to talk about distance, for example to say how far it is between two places. *Dublin is 60 miles from the Ulster border.* ■ **From** is used to talk about a reduction in something. *This amount will be deducted from your pension.* ■ **From** is used to mention the cause of something. *My eyes hurt from the wind.* ■ If someone returns **from** doing something, they return after doing it. *The men had not yet come back from fishing.* ■ **From** is used to talk about a range of possibilities. *The process takes from two to five weeks.*

frond The leaves of a fern or palm tree are called **fronds.**

front The **front** of something is the part which is facing you or facing forward. ■ The **front** page of a newspaper is the first page, containing the main stories. ■ You say someone is **in front** when they are ahead of other people going the same way, especially in a competition. ■ The **front** or **front line** is the place where two opposing armies are fighting each other. ■ A **front** is a place where a mass of cold air meets a mass of warm air. ■ If something is happening on a certain **front**, it is happening in a certain situation or field of activity. *On the intellectual front, little advance has been made.* ■ If someone puts on a certain kind of **front**, they pretend to have a particular quality. *We must present a united front.* ■ If an organization or activity is a **front** for something illegal or secret, it hides what is going on. ■ The person who **fronts** an organization is the most senior person in it.

frontage A **frontage** of a building is a side facing a street.

frontal A **frontal** or **full-frontal** attack is made directly at the main part of something. *...a frontal attack on the camp.* ■ A **frontal** or **full-frontal** attack criticizes or threatens someone or something in a strong, direct way. *...his frontal attack on the conservatives.* ■ **Full-frontal** is used to describe the front view of a nude person. *...the first full-frontal male nude to appear in a play here.* ■ In biology, **frontal** is used to talk about things to do with the front of the brain. *...the frontal lobes.*

front bench (**frontbencher**) In Parliament, the **front bench** or **front benches** refers to MPs who are ministers in the government or who hold official positions in the opposition. These MPs are called **frontbenchers.**

frontier A **frontier** is a border between two countries. ■ **Frontier** is used to describe places at the edge of the settled area of a country. *...a frontier town.* ■ The **frontiers** of a branch of knowledge or activity are its normally recognized limits. *...helping us to advance the frontiers of medical science.*

frontispiece The **frontispiece** of a book is a picture at the beginning, opposite the title page.

front runner The **front runner** in a competition is the person most likely to win.

frost When there is a **frost**, the ground is covered with powdery white ice crystals because the temperature has fallen below freezing.

frostbite (**frostbitten**) **Frostbite** is a painful condition caused by severe cold. It can damage a person's fingers, toes, nose, or ears. *...a frostbitten hand.*

frosted glass has an uneven and slightly rough surface on one side, to stop people seeing through it. ■ **Frosted** means covered with something which looks like frost. *...frosted fruit.*

frosty (**frostily**) If the weather is **frosty**, the temperature has fallen below freezing. ■ If you call someone's behaviour **frosty**, you mean they are being unfriendly. *She smiled frostily.*

froth (**frothy, frothing**) When a liquid **froths** or there is **froth** on it, a mass of small bubbles appears on its surface. ■ You can use **froth** to describe something which appears exciting or attractive, but has very little real value or importance. *The government may want to remove the political froth from public-spending plans.*

frown When someone **frowns**, they draw their eyebrows together and wrinkle their forehead, because they are worried, annoyed, or concentrating. You call their expression a **frown.** ■ If people **frown on** something, they disapprove of it.

froze (**frozen**) See **freeze.**

fructose is a kind of sugar which you get in honey and some fruit.

frugal (**frugally, frugality**) You say someone is **frugal** when they do not eat much or spend much money on themselves. *...three years of living frugally. ...frugality and economy.*

fruit (*usual plural:* **fruit**) A **fruit** is something which grows on a tree or bush and which often contains seeds or a stone covered by a substance you can eat. ■ The **fruits** of someone's work are the good things which come from it. ■ If something you do **bears fruit**, it produces good results.

fruit cocktail A **fruit cocktail** is a mixture of pieces of different kinds of fruit, eaten as part of a meal.

fruitful (**fruitfully**) You say something is **fruitful** when it produces good results. *The talks had been fruitful.*

fruition (*pron:* froo-**ish**-on) If something you have done or planned comes to **fruition,** it produces the results you want.

fruitless (**fruitlessly**) You say something is **fruitless** when it does not achieve what you want.

fruit machine A **fruit machine** is a machine for gambling. You put a coin in a slot, and the machine pays out money if a particular pattern of symbols appears on its screen.

fruit salad is a mixture of pieces of different kinds of fruit, usually eaten as dessert.

fruity (**fruitiness**) **Fruity** things taste or smell of fruit.

frustrate (**frustrating, frustrated; frustration**) If something **frustrates** you or is **frustrating,** it makes you angry or upset, because it stops you doing what you want. You call your feelings **frustration.** ■ If you **frustrate** someone's hopes or plans, you stop them being fulfilled. ■ You use **frustrated** to describe someone who has not succeeded in being what they wanted to be. *...an enthusiastic English teacher who I suspect was a frustrated actor.*

fry (**fries, frying, fried**) When you **fry** food, you cook it in a pan with hot fat. A **fry-up** is a meal of fried food. ■ **Fries** or **French fries** are chips cut very thin. ■ **small fry:** see **small.**

frying pan A **frying pan** is a shallow metal pan with a long handle, for frying food.

ft See **foot.**

FTSE Index The **FTSE Index** or **FTSE** (*pron:* **foot**-sie) is an indicator of share values. It gives the average price of 100 leading shares on the stock market during each day of trading. 'FTSE Index' stands for 'Financial Times Stock Exchange 100 Index'.

fuchsia (*pron:* **fyew**-sha) **Fuchsias** are a kind of shrub with pink, purple, or white flowers. ■ **Fuchsia** is a bright pinky-purple colour.

fuddled If someone is **fuddled,** they cannot think clearly, often because they have been drinking.

fudge (**fudging, fudged**) **Fudge** is a soft brown sweet made from butter, milk, and sugar. ■ If you **fudge** something, you avoid making a clear and definite decision or statement about it. *They were inclined to fudge the issue of right and wrong.*

fuel (**fuelling, fuelled**) (*Am:* **fueling, fueled**) **Fuel** is a substance like wood, coal, or petrol which is burned to give heat or power. ■ If a machine or vehicle is **fuelled** by a particular substance, it uses it as a fuel. ■ If something is **fuelled** by something else, it gets stronger or more intense because of it. *Hugh's anger was fuelled by resentment.*

fuel injection is a system for introducing liquid fuel under pressure directly into a vehicle's engine without the use of a carburettor.

fug You can say there is a **fug** in a place when the atmosphere there is smoky and stale.

fugitive A **fugitive** is someone who is running away or hiding from the police.

fugue (*pron:* **fyewg**) A **fugue** is a piece of music that begins with a simple tune which is then repeated by other voices or instrumental parts with small variations; a technical term in music.

fulcrum The **fulcrum** of something is its most important part, which everything else depends on. *...the historical fulcrum of western economic development.* ■ In physics, a **fulcrum** is a point where something balances or pivots.

fulfil (*Am:* **fulfill**) (**fulfils, fulfilling, fulfilled; fulfilment**) If you **fulfil** a promise, task, or ambition, you carry it out or achieve it. ■ If something you do **fulfils** you, it makes you happy and satisfied. *...a hobby that fulfilled her.*

full If something is **full** or **full up,** there is no room inside it for anything or anyone else. You say you feel **full** when you have had enough to eat or drink. ■ A **full** skirt or sleeve has been made using a lot of material. ■ If you are affected very strongly by a feeling, you can say you are **full** of it. *I was full of confidence.* ■ **Full** is used to talk about the whole of something. *...the full impact of the opinion polls.* ■ When there is a **full** moon, you can see the whole face of the moon. ■ If you do or use something **to the full,** you do or use it to the maximum extent. *How can we be sure we exploit this opportunity to the full?* ■ If someone leads a **full** life, they are always busy doing a lot of different things. ■ If there is **full** employment, there is work for everyone. ■ If you get **full marks** in a test, you are given the maximum number of marks. ■ If machinery is at **full** capacity, it is working at its greatest power. ■ If food or drink has a **full** flavour, it has a rich strong flavour. ■ See also **fully.**

full back A **full back** is a defender in football or hockey.

full-blooded actions or behaviour are carried out with great intensity or enthusiasm. *The performance was admirably full-blooded.*

full-blown You use **full-blown** to emphasize that you are talking about something in its most complete form. *...full-blown AIDS.*

full board If a hotel or guest house provides **full board,** you can get all your meals there.

full-frontal See **frontal.**

full-grown See **fully-grown.**

full-length things are the normal length, as distinct from shorter things of the same kind. *...his first full-length play.*

full-page A **full-page** advertisement or article takes up a whole page in a newspaper or magazine.

full-scale You use **full-scale** to emphasize that something is as complete or intense as possible. *...a full-scale war.*

full-size (**full-sized**) **Full-size** or **full-sized** things are the normal size, as distinct from smaller things of the same kind. *...a full-size grand piano.* ■ A **full-size** model is the same size as the original.

full stop A **full stop** is the punctuation mark . used at the end of a sentence.

full-time work or study takes up the whole of a normal working week. ■ In games like football, **full time** is the end of the match.

fully is used to mean 'completely'. ■ If something is done **fully,** it is done to the greatest possible extent. *...a willingness to participate fully in such activities.*

fully-fledged (*Am:* **full-fledged**) You use **fully-fledged** to describe people or things that have developed completely. *...his first film as a fully-fledged producer.*

fully-grown or **full-grown** animals and plants have reached their natural size and stopped growing.

fulminate (**fulminating, fulminated; fulmination**) If you **fulminate** against someone or something, you criticize them angrily.

fulsome (**fulsomely**) You use **fulsome** to describe praise, apologies, or thanks which you think are exaggerated and insincere. *The IMF has, rather fulsomely, praised Vietnam's economic policies.*

fumble (**fumbling, fumbled**) If you **fumble** for something, you reach or feel for it in a clumsy way. ■ If you **fumble** with something, you fiddle clumsily with it. ■ If you **fumble** what you are trying to do or say, you make mistakes and do it badly.

fume (**fuming, fumed**) **Fumes** are smoke or gases given off by chemicals or something burning. ■ If you say someone is **fuming,** you mean they are extremely angry.

fumigate (**fumigating, fumigated; fumigation**) If you **fumigate** something, you disinfect it using special chemicals, usually to get rid of germs or insects.

fun If something is **fun,** it is enjoyable and entertaining. *It's fun working for him.* You can also say someone is **fun.** ■ If you do something **for fun,** you do it just because you enjoy it. ■ If you **make fun** of someone, or **poke fun** at them, you tease them or make unkind jokes about them.

function (**functioning, functioned**) The **function** of a person or thing is their purpose or role. *The essential function of trade unions is to bargain with employers.* ■ If something **functions** as a particular thing, that is what it is used for. *The room had previously functioned as a playroom.* If someone **functions** as a particular thing, that is their role or job. ■ The way something **functions** is the way it works. If something like a machine is **functioning,** it is working. ■ A **function** is a sequence of operations performed by a computer when a single key is pressed. ■ A **function** is a formal social event like a dinner.

functional (**functionally**) **Functional** things are useful and practical rather than attractive. ■ When something like a machine or system is **functional,** it is working and ready to be used. ■ If someone is **functionally illiterate,** they cannot read or write enough to cope in everyday situations.

functionary (**functionaries**) A **functionary** is an official who does administrative work, especially for a political party.

fund **Funds** are money available for spending. *The Home Office would be forced to seek extra funds.* ■ If a person or organization **funds** something or provides **funding** for it, they provide the money for it. ■ A **fund** is money being collected for a particular purpose. *...our campaign fund.* ■ If someone has a **fund** of knowledge or experience, they have a lot of it.

fundamental (**fundamentally**) **Fundamental** is used to describe things of the most basic and important kind. *...the fundamental cause of the crisis. ...The project is fundamentally flawed.* ■ The **fundamentals** of something are its most basic or important parts. *...the fundamentals of police work.*

fundamentalism (**fundamentalist**) **Fundamentalism** is belief in the original form of a religion, and rejection of all later forms. *...Hindu fundamentalists.*

fund-raising (**fund-raiser**) **Fund-raising** is collecting money for a charity, a political party, or some other organization.

funeral A **funeral** is a ceremony for the burial or cremation of a dead person.

funereal (*pron:* fyoo-**neer**-ee-al) You use **funereal** to describe things which are very sombre and serious.

funfair A **funfair** is a place or an event with things such as amusement arcades and rides.

fungal means to do with fungus. *...fungal spores.*

fungi See **fungus.**

fungicide is a chemical used to kill fungus or stop it growing.

fungus (*plural:* **fungi**) **Fungi** are organisms such as mushrooms and toadstools which have no leaves, flowers, or roots.

funk is a type of dance music based on jazz and blues, with a strong bass part.

funnel (**funnelling, funnelled**) (*Am:* **funneling, funneled**) A **funnel** is a device for pouring substances through small openings. It has a wide open top which narrows to a tube at the bottom. ■ If people or things are **funnelled** somewhere, they are made to pass through a narrow space. *Visitors are funnelled in to see the painting.* ■ If money is **funnelled** into an organization, it is directed there from different places. ■ A **funnel** is a metal chimney on a ship or steam-powered railway engine.

funnily You say **funnily enough** when you are mentioning something which is surprising but true.

funny (**funnier, funniest**) You say people or things are **funny** when they make you smile or laugh. ■ You say something is **funny** when it is surprising or puzzling. *Shock does funny things to people.*

fur An animal's **fur** is its thick hair. ■ **Fur** is the fur-covered skins of animals which is used to make clothes and rugs. Some artificial materials are also called **fur.** ■ A **fur** is a coat or stole made from fur.

furious (**furiously**) If someone is **furious,** they are extremely angry. ■ **Furious** is used to say something is done with a lot of energy, speed, or violence. *They are working furiously to cut costs.*

furlong A **furlong** is 220 yards (about 201.2 metres). Nowadays, this measurement is used only in horseracing.

furnace A **furnace** is an enclosed space for a very hot fire used, for example, to heat metal.

furnish (**furnishes, furnishing, furnished**) If you **furnish** a room or house, you put furniture in it. ■ **Furnished** is used to describe the furniture in a room or house. *...his elegantly furnished house.* ■ **Furnished** accommodation is let with furniture already in it. ■ If you **furnish** someone with something, you provide or supply it for them.

furnishings The **furnishings** in a room are the furniture and fittings.

furniture is objects like tables and chairs.

furore (*Am:* **furor**) (*pron:* fyew-**ror**-ee *or* fyew-**ror**) If there is a **furore** about something, people get excited and angry about it.

furrier A **furrier** is a person or firm that makes or sells clothes made from fur.

furrow A **furrow** is a long groove made in the earth, for planting seeds. ■ If someone's brow is **furrowed,** they are frowning.

furry A **furry** animal has thick soft hair. ■ A **furry** object is covered with fur, or something like fur.

further (**furthering, furthered; furtherance**) See **far.** ■ A **further** thing, person, or amount is an additional one. *...the release of further American hostages.* ■ If you **further** something, you help it make progress or succeed. *Hall helped to further the careers of several future stars... £5,000 is to be spent on the* *furtherance of the winning project.* ■ If you go **further** with something or take it **further,** you take it to a more advanced stage.

further education is education after leaving school, at a college rather than a university.

furthermore You say **furthermore** when you are adding information to what you have just said. *Furthermore, they claim that any such interference is completely ineffective.*

furthest See **far.**

furtive (**furtively**) If you do something in a **furtive** way, you try not to be noticed doing it.

fury is very great anger.

fuse (**fusing, fused; fusion**) A **fuse** is a wire which acts as a safety device in an electrical circuit. If an appliance **fuses,** a fault causes the wire to melt, breaking the circuit. ■ A **fuse** is part of an explosive device which delays the explosion, so people can move to safety. ■ If you say someone has a **short fuse,** you mean they lose their temper easily. ■ If objects **fuse** or are **fused,** they are joined together by heat or a biological process. ■ If people **fuse** things like ideas or methods, they combine them successfully. You can talk about a **fusion** of ideas or methods.

fuse box A **fuse box** is a box, usually on an inside wall, with fuses in it for all the electrical circuits in a building.

fuselage (*pron:* **fyew**-zil-lahzh; *the 'zh' sounds like 's' in 'pleasure'*) The **fuselage** of a plane is the main part, which the wings and tail are attached to.

fusillade (*pron:* fyew-zil-**laid**) A **fusillade** of shots is a lot of them fired at the same time.

fusion See **fuse, nuclear.**

fuss (**fusses, fussing, fussed**) If you say someone is **fussing,** you mean they are behaving in an unnecessarily anxious way. You call behaviour like this **fuss.** ■ If someone **fusses over** you or **makes a fuss** of you, they keep showing concern for your well-being. ■ If someone **makes a fuss** or **kicks up a fuss,** they object strongly to something.

fussy (**fussier, fussiest; fussiness**) You say someone is being **fussy** when they are too concerned with unimportant details and are difficult to please. ■ You can say something like a building is **fussy** when it is too full of decoration.

fusty (**fustier, fustiest**) If you say people or ideas are **fusty,** you think they are old-fashioned. ■ If something smells **fusty,** it smells stale because it is old or neglected.

futile (**futility**) You say something is **futile** when it does not achieve anything.

futon (*pron:* **foo**-tonn) A **futon** is a thin mattress which can be laid on the floor as a bed, or folded up and placed on a frame as a sofa.

future The **future** is the time which has not yet happened. Future is used to talk about a time in the future, or about something that will happen in the future. *Let's meet again at some future date.* ■ You say **in future** when you are saying what will happen from now on. *I asked her to be more careful in future.* ■ If you say something has a **future,** you mean it is likely to be successful. ■ **Futures** are goods or shares bought or sold on the stock market at an agreed price and paid for at a later date.

futuristic is used to describe unusual-looking things which seem to belong to some time in the future. *...a futuristic office development.*

fuzzy (**fuzzier, fuzziest**) A **fuzzy** picture or sound is blurred or indistinct. ■ **Fuzzy** hair sticks up in a soft curly mass. ■ **Fuzzy** logic is a type of computer logic that is supposed to imitate the way that humans think, for example by adapting to changing circumstances rather than by always following the same procedure.

G g

g See **gram.**

G-7 The **G-7** is a group of seven major industrial countries which meets to seek agreement on economic matters. The seven countries are Canada, France, Germany, Italy, Japan, Great Britain, and the USA. G-7 stands for 'Group of Seven'.

gab People who have **the gift of the gab** can speak confidently and persuasively.

gabardine (*or* **gaberdine**) is a thick cloth used for making coats.

gabble (**gabbling, gabbled**) If someone **gabbles,** they talk so fast it is difficult to make out what they are saying.

gaberdine See **gabardine.**

gable (**gabled**) A **gable** is the pointed top of an outside wall of a building, made by two sloping sides of a roof. ■ A **gabled** house has a noticeable gable or gables.

gadfly (**gadflies**) Gadflies are flies which bite and annoy horses and cattle. ■ Someone who annoys people by criticizing them publicly is sometimes called a **gadfly.**

gadget (**gadgetry**) A **gadget** is a small device which does a useful job. When you are talking about several gadgets, you can call them **gadgetry.**

Gaelic (*pron:* **gay**-lic *or* **gal**-lic) is a language spoken in parts of Scotland. A similar language spoken in parts of Ireland is called **Irish** or **Irish Gaelic.**

gaff If you **blow the gaff** or **blow the gaffe,** you reveal someone's secret. ■ On a boat, a **gaff** is a pole which is attached to a mast to support a particular kind of sail. ■ A **gaff** is a pole with a spike or hook at the end, which is used for catching large fish.

gaffe If someone commits a **gaffe,** they cause embarrassment by saying or doing the wrong thing in public. ■ **blow the gaffe:** see **gaff.**

gag (**gagging, gagged**) If someone is **gagged,** a piece of cloth is tied round their mouth to stop them speaking or crying out. The cloth is called a **gag.** ■ You say someone is being **gagged** when someone in authority stops them speaking out about something. ■ A **gag** is a joke.

gaggle A **gaggle** of people is a bunch of them doing something together.

gaiety is liveliness and fun.

gaily If something is **gaily** decorated, it is brightly and prettily decorated. ■ If you do or say something **gaily,** you do it in a lively happy way. ■ You use **gaily** to say someone does something without realizing how silly or inappropriate it is. *That was in the days when people still gaily demolished old buildings.*

gain (**gaining, gained; gainer**) If you **gain** something, you get it. *...a chance to gain valuable skills and experience... Victory over Italy was not enough to gain Britain a medal.* ■ If someone **gains from** something, they benefit from it. The person who benefits can be called the **gainer.** ■ If you **gain on** someone, you gradually catch them up. ■ A **gain** is an improvement or increase. *...further gains in productivity.* ■ If you do something for **gain,** you do it for profit. ■ **gain ground:** see **ground.**

gait Your **gait** is the way you walk. *...his ambling gait.*

gaiter – **Gaiters** are coverings worn around each leg below the knee.

gala (*usual pron:* **gah**-la) events are put on as part of a public festival. *...a gala dinner.*

galactic is used to talk about things connected with a galaxy or galaxies. *...galactic dust.*

galaxy (**galaxies**) A **galaxy** is a huge group of stars and planets. The group the Earth and solar system belong to is called the **Galaxy.** ■ You can talk about a **galaxy** of famous people when they are together in one place.

gale A **gale** is a very strong wind. ■ If people are laughing noisily, you can say there are **gales** of laughter.

gall (*pron:* **gawl**) (**galling**) If something **galls** you or you find it **galling,** it makes you angry or annoyed. ■ If someone does something which is obviously unfair or dishonest, you can say they have the **gall** to do it. *Few institutions would have the gall to charge £15 for a sandwich.*

gallant (**gallantly, gallantry**) If someone is **gallant,** they show determination and courage in a difficult or dangerous situation. Behaviour like this is called **gallantry.** ■ You say someone is **gallant** when they are kind, polite, and considerate towards other people, especially women.

gall bladder The **gall bladder** is the organ next to the liver which stores bile.

galleon A **galleon** was a type of three-masted sailing ship, in use from the 15th to the 18th century.

gallery (**galleries; galleried**) A **gallery** or **art gallery** is a large building in which there are permanent exhibitions of works of art. The rooms in an art gallery or museum are sometimes called **galleries.** ■ A place where works of art are sold is sometimes called a **gallery.** ■ A **gallery** in a room, hall, or church is a raised area like a long balcony at the back or sides. A **galleried** room or hall has an area like this. ■ The **gallery** in a theatre is an upper floor at the back, where the cheapest seats are. ■ If you say someone is **playing to the gallery,** you mean they are trying to impress the public, rather than dealing with an issue seriously.

galley The **galley** in a ship or plane is the part where food is prepared. ■ A **galley** kitchen is very small. ■ Originally, a **galley** was a ship with sails and many oars, rowed by slaves.

Gallic means to do with French people. *...Gallic charm. ...Gallic passion.*

gallon The volume of an amount of liquid can be expressed in **gallons.** A British gallon is about 4.5 litres, and a US gallon is about 3.79 litres.

gallop (**galloping, galloped**) When a horse **gallops** or moves at a **gallop,** it moves very fast, so that all its legs are off the ground at the same time. ■ You say someone **gallops** when they run somewhere quickly. ■ If a situation, activity, or process **gallops** ahead, it is dealt with very quickly. *Parliament had galloped through the remaining business.* ■ **Galloping** is used to describe something which is increasing or developing so fast that it is difficult to control. *...galloping inflation.*

gallows A **gallows** was a wooden frame which criminals were hanged from. ■ **Gallows humour** finds something humorous in grim situations.

gallstone A **gallstone** is a painful lump which can develop in your gall bladder.

galore is used to emphasize that something exists in very large quantities. *There's fun and games galore!*

galvanize (*or* **galvanise**) (**galvanizing, galvanized**) If something **galvanizes** you into taking some action, it motivates you to suddenly go ahead and do it. ■ **Galvanized** metal has been covered with zinc to protect it from rust.

gambit A **gambit** is something someone says or does to get an advantage. ■ A conversational **gambit** is a way of starting a conversation.

gamble (**gambling, gambled; gambler**) When someone **gambles** or takes a **gamble,** they do something risky in the hope of gaining an advantage. ■ If you **gamble** on something happening, you take action as if you expect it to happen, although you cannot be sure it will. *The City gambled on an early cut in base rates.* ■ If you **gamble,** you bet money on the result of a game or competition.

gambol (**gambolling, gambolled**) (*Am:* **gamboling, gamboled**) If animals or people **gambol,** they run and jump around playfully.

game (**gamey, gamely**) A **game** is a sport or other activity with rules, which people play for enjoyment or to entertain other people. ■ In sport, a **game** is a match or part of a match. *Mackay was hav-*

ing a good game. ■ **Games** are sports played at school. *I was hopeless at games.* ■ Large sporting events such as international athletics are sometimes called **games.** *...the World Student Games.* ■ A **game** is a set of bits and pieces for playing a game at home. ■ If you say **the game is up,** you mean someone's secret plans or activities have been discovered. ■ **Game** is wild animals or birds hunted for sport or food. See also **big game.** ■ In Africa, a **game reserve** or **game park** is an area where wild animals can roam freely and are protected. ■ If you say someone is **game,** you mean they are willing to try something new, unusual, or risky. ■ If you say someone does something **gamely,** you mean they keep doing it in spite of difficulties. ■ **fair game:** see **fair.**

gamekeeper A **gamekeeper** is a person employed to look after the game on someone's land.

game show A **game show** is a TV show in which people play games for prizes.

gamesmanship is a way of winning a game by using methods which are not against the rules, but are unsporting.

gamey food has the smell or flavour of game such as pheasant, especially over-ripe game.

gamine (*pron:* **gam**-een) is used to describe a woman or girl who is attractive in a boyish way.

gaming is the same as gambling.

gamma is Γ or γ, the third letter of the Greek alphabet. ■ **Gamma rays** are a form of electromagnetic radiation which are similar to X-rays, but have a shorter wavelength.

gammon is smoked or salted meat from the hindquarters of a pig.

gammy A **gammy** leg is crippled or injured.

gamut (*pron:* **gam**-ut) You use **gamut** to talk about the whole range of something. *...reactions run the gamut from agony to ecstasy.*

gander A **gander** is a male goose.

gang A **gang** is (a) a group of criminals who work together. (b) a group of people who go around together, often causing trouble. ■ A **gang** of workmen is a group who work together. ■ If people **gang up** on you, they get together to oppose you.

gangland is used to talk about organized crime and the people involved in it.

ganglia See **ganglion.**

gangling (*or* **gangly**) is used to describe someone who is tall, thin, and clumsy.

ganglion (*plural:* **ganglia**) A **ganglion** is (a) a group of nerve cells. (b) a small harmless tumour.

gangly See **gangling.**

gangplank A **gangplank** is a short bridge between a ship and the quay, for people to get on and off.

gangrene (**gangrenous**) **Gangrene** is decay in a part of a person's body, caused by a loss of blood supply to that part as a result of disease or injury. You say the affected part is **gangrenous** (*pron:* **gan**-grin-uss).

gangster A **gangster** is a member of a violent criminal gang.

gangway A **gangway** is (a) a passage between rows of seats, for people to get through. (b) a ship's gangplank.

ganja is the same as marijuana.

gannet — Gannets are large white seabirds. ■ If you call someone a **gannet,** you mean they are greedy.

gantry (**gantries**) A **gantry** is a high metal structure supporting something like a crane.

gaol (**gaoler**) See **jail.**

gap A **gap** is a space between two things, or a hole through something. ■ A **gap** is a period of time when there is a break between events or activities. *After a gap of two years, she went back to college.* ■ You can say there is a **gap** in a situation when you feel someone or something is missing from it. *Her death has left a gap in my life. ...a gap in the market.* ■ A **gap** is a great difference between two things, ideas, or groups. ■ **credibility gap:** see **credible. generation gap:** see **generation.**

gape (**gaping, gaped**) If you **gape** at someone or something, you look at them in surprise. ■ **Gaping** is used to emphasize how wide a hole or opening is.

garage A **garage** is (a) a building you keep a car in. (b) a place where you can get your car repaired, buy a car, or buy petrol.

garb (**garbed**) Someone's **garb** is the clothes they are wearing. *...regulation prison garb. ...garbed only in swimming shorts.*

garbage is the usual American word for rubbish. ■ If you call someone's opinion **garbage,** you mean it is nonsense.

garbled If something written or spoken is **garbled,** the details are confused or wrong.

garda The **Garda** is the police force of the Irish Republic. A member of the force is called a **garda** (*plural:* **gardai**).

garden (**gardening, gardened; gardener**) A **garden** is an area of land next to a house, with plants and sometimes a lawn. When someone tends the plants, you say they are **gardening. A gardener** is someone who tends a garden, either for pleasure or as a job. ■ Large parks are sometimes called **gardens.**

garden centre A **garden centre** is a place which sells plants and other garden requirements.

garden city A **garden city** is a planned town with a lot of open spaces, trees, and grass.

gardenia (*pron:* gar-**deen**-ya) **Gardenias** are shrubs which have large white or yellow pleasant-smelling flowers.

garden party A **garden party** is a formal afternoon party held in a large private garden.

gargantuan (*pron:* gar-**gan**-tyoo-an) is used to emphasize that something is very large.

gargle (**gargling, gargled**) When you **gargle,** you wash your throat by filling your mouth with liquid, tilting your head back, and making a bubbling noise.

gargoyle A **gargoyle** is a stone carving of an ugly creature on the outside of an old building. Water from the roof drains through its open mouth.

garish (*pron:* **gair**-ish) (**garishly**) You say something like a colour is **garish** when it is unpleasantly bright.

garland (**garlanded**) A **garland** is a circular decoration made from flowers and leaves. When someone or something is **garlanded,** they have a garland hung round them.

garlic (garlicky) Garlic is the small white bulb of an onion-like plant. It has a strong smell and taste and is used to flavour food. **Garlicky** things taste or smell of garlic.

garment A **garment** is a piece of clothing.

garner (garnering, garnered) If someone succeeds in collecting or gaining something, you can say they **have garnered** it. *His Channel 4 series has garnered impressive reviews.*

garnet A **garnet** is a hard shiny stone used in jewellery. It is usually red.

garnish (garnishes, garnishing, garnished) A **garnish** is a small amount of food like herbs or salad, used to decorate cooked or prepared food. If food is **garnished,** it is decorated with a garnish.

garotte See **garrotte.**

garret A **garret** is a very small room at the top of a house.

garrison (garrisoned) A **garrison** is a group of soldiers stationed in a town or building, to guard it. You say the town or building **is garrisoned** by the soldiers, or they are **garrisoned** there.

garrotte (*or* garotte) (*pron:* ga-**rot**) **(garrotting, garrotted)** If someone is **garrotted,** a piece of wire or a metal collar is used to strangle them or break their neck. The wire or collar is called a **garrotte.**

garrulous A **garrulous** person is very talkative.

garter A **garter** is a piece of elastic worn round the top of a stocking or sock, to keep it up. ■ **Garter** is the American word for a suspender.

gas (*plural:* gases) **(gasses, gassing, gassed) Gas** is the inflammable air-like substance used for cooking and heating. ■ **Gas** fires and cookers use gas as fuel. ■ A **gas** is any air-like substance, for example oxygen. ■ When a person or animal is **gassed,** they are killed by poisonous gas. ■ **Gas** is the usual American word for petrol.

gas chamber A **gas chamber** is a room designed to be filled with poisonous gas, to kill people or animals.

gaseous (*pron:* gas-yus *or* gay-shus) is used to talk about things which contain or consist of a gas.

gas field A **gas field** is an area under the earth or seabed from which natural gas is taken.

gash (gashes, gashing, gashed) A **gash** is a long deep cut in the surface of something. If something is **gashed,** it accidentally gets a cut like this.

gasket A **gasket** is a flat piece of material placed between two joined surfaces in a pipe or engine, to stop gas or liquid escaping. ■ If someone **blows a gasket,** they lose their temper violently.

gas lamp A **gas lamp** produces light by burning gas.

gaslight is the light given off by gas lamps.

gas mask A **gas mask** is a device worn over the face to protect against poisonous gas.

gas meter A **gas meter** is a device which measures and records the amount of gas going through it.

gasoline is an American word for petrol. See also **gas.**

gasometer (*pron:* gas-**som**-it-er) A **gasometer** is a very large metal cylinder used to store gas before it is piped to people's homes.

gasp If you **gasp,** you take in breath quickly, out of pain or surprise. You call this intake of breath a **gasp.** ■ **Last gasp** means done at the last possible moment. *...a last-gasp goal.*

gas rig A **gas rig** is a structure used as a base for obtaining offshore natural gas.

gas ring A **gas ring** is a circular device, for example on a cooker, which gives out jets of gas.

gas station Americans call a petrol station a **gas station.**

gassy drinks have lots of bubbles.

gastric means to do with the stomach. *...a gastric complaint.*

gastritis is an illness causing inflammation of the stomach.

gastroenteritis is an illness causing inflammation of the stomach and intestines.

gastroenterology (gastroenterologist) Gastroenterology is the study of diseases of the stomach and intestines. A **gastroenterologist** is a specialist in this field.

gastronome See **gastronomy.**

gastronomic (gastronomical) Gastronomic and **gastronomical** mean connected with good food.

gastronomy (gastronome) Gastronomy is the preparation and enjoyment of good food. A **gastronome** enjoys good food.

gasworks (*plural:* gasworks) A **gasworks** is a place where gas is produced.

gate (gated) A **gate** is a door-like structure at the entrance to an area of land. ■ A **gated** road has a gate across it. ■ At an airport, a **gate** is an exit you go through to get to your plane. ■ The **gate** at a sporting event is the number of spectators. The **gate money** is the total amount they pay to watch. ■ When there is a political scandal, people sometimes invent a new word to talk about it by adding **-gate** to the name of a place or person. *...Whitewatergate.*

gateau (*pron:* gat-toe) (*plural:* gateaux) A **gateau** is a rich cream cake.

gatecrash (*or* gate-crash) **(gatecrasher)** If you **gatecrash** a party, you go there uninvited.

gated See **gate.**

gatehouse A **gatehouse** is a building next to a large entrance gate, where someone like a porter lives.

gatepost A **gatepost** is one of the posts on either side of a gate.

gateway A **gateway** is an entrance with a gate. ■ A place is called the **gateway** to a country or region when people often enter the country or region there. ■ If something is a means of achieving something else, you can say the first thing is a **gateway** to the second. *Science A levels are not always a gateway to a successful career.*

gather (gathering, gathered; gatherer) If people **gather** somewhere, they arrive from different places. You can also say someone **gathers** people together. A **gathering** is a group of people meeting for a special purpose. ■ If you **gather** objects, you collect them, or bring them together in one place. Similarly, if you **gather** information, you collect it. ■ You use **gather** to talk about an increase in something. *The plane was gathering speed to take off.*

■ You use **gather** to say someone gets to hear a bit of information. *I gather she plans a short visit.* ■ If you **gather** material, you make small folds in it by sewing a thread through it and pulling the thread tight.

gauche (*pron:* **gohsh**) If you say someone is **gauche,** you mean they are awkward and shy.

gaucho (*pron:* **gow**-choh) (**gauchos**) A **gaucho** is a South American cowboy.

gaudy (**gaudily**) If you call something **gaudy,** you mean it is brightly coloured and rather vulgar. *...her gaudy floral hat.*

gauge (*pron:* **gayj**) (**gauging, gauged**) If you **gauge** something, you work out what it is, using tests, instruments, or your own judgment. ■ A **gauge** is a device which shows the amount of something. *...a fuel gauge.* ■ A **guage** is something people use to judge the success or degree of something. *Another good gauge of quality is the amount of carving.* ■ The **gauge** of a railway is the distance between the rails. ■ A **gauge** is the thickness of something, especially metal or wire.

gaunt people look thin and unhealthy.

gauntlet – Gauntlets are long thick protective gloves. ■ If someone **throws down the gauntlet,** they do something which is seen as a challenge. If someone **picks up the gauntlet,** they show they are prepared to compete with someone. ■ If you **run the gauntlet,** you risk attack by going somewhere or doing something.

gauze is (a) light soft cloth with tiny holes in it. (b) fine wire mesh.

gave See **give.**

gavel (*pron:* **gav**-el) A **gavel** is small hammer which a judge or the chairman of a meeting bangs on the table to get attention.

gawky If you say someone is **gawky,** you mean they are awkward and clumsy.

gawp If people **gawp** at something, they stare at it stupidly.

gay (**gayness**) If someone is **gay** or a **gay,** they are homosexual. You can talk about a homosexual's **gayness.** ■ In the past, **gay** was used to describe bright and cheerful things.

gaze (**gazing, gazed**) If you **gaze** at something, you look at it for a long time. When someone does this, you can talk about their **gaze.** ■ If you do something under someone's **gaze,** they watch you while you do it.

gazebo (*pron:* gaz-**zee**-boh) (**gazebos**) A **gazebo** is a small open-sided building, put up so people can enjoy the view.

gazelle – Gazelles are a kind of small antelope.

gazette (**gazetting, gazetted**) Gazette appears in the names of many newspapers and journals. *...Antiques Trade Gazette.* ■ A **gazette** is an official journal in which honours and public appointments are announced. When an honour or appointment **is gazetted,** it appears in a journal like this.

gazetteer A **gazetteer** is a book or part of a book which lists and describes places.

gazump If you **are gazumped,** someone agrees to sell you their house, then sells it to someone offering a higher price.

GBH See **grievous bodily harm.**

GCE 'A' level exams are taken by young people in England, Wales, and Northern Ireland at the age of 17 or 18. **GCE** 'O' level exams were replaced by GCSEs in 1988. GCE stands for 'General Certificate of Education'.

GCSE exams are taken by English, Welsh, and Northern Irish school students at the age of 15 or 16. GCSE stands for 'General Certificate of Secondary Education'.

gear (**gearing, geared**) The **gear** or **gears** on a machine or vehicle are a device for changing the rate at which energy is converted to motion. When this rate is at a particular level, you say the machine or vehicle is in a particular **gear.** ■ The **gear** for an activity is the clothes or equipment needed for it. ■ If something is **geared** to a type of person or a particular purpose, it has been designed specially for that person or purpose. ■ If someone **gears up** for something, they get ready to deal with it. When they are **geared up,** they are ready.

gearbox (*or* **gear box**) The **gearbox** is the system of gears in an engine or vehicle.

gear lever The **gear lever** in a vehicle is the lever you use to change gear.

gearshift is the American word for a gear lever.

gecko (**geckos**) Geckos are small lizards.

geek If you call a man a **geek,** you mean he is boring and unattractive.

geese See **goose.**

Geiger counter (*pron:* **guy**-ger) A **Geiger counter** is a device for detecting and measuring radioactivity.

geisha (*pron:* **gay**-sha) A **geisha** or **geisha girl** is a Japanese woman specially trained in music, dancing, and the art of conversation, whose job is to entertain men.

gel (*pron:* **jell**) (**gelling, gelled**) A **gel** is a smooth soft jelly-like substance. Toiletries are often produced in this form. *...hair gel. ...shower gel.* ■ If people or things **gel,** they work well together. *Arsenal are lacking a midfield player who can make their team gel.*

gelatine (*pron:* **jel**-at-teen) (*or* **gelatin**) (*pron:* **jel**-at-tin) is a clear tasteless powder used to make liquids set, for example when making jellies.

gelatinous (*pron:* jel-**at**-in-uss) substances have the consistency of jelly.

geld If a male animal is **gelded,** it is castrated.

gelding A **gelding** is a castrated male horse.

gelignite is a type of dynamite.

gem – Gems are jewels. ■ If you call something a **gem,** you mean it is especially pleasing.

gemstone A **gemstone** is a precious stone which can be cut and polished to make a jewel.

gendarme (*pron:* **zharn**-darm; *the 'zh' sounds like 's' in 'pleasure'*) (**gendarmerie**) A **gendarme** is a member of a military-type police force in France and some other countries. The members of a force like this can be called the **gendarmerie** (*pron:* zharn-**darm**-er-ee).

gender A person's **gender** is the fact that they are male or female.

gene (*pron:* **jean**) **Genes** are the parts of a cell which determine a living thing's physical characteristics, growth, and development. You inherit your genes from your parents. When a group of living things breed among themselves, the total set of genes they share is called a **gene pool.**

genealogy (**genealogies; genealogical, genealogist**) **Genealogy** (*pron:* jean-ee-**al**-a-gee) is the study of the history of families. **Genealogical** (*pron:* jean-ee-a-**lodge**-i-cal) is used to talk about things connected with this study. ...*genealogical data.* ■ A person's **genealogy** is the history of their family.

genera See **genus.**

general (**generally**) **General** is used to talk about something as a whole, rather than in detail. *In general, the policies will receive overwhelming agreement... His account was generally accurate.* ■ **General** is used to talk about people as a whole, or most of the people in a group. *There was a general movement to leave the table... When will this material become generally available?* ■ **General** is used to talk about something which covers a wide range of things. *...unskilled general labourers. ...general costs.* ■ A **general** is a high-ranking officer in the army.

general anaesthetic A **general anaesthetic** is one which makes you unconscious. See also **local anaesthetic.**

general election A **general election** is one to elect a new parliament, in which every parliamentary seat is contested.

generalise (**generalisation**) See **generalize.**

generalist A **generalist** is someone with a wide range of skills or knowledge.

generality (**generalities**) **Generalities** are statements which are so general they do not tell you anything interesting or useful. ■ The **generality** of something is most of it.

generalize (*or* **generalise**) (**generalizing, generalized; generalization**) If you **generalize** or make a **generalization,** you say something which is true in most cases. ■ **Generalized** means involving a wide range of people or things. ...*generalized research.*

generally See **general.**

general practice (**general practitioner**) **General practice** is the work of a non-specialist doctor who treats people at a local surgery or in their own homes. A doctor who does this is called a **general practitioner** or **GP.** The organization he or she runs is called a **general practice.**

general public You refer to people in general as the **general public,** especially when you are comparing them to a specific social group.

general-purpose things have a wide range of uses, rather than one particular use.

general staff A country's **general staff** are a group of senior military advisers.

general strike When there is a **general strike,** large numbers of workers from many different occupations go on strike together.

generate (**generating, generated; generation**) If something is **generated,** it is produced or created. *Her work has generated much interest. ...the generation of wealth.*

generation (**generational**) A **generation** is all the people of a similar age in a country or group. *Few actresses of her generation could play the part well.* ■ When people talk about the **generation gap,** they mean the differences in attitudes and behaviour between older and younger people. ■ When a new stage is reached in the development of a type of product, people talk about a new **generation** of products of that kind. *...a new generation of microprocessors.* ■ A **generation** is an approximate period of time, roughly the time it takes for children to grow up and have children of their own. ■ See also **generate.**

generator A **generator** is a machine for producing electricity.

generic (*pron:* jin-**ner**-ik) (**generically**) **Generic** is used to say something has the typical features of a particular kind of thing. *The music is generic heavy metal.* ■ A **generic** term is a single term used to refer to a group of similar things. *Silver halide is a generic term for silver chloride, bromide and iodide.*

generous (**generously, generosity**) You say people are **generous** when they give more money, or more of something else, than is usual or expected. ...*an act of extreme generosity.* ■ You say people are **generous** when they are helpful or willing to see good qualities in other people or things. ■ A **generous** amount of something is rather a lot of it. ...*a generous portion of fish.*

genesis If you talk about the **genesis** of something, you are talking about what started it or brought it into existence. *It is difficult to pinpoint the genesis of any idea.*

genetic (*pron:* jin-**net**-tik) (**genetically; genetics, geneticist**) **Genetic** means to do with genes. ...*genetic tests.* ■ **Genetics** is the study of how characteristics are passed on by genes. A **geneticist** is an expert in this subject.

genetically modified (*or* **GM**) Genetically modified plants and animals have had their DNA altered by scientists to remove defects or make improvements.

genetic engineering consists of changing the genetic structure of a living thing, to correct something which is wrong or to make the thing develop in a different way.

genetic fingerprinting (**genetic fingerprint**) **Genetic fingerprinting** is a way of identifying someone by the DNA molecules in their blood, saliva, hair, or skin tissue. Everyone has their own particular **genetic fingerprint.**

genial (*pron:* **jean**-ee-al) (**genially**) **Genial** people are good-humoured and friendly.

genie (*pron:* **jean**-ee) In fairy stories, a **genie** is a magical being which obeys the orders of the person who has control over it.

genitals (**genitalia, genital**) A person's or animal's **genitals** or **genitalia** are their external sexual organs. **Genital** is used to talk about things relating to the genitals. ...*genital diseases.*

genius (**geniuses**) A **genius** is an exceptionally intelligent or talented person. You call their talents or abilities **genius.** ■ If someone has a **genius** for something, they are unusually good at it.

genocide (*pron:* **jen**-no-side) (**genocidal**) Genocide is the murder of a whole community or race. **Geno-**

cidal is used to describe people or things involved in something like this. ...*the Third Reich's genocidal barbarism.*

genre (*pron:* **zhahn**-ra; *the 'zh' sounds like 's' in 'pleasure'*) A **genre** is a type of literature, art, music, or film.

gent (**gents**) A **gent** is a gentleman. ■ A **gents** is a men's public toilet.

genteel people are respectable and refined. Their way of life and the places they live in can also be called **genteel.**

gentian (*pron:* **jen**-shun) **Gentians** are mountain plants with blue flowers.

Gentile Non-Jewish people are sometimes called **Gentiles.**

gentility is (a) the social status and way of life of upper-class people. (b) well-mannered behaviour.

gentle (**gentler, gentlest; gently, gentleness**) **Gentle** people are kind and calm. ■ A **gentle** action is done carefully, with little force. ■ **Gentle** activities are not strenuous or difficult. ■ You can use **gentle** to talk about the weather when it is not rough or stormy. ...*gentle rain.* ■ A **gentle** slope or curve is gradual, not steep. ...*gentle rolling hills.*

gentlefolk is an old-fashioned word for upper-class people.

gentleman (**gentlemen; gentlemanly**) **Gentleman** is a polite word for a man. ■ A **gentleman** is an upper-class man. ■ If you say a man is a **gentleman,** you mean he is polite and well-educated. You can call his behaviour **gentlemanly.** ■ A **gentleman's agreement** is an unwritten one in which people trust one another to do what they have promised.

gentleness See **gentle.**

gentlewoman (**gentlewomen**) A **gentlewoman** is an upper-class woman.

gently See **gentle.**

gentrify (**gentrifies, gentrifying, gentrified; gentrification**) If you say a working-class area has been **gentrified,** you mean middle-class people have moved in and changed the appearance and character of the area to fit their lifestyle. This process is called **gentrification.**

gentry Upper-class people used to be called the **gentry.**

genuflect (**genuflection**) In church, when people **genuflect,** they bend one or both knees, to show respect. An action like this is called a **genuflection.**

genuine (**genuinely, genuineness**) You use **genuine** and **genuinely** to describe things which are what they appear to be, and are not imitations. ■ You say feelings or beliefs are **genuine** when they are real and not pretended. ■ If you say someone is **genuine,** you mean they are sincere.

genus (*pron:* **jean**-uss) (*plural:* **genera**) (*pron:* **jen**-er-a) A **genus** is a class of similar things, especially a group of animals or plants consisting of one or more species.

geography (**geographer; geographical, geographic, geographically**) **Geography** is the study of different countries and the natural features of the earth's surface. A **geographer** is an expert on this. **Geographical** and **geographic** are used to talk

about things to do with geography. ■ The **geography** of a place is the location of such things as its rivers, mountains, and cities. **Geographical, geographic,** and **geographically** are used to talk about things connected with the geography of a place. ■ **Geographical** and **geographic** are used to talk about the position of a place in relation to other places. ...*the country's geographical remoteness.*

geology (**geologist; geological**) **Geology** is the study of the Earth's structure, surface, and origins. **Geological** means to do with geology.

geometry (**geometric, geometrical; geometrics**) **Geometry** is the branch of maths dealing with lines, angles, curves, and shapes. **Geometric** and **geometrical** are used to talk about things to do with geometry. ■ **Geometric** or **geometrical** designs are made up of regular shapes and lines, often with sharp angles. These shapes and lines are sometimes called **geometrics.**

geophysics (**geophysicist; geophysical**) **Geophysics** is the branch of geology which uses physics to examine the Earth's structure, climate, and oceans. **Geophysical** means to do with geophysics.

geopolitics (**geopolitical**) **Geopolitics** is the study of politics on a worldwide scale, especially as it affects the relations between countries. **Geopolitical** means to do with global international relations.

Geordie A **Geordie** is someone from Tyneside. ■ **Geordie** is a dialect of English spoken on Tyneside.

George Cross The **George Cross** is a medal awarded to civilians for acts of great heroism.

Georgian The **Georgian** period was from 1714 to 1830, when the kings George I to George IV reigned. **Georgian** is used to describe people or things from that time.

geranium – Geraniums are plants with small red, pink, or white flowers. They are also called 'pelargoniums'.

gerbil – Gerbils are small furry rodents, often kept as pets.

geriatric means to do with old people and their illnesses. ...*geriatric medicine.*

germ – Germs are very small organisms which cause disease. ■ **Germ warfare** is the deliberate spreading of harmful germs during a war to cause disease. ■ The **germ** of something like an idea is the thing it develops from.

German is used to describe people and things in or from Germany. ■ A **German** is someone who comes from Germany. ■ **German** is the language used in Germany and Austria.

germane (*pron:* ger-**mane**) If something is **germane** to what is being done or considered, it is relevant to it.

Germanic If you describe someone or something as **Germanic,** you think their appearance or behaviour is typical of German people or things. ■ **Germanic** is used to describe the ancient culture and language of the peoples of northern Europe. ...*Germanic tribes.*

German measles is a disease similar to measles which gives you a cough, a sore throat, and spots. Its medical name is **rubella.**

German shepherd dog A **German shepherd dog** or **German shepherd** is the same as an alsatian.

germinate (**germinating, germinated; germination**) When seeds **germinate,** they start to grow. If you **germinate** seeds, you get them to grow. ■ If an idea **germinates,** it starts to develop.

gerontology is the study of the ageing process and problems faced by old people.

gerrymandering is the changing of political boundaries, to give an unfair advantage to one party in an election.

gestation is the development of a baby inside its mother's body. ■ **Gestation** is used to talk about the development of an idea.

gesticulate (**gesticulating, gesticulated; gesticulation**) If you **gesticulate,** you make movements with your hands and arms, often while you are talking. These movements are called **gesticulations.**

gesture (**gesturing, gestured**) If you describe something someone does as a **gesture,** you mean it is done to show their attitude or intention. *He offered to repair the property, as a gesture of goodwill.* ■ A **gesture** is a movement you make with your hands, or head to express your feelings. *He spread his hands in a gesture of despair.* ■ If you **gesture,** you use movements of your hands or head to tell someone something or draw their attention to something.

get (**getting, got**) If you **get** something, you fetch it, receive it, or are given it. ■ If you **get** a train or bus, you catch it. ■ **Get** is used to mean 'become'. *As women get older, the risk increases.* ■ If you **get** into a particular situation, you find yourself in that situation. *I have got into debt.* ■ If you **get** something done, you do it, or persuade someone to do it. ■ If you **get** somewhere, you go there or arrive there. *They eventually got home exhausted.* ■ **Get** is used to say what stage has been reached in something. *Policy makers have not got very far in working out how this might be done.* ■ If you **get** something right, you produce a correct answer, description, or forecast. ■ If you **get** a joke or **get** the point of something, you understand it. ■ If you **get to** do something, you eventually do it. *Miller and Ferlinghetti got to be friends.* ■ If you **get to** do something, you have the opportunity to do it, and you do it. *Men get to run things more often than women.* ■ If someone **gets away with** something, they do something wrong and escape being punished. You can also say they **get off** without being properly punished. *He got off with a £50 fine.* ■ If you **get out of** doing something, you avoid doing it. ■ If you **get round** a problem, you find a way of overcoming it. ■ If you **get by,** you manage with fewer resources than you really need. ■ If you **get back at** someone or **get them back,** you do something unpleasant to them because they have done something unpleasant to you. ■ If you **get round to** doing something, you eventually do it. *It took her two years to get around to buying a car.* ■ If you **get at** something, you manage to reach or obtain it. *...a determination to get at the facts.* ■ If you **get down to** something, you start doing it seriously. If you **get on with** it, you keep doing it. ■ If you **get on** in

something you are doing, you are successful at it. *Livy's getting on very well in Russian.* ■ If someone is **getting on,** they are old. ■ When people **get together,** they meet to discuss something or to spend time together. You call a meeting like this a **get-together.** ■ If you **get on with** someone or **get along with** them, you have a friendly relationship. ■ If you **get** a message **across** or **get** it **over,** you succeed in communicating it. If you **get through** to someone, they understand what you are trying to communicate. ■ If you ask what someone is **getting at,** you want to know what they mean. ■ If an experience **gets** to you, it affects you strongly. *Will the pressure get to him?* ■ If something **gets you down,** it makes you unhappy. ■ **Getting on for** in front of a number means 'nearly'. *I've been trying to pack up for getting on for two years now.* ■ **get going:** see **going.** See also **got, gotten.**

getaway When criminals make a **getaway,** they escape from the scene of a crime.

get-up If someone is wearing unusual clothes, you can call these clothes their **get-up.**

gewgaw (*pron:* **gyoo**-gaw) Gewgaws are cheap bright ornaments and jewellery.

geyser (*pron:* **geez**-er) A **geyser** is a hole in the Earth's surface which hot water and steam are forced out of.

ghastly (**ghastlier, ghastliest; ghastliness**) People use **ghastly** to describe (a) things which are extremely unpleasant. (b) people or things they dislike very much. ■ If someone looks **ghastly,** they look very pale and ill.

ghee is clarified butter used in Indian cookery.

gherkin – Gherkins are small cucumbers pickled in vinegar.

ghetto (**ghettos** or **ghettoes**) A **ghetto** is part of a city, often a poor area, inhabited mostly by people of the same nationality, religion, or ethnic group.

ghetto-blaster Large portable stereos can be called **ghetto-blasters.**

ghost A **ghost** is the spirit of a dead person believed to haunt a person or place. ■ **Ghost** is used to talk about memories people would rather forget. *...the ghost of their colonial dirty war.* ■ If you **lay the ghost** of something which has gone wrong in the past, you do something which makes up for it. ■ If something like a machine **gives up the ghost,** it breaks down completely.

ghostly describes things to do with ghosts, or things which seem unreal and make you think of ghosts.

ghost town You call a town a **ghost town** when it used to be busy and prosperous but is now deserted.

ghost-write (**ghost-writer** or **ghostwriter**) If a book or article is **ghost-written,** it is supposed to be by someone famous but is actually written by a professional writer called a **ghost-writer.**

ghoul (*pron:* **gool**) (**ghoulish**) A **ghoul** is an imaginary evil spirit, especially one which eats dead bodies. ■ If you call someone a **ghoul** or say they are **ghoulish,** you mean they are interested in things like dead bodies.

GHQ is a place which military operations are organized from. GHQ stands for 'General Headquarters'.

GI A **GI** is a soldier in the US Army.

giant In children's stories, a **giant** is an impossibly big person. ■ A very tall person is sometimes called a **giant**. ■ People thought to be better than anyone else in their field can be called **giants**. *At the time Camus and Sartre were the two literary giants.* ■ Very large firms are called **giants**. *...the car giants.* ■ **Giant** is used to describe unusually large objects. *...a giant Christmas pudding.*

giantess (**giantesses**) A **giantess** is a female giant.

giant-killer (**giant-killing**) In sport, lowly-rated teams who beat famous ones are called **giant-killers**. Their victories are described as **giant-killing**.

giant panda See **panda**.

gibber (*pron:* **jib**-ber) (**gibbering, gibbered**) If someone **gibbers,** they talk very fast in a confused way.

gibberish If you say someone is talking **gibberish**, you mean what they say does not make sense.

gibbet (*pron:* **jib**-bit) A **gibbet** was (a) a gallows. (b) a wooden structure for exhibiting the bodies of executed criminals.

gibbon – **Gibbons** are a kind of ape with very long arms. They live in forests in southern Asia.

gibe See **jibe**.

giblets The **giblets** of a chicken or other bird are parts like the heart which are taken out before the bird is cooked.

giddy (**giddiness**) If you feel **giddy**, you feel you are about to fall over, usually because you are ill. ■ You can use **giddy** to describe happy excited behaviour. *He worked the crowd to a giddy high.*

gift (**gifted**) A **gift** is something you give someone. ■ **Gift** and **gifted** are used to say someone is naturally very good at something. *...a gift for teaching... He was gifted with a sharp business brain.* A **gifted** child is naturally good at several things.

giftware is objects made specially to be sold as gifts.

gift-wrapped A **gift-wrapped** present is wrapped in pretty paper.

gig A **gig** is a live performance by a pop musician. ■ A **gig** used to be a kind of open two-wheeled carriage, pulled by a single horse.

giga- (*pron:* **gig**-a) is added to words to talk about very large amounts of something. **Giga-** usually means 1000 million. For example, a **gigawatt** is 1000 million watts. However, in computing, **giga-** means 2^{30} (about 1074 million). A **gigabyte** is 2^{30} bytes.

gigantic things are extremely large.

gigawatt See **giga-**.

giggle (**giggling, giggled; giggly**) If someone **giggles**, they laugh in a silly or nervous way. If they do it often, you say they are **giggly**.

gigolo (*pron:* **jig**-a-lo) (**gigolos**) A **gigolo** is a man paid to be the lover and companion of an older woman.

gild (**gilding, gilded; gilt**) When someone **gilds** an object, they cover it with a thin layer of gold paint. The paint on them is called **gilding** or **gilt**. *...gilded*

statues. ■ If someone **gilds the lily,** they try to improve something which is good enough already.

gill A fish's **gills** (*pron:* **gills**) are the organs at the sides of its body which it breathes through. ■ A **gill** (*pron:* **jill**) is a quarter of a pint.

gilt See **gild, gilt-edged**.

gilt-edged stocks and securities (also called **gilts**) are issued by the government for people to invest in for a fixed time at a fixed rate of interest.

gimcrack (*pron:* **jim**-krak) things look attractive but are badly made and are not of much use or value.

gimlet (*pron:* **gim**-let) If you say someone has **gimlet** eyes, you mean they look at things very intently, because they are determined to find out the truth.

gimmick (**gimmicky, gimmickry**) If you call something a **gimmick**, you mean it has no real value and is just done to attract interest. You can say something like this is **gimmicky**. A lot of gimmicks can be called **gimmickry**.

gin is a colourless alcoholic drink distilled from grain and flavoured with juniper berries.

ginger (**gingery**) **Ginger** is a tropical plant grown for its root. This root, also called **ginger,** has a spicy hot flavour and is used in cooking. **Ginger wine** is an alcoholic drink made partly from fermented ginger. **Ginger ale** and **ginger beer** are sweet non-alcoholic drinks flavoured with ginger. ■ A **ginger group** is a group of people within an organization who have strong ideas which they try to get other people in the organization to accept. ■ **Ginger** is a bright orange-brown colour. If something has this colour to some extent, you say it is **gingery**.

gingerbread is a kind of sweet biscuit flavoured with ginger.

gingerly If you do something **gingerly,** you do it cautiously and rather nervously.

gingham (*pron:* **ging**-am) is cotton cloth with a woven pattern of small squares, usually in white and one other colour.

gingivitis (*pron:* jin-jiv-**vite**-iss) is an inflammation of the gums.

ginseng (*pron:* **jin**-seng) is a plant from China, Korea, and North America. Its root is also called **ginseng,** and is thought by some people to be good for your health.

gipsy See **gypsy**.

giraffe The **giraffe** is a central African animal with very long legs and a long neck.

gird If people **gird themselves** or **gird their loins,** they prepare to tackle something difficult.

girder A **girder** is a long thick piece of steel or iron used in the frameworks of buildings and bridges.

girdle (**girdling, girdled**) A **girdle** is a piece of women's underwear which fits tightly round the stomach and hips.

girl A **girl** is a female child. ■ Young women are sometimes called **girls.**

girlfriend (*or* **girl friend**) Someone's **girlfriend** is a girl or woman they are having a romantic or sexual relationship with. ■ A **girlfriend** is a female friend.

girlhood A woman's **girlhood** is the time when she was a girl.

girlie magazines and calendars have photos of naked or almost naked women, to please men.

girlish is used to describe things which are typical of a young girl. ...*her girlish excitement.*

giro (**giros**) Giro is a system for paying money to people who might not have a bank account. A **giro cheque** can be cashed at a post office. A giro cheque for unemployment money is often called a **giro.**

girth The **girth** of an object or person's body is the distance round it. ...*gentlemen of ample girth.*

gist (*pron:* **jist**) The **gist** of what someone says is its general meaning.

give (**giving, gave, have given**) Give is used to describe something someone does. For example, if you **give** something a push, you push it. ■ If you **give** someone something, you hand it to them, provide them with it, or allow them to have it. *She gave them the keys... He gave her a lift... The Parliament gave him two weeks to come up with a solution.* ■ If you **give** something **away,** you give it to someone, rather than selling it. A **give-away** is a free gift. ■ If you **give away** something someone is trying to keep secret, you tell people about it. ■ A **giveaway** is something which makes you realize the truth about something. *The only giveaway was the look of amusement in her eyes.* ■ If you **give up** something, you stop doing or having it. *The prisoners gave up their protest... He almost gave up hope.* ■ When criminals **give themselves up,** they surrender to the police. ■ If you **give in** or **give way** to a demand, you agree to do something you do not want to. ■ When one thing is replaced or followed by another, you can say the first thing **gives way** to the second. *The rain gave way to sunshine.* ■ If something **gives off** or **gives out** heat, gas, or a smell, it produces it. ■ If something **gives way,** it collapses because of the weight pressing on it. ■ **Give and take** is willingness to listen to other people's opinions and make compromises. ■ **give birth:** see **birth. give evidence:** see **evidence. give rise to:** see **rise.** See also **given.**

giveaway See **give.**

given See **give.** ■ **Given** is used to say something is being taken into account. *This may seem an odd view to take, given that I am strongly in favour of the treaty.* ■ If someone is **given** to doing something, they keep doing it. *Darvell was given to making false confessions.* ■ If a place is **given over to** something, that is what it is used for. ■ If a book or meeting is **given over to** something, that is what is discussed in it. ■ If you talk about a **given** position or time, you mean the particular position or time which is specified or arises. *Each company is required to finish cabling by a given date... In chess there are typically about 36 legal moves from any given board position.*

given name Your **given names** are all your names except your surname.

gizmo A **gizmo** is a device which performs a particular task, usually in a new and efficient way. ■ People use **gizmo** to talk about a device when they do not know what it is really called. ...*the plastic gizmo for holding a coffee cup on the dashboard.*

gizzard A bird's **gizzard** is a part of its digestive system where hard food is broken up.

glacé (*pron:* **glass**-ay) cherries have been preserved in a thick sugary syrup.

glacial (*pron:* **glay**-shal) (**glacially**) Glacial means to do with glaciers. ...*glacial ice.* ■ You call people's behaviour **glacial** when they show no signs of warmth or friendliness. ■ A **glacial** pace is very slow.

glacier A **glacier** is a huge mass of ice which moves very slowly, often down a mountain valley.

glad (**gladly**) If you are **glad** about something, you are pleased, thankful, or relieved because of it. *I was glad to get inside... I gladly accepted the offer of a lift.* ■ If you are **glad of** something, you are pleased you have it. *Party officials are glad of the chance to speak out.*

gladden (**gladdening, gladdened**) If you say something will **gladden** someone or **gladden** their heart, you mean they will be delighted with it.

glade A **glade** is an open area in a wood or forest.

glad-handing You say a politician is **glad-handing** when he or she mingles with people and chats to them in a friendly way.

gladiator (**gladiatorial**) In ancient Rome, a **gladiator** was a man trained to fight with weapons in an arena, to entertain people. ■ **Gladiatorial** is used to describe an intense struggle between two people. ...*a gladiatorial contest.*

gladiolus (*plural:* **gladioli**) The **gladiolus** is a plant with sword-shaped leaves and spikes of brightly-coloured flowers.

glamor See **glamour.**

glamorize (*or* **glamorise**) (**glamorizing, glamorized**) If a book or film **glamorizes** something like crime or violence, it makes it seem exciting and attractive.

glamorous people are very attractive in a stylish way. ■ A **glamorous** job or way of life is one which people find attractive and exciting.

glamour (*Am:* **glamor**) You say a place or way of life has **glamour** when people find it very attractive and exciting.

glance (**glancing, glanced**) If you **glance** at something or cast a **glance** at it, you look at it quickly, then look away. ■ If you **glance** through something like a magazine, you look at it quickly without reading it properly. ■ If you can see something **at a glance,** you can see it immediately. ■ You say **at first glance** to talk about a first impression of someone or something. *At first glance the shop looks empty.* ■ If one object **glances off** another, or strikes it a **glancing** blow, it hits it at an angle and bounces away in another direction.

gland – **Glands** are organs which produce substances the body needs in order to function.

glandular fever is an infectious disease which causes fever, a sore throat, and a painful swelling of the lymph glands.

glare (**glaring, glared; glaringly**) If you **glare** at someone, you stare angrily at them. An angry stare is called a **glare.** ■ When a light shines very brightly, making it difficult to see, you can talk about its **glare.** ■ When someone's actions are constantly being watched and reported by the media, you can say they are in **the glare of** publicity. ■ A **glaring** mistake is very obvious. ■ If something is **glaringly** obvious, it is very obvious.

glasnost is a policy introduced by President Gorbachev in the former Soviet Union. It involved greater openness and accountability by the Soviet government, and an improvement in relations with other countries.

glass (**glasses**) Glass is the hard transparent substance windows are made from. ■ A **glass** is a glass drinks container. ■ A person's **glasses** are two lenses in a frame which they wear in front of their eyes, to see better.

glass-blowing (**glass-blower**) Glass-blowing is the activity of shaping molten glass by blowing air into it. A **glass-blower** is someone whose job is to make round glass objects by shaping molten glass in this way.

glass fibre is the same as fibreglass.

glasshouse (*or* **glass house**) A **glasshouse** is a large greenhouse.

glassware is objects made of glass, such as drinking glasses.

glassworks (*plural:* **glassworks**) A **glassworks** is a factory where glass is made.

glassy objects are hard, smooth, and shiny, like glass. ■ If you say someone is **glassy-eyed**, or that their eyes are **glassy**, you mean that their eyes are expressionless.

glaucoma (*pron:* glaw-**koh**-ma) is an eye disease which can lead to blindness.

glaze (**glazing, glazed**) The **glaze** on a piece of pottery is a thin layer of a hard shiny substance on its surface. You say pottery like this is **glazed**. ■ If you **glaze** food, you spread a layer of beaten egg, milk, or other liquid on it before you cook it, to give it a shiny surface. This layer is called a **glaze**. ■ When windows are **glazed**, glass is put into them. ■ If someone's eyes **glaze over**, they become dull and expressionless, often because the person is bored. You say someone like this has a **glazed** look.

glazier A **glazier** is someone whose job is fitting glass into windows.

gleam (**gleaming, gleamed**) If a light **gleams**, it shines brightly. A **gleam** of light is a glow of light. If an object or surface **gleams**, it shines because it is reflecting light. You can talk about the **gleam** of an object or surface when it reflects light. ...*the gleam of brass and polished leather.* ■ A **gleam** of something is a faint sign of it. ...*a gleam of hope for peace.* ■ If you say there is a **gleam** in someone's eye or their eyes **gleam**, you mean their eyes seem to shine. ■ If you say something is no more than a **gleam** in someone's eye, you mean it is just an idea they have, and has not yet been properly developed.

glean (**gleaning, gleaned**) If you **glean** information about something, you obtain it with difficulty.

glee (**gleeful, gleefully**) Glee is great delight at something. You can also talk about someone's **gleeful** behaviour. *These remarks have been gleefully seized on by the opposition.*

glen A **glen** is a deep narrow valley, especially in Scotland.

glib (**glibly, glibness**) You say someone is being **glib** when they try to mislead people by making something out to be more straightforward than it really is.

glide (**gliding, glided; glider**) If a vehicle **glides** somewhere, it moves smoothly and quietly. ■ When a bird or plane **glides**, it floats on air currents. ■ **Gliding** is the sport of flying in a plane called a **glider**, which has no engine and flies by floating on air currents.

glimmer (**glimmering, glimmered**) A **glimmer** of something is a faint sign of it. ...*a glimmer of hope.* ■ When a light **glimmers**, it shines in a faint unsteady way. You can talk about a **glimmer** of light.

glimpse (**glimpsing, glimpsed**) If you **glimpse** something or catch a **glimpse** of it, you see it briefly. ■ You can say you **glimpse** something or are given a **glimpse** of it when you experience it briefly. ...*breathless tourists eager for a glimpse of the future.*

glint If an object or surface **glints**, it gives out little flashes of reflected light. Each flash is called a **glint**. ■ You say someone's eyes **glint** or talk about a **glint** in their eyes, when their eyes seem to shine with eagerness, expectation, or pleasure.

glisten (**glistening, glistened**) If something **glistens**, it shines, because it is smooth, wet, or oily.

glitch (**glitches**) A **glitch** is (a) a small problem which stops something working properly or being successful. (b) a false electronic signal caused by a sudden increase in power.

glitter (**glittering, glittered; glittery**) If something **glitters**, it shines and sparkles. ■ A **glittering** occasion is attended by rich and glamorous people. ■ A **glittering** career is very successful. ■ When people talk about **the glittering prizes**, they mean things like well-paid jobs which are available to certain people because of their education or social status. ■ If something is attractive in a superficial way, you can talk about its **glitter** or call it **glittery**. ...*a glittery nightspot.*

glitterati (*pron:* glit-ter-**ah**-tee) The fashionable celebrities in a place are sometimes called its **glitterati**.

glitzy (**glitzier, glitziest; glitz**) Glitzy means attractive in a showy and rather superficial way. When something is like this, you can talk about its **glitz**.

gloaming Twilight is sometimes called the **gloaming**.

gloat (**gloating, gloated; gloatingly**) If someone **gloats** over something, they show pleasure at their own success or someone else's failure.

global (**globally**) Global means involving the whole world. ...*firms that want to compete globally.* ■ People sometimes call the world **the global village** as a way of emphasizing how closely linked the parts of the modern world are. ■ **Global warming** is the gradual rise in temperature thought to be taking place in the Earth's atmosphere because of the 'greenhouse effect', in which heat absorbed from the sun cannot escape from the atmosphere, due to a build-up of carbon dioxide and other gases.

globalize (or **globalise**) (**globalizing, globalized; globalization**) If something is **globalized,** it is changed so that it involves or affects the whole world.

globe People sometimes call the world the **globe.** ■ A **globe** is a ball-shaped object with a map of the world on it.

globetrotter (**globetrotting**) You say someone is a **globetrotter** when they are always visiting different parts of the world.

globular objects are round like a ball.

globule A **globule** of liquid is a tiny round drop.

glockenspiel The **glockenspiel** is a musical instrument consisting of a row of tuned metal plates which you hit with a pair of small hammers.

gloom is (a) a feeling of unhappiness. (b) a state of semi-darkness.

gloomy (**gloomier, gloomiest; gloomily**) You say someone is **gloomy** when they are unhappy and pessimistic. *He shook his head gloomily.* ■ You say a situation is **gloomy** when it is likely to make people disappointed and unhappy. ■ **Gloomy** places are dark and depressing.

glorify (**glorifies, glorifying, glorified; glorification**) When something is **glorified,** attempts are made to convince people that it is wonderful and desirable. *...the glorification of speed in car ads.* ■ **Glorified** is used to say someone or something is not as grand as they are reckoned to be. *She was just a glorified Personal Assistant.*

glorious (**gloriously**) You call something you see or hear **glorious** when it is very beautiful and impressive. *...a gloriously picturesque village.* ■ **Glorious** weather is very sunny. ■ A **glorious** time in someone's life is one when they have many successes. ■ You call something someone does **glorious** when they do it exceptionally well. *...a glorious goal.* ■ People sometimes use **gloriously** to say something is so bad or absurd that they find it amusing or delightful. *The Panthermal Therapy Bath is a gloriously absurd contraption.*

glory (**glories, glorying, gloried**) **Glory** is the fame and admiration someone gets when they have done something remarkable. ■ If you say someone is basking in someone else's **reflected glory,** you mean they are enjoying the attention they are getting as a result of being connected with that other person. ■ If you talk about someone's **past glories** or their **glory days,** you mean the occasions in the past when they did something remarkable. ■ The **glories** of a culture or place are the things people find most impressive about it. ■ If you **glory in** something, you thoroughly enjoy it.

gloss (**glosses, glossing, glossed**) **Gloss** is a bright shine on a surface. ■ **Gloss** paint looks shiny when it is dry. ■ If someone puts a **gloss** on something, they make it seem better than it is. ■ If someone **glosses over** a problem, they try to make it seem less serious. ■ If something **takes the gloss off** an achievement, it makes it seem less satisfactory.

glossary (**glossaries**) A **glossary** in a book is an alphabetical list of special or technical words used in the book, with explanations of their meanings.

glossy (**glossier, glossiest; glossies**) If something is **glossy,** it is smooth and shiny. *...black glossy hair.* ■ **Glossy** photographs and booklets are produced on expensive shiny paper. ■ **Glossy magazines** or **glossies** are printed on shiny paper and typically have pictures of fashionable clothes, famous people, and expensive houses.

glove (**gloved**) **Gloves** are items of clothing worn over a person's hands and wrists with separate sections for each finger. **Gloved** is used to say someone is wearing gloves. *...a gloved hand.* ■ If something **fits like a glove,** it fits exactly. ■ You say people are working **hand in glove** with each other when they are closely involved in something together. ■ You say the **gloves are off** when people start criticizing each other in an unrestrained way.

glove compartment A car's **glove compartment** is a small cupboard or shelf just below the windscreen.

glow (**glowing, glowingly**) If something **glows,** it produces a gentle steady light, or looks bright because of reflected light. You call this effect a **glow.** ■ If someone is **glowing,** their face is pink as a result of exercise, excitement, or pleasure. ■ A **glow** is a strong feeling of pleasure or satisfaction. *...a song to send everyone home with a warm glow in their hearts.* ■ If you give a **glowing** description of someone or something, you praise them highly. *His obituary notice glowingly describes him as 'a great Englishman'.*

glower (rhymes with 'power') (**glowering, glowered**) If someone **glowers** at you, they look at you with anger or hostility. You call their expression a **glower.**

glow-worm — Glow-worms are a kind of beetle. Females and young glow-worms have organs on their bodies which produce a greenish light.

glucose is a type of sugar which gives you energy.

glue (**glueing** or **gluing, glued**) **Glue** is a sticky substance used for joining things together. If you **glue** one thing to another, you stick them together using glue. ■ You say objects are **glued** together when they are stuck firmly together, as if by glue. ■ If you say someone is **glued** to their TV screen, you mean they are watching it very closely and are not interested in anything else.

glum (**glummer, glummest; glumly**) You say someone is **glum** when they are sad because they have had a disappointment.

glut If there is a **glut** of something like a type of goods, there is more than can be sold or used.

gluten is a protein which occurs in cereal grains, especially wheat.

glutinous A **glutinous** substance has the texture of glue.

glutton (**gluttonous, gluttony**) A **glutton** is a greedy person who eats too much. Behaviour like this is called **gluttony.** ■ If someone is a **glutton** for something, they like a lot of it. *...a glutton for detail. ...a glutton for punishment.*

glycerine (*or* **glycerin**) is a thick colourless liquid, used in medicines and explosives.

gm See **gram.**

GM See **genetically modified.**

GMT or **Greenwich Mean Time** is the standard time in Britain, and is used to calculate the time in the rest of the world.

gnarled A **gnarled** tree is old, twisted, and misshapen. You can also describe a person as **gnarled.**

gnash (**gnashes, gnashing, gnashed**) When people get very angry and frustrated about something, you can say they **gnash their teeth.**

gnat – **Gnats** are small flying insects which bite.

gnaw If an animal or person **gnaws** something, they bite into it repeatedly. ■ If something gradually damages something else, you can say it **gnaws** at it. *The recession is going to gnaw away at all segments of the economy.* ■ If something like a feeling **gnaws at** you, it keeps troubling you.

gnome In children's stories, a **gnome** is a little old man with a beard and a pointed hat.

gnomic You can describe something someone says as **gnomic** when it is odd and hard to understand.

GNP A country's **GNP** or **gross national product** is the total value of all the goods it has produced and services it has provided, plus its income from abroad, during one year.

gnu (*pron:* **noo**) The **gnu** or **wildebeest** is a large African antelope.

GNVQ – **GNVQs** or 'General National Vocational Qualifications' are qualifications taken at college or in the sixth form which are intended to provide students with skills related to particular jobs.

go (**goes, going, went, have gone**) **Go** is used to talk about movement or travel from one place to another. *She went into the sitting-room... We can go up in the elevator.* ■ **Go** is used to talk about leaving a place. *Our train went at 2.25... They went away empty-handed.* ■ **Go** is used to talk about leaving a place temporarily in order to do something. *Let's go fishing.* ■ **Go** is used to talk about attending a place regularly. *She went to London University.* ■ **Go** is used to talk about something being in a particular state. *Interest rates went up by 4%... The phone went dead.* ■ **Go** is used to talk about the way that something happens, especially the extent to which it is successful. *Sales are going well... The ref's decision went against us.* ■ If you talk about what is **going on,** you are talking about what is happening. ■ If something **goes on** happening, it continues happening. *'What a strange idea,' she went on.* ■ If you **go on to** do something new, you do it after doing something else. If you **go back** to something you have done before, you do it again after doing something else. ■ If something **goes ahead** or **goes through,** it happens as planned. ■ If you **go through with** or **go ahead with** something you have been planning to do, you do it. The way you **go about** something is your method of dealing with it. ■ **Go** is used to talk about examining or describing something in detail. *I went through the booklet of instructions.* ■ If something **goes** away, it disappears. *The problem won't go away.* ■ **Go** is used to talk about something being allocated or awarded in a particular way. *Most of my*

money goes on bills... *Victory went to her arch-rival.* If something will **go round,** there is enough of it for everyone to have some. ■ **Go** is used to talk about things that are connected with each other or can exist or operate together. *...the house that goes with the job... I've taught them what ingredients go well together.* ■ If you say a statement about one person or thing **goes for** another person or thing, you mean it also applies to the second person or thing. ■ **Go** is used to talk about time passing. *The day went slowly... There's still a year to go.* ■ **Go** is used with 'back' to talk about a period of time measured back from the present. *He has been accused of widespread fraud going back a number of years.* ■ **Go** is used to say where something belongs or fits. *The shoes go on the shoe shelf.* ■ You say a machine or device is **going** when it is operating. ■ If you **go for** something, you choose it. If you **go in for** something, you choose to do or use it. *Students are not going to go in for elaborate recipes.* ■ If you **go by** or **go on** something, you use it as a basis for a judgment or action. *I go by my own eyes.* ■ If you **go along with** a decision or idea, you accept it and obey it. If you **go against** it, you do something which conflicts with it. ■ If you **go back on** a promise, you do not do what you promised. ■ If you **go through** a difficult time, you experience it. ■ If you **go without** something for a time, you do not have it. ■ If you **go down** with an illness, you catch it. ■ If you are **going out** with someone, you are having a romantic or sexual relationship with them. ■ You use **go** with 'as' when comparing something to other things of the same kind. *As comets go, Chiron is enormous.* ■ If you have a **go** at something or give it a **go,** you try it out. If it is your **go,** it is your turn to try something. ■ If you have a **go** at someone, you criticize them. ■ **goes without saying:** see **say.** See also **going, gone.**

goad (**goading, goaded**) If someone is **goaded** into doing something, they do it as a result of being made angry.

go-ahead A **go-ahead** person or organization deals with things in an enterprising way, often trying out new methods.

goal In games such as football, the **goal** is the space into which the players try to get the ball in order to score points. The points are also called **goals.** ■ A person's **goal** is what they are hoping to achieve.

goalie A **goalie** is a goalkeeper.

goalkeeper In a sports team, the **goalkeeper** is the person who guards the goal.

goalmouth In games like football and hockey, the **goalmouth** is the area in front of the goal.

goalpost In games like football and hockey, the **goalposts** are the two upright posts the ball passes between when a goal is scored. ■ If you accuse someone of **moving the goalposts,** you mean they have changed an agreed objective, making it easier for them to achieve it, or harder for someone else.

goat – **Goats** are sheep-like animals with long horns and often a beard.

goatee A **goatee** is a short pointed beard which covers a man's chin only.

gobbet

gobbet A **gobbet** of something such as food is a small piece of it.

gobble (**gobbling, gobbled**) When something like an organization **gobbles up** a smaller one, they take control of it. ■ You say something **gobbles up** things like money, when it is expensive to operate. ■ If a person or animal **gobbles** their food or **gobbles** it **up,** they eat it quickly and greedily.

gobbledegook (*or* **gobbledygook**) When something official is expressed in language no one can understand, people say it is **gobbledegook.**

go-between A **go-between** is someone who takes messages between people who are not able or willing to meet each other.

goblet A **goblet** is a long-stemmed cup without handles.

goblin A **goblin** is a small ugly creature in fairy stories.

gobsmacked If you are **gobsmacked** by something, you are amazed by it.

god In Christianity, Judaism, and Islam, **God** is the being worshipped as the creator and ruler of the universe. ■ In some religions, there are many **gods.** They are spiritual beings believed to have power over an aspect of life. *...the pagan god Vaval, symbol of evil.*

godchild (**godchildren; goddaughter, godson**) A person's **godchild** is a child, who at his or her baptism, they have promised to help bring up as a Christian. The child then becomes their **goddaughter** or **godson.**

goddaughter See **godchild.**

goddess (**goddesses**) A **goddess** is a female god.

godfather See **godparent.**

god-fearing is used to describe people who believe in God and apply the principles of their religion to their lives.

godless People who do not have any religion are sometimes called **godless.**

godly (**godliness**) **Godly** is used to describe people who believe in God and lead a good life. You call their behaviour **godliness.**

godmother See **godparent.**

godparent (**godfather, godmother**) A child's **godparents** are people who attend its baptism and promise to help bring it up as a Christian. A man is known as a child's **godfather** and a woman as its **godmother.**

godsend If something good comes your way unexpectedly when things are not going well, you can call it a **godsend.**

godson See **godchild.**

go-getter You say someone is a **go-getter** when they are ambitious and enterprising.

goggle (**goggling, goggled**) If you **goggle** at a person or thing, you stare at them because you are amazed or fascinated.

goggles are large close-fitting protective glasses.

go-go dancers dance to pop-music in nightclubs, wearing very few clothes.

going See **go.** ■ **Going to** is used to make statements about what will happen in the future. *She is going to vote for him.* ■ In horseracing, **the going** is the condition of the ground. You can also use **go-**ing to describe how easy or difficult it is to do something. *They found the going tough.* ■ If you call a business a **going** concern, you mean it is making a profit, and not likely to fail. ■ The **going** rate for something is the usual and expected rate. ■ When someone or something **gets going,** they start doing something, often after a delay.

goings-on If you describe activities as **goings-on,** you mean they are strange or shocking. *...last week's crazy goings-on in Downing Street.*

goitre (*Am:* **goiter**) (*pron:* **goy**-ter) is a swelling of the thyroid gland in the neck.

go-kart A **go-kart** is a very small racing car with a low-powered engine.

gold is a valuable yellow metal used in jewellery and as an international currency. ■ **Gold** is a bright yellow colour. ■ The winner of a race or competition often gets a **gold** medal, made either of gold or a gold-coloured metal. *The Italians won the gold.*

golden things are gold-coloured or made of gold. ■ You use **golden** to describe something which is special or particularly important. *...a golden opportunity. ...a golden rule.* ■ If a senior employee gets a **golden handshake,** he or she is given a large sum of money at the end of their term of service. ■ The **golden age** of something is the time when it was at its best. ■ If you celebrate a **golden** jubilee or wedding, you are celebrating a 50th anniversary.

golden eagle The **golden eagle** is a eagle which lives in mountains in northern Europe.

goldfinch (**goldfinches**) The **goldfinch** is a common European seed-eating bird which has a red and black face and a black, yellow, white, and brown body.

goldfish (*usual plural:* **goldfish**) **Goldfish** are small orange-coloured ornamental fish.

gold leaf is paper-thin gold sheet used for gilding statues and woodwork.

goldmine A **goldmine** is a place where gold ore is dug out of the ground. ■ If you say a business or idea is a **goldmine,** you mean it is very profitable.

gold-plated objects are covered with a very thin layer of gold.

gold rush A **gold rush** is a large-scale migration of people to an area where gold has been found.

golf (**golfer, golfing**) **Golf** is an outdoor game in which a player tries to hit a ball into a series of small holes in the ground. *...a golfing holiday in Spain.*

golf club A **golf club** is an organization for people who play golf, with its own golf course and clubhouse. ■ A **golf club** is a stick for hitting the ball in golf.

golf course A **golf course** is an area of land where golf is played.

gonad (*pron:* **goh**-nad) **Gonads** are reproductive organs, such as the testicles or ovaries.

gondola (**gondolier**) A **gondola** (*pron:* **gon**-do-lah) is a long narrow canal boat in Venice. It is propelled by a man called a **gondolier** (*pron:* gon-do-**leer**), using a pole. ■ A **gondola** is a small cable car.

gone See **go.** ■ If you say something is **gone,** you mean it is no longer there. ■ If it is **gone** a certain time, it is later than that time. *I didn't get off till gone four.*

gong A **gong** is a flat metal disc, suspended vertically, which makes a loud noise when hit. ■ Awards are sometimes called **gongs.**

gonorrhoea (*or* **gonorrhea**) (*pron:* gon-or-**ree**-a) is a type of venereal disease.

good (**goodness**) **Good** is used to describe things which are pleasing, acceptable, or of high quality. *...good food. ...a good idea.* ■ If you are **good** at something, you are skilful and successful at it. ■ A **good** person is kind or thoughtful. ■ **Good** is moral or spiritual correctness. *...a struggle between the forces of good and evil.* ■ Something that is **good for you** or **does you good** benefits you in some way. ■ **Good** is used to add emphasis. *...a good while ago.* ■ If something has gone **for good,** it has gone permanently. ■ **Goods** are things to be sold. ■ If someone **delivers** or **comes up with the goods,** they do what is expected of them, or what they promised to do. ■ You use **as good as** to say something is practically true. *The game was as good as over.* ■ If someone **makes good** some damage or a loss, they repair or replace the damaged or lost thing.

goodbye (*or* **good-bye**) People say **'Goodbye'** to each other when parting. You call what they say a **goodbye.**

Good Friday is the Friday before Easter, when the Crucifixion is commemorated.

good-humoured people are happy and cheerful.

goodie See **goody.**

good-looking (**good looks**) You say someone is **good-looking** or talk about their **good looks** when they have an attractive face.

good-natured people are kind and even-tempered.

goodness See **good.**

goodnight (*or* **good night**) People say **'Goodnight'** late in the evening before parting or going to bed.

goods See **good.**

Good Samaritan In the Bible, the **Good Samaritan** was a man who helped someone who had been beaten and robbed. You say someone is a **good samaritan** when they go out of their way to help someone in trouble.

goods train A **goods train** is the same as a freight train.

goodwill When people show **goodwill,** they are friendly and helpful. ■ A firm's **goodwill** consists of things like its reputation and its regular customers, as distinct from other assets like buildings and machinery.

goody (*or* **goodie**) (**goodies**) **Goodies** are things for people to enjoy, especially food. *...a Christmas hamper packed with goodies.* ■ The good characters in a story or film are sometimes humorously called the **goodies.**

goody-goody (**goody-goodies**) If you call someone a **goody-goody,** you dislike the way they are always on their best behaviour when people in authority are around.

gooey substances are soft and sticky.

goof (**goofing, goofed**) If someone **goofs,** they make a mistake. A **goof** is a mistake.

goofy (**goofier, goofiest**) If you say someone is **goofy,** you mean they are rather silly.

goose (**geese**) **Geese** are large duck-like birds with long necks.

gooseberry (**gooseberries**) **Gooseberries** are small round green fruit which grow on bushes.

goose-pimples If someone gets **goose-pimples,** their skin comes out in tiny bumps, because they are cold or nervous.

goose-step When soldiers **goose-step,** they march slowly, kicking their feet high without bending their knees.

gopher (*pron:* go-fer) The **gopher** is a North American burrowing animal. It has short legs and cheek pouches.

gore (**goring; gored; gory**) If someone is **gored** by an animal, it wounds them badly with its horns. ■ **Gore** is a lot of blood from a wound. ■ You describe a situation as **gory** when it involves a lot of bloodshed.

gorge (**gorging, gorged**) A **gorge** is a narrow steep-sided valley. ■ If you **gorge** yourself on something, you eat a lot of it greedily.

gorgeous (**gorgeously**) If you say someone or something is **gorgeous,** you are emphasizing that they are strikingly attractive.

Gorgonzola is a sharp-flavoured blue-veined Italian cheese.

gorilla – **Gorillas** are the largest members of the ape family. They live in forests in central West Africa.

gormless If you say someone is **gormless,** you mean they are stupid.

gorse is a spiny-leaved yellow-flowered evergreen shrub.

gory See **gore.**

gosling A **gosling** is a young goose.

go-slow If workers are on a **go-slow,** they are deliberately working slowly as a protest.

gospel The **Gospels** are the first four books of the New Testament, which describe the life of Jesus. ■ **Gospel** or **gospel music** is black religious music which originated in the churches of the southern United States. ■ If you say someone preaches a particular **gospel,** you mean they urge other people to adopt their standards, or follow their beliefs. *...spreading the gospel of capitalism.* ■ If something is taken as **gospel,** it is accepted as unquestionably true.

gossamer is used to describe things which are light, thin, and delicate. *...a gossamer-thin veil.*

gossip (**gossiping, gossiped; gossipy**) **Gossip** is casual or malicious talk about people's private lives. When someone talks like this, you say they are **gossiping.** If they do it a lot, you call them a **gossip.** ■ You say books or articles are **gossipy** when they give details of people's private lives.

gossip column (**gossip columnist**) The **gossip column** in a newspaper or magazine is the part dealing with the social or private lives of famous people. The person who writes it is called a **gossip columnist.**

got See **get.** ■ If you have **got** something, you have it. *He's got a lovely smile... She's got two sisters... I've* *got a date.* ■ If you ask what has **got into** someone, you want to know why they are behaving strangely.

Goth The **Goths** were an East Germanic people who invaded the Roman Empire. ■ Nowadays, **goths** are young people who wear black clothes and heavy black eye make-up.

gothic The **Gothic** style of architecture dates from the Middle Ages and is characterized by tall pillars, high curved ceilings, and pointed arches. ■ **Gothic** stories involve mysterious happenings in dark and lonely places such as castles. ■ **Gothic** is a kind of heavy ornate lettering.

gotten Americans often say **have gotten** rather than 'have got'. *His leg may have gotten tangled in a harpoon line.*

gouache (*pron:* goo-ash) is a painting technique using thick non-transparent watercolours; the watercolours are also called **gouache.** A **gouache** is a painting done this way.

Gouda (*pron:* gow-dah) is a mild Dutch cheese.

gouge (*pron:* gowj) (**gouging, gouged**) If you **gouge** something, you make a hole or long cut in it, usually with a pointed object. ■ A **gouge** is a tool used for cutting and shaping wood.

gourd (*pron:* goord) A **gourd** is a large marrow-like fruit. Gourds are sometimes dried and used as containers.

gourmand (*pron:* goor-mand) A **gourmand** is someone who enjoys eating and drinking, especially in large quantities.

gourmet (*pron:* goor-may) A **gourmet** is someone who knows a lot about good food and wine. ■ **Gourmet** food is nicer or more unusual and sophisticated than ordinary food.

gout is a disease which causes painful swollen joints, especially in a person's foot.

govern The people who **govern** a country are the ones who make its laws and look after its affairs. ■ If something is **governed** by a set of regulations, it is controlled by them. ■ **Governing** is used to describe a group of people officially responsible for making and enforcing regulations. ...*the zoo's governing council.* ■ If something **governs** a situation, it controls it. *The family's lives are governed by his sporting demands.*

governance The **governance** of a country, industry, or institution is the way it is governed or managed. ...*the CBI's conference on corporate governance.*

governess (**governesses**) A **governess** is a woman who lives with a family and teaches its children.

government The **government** of a country is the group of people responsible for governing it. ■ **Government** is the organization and administration involved in governing a country or smaller area. ...*local government.*

governmental means to do with government or governments. ...*governmental affairs.*

governor A **governor** is the person in charge of the political administration of an area. American states have governors. ■ In British colonies, the **governor** is the representative of the monarch. ■ In Britain, the heads of prisons and some other large institutions are called **governors.** ...*the Governor of the Bank of England.* ■ The members of the committees which control schools and some other organizations are called **governors.**

governor general (**governor generals** *or* **governors general**) Some former British colonies have a **governor general,** who is the chief representative of the British monarch.

governorship If someone is appointed or elected to the **governorship** of an area or institution, they become its governor.

gown A **gown** is a long dress worn on formal occasions. ■ A **gown** is a long loose coat worn by judges, lawyers, and academics. ■ The protective outer garment worn by nurses and doctors in an operating theatre is called a surgical **gown.**

GP See **general practice.**

grab (**grabbing, grabbed**) If you **grab** something, you take hold of it quickly. If you **grab** at something or make a **grab** for it, you try to get hold of it. ■ If you **grab** an opportunity, you take it eagerly. ■ In sport, if someone **grabs** a victory, they win at the last moment. ■ If something **grabs** your attention, you immediately notice it and become interested in it. ■ If something is **up for grabs,** it is available to anyone who wants it.

grace (**gracing, graced**) If someone moves with **grace,** they move smoothly and elegantly. ■ If someone behaves with **grace,** they are dignified, even if things are not going well for them. ■ If you say someone **graced** an event, you mean they were present at it, and their presence made a very pleasing contribution. ...*Frank Worthington, whose talents graced the Wembley turf in 1974.* ■ If someone does something with **good grace,** they do it willingly. ■ If you say someone has **fallen from grace,** you mean they are suddenly out of favour with the public, or with people in power. ■ **Grace** is used to talk about the extra time someone is given to do something. *She wanted a couple of days grace to get the house cleaned.* ■ In Christianity, **grace** is the special goodwill of God towards man. *Holiness was only possible by the grace of God.* ■ If you say **grace,** you say a short prayer before or after a meal. ■ You say **Your Grace** when talking to a duke, duchess, or archbishop. ■ A **grace and favour** house is let rent-free to someone by the monarch, the government, or an institution, as a special privilege. A **grace and favour** appointment is one which relies on the goodwill of whoever is in charge. ■ **saving grace:** see **saving.**

graceful (**gracefully, gracefulness**) If something is **graceful,** it has simple elegant beauty. ...*a graceful gesture.* ...*graceful sailing boats.* ■ **Graceful** behaviour is polite and dignified. ...*a graceful apology.*

graceless You say something is **graceless** when it is unattractive and has no interest or charm. ■ You say someone's behaviour is **graceless** when they are rude or thoughtless, especially to someone who has been kind to them.

gracious (**graciously, graciousness**) You say someone is **gracious** when they behave politely and unselfishly. ■ **Gracious** is used to describe the comfortable way of life of wealthy people. ...*a monument to 1930s gracious living.*

gradation – **Gradations** are small differences or variations. *...a subtle gradation of colour.*

grade (**grading, graded**) When a group of things or people is divided into **grades,** it is split into smaller groups, based on things like size, quality, or rank, with each group being given a name, number, or letter. *...high grade VHS tape.* When a group is divided up like this, you say the people or things are **graded** or given a **grading.** ■ Your **grade** in an examination or piece of written work is the mark you get. ■ If you say someone **makes the grade,** you mean they succeed in something, or reach a required standard.

gradient A **gradient** is a slope, or the angle of a slope. *The railway climbs up a 1 in 100 gradient.*

gradual (**gradually**) A **gradual** change happens slowly.

graduate (**graduating, graduated**) When someone **graduates,** they successfully complete a first degree at a university. Someone who has done this is called a **graduate.** ■ In the United States and Canada, young people also **graduate** from high school. ■ When someone goes from doing something easy to something harder, you can say they **graduate** to the second thing. ■ **Graduated** is used to describe something that increases by regular amounts. *...graduated physical exercises.* ■ If an object is **graduated,** it is marked with lines for measuring something.

graduation is (a) the successful completion of a course at a university or North American high school. (b) the ceremony at which students receive their certificates.

graffiti is words or drawings scribbled or sprayed on walls.

graft When doctors **graft** a piece of healthy tissue or an organ onto someone's body, they surgically attach it, to replace or repair a damaged part. Tissue or organs attached like this are called **grafts** or **transplants.** ■ When one plant is **grafted** onto another, a shoot from one is joined to the stem and root system of the other, so they grow as one plant. ■ If something new is **grafted** onto something which already exists, the two things are combined successfully. *His challenge is to graft Japanese production methods onto the American talent for innovation.* ■ **Graft** is hard unglamorous work. If a person **grafts,** they work hard. ■ **Graft** is obtaining money dishonestly by misusing a position of authority.

grain is a cereal crop like wheat or rice. The **grains** from a cereal crop are its seeds. ■ A **grain** of something like sand or pollen is a small particle. ■ If you say there is a **grain** of truth in what someone says, you mean there is some truth in it. ■ The **grain** in wood is the pattern and direction of lines on its surface. ■ You say something **goes against the grain** when it conflicts with tradition or popular belief.

grainy You say something is **grainy** when it has a rough surface or texture as if it were made up of a lot of small grains. ■ A **grainy** photograph or film looks as if it is composed of grains of colour.

gram (*or* **gramme**) The weight of something can be expressed in **grams.** There are 1000 grams in a kilogram. A gram is about 0.035 of an ounce. **Grams** is usually written 'g' or 'gm'.

grammar The **grammar** of a language consists of rules which say how sentences should be formed. ■ A **grammar** is a book which describes the rules of a language. ■ A person's **grammar** is the way they apply or misapply the rules of a language.

grammarian A **grammarian** studies and writes about grammar.

grammar school A **grammar school** is a school for children who have shown high academic ability at age 11.

grammatical (**grammatically**) Grammatical means connected with grammar. *...grammatical errors.* ■ If what someone says is **grammatical,** it follows the accepted rules of a language.

gramme See **gram.**

gramophone A **gramophone** is a record player.

granary (**granaries**) A **granary** is a building for storing grain. ■ **Granary** bread contains whole grains of malted wheat. 'Granary' is a trademark. ■ You can refer to a place where a large amount of grain is grown as the **granary** of a particular region.

grand (**grandly**) You use **grand** to describe things which are splendid, impressive, or important. *...one of the grandest castles in England. ...a grand plan to unify the sport.* ■ When you add together a series of totals, you get a **grand** total.

grandad (*or* **granddad**) Your **grandad** is your grandfather.

grandchild (**grandchildren**) A person's **grandchild** is their son's or daughter's child.

granddaughter A person's **granddaughter** is the daughter of their son or daughter.

grandee In Spain and Portugal, a **grandee** is a nobleman of the highest rank. ■ Powerful or influential people, especially in politics, are sometimes called **grandees.**

grandeur When something is splendid or magnificent, you can talk about its **grandeur.** ■ If someone has **delusions of grandeur,** they think they are more important than they really are.

grandfather Your **grandfather** is the father of your mother or father.

grandfather clock A **grandfather clock** is a clock with a pendulum in a very tall wooden case.

grandiloquent (**grandiloquence**) If someone is **grandiloquent,** they try to impress people by speaking in a pompous or unnecessarily complicated way.

grandiose is used to describe something which is large and elaborate and meant to be impressive.

grand jury In the US and Canada, a **grand jury** is a group of people summoned to decide whether there is enough evidence to bring a criminal case to trial.

grandma Your **grandma** is your grandmother.

grandmaster is the title awarded to people who reach the highest international standard in chess.

grandmother Your **grandmother** is the mother of your father or mother.

grandpa Your **grandpa** is your grandfather.

grandparent Your **grandparents** are the parents of your mother or father.

grand piano A **grand piano** is a large harp-shaped piano with horizontal strings.

Grand Prix (*pron:* gron **pree**) (*plural:* **Grands Prix** *or* **Grand Prix**) A **Grand Prix** is one of a series of international motor races for powerful racing cars.

grand slam If a sports team achieves a **grand slam,** it wins all its major matches or competitions in a season. ■ In tennis, a **grand slam** tournament is one of a series of top international championships.

grandson A person's **grandson** is the son of their daughter or son.

grandstand A **grandstand** is a terraced block of seats which give the best view of a sporting event. ■ If a sporting event has a **grandstand finish,** it finishes in an exciting way, often with the result being decided at the very end.

granite is a very hard rock used for building.

granny (*or* **grannie**) (**grannies**) Your **granny** is your grandmother.

grant When the government or a public body **grants** money or makes a **grant,** it gives money for a particular purpose. ■ If someone in authority **grants** an application or request, they agree to it. ■ When someone receives something like an honour, you say they have been **granted** it. ■ If you **take** something **for granted,** you accept it as being the case. ■ If a person is **taken for granted,** the things they do are not appreciated. ■ People sometimes say **granted** when admitting something is true. *Granted, he doesn't look too bad for his age.*

granulated sugar is coarsely ground white sugar.

granule (**granular**) A **granule** is a small grain of something. A **granular** substance is made up of granules.

grape – **Grapes** are green or purple berries used to make wine. They can also be eaten raw, or dried to make raisins, currants, or sultanas.

grapefruit (*usual plural:* **grapefruit**) are large round yellow sharp-tasting citrus fruit.

grapevine A **grapevine** is the plant grapes grow on. ■ If you hear something on the **grapevine,** you hear it as a result of news or gossip being passed around.

graph A **graph** is a way of showing how amounts increase or decrease in relation to each other. It is usually based on two lines called 'axes' drawn at right angles.

graphic (**graphically**) If someone gives a **graphic** account of something, they describe it in vivid detail. ■ **Graphics** are the drawings, photographs, and art work associated with the production of books, magazines, and TV programmes. **Graphic** means connected with this kind of work. *...a graphic designer.* ■ Computer **graphics** are pictures, graphs, and diagrams produced on a computer.

graphite is a soft black form of carbon, used to make pencil leads.

graphology (**graphologist**) **Graphology** is the study of how handwriting relates to a person's character. A **graphologist** is an expert on this.

graph paper is paper printed with small squares to make drawing graphs easier.

grapple (**grappling, grappled**) If you **grapple** with a problem, you try hard to solve it. ■ If two people **grapple,** they take hold of one another and struggle or fight.

grasp If you **grasp** something, you grip it firmly. When someone is gripping something, you can talk about their **grasp** of it. ■ If you **grasp** something difficult, you understand it. You can talk about someone's **grasp** of something like this. ■ If you **grasp** an opportunity, you take it. ■ If something is **within your grasp,** it is likely you will get it or achieve it. ■ If you describe someone as **grasping,** you mean they are selfish and greedy.

grass (**grasses, grassing, grassed; grassy**) **Grass** is the green narrow-leaved plant which grows naturally over large areas and is used to create lawns. Bamboo and cereals like wheat and rice are also types of grass. ■ A **grassed** or **grassy** area is covered with grass. ■ If a person is **put out to grass,** they are made to retire. ■ If someone **grasses** on a criminal, they tell people in authority what he or she has done or is planning to do. Someone who does this is called a **grass.** ■ Marijuana is sometimes called **grass.**

grasshopper The **grasshopper** is a jumping insect with long hind legs.

grassland is land covered with wild grass.

grass roots (*or* **grassroots**) The **grass roots** of an organization are its ordinary members.

grass snake The **grass snake** is a brownish-green non-poisonous European snake.

grate (**grating, grated; grater**) If you **grate** food, you shred it into small pieces by rubbing it on the rough metal surface of a device called a **grater.** ■ If things **grate,** they rub against each other, producing a harsh sound. ■ A **grating** sound is harsh and unpleasant. ■ If something **grates** on you, you find it very irritating. ■ A **grate** is a metal framework for holding coal or logs in a fireplace. ■ A **grating** is a framework of wire or metal covering a hole.

grateful (**gratefully**) If you are **grateful** for someone's help or kindness, you appreciate what they have done.

gratify (**gratifies, gratifying, gratified; gratifyingly, gratification**) If you are **gratified** by something or find it **gratifying,** it gives you pleasure and satisfaction. ■ If someone's desire for something is **gratified,** it is satisfied.

grating See **grate.**

gratis If something is done or provided **gratis,** you do not have to pay for it.

gratitude is the feeling of being grateful for someone's kindness or help.

gratuitous (**gratuitously**) **Gratuitous** is used to describe something harmful or upsetting which is done without justification. *TV is saturated with gratuitous sex and violence.*

gratuity (**gratuities**) Money given as a tip is sometimes called a **gratuity.** ■ A **gratuity** is an amount of money given to a member of the armed forces when he or she leaves after many years of service.

grave (**gravely**) **Grave** is used to describe (a) events or situations which are very serious. *...a grave crisis.* (b) people's feelings when they are very worried

about something. *The government expressed its grave concern.* ■ **Grave** behaviour is quiet and serious.
■ A **grave** is a place where a dead person is buried.
■ The **grave** accent (*pron:* **grahv**) is a symbol sometimes written over 'a' or 'e' in French, indicating a change in its pronunciation, as in 'Sèvres porcelain'.

gravedigger A **gravedigger** is someone whose job is digging graves.

gravel consists of small stones.

gravelly A **gravelly** voice is low and rough. ■ **Gravelly** land is covered in gravel.

graveside If you are at someone's **graveside**, you are standing next to their grave at their funeral.

gravestone A **gravestone** is a large stone marking a grave, giving information about the person buried there.

graveyard A **graveyard** is a burial ground, especially one next to a church.

gravitas (*pron:* **grav**-it-ass) Someone who has **gravitas** is respected for their seriousness and intelligence.

gravitate (**gravitating, gravitated**) You can say you **gravitate** towards something or someone when you are drawn towards them. *When Brett was 14, he gravitated towards Brighton... Younger audiences gravitate to younger musicians.*

gravitational The effect gravity has on something is called the **gravitational** force or pull.

gravity is the force which pulls things towards the centre of a planet, star, or moon. The Earth's gravity causes things to fall when you drop them. See also **centre of gravity**. ■ If you talk about the **gravity** of a situation, you mean it is very serious.

gravy is a hot savoury brown sauce, served with meat. ■ If you say people are on the **gravy train**, you mean they are part of an organization which gives them a lot of money for very little effort.

gray is the usual American spelling of 'grey'.

graze (**grazing, grazed**) When animals **graze** they eat grass. The land or grass they graze on is called **grazing**. ■ If something **grazes** another thing, it touches it lightly. *His header grazed the top of the bar.* ■ If you **graze** yourself, you injure your skin by scraping it against something. Your injury is called a **graze**.

grease (**greasing, greased**) **Grease** is soft or melted animal fat. ■ If you **grease** something like a pan, you put oil or grease on it, to stop food sticking to it. ■ **Grease** is the thick oil that is used to lubricate machinery. If you **grease** machinery, you lubricate it with grease.

greasepaint is the oily make-up worn by actors in the theatre.

greaseproof paper does not absorb grease. It is often used to line baking tins.

greasy things contain grease or are covered in grease.

great (**greater, greatest; greatly, greatness**) **Great** is used to say something is very large, very important, or outstandingly good. *Butterflies are out in great numbers... The greatest threat is the onset of winter. ...one of the world's greatest sopranos.* ■ **Great** and **greatly** are used to emphasize the degree or

scope of something. *Movie stars go to great lengths to protect their privacy.* ■ **Great-** is added to words like 'uncle' and 'niece' to talk about relatives a generation further away. For example, your **great-aunt** is your mother's or father's aunt. ■ **Greater** is used in front of the name of a city to talk about the city and its suburbs. *...Greater Manchester.*

Great Britain is the island consisting of England, Scotland, and Wales, which together with Northern Ireland make up the United Kingdom.

greatcoat A **greatcoat** is a thick overcoat, especially one worn by people in the armed forces.

Great Dane – **Great Danes** are very large dogs with short hair.

grebe – **Grebes** are diving birds which live in lakes and ponds.

Grecian is used to talk about (a) things to do with Ancient Greece. *...a Grecian urn.* (b) things copied from the style of Ancient Greece. *...the club's elegant Grecian columns.*

greed is the desire for more money or possessions than is necessary or fair.

greedy (**greedily**) You say someone is being **greedy** when they try to get more of something than is necessary or fair.

Greek is used to talk about people and things in or from Greece. ■ A **Greek** is a person from Greece. The inhabitants of ancient Greece are sometimes called the **Greeks.** ■ The languages of modern Greece and ancient Greece are both called **Greek.**

green (**greener, greenest**) **Green** is the colour of grass. ■ **Green** issues are concerned with protecting the environment. ■ **Green** places are covered with grass or trees and shrubs. ■ A **green** is a public area of grass in a town or village. ■ The **greens** on a golf course are the areas of close-cut grass around each hole. ■ **Greens** are the cooked leaves of vegetables like cabbage. ■ If you say someone is **green**, you mean they are inexperienced or naive. ■ If someone has **green fingers**, they are good at gardening.

greenback A **greenback** is a US dollar bill.

green belt A **green belt** is an area of countryside surrounding a city, where new building is limited by law.

Green Beret British and American commandos are sometimes called **Green Berets.**

green card If you have a **green card**, your motor insurance covers accidents abroad. ■ In the US, a **green card** is a document giving immigrants the right to live and work there temporarily.

greenery Plants that make a place look attractive are referred to as **greenery.**

greenfly (*plural:* **greenfly** *or* **greenflies**) **Greenfly** are tiny green insects which damage plants.

greengrocer A **greengrocer** or **greengrocer's** is a fruit and vegetable shop. The person who runs it is also called a **greengrocer.**

greenhouse A **greenhouse** is a transparent building, usually of glass, for growing plants in controlled conditions. ■ The **greenhouse effect** is used to describe what happens when heat absorbed from the sun cannot escape from the atmosphere, due to a build-up of carbon dioxide and other gases producing 'global warming'. ■ **Greenhouse** is used to talk about things to do with the greenhouse effect. *...the main greenhouse gas.*

greenish If something is **greenish,** it is slightly green.

green paper A **green paper** is a document containing policy proposals to be discussed by Parliament and other groups.

Greenwich Mean Time See **GMT.**

greet (greeting, greeted) When you **greet** someone, you welcome them by saying pleasant or polite things. The things you say are called **greetings.** ■ When a crowd **greets** someone, they welcome them with applause or cheers. ■ You can describe people's reaction to something by saying it is **greeted** in a particular way. *The news was greeted with dismay.* ■ If you arrive somewhere and see something surprising or impressive, you can say you are **greeted** by the sight of it.

gregarious people like being with others.

gremlin – **Gremlins** are imaginary beings blamed for mechanical problems.

grenade A **grenade** is a small bomb which can be thrown by hand or fired from a rifle.

grew See **grow.**

grey (*Am:* **gray**) **(greying; greyness)** Any colour between black and white can be called **grey.** ■ If you are **greying** or **going grey,** your hair is going grey. ■ A **grey** is a grey or white horse. ■ If the weather is **grey,** the sky is covered with cloud and it is very dull. ■ You use **grey** to describe things which are boring and unattractive. ■ You say there is a **grey area** when there is no clear dividing line between two things.

greyhound – **Greyhounds** are thin dogs which can run very fast and are bred for racing.

greyish If something is **greyish,** it is slightly grey.

grid A **grid** is a pattern of straight lines crossing each other to form squares. **Grid** is used to talk about various things which have this pattern, for example metal objects or the layout of a city's streets. *...a wire grid.* ■ A **grid** reference is a series of numbers which help pinpoint a place on a map. ■ An electricity **grid** is a network of power lines supplying electricity to an area. ■ In a car or motorcycle race, the starting **grid** is the place where the vehicles are positioned ready to begin.

griddle A **griddle** is a flat heavy piece of metal with a handle over the top, which is placed on a stove and used for cooking.

gridlock is the situation that exists when all the roads in a place are so full of vehicles that none of them can move. ■ You can use **gridlock** to talk about a situation in which neither side in a dispute is prepared to give in, so no agreement can be reached. *...the gridlock in the Senate.*

grief is extreme sadness, often caused by someone's death. ■ If something **comes to grief,** it ends disastrously.

grievance If you have a **grievance,** you feel resentful because you think you have been unfairly treated.

grieve (grieving, grieved) When people **grieve,** they feel very sad about something, especially someone's death. ■ If something **grieves** you, it annoys or upsets you.

grievous (grievously) If something is **grievous,** it is very serious. *...grievous doubts.*

grievous bodily harm If someone is charged with **grievous bodily harm** or **GBH,** they are charged with seriously injuring someone deliberately.

griffin The **griffin** was a mythological creature with an eagle's head and wings, and a lion's body.

grill If you **grill** food, you cook it over or under a strong heat. The part of a cooker where you do this is called a **grill,** and so is the metal grid the food is placed on. ■ A **grill** is food cooked on a grill. *...a mixed grill.* ■ Some restaurants serving grilled food are also called **grills.** ■ If someone is **grilled** or given a **grilling,** they are questioned intensively about something. ■ See also **grille.**

grille (*or* **grill**) A **grille** is a protective framework of wire or metal bars in front of a window or machine.

grim (grimmer, grimmest; grimly, grimness) A **grim** situation is harsh, unpleasant, or depressing. You can also say news or a description of something is **grim.** ■ A **grim** place is unattractive and depressing. ■ If someone looks **grim,** they look serious or stern. You can also say someone is in a **grim** mood or does something **grimly.** ■ **Grim** humour consists of finding something to laugh at in serious or sad situations. ■ If you **hang on grimly,** you continue with a course of action despite all difficulties.

grimace (*pron:* **grim**-uss) **(grimacing, grimaced)** If someone **grimaces,** their face twists into an ugly expression because they are in pain or annoyed. You call their expression a **grimace.**

grime (grimy, grimier, grimiest) **Grime** is dirt which has built up over a long time. If something is **grimy,** it is covered in dirt.

grin (grinning, grinned) If you **grin,** you smile broadly. A smile like this is called a **grin.** ■ If you say someone will have to **grin and bear** something, you mean they have no choice but to accept it.

grind (grinding, ground) If you **grind** something or **grind** it **up,** you crush it to a powder. ■ If someone tries to **grind down** an opponent, they try to break their resistance by continually putting pressure on them. ■ If two hard things **grind** against each other, they rub together, often making a harsh noise. ■ If something **grinds on,** it carries on slowly. If it **grinds to a halt,** it slows down and eventually stops. ■ Hard dull routine work is sometimes called **the daily grind.**

gringo (gringos) Latin Americans sometimes call foreigners, especially North Americans, **gringos.**

grip (gripping, gripped; grippingly) If you **grip** something, you take hold of it firmly. Your hold is called your **grip.** ■ If you have a **grip** on something, it is under your control. ■ If you have a **grip** on a subject, you understand it. ■ If people are in the **grip** of something unpleasant, they are seriously affected by it. ■ If people are **gripped** by a strong feeling, they experience it. ■ If a story **grips** you, it holds your attention. You say a story like this is **gripping**. ■ If you **get to grips** with something like a problem, you begin to deal with it effectively.

gripe (**griping, griped**) If someone keeps protesting or complaining about something, you can say they have a **gripe** or are **griping**.

grisly A **grisly** murder or story is a particularly horrible one.

grist If you say something is **grist to the mill,** you mean you can use it to your advantage.

gristle is tough strands of cartilage in meat.

grit (**gritting, gritted**) If you say someone has **grit,** you mean they have a lot of courage. ■ When people prepare to carry on in a difficult situation, you can say they **grit their teeth**. ■ **Grit** is tiny pieces of stone. ■ When lorries **grit** roads during very cold weather, they sprinkle them with grit.

gritty (**grittier, grittiest**) **Gritty** people are courageous and determined. ■ A **gritty** description of something is harsh and unsentimental. ■ If something is **gritty,** it is covered in grit, or has a texture like grit.

grizzle (**grizzling, grizzled**) If a baby or child **grizzles,** it keeps crying and whining. You say an adult **grizzles** when they complain about something in an irritating way.

grizzled people have grey or grey-streaked hair.

grizzly (**grizzlies**) **Grizzlies** or **grizzly bears** are large fierce greyish-brown North-American bears.

groan (**groaning, groaned**) If you **groan,** you make a long low sound out of pain or disappointment. A sound like this is called a **groan.** ■ When people complain about something, you can say they **groan** about it. ■ If wood **groans,** it makes a deep straining sound as it moves. ■ You can say something is **groaning** when it is very heavily loaded.

grocer A **grocer** or **grocer's** is a small local shop which sells food and other household goods.

grocery (**groceries**) A **grocery** shop or **grocery** is the same as a grocer's. ■ **Groceries** are things like flour, tea, and tinned foods.

grog is a drink made by diluting a spirit like rum with water.

groggy (**grogginess**) If you feel **groggy,** you feel weak and dizzy.

groin Your **groin** is the area between your legs where they join your body.

grommet A **grommet** is a plastic tube put into the eardrum of someone who has an ear infection. The grommet allows air to enter and dry out the ear.

groom (**grooming, groomed**) If a person is **groomed** for a possible future job, they are given special training or experience which will help them. ■ At a wedding, the **groom** is the bridegroom. ■ If a person is **well-groomed,** their appearance is very neat and tidy. ■ **Grooming** is the things people do to keep their skin and hair clean and healthy. ■ If you **groom** a horse, you clean and brush it. A person whose job is to look after horses is called a **groom.** ■ When animals **groom** each other, they clean each other's fur.

groove A **groove** is a narrow channel cut into a surface. ■ The **groove** of pop music is its rhythm.

groovy If you say something is **groovy,** you mean it is cool and fashionable.

grope (**groping, groped**) If you **grope** for a solution to a problem, you try hard to think of one. ■ If you **grope** for something, you feel about, to try to find it. ■ If one person **gropes** another, they touch or grab their body in a rough sexual way.

gross (**grosses, grossing, grossed; grossly**) A **gross** amount is a total amount before deductions such as tax. *The bond will pay 8.2% net, 10.9% gross.* See also **net.** ■ If a person or business **grosses** an amount of money, they earn that amount before deductions are made for tax or expenses. ■ The **gross** weight of something is its weight including packaging. ■ You use **gross** to emphasize how bad something is. *...a gross miscarriage of justice... Many public services are still grossly inefficient.* ■ **Gross** speech or behaviour shows a lack of taste, or is very rude. ■ A **gross** (*plural:* **gross**) is a dozen dozen, or 144.

gross national product See **GNP.**

grotesque (*pron:* grow-**tesk**) (**grotesquely**) You say something is **grotesque** when it is so unnatural, unpleasant, and exaggerated that it upsets or shocks you.

grotto (**grottoes**) A **grotto** is a small pretty cave.

grotty is used to describe things and places which are unpleasant and of poor quality.

grouch (**grouches; grouchy**) If you **grouch** about something, you complain about it. ■ A **grouchy** person is bad-tempered and always complaining.

ground The **ground** is the surface of the Earth. ■ If aircraft or pilots are **grounded,** they are not allowed to fly. ■ **Ground** is (a) an area of open land. *...derelict ground.* (b) land used for a particular purpose. *...a camping ground.* ■ The **grounds** of a large building are the land surrounding it and belonging to it. ■ **Grounds** for something are reasons for it. *He has called for their release on humanitarian grounds... There are grounds for optimism.* If a feeling is **well-grounded,** there are strong reasons for having it. ■ If something is **grounded** in something else, it is based on it. *His cuisine is grounded in the rustic traditions of his homeland.* ■ If someone **gains ground** in a competition, they improve their position. ■ The **ground** you cover when you are discussing something is the range of things you talk about. ■ **Ground** is used to talk about a place or situation where particular ideas or attitudes can develop. *Depression may make the village a fertile ground for ethnic hatred.* ■ You use **on the ground** when talking about the actual place where something is happening. *...the troops on the ground.* ■ If you **go to ground,** you hide somewhere for a time. See also **grind.**

ground floor The **ground floor** of a building is the one which is level with the ground.

grounding If you are given a **grounding** in a subject, you are taught the basic principles.

groundless If you say a fear or suspicion is **groundless,** you mean there is no good reason for having it.

groundnut – Groundnuts are peanuts.

ground plan A **ground plan** is a plan of the ground floor of a building.

ground rent is rent paid by the owner of a house or flat to the owner of the land on which it is built.

ground rules are basic principles by which a system is supposed to operate.

groundsman (**groundsmen**) A **groundsman** is someone whose job is to look after a sports ground.

ground staff are (a) people employed to look after sports grounds. (b) people whose job is to help maintain aircraft and runways, and to deal with passengers at airports.

groundswell If you say there is a **groundswell** of feeling or opinion about something, you mean a particular view of things is growing among people.

ground-to-air missiles are fired from the ground at aircraft or other missiles in the air.

groundwork If you do the **groundwork** for something, you do the early work on which later work is based.

group A **group** of people or things is (a) a number of them with something in common. *The scheme will be directed at the 13-17 age group.* (b) a number of them close together. *...an interesting group of trees.* ■ When people or things are **grouped,** they are divided into groups. ■ If people **group together,** they join together to achieve a particular aim. ■ A **group** is a small number of singers and musicians who perform pop songs together. ■ A **group** is a number of associated companies owned and controlled by one person or organization.

group captain A **group captain** is a high-ranking officer in the RAF.

groupie – **Groupies** are people, especially young women, who follow a rock star or other famous person around when they are on tour.

grouping A **grouping** is an organized set of people working together towards the same objectives. *...a grouping of fifteen developing countries.*

group therapy is a form of psychological counselling in which people discuss their problems with others in a group.

grouse (**grousing, groused**) The **grouse** (*plural: grouse*) is a small fat game bird. ■ If people are **grousing,** they are complaining in a bad-tempered way.

grout is a thin mortar for filling the joins between tiles and bricks.

grove A **grove** is (a) a plantation of olives, bananas, or citrus fruits. (b) a group of trees growing close together, without undergrowth.

grovel (**grovelling, grovelled**) (*Am: groveling, groveled*) You say someone **grovels** when they behave humbly towards someone and try to please them.

grow (**growing, grew, have grown; -grown**) If something **grows,** it increases or gets stronger. *There is growing concern about the level of violence in schools.* ■ When people or animals **grow,** their bodies mature and get bigger. A **grown** person is fully developed and mature. ■ **-grown** is added to words like 'full' and 'half' to say what stage an animal has reached in its development. *...fully-grown fish.* ■ When someone **grows up,** they gradually change

from a child to an adult. When they become an adult, you say they are **grown-up.** ■ When someone's hair or nails **grow,** they get longer. When a man **grows** a beard, he allows it to grow. ■ If a plant or tree is **growing** somewhere, it is alive there. If you **grow** plants or crops, you plant them and look after them. ■ **Grow** is sometimes used to mean 'become'. *She grew distraught.* ■ When people or things **grow** into something else, they develop into that thing. *This row threatens to grow into a full-blown crisis.* ■ When young people give up a childish interest or habit, you say they **grow out of** it.

grower A **grower** is someone who grows and sells large quantities of a plant or crop.

growing pains are (a) pains children get in their muscles and joints, which some people think are the result of growing. (b) the temporary difficulties new organizations experience during the early stages of their development.

growl (**growling, growled**) When an animal **growls** or gives a **growl,** it makes a low noise in its throat, usually because it is angry. ■ You can say someone **growls** something when they say it in a low rough angry voice.

grown See grow.

grown-up See grow.

growth When economists talk about **growth,** they mean the increase in the amount of things a country or industry produces and sells at a profit. ■ A **growth** in something is an increase in it. *...the growth of public expenditure.* ■ **Growth** in a person, animal, or plant, is an increase in size and development. ■ A **growth** is an abnormal lump which grows on or inside a person, animal, or plant.

grub (**grubbing, grubbed**) **Grub** is food. ■ A **grub** is the worm-like young of an insect. ■ If you **grub** something **up** or **grub** it **out,** you dig it out of the ground.

grubby (**grubbiness**) **Grubby** things are rather dirty. ■ If you say behaviour or an activity is **grubby,** you mean it is not completely honest or respectable.

grudge (**grudging, grudgingly**) If you have a **grudge** against someone, you go on feeling bitter towards them for harm they have done you in the past. ■ A **grudging** feeling or action is one you hold or do in spite of other feelings. For example, you might dislike someone, but have a **grudging** admiration for them. *His athletic status is somewhat grudgingly acknowledged.* ■ If you say you do not **grudge** someone something, you mean you do not mind them having it.

gruel is a dish made by boiling oats or another cereal with milk or water.

gruelling (*Am: grueling*) activities are extremely difficult and tiring.

gruesome (**gruesomely**) **Gruesome** activities, stories, or pictures are to do with death or dying and are horrible and shocking.

gruff (**gruffly**) A **gruff** voice is low, rough, and unfriendly.

grumble (**grumbling, grumbled**) When people **grumble,** they complain about something. **Grumbles** or **grumblings** are complaints.

grumpy (**grumpily**) A **grumpy** person is bad-tempered and miserable.

grunge is a type of rock music which started in Seattle. The fashion associated with this type of music is also called **grunge** and involves wearing scruffy or old clothes.

grunt If someone or something **grunts** or makes a **grunt,** they make a short low noise. You call this noise a **grunt.** ■ You say someone **grunts** something when they say it in a low rough voice, usually because they are annoyed.

Gruyère (*pron:* **grew**-yair) is a hard yellow Swiss cheese with holes.

G-string A **G-string** is a narrow piece of cloth worn to cover a person's genitals and held up by a string round the waist.

guano (*pron:* **gwah**-no) is dried sea-bird droppings. It is used as a fertilizer.

guarantee (**guaranteeing, guaranteed**) If one thing **guarantees** another or is a **guarantee** of it, it is certain to make it happen. *Artistic talent was no guarantee of success.* ■ If you **guarantee** something, you promise it will definitely happen, or that you will do it or provide it. A promise like this is called a **guarantee.** ■ If a company **guarantees** their work or gives a **guarantee,** they give a written promise that any faults occurring within a certain time will be repaired or the goods replaced free of charge.

guarantor A **guarantor** of a policy is someone who guarantees to see it is carried out. ■ A **guarantor** of a loan is someone who promises to repay it if the borrower fails to do so.

guard If you **guard** a person, place, or object, you watch over them to protect them. You say soldiers are **on guard** when they are protecting a person or place. ■ If prisoners are being **guarded** or are **under guard,** they are being watched over by soldiers or police, to make sure they do not escape. ■ A **guard** is someone whose job it is to protect someone or something, or prevent someone from escaping. ■ A **guard** is a railway official who collects tickets and ensures safety on a train. ■ A **guard** is a protective cover over a dangerous part of a machine. ■ If you are **on your guard** or **guard against** something happening, you take precautions to prevent it. ■ If you catch someone **off guard,** you do something unexpected, which puts them at a disadvantage. ■ When people talk about the **old guard,** they mean a group who have been powerful within an organization for some time, but whose ideas now seem out of date.

guarded (**guardedly**) You say people's behaviour is **guarded** when they are careful not to show their feeling or give away information. *They expressed guarded optimism about a peaceful outcome.*

guardian (**guardianship**) If you say someone is a **guardian** of something, you mean they are a protector or defender of it. ■ If something is under someone's **guardianship,** they are responsible for looking after it. ■ A **guardian** is someone who is named by the courts to look after a child. ■ A person's **guardian angel** is a spirit who is believed to guide and protect them.

guardsman (**guardsmen**) Soldiers belonging to some regiments are called **guardsmen.**

guava (*pron:* **gwah**-va) **Guavas** are round yellow tropical fruit with pink or white flesh.

gubernatorial (*pron:* gyoo-ber-nat-**tor**-i-al) means connected with the post of governor. *...the Republican gubernatorial candidates.*

guerrilla (*or* **guerilla**) A **guerrilla** is a person who fights for a political cause with an unofficial army, usually against regular forces.

guess (**guesses, guessing, guessed**) If you **guess** something or make a **guess,** you give an opinion without certainty, because you do not have all the facts. ■ You say someone **guesses** something when they give a correct answer or make a correct assumption without having all the facts. *As you have probably guessed, the problem was electrical.* ■ If you say something is **anybody's guess,** you mean nobody really knows what the true situation is. ■ If you **keep someone guessing,** you do not tell them what they want to know.

guesstimate A **guesstimate** is an estimate based partly on guesswork.

guesswork is working something out by guessing, because you do not have all the facts.

guest A **guest** is someone you have invited to your home. ■ A **guest** is someone specially invited to appear or perform somewhere. ■ A **guest** at a hotel is someone staying or eating there.

guest house (*or* **guesthouse**) A **guest house** is a small hotel.

guest of honour (**guests of honour**) The **guest of honour** is the most important guest at a dinner or other occasion.

guest worker — Guest workers are people from poorer countries who are allowed into a developed country to work for a limited time.

guff You can describe statements which you think are nonsense as **guff.** *...a lot of guff about horizontal management.*

guffaw If you **guffaw,** you laugh loudly and heartily. This type of laugh is called a **guffaw.**

guidance is help and advice from someone who knows more about a subject than you do. *...parents who want more guidance in choosing a school.* ■ The **guidance** system on an aircraft or missile controls its course.

guide (**guiding, guided**) A **guide** is someone who shows people round places like museums or leads the way through difficult country. You can say someone **guides** people through places like these. ■ A **guide** or **guidebook** is a book which gives information about places like museums or hotels. ■ A **guide** is a book which gives you information or instructions to help you do or understand something. *...a guide on how to sell a story to a national paper.* ■ If you **guide** something, you control or influence what happens to it. *He became the guiding force behind the reforms.* ■ If you are **guided** by something, it controls or influences what you do. *...Lenin's guiding principles.* ■ If something acts as a **guide,** it helps you understand something or predict what will happen. *If previous recoveries are any guide, unemployment may rise for two years after out-*

put touches bottom. ■ A **guide** is a girl aged 10 to 15 who belongs to the Guides Association.

guided missile A **guided missile** is one whose course can be controlled while it is in the air.

guide dog A **guide dog** is a dog which is specially trained to help a blind person get about.

guideline – **Guidelines** are official advice about how something should be done.

guild A **guild** is an organization of people who do the same job or share an interest. *...the Townswomen's Guild.*

guilder The **guilder** is the unit of currency in the Netherlands (Holland).

guile is crafty behaviour.

guileless You say someone is **guileless** when they are innocent and trusting.

guillemot (*pron:* gil-lee-mot) The **guillemot** is a black and white sea bird.

guillotine (*pron:* gil-o-teen) (**guillotining, guillotined**) The **guillotine** was a device which was used to execute people by cutting off their heads. When someone was **guillotined,** they were executed in this way. ■ In parliament, if the government **guillotines** a debate or imposes a **guillotine** on it, it officially limits the amount of time for discussion before a vote. ■ A **guillotine** is a device for cutting and trimming paper.

guilty (**guiltily, guilt**) If you feel **guilty** about something, you realize you have done something wrong and are sorry about it. You call this feeling **guilt.** ■ If someone has committed a crime, you say they are **guilty** of it.

guinea A **guinea** is an old British unit of money worth 21 shillings, or £1.05.

guinea fowl (*plural:* guinea fowl) **Guinea fowl** are plump grey birds related to the pheasant.

guinea pig – **Guinea pigs** are small furry animals, originally from South America and often kept as pets. ■ People used in experiments are sometimes called **guinea pigs.**

guise (*rhymes with 'size'*) If someone or something is **in the guise** of something, they appear or are pretending to be something they are not. *Under the guise of 'scientific whaling' some have continued to hunt.*

guitar (**guitarist**) A **guitar** is a six-stringed instrument played by plucking or strumming.

gulag A **gulag** was a prison or labour camp in the former Soviet Union, often used for political prisoners.

gulf A **gulf** is a very large bay. *...the Gulf of Mexico.* ■ The **Gulf** is the Persian Gulf and the countries around it, including Iran, Iraq, Kuwait, and Saudi Arabia. ■ A **gulf** is a large gap or difference, especially between people's views. *The gulf between the moderates and the fundamentalists is as wide as ever.*

Gulf Stream The **Gulf Stream** is a warm ocean current flowing from the Gulf of Mexico towards north-west Europe.

gull – **Gulls** are common long-winged sea birds.

gullet Your **gullet** is the muscular tube connecting your mouth to your stomach.

gulley (*or* gully) A **gulley** is a long narrow steep-sided valley.

gullible (**gullibility**) A **gullible** person is easily tricked.

gully (**gullies**) See **gulley.**

gulp If you **gulp** food or drink, you eat or drink it quickly, swallowing large quantities at a time. Each swallow can be called a **gulp.** ■ If you **gulp,** you swallow air, often because you are surprised or nervous.

gum (**gumming, gummed**) **Gum** is a type of glue for sticking paper. If you **gum** things together, you stick them together using gum. ■ Chewing gum is often called **gum.** ■ A person's **gums** are the firm pink flesh which their teeth grow out of.

gun (**gunning, gunned**) A **gun** is a weapon which fires bullets, shells, or missiles. ■ If someone is **gunned down,** they are shot and fall to the ground. ■ If someone is **gunning for** you, they are trying to harm you or make trouble for you. ■ If you say someone has **jumped the gun,** you mean they have done something before they were supposed to. ■ If you **stick to your guns,** you do not change your views, in spite of pressure from other people.

gunboat A **gunboat** is a small warship with several large guns.

gunfire is the repeated shooting of guns.

gung-ho If someone has a **gung-ho** attitude, they are very keen on getting involved in something, especially a war. *He scoffs at the gung-ho attitude of many firemen.*

gunman (**gunmen**) A **gunman** is an armed criminal.

gunner A **gunner** is an ordinary soldier in an artillery regiment. ■ A **gunner** is a member of a ship's or aircraft's crew responsible for firing its guns.

gunpoint If someone is forced to do something at **gunpoint,** they are threatened with a gun and told to do it.

gunpowder is an explosive mixture of potassium nitrate, sulphur, and charcoal.

gun-running (**gun-runner**) **Gun-running** is smuggling weapons and ammunition.

gunship See **helicopter.**

gunshot A **gunshot** is a single shot fired from a gun.

gurgle (**gurgling, gurgled**) When liquids **gurgle,** they make a bubbling sound. ■ When a baby **gurgles** or produces **gurgles,** it makes happy bubbling noises in its throat.

Gurkha A **Gurkha** is a member of a Hindu people from Nepal. Gurkha men are often soldiers in the British Army.

guru A **guru** is a Hindu or Sikh spiritual leader or teacher. ■ The chief thinker of an intellectual or political movement can be called its **guru.** ■ An expert on a subject is sometimes called a **guru.**

gush (**gushes, gushing, gushed**) When liquid **gushes** out of something or comes out in a **gush,** a lot of it flows out quickly. ■ If someone **gushes,** they express admiration or pleasure in an exaggerated way.

gusset A **gusset** is a piece of material sewn into clothes to make them stronger, wider, or more comfortable, especially the piece of material sewn into the crotch of underwear.

gust (**gusty**) A **gust** of wind is a sudden strong burst of it. You can talk about winds being **gusty** or say they **gust**. ...*violent winds, which at times gusted up to 138 mph.*

gusto If you do something with **gusto**, you do it with energy and enthusiasm.

gut (**gutting, gutted**) The **gut** is the tube inside the body which food passes through as it is being digested. ■ If you talk about a person's or animal's **guts,** you mean their intestines, or all their internal organs. ■ If you **gut** an animal or fish, you take out its internal organs. ■ A **gut** feeling is one based on instinct or emotion rather than reason. ■ If you say someone has **guts,** you mean they are brave and determined. ■ If a building or vehicle is **gutted,** the inside is destroyed by fire.

gutless A **gutless** person lacks courage and determination.

gutsy A **gutsy** person is brave and determined.

gutter A **gutter** is (a) a channel at the side of a road for carrying away rainwater. (b) a long trough along the edge of a roof for taking rainwater to a drainpipe. ■ If you say someone is in the **gutter,** you mean they are homeless or very poor. ■ Newspapers which rely on sensational stories rather than serious news are sometimes called the **gutter press.**

guttural sounds are harsh sounds produced at the back of a person's or animal's throat. ..*a guttural growl.*

guy Men are sometimes called **guys.** ■ A **guy** is a model of Guy Fawkes, burned on November 5th.

guzzle (**guzzling, guzzled; guzzler**) If you **guzzle** liquid, you drink it quickly and eagerly. You can also say a car **guzzles** fuel.

gym A **gym** is the same as a gymnasium.

gymkhana (*pron:* jim-**kah**-na) A **gymkhana** is an event involving various horse riding competitions.

gymnasium A **gymnasium** is a large room with exercise equipment.

gymnastics (**gymnast; gymnastic**) Gymnastics (*pron:* jim-**nas**-tiks) are physical exercises involving things like ropes and wooden bars. People who take part in gymnastic competitions are called **gymnasts** (*pron:* **jim**-nasts). ■ **Gymnastic** means to do with gymnastics. ...*gymnastic ability.*

gynaecology (*or* gynecology) (*pron:* guy-nee-**kol**-la-jee) (**gynaecologist; gynaecological**) Gynaecology is the branch of medicine dealing with diseases and illnesses suffered only by women, particularly those affecting the reproductive system. A doctor who specializes in this is called a **gynaecologist.** ...*gynaecological investigations.*

gypsum is a chalk-like mineral used for making plaster of paris.

gypsy (*or* gipsy) (**gypsies**) Gypsies are a race of travelling people found throughout Europe.

gyrate (**gyrating, gyrated; gyration**) If something **gyrates,** it turns round and round in a circle, usually very fast. A movement like this is called a **gyration.** ■ When people who are dancing **gyrate,** they make circular movements with their hips.

gyroscope A **gyroscope** is a device that contains a disc rotating on an axis that can turn freely in any direction, so that the disc maintains the same position whatever the position or movement of the surrounding structure.

H h

ha See **hectare.**

habeas corpus (*pron:* hay-bee-ass **kor**-puss) A writ of **habeas corpus** is a legal document ordering that an arrested person be brought before a court, so that the court can decide if it is lawful to keep them in custody.

haberdashery (**haberdasher**) Haberdashery is small articles like thread, buttons, and zips, used in sewing. A shop which sells haberdashery is called a **haberdasher** or **haberdasher's.**

habit A **habit** is something you do often. ■ A **habit** is something which is bad for you but which it is difficult to stop doing. ...*a serious drug habit.* ■ A monk's or nun's **habit** is the long loose robe which they wear.

habitable If a building is **habitable,** it is fit to live in.

habitat The **habitat** of an animal or plant is its natural environment.

habitation is the fact of living somewhere. If you say a building is unfit for **habitation,** you mean it is not fit to live in.

habitual (**habitually**) Habitual and **habitually** are used to talk about things a person keeps on doing. *They habitually use all sorts of drugs.*

habituated If you are **habituated** to something, you are used to it.

habitué (*pron:* hab-**it**-yew-ay) A **habitué** of a place is someone who goes there regularly.

hacienda (*pron:* hass-ee-**end**-a) A **hacienda** is a ranch or large estate in Latin America.

hack (**hacker, hacking**) If you **hack** something, you cut it with a sharp tool, using rough strokes. ■ If you call a writer a **hack,** you mean they work quickly without worrying about the quality of their work. ■ If someone **hacks** into a computer, they get unauthorized access to it. Someone who does this is called a **hacker;** what they do is called **hacking.**

hackles are the hairs on the back of a dog's neck, which rise when the dog gets angry. If something **makes your hackles rise,** it makes you angry.

hackneyed If you call something **hackneyed,** you mean it has lost a lot of its meaning or impact because it has been overused. ...*hackneyed music-hall gags.*

hacksaw A **hacksaw** is a small saw for cutting metal.

had See **have.**

haddock (*plural:* **haddock**) **Haddock** are large fish caught in the North Atlantic.

Hades (*pron:* hay-deez) In Greek mythology, **Hades** is the home of the dead.

haematology (*or* hematology) (*pron:* hee-ma-**tol**-o-jee) (**haematologist**) **Haematology** is the branch of medicine concerned with diseases of the blood.

haemoglobin (*or* hemoglobin) (*pron:* hee-moh-**globe**-in) is a protein in red blood cells which carries oxygen from the lungs.

haemophilia (*or* hemophilia) (*pron:* hee-moh-**fill**-lee-a) (**haemophiliac**) **Haemophilia** is a disease in which the blood does not clot, so the sufferer bleeds for a long time when cut or injured. Someone who has this disease is called a **haemophiliac.**

haemorrhage (*or* hemorrhage) (*pron:* **hem**-or-ij) (**haemorrhaging, haemorrhaged**) A **haemorrhage** is serious bleeding in part of someone's body. If someone is bleeding like this, you say they are **haemorrhaging.** ■ If a place or group is rapidly losing people or resources, you can say it is **haemorrhaging.** You can also say there is a **haemorrhage** of people or resources.

haemorrhoids (*or* hemorrhoids) (*pron:* hem-or-oydz) **Haemorrhoids** are painful swollen veins in and around the anus. They are also called 'piles'.

hag When people dislike a woman very much, they sometimes call her a **hag.**

haggard If someone is **haggard,** they look tired and ill.

haggis (**haggises**) A **haggis** is a Scottish dish made from oatmeal, onion, and offal, boiled inside the skin of a sheep's stomach.

haggle (**haggling, haggled**) If someone **haggles,** they argue about something before reaching agreement, especially about the cost of something they want to buy.

hail (**hailing, hailed; hailstone**) You say someone or something is **hailed** as important or successful when they are praised publicly. *The agreement was hailed as a breakthrough.* ■ When it **hails,** tiny balls of ice called **hailstones** fall from the sky. **Hail** is a shower of **hailstones.** ■ A **hail** of objects is a large number of them falling together. ■ If you **hail** from a place, that is where you come from. ■ If you **hail** a taxi, you wave to the driver to stop so you can get in.

hair (**-haired**) **Hair** consists of the threadlike strands which grow from the skin of animals and humans. Your **hair** is the mass of fine strands which grow out of the skin on your head. **-haired** is used to say what kind of hair a person or animal has. ...*a long-haired poet.* ■ If something comes within a **hair's breadth** of happening, it nearly happens.

hairbrush (**hairbrushes**) A **hairbrush** is a brush for your hair.

haircut A person's **haircut** is the style in which their hair has been cut. ■ If you have a **haircut,** someone cuts your hair for you.

hairdo (**hairdos**) Someone's **hairdo** is the way their hair has been cut and styled.

hairdressing (**hairdresser**) **Hairdressing** is cutting and styling hair. A person who does this for a living is called a **hairdresser.** A place where people go to get their hair cut and styled is called a **hairdresser's.**

hairdryer (*or* hairdrier) A **hairdryer** is a machine for drying hair.

hairline Your **hairline** is the edge of your hair next to areas of smooth skin.

hairpiece A **hairpiece** is a piece of false hair used to make natural hair look thicker or longer.

hairpin bend A **hairpin bend** is a sharp U-shaped bend in a road.

hair-raising A **hair-raising** experience, event, or story is very frightening but can also be exciting.

hair-shirt If you say someone is wearing a **hair-shirt,** you mean they are trying to punish themselves to show they are sorry for something they have done. *No one is asking you to put on a hair shirt and give up all your luxuries.* ■ A **hair-shirt** was an uncomfortably rough shirt made of horsehair cloth and worn by some Christians to punish themselves.

hairstyle Someone's **hairstyle** is the way their hair has been cut and styled.

hairy (**hairier, hairiest**) A **hairy** person or animal is covered with hair. ■ If you call a situation **hairy,** you mean it is dangerous.

hake (*plural:* **hake**) **Hake** are large fish similar to cod.

halal (*pron:* hal-**lahl**) If something is **halal,** it is approved by the laws of the Muslim religion. **Halal** meat is from animals slaughtered according to Muslim law.

halcyon (*pron:* **hal**-see-on) A **halcyon** time is a time in the past which was peaceful or happy.

half (**halves**) A **half** is one of two equal parts of something. If something is divided in **half,** it is divided into two equal parts. ■ A **half** or **one half** is the fraction $\frac{1}{2}$. ■ **Half past** means thirty minutes after the hour. ■ You use **half** to show that something is only partly the case or happens to a limited extent. *They half expected this to happen.* ...*half-closed blinds.*

half-baked ideas or plans are poorly thought out, and are likely to fail.

half board means hotel accommodation which includes breakfast and an evening meal but not lunch.

half-brother If someone is your **half-brother,** he has the same father as you or the same mother, but not both.

half-caste is an offensive word for someone who has parents of different races.

half-hearted (**half-heartedly**) If someone is **half-hearted** about something, they do not show any enthusiasm for it.

half-life The **half-life** of something radioactive is the time it takes to lose half its radioactivity.

half-mast If a flag is at **half-mast,** it is flying halfway down the pole, as a sign of mourning.

half-moon A **half-moon** shape is a semi-circle.

half-sister If someone is your **half-sister,** she has the same father as you or the same mother, but not both.

half-term is a short holiday in the middle of a school term.

half-timbered buildings have a visible framework of wooden beams.

half-time is the rest break for players between the two halves of a sports match.

halfway means in the middle of a period of time or of an event. ■ If something is **halfway** between two places, it lies the same distance between each of them. ■ If you **meet someone halfway,** you compromise on some points to reach an agreement. A compromise position can be called a **halfway house.**

halibut (*plural:* **halibut**) The **halibut** is a large flatfish caught in the North Atlantic.

halite is the mineral from which 'rock salt' is obtained.

halitosis is bad breath.

hall A **hall** is a large room used for public events like concerts. ■ A **hall** is an entrance area just inside the front door of a house.

hallmark The **hallmark** of someone or something is their most typical quality or feature. *Believing in greater equality is the traditional hallmark of the socialist.* ■ A **hallmark** is an official mark on a gold, platinum, or silver object which shows its quality.

hallo See **hello.**

hall of residence – **Halls of residence** are blocks of rooms owned by universities for students to live in.

hallowed things are greatly respected.

Halloween (*or* **Hallowe'en**) is October 31st, the night when witches and ghosts are supposed to be about.

hallucinate (**hallucinating, hallucinated; hallucination**) If someone **hallucinates** or has **hallucinations,** they see things which are not really there, because they are ill or on drugs.

hallucinatory is used to describe something that is like a hallucination or is the cause of hallucinations. *...hallucinatory drugs.*

hallucinogenic drugs make people hallucinate.

hallway The **hallway** of a building is its entrance hall.

halo (**haloes** *or* **halos**) A **halo** is a ring of light round a star, planet, or other object. ■ In religious pictures, **haloes** are the circles of light round the heads of holy figures.

halogen (*pron:* **hal**-oh-jen) is the name given to a group of nonmetallic chemical elements including fluorine and chlorine. **Halogen** bulbs contain halogens which give off a bright light.

halt If growth, development, activity, or movement is **halted,** it stops completely. You can also say it **comes to a halt** or **grinds to a halt.** ■ If someone **calls a halt** to something, they decide not to continue with it.

halter A **halter** is a strap round an animal's head with a lead attached to it. ■ A **halter neck** top is a sleeveless and backless woman's garment which is fastened at the back of the neck.

halting (**haltingly**) **Halting** speech has many pauses and hesitations.

halve (**halving, halved**) If something **halves** or is **halved,** it is reduced to half its original size. ■ When you **halve** something like an orange, you cut it into two equal parts.

ham (**hamming, hammed**) **Ham** is smoked or salted meat from a pig's thigh. A **ham** is a joint of this meat. ■ A **ham** is an amateur radio operator. ■ If you say actors are **hamming it up,** you mean they are overacting.

hamburger A **hamburger** is a flat round cake of fried or grilled minced beef, often served in a bread roll.

ham-fisted If you say someone is **ham-fisted,** you mean they are clumsy in the way they use their hands.

hamlet A **hamlet** is a small village.

hammer (**hammering, hammered**) A **hammer** is a tool with a heavy head for hitting things. If you **hammer** something somewhere, you force it there with a hammer. ■ If you **hammer** on a surface, you keep hitting it with your fists. ■ In sport, if someone is **hammered** or takes a **hammering,** they are heavily defeated. ■ If someone **hammers away** at a point or **hammers** it **home,** they keep mentioning it, to get people to think about it. ■ When people **hammer out** an agreement, they reach it after long and difficult discussions. ■ If something is **under the hammer,** it is being sold by auction. ■ The **hammer** is a field event in athletics. Competitors throw a metal ball on the end of a wire as far as they can.

hammock A **hammock** is a hanging bed made of string or canvas.

hamper (**hampering, hampered**) If someone or something **hampers** you, they make it difficult for you to do what you are trying to do. ■ A **hamper** is a large food basket with a lid, often used for picnics.

hamster – **Hamsters** are small mouse-like animals with cheek pouches, often kept as pets.

hamstring (**hamstringing, hamstrung**) A person's **hamstrings** are the tendons at the back of their knees. ■ If someone is **hamstrung,** the actions they can take in a situation are very limited.

hand Your **hands** are the parts of your body attached to your arms. ■ If you do something **by hand,** you do it using your hands rather than a machine. ■ **Hand** is used to describe a small version of an object, designed to be held in the hand. *...a hand mirror.* ■ If you **hand** something to someone, you give it to them. If you **hand out** a set of things, you give one to each person. See also **handout.** ■ When people in authority **hand out** advice or punishment, they give it. ■ When a judge **hands down** a sentence, he or she announces what it will be. ■ If you **hand in** something, you give it to someone in authority. *Lobbyists will hand in a 50,000-signature petition.* ■ If you **hand over** to someone, you pass the responsibility you had for something to them. ■ If possessions are **handed down,** they are given or left to younger family members. ■ If something **changes hands,** it goes from one person to another. ■ If you **have a hand in** something, you are actively involved in it. ■ If you **give** someone **a hand,** you help them. ■ If you give someone a **free hand,** you let them deal with something exactly as they want. ■ If you have a problem **on your hands,** you have to deal with it. ■ If you **wash your hands of** a problem, you refuse to take any more responsibility for it. ■ The task **in hand** is the one you are dealing with now. ■ If a sports team has games **in hand,** they have played fewer games than their opponents. ■ If you have something **to hand,** you have it ready to use when needed. ■ Something which is **at hand** is close by or is going to happen soon. ■ If someone is **on hand,** they are near and ready to help. ■ If you reject an idea **out of hand,** you reject it immediately and completely. ■ If a situation **gets out of hand,** it is no longer controllable. ■ A **hand** of cards is all the cards dealt to a player in a game. ■ The **hands** of a watch or clock are the pointers which show the time. ■ Factory or farm workers are sometimes called **hands.** ■ You say **on the one hand** and **on the other hand** when mentioning contrasting aspects of a situation. ■ **hand in glove: see glove.**

handbag A **handbag** is a small bag used for carrying things like keys.

hand baggage See **hand luggage.**

handball is a team game in which a ball is hit with the palm of the hand. ■ In football, if anyone except the goalkeeper handles the ball, it is an offence called **handball.**

handbook A **handbook** is a book giving advice or instructions on something.

handbrake In a car, the **handbrake** is a brake operated with your hand.

handcart A **handcart** is a small two-wheeled goods cart.

handcuff If someone is **handcuffed** or is wearing **handcuffs,** they have two metal rings linked by a short chain locked round their wrists, to prevent them escaping.

handful A **handful** of people or things is a small number of them. ■ A **handful** is a small amount, or the amount you can hold in one hand.

handgun (*or* hand gun) A **handgun** is a gun you can hold and fire with one hand.

hand-held machines are small enough to carry in your hand.

handicap (**handicapping, handicapped**) If someone is **handicapped** or has a **handicap,** they have a physical or mental disability. People who are handicapped are sometimes called the **handicapped.** ■ If something makes things difficult for you, you can say you are **handicapped** by it or call it a **handicap.** ■ A **handicap** is a disadvantage given to someone who is good at a sport, to make the competition between them and others more equal. A game or race in which this happens is called a **handicap.**

handicraft – **Handicrafts** are objects made skilfully by hand. **Handicraft** means things connected with handicrafts. ...*handicraft material.*

handiwork A person's **handiwork** is something they have made or created. ■ If you say something bad is someone's **handiwork,** you mean they did it.

handkerchief (**handkerchiefs**) A **handkerchief** is a small square of material or paper for blowing your nose into.

handle (**handling, handled**) If you **handle** a task or problem, you deal with it. ■ If you **handle** a piece of equipment well, you use it or control it effectively. Equipment which **handles** well is easy to use. *The car handles very neatly.* ■ When you **handle** something, you hold or touch it with your hands. ■ An object's **handle** is the part you hold when you are carrying it, using it, or opening it.

handlebar The **handlebars** on a bicycle are the metal bars used to steer it.

handler A **handler** is someone who controls an animal. ...*dog handlers.* ■ A **handler** is someone whose job is to deal with a particular type of object. ...*baggage handlers.*

hand luggage or **hand baggage** is the bags or cases you keep with you during a coach or plane journey.

handmade If something is **handmade,** it is made by hand rather than by machine.

handmaiden In the past, female servants were sometimes called **handmaidens.**

hand-me-downs are clothes passed from one person to another when the first person has finished with them.

handout A **handout** is money, clothing, or food given free to poor people. ■ A **handout** is a copy of a document given to people in a class or meeting.

hand-picked If someone is **hand-picked,** they are carefully chosen for a particular job.

handrail A **handrail** is a rail next to a stairway.

handset The **handset** of a telephone is the part you listen to and speak into.

handshake When people shake hands, you call their action a **handshake.** ■ **golden handshake: see golden.**

hands-off If you have a **hands-off** approach to a situation, you let it develop by itself, and intervene as little as possible.

handsome (**handsomely**) A **handsome** person is attractive to look at. ■ A **handsome** amount of money is fairly large.

hands-on instruction involves being taught whilst doing a particular thing, rather than just being told about it. ■ If you have a **hands-on** approach to a situation, you involve yourself directly in dealing with it.

hand-to-hand fighting involves direct confrontation using weapons such as fists or swords.

hand-to-mouth If you live **hand-to-mouth,** you are very poor and have barely enough food.

handwriting (**handwritten**) Your **handwriting** is your style of writing with a pen or pencil. If something is **handwritten,** it is written with a pen or pencil rather than typed.

handy (**handier, handiest; handily**) **Handy** things are useful and easy to use. ■ You say something is

handy when it is nearby or conveniently placed. *...jumping off the train at a handy station.* ■ Someone who is **handy** with something is skilful at using it.

handyman (**handymen**) A **handyman** is someone who is good at making and repairing things.

hang (**hanging, hung** *or* **hanged;** *you say an object is 'hung' but a person is 'hanged'*) If you **hang** something somewhere, you place it so the highest part is supported and the rest is not. *The sacks were hung from the roof... His jacket was hanging up in the hallway. ...hanging out washing.* ■ If someone is **hanged,** they are executed by having a rope tied around their neck and the support under their feet removed. ■ If you **hang on to** something, you do not get rid of it or give it up. ■ If you **hang on,** you wait. ■ If one thing **hangs on** another, it depends on it. *So much hangs on customer service.* ■ If a problem is **hanging over** you, it is a constant worry. ■ If you **hang around** or **hang about** somewhere, you wait there, doing very little. ■ If you **hang out** in a place or use it as a **hang-out,** you spend a lot of leisure time there. ■ When you **hang up** the phone, you end the call by putting the receiver back. If you **hang up** on someone, you hang up the phone unexpectedly.

hangar A **hangar** is a large building for storing aircraft.

hangdog If you say someone has a **hangdog** expression, you mean they look miserable or guilty.

hanger A **hanger** is a curved piece of metal or wood for hanging clothes on.

hanger-on You can call people **hangers-on** when they hang around with a rich or famous person, hoping to gain some advantage for themselves.

hang-glider (**hang-gliding**) A **hang-glider** is a lightweight kite-shaped glider. The pilot hangs underneath it in a harness. Flying a hang-glider is called **hang-gliding.**

hangman (**hangmen**) A **hangman** is a man whose job is to execute people by hanging.

hangover If you wake up with a **hangover,** you feel ill or have a headache as a result of drinking a lot of alcohol the day before. ■ If you say ideas are a **hangover** from the past, you mean they have continued into the present even though they are no longer useful.

hang-up If you have a **hang-up** about something, you feel anxious or embarrassed about it. *...sexual hang-ups.*

hanker (**hankering, hankered**) If you **hanker** after something or have a **hankering** for it, you want it a lot.

hankie (*or* **hanky**) (**hankies**) A **hankie** is the same as a handkerchief.

hanky-panky Suspicious or illegal goings-on are sometimes called **hanky-panky.** ■ Sexual activity is sometimes called **hanky-panky.**

haphazard (**haphazardly**) If something is **haphazard,** it is not organized according to a plan.

hapless is used to describe someone who is unlucky. *...hapless motorists trapped in the blockade.*

happen (**happening, happened**) When something unplanned takes place, you say it **happens.** *The explosion happened at noon.* Something unplanned like this is called a **happening.** ■ If you **happen** to do something, you do it by chance. ■ When something **happens** to you, it takes place and affects you. ■ You say **as it happens** when you are mentioning a new or surprising piece of information. *As it happens, most Labour Party members favour such reform.*

happy (**happier, happiest; happily, happiness**) If you are **happy,** you have feelings of joy or contentment. ■ If you say someone is **happy-go-lucky,** you mean they enjoy life and do not worry about the future. ■ If you say you are **happy** to do something, you mean you are willing to do it. ■ A **happy** chance or coincidence is a lucky one.

harangue (**haranguing, harangued**) If you **harangue** someone, you speak to them angrily or forcefully, often to try to persuade them of something. *She launched into an harangue against the Bishop.*

harass (**harasses, harassing, harassed; harassment**) If someone **harasses** you, they keep interfering with you in an annoying or upsetting way. *He decides to sue for sexual harassment.* ■ You say someone is **harassed** when they are upset or worried because they have more work or problems than they can handle.

harbinger (*pron:* har-bin-jer) A **harbinger** of something is a sign that it is going to happen. *The industrial action could be a harbinger of further troubles.*

harbour (*Am:* **harbor**) (**harbouring, harboured**) A **harbour** is a sheltered area of water used for mooring boats. ■ If you **harbour** someone, you give them shelter and protection. ■ If someone **harbours** certain feelings, they have them but do not talk about them.

hard (**hardness**) If you work **hard,** you put a lot of effort into your work. ■ If something is **hard** to do, it cannot be done easily. ■ If an object or surface is **hard,** it is firm, rather than soft or yielding. ■ **Hard** water contains fairly large amounts calcium and magnesium, and does not lather easily. See also **soft.** ■ **Hard** is used to say something is done with a lot of force. *He hit the ball too hard.* ■ A **hard-hitting** speech is tough or critical. ■ If you say someone is **hard,** you mean they show little kindness or pity. If you are **hard on** someone, you treat them unkindly or unfairly. ■ If a period of your life is **hard,** it is unpleasant and difficult. ■ A **hard** winter or frost is very severe. ■ **Hard** is used to talk about strong alcohol or drugs. **Hard** drink is drink such as whisky. **Hard** drugs are drugs such as heroin. ■ **Hard** or **hard-core** pornography shows explicit sex scenes. ■ **Hard** facts are definitely true. ■ **Hard and fast** is used to describe things which are definite or fixed. *There are no hard and fast answers.* ■ If you are **hard up,** you have very little money. ■ If you feel **hard done by,** you feel you have been unfairly treated. ■ **hard of hearing:** see **hearing.**

hardback A **hardback** is a book with a stiff cover.

hard-bitten If you say someone is **hard-bitten,** you mean they are tough and unsentimental.

hardboard is thin stiff board made of compressed woodchips.

hard-boiled A **hard-boiled** egg has been boiled until the yolk is solid. ■ If you say a person is **hard-boiled,** you mean they are tough and unemotional.

hard cash is notes and coins, as opposed to cheques or credit.

hard copy is computer output printed on paper.

hard core (or **hardcore**) The **hard core** of a group of people are the ones most involved in its activities. ■ You can talk about types of rock and dance music as **hardcore** when you mean they are an uncompromising and uncommercial example of their type. ■ **Hard-core** pornography: see **hard.** ■ **Hardcore** is pieces of broken stone used as a base on which to build something.

hard currency A **hard currency** is one which can be bought and sold on the international money markets, and for which demand is high because it is unlikely to lose its value.

hard disk (or **hard disc**) A **hard disk** is a piece of stiff plastic coated with a magnetic substance on which computer information can be stored.

harden (**hardening, hardened**) If your attitude **hardens** or you become **hardened** by things, your attitude becomes tougher and less sympathetic. ■ If people have become **hardened** to something unpleasant, it no longer affects them, because they have experienced it so much. ■ If a substance **hardens,** it becomes firm.

hard-headed people are practical and determined.

hard-hearted If you say someone is **hard-hearted,** you mean they are unfeeling.

hard-hitting See **hard.**

hard labour is hard physical work.

hard line (**hardline, hardliner**) If you take a **hard line** on something, you have a firm policy which you refuse to change. ■ A **hardline** approach is strict and often extreme. Someone with this approach is called a **hardliner.**

hardly is used (a) to say something is only just true, or someone is only just able to do something. *I hardly slept last night... The police and courts can hardly cope.* (b) to say one thing happened immediately after another. *He had hardly begun speaking when he was again interrupted by the president.* ■ **Hardly** is used with 'without' to emphasize how often something happens. *Hardly a day passes without bad news about the NHS.* ■ If something **hardly ever** happens, it almost never happens. ■ **Hardly** is sometimes used jokingly: For instance, if you say something is **hardly** a surprise, you mean it is not a surprise at all.

hard-nosed If you say someone is **hard-nosed,** you mean they are tough and realistic.

hard-pressed If you are **hard-pressed,** you are under a great deal of strain and worry. ■ If you are **hard-pressed** to do something, you have great difficulty doing it.

hard sell If salespeople give a product the **hard sell,** they use sales techniques which put pressure on people to buy it.

hardship If someone suffers **hardship,** they have difficulties and problems caused by lack of money.

hard shoulder The **hard shoulder** of a motorway is the strip of road along the edge where you can stop in an emergency.

hardware Military **hardware** is the weapons and equipment used in war. ■ Computer **hardware** is the machinery itself, rather than the software. ■ A **hardware** shop sells tools and equipment for the home and garden.

hard-wearing things are tough and long-lasting.

hard-won A **hard-won** victory is one which was difficult to achieve.

hardwood – **Hardwoods** are trees like oak which produce strong hard timber. Timber of this type is called **hardwood.**

hardy (**hardier, hardiest; hardiness**) **Hardy** things are able to survive in difficult conditions.

hare A **hare** is a wild animal like a rabbit but with longer ears and legs.

harebell – **Harebells** are blue bell-shaped wild flowers.

hare-brained You say a scheme is **hare-brained** when you think it is badly thought out or silly.

hare-coursing is a sport in which two greyhounds chase a hare by sight rather than scent.

Hare Krishna (pron: har-ee **krish**-na) The **Hare Krishna** movement is a Hindu religious sect devoted to the worship of the god Krishna.

harelip If someone has a **harelip,** they were born with a split in their upper lip.

harem (pron: har-**eem**) In many Muslim countries in former times, a **harem** was the women's section of a wealthy man's house. The wives or concubines who lived there were also called a **harem.**

haricot bean (pron: **har**-rik-oh) **Haricot beans** are small white beans.

hark If you **hark back** to a topic, you keep returning to it.

harlot A **harlot** is a prostitute.

harm If you **harm** someone or something or cause them **harm,** you injure or damage them. ■ If you are **out of harm's way,** you are out of danger.

harmful Something **harmful** has a bad effect on people or things.

harmless (**harmlessly**) Something **harmless** does not harm anyone or anything.

harmonic means connected with harmony. *...the music's harmonic structure.* ■ A **harmonic** is an additional higher sound produced when a note is played on a musical instrument. A sound like this can be produced as a separate note on some instruments.

harmonica A **harmonica** is a small hand-held musical instrument played by blowing and sucking air through it.

harmonious (**harmoniously**) A **harmonious** environment is friendly and peaceful. ■ **Harmonious** is used to describe things which go well together. *...a combination of vibrant shades that blend harmoniously with your natural colour.*

harmonise See **harmonize.**

harmonium A **harmonium** is a keyboard instrument like a small organ.

harmonize (or **harmonise**) (**harmonizing, harmonized; harmonization**) If two or more things **har-**

monize, they fit in well with each other. When things are **harmonized,** they are made to fit in with each other or operate smoothly together. ■ When people **harmonize,** they sing or play notes which are different from the main tune, but which sound nice with it.

harmony If people are living in **harmony,** they are living peacefully together. ■ **Harmony** can be used to talk about a pleasant and satisfying arrangement of things, especially buildings. ■ In music, **harmony** is a pleasant effect produced by different notes being played at the same time.

harness (harnesses, harnessing, harnessed) If you **harness** something, you bring it under your control, to use its energy. ■ A **harness** is a set of straps for attaching an animal to a plough, cart, or carriage. If you **harness** an animal, you attach it to one of these vehicles with a harness. ■ A **harness** is a set of straps fastened around your body to hold something on, or to keep you safely attached to something.

harp (harpist) A **harp** is a large triangular musical instrument with vertical strings which are plucked by hand. ■ If you keep **harping on** about something, you keep talking about it, irritating other people.

harpoon (harpooning, harpooned) A **harpoon** is a barbed spear attached to a rope, used to catch whales. If you **harpoon** a whale, you fire a harpoon into it.

harpsichord A **harpsichord** is a keyboard instrument like a small piano.

harrow A **harrow** is a tool used to break up the soil after land has been ploughed.

harrowing experiences are extremely upsetting or disturbing.

harry (harries, harrying, harried) If you **harry** someone, you keep asking them to do something. ■ If you **harry** your enemy, you attack them repeatedly.

harsh (harshly; harshness) Harsh actions are cruel or severe. *The Police Department has been harshly criticized for its handling of the case.* ■ If you live in **harsh** conditions, they are difficult or extreme. ■ A **harsh** light or sound is unpleasantly bright or loud.

harvest A **harvest** is a crop of grain or fruit when it is gathered at the end of the growing season. The **harvest** is the gathering of this crop. When it is gathered, you say it is **harvested.**

harvester A **harvester** is (a) a machine for gathering crops. (b) a person who helps with the harvest.

harvest festival A **harvest festival** is a Christian service of thanksgiving for the harvest.

has See **have.**

has-been If you say someone is a **has-been,** you mean they are no longer important or successful.

hash If you say someone has **made a hash** of a job, you mean they have done it very badly. ■ **Hash** is a dish of cooked meat and vegetables mixed together and fried or baked. ■ **Hash** is short for 'hashish'.

hashish (pron: hash-eesh) is cannabis resin, which some people smoke for its intoxicating effects. Hashish is an illegal drug in Britain.

hassle (hassling, hassled) Hassle or a **hassle** is something which causes trouble or difficulty. ■ If someone **hassles** you, they pester you to do something.

hassock A **hassock** is a cushion for kneeling on in church.

haste If you do something in **haste,** you do it quickly and hurriedly. ■ If you **make haste,** you get on with something as quickly as you can.

hasten (hastening, hastened) If you **hasten** something, you make it happen sooner. ■ If you **hasten** to do something, you do it as quickly as you can. ■ If you **hasten** somewhere, you hurry there.

hasty (hastily) Hasty means done or arranged in a hurry, or without proper thought. *His mother complained that police had acted hastily.*

hat A **hat** is a covering for the head. ■ If you say you **take your hat off** to someone, you mean you admire them for something they have done. ■ If you **pass the hat around,** you collect money from people in order to pay for something. ■ If you **throw your hat into the ring,** you enter a contest. ■ If you say something is **old hat,** you mean it is no longer interesting, or has become unfashionable.

hatch (hatches, hatching, hatched) When an egg **hatches,** it breaks open and a baby creature comes out. ■ If you **hatch** a plot, you think it up and plan it. ■ A **hatch** is (a) an opening in a ship or spacecraft which people or things can get in and out through. (b) a small opening in a wall or door through which things can be passed.

hatchback A **hatchback** is a car with a door at the back which opens upwards.

hatchery (hatcheries) A **hatchery** is a place where eggs are hatched under artificial conditions.

hatchet A **hatchet** is a small axe. ■ If people **bury the hatchet,** they become friendly again after a quarrel. ■ If someone does a **hatchet job** on a person, they make a violent written or spoken attack on them. ■ A **hatchet man** is someone employed to do unpleasant tasks.

hate (hating, hated) Hate is intense dislike. If you **hate** someone, you dislike them intensely.

hateful is used to describe extremely unpleasant things.

hatred is intense dislike.

hat-trick In sport, a **hat-trick** is a series of three achievements, for example three goals scored by the same person in a football match.

haughty (haughtily, haughtiness) You say someone is **haughty** when they behave as if they are superior to others.

haul (hauling, hauled) If you **haul** something somewhere, you pull or drag it there. ■ If a person is **hauled** somewhere, they are made to go there unwillingly. ■ A **haul** is the quantity of fish caught in a net. ■ A **haul** of drugs or stolen goods is the amount recovered by police or stolen by criminals. ■ **Long-haul** flights are long journeys by air, usually between continents. **Short-haul** flights cover shorter distances. ■ If a journey or struggle is a **long haul,** it takes a long time and lots of effort.

haulage companies transport goods by road.

haulier A **haulier** runs a haulage company.

haunches Your **haunches** are your buttocks and the tops of your thighs.

haunt (**haunting, hauntingly**) If a ghost is said to **haunt** a place, it is believed to regularly appear there. ■ If unpleasant memories or thoughts **haunt** you, they keep coming back to you. ■ You can say something **haunts** you when it keeps making difficulties for you and you do not seem to be able to get away from it. *Oakland is haunted by its reputation for drugs, violent crime and poor schooling.* ■ You call something **haunting** when it stays in your thoughts because it is very beautiful or sad. *...the hauntingly beautiful 'Smokehouse Blues'.* ■ Your **haunts** are places you visit regularly.

haute couture (*pron:* **oat** koo-**ture**) refers to expensive fashionable clothes made by exclusive designers.

hauteur (*pron:* oat-**ur**) If someone behaves with **hauteur,** they behave as if they are superior to others.

have (**has, having, had**) **Have** is used in front of words like 'been' and 'done' to mention something which happened recently. *A curfew has been imposed in the town... 5,000 workers have lost their jobs.* **Have** is used after words like 'might' and 'would' to talk about possibilities. *If I had sat in the flat every day I would have gone mad.* ■ If you **have to** do something, you must do it. ■ If you **have** something, you own or possess it. *He had a tiny mews house full of antiques.* ■ If you **have** something, you experience it or you are affected by it. *I had breakfast with my father... He has a cold.* ■ If a woman **has** a baby, she gives birth to it. ■ If someone **has it in for** you, they are determined to make trouble for you because they dislike you. ■ If someone or something has **had it,** they are in very serious trouble and cannot be saved. ■ People talk about the **haves** and the **have-nots** when they are comparing people who have a high standard of living with those who do not.

haven A **haven** is a place where a person or animal is safe from trouble or danger. ■ **tax haven:** see **tax.**

haversack A **haversack** is a canvas bag worn on your back or shoulder.

havoc is disorder or destruction. You can say something **plays** or **wreaks havoc** with something else. *Storms wreaked havoc in many parts of Britain.*

hawk (**hawkish, hawker**) **Hawks** are birds of prey with strong claws, short rounded wings, and long tails. ■ Politicians who favour war or aggressive policies are sometimes called **hawks;** their behaviour is described as **hawkish.** See also **dove.** ■ If you **hawk** something, you try hard to sell it, often by taking it from place to place. People who sell things on the street or door-to-door are called **hawkers.**

hawser A **hawser** is a large rope used on a ship.

hawthorn The **hawthorn** is a small thorny tree or bush with white or pink flowers in spring and red berries in autumn.

hay is dried grass used to feed animals. ■ If you **make hay while the sun shines,** you make the most of an opportunity because it is unlikely to last.

hayfever is an allergy to pollen, which causes sneezing and runny eyes.

haystack A **haystack** is a large pile of stored hay.

haywire If something goes **haywire,** it goes badly wrong or gets out of control.

hazard (**hazardous**) If something is a **hazard,** it can cause disease, injury, or death. You say something like this is **hazardous.** ■ A **hazardous** activity is one where things can easily go wrong. ■ If you **hazard** a guess, you make one.

haze (**hazy**) A **haze** is a mist caused by heat or by dust in the air. When there is a haze, you say the sky or view is **hazy.** ■ If you are in a **haze,** your thoughts are unclear or confused. ■ If a memory of something is **hazy,** it is not at all clear.

hazel (**hazelnut**) The **hazel** is a small tree or bush with edible nuts called **hazelnuts.** ■ **Hazel** eyes are greenish-brown.

H-bomb See **hydrogen bomb.**

he You use **he** to talk about a man or boy you have already mentioned. You can also use **he** to talk about a male animal. *He was known to all as Eddie.* ■ Writers sometimes use **he** to refer to a person without saying whether that person is a man or a woman. *A doctor who prescribed drugs only because he was paid by the drug company would deserve to be struck off.*

head (**heading, headed; header**) Your **head** is the part of your body above your neck. ■ If something costs a certain amount **per head** or a **head,** it costs that amount for each person. ■ If you are playing football and you **head** the ball, you hit it with your head. This action is called a **header.** ■ If you have a **head start** on someone, you have an advantage over them in a competition. ■ If you **give** someone **their head,** you let them do what they want to do. ■ If two people or groups go **head-to-head,** they compete fiercely for something. ■ If you toss a coin and it comes down **heads,** the side uppermost has a person's head on it. ■ You can use **head** to refer to your mind or your mental abilities. *I do not have the figures in my head.* ■ If someone **keeps their head,** they do not panic. ■ The **head** of an organization is the person in charge. You can say someone **heads** an organization. ■ The **head** of something is the top, start, or most important part of it. *...the mast-head... He increased his lead at the head of the table.* ■ If you **head** in a particular direction, you go in that direction. ■ If you are **heading for** something, it is going to happen to you. *We are heading for trouble.* ■ If a situation **comes to a head,** it reaches a state where something has to be done urgently. ■ If you **head off** something unpleasant, you stop it happening. ■ **Headed** notepaper has the name and address of the sender printed at the top. ■ See also **heading.**

headache If you have a **headache,** you have a pain in your head. ■ If you say something is a **headache,** you mean it causes you difficulty.

headband A **headband** is a narrow strip of material worn round a person's head.

headboard The **headboard** of a bed is an upright board fixed at the end where you lay your head.

head boy (head girl) The **head boy** or **head girl** of a school is the leader of the prefects.

headdress (*or* **head-dress**) **(headdresses)** A **headdress** is something worn on a person's head for decoration.

header See **head.**

headgear You can call anything worn on a person's head their **headgear.**

head girl See **head boy.**

head-hunt (head-hunter) If a person is **head-hunted** by a company, he or she is offered an incentive to leave their present job and work for that company. ■ Originally, **head-hunting** meant cutting off the heads of dead enemies and preserving them as trophies.

heading A **heading** is a piece of writing, written or printed at the top of a page.

headlamp A **headlamp** is the same as a headlight.

headland A **headland** is a narrow piece of land sticking out into the sea.

headlight A car's **headlights** are the bright lights at the front.

headline A **headline** is the title of a newspaper story, printed in large letters at the top. You can say a story is **headlined** in a particular way. ■ The **headlines** are the main points of the news given on the TV or radio. ■ If a person **hits the headlines,** they attract a lot of media attention because of something they have done.

headlong If you rush **headlong** into something, you do it without stopping to think about the consequences. ■ If you move **headlong** in a particular direction, you move there very quickly.

headman (headmen) A **headman** is a chief or tribal leader in a village.

headmaster (headmistress) A **headmaster** or **headmistress** is a person who is the head teacher of a school.

head office The **head office** of a company is its main office.

head of state (heads of state) The **head of state** is the leader of a country, for example its president or queen.

head-on A **head-on** conflict is strong and direct, without any compromise. ■ If two vehicles hit each other **head-on,** their front parts collide.

headphones are small speakers connected by a headband and worn over someone's ears, so they can listen to a radio, record player, or tape recorder without other people hearing.

headquarters (headquartered) The **headquarters** of an organization is the main centre where it is run from. You can say an organization is **headquartered** in a certain place. 'Headquarters' is often shortened to 'HQ'.

headrest A **headrest** is a support for a person's head on the back of a seat.

headroom is the amount of space below a ceiling, arch, or bridge.

headset A **headset** is a pair of headphones, often with a microphone attached. Virtual reality **headsets** are helmets which include earphones and a video screen.

headship A **headship** is the position of being the head of a school, college, or department.

headstand If you do a **headstand,** you balance upside down on your head and hands with your legs up in the air.

headstone A **headstone** is a large stone at one end of a grave, showing the name of the dead person.

headstrong If you say someone is **headstrong,** you mean they are very determined to do what they want.

head teacher A **head teacher** is the teacher in charge of a school.

headway If you **make headway,** you make progress towards achieving something.

headwind A **headwind** is a wind which blows against the direction you are moving in.

heady (headier, headiest) A **heady** atmosphere or experience strongly affects people's feelings. *...the heady days of the Swinging Sixties.*

heal (healing, healed; healer) When an injury **heals,** the injured part becomes healthy again. ■ You can talk about **healing** wounds or a rift when a situation which has been damaged is restored to its former state. *...a desperate bid to heal the rift in the Tory Party.*

health Your **health** is the condition of your body. ■ **Health** or **good health** is being fit and well. **Ill health** is being ill. ■ The **health** of an organization or system is how well it is working.

health care is the services provided, either by the NHS or private health schemes, to advise people about their health or to treat them when they are ill.

health centre A **health centre** is a building where a group of GPs and other NHS staff provide health treatment and advice for the local community.

health food — **Health foods** are natural foods without artificial ingredients.

Health Service The **Health Service** is the same as the NHS.

health visitor A **health visitor** is a trained nurse employed to visit people in their homes and give help and advice.

healthy (healthier, healthiest; healthily) A **healthy** person is not suffering from any illness. ■ **Healthy** things are good for you and likely to make you fit and strong. ■ You say someone has **healthy** skin or a **healthy** appetite when these things show they are fit and well. ■ A **healthy** organization or system is working well. ■ A **healthy** amount of something is a large amount that shows success. *...healthy profits.* ■ If you have a **healthy** attitude to something, you show good sense.

heap (heaping, heaped) A **heap** of things is a pile of them lying one on top of the other, especially an untidy pile. When someone makes a pile like this, you say they **heap** things together or **heap** them **up.** ■ If you **heap** praise or criticism on someone, you praise or criticize them a lot.

hear (hearing, heard) When you **hear** a sound, you become aware of it through your ears. ■ If you **hear** something like a piece of music, you listen to it. ■ If you **hear** some information, you are told about it. ■ If you **hear** from someone, you receive a letter or phone call from them. ■ When a court or judge **hears** a case or **hears** evidence, they listen to it.

hearing is one of the five senses. It makes it possible for you to be aware of sounds. ■ If someone is **hard of hearing,** they cannot hear well, but are not completely deaf. ■ A **hearing** is an official meeting held to collect facts about an incident or problem. ■ If someone gives you a **hearing,** they listen to your point of view.

hearing aid A **hearing aid** is a device which people with hearing difficulties wear in their ear to enable them to hear better.

hearsay is information which you have been told by someone else, but which you do not personally know to be true.

hearse A **hearse** is a funeral car used to carry a coffin.

heart Your **heart** is the organ which pumps blood around your body. ■ People sometimes talk about their **heart** when they mean their feelings. *I cannot find it in my heart to think harshly of her. ...a man who speaks from the heart.* ■ If you believe something **in your heart of hearts,** you know it is true though you may be reluctant to admit it. ■ If you have **set your heart** on something, you will be very disappointed if you cannot have it. ■ If something **gives you heart** or you **take heart** from it, it makes you feel encouraged and optimistic. ■ If you **take** something **to heart,** you take it seriously and are deeply affected by it. ■ If you have someone's interests **at heart,** you are acting in a way which is intended to help them. ■ If you say someone is a particular kind of person **at heart,** you mean that is what they are really like, though they may give a different impression. ■ If you learn a piece of writing **by heart,** you memorize it so you can repeat it without looking at it. ■ The **heart** of a place is its centre. *...Magdalen Chapel, in the heart of Edinburgh's Old Town.* ■ The shape ♥ is called a **heart** and is often used as a symbol of love. ■ **Hearts** is one of the four suits in a pack of playing cards. All cards in this suit have the symbol ♥ on them.

heartache is very great sadness and emotional suffering.

heart attack If someone has a **heart attack,** their heart begins to beat very irregularly or comes to a complete stop.

heartbeat Your **heartbeat** is the regular movement of your heart as it pumps blood round your body. Each movement of the heart is called a **heartbeat.**

heartbreak (**heartbroken, heartbreaking**) **Heartbreak** is very great sadness or disappointment. If someone has this feeling, you say they are **heartbroken.** ■ If you say something is **heartbreaking,** you mean it is extremely sad and upsetting.

heartburn is a painful burning sensation in the chest, caused by indigestion.

hearten (**heartening, heartened**) If you are **heartened** by something, it makes you more cheerful and optimistic.

heart failure is a serious medical condition in which the heart fails to pump enough blood round the body.

heartfelt emotions are sincerely and deeply felt.

hearth (*pron: harth*) A **hearth** is the floor of a fireplace. People sometimes talk about the **hearth** when they mean the comforts of home. *...the strong pull of hearth and home.*

heartland People sometimes talk about the **heartland** of a particular activity or belief when they mean the area where it is most common or significant. *...Sao Paulo, the industrial heartland of Brazil. ...the Labour heartlands of Scotland.* ■ You can call the central area of a place its **heartland.** *The drive takes you into the heartland of Sicily.*

heartless (**heartlessly**) You say someone is **heartless** when they are cruel and show no pity.

heart-rending If something is **heart-rending,** it makes you feel great sadness and pity.

heartstrings If sights or sounds tug at your **heartstrings,** they make you feel very emotional.

heart-throb You can call a male actor or singer a **heart-throb** if women find him very attractive.

heart-to-heart If two friends have a **heart-to-heart,** they discuss their feelings and problems openly with each other.

heart-warming You can say a situation is **heartwarming** when it makes you feel happy because it involves good things happening to someone.

hearty (**heartier, heartiest; heartily**) You can describe people as **hearty** if they are loud, cheerful, and enthusiastic. ■ You use **heartily** to emphasize the way you feel about something. *People are heartily sick of teenage louts.* ■ A **hearty** meal is large and satisfying.

heat (**heating, heated; heatedly**) When you **heat** something or **heat** it **up,** you raise its temperature. ■ **Heat** is high temperature. *The rail line buckled in the heat.* ■ Your **heating** is the system and equipment you use for warming your house. See also **central heating.** ■ If you **turn up the heat** on someone, you try to make life difficult for them. ■ You use **heat** to talk about strong feelings, especially anger or excitement. *...getting carried away in the heat of the moment. ... The SFA spoke heatedly with the referee.* ■ A **heat** is an early round in a competition. See also **dead heat.**

heater A **heater** is a piece of equipment for warming a room or heating water.

heath A **heath** is an area of open land covered with rough grass or heather.

heathen Christians used to call people who were not Christians **heathens.**

heather is a low spreading plant with small purple, pink, or white flowers. It grows wild on hills and moorland.

heat-seeking missiles can detect sources of heat and are used to destroy fighter planes.

heat-stroke is an illness caused by the body getting very hot.

heatwave A **heatwave** is a fairly long period of unusually hot weather.

heave (**heaving, heaved**) If you **heave** something or give it a **heave,** you pull, push, or lift it using a lot of effort. ■ If someone throws something heavy, you can say they **heave** it. ■ If you say someone **heaves a sigh of relief,** you mean they are very relieved. ■ If someone **heaves,** they vomit or feel sick.

heaven is the place where God is believed to be and where the souls of the dead are believed to live in everlasting happiness. ■ When people talk about **the heavens,** they mean the sky. ■ If you say **the heavens opened,** you mean it started to rain heavily. ■ If you say an experience is **heaven,** you mean it is wonderful. ■ If you say you are **in heaven,** you mean you are extremely happy. ■ A **heaven-sent** opportunity is very welcome because it comes just at the right time.

heavenly If you say something is **heavenly,** you mean it is very pleasant and enjoyable. ■ **Heavenly** means connected with heaven. *Being a Christian is no longer about mere heavenly rewards.* ■ A **heavenly body** is a planet, star, moon, or other natural object in space.

heavenwards If you look **heavenwards** or **heavenward,** you look up towards the sky or heaven.

heavy (heavier, heaviest; heavily, heaviness; heavies) Heavy things weigh a lot. ■ **Heavy** work requires a lot of physical effort. ■ **Heavy** is used to say something is great in amount or intensity. *...heavy drinking. ...heavy traffic... She has a heavy schedule on this trip. ...heavily advertised brands.* ■ If something is **heavy,** it is thick and solid. *...a heavy black outline.* ■ **Heavy** weapons or machinery are large and powerful. ■ **Heavy** seas are rough with big waves. ■ If you say someone is **making heavy weather** of a task, you mean they are making it more difficult by not doing it efficiently. ■ Large strong men employed for protection are sometimes called **heavies.** ■ If someone is **heavily built,** their body is large, solid, and strong. ■ If someone moves **heavily,** they move as if their body weighs a lot. ■ If you do something with a **heavy heart,** you do it sadly. ■ If you say a piece of writing is **heavy,** you mean it is complicated and difficult to understand.

heavy-duty machines and equipment are strong and made to last.

heavy-handed actions are clumsy, forceful, and thoughtless.

heavy industry is industries such as steel-making and shipbuilding, where raw materials, the machinery, and the end product are all bulky and heavy.

heavy metal is a type of loud rock music with a fast beat.

heavyweight If you say someone is a **heavyweight,** you mean they have a lot of experience and influence in a particular field. *...jazz heavyweights.*

Hebrew was the language spoken by the Israelites. A modern form of Hebrew is now spoken in Israel.

heckle (heckling, heckled; heckler) When people **heckle** a public speaker, they interrupt them by shouting questions, comments, or rude remarks.

hectare (*pron:* **hek**-tair) Area is often expressed in **hectares.** A hectare is 10,000 square metres (about 2.5 acres). 'Hectares' is usually written 'ha'.

hectic activities are busy, rushed, and rather confused.

hector (hectoring, hectored) If someone **hectors** you, they talk to you in a bullying and critical way.

hedge (hedging, hedged) A **hedge** is a row of bushes along the edge of a garden, field, or road. ■ If you **hedge** against something unpleasant happening, you take action to protect yourself from its effects. *Gold is traditionally a hedge against inflation.* ■ If you **hedge your bets,** you minimize the chances of losing by backing more than one thing or person. ■ If you **hedge,** you avoid answering a question or committing yourself to something. ■ If an agreement is **hedged about** with conditions, the conditions make the agreement less effective.

hedgehog – **Hedgehogs** are small brown mammals with sharp spines on their backs.

hedgerow A **hedgerow** is a row of bushes, trees, and plants, usually growing around the edges of fields.

hedonism (hedonist, hedonistic) Hedonism is the belief that pleasure is the most important thing in life. A **hedonist** is someone who believes this, or acts as though they do. *...the hedonistic pleasures of partying until dawn.*

heed (heeding, heeded) If you **heed, take heed of,** or **pay heed to** what someone says, you do what they advise or suggest.

heedless If you are **heedless** of advice or of a situation, you ignore it.

heel A person's **heel** is the back part of their foot, below their ankle. ■ The **heel** of a sock or shoe is the part around the heel. ■ If one situation follows **on the heels** of another, it happens very soon after it. ■ If you **bring** someone **to heel** or if they **come to heel,** you bring them under your control. ■ If you **dig in your heels,** you refuse to be persuaded to do something. ■ See also **down-at-heel, well-heeled.**

hefty people or amounts of something are large. *...a hefty Labour majority.* ■ If someone gives you a **hefty** kick or shove, they kick or shove you with a lot of force.

hegemony (*pron:* hig-**em**-on-ee *or* hij-**em**-on-ee) If a country, organization, or group has **hegemony** over others within the same group or area, it is dominant or in control. *...the growth of German hegemony in Europe.*

Hegira (*pron:* **hej**-ira) was Mohammed's flight from Mecca to Medina in 622 AD. The Muslim calendar dates from this event.

heifer (*pron:* **hef**-fer) A **heifer** is a young cow which has not yet had a calf.

height The **height** of a person or thing is the measurement from their lowest part to their highest. ■ If something is at a particular **height,** it is that distance above something such as the ground or sea level. ■ If you say something is at a **height,** you mean it is a long way above the ground. *They fish by diving from a height.* ■ If something is at its **height,** it is at its most successful, powerful, or intense. *...at the height of the summer season.* ■ **Height** is used to talk about the greatest extreme of something. For example, the **height** of luxury, means the greatest luxury possible.

heighten (*pron:* **high**-ten) (**heightening, heightened**) If a feeling **heightens** or is **heightened,** it becomes stronger and more intense.

heinous (*pron:* **hee**-nuss *or* **hay**-nuss) A **heinous** crime is evil.

heir (*pron:* **air**) Someone's **heir** is the person who will inherit their money, property, or title when they die. ■ Someone's **heir apparent** is the person who is expected to take their place, for example as leader of a political party.

heiress (**heiresses**) An **heiress** is a woman who has inherited, or will inherit, property, money, or a title.

heirloom An **heirloom** is an object which has been handed down within the same family over several generations.

heist (*rhymes with 'sliced'*) A **heist** is a carefully planned robbery, often of large amounts of money.

held See **hold.**

helicopter A **helicopter** is an aircraft with overhead propellers which rotate horizontally. ■ A **helicopter gunship** is a military helicopter with large guns.

heliport A **heliport** is a place where helicopters land and take off.

helium (*pron:* **heel**-ee-um) is a colourless gas which is lighter than air.

helix (*pron:* **heel**-iks) (*plural:* **helixes** *or* **helices**) A **helix** is a spiral shape.

hell (**hellish**) **Hell** is the place where Christians believe the souls of wicked people go to be punished when they die. ■ If you describe something as **hell** or **hellish,** you mean it is very unpleasant. ...*hellish desert camps.* ■ Some people use **hell** to add emphasis to what they are saying. ...*a hell of a lot of money.* ■ If you do something **for the hell of it,** you do it for fun, or for no particular reason. ■ If you go for something **hell for leather,** you press ahead with it in a determined way. ■ If you are **hell-bent** on doing something, you are determined to do it, whatever the consequences.

Hellenic is used to describe things to do with Ancient Greece.

hello (*or* **hallo** *or* **hullo**) People say **'Hello'** to each other when they meet or start talking on the telephone.

helm The **helm** of a boat is the place where the tiller or wheel is. ■ You say someone is **at the helm** when they are in control or in a position of leadership.

helmet (**helmeted**) **Helmets** are hard protective hats. A **helmeted** person is wearing a helmet.

helmsman (**helmsmen**) The **helmsman** of a boat is the person steering it.

help If you **help** someone, you make things easier for them, for example by doing some of their work or giving them advice or money. You can also say you **help** someone **out** or give them **help.** When someone is in difficulties, you can talk about giving them a **helping hand.** ■ **Help** is assistance given to someone in danger or difficulty. ■ If something **helps** or is a **help,** it makes a situation easier to deal with. *Facilities like piped water would be a big help.* ■ If you **cannot help** the way you feel or behave, you cannot change or stop it. ■ If you **help**

yourself, you serve yourself with food or drink. ■ If someone **helps** themselves **to** something which does not belong to them, they steal it.

helper A **helper** is someone who helps another person or group with what they are doing.

helpful (**helpfully, helpfulness**) If someone is **helpful,** they help you by doing something for you or giving you advice, information, or support. ...*a system to encourage helpfulness to the public.* ■ If something is **helpful,** it makes a situation more pleasant or easier to deal with.

helping See **help.** ■ A **helping** of food is the amount you get in a single serving.

helpless (**helplessly; helplessness**) If you are **helpless,** you cannot do anything for yourself or cannot protect yourself.

helpline A **helpline** is a telephone line for contacting counsellors or specialists to get advice.

helter-skelter If something happens **helter-skelter,** it happens very quickly and is difficult to control. ■ A **helter-skelter** is a tower with a spiral-shaped slide around the outside for people to slide down on a mat for fun.

hem (**hemming, hemmed**) The **hem** of a piece of material is the part at the edge which is turned under and sewn down. ■ If you are **hemmed in,** you are surrounded and cannot move.

he-man (**he-men**) A **he-man** is a strong muscular man.

hematology See **haematology.**

hemisphere (**hemispherical**) A **hemisphere** is a shape like half a sphere. Something shaped like this is called **hemispherical.** The Earth is often considered as two hemispheres, usually the northern and southern hemispheres separated by the equator. ■ The two halves of the brain are called the left and right **hemispheres.**

hemline The **hemline** of a skirt or dress is the bottom edge.

hemlock is a poisonous plant with small white flowers and a spotted stem.

hemoglobin See **haemoglobin.**

hemophilia See **haemophilia.**

hemorrhage See **haemorrhage.**

hemorrhoids See **haemorrhoids.**

hemp is an Asian plant used for making rope and in the production of cannabis.

hen A **hen** is a female chicken. ■ A **hen** is a female bird of any species. ■ Women only social events are sometimes called **hen parties** or **hen nights.**

hence means for the reason just mentioned. *The United States is a much larger and hence more self-reliant economy.* ■ If something is going to happen a certain length of time **hence,** it will happen that length of time from now. *They are not talking about tomorrow, but about 400 years hence.*

henceforth or **henceforward** means from this time on. *Henceforth, all applicants will have to pass a test.*

henchman (**henchmen**) A powerful and unpleasant person's supporters are sometimes called their **henchmen.**

henna is a reddish-brown dye made from the leaves of a shrub, used for colouring hair or skin.

henpecked If you say a man is **henpecked,** you mean he is dominated and controlled by his wife.

hepatitis (*pron:* hepa-**tie**-tis) is a serious liver disease.

heptagon (**heptagonal**) A **heptagon** is a geometric shape with seven straight sides.

heptathlon The **heptathlon** is an athletics competition, usually for women, in which each competitor completes seven different events.

her You use **her** to talk about a girl or woman you have already mentioned. *I was at school with her.* ■ You use **her** when talking about something belonging to or connected with a girl or woman you have mentioned. *...her son.*

herald If something **heralds** something else or is a **herald** of it, it is a sign it has started to happen, or will happen soon. *These sales heralded a reawakening of interest in stained glass.* ■ If something new is **heralded** as a particular thing, people say it is that thing. *America's common market agreement has been heralded as a rival to the EU.* ■ In the past, a **herald** was a man who delivered and announced important news.

heraldic jewellery and flags have coats of arms on them.

heraldry is the study of coats of arms, and of the history of the families who have them.

herb (**herbal**) A **herb** is a plant used to flavour food, or as a medicine. **Herbal** teas and medicines are made using herbs.

herbaceous (*pron:* her-**bay**-shus) is commonly used to describe plants which die down in winter and reappear in spring. In botany, **herbaceous** is used to describe plants which are soft and fleshy rather than hard and woody.

herbalist A **herbalist** is a person who grows or sells medicinal herbs or makes herbal medicines.

herbicide A **herbicide** is a chemical used to destroy plants, especially weeds.

herbivore (**herbivorous**) A **herbivore** is an animal which only eats plants. You say an animal like this is **herbivorous** (*pron:* herb-**biv**-or-uss).

herculean (*pron:* her-kew-**lee**-an) A **herculean** task is on a very large scale and requires great effort and determination.

herd A **herd** of animals is a large group of them living and feeding together. ■ If you **herd** people or animals somewhere, you move them there as a group.

herdsman (**herdsmen**) A **herdsman** is a person who looks after a herd of animals.

here You use **here** to talk about the place where you are. *Will you be here tomorrow?* ■ You use **here** to say you have something with you. *I have here a very important message.* ■ **Here** is used to mean 'in this situation'. *The problem here is the price.* ■ **Here** is used to introduce a person or subject, especially on TV or radio. *Here's our South East Asia correspondent.* ■ **Here and there** is used to say something happens or exists in several places. *Here and there, banners left over from the festival sadly drooped.*

hereabouts If you say something is **hereabouts,** you mean it is not far away.

hereafter The **hereafter** is life after death. ■ **Hereafter** means 'from now on'.

hereby If you use **hereby** in a statement, you are indicating that by making the statement you are doing the thing mentioned. *I hereby challenge my opponent to a debate.*

hereditary (*pron:* hir-**red**-it-tree) A **hereditary** disease or characteristic is passed on in the genes from parent to child. ■ A **hereditary** title or position is passed on from parent to child.

heredity (*pron:* hir-**red**-it-ee) is the biological process by which characteristics are passed on in the genes from parent to child.

herein You use **herein** to draw attention to a feature or consequence of the thing you have just mentioned. *Most of the jobs available to welfare recipients pay minimum wage, and herein lies another big obstacle.* ■ **Herein** means 'in this place' or 'in this document'. *The statements and views expressed herein are those of the author.*

heresy (**heresies; heretic, heretical**) If a religious person commits **heresy,** they say something which goes against the accepted beliefs of their religion. A person like this is called a **heretic.** *They denounced the translation as heretical.* ■ You call what someone says **heresy** when it goes against generally accepted beliefs.

herewith is used in letters to say something is enclosed. *A schedule of the event is appended herewith.*

heritage A country's **heritage** is things from its past which are still valued, such as its buildings, monuments, and traditions. ■ Anything left over from an earlier time can be called a **heritage.** *The present legal system, a heritage of the Ceausescu regime, is badly suited to the task.*

hermaphrodite (*pron:* her-**maf**-roe-dite) A **hermaphrodite** is an animal, plant, or person that has both male and female reproductive organs.

hermetic (**hermetically**) If a container is **hermetic** or **hermetically sealed,** no air can get in or out. ■ If you say a place or culture is **hermetically sealed,** you mean no outside influences are allowed into it.

hermit In early Christian times, a **hermit** was a person who lived alone in an isolated place in order to pray and meditate.

hernia A **hernia** is a medical condition in which an inner organ pushes out through a weak point in the surrounding muscle.

hero (**heroes**) A **hero** is someone brave or good who is much admired. If you say a man is your **hero,** you mean he is the person you most admire. ■ The **hero** of a book, play, or film is its main male character.

heroic (**heroically; heroics**) You say a person is **heroic** when they show great courage or determination. ■ **Heroics** are brave actions.

heroin is a highly addictive drug which is made from morphine.

heroine The **heroine** of a book, play, or film is its main female character. ■ A **heroine** is a much-admired brave or good woman. If you say a woman is your **heroine,** you mean she is the person you most admire.

heroism (*pron:* **herr**-oh-izz-um) is courageous behaviour in a dangerous situation.

heron The **heron** is a large wading bird.

herpes (*pron:* **her**-peez) is the name given to several inflammatory skin diseases. When people talk about **herpes**, they usually mean **herpes simplex**, a disease that affects the lips, nostrils, and genitals.

herring (*plural:* **herring** *or* **herrings**) **Herring** are long silvery fish which swim in large shoals.

herringbone is a pattern in things like fabrics and brickwork; it consists of rows of V shapes.

hers You use **hers** to say something belongs to a girl or woman you have just mentioned. *She says her husband's belongings are now hers.*

herself You use **herself** to say something done by a woman or girl affects that same woman or girl. *She is financially able to support herself.* ■ You use **herself** to emphasize that your statement really does apply to the woman or girl you are talking about. *The Order of Merit is awarded by the Queen herself.*

hertz (*plural:* **hertz**) Frequency is sometimes expressed in **hertz**. A hertz is equal to one cycle per second. 'Hertz' is usually written 'Hz'.

hesitate (**hesitating, hesitated; hesitation; hesitant, hesitantly; hesitancy**) If you **hesitate**, you pause while you are doing something or just before you do it, because you are uncertain or worried. You say someone who pauses like this is **hesitant;** you also talk about their **hesitancy.** Each occasion when someone pauses is called a **hesitation.** ■ If someone does not **hesitate** to do something, they do it and are not at all worried or unsure about it.

hessian is a thick rough cloth, used for making sacks.

heterodox beliefs are different from the ones people usually have.

heterogeneous (*pron:* het-er-oh-**jean**-ee-us) You say something is **heterogeneous** when it consists of many different types of things or people. *...modern societies with heterogeneous populations.* See also **homogeneous.**

heterosexual (**heterosexuality**) A **heterosexual** is someone who is sexually attracted to people of the opposite sex, rather than their own sex. This kind of attraction is called **heterosexuality.** A **heterosexual** relationship is a sexual relationship between a man and a woman.

heuristic (*pron:* **hew**-rist-ik) methods of learning involve reasoning and experiments rather than rules or formulae.

hew If someone **hews** wood or stone, they chop or carve it roughly.

hexagon (**hexagonal**) A **hexagon** is a geometric shape with six straight sides.

heyday You can call the time when a person or thing was most successful or popular their **heyday.**

hey presto People say **hey presto** when they are talking about something producing an instant result, as if by magic.

hiatus (*pron:* hie-**ay**-tuss) (*usual plural:* **hiatuses**) A **hiatus** is a pause in which nothing happens. *There was a 24-hour hiatus before a message came back from Iran.*

hibernate (**hibernating, hibernated; hibernation**) Animals which **hibernate** spend the winter in a state like a deep sleep.

hibiscus (**hibiscuses**) The **hibiscus** is plant with large bell-shaped flowers and long stamens.

hiccup (*or* **hiccough**) (*both pron:* **hik**-kup) (**hiccupping, hiccupped**) A **hiccup** is a minor problem or difficulty. ■ If you **hiccup** or have **hiccups**, you keep making a 'hup' sound because of a spasm in your diaphragm.

hick If you call someone a **hick,** you think they seem stupid and naive because they come from the country. You can also call somewhere a **hick** place.

hickory is a North American tree.

hid See **hide.**

hidden See **hide.** ■ **Hidden** things are not easily noticed. ■ **Hidden** places are difficult to find. ■ If you say someone has a **hidden agenda,** you mean they are keeping some of their intentions secret. *...a hidden agenda to divide the unions.*

hide (**hiding, hid, have hidden**) If you **hide** something, you put it somewhere where it cannot be seen. ■ If you **hide,** you go somewhere where you cannot easily be seen or found. ■ If you **hide** what you feel or know, you keep it a secret. ■ A **hide** is a skin taken from the dead body of a large animal. ■ A **hide** is a place built to look like its surroundings, from which people watch animals or birds.

hide-and-seek is a children's game in which one child tries to find others who are hiding.

hideaway A **hideaway** is a place where you go to avoid other people.

hidebound You say people are **hidebound** when they are unwilling to change or to accept new ideas.

hideous (**hideously**) If you say something is **hideous,** you mean it is extremely unpleasant or ugly.

hideout A **hideout** is a hiding place for someone who is trying to avoid being caught by the police or by soldiers.

hiding If someone is **in hiding,** they have gone somewhere where they hope they cannot be found. ■ A **hiding place** is a place where people or things are hidden. ■ If a child is given a **hiding,** it is hit repeatedly as a punishment.

hierarchy (*pron:* **hire**-ark-ee) (**hierarchies; hierarchical, hierarchically**) A **hierarchy** is a system in which people have different ranks or positions depending on how important they are. A system like this is called **hierarchical.**

hieroglyphics (*pron:* hire-oh-**gliff**-iks) (*or* **hieroglyphs**) **Hieroglyphics** are symbols used in some writing systems, for example in ancient Egypt.

hi-fi A **hi-fi** is a set of stereo equipment on which you can play records, tapes, or CDs.

higgledy-piggledy If you say something is **higgledy-piggledy,** you mean it is untidy or disordered.

high is used to say something contains or involves a lot of something. *...high-tar tobacco... Yachting is a high risk sport.* ■ If something is **high,** it is a long way up or extends a long way upwards. *I looked down from the high window. ...high mountains.* ■ **High** is used to talk about measurements from bottom to top. *...only nine inches high.* ■ **High** is used to talk about the top of a scale. *...high pressure.* A **high** is the greatest level something reaches. *Wall Street rose to an all-time high.* ■ The **high point** of an occasion is the most exciting or enjoyable part. ■ If you have a **high** opinion of someone or something, you admire or respect them. *I am sure his teachers think highly of him.* ■ If someone is **high** on drugs, they are under their influence. ■ If someone enjoys the **high life,** they have an exciting and luxurious lifestyle. ■ **High summer** is the middle of summer. ■ **High season** is the time of year when holiday resorts and attractions are most busy. ■ **High noon** is used to refer to a time when a conflict or crisis will come to a head and a dispute will be settled.

highbrow is used to describe activities which are thought to be serious and intellectual.

high chair A **high chair** is a chair for very young children. It has extra long legs and a tray at the front.

High Church The **High Church** group within the Church of England is concerned to keep the authority of bishops and the ceremony and ritual which come from the Catholic tradition.

high command The **high command** of a country's armed forces is its commander-in-chief and senior officers.

High Commissioner (**High Commission**) Members of the Commonwealth have **High Commissioners** in each other's countries instead of ambassadors. The building where a High Commissioner and his or her staff work is called a **High Commission.**

High Court The **High Court** is a law court which deals mainly with important civil cases.

higher A **higher** plant or animal is one with a complex biological form. ■ A **higher** exam or qualification is of an advanced standard or level. *...the Higher National Certificate.* ■ In Scotland, **highers** are the advanced level of the Certificate of Education. They are taken at 17 or 18.

higher education is education involving degree courses and other courses of a more advanced standard than 'A' levels or highers.

high explosive is an extremely powerful explosive substance such as TNT.

high-flier See **high-flying.**

high-flown language is unnecessarily grand or literary.

high-flying (**high-flyer** *or* **high-flier**) **High-flying** people or **high-flyers** are very talented, and are likely to succeed in their careers.

high-handed (**high-handedness**) A **high-handed** person uses their authority in an unnecessarily forceful way without considering other people's ideas or feelings.

high heels (**high-heeled**) **High heels** or **high-heeled** shoes are women's shoes with high narrow heels.

high jinks See **jink.**

high jump The **high jump** is an athletics event which involves jumping over a raised bar.

highlands (**highland; Highlander**) **Highlands** are mountainous areas. **Highland** is used to talk about people and things connected with these areas. *...the central highland city of Huambo.* ■ A **Highlander** is someone who comes from the Highlands of Scotland.

highlight If you **highlight** a point, you draw attention to it. ■ The **highlight** of an occasion is the most interesting or exciting part of it. ■ **Highlights** are light-coloured streaks in someone's hair.

highly is used in front of some words to mean 'very'. *He was highly critical of the referee.* ■ If something or someone is **highly** praised, they receive a lot of praise.

highly-strung people or animals are nervous and easily upset.

high-minded people have strong moral principles.

Highness (**Highnesses**) Expressions such as 'Your Highness' and 'His Highness' are used when talking to or about a royal person other than a king or queen.

high-pitched A **high-pitched** sound is high and shrill.

high-powered A **high-powered** person has a career in which they are powerful and successful. You can also say their job is **high-powered.** ■ A **high-powered** machine or other piece of equipment is powerful.

high priest (**high priestess**) If you call someone the **high priest** or **high priestess** of something, you mean they are recognized as being the person who knows most about it.

high-rise buildings are many storeys high.

high school In Britain, some schools for students aged 11 to 18 have **High School** as part of their name. ■ In the US, a **high school** is a school for students aged 15 to 18.

high-sounding statements seem very grand and important but do not actually mean very much.

high-spirited people are very lively.

high street shops and banks are the branches of major companies in main shopping areas.

high tea is a meal eaten in the early evening, often with tea to drink.

high technology equipment uses advanced electronics and computers or is developed using such techniques. 'High technology' is often shortened to 'high-tech' or 'hi-tech'.

high tide is the time when the sea is at its highest level on the coast.

high treason See **treason.**

high water — **High water** is the same as high tide. A **high-water mark** is the level reached by the sea at high tide. ■ The **high-water mark** of something is the point at which it is most successful, after which there is a decline.

highway In the US, a **highway** is a main road.

Highway Code The **Highway Code** is an official booklet containing the rules relating to driving and public safety on the roads.

highwayman (**highwaymen**) A **highwayman** was a robber, usually on horseback, who held up and robbed travellers.

hijack (**hijacker**) If someone **hijacks** a plane or other vehicle, they take control of it by force. This is called a **hijack** or **hijacking.** A person who hijacks a plane or vehicle is called a **hijacker.**

hike (**hiking, hiked; hiker**) A **hike** in prices or interest rates is a large increase. If things like these are **hiked,** they are increased. ■ A **hike** is a long walk in the countryside for pleasure. If you **hike** or go **hiking,** you go for a walk of this kind. People who do this are called **hikers.**

hilarious (**hilariously**) If something is **hilarious,** it is extremely funny.

hilarity If something causes **hilarity,** it causes a lot of amusement and laughter.

hill (**hilly**) A **hill** is a rounded area of land higher than its surroundings. A **hilly** area has many hills.

hillbilly (**hillbillies**) In the US, a **hillbilly** is someone from a remote mountain area who is thought by townspeople to be uneducated and stupid.

hillock A **hillock** is a small hill.

hilly See **hill.**

hilt If you support someone **to the hilt,** you give them all the support you can. ■ The **hilt** of a sword is its handle.

him You use **him** to talk about a boy or man you have already mentioned. *No one could accuse him of indifference.*

himself You use **himself** (a) to say something done by a man or boy affects that same man or boy. *He cut himself shaving.* (b) to emphasize that your statement really does apply to the man or boy you are talking about. *The President himself would be there.*

hind An animal's **hind** legs are its back ones. ■ A **hind** is a female deer.

hinder (**hindering, hindered**) If something **hinders** you, it makes it difficult for you to do what you are trying to do. ■ If people **hinder** something, they get in the way and delay it.

hindquarters An animal's **hindquarters** are its back parts and two back legs.

hindrance A **hindrance** is a person or thing that makes it more difficult for you to do something. ■ If you do something **without hindrance,** you do it without interference.

hindsight If you say with **hindsight** you would have acted differently, you mean you would not have acted the way you did if you had known what would happen.

Hinduism (**Hindu**) Hinduism is an Indian religion, which has many gods and teaches that people have another life on earth after they die. **Hindu** means connected with this religion. *...Hindu temples.* Someone who practises Hinduism is called a **Hindu.**

hinge (**hinging, hinged**) If something **hinges on** something else, it depends on it. ■ A **hinge** is a device for joining things like doors and windows to their frames while allowing them to be opened and closed.

hint If you **hint** something or give a **hint,** you indicate your attitude or reveal information in an indirect way. If you **take a hint,** you act on something which has been communicated to you indirectly. ■ If something **hints** that something may happen, it suggests it may happen. ■ A **hint** is a helpful piece of advice. ■ A **hint** of something is a very small amount of it.

hinterland The **hinterland** of a coast is the inland area close to it. ■ You can describe any remote or underdeveloped area as a **hinterland.**

hip A person's **hips** are the sides of their body between their waist and the tops of their legs. ■ If you say someone or something is **hip,** you mean they are very modern and fashionable. ■ If you say someone **shoots from the hip,** you mean they make quick replies or decisions without careful thought.

hip flask A **hip flask** is a small metal bottle for spirits.

hip-hop is a form of black popular culture which includes rap music and graffiti art.

hippie See **hippy.**

hippo (**hippos**) A **hippo** is a hippopotamus.

Hippocratic oath The **Hippocratic oath** is a solemn promise made by new doctors to try to save life and uphold the standards of their profession.

hippopotamus (**hippopotamuses**) The **hippopotamus** is a large African animal with short legs and thick wrinkled skin which lives near rivers.

hippy (*or* **hippie**) (**hippies**) In the 1960s and 1970s, **hippies** were people who rejected conventional society and tried to live a life based on peace and love. Young people today with similar attitudes are sometimes called **hippies.**

hire (**hiring, hired**) If you **hire** a vehicle or piece of equipment, you pay to use it for a time. When an owner makes something available for use like this in return for money, you say they **hire** it **out.** Hiring things out can be called, for example, **car hire** or **plant hire.** If something is **for hire,** you can hire it. ■ If you **hire** a person, you employ them to do a job.

hireling A **hireling** is someone who is hired to do something, especially someone who does not care what they do as long as they are paid.

hire purchase is a way of buying something by making small regular payments rather than paying the full cost straight away. 'Hire purchase' is often shortened to 'HP'.

hirsute (*pron:* **her**-suit) men are very hairy.

his means belonging to or connected with the boy or man you have just mentioned. *David Lodge will be there to answer questions about his work.* ■ You use **His** when you are talking formally about a royal or titled man. *...His Royal Highness Prince Edward.*

Hispanic people come from Spain or a Spanish-speaking country.

hiss (**hisses, hissing, hissed**) If something **hisses,** it makes a long 'sss' sound. The sound is called a **hiss.** ■ If a crowd **hisses,** they make long 'sss' sounds to show disapproval. ■ If you **hiss** something, you say it in a strong whisper.

histamine is a substance produced by the body and released during allergic reactions, causing irritation.

historian See **history**.

historic An **historic** occasion is one which will continue to be regarded as important for a very long time. ■ **Historic** places are ones where important things happened in the past.

historical (**historically**) **Historical** people, things, or events are known to have existed or taken place in the past. ...*famous historical figures.* ■ If the feelings shared by a group of people are **historical,** they have existed for a very long time. ■ You say **historically** when you are making a statement about a long period of history, rather than just recent times. *Historically, most women have been working women.* ■ **Historical** means to do with the study of history. ...*the Royal Historical Society.* ■ **Historical** places are associated with important past events. ■ **Historical** novels are set in the past.

history (**histories; historian**) **History** is the study of the past. A **history** is an account of things which happened in the past over a period of time. Someone who studies and writes about the past is called a **historian.** ■ If you say someone or something will **go down in history,** you mean they are so remarkable they will be remembered in the future. ■ If someone **makes history,** they do something remarkable which will be remembered for a long time, often because it is the first time it has been done. ■ If you say a person or place has a **history** of something, you mean things of that kind have taken place in their past. ...*a history of heart trouble.*

histrionic (**histrionics**) **Histrionic** behaviour is dramatic and over-emotional. Behaviour like this can be called **histrionics.** ■ **Histrionic** is used to talk about a person's ability and achievements as an actor. ...*her histrionic talents.*

hit (**hitting, hit**) If places and businesses are **hit** by things like bad weather, strikes, or economic recession, they are badly affected by them. ■ If you **hit** someone, you strike them with your hand or with a weapon. You can also say a moving object **hits** a person or thing. If an object like a missile hits its target, this is called a **hit.** ■ If a moving vehicle **hits** something, it runs into it. ■ If you **hit out** at someone, you criticize them strongly. If they **hit back** at you, they respond by criticizing or attacking you. ■ If you **hit on** a solution to a problem, you suddenly think of it. ■ If something **hits** a high or low point on a scale, it reaches it. ■ A **hit** is a very successful record, play, or film. ■ If a website gets a lot of **hits,** many people visit it. ■ If two people **hit it off** when they meet, they immediately get on well together. ■ If something you do is **hit and miss,** it involves a lot of guesswork. ■ A **hit man** is a hired killer. ■ A **hit list** is (a) a list which terrorists have of people they intend to kill. (b) a list of people or things that someone means to take action against.

hit-and-run A **hit-and-run** car accident is one where the driver responsible does not stop. ■ In warfare, a **hit-and-run** attack is a surprise raid on an enemy position, after which the attackers quickly withdraw.

hitch (**hitches, hitching, hitched**) A **hitch** is a slight problem. ■ If you **hitch** a lift, you hitch-hike. ■ If you **hitch up** a trailer to a vehicle or **hitch** them together, you connect them so the vehicle can tow the trailer. ■ If you **hitch up** a piece of clothing, you pull it up to a higher level.

hitch-hike (*or* **hitchhike**) (**hitch-hiking, hitchhiker**) If you **hitch-hike,** you travel around by getting free lifts from passing vehicles.

hi-tech see **high technology.**

hither means towards the place where you are. ■ If something moves **hither and thither,** it moves in all directions.

hitherto If something has been happening **hitherto,** it has been happening up until now.

HIV is the virus which can cause AIDS. If someone is **HIV positive,** they have this virus. **HIV** stands for 'human immunodeficiency virus'.

hive (**hiving, hived**) A **hive** is the same as a beehive. ■ If you say a place is a **hive** of activity, you mean there is a lot of activity there. ■ If part of a business in **hived off,** it is separated from the rest by being sold or put under new ownership.

HM is short for 'Her Majesty's' or 'His Majesty's' in the names of organizations.

HMS is used in the names of ships in the Royal Navy. It stands for 'Her Majesty's Ship' or 'His Majesty's Ship'.

HNC An **HNC** is a qualification in technical and practical subjects. HNC stands for 'Higher National Certificate'.

HND An **HND** is a higher qualification in technical and practical subjects. It is equivalent to a university degree without honours. HND stands for 'Higher National Diploma'.

hoard (**hoarder**) If you **hoard** things, you store them, often secretly. A **hoard** is a collection of things saved and stored like this. You call someone who hoards things a **hoarder.**

hoarding A **hoarding** is a large advertising board, usually at the side of a road.

hoarse (**hoarsely**) If you are **hoarse,** your voice is rough and harsh.

hoary is used to describe things like jokes which are old and familiar.

hoax (**hoaxes; hoaxer**) A **hoax** is an attempt to deceive people, as a joke. The person responsible is called a **hoaxer.**

hob A **hob** is the part of a cooker with gas or electric cooking rings.

hobble (**hobbling, hobbled**) If you **hobble,** you walk awkwardly, because you are injured or in pain.

hobby (**hobbies**) A **hobby** is something you enjoy doing in your spare time.

hobby-horse You can call a topic someone's **hobby-horse** when they have strong feelings on it and like talking about it. ■ A **hobby-horse** is a toy consisting of a horse's head on a stick, which a child can pretend to ride.

hobnob (**hobnobbing, hobnobbed**) If someone spends time with rich or famous people, you can say they are **hobnobbing** with them.

hobo (**hobos** or **hoboes**) In the US, a **hobo** is someone who has no home or work and often travels from town to town.

Hobson's choice You describe a situation as **Hobson's choice** when there appear to be alternatives but really there is only one thing you can do.

hock If you are **in hock** to a bank or other lender, you owe them money. ■ An animal's **hock** is the angled joint in its back leg. ■ **Hock** is a type of white wine from the Rhineland.

hockey is a game in which two teams of 11 players try to score goals by hitting a ball with long curved sticks.

hocus-pocus If you say something is **hocus pocus**, you mean it is intended to seem mysterious or important, but is really a load of nonsense.

hod A **hod** is a V-shaped container on a stick used to carry bricks on a building site.

hodge-podge You can call a confused mixture of things a **hodge-podge.**

hoe (**hoeing, hoed**) A **hoe** is a long-handled gardening tool, used to remove small weeds and break up the soil. When you use a hoe, you say you are **hoeing.**

hog (**hogging, hogged**) If you **hog** something, you take more than your fair share, or keep it for too long. ■ If you **go the whole hog**, you do something thoroughly or completely. ■ In the US, a **hog** is a pig. ■ In the UK, a **hog** is a castrated male pig.

Hogmanay is New Year's Eve in Scotland.

hogwash If you say an idea is **hogwash**, you mean it is absolute nonsense.

hoi polloi (pron: hoy pol-**loy**) Ordinary people are sometimes called **hoi polloi.** *Wimbledon is no longer glamorous. You get the hoi polloi there now.*

hoist If you **hoist** something into position, you lift or pull it up. A machine for lifting heavy things is called a **hoist.** ■ **hoist with their own petard:** see **petard.**

hokum If you call something **hokum**, you mean it is nonsense. *The book is enjoyable hokum.*

hold (**holding, held**) When you **hold** something, you carry, support, or grasp it. If you **hold onto** something, you grasp it tightly. ■ If you **hold on to** something you have, you keep it in your possession. ■ If something **holds** an object, the object is in it or on it. ■ If something is **held** in a certain position or situation, it is kept in that position or situation. ■ If a container **holds** a particular amount of something, it can or does contain that amount. ■ If you have a **hold over** someone, you have control over them. ■ If you **hold** something, you have it or own it. ■ If someone **holds** something like a meeting, they organize it and it takes place. ■ If you **hold** something to be true, you believe and state that it is true. *The Supreme Court held that Congress could insist on the inspection of steamships... If anything happens to the hostages we hold you responsible.* ■ If an idea or belief **holds good**, it remains useful or true despite changing circumstances. ■ If you **hold off** from doing something, you delay doing it. ■ If you put something **on hold**, you stop it temporarily. ■ If you **hold back**, you do not do something you had planned to do. ■ If

something **holds** you **up,** it delays you. A **hold-up** is a delay. ■ A **hold-up** is an armed robbery. If someone **holds up** something like a shop, they rob it at gunpoint. ■ If people are **held back,** they are physically prevented from getting somewhere. ■ If you **hold off** a challenge, you manage to prevent someone beating you. ■ If you **hold your own,** you do something as well as other people around you. ■ If someone **holds forth** on something, they speak at length about it. ■ When something **takes hold,** it starts to have an effect. ■ If you **get hold of** someone or something, you manage to get them or find them. ■ If you **hold down** a job, you manage to keep it. ■ If you **hold out,** you refuse to give in. If you **hold out for** something, you keep insisting you are given it. ■ The **hold** of a ship or plane is the part where the cargo is stored.

holdall A **holdall** is a large bag for carrying clothes and other belongings on a journey.

holder The **holder** of something is the person who has it or owns it. ■ A **holder** is a container which protects something or keeps it in position.

holding See **hold.** ■ A **holding** operation is a temporary measure designed to keep a difficult situation under control. ■ A **holding** is an area of farmland rented or owned by the person who farms it.

hold-up See **hold.**

hole (**holing, holed**) A **hole** is an opening or hollow area in something solid. ■ If something is **holed,** holes are made in it. ■ If someone is **holed up** somewhere, they are hiding there to avoid trouble. ■ If you call a place a **hole,** you mean it is very unpleasant. ■ If you **pick holes** in an argument or theory, you find small faults or weak points in it.

holiday A **holiday** is time spent enjoying yourself away from home, or a period of time when you are not working.

holiday camp A **holiday camp** is a place which provides accommodation and entertainment for large numbers of holidaymakers.

holidaymaker A **holidaymaker** is a person who is away from home on holiday.

holiness See **holy.**

holistic A **holistic** approach to something treats it as a whole. For example, holistic medicine treats the whole person, not just different parts of the body.

holler (**hollering, hollered**) If you **holler** something, you shout it loudly.

hollow (**hollowness**) If something is **hollow** or it has been **hollowed out,** it has a hole or space inside it. ■ A **hollow** is an area which is lower than the surrounding surface. ■ If you describe something as **hollow,** you mean it has no real value or significance. *...a hollow victory.* ■ A **hollow** sound is dull and echoing. ■ If someone is **hollow-eyed,** they look very tired.

holly is an evergreen shrub with spiky leaves and, in winter, red berries.

hollyhock — **Hollyhocks** are plants with tall spikes of colourful flowers.

Hollywood is used to talk about the American film industry in Los Angeles. *...Hollywood stars.*

holocaust The **Holocaust** was the mass murder of Jews by the Nazis. ■ Any loss of life on a huge scale can be called a **holocaust**. ...*the nuclear holocaust.*

hologram A **hologram** is a three-dimensional photographic image created by lasers.

hols Some people call their holidays their **hols.**

holster A **holster** is a holder for a gun, worn at the waist or under the arm.

holy (**holier, holiest; holiness**) A **holy** place or thing has special significance for the followers of a particular religion. ■ A **holy** person is religious and leads a good and pure life. ■ People sometimes call a religious leader like the Pope or the Dalai Lama **His Holiness.**

Holy Father Roman Catholics often call the Pope the **Holy Father.**

Holy Ghost The **Holy Ghost** is the same as the Holy Spirit.

Holy Grail In medieval legend, the **Holy Grail** was the cup used by Jesus at the Last Supper. ■ You can call the solution to a problem a **holy grail,** especially when it is difficult to find.

Holy Spirit In Christianity, the **Holy Spirit** is the third aspect of God, the other two being God the Father and God the Son.

Holy Week is the week before Easter.

homage (*pron:* **hom**-ij) If you pay **homage** to someone, you show your respect or admiration for them.

home (**homing, homed**) Your **home** is the place where you live or come from. Your **home** town is the town you come from. ■ If you feel **at home** somewhere or with a subject, you feel comfortable because it is familiar. ■ If you call a place the **home** of something, you mean that is where it started or where most of it comes from. ■ A **home** is a place where people or animals who cannot care for themselves are looked after. ...*a children's home.* ■ If something **homes in** on a target, it moves directly and quickly towards it. ■ If you drive **home** a message, you emphasize it. ■ If something is brought **home** to you, you are made to realize it. ■ **Home truths** are unpleasant facts about yourself revealed to you by someone else.

homecoming Someone's **homecoming** is their return to their home or country after they have been away a long time.

home economics is a school subject dealing with how to run a home, especially how to cook.

home-grown If something is **home-grown,** it develops in your own country or area. *They will have to rely more on their home-grown talent.* ■ **Home-grown** fruit and vegetables come from your own garden.

home help A **home help** is a person employed by a local authority to help elderly or disabled people look after themselves in their own homes.

homeland Your **homeland** is your native country. ■ In South Africa, **homelands** were regions allocated under the apartheid system to the black population.

homeless (**homelessness**) If someone is **homeless,** they have nowhere to live.

homely (**homeliness**) If something is **homely,** it is simple, ordinary, and comfortable. ■ When Americans say a person is **homely,** they mean they are not very attractive.

home-made If something is **home-made,** it has been made at someone's own home, shop, or restaurant, rather than in a factory.

Home Office The **Home Office** is the government department responsible for immigration, law and order, and broadcasting.

homeopathy (*or* **homoeopathy**) (*pron:* home-ee-**op**-ath-ee) (**homeopathic, homeopath**) **Homeopathy** is a way of treating illness using minute amounts of a substance which would in large doses cause symptoms similar to the illness. **Homeopathic** medicine (*pron:* home-ee-oh-**path**-ic) follows these principles. A person who practises homeopathy is called a **homeopath** (*pron:* home-ee-oh-path).

Home Secretary The **Home Secretary** is the government minister in charge of the Home Office.

homesick (**homesickness**) If you are **homesick,** you feel lonely and unhappy because you are away from home.

homespun advice and ideas are simple and unsophisticated.

homestead In America, a **homestead** is a family-run farmhouse and its surrounding land.

homeward (**homewards**) If you travel **homeward** or **homewards,** you travel towards your home.

homework is work given to pupils to do at home. ■ If you say someone has done their **homework,** you mean they have researched something thoroughly.

homicide (**homicidal**) In the US, the killing of one person by another is called **homicide.** Someone who is likely to commit murder can be described as **homicidal.**

homily (**homilies**) A **homily** is a speech telling someone how to behave.

homing pigeon – Homing pigeons are pigeons trained to return to a place.

hominid Man and his extinct ancestors are called **hominids.**

homoeopathy See **homeopathy.**

homogeneous (*pron:* hom(e)-oh-**jean**-ee-uss) (*or* **homogenous**) (*pron:* hom-**moj**-in-uss) (**homogeneity**) If you say something is **homogeneous** or talk about its **homogeneity** (*pron:* hom-moj-in-**ay**-ity), you mean it consists of things or people that are very similar to each other. See also **heterogeneous.**

homogenize (*or* **homogenise**) (*pron:* hom-**moj**-in-ize) (**homogenizing, homogenized**) If you say something is **homogenized,** you mean all its parts are very similar and there are no interesting differences. ■ **Homogenized** milk has been treated to distribute the cream evenly through the milk.

homogenous See **homogeneous.**

homophobia (**homophobic**) **Homophobia** is hatred or fear of homosexuals. People who have these feelings are described as **homophobic.**

homo sapiens (*pron:* **hoe**-moh **sap**-ee-enz) is the scientific name for human beings.

homosexual (**homosexuality**) If someone is **homosexual** or a **homosexual**, they are sexually attracted to people of their own sex. This kind of attraction is called **homosexuality**. **Homosexual** behaviour is sexual behaviour between people of the same sex.

Hon is short for 'honourable' or 'honorary' in people's titles.

hone (**honing, honed**) If you **hone** something, you carefully develop it until it is exactly right for a special purpose.

honest (**honestly; honesty**) You say people are **honest** or talk about their **honesty** when they do not try to deceive other people. ■ If someone acts as **honest broker,** they negotiate with both sides in a conflict to try and bring peace.

honey is an edible sweet sticky substance made by bees.

honeycomb A **honeycomb** is a wax structure made by bees, consisting of hundreds of cells for storing honey and eggs. ■ Structures with a lot of holes or spaces can be called **honeycombs.**

honeyed If you say someone is using **honeyed** words, you mean what they say is soothing and pleasant but they are probably trying to deceive you.

honeymoon A **honeymoon** is a holiday taken by a newly-married couple. ■ A **honeymoon** period is a time when someone is treated kindly because they are beginning something like a new job.

honey-pot You can call a place a **honey-pot** when it attracts a lot of people.

honeysuckle is a climbing plant with sweet-smelling cream or pink flowers.

honk If you **honk** a car horn, you make a short loud sound with it.

honky-tonk In the US, a **honky-tonk** is a cheap shabby bar or nightclub. ■ **Honky-tonk** is a style of ragtime piano-playing using a tinny-sounding piano called a **honky-tonk** piano.

honor See **honour.**

honorable See **honourable.**

honorary An **honorary** title is given as a mark of respect to someone who does not qualify for it in the normal way. *He was made an honorary citizen of Berlin.* ■ An **honorary** position is not paid. *He was honorary secretary of the Burma Star Association.*

honorific An **honorific** title is given to someone as a mark of respect.

honour (*Am:* **honor**) (**honouring, honoured**) Your **honour** is your good reputation and the respect people have for you. ■ If someone is **honoured,** they are given public praise or an award. An award like this is called an **honour.** ■ If something is held **in** someone's **honour,** it is arranged to show appreciation for them. ■ If someone says something is an **honour** or that they feel **honoured** by it, they mean they are proud it has happened to them. ■ If you **honour** a promise, you keep it. ■ **Honours** is a class of university degree which is higher than an ordinary or pass degree. 'Honours' is usually written 'Hons' after the name of a degree. ■ **Honour** is used in the titles of judges. *...His Honour Judge Patrick Medd, QC.*

honourable (*Am:* **honorable**) (**honourably**) If you call a person or action **honourable,** you mean they deserve respect and admiration. ■ If you get an **honourable mention** in a competition, you are praised but do not win a prize. ■ **Honourable** is used as a title in front of the names of government ministers, High Court judges, and some members of the nobility. In writing, it is usually shortened to 'Hon'.

honours list The **honours list** is a list of people who are to receive official honours from the Queen.

Hons See **honour.**

hood (**hooded**) A **hood** is a loose covering for the head, usually part of a coat. **Hooded** clothing has a hood. ■ A **hooded** person is wearing a hood which covers most of their face, to hide their identity. ■ Someone with **hooded** eyes has large eyelids which are partly closed. ■ In the US, the bonnet of a car is called the **hood.**

hoodlum A **hoodlum** is a gangster or a young violent criminal.

hoodwink If someone is **hoodwinked,** they are tricked.

hoof (*plural:* **hooves** or **hoofs**) The **hooves** of an animal like a horse are the hard horny parts of its feet. ■ If you do something **on the hoof,** you do it while you are doing something else. *You can grab a snack on the hoof.*

hoo-ha A **hoo-ha** is a fuss or commotion.

hook (**hooking, hooked**) A **hook** is a curved piece of metal or plastic for holding things or hanging things on. If you **hook** things together, you attach them to each other using hooks. If you **hook** a fish, you catch it using a hook. ■ If someone is **hooked** on drugs, they are addicted to them. You can also say people are **hooked** on other things. *He is hooked on railways.* ■ If someone gets **off the hook,** they manage to get out of a difficult situation. ■ If you **hook up** a computer or other electronic machine, you connect it to other similar machines or to a central power supply.

hooker In the US, a **hooker** is a prostitute.

hooligan (**hooliganism**) Noisy and destructive young people are sometimes called **hooligans.**

hoop A **hoop** is a large ring made of wood, metal, or plastic. ■ If someone is made to **jump through hoops,** they are made to go through a lot of unnecessary procedures.

hoopla (*or* **hoop-la**) Fuss and excitement is sometimes called **hoopla.** *The world's media has delivered all the usual hype and hoopla.*

Hooray Henry (**Hooray Henries**) Upper-class young men are sometimes called **Hooray Henries,** especially when they are loud and arrogant.

hoot (**hooting, hooted**) If you **hoot** a car horn, you make a short loud sound with it. ■ If someone **hoots** or lets out a **hoot,** they laugh in a noisy way. ■ You can say something very funny is a **hoot.** ■ If you say someone **could not give a hoot** about something, you mean they do not care about it at all.

hooter A **hooter** is a device which makes a loud noise as a warning or signal.

hoover (hoovering, hoovered) A **hoover** is a vacuum cleaner. If you **hoover** a carpet, you vacuum it in. 'Hoover' is a trademark.

hooves See **hoof.**

hop (hopping, hopped) If you **hop,** you jump along on one foot. ■ When birds or small animals **hop,** they make a series of small jumps. ■ If you **hop** somewhere, you get there quickly. *The president hopped from one airport rally to another.* ■ If you **catch** someone **on the hop,** you take them by surprise. ■ **Hops** are the dried flowers of the hop plant, used to flavour beer.

hope (hoping, hoped) If you **hope** something happens or is true, you want it to happen or be true. Your **hopes** are all the things you want to happen in the future. ■ **Hope** is a feeling that something good will happen in the future. ■ If you do something **in the hope** that something will happen, you do it because it might lead to that thing happening. *He is going to America in the hope of meeting Darlene.* ■ If you are **pinning your hopes** on something happening, you want it to happen, because you think it will solve a difficulty for you. ■ If something **raises your hopes,** it makes you more confident that something you are hoping for will happen. ■ If there is a **hope** of something you want happening, there is a chance it might happen. If you give up **hope** of something happening, you decide there is no chance it will happen.

hopeful If you are **hopeful** about something, you think there is a good chance things will turn out well. A **hopeful** sign is something which encourages you to think like this. ■ People who are hoping to achieve something are sometimes called **hopefuls.** *...Olympic medal hopefuls.*

hopefully People say **hopefully** when mentioning something they hope will happen. *Hopefully they'll be happy here.* ■ If you do something **hopefully,** you do it hoping that something you want will happen.

hopeless (hopelessly, hopelessness) If a situation is **hopeless,** there is no chance of things turning out the way you want. ■ If an attempt to achieve something is **hopeless,** there is no chance of it succeeding. ■ If people are **hopeless,** they see no hope of their situation improving. ■ If you say something is **hopeless,** you mean it is no good at all. ■ If you are **hopeless** at something, you are no good at it.

hopper A **hopper** is a large funnel-shaped device for temporarily storing things like grain or cement before directing them into containers below.

horde If you say there are **hordes** of people somewhere, you mean there are extremely large numbers of them.

horizon The **horizon** is the distant line where the sky seems to meet the land or sea. ■ If you say something is **on the horizon,** you mean it is likely to happen soon. ■ Your **horizons** are the limits of your ambitions. *His horizons had begun to broaden.*

horizontal (horizontally) If something is **horizontal,** it is flat and level with the ground, rather than at an angle to it.

hormone (hormonal) Hormones are chemicals produced by glands to stimulate certain organs in the body. *...normal hormonal levels.* ■ **hormone replacement therapy:** see **HRT.**

horn (-horned) Horns are the hard pointed growths on the heads of animals like cows and goats. The substance horns are made of is called **horn.** ■ If you **lock horns** with someone, you argue or compete with them. ■ A **horn** or **French horn** is a fairly large valved brass instrument played in orchestras and bands. In jazz, any brass instrument can be called a **horn.** ■ A car **horn** is a device which makes a loud noise as a signal or warning.

hornet – Hornets are large wasps with a painful sting. ■ If you say someone stirs up a **hornets' nest,** you mean they do something which causes controversy.

horny If someone feels **horny,** they feel like having sex.

horoscope Your **horoscope** is a prediction about what is supposedly going to happen to you, based on the position of the stars and planets when you were born.

horrendous (horrendously) Horrendous is used to describe things which (a) are extremely unpleasant and shocking. (b) people find worrying or alarming.

horrible (horribly) People use **horrible** to describe things which they find unpleasant, frightening, or disgusting. ■ **Horribly** is used to stress how bad something is. *The agreement could still go horribly wrong.*

horrid is used in the same way as 'horrible'. *They were horrid to each other. ...a horrid smell.*

horrific (horrifically) Horrific is used to describe things which are extremely unpleasant, especially things involving violence.

horrify (horrifies, horrifying, horrified; horrifyingly) If you are **horrified** by something, you are very shocked and upset by it. You say something is **horrifying** when it makes people feel like this.

horror is a strong feeling of alarm, dismay, and disgust. You can talk about the **horror** of something when it makes you feel like this. *...the sheer horror of this week's killings.* Incidents which give you this feeling can be called **horrors.** *...the horrors of the last war.* ■ If you have a **horror** of something, it frightens or disgusts you. ■ A **horror** film or story is meant to frighten people.

hors d'oeuvre (hors d'oeuvres) (both pron: ore **durv**) Hors d'oeuvres are a variety of foods served in small portions to be eaten before the main course of a meal.

horse – Horses are four-legged animals with manes, which can be ridden or used to pull a cart or plough. ■ In gymnastics, a **horse** is a piece of equipment with four legs or a solid base, for jumping over.

horseback If someone is **on horseback,** they are riding a horse.

horsebox (or horse-box) (horseboxes) A **horsebox** is a vehicle for transporting horses.

horse chestnut The **horse chestnut** is a large tree with white or pink flowers in spring and large nuts called conkers in the autumn. See also **chestnut.**

horse-drawn A **horse-drawn** vehicle is pulled by one or more horses.

horseflesh is used to talk about horses as a group.

horseman (horsewoman) A **horseman** is a man who rides a horse or who rides horses well.

horsemanship is the skill of riding horses well.

horseplay between friends is rough play or silly antics done for fun.

horsepower The power of an engine can be expressed in **horsepower.** One horsepower is about 746 watts. 'Horsepower' is sometimes written 'hp'.

horseracing is a sport in which horses ridden by jockeys run in races.

horseradish is the sharp-tasting root of the horseradish plant. It is often made into a sauce.

horseshoe A **horseshoe** is a U-shaped piece of metal fixed to a horse's hoof to strengthen it.

horse-trading is unofficial bargaining to try to reach an agreement about something. ...*the reported horse-trading between trade union leaders and the party leadership.*

horsey (or **horsy**) people are keen on horses and riding.

horticulture (horticultural, horticulturalist or **horticulturist)** **Horticulture** is growing flowers, fruit, or vegetables for a living. An expert on this is called a **horticulturalist** or **horticulturist. Horticultural** means connected with horticulture. ...*horticultural products.*

hose (hosing, hosed) A **hose** is a long flexible pipe made of rubber or plastic. ■ If you **hose** something, you wash or water it using a hose. ■ If you **hose** something **down,** you spray water on it through a hose, to clean it. ■ In the past, **hose** were men's skin-tight trousers worn with a close-fitting jacket called a doublet.

hosepipe A **hosepipe** is the same as a hose.

hosiery is used to refer to tights, stockings, and socks.

hospice A **hospice** is a special nursing home for the dying.

hospitable people or places are friendly and welcoming.

hospital A **hospital** is a place where patients are looked after by doctors and nurses.

hospitalise See **hospitalize.**

hospitality is (a) friendly welcoming behaviour. (b) food and drink provided by companies for their guests or clients.

hospitalize (or **hospitalise**) **(hospitalizing, hospitalized; hospitalization)** If someone is **hospitalized,** they are admitted to a hospital and kept there for treatment.

host The **host** at a dinner or other gathering is the person who invited the guests and looks after them while they are there. ■ The **host** of a TV or radio show introduces it and talks to the people taking part. ■ If a town or country **hosts** an event or is the **host,** it provides the facilities for it. ■ The **host** of a parasite is the animal or plant it feeds on. ■ A **host** of things or people is a lot of them. ■ The **Host** is the consecrated bread used in Holy Communion.

hostage A **hostage** is a person who is illegally held prisoner and threatened with injury or death unless certain demands are met by other people. You say people are **taken hostage** or **held hostage.** ■ If you are a **hostage** to something, your freedom to do things is limited by previous arrangements, or by things you cannot control. ...*but future growth will clearly be hostage to improvements in the country's physical condition.*

hostel A **hostel** is a building providing cheap temporary accommodation.

hostelry (hostelries) **Hostelry** is an old or jokey name for a pub.

hostess (hostesses) The **hostess** at a dinner or other gathering is the woman who invited the guests and looks after them while they are there. ■ A **hostess** at a night club is a woman paid by a man to be his companion for the evening. ■ See also **air hostess.**

hostile (hostility, hostilities) **Hostile** people are unfriendly and aggressive. You call their behaviour **hostility.** ■ If you are **hostile** towards a person or idea or feel **hostility** towards them, you oppose or mistrust them. ■ In a war, **hostile** is used to describe things to do with the enemy. ...*hostile forces.* ■ Fighting between countries is often called **hostilities.** ■ A **hostile** environment is one which humans find it difficult to live or work in. ...*hostile climatic conditions.* ■ A **hostile** takeover bid is one where a larger company tries to buy a smaller company against its wishes.

hot (hotter, hottest; hotly) If something is **hot,** it has a high temperature. If you are **hot,** you feel as if your body temperature is unpleasantly high. ■ **Hot** food contains chilli or pepper. ■ You describe news as **hot** when it is recent and exciting. ...*a hot political issue.* ■ In a competition, the **hot** favourite is the competitor people think is most likely to win. ■ **Hot** is used in expressions like **in hot pursuit** to say something is being done with great effort or speed. ■ If you say someone is **hot on** a subject, you mean they know a lot about it. ■ **Hotly** is used to say someone expresses strong disagreement with something. *The allegation has been hotly denied by the opposition.* ■ If you say someone is in the **hot seat,** you mean they are in a position of responsibility and have to make important decisions. ■ **hot potato:** see **potato.**

hot-air balloon See **balloon.**

hotbed If you call a place a **hotbed** of some illegal or undesirable activity, you mean a lot of it goes on there.

hot-blooded If you say someone is **hot-blooded,** you mean they are quick to express their emotions, especially anger or love.

hotchpotch (hotchpotches) A **hotchpotch** is a jumbled mixture of things.

hot dog A **hot dog** is a sausage served hot in a long roll.

hotel A **hotel** is a place which provides overnight accommodation and food in return for payment.

hotelier A **hotelier** is a person or company that owns or runs a hotel.

hot flush A **hot flush** is a sudden hot feeling in the skin, often experienced by women during the menopause.

hotfoot (hotfooting, hotfooted) If you **hotfoot** it somewhere, you go there in a hurry.

hot-headed (hothead) A **hot-headed** person acts hastily and angrily, without considering the consequences. You call someone like this a **hothead.**

hothouse A **hothouse** is a heated greenhouse. ■ You call a place a **hothouse** when there is intense activity there. ...*an academic hothouse.*

hot line A **hot line** is (a) a direct telephone link between governments. (b) a similar link for the public to contact emergency or information services.

hotplate A **hotplate** is a heated flat surface on a cooker.

hot-tempered people get angry very easily.

hot-water bottle A **hot-water bottle** is a rubber container which is filled with hot water and used to warm a bed.

hot-wire If thieves **hot-wire** a car, they start the engine without using the key.

hound A **hound** is a dog, especially one used in hunting or racing. ■ If someone **hounds** you, they keep criticizing you or troubling you.

hour (hourly) An **hour** is a period of sixty minutes. In writing, 'hour' can be shortened to 'hr'. ■ If something happens **hourly,** it happens every hour. If it happens **on the hour,** it happens every hour at exactly one o'clock, two o'clock, and so on. ■ A person's **hourly** pay is what they earn each hour they work. ■ **Hour** is used to talk about a particular time of day. *Even at that late hour, open-air cafes are busy.* ■ **Hour** is used to talk about a special time for someone. ...*their hour of triumph.* ■ **Hours** is used to talk about periods during which something regularly happens. ...*shorter opening hours.* ■ **eleventh hour:** see **eleven.** See also **rush hour.**

house (housing, housed) A **house** is a building where people live. ■ If people are **housed,** they are given a place to live. ■ If something is **housed** in a building, it is kept there. ■ A country's parliament is often divided into separate assemblies called **Houses.** ■ **House** appears in the names of some large buildings. ...*the Royal Opera House.* ■ **House** music is a type of electronic dance music with a fast repetitive beat. ■ **House** wine is an unnamed wine sold at a restaurant, at a lower price than the other wines on the wine list.

house arrest If someone is under **house arrest,** they are officially forbidden to leave their home.

houseboat A **houseboat** is a boat which people live in, moored on a river or canal.

housebound If someone is **housebound,** they are unable to leave their home, usually because they are ill or cannot walk far.

housebreaking (housebreaker) Housebreaking is the crime of entering another person's house to steal things.

household A **household** is all the people living in a house or flat. ■ **Household** means to do with the home. ...*household appliances.* ■ If someone or something is a **household name,** they are well-known.

householder A **householder** is the legal owner or tenant of a house.

house husband (or househusband) A **house husband** is a married man who does not have a paid job but instead looks after his home and children.

housekeeper Someone's **housekeeper** is a person employed to cook and to look after their house.

housekeeping is (a) the work involved in running a home. (b) money used to buy food and household necessities.

housemaid In a large house, a **housemaid** is a female servant who does the housework.

houseman (housemen) A **houseman** is a junior doctor in a hospital.

house martin – House martins are small black and white birds with slightly forked tails.

housemaster A **housemaster** is a teacher, usually in a boarding school, who is in charge of the pupils in one of the school's houses.

House of Commons The **House of Commons** is the more powerful of the two parts of Parliament. It is elected by the public.

House of Lords The **House of Lords** is the less powerful of the two parts of Parliament. Its members have the right to belong because they come from noble families or hold a special office.

House of Representatives The **House of Representatives** is one of the two parts of the US Congress, or a similar part of the system of government in some other countries.

house party A **house party** is a party held at a big house in the country, where the guests stay for a few days.

houseplant A **houseplant** is a plant which grows in a pot indoors.

Houses of Parliament The **Houses of Parliament** are the buildings in London where MPs and Lords work. See **House of Commons, House of Lords.**

house-to-house A **house-to-house** search or enquiry involves going to all the houses in an area one after another.

house-trained If a dog or cat is **house-trained,** it has been trained to urinate or defecate outside or in a particular place.

house-warming A **house-warming** is a party you give when you move into a new home.

housewife (housewives) A **housewife** is a married woman who does not have paid work but looks after her home and children.

housework is work like cleaning and cooking, done in the home.

housing is buildings for people to live in. ■ A **housing association** is an organization which owns low-cost homes for people to rent or buy.

hovel A **hovel** is a small hut or house which is dirty or in poor condition.

hover (hovering, hovered) When a bird, insect, or helicopter **hovers,** it stays in the same position in the air. ■ If someone **hovers** somewhere, they wait there, because they are not sure what to do. ■ If something **hovers** at a particular level on a scale, it stays roughly at that level.

hovercraft (*plural:* **hovercraft** *or* **hovercrafts**) A **hovercraft** is a vehicle which can travel across land or water on a cushion of air.

how is used to talk or ask about the way something is done. *He outlines how they operated in Poland at that time.* ■ **How** is used to talk or ask about the effects of something. *How did that affect you?* ■ **How** is used to talk or ask about the state of something, especially a person's health. *How is she this morning?* ■ **How** is used with words like 'long' or 'far' to talk or ask about a measurement or quantity. *They are unsure how far they want to go.* ■ **How** is used to talk or ask about the extent to which something has a quality, especially a good one. *How useful were these lessons?*

however You say **however** when you are adding a comment which contrasts with what has just been said. *Higher sales have not helped profits, however.* ■ You use **however** to say something makes no difference to the main point you are making. *No machine is infallible, however advanced the technology may be.*

howitzer A **howitzer** is a large gun which fires shells high up into the air, so they will drop on the target.

howl If an animal like a dog **howls,** it makes a loud wailing sound. This sound is called a **howl.** ■ If a person **howls** or lets out a **howl,** they make a loud noise, because they are angry or distressed. ■ If you **howl** with laughter, you laugh very loudly. ■ When the wind **howls,** it blows hard and makes a loud noise.

howler A **howler** is a stupid mistake.

HP See **hire purchase.**

hp See **horsepower.**

HQ See **headquarters.**

hr (**hrs**) See **hour.**

HRH is a short way of writing 'His Royal Highness' or 'Her Royal Highness'.

HRT is a treatment for symptoms of the menopause and for the brittleness of bones common in older women. HRT stands for 'hormone replacement therapy'.

hub The **hub** of an organization is the place where its most important activities are based. ■ The **hub** of a wheel is the part at the centre.

hubbub A **hubbub** is great noise or confusion.

hubcap A **hubcap** is a metal or plastic disc which covers and protects the hub of a car wheel.

hubris (*pron:* **hew**-briss) is arrogance which leads to someone's downfall.

huddle (**huddling, huddled**) If you **huddle** somewhere, you crouch or curl up, usually because you are cold or frightened. ■ A **huddle** of people or things is a small group of them close together.

hue A **hue** is a colour, or a shade of a colour. ■ When people talk about politicians of all **hues,** they mean politicians with views ranging from extreme left to extreme right. ■ If people make a **hue and cry** about something, they make a lot of fuss and protest.

huff (**huffy, huffily**) If someone **huffs and puffs** about something which goes against their wishes, they say a lot of angry things but do not actually do anything. ■ If someone is **huffy** or **in a huff,** they are bad-tempered because they have been annoyed or offended.

hug (**hugging, hugged**) If you **hug** someone or give them a **hug,** you put your arms round them and hold them close. ■ If a road **hugs** something, it stays close to it. ■ If clothes **hug** a person's body, they fit closely to it.

huge (**hugely**) If something is **huge,** it is extremely large.

hulk (**hulking**) You can call a large building or ship a **hulk,** especially when it is in a ruined state. ■ You can call a person a **hulk** or describe them as **hulking** when they are unusually large and heavy.

hull (**-hulled**) The **hull** of a boat is the main curved part which rests in the water. *...steel-hulled trawlers.* ■ If you **hull** strawberries, you pull out the central core and top leaves.

hullo See **hello.**

hum (**humming, hummed**) If you **hum,** you sing a tune with your lips closed. ■ If something like a motor **hums** or makes a **hum,** it makes a continuous low noise. ■ If a place **hums** with activity, there is a lot of it there.

human A **human** or **human being** is a man, woman, or child. **Human** means relating to humans. *...the human body. ...human rights.*

humane (**humanely**) If you treat people or animals in a **humane** way, you avoid causing them unnecessary suffering.

humanise See **humanize.**

humanism (**humanist, humanistic**) **Humanism** is the belief that people can achieve happiness and fulfilment without religion.

humanitarian (**humanitarianism**) **Humanitarian** is used to describe concern for people's sufferings, and attempts to help them. *...humanitarian aid.* Concern for people's sufferings is sometimes called **humanitarianism.**

humanities The **humanities** are subjects like literature and history, as opposed to scientific subjects.

humanity is people in general. *...research that could benefit humanity.* ■ Your **humanity** is the fact that you are a human, rather than an animal or a thing. ■ If someone behaves with **humanity,** they show kindness and compassion.

humanize (*or* **humanise**) (**humanizing, humanized**) If you **humanize** a system, you make it less harsh and unfeeling. *...programmes to humanize the prison system.*

humankind is the same as mankind.

humanly If you do what is **humanly possible,** you do everything which can possibly be done. ■ **Humanly** means relating to human beings.

humble (**humbly; humbling, humbled**) If someone behaves in a **humble** way, they behave as if they are unimportant, or they show they are ashamed of something they have done. ■ You say someone is **humbled** when they are humiliated or made to feel unimportant. ■ If someone has to eat **humble pie,** they have to behave humbly and admit they have made a mistake. ■ **Humble** can be used to describe people, places, or things which are ordinary or of low status. *He rose from humble salesman to editorial director. ...a humble country cottage.*

humbug If you accuse someone of **humbug**, you mean they say things which sound impressive but are actually dishonest or meaningless.

humdrum things are ordinary and dull.

humerus (*pron:* **hew**-mer-uss) The **humerus** is the bone which extends from the shoulder to the elbow.

humid If it is **humid**, the air is damp and warm.

humidifier A **humidifier** is a device for putting moisture into the air in a room.

humidity is the amount of moisture in the air.

humiliate (**humiliating, humiliated; humiliatingly, humiliation**) If you are **humiliated**, you are made to feel stupid or ashamed.

humility is humble behaviour.

hummingbird The **hummingbird** is a tiny brightly-coloured bird which lives mainly in Mexico and the southern US. It hovers when feeding, beating its wings very rapidly, making a humming sound.

humor See **humour**.

humorist A **humorist** is a writer or entertainer who makes jokes and tells funny stories.

humorless See **humourless**.

humour (*Am:* **humor**) (**humorous, humorously; humouring, humoured**) If you have a sense of **humour**, you can see the funny side of things. ■ If something is **humorous**, it is amusing and makes you want to laugh. You can talk about the **humour** of something like this. ■ If you are in a good **humour**, you are happy and cheerful. ■ If you **humour** someone, you try to please them to avoid trouble.

humourless (*Am:* **humorless**) If someone is **humourless**, they do not have a sense of humour.

hump A **hump** is a small rounded lump or mound. ■ If you **hump** a heavy object somewhere, you carry it there.

humus is decaying plant and animal matter in the soil.

hunch (**hunches**) A **hunch** is a feeling or suspicion about something, not based on facts or evidence. ■ If you are **hunched** over something, you are sitting close to it with your shoulders drawn forward and your back curved.

hunchback A **hunchback** is someone with a deformity of the spine which causes a hump on their back. 'Hunchback' is an offensive word.

hundred (**hundredth**) A **hundred** is the number 100.

hundredweight (*plural:* **hundredweight** or **hundredweights**) Weight is sometimes expressed in **hundredweights**. In Britain, a hundredweight is 112 pounds (about 50.8 kilograms); in the US, it is 100 pounds (about 45.4 kilograms). 'Hundredweights' is usually written 'cwt'.

hung See **hang**. ■ A **hung** parliament or council is one in which no party has a clear majority. ■ If someone is **hung over**, they feel ill or have a headache as a result of drinking a lot of alcohol the day before.

hunger (**hungering, hungered**) **Hunger** is a serious lack of food which can lead to illness or death. ■ **Hunger** is the feeling you get when you are hun-

gry. ■ If you **hunger** for something or have a **hunger** for it, you want it very much.

hunger strike (**hunger striker**) If someone goes on **hunger strike,** they refuse to eat as a protest.

hungry (**hungrier, hungriest; hungrily**) If you are **hungry,** your stomach feels empty and you want food. ■ If you are **hungry** for something, you want it very much.

hunk A **hunk** of something like bread or cheese is a large piece of it. ■ Some people call a big strong man a **hunk** when they find him attractive.

hunker (**hunkering, hunkered**) If you **hunker** down, you squat or crouch.

hunt (**hunting, hunter**) When people or animals **hunt,** they chase and kill wild animals for food or as a sport. A person who does this is called a **hunter.** ■ In Britain and Ireland, a **hunt** is a group of people who go fox-hunting regularly. A **hunter** is a fast strong horse used for hunting. ■ If you **hunt** for someone or something, you try to find them. You can call your search a **hunt.** People who search for things of a particular kind are called **hunters.** *...a souvenir hunter.* A **hunting ground** is a place where you are likely to find what you are looking for. ■ If the police **hunt** someone **down,** they try to find and catch them.

huntsman (**huntswoman**) A **huntsman** or **huntswoman** is a man or woman who hunts foxes as a member of a hunt.

hurdle (**hurdling, hurdled; hurdler**) The **hurdles** is an athletic event. Runners called **hurdlers** jump obstacles which are also called **hurdles.** ■ When someone who is running jumps over an obstacle, you can say they **hurdle** it. *Morris hurdled safety barriers to grab the distraught 24-year-old.* ■ A **hurdle** is a difficulty which has to be overcome to achieve something.

hurl If you **hurl** something somewhere, you throw it with a lot of force. ■ If people **hurl** abuse at someone, they shout it at them repeatedly. People can also **hurl** questions at someone.

hurling is an Irish game resembling hockey played between two teams of fifteen players.

hurly-burly The **hurly-burly** of a place is all the noise and activity there.

hurricane A **hurricane** is a fierce tropical storm.

hurry (**hurries, hurrying, hurried; hurriedly**) If you **hurry** somewhere or go somewhere **in a hurry,** you go there quickly because you do not have much time. You can also say you do something in a **hurry** *...the Pope's hurriedly arranged schedule.* ■ If you **hurry** to do something, you do it as soon as possible. ■ If you tell someone to **hurry up,** you are telling them to do something more quickly. ■ If you **hurry** something **up,** you make it happen more quickly.

hurt (**hurtful**) If someone **hurts** you, they do something which makes you feel pain. If you **hurt** yourself, you injure yourself. If you have been injured, you can say you are **hurt.** ■ If a part of your body **hurts,** you feel pain there. ■ You say someone **hurts** you when they upset you by being unkind. When this happens, you can say you feel **hurt;** you can also call a person's behaviour **hurtful.** ■ If organizations are **hurt** by something, they are badly affected by it.

hurtle (**hurtling, hurtled**) If something **hurtles** along, it moves very fast, in an uncontrolled way.

husband A woman's **husband** is the man she is married to. ■ If people **husband** resources, they manage them carefully to make them last a long time.

husbandry is (a) farming. (b) careful management of land or other resources.

hush (**hushes, hushing, hushed**) If there is a **hush**, everything is quiet. **Hushed** is used to describe a quiet sound or a quiet place. *...his hushed tones.* ■ If something is **hush-hush**, it is secret. ■ If some wrongdoing is **hushed up**, people in authority deliberately keep it secret.

husk The **husk** of a grain or seed is its outer covering.

husky (**huskies**) If someone's voice is **husky**, it sounds a little hoarse, often in an attractive way. ■ **Huskies** are strong furry dogs, used to pull sledges.

hustings When politicians are on the **hustings**, they are campaigning and making speeches before an election.

hustle (**hustling, hustled; hustler**) If someone is **hustled** into doing something, they are hurried into doing it. In the US, someone who gets people to do things by persuasive and perhaps dishonest talk is called a **hustler**. ■ If someone is **hustled** somewhere, they are made to move there quickly. ■ **Hustle and bustle** is a lot of noise and activity.

hut A **hut** is a small simple building.

hutch (**hutches**) A **hutch** is a box made from wire mesh and wood, for keeping pets like rabbits in.

hyacinth – **Hyacinths** are plants which grow from bulbs. They have a lot of small sweet-smelling flowers on a single stem.

hybrid A **hybrid** is an animal or plant bred from two different types of animal or plant. ■ Anything which is an unusual mixture of different things can be called a **hybrid.**

hybridize (*or* **hybridise**) (**hybridizing, hybridized**) If animals or plants of different kinds **hybridize**, they breed and produce a hybrid. *Wild boar readily hybridize with the domestic pig.*

hydra The **Hydra** was a mythical many-headed water serpent which grew two new heads for each one cut off. ■ You can call any persistent problem a **hydra.** *Killing the hydra of drug production is impossible.* ■ A **hydra** is a very small freshwater creature with a slender tubular body and tentacles round its mouth.

hydrangea (*pron:* high-**drain**-ja) **Hydrangeas** are garden shrubs which have large clusters of blue or pink flowers.

hydrant A **hydrant** is a pipe in a street which supplies water for use in emergencies.

hydraulic (**hydraulically**) A **hydraulic** machine or device is operated by oil, water, or some other fluid under pressure.

hydrocarbon A **hydrocarbon** is a chemical compound of hydrogen and carbon.

hydrochloric acid is a very strong, colourless acid.

hydro-electric (*or* **hydroelectric**) (**hydroelectricity**) **Hydro-electric** power or **hydroelectricity** is electrical power created from the energy of running water.

hydrofoil A **hydrofoil** is a boat which has fins like skis which raise the hull above the water when it is moving at speed.

hydrogen is a colourless gas that is the lightest and most common chemical element.

hydrogen bomb A **hydrogen bomb** or **H-bomb** is a nuclear bomb in which energy is released from hydrogen atoms.

hydrogen peroxide is a colourless liquid used as a bleach and an antiseptic.

hydrology (**hydrological**) **Hydrology** is the study of the earth's water resources and their management. **Hydrological** means to do with hydrology.

hydroponics is a way of growing plants without soil, either in water or in something like sand or gravel.

hydropower is the same as hydro-electric power.

hydrotherapy is a way of treating sick or injured people by getting them to swim and exercise in water.

hyena – **Hyenas** are dog-like animals in Africa and Asia that make a loud noise like high-pitched laughter.

hygiene (**hygienic, hygienically**) **Hygiene** is keeping yourself and your surroundings clean, especially to prevent the spread of disease. **Hygienic** things are clean and unlikely to cause disease.

hymen (*pron:* **high**-men) A woman's **hymen** is the piece of skin which partly covers her vagina. It is usually broken when she first has sex.

hymn A **hymn** is a Christian song sung in praise of God.

hymnal A **hymnal** is a book of hymns.

hype (**hyping, hyped**) **Hype** is the advertising of someone or something using intensive or extravagant methods of publicity. If someone or something is **hyped** or **hyped up**, they are promoted in this way. ■ You can say a person is **hyped up** when they are very excited or nervous.

hyper- is added in front of words to talk about an extreme form of something. *...hyper-inflation.*

hyperactive (*or* **hyper-active**) (**hyperactivity**) A **hyperactive** person is unable to relax and is always in a state of restless activity. You say someone like this suffers from **hyperactivity.**

hyperbole (*pron:* hie-**per**-bol-ee) is using deliberate exaggeration in speech or writing.

hypermarket A **hypermarket** is a very large supermarket.

hypersensitive If you say someone is **hypersensitive,** you mean they are easily annoyed or offended. ■ You can say someone is **hypersensitive** when they are extremely sensitive to certain drugs or chemicals.

hypertension is abnormally high blood pressure.

hypertext In computing, **hypertext** is a way of organizing a database, so that users can find particular information without reading from beginning to end.

hyperventilate (**hyperventilation**) If someone **hyperventilates,** their breathing rate increases uncontrollably, usually because of stress. An increase in someone's breathing is called **hyperventilation.**

hyphen (**hyphenated**) A **hyphen** is a punctuation mark used to link words or parts of words. Words with hyphens between the parts are called **hyphenated** words.

hypnosis is the technique of hypnotizing people.

hypnotic (**hypnotically**) If you call something **hypnotic,** you mean it is so fascinating you cannot stop watching it or listening to it.

hypnotise See **hypnotize.**

hypnotism (**hypnotist**) **Hypnotism** is the same as hypnosis. A **hypnotist** is someone who hypnotizes people.

hypnotize (*or* **hypnotise**) (**hypnotizing, hypnotized**) If someone **hypnotizes** you, they use a special technique to put you into a trance, during which you are very receptive to suggestions. ■ If you are **hypnotized** by something, you are so fascinated by it you have to keep watching it or listening to it.

hypoallergenic jewellery and cosmetics are made from materials which are unlikely to cause an allergic reaction.

hypochondriac (**hypochondria**) A **hypochondriac** is someone who continually worries about their health, although there is nothing physically wrong with them. Behaviour like this is called **hypochondria.**

hypocrisy (*pron:* hip-**pok**-rass-ee) (**hypocritical, hypocritically; hypocrite**) If you accuse someone of **hypocrisy,** you mean they pretend to have certain beliefs, while behaving in a way which goes against them. You say someone like this is being **hypocritical;** you can also call them a **hypocrite.**

hypodermic A **hypodermic** needle or syringe is used for giving injections.

hypotension is abnormally low blood pressure.

hypotenuse (*pron:* hie-**pot**-a-news) The **hypotenuse** of a right-angled triangle is its longest side.

hypothermia is a condition in which a person's body temperature is very low as a result of being in cold conditions for a long time.

hypothesis (*pron:* high-**poth**-iss-iss) (*plural:* **hypotheses**) A **hypothesis** is a theory which has not yet been proved to be correct.

hypothesize (*or* **hypothesise**) (**hypothesizing, hypothesized**) If you **hypothesize** about something, you put forward a theory.

hypothetical (**hypothetically**) A **hypothetical** situation is a possible one, which you imagine happening in order to consider the possible consequences.

hysterectomy A **hysterectomy** is an operation to remove a woman's womb.

hysteria (**hysterical, hysterically; hysterics**) **Hysteria** is uncontrolled excitement, anger, or panic among a group of people. ■ If an individual person is **hysterical** or suffering from **hysteria,** they are in an uncontrolled emotional state as a result of shock. You can also say someone in this state is in **hysterics** or having **hysterics.**

I i

I A speaker or writer uses **I** to refer to himself or herself.

ice (**icing, iced**) **Ice** is frozen water. ■ If something **ices up,** ice forms around it or inside it. ■ **Ice** is pieces of ice used to keep food or drink cool. ■ An **iced** drink has been made very cold. ■ If you **break the ice,** you do something to make people feel relaxed. ■ If something **cuts no ice** with someone, it does not impress or influence them. ■ If you **ice** a cake, you cover it with icing. ...*iced buns.* ■ If you put a project **on ice,** you delay it.

ice age When people talk about the **ice age,** they mean a period in the Earth's history during which a large part of its surface was covered with ice.

ice axe An **ice axe** is an axe-like tool used by mountaineers.

iceberg An **iceberg** is a large tall mass of ice floating in the sea.

ice-breaker An **ice-breaker** is a ship designed to break a channel through ice.

ice-cap An **ice-cap** is a layer of thick ice and snow which permanently covers an area of land.

ice cream is a food made from frozen milk, fats, and sugar. An **ice cream** is a portion of ice cream.

ice cube An **ice cube** is a small block of ice put into a drink to make it cold.

ice floe An **ice floe** is a large area of ice floating in the sea.

ice hockey is a game like hockey played on ice.

ice rink An **ice rink** is an area of ice deliberately created for skating on.

ice-skate – Ice-skates are boots with metal blades, for skating on ice.

ice-skating (**ice-skater**) **Ice-skating** is skating on ice, for amusement or as a sport.

icicle An **icicle** is a long pointed piece of ice hanging from a surface.

icily See **icy.**

icing is a sweet substance used to cover and decorate cakes. ■ If you say something is the **icing on**

the cake, you mean it makes a good thing even better, but is not essential.

icon (*pron:* **eye**-kon) (**iconic**) An **icon** is a picture of a religious figure painted on a wooden panel and is regarded as holy. ■ An **icon** is someone or something that is greatly admired, often because they are seen as a perfect example of something. You say someone or something like this is **iconic.** ■ An **icon** is a small sign on a computer screen, representing a function.

iconoclast (**iconoclastic, iconoclasm**) An **iconoclast** is someone who criticizes generally accepted beliefs. You describe what they say or write as **iconoclastic** or call it **iconoclasm.**

icy (**icier, iciest; icily**) Icy air or water is extremely cold. ■ An **icy** road has ice on it. ■ You say someone's behaviour is **icy** when they are unfriendly or show anger in a quiet controlled way.

ID cards or badges show a person's identity. ID is short for 'identity' or 'identification'.

idea An **idea** is a plan, suggestion, or a possible course of action which comes into your mind. ■ The **idea** of an activity is its purpose. *The idea is to build confidence and reduce suspicion.* ■ Your **idea** of something is what you know or believe about it, but are not sure. *I had an idea that he joined the army... No one has any real idea how much the company will make next year.*

ideal An **ideal** is a principle, idea, or standard which you believe in and try to achieve. ■ You say someone or something is **ideal** when they are just what is wanted for a particular purpose. *...the ideal candidate.* ■ Your **ideal** of something is the person or thing that you think is a perfect example of it.

idealise See **idealize.**

idealism (**idealist, idealistic**) Idealism is having ideals. A person who has ideals and tries to achieve them is called an **idealist.** You call their ideas and behaviour **idealistic.**

idealize (*or* **idealise**) (**idealizing, idealized; idealization**) If you **idealize** someone or something, you think they are much better than they really are.

ideally If you say **ideally** something should happen, you mean it would be the best thing that could happen, although it is not really likely. *Ideally, the amounts of money raised and spent would be the same.* ■ If someone or something is **ideally** suited for something, they are just right for it. *The hotel is ideally situated for country walks.*

identical (**identically**) If things are **identical,** they are exactly the same. ■ **Identical twins** are two people who were conceived from a single egg and look exactly alike.

identifiable If someone or something is **identifiable,** you can tell who or what they are.

identify (**identifies, identifying, identified; identification**) If you **identify** someone or something, (a) you establish who or what they are. *The positive identification was made from dental records.* (b) you reveal who or what they are to other people. *...a state organisation which he refused to identify.* ■ Your **identification** is a document like your passport which proves who you are. ■ An **identification parade** is the same as an identity parade. ■ If something is

identified with a particular thing, (a) people associate it with that thing. *The area is now identified with quality wines.* (b) people see them as amounting to the same thing. *...the need to identify nationhood with language.* ■ If you can **identify with** someone, you can understand their feelings or imagine yourself in their situation.

identikit is a collection of pictures of facial features, from which pictures of complete faces can be constructed. The police use identikit to construct faces of criminals from witness's descriptions. 'Identikit' is a trade mark. **Identikit** is also used to describe someone or something that gives the impression of having been put together in this way. *...identikit shopping precincts.*

identity (**identities**) Your **identity** is who you are. *Her accomplice has still not revealed his identity.* ■ The **identity** of a group of people is all the unique things about them which distinguish them from other groups. ■ If you say there is an **identity** of interests or aims, you mean two groups of people have the same interests or aims.

identity parade When the police hold an **identity parade,** they get together a line of people, including one who is a suspected criminal, to see if a victim or witness of a crime identifies them.

ideologist (**ideological**) See **ideology.**

ideologue (*pron:* **eye**-dee-a-log) An **ideologue** is the same as an ideologist.

ideology (**ideologies; ideologist, ideological, ideologically**) An **ideology** is a set of political beliefs. An **ideologist** is someone who develops or supports an ideology, and works out how it can be turned into action. **Ideological** is used to talk about things to do with ideologies.

idiocy See **idiotic.**

idiom An **idiom** is a group of words whose meaning cannot be worked out from the words taken separately. For example, 'let the cat out of the bag' is an idiom. ■ An **idiom** is a style of speech, writing, or music. *He skilfully fused the jazz idiom with classical music.*

idiomatic language is the kind of language you use in conversation.

idiosyncrasy (*pron:* id-ee-o-**sin**-krass-ee) (**idiosyncrasies; idiosyncratic**) A person's **idiosyncrasies** are their unusual habits or characteristics; you can say someone's habits and characteristics are **idiosyncratic.**

idiot If you call someone an **idiot,** you mean they are very stupid, or have done something stupid. ■ In the past, a person with a severe mental handicap was often referred to as an **idiot.**

idiotic (**idiocy, idiocies**) If you say something is **idiotic,** you mean it is very stupid. You can talk about the **idiocy** of something like this. **Idiocies** are stupid actions.

idle (**idling, idled; idly, idleness, idler**) If workers, factories, or machines are **idle,** they are not being used because their is no work available. ■ If a car engine is **idling,** it is running slowly and is not in gear. ■ You say someone is **idle** when they are too lazy to do any work. A person who spends their time doing nothing is called an **idler.** ■ Idle is used to describe things people do to pass the time. *...idle curiosity.* ■ If you call what people are saying **idle** talk, you mean it is not based on facts and should not be taken seriously. *...idle rumours.* ■ If you say it would be **idle** to do something, you mean nothing useful would come of it.

idol (**idolatry**) (*pron:* ide-**ol**-a-tree) An **idol** is someone like a pop star who is greatly admired by many people. Obsessive admiration for a person can be called **idolatry.** ■ An **idol** is a statue worshipped by people who believe it is a god. Worshipping statues is called **idolatry.**

idolize (*or* **idolise**) (**idolizing, idolized; idolization**) If you **idolize** someone, you admire them greatly.

idyll (*pron:* id-ill) (**idyllic**) An **idyll** is a simple life of peace and happiness. **Idyllic** (*pron:* id-**dill**-ik) is used to describe a life like this.

i.e. You write **i.e.** when you are putting something you have just mentioned in a different way, to make your meaning clearer. *...remand prisoners, ie, people who are awaiting trial.*

if is used to say one thing happens or is true, depending on whether another thing happens or is true. *She has threatened to kick me out of the home if I keep the baby.* ■ **If** is used when mentioning a question someone has asked. *He asked if we were still interested.* ■ **If not** is used to suggest something might be larger, earlier, etc than you have just said. *I will be ready in a couple of weeks, if not sooner.* ■ **If only** is used when mentioning a reason for something, to suggest there may be other reasons. *See your doctor, if only to put your mind at rest.* ■ **If** is used to say something has a quality which contrasts with the one you have just mentioned. *...a dramatic, if temporary, worsening of Britain's overseas trade position.*

iffy If you say something is **iffy,** you mean it is uncertain or not very good.

igloo An **igloo** is a dome-shaped house, made from blocks of snow.

igneous rock is formed by hot liquid rock cooling and going hard.

ignite (**igniting, ignited; ignition**) If something **ignites,** it starts burning. ■ A car's **ignition** is (a) the part of the engine which ignites the fuel and starts the car. (b) the keyhole where you turn on the ignition. ■ If something **ignites** a conflict, it starts it off.

ignoble (**ignobly**) If you describe someone's behaviour or circumstances as **ignoble,** you mean they are shameful or dishonourable.

ignominious (*pron:* ig-no-**min**-ee-uss) (**ignominiously; ignominy**) **Ignominious** is used to describe things which are shameful or embarrassing. *...an ignominious FA cup defeat.* **Ignominy** (*pron:* ig-nom-in-ee) is shame or public disgrace.

ignorant (**ignorantly, ignorance**) If you are **ignorant** of something, you do not know about it. *The public is kept in ignorance about potential disasters.* ■ If you say someone is **ignorant,** you mean they are rude or inconsiderate.

ignore (**ignoring, ignored**) If you **ignore** someone or something, you deliberately take no notice of

them. ■ If something **ignores** an aspect of a situation, it fails to take it into account.

ikon See **icon.**

ilk means the same kind of person or thing as others already mentioned. *...journalists and their ilk.*

ill (**illness, illnesses**) If you are **ill** or have an **illness,** you are suffering from a health problem. If you **fall ill** or are **taken ill,** you become ill suddenly. ■ **Ill** is evil or harm. *Information can be used for ill as well as for good.* ■ **Ills** are difficulties. ■ **Ill** is used to say something is bad or unpleasant. *He bears no ill feelings towards Johnson.* ■ If you speak **ill** of someone, you criticize them. ■ **ill at ease:** see **ease. ill afford:** see **afford.**

ill-advised An **ill-advised** action is not sensible or wise.

illegal (**illegally; illegality, illegalities**) If something is **illegal,** it is against the law. **Illegality** is having or doing something illegal. **Illegalities** are illegal acts. ■ An **illegal** immigrant is someone who has entered a country without official permission.

illegible writing is so bad that you cannot read it.

illegitimate (**illegitimacy**) An **illegitimate** person's parents were not married to each other at the time he or she was born. **Illegitimacy** is being born to parents who were not married to each other. ■ **Illegitimate** activities are against the law.

ill-equipped If you are **ill-equipped** for something, you do not have the right ability, qualities, or equipment for it.

ill-fated is used to describe things which end in a tragic or unfortunate way.

ill-founded See **found 4.**

ill-gotten amounts of money have been obtained illegally. *...criminals' ill-gotten gains.*

ill health See **health.**

illiberal If you call a law or system of government **illiberal,** you mean it restricts people's freedom.

illicit (**illicitly**) An **illicit** activity or substance is not allowed by law. *...illicit drugs.* ■ **Illicit** is used to describe activities which are unacceptable according to the customs of a country. *...illicit sex.*

illiterate (**illiteracy**) An **illiterate** person cannot read or write. **Illiteracy** is not being able to read or write. Illiterate people are sometimes called **illiterates.**

ill-mannered people are rude and inconsiderate.

illness See **ill.**

illogical (**illogically**) If something is **illogical,** it is not reasonable or sensible.

ill-starred means the same as 'ill-fated'.

ill-tempered If you describe someone as **ill-tempered,** you mean they are angry or hostile. *...an ill-tempered debate.*

ill-timed If something is **ill-timed,** it is done at the wrong time.

ill-treat (**ill-treatment**) If someone is **ill-treated,** they are treated badly.

illuminate (**illuminating, illuminated; illumination**) If a light **illuminates** something, it shines on it and makes it bright. If something is **illuminated,** it has lights shining on it, or lights placed on it. The **illumination** in a place is the lighting there. ■ **Illuminations** are coloured lights put up in a town for decoration. ■ If you **illuminate** something which is difficult to understand, you make it clearer. If you say something is **illuminating,** you mean it helps you understand something. ■ **Illuminated** books and manuscripts have brightly-coloured drawings and designs round the writing.

illusion An **illusion** is a false idea or belief. You say someone is **under an illusion** about something. ■ An **illusion** or **optical illusion** is something which looks like one thing, but is really something else or not there at all.

illusionist An **illusionist** is a magician who tries to make people believe they have seen things which have not really happened.

illusory things seem to exist but do not really exist at all.

illustrate (**illustrating, illustrated; illustration, illustrator**) If something **illustrates** a situation or is an **illustration** of it, it is an example of it, and proves it exists. ■ If you **illustrate** a point you are making, you provide an example which shows the kind of thing you mean. ■ If someone **illustrates** a book, they draw the pictures or diagrams which go into it. An **illustration** is a picture or diagram in a book. An **illustrator** is an artist who draws pictures for books.

illustrative If something is **illustrative** of a thing, it provides an example of that thing, or shows what it is like. *The following excerpt is illustrative of her interaction with students.*

illustrator See **illustrate.**

illustrious You say someone is an **illustrious** person or has an **illustrious** career when they are famous and greatly admired. *...an illustrious career.*

image (**imagery; imaging, imaged**) If you have an **image** of someone or something, you have a picture or idea of them in your mind. ■ An **image** in a film or book is something which catches your attention and is meant to stand for something important or significant. *A handful of recent films capture raw and contemporary images of Latin America.* The images in a film or book can also be called its **imagery.** ■ Your **image** is the way you appear to other people. ■ Your **image** is your reflection in something. See also **mirror image.** ■ An **image** of an object, especially one which you cannot see with the naked eye, is a picture of it produced, for example, by photography or radar. **Imaging** equipment is used to produce pictures like this. *...a thermal imaging camera.*

imaginable The best or worst thing **imaginable,** is the best or worst thing you can think of.

imaginary See **imagine.**

imagination (**imaginative, imaginatively**) Your **imagination** is your ability to form new ideas and think about things which do not exist. If someone has this ability, you say they are **imaginative** or have **imaginative** ideas.

imagine (**imagining, imagined; imaginary**) If you **imagine** something, you form a picture or idea of it in your mind. ■ **Imagined** or **imaginary** things exist only in people's minds; such things can also be called **imaginings.** *...the imaginings of young chil-*

dren. ■ If you **imagine** something is true, you suppose it is true. *I imagine this happens a lot.*

imam (*pron:* im-**mahm**) An **imam** is a Muslim prayer-leader at a mosque.

imbalance (**imbalanced**) If there is an **imbalance** in a situation, things are not evenly or fairly arranged.

imbecile If you call someone an **imbecile,** you mean they are stupid, or have done something stupid.

imbibe (**imbibing, imbibed**) If you **imbibe** alcohol, you drink it. ■ When people **imbibe** ideas or arguments, they listen to them and accept them.

imbroglio (*pron:* imb-**role**-lee-oh) (**imbroglios**) An **imbroglio** is a confusing or complicated situation.

imbue (**imbuing, imbued**) If something is **imbued** with a quality, it is filled with it. *...a record imbued with a love of life.*

IMF The **IMF** or 'International Monetary Fund' is an international agency which is part of the United Nations. It exists to promote trade and economic development in the countries belonging to it.

imitate (**imitating, imitated; imitative, imitator**) If you **imitate** someone, you copy what they do. Behaviour like this is called **imitative** behaviour. People who copy what a well-known person does are called that person's **imitators.**

imitation is copying what someone else does. ■ If you give an **imitation** of someone, you copy the way they speak or behave, to amuse people. ■ **Imitations** are things which are not genuine but are made to look as if they are. *...an imitation pearl necklace.*

immaculate (**immaculately**) You say someone or something is **immaculate** when they are exceptionally clean and tidy. ■ **Immaculate** is used to describe things which are done perfectly, without any mistakes. *The orchestra plays immaculately.*

immaterial If you say something is **immaterial,** you mean it is irrelevant or makes no difference. *Who is elected is immaterial to us.*

immature (**immaturity**) **Immature** things are not yet fully developed. *...ovary tissue containing immature eggs.* ■ If you call a person **immature** or talk about their **immaturity,** you mean they do not behave in a sensible and adult way.

immeasurable (**immeasurably**) If something is **immeasurable,** people cannot measure or appreciate how great it is. *The war is causing immeasurable suffering.*

immediacy If you talk about the **immediacy** of something, you mean it seems very real and makes you feel closely involved with what is going on. *...the immediacy of television news reporting.*

immediate (**immediately**) **Immediate** is used to say something happens straight away. *The news immediately pushed up share values.* ■ If something happens **immediately** before or after something else, it happens just before or after it. **Immediately** is used to say something happens as soon as something else happens. *They would fly out immediately after the President gave the order.* ■ **Immediate** needs or concerns must be attended to straight away. ■ **Immediate** is used to say something is just next to something else. *...Iraq's immediate* *neighbours.* ■ Your **immediate** family are your closest relatives.

immemorial If you say something has been happening **since time immemorial,** you mean it has been happening for longer than anyone can remember.

immense (immensely, immensity) If you say something is **immense** or talk about its **immensity,** you mean it is extremely large or great.

immerse (immersing, immersed; immersion) If you **immerse** yourself in something, you become completely involved in it. *She immersed herself in music and dance.* ■ If you **immerse** something in a liquid, you put it in the liquid so that it is completely covered.

immigrant (immigration) **Immigrants** are people who come to live and work in a country. Coming to live and work in a country is called **immigration.** ■ At a port, airport, or border, **immigration** is the place where the passports of people entering the country are checked. ■ See also **emigrate.**

imminent (imminently, imminence) If something is **imminent,** it will happen very soon.

immobile (immobility) If someone or something is **immobile,** they are not moving. ■ You say someone is **immobile** when they are unable to move, for example because of serious injury.

immobilize (or immobilise) (immobilizing, immobilized; immobilization) If something is **immobilized,** it is prevented from working or moving.

immoderate (immoderately) **Immoderate** behaviour is extreme or excessive.

immodest (immodesty) An **immodest** person is boastful. **Immodesty** is boastful behaviour.

immolation is killing someone as a sacrifice, especially by burning them alive. If people die by **self-immolation,** they burn themselves alive, usually for religious or political reasons.

immoral (immorality) If you say someone is **immoral** or their behaviour is **immoral,** you mean they do things which are morally wrong. *...the immorality of drink driving.*

immortal (immortality) You can say someone is **immortal** or talk about their **immortality** when they are famous and will be remembered for a very long time. *...sporting immortals such as boxer Muhammad Ali.* ■ When a religious person talks about being **immortal** they mean living forever in Heaven.

immortalize (or immortalise) (immortalizing, immortalized) If someone or something is **immortalized** in something like a book or film, they are made famous and will be remembered because of it.

immovable (immovably) An **immovable** object cannot be moved. ■ You say a person is **immovable** when they will not change their mind about something.

immune (immunity) If you are **immune** to a disease or have **immunity** to it, you cannot be made ill by it. ■ The body's **immune system** is the way it fights infection, especially by producing antibodies to destroy disease-carrying substances. ■ If you are **immune** to things happening around you, you are not affected by them. ■ **Immune** is used to say some action cannot be taken against someone. *He demanded immunity from prosecution.* ■ **diplomatic immunity:** see **diplomatic.**

immunize (or immunise) (immunizing, immunized; immunization) If you are **immunized** against a disease, you are made immune to it, usually by an injection.

immunodeficiency (immunodeficiencies) An **immunodeficiency** is a breakdown or serious weakness in the body's immune system. See also **AIDS, HIV.**

immunology (immunologist, immunological) The study of immunity to disease is called **immunology.** An expert on this is called an **immunologist.** **Immunological** means to do with immunity to disease. *...the immunological system.*

immutable (immutably) If something is **immutable,** it cannot be changed.

imp In fairy tales, an **imp** is a small mischievous creature with magical powers.

impact If something has an **impact** on a person or situation or **impacts** (*pron:* im-pakts) on them, it has a strong effect on them. ■ The **impact** of one object on another is the force with which it hits it. If an object **impacts** with something, it collides with it.

impair (impairing, impaired; impairment) If something is **impaired,** it is damaged or weakened, and this stops it being effective or working properly.

impale (impaling, impaled) If you **impale** something, you stick a pointed object through it.

impart If you **impart** information to someone, you give it to them. ■ If something **imparts** a quality to something else, it gives that quality to it.

impartial (impartially, impartiality) If you are **impartial,** you act fairly and do not take sides in a situation or argument. When someone behaves like this, you talk about their **impartiality.**

impassable If a road is **impassable,** you cannot get along it, because it is blocked or in a bad condition.

impasse (*pron:* am-pass) An **impasse** is a difficult situation where no progress can be made.

impassioned If you make an **impassioned** plea, you express your strong feelings about an issue in a forceful way.

impassive (impassively) If you are **impassive,** you do not show any emotion.

impatient (impatiently, impatience) If you are **impatient,** you are annoyed because you have to wait for something. *He repeated his question impatiently.* ■ If you are **impatient** to do something, or **impatient** for something to happen, you are eager to do it, or for it to happen. ■ **Impatient** people have very little patience.

impeach (impeaches, impeaching, impeached; impeachment) If a politician is **impeached,** they are charged with committing a serious crime in connection with their job.

impeccable (impeccably) If someone's behaviour or dress is **impeccable,** it is perfect in every detail.

impecunious If someone is **impecunious,** they have very little money.

impede (**impeding, impeded; impediment**) If you are **impeded** by something, it makes it difficult for you to move or make progress. Something which has this effect is called an **impediment.** ■ A speech **impediment** is a disability like a stammer which makes speaking difficult.

impel (**impelling, impelled**) If something **impels** you to do something, it forces you to do it.

impending is used to describe things which are going to happen soon. ...*the impending elections.*

impenetrable (**impenetrability, impenetrably**) If an area is **impenetrable,** it is impossible to get through it or into it. ■ If something written or spoken is **impenetrable,** it is impossible to understand it. ...*impenetrably detailed reports.*

imperative If you say it is **imperative** that something is done, you mean it must be done. ■ If there is an **imperative** need for something, it is needed urgently. ■ An **imperative** is something you must do or have. ...*the political imperative of cutting waiting lists.*

imperceptible (**imperceptibly**) If something is **imperceptible,** it is too small to notice.

imperfect (**imperfectly, imperfection**) If a system is **imperfect,** it has faults or weaknesses. You call these faults or weaknesses **imperfections.** ■ If an object is **imperfect,** it has been made with a slight fault, or has been damaged. You call the fault or damage an **imperfection.** ■ If something has been done **imperfectly,** it has not been done correctly.

imperial is used to talk about things to do with an emperor, empress, or empire. ...*the first ever imperial visit to South Korea.* ■ The **imperial** system of measurement uses miles, feet and inches, pounds and ounces, gallons and pints.

imperialism (**imperialist, imperialistic**) Imperialism is a system in which a rich and powerful country controls other countries. **Imperialist** and **imperialistic** are used to talk about things to do with imperialism.

imperil (**imperilling, imperilled** (*Am:* **imperiling, imperiled**) If something **imperils** something else, it puts it in danger.

imperious (**imperiously**) An **imperious** person is proud and expects to be obeyed. *He held up his hand imperiously.*

imperishable If something is **imperishable,** it cannot be removed or destroyed.

impermeable If a layer of something is **impermeable,** liquid cannot get through it.

impermissible If something is **impermissible,** it is not allowed.

impersonal is used to describe treatment of people in which they are made to feel they are unimportant, and that their feelings and opinions do not matter. A place where people are treated like this can also be called **impersonal.** ■ **Impersonal** is used to describe things which cannot be identified with any particular person. ...*impersonal market forces.*

impersonate (**impersonating, impersonated; impersonation, impersonator**) If you **impersonate** someone or do an **impersonation** of them, you pretend to be them, either to deceive or entertain

people. An **impersonator** is an entertainer who impersonates famous people.

impertinent (**impertinence**) If you say someone's behaviour is **impertinent,** you mean it is rude and disrespectful.

imperturbable If someone is **imperturbable,** they remain calm in a disturbing situation.

impervious (**imperviousness**) If you are **impervious** to what people say or do, you do not let it affect you. ■ If something is **impervious** to liquids or heat, it does not let them pass through it.

impetuous (**impetuosity**) You say someone is **impetuous** when they act suddenly without thinking. Behaviour like this is called **impetuosity.**

impetus If something is given **impetus,** it is made more powerful or effective. ■ The **impetus** of a moving object is the force it exerts when it hits something.

impinge (**impinging, impinged**) If something **impinges** on you or on your life, it makes a difference to the way you live. ■ If something **impinges** on your rights, it has a serious effect on them. Similarly, something can **impinge** on something you are trying to achieve.

impish An **impish** person is cheeky and mischievous.

implacable (**implacably**) You say someone is **implacable** when their attitude to something is firm and shows no sign of changing. *The Socialist Party is implacably opposed to any constitutional change.*

implant (**implantation**) If something is **implanted** in a person's or animal's body, it is put there, usually by an operation. The process is called **implantation;** the thing placed in the body is called an **implant.**

implausible (**implausibly, implausibility**) If something is **implausible,** it is difficult to believe and therefore unlikely to be true. ...*$72.5 billion, which is meant, rather implausibly, to come out of defence cuts.*

implement (**implementation**) When a plan or decision is **implemented,** it is put into practice. ■ An **implement** is a tool or other piece of equipment.

implicate (**implicating, implicated**) If someone is **implicated** in something like a crime, they are shown to have been involved in it.

implication The **implications** of something are its indirect effects. ■ If something is true **by implication,** it follows indirectly from what has just been said. *The findings have increased fears that transmission between species and, by implication, to man, is possible.*

implicit (**implicitly**) If something is **implicit** in a statement or attitude, it is there but not stated openly. *The desire to maintain a nuclear policy seems implicit in official remarks.* ■ If you have **implicit** faith in someone or something, you believe in them completely.

implode (**imploding, imploded; implosion**) If an object **implodes,** it collapses inwards because the pressure inside is less than the pressure outside. ■ If a system or organization **implodes,** it collapses as a result of internal faults.

implore (**imploring, implored**) If you **implore** someone to do something, you beg them to do it.

implosion See **implode.**

imply (**implies, implying, implied**) If you **imply** that something is true, you suggest it is true without actually saying so. ■ If what someone says **implies** an attitude or opinion, it suggests they have it. ■ If one thing **implies** another, you are likely to get the second thing when you get the first. *Experimentation implies taking risks.*

impolite behaviour is rude and offends people.

impolitic An **impolitic** action is unwise and likely to cause difficulty or embarrassment.

imponderable things are impossible to assess or estimate. Things like these can be called **imponderables.**

import (**importation, importer**) If a person, country, or business **imports** goods, they buy them from another country and bring them into their own country. You talk about the **import** or **importation** of goods. A person, country, or business that does this is called an **importer;** the goods imported are called **imports.** ■ If ideas or values are **imported** into a place, they are introduced from outside. ■ The **import** of something is its importance. *...a matter of such life-changing import.*

important (**importantly, importance**) If something is **important,** it has special significance, or is very useful or valuable. ■ An **important** person has a lot of influence or power.

importation (**importer**) See **import.**

importunate An **importunate** person is persistent in trying to get something they want.

importune (*pron:* im-por-**tune**) (**importuning, importuned**) If you **importune** someone, you pester them for something or urge them to do something.

impose (**imposing, imposed; imposition**) If something like a rule is **imposed** on people, they are forced to obey it. ■ If someone **imposes** on you, they unreasonably expect you to do something for them.

imposing (**imposingly**) You say someone or something is **imposing** when they have an impressive appearance or manner.

imposition See **impose.**

impossible (**impossibly; impossibility, impossibilities**) If something is **impossible,** it cannot be done, cannot happen, or cannot be true. You say something like this is an **impossibility.** ■ An **impossible** situation is one which cannot be dealt with satisfactorily. ■ If you say someone is **impossible,** you mean they are very difficult to deal with.

impostor (*or* **imposter**) An **impostor** is someone who tricks people by pretending to be someone else.

impotent (**impotently, impotence**) You say someone is **impotent** when they have no control over what is going on. ■ If a man is **impotent,** he is unable to have or maintain an erection during sex. This condition is called **impotence.**

impound If something is **impounded** by police or other officials, they officially take possession of it because a law has been broken.

impoverish (**impoverishes, impoverishing, impoverished; impoverishment**) If something **impoverishes** people, it makes them poor. ■ If something becomes **impoverished,** it suffers a loss in quality.

impracticable If a course of action is **impracticable,** it cannot be carried out.

impractical If an idea or course of action is **impractical,** it is not sensible or practical.

imprecise (**imprecision**) If something is **imprecise,** it is too general or vague.

impregnable If a building is **impregnable,** it cannot be broken into. ■ If a ruler is **impregnable,** he or she cannot be removed from power.

impregnate (**impregnating, impregnated**) If something is **impregnated** with a substance, the substance is made to spread through it. ■ If a man **impregnates** a woman, he makes her pregnant.

impresario (*pron:* im-pris-**sar**-ee-oh) (**impresarios**) An **impresario** is someone who arranges for plays, concerts, and other entertainments to be performed.

impress (**impresses, impressing, impressed; impressive, impressively**) If something **impresses** you or you find it **impressive,** you are struck by how admirable it is. ■ If you try to **impress** someone, you try to get them to admire you. ■ If you **impress** something on someone, you get them to see how important it is.

impression Your **impression** of someone or something is the way they look or seem to you. You can say someone or something creates a certain **impression.** *The new Prime Minister has created a favourable impression.* ■ If you **make an impression,** people notice you and remember you. ■ If you are **under the impression** that something is true, you believe it is true, usually when it is not. ■ An **impression** of a well-known person is an amusing imitation of them. ■ An **impression** of an object is a mark or outline left after it has been pressed hard against a surface.

impressionable people are easy to influence.

Impressionism (**impressionist**) Impressionism is a style of painting developed in France between 1870 and 1900 which depicted the effects of light, rather than realistic details. Artists who painted in this style are called **impressionists.**

impressionistic is used to describe music, painting, or writing which gives pleasing or interesting impressions, rather than being concerned with accurate representation.

impressive See **impress.**

imprimatur (*pron:* imp-rim-**ah**-ter) If you have an important person's **imprimatur** to do something, you have their approval.

imprint If something is **imprinted** on your mind or memory, or leaves an **imprint** on your mind or memory, you cannot forget it. ■ If an object is **imprinted** onto a surface, it is pressed hard onto it, leaving a mark or outline called an **imprint.** ■ An **imprint** is the name of a publisher printed in a book.

imprison (**imprisoning, imprisoned; imprisonment**) If someone is **imprisoned,** they are sent to prison. *They were sentenced to life imprisonment.* ■ You say someone is **imprisoned** when they are trapped in an enclosed space.

improbable (**improbably; improbability, improbabilities**) If something is **improbable**, it is unlikely to be true or to happen. ■ You can describe something as **improbable** when you find it surprising. *Squat and balding, he was an improbable hero.*

impromptu things are not planned in advance. *...an impromptu news conference.*

improper (**improperly**) **Improper** is used to describe things which are illegal, dishonest, or unacceptable. *...improper share dealing.* ■ **Improper** is used to describe rude or shocking behaviour. *He accused me of making improper suggestions to his wife.*

impropriety (pron: im-proe-**pry**-a-tee) (**improprieties**) **Impropriety** is improper behaviour. *...allegations of financial improprieties.*

improve (**improving, improved; improvement**) If something **improves** or there is an **improvement** in it, it gets better.

improvident If someone is **improvident**, they are wasteful and do not think about what they might need in the future.

improvisation (**improvisational, improvisatory**) **Improvisation** is making up what you do or perform as you go along. **Improvisational** and **improvisatory** are used to talk about things to do with improvising. *...improvisational jazz. ...the improvisatory nature of events between 1939 and 1945.*

improvise (**improvising, improvised**) If you **improvise**, you make or do something without planning it in advance, using whatever materials are available. ■ If an actor or musician **improvises**, they make up what they perform as they go along.

imprudent (**imprudently, imprudence**) **Imprudent** behaviour is not sensible or careful.

impudent (**impudence**) If someone is **impudent**, they behave in a rude and disrespectful way.

impugn (pron: imp-**yoon**) If you **impugn** someone's motives or character, you suggest that they are not entirely honest or honourable.

impulse (**impulsive, impulsively**) An **impulse** is a sudden desire to do something. You call behaviour like this **impulsive**. *Impulsively, he took her hand in his.* ■ If you talk about a person's **impulses**, you mean their tendency to behave in certain ways. *His creative impulses have vanished.* ■ An **impulse** is a short electrical signal sent along a wire, a nerve, or through the air.

impunity If you do something wrong with **impunity**, you do it without fear of being punished.

impure (**impurity, impurities**) If a substance is **impure**, its quality is inferior, because it has small amounts of other substances called **impurities** in it.

impute (**imputing, imputed; imputation**) If you **impute** a quality to someone or something, you say they possess it.

in is added to some words to form a word with the opposite meaning. For example, 'incorrect' means 'not correct'.

in is used to say where something is, or where it happens. *There are all the usual drinks in the cupboard... His aircraft crashed in Mongolia.* ■ If you are **in**, you are at your home or place of work. ■ When someone comes **in**, they enter a room or building.

■ When a train, boat, or plane comes **in**, it arrives. ■ When the sea or tide comes **in**, the sea gradually moves further towards the shore. ■ **In** is used to say what someone is wearing. *...people in rags, with no shoes.* ■ If something happens **in** a particular century, year, or month, it happens then. ■ **In** is used to say something will happen after a certain length of time. *The meeting is to be held in three weeks' time.* ■ **In** is used to say that someone is involved with an activity or organization. *He is going to be in the school play.* ■ **In** is used to say what subject or field of activity you are talking about. *...a distinguished career in journalism. ...advances in computer technology.* ■ **In** is used to say what aspect of something you are talking about. *The whales grow to about ten metres in length.* ■ **In** is used to say in what way something is true. *We are no different from other manufacturers in that we offer discounts to our employees.* ■ You talk about something being **in** a particular state or situation. *The ship was never in any danger of sinking... She's in love.* ■ If something happens **in** a particular situation, it happens during it and as a result of it. *Eight people have been killed in unrest.* ■ **In** is used to say how many people or things do something. *People vote in greater numbers if they feel their vote is going to count.* ■ **In** is used to say how something is communicated. *The opera was sung in English.* ■ **In** is used to show approximate ages or temperatures. *...a couple in their seventies.* ■ **In** is used to express a ratio, proportion, or probability. *Doctors gave him a one in ten chance of survival.* ■ **In** is used to talk about strong reactions to something. *The country recoiled in horror at the bombing campaign.* ■ If you say someone is **in for** a shock or other unwelcome experience, you mean they are going to experience it. *The President is in for a rough ride.* ■ If you are **in on** something, you are involved in it. *He was in on the crucial planning stages of the restaurant.* ■ If something is **in**, it is fashionable. ■ If you discuss the **ins and outs** of something, you discuss all its detailed points.

in. See **inch**.

in absentia If something concerning a person is done **in absentia**, it is done when they are not there.

inaccessible (**inaccessibility**) An **inaccessible** place is impossible or very difficult to reach. ■ If something like music is **inaccessible**, it is hard for people to understand or appreciate.

inaccurate (**inaccurately; inaccuracy, inaccuracies**) If something is **inaccurate**, it is not correct. When something is not correct, you talk about its **inaccuracy;** its incorrect parts can be called **inaccuracies.**

inaction If you accuse someone of **inaction,** you mean they are failing to do something they should be doing.

inactivate (**inactivating, inactivated**) If something like a virus is **inactivated**, it is made harmless.

inactive means not functioning or doing anything.

inadequate (**inadequately; inadequacy, inadequacies**) If something is **inadequate**, there is not enough of it, or it is not good enough. You talk about the **inadequacy** of something like this. ...*inadequately trained riders.* **Inadequacies** are aspects of something which are wrong or not good enough. ...*the inadequacies of security measures.* ■ If you say a person is **inadequate** or talk about their **inadequacy,** you mean they do not have the qualities necessary to do something or to cope with life.

inadmissible If something is **inadmissible,** it is not allowed or acceptable. ...*inadmissible evidence.*

inadvertent (inadvertently) Inadvertent is used to describe something you do without intending to. *You may have inadvertently pressed the wrong button.*

inadvisable If you say it would be **inadvisable** to do something, you mean it would not be a good idea.

inalienable rights are ones which cannot be taken away from you.

inane (inanely; inanity, inanities) An **inane** remark or action is a particularly silly one. An **inanity** is a remark or action like this.

inanimate can be used to describe anything which is not a living thing.

inanity See inane.

inarticulate If you are **inarticulate,** you cannot express yourself easily.

in as much (*or* **inasmuch) In as much as** means 'seeing that' or 'because'. *I am extremely lucky in as much as I have a very strong and loving wife.*

inattentive (inattention) If you are **inattentive,** you are not paying attention. **Inattention** is lack of attention.

inaudible If a sound is **inaudible,** it is not loud enough to be heard.

inaugural An **inaugural** meeting is the first meeting of a new organization. An **inaugural** speech is a speech given on an occasion like this, or the first speech given by a new leader.

inaugurate (inaugurating, inaugurated; inauguration) When a new leader is **inaugurated,** he or she officially takes up their new position at a special ceremony. ■ If a system is **inaugurated,** it is introduced and put into action.

inauspicious (inauspiciously) You say something has an **inauspicious** start when it begins in a way that suggests things are not going to turn out well. *The talks began inauspiciously with a meeting lasting less than half an hour.*

inborn qualities are natural ones you are born with.

inbred (inbreeding) Inbred means the same as '**inborn'.** ■ **Inbreeding** is the repeated breeding of closely related people or animals. People or animals born as a result of inbreeding are described as **inbred.**

inbuilt An **inbuilt** quality is one that someone or something has from the time they were born or produced. *We all have an inbuilt curiosity to discover what lies beyond.* ...*an answering machine with inbuilt fax and printer.*

incalculable You say something is **incalculable** when it is too great to be counted or estimated.

incandescent substances or devices give out a lot of light when heated. ■ If someone is **incandescent** with fury, they are extremely angry.

incantation An **incantation** is a magic spell which is chanted or sung.

incapable If someone is **incapable** of doing something, they are unable to do it. ■ An **incapable** person is unable to do anything satisfactorily.

incapacitate (incapacitating, incapacitated) If an illness or injury **incapacitates** you, it prevents you from doing certain things.

incapacity Someone's **incapacity** to do something is their inability to do it.

incarcerate (incarcerating, incarcerated; incarceration) If someone is **incarcerated,** they are put in prison.

incarnate (incarnating, incarnated) You use **incarnate** to say that something, especially a god or spirit, is represented in human form. *He was the god Vishnu incarnated on earth as a just and righteous king.* ■ If you say someone is a certain quality **incarnate,** you mean they represent that quality or are typical of it in an extreme form. *The Rolling Stones were thought to be devils incarnate.*

incarnation According to some religions, an **incarnation** is one of the lives a person has. ■ If you say someone is the **incarnation** of someone or something, you mean they are a typical example of that person or thing. *He is the incarnation of the American dream.* ■ When someone or something has appeared in several different forms or roles, you can refer to each of them as an **incarnation.** ...*the latest incarnation of the Australian book fair.* ...*her previous incarnation as a newsreader.*

incautious (incautiously) An **incautious** action is done without careful consideration of the possible consequences.

incendiary (incendiaries) Incendiary weapons or attacks are ones which cause large fires. This type of weapon is called an **incendiary.**

incense (incensing, incensed) Incense (*pron:* in-sense) is a substance burned for its sweet smell. ■ If you are **incensed** (*pron:* in-senst) by something, it makes you extremely angry.

incentive An **incentive** is something which encourages you to do something.

inception The **inception** of an organization or activity is its start.

incessant (incessantly) You use **incessant** to describe things which bother you because they go on without stopping.

incest (incestuous) If someone commits **incest,** they have sex with a close relative, such as their brother or daughter. **Incestuous** means to do with incest. ■ If you describe a group of people as **incestuous,** you mean they are not interested in ideas and people from outside the group.

inch (inches, inching, inched) Length is often expressed in **inches.** An inch is about 2.54 centimetres. There are 12 inches in a foot. 'Inches' can be written 'in.' or 'ins.' ■ If you **inch** somewhere, you get there a bit at a time.

inchoate (*pron:* in-koe-ate) ideas or attitudes are newly formed and not yet properly developed.

incidence An **incidence** of something unpleasant is a case of it, or an occasion when it happens. ...*incidences of leukaemia.* ...*the rising incidence of car fires.*

incident An **incident** is something which happens, especially something unpleasant. ...*a shooting incident.*

incidental If one thing is **incidental** to another, it is less important than the other thing. ■ **Incidental music** is background music for a play or film.

incidentally You say **incidentally** when you are adding an extra piece of information. *Attendance at mosques has dropped sharply (so, incidentally, has worship in churches).*

incident room An **incident room** is a room used by the police as a base while investigating a major crime or accident.

incinerate (**incinerating, incinerated; incineration, incinerator**) If you **incinerate** something, you get rid of it by burning it. An **incinerator** is a furnace for burning things.

incipient is used to talk about things which are just starting to happen. ...*incipient middle age.*

incise (**incising, incised; incision**) If an object is **incised** with a design, the design is cut into its surface. ...*stone decorated with carefully incised geometric lines.* ■ An **incision** is a sharp cut made in something's surface, especially by a surgeon.

incisive speech or writing is clear and forceful.

incisor Your **incisors** are the teeth at the front of your mouth.

incite (**inciting, incited; incitement**) If someone **incites** people to behave in a violent or unlawful way, they encourage them to behave in that way, usually by making them angry or excited. ...*incitement to religious hatred.*

inclement weather is unpleasantly cold or stormy.

incline (**inclining, inclined; inclination**) If someone is **inclined** to behave in a certain way, they tend to behave like that or they want to do so. You can also say someone has an **inclination** to behave in a certain way. ■ You can say you are **inclined** to have a certain opinion when you have that opinion but do not feel strongly about it. *She was inclined to accept the lawyer's advice.* ■ If someone is for example artistically **inclined,** they have a natural ability for art. ■ If you **incline** your head, you move it downwards and forwards. ■ An **incline** (*pron:* **in-**kline) is a slope.

include (**including, included; inclusion**) If something **includes** something else, it has it as one of its parts. If you **include** one thing in another, you make it part of it. ■ When you mention a group of things or people, you can use **including** or **included** to say who some of them are. ...*a five-channel service, including two film channels... Many African countries, Nigeria included, broke off diplomatic ties.*

inclusive is used to say everything is included in the price you pay for something. ...*a fully inclusive holiday.* ■ You use **inclusive** when you are talking about a range of things, to show it includes the first and last one you mention. ...*August 17-20 inclusive.*

incognito You say someone is **incognito** when they are using a false name or wearing a disguise, so they will not be recognized.

incoherent (*pron:* in-koe-**heer**-rent) (**incoherently, incoherence**) If something is **incoherent,** it is un-

clear and difficult to understand. ■ If someone is **incoherent,** they are not talking clearly.

income A person's **income** is the money they earn or regularly receive.

income tax is a percentage of your income paid regularly to the government.

incoming is used to talk about things coming into a place. ...*the incoming tide. ...incoming calls.* ■ An **incoming** government or official has just been elected or appointed.

incommunicado If you are being held **incommunicado,** you are not allowed to talk to anyone from outside the place where you are. ■ If someone is **incommunicado,** they do not want to be disturbed or are in a place where they cannot be contacted. *He is incommunicado in a secluded cottage in Wales.*

incomparable (**incomparably**) If you say something is **incomparable,** you mean it is so good nothing else can be compared with it. ■ **Incomparably** is used to say something has much more of a quality than anything else. *South Africa seems incomparably richer than the rest of Africa.*

incompatible (**incompatibility**) If two things are **incompatible,** they cannot exist or be used together, because of the differences between them. ...*incompatibility between the two railway systems.* ■ If a couple are **incompatible,** they cannot have a satisfactory relationship, because of differences in their character or outlook.

incompetent (**incompetently, incompetence**) You say someone is **incompetent** or talk about their **incompetence** when they keep doing things badly. Someone who is incompetent can be called an **incompetent.**

incomplete If something is **incomplete,** it does not have all the parts it should have, or it is not finished.

incomprehensible (**incomprehension**) If something is **incomprehensible,** it is impossible to understand. **Incomprehension** is being unable to understand something.

inconceivable If you say something is **inconceivable,** you mean you cannot believe it could happen or be true.

inconclusive (**inconclusively**) If something like a discussion is **inconclusive,** it fails to settle something. ■ If evidence or an experiment is **inconclusive,** it fails to prove anything.

incongruous (**incongruously; incongruity, incongruities**) If something is **incongruous,** it seems strange because it does not fit in with things around it, or with things happening at the same time. You talk about the **incongruity** of something like this. Incongruous things can be called **incongruities.**

inconsequential If something is **inconsequential,** it is unimportant.

inconsiderable A **not inconsiderable** amount of something is a rather large amount.

inconsiderate people do not care how their behaviour affects other people.

inconsistent (**inconsistency, inconsistencies**) If someone is **inconsistent,** they behave differently in similar situations at different times. Behaviour like this is called **inconsistency.** ■ If two or more statements are **inconsistent** or there is an **inconsistency** between them, they contradict each other. ■ If something is **inconsistent** with a set of ideas, values, or requirements, it is not in accordance with them.

inconsolable If you are **inconsolable,** you are very sad, and cannot be comforted.

inconspicuous (**inconspicuously**) If something is **inconspicuous,** it does not stand out, or is not noticeable at all.

incontestable (**incontestably**) If something is **incontestable,** it is obviously true and cannot be denied.

incontinent (**incontinence**) You say someone is **incontinent** when they have no control over their bladder or their bowels, or both. This condition is called **incontinence.**

incontrovertible (**incontrovertibly**) **Incontrovertible** evidence or proof shows something is definitely true.

inconvenient (**inconveniently; inconvenience, inconveniencing, inconvenienced**) If something is **inconvenient** or causes **inconvenience,** it causes problems. You can also say something **inconveniences** someone or is an **inconvenience.**

incorporate (**incorporating, incorporated; incorporation**) If one thing **incorporates** another, it includes the other *The new car will incorporate a number of major improvements.* ■ If something is **incorporated** into a large group or system, it becomes a part of it. *...the incorporation of women into the priesthood.*

incorrigible (**incorrigibly**) If you tell someone they are **incorrigible,** you are saying, often humorously, that they have faults which will never change.

incorruptible (**incorruptibility**) If someone is **incorruptible,** they cannot be bribed or persuaded to do things they should not do. *His incorruptibility makes him a possible winner.*

increase (**increasing, increased**) If something **increases,** it gets bigger. If something is getting bigger, you can say it is **on the increase.** If it has got bigger, you say there has been an **increase** in it.

increasingly is used to say that something is happening more and more often or a quality is becoming more noticeable. *Investors have become increasingly jittery.*

incredible (**incredibly**) If something is **incredible,** it is hard to believe. *...their incredible story.* ■ **Incredible** is used to say how big something is, or what a lot of it there is. *There was an incredible bang.* ■ People use **incredible** to express great delight or admiration at something. *The view was incredible.*

incredulous (**incredulously, incredulity**) If you are **incredulous,** you have difficulty believing what you have just heard or seen, because it is very surprising or shocking. You can also say you react to something with **incredulity.**

increment (**incremental, incrementally**) An **increment** in something is an increase, especially one in a series of increases. **Incremental** and **incrementally** are used to talk about things which increase like this. ■ An **increment** is an amount by which someone's salary automatically increases after a fixed period of time.

incriminate (**incriminating, incriminated**) If something **incriminates** someone, it suggests they are responsible for a crime. *...incriminating evidence.*

incubate (**incubating, incubated; incubation**) When eggs are **incubated,** they are kept warm until they are ready to hatch. ■ The **incubation** period for a disease is the period from when the infection enters your body to the time when symptoms first appear.

incubator An **incubator** is a device in which weak premature babies are kept until they are healthy.

incubus (*pron:* in-cube-uss) (*plural:* **incubuses** *or* **incubi**) An **incubus** is something which brings you problems and which you would like to get rid of. *...the incubus of debt.*

inculcate (**inculcating, inculcated**) If you **inculcate** an idea in someone, you teach it to them so it becomes fixed in their minds.

incumbent (**incumbency, incumbencies**) The person who holds a post at a particular time can be called the **incumbent.** You call the period when they hold the post their **incumbency.** ■ If it is **incumbent on** or **upon** you to do something, it is your duty to do it.

incur (**incurring, incurred**) If you **incur** something undesirable, it happens to you because of what you do. *...debts incurred by state companies.*

incurable (**incurably**) An **incurable** disease cannot be cured. ■ **Incurable** is used to describe people with fixed attitudes or habits. *Alistair was an incurable romantic.*

incursion An **incursion** is a sudden invasion, attack, or raid.

indebted (**indebtedness**) **Indebted** is used to describe people who owe money. *...heavily indebted countries.* ■ If you say you are **indebted** to someone, you mean you are grateful to them for something they have done.

indecent (**indecently, indecency**) **Indecent** is used to describe things involving sex or nakedness which people find shocking. ■ **Indecent assault** is a sexual attack which does not include rape. **Indecency** is illegal sexual behaviour. *He denied touching the women indecently.* ■ **Indecent** is used to describe things which break rules of good behaviour or morality. *...the indecent haste of the leadership election.*

indecipherable If writing is **indecipherable,** you cannot read it.

indecisive (**indecision, indecisiveness**) If you are **indecisive,** you cannot decide what to do. Uncertainty about what to do is called **indecision** or **indecisiveness.** ■ If a vote is **indecisive,** there is no clear result one way or the other.

indeed You use **indeed** when you are confirming or agreeing with something that has been said. *He admitted that there is indeed a 'territorial dispute' between the two countries.* ■ You use **indeed** for extra emphasis. *...a very big iceberg indeed.*

indefatigable (**indefatigably**) If someone is **indefatigable,** they keep on with something and never get tired of it. *He worked indefatigably to interest the young in music.*

indefensible If a wrong action is **indefensible**, it cannot be justified.

indefinable An **indefinable** quality or feeling is hard to describe. *...that indefinable magical appeal of Paris.*

indefinite (**indefinitely**) If something is **indefinite** or will go on for an **indefinite** time, no decision has been taken about when it will end. *...an indefinite general strike.*

indefinite article The **indefinite article** is 'a' or 'an'.

indelible (**indelibly**) **Indelible** dye or ink cannot be removed or washed out. ■ **Indelible** is used to say the bad effects of something are permanent. *The experience left an indelible mark on him.*

indelicate behaviour is rude or offensive.

indemnify (**indemnifies, indemnifying, indemnified**) If you are **indemnified** against losing or damaging something, you will receive financial compensation if you lose or damage it.

indemnity (**indemnities**) If something provides **indemnity,** it provides insurance or protection against loss or damage, especially in the form of financial compensation. An **indemnity** is money or goods received as compensation for loss or damage.

indent (**indentation**) When you **indent** a line, you position it further away from the margin than the other lines. ■ If something is **indented**, or there is an **indent** or **indentation** in it, there is a mark where its surface or edge has been cut away, or looks as if it has been cut away. *...the deeply indented coastline.*

independent (**independently, independence**) **Independent** is used to describe things you do on your own, rather than jointly with other people. *France was pursuing an independent foreign policy.* ■ If someone is **independent,** they look after their own affairs, without help. ■ An **independent** hospital, school, or other organization does not receive money from the government or a local authority, and is not controlled by them. ■ If a country or state becomes **independent** or gains **independence,** it elects its own government and is no longer ruled by another country. ■ An **independent** inquiry is held by people who are not involved in a situation and so are able to make a fair judgment. Similarly, you can say someone gives an **independent** opinion about something.

in-depth An **in-depth** investigation is thorough and detailed.

indescribable (**indescribably**) If you say something is **indescribable,** you mean it is so bad no words can properly describe it.

indestructible If something is **indestructible,** it cannot be destroyed.

indeterminate You use **indeterminate** to describe things which are not certain or fixed. *...prisoners serving indeterminate sentences. ...a woman of indeterminate age.*

index (**indexes, indexing, indexed; indices**) An **index** is an alphabetical list at the back of a book

saying where you can find things in the book. ■ An **index card** is a card on which you write information for future reference. See also **card index.** ■ If something is used as an **index** of something else, it is used as a way of measuring it. (*For this and the following meanings, the usual plural of 'index' is 'indices', ind*-diss-ezz). ■ An **index** is a system by which changes in the value of something can be compared or measured. *...stockmarket indices.* ■ If one thing is **indexed** to another, things are arranged so that when the second thing increases or decreases, the first one does too. *...a price indexed to inflation.* ■ In maths, **indices** are the little numbers showing how many times a number is to be multiplied by itself. For example, in the equation $3^2 = 9$, 2 is an index.

indexation is the same as index-linking.

index finger Your **index finger** is the one next to your thumb.

index-linked (**index-linking**) **Index-linked** wages, pensions, and interest rates are linked to an index measuring inflation or the cost of living. This system is called **index-linking.**

Indian people and things are in or from India. An **Indian** is someone who comes from India. ■ An **Indian** is someone descended from the earliest inhabitants of North, South, and Central America. **Indian** means connected with these people. *...Nevada's Indian reservations.*

Indian summer An **Indian summer** is a period of warm weather during the autumn. ■ If someone has an **Indian summer,** they have a period of success towards the end of their life or career.

indicate (**indicating, indicated**) If something **indicates** that a certain thing is the case, it shows it is the case. ■ If you **indicate** a fact, opinion, or intention, you make it known. *He indicated he was willing to help.* ■ If you **indicate** something to someone, you show them where it is, usually by pointing to it. ■ If you **indicate** when you are driving, you show which way you are going to turn.

indication An **indication** is a sign giving an idea of what the situation is. *There is no clear indication of when those arrested will be brought to trial.*

indicative (*pron:* in-dik-a-tiv) If something is **indicative** of something else, it is a sign of it.

indicator An **indicator** is something which acts as a sign, telling you what the situation is. *Dehydration is a common indicator of a lack of fat in the diet.* ■ A car's **indicators** are the lights that show which way it is turning.

indices See **index.**

indict (*pron:* in-dite) (**indictment, indictable**) If someone is **indicted** for a crime, they are officially charged with it. An **indictment** is a criminal charge. An **indictable** offence is one you can be charged with. ■ If one thing is an **indictment** of another, it shows how bad it is.

indie music is pop music produced by small independent record companies, often considered more interesting and creative than mainstream pop.

indifferent (**indifferently, indifference**) You say people are **indifferent** to something when they show no interest in it. ■ If you say something is **in-**

indigence   326   indulge

different, you mean it is of a rather low standard. *...indifferent cooking.*

indigence See **indigent.**

indigenous (*pron:* in-**dij**-in-uss) The **indigenous** inhabitants of a country are the ones who have been there from earliest times, rather than people who arrived later. ■ If a type of plant or animal is **indigenous** to a place, it grows or lives there naturally, rather than being introduced from outside.

indigent (*pron:* **in**-dij-ent) (**indigence**) If someone is **indigent,** they are very poor. **Indigence** is poverty.

indigestible food is difficult to digest.

indigestion is pain caused by difficulty in digesting food.

indignant (**indignantly, indignation**) If you are **indignant,** you are shocked and angry at the way someone has behaved. You call this feeling **indignation.**

indignity (**indignities**) If you suffer an **indignity,** you are made to feel humiliated.

indigo is a dark violet-blue colour.

indirect (**indirectly**) **Indirect** effects are not caused immediately and obviously by a person or thing, but happen because of something else they have done. ■ If people have **indirect** contact, they deal with each other through someone else. ■ If you say something in an **indirect** way, you do not mention it directly, but say other things which refer to it.

indirect tax – **Indirect taxes** are taxes added to the price of goods and services. VAT and import duty are indirect taxes.

indiscipline (**indisciplined**) **Indiscipline** is a lack of discipline. If people are **indisciplined,** they behave badly, because they are not used to obeying rules.

indiscreet (**indiscretion**) If you are **indiscreet,** you do things openly, or talk about things openly, which you ought to keep secret. Behaviour like this is called **indiscretion. Indiscretions** are indiscreet acts.

indiscriminate (**indiscriminately**) You say an action is **indiscriminate** when it does not involve any kind of selection, and can affect anyone or anything. *...indiscriminate arrests.*

indispensable If something is **indispensable,** you cannot do without it.

indisposed If someone is **indisposed,** they are ill, and unavailable to do something.

indisputable (**indisputably**) If something is **indisputable,** there is no question that it is true.

indissoluble (**indissolubly**) An **indissoluble** relationship is so strong it can never be broken.

indistinct If something is **indistinct,** it is difficult to see, hear, or recognize, because it is faint or unclear.

indistinguishable If two or more things are **indistinguishable,** they are so similar you cannot tell them apart.

individual (**individually**) **Individual** means relating to one person or thing, rather than to a large group. *Australia won both the team and individual gold medals... He will meet them individually.* ■ When people talk about **the individual,** they mean every person, considered as someone special and different from every other person. *...the freedom of the individual.* ■ **Individual** is used to say something has a special character which makes it unique. *...strongly individual buildings.*

individualise See **individualize.**

individualist (**individualistic, individualism**) An **individualist** is someone who likes to do things their own way. You talk about the **individualism** of someone like this, or say they are **individualistic.**

individuality A person's or thing's **individuality** is all the things about them which make them different from other people or things.

individualize (*or* **individualise**) (**individualizing, individualized**) If you **individualize** something, you make it recognizably different from other things of that kind.

indivisible If something is **indivisible,** it cannot be split up into separate parts. ■ If something is **indivisible** from something else, the two things cannot be regarded as separate.

Indo- is joined to other words to talk about things involving India and another country. *...a new Indo-British venture.*

indoctrinate (**indoctrinating, indoctrinated; indoctrination**) When people are **indoctrinated** with a belief, they are made to accept it unquestioningly.

indolent (**indolence**) If someone is **indolent,** they are lazy. **Indolence** is laziness.

indomitable (**indomitably**) If you say someone is **indomitable,** you mean they never give up. ■ **Indomitable** is used to describe qualities which never change or disappear. *...his indomitable courage.*

indoor (**indoors**) **Indoor** is used to describe things inside a building. *...an indoor market.* ■ If something happens **indoors,** it happens inside a building.

indubitable (**indubitably**) **Indubitable** is used to say there is no doubt that something exists or is true. *His behaviour was indubitably ill-judged.*

induce (**inducing, induced; inducement**) If something **induces** a situation, it brings it on. ■ If doctors **induce** labour or birth, they give a pregnant woman drugs to make the birth begin. ■ If you are **induced** to do something, you are persuaded to do it. An **inducement** is something like a gift or bribe, which is offered to someone to persuade them to do something.

induct (**induction**) When someone is **inducted** into an exclusive group, they are made a member of it. ■ **Induction** is a procedure or ceremony for introducing someone to a new job or way of life. *...a four-week induction course.* ■ The act of inducing labour in pregnant women is called **induction.** ■ **Induction** is the process by which electricity or magnetism is passed between two objects or circuits without them touching each other.

induction coil An **induction coil** is a transformer used to produce a high voltage from a low one.

indulge (**indulging, indulged; indulgence, indulgent, indulgently**) If you **indulge** in something you enjoy doing or **indulge** your passion for it, you do it. The thing you do can be called an **indulgence.** *He still indulges one of his great passions, motor-mechanics.* See also **self-indulgent.** ■ If you **indulge** someone else, you let them have what they want, even if it is not good for them. An **indulgent** person behaves like this to others. ■ If you are **indulgent,** you are kind to people and do not criticize their weaknesses.

industrial (**industrially**) Industrial means to do with industry. *...French industrial policy.* ■ An **industrial** area is one where industry is important or highly developed. ■ An **industrial estate** is an area, often on the edge of a town, specially designed for industry and business. ■ **Industrial relations** are the relations between employers and workers. ■ If workers take **industrial action,** they go on strike or protest in some other way.

industrialise See **industrialize.**

industrialist An industrialist is a person who owns or controls large amounts of money or property in industry.

industrialize (or **industrialise**) (**industrializing, industrialized; industrialization**) When a country **industrializes** or is **industrialized,** industry is introduced there on a large scale.

industrial revolution The **Industrial Revolution** was the period from about 1750 to 1850 when Britain became an industrial nation. Any similar period in a country's history can be called an **industrial revolution.**

industrious If you are **industrious,** you work hard.

industry (**industries**) Industry is the work and processes involved in making things in factories. ■ An **industry** consists of all the people and processes involved in manufacturing or producing a particular type of product. *...the car industry.*

inebriated (*pron:* in-**nee**-bree-ate-ed) If you are **inebriated,** you are drunk.

inedible (**inedibility**) If something is **inedible,** it is poisonous, or too unpleasant to eat.

ineffable (**ineffably**) Ineffable is used to say something has more of a quality than can be expressed in words. *There is something ineffably sad about Updike's novel.*

ineffective (**ineffectively, ineffectiveness**) If something you do is **ineffective,** it does not produce the effect you want.

ineffectual (**ineffectually**) If something you do is **ineffectual,** it does not produce the results you want. ■ An **ineffectual** person fails to get things done.

inefficient (**inefficiency, inefficiencies**) You say a person, system, or machine is **inefficient** or talk about their **inefficiency** when they do not use time, energy, or other resources in the best way. Inefficient parts of a system are called **inefficiencies.**

inelegant (**inelegance**) If you say something is **inelegant** or talk about its **inelegance,** you mean it is not attractive or graceful.

ineligible (**ineligibility**) If you are **ineligible** for something, you are not qualified for it or not entitled to have it.

ineluctable If something is **ineluctable,** there is no escape from it.

inept (**ineptly, ineptitude**) You say someone is **inept** or talk about their **ineptitude** when they do something in a clumsy and unskilful way.

inequality (**inequalities**) If there is **inequality** somewhere, there are differences in wealth and opportunity between different social or racial groups. An **inequality** is a difference like this.

inequitable (**inequity, inequities**) If you say something is **inequitable** or talk about its **inequity,** you mean it is unfair or unjust. **Inequities** are things which are unfair or unjust.

ineradicable If something is **ineradicable,** it cannot be removed or destroyed.

inert If someone or something is **inert,** they are not moving. ■ **Inert** is used to describe substances, especially gases, which do not react chemically with other substances.

inertia (*pron:* in-**ner**-sha) If you have a feeling of **inertia,** you feel very lazy and unwilling to do anything. ■ **Inertia** is an organization's lack of energy or initiative in dealing with a problem. *Governmental inertia ensured that nothing was done.* ■ In physics, **inertia** is the tendency of an object to remain still or continue moving, unless a force is applied to it.

inertia selling is sending goods to people who have not ordered them, then sending a bill if the goods are not returned.

inescapable (**inescapably**) If something is **inescapable,** it cannot be avoided.

inessential If something is **inessential,** it is not needed.

inestimable If you say something is of **inestimable** value, you mean it is of very great value.

inevitable (**inevitably, inevitability**) If something is **inevitable,** it cannot be prevented or avoided.

inexact If something is **inexact,** it is not accurate or precise.

inexcusable (**inexcusably**) If you say something is **inexcusable,** you mean it is so bad that it cannot be justified or tolerated.

inexhaustible If something is **inexhaustible,** there is so much of it that it can never be used up.

inexorable (**inexorably**) If a process is **inexorable,** nothing can stop it.

inexpensive (**inexpensively**) Inexpensive things do not cost much.

inexperienced (**inexperience**) If you are **inexperienced** at something, you have little knowledge or experience of it. **Inexperience** is lack of experience.

inexpert If you are **inexpert** at something, you have very little skill at it.

inexplicable (**inexplicably**) If something is **inexplicable,** there seems to be no explanation for it.

in extremis is used to talk about someone being in a very difficult situation in which they have to use extreme methods to solve their problems. *The use of antibiotics was permitted only in extremis.*

inextricable (**inextricably**) If there is an **inextricable** connection between things, they cannot be considered separately. *Economic and political reform are inextricably bound together.*

infallible (**infallibility**) If you claim a person or thing is **infallible** or talk about their **infallibility**, you mean they are never wrong. ■ If you say someone or something is **not infallible,** you mean they are capable of making mistakes.

infamous (*pron:* in-fam-uss) (**infamously, infamy**) **Infamous** people and things are well-known for bad reasons. You can talk about the **infamy** of wicked people or their deeds.

infant (**infancy**) An **infant** is a very young child or baby. **Infancy** is the period of someone's life when they are a very young child. ■ An **infant** organization or movement is new and has not yet developed properly. *...Poland's infant stock exchange.* You say something like this is **in its infancy.**

infanticide is the killing of a baby.

infantile means to do with very young children. *Much infantile unhappiness is attributed to teething.* ■ If you say someone is being **infantile**, you mean they are behaving in a silly childish way.

infantry (**infantryman, infantrymen**) The **infantry** are soldiers who fight on foot. An **infantryman** is a soldier in an infantry regiment.

infant school An **infant school** is one for children aged about 4 to 7.

infatuated (**infatuation**) If you are **infatuated** with someone or something, you have such strong feelings for them that you cannot think clearly or sensibly about them.

infect (**infected, infection**) If someone or something **infects** you, they give you a disease. An **infection** is a disease caused by germs. ■ When food or some other substance is **infected**, it becomes contaminated by germs or dirt. ■ If something bad **infects** people, places, or things, it spreads to them and affects them as if it were a disease. *I was infected by her fear.*

infectious If you have an **infectious** disease, other people can catch it from you, especially by breathing in the germs. ■ If something like a feeling is **infectious,** it spreads easily to other people.

infective is used to describe things like viruses which can cause an infection. *...the infective organism that caused BSE.*

infer (**inferring, inferred; inference**) If you **infer** something, you decide it is true on the basis of the information you have. An **inference** (*pron:* in-fer-renss) is a conclusion you draw about something.

inferior (**inferiority**) If you feel **inferior,** you feel other people are better than you in some way. You say someone who feels like this has a sense of **inferiority.** People can also regard other people as **inferior** or treat them as their **inferiors.** ■ If something is **inferior** to something else, it is not as good.

inferiority complex If someone has an **inferiority complex,** they feel they are less important or less worthwhile than other people.

inferno (**infernos**) An **inferno** is a large dangerous fire.

infertile (**infertility**) If people or animals are **infertile,** they cannot produce babies. *...infections which can lead to infertility.* ■ If land or soil is **infertile,** very few plants can grow there.

infest (**infestation**) If a place is **infested** with insects, rats, or other unwelcome animals, they are there in large numbers. *...mouse infestations.* Similarly, you can say a place is **infested** with dangerous people or things. *...drug-infested ghettos.*

infidel Some people with strong religious beliefs call other people **infidels** when they belong to a different religion or have no religion at all.

infidelity (**infidelities**) **Infidelity** is being unfaithful to a husband, wife, or lover. A person's **infidelities** are the occasions when they are unfaithful.

in-fighting (*or* **infighting**) is rivalry or quarrelling between members of the same organization.

infill If a gap or hole is **infilled,** it is closed up or filled in. ■ **Infill** or **infilling** is something which fills a hole or gap.

infiltrate (**infiltrating, infiltrated; infiltration, infiltrator**) If people **infiltrate** a place or organization, they enter it in order to spy on it or influence it. People who do this are called **infiltrators.**

infinite (**infinitely**) **Infinite** is used to describe things which have no end or limit, or seem as if they have no end or limit.

infinitesimal (*pron:* in-fin-i-**tess**-i-mal) (**infinitesimally**) If something is **infinitesimal,** it is extremely small.

infinitive In grammar, the **infinitive** is the base form of a verb, usually with 'to' in front of it. A **split infinitive** is one where another word is put between 'to' and the verb; for example 'to boldly go'.

infinity In maths, **infinity** is the number which is larger than any other number. It is represented by the symbol ∞. ■ You say there is an **infinity** of things or they stretch to **infinity** when there seems to be an endless number of them.

infirm (**infirmity, infirmities**) If someone is **infirm,** they are weak or ill.

infirmary (**infirmaries**) Some older hospitals are called **infirmaries.**

infirmity See **infirm.**

in flagrante delicto (*pron:* in fla-**grant**-eh de-**lict**-toh) If a couple are caught **in flagrante delicto,** they are caught having sex.

inflame (**inflaming, inflamed; inflammation**) If something **inflames** a difficult situation or a bad feeling, it makes it worse. ■ If part of your body is **inflamed,** it is red or swollen because of an infection or injury. When this happens, you say there is **inflammation.**

inflammable An **inflammable** material or chemical catches fire easily. ■ An **inflammable** situation could easily become violent.

inflammation See **inflame.**

inflammatory comments are likely to make people angry or hostile. ■ **Inflammatory** diseases make parts of the body become inflamed.

inflatable objects are objects like balloons which are filled with air or some other gas to get them to their full size. ■ An **inflatable** is an inflatable dinghy.

inflate (**inflating, inflated**) If you **inflate** something like a balloon, you fill it with air or some other gas, to get it to its full size. ■ If something **inflates** prices or costs, it sends them up to a high level. ■ You say someone **inflates** something when they make it out to be bigger or more important than it really is. *She has an inflated sense of her own worth.*

inflation (**inflationary**) **Inflation** is a general increase in prices in a country. **Inflationary** means to do with inflation, or things which cause inflation.

inflection (*or* **inflexion**) The **inflection** of your voice is the way it sounds, for example the way you emphasize certain words.

inflict If you **inflict** something unpleasant on someone, you make them suffer it.

in-flight is used to describe things which are used or provided on a plane when it is in the air. *...in-flight entertainment.*

inflow The **inflow** of people or things into a place is the numbers arriving there.

influence (**influencing, influenced**) If someone has **influence,** they have the power to affect other people's actions. ■ Someone's or somethings **influence** is their ability to affect what you say or do. *...driving under the influence of alcohol.* If someone or something is **influenced** by another person or thing, they are affected by them. ■ You can describe the effect someone has on other people by saying they are a particular kind of **influence.** *He accused them of being a disruptive influence.* ■ In music or art, an **influence** is a style used or adapted by a musician or artist in their own work. *The band's fusion of reggae and jazz influences worked well.*

influential people and things have a lot of influence over people.

influenza is the same as flu.

influx (**influxes**) If there is an **influx** of people or things into a place, they arrive in large numbers.

info is the same as information.

inform (**informed**) If you **inform** someone of something, you tell them about it. ■ An **informed** opinion is based on good knowledge of a subject or situation. ■ If you **inform** on someone, you tell the police about a crime they have committed.

informal (**informally, informality**) **Informal** means relaxed and casual. *...an informal supper party. ...an informal dress code.* ■ An **informal** arrangement is not officially established, and works on a casual basis.

informant An **informant** is (a) someone who provides you with information. (b) an informer.

information is facts or news.

information technology or **IT** is the theory and practice of using computers to transmit information.

informative If something is **informative,** it gives you useful information.

informer An **informer** is someone who gives information about a crime to the police.

infotainment You can call radio or TV programmes that are intended to be entertaining while providing useful information at the same time as **infotainment.**

infra-red light is below the colour red in the spectrum and cannot be seen.

infrastructure The **infrastructure** of a country is the structure which enables it to function effective-

ly, for example its public services and communications.

infrequent (**infrequently**) If something is **infrequent,** it does not happen often.

infringe (**infringing, infringed; infringement**) If a law or agreement is **infringed** or there is an **infringement** of it, it is broken. ■ If something **infringes** people's rights or is an **infringement** of them, it interferes with them.

infuriate (**infuriating, infuriated; infuriatingly**) If something **infuriates** you, it makes you angry or frustrated.

infuse (**infusing, infused; infusion**) If people or things are **infused** with a quality, they are full of it. *The meeting was infused with goodwill.* ■ If a patient is given an **infusion** of a fluid, they are given it slowly from a drip. ■ If you **infuse** a medicine or a drink such as tea, you make it by pouring hot water onto herbs or leaves, letting it stand, and straining it. An **infusion** is a drink or medicine prepared like this.

ingenious (*pron:* in-**jeen**-ee-uss) (**ingeniously, ingenuity**) If you call a device or plan **ingenious,** you mean it has been cleverly designed or thought out. ■ If you call a person **ingenious,** you mean they are able to invent things, or think of clever ways of doing things. You talk about the **ingenuity** (*pron:* in-jen-**new**-it-ee) of someone like this.

ingenue (**ingenu**) (*both pron:* **an**-zhay-new; the 'zh' sounds like 's' in 'pleasure'*) In a play or film, an **ingenue** is a young innocent female character. An **ingenu** is a similar role for a man.

ingenuity See **ingenious.**

ingenuous (*pron:* in-**jen**-new-uss) (**ingenuousness**) An **ingenuous** person is innocent, trusting, and honest.

ingest (**ingestion**) If you **ingest** a substance, you eat or drink it.

inglenook An **inglenook** is a corner by a large open fireplace.

inglorious (**ingloriously**) **Inglorious** behaviour is shameful and disgraceful.

ingot An **ingot** is a lump of metal, usually shaped like a brick.

ingrained (*or* **engrained**) habits and beliefs are difficult to change.

ingratiate (*pron:* in-**gray**-shee-ate) (**ingratiating, ingratiated**) If someone **ingratiates** themselves with you, they try to make you like them.

ingratitude is a lack of gratitude, shown in the way someone behaves to a person who has helped them.

ingredient The **ingredients** of something like a cake are the things it is made from. ■ The factors which lead to something happening can be called **ingredients.** *A key ingredient for success is the ability to have fun.*

ingrowing (**ingrown**) An **ingrowing** or **ingrown** toenail is growing into the toe, often causing infection and pain.

inhabit (**inhabiting, inhabited; inhabitant**) The people or animals that **inhabit** a place are the ones that live there; you can also call them its **inhabitants.**

inhale (**inhaling, inhaled; inhalation**) When you **inhale,** you breathe in. If you **inhale** something like smoke, you breathe it in.

inhaler An **inhaler** is a device for inhaling vaporized medicines, especially ones which make breathing easier.

inherent (**inherently**) If a characteristic is **inherent** in something, it is built into it, or part of its nature.

inherit (**inheriting, inherited; inheritance, inheritor**) If you **inherit** money or property, you get it from someone when they die. The money or property is called an **inheritance;** you are called the **inheritor.** ■ You can say you **inherit** traditions or problems when they are handed down to you from people who have gone before you. ■ If you **inherit** a characteristic or disease, you are born with it because your parents or ancestors had it.

inhibit (**inhibiting, inhibited; inhibition**) If something **inhibits** a process, it slows or stops it. ■ If you **inhibit** someone from doing something, you make it difficult for them to do it. ■ If someone is **inhibited** or has **inhibitions,** they find it difficult to behave naturally and show their real feelings, because they worry too much about what people might think.

inhibitor An **inhibitor** is a substance which slows or stops a chemical reaction.

inhospitable An **inhospitable** place is unpleasant to be in, for example because of bad weather conditions. ■ You say a person is **inhospitable** when they do not make visitors feel welcome.

in-house is used to talk about things being done within an organization, rather than being subcontracted to someone else. *...in-house caterers.*

inhuman behaviour is extremely cruel.

inhumane (**inhumanity**) You say treatment of people or animals is **inhumane** when it involves cruelty.

inimical If conditions are **inimical** to something, they are not favourable to it.

inimitable (**inimitably**) **Inimitable** is used to describe something special about a person which others cannot copy. *...his inimitable culinary skills.*

iniquitous (**iniquity, iniquities**) If you say something is **iniquitous** or an **iniquity,** you mean it is very bad and unfair.

initial (**initially; initialling, initialled**) (*Am:* **initialing, initialed**) **Initial** is used to say what happens at the beginning of something, in contrast to what happens later. *His criticism initially went unheeded.* ■ Your **initials** are the first letters of each of your names. If you **initial** a document, you write your initials on it as a signature.

initiate (**initiating, initiated; initiation, initiator**) If you **initiate** something, you start it, or make it happen. Someone who initiates something can be called its **initiator.** ■ If you **initiate** someone into something, you introduce them to it and teach them about it. *Swallow initiated him into the art of film-making.* ■ If someone is **initiated** into a group or society, a ceremony is held to make them a member or to teach them secrets or skills. The ceremony is called an **initiation** ceremony; the person being initiated is called an **initiate.**

initiative An **initiative** is something positive someone does in an attempt to resolve a problem. ■ If you **take the initiative** in a situation, you do not wait to see what others do, but take some action yourself. ■ If you have the **initiative,** you are in a stronger position than your opponents. ■ Someone who has **initiative** has the ability to take action without being told what to do.

initiator See **initiate.**

inject (**injectable, injection**) If you are **injected** with a medicine or have an **injection,** the medicine is put into your body using a syringe. **Injectable** medicines are ones which can be injected into someone. Addicts also **inject** themselves with drugs. ■ If you **inject** a quality such as excitement into a situation, you add it. ■ If money is **injected** into a business, additional money is provided in order to keep it going.

injudicious (**injudiciously**) **Injudicious** behaviour is unwise and shows poor judgment.

injunction An **injunction** is (a) a court order making someone do something, or stopping them doing it. (b) an instruction to behave in a certain way.

injure (**injuring, injured; injury, injuries**) If you are **injured** or receive an **injury,** a part of your body is damaged in a battle or accident. **Injury** is being injured. ■ **Injury time** is time added at the end of a football match to make up for time lost when players were injured. ■ If your feelings are **injured,** you are offended about something. ■ In a dispute, if you claim you are the **injured party,** you say you are the one who has been treated unfairly.

injurious If something is **injurious,** it is harmful or damaging.

injury See **injure.**

injustice is a lack of fairness or justice in a situation. ■ If you say you do not want **to do** someone **an injustice,** you mean you do not want to say something critical about them which might not be true.

ink is black or coloured liquid for writing, drawing, or printing. If you **ink in** something which has been written in pencil, you go over the letters in ink.

inkling If you **have an inkling** of something, you have a vague idea or suspicion about it.

inky things are covered in ink, or very dark like ink.

inlaid (**inlay**) An **inlaid** object has a design on it made by putting thin pieces of a substance into grooves made to hold them. A design like this is called an **inlay.**

inland means away from the coast.

Inland Revenue The **Inland Revenue** is the government authority which collects income tax and some other taxes.

in-laws Your **in-laws** are your husband's or wife's close relatives, especially their parents.

inlay See **inlaid.**

inlet An **inlet** is a narrow strip of sea water stretching into the land or lying between two islands.

in loco parentis If you are **in loco parentis,** you are temporarily acting as a parent towards someone else's child.

inmate The **inmates** of a prison or psychiatric hospital are the people being kept there.

inmost See **innermost.**

inn An **inn** is a pub or small hotel.

innards A person's or animal's **innards** are the organs inside their body.

innate (**innately**) An **innate** quality or ability is one you seem to have been born with. ...*an innately courteous man.*

inner The **inner** one of two things is the one which is inside the other. ...*the inner perimeter fence.* ■ **Inner** is used to talk about the central part of a large city, or areas close to the centre of a city. ...*Inner London.* ■ **Inner** is used to talk about a person's thoughts and feelings, as distinct from their outward behaviour. ...*her inner turmoil.* ■ An **inner circle** is a powerful group of people who strongly influence an organization, often secretively.

inner ear The **inner ear** is a part inside the head which is essential for hearing and balance.

innermost Your **innermost** or **inmost** feelings are your most personal and private ones.

inner tube An **inner tube** is the rubber tube containing air inside a tyre.

inning (**innings**) In a cricket match, an **innings** is a period during which one or other team is batting. The time each batsman spends on the field is also called his or her **innings.** ■ In a baseball game, an **inning** is a period during which both teams have a turn at bat. Each team's turn is called a **half-inning.**

innkeeper is an old word for someone who looks after an inn.

innocent (**innocently, innocence**) If an accused person is **innocent,** they are not guilty of the crime they are accused of. ■ You say people are **innocent** when they suffer in a crime or conflict they are not involved in. ...*innocent bystanders.* ■ You say someone is **innocent** when they are inexperienced and ignorant about the more unpleasant side of people's behaviour. ■ An **innocent** remark or action is not meant to offend or upset anyone.

innocuous (**innocuously**) If you say something is **innocuous,** you mean it is harmless or inoffensive, or appears to be. *Bush grinned innocuously.*

innovate (**innovating, innovated; innovation, innovator, innovative, innovatory**) If someone **innovates,** they introduce changes and new ideas to the way something is done or made. The changes are called **innovations.** A person who introduces something new is called an **innovator;** you also say they are being **innovative. Innovative** or **innovatory** things are new and original.

innuendo (**innuendoes** or **innuendos**) Innuendo is indirect reference to something rude or unpleasant.

innumerable means very many. ...*his innumerable appearances on television.*

innumerate people have no understanding of basic arithmetic.

inoculate (**inoculating, inoculated; inoculation**) If you are **inoculated** against a disease or are given an **inoculation,** you are injected with a weak form of the disease, to protect you against it.

inoffensive If something you say or do is **inoffensive,** it is not likely to offend or upset anyone. An **inoffensive** person is never likely to offend anyone.

inoperable If a medical condition is **inoperable,** it cannot be removed or cured by an operation. ■ If something like a piece of equipment is **inoperable,** it cannot be made to work.

inoperative If a system is **inoperative,** it does not work any more or cannot be made to work.

inopportune If something happens at an **inopportune** time, it happens at an unsuitable time and causes trouble or embarrassment.

inordinate (**inordinately**) An **inordinate** amount of something is much greater than you would normally expect.

inorganic matter has never at any time been part of a living thing.

in-patient An **in-patient** is someone who stays in hospital while they receive treatment.

input (**inputting, inputted**) Input is money and resources put into a project to make it work. ■ Your **input** into a discussion or activity is your contribution to it. ■ If you **input** information into a computer, you feed it in, for example by typing it on a keyboard. This information is called **input.** See also **output.**

inquest An **inquest** is an official inquiry to investigate something in detail, especially one held by a coroner to investigate a suspicious death.

inquire (or **enquire**) (**inquiring, inquired; inquiry, inquiries; inquirer**) If you **inquire** about something, you ask for information about it. **Inquiry** is asking about something. *This is the line of inquiry being taken... I am making enquiries into my father's death.* A person who is asking for information can be called an **inquirer.** ■ If you **inquire into** something, you investigate it thoroughly. An **inquiry** is an official investigation. ■ If you have an **inquiring** mind, you are always interested in learning new things.

inquisition (**inquisitorial, inquisitor**) People sometimes call an official investigation an **inquisition** when it is very thorough and uses harsh methods of questioning. The person asking the questions can be called an **inquisitor. Inquisitorial** is used to describe harsh methods of questioning. ■ An **inquisitorial** system of justice is one which involves an accused person being questioned directly by a judge or magistrate.

inquisitive (**inquisitiveness**) If you are **inquisitive,** you are always wanting to find out about things.

inquisitor (**inquisitorial**) See **inquisition.**

inquorate (pron: in-**kwor**-it) If something like a meeting is **inquorate,** there are not enough members present to meet the minimum number officially required before decisions can be made.

inroads If one thing **makes inroads** into another, the first thing starts affecting the second. *Television has made inroads into cinema.*

insane (**insanely, insanity**) If someone is **insane,** their mind does not work in a normal way, and this makes their behaviour strange. This condition is called **insanity. The insane** are people who are insane. ■ If you call someone's plans or actions **in-**

sane, you mean they are extremely foolish. You can talk about the **insanity** of such plans or actions. ...*the insanity of the war.*

insanitary If something is **insanitary,** it is so dirty it is likely to have a bad effect on people's health.

insanity See **insane.**

insatiable (*pron:* in-saysh-a-bl) If someone's desire for something is **insatiable,** it can never be satisfied.

inscribe (**inscribing, inscribed; inscription**) If words are **inscribed** on an object or if the object is **inscribed** with them, they are written or carved on it. An **inscription** is words written or carved on something.

inscrutable (**inscrutably**) If you say someone is **inscrutable,** you mean you cannot tell what they are thinking.

insect An **insect** is a small creature with six legs.

insecticide An **insecticide** is a chemical used to kill insects.

insecure (**insecurity, insecurities**) If you feel **insecure** or have feelings of **insecurity,** you lack confidence and do not think other people like you or respect you. ■ Something that is **insecure** is not safe or protected. ...*low-paid insecure jobs.*

inseminate (**inseminating, inseminated; insemination**) If a woman or female animal is **inseminated,** sperm is put inside her to make her pregnant. See also **artificial insemination.**

insensitive (**insensitively, insensitivity**) If someone is **insensitive,** they behave in a way which shows they are unaware of other people's feelings, or do not care about them. Behaviour like this is called **insensitivity.** ■ If you are **insensitive** to something, you are not aware of it, or not interested in it. ...*insensitivity to the environmental consequences.*

inseparable (**inseparably**) If two things are **inseparable,** they are so closely connected they cannot be separated. ...*liberty is inseparable from social justice.* ■ **Inseparable** friends are always together.

insert (**insertion**) If you **insert** an object into something, you put it inside it. ...*the insertion of acupuncture needles.* ■ An **insert** (*pron:* in-sert) is something inserted somewhere, especially a piece of paper with an advert on it placed inside a magazine or newspaper. ■ If something is **inserted** into a speech or piece of writing, it is put in at a late stage.

inset If an object is **inset** with something like jewels, they are fixed into its surface.

inshore waters are the parts of the sea which are close to land.

inside (**insider**) **Inside** is used to talk about things being in an enclosed space or surrounded by something else. *Inside the passport was a slip of paper. ...a house inside the embassy compound... Some demonstrators have got inside the building.* ■ If clothing is **inside out,** the inside part has been turned so it faces outwards. ■ If you know someone or something **inside out,** you know them extremely well. ■ **Inside** is used to talk about feelings someone has without showing them. *I was furious inside.* ■ If something happens **inside** an organization, it

involves members of the organization and nobody else. People from within an organization can be called **insiders.** See also **insider dealing.** ■ On a road, the **inside** lane is the lane closest to the edge of the road. ■ If you do something **inside** a particular time, you do it before that time is finished.

insider dealing or **insider trading** is the illegal buying or selling of shares by someone with special knowledge of the companies concerned. People who do this are called **insider dealers.**

insidious (**insidiously**) **Insidious** is used to describe harmful things which develop gradually without being noticed.

insight (**insightful**) If something gives you an **insight** into a situation, it helps you to understand it better. If you call something like a book **insightful,** you mean it makes you realize things you had not thought of before.

insignia (*plural:* insignia) An **insignia** is an official badge or sign showing that a person, vehicle, etc belongs to a particular organization. ...*transport planes bearing the insignia of the Red Cross.*

insignificant (**insignificance**) If something is **insignificant,** it is so small or unimportant it is not worth bothering about. *The party committee has been reduced to insignificance.*

insincere (**insincerity**) If someone is **insincere,** they pretend to have feelings they do not have. Behaviour like this is called **insincerity.**

insinuate (**insinuating, insinuated; insinuation**) If you say someone **insinuates** that something is true, you mean they hint at it in an unpleasant way. This is called making an **insinuation.** ■ When people **insinuate** themselves into positions of power or influence, they manage to get there using patience and cunning.

insipid If you call someone or something **insipid,** you mean they are dull and boring. ■ **Insipid** food or drink has very little taste.

insist If you **insist** that something must happen, you say very firmly it must happen. You can also **insist** on doing something or **insist** that something is true. *He insists he is innocent.*

insistent (**insistently, insistence**) If you are **insistent,** you say very firmly that something must be done. ...*Raeder's insistence that naval uniform be worn.* ■ If a noise is **insistent,** it continues for a long time and you cannot help being aware of it.

in situ If something stays **in situ,** it stays where it is. *The platform and track were still in situ but the buildings had been demolished.*

insofar as (*or* **in so far as**) is used to say in what way something is true. *She was not ashamed of it, except insofar as it troubled her husband.*

insole The **insole** of a shoe is the soft layer of material which the sole of your foot rests on.

insolent (**insolence**) An **insolent** person is rude and disrespectful. **Insolence** is behaviour like this.

insoluble An **insoluble** problem cannot be solved. ■ An **insoluble** substance cannot be dissolved.

insolvent (**insolvency, insolvencies**) If a person or organization is **insolvent,** they do not have enough money to pay their debts. Being in this position is called **insolvency.**

insomnia (**insomniac**) If someone suffers from **insomnia,** they find it difficult to get to sleep or to stay asleep. You say someone like this is an **insomniac.**

insouciant (*pron:* in-**soo**-si-ant) (**insouciantly, insouciance**) **Insouciant** behaviour shows a lack of concern. *The UN treats the kidnappings with apparent insouciance.*

inspect (**inspection; inspector, inspectorate**) If you **inspect** something, you examine it carefully, to find out about it or to check that it is all right. An **inspection** is an examination like this. ■ If an official **inspects** a place or carries out an **inspection,** he or she visits the place and looks at it carefully, to find out if regulations are being obeyed. Someone who does this is called an **inspector.** A group of inspectors with a particular responsibility is sometimes called an **inspectorate.** ■ An **inspector of taxes** is employed by the government to calculate the amount of tax people should pay. ■ An **inspector** is a police officer, ranked above a sergeant and below a superintendent.

inspire (**inspiring, inspired; inspiration, inspirational**) If someone or something **inspires** you or is an **inspiration** to you, they make you want to do something by giving you new ideas and enthusiasm. You say people and things that have this effect are **inspiring** or **inspirational.** ■ If you say something someone does is **inspired,** you mean they do it especially well. *India played inspired hockey.* ■ If you have an **inspiration,** you suddenly have a good idea. **Inspiration** is having a good idea. ■ If something **inspires** an emotion in you, it makes you feel it. *It inspires confidence.*

instability (**instabilities**) **Instability** is a lack of stability in a place, situation, or person.

install (**installation**) When a machine or piece of equipment is **installed** in a place, it is placed or fitted there, ready for use. ■ An **installation** is a place containing equipment and machinery for a particular purpose. *...oil installations.* ■ You say someone is **installed** in a new job or position when they are officially given the job or position, often at a special ceremony.

instalment (*Am:* **installment**) If you pay for something in **instalments,** you pay small sums at regular intervals over a period of time. ■ An **instalment** of a story or plan is one of its parts that are published or carried out separately one after the other.

instance You say **for instance** when giving an example. *Subsidies for the arts, for instance, will be slashed.* ■ An **instance** is a case of something happening. *The report details many instances of financial mismanagement.* ■ You say **in the first instance** when you are mentioning the first in a series of steps or actions. *The two men then agreed to meet privately for, in the first instance, fifteen minutes.*

instant (**instantly**) **Instant** is used to say something happens immediately. *They were instantly obeyed.* ■ **Instant** food can be prepared quickly and easily, for example by just adding boiling water. ■ An **instant** is an extremely short period of time.

instantaneous (**instantaneously**) You say something is **instantaneous** when it happens immediately.

instead is used to say one thing happens or is done rather than another. *Use oil instead of butter.*

instep Your **instep** is the middle part of the sole of your foot, where it arches upwards. The part of a shoe which supports this area is called the shoe's **instep.**

instigate (**instigating, instigated; instigator, instigation**) If someone **instigates** something or they are the **instigator** of it, they are responsible for starting it.

instil (*Am:* **instill**) (**instilling, instilled**) If an idea is **instilled** into someone, measures are taken to ensure they accept it.

instinct (**instinctive, instinctively**) **Instinct** or an **instinct** is a natural tendency in people or animals to behave in a certain way, without thinking about it. You call feelings or actions **instinctive** when people have them or do them without necessarily being able to explain them. *I am instinctively anti-establishment.*

institute (**instituting, instituted; institution**) An **institute** is an organization set up to do a particular type of work, especially research or teaching. ■ If someone **institutes** a system, rule, or course of action, they introduce it. *...demands for the institution of multi-party democracy...*

institution (**institutional**) An **institution** is (a) a large organization like a university or a bank. (b) a building where people of a certain kind are kept or looked after. *...mental institutions. ...institutional care.* ■ You call something an **institution** or describe it as **institutional** when it is a well-established feature somewhere. *...that great British institution, the pub.* ■ See also **institute.**

institutionalize (*or* **institutionalise**) (**institutionalizing, institutionalized; institutionalization**) If something is **institutionalized,** it becomes an accepted part of a social system. *...institutionalised racism.* ■ If a person is **institutionalized,** they are put in an institution like a mental hospital. If they become **institutionalized,** they get so used to living in an institution they can no longer cope on their own.

instruct (**instruction, instructional, instructor**) If you **instruct** someone to do something, you tell them to do it. What you say is called an **instruction.** ■ If you **instruct** someone in a subject or skill, you teach it to them. An **instructor** is someone who does this as their job. **Instructions** are information, often written, on how to do something. *...an instructional video.*

instructive If you say an experience is **instructive,** you mean you can learn something from it.

instructor See **instruct.**

instrument (**instrumental, instrumentalist**) An **instrument** is (a) a tool designed to do a particular task, especially delicate work. *...surgical instruments.* (b) a device for taking measurements, for example of speed or height. *...navigational instruments.* ■ A musical **instrument** is an object like a piano, guitar, or flute, used to produce music. **Instrumental**

music is written to be played on instruments, rather than sung. ■ Anything which is used to achieve a particular aim can be called an **instrument**. *Devaluation is an overrated economic instrument.* ■ If you are **instrumental** in getting something done, you play an important part in it.

instrumentation The **instrumentation** in a place, for example in the cabin of a plane, is all the instruments there. ■ The **instrumentation** of a piece of music is the the way in which it is written for different instruments.

insubordinate (insubordination) Insubordinate people disobey orders. Behaviour like this is called **insubordination.**

insubstantial You say something is **insubstantial** when it is not large, solid, or strong.

insufferable (insufferably) If you call someone or something **insufferable,** you mean they are very unpleasant or annoying.

insufficient (insufficiently, insufficiency) If something is **insufficient** or there is an **insufficiency** of it, there is not enough of it.

insular (insularity) If you say a group of people are **insular** or talk about their **insularity,** you mean they are suspicious of people or ideas from outside their group.

insulate (insulating, insulated; insulation, insulator) If something **insulates** you from some harm, it protects you from it. *They live in a cosy, insulated world.* ■ If something is **insulated,** it is covered with a thick layer of a substance, to stop heat escaping. A substance used for this purpose is called an **insulator.** ■ If an electrical device is **insulated,** parts of it are covered with a substance such as rubber, to stop people touching them and getting a shock.

insulin is a substance in the body which controls the level of sugar in the blood.

insult (insulting, insultingly) If you **insult** someone, you offend them by behaving rudely or saying unpleasant things about them. What you say or do is called an **insult.**

insuperable If you say a problem is **insuperable,** you mean there is no way in which it can be dealt with successfully.

insupportable If you find something **insupportable,** it is so unpleasant you cannot tolerate it.

insure (insuring, insured; insurance) If you **insure** yourself or your property or take out **insurance,** you pay money to an insurer so that, if you become ill or your property is stolen or damaged, the company will pay you a sum of money. ■ If you do something to **insure** against something undesirable, you do it to protect yourself in case it happens. *Owning land is no insurance against poverty.* ■ Americans sometimes use **insure** to mean 'ensure'.

insurer An **insurer** is a company which sells insurance.

insurgent (insurgency, insurgencies) Insurgents are people rebelling against the government or army in their own country. A rebellion of this sort is called an **insurgency.**

insurmountable If you say a task or problem is **insurmountable,** you mean there is no way it can be dealt with successfully.

insurrection An **insurrection** is violent action taken by a group of people against the rulers of their own country.

intact If something is **intact,** it is complete and has not been damaged or changed.

intake Your **intake** of food, drink, or air is the amount you eat, drink, or breathe. ■ If you say something like an announcement is followed by an **intake of breath,** you mean people are shocked by it. ■ The **intake** of an institution or organization is the number of people or things accepted into it at a particular time.

intangible If something is **intangible,** it exists but cannot be seen, touched, or easily explained. ■ A company's **intangible assets** or **intangibles** are things like customer goodwill which cannot be seen or given an exact value, but are nevertheless important for the company's success.

integer (*pron:* in-ti-jer) An **integer** is a whole number like 5 or 23, as opposed to a fraction.

integral If something is an **integral** part of something else, it is an essential part of it.

integrate (integrating, integrated; integration) If people **integrate** into a social group, they become a part of it. ■ If something like an institution or activity is **integrated,** it is open to people of all races and groups. ■ If you **integrate** things, you combine them to form one thing. *We integrate contemporary dance with acrobatics.*

integrity If you talk about someone's **integrity,** you mean they are honest and firm in their moral principles. ■ If you talk about the **integrity** of a group of people, you mean they are united and form a whole.

intellect A person's **intellect** is their ability to think intelligently and logically.

intellectual (intellectually, intellectualism) Intellectual activities involve the use of a person's intellect. The development of someone's intellect can be called **intellectualism.** ■ You say someone is **intellectual** or an **intellectual** when they are interested in, and have an understanding of, complex ideas.

intelligent (intelligently, intelligence) An **intelligent** person has the ability to understand, learn, and think quickly and well. A person's **intelligence** is the extent to which they have this ability. ■ **Intelligence** is information gathered by a government about its country's enemies. The people responsible for gathering this information are also called **intelligence.** *In the war he served with British Intelligence.* ■ **intelligence quotient:** see **IQ.**

intelligentsia The **intelligentsia** in a country or community are the most educated people there, especially those interested in the arts, philosophy, and politics.

intelligible (intelligibly) If something is **intelligible,** it can be understood.

intend If you **intend** to do something, you are planning to do it. ■ If you **intend** something to happen or to have a particular function, that is what you

have planned. *...moves intended to stop the violence.*
■ If something is **intended** for a particular person, they are meant to have it.

intense (**intensely, intensity**) Intense is used to describe things which are very powerful or extreme. *Media interest was intense. ...the intensity of their love.* ■ If you say a person is **intense,** you mean they are very serious and do not show much sense of humour.

intensify (**intensifies, intensifying, intensified; intensification**) If something is **intensified,** the level of activity in it is increased. *...intensified fighting.*

intensity See **intense.**

intensive (**intensively**) An **intensive** activity involves a great concentration of energy, resources, or people on one task. *...an intensive advertising campaign.* ■ **Intensive care** is extremely thorough care provided for seriously ill people in hospital.

intent (**intently**) Intent is used with a similar meaning to 'intention'. *It was our intent to provide a general-purpose research facility.* ■ In law, **intent** is the intention to commit a crime. *He admitted communicating false information with intent.* ■ If you are **intent** on doing something, you are determined to do it. ■ If you are **intent** on what someone is saying, you are paying close attention to it. *She listened intently.* ■ **To all intents and purposes** means something is not exactly true, but is true in all important respects.

intention If it is your **intention** to do something, you are planning to do it.

intentional (**intentionally**) If something you do is **intentional,** you do it deliberately.

inter (**interring, interred**) When a dead body is **interred,** it is buried.

inter- is used to form words which describe something as existing or happening between places, things, or groups of people. For example, intergovernmental relations are relations between governments. *...intercontinental.*

interact (**interaction**) If people **interact,** they cooperate or exchange ideas. ■ If one thing **interacts** with another, the two things react together and affect each other.

interactive You say a computer program is **interactive** when it involves the user communicating directly with the computer. **Interactive** is used to talk about other machines or systems which the user can communicate with in this way. *...interactive television.*

inter alia (*pron:* **ay**-lee-a) means 'among other things'.

interbreed (**interbreeding, interbred**) When plants or animals of different groups **interbreed,** they produce offspring combining the characteristics of both groups. Similarly, you can talk about people from different societies **interbreeding.** *Farmers spreading across Europe would have interbred with the people they were overrunning.* ■ **Interbreeding** is sometimes used to mean inbreeding.

intercede (**interceding, interceded; intercession**) If someone **intercedes** in a dispute, they try to settle it, by talking to both sides. Trying to settle a dispute like this is called **intercession.** ■ If someone **intercedes** on behalf of someone in trouble, they try to help them by talking to someone in authority.

intercept (**interception**) If you **intercept** someone or something when they are travelling somewhere, you stop them before they get there.

interceptor An **interceptor** is a fighter aircraft or ground-based missile system designed to intercept and attack enemy planes.

intercession See **intercede.**

interchange (**interchanging, interchanged; interchangeable, interchangeably**) If there is an **interchange** of ideas or information between groups, they pass these things on to each other. ■ If things can be **interchanged,** one can be substituted for the other without making any real difference. You say things like these are **interchangeable.** ■ An **interchange** is a junction where a motorway meets a main road or other motorway.

inter-city trains are fast trains travelling between major towns and cities.

intercom An **intercom** is a device consisting of a microphone and a loudspeaker, for talking to people in another room.

interconnect (**interconnection**) If things **interconnect** or are **interconnected,** they are joined together, so people or things can get from one to the other. **Interconnections** are links between things. ■ If events are **interconnected,** they are related in some way. *...interconnected economic and social problems.*

intercourse If people have **intercourse** or **sexual intercourse,** they have sex. ■ Social **intercourse** is meeting other people and having conversations with them.

intercut (**intercutting, intercut**) In a film, if one scene or image is **intercut** with another, the film keeps going backwards and forwards between them.

interdependent (**interdependence**) If people or things are **interdependent,** they depend on each other.

interdiction is preventing a supply of something, especially illegal drugs, from reaching a place.

interdisciplinary means involving more than one academic subject. *...the Interdisciplinary Research Centre.*

interest (**interesting, interested; interestingly**) If something **interests** you, you want to know more about it; you can also talk about your **interest** in it. ■ Your **interests** are the things you concern yourself with or enjoy doing. *Her varied interests range from horse-racing to humanitarian causes.* ■ If you are **interested** in doing something, you are keen to do it. If you **interest** someone else in something, you persuade them to do it or buy it. ■ If you have an **interest** in something, you want it because it will benefit you. *The United States and Israel have a long-term strategic interest in maintaining friendly regimes on the Red Sea coast.* A group of people who have an interest in something is called an **interest group.** ■ If something is in the **interests** of a person or group, it will benefit them in some way. ■ If a person or large organization has **interests** in a type of business, they own shares or companies in it. *The company may float off its leisure and hotel interests.* ■ **Interest** is a sum of money paid as a percentage of a larger sum which has been borrowed or invested. You receive interest on money you invest and pay interest on money you borrow. See also **compound interest, simple interest.**

interface (**interfacing, interfaced**) The **interface** between two groups or systems is the area in which they affect each other or have links with each other. ■ The user **interface** of a piece of computer software is its presentation on screen and how easy it is to operate. ■ If one thing **interfaces** with another or if two things **interface,** they have connections with each other or interact.

interfere (**interfering, interfered; interference**) If you say someone is **interfering** in something, you mean they have become involved in it and it has nothing to do with them. ■ If someone **interferes** with a process or system, they damage it or stop it working properly. ■ If you get **interference** when you are listening to the radio, you cannot hear a programme properly because you can hear another station broadcasting at the same time.

interim is used to describe (a) something established on a temporary basis. *...the interim government.* (b) the first part of something which will be given in full later. *...an interim payment.* ■ **In the interim** means in the period between two events.

interior The **interior** of something is its inside part. *...the interior of the Earth.* ■ The **interior** of a country is its central area. ■ An **interior** minister or ministry deals with affairs within their country.

interior decorator An **interior decorator** is a person or firm that decorates the insides of buildings.

interior designer An **interior designer** is a person who gives advice on the way the inside of a building can be decorated and furnished.

interject (**interjection**) If you **interject** or make an **interjection,** you say something when someone else is speaking.

interlace (**interlacing, interlaced**) If two things are **interlaced,** they are joined together closely as if they are woven.

interlink (**interlinked**) If things are **interlinked,** they are connected up to each other. *...a system of interlinked databases.*

interlock (**interlocking, interlocked**) If objects **interlock,** they fit together and are firmly joined to each other. ■ If systems or plans **interlock,** they operate in conjunction with each other.

interlocutor (*pron:* in-ter-**lok**-yew-ter) Your **interlocutor** is the person you are having a conversation with.

interloper (*pron:* **in**-ter-lope-er) An **interloper** is a person who interferes in something, or is in a place where they are not supposed to be.

interlude An **interlude** is a short period of time when an activity or event stops.

intermarry (**intermarries, intermarrying, intermarried; intermarriage**) If two social, racial, or religious groups **intermarry,** people from one group

marry people from the other. When this happens, you say there is **intermarriage** between the groups.

intermediary (**intermediaries**) An **intermediary** is someone who tries to get two groups to come to an agreement, by negotiating with both sides.

intermediate An **intermediate** stage or level comes between two others.

interminable (**interminably**) If you say something is **interminable,** you mean it seems as if it will never end.

intermingle (**intermingling, intermingled**) If people or things **intermingle,** they move around among each other.

intermission An **intermission** is an interval between two parts of something like a play.

intermittent (**intermittently**) If something is **intermittent,** it happens occasionally rather than all the time.

intern (**internment; internee**) If someone is **interned,** they are put in prison or confined somewhere for political reasons. Interning people is called **internment;** a person who is interned is called an **internee.** ■ In the US, an **intern** (*pron:* **in**-tern) is a senior student or graduate doing supervised work, especially in medicine.

internal (**internally**) **Internal** is used to talk about things inside a building, an object, or a person's body. *...an internal wall. ...internal bleeding.* ■ **Internal** is used to talk about things happening or existing inside a country or organization. *...internal security.*

internal combustion engine An **internal combustion engine** is an engine with one or more cylinders, such as the one in a car, which creates energy by burning fuel inside the cylinders.

internalize (*or* **internalise**) (**internalizing, internalized**) If you **internalize** something like a belief, it becomes a part of your way of thinking.

international (**internationally**) **International** means involving more than one country. ■ In sport, an **international** is a match between teams from different countries. A player who plays in one of these matches is also called an **international.**

internationalise See **internationalize.**

internationalism is the belief that countries should co-operate with one another and try to understand each other better.

internationalize (*or* **internationalise**) (**internationalizing, internationalized**) If a crisis or issue is **internationalized,** it becomes the concern of many countries.

internecine (*pron:* in-ter-**nee**-sine) An **internecine** conflict is one between opposing groups within the same country or organization.

Internet (*or* **Net**) **The Internet** is the worldwide network of computer links which allows computer users to connect with computers all over the world, and which carries electronic mail.

internment (**internee**) See **intern.**

interpersonal is used to talk about people's ability to communicate with other people. *...interpersonal skills.*

interplay The **interplay** between things is the way they affect or influence each other.

Interpol is an international police organization which co-ordinates national police forces to fight international crime.

interpose (**interposing, interposed**) If you **interpose** something between two people or things, you place it between them.

interpret (**interpreting, interpreted; interpretation, interpreter**) If you **interpret** what someone says or does in a particular way, you decide that is its meaning or significance. *There are two distinct interpretations of the purpose of his visit.* ■ If you **interpret** something like a set of figures or the result of an experiment, you say what it shows or proves. ■ When an actor **interprets** a part or a musician **interprets** a piece of music, he or she performs it in a particular way. *...one of the greatest interpreters of Wagner.* ■ If you **interpret** what someone is saying, you immediately translate it into another language. An **interpreter** is someone who does this as their job.

interpretative is used to talk about things which provide an interpretation of something. *...interpretative notes.*

interpreter See **interpret.**

interpretive means the same as 'interpretative'.

interregnum (*plural:* **interregnums** *or* **interregna**) An **interregnum** is a period of time between the end of one ruler's reign and the beginning of the next one's.

interrelate (**interrelating, interrelated; interrelation**) If two things are **interrelated** or there is an **interrelation** between them, there are connections between them or they have an effect on each other.

interrogate (**interrogating, interrogated; interrogation, interrogator**) If someone **interrogates** you or you are under **interrogation,** you are questioned thoroughly, to get information from you; the person asking questions is called an **interrogator.**

interrupt (**interruption**) If someone **interrupts** you, they say or shout something while you are speaking. *He was subjected to a stream of interruptions.* ■ If something **interrupts** something else, it stops it for a time. *The game continued without further interruption.*

intersect (**intersection**) If lines or roads **intersect,** they cross each other. An **intersection** is a place where roads cross.

intersperse (**interspersing, interspersed**) If something is **interspersed** with other things, these things occur in it here and there. Similarly, you can **intersperse** one thing with another. *He has interspersed negotiations with his legal advisers with media interviews.*

interstate In the US, an **interstate** is a main road running through several states. ■ **Interstate** means happening between states. *...interstate banking.*

interstellar is used to talk about things which exist or happen between stars. *...interstellar travel.*

intertwine (**intertwining, intertwined**) If two things are **intertwined,** they are threaded through each other or wrapped around each other. ■ If things like systems are **intertwined,** there are many connections between them.

interval An **interval** is a period of time between two events or dates. *...an interval of 25 years.* ■ If something happens **at intervals,** it happens from time to time. ■ If things are placed **at intervals,** they are placed somewhere with gaps between them. *Barriers marked the road at intervals of about a mile.* ■ An **interval** is a short break during a play, film, or concert. ■ In music, an **interval** is the difference in pitch between two notes.

intervene (**intervening, intervened; intervention**) If someone **intervenes** in a situation, they become involved in it and try to change it. Becoming involved in a situation like this is called **intervention.** *...a personal intervention by the President.* ■ If an event **intervenes,** it happens unexpectedly and stops something happening. ■ The **intervening** period between two events is the time between them.

interventionism (**interventionist**) **Interventionism** is a government's policy when it intervenes either in the affairs of other countries or in the economic affairs of its own country. A policy like this is called **interventionist.**

interview (**interviewer, interviewee**) When journalists or broadcasters **interview** someone, they ask them questions about their work or their lives. The conversation is called an **interview.** A person who interviews people on TV or radio is called an **interviewer.** ■ If an employer **interviews** you for a job or gives you an **interview,** he or she asks you questions, to see if you are suitable for the job. People being interviewed for a job are called **interviewees.** ■ If the police **interview** someone, they question them about a crime.

interweave (**interweaving, interwove, have interwoven**) If two things **interweave** or are **interwoven,** they are threaded through each other or wrapped round each other. ■ If you say things like systems are **interwoven,** you mean there are many connections between them.

intestate If someone dies **intestate,** they die without having made a will.

intestine (**intestinal**) Your **intestines** are the tubes which food passes through when it has left your stomach. **Intestinal** means to do with the intestines.

intifada The **intifada** was the Palestinian uprising against Israel in the West Bank and Gaza Strip between 1987 and 1994.

intimacy (**intimacies**) When there is **intimacy** between people, they have a very close relationship. **Intimacies** are things people do together and say to each other when they have a close relationship.

intimate (**intimately; intimating, intimated, intimation**) If you have an **intimate** friendship with someone, you are close friends. Your **intimates** are your close friends. ■ You say people are **intimate** when they have a romantic or sexual relationship with each other. ■ **Intimate** is used to describe things which are personal and private. *...an intimate conversation.* ■ If you have an **intimate** knowledge of something, you know it in great detail. ■ An **intimate** connection between things is a very close one. *There is an intimate connection between a healthy economy and a healthy environment.* ■ If you

intimate (*pron:* **in**-ti-mate) something, you suggest it is true without actually saying so. An **intimation** is an indirect suggestion or sign of something.

intimidate (**intimidating, intimidated; intimidatingly, intimidation**) If someone **intimidates** you, they frighten you by making threats. ■ If you find someone or something **intimidating,** they make you feel nervous and lose confidence in yourself.

intimidatory behaviour is meant to make people frightened.

into If someone or something goes **into** something, they go in or inside it. ■ If someone or something comes **into** a place, they arrive there. ■ If someone or something crashes **into** something, they collide with it. ■ **Into** is used to talk about a change of state or function. *The whole city was plunged into darkness. Cinemas were turned into bingo halls.* ■ **Into** is used when mentioning the subject of an investigation. *...research into fish farming.* ■ If something continues **into** a period of time, it continues after that period has begun. *Officials argued into the small hours.* ■ **Into** is used to talk about dividing numbers or amounts. *The estate has been split into five areas.* ■ If you are **into** something, you are very interested in it or involved with it.

intolerable (**intolerably**) If something is **intolerable,** it is so bad people cannot tolerate it or accept it.

intolerant (**intolerance**) Intolerant people disapprove of behaviour and opinions which are different from their own.

intonation Your **intonation** is the way your voice rises and falls in pitch when you speak.

intone (**intoning, intoned**) If you **intone** something, you speak or recite it slowly and clearly, with little variation in the pitch of your voice.

intoxicant An **intoxicant** is a substance like alcohol which can affect your behaviour or body processes.

intoxicated (**intoxicating; intoxication**) If someone is **intoxicated,** they are drunk. **Intoxication** is being in this state. **Intoxicating** drinks can make people drunk. ■ If you are **intoxicated** by something, it makes you so excited that you are unable to think clearly or sensibly. If something has this effect on you, you can say it is **intoxicating.** *...a climber intoxicated with danger.*

intra- is used to form words which describe something within or inside something else. For example, intra-European trade is trade carried on inside Europe. *...intramuscular fat.*

intractable (**intractability**) An **intractable** problem is hard to deal with. ■ An **intractable** person is stubborn and hard to influence.

intranet An **intranet** is a network of computer links, that makes use of Internet technology, within a business or organization.

intransigent (**intransigence**) If someone is **intransigent,** they refuse to change their behaviour or opinions. *The Australian Trade Minister is blaming EU intransigence for the present stalemate.*

intra-uterine device See **IUD.**

intravenous (*pron:* in-tra-**vee**-nuss) (**intravenously**) **Intravenous** treatment involves giving blood, food,

or medicine to sick people through their veins by a drip. *She is being treated intravenously with antibiotics.* ■ An **intravenous** drug user is someone who injects addictive drugs into their veins.

in-tray An **in-tray** is a tray or basket used in an office to put letters and documents in when they arrive, or when they are waiting to be dealt with.

intrepid An **intrepid** person is brave and daring.

intricate (**intricately; intricacy, intricacies**) If something like a design is **intricate,** it has many small parts or details, often as a result of skilful artistic work. *...intricately quilted satin.* ■ If a system is **intricate,** it works in a complicated way. You can talk about the **intricacies** of a system like this.

intrigue (**intriguing, intrigued; intriguingly**) Intrigue (*pron:* in-treeg) is making secret plans, to harm or deceive people. An **intrigue** is a plan like this. ■ If something **intrigues** you (*pron:* in-**treegs**), it interests and makes you curious about it. You can say something like this is **intriguing.**

intrinsic (**intrinsically**) If something has **intrinsic** value or **intrinsic** interest, it is valuable or interesting because of its basic nature or character, rather than because of its connection with something else. *It is of little intrinsic value, yet one of the most priceless objects in the world is an Olympic gold medal.*

introduce (**introducing, introduced; introduction**) If you **introduce** one person to another, you tell them each other's names, so they can get to know each other. This is called making an **introduction.** ■ If you **introduce** someone to something, you tell them about it or get them involved in it for the first time. The first time someone becomes involved in something can be called their **introduction** to it. ■ When something is **introduced** in a place, it is done or used there for the first time. *...the introduction of 20mph zones in residential areas.* ■ When the government **introduces** a bill in the House of Commons, they present it formally for discussion. ■ The **introduction** to a book is a part at the beginning which tells you what the book is about.

introductory An **introductory** remark or book gives a small amount of general information about a certain subject, without going into details. ■ An **introductory** offer or price on a new product is something like a free gift or a low price, intended to attract new customers.

introspective (**introspection**) Introspective people spend a lot of time examining their own thoughts, ideas, and feelings. Behaviour like this is called **introspection.**

introvert (**introverted; introversion**) If you say a person is **introverted** or an **introvert,** you mean he or she is wrapped up in their own affairs and finds it difficult to talk to people. Being introverted is called **introversion.**

intrude (**intruding, intruded; intrusion**) If something **intrudes** on your mood or your life, it disturbs it or has an unwanted effect on it. You say something which has this effect is an **intrusion.** ■ If someone **intrudes** into a certain place or situation, they are not wanted or welcome there. You call this an **intrusion.**

intruder An **intruder** is someone who goes into a place where they are not supposed to be.

intrusion See **intrude.**

intrusive (**intrusiveness**) You say something is **intrusive** when it has an unwelcome or unpleasant effect on your mood or your life.

intuition (**intuitive, intuitively**) Your **intuition** is an unexplained feeling you have that something is true although you have no evidence or proof of it. You say feelings of this kind are **intuitive.**

Inuit (*pron:* **in**-yoo-it) **Inuits** are the native people of North America or Greenland.

inundate (**inundating, inundated; inundation**) If you are **inundated** with things, you receive so many you cannot deal with them all. ■ If an area of land is **inundated,** it becomes covered with water.

inure (*pron:* in-**yoor**) (**inuring, inured**) If you become **inured** to something unpleasant, you become used to it, so that it no longer affects you.

invade (**invading, invaded; invasion, invader**) If an army **invades** a country, it enters it by force. *...the invasion of Czechoslovakia.* The soldiers invading a country can be called **invaders.** You can refer to an invading country or army as an **invader.** ■ When people or animals arrive in large numbers in a place, you can say they **invade** it, especially when their arrival is unwelcome. ■ If someone **invades** your privacy, they disturb you when you want to be alone. You call this an **invasion** of your privacy.

invalid (**invaliding, invalided; invalidity**) An **invalid** is someone who is very ill or disabled and needs to be cared for by someone else. ■ If someone is **invalided** out of the armed forces, they have to leave because of poor health. ■ If something like an action, procedure, or document is **invalid** (*pron:* in-**val**-id), it cannot be accepted because it breaks the law or an official rule. You can talk about the **invalidity** of any of these things. ■ If a result or argument is **invalid,** it is not acceptable because it is based on a mistake.

invalidate (**invalidating, invalidated**) If a fault in an agreement **invalidates** the agreement, it prevents the agreement being legal. Similarly, a mistake in an experiment or line of reasoning can **invalidate** the result.

invalidity See **invalid.**

invaluable If you say someone or something is **invaluable,** you are emphasizing how useful they are.

invariable (**invariably**) If something is **invariable,** it never changes. ■ If something **invariably** happens or is **invariably** true, it always happens or is true in particular circumstances. *Economic liberalisation invariably leads to demands for political reform.*

invasion See **invade.**

invasive surgery involves entering the body in some way, for example by cutting it open or inserting something into it. ■ **Invasive** is used to describe things which keep getting into a place where you do not want them. *...invasive weed roots.*

invective is unpleasant and sarcastic things said about someone.

inveigh (*pron:* in-**vay**) If you **inveigh** against something, you criticize it strongly.

inveigle (*pron:* in-**vay**-gl *or* in-**vee**-gl) (**inveigling, inveigled**) If you **inveigle** someone into doing something, you cleverly persuade them to do it when they do not really want to.

invent (**invention, inventor**) If you **invent** something, you are the first person to think of it or make it. The thing you invent is called an **invention;** you are called its **inventor.** ■ **Invention** is the ability to come up with clever and original ideas. *...the richness of Purcell's musical invention.* ■ If you **invent** a story or excuse, you make it up, hoping people will believe it is true.

inventive (**inventively, inventiveness**) An **inventive** person has clever and original ideas.

inventor See **invent.**

inventory (*pron:* **in**-ven-tree) (**inventories**) An **inventory** is a written list of the things in a room or building.

inverse (**inversely**) If there is an **inverse** relationship between two things, one of them decreases as the other increases. *Stress is inversely related to job satisfaction.*

inversion If there is an **inversion** of something, it is changed so it is the opposite way round to normal.

invert (**inverted**) If you **invert** something, you turn it upside down or back to front. ■ **Inverted snobbery** is looking down on things which are favoured by educated or upper class people.

invertebrate An **invertebrate** is a creature without a spine, for example an insect.

inverted commas are the set of punctuation marks ' ' or " ". They are used to show where speech or a quotation begins and ends.

invest (**investment, investor**) If you **invest** money or make an **investment,** you use your money in a way which you hope will increase its value, for example by buying shares or property. ■ If a government or organization **invests** in something, it spends money on something it considers useful or profitable. *We must invest in new roads.* ■ If you spend a lot of time trying to make something successful, you can say you **invest** time in it. ■ If someone is **invested** with certain rights or responsibilities, they are given them legally or officially. ■ If someone is **invested** with a title or honour, they are given it during a special ceremony.

investigate (**investigating, investigated; investigation, investigator**) If someone **investigates** something or conducts an **investigation** into it, they find out all the facts about it, to try to get at the truth. You can call someone who does this an **investigator.**

investigative activities involve finding out the facts about something. *...investigative journalism.*

investigator See **investigate.**

investigatory means the same as 'investigative'.

investiture An **investiture** is a ceremony in which someone is given an official title.

investment (**investor**) See **invest.**

inveterate is used to say someone has been doing something for a long time, and is unlikely to stop. *...an inveterate gambler.*

invidious If you are in an **invidious** position, whatever you do will be judged to be wrong. ■ An **in-**

vidious comparison or choice is unfair or pointless, because the things in question are equally good or bad, or cannot really be compared.

invigilate (**invigilating, invigilated; invigilator**) If someone **invigilates** an exam, they supervise the people taking it, making sure they keep to the rules. A person who does this is called an **invigilator.**

invigorate (**invigorating, invigorated**) If something **invigorates** you, it makes you feel more energetic. ■ If a system or activity is **invigorated,** it is made more lively or successful.

invincible (**invincibility**) If a person or thing is **invincible,** they cannot be beaten.

inviolable (**inviolability**) If you say something like a right is **inviolable,** you mean it cannot or must not be taken away.

inviolate If something is **inviolate,** it has not been harmed, or cannot be harmed.

invisible (**invisibly, invisibility**) If something is **invisible,** you cannot see it, for example because it is hidden or very small. ■ In stories, **invisible** people or things are present but cannot be seen. ■ **Invisible** earnings are the money a country makes from services like banking or tourism, rather than by producing goods. ...*invisible exports.*

invite (**inviting, invited; invitingly, invitation**) If you **invite** someone to something like a party, you ask them to come. This is called making an **invitation.** If you ask someone in writing, the note you send is also called an **invitation.** ■ If you **invite** someone to do something, you formally ask them to do it. *He has accepted an invitation to become honorary president.* ■ If someone or something **invites** another thing, they encourage it or make it more likely to happen. *Don't invite trouble by going out again today.* ■ If you say something is **inviting,** you mean it is attractive and desirable. *The democratic future beckoned invitingly.*

in vitro See **IVF.**

invocation See **invoke.**

invoice (**invoicing, invoiced**) An **invoice** is a document listing goods or services you have received, and saying how much you owe for them. If someone **invoices** you, they send you an invoice.

invoke (**invoking, invoked; invocation**) If someone **invokes** a law, they make use of it to get what they want. This is called an **invocation** of the law. ■ If someone **invokes** something like a saying or idea, they mention it to justify their actions, or to persuade people to do something. ■ If something **invokes** a reaction, it produces it. *This would inevitably invoke protests from Brussels.* ■ If someone **invokes** a god, they appeal to him or her for help. An appeal like this is called an **invocation.**

involuntary (**involuntarily**) If you make an **involuntary** movement, you do it suddenly and unintentionally, because you are unable to control yourself. ■ **Involuntary** is used to describe a situation which is forced on someone. *De Gaulle was an involuntary exile.*

involve (**involving, involved; involvement**) If people or things are **involved** in something or it **involves** them, they are connected with it or are a

necessary part of it. ...*a bribe scandal involving referees.* ...*the responsibilities involved in caring for a pet.* ■ If you **involve** yourself in something which is happening or get **involved** in it, you take part in it. ■ If you are **involved** with someone or have an **involvement** with them, you have some sort of relationship with them, especially one in which you are trying to achieve something together. ■ You say someone is **involved** with someone else when they are having an affair with them. ■ You say a situation is **involved** when it is very complicated.

invulnerable (**invulnerability**) If someone or something is **invulnerable,** they cannot be harmed or damaged. ...*the invulnerability of laser-guided bombs.*

inward (**inwards, inwardly**) Your **inward** thoughts or feelings are ones which you do not express or show to other people. ■ If something moves or faces **inward** or **inwards,** it moves or faces towards the inside or centre of something. ■ **Inward-looking** people or societies are only interested in themselves and not in other people or societies.

iodine (*pron:* **eye**-oh-deen) is a dark-coloured substance used in medicine and photography.

ion (*pron:* **eye**-on) **Ions** are electrically charged atoms.

ionize (*or* **ionise**) (**ionizing, ionized; ionization**) If a substance **ionizes** or is **ionized,** the atoms it consists of are changed into ions. This process is called **ionization.**

ionizer (*or* **ioniser**) An **ionizer** is a device which is meant to make the air in a room more healthy by producing negative ions.

ionosphere The **ionosphere** is an area of ionized air in the Earth's upper atmosphere which reflects radio waves.

iota (*pron:* eye-**oh**-ta) An **iota** of something is an extremely small amount of it.

IOU An **IOU** is a written note promising to pay back some money which is owed. IOU is short for 'I owe you'.

ipso facto means 'by that very fact'. You use it to say something automatically follows from the thing you have just mentioned. *A law whose operations cannot be scrutinised by any court is, ipso facto, bad law.*

IQ Your **IQ** or **intelligence quotient** is your level of intelligence, measured by a special test.

irascible An **irascible** person becomes angry very easily.

irate If you are **irate,** you are very angry.

ire is anger.

iridescent If something is **iridescent,** it has many bright colours which seem to keep changing.

iridium (*pron:* eye-**rid**-ee-um) is a very hard yellowish-white metallic element which occurs in platinum ores.

iris (**irises**) The **iris** is the round coloured part of your eye. ■ **Irises** are flowers with long pointed leaves and large purple, blue, yellow, or white petals.

Irish is used to talk about people or things in or from Ireland. ■ The **Irish** are the Irish people. ■ **Irish** is a language spoken in Ireland.

Irishman (Irishwoman) An **Irishman** or **Irishwoman** is a person who comes from Ireland.

irk (irksome) If something **irks** you, it irritates or annoys you. You say something like this is **irksome.**

iron (ironing, ironed) Iron is a strong hard metallic element. It is also an important component of blood. ■ **Iron** is used in expressions such as **iron grip** and **iron discipline** to talk about determined or ruthless behaviour. ...*the iron-fist methods employed by the security forces.* ■ An **iron** is an electrical device for smoothing out creases from fabric. *She used to iron his shirts.* ■ An **iron** is one of a set of nine golf clubs.

Iron Age The **Iron Age** was the period in history when iron tools and weapons were first made.

Iron Curtain The border between the former USSR and its allies and Western Europe used to be called the **Iron Curtain.**

ironic (ironical, ironically) See **irony.**

ironmonger (ironmongery) An **ironmonger** or **ironmonger's** is a shop selling tools, nails, pans, and other things for doing jobs around the house or garden. **Ironmongery** is the things sold in an ironmonger's.

ironwork is iron objects like gates and balconies made in a skilful and attractive way.

ironworks An **ironworks** is a factory where iron is smelted or cast.

irony (pron: eye-ron-nee) (ironies; ironic, ironical, ironically) Irony is a form of humour, or an indirect way of conveying meaning, in which you really mean the opposite of what you say. You call remarks like this **ironic** or **ironical.** ■ An **irony** is a situation involving two factors which contrast in an unexpected or amusing way. You talk about the **irony** of a situation like this, or say it is **ironic** or **ironical.** You say **ironically** when you are mentioning a situation like this. *Ironically, for a man who hated war, he would have made a superb war cameraman.*

irradiate (irradiating, irradiated; irradiation) If you are **irradiated,** you are exposed to a large amount of radiation. ■ If food is **irradiated,** it is exposed to radiation to kill bacteria and make it safe to eat for a longer period of time. This process is called **irradiation.**

irrational (irrationally, irrationality) If you call something **irrational,** you mean it has not been thought out in a logical way. *She became frustrated at the irrationality of his behaviour.*

irreconcilable If two opinions are **irreconcilable,** nobody could have both of them at the same time. Similarly, if two objectives are **irreconcilable,** they cannot both be achieved. ■ An **irreconcilable** disagreement is so serious it cannot be settled.

irrecoverable If a bad situation is **irrecoverable,** it cannot be put right.

irredeemable (irredeemably) An **irredeemable** fault cannot be corrected.

irredentism (pron: i-ri-dent-iz-um) (irredentist) Irredentism is a country's policy of regaining territory which once belonged to it, or is thought to have belonged to it. **Irredentist** is used to describe things to do with this policy.

irreducible If something is **irreducible,** it cannot be modified or made simpler. ...*the irreducible complexity of human life.*

irrefutable If something is **irrefutable,** it cannot be denied or disproved.

irregular (irregularly; irregularity, irregularities) If something is **irregular,** it is not smooth or straight, or does not form a regular pattern. ■ **Irregular** means not happening at regular intervals. ■ **Irregular** behaviour breaks accepted rules or procedures. *About half the results were cancelled because of electoral irregularities.* ■ **Irregulars** are soldiers who fight in a war but do not belong to an official national army.

irrelevant (irrelevance; irrelevancy, irrelevancies) If a fact or remark is **irrelevant** to what is being discussed or dealt with, it is not connected with it, or does not make any real difference to it. You can say something like this is an **irrelevance** or an **irrelevancy.** *His party's landslide victory in the elections makes a multi-party system something of an irrelevance.*

irreligious People who do not have a religion are sometimes called **irreligious.**

irremediable (pron: i-ri-mee-di-a-bl) (irremediably) If a situation is **irremediable,** it cannot be put right.

irreparable (pron: ir-rep-ir-a-bl) (irreparably) Irreparable damage cannot be put right.

irreplaceable If someone or something is **irreplaceable,** they are so special they cannot be replaced if they are lost or destroyed.

irrepressible (irrepressibly) Irrepressible people are lively and energetic, and never let things get them down.

irreproachable (irreproachably) If you say someone's behaviour or character is **irreproachable,** you mean there is nothing anyone could find wrong with it.

irresistible (irresistibly) You say someone or something is **irresistible** when you find them very attractive, entertaining, or amusing. ■ If you have an **irresistible** urge to do something, you want to do it so much you cannot stop yourself. ■ An **irresistible** force cannot be stopped or prevented.

irresolute (irresolution) If you are **irresolute,** you cannot decide what to do. Behaviour like this is called **irresolution.**

irrespective of is used to say something is not taken into account when imposing a rule or deciding about something. *You pay the same fare irrespective of the length of the vehicle.*

irresponsible (irresponsibly, irresponsibility) If you call someone **irresponsible,** you mean they say or do things without considering their possible consequences. You can also call the things they say or do **irresponsible.** *He has been accused of incompetence and irresponsibility.*

irretrievable (irretrievably) If damage or a situation is **irretrievable,** it is so bad it cannot be put right.

irreverent (irreverence) If someone is **irreverent,** they do not show the same respect for someone or something that others do.

irreversible (**irreversibly, irreversibility**) If a decision or process is **irreversible**, it cannot be changed or stopped. ■ If damage is **irreversible**, it cannot be put right.

irrevocable (*pron:* ir-**rev**-oke-a-bl) (**irrevocably**) If something **irrevocable** happens, you cannot afterwards change things back to the way they were before.

irrigate (**irrigating, irrigated; irrigation**) When land is **irrigated,** a system of ditches or pipes is introduced to make sure water reaches all parts of it. *...an irrigation canal.*

irritable (**irritably, irritability**) Someone who is **irritable** is easily annoyed. *She shrugged irritably... His irritability seemed to increase.*

irritant An **irritant** is (a) something which keeps annoying someone. (b) a substance which makes part of your body itch or feel sore.

irritate (**irritating, irritated; irritatingly, irritation**) If something **irritates** you or you feel **irritated** by it, it keeps annoying you. *...irritatingly familiar tunes.* You can talk about your **irritation** with something, or call it an **irritation**. ■ If something **irritates** part of your body, it makes it itch or feel sore.

is See **be.**

ISA (*pron:* **eye**-sa) An **ISA** is a type of account which allows you to save and invest a limited amount of money without paying tax. **ISA** stands for 'Individual Savings Account'.

Islam (**Islamic, Islamist**) **Islam** is the Muslim religion, which teaches that Allah is the only God and that Mohammed is his prophet. **Islamic** means to do with Islam. ■ An **Islamic** state is run on traditional Islamic principles, with religious leaders playing an important part in its affairs. An **Islamist** is in favour of this kind of government.

island (**islander**) An **island** is a piece of land surrounded by water. Someone who lives on an island can be called an **islander.** ■ You can call a person or place an **island** if they differ in some way from the people or area surrounding them. *She was an island of calm.*

isle An **isle** is an island.

islet An **islet** is a very small island.

isobar An **isobar** is a line on a map joining points of equal atmospheric pressure.

isolate (**isolating, isolated; isolation**) If something **isolates** you or you **isolate** yourself, you become physically or socially separated from others. ■ If you are kept **in isolation,** you are kept away from others. ■ When a country or government is **isolated,** it is cut off politically from other countries or governments. ■ An **isolated** place is a long way away from any town or village. ■ If a scientist **isolates** something, he or she separates it from other things, so it can be examined in detail. ■ An **isolated** example or incident comes on its own and is not part of a general pattern. *...an isolated case of cheating.* ■ If you do something **in isolation,** you do it on your own.

isosceles triangle (*pron:* ice-**soss**-ill-eez) An **isosceles triangle** has two equal sides.

isotherm An **isotherm** is a line on a map joining points of equal average temperature.

isotope – **Isotopes** are atoms of the same substance which have different properties because they have a different number of neutrons.

issue (**issuing, issued**) An **issue** is something important which people are discussing or arguing about. ■ If you talk about what is **at issue,** you mean what it is that needs to be settled. Similarly, you can say something is **the issue.** ■ If you **take issue** with a person or what they say, you disagree with them. ■ If someone **issues** a statement, warning, or document, they officially make it public. *...a special issue of postage stamps.* ■ An **issue** is an edition of a newspaper or magazine. ■ If you are **issued** with something, it is officially given to you. ■ If something **issues** from a place, it comes out of it. ■ If someone dies **without issue,** they have no living descendants at the time of their death.

isthmus (*pron:* **iss**-muss) (**isthmuses**) An **isthmus** is a strip of land with sea on either side, joining two large areas of land.

IT See **information technology.**

it is used (a) to talk about an object, animal, or other thing which has already been mentioned. *Meat is cooked over a wood fire and potatoes are baked in it.* (b) to talk about a child whose sex is unknown, or to talk about any child, male or female. (c) to talk about a situation you have just described or are about to describe. *The windows are traversed by a broad bar which makes it extremely awkward to see out.* (d) to talk about things like the weather or the time. *It was raining hard... It is nine o'clock in the evening.*

Italian means in or from Italy. *...Italian wines.* ■ An **Italian** comes from Italy. ■ **Italian** is the main language spoken in Italy.

italics (**italic**) **Italics** are letters printed or written sloping to the right. **Italic** is used to describe writing like this. *...italic type.*

itch (**itches, itching, itched; itchy**) If you **itch** or a part of your body **itches,** you have an unpleasant feeling on your skin which makes you want to scratch. You can also say you are **itchy** or have an **itch.** ■ If you are **itching** to do something or have an **itch** to do it, you are impatient to do it.

item An **item** is (a) one of a collection or list of objects, for example one you are buying or selling. *The only really essential item is a good pair of shoes.* (b) one of a number of matters to be dealt with. *Regional security is the main item under discussion.* ■ An **item** in a newspaper or magazine is a report or article.

itemize (*or* **itemise**) (**itemizing, itemized**) If you **itemize** something, you make a list of the things included in it. *...an itemized bill.*

iteration An **iteration** of something is a repetition of it.

itinerant (*pron:* eye-**tin**-er-ant) people travel around, living and working for short periods in different places.

itinerary (**itineraries**) An **itinerary** is a plan of a journey, showing the route to be taken and the places to be visited.

its is used to talk about something to do with an object, animal, child, or something else. *We liked the house and its position... As the child ages, its wishes must be taken into account.*

it's is short for 'it is' or 'it has'.

itself You use **itself** to say something done by an object or substance affects that same object or substance. *For fertilisation to begin, a sperm has to attach itself to the outside of an egg cell.* You use **itself** in a similar way to talk about a baby, an animal, an organization, or anything else which can be referred to using 'it'. ■ You use **itself** after a word or phrase to make it clear that you are talking about the thing the word or phrase refers to. *In Athens itself, the decision was greeted with scenes of disbelief.* ■ If you say something has a quality or effect **in itself,** you mean it has it on its own, without taking into account other things.

ITV or **Independent Television** is a group of TV companies funded by advertising.

IUD An **IUD** or **intra-uterine device** is a contraceptive device, consisting of a piece of plastic or metal put inside a woman's womb. It is also known as the **coil.**

IVF or **in vitro fertilization** (*pron:* **vee**-troh) is a process in which an egg is taken from a woman, fertilized with a man's sperm in a laboratory, then returned to her body.

ivory is the valuable creamy-white bone which elephants' tusks are made of. ■ When people talk about intellectuals living in an **ivory tower,** they mean they spend their lives cut off from reality and the problems of everyday life. ■ **Ivory** is a creamy-white colour.

ivy is an evergreen climbing plant.

Ivy League In the US, the **Ivy League** is a group of eight prestigious universities in the east of the country, including Yale and Harvard.

J j

jab (jabbing, jabbed) If you **jab** something somewhere, you push it there with a quick sudden movement and with a lot of force. ■ A **jab** is a sudden sharp punch. If a boxer **jabs** his opponent, he hits him with a punch like this. ■ A **jab** is an injection.

jabber (jabbering, jabbered) If you say someone is **jabbering,** you mean they are talking rapidly so you cannot understand them.

jack A **jack** is a device for lifting a heavy object off the ground. ■ The **jack** in a pack of cards is the lowest-ranking picture card. ■ In a game of bowls, the **jack** is the small white ball the players aim at.

jackal – **Jackals** are wild dog-like animals in parts of Africa and Southern Asia. ■ People who take advantage of other people's misfortunes are sometimes called **jackals.**

jackboot – **Jackboots** are knee-length leather boots worn by some soldiers. ■ If people are **under the jackboot,** they are suffering under an authoritarian government.

jackdaw – **Jackdaws** are small birds like crows.

jacket (-jacketed) A **jacket** is a short coat. *...the leather-jacketed security guard.* ■ A potato baked in its skin can be called a **jacket** potato. ■ The **jacket** of a book is its paper cover.

jack-knife If a lorry **jack-knifes,** the trailer swings round at a sharp angle to the cab. ■ A **jack-knife** is a knife with a blade which can be folded into the handle.

jack-of-all-trades If you call someone a **jack-of-all-trades,** you mean they are able to do many kinds of work.

jackpot The **jackpot** is the biggest prize you can win in a competition. ■ You say someone **hits the jackpot** when they have great success or good luck.

Jacobean (*pron:* jak-o-**bee**-an) The **Jacobean** period was from 1603 to 1625. **Jacobean** is used to describe buildings, furniture, and other work dating from that time.

Jacuzzi (*pron:* jak-**oo**-zee) A **Jacuzzi** is a large circular bath fitted with a device which makes the water swirl. 'Jacuzzi' is a trademark.

jade is a hard stone, usually green, which is carved to make jewellery and ornaments.

jaded If you are **jaded,** you feel bored and tired.

jagged (*pron:* **jag**-gid) A **jagged** object has a lot of sharp projecting points.

jaguar (*pron:* **jag**-yoo-ar) **Jaguars** are large wild cats with spotted fur. They live in Central and South America.

jail (*or* **gaol**) **(jailing, jailed; jailer)** **Jail** is another word for prison. If someone is **jailed,** they are sent to prison.

jam (jamming, jammed) **Jam** is a sweet food made from fruit boiled with sugar that you spread on bread. ■ If you **jam** something somewhere, you push it there firmly. ■ If something **jams,** it gets stuck and cannot move freely or work properly. ■ If a lot of people are **jammed** somewhere, they are pressed together tightly and can hardly move. If vehicles **jam** a road, there are so many of them that they cannot move. ■ If someone is in a **jam,** they are in a difficult situation. ■ When people **jam** a radio or electronic signal, they interfere with it, and prevent it being received clearly. ■ You say a telephone switchboard becomes **jammed** when so many people ring in that nobody else can get through. ■ When jazz or rock musicians **are jamming** or have a **jam session,** they are informally playing music which has not been written down or planned in advance.

jamb (*pron:* **jam**) A **jamb** is the upright part of a door frame or window frame.

jamboree A **jamboree** is a large party or celebration.

jangle (**jangling, jangled**) When metal objects strike against each other, you can say they **jangle.** The sound they make is called a **jangle.** ■ You say your nerves are **are jangling** when you feel very anxious or upset.

janitor A **janitor** is a person paid to look after a building.

Japanese is used to talk about things to do with Japan or its people.. *...the Japanese government.* ■ **Japanese** is the main language spoken in Japan. ■ The **Japanese** are the people who live in or come from Japan.

jar (**jarring, jarred**) A **jar** is a glass container with a lid. ■ If your body **is jarred,** it is jolted or shaken, often as a result of colliding with something. *Netball jarred my knee too much.* ■ If something **jars** on you, you find it unpleasant or shocking. *...the jarring quality of his voice.* ■ If two things **jar** with each other, they disagree or clash. *The report jars with the government figures.*

jargon is the specialist language of a subject or group of people. *...cricketing jargon.*

jasmine is a shrub with sweet-smelling yellow or white flowers.

jaundice is a blood condition in which a person's skin and the whites of their eyes turn yellow because of an illness affecting the liver.

jaundiced If someone takes a **jaundiced** view of something, they see only the bad side of it.

jaunt A **jaunt** is a short trip taken for pleasure.

jaunty (**jauntily, jauntiness**) **Jaunty** behaviour is bright and cheerful.

javelin The **javelin** is a field event in athletics. Competitors throw a kind of spear (the **javelin**) as far as they can.

jaw (**jawing, jawed**) Your **jaw** is the lower part of your face below your mouth. ■ A person's or animal's **jaws** are the two bones in their head which their teeth are attached to. ■ If you say people are **jawing,** you mean they are doing a lot of talking.

jawbone A person's or animal's **jawbone** is their lower jaw.

jay – Jays are large birds of the crow family.

jaywalking (**jaywalker**) **Jaywalking** is walking across a road in a careless or dangerous way.

jazz (**jazzes, jazzing, jazzed**) **Jazz** is a style of music invented by black American musicians in the early part of the twentieth century. It has very strong rhythms and often involves improvisation. ■ If music is **jazzed-up,** it is played in a faster and more syncopated way. ■ If you **jazz up** a place or thing, you make it more colourful or exciting.

jazzy (**jazzier, jazziest**) **Jazzy** clothing is bright and eye-catching. ■ **Jazzy** music sounds like jazz.

JCB A **JCB** is a construction vehicle for digging earth. 'JCB' is a trademark.

jealous (**jealously; jealousy, jealousies**) If you are **jealous** of someone, you envy them because they have something you would like to have yourself. This feeling is called **jealousy.** ■ You say a person

is **jealous** when he or she worries that another person is trying to take someone or something away from them. *...an insanely jealous girlfriend.* ■ If people are **jealous** of something like a right or privilege, they value it and are not willing to give it up. *In America, the right to jury trial is jealously guarded in civil cases.*

jeans are casual trousers, usually made of denim.

Jeep – Jeeps are small four-wheeled vehicles which can travel over rough ground. 'Jeep' is a trademark.

jeer (**jeering, jeered**) If people **jeer** at someone, they shout out rude things about them.

Jehovah is another name for God.

Jehovah's Witness The **Jehovah's Witnesses** are a Christian sect who believe that the world is going to end very soon.

jelly (**jellies, jellied**) **Jelly** is (a) a clear fruit-flavoured dessert made with gelatine. (b) a type of clear jam. ■ **Jelly** is a clear substance added to savoury food to preserve it and keep its flavour. **Jellied** food is prepared and served in this substance. ■ If you say your arms or legs feel like **jelly,** you mean they seem to have lost their strength, because you are frightened or exhausted.

jellyfish (*or* **jelly-fish**) (*plural:* **jellyfish**) Jellyfish are sea creatures with soft transparent bodies and tentacles that can sting.

jemmy (**jemmies**) A **jemmy** is a short crowbar used by criminals.

jeopardize (*pron:* **jep**-pa-dize) (*or* **jeopardise**) (**jeopardizing, jeopardized**) If one thing **jeopardizes** another, it makes the other thing less likely to happen, continue, or succeed.

jeopardy (*pron:* **jep**-pa-dy) If something is **in jeopardy,** it is in danger of not continuing or of not taking place.

jerk If something **jerks** or is **jerked,** it makes a sudden short movement. A **jerk** is a movement like this.

jerky (**jerkily**) If something moves in a **jerky** way, it moves in short quick bursts.

jerry-built You say a building or machine is **jerry-built** when it has been built quickly, cheaply, and carelessly.

jerry can A **jerry can** is a flat-sided petrol can.

jersey is a stretchable material used to make clothing. ■ A **jersey** is (a) a sweater. (b) a football shirt.

jest A **jest** is a joke. If you say something **in jest,** you say it as a joke.

jester – Jesters were clowns who had the job of entertaining kings and queens.

Jesuit (*pron:* **jez**-yoo-it) **Jesuits** are members of a Roman Catholic order called the Society of Jesus.

Jesus or **Jesus Christ** is the man Christians believe is the Son of God. Jesus's teachings are the basis of Christianity.

jet (**jetting, jetted**) A **jet** engine propels a plane or other vehicle by shooting out a stream of hot gas. ■ A **jet** is a plane with a jet engine. ■ If you **jet** somewhere, you fly by jet. *...jetting around the world.* ■ A **jet** of liquid or gas is a thin powerful stream forced out through a small opening. ■ **Jet** is a hard black stone used in jewellery.

jet-black If you say something is **jet-black,** you are emphasizing that it is completely black.

jet lag (*or* **jetlag**) (**jet-lagged**) If you have **jet lag** or you feel **jet-lagged,** you feel tired and disorientated after a long flight through different time zones.

jetsam is things thrown from a ship, which float on the sea or get washed onto the shore. See also **flotsam.** ■ Anything which has been thrown away can be called **jetsam.**

jet set (**jet-setter, jet-setting**) Rich and fashionable people are sometimes called **jet-setters** or the **jet set,** especially when they fly around the world, staying in glamorous places. *...jet-setting superstars.*

jet ski (**jet-skier, jet-skiing**) A **jet ski** is a small sea-going vehicle which looks like a motor-bike with skis instead of wheels.

jet stream The **jet stream** is a stream of air which moves over the earth at a great height and speed, affecting the weather.

jettison (**jettisoning, jettisoned**) When a ship **jettisons** something, it gets rid of it, to lighten its load. ■ When people **jettison** an idea or plan, they decide to do without it.

jetty (**jetties**) A **jetty** is a wide stone wall or wooden platform sticking out into the sea, a lake, or a river, where boats can pull up to let people on and off.

Jew A **Jew** is a person who practises the religion of Judaism, or is descended from the ancient Israelites.

jewel (**jewelled**) (*Am:* **jeweled**) A **jewel** is a precious stone, often in something like a ring or necklace. A **jewelled** object has jewels in it. ■ A person's **jewels** are the things they have with jewels in them, like rings and necklaces. ■ If you call something a **jewel,** you mean it stands out from the things around it because it is so attractive. *On the other side is Portbraddan, a little jewel of a village.*

jeweller (*Am:* **jeweler**) A **jeweller** is a person who makes, sells, and repairs jewellery and watches. ■ A shop which sells and repairs jewellery and watches is sometimes called a **jeweller** or **jeweller's.**

jewellery (*Am:* **jewelry**) is rings, necklaces, and other valuables which people wear.

Jewish A **Jewish** person is a Jew. **Jewish** means to do with Jewish people. *...Jewish schools.*

Jewry is all the people who are Jewish, through religion or ancestry.

jib (**jibbing, jibbed**) If people **jib at** something, they object to it. ■ The **jib** of a crane or derrick is its projecting arm. ■ A sailing boat's **jib** is the triangular sail in front of the mainmast.

jibe (*or* **gibe**) A **jibe** is a rude or insulting remark.

jiffy A **jiffy** is a very short period of time. *I'll be back in a jiffy.*

jig (**jigging, jigged**) A **jig** is a lively traditional dance in which people make small kicks and leaps. ■ A **jig** is a lively tune people can dance to, usually played on the violin. ■ When someone does a little dance to show they are pleased about something, this is often called a **jig.** ■ A **jig** is a device for holding things steady while they are being cut

or drilled, and for guiding the tool to the correct place.

jiggery-pokery is mischief, trickery, or dishonesty.

jiggle (**jiggling, jiggled**) If something **jiggles** or is **jiggled,** it shakes up and down or from side to side.

jigsaw A **jigsaw** or **jigsaw puzzle** is a picture on cardboard or wood, cut into small interlocking pieces and sold in a box, so people can amuse themselves by putting the picture together again. ■ You can call a complicated situation or issue a **jigsaw.** *This finding is a crucial piece in the jigsaw of understanding cancer.* ■ A **jigsaw** is a hand-held power saw.

jihad (*pron:* ji-had) A **jihad** is a holy war which Islam allows Muslims to fight against its enemies.

jilt If someone **jilts** the person they are having a relationship with, they end the relationship suddenly.

jingle (**jingling, jingled**) When something **jingles** or is **jingled,** it makes a gentle ringing noise, like tiny bells. You call a noise like this a **jingle.** ■ A **jingle** is a short catchy song used to advertise a product or radio programme.

jingoism (**jingoistic**) When people show they believe their country is better than other countries, especially during a war, you call this **jingoism.** *...a certain jingoistic flag-waving section of the population.*

jink When a person or animal **jinks,** they make a sudden turn to left or right, usually to avoid an obstacle. ■ You say there are **high jinks** when people do things for fun or pleasure which are not generally approved of. *...accusations of sexual high jinks with teenage girls.*

jinx (**jinxes, jinxed**) If you say someone has a **jinx** or is **jinxed,** you mean things keep going wrong for them.

jitters (**jittery**) If something gives you the **jitters** or makes you **jittery,** it makes you very nervous.

jiujitsu See **jujitsu.**

jive (**jiving, jived**) The **jive** is a lively dance performed by couples to rock and roll music. When people do this dance, you say they **jive.**

job A **job** is regular paid work available for one person to do. ■ If you talk about **jobs for the boys,** you mean people are unfairly giving jobs to their friends, or to influential people in return for their support. ■ If you learn a skill **on the job,** you learn it while you are actually working, rather than at a school or college. ■ A task is often called a **job.** *There are plenty of jobs to be done around here.*

jobber A **jobber** or **stockjobber** is someone whose job is to arrange the buying and selling of commodities between stockbrokers.

jobbing A **jobbing** worker does not have a regular employer, but is hired by people to do individual jobs. *...a jobbing builder.*

job club A **job club** is a place where people who have been unemployed for some time are given help to find a job.

job lot A **job lot** is an assortment of things, sold together.

job seeker's allowance is the money paid by the government to some unemployed people who are looking for work.

jock A **jock** is a young man who is very enthusiastic about a particular sport, and spends a lot of time doing it or involved with it. *...football jocks.* ■ A **jock** is the same as a disc jockey. *...a local radio jock.*

jockey (jockeying, jockeyed) **Jockeys** are people who ride racehorses for a living. ■ If people who are after the same thing **jockey for position,** they try to get an advantage over each other.

jockstrap A **jockstrap** is a piece of underwear worn by sportsmen to support their genitals.

jocose (*pron:* joke-**kohss**) people are cheerful and always making jokes.

jocular (jocularity) A **jocular** remark is made as a joke. When someone is making jokes, you can say they are being **jocular** or talk about their **jocularity.**

jodhpurs are close fitting trousers, worn by horse riders.

jog (jogging, jogged; jogger) A **jog** is a gentle run. When someone **jogs,** they run at a gentle pace, usually for exercise. This kind of exercise is called **jogging;** the people who do it are called **joggers.** ■ If you **jog** someone or something, you give them a slight push. ■ If something **jogs your memory,** it reminds you of something you had forgotten.

joie de vivre (*pron:* jwah de **veev**-ra) is enjoyment at being alive.

join (joining, joined) If you **join** someone somewhere, you travel somewhere to meet them. ■ If you **join** an organization, you become a member. ■ If you **join** something which is already happening or **join in,** you take part in it. ■ When people **join up,** they enlist in the armed services. ■ If two roads or rivers **join,** or if one joins the other, they come together. ■ If you **join** two things together, you attach them to each other. The place where they are attached is called a **join.** ■ **join forces:** see **force.**

joiner (joinery) A **joiner** makes wooden fixtures, such as window and door frames, doors, and cabinets. A joiner's work is called **joinery.** See also **carpenter.**

joint (jointly, jointed) **Joint** means shared by two or more people. *It is operated jointly by the police and the army.* ■ **Joints** are the parts of your body where certain bones meet, and which allow you to do things like bend your knees. ■ If a structure is **jointed,** it can bend at certain places. ■ A **joint** is a place where two things, such as pieces of pipe, are fixed together. ■ A **joint** of meat is a large piece, suitable for roasting. ■ Americans call a disreputable bar or nightclub a **joint.** ■ A **joint** is a marijuana cigarette. ■ If you say things are **out of joint,** you mean they do not seem quite right.

joint-stock company A **joint-stock company** is a business whose shares can be bought by the public.

joist – Joists are long thick beams of wood, metal, or concrete, used to support floors and roofs.

jojoba (*pron:* hoe-**hoe**-ba) is an American shrub. Its seeds contain an oil used in cosmetics.

joke (joking, joked; jokingly) If you tell a **joke,** you tell a funny story or make a funny remark. If you **joke,** you say funny things to make people laugh. ■ If you say something **jokingly,** you mean it as a joke. ■ If you **play a joke** on someone, you do something to mislead them and make them look foolish. See also **practical joke.** ■ If you say someone or something is a **joke,** you mean you cannot take them seriously.

joker A **joker** likes telling or playing jokes. ■ In a pack of playing cards, the **joker** is an extra card, usually with a picture of a jester. There are two jokers in a pack. ■ When people say someone or something is the **joker in the pack,** they mean they are unpredictable.

jokey (*or* **joky**) things are not intended to be taken seriously.

jollity is cheerful behaviour.

jolly (jollier, jolliest; jollies, jollying, jollied) A **jolly** person is happy and cheerful. ■ **Jolly** means attractive, enjoyable, or lively. *...a particularly jolly party.* ■ People use **jolly** and **jolly well** for emphasis. *What a jolly good idea... I jolly well hope not.* ■ If you **jolly** someone **along,** you keep them in a good mood.

jolt If something is **jolted** or given a **jolt,** it is shaken by a sudden bump or tremor. ■ If something which happens **jolts** you or gives you a **jolt,** it gives you a nasty surprise or shock.

jostle (jostling, jostled) When people in a crowd **jostle,** they push, knock, and elbow each other, competing for space, or a good position. If someone is being roughly treated like this, you can say they are being **jostled.**

jot (jotting, jotted) A **jot** is a very small amount. ■ If you **jot** something down, you write it in the form of a short note, so you will not forget it. ■ **Jottings** are ideas and thoughts, written down as short notes.

jotter A **jotter** is a pad or notebook.

joule (*pron:* jool) In physics, energy is expressed in **joules.** A joule is the work done when a force of 1 newton is moved 1 metre in the direction of the force. 'Joules' is usually written 'J'.

journal A **journal** is a magazine which covers a particular subject. *...a medical journal.* ■ **Journal** is an old word for a diary.

journalese is a kind of lazy writing used by some journalists, which makes use of a lot of clichés.

journalism (journalist, journalistic) **Journalism** is the writing of news and features for newspapers, magazines, TV, or radio. The news and features themselves are also called **journalism. A journalist** is someone who writes news and features. **Journalistic** means to do with journalism and journalists. *...journalistic ethics.*

journey If you **journey** somewhere, or make a **journey** there, you travel there.

journeyman (journeymen) A **journeyman** is a qualified craftsman who works for someone else. ■ You can call someone a **journeyman** when they are competent at their job, but not outstanding. *...a journeyman boxer.*

joust (*pron:* **jowst**) (**jousting, jousted**) In medieval times, a **joust** was an organized fight on horseback between two knights using lances; this was called **jousting.** ■ Any contest in which one person tries to demonstrate their superiority over another can be called a **joust.** You can talk about people **jousting** with each other.

jovial (**jovially; joviality**) **Jovial** people are cheerful and good-humoured. You say their behaviour is **jovial** or talk about their **joviality.**

jowl (**jowly**) Flabby lower cheeks covering someone's jawbone are called **jowls. Jowly** is used to describe people with cheeks like this.

joy is a feeling of great happiness. ■ If you say someone or something is a **joy,** you mean they give you a lot of pleasure. *She was a joy to behold.* ■ **Joy** is sometimes used to mean 'success'. *She wanted a boyfriend and had no joy with ordinary agencies.*

joyful (**joyfully**) A **joyful** occasion is one where people are very happy and enjoy themselves. You can say people are **joyful** on occasions like these.

joyless activities have no pleasure in them, or give no pleasure.

joyous means the same as 'joyful'.

joyride (*or* **joy-ride**) (**joyriding, joyrider**) When people **joyride,** they steal a car, and drive it recklessly at high speed. People who do this are called **joyriders;** what they do is called **joyriding.**

joystick A **joystick** is (a) the lever a pilot uses to steer a plane. (b) a lever connected to a computer, which lets you control the movements of characters on screen.

JP A **JP** is a local magistrate. JP stands for 'Justice of the Peace'.

jubilant (**jubilantly; jubilation**) If someone is **jubilant,** they are happy and triumphant, because they have had a great victory or success. You can talk about the **jubilation** of people like this.

jubilee A **jubilee** is a special anniversary of an important occasion.

Judaism (**Judaic**) **Judaism** (*pron:* **joo**-day-iz-um) is the religion of the Jewish people, based on the teachings of the Old Testament of the Bible, and the Talmud. **Judaic** (*pron:* joo-**day**-ik) means to do with Judaism. *...Judaic law.*

Judas was the disciple who betrayed Jesus Christ. If you call someone a **Judas,** you mean they have betrayed a friend.

judder (**juddering, juddered**) If something **judders,** it shakes and vibrates violently. A movement like this is called a **judder.**

judge (**judging, judged**) A **judge** is the person in a law court who decides how the law should be applied to the people who appear in court. ■ A **judge** is a person who decides the winner of a contest; you say he or she **judges** the contest. ■ If you **judge** someone or something, you form an opinion about them. *The experiment was judged a success.* ■ If you **judge** something like speed or distance, you estimate what it is likely to be. ■ If you say someone is a **good judge** of something, you mean their

opinion can be relied on. ■ You can say something is **well-judged** when it is done or said in just the right way.

judgment (*or* **judgement**) A **judgment** is a ruling by a judge on a legal matter. ■ **Judgment** is the ability to make sensible guesses about a situation and sensible decisions about what to do. ■ **Judgment** is the ability to form an opinion about someone or something. A **judgment** is an opinion. ■ If you **pass judgment** on someone or something, you give your opinion of them. If you **reserve judgment,** you do not give an opinion until you know more about something. ■ In Judaism, Christianity, and Islam, **Judgment Day** is the day of God's final judgment on the world.

judgmental (*or* **judgemental**) If you say that someone is **judgmental,** you mean they are quick to criticise other people or things.

judicial (*pron:* joo-**dish**-al) (**judicially**) **Judicial** means involving the law.

judiciary (*pron:* joo-**dish**-ar-y) (**judiciaries**) A country's **judiciary** is its legal system.

judicious (*pron:* joo-**dish**-us) (**judiciously**) **Judicious** activities or decisions are sensible and show good judgment.

Judo is a modern Japanese martial art which is based on jujitsu.

jug A **jug** is a container for liquids, with a handle and a small spout.

juggernaut A **juggernaut** is a large lorry. ■ A large organization or system can be called a **juggernaut.**

juggle (**juggling, juggled; juggler**) If you **juggle,** you keep several objects in the air at the same time, without dropping them; this activity is called **juggling.** ■ If you say you **juggle** two or more activities, you mean you arrange them to fit your needs or so that you can deal with them at the same time. *Her career involved constant juggling of home and work... They juggle their debts to get by from day to day.* When someone does something like this, you can say they are performing a **juggling act.**

jugular The **jugular** veins are the veins in your neck which carry blood from your head back to your heart. ■ If someone **goes for the jugular,** they ruthlessly attack an opponent's weak points.

juice is the liquid in fruit and vegetables. ■ The **juice** of a piece of meat is the liquid which seeps out while it is cooking. ■ The **digestive juices** in a person's stomach are the fluids which help them digest food.

juicy (**juicier, juiciest**) **Juicy** food has a lot of juice in it. ■ You use **juicy** to describe things which are interesting, exciting, or scandalous. *...a juicy part for an actor. ...juicy rumours.*

jujitsu (*or* **jiujitsu**) is a traditional Japanese martial art. See also **Judo.**

jukebox A **jukebox** is an automatic coin-operated record player, usually found in pubs and cafées.

jumble (**jumbling, jumbled**) A **jumble** of things is a confused mixture of them. If things are **jumbled** or **jumbled up,** they are mixed together carelessly and untidily. ■ A **jumble sale** is a sale of cheap second-hand goods donated by the public, to raise money for charity. The goods are called **jumble.**

jumbo A **jumbo** or **jumbo jet** is a large wide-bodied jet plane. ■ **Jumbo** is used to describe things which are very large.

jump (jumping, jumped) When you **jump**, you use the strength in your legs to move yourself off the ground into the air. A movement like this is called a **jump**. ■ If you **jump** an obstacle, you move quickly up and through the air over it. The obstacle can be called a **jump**. ■ If you **jump** somewhere, you move there quickly and suddenly. ■ If you **jump** at an offer or opportunity, you accept it eagerly, as soon as it is offered to you. ■ If something **makes you jump**, it causes you to make a sudden movement, because you are startled. ■ If an amount or level **jumps**, it rises sharply. A sudden rise like this is called a **jump**. ■ **jump the gun:** see **gun. jump to conclusions:** see **conclusion.**

jumped-up is used to describe people who think they are more important than they really are.

jumper A **jumper** is a sweater or pullover. ■ A **jumper** is an athlete who takes part in a particular jumping event.

jump jet A **jump jet** is a jet plane which can take off and land vertically.

jump leads are a pair of thick electrical cables with clips at each end, for starting a vehicle with a flat battery. The battery is connected by the leads to the battery of another vehicle, to provide enough power to start the engine.

jump-off In a show jumping competition, a **jump-off** is an extra round, to decide the winner when two or more horses are equal first.

jump-start If you **jump-start** a vehicle, you get the engine to start, either by using jump leads, or by pushing the car while it is in gear and then releasing the clutch. Either method can be called a **jump start.** ■ If an activity or process is **jump-started**, someone or something gets it going. *He decided to jump-start his career by making a few martial art movies.*

jumpsuit A **jumpsuit** is a one-piece garment, combining trousers and top.

jumpy (jumpier, jumpiest) You say someone is **jumpy** when they are nervous or worried.

junction A **junction** is a place where roads or railway lines meet or cross.

junction box A **junction box** is a box where electrical wires or cables meet, and are joined together.

juncture A **juncture** is a point in time which is important to a process or series of events. *They take over the EU leadership at a crucial juncture.*

jungle A **jungle** is a dense tropical forest. ■ You say something is a **jungle** when there is a lot of it and you cannot find what you want. *...a jungle of complex rules.* ■ You call a situation a **jungle** when people there behave in a ruthless way. *...the political jungle.*

junior If someone has a **junior** position in an organization or profession, they are of lesser rank or importance than other people in it. *...a junior minister in the Foreign Office.* ■ If you are someone's **junior,** you are younger than they are. ■ British schoolchildren aged 7 to 11 are sometimes called **juniors.**

junior school A **junior school** is one for children aged 7 to 11.

juniper is an evergreen shrub with purple berries.

junk is discarded objects of little or no value. ■ A **junk shop** sells cheap secondhand goods. ■ **Junk** is used to describe things of poor quality. *...junk books.* ■ If you **junk** something you no longer want, you get rid of it. ■ A **junk** is a Chinese sailing boat with a flat bottom and square sails. ■ **junk mail:** see **direct mail.**

junket A **junket** is a trip taken for pleasure and paid for by someone else, especially one taken by public officials and paid for from public funds. ■ A **junket** is a blancmange-like pudding.

junketing – **Junketings** are expensive events, put on to celebrate something or for the benefit of important visitors.

junk food If you refer to food as **junk food,** you mean it is quick and easy to prepare but is not healthy.

junkie A **junkie** is a drug addict. ■ Someone who is obsessively interested in something can be called a **junkie.** *...a computer junkie.*

junta A **junta** is a small group of powerful people, usually military officers, who rule a country, having taken control of it by force.

Jurassic The **Jurassic Age** began about 200 million years ago and ended about 140 million years ago. The Jurassic Age was the period when many life forms evolved and dinosaurs existed.

juridical (*pron:* joor-**rid**-ik-al) is used to talk about things connected with the law and the administration of justice.

jurisdiction The **jurisdiction** of a court is the power it has to deal with a particular matter. *He claimed that the High Court had no jurisdiction to review the decision.* ■ If a territory comes under the **jurisdiction** of a country, that country's laws apply there.

jurisprudence is the study of law and the principles the laws are based upon.

jurist A **jurist** is an expert on jurisprudence.

juror A **juror** is a member of a jury.

jury (juries) A **jury** is a panel of 12 people, summoned to a court to listen to the facts of a case, then give a verdict on whether the accused person is innocent or guilty. ■ The panel of judges in a competition is called the **jury.**

jury box The **jury box** is the place in a court where the jury sits.

just (justly) **Just** is used with amounts to emphasize that they are not very big. *He was just 15 at the time.* ■ **Just** means 'simply' or 'only'. *Cutting down on fat is just one aspect of changing to a healthier lifestyle... It's just a suggestion.* ■ **Just** is used to say something happened a short time ago, or at the same moment as something else. *She put the telephone down just as the doorbell rang.* ■ **Just** means exactly. For example, if you say something is **just** what is required, you mean it is exactly what is required. ■ **Just** is used with 'as' to emphasize that the first person or thing mentioned has as much of a quality as the second thing mentioned. *A woman can be just as competitive as a man.* ■ If a situation, action, or belief is **just,** it is fair and morally right.

...a just war. ■ **Justly** is used to say that something deserves its reputation. *Australians are justly proud of their native wildlife.*

justice is the principle that someone accused of a crime should get a fair hearing. **Justice** is also fairness in the way people are treated. ■ A **justice** is a judge or magistrate. **Justice** in front of someone's name means they are a judge. ■ A country's **justice** system is its legal system. ■ The **justice** of a cause or claim is its quality of being morally right. *They were confident in the justice of their cause.* ■ If you **do justice** to something, you deal with it properly or completely. *The official statement hardly does justice to the feelings of outrage here.*

Justice of the Peace See **JP.**

justify (**justifies, justifying, justified; justifiable, justifiably; justification**) If someone or something **justifies** an action or point of view, they prove it is reasonable or necessary. *A reduction in inflation justifies a small reduction in interest rates.* When there is a good reason for an action or point of view, you say it is **justified, justifiable,** or there is **justifica-**

tion for it. ■ If printed text is **justified,** it is adjusted to make it fit a space exactly. If a column is right justified, each line finishes at the same distance from the edge of the page, like the columns in this book.

jut (**jutting, jutted**) If something like a rock **juts** out, it sticks out sharply.

jute is a fibre, used to make rope and sacks. It comes from a plant called **jute.**

juvenile A **juvenile** is a young person or child. ■ **Juvenile** means connected with young people, rather than adults. *...a juvenile court.* ■ **Juvenile** behaviour is silly and immature.

juvenilia is work produced by an author in his or her youth.

juxtapose (**juxtaposing, juxtaposed; juxtaposition**) If you **juxtapose** two things or ideas, you put them side by side, usually to contrast the difference between them. *...the juxtaposition of curves and angles.*

K k

kaftan See **caftan.**

kale is a cabbage-like vegetable with curly green leaves.

kaleidoscope (*pron:* kal-**lie**-de-scope) (**kaleidoscopic**) A **kaleidoscope** is a toy in the shape of a tube which you hold in your hand. When you look through one end and turn the tube, you see a changing pattern of colours. ■ Any pattern of colours which keeps changing can be called a **kaleidoscope.** You can describe the patterns as **kaleidoscopic** (*pron:* kal-lie-de-**scop**-ik.) ■ A constantly changing situation can be called a **kaleidoscope.** *...the traditional parties whose kaleidoscopic coalitions have formed 50 governments in the past 45 years.*

kamikaze (*pron:* kam-mee-**kah**-zee) In the Second World War, Japanese **kamikaze** pilots undertook suicide missions by deliberately crashing their planes, loaded with explosives, into enemy targets. ■ **Kamikaze** is used to talk about actions in which someone sacrifices their life or career, or risks injury, in order to achieve something.

kangaroo — Kangaroos are large Australian animals. They move by jumping on their powerful back legs. Female kangaroos carry their babies in a pouch on their stomachs. ■ If you say an unofficial trial or tribunal is a **kangaroo court,** you mean that the accused person will be found guilty whatever the evidence.

kaolin (*pron:* **kay**-oh-lin) is a type of fine white clay used to make bone china and some medicines.

karaoke (*pron:* ka-ree-**oh**-kee) is a form of entertainment in some bars and clubs in which customers

sing well-known songs to a pre-recorded backing tape.

karat See **carat.**

karate (*pron:* ka-**rah**-tee) is a sport and martial art in which two people fight each other using their hands, elbows, feet, and legs.

karma In the Buddhist and Hindu religions, **karma** is the belief that a person's actions in one life have an effect on all their later lives.

kasbah (*or* **casbah**) In many north African cities, the **kasbah** is the oldest part, surrounding a castle or citadel.

kayak (*pron:* **kie**-ak) A **kayak** is a covered canoe with a small opening for the canoeist. Kayaks are used by Inuits (eskimos), and also in the sport of canoeing.

kebab (*pron:* ke-**bab**) A **kebab** consists of grilled meat prepared in one of two ways. A **shish kebab** is pieces of grilled meat stuck on a stick. A **doner kebab** is slices of grilled meat served with salad in pitta bread.

keel (**keeling, keeled**) The **keel** of a boat is a long piece of shaped wood or metal along its bottom. It is there to strengthen the boat and keep it steady. ■ If something is **on an even keel,** it is working or progressing smoothly and satisfactorily. ■ If someone or something **keels over,** they fall over sideways.

keen (**keener, keenest; keenly, keenness**) If someone is **keen** to do something, they are eager to do it. *There has never been any doubt about Harvey's keenness to make changes.* You can also say someone is

keen for something to happen. ■ **Keen** is used to say someone enjoys doing something or is very interested in it. ■ If people are watching something **keenly,** they are paying a lot of attention to it. ■ **Keen** senses let you see, hear, taste, or smell things clearly. Similarly, you can say someone has a **keen** understanding or appreciation of something. ■ In a **keen** contest, the competitors take part in a very determined way, making the outcome difficult to predict. ...*a keenly contested football match.*

keep (**keeping, kept**) If you **keep** in a place or position or if someone **keeps** you there, you stay there. *They kept away from the forest.* ■ If you **keep** something in a particular place, you have it there. ■ If someone or something is **kept** in a particular state, they remain in that state. *They had been kept awake by nightingales.* ■ **Keep** is used to say someone continues to do or have something. *The question is whether the Democrats can keep hold of this advantage.* ■ If you decide to **keep** something, you hold on to it, rather than getting rid of it. ■ If you **keep** part of something **back,** you do not use it all or give it all away. ■ If you **keep** something from someone, you do not tell them about it. ■ If someone or something **keeps** you from doing something, they stop you or delay you doing it. ■ If you **keep** something **off** or **keep** it **away,** you stop it reaching you. *They built a bamboo shelter to keep the rain off.* ■ If something is **kept** to a particular amount, it is limited to that amount. ■ If you **keep** something like a promise, you do what you said you would do. ■ If you **keep to** a rule, plan, or agreement, you do what is required. ■ If you **keep** a record of something, you write things down as they happen. Similarly, you can **keep** a diary. ■ People who **keep** animals own them and take care of them. ■ If you **keep up** with a moving person or thing, you stay with them by going at the same speed. ■ If you **keep up** with what is going on, you make sure you know about it. ■ If someone **keeps on** about something, they talk about it repeatedly or without stopping. If someone **keeps on** at you, they repeatedly tell you to do something. ■ A person's **keep** is the cost of food and other things they need each day. ■ **keep** someone **guessing: see guess. keep your head: see head.** See also **keeping.**

keeper A **keeper** is someone who looks after or is in charge of something. ...*lighthouse keepers.*

keep-fit is keeping fit by doing regular exercise.

keeping If something is **in keeping with** something else, it is appropriate or suitable in relation to it. *The builders are looking at alternatives that may be visually more in keeping.*

keg A **keg** is a small barrel for storing alcoholic drinks. ■ **Keg** beer is kept under pressure in a metal barrel.

kennel A **kennel** is a small hut for a dog to sleep in. ■ **Kennels** are a place where dogs are kept and looked after, for example while their owners are on holiday.

kept See **keep.**

kerb (*or* **curb**) The **kerb** is the edge of the pavement, next to the road.

kerb-crawling is the illegal activity of driving slowly next to a pavement to try and hire a prostitute.

kerfuffle You say there is a **kerfuffle** when there is a disagreement or argument about something.

kernel The **kernel** of a nut is the part inside the shell. ■ The **kernel** of what a person says or does is its most important part.

kerosene is another name for paraffin.

kestrel The **kestrel** is a small falcon.

ketch (**ketches**) A **ketch** is a sailing ship with two masts.

ketchup (*Am:* **catsup**) is a thick cold sauce usually made from tomatoes.

kettle A **kettle** is a container with a handle and a spout, for boiling water in.

key A **key** is a shaped piece of metal which fits into a lock and opens it. ■ If you say something is the **key** to something puzzling or desirable, you mean it is the way to solve or obtain it. *Hard training is the key to success.* ■ The **key** to a map, diagram, or technical book is an explanation of the symbols or abbreviations used in it. ■ The **key** things or people in a group are the most important ones. ...*key personnel.* ■ The **keys** on a typewriter, computer keyboard, or cash register are the buttons you press to make it work. ■ If you **key** information into a computer, you enter it using the keyboard. ■ The **keys** on a musical instrument are the bars or buttons you press to play different notes. ■ If a piece of music is in a particular **key,** it is based on a particular scale of notes. ■ If someone is **keyed up,** they are excited and nervous about a forthcoming event.

keyboard The **keyboard** of something like a typewriter or computer is the set of keys you press to make it work. ■ The **keyboard** of an instrument like a piano is the set of black and white keys you press to play it.

keyhole A **keyhole** is the hole you put a key in to operate a lock. ■ **Keyhole** surgery involves operating on someone through a very small cut in their body.

keynote A **keynote** speech is a very important one, dealing with fundamental issues. ■ If you say something is the **keynote,** you mean that is what is important. *Simplicity is the keynote.*

keystone A **keystone** is a stone at the top of an arch which keeps the other stones in place. ■ The **keystone** of something like a system is the most important part, on which all the rest depends.

kg See **kilogram.**

KGB The **KGB** was the government organization in the USSR responsible for the country's internal security, and for obtaining secret information about the political and military affairs of other countries.

khaki is a yellowish-brown colour.

kHz See **kilohertz.**

kibbutz (*plural:* **kibbutzim** *or* **kibbutzes**) A **kibbutz** is a farm or factory in Israel, where the workers live together and share all the duties.

kick If you **kick** something or give it a **kick,** you hit it sharply with your foot. ■ If you **kick** a habit, you successfully give it up. ■ If someone is **kicked out** of a place, they are made to leave. ■ If someone **kicks up** a fuss, they complain strongly about something. ■ When a football match **kicks off,** it starts. The time it starts is called the **kick-off.** ■ If people or events **kick off** with something, they start with it. ■ If you get a **kick** from something, you find it exciting.

kickback A **kickback** is a sum of money paid for illegally helping someone make a profit.

kick-off See **kick.**

kick-start If you **kick-start** something or give it a **kick-start,** you start it working.

kid (kidding, kidded) A **kid** is a child. ■ Young people who are no longer children are also sometimes called **kids.** ...*college kids.* ■ Your **kid brother** or **kid sister** is your younger brother or sister. ■ A **kid** is a young goat. **Kid** is soft leather made from a young goat's skin. ■ If you handle someone **with kid gloves,** you are careful not to annoy or upset them. ■ If you **kid** someone, you tease them or try to make them believe something which is not true.

kiddie – **Kiddies** are very young children.

kidnap (kidnapping, kidnapped; kidnapper) If someone is **kidnapped,** they are taken away by force, usually to get money from their family, employer, or government. **Kidnap** is the crime of kidnapping someone. A **kidnapper** is someone who does it.

kidney A person's or animal's **kidneys** are the two organs which filter waste matter from their bloodstream, and send it out of their body in their urine.

kidney bean – **Kidney beans** are reddish-brown kidney-shaped beans.

kidney machine A **kidney machine** is a machine which does the work of a kidney for someone whose own kidneys do not work properly.

kill If someone or something **kills** a person or animal, they cause them to die. ■ When there is a **kill,** a wild animal is killed by hunters or by another animal. ■ If you **kill** or **kill off** something, you bring it to an end. ■ If you do something to **kill time,** you do it while you are waiting for something else to happen.

killer A **killer** is someone or something that has killed people. *Heart disease is the biggest killer in Britain.* ■ If someone has the **killer instinct,** they are very determined to defeat their opponents, and are more likely to win because of this.

killing When there is a **killing,** someone deliberately kills someone else. ■ If someone has **made a killing,** they have made a large profit quickly and easily.

killjoy A **killjoy** is someone who tries to stop people enjoying themselves.

kiln A **kiln** is an oven for baking things like bricks or pottery.

kilo (kilos) A **kilo** is the same as a kilogram.

kilobyte Computer memory can be expressed in **kilobytes.** A kilobyte is 1000 bytes.

kilogram (or kilogramme) Weight is often expressed in **kilograms.** A kilogram is 1,000 grams (about 2.2 pounds). 'Kilograms' is usually written 'kg'.

kilohertz (plural: kilohertz) The frequency of radio waves is often expressed in **kilohertz.** A kilohertz is equal to 1,000 cycles per second. 'Kilohertz' is usually written 'kHz'.

kilometre (Am: kilometer) Distance is often expressed in **kilometres.** A kilometre is 1,000 metres (about 0.62 miles). 'Kilometres' is usually written 'km'.

kilowatt Power is often measured in **kilowatts.** A kilowatt is 1,000 watts. 'Kilowatts' is usually written 'kW'.

kilowatt hour Energy is often measured in **kilowatt hours.** One kilowatt hour is the energy generated by 1,000 watts in one hour. 'Kilowatt hours' is usually written 'kWh'.

kilt A **kilt** is a short pleated tartan skirt. Kilts are worn by men as part of Scottish Highland dress.

kilter If a system is **out of kilter,** it is not working properly. ■ If something is **out of kilter** with something else, it does not fit in with it.

kimono (pron: kim-moan-no) (kimonos) A **kimono** is a long loose Japanese garment with wide sleeves and a sash.

kin Your **kin** are your relatives. See also **next of kin, kith and kin.**

kind A particular **kind** of thing is a sort or type of that thing. ■ A **kind** person is caring, gentle, and helpful. See also **kindly, kindness.** ■ If you pay someone **in kind,** you pay them with goods or services rather than money. ■ If you react to someone's action by doing something **in kind,** you do the same thing to them. *Our troops would retaliate in kind if attacked with chemical agents.*

kindergarten A **kindergarten** is the same as a nursery school.

kindle (kindling, kindled) If something **kindles** a feeling, it brings it on. *The war kindled his enthusiasm for politics.* ■ If you **kindle** a fire, you start it by lighting wood or paper. The wood or paper is called **kindling.**

kindly (kindlier, kindliest; kindliness) **Kindly** people are gentle and caring. *His kindliness made him particularly effective with handling personal problems.* ■ If you say someone **kindly** did something, you mean they helped you in some way and you are grateful for it. ■ If someone does not **take kindly** to something, they are not willing to accept it. ■ If you **look kindly** on something, you are sympathetic towards it.

kindness (kindnesses) **Kindness** is kind behaviour. A **kindness** is a kind act.

kindred If you call someone a **kindred spirit,** you mean they have the same view of life as yourself.

kinetic (pron: kin-net-tik) **Kinetic energy** is the energy an object has when it is moving. ■ **Kinetics** is a branch of mechanics dealing with moving objects.

king The **king** of a country is the male member of its royal family who is the head of state. ■ A man is sometimes called the **king** of something when people think he is better at it than anyone else. ...*the King Of Rock.* ■ The **king** is a piece in chess. ■ A **king** is a playing card with a picture of a king on it.

kingdom A **kingdom** is a country or region ruled by a king or queen. ■ The **animal kingdom** is all animals, including birds, insects, and fish.

kingfisher The **kingfisher** is a small brightly-coloured bird which lives near fresh water and catches fish.

kingpin The **kingpin** of an organization is the most important person in it.

king-size or **king-sized** things are larger than the normal size. ...*a king-sized bed.*

kink A **kink** is a twist or curve in something which is otherwise straight. ■ A **kink** is an interruption in the smooth progress of something.

kinky is used to describe strange sexual practices and the people who take part in them. ■ **Kinky** hair is full of tight curls.

kinship is the relationship between people from the same family. ■ If you have a feeling of **kinship** with someone, you have similar ideas or feelings and so feel close to them.

kinsman (**kinsmen**) A person's **kinsmen** are their relations, or people from the same ethnic group.

kiosk A **kiosk** is a covered stall where things like sandwiches or newspapers are sold. ■ A telephone **kiosk** is the same as a telephone box.

kip If you have a **kip,** you sleep for a short time.

kipper A **kipper** is a smoked herring.

kirk is a Scottish word for a church.

kirsch (*pron:* **key-**ersh) is a brandy made from cherries.

kiss (**kisses, kissing, kissed**) If you **kiss** someone or give them a **kiss,** you press your lips against them to show affection or desire. ■ If you give the **kiss of life** to someone whose breathing has stopped, you put your mouth over theirs and breathe into their lungs, to start them breathing again. ■ If something is the **kiss of death** to a plan or organization, it is guaranteed to make it fail disastrously.

kit (**kitting, kitted**) A **kit** is a piece of equipment or group of items kept together and used for a particular purpose. ...*a first aid kit.* ■ A **kit** is a set of parts which you put together to make something. ...*DIY kits.* ■ If you say someone is **kitted out** in a certain way, you are describing the clothes they are wearing. ...*kitted out in smart new overalls.* ■ Someone's **kit** is the clothes they wear for a particular activity, especially a sport. ■ When a building or room is **kitted out,** it is furnished or equipped in some way.

kitbag A **kitbag** is a large cylindrical bag used, especially by people in the armed forces, for carrying clothes and personal possessions.

kitchen A **kitchen** is a room used for cooking and washing up.

kitchen garden A **kitchen garden** is the part of a large garden where vegetables, herbs, and fruit are grown, but not flowers.

kite A **kite** is a lightweight object made to float in the air on the end of a long string. It consists of a frame covered with paper or cloth. ■ The **kite** is a type of hawk with long narrow wings and a forked tail.

kitemark In Britain, the **kitemark** is a symbol displayed on products which meet certain safety and quality standards.

kith and kin Your **kith and kin** are your friends and relatives.

kitsch You use **kitsch** to describe things which are meant to be appealing, but which you think are vulgar or sentimental.

kitten A **kitten** is a very young cat.

kitty (**kitties**) A **kitty** is an amount of money which several people contribute to and which is spent on things they can all use.

kiwi The **kiwi** is the national bird of New Zealand. It has short thick legs and a long beak. It cannot fly. ■ People from New Zealand are sometimes called **kiwis.**

kiwi fruit (plural: **kiwi fruit** or **kiwi fruits**) Kiwi **fruit** are fruit with brown hairy skins and green flesh.

Kleenex (plural: **Kleenexes** or **Kleenex**) Kleenex is soft tissue paper used as a handkerchief. A **Kleenex** is a single tissue of this kind. 'Kleenex' is a trademark.

kleptomania (**kleptomaniac**) Kleptomania is a form of mental illness which makes people want to keep stealing things. A **kleptomaniac** is someone with this illness.

km See **kilometre.**

knack If you have the **knack** of doing something, you are able to do it, though other people may find it difficult.

knacker A person who buys up old horses and then kills them for their meat, bones, or leather is sometimes called a **knacker.**

knackered If you say you are **knackered,** you mean you feel very tired.

knacker's yard A place where old horses are slaughtered for their meat, bones, and leather is sometimes called a **knacker's yard.**

knapsack A **knapsack** is a canvas or leather bag you carry on your back or over your shoulder.

knave A dishonest man is sometimes called a **knave.**

knead (**kneading, kneaded**) If you **knead** food like dough, you press and squeeze it to make it smooth.

knee (**kneeing, kneed**) Your **knees** are the joints where your legs bend. ■ If someone **knees** you, they hit you with their knee. ■ If someone is on their **knees,** they are kneeling. ■ You say a person, organization, or country is **on their knees** when they are in a very bad state.

kneecap (**kneecapping, kneecapped**) Your **kneecaps** are the flat bones at the front of your knees. ■ If someone is **kneecapped,** they are shot through the kneecap.

knee-deep If you are **knee-deep** in something like water or mud, it reaches your knees.

knee-high If grass is **knee-high,** it reaches your knees.

knee-jerk reactions are automatic and unthinking. ...*their knee-jerk hostility to the reforms.*

kneel (**kneeling, knelt** or **kneeled**) If someone **kneels** or **kneels down,** they bend their legs and lower their body until their knees are on the ground, supporting the rest of their body.

knelt See **kneel.**

knew See **know.**

knickerbockers are loose trousers fastened with a band at the knee or above the ankle.

knickers are women's underpants.

knife (**knifing, knifed**) A **knife** (*plural:* **knives**) is a tool with a handle and a blade, for cutting things. ■ If one person **knifes** another, they attack and injure them with a knife. When this happens, you say there has been a **knifing.**

knife-edge If you say a contest is on a **knife-edge,** you mean things are very equal and the result could go either way. ■ If you say people are on a **knife-edge,** you mean they are anxiously waiting for the outcome of something.

knight (**knighthood**) If a man is **knighted,** he is given an honour called a **knighthood** by the king or queen for outstanding achievements or services to his country. A man who has this honour is called a **knight** and puts the title 'Sir' in front of his name. ■ In historical times, a **knight** was a man of noble birth who served his king or queen in battle on horseback. ■ A **knight** is a piece in chess.

knit (**knitting, knitted; -knit**) If you **knit** something, you make it from wool, using knitting needles or a machine. A person's **knitting** is something they are making in this way. ■ If you **knit** things together, you get them to fit together closely. *She was helping to knit the two businesses together.* ■ **Knit** or **-knit** is used with 'tightly', 'closely', or 'loosely' to say how strong the connection is between the people or countries in a group. *...a tightly knit community. ...a loose-knit confederation.*

knitting needle – Knitting needles are long pointed plastic or metal rods for knitting with.

knitwear is clothing which has been knitted.

knives See **knife.**

knob A **knob** is (a) a round handle on a door or drawer. (b) a round switch on a piece of machinery or equipment. ■ A **knob** is a small rounded lump of something. *...a knob of butter.*

knobbly things have lumps on them.

knock If you **knock** or give a **knock** on a door or window, you hit it, to attract someone's attention. ■ If you **knock** a ball somewhere, you hit it with something like a bat. ■ If you **knock** against something, you collide with it. ■ If someone or something is **knocked,** they are hit hard by a person or by something such as a car. *A drunk driver knocked down and killed two girls.* ■ If someone **knocks** you **out,** they hit you so hard you become unconscious. ■ If a building is **knocked down,** it is deliberately destroyed. ■ If a person or team is **knocked out** of a competition, they lose in a match or race and can take no further part in the competition. ■ If you **knock** a person or thing, you criticize them. ■ If someone or something receives a **knock,** they become less confident or less fortunate than they were. *The art world has suffered some severe knocks in the last two years.* ■ If an amount is **knocked off** the price of something, the price is reduced by that

amount. ■ If someone **knocks back** a drink, they drink it quickly.

knockabout is used to describe a type of comedy in which there is a lot of physical action.

knockdown (*or* **knock-down**) If something is sold at a **knockdown** price, it is sold for much less than usual.

knocker A **knocker** is a piece of metal attached to the door of a building. You bang it on the door to attract the attention of the people inside.

knock-on If something you do has a **knock-on** effect, it makes something else happen.

knockout In boxing, you say there is a **knockout** when one of the boxers falls after being hit and cannot get up before a count of ten. ■ In a **knockout** competition, the winner of each match or race goes on to the next round until one competitor or team is the overall winner.

knoll A **knoll** is a small hill.

knot (**knotting, knotted**) If you tie a **knot** in something like a rope, you make a loop in it and pass one end through, pulling the rope tight. If you **knot** something, you tie a knot in it. ■ A **knot** of people is a group of them standing close together. ■ The speed of ships, aircraft, and the wind is usually expressed in **knots.** A knot is one nautical mile per hour (about 1.85kph or 1.15mph).

knotty A **knotty** problem is difficult to solve.

know (**knowing, knew, have known**) If you **know** something like a fact, it is in your mind and you do not need to learn it. *I knew that she had recently graduated from law school.* ■ If you **let** someone **know** about something, you tell them about it. ■ If you **know** a place or thing, you are familiar with it. *He knew London well.* ■ If you **know** a person, you are familiar with them because you have met them before. ■ If you **get to know** someone, you find out what they are like, as a result of spending time with them. ■ If you **know** how to do something, you are able to do it. ■ **Known as** is used to say what someone or something is usually called. *...a professional caddie known as Big Brian.* ■ When only a small number of people know about something, you can call them the people **in the know.** ■ See also **knowing, well-known.**

know-how is specialized knowledge of methods or techniques. *They now had the facilities and know-how to produce advanced weapons.*

knowing (**knowingly**) If you give someone a **knowing** look, you show that you are aware of something even though it has not been mentioned directly. ■ If someone **knowingly** does something wrong, they are aware it is wrong when they do it.

knowledge is things people know. Your **knowledge** of something is what you know about it.

knowledgeable (*or* **knowledgable**) (**knowledgeably**) A **knowledgeable** person knows a lot about a subject, or about many different things.

knuckle (**knuckling, knuckled**) A person's **knuckles** are the rounded pieces of bone where their fingers bend. ■ **White knuckle** is used to describe thrilling things like fairground rides. ■ If someone **knuckles down** to something, they begin to work hard. ■ If someone **knuckles under,** they give way to pressure and do what someone else tells them to.

koala The **koala** is an Australian animal which looks like a small bear with grey fur. Koalas live in trees and eat leaves.

kookaburra The **kookaburra** is a large Australian bird of the kingfisher family. It makes a loud noise like a person laughing.

kopeck (or **kopek**) The **kopeck** is a unit of money in Russia and in other countries formerly in the USSR. There are 100 kopecks in a rouble.

Koran (*pron:* kor-**rahn**) (**Koranic**) The **Koran** (or **Qur'an**) is the sacred book on which the religion of Islam is based. **Koranic** means connected with the Koran. ...*Koranic law.*

Korean A **Korean** is a person from North or South Korea. ■ **Korean** means to do with North or South Korea or their people. ■ **Korean** is the main language spoken in Korea.

kosher (*pron:* **koh**-sher) food is made in a way approved by the laws of the Jewish religion.

kow-tow (or **kowtow**) If you say a person **kow-tows** to someone in authority, you mean they behave in a very humble or respectful way, usually because they hope to get something from them.

kph stands for 'kilometres per hour'. It is written after a number to give the speed at which something is moving. 100kph is about 62mph.

kraal A **kraal** is a village in southern Africa surrounded by a wooden fence.

Kremlin The **Kremlin** is a group of buildings in the centre of Moscow, now used as the government offices of the Russian Federation. In the past, **the Kremlin** was used to talk about the central government of the Soviet Union.

krill (*plural:* **krill**) are small shrimp-like shellfish.

krona (*pron:* **kroh**-na) (*plural:* **kronor**) The **krona** is the main unit of currency in Sweden.

krone (*pron:* **kroh**-na) (*plural:* **kroner**) The **krone** is the main unit of currency in Norway and Denmark.

kudos (*pron:* **kyew**-doss) is fame or admiration someone gets because of something they have done.

Ku Klux Klan The **Ku Klux Klan** is a secret organization of white Protestant Americans who use violence against Blacks, Jews, and members of other minority groups.

kulak – **Kulaks** were rich independent peasants in Russia before the 1917 revolution.

Kung Fu is a traditional Chinese martial art. In most kinds of kung fu, the fighters use only their hands and feet.

kW See **kilowatt.**

kWh See **kilowatt hour.**

L l

lab A **lab** is a laboratory.

label (**labelling, labelled**) (*Am:* **labeling, labeled**) A **label** is a piece of paper, cloth, or plastic attached to an object, with information written on it about the object. If you **label** something, you attach a label to it. ■ If someone is **labelled** as a particular kind of person, people say they are that kind of person, although this may not be true. *They have found themselves labelled 'subversive'.* ■ You can talk about a record company as a particular **label.** ...*a series of hits on the Stax record label.*

labor See **labour.**

laboratory (**laboratories**) A **laboratory** is a building or room where scientific experiments are carried out.

laborious (**laboriously**) A **laborious** task takes a lot of time and effort.

labour (*Am:* **labor**) (**labouring, laboured**) **Labour** is used to talk about the Labour Party. *Labour condemned the move.* ■ **Labour** is hard work. Someone's **labours** are the hard work they do. ...*a pleasant distraction from his political labours.* ■ If you **labour** at something, you work hard at it. ■ You can refer to workers as **labour.** ...*the city's supply of cheap labour.* ■ **Labour** is the work a group of workers does. *They are threatening a withdrawal of labour.* ■ If you say someone is **labouring** under a misapprehension, you mean they believe something which is not true. ■ If someone **labours** a point, they talk about it more than is necessary. ■ If a

woman is **in labour,** she is in the last stage of pregnancy.

labour camp A **labour camp** is a prison camp where prisoners do hard physical work.

labourer A **labourer** is a person who does a job involving hard physical work.

labour-intensive industries or activities involve a lot of workers.

Labour Party The **Labour Party** is the main left-of-centre party in the United Kingdom.

labrador – **Labradors** are fairly large dogs with black or pale gold coats.

laburnum The **laburnum** is a small tree with long stems of yellow flowers.

labyrinth (*pron:* **lab**-er-inth) (**labyrinthine**) You call a complicated series of paths or passages a **labyrinth** or describe them as **labyrinthine** when it is difficult to find your way through them. ■ You can call something you have to deal with a **labyrinth** when it is complicated and difficult to understand. ...*the labyrinthine complexity of the case.*

lace (**lacing, laced**) **Lace** is a kind of delicate cloth with a pattern of holes in it. ■ **Laces** are pieces of cord used to fasten things like shoes. If you **lace** something **up,** you fasten it with a lace or laces. ■ If you **lace** food or drink with a drug or alcohol, you put a small amount in. ■ You can say something is **laced** with a feature when it has that feature to some extent. *The current power struggle is laced with confusion and uncertainty.*

lacerate (*pron:* **lass**-er-ate) (**lacerating, lacerated; laceration**) If something **lacerates** a part of your body, it cuts the skin deeply. A **laceration** is a deep cut in someone's skin. ■ You say someone makes a **lacerating** attack on something when they criticize it fiercely and bitterly.

lachrymose (*pron:* **lack**-ree-moass) A **lachrymose** person cries often and easily.

lack If there is a **lack** of something or it is **lacking,** there is not enough of it, or none at all. *Vital information is still lacking.* ■ If you **lack** something, you do not have it, or do not have enough of it.

lackadaisical A **lackadaisical** person is careless and not sufficiently interested in what they are doing.

lackey If you say someone is another person's **lackey,** you mean they do whatever that person tells them, as if they were their servant.

lacklustre (*Am:* **lackluster**) If you say a person's or thing's performance is **lacklustre,** you mean it is dull and lacks energy.

laconic (**laconically**) If you describe someone as **laconic,** you mean they use few words to say something, so they seem casual or unfriendly.

lacquer (**lacquered**) **Lacquer** is a clear liquid spread on wood or metal to protect it and make it shiny. **Lacquered** wood or metal has been covered with this liquid. ■ **Lacquer** is a clear liquid some people spray on their hair to hold it in place.

lacrosse (*pron:* lak-**kross**) is a team game in which players try to score goals using long sticks with a net at one end to catch, throw, and carry the ball.

lactation is the production of milk by women and female mammals.

lactic acid is a type of acid found in sour milk and produced by your muscles during vigorous exercise.

lactose is a type of sugar found in milk.

lacuna (*plural:* **lacunae** or **lacunas**) A **lacuna** is a missing part in something like a piece of writing.

lacy clothes are made from lace or have pieces of lace attached to them.

lad A **lad** is a boy or young man.

ladder (**laddering, laddered**) A **ladder** is a piece of equipment for climbing up or down something, consisting of two long pieces of wood, metal, or rope with steps fixed between them. ■ **Ladder** is used to talk about progress in a career. For example, if you say someone has reached the top of the **ladder,** you mean they have reached a very high position in their profession. ■ If tights or stockings are **laddered** or they have a **ladder** in them, they have a torn part where some of the vertical threads have broken, leaving only horizontal threads.

laden If a person, animal, or vehicle is **laden** with heavy things, they are carrying a lot of them. ■ You say a person or thing is **laden** with something when they have an unusually large amount of it. *This meeting is laden with significance.*

ladies' man If you say a man is a **ladies' man,** you mean he gets on well with women and enjoys flirting with them.

ladle (**ladling, ladled**) A **ladle** is a large round deep spoon with a long handle, for serving soup or stew. If someone **ladles** food, they serve it using a ladle.

lady (**ladies**) Women are sometimes called **ladies.** ■ People sometimes say a woman is a **lady** when she is polite and dignified. ■ **Lady** is a title used in front of a woman's name, either because she is a member of the aristocracy or the House of Lords, or because she is married to a man who has been knighted. *...Lady Antonia Fraser.* ■ A **ladies** is a women's public toilet.

ladybird – **Ladybirds** are small round beetles, usually red with black spots.

ladybug is the usual American word for a ladybird.

lady-in-waiting (**ladies-in-waiting**) A **lady-in-waiting** is a woman from the upper classes who acts as a companion to a female member of the royal family.

lady killer (*or* **ladykiller**) If you say a man is a **lady killer,** you mean that he succeeds in attracting the sexual interest of a lot of women, but that he is never faithful.

ladylike If you say a woman or girl is **ladylike,** you mean she is polite and dignified.

Ladyship When a woman has the title 'Lady', people refer to her as **Her Ladyship.**

lag (**lagging, lagged**) You say a person or thing **lags** when they fail to keep up with other people or things. *Statistics lag a long way behind what's happening in the real economy.* ■ A time **lag** is a period of time between the ending of one thing and the beginning of another. ■ If you **lag** something like a hot water pipe or the inside of a roof, you cover it with a fibreglass material to stop heat escaping. ■ See also **jet lag.**

lager is a kind of light beer.

lager lout Noisy violent drunken young men are sometimes called **lager louts.**

laggard If you call someone a **laggard,** you mean they are slow at dealing with something.

lagoon A **lagoon** is an area of calm sea water separated from the ocean by reefs or sandbanks.

laid See **lay.**

laid-back people are calm and relaxed, as if nothing ever worries them.

lain See **lie.**

lair A wild animal's **lair** is the place where it lives. A lair is usually underground or well-hidden. ■ Someone's **lair** is the room or hiding place they go to, especially when they want to be alone.

laird A **laird** is a landowner in Scotland who owns a large area of land.

laissez-faire (*pron:* lay-say-**fair**) is a policy based on the idea that government should not interfere with the workings of business such as prices or wages.

laity (*pron:* **layi**-tee) The **laity** are all the people involved in the work of a church who are not clergy, monks, or nuns.

lake A **lake** is a large area of fresh water, surrounded by land.

lama (*pron:* **lah**-ma) A **lama** is a Buddhist priest or monk in Tibet or Mongolia.

lamb (**lambing**) A **lamb** is a young sheep. ■ **Lambing** is one of several times in a year when a large number of lambs are born on a farm. ■ **Lamb** is the meat of a sheep or lamb.

lambast (**lambasting**) If someone **lambasts** a person or organization, they criticize them severely.

lambswool is the soft hair of young sheep, used mainly in knitwear.

lame (**lamely, lameness**) If a person or animal is **lame,** they cannot walk properly because of a leg injury. ■ If you say a person or organization is a **lame duck,** you mean they are not successful, and need a lot of help. ■ If you say something like an excuse or remark is **lame,** you mean it very weak.

lamé (*pron:* **lah**-may) is cloth with threads of gold or silver woven into it. *...a gold lamé shirt.*

lament (*pron:* la-**ment**) If someone **laments** something, they say how sad they are about it, or how much they regret it. You call what they say a **lament.** ■ A **lament** is a poem or song written to show sadness about someone's death.

lamentable (**lamentably**) If you say something is **lamentable,** you mean it is very unfortunate or disappointing.

lamentation – **Lamentations** are expressions of grief or disappointment.

laminated (**laminate**) A **laminated** substance or material is made from thin layers of wood or plastic stuck together. A substance like this is called a **laminate.** ■ If a product is **laminated,** it is covered with a thin sheet of clear plastic to protect it.

lamp A **lamp** is a light which works by electricity or by burning something like oil.

lampoon (**lampooning, lampooned**) If you **lampoon** a person or thing, you criticize them by making fun of them. What you say or write is called a **lampoon.**

lamp-post A **lamp-post** is a tall pole beside a road with a light on top.

lamprey The **lamprey** is an eel-like fish with a round sucking mouth.

lampshade A **lampshade** is a decorative cover over an electric light bulb.

lance (**lancing, lanced**) If a doctor **lances** something like a boil, he or she pierces it to let the pus drain out. ■ A **lance** is a long spear.

lance-corporal A **lance-corporal** is an NCO of the lowest rank in the army.

lancet A **lancet** is a surgeon's small, pointed knife with two sharp edges.

land (**landed**) You use **land** to talk about an area of ground. **Landed** people own large areas of land. ■ **Land** is used to talk about solid ground, as distinct from the sea or air. *We turned away from land and headed out to sea.* ■ If something which has been moving through the air **lands** somewhere, it comes down to earth. ■ If a ship calls at a place to unload passengers or cargo, you say it **lands** there. ■ **Land** is sometimes used to mean 'country'. *Australia is a land of opportunities.* ■ When people talk about **the land,** they mean farming and its way of life. ■ If you **land** a job, you succeed in getting it. ■ If someone **lands** you with an unpleasant situation, they put you in a position where you have to deal with it.

landfall is the first sighting of land after a long sea voyage.

landfill A **landfill** or **landfill site** is a place where large amounts of waste are disposed of by burying them in a large deep hole. Disposing of waste like this is called **landfill.**

landing A **landing** is an area at the top of a staircase with rooms leading off it. ■ If the pilot of an aircraft makes a **landing,** he or she brings the aircraft down to the ground. ■ A **landing** is the arrival of troops by boat from the sea.

landing craft A **landing craft** is a boat or ship designed to land troops and military equipment on a beach.

landing gear The **landing gear** of a plane is the part, including the wheels, which supports the aircraft when it is on the ground.

landing stage A **landing stage** is a wooden platform extending over an area of water for landing goods and passengers from a boat.

landing strip A **landing strip** is a long flat piece of land where aircraft can take off and land.

landlady (**landlord**) A **landlady** or **landlord** is a person who owns a house, flat, or room which she or he rents out to people. ■ The **landlady** or **landlord** of a pub is the person who owns it or runs it on behalf of a brewery.

landlocked A **landlocked** country is surrounded by other countries and has no sea coast.

landlord See **landlady.**

landlubber People who are not used to travelling on water and know very little about the sea are sometimes humorously called **landlubbers.**

landmark A **landmark** is something like a hill which you can see from a lot of places and which can help you work out where you are. ■ A **landmark** is an important stage in the development of something.

land mass A **land mass** is a very large area of land, such as a continent.

landmine A **landmine** is an explosive device put on or under the ground which explodes when touched.

land registry A **land registry** is a government office where records are kept about the size, location, and ownership of each piece of land in a country or region.

landscape (**landscaping, landscaped**) The **landscape** is everything you can see when you look across an area of land. ■ A **landscape** is a painting of the countryside. ■ If someone **landscapes** an area of land, they alter it to make it look attractive, for example by planting trees. A person who designs schemes of this kind is called a **landscape gardener** or a **landscape architect.** ■ The **landscape** of a situation is its background and everything which affects it. *...the bewildering political landscape of post-communist Russia.*

landslide If a political party wins a general election by a **landslide,** they win by a very large number of votes. ■ A **landslide** is a large amount of earth and rocks falling down the side of a mountain.

landslip A **landslip** is a small movement of earth and rocks down a slope.

landward The **landward** side of something on the coast is the side which faces away from the sea or is furthest from the sea.

lane A **lane** is a narrow road in the country. ■ Roads, race courses, and swimming pools are sometimes divided into **lanes.** These are parallel strips separated by lines. ■ You use **lane** to talk about a well-defined route used by ships or aircraft, which smaller or privately owned craft may not use. *...the vital sea lanes.*

language A **language** is a system of sounds and written symbols used by the people of a country or area to communicate with each other. ■ **Language** is the use of words to communicate with other people. *This research helps teachers to understand how children acquire language.* ■ **Language** is used to talk about non-verbal systems of communication, for example sign language. ■ The **language** of a subject is the special words and phrases used to talk about it. *...obscure legal language.* ■ **Language** is used to talk about the style in which something is written or spoken. *...a booklet summarizing it in plain language.* You can talk about someone's use of rude words as bad **language** when it offends you.

language laboratory A **language laboratory** is a classroom equipped with tape recorders and headphones where people can improve their foreign language skills.

languid (languidly) If you say someone is **languid,** you mean they behave as though they have no energy or little interest in what they are doing.

languish (languishes, languishing, languished) If someone is forced to remain in a place where they are suffering, you can say they are **languishing** there. ■ You say something is **languishing** when it is not successful. *New products languish on the drawing board.*

languor (*pron:* lang-or) **(languorous)** **Languor** is a pleasant feeling of being relaxed and not having much interest in anything. You can talk about feelings like these as **languorous.** *...the languorous hot summer.*

lank hair is long, greasy, and unattractive.

lanky people are very tall and thin.

lantern A **lantern** is a lamp in a metal frame with glass sides.

lap (lapping, lapped) In a race, if you have completed a **lap,** you have gone round the course once. If you **lap** someone else, you pass them while they are still on the previous lap. ■ A person's **lap** is the flat area formed by their thighs when they are sitting down. ■ If water **laps** against something, it touches it gently and makes a soft slapping sound. ■ If an animal **laps** a drink, it uses its tongue to flick the liquid into its mouth.

lapdog A **lapdog** is a small quiet well-behaved pet dog. ■ If you say someone is a person's **lapdog,** you mean they do whatever that person wants them to do.

lapel (*pron:* lap-**pel**) The **lapels** of a jacket are the two parts at the front which are folded back on each side and join the collar.

lapis lazuli (*pron:* **lap**-iss **lazz**-yoo-lie) is a bright blue semi-precious stone, used in making jewellery.

lapse (lapsing, lapsed) The **lapse** of time between two events is the period between them. ■ If a period of time **lapses,** it passes. ■ If something like a legal contract **lapses,** it is not renewed and becomes invalid. ■ If someone has a **lapse** of some kind, they fail to do something or do not do it as well as normal. *...a serious security lapse.* ■ If someone starts behaving in a way you do not approve of, you can say they **lapse** into this behaviour. A **lapse** is a piece of bad behaviour by someone who normally behaves well.

laptop A **laptop** computer is small enough to be carried around and used without a desk.

lapwing The **lapwing** or **peewit** is a black and white bird with a crested head.

larceny is the crime of theft.

larch (larches) The **larch** is a tree which produces cones and has needle-shaped leaves.

lard is soft white fat from a pig, used for cooking. ■ If you say someone's speech or writing is **larded** with unnecessary or unconvincing words or ideas, you mean they use them a lot.

larder A **larder** is a room or cupboard where food is kept.

large (larger, largest) **Large** is used to say something is of great size. *...a large cloud.* ■ **By and large** is used to say something is generally true, but not completely true. *By and large, they were free to do as they wished.* ■ **At large** is used to talk about all the people in a country or community, as distinct from one group. *This anxiety is felt not only by MPs but by the people at large.* ■ If a dangerous person or animal is **at large,** they are moving around freely and have not been captured.

largely is used to say something is mostly true, but not completely true. *The radio's casualty figures were largely confirmed by hospitals.*

large-scale is used to describe something which exists over a wide area, or involves a lot of people or things. *...a large-scale refugee problem.* ■ A **large-scale** map is drawn to a larger scale than usual.

largesse (*pron:* lar-**zhess;** the 'zh' sounds like 's' in 'pleasure')* is generosity, especially in giving away large amounts of money.

largish things are fairly large.

lark The **lark** or **skylark** is a small brown bird with a pleasant song. ■ If you say someone is **larking about** or doing something for a **lark,** you mean they are enjoying themselves doing silly or mischievous things.

larva (larval) A **larva** (*plural:* **larvae**) is an insect at the stage before it becomes an adult. It looks like a short fat worm. **Larval** means to do with insect larvae. *...the larval stage.*

laryngitis is a throat infection in which a person's larynx becomes swollen and painful, making speech difficult for them.

larynx (*plural:* **larynxes** or **larynges**) Your **larynx** is the top part of the passage from your throat to your lungs. It contains your vocal cords.

lasagne

lasagne is (a) a type of pasta made in wide flat sheets. (b) a cooked dish made from this pasta together with meat or vegetables.

lascivious If someone is **lascivious,** they are eager for sex.

laser A **laser** is a narrow beam of concentrated light. ■ A **laser** is a machine which produces laser beams. ■ A **laser printer** is a printer connected to a computer which produces very clear print or pictures using laser light.

lash (**lashes, lashing, lashed**) If someone **lashes** a person or animal or gives them a **lashing,** they hit them with a whip. **Lashes** are blows with a whip, especially blows on someone's back given as a punishment. ■ If someone **lashes out,** they suddenly try to hit someone else. ■ You say someone **lashes out** at someone when they attack them fiercely in speech or writing. ■ If the rain or wind **lashes** something, it hits it violently. ■ If you **lash** an object to something, you tie it there tightly. ■ A person's **lashes** are the hairs growing on the edge of their eyelids. ■ **Lashings** of something means a lot of it. ...*hot-dogs served with lashings of mustard.*

lass (**lasses**) A **lass** is a girl or young woman.

lassie In Scotland, a **lassie** is a girl or young woman.

lassitude is tiredness, laziness, or lack of interest.

lasso (*pron:* lass-**soo**) (**lassoes, lassoing, lassoed**) A **lasso** is a long rope with a noose at one end. If someone **lassoes** an animal, they catch it using a lasso.

last is used to talk about the most recent period or event of a particular type, or the most recent time something happened. ...*last December.* ...*the last general election... They last saw their homeland nine years ago.* ■ **The last** is used to say something did not happen or exist again after a particular time. *That was the last I ever saw of Northcliffe.* ■ When something you have been waiting for finally happens, you can say it happens **at last.** ■ The **last** thing of a particular kind is the one which comes at the end, after all the others. *He missed the last bus.* ■ The **last** of something or the **last** parts of it are the remaining parts. *She removed the last traces of make-up.* ■ If something **lasts** for a certain time, that is how long it goes on for before it finishes or can no longer be used. ■ If something **lasts,** it is around for a long time. ...*a plan to bring lasting peace to the Middle East.* ■ **the last word:** see **word. the last straw:** see **straw.**

last-ditch is used to talk about a final attempt to prevent something bad happening. ...*a last ditch appeal for peace.*

Last Judgement For Christians, the **Last Judgement** is the end of the world, when God will judge everyone.

lastly You use **lastly** when you are making a final point or mentioning a final item in a list. *Lastly, there is the vexed question of the ownership of guns.*

last post The **last post** is an army bugle-call played at sunset and military funerals.

last rites If a Christian priest gives the **last rites** to a dying person, he holds a special religious ceremony for them.

latch (**latches, latching, latched**) A **latch** is a fastening on a door or gate. It consists of a metal bar which slots into a catch. ■ If you **latch onto** something like an idea, you make use of it as a way of dealing with something.

late (**later, latest; lately, lateness**) **Late** is used to say something happens towards the end of a period of time or a person's life. ...*late September.* ...*Picasso's late work.* ■ If you are **late** for something or arrive somewhere **late,** you should have been there earlier. ■ If it is **too late** to do something, it is no longer possible to do it. If you say something happens **too late,** you mean it happens after the time when it would have been useful. ■ **Late** is used to say someone does something after the time they normally do it. *We had a late lunch.* ■ **Lately** and **of late** are used to talk about things which have happened recently. *Business has not been so good lately.* ■ **Late** is used to say someone has died recently. ...*the late Walter Mathau.* ■ The **latest** thing of a particular kind is the most recent one. ...*her latest book.* ■ You use **later** or **later on** to talk about a time coming fairly soon. *Later on, we shall have some music.* ■ You use **later** to talk about a time coming after the one you have been talking about. *I returned four weeks later.*

latecomer You can call people **latecomers** when they (a) arrive late for an organized event. (b) get involved in something at a later stage than other people. *The National Health Service is a relative latecomer to modern management training.*

latent If someone has **latent** qualities or feelings, these qualities or feelings have not yet shown themselves, but may do so in the future.

lateral movement is sideways, rather than upwards or forward. ■ **Lateral thinking** is a way of solving problems in an imaginative way, rather than by using logic or accepted ways of thinking.

latex is a substance obtained from trees such as the rubber tree and used to make rubber and glue.

lath is strips of thin wood put onto the inside walls of buildings before covering them with plaster.

lathe A **lathe** is a machine used for shaping wood or metal.

lather When a substance such as soap **lathers** or produces a **lather,** it produces a white mass of bubbles when mixed with water. When you **lather** an object, you rub soap on it and produce a lather. ■ If you say someone **gets in a lather,** you mean they get upset, angry, or agitated over something insignificant.

Latin is the language of the ancient Romans. ■ **Latin** is sometimes used to describe dark-haired, dark-eyed people who come from countries where French, Italian, Spanish, or Portuguese are spoken.

Latin America (**Latin American**) The countries of South and Central America where Spanish or Portuguese is spoken are called **Latin America. Latin American** is used to describe people and things from these countries. A **Latin American** is a person from Latin America.

latitude The **latitude** of a place is how far north or south it is from the equator, measured in degrees.

■ **Latitude** is the amount of freedom people have in choosing how to do things. *Actors say he allows them great latitude in interpreting his characters.*

latrine (*pron:* la-**treen**) **Latrines** are toilets, especially temporary ones.

latter is used to talk about the second of two people or things that have already been mentioned. *Buy your mineral water in glass, not plastic. The latter can affect the taste.* ■ The **latter** half of something is the second half. *...the latter half of the century.*

latter-day things or people are the modern equivalents of things or people in the past. *...a latter-day Don Juan.*

latterly means having happened recently.

lattice A **lattice** is a structure made of strips of wood which cross over each other diagonally leaving holes in between.

laud (**lauding, lauded**) If you **laud** someone, you praise them.

laudable (**laudably**) If you call someone's efforts or goals **laudable,** you mean they deserve to be praised and admired.

laudatory A **laudatory** speech or piece of writing expresses praise for someone.

laugh When you **laugh,** you make a noise which shows you are happy or amused. The noise you make is called a **laugh.** ■ If people refuse to take something seriously, you can say they **laugh at** it or **laugh** it **off.**

laughable (**laughably**) If you say someone or something is **laughable,** you mean they appear ridiculous and cannot be taken seriously.

laughing stock If a person or organization has become a **laughing stock,** they have been made to appear ridiculous.

laughter is the act of laughing, or the sound of people laughing.

launch (**launches, launching, launched**) If someone **launches** something like a political movement, they start it. You can talk about the **launch** of something like this. ■ When a company **launches** a new product, it makes it available for the first time. You call this the **launch** of the product. A **launch** is also a social event to publicize a new product. ■ If you **launch into** a speech, fight, or something else, you enthusiastically start it. ■ When a ship is **launched,** it is put into water for the first time. ■ When a rocket is **launched,** it is sent into space. You call this its **launch.** ■ A **launch** is a large motorboat.

launcher A **launcher** is (a) a device for holding a rocket, missile, or satellite before it is launched. (b) a rocket from which a satellite is released into orbit.

launching pad A **launching pad** is the same as a launch pad.

launch pad A **launch pad** is a platform from which rockets, missiles, or satellites are launched. ■ If you say something is a **launch pad** for something else, you mean people use it as a means of going on to something better.

launder (**laundering, laundered; launderer**) When things like clothes and sheets are **laundered,** they are washed and ironed. ■ If someone **launders** money obtained illegally, they invest it legitimately, so that no-one knows it was illegally obtained. Someone who invests money like this for people is called a **money launderer.**

launderette A **launderette** is a place with washing machines and dryers which people can pay to use.

laundry (**laundries**) A person's **laundry** consists of things like clothes, sheets, and towels which need to be washed, or have just been washed. ■ A **laundry** is a firm which washes and irons clothes, sheets, and towels for people.

laureate (*pron:* **lor**-ee-at) A **laureate** is someone who has been honoured with an award for their work in art or science. See also **poet laureate.**

laurel The **laurel** is an evergreen tree with shiny leaves. ■ If you say someone is **resting on their laurels,** you mean they are satisfied with what they have achieved and are not making any more effort.

lava (*pron:* **lah**-va) is hot liquid rock which comes out of a volcano and becomes solid as it cools.

lavatory (**lavatories**) A **lavatory** is the same as a toilet.

lavender is a garden plant with sweet-smelling bluish-purple flowers.

lavish (**lavishes, lavishing, lavished; lavishly**) If you describe something as **lavish,** you mean it is extravagant. *They enjoy a lavish lifestyle.* ■ If you **lavish** something like money or affection on someone or something, you spend a lot of money on them or give them a lot of affection.

law The **law** is a system of rules developed by the government of a country for dealing with crime, business agreements, and social relationships. Each rule is called a **law.** ■ **Law** is used to talk about a particular branch of the law. *...company law.* ■ Rules of behaviour are sometimes called **laws.** *Children soon accept social laws.* ■ In science, a **law** is a general rule which says something will always happen in certain conditions. ■ See also **criminal law, civil law.**

law-abiding people obey the law.

law and order If you say there is **law and order** in a country, you mean the laws there are generally accepted and obeyed.

law-breaking (**law-breaker**) **Law-breaking** is doing something illegal. People who do illegal things are called **law-breakers.**

law court A **law court** is a place where legal matters are decided by a magistrate, or by a judge and jury.

law-enforcement is the methods used in a country to make sure its laws are obeyed.

lawful (**lawfully**) If something like an activity or organization is **lawful,** it is allowed by law.

lawless (**lawlessness**) You say people are **lawless** when they do not respect the law, especially when they commit violent crimes.

Law Lord The **Law Lords** are the Lord Chancellor and other members of the House of Lords who belong to the legal profession.

lawmaker A country's **lawmakers** are the people who propose and pass new laws.

lawn A **lawn** is an area of short grass in a garden.

lawnmower A **lawnmower** is a machine for cutting a lawn.

lawn tennis is tennis played on grass, rather than on clay or hard courts.

lawsuit A **lawsuit** is a civil court case brought by one person or organization against another.

lawyer A **lawyer** is a person qualified to advise people about the law and represent them in court. See also **barrister, solicitor, attorney, advocate.**

lax (**laxity**) If you say a system is **lax,** you mean the rules are not being obeyed or standards are not being maintained. You can say the people involved are **lax,** or talk about their **laxity.**

laxative A **laxative** is a medicine for curing constipation.

laxity See **lax.**

lay (**laying, laid**) See **lie.** ■ If you **lay** something somewhere, you place it there. ■ If you **lay** the table, you put out the knives, forks, etc before a meal. ■ When a bird **lays** an egg, the egg comes out of its body. ■ If someone **lays on** food, entertainment, or a service, they provide it. ■ If someone **lays** the basis for something, they do something in preparation for it. ■ If someone **lays out** a garden or a new development, they plan or design it. ■ If someone **lays down** something like a requirement, they insist it must be done. ■ If workers are **laid off,** they are told to leave their jobs, usually because there is no more work. ■ A **lay-off** is a period of time when someone does not take part in their normal activities. ...*a lengthy lay-off through injury.* ■ If a criminal charge or a criticism is **laid against** someone, they are accused of doing something illegal or wrong. ■ **Lay** is used to describe (a) people involved with the Christian church but who are not members of the clergy, or monks or nuns. (b) people who are not experts in a particular subject or activity. ■ **lay claim to** something: see **claim. lay** something **bare:** see **bare. lay** something **to rest:** see **rest. lay** something **at someone's door:** see **door.**

layabout If you call someone a **layabout,** you mean they are lazy and do no work.

lay-by A **lay-by** is a short strip of road by the side of a main road, where vehicles can stop for a while.

layer (**layering, layered**) A **layer** is a single thickness of something, either on top of or between other things. If something consists of layers, you can say it is **layered.**

layman (**laymen**) A **layman** is someone who has no specialized knowledge of a subject.

lay-off (or **layoff**) See **lay.**

layout The **layout** of something is the way its different parts are arranged.

laze (**lazing, lazed**) If you **laze** somewhere or **laze** around, you relax and do no work.

lazy (**lazier, laziest; lazily, laziness**) You say people are **lazy** when they try to avoid work. *He had a reputation for laziness.* ■ **Lazy** actions are done slowly, without much effort. *He drew lazily on his cigarette.*

lb See **pound.**

lbw In cricket **lbw** is an abbreviation for 'leg before wicket', which is the way in which a batsman is dismissed when his legs prevent the ball from hitting the wicket.

LCD An **LCD** or **liquid crystal display** is a display of information on a screen. It uses liquid crystals which become visible when electricity is passed through them.

leach (**leaches, leaching, leached**) If something **leaches** from a substance, it is washed out by water passing through it or over it. ...*the pesticides that leach into rivers.*

lead (**leading, led**) In a contest, if someone is **leading** or in the **lead,** they are winning. ■ If you **lead** someone somewhere, you show them where it is by taking them there. ■ If something like a road **leads** somewhere, it goes there. ■ If someone **leads** a group or organization, they are in charge it. ■ The person who **leads off** is the first one to do something. *The chairman led off with a financial statement.* ■ If one thing **leads** to another, the second thing happens as a result of the first. ■ The **lead** in a play or film is the most important acting role. ■ The **lead** story in a newspaper is the piece of news thought to be most important and given the most space. ■ If someone **leads** a particular type of life, they live that way. *He leads a life of considerable luxury.* ■ A dog's **lead** is the same as a dog's leash. ■ **Lead** (pron: **led**) is a soft grey heavy metal. ■ The **lead** in a pencil is the part in the middle which makes a mark when you write.

leaded petrol has had a small amount of lead added to it. ■ **Leaded** windows are made of small pieces of glass held together by strips of lead.

leaden (pron: **led**-en) If you say conversation or writing is **leaden,** you mean it is very dull. ■ If your movements are **leaden,** you are moving slowly and heavily, because you are very tired. ■ A **leaden** sky or sea is dark grey.

leader The **leader** of a country, organization, or group of people is the person in charge. ■ The **leader** in a contest is the person who is winning. ■ The **leader** in a commercial activity is the firm which is most successful at it. ■ The **leaders** or **leading articles** in a newspaper are a small group of articles expressing views on the main news of the day.

leadership The people in charge of a country or organization are often called the **leadership.** ■ **Leadership** is used to talk about the position of being leader, or to comment on a leader's methods or performance. *Opponents grumble about her hard-nosed style of leadership.*

lead-free petrol is the same as unleaded petrol.

lead-in A **lead-in** is an introduction to something like a talk or a TV report.

leading is used to talk about the most important or successful people in a particular activity or area. ...*a leading Albanian intellectual.* ■ The **leading** role in a play or film is the main one. ■ If someone plays a **leading** role in getting something done, they have a lot to do with it. ■ **leading light:** see **light.**

leading article See **leader.**

lead-up The **lead-up** to an event is the time before it, when preparations are being made.

leaf (plural: **leaves**) (**leafs, leafing, leafed**) The **leaves** of a plant are the thin flat parts growing on its branches or stalks; they are usually green. ■ In a book, a **leaf** is a single sheet of paper. ■ If you **leaf through** a book, you turn the pages quickly, without looking at anything carefully.

leaflet (**leafleting, leafleted**) A **leaflet** is a piece of paper or booklet giving information or advertising something. If you **leaflet** a place, you distribute leaflets there.

leafy trees and plants have a lot of leaves. **Leafy** places have a lot of trees and plants.

league A **league** is a group of people, organizations, or countries that have joined together because they share a common interest. ...*the National League for Democracy.* ■ A **league** is a group of sports clubs which play in competition with each other. ■ If you say someone is **in league with** someone else, you mean they are secretly working together.

league table A **league table** is a list of people, teams, or organizations arranged with the most successful at the top and the least successful at the bottom.

leak (**leaking, leaked**) If a container or other object **leaks** or has a **leak**, it has a small hole or crack through which liquid or gas escapes. ■ If someone **leaks** a piece of confidential information, they let other people know about it. When this happens, you say there is a **leak.**

leakage If there is a **leakage** of liquid or gas, some of it escapes from a pipe or container through a hole or crack. ■ If there is a **leakage** of secret information, it is passed on to someone who is not supposed to know about it.

leaky things have holes or cracks which let liquids in or out.

lean (**leaning, leaned** *or* **leant; leaner, leanest**) If you **lean** in a particular direction, you bend your body that way. ■ If a person or thing **leans** on or against something, they rest against it. ■ If someone **leans on** you, they try to get you to do something, by threatening you. ■ You say one person **leans on** or **upon** another when they depend on them. *They lean heavily upon each other for support.* ■ If you **lean towards** a particular point of view or a course of action, you tend to sympathize with it and may adopt it. *Her socialist leanings were not to the liking of her family.* ■ **Lean** people are thin, but also look fit and healthy. ■ **Lean** meat has very little fat on it. ■ In a **lean** period, people do not have much food, money, or success.

leap (**leaping, leapt** *or* **leaped;** *both pron:* **lept**) If you **leap,** you jump a long way. A jump like this is called a **leap.** ■ You say someone **leaps** somewhere when they move there quickly and suddenly. *She leapt into a taxi.* ■ If something **leaps,** it suddenly increases by a large amount. ...*a leap in oil prices.* ■ A **leap** is a sudden and important change, increase, or advance in someone's position or way of thinking. *Contemporary Art has taken a huge leap forward.* ...*a giant leap in productivity.* ■ If you **leap at** a chance, you accept it eagerly.

leapfrog (**leapfrogging, leapfrogged**) If something **leapfrogs** something else, it overtakes it and gets ahead of it. ■ **Leapfrog** is a game for children in which some of them bend over and others jump over their backs.

leapt See **leap.**

leap year A **leap year** is the one year in every four which has 366 days.

learn (**learning, learnt** *or* **learned; learner**) If you **learn** something, you gain knowledge or a skill, especially by studying or training. *Learner drivers must be supervised.* ■ **Learned** people (*pron:* **ler**-nid) have studied a lot and gained a lot of knowledge. The books and papers they write can also be called **learned.** ■ If you **learn** of something, you find out about it. ■ If you **learn** to do something, you gradually start doing it, because you realize it needs to be done. *You have to learn to face your problem.*

lease (**leasing, leased; lessor, lessee**) If you **lease** property, you make a legal agreement with the owner and pay to be allowed to use it for a period of time. The agreement is called a **lease;** the owner is called the **lessor;** you are called the **lessee.** ■ If someone or something is given a new **lease of life,** they become unexpectedly useful or successful again. *After a career as a comedian, he found a new lease of life as an actor.*

leasehold (**leaseholder**) A **leasehold** property is one which can be leased. If you lease property from someone, you are called the **leaseholder.** See also **freehold.**

leash (**leashes**) A dog's **leash** is a chain or strip of leather attached to its collar, to keep it under control.

least You use **least** to say that something is as small in amount or extent as it could be, or smaller than other things of the same kind. *He came out when I least expected it... They're the ones who need it the least... ...one of the least powerful of the African states... That was the least of her worries.* ■ You use **at least** or **at the least** to say that something is the minimum possible or the minimum that someone should do. *At least 32 people were injured... At the very least they could make donations.* ■ You use **at least** (a) to draw attention to a good point in something. *The process looks rather laborious but at least it's not dangerous.* (b) to correct something you have just said. *A couple of days ago I spotted my ex-wife – at least I thought I did.* ■ If something is not true **in the least,** it is not true at all. ■ **Not least** is used to mean 'especially', when you are giving an example of something, or a reason for it. *I happen to be a fan of hers, not least because she has the courage to hold steadfastly to her belief.* Similarly, **least of all** is used to mean 'especially not'. *Nobody seemed amused, least of all Jenny.*

leather is specially treated animal skin used to make things like shoes, clothes, and bags.

leathery things have a tough texture like leather.

leave (**leaving, left**) If you **leave** a place, you go away from it. ■ If you **leave** an organization or institution, you end your connection with it, usually for good. ■ If you **leave** your husband or wife or the person you are living with, you end your relationship with them and move out. ■ If you **leave** someone or something somewhere or **leave** them

behind, you do not take them with you when you go. ■ If you **leave** someone or someone to do something, you let them get on with it on their own. ■ If you **leave** a decision to someone, you let them make it. ■ If something **leaves** you in a particular state, you are in that state as a result of it. *This has left everyone dissatisfied.* ■ If someone or something **leaves** something like a mark or impression, it is there as a result of what they have done. *The explosion left a crater as wide as the road.* ■ If you **leave** something until a particular time, you wait until then before dealing with it. ■ If you continue with something **from where you left off,** you start again from the point where you stopped. ■ If you **leave** an amount of something, you do not use it. If an amount is **left** or **left over,** it is still there after the rest has gone or been used. ■ If someone **leaves** you money or other property, you get it when they die. ■ If someone is **left out** of something, or **left off** it, they are not included in it. ■ If someone in authority gives you **leave** to do something, they give you permission. ■ **Leave** is a period when you are on holiday from your job or allowed to be absent for some other reason.

leaven (*pron:* lev-en) (**leavening, leavened**) If you say someone **leavens** the group of people they belong to, you mean they are different from the other people in the group, and make it seem less dull or extreme. You can say someone like this provides a **leavening.**

lecherous (**lecher, lechery**) If you say someone is **lecherous** or a **lecher,** you mean they are greedy for sex. You call their behaviour or inclinations **lechery.**

lectern A **lectern** is a high sloping desk for putting a book or notes on when you are standing up and talking to an audience.

lecture (**lecturing, lectured**) A **lecture** is a talk given to an audience on a subject. If someone **lectures** on a subject, they give a lecture or series of lectures on it. ■ If someone **lectures** you or gives you a **lecture,** they tell you off, or tell you how to behave.

lecturer (**lectureship**) A **lecturer** is a university or college teacher. His or her post is called a **lectureship.**

led See **lead.**

ledge A **ledge** is (a) a narrow flat area on the side of a cliff or mountain. (b) a narrow shelf along the bottom edge of a window.

ledger A **ledger** is a book in which an organization keeps a record of the amounts of money it receives and spends.

leech (**leeches**) Leeches are small worms which live in or near water and feed by attaching themselves to other animals and sucking their blood.

leek The **leek** is a vegetable consisting of a white part with a cluster of straight green leaves growing out of it.

leer (**leering, leered**) If someone **leers** at you, they smile suggestively; a smile like this is called a **leer.**

leery If someone is **leery** of something, they are suspicious or worried about it.

leeway is used to talk about the amount of freedom or flexibility someone has in dealing with something. *They have little leeway to increase their exports.*

left See **leave.** ■ **Left** is one of two opposite sides or directions. If you turn to the left, you turn quarter of a circle in an anticlockwise direction. ■ **The left** are people who support socialism rather than capitalism.

left-handed (**left-hander**) Left-handed people use their left hand rather than their right for things like writing or throwing a ball. In sport, people like these are called **left-handers.**

leftist A person with socialist or communist views is sometimes called **leftist.**

left-luggage office A **left-luggage office** is a place at a station or airport where you can pay to leave your luggage.

left-of-centre organizations have moderate political views which are closer to socialism than to conservatism or capitalism.

leftover The **leftovers** from a meal are the food which has not been eaten. ■ If you say a thing or person is a **leftover** from an earlier time, you mean they were important or useful then, but are not so any more.

left-wing (**left-winger**) Left-wing people have socialist ideas and opinions. People like these are sometimes called **left-wingers.** ■ The **left wing** of a party consists of the members whose beliefs are closest to socialism.

lefty (*or* **leftie**) (*plural:* **lefties**) People who do not like left-wing people sometimes call them **lefties.** ■ Americans call left-handed people **lefties.**

leg (**-legged**) A person's **legs** are the parts of their body between their hips and their feet. An animal's, bird's, or insect's **legs** are the parts it uses to stand on or move across the ground. ■ **-legged** is used to describe a person's or animal's legs, or to say how many legs they have. *...a one-legged man.* ■ If you say someone is **pulling your leg,** you mean they are telling you something untrue as a joke. ■ The **legs** of a table or chair are the thin vertical parts which support it. ■ If you say something is **on its last legs,** you mean it is in bad condition and likely to stop working, break, or fall to pieces. ■ A **leg** of something like a tour, journey, or visit is one part of it. Similarly, a **leg** of a race or competition is one stage or part of it.

legacy (**legacies**) A **legacy** is money or property which someone leaves you in their will. ■ Anything left over from an earlier time which people have to put up with or deal with can be called a **legacy.**

legal (**legally**) Legal means to do with the law. *...the legal implications.* ■ If something is **legal,** it is allowed by law. *The settlers say they are there legally.* ■ If a coin or note is **legal tender,** it is officially a part of a country's currency and can be used to buy things there.

legal aid is financial help given by the government to people who cannot afford a lawyer.

legalise See **legalize.**

legalistic If you say something like an argument is **legalistic,** you mean it concentrates too much on the legal side of things and is therefore unhelpful.

legality (legalities) If you talk about the **legality** of something, you are talking about whether it is legal or not. ■ The **legalities** of something are its legal aspects.

legalize (or legalise) (legalizing, legalized; legalization) When something is **legalized,** it is made legal.

legation A **legation** is (a) a group of government officials and diplomats who work in a foreign country as representatives of their government. (b) the place where they work.

legend (legendary) A **legend** is a very old story which may be based on real events. **Legendary** is used to talk about people and things in legends. *...the legendary King Lud.* ■ You call a living person **legendary** or a **legend** when they are very famous and much admired. *...the legendary Tina Turner.*

leggings are (a) skintight trousers, often made with stretchy material. (b) an outer covering worn over a normal pair of trousers to protect them.

leggy A **leggy** woman has very long legs.

legible writing is clear enough to be read.

legion A **legion** was a large military unit in the Roman army. ■ **Legion** appears in the names of some modern military forces. *...the French Foreign Legion.* ■ A **legion** of people or things is a large number of them. ■ If you say things are **legion,** you mean there are a lot of them. *The examples of anti-social behaviour today are legion.*

legionnaire – Legionnaires are soldiers who are members of a legion.

Legionnaires' disease is a serious lung infection.

legislate (legislating, legislated; legislation) When a government **legislates,** it passes new laws. Laws are sometimes called **legislation.**

legislative A **legislative** council is one which has the authority to make laws. ■ **Legislative** means to do with making laws. *...the Government's legislative programme.*

legislator A **legislator** is a person involved in making or passing laws, for example an MP.

legislature A **legislature** is a group of people with the authority to make laws.

legitimate (legitimately, legitimacy) If something is **legitimate,** it is allowed by law. *He did not acknowledge the legitimacy of his imprisonment.* ■ If you say a claim is **legitimate,** you mean it is reasonable or justified. ■ If a child is **legitimate,** it was born to married parents.

legitimize (or legitimise) (legitimizing, legitimized) If something is **legitimized,** it is made legal.

legless You can say someone is **legless** when they are extremely drunk.

legumes (pron: leg-yooms) (leguminous) Legumes are a group of plants, including clover, peas, and beans, whose seeds grow in pods. **Leguminous** plants are members of this group.

leisure (leisured) Your **leisure** time is the time when you do not have to work and can do things you enjoy. You can call these things **leisure** activities. ■ The **leisured** classes are people who have so much money they never need to work. ■ If you are allowed to do something **at leisure,** you can do it when you want to, rather than having to do it immediately.

leisure centre A **leisure centre** is a large building with facilities for leisure activities, for example a sports hall, swimming pool, and meeting rooms.

leisurely is used to say something is done in a relaxed and unhurried way. *...a leisurely walk.*

leitmotif (or leitmotiv) (pron: lite-mote-eef) A **leitmotif** is a musical phrase which occurs many times in a piece of music and represents a particular person or idea. Similarly, an object can be used as a **leitmotif** in a novel or film.

lemming The **lemming** is an animal which looks like a rat with thick fur. Lemmings sometimes migrate in large groups. ■ If you say people are behaving like **lemmings,** you mean they are behaving as a mindless group in a stupid or self-destructive way.

lemon – Lemons are yellow citrus fruit with sour juice.

lemonade is (a) a clear sweet fizzy drink. (b) a drink made from fresh lemons with water and sugar.

lemon curd is a sweet paste made from sugar, butter, eggs, and lemons.

lemur – Lemurs are long-tailed monkey-like animals from Madagascar.

lend (lending, lent) If you **lend** someone something you own, you let them use it for a time. ■ When banks **lend** money to someone, they give them a sum of money, which has to be paid back with interest over a given period of time. ■ If you **lend** your support to someone, you show you agree with them and support them. ■ If something **lends** a quality to something else, it gives it that quality. *The decorations have lent a splash of colour to an otherwise drab city.* ■ If something **lends** itself to being dealt with in a certain way, it has features which make it easy to deal with in that way. *Puccini's opera does not lend itself easily to concert performance.*

lender – Lenders are people or institutions like banks that lend money to people.

length The **length** of something is the distance from one end to the other. ■ In a horse or boat race, a **length** is the distance from the front to the back of a horse or boat. *...a victory by half a length.* ■ A **length** of something is a piece of it *...a short length of chain.* ■ The **length** of a book or other piece of writing is the number of pages or the amount of writing in it. ■ **Length** is used to talk about how long something lasts. *...the length of time people have to wait for operations.* ■ If you discuss something **at length,** you discuss it for a long time or in great detail. ■ **At length** is used to say something happens eventually, after a long time. *At length, his obsessive desire destroyed his marriage.* ■ If you **go to great lengths** to achieve something, you try very hard and do things you would not normally do to achieve it.

lengthen (lengthening, lengthened) If something **lengthens** or is **lengthened,** it becomes longer.

lengthways means the same as 'lengthwise'.

lengthwise (*or* **lengthways**) If you cut something **lengthwise** or **lengthways,** you cut it along its length rather than across its width.

lengthy If something is **lengthy,** it takes a long time.

lenient (**leniently, leniency**) If someone in authority is **lenient** with wrongdoers, they are not as strict or severe as they might be. ...*the judge's leniency.*

lens (**lenses**) A **lens** is a thin curved piece of glass or plastic which makes things look bigger, smaller, or clearer when you look through it. Lenses are used in cameras, telescopes, and glasses. ■ The **lens** in your eye is the part behind the iris, which focuses light.

lent See **lend.** ■ **Lent** is the period of 40 days before Easter when many Christians give up something they enjoy.

lentil – **Lentils** are small round brown or orange seeds from the lentil plant. They are dried then boiled and eaten in curries and soups.

leopard The **leopard** is a large member of the cat family. It has yellow fur and black spots. Leopards live in Africa and Asia.

leotard A **leotard** is a thin tight-fitting piece of clothing covering the body but not the legs, worn for things like dance and aerobics.

leper – **Lepers** are people who suffer from leprosy. ■ If someone is treated as a **leper,** people avoid them or are unfriendly towards them, because they have done something shocking or offensive.

leprechaun (*pron:* **lep**-rik-kawn) In Irish folk tales, **leprechauns** are tiny people with magical powers who play tricks on people.

leprosy is a serious infectious disease which damages the flesh.

leprous means affected by leprosy. ...*leprous hands.*

lesbian (**lesbianism**) **Lesbians** are women who are sexually attracted to other women, rather than men. **Lesbianism** is sexual attraction and sexual activity between women.

lèse-majesté (*pron:* lezz-**maj**-est-ee) is behaviour likely to cause offence to a king or other ruler.

lesion A **lesion** is an injury or wound.

less is used to say an amount is below a certain level. *We had less than three miles to go.* ■ **Less** is used to say something does not have a quality to the degree that it used to, or to the degree that something else has. *The future looks less secure.* ■ **Less** is used to say one number is subtracted from another. *He earns £53,200 a week, less tax.*

lessee See **lease.**

lessen (**lessening, lessened; lessening**) If something **lessens** or is **lessened,** there is less of it than there was before.

lesser is used to say something is not as large, not as serious, or not as good as something else. ...*a new exam that did not exclude children of lesser ability.*

lesson A **lesson** is a short period of time when children are taught a subject at school. ■ If you learn a **lesson** from something that happens, it acts as a warning or example from which you learn something.

lessor See **lease.**

lest is used to give reasons for someone's feelings or behaviour when they are anxious to prevent something happening. *I was afraid to open the door lest he should follow me.*

let (**letting, let**) If you **let** something happen, you allow it to happen. If you **let** someone do something, you allow them to do it. ■ **Let** is used to make suggestions. *Let us give them the benefit of the doubt.* ■ If you **let** someone or something into a place, you allow them to go in. ■ If you **let** your house or land to someone, you allow them to use it in exchange for regular payments. ■ If you **let** someone **in on** a secret, you tell them about it. ■ If someone is **let off,** they are not punished for something they have done, or not made to do a task. ■ If you **let out** a sound, you utter it. ■ If you wonder what you have **let** yourself **in for,** you begin to think you may be getting involved in something difficult or unpleasant. ■ See also **let-up.**

let-down If you say something you have been looking forward to is a **let-down,** you mean it is disappointing.

lethal (**lethally**) If something is **lethal,** it causes death.

lethargic (*pron:* lith-**ar**-jick) (**lethargy**) If someone is **lethargic,** they have no energy or enthusiasm. This condition is called **lethargy** (*pron:* **leth**-ar-jee).

let's is short for 'let us' when you are making a suggestion. See **let.**

letter A **letter** is a message you write and send to someone, usually through the post. ■ **Letters** are the written symbols which stand for the sounds of a language. ■ If you keep to the **letter of the law,** you do nothing to break it, although you may go against its general principles.

letterbox (**letterboxes**) A **letterbox** is (a) a rectangular hole in a door which letters and small parcels are delivered through. (b) a large metal box in the street or at a post office with a rectangular hole for letters to be posted in.

letterhead A **letterhead** is the printed section at the top of a letter, giving the writer's name and address.

lettering is writing, especially when the letters are in a particular style or colour. ...*gilt lettering.*

lettuce – **Lettuces** are salad vegetables with large green leaves.

let-up If there is no **let-up** in something, it continues at the same level. *He warned there would be no let-up in the war on inflation.*

leukaemia (*or* **leukemia**) (*pron:* loo-**kee**-mee-a) is a type of cancer which results in abnormal white blood cells being produced, causing weakness and sometimes death.

levee (*pron:* **lev**-vee) In the US, a **levee** is a ridge or bank built next to a river to stop floods. ■ A **levee** is a formal reception held by a king or queen at their palace.

level (**levelling, levelled**) (*Am:* **leveling, leveled**) A **level** is a point or stage on a scale. *The FT-SE 100 index dipped below the 2,400 level.* ...*top-level meetings.* ■ The **level** of something is its height or position. ...*the ground-level concourse.* ...*dive-bombing at low level.* ■ When people talk about the different **levels**

of a story or film, they mean the different ways of thinking about it or understanding it. *On one level it's a comic romp, and on another it's a strong psychological story.* ■ If something is **level,** it is flat and no part is higher than the rest. If an area of land is **levelled,** it is made flat. ■ If something which has been increasing or decreasing **levels off** or **levels out,** it stops increasing or decreasing. *Inflation is finally levelling out at around 11% a month.* ■ If two amounts are **level,** they are equal. If you **draw level** with someone, you move towards them from behind until you are in an equal position. ■ When someone is criticized, you can say criticisms are **levelled** at them. ■ See also **A level, O level.**

level crossing A **level crossing** is a place where a railway line and a road cross each other at the same level. There are usually gates to block off the road when a train is passing.

level-headed If you say someone is **level-headed,** you mean they are calm and sensible in difficult situations.

lever (levering, levered) A **lever** is a bar or handle you pull or push to make a piece of machinery work. ■ A **lever** is a bar. You push one end under a heavy object. When you push down on the other end, you can move the object. If you **lever** something, you move it in this way. ■ You can call something a **lever** when you use it as a way of getting someone to do what you want. *...using the hostages as a lever to gain concessions.*

leverage If you have **leverage** over someone, you have the power to make them do what you want, for example because you have control over something they need.

leveret (pron: **lev**-er-it) A **leveret** is a young hare, especially one less than a year old.

leviathan (pron: lev-**vie**-ath-an) In the Bible, the **leviathan** is a sea monster, sometimes thought to be a whale and sometimes a crocodile. ■ Anything which is large, powerful, and frightening can be called a **leviathan.** *...Tokyo's leviathan banks.*

levitate (levitating, levitated; levitation) Some people claim to be able to **levitate.** This means making their whole body rise up in the air, with nothing supporting it. Some people also claim to be able to **levitate** objects.

levity is treating serious matters light-heartedly.

levy (levies, levying, levied) When a government **levies** a tax on something, it charges it. The tax can be called a **levy.**

lewd behaviour involves sex and is crude and unpleasant.

lexicographer (lexicography) A **lexicographer** is someone whose job involves writing and editing dictionaries. This kind of work is called **lexicography.**

lexicon A **lexicon** is an alphabetical list of the words of a language, or of words used in connection with a subject. ■ The words a group of people use among themselves can be called a **lexicon.** *A more recent addition to upper-class slang is 'brill'.*

LGV Someone who has an **LGV** licence is authorized to drive lorries. LGV stands for 'Large Goods Vehicle'.

liability (liabilities) Liability for a debt or accident is legal responsibility for it. *The driver admitted liability.* ■ **Liabilities** are debts. ■ If someone or something is a **liability,** they cause problems rather than being a help.

liable If someone is **liable** for something like a debt or an accident, they are legally responsible for it. ■ If a criminal is **liable** to a certain punishment, the authorities are entitled to punish them that way. ■ If someone or something is **liable** to do something, they are likely to do it. ■ If you are **liable** to something unpleasant, it is likely to happen to you. *Any vehicles moving during curfew are liable to be attacked.*

liaise (pron: lee-**aze**) **(liaising, liaised)** If people **liaise** with each other, they communicate and exchange information. If someone **liaises** between people, they act as a means of communication between them.

liaison (lee-aze-on) is communication and the exchange of information between people. ■ A **liaison** is a sexual relationship, especially a secret one.

liar A **liar** is a person who tells lies.

Lib Dem A **Lib Dem** is a member of the Liberal Democrats.

libel (libelling, libelled; libellous) (*Am:** libeling,* *etc)* If someone **libels** you, they write something untrue which damages your reputation and is therefore against the law. This offence is called **libel.** You can say a piece of writing is **libellous.**

liberal (liberalism, liberally) In the UK, **Liberals** were members or supporters of the former Liberal Party. ■ A **liberal** is a person who believes in individual freedom, is tolerant of other people's beliefs, and is ready to accept change. *...a more liberal approach to teaching.* ■ **Liberal** is used to say something is used or given freely in large amounts. *Sprinkle the wheat grains liberally over the soil.*

Liberal Democrat The **Liberal Democrats** are the third largest political party in the UK and the main centre party.

liberalize (or liberalise) (liberalizing, liberalized; liberalization) If a country or organization **liberalizes** its laws or attitudes, it makes them less strict and allows more freedom.

Liberal Party In Britain, the **Liberal Party** was a political party which merged with the Social Democratic Party in 1988 to form the Liberal Democrats.

liberate (liberating, liberated; liberation) If a place is **liberated,** it is freed from the control of another country or from a repressive government. ■ If people are **liberated,** they are freed from captivity or from a situation in which they are cruelly or unjustly treated. ■ If you say someone is **liberated,** you mean their attitude to things like sexual behaviour and the roles of men and women is more tolerant than that of most of the people where they live.

liberation theology is the belief that the Church should become actively involved in politics to bring about social change.

liberator You call someone a **liberator** when they do something to free people from oppression or foreign occupation.

libertarian A **libertarian** is someone who believes people should be free to think and behave as they want.

libertine (*pron:* **lib**-er-teen) A man is sometimes called a **libertine** when it is thought that he leads an immoral life, especially in his sexual behaviour.

liberty (**liberties**) **Liberty** is the freedom to live or behave as you want. **Liberties** are the freedom to do particular things. ...*religious liberties.* ...*political liberties.* See also **civil liberties.** ■ **Liberty** is the freedom to go where you want, rather than being imprisoned somewhere. ■ If you say you are not **at liberty** to do something, you mean you are not allowed to do it. ■ If you say someone is **taking liberties,** you mean they are being cheeky, or doing something they are not entitled to do.

libidinous people have strong sexual feelings.

libido (*pron:* lib-**ee**-doe) (**libidos**) A person's **libido** is their sexual desires.

librarian A **librarian** is a person who works in, or is in charge of, a library.

library (**libraries**) A **library** is a place where a collection of books and other publications is kept for people to read or borrow. The collection is also called a **library.** ■ A **library** is a collection of objects, such as films or records.

libretto (*plural:* **librettos** *or* **libretti**) (**librettist**) The **libretto** of an opera is the words sung and spoken in it. The person who wrote the libretto is called the **librettist.**

lice See **louse.**

licence (*Am:* **license**) A **licence** is an official document giving you permission to have, do, or use something. ■ If you do something **under licence,** you do it using someone else's patent, trademark, or copyright, with their permission. ■ If you call something a **licence** to act badly, you mean it makes people think they can behave badly and get away with it. ■ If you say a writer is using **poetic licence,** you mean he or she is not obeying the conventional rules of language or is misrepresenting the truth in some way to achieve an artistic goal. You use **artistic licence** in a similar way when you are talking about art.

license (**licensing, licensed**) When someone is **licensed** to do something, they are given official permission to do it. ...*a licensed beautician.* ■ If a drug is **licensed,** official permission has been given for it to be available. ■ If something like a restaurant or bar is **licensed,** it has permission to sell alcohol. ■ See also **licence.**

licensee A **licensee** is someone who holds a licence, especially a licence to sell alcohol.

license plate (*or* **licence plate**) A vehicle's number plate is called its **license plate,** especially in the US.

licentious (*pron:* lice-**sen**-shuss) (**licentiousness**) **Licentious** behaviour is sexual behaviour which is considered to be shocking and immoral.

lichen (*pron:* **lie**-ken) is a crusty or moss-like plant which grows on rocks or tree trunks.

lick When you **lick** something, you stroke your tongue across its surface. ■ If someone is **licking their wounds,** they are recovering from a defeat or humiliation. ■ If you **lick** someone or something, you defeat that person or overcome that thing.
■ When people talk about a **lick of paint,** they are talking about a building or room being decorated.
■ When flames or a large fire **lick** somewhere or something, the fire begins to reach that place or thing and the flames touch it lightly and briefly. *Flames were licking at the bedroom door.* ■ A **lick** is a short piece of music which is part of a song and played on a guitar.

licorice See **liquorice.**

lid A **lid** is a cover for a container. ■ If you **keep the lid** on something, or **keep a lid** on it, (a) you restrict it. *The soldiers' presence seemed to keep a lid on the violence.* (b) you prevent people finding out about it. *Britain tried to keep the lid on the expulsion.*
■ Your **lids** are your eyelids.

lido A **lido** is (a) an outdoor swimming pool. (b) part of a beach used for swimming, sunbathing, or water sports.

lie (**lying, lay, have lain; lying, lied**) (*If you are talking about the past, you say, for example, 'She lay on the beach' but 'She lied to the police.'*) If you **lie** somewhere, you place yourself in a horizontal position.
■ If you **lie around,** you spend time relaxing.
■ You say an object is **lying** somewhere when it is on the ground or on some other horizontal surface.
■ You use **lie** when you are saying something about the state of a building or piece of land. For example, you say a house is 'lying empty'. ■ You use **lie** when you are saying where something is situated. *The house lies within a conservation area... The French are lying third.* ■ **Lie** is used to talk about things happening in the future. ...*the political bargaining that lies ahead.* ■ **Lie** is used (a) when mentioning the cause of a problem. *Lack of money lies at the root of their problems... Some of the blame lies with the president.* (b) when saying where the answer to a problem can be found. *The key may lie in dental records held by Scotland Yard.* ■ If someone **lies** or tells a **lie,** they deliberately say something which is untrue. ■ **lie low:** see **low.**

lie-in If you have a **lie-in,** you stay in bed late.

lieu (*pron:* **lyew** *or* **loo**) If you are given something **in lieu of** the thing you are expecting, you are given it instead of the other thing.

lieutenant (*pronounced* lef-**ten**-ant *in British English and* loo-**ten**-ant *in American*) A **lieutenant** is (a) a junior officer in the army. (b) a middle-ranking officer in the Royal Navy. ■ Someone who works closely with an important person, often acting as their assistant, can be called their **lieutenant.**
■ See also **flight lieutenant.**

life (**lives**) A person's **life** is the time from their birth to their death. ■ **For life** is used to say something lasts for the rest of a person's life. *The accident left her scarred for life.* ■ A person's **life** is their circumstances and their daily activities. **Life** is also used to talk about particular activities. ...*his sex life... Football is my whole life.* ■ If someone **takes** a person's **life,** they kill them. You can also say someone **takes** their own **life.** ■ If there is **life** somewhere, there are living things there. ■ The **life** in a place is all the activities that go on there.

You can say that a film, book, or play **comes to life,** when it becomes lively or interesting. ■ The **life** of a machine is the length of time it can be used before it needs to be replaced or scrapped. ■ If something takes on a **life of its own,** it becomes independent and important in its own right. ■ **fact of life:** see fact. **facts of life:** see fact. **See also shelf-life, still life, walk of life, way of life.**

life assurance is the same as life insurance.

lifebelt A **lifebelt** is a large ring thrown to people to keep them afloat.

lifeblood If you say something is the **lifeblood** of a person or group, you mean their happiness, success, or survival depends on it.

lifeboat A **lifeboat** is (a) a boat which is sent out from shore to rescue people in danger at sea. (b) a boat kept on a ship, which can be launched if the ship is in danger of sinking.

life cycle The **life cycle** of an animal is the stages of development it goes through from birth to death.

life expectancy A person's **life expectancy** is the length of time they can normally be expected to live.

life form A **life form** is any kind of living thing.

lifeguard A **lifeguard** is a person at a beach or swimming pool whose job is to save people from drowning.

life insurance is an insurance on your own or a relative's life. In return for regular payments, the insurance company pays a sum of money to the family either when the person dies, or sometimes after a certain number of years.

life jacket (or **lifejacket**) A **life jacket** is a sleeveless jacket which you wear to keep afloat.

lifeless If you say something is **lifeless,** you mean it lacks excitement, liveliness, or interest. ■ You can say a dead body is **lifeless.**

lifelike You say a portrait or statue is **lifelike** when (a) it is so like a real person that it almost seems to be alive. (b) it is extremely like the person it represents.

lifeline If you call something a **lifeline,** you mean it provides a link needed for someone's survival. ■ If you **throw** someone **a lifeline,** you help them out of a difficult situation.

lifelong means lasting the rest of your life. ...a vaccine which will give lifelong protection. ■ A **lifelong** ambition is one you have had since you were a child.

life peer (**life peerage**) A **life peer** is a member of the House of Lords who has been given a title but cannot pass it on to his or her descendants. When someone is awarded a title like this, you say they are given a **life peerage.**

lifer A **lifer** is a criminal who has been sent to prison for the rest of his or her life.

life raft A **life raft** is an inflatable boat carried on a ship or aircraft for use in an emergency.

life science The **life sciences** are sciences like zoology, biology, and botany, which deal with living things.

lifespan (or **life span**) The **lifespan** of a living thing is the length of time they live for. ■ The **lifespan** of a product is the length of time it is in use, before it is replaced or thrown away.

lifestyle Your **lifestyle** is the way you live, for example your living conditions or your typical behaviour.

life support A **life support** machine is a piece of hospital equipment used to keep dangerously ill people alive.

lifetime A person's **lifetime** is the period during which they are alive. ■ The **lifetime** of something is the period of time it lasts for.

lift If you **lift** something or **lift** it **up,** you raise it upwards. ■ A **lift** is a box-like device for carrying people or goods from one floor of a building to another. ■ If something **lifts** your spirits or gives you a **lift,** it makes you more cheerful and confident. ■ If you **lift yourself** out of a bad situation, you get out of it by your own efforts. Mr Bush soon lifted himself out of the gloom. ■ If a restriction is **lifted,** it is removed. ■ If fog or mist **lifts,** it goes away. ■ If someone asks you for a **lift,** they ask you to take them somewhere in your car. ■ When a rocket **lifts off,** it leaves its launch pad and rises into the air. The moment when this happens is called **lift-off.**

ligament – Ligaments are the bands of strong tissue which connect bones at the joints. He damaged ankle ligaments in a pre-season friendly.

light (**lighting, lit** or **lighted; lightly, lightness**) **Light** is brightness from things like the sun or a lamp which allows you to see things. ■ If something **lights** up an area, it makes it bright with light. ■ If something is **lit** in a particular way, that is how it gets its light. ...a gas-lit passage. ■ A **light** room or building is bright with natural light. ■ A **light** is anything which provides artificial light. The **lighting** in a place is the lights there or the way it is lit. ■ If you **light** something like a fire, you start it burning. ■ A **light** is something like a match, used to start a cigarette burning. ■ **Light** colours are pale. ■ **Light** people or objects do not weigh much. ■ **Light** is used to say something is not very great in extent or degree. Traffic was relatively light. ...a light breeze. ■ **Light** entertainment is not serious, and does not require much thought. You can also refer to a film or book which is not serious as **light.** ■ If you say something should not be done **lightly,** you mean people should think carefully before doing it. ■ If you **light on** someone or something, you suddenly notice them or find them. ■ If someone is a **leading light** in an organization, they are one of the most important people in it. ■ **In the light of** is used to mention circumstances which might affect a choice or decision. He believes that in the light of recent reforms the time has come to relax sanctions. ■ If you **make light of** something, you pretend you do not think it is important.

lighten (**lightening, lightened**) If the sky **lightens,** it becomes less dark. ■ If someone's mood **lightens** or they **lighten up,** they become less serious and more cheerful. ■ If something like a burden is **lightened,** it is reduced.

lighter A **lighter** or **cigarette lighter** is a small device for lighting cigarettes.

light-hearted (**light-heartedly**) **Light-hearted** behaviour is not at all serious.

lighthouse A **lighthouse** is a tower by the sea, which sends out a powerful light to guide ships or warn them of danger.

light industry is the manufacture of goods without using heavy machinery. See also **heavy industry.**

lighting See **light.**

lightly See **light.**

lightning – **Lightning** is electricity seen as bright flashes of light in the sky during a thunderstorm. ■ **Lightning** is used to describe things which happen very quickly or last for a very short time. *In May I paid a lightning visit to the south.*

lightning conductor A **lightning conductor** is a metal rod fixed to the top of a tall building and down its side running into the ground. It guides lightning to the ground and prevents damage to the building.

light pen A **light pen** is a device for electronically reading bar codes on items you buy in a shop.

lightweight A **lightweight** object or material weighs less than things of its type usually do. ■ A **lightweight** book or play is not meant to be serious. ■ If you call someone a **lightweight**, you mean they are not capable of thinking deeply, or do not have much power. ■ **Lightweight** is a category in some sports such as boxing or rowing. A **lightweight** is someone who is in this category.

light year Very long distances in space are measured in **light years.** One light year is the distance light travels in a year. ■ If you talk about things being **light years** apart, you are saying how different they are from each other. *She says the French education system is light years ahead of the English one.*

lignite is a brown mineral with a woody texture. It is burned as a fuel.

likable See **likeable.**

like (**liking, liked**) If you **like** someone or something, you find them pleasant or attractive, or you approve of them. ■ A person's **likes** are the things they enjoy or find pleasant. ■ If you **like** to do something in a certain way, you prefer to do it that way. *Big Japanese firms like to recruit graduates straight from university.* ■ If one person or thing is **like** another, they have similar characteristics or behave in similar ways. ■ **Like** can be used to mean 'in the same way that' or 'in the same way as'. *The firm cannot afford to miss out like they did last year... He was wooed like visiting royalty.* ■ **Like** can be used to give an example of something. *...big-spending countries like Holland and Canada.* ■ **Like this** and **like that** are used when describing how something is done. *Eels and river fish are cooked like this.* ■ You say **the likes of** when you are mentioning someone as an example of a type of person. *...successful producers for the likes of Liza Minelli and Dusty Springfield.* ■ You add **and the like** after a list to indicate that there are other things which could be included in it. *The castles have a variety of new careers as hotels, museums, offices, and the like.*

-like is added to a word to say someone or something is similar to the thing described by the word. *...a tiny worm-like creature.*

likeable (*Am:* **likable**) If you say someone or something is **likeable,** you mean they are pleasant and easy to like.

likelihood If you talk about the **likelihood** of something, you are talking about the chances of it happening or being true.

likely (**likelier, likeliest**) If something is **likely** to happen, it will probably happen.

like-minded people have similar ideas or opinions.

liken (**likening, likened**) If you **liken** one person or thing to another, you say they are similar.

likeness (**likenesses**) If you talk about someone's **likeness** to another person, you mean they look like them. ■ A **likeness** of someone is a drawing or statue of them.

likewise You use **likewise** when highlighting the similarities between people or things. *The long jumper who fouls his first effort has two more; the javelin thrower likewise; but a sprint hurdler pays for his first mistake.* ■ If you do something and another person does **likewise,** they do the same thing as you.

liking See **like.** ■ If you have a **liking** for something, you enjoy it. ■ If something is **to your liking,** (a) it is the way you like it. *Cook for about 8-10 minutes until the fish is to your liking.* (b) you are pleased about it. *Mrs Parsons' early socialist leanings were not to the liking of her family.*

lilac The **lilac** is a tree with large clusters of sweet-smelling flowers. ■ **Lilac** is a pale mauve colour.

Lilo (**Lilos**) A **Lilo** is an inflatable mattress. 'Lilo' is a trademark.

lilt (**lilting**) If a voice or tune is **lilting** or has a **lilt,** its pitch rises and falls pleasantly.

lily (**lilies**) **Lilies** are plants with large flowers which are often white.

lily of the valley (**lilies of the valley**) The **lily of the valley** is a small plant with large leaves and clusters of bell-shaped white flowers.

limb (**-limbed**) A person's **limbs** are their arms and legs. *...long-limbed ballerinas.* ■ The **limbs** of a tree are its branches. ■ If you are **out on a limb,** you have taken a risk by taking a different stance on something from other people.

limber (**limbering, limbered**) If you **limber up** for an activity such as running, you prepare for it by doing stretching exercises.

limbo If you are **in limbo,** you are in a situation where you do not know what will happen next and you have no control over things. ■ The **limbo** is a West Indian dance in which the dancers pass under a low bar while leaning backwards.

lime The **lime** is a large European tree with pale green leaves. ■ The **lime** is a small Asian tree which has small green citrus fruit called **limes.** ■ **Lime** or **lime-green** is a pale yellowish-green colour. ■ **Lime** is a white powder used in cement and whitewash, and as a fertilizer.

limelight If someone or something is in the **limelight,** they are getting a lot of attention, because they are famous or have done something exciting.

limerick A **limerick** is a humorous poem with five lines and a distinctive rhythm. One limerick goes: 'There was a young lady of Ryde – Who ate some green apples and died – The apples fermented – Inside the lamented – And made cider inside her inside.'

limestone is a white rock used for building and making cement.

limit (**limiting, limited**) A **limit** is the greatest amount, extent, or degree of something which is allowed or possible. ...*a speed limit of 75mph.* ■ If something is **limited**, restrictions are put on it. ■ If something is **limited** to a particular place or group of people, it is only found in that place, or it is only owned or used by those people. ■ If you **limit** yourself to a range of things, you keep within that range. ■ A **limited** company is a company owned by shareholders. If it becomes insolvent, the shareholders' liability for its debts is limited to the money they have invested in shares. ■ The **limits** of an area are its boundaries or edges.

limitation – **Limitations** on something are restrictions on how much someone is allowed to have. ■ A person's **limitations** are the limits of what they are capable of doing.

limo (**limos**) A **limo** is the same as a limousine.

limousine (*pron:* **lim**-o-zeen) A **limousine** is a large luxurious car.

limp If someone **limps** or walks with a **limp,** they walk in an uneven way, because they have injured their foot or leg. ■ You say someone or something **limps** when they make slow progress, because of the poor state they are in. *America limped out of recession in the second quarter.* ■ A **limp** object lacks stiffness or firmness.

limpet – **Limpets** are shellfish which attach themselves firmly to rocks.

limpid If the water in a lake or the sea is **limpid,** it is so clear you can see to the bottom. ■ If you describe writing or singing as **limpid,** you are praising its clarity.

linchpin (*or* **lynchpin**) The **linchpin** of an organization or process is the most important person or thing in it.

linctus (**linctuses**) A **linctus** is a syrupy medicine for a cough or sore throat.

linden The **linden** is the same as the European lime tree.

line (**lining, lined**) A **line** is a long thin mark on a surface. ■ A **line** of people or things is a row of them. If people **line up** or are **lined up,** they form a queue or row. If people or things **line** something like a road, they are present in large numbers along its edges. ■ A line is a route along which someone or something moves. ...*a railway line.* ■ A **line** is a company which provides services for transporting people or goods by sea, air, bus, or rail. ...*the Cunard shipping line.* ■ The words an actor learns are called his or her **lines.** ■ A length of string, wire, or cable used for a particular purpose can be called a **line.** ...*a fishing line.* ...*a telephone line.* ■ The **line** someone takes on an issue or problem is the attitude or policy they adopt towards it. *UEFA will take a tough line with offending*

clubs. ■ A **line** is a type of product made by a particular company. ...*its long-awaited new line of personal computers.* ■ Imaginary boundaries between groups of people or things are sometimes called **lines.** *Many children live below the poverty line.* ...*the dividing line between success and failure.* ■ Your **line** of work is the kind of work you do. ■ If someone is **in line** for something, they are likely. to get it. *Britain may be in line for a medal.* ■ If you say something like a policy is **on the right lines,** you mean it is generally correct and likely to succeed. ■ If something is **on the line,** it is at risk. *His job is on the line.* ■ If you **line** someone or something **up,** you arrange for them to be available. *The organisers are trying to line up a replacement.* ■ If you **line** a container, you cover its inside surface with paper or some other material. Similarly, a piece of clothing can be **lined** with a fabric. ■ **line** your **pockets:** see **pocket. toe the line:** see **toe. front line:** see **front. firing line:** see **fire.** See also **party line, on-line.**

lineage (*pron:* **lin**-ee-ij) A person's **lineage** is the line of people they are descended from through one of their parents.

linear A **linear** process is one where things happen one after another, each developing from the previous one. ■ **Linear** is used to describe things which form a long line or are in a long narrow shape. ...*linear islands.*

line dancing is a type of dancing performed by rows of people to country and western music.

linen is a fabric made from flax and used to make clothes, tablecloths, and sheets. Things like tablecloths and sheets are often called **linen.**

liner A **liner** is a large passenger ship. ■ You can call anything you use to line something a **liner.** ...*bin liners... ...nappy liners.*

linesman (**linesmen**) A **linesman** is an official in a game like football who indicates when the ball goes over the boundary line or when a rule is broken.

line-up (**line-ups**) A **line-up** is a group of people or series of things brought together for an activity or event. *The line-up includes three former winners.* ■ A police **line-up** is the same as an identity parade.

linger (**lingering, lingered**) If something **lingers,** it stays around for a long time. ...*lingering smells.* ■ If you **linger** somewhere, you stay longer than necessary. *I lingered in the courtyard... Customers are welcome to linger over coffee.*

lingerie (*pron:* **lan**-zher-ee; the *'zh'* sounds like *'s'* in *'pleasure'*) **Lingerie** is women's underwear and nightclothes.

lingo (**lingos**) People sometimes call a foreign language a **lingo.** ■ The **lingo** of a group of people is the special language they use. ...*academic lingo.*

lingua franca (*pron:* **ling**-wa **frang**-ka) A **lingua franca** is a language which is widely used as a means of communicating between people who speak different languages.

linguist A **linguist** is (a) someone who speaks several languages. (b) someone who studies or teaches linguistics.

linguistic (**linguistically; linguistics**) **Linguistic** means to do with languages. ...*his linguistic ability.*

■ **Linguistics** is the scientific study of the way language works.

liniment A **liniment** is a medicated liquid you rub into your skin to reduce pain or stiffness.

lining The **lining** of your stomach or other organ is a layer of tissue on the inside. ■ The **lining** of a piece of clothing is material attached to its inside, to make it warmer or more comfortable. ■ You can use **lining** to talk about a layer of paper, plastic, metal, or other substance that is attached to something to insulate or protect it. ■ **silver lining:** see **silver.**

link (**-linked**) If two things are **linked** or there is a **link** between them, they are connected in some way. ■ When a connection is made between two organizations or other things, you can say there is a **link-up** between them, or one thing is **linked up** to the other. ■ If there are **links** between two groups of people, they have a friendly relationship with each other. ■ If two objects are **linked,** they are joined together, or connected by something like a power cable. When a connection like this is made, you can say there is a **link-up** between the objects, or one object is **linked up** to the other. ■ If two places are **linked** by a road or railway, the road or railway runs between them. You can talk about road or rail **links** between places. Similarly, you can talk about telephone or postal **links.** ■ A **link** of a chain is one of the rings in it. ■ If several people **link** hands, they form a chain, each person holding the next person's hand. ■ A golf **links** is a golf course, especially one close to the sea.

linkage If you say there is **linkage** between two things, you mean they are connected in some way. ■ **Linkage** is the connecting of two separate issues, so that someone agrees to do one thing only if something else is done. *The letter urged against any linkage between chemical and nuclear disarmament.*

link-up See **link.**

linnet The **linnet** is a small songbird of the finch family.

linoleum or **lino** is a floor covering made of cloth covered with a hard shiny substance.

Linotype A **Linotype** is an old-fashioned typesetting machine operated by a keyboard. It casts each line on a piece of metal called a slug. 'Linotype' is a trademark.

linseed is the seed of the flax plant. The oil from this seed is used to make paints, varnishes, and inks, or rubbed into wooden surfaces to protect them.

lint is a soft cotton or linen fabric used for dressing wounds.

lintel A **lintel** is a piece of stone or wood over a door or window. It supports the bricks or stones above it.

lion — **Lions** are large wild members of the cat family. They have yellowish fur; the male has a long shaggy mane. Lions live mainly in Africa. ■ If you get the **lion's share** of something, you get most of it.

lioness (**lionesses**) A **lioness** is a female lion.

lionize (or **lionise**) (**lionizing, lionized**) If someone is **lionized,** they are treated as a celebrity.

lip A person's **lips** are the top and bottom fleshy edges of their mouth. ■ If you say someone is keeping a **stiff upper lip,** you mean they are hiding their emotions even though this may be difficult for them. ■ If you say a word or name is **on everyone's lips,** you mean you keep hearing it everywhere. ■ **Lip-reading** is understanding what someone is saying by watching their lip movements. ■ If you **curl your lip** at something, you sneer at it and show your contempt for it. ■ If someone **pays lip service** to an idea, they pretend they approve of it, but in fact do nothing to support it.

lipid — **Lipids** are substances like fats and oils which are insoluble in water but soluble in alcohol and ether. They are important structural materials in living things.

liposuction is a way of removing excess body fat by sucking it out with a machine.

lipstick is a cosmetic in the form of a small stick, which women put on their lips.

liquefaction is the process of making something liquid.

liquefied (or **liquified**) A **liquefied** substance is one which is normally solid or a gas, but has been changed to liquid form.

liqueur (*pron:* lik-**cure**) **Liqueurs** are strong sweet alcoholic drinks.

liquid A **liquid** is any substance which is not a solid or a gas and which can be poured. ■ **Liquid** assets can be quickly turned into cash if necessary.

liquidate (**liquidating, liquidated; liquidation, liquidator**) When a company **is liquidated,** it is closed down by a procedure called **liquidation,** in which its assets are sold off to help repay its debts. A **liquidator** is someone brought in to supervise this procedure. ■ You can say someone **liquidates** their assets when they sell off property such as buildings or machinery, to get money. ■ If someone **liquidates** another person, they kill them.

liquid crystal A **liquid crystal** is a liquid which has some of the qualities of crystals, for example reflecting light from different directions in different ways. ■ **liquid crystal display:** see **LCD.**

liquidity is having enough cash or liquid assets to pay any debts or cover any emergencies.

liquidize (or **liquidise**) (**liquidizing, liquidized; liquidizer**) When you **liquidize** food, you blend it in an electrical machine called a **liquidizer,** to make it into a pulp or liquid.

liquified See **liquefied.**

liquor is strong alcoholic drink, especially spirits.

liquorice (or **licorice**) (*usual pron:* lik-ker-ish) is a black substance used to make sweets.

lira (*plural:* **lire**) The **lira** is the unit of currency in Italy and Turkey.

lisp If someone **lisps** or has a **lisp,** they pronounce 's' and 'z' as 'th'.

lissom people are slim and graceful.

list (**listing**) A **list** is a series of things or names written one below the other. When a document contains a list, you can say it **lists** a number of things or people. ■ If something is **listed,** it is included as an item on a list, especially an official list. The items in a list are sometimes called **listings**. ■ A **listed** building is included in a list of buildings of architectural or historic interest which are protected by law from being demolished or altered. ■ If a person **lists** something, they mention a series of things or names. *She was asked to list her engagements.* ■ A **listed company** is one whose shares have been approved and quoted for trading on a stock market. When this happens, you say the company is given a **listing**. ■ The **list price** of something is the price suggested by the manufacturers in their catalogue, price list, or advertisements. You say something is **listed** at a particular price. ■ If a ship **lists**, it leans to one side.

listen (listening, listened) If you **listen** to someone who is talking, you pay attention to what they are saying. Similarly, you can **listen** to music or other sounds. ■ You say someone **listens** to someone else when they take account of what they say. *The commission has listened to its critics.* ■ If someone **listens in** on a private conversation, they listen without the people concerned knowing about it.

listener Anyone who listens to something can be called a **listener**.

listeria is a kind of bacteria which causes severe food poisoning.

listing See **list**.

listless (listlessly, listlessness) If someone is **listless,** they are weary and lacking in energy or enthusiasm.

lit See **light**.

litany (litanies) The **litany** is part of a church service in which the priest says a set group of prayers and the congregation replies with set responses. ■ You can call a list of tedious or unpleasant things a **litany**. *...a mounting litany of complaints.*

liter See **litre**.

literacy is the ability to read and write.

literal (literally) The **literal** meaning of a word is its most basic meaning. *It could be said that Venice is literally sinking under the weight of visitors.*

literary people and things are connected in some way with literature. *...a prominent literary critic.* ■ **Literary** words and expressions are used in novels and poems, but are not usually used in conversation, except in a humorous way.

literate people can read and write. You can also describe a well-written piece of writing as **literate**. *...Waller's literate financial thriller.* You can use **literate** when talking about other skills. *...computer-literate film makers... Become financially literate.*

literati are well-educated people who are interested in literature.

literature is creative writing such as novels, plays, and poetry. ■ **Literature** is any kind of printed information. *The opposition parties had difficulty in distributing campaign literature.*

lithe If you say someone is **lithe,** you mean they move easily and gracefully.

lithium is the lightest known metal.

lithography (lithograph, lithographic) Lithography is a method of printing in which a piece of metal or plastic is specially treated so ink sticks to

some parts and not to others. *...lithographic plates.* A **lithograph** is a printed picture made by this method.

litigant – **Litigants** are the people, other than the lawyers, who are fighting or defending a civil law case.

litigate (litigating, litigated; litigation, litigator) If someone **litigates,** they take a dispute to a civil court for a decision. This process is called **litigation**. A **litigator** is a lawyer who fights or defends civil lawsuits.

litigious *(pron:* li-**tij**-uss) people are always taking issues to court.

litmus is a chemical which is turned red by acids and blue by alkalis. ■ Any simple but effective way of determining something can be called a **litmus test**. *Mr Weld's status within his party may prove a good litmus test of its electoral chances.*

litre *(Am: liter)* The volume of liquids and gases is often expressed in **litres**. A litre is 1,000 cubic centimetres (about 1.76 pints).

litter (littering, littered) **Litter** is small pieces of rubbish, for example bits of paper, left lying around in a public place. You can say rubbish **litters** a place or the place is **littered** with it. ■ You can say something is **littered** with things when it contains a lot of them. *The book is littered with verbless sentences.* ■ A **litter** is a group of baby animals born at the same time to the same mother.

little is used to describe things which are smaller in size or shorter in duration than usual. *...a little man. ...a little chat.* ■ **Little** is used to describe things which are unimportant. *He complained a lot about little things.* ■ A **little** is a short time. *Frido stood still for a little.* ■ A **little** of something is a small amount of it. *I know a little French.* ■ A **little** means to a small degree. *He tapped a little harder.* ■ **Little** is used to say there is not much of something. *He has shown little interest in Mexico.* ■ If someone does **little** or says **little,** they do not do or say much.

littoral The area along a coast is sometimes called the **littoral**. *...the Black Sea littoral.*

liturgical means connected with religious services. *...liturgical music.*

liturgy (liturgies) A **liturgy** is a traditional form of service in some churches.

live *(pron:* liv) *(living, lived)* If you **live** in a place, it is your home. *She lived in Hollywood for 48 years.* ■ If someone **lives** for a certain length of time, they are alive for that time. ■ The way you **live** is the kind of lifestyle you have. *The Lynch family lived a conventional, lower-middle-class life.* ■ If you **live on** something or **live off** it, it provides you with money for the everyday things you need. *He lives off state benefits.* ■ If you **live off** a kind of food or **live on** it, it is the only kind you eat. ■ If you **live by** a set of standards or rules, you behave the way they say you should. ■ If you do not **live up to** something, you fail to do what is expected of you. *The show failed to live up to expectations.* ■ If you have to **live with** an unpleasant situation, you have to accept it and carry on with your life or work. ■ If you are trying to **live down** something embarrassing which has happened to you, you are hoping people will forget about it. ■ If you say someone will **live** to regret something they have done, you mean they will eventually be sorry they did it. ■ If you **live for** something, it is the most important thing in your life. ■ If you **live it up,** you have a good time, for example by going to parties.

live If a TV or radio programme is **live,** what you see or hear is happening now, and has not been recorded beforehand. ■ A **live** performance takes place in front of an audience. *Much of today's best acting is to be found on the small screen, not in live theatre.* ■ A **live** animal is one which is alive in circumstances where you would expect it to be dead. *One applicant sent us a box containing a live locust.* ■ **Live** bombs or shells have not yet exploded. ■ If something electrical is **live,** it is directly connected to a source of electricity, and will give you a shock if you touch it.

livelihood Your **livelihood** is your job, or whatever provides your income.

lively (livelier, liveliest; liveliness) Lively people are active, enthusiastic, and cheerful. ■ If people have a **lively** discussion, they discuss things enthusiastically, because they are strongly interested in the topic.

liven (livening, livened) If something **livens up** a place or event, it makes it more interesting and exciting.

liver A person's or animal's **liver** is a large organ in their body which processes and cleans their blood.

livery (liveries) A company's **livery** is a design or set of colours associated with it, appearing, for example, on its vehicles. ■ A servant's **livery** is the uniform he or she wears.

livestock is farm animals like cattle and sheep.

livid If you are **livid,** you are extremely angry. ■ If something is **livid,** it is an unpleasant dark colour.

living A **living** person is alive now. ■ If you earn your **living** in a particular way, you get the money you live on by doing that kind of work. ■ If you are paid a **living wage,** you are paid just enough money to buy food, clothing, and other necessary things. ■ **Living** is used to talk about (a) places where people live, especially when they are attached to their workplace. *...the crews' living quarters.* (b) a particular way of life. *...the stresses of urban living.* ■ When you talk about **living standards,** you mean the level of comfort in which people live, which usually depends on how much money they have.

living room The **living room** is the room in a house where people sit and relax.

lizard — Lizards are reptiles with short legs, dry scaly skin, and long tails.

llama The **llama** is a South American pack animal with thick hair. It looks like a small camel without a hump.

LLB after someone's name means they have a university degree in law. LLB stands for 'Bachelor of Laws'.

lo People sometimes say **lo** or **lo and behold** when they are mentioning something surprising.

load (loading, loaded) When people **load** a vehicle or container, they put things into it. ■ A **load** of something is a quantity of it being carried somewhere. *...a lorry-load of sheep.* ■ If you **load** a weapon, you put ammunition into it, so it is ready to be fired. ■ If you **load** a camera, you put film into it. Similarly, you can **load** a tape or disk into a cassette player or computer. ■ A **loaded question** has more meaning than it appears to have, because it is intended to cause a particular reaction. ■ If something is **loaded** in someone's favour, it works unfairly to their advantage. Similarly, something can be **loaded** against someone. ■ A **load** of things or people means a lot of them. *I received loads of letters.* ■ If someone is **loaded,** they have a lot of money.

loaf (loafing, loafed) A **loaf** (*plural:* **loaves**) is bread baked in one large shape which can be sliced. ■ If you **loaf** around, you spend time doing nothing.

loafer — Loafers are casual shoes, similar to moccasins. ■ If you call a person a **loafer,** you mean they spend their time lazing around.

loan (loaning, loaned) A **loan** is an amount of money you borrow, for example from a bank, and have to pay back with interest. ■ A **loan shark** is someone who lends people money at very high interest rates. ■ If you **loan** something to someone, you lend it to them. If you offer someone the **loan** of something, you offer to lend it to them. If a book or picture is **on loan,** it has been lent to someone.

loath (or loth) If you are **loath** to do something, you are unwilling to do it.

loathe (loathing, loathed) If you **loathe** someone or something, you dislike them intensely. *...his loathing of Communism.*

loathsome If you say someone or something is **loathsome,** you mean they are very unpleasant.

lob (lobbing, lobbed) If you **lob** something somewhere, you get it to land there by throwing it high in the air. *Police lobbed tear gas shells into the house.* ■ If you **lob** the ball in tennis, you hit it high in the air so it lands behind your opponent. This kind of shot is called a **lob.**

lobby (lobbies, lobbying, lobbied; lobbyist) A **lobby** is a group of people who try to persuade a government or organization to do or prevent something. *...the anti-abortion lobby.* ■ If you **lobby** people like government ministers, you try to get them to do something. People who lobby are called **lobbyists.** ■ The **lobby** of a large building is the main entrance area, with corridors and staircases leading off it.

lobe The **lobe** of your ear is the soft fleshy part at the bottom. ■ Rounded parts of some parts of the body are called **lobes,** for example parts of the brain, the lungs, and the liver.

lobelia The **lobelia** is a bedding plant covered with small blue flowers.

lobotomy A **lobotomy** is a surgical operation in which some of the nerves in the brain are cut to treat severe mental illness.

lobster The **lobster** is a sea creature with a hard shell, two front claws, and eight legs. ■ A **lobster pot** is a basket-like trap for catching lobsters.

local (**locally**) **Local government** is the organization and administration of public services on a local rather than a national basis. The **local authority** in an area is the council responsible for running the services there. **Local** means connected with local government. *...the local council.* ■ You use **local** to talk about things in the area where you live or work. *...a local restaurant... These facilities weren't available locally.* ■ You can call the people who live in an area the **locals**. ■ Your **local** is a pub near where you live, where you often go for a drink. ■ **Local colour** is the features of a place which are special to that place.

local anaesthetic A **local anaesthetic** stops the feeling in only one part of your body, and does not make you unconscious. See also **general anaesthetic.**

local authority See **local.**

locale (*pron:* loh-**kahl**) The **locale** for something is the place chosen for it.

local government See **local.**

locality (**localities**) If you talk about something happening **in the locality,** you mean it happens in the general area you have been talking about.

localized (*or* **localised**) things are limited to a small area. *...localized pain.*

locate (**locating, located**) If you **locate** someone or something, you succeed in finding them. ■ If something is **located** somewhere, that is where it is.

location Something's **location** is the place where it is. ■ If a film or TV programme is made **on location,** it is made in real surroundings away from the studio.

loch In Scotland, a **loch** is a large area of water completely or almost completely surrounded by land. In Ireland, an area of water like this is called a **lough.**

lock The **lock** on a door is the device you turn a key in, to fasten the door. If you **lock** a door, you fasten it like this. ■ If you **lock** something **in** a cupboard, drawer, or safe, or **lock** it **away** there, you put it there and lock the door. ■ If something is **under lock and key,** it is in a locked room or container. ■ If someone is **locked in** a room or other place, the door is locked and they cannot get out. If someone is kept somewhere like this as a prisoner, you say they are **locked up.** ■ If you **lock up,** you close and lock all the outside doors of a building. ■ If someone is **locked out,** they are prevented from getting into a place by the doors being locked. ■ If you **lock** yourself **out** of a place, you cannot get in because the door is locked and you have left your keys inside. ■ If the management of a factory **locks out** the workers, it closes the factory and prevents the workers from coming in, because they refuse to accept the management's conditions. A situation like this is called a **lock-out** or **lockout.** ■ If people are **locked** in a fight or argument, they are fighting or arguing fiercely, and determined not to give in to their opponent. ■ A **lock** on a canal is a short stretch of water between two barriers, where the water level can be raised or lowered to allow boats to move between higher

and lower sections of the canal. ■ A **lock** of hair is a small bunch of someone's hair. ■ A person's hair can be called their **locks.**

locker A **locker** is a small cupboard with a lock, where you put your personal belongings temporarily. ■ A **locker room** is a room in a sports club where people change their clothes and store their belongings in lockers.

locket A **locket** is a piece of jewellery containing a picture, worn on a chain around the neck.

lockout See **lock.**

locksmith A **locksmith** makes and repairs locks as their job.

lock-up garage A **lock-up garage** is not within the boundaries of your house, but is in a block of garages somewhere nearby.

locomotion is moving from one place to another. *There was no mention of her means of locomotion.*

locomotive A **locomotive** is a railway engine.

locum A **locum** is a doctor or priest who temporarily takes over the work of another doctor or priest while he or she is absent.

locus The **locus** of something is (a) the place where it happens. (b) the most important area or point with which it is associated. *...Barcelona, the locus of Spanish industry.*

locust – Locusts are large grasshopper-like insects.

lodge (**lodging, lodged; lodger, lodgings**) If you **lodge** something like a complaint, you make it formally. ■ If you **lodge** money or other valuables somewhere, you leave them there. ■ If something **lodges** somewhere or is **lodged** there, it becomes stuck. ■ If someone **lodges** in your house, they live there for a time, usually paying rent. You refer to them as your **lodger;** they call your house their **lodgings.** ■ A **lodge** is (a) a small house at the entrance to the grounds of a large one. (b) a building where people stay on holiday, especially when they are taking part in sports like hunting or fishing. ■ Some organizations have local branches or meeting places called **lodges.** *...a masonic lodge.*

loft A **loft** is the space inside the roof of a house, often used for storing things.

lofty (**loftier, loftiest; loftily**) A **lofty** building is very high. ■ **Lofty** ideals or ambitions are noble and admirable. ■ You can say someone is **lofty** when they are rather too proud and haughty.

log (**logging, logged; logger**) A **log** is a piece of wood cut from a thick branch or from the trunk of a tree. ■ If an area of forest is **logged,** trees are cut down for timber. A **logger** is a person whose job is cutting down trees in a forest. ■ A **log** is an official written record of something. If you **log** something, you officially make a record of it. ■ If you **log into** a computer system, you gain access to it, usually by typing your name or identity code and a password.

loganberry (**loganberries**) **Loganberries** are small purplish-red fruit, similar to large raspberries.

logarithm The **logarithm** of a number is a number that it can be represented by to make a difficult multiplication or division sum simpler.

log book A **log book** is a book in which you record details and events, especially to do with your car.

logger See **log.**

loggerheads You say people are **at loggerheads** when they disagree strongly about something.

logic is a method of reasoning which involves a progression of statements, each of which must be true if the statement before it is true.

logical (**logically**) You say an argument is **logical** when each step follows from the one before. ∎ A **logical** course of action seems sensible in the circumstances.

logistics (**logistic, logistical, logistically**) In the armed forces, **logistics** is the organization of transport, supplies, and maintenance for troops and equipment. ∎ You can talk about the **logistics** of anything which needs careful organization. ...the logistics of big-budget film-making... For logistical simplicity, the Americans want these negotiations to stay in Madrid.

log-jam (or **logjam**) If you say there is a **log-jam**, you mean many things are waiting to be dealt with, because they have been appearing faster than people can deal with them.

logo (**logos**) The **logo** of a company or other organization is the unique symbol or lettering it puts on its products and publicity material.

loin is a piece of meat from the back or sides of an animal. ∎ A person's **loins** are the front part of their body between their waist and thighs, especially their genitals. ∎ If you **gird your loins**, you prepare to do something difficult or dangerous.

loincloth A **loincloth** is a piece of cloth sometimes worn by men to cover their genitals, especially in hot countries.

loiter (**loitering, loitered**) If you **loiter** somewhere, you hang around with no real purpose.

loll If you **loll** somewhere, you sit or lie there in a very relaxed position. ∎ If your head or tongue **lolls**, it hangs loosely.

lollipop A **lollipop** is a sweet on the end of a stick.

lollipop lady (**lollipop man**) A **lollipop lady** or **lollipop man** is a person whose job is to stop traffic to allow children to cross a busy road. The official job title is 'school crossing patrol'.

lolly (**lollies**) A **lolly** is (a) a piece of flavoured ice or ice cream on a stick. (b) a lollipop. ∎ **Lolly** is money.

lone A **lone** person or thing is the only one of their kind, or the only one in a particular place. Britain has often been perceived as a lone voice against a single European currency.

lonely (**lonelier, loneliest; loneliness**) If someone is **lonely**, they are unhappy because they are alone or do not have any friends. ∎ A **lonely** place is one where few people go.

lonely hearts The **lonely hearts** section of a newspaper or magazine consists of adverts placed by people who want to find a friend or lover.

loner A **loner** is a person who likes being on their own.

lonesome is the usual American word for 'lonely'.

long is used to talk about a great deal of time. ...a long period of low interest rates... They queued outside long before opening time. ∎ **Long** is used when mentioning the time something lasts. 'Don Carlos' is well over five hours long... How long will the journey take? ∎ If something **no longer** happens, it used to happen but does not happen now. ∎ If something is true **as long as** something else is true, the first thing is true only if the second one is. The tax advantages apply only so long as the money remains invested. ∎ If something is **long,** it measures a large distance from one end to the other. ...a long corridor. ∎ **Long** is used when mentioning the length of something. The lake is 150 metres long. ∎ If you say someone has a **long face,** you mean they are sad or worried. ∎ If you **long** for something, you want it very much.

long- is added to words to describe things which go on for a long time. ...the firm's long-awaited stockmarket flotation.

longboat A **longboat** was a narrow uncovered boat powered by oars and sails, used by the Vikings.

longbow The **longbow** was a large bow used by English and Welsh medieval archers.

longevity (pron: lon-**jev**-it-ee) is long life.

longhand If you write something in **longhand,** you write it by hand using complete words and normal letters, rather than typing it or using shortened forms or special symbols.

longing (**longingly**) A **longing** is a rather sad feeling of wanting something you know you are unlikely to get.

longitude The **longitude** of a place is how far east or west it is, measured in degrees from a north-south line passing through Greenwich.

longitudinal A **longitudinal** measurement, axis, or cross-section runs from one end of a thing to the other, rather than across it from side to side.

long johns are underpants with long legs.

long jump The **long jump** is an athletics event in which competitors jump as far as they can.

long-life things are made or treated so that they last longer than other things of the same kind. ...long-life milk.

long-lived If people of a particular kind are **long-lived,** they tend to live longer than most other people.

long-lost is used to describe people, especially friends and relatives, who have not been seen for a very long time. ...a long-lost uncle.

long-range is used to describe things, especially weapons, which operate over long distances. ...long-range missiles. ∎ A **long-range** forecast or plan covers a period extending well into the future.

long-sighted (**long-sightedness**) If you are **long-sighted,** you cannot see things near you clearly.

long-standing A **long-standing** situation has existed for a long time. ...a long-standing row.

long wave is used to talk about the range of radio waves from 1,000 metres upwards.

long-winded remarks are boring because they are longer than necessary.

loo Some people call the toilet the **loo.**

look (**looking, looked**) If you **look** in a certain direction, you direct your eyes that way, to see what is there. ∎ If you **look** at something or take a **look** at it, you watch it or examine it. ∎ If you **look on** while something happens, you watch it and do nothing about it. ∎ **Look** is used to say how someone or something appears or to describe their expression. *His blue bri-nylon anorak gave him the look of a warehouse foreman. ...Mr Stephens looked puzzled.* ■ When you talk about someone's good **looks**, you are talking about how attractive they are. ■ A particular **look** is a style in something like clothes. *...the new look for winter.* ■ If you **look up to** someone, you respect and admire them. If you **look down on** someone, you think they are inferior to you. ■ If something **looks like** happening, it seems likely to happen. ■ If a situation is **looking up**, it is improving. ■ If you **look after** someone or something, you take care of them. ■ If you **look for** someone or something, you try to find them. ■ If you **look into** something, you investigate it. ■ If you **look** something **up**, you consult a book to find out what you want to know. ■ If you **look in on** a person or place, you visit them for a short time. ■ **look forward to:** see **forward.**

lookalike Someone's **lookalike** is a person who looks very like them. *...a Marlene Dietrich lookalike.*

look-in If you do not get a **look-in,** you do not get a chance to do something, because so many other people are doing it.

-looking You add **-looking** to a word to say how someone or something appears. *...a dreary-looking place near Euston Station.* ■ You add **-looking** to a word to describe someone's attitudes. *...forward-looking countries such as Norway, Sweden, Canada.*

looking glass A **looking glass** is the same as a mirror.

lookout (*or* **look-out**) If you are **on the lookout** for something or **keeping a lookout** for it, you are watching out for it. ■ A **lookout** is a place from which you can see clearly in all directions or a person who is watching for danger.

loom (**looming, loomed**) If you talk about something unpleasant **looming,** you mean it is going to happen soon. *...the threat of another recession looms.* ■ If an object **looms** in front of you, it appears as a tall, unclear, and often frightening shape. *Great rectangular pillars of hard rock loom above the clifftop.* ■ A **loom** is a device for weaving thread into cloth.

loony (**loonies**) If you call an idea or plan **loony,** you mean it is extremely silly.

loop (**looping, looped**) A **loop** in something like a rope is a part where it has been bent until it crosses over itself. ■ If you **loop** a piece of rope round something, you tie it in a circle round it. ■ If something like a road **loops** somewhere, it goes round there in a circle.

loophole A **loophole** in the law is a small mistake or omission which allows you to do something the law was meant to prevent.

loopy If you say someone is **loopy,** you mean they are mad or highly eccentric.

loose (**looser, loosest; loosely, looseness; loosing, loosed**) If something is **loose,** it is not firmly held or fixed in place. ■ **Loose** clothes do not fit your body closely. ■ A **loose** grouping or arrangement is not rigidly controlled. *...a loosely organised group.* ■ If something is **loosely** based on something else, it takes its main idea from it, but is different in

many details. ■ If you let an animal **loose,** you release it from captivity. ■ If someone **looses off** a weapon, they fire it. ■ If you are **at a loose end,** you have nothing to do and are bored.

loosen (**loosening, loosened**) If the authorities **loosen** laws, they make them less strict. ■ If something **loosens** links between people, it makes them less close. ■ If something is **loosened,** it becomes less firmly held in place. ■ If you **loosen up,** you become more relaxed.

loot (**looting, looted; looter**) When people **loot** shops or houses, they steal things from them during a riot or other disturbance. People who do this are called **looters.** ■ **Loot** is money or goods stolen in a robbery.

lop (**lopping, lopped**) If you **lop** something **off,** you cut it off in a quick movement. ■ If you **lop** a certain amount **off** something, you reduce it by that amount. *Nationwide announced that it was lopping an average of 0.4% gross off its savings accounts.*

lope (**loping, loped**) When people or animals **lope,** they run in a relaxed way with long strides.

lopsided (*or* **lop-sided**) If an object is **lopsided,** it looks odd, because one side is bigger or higher than the other.

loquacious (**loquacity**) If you say someone is **loquacious** or talk about their **loquacity,** you mean they talk a lot.

lord is a title used in front of the name of a male member of the aristocracy or House of Lords, or a senior male judge. ■ A **lord** is a high-ranking British nobleman. ■ People who have a great deal of power are sometimes called **lords.** *...press lords.* ■ If someone **lords it over** you, they order you around. ■ When Christians talk about **the Lord,** they mean God.

lordly is used to describe something done in a proud and arrogant way. *Their usual lordly indifference to patients.* ■ **Lordly** is used to talk about things to do with lords. *Lordly eyebrows have been raised in the Upper Chamber.*

Lordship is used when talking respectfully to a lord, bishop, or senior male judge, or when talking about him in a formal way.

Lord's Prayer The **Lord's Prayer** is the most important Christian prayer. According to the Bible, Jesus Christ taught it to his disciples.

lore The **lore** of a region, group, or nation is its traditional stories and customs.

lorry (**lorries**) A **lorry** is a large motor vehicle for transporting goods by road.

lose (**losing, lost**) If you **lose** something, you cannot find it. ■ If you **lose** someone or something, you no longer have them, because they have been taken from you or destroyed. ■ If you **lose** a contest or argument, you are beaten. ■ If you **lose** time, you get behind with a task you are doing. ■ If a clock **loses** time, it goes too slowly and shows the wrong time. ■ If you **lose** something such as weight, you have less of it. ■ If a business **loses** money, it earns less than it spends. ■ **lose sight** of something: see **sight.**

loser The **loser** of a contest is the person who is beaten. ■ If you are the **loser** as a result of something, you are worse off because of it. *These institutes have been the country's greatest losers in the recession.* ■ If you call someone a **loser,** you think they are never successful, and never likely to be so.

loss (**losses**) When something is destroyed or ceases to exist, you can talk about its **loss.** *...the loss of 500 jobs.* ■ If a company makes a **loss,** it earns less money than it spends. ■ If a business sells something **at a loss,** they sell it for less than it cost them to make it or buy it. ■ The **loss** of a relative or friend is their death. ■ If you are **at a loss,** you do not know what to do in a particular situation. ■ If you **cut your losses,** you stop doing something which is unsuccessful, to prevent a bad situation becoming worse.

loss leader A **loss leader** is a product which is sold at much lower than cost price, to attract customers.

lost See **lose.** ■ If you are **lost,** you do not know where you are, or you are unable to find your way. ■ If something is **lost,** you cannot find it or you no longer have it. ■ If you say you would be **lost** without someone or something, you mean you would be unhappy or unable to do something properly without them. ■ If something is **lost** on someone, they do not understand it.

lost property is things people have accidentally left behind in a public place, which is kept for a time in case they claim it.

lot – A **lot** of something or **lots** of it means a large amount of it. ■ A **lot** means 'very much'. *It was a lot more fun than college.* ■ If you do something **a lot,** you do it often. ■ You can use **lot** to talk about a group of people or things. *There's hardly any of the old lot left now.* ■ The **lot** means all of the thing you have just mentioned. *When his first wage packet arrived, he went to a betting shop and lost the lot in half an hour.* ■ At an auction, a **lot** is one of the items being sold. ■ A person's **lot** is the kind of life they lead. *The WI aims to improve the lot of all women.* ■ If you **throw in your lot** with someone, you decide to join them in what they are doing and stay with them whatever happens. ■ If people **draw lots** to decide who will do something, they each take a piece of paper from a container. One or more pieces of paper is marked, and the people who take marked pieces are chosen.

loth See **loath.**

lotion A **lotion** is a liquid you use on your skin or hair to clean, protect, or improve it.

lottery (**lotteries**) A **lottery** is a gambling game in which large numbers of people buy numbered tickets. Several numbers are chosen at random, and the people with those numbers on their tickets win a prize. ■ If you say something is a **lottery,** you mean what happens depends entirely on chance.

lotus (**lotuses**) The **lotus** is a type of water-lily in Africa, Asia, and America.

louche (*pron:* loosh) is used to describe people and places which are seedy or disreputable.

loud (**louder, loudest; loudly, loudness**) A **loud** noise is one in which the volume of sound is very high. ■ If you are **loud** in your support or condem-

nation of something, you express your opinion forcefully. ■ If you say something **out loud,** you say it so people can hear it, rather than just thinking it. ■ If you call a piece of clothing **loud,** you mean it has bright colours or patterns, and looks vulgar.

loudhailer (*or* loud-hailer) A **loudhailer** is a hand-held loudspeaker which contains its own microphone and amplifier.

loudmouth (**loud-mouthed**) If you call someone a **loudmouth** or describe them as **loud-mouthed,** you mean they talk a lot in an unpleasant or stupid way.

loudspeaker A **loudspeaker** is a piece of equipment, for example part of a hi-fi system, through which sound comes out.

lough See **loch.**

lounge (**lounging, lounged**) The **lounge** in a house or hotel is a room where people can sit and relax. ■ The **lounge** or **lounge bar** in a pub is a comfortably furnished bar. ■ If you **lounge** somewhere, you sit or stand around in a relaxed way. If you **lounge about** or **lounge around,** you spend your time idly.

lounge lizard If you describe someone as a **lounge lizard,** you mean they are an idler who regularly frequents the places where rich and famous people gather.

lounge suit A **lounge suit** is a man's suit with matching jacket and trousers.

louse (*plural:* lice) **Lice** are small insects which live on the bodies of people or animals.

lousy (**lousier, lousiest**) If you say something is **lousy,** you mean it is very bad. ■ You can say someone or something is **lousy** when they are covered in lice.

lout (**loutish**) A **lout** is a man who behaves in a rude or aggressive way. **Loutish** behaviour is rude and aggressive.

louvre (*pron:* loo-ver) (**louvred**) **Louvres** are horizontal sloping slats in a door or window. *...louvred blinds.*

lovable (*or* loveable) If you say someone is **lovable,** you mean they are easy to like.

love (**loving, loved**) **Love** is a very strong feeling of affection for someone you are romantically and sexually attracted to. If you **love** someone, you feel like this about them; you can say they are your **love.** ■ If you are **in love** with someone, you are romantically and sexually attracted to them. ■ When two people **make love,** they have sex. ■ **Love** is caring deeply about friends and members of your family. You can say you **love** someone like this. Your **loved ones** are the people you care about. ■ If someone **loves** their country, they care deeply about it. You can talk about someone's **love** for their country. ■ If you **love** something, or have a **love** of it, you like it very much. *...their love of gambling.* ■ If you would **love** to do something, you want the chance to do it. ■ In tennis, **love** is a score of zero.

loveable See **lovable.**

love affair A **love affair** is a sexual or romantic relationship between two people who are not married to each other. ■ When people involve themselves enthusiastically with something, you can say they have a **love affair** with it. ...*his love affair with Venice.*

lovebird – Lovebirds are a type of small African parrot. ■ You can refer humorously to two people as **lovebirds** when they are obviously very much in love.

love child A **love child** is someone who was born to parents who were not married to each other.

love-hate If you have a **love-hate** relationship with someone or something, your attitude to them keeps changing from love to hate.

love life A person's **love life** is their romantic and sexual relationships.

lovelorn If someone is **lovelorn,** they are miserable because the person they love does not love them.

lovely (**lovelier, loveliest**) You use **lovely** to describe people and things that are beautiful and therefore very pleasing to look at or listen to. ■ You can use **lovely** to describe people or things which give you pleasure. *The meal was lovely.*

love-making (*or* **lovemaking**) is sexual activity between two people.

love nest A **love nest** is a place where a couple meet, often secretly, to carry on a love affair.

lover Someone's **lover** is a person they are having an affair with. When people are having an affair, you say they are **lovers.** ■ If you are a **lover** of something, you like it very much. ...*lovers of good food.*

loving (**lovingly**) A **loving** person feels and shows love for someone, or for people generally. ...*his loving concern for abandoned children... She looked at her husband lovingly.* ■ You describe someone's actions as **loving** when they do something carefully and thoroughly, because they enjoy it. ...*his lovingly restored MGB Roadster.*

low If something is **low,** it is below what is normal or average. ...*low pay. ...low temperatures.* ■ A **low** is the lowest level something reaches. *The pound crashed to a post-war low.* ■ If something is **low,** it does not extend upwards very far. ...*a low wall. ...low hills.* ■ If you are feeling **low,** you are unhappy. ■ If a light is **low,** it is dim. ■ If someone is **lying low,** they are in hiding, or keeping out of sight. ■ If you are **laid low** by disease or injury, it makes you weak or ill. ■ **Low season** is the time of year when holiday resorts and attractions are least busy.

lowbrow is used to describe activities and forms of entertainment which are not thought to be serious or intellectual.

Low Church The **Low Church** group within the Church of England is opposed to excessive ceremony and ritual, and holds evangelical beliefs.

low-cut A **low-cut** dress or blouse leaves a woman's neck, shoulders, and the top of her chest bare.

lower (**lowering, lowered**) **Lower** is used to talk about (a) the bottom part of something. ...*the lower part of the slope.* (b) the bottom one of a pair of things. ...*the lower lip.* ■ **Lower** is used to talk about an institution whose status is below that of a similar institution. *It upheld a ruling by a lower court.* ■ If you **lower** an amount, you decrease it.

■ If you **lower** an object, you move it slowly downwards. ■ If you **lower** your voice, you speak more quietly.

lower case letters are small letters, rather than capitals.

lower class (**lower classes**) People whose social status is thought to be lower than that of other people are sometimes called the **lower classes. Lower-class** is sometimes used to describe things associated with such people. *Horse-racing was once considered vulgar and lower-class in Japan.*

lowest common denominator You can accuse people of appealing to the **lowest common denominator** when they reduce something to its most basic and simple level so it will appeal to the greatest number of people. ■ The **lowest common denominator** of a group of fractions is the smallest number all their denominators can go into.

low-key If an event is **low-key,** things are done in a restrained way, without much publicity.

lowland The **lowlands** of a country are the parts which are flat or hilly rather than mountainous. ...*lowland bogs.*

low-life The people in a place who are involved in crime or immoral activities are sometimes called its **low-life.**

lowly (**lowlier, lowliest**) You call someone or something **lowly** when they are of low status.

low-lying land is at, near, or below sea level.

low profile If someone keeps a **low profile,** they avoid publicity.

low-rise buildings are of normal height, as distinct from tower blocks. See also **high-rise.**

low-tech systems or practices do not make use of the most up-to-date methods or equipment.

low tide (*or* **low water**) is the time when the sea is at its lowest level on the coast.

loyal (**loyally**) If you are **loyal** to someone or something, you remain firm in your support for them.

loyalist In Northern Ireland, a **loyalist** is someone who wants to keep Northern Ireland as part of the United Kingdom and is opposed to the unification of Ireland. ■ People can be called **loyalists** when they are firm in their support for their government, party, or ruler.

loyalty (**loyalties**) Loyalty is being firm in your support for someone or something. ■ **Loyalties** are feelings of friendship and duty.

loyalty card A **loyalty card** is a swipe card which records credit points awarded for the amount of money you spend in a supermarket or chain store.

lozenge A **lozenge** is a medicated tablet which you suck, for example when you have a sore throat.

LP An **LP** is a record with about 25 minutes of music on each side. LP is short for 'long player'.

L-plate – L-plates are small signs with an 'L' on them which you must attach to your car when you are learning to drive.

LSD is a powerful illegal drug which can cause hallucinations. It is also known as 'acid'. LSD is short for 'lysergic acid diethylamide'.

Ltd after a company's name means 'Limited'.

lubricate (**lubricating, lubricated; lubrication, lubricant**) If you **lubricate** something, you put a substance like oil on its moving parts, to make sure they operate smoothly. A substance used for this purpose is called a **lubricant.**

lucerne See **alfalfa.**

lucid (**lucidly, lucidity**) **Lucid** writing or speech is clear and easy to understand. ■ If a sick person is **lucid,** their mind is unaffected by their illness and they are able to think clearly and logically.

luck is used to talk about things happening to you which are not the result of your own efforts, or not your fault. If you have **luck** or **good luck,** the things which happen are desirable. If you have **bad luck,** the things which happen are unpleasant.

luckily You add **luckily** to a statement to say something is fortunate. *Luckily I have a housekeeper to look after the children.*

luckless is used, often humorously, to describe people who have been unlucky.

lucky (**luckier, luckiest**) You say someone is **lucky** when they are in a desirable situation or things go well for them. *I was lucky enough to be one of the first customers... We were lucky to come out of it alive.* ■ You say someone is **lucky** when they always seem to have good luck. ■ **Lucky** is used to describe things which people believe bring them luck. *Seven is his lucky number.* ■ If you say a situation is a **lucky dip,** you mean the result depends on chance rather than on any plan you might have.

lucrative A **lucrative** business or activity earns someone a lot of money.

lucre (*pron:* **loo**-ker) is another word for money. People call money **filthy lucre** when they do not approve of the way it has been acquired.

ludicrous (**ludicrously**) If you say something is **ludicrous,** you mean it is totally silly or unreasonable.

lug (**lugging, lugged**) If you **lug** something heavy from one place to another, you carry it there with difficulty.

luge (*pron:* **loozh;** *the 'zh' sounds like 's' in 'pleasure'*) A **luge** is a kind of toboggan used for racing. The rider lies on his or her back on the luge and goes down the course feet first.

luggage Your **luggage** is the suitcases and bags you take with you when you travel.

lugubrious (*pron:* loo-**goo**-bree-uss) (**lugubriously**) You say someone is **lugubrious** when they are sad and gloomy.

lukewarm If someone's attitude to something is **lukewarm,** they do not show much enthusiasm or interest. ■ If something is **lukewarm,** it is only slightly warm.

lull A **lull** is a period of quiet or little activity. *The upsurge of fighting follows a lull of several weeks.* ■ If you are **lulled** into feeling safe, you are made to feel safe, usually in a situation where you are not.

lullaby (**lullabies**) A **lullaby** is a quiet song which you sing to help a child go to sleep.

lumbar means to do with the lower part of the back. *...the lumbar vertebrae.*

lumber (**lumbering, lumbered**) If someone or something **lumbers** somewhere, they move there slowly and clumsily. ■ You can use **lumbering** to describe a large inefficient organization. *...a lumber-*

ing, outdated company. ■ If you are **lumbered with** something you do not want, you have to have it or deal with it. *They are lumbered with a building that they cannot sell.* ■ **Lumber** is large roughly cut pieces of trees.

lumberjack A **lumberjack** is a person whose job is to cut down trees.

luminary (**luminaries**) A **luminary** is a famous person, or an expert in a particular field.

luminosity is bright light.

luminous If something is **luminous,** it shines or glows in the dark.

lump A **lump** of something solid is an irregularly-shaped piece of it. ■ A **lump** of sugar is a small cube of it. ■ A **lump** in or on someone's body is a small hard swelling caused by injury or illness. ■ If you have a **lump in your throat,** you have a tight feeling there, as if you are going to cry, because of strong emotion. ■ If you **lump** people or things together, you treat them as a group, ignoring any differences between them. ■ If you say someone will have to **lump it,** you mean they will have to accept a situation whether they like it or not.

lumpectomy A **lumpectomy** is an operation in which a woman has a lump such as a tumour removed from one of her breasts, rather than having the entire breast removed.

lump sum A **lump sum** is a large sum of money paid all at once, rather than in instalments.

lumpy (**lumpiness**) If something is **lumpy,** it is full of lumps or covered in lumps.

lunacy You can call an idea or action **lunacy** when you think it is stupid or dangerous. ■ In the past, severe mental illness was sometimes called **lunacy.**

lunar means relating to the moon. *...a lunar eclipse.*

lunatic When a person behaves stupidly or recklessly, people sometimes call them a **lunatic.** ■ In the past, mentally ill people were called **lunatics.**

lunatic asylum In the past, a **lunatic asylum** was a place where mentally disturbed people were locked up.

lunch (**lunches, lunching, lunched**) **Lunch** is a meal in the middle of the day. When people **lunch,** they have this meal. **Lunch** or **lunchtime** is the time when people have lunch.

lunchbox (**lunchboxes**) A **lunchbox** is a container for taking cold food to school or work to eat for lunch.

luncheon is a formal meal in the middle of the day.

lunchtime See **lunch.**

lung Your **lungs** are the two organs inside your chest which fill with air when you breathe in.

lunge (**lunging, lunged**) If you **lunge** or make a **lunge,** you make a sudden violent movement towards something.

lupin – Lupins are garden plants with tall spikes of brightly coloured flowers.

lurch (**lurches, lurching, lurched**) A **lurch** is a sudden jerky movement, especially forwards. If someone **lurches** somewhere, they move suddenly like this. ■ If someone or something **lurches** from one thing to another, they move on to the second thing suddenly and clumsily. *The government has lurched* from one crisis to the next. ■ If someone **leaves you in the lurch,** they let you down at a difficult time.

lure (luring, lured) If you are **lured** somewhere, you are persuaded to go there by the promise of something attractive. You can also say you are **lured** into doing something.

lurid (luridly) Lurid is used to talk about things which attract a lot of attention because they involve sex or violent death. ...the most lurid sex scandal since the Profumo affair. ■ **Lurid** colours are unpleasantly bright and vivid.

lurk If you talk about feelings or dangers **lurking** somewhere, you mean they are present, but people are not yet completely aware of them. ■ If someone **lurks** somewhere, they wait there secretly.

luscious People use **luscious** to describe someone or something they find very attractive and desirable. ...a luscious blonde. ■ **Luscious** fruit is juicy and delicious.

lush (lushness) Lush fields or gardens have a lot of healthy grass or plants.

lust is a strong feeling of sexual desire. When someone has this feeling, you can say they **lust after** someone. ■ A **lust** for something like power or money is a strong desire to get hold of it.

luster See **lustre.**

lustful means feeling or expressing strong sexual desire. ...lustful glances.

lustre (Am: **luster**) **(lustrous) Lustre** is a gentle shining light reflected from a smooth or polished surface. You say a surface like this is **lustrous.** ■ If you say something has lost its **lustre,** you mean it is no longer interesting or exciting.

lusty (lustily) Lusty is used to talk about people doing things with a lot of physical strength or vocal power. ...a lusty guffaw. ■ **Lusty** means lustful. ...lusty executives leering at secretaries.

lute A **lute** is an old-fashioned musical instrument with strings, played like a guitar.

Lutheran A **Lutheran** is a member of the Lutheran Church, a Protestant church founded in the 16th century.

luxuriant (luxuriantly) Luxuriant plants or gardens are very green and healthy. ■ **Luxuriant** hair is thick and healthy.

luxuriate (luxuriating, luxuriated) If you **luxuriate** in something, you relax and enjoy it thoroughly. Pemberton lay luxuriating in a bath.

luxurious (luxuriously) Luxurious is used to describe things which are comfortable and expensive. The offices were luxuriously refitted.

luxury (luxuries) Luxury is great comfort among attractive and expensive surroundings. ...a life of luxury. ■ **Luxury** things are more expensive and comfortable than other things of the same kind. ...a luxury hotel. ■ **Luxuries** or **luxury goods** are fairly expensive things which bring pleasure but are not essential. ■ You can call a pleasure or advantage a **luxury** when it is not often available. Wilkinson had the luxury of 11 free days to work on the problem.

lychee – Lychees are Chinese fruit with soft white flesh.

Lycra is a man-made elasticated fibre, or the fabric made from this fibre, used in sportswear and underclothes. 'Lycra' is a trademark.

lymph is a colourless fluid which contains white blood cells.

lymphatic system The **lymphatic system** is the network of capillaries which transports lymph into the bloodstream.

lymph gland The **lymph glands** are small masses of tissue in various parts of the body, where white blood cells are formed.

lymph node is the medical term for a lymph gland.

lynch (lynches, lynching, lynched) If someone is **lynched,** a crowd drags them off and kills them by hanging because they are thought to have committed a crime. A killing like this is called a **lynching;** the people who carry it out are called a **lynch mob.**

lynchpin (or **lynch-pin**) See **linchpin.**

lynx (lynxes) The **lynx** is a large wild member of the cat family, with a short tail.

lyric The **lyrics** of a song are its words. ■ **Lyric** poetry is written in a simple and direct style, usually expressing personal emotions such as love. A **lyric** is a poem written in this style.

lyrical (lyrically) Lyrical is used to talk about things being expressed in a poetic way. Each dish is lyrically described. ■ If you **wax lyrical** about something, you speak very enthusiastically about it.

lyricism is gentle and romantic emotion expressed in poetry, writing, or music.

lyricist A **lyricist** is someone who writes the words for songs or musicals.

M m

m See **metre, mile.**

M.A. An **M.A.** is a higher degree in an arts or social science subject. M.A. stands for 'Master of Arts'.

ma'am People sometimes say **ma'am** as a formal way of addressing a high-ranking woman.

mac A **mac** is a mackintosh.

macabre (*pron:* mak-**kahb**-ra) A **macabre** event or story is very strange and horrible.

macaroni is a kind of pasta made in the shape of short hollow tubes.

mace A **mace** is an ornamental stick carried by an official or placed somewhere as a symbol of authority.

Mach (*pron:* mak) is a unit of measurement for very high speeds. If an aircraft is travelling at **Mach 1**, it is travelling at the speed of sound.

machete (*pron:* mash-**ett**-ee) A **machete** is a large knife with a broad blade.

Machiavellian (*pron:* mak-ee-a-**vel**-yan) If you describe someone as **Machiavellian,** you mean they use cunning and deceitful methods to get what they want. *...Machiavellian schemes.*

machinations (*pron:* mak-in-**nay**-shunz) are secret and complicated plans to gain power, especially when they harm someone. *...innocent people caught up in their machinations.*

machine (**machining, machined**) A **machine** is a piece of equipment with moving parts, powered by electricity or an engine. ■ A well-controlled system or organization can be called a **machine.** ■ **Machine code** is a way of expressing instructions and information in a numerical form which can be understood by a computer or microchip.

machine gun A **machine gun** is a gun which fires a lot of bullets very quickly one after the other.

machinery is machines in general. The **machinery** in a place is all the machines there. ■ The **machinery** of a piece of equipment is the parts which move when it is working. ■ The **machinery** of a government or other organization is the system it uses to deal with things.

machine tool A **machine tool** is a power-driven machine which cuts, shapes, or finishes metal or other materials.

machinist A **machinist** is a person whose job is to operate a machine, especially in a factory.

machismo (*pron:* mak-**izz**-moh) is aggressively masculine behaviour or attitudes.

macho (*pron:* **match**-oh) You call a man **macho** if he behaves in an aggressively masculine way.

mackerel (*plural:* mackerel *or* mackerels) **Mackerel** are a kind of sea fish.

mackintosh (**mackintoshes**) A **mackintosh** is a raincoat.

macro is used to show something relates to a general area, rather than being detailed or specific. *...working for social change on the macro level.* ■ **Macro** lenses and other devices are used for photographing or filming things at close range.

■ A **macro** is a single computer command which makes the computer carry out a set of actions.

macro- Words beginning with **macro-** describe things which are much larger in scope than usual. *...macropolitical issues.* See also **micro-.**

macroeconomics (**macroeconomic**) **Macroeconomics** is the study of the economic systems of countries or groups of countries, rather than those of companies or industries. **Macroeconomic** means connected with the economy of a country or group of countries. See also **microeconomics.**

mad (**madder, maddest; madly, madness**) If someone is **mad,** they behave strangely or dangerously because they are mentally ill. ■ You say someone is **mad** when they do or say things you think are very silly. ■ **Mad** is used to describe wild uncontrolled behaviour. *He ran madly around.* ■ You say someone is **mad** when they are very angry. ■ If someone is **mad** about something, they like it very much and spend a lot of time on it. *...a horse-mad girl.* ■ If you are **madly** in love with someone, you are very much in love with them.

madam Some people call a woman **Madam** when they are being very polite. ■ **Madam** is used when addressing a woman in a position of authority. *...Madam Chairman.* ■ A **madam** is a woman in charge of a brothel.

madcap A **madcap** plan is silly and unlikely to succeed.

mad cow disease is a fatal brain disease which affects cattle. It is also known as 'bovine spongiform encephalopathy', or BSE.

madden (**maddening, maddened; maddeningly**) If something **maddens** you, it irritates or angers you.

made See **make.**

madhouse If you say a place or situation is a **madhouse,** you mean it is full of noise and confusion. ■ People used to call a mental hospital a **madhouse.**

madman (**madmen**) If you call a man a **madman,** you mean he is insane.

Madonna The **Madonna** is Mary, the mother of Jesus. ■ A **Madonna** is a painting or sculpture of Mary.

maelstrom (*pron:* male-strom) You can call a confused or violent situation a **maelstrom.**

maestro (*pron:* **my**-stroh) (**maestros**) People call a man a **maestro** when he is very skilful at something, especially conducting or playing music.

mafia (**mafioso, mafiosi**) The **Mafia** is a large criminal organization which operates in Sicily, Italy, and the US. A member of this organization is called a **mafioso** (*plural:* mafiosi). ■ When a group of people seem to dominate an organization or activity, people sometimes call them a **mafia.**

mag A **mag** is a magazine.

magazine A **magazine** is a regular publication, usually weekly or monthly, which carries articles, stories, photographs, and advertisements. ■ On radio or television, a **magazine** is a regular programme consisting of several items about different topics or people. ■ The **magazine** in a gun is a metal case which holds several cartridges.

magenta (*pron:* maj-**jen**-ta) is a dark reddish-purple colour.

maggot – Maggots are tiny creatures which look like very small worms and turn into flies.

magic (**magical, magically**) Magic is the power to use supernatural forces to make apparently impossible things happen. **Magic** and **magical** mean connected with magic. ...*a woman with magical powers.* ■ **Magic** is the art of performing tricks to entertain people, for example making things seem to appear and disappear. ■ The **magic** of something is a special quality which makes it seem wonderful and exciting. You call things which have this quality **magical.** ...*magical countryside.*

magic carpet In stories, a **magic carpet** is a carpet which can carry people through the air.

magician A **magician** is a person who performs tricks as a form of entertainment. ■ In stories, a **magician** is a man with magic powers.

magic lantern A **magic lantern** was an old-fashioned type of projector which used large pieces of glass as slides to project a picture onto a screen.

magisterial (*pron:* maj-is-**teer**-rial) If you describe someone as **magisterial,** you mean they are impressive and in complete control.

magistrate A **magistrate** is an official, usually a selected member of the public who has volunteered and had special training, who acts as a judge in a law court dealing with minor crimes or disputes.

magma is molten rock below the earth's surface.

magnanimous (**magnanimously, magnanimity**) If you are **magnanimous** or show **magnanimity,** you are generous or forgiving to someone, especially after you have beaten them in a contest.

magnate A **magnate** is a person with a lot of power, especially in business.

magnesium is a light silvery-white metallic element which burns with an intense white flame.

magnet (**magnetic, magnetism**) A **magnet** is a piece of iron which attracts iron or steel towards itself. The surrounding area where it has this effect is called its **magnetic field.** Its power to attract things is called **magnetism;** a **magnetic** object is one which has this power. ■ If a person is **magnetic** or has **magnetism,** they have qualities which attract people to them.

magnetic north is the direction in which a compass needle points.

magnetic tape is narrow plastic tape covered in a magnetic substance. It is used to record sound or video signals, or to store information in computers.

magnetise See **magnetize.**

magnetism See **magnet.**

magnetize (*or* **magnetise**) (**magnetizing, magnetized**) If a substance or object is **magnetized,** it is made magnetic.

magnificent (**magnificently, magnificence**) If you say something is **magnificent,** you mean it is beautiful and impressive.

magnify (**magnifies, magnifying, magnified; magnification**) If an object is **magnified,** it is made to appear bigger than it really is, for example because you are looking at it through a microscope. *This tiny creature is visible only under magnification.* ■ The **magnification** of a microscope, telescope, or pair of binoculars is the degree to which it magnifies things. ■ If a feeling or problem is **magnified,** it is increased.

magnifying glass A **magnifying glass** is a hand-held object with a lens which makes things appear bigger when you look through it.

magnitude The **magnitude** of something is how big it is. *I was underestimating the magnitude of the task.*

magnolia The **magnolia** is a type of oriental tree with large white or pink flowers. ■ **Magnolia** is a very pale pink colour.

magnum A **magnum** is a wine bottle which holds the equivalent of two normal bottles (about 1.5 litres).

magnum opus The **magnum opus** of a writer, painter, or composer is their greatest single work.

magpie The **magpie** is a black and white bird from the crow family.

maharaja (*or* **maharajah**) A **maharaja** is the head of one of the royal families which used to rule parts of India.

mahogany is the dark reddish-brown wood of several kinds of tropical trees.

maid A **maid** is a female servant. ■ In the past, a young unmarried woman was sometimes called a **maid.**

maiden In the past, a **maiden** was a young unmarried woman. ■ A married woman's **maiden name** is her parent's surname. ■ Someone's **maiden aunt** is an aunt who has never married. ■ The **maiden** voyage or flight of a ship or plane is its first official journey. ■ In cricket, a **maiden over** is one in which no runs are scored.

mail (**mailing, mailed**) Mail is letters and parcels delivered to you. The system of collecting and delivering parcels and letters is called **the mail.** If you **mail** something, you send it by post.

mailbag A **mailbag** is a large bag used by the post office for carrying letters and parcels.

mailbox (**mailboxes**) In the US, a **mailbox** is (a) a box outside a house, where letters are delivered. (b) a post-box.

mailing list A **mailing list** is a list of names and addresses which is kept by an organization so it can send people information.

mail order is a system of buying goods by post.

mailshot When an organization sends out a **mailshot,** it sends information to a large number of selected people at the same time.

maim (**maiming, maimed**) If someone is **maimed,** they are permanently injured.

main (**mainly**) The **main** thing in any situation is the most important one. ■ **Mainly** is used to say a statement is true in most cases or to a large extent. *The disease is carried mainly by foxes and by dogs.*

■ If something is true **in the main,** it is generally true, although there may be exceptions. ■ The **mains** are the pipes or cables which carry gas, water, electricity, or sewage.

mainframe A **mainframe** is a large computer which can be used by many people at the same time.

mainland The **mainland** is the major part of a country or continent, in contrast to islands around its coast.

mainline A **mainline** station is one on an important railway line.

mainly See **main.**

mainstay The **mainstay** of something like an organization is the part which gives it most of its strength or effectiveness. *Orange trees, the mainstay of local agriculture, are withering away for lack of irrigation.*

mainstream is used to describe people or ideas which are typical or conventional. *...mainstream theatre. ...the mainstream of the Labour Party.*

maintain (**maintaining, maintained; maintenance**) If you **maintain** something, you keep it up or keep it at a particular rate or level. *A resolution calling for the maintenance of sanctions was adopted... The government was right to maintain interest rates at a high level.* ■ If you **maintain** someone, you provide them with money for the things they need. Money paid like this is called **maintenance.** ■ When people **maintain** a building, road, or machine, they keep it in good condition. ■ If you **maintain** something is true, you state firmly that it is so. *Police sources maintain that the situation is now under control.*

maisonette A **maisonette** is a flat on two floors of a larger building.

maître d'hôtel (*pron:* **met**-ra doh-**tell**) In some restaurants, the head waiter or restaurant manager is called the **maître d'hôtel.**

maize is a tall cereal plant which produces sweetcorn.

majestic (**majestically**) **Majestic** is used to describe things which are beautiful, dignified, and impressive.

majesty (**majesties**) When you begin talking to a king or queen, you are supposed to say **Your Majesty.** If you are talking about a king or queen in a formal way, you say **His Majesty** or **Her Majesty.** ■ When you talk about the **majesty** of something, you mean it is impressive and dignified. *...the majesty of the mainland mountains.*

major (**majoring, majored**) You use **major** to talk about something which is more important, serious, or significant than other things of its kind. *...a major social problem.* ■ A **major** is a middle-ranking army officer. ■ In the US, if someone **majors** in a subject, they study it as their main subject at university.

majorette – **Majorettes** or **drum majorettes** are young women who march, often twirling batons, in front of a band.

major-general A **major-general** is a senior army officer.

majority (**majorities**) The **majority** of a group of people or things is more than half of it. *Women students are in a majority in universities and colleges in all parts of Britain except Scotland.* ■ In a vote, a **majority** is the difference between the number of votes gained by the winner and the number gained by the loser or losers. ■ When people talk about **majority rule,** they mean a system in which a government is seen as representing the majority of people, rather than a minority. ■ **overall majority:** see **overall. simple majority:** see **simple.** See also **absolute majority.**

make (**making, made**) **Make** is used to say someone does something. *She made me an offer... He made a brief visit to Kenya.* ■ If you **make for** a place or **make** your way there, you go to it, or towards it. ■ If you **make off** with something, you steal it and run away. ■ **Make** is used to say someone or something is caused to be in a particular state, or to become a particular thing. *He says the charges have made him ill... He was made editor.* ■ If someone or something **makes** you do something, they force you to do it. ■ If you **make** something, you create it or produce it. ■ If you can **make** something **out,** you can see it, hear it, or understand it. *I don't think there were any injuries, as far as I can make out.* ■ If you **make out** that something is true, you try to persuade people to believe it. ■ You use **make** to say someone or something is suitable for a particular task or role. *She'll make a good actress.* ■ If you say something has the **makings** of a particular thing, you mean it is likely to become it. *This dispute is not yet a war but has the makings of one.* ■ You use **make** when you are talking about the result of a calculation. *Two and two makes four.* ■ The **make** of something like a car is the name of the company that manufactured it. ■ If you have to **make do with** something, you have to manage with it because you cannot have what you really want. ■ If you **make up** a story, you invent it. ■ If two people **make up,** they become friends again after a disagreement. ■ **make up your mind:** see **mind. make good:** see **good.** See also **make-up.**

make-believe is pretending things are better or more exciting than they really are.

maker The **maker** of something is the person or company that makes it.

makeshift things are temporary and usually of poor quality.

make-up is things like lipstick which people use on their face, to make themselves more attractive. ■ A person's **make-up** is the combination of qualities in their character. *There was a lot of the hippy in her make-up.* ■ The **make-up** of something consists of its various parts and the way they are arranged.

maladjusted You say people are **maladjusted** when they have psychological problems and behave in socially unacceptable ways.

maladministration is inefficient or dishonest administration.

maladroit (*pron:* mal-a-**droyt**) is used to say something is done clumsily or tactlessly. *...the government's maladroit handling of the issue.*

malady (*pron:* **mal**-a-dee) (**maladies**) A **malady** is an illness.

malaise (*pron:* mal-**laze**) is a vague feeling of ill-health, often indicating the beginning of a more serious illness. ■ **Malaise** is a state in which people feel dissatisfied or unhappy but do not know exactly what is wrong.

malapropism If someone says a word which is similar to the one they mean to say but has completely the wrong meaning, you call this a **malapropism.** For example, an old lady once went into an optician's and asked for 'a pair of bisexual glasses'.

malaria (**malarial**) Malaria is a serious disease carried by mosquitoes. It causes periods of fever and intense shivering. **Malarial** means to do with malaria. ...*anti-malarial drugs.*

malcontent People who criticize the way society is run are sometimes called **malcontents** by people who think everything is all right.

male (**maleness**) A **male** is a person or animal belonging to the sex which cannot have babies or lay eggs. ...*male attitudes.* ...*male athletes.*

malevolent (*pron:* mal-**lev**-o-lent) (**malevolently, malevolence**) A **malevolent** person deliberately tries to cause harm or evil.

malformed (**malformation**) If a part of someone's body is **malformed,** it does not have a normal shape, and usually has been that way from birth.

malfunction (**malfunctioning, malfunctioned**) If something **malfunctions,** it fails to work properly. When this happens, you say there is a **malfunction.**

malice (*pron:* mal-**liss**) (**malicious, maliciously**) **Malice** is a desire to harm people. If an action is **malicious,** it is meant to cause harm.

malign (*pron:* mal-**line**) If someone **maligns** you, they say unpleasant and untrue things about you. ■ If something has **malign** effects, it is harmful.

malignant (*pron:* mal-**lig**-nant) (**malignancy**) A **malignant** disease spreads rapidly, causing death unless quickly treated. ■ **Malignant** behaviour is cruel and intended to cause harm.

mall (*pron:* **mawl** *or* **mal**) A **mall** is a large indoor shopping area.

mallard The **mallard** is a very common kind of wild duck.

malleable (*pron:* mal-**lee**-a-bl) (**malleability**) **Malleable** people are easily influenced and controlled by other people. ■ If a substance is **malleable,** it can be beaten or pressed into different shapes easily.

mallet A **mallet** is a hammer with a head made of wood, rubber, or plastic.

malnourished (**malnutrition**) If someone is **malnourished** or suffering from **malnutrition,** they are weak because they have not been eating enough food or have not had a balanced diet.

malodorous (*pron:* mal-**lode**-or-uss) If something is **malodorous,** it smells nasty.

malpractice Someone like a doctor or lawyer is guilty of **malpractice** when they break the law or the rules of their profession for personal advantage.

malt is a substance made from grain and used in making beer and whisky. ■ A **malt** is a malt whisky.

malted milk is a drink made from milk and a powder containing malt.

maltreat (**maltreating, maltreated; maltreatment**) If people or animals are **maltreated,** they are treated badly, especially physically.

mammal (**mammalian**) Mammals are animals whose females generally give birth to live young rather than eggs, and feed their young with milk. Humans, lions, mice, and whales are all mammals. **Mammalian** means to do with mammals. ...*papers on mammalian reproduction.*

mammary means to do with the breasts. ...*mammary cancers.*

Mammon is used to talk about wealth and the pursuit of it. ...*socialists sacrificing their convictions to Mammon.*

mammoth is used to describe things which are extremely large. ...*a mammoth task.* ■ **Mammoths** were very large elephant-like animals which became extinct a long time ago.

man (*plural:* **men**) (**manning, manned**) A **man** is an adult male human being. ■ A **man-to-man** conversation involves two men talking openly and treating each other as equals. ■ **Man** is used to talk about human beings in general. ...*man's inhumanity to man.* ■ When people **man** a position or machine, they supervise it or operate it. ...*an information centre manned by knowledgable advisors.* ■ If you say something is, for example, a **two-man** operation, you mean it involves that number of people.

manacle (*pron:* man-a-kl) (**manacling, manacled**) **Manacles** are metal devices fastened round prisoners' wrists or ankles to stop them moving easily or escaping. **Manacled** prisoners are immobilized in this way.

manage (**managing, managed**) If you **manage** a business, you run it. ■ If you **manage** to do something, you succeed in doing it. *He managed to free one hand.* ■ If someone **manages,** they succeed in living or doing something on limited resources. *His poor wife just can't manage on her pitiful pension.*

manageable If something is **manageable,** it can be dealt with, because it is not too big or complicated.

management The running of an organization is called **management.** ...*the management of schools... These losses have arisen partly out of bad management.* ■ The people who run an organization are called the **management.**

manager A **manager** is a man or woman responsible for running a business or part of an organization. ■ The **manager** of an entertainer is the person who looks after their business interests. ■ The **manager** of a sports team is the person responsible for organizing and training it.

manageress (**manageresses**) A **manageress** is a woman who runs a business such as a shop or restaurant.

managerial means to do with the work of a manager. ...*managerial incompetence.*

managing director The **managing director** of a company is the director in charge of it.

mandarin A **mandarin** is a small orange. ■ Important civil servants are sometimes called

mandarins. ■ Originally, a **mandarin** was an important government official in China.

Mandarin Chinese is the official language of China.

mandate (**mandating, mandated; mandatory**) A government's **mandate** is the authority it has to carry out policies as a result of winning an election. ■ When someone is **mandated** to do something or given a **mandate** to do it, they are authorized or instructed to do it. ■ If something is **mandated** or **mandatory,** the law states that it must be done. *Extended re-tests will be mandatory for drivers convicted of serious offences.*

mandolin A **mandolin** is a musical instrument like a small guitar with four pairs of strings.

mane The **mane** of an animal like a horse or lion is the long thick hair growing from its neck.

maneuver (**maneuvring, maneuvred; maneuvrable**) See **manoeuvre.**

manfully If you do something **manfully,** you do it in a very determined way.

manganese is a greyish-white metal used in making steel.

manger (*pron:* **mane**-jer) A **manger** is a feeding box for horses or cattle in a stable or barn.

mangetout (*pron:* **mawnzh**-too; *the 'zh' sounds like 's' in 'pleasure'*) are a variety of pea with an edible pod.

mangle (**mangling, mangled**) If something is **mangled,** it is crushed and twisted. ■ A **mangle** is a device for wringing water out of laundry. You pass the clothes between two heavy rollers in a metal frame.

mango (**mangoes** *or* **mangos**) **Mangoes** are large sweet yellowish tropical fruit.

mangrove The **mangrove** is a tree which grows along coasts and riverbanks in tropical countries. Its roots grow above the water.

mangy (*pron:* **main**-ji) animals have lost a lot of their hair through disease.

manhandle (**manhandling, manhandled**) If someone **manhandles** you, they physically push you around.

manhole A **manhole** is a covered hole in the ground leading to a drain or sewer.

manhood is (a) the state of being a man. *...the training boys receive for manhood.* (b) the period of a man's adult life. *...his early manhood.*

man-hour A **man-hour** is the amount of work one person can do in an hour.

manhunt A **manhunt** is a search for someone who has escaped or disappeared.

mania A **mania** is a very strong interest in something, especially one shared by a lot of people. *...the mania for DIY.* ■ Some kinds of mental illness are called **manias.**

maniac (**maniacal**) A **maniac** is a psychologically disturbed person who is violent and dangerous. **Maniacal** behaviour (*pron:* man-**eye**-ak-l) is violent, uncontrolled, and dangerous.

manic (*pron:* **man**-ik) behaviour is very energetic because the person concerned is highly excited or anxious. *...manic laughter.*

manic depression (**manic depressive**) **Manic depression** is a mental illness in which sufferers are over-excited and confident some of the time and very depressed at other times. A person who has this illness is called a **manic depressive.**

manicure (**manicuring, manicured; manicurist**) If you have a **manicure** or your nails are **manicured,** the skin on your hands is moisturized and your nails are cut and varnished. A person who does this for a living is called a **manicurist.** ■ If a lawn is **manicured,** it has been neatly trimmed in a rather fussy way.

manifest (**manifesting, manifested; manifestly**) If something is **manifest,** it is obvious to everyone. *The decision was manifestly unfair.* ■ If you **manifest** something, you make people aware of it. If something **manifests** itself, it becomes apparent.

manifestation A **manifestation** of something is a sign that it exists.

manifesto (**manifestos** *or* **manifestoes**) A **manifesto** is a written statement in which a political party sets out its aims and policies.

manifold things are of many different kinds. *...the manifold benefits of a healthy diet.*

manipulate (**manipulating, manipulated; manipulation, manipulative, manipulator**) If someone **manipulates** people, they control them to their own advantage. You can also talk about someone **manipulating** a situation or system. ■ If you say someone is **manipulative** or a **manipulator,** you mean they try to control people or situations to their own advantage. ■ If you **manipulate** a piece of equipment, you control it skilfully.

mankind is the whole human race.

manly (**manliness**) **Manly** is used to describe behaviour which is thought to be typical of a man.

man-made things are constructed by people rather than formed naturally.

manna If something appears like **manna** or **manna from heaven,** it appears suddenly as if by a miracle.

mannequin A **mannequin** is (a) a life-sized model of a person, used to display clothes, especially in a shop window. (b) a woman who models clothes.

manner The **manner** in which you do something is the way you do it. ■ If you say a piece of art or writing is **in the manner of** someone, you mean it is done in a style typical of them. ■ A person's **manner** is the way they behave and talk. *...his aggressive manner.* ■ If someone has good **manners** or is **well-mannered,** they behave and speak politely. You can also say someone has bad **manners** or is **bad-mannered** or **ill-mannered.**

mannered If someone's speech or writing is **mannered,** it seems artificial, as though they are trying to impress someone.

mannerism A **mannerism** is a gesture or way of speaking which is characteristic of a person.

manning The level of **manning** in a company or operation is the number of employees.

manoeuvre (*Am:* **maneuver**) (**manoeuvring, manoeuvred; manoeuvrable**) If you **manoeuvre** an object into or out of an awkward position, you move it skilfully. If something is **manoeuvrable,** it is easy to move about. ■ A **manoeuvre** is something clever you do to turn a situation to your own advantage.

His offer is being seen as a political manoeuvre to weaken his opponents. ■ If you have **room for manoeuvre,** you have the opportunity to change your plans if it becomes necessary. ■ Military **manoeuvres** are training exercises over large areas of countryside.

manor (**manorial**) A **manor** is a large country house and the land belonging to it. The house is called the **manor house. Manorial** means connected with a manor. *...manorial estates.*

manpower People sometimes call workers **manpower.**

manqué (*pron:* **man**-kay) is used to talk about someone's failure to become something. For example, an actor **manqué** is a person who wanted to be an actor, but who never succeeded. *...a playwright manqué.*

manse A **manse** is a house provided for the minister in certain Christian churches.

mansion A **mansion** is a very large house.

manslaughter is the crime of killing someone when this is not legally considered to be murder, for example because the killing was unintentional.

mantelpiece (*or* **mantlepiece**) A **mantelpiece** is a shelf over a fireplace.

mantle A **mantle** is a sleeveless cloak. ■ If you take on the **mantle** of something, you take on its responsibilities. *She has the intellectual form to take up the mantle of leadership.* ■ A **mantle** is a layer of something covering a surface. *...the atmosphere's protective ozone mantle.* ■ The Earth's **mantle** is the part between the crust and the core.

mantlepiece See **mantelpiece.**

mantra In Hinduism or Buddhism, a **mantra** is a sacred word or sound which is repeated continually to aid religious contemplation.

manual (**manually**) **Manual** work involves using physical strength rather than mental skills. ■ **Manual** is used to describe things which are operated by hand. *...a six-speed manual gearbox... Everything had to be done manually.* ■ A **manual** is a book which tells you how to do something.

manufacture (**manufacturing, manufactured; manufacturer**) **Manufactured** things are made in a factory. You can talk about the **manufacture** of things in a factory. A **manufacturer** is a person or business that manufactures things. ■ If someone **manufactures** information, they invent it.

manure is animal dung used as fertilizer.

manuscript A **manuscript** is (a) the author's typed or handwritten version of a book before it is printed. (b) a document which was written by hand before the printing press was invented.

Manx means in or from the Isle of Man. *...the Manx Parliament.* ■ The **Manx** are the Manx people. ■ **Manx** is the language formerly spoken in the Isle of Man.

many is used to talk about a lot of people or things. *There were many casualties on both sides... Many feel trapped.* ■ **How many** is used (a) to ask about a number of people or things. *How many of these can you turn out in an hour?* (b) to talk about an unknown number of people or things. *Nobody knows how many spiders there are in Britain.*

map (**mapping, mapped**) A **map** is a detailed representation of an area as it appears from above. When an area is **mapped,** a map is made of it. ■ If you **map out** a route, you plan how to get somewhere, using a map. ■ If you **map out** a strategy, you plan it.

maple The **maple** is a tree with large five-pointed leaves. Its wood is used to make furniture and flooring.

maple syrup is a very sweet syrup made from the sap of a type of maple tree.

mar (**marring, marred**) If you **mar** something, you spoil it.

maraca (*pron:* mar-**rak**-a) **Maracas** are percussion instruments traditionally made from hollow gourds filled with pebbles or beans.

marathon A **marathon** is a road race of about 26.2 miles (42.2 km). ■ A **marathon** task takes a long time to complete. *...marathon negotiations.*

marauding (**marauder**) **Marauding** people are looking for something to steal or kill. You can also talk about **marauding** animals. People and animals like these can be called **marauders.**

marble (**marbled**) **Marble** is a very hard rock used to make statues, fireplaces, and floors. It often has a pattern of irregular lines and patches of colour. **Marbled** is used to describe rooms and buildings where many of the surfaces are marble. *...marbled halls.* ■ **Marbles** is a children's game played with small glass balls called **marbles.** ■ If you say someone has **lost their marbles,** you mean they have gone mad.

march (**marches, marching, marched; marcher**) When soldiers **march,** they walk with quick regular steps in time with each other. This way of walking is called a **march.** ■ A **march** is a piece of music written with a regular rhythm which you can march to. ■ When a large group of people **march** or go on a **march,** they walk together somewhere, usually to protest about something. ■ If you **march** somewhere, you walk there quickly and purposefully. ■ The **march** of something is its steady progress. *...the march of science.* ■ If you **steal a march** on someone, you start doing something before they do, to get an advantage over them.

marchioness (*pron:* marsh-on-**ness**) (**marchionesses**) A **marchioness** is the wife of a marquess, or a woman who holds the rank of a marquess.

mare A **mare** is an adult female horse.

margarine is a butter-like substance made from vegetable oil or animal fat.

margin A **margin** is the difference between two amounts, especially the difference in the number of votes or points between the winner and the loser in a contest. *They rejected the treaty by a narrow margin.* ■ If there is a **margin** for something in a situation, there is some freedom to choose what to do. *There was no margin for error.* ■ On a written or printed page, the **margins** are the blank spaces down each side. ■ The **margins** of a place are its edges. *...the margins of the lake.* ■ If you are **on the margin** of a group or situation, you are only just included in it. *...on the margins of political life.*

marginal is used to describe people or things that are unimportant or insignificant. ...*a marginal improvement.* ■ In politics, a **marginal** seat is won by a small margin. ■ **Marginal** land is on the edge of a fertile area and is less suitable for growing food.

marginalize (*or* **marginalise**) (**marginalizing, marginalized; marginalization**) If people or things are **marginalized,** they are made to seem isolated and unimportant.

marginally means to only a small extent.

marigold The **marigold** is a yellow or orange garden flower.

marijuana (*pron:* mar-ri-**wah**-na) is an illegal drug made from the dried flowers and leaves of the hemp plant. It is usually smoked.

marimba The **marimba** is a percussion instrument which looks like a large xylophone.

marina A **marina** is a small harbour for pleasure boats.

marinade A **marinade** is a mixture of oil, wine, vinegar, herbs, and spices. You soak meat or fish in a marinade before cooking it, to add flavour or to make it more tender. ■ If you **marinade** something, you soak it in a marinade before cooking it.

marinate (**marinating, marinated**) If you **marinate** meat or fish, you soak it in a marinade before cooking it.

marine A **marine** is a soldier in the Royal Navy or the Marine Corps. ■ **Marine** means to do with the sea. ...*marine life.*

Marine Corps The **Marine Corps** is a corps of soldiers which is part of the US Navy.

mariner A **mariner** is a sailor.

marionette A **marionette** is a puppet controlled by strings or wires.

marital is used to talk about things to do with a marriage. ...*marital difficulties.* Your **marital status** is whether you are single, married, widowed, or divorced.

maritime means to do with the sea and ships.

marjoram is a herb used in cooking as a flavouring.

mark A **mark** is a small stain or damaged area on a surface. If something **marks** a surface, it damages it in some way. ■ A **mark** is a number or letter indicating someone's score in a test or examination. When a teacher **marks** a student's work, he or she decides its grade. ■ A **mark** is a written or printed symbol. If you **mark** something, you write a particular symbol on it. *My letter was returned, marked 'gone away'.* ■ If something reaches a particular **mark,** it reaches a particular level. *Sales edged past the million mark.* ■ If something **marks** a position, it shows where something is or was. ...*a monument marking the spot where they died.* ■ If something **marks** an important occasion or change, it shows it is taking place. *Sunday's elections are meant to mark a return to the old traditions.* ■ A **mark** of something is a sign or typical feature of it. *As mark of respect, riders wore black armbands.* ■ If something **marks** you as a certain type of person, it shows you are that type of person. *She would now be marked as a troublemaker.* ■ If you are **marking time,** you are waiting for something to happen. ■ When prices are **marked up,** they are increased. When they are

marked down, they are reduced. ■ In sports such as football, when a player **marks** their opposing player, he or she stays close to them, to prevent them having a lot of space to play in. ■ The **mark** is the unit of currency in some European countries, for example Finland. People often refer to Deutschmarks as **marks.** ■ See also **marked, marking.**

marked (**markedly**) (*pron:* markt, mark-id-ly) A **marked** quality or change is obvious.

marker A **marker** is an object showing the position of something. ■ If a person or organization **puts down a marker,** they do something to signal what they want to happen or intend to do. ■ A **marker** or **marker pen** is a pen with a thick felt tip.

market (**marketing, marketed**) A **market** is an event at which people buy and sell goods, usually in the open air. The place where a market is held is also called a **market.** ■ A **market** for a product is the number of people who want to buy it, or a part of the world where it can be sold. *The British market is still the company's biggest source of profits.* ■ When a company **markets** a product, they organize its sale by deciding on its price, where it should be sold, and how it should be advertised. This process is called **marketing.** ■ When people talk about **the market** or a **market economy,** they mean a situation where the price of things is decided by availability and demand. ■ See also **black market.**

marketable If something is **marketable,** it can be sold, because people want to buy it.

market forces are the economic factors which affect the availability of goods and the demand for them.

market garden A **market garden** is a small farm where fruit, vegetables, and sometimes flowers are grown for sale.

market place In business, **the market place** is the activity of buying and selling products. *Many small businesses have entered the market place.* ■ A **market place** is an area in a town where a market is held.

market research (**market researcher**) Market research is research into what people want, need, and buy.

marking – **Markings** are shapes on the surface of something.

marksman (**marksmen; marksmanship**) A **marksman** is a person who can shoot very accurately. **Marksmanship** is the ability to shoot accurately.

marmalade is a jam-like food made from citrus fruits such as oranges.

marmoset – **Marmosets** are very small South American monkeys with claws on their fingers and toes.

maroon (**marooning, marooned**) If you are **marooned** somewhere, you cannot get away. ■ **Maroon** is a dark reddish-purple colour.

marque (*pron:* mark) A **marque** is a particular make of a product. *Grande Marque champagnes.*

marquee (*pron:* mar-**kee**) A **marquee** is a large tent.

marquess (*pron:* mark-wiss) (**marquesses**) A **marquess** is a British nobleman ranking below a duke and above an earl.

marquetry (*pron:* mark-it-ry) is the technique of decorating furniture with a pattern of inlaid pieces of wood, ivory, or other substances.

marquis (**marquises**) A **marquis** (*pron:* **mark**-wiss) is the same as a marquess.

marriage A **marriage** is the act of getting married or the state of being married. A **marriage** is also the relationship between a husband and wife. ■ When two skills or methods are combined, you can call this a **marriage** of skills or methods.

marriageable You can describe someone as **marriageable** when they are old enough to marry or if you think they would be a good prospect as a husband or wife.

marriage of convenience (**marriages of convenience**) If someone marries another person for social, financial, or political reasons rather than for love, you call this a **marriage of convenience.**

married If you are **married,** you have a husband or wife. ■ **Married** means to do with marriage. *...all his married life.*

marrow or **bone marrow** is the fatty substance at the centre of bones. ■ **Marrows** are long thick green vegetables.

marry (**marries, marrying, married**) When a man and a woman **marry,** they become husband and wife during a special ceremony. You also say the person who conducts the ceremony **marries** the couple.

marsh (**marshes**) A **marsh** is a wet muddy area of land.

marshal (**marshalling, marshalled**) (*Am:* **marshaling, marshaled**) If you **marshal** things or people, you gather them together and organize them. A **marshal** is a person who helps organize a public event. ■ A **marshal of the RAF** is an officer of the highest rank in the RAF. ■ In the US, a **marshal** is (a) a police officer in a small town with the same powers and duties as a sheriff. (b) a federal officer appointed to carry out court orders.

marshland is land consisting mainly of marshes.

marshmallow — **Marshmallows** are soft spongy sweets.

marshy land is wet and muddy.

marsupial (*pron:* mar-**soop**-ee-al) **Marsupials** are animals such as kangaroos and koalas which carry their young in a pouch on their bodies.

martial means to do with war or soldiers. *...martial music.* See also **court martial.**

martial arts are the techniques of self-defence from the Far East, such as judo and karate.

martial law If a place is under **martial law,** it is controlled by the armed forces, rather than civilians.

Martian means to do with the planet Mars. *...Martian weather.* ■ A **Martian** is an imaginary creature from the planet Mars.

martin See **house martin.**

martinet (*pron:* mar-tin-**net**) You call someone a **martinet** when they believe in strict discipline and expect all their orders to be obeyed.

martini A **martini** is a cocktail made from gin and vermouth. 'Martini' is a trademark for a brand of vermouth.

martyr (**martyred; martyrdom**) When someone is killed or made to suffer for their religious or political beliefs, people call them a **martyr** or say they

are **martyred;** they also talk about their **martyrdom.** ■ If someone plays the **martyr,** they exaggerate their sufferings to get sympathy, praise, or support.

marvel (**marvelling, marvelled**) (*Am:* **marveling, marveled**) If you **marvel** at something, it fills you with amazement or admiration. Something which has this effect on people can be called a **marvel.**

marvellous (*Am:* **marvelous**) (**marvellously**) You use **marvellous** to describe things you think are very impressive or enjoyable.

Marxism (**Marxist**) **Marxism** is a political philosophy based on the writings of Karl Marx. Marx's view was that society would develop towards communism through the struggle between different social classes. *...Marxist ideas.* A **Marxist** is a person who believes in Marxism.

marzipan is a paste made of almonds, sugar, and egg.

mascara is a substance used to colour and thicken eyelashes.

mascot A **mascot** is a person, animal, or toy thought to bring good luck.

masculine (**masculinity**) **Masculine** characteristics or qualities are thought to be typical of men. *The old ideas of masculinity do not work for most men.*

mash (**mashes, mashing, mashed**) If you **mash** vegetables, you crush them after cooking them.

mask A **mask** is something you wear over your face as a protection or disguise. A **masked** person is wearing a mask. ■ If one thing **masks** the true nature of another, it hides it. *There is little of substance behind their mask of authority.*

masking tape is paper sticky-tape which can be peeled off easily after use.

masochism (*pron:* **mass**-oh-kiz-m) (**masochist, masochistic**) **Masochism** is getting pleasure from your own mental or physical suffering. A **masochist** is someone who gets pleasure this way. If someone's behaviour is **masochistic,** they suffer pain deliberately to get pleasure from it.

mason A **mason** is a person who is skilled at building things out of stone. ■ A **Mason** is a Freemason.

masonic means to do with Freemasons. *...masonic symbols.* A **masonic lodge** is a local branch of the Freemasons.

masonry is the bricks or stones in a wall or building.

masquerade (*pron:* mask-er-**aid**) (**masquerading, masqueraded**) In the past, a **masquerade** was a costume ball where masks were worn. ■ If you say something is a **masquerade,** you mean it is a show got up to deceive people. *He told a news conference that the elections would be a masquerade.* ■ If you **masquerade** as something, you pretend to be that thing.

mass (**masses, massing, massed**) A **mass** of things is a very large amount of them. *It has masses of flowers each year.* ■ **Mass** is used to talk about something involving a very large number of people. *...a mass airlift.* ■ If people or animals **mass,** they gather to form a large crowd. ■ The **masses** are ordinary people. *His music is aimed at the masses.* ■ In science, the **mass** of an object is how much physical matter there is in it. ■ In some Christian churches, **Mass** is a ceremony in which bread and wine are shared by the congregation in remembrance of Christ's death and resurrection. The special words used in this ceremony are called the **Mass**. A **Mass** is a piece of music written to these words.

massacre (**massacring, massacred**) If there is a **massacre** or if people are **massacred,** large numbers are deliberately killed.

massage (**massaging, massaged**) If you **massage** someone or give them a **massage,** you rub their body to help them relax or to stop their muscles hurting. ■ If someone **massages** statistics or evidence, they alter them to deceive people.

masse See **en masse.**

masseur (*pron:* mass-**sur**) A **masseur** is a person whose job is to give people massages.

masseuse A **masseuse** is a female masseur.

massif (*pron:* mass-eef) A **massif** is a group of mountains or a high plateau.

massive (**massively**) If something is **massive,** it is extremely large.

mass-market products are designed to appeal to large numbers of people.

mass media The **mass media** are TV, radio, and popular newspapers.

mass produce (**mass production**) If a product is **mass produced,** it is manufactured in large quantities by machine.

mast The **masts** of a boat are the tall upright poles which support its sails. ■ A radio or TV **mast** is a tall pole used as an aerial to transmit sound or TV pictures.

mastectomy A **mastectomy** is a surgical operation to remove a woman's breast.

master (**mastering, mastered**) If you **master** a situation, you succeed in taking control of it. ■ If you **master** something like a skill, you learn it. ■ If you say someone is the **master** of something, you mean they are very good at it, or the best in their field. *Evans had become the master of the single telling phrase... The Georgian leader is a master tactician.* ■ A **master plan** is a clever plan intended to help someone succeed in a very difficult or important task. ■ In the past, the man a servant or slave worked for was called his or her **master.** ■ A **master** is a male teacher. ■ The captain of a merchant ship is called the **master.**

master bedroom The **master bedroom** is the largest bedroom in a house.

masterclass (**masterclasses**) A **masterclass** is a class for trained musicians given by a famous musician.

masterful (**masterfully**) A **masterful** person behaves in a powerful and dominating way. ■ If something is done in a **masterful** way, it is done with great skill.

master key A **master key** is a key that will open any of a particular set of locks.

masterly is used to describe things done in a very skilful way.

mastermind (**masterminding, masterminded**) If someone **masterminds** a complicated activity or is the **mastermind** behind it, they plan it and make sure it is carried out successfully.

Master of Arts See **M.A.**

master of ceremonies At events such as formal dinners and variety shows, the **master of ceremonies** is the person who introduces the speakers or performers. 'Master of Ceremonies' is often shortened to 'MC'.

Master of Sciences See **M.Sc.**

Master of the Rolls The **Master of the Rolls** is the President of the Court of Appeal, the senior civil judge in the country, and the Keeper of the Records at the Public Records Office.

masterpiece If you call a work of art a **masterpiece,** you mean it is one of the greatest of its kind. ■ An artist's **masterpiece** is his or her greatest work.

master's degree A **master's degree** is a higher degree, such as an M.A. or M.Sc.

masterstroke A **masterstroke** is a very clever move which helps you to achieve what you want.

mastery If you achieve **mastery** of something, you become an expert at it. *...mastery of a foreign language.* ■ **Mastery** is complete power or control over something. *...the mastery of space.*

masthead The **masthead** of a ship is the highest part of its mast. ■ The **masthead** of a newspaper is its name as it appears at the top of the front page.

masticate (**masticating, masticated; mastication**) When you **masticate** food, you chew it.

mastitis is an infection which causes inflammation of a woman's breast or an animal's udder.

mastodon – **Mastodons** were large elephant-like animals which became extinct during the Stone Age.

masturbate (**masturbating, masturbated; masturbation**) If someone **masturbates,** they rub or stroke their genitals for sexual pleasure. This is called **masturbation.**

mat A **mat** is a piece of fabric or other material used as a floor covering or to protect a surface.

matador In a bullfight, the **matador** is the person who tries to kill the bull.

match (**matches, matching, matched**) A **match** is an organized game of football, tennis, or other sport. ■ A **match** is a little wooden stick which produces a flame when you strike it on a rough surface. ■ If one thing **matches** another, it is the same or very similar. *Overseas sales matched last year's record levels.* You also say one thing **matches** another when they go well together. *...a matching blouse and skirt.* You can say things like these are a good **match.** ■ If you **match** things or **match** them **up,** you choose ones which correspond to each other. ■ If two people are well **matched** or a good **match,** they are suited to each other. ■ If two people or teams are **matched** against each other, they have to play each other in a contest. ■ If you **meet your match,** you find you are competing against someone you cannot beat. ■ If you **match** something which someone else has done, you do the same thing, or something else as good. ■ If one thing **matches up** to another, it reaches the same standard.

matchbox (**matchboxes**) A **matchbox** is a small box sold with matches in it.

matchless If you say something is **matchless**, you mean nothing else is as good.

matchmaking (**matchmaker**) **Matchmaking** is encouraging people you know to form a relationship or get married. Someone who does this is called a **matchmaker.**

match point is a situation in a game like tennis in which the player in the lead will win the match if he or she wins the next point.

matchstick A **matchstick** is the wooden part of a match.

mate (**mating, mated, -mate**) Some people call their friends their **mates.** ■ **-mate** is added to a word to talk about someone who has something in common with you. For example, your 'team-mate' belongs to the same team as you. See also **running mate, soulmate.** ■ The **mate** or **first mate** of a merchant ship is the officer next-in-command to the captain. ■ An animal's **mate** is its sexual partner. ■ When animals **mate,** they have sex. If you **mate** captive or domestic animals, you bring them together so they will breed.

material (**materially**) A **material** is a solid substance. ...*explosive material.* ■ Cloth is often called **material.** ■ **Materials** are the things you make something out of. ■ If you say, for example, someone is officer **material,** you mean they have the potential to be a good officer. ■ If someone is collecting **material** for a book or film, they are gathering information they can use in it. ■ **Material** wealth and possessions are related to the physical world, rather than the spiritual. ■ You say something is **material** when it is relevant or significant.

materialise See **materialize.**

materialism (**materialist, materialistic**) **Materialism** is regarding money and possessions as more important than other things. People who have this view of life are called **materialists.**

materialize (*or* **materialise**) (**materializing, materialized**) If someone you are expecting to come does not **materialize,** they do not turn up. Similarly, if an expected event fails to **materialize,** it does not happen.

maternal is used to describe (a) feelings or actions which are typical of those of a mother towards her child. ...*maternal love.* (b) things relating to the mother of a baby. ...*maternal diet.* ■ Your **maternal** grandparents are your mother's parents.

maternity means to do with pregnancy and birth. ...*maternity units.* ■ **Maternity** is the state of being a mother. ...*her first months of maternity.*

matey If someone is being **matey,** they are behaving in a friendly way, sometimes insincerely.

mathematical (**mathematically**) **Mathematical** means involving numbers and calculations. ...*mathematical equations.*

mathematics (**mathematician**) **Mathematics** is the study of numbers and shapes. A **mathematician** is someone who has studied this subject to an advanced level.

maths is the same as mathematics.

matinee (*or* **matinée**) (*pron:* **mat**-in-nay) A **matinee** is an afternoon performance of a play, or a morning or afternoon showing of a film.

matins is an Anglican religious service held in the morning.

matriarch (*pron:* **mate**-ree-ark) (**matriarchal, matriarchy**) A **matriarch** is an old female member of a family who exerts power over all the other members. A woman like this can be described as **matriarchal.** ■ A **matriarchal** society or **matriarchy** is one where the women exert a lot of power in their families.

matriculate (**matriculating, matriculated; matriculation**) In some countries **matriculation** is the exams a student takes at the end of high school to enable him or her to study at university. If the student passes, he or she is said to **matriculate.**

matrimonial means to do with marriage. ...*matrimonial law.*

matrimony is the state of being married.

matrix (*pron:* **may**-triks) (*plural:* **matrices,** *pron:* **may**-triss-eez) A **matrix** is the environment or framework within which something develops. ■ In maths, a **matrix** is an arrangement of numbers, symbols, or letters in rows and columns, used in solving certain problems.

matron (**matronly**) The **matron** is the senior nurse in a hospital or nursing home. Hospital matrons are now usually called **chief nursing officers.** ■ At a boarding school, the **matron** is a woman who looks after pupils' welfare. ■ A **matron** is a dignified middle-aged married woman, especially one with children. You describe a woman like this as **matronly.**

matt (*or* **matte**) surfaces are dull rather than shiny.

matted means twisted and stuck together untidily. ...*matted hair.*

matter (**mattering, mattered**) A **matter** is a situation which has to be dealt with. ...*a personal matter.* ■ **Matters** means the situation you are talking about. *Recent Government policy has made matters worse.* ■ If you say something is just **a matter of** doing something, you mean it can be achieved just by doing that thing. ■ If you say something is only **a matter of time,** you mean it is certain to happen at some time in the future. ■ If you talk about something being done in **a matter** of days or weeks, you are emphasizing how quickly it is done. ■ If you say something is **a matter of opinion,** you mean it is not necessarily true. ■ You say **for that matter** when you are saying that something applies equally to another situation or person. *We're not used to violent demonstrations, or demonstrations of any sort for that matter.* ■ If something **matters,** it is important. ■ **No matter** is used to say something happens or is true in all circumstances. ■ **Matter** is physical substances generally. ...*solid matter.* ...*living matter.* ■ Books and magazines are often called **reading matter.** ■ The **subject matter** of a book or film is the topic it deals with. ■ **as a matter of course:** see **course.**

matter-of-fact (**matter-of-factly**) If you say someone is **matter-of-fact,** you mean they show no emotion, especially in a situation where you would expect them to be emotional. *'We played better football than they did,' Reilly said matter-of-factly.*

matting is a floor covering woven from coarse fibre like rope.

mattress (mattresses) A **mattress** is a thick rectangular pad filled with soft material or springs, which is put on a bed to make it comfortable to sleep on.

mature (maturing, matured; maturity, maturation) When a child or young animal **matures** or reaches **maturity**, it becomes an adult. ■ You say people are **mature** when they behave sensibly and responsibly. ■ You use **mature** to describe things which are fully developed and established. ...*a mature garden*. ■ When something like cheese or wine is **matured**, it is left for a time to allow its full flavour to develop. This process is called **maturation**. ■ When an investment or insurance policy **matures**, it becomes due for repayment.

mature student A **mature student** is someone who begins their studies at university or college when they are over 21.

maudlin If someone becomes **maudlin**, they start being sad and sentimental when they are drunk.

maul (mauling, mauled) If someone is **mauled** by an animal, they are attacked and badly injured by it. ■ You say someone is **mauled** or given a **mauling** when they are heavily criticized or defeated.

mausoleum (*pron:* maw-so-**lee**-um) A **mausoleum** is a building containing the grave of someone rich or famous.

mauve is a pale purple colour.

maverick If you say someone is a **maverick**, you mean they are unconventional and independent.

maw You call something a **maw** when it seems to swallow things up like a giant mouth. *The hard currency gained by oil sales disappeared down the Soviet maw.*

mawkish (mawkishness) If you describe something as **mawkish**, you mean it is over-sentimental and silly. ...*a sentimental plot, with an inevitable mawkish ending.*

maxim A **maxim** is a short saying recommending a particular form of behaviour.

maximize (or **maximise**) **(maximizing, maximized)** If you **maximize** something, you make it as large or extensive as you can.

maximum The **maximum** amount of something is the largest amount possible.

may You use **may** to say something is possible. *The two sides may be close to reaching an agreement.* ■ You use **may** to say something is allowed. *They may stay as long as they wish.* ■ You use **may** when saying that, although one thing is true, another contrasting thing is also true. *He may look fierce, but he's a big softie really.* ■ **May** is sometimes used to express a wish that something will happen. *May we have many more projects of this quality.*

maybe You use **maybe** when stating a possibility you are not certain about. *Maybe it will happen one day, but not today.* ■ You use **maybe** to say that though a comment is possibly true, there is another side to be considered. *Maybe he is the right candidate but this is the wrong way to choose a leader.* ■ You use **maybe** when you are making a guess at an amount. *Once, maybe 100,000 people would watch a race. Now it's millions.*

May Day is May 1st. It is celebrated as a festival in many countries.

mayday If someone in a plane or ship sends out a **mayday** call, they send out a radio message calling for help, because they are in serious difficulty.

mayhem is an uncontrolled and confused situation.

mayonnaise is a thick salad dressing made from raw egg yolks, vinegar, and oil.

mayor (mayoress, mayoresses; mayoral) The **mayor** of a town is a person elected to represent it for a fixed period of time. If the mayor is a man, his wife is called the **mayoress**. If the mayor is a woman, she can call herself either the **mayor** or the **mayoress**. **Mayoral** is used to talk about things to do with a mayor or mayoress. ...*mayoral elections.*

maypole A **maypole** is a tall pole which people dance round while holding streamers attached to the head of the pole.

maze A **maze** is a complicated system of passages which is difficult to find your way through.

MBE An **MBE** is an honour granted by the monarch for a special achievement. MBE stands for 'Member of the Order of the British Empire'.

MC See **Master of Ceremonies.**

McCoy If you describe something as the real **McCoy**, you mean it is the genuine article and not an imitation.

MD The **MD** of a company is its managing director.

ME is a medical condition involving chronic fatigue and muscular pain. ME stands for 'myalgic encephalomyelitis'. This condition is also called **post-viral syndrome** and **chronic fatigue syndrome**.

me A speaker or writer uses **me** to talk about himself or herself.

mead is an alcoholic drink made of honey, spices, and water.

meadow A **meadow** is a field of grass and wild flowers.

meagre (*Am:* **meager**) A **meagre** amount of something is very small or too small.

meal A **meal** is an occasion when people eat, or the food they eat on that occasion. ■ **Meal** is a coarse powder made of crushed grain.

meals-on-wheels is a service organized by the local authority or charities to provide hot meals to old or sick people in their own homes.

mealy-mouthed If you say someone is being **mealy-mouthed**, you mean they are avoiding talking openly or directly about something unpleasant.

mean (meaning, meant; meaner, meanest; meanness) If you talk about the **meaning** of a word, expression, or gesture, or what it **means**, you are talking about what it refers to or stands for. ■ If one thing **means** another, it shows the second thing exists or is true. *Caring means cheering her up when she's down.* ■ If you **mean** to do something, you intend to do it. If you **mean** what you say, you are serious about it. ■ If something is **meant** for a particular purpose, it is intended for that purpose. ■ If something is **meant** to be true, it is supposed to be true. ■ If something has **meaning**, it seems to be worthwhile and to have real purpose. If something **means** a lot to you, it is very important to you. ■ A **mean** person is unwilling to spend money. *They* *were famous for their meanness.* ■ If someone is **mean** to you, they are cruel or unkind. ■ In maths, the **mean** is the average of a set of numbers. ■ See also **means.**

meander (*pron:* me-**and**-er) (**meandering, meandered**) If a river or road **meanders,** it has a lot of bends. ■ If you **meander** somewhere, you move there slowly and aimlessly.

meaning See **mean.**

meaningful (**meaningfully**) If you describe something as **meaningful,** you mean it is serious, important, or useful in some way. *There was no meaningful progress towards political reform.* ■ A **meaningful** look or gesture is one intended to show what you feel. *He gave the goalkeeper a long and meaningful stare after Quinn scored.*

meaningless (**meaninglessly**) If something which someone says or writes is **meaningless,** it has no meaning, or seems to have no meaning. *...a meaningless piece of jargon.* ■ You use **meaningless** to say something is pointless, because it will not achieve anything. *Their attempt at a ceasefire is meaningless.*

means is used to talk about the amount of money you have for spending. *We have to live within our means.* ■ A **means** of doing something is a method, instrument, or process which can be used to do it. ■ You say **by no means** to emphasize that something is not true. *It is by no means a poor restaurant.* ■ You say **by all means** to emphasize that it is all right for someone to do something. *By all means let him have his way.*

means test (**means-tested**) A **means test** is an official government assessment of your income, to see if you are eligible for grants or benefits.

meant See **mean.**

meantime – In the meantime means in the period of time between two events. ■ **For the meantime** means for a period from now until something else happens.

meanwhile means while a particular thing is happening. ■ **Meanwhile** can mean 'in the meantime'. *Another meeting is planned next week, meanwhile, rebels are insisting there must be no compromise.*

measles is an infectious illness which gives you red spots.

measly A **measly** amount of something is very small and inadequate.

measurable If something is **measurable,** it can be measured.

measure (**measuring, measured; measurement**) If you **measure** something, you find out how big it is, using an instrument of some kind. The numbers you get when you measure something are called **measurements.** ■ You can say how big something is by saying it **measures** a certain amount. *The vole measures 170mm from nose to tail.* ■ If something like progress is **measured,** it is assessed. ■ If you say something is a **measure** of a certain thing, you mean it can be used to judge it. *How states treat their minorities is a measure of their democracy.* ■ If something **measures up** to expectations or standards, it meets them. ■ A **measure** of something is a certain amount of it. *The idea has a measure of support.* ■ **Measures** are actions taken by people in authority to try to achieve something. *...cost-cutting measures.*

measured behaviour or speech is careful and restrained.

meat is the flesh of an animal which is cooked and eaten.

meaty (**meatier, meatiest**) If you say something like a book is **meaty,** you mean it is full of interesting or useful information. ■ **Meaty** food contains a lot of meat.

Mecca is a city in Saudi Arabia. It is a place of pilgrimage for Muslims. ■ If you say a place is a **mecca** for certain people, you mean they go there in large numbers, because there is something about it which interests them. *Wembley is a mecca for football fans.*

mechanic (**mechanics**) A **mechanic** is someone whose job is to repair and maintain engines and machines. ■ If you talk about the **mechanics** of something, you are talking about how it works or is done. *...the mechanics of implementing the agreement.* ■ **Mechanics** is the branch of science which deals with forces acting on moving or stationary objects.

mechanical (**mechanically**) **Mechanical** devices have moving parts and are often powered by electricity or an engine. ■ **Mechanical** means involving machines. *...a mechanical failure.* ■ A **mechanical** action is done automatically, without thinking about it. *The criteria should not be applied mechanically.*

mechanise See **mechanize.**

mechanism A **mechanism** is a part of a machine which does a specific task. *...the locking mechanism.* ■ A **mechanism** is a procedure for getting something done. *The party has no mechanism by which to appoint a new leader.* ■ A **mechanism** is an automatic part of your behaviour which helps you cope in difficult situations. *...a primitive survival mechanism.*

mechanistic A **mechanistic** view is one which tries to explain human behaviour and natural processes as if they were machines.

mechanize (*or* **mechanise**) (**mechanizing, mechanized; mechanization**) When a type of work is **mechanized,** machines are introduced to do things previously done by hand.

medal A **medal** is a small metal disc given as an award for bravery or as a prize in a sporting event.

medalist See **medallist.**

medallion A **medallion** is a round metal disc worn as an ornament on a neck chain.

medallist (*or* **medalist**) A **medallist** is a person who has won a medal in a sporting event.

meddle (**meddling, meddled; meddler, meddlesome**) If someone **meddles** in something, they try to influence or change it without being asked to. You call someone who behaves like this a **meddler** or say they are being **meddlesome.**

media Television, radio, and newspapers are often called the **media.** ■ See also **medium.**

mediaeval See **medieval.**

median The **median** value of a set of values is the middle one when they are arranged in order.

mediate

mediate (mediating, mediated; mediation, mediator) If someone **mediates** between two people, they try to help them settle a dispute. A person who does this is called a **mediator.**

medic A **medic** is a doctor or a medical student.

medical (medically) **Medical** means connected with the treatment of illness or injury. ...*medical equipment.* ■ A **medical** is a thorough examination of your body by a doctor.

medicament A **medicament** is a medicine or ointment.

medication is the medicine someone takes or is given.

medicinal If something has **medicinal** properties, it can be used to treat illness.

medicine is the treatment of illness and injury by doctors and nurses. *He gave up medicine and retired to the country.* ■ A **medicine** is a substance you take to cure an illness.

medieval (*or* mediaeval) (*pron:* med-ee-**eve**-al) The **medieval** period in European history began with the end of the Western Roman Empire in 476 AD and ended about 1500 AD.

mediocre (*pron:* mee-dee-**oak**-er *or* mee-dee-oak-er) (**mediocrity, mediocrities**) If you call something **mediocre** or talk about its **mediocrity** (*pron:* mee-dee-**ok**-rit-ee), you mean it is not particularly good.

meditate (meditating, meditated; meditation) If you **meditate** on something, you think about it carefully and deeply for a long time. A **meditation** on something is a piece of writing which examines it carefully and thoughtfully. ■ If you **meditate,** you spend time in a calm state of concentration, especially as part of religious training or practice. Being in this state is called **meditation**.

meditative means to do with meditation. ...*the Chinese meditative practice of tai chi.* ■ You can describe someone as **meditative** when they are thinking deeply about something. **Meditative** is also used to describe things people say or write as a result of deep thought. ...*meditative poetry.*

Mediterranean The **Mediterranean** is the area surrounding the Mediterranean Sea, the sea between Europe and North Africa. ■ **Mediterranean** is used to describe things thought to be typical of the Mediterranean. ...*Mediterranean weather.*

medium is used to describe things which are about halfway between two extremes. ...*medium-sized businesses.* ■ A **medium** (*plural:* media) is a means of communicating or teaching something. *In the National University of Singapore, English was the medium of instruction.* See also **media.** ■ A **medium** (*plural:* mediums) is a person who claims to be able to communicate with the dead.

medium wave is the range of radio waves from 100 to 1,000 metres.

medley A **medley** is a selection of tunes or songs played one after another as a continuous piece of music. ■ A **medley** is a swimming race in which the four main strokes are used one after another. ■ Any assortment of different things can be called a **medley.** *The city is a raucous medley of sights and sounds.*

meek (meekly) A **meek** person is gentle and quiet and usually does what other people tell them to.

meet (meeting, met) If you **meet** someone, you happen to be in the same place and start talking to them. ■ If you arrange to **meet** someone, you arrange to be in the same place at the same time, so you can do something together. ■ If you **meet** someone from a train or plane, you collect them when they arrive on it. ■ You can say you **meet** someone when you are introduced to them for the first time. ■ When people **meet,** they get together to discuss things and make decisions. ■ In sport, when two players **meet,** they compete against each other. ■ If something **meets** a requirement, it fulfils the requirement. ■ If you **meet** a problem or challenge, you deal with it satisfactorily. ■ If you **meet** the cost of something, you pay for it. ■ If something **meets with** a particular reaction, that is how people react to it. ■ **make ends meet:** see **end.**

meeting A **meeting** is an occasion when people get together to discuss things and make decisions. The people at a meeting can be called the **meeting.** *The meeting decided that further efforts were needed.* ■ A **meeting** is an occasion when you meet someone, such as a friend.

mega- at the beginning of a unit of measurement means it is a million times greater than another unit. For example, a megawatt is 1,000,000 watts. ■ **Mega-** is added to words to say something is very large or important. *Valium became the drug industry's first mega-hit.*

megabyte Computer memory is often expressed in **megabytes.** A megabyte is 1,048,576 bytes. 'Megabytes' is usually written 'Mb'.

megahertz (*plural:* megahertz) The frequency of radio waves is often expressed in **megahertz.** One megahertz is 1,000,000 cycles per second. 'Megahertz' is usually written 'MHz'.

megalith (megalithic) A **megalith** is a large upright stone or group of stones, placed in its position in prehistoric times. **Megalithic** means connected with stones like these. ...*the megalithic site of Lagatjar.*

megalomaniac (megalomania) If you call someone a **megalomaniac** or talk about their **megalomania,** you mean they do things just because of the feeling of power it gives them. ■ **Megalomania** is a form of mental illness in which someone believes they are much more powerful than they really are.

megaphone A **megaphone** is a cone-shaped device for making your voice sound louder in the open air.

megaton The explosive power of a nuclear weapon is often expressed in **megatons.** One megaton is equal to the explosive power of 1,000,000 tons of TNT.

megawatt Power is often expressed in **megawatts.** A megawatt is 1,000,000 watts. 'Megawatts' is usually written 'MW'.

melancholy (melancholic) **Melancholy** is an intense feeling of sadness. If you are **melancholy** or **melancholic,** you feel like this.

mélange (*pron:* **may**-lanzh; *the 'zh' sounds like 's' in pleasure*) A **mélange** is a mixture of people or things.

melanin is a dark substance in the skin, eyes, and hair of people and animals, which gives them colour and protects them against strong sunlight.

melanoma (*pron:* mel-a-**nome**-a) is a malignant form of skin cancer. The tumour is marked by an irregular dark blotch on the skin.

meld If you **meld** a number of things together, you combine them.

mêlée (*pron:* **mel**-lay) A **mêlée** is a crowd of people rushing about in different directions, doing different things. ■ A **mêlée** is a fight involving a crowd of people.

mellifluous A **mellifluous** voice or sound is very pleasant.

mellow colours are soft and gentle. ■ **Mellow** music is pleasant and relaxing. ■ If someone **mellows** or if something **mellows** them, they become gentler and more relaxed, or less extreme in their opinions.

melodious A **melodious** sound is pleasant to listen to.

melodrama (**melodramatic, melodramatically**) A **melodrama** is a dramatic and sensational story or play in which people's behaviour is exaggerated and emotional. Anything in fiction or real life which has features like this can be called **melodramatic.** *He talked melodramatically about the need to combat an American plot.*

melody (**melodies; melodic**) A **melody** is a tune. **Melodic** means to do with writing tunes. *...melodic invention.* A **melodic** piece of music has a definite tune or tunes in it.

melon – **Melons** are large juicy fruit with yellow or green skins.

melt When a solid substance **melts**, it changes to a liquid, as a result of being heated. ■ If you **melt down** a metal or glass object, you heat it until it melts. ■ If something **melts** or **melts away,** it gradually disappears. *The crowd melted away.*

meltdown If there is a **meltdown** in a nuclear reactor, a fault allows the core to overheat and melt, sometimes leading to a radiation leak. ■ Any sudden dramatic collapse in a system can be called a **meltdown.** *Share prices plunged to a six-year low, fuelling concern about a financial meltdown.*

melting pot A **melting pot** is a place or situation where different people, cultures, and ideas get mixed together.

member A **member** of a group is one of the people or things belonging to it. ■ The **member** for a place is its MP.

Member of Parliament See **MP.**

membership of an organization is belonging to it. *He was stripped of his party membership.* ■ The **membership** of an organization is the people who belong to it. *Documents were distributed to the entire membership.*

membrane A **membrane** is a thin piece of skin covering or connecting parts of a person's or animal's body.

memento (**mementoes** *or* **mementos**) A **memento** is an object you keep to remind you of a person or special occasion.

memento mori (*pron:* **more**-ee) A **memento mori** is something which reminds you of death or mortality.

memo (**memos**) A **memo** is an official note written from one person to another within the same organization. 'Memo' is short for 'memorandum'.

memoir A person's **memoirs** are a book they have written about their life and experiences. ■ A **memoir** is a book or article about a well-known person written by someone who knew them well.

memorabilia are things you collect because they are connected with a person or event that interests you. *...Elvis memorabilia.*

memorable (**memorably**) **Memorable** things are likely to be remembered because they are special or unusual.

memorandum (*plural:* **memoranda** *or* **memorandums**) A **memorandum** is (a) a written report prepared for a person or committee. (b) an informal diplomatic communication from one government to another. ■ See also **memo.**

memorial A **memorial** is a structure built to remind people of a famous person or event. ■ A **memorial** event is held in honour of someone who has died. ■ If something someone has achieved continues to be remembered after their death, you can say it is a **memorial** to them.

Memorial Day In the US, **Memorial Day** is a public holiday, usually at the end of May, when Americans who have been killed in wars are remembered.

memorize (*or* **memorise**) (**memorizing, memorized**) If you **memorize** a piece of writing, you learn it so you can remember it without having to look at it again.

memory (**memories**) Your **memory** is your ability to remember things. ■ A **memory** is something you remember from the past. ■ A computer's **memory** is its capacity to store information.

men See **man.**

menace (**menacing, menaced; menacingly**) If you call something a **menace,** you mean it is likely to cause serious harm. *Excessive drinking is a social menace.* ■ If someone **menaces** you, they threaten to harm you. *He dropped menacing hints about 'retaliatory measures'.* ■ **Menace** is something in a person's behaviour or the atmosphere of a place which seems dangerous or threatening. *There is a real feeling of menace on the streets.* ■ You call someone or something a **menace** when they cause trouble or annoyance.

ménage (*pron:* **may**-nazh; *the 'zh' sounds like 's' in pleasure*) A **ménage** is a group of people living together in one house.

ménage à trois (*pron:* **may**-nazh ah twah) A **ménage à trois** is a situation in which three people live together and one of them is having a sexual relationship with both the others.

menagerie (*pron:* min-**naj**-er-ee) A **menagerie** is a collection of wild animals.

mend If you **mend** something which is damaged or broken, you repair it. ■ If you are **on the mend,** you are recovering after an illness or injury. If a situation is **on the mend,** it is improving after a difficult period. *Relations with Moscow are on the mend.* ■ If someone who has been behaving badly **mends their ways,** they start to behave better.

mendacious (mendacity) A **mendacious** statement is not truthful. **Mendacity** is telling lies.

menfolk When women talk about their **menfolk,** they mean the men in their family or community.

menial work is boring and tiring, and is regarded as having low status.

meningitis is a serious infectious illness which causes inflammation of the membranes surrounding the brain and spinal cord. It can be caused by a virus or by bacteria.

menopause (menopausal) The **menopause** is the time when a woman stops having periods. **Menopausal** means to do with this time.

menstruate (menstruating, menstruated; menstrual, menstruation) When a woman **menstruates,** blood comes from her womb. Women who are fertile menstruate once a month unless they are pregnant. **Menstrual** means to do with menstruation. *...the menstrual cycle.*

menswear is men's clothing.

mental (mentally) **Mental** means to do with the mind and the process of thinking. *He is a man of mental as well as physical courage.* ■ **Mental** is used to talk about the health of a person's mind. *...mentally disturbed prisoners.*

mental hospital A **mental hospital** is a hospital for people suffering from mental illness.

mentality (mentalities) Your **mentality** is your attitude or way of thinking.

menthol is a substance which smells like peppermint and is used to flavour things like toothpaste.

mention (mentioning, mentioned) If you **mention** something, you say something about it, usually briefly. ■ A **mention** is a reference to someone or something. *Economic pundits tremble at the mere mention of his name.*

mentor Your **mentor** is someone who teaches you and gives you advice.

menu A **menu** is a list of the food you can order in a restaurant. ■ On a computer, a **menu** is a list of choices. Each choice represents something you can do using the computer.

MEP An **MEP** is a person who has been elected to the European Parliament. MEP stands for 'Member of the European Parliament'.

mercantile means to do with merchants and trading. *...the mercantile system. ...mercantile wealth.*

mercenary (mercenaries) **Mercenaries** are soldiers paid to fight for a foreign country. ■ If you say someone is **mercenary,** you mean they are only interested in obtaining money from a situation.

merchandise is goods which are bought, sold, or traded.

merchandizing is (a) producing a range of goods closely connected with someone or something famous, for example a film. (b) promoting the sales of products generally.

merchant A **merchant** is someone who buys or sells goods in large quantities, especially someone who imports and exports goods.

merchant bank A **merchant bank** is a bank which deals mainly with businesses and investment.

merchant navy A country's **merchant navy** consists of its merchant ships and the people who man them.

merchant ship A **merchant ship** is a ship which carries cargo and sometimes passengers.

merciful (mercifully) A **merciful** person is kind and forgiving to people in their power. ■ You say something that happens is **merciful** when it puts an end to suffering. ■ **Mercifully** is used to express pleasure or relief that something unpleasant does not exist, or has been stopped or avoided. *Crime is mercifully rare here.*

merciless (mercilessly) A **merciless** person is cruel and shows no pity.

mercurial If you say someone is **mercurial,** you mean they change their mind often and without warning.

mercury is a heavy silvery-white liquid metal which is highly toxic.

mercy (mercies) If someone shows **mercy,** they show kindness and forgiveness. ■ If you are **at** someone's **mercy,** they have complete power over you.

mercy killing is painlessly killing someone who is very ill to stop their suffering.

mercy mission If someone goes on a **mercy mission,** they try to help people in great need.

mere (merest) **Mere** is used to emphasize how small or unimportant something is. *This time there was not the merest hint of dissent.*

merely You use **merely** to emphasize that something is only what you say, and not something bigger, better, or more important. *The time difference between the drivers is merely a tenth of a second.*

meretricious If something is **meretricious,** it seems attractive on the surface but has little real value.

merge (merging, merged; merger) When one organization is **merged** with another one, they are joined together to form a single organization. You call this a **merger.** ■ If one colour, sound, or object **merges** into another, they are so similar you cannot distinguish between them.

meringue (*pron:* mer-**rang**) A **meringue** is a type of crisp sweet food made with sugar and whipped egg white.

merit (meriting, merited) If something has **merit,** it is good or worthwhile. ■ The **merits** of something are its advantages or good qualities. ■ If something **merits** particular treatment, it deserves to be treated that way.

meritocracy (meritocracies; meritocratic) A **meritocracy** is a social system in which people have power or prestige because of their intelligence and abilities, rather than because of their wealth or social status. You say a system like this is **meritocratic.**

meritorious If something is **meritorious,** it has good or worthwhile qualities.

mermaid In stories, a **mermaid** is a woman with a fish's tail instead of legs, who lives in the sea.

merrily See **merry.**

merriment If something causes **merriment,** it makes people laugh.

merry (merrier, merriest; merrily) Merry is used to describe things which are happy and cheerful. ...*merry reminiscences.* ■ **Merry** means slightly drunk. ■ **Merrily** is used to say something is done without people thinking properly about it. *Government spending has gone on merrily unchecked, driving inflation well into four digits.*

merry-go-round A **merry-go-round** is a large revolving platform with models of animals or vehicles on it, which children can ride on. ■ You can refer to a continuous series of activities as a **merry-go-round,** especially if nothing much is being achieved.

merry-making is enjoying yourself in a happy way with other people.

mesh (meshes, meshing, meshed) Mesh is a net-like material made from wire, thread, or plastic. ■ You say things like gears **mesh** when they operate by fitting precisely into each other. ■ You talk about things **meshing** when they correspond exactly. *This story never quite meshed with the facts.*

mesmeric If something is **mesmeric,** it holds your attention, hypnotically.

mesmerize (or mesmerise) (mesmerizing, mesmerized) If you are **mesmerized** by something, you are so fascinated by it that it holds your attention completely. *She had a mesmerizing smile.*

Mesolithic (*pron:* mess-o-**lith**-ik) The **Mesolithic** period was the middle period of the Stone Age, when people were hunters and fishermen and first began using boats. See also **Palaeolithic, Neolithic.**

mess (messes, messing, messed) If a place is very untidy, dirty, or disorganized, you can say it is a **mess.** ■ If you call a situation a **mess,** you mean things have gone badly wrong. ■ If you **mess about** or **mess around,** you do things without any particular aim. ■ If you **mess** someone **around** or **mess** them **about,** you treat them badly, for example by continually changing plans which affect them. ■ If you **mess** something **up,** you spoil it. ■ A **mess** is a room or building where members of the armed forces eat.

message A **message** is a piece of information or a request which you send to someone, or leave for them. ■ The **message** in a speech or piece of writing is what the speaker or writer is trying to convey.

messenger A **messenger** is a person who takes a message to someone, or delivers messages as their job.

messiah For Jews, the **Messiah** is the king or leader promised in their holy writings by God. ■ For Christians, the **Messiah** is Jesus Christ. ■ Someone who promises to rescue, or succeeds in rescuing, people from a difficult or dangerous situation can be called a **messiah.** *He sees himself as a messiah of the Slavia world.*

messianic is used to describe things connected with the belief that a divine being or a great human leader has been born, or will be born, who will change the world. *Jesus' appreciation of his messianic task is repeatedly found in the gospels.*

Messrs (*pron:* **mess**-erz) is used before the names of two or more men, often as part of the name of a business. ...*Messrs Lindt Sprungli.*

messy (messily) Messy things are dirty or untidy. ■ A **messy** person or activity makes things dirty or untidy. ■ A **messy** situation is confused or complicated and makes trouble for people.

met See **meet.**

metabolise See **metabolize.**

metabolism (*pron:* met-**tab**-oh-liz-zum) **(metabolic)** Your **metabolism** is the chemical process in your body which causes food to be absorbed and used for growth and energy. **Metabolic** (*pron:* met-tab-**bol**-lik) is used to talk about things to do with this process.

metabolize (*or* **metabolise**) **(metabolizing, metabolized)** When you **metabolize** food, your body breaks it down chemically so it can be used for growth and energy.

metacarpal The **metacarpals** are the five bones connecting the wrist to the fingers.

metal is a hard substance which has special properties, such as being a good conductor of heat and electricity. Some metals are chemical elements, for example iron; others are alloys, such as steel.

metal fatigue is a weakening of a metal part through repeated movement which might cause it to break.

metallic things are made of metal. ■ A **metallic** sound is like one piece of metal hitting another. ■ **Metallic** colours shine like metal.

metallurgy (metallurgical, metallurgist) Metallurgy is the science and technology of extracting metals from their ores and preparing them for use. A **metallurgist** is an expert on this. **Metallurgical** is used to describe things connected with the refining of metals. ...*metallurgical industries.*

metalwork is making things out of metal as a craft or hobby. **Metalwork** is also things made out of metal in this way. *The Armenian pottery and metalwork sold well.*

metamorphose (metamorphosing, metamorphosed; metamorphosis) When something **metamorphoses,** it changes to something completely different. *The tadpoles metamorphose and emerge onto land.* A change like this is called a **metamorphosis** (*plural:* **metamorphoses**).

metaphor (metaphorical, metaphorically) A **metaphor** is a way of describing something by calling it something else which has a well-known quality or characteristic. For example, if you have to deal with something which is full of hidden dangers, you can call it a minefield. This is called a **metaphorical** use of language.

metaphysics (metaphysical) Metaphysics is the part of philosophy which deals with theories about what exists and how we know it exists. ...*metaphysical ideas about life.*

mete (meting, meted) The kind of punishment or treatment **meted out** to someone is the kind they receive.

meteor A **meteor** is a piece of rock which burns very brightly when it enters the Earth's atmosphere from space. Meteors are often called 'shooting stars'.

meteoric A **meteoric** rise to power or fame happens very quickly.

meteorite A **meteorite** is a piece of rock which lands on Earth from space.

meteorology (**meteorologist, meteorological**) **Meteorology** is the study of the processes in the Earth's atmosphere which cause weather conditions. A **meteorologist** is someone who studies and interprets these processes. ...*meteorological conditions.*

meter (**metering, metered**) A **meter** is a device which measures and records something. ...*a gas meter.* When something is measured and recorded in this way, you say it is **metered**. ■ See also **metre**.

methane is a colourless flammable gas which has no smell. Natural gas consists mainly of methane.

methanol is a colourless flammable poisonous liquid. It is used as an antifreeze, a solvent, and a fuel.

method A **method** is a particular way of doing something.

methodical (**methodically**) A **methodical** person does things carefully and in a logical order.

Methodist (**Methodism**) **Methodists** are Protestants who follow the teachings of John Wesley. Their beliefs and practices are called **Methodism**. **Methodist** is used to describe things connected with this Church.

methodology A **methodology** is a system of methods and principles for doing something, for example carrying out research.

methylated spirit is a poisonous liquid made from alcohol and other chemicals. It is used as a solvent and a fuel. It is often called 'meths'.

meticulous (**meticulously**) A **meticulous** person does things very carefully and with great attention to detail.

métier (*pron: met-ee-ay*) Your **métier** is the type of work for which you have a natural talent.

metre (*Am: meter*) Distance is often expressed in **metres**. A metre is 100 centimetres (about 39.4 inches). 'Metres' is usually written 'm'. ■ In poetry, **metre** is the regular and rhythmic arrangement of words and syllables.

metric The **metric** system is the system which uses metres, kilograms, and litres. See also **imperial**.

metrication is the process of changing from measuring things in imperial units to measuring them in metric units.

metric ton Heavy weights are sometimes expressed in **metric tons**. A metric ton is 1,000 kilograms (about 2,200 pounds). Metric tons are also called **tonnes**.

metro Some cities, for example Paris, have an underground railway system called the **metro**.

metronome A **metronome** is a device used by musicians to help them play a piece at a constant speed. It makes a regular clicking sound and can be adjusted to go faster or slower.

metropolis (**metropolises**) A **metropolis** is a very large city.

metropolitan is used to talk about things relating to a large busy city.

mettle is used to talk about people being made to show how good they are at handling something difficult. You say, for example that something 'tests their mettle' or 'puts them on their mettle'.

mews A **mews** is a yard or street surrounded by houses which were originally built as stables.

mezzanine (*pron: mez-zan-neen*) A **mezzanine** floor is a partial floor built between two storeys in a building.

mezzo-soprano (*pron: met-so*) A **mezzo-soprano** or **mezzo** is a female singer who sings with a higher range than a contralto but a lower range than a soprano.

mg See **milligrams**.

Mgr in front of a priest's name stands for 'Monsignor'.

MHz See **megahertz**.

MI5 is a British government organization which is concerned with protecting British national security. Its official title is 'The Security Service'.

MI6 is a British government organization which tries to obtain secret information about the affairs of other countries. Its official title is 'The Secret Intelligence Service'.

miasma (*pron: mee-az-ma*) A **miasma** is an unpleasant or unhealthy atmosphere caused by decaying things.

mica (*pron: my-kah*) is a hard mineral which can be split into thin sheets. It has a great resistance to heat and electricity.

mice See **mouse**.

Michaelmas (*pron: mik-kl-mass*) is a Christian festival celebrated on the 29th of September in honour of the archangel Michael.

mickey If you **take the mickey** out of someone, you make fun of them.

micro A **micro** is the same as a microcomputer.

micro- is used at the beginning of words to talk about very small versions of things. ...*micronutrients.*

microbe (**microbial**) **Microbes** are very small living things like bacteria, which you can only see with a microscope. ...*microbial contamination.*

microbiology (**microbiologist, microbiological**) **Microbiology** is the study of microbes. A **microbiologist** is an expert in this field. ...*the Microbiological Research Centre.*

microchip A **microchip** is a small piece of silicon inside a computer with electronic circuits printed on it.

microcomputer A **microcomputer** is a small computer, often used for word-processing.

microcosm If you say a place or event is a **microcosm** of a larger one, you mean it is like a smaller version of it with all the typical features.

microeconomics (**microeconomic**) **Microeconomics** is the study of the economics of a small-scale system, for example a family or a small business. **Microeconomic** theories or policies are concerned with systems like these. See also **macroeconomics**.

microelectronics (microelectronic) Microelectronics is the branch of electronics which deals with very small circuits and components. **Microelectronic** devices are made up of these very small components.

microfiche (*pron:* **my**-kro-feesh) A **microfiche** is a small sheet of film on which information is stored in very small print.

microfilm is film used for photographing information and storing it in a reduced form.

micrometre (*Am:* **micrometer**) A **micrometre** is the same as a micron.

micron Very small distances are often expressed in **microns**. A micron is one millionth of a metre.

microorganism A **microorganism** is the same as a microbe.

microphone A **microphone** is a device for picking up sounds so that they can be amplified or recorded.

microprocessor A **microprocessor** is a microchip which can be programmed to do a large number of tasks in a computer or other piece of equipment.

microscope A **microscope** is an instrument which magnifies very small objects so they can be studied.

microscopic (microscopically) If something is **microscopic**, it is extremely small. *...a microscopically thin layer of tissue.* ■ A **microscopic** examination of something is very detailed.

microsurgery is intricate surgery using a microscope and very small instruments.

microwave (microwaving, microwaved) A **microwave** or **microwave oven** is a cooker which cooks food very quickly using short-wave electromagnetic radiation rather than heat. If you **microwave** food, you cook it in this kind of oven.

mid is used to talk about the middle part of a region or period of time. *...mid-Wales. ...mid September.*

midday is (a) the same as noon. (b) used to describe things which happen around noon. *...midday meals.*

middle The **middle** of something is the part farthest from its edges, ends, or outside surface. ■ The **middle** thing in a series is the one with an equal number of things on each side of it. ■ Your **middle** is the front part of your body at your waist. ■ If you take a **middle** course, you choose a moderate course of action which lies between two extremes.

middle age (middle-aged) **Middle age** is the middle part of a person's life, when they are neither old nor young. *Mick is middle-aged.*

Middle Ages In European history, the **Middle Ages** was the period between the end of the Western Roman Empire in 476 AD and about 1500 AD.

middle-brow (*or* **middlebrow**) people are educated but have conventional tastes. **Middle-brow** programmes and newspapers are aimed at people like these.

middle-class (middle classes) The **middle classes** are people who are neither working class nor upper class, for example teachers, doctors, and lawyers.

middle distance races are athletics events like the 800 metres, the 1,500 metres, and the mile.

Middle East The **Middle East** consists of Iran and the countries in Asia to the west and south-west of Iran.

middleman (middlemen) A **middleman** is someone who buys things from the people who produce them and re-sells them at a profit. ■ A **middleman** is someone who acts as an intermediary between the parties in a dispute.

middle-of-the-road is used to describe things such as political views which are moderate, rather than extreme.

middle school A **middle school** is for children from the age of 8 or 9 to the age of 12 or 13.

middling things are of average level or quality.

midfield (midfielder) In football, the **midfield** is the part of the pitch about halfway between the two goalmouths. A **midfielder** is a player who normally plays in this part of the pitch.

midge – **Midges** are very small flying insects which bite.

midget Some people refer to very small people as **midgets**. ■ **Midget** is used to describe things which are very small. *...a midget submarine.*

midnight is 12 o'clock in the middle of the night. **Midnight** is used to describe things which happen around the middle of the night. *...a midnight raid.*

midpoint (*or* **mid-point**) The **midpoint** of a line or scale is the point which is an equal distance from each end. ■ The **midpoint** of an event or period of time is the point halfway between the beginning and the end.

midriff Your **midriff** is the middle of your body, particularly your waist and the area just above it.

midshipman (midshipmen) A **midshipman** is a naval officer of the lowest rank.

midst If you are **in the midst** of doing something, you have started doing it and have not yet finished. ■ If something happens **in the midst** of an event, it happens during it. ■ If you are **in the midst** of a group of people, you are among them.

midstream is the middle of a river, where the current is strongest.

Midsummer's Day is the 24th of June.

midtown (*or* **mid-town**) is the central part of a city.

midway If something is **midway** between two places or a period of time, it is in the middle.

midweek means happening in the middle of a week. *...England's last two midweek games.*

Mid-west (*or* **Midwest**) (Mid-western) The **Mid-west** is the northern central part of the US. **Mid-western** means in or from the Mid-west.

midwife (midwives; midwifery) A **midwife** is a specially qualified nurse who advises pregnant women and helps them give birth. **Midwifery** (*pron:* **mid**-wiff-er-ree) is the work of a midwife and the skills it involves.

mien (*pron:* **mean**) Someone's **mien** is their general appearance and manner, especially their facial expression.

miffed If you are **miffed,** you are slightly annoyed and hurt because of something someone has said or done.

might If something **might** happen, it is possible that it happened, will happen, or could have happened but did not. *Smoking might be banned totally in most government buildings... Outside intervention might have prevented the fighting.* ■ You use **might** to make a suggestion or request something. *You might want to try freelance work... I wonder if I might add a word.* ■ **Might** is power or strength.

mightily means to a large extent or degree. *I was mightily impressed.*

mighty (**mightier, mightiest**) **Mighty** is used to describe people and organizations that are very powerful. *...the once mighty trade unions.* ■ **Mighty** is used for emphasis. *I'm mighty glad you're here.*

migraine A **migraine** is a severe headache which makes you feel very ill.

migrant A **migrant** is someone who moves from one place to another, usually to find work. ■ **Migrant** birds or animals go to a different area for part of the year to find food or breed.

migrate (**migrating, migrated; migration, migratory**) When people **migrate,** they move from one place to another, often looking for work. **Migratory** is used to describe people who move around like this. *...migratory workers.* ■ **Migratory** birds and animals journey to a different area at the same time each year, to find food or breed. When they make this journey, you say they **migrate.**

mike A **mike** is a microphone.

mild (**mildly, mildness**) If something is **mild,** it is not strong and does not have any powerful effects. *...a mild sedative.* ■ **Mild** weather is warmer than usual. ■ **Mild** people are gentle and kind. ■ **Mild** means not very great or extreme. *...a mildly successful film.*

mildew is various types of powdery fungus which grow in warm damp places on things like plants, books, and cloth.

mild-mannered people are gentle and polite.

mile Distance is often expressed in **miles.** A mile is 1,760 yards (about 1.6 kilometres). 'Miles' is sometimes written 'm'.

mileage The **mileage** someone covers is the distance they travel in miles. ■ The **mileage** you get out of something is what you gain from it.

mileometer A vehicle's **mileometer** is a device which shows how many miles it has travelled.

milestone If you say something is a **milestone,** you mean it represents an important stage in the history or development of something. ■ A **milestone** is a stone by the side of a road showing the distances to different places.

milieu (*plural:* **milieux**) (*both pron:* **meel**-yer) Your **milieu** is your surroundings and the people you live or work with.

militancy (**militant, militantly**) **Militancy** is the behaviour and attitudes of people who try to bring about political or social change using forceful methods which other people find unacceptable. You call methods like these **militant;** you say the people who use them are **militants.**

militarised See **militarized.**

militarism (**militarist, militaristic**) **Militarism** is a policy of having powerful armed forces and using them to threaten other countries. People who sup-

port this policy are called **militarists;** you say their ideas are **militarist** or **militaristic.**

militarized (*or* **militarised**) (**militarization**) A **militarized** place has members of the armed forces and their equipment in it.

military (**militarily**) **Military** means to do with a country's armed forces. *...France's military strength... The administration is adamant that America will not intervene militarily.* ■ The **military** are the armed forces of a country.

militate (**militating, militated**) If something **militates against** something else, it makes it less likely to happen or succeed.

militia (**militiaman, militiamen**) A **militia** is an armed force made up of people who live in an area, and who can be called on to fight if necessary. Its members are called **militiamen.**

milk (**milky**) **Milk** is the white liquid produced by cows, goats, and ewes, which people drink and make into butter, cheese, and yoghurt. If you **milk** one of these animals, you get milk from it by pulling its udders. ■ **Milky** food or drink contains a lot of milk. ■ **Milk** is the white liquid from a woman's breasts which babies drink. ■ If something is **milky,** it is the colour of milk. ■ If someone **milks** a situation or place, they get as much personal gain from it as possible.

milk float A **milk float** is a small electric van for delivering milk to people's houses.

milkman (**milkmen**) A **milkman** is a person who delivers milk to people's houses.

milk round A **milk round** is the houses a milkman delivers milk to each day. ■ The **milk round** is the yearly series of interviews conducted by large companies wishing to recruit graduates.

milkshake (*or* **milk shake**) A **milkshake** is a cold drink made by mixing milk with flavouring and sometimes with ice-cream, then whisking it.

milk tooth A child's **milk teeth** are their first set of teeth.

Milky Way The **Milky Way** is the pale strip of light consisting of many stars which stretches across the sky at night.

mill A **mill** is a building where grain is crushed to make flour. ■ Various kinds of factories are called **mills,** for example steel mills. ■ **Milled** pepper has been ground using a device called a **pepper mill** or a pestle. ■ When a crowd of people **mill around** or **mill about,** they move around aimlessly.

millennium (*plural:* **millennia** *or* **millenniums**) A **millennium** is a period of one thousand years. ■ People sometimes call the year 2000 the **millennium.**

miller A **miller** is a person or firm that makes flour in a mill.

millet is a tall grass cultivated for its edible seeds or for hay.

milli- at the beginning of a unit of measurement means it is one thousandth of a larger unit.

millibar Atmospheric pressure is usually expressed in **millibars.** A millibar is one thousandth of a bar (or 100 newtons per square metre). 'Millibars' is usually written 'mb'.

milligram (*or* **milligramme**) Very small weights are often expressed in **milligrams.** A milligram is one thousandth of a gram. 'Milligrams' is usually written 'mg'.

millilitre (*Am:* **milliliter**) Volume is sometimes expressed in **millilitres.** A millilitre is one thousandth of a litre. 'Millilitres' is usually written 'ml'.

millimetre (*Am:* **millimeter**) Small lengths are often expressed in **millimetres.** A millimetre is one thousandth of a metre. 'Millimetres' is usually written 'mm'.

milliner (**millinery**) A **milliner** makes or sells women's hats. **Millinery** is making hats, or the hats made or sold by a milliner.

million (**millionth**) A **million** is the number 1,000,000.

millionaire (**millionairess, millionairesses**) A **millionaire** is a person who has money, investments, or property worth at least a million pounds or dollars. A female millionaire is sometimes called a **millionairess.**

millipede A **millipede** is a creature with a long thin body divided into many segments, each with two pairs of legs.

millstone A **millstone** is a problem or responsibility which makes it difficult for you to do the things you want to. ■ Originally, **millstones** were two large flat round stones used to grind grain into flour.

mime (**miming, mimed**) Mime is the use of movements and gestures to express something or tell a story without using speech. ■ If you **mime** something, you describe or express it using movements and gestures. ■ You say people **mime** when they pretend to be singing or playing a musical instrument, when the music is in fact coming from a recording.

mimic (**mimicking, mimicked; mimicry**) If you **mimic** someone's actions or voice, you imitate them in an amusing way. Imitating people like this is called **mimicry.** Someone who does it well is called a **mimic.** ■ If something **mimics** something else, it has the same characteristics and behaviour.

min is short for 'minute' or 'minutes'.

minaret (*pron:* min-ar-**ret**) A **minaret** is a tall slender tower which is part of a mosque.

mince (**mincer; mincing, minced**) Mince is meat cut into very small pieces by a device called a **mincer.** If you **mince** meat, you cut it up using a mincer. ■ If you say someone **minces** somewhere, you mean they walk with small quick steps. ■ If you **do not mince your words,** you say what you think in a straightforward way, without worrying about upsetting people.

mincemeat is a sticky mixture of dried fruit, apples, sugar, and suet. ■ When Americans talk about **mincemeat,** they usually mean minced meat. ■ If you **make mincemeat** of someone, you defeat them easily and completely in a contest.

mince pie A **mince pie** is a small pie containing mincemeat.

mind (**-minded**) Your **mind** is your ability to think, reason, and imagine things. ■ If something is **on your mind,** you are worried about it and think

about it a lot. ■ You say, for example, that you are **in two minds** about something or that you have **made up your mind** about it to talk about a decision that you need to make or have made. ■ You use **mind** in expressions such as **to my mind** or to **speak your mind** when you mean that you are giving your opinion about something. ■ If you do not **mind** something, you do not object to it. ■ You say **never mind** (a) to indicate that something is not important. *Never mind, it's only money.* (b) when you have talked about something not being achieved and you are going on to mention something even harder to achieve. *Many young people in Wales cannot afford their first home, never mind a second.* ■ If you **mind** something for someone, you look after it for them. ■ **-minded** can be added to words to describe a person's character, attitude, or aims. *...single-minded.* *...liberal-minded.* *...career-minded.* ■ See also **state of mind.**

mind- is used with various words to say something is so extreme it is difficult to take in. *...a mind-blowing array of treatments. ...a mind-boggling £286m.*

minder A **minder** is (a) someone who looks after a person who cannot look after himself or herself. (b) someone whose job is to protect an important person.

mindful If you are **mindful** of something, you are aware of it and take account of it when you do something.

mindless You say a destructive action is **mindless** when there seems to be no reason for it.

mind-numbing See **numb.**

mind-set If you talk about someone's **mind-set,** you mean their fixed way of looking at things.

mine (**mining, mined; miner**) You use **mine** to talk about things to do with yourself, or things belonging to you. *...a friend of mine... The only raised voice was mine.* ■ A **mine** is a place where people dig deep holes or tunnels to get coal, diamonds, or other minerals out of the ground. When minerals are **mined,** they are got out in this way; the industry concerned is called **mining.** A **miner** works down a mine. ■ A **mine** is a bomb hidden in the ground or floating on water, which explodes when touched. If a place is **mined,** mines are planted there.

minefield A **minefield** is an area of land or water where mines have been laid. ■ If you say a situation is a **minefield,** you mean it is full of hidden dangers or problems.

mineral – Minerals are substances such as tin, salt, uranium, or sulphur, which are formed naturally in rocks and in the earth. Minerals are also found in small quantities in food and drink.

mineralogy (**mineralogist**) **Mineralogy** is the scientific study of minerals. A **mineralogist** is an expert on this.

mineral water is water which contains dissolved mineral salts.

minestrone is a soup containing small pieces of vegetables and pasta.

minesweeper A **minesweeper** is a ship used to clear away mines.

mingle (**mingling, mingled**) If things like sounds, smells, or feelings **mingle,** you get several of them at the same time. ■ If you **mingle,** you move around at a party, chatting to people.

mini See **miniskirt.**

mini- at the beginning of a word means it is a small version of something. *...a mini-submarine.*

miniature (**miniaturist**) A **miniature** version of something is much smaller than usual. ■ A **miniature** is a very small detailed painting, often of a person. An artist who paints miniatures is called a **miniaturist.**

miniaturize (*or* **miniaturise**) (**miniaturizing, miniaturized; miniaturization**) When a product is **miniaturized,** very small versions of it are made.

minibus (*or* **mini-bus**) (**minibuses**) A **minibus** is a van with seats in the back, used as a small bus.

minicab A **minicab** is an ordinary car used as a taxi.

minim A **minim** is a musical note with the same time value as two crotchets.

minimal (**minimally**) **Minimal** means as little as possible. *It requires minimal effort. ...a minimally-equipped kitchen.* ■ A **minimal** amount of something is very small.

minimalism (**minimalist**) **Minimalism** is an artistic movement which aims to show everything in as simple a form as possible. **Minimalist** art or music is produced by artists or musicians called **minimalists.**

minimize (*or* **minimise**) (**minimizing, minimized**) If you **minimize** something, you reduce it to the lowest level possible. *Many of these problems can be minimized by sensible planning.* ■ You say you **minimize** something when you make it seem smaller or less important than it really is. *It would be in their interests to minimize their differences.*

minimum The **minimum** of something is the smallest amount possible or necessary.

mining See **mine.**

minion If you talk about a person's **minions,** you mean people with low status who carry out their orders for them.

mini-series A **mini-series** is a TV drama in parts, shown on consecutive days or weeks.

miniskirt (*or* **mini-skirt**) A **miniskirt** or **mini** is a very short skirt.

minister (**ministering, ministered**) A **minister** is a person in charge of a government department. ■ A **minister** is a member of the clergy in a Nonconformist church. ■ If a member of the clergy **ministers** to a community or congregation, he or she conducts religious services for them. ■ If you **minister** to someone's needs, you make sure they have everything they need or want.

ministerial means to do with a government minister or ministry. *...ministerial approval.*

ministrations A person's **ministrations** are the things they do to help someone.

ministry (**ministries**) A **ministry** is a government department. ■ The **ministry** of a member of the clergy is the work they do. ■ Members of the clergy in some Christian churches are called the **ministry.**

mink (*plural:* **mink** *or* **minks**) **Mink** are small furry animals. Their fur, which is called **mink,** is used to make articles of clothing.

minnow – **Minnows** are very small freshwater fish.

minor things are not as important, serious, or significant as other things of the same kind. ■ A **minor** is a person who is still legally a child. In Britain, young people are minors until the age of 18.

minority (**minorities**) If you talk about a **minority** of the people or things in a group, you mean less than half the whole group. ■ A **minority** is a group of people of a particular race or religion who live in a place where most of the people are of another race or religion. *...the country's white minority.*

minster A number of large churches and cathedrals are called **minsters.**

minstrel In medieval times, a **minstrel** was a singer and musician who used to travel round performing for noble families.

mint is a type of herb used in cooking. ■ A **mint** is a peppermint flavoured sweet. ■ When a country's coins or medals are **minted,** they are made in a building called a **mint.** ■ If something is in **mint** condition, it is in very good condition, as if it was new.

minus (**minuses**) You use **minus** to show one number is being subtracted from another. You represent this in figures as (–), as for example in '5 – 3'. The sign between the 5 and 3 is called a **minus sign.** ■ **Minus** is used to show a number is less than zero. *The temperature often falls to minus 20.* ■ You use **minus** to talk about the absence of something. *A neighbour who swapped his GTI for a diesel swears he gets there just as quickly, minus the stress.*

minuscule If something is **minuscule,** it is very small indeed.

minute (**minutely**) A **minute** is one of the sixty equal parts of an hour. ■ The **minutes** of a meeting are the written records of what is said and decided. ■ If something is **minute** (*pron:* my-**newt**), it is extremely small. ■ In a **minute** examination or study, great attention is paid to every detail. *The Americans will scrutinize this proposal minutely.*

minutiae (*pron:* my-**new**-shee-eye) The **minutiae** of something like a system are its small details.

miracle (**miraculous, miraculously**) If something very surprising and fortunate happens, you can call it a **miracle** or say it is **miraculous.** ■ When people with strong religious beliefs talk about a **miracle,** they mean a surprising and wonderful event caused by God.

mirage A **mirage** is an image which you see in the distance in very hot weather, and which appears to be close but is actually a long way away or does not really exist.

mire (**mired**) You call an unpleasant situation a **mire** when any attempt to get out of it seems to fail or make things worse. You can talk about people being **mired** in an unpleasant situation.

mirror (**mirroring, mirrored**) A **mirror** is a piece of glass with a metallic backing in which you can see your reflection. ■ If something is **mirrored** in water or a shiny surface, you see it reflected in it. ■ If something is a **mirror image** of something else, it is identical to it, but the other way round. ■ If one thing **mirrors** another, it reproduces many of its features, and seems like a copy of it. *His own shock was mirrored on her face.*

mirth is amusement or laughter.

mis- is used to form words which describe things being done badly or wrongly. *...a serious misallocation of resources.*

misadventure A **misadventure** is something unfortunate which happens to someone. *...death by misadventure.*

misanthrope (**misanthropic, misanthropy**) A **misanthrope** is someone who does not like other people. You talk about the **misanthropy** of someone like this or say they are **misanthropic.**

misanthropist A **misanthropist** is the same as a misanthrope.

misapply (**misapplies, misapplying, misapplied; misapplication**) If you **misapply** something, you use it in a way it is not meant to be used. *The report accused them of misapplication of funds.*

misapprehension If you are under a **misapprehension** about something, you have a wrong idea or impression about it.

misappropriate (**misappropriating, misappropriated; misappropriation**) If someone **misappropriates** money or other valuable things, they take them and use them for their own purposes. *The promotions director has been charged with misappropriation of funds.*

miscalculate (**miscalculating, miscalculated; miscalculation**) If you **miscalculate** or make a **miscalculation,** you make a mistake in judging a situation.

miscarriage If a woman has a **miscarriage,** she gives birth to a foetus before it is properly formed and it dies. ■ If there is a **miscarriage of justice,** a wrong decision is given by a court, with the result that an innocent person is punished.

miscarry (**miscarries, miscarrying, miscarried**) If a woman **miscarries,** she has a miscarriage.

miscast If you say an actor or actress is **miscast,** you mean they are playing a role which is not suitable for them.

miscellaneous (*pron:* miss-sell-**lane**-ee-uss) A **miscellaneous** group is made up of people or things of different kinds.

miscellany (*pron:* miss-**sell**-a-nee) A **miscellany** is a collection of things which are different from each other.

mischievous (**mischievously; mischief**) If you call something a person does **mischievous,** you mean it is intended to cause trouble. Causing trouble like this is called **mischief;** the trouble caused is also called **mischief.** ■ You say someone, especially a child, is **mischievous** when they are eager to have fun, especially by playing tricks. Eagerness to have fun can be called **mischief.** *She is rarely still, her eyes perpetually dancing with mischief.*

misconceived A **misconceived** plan is based on a mistake and is not likely to succeed.

misconception A **misconception** is a wrong idea about something.

misconduct is bad or unacceptable behaviour, especially by a professional person.

misconstrue (**misconstruing, misconstrued**) If you **misconstrue** something which happens or is said, you interpret it wrongly.

miscreant (*pron:* **miss**-kree-ant) A **miscreant** is someone who has done something wrong, especially a criminal.

misdeed A **misdeed** is a bad or evil act.

misdemeanour (*Am:* **misdemeanor**) A **misdemeanour** is an act some people consider to be shocking or unacceptable. ■ In countries where the legal system distinguishes between very serious crimes and less serious ones, a **misdemeanour** is a less serious one.

misdirect (**misdirection**) If you say someone's energies are **misdirected,** you mean they are used wrongly or inappropriately. Similarly, public money or other resources can be **misdirected.** *It would be a horrible misdirection of scarce government resources.* ■ If something is **misdirected,** it is sent to the wrong place.

miser A **miser** is someone who enjoys saving money and hates spending it.

miserable (**miserably**) If you are **miserable,** you are depressed. You call something which makes you feel like this **miserable.** *...two days of miserable weather.* ■ You say someone is **miserable** when they are bad-tempered or unfriendly. ■ You describe something as **miserable** when it is disappointing. *The Tories trailed in a miserable third.*

miserly (**miserliness**) A **miserly** person enjoys saving money and hates spending it. ■ A **miserly** amount of something is very small. *...miserly grants.*

misery (**miseries**) Misery is great unhappiness. **Miseries** are unhappy experiences. ■ If you **put** an animal **out of its misery,** you kill it because it is fatally ill or injured. ■ If you **put** a person **out of their misery,** you tell them something they are very anxious to know.

misfire (**misfiring, misfired**) If a plan **misfires,** it goes wrong. ■ If a gun **misfires,** it fails to go off when fired. ■ If an engine **misfires,** the fuel does not ignite when it is started.

misfit A **misfit** is a person who is not easily accepted by other people, because their behaviour or beliefs are different from everyone else's.

misfortune Your **misfortunes** are the bad things which happen to you. *She had the misfortune to be pregnant by another man.*

misgiving If you have **misgivings** about something, you are worried or unhappy about it.

misguided If you say someone's behaviour is **misguided,** you mean they are doing the wrong thing, because they have not understood the situation they are dealing with.

mishandle (**mishandling, mishandled**) If you **mishandle** something, you deal with it badly.

mishap A **mishap** is a minor accident.

mish-mash (*or* mishmash) A **mish-mash** is a confused mixture of things.

misinform (**misinformation**) If you are **misinformed** about something, you are given wrong information about it. Wrong information is called **misinformation.** See also **disinformation.**

misinterpret (**misinterpreting, misinterpreted; misinterpretation**) If you **misinterpret** something, you understand it wrongly.

misjudge (**misjudging, misjudged; misjudgment** or **misjudgement**) If you **misjudge** someone or something, you form an inaccurate opinion of them, and often make a wrong decision as a result. Getting something wrong like this is called a **misjudgment.**

mislay (**mislaying, mislaid**) If you have **mislaid** something, you cannot remember where you have left it.

mislead (**misleading, misled; misleadingly**) If you **mislead** someone, you get them to believe something which is untrue. *...a misleadingly high figure.*

mismanage (**mismanaging, mismanaged; mismanagement**) If a system or organization is **mismanaged,** it is managed badly or dishonestly.

misnomer A **misnomer** is a word or phrase which describes someone or something incorrectly.

misogyny (*pron:* miss-**soj**-i-nee) (**misogynist, misogynistic**) Misogyny is hatred of women. A **misogynist** is a man who hates women. You say men like this are **misogynistic.**

misplaced A **misplaced** feeling is inappropriate, or directed towards the wrong person or thing.

misprint A **misprint** is a printing error.

misquote (**misquoting, misquoted**) If you **misquote** what someone has said or written, you repeat it inaccurately.

misread (**misreading, misread**) If you **misread** a situation or a person's behaviour, you do not understand it properly and often make a wrong decision as a result. A wrong understanding of a situation can be called a **misreading** of it. ■ If you **misread** a piece of writing, you think it says something which it does not say.

misrepresent (**misrepresentation**) If you **misrepresent** a person or what they say, you give a misleading or inaccurate account of what they say. An account like this is called a **misrepresentation.**

misrule (**misruling, misruled**) If a country is **misruled,** it is badly or inefficiently governed. **Misrule** is bad or inefficient government.

miss (**misses, missing, missed**) If you **miss** something you are trying to hit, you fail to hit it. A failure to hit or catch something is called a **miss.** ■ If you **miss** a bus, train, or plane, you fail to catch it. ■ If you **miss** a chance, you fail to take advantage of it. ■ If you **miss out** on something worth having, you do not get it when other people do. ■ If you **miss** something, you fail to notice or understand it. *You're missing my point.* ■ If you **miss** something **out,** you do not include it in what you say or do. ■ If you **miss** someone or something, you feel sad because you no longer see that person or have that thing. ■ You say you **miss** someone when you notice they are not where you expect them to be. *No-one had missed us yet at home.* ■ **Miss** is used in front of a girl's or unmarried woman's name. ■ **near miss:** see **near.** See also **missing.**

misshapen If something is **misshapen,** it is an unusual and unattractive shape.

missile A **missile** is a weapon which travels long distances and explodes when it reaches its target. ■ Anything thrown as a weapon can be called a **missile.** *...a shower of stones, bricks, and other missiles.*

missing If something is **missing,** it is not there. ■ You say something is **missing** when nobody has been able to find it. *...Casey's missing passport.* ■ A **missing** person has disappeared completely and nobody knows where they are. ■ The **missing link** is a theoretical creature, half-ape and half-human, whose existence is necessary to support the theory of evolution.

mission A **mission** is an important task someone is given to do, especially one which involves travelling abroad. A group of people given a task like this can also be called a **mission.** *A trade mission will visit Britain in September.* ■ A **mission** is a journey made by a military aircraft or space rocket for a particular purpose. ■ If you have a **mission,** you have a task which you feel it is your duty to carry out. ■ A **mission** is (a) the activities of a group of Christians who have been sent to a place to teach people about Christianity. (b) the building or buildings they live and work in.

missionary (**missionaries**) A **missionary** is a Christian who has been sent to a foreign country to try and convert people to Christianity.

missive A **missive** is a letter.

misspend (**misspending, misspent**) If money or someone's time is **misspent,** it is wasted or used inappropriately.

mist is tiny drops of water suspended in the air. ■ If a piece of glass **mists over** or **mists up,** it becomes covered in drops of moisture.

mistake (**mistaking, mistook, have mistaken**) If you make a **mistake,** you do something you did not intend to, or something which produces a result you did not want. ■ If you **mistake** one person or thing for another, you wrongly think they are the other person or thing.

mistaken (**mistakenly**) If you are **mistaken** about something, you are wrong. A **mistaken** belief or decision is an incorrect one. *Some of the crew mistakenly believed the ship was under attack.* ■ If someone thinks they recognize a person, but it turns out to be a different person, you call this a case of **mistaken identity.**

mister See **Mr.**

mistime (**mistiming, mistimed**) If you **mistime** something, you do it at the wrong time and it does not have the effect you want.

mistletoe is an evergreen plant with white berries which grows on trees and is traditionally used in Britain as a Christmas decoration.

mistreat (**mistreating, mistreated; mistreatment**) If someone **mistreats** a person or animal, they treat them badly.

mistress (**mistresses**) A married man's **mistress** is a woman who is not his wife and who he is having a sexual relationship with.

mistrial A **mistrial** is a trial which has been declared void because of some error in procedure.

mistrust (**mistrustful**) If you **mistrust** someone or something or are **mistrustful** of them, you do not trust them. **Mistrust** is the feeling you have about someone you do not trust.

misty If it is **misty,** there is a lot of mist in the air.

misty-eyed If you say someone is **misty-eyed,** you mean they are very emotional about something, and seem about to cry.

misunderstand (**misunderstanding, misunderstood**) If you **misunderstand** something someone says or does, you do not understand it properly. *There has been some misunderstanding of our publishing aims.* ■ If two people have a **misunderstanding,** they have a minor disagreement.

misuse (**misusing, misused**) If you **misuse** something (*pron:* miss-**yewz**), you use it incorrectly, carelessly, or dishonestly. When something is wrongly used, you talk about its **misuse** (*pron:* miss-**yewss**). *...the misuse of power.*

mite – A **mite** means 'a bit' or 'rather'. *I admit to feeling a mite insulted.* ■ **Mites** are microscopic creatures which live in places such as the fur of animals.

miter See **mitre.**

mitigate (**mitigating, mitigated; mitigation**) If the bad effects of something are **mitigated,** they are made less unpleasant or serious. ■ **Mitigating** circumstances are circumstances which partly explain why a crime was committed. They are told to the court in the hope that the person who committed the crime will get a lighter punishment. You say things like these are told to the court **in mitigation.**

mitre (*Am:* **miter**) A **mitre** is a tall crown worn by bishops and archbishops on ceremonial occasions.

mitten – **Mittens** are gloves which have one section for all your fingers and another for your thumb.

mix (**mixes, mixing, mixed**) When two or more things are **mixed,** they are combined. *Designers are mixing loose and tight clothing in new ways.* A **mix** is a combination of two or more things. ■ **Mixed** is used to talk about a combination of good and bad things. *The two newcomers had mixed fortunes.* ■ **Mixed** means involving two or more races or religions or both males and females. *In 1945 one-tenth of its marriages were mixed; now it is one in three... He found himself playing against a mixed students' soccer eleven.* ■ If you **mix** with other people, you meet them socially. ■ If you say someone is **mixed up** in something bad or with someone you disapprove of, you mean they are involved in or with them. ■ If you **mix up** two things or people, you confuse them and think one is the other. If someone is **mixed up,** they are confused. ■ If things get **mixed up,** they get out of order. ■ When people **mix** a recording, they blend several sound tracks, such as the singing and the backing, to make a single balanced track. A **mix** is a particular production of a recording.

mixer A **mixer** is a machine for mixing things together. *...a cement mixer.* ■ A **mixer** is a soft drink such as tonic, used to dilute an alcoholic drink.

mixture A **mixture** of different things is several of them together. *United Airlines is unusual in having a mixture of European and American cabin crew.* ■ A **mixture** is a substance made up of other substances shaken or stirred together.

mix-up A **mix-up** is a mistake which happens because of a misunderstanding or bad organization.

ml See **millilitre.**

mm See **millimetre.**

mnemonic (*pron:* ni-**mon**-ik) A **mnemonic** is a word, phrase, or rhyme which helps you remember something like a scientific law or spelling rule. For example, 'i before e except after c' is a mnemonic to help people remember how to spell words like 'believe' and 'receive'.

MO An **MO** is a doctor who works in the armed forces. MO stands for 'medical officer'.

moan (**moaning, moaned; moaner**) When people **moan** about something, they complain about it. You call their complaints **moans.** Someone who complains a lot can be called a **moaner.** ■ A **moan** is a low miserable sound made by someone who is unhappy or in pain. If someone **moans,** they make a sound like this.

moat (**moated**) A **moat** is a deep wide water-filled ditch round a fort or castle for protection.

mob (**mobbing, mobbed**) A **mob** is a disorganized, often violent crowd of people. ■ If a crowd **mobs** someone, they crowd round them in a disorderly way. ■ In the US, the **mob** is the Mafia.

mobile (**mobility**) You use **mobile** when you are talking about someone's ability to move around. *The Pakistani was much more mobile than his opponent.* ■ If you are **mobile,** you are able to travel or move to another place. *...a mobile workforce.* See also **upwardly mobile.** ■ **Mobile** is used to describe facilities like libraries when they are based in a van which can be driven around from place to place. ■ A **mobile** is a mobile phone. ■ A **mobile** is a light structure which hangs from the ceiling as a decoration and moves gently in the air.

mobile home A **mobile home** is a large caravan for people to live in. It can be towed around, but usually remains in one place.

mobile phone (*or* **mobile**) A **mobile phone** is a portable phone which uses radio waves to transmit signals instead of wires.

mobilize (*or* **mobilise**) (**mobilizing, mobilized; mobilization**) If you **mobilize** a group of people, you organize them to do something. *Health brigades were being mobilized to try and prevent the spreading of the disease.* ■ If you **mobilize** resources, you make them available for a particular task. ■ When a country **mobilizes,** it prepares for war.

mobster In the US, a **mobster** is a member of a violent criminal organization.

moccasin – **Moccasins** are soft leather shoes with low heels and a raised seam round the top.

mock (**mocking, mockingly; mockery**) If you **mock** someone, you make fun of them, unkindly. This sort of behaviour is called **mockery.** ■ **Mock** is used to describe things which are an imitation or pretence, rather than the real thing. *...mock Gothic. ...a mock execution.*

mock-up A **mock-up** of a structure or machine is a model of it made for a special purpose, such as to perform tests.

MOD The **MOD** or **Ministry of Defence** is the government department which deals with things connected with the defence of the United Kingdom.

mod In the 1960s and 1970s, **mods** were young people who wore smart clothes, rode motor-scooters, and liked soul music.

mod cons If a house has all **mod cons,** it has all the facilities which make it pleasant and comfortable to live in.

mode A **mode** is a particular way of doing something. *...the capitalist mode of production.* ■ If a device is in a particular **mode,** it is ready to operate in a particular way. *...when the camera is in manual mode.* ■ A **mode** is a style in art, literature, or fashion. *...a building in Byzantine mode.*

model (**modelling, modelled**) (*Am:* **modeling, modeled**) A **model** is a three-dimensional copy of something that shows what the original looks like or how it works. ■ If you **model** shapes or figures, you make them out of a substance like clay or plasticine. ■ A **model** of a system or process is a theoretical representation which helps you understand how it works, or predicts its effects. *Geophysicists are modelling in the lab what actually happens in an earthquake.* ■ If you **model** yourself or your behaviour on someone you admire, you copy them. ■ **role model:** see **role.** ■ If you say someone or something is a **model** of a particular quality, you mean they have that quality to a high degree. *His approach has been a model of diplomacy.* A perfect example of something can also be called a **model.** *...a model pupil.* ■ A **model** is someone who poses for an artist or photographer. You say someone like this **models** for the artist or photographer. ■ A **model** is someone whose job is to display clothes by wearing them. You say he or she **models** clothes. ■ A **model** of something like a car is a particular version of it.

modem (*pron:* **moe**-dem) A **modem** is an electronic device which allows data to be sent from one computer to another using telephone lines.

moderate (**moderating, moderated; moderately**) **Moderate** behaviour or views are not extreme. *People who drink moderately have less heart disease.* Politicians who hold moderate views are called **moderates.** ■ If something **moderates** (*pron:* **mod**-er-ates) it becomes less extreme. *The wind moderated.* ■ A **moderate** amount of something is neither large nor small.

moderation is self-control and restraint. ■ If you do something **in moderation,** you do not do it too much. *Exercise is good in moderation.*

moderator In Protestant churches, a **moderator** is a minister appointed to take charge at important church meetings. ■ A **moderator** is someone who helps people settle their disputes.

modern (**modernity**) **Modern** is used to describe things which exist or happen now, rather than in the past. *...modern industrial relations.* ■ **Modern** is used to describe things which make use of the latest ideas or technology. *...a modern railway system.* You talk about the **modernity** of things like these. ■ People are sometimes described as **modern** when they have opinions which are ahead of those of other people. *...her modern views on sexual equality.*

modern-day is used to refer to the new or modern aspects of a place, an activity, or a society. *...modern-day photography. ...a modern-day gold rush.*

modernise See **modernize.**

modernism (**modernist**) **Modernism** was an early 20th-century movement in the arts which moved away from traditional subject areas and means of expression, using artistic form and language to express intellectual and emotional states of mind.

modernity See **modern.**

modernize (*or* **modernise**) (**modernizing, modernized; modernization**) When something like a system or factory is **modernized,** new methods or equipment are introduced into it.

modern languages You can refer to the modern European languages such as French and German as **modern languages,** especially when considering them as subjects studied at school or university.

modest (**modestly, modesty**) If something is **modest,** it is quite small. *...a modest improvement.* ■ If you are **modest,** you do not boast about yourself. When someone is like this, you can talk about their **modesty.** ■ If you describe a woman as **modest,** you mean she avoids doing or wearing anything to arouse men's sexual feelings towards her. When women behave like this, you can talk about their **modesty.**

modicum A **modicum** of something is a small amount of it.

modify (**modifies, modifying, modified; modification**) If you **modify** something, you improve it by making a slight change to it. The change is called a **modification.**

modish (*pron:* **moe**-dish) If something is **modish,** it is fashionable.

modular See **module.**

modulate (**modulating, modulated; modulation**) If you **modulate** your voice, you vary the way it sounds according to the effect you want to create. ■ If you **modulate** an activity or process, you alter it, to make it more suitable to a particular set of circumstances.

module (**modular**) A **module** is one of a number of standard parts fitted together to form a structure. A **modular** structure is put together in this way. ■ A **module** is part of a machine or system, which performs a particular function. ■ Some university or college courses consist of separate units called **modules.** A **modular** course is made up of units like these.

modus operandi (*pron:* mode-uss op-per-**and**-die) A **modus operandi** is a way of doing something.

modus vivendi (*pron:* mode-uss vie-**ven**-die) If people with different beliefs or attitudes find an acceptable way of living or working together, you can say they establish a **modus vivendi.**

mogul The **Moguls** were Muslim rulers in India in the 16th to 18th centuries. ■ A **mogul** is a rich and powerful businessman, especially one in the film or TV industry.

mohair is a kind of soft wool from Angora goats.

moist If something is **moist,** it is slightly wet.

moisten (moistening, moistened) If you **moisten** something, you make it slightly wet.

moisture consists of tiny drops of water in the air or on a surface.

moisturize (or **moisturise**) **(moisturizing, moisturized; moisturizer)** If you **moisturize** your skin, you put a cream called a **moisturizer** on it, to soften it.

molar Your **molars** are the large teeth at the back of your mouth.

molasses is a sweet thick dark brown syrup produced when sugar is refined.

mold See **mould.**

molder See **moulder.**

mole A **mole** is a natural dark spot on your skin. ■ The **mole** is a small black furry animal which lives in tunnels underground. The small piles of earth left by moles digging are called molehills. ■ A member of an organization who secretly reveals information can be called a **mole.**

molecule (pron: **moll**-lik-yule) **(molecular)** A **molecule** is the smallest amount of a chemical substance which can exist without breaking apart into other substances. **Molecular** (pron: moll-**lek**-you-lar) means to do with molecules.

molest (molestation, molester) If a person **molests** someone, they touch them in a sexual way against their will. Behaviour like this is called **molestation;** a person who does it is called a **molester.**

moll A gangster's **moll** is his girlfriend.

mollify (mollifies, mollifying, mollified) If you **mollify** someone, you make them less upset or angry.

mollusc A **mollusc** is an animal like a snail, slug, clam, or octopus, which has a soft body and no backbone. Many molluscs have hard shells.

Molotov cocktail A **Molotov cocktail** is a petrol bomb.

molt See **moult.**

molten rock or metal has been heated to a very high temperature and has become a hot thick liquid.

molybdenum (pron: mol-**lib**-din-um) is a very hard silvery-white metallic element. It is used in alloys, especially to harden and strengthen steel.

mom See **mum.**

moment A **moment** is a very short period of time. ■ A **moment** is a particular point in time. *Many people still remember the moment when they heard that President Kennedy had been assassinated.* ■ If you say something will happen **in a moment,** you mean it will happen very soon. ■ If something is happening **at the moment,** it is happening now. ■ If you say a problem has been dealt with **for the moment,** you mean it has been dealt with temporarily. ■ If you say something happens **the moment** something else happens, you are emphasizing it happens immediately after the other thing. *The moment he arrived in Japan he fell in love with it.*

momentarily If something happens **momentarily,** it happens for only a short time. ■ In the US, mo-

mentarily is used to say something will happen soon. *We are expecting a statement from him momentarily.*

momentary If something is **momentary,** it lasts for only a short time.

momentous A **momentous** event is a very important one.

momentum If a process or movement gains **momentum,** it steadily increases. ■ **Momentum** is the ability of a moving object to keep moving because of the speed it already has.

monarch (monarchical) A **monarch** is a reigning queen or king. **Monarchical** means to do with a monarch.

monarchist A **monarchist** is a person who thinks their country should have a monarch.

monarchy (monarchies) The **monarchy** is a country's royal family. ■ A **monarchy** is (a) a system in which a monarch reigns over a country. (b) a country which has a king or queen.

monastery (monasteries) A **monastery** is a building where monks live.

monastic (monasticism) **Monastic** means to do with monks or monasteries. *...a monastic community.* **Monasticism** is the system of having monasteries.

monetarism (monetarist) **Monetarism** is the control of a country's economy by regulating the total amount of money which is available and in use. A **monetarist** is someone who favours this policy. **Monetarist** means to do with monetarism.

monetary means to do with money, especially the finances of a country.

money (monies) **Money** is coins and bank notes or the sum you have in a bank account. ■ **Monies** is sometimes used to refer to separate sums of money forming part of a larger amount. *...a substantial reduction in monies available for other services.*

money-box A child's **money-box** is a small box for saving coins in.

money changer A **money changer** is a person who converts money from one currency to another, often illegally.

moneyed people have a lot of money.

moneylender (or **money-lender**) A **moneylender** is a person who lends money to people and charges a high rate of interest.

money market A country's **money market** consists of its commercial banks and all other institutions including the government which deal with short-term loans and foreign exchange.

moneymen (or **money men**) You can talk about the people who deal with an organization's finances as **moneymen.**

money order In Canada and the US, a **money order** is a postal order.

money-spinner (money-spinning) If an activity or event is a **money-spinner,** it makes a lot of money for someone.

mongoose — Mongooses are stoat-like animals from Africa and Asia which kill snakes.

mongrel A **mongrel** is a dog with parents of different breeds.

monies See **money.**

monitor (**monitoring, monitored**) If you **monitor** something, you regularly check its condition. ■ If someone **monitors** radio broadcasts, they record them or listen carefully to them to get information. ■ A **monitor** is a machine used to check or record things. ■ A person who checks that something is done correctly can be called a **monitor.** ■ The visual display unit of a computer is sometimes called a **monitor.**

monk A **monk** is a member of a male religious community.

monkey – **Monkeys** are long-tailed tree-climbing animals which live mainly in hot countries.

monkey nut – Monkey nuts are peanuts.

mono (**mono-**) On a **mono** recording or sound system, all the sound is directed through one speaker. ■ **Mono** or **mono-** is used at the beginning of other words to mean 'one' or 'single'. ...*mono-unsaturates.* ...*monolingual dictionaries.*

monochrome A **monochrome** painting is done using various shades of only one colour. ■ **Monochrome** film is in black and white.

monocle A **monocle** is a glass lens worn in front of one eye only.

monoculture A **monoculture** is an agricultural system producing only one type of crop.

monogamy (*pron:* mon-**nog**-a-mee) (**monogamous**) **Monogamy** is the state or custom of having only one sexual partner. A **monogamous** person or animal has only one sexual partner at a time. See also **polygamy.**

monogram (**monogrammed**) A **monogram** is a design based on someone's initials which is used to mark the things they own.

monograph A **monograph** is a book which is a detailed study of one subject.

monolith A **monolith** is a very large, upright block of stone, especially one erected in ancient times.

monolithic A **monolithic** building is very tall and featureless, like a monolith. ■ If you say an organization or system is **monolithic,** you mean it is very large and slow to change, with no distinct parts.

monologue A **monologue** is a long speech by one person.

monopolise See **monopolize.**

monopolistic If you refer to a business or its practices as **monopolistic,** you mean it tries to control as much of an industry as it can and does not allow fair competition.

monopolize (*or* monopolise) (**monopolizing, monopolized**) If someone **monopolizes** something, they control it completely and prevent other people from having a share in it.

monopoly (**monopolies**) If a person or a firm has a **monopoly** on something, they are in complete control or possession of it. *The party has relinquished its monopoly on power.* ■ A **monopoly** is a company which is the only provider of a particular product or service and therefore has complete control over what it offers or charges.

monorail A **monorail** is a system of transport in which trains travel along a single rail, usually high above the ground.

monosodium glutamate is a white crystalline substance added to food to make the flavours stronger.

monosyllable (**monosyllabic**) A **monosyllable** is a word with only one syllable, for example 'no' or 'why'. If someone is **monosyllabic,** they tend to talk in monosyllables.

monotheism (**monotheistic**) **Monotheism** is the belief that only one God exists. A **monotheistic** religion is founded on belief in only one God.

monotone If someone speaks in a **monotone,** the sound of their voice does not vary at all.

monotonous (**monotonously, monotony**) If you call something **monotonous,** you mean it is has no variety and is boring. You talk about the **monotony** of something like this.

Monsignor is the title of a priest of high rank in the Catholic Church.

monsoon The **monsoon** is the season of very heavy rain in Southern Asia.

monster A **monster** is a large frightening imaginary creature. ■ People sometimes call a cruel, frightening, or evil person a **monster.** ■ **Monster** is used to describe things which are extremely large.

monstrosity (**monstrosities**) You call something a **monstrosity** when it is large and very ugly.

monstrous (**monstrously**) A **monstrous** act is very cruel and shocking. ■ If you say something unpleasant is **monstrous,** you mean it is extremely large in size or extent. ...*a monstrous invasion of privacy.* ■ If you say an object is **monstrous,** you mean it is very large and ugly.

montage (*pron:* mon-**tazh**; *the 'zh' sounds like 's' in 'pleasure'*) A **montage** is a picture, film, or piece of music made up of several different elements.

month A **month** is one of the twelve periods a year is divided into.

monthly (**monthlies**) **Monthly** is used to describe something which happens every month. ...*monthly broadcasts... He paid monthly interest on the deal.* ■ A **monthly** is a magazine published once a month.

monument A **monument** is a large structure, put up as a memorial. ■ A **monument** is something like an old castle thought to be important because of its historical interest. ■ If you say something is a **monument to** something else, you mean it shows how important and powerful that thing is. *The average supermarket is a monument to the power of consumer choice.*

monumental (**monumentally**) A **monumental** building or work of art is very large and impressive. ■ You can use **monumental** to emphasize the size or extent of something. ... *a monumental task.*

mooch (**mooches, mooching, mooched**) If you **mooch** around, you wander around aimlessly.

mood Your **mood** is the way you feel at a particular time. ■ If you are in a **mood,** you are angry, sulking, or impatient. ■ The **mood** of a group of people is the way they feel or think about something.

moody (**moodily**) You say a person is **moody** (a) when their mood changes quickly and unpredictably. (b) when they are gloomy and depressed.

moon The **moon** is the object moving round the Earth which you see as a shining circle or crescent in the night sky. Some other planets have **moons.** ...*one of Jupiter's moons.*

moonbeam A **moonbeam** is a ray of light from the moon.

moonlight (**moonlit**) **Moonlight** is the light which shines from the moon. If something is **moonlit,** it is lit by moonlight. ■ If someone is **moonlighting,** they have a second job, often without informing their main employer or the tax office.

moonscape If you describe an area of land as a **moonscape,** you mean it looks desolate, like the surface of the moon.

moonshine is illegally distilled spirits. ■ **Moonshine** is foolish talk and ideas.

Moor (**Moorish**) The **Moors** were a Muslim people who established a civilization in North Africa and Spain between the 8th and 15th centuries. **Moorish** is used to describe things connected with these people and their culture.

moor (**mooring, moored**) A **moor** is an area of high open ground covered mainly with rough grass and heather. ■ If a boat is **moored,** it is tied up to something on land to stop it drifting away. A place where a boat can be tied up is called a **mooring.**

moorhen The **moorhen** is a water bird with black feathers and a red bill.

mooring See **moor.**

Moorish See **Moor.**

moorland is land consisting of moors.

moose (*plural:* **moose**) is the North American name for an elk.

moot (**mooting, mooted**) If you say something is **moot** or a **moot point,** you mean it is open to doubt or argument. ■ If an idea is **mooted,** it is put forward for discussion.

mop (**mopping, mopped**) A **mop** is a tool for washing floors, consisting of a sponge or string head attached to a long handle. If you **mop** a floor, you clean it with a mop. ■ If you **mop** a surface or **mop up** liquid from it, you wipe it with a dry cloth to remove the liquid. ■ If someone has a **mop** of hair, they have a lot of untidy hair.

mope (**moping, moped**) If you **mope** or **mope about,** you feel miserable and are not interested in anything.

moped A **moped** is a lightweight motorbike with a small engine.

moral (**morally**) **Moral** means connected with right behaviour. ...*moral dilemmas... Such behaviour is morally indefensible.* ■ If you do something because it is your **moral** duty or **moral** responsibility, you do it because you believe it is right, rather than because you are legally obliged to do it. ■ A **moral** person has moral principles and tries to stick to them. Principles like these are called **morals.** ■ If you give someone **moral support,** you give them encouragement, rather than practical help. ■ If the loser of a dispute or contest claims to have won a **moral** victory, they mean they have shown they were right about something, in spite of the result. ■ The **moral** of a story is what it teaches you about what you should or should not do. ■ **Moral fibre:** see **fibre.**

morale (*pron:* mor-**rahl**) When you talk about the **morale** of a group of people, you mean the amount of confidence and optimism they have in what they are doing.

moralise See **moralize.**

moralist (**moralistic**) A **moralist** is someone with strong ideas about right and wrong, which they try to get other people to accept. You say someone who behaves like this is **moralistic.**

morality is the belief that some behaviour is right and acceptable and other behaviour is wrong. ■ The **morality** of something is how right or acceptable it is.

moralize (*or* **moralise**) (**moralizing, moralized**) If someone **moralizes** about something, they draw conclusions about the rights and wrongs of it, often based solely upon their own opinions.

morass (*pron:* mor-**rass**) (**morasses**) A **morass** is a complicated and confused situation which is difficult to get out of.

moratorium (*plural:* **moratoriums** *or* **moratoria**) If there is a **moratorium** on some kind of activity, people or governments agree that they will stop doing it for a certain period.

morbid (**morbidly, morbidity**) If you say something like a book or conversation is **morbid,** you mean it is too concerned with unpleasant things, especially death. You can talk about the **morbidity** of something like this. ■ **Morbidity** is used to talk about disease, for example the number of cases of a particular disease. ...*statistics on morbidity.*

mordant humour is sarcastic and sharply critical.

more If there is **more** of one thing than another, or **more** of something than there was before, there is a greater amount of it. ■ You use **more** when you are talking about an additional thing or amount. *The shuttle has enough fuel on board to remain in orbit for at least two more days... Add a little more olive oil.* ■ **More** means to a greater extent. *Few countries have been more closely identified with Catholicism than Spain.* ■ You use **more** when you are comparing things, for example when you say one thing is more important than another. ■ You use **no more** or **not any more** to say something has stopped happening or existing, or is no longer true. *In five years, this ancient culture won't exist any more.*

moreover You say **moreover** when you are adding more information or making a further point.

mores (*pron:* more-rayz) The **mores** of a place are the customs and habits there.

morgue A **morgue** is a place where dead bodies are kept until they are released for burial.

moribund If something is **moribund,** it is about to come to an end because it no longer has any useful function.

Mormon The **Mormons** are a Christian group founded in the US in the 19th century. Their church is called the Church of Jesus Christ of Latter-day Saints.

morning When people talk about the **morning,** they usually mean the time between sunrise and the middle of the day. However, a particular time **in the morning** means a time between midnight and noon. *I stayed up till 4.30 in the morning.* ■ **Morning**

sickness is the feeling of sickness some women have in the mornings during early pregnancy.

moron (**moronic**) If you call someone a **moron** or say they are **moronic,** you mean they are very stupid.

morose (**morosely**) If someone is **morose,** they are miserable and unwilling to talk.

morphine is a painkilling drug manufactured from opium poppies.

morphology (**morphological**) **Morphology** is used to talk about the structure or formation of various things. For example, in biology, **morphology** is the study of the physical structure of plants and animals. The **morphology** of a language is the way words are constructed, for example adding prefixes or suffixes. In geography, the **morphology** of a town or landscape is its physical development. You use **morphological** to talk about things connected with any of these kinds of morphology.

morris dancing (**morris dancer**) Morris dancing is a type of old English country dancing, traditionally performed by men with handkerchiefs, sticks, and bells. The people who perform these dances are called **morris dancers.**

Morse or **morse code** is an international code for sending messages. It uses a system of written dots and dashes or short and long sounds to represent the letters of the alphabet.

morsel A **morsel** is a small piece of something, especially food.

mortal (**mortally**) Anything that dies is said to be **mortal.** ■ When you are talking sarcastically about someone who is supposed to be very important or clever, you can call other people **mere mortals** or **lesser mortals.** ■ A **mortal** wound causes death. *He was mortally wounded in an exchange of fire with police.* ■ If someone is your **mortal** enemy, they are trying to kill you. ■ If you are in **mortal** danger, you are in danger of being killed. ■ In the Catholic Church, a **mortal sin** is a very serious and deliberate one which will result in the person being damned if he or she does not confess and fully repent.

mortality is the fact that everyone has to die sometime. ■ **Mortality** is used to talk about the numbers of people who die at a particular age or from a particular cause. *...the infant mortality rate.*

mortar A **mortar** is a short cannon which fires shells high into the air for a short distance. Shells fired from a mortar can also be called **mortars.** ■ **Mortar** is a mixture of sand, water, and cement used to hold bricks firmly together. ■ A **mortar** is a bowl in which you crush dried grains or spices with a tool called a pestle.

mortarboard (*or* **mortar board**) A **mortarboard** is a stiff black cap with a flat square top and a tassel hanging from it.

mortgage (*pron:* **more**-gij) (**mortgagor, mortgagee; mortgaging, mortgaged**) A **mortgage** is a loan you get from a bank or building society to enable you to buy a house. In an arrangement like this, you are called the **mortgagor** and the bank or building society is called the **mortgagee.** ■ If you **mortgage** your house or land, you use it as a guarantee to a company so they will lend you money.

mortice (*or* **mortise**) A **mortice** is a slot cut in a piece of wood or stone. Another piece, called a **tenon,** fits into the slot.

mortician A **mortician** is the same as an undertaker.

mortify (**mortifies, mortifying, mortified; mortification**) If you are **mortified,** you feel great shame or embarrassment.

mortise A **mortise lock** is a lock which fits into a hole cut in the edge of a door rather than being fixed to one side of it. ■ See also **mortice.**

mortuary (**mortuaries**) A **mortuary** is a place where dead bodies are kept before they are buried or cremated.

mosaic A **mosaic** is a design made up of small pieces of coloured stone or glass set in concrete or plaster.

Moslem See **Muslim.**

mosque A **mosque** is a Muslim temple.

mosquito (**mosquitoes** *or* **mosquitos**) Mosquitoes are bloodsucking flying insects which live in damp areas.

mosquito net A **mosquito net** is a curtain made of very fine material which is hung round a bed as protection against mosquitoes and other insects.

moss (**mosses; mossy**) **Moss** is a soft green covering on damp soil, wood, or stone. It is made up of dense clusters of a tiny plant. **Mossy** things have moss growing on them.

most You use **most** to talk about the majority of a group of people or things, or the largest part of something. *Most New Yorkers would leave the city if they could... I spent most of my time studying.* ■ **Most** or **the most** means the largest amount. *The two groups most involved... The smaller cars cost the most to service.* ■ You use **most** to say someone or something possesses a quality to a very high degree, or has more of a quality than anyone or anything else. *...a masterful work of contemporary history based on the most careful scholarship... He is France's most popular politician.* ■ If you talk about what happens or matters **most** or **most of all,** you mean what happens or matters more than anything else. You can also use **most** or **most of all** to talk about something having more of an effect than other things. *It was his eyes that attracted her most of all.* ■ If you **make the most** of something, you get the maximum use from it.

most-favoured-nation If there is a **most-favoured-nation** agreement between two countries, they have agreed to apply their lowest tariff rates when they import each other's goods.

mostly is used to say something is generally true, for example true of the majority of a group of people, or true most of the time. *...70,000 refugees, mostly Muslims, fleeing from Bosnia.*

MOT An **MOT** or **MOT test** is a compulsory annual test on road vehicles over three years old, to make sure they are roadworthy. MOT stands for 'Ministry of Transport'.

motel A **motel** is a hotel intended for people travelling by car.

motet A **motet** is a piece of unaccompanied choral music usually based on a religious text.

moth – **Moths** are insects like butterflies which usually fly at night.

mothball If a project is **mothballed,** work on it is postponed for a time. ■ **Mothballs** are small white balls made of a chemical such as naphthalene which are put among clothes to keep moths away.

moth-eaten things look very old and tattered.

mother (**mothering, mothered**) Your **mother** is your female parent. ■ If a woman **mothers** someone, she cares for them like a mother. ■ A person's **mother country** is the country where they or their ancestors were born, and which they feel emotionally linked to. ■ Your **mother tongue** is your native language. ■ People sometimes use **the mother of all** to emphasize the size or extent of something. ...*the mother of all battles.*

motherhood is the state of being a mother.

mother-in-law (**mothers-in-law**) Your **mother-in-law** is the mother of your husband or wife.

motherland A person's **motherland** is the country where they or their ancestors were born.

motherly A **motherly** woman is kind and protective.

mother-of-pearl is the pearly layer on the inside of some shells. It is used to make decorative objects.

Mother's Day or **Mothering Sunday** is a special day when children give cards and gifts to their mothers. In Britain, it is the fourth Sunday in Lent.

Mother Superior The **Mother Superior** is the nun in charge of a convent.

mother-to-be (**mothers-to-be**) A **mother-to-be** is a pregnant woman.

motif (*pron:* mo-**teef**) A **motif** is a theme or idea repeated frequently throughout a piece of literature or music. ■ A **motif** is a shape repeated in a pattern.

motion (**motioning, motioned**) **Motion** is the process of continually moving or changing position. ■ If something is **in motion,** it is moving or happening. *His World Cup campaign is in motion.* ■ A **motion** is an action, gesture, or movement. If you **motion** for someone to do something, you make a gesture which shows you want them to do it. ■ In a meeting or debate, a **motion** is a formal proposal which is discussed and voted on.

motionless If something is **motionless,** it is not moving.

motion picture A **motion picture** is a film.

motivate (**motivating, motivated; motivation**) If you **are motivated** by something, it causes you to behave in a particular way. ■ If you **motivate** someone, you make them determined to do something. ...*a highly-motivated workforce.*

motive Your **motive** for doing something is your reason for doing it.

motley A **motley** collection is made up of people or things of very different types.

motocross is motorcycle racing over a cross-country course.

motor (**motoring, motored**) The **motor** of a car or other vehicle is its engine. ■ **Motor** means to do with cars and other powered vehicles. ...*a motor mechanic.* ...*the Birmingham International Motor Show.* ■ **Motoring** is driving in a car. If you **motor** some-

where, you drive there in a car. ■ The **motor** of a machine is the part which provides the power to make it work.

motorbike A **motorbike** is the same as a motorcycle.

motorcade A **motorcade** is a procession of cars.

motor car A **motor car** is the same as a car.

motorcycle (*or* **motor cycle**) (**motorcyclist, motorcycling**) A **motorcycle** is a two-wheeled vehicle powered by an engine.

motorist A **motorist** is someone who drives a car.

motorized (*or* **motorised**) If something is **motorized,** it is powered by a motor.

motor scooter A **motor scooter** is a two-wheeled motor vehicle like a motorcycle, but with smaller wheels and an enclosed engine.

motorway A **motorway** is a major road with several lanes, specially built to allow fast travel over long distances.

mottled If something is **mottled,** it is covered in irregular patches of different colours.

motto (**mottoes** *or* **mottos**) A **motto** is a short sentence or phrase which gives a rule for sensible behaviour.

mould (*Am:* **mold**) (**moulding, moulded**) The things which **mould** someone or something, are the things which influence them to develop in a particular way. ...*the generation of politicians moulded by the Second World War.* ■ You can describe a person by saying they are in a certain **mould.** ...*mega-stars in the mould of Elvis Presley.* ■ If you **mould** a substance like clay, you make it into a particular shape. ■ A **mould** is a container for making substances into a particular shape. You put the liquid substance into the mould; when it is set, its shape is the same as the mould. ■ **Mould** is a soft grey, green, or blue substance which sometimes grows on old food or damp walls.

moulder (*Am:* **molder**) (**mouldering, mouldered**) If something is **mouldering,** it is crumbling and decaying.

mouldy (*Am:* **moldy**) If something is **mouldy,** it has mould growing on it.

moult (*Am:* **molt**) When an animal or bird **moults,** it loses its hair or feathers to make way for new growth.

mound A **mound** is a small hill. ■ A **mound** of things is a large pile of them.

mount If someone **mounts** a campaign or event, they organize it and carry it out. *He will mount a challenge to the leadership of the party.* ■ If something **mounts,** it increases. ...*mounting crime.* ■ If something **mounts up,** it gets bigger because more is being added to it. ■ If you **mount** a horse, you get onto its back. ■ A **mounted** person is on horseback. Someone's horse can be called their **mount.** ■ If something is **mounted** somewhere, it is fixed there. ■ Some mountains have **Mount** as part of their name. ...*Mount Everest.*

mountain A **mountain** is a high area of land with steep sides. ■ A **mountain** of something is a very large amount of it.

mountaineer (**mountaineering**) A **mountaineer** is someone who climbs mountains as a hobby.

Mountaineering is the activity of climbing mountains.

mountain lion The **mountain lion** is the same as the puma.

mountainous A **mountainous** place has a lot of mountains.

mountainside A **mountainside** is one of the steep slopes of a mountain.

Mountie The **Mounties** is the popular name for the Royal Canadian Mounted Police.

mourn If you **mourn** someone who has died, you express your sadness about their death. ■ If someone is **in mourning**, they are wearing special clothes or behaving in a certain way, because someone they love or respect has died. ■ If you **mourn** the loss of something, you are sad because it is no longer there.

mourner The people attending a funeral are called the **mourners.**

mournful (mournfully) Mournful means very sad.

mouse – Mice are small furry mammals with long tails and whiskers. ■ A **mouse** (*plural:* **mice** *or* **mouses**) is a hand-held electronic device used with a computer system. By moving it over a flat surface and pressing its buttons, you can move the cursor around the screen and perform certain operations without using the keyboard.

mousetrap A **mousetrap** is a small device for catching or killing mice.

mousse (*pron:* **moose**) is (a) a type of light frothy food made from whisked egg white with some sweet or savoury ingredients. (b) a light frothy substance you can use to style your hair.

moustache (*or* **mustache**) (**moustached**) A man's **moustache** is the hair he allows to grow on his upper lip. A **moustached** man has a moustache.

mouth Your **mouth** is your lips, or the space behind your lips where your teeth and tongue are. ■ If you **mouth** something, you form the words with your lips, without making any sound. ■ If someone **mouths** something like a slogan, they say it because they have to, and not because they really believe it. ■ The **mouth** of a harbour or a river is the place where it opens into the sea. ■ The **mouth** of a cave, hole, or bottle is its entrance or opening.

mouthful A **mouthful** of food or drink is the amount you put or have in your mouth. ■ If you say a word or phrase is a **mouthful,** you mean it is long and difficult to say.

mouth organ A **mouth organ** is the same as a harmonica.

mouthpiece The **mouthpiece** of an organization is the person who publicly presents their opinions and policies. A newspaper or radio station can also function as a mouthpiece. ■ The **mouthpiece** of a musical instrument is the part that you blow into. ■ The **mouthpiece** of a telephone is the part that you speak into.

mouthwash is a liquid you rinse your mouth with to freshen your breath.

mouth-watering food looks or smells delicious.

movable (*or* **moveable**) If something is **movable,** it can be moved from one place to another.

move (moving, moved; movingly, mover) If someone or something **moves,** they change their position or go to a different place. *The doctor made a move towards the door.* ■ If you **move,** you take action or begin to do something. *It was a wise move.* ■ In games like chess, each change of position of a piece is called a **move.** ■ If you **move** or **move house,** you go to live in a different house. Going to live in another house is called a **move.** ■ If you say someone **moves** in particular circles, you are talking about the people they socialize with. ■ If people are **moving** towards a new system, they are gradually introducing it. *The proposals coincide with moves to reform the training of primary teachers.* ■ If something **moves** you, it makes you feel sadness or sympathy. *It was a moving moment for Marianne.* ■ If you **move** a motion at a meeting, you propose it so people can vote for or against it. *...the mover of the resolution, Mr. T. J. Gray.* ■ If the date of an event is **moved,** the date when it will take place is changed.

moveable See **movable.**

movement A **movement** is a group of people who share the same beliefs or aims. *...the Civil Rights movement.* ■ **Movement** is the process by which someone or something changes position or goes to a different place. ■ Your **movements** are everything you do during a certain period. *He was questioned about his movements by police.* ■ If there is **movement** in people's attitudes, there are signs that they are beginning to change. *There's a movement away from this idea.* ■ A **movement** is one of the sections of a piece of classical music.

mover The most powerful and influential people in an industry are sometimes called its **movers and shakers.**

movie A **movie** is a film.

moving (movingly) See **move.**

moving picture In the past, films were sometimes called **moving pictures.**

mow (mowing, mowed, have mowed *or* **have mown)** If you **mow** a lawn, you cut the grass. ■ If a group of people are **mown down,** they are killed at the same time, for example by machine-gun fire.

mower A **mower** is a machine for cutting grass, corn, or wheat.

mozzarella (*pron:* mot-sa-**rel**-la) is a type of white Italian cheese originally made using buffalo milk.

MP An **MP** or **Member of Parliament** is a person who has been elected to represent people in their country's parliament.

MP3 – MP3 is a technology that allows you to download and play music and other audio files from the Internet. MP3 stands for 'Mpeg-1 layer3'.

mpg is short for 'miles per gallon'. It is used to say how far a vehicle can travel on a gallon of fuel.

mph Speed is often expressed in **mph** or 'miles per hour'.

Mr is used in front of a man's name. It is short for 'Mister'.

Mrs is used in front of a married woman's name.

MS See **multiple sclerosis.**

Ms is used in front of a woman's name when it is not known whether she is married, or when she does not want to be identified as married or single.

M.Sc. An **M.Sc.** is a higher degree in a scientific subject. M.Sc. stands for 'Master of Science'.

MSP In Scotland, an **MSP** is a person who has been elected to represent people in the Scottish parliament. MSP stands for 'Member of the Scottish Parliament'.

much is used to say something is true to a great extent. *It depends very much on the individual... He speaks English, but not very much.* ■ **Much** is used to ask questions about quantity or give information about the size or amount of something. *How much money can I afford?.. They are grown in full sun, without much water.* ■ **Much** of something means a lot of it. **Nothing much** means very little. *Much of the blame lies with the Americans... Nothing much will happen before the new year.* ■ If you say **so much for** a particular thing, you are commenting on how useless or meaningless it has turned out to be. ■ You say **so much for** something to show you have finished talking about it. *So much for the policy goal; what about the ends for achieving it?*

muchness If you say a number of things are **much of a muchness**, you mean there is not much difference between them.

muck is dirt, sewage, or manure. ■ If you **muck out** a stable, pigsty, or cowshed, you clean it. ■ If you **muck** something **up**, you do it very badly. ■ If you say someone is **mucking about,** you mean they are behaving stupidly and wasting time.

muck-raking is finding out details about the personal lives of public figures, and spreading scandal about them.

mucky If something is **mucky,** it is very dirty or muddy.

mucus (*or* **mucous**) (*pron:* mjew-kus) is liquid produced in some parts of the body. For example, it is produced in the throat to aid swallowing.

mud is a sticky mixture of earth and water.

muddle (**muddling, muddled**) If something is in a **muddle,** it is in a confused state. ■ If someone is **muddled,** they are not thinking clearly. *...the muddled reaction of the authorities.* ■ If you **muddle** things or **muddle** them **up,** you mix them up or get them in the wrong order. ■ If you **muddle through,** you manage to do something even though you do not really know how to do it properly. ■ If you **muddle along,** you live or exist without purpose.

muddy (**muddier, muddiest; muddies, muddying, muddied**) If something is **muddy,** it is full of mud, or covered with mud. ■ If something **muddies** a situation, it makes it more difficult to understand or sort out. You can also talk about something **muddying the waters.**

mudflat – Mudflats are flat muddy areas of coastal land which are covered by sea when the tide is in.

mudguard The **mudguards** on a bicycle or other vehicle are metal or plastic parts above the wheels which stop the rider or vehicle getting splashed with mud.

mud-slinging is trying to damage someone's reputation by accusing them of immoral or dishonest behaviour.

muesli (*pron:* mews-lee) is a mixture of grains and dried fruit, eaten as a breakfast cereal.

muezzin (*pron:* moo-**ez**-in) The **muezzin** is the official in a mosque who calls the faithful to prayer five times a day.

muff If you are given the opportunity to do something and you do it badly, you can say you **muff** it or **muff your chances.**

muffin A **muffin** is (a) a small American-style cake, usually with fruit or some other flavouring in it. (b) a small flat round bread roll, which you eat toasted.

muffle (**muffling, muffled**) If you **muffle** a sound, you make it quieter. *...a muffled cough.* ■ If you are **muffled,** you are wearing a lot of warm clothes.

muffler A **muffler** is the same as a scarf. ■ Americans call a car's silencer a **muffler.**

mug (**mugging, mugged; mugger**) A **mug** is a large deep straight-sided cup. ■ A person's face is sometimes humorously called their **mug.** ■ If you say someone would be a **mug** to do something, you mean they would be very foolish to do it. Similarly, if you say something is a **mug's game,** you mean anyone who gets involved in it is bound to come off badly. ■ If you are **mugged,** you are attacked and robbed in a public place. A robbery of this kind is called a **mugging;** the person who does it is called a **mugger.** ■ If you **mug up** on something, you learn as much as you can about it.

muggy If the weather is **muggy,** the air is unpleasantly warm and damp.

mugshot A **mugshot** is a photograph taken by the police of someone who has been charged with a crime.

mulberry (**mulberries**) The **mulberry** is a tree which bears purple or white berries, also called **mulberries.**

mulch (**mulches, mulching, mulched**) Mulch is a mixture of rotting plant material put round the roots of plants to protect and feed them. If you **mulch** plants, you put mulch around them.

mule A **mule** is the sterile offspring of a female horse and a male donkey.

mull If you **mull** something **over,** you think about it for a long time, before deciding what to do. ■ **Mulled** wine is served hot with sugar and spices added to it.

mullah A **mullah** is a Muslim religious leader.

mullioned windows are divided into panes by vertical strips.

multi- is added to words to indicate that something involves several people or things. *...multi-candidate elections. ...a multi-faith society.*

multi-ethnic countries or societies have people from several different ethnic backgrounds living in them.

multifarious things are of many different kinds. *...his wife's multifarious interests.*

multilateral means involving several countries or groups. *...multilateral talks.*

multi-lingual (*or* **multilingual**) If someone is **multi-lingual,** they can speak several languages. A **multi-lingual** book is written in several languages.

multimedia In computing, you use **multimedia** to talk about products which use sound, pictures, film, and ordinary text to convey information. ■ People talk about the use of television and other different media in the classroom as **multimedia.**

■ The use of different kinds of material in a painting or sculpture is called **multimedia.**

multinational (or **multi-national**) means involving several countries. *...the multinational relief effort in Somalia.* ■ A **multinational** or **multinational** company owns smaller companies in several countries.

multi-party If a country has a **multi-party** electoral system, it has regular elections contested by a number of parties.

multiple is used to say something involves many things. *...multiple injuries.* ■ If a number is a **multiple** of a smaller number, the smaller one can be divided into the larger one an exact number of times. For example, 24 is a multiple of 6.

multiple choice In a **multiple choice** test, you are given a number of possible answers to each question, and you have to choose the correct one.

multiple sclerosis or **MS** is a serious disease of the nervous system which can eventually lead to paralysis and can also affect a person's speech and vision.

multiplex (**multiplexes**) A **multiplex** is a cinema complex with several screens.

multiplication See **multiply.**

multiplication sign A **multiplication sign** is the sign ✕ which is put between two numbers to show they are being multiplied.

multiplication table When children learn their **multiplication table,** they learn by heart all possible multiplications of numbers between 1 and 12.

multiplicity A **multiplicity** of things is a large number of them.

multiply (**multiplies, multiplying, multiplied; multiplication**) When things **multiply,** the number of them keeps increasing. ■ If you **multiply** one number by another, you calculate the total you would get if you added the first number to itself a certain number of times. For example, 2 multiplied by 3 is 2 plus 2 plus 2 which equals 6. Multiplying numbers is called **multiplication.**

multi-tasking If a computer is capable of **multi-tasking,** it can do several tasks at the same time, usually with each task being shown in a different window.

multitude A **multitude** of people or things is a very large number of them.

mum (**mummy**) Some people call their mother **mum, mummy,** or **mom.** ■ If you **keep mum** about something, you do not tell anyone about it.

mumble (**mumbling, mumbled**) If you **mumble** something, you say it quietly and indistinctly.

mumbo-jumbo If something is **mumbo-jumbo** to you, it does not make any sense.

mummify (**mummifies, mummifying, mummified; mummification**) When a dead body is **mummified,** it is preserved, usually by embalming it or drying it and wrapping it in cloth. This process is called **mummification.**

mummy (**mummies**) A **mummy** is a mummified dead body. ■ See **mum.**

mumps is an infectious disease which causes a mild fever and painful swelling of the glands in the neck and jaw.

munch (**munches, munching, munched**) If you **munch** food, you chew it steadily and thoroughly.

mundane things are very ordinary and not particularly interesting. *...mundane tasks.*

municipal means connected with local government.

municipality (**municipalities**) A **municipality** is a city or town which has a local council and local officials to administer its internal affairs.

munificent (**munificence**) A **munificent** gift is a very generous one. When someone gives a gift like this, you can talk about their **munificence.**

munitions are military equipment or supplies, especially weapons and ammunition.

mural A **mural** is a large picture painted on a wall.

murder (**murdering, murdered; murderer**) Murder is the crime of deliberately killing someone. If someone **murders** someone or commits a **murder,** they kill someone deliberately. A person who has murdered someone is called a **murderer.** ■ If you say someone is **getting away with murder,** you mean they are doing something wrong, and not being punished or stopped. ■ You say something is **murder** when you want to emphasize how difficult, dangerous, or unpleasant it is.

murderous (**murderously**) If you say someone is **murderous,** you mean they have murdered someone, or are likely to. ■ If you call something **murderous,** you mean it has caused death, or is capable of it. *He made a murderous attack on his wife.*

murk is (a) darkness or thick mist which you cannot see through. (b) something which confuses or obscures a situation. *...the political murk in Belgrade.*

murky (**murkier, murkiest**) Murky water is so dark or dirty you cannot see through it. ■ **Murky** places are dark and unpleasant. ■ You use **murky** to describe something which you suspect is dishonest or morally wrong. *...the loan sharks whose murky business is booming in our inner cities.*

murmur (**murmuring, murmured**) If you **murmur** something, you say it very quietly. The sound of people speaking quietly can be called a **murmur.**

muscle (**muscling, muscled**) A **muscle** is a piece of tissue inside your body which is able to get bigger and smaller to enable your body to move. ■ If you talk about someone having **muscle,** you mean they have the power to achieve what they want. ■ If you talk about someone **muscling in** on a situation, you mean they are intervening without being asked to.

muscular means involving or affecting the muscles. *...muscular pain.* ■ **Muscular** people have strong firm muscles.

muscular dystrophy is a serious hereditary disease which makes a person's muscles gradually get weaker.

muse (**musing, mused**) If you **muse** about something, you think about it for a long time. ■ When writers talk about their **muse,** they mean an imaginary force which is supposed to give them their inspiration.

museum A **museum** is a building where old, interesting, or valuable objects are kept on public display. ■ If you call something a **museum piece,** you mean it is old and out of date.

mush You call a substance a **mush** when it is like a thick soft paste.

mushroom (mushrooming, mushroomed) A **mushroom** is a fungus, usually with a short stem and a round top. ■ If something **mushrooms,** it grows very rapidly.

mushy You say food is **mushy** when it is too soft and has lost its shape or texture. ■ **mushy** books or films are over-sentimental.

music is the pattern of sounds created by people singing or playing instruments. When music is written down, the symbols representing sounds are also called **music.**

musical (musically) Musical means to do with music. ...a musical recital. ■ If someone is **musical,** they have a natural ability and interest in music. ■ A **musical** sound is pleasant to listen to. ...a soft almost musical voice. ■ A **musical** is a play or film which uses singing and dancing in the story.

musical chairs is a game children play in which they run round a row of chairs while music is played and try to sit down when it stops. ■ You can say people like politicians are playing **musical chairs** when they keep changing jobs or positions.

musical instrument See **instrument.**

music hall In the past, a **music hall** was a theatre where you could see shows consisting of performances by comedians, singers, and dancers. This type of entertainment was called **music hall.**

musician A **musician** is someone who plays a musical instrument as their job or hobby.

musicianship is the skill involved in playing a musical instrument.

musicology (musicologist) Musicology is the scientific and historical study of music. A **musicologist** is an expert in this field.

musk is a substance with a strong persistent smell which is used to make perfume.

musket (musketeer) A **musket** is an old-fashioned gun with a long barrel. A **musketeer** was a soldier armed with a musket.

muskrat The **muskrat** is a large rat-like North American animal with brown fur. Its fur, usually called **musquash,** is sometimes used to make coats.

musky If something is **musky,** it smells like musk.

Muslim (or Moslem) A **Muslim** is a person who believes in Islam and lives by its rules. ■ **Muslim** means connected with Islam.

muslin is a soft loosely-woven cotton material.

musquash (musquashes) See **muskrat.**

mussel – Mussels are a kind of edible shellfish with black shells.

must If something **must** happen, it is very important or necessary that it happens. ■ If you say something is **a must,** you mean it is absolutely necessary to have it or do it. A meal in the Stables restaurant is a must. ■ If you say something **must** have happened or **must** be true, you mean you feel sure it happened or is true. The snow must have softened the impact.

mustache See **moustache.**

mustang – Mustangs are wild horses in North America, descended from escaped Spanish ponies.

mustard is a yellow or brown spicy mixture made from the seeds of the mustard plant. It is used to flavour food. ■ **Mustard** is a brownish-yellow colour.

mustard gas is a poisonous substance used as a chemical weapon.

muster (mustering, mustered) If you **muster** something such as strength or support, you gather as much of it as you can, in order to do something. The next generation of leaders will gain legitimacy only if they can muster popular support. ■ If you say someone or something **passes muster,** you mean they are good enough for their purpose.

musty If something is **musty** or has a **musty** smell, it smells stale and damp.

mutant A **mutant** animal or plant is physically different from the rest of its species, because of a change in its genetic structure. An animal or plant like this is called a **mutant.**

mutate (mutating, mutated; mutation) If an animal or plant **mutates,** it develops different characteristics as a result of a genetic change.

mute (mutely; muting, muted) If someone is **mute** they choose not to say anything. ■ If you **mute** a sound, you make it quieter. ■ A **mute** is a device fitted into or onto a musical instrument to make it play more quietly. ■ A **muted** reaction or emotion is not strong. ■ A **muted** colour is soft and gentle.

mutilate (mutilating, mutilated; mutilation) If someone is **mutilated,** their body is severely and permanently damaged. ■ If someone **mutilates** something like a statue, they damage its appearance.

mutiny (mutinies; mutinous, mutineer) A **mutiny** is a rebellion by a group of people, especially members of the armed forces, against the people in authority over them. You say people who rebel like this are **mutinous;** you can also call them **mutineers.**

mutter (muttering, muttered) If someone **mutters,** they speak very quietly so other people can hardly hear them. People sometimes do this when they are complaining about something or talking to themselves. ...a mutter of protest. ■ If there are **mutterings** about something, people are talking about it, but not openly.

mutton is meat from an adult sheep.

mutual means something that two or more people share or do to each other. His relations with the press are full of mutual fear and loathing... Lithuania and Moscow have a mutual interest in peaceful compromise.

mutually is used to talk about something which affects two or more people in the same way. ...Elizabeth's and Mary's mutually beneficial relationship. ■ If two things are **mutually exclusive** or **mutually contradictory,** they cannot both happen or be true at the same time.

Muzak is recorded background music played in places like supermarkets. 'Muzak' is a trademark.

muzzle (muzzling, muzzled) An animal's **muzzle** is its nose and mouth. ■ If you **muzzle** a dog, you put a device called a **muzzle** over its nose and mouth, to stop it biting. ■ If a person or group of people is **muzzled,** they are prevented from speaking out about something. ■ The **muzzle** of a gun barrel is the end where the bullets come out.

MW is short for (a) 'medium wave'. (b) 'megawatts'.

my You use **my** when you are talking about something belonging to or connected with yourself.

mycology (*pron:* my-**kol**-o-jee) (**mycologist**) **Mycology** is the study of fungi. A **mycologist** is an expert on fungi.

myopia (**myopic**) **Myopia** is the medical term for short-sightedness. You say someone is **myopic** when they are short-sighted.

myriad If you talk about **myriad** things of a particular kind, you mean there are very many of them. *...the myriad peoples and cultures of South Africa.*

myrrh (*pron:* **murr**) is an aromatic resin used in incense and perfume.

myself You use **myself** to say something you do affects you rather than anyone else. *I made a fool of myself.* ■ You use **myself** to emphasize that a statement really does apply to you. *I can't say I fancy it myself.*

mysterious (**mysteriously**) If something is **mysterious,** it is strange and not easily explained or understood. *A mysterious illness confined him to bed.* ■ If you say someone is being **mysterious,** you mean they are being secretive.

mystery (**mysteries**) If you say something is a **mystery,** you mean it cannot be explained or understood. ■ A **mystery** person or thing is one whose identity or nature is not known. *...the wife's mystery lover.* ■ A **mystery** is a story in which strange things happen which are not explained until the end.

mystery play A **mystery play** is a medieval play based on incidents in the Bible, especially the life, death, and resurrection of Jesus.

mystic (**mystical, mysticism**) **Mystic** and **mystical** are used to talk about experiences people claim to have which involve spiritual powers and influences that cannot be understood by reasoning. *...mystical visions.* ■ **Mysticism** is a religious practice in which people search intensely for truth, knowledge, and God through meditation and prayer. A **mystic** is someone who practises mysticism.

mystify (**mystifies, mystifying, mystified; mystification**) If something **mystifies** you, you cannot understand it.

mystique (*pron:* miss-**teek**) The **mystique** of something is the atmosphere of mystery and secrecy associated with it. *...the mystique of monarchy.*

myth (**mythical**) If you say something which is widely believed is **mythical** or a **myth,** you mean it is untrue. *...the myth of cheap nuclear power.* ■ A **myth** is a story which has been made up in the past to explain natural events or justify religious beliefs. **Mythical** is used to describe people, creatures, and other things in myths. *The sky dragon is the mythical ruler of the empire.*

mythic is used to describe people and things that are like something in a myth, because they are fantastic or extreme. *Struggles between film-makers and studio bosses have, at times, escalated to mythic proportions.*

mythological is used to talk about things to do with myths, or things which remind you of myths. *...the mythological beast that was part lion and part goat.*

mythologize (*or* **mythologise**) (**mythologizing, mythologized**) If someone or something is **mythologized,** myths are created about them.

mythology is stories made up in the past to explain natural events or justify religious beliefs. ■ The **mythology** of an activity is the stories and beliefs connected with it, many of which may not be true. *...British food mythology.*

myxomatosis is an infectious disease which affects rabbits and usually kills them.

N n

n/a (*or* **N.A.**) You write **n/a** on a form to show that a question or category does not apply to you. n/a stands for 'not applicable'.

nab (**nabbing, nabbed**) If the police **nab** someone, they catch them doing something wrong, or they arrest them.

nadir (*pron:* **nay**-dear) If someone or something reaches their **nadir,** they reach their lowest point.

naff If you say something is **naff,** you mean it is inappropriate or in bad taste, because it is showy, old-fashioned, or of poor quality.

nag (**nagging, nagged**) If something like a problem **nags** at you, it keeps troubling you. You use **nagging** to describe things like this. *...nagging doubts.* ■ If someone **nags** you, they keep complaining or asking you to do something. ■ A **nag** is a horse, especially an old one.

nail (**nailing, nailed**) A **nail** is a small sharp piece of metal which you hammer through something, to fasten it to something else. If you **nail** something to a surface, you fix it there with a nail or nails. ■ If someone **nails their colours to the mast,** they make their intentions clear and show they do not intend to change their mind. ■ If you **nail** someone, you catch them and prove that they have been breaking the law. ■ If you **nail** something false someone has said or written, you show it is a lie. ■ Your **nails** are the thin hard areas covering the ends of your fingers and toes. ■ a **nail** in someone's **coffin:** see **coffin.**

nail-biting If you describe something such as a story or sports match as **nail-biting,** you mean that it makes you feel very excited or nervous because you do not know how it is going to end. *...the nail-biting climax.*

naive (*pron:* nye-**eev**) (**naively**) If you say someone is being **naive,** you mean they are behaving as if a situation was simpler than it really is, or as if people were nicer or more co-operative than they really are. A **naive** person tends to behave like this all the time, because of lack of experience. ■ **Naive** art involves the use of unsophisticated or primitive techniques. *...naive sculptures.*

naivety (*pron:* nye-**eev**-i-tee) is behaviour which shows simple and naive beliefs and a lack of knowledge or experience of life.

naked (**nakedly, nakedness**) If someone is **naked,** they are not wearing any clothes. ■ You use **naked** to describe things which have no covering. *...naked light bulbs.* ■ If you can see something with the **naked** eye, you can see it without something such as a telescope or microscope. ■ You use **naked** to describe actions, emotions, or behaviour which are open and undisguised. *...naked greed... ...a nakedly ambitious man.*

namby-pamby You say people are **namby-pamby** when they are weak and timid and unwilling to expose themselves to risk or danger.

name (**naming, named**) The **name** of a person, animal, place, or thing is the word or words used to identify them. ■ When a child is **named,** it is given a name. ■ If you **name** something like a team, you say who will be in it. *India's new Prime Minister is expected to name his Cabinet today.* ■ If you **name** the person responsible for something, you say who they are. ■ If you **name** a date, you say when something will take place. ■ The **name** of a person or thing is their reputation. *He wants to restore the good name of his family.* ■ If someone **calls** you **names,** they insult you by saying unpleasant things to you or about you. ■ If something is done **in the name of** an organization or ideal, it is done by people claiming to represent that organization or ideal. *They called for sacrifice in the name of the revolution.* ■ **big name:** see **big.** See also **Christian name, first name, given name.**

name-dropping is the habit of talking about famous people as though they were your friends, to impress people.

nameless is used to describe people or things whose name is unknown, or that do not have a name. ■ If you say someone will remain **nameless,** you mean you will not mention their name, even though you know it, because you do not want to embarrass them.

namely You use **namely** to say more exactly what you mean, when you have just mentioned something indirectly. *The conference is far from achieving its aim, namely to break the deadlock.*

nameplate A **nameplate** is a small sign on or by the door of a room or a building, showing the name of the person or organization that uses it.

namesake Your **namesake** is someone who has the same name as you.

nanny (**nannies**) A **nanny** is a woman who is paid by parents to look after their children and sometimes lives in the family home. ■ When people talk

about a **nanny** state or society, they mean one where people are over-protected by the authorities.

nano- is used (a) in words like 'nanotechnology' and 'nanocomputer' to indicate extreme smallness. (b) in measurement words to represent a thousandth of a millionth part of something. *...12.5 nanograms.*

nap (**napping, napped**) A **nap** is a short sleep. If you **nap,** you have a short sleep. ■ If you are caught **napping,** something happens to you when you are not prepared for it. ■ In horse-racing, a **nap** is a tip given by a tipster for an almost certain winner.

napalm (*pron:* **nay**-parm) is a substance which is mixed with petrol to make bombs which burn and destroy people and plants.

nape Your **nape** is the back of your neck.

napkin A **napkin** is a small piece of cloth or paper used to protect your clothes when you are eating, or to wipe your face and hands.

nappy (**nappies**) A **nappy** is a piece of soft thick cloth or padded paper fastened round a baby's bottom to soak up urine and faeces.

narcissi See **narcissus.**

narcissistic (*pron:* nar-siss-**siss**-tik) (**narcissism**) If someone is **narcissistic,** they behave in a self-admiring way. Behaviour like this is called **narcissism** (*pron:* **nar**-si-siz-um).

narcissus (*plural:* **narcissi**) The **narcissus** is a type of daffodil, often white, with a short trumpet. **Narcissus** is also the scientific name for the whole daffodil family.

narco- is used to indicate a connection with narcotic drugs. *...narco-terrorism.*

narcolepsy is a rare medical condition which causes the sufferer to fall into a deep sleep at any time without warning.

narcotic – Narcotics are addictive drugs like opium and morphine which make you sleepy and unable to feel pain. **Narcotic** is used to talk about substances having this effect or being used to obtain it. *...narcotic drugs.*

narrate (**narrating, narrated; narration, narrator**) If a story is **narrated** by someone, they tell it; they are called the story's **narrator.** ■ If something like a film or TV documentary is **narrated,** someone gives a spoken commentary, to explain and accompany the pictures. This commentary is called the **narration.**

narrative A **narrative** is a story, or an account of events or experiences. ■ The **narrative** in a novel is the way the events are presented. ■ **Narrative** is used to describe songs or poems which tell a story. *...Masefield's narrative verse.*

narrow (**narrowly, narrowness**) If something is **narrow,** the distance between its sides is very small. ■ If something **narrows,** it becomes less wide. *The road now narrows to a single track.* ■ If you **narrow down** a range of possibilities, you reduce it by getting rid of some of them. ■ If you have a **narrow** victory or defeat, you only just win or lose. ■ If you have a **narrow** escape, you only just miss having something unpleasant happen to you.

narrow boat A **narrow boat** is a long low boat, used on canals.

narrow-minded If you say someone is **narrow-minded,** you mean they are unwilling to consider new ideas or other people's opinions.

NASA is an American government organization concerned with research and development in the field of aeronautics and space flight. NASA stands for 'National Aeronautics and Space Administration'.

nasal (pron: **nay**-zal) is used to talk about things to do with the nose. ...nasal ulcers. ...nasal sprays. **Nasal** sounds are produced by air passing through your nose as well as your mouth when you speak.

nascent (pron: **nass**-sent or **nace**-sent) things or processes are just beginning, and are expected to increase and grow stronger. ...nascent Russian capitalism.

nasturtium (pron: nas-**tur**-shum) **Nasturtiums** are garden plants with round leaves and red, orange, or yellow flowers.

nasty (**nastier, nastiest; nastily, nastiness; nasties**) If you say something is **nasty,** you mean it is very unpleasant, unattractive, or harmful. ■ Unpleasant people, creatures, or things are sometimes called **nasties.** It contains some stimulants and other nasties linked with cancer. ■ See also **video nasty.**

natal is used to talk about things to do with birth. **Pre-natal** and **ante-natal** both mean 'before birth'; **post-natal** means 'after birth'. ...an ante-natal clinic. ...post-natal depression.

nation (**national, nationally**) A **nation** is a country, together with its social and political structures. **National** means involving one country, rather than several countries. ...national and international competitions. **National** also means to do with the whole of a country, rather than part of it. ...national and local elections. ■ The **nation** is all the people who live in a country. **National** means to do with these people. ...the Czech national character. ■ A country's **nationals** are its citizens.

national anthem A country's **national anthem** is its official song.

national government A **national government** is a coalition government, especially one formed during a crisis.

national grid The **national grid** is a network of high-voltage power lines connecting major power stations.

National Health Service See **NHS.**

national insurance is the system by which a government collects money regularly from employers and employees to pay to people who are ill, unemployed, or retired. 'National insurance' is sometimes shortened to 'NI'.

nationalise See **nationalize.**

nationalism (**nationalist, nationalistic**) **Nationalism** is a love for your country and a belief in its importance, often accompanied by a belief that it is better than other countries. Beliefs of this kind are called **nationalist** or **nationalistic.** ■ **Nationalism** is the desire for political independence by a group of people sharing the same language, religion, or culture. ...a growing nationalist movement. A **nationalist** is someone with nationalist beliefs.

nationality (**nationalities**) **Nationality** is used to say what country a person legally belongs to. He was given British nationality. ■ A **nationality** is a group of people who have the same racial origins, especially a group which does not have a country of its own. The republic is a melting pot of different nationalities.

nationalize (or **nationalise**) (**nationalizing, nationalized; nationalization**) If a government **nationalizes** an industry, institution, or resource, it takes it out of private hands and places it under state control.

national park A **national park** is a large area of land protected by the government of a country because of its natural beauty or wildlife.

national service is a period of compulsory service in a country's armed forces.

nationhood is a country's status as a nation. This brought Canada to independent nationhood.

nation state A **nation state** is an independent state inhabited by people from the same national group.

nationwide is used to describe things which happen or exist throughout a country. ...a nationwide general strike.

native Your **native** country, town, or village is the one you were born in. You can also say someone is a **native** of a country or other place. ■ Your **native** language is the one you learned first. ...a conversation in their native tongue. ■ A **native** plant or animal has existed in a place from earliest times, and was not introduced by man. ■ A **native** ability or quality is one you possess naturally without having to learn it. ■ The descendants of the people who lived in a country before it was settled and colonized are sometimes called the **natives.** This use of 'native' is offensive and old-fashioned. ■ If a visitor to a country **goes native,** he or she begins to act and live like the people who live there.

Native American A **Native Indian** is the same as an American Indian.

native speaker A **native speaker** of a language has it as their first language, rather than having learned it as a foreign language.

Nativity The **Nativity** is the birth of Jesus, celebrated by Christians at Christmas.

NATO is an international organization which was founded to provide joint defence for its members. These are the US, Canada, the UK, and other European countries. NATO stands for 'North Atlantic Treaty Organization'.

natty (**nattier, nattiest**) If you call things like clothes **natty,** you mean they are smart or fashionable.

natural (**naturally, naturalness**) If you say something is **natural,** you mean it is normal and to be expected. It is only natural that he should resent you. ■ Someone with a **natural** ability was born with it and did not have to learn it. You can say someone like this is a **natural.** ■ **Natural** is used to talk about things which exist in nature, rather than being made or caused by man. ...a natural amphitheatre. ■ If someone's behaviour is **natural,** it is relaxed and not affected or artificial. ■ A person's **natural** parents are their real parents, rather than people who have adopted them. ■ If someone has died of **natural causes,** they have died because they were ill, and not as a result of an accident, suicide, or murder. ■ In music, **natural** is used to say a note is not sharp or flat. 'Natural' is usually written ♮.

natural gas is gas, mainly methane, which is found underground or under the sea. It is collected and stored, then piped into people's houses to be used for cooking and heating.

natural history is the study of plants and animals. ■ The **natural history** of a place is the plants and animals there.

naturalise See **naturalize.**

naturalism (**naturalistic**) Naturalism is a movement in literature and art which aims to show people and objects as they really are, rather than in an idealistic or unnatural way. A **naturalistic** novel or painting shows people or things in this way.

naturalist A **naturalist** is a person who studies plants and animals.

naturalize (or **naturalise**) (**naturalizing, naturalized; naturalization**) If someone is **naturalized,** they legally become a citizen of a country they were not born in.

natural resources are useful things like forests, minerals, and sources of energy, which occur naturally.

natural science is the study of the whole physical world, including biology, chemistry, and physics. These sciences are sometimes called the **natural sciences.**

natural selection is the process by which plants and animals which are best adapted to their environment survive and reproduce, while those which are less well adapted die out.

natural wastage If a company or other organization reduces its workforce by **natural wastage,** it does it by not replacing employees who leave or retire, rather than by sacking people.

nature (**-natured**) Nature is all living things, and all events and processes not caused by man. ■ The **nature** of something is its basic character. *This experiment raises important questions about the nature of the disease... He will claim that charges against him are political in nature.* ■ A person's **nature** is their character, which shows in the way they behave. *...Nicholas's gentle nature... Some ill-natured fools will call this egotism.* ■ If something is **second nature** to you, you can do it easily, because you are used to doing it. *Cooking is second nature to me now.*

nature trail A **nature trail** is a route through an area of countryside with signposts indicating interesting features.

naturism (**naturist**) Naturism is the practice of not wearing any clothes, which some people do on particular beaches or in other special areas. A **naturist** is a person who does this.

naught See **nought.**

naughty (**naughtier, naughtiest; naughtiness**) A **naughty** child is badly behaved. ■ **Naughty** is used

to describe things which are slightly rude or related to sex. *...naughty lingerie.*

nausea is a feeling of sickness as though you are going to vomit.

nauseam See **ad nauseam.**

nauseate (**nauseating, nauseated; nauseous**) If you are **nauseated** by something or it makes you **nauseous,** it gives you the feeling of wanting to vomit. ■ You say you are **nauseated** by something when it disgusts you. *He accused them of nauseating hypocrisy.*

nautical means to do with ships and the sea. *...their nautical adventures.*

nautical mile A **nautical mile** is about 1852 metres or 2025 yards and is used to express distances at sea.

naval See **navy.**

nave The **nave** of a church is the long central part where the congregation sits.

navel A person's **navel** is the small hollow in the middle of their stomach where the umbilical cord was attached. ■ If you say someone is **navel-gazing** you mean they are spending a lot of time examining their own thoughts and feelings.

navigable A **navigable** waterway is wide enough and deep enough for a boat to travel along.

navigate (**navigating, navigated; navigation, navigational**) When someone **navigates,** they work out the direction in which a car, ship, or aircraft should go, using maps or instruments. **Navigational** means to do with navigating ships or aircraft. ■ If you **navigate** your way somewhere, you get there with difficulty, because you have to take an indirect route, or because there are things in the way. ■ If you **navigate** your way through difficulties, you deal with them skilfully.

navigator A **navigator** is someone in a car, ship, or aircraft who works out which way it should go.

navvy (**navvies**) A **navvy** is a person employed to do hard physical work, for example building roads.

navy (**navies; naval**) A country's **navy** is the part of its armed forces which is trained to fight at sea. **Naval** means connected with a navy. *...a naval family.* ■ **Navy** or **navy blue** is a dark blue colour.

nay is an old or dialect word for 'no'.

Nazi (**Nazism**) The **Nazis** were members of the National Socialist Party, which seized power in Germany in 1933 under Adolf Hitler. These people believed in **Nazism,** which meant especially the racial supremacy of the German people, and the expansion of Germany's borders. Today, groups of people with strong racist views in Germany and other parts of the world are sometimes called **neo-Nazis.**

NB You write **NB** to draw people's attention to what follows. NB stands for 'nota bene', which is Latin for 'note well'.

NCO An **NCO** is a member of the armed forces who has a higher rank than a private, seaman, or aircraftsman, but does not have a commission. NCO stands for 'non-commissioned officer'.

Neanderthal (*pron:* nee-**ann**-der-tahl) man was an early type of man living in Europe about 35,000 to 70,000 years ago.

near (**nearer, nearest; nearing, neared**) If something is **near** a place or thing, it is a short distance away from it. ■ If you are **nearing** something, you are approaching it and will soon reach it. ■ In front of a number, **near** means 'almost'. *We achieved near 100 per cent participation in this study.* ■ **Near-** and **as near as** are used to say someone or something is very close to being a particular thing. *...Intel's near-monopoly of the PC microprocessor market... Peter Rice is as near an artistic genius as the world of engineering has produced in half a century.* ■ **Nowhere near** is used to say something is a long way from being achieved. *The guerrillas are nowhere near victory.* ■ A **near miss** is (a) an attempt to do something which almost succeeds. (b) an incident in which there is almost an accident.

nearby things are only a short distance away.

Near East The **Near East** is the same as the Middle East.

nearly If someone or something is **nearly** a particular thing, they are close to being that thing. *The food they receive each month is not nearly enough.* ■ **Nearly** an amount or number means slightly less than that amount or number. *The book has sold nearly 20,000 copies.* ■ If something **nearly** happens, it comes close to happening.

nearside The **nearside** of a vehicle is the side normally nearest to the edge of the road. See also **offside.**

neat (**neater, neatest; neatly, neatness**) A **neat** place, person, or thing is tidy and smart. ■ Someone who is **neat** does things in a tidy way or keeps their possessions tidy. *...neat handwriting.* ■ A **neat** way of doing something is simple, clever, and efficient. ■ A **neat** alcoholic drink has nothing added to it.

nebula (*plural:* **nebulas** or **nebulae**) A **nebula** is an area of gas and dust in space. You see it as a patch of pale light in the night sky.

nebulous things are vague and not precise.

necessarily If you say something is **not necessarily** true, you mean it is not always true. *Economic progress does not necessarily solve human problems.*

necessary If something is **necessary,** you must have it, or it must be done. *It was necessary to introduce blood testing.* ■ If something is **necessary** to achieve a certain result, you must have it to get that result. *They failed to win the support necessary to bring the government down.* ■ A **necessary** consequence is one which cannot fail to happen. *No one can say if this is a necessary side-effect of galaxy formation.*

necessitate (**necessitating, necessitated**) If something **necessitates** an action, it makes it necessary.

necessity (**necessities**) If there is a **necessity** for something, it must be done, provided, or obtained. *...the necessity for an exit visa.* ■ **Necessities** are the things you must have in order to do something or in order to survive. ■ **Of necessity** is used to say that in particular circumstances something must happen or be the case. *The motorist's concentration must of necessity be less at these times.*

neck (**-necked**) A person's or animal's **neck** is the part of their body which joins their head to the rest of their body. **-necked** is added to a word to say what kind of neck someone or something has. *...a long-necked dinosaur.* ■ The **neck** of a piece of clothing is the part round your neck or just below it. *...an open-necked shirt.* ■ In a race or contest, if two people are **neck and neck,** they are level with each other. ■ If someone is **breathing down your neck,** they are watching you and checking what you do very carefully. ■ If you **stick your neck out,** you bravely do or say something which makes it likely you will be criticized or harmed. ■ The **neck** of something like a bottle is the long narrow part at the top.

neckerchief A **neckerchief** is a piece of cloth folded and worn round the neck.

necklace A **necklace** is a piece of jewellery worn round the neck.

neckline The **neckline** of a dress or blouse is the top edge at the front.

necktie A man's tie can be called a **necktie.**

necromancy is black magic or witchcraft.

necrophilia (**necrophiliac**) **Necrophilia** is the act of having sexual intercourse with a dead body, or the desire for it. Someone who feels this desire is called a **necrophiliac.**

necropolis (*pron:* neck-**rop**-pol-liss) (**necropolises**) A **necropolis** is a burial site.

nectar is a sweet liquid produced by flowers, which bees and other insects collect.

nectarine A **nectarine** is a type of smooth-skinned peach.

née is used to mention the maiden name of a married woman. *...Elizabeth Fowles (née Whitton).*

need (**needing, needed**) If you **need** something, you believe you must have it or do it. ■ A **need** is a strong feeling that you must have or do something. ■ If you say something **needs** doing, or there is a **need** for it, you mean it ought to be done. You can also say something **needs** to happen. *The production of rice needs to rise by 45 percent.* ■ People's **needs** are the things they must have to survive or to improve their situation. *...the basic needs of life... Find out what courses are on offer to suit your needs and abilities.* ■ People who are **in need** are very poor or require help of some kind. ■ If something **needs** something else, it needs that thing to improve it or make it work properly. *A few details need some attention... It doesn't need a lot of maintenance.*

needle (**needling, needled**) A **needle** is a small thin piece of metal with a hole at one end, for sewing. ■ A **needle** is a sharp piece of hollow metal attached to a syringe, for giving injections. ■ On a measuring instrument, the **needle** is the thin pointer which moves backwards and forwards on the dial. ■ The **needle** on a record player is the stylus. ■ The **needles** on a conifer are its thin hard pointed leaves. ■ If someone **needles** you, they annoy you by constantly criticizing you. ■ See also **pins and needles, knitting needle.**

needlepoint is embroidery done on canvas.

needless (**needlessly**) **Needless** is used to say something bad is completely unnecessary. *More jobs will be needlessly lost.* ■ People say **'needless to say...'** to emphasize they are saying something obvious or unsurprising. *The army needless to say was furious.*

needlework is sewing or embroidering by hand. A person's **needlework** is a piece of work of this kind.

needy (needier, neediest) Needy people are very poor and do not have enough food or clothing or decent housing. People like these are called **the needy.**

nefarious If you describe an activity as **nefarious,** you mean it is wicked and immoral.

negate (negating, negated; negation) If one thing **negates** another, it cancels it out. *These weaknesses negated his otherwise progressive attitude towards the staff.* ■ If you **negate** something, you deny the truth of it. *He warned that to negate the results of elections would only make things worse.*

negative (negatively) A **negative** reply or decision means 'no'. ■ **Negative** is used to describe something which is unpleasant or damaging. *The car tax was having a very negative effect on car sales.* ■ When a person concentrates on the bad aspects of something, you can say they are being **negative** or talk about their **negative** attitude. *...a negative view of the world.* ■ If a medical or other scientific test is **negative,** it shows no evidence of the condition or substance you are testing for. *The drug tests proved negative.* ■ A **negative** is the image first produced when you take a photograph and which the final photograph is developed from. ■ A **negative** number is less than zero. ■ A **negative** electric charge is one of two opposite kinds of charge, the other one being a positive charge.

negative equity If a person with a mortgage on their home has **negative equity,** the amount of money they owe to the mortgage company is greater than the value of their home.

neglect (neglectful) If you **neglect** someone or something, you do not look after them properly. **Neglect** is failing to look after someone or something. You say someone who behaves like this is **neglectful.** *...a neglectful parent.* ■ If you **neglect** to do something, you fail to do it. ■ If you say someone or something is **neglected,** you mean they do not receive the attention or recognition they deserve. *...long neglected poems.*

negligee (*or* **negligée**) (*pron:* **neg**-lee-zhay, *the 'zh' sounds like 's' in 'pleasure'*) A **negligee** is a woman's dressing gown made of very thin material.

negligent (negligently, negligence) If someone is **negligent,** they fail to do something which it is their duty or responsibility to do. You talk about the **negligence** of someone like this.

negligible A **negligible** amount or effect is so small that it is not worth bothering about.

negotiable If something is **negotiable,** it can be changed or agreed upon as the result of discussion about it. *The conference insisted that human rights are not negotiable.*

negotiate (negotiating, negotiated; negotiation, negotiator) When people **negotiate** with each other, they talk about a problem or situation to try and reach agreement. Talks like these are called **negotiations;** the people taking part are called **negotiators.** ■ If something is **negotiated,** it is

brought about by negotiating. *...a negotiated settlement.* ■ When people get round **the negotiating table,** they have serious discussions, to try and resolve their differences. ■ If you **negotiate** an obstacle, you succeed in getting through it or round it.

Negro (*or* **negro**) (**Negroes**) Negro is a word, considered offensive by many people, for a person with black skin.

neigh When a horse **neighs,** it makes a loud quavering high-pitched noise. This noise is called a **neigh.**

neighbour (*Am:* **neighbor**) (**neighbouring**) Your **neighbours** are the people who live near you. ■ You can call the person standing or sitting next to you your **neighbour.** ■ **Neighbouring** places or things are near others of the same kind. *...the neighbouring shop.* You can call places or things like this **neighbours.**

neighbourhood (*Am:* **neighborhood**) A **neighbourhood** is one of the parts of a town where people live. ■ The **neighbourhood** of someone or something is the area or the people around them. *...excited crowds in the neighbourhood of the park.* ■ If something is **in the neighbourhood of** an amount or rate, it is close to it. *...in the neighbourhood of 380 mph.*

Neighbourhood Watch A **Neighbourhood Watch** scheme involves getting residents to co-operate with each other and with the police, to try to reduce crime in their area.

neighbourly (*Am:* **neighborly**) (**neighbourliness**) **Neighbourly** means things involving neighbours. *...neighbourly quarrels.* ■ If someone living near you behaves in a **neighbourly** way, they are friendly and helpful. *...the neighbourliness of the old urban communities.*

neither is used to say something is not true of two or more people, things, or groups. *Neither the people nor the state would tolerate such acts... Neither was badly injured.* ■ If you have made a statement using a word like 'not' or 'never', you can make it apply to someone or something else by using **neither.** *You will not be getting everything you want. Neither will we.*

nemesis (*pron:* nem-miss-iss) The **nemesis** of a person or group of people is someone or something that brings about their downfall or defeat.

neo- is used to form words which refer to modern versions of earlier beliefs and styles. *...neo-fascists. ...a neo-classical mansion.*

neo-colonialism is domination by a powerful country of another country which is supposed to be independent, by controlling its businesses or financial institutions.

Neolithic The **Neolithic** period or **New Stone Age** was the last period of the Stone Age, when the earliest kind of farming began, and people used polished flint tools and weapons. See also **Palaeolithic, Mesolithic.**

neologism (*pron:* nee-ol-a-jiz-zum) A **neologism** is a new word or expression, or a familiar one being used with a new meaning.

neon is a colourless odourless gas which is used in glass tubes to make lights and signs.

neonate (**neonatal**) A **neonate** is a new-born baby. **Neonatal** means to do with new-born babies. ...*a neonatal unit.*

neophyte A **neophyte** is someone who is new to an activity. ...*neophyte actors.*

nephew Your **nephew** is the son of your sister or brother, or of your husband's or wife's sister or brother.

nepotism If you accuse someone of **nepotism,** you mean they have used their power or influence to get jobs or other benefits for members of their family.

nerd If you call a man a **nerd,** you mean he is boring and unfashionable.

nerve A **nerve** is one of the fibres which carry messages between your brain and the rest of your body. ■ If you talk about someone's **nerves,** you mean their ability to stay calm in difficult situations. *Mortar explosions shatter the nerves of those who have to stay.* ■ **Nerve** is the courage to do something difficult or dangerous. ■ If you say someone has a **nerve,** you mean they are doing something they have no real right to do. ■ If something **gets on your nerves,** it annoys or irritates you. ■ If something like a remark **touches a raw nerve,** it upsets you because it concerns something you are sensitive about.

nerve centre The **nerve centre** of an organization is the place its activities are controlled from.

nerve gas is a poisonous gas which affects people's nervous systems, paralysing them and eventually killing them.

nerve-wracking (*or* **nerve-racking**) A **nerve-wracking** experience is worrying and upsetting, because it is full of uncertainty and danger.

nervous (**nervously; nervousness**) If you are **nervous,** you are anxious and this shows in your behaviour. ■ If you are **nervous** about something, you are afraid to do it, or afraid to become involved with it. ...*nervousness about new technology.* ■ **Nervous** people are easily frightened or upset. ■ Your **nervous system** is all the nerves in your body, together with your brain and spinal cord. It controls your movements and reflexes as well as your thoughts and feelings. ■ If someone has a **nervous breakdown,** they suffer from severe depression and need medical treatment.

nervy people are anxious, and easily upset.

nest A bird's **nest** is a structure it builds to lay its eggs in. Some insects and other animals build nests as places to rear their young in. When a bird **nests** somewhere, it builds a nest there. ■ **hornets' nest:** see **hornet.** See also **love nest.**

nest-egg A **nest-egg** is a sum of money someone is saving for a particular purpose.

nestle (**nestling, nestled**) If a building, place, or thing **nestles** somewhere, it is in a place that seems safe or sheltered.

net (**netting, netted**) **Net** or **netting** is material made of pieces of string, wire, or thread, woven together with spaces in between. ...*net curtains.* ...*plastic netting.* A **net** is a piece of this material used, for example, to catch fish. If you **net** a fish, you catch it in a net. See also **safety net.** ■ If you

net an amount of something, you obtain it as a result of something you do. ...*a robbery which netted some £25,000.* ■ A **net** amount is the final amount after all deductions have been made. ...*a net profit margin of more than 2%.* See also **gross.** ■ The **net** weight of something is its weight without its container or wrapping. See also **gross.** ■ The **net** result of a series of events is the final result when some effects have cancelled each other out.

Net The **Net** is the internet.

netball is a game played by two teams in which goals are scored by throwing a ball through a net on top of a pole at their opponents' end of the court.

nether means 'lower'. The lower part of a person's torso, including their buttocks, is sometimes humorously called their **nether regions.** ■ Ways of life which are not considered respectable, can be referred to as a **nether world.** ...*a nether world of drugs.*

nett has the same meaning as 'net' when talking about an amount or weight.

nettle (**nettling, nettled**) A **nettle** is a wild plant covered with little hairs which sting. ■ If you **grasp the nettle,** you deal with something difficult in a determined way. ■ If someone is **nettled,** they are annoyed or offended.

network (**networking, networked**) A **network** is a number of people, things, or organizations in different places working together as a system. *A car factory is part of a much wider network of manufacturers, deliverers, suppliers and designers.* ...*a telephone network.* ■ A TV **network** is a company or group of companies which broadcasts the same programmes at the same time in different parts of the country. You say programmes broadcast like this are **networked.** ■ When a computer is **networked,** it is connected to other computers so they can exchange information and work together as a system. ■ When a group of professional people try to help each other out in their careers, this is called **networking.** If they went to the same public school, or knew each other at Oxford or Cambridge, you can say they are operating **the old-boy network.**

neural (*pron:* **nyoor**-ral) is used to talk about things relating to nerves or the nervous system.

neuralgia (*pron:* nyoor-**ral**-ja) is severe pain along the whole length of a nerve.

neural network In computing, a **neural network** is a program or system which is designed to imitate the human brain's method of functioning, particularly the process of learning.

neuro- at the beginning of a word means it has something to do with nerves or the nervous system. ...*a neuro-psychiatrist.*

neurology (**neurological; neurologist**) **Neurology** is the medical study of the structure, function, and diseases of the nervous system. ...*neurological disorders.* A person who specializes in neurology is called a **neurologist.**

neuron (*or* **neurone**) A **neuron** is a cell which is part of the nervous system and carries messages from one part of the body to another.

neurosis (*pron:* nyoor-**roh**-siss) (**neuroses; neurotic, neurotically**) Neurosis is a mental disorder which causes people to be depressed and obsessive, and to have unreasonable fears and worries. **Neurotic** is used to describe a person suffering from this disorder, or to talk about behaviour connected with it. *...a neurotic delusion... These patients are not neurotics.* ■ **Neurotic** is used to describe people who are not actually ill but show a lot of unreasonable anxiety about something. *Hollywood seems to be more neurotic than ever about its intellectual image.*

neurotransmitter A **neurotransmitter** is a chemical by which a nerve cell communicates with another nerve cell or with a muscle.

neuter (**neutering, neutered**) When an animal is **neutered,** its reproductive organs are removed. ■ If an organization or system is **neutered,** something is done to it which reduces its effectiveness. *The Government's 'hidden agenda' to neuter local authorities.*

neutral (**neutrality**) A **neutral** person or country does not support either side in a war or dispute. *...neutral observers.* Neutral countries and people can also be called **neutrals.** Not supporting either side in a war or dispute is called **neutrality.** ■ A **neutral** zone is an area of land, usually between two opposing armies, where it has been agreed that no fighting shall take place. ■ **Neutral** is used to describe things which do not show any bias, preference, or opinion. *...the neutrality of the interview form.* ■ **Neutral** colours or **neutrals** are colours like grey or brown which are not bright and which harmonize with most other colours. ■ **Neutral** is the position between the gears of a vehicle, in which the gears are not connected to the engine.

neutralize (*or* **neutralise**) (**neutralizing, neutralized; neutralization**) If you **neutralize** something, you prevent it from having any effect or from working properly. *The devices are neutralized by a card key.*

neutron A **neutron** is an atomic particle which has no electrical charge.

neutron bomb The **neutron bomb** is a nuclear weapon designed to kill all living things within a certain area without a large explosion and without long-lasting radioactive contamination.

never means at no time in the past or future. *This feat has never before been attempted.* ■ **Never** is used to mean 'not in any circumstances'. *Destroying life could never be justified.* ■ **never mind:** see **mind.**

never-never land When people talk about a **never-never land,** they mean an imaginary place where everything is pleasant.

nevertheless means in spite of what has just been said. *The Plaza is dominated mainly by tourist shops, but nevertheless the town has a welcoming feel to it.*

new (**newly, newness**) New things have been recently made or created, or are in the process of being made or created. *...a new 10 per cent tax on luxuries.* ■ If something is **new** to you or you are **new** to it, you have never experienced it or done it before. ■ **New** potatoes or carrots have been produced early in the season, and are usually small with a sweet flavour.

New Age travellers are people who travel from place to place, living in tents and caravans, and who reject many of the values of modern society. ■ **New Age** is used to talk about activities like meditation, astrology, and alternative medicine, or to describe people involved in them. *...New Age mystics.*

newborn A **newborn** baby has been born very recently.

newcomer People who have only recently arrived in a place or become involved in an activity are sometimes called **newcomers.**

newel A **newel** or **newel post** is the thick post at the top or bottom of a staircase which supports the hand rail.

new-fangled Some people use **new-fangled** to describe new ideas or inventions which they do not like or do not trust.

new-found is used to describe interests or beliefs which someone has recently acquired. *...her new-found enthusiasm for sailing.*

newly See **new.**

New Man When people talk about the **New Man,** they mean men who have modern ideas about relationships between men and women and who believe in sharing the childcare and housework with their partners.

new moon The moon is called a **new moon** when it is seen as a thin crescent shape, after not appearing the previous night.

news is information about recent events. *He is wondering how he can face his friends with the news.* ■ **News** is information about recent events given in newspapers and on TV and radio. A regular news programme is often called **the news.**

news agency A **news agency** is an organization which collects news stories from all over the world and sells them to newspapers and TV and radio stations.

newsagent A **newsagent** or **newsagent's** is a shop which sells newspapers, magazines, sweets, and cigarettes. The person who runs this type of shop can also be called a **newsagent.**

newscast (**newscaster**) A **newscast** is a TV or radio programme which gives news about recent events in the world. The person who reads the news on a newscast is called a **newscaster.**

news conference A **news conference** is a meeting held by a famous or important person in which they answer journalists' questions.

newsflash (**newsflashes**) A **newsflash** is an interruption in a TV or radio programme, to announce an important piece of news.

newshound A **newshound** is a very eager newspaper reporter who is always looking for new and exciting stories.

newsletter A **newsletter** is a printed sheet or small magazine containing information about an organization. It is sent out regularly to people, especially members of the organization.

newsman (**newsmen**) News reporters or presenters are sometimes called **newsmen.**

newspaper A **newspaper** consists of several large sheets of folded paper with things like news reports, articles, and adverts printed on them. ■ A **newspaper** is an organization which produces a newspaper. *A short time later, a man called a newspaper.* ■ **Newspaper** is old newspapers, especially when they are used for a purpose such as wrapping things up.

newspaperman (**newspapermen**) A **newspaperman** is a reporter or photographer who works for a newspaper.

newsprint is (a) the cheap paper on which newspapers are printed. (b) the ink used to print newspapers. (c) the text printed in newspapers. *The papers are still devoting pages of newsprint to the crisis.*

newsreader A **newsreader** is a person who reads the news on TV or radio.

newsreel In the past, **newsreels** were short films about recent events, shown in cinemas.

newsroom A **newsroom** is (a) a TV or radio studio where news reports are prepared and broadcast. (b) a newspaper office where news reports are written and edited before they are printed.

news-stand (or **newsstand**) A **news-stand** is a movable stall in the street or at a railway station, where you can buy newspapers.

newsworthy If you say something which has happened is **newsworthy**, you mean it is interesting or important enough to be in the news.

newt The **newt** is a small lizard-like creature with a moist skin. Newts usually live in water.

New Testament The **New Testament** is the part of the Bible which deals with the life of Jesus and with Christianity in the early Church.

new town A **new town** is a town which has been planned and built as a whole, rather than developing gradually in an unplanned way.

new wave A **new wave** is a movement in art, music, or film which introduces many new ideas.

New World The **New World** is the whole of the American continent.

New Year is the time when people celebrate the start of a year.

New Year's Day is the first day of the year, which in Western countries is January 1st.

New Year's Eve is the last day of the year.

next You say **next** when you are mentioning what happened or what should happen after the thing you have just described. *Next, stir in the gelatine.* ■ The **next** thing of a particular kind means the first one after the present one, or the first one since the last one. *...the next problem. ...her next book.* ■ If you are among a group of people or things, the **next** person or thing is the one nearest to you. *...in the next room. ...a man in the next row.* Similarly, you say one person or thing is **next to** another one. ■ If a house or flat is **next door** to yours, there are no other houses or flats in between. ■ The **next** best thing of a particular kind is better than all the others except the best one. ■ **Next to nothing** means hardly anything. *They say next to nothing about real women.*

next of kin Your **next of kin** are your closest relatives.

nexus (*plural:* **nexus**) A **nexus** is a connection or system of connections linking things closely together. *...the nexus of money and politics.*

NHS In Britain, the **NHS** or **National Health Service** is a publicly-funded system which provides free or inexpensive medical care for everyone.

nib The **nib** of a fountain pen is the small pointed piece of metal at the end which releases ink onto the paper when you write.

nibble (**nibbling, nibbled**) Light snacks like crisps and nuts are sometimes called **nibbles**. ■ If a person or animal **nibbles** something, they take small repeated bites out of it.

nice (**nicer, nicest; nicely, niceness**) If you say something is **nice**, you mean it is enjoyable, pleasant, welcome, or reassuring. *...a nice cup of tea... It's nice to know that you can speak to an expert if you get stuck.* ■ **Nice** can be used to say something looks neat and attractive. *...nice clothes... The tables are nicely laid.* ■ If you say someone is **nice,** you mean they are friendly, pleasant, and polite. ■ If something is working **nicely,** it is working very satisfactorily.

nicety (**niceties**) Niceties are the small details of something, especially the finer points of polite behaviour.

niche (*pron:* **neesh**) A **niche** is a hollow area in a wall, or a natural hollow in a rock. ■ If you find a **niche,** you find a job or position which is exactly right for you.

nick If someone **nicks** something, they steal it. ■ If the police **nick** someone, they arrest them. ■ Prison is sometimes called the **nick.** ■ If you **nick** something, you make a small cut in it. A **nick** is a small cut in something. ■ If something is **in good nick,** it is in good condition. ■ If something happens **in the nick of time,** it happens just in time for something bad to be prevented.

nickel is a silvery-white metal which is resistant to corrosion. ■ A **nickel** is an American or Canadian coin worth five cents.

nickname (**nicknamed**) A **nickname** is an informal name given to someone or something.

nicotine is a poisonous addictive substance found in tobacco.

niece Your **niece** is the daughter of your sister or brother, or of your husband's or wife's sister or brother.

nifty If something is done in a **nifty** way, it is done skilfully. ■ A **nifty** device is cleverly designed to make something easy for you.

niggardly If someone is **niggardly,** they are not generous with something, especially money.

nigger is an offensive word for a black person.

niggle (**niggling, niggled**) A **niggle** is a minor problem which keeps worrying you. You can say a problem like this **niggles** you. *Niggling doubts remain.*

nigh If you say something is **nigh,** you mean it is going to happen soon. ■ **Nigh, well-nigh,** and **nigh on,** are used in front of words like 'impossible' to mean 'almost'. *His behaviour has become well-nigh intolerable.*

night The **night** is the period each twenty-four hours when it is dark. ■ If you have an **early night,**

you go to bed early. If you have a **late night,** you do not go to bed until late. ■ **Night** is used to mean 'evening'. *He is injured so he'll miss Wednesday night's replay.* **Last night** means yesterday evening.

nightcap A **nightcap** is a drink, usually alcoholic, which you have just before going to bed. ■ In the past, a **nightcap** was a kind of hat people wore in bed.

nightclothes are the clothes you wear in bed.

nightclub A **nightclub** is a place people go to late in the evening to drink and dance or see a show.

nightdress (nightdresses) A **nightdress** is a loose dress worn by women or girls in bed.

nightfall is the time of day when it starts to get dark.

nightgown In the US, a nightdress is usually called a **nightgown.**

nightie A **nightie** is the same as a nightdress.

nightingale The **nightingale** is a small brown European bird. The male bird sings beautifully, especially in the evening.

nightlife The **nightlife** in a town or city is the entertainment available at night.

nightlight A **nightlight** is a very dim light which is left on at night.

nightly A **nightly** event happens every night or every evening. *...performing nightly in front of local audiences.*

nightmare (nightmarish) A **nightmare** is a frightening dream. You can also say a situation that is very frightening or unpleasant is a **nightmare** or **nightmarish.** *Since then our lives have been a nightmare.* ■ If you say something is someone's **nightmare,** you mean it is the thing they are most afraid of happening.

night school is an institution where adults can go to take educational courses in the evenings.

nightspot A **nightspot** is the same as a nightclub.

night-time is used to talk about things connected with the period between sunset and sunrise. *...night-time temperatures.*

nightwatchman (or night watchman) (nightwatchmen) A **nightwatchman** is a man whose job is to guard buildings at night.

nightwear is clothing worn in bed, such as pyjamas and nightdresses.

nihilism (pron: nye-ill-liz-zum) (nihilistic; nihilist) **Nihilism** is the belief that there is no justification for any existing authorities, institutions, or values, and that they should all be rejected or destroyed. Someone who takes this view is called a **nihilist;** you say his or her opinions are **nihilistic.**

Nikkei (pron: nik-kay) The **Nikkei index** or **Nikkei average** is an index of share prices based on the average price of shares in 225 Japanese companies on the Japanese Stock Exchange. It is used to check general changes in share prices.

nil means zero or nothing.

nimble (nimbler, nimblest; nimbly, nimbleness) A **nimble** person is quick and agile. ■ Someone who has a **nimble** mind is able to take things in quickly and make rapid decisions and judgments.

nimbus A **nimbus** is a large dark grey cloud which brings rain or snow.

nimby (or NIMBY) stands for 'Not In My Back Yard'. It is used to talk about people who object to something (for example a probation hostel) being sited near their home. *Local MPs have met with a barrage of NIMBY fury.*

nine (ninth) Nine is the number 9.

ninepin – Ninepins is another name for the game of skittles. Each skittle can be called a **ninepin.** ■ If you say people or things are going down like **ninepins,** you mean they are being injured or destroyed one after the other.

nineteen (nineteenth) Nineteen is the number 19.

ninety (ninetieth, nineties) Ninety is the number 90. ■ The **nineties** is the period from 1990 to 1999. ■ If someone is in their **nineties,** they are aged 90 to 99.

ninny (ninnies) If you call someone a **ninny,** you mean they are rather silly.

nip (nipping, nipped) If an animal or insect **nips** you or gives you a **nip,** it takes a small bite at you. ■ **nip** something **in the bud:** see bud. ■ If you **nip** somewhere, you go there quickly or briefly, to do something or get something. *She nipped out for extra supplies of milk.*

nipple A person's **nipples** are the two round pieces of darker-coloured flesh on their chest. Babies suck milk through their mother's nipples.

nippy A **nippy** person or vehicle moves around quickly among other people or vehicles.

nirvana (pron: near-vah-na) For Buddhists and Hindus, **nirvana** is the highest state of spiritual enlightenment which can be achieved. ■ People sometimes talk about a state of complete happiness or peace as **nirvana.**

nit – Nits are the tiny eggs of a louse which have been laid in someone's hair.

nit-picking If you say someone is **nit-picking,** you mean they keep finding fault with something by concentrating on small and unimportant details.

nitrate – Nitrates are chemical compounds that include nitrogen and oxygen. Nitrates are used as fertilizers.

nitrogen is a colourless gas with no smell. It forms about 78% of the earth's atmosphere.

nitroglycerine is a powerful liquid explosive.

nitrous oxide is a colourless gas used as a mild anaesthetic. It is also called 'laughing gas'.

nitty-gritty If you get down to the **nitty-gritty** of something, you deal with the most important and basic part of it.

no (noes) No is used to give a negative answer to a question, to refuse an offer, or to refuse permission for something. ■ In Parliament, the **noes** are the people who vote against a motion. The people who vote in favour are called the 'ayes'. ■ **No** is used to say there is nothing of a particular kind. *Mrs Brown, a widow, had no children.* ■ **No** is often used when making comparisons between things. For example, if you say something is **no** bigger than something else, you mean it is the same size or smaller. *The risks are no greater than for any other new treatment.* ■ If you say **there's no** doing a particular thing, you mean it is impossible to do it. *There's no going back to the old days.*

No. (Nos.) No. is short for 'number'. ...*Nos. 3 and 4.*

nob Upper-class people are sometimes called **nobs.**

no-ball In cricket, if a bowler bowls a **no-ball,** he or she bowls in a way which is against the rules.

nobble (nobbling, nobbled) If a racehorse is **nobbled,** it is deliberately harmed, often by giving it a drug, to prevent it from winning.

Nobel Prize (Nobel prizewinner) Nobel Prizes are annual prizes awarded by an international committee for outstanding achievements in various fields.

noble (nobler, noblest; nobly, nobility) Noble behaviour is honest, brave, and unselfish. ■ A **noble** is someone of high social class who has a title. You say someone like this belongs to the **nobility** or comes from a **noble** family. ■ **Noble** is sometimes used to describe things which are grand and impressive. ...*the great parks with their noble trees.*

nobleman (noblewoman) A **nobleman** or **noblewoman** is a member of the nobility.

noblesse oblige *(pron:* no-bless oh-**bleezh;** *the 'zh' sound is like 's' in 'pleasure')* is the idea that privileged people, for example the nobility, should act honourably and use their privileges to help other people.

noblewoman See **nobleman.**

nobody (nobodies) Nobody or **no one** means not a single person. ■ A **nobody** is someone who is not considered important.

no-claims A **no-claims bonus** is a reduction in an insurance premium if no claims have been made within a certain period.

nocturnal means happening or active during the night. ...*nocturnal noise.* ...*nocturnal creatures.*

nod (nodding, nodded) If you **nod** or give a **nod,** you move your head up and down quickly, as a way of saying 'yes'. ■ If you **nod** towards something, you indicate where it is by making a quick movement of your head. ■ If someone **gets the nod** or is **given the nod,** they are given permission to do something. ■ If you **nod off,** you fall asleep. ■ If a footballer **nods** the ball in a particular direction, they hit it there with their head. ■ **nodding acquaintance:** see **acquaintance.**

node On a plant, a **node** is one of the places on the stem which a leaf grows from. ■ A **node** in someone's body is a swelling or roundish lump.

nodule A **nodule** is a small round lump on something.

Noel is another word for Christmas.

no-go A **no-go area** is (a) a place which has a reputation for violence and crime which makes people frightened to go there. (b) a place controlled by people who use force to prevent other people from entering it.

noise A **noise** is a sound, especially an unpleasant one. ■ If someone makes **noises** of a certain kind about something, they say things which indicate their attitude towards it. *He took care to make encouraging noises about the future.* ■ If you say someone is **making the right noises,** you mean they are behaving in a certain way because they feel they ought to, rather than because they really want to.

At the annual party conference he always made the right noises.

noiseless is used to describe things which do not make a noise, or things which happen without any noise being made.

noisy (noisier, noisiest; noisily) You say someone or something is **noisy** when they make a lot of noise. A **noisy** place is full of noise. ■ You call someone's actions **noisy** when they make a lot of fuss to draw attention to something.

nomad (nomadic) A **nomad** is a member of a tribe which travels from place to place, rather than living in one place all the time. **Nomadic** is used to describe people like these and their way of life.

no-man's land is an area of land which is not owned or controlled by anyone, for example the area of land between two opposing armies.

nom de guerre *(plural:* **noms de guerre)** *(pron:* nom duh **gair)** A **nom de guerre** is a false name someone uses for something they do.

nom de plume *(plural:* **noms de plume)** *(pron:* nom duh **ploom)** A **nom de plume** is the same as a pen name.

nomenclature *(pron:* no-**men**-klatch-er) A **nomenclature** is a system of naming a particular set of things. ...*botanical nomenclature.* ...*the nomenclature of woody plants.*

nominal (nominally) Nominal is used to talk about a characteristic someone or something is supposed to have, but which they may not have in reality. *The two states are nominal allies.* ■ A **nominal** price or sum of money is very small in comparison with the real value of the thing being bought or sold. *You will be charged only a nominal fee.*

nominate (nominating, nominated; nomination, nominee) If someone is **nominated** for a position or job, they are officially appointed to do it, or their name is put forward as a candidate. You say they are a **nominee** for the position or job. *Leadership nominations close at noon next Thursday.* ■ If someone or something is **nominated** for an award, someone formally suggests that person or thing is considered for it. You say they are a **nominee** for the award. ...*an Oscar nomination.*

non- is added to a word to say someone or something does not have a certain quality or characteristic. ...*a non-cancerous condition.* ...*a non-custodial sentence.* ■ **Non-** is added to words to say someone does not do something. ...*non-payers.* ...*the non-attendance of the two men.*

nonagenarian *(pron:* no-nej-jin-**nair**-ee-an) A **nonagenarian** is a person in their nineties.

non-aggression A **non-aggression** pact is an agreement between countries that they will not attack or harm each other.

non-aligned (non-alignment) A **non-aligned** country does not belong to any politically linked group of countries. You say a country like this is following a policy of **non-alignment.**

nonchalant *(pron:* non-shall-ant) **(nonchalantly, nonchalance)** You say someone is **nonchalant** when they are very calm and seem not to worry or care about things. You talk about the **nonchalance** of someone like this.

non-combatant troops are members of the armed forces whose duties do not include fighting. ■ In a war, **non-combatants** are people who are not members of the armed forces.

non-commissioned officer See **NCO.**

non-committal You can describe someone as **non-committal** when they deliberately do not express their opinion or reveal their intentions clearly. *He is non-committal about the level of support for a UN resolution.*

non-conformist (*or* **nonconformist**) (**non-conformity**) **Non-conformist** churches are Protestant churches which are not part of the Church of England. A **non-conformist** is a member of a non-conformist church. ■ A **non-conformist** is someone who behaves or thinks in an unusual, original, or rebellious way. You talk about the **non-conformity** of someone like this.

nondescript people and things are dull and uninteresting.

none means not a single person or thing, or not even a small amount of something. ■ **None too** is used in front of words like 'sure' and 'easily' to emphasize that the quality mentioned is not present. *The City is none too keen on tycoons at present.* ■ If you say you will **have none of** something, you mean you will not tolerate or accept it. *He was looking for a penalty, but the referee would have none of it.* ■ **none the less:** see **nonetheless.**

nonentity (**nonentities**) If you call someone a **nonentity,** you mean they are not special or important in any way.

nonetheless (*or* **none the less**) means the same as 'nevertheless'.

non-event If you say something was a **non-event,** you mean it turned out to be not as exciting or significant as people were expecting.

non-existent (**non-existence**) If you say something is **non-existent** or talk about its **non-existence,** you mean it does not exist.

non-fiction is writing which provides information or describes real events, rather than telling a story.

non-interference is the same as non-intervention.

non-intervention (**non-interventionist**) If a country has a policy of **non-intervention,** it purposely does not become involved in wars or disputes between other countries. People, especially politicians, who favour a policy like this are called **non-interventionists.**

no-nonsense people are firm, straightforward, and efficient.

non-partisan is used to describe people and organizations that do not support any particular political party. *...a non-partisan head of state.* A **non-partisan** approach to a problem involves co-operation between political parties who would normally be opposing each other.

non-person If someone becomes a **non-person,** people reject them, because they have done something wrong or fallen out of favour with the authorities.

nonplussed If you are **nonplussed** by something, you do not know what to do or say.

non-proliferation A **non-proliferation** treaty is one in which countries agree to limit the production and spread of nuclear weapons.

non-sectarian organizations are not connected with any particular religion.

nonsense (**nonsensical**) If you say something is **nonsense** or describe it as **nonsensical,** you mean it is untrue or silly. ■ If you say someone in authority will stand **no nonsense,** you mean they will not tolerate any indiscipline or awkward behaviour. ■ **Nonsense** is a kind of humorous writing, especially for children. It deals with imaginary creatures or impossible situations.

non-sequitur (*pron:* non sek-wit-tur) If you say a statement is a **non-sequitur,** you mean it does not follow logically from what was said before.

non-starter If you say something is a **non-starter,** you mean it has no chance of being accepted or succeeding.

non-stick A **non-stick** pan is coated with a substance which prevents food sticking to it.

non-stop is used to describe things which continue without any breaks or pauses. *...a non-stop flight.*

non-verbal communication does not involve the use of words.

noodle – **Noodles** are long thin pieces of pasta which are cooked in soup or boiling water.

nook If you talk about every **nook and cranny** in a place, you mean every part of it.

nooky (*or* **nookie**) is a humorous word for sexual intercourse.

noon is twelve o'clock in the middle of the day.

noonday is used to talk about things happening in the middle of the day. *...the noonday sun.*

no one means the same as 'nobody'.

noose A **noose** is a loop at the end of a piece of rope, especially one used to hang someone.

nor See **neither.** ■ **Nor** is used to link two negative statements which have something in common. *We have certainly not lost a battle, nor do we plan to do so in the future.*

Nordic People are sometimes described as **Nordic** when they are fairly tall and have blond or fair hair, blue eyes, and fair skin.

norm If you say something is the **norm,** you mean it is what usually happens. ■ A **norm** is an official standard or level which people are supposed to achieve or conform to. *...a national pay norm.* ■ **Norms** are rules of behaviour which are considered normal in a society or group.

normal (**normally**) If you say someone or something is **normal,** you mean they conform to what is usual and expected. *Life in the city was beginning to return to normal... It is not something I would normally do.*

normalcy is the same as normality.

normalise See **normalize.**

normality is a situation where everything is normal. *Life was returning to somewhere near normality.*

normalize (*or* **normalise**) (**normalizing, normalized; normalization**) If a country **normalizes** relations with another country, it restores them to the way they were before they had a quarrel or conflict.

■ When a situation is **normalized,** it returns to normal. *...the normalization of the blood-sugar levels.*

Norman The **Normans** were a people from northern France who successfully invaded England in 1066.

normative is used to describe things which impose a standard for people to follow. *...normative guidelines for action.*

Norse The **Norse** people were the people who lived in Scandinavia in ancient and medieval times.

north (**northern**) **North** is one of the four main points of the compass. ■ The **north** is the direction on your left when you look towards the place where the sun rises. If you go in that direction, you go **north;** a place in that direction is **north of** the place where you are now. ■ The **north** or **northern** part of a place is the part north of its centre. *...Turkey, Iraq's northern neighbour.* ■ **North** winds blow from the north.

North Atlantic Treaty Organization See **NATO.**

northbound traffic is heading towards the north.

north-east (*or* **northeast**) (**north-eastern**) The **north-east** is the direction halfway between north and east. ■ The **north-east** or **north-eastern** part of a place is the part north-east of its centre.

north-easterly A **north-easterly** wind blows from the north-east. ■ If you travel in a **north-easterly** direction, you travel towards the north-east.

north-eastern See **north-east.**

northerly winds blow from the north. ■ If you travel or face in a **northerly** direction, you travel or face towards the north. ■ The most **northerly** part of a place is the part furthest to the north. Similarly, the most **northerly** place of a group of places is the one furthest to the north.

northern See **north.**

northerner A **northerner** is a person who was born or lives in the northern part of a country or region.

northernmost The **northernmost** part of a place is the part furthest to the north.

northward (**northwards**) If you go **northward** or **northwards,** you go towards the north.

north-west (*or* **northwest**) (**north-western**) The **north-west** is the direction halfway between north and west. ■ The **north-west** or **north-western** part of a place is the part north-west of its centre.

north-westerly A **north-westerly** wind blows from the north-west. ■ If you travel in a **north-westerly** direction, you travel towards the north-west.

north-western See **north-west.**

Norwegian is used to talk about people and things in or from Norway. *...a Norwegian economist.* ■ A **Norwegian** is someone who comes from Norway. ■ **Norwegian** is the main language spoken in Norway.

Nos. See **No.**

nose (**nosing, nosed**) Your **nose** is the organ which enables you to smell things. ■ If you **nose around,** you search for something. ■ If you have a **nose** for something, you have an instinctive ability to find or recognize it. *Barbara has a good nose for a story.* ■ The **nose** of a wine is its smell. ■ The **nose** of a plane is the part at the front.

nosebag A **nosebag** is a bag containing food for a horse, hung over the horse's head.

nosebleed If you have a **nosebleed,** blood runs out of the inside of your nose.

nosedive (*or* **nose-dive**) (**nosediving, nosedived**) If a plane **nosedives** or goes into a **nosedive,** it dives steeply, nose first, towards the ground. ■ If something like a share price **nosedives** or goes into a **nosedive,** it falls suddenly and rapidly. ■ If a situation **nosedives,** it takes a sudden bad turn.

nosey See **nosy.**

nostalgic (**nostalgically, nostalgia**) If you are **nostalgic** for something in the past or feel **nostalgia** for it, you think of it with pleasure and affection.

nostril Your **nostrils** are the two openings at the lower end of your nose.

nostrum A **nostrum** is a simple remedy for dealing with a problem, especially one which can be summed up in a few words.

nosy (*or* **nosey**) (**nosier, nosiest**) If you say someone is being **nosy,** you mean they are trying to find out about something which is none of their business.

not is used to give a sentence its opposite meaning. *It is not like that in real life.* After words like 'is' and 'do', **not** is often shortened to **n't.** *It didn't make any difference.* ■ **Not** is used to say there are exceptions to something which is generally true. *The news is not all bad.*

notable (**notably**) **Notable** is used to say something is significant or interesting. *Britain's richest are slow to give to charity, with some notable exceptions... The fish and shellfish are notably fresh.* ■ **Notables** are people who have an important position of some kind. *...the local notables.*

notary (**notaries**) A **notary** or **notary public** is a person, usually a lawyer, who has legal authority to witness the signing of documents so they are legally valid, especially for use overseas.

notation A **notation** is a set of written symbols used in something like maths, music, or chess.

notch (**notches, notching, notched**) A **notch** is a small cut, usually V-shaped, in the surface or edge of something. ■ If something is raised or lowered a **notch,** it is raised or lowered by a small amount. ■ If you **notch** a victory or **notch** it **up,** you achieve it. ■ See also **top-notch.**

note (**noting, noted**) A **note** is a short letter. ■ A **note** in a book or other document is a short piece of additional information. ■ If you **make a note** of something or **note it down,** you write it down, so you have the information when you need it. ■ If you **note** something, you become aware of it. *He noted that the majority of women who work there were pretty.* ■ A person or thing **of note** is important or well-known. *He has published nothing of note.* ■ If someone is **noted** for something, they are well-known for it. *...a highly respected priest who is noted for his work with the poor.* ■ In music, a **note** is a sound with a particular pitch, or a written symbol representing this sound. ■ A particular **note** is a feeling, atmosphere, or quality. *Do I detect a note of panic in your voice?* ■ A **note** is a banknote.

notebook A **notebook** is a small book for writing notes in. ■ A **notebook** computer is a portable computer, the size of a small book.

notepad A **notepad** is a small pad of paper for writing notes on. ■ A **notepad** computer is a small portable computer and personal organizer.

notepaper is paper for writing letters on.

noteworthy is used to describe things which are significant or remarkable in some way. *The most noteworthy incident occurred in the thirtieth minute.*

nothing means 'not anything'. *Nothing is being done... I think there is nothing better than English roast beef.*

nothingness is complete non-existence or emptiness. *He wanted evidence that there might be something beyond the grave and not nothingness.*

notice (**noticing, noticed**) A **notice** is a written sign or announcement, placed where people can read it. ■ **Notice** is advanced warning about something. If something happens at an hour's **notice,** you are warned one hour in advance that it is going to happen. ■ If an employer **gives** someone their **notice,** he or she warns them they have a specified period of time before they have to leave their job. Similarly, an employee can **hand in their notice** to their employer. ■ If you **notice** someone or something, you become aware of them. ■ If you **take notice of** someone or something, you pay attention to them. ■ If a performance or book gets good **notices,** critics write approving things about it.

noticeable (**noticeably**) If something is **noticeable,** it is obvious and easily noticed.

noticeboard (*or* **notice board**) A **noticeboard** is a board on a wall where people pin notices.

notifiable A **notifiable** disease is one which must be reported to the authorities whenever it occurs, because it is dangerous or can spread rapidly.

notify (**notifies, notifying, notified; notification**) If you **notify** someone of something you are going to do or give them **notification** of it, you officially inform them of it.

notion A **notion** is an idea or belief. *Most creative people object to the notion that the work they do comes easily.*

notional (**notionally**) **Notional** is used to describe something which exists for theoretical purposes only, and which may be very different from what really exists. *Both committees are notionally chaired by the president, but the effective chairman is always the attorney-general.*

notorious (**notoriously; notoriety**) If someone or something is **notorious** for something bad, they are well-known for it. Being well-known for something bad is called **notoriety.**

notwithstanding If you say something is the case **notwithstanding** something else, you mean it is so in spite of it. *He despised William Pitt, notwithstanding the similar views they both held.*

nougat (*pron:* **noo**-gah *or* **nug**-gut) is a kind of firm chewy sweet, usually with nuts in it.

nought is the number zero.

noun – **Nouns** are names and other words you use to refer to people, places, and things. 'James', 'engineer', and 'love' are all nouns.

nourish (**nourishes, nourishing, nourished; nourishment**) You say food **nourishes** people or animals or provides **nourishment** for them when it keeps them alive and healthy. **Nourishing** food is particularly good at this. You say people are **well-nourished** when they have been eating plenty of healthy food. ■ If something **nourishes** your mind, it keeps it active.

nous (*rhymes with* 'house') is common sense or good judgment in practical matters. *...commercial nous.*

nouveau riche (*plural:* **nouveaux riches**) (*both pron:* noo-voh **reesh**) When people talk about the **nouveaux riches,** they mean people who have made a lot of money and spend it on expensive things without showing much taste.

nouvelle cuisine (*pron:* **noo**-vell kwi-**zeen**) is a style of French cooking known for its light sauces, fresh ingredients, and careful presentation.

novel (**novelist, novelistic**) A **novel** is a long book which tells a story. A person who writes novels is called a **novelist.** ■ If you say something is **novel,** you mean it is new, fresh, or original. *...a novel attempt to attract customers to high culture.*

novelette A **novelette** is a short novel intended for light reading.

novella A **novella** is a short novel.

novelty (**novelties**) A **novelty** is something which is interesting because it is new or unusual. *...the days when a motor car was a novelty... Changing styles cater to a desire for novelty and individualism.* ■ **Novelty** objects are designed to appeal to people because they are curious and original. *...a novelty telephone shaped like a Jaguar car.* Objects like these are sometimes called **novelties.**

novice (*pron:* **nov**-viss) A **novice** is someone who is new to an activity. *...a novice parachutist.* ■ In a monastery or convent, a **novice** is a person preparing to be a monk or nun.

now is used to talk about a situation in the present, usually in contrast to one in the past. *The couple now have three children.* ■ **Now** is used to give the reason for a situation which exists at present. *In the former Soviet Union, few mines look viable now that the state no longer pays their bills.* ■ **Just now** is used to talk about something which happened a very short time ago. *You were showing it me just now on a computer terminal.* ■ If something happens **now and then** or **now and again,** it happens occasionally, but not regularly. ■ If you say something will happen **any day now** or **any time now,** you mean it will happen very soon.

nowadays is used to talk about the present, in contrast to the past. *Kids nowadays know how babies are born.*

nowhere means 'not anywhere'. *There was nowhere to sit.* ■ If something is in the **middle of nowhere,** it is far away from other places and is usually difficult to get to. ■ If you say someone or something came **from nowhere,** you mean they appeared suddenly and unexpectedly. ■ If you say someone or something is **getting nowhere,** you mean they are not achieving anything. ■ **nowhere near:** see **near.**

noxious substances are poisonous or harmful. *...noxious chemicals.* ■ You can call unpleasant things and people **noxious.** *...a noxious smell.*

nozzle A **nozzle** is a narrow piece on the end of something like a hose, which controls the flow of whatever goes into it or out of it.

nuance (*pron:* **new**-ahnss) (**nuanced**) The **nuances** in something someone says, writes, or performs, are its small and subtle differences in sound, feeling, appearance, or meaning. ...*his delicately nuanced performance.*

nub The **nub** of a problem or argument is its most basic and central part.

nubile (*pron:* **new**-bile) women are young, physically mature, and sexually attractive.

nuclear is used to talk about things to do with the nuclei of atoms, or with the energy produced when they are split or combined. ...*nuclear power stations.* ■ A **nuclear reactor** is a device which uses a nuclear reaction to produce nuclear energy. ■ **Nuclear fission** is a way of producing massive amounts of energy by splitting the nuclei of atoms of materials such as uranium. Similarly, **nuclear fusion** produces massive amounts of energy by combining pairs of atoms of a substance such as tritium. ■ A **nuclear** weapon produces an explosion by nuclear fission or fusion. ...*nuclear missiles.* ...*the nuclear arms race.* ■ A country which has nuclear weapons is called a **nuclear power.**

nuclear family A **nuclear family** consists of a father and mother and their children.

nuclear-free zones are areas where anything to do with nuclear weapons or nuclear energy is forbidden.

nuclear winter is a possible after-effect of a large nuclear explosion. It is thought that dust in the atmosphere could shut out the sunlight, and this would result in very low temperatures for a long time.

nucleus (*pron:* **nyoo**-klee-uss) (*plural:* **nuclei**) The **nucleus** of a cell or atom is its central part, consisting of protons and neutrons. ■ The **nucleus** of something is its central or most important part. *This collection formed the nucleus of the British Library.*

nude (**nudity**) If someone is **nude** or **in the nude,** they are not wearing any clothes. **Nudity** is being without any clothes. ■ A **nude** is a picture or statue of someone not wearing clothes.

nudge (**nudging, nudged**) If something is **nudged** or given a **nudge,** people try gently to get it to change in a certain way. *British companies are nudging clients to travel further afield.* ■ If you **nudge** someone or give them a **nudge,** you give them a gentle push with your elbow, usually to draw their attention to something. ■ If something is **nudging** a level or figure, it is getting close to it. *The temperature was nudging 80 degrees.*

nudist A **nudist** is the same as a naturist.

nudity See **nude.**

nugatory (*pron:* **new**-gat-tree) things are without value. *If the Secretary of State's powers were limited in this way, they would be wholly nugatory.*

nugget A **nugget** is a small rough lump of something, especially gold. ■ A **nugget** of information is a small piece of it which is especially interesting or valuable.

nuisance If you say someone or something is a **nuisance,** you mean they are annoying you.

nuke (**nuking, nuked**) A **nuke** is a nuclear weapon. If one country **nukes** another, it attacks it with nuclear weapons.

null If something is declared **null and void,** it is not legally valid.

nullify (**nullifies, nullifying, nullified**) If one thing **nullifies** another, it makes it lose its effect. *Painkillers nullified the effect of preventive medicines.* ■ If something like a contract is **nullified,** it is declared not valid.

numb (**numbing, numbingly, numbness**) If part of your body is **numb,** you have no feeling there. ■ If an experience **numbs** you or leaves you feeling **numb,** you are so upset by it that you cannot think clearly or feel any emotion. ■ If you say something is **numbing** or **mind-numbing,** you mean it is very dull and uninteresting.

number (**numbering, numbered**) A **number** is a word or symbol used for counting or to say where something comes in a series. ...*Room Number 118.* If you **number** something you give it a number. ■ The **number** of people or things involved in a situation is how many there are. You can say people or things **number** a particular amount. ...*a crowd which numbered some four thousand.* ■ If you talk about a **number of** people or things, you mean several of them. ■ If someone or something **is numbered** among a particular group, they are believed to belong in it. *She is still to be numbered among the best vocalists in jazz.* ■ If you say someone's **days are numbered,** you mean they will not live much longer. ■ A **number** is a song or other short piece of music. ■ **opposite number:** see **opposite.**

number-crunching is doing large numbers of calculations, for example in finance, statistics, or computing.

number-plate A vehicle's **number-plates** are the signs on its front and back showing its registration number.

Number Ten is 10 Downing Street, London, the official address of the Prime Minister. **Number Ten** is often used to talk about the position of Prime Minister.

numeral – **Numerals** are written symbols used to represent numbers. Symbols like 3 and 7 are called Arabic numerals. Symbols like V and XII are called Roman numerals.

numerate (*pron:* **nyoo**-mer-rit) (**numeracy**) A **numerate** person is able to do arithmetic. **Numeracy** is having this ability.

numerical (**numerically**) **Numerical** means expressed in numbers or relating to numbers. *Numerically, there are a lot of young people involved in crime.*

numerous is used to say there are a lot of things of a certain kind.

numinous is used to describe things which are holy, awe-inspiring, and mysterious.

numismatics (**numismatic**) **Numismatics** is studying or collecting coins and medals. ...*numismatic dealers.*

nun A **nun** is a female member of a religious order.

nuncio (**nuncios**) In the Roman Catholic church, a **nuncio** is an official who represents the Pope in a foreign country.

nunnery (**nunneries**) **Nunnery** is an old word for a convent.

nuptial (**nuptials**) A person's **nuptials** are their wedding celebrations. ■ **Nuptial** is used to refer to things relating to a wedding or to marriage. *...the nuptial contract. ...nuptial harmony.*

nurse (**nursing, nursed**) A **nurse** is a person whose job is to care for sick people, usually in a hospital. ■ If you **nurse** a sick person or animal, you care for them when they are ill. ■ If you **nurse** an injury or illness, you allow it to get better by resting as much as possible. ■ You say a mother is **nursing** her baby when she is breast-feeding it. You can also say someone is **nursing** a baby when they are cradling it in their arms. ■ If you **nurse** something like an emotion or desire, you feel it strongly for a long time. *She still nurses an ambition to appear in films.*

nursemaid In the past, a **nursemaid** was a girl or woman paid to look after young children.

nursery (**nurseries**) A **nursery** is a place where very young children can be looked after, usually while their parents are at work. ■ A **nursery** is a room in a house where young children sleep or play. ■ **Nursery** education is education at a nursery school. ■ A **nursery** is a place where plants are grown to be sold.

nurseryman (**nurserymen**) A **nurseryman** is a person who works in a place where plants are grown for sale.

nursery rhyme A **nursery rhyme** is a poem or song for young children, especially one which is old or well-known.

nursery school A **nursery school** is a school for young children who are not yet old enough for primary school.

nursery slope A **nursery slope** is a gentle slope on a mountain used by people learning to ski.

nursing is the activity or profession of looking after people who are ill.

nursing home A **nursing home** is a hospital providing long-term medical care, especially for old people.

nursing officer A **nursing officer** is a senior nurse in a hospital whose job involves the management of nursing services.

nurture (**nurturing, nurtured**) **Nurture** is care and encouragement given to someone while they are growing and developing. If you **nurture** a young child or a plant, you care for it in this way. ■ If you **nurture** plans, ideas, or people, you actively encourage their development and success. *Genuine change needs careful nurturing.*

nut – **Nuts** are the firm shelled fruit of some trees and bushes. ■ If you say someone is **nuts** or call them a **nut,** you mean they are mad, or extremely silly. ■ If you say someone is **nuts** about someone or something, you mean they like that person or thing very much. You can refer to someone as a **nut** when they are extremely enthusiastic about a subject or activity. *...a video games nut.* ■ A **nut** is a small piece of metal with a hole through which you screw a bolt. ■ If you talk about the **nuts and bolts** of something, you mean its practical aspects.

nutcase If you call someone a **nutcase,** you mean they are mad, or do extremely silly things.

nutcracker A **nutcracker** is a tool for cracking nuts open.

nutmeg is a spice made from the nut-like seeds of a tropical tree called a **nutmeg.**

nutrient (*pron:* **new-tree-ent**) **Nutrients** are substances which are necessary for plants and animals to grow.

nutrition (*pron:* new-**trish**-shun) (**nutritional; nutritionist**) **Nutrition** is the process of providing or obtaining nutrients from food which the body needs to be healthy. **Nutritional** means things to do with nutrition. *...nutritional deprivation.*

nutritious food contains the proteins, vitamins, and minerals which help your body to be healthy.

nutshell You say **in a nutshell** when you are summing something up in a few words. *In a nutshell, the City is saying the recession is over.*

nutter If you call someone a **nutter,** you mean they are mad or very foolish.

nutty If you call a plan or proposal **nutty,** you mean it is very foolish or impractical. ■ If a food or a drink has a **nutty** flavour, it tastes of nuts.

nuzzle (**nuzzling, nuzzled**) If a person or animal **nuzzles** you, they gently rub their nose and mouth against you to show affection.

nylon is a strong flexible man-made fibre.

nymph In Greek and Roman mythology, a **nymph** was a spirit of nature who took the form of a young woman.

nymphomaniac A woman who keeps wanting to have sex is sometimes called a **nymphomaniac.**

O o

oaf (**oafish**) You can call a stupid, clumsy, or rude person an **oaf** or describe them as **oafish.**

oak The **oak** is a large deciduous tree which produces acorns.

OAP An **OAP** or **old-age pensioner** is a man over the age of 65 or a woman over the age of 60.

oar – **Oars** are long poles with flattened ends used for rowing a boat.

oarsman (**oarswoman**) Someone rowing a boat, especially a racing boat, can be called an **oarsman** or **oarswoman.**

oasis (*pron:* oh-**ay**-siss) (*plural:* **oases,** *pron:* oh-**ay**-seez) An **oasis** is a small area with water and trees in the middle of a desert. ■ Any place which is pleasantly different from the area around it can be called an **oasis.** *The country has had a reputation as one of the continent's few oases of political stability.*

oast-house An **oast-house** is a building, usually with a cone-shaped roof, which contains large ovens for drying hops.

oatcake – **Oatcakes** are thin flat oatmeal biscuits.

oath If you take an **oath,** you make a formal promise to do something, usually in front of witnesses. ■ When someone **takes the oath** in court, they promise to tell the truth by swearing on the New Testament or the holy book of another religion.

oatmeal is a coarse flour made by grinding oats.

oats are a kind of tall cereal grass.

obdurate (*pron:* ob-joor-it) (**obduracy**) You say someone is **obdurate** or talk about their **obduracy** when they refuse to change their mind about something.

OBE An **OBE** is an honour granted by the British monarch for a special service or achievement. OBE stands for 'Officer of the Order of the British Empire'.

obedient (**obediently, obedience**) If someone is **obedient,** they do what they are told.

obeisance (*pron:* ob-**bay**-sanss) is holding someone in great respect and being prepared to carry out all their commands.

obelisk (*pron:* **ob**-bill-isk) An **obelisk** is a tall tapering four-sided pillar, often with a pyramid-shaped point at the top. Obelisks are usually put up in honour of a person or an important event.

obese (*pron:* oh-**beess**) (**obesity**) If someone is **obese,** they are very fat. **Obesity** is being very fat.

obey If you **obey** a person or order, you do what you are told.

obfuscate (*pron:* ob-fuss-kate) (**obfuscating, obfuscated; obfuscation**) If someone **obfuscates** something, they make it more difficult to understand, for example by expressing it in a complicated, long-winded way.

obituary (**obituaries**) An **obituary** is a short article in a newspaper or magazine about someone who has just died, giving an account of their life and achievements.

object An **object** is anything solid which you can touch and see, and which is not alive. ■ The **object** of something is its aim or purpose. ■ If you are the **object** of certain feelings, someone has those feelings about you. *Bad guys began to look more like objects of pity than of fear.* Similarly, you can be the **object** of certain actions. *He is himself the object of an internal police inquiry.* ■ If you say money is **no object,** you mean someone can spend as much money as necessary. ■ An **object lesson** is a very clear example of something. *It was an object lesson for me on just how to conduct oneself on such an occasion... Each piece of flotsam in the North Sea is an object lesson in how we mistreat our coastline.* ■ If you **object** (*pron:* ob-**ject**) to something, you express your disapproval of it.

objection If you have an **objection** to something, you have reasons for disapproving of it. ■ If you make an **objection** to something, you tell people you are against it.

objectionable If you say someone or something is **objectionable,** you mean they are unpleasant and offensive.

objective (**objectively; objectivity**) Someone's **objective** is what they are trying to achieve. ■ If you are being **objective,** you are deciding about something purely by considering the facts, and are not letting your feelings influence you in any way. When someone makes a decision in this way, you can talk about their **objectivity.** *The jury was asked to look at every bit of the evidence fairly and objectively.*

objector People who openly object to something are called **objectors.** *Construction was delayed for years by environmental objectors.* See also **conscientious objector.**

objet d'art (*plural:* **objets d'art**) (*pron:* ob-jay **dar**) An **objet d'art** is an ornament or other small decorative object which is of interest to collectors.

obligation If you have an **obligation** to do something, you are required to do it. *Water companies have a legal obligation to supply their consumers.*

obligatory (*pron:* ob-**lig**-a-tree) If something is **obligatory,** there is a law or rule stating that it must be done. ■ You use **obligatory** to describe things which are done from habit or custom rather than any sense of enthusiasm. *They forgot to take the obligatory snapshots.*

oblige (**obliging, obliged; obligingly**) If something **obliges** you to do something, it makes it necessary for you to do it. *He felt obliged to speak out.* ■ If you **oblige** someone who has asked you to do something, you do it. An **obliging** person is always willing to do things for people. *The spectator obligingly moved further back.*

oblique (*pron:* oh-**bleak**) If something like a line is **oblique,** it is sloping or diagonal rather than straight. ■ An **oblique** comment or remark expresses something in an indirect way.

obliterate (obliterating, obliterated; obliteration) If something is **obliterated**, it is completely destroyed.

oblivion If someone or something passes into **oblivion**, they become forgotten or ignored.

oblivious (obliviously) If someone is **oblivious** to what is happening around them, they are not aware of it.

oblong An **oblong** is a shape with two long sides, two short ones, and four right angles.

obnoxious If you call someone or something **obnoxious**, you mean they are extremely unpleasant.

oboe (oboist) An **oboe** is a woodwind instrument with a double reed.

obscene (pron: ob-seen) (obscenity, obscenities) If you say something is **obscene**, you mean it is indecent or pornographic. ...an obscene telephone call. ...an obscene gesture. **Obscenity** (pron: ob-sen-it-tee) is indecent language or behaviour. An **obscenity** is an obscene word or action. They screamed obscenities at each other. ■ You can say something is **obscene** when you feel it is utterly wrong. ...the obscenity of 40,000 children dying every day, mainly from preventable diseases.

obscurantism (pron: obs-cure-ran-tiz-um) (obscurantist) **Obscurantism** is deliberately making something vague and difficult to understand, especially to prevent people finding out the truth. You say someone who behaves like this is being **obscurantist.**

obscure (obscuring, obscured; obscurity) **Obscure** is used to describe people and places that are not well known. ...an obscure little town on the Kansas plains. ...the man who rose from obscurity to fame within a few months. ■ **Obscure** is used to describe things which are puzzling or unclear. Their political objectives still remain obscure. ■ If something is **obscured** by something else, you cannot see it because the other thing is in the way.

obsequious (pron: ob-seek-wee-uss) people are always trying to please people they think are important, by doing small favours for them or agreeing with everything they say.

observable If something is **observable**, it can be seen or noticed. The drug was being given in doses too low to have an observable effect.

observance See observe.

observant An **observant** person pays close attention to everything and notices things which other people might miss.

observation (observational) **Observation** is watching someone or something carefully. He was taken to hospital for observation. ■ An **observation** is a comment or remark.

observational writing or comedy involves noticing details of people's behaviour and describing or imitating them.

observatory (observatories) An **observatory** is (a) a building equipped with large telescopes to observe the sun, moon, and stars. (b) a building equipped to observe and record weather conditions.

observe (observing, observed; observance) If you **observe** something, you watch it carefully. They spent months living in the bush observing the animals and birds. ■ You say you **observe** something when you notice it. We have observed a similar pattern in populations of smooth and palmate newts. ■ If you **observe** something like a law or custom, you obey it or follow it. ...the observance of a minute's silence. ■ If you **observe** that something is the case, you say it. He observed that a week is a long time in politics.

observer You can refer to someone who notices or sees something as an **observer.** ■ People who watch and analyse current events and situations are called **observers.** Political observers believe a new cabinet may be formed shortly. ■ An **observer** is a person officially sent to monitor something like an election or ceasefire and make sure it is carried out fairly.

obsessed (obsession, obsessional, obsessive) If you are **obsessed** by something, you think about it all the time and find it difficult to think of anything else. When someone feels like this, you can say they have an **obsession** with something; you can describe their behaviour as **obsessional** or **obsessive.**

obsolescent (obsolescence) If something is **obsolescent**, it is no longer needed because something better has been invented.

obsolete If something is **obsolete**, it is out of date and no longer in use.

obstacle An **obstacle** is an object which makes it difficult for you to go where you want to, because it is in your way. ■ You can refer to anything which makes it difficult for you to do something as an **obstacle.** ...obstacles blocking progress towards the resumption of diplomatic relations.

obstetrics (obstetric; obstetrician) **Obstetrics** is the branch of medicine concerned with pregnancy and childbirth. **Obstetric** means things to do with obstetrics. A doctor who specializes in obstetrics is called an **obstetrician.**

obstinate (obstinacy) If someone is being **obstinate**, they are determined to do what they want, and cannot be persuaded to change their mind. You talk about the **obstinacy** of someone like this.

obstreperous people are noisy and difficult to control.

obstruct (obstruction; obstructive) If something **obstructs** a road or path, it blocks it so people or vehicles cannot get past. You call something like this an **obstruction.** ■ An **obstruction** is something which blocks a passage in your body. ...an obstruction of the coronary arteries. ■ If someone or something **obstructs** a process, they prevent it from taking place. The war is obstructing distribution of famine relief. When someone deliberately obstructs the progress of something, you say they are being **obstructive.**

obstructionism (obstructionist) **Obstructionism** is deliberately delaying or preventing legal, business, or parliamentary matters. You say someone who behaves like this is being **obstructionist.**

obtain (obtaining, obtained; obtainable) If you **obtain** something you want, you succeed in getting it or achieving it. If something is **obtainable**, it is possible to obtain it. ■ If a situation **obtains**, it exists. *The longer this situation obtains, the more extensive the problems become.*

obtrusive If someone or something is **obtrusive,** they are noticeable in an unpleasant way.

obtuse (**obtuseness**) If someone is **obtuse,** they have difficulty understanding things or make no effort to understand.. ■ An **obtuse** angle is any angle between 90 degrees and 180 degrees. See also **acute, reflex.**

obverse The **obverse** of a situation or argument is its other side, which contrasts with it. *The obverse of rising unemployment is continued gains in productivity.* ■ The **obverse** of a coin or medal is the side which has the main design, usually the side which shows a head. See also **reverse.**

obviate (**obviating, obviated**) If something **obviates** the need for something else, it removes it. *The adoption of the resolution would obviate the need for force.*

obvious (**obviously**) If something is **obvious,** you can clearly see it or understand it. ■ If you describe what someone says as **obvious,** you mean it is unnecessary or unimaginative. *'We've got to turn!' I shouted, foolishly stating the obvious.*

occasion An **occasion** is a time when something happens. ■ An **occasion** is an important event, ceremony, or celebration. *This semi-final is a big occasion.* ■ An **occasion** for doing something is an opportunity to do it. *Many delegates view these meetings as an occasion to share intellectual ideas.* ■ If someone **rises to the occasion,** they deal with a difficult situation well. ■ If something happens **on occasion,** it happens sometimes but not often.

occasional (**occasionally**) **Occasional** means happening sometimes but not regularly or often.

occidental (*pron:* ok-sid-**dent**-al) is used to talk about European and American people and customs, as distinct from those of the Far East. See also **orient.**

occult – The occult is the knowledge and study of supernatural or magical forces.

occupancy is used to say that someone lives or works in a particular building or on a particular area of land. *...an average occupancy of two people per dwelling.*

occupant The **occupants** of a building are the people who live or work there. ■ The **occupants** of a place such as a room, bed, or car are the people who happen to be in it at a particular time.

occupation A person's **occupation** is their job or profession. ■ An **occupation** is something you do for pleasure or as part of your daily life. *...their favourite occupations: eating and making money.* ■ If you talk about the **occupation** of a building, you mean the people who live or work there. *...a private dwelling for owner occupation.* ■ The **occupation** of a country is its invasion and control by a foreign power.

occupational means things to do with someone's work or profession. *...an occupational hazard. ...an occupational pension.*

occupational therapy (**occupational therapist**) **Occupational therapy** is a method of helping people recovering from an illness or injury to develop or regain skills by giving them activities to do.

occupy (**occupies, occupying, occupied; occupier**) The people who **occupy** a building are those who live or work there. They can also be called its **occupiers.** ■ When people **occupy** a place, they move into it and take control of it. ■ If something **occupies** a particular area, it fills it or exists there. If something such as a journey **occupies** a particular period of time, it takes that amount of time to complete. ■ You say a room or something like a seat is **occupied** when it is in use and not free for anyone else. ■ If someone **occupies** a certain job or position, they have it. ■ If you **occupy** yourself in doing something, you are busy doing it. ■ If you are **occupied** with someone or something, they are taking up your attention or time.

occur (**occurs, occurring, occurred; occurrence**) When something **occurs,** it happens. An **occurrence** is something that happens. *Food queues have become a daily occurrence.* ■ When something **occurs** in a particular place, it exists or is present there. *This species occurs in wooded habitats.* ■ The **occurrence** of something is the fact that it happens or is present. *The greatest occurrence of coronary heart disease is in those over 65.* ■ If something **occurs** to you, you suddenly think of it.

ocean (**oceanic**) An **ocean** is a very large stretch of sea.**Oceanic** (*pron:* oh-shee-**an**-ik) is used to describe things to do with oceans. **Ocean-going** ships are designed to travel on the open sea. ■ **Oceans** of something means a huge amount of it.

oceanography (**oceanographer; oceanographic**) **Oceanography** is the scientific study of oceans and their plant and animal life. **Oceanographic** (*pron:* oh-shun-oh-**graff**-ik) means things to do with oceanography.

ocelot (*pron:* **oss**-il-lot) The **ocelot** is a wild cat with brown spotted fur. Ocelots live in the forests of Central and South America.

ochre (*pron:* **oh**-kur) is (a) a yellowish or reddish-brown earth used for making paints and dyes. (b) a golden-yellow colour.

o'clock is used to say what time it is.

octagon (**octagonal**) An **octagon** is a geometric shape with eight straight sides. Something with this shape is called **octagonal.**

octane is a chemical substance which exists in petrol and is used to measure the quality of petrol; the best quality is **high-octane.** ■ **High-octane** is used to describe things which are done with great energy and enthusiasm. *He is renowned for his high-octane lifestyle.*

octave An **octave** is a musical interval between the first note and the eighth note of a scale.

octet An **octet** is (a) a piece of music for eight instruments. (b) a group of eight singers or musicians.

octogenarian (*pron:* ok-toe-jin-**nair**-ee-an) An **octogenarian** is a person in their eighties.

octopus (**octopuses**) The **octopus** is a sea creature with eight long tentacles which it uses to catch its food.

odd (**oddly, odds**) **Odd** is used to describe things which are strange or unusual. *It seemed odd that he said so little. ...oddly dressed people.* ■ **Odd** numbers are numbers like 7 and 53 which cannot be divided exactly by 2. ■ You use **odd** after a round number like 40 or 100, to show you are talking about an amount which is approximately that number. *I travel 60-odd miles every day.* ■ You use **odd** to talk about things which are random or unimportant. *She hoards odd bits of string for future use.* ■ If someone or something is the **odd one out,** they are the only one that does not fit in among a group of people or things. ■ In gambling, the **odds** show how much money you stand to win compared with the amount you bet. ■ If you say someone or something is **odds on** to win something, you mean they are very likely to win. ■ If you pay **over the odds** for something, you pay more than it is worth. ■ If you are **at odds** with someone, you disagree with them.

oddball people or things are unusual or peculiar. *...oddball humour.* Someone who behaves in an unusual way can be called an **oddball.**

oddity (**oddities**) A strange or unusual person or thing can be called an **oddity.**

oddments are objects which do not seem to belong to any particular set or group.

odds See **odd.**

ode An **ode** is a poem written in praise of someone or something.

odious is used to describe people or things that are extremely unpleasant.

odium is having people dislike you for something you have done. *The complainant has been exposed to public odium.*

odour (*Am: odor*) An **odour** is a smell, especially a strong one.

odourless (*Am: odorless*) If something is **odourless,** it has no smell.

odyssey (*pron: od*-i-see) An **odyssey** is a long and eventful journey. You can also call something like a long-term project an **odyssey.** *...a six-year odyssey of reform.*

oedema (*plural: oedemata*) (*Am: edema, edemata*) An **oedema** (*pron: id-eem-ah*) is an abnormal swelling of part or all of a person's body, caused by the body retaining too much water.

oesophagus (**oesophaguses**) (*Am: esophagus, esophaguses*) A person's **oesophagus** (*pron: ee-soff-ag-uss*) is the tube which carries food from their throat to their stomach.

oestrogen (*Am: estrogen*) Oestrogen (*pron: ee-stra-jen*) is a hormone produced in the ovaries of female humans and animals. It controls female sexual development and the reproductive cycle.

of is used to show who or what a person or thing is connected with or belongs to. *...the director of the Imperial War Museum.* ■ **Of** is used to say what a feeling or thought relates to. *...fears of an economic slump.* ■ **Of** is used to say what something contains or is made up with. *...a cup of tea. ...a pane of glass.* ■ **Of** is used when talking about amounts and quantities. *...the amount of carbon dioxide in the atmosphere.* ■ **Of** is used to talk about a characteristic or quality that someone has. *...a man of the highest principles.*

of course See **course.**

off is used to say someone moves away from something or out of something. *Alison wandered off to find us somewhere to stay... They had just stepped off the plane.* ■ **Off** is used to talk about something being removed or separated from other things. *Travellers in groups of 25 or more get 30% off the standard fare.* ■ **Off** is used to say something is a little way from something like a road or shore. *...an island off the coast of Greece.* ■ **Off** is used to say how far away something is. *It ought to be spotted a mile off.* ■ If you have time **off,** you stop working for a period. ■ If you have gone **off** something, you do not like it any more. ■ When food or drink **goes off,** it goes bad. ■ If an electrical device is **off,** it is not switched on. ■ If an event is **off,** it has been cancelled or postponed.

offal The liver, kidneys, and other internal organs of an animal are called **offal** when they are used for food.

off-balance See **balance.**

off-beat (*or offbeat*) is used to describe entertainment which is unconventional or unusual. *...an off-beat comedy.*

off-centre If something is **off-centre,** it is not exactly in the middle of a space or surface.

off-chance If you do something **on the off-chance,** you do it hoping things will go the way you want, although this may be unlikely.

off-colour If you say someone is **off-colour,** you mean they are slightly ill.

off-day If you have an **off-day,** you do not do something as well as usual.

offence (*Am: offense*) When someone commits an **offence,** they break a law or rule. ■ If someone **takes offence,** they are upset or annoyed by something.

offend (**offending**) If something **offends** people, it upsets or embarrasses them. ■ If a person **offends,** they break a law or rule. *She wanted the offending players punished.*

offender An **offender** is a person who has committed a crime. *...a prison for young offenders.* ■ People or things that cause harm are sometimes called **offenders.** *Coal-fired power stations are among the worst offenders in the production of sulphur gases.*

offense See **offence.**

offensive (**offensively**) If someone's behaviour is **offensive,** it is rude and unpleasant. ■ In war, an **offensive** is a strong determined attack. ■ **Offensive** weapons are used for attack, rather than defence. ■ A positive attempt to take the initiative in a situation can be called an **offensive.** *The Security Council stepped up the diplomatic peace offensive.*

offer (**offering, offered**) If you **offer** something to someone or make them an **offer** of it, you say they can have it if they want it. ■ If you **offer** advice or information, you provide it. ■ If you **offer** to do something, you say you are willing to do it. ■ If something is **on offer,** it is available to be bought, won, or used. ■ If you make an **offer** for something, you say you will pay a certain sum of money for it. ■ If something **offers** an advantage of some kind, it provides it. *New diesel engines will offer outstanding fuel economy and less pollution.*

offering An **offering** is something someone produces and makes available. *Critics see the movie as another offering from a film-maker who likes to play it safe.* ■ An **offering** is a gift or sacrifice to a god.

off-guard If someone is caught **off-guard,** they are taken by surprise.

offhand (*or* **off-hand**) If someone's manner is **offhand,** they show little interest in what people are saying to them.

office An **office** is (a) a room or part of a building where people work sitting at desks. (b) a small building or room where people go for things like information, tickets, or a service. *...the local tourist office.* ■ **Office** appears in the names of some government departments and other government organizations. *...the Foreign Office.* ■ Someone who holds **office** has an important position in a government or other organization.

officer An **officer** in the armed forces is a person who holds a commission and has authority over other ranks. ■ People who work in local government are called local government **officers.** *...Barnet's chief education officer.* ■ Members of the police force are sometimes called **officers.** *...senior police officers.*

official (**officially**) **Official** is used (a) to describe things published or approved by the government or by someone else in authority. *...the government's official figures.* (b) to describe things done or used by people in authority as part of their job or position. *...an official visit.* ■ An **official** is a person who holds a position of authority in an organization. *...a Foreign Office official.*

officialdom is used to talk about government officials, usually disapprovingly.

Official Receiver The **Official Receiver** is an officer appointed by the Department of Trade and Industry to manage the affairs of a bankrupt or a company which is being wound up.

officiate (**officiating, officiated**) When someone **officiates** at something like a ceremony, they are in charge and perform the main part of it. ■ When someone **officiates** in a game, they are there to make sure the rules are followed.

officious (**officiously**) If you say someone is being **officious,** you mean they are being bossy and interfering.

offing If something is **in the offing,** it is likely to happen soon.

off-key If music is **off-key,** it is not in tune.

off-licence An **off-licence** is a shop which sells alcohol.

off-limits If a place is **off-limits** to certain people, they are not allowed to go there.

offload (*or* **off-load**) When goods are **offloaded** from a container or vehicle, they are removed from it. ■ If someone **offloads** something they cannot sell or do not want, they get rid of it by selling it off cheaply or giving it away.

off-peak things are available at times when there is less demand, and are cheaper than usual. *...off-peak electricity.*

off-putting If you say something is **off-putting,** you mean it makes you feel uncomfortable or distracts you from what you are doing, or makes you dislike a particular thing.

off-road — **Off-road** vehicles are designed to be driven over rough ground.

offset (**offsetting, offset** *not* '**offsetted**') You say two things **offset** each other when the effects of one are balanced out by the effects of the other. ■ See also **lithography.**

offshoot If something is an **offshoot** of something else, it has developed from it.

offshore is used to describe (a) things which take place or are situated in the sea near to a coast. *...offshore races. ...offshore oil rigs.* (b) things which are based abroad in places where the tax system is more advantageous than in the home country. *...offshore tax havens.*

offside The **offside** of a vehicle is the side normally furthest from the edge of the road. See also **nearside.** ■ Several games played by two teams on a pitch have an **offside** rule. A footballer is given **offside** when the ball is being played towards his opponents' goal and he is nearer to this goal than any of their defenders, except the goalkeeper.

offspring (*plural:* **offspring**) You can refer to a person's children or an animal's young as their **offspring.**

off-stage (*or* **offstage**) is used to describe things which take place behind the stage during the performance of a play and which the audience cannot see.

off-the-cuff comments have not been planned in advance.

off-the-peg clothing is ready-made, rather than made specially for you.

off-the-record remarks are made unofficially, and are not intended to be made public.

off-the-wall If you describe something as **off-the-wall,** you mean it is unusual and rather strange. *...surreal off-the-wall humor.*

off-white things are not pure white, but slightly yellow or grey.

oft- is added to words to say something has happened often. *...his oft-repeated statement.*

often If something happens **often,** it happens many times. ■ If something happens **every so often,** it happens occasionally.

ogle (**ogling, ogled**) When one person **ogles** another, they stare at them in a way which shows sexual interest.

ogre An **ogre** is a cruel frightening giant in a fairy story.

ohm Electrical resistance is expressed in **ohms.** When there is a resistance of one ohm, each volt of electrical force produces one amp of current.

O.H.M.S. (*or* **OHMS**) is printed on stationery used for official government business. It stands for 'On Her Majesty's Service'.

oil (**oiling, oiled**) **Oil** is a smooth thick sticky liquid found underground and used as a fuel or to lubricate machinery. If you **oil** something like a machine, you lubricate it with oil. ■ **Oil** is the name given to various thick greasy liquids produced by plants and animals and used in cooking or cosmetic products. *...olive oil. ...moisturizing oil.* ■ Oil paints and oil paintings are often called **oils.** ■ **essential oils:** see **essential.**

oilfield An **oilfield** is an area under the earth or seabed where oil is found and extracted.

oil-fired systems use oil as a fuel.

oilman (**oilmen**) **Oilmen** are (a) the owners and senior staff of oil companies. (b) the workers who do the actual drilling.

oil paint (**oil painting**) **Oil paint** is a thick paint made from coloured powder mixed with linseed oil. An **oil painting** is a picture painted with oil paints.

oil platform An **oil platform** is a structure built up from the sea bed or floating on the sea and used to support an offshore oil rig.

oil rig An **oil rig** is a structure on land or in the sea which is used as a base when drilling for oil.

oilseed rape See **rape.**

oilskins are waterproof clothes worn by people like sailors.

oil slick An **oil slick** is a layer of oil floating on the sea, caused by oil tankers being wrecked or damaged, or being careless with waste oil.

oil well An **oil well** is a hole bored into the earth or seabed to extract oil.

oily is used to describe things which are covered in oil, or feel or look like oil. ■ If you call a person **oily,** you mean you do not like them, because they keep flattering people or behaving in an exaggeratedly polite way.

ointment is a smooth thick medicated substance put on the skin to heal or protect it.

okay (or **OK**) If you say something is **okay,** you mean it is all right.

okra (*pron:* **oh**-kra) is a tropical plant with long green edible pods.

old An **old** person has lived a long time. Old people are sometimes called **the old.** ■ **Old** is used to describe things which have existed or been in use for a long time. *...the old custom of reading aloud.* ■ **Old** is used to talk about the age of someone or something. *...a 13-year-old girl.* ■ **Old** is used to describe things which are no longer used or exist, or have been replaced by something else. *The old economic system has disintegrated.* ■ **Old** is used to show pity or affection for someone or something. *The poor old taxman is, it seems, universally unpopular.* ■ **Of old** is used to talk about things which existed in the past. *...the cartoon heroes of old.* ■ You use **of the old school** to describe someone who has been doing something for a long time and does it in an older way which you prefer to more recent ways.

old-age pensioner See **OAP.**

old boy An **old boy** of a school or college is a man who used to be a pupil there. ■ Old men are sometimes called **old boys.** ■ **old-boy network:** see **network.**

old-fashioned If you describe something as **old-fashioned,** you mean it belongs to the past and has now been replaced by something more mod-

ern. *...old-fashioned zinc buttons.* You can say a person is **old-fashioned** when they think or behave in a way which is uncommon or inappropriate in the modern world.

old girl An **old girl** of a school or college is a woman who used to be a pupil there.

oldie An **oldie** is (a) an old person. (b) an old record or film.

old master The great European painters of the period 1500 to 1800 are called **old masters.** Their paintings are also called **old masters.**

old school tie When people talk about the **old school tie,** they mean the unofficial system by which men who have been to the same public school or university use their positions of influence to help each other.

old-style means the same as 'old-fashioned'. *...old-style phone kiosks.*

Old Testament The **Old Testament** is the first part of the Bible, containing writings relating to the history of the Jews.

old timer You say someone is an **old timer** when they have been in the same place or doing the same thing for along time. ■ In the US, an **old timer** is any old man.

old wives' tale If you call a popular belief an **old wives' tale,** you mean it is based on ignorance or superstition and has no truth in it.

Old World The **Old World** is the continents of Europe, Asia, and Africa, as opposed to America.

O-Level – **O-levels** were the exams English, Welsh, and Northern Irish school students used to take at 15 or 16 before GCSEs were introduced in 1988. 'O-level' stands for 'Ordinary Level'.

olfactory means to do with the sense of smell. *...the olfactory nerves.*

oligarchy (*pron:* ol-ig-gar-kee) (**oligarchies; oligarch**) An **oligarchy** is a small group of people who control and run a country or state. This system of government is called **oligarchy.** A member of the government is called on **oligarch.**

olive – **Olives** are the small green or black fruit of a Mediterranean tree called an **olive tree.** ■ If someone offers you an **olive branch,** they say or do something to show they want to end a quarrel. ■ **Olive** is a dark yellowish-green colour.

olive oil is an oil obtained by pressing olives. It is used as a salad dressing or for cooking food.

Olympiad Each staging of the modern Olympic Games is called an **Olympiad.** ■ An international contest in a game like chess or bridge is called an **Olympiad.**

Olympian is used to describe things which are very large. *Getting his book into print was an Olympian task.* ■ Athletes who take part in the Olympic Games are sometimes called **Olympians.**

Olympic The **Olympic Games** or **Olympics** are a series of international sports competitions which take place every four years. **Olympic** means to do with the Olympic Games. *...the Olympic movement.*

OM An **OM** is an honour awarded to people for special achievements in a particular field. OM stands for 'Order of Merit'.

ombudsman (**ombudsmen**) An **ombudsman** is an independent official who investigates complaints by the public in a particular field. ...*the Insurance Ombudsman.*

omega is Ω or ω, the last letter of the Greek alphabet.

omelette (*Am:* **omelet**) An **omelette** is a pancake-shaped food made by whisking eggs and then frying them.

omen If you say something is an **omen,** you mean it is a sign of what may happen in the future.

ominous (**ominously**) If something is **ominous,** it is worrying, because it suggests that something unpleasant is going to happen. ...*ominous black clouds.*

omit (**omits, omitting, omitted; omission**) If something is **omitted** from a broadcast or piece of writing, it is left out. The part which is left out is called an **omission.** ■ If you **omit** to do something, you do not do it.

omnibus (**omnibuses**) An **omnibus** is a collection of stories or articles, often by the same person or about the same subject. ...*the Sherlock Holmes omnibus.* ■ An **omnibus** edition of a TV or radio programme contains two or more episodes or programmes which have already been broadcast separately. ■ **Omnibus** is an old word for a bus.

omnipotent (*pron:* om-**nip**-o-tent) (**omnipotence**) If someone is **omnipotent,** they have unlimited power.

omnipresent (*pron:* om-ni-**prez**-ent) (**omnipresence**) If someone or something is **omnipresent,** they are everywhere, or seem to be everywhere.

omniscient (*pron:* om-**niss**-ee-ent) (**omniscience**) If you say someone is **omniscient** or talk about their **omniscience,** you mean they know everything, or seem to know everything.

omnivorous If a person or animal is **omnivorous,** they eat different kinds of food, including meat and plants. ■ You can say someone is **omnivorous** when they absorb or take an interest in a wide variety of subjects.

on is used to say where someone or something is, where something is put, or where something happens. ...*posters on his bedroom wall... They must be prepared to play on the same pitch.* ■ When you put your clothes **on,** you get dressed. ■ You say something happens **on** a certain day or date. ■ If a programme is **on** TV or the radio, it is being broadcast. You also say something like a play or a film is **on** when it is being shown or performed. ■ If an event is **on,** it is happening or taking place. ■ If someone is **on** a medicine or drug, they are taking it regularly. ■ If something like a book is **on** a certain subject, that is what it is about. ■ You say something has an effect **on** someone or something else. ■ If something is done **on** a type of machine or instrument, it is done using it. ■ If you are **on** a committee, you are a member of it. ■ If a machine or light is **on,** it is functioning. ■ **On** is used to say someone or something keeps doing something. *Prices kept on rising... We drove on to the border.* ■ If you are very busy, you can say you have a lot **on.** ■ If you say something is **not on,** you mean it is not acceptable.

once If something happens **once,** it happens just one time. ■ **Once** is used to say something used to be true, but is no longer true. *Bristol was once England's most important provincial city.* ■ If something happens **once** something else has happened, it happens as soon as the other thing has happened. *Once they have money in their hands, they spend it quickly.* ■ If you do something **at once,** you do it immediately. ■ When several things happen at the same time, you can say they happen **at once.** ■ **For once** is used to say something has happened which is very different from what normally happens. *For once, the good guys really do win.* ■ **Once again** and **once more** are used to talk about something happening which has happened many times before. *Press freedom is once again under threat.*

oncoming is used to describe something which is moving towards you. ...*oncoming traffic.*

one is the number 1. ■ **One day** means at some unspecified time in the future or past. *Lasers can be very powerful, and may one day make formidable weapons... One day a blonde woman walked into the shop... Late one night the phone rang.* ■ If you are **at one** with someone, you are in complete agreement with them. ■ If you are **at one** with something like the environment, you have a sense of unity with it. ■ If you are **one up** on someone, you have gained an advantage over them. ■ **One** is sometimes used to mean people in general, or to mean the speaker or writer themselves. *One does not cure this problem by throwing money around... One knows that one is growing older.*

one-armed bandit A **one-armed bandit** is a gambling machine operated by pulling down a lever at the side.

One-hundred Share Index The **One-hundred Share Index** is the same as the FTSE.

one-liner A **one-liner** is a short joke or witty remark.

one-man is used to describe (a) things done by just one man. ...*a one-man show.* (b) things intended for one person. ...*a one-man submarine.* ■ A **one-man band** is a street entertainer who plays a lot of musical instruments at the same time. ■ If all the decisions in an organization are taken by one person, you can call it a **one-man band** or **one-man show.**

oneness is a sense of unity with other people or creatures.

one-night stand A **one-night stand** is something like a play performed at a place on one evening only. ■ A **one-night stand** is a brief sexual relationship, usually involving a couple having sex with each other on one occasion only.

one-off is used to describe (a) things which happen only once. ...*a one-off fee of £95.* (b) items made individually as required. *Special one-off items will be ordered direct from the manufacturers.*

one-piece is used to describe something made in one complete piece instead of two or more separate parts. ...*a blue one-piece bathing suit.*

onerous (*pron:* ohn-er-uss) If something is **onerous,** it involves very hard work or heavy responsibilities.

oneself A speaker or writer uses **oneself** to talk about himself or herself or about people in general, in a formal way. *One can only speak for oneself... One should be cared for when one cannot care for oneself.*

one-sided If an activity or relationship is **one-sided,** one of the people or groups involved is much more active or much stronger that the other. *...a one-sided conversation.* ■ A **one-sided** account of a situation shows things from one point of view only.

one-time is used when mentioning something that a person or place used to be in the past. *...a one-time actress.*

one-to-one In a **one-to-one** relationship or situation, you deal with only one other person. *...one-to-one tuition.*

one-upmanship is trying to appear better than someone else, for example by owning something unusual they have not got.

one-way In a **one-way** street, vehicles can travel in one direction only. ■ A **one-way** ticket enables you to travel to a place, but not to come back again. ■ A **one-way** communications device, for example a pager, can either send signals or receive them, but not both.

one-woman is used to describe something done by just one woman. *...her one-woman show.*

ongoing is used to describe things which are continuing to happen. *...ongoing talks.*

onion — Onions are round strong-tasting vegetables with papery skin and layers of white flesh.

on-line (*or* **on line**) is used to talk about things which are directly connected to or controlled by a computer and to describe services or facilities which are available as a result. *...an on-line service offering news and information.*

onlooker An **onlooker** is a person who watches something happening without taking part.

only is used to talk about something being limited to one person, thing, or group. *He is now the only potential owner.* ■ If you are an **only** child, you have no brothers or sisters. ■ **Only** and **only too** are used for emphasis. *It only lasted 10 seconds... It is only right that the court should decide... Young people are only too well aware of the dangers of AIDS.* ■ If you say something will happen **only if** something else happens, you mean it will not happen unless that thing happens. ■ If you say someone **has only** to do one thing in order to achieve something, you mean that is all they have to do to achieve it. *Mackay had only to pick up the loose ball to score.* ■ You use **only** to say one thing followed another, and was a disappointment or anti-climax. *Hopes of recovery have come before, only to be dashed.* ■ You use **only** when you are pointing out the difference between two things of the same kind. *Leaders of the two main parties also have big cars, only theirs are provided by the state.* ■ **if only:** see **if.**

onomatopoeic (*pron:* on-o-mat-o-**pee**-ick) (**onomatopoeia**) **Onomatopoeic** words sound like the noise they are describing; for example, 'hiss' and 'buzz' are onomatopoeic. This feature of language is called **onomatopoeia.**

onrush If there is an **onrush** of something, it develops or increases suddenly and quickly. *...the onrush of new members.*

onrushing is used to describe someone or something that is moving quickly towards you. *...flicking the ball past the onrushing goalkeeper.*

on-screen is used to talk about things displayed on the screen of a computer or word-processor. *...on-screen graphics.*

onset The **onset** of something, especially something unpleasant, is its beginning. *...the onset of war.*

onshore An **onshore** wind reaches the land from the sea. ■ **Onshore** is used to describe things which are on land, rather than out at sea. *...onshore jobs in the oil industry.*

onslaught An **onslaught** is a violent attack. ■ Strong and repeated criticism can be called an **onslaught.** *He kept up Labour's onslaught on the government's handling of the economy.*

onstage is used to talk about things happening on the stage in a theatre.

onstream When an oil well comes **onstream,** it starts producing oil.

on-the-job training or experience is given while you are doing the job you are being trained for.

on-the-spot is used to describe things done or provided as an immediate response to something. *...on-the-spot fines.* ■ **On-the-spot** investigations are carried out in the place where something is actually happening, rather than from somewhere else.

onto If you go **onto** something, you change your position so you are standing on it or inside it. *Eleven prisoners have climbed onto the roof... He got onto the plane.* Similarly, an object can fall **onto** something. ■ **Onto** is used to say something is attached somewhere. *Those last sequins are being sewn onto the costumes.* ■ **Onto** is used to say something like a light is directed somewhere. *The image is projected onto a screen.*

onus (*pron:* **own**-uss) If the **onus** is on you to do something, it is your duty or responsibility to do it.

onward (**onwards**) **Onward** and **onwards** are used to talk about the continuation of a journey. *...a flight to Frankfurt with an onward flight to New York.* ■ **Onward** is used to talk about the development or progress of something. *...the onward march of technology.* ■ If something happens from a certain time **onwards,** it starts at that time and goes on happening.

onyx (*pron:* **on**-iks) is a semiprecious stone with layers of different colours, used for making ornaments and jewellery.

oodles of something means a lot of it. *He's got oodles of money.*

oomph If you say someone or something has **oomph,** you mean they create an impression of liveliness and vigour. *Backbenchers are depressed by their leader's lack of oomph.*

ooze (**oozing, oozed**) If a thick sticky liquid **oozes** out of something, it flows out slowly. *...a handful of cars oozing oil.* ■ **Ooze** is the fine mud found on the sea bed. ■ If you say a person **oozes** a quality, you mean they are full of it. *They ooze vitality.*

op An **op** is (a) a surgical operation. *...breast cancer ops.* (b) a military operation. *...night fighter ops from British bases.*

opacity See **opaque.**

opal – **Opals** are gemstones which show flashes of many colours. They are used for making jewellery.

opaque (*pron:* oh-**pake**) (**opacity,** *pron:* ope-**ass**-it-tee) If something is **opaque,** you cannot see through it. ■ You say something is **opaque** if it is hard to understand. *His article was deliberately opaque.*

op. cit. (*pron:* op sit) When a book is mentioned more than once in a piece of writing, **op. cit.** is used after the author's name on each occasion apart from the first, to save repeating the title.

OPEC (*pron:* oh-pek) is an organization of oil-producing countries. OPEC stands for 'Organization of Petroleum-Exporting Countries'.

open (**opening, opened; openly**) When you **open** something, you move it so that it is no longer closed. When you have done this, you say it is **open.** *His mouth was open.* ■ **Open** things are not covered or enclosed. *...an open fireplace.* ■ When something like a shop **opens,** work or business starts for the day. ■ When a new facility or event **opens,** it starts or becomes available. ■ If a country **opens** its borders, it allows people to move into and out of it freely. ■ If someone is **open,** they are honest and frank about something. ■ If something is brought **into the open,** people are told about it and it is no longer a secret. ■ If someone is **open** to suggestions or new ideas, they are willing to consider them. You say someone like this is **open-minded.** ■ If a course of action is **open** to you, you can take it if you want to. ■ **Open** is used to describe something like a meeting or competition which anyone can take part in. *...the British Golf Open Championship.* ■ If someone or something is **open** to something bad, it could happen to them. *They have formed associations which lay them open to blackmail.* ■ If a situation is left **open,** no final decision is made about it. ■ If someone keeps **open house,** friends and visitors are welcome at their house at any time without needing invitations. ■ An **open** area of sea or land is a large empty area. ■ If you do something **in the open air,** you do it out of doors. ■ If you **open** an account with a bank, you start to use their services by depositing some of your money with them. ■ When something like a share **opens** at a certain value, it has that value at the start of the day's trading.

open-and-shut An **open-and-shut** case is a matter which is easily decided or solved because the facts are very clear.

open-cast In an **open-cast** mine, the coal or mineral deposits are near the surface, and can be dug out without tunnelling underground.

open day An **open day** is a special day when something like a school or university is open to the public.

open-ended agreements are ones you enter into without placing any limits on what you are prepared to do.

opener In cricket, the batsman who goes in first to play for his or her team is called an **opener.**

open-heart surgery is performed on the heart while blood circulation is maintained by a machine.

opening The **opening** one of a series of things is the first one. *...the opening day of the baseball season.* ■ The **opening** of a book or film is the beginning. ■ An **opening** is a hole or space which things can pass through. ■ An **opening** is an opportunity to do something. *Anderson created the openings for the first three goals.*

open learning is a system in which people with few or no qualifications can study by taking a correspondence course.

open letter An **open letter** is a letter, especially a protest, addressed to an important person or an organization but also made public, for example in a newspaper.

open-minded See **open.**

open-necked shirts are unbuttoned at the collar and worn without a tie.

open-plan buildings or rooms have only a few interior walls to divide up the living or working space.

open prison An **open prison** is a minimum security prison.

open season In hunting, fishing, and shooting, the **open season** is the time of the year when certain birds, animals, and fish can legally be killed. ■ If you say it is **open season** on someone, you mean a lot of people are criticizing them or making fun of them.

Open University The **Open University** is a university founded in 1969 for students wishing to study part-time mainly at home. Lectures are broadcast on TV and radio.

open verdict At an inquest, an **open verdict** is recorded when the cause of death has not been established.

opera (**operatic**) An **opera** is a musical work performed in a theatre. It is acted like a play, but most or all of the words are sung. This kind of music is called **opera. Operatic** means to do with opera. *...Rossini's operatic career.*

operate (**operating, operated**) When you **operate** a machine, you make it work. ■ If you **operate** a business, you run it. **Operating** means to do with running a business. *...operating costs.* You say a business or system **operates** in a particular way or in a particular place. *His company would continue to operate as an independent business.* ■ When a surgeon **operates,** he or she cuts open a patient's body to remove or treat a damaged part.

operating system The **operating system** of a computer is the software program which controls things like the function of the keyboard, screen, printer, and disks.

operating theatre An **operating theatre** is a specially equipped room in a hospital where surgery is carried out.

operation (operational, operationally) An **operation** is a complex event or action which needs careful planning. ...*military operations*. **Operational** means to do with operations like these. ...*operational headquarters*... *The rocket has never been used operationally*. ■ If something is **in operation** or **operational**, it is working or being used. ■ Businesses can be called **operations**. ■ An **operation** is medical treatment in which a surgeon cuts open a patient's body to remove or treat a damaged part.

operative If something like a system or machine is **operative**, it is working. ■ If you say a word you have just used is **the operative word**, you mean it sums up the most important aspect of a situation. ■ **Operative** means to do with surgical operations. ...*post-operative recovery*. ■ An **operative** is a person who works for a government's secret service or for a detective agency.

operator A person who controls or operates a machine is called an **operator**. ...*computer operators*. ■ Someone who runs a business can be called an **operator**. ...*ferry operators*. ■ If you say someone is, for example, a clever **operator**, you mean they are skilled at getting what they want. ...*one of the few smart operators in the business*.

operetta An **operetta** is a light-hearted comic opera.

ophthalmic (*pron*: off-**thal**-mik) means to do with the medical care of your eyes. ...*ophthalmic equipment*. ■ **ophthalmic optician**: see **optician**.

ophthalmology (*pron*: off-thal-**moll**-o-gee) (**ophthalmologist**) **Ophthalmology** is the branch of medicine concerned with the eye and its diseases. A doctor who specializes in this is called an **ophthalmologist**.

opiate (*pron*: oh-pee-ate) An **opiate** is a drug containing opium.

opine (opining, opined) To **opine** means to express your opinion. *The foreign minister opined that peace negotiations could be at a decisive stage*.

opinion An **opinion** is a personal belief or judgment about something. You can talk, for example, about **public opinion** or **medical opinion** when you are referring to views generally held by groups of people.

opinionated If you say someone is **opinionated**, you mean they have strong opinions and are fond of expressing them.

opinion poll An **opinion poll** is a way of finding out what people think about something by questioning a representative sample.

opium is a drug made from the seed pods of a type of poppy called the **opium poppy**.

opossum The **opossum** is a small long-tailed animal which carries its young in a pouch on its body, found in North and South America and in Australia.

opponent Your **opponent** is the person you are trying to beat in an contest or argument. ■ If you are an **opponent** of something, you are against it. ...*opponents of whaling*.

opportune If something is **opportune**, it comes at just the right time. *The visit is seen as particularly op-portune*... *The commission's proposals come at an opportune moment*.

opportunist (opportunistic, opportunism) You say someone is **opportunistic** or an **opportunist** when they are prepared to take advantage of any opportunity which comes along, to get money or power. This kind of behaviour is called **opportunism**. ■ **Opportunist** actions are not planned, but take advantage of something which happens. *They knocked in three opportunist goals in the second half*. ■ An **opportunistic** infection is caused by germs which are harmless to a healthy person but which affect someone whose immune system is weakened by disease or drug treatment.

opportunity (opportunities) If there is an **opportunity** for you to do something, a situation arises when you can do it. ■ If there is **opportunity** for something in a place, it is possible to achieve it there. If there is **equal opportunity**, nobody is put at a disadvantage because of things like their sex or race.

oppose (opposing, opposed) If you **oppose** something or are **opposed** to it, you are against it. ■ **Opposed** or **opposing** views are totally different and conflict with each other. ■ **Opposing** is used to describe groups of people who are fighting, arguing with, or competing against each other. *The sisters play in opposing teams*. ■ You say **as opposed to** when you are distinguishing one thing from another. ...*interim results as opposed to the final figures*.

opposite is used to describe things of the same kind which are completely different in some way. *We were moving in opposite directions*... *Daniel Johnson, in The Times, presented the opposite view*... *Puttsborough Sands is the complete opposite of Blackpool*. ■ You use **opposite** to talk about two things being on either side of the same thing and facing each other. ...*two high arches on opposite sides of the hall*... *I was sitting opposite him*. ■ You use **opposite** to describe the part of something which is farthest away from you. ...*the opposite end of the street*. ■ When two actors perform **opposite** each other, they have the leading male and female roles. ■ Your **opposite number** is someone who has the same position as you in a different place or organization. *The British Foreign Secretary telephoned his German opposite number*.

opposition If there is **opposition** to something like a policy, a number of people are against it. ■ In parliament, the **opposition** are the politicians who do not belong to the government. ■ You can call a person or group you are competing against the **opposition**.

oppress (oppresses, oppressing, oppressed; oppression, oppressor) When people are **oppressed**, they are treated cruelly and unfairly by their rulers. People treated like this can be called the **oppressed**; their rulers are called their **oppressors**.

oppressive (oppressively) An **oppressive** government or system treats people cruelly and unfairly. ■ When the weather is unpleasantly hot and humid, you can say it is **oppressive**.

oppressor See **oppress**.

opprobrium (*pron:* op-**pro**-bree-um) is strong public disapproval brought on someone by their own actions.

opt If you **opt** for something, you choose it. *Voters opted for independence by a massive majority... They have opted to make the long journey by road.* ■ If you **opt out** of something like a system, you choose not to be involved in it. An **opt-out** is something like a clause in an agreement which allows you to opt out of a particular part of it.

optic (**optics**) **Optic** means to do with the eyes. *...the optic nerve.* ■ **Optics** is the branch of physics and engineering concerned with the properties of light. See also **fibre optics.** ■ An **Optic** is a device attached to an upside-down bottle for dispensing measured amounts of spirits such as whisky, used especially in bars.

optical means to do with vision, light, and images. *...optical instruments.* ■ **optical illusion:** see **illusion.**

optical fibre is a telecommunications cable consisting of a thin flexible glass fibre in a protective coating, used to transfer messages using light flashed by lasers.

optician An **optician** is a person who supplies glasses. A **dispensing optician** supplies and fits glasses and contact lenses, but is not qualified to prescribe them. An **ophthalmic optician** is qualified to examine eyes and prescribe and supply glasses and contact lenses.

optimal means the same as 'optimum'.

optimise See **optimize.**

optimist (**optimism; optimistic, optimistically**) An **optimist** is a person who looks on the bright side of life and is hopeful about the future. You can talk about the **optimism** of someone like this or describe their behaviour as **optimistic.**

optimize (*or* **optimise**) (**optimizing, optimized**) If you **optimize** something, you make the best use of it or develop it to the highest possible standard. *I would welcome the chance to optimise my potential.*

optimum An **optimum** level or situation is one which produces the best results. *...providing muscles with the optimum amount of oxygen. ...the optimum conditions for developing embryos.*

option (**optional**) An **option** is one of a number of available choices. ■ If something is **optional,** you can choose whether or not to have it or do it. ■ An **option** is an agreement which gives someone the right to buy or sell something at a fixed price within a certain period.

opulent (*pron:* op-yool-nt) (**opulence**) If you call something **opulent** or talk about its **opulence,** you mean it is luxurious or expensive-looking. *...an opulent mansion.*

opus (*pron:* oh-puss) (**opuses**) **Opus** numbers show the order in which the works of a classical composer were published. So, for example, a composer's first published work is usually called his or her Opus 1. 'Opus' is often shortened to **Op.** ■ A book or film on a large scale is sometimes called an **opus.** ■ See also **magnum opus.**

or You use **or** when mentioning alternatives. *...national, regional or local authorities... It doesn't matter whether this is true or false.* ■ You use **or** between numbers when you are giving an approximate amount. *...two or three days.* ■ You use **or** to warn what will happen if something is not done. *We must resist aggression, or it will destroy our freedoms.* ■ You use **or** to say why you think something is true. *The myths have an astonishing appeal, or they would not have lasted so long.* ■ You use **or** when you are correcting something you have just said. *I did the illustrations, or at least some of them.*

oracle In ancient Greece, an **oracle** was a prediction about the future, revealed by a priest or priestess at the shrine of a god. The priest or priestess was also called an **oracle,** and so was the shrine. ■ Anyone who has a reputation for predicting future events accurately can be called an **oracle.**

oral (**orally**) **Oral** is used to describe things to do with the mouth, or things taken through the mouth. *...oral hygiene... She could not have taken these massive doses orally.* ■ **Oral** is used to describe things which are spoken rather than written. *...oral evidence.* ■ An **oral** is an exam which is spoken rather than written.

orange is a reddish-yellow colour. ■ **Oranges** are large round juicy citrus fruit with thick orange-coloured peel. They grow on trees called **orange trees.**

Orangeman (**Orangemen**) An **Orangeman** is a member of a society founded in Ireland in 1795 to uphold the Protestant religion and cause.

orang-utan (*or* **orang-outang**) **Orang-utans** are large apes with long reddish-brown hair. They live in the forests of Borneo and Sumatra.

oration An **oration** is a formal speech.

orator (*pron:* or-rat-tor) (**oratory, oratorical**) If someone is good at making powerful speeches, you can call them an **orator** or talk about their **oratory.** *...a vivid oratorical style.*

oratorio (*pron:* or-rat-tor-ee-oh) (**oratorios**) An **oratorio** is a piece of religious music for solo singers, a choir, and an orchestra.

orb An **orb** is a small ornamental sphere with a cross on top, carried by a king or queen as a symbol of their power.

orbit (**orbiting, orbited**) When an object in space **orbits** a planet, a moon, or the sun, it goes round and round it. Its curved path is called an **orbit.**

orbital means to do with an orbit. *The comet moves in its orbital path roughly between Saturn and Uranus.* ■ An **orbital** road goes all the way round a large city.

orchard An **orchard** is a piece of land where fruit trees are grown.

orchestra (**orchestral**) An **orchestra** is a large group of musicians who play a variety of musical instruments together. *...orchestral music.* ■ In a theatre, the **orchestra pit** is a space reserved for musicians, immediately in front of or below the stage.

orchestrate (**orchestrating, orchestrated; orchestration**) If something is **orchestrated,** it is carefully organized in advance to achieve a desired result. *...a well-orchestrated demonstration.* ■ When someone **orchestrates** a piece of music, they rewrite it

orchid

441

so it can be played by an orchestra. This new version is called an **orchestration.**

orchid – Orchids are plants with colourful and unusually shaped flowers.

ordain (**ordaining, ordained; ordination**) When someone is **ordained,** they are made a member of the clergy during a religious ceremony. This is called their **ordination.** ■ If someone in authority **ordains** something, they order that it shall happen.

ordeal An **ordeal** is a difficult and extremely unpleasant experience.

order (**ordering, ordered**) If a person in authority **orders** you to do something or gives you an **order,** they tell you to do it. ■ When you **order** something, you ask for it to be sent or brought to you. Your request is called an **order.** *The waiter returned with their order.* ■ If a set of things is arranged or done in a certain **order,** they are arranged or done according to a system. *...lists of words in alphabetical order.* ■ **Order** is a situation in which everything is in the correct place or done at the correct time. See also **law and order.** ■ If you say something is **of a high order,** you mean it is very good. ■ You say **in** or **of the order of** when you are mentioning an approximate figure. *The discrepancy was of the order of 20%.* ■ A religious **order** is a group of monks or nuns who live according to certain rules, often in a religious community. ■ Some honours are called **Orders.** *...the Order of the Garter.* ■ If you do something **in order to** achieve something else, you do it for that reason. *Most schools are extremely unwilling to cut down on staff in order to cut costs.*

orderly (**orderliness; orderlies**) **Orderly** things are well organized or arranged. *...an orderly transfer of power.* ■ In the past, hospital attendants who carried out routine non-nursing tasks were called **orderlies.**

Order of Merit See **OM.**

ordinal number An **ordinal number** is a number like 'third' or '17th' which tells you what position something has in a series. See also **cardinal number.**

ordinance An **ordinance** is an official rule or order.

ordinand An **ordinand** is a person training to be a priest.

ordinary (**ordinarily; ordinariness**) **Ordinary** people, things, or situations are not special or unusual in any way. *...an ordinary working week.*

ordination See **ordain.**

ordnance is military supplies, especially weapons and ammunition.

Ordnance Survey The **Ordnance Survey** is the official organization which produces detailed maps of Britain and Ireland.

ordure (*pron:* ord-yoor) is excrement.

ore is rock from which metal can be extracted, for example iron ore.

oregano is a herb used in cooking. It is a type of wild marjoram.

organ (**organist**) An **organ** is a part of the body with a particular function, for example the heart. ■ The **organ** is a large musical instrument with a keyboard and pipes of different lengths. ■ The newspaper or journal of an organization or profession can be called its **organ.** *...the British Medical Journal, the organ of the British medical establishment.*

organdie (*Am:* **organdy**) is a sheer, slightly stiff cotton fabric used for making women's or children's clothes.

organic (**organically**) **Organic** is used to describe things produced by or found in plants or animals. *The Viking craft that landed on Mars reported that there was no organic material there.* ■ **Organic** methods of farming and gardening use only natural animal and plant products as fertilizers or pesticides. Food produced by these methods is also called **organic.** ■ You say something is **organic** when it develops naturally without any outside help. *A more buoyant economy will generate tax revenues organically.* ■ If a community or structure is an **organic** whole, each part of it is necessary and works with the other parts. *City planning treats the city as a unit, as an organic whole.*

organisation (**organisational**) See **organization.**

organise See **organize.**

organiser See **organizer.**

organism An **organism** is any living animal or plant.

organist See **organ.**

organization (*or* **organisation**) (**organizational**) An **organization** is an organized group, for example a business or a charity. ■ The **organization** of a system is the way it is planned and run. *...the party's organizational structure.* ■ When someone is good at organizing things, you can talk about their **organizational** ability. ■ The **organization** of something like an activity or event is the planning and making of arrangements.

organize (*or* **organise**) (**organizing, organized**) If you **organize** an event, you plan it and make all the arrangements. ■ **Organized** activities involve a number of people doing something together in a structured way. *...organized crime.* ■ **Organized** is used to describe the way something is run. For example, you say something is 'well-organized' or 'badly-organized'. ■ When employees **organize,** they form an organization like a union. *...organized labour.* ■ If you **organize** a number of people or objects, you arrange them into some kind of order or system. *The employees were organized into teams.*

organizer (*or* **organiser**) The **organizer** of an activity or event is the person who organizes it. ■ See also **personal organizer.**

organza is a sheer stiff fabric, made from cotton and silk or cotton and nylon. It is used to make evening dresses.

orgasm An **orgasm** is the moment of greatest pleasure and excitement during sexual activity.

orgy (*pron:* or-jee) (**orgies**) An **orgy** is a wild uncontrolled party involving a lot of drinking and sexual activity. ■ If there is an **orgy** of something, people indulge in a lot of it. *...an orgy of destruction.*

oriel (*pron:* aw-ree-ul) An **oriel** window projects from an upper wall of a building.

orient (**oriental; oriented, -orientated**) The **Orient** is eastern and south-eastern Asia. **Oriental** means to do with the Orient. *...oriental art.* ■ If you **orient** yourself to a new situation, you adjust to it and become familiar with it. ■ If a person or thing is **ori-**

ented towards something, that is what they are interested in or concerned with. *...American policies oriented towards maintaining the status quo in Latin America.* ■ **Oriented** or **orientated** is used to show who or what something is designed for. *...adult-oriented films. ...family orientated holidays.*

orientalist (**orientalism**) An **orientalist** is a person from the West who is interested in and knowledgeable about the Orient.

orientated See **orient.**

orientation The **orientation** of a structure or object is the direction it faces. ■ You can talk about people's **orientation** when you mean their aims, interests, or preferences. For example, someone's **sexual orientation** is whether they are attracted to people of their own sex or the opposite sex. *NATO's orientation is becoming less military and more political.*

orienteering is a competitive sport in which people run from one place to another across country, using a map and compass to guide them between checkpoints.

orifice (*pron:* **or**-if-iss) An **orifice** is an opening or hole, especially one in the body.

origami (*pron:* or-rig-**gah**-mee) is the Japanese art of folding paper to make models of people, animals, or objects.

origin If you talk about the **origin** of something, you mean the way it started, or what first caused it. *The origins of her defeat went back a long way.* ■ If you talk about a person's **origins,** you mean their family background. *...a man of humble origins.*

original (**originally, originality**) The **original** version of something is the first version. *His original idea was to use it as his company headquarters. ...the number of planes they originally planned to buy.* ■ The **original** of something like a document is the first version, rather than a copy. ■ If you say someone's work or ideas are **original** or talk about their **originality,** you mean they are unlike anything there has been before. ■ You can call someone an **original** when (a) they keep having original ideas. (b) their behaviour or way of life is strange and unlike anyone else's. ■ For Christians, **original sin** is the state of human imperfection everyone is born with as a result of Adam's and Eve's disobedience to God.

originate (**originating, originated; originator**) If something **originated** in a place, that is where it started or came from. ■ If someone **originates** a new idea, they think it up. You say they are the **originator** of the idea.

ormolu (*pron:* **or**-mul-oo) is a gold-coloured alloy of copper, tin, or zinc, used to decorate furniture, picture frames, and clocks.

ornament (**ornamented, ornamental, ornamentation**) An **ornament** is a small attractive object you display in your home. You can also call a piece of jewellery an **ornament.** ■ If something is **ornamented,** it is decorated to make it look more attractive. *...heavily ornamented clothes... In the 1920s and 1930s typeface designers dispensed with ornamentation.* ■ **Ornamental** things are intended to be attractive rather than useful.

ornate buildings and other objects are highly decorated.

ornithology (**ornithological, ornithologist**) **Ornithology** is the study of birds. *...ornithological reference works.*

orphan (**orphaned**) You call a child an **orphan** or say it has been **orphaned** when its parents have died.

orphanage An **orphanage** is a place where orphans are looked after.

orthodontic (**orthodontist**) **Orthodontics** is the branch of dentistry concerned with straightening and correcting crooked or irregular teeth. A dentist who specializes in this is called an **orthodontist.** *...orthodontic care.*

orthodox (**orthodoxy, orthodoxies**) **Orthodox** beliefs or methods are ones which most people have or use and which are considered standard. An **orthodoxy** is an accepted view about something. ■ The **orthodox** form of a religion or ideology is the older, more traditional form. **Orthodoxy** is traditional and accepted beliefs. ■ The **Orthodox Church** is the part of the Christian Church which separated from the western European church in the eleventh century. It is the main church in Greece, the former USSR, and some other countries.

orthography (*pron:* or-**thog**-graff-ee) is spelling, especially the spelling system of a particular language.

orthopaedic (*Am:* **orthopedic**) (*pron:* orth-op-**pee**-dik) **Orthopaedic** means to do with the medical care of bones and muscles, especially the treatment or prevention of injuries or defects. *...an orthopaedic surgeon. ...orthopaedic shoes.*

Orwellian You use **Orwellian** to talk about things which remind you of the kind of totalitarian society described in George Orwell's novel '1984'. *There is something grim and Orwellian in the spectacle of kids clocking in to school.*

oryx (*plural:* **oryx** or **oryxes**) The **oryx** is an long-horned African antelope.

OS is short for 'Ordnance Survey'.

Oscar An **Oscar** is a statuette given as an award for an outstanding performance or achievement in films. Oscars are also called Academy Awards.

oscillate (*pron:* **oss**-ill-late) (**oscillating, oscillated; oscillation**) If something **oscillates,** it repeatedly moves backwards and forwards or from side to side. *...an oscillating sprinkler.* ■ If someone **oscillates** between two moods, they keep changing from one to the other. ■ An **oscillating** electric current changes its direction of flow at rapid regular intervals.

osier (*pron:* **oh**-zee-er) The **osier** is a kind of willow tree. Its twigs are used for making baskets.

osmosis (*pron:* oz-**moh**-siss) is a process by which a liquid passes through the thin outer layer of something and is soaked up by what is on the other side, for example the way moisture is soaked up through the roots of a plant. ■ When someone acquires knowledge or skills gradually, without any obvious effort, people sometimes say they acquire them by **osmosis.**

osprey (*usual pron:* **oss**-pray) The **osprey** is a large bird of prey which feeds on fish.

ossified If a soft object **ossifies**, it gradually becomes hard like bone. ■ You can say things **ossify** when they become fixed and difficult to change. *The time had come to reform Britain's ossified education system.*

ostensible (**ostensibly**) The **ostensible** purpose of something is the official or apparent purpose, which may not be the real one. *The pass has recently been closed, ostensibly because of landslides.*

ostentatious (**ostentatiously; ostentation**) **Ostentatious** things are expensive and showy, and intended to impress people. ■ You say people are **ostentatious** when they show off their wealth. Behaviour like this is called **ostentation.** ■ If you do something in an **ostentatious** way, you do it in an exaggerated way, to make sure someone notices it.

osteopath (*pron:* **oss**-tee-oh-path) (**osteopathy**) An **osteopath** is a person who carries out a method of medical treatment based on the manipulation of joints, especially in the spine. This kind of treatment is called **osteopathy** (*pron:* oss-tee-**op**-path-ee).

osteoporosis (*pron:* oss-tee-oh-pore-**roh**-siss) is a condition in which the bones become very brittle.

ostracize (*or* **ostracise**) (**ostracizing, ostracized; ostracism**) If someone is **ostracized,** people are deliberately unfriendly towards them and do not let them join in with what they are doing. Behaving like this towards someone is called **ostracism.**

ostrich (**ostriches**) The **ostrich** is a large flightless African bird with a long neck. ■ If you say someone is like an **ostrich,** you mean they refuse to accept the truth about something, just as an ostrich is supposed to bury its head in the sand when there is danger.

other If you have mentioned some of the things or people in a group, you use **other** or **others** to talk about some or all of the remaining ones. *Some defendants were given bail, while others were remanded in custody.* ■ If you say something happened the **other** day or the **other** week, you mean it happened recently. ■ If something happens **every other** day, it happens on alternate days. *The election is held every other year.* ■ You use **other than** to introduce an exception to what you have just mentioned. *The latest round of talks made little progress, other than to set a date for another meeting.* ■ **each other:** see **each.**

otherwise You use **otherwise** to say what will happen if something is not done. *Local authorities will have to stay within spending limits, otherwise they will be capped.* ■ You use **otherwise** to talk about the opposite possibility from the one you have just mentioned. *He may be right, but history suggests otherwise.* ■ **Otherwise** means apart from the thing just mentioned. *The tourists were tired and dusty but otherwise unharmed.*

otherworldly You say something is **otherworldly** when it seems to belong to a world of ghosts or fairies, rather than the real world. *...their otherworldly music.*

otiose (*pron:* **oh**-tee-oze) If you say something is **otiose,** you mean it is meaningless or pointless.

otter The **otter** is a small animal with thick smooth dark-brown fur, a long tail, and webbed feet. Otters are extremely good swimmers and feed on fish.

ottoman An **ottoman** is a long low upholstered seat. Some ottomans have a storage space under the seat. ■ The **Ottoman Empire** was the Turkish empire in parts of Europe, Asia, and Africa which lasted from the 13th century to the end of World War I. *...Ottoman architecture.*

ought If you say something **ought to** happen, you mean you think it is right or a good idea. *If he's done wrong, he ought to be punished.* ■ You say something **ought to** happen when you are expecting it to happen. *She ought to win.* ■ If you say something **ought to have** happened, you mean it would have been right or a good thing if it had happened, but it did not in fact happen. *I ought to have been a footballer.*

Ouija (*pron:* **wee**-ja) A **Ouija board** is a board marked with the letters of the alphabet. Some people think messages from the dead can be spelled out by a pointer moving from letter to letter. 'Ouija' is a trademark.

ounce Weight is often expressed in **ounces.** An ounce is about 28.35 grams. There are sixteen ounces in a pound. 'Ounces' is usually shortened to 'oz.' ■ An **ounce** of something is a small amount of it. *If only my father had possessed an ounce of business sense.*

our (**ours**) You use **our** or **ours** when you are talking about something belonging to or connected with two or more people including yourself. *...our two children... Many carriages were empty, but ours was packed.*

ourselves You use **ourselves** to say something which is done by you and other people affects only you and those people. *We committed ourselves to this decision a long time ago.* ■ You use **ourselves** to emphasize that your statement really does apply to you and the other people you have been talking about. *Change would only be possible if we ourselves wanted it.*

oust If someone is **ousted** from a job or place, they are forced to leave.

out When you go **out** of a place or get **out** of a vehicle, you leave it. ■ If you are **out,** you are not at home. ■ **Out** is used to talk about an object being removed from an enclosed space. *He takes an apple out of his pocket.* ■ You say something is **out** when it is available to customers. *His book is now out in paperback.* ■ If a light is **out,** it is not shining. ■ If a fire is **out,** it is not burning. ■ If someone is **out** of a contest, they have been eliminated. ■ If a calculation or measurement is **out,** it is incorrect. ■ When something is no longer fashionable, you can say it is **out.** ■ **Out** is used to talk about a period of time coming to an end. *Those numbers could double before the week is out.* ■ If someone is **out to** do something, they intend to do it. ■ If you see something **out of** a window, you see it through the window from the inside of a building or vehicle. ■ If you are **out of** something, you no longer have any of it. ■ If something is made **out of** a certain material, it is made from it. ■ **Out of** is used to express proportions. *Leicester had lost seven out of eight matches.* ■ **Out of** is used to say why someone does something. *She must have deprived him of it out of sheer spite.* ■ If something gives you pleasure, you can say you get pleasure **out of** it. ■ If someone famous is **outed,** their homosexuality is made public knowledge against their wishes.

out- is used to form words which describe someone doing something better than someone else and beating them at it. *He outboxed Thompson for the first three rounds. The bank outperformed its rivals.*

out-and-out is used to say someone or something has all the characteristics of a certain type of person or thing. *He is an out-and-out winner.*

outback The remote areas of Australia are called the **outback.**

outbid (**outbidding, outbid** not 'outbidded') If you **outbid** someone, you offer more than them for something you both want to buy. ■ You can say someone **outbids** someone else when they make a more attractive offer. *Banks are trying to outbid each other's interest rates.*

outboard motor An **outboard motor** is a portable motor with a propeller, for attaching to a small boat.

outbox See **out-.**

outbreak An **outbreak** of something unpleasant is a sudden widespread occurrence of it. *...an outbreak of violence. ...cholera outbreaks.*

outbuilding An **outbuilding** is a building like a garage or barn which belongs to a house but is not part of the main living area.

outburst An **outburst** is a sudden strong expression of anger or some other emotion. *...an outburst of fury.* ■ If there is an **outburst** of an activity, there is suddenly a lot of it going on. *...a sudden outburst of price-cutting.*

outcast You say someone is an **outcast** when people refuse to have anything to do with them. *The senator was a virtual outcast among his fellow Republicans.*

outclass (**outclasses, outclassing, outclassed**) If you **outclass** someone, you do something much better than they do.

outcome The **outcome** of something is its result.

outcrop An **outcrop** is a large area of rock sticking up out of the ground.

outcry (**outcries**) If there is an **outcry** about something, a lot of people get angry about it.

outdated If something is **outdated,** it is old-fashioned and no longer useful. *...outdated industries.*

outdistance (**outdistancing, outdistanced**) If you **outdistance** someone, you progress faster or more successfully than they do and leave them behind.

outdo (**outdoes, outdoing, outdid, have outdone**) If you **outdo** someone, you are more successful at something than they are.

outdoor (**outdoors**) **Outdoor** is used to describe things which take place or are used in the open air, rather than in a building. *...outdoor festivals. ...outdoor shoes.* ■ If something happens or is located **outdoors,** it happens or is located in the open air.

■ The **outdoors** is the open air. *She loved the outdoors and had a sense of adventure.*

outer The **outer** parts of something are the parts furthest from its centre. *...the rundown areas between the city centre and the outer suburbs. ...the prison's outer wall.*

outermost The **outermost** of several things is the one furthest from the centre of something. *...Saturn's outermost ring.*

outer space is any region of space beyond the Earth's atmosphere.

outfall An **outfall** is the end of a drain, where water pours out.

outfit An **outfit** is (a) a set of clothes. *His outfit consisted of a T-shirt and trousers.* (b) an organization or group of people. *...a merchant-banking outfit.*

outfitter A gentlemen's **outfitter** or **outfitters** is a shop which sells men's clothes. Some other clothes shops are also called **outfitters.** *...sports outfitters.*

outflank If one army **outflanks** another, it manages to get round its side, to make an attack. ■ If you **outflank** someone, for example in an argument, you defeat them.

outflow When there is an **outflow** of money or resources, large amounts are transferred from one place or organization to another. *The group expected a cash outflow of £350m over the next four months.* ■ The movement of large numbers of people out of a place can be called an **outflow.** *...a massive outflow of refugees.*

outfox (**outfoxes, outfoxing, outfoxed**) If you **outfox** someone, you manage to beat them by being more clever or cunning.

outgoing is used to describe someone who will shortly be leaving their job or position. *...the outgoing chairman.* ■ **Outgoing** is used to describe something which is going out of a place. *The system allows only outgoing calls.* ■ A person's or organization's **outgoings** are the amounts of money they pay out. ■ An **outgoing** person is friendly and likes meeting people.

outgrow (**outgrowing, outgrew, have outgrown**) When a child **outgrows** an item of clothing, the child gets bigger and can no longer wear it. ■ When people **outgrow** a place, the size of their family or business increases and there is no longer enough room for them. ■ If you **outgrow** a type of behaviour, you become more mature and no longer behave in that way. *She outgrew her little-girl awkwardness.*

outgrowth If one thing is an **outgrowth** of another, it begins by being part of the other thing, then gradually develops into a separate thing. *The Actors' Studio was an outgrowth of the Group Theatre.*

outgun (**outgunning, outgunned**) In war, if an army is **outgunned,** their opponents have a greater number of guns. ■ If someone is **outgunned** in a sporting contest, they are beaten, because their opponents have greater strength, speed, or ability.

outhouse An **outhouse** is a small building attached to a house or in its garden.

outing An **outing** is a pleasure trip. ■ When a sportsperson or team takes part in an event, this is sometimes called an **outing.**

outlandish (**outlandishly**) If you say something is **outlandish,** you mean it is strikingly unusual or strange.

outlast If something **outlasts** something else, it is still there when the other thing has gone.

outlaw When something is **outlawed,** it is made illegal. ■ In the past, a criminal on the run was called an **outlaw.**

outlay An **outlay** is an amount of money spent on something by a company or other organization. *Their total outlay on players is close to ten and a half million pounds.*

outlet An **outlet** is a means of releasing or expressing something like feelings. *The house became an outlet for her own creativity.* ■ An **outlet** is a shop or commercial organization selling goods made by a particular manufacturer. ■ Something which provides a way out of a place can be called an **outlet.** *For years Assab has been Ethiopia's main outlet to the sea.* ■ An **outlet** is something like a hole or pipe which water or air can flow out of. *...a sewage outlet.*

outline (**outlining, outlined**) If you **outline** an idea or plan, you explain it in a general way without going into details. A general explanation can be called an **outline.** ■ If you can see the **outline** of something, you can see its general shape or silhouette, but no other details. You can also talk about seeing something **outlined** against something else.

outlive (**outliving, outlived**) If someone or something **outlives** someone or something else, they live or last longer than the other person or thing.

outlook A person's **outlook** is their general attitude towards life. ■ The **outlook** in a situation is the way things seem likely to develop. *The economic outlook appeared similarly bleak.*

outlying The **outlying** parts of a place are the parts a long way from its centre.

outmanoeuvre (**outmanoeuvring, outmanoeuvred**) (*Am:* **outmaneuver,** *etc*) If you **outmanoeuvre** someone, you gain an advantage over them by being more clever or skilful.

outmatch (**outmatches, outmatching, outmatched**) If you **outmatch** a person or what they do, you are more successful than they are at something.

outmoded things are old-fashioned and no longer useful.

outnumber (**outnumbering, outnumbered**) If one group **outnumbers** another, it has more people or things in it.

out-of-date See **date.**

out-of-the-way places are remote and seldom visited.

out-of-touch See **touch.**

outpace (**outpacing, outpaced**) If someone or something **outpaces** someone or something else, they move or grow faster than the other person or thing.

out-patient An **out-patient** is a hospital patient who does not stay overnight.

outperform See **out-.**

outplacement firms offer counselling and careers advice to redundant executive or professional staff, or advice to businesses dealing with redundancy.

outpoll (*pron:* out-**pole**) If someone **outpolls** someone else in an election, they get more votes than the other person.

outpost An **outpost** is a small settlement a long way from a main centre, usually set up as a branch of a large organization. *...a government outpost.*

outpouring An **outpouring** of an emotion is the expression of it in an uncontrolled way. *...the national outpouring of grief which greeted his death.*

output The **output** of something is the amount which is made or produced. *...oil output. ...industrial output.* ■ The **output** from a TV or radio channel is the programmes it broadcasts. ■ The **output** of a computer is the information it sorts and produces as a result of a program or operation. See also **input.**

outrage (**outraging, outraged; outrageous, outrageously**) If you are **outraged** at something which has happened, you are very shocked and angry about it. You say something like this is **outrageous** or an **outrage;** you can also call your feelings about it **outrage.** *The proposals have caused outrage in the German press.* ■ You say someone's behaviour is **outrageous** when it goes beyond what is normally acceptable.

outran See **outrun.**

outrank If one person or organization **outranks** another, they have a higher level of success or power.

outré (*pron:* **oo**-tray) is used to describe things which are very unusual and rather shocking. *...Vivienne Westwood's outré designs.*

outreach is a system in which an organization deliberately sets out to make its services or facilities known and available to people who may otherwise be unaware of what it has to offer.

outrider An **outrider** is a member of the armed forces or police who rides on a motorbike or horse alongside or in front of an official vehicle to protect and escort the people in it.

outright is used to describe something which is complete and absolute. *...an outright victory.* ■ If you come out with something **outright,** you say it in an open and direct way, rather than just hinting at it. ■ If someone is **killed outright,** they die immediately from their injuries.

outrun (**outrunning, outran**) If someone or something **outruns** someone or something else, they run or develop faster than the other person or thing.

outsell (**outselling, outsold**) If one product **outsells** another, it is sold in larger quantities.

outset The **outset** of something is its very beginning.

outshine (**outshining, outshone**) If you **outshine** someone at something, you are better at it than them.

outside The **outside** of something like a building or container is the part which faces outwards. ■ If you are **outside** a building, you are close to its outside. *A few students demonstrated outside parliament.* ■ If something happens **outside** a country, it happens somewhere else. *He said he would be forced to work outside Britain.* ■ If someone is **outside** an organization, they do not belong to it. *...outside suppliers.* ■ If someone operates **outside** the law or **outside** someone's authority, they are not controlled by it. ■ If something happens **outside** certain hours, it happens at some other time. *Emergency cover will be provided outside surgery hours.* ■ If you say there is an **outside chance** of something happening, you mean there is a remote possibility it might happen.

outside broadcast An **outside broadcast** is a TV or radio programme which is not filmed or recorded in a studio.

outsider Someone who does not belong to a particular group can be called an **outsider.** ■ A horse which is considered unlikely to win a race is called an **outsider.**

outsize or **outsized** things are much larger than the usual size.

outskirts The outskirts of a city or town are the parts farthest from the centre.

outsmart If you **outsmart** someone, you get the better of them.

outspoken (**outspokenness**) If someone is **outspoken,** they tend to say what they think, even if it shocks people.

outstanding (**outstandingly**) You say someone or something is **outstanding** when they are extremely impressive or remarkable. ■ An **outstanding** issue or problem has not yet been resolved. ■ If a debt is **outstanding,** it has not been paid off.

outstay If you **outstay your welcome,** you stay longer than your host wishes.

outstretched is used to describe a part of the body which is stretched out as far as it will go. *...an eagle with outstretched wings.*

outstrip (**outstripping, outstripped**) If something **outstrips** another, it becomes greater or more successful. *Demand is outstripping supply... He outstrips his rival in all the opinion polls.*

out-take An **out-take** is a piece of film or part of a recorded TV programme which is not included in the final version.

outvote (**outvoting, outvoted**) If someone is **outvoted,** they are defeated because their opponents get more votes than they do.

outward (**outwardly, outwards**) If something moves or faces **outward** or **outwards,** it moves or faces towards the outside. ■ If you go to a place and come back, your **outward** journey is your journey there. ■ **Outward-looking** people are interested in other people and things. ■ **Outward** and **outwardly** are used to talk about the way people and things appear, which may be different from the way they really are. *There are no outward signs of political discontent.*

outward bound courses provide training in adventurous outdoor pursuits, usually for young people.

outweigh If the bad things in a situation **outweigh** the good ones, there are more bad things than good ones.

outwit (**outwitting, outwitted**) If you **outwit** someone, you cleverly get the better of them.

outworn beliefs or customs are old-fashioned and no longer have any meaning.

ova See **ovum.**

oval An **oval** is a round two-dimensional shape, like a circle but wider in one direction than the other.

ovary (*pron:* **oh**-var-ree) (**ovaries; ovarian**) A woman's **ovaries** are the two small organs in her body which produce eggs. **Ovarian** (*pron:* oh-**vair**-ee-an) means to do with the ovaries. *...ovarian cancer.*

ovation An **ovation** is a long and enthusiastic round of applause from an audience.

oven An **oven** is the box-shaped part of a cooker, which food can be heated up or cooked in.

oven-proof dishes are made from materials which are not damaged by heat in an oven.

oven-ready foods are bought already prepared for cooking in an oven.

over If something is **over** something else, it is on top of it or directly above it. ■ If you go **over** something, you cross from one side to the other. The view **over** an area is what you can see from one side to the other. ■ **Over** is used to talk about the other side of something. *There is a big park over the road... I rolled over in bed.* ■ **Over** is used to talk about a position away from something or something. *See that box over there?* ■ **Over** is used to talk about the extent of something. *Crops have been damaged over a wide area.* ■ If something is **over** an amount, it is beyond it. *...driving while over the alcohol limit.* ■ If something happens **over** a period of time, it happens during that time. ■ **Over** is used to talk about ways of sending or receiving a message. *...talking over a digital telephone link.* ■ If something is **over,** it is finished. ■ If something is left **over,** it is still there when other things have been removed. ■ **Over** is used to mention a topic that causes discussion or concern. *The ministers were trying to reach a compromise over a plan put forward by the EU Commission.* ■ In cricket, an **over** is six consecutive balls bowled from the same end of the pitch.

over- Some words beginning with 'over' can be spelled with a hyphen after the 'r'. See, for example, entries at **overestimate, overreach.** ■ **over-** or **over** is used to form words which say there is too much of something, or that something is done to too great an extent. *The oversupply of commercial property has pushed down rents. ...over-production of cereals.*

overact If you say an actor is **overacting,** you mean he or she is playing a part in an exaggerated and unconvincing way.

overall You use **overall** when you are talking about the whole of something, rather than just parts of it. *He was still in overall charge.* ■ If a political party wins an **overall majority** in an election, they win more votes or seats than the total number gained by all their opponents put together. ■ An **overall** is a loose lightweight coat which you wear to protect your clothes while working. ■ **Overalls** are a single item of clothing consisting of a top and loose trousers joined together and worn over ordinary clothes to protect them.

overarm If you throw or hit a ball **overarm,** your arm is raised above your shoulder and moves forward and down.

overawe (**overawing, overawed**) If you are **overawed** by someone or something, you are impressed and a little afraid of them.

overbalance (**overbalancing, overbalanced**) If you **overbalance,** you fall over or nearly fall over, because you have got into an unstable position.

overbearing An **overbearing** person is unpleasant and domineering.

overblown If you say something is **overblown,** you mean it is exaggerated or excessive. *Warnings of disaster may be overblown.*

overboard If someone falls **overboard,** they fall over the side of a ship into the water.

overburdened If you are **overburdened** with something like work or problems, you have more than you can cope with.

overcame See **overcome.**

overcast If the sky is **overcast,** it is covered with clouds.

overcharge (**overcharging, overcharged**) If someone **overcharges** you, they charge you too much for something.

overcoat An **overcoat** is a thick warm coat.

overcome (**overcoming, overcame, have overcome**) If you **overcome** a problem or a feeling, you deal with it successfully. ■ If you are **overcome** by a feeling, you feel it very strongly. *She was overcome by horror.* ■ If you are **overcome** by something like heat or smoke, you are seriously affected by it and collapse.

overcrowded (**overcrowding**) If a place is **overcrowded,** there are too many people or things there.

overdo (**overdoes, overdoing, overdid, have overdone**) If you **overdo** something, you do it in an exaggerated way, or you do it too much. *While an occasional drink can be pleasant, overdoing it depresses the central nervous system.* ■ You say someone **overdoes** things when they try to do more than they can physically manage. ■ You say food is **overdone** when it has been cooked for too long.

overdose (**overdosing, overdosed**) If someone **overdoses** or takes an **overdose,** they take more of a drug than is safe, and may die.

overdraft If someone has an **overdraft,** their bank has allowed them to draw out more money than they have in their account.

overdrawn If a person is **overdrawn,** they have drawn more money out of the bank than they have in their account. You also say their account is **overdrawn.**

overdressed If you say someone is **overdressed,** you mean they are dressed too elaborately or formally.

overdrive If something goes into **overdrive,** it operates in an unusually rapid or intense way. *His imagination went into overdrive.* ■ **Overdrive** in a motor vehicle is an additional higher gear used at high speeds to reduce engine wear and save petrol.

overdue If you say something is **overdue,** you mean it should have happened before now. *...an overdue visit to my mother.* ■ If someone or something is late, you can say they are **overdue.** *...a long-overdue train... Payments were more than 90 days overdue.*

overeat (**overeating, overate, have overeaten**) If you **overeat,** you eat too much.

overestimate (or **over-estimate**) (**overestimating, overestimated**) If you **overestimate** someone or something, you think they are bigger, better, or more important than they really are.

overflow When a liquid **overflows,** it flows over the edges of the container it is in. ■ An **overflow** is a hole or pipe through which liquid can flow out of a container when it gets too full. ■ If something is **overflowing** with things, it is full of them. *The street stalls are overflowing with fresh fruit and vegetables.* ■ If someone is **overflowing** with a feeling, they are full of it and this shows in their behaviour. *She was overflowing with optimism.*

overfly (**overflies, overflying, overflew, have overflown; overflight**) When an aircraft **overflies** an area, it flies over it without landing. This is called an **overflight.**

overgrown You say an area is **overgrown** when it is thickly covered with plants because it has not been looked after. ■ You can call an adult who behaves childishly an **overgrown** child. *...an overgrown schoolboy.*

overhang (**overhanging, overhung**) If one thing **overhangs** another, part of it sticks out over the other thing. *There are shady trees overhanging the garden.* The part which sticks out can be called an **overhang.**

overhaul (**overhauling, overhauled**) If you **overhaul** a piece of equipment or give it an **overhaul,** you clean and check it thoroughly and repair it if necessary. You can also say a system is **overhauled** when it is examined carefully with a view to making changes.

overhead If something is **overhead,** it is above you, or above the place you are talking about. *A helicopter circled overhead.* ■ The **overheads** of a business are its regular essential expenses, for example rent and telephone bills.

overhear (**overhearing, overheard**) If you **overhear** a conversation, you hear what the people are saying without them realizing it.

overjoyed If you are **overjoyed,** you are extremely pleased about something.

overkill You say there is **overkill** when something is spoiled by being done too much.

overland is used to talk about journeys made across land rather than by plane or boat.

overlap (**overlapping, overlapped**) If two things **overlap** or there is an **overlap,** part of one covers part of the other. ■ If two ideas or activities **overlap,** they involve some of the same subjects, people, or periods of time. *...the overlap between civil and military technology.*

overlay (**overlaying, overlaid**) If one thing is **overlaid** with another, the second thing forms a cover over the first. You call the thing which forms the cover an **overlay.** *She peeled back the overlay to reveal* the illustration beneath. ■ If you say one characteristic in a book or film is **overlaid** with another, you mean both are present at the same time. ...*bitter humour overlaying stark tragedy.*

overleaf is used to say something is on the next page. *Look at chart 22 overleaf.*

overload (overloading, overloaded) When a vehicle is **overloaded,** there are too many people or things in it. Similarly, you can talk about a place being **overloaded** with people, or an organization being **overloaded** with problems. ■ If an electrical system is **overloaded,** too many electrical appliances are being used, and the system is likely to be damaged.

overlook (overlooking, overlooked) If a building **overlooks** a place, you get a view of the place from it. ■ If you **overlook** a feature of something or a fact about it, you ignore it, do not notice it, or do not realize its importance. ■ If you **overlook** someone's faults or bad behaviour, you decide to ignore them. ■ You say a person is **overlooked** when they are not chosen for a job or position.

overlord In the past, an **overlord** was a person who had power over many people.

overly is used to talk about the strength of someone's feelings. For example, if you say someone is **overly** excited, you mean they are too excited; if you say they are not **overly** pleased, you mean they are not very pleased.

overmanning (overmanned) If there is **overmanning** in a workplace or it is **overmanned,** it has more workers than necessary.

overmuch means the same as 'too much'. *It did not really matter overmuch.*

overnight is used to describe (a) things which last all night. ...*an overnight curfew.* (b) things which happen during the night. ...*overnight rain.* ■ An **overnight** bag is one you carry your clothes and belongings in when you go away for one or two nights. ■ **Overnight** is used to describe something which happens suddenly. ...*an overnight success.*

overpay (overpaying, overpaid) If you say someone is **overpaid,** you mean they are paid more than they deserve.

overplay If you **overplay** something, you make it seem more important than it really is.

overpopulated (overpopulation) An **overpopulated** city or country has too many people living in it.

overpower (overpowering, overpowered) If you **overpower** someone in a fight or struggle, you get control of them, because you are stronger than they are. ■ If one sportsperson or team **overpowers** another, they play better and manage to defeat them. ■ You say something is **overpowering** when it affects you very strongly. ...*an overpowering stench.*

overpriced things cost more than they are worth.

overran See **overrun.**

overrated If you say something is **overrated,** you mean people think it is better or more important than it really is.

overreach (*or* **over-reach) (overreaches, overreaching, overreached)** If you **overreach** yourself, you fail to achieve something because you try to be too clever or to do too much.

override (overriding, overrode, have overridden) If something **overrides** other things, it is regarded as more important than them. *The overriding need was to find a leader who could unite the party.* ■ If someone **overrides** an order or decision made by someone else, they cancel or change it. ■ If you **override** the automatic controls of a device, you operate it by hand.

overrule (overruling, overruled) If a decision is **overruled,** someone in authority officially decides it is incorrect or invalid.

overrun (overrunning, overran, have overrun) If an army **overruns** a place, it captures every part of it. ■ You can say a place is **overrun** by people or things when there are too many of them there. *Britain has never been so overrun with big outdoor rock concerts as it is this summer.* ■ If an event **overruns,** it goes on longer than it was intended to.

oversaw See **oversee.**

overseas means connected with countries across the sea. ...*overseas aid.* ...*overseas visitors.*

oversee (overseeing, oversaw, have overseen; overseer) When someone **oversees** something or acts as an **overseer,** they watch it being done, to make sure it is done properly.

oversell (overselling, oversold) If you **oversell** something, you exaggerate its quality or importance.

overshadow If one thing is **overshadowed** by another, people are less aware of it because of the other thing. *Stewart's deeds were overshadowed by the contribution of Carl Hooper.* ■ If something unpleasant **overshadows** a situation or event, it makes it less enjoyable or successful. ■ If a mountain or tall building **overshadows** a place, it is close to it or in the middle of it and is very noticeable.

overshoot (overshooting, overshot) If something **overshoots** a target or a place where it is supposed to stop, it goes beyond it. ■ When an organization **overshoots** its estimated budget, the amount it spends goes beyond its original estimate. ...*a £67m overshoot in expenditure.*

oversight If there has been an **oversight,** someone has forgotten to do something which they should have done.

oversimplify (oversimplifies, oversimplifying, oversimplified; oversimplification) If you **oversimplify** something, you make it seem simpler than it really is. *It would be an oversimplification to describe Radio 3 and Classic FM as direct competitors.*

oversized things are too big, or bigger than usual. ...*oversized clothes.*

oversleep (oversleeping, overslept) If you **oversleep,** you sleep longer than you meant to and are late getting up.

overspill is used to talk about people from crowded cities who have been rehoused in smaller towns.

overstate (overstating, overstated; overstatement) If you **overstate** something, you make it out to be greater or more important than it really is. Making a claim like this is called **overstatement;** the claim you make is called an **overstatement.**

overstep (**overstepping, overstepped**) If someone **oversteps** something like the rules of a system or **oversteps the mark**, they go beyond what is allowed or acceptable.

overstretch (**overstretches, overstretching, overstretched**) If someone or something is **overstretched**, they have been forced to take on more work or commitments than they can cope with.

oversubscribed If an event or educational course is **oversubscribed**, there are not enough places for the number of people who want to attend. ■ If a sale of shares in a company is **oversubscribed**, too many people want to buy them.

overt (**overtly**) **Overt** attitudes and intentions are open and obvious. ...*overt hostility.* ...*an overtly military role.*

overtake (**overtaking, overtook, have overtaken**) If you **overtake** a vehicle or person moving in the same direction as yourself, you pass them because you are moving faster than they are. ■ You say someone or something **overtakes** someone or something else, when they become more successful, greater, or more important than them. *Shanghai reckons that it will overtake Hong Kong as a financial centre within the next 10-15 years.* ■ If you are **overtaken** by something which happens, it happens unexpectedly or suddenly, before you are ready to deal with it. *The biggest sex scandal for years was about to overtake the government.*

overtax (**overtaxes, overtaxing, overtaxed**) If someone or something is **overtaxed,** they have too great a strain placed on them. ■ If a government **overtaxes** people, it makes them pay too much tax.

overthrow (**overthrowing, overthrew, have overthrown**) If a government or leader is **overthrown,** they are removed from power by force. You call this their **overthrow.** ■ If something like a rule is **overthrown,** it is replaced by something else.

overtime is time someone spends working in addition to their normal working hours. ■ If you say someone is **working overtime** to achieve something, you mean they are putting a lot of effort, energy, or enthusiasm into it.

overtone If you say something has certain **overtones,** you mean there are further aspects to it apart from the obvious ones. ...*a new financial scandal with political overtones.*

overtook See **overtake.**

overture An **overture** is a piece of music played as the introduction to an opera or play. ■ If you **make overtures** to someone, you try to start a friendly, romantic, or business relationship with them.

overturn If something **overturns** or is **overturned,** it turns upside down or on its side. ■ If someone in authority **overturns** a decision, they cancel it. ■ If something **overturns** a belief, it shows it is wrong. ■ In an election, when someone wins a seat which had previously been held by a different party, you can say they **overturn** that party's majority.

overview If you have an **overview** of a situation, you have a good general understanding of it. Similarly, if you give someone an **overview** of something, you give a good general description of it.

overweening is used to say someone or something has too much of something. ...*a man of overweening ambition.*

overwhelm (**overwhelming, overwhelmingly**) If one person or group **overwhelms** another, they defeat them completely, usually by superior strength or ability. ■ If you are **overwhelmed** with something, or **overwhelmed** by it, you have more of it than you can cope with. *They're overwhelmed with paperwork.* ■ **Overwhelming** is used to describe things which are much greater or more powerful than other things of their kind. *My overwhelming feeling has become one of anger.*

overwrought (*pron:* over-**rawt**) people are nervous, worried, and upset.

ovulate (*pron:* ov-yew-late) (**ovulating, ovulated; ovulation**) When a woman or female animal **ovulates,** she produces eggs from her ovary. This process is called **ovulation.**

ovum (*pron:* oh-vum) (*plural:* **ova**) The eggs produced in the ovaries of a woman or female animal are called **ova.**

owe (**owing, owed**) If someone **owes** you money, they have not paid back money they have borrowed from you. ■ If you **owe** some advantage to someone or something, it is because of them that you have it. *She owed her long life to healthy eating.* ■ If you say you **owe** gratitude, respect, or loyalty to someone, you mean they deserve it from you or have a right to expect it. *There are literally hundreds of people to whom I owe my thanks.* ■ **Owing to** means 'because of'. *They are facing higher costs owing to rising inflation.*

owl – **Owls** are birds of prey which hunt at night. They have large eyes, short hooked beaks, and strong sharp claws.

owlish people look very serious and studious.

own You use **own** (a) to emphasize that something belongs to a certain person or thing. ...*a house of his own.* (b) to talk about someone doing something without help. *She couldn't cope on her own.* ■ If someone is **on their own,** they are alone. ■ If you **get your own back** on someone, you pay them back for something unpleasant they have done to you. ■ If you **own** something, it is your property. You add **-owning** to a word to say what someone owns. ...*home-owning voters.* You add **-owned** to a word to show who something belongs to. ...*state-owned airlines.* ■ If you say that someone has something they can **call** their **own,** you mean it belongs to them personally, rather than, for example being controlled by or shared with someone else. *I would like a place I can call my own.* ■ If you **own up** to something wrong you have done, you admit you did it. ■ **hold your own:** see **hold.**

own-brand See **brand.**

owner (**ownership**) The **owner** of something is the person it belongs to. **Ownership** is owning something. ...*the rise in car ownership.*

own goal In sport, if someone scores an **own goal,** they accidentally send the ball into their own goal. ■ You say someone scores an **own goal** when they do something unwise which turns out badly for them.

ox (*plural:* **oxen**) An **ox** is a castrated bull.

Oxbridge is the universities of Oxford and Cambridge.

oxidation See **oxidize.**

oxide An **oxide** is a compound of oxygen and another chemical element.

oxidize (*or* **oxidise**) (**oxidizing, oxidized; oxidation**) When a substance **oxidizes,** it reacts chemically with another substance to form an oxide. This process is called **oxidation.**

oxtail is a cow's or bullock's tail when it is used in soups and stews.

oxyacetylene is a mixture of oxygen and acetylene used for cutting or welding metals at high temperatures.

oxygen is a colourless gas which all plants and animals need to live.

oxygenate (**oxygenating, oxygenated**) If something is **oxygenated,** oxygen is added to it.

oxygen mask An **oxygen mask** is a mask connected to an oxygen container, placed over the nose and mouth of a person to help them breathe more easily, for example if they are ill or working at high altitudes.

oxygen tent An **oxygen tent** is a clear plastic tent placed over a very ill patient in hospital and filled with pure oxygen to help them breathe more easily.

oxymoron An **oxymoron** is a combination of words which appear to contradict each other, for example 'strangely familiar'.

oyster – **Oysters** are large flat shellfish. ■ If you say **the world is your oyster,** you mean you can go anywhere or do anything you want.

oystercatcher – **Oystercatchers** are large black-and-white wading birds with long red bills which they use to catch shellfish and worms.

oz. See **ounce.**

ozone is a strong-smelling poisonous form of oxygen. The **ozone layer** is a layer of ozone in the upper part of the Earth's atmosphere which protects living things from the sun's radiation.

P p

p See **pence.**

p. (**pp.**) **p.** is short for 'page'. **pp.** is short for 'pages'. *...see pp. 209-14.*

PA See **personal assistant.** ■ **PA** stands for 'public address system'.

p.a. See **per annum.**

pace (**pacing, paced**) A **pace** is one step. *His father followed a few paces behind.* ■ If you **pace** up and down, you walk up and down continually, because you are anxious or impatient. ■ Your **pace** is the speed you walk or run at. *We went at a leisurely pace.* You can also talk about the **pace** at which something happens or is done. *...the pace of reform. ...a fast-paced political thriller.* ■ If you **put** someone or something **through their paces,** you test their ability.

pacemaker A **pacemaker** is a device attached to a person's heart to help it beat normally. ■ In athletics, a **pacemaker** is a runner who keeps ahead of the other competitors for the first part of a race and sets the pace for them.

pacey See **pacy.**

pacifier In Canada and the US, a **pacifier** is a child's dummy.

pacifism (**pacifist**) **Pacifism** is the belief that violence is always wrong. People who believe this are called **pacifists;** because of their beliefs, they often refuse to fight in wars.

pacify (**pacifies, pacifying, pacified; pacification**) If you **pacify** someone who is angry or upset, you calm them down. ■ If an army **pacifies** people, it uses force to overcome their resistance or protests.

pack (**packer**) A **pack** of things is a set of them, often sold together in a packet. *...a free information pack. ...a pack of cigarettes.* ■ A **pack** is a rucksack. ■ A **pack animal** is an animal like a horse or donkey, which is used to carry loads. ■ A **pack** of dogs or wolves is a group of them which hunt together. ■ A group of people who go around together can be called a **pack.** *...a pack of journalists.* ■ When you **pack** or do your **packing,** you put clothes and belongings into a bag or suitcase. ■ When goods are **packed,** they are put into boxes ready to be transported. Any protective material put around them is called **packing.** A **packer** is a person or company whose job or business is packing goods. ■ If someone is **packed off** somewhere, they are sent there. ■ If someone is **sent packing,** they are told firmly to leave. ■ When people **pack** a place, they fill it until it becomes crowded. *...a packed hall.* ■ If someone **packs** a meeting, they fill it with their supporters, to make sure things go the way they want. ■ If something is **packed** with things, it is full of them. *Their catalogue is packed full of attractive gift ideas.* ■ If you **pack** something **in,** you stop doing it.

package A **package** is a small parcel. ■ A **package** is a set of proposals or arrangements which are offered together, or have to be taken together. ■ A **package holiday** is a holiday in which everything is arranged by one company, for a fixed price.

packaging A product's **packaging** is the wrapping or container it is sold in.

packet A **packet** is a small box or bag in which something is sold. ■ A **packet** is a small parcel. ■ If something costs a **packet,** it costs a lot of money.

pack ice is large masses of ice floating in the sea.

packing case A **packing case** is a large wooden box in which things are stored or transported.

pact A **pact** is a formal agreement, especially one in which people agree to help each other.

pacy (*or* **pacey**) If you call a sportsperson **pacy,** you mean they move around at a fast pace. Similarly, if a book or film is **pacy,** the plot moves at a fast pace.

pad (**padding, padded**) A **pad** is a thick soft piece of material such as foam rubber. Pads are used, for example, to clean things, protect things, or fill out their shape. ■ **Padding** is thick soft material placed inside something to make it more comfortable, fill out a shape, or give protection. If something contains padding, you say it is **padded.** ■ If you **pad out** a piece of writing, you put in unnecessary extra information, to get it up to a certain length. ■ A **pad** is a number of sheets of paper fastened together at one end, for writing on. ■ A landing **pad** is an area of flat hard ground where helicopters can land and take off. ■ The **pads** of an animal are the soft fleshy parts on the bottom of its paws. ■ If you **pad** somewhere, you walk there with soft steps. ■ A lily **pad** is the large floating leaf of a water lily. ■ People sometimes call the place where they live their **pad.** ■ See also **launching pad.**

padded cell A **padded cell** is a small room with padded walls in a psychiatric hospital, where patients are put when it is thought they are in danger of harming themselves.

paddle (**paddling, paddled**) A **paddle** is a short pole with a wide flat part at one or both ends, for propelling a canoe. When you **paddle** a canoe, you propel it using a paddle. ■ When a bird or animal **paddles,** it swims using its legs or feet. ■ When people **paddle** or have a **paddle,** they walk, stand, or splash around with bare feet in shallow water.

paddle steamer A **paddle steamer** is a steam-powered ship propelled by a large wheel or wheels.

paddock A **paddock** is a small field where horses are kept. ■ At a racecourse, the **paddock** is an area where horses walk around before a race. ■ In motor racing, the **paddock** is an area where the cars assemble before a race.

paddy (**paddies**) A **paddy** or **paddy field** is a flooded field where rice is grown.

padlock (**padlocked**) A **padlock** is a removable lock with a hinged U-shaped bar which clicks shut. If something is **padlocked,** it is locked with a padlock.

padre (*pron:* pah-dray) A **padre** is a chaplain in the armed forces.

paean (*pron:* pee-an) A **paean** is something spoken, sung, or written in praise of a person or thing.

paediatrician (*Am:* **pediatrician**) A **paediatrician** (*pron:* peed-ya-**trish**-un) is a doctor who specializes in treating sick children.

paediatrics (**paediatric**) (*Am:* **pediatrics, pediatric**) **Paediatrics** (*pron:* pee-dee-**ya**-triks) is the branch of medicine which deals with children's diseases. ...*a paediatric surgeon.*

paedophile (**paedophilia**) (*Am:* **pedophile, pedophilia**) A **paedophile** (*pron:* **pee**-do-file) is an adult who is sexually attracted to children. This kind of attraction is called **paedophilia** (*pron:* pee-do-**fill**-ya).

paella (*pron:* pie-**ell**-a) is a Spanish dish of rice, chicken, shellfish, and vegetables.

pagan (**paganism**) **Pagan** beliefs and practices do not belong to any of the main world religions and are based in nature and belief in many gods. People involved in these practices are sometimes called **pagans;** their beliefs and worship are called **paganism.**

page (**paging, paged**) A **page** is one of the sheets in a book, newspaper, or magazine, or a side of one of these sheets. ■ If you **page** someone, you summon them over a loudspeaker or through a pager. ■ A **page** or **pageboy** is a small boy who attends a bride at her wedding.

pageant A **pageant** is a show or parade, especially one with a historical theme. ■ A **beauty pageant** is the same as a beauty contest.

pageantry is the elaborate and colourful ceremonies you get at certain state occasions.

pageboy See **page.** ■ A **pageboy** is a medium-length hairstyle in which the hair is curled under at the ends.

pager A **pager** is a small portable electronic device which bleeps when there is a message for you.

pagoda A **pagoda** is a tall ornately decorated tower where Buddhists worship, or a non-religious building in this style.

paid See **pay.**

paid-up You can say someone is a **paid-up** member of a group when they are a recognized or enthusiastic member of it. *She is now a paid-up member of the celebrity circuit.*

pail A **pail** is a bucket, especially a metal or wooden one.

pain (**paining, pained**) Pain or a **pain** is an unpleasant feeling in part of your body caused by an illness or injury. ■ **Pain** is a feeling of deep unhappiness. ■ If something **pains** you, it hurts or upsets you. ■ If you **take pains** to do something, you try hard to do it. ■ If someone is ordered not to do something **on pain of** a certain punishment, they must not do it or they will suffer that punishment.

painful (**painfully**) If a part of your body is **painful,** it hurts. ■ If something is **painful,** it causes you physical pain. ■ A **painful** experience is upsetting and difficult to cope with.

painkilling (**painkiller**) A **painkilling** drug reduces pain. Drugs like these are called **painkillers.**

painless If a medical treatment is **painless,** it does not cause physical pain. ■ You say something is **painless** when it is managed without difficulty.

painstaking (**painstakingly**) **Painstaking** work is very careful and thorough.

paint (**painting**) **Paint** is a coloured liquid you put onto a surface to protect it or decorate it, or which you use to make a picture. ■ If you **paint** a wall or an object, you cover it with paint. ■ If you **paint** something or **paint** a picture of it, you make a picture using paint; the picture is called a **painting.** ■ If a woman **paints** her lips or nails, she puts lipstick or nail varnish on them. ■ When someone describes a situation, you can say they **paint a pic-**

ture of a certain kind. *The report paints an alarming picture.*

paintbox (**paintboxes**) A **paintbox** is a flat box containing small blocks of dry paint used for painting pictures.

paintbrush (**paintbrushes**) A **paintbrush** is a brush you use for painting.

painter (**painterly**) A **painter** is an artist who paints pictures. **Painterly** means things to do with painters or painting. *Lawrence had painterly ambitions.* ■ A **painter** is someone whose job is painting the insides or outsides of buildings.

painting See **paint.**

paintwork The **paintwork** of a building or vehicle is the paint on it.

pair (**pairing, paired**) A **pair** is a set of two matching things. ■ **Pair** is used to talk about objects made up of two matching parts. *...a pair of jeans.* ■ You can refer to two people as a **pair,** either when they have a relationship with each other, or when they happen to be together at a particular time. ■ If one person or thing is **paired** with another, they are put together or considered together. You can talk about the **pairing** of two people or things. ■ If you **pair up** with someone, you join with them to do something. ■ When people **pair off,** they split up into pairs. ■ See also **au pair.**

paisley is a pattern of curving shapes usually in bright colours, used especially on fabrics.

pajamas See **pyjamas.**

Pakistani is used to talk about people or things in or from Pakistan. ■ A **Pakistani** is someone who comes from Pakistan.

pal Your **pals** are your friends.

palace A **palace** is a large splendid house, especially the home of a king, queen, or president.

Palaeolithic (*Am:* **Paleolithic**) The **Palaeolithic** period was the earliest period of the Stone Age when man began to walk upright and to use speech, fire, and tools. See also **Mesolithic, Neolithic.**

palaeontology (*Am:* **paleontology**) (**palaeontologist**) **Palaeontology** (*pron:* pal-ee-on-**tol**-a-jee) is the study of the fossils of extinct animals and plants.

palatable You say food or drink is **palatable** when it is pleasant to eat or drink. ■ You say things are **palatable** when they are easy to accept.

palate Your **palate** is the roof of your mouth. ■ Your **palate** is your ability to judge and appreciate good wine or food.

palatial A **palatial** building is large and splendid like a palace.

palaver (*pron:* pah-**lah**-ver) is unnecessary fuss.

palazzo (*pron:* pal-**lats**-so) (*plural:* **palazzi**) A **palazzo** is a very large and grand Italian house.

pale (**paleness; paling, paled**) **Pale** colours are not strong or bright. ■ If someone **pales** or if they are **pale,** their face looks lighter than usual, because they are ill or shocked. ■ If one thing **pales** when compared to another, it is made to seem much less important or exciting. ■ If you say someone's behaviour is **beyond the pale,** you mean that it is unacceptable.

Paleolithic See **Palaeolithic.**

paleontology See **palaeontology.**

palette A **palette** is a flat board on which an artist mixes paints.

palette knife A **palette knife** is a knife with a broad flat flexible blade. It is used in cookery and in oil painting.

palimony In the US, **palimony** is alimony awarded to a non-married partner after the break-up of a long term relationship.

palindrome A **palindrome** is a word or phrase which is the same whether you read it forwards or backwards, for example the word 'refer'.

palings are a fence made up of a row of narrow upright posts.

palisade A **palisade** is a fence of upright posts to protect people from attack.

pall (*pron:* **pawl**) A **pall** of smoke is a thick cloud of it hanging over a place. ■ A **pall** is a cloth covering a coffin, or the coffin itself. ■ If something **palls,** it becomes less interesting or enjoyable.

pallbearer The **pallbearers** at a funeral are the people who carry the coffin or walk beside it.

pallet A **pallet** is a wooden platform on which goods are stacked, so they can be moved using a fork-lift truck.

palliative (*pron:* pal-lee-a-tiv) A **palliative** is a drug or medical treatment which relieves suffering without treating the cause. ■ A **palliative** is something done to relieve a problem, without tackling its cause.

pallid If someone is **pallid,** they are extremely pale. ■ **Pallid** is used to describe people and things that have little power or vigour.

pallor Someone's **pallor** is an unhealthy paleness of their skin.

palm A **palm** or **palm tree** is a tall tropical tree with no branches and a crown of long leaves. ■ The **palm** of your hand is the flat part which your fingers bend towards. ■ If someone **palms** something **off** on you, they get you to accept something you do not want. ■ If someone **palms** you **off with** a lie or excuse, they tell you something just to get rid of you.

palmistry (**palmist**) **Palmistry** is telling people's fortunes by examining their palm.

palm oil is a thick yellow oil from the fruit of certain palm trees. It is used in the manufacture of some foods and cosmetics.

Palm Sunday is the Sunday before Easter.

palmtop A **palmtop** computer is a very small one. You can operate it with one hand while resting it on the palm of the other.

palomino (**palominos**) A **palomino** is a golden-coloured horse with a white mane and tail.

palpable (**palpably**) You describe something as **palpable** when it is obvious.

palpitation (**palpitations**) If someone has **palpitations,** they feel their heart beating very fast or with an irregular beat.

palsy (*pron:* **pol**-zee) is paralysis, or an illness which causes paralysis. See also **cerebral palsy.**

paltry If something, especially a sum of money, is **paltry,** it is disappointingly small.

pampas The **pampas** is a large area of flat grassy land in South America.

pamper (**pampering, pampered**) If you **pamper** someone, you are very kind to them and do a lot of nice things for them.

pamphlet (**pamphleteer**) A **pamphlet** is a thin book with a paper cover, giving information about something. A **pamphleteer** is a person who writes pamphlets, especially on political subjects.

pan (**panning, panned**) A **pan** is a metal container with a long handle, used for cooking things on top of a cooker. ■ When people **pan** for gold, they search for it in a river by washing mud or sand in a shallow metal dish. ■ If a critic **pans** something, he or she criticizes it severely. ■ When a film camera **pans**, it follows a moving object or turns slowly to give a panoramic effect.

pan- at the beginning of a word means it refers to the whole of something, or every one of the things in a group. ...*a pan-European advertising campaign.* ...*a pan-Islamic movement.*

panacea (*pron:* pan-a-**see**-a) A **panacea** is something which is supposed to be a remedy for all problems.

panache (*pron:* pan-**ash**) If you do things with **panache,** you do them with style and confidence.

panama A **panama** or **panama hat** is a straw hat with a fairly wide brim.

pancake – Pancakes are flat thin circular pieces of fried batter, usually folded and eaten hot with a sweet or savoury filling.

Pancake Day See **Shrove Tuesday.**

pancreas (*pron:* pan-kree-ass) (**pancreases, pancreatic**) Your **pancreas** is a large gland behind your stomach, which produces insulin and helps with digestion. **Pancreatic** means to do with the pancreas. ...*pancreatic cancer.*

panda The **panda** or **giant panda** is a bear-like animal with black and white fur, which lives in the bamboo forests of China and Tibet.

panda car A **panda car** is a small police patrol car.

pandemic A **pandemic** is a disease which affects people over a very wide area.

pandemonium is noisy confusion.

pander (**pandering, pandered**) If you **pander** to someone, you give them what they want, often to get their support.

Pandora's box If you say someone has opened a **Pandora's box,** you mean they have started something which will bring a lot of trouble.

pane A **pane** is a flat sheet of glass in a window or door.

panegyric (*pron:* pan-i-**jir**-ik) A **panegyric** is a formal speech or piece of writing in praise of someone or something.

panel (**panellist**) (*Am:* **panelist**) A **panel** is a flat rectangular piece of wood or other material, which forms part of a larger object, such as a door. ■ A control or instrument **panel** is a surface containing switches and controls. ■ A **panel** is a small group of people who have been chosen to do something such as answer questions on television. A **panellist** is a member of a panel.

panelling (**panelled**) (*Am:* **paneling, paneled**) **Panelling** is rectangular pieces of wood covering a building's inside walls. A **panelled** room has walls like this.

panellist See **panel.**

pang A **pang** of hunger or guilt is a sudden feeling of it.

panic (**panics, panicking, panicked**) **Panic** is a sudden feeling of fear or anxiety, which can make someone act without thinking sensibly. When someone behaves like this, you say they **panic** or are **panicked;** if a lot of people do it, you say there is a **panic.** A **panic button** is a button you press in an emergency, which rings an alarm. When someone takes sudden emergency measures, you can say they **press the panic button.**

panicky is used to describe people who are panicking, or things they do when they panic. ...*panicky decisions.*

pannier A **pannier** is a bag, box, or basket, especially one of a pair on either side of a bicycle or pack animal such as a donkey.

panoply A **panoply** of things is a large number of them, of different kinds.

panorama (**panoramic**) A **panorama** or **panoramic view** is a view over a wide area. ■ A **panorama** is a detailed and wide-ranging description of something.

pan-pipes are a musical instrument made of wooden pipes of different lengths tied together.

pansy (**pansies**) **Pansies** are small garden flowers with large round velvety petals. ■ **Pansy** is an offensive word for an effeminate or homosexual man.

pant – Pants are the same as underpants. ■ In the US and some parts of Britain, trousers are called **pants.** ■ When you **pant,** you breathe quickly and loudly, because you have been doing something energetic.

pantaloons are long trousers with wide legs, gathered at the ankle.

pantechnicon A **pantechnicon** is a large covered lorry, especially one used for moving equipment or furniture.

pantheism (**pantheist, pantheistic**) **Pantheism** is the belief that God is present in everything in nature. Someone who believes this is called a **pantheist;** you say their beliefs are **pantheistic.**

pantheon A **pantheon** is a building or monument commemorating a nation's dead heroes. ■ In ancient Greece and Rome, a **pantheon** was a temple to all the gods. ■ People sometimes use **pantheon** to mean the best people ever in a particular field. ...*the pantheon of champion golfers.*

panther A **panther** is a leopard with black fur.

panties are underpants worn by women.

pantile – Pantiles are roofing tiles with an S-shaped cross-section.

pantomime A **pantomime** or **panto** is a type of traditional musical play for children, performed at Christmas.

pantry (**pantries**) A **pantry** is a room or cupboard for storing food.

pantyhose are women's tights.

pap is soft or mushy food, especially food for babies or sick people. ■ If you call something **pap,** you mean it has no value.

papacy (*pron:* **pay**-pa-see) The **papacy** is the position of being Pope.

papal (*pron:* **pay**-pal) means connected with the Pope. ...*a papal visit.*

paparazzi (*pron:* pap-a-**rat**-see) The **paparazzi** are photographers who follow celebrities around.

papaya (*pron:* pa-**pie**-ya) **Papayas** are West Indian fruit with yellowish skins, sweet pinkish flesh, and black seeds. They are also called 'pawpaws'.

paper (**papering, papered**) **Paper** is a material made from wood pulp, used for example for writing on. ■ **On paper** means in theory, as opposed to fact. *On paper, the two sides are closer than ever before.* ■ **Papers** are sheets of paper with information on them. ■ Your **papers** are your identification documents, such as your passport. ■ A **paper** is (a) one part of a written examination. (b) an article or essay on an academic or scientific subject. ■ A **paper** is a newspaper. ■ If you **paper** a wall, you put wallpaper on it. ■ If you **paper over** a difficulty, you try to hide it by giving the impression that things are going well. ■ If you call someone or something a **paper tiger,** you mean they do not have any real power although they may seem powerful.

paperback A **paperback** is a book with a thin cardboard cover.

paper clip A **paper clip** is a small piece of bent wire, used to fasten sheets of paper together.

paperweight A **paperweight** is a small heavy object, placed on top of loose papers to stop them blowing away.

paperwork is things like letters, records, and reports which have to be dealt with as part of a job.

papery If something is **papery,** it is thin and dry like paper.

papier-mâché (*pron:* **pap**-yay **mash**-ay) is a mixture of pieces of paper and paste which hardens when it dries, used to make models.

papist (*pron:* **pape**-ist) is an offensive word for a Roman Catholic.

paprika is a mild red pepper made from capsicums.

papyrus (*pron:* pap-**ire**-uss) (**papyruses**) **Papyrus** is a tall reed-like African water plant. A type of paper made from its stems is also called **papyrus.** A **papyrus** is an ancient document written on papyrus.

par is the normal standard of something. *His performance was not up to par.* ■ If one thing is **on a par** with another, it is of a similar standard or at a similar level. ■ On a golf course, **par** is the number of strokes a good golfer should take to complete a hole or course.

para See **paratroop.**

parable A **parable** is a story which makes a moral or religious point.

parabola (*pron:* pa-**rab**-bol-a) (**parabolic**) A **parabola** is a curve like the path of a ball when it is thrown. If something is **parabolic,** it has a curve or curves like this.

paracetamol is a mild pain-relieving drug.

parachute (**parachuting, parachuted; parachutist**) A **parachute** is an apparatus which enables a person or package to float safely to the ground from an aircraft. It consists of a large umbrella-shaped piece of fabric, which is attached to the person or package by long cords. If you **parachute** somewhere, you jump from an aircraft and float down using a parachute. Someone who does this regularly is called a **parachutist.**

parade (**parading, paraded**) A **parade** is a procession of people or things, held to celebrate a special event. ■ A **parade** is a formal occasion when members of the armed forces assemble for inspection. ■ When soldiers or other people **parade** somewhere, they march or walk together in a group. ■ If you **parade** something, you display it in public. *He paraded the trophy around Liverpool.* ■ A **parade** is a short row of shops.

parade ground A **parade ground** is an area where soldiers practise marching and assemble for parades.

paradigm (*pron:* **par**-a-dime) (**paradigmatic**) A **paradigm** is a model or example of something. If someone or something is **paradigmatic** (*pron:* para-dig-**mat**-tik), they serve as a model or example.

paradise is another name for heaven.

paradox (**paradoxes; paradoxical, paradoxically**) A **paradox** is a situation which is puzzling, because it seems to involve a contradiction. You say something like this is **paradoxical.**

paraffin is a strong-smelling flammable liquid, used as fuel.

paragliding (**paraglider**) **Paragliding** is the sport of cross-country gliding using a specially designed rectangular parachute. Someone who takes part in this sport is called a **paraglider.**

paragon If you say someone is a **paragon** of a particular quality, you mean they are a perfect example of it. ...*Aristotle, that paragon of genius.*

paragraph A **paragraph** is one of the sections a piece of writing is divided into. Each paragraph begins on a new line.

parakeet A **parakeet** is a small long-tailed parrot.

parallel (**paralleling, paralleled**) If there are **parallels** between two things, there are similarities between them. You can say one thing **parallels** another. ■ If you draw a **parallel** between two things, you say they are similar. ■ If two lines are **parallel,** they are the same distance apart along the whole of their length. ■ A **parallel** is any of the lines of latitude which circle the earth parallel to the equator.

parallelogram A **parallelogram** is a four-sided shape in which each side is parallel to the one opposite.

paralyse (*Am:* **paralyze**) (**paralysing, paralysed; paralysis**) If something, especially an illness or accident, **paralyses** you, it causes loss of movement in your body and usually loss of feeling. This condition is called **paralysis.** ■ If something **paralyses** a process, place, or organization, it brings it to a standstill.

paralytic A **paralytic** disease or condition causes paralysis.

paramedical (paramedic) **Paramedical** staff or **paramedics** are medical support staff, especially the crews of some emergency ambulances who have been trained to use life-saving equipment.

parameter (pron: par-**am**-it-er) The **parameters** affecting something are the factors limiting how it can be done, made, or operated.

paramilitary (paramilitaries) A **paramilitary** organization is an armed group which is organized along military lines, but is not part of a country's armed forces. Members of a group like this are called **paramilitaries**.

paramount (paramountcy) If something is **paramount** or of **paramount** importance, it is more important than anything else. You talk about the **paramountcy** of something like this.

paramour (pron: **par**-a-moo-er) Someone's **paramour** is their lover.

paranoia (paranoid, paranoiac) **Paranoia** is a mental illness which makes someone believe that other people are trying to harm them, or that they are much more important than they really are. You say someone with this illness is **paranoid** or **paranoiac**. ■ **Paranoia** is a tendency to suspect or mistrust other people.

paranormal The **paranormal** is things like telepathy, clairvoyance, and the appearance of ghosts and poltergeists, for which there is no scientific explanation.

parapet A **parapet** is a low wall along the edge of a bridge, roof, or balcony.

paraphernalia is various objects connected with a particular activity. ...kitchen paraphernalia. ...sporting paraphernalia.

paraphrase (paraphrasing, paraphrased) If you **paraphrase** what someone has said or written, you express it differently. What you say or write is called a **paraphrase**.

paraplegic (pron: par-a-**pleej**-ik) (paraplegia) If someone is **paraplegic**, they are paralysed from somewhere in the region of their waist downwards. This condition is called **paraplegia**. See also **quadriplegic**.

parapsychology is the study of mental abilities beyond normal explanation, such as ESP.

parasite (parasitic, parasitical, parasitism) A **parasite** is an animal, plant, or organism which lives on or inside a larger one and gets its food from it. You say an animal, plant, or organism like this is **parasitic**. Parasitic diseases are caused by parasites. ■ If you call someone a **parasite**, you mean they live off other people without doing anything in return. You say people like this are **parasitic** or **parasitical**. You call their behaviour **parasitism**.

parasol A **parasol** is a light umbrella for providing shade from the sun.

paratroop (paratroops; paratrooper, para) **Paratroops** are soldiers trained to drop into battle by parachute. A soldier of this kind is called a **paratrooper** or **para**.

parboil (parboiling, parboiled) If you **parboil** vegetables, you boil them until they are partly cooked.

parcel (parcelling, parcelled) (Am: parceling, parceled) A **parcel** is something wrapped up in paper and secured with string or tape. If you **parcel** something **up**, you make it into a parcel. ■ A **parcel** of land is a piece of it with definite boundaries. ■ If you **parcel** something **out**, you divide it among several people or groups.

parched If the ground is **parched**, it is very dry, because the sun has been hot and there has been no rain. ■ If you are **parched**, you are very thirsty.

parchment was a type of paper made from goat or sheep skin. **Parchments** are writings on parchment. A modern type of stiff paper is also called **parchment**.

pardon (pardoning, pardoned) When a monarch, president, or government **pardons** someone, they free them from prosecution or a death sentence, or release them from prison. The order requiring this to be done is called a **pardon**. ■ If you say someone could be **pardoned** for doing something, you mean you would not blame them if they did it.

pardonable If you say something is **pardonable**, you mean it can be excused in the circumstances.

pare (paring, pared) When you **pare** something, you trim or peel it. ■ A **paring** is a thin piece cut off something, such as a fingernail. ■ If you **pare** something **back** or **pare** it **down**, you reduce it to a minimum.

parent (parental) Your **parents** are your mother and father. A **parent** is someone who has a child or children. **Parental** means to do with parents. ...parental rights.

parentage If you talk about someone's **parentage**, you are talking about who their parents are or were. He is of Zambian parentage.

parental See parent.

parent company A company's **parent company** is a larger company which owns it or holds over half of its shares.

parenthesis (parentheses) (pron: par-**en**-thiss-iss, par-**en**-thiss-eez) A **parenthesis** is a word or phrase inserted into a sentence inside brackets, dashes, or commas. ■ Brackets are sometimes called **parentheses**.

parenthood is being a parent.

parenting is bringing up children.

par excellence (pron: par ek-sel-**lons**) is used to say someone or something is the best possible example of a kind of thing. ...a travel writer par excellence.

pariah (pron: par-**rye**-a) You say a person or country is a **pariah** when other people or countries will have nothing to do with them, because of something they have done.

parish (parishes) A **parish** is (a) the area served by an Anglican or Catholic church. (b) one of the small areas a district council is divided into.

parishioner A priest's **parishioners** are the people who live in his or her parish and attend the church there.

parity (parities) If there is **parity** between two things, they have equal power, status, or value. ■ In finance, a currency's **parity** is its exchange-rate value.

park A **park** is (a) an area of public land with grass and trees. (b) an area of private land with grass and trees, surrounding a large country house. ■ Various areas used for a particular purpose are called **parks,** for example business parks or theme parks. ■ When you **park** a vehicle, you drive it into a position where it can be left. ■ See also **national park.**

parka A **parka** is a warm jacket with a quilted lining and a hood.

parking lot In the US, a **parking lot** is an outdoor car park.

Parkinsonism is Parkinson's disease, or one of several similar disorders.

Parkinson's disease is a brain disease which causes a person to tremble uncontrollably, and makes walking difficult.

parkland is land with grass and trees, especially around a country house.

parlance If you say something in a particular **parlance,** you use a word or phrase which is special to a trade or group of people. *It is, in cricketing parlance, a 'result' pitch.*

parley When people **parley** or have a **parley,** they have a discussion, usually to try to settle a dispute.

parliament A country's **parliament** is an assembly of representatives which makes its laws. In Britain, **Parliament** consists of the House of Commons and the House of Lords.

parliamentarian A **parliamentarian** is an MP. ■ **Parliamentarian** is used to talk about someone's skill at debating in Parliament. *John is a brilliant parliamentarian.* ■ In the English Civil War, the **Parliamentarians** were the people who supported Parliament and opposed the King.

parliamentary means to do with a parliament. *...parliamentary elections.*

parlour (*Am:* **parlor**) is an old word for a living room. ■ **Parlour** is used in the names of some shops and businesses. *...pizza parlours. ...funeral parlours.*

parlour game A **parlour game** is a game played indoors by families or at parties, for example a guessing game or a word game.

parlourmaid (*or* **parlour maid**) A **parlourmaid** was a female servant whose job included serving food at mealtimes.

parlous If something is in a **parlous** state, it is in a very poor state indeed.

Parmesan is a hard Italian cheese, usually served grated over food.

parochial (**parochially, parochialism**) If you call someone **parochial** or talk about their **parochialism,** you mean they take too narrow a view of things and are only interested in their own country or area. ■ **Parochial** means relating to a priest's parish. *...his parochial duties.*

parody (**parodies, parodying, parodied**) A **parody** is an exaggerated and amusing imitation of someone or something. If you **parody** someone or something, you imitate them like this. ■ If something fails badly to be the thing it is supposed to be, you can say it is a **parody** of it. *...a parody of justice.*

parole (**paroling, paroled**) When prisoners are **paroled** or let out **on parole,** they are released early on condition that they behave well.

paroxysm – **Paroxysms** are spasms or convulsions. ■ If you say someone goes into **paroxysms** of rage, you mean they get so angry they lose control.

parquet (*pron:* **par**-kay) A **parquet** floor is made of small rectangular blocks of wood, fitted together in a pattern.

parrot (**parroting, parroted**) A **parrot** is a tropical or sub-tropical bird with a large curved beak and brightly-coloured or grey feathers. Some parrots can imitate human speech. ■ If you **parrot** something you have heard or read, you repeat it without really understanding it.

parry (**parries, parrying, parried**) If you **parry** a question, you cleverly avoid answering it.

parsimonious (**parsimony**) If you say someone is **parsimonious** or talk about their **parsimony,** you mean they are reluctant to spend money.

parsley is a herb with curly leaves.

parsnip – **Parsnips** are long thick cream-coloured root vegetables.

parson A **parson** is a member of the clergy, especially a Church of England vicar.

parsonage A **parsonage** is a parson's house.

part A **part** of something is one of the pieces, sections, or aspects which it consists of. ■ A **part** in a play or film is one of the roles in it. ■ Behaviour **on** someone's **part** is behaviour by that person. *He said that the delay was caused by the need to modify legislation, not by a lack of political will on his part.* ■ If you take **part** in something or play a **part** in it, you are involved in it. ■ When things which are touching **part** or are **parted,** they move away from each other. *Her lips parted.* ■ If you **part with** something, especially something you would rather keep, you give it or sell it to someone else. ■ When people **part,** they leave each other. ■ If your hair is **parted,** it is combed into two different directions, so that a line of scalp is left showing between. This line is called a **parting.** In the US, it is called a **part.**

partake (**partaking, partook, have partaken**) If you **partake** of food or drink, you eat it or drink it. ■ If you **partake** in an activity, you take part in it.

part-exchange If an item is taken in **part-exchange** for something else, it is taken as part of the payment towards it.

partial (**partially; partiality**) **Partial** means not complete or total. *...partial deafness.* ■ If you are **partial** to something, especially a kind of food or drink, you enjoy it very much. ■ If you accuse someone of being **partial** or showing **partiality** in a dispute, you mean they are showing favouritism towards one side.

participant The **participants** in an activity are the people taking part.

participate (**participating, participated; participation**) If you **participate** in something, you take part in it.

participatory A **participatory** activity is one you take part in yourself, rather than just watching. *Fishing is the most popular participatory sport in the United Kingdom.*

particle A **particle** of something is a very small piece of it. ■ In physics, a **particle** is a piece of matter smaller than an atom, for example a proton, neutron, or electron.

particular You use **particular** to emphasize that you are talking about just one thing, and not others of the same kind. *In this particular case, the bank did in fact refund the money.* ■ If a person or thing has a **particular** quality, it is a quality that other people or things do not tend to have. *It turns out that cotton has a particular advantage.* ■ If something is of **particular** interest or concern, people are especially interested in it or concerned about it. ■ **In particular** means especially. *Britain, in particular, is opposed to the idea.* ■ **Particulars** are details about something. *Once you have registered your particulars, the process begins.* ■ If someone is **particular** about something, they like it to be a certain way, and are not satisfied with anything else.

particularly You use **particularly** to indicate that what you are saying applies more to one person or thing than others. *There was a need for more relief supplies, particularly blankets.* ■ **Particularly** means more than usually. *Her chances are particularly good this year.*

partisan (**partisanship**) If you say someone is being **partisan**, you mean they are prejudiced in favour of one side in a dispute or game. Showing prejudice like this is called **partisanship.** ■ A **partisan** is a member of a resistance movement, especially one which fought occupying German troops during the Second World War.

partition (**partitioning, partitioned**) A **partition** is a thin wall or screen dividing one part of a room from another. You can say part of the room is **partitioned off.** ■ When a country is **partitioned**, it is divided into two or more independent countries.

partly means to some extent, but not completely. *There were delays at the main airports, partly due to action by air traffic controllers.*

partner (**partnering, partnered; partnership**) Your **partner** is the person you are married to or having a relationship with. ■ When an activity involves people doing something in pairs, you call the person you do it with your **partner.** You also say you **partner** the other person. ■ If people are **partners** in a business, they run it together and share the profits. An arrangement like this is called a **partnership.**

partridge – **Partridges** are game birds with round bodies and short tails.

part-time (**part-timer**) If someone is a **part-time** worker or has a **part-time** job, they work for less than the usual number of hours. Someone like this can be called a **part-timer.**

party (**parties, partying, partied**) A **party** is a social gathering with food and drink, usually held to celebrate something. When people **party,** they have a party or go to a party. ■ A political **party** is an organization of people with similar political views, who try to win power. ■ A **party** of people is a group of them doing something together. *...a party of French tourists.* ■ The **parties** in an agreement or dispute are the people involved in it. ■ If you are a

party to something, you are involved in it. *He said that he had not been a party to the attacks.* ■ See also **third party.**

party line The **party line** is the official view on something taken by a political party. ■ A **party line** is a telephone line that is shared by two or more subscribers.

party piece Someone's **party piece** is something like a trick which they often do to entertain people.

party political activities are aimed at getting people to support a particular political party.

party politics If you say a political party is indulging in **party politics,** you mean it is doing something to get an advantage over other parties, rather than for the benefit of the country.

party pooper You call someone a **party pooper** when they spoil people's fun.

party wall A **party wall** is the wall between two adjoining houses.

parvenu (*pron:* **par**-ven-new) People who have recently become rich or important but are not very cultured or educated are sometimes called **parvenus.**

pas de deux (*plural:* **pas de deux**) (*pron:* **pah** duh **duh**) In a ballet, a **pas de deux** is a dance for two people.

pass (**passes, passing, passed**) If you **pass** someone or something, you go past them. ■ If you **pass** through a place, you go through it. ■ If someone or something is **passed over,** they are ignored or disregarded. *She claims she was repeatedly passed over for promotion.* ■ If you **pass** something to someone, you give it to them. ■ If you **pass** the ball in a ballgame, you throw, hit, or kick the ball to another player in your team. This action is called a **pass.** ■ When a period of time **passes,** it happens and finishes. ■ When someone **passes away,** they die. ■ **Passing** is used to describe things which do not last very long. *This awareness about the environment might be a passing phenomenon.* ■ If you **pass** a test or gain a **pass** in it, you reach an acceptable standard. ■ If a new law or proposal is **passed,** it is formally approved. ■ When a judge **passes sentence** on someone, he or she states what the punishment will be. ■ If someone makes a **pass** at you, they make sexual advances towards you. ■ If someone or something **passes for** a certain thing or **passes as** it, people believe they are that thing. ■ If you **pass** something **off** as something else, you convince people it is that thing. ■ If you **pass out,** you faint. ■ If you **pass up** an opportunity, you do not take advantage of it. ■ A **pass** is an official document which allows you to do something. ■ A **pass** is a narrow route between mountains. ■ When you **pass** water, you urinate. ■ **pass judgment:** see **judgment.**

passable (**passably**) If something is **passable,** it is of an acceptable standard. *Most resorts are passably well equipped.* ■ If a road is **passable,** it is possible to get along it.

passage A **passage** is a narrow corridor or space which allows movement between two areas. ■ **Passage** is the act of moving somewhere. *They negotiated the safe passage of 300 people from Bos-*

nia... Psyllium slows down the passage of digested food through the gut. ■ A **passage** is a journey, especially by ship. ■ A **passage** in a book, speech, or piece of music is a short section of it.

passageway A **passageway** is a narrow corridor or space connecting one room or place with another.

passé (*pron:* pas-say) If you say something is **passé,** you mean it is no longer fashionable.

passenger A **passenger** is a person travelling in a vehicle, aircraft, or ship.

passer-by (**passers-by**) A **passer-by** is a person who happens to be walking past when something happens.

passim is used to indicate that something is referred to throughout a book or other piece of writing. *...Fox, pp. 16-17 and passim.*

passion is a very strong feeling, especially anger or sexual desire. *Passions are running high. ...a night of passion.* ■ If you have a **passion** for something, you have a great liking for it. *His passions were cricket and birdwatching.* ■ For Christians, Jesus Christ's **Passion** is his suffering from his arrest until his death on the Cross.

passionate (**passionately**) If someone is **passionate** about something, they have very strong feelings about it. *The French feel passionately about their native tongue.* You call something like a speech **passionate** when it expresses strong feelings. *...a passionate debate.* ■ You call people's sexual behaviour **passionate** when it is full of desire. *She kissed him passionately.*

passion fruit (*plural:* **passion fruit**) **Passion fruit** are the small egg-shaped fruit of certain tropical plants.

passive (**passively, passivity**) You say someone is being **passive** when they accept what is going on without protesting or taking any action. *He said that the international community could not passively allow the genocide to go on.* ■ A **passive** activity involves just watching or listening, rather than taking part in something. *Rock is essentially a passive experience.*

passive resistance is non-violent protest, such as fasting, demonstrating peacefully, or refusing to co-operate.

passive smoking is breathing other people's tobacco smoke.

Passover is a Jewish festival lasting seven or eight days in late March or early April. It commemorates the sparing of the Jewish first-born when the first-born of Egypt were slain by the Angel of Death.

passport Your **passport** is an official document issued by the government, containing your name, photograph, and personal details. You show your passport when you enter or leave a country. ■ If something is a **passport** to something you want, it enables you to get it. *Divorce may not be a passport to happiness.*

password A **password** is a secret word or phrase which enables you to enter a place or use a computer system.

past The **past** is the period of time before the present. ■ **Past** things happened or existed in the past. *...past governments. ...past attempts at reform.* ■ **Past** is used to talk about a period of time leading up to

the present. *In the past eight days, at least 170 people have been killed.* ■ If you go **past** something, you go up to it and beyond it. ■ If you say something is **past** something else, you mean it is beyond it. *Past the stables there is a beautiful little chapel.* ■ If you say someone is **past it,** you mean they no longer have the strength or energy to do something because they are too old. ■ If you are a **past master** at something, you are very skilful at it because you have had a lot of experience of it.

pasta is a type of food made from flour, eggs, and water. Spaghetti and macaroni are types of pasta.

paste (**pasting, pasted**) A **paste** is a soft mixture which spreads easily. Some pastes are foodstuffs and some are used as adhesives. *...fish paste. ...wallpaper paste.* If you **paste** something to a surface, you stick it there with paste or glue. ■ If someone is given a **pasting,** (a) they are beaten soundly in a game or fight. (b) they suffer badly as a result of something which happens. *Merchant banks took a terrible pasting during the recession.*

pastel colours or **pastels** are pale and soft. *...timber-framed houses painted in faded pastels.* ■ **Pastels** are small coloured sticks of chalk-like crayon, used for drawing. A drawing made with pastels is also called a **pastel.**

pasteurized (*or* **pasteurised**) milk or cheese has been treated in a special heating process to kill bacteria.

pastiche (*pron:* pass-**teesh**) In the arts, **pastiche** is combining several elements, or copying something else, usually for humorous effect. A **pastiche** is something produced like this. *...a delicious pastiche of a true-crime documentary.*

pastime A **pastime** is something you do for pleasure.

pastor A **pastor** is a clergyman in charge of a congregation in some Protestant churches.

pastoral means things relating to the duties of the clergy in caring for the needs of their parishioners. ■ **Pastoral** is used to describe things to do with a peaceful country life. *...a pastoral scene.*

pastrami (*pron:* pass-**trah**-mee) is strongly seasoned smoked beef.

pastry (**pastries**) **Pastry** is a dough made of flour, fat, and water and used to make pies and flans. ■ A **pastry** is a small cake made of pastry.

pasture is grassy land for farm animals to graze on. ■ If you move to **pastures new,** you move to a different place or job, looking for fresh opportunities.

pasty (**pasties**) A **pasty** (*pron:* past-tee) is a pie made of pastry folded around a savoury filling. ■ If someone looks **pasty** (*pron:* pay-stee), they look pale and unhealthy.

pat (**patting, patted**) If you **pat** something or give it a **pat,** you tap it lightly with the flat of your hand. ■ A **pat** of butter is a small portion of it. ■ If you call what someone says **pat,** you mean it sounds too simple and may not be true or sincere. ■ If you have something **off pat,** you have memorized it and can repeat it exactly.

patch (**patches, patching, patched**) A **patch** is a small piece of material, for example one used to cover a hole. If you **patch** something, you mend it with a patch. ■ If you **patch** something **up**, you repair it in a makeshift way. ■ If you **patch up** a quarrel or relationship, you try to be friendly again and not to quarrel any more. ■ If people **patch up** a deal or **patch** it **together,** they manage to agree on it after difficult discussions. ■ A fog or mist **patch** is a small dense area of it. ■ A **patch** is a small part of a surface or area which looks different from the rest. ■ Someone's **patch** is their territory, or their area of responsibility. ■ A bad **patch** is a period of difficulties or problems. ■ If you say something is **not a patch** on something else, you mean it is nothing like as good as it.

patchwork A **patchwork** quilt is made from many small pieces of material sewn together. Sewing like this is called **patchwork.** ■ If you call something a **patchwork,** you mean it is made up of many different things. ...*a patchwork of rules and regulations.*

patchy (patchily) If you say something is **patchy,** you mean (a) some parts of it are better than others. (b) it is incomplete.

pate Your **pate** is the top of your head.

pâté (*pron:* **pat**-ay) is a savoury paste, usually made from meat or fish.

patella The **patella** is the small flat bone which protects the human knee joint. It is commonly known as the **kneecap.**

patent (patently) A **patent** is an official right to be the only person or company allowed to make or sell a new product for a certain period of time. If you **patent** something, you obtain a patent for it. ■ If you use **patent** to describe something, you are emphasising that it is obvious. ...*patently true.*

patent leather is leather with a very shiny surface.

paternal is used to describe feelings or actions which are typical of those a father feels towards his child. ■ Your **paternal** grandparents are your father's parents.

paternalist (paternalistic, paternalism) You say a government or company is **paternalist** or **paternalistic** when it takes all the decisions for the people it governs or employs, giving them no responsibility. Treating people like this is called **paternalism.**

paternity means the state or fact of being a father. ■ **Paternity leave** is time allowed off work for a man whose child has just been born. ■ A **paternity suit** is a lawsuit brought by a woman to prove that a man is the father of her child, often to claim financial support from him.

path A **path** is a strip of ground which people walk on. ■ Your **path** is the space ahead of you as you move along. ■ If something is in your **path,** it is preventing you from doing or achieving what you want. ■ The **path** of something is the line it moves along in a particular direction. ■ A course of action can be called a **path.**

pathetic (pathetically) You say someone or something is **pathetic** when they seem weak or helpless and make you feel sorry for them. ■ You say something is **pathetic** when it is hopelessly unsatisfactory.

pathfinder You call someone a **pathfinder** when they lead the way through unexplored territory or a new area of knowledge.

pathogen (pathogenic) Pathogens are very small organisms which cause disease. You say organisms like these are **pathogenic.**

pathologist A **pathologist** is a person who studies or investigates diseases and illnesses, and examines dead bodies to find out the cause of death.

pathology (pathological) Pathology is the study of the way diseases and illnesses develop. **Pathological** means things to do with pathology. ■ **Pathological** is used to describe behaviour which is extreme and uncontrollable. ...*a pathological liar.*

pathos (*pron:* **pay**-thoss) is a quality in a situation which makes people feel sadness and pity.

pathway A **pathway** is the same as a path.

patient (patiently, patience) A **patient** is someone receiving professional medical care. ■ If you are **patient** or have **patience,** you stay calm when something takes a long time or when someone is not doing what you want them to. ■ **Patience** is a card game for one player.

patina A **patina** is a fine layer of something on a surface. ...*a patina of gold.* ■ The **patina** of an antique or other old object is the sheen which develops on its surface as it ages.

patio (patios) A **patio** is a paved area adjoining a house.

patisserie (*pron:* pat-**tiss**-er-ee) is pastries. A **patisserie** is a shop selling fancy cakes and pastries.

patois (*pron:* **pat**-wah) (*plural:* **patois**) A **patois** is an unwritten dialect form of a language, especially French. ■ A **patois** is a language which has developed from a mixture of other languages.

patriarch A **patriarch** is the male head of a family or tribe. ■ A **patriarch** is a bishop who is the head of one of the Orthodox Churches.

patriarchal (patriarchy) A **patriarchal** society or system is one where men have the power. A society or system like this can be called a **patriarchy.**

patrician people come from a family with high social rank.

patrimony Someone's **patrimony** is the property they have inherited from their father or ancestors. ■ A country's **patrimony** is its national treasures and works of art.

patriotic (patriot, patriotism) If someone is **patriotic** or a **patriot,** they love their country and feel loyal towards it. You talk about the **patriotism** of someone like this.

patrol (patrolling, patrolled) When soldiers, police, or guards **patrol** a place or carry out a **patrol,** they move round it, to make sure there is no trouble. A **patrol** is a group of people or vehicles doing this.

patrolman (patrolmen) A **patrolman** is a person employed by a motorists' association to assist members when their cars break down. ■ In the US, a **patrolman** is a uniformed policeman who patrols a particular area.

patron A **patron** is a person who supports and gives money to artists, writers, or musicians. ■ The **patron** of a charity, group, or campaign is an important person who allows his or her name to be used in its publicity. ■ The **patron** of a restaurant is its owner. ■ The **patrons** of a shop, pub, or place of entertainment are its customers.

patronage is (a) the support given by a patron. (b) the power someone has to appoint people to important jobs, regardless of whether they are suitable or not.

patroness (**patronesses**) A **patroness** is a female patron.

patronize (*or* **patronise**) (**patronizing, patronized; patronizingly**) If someone **patronizes** you, they treat you in a way which seems friendly, but which shows they feel superior to you. ■ If you **patronize** a shop, pub, or place of entertainment, you are one of its customers. ■ When a public figure **patronizes** a charity, group, or campaign, they support it and allow their name to be used in its publicity.

patron saint The **patron saint** of a place or group of people is a saint who is believed to give them special help and protection.

patter (**pattering, pattered**) If something **patters** on a surface, it makes light tapping sounds. You talk about the **patter** of something on a surface. *...the patter of the rain on the roof.* ■ Someone's **patter** is something they have learned to say quickly and easily, to entertain people or persuade them to buy something.

pattern (**patterned**) A **pattern** is a decorative design of repeated lines, shapes, or colours. If something is **patterned**, it has a pattern on it. ■ If something fits a particular **pattern,** it has similar features to something which has occurred before. ■ Behaviour **patterns** are regular ways of behaving. ■ A **pattern** is a set of instructions and diagrams for making something, for example a knitting pattern.

patterning is the forming of fixed ways of behaviour or of doing things by constantly repeating or copying an action. ■ The **patterning** on something is its pattern.

patty (**patties**) A **patty** is (a) a small pie. (b) a small flat cake of minced food.

paucity (*pron:* **paw**-si-tee) If you say there is a **paucity** of something, you mean there is an insufficient amount of it.

paunch (**paunches; paunchy**) If a man has a **paunch,** he has a fat stomach. You say a man like this is **paunchy.**

pauper A **pauper** is someone who is very poor.

pauperize (*or* **pauperise**) (**pauperizing, pauperized**) If something **pauperizes** people, it makes them poor.

pause (**pausing, paused**) If you **pause** while you are doing something, or **pause** before doing it, you stop for a moment. This stop is called a **pause.** ■ If something **gives** you **pause,** it makes you stop and think carefully about what you were intending to do.

pave (**paving, paved**) When an area of ground is **paved** or **paved over,** it is covered with blocks of stone, bricks, or concrete. **Paving** is a paved area or surface. ■ If something **paves the way** for something else, it makes it possible.

pavement A **pavement** is a paved path for pedestrians along the roadside.

pavilion A **pavilion** is (a) a building at the edge of a sports ground, where players can wash and change. (b) a building put up to house an exhibition.

paving stone — **Paving stones** are flat square or rectangular pieces of stone or concrete, used to pave surfaces.

Pavlovian You say someone's behaviour is **Pavlovian** when they respond in an automatic way to something each time it happens.

paw A dog's, cat's, or bear's **paws** are its feet, which have claws for gripping things and soft pads for walking and running. ■ If an animal **paws** something, it scrapes it with its paw or hoof.

pawn A **pawn** is the least valuable piece in chess. ■ You say someone is a **pawn** when they are being used by other people rather than making their own decisions. ■ If you **pawn** something, you leave it with a person called a **pawnbroker** in return for a loan. If you do not pay back the loan within a certain time, the pawnbroker can sell the item. A pawnbroker's premises are sometimes called a **pawnshop.**

pawnbroker See pawn.

pawpaw See papaya.

pay (**paying, paid** *not 'payed'*) When you **pay** money to someone, you give it to them because you are buying something or owe it to them. ■ When your employers **pay** you, they give you your wages or salary. Your **pay** is what they give you. You can say a job or investment **pays** a certain amount. ■ If you say someone is **in the pay** of someone else, especially someone bad or crooked, you mean they are working for them. ■ If it **pays** to do something, it is to your benefit or advantage. *It pays to shop around.* ■ If something **pays off,** it results in success. *Her determination paid off.* ■ If you **pay** for something, you suffer because of it. *Throughout his life, he was made to pay for his political convictions.* ■ If something **puts paid** to someone's hopes or plans, it prevents them being fulfilled. ■ If you **pay** someone a visit or a call, you visit them. ■ **pay a compliment:** see **compliment. pay your respects:** see **respect.**

payable If an amount of money is **payable,** it has to be paid or it can be paid. *The death duties payable on the estate could top £4 million... The money is payable in three instalments.* ■ If a cheque is made **payable** to you, it is made out to you.

pay award A **pay award** is an increase in pay for a group of people, especially people employed by the government or by local authorities.

payback A **payback** is a return on an investment.

PAYE is a system of paying income tax used in the UK, in which your employer deducts income tax from your wages, and pays it directly to the government. PAYE stands for 'pay as you earn'.

payee The **payee** of a sum of money is the person you are paying it to. ■ The **payee** of a cheque or banker's order is the person it is made out to.

payer The **payer** of a sum of money is the person paying it. *...tax payers.*

paying-in A **paying-in** slip is a form you fill in when you pay cash or cheques into a bank account. A **paying-in** book is a book of paying-in slips.

payload An aircraft's or spacecraft's **payload** is its passengers or cargo. ■ A missile's **payload** is the amount of explosives it carries.

paymaster Someone's **paymaster** is the person or organization that pays their wages. *...the ruling party's paymasters in business and banking.*

payment is paying money for something. *Payment must be made by cheque.* A **payment** is an amount of money paid for something.

payoff (*or* pay-off) The **payoff** from an action is the advantage or benefit you get from it. ■ A **payoff** is a payment, especially a payment made to an executive who leaves or loses their job.

payola is another name for bribery or a bribe.

payout A **payout** is a sum of money an organization gives to someone because it is required to.

pay packet Your **pay packet** is (a) the envelope containing your wages. (b) the amount you earn.

payphone A **payphone** is a coin-operated telephone.

payroll An organization's **payroll** is (a) its list of paid employees. (b) the amount it spends paying its employees.

PC See (a) **police constable.** (b) **personal computer.** (c) **politically correct.**

PCB – **PCBs** are extremely poisonous chemical compounds formerly used in industry. PCB stands for 'polychlorinated biphenyl'.

PE is a school lesson in which pupils do physical exercises, or take part in games or sports. PE stands for 'physical education'.

pea – **Peas** are round green seeds which grow in pods and are eaten as a vegetable.

peace is a state of undisturbed calm and quiet. ■ **Peace** is a time of not being at war. When a country or region is **at peace,** it is not involved in a war. A **peace treaty** is a treaty ending a war. ■ **Peace** is harmony between people. *For the sake of peace, she had never complained.* ■ **The peace** is sometimes used to mean public order. *...behaviour likely to cause a breach of the peace.*

peaceable (peaceably) A **peaceable** person, group, or country tries to avoid quarrelling or fighting. ■ A **peaceable** event or process takes place without any trouble or violence.

peace dividend When people talk about the **peace dividend,** they mean the money saved on defence since the end of the Cold War.

peaceful (peacefully, peacefulness) A **peaceful** place or time is quiet and free from disturbance. ■ If you feel **peaceful,** you feel free from worry or anxiety. ■ If something is **peaceful,** it does not involve violence or war. *...a peaceful transition to civilian rule.* ■ A **peaceful** person, group, or country tries to avoid quarrelling or fighting.

peacekeeping (*or* peace-keeping) (peacekeeper) **Peacekeeping** is attempting to stop war or fighting in a place. Organizations or troops which attempt this are called **peacekeepers.**

peacemaking (*or* peace-making) (peacemaker) **Peacemaking** is trying to restore peace between groups of people who are fighting or quarrelling. A person who tries to do this is called a **peacemaker.**

peacetime is a period during which a country is not at war.

peach (peaches, peachy) **Peaches** are soft round juicy fruit with fuzzy yellow and red skins. If something is **peachy,** it has the colour or flavour of peaches. ■ **Peach** is a pinky-orange colour.

peacock (peahen, peafowl) **Peacocks** are large birds with shiny blue and green feathers. Male peacocks have long tail feathers which they spread out in a fan shape. Female peacocks are called **peahens.** A group of male and female peacocks together can be called **peafowl.**

peak (peaking, peaked) When something **peaks** or reaches its **peak,** it reaches its highest level. *Unemployment reached 3.2 million at its peak... The peak years of deforestation came in 1983-87.* ■ In broadcasting, **peak time** is the same as prime time. ■ When a person **peaks** or reaches their **peak,** they reach the height of their powers. ■ A **peak** is a mountain, or the top of a mountain. ■ The **peak** of a cap is the part at the front which sticks out over your eyes. A **peaked** cap has a peak.

peaky If someone looks **peaky,** they look pale and ill.

peal (pealing, pealed) When church bells ring, you can say they **peal,** or there is a **peal** of bells. ■ A **peal** of laughter is a loud burst of it.

peanut – **Peanuts** are small nuts, often eaten roasted or salted as a snack. ■ You can call a very small amount of money **peanuts.**

peanut butter is a paste made from ground roasted peanuts.

pear – **Pears** are a fruit with white flesh and yellow or green skins. They are narrow at the top and wider and rounded at the bottom. ■ If something goes **pear-shaped** it fails or goes badly wrong. *Let's hope the economy doesn't go pear-shaped.*

pearl – **Pearls** are hard shiny objects which grow in the shells of some molluscs, especially oysters. They are used in jewellery. See also **mother-of-pearl.** ■ You can call a small thing of great value a **pearl.** *...pearls of wisdom.*

pearl barley is barley grains with the husks removed. It is used in soups and stews.

pearly is used to describe things which remind you of pearls, especially a person's teeth. *...pearly smiles.*

peasant (peasantry) In some countries, small farmers and people who work as agricultural labourers are called **peasants.** A country's peasants can also be called its **peasantry.**

peat is a kind of rich dark earth found in boggy areas, which is used in compost or as a household fuel.

peaty soil, land, or water contains a lot of peat.

pebble A **pebble** is a small smooth round stone.

pebble-dash (pebble-dashed) Pebble-dash is a coating for the outside walls of a house, made of small stones set in plaster. A **pebble-dashed** house has its outside walls coated in pebble-dash.

pebbly A **pebbly** beach or river bed is covered in pebbles.

pecan (*pron:* **pee**-kan) **Pecans** or **pecan nuts** are edible nuts similar to walnuts but with oval reddish shells.

peccadillo (**peccadillos** *or* **peccadilloes**) A **peccadillo** is a small unimportant misdeed.

peck When a bird **pecks** something, it takes a bite at it with a sudden forward movement of its beak. A bite like this is called a **peck.** ■ If you **peck** someone or give them a **peck,** you give them a quick light kiss, usually on the cheek. ■ If you talk about the **pecking order** in an organization, you mean the order of seniority or power within it.

peckish If you feel **peckish,** you feel hungry.

pecs See **pectoral.**

pectin is a substance which helps jam to set.

pectoral Your **pectorals** are the large chest muscles used to move your shoulders and arms. 'Pectorals' is often shortened to 'pecs'. ■ **Pectoral** means to do with the chest, or worn on the chest. *...a pectoral cross.*

peculiar (**peculiarly**) If something is **peculiar,** it is strange or puzzling. *One of the eggs was peculiarly marked.* ■ If something is **peculiar** to a person, place, or thing, it applies only to them. *The problem is by no means peculiar to Jamaica.*

peculiarity (**peculiarities**) A **peculiarity** is a characteristic or habit, especially an unusual one. *One of his distinguishing peculiarities is his extreme fairness.*

pecuniary means to do with money. *He denies obtaining a pecuniary advantage by deception.*

pedagogue (**pedagogy, pedagogic, pedagogical**) **Pedagogue** (*pron:* **ped**-a-gog) is an old word for a teacher. **Pedagogy** (*pron:* ped-a-**goj**-ee) is the principles and methods of teaching. **Pedagogic** (*pron:* ped-a-**goj**-ik) or **pedagogical** means related to teaching. *...immense pedagogic experience.*

pedal (**pedalling, pedalled**) (*Am:* **pedaling, pedaled**) The **pedals** on a bicycle are the two parts you push with your feet to make it move. When you **pedal** a bicycle, you make it move in this way. ■ Various kinds of levers which you push with your foot are called **pedals,** for example the brake pedal in a car.

pedal bin A **pedal bin** is a waste bin with a lid which is raised by a pedal.

pedalo (**pedalos** *or* **pedaloes**) A **pedalo** is a small pleasure boat, driven by paddle wheels which you operate by pedals.

pedant (**pedantic, pedantry**) If you call someone a **pedant** or describe them as **pedantic,** you mean they are too concerned with small details or correct procedure. You can talk about the **pedantry** of someone like this.

peddle (**peddling, peddled; peddler**) If someone **peddles** something, especially something illegal or of poor value, they sell it. *...drug peddling.* ■ A **peddler** or **pedlar** is a person who sells things from place to place, or door-to-door. ■ If someone **peddles** silly ideas or unreliable pieces of information, they try to interest people in them. *...peddlers of malicious gossip.*

pederasty (**pederast**) **Pederasty** is sexual relations between a man and a boy. Men who have sexual relations with boys are called **pederasts.**

pedestal The **pedestal** of a statue or column is the base it stands on. ■ If you **put** someone **on a pedestal,** you admire them greatly and cannot accept that they have any faults.

pedestrian A **pedestrian** is a person who is walking somewhere, especially along a street. ■ If you call something **pedestrian,** you mean it is dull and ordinary. *...a pedestrian performance.*

pedestrian crossing A **pedestrian crossing** is a place on a road where motorists have to stop when pedestrians want to cross.

pedestrianize (*or* **pedestrianise**) (**pedestrianizing, pedestrianized; pedestrianization**) If a street is **pedestrianized,** it is closed to traffic so only pedestrians can use it.

pediatrician See **paediatrician.**

pediatrics See **paediatrics.**

pedicure If you have a **pedicure,** you have your toenails cut and the skin on your feet softened by a chiropodist or a beautician.

pedigree A **pedigree** animal is descended only from animals of the same breed, and so is considered to be of high quality. ■ An animal's **pedigree** is the list of its ancestors. ■ You can call a person's background or ancestry their **pedigree.**

pediment A **pediment** is a piece of stone or wood, usually triangular, built over a door or window as a decoration.

pedlar See **peddle.**

pedometer (*pron:* pid-**dom**-it-er) A **pedometer** is a device which gives a rough measurement of the distance you walk, based on the number of paces you take.

pedophile (**pedophilia**) See **paedophile.**

pee (**peeing, peed**) **Pee** is urine. When someone **pees** or has a **pee,** they urinate.

peek (**peeking, peeked**) If you **peek** at something or take a **peek** at it, you have a quick look at it.

peel (**peeling, peeled**) The **peel** of a fruit or vegetable is its skin. When you **peel** a fruit or vegetable, you remove its peel with a knife. **Peelings** are strips of peel removed like this. ■ If paint is **peeling** off a surface, it is coming off in flakes. If your skin **peels,** it comes off in flakes. ■ If you **peel** something **off** a surface, you pull it off gently in one piece.

peep (**peeping, peeped**) If you **peep** at something or take a **peep** at it, you have a quick look at it. ■ If something **peeps** out from somewhere, it just becomes visible. *...the moon peeping through a cloud.* ■ If you say there is not a **peep** from someone, you mean they do not say anything or make any noise.

peep-hole A **peep-hole** is a small hole in a door or wall through which you can look secretly at what is happening on the other side.

Peeping Tom A **Peeping Tom** is a man who spies on women getting undressed.

peer (**peering, peered**) If you **peer** at something, you look very hard at it, because it is difficult to see clearly. ■ A **peer** or **peer of the realm** is a member of the nobility. ■ Your **peers** or **peer group** are people of the same age or status as yourself.

peerage A **peerage** is the rank or position of a peer. *He received his peerage in 1965.* The system of having peers is also called the **peerage.**

peeress (peeresses) A **peeress** is a female peer.

peerless If you say something is **peerless,** you mean it is so beautiful or wonderful that nothing can equal it. *...a peerless view across the bay.*

peeved If you are **peeved** about something, you are annoyed about it.

peevish (peevishly) If someone is **peevish,** they are bad-tempered and irritable. *She frowned peevishly.*

peewit A **peewit** is the same as a lapwing.

peg (pegging, pegged) A **peg** is a small hook or knob for hanging something on. ■ If you say something is a **peg** on which to hang something else, you mean it gives an opportunity or excuse for doing something. ■ A **peg** is a metal or wooden pin for securing something in place. ■ If a price or amount of something is **pegged** at a certain level, it is fixed at that level. ■ If someone is brought **down a peg,** they are made to realize they are not as important as they think. ■ When someone **pegs out,** they die.

pejorative (*pron:* pij-**jor**-a-tiv) A **pejorative** word or phrase shows disapproval of someone or something.

Peke A **Peke** is the same as a Pekinese.

Pekinese (*usual plural:* **Pekinese**) **Pekinese** are small dogs with long hair, short legs, and short flat noses.

pelargonium – Pelargoniums are garden plants with scented leaves and clusters of flowers. Geraniums are a type of pelargonium.

pelican The **pelican** is a large water bird with a pouch beneath its beak in which it stores fish.

pelican crossing A **pelican crossing** is a place where you can cross a road by pressing a button which operates traffic lights.

pellagra is a disease caused by lack of vitamin B. The symptoms are tiredness, weight loss, and disorders of the skin and digestive system.

pellet A **pellet** is a small ball of something.

pell-mell If you move **pell-mell** somewhere, you move there in a hurried and uncontrolled way.

pellucid If something is **pellucid,** it is extremely clear. *...the pellucid waters of the harbour.*

pelmet A **pelmet** is a long narrow piece of wood or fabric fixed at the top of a window for decoration and to hide the curtain rail.

pelt If you are **pelted** with things, people throw them at you. ■ If you go somewhere **full pelt,** you go as fast as you can. ■ The **pelt** of an animal is its whole skin and fur.

pelvis (pelvises; pelvic) Your **pelvis** or **pelvic girdle** is the large bone structure at the level of your hips. **Pelvic** means things to do with the pelvis.

pen (penning, penned) A **pen** is an instrument for writing in ink. ■ If you **pen** something, you write it. ■ A **pen** is a small fenced area where animals are kept. ■ If people or animals are **penned** somewhere or **penned up,** they are forced to remain in a very small area. ■ A female swan is called a **pen.**

penal (*pron:* **pee**-nal) means things to do with the punishment of criminals. ■ A country's **penal code**

is its system of laws for dealing with crime and punishment.

penalize (*or* **penalise**) (**penalizing, penalized**) If someone is **penalized** for something, they are made to suffer some disadvantage because of it.

penalty (penalties) A **penalty** is a punishment for breaking a law or rule. ■ If you **pay the penalty** for an action or decision, you suffer the consequences of it. ■ In sports like football, hockey, and rugby, a **penalty** is a free kick or hit at goal, given to the attacking team if the defending team commit a foul near their own goal. ■ **death penalty:** see **death.**

penalty area The **penalty area** is a rectangular area on a football pitch in front of the goal.

penalty box In football, the **penalty box** is the same as the penalty area. ■ In ice hockey, the **penalty box** is the area where players who have been sent off sit until they are allowed back onto the ice.

penance If you do **penance** or a **penance,** you do something that you find unpleasant to show you are sorry for something wrong you have done.

pence The pound sterling is divided into 100 **pence.** 'Pence' is usually shortened to 'p'.

penchant (*pron:* **pon**-shon) If you have a **penchant** for something, you have a special liking for it, or a tendency to do it.

pencil (pencilling, pencilled) (*Am:* **penciling, penciled**) A **pencil** is an object used for writing and drawing. It consists of a thin piece of wood with a rod of graphite down the centre which is exposed and sharpened at one end. If you **pencil** something, you write or draw it in pencil. ■ If an event or appointment is **pencilled in,** it is agreed but not yet confirmed.

pen computer A **pen computer** is a computer which you enter commands into by writing on the screen with a special pen.

pendant A **pendant** is an ornament on a chain you wear round your neck.

pending If something is **pending,** it is going to happen soon. ■ You say something is **pending** when it is waiting to be decided or settled. ■ If something is done **pending** a future event, it is done until that event happens or is over. *The pool has been closed pending an investigation.*

pendulous is used to describe things which hang downwards swinging freely.

pendulum The **pendulum** in a clock is a rod with a weight at one end which swings regularly from side to side to control the clock. ■ You can refer to regular changes in a situation or in people's opinions as a **pendulum.** *The political pendulum is starting to swing away from them.*

penetrate (penetrating, penetrated; penetration) If someone or something **penetrates** a physical object or an area, they succeed in getting into it or passing through it. *X-rays can penetrate many objects.* ■ If someone **penetrates** an organization, a group, or a profession, they succeed in entering it although it is difficult. *...the failure of women to penetrate the higher levels of engineering.* ■ If someone **penetrates** an enemy organization, they succeed in joining it to gather information about it. ■ If a company **penetrates** a market or area, it succeeds in selling its products there. ■ If you **penetrate** something which is difficult to understand, you succeed in understanding it. ■ If someone has a **penetrating** mind, they are able to grasp things quickly and thoroughly. ■ If someone gives you a **penetrating** look, it makes you feel they can see into your mind. ■ A **penetrating** sound is loud and piercing.

penetrative sex involves a man inserting his penis into his partner's vagina or anus.

pen-friend A **pen-friend** is someone, often in a foreign country, who you write to regularly and get to know through your letters.

penguin – Penguins are flightless black and white seabirds with webbed feet and flipper-like wings, mainly found in the Antarctic.

penicillin is a powerful antibiotic used to treat a variety of infections.

penile See **penis.**

peninsula (**peninsular**) A **peninsula** is a large area of land surrounded by water on three sides. **Peninsular** means things on or relating to a peninsula. ...*peninsular Malaysia.*

penis (**penises; penile**) A man's or male animal's **penis** is the part of the body used for urinating and having sex. **Penile** means involving the penis.

penitent (**penitence**) If someone is **penitent,** they are very sorry. You can talk about their **penitence** or call them a **penitent.**

penitentiary (**penitentiaries**) In the US, some prisons are called **penitentiaries.**

penknife (**penknives**) A **penknife** is a small knife with a folding blade or blades.

pen name A **pen name** is a name used by an author instead of their real name.

pennant A **pennant** is a long narrow flag.

penniless If someone is **penniless,** they have no money.

penny (**pennies**) A **penny** is a coin worth 1p. ■ Before the change to decimal currency in 1971, a **penny** was a coin worth one twelfth of a shilling. ■ In the US, a **penny** is a cent coin.

penny-farthing The **penny-farthing** is an old-fashioned bicycle with a large front wheel and a small back one.

penny-pinching is unwillingness to spend money.

penny whistle A **penny whistle** is a simple wind instrument consisting of a straight metal tube with holes in it and a mouthpiece.

pen-pal A **pen-pal** is the same as a pen-friend.

pen-pusher People who sit behind a desk doing paperwork are sometimes called **pen-pushers.**

pension (**pensioning, pensioned**) A **pension** is a sum of money paid regularly to someone who is old, retired, widowed, or disabled. ■ If someone is **pensioned off,** they are made to retire and given a pension. ■ A **pension** (*pron:* **pon**-see-on) is a boarding house in France and some other countries.

pensionable If you are of **pensionable** age, you are at an age at which you are entitled to a pension from the state. ■ **Pensionable** employment provides you with a works pension when you retire.

pensioner A **pensioner** is a person who is entitled to a state pension.

pension fund A **pension fund** is a fund paid into by employers and employees. The money is invested to provide pensions for the employees.

pension scheme A **pension scheme** is a scheme which provides you with a pension after you have contributed to it for a certain period.

pensive (**pensively**) If someone is **pensive,** they are deep in thought.

pentacle A **pentacle** is a five-pointed star.

pentagon (**pentagonal**) A **pentagon** is a geometric shape with five straight sides. If something is **pentagonal,** it is shaped like a pentagon. ■ The **Pentagon** is the headquarters of the US Defense Department in Washington. The Defense Department is itself often called the **Pentagon.** *The Pentagon is urging caution.*

pentamidine (*pron:* pen-**tam**-i-deen) is a drug used to treat a type of pneumonia suffered by people with AIDS.

pentathlon The **pentathlon** is an athletics contest in which competitors take part in five different events.

Pentecost In the Jewish religion, **Pentecost** is a festival held 50 days after Passover, to celebrate the harvest and the giving of the law to Moses. ■ In the Christian religion, **Pentecost** is a festival held on the seventh Sunday after Easter, to celebrate the sending of the Holy Spirit to Jesus's disciples.

Pentecostal (**Pentecostalist, Pentecostalism**) **Pentecostal** Christians or **Pentecostalists** believe strongly in the power of the Holy Spirit and in a literal interpretation of the Bible.

penthouse A **penthouse** is a flat or maisonette built onto the top floor or roof of a building.

pent-up emotions have been held back for a long time.

penultimate The **penultimate** thing in a series is the last but one. ...*the penultimate lap.*

penumbra (*plural:* **penumbras** or **penumbrae**) A **penumbra** is a partial shadow.

penury (**penurious**) **Penury** is extreme poverty. **Penurious** people are extremely poor.

peony (**peonies**) **Peonies** are garden plants with large red, pink, or white flowers.

people (**peopled**) **People** is the usual plural of 'person'. ■ A **people** is a race or nation. ...*India's many peoples.* ■ The **people** are the ordinary men and women of a country. *British politicians like to think they are in touch with the people.* ■ You use **peopled** to say what kind of people live in a place. ...*a Caribbean island peopled by Americans.*

people mover (*or* **people carrier**) A **people mover** is a large car that looks like a van and can carry up to eight people.

pep (**pepping, pepped**) **Pep** is energy and enthusiasm. ■ A **pep** talk is designed to give people encouragement. ■ If you **pep** something **up,** you make it more lively or interesting.

pepper (**peppering, peppered**) **Pepper** is a hot-tasting powder used to season food. ■ **Peppers** are hollow green, red, or yellow vegetables. ■ If something is **peppered** with things, there are a lot of them in it, on it, or hitting it. *...speeches peppered with glowing compliments... The airport was peppered with sniper fire.*

peppercorn – Peppercorns are the small dried berries which pepper is made from. ∎ A **peppercorn** rent is very low.

peppermint is a plant grown for its oil, which is used in medicines and flavourings. ∎ A **peppermint** is a peppermint-flavoured sweet.

pepperoni is a kind of spicy sausage.

peppery If something is **peppery,** it tastes strongly of pepper.

peppy If someone or something is **peppy,** they are full of energy and enthusiasm.

peptic ulcer A **peptic ulcer** is an ulcer in the stomach, the duodenum, or the lower end of the oesophagus.

peptide – Peptides are small protein molecules.

per is used to mean 'each' when giving rates and ratios. *The membership fee is £650 per year. ...four ounces of dried pasta per person.*

perambulate (perambulating, perambulated) If you **perambulate,** you walk about for pleasure.

per annum A particular amount **per annum** means that amount each year. 'Per annum' is often shortened to 'p.a.'. *...a service charge of £50 per annum.*

per capita A **per capita** amount is the amount, on average, for each member of the population. *In 1990 we spent £582 per capita on health.*

perceive (perceiving, perceived) If you **perceive** something, you see, notice, or realize it. *They could perceive no sign of life below.* ∎ If something is **perceived** as a certain thing, that is how people regard it. *Yacht racing is perceived as an elitist sport.*

per cent You use **per cent** to talk about amounts as a proportion of a hundred. For example, if an amount is 10 per cent of a larger amount, it is equal to 10 hundredths of the larger amount. 'Per cent' is usually written **%** .

percentage is used to say roughly how large or small an amount is as a proportion of a whole. *A high percentage of the members are in the older age bracket.* ∎ A **percentage point** is one per cent.

perceptible (perceptibly) If something is **perceptible,** it is large or intense enough to be seen or noticed. *The mood was perceptibly lightened by the announcement.*

perception is recognizing things by means of your senses, especially your sight. *...visual perception.* ∎ Your **perception** of something is your understanding or opinion of it.

perceptive (perceptively; perceptiveness) A **perceptive** person is good at noticing or realizing things which are not obvious.

perceptual is used to talk about people's ability to recognize things through their senses, especially their sight. *...perceptual skills.*

perch (perches, perching, perched) If you **perch** on something, you sit on the edge of it. You can call the place where you sit your **perch.** ∎ If something is **perched** on something else, it is on top of it or on the edge of it. *The castle is perched on cliffs overlooking the Bristol Channel.* ∎ When a bird **perches** on something like a branch, it stands there. ∎ A

perch is a place for a bird to stand, especially a short horizontal rod in a pet bird's cage. ∎ The **perch** *(plural:* **perch)** is an edible freshwater fish.

perchance is an old word meaning 'perhaps'.

percolate (percolating, percolated) If a liquid **percolates** somewhere, it makes its way there slowly through small holes or gaps. ∎ **Percolated** coffee is coffee made in a percolator. ∎ If information **percolates** to people, it gradually gets through to them.

percolator A **percolator** is a pot in which coffee is made by circulating boiling water over ground coffee beans.

percussion (percussionist) Percussion instruments are musical instruments which you hit to produce sounds.

percussive sounds are the sounds made when one object hits against another.

perdition is a state of never-ending punishment after death.

peregrination A **peregrination** is a long rambling journey.

peregrine The **peregrine** or **peregrine falcon** is a large bird of prey, which has a dark-coloured back and is lighter coloured underneath.

peremptory (peremptorily) If someone says something in a **peremptory** way, they show they expect to be obeyed immediately.

perennial is used to describe things which keep happening or seem to go on for ever. *...one of those perennial European problems.* ∎ **Perennial** plants live for several years, flowering each year. Plants like these are called **perennials.**

perestroika was the policy of economic and political reform in the former Soviet Union in the late1980s.

perfect (perfectly, perfection) If something is **perfect,** it is as good as it could possibly be. You talk about the **perfection** of something like this. ∎ You use **perfect** to emphasize that something really is a particular thing. *...a perfect stranger.* ∎ If you **perfect** something *(pron:* per-**fekt**), you make it as good as it could possibly be.

perfectible (perfectibility) If something is **perfectible,** it can be made perfect.

perfection See **perfect.**

perfectionist (perfectionism) If you say someone is a **perfectionist,** you mean they are never satisfied with what they do and are always trying to improve it. You can talk about their **perfectionism.**

perfect pitch If someone has **perfect pitch,** they can identify or sing musical notes correctly.

perfidious (perfidy) If you describe someone as **perfidious,** you mean they are treacherous and untrustworthy. **Perfidy** is treachery.

perforate (perforating, perforated; perforation) If something is **perforated,** small holes are made in it. These holes are called **perforations.**

perforce is used to say something happens because it is unavoidable, rather than because it is intended or desired. *New immigrant groups settle perforce in the areas of poorest housing.*

perform (performance) If you **perform** a task or action, you do it. If something **performs** a function, it has that function. You can talk about the **performance** of these things. *...the performance of his public duties.* ■ You can use **perform** to say how well someone or something does a task or job or talk about their **performance.** *Women pilots often perform better than men.* ■ If you **perform** a play, a piece of music, or a dance, you do it in front of an audience. A **performance** of something like this is an occasion when it is performed.

performer A **performer** is a person who does something to entertain an audience. ■ You can use **performer** when describing someone or something in a way that shows how well they do a particular thing. *...United's star performer.*

performing arts The **performing arts** are dance, drama, music, and other forms of entertainment usually performed live to an audience.

perfume (**perfumed**) **Perfume** is a pleasant-smelling liquid you put on your body. ■ A **perfume** is a pleasant smell. If something is **perfumed,** it has a pleasant smell.

perfunctory (**perfunctorily**) A **perfunctory** action is done quickly and carelessly, and shows a lack of interest. *The applause was perfunctory.*

pergola (*pron:* **per**-go-la) A **pergola** is an arch-like framework for climbing plants to grow on.

perhaps is used to say something may be the case. *Perhaps she was right.*

peril is great danger. ■ The **perils** of a particular course of action, are the dangers or problems which can arise from doing it. ■ If you say someone does something **at** their **peril,** you are warning them they will probably suffer as a result of doing it. *Those who underestimate him do so at their peril.*

perilous (**perilously**) **Perilous** is used to describe things which are very dangerous.

perimeter (*pron:* per-**rim**-it-er) The **perimeter** of an area of land is the whole of its outer edge. *...the perimeter fence.*

perinatal means in the period shortly before or after birth.

period A **period** is (a) a length of time. *...a period of two years.* (b) a particular time. *...the Edwardian period.* ■ **Period** costumes, objects, and buildings were made at an earlier time in history, or look as if they were made then. ■ A woman's **period** is the monthly bleeding from her womb. ■ In the US, a full stop is called a **period.**

periodic events or occurrences take place at regular intervals.

periodical (**periodically**) **Periodical** means the same as 'periodic'. *Jets fly over periodically.* ■ A **periodical** is a magazine.

peripatetic (*pron:* per-rip-a-**tet**-ik) workers have jobs which involve them travelling from place to place. *...peripatetic teachers.* You say someone has a **peripatetic** life when they travel around, living in places for only short periods of time.

peripheral (*pron:* per-**if**-er-al) (**peripherally**) **Peripheral** means on or relating to the edge of something. ■ If something is **peripheral,** it is not very important compared to something else. ■ **Peripherals** or **peripheral** devices are extra devices that can be attached to or put in a computer, such as printers and modems.

periphery (*pron:* per-**if**-er-ee) (**peripheries**) The **periphery** of something is its edge. ■ The **periphery** of a field of activity is the parts which are not as important or basic as the main part.

periscope A submarine's **periscope** is a vertical tube which can be raised so that the people inside can see above the surface of the water.

perish (**perishes, perishing, perished**) If people or animals **perish,** they die. ■ If a food, substance or material **perishes,** it rots and becomes useless. ■ If you say **perish the thought,** you are emphasizing that a suggestion or possibility seems unpleasant or ridiculous.

perishable food goes bad quite quickly.

peritonitis (*pron:* per-rit-tone-**ite**-iss) is a painful and serious inflammation of the membrane lining the abdomen, often following a burst appendix.

periwinkle – Periwinkles are evergreen plants with trailing stems and blue flowers. ■ Winkles are sometimes called **periwinkles.**

perjure (**perjuring, perjured; perjury**) If you **perjure** yourself or commit **perjury,** you commit an offence by deliberately telling lies in court while under oath.

perk A **perk** is something extra you get in addition to your salary, for example a company car. ■ If someone or something **perks up,** they become more cheerful or lively.

perky (**perkier, perkiest; perkily, perkiness**) If someone is **perky,** they are cheerful and lively.

perm If you have a **perm** or have your hair **permed,** your hair is treated with chemicals and then curled so the curls last for several months.

permafrost is land which is permanently frozen to a great depth.

permanent (**permanently, permanence**) If something is **permanent,** it lasts forever. You talk about the **permanence** of something like this. ■ You say something is **permanent** (a) when it is there all the time. (b) when it is not expected to change. *...a permanent address.*

permeable (**permeability**) If something is **permeable,** it is possible for something like light or liquid to pass through it.

permeate (**permeating, permeated**) If something like an idea or attitude **permeates** a place or institution, everyone is affected by it. ■ If a liquid, smell, or flavour **permeates** a place, it spreads throughout it.

permissible If something is **permissible,** you are allowed to do it.

permission If you give someone **permission** to do something, you allow them to do it.

permissive (**permissiveness**) People can be described as **permissive** when they allow other people a great deal of freedom in the way they behave, especially in sexual matters. *...permissive parents.* *...the permissive Sixties.*

permit (**permitting, permitted**) If you are **permitted** to do something, you are allowed to do it. ■ A **permit** (*pron:* **per**-mit) is an official document allowing you to do something. *...work permits.* ■ If circumstances **permit** something, they make it possible.

permutation A **permutation** is one of the ways in which a number of things can be ordered or arranged. *She now makes necklaces and bracelets in endless permutations of colours, designs and styles.*

pernicious If you say something is **pernicious,** you mean it is very harmful.

pernicious anaemia is a type of anaemia caused by lack of vitamin B12.

pernickety If you call someone **pernickety,** you mean they are too concerned with small or unimportant details.

peroration A **peroration** is (a) a speech. (b) the summing-up at the end of a speech.

peroxide or **hydrogen peroxide** is a chemical used for bleaching hair. It is also used as an antiseptic.

perpendicular If something is **perpendicular,** it stands or rises straight up from the ground. *...a virtually perpendicular slope.* ■ If something is **perpendicular** to a line or surface, it is at right angles to it.

perpetrate (**perpetrating, perpetrated; perpetration, perpetrator**) If someone **perpetrates** a crime or some other wrong or harmful act, they commit it. You say they are the **perpetrator** of the crime or act.

perpetual is used to describe things which go on forever or happen all the time. *...perpetual motion... Nearly a quarter of women are perpetually on a diet.*

perpetuate (**perpetuating, perpetuated; perpetuation**) If someone or something **perpetuates** an undesirable situation, they cause it to continue.

perpetuity If something is meant to last **in perpetuity,** it is meant to last for ever.

perplex (**perplexes, perplexing, perplexed; perplexity, perplexingly**) If you are **perplexed,** you are confused and puzzled. *Most of the audience left in perplexity.*

perquisite A **perquisite** is the same as a perk.

perry is an alcoholic drink made from fermented pears.

per se (*pron:* **per say**) You use **per se** to say you are talking about a thing in itself, rather than, for example, the way it is presented or used. *Violence in art and entertainment is neither good nor bad per se.*

persecute (**persecuting, persecuted; persecution, persecutor**) If someone **persecutes** you, they treat you cruelly and unfairly over a long period. You call someone like this your **persecutor.**

persevere (**persevering, persevered; perseverance**) If you **persevere** with something difficult, you do not give up. *Her perseverance has paid off.*

Persian means to do with ancient Persia or modern Iran. *...Persian antiques.* The **Persians** were citizens of ancient Persia. ■ **Persian** is the main language spoken in Iran. It is also called **Farsi.**

Persian cat – Persian cats are a breed of long-haired cats with round flat faces.

persimmon – Persimmons are a sweet orange-coloured fruit, grown in the US and the Far East.

persist (**persistent, persistently, persistence**) If something undesirable **persists,** it continues to exist. You say something is **persistent.** *...persistent rumours. ...the persistence of anti-Jewish sentiment.* ■ If

you **persist** in doing something, you keep doing it in spite of opposition or difficulty. You say someone who behaves like this is **persistent.**

person (*plural:* **people** or **persons**) A **person** is a man, woman, or child. ■ Your **person** is your body. ■ If you do something **in person,** you do it yourself, rather than getting someone else to do it.

persona (*pron:* per-**soh**-na) (*plural:* **personae** or **personas**) Your **persona** is the image of yourself that you present to other people. *...his stage persona.*

personable Someone who is **personable** has a pleasant appearance and character.

personage A **personage** is a person, especially an important or distinguished one. *...no less a personage than Henry the Eighth.*

personal A **personal** opinion, quality, or thing belongs or relates to a particular person. *It was his personal view that workers had little need for unions. ...the Prime Minister's personal authority.* ■ If you give something your **personal** attention, you do it yourself, rather than getting someone else to do it. ■ **Personal** matters relate to your feelings, relationships, or health. *He had to return to the United States for personal reasons.* ■ **Personal** remarks or comments refer critically or offensively to someone's appearance or character.

personal assistant Someone's **personal assistant** or **PA** is a person in charge of their secretarial and administrative work.

personal column The **personal column** of a newspaper is a column containing personal messages and advertisements.

personal computer A **personal computer** or **PC** is a small computer used by one person.

personalise See **personalize.**

personality (**personalities**) Your **personality** is your character and nature. ■ A **personality** is a famous person.

personalize (*or* **personalise**) (**personalizing, personalized; personalization**) If you **personalize** a campaign, issue, or argument, you focus it on a particular person. ■ **Personalized** is used to describe (a) something designed to a particular person's requirements. *...24-hour personalised nursing.* (b) something with a person's name or initials on it. *...personalized envelopes.*

personally You use **personally** to emphasize that what you are saying is your own opinion. *Personally, I think she's gone too far.* ■ If you do something **personally,** you do it yourself, rather than getting someone else to do it. Similarly, you can be **personally** responsible for something. ■ If you take a remark or criticism **personally,** you take it as referring to yourself. ■ If you know someone **personally,** you have met them several times, and have not just heard about them from other people.

personal organizer (*or* **personal organiser**) A **personal organizer** is a personal filing system. It can be either a small ring-bound book or a small computer.

personal stereo A **personal stereo** is a small portable cassette player with headphones.

persona non grata If someone is **persona non grata,** they are not welcome somewhere.

personify (**personifies, personifying, personified; personification**) If you say someone **personifies** a particular quality, you mean they are a perfect example of it. *He can be charm personified.*

personnel An organization's **personnel** are the people who work for it.

perspective In art, **perspective** is drawing objects as they appear to the human eye, so that things which are further away appear smaller than things which are close. ■ A person's **perspective** is the way they view a situation. ■ If you get something into **perspective,** you judge its proper importance by considering it in relation to other things. *The incident needs to be kept in perspective.*

Perspex is a strong clear plastic sometimes used instead of glass. 'Perspex' is a trademark.

perspicacious (**perspicacity**) If you say someone is **perspicacious** or talk about their **perspicacity,** you mean they notice or understand things quickly.

perspire (**perspiring, perspired; perspiration**) When you **perspire,** you sweat. **Perspiration** is sweat.

persuade (**persuading, persuaded; persuasion, persuader**) If you **persuade** someone to do something, you get them to do it, either by coaxing them or by convincing them it is a good idea. **Persuasion** is persuading someone to do something. A **persuader** is someone or something that persuades people to do something. ■ If you **persuade** someone of something, you convince them that it exists or is true. *...a campaign to persuade people of the benefits of gas.* ■ A **persuasion** is a belief. *...local politicians of all political persuasions.*

persuasive (**persuasively; persuasiveness**) If someone or something is **persuasive,** they are likely to make you believe something is true or a good idea. *...persuasive evidence... He argued persuasively.*

pert A young woman is sometimes described as **pert** when she is lively and cheeky. ■ If you say someone has, for example, a **pert** bottom, you mean it is small, neat, and attractive.

pertain (**pertaining, pertained**) If something **pertains** to something else, it belongs to it or is connected with it. *...vital military secrets pertaining to the Gulf War.* ■ The situation that **pertains** at a particular time or in a particular place is the one that exists at that time or in that place. *...the circumstances that pertained at the year end.*

pertinent (**pertinently, pertinence**) If something is **pertinent,** it is important and relevant.

perturb (**perturbation**) If something **perturbs** you, it worries you. **Perturbation** is worry and anxiety.

peruse (**perusing, perused; perusal**) If you **peruse** something, you read it. Reading something can be called a **perusal** of it.

pervade (**pervading, pervaded; pervasive, pervasiveness**) If something like a smell **pervades** a place, you can smell it everywhere. Similarly, you can talk about a feeling or attitude **pervading** a group of people. You call something like this **pervasive.** *...pervasive corruption.*

perverse (**perversely; perversity**) If you say someone is being **perverse** or talk about their **perversity,** you mean they are deliberately being unreasonable. ■ You say **perversely** when you are talking about something working out the opposite way to what is intended or expected. *Perversely, it was the 1980-81 recession that caused an upturn in spirits.*

pervert (**perversion**) If someone **perverts** something (*pron:* per-**verts**), they interfere with it so it is not what it should be. *...the perversion of justice.* ■ People with abnormal sexual desires are sometimes called **perverts** (*pron:* **per**-verts); their behaviour is described as **perverted.** A **perversion** is an abnormal sexual act or desire.

peseta (*pron:* pe-**say**-ta) The **peseta** is the unit of money in Spain.

pesky is used to describe people or things that are troublesome or a nuisance.

peso (*pron:* **pay**-so) (**pesos**) The **peso** is the unit of money in a number of countries including Mexico and the Philippines.

pessary (**pessaries**) A **pessary** is (a) a solid block of medicine or contraceptive which a woman inserts into her vagina, where it melts. (b) a device placed in the vagina to support the womb.

pessimistic (**pessimist; pessimism, pessimistically**) If someone is **pessimistic** about a situation, they do not expect things to turn out well. You can talk about the **pessimism** of someone like this. A **pessimist** is someone who always expects things to turn out badly.

pest (**pestilential**) A **pest** is an insect or small animal which damages plants or food supplies, harms livestock, or is a hazard to health. ■ You can call an annoying person a **pest.**

pester (**pestering, pestered**) If someone **pesters** you, they keep bothering or annoying you.

pesticide – **Pesticides** are chemicals for killing insect pests.

pestilence is any disease that spreads quickly, killing lots of people.

pestilential is used to describe things that cause disease or are related to disease.

pestle A **pestle** is a tool like a small club, used for grinding things to powder in a bowl called a mortar.

pesto is an Italian sauce made from basil, garlic, pine nuts, cheese, and olive oil.

pet (**petting, petted**) **Pets** are animals people keep for pleasure and companionship. ■ If you **pet** an animal, you pat or stroke it affectionately. ■ You can call someone's favourite their **pet.** *...teacher's pet.* ■ Your **pet name** is the name people close to you call you instead of your real name. ■ Someone's **pet** project or theory is one they particularly support or favour. Similarly, you can talk about someone's **pet** subject or their **pet** concerns or hates. ■ **Petting** is used to describe a couple kissing and caressing each other.

petal (**-petalled**) A flower's **petals** are the coloured outer parts of its head. **-petalled** is used to describe the colour or number of a flower's petals. *...five-petalled flowers.*

petard If you have planned to harm someone and are **hoist with your own petard,** your plan backfires and you only succeed in harming yourself.

peter (**petering, petered**) If something **peters out,** it gradually comes to an end.

pethidine (*pron:* peth-i-deen) is a pain reliever given to women in labour.

petite women are small and dainty.

petition (**petitioning, petitioned; petitioner**) A **petition** is a document signed by many people, demanding that a particular action be taken. The people who sign it are called **petitioners.** ...*a petition calling on the Government to ban hunting.* ■ A **petition** is a formal application to a court of law for permission to do something. The person who makes the application is called a **petitioner.** ...*a divorce petition.* ■ If you **petition** someone in authority, you make a formal request to them.

petrel – Petrels are long-winged seabirds.

petri dish (**petri dishes**) Petri dishes are flat shallow laboratory dishes.

petrify (**petrifies, petrifying, petrified**) If you are **petrified,** you are very frightened. ■ When an object **petrifies,** it turns to stone.

petrochemical (*or* **petro-chemical**) Petrochemicals are chemicals obtained from petroleum or natural gas.

petrodollar (*or* **petro-dollar**) Petrodollars are the dollars a country earns from its oil exports.

petrol is a flammable liquid obtained from petroleum and used as fuel.

petrol bomb A **petrol bomb** is a bomb made from a bottle filled with petrol with a piece of cloth stuffed into its neck. If something is **petrolbombed,** petrol bombs are thrown at it.

petroleum is the oil which petrol and paraffin are obtained from.

petroleum jelly is a soft clear greasy substance obtained from petroleum, used in ointments and as a lubricant.

petrol station A **petrol station** is a garage by the side of the road where you can obtain petrol.

petticoat A **petticoat** is an item of women's underwear similar to a thin skirt.

pettifogging means too concerned with small or insignificant details.

petty (**pettiness**) Petty is used to describe minor criminals and offences. ...*petty thieves.* ■ **Petty** matters are small and unimportant. ■ If you say someone's behaviour is **petty,** you mean they behave in a mean or selfish way over some small matter. *He was instantly sorry for his pettiness.*

petty cash is money kept in an office to make small payments.

petty officer A **petty officer** is an NCO in the Royal Navy.

petulant (**petulantly, petulance**) You say someone's behaviour is **petulant** when they are childishly bad-tempered or irritable.

petunia – Petunias are garden plants with large pink, white, or purple trumpet-shaped flowers.

pew – Pews are the long wooden benches people sit on in church.

pewter is a grey metal made by mixing tin and lead. In the past it was used to make things like plates and tankards.

pfennig (*pron:* fen-ig) The **pfennig** is a unit of money in Germany.

PGCE The **PGCE** is a teaching qualification for graduates. PGCE stands for 'Postgraduate Certificate in Education'.

pH The **pH** of a solution indicates how acidic or alkaline it is. Acid solutions have a pH less than 7, alkaline solutions a pH greater than 7.

phalanx A **phalanx** of soldiers or police is a group of them standing or marching close together. ■ Any group of people of the same kind gathered together can be called a **phalanx.** ...*a phalanx of photographers.* ■ A **phalanx** is any of the bones in the fingers or toes.

phallic means shaped like a penis or meant to represent a penis. ...*a phallic symbol.*

phallus (**phalluses**) A **phallus** is a penis or a representation of one.

phantasmagoria A **phantasmagoria** is a series of confused images of real or imaginary things.

phantasmagorical means dream-like or bizarre.

phantasy is an older spelling of 'fantasy'.

phantom A **phantom** is a ghost. ■ **Phantom** is used to describe things which are thought to exist for a time, but turn out not to exist. ...*phantom pregnancies.* ...*phantom companies.*

pharaoh (*pron:* fare-oh) The **pharaohs** were the kings of ancient Egypt.

Pharisee The **Pharisees** were an ancient Jewish sect, mentioned in the Bible, who believed in strictly obeying the laws of Judaism.

pharmaceutical means connected with the production of medicines and medical products. ...*pharmaceutical companies.* **Pharmaceuticals** are medicines.

pharmacist A **pharmacist** is a person qualified to prepare and sell medicines.

pharmacology (**pharmacological, pharmacologist**) **Pharmacology** is the study of drugs and their effects. **Pharmacological** means connected with drugs or the study of drugs. **Pharmacologists** are researchers who test the effects of drugs.

pharmacy (**pharmacies**) **Pharmacy** is the preparation and giving out of drugs and medicines. ■ A **pharmacy** is a shop where medicines are sold, or a hospital department where they are prepared or kept.

pharyngitis (*pron:* far-rin-**jite**-iss) is inflammation of the pharynx.

pharynx (*pron:* **far**-rinks) (*plural:* **pharynges** or **pharynxes**) The **pharynx** is the back of the throat.

phase (**phasing, phased**) A **phase** is a stage in a process or in the development of something. ■ If something is **phased,** it is carried out in stages. ...*a phased withdrawal of the troops.* ■ If something is **phased in,** it is introduced gradually. If something is **phased out,** people gradually stop using it.

PhD A **PhD** is a degree awarded to someone who has done advanced postgraduate research in a subject. 'PhD' is short for 'Doctor of Philosophy'.

pheasant – **Pheasants** are large long-tailed game birds.

phenobarbitone is a drug used as a sedative.

phenol is another name for carbolic acid.

phenomenal (**phenomenally**) If something is **phenomenal,** it is extraordinarily good.

phenomenon (plural: **phenomena**) A **phenomenon** is something which happens or exists, especially something remarkable or something being considered in a scientific way. ■ A person who is remarkable in some way is sometimes called a **phenomenon.**

pheromone Some animals and insects produce chemicals called **pheromones** which affect the behaviour of other animals and insects of the same type, for example by attracting them sexually.

phial A **phial** is a small tube-shaped glass bottle.

philandering (**philanderer**) A **philandering** man has casual love affairs with many women. You call a man like this a **philanderer.**

philanthropic (**philanthropy; philanthropist**) A **philanthropic** person or organization gives money or help to people who need it. You talk about their **philanthropy.** Someone who helps people like this is called a **philanthropist.**

philately (pron: fill-**lat**-a-lee) (**philatelist, philatelic**) **Philately** is stamp collecting. **Philatelic** means things to do with stamps and stamp collecting.

philharmonic A **philharmonic** orchestra is a large orchestra which plays classical music.

philistine (**philistinism**) If you call someone a **philistine** or talk about their **philistinism,** you mean they have no appreciation of art, literature, or music.

philology (**philologist**) **Philology** is the study of languages and their development.

philosopher See **philosophy.**

philosophic means the same as 'philosophical'.

philosophical (**philosophically**) **Philosophical** is used to describe things to do with philosophy. ■ If you are **philosophical** or take things **philosophically,** you do not get upset when disappointing or disturbing things happen.

philosophize (or **philosophise**) (**philosophizing, philosophized**) If someone **philosophizes,** they talk about theories of life in general.

philosophy (**philosophies; philosopher**) **Philosophy** is the study or creation of theories about the nature of existence, knowledge, beliefs, or behaviour. A **philosophy** is a set of theories of this kind. A person who studies or creates theories like these is called a **philosopher.**

phlegm (pron: **flem**) is the thick yellowish substance that develops in your throat when you have a cold.

phlegmatic (pron: fleg-**mat**-ik) (**phlegmatically**) If someone is **phlegmatic,** they stay calm even when exciting or upsetting things happen.

phlox is a garden plant with clusters of sweet-smelling flowers.

phobia (**phobic**) A **phobia** is an irrational fear or hatred of something. You say someone who has a feeling like this is **phobic** or a **phobic.**

phoenix (**phoenixes**) A **phoenix** is an imaginary bird which, according to ancient myths, burns itself to ashes every five hundred years and is then born again.

phone (**phoning, phoned**) **Phone** is short for 'telephone'. ■ If you **phone** someone, you telephone them. If you are **on the phone** to someone, you are speaking to them by telephone. ■ You say someone is **on the phone** when they have a telephone in their home.

phonecard (or **phone card**) A **phonecard** is a plastic card you can use to make telephone calls from certain public telephones.

phone-in A **phone-in** is a live radio or TV programme in which people telephone with their comments and their calls are broadcast.

phonetic (**phonetically**) **Phonetics** is the study of speech sounds. **Phonetic** means things connected with this study. ■ **Phonetic** systems of spelling use a particular symbol to represent each sound.

phoney (or **phony**) If something is **phoney,** it is fake or false. ■ If you say a person is **phoney** or a **phoney,** you mean they are insincere.

phonics (**phonic**) **Phonics** is a way of teaching people to read by matching sounds to letters. **Phonic** means things connected with this method.

phonograph In the US, a record player is sometimes called a **phonograph.**

phony (**phonies**) See **phoney.**

phosphate – **Phosphates** are chemical compounds containing phosphorus, which are often used in fertilizers.

phosphorescent (**phosphorescence**) If something is **phosphorescent,** it glows faintly in the dark. This glow is called **phosphorescence.**

phosphorus is a colourless chemical which glows faintly in the dark. It burns in contact with the air, giving off white fumes.

photo (**photos**) A **photo** is the same as a photograph.

photo-call A **photo-call** is a session arranged for someone to be photographed by the press.

photocopier A **photocopier** is a machine which quickly copies documents by photographing them.

photocopy (**photocopies, photocopying, photocopied**) If you **photocopy** a document, you make a copy of it using a photocopier. A copy made like this is called a **photocopy.**

photo-finish If the end of a race is a **photo-finish,** competitors cross the finishing line so close together that a photograph has to be examined to decide the winner.

photofit A **photofit** of someone wanted by the police is a picture of them, made up from photographs of different facial features. 'Photofit' is a trademark.

photogenic If someone is **photogenic,** they look nice in photographs.

photograph A **photograph** is a picture taken with a camera. When you **photograph** someone or something, you take a picture of them.

photographer A **photographer** is someone who takes photographs as a job or hobby.

photographic means things to do with photography. ■ If you have a **photographic memory,** you can remember things in great detail after you have seen them.

photography is the art of taking photographs.

photo-journalism (**photo-journalist**) When news stories are presented mainly in photographs, you call it **photo-journalism.**

photomontage is making a picture by sticking together bits of different photographs. A picture like this is called a **photomontage.**

photon – **Photons** are particles of light.

photo-opportunity A **photo-opportunity** is a session arranged for someone famous to be photographed or filmed by the media.

photosensitive things are sensitive to light.

photostat A **photostat** is a type of photocopy. 'Photostat' is a trademark.

photosynthesize (or **photosynthesise**) (**photosynthesizing, photosynthesized; photosynthesis**) When a plant **photosynthesizes**, it uses sunlight to convert chlorophyll into the food it needs. This process is called **photosynthesis.**

phrase (**phrasing, phrased**) A **phrase** is a group of words often used together, whose meaning is not always obvious from the individual words. *The phrase 'man in the street' must now become 'people in general'.* ■ The way you **phrase** something is the way you express it in words. ■ If someone has a particular **turn of phrase,** they have a particular way of expressing themselves in words. *...a clever turn of phrase.*

phrase book A **phrase book** is a book for travellers to a foreign country, containing useful words and expressions, with translations.

phraseology Your **phraseology** is the words you use to express something.

phrenology is the study of the size and shape of people's skulls in the belief that it can reveal their character or intelligence.

phylum (*plural:* **phyla**) A **phylum** is a group of animal or plant species.

physical (**physically**) **Physical** qualities, actions, or experiences are to do with a person's body, rather than their mind. ■ **Physical** is used to describe things you can see or touch. ■ **Physical** means concerning the laws of physics.

physical education See **PE.**

physical geography is the branch of geography dealing with natural features of the earth's surface, such as mountains and rivers.

physicality The **physicality** of a person or thing is their physical nature or appearance.

physical science The **physical sciences** are sciences like physics, chemistry, and geology, which deal with non-living things and natural forces.

physical training is the same as PE.

physician A **physician** is a person legally qualified to practise medicine.

physics (**physicist**) **Physics** is the scientific study of forces such as heat, pressure, and electricity. A **physicist** is a scientist who studies physics.

physio See **physiotherapy.**

physiognomy (*pron:* fiz-ee-**on**-om-ee) (**physiognomies**) A person's **physiognomy** is their face.

physiological (**physiologically**) **Physiological** means to do with the body. *...physiological changes.*

physiology (**physiologist**) **Physiology** is the scientific study of how the bodies of living things work. A **physiologist** is a scientist who studies this. ■ Your **physiology** is the way your body works.

physiotherapy (**physiotherapist**) **Physiotherapy** is the treatment of disease or injury by means such as exercise, heat treatment, or massage. A person who treats people in these ways is called a **physiotherapist.** 'Physiotherapy' and 'physiotherapist' are both often shortened to 'physio'.

physique Your **physique** is your body's build and muscular development.

pi is π, the sixteenth letter of the Greek alphabet. π is used as a mathematical symbol for the ratio of the circumference of a circle to its diameter, approx 3.142.

pianistic means connected with piano playing. *...his pianistic skills.*

piano (**pianos; pianist**) A **piano** is a large musical instrument with a row of black and white keys which you press with your fingers.

pianoforte A **pianoforte** is the same as a piano.

pianola A **pianola** is a mechanical piano which plays a tune when you press its pedals. 'Pianola' is a trademark.

piazza (*pron:* pee-**ats**-a) A **piazza** is a public square, especially in Italy.

picaresque A **picaresque** novel is one in which a slightly immoral but likeable hero travels around having exciting adventures.

piccolo (**piccolos**) A **piccolo** is a musical instrument like a very small flute.

pick If you **pick** someone or something, you choose them. Your **pick** is your choice. ■ If you **pick** an object **up, you lift it off the ground or some other surface.** ■ If you **pick** a flower or fruit, or **pick** something from a place, you remove it with your fingers. ■ If you **pick at** some food which is in front of you, you eat only small amounts of it. ■ If someone **picks** a fight or quarrel with you, they deliberately start it. ■ If someone **picks on** you, they single you out for criticism or harassment. ■ If you **pick** a lock, you open it without a key, for example using a piece of wire. ■ If you **pick your way** across something, you walk carefully, avoiding any obstacles. ■ If you **pick** someone or something **up,** you collect them from a place as arranged. ■ If you **pick up** someone you have not met before, you get talking to them and start a romantic or sexual relationship with them. ■ If someone is **picked up** by the police, they are arrested. ■ If you **pick up** a skill, you acquire it gradually. ■ If a piece of equipment **picks up** a signal or sound, it receives it or detects it. ■ If things **pick up,** they improve. ■ If a vehicle **picks up** speed, it goes faster. ■ A **pick** is a pickaxe. ■ **pick holes in** something: See **hole.** pick someone's **pocket:** See **pocket.** See also **picker, pickings.**

pickaxe (*Am:* **pickax**) A **pickaxe** is a tool for breaking up rocks or the ground. It consists of a curved iron bar, pointed at both ends, attached in the middle to a long wooden handle.

picker People paid to pick crops are called **pickers**. ...*cotton pickers.*

picket (**picketing, picketed**) When strikers **picket** a place of work during industrial action, they stand outside and try to persuade other workers not to go in to work. You say they form a **picket** or **picket line**. An individual member of a picket is also called a **picket**. ■ **Pickets** are pointed wooden stakes used to make fences.

pickings You can call the money made from an activity the **pickings**, especially when the activity is an illegal one.

pickle (**pickling, pickled**) When food is **pickled**, it is put into vinegar or salt water, to preserve it. **Pickles** are vegetables or fruit preserved in this way. ■ An awkward situation can be called a **pickle**. *This put the British government in a pickle.*

pick-me-up A **pick-me-up** is something which restores your energy, especially a drink.

pickpocket (**pickpocketing**) **Pickpockets** are thieves who steal things from people's pockets or bags. Stealing things in this way is called **pickpocketing.**

pickup A **pickup** or **pickup truck** is a truck with low sides.

picky You say someone is **picky** when they are difficult to please and only like a small range of things. ...*picky eaters.*

picnic (**picnicking, picnicked; picnicker**) When people **picnic** or have a **picnic**, they eat an informal meal in the open air. People doing this are called **picnickers.**

Pict The **Picts** were a race of people who lived in northern Britain in ancient times.

pictorial (**pictorially**) **Pictorial** means involving or using pictures. ...*a pictorial record of city life down the ages.*

picture (**picturing, pictured**) A **picture** is a drawing, painting, or photograph. You also call the image you see on a TV screen the **picture**. ■ When someone is **pictured** in a newspaper or magazine, a photograph of them is printed in it. ■ If you go to the **pictures,** you go to see a film at the cinema. ■ If you **picture** something or have a **picture** of it, you have a mental image of it. ■ The general situation is sometimes called the **picture**. *The economic picture is now grim.* If you **put** someone **in the picture,** you fill them in on a situation. ■ If you are a **picture** of something, you are a perfect example of it. *She was the picture of health.*

picturesque (**picturesquely**) A **picturesque** place is attractive and unspoilt.

picture window A **picture window** is a large window consisting of a single pane of glass.

piddling means small or unimportant. ...*piddling amounts of money.*

pidgin A **pidgin** or **pidgin** language is a mixture of two or more languages, used by people who speak different languages to communicate with each other. ...*pidgin English.*

pie A **pie** is a dish of meat, fruit, or vegetables baked in pastry.

piebald A **piebald** horse or other animal is partly white and partly a dark colour, especially black.

piece (**piecing, pieced**) A **piece** of something is a portion, part, or section of it. ■ A **piece** is something written or created, such as an article or musical composition. ...*his piece in the New York Times.* ■ You can use **piece** to refer to specific coins. ...*a 50p piece.* ■ In a board game, the **pieces** are the objects you move around the board. ■ If you **piece together** information about something which has happened, you try to work out the actual sequence of events. ■ **piece of cake:** See **cake.**

pièce de résistance (*pron:* **pyess** de ray-**ziss**-tonss) The **pièce de résistance** is the most impressive thing in a series or collection of things.

piecemeal A **piecemeal** process happens a bit at a time.

piecework is work you are paid for according to how much you do, rather than how long you work.

pie chart A **pie chart** is a circular diagram divided into sections to show proportional amounts of something.

pied Some birds whose feathers are in two contrasting colours, especially black and white, have **pied** as part of their name, for example the pied wagtail.

pied-à-terre (**pieds-à-terre**) (*both pron:* pyayd-da-**tair**) A **pied-à-terre** is a small flat or house for occasional use.

pier A **pier** is a large platform sticking out into the sea, along which people can walk.

pierce (**piercing, pierced; piercingly**) If a sharp object **pierces** something, it goes through it, making a hole. ■ If you **pierce** someone's defences, you succeed in getting through them. ■ A **piercing** sound is shrill and high-pitched. ■ If you talk about someone's **piercing** eyes, you mean they seem to look at you very intensely.

pierrot (*pron:* **pier**-roe) A **pierrot** is a clown or entertainer who wears a white costume and whose face is covered with white make-up.

pietà (*pron:* pee-et-**ah**) A **pietà** is a painting, drawing, or sculpture of the Virgin Mary holding the dead body of Jesus and mourning over it.

piety is strong religious belief.

piffle If you say something is **piffle,** you mean it is nonsense.

piffling means small or unimportant. ...*a piffling achievement.*

pig A **pig** is a farm animal with a snout and a bristle-covered skin.

pigeon – **Pigeons** are fat birds with short legs, often seen in towns.

pigeon-hole (*or* **pigeonhole**) (**pigeon-holing, pigeon-holed**) A **pigeon-hole** is one of several sections in a frame on a wall, where letters and messages can be left. ■ If you **pigeon-hole** someone, you regard them as a particular type of person, rather than thinking of them as an individual. *He resisted being pigeon-holed as either a serious or popular composer.*

pigeon-toed If someone is **pigeon-toed,** their feet turn inwards.

piggery (**piggeries**) A **piggery** is a place where pigs are kept and bred.

piggy-back (or **piggyback**) If you give someone a **piggy-back**, you carry them on your back, supporting them under their knees.

piggy bank A **piggy bank** is a child's money box, usually shaped like a pig.

pig-headed If you call someone **pig-headed,** you mean they are stubborn or obstinate.

pig-iron is crude iron produced in a blast furnace.

piglet A **piglet** is a young pig.

pigment or a **pigment** is the substance which gives something its colour.

pigmentation The **pigmentation** of a person's or animal's skin is its natural colour.

pigmy See **pygmy.**

pigpen A **pigpen** is the same as a pigsty.

pigskin is a kind of leather made from the skin of a pig.

pigsty (**pigsties**) A **pigsty** is a hut with a yard where pigs are kept. ■ If you call a place a **pigsty,** you mean it is very dirty or untidy.

pigtail A **pigtail** is a length of hair which has been divided into three and then plaited.

pike The **pike** (plural: **pike**) is a large freshwater fish with a long narrow snout and sharp teeth. ■ In the past, a **pike** (plural: **pikes**) was a weapon consisting of a pointed metal blade attached to a long pole.

pilaster A **pilaster** is a rectangular column set into a wall.

pilchard – Pilchards are small edible sea fish.

pile (**piling, piled**) A **pile** of things is a quantity of them lying one on top of another. If you **pile** things somewhere, you put them there in a pile. ...tables piled high with leaflets. ■ If people **pile** into or out of a place, they all go in or out in a disorganized way. ■ If things **pile up**, more and more of them keep arriving or happening. Throughout the day the phone calls start to pile up. ■ A **pile** of something is a large amount of it. Boxing has made him a pile of money. ■ A large building is sometimes called a **pile.** ...St Donat's Castle, a thirteenth-century pile. ■ The **pile** of a carpet is its soft surface, consisting of many small threads standing on end. ■ See also **haemorrhoids.**

pile-up A **pile-up** is a road accident involving several vehicles.

pilfer (**pilfering, pilfered**) If someone **pilfers** things, they steal them.

pilgrim – Pilgrims are people making a journey to a holy place for religious reasons.

pilgrimage A **pilgrimage** is a journey to a holy place, made for religious reasons. ■ You can say someone goes on a **pilgrimage** when they make a journey to a place connected with someone or something they are especially interested in.

pill – Pills are small solid round masses of medicine or vitamins which you swallow without chewing. ■ If a woman is on **the pill**, she regularly takes a pill which prevents her becoming pregnant. ■ You can say a failure or humiliation is a **bitter pill.**

pillage (**pillaging, pillaged**) If people like soldiers **pillage** a place, they steal property from it using force and violence. ■ You can say money is **pillaged** when it is dishonestly and unfairly taken from its owners. £400 million has been pillaged from their pension funds.

pillar (**pillared**) A **pillar** is a tall solid post used in building as a support or decoration. If a building is **pillared**, it has pillars round it, or it is supported by pillars. ■ If you say something is a **pillar** of an organization or system, you mean it is one of the features which make it strong or successful. The pillar of her economic policy was keeping tight control over money supply. ■ If you say someone is **a pillar of the community,** you mean they play an active, important, and respected role in society.

pillar box A **pillar box** is an upright red cylinder in the street into which you post letters.

pillbox (or **pill box**) (**pillboxes**) A **pillbox** is a small tin or box for keeping pills in. ■ A **pillbox** is a small, usually circular concrete shelter with narrow slits from which guns can be fired.

pillion If you ride **pillion** on a motorbike, you sit behind the person controlling it.

pillory (**pillories, pillorying, pilloried**) The **pillory** was a wooden frame with holes for the neck and wrists. People convicted of minor crimes were sometimes locked in the pillory in a public place as a punishment. ■ Nowadays, you say someone is **pilloried** when they are publicly ridiculed and criticized, especially in the newspapers or on TV.

pillow – Pillows are the cushions you rest your head on in bed. ■ **Pillow talk** is conversation between people who are in bed together, especially about secret subjects.

pillowcase A **pillowcase** is a cover for a pillow.

pillowslip A **pillowslip** is the same as a pillowcase.

pilot (**piloting, piloted**) A **pilot** is a person trained to fly an aircraft. When someone **pilots** an aircraft, they fly it. ■ A **pilot** is a person who steers a ship through a difficult stretch of water, for example the entrance to a harbour. He regularly piloted ships through Rhode Island Sound. ■ If a government minister **pilots** a new bill through parliament, he or she makes sure it is approved. ■ A **pilot** scheme or project is one used to test an idea before introducing it on a larger scale. ■ A **pilot** or **pilot episode** is a single TV programme shown to find out whether a series is likely to be popular.

pilot light A pilot light is a small flame in a gas boiler or cooker which burns continuously and lights the burner when the appliance is turned on.

pilot officer A **pilot officer** is an officer of the lowest rank in the RAF.

pimp A **pimp** is a man who gets clients for prostitutes and takes a large part of the money they earn.

pimple (**pimply**) Pimples are small red spots, usually on the face, which most commonly appear during adolescence. If you call someone **pimply,** you mean they have pimples, and you are using this as a way of saying they are very young. ...a book written while he was a pimply student at Leeds University.

pin (**pinning, pinned**) Pins are small thin pieces of metal with a point at one end, used to fasten pieces of material together. ■ Various long narrow pieces of metal or wood are called **pins,** especially when they are used to fasten things together. ■ In the US, a brooch is called a **pin.** ■ If you **pin** something somewhere, you attach it there with a pin or drawing pin. ■ If you **pin** your hopes on something, you rely on it as your best or only chance of getting what you want. ■ If someone **pins** the blame on you for something, they say it is your fault. ■ If you try to **pin** something **down,** you try to give an exact description of it. *The unique quality of Fonteyn's dancing has never been easy to pin down.* If you **pin** someone **down,** you get them to give you exact information. *She couldn't pin him down to a date.* ■ You say someone is **pinned down** when they are unable to move, for example because people are shooting at them. *Government troops were pinned down around the presidential mansion.* ■ **Pin money** is small amounts of extra money you earn to buy luxury items. ■ Someone's **PIN** number is the secret number they use to withdraw money from a cash machine. PIN stands for 'personal identification number'.

pinafore A **pinafore** is an apron. ■ A **pinafore dress** is a sleeveless dress usually worn over a blouse or sweater.

pinball is an electronic game in which you press buttons to flick a ball up a slope so that it hits objects, lights lights, and rings bells to score points.

pince-nez (*pron:* panss-**nay**) are an old-fashioned kind of spectacles. They consisted of a pair of lenses which fitted tightly onto the top of the nose, with no ear pieces.

pincer – **Pincers** are a tool for gripping or pulling things. They consist of two pieces of metal hinged in the middle. ■ The **pincers** of an animal like a crab are its front claws, which it uses for gripping, squeezing, and tearing. ■ A **pincer movement** is a move by an army in which they divide into two columns as they approach an enemy, to try to surround them.

pinch (**pinches, pinching, pinched**) If you **pinch** someone, you use your forefinger and thumb to give their skin a short squeeze. ■ A **pinch** of something is the amount you can hold between your thumb and finger. *...a pinch of salt.* ■ If something is possible **at a pinch,** it can be done if it is really necessary, although it will not be easy. *My car will accommodate four people, five at a pinch.* ■ If people are **feeling the pinch,** they can no longer afford to buy things as easily as they could in the past. ■ If someone **pinches** something, they steal it.

pincushion A **pincushion** is a small padded object you stick pins and needles into, ready for when you need them.

pine (**pining, pined**) **Pines** are various kinds of tall trees which produce cones and have needle-shaped leaves. ■ If you are **pining** for someone or something, you feel very sad because you no longer have them with you.

pineapple – **Pineapples** are large oval fruit with sweet yellow flesh and thick lumpy, pale brown skin.

pine marten The **pine marten** is a weasel-like animal which lives in coniferous woods in northern Europe and Asia.

pinewood A **pinewood** is a wood which consists mainly of pine trees. ■ See also **pine.**

ping If something **pings** or goes **ping,** it makes a short, high-pitched, metallic sound.

ping-pong is the same as table tennis.

pinhead A **pinhead** is the small ball-shaped part at the top of a pin.

pinion (**pinioning, pinioned**) If someone is **pinioned,** they are tied or held firmly by their arms, so they cannot move.

pink is the colour between red and white. ■ **Pinks** are small garden flowers with pink or white petals.

pinking shears are special scissors whose blades have V-shaped teeth which give a zig-zag edge when they cut.

pinnacle A **pinnacle** is (a) a sharp rock pointing upwards, high up a mountain. (b) a cone-shaped stone high up on a building. ■ When someone has reached the **pinnacle** of their career, they have reached its highest point.

pinny (**pinnies**) A **pinny** is an apron.

pinpoint If you **pinpoint** something, you discover or show exactly what it is or where it is. *It was impossible to pinpoint the cause of death.*

pinprick A **pinprick** of something is a small spot of it. *...pinpricks of light.*

pins and needles When you get **pins and needles,** you feel sharp tingling pains in your fingers, toes, or legs for a short while, caused by the return of normal blood circulation after being in an awkward position.

pinstriped (**pinstripes**) **Pinstriped** suits or trousers are dark with very narrow vertical stripes. Pinstriped suits and trousers are sometimes called **pinstripes.**

pint The volume of an amount of liquid can be expressed in **pints.** A British pint is one eighth of an imperial gallon (0.568 litres). A US pint is one eighth of an US gallon (0.473 litres). ■ A **pint** is a pint of beer.

pint-sized A **pint-sized** person or thing is very small.

pin-up A **pin-up** is an attractive man or woman who appears on posters or in newspapers, usually scantily dressed.

pioneer (**pioneering, pioneered**) **Pioneers** are people who settle, colonize, or explore a new country or region. ■ If someone **pioneered** something or was a **pioneer** of it, they were one of the first people to be involved with it and develop it.

pious (**piously**) A **pious** person is very religious and moral. ■ **Pious** is sometimes used rather sarcastically to suggest that someone's righteous moral stance or good intentions are insincere, or unlikely to result in anything useful. *Some speculated that the president was getting pious in his old age. ...pious platitudes.* ■ **Pious** hopes are unlikely to be fulfilled.

pip (**pipping, pipped**) **Pips** are the small hard seeds in a fruit like an apple. ■ If someone is **pipped** in a competition, they are beaten by a narrow margin. ■ **Pips** are short high-pitched sounds, for example the ones you hear on a public phone as a signal to put more money in.

pipe (**piping, piped; piper**) A **pipe** is a long hollow object designed for liquid or gas to flow through. ■ If liquid or gas is **piped** somewhere, it is transferred from one place to another through a pipe. ■ **Piped** music is quiet background music played through speakers in public places. ■ A **pipe** is an object for smoking tobacco, consisting of a cup-shaped part at the end of a tube. ■ Small simple wind instruments such as penny whistles are sometimes called **pipes.** ■ Bagpipes are often called **pipes.** A person who plays the bagpipes is called a **piper.**

pipe-dream If you call a hope or plan a **pipe-dream,** you mean it has no chance of becoming a reality.

pipeline A **pipeline** is a large pipe used for carrying oil or gas over a long distance. ■ If you say something is **in the pipeline,** you mean it has already been planned or begun.

piper See **pipe.**

pipette (*pron:* pip-**et**) A **pipette** is a thin glass tube used in chemistry for measuring and dispensing small amounts of liquid.

pipework is pipes generally, or the pipes in a particular machine or other construction.

piping is (a) lengths of pipe. ...*bits of metal piping.* (b) cloth made into a narrow tube and used to decorate the edges of things like clothing and cushions. ...*a fawn anorak with red piping.*

pipit – Pipits are small songbirds with brownish speckled feathers and long tails.

piquant (*pron:* **pee**-kant) (**piquancy**) If food is **piquant,** it has a pleasantly spicy taste. ■ You say things are **piquant** when they are interesting and curious. *The pupils' neat appearance is in piquant contrast to the squalor from which they emerge.* When something brings this quality to something else, you can say it adds **piquancy** to it.

pique (*pron:* **peek**) (**piqued**) If someone does something out of **pique,** they do it because their pride has been hurt, rather than for any sensible reason. *In a fit of pique he stuck his hand through the dressing-room door and lacerated his arm.* ■ If someone is **piqued** at something, they are angry and resentful, because their pride has been hurt.

piracy See **pirate.**

piranha (*pron:* pir-**rah**-nah) **Piranhas** are small fierce fish with sharp teeth. They live in rivers in South America.

pirate (**pirating, pirated; piracy**) **Pirates** are sailors who attack and rob other ships. This practice is called **piracy.** ■ Someone who **pirates** things like video cassettes or computer software makes and sells illegal copies of them.

pirate radio is the illegal broadcasting of radio programmes.

pirouette (*pron:* pir-roo-**et**) (**pirouetting, pirouetted**) When a ballet dancer **pirouettes** or does a **pirouette,** he or she balances on one foot and spins round.

pistachio nuts (*pron:* pis-**tash**-ee-oh) come from a Mediterranean and Middle Eastern tree. They have greenish kernels and smooth pale-brown shells.

piste (*pron:* **peest**) A **piste** is a route through snow which has been flattened in order to make it suitable for skiing.

pistol A **pistol** is a handgun with a short barrel.

piston In a machine, a **piston** is a part which is forced backwards and forwards by expanding gases.

pit (**pitting, pitted**) A **pit** is a large hole dug in the ground. ■ If a surface is **pitted,** it is covered with holes. ■ A **pit** is a coal mine. ■ In the US, the stones in fruit are called **pits.** If you **pit** a fruit, you remove its stone. ■ In motor-racing, the **pits** are the areas where drivers stop for refuelling and repairs. ■ If you are **pitted** against someone, you are competing against them.

pitch (**pitches, pitching, pitched**) A **pitch** is an area of ground marked out for playing a game like football. ■ If you **pitch** an object somewhere, you throw it there forcefully. ■ A **pitched** roof is sloping. ■ If a boat **pitches,** it moves violently up and down with the movement of the waves. ■ The **pitch** of a sound is how high or low it is. ■ If something reaches a particular **pitch,** it reaches that level or intensity. *The conflict reached its highest pitch so far.* ■ If something is **pitched** at a certain level, it is set at that level. *The share price was pitched at 240p, valuing the industry at £5 billion.* ■ When people **pitch in,** they join in and help with something. ■ When you **pitch** a tent, you put it up. ■ **Pitch** is a black substance used to waterproof things like roofs and boats. ■ Someone's **sales pitch** is the things they say to try to persuade you to buy a product. ■ A **pitched battle** is a violent fight involving many people.

pitcher In the US, a **pitcher** is a jug. ■ A **pitcher** is a large container made of clay. Pitchers are usually round with a narrow neck and two ear-shaped handles. ■ In baseball, the **pitcher** is the person who throws the ball to the batter.

pitchfork A **pitchfork** is a large fork with a long handle and two prongs, used for lifting hay or grass.

piteous (**piteously**) You call something you see or hear **piteous** when it involves suffering and makes you feel pity. ...*piteous wailing.*

pitfall The **pitfalls** of doing something are the things which may go wrong.

pith The **pith** of an orange or other citrus fruit is the white substance between the peel and the inside of the fruit.

pithead At a coal mine, the **pithead** is all the above-ground buildings and machinery.

pithy (**pithily**) A **pithy** comment or piece of writing is short, direct, and memorable.

pitiable You call someone **pitiable** when they are in such a sad or weak state that you feel sorry for them. *Thirty years of civil war left Ethiopia in a pitiable condition.*

pitiful (**pitifully**) You call someone **pitiful** when they are in such a sad or weak state that you feel sorry for them. ...*a pitiful queue of prisoners.* ■ You use **pitiful** to describe things which are completely inadequate or of very poor quality. ...*pitiful wages.* ...*a pitiful batting performance.*

pitiless (**pitilessly**) If someone is **pitiless,** they show no pity or mercy.

piton (*pron:* **peet**-on) **Pitons** are metal spikes used by climbers. They are driven into rock crevices or ice and used to secure ropes.

pitta bread is flat ovals of slightly leavened bread, originally from the Middle East, with a hollow inside like a pocket, which can be filled with food.

pittance If you say someone is paid a **pittance,** you mean they are paid only a very small amount of money.

pitted See pit.

pituitary (**pituitaries**) The **pituitary** or **pituitary gland** is a gland attached to the base of the brain. It produces hormones which affect things such as growth and sexual development.

pity (**pities, pitying, pitied**) If you **pity** someone or feel **pity** for them, you feel sorry for them. If you **take pity** on someone, you help them because you are sorry for them. ■ You say '**It's a pity...**' when you are expressing regret about something.

pivot (**pivoting, pivoted**) A **pivot** is the pin or central point on which something balances or turns. You can say something is **pivoted** on a particular point. ■ The **pivot** in a situation or the thing it **pivots on** is the most important person or thing in it, which everything else is based on or arranged around. *The production pivots on Ron Cook's Odysseus.*

pivotal If a person or thing plays a **pivotal** role in something, they are extremely important to its success.

pixel A **pixel** is the smallest size of spot making up the image on a computer screen.

pixie In children's stories, **pixies** are little creatures who have pointed ears and wear pointed hats.

pizza A **pizza** is a flat round piece of dough covered with tomatoes, cheese, or other food, and then baked in an oven.

pizzazz (*or* **pzazz**) is an attractive combination of energy, style, vitality, and glamour. *It has all the pizzazz of a continental fiesta.*

pizzicato (*pron:* pit-see-**kah**-toe) If a stringed instrument is played **pizzicato,** it is played by plucking the strings with the fingers rather than using the bow.

placard A **placard** is a large notice carried in a demonstration or displayed in a public place.

placate (**placating, placated; placatory**) If you **placate** someone, you stop them feeling angry or resentful by doing or saying things which please them. The things you do or say can be described as **placatory.**

place A **place** is any point, building, town, country, etc. ■ Your **place** is the house or flat where you live. ■ A **place** is a seat or position which is available for someone to occupy. *I found a place right at the back.* ■ You call the position where something belongs its **place.** *Sean returned the album to its place on the shelf.* ■ If you have a **place** in a group or at a college, you are a member or are accepted as a student. ■ A person's **place** in a system or organization is their position or role in it. ■ Your **place** in a competition is your position at the end of it. ■ If you **place** something somewhere, you put it there.

■ If you **place** an order, you order something. ■ If you cannot **place** someone, you cannot remember exactly who they are, or where you met them before. ■ When something **takes place,** it happens. *The show is set to take place on April 3.*

placebo (*pron:* plas-**see**-bo) (**placebos**) A **placebo** is a harmless inactive substance given to a patient in place of a drug. Placebos are used when testing new drugs or when a patient is not really ill. The **placebo effect** is the fact that some patients' health improves after taking what they believe is an effective drug but which is in fact only a placebo.

placeman (**placemen**) If you call a public official a **placeman,** you mean he uses his position for personal benefit, or has been given it by people who knew they could rely on him for political support.

placement The **placement** of someone in a job, home, or school is the process of putting them there. ■ When someone who is being trained gets a **placement,** they get a temporary job intended to give them practical experience.

placenta (**placental**) The **placenta** is the mass of blood vessels and tissue inside the womb of a pregnant woman or animal, which the foetus is attached to. **Placental** means to do with the placenta. *...the placental barrier.*

place setting A **place setting** at a table is an arrangement of knives, forks, spoons, and glasses laid out for the use of one person.

placid A **placid** person is calm and does not easily get excited, angry, or upset. ■ A **placid** stretch of water is calm and still.

plagiarize (*or* **plagiarise**) (*pron:* **play**-jer-ize) (**plagiarizing, plagiarized; plagiarism**) If someone **plagiarizes** another person's idea or work, they use it or copy it, claiming it is their own. You say someone who does this is a **plagiarist** or is guilty of **plagiarism.**

plague (**plaguing, plagued**) A **plague** is an infectious disease which spreads quickly and kills large numbers of people. ■ If there is a **plague** of unpleasant things, a large number of them arrive or happen at the same time. *Last year there was a plague of robbery and housebreaking.* ■ If you are **plagued** by unpleasant things, they continually cause you a lot of trouble. *The city has been plagued by strikes for the past two years.*

plaice (*plural:* **plaice**) are a type of edible flatfish.

plaid (*usual pron:* **plad**) is material with a tartan or other check design on it. The design itself is also called **plaid.** *...a plaid flannel shirt.* **Plaids** are plaid clothes. ■ A **plaid** is a long piece of tartan material worn over the shoulder as part of Scottish Highland national dress.

Plaid Cymru (*pron:* **plide kum**-ri) is the Welsh Nationalist Party, set up in 1925 to try to achieve Welsh home rule. 'Plaid Cymru' is Welsh for 'Party of Wales'.

plain (**plainer, plainest; plainly, plainness**) A **plain** object, surface, or fabric is entirely in one colour and has no pattern, design, or writing on it. ■ If something is **plain,** it is simple in style and rather dull. *I was surprised at the plainness of the room.* ■ In knitting, **plain** is the most basic type of stitch. ■ A person is sometimes described as **plain** when they are not good-looking in any way. ■ You say something is **plain** when you think it is obvious and people cannot fail to understand or be aware of it. ■ **Plain speaking** is saying exactly what you think, even when it may not please other people. A **plain-speaking** person is someone who tends to speak like this. ■ **Plain** is used in front of some words for emphasis. *I think that's plain stupid.* ■ A **plain** is a large flat area of land with very few trees.

plain clothed (**plain clothes**) (*or* **plainclothed, plainclothes**) **Plain clothed** or **plain clothes** police officers are wearing ordinary clothes, so they will not be recognized as police.

plain flour is flour which does not make cakes and biscuits rise when they are baked.

plainsong is a type of medieval church music in which a group of people sing one tune together with no harmony and without accompaniment.

plaintiff In court, a **plaintiff** is someone who has brought a legal case against someone else.

plaintive (**plaintively**) A **plaintive** sound or voice is sad or mournful.

plait (*pron: plat*) (**plaiting, plaited**) If you **plait** three or more lengths of hair, rope, or other material together, you twist them over and under each other to make one thick length. **Plaits** are plaited lengths of hair.

plan (**planning, planned**) A **plan** is a method of making or achieving something which has been worked out in advance. *...the American peace plan.* If you **plan** something, you work out a method like this. ■ If you are **planning** to do something or are **planning on** doing it, you are intending to do it.

plane (**planing, planed**) A **plane** is an aircraft with wings and one or more engines. ■ In science and geometry, a **plane** is a real or imagined flat surface at any angle. ■ A **plane** is a flat-bottomed tool with a sharp blade in it, which is moved over wood to make it smaller or smoother. This is called **planing** the wood.

planet A **planet** is a large object in space which orbits around a star.

planetarium (*plural: planetariums or planetaria*) A **planetarium** is a building where lights are shone on a curved ceiling to represent the planets and the stars and to show how they appear to move.

planetary means to do with planets. *...planetary exploration.*

plane tree – **Plane trees** are large trees with broad leaves which often grow in towns.

plangent (*pron: plan-jent*) A **plangent** sound is deep, loud, resonant, and slightly mournful.

plank A **plank** is a long thin rectangular piece of wood. ■ The central **plank** of a policy is its main principle or aim.

plankton is a mass of microscopic animals and plants living in the surface layer of the sea.

planner – **Planners** are people whose job is to make decisions about what is going to be done in the future. *...town planners.*

planning permission is official permission from the local authority which is required before you can put up a new building or extend an existing one.

plant – **Plants** are living things which typically grow in the earth and have a stem, leaves, and roots. Flowers, vegetables, and trees are all plants. ■ When you **plant** seeds, garden plants, or young trees, you put them into the ground so they will grow there. You can also talk about **planting** land with crops. ■ If you **plant** something somewhere, you put it there firmly, deliberately, or secretly. *She admitted planting a bomb on the plane.* ■ If an organization **plants** an informer or spy somewhere, they send that person there so they can do something secretly. A person like this is sometimes called a **plant.** ■ A **plant** is a factory, or a place where power is generated. *...the Sellafield nuclear plant.* ■ **Plant** is large industrial or construction machinery.

plantain – **Plantains** are (a) large green banana-like fruit. (b) wild plants with broad leaves and a small head of tiny green flowers on a long stem.

plantation A **plantation** is (a) a large piece of land, especially in a tropical country, where a crop such as rubber, tea, or sugar is grown. (b) a large number of trees which have been planted together. *...conifer plantations.*

planter – **Planters** are people who own or manage plantations in tropical countries. ■ A **planter** is a decorative pot for house plants.

plaque A **plaque** is a flat piece of metal, wood, or stone, fixed to a wall in memory of a famous person or event. ■ **Plaque** is a sticky substance which forms on your teeth and can damage your teeth and gums. It consists of saliva, bacteria, and food.

plasma is the clear fluid part of blood which the blood cells are suspended in.

plaster (**plastering, plastered**) **Plaster** is a smooth paste usually made of sand, gypsum, and water, which dries and forms a hard layer. It is used to cover walls and ceilings, and to make sculptures. ■ If you **plaster** a wall or ceiling, you cover it with a layer of plaster. ■ If a surface has things like posters or writing all over it, you can say it is **plastered** with them. ■ A **plaster** is a strip of sticky material used for covering small cuts or sores on your body. ■ If you have your leg or arm **in plaster,** you have a cast made of plaster of Paris around it to protect a broken bone and allow it to mend.

plasterboard is thin rectangular sheets of cardboard held together with plaster, used for covering walls and ceilings as an alternative to plaster.

plasterer A **plasterer** is a person whose job is plastering walls and ceilings.

plaster of Paris is a type of quick-drying plaster made from white powder and water.

plasterwork is a covering of plaster on an inside wall or ceiling.

plastic is a strong, light, flexible material produced by a chemical process and used to make many objects. ■ If you pay for something using **plastic,** you pay by credit card.

plastic bullet – **Plastic bullets** are bullets made of plastic which are intended to disperse crowds in riots, rather than to kill people.

plastic explosive is an explosive substance used to make small bombs.

Plasticine is a soft coloured clay-like substance which children use for making small models. 'Plasticine' is a trademark.

plastic surgery (plastic surgeon) Plastic surgery is carrying out operations to repair or replace damaged skin and tissues, or to improve a person's appearance. A doctor who performs plastic surgery is called a **plastic surgeon.**

plate (**plating, plated**) A **plate** is a round or oval flat dish, used to hold food. ■ **Plate** is dishes, bowls, cups, and ornaments made of silver or gold. ■ **-plated** is used to say something made of metal is covered with a thin layer of another metal. *...gold-plated taps.* The process of adding the layer of metal is called **plating.** ■ A **plate** is a flat piece of metal, for example one on the wall of a building with someone's name on. ■ A **plate** is a full-page illustration or photograph in a book, usually printed on better quality paper than the rest of the book. ■ A dental **plate** is a piece of plastic shaped to fit inside a person's mouth, with a set of false teeth attached to it. ■ In geology, **plates** are large pieces of the earth's surface, which are believed to be drifting extremely slowly on the molten rock beneath. ■ If something is **handed to you on a plate,** you get it very easily, without having to work for it.

plateau (*plural:* **plateaus** *or* **plateaux**) A **plateau** is a flat area of high-lying land. ■ If something which has been increasing reaches a **plateau,** it stops increasing and stays at the same level.

plate glass is thick, highly polished glass made in large flat pieces.

platelet — **Platelets** are a type of blood cell involved in the formation of clots.

plate tectonics See **tectonic.**

platform A **platform** is a flat raised structure, especially one people stand on to give speeches. ■ When people talk about the **platform** of a political party, they mean the basic policies and principles it presents to the people during its election campaign. ■ If someone has a **platform,** they have an opportunity to get their views across to large numbers of people. *The law and order debate was a platform for the old style hardliners.* ■ A **platform** at a railway station is an area next to the rails, where you get on or off a train. ■ A **platform** is a structure built over the sea for people to work and live on while they are extracting oil or gas.

plating See **plate.**

platinum is a valuable silvery-white metal which is very resistant to heat and other chemicals. It is used for making jewellery, precision tools, and electrical equipment. ■ A **platinum** record is one which has sold over 300,000 or 600,000 copies in Britain, or over one million copies in the US.

platitude A **platitude** is a statement which is boring and almost meaningless because so many people have made it before.

platonic relationships and feelings do not involve sex.

platoon A **platoon** is a small group of soldiers commanded by a lieutenant.

platter A **platter** is a large flat plate for serving food.

platypus (**platypuses**) The **platypus** or **duck-billed platypus** is an egg-laying mammal which lives in Australia, partly in water. It has brown fur, webbed feet, and a snout like a duck's bill.

plaudit If you receive **plaudits** for something you do, you are praised for it.

plausible (**plausibly, plausibility**) If a statement or theory is **plausible,** it seems convincing and is likely to be true or correct. ■ If you say a person is **plausible,** you mean the things they say sound convincing, although they are probably not true.

play When children **play,** they do things they enjoy, such as taking part in games or doing things with toys. ■ When you **play** a sport or game, you take part in it. ■ If you **play** a musical instrument, you produce music from it. ■ If you **play** a record, you put it on the record-player and listen to it. Similarly, you can **play** a tape or CD. ■ A **play** is a piece of drama written to be performed in a theatre, or on radio or TV. ■ If an actor **plays** a character in a play or film, he or she performs that part. ■ **Play** is used to describe someone's behaviour when they try to create a certain impression, especially a false one. For example, if someone **plays** the innocent, they pretend to be innocent. ■ If you **play** a role in something, you are actively involved in it. *...a family which played a major role in Kashmir's politics.* ■ If someone **plays** a joke or trick on you, they deceive or surprise you in a way they think is funny, but which may annoy or inconvenience you. ■ If a situation is being **played out** somewhere, it is happening there. *...the battle now being played out in the foreign exchanges.* ■ If you **play on** people's fears, you deliberately use them to get what you want. ■ When something **comes into play,** it begins to be used or to have an effect. *Strength comes into play whenever you lift a child or push open a heavy door.* ■ If you are **playing for time,** you are delaying doing something, to give yourself a chance to think how best to deal with it. ■ A **play on words** is the same as a pun.

play-acting If you say someone is **play-acting,** you mean they are pretending to have attitudes or feelings they do not really have.

playboy A **playboy** is a rich man who lives a life of expensive pleasure.

player The **players** in a sport or game are the people taking part. ■ Musicians can be called **players.** For example, a tuba player is someone who plays the tuba. ■ Actors are sometimes called **players.** ■ The people, organizations, or countries involved in some type of activity can be called the **players** in it. *The three big players in the video game magazine sector are Emap Images, Future and Europress.*

playful (**playfully, playfulness**) **Playful** behaviour is lively and mischievous, without meaning any real harm. *He aimed a playful punch at Gutteridge.*

playground A **playground** is a piece of land where children can play, for example at a school or in a public park. ■ If you describe a place as a **playground** for a certain group of people, you mean they like to enjoy themselves there. *This is the Riviera, a holiday playground for the rich and famous.*

playgroup A **playgroup** is a kind of nursery where young children learn things by playing.

playing card See **card.**

playing field A **playing field** is a large area of grass where people play sports.

playmate A child's **playmate** is another child who often plays with him or her.

play-off A **play-off** is an extra game to decide the result of a competition when two competitors have finished on the same score.

playpen A **playpen** is a small structure designed for a baby or young child to play safely in.

playroom A **playroom** is a room in a house for children to play in.

playschool A **playschool** is the same as a playgroup.

plaything A **plaything** is a toy, or any object a child plays with. ■ You can say a person is someone's **plaything** when they use them for their enjoyment or advantage. *He was an unfaithful husband who treated women as playthings.*

playtime is what young children call the period of time between school lessons when they can play.

playwright A **playwright** is a person who writes plays.

plaza A **plaza** is an open square in a city.

plc A **plc** is a public limited company, meaning a company whose shares can be bought by the public. Companies like this must have 'plc' at the end of their official names. *...Barclays Bank plc.*

plea A **plea** is an intense emotional request. *...a plea for help.* ■ In court, a **plea** is the answer given by the person accused of a crime as to whether they are guilty or not guilty. *They entered a plea of not guilty.* ■ A **plea** is someone's excuse for doing something. *...his plea that he'd been provoked into killing his wife by her drunken, nagging behaviour.*

plead (pleading, pleaded) If you **plead** for something, you ask for it in an intense emotional way. *He pleaded for patience.* The things you say are called **pleadings.** ■ If you **plead** someone's case or cause, you speak out in their support or defence. ■ In court, when someone charged with a crime **pleads** guilty or not guilty, they make an official statement saying they are guilty or not guilty. ■ If you **plead** something as the reason for doing or not doing something, you give it as your excuse. *They avoided death sentences by pleading insanity.*

pleasant (pleasantly) You say something is **pleasant** when it is likeable, enjoyable, or pleasing.

pleasantry (pleasantries) Pleasantries are friendly remarks people make to be polite.

please (pleasing, pleased) You say **please** when you are asking for something or inviting someone to do something. *Can we have the bill please?... Please come in.* You say **'Yes, please'** when you are accepting an offer. ■ If you are **pleased** with something, it makes you happy or satisfied, because it is what you want. ■ **Please** is used to indicate people can do or have whatever they want. *People are free to come and go as they please.*

pleasurable (pleasurably) Pleasurable experiences or sensations are pleasant and enjoyable.

pleasure If something gives you **pleasure,** you get a feeling of happiness, satisfaction, or enjoyment from it. If something makes you feel like this, you can say it is a **pleasure.** *Mr Frankland's book is a pleasure to read.* ■ You use **pleasure** to talk about things people do for enjoyment, rather than because it is their work or duty. *...mixing business and pleasure. ...a pleasure trip.* ■ **Pleasure** boats are boats people take trips on for relaxation and enjoyment.

pleat (pleated) A **pleat** is a permanent fold in a piece of clothing, made by folding one part over the other and sewing across the top end of the fold. If a piece of clothing is **pleated,** it has folds in it like this. *...a pleated skirt.*

plebeian (*pron:* pleb-**ee**-an) In the past, people of a low social class and things associated with them were sometimes described as **plebeian.** *...a man with a cockney accent and a plebeian manner.*

plebiscite (*usual pron:* **pleb**-iss-it) A **plebiscite** is a vote by all the people of a country or region on a particular issue, for example whether a region should become an independent state.

plectrum A **plectrum** is a small thin piece of plastic or other material, used to pluck or strum a stringed instrument such as a guitar.

pledge (pledging, pledged) If you **pledge** to do something or make a **pledge,** you promise to do something. ■ If you **pledge** something valuable, you leave it with someone as a guarantee that you will repay money you have borrowed.

plenary (*usual pron:* **pleen**-na-ree) A **plenary** session or meeting is one attended by everyone who has the right to attend.

plenipotentiary (plenipotentiaries) A **plenipotentiary** is a person who has full power to act on behalf of their government, especially in a foreign country.

plentiful (plentifully) If something is **plentiful,** there is more than enough of it for people's wants or needs.

plenty If there is **plenty** of something, there is a lot of it, or more than enough to satisfy people's wants or needs.

plenum (*pron:* **plee**-num) A **plenum** is a meeting which all the members of a committee or assembly are expected to attend.

plethora (*pron:* **pleth**-or-a) If there is a **plethora** of things of a certain kind, there are far more than you need, want, or can cope with. *...the bewildering plethora of new products.*

pleurisy (*pron:* **ploor**-ris-see) is a painful inflammation of the lungs, often connected with pneumonia.

pliable If something is **pliable,** it bends easily without cracking or breaking. ■ A **pliable** person is easily influenced and controlled by other people.

pliant people are easily influenced and controlled by others.

pliers are a small tool with metal jaws for holding small objects and bending wire.

plight If you talk about someone's **plight,** you mean the difficult or distressing situation they are in. ...*the country's economic plight.*

plimsoll – **Plimsolls** are canvas shoes with flat rubber soles.

Plimsoll line – **Plimsoll lines** are a series of markings on the outside of a ship. When the appropriate Plimsoll line is level with the water, no more cargo should be taken on board.

plinth A **plinth** is a rectangular block of stone on which a statue or pillar stands.

plod (**plodding, plodded**) If someone **plods** somewhere, they walk slowly and heavily. A long tiring walk can be called a **plod.** ■ If you **plod on** with something, you keep doing it, although you are making very slow progress.

plodder If you call someone a **plodder,** you mean they work slowly and steadily at something.

plonk If you **plonk** something somewhere, you put it or drop it there heavily and carelessly. ■ **Plonk** is cheap wine.

plop (**plopping, plopped**) If something **plops** somewhere, it drops there with a soft gentle sound.

plot (**plotting, plotted; plotter**) If people **plot** together, they secretly plan to do something wrong or illegal. Their plan is called a **plot.** They are called **plotters.** ■ The **plot** of a novel, play, or film is the connected series of events which make up the story. ■ If you **plot** a line on a graph, you mark a series of points then join them up. ■ When someone **plots** the position or course of a plane or ship, they mark it on a map using instruments to obtain accurate information. ■ A **plot** of land is a small piece of it, especially one marked out for a special purpose. ...*a vegetable plot.*

plough (*Am:* **plow**) A **plough** is a large farming implement with sharp blades, used to turn the soil. ■ When fields are **ploughed,** the soil is turned over using a plough. ■ If a vehicle **ploughs into** something, it crashes into it, out of control. ■ If money is **ploughed into** something, a large amount is invested in it or spent on improving it. ■ If you **plough on** with something, you continue doing it even though it may be difficult or unwise to do so. ■ The **Plough** is a group of seven bright stars in the northern hemisphere which are thought to look like a plough.

ploughman (*Am:* **plowman**) (**ploughmen**) A **ploughman** is a man whose job is guiding a plough. ■ A **ploughman's lunch** is a simple midday meal often served in pubs. It consists of bread, cheese, pickle, and sometimes onion and salad.

ploughshare (*Am:* **plowshare**) A **ploughshare** is the blade on a plough.

plover (*rhymes with 'cover'*) **Plovers** are long-winged wading birds that live by the seashore or in marshland.

plow See **plough.**

ploy If you call something someone does a **ploy,** you mean it is a cunning way of getting something they want.

pluck (**plucky**) If you **pluck** something or **pluck at** it, you take it between your fingers and pull it sharply away from the place where it is. ■ If you **pluck** a

chicken or other dead bird, you pull its feathers out to prepare it for cooking. ■ If you are **plucked** from an unpleasant or dangerous situation, you are removed from it. *A Royal Navy helicopter plucked the boy from the water.* ■ If someone unknown is given an important job or role and quickly becomes famous, you can say they were **plucked** from their former position. ...*beautiful girl gets plucked from obscurity and makes it to the top.* ■ **Pluck** is courage. If you admire someone's courage or determination, you can call them **plucky.**

plug (**plugging, plugged**) The **plug** on a piece of electrical equipment is a small plastic object with two or three metal pins which fit into the holes of an electric socket. The socket itself is sometimes called a **plug.** ■ If you **plug in** a piece of electrical equipment, you connect it to the mains or to another piece of electrical equipment, by pushing its plug into a socket. ■ A **plug** is a thick circular piece of rubber or plastic used to block the hole in a bath or sink. ■ If you **plug** a hole, gap, or leak, you block or stop it with something. Something blocking a hole like this is called a **plug.** ■ **Plugs** are small hollow plastic cylinders designed to hold screws in masonry. ■ If someone **plugs** a new product like a film or book, or gives it a **plug,** they give it publicity by mentioning it or praising it, especially on TV or the radio. ■ If you **plug away** at something, you keep trying hard to make it succeed.

plum – **Plums** are small sweet yellow or reddish-purple fruit with a stone in the middle. ■ A **plum** job is one which a lot of people would like.

plumage A bird's **plumage** is its feathers.

plumb (**plumbing, plumber**) When someone **plumbs in** a device like a washing machine, they connect it to the water and drainage pipes in a building. ■ The **plumbing** in a building consists of its water and drainage pipes, baths, and toilets. The work of connecting and repairing things like these is also called **plumbing.** A person who does it is called a **plumber.** ■ A **plumb line** is a piece of string with a weight attached to the end, used to check that something like a wall is vertical. ■ If you say someone is **plumbing the depths,** you mean they have reached a very low level in their life or in something they are involved in.

plume A **plume** of smoke, dust, or water is a large quantity of it rising into the air in a column. ■ A **plume** is (a) a large soft feather. (b) a bunch of long thin strands of material, tied at one end and flowing loosely at the other. ■ If something is **plumed,** it is decorated with a plume or plumes.

plummet (**plummeting, plummeted**) If something **plummets** it falls swiftly.

plummy If you say someone has a **plummy** voice, you mean they speak in a rather old-fashioned upper-class English way.

plump You say a person or thing is **plump** when they are rather fat or rounded. ...*plump, juicy olives.* ■ If you **plump** a pillow or cushion, you shake it and pat it to get it back in a rounded shape. ■ If you **plump for** someone or something, you choose them, often after some hesitation.

plum pudding is an old name for a Christmas pudding.

plum tomato – Plum tomatoes are long egg-shaped tomatoes used mainly in cooking.

plunder (**plundering, plundered**) If someone **plunders** a place or **plunders** things from it, they steal things from it. Stealing things like this is called **plunder.** *...the systematic plunder of Egypt's ancient treasures.* The stolen property is also called **plunder.** ■ You say people **plunder** a place when they make heavy use of its resources.

plunge (**plunging, plunged**) If you **plunge** into something, you fall, rush, or throw yourself into it. ■ If you **plunge** a knife into something, you push it in quickly and violently. ■ If an amount or level **plunges** or there is a **plunge** in it, it decreases suddenly and rapidly. *...the plunge in interest rates.* ■ If you say someone or something **plunges** or is **plunged** into an unpleasant situation, you mean they are suddenly put into it. *Ethnic conflicts could plunge the country into chaos.* ■ If you **plunge** into an activity or take a **plunge** into it, you suddenly get involved in it. *...investors wondering whether to take the plunge into the stock market.* ■ A dress or blouse with a **plunging** neckline is cut in a very low V-shape at the front.

plunger A **plunger** is a device for unblocking sinks, consisting of a rubber cup on the end of a stick.

plural The **plural** form of a word is the form used when referring to more than one person or thing. ■ A **plural** society is the same as a pluralist society.

pluralist (**pluralistic, pluralism**) A **pluralist** or **pluralistic** society is one where people of different races, religions, and cultures exist together and are allowed to have their own practices and customs. Having a society like this is called **pluralism.**

plurality A **plurality** of things means several of them, rather than just one. *The alliance now represents a plurality of views.* ■ **Plurality** is a situation where more than one political group is allowed to exist.

plus (*plural:* **pluses** or **plusses**) You use **plus** to say one number is being added to another. *Two plus two equals four.* In maths, 'plus' is represented by the sign **+.** ■ You can use **plus** when you mention an additional item. *She lives with her husband and five children plus her brother in this one tiny room.* ■ You use **plus** after a number (a) to show you are referring to this number or any number greater than it. *For sums of £20,000-plus, the rate is 10.6% gross.* (b) to show you cannot be exact about an amount but it is greater than the number you have mentioned. *...seventy thousand-plus spectators.* ■ A **plus** is an advantage or benefit.

plus-fours are short baggy trousers fastened below the knees which men used to wear when playing golf.

plush If you describe something as **plush,** you mean it is smart and luxurious. ■ **Plush** fabrics have a thick soft texture similar to velvet.

plutocrat If you describe someone as a **plutocrat,** you mean they are powerful only because they are very rich.

plutonium is a radioactive element used in nuclear weapons and to generate nuclear power.

ply (**plies, plying, plied**) If someone **plies** you with food or drink, they keep offering you more of it. ■ If you **ply** a trade, you do a particular kind of work regularly as your job, especially one which involves selling goods or services. ■ If a ship, aircraft, or road vehicle **plies** a route, it makes regular journeys along it. ■ **Ply** is the thickness of wool or thread, measured by the number of strands it is made from. *...a two-ply cashmere sweater.*

plywood is board made from several thin layers of wood stuck together.

PM The **PM** is the Prime Minister.

p.m. is used when stating a time between noon and midnight. **p.m.** stands for 'post meridiem', which is Latin for 'after noon'.

PMS See premenstrual syndrome.

PMT See premenstrual tension.

pneumatic (*pron:* new-**mat**-ik) (**pneumatically**) If something is **pneumatic,** it is operated by or filled with compressed air.

pneumonia (*pron:* new-**moan**-ee-ah) is a serious disease which affects the lungs.

poach (**poaches, poaching, poached; poacher**) If someone **poaches** animals, birds, or fish, they catch or shoot them illegally. A person who does this is called a **poacher.** ■ If an organization **poaches** members or customers from another organization, it secretly or dishonestly persuades them to join it or become its customer instead. ■ If you **poach** food, you cook it gently in hot liquid.

PO Box is used before a number as a kind of address. The Post Office keeps letters addressed to a PO Box until they are collected by the person who has paid for the service.

pocked means the same as 'pockmarked'.

pocket (**pocketing, pocketed**) A **pocket** is a small bag or pouch which forms part of a piece of clothing. ■ If you **pocket** something, you put it in your pocket. ■ **Pocket** is used to describe something which is small enough to fit in your pocket, especially a smaller version of a large item. *...a pocket bible.* ■ If someone in possession of something valuable **pockets** it, they take it for themselves, even though it does not belong to them. ■ If you are **out of pocket,** you have less money than you should have. ■ If you say someone is **in** another person's **pocket,** you mean they are willing to do whatever the other person tells them, for example because they are weak or are being paid by the other person. ■ If someone **picks your pocket,** they steal something from your pocket. ■ A **pocket** of something is a small area of it.

pocketbook In the US, a **pocketbook** is a small handbag or wallet.

pocket knife A **pocket-knife** is the same as a pen-knife.

pocket money is a small amount of money which someone is given regularly to spend as they like.

pockmarked If a surface is **pockmarked,** it is covered with shallow holes and dents.

pod The **pods** of plants like peas and beans are their long narrow seed containers.

podgy people are rather short and fat.

podiatry (*pron:* pod-**eye**-it-tree) (**podiatrist**) **Podiatry** is the professional care and treatment of people's feet.

podium A **podium** is a small platform on which someone stands to give a lecture, conduct an orchestra, or receive an award.

poem A **poem** is a piece of writing in which the words are chosen mainly for their sound and are carefully arranged, often in short lines which rhyme.

poesy is an old-fashioned word for poetry or the art of writing poetry.

poet A **poet** is a person who writes poetry.

poetess (**poetesses**) You can refer to a female poet as a **poetess**, although most prefer to be called 'poets'.

poetic (**poetical, poetically**) **Poetic** and **poetical** means relating to poetry. ■ If you describe something like a film or novel as **poetic** or **poetical,** you mean it is beautiful and expressive. ■ If you say something bad which happens to someone is **poetic justice,** you mean it is exactly what they deserve, because of the things they have done.

poet laureate The **poet laureate** is the officially appointed poet who is given a lifetime post as a member of the Royal Household and often writes poems for special national occasions.

poetry is poems considered as a form of literature. ■ If you talk about the **poetry** of something, you mean the things about it which are beautiful and evoke powerful feelings.

po-faced If you think someone is being unnecessarily serious about something, you can describe them as **po-faced.**

pogo stick A **pogo stick** is a pole with a step for your feet and a spring at the bottom. You hold the top, stand on the step, and bounce up and down for fun.

pogrom A **pogrom** is an organized official persecution for racial or religious reasons, which usually leads to the mass killing of a group of people.

poignant (**poignancy**) If something is **poignant,** it affects you with a deep feeling of sadness. You can talk about the **poignancy** of something like this.

point A **point** is a fact or opinion expressed by someone. ■ A **point** is a detail, aspect, or quality. *...the finer points of photography.* ■ The **point** of something is its purpose or importance. *What is the point of being bitter?* ■ If what someone says is **to the point,** it is brief and relevant. If what they say is **beside the point,** it is not relevant. ■ If you **make a point of** doing something, you do it in a deliberate or obvious way. ■ A **point** is a particular position or time. *The pain originated from a point in his right arm... It was at that point pandemonium broke out.* ■ If you are **on the point of** doing something, you are just about to do it. ■ If you **point** at something, you stick out your finger to show where it is. ■ If something **points** in a particular direction, it faces that way. ■ If you **point** something **out,** you draw attention to it. ■ If you use something as a

point of reference, you use it as a standard to compare other things with. ■ The **point** of something like a pin or a knife is its thin sharp end. ■ The **decimal point** in a number is the dot which separates the whole number from the fraction. ■ In competitions, **points** are the units in which competitors' scores are measured. ■ The **points** of a compass are the 32 directions marked on it. ■ On a railway line, the **points** are the levers and rails which enable a train to move from one track to another. ■ A **power point** is an electric socket. ■ When builders **point** a wall, they put mortar into the gaps between the bricks. The mortar between the bricks is called **pointing.**

point-blank If someone is shot **point-blank** or at **point-blank range,** the gun is touching them or extremely close to them when it is fired. ■ If someone refuses **point-blank** to do something, they firmly and absolutely refuse to do it.

pointed (**pointedly**) A **pointed** object has a point at one end. ■ A **pointed** comment or **pointed** behaviour expresses disapproval or criticism in an obvious way. *They pointedly refused to support him.*

pointer You say something is a **pointer** to another thing when it helps you understand the other thing, or indicates how it will develop. *The elections should be a pointer to the public mood.* ■ A **pointer** is a long thin stick used to point at something like a chart on a wall. ■ The **pointer** on a measuring instrument is the thin piece of metal which points to the numbers. ■ **Pointers** are a type of large dog.

pointless (**pointlessly, pointlessness**) If you say something is **pointless,** you mean it has no sense or purpose. *Violence is always pointless.*

point of order (**points of order**) In a formal debate, a **point of order** is an objection someone makes because the rules governing procedures have been broken.

point of view (**points of view**) Your **point of view** is your opinion about something or your attitude towards it. ■ A **point of view** is one aspect of something. *From a financial point of view the day was a great success.*

point-to-point A **point-to-point** is a steeplechase for amateur jockeys riding horses regularly used for hunting.

pointy means the same as 'pointed'.

poise If someone has **poise,** they are calm and dignified. ■ **Poise** is graceful and controlled posture and movement. *Ballet classes are important for poise and grace.*

poised If you are **poised** to do something, you are ready to do it at any moment. ■ If a situation is **poised,** it is delicately balanced. *The economy is poised on a knife-edge.* ■ If someone is **poised,** they are calm and dignified.

poison (**poisoning, poisoned; poisoner**) **Poison** is a substance which kills people or animals or makes them ill if they swallow or absorb it. If someone is **poisoned,** they are killed or made ill by poison. A person who kills someone with poison is called a **poisoner.** ■ If food, drink, or a weapon is **poisoned,** it has had poison added to it so it can be used to kill someone. ■ If water, land, or air is **poisoned,** it has been damaged by harmful substances. ■ If something **poisons** a situation or relationship, it spoils it. ■ See also **food poisoning, blood poisoning.**

poisonous substances make you ill or kill you if you swallow or absorb them. ■ A **poisonous** animal injects poison with its bite or sting. ■ If something spoils a situation or relationship by making people quarrel or disagree, you can describe it as **poisonous.** ...*poisonous comments.*

poison-pen letter A **poison-pen letter** is an anonymous letter containing malicious remarks and sent to upset someone or cause trouble.

poke (poking, poked) If you **poke** someone or something, you push them sharply with your finger or a pointed object. If you **poke** one thing into another, you push the first thing into the second. ■ If something **pokes out of** or **through** something else, you can see part of it appearing from behind or underneath the other thing. ■ If you **poke around** for something, you search for it, usually by moving lots of objects around. ■ **poke fun at:** see **fun‘.**

poker is a card game usually played for money. ■ A **poker** is a metal stick used to move coal or wood on a fire so it burns better.

poker-faced If someone is **poker-faced,** their face shows no emotion.

poky A **poky** house or room is uncomfortably small.

polar The **polar** regions are the areas around the North and South Poles. ...*a polar expedition.*

polar bear The **polar bear** is a large white bear found near the North Pole.

polarise See **polarize.**

polarity (polarities) If there is a **polarity** between two people or things, they are completely different. ...*the polarities of good and evil.*

polarize (or **polarise**) **(polarizing, polarized; polarization)** If people or things are **polarized,** two separate groups are formed with opposite positions or opinions. ...*the country's growing political polarization.*

Polaroid A **Polaroid camera** is a small camera which can take, develop, and print a photo in a few seconds. A **Polaroid** is a photo taken with a Polaroid camera. 'Polaroid' is a trademark.

pole A **pole** is a long rounded piece of wood or metal, used especially for supporting things. ■ The earth's **poles** are the two opposite ends of its axis. ■ A magnet's **poles** are its two ends, where opposite magnetic forces are concentrated. ■ The **poles** of a range of qualities, opinions, or beliefs are its opposite extremes. ...*opposite poles of the political spectrum.* If you say two people are **poles apart,** you mean they have completely different opinions.

poleaxe (poleaxing, poleaxed) If someone is **pole-axed** (a) they are knocked unconscious. (b) they are so surprised or shocked they do not know what to say or do.

polecat – **Polecats** are a type of large weasel with an unpleasant smell.

polemic (*pron:* pole-**lem**-ik) **(polemical, polemicist)** A **polemic** is a strongly worded criticism or defence of a belief. **Polemical** is used to describe written or

spoken statements like this. A **polemicist** (*pron:* pole-**lem**-iss-ist) is someone skilled at arguing passionately for or against a belief.

pole position When a racing car is in **pole position,** it is in front of the other cars at the start of a race.

pole vault (pole vaulter) The **pole vault** is an athletics event in which contestants use a long flexible pole to help them jump over a high bar.

police (policing, policed) The **police** are the official organization responsible for enforcing the law. ■ If police or military forces **police** an area or event, they make sure law and order is preserved in that area or at that event. **Policing** is the system and methods used to keep law and order in a place. ■ If a system is **policed,** someone makes sure its laws or rules are not broken. *Such deals are policed by the country's national merger authorities.* ■ See also **secret police.**

police constable A **police constable** is a police officer of the lowest rank. 'Police Constable' is often shortened to 'PC'.

police force A **police force** is the police organization in a particular country or area.

policeman (policewoman) A **policeman** or **policewoman** is a member of the police force.

police officer A **police officer** is a policeman or policewoman.

police state You call a country a **police state** when the government controls people's freedom by means of the police, especially secret police.

police station A **police station** is a building where local police are stationed.

policewoman See **policeman.**

policing See **police.**

policy (policies) A **policy** is a set of ideas or plans used as a basis for making decisions, especially in politics, economics, or business. In politics, the process of deciding new policies is called **policy-making.** ■ An insurance **policy** is a document showing the agreement you have made with an insurance company. Someone who has an insurance policy is called a **policyholder.**

polio or **poliomyelitis** is an infectious disease which sometimes causes paralysis.

polish (polishes, polishing, polished) Polish is a substance you put on an object to clean it and make it shine. ■ If you **polish** something, you put polish on it or rub it with a cloth, to clean it and make it shine. ■ If you call a performance **polished,** you mean it is of a high standard. ■ If you say a person is **polished,** you mean they are confident and sophisticated. ■ If you **polish** your technique or image, you work on improving it. ■ If you **polish off** some food or drink, you eat or drink all of it.

Politburo In a communist country or party, the **Politburo** is the chief committee, which makes policies and decisions.

polite (politely, politeness) A **polite** person has good manners and shows consideration for others. ■ If you talk about **polite society** or **polite company,** you mean people who consider themselves to be socially superior and to set standards of behaviour for everyone else.

politic If you decide it is **politic** to do something, you decide it is the most sensible thing to do in the circumstances.

political (**politically**) **Political** means to do with politics. ...*political parties*.

political asylum When someone seeks **political asylum** in a country, they ask the government for permission to live there, because they have been forced to leave their own country for political reasons.

politically correct (**political correctness**) If you say someone or something is **politically correct** or talk about their **political correctness**, you mean they reflect the attitudes and language typical of people who hold left-wing or liberal views. 'Politically correct' and 'political correctness' are often shortened to 'PC'.

political prisoner A **political prisoner** is someone who has been imprisoned for criticizing their own government.

political science (**political scientist**) **Political science** is the study of politics.

politician A **politician** is someone whose job is in politics, especially an MP.

politicize (*or* **politicise**) (**politicizing, politicized; politicization**) If you **politicize** someone or something, you make them more interested in politics or more involved with politics.

politicking If you describe someone's political activity as **politicking,** you think they are engaged in it to gain votes or personal advantage for themselves.

politico (**politicos**) Politicians are sometimes called **politicos.**

politico- is added to words to describe something which involves politics and another thing. ...*another politico-financial scandal.*

politics is all the things politicians do to try to achieve or hold onto power or make sure it is used in a certain way. You can also call things people do to achieve or hold onto power in other situations **politics.** ...*office politics.* ■ **Politics** is the study of the ways political power is achieved and how countries are governed. ■ Your **politics** are your beliefs about how a country should be governed.

polity (**polities**) A **polity** is a system of government, or a country with a particular political system.

polka The **polka** is a fast lively dance in which couples dance together in circles around a room.

polka dot A **polka dot** pattern consists of regularly-spaced spots on a plain background.

poll (*pron:* **pole**) A **poll** is the same as an opinion poll. If a group of people are **polled,** they are asked their opinions about something as part of an opinion poll. See also **exit poll, straw poll.** ■ An election is often called **the polls. Polling** is voting in an election. *The capital was reported calm during the polling.* ■ If a candidate **polls** a certain number of votes, they get that number.

pollen is a fine yellow powder produced by flowers. Each grain contains a male reproductive cell which can fertilize other flowers of the same species.

pollinate (**pollinating, pollinated; pollination**) When a plant is **pollinated,** it is fertilized with pollen.

polling See **poll.**

polling booth A **polling booth** is a small cubicle at a polling station where you vote in private.

polling day is the day when people vote in an election.

polling station A **polling station** is a place like a school or church hall where people go to vote in an election.

pollster – **Pollsters** are people or organizations that carry out opinion polls and try to make predictions from their results.

poll tax A **poll tax** is a tax which every adult in a country must pay. ■ The **Poll Tax** was the Community Charge.

pollute (**polluting, polluted; pollution, pollutant, polluter**) If a substance **pollutes** the air, water, or the environment, it makes it dirty and dangerous to use or live in. Substances that do this are called **pollutants.** When they are present, you say there is **pollution.** A **polluter** is a company which causes pollution.

polo is a game played on horseback by two teams of players who try to score goals by hitting a ball with long-handled wooden hammers.

polo-necked (**polo-neck**) A **polo-necked** sweater has a thick fold of material at the top covering most of your neck. Sweaters like these are sometimes called **polo-necks.**

polo shirt A **polo shirt** is a T-shirt with a collar.

poltergeist (*pron:* **pol**-ter-guyst) A **poltergeist** is an invisible force believed to move objects around. Poltergeists are often thought of as a type of ghost.

poly (**polys**) A **poly** was the same as a polytechnic.

polyandry is a custom in some places in which a woman can be married to more than one man at the same time. See also **polygamy, polygyny.**

polychrome (**polychromatic**) If something is **polychrome** or **polychromatic,** it has many colours.

polyester is a man-made fibre which is often blended with natural fibres to make clothes and bedclothes.

polyethylene is another name for polythene, especially in the US.

polygamy (*pron:* pol-**lig**-gam-ee) (**polygamous**) **Polygamy** is a custom in some places in which people can be married to more than one person at the same time, especially the custom of a man having more than one wife. **Polygamous** means having or involving this custom. ...*a polygamous country.* See also **polyandry, polygyny.**

polyglot A **polyglot** is a person who speaks several different languages. You say a group of people are **polyglot** when they speak several different languages between them. ...*a polyglot UN force.*

polygon A **polygon** is any two-dimensional shape with three or more straight sides, for example a triangle or a pentagon.

polygraph A **polygraph** or **polygraph test** is a test in which someone asks you questions and a machine records any changes in your blood pressure, temperature, or breathing to find out if you are telling the truth.

polygyny (*pron:* pol-**lidj**-in-ee) is a custom in some places in which a man can have more than one wife at the same time. See also **polyandry, polygamy.**

polymath A **polymath** is someone who knows a lot about many different subjects.

polymer A **polymer** is a type of chemical compound consisting of large molecules made up of smaller ones.

polyp (*pron:* pol-lip) A **polyp** is a tiny sea creature with a hollow cylindrical body and tentacles around its mouth. ■ **Polyps** are small unhealthy growths on a surface inside the body.

polyphony (**polyphonic**) **Polyphony** (*pron:* pol-**lif**-fon-nee) is the singing or playing of several different melodies at the same time in a piece of music. You call music like this **polyphonic** (*pron:* pol-lee-**fon**-nik).

polypropylene is a tough heavy-duty plastic used to make things like bottles and pipes.

polystyrene is a light plastic substance, used as packaging or insulating material.

polytechnic Some universities, especially ones where you can study for vocational qualifications, used to be called **polytechnics.**

polythene is a type of plastic which is made into thin sheets or bags.

polyunsaturated fats are fats thought to be healthier than saturated fats because they are less likely to be converted into cholesterol in the body. They are mostly found in vegetable and fish oils.

polyurethane is a plastic material used, for example, to make water-resistant paints and varnishes.

Pom Australians sometimes call English people **Poms.**

pomegranate – **Pomegranates** are round apple-sized fruit with thick gold-red skins. They contain a lot of small seeds with juicy flesh around them.

pommel The **pommel** of a sword is the knob on the end of the handle. ■ The **pommel** of a saddle is the part which rises up at the front.

pomp or **pomp and circumstance** is the use of ceremony, fine clothes, and decorations on special or official occasions.

pom-pom A **pom-pom** is a ball of woollen threads used as a decoration, for example on a hat.

pompous (**pompously, pomposity**) If you say someone is **pompous** or talk about their **pomposity,** you mean they are too serious and self-important.

poncho (**ponchos**) A **poncho** is a piece of clothing consisting of a long piece of material with a hole cut in the middle to put your head through.

pond A **pond** is a small, usually man-made, area of water. ■ In the US, a **pond** is a lake.

ponder (**pondering, pondered**) If you **ponder** something, you think about it carefully.

ponderous (**ponderously**) If you say someone or something is **ponderous,** you mean they move or operate slowly and with difficulty, because of their size or weight. ■ If you say a speech or piece of writing is **ponderous,** you mean it uses long words and sentences to express something fairly simple.

pong A **pong** is an unpleasant smell.

pontiff The **pontiff** is the Pope.

pontificate (**pontificating, pontificated**) You say someone **pontificates** when they state their opinions in a pompous way.

pontoon A **pontoon** is a floating platform, often used to support a bridge. ■ **Pontoon** is a card game in which players try to collect a set of cards which add up to twenty-one. Pontoon is also called **blackjack** or **vingt-et-un.**

pony (**ponies**) A **pony** is a type of small horse.

ponytail (*or* pony-tail) (**ponytailed**) If someone has their hair in a **ponytail,** it is tied at the back of their head. *...a pony-tailed man.*

pony trekking is the pastime of riding ponies cross-country.

pooch (**pooches**) Dogs are sometimes called **pooches.**

poodle – **Poodles** are a type of dog with thick curly hair.

pooh-pooh If you **pooh-pooh** an idea, you show contempt for it.

pool (**pooling, pooled**) A **pool** is a small area of still water. ■ A **pool** of liquid is a puddle of it. *...a pool of blood.* ■ A swimming pool is often just called a **pool.** ■ A **pool** of light is a small area of it. ■ If a group of people **pool** their money, knowledge, or equipment, they allow it to be used or shared by everyone in the group. ■ A **pool** of people, money, or things is a supply of them used or shared by several people. ■ If you do the football **pools,** you take part in a gambling competition in which people try to win money by guessing the results of several football matches. ■ **Pool** is a game similar to snooker but played on a smaller table.

poolside means situated or happening next to a swimming pool. *...poolside frolics.*

poop The **poop** of an old-fashioned sailing ship was the raised deck at the back.

pooper-scooper A **pooper-scooper** or **poop-scoop** is a small device like a shovel used by dog owners to pick up their dogs' excrement from public places.

poor (**poorer, poorest; poorly**) If you are **poor,** you have very little money and few possessions. The **poor** are poor people. ■ If a place is **poor** in something, it has very little of it. *The south of the country was desperately poor in natural resources.* ■ **Poor** is used to describe things which are of low standard or quality. *He suffered from poor eyesight.* ■ If you are **poorly,** you are ill. ■ People use **poor** to show sympathy for someone. *The poor chap died at the age of twenty five.*

poorhouse A **poorhouse** was an institution where very poor people were housed if they could not support themselves.

poorly See **poor.**

pop (**popping, popped**) **Pop** is modern music written mainly for young people. ■ If something **pops** or goes **pop,** it makes a sound like a cork being pulled out of a bottle. ■ If you say someone's eyes are **popping,** you mean they are very surprised or excited. ■ If you **pop** something somewhere, you put it there. ■ If you **pop** somewhere, you go there for a short time. ■ If someone or something **pops** out from a place where they could not be seen, they suddenly appear. *A woman's head popped up from behind the hedge.* ■ Flavoured fizzy drinks are sometimes called **pop.**

pop art is a style of modern art which became well-known in the 1960s. It uses bright colours, copies styles of drawing from advertising and comics, and features everyday objects like Coca-Cola bottles.

popcorn is the grains of a type of maize, which have been heated until they have burst and become large and light.

Pope The **Pope** is the head of the Roman Catholic Church.

poplar The **poplar** is a tall thin tree with triangular leaves.

poppadom (*or* **poppadum**) **Poppadoms** are large thin crisp pieces of Indian bread fried in oil.

poppy (**poppies**) The **poppy** is a flower with large delicate petals, usually red, and a hairy stem. ■ A **poppy** is an artificial red poppy worn in Britain on Remembrance Day in memory of those who died in the two World Wars.

poppycock If you say something is **poppycock,** you mean it is nonsense.

populace The **populace** of a town or country are the people who live there.

popular (**popularly, popularity**) If someone or something is **popular,** they are liked or enjoyed by many people. ...*the growing popularity of classical music.* ■ **Popular** is used to describe ideas or attitudes held by large numbers of people. ...*popular support for independence.* ■ **Popularly** is used to show (a) that an idea is believed by many people, although it may not be true. *The Great Wall of China is longer than popularly thought.* (b) that a name is used by many people, although it is not the official one. *Popularly, dyslexia is known as 'word blindness'.* ■ Newspapers aimed at the widest possible audience are sometimes called the **popular** press.

popularize (*or* **popularise**) (**popularizing, popularized; popularization**) If something is **popularized,** a lot of people become interested in it and start to enjoy it.

populate (**populating, populated**) The people or animals that **populate** an area live there.

population The **population** of a place is (a) the people living there. ...*the local population.* (b) the number of people living there. ...*a country with a population of 1.2 billion.* ■ You use **population** to talk about one section of the people or animals living in a place. ...*the country's civilian population.*

populist (**populism**) A **populist** is a politician who claims to represent the interests of ordinary people and who tries to get their support, often by exploiting their fears and prejudices. This kind of politics is called **populism.**

populous countries or areas have a lot of people living in them.

pop-up books have pictures which stand up when the book is opened.

porcelain is (a) delicate, high quality china used especially for making tea services and ornaments. (b) things made of porcelain.

porch (**porches**) A **porch** is a sheltered area at the entrance to a building. ■ In the US, a veranda is called a **porch.**

porcine (*pron:* **por**-seen) is used to talk about things to do with pigs, or which remind you of a pig.

porcupine The **porcupine** is a large rodent with long spines on its back.

pore (**poring, pored**) **Pores** are (a) very small holes in your skin or the surface of a plant, which allow moisture to pass through. (b) tiny gaps or cracks in rocks and soil. ■ If you **pore over** a piece of writing, you study it carefully.

pork is meat from a pig.

porker A **porker** is a pig raised or fattened for its meat.

porky (**porkies**) If you call someone **porky,** you mean they are fat. ■ If you say someone is telling a **porky,** you mean they are telling a lie.

porn is the same as 'pornography'.

porno means the same as 'pornographic'. ...*porno films.*

pornography (**pornographic; pornographer**) **Pornography** is magazines, pictures, or films designed to cause sexual excitement by showing naked people and sexual acts. You say things like these are **pornographic.** Someone who produces pornographic material is called a **pornographer.**

porous (**porosity**) If something is **porous,** it has many small holes in it, which air and water can pass through. You talk about the **porosity** of something like this.

porpoise – **Porpoises** are sea mammals with short rounded snouts, related to dolphins.

porridge is a thick sticky food made from oats cooked in milk or water.

port A **port** is (a) a town which has a harbour or docks. (b) a harbour area where ships load and unload. ■ The **port** side of a ship is the left side when you are facing the front. ■ **Port** is a type of sweet fortified red wine.

portable (**portability**) A **portable** machine or device is designed to be easily carried.

portal A **portal** is a large impressive entrance.

portcullis (**portcullises**) A **portcullis** is a strong metal gate above an entrance to a castle, which was lowered to keep out enemies.

portend (**portent**) If something **portends** something else or is a **portent** of it, it shows it is likely to happen. *The civil war in Yugoslavia could be a portent of what's to come in the rest of the region.*

portentous (*pron:* por-**tent**-uss) (**portentously, portentousness**) If something is **portentous,** it shows something is about to happen. ■ You say someone is **portentous** when they try to impress people by behaving in a serious and self-important way.

porter A **porter** is (a) someone whose job is to carry things. (b) the person in charge of the entrance of a building like a hotel.

portfolio (**portfolios**) A cabinet minister's **portfolio** is the area of government he or she has responsibility for. ■ You call the various shares and other investments owned by an investor their **portfolio.** ■ A **portfolio** is a thin flat case for carrying large papers or drawings. ■ An artist's **portfolio** is a selection of his or her work, used, for example, to show a prospective employer.

porthole A **porthole** is a small round window in the side of a ship or aircraft.

portico (**porticoes** or **porticos**) A **portico** is a large covered area at the entrance to a building, with pillars supporting its roof.

portion (**portioning, portioned**) A **portion** of something is a part of it. *The contractor removed a portion of the roof.* ■ A **portion** of food is the amount given to one person at a meal. *...a portion of chips.* ■ If you **portion** something **out,** you give a share of it to each person in a group.

portly (**portlier, portliest**) A **portly** person is quite fat.

portmanteau (*plural:* **portmanteaux**) (*both pron:* port-man-toe) A **portmanteau** is a large old-fashioned travelling case which opens into two compartments. ■ **Portmanteau** is used to describe something which combines several things or features.

portrait (**portraitist**) A **portrait** is a painting, drawing, or photograph of a person, often showing only their face. An artist who specializes in portraits is called a **portraitist.** See also **self-portrait.** ■ You can call a film or piece of writing a **portrait** when it shows what someone or something is like. *...a fascinating portrait of the East End underworld.*

portraiture is the art of painting or drawing portraits.

portray (**portrayal**) When an actor or actress **portrays** someone, he or she plays that person in a film or play. You talk about their **portrayal** of the person. ■ If a writer **portrays** a person or thing, he or she shows what they are like. ■ If you **portray** someone or something in a particular way, you make them appear to be a certain kind of person or thing. *The government has portrayed him as a traitor.*

Portuguese is used to talk about people and things in or from Portugal. *...the Portuguese president.* ■ A **Portuguese** is someone who comes from Portugal. ■ **Portuguese** is the main language spoken in Portugal, and also in Brazil.

pose (**posing, posed; poseur**) If something **poses** a problem, it causes that problem. ■ If you **pose** a question, you ask it. ■ If you **pose** as someone, you pretend to be them, to deceive people. ■ If you call someone's behaviour a **pose,** you mean they are trying to create an impression which is different from their real character. You call someone who behaves like this a **poseur.** ■ If you **pose** for a photograph or painting, you stay in one position, so someone can photograph or paint you. Your position is called a **pose.**

poser A **poser** is a puzzling question or problem.

poseur See **pose.**

posh You say something is **posh** when it is smart, fashionable, and expensive. *...a posh restaurant.*

■ You say people are **posh** when they come from a high social class.

posit (*pron:* pozz-it) (**positing, posited**) If you **posit** something, you put it forward as a possible way of dealing with a situation. *The IMF are positing a new austerity regime.*

position (**positioning, positioned; positional**) The **position** of a person or thing is the place where they are in relation to other things. ■ If you **position** something somewhere or put it **in position,** you put it where it is meant to be. ■ If you are in a particular **position,** you are sitting, standing, or lying in a particular way. *She was forced to crouch in a sitting position.* ■ Your **position** is the situation you are in at a particular time. *Norway is in a difficult position over Lithuania.* ■ Your **position** is your job. *...middle to upper management positions.* ■ Your **position** is your status. *...the once privileged position of the Russians.* ■ Your **position** on an issue is your attitude towards it. *The United States has changed its position on moves to protect the Antarctic.*

positive (**positively**) **Positive** is used to describe something which concentrates on the good aspects of something. *...positive thinking. ...positive images of old age.* ■ If you give a **positive** response, you say 'yes', or something which means yes. ■ If you take **positive** action, you do something which significantly affects a situation. ■ If you are **positive** about something, you are completely sure about it. ■ If a medical or scientific test is **positive,** it shows something like a disease or substance is present. *Three competitors have been positively tested for banned drugs.* ■ **Positive** is used to say something is true, where you might expect the opposite. *His youth may be a positive advantage.* ■ A **positive** number is greater than zero. ■ A **positive** electric charge is one of two opposite kinds of charge, the other being a negative charge. ■ **HIV positive:** see **HIV.**

positive discrimination is the policy of deliberately treating one group of people better than others, because it is thought they are often treated unfairly.

positron A **positron** is a tiny particle of matter. It is like an electron, but has a positive electrical charge.

posse (*pron:* poss-ee) In the American West, a **posse** was a group of men brought together by a sheriff to help chase and capture a criminal. ■ Any group of people arriving somewhere to do something together can be called a **posse.** *...a posse of reporters.*

possess (**possesses, possessing, possessed; possession**) If you **possess** something or it is in your **possession,** you have it or own it. Your **possessions** are things you have or own. ■ If someone is **possessed,** their mind and body are supposed to be controlled by an evil spirit or the devil. ■ If you are **possessed** by something, you are very interested in it and keep thinking about it. *The young Russell was so possessed by theories that he had little time for anything else.* ■ If you ask **what possessed** someone to do something, you are expressing surprise because they have done something silly or dangerous.

possessive (possessiveness) You say someone is **possessive** when (a) they want all of another person's love and attention. (b) they do not like other people using their things. ■ **Possessive adjectives** or **determiners** are words like 'my' and 'your'. **Possessive pronouns** are words like 'mine' and 'yours'.

possessor The **possessor** of something is the person who has it or owns it.

possible (possibly; possibility, possibilities) If it is **possible** to do something, it can be done. ■ A **possibility** is something you are able to do and might do. *One possibility being considered is to cut the defence budget.* ■ **Possible** is used to say something might be true or correct, or might happen. *The army was prepared for all possible developments.* *...a difficult and possibly dangerous time.* You can call something like this a **possibility.** *...a contract to cover all possibilities.* ■ A **possible** is one of several people or things that could be chosen for something. *He had been on the Nobel committee's list of possibles.* ■ If you say something has **possibilities,** you mean it could be developed into something useful or profitable in the future.

possum In Australia and New Zealand, a **possum** is a long-tailed furry animal which lives in trees and carries its young in a pouch on its body. ■ In the US, a **possum** is the same as an opossum.

post (postal, posting) The **post** is the public service by which letters and parcels are collected and delivered. The letters and parcels are called **post.** *...a pile of post.* **Postal** means to do with the post. *...postal deliveries.* If you **post** something, you send it through the post. ■ A **post** is an upright pole fixed into the ground. ■ A **post** is a job or official position. *...the newly-created post of vice president.* ■ A **post** is a place where someone like a soldier is commanded to be to do their job. You talk about a soldier being **posted** somewhere. ■ If you are **posted** to another town or country, you are sent to work there by your employer. The place you are sent to is called a **posting.** ■ If you **post** a notice somewhere, you fix it to a wall or noticeboard.

post- is used to form words which describe something taking place after a particular time or event. *...post-apartheid South Africa.*

postage is the money you pay for sending letters and parcels through the post.

postage stamp A **postage stamp** is a small piece of paper you buy and stick on an envelope or parcel before posting it.

postal See **post.**

postal order A **postal order** is a piece of paper representing a sum of money, which you buy at a post office and send to someone as a secure way of sending money by post.

postbag A **postbag** is a bag in which a postman carries letters and parcels. ■ The **postbag** of an important person is the letters they get from the general public.

post box A **post box** is a large metal container you put letters into for collection.

postcard A **postcard** is a piece of card, often with a picture on one side, which you write on and post to someone.

postcode A **postcode** is a short series of letters and numbers at the end of an address which aids sorting and delivery of letters.

post-dated On a **post-dated** cheque the date is a later one than the date the cheque was actually written, so it cannot be cashed before a certain time.

poster A **poster** is a large picture or notice stuck on a wall or board.

poste restante is a service by which someone's post is sent to a particular post office to await collection.

posterior Your **posterior** is your bottom.

posterity means future generations of people. *...a collection preserved for posterity.*

poster paint is a type of thick brightly-coloured paint containing no oil, used for painting pictures.

postgraduate study or research is done by a student who has a first degree and is studying or doing research at a more advanced level. The student is called a **postgraduate.**

post-haste (*or* post haste) If you go somewhere or do something **post-haste,** you go there or do it as quickly as you can.

posthumous (*pron:* poss-tume-uss) **(posthumously)** **Posthumous** is used to describe something happening or awarded after a person's death. *...posthumously published diaries.*

post-impressionism (post-impressionist) Post-**impressionism** is a style of painting developed as a reaction against impressionism. Artists who painted in this style are called **post-impressionists.**

post-industrial is used to describe the present state of many Western countries, especially the move from heavy industry to service industries, and the production of consumer goods.

posting See **post.**

postman (postmen) A **postman** is a man who collects and delivers the post.

postmark A **postmark** is a mark printed on letters and parcels showing where and when they were posted.

postmaster (postmistress) A **postmaster** or **postmistress** is a person in charge of a post office.

post-modernism (post-modern, post-modernist) **Post-modernism** is a late 20th century style in art, literature, and architecture which rejects the rules of modernism and mixes old and new influences in unusual ways. You say art, literature, and architecture in this style is **post-modern** or **post-modernist.** An artist, writer, or architect who uses this style is called a **post-modernist.**

post-mortem A **post-mortem** is the same as an autopsy. ■ You can call an examination of something which has recently happened a **post-mortem,** especially something which has gone wrong.

post-natal (*or* postnatal) means happening soon after the birth of a baby. *...a post-natal check-up.*

post office The **Post Office** is the national organization responsible for postal services. ■ A **post office** is a place where you can buy stamps, post letters and parcels, and use other Post Office services.

post-operative means happening after and relating to a surgical operation. *...post-operative care.*

postpone (**postponing, postponed; postponement**) If you **postpone** an event, you arrange for it to take place later than was originally planned.

post-prandial is used to talk about things you do or have after a meal. *...a post-prandial cigar.*

post-production is work like editing or dubbing which is carried out on a film or TV programme after the filming has been done.

postscript A **postscript** is an additional message written at the end of a letter after you have signed it. You write 'PS' in front of it.

post traumatic stress disorder (*or* **PTSD**) is a psychological condition, characterized by symptoms such as anxiety, withdrawal, and a tendency towards physical illness, which some people suffer following a traumatic experience.

postulate (**postulating, postulated**) If you **postulate** something, you assume it or suggest it as the basis for a theory or calculation. *His theory postulated the existence of a lost manuscript.*

posture (**posturing, postured**) Your **posture** is the way you hold your body when you are standing or sitting. ■ Your **posture** is the attitude you adopt towards a particular issue. *...their puritanical posture.* ■ If you say someone is **posturing,** you mean they are trying to give a particular impression to people. You can talk about someone's **posturing** or **posturings.**

post-war is used to describe something which happens or exists in the period after a war, especially the Second World War.

postwoman (**postwomen**) A **postwoman** is a woman who collects and delivers the post.

posy (**posies**) A **posy** is a small bunch of flowers.

pot (**potting, potted**) A **pot** is a deep round container. ■ If you **pot** a plant, you put it into a flower pot filled with earth. A **potted** plant is growing in a flower pot. ■ **Potted** meat or fish has been cooked and put into a small sealed container. ■ A **potted** biography or history contains the main facts about someone or something in a short simplified form. ■ When you **pot** a ball in snooker, you hit it into one of the pockets. ■ If you **pot** a small animal like a rabbit, you shoot and kill it. ■ If you say something has **gone to pot,** you mean it has deteriorated, because it has been neglected. ■ If you take **pot luck,** you decide to do something even though you do not know what you will get as a result. ■ **Pot** is another name for cannabis.

potash is a white powdery substance, obtained from the ashes of burnt wood. It is used as a fertilizer and to make soap and glass.

potassium is a soft silvery-white chemical element, used in making soap, detergents, fertilizers and glass.

potato (**potatoes**) **Potatoes** are round white root vegetables with a brown or red skin. ■ You can call a controversial problem or issue a **hot potato.**

potato chip In the US, crisps are called **potato chips.**

pot belly (**pot-bellied**) If someone has a **pot belly** or is **pot-bellied,** their stomach sticks out noticeably.

potboiler If you call a book or film a **potboiler,** you mean it has been created to earn money quickly, and may have no artistic merit.

potent (**potently, potency**) If something is **potent,** it is effective and powerful. You talk about the **potency** of something like this. ■ If a man is **potent,** he is able to have an erection and keep it during sex.

potentate A **potentate** is a ruler who has absolute power over his people.

potential (**potentially; potentiality, potentialities**) You use **potential** to say someone or something is capable of developing into the particular kind of person or thing mentioned. *...potential customers.* ■ If you say someone or something has **potential** or talk about their **potentiality,** you mean they have the necessary abilities or qualities to be useful or successful in the future. ■ If there is **the potential for** something, it may happen. *...the potential for conflict is great.*

pothole (**potholing, potholer**) A **pothole** is a large hole in the surface of a road. ■ A **pothole** is a deep hole in the ground in a limestone area, often leading to a network of underground caves and tunnels. **Potholing** is going down potholes to explore caves; a person who does this is called a **potholer.**

potion A **potion** is a drink containing medicine, poison, or something which is supposed to have magic powers.

pot plant A **pot plant** is a plant suitable for growing indoors in a flowerpot.

pot pourri (*pron:* po **poo**-ree) is a mixture of dried petals and leaves in a bowl, used to make rooms smell pleasant. ■ A **pot pourri** of things is a collection of different items not originally intended to go together.

pot roast A **pot roast** is a piece of meat, usually beef, cooked very slowly with a small amount of liquid in a covered pot.

pot-shot If you take a **pot-shot** at someone or something, you shoot at them without taking very careful aim.

potted See **pot.**

potter (**pottering, pottered**) A **potter** is someone who makes pottery. ■ A **potter's wheel** is a piece of equipment consisting of a flat disc which spins round, on which a potter puts soft clay to shape it into a pot. ■ If you **potter** about, you pass the time in an unhurried way, doing pleasant but unimportant things.

pottery (**potteries**) **Pottery** is pots, dishes, and other objects made from clay. The craft of making things like these is called **pottery.** ■ A **pottery** is a factory or workshop where pottery is made.

potting compost is soil specially prepared to help young plants grow.

potting shed A **potting shed** is a garden shed.

potty (**potties**) A **potty** is a deep bowl a small child uses as a toilet. **Potty-training** is teaching a child to use a potty. ■ If you say someone is **potty,** you mean they are mad or very silly.

pouch (**pouches**) A **pouch** is a flexible container like a small bag. ■ The **pouch** of an animal like a kangaroo is the pocket of skin on its stomach in which its baby grows.

pouffe (*pron:* **poof**) A **pouffe** is a low, soft piece of furniture for sitting or resting your feet on.

poultice (*pron:* **pole**-tiss) A **poultice** is a pad with heated ointments in it which is put over a swollen or painful part of the body.

poultry is birds like chickens and ducks kept for their eggs and meat.

pounce (**pouncing, pounced**) If an animal or person **pounces** on something or someone, they leap forward and grab them. ■ If you **pounce** on something like a mistake, you notice it and quickly take advantage of it in some way.

pound (**-pounder, pounding**) The **pound** or **pound sterling** is the unit of currency in Britain. Some other countries, for example Cyprus and Egypt, have a unit of currency called a **pound.** ■ Weight is often expressed in **pounds.** A pound is 16 ounces (about 0.454 kilograms). 'Pounds' is usually written 'lbs'. ■ **-pounder** is used to describe (a) a fish weighing a certain number of pounds. *...a 27-pounder.* (b) a gun which fires a shell weighing a certain number of pounds. *...a 32-pounder cannon.* ■ If something is **pounded** by something else, it is hit by it repeatedly. *Long-range artillery continued to pound the city.* ■ If you **pound** something, you crush it into a paste or powder. ■ When your heart or some other part of your body **pounds,** it beats or throbs with a strong fast rhythm. Similarly, you can talk about music **pounding.** ■ If you **pound** somewhere, you run there with heavy noisy steps.

pour (**pouring, poured**) If you **pour** a liquid, you make it flow out of a container by holding the container at an angle. ■ If a liquid **pours** somewhere, it flows there quickly and in large quantities. *Sweat was pouring down his face.* ■ When it **pours** with rain, it rains heavily. ■ If people **pour** into a place, they go there in large numbers. Similarly, if something like mail **pours** into a place, a lot of it is received. ■ If someone **pours** money into an activity or organization, they keep spending money on it. ■ **pour scorn:** see **scorn.**

pout (**pouting, pouted**) If someone **pouts,** they stick their lips out, because they are annoyed or because they want to look sexually attractive. An expression like this is called a **pout.**

poverty is being very poor.

POW (*or* **pow**) (*pronounce each letter separately*) A **POW** is a prisoner of war.

powder (**powdering, powdered**) **Powder** is tiny particles of a solid substance. A **powdered** substance comes in the form of a powder. *...powdered milk.* ■ If you **powder** something, you cover it with powder. ■ If you call a situation or place a **powder keg,** you mean things could become violent at any time.

powder room A **powder room** is a women's toilet in a place like a department store.

powdery substances look or feel like powder.

power (**powering, powered**) If someone has **power,** they have control over other people and their activities. ■ If someone in authority has the **power** to

do something, they have the legal right to do it. ■ A **power** is a very rich or important country, or one with strong military forces. *...world powers such as the United Kingdom and France.* ■ A country's **air power** is its military aircraft. Similarly, its **naval power** is its warships. ■ Your **power** to do something is your ability to do it. ■ **Power** is energy, for example electricity or the energy of the sun or wind. ■ If a machine is **powered** in a certain way, that is how it gets the fuel or energy it needs to work. *...a wind-powered generator.* ■ A **power** tool is electrically operated. ■ The **power** of something is its physical strength. *...the power of the sea.*

power base A politician's **power base** is the supporters who provide him or her with power and influence.

powerboat A **powerboat** is a fast powerful motorboat.

power-broker A **power-broker** is someone who can influence people in political power.

powered See **power.**

powerful (**powerfully**) A **powerful** person or organization has a lot of power. ■ A **powerful** machine, device, or substance is very strong and effective. *...a powerful laser.* ■ If your body is **powerful,** it is physically strong. *He was very powerfully built.* ■ A **powerful** voice is strong and easily heard. ■ A **powerful** smell or flavour is strong and very noticeable. ■ You say something is **powerful** when it has a strong effect on people. *...a powerful and original novel.*

powerhouse If you call an industrial area the **powerhouse** of a region, you mean it is the part which creates the region's wealth.

powerless (**powerlessly, powerlessness**) If you are **powerless,** you are unable to control or influence events. ■ If you are **powerless** to do something, you are unable to do it.

power of attorney In law or business, **power of attorney** is the right to appoint someone, for example a solicitor, to perform certain acts on your behalf.

power point See **point.**

power station A **power station** is a place where electricity is generated.

power steering or **power-assisted steering** is a way of making steering lighter and easier by using power from the vehicle's engine.

pow-wow People sometimes call a meeting or conference a **pow-wow.**

pox The **pox** is syphilis.

pp You write **pp** in front of someone's name at the end of a letter to show you have signed it for them. **pp** means 'for and on behalf of'. ■ See also **p.**

PR See (a) **public relations.** (b) **proportional representation.**

practicable (**practicability**) If a course of action is **practicable,** it can be carried out successfully.

practical (**practicality, practicalities**) **Practical** is used to talk about problems and situations which actually arise, and ways of dealing with them. *Selling the stock remains the only practical alternative for most investors.* The practical aspects of something can be called **practicalities.** ■ If you call a plan or method **practical** or talk about its **practicality,** you mean it is capable of being carried out successfully. ■ **Practical** exams or lessons are ones in which students make things or do experiments, rather than just doing theoretical work. ...*practical subjects.* ■ A **practical** person deals with problems sensibly and effectively. ■ **Practical** clothes or household objects are useful rather than fashionable or attractive.

practical joke (practical joker) A **practical joke** is a trick played on someone to make them look silly. Someone who plays tricks like this is called a **practical joker.**

practically (practicality) **Practically** means almost. *I've lived here practically all my life.* ■ You use **practically** to describe something which has been done in a practical way.

practice A **practice** is something people do regularly. ...*the practice of pairing birds of the same strain together.* ■ **Practice** is regular training or exercise in something. ...*piano practice.* ■ A doctor's or lawyer's **practice** is their business, often shared with other doctors or lawyers. ■ What happens **in practice** is what actually happens, as distinct from what is supposed to happen. ■ If you put an idea or method **into practice,** you carry it out.

practise (*Am:* practice) (practising, practised) If you **practise** something, you keep doing it regularly to improve your skill at it. If you are **practised** at something, you are good at it, because you have had a lot of experience of it. ■ If someone **practises** medicine, they work as a doctor. People can also **practise** other professions. ...*a practising engineer.* ■ When people **practise** something like a custom, an activity, or religion, they take part in the activities associated with it. ...*practising Catholics.*

practitioner People in some professions, for example medicine or the law, can be called **practitioners.** ...*a dental practitioner.* ■ A **practitioner** of something involving skill is someone who does it regularly. ...*judo practitioners.*

praesidium See presidium.

pragmatic (pragmatically; pragmatism, pragmatist) You say people are being **pragmatic** or showing **pragmatism** when they disregard theories or ideologies and do what they think is best. Someone who regularly behaves like this is called a **pragmatist.**

prairie A **prairie** is a large area of flat grassy land in North America.

praise (praising, praised) If you **praise** someone or something, you speak highly of them. *Musically, this production deserved high praise.*

praiseworthy If you say something is **praiseworthy,** you mean it is very good and deserves to be praised.

pram A **pram** is a vehicle like a cot with wheels, for pushing a small baby around.

prance (prancing, pranced) If someone **prances** around, they move around with exaggerated movements. ■ If a horse **prances,** it moves with quick high steps.

prank (prankster) **Pranks** are childish tricks. You call someone who plays tricks like these a **prankster.**

prat If you call someone a **prat,** you mean they are stupid.

prattle (prattling, prattled) If you say someone is **prattling** on about something, you mean they are talking a lot without saying anything important.

prawn — **Prawns** are small shellfish. They are similar to shrimps, but larger.

pray When people **pray,** they speak to the God they believe in, giving thanks to him or asking for help. ■ You can say someone is **praying** something will happen when they are hoping very much it is going to happen.

prayer is the practice of praying. A **prayer** is the words someone says when they pray. ■ If you say someone **hasn't got a prayer,** you mean they have no hope of succeeding.

pre- is used to form words which describe something as taking place before a particular date or event. ...*pre-1900 literature.* ...*pre-Olympic trials.* ■ **Pre-** is used to form words which describe something being done in advance. For example, you say something is 'pre-planned' or 'pre-arranged'.

preach (preaches, preaching, preached) When someone, especially a member of the clergy, **preaches,** they give a talk on a religious subject as part of a church service. ■ If you **preach** a set of ideas or beliefs, you try to persuade people to accept them. *The industrial countries have been preaching free trade to the third world for years.* ■ If you **preach at** someone, you give them unwanted advice in a moralizing way.

preacher Members of the clergy are sometimes called **preachers.**

preamble (*pron:* pree-am-bl) The **preamble** of a speech or piece of writing is an introductory part at the beginning.

prebendary (*pron:* preb-en-der-ee) (prebendaries) A **prebendary** is a member of the clergy on the staff of a cathedral.

precarious (precariously, precariousness) If a situation is **precarious,** things could go badly wrong at any time. ■ **Precarious** is used to talk about situations in which a person or thing is likely to fall because they are not well-balanced or secure. *They were precariously close to the edge.*

precaution (precautionary) If you do something as a **precaution,** you do it to reduce the risk of something dangerous or unpleasant happening. *The local administration says the curfew is purely a precautionary measure.*

precede (preceding, preceded) If one event **precedes** another, it happens before it. ■ The person who **preceded** you in your job was the one who had it before you. ■ If you **precede** someone somewhere, you go in front of them. *Now and again through the crowd would rush a runner, preceded by a torch-bearer.*

precedence (*pron:* press-ee-denss) If one thing **takes precedence** over another, it is seen as more important than the other thing.

precedent (*pron:* **press**-ee-dent) You say something sets a **precedent** when the fact that it has happened once makes it likely that it will happen again, perhaps several times. *Some would say that the airport affair has set a dangerous precedent for the future... There are precedents for meetings at short notice at times of international tension.* ■ **Precedent** is used to talk about the way something has always been done, which is therefore considered to be correct. *He has broken with precedent by refusing to go to the lunches.*

preceding See **precede.**

precentor (*pron:* pree-**sen**-ter) In some cathedrals and churches, the **precentor** is a member of clergy responsible for the music sung there.

precept (*pron:* **pree**-sept) A **precept** is a general rule which helps you decide how you should behave in particular circumstances.

precinct A shopping **precinct** or pedestrian **precinct** is a shopping area in which cars are not allowed. ■ The **precincts** of a property are the land and buildings within its boundaries. ■ In the US, a **precinct** is a division of a city for police purposes, or a subdivision of a county or ward for electoral purposes.

precious If something is **precious,** it is valuable or very important and should be looked after or used carefully. ■ **Precious metals** are valuable metals like gold and silver. ■ **Precious stones** are valuable gemstones like diamonds and rubies. See also **semi-precious.** ■ If there is **precious little** of something, there is very little of it. ■ If you say a person is **precious,** you mean their behaviour is very formal and unnatural.

precipice (*pron:* **press**-sip-iss) A **precipice** is a very steep rock face. ■ If you say someone is close to a **precipice,** you mean they are in a dangerous situation where disaster or failure could easily happen.

precipitate (**precipitating, precipitated; precipitately**) If something **precipitates** (*pron:* pris-**sip**-i-tates) a happening or change, it makes it happen sooner than expected. *Her resignation was precipitated by her failure to win a decisive majority in the first round of voting.* ■ **Precipitate** (*pron:* pris-**sip**-i-tet) is used to describe things which happen suddenly and rapidly. *...a precipitate rush towards monetary union.*

precipitation In meteorology, **precipitation** is rain, snow, or hail.

precipitous (**precipitously**) A **precipitous** slope is very steep. ■ **Precipitous** events happen suddenly and rapidly. *Living standards are falling precipitously.*

précis (*pron:* **pray**-see) (*plural:* **précis**) A **précis** is a short piece of writing summarizing the main points of a book or report.

precise (**precisely**) **Precise** is used to talk about something happening exactly at a particular time. *At that precise moment we were struck by the car.* ■ **Precise** is used to emphasize that something is a particular thing in every detail. *That is precisely what she has done.* ■ If a measurement is **precise,** it is exact rather than approximate.

precision If something is done with **precision,** it is done very accurately. ■ **Precision** equipment is very accurate. *...high-precision radar.*

preclude (**precluding, precluded**) If one thing **precludes** another, it makes it impossible for the other thing to happen.

precocious (**precociously; precocity**) If you call a child **precocious** or talk about its **precocity** (pree-**koss**-it-tee), you mean it does or says things which are very advanced for its age.

preconception (**preconceived**) If you say someone has **preconceptions** about something or **preconceived** ideas about it, you mean they have made up their mind about it before they have had enough information or experience to form a fair opinion.

precondition (*or* **pre-condition**) If one thing is a **precondition** of another, it must happen or be done before the other thing can happen. *Both sides are expected to lay down preconditions before more substantial negotiations can take place.*

precursor If one thing is a **precursor** of another, it happens before the other thing and acts as a signal or warning that it is going to happen. *The deal should not be seen as a precursor to a merger.*

predate (*or* **pre-date**) (**predating, predated**) If one thing **predates** another, it happened or was made before it. *The monument predates the arrival of the druids in Britain.*

predator (**predatory; predation**) A **predator** is an animal which kills and eats other animals. You say an animal like this is **predatory. Predation** is killing and eating other animals. ■ You say a person or organization is **predatory** or call them a **predator** when they are eager to gain something out of someone else's weakness or suffering.

predecease (**predeceasing, predeceased**) If someone **predeceases** you, they die before you.

predecessor Your **predecessor** is the person who had your job before you. ■ The **predecessor** of something like a machine is the one it replaced or the one from which it developed.

predestined (**predestination**) If you say something was **predestined** to happen, you mean it could not have been prevented, because it had already been decided by God or by fate. People who believe in **predestination** believe that events are controlled in this way.

predetermined (*or* **pre-determined**) If something is **predetermined,** it is decided beforehand.

predicament A **predicament** is an unpleasant situation which is difficult to get out of.

predicate (**predicating, predicated**) If one thing is **predicated** on another, it is based on the assumption that the other thing will happen or exist. *The whole process of unification is predicated on this hope of economic growth.*

predict (**prediction, predictor**) If you **predict** that something will happen, you say you believe it will happen. This is called making a **prediction.** You call something a **predictor** when it helps you make a prediction. *The most reliable predictor of voting is education and age.*

predictable (**predictably, predictability**) You say something is **predictable** when it is obvious in advance what is going to happen.

prediction See **predict.**

predictor See **predict.**

predilection (pron: pree-dil-**lek**-shn) If you have a **predilection** for something, you like it. ...his predilection for fast cars.

predispose (**predisposing, predisposed; predisposition**) If you are **predisposed** to a medical condition or have a **predisposition** to it, you are likely to be affected by it. US scientists have discovered a gene that predisposes people to alcoholism. ■ If something **predisposes** you to behave in a certain way, it makes it likely you will behave that way.

predominant (**predominantly, predominance**) If certain things are **predominant** or there is a **predominance** of them, there are more of them, or they are more noticeable, than other things. There is a predominance of civilian employees here. ■ You say someone or something is **predominant** or has **predominance** when they are more powerful or important than other people or things. ■ **Predominantly** means 'mainly'. Pakistan is a predominantly agricultural country.

predominate (**predominating, predominated**) If one type of person or thing **predominates** in a group, there are more of that type than any other. US and European cyclists predominate and they usually lead the field.

pre-eminent (**pre-eminently, pre-eminence**) If someone is **pre-eminent** in a group, they are more important, powerful, or capable than other people in the group. ■ **Pre-eminently** is used to say something is more true of one person or thing in a group than others. America is the pre-eminently religious nation of the West.

pre-empt (**pre-emptive, pre-emptively**) If you **pre-empt** something, you stop it happening by doing something in advance which makes it pointless or impossible. He resigned from the Communist party last week, pre-empting a decision to expel him. **Pre-emptive** is used to describe actions done in advance like this. ...pre-emptive strikes against terrorists.

preen (**preening, preened**) When a bird **preens** itself, it cleans and arranges its feathers. ■ If you talk about people **preening** themselves, you mean they spend a lot of time and effort making themselves look neat and attractive.

pre-existing situations and things exist already or existed before something else you are talking about. In some athletes the training may trigger a pre-existing condition.

prefab A **prefab** is a prefabricated building, especially a house.

prefabricated buildings are built from ready-made sections which are easily put together.

preface (pron: **pref**-fiss) (**prefacing, prefaced**) A **preface** is an introduction at the beginning of a book, explaining what the book is about or why it was written. ■ If you **preface** an action or speech with something else, you do or say the other thing first.

prefect (**prefecture**) In some countries, a **prefect** is the chief administrator of a government department or region. The area a prefect deals with is called a **prefecture.** ■ In some schools, a **prefect** is an older pupil who has been given special duties.

prefer (**preferring, preferred**) If you **prefer** one thing to another, you like the first thing better. ■ If the police **prefer** charges against someone, they make a formal accusation against them which then has to be decided in court.

preferable (pron: **pref**-fer-a-bl) (**preferably**) If you say one thing is **preferable** to another, you mean it is more worthwhile or desirable.

preference (pron: **pref**-fer-enss) If you have a **preference** for something, you like it better than other things. ■ If you give **preference** to someone, you choose them rather than someone else.

preference share — Preference shares pay a fixed dividend and are safer than ordinary shares.

preferential If you get **preferential** treatment, you are deliberately treated better than other people, and therefore have an advantage.

preferment is promotion to a better and more influential job.

preferred See **prefer.**

prefigure (**prefiguring, prefigured**) If one thing **prefigures** another, it shows or suggests that the other thing will happen.

prefix (**prefixes, prefixing, prefixed**) A **prefix** is a group of letters added at the beginning of a word to make a new word with a different meaning. 'semi-', 'pre-', and 'un-' are prefixes. ■ If a word or number is **prefixed** by another word or number, the other word or number comes before it. All telephone numbers should be prefixed by 010 33.

pregnant (**pregnancy**) If a woman or female animal is **pregnant,** a baby is developing in her womb. A woman's **pregnancy** is the time during which she is pregnant. ■ If you say there is a **pregnant** pause or silence, you mean nothing is said for a while, but this in itself seems to convey a special meaning.

prehistoric (**prehistory**) Prehistoric is used to describe things which happened or existed a long time ago, before writing was invented. This time is called **prehistory.**

prejudge (**prejudging, prejudged**) If you **prejudge** a situation, you form an opinion about it before you know all the facts.

prejudice (**prejudicing, prejudiced**) Prejudice is an unreasonable dislike for someone or something, especially a group of people. ...prejudice against gays and lesbians. You say people who have unreasonable dislikes are **prejudiced.** ■ If one thing **prejudices** the chances of another thing succeeding, it makes the other thing less likely to succeed.

prejudicial If an action, comment, or situation is **prejudicial** to someone or something, it is harmful to them. ...prejudicial media reporting.

prelate (pron: **prel**-it) A **prelate** is a high-ranking member of the clergy, for example a bishop.

preliminary (**preliminaries**) Preliminary is used to describe things which are the first of their kind and serve as a preparation for others which are to follow. Things like these are also called **prelimi-**

naries. ...*a preliminary agreement on fishing rights...* *The Japanese went straight onto the offensive without lengthy preliminaries.*

prelude (*pron:* **prel**-yewd) If you say one thing is a **prelude** to another, you mean it comes before the other thing and serves as an introduction to it. *The interest-rate cut is a prelude to other economy-boosting measures.* ■ A **prelude** is a short piece of music, usually for piano or organ.

premature (**prematurely**) **Premature** is used to describe things which happen earlier than usual, or earlier than expected. ...*premature arthritis.* ...*prematurely white hair.* ■ A **premature** baby weighs less than 2,500 grams (about 5½ lb) when it is born and is usually born earlier than expected. ■ If you describe something someone has done as **premature,** you mean they have done it too soon, at an inappropriate time.

premeditated (**premeditation**) A **premeditated** action, especially a crime, is planned or thought about beforehand.

premenstrual syndrome If a woman suffers from **premenstrual syndrome** or **PMS,** changes in her hormone levels in the days before her periods start make her feel irritable and unwell.

premenstrual tension Premenstrual syndrome is sometimes called **premenstrual tension** or **PMT.**

premier (*pron:* **prem**-ee-er) (**premiership**) A country's prime minister is sometimes called its **premier.** The **premiership** is the job or position of being prime minister. ■ **Premier** is sometimes used to describe the most important thing of a particular kind. ...*the Premier Division.* ...*the premier power in Central Asia.*

premiere (*pron:* **prem**-mee-air) (**premiering, premiered**) The **premiere** of something like a new play is its first public performance. When this performance takes place, you say the play is **premiered.**

premiership See **premier.**

premise (*pron:* **prem**-iss) The **premises** of a business are all the buildings and land it occupies. ■ A **premise** or **premiss** is something which you suppose is true and which you use as a basis for an idea. ...*a series of laws based on the premise that a human embryo has certain basic rights.*

premiss (**premisses**) See **premise.**

premium A **premium** is (a) an extra sum of money paid in addition to the normal cost of something. (b) a sum of money you pay regularly to an insurance company when you have taken out a policy with them. ■ If something is **at a premium,** it is hard to get because it is in short supply. ■ **Premium** prices are higher than usual. ■ **Premium** is used to describe things which are of high quality. ...*premium lager.* ■ If you put or place a **premium** on something, you consider it to be especially important.

premium bond – **Premium bonds** are numbered bonds sold by the government at post offices. You do not earn interest on them, but every month there is a draw for cash prizes.

premonition If you have a **premonition,** you have a feeling that something is going to happen, often something unpleasant.

prenatal (*or* **pre-natal**) means to do with the medical care of pregnant women. ...*pre-natal screening.*

preoccupy (**preoccupies, preoccupying, preoccupied; preoccupation**) If something **preoccupies** you or you are **preoccupied** with it, you pay a lot of attention to it. ...*Moscow's preoccupation with its economic crisis.* ■ A **preoccupation** is something you think about a lot because it is important to you.

pre-ordained (*or* **preordained**) When people talk about something being **pre-ordained,** they mean it has been decided in advance that it will happen, for example by God or fate.

pre-packaged goods are packed or wrapped before they are sold.

preparation See **prepare.**

preparatory is used to describe things which are done in preparation for something. ...*preparatory talks on ending the civil war...* *Sloan cleared his throat preparatory to speaking.*

preparatory school A **preparatory school** is the same as a prep school.

prepare (**preparing, prepared; preparation**) If you **prepare** something, you get it ready, or put it together. *The site is being prepared for a rock concert.* ■ **Preparations** are all the things done and arrangements made for a forthcoming event. ■ If you **prepare** for an event, action, or situation, you get ready to deal with it. ■ If you **prepare** someone else for something, you make sure they are able to deal with it when it happens. *The system failed to prepare students for the harsh realities of being a working architect.* ■ If you **prepare** something like a report, you write it, putting in everything that is needed. ■ A **preparation** is a mixture prepared for use as a food, medicine, or cosmetic. ...*anti-ageing creams and sensitive-skin preparations.*

prepared (**preparedness**) If you are **prepared** to do something, you are willing to do it. ■ If you are **prepared** for something which may happen, you are ready to deal with it when it happens. ■ **Prepared** is used to describe things which have been done or made in advance. ...*a prepared statement.*

preponderance (**preponderant**) If there is a **preponderance** of one type of person or thing in a group or if they are **preponderant,** there are more of them than other types, or they are more important or powerful.

preposition – **Prepositions** are words like 'by', 'for', 'into', and 'with', which are usually followed by a noun. Prepositions usually provide information about time or place, or the relationship of people to things.

preposterous (**preposterously**) If you call something **preposterous,** you mean it is extremely unlikely or unreasonable.

preppy (*or* **preppie**) (**preppies**) In the US, a **preppy** is a student or former student of an expensive private school. Preppies are well known for wearing expensive conservative clothes.

pre-prandial is used to describe things which happen before a meal, especially dinner. ...*pre-prandial drinks.*

prep school A **prep school** is a private school for children up to 11 or 13. ■ In the US, a **prep school** is a secondary school, usually private, to prepare students to enter college.

pre-pubescent girls or boys are at the age just before puberty.

Pre-Raphaelite The **Pre-Raphaelites** were a group of 19th century English artists and writers who based their work on themes from medieval literature, Shakespeare, and the Bible.

pre-recorded If something is **pre-recorded,** it has been recorded in advance. ...*a pre-recorded interview.* ■ **Pre-recorded** cassettes already have music on them, rather than being blank for you to record on them yourself.

prerequisite If one thing is a **prerequisite** of another, the first thing must happen or exist before the second thing is possible.

prerogative If something is a **prerogative** of a particular person or group, it is a privilege or right which only they have.

presage (*pron:* **press**-ij) (**presaging, presaged**) If something **presages** a situation or event, it is seen as a sign or warning that it is about to happen.

Presbyterian The **Presbyterian** Church is a Protestant church based on Calvinism. Its members are called **Presbyterians.**

presbytery (**presbyteries**) In the Presbyterian Church, a **presbytery** is a local church court composed of ministers and elders. ■ A **presbytery** is the house in which a Roman Catholic priest lives.

pre-school means to do with the care and education of children before they reach school age. ...*pre-school facilities.*

prescient (*pron:* **press**-ee-ent) (**prescience**) If someone is **prescient,** they foresee what is going to happen in the future. You talk about the **prescience** of someone like this.

prescribe (**prescribing, prescribed; prescription**) If a doctor **prescribes** treatment or a medicine, he or she decides what treatment or medicine you should have, and arranges for the treatment or writes out an order for the medicine. The medicine a doctor prescribes is called a **prescription;** the form it is ordered on is also called a **prescription.** ■ If someone in authority **prescribes** something, they give instructions that it shall be done. *They fear fines for having more than the prescribed one child per family.*

prescriptive If something is **prescriptive,** it sets down rules about what should be done. ...*a prescriptive curriculum.*

presence Your **presence** somewhere is the fact that you are there. ■ If you are **in** someone's **presence,** you are in the same place as them. ■ If a country has a military **presence** somewhere, it has soldiers stationed there. ■ If you say someone has **presence,** you mean they have an impressive appearance and manner. ■ **Presence of mind** is the ability to act quickly and sensibly in a difficult situation.

present (**presentation, presenter**) The **present** is the period of time taking place now. **Present** is used to describe people and things that exist now. ...*the present government.* ■ If someone or something is **present** in a place, they are there. ■ A **present** is something you give to someone, for example on their birthday. ■ If you **present** someone with something like information or an award, you give it to them formally. ■ When people **present** something like a performance, they put it on, so the public can come and see it. ■ If you talk about the **presentation** of a piece of work, you are talking about the way it looks or is set out, and the impression it gives. *The standard of presentation is dire.* ■ If you **present** yourself somewhere, you arrive there, for example to keep an appointment. ■ If something **presents** a difficulty, challenge, or opportunity, it causes or provides it. ■ If you **present** yourself as a particular thing, you try to get people to believe you are that thing. *He presents himself as a man of the people.* ■ When someone **presents** a TV or radio programme, they introduce each part of it or each person on it. Someone who does this is called a **presenter.**

presentable If you talk about someone or something being **presentable,** you mean they are suitable for people to see.

presentation (**presenter**) See **present.**

presently is used to say something is happening now. *She is presently developing a number of projects.*

preservation See **preserve.**

preservative A **preservative** is a chemical which prevents things from decaying. Some preservatives are added to food; others are used to treat wood or metal.

preserve (**preserving, preserved; preserver; preservation, preservationist**) If you **preserve** something, you take action to save it or protect it from damage, loss, or decay. People involved in preserving things are called **preservationists.** ■ A **preserve** is an area of land or water where animals are protected. ■ If you **preserve** a desirable situation, you make sure it stays as it is. *The pact was vital for preserving peace and stability in Asia.* You can say someone is a **preserver** of a desirable situation. ■ If you **preserve** food, you treat it in a way which prevents it from decaying, for example by freezing it or using sugar or salt. ■ **Preserves** are foods such as bottled fruit, jams, marmalades, and chutneys. ■ If something is the **preserve** of a group of people, it is restricted to that group. *Mobile phones, once the preserve of businessmen, are now being pitched at the general public.*

pre-set is used to describe (a) things which have been decided in advance. ...*a pre-set rate of return.* (b) equipment whose controls have been set in advance. ...*pre-set radio stations.*

preside (**presiding, presided**) The person who **presides** over a meeting is the person in charge of it. ■ If someone **presides** over something which is taking place, they are responsible for it and in control of it. *The new cabinet would preside over the reconstruction of the country.*

presidency (**presidencies**) The **presidency** is the job or position of being a president. A person's **presidency** is the time during which they are president.

president The **president** of a country which is not a monarchy is the head of state there. In the US and some other countries, the president is also the person with the highest political position. ■ The **president** of an organization is the person with the highest position in it.

president-elect The **president-elect** is the person who has been elected as the next president, but who has not yet taken up the post.

presidential means to do with a country's president. ...*presidential elections.*

presidium (*or* **praesidium**) In communist countries, the **presidium** is a committee or other body which takes policy decisions on behalf of a larger group, for example a parliament.

press (**presses, pressing, pressed**) If you **press** something, you push it or hold it firmly against something else. ■ If you **press** clothes, you iron them. ■ A **press** is a machine or device which puts pressure on something, for example to squeeze liquid from it. ...*garlic presses.* ■ If you **press** someone to do something, you try hard to get them to do it. ■ If you **press** charges against someone, you make an official accusation which has to be settled in court. ■ Newspapers and journalists are often called the **press.** ■ A printing **press** is a machine for printing books and papers. ■ If you **press on** or **press ahead** with an activity, you continue doing it in a determined way, regardless of any difficulties.

press box A **press box** is a room at a sports ground reserved for journalists.

press conference A **press conference** is the same as a news conference.

press corps (*pron:* **kor**) The **press corps** is a group of reporters from different papers all working in the same place.

press cutting A **press cutting** is an article which you cut out of a paper and keep, usually because it is about you.

press-gang In the past, when someone was **press-ganged** into the navy, they were captured and forced to join it. The group of people who did the capturing were called a **press gang.** These days, if someone is **press-ganged** into doing something, they are made to do it, although they do not really want to.

pressing See **press.** ■ If something is **pressing,** it needs to be dealt with immediately. ...*pressing economic problems.* ■ A **pressing** is a batch of CDs or LPs made from a master recording.

pressman (**pressmen**) A **pressman** is a journalist, especially a man, who works for a newspaper or magazine.

press office The **press office** of a large organization or government department is the section which gives information about its activities to the press.

press officer A **press officer** is someone employed by an organization to give information about it to the press.

press release A **press release** is a written statement about a matter of public interest given to journalists by the organization involved in it.

press secretary A **press secretary** is the same as a press officer.

press stud A **press stud** is a small device in two pieces for fastening clothes. One piece has a knob which snaps into a hole on the other piece.

press-up – **Press-ups** are exercises for strengthening the arm and chest muscles. They are done by lying with your face towards the floor and pushing with your hands until your arms are straight.

pressure (**pressuring, pressured**) **Pressure** is the force of something pushing on something else. ■ If someone **pressures** you or puts **pressure** on you, they try to persuade you to do something. ■ **Pressure** is tension and stress.

pressure cooker A **pressure cooker** is a large saucepan with an air-tight lid in which you can cook food quickly using steam at high pressure.

pressure group A **pressure group** is an organization which campaigns to get a government or other authority to take a particular course of action.

pressurize (*or* **pressurise**) (**pressurizing, pressurized**) If you are **pressurized** to do something, people try hard to persuade or force you to do it. ■ If a container or area is **pressurized,** the pressure inside it is different from the pressure outside.

prestige (**prestigious**) If a person or thing has **prestige,** people admire and respect them, because they are important or successful. You can also say something is **prestigious.** ...*the world's most prestigious cycle race.* **Prestige** is used to describe things which have prestige. ...*prestige projects.*

presto See **hey presto.**

presumably You use **presumably** to say you think something is true, although you cannot be certain of it. *People in Yorkshire eat the most fish, and presumably chips.*

presume (**presuming, presumed; presumption, presumptuous**) If something is **presumed** to be true or there is a **presumption** that it is true, people suppose it is true or behave as if it is true, although they have no proof and cannot be certain about it. ■ If you talk about someone **presuming** to do something, you mean they do it even though they have no right to. *They're resentful that outsiders presume to meddle in their affairs.* You say someone who behaves like this is **presumptuous;** you call their behaviour **presumption.**

presuppose (**presupposing, presupposed**) If one thing **presupposes** another, it cannot happen or be true unless the other thing happens or is true. *All your arguments presuppose that he's a rational, intelligent man.*

pre-tax is used to talk about a company's profits or a person's earnings before tax has been deducted.

pretend (**pretence**) (*Am:* **pretense**) If you **pretend** something is true, you try to make people believe it is true. Behaviour like this is called a **pretence.** ■ If a child **pretends** to do something, they behave as if they are doing it, often as part of a game. **Pretend** things are imaginary. *To a child a pretend playmate is for real.*

pretender A **pretender** to a throne or title is someone who claims the right to it, but whose claim is disputed in some way.

pretense See **pretend.**

pretension (**pretentious, pretentiously, pretentiousness**) **Pretension** is trying to make people believe you are very important or sophisticated. When someone behaves like this, you say they are being **pretentious.** You can also call something like a play or book **pretentious.** ■ If someone has **pretensions** to something, they claim to be able to do it or be it. *...Madrid's pretension to the title of cultural capital of Europe.*

pre-term A **pre-term** baby is born prematurely.

preternaturally is used to say something is so unusual or exceptional that it seems unnatural. *The stars were preternaturally bright and clear.*

pretext If you use something as a **pretext** for doing something you want or intend to do, you use it as an excuse for doing it.

prettify (**prettifies, prettifying, prettified**) If someone **prettifies** something ugly or unpleasant, they try to make it look pretty or pleasant. *...just a clever effort to prettify animal slaughter.*

pretty (**prettier, prettiest; prettily, prettiness**) A **pretty** woman or girl is attractive in a delicate way. ■ A **pretty** place or building has many attractive features, and is pleasant to look at. ■ **Pretty** is used to mean 'quite' or 'rather'. *The situation is pretty bad.* ■ If you say someone is **sitting pretty,** you mean they are in a comfortable position while other people are suffering or having to work hard.

pretzel A **pretzel** is a type of brittle salted biscuit made in the shape of a loose knot.

prevail (**prevailing, prevailed**) If something like a principle **prevails,** it emerges as the strongest factor in a situation. *We hoped that common sense would prevail.* Similarly, you say a person **prevails** if their ideas are accepted. ■ If you **prevail upon** someone to do something, you persuade them to do it. ■ If you talk about the **prevailing** wind in a place, you are saying which direction the wind usually blows from.

prevalent (**prevalence**) If something is **prevalent,** it exists or happens very commonly. *The authorities admit that torture is prevalent throughout the country.*

prevaricate (**prevaricating, prevaricated; prevarication**) If you **prevaricate,** you avoid making a firm decision or giving a direct answer.

prevent (**prevention**) If you **prevent** someone from doing something, you make it impossible for them to do it. If you **prevent** something happening, you make sure it does not happen.

preventable If something is **preventable,** it can be prevented.

preventative means the same as 'preventive'.

prevention See **prevent.**

preventive actions are intended to stop something undesirable happening. *...preventive dentistry.*

preview When something like a film is **previewed** or there is a **preview** of it, a limited number of people are allowed to see it before it opens to the general public.

previous (**previously**) **Previous** is used when mentioning a time or event which came before the one you are talking about. *They had lost three of the previous four matches. Two years previously, the company had lost £18 million.*

pre-war is used to describe something which happened or existed in the period just before a war, especially the Second World War. *...pre-war Romania. ...the pre-war years.*

prey An animal's or bird's **prey** are the creatures it hunts and eats. You say it **preys on** those creatures. ■ If someone **preys on** other people, they get money from them by tricking them or taking advantage of their weaknesses. *At the airport, visitors are regularly preyed on by greedy taxi drivers.* ■ If you **fall prey to** something unpleasant, you are affected by it. *She then fell prey to drugs.*

priapic (*pron:* pry-**ap**-pik) means involving lustful male sexuality. *...the priapic antics of the president.*

price (**pricing, priced**) The **price** of something is the amount you have to pay to buy it. You can also say something is **priced** at a particular amount. ■ You can talk about the **price** of something when you mean its consequences. *Fame comes at a price.*

priceless If something is **priceless,** it is so valuable it is impossible to say how much it is worth. ■ Some people use **priceless** to say they find something very amusing. *...a priceless remark.*

pricey If something is **pricey,** it is expensive.

prick If you **prick** something, you make a small hole in it with a sharp object. ■ If something **pricks** your conscience, it makes you feel guilty. ■ If you **prick up** your ears, you start listening eagerly.

prickle (**prickling, prickled**) **Prickles** are sharp points on the leaves or stalks of plants. ■ If your skin **prickles,** it tingles, because you are afraid or excited.

prickly (**prickliness**) A **prickly** plant has a lot of prickles on it. ■ A **prickly** person loses their temper easily. ■ If a **prickly** problem or issue is difficult to deal with. ■ **Prickly heat** is a condition caused by very hot weather, in which your sweat ducts are blocked and your skin comes up in a hot itchy rash.

pride (**priding, prided**) **Pride** is (a) a feeling of satisfaction because you have done something well. (b) a feeling of dignity and self-respect. (c) a feeling of being superior to other people. ■ If you **pride yourself** on a quality or skill, you are proud of having it, and usually make sure other people know about it too. ■ If something you have is your **pride and joy,** you are very pleased with it and it is important to you. ■ If something has **pride of place,** it is treated as the most important thing in a group of things. ■ A **pride** of lions is a group of them.

priest (**priestess, priestesses**) A **priest** is an ordained Christian minister. ■ In some non-Christian religions, a **priest** is a man with special duties and responsibilities in a place where people worship. A **priestess** is a woman with similar duties and responsibilities.

priesthood The **priesthood** is the position and office of being a priest. *He thought of going into the priesthood.* ■ The **priesthood** is all the members of the Christian clergy, especially in a particular Church.

priestly means to do with a priest. *...priestly duties.*

prig (**priggish**) If you call someone a **prig** or say they are **priggish,** you mean they are irritatingly proud of their good behaviour and think they are better than other people.

prim (**primly**) A **prim** person is easily shocked by anything rude or improper. ■ If something is **prim,** it is very neat and tidy. ...*prim white blouses.*

prima ballerina (*pron:* **pree**-ma) In a ballet or ballet company, the **prima ballerina** is the most important female dancer.

primacy (*pron:* **prime**-a-see) If something has **primacy** in a certain situation, it is the most important or powerful thing in it. ...*the growing primacy of television in broadcasting.*

prima donna A **prima donna** is a famous female opera singer. ■ If you call someone a **prima donna,** you mean they are temperamental and difficult to deal with.

primaeval See **primeval.**

prima facie (*pron:* **prime**-a fay-shee) is used to describe something which seems to be true when you consider it for the first time. 'Prima facie' is Latin for 'as it seems at first'. ...*a prima facie case of libel.*

primal means to do with the basic causes or origins of things. ...*primal fears and urges.*

primarily is used to say what is the most important aspect of something. *Miró was primarily a painter.*

primary (**primaries**) The **primary** thing in a situation is the main one. *The primary aim of economic policy, the government says, is to reduce inflation.* ■ **Primary** is used to talk about the first stage of a process. ...*the primary treatment of sewerage.* ■ **Primary** education is for children aged between 4 or 5 and 11. ■ In the US, various kinds of preliminary elections and selection procedures are called **primaries.** Their purpose is to choose convention delegates and candidates for political office.

primary colour The **primary colours** in light are red, green, and blue, which combine to produce all other colours, including white but not black. ■ In art, the **primary colours** are red, yellow, and blue, which can be mixed to make other colours.

primary health care is the treatment or advice you get from a GP, district nurse, or health visitor, as distinct from hospital treatment.

primary school A **primary school** is for children aged between 4 or 5 and 11.

primate A **primate** is a member of the group of mammals which includes humans, monkeys, and apes. ■ A **primate** is an archbishop.

prime (**priming, primed**) The **prime** thing in any situation is the most important one. ...*the prime reason for their journey.* ■ **Prime** is used to describe things which are of the best possible quality. ...*prime cuts of venison.* ■ If someone or something is a **prime mover** in a plan or situation, they have an important influence in starting it. ■ You say someone is in their **prime** when they are at the most active or successful stage of their life. ■ If you **prime** someone, you prepare them for something by giving them information about it. ■ If a person or thing is **primed** to do something, they are ready to do it. *Cruise stands stripped to the waist, muscles primed for boxing.*

Prime Minister (**prime ministerial**) The leader of the government in the UK and many other countries is called the **Prime Minister. Prime ministerial** means to do with being a prime minister. ...*his prime ministerial duties.*

prime number A **prime number** is a whole number greater than 1 which cannot be divided exactly by any whole number except itself and 1. So, for example, 2, 3, 7, and 11 are prime numbers.

primer is a type of paint put onto wood or metal to prepare it for the main layer of paint. ■ A **primer** is a beginners book on a subject.

prime time TV or radio programmes are broadcast in the evening, the most popular time for watching TV or listening to the radio.

primeval (*or* **primaeval**) (*pron:* prime-**ee**-val) means belonging to a very early period in history. ...*primeval forests.*

primitive In **primitive** societies, people live in a simple way, usually without industries or a writing system. ■ You say something is **primitive** when it is very basic or old-fashioned, or at an early stage of its development. ...*primitive sound equipment.*

primly See **prim.**

primogeniture is a system in which the eldest son or eldest child inherits all their parents' property.

primordial means existing at the beginning of time. ...*the primordial sea.*

primrose – Primroses are small pale yellow flowers which come out in Spring.

prince A **prince** is (a) a male member of a royal family, especially the son of a king or queen. (b) a male royal ruler of a small country or state.

princeling In the past, rulers of very small territories were sometimes called **princelings.**

princely means belonging to a prince or suitable for a prince. ■ A **princely** sum of money is very large.

princess (**princesses**) A **princess** is (a) a female member of a royal family, especially a daughter of a king or queen, or the wife of a prince. (b) a female royal ruler of a small country or state.

Princess Royal is a title sometimes given to the British monarch's eldest daughter.

principal The **principal** person or thing is the main or most important one. *Rubber became the small country's principal cash crop.* ■ The **principal** of a school or college is the person in charge of it.

principality (**principalities**) A **principality** is a country ruled by a prince or princess.

principally is used when mentioning the main thing to which something applies. *He built up a considerable reputation, principally in civil cases.*

principle (**principled**) A person's **principles** are their beliefs about the way they should behave. **Principled** behaviour is based on moral beliefs. ■ A **principle** is a general rule which provides a basis for people's actions or for the way society is organized. ...*the fundamental principle of one-person-one-vote.* ■ If you agree to something **in principle,** you agree to the idea of it, but may be unable or unwilling to support it in practice. ■ A **principle** is a scientific law explaining how something happens or works.

print When something like a book, newspaper, or money is **printed,** it is produced in large quantities by a mechanical process. ■ When something like a speech or piece of writing is **printed,** it is included in a paper, magazine, or book. ■ If a book is **in print,** it is available from a publisher. ■ The letters and numbers on the pages of a book, newspaper, or other document are called the **print.** ■ If you say something is a **licence to print money,** you mean it cannot fail to earn someone a very large amount of money. ■ When information from a computer is **printed out,** it is reproduced on paper called **print-out.** ■ A **print** is the pattern printed on a piece of material. ■ A **print** is (a) a photographic copy of a painting. (b) a photograph. ■ A **print** is an outline made by something pressing onto a surface. *...a palm print.* ■ If you **print,** you write in letters which are not joined together.

printed circuit board A **printed circuit board** is an electronic circuit which uses lines of copper on a fibreglass base to conduct electricity, instead of wire.

printer A **printer** is (a) a person or firm that prints books or newspapers. (b) a machine for printing information from a computer.

printing press A **printing press** is a machine for printing books and papers.

print-out See print.

print run A **print run** is all the copies of something produced by a printing press at one time.

prior If something happens **prior** to a time or event, it happens before it. ■ **Prior** is used to describe something which has happened or been provided before another event takes place. *Demonstrations are illegal without prior permission.* ■ A **prior** claim or duty is more important than other claims or duties. ■ A **prior** is a monk in charge of a priory, or one who is an abbot's deputy in a monastery.

prioress (**prioresses**) A **prioress** is a nun in charge of a priory, or one who is an abbess's deputy.

prioritize (*or* **prioritise**) (**prioritizing, prioritized**) If you **prioritize** a set of tasks, you decide which are the most important and do those first.

priority (**priorities**) If something is a **priority,** it must be done or dealt with as soon as possible. ■ If you **give priority** to something, you treat it as more important than other things. ■ Your **priorities** are the things you consider to be most important.

priory (**priories**) A **priory** is a place where a small group of monks or nuns live.

prise (*or* **prize**) (**prising, prised**) If you **prise** one thing away from another, you force it away from the other thing. Similarly, you can **prise** something **open.**

prism In maths, a **prism** is a solid shape with two identical parallel ends and the same cross-section throughout. ■ A **prism** is an object made of clear glass with many flat sides. It separates light passing through it into the colours of the rainbow.

prison A **prison** is a building where criminals and people awaiting trial are kept.

prison camp A **prison camp** is a guarded camp where prisoners of war or political prisoners are kept.

prisoner A **prisoner** is (a) someone kept in a prison because they have committed a crime or are waiting to be tried for one. (b) someone captured by an enemy in a war. ■ If you describe yourself as a **prisoner** of a situation, you mean you feel trapped by it. *She is a prisoner of her own celebrity.*

prisoner of conscience (**prisoners of conscience**) A **prisoner of conscience** is someone imprisoned by a government for their religion, race, or political views, rather than because they have committed a crime.

prisoner of war (**prisoners of war**) A **prisoner of war** is a member of the armed forces who has been captured during a war.

prison officer A **prison officer** is someone who supervises the prisoners in a prison.

prissy If you say someone is **prissy,** you mean they are easily shocked by anything slightly rude or improper.

pristine things are completely new and clean.

privacy (*usual pron:* **priv**-a-see) is being alone, so you can do things without being seen or disturbed.

private (**privately**) **Private** is used to describe (a) things or places which are for the use of one person or group, rather than the general public. *...a private jet.* (b) services or industries which are owned and controlled by an individual or organization, rather than by the state. *...private medicine.* ■ **Private** discussions take place between a small group of people and are kept secret from others. *...a private meeting.* ■ If you say something **privately** or **in private,** you say it to one person or group rather than the general public, because you do not want it to be generally known. You can also talk about things being done **privately** or **in private.** *Evidence will be heard in private.* ■ Your **private** activities are connected with your personal life. *...a private telephone call.* ■ If you describe someone as a **private** person, you mean they are very quiet and do not share their thoughts and feelings with others. ■ A **private** is a soldier of the lowest rank in the British army.

private company A **private company** is a limited company which does not issue shares to the public.

private detective A **private detective** is a detective who is not in the police force and who can be hired to carry out investigations.

private eye A **private eye** is the same as a private detective.

private member's bill A **private member's bill** is a law proposed by a backbench MP acting as an individual rather than as a member of a political party.

private parts Someone's **private parts** are their outer sex organs.

private school A **private school** is a school which is not supported financially by the government and charges fees. Private schools are now usually called 'independent schools'.

private secretary (**private secretaries**) A **private secretary** is a secretary working for just one person.

private sector The **private sector** is the part of a country's economy which is not controlled or supported financially by the state.

privation If you suffer **privations,** you are deprived of the basic things you need to live a normal life. *The privations of the coming winter will be great.*

privatize (*or* **privatise**) (**privatizing, privatized; privatization**) If a state-owned organization is **privatized,** the government sells it by offering shares in it to private individuals or groups.

privet (*pron:* **priv**-it) is an evergreen shrub, often used to make hedges.

privilege (**privileged**) A **privilege** is a special right or advantage which puts one person or group in a better position than others. **Privileged** is used to describe a right or advantage like this. *...Germany's privileged access to central Europe.* ■ **Privilege** is the power and advantages belonging to a small group of people, usually because of their wealth or social class. You say people like these are **privileged.** ■ If you say something involving yourself is a **privilege,** you mean you recognize that you have been given an advantage or opportunity which not many people have, and you are pleased and grateful about it.

privy (**privies**) If you are **privy** to something secret, you are allowed to know about it. ■ A **privy** was a toilet, especially an outside one.

Privy Council In Britain, the **Privy Council** is a group of people appointed to advise the monarch on political affairs.

prize (**prizing, prized**) A **prize** is something of value, for example money or a trophy, given to the winner of a game or contest, or as a reward for doing good work. ■ **Prize** is used to describe something which is of such high quality that it has won prizes, or deserves to. *...prize leeks.* ■ If you **prize** something, you consider it to be very valuable and important. ■ See also **prise.**

prize-fighter (**prize fight**) A **prize-fighter** is a boxer who fights to win money. The matches he takes part in are called **prize fights.**

prize-winning (**prize-winner**) **Prize-winning** is used to describe a person or thing that has won a prize. *...a prize-winning poet.* A **prize-winner** is someone who has won a prize.

pro A **pro** is someone who does something, especially sport, professionally. *...a pro baseball team.* ■ The **pros and cons** of something are its advantages and disadvantages.

pro- (*or* **pro**) is used to form words which say who or what someone supports. *...pro-abortion groups. ...pro government forces.*

proactive (*or* **pro-active**) policies involve taking the initiative and making things happen, rather than simply reacting to things.

probable (**probably; probability, probabilities**) If you say something is **probable** or talk about its **probability,** you mean it is likely to be true or correct, or likely to happen. *Once the fit is over, your child will probably want to sleep.* ■ You say **in all**

probability when you are confident that something is true or correct, or likely to happen. ■ A **probability** is a mathematical measurement of how likely it is that something will happen.

probate In law, **probate** is the process of proving that a will is valid and can be carried out.

probation (**probationary**) **Probation** is a period of time during which a convicted person is not sent to prison but has to fulfil certain conditions and is supervised by a probation officer. During this time, you say the person is **on probation.** ■ **Probation** is a period of time during which someone's work is assessed before they are given a permanent job. This period is called a **probationary** period. **Probationary** is also used to describe the person being assessed. *...probationary teachers.*

probationary See **probation.**

probation officer A **probation officer** is someone who supervises and helps people on probation.

probe (**probing, probed**) If you **probe** something, especially something people want to keep secret, you investigate it. An investigation like this is called a **probe.** ■ A **probe** is a thin metal object used by a surgeon to examine a patient's body during an operation. ■ See also **space probe.**

probity is honest and trustworthy behaviour.

problem A **problem** is an unsatisfactory situation which causes difficulties. ■ **Problem** children continually cause difficulties for themselves and other people, often because they have had unhappy experiences. ■ A **problem** is a puzzle for people to solve.

problematic (**problematical**) If something is **problematic** or **problematical,** it involves problems and difficulties.

proboscis (*pron:* pro-**boss**-iss) (**proboscises**) A **proboscis** is a long flexible tube which some insects use as a mouth. ■ An elephant's trunk can be called its **proboscis.** ■ People sometimes humorously call a person's nose their **proboscis.**

procedure (**procedural**) A **procedure** is a way of doing something, especially the accepted or correct way. *...a breakdown in safety procedures.* **Procedural** means involving a procedure. *...procedural errors.*

proceed (**proceeding, proceeded**) If you **proceed** to do something, you start doing it, or continue doing it. *He proceeded to break records at an amazing rate.* ■ When you are talking about a series of events, especially organized ones, you can refer to them as the **proceedings.** *The entire proceedings can be watched from the comfort of the shore.* ■ Legal **proceedings** are legal actions taken against someone. *...bankruptcy proceedings.* ■ If you **proceed** in a certain direction, you go in that direction. ■ The **proceeds** (*pron:* pro-seeds) of an event or activity are the money obtained from it.

process (**processes, processing, processed**) A **process** is a series of actions or events aimed at achieving a particular result. *...the Middle East peace process.* ■ If you are doing one thing and you do something else **in the process,** you do the second thing as a result of doing the first. ■ If you are **in the process of** doing something, you are in the middle of doing it. ■ When foods or materials are

processed, they are treated in some way. ■ When information is **processed,** it is dealt with systematically.

procession (processional) A **procession** is a line of people or vehicles moving together, for example as part of a ceremony. **Processional** means to do with processions. *...the processional routes to Buckingham Palace.* ■ A **procession** of things is a long series of them.

processor A **processor** is a company which processes something. *...a cocoa processor.* ■ In computing, a **processor** is the same as a central processing unit. ■ See also **word processor.**

proclaim (proclaiming, proclaimed; proclamation) If someone **proclaims** something or makes a **proclamation,** they make an important public announcement. See also **self-proclaimed.**

proclivity (proclivities) If you talk about someone's **proclivities,** you mean their tendency to behave in certain ways. *...his sexual proclivities.*

procrastinate (procrastinating, procrastinated; procrastination) If you **procrastinate,** you keep leaving something until later.

procreate (procreating, procreated; procreation, procreative) When animals or people **procreate,** they produce offspring. **Procreative** means to do with procreating. *...women's procreative powers.*

procurator Some countries have senior legal officials or administrators called **procurators.**

procurator fiscal In Scotland, the **procurator fiscal** is a legal officer who performs the functions of a public prosecutor and coroner in a particular district.

procure (procuring, procured) If you **procure** something, especially something difficult to get, you obtain it.

procurement is buying or obtaining something, especially supplies for a large organization like the army.

prod (prodding, prodded) If you **prod** someone or something or give them a **prod,** you push them quickly with your finger or a pointed object. ■ A **prod** or **cattle prod** is a long pointed metal stick, often electrified, used to poke animals to make them move along. ■ If you **prod** someone into doing something, you get them to do it by continually reminding them about it or urging them to do it.

prodigal You call someone a **prodigal** or a **prodigal son** when they have gone away or done something wrong, but are now sorry for it and have been welcomed back or forgiven.

prodigious (prodigiously) If something is **prodigious,** it is amazingly large or extensive. *...her prodigious memory.*

prodigy (prodigies) A **prodigy** or **child prodigy** is someone who shows extraordinary natural ability for something such as music at an early age.

produce (producing, produced) If one thing **produces** another, it causes the other thing to happen or exist. *The crisis has produced a new refugee problem.* ■ When foodstuffs or goods are **produced,** they are grown or manufactured on a large scale. ■ **Produce** (*pron:* **prod**-juice) is food produced by farming. *There was almost no fresh produce in the shops.* ■ A

producer of a food or material is a company or country which grows or provides a large amount of it. *...the world's largest steel producer.* ■ If you **produce** an object from somewhere, you bring it out so it can be seen. *The assailant produced a knife and snatched the briefcase.* ■ If someone **produces** a play, film, or record, they organize it and decide how it should be done. A person who does this is called a **producer.**

product A **product** is something a company makes and sells, often in large quantities. ■ If someone is the **product** of something like a type of education, their attitudes and behaviour result from it. *He speaks and acts as if he is the product of a Victorian rather than a 20th-century upbringing.* ■ In maths, the **product** of two or more numbers is the result of multiplying them together.

production is growing or manufacturing something in large quantities. *...the production and export of cocaine.* ■ When something is created as a result of a natural process, you can talk about its **production.** *These proteins stimulate the production of blood cells.* ■ **Production** is the organization and preparation of a play, film, TV programme, or record. *This film went very wrong during production.* ■ A **production** is a performed version of a play or opera. *...the London production of 'Phantom of the Opera'.*

production line A **production line** is a system in a factory in which individual machines make one part of a product before passing it on to the next machine.

productive (productively) If you say someone or something is **productive,** you mean they produce a lot of goods or do a lot of work. ■ If something like a meeting is **productive,** useful things come out of it.

productivity is the rate at which goods are produced, and how efficiently they are produced. *...a reorganisation to boost productivity by 60%.*

Prof in front of someone's name means 'Professor'. *...Prof Michael Dummett.*

profane (profanity) If you say someone is **profane** or accuse them of **profanity,** you mean they show disrespect for religion and are sinful. ■ **Profane** is used to talk about non-religious things, as opposed to religious ones. *...the sacred and profane pleasures of Kathmandu.*

profess (professes, professing, professed) If someone **professes** to do or have something, they claim to do or have it, although they may not be telling the truth. *He professes to loathe media attention.* ■ You say someone **professes** something when they openly express it. *He openly professed his ambition to become Prime Minister. ...a professed liberal.*

profession A **profession** is a job which requires advanced education or training and has a fairly high status. ■ When someone claims to have certain beliefs or feelings, you can talk about their **professions** of these beliefs or feelings. *The paper noted his professions of loyalty to the Republic.*

professional (professionally, professionalism) **Professional** means to do with professions. *...professional qualifications.* A **professional** person is someone who has a profession. ■ **Professional** means to do with people's work, as distinct from their private lives. *He spent the whole of his professional life working as a librarian.* ■ A **professional** is someone who does something as a job which many people do as a hobby. *...a professional actress.* ■ **Professional** is used to praise things which are done skilfully or to a very high standard. *The coalition appeared to run a highly professional campaign... He praised the newscaster's unruffled professionalism.*

professionalize (*or* **professionalise**) (**professionalizing, professionalized; professionalization**) If an activity is **professionalized**, people start to earn money from doing it, rather than doing it as a hobby.

professionally See **professional.**

professor In a British university, a **professor** is a person with the highest academic rank, especially a person in charge of a department. ■ In an American university or college, a **professor** is a teacher.

professorial is used to describe someone who looks or behaves like a professor. *He cuts an unlikely, almost professorial, figure.* ■ **Professorial** means to do with the work of a professor. *...professorial departments.*

professorship A **professorship** is the post of professor in a university.

proffer (**proffering, proffered**) If you **proffer** something to someone, you offer it to them.

proficient (**proficiency**) If you are **proficient** at something, you are very good at it. **Proficiency** is the ability to do something well.

profile (**profiling, profiled**) Your **profile** is the outline of your face seen from the side. ■ A person's or thing's **profile** is their public image. You say they have a **high profile** when they are well known. ■ If a journalist **profiles** someone or writes a **profile** of them, he or she writes a short description of their life and character.

profit (**profiting, profited**) If you make a **profit,** you sell something for more than it cost you. ■ If you **profit** from something, you gain an advantage or benefit from it.

profitable (**profitably, profitability**) A **profitable** organization makes a profit. ■ If something you do is **profitable,** it results in some advantage or benefit. *...a very profitable discussion.*

profiteering (**profiteer**) Profiteering is making large profits by charging high prices for goods which are hard to get. People who make money like this are called **profiteers.**

profit margin A **profit margin** is how much greater the selling price of a product is than its cost.

profit-sharing is a system by which all the people who work in a company have a share in its profits.

profligate (**profligately, profligacy**) If you call someone **profligate** or talk about their **profligacy,** you mean they are extravagant and wasteful.

pro forma In banking, a company's **pro forma** balance or earnings are their expected balance or earnings.

profound (**profoundly; profundity**) Profound is used to emphasize how great or intense something is. *...profound embarrassment. ...profoundly deaf peo-*

ple. ■ If you say something is **profound** or talk about its **profundity,** you mean it shows great intellectual depth and understanding. *...profound philosophical questions.*

profuse (*pron:* pro-**fyooss**) (**profusely, profusion**) If something is **profuse,** there is a lot of it. *...profuse apologies... He was bleeding profusely.* You can also say there is a **profusion** of something.

progenitor A **progenitor** of someone is a direct ancestor of theirs. ■ The **progenitor** of an idea is the person who first thought of it.

progeny (*pron:* **proj**-in-ee) The **progeny** of people or animals are their offspring.

progesterone (*pron:* pro-**jest**-er-ohn) is a hormone secreted in the ovaries of female mammals, which prepares the uterus for pregnancy. It is also used in the birth control pill.

prognosis (*plural:* **prognoses**) A **prognosis** is a prediction, especially about what course an illness will take.

prognostication A **prognostication** is a prediction.

program (**programming, programmed; programmer**) If you **program** a computer, you give it a set of instructions called a **program.** A person who writes programs is called a computer **programmer.** ■ **Program** is the American spelling of 'programme'.

programme (*Am:* **program**) (**programming, programmed**) A **programme** is a series of actions or events which are planned to take place. *...a programme to combat AIDS.* ■ If something has been **programmed** to happen, it has been planned in advance. ■ A TV or radio **programme** is something like a show, play, or game broadcast on TV or radio. **Programming** is choosing and organizing what is going to be broadcast. ■ The **programme** for a concert or show is (a) the items performed in it. (b) a booklet or sheet of paper giving information about the play or concert you are attending. ■ If you **programme** a machine or system, you set its controls so it will work in a particular way. ■ If someone is **programmed** to behave in a certain way, they are likely to behave in that way, because of social or biological factors they cannot control. *People are going to be the weight they were genetically programmed to be.*

programmer See **program.**

progress (**progresses, progressing, progressed**) If you **progress** (*pron:* pro-**gress**), you get better at something or move on to a more advanced stage of it. *They progressed to the semi-finals.* ■ **Progress** (*pron:* **pro**-gress) is the process of gradually improving or getting near to achieving something. *Their talks made little progress.* ■ The **progress** of something or the way it **progresses** is the way it develops or continues. ■ If something is **in progress,** it is happening. ■ When someone or something is moving in a certain direction, you can talk about their **progress** in that direction. *...our slow progress towards Cape Town.*

progression A **progression** is a gradual development from one thing to another.

progressive (**progressively**) If someone is **progressive,** they have modern ideas and are eager to change the way things are done. Someone like this is called a **progressive.** ■ A **progressive** change happens gradually.

prohibit (**prohibiting, prohibited; prohibition**) If a law or rule **prohibits** people from doing something, it forbids them to do it. ■ In the US, **Prohibition** was the official banning of alcohol between 1920 and 1933.

prohibitive (**prohibitively**) If the cost of something is **prohibitive,** it is so high people cannot afford it.

project (**projection**) A **project** (*pron:* **proj**-ekt) is a carefully planned scheme to achieve something or a detailed study of something, carried out over a period of time. *...road construction projects.* ■ If something is **projected** (*pron:* pro-**jekt**-id), it is planned or expected. A **projection** of a future amount is an estimate of it. *Projections of the result are already coming in.* ■ If you **project** a film or slide onto a screen, you make it appear there. ■ If you **project** something or someone in a certain way, you try to give people a particular impression of them. *He had tried to project himself as a wise, avuncular leader.* ■ If you **project** your feelings on other people, you imagine they have the same feelings as you. *She tends to project her fears onto strangers.* ■ If something **projects,** it sticks out beyond a surface or edge. A **projection** is something which sticks out like this.

projectile A **projectile** is an object fired from a gun or thrown at something.

projection See **project.**

projectionist A **projectionist** is someone whose job is to operate a projector in a cinema.

projector A **projector** is a machine which projects films or slides onto a screen.

prolapse A **prolapse** is a medical condition in which an organ of the body sags or slips down from its proper position.

prole A **prole** is a member of the proletariat.

proletariat (*pron:* pro-lit-**air**-ee-at) (**proletarian**) Working-class people are sometimes called the **proletariat. Proletarian** means things to do with the proletariat. *...a proletarian revolution.*

proliferate (**proliferating, proliferated; proliferation**) You say things **proliferate** when the number of them increases rapidly.

prolific A **prolific** writer, artist, or composer produces a large number of works. ■ An animal or person that produces a large number of offspring can be called **prolific.**

prolix If a speech or piece of writing is **prolix,** it is so long as to be boring.

prologue A **prologue** is a speech or piece of text which introduces a play or book.

prolong (**prolonged; prolongation**) If you **prolong** something, you make it last longer. ■ A **prolonged** event or situation continues for a long time, or for longer than expected.

prom The **proms** are the series of promenade concerts held each summer in the Royal Albert Hall, London. ■ In the US, a **prom** is a formal dance held for students at a high school or college. ■ In a seaside town, the **prom** is the promenade.

promenade (**promenading, promenaded**) In a seaside town, a **promenade** is a road or path along the sea front. ■ If you **promenade,** you go for a stroll, especially in a public place. A walk like this can be called a **promenade.** ■ A **promenade** concert is one at which some of the audience stand rather than sit.

prominent (**prominently, prominence**) A **prominent** person is important and well-known. *...prominent lawyers.* ■ If something is **prominent,** it is very noticeable, or it is an important part of something. ■ If something is **given prominence,** a lot of attention is paid to it. ■ You say an object is **prominent** when it sticks out. *...prominent teeth.*

promiscuous (**promiscuity**) If someone is **promiscuous,** they have sex with many different people. Behaviour like this is called **promiscuity.**

promise (**promising, promised**) If you **promise** to do something, you say you will definitely do it. If you **promise** something to someone, you guarantee they will get it. This is called making a **promise.** ■ If something **promises** to have a particular quality, it shows signs that it will have that quality. *The hearings promise to be lively and informative.* ■ If someone or something shows **promise** or looks **promising,** they seem likely to be very good or successful. *...a promising political career.*

promo (*pron:* **proe**-moe) (**promos**) A **promo** is a short video made to promote a pop record.

promontory (**promontories**) A **promontory** is a high part of the coast which juts out into the sea.

promote (**promoting, promoted; promotion, promoter**) If you **promote** something, you help it to develop or succeed. Someone who promotes something can be called a **promoter** of it. ■ If a company **promotes** a product, it tries to increase its sales and popularity. ■ If someone **promotes** a public event, they organize and finance it. Someone who does this is called a **promoter.** ■ If you are **promoted** or given a **promotion,** you are given a more important job in the organization you work for. ■ When a football team is **promoted,** it goes up into a higher division.

promotional events or ideas are designed to increase the sales of a product or service.

prompt (**promptly, promptness, prompter**) If something **prompts** an event or action, it causes it to happen. ■ If something **prompts** you to do something, it makes you decide to do it. If you **prompt** someone to do something, you urge them to do it. ■ If you **prompt** an actor, you remind them of the next words they are supposed to say. The person who does this during a performance is called the **prompt** or **prompter.** ■ A **prompt** action is taken without delay. ■ If you do something **promptly at** a particular time, you do it at exactly that time. *It had started promptly at 8.45.*

promulgate (**promulgating, promulgated; promulgation**) When a new law is **promulgated,** it is announced publicly.

pron is short for 'pronounced'.

prone If someone or something is **prone** to something, they have a tendency to be affected by it. **-prone** is added to words to say someone or something is frequently affected by something bad. ...*an accident-prone family.* ■ If you are lying **prone**, you are lying flat on your stomach. See also **supine.**

prong (-pronged) The **prongs** of a fork are the thin pointed parts. ■ -**prong** and -**pronged** are used to say an action is divided into a number of separate parts. ...*a three-pronged attack.*

pronoun A **pronoun** is a word you use instead of a noun. 'She', 'them', and 'something' are pronouns.

pronounce (**pronouncing, pronounced; pronunciation**) The way you **pronounce** a word or sound is the way you say it. *Feng shui (pronounced fung schway) is the ancient Chinese art of placing things.* The **pronunciation** of a word or sound is the way it is pronounced. ■ When someone **pronounces** a verdict or their opinion, they state or announce it formally. *A team of observers pronounced the election free and fair.* ■ If something is **pronounced,** it is noticeable. *Attitudes are changing now, as nationalism becomes more pronounced.*

pronouncement A **pronouncement** is a public or official statement on an important topic.

pronunciation See **pronounce.**

proof is evidence which shows something is true or exists. ■ If a person or thing is **proof** against something, they cannot be harmed or affected by it. *The fortress was proof against the techniques of attack then in use.* ■ A **proof** is a first printed copy of a text. It is produced so mistakes can be corrected before more copies are printed. ■ **Proof** is a measure of the alcoholic strength of drinks like whisky and brandy. *Whisky sold in the UK is usually 70% proof.*

-**proof** (-**proofing, -proofed**) -**proof** is added to words to describe things which have been specially designed to prevent something harmful passing through them. ...*bullet-proof vests.* ...*draught-proofing.* See also **oven-proof.**

proof-reading (**proof-reader**) **Proof-reading** is reading a text which is going to be printed, to check for any mistakes which need to be corrected by the printer. Someone who does this as their job is called a **proof-reader.**

prop (**propping, propped**) If you **prop** an object against something, you put it in a position where it is supported by that thing. *The lunch menu board had been propped on the counter.* ■ A **prop** is a stick or some other object used to support something. ...*a clothes prop.* ■ If a government **props up** something like a system, it supports it and helps it to survive. ...*emergency measures to prop up the housing market.* Something that helps keep a system or organization going can be called a **prop.** ■ The **props** in a play are the objects used in it. ■ The **prop** on a plane or boat is its propeller.

propaganda (**propagandist**) **Propaganda** is information, often inaccurate or biased, which is published or broadcast by an organization to influence people. Someone who produces propaganda is called a **propagandist.**

propagate (**propagating, propagated; propagation**) If you **propagate** plants, you grow more of them from the original ones, for example by taking cuttings or sowing seeds. This process is called

propagation. ■ If people **propagate** an idea, they spread it so that it will influence other people.

propane is a gas which comes from petroleum and is used for cooking and heating.

propel (**propelling, propelled**) If something is **propelled,** it is made to move forward. ...*a rocket-propelled grenade.* ■ If something **propels** someone to victory, it makes them the winner in a competition.

propellant A **propellant** is (a) a substance burned in a rocket motor, which gives the rocket its thrust. (b) an explosive in a gun which forces out the ammunition.

propeller A **propeller** on a boat or aircraft is a device with rotating blades mounted on a shaft, which causes the boat or aircraft to move.

propensity (**propensities**) If you have a **propensity** to behave in a certain way, you have a natural tendency to behave that way.

proper (**properly**) **Proper** is used to describe things which are of an acceptable standard. *No proper investigation had been carried out.* ■ **Proper** is used to emphasize that you are talking about a particular thing, and not about something similar connected with it. *The election proper is not until April.* ■ **Proper** is used to mean 'correct'. *Its proper place is in a museum.* ■ **Proper** behaviour is socially and morally acceptable.

proper noun A **proper noun** or **proper name** is the name of a person, place, or individual thing, for example 'Tony Blair', 'Cardiff', or 'the Statue of Liberty'.

property (**properties**) Your **property** is all the things you own. If something is your **property,** it belongs to you. ■ **Property** is buildings and land. ...*a tax on residential property.* A **property** is a building and the land that goes with it. ■ The **properties** of a substance or object are its characteristics or qualities. ...*a light-weight plastic foam with good insulating properties.*

prophesy (**prophesies, prophesying, prophesied; prophecy, prophecies**) If you **prophesy** (pron: prof-iss-eye) something, you say it will happen. A **prophecy** (pron: prof-iss-see) is a statement saying something will happen.

prophet A **prophet** is a person believed to have been chosen by God to pass on the things God wants to tell people. ■ A **prophet** is (a) someone who predicts that a particular thing will happen. *The climate prophets are predicting that this could cause global warming.* (b) someone who strongly and actively supports a particular idea. ...*a prophet of a fairer and more tolerant society.*

prophetic (**prophetically**) You say something was **prophetic** when it correctly described what later happened. ...*prophetic dreams.*

prophylactic A **prophylactic** drug or treatment is concerned with preventing disease, rather than curing it.

propitious If something is **propitious,** it is likely to lead to success. *This is not the most propitious time to take over as Chancellor.*

proponent A **proponent** of an idea or policy is someone who actively supports it.

proportion (**proportioned**) A **proportion** of an amount or group is a part of it. *A high proportion of Americans in Germany are there as members of the forces.* ■ The **proportion** of one amount to another is its size in comparison with the other amount. *In 1965 the proportion of European to non-European immigrants was nine to one.* ■ If something increases or decreases **in proportion** to something else, it goes up or down at the same rate. *Cities expanded in proportion with the growth in industry.* ■ If a part of something is **in proportion** to the whole, it is the correct size in comparison with the whole. ■ You can talk about the **proportions** of something when you mean its size. *Farming subsidies have reached absurd proportions.* ■ If you say someone is getting things **out of proportion**, you mean they are behaving as if something is more important or more worrying than it really is.

proportional (**proportionally**) **Proportional** is used to say how large or small something is when compared to something else. *In the past Sweden has taken a proportionally higher number of refugees than any other country.* ■ If one thing is **proportional to** another, it remains the same size in comparison with the other thing.

proportional representation or **PR** is a system of voting in elections in which each party is represented in parliament according to the number of votes it wins. See also **first-past-the-post**.

proportionate (**proportionately**) **Proportionate** means the same as 'proportional'.

propose (**proposing, proposed; proposal, proposer**) If you **propose** something, you suggest that it should be done. A **proposal** is a suggested course of action. ■ If you **propose** to do something, you intend to do it. ■ In a meeting, if you **propose** a person or **propose** a motion, you suggest them for people to vote for. You are called the proposer of the candidate or motion. ■ If you **propose** someone in an election, you suggest them as a candidate. You are called a **proposer** of the person. ■ If you **propose** a motion in a debate, you introduce it and say why people should agree with it. You are called the **proposer** of the motion. ■ If you **propose** to someone, you ask them to marry you. This is called a marriage **proposal**.

proposition (**propositioning, propositioned**) A **proposition** is a statement put forward for discussion. *The proposition is that man is basically selfish.* ■ A **proposition** is an offer or suggestion. *I have a proposition to make.* ■ If someone **propositions** another person, especially a person they are not in a relationship with, they ask that person to have sex with them.

propound If you **propound** an idea or opinion, you put it forward for people to consider.

proprietary products can only be made and sold by a certain person or group of people.

proprietor The **proprietor** of a business is its owner.

proprietorial If your behaviour is **proprietorial**, you behave in a way which shows you are, or think you are, the owner of something.

propriety (**proprieties**) **Propriety** is behaviour which is socially or morally acceptable. *He is no respecter of proprieties.*

propulsion is the power which moves something, especially a vehicle, in a forward direction. *...rocket propulsion.*

pro rata If someone is paid **pro rata** for something they do, they are paid a proportionate amount. For example, if the wage for a job is £300 for a 40-hour week, and someone is paid **pro rata** for working a 30-hour week, they receive £225.

prorogue (**proroguing, prorogued; prorogation**) If parliament is **prorogued**, it is suspended for a period of time, but not dissolved.

prosaic (*pron:* pro-**zay**-ik) (**prosaically**) If you say something is **prosaic**, you mean it is unimaginative and dull.

proscenium (*pron:* pro-**seen**-i-um) (*plural:* **prosceniums** or **proscenia**) A **proscenium** or **proscenium arch** is an arch in a theatre separating the stage from the audience.

proscribe (**proscribing, proscribed; proscription**) If people in authority **proscribe** something, they ban it. If something is **proscribed**, it is forbidden. *...the proscription of his records.*

prose is language, especially literary writing, which is not poetry.

prosecute (**prosecuting, prosecuted; prosecution**) If someone is **prosecuted** or a **prosecution** is brought against them, they are charged with a crime and put on trial. ■ In court, the lawyer who **prosecutes** is the one who tries to prove that the accused person is guilty. This lawyer and his or her assistants are also called the **prosecution**. *...a key prosecution witness.*

prosecuting attorney In the US, a **prosecuting attorney** is an official who conducts criminal prosecutions on behalf of the state and people.

prosecution See **prosecute**.

prosecutor A **prosecutor** is a lawyer or official who brings charges against someone and tries to prove they are guilty in a trial.

proselytize (*or* **proselytise**) (*pron:* **pross**-ill-it-ize) (**proselytizing, proselytized**) If you **proselytize**, you try to persuade people to leave their religious faith or political party and join yours.

prospect (**prospector**) If there is a **prospect** of something happening, there is a possibility it will happen. ■ A particular **prospect** is something you expect or know is going to happen. *...the prospect of a recession.* ■ Your **prospects** are your chances of being successful in your career. ■ If someone **prospects** (*pron:* pross-**pekts**) for a valuable substance like gold, they look for it in a particular place. A person who does this is called a **prospector**.

prospective is used to describe a person who intends to be a particular thing or is likely to become one. *The Labour Party has four prospective candidates.* ■ **Prospective** is used to describe things which are expected to happen. *...prospective earnings.*

prospector See **prospect**.

prospectus (**prospectuses**) A **prospectus** is a booklet produced by a university, school, or company giving details about it.

prosper (**prospering, prospered; prosperous, prosperity**) When people or businesses **prosper,** they are successful. When this happens, you say they are **prosperous** or talk about their **prosperity.** ...*Japan's economic prosperity.*

prostate The **prostate** or **prostate gland** is an organ situated just below the bladder in male mammals. It produces a liquid which forms part of the semen.

prosthesis (pron: pross-**theess**-siss) (**prosthetic**) A **prosthesis** (plural: **prostheses**) is an artificial body part, for example a limb or a breast. A part like this can also be called a **prosthetic** limb or breast (pron: pross-**thet**-tik).

prostitute (**prostituting, prostituted; prostitution**) A **prostitute** is a person, especially a woman, who has sex with men in exchange for money. This practice is called **prostitution.** ■ If you **prostitute** yourself, you use your talents for unworthy purposes, usually for money.

prostrate (**prostrating, prostrated**) If you **prostrate** yourself (pron: pross-**strate**), you lie face down on the ground, especially as an act of worship or submission. If you are in this position, you say you are **prostrate** (pron: **pross**-strate).

protagonist The **protagonists** in a play or novel are the main characters. ■ A **protagonist** of an idea or movement is a supporter of it. ...*Labour's anti-EU protagonists.*

protean (pron: pro-**tee**-an) If something is **protean,** it has the ability to keep changing its nature, appearance, or behaviour. ...*a protean virus.*

protect (**protection; protectionism, protectionist**) If you **protect** someone or something or give them **protection,** you keep them safe from harm. ■ A **protected species** of animal, bird, or plant is one you are not allowed to kill or interfere with, because it is in danger of becoming extinct. ■ If criminals extort **protection money** from people like shopkeepers, they demand money and in return promise not to hurt them or damage their property. ■ If a government **protects** an industry, it helps it by limiting imports or by putting a heavy tax on imported goods. Helping industries in this way is called **protectionism. Protectionist** means to do with protectionism; a **protectionist** is someone who favours a policy like this.

protective (**protectively, protectiveness**) A **protective** object or action is intended to protect someone or something from harm. ...*protective clothing.* ■ If someone is **protective** towards you, they show a strong desire to keep you safe from things which could hurt or frighten you.

protector A **protector** of a person or thing is someone or something which protects them. ...*ear protectors.*

protectorate A **protectorate** is a country controlled and protected by a more powerful country.

protégé (**protégée**) (both pron: **pro**-ti-zhay; the 'zh' sounds like 's' in 'pleasure') If someone helps and guides a young person, especially in his or her career, you say he or she is the person's **protégé.** You can also refer to a female protégé as a **protégée.**

protein (pron: **pro**-teen) A **protein** is a complex compound consisting of amino acid chains, found in many foods, for example meat and eggs, and essential for all living things.

protest (**protester, protestor**) If you **protest** about something (pron: pro-**test**), you say or show publicly that you do not approve of it. A **protest** (pron: **pro**-test) is a demonstration or statement like this. A **protester** or **protestor** is someone who protests in public about something. ■ If you **protest** when someone says or does something, you interrupt them to say you disagree with them or object to what they are doing. What you say is called a **protest.** *Despite his protests, six plainclothes officers searched the office.* ■ If you **protest** that something is the case, you insist it is the case. *He strenuously protested his innocence.*

Protestant (**Protestantism**) **Protestants** are Christians who are not Roman Catholics or members of one of the Orthodox churches.

protestation A **protestation** is a strong declaration that something is true or not true. *Protestations of peaceful intention on both sides are becoming louder.*

protester (**protestor**) See **protest.**

proto- is used to form words which describe things as being the first of their type. ...*proto-galaxies.*

protocol is a system of rules about the correct way to act on important formal occasions, for example at meetings between governments of different countries. ■ A **protocol** is the written record of a treaty or agreement.

proton A **proton** is a particle which forms part of the nucleus of an atom and which has a positive electrical charge.

prototype The **prototype** of something like a new vehicle is the first of its kind to be produced.

protozoan (pron: pro-toe-**zoe**-an) (plural: **protozoa**) A **protozoan** is a microscopic one-celled creature.

protract If something is **protracted,** it lasts longer than is usual or expected.

protractor A **protractor** is a flat semicircular piece of plastic, wood, or metal used for measuring angles.

protrude (**protruding, protruded; protrusion**) If something **protrudes** from somewhere, it sticks out. ...*protruding front teeth.* Something which sticks out can be called a **protrusion.**

proud (**prouder, proudest; proudly**) If you are **proud** of something you own or have done, it gives you a feeling of pleasure and satisfaction, and you show this in the way you behave. ■ If someone **does you proud,** they do something very well, so you can feel proud of them. ■ You say people are **proud** when they have great dignity and self-respect. ■ You say people are **proud** when they believe they are superior to other people.

provable If statements are **provable,** they can be proved to be true or correct.

prove (**proving, proved, have proved** or **have proven**) If you **prove** something is true, you show conclusively that it is true. ■ If someone or something **proves** to have a certain quality, it becomes clear that they have it. *The first half of the course proved difficult.* ...*young musicians of proven talent.*

provenance The **provenance** of something, especially a work of art, is the place it originally came from.

proverb (proverbial, proverbially) A **proverb** is a short well-known saying which is supposed to sum up an important truth about life. 'A stitch in time saves nine' is a typical proverb. ■ **Proverbial** is used when mentioning a proverb or some other well-known expression. ...*the proverbial man-in-the-street.* ■ If something is **proverbial,** it is well known or widely believed. *His generosity is proverbial.*

provide (providing, provided; provider) If you **provide** someone with something they need or want, you give it to them or make it available to them. A person or organization which does this can be called a **provider.** ...*Japan, China's biggest provider of foreign aid.* ■ If you **provide** for someone, you give them the things they need. *He had neglected to provide for his children.* ■ If something **provides** a useful or desirable feature or quality, it has it or gives it. *The war provided him with extraordinary opportunities.* ■ If you **provide** for a possible future event, you take it into account when you plan or do something. ■ If a law or decision **provides** that something will happen, it states that it will happen. *The treaty provides that, by the end of the century, the United States must have removed its bases.* ■ If you say something will happen **provided or providing** something else happens, you mean the first thing will happen only if the second one does. *The other proposal was to promise to cut income taxes, providing that spending was cut by an equal amount.*

providence (or Providence) is God, or a force believed to control the things which happen to people, especially in a positive way.

providential (providentially) If you say something which happens is **providential,** you mean it is very lucky.

providing (provider) See **provide.**

province A **province** is a large section of a country with its own administration. ■ The **provinces** are the parts of a country away from its capital. ■ If a subject or activity is someone's **province,** they have a special interest in it or responsibility for it.

provincial (provincialism) Provincial things and areas of a country are away from its capital. ...*provincial theatres.* ■ People who live in a country's capital sometimes call people from other parts of the country **provincials** or talk about their **provincialism,** implying that they are unsophisticated and perhaps narrow-minded.

provision (provisioning, provisioned) When something is provided for people, you talk about its **provision.** ...*childcare provision.* ■ A **provision** in an agreement is a condition which must be fulfilled. ■ **Provisions** are supplies of food. If a place is well **provisioned,** it has all the food or supplies people need.

provisional (provisionally) Provisional things are temporary and may be changed in the future. ...*a provisional government.*

proviso (pron: pro-**vize**-oh) **(provisos)** A **proviso** is a condition in an agreement. You agree to do something if this condition is fulfilled.

provocateur A **provocateur** is the same as an agent provocateur.

provocative (provocatively, provocation) If something is **provocative** or a **provocation,** it is intended to provoke an angry reaction. ■ Certain things can be described as **provocative** when they produce feelings of sexual desire. ...*sexually provocative newspaper advertising.*

provoke (provoking, provoked) If you **provoke** someone, you deliberately annoy them and try to make them react aggressively. ■ If something **provokes** an unpleasant reaction, it causes it. *News of his death provoked widespread anger.*

provost Some colleges have a head called a **provost,** for example the university colleges at Oxford and Cambridge. ■ In Scotland, a **provost** is the chairman and civic head of a district council. ■ In the Catholic and Anglican Churches, a **provost** is the person in charge of the administration of a cathedral or collegiate church.

prow The **prow** of a ship or boat is its front part.

prowess Someone's **prowess** is their ability to do something extremely well. ...*sporting prowess.*

prowl When an animal or person **prowls,** they move around quietly, usually when hunting. ■ You can say someone is **on the prowl** when they are looking for something like a sexual partner or a business deal.

prowler A **prowler** is someone who creeps around outside houses at night, usually intending to harm someone or commit a robbery.

proximity to a place is nearness to it. ...*Greece's proximity to the Balkans.*

proxy (proxies) If you do something **by proxy,** you arrange for someone to act on your behalf when you are not present, for example at an election; the person is called your **proxy.** ■ **Proxy** is used to describe other things carried out by someone on another person's behalf. *The Cambodian conflict was a proxy war between China and Vietnam.*

Prozac (pron: **pro**-zack) is the drug fluoxetine, and is taken to treat depression. 'Prozac' is a trademark.

prude See **prudish.**

prudent (prudently, prudence) If you are **prudent,** you are sensible and careful.

prudish (prude, prudishness, prudery) If you say someone is **prudish** or call them a **prude,** you mean they are easily shocked by things to do with nudity and sex. You talk about the **prudishness** or **prudery** of someone like this.

prune (pruning, pruned) A **prune** is a dried plum. ■ When you **prune** a tree or bush, you trim back some of its branches to make it look neater, or to get it to produce better fruit or flowers. ■ If an organization is **pruned,** it is made smaller, for example by reducing staff or spending.

prurient (pruriently, prurience) If someone or something is **prurient,** they are excessively interested in things to do with sex.

pry (pries, prying, pried) If you accuse someone of **prying,** you mean they keep poking their nose into other people's affairs.

PS is written before a message which has been added at the end of a letter. PS stands for 'postscript'.

psalm (*pron:* **sahm**) The **psalms** are the 150 songs, poems, and prayers which form the Book of Psalms in the Bible.

psalter (*pron:* **sawl**-ter) A **psalter** is a book containing a collection of psalms.

PSBR See **public sector**.

psephology (*pron:* sif-**fol**-loj-ee) (**psephologist, psephological**) **Psephology** is the study of elections and how people vote in them. ...*psephological research*.

pseud (*pron:* **syood**) If you say someone is a **pseud**, you mean they pretend to be knowledgeable or artistic, when in fact they are not.

pseudo- is put at the beginning of a word to describe something which is not what it is claimed to be. ...*pseudo-scientific theories*.

pseudonym (*pron:* **syoo**-doe-nim) A **pseudonym** is a name used by someone, especially a writer, instead of his or her real name.

psoriasis (*pron:* so-**rye**-a-siss) is a skin disease which produces red patches covered with silvery scales.

psych (*pron:* **sike**) If you **psych** yourself **up** to do something, you prepare yourself mentally, especially by telling yourself you can succeed.

psyche (*pron:* **sigh**-kee) Your **psyche** is your mind and your deepest feelings and attitudes.

psychedelic (*pron:* sigh-ked-**del**-lik) (**psychedelia**) **Psychedelic** drugs are drugs like LSD which have a strong affect on your mind, sometimes producing hallucinations. ■ **Psychedelic** means associated with the effects of drugs like LSD. ...*walls painted in psychedelic colours*. You can call things like this **psychedelia** (*pron:* sigh-ked-**dee**-lee-a).

psychiatry (**psychiatric, psychiatrically, psychiatrist**) **Psychiatry** is the branch of medicine concerned with the treatment of mental illness. **Psychiatric** means to do with psychiatry. ...*a psychiatric hospital*. A **psychiatrist** is a doctor who treats people suffering from mental illness.

psychic If someone is thought to be a **psychic** or to have **psychic** powers, they are supposed to have unusual mental abilities, such as being able to communicate with spirits or see into the future.

psycho (**psychos**) A **psycho** is the same as a psychopath.

psycho- is used to form words which describe things to do with the mind or mental processes. ...*a psycho-thriller*.

psychoactive drugs are drugs such as LSD which affect your mind.

psychoanalyse (*Am:* **psychoanalyze**) (**psychoanalysing, psychoanalysed**) When a psychiatrist or psychotherapist **psychoanalyses** someone, they examine or treat them using psychoanalysis.

psychoanalysis (**psychoanalyst; psychoanalytic, psychoanalytical**) **Psychoanalysis** is a method of treating someone who has mental problems by asking them about their feelings and their past to discover the cause of their problems. Someone who is trained to do this is called a **psychoanalyst**. ...*a psychoanalytical investigation*.

psychoanalyze See **psychoanalyse**.

psychobabble Some people call the technical language which is used in psychology, especially in psychotherapy, **psychobabble**.

psychological (**psychologically**) **Psychological** means to do with people's minds and thoughts. ...*psychological problems*. ...*psychological warfare*. ■ **Psychological** means to do with psychology. ...*the British Psychological Society*.

psychology (**psychologist**) **Psychology** is the scientific study of the mind and of the reasons for people's behaviour. An expert in this field is called a **psychologist**. ■ Your **psychology** is the kind of mind you have and the way you think.

psychometric tests are designed to assess things like your personality, mental abilities, and suitability for certain kinds of work.

psychopath (**psychopathic**) A **psychopath** is a person with a severe mental disorder who behaves in a violent anti-social way. You say someone like this is **psychopathic**.

psychosis (**psychotic**) A **psychosis** (*plural:* **psychoses**) is a severe mental illness. You say a person with an illness like this is **psychotic** or a **psychotic**.

psychosomatic A **psychosomatic** illness is a physical condition brought on by a person's mental or emotional problems.

psychotherapy (**psychotherapist**) **Psychotherapy** is using psychological methods to treat mentally ill people, rather than physical methods such as drugs. A person who treats people in this way is called a **psychotherapist**.

psychotic See **psychosis**.

psychotropic (*pron:* sigh-ko-**trope**-ik) drugs are drugs such as sedatives, anti-depressants, and stimulants which affect people's mental states.

PTA A **PTA** or **parent-teacher association** is a school organization run jointly by teachers and parents to discuss school matters and to try to improve school facilities.

pterodactyl (*pron:* terr-roe-**dak**-til) **Pterodactyls** were prehistoric reptiles with bat-like wings.

PTO is short for 'please turn over'. It is written at the bottom of a page to show the writing continues on the other side.

pub A **pub** is a building where people go to buy and drink alcohol or soft drinks and meet friends. ■ If you go on a **pub crawl**, you go from one pub to another, having a drink in each one.

puberty (*pron:* **pew**-ber-tee) is the stage in your life when your body changes from that of a child to that of an adult.

pubescent A **pubescent** girl or boy is one who has reached puberty.

pubic is used to talk about things to do with the area just above the genitals. ...*pubic hair*.

public (**publicly**) The **public** is people in general, or the people in a particular place. ...*members of the public*. ...*the American public*. **Public** is used to talk about the feelings and behaviour of people in general. ...*public enthusiasm for environmental issues*. ■ **Public** things and places are provided for everyone to use, or are open to anyone. ...*public libraries*. ■ If someone is a **public** figure or is in **public** life, they are well-known. You say someone like this is

in the public eye. ■ If someone holds **public office,** they have been elected or appointed to an important position in central or local government. ■ **Public** is used to talk about things being said or done so that everyone can hear them or see them. *The treasures will go on public display tomorrow... The police chief publicly apologised for the corruption case.* ■ If a company **goes public,** it starts selling shares to the public.

public address system The **public address system** or **PA** in a place is electrical audio equipment which enables a speaker or music to be heard by a large number of people.

publican A **publican** is someone who owns or manages a pub.

publication When a book, magazine, or newspaper is printed and made available, this is called its **publication.** A **publication** is a book, magazine, or newspaper.

public bar A **public bar** is a room in a pub where the furniture is plain and the drinks are cheaper than in the other bars.

public convenience A **public convenience** is a public toilet.

public domain If information, news, or computer software is in the **public domain,** it is not secret or copyright and can be used or discussed by anyone.

public house A **public house** is the same as a pub.

publicise See **publicize.**

publicist A **publicist** is someone whose job is to publicize things.

publicity is advertising, information, or actions intended to attract the public's attention to someone or something. ■ **Publicity** is the attention paid to someone or something by the media. *The meat industry has had to contend with a lot of bad publicity lately.*

publicize (*or* **publicise**) (**publicizing, publicized**) If you **publicize** something, you make it widely known to the public. *...a much-publicized meeting.*

public limited company See **plc.**

public order is a situation in which people are going about their business normally and there is no fighting or other trouble. *...displays of Islamic fervour which were regarded as a threat to public order.*

public prosecutor In some countries, a **public prosecutor** is an official who carries out criminal prosecutions on behalf of the government and people.

public relations or **PR** is the work of presenting a good image of an organization or well-known person to the public. ■ The relationship between an organization and the public is called **public relations.** *They are taking slightly more positive steps to try to polish up their public relations.* If you say something is a **public relations exercise,** you mean it is done to create a good impression, rather than for any practical reason.

public school In England and Wales, a **public school** is a private school providing secondary education. Public schools are also called 'independent schools'.

public sector The **public sector** is the part of a country's economy which is controlled or support-

ed financially by local or central government. ■ In Britain, the **public sector borrowing requirement** or **PSBR** is the difference between the money the government collects, for example through taxation, and the money it spends.

public service (**public servant**) A **public service** is a service provided for the community, for example transport. ■ If you work in **public service,** you work for national or local government. A **public servant** is a civil servant or local government officer.

public-spirited (**public-spiritedness**) If you say someone is **public-spirited** or talk about their **public-spiritedness,** you mean they try to help other people or the community they belong to.

public works are things like roads which are built by the government for use by the public.

publish (**publishes, publishing, published; publisher**) When a company **publishes** a book, magazine, or newspaper, it prints copies of it for sale in the shops. ■ **Publishing** is the business of publishing books. A **publishing house** is a company that publishes books. A **publisher** is a person or company that publishes books. ■ When a piece of writing is **published** in a newspaper or magazine, it appears in it.

puce is a dark reddish-purple colour.

puck In ice hockey, the **puck** is the small rubber disc used instead of a ball.

puckered If someone's face is **puckered,** it is wrinkled or creased.

puckish A **puckish** person is mischievous and enjoys playing tricks on people.

pudding A **pudding** is a hot sweet cooked food, usually boiled or baked. **Pudding** is also the dessert course of a meal. ■ Some boiled savoury dishes are called **puddings.** *...steak and kidney pudding.*

pudding basin A **pudding basin** is a deep round bowl used especially for boiling or steaming puddings in.

puddle A **puddle** is a small shallow pool of liquid on the ground.

pudgy A **pudgy** person is fairly fat.

puerile (*pron:* **pyoo**-rile) If you say something is **puerile,** you mean it is silly and childish.

puff If you **puff** a cigarette, cigar, or pipe, you smoke it. ■ A **puff** of smoke is a small amount of it. ■ If you are **puffing,** you are breathing loudly and quickly because you are out of breath. ■ If something **puffs out** or **puffs up,** it swells and becomes larger. ■ If you say a person is **puffed up,** you mean they are proud and self-important. ■ A **puff** is a type of cake made of puff pastry filled with cream, fruit, or jam. *...a cream puff.*

puffin – **Puffins** are black and white seabirds with large brightly-coloured striped beaks.

puff pastry is a type of very light pastry which consists of many thin layers.

puffy If something is **puffy,** it is round and swollen.

pug – **Pugs** are small short-haired dogs with flat noses.

pugilism (*pron:* **pew**-jil-iz-zum) (**pugilist**) Boxing is sometimes called **pugilism.** A **pugilist** is a boxer.

pugnacious (**pugnacity**) If someone is **pugnacious,** they are always ready to quarrel or start a fight. You can talk about the **pugnacity** of someone like this.

puke (**puking, puked**) If you **puke,** you vomit.

pukka Things are sometimes described as **pukka** when they are rather superior and posh. *He speaks in the pukka tones of the ruling class.*

pull If you **pull** something, you hold it and move it towards you. ■ If you **pull** something like a cart, you move forward holding on to it, so that it moves along behind you. ■ If you **pull** a muscle, you injure it by stretching it too much. ■ If a building is **pulled down,** it is demolished. ■ The **pull** of something like a magnet is the force it exerts which draws things towards it. *...the earth's gravitational pull.* ■ When a vehicle **pulls away, pulls out,** or **pulls in,** it moves in the direction indicated. ■ If you **pull out** of something you are involved in, you withdraw from it. ■ If someone has succeeded in something, you can say they have **pulled** it **off.** ■ If you **pull through** a difficult situation, you manage to survive it. ■ **pull** someone's **leg:** see **leg. pull punches:** see **punch. pull rank:** see **rank. pull strings:** see **string. pull your weight:** see **weight.**

pullet A **pullet** is a young hen.

pulley (**pulleys**) A **pulley** is a device for lifting heavy weights. It consists of one or more wheels with rims over which a rope passes.

Pullman A **Pullman** is a luxurious type of train or railway carriage.

pull-out A **pull-out** is a section of a magazine which you can easily remove and keep.

pullover A **pullover** is a woollen piece of clothing which covers the upper part of the body.

pulmonary means things to do with the lungs. *...pulmonary TB.*

pulp If something is **pulped** or turned into a **pulp,** it is crushed until it is soft, smooth, and moist. ■ **Pulp** is a substance made from crushed wood and fibres which is used to make paper. ■ People refer to books and magazines as **pulp** fiction when they consider them to be of poor quality, because they are sensational or shocking.

pulpit The **pulpit** in a church is a small raised platform with a rail or barrier around it, where a member of the clergy stands to preach.

pulsar – **Pulsars** are small, very dense stars which give out regular bursts of radio waves. They are thought to be the remains of larger stars which have exploded.

pulsate (**pulsating, pulsated; pulsation**) If something **pulsates,** it moves in and out or vibrates with strong regular movements.

pulse (**pulsing, pulsed**) Your **pulse** is the regular beating of blood through your body which you can feel, for example, at your wrists and neck. ■ If you have your **finger on the pulse** of something, you know all the latest opinions and developments. ■ In music, a **pulse** is a regular beat. ■ If something **pulses,** it has a strong regular tempo. ■ **Pulses** are the dried edible seeds of certain plants, for example lentils and peas.

pulverize (*or* **pulverise**) (**pulverizing, pulverized**) If something is **pulverized,** it is crushed into a powder. ■ If a place is **pulverized,** it is destroyed by bombs or gunfire. ■ If someone is **pulverized** in a contest, they are beaten by a large margin.

puma The **puma** is a large American wild cat. It is also called a 'cougar' or 'mountain lion'.

pumice (*pron:* **pum**-iss) is a lightweight grey stone which can be used to remove areas of hard skin.

pummel (**pummelling, pummelled**) (*Am:* **pummeling, pummeled**) If you **pummel** someone or something, you beat them with your fists. ■ You can say a place is **pummelled** when it is repeatedly bombed or shelled.

pump If a liquid or gas is **pumped** somewhere, it is forced there using a device called a **pump.** ■ If you **pump** a tyre, you fill it with air using a **pump.** ■ A petrol **pump** is a machine with a hose attached, for putting fuel into a car. ■ If you **pump** money or energy into something, you put a lot of money or energy into it. ■ You can say something is **pumped out** when it is produced or supplied continually in large amounts. *...the 300 hours of storytelling pumped out annually by Radio 4.* ■ Plimsolls are sometimes called **pumps.**

pumpernickel is a kind of dark brown bread made from rye.

pumping station A **pumping station** is a place with pumps, where a substance like water, sewage, or oil is pumped away to another area.

pumpkin – **Pumpkins** are large round orange-coloured vegetables.

pun (**punning, punned**) A **pun** is a clever and amusing use of a word with more than one meaning, or a word which sounds like another word, so that what you say has two different meanings. If you **pun,** you make a pun. *There are countless nicknames (forgive the pun) for prison.*

punch (**punches, punching, punched**) If someone **punches** you or gives you a **punch,** they hit you hard with their fist. ■ If you do not **pull** your **punches** when you criticize someone, you say exactly what you think, without softening your criticism. ■ If you **punch** holes in something, you make holes in it using a sharp tool called a **punch.** ■ **Punch** is a drink which consists of a mixture of fruit juice and alcohol.

Punch and Judy show A **Punch and Judy show** is a traditional puppet show for children.

punchbag A **punchbag** is a heavy leather bag stuffed with something like horsehair. It hangs from a rope and is used by boxers for training and exercise.

punchball A **punchball** is a large leather ball fixed on a spring which is punched by boxers for training and exercise.

punchbowl A **punchbowl** is a large bowl in which punch is mixed and served.

punch-drunk If a boxer is **punch-drunk,** he shows signs of brain damage, for example unsteadiness and inability to think clearly, after suffering too many blows to the head. ■ You can say someone is **punch-drunk** when they are dazed and confused.

punch line The **punch line** of a joke is the part at the end which makes it funny.

punch-up A **punch-up** is a fight in which people hit each other with their fists.

punchy (**punchier, punchiest**) If you describe something as **punchy**, you mean it conveys a meaning or creates an effect forcefully and effectively.

punctilious You say people are **punctilious** when they are very careful to behave correctly.

punctual (**punctually, punctuality**) If someone or something is **punctual**, they arrive somewhere or do something at the right time, and are not late.

punctuate (**punctuating, punctuated**) If an activity is **punctuated** by something, it is regularly interrupted by it. *The game was punctuated by disputes involving umpires and scorers.*

punctuation The marks in writing such as commas, full stops, and question marks are called **punctuation** or **punctuation marks.**

puncture (**puncturing, punctured**) A **puncture** is a small hole in a tyre made by a sharp object. ■ If you **puncture** something, you make a small hole in it.

pundit (**punditry**) A **pundit** is someone who knows a lot about a subject and is often asked to give an opinion about it on TV or radio.

pungent (**pungently, pungency**) If something is **pungent**, it has a strong bitter smell or taste. ■ **Pungent** speech or writing is direct, powerful, and critical.

punish (**punishes, punishing, punished; punishable**) If someone is **punished**, they are made to suffer because they have done something wrong. ■ If an offence is **punished**, people who commit it are made to suffer. You can say that the offence is **punishable** by a particular penalty. *...high treason, a crime punishable by death.* ■ **Punishing** is used to describe things which make you very weak and tired. *...a punishing schedule.*

punishment A **punishment** is a particular way of punishing someone. See also **capital punishment, corporal punishment.** ■ Severe treatment of any kind can be called **punishment.**

punitive (*pron:* pew-nit-iv) (**punitively**) Punitive actions are intended to punish people. ■ You can say things which make people suffer are **punitive.** *...punitive economic measures.*

punk or **punk rock** is a type of aggressive rock music which began in the late 1970s as a form of protest. A **punk** is a follower of punk rock.

punnet A **punnet** is a small light box for soft fruits.

punt A **punt** is a long shallow flat-bottomed boat, square at both ends. You move it along by standing in it and pushing a long pole against the bottom of the river. ■ The **punt** is the unit of currency in the Republic of Ireland.

punter A **punter** is someone who bets money, especially on horse races. ■ Some people call their customers or clients **punters.**

puny (**punier, puniest**) If someone or something is **puny**, they are small and weak.

pup A **pup** is a young dog. ■ The young of some animals, for example seals, are called **pups.** ■ If you

are **sold a pup,** you are persuaded to accept something which turns out to be worthless.

pupa (*pron:* pew-pa) (*plural:* pupae) A **pupa** is an insect at the stage of development between a larva and a fully developed adult.

pupil The **pupils** at a school are the children there. You can also call someone who studies with someone such as an artist or musician their **pupil.** ■ The **pupils** of your eyes are the black parts at the centre.

puppet (**puppetry**) A **puppet** is a doll or toy animal which performs actions when you pull strings attached to it or put your hand inside it. **Puppetry** is the art of making puppets or operating them. ■ You can call a country a **puppet state** when it is controlled by a more powerful country.

puppy (**puppies**) A **puppy** is a young dog. ■ **Puppy fat** is fat which children have on their bodies when they are young but which disappears as they grow.

purchase (**purchasing, purchased; purchaser**) When you **purchase** something, you buy it. You can call things you have bought your **purchases.** A **purchaser** is a person who buys something. ■ If you get a **purchase** on something, you get a firm grip on it.

purdah In some Muslim societies, **purdah** is the custom by which women conceal themselves from public view.

pure (**purity**) If something is **pure**, it is not mixed with anything else. *...pure gold.* You talk about the **purity** of something like this. ■ You say something is **pure** when it is clean and free from harmful substances. *...pure mountain air.* ■ You say someone is **pure** when they have never done anything bad or sinful. ■ **Pure** science is concerned only with increasing knowledge rather than putting it to practical use. ■ **Pure** is used to mean 'complete and total'. *We found out about these changes by pure accident.*

puree (*or* **purée**) (*pron:* pure-ray) **Puree** is food which has been sieved or liquidized so that it forms a thick smooth pulp. *...tomato puree.*

purely is used to emphasize that something is restricted in some way. *The troops' role will be purely defensive.*

purgative A **purgative** is a medicine which helps clear the bowels.

purgatory is the place where Roman Catholics believe the spirits of some dead people are sent, to suffer for their sins before they can go to heaven. ■ Any unpleasant experience which people have to suffer can be called **purgatory.**

purge (**purging, purged**) If an organization is **purged** of unacceptable members, they are removed from it. This is called a **purge** of the members. ■ If you **purge** something of undesirable things, you get rid of them. *Millroy has a vision of a modern America purged of ill-health and unhappiness.*

purify (**purifies, purifying, purified; purification**) When a substance is **purified**, it is made pure by removing any harmful, dirty, or inferior substances.

purist (**purism**) A **purist** is someone who believes in sticking strictly to the correct way of doing something. *...jazz purists. ...Communist purism.*

puritan (**puritanical, puritanism**) The **Puritans** were a group of English Protestants in the 16th and 17th centuries who believed in strict religious discipline. ■ If you say someone is a **puritan,** you mean they live according to strict moral or religious principles, especially by avoiding physical pleasures. *He does not hold puritanical views about sex.*

purity See **pure.**

purl is a knitting stitch in which you put the needle into the back rather than the front of the stitch on the other needle.

purlieus (*pron:* **per**-lyooz) The **purlieus** of a place are the areas immediately surrounding it.

purloin (**purloining, purloined**) If you **purloin** something, you steal it or borrow it without asking the owner's permission.

purple is a dark reddish-blue colour.

purport (**purported, purportedly**) If you say something **purports** to be a particular thing, you mean it is claimed to be that thing. *He was given a letter purportedly signed by the Deputy Commissioner.*

purpose The **purpose** of something is the reason why it is made, created, or done. ■ If you have a sense of **purpose,** you have a definite aim which you are determined to achieve. Your **purpose** is the thing you want to achieve. ■ If you do something **on purpose,** you do it deliberately.

purpose-built If something is **purpose-built,** it has been specially designed and built for a particular use. *...the first purpose-built Olympic stadium.*

purposeful (**purposefully**) You say someone is **purposeful** when they have a definite aim and a strong desire to achieve it.

purposeless If you say something is **purposeless,** you mean it does not seem to have a sensible purpose.

purposely If you do something **purposely,** you do it deliberately.

purr When a cat **purrs,** it makes a low vibrating sound in its throat. ■ You can say a person **purrs** when they speak in a soft gentle voice. *'You can tell me the truth,' she purred.* ■ When an engine or machine **purrs,** it makes a quiet continuous vibrating sound.

purse (**pursing, pursed**) A **purse** is an object like a small bag used to keep money in. ■ The **purse** in a contest, especially a boxing match, is the prize money. ■ In the US, a handbag is called a **purse.** ■ If you **purse** your lips, you draw them together to make a small rounded shape.

purser The **purser** on a ship is an officer who deals with the accounts and official papers. On a passenger ship, the **purser** is also responsible for the welfare of the passengers.

pursuance If you do something **in pursuance** of a particular aim, you do it to achieve that aim.

pursuant If something is done **pursuant to** a law, it is done in accordance with it.

pursue (**pursuing, pursued; pursuer, pursuit**) If someone is **pursuing** you or is in **pursuit** of you, they are trying to catch you. You can call this person your **pursuer.** ■ If you **pursue** something, you try to achieve it. *Mexico is eagerly pursuing a free-trade*

agreement with the United States... Electricity workers have voted for industrial action in pursuit of a pay claim.* ■ If you **pursue** something like a plan, you go ahead with it. *The committee is to pursue its enquiry into the Maxwell pension funds.* ■ If you **pursue** a topic, you try to find out more about it by asking questions. *The Democrats vowed to pursue the matter when the President returns from his trip.* ■ **Pursuits** are activities you take part in, especially for enjoyment. *Music is often seen as a middle-class pursuit.*

purvey (*pron:* per-**vay**) (**purveyor**) If someone **purveys** goods or services, they provide them. *BMW has just become the country's biggest purveyor of luxury cars.*

purview The **purview** of an organization or law is the range of things it deals with.

pus is a thick yellowish liquid which forms in abscesses and infected wounds.

push (**pushes, pushing, pushed; pusher**) If you **push** someone or something or give them a **push,** you press hard against them, to get them to move. ■ If you **push ahead** with something you are intending to do, you start doing it. If you **push on** with it, you continue with it. ■ If you **push** someone into doing something, you force or persuade them to do it. ■ If you **push** for something to happen, you try hard to get it to happen. ■ If you **push** an idea or belief, you try to get people to accept it. ■ Someone who **pushes** drugs sells them illegally. A person who does this is called a drug **pusher.** ■ If someone is **given the push,** they are dismissed from their job. ■ If you are **pushing** a particular age, you are nearly that age. *I'm pushing forty.*

push bike People sometimes call a bicycle a **push bike.**

pushchair A **pushchair** is a chair on wheels in which a small child can sit and be wheeled around.

pusher See **push.**

pushiness See **pushy.**

pushover If you say something is a **pushover,** you mean it is easy to do or easy to get. ■ You say someone is a **pushover** when you find it easy to persuade them to do what you want.

pushy (**pushiness**) You say someone is **pushy** when they are very forceful about getting what they want, often at other people's expense.

pusillanimous You say someone is **pusillanimous** when they are too timid to take risks.

pussy (**pussies**) People often call cats **pussies** or **pussy cats.** ■ If you call a person a **pussy cat,** you mean they are kind and gentle.

pussyfoot (**pussyfooting, pussyfooted**) If you accuse people of **pussyfooting around,** you mean they are behaving cautiously and will not commit themselves to a course of action.

pustule A **pustule** is a pimple containing pus.

put (**putting, put, have put**) If you **put** something somewhere, you move it into that place or position. ■ You can use **put** to express an estimate of the size or importance of something. *I would put her age at about 50.* ■ If you **put** someone in a particular state or situation, you cause them to be in it. *...an economic policy that put 1.9 million people out of* *work.* ■ If you **put** a remark or idea in a particular way, you express it in that way. *To put it politely, they failed to cope.* ■ The manner in which you **put** an opinion **across** or **over** is the way you describe or explain it. ■ If you **put** money **by, you save it.** ■ If the authorities **put down** a rebellion, they use force to stop it. ■ If someone **puts** you **down,** they criticize you or make you appear silly. A **put-down** is a remark which makes someone appear silly. ■ If you **put** something **down to** a particular thing, you believe it is caused by that thing. ■ If an animal is **put down,** it is killed humanely. ■ If you **put forward** a plan, you suggest it should be considered. If you **put** someone's name **forward** for a job, you suggest they should be given the job. ■ If you **put in** a request or application, you make it. ■ If you **put** time, money, or effort **into** something, you invest time, money, or effort in it. ■ If you **put** something **off,** you delay doing it. If you **put** someone **off,** you delay giving them what they want. ■ If something **puts** you **off** something, it makes you dislike it. ■ If you **put on** a show or event, you perform or arrange it. ■ If you **put on** weight, you become heavier. ■ If you **put on** electrical equipment, you switch it on to start it operating. ■ If you are **put out** by something, you are upset by it. ■ If you **put** yourself **out** for someone, you go to a lot of trouble to help them. ■ If you **put up** resistance to something, you oppose it. ■ If you **put** someone **up,** you let them stay at your house on a temporary basis. ■ If someone **puts** you **up** to doing something wrong, they encourage you to do it. ■ If a wall or building is **put up,** it is built. ■ If the cost of something is **put up,** it is increased. ■ If you **put up** with something, you tolerate it reluctantly.

putative (*pron:* **pew-**tat-iv) is used to say someone or something is generally thought to be a particular thing. *...the putative father of her child.*

put-down See **put.**

putrefy (*pron:* **pew-**tri-fie) (**putrefies, putrefying, putrefied**) If something **putrefies,** it rots, producing a disgusting smell.

putrid (*pron:* **pew-**trid) If something is **putrid,** it is rotten and smells disgusting.

putsch A **putsch** is a violent attempt to overthrow a government.

putt In golf, if you **putt** the ball, you hit it gently when it is near the hole. A stroke like this is called a **putt.**

putter (**puttering, puttered**) A **putter** is a type of golf club. ■ **Puttering about** means the same as pottering about.

putting green A **putting green** is a small golf course with short grass and no obstacles.

putty is a paste used to fix glass panes into frames.

puzzle (**puzzling, puzzled; puzzlingly, puzzlement**)

If something **puzzles** you or you find it **puzzling,** you do not understand it. You can talk about your **puzzlement** at something like this. ■ You can call something which is hard to understand a **puzzle.** ■ A **puzzle** is a question, game, or toy which requires a lot of thought to complete or solve. ■ If you **puzzle over** something, you try to think of the answer or explanation for it. If you **puzzle** it **out,** you succeed in finding the answer.

PVC is a plastic used for making things like clothing, pipes, and tiles. PVC is short for 'polyvinyl chloride'.

pygmy (or **pigmy**) (**pygmies**) **Pygmy** is used to describe the smallest of a group of related things. *...pygmy chimpanzees.* ■ A **pygmy** is a very small person, especially one who belongs to a racial group in which all the people are small.

pyjamas (*Am:* **pajamas**) consist of loose trousers and a top which you wear in bed.

pylon A **pylon** is a tall metal structure for carrying overhead electric cables.

pyramid (**pyramidal**) A **pyramid** is a three-dimensional shape with a square base and four flat triangular sides sloping upwards to a point. **Pyramidal** is used to describe things shaped like this. ■ The **Pyramids** are ancient pyramid-shaped stone structures built over the tombs of Egyptian kings and queens. ■ **Pyramid selling** is a method of selling goods which is illegal in the UK. Manufacturers sell their goods to distributors, who then sell batches of these goods at an increased price to further distributors. The process continues until the final distributors are left with stock they can only sell at a loss.

pyre A **pyre** is a high pile of wood on which a corpse or a religious offering is burned.

Pyrex is a type of strong glass used for making dishes which can withstand high temperatures. 'Pyrex' is a trademark.

pyromaniac (**pyromania**) A **pyromaniac** is someone who gets uncontrollable urges to set fire to things. This condition is called **pyromania.**

pyrotechnics (**pyrotechnic**) **Pyrotechnics** is the making or display of fireworks. **Pyrotechnic** is used to talk about things to do with fireworks. ■ **Pyrotechnics** is sometimes used to talk about a brilliant display of skill. *...vocal pyrotechnics.*

Pyrrhic (*pron:* **pir**-ik) If you call a result a **Pyrrhic** victory, you mean that, although someone has won something, it was not worth the sacrifices they had to make.

python — Pythons are large snakes which kill their prey by squeezing it.

pzazz See **pizzazz.**

Q q

QC A **QC** is a senior British barrister. QC stands for 'Queen's Counsel'.

QED People sometimes say **'QED'** when they think they have just shown logically that something must be true.

quack A **quack** is the sound a duck makes. When it makes this noise, you say it **quacks.** ■ A **quack** is someone who claims dishonestly to be able to cure people of their illnesses.

quad See (a) **quadrangle.** (b) **quadruplet.**

quad bike A **quad bike** is a vehicle that is like a motorcycle but has four large wheels so it can be used on very rough ground.

quadrangle A **quadrangle** or **quad** is a courtyard with buildings all round it.

quadrant A **quadrant** is a quarter of a circle.

quadrilateral A **quadrilateral** is any shape with four straight sides.

quadrille (*pron:* kwod-**reel**) The **quadrille** is a dance for four couples.

quadriplegic (*pron:* kwod-ri-**pleej**-ik) (**quadriplegia**) If someone is **quadriplegic** they are paralysed in their body, arms, and legs, usually because they have broken their neck. This condition is called **quadriplegia.** See also **paraplegic.**

quadruped A **quadruped** is any four-legged animal.

quadruple (**quadrupling, quadrupled**) When an amount or number **quadruples,** it becomes four times as large.

quadruplet – Quadruplets or **quads** are four children born to the same mother at the same time.

quaff (*pron:* **kwoff**) When you **quaff** something alcoholic, you drink it.

quagmire A **quagmire** is (a) a soft wet area of land which you sink into if you try to walk on it. (b) a complicated situation which is difficult to get out of.

quail (**quailing, quailed**) **Quails** are small game birds with round bodies and short tails. ■ If something makes you **quail,** it makes you very afraid.

quaint (**quaintly; quaintness**) If you say something is **quaint,** you mean it is attractively old-fashioned or unusual. *...what are quaintly termed 'gents outfitters'.*

quake (**quaking, quaked**) An earthquake is sometimes called a **quake.** ■ If you talk about a person **quaking,** you mean they are very frightened or concerned about something which may happen to them.

Quaker – Quakers are members of a pacifist Christian group, the Religious Society of Friends.

qualify (**qualifies, qualifying, qualified; qualification, qualifier**) When someone **qualifies,** they pass the exams they need for a particular job. An examination pass which helps you in your career is called a **qualification.** ■ If you are **qualified** to do something, you have the qualities, knowledge, or skills necessary for it. ■ If you **qualify** for something like a grant, you are entitled to it. ■ If you **qualify** in a competition, you are successful in an early round and go on to the next one. People or teams who do this are called **qualifiers.** The early rounds of a competition are sometimes called **qualifying** rounds or **qualifiers.** ■ If you **qualify** something you have said, you add something which makes it less strong or less general. ■ **Qualified** is used to say something is not complete. *Israelis have given the plan a qualified welcome.*

qualitative is used to talk about things to do with quality. For example, if you talk about a **qualitative** change in something, you mean its quality has improved or declined.

quality (**qualities**) The **quality** of something is how good or bad it is. ■ **Quality** goods and services are of a high standard. High standards in general are sometimes called **quality.** *All their towels carry the USA Cotton Mark as an assurance of quality.* ■ **Quality control** in a factory is a process in which products are checked, to make sure they are satisfactory before they are sent out to be sold. ■ A person's or thing's **qualities** are their good characteristics. ■ The **quality** press are the larger, more serious newspapers.

qualm If you have **qualms** about what you are doing, you are worried that it may not be right or safe.

quandary (**quandaries**) If you are in a **quandary,** you cannot decide what to do.

quango (**quangos**) A **quango** is any partly independent official organization or committee set up by the government.

quantifiable If something is **quantifiable,** it can be expressed as a number or amount.

quantify (**quantifies; quantifying, quantified**) If you **quantify** something, you express it as a number or amount.

quantitative is used to talk about the size or amount of something. For example, if you say there has been a **quantitative** change in something, you mean there is more or less of it.

quantity (**quantities**) A **quantity** of something is an amount of it. *...a small quantity of explosives.* ■ If something is present **in quantity,** there is a lot of it. ■ If you say someone or something is an **unknown quantity,** you mean you do not know much about them.

quantity surveyor A **quantity surveyor** is someone whose job is to estimate how much new building works will cost.

quantum means to do with the properties and behaviour of atomic particles. *...quantum theory.* ■ A **quantum leap** is a very great advance or increase.

quarantine (**quarantining, quarantined**) If a person or animal is **quarantined** or kept in **quarantine,** they are kept separate from other people or animals, in case they have an infectious disease.

quark – Quarks are very tiny particles which neutrons and protons are thought to consist of.

quarrel (**quarrelling, quarrelled**) (*Am:* **quarreling, quarreled**) If you **quarrel** with someone or have a **quarrel** with them, you have an angry argument with them. ■ If you say you have **no quarrel** with what someone is doing, you mean you do not object to it.

quarrelsome people are always quarrelling.

quarry (**quarries, quarrying, quarried**) When stone is **quarried**, it is dug or blasted out of the ground in large quantities. A **quarry** is a place where this is done. ■ Someone's **quarry** is (a) the animal or animals they are hunting. (b) the person they are trying to find and catch.

quart The amount of liquid in a container is sometimes expressed in **quarts.** In Britain, a quart is two pints (about 1.136 litres). A US quart is about 0.946 litres. 'Quarts' is often written 'qt'.

quarter A **quarter** is one of four equal parts of something. ■ A **quarter** or **one quarter** is the fraction $\frac{1}{4}$. ■ In the US, a **quarter** is a coin worth 25 cents. ■ In a city, a **quarter** is an area where a particular group of people live or work. *...the Jewish quarter of Paris.* ■ A soldier's or servant's **quarters** is the house or set of rooms where he or she lives. ■ If you talk about feelings or reactions from a certain **quarter,** you mean the feelings or reactions of a group of people. ■ If you see someone or something **at close quarters,** you are close enough to see them very clearly.

quarterback In American football, a **quarterback** is a player who directs the other players in his team.

quarter-final (**quarter-finalist**) A **quarter-final** is one of the four games, matches, or races in a competition which decide who will take part in the semi-finals. The people or teams taking part in a quarter-final are called **quarter-finalists.**

quarterly (**quarterlies**) **Quarterly** is used to describe something which happens every three months. *...quarterly dividend payments... Interest is paid quarterly.* ■ A **quarterly** is a magazine or journal that is published four times a year, at intervals of three months.

quartermaster In the army, a **quartermaster** is an officer responsible for housing, food, and equipment.

quartet A **quartet** is a piece of music for four musicians. ■ A **quartet** is a group of four people who do something together, for example sing or play music.

quartz is a hard shiny crystalline mineral.

quasar (*pron:* **kway**-zar) **Quasars** are distant starlike objects in space which produce very bright light and other forms of energy.

quash (**quashes, quashing, quashed**) If a decision is **quashed,** it is overturned and is no longer valid. ■ If you **quash** a rumour, you put an end to it. ■ If an uprising is **quashed,** it is put down by force.

quasi- (*pron:* **kwaze**-eye) is used in front of a word to say something has many of the features of the thing described by that word. *...quasi-military rule.*

quaver (**quavering, quavered**) A **quaver** is a musical note with half the time value of a crotchet. ■ If your voice **quavers,** it is unsteady, because you feel nervous or emotional.

quay (*pron:* **kee**) A **quay** is a long platform beside the sea or a river, where boats can load and unload.

queasy (**queasier, queasiest; queasiness**) If you feel **queasy,** (a) you feel as though you are going to be sick. (b) you are uneasy and worried about something. *...a gamble needing firm leadership and no queasiness.*

queen A **queen** is a female monarch or a woman married to a king. ■ A woman is sometimes called the **queen** of something when she is more successful at it than any other woman. *...the undisputed queen of archery.* ■ A **queen** is a female bee or ant which can lay eggs. ■ In chess, the **queen** is the most powerful piece, which can move in any direction. ■ A **queen** is a playing card with a picture of a queen on it.

Queen's Counsel See **QC.**

queer (**queerest**) If you say something is **queer,** you mean it is strange or peculiar. ■ Homosexual men are sometimes called **queers.** This use of 'queer' is generally considered offensive, but some homosexual men use it to talk about themselves.

quell If someone in power **quells** opposition or an uprising, they put an end to it using force. ■ If someone **quells** something harmful, they succeed in stopping it.

quench (**quenches, quenching, quenched**) If you **quench** your thirst, you drink something and no longer feel thirsty. ■ If you **quench** a fire, you put it out. ■ If something **quenches** people's feelings, it makes them disappear. *Nothing can quench the high spirits of the cast.*

querulous (*pron:* **kwer**-yoo-luss) A **querulous** person is always complaining.

query (**queries, querying, queried**) A **query** is a question about a particular aspect of something. ■ If you **query** something, you ask if it is correct or you express doubt about it. ■ **Query** is sometimes used to say someone asks a question. *'What did he get it for?' she queried.*

quest (**questing**) A **quest** is a long difficult search for something. ■ **Questing** is used to describe people who are searching for something, especially something like wisdom or understanding. *...a questing young intellectual.*

question (**questioning, questioned; questioner**) If you ask a **question,** you ask someone to tell you something you want to know. The person who is asking a question can be called the **questioner.** ■ If you **question** someone, you ask them questions. ■ In an exam, a **question** is a problem set to test your knowledge or ability. ■ A **question** is a matter which needs to be considered. *What's at stake here is a question of power.* ■ The person or thing **in question** is the one you are talking about. ■ If you **question** something, you express doubts about it. ■ You say something is **in question** when there is doubt about whether it will happen or continue. *Italy's participation is also in question.* ■ If you say there is **no question** of something happening, you are saying emphatically that it will not happen. *There was no question of him resigning, he said.* Similarly, you can say something is **out of the ques-**

tion. ■ If you say a statement **begs the question,** you mean it assumes something is true, when there are no real grounds for assuming it is true at all.

questionable If you say something is **questionable,** you mean there is some doubt about it. ■ You use **questionable** to describe things people do which may be improper or illegal. *He has been dogged by allegations of questionable business practices.*

question mark A **question mark** is the punctuation mark **?** which you write after a question. ■ If you say there is a **question mark** over something, you mean there is some doubt about it.

questionnaire A **questionnaire** is a list of questions you are asked to answer, to provide information for a report or survey.

queue (**queuing** *or* **queueing, queued**) A **queue** is a line of people or vehicles, one behind the other, waiting for something. When people form a line like this, you say they are **queuing** or **queuing up.**

quibble (**quibbling, quibbled**) A **quibble** is a small objection to something. If someone keeps making small objections, you say they are **quibbling.**

quiche (*pron:* **keesh**) A **quiche** is a pastry case filled with a savoury mixture of eggs and things like cheese or onion.

quick (**quickly, quickness**) **Quick** is used to describe things which take or last a very short time. *...a quick drink after work.* ■ **Quick** is used to describe things which move at speed or are done at speed. *I'd never driven anything as quick as a Formula One car... The women worked quickly.* ■ The **quick** on your fingernails is the area around the edge where the nail joins the finger.

quicken (**quickening, quickened**) If something **quickens,** it gets quicker.

quick-fire is used to describe something which involves several things happening quickly, one after another. *...his quick-fire repartee.*

quick-fix A **quick-fix** solution to a problem works in the short term but is unlikely to last long.

quicksand is deep wet sand you sink into when you try and walk on it.

quicksilver is used to describe people who are very quick and agile. *...the quicksilver young forward.* ■ **Quicksilver** is an old word for mercury.

quick-tempered people get angry very easily.

quick-witted people are able to think quickly and do the right thing in difficult situations.

quid (*plural:* **quid**) A pound is sometimes called a **quid.** *...twenty quid.*

quid pro quo A **quid pro quo** is something you agree to give someone, to get them to do what you want. *It isn't clear what quid pro quo the kidnappers want.*

quiescent (*pron:* kwee-**ess**-ent) (**quiescence**) You say people or places are **quiescent** when they are calm and inactive.

quiet (**quieter, quietest; quietly, quietness**) **Quiet** people or things make very little noise. ■ **Quiet** is used to say there is not much activity in a place. *The high streets have been quiet this year.* ■ If some-

one does something **on the quiet,** they do it secretly.

quieten (**quietening, quietened**) If you **quieten** someone's fears, you do something to make them less worried or afraid. ■ If a place **quietens down,** things become quiet after there has been a lot of noise or trouble.

quietist A **quietist** approach to life involves calmly accepting what happens.

quiff If a man has a **quiff,** his hair is swept upwards and backwards from his forehead.

quill A bird's **quills** are the large stiff feathers on its wings and tail. A **quill** is a pen made from one of these feathers. ■ A porcupine's or hedgehog's **quills** are the long sharp spines on its back.

quilt A **quilt** is a bed covering filled with feathers or other warm soft material.

quilted clothes or coverings are made up of two layers of fabric with a layer of thick soft material between them. The layers are held together and decorated by lines of stitching. *...a quilted jacket.*

quin See quintuplet.

quince – **Quinces** are hard yellow fruit which look like large pears.

quinine (*pron:* **kwin**-neen) is a drug sometimes used to treat leg cramps and malaria.

quintessential (**quintessentially, quintessence**) **Quintessential** is used to describe someone or something that seems to sum up what is most typical of a place, or of a kind of person or thing. *Mars bars are one of the few things that are quintessentially British, like HP Sauce and Birds Eye.* You say someone or something like this is the **quintessence** of the place, person, or thing.

quintet A **quintet** is a piece of music written for five musicians. ■ A **quintet** is a group of five musicians who play together.

quintuple (**quintupling, quintupled**) When an amount **quintuples,** it becomes five times as large.

quintuplet – **Quintuplets** or **quins** are five children born to the same mother at the same time.

quip (**quipping, quipped**) If someone **quips** or makes a **quip,** they make a clever amusing remark.

quirk A **quirk** is something strange that happens by chance. *...a tantalising quirk of fate.* ■ A **quirk** is an odd or unusual habit or characteristic.

quirky (**quirkier, quirkiest; quirkily, quirkiness**) If you call a person or thing **quirky,** you mean their behaviour, character, or appearance is odd or unusual.

quisling A **quisling** is a traitor who helps an enemy that is occupying his or her country.

quit (**quitting, quit** *not* '**quitted**') If you **quit** your job, you resign. ■ If you **quit** doing something, you stop doing it. ■ If you **quit** a place, you leave it.

quite is used to say someone or something has a quality or characteristic to some extent. *Bangor is quite small.* ■ In front of words like 'sure' and 'different', **quite** means 'completely'. *I am quite sure that there's no truth in it.* ■ **Quite** is used in front of words like 'how' and 'who' to mean 'exactly'. *Quite how popular Latin could become is an interesting question.* ■ **Quite** is used with 'a' or 'an' to emphasize how big something is. *It was quite a blunder.* ■ If you are very impressed with something you can say it is **quite something.**

quitter You call someone a **quitter** when you think they are giving up too easily.

quiver (**quivering, quivered**) A **quiver** is a slight trembling movement. When something **quivers,** it moves like this. *His lower lip quivered.* ■ A **quiver** is a container for carrying arrows.

quixotic (*pron:* kwik-**sot**-ik) If you describe someone's ideas or plans as **quixotic,** you mean they are imaginative or noble but unrealistic.

quiz (**quizzes, quizzing, quizzed**) A **quiz** is a contest in which people are asked questions which test their knowledge. ■ If you are **quizzed** about something, you are questioned about it.

quizzical If someone's expression is **quizzical,** they look surprised or amused at what has been said.

quoits (*pron:* **koyts**) is a game in which people try to throw rings over a small post.

quorum A **quorum** is the minimum number of members of a committee that must be present before a meeting can carry out its business officially.

quota A **quota** is the number of people or things allowed or required in a particular situation. *The quota of four tickets per person has been reduced to two.*

quotable A **quotable** phrase in a speech or piece of writing is one suitable to be quoted, for example because it is brief and interesting or amusing.

quotation A **quotation** is a passage or phrase from a book, poem, or play, especially one used to support a point or argument. ■ If someone gives you a **quotation,** they tell you how much they will charge you for doing a piece of work.

quotation marks are the punctuation marks ' ' or " " used to show where speech or a quotation begins and ends.

quote (**quoting, quoted**) A **quote** from a book or speech is a passage or phrase from it. ■ If you **quote** someone or **quote** what they have said or written, you repeat the exact words they used. ■ If you **quote** an example or a fact, you mention it, because it supports what you are saying. ■ If someone **quotes** you for a piece of work or gives you a **quote** for it, they tell you how much they will charge you for it. ■ A **quoted** company is one whose shares are traded on the Stock Exchange.

quotient (*pron:* kwoh-shent) is used to say how much of something a person or thing has. *No game in the world has a greater arrogance quotient.* ■ In arithmetic, a **quotient** is the number you get when you divide one number into another.

Qur'an (**Qur'anic**) The **Qur'an** is the Koran. **Qur'anic** means 'Koranic'.

Qwerty A **Qwerty** typewriter or computer keyboard is the standard English language keyboard, on which the top line of letter keys begins with q, w, e, r, t, and y.

R r

R See **three Rs.**

RA after an artist's name means he or she is a member of the Royal Academy of Arts. RA stands for 'Royal Academician'.

rabbi (*pron:* rab-bye) (**rabbinic, rabbinical**) A **rabbi** is a Jewish religious teacher, often the leader of a congregation. **Rabbinic** (*pron:* rab-**bin**-ik) and **rabbinical** are used to talk about things involving rabbis. *...the rabbinic tradition.*

rabbit – Rabbits are small furry animals with long ears.

rabble A crowd of noisy disorderly people can be called a **rabble.**

rabble-rouser (**rabble-rousing**) A **rabble-rouser** is a speaker who can persuade a group of people to behave violently, often for his or her own advantage.

rabid (*pron:* rab-bid *or* ray-bid) (**rabidly**) A **rabid** animal is infected with rabies. ■ **Rabid** is used to describe people whose views or behaviour are considered to be unreasonable and extreme.

rabies (*pron:* **ray**-beez) is an infectious disease which causes people and animals to go mad and die.

RAC The **RAC** is a motoring organization which helps members when their cars break down. RAC stands for 'Royal Automobile Club'.

raccoon (*or* **racoon**) The **raccoon** is a small furry animal with a long striped tail. Raccoons live in forests in America and the West Indies.

race (**racing, raced**) A **race** is a competition to see who is the fastest, for example in running or driving. If you **race,** you take part in a race. ■ Any competitive situation can be called a **race.** *...the race for the party leadership.* ■ If you **race** somewhere, you go there very quickly. ■ A **race** is one of the groups which human beings can be divided into according to their physical characteristics.

racecourse A **racecourse** is a track where horses race.

racehorse A **racehorse** is a horse bred and trained to be ridden in races.

race meeting A **race meeting** is an occasion when a series of horse races are held at the same racecourse.

racer A **racer** is (a) a person or animal that takes part in races. (b) a vehicle such as a car or bicycle designed to be used in races.

racetrack A **racetrack** is a track for races.

racial (**racially**) Racial means relating to people's race. ...*racial segregation.*

racialism (**racialist**) Racialism is the same as racism. A **racialist** is a racist.

racism (**racist**) Racism is believing that people of some races are inferior to others, and treating them differently because of this. **Racist** is used to describe beliefs and behaviour like this. A **racist** is a person who holds racist beliefs.

rack A **rack** is a piece of equipment for holding things or hanging things on. ■ The **rack** was a piece of torture equipment which stretched the victim's body. ■ If you say someone is **on the rack,** you mean someone or something is causing them great pain or anxiety. ■ If someone is **racked** or **wracked** by something unpleasant, they are suffering because of it. ■ If you **rack up** a large amount of something, you build it up over a period of time. ■ If you **rack** your **brains,** you try very hard to think of something.

racket A **racket** or **racquet** is a bat consisting of strings stretched across a frame with a handle. Rackets are used in games like tennis, badminton, and squash. ■ An illegal way of making money can be called a **racket.** ■ A loud unpleasant noise can be called a **racket.**

racketeer (**racketeering**) A **racketeer** is someone who makes money illegally. Making money like this is called **racketeering.**

raconteur (*pron:* rak-on-**tur**) A **raconteur** is a person who can tell stories in an interesting or amusing way.

racoon See **raccoon.**

racquet See **racket.**

racy (**racier, raciest**) If you describe a book, a film, or someone's behaviour as **racy,** you mean it is exciting and slightly shocking. *These scenes will only add to her racy reputation.*

radar is a way of tracking vehicles, ships, or aircraft that are out of sight by using radio signals. 'Radar' stands for 'radio detecting and ranging'.

raddled If you describe someone as **raddled,** you mean they have lost their good looks as a result of old age and leading a debauched life.

radial is used to describe things which form a pattern like straight lines spreading out from the centre of a circle.

radiant (**radiantly, radiance**) If someone is **radiant,** they are so happy it shows in their face. You can talk about their **radiance.** ■ A **radiant** light shines brightly.

radiate (**radiating, radiated**) If things **radiate** from a place, they form a pattern like lines spreading outwards from the centre of a circle. ■ If something **radiates** heat or light, it gives it off. ■ If you **radiate** a quality or emotion, it shows clearly in your face and manner.

radiation is (a) particles of radioactive material. (b) the giving off of energy in the form of electromagnetic waves such as X-rays, infra-red rays, or ultra-violet rays.

radiation sickness is an illness caused by exposure to high levels of radiation.

radiator A **radiator** is a hollow metal device, usually connected to a central heating system, used for heating a room. ■ The **radiator** in a car is a device for cooling the engine.

radical (**radicalism, radically**) A **radical** or someone with **radical** beliefs is a person who thinks there should be major changes in society, and tries to make them happen. **Radicalism** is the beliefs and behaviour of someone like this. ■ **Radical** is used to describe things which involve the most basic aspects of something. ...*radically different opinions.*

radicalize (*or* **radicalise**) (**radicalizing, radicalized; radicalization**) If a process, situation or person is **radicalized,** something makes them more radical.

radii See **radius.**

radio (**radios, radioing, radioed**) Radio is a system of sending sound over a distance by electromagnetic waves. If you **radio** someone, you send them a message by radio. ■ **Radio** is the broadcasting of programmes to the public by sending out signals from a transmitter. A **radio** is a device for listening to radio programmes.

radioactive (**radioactivity**) If something is **radioactive,** it gives off powerful rays which can be harmful. This energy is called **radioactivity.**

radiocarbon dating is the same as carbon dating.

radio-controlled If something is **radio-controlled,** it is operated from a distance using radio signals.

radiographer (*pron:* ray-dee-**og**-raf-fer) A **radiographer** is a person trained to take X-rays.

radiology (*pron:* ray-dee-**ol**-a-jee) (**radiologist**) is the branch of medical science which uses X-rays and other forms of radiation.

radio telephone A **radio telephone** is a telephone which sends out and picks up sound using radio signals rather than wires.

radio telescope A **radio telescope** is a huge dish-shaped device which receives radio waves from space, enabling it to detect stars and other objects which cannot be seen using optical instruments.

radiotherapy is the treatment of diseases, especially cancer, using radiation.

radish (**radishes**) Radishes are small red and white root vegetables which are eaten raw in salads.

radium is a highly radioactive element, formerly used in the treatment of cancer.

radius (*plural:* **radii**) The **radius** of a circle is the distance from its centre to its outside edge. ■ The area within a certain **radius** of a particular point is all the places not more than that distance from it. ■ The **radius** is the shorter of the two bones in the human forearm, extending from the elbow to the wrist.

radon is a radioactive gas formed by the disintegration of radium.

RAF The **RAF** or **Royal Air Force** is the air force of the UK.

raffia is a strawlike fibre made from palm leaves. It is used to make mats and baskets.

raffish If you describe someone as **raffish,** you mean they are not very respectable, but you find them rather stylish and likeable.

raffle A **raffle** is a competition in which you buy numbered tickets and win a prize if yours is chosen.

raft (**rafting**) A **raft** is a floating platform, usually made of wood. ∎ A **raft** is a large inflatable boat. If you go **rafting**, you travel down a river on a boat like this.

rafters are the sloping pieces of wood which support a roof.

rag A **rag** is a piece of old cloth which you can use, for example, to clean things. ∎ If someone is dressed in **rags,** their clothes are old and torn. ∎ When people are talking about a newspaper they do not like, they sometimes call it a **rag.** ∎ If something is a **red rag** to you, it makes you angry.

rag-and-bone man A **rag-and-bone man** is a man who goes from street to street asking for things like old clothes and furniture and makes money by selling them.

ragbag A **ragbag** is an unusual collection of things which do not have much in common. *The opposition is a ragbag of right-wing liberals, Flemish nationalists and greens.*

rag doll A **rag doll** is a soft doll made from pieces of cloth.

rage (**raging, raged**) **Rage** is a strong feeling of anger which is difficult to control. If you **rage** about something, you speak angrily about it. ∎ **Raging** is used to describe unpleasant feelings which are persistent and powerful. *...a raging hangover.* ∎ If something like a storm, a fire, or an argument **rages**, it goes on with great force or violence. ∎ If something is **all the rage,** it is popular or fashionable.

ragga is a type of pop music originating in Jamaica which combines aspects of reggae and rap.

ragged (*pron:* **rag**-gid) If you say a performance by a group of people is **ragged,** you mean the performers do not always keep together. ∎ If someone is **ragged,** their clothes are torn and dirty.

ragout (*pron:* rag-**goo**) is a richly seasoned stew.

ragtime is a type of jazz piano music which was popular in the 1920s.

rag trade The business of making and selling clothes is sometimes called the **rag trade.**

raid (**raiding, raided; raider**) When soldiers, police, or criminals **raid** a place, they make a sudden quick attack on it, or enter it by force to look for someone or something. An attack or search like this is called a **raid.** *Armed raiders have shot and killed a sub-postmaster in East London.* See also **ram-raid.**

rail (**railing, railed**) Rail is used to talk about transport by train. *...rail traffic.* The steel bars which trains run on are called **rails.** ∎ A **rail** is a horizontal bar used as part of a fence, as a support, or for hanging things on. ∎ If you **rail** against someone or something, you complain bitterly about them.

railcard A **railcard** is an identity card which allows its owner to buy train tickets at a lower price than usual.

railing A fence made from metal bars can be called **railings** or a **railing.**

railroad (**railroading, railroaded**) **Railroad** is the usual American word for a railway. ∎ If someone is **railroaded** into something, they are hurried into doing it using unfair pressure.

railway A **railway** or **railway line** is a route along which trains travel. The steel rails on which the trains run can be called **railway tracks** or **railway lines.**

railwayman (**railwaymen**) **Railwaymen** are people such as engine drivers, guards, and signalmen who work on a railway.

rain (**raining, rained**) **Rain** is water which falls from the clouds in drops. When rain falls, you say it is **raining.** ∎ In countries where rain tends to fall only during certain seasons, this rain is called **the rains.** ∎ If an event is **rained off,** it is cancelled because of rain. ∎ If things **rain** down on a place, they fall in large quantities. *Home-made mortars rained down on the camp.*

rainbow A **rainbow** is an arch of different colours you sometimes see in the sky when it is raining and the sun is shining at the same time. ∎ A **rainbow** coalition or alliance is a political group made up of several smaller groups with a wide range of different principles.

raincoat A **raincoat** is a long waterproof coat.

raindrop A **raindrop** is a single drop of rain.

rainfall The **rainfall** in a place is the amount of rain which falls during a certain period.

rainforest A **rainforest** is a thick forest of tall trees in a place where the climate is very warm and wet.

rainstorm A **rainstorm** is a heavy fall of rain.

rainswept You say a place is **rainswept** when it is very windy and it is raining hard.

rainwater is water which has fallen as rain.

rainy A **rainy** period is one when it rains a lot.

raise (**raising, raised**) If you **raise** something, you move it to a higher position. *He defiantly raised a clenched fist... He raised interest rates from 10% to 12%. ...a raised platform.* ∎ If you **raise** your voice, you speak louder. ∎ If you **raise** money for a charity, you organize an event which results in money being collected for the charity. ∎ When someone **raises** a child, they care for it while it is growing up. ∎ If you **raise** a subject, you introduce it into a discussion. ∎ If you **raise** an objection, you object to something which is being proposed.

raisin – **Raisins** are dried grapes, used in cooking.

raison d'être (*pron:* **ray**-zon det-ra) The **raison d'être** of something is the reason for its existence.

Raj (*pron:* rahj) The **Raj** was the period of British rule in India before 1947.

rajah A **rajah** is an Indian king or prince.

rake (**raking, raked**) A **rake** is a garden tool consisting of a row of metal or wooden teeth on the end of a long handle. You use it, for example, to scrape leaves into a pile. This is called **raking** the leaves. ∎ If you say someone is **raking in** money, you mean they are earning a lot of it. ∎ If you **rake up** something unpleasant from the past, you remind people of it. ∎ In the past, a man who was rather immoral could be referred to as a **rake.**

rake-off A **rake-off** is a share in profits taken by someone who has helped to arrange a business deal. Rake-offs are often illegal.

rakish (**rakishly**) If someone wears a hat at a **rakish** angle, it is tilted in a casual and confident way.

rally (**rallies, rallying, rallied**) A **rally** is a large public meeting held, for example, in protest at something. ■ If people **rally** to a cause, they unite to support it. If someone **rallies** support for a cause, they get people to support it. If something is a **rallying cry** or a **rallying call**, it inspires people to unite in support of a cause. ■ When people **rally round** a person, they support them in a time of difficulty. ■ If a sick person **rallies**, they start to get better. ■ If prices **rally**, they start increasing after a fall. An increase like this is called a **rally.** ■ A **rally** is a competition in which vehicles are driven in timed stages over roads. Taking part in competitions like this is called **rallying.** ■ In racket games like tennis, a **rally** is a continuous series of shots.

RAM is the part of a computer in which information is kept temporarily for immediate use. RAM is an abbreviation for 'Random Access Memory'.

ram (**ramming, rammed**) If one vehicle **rams** another, it is driven into it with great force, usually deliberately. ■ If you **ram** something somewhere, you push it there with great force. ■ If a fact is **rammed home**, people are made aware of it in a forceful way. *The polls ram home the depth of public unease about the economy.* ■ A **ram** is an uncastrated adult male sheep.

Ramadan is the ninth month of the Muslim year, during which Muslims must go without food and drink from sunrise to sunset.

ramble (**rambling, rambled; rambler**) A **ramble** is a long walk in the countryside. If you go **rambling**, you go for walks like this. People who go rambling regularly are called **ramblers.** ■ A **rambling** building is large and old with an irregular shape. ■ If someone **rambles** or **rambles on**, they talk about something for a long time in a confused way. You can call the things they say their **ramblings.**

ramekin (*pron:* ram-ik-in) A **ramekin** is a savoury dish for one person baked in a small fire-proof container called a **ramekin.**

ramifications The **ramifications** of a situation are all its consequences and effects.

ramp A **ramp** is (a) a sloping surface between two places which are at different levels. (b) a short section of road which has been made higher than the rest, to slow the traffic down.

rampage (**rampaging, rampaged**) When people or animals **rampage** through a place or **go on the rampage**, they rush about wildly, causing damage and destruction.

rampant If something undesirable is **rampant**, it is growing and spreading rapidly. *...rampant corruption.*

ramparts are mounds of earth, usually with walls along the top, built to protect a town or castle.

ram-raid (**ram-raiding, ram-raider**) A **ram-raid** is a robbery in which people drive a stolen car through a shop front. Committing robberies like this is called **ram-raiding.** The people who do it are called **ram-raiders.**

ramrod is used to describe people who are holding their bodies straight and stiff. *...ramrod stiff soldiers.*

ramshackle A **ramshackle** building is in a very bad state of repair. ■ You describe things as **ramshackle** when they are very badly organized.

ran See **run.**

ranch (**ranches; ranching, rancher**) A **ranch** is a large farm on which sheep, cattle, or horses are bred. Running a ranch is called **ranching.** A person who owns, manages, or works on a ranch is called a **rancher.**

rancid If fatty foods like butter or bacon go **rancid**, they go bad and taste unpleasant.

rancour (*Am:* rancor) (**rancorous**) **Rancour** is a deep bitter feeling of anger. If something is **rancorous**, it involves people having feelings like this.

rand (*plural:* rand *or* rands) The **rand** is the unit of currency in South Africa.

random (**randomly, randomness**) **Random** is used to say that people or things are not chosen according to any plan or pattern. *...names picked at random from telephone directories.*

randy If someone is **randy**, they are eager to have sex.

rang See **ring.**

range (**ranging, ranged**) The **range** of something like a gun is the greatest distance at which it can be used effectively. ■ The **range** of a singer or musical instrument is all the notes they are capable of producing, from the lowest to the highest. ■ A **range** of things is a number of different ones of the same general kind. *...a range of water sports including wind-surfing and water-skiing.* ■ If you want to show how varied a group of things is, you can say they **range** from one thing to another. *Reactions ranged from amusement to horror.* ■ If you talk about things in a particular **range**, you are talking about all the things between two points on a scale. *...the age range forty-five to fifty-five.* ■ If a large number of people are **ranged** against you, they are all attacking you or criticizing you together. ■ A **range** of hills or mountains is a group of them together. ■ A **range** is a place where people can practice shooting or where rockets are tested.

rangefinder A **rangefinder** is an instrument which tells you how far away something is when you want to shoot or photograph it.

ranger A **ranger** is a person whose job is to look after a forest.

rangy If you call a person or animal **rangy**, you mean they have long slender limbs.

rank A person's **rank** is their position or grade in an organization. **-ranking** is used after a word like 'high' to describe someone's rank. *...high-ranking army officers.* ■ If someone **pulls rank**, they use the fact that they are more senior or powerful to make someone do something. ■ The **ranks** or **rank and file** are the ordinary members of an organization, rather than its officers or leaders. ■ If you become a member of a large group of people, you can say you **join its ranks.** ■ If people **close ranks**, they respond to a difficult situation by supporting each other, to protect themselves from attack or criticism. ■ If someone **breaks ranks**, they are disloyal or fail to support a group of which they are a member. ■ When you say where someone or something

ranks or is **ranked,** you are describing their position on a scale. A position like this can be called a **ranking.** ■ A **rank** smell is strong and unpleasant. ■ A **rank outsider** in a competition is someone who is not expected to win.

rank and file See **rank.**

rankle (rankling, rankled) If something **rankles,** it makes you feel bitter and angry.

ransack If you **ransack** a building or room, you disturb a lot of the things in it and leave it in a mess because you are looking for something.

ransom (ransoming, ransomed) A **ransom** is an amount of money demanded for the return of someone who has been kidnapped. When someone is kidnapped and money is demanded, you can say they are **ransomed** or **held to ransom.** ■ You can say a government or other group of people is **held to ransom** when they are forced to agree to the demands of people who have something they need.

rant (ranter) If someone talks about something loudly and angrily, you can say they are **ranting** or having a **rant.** If they make a habit of doing it, you can call them a **ranter;** you call what they say their **rantings.**

rap (rapping, rapped; rapper) If you **rap** on something or give it a **rap,** you hit it quickly and firmly. ■ If you **take the rap** for something, you are blamed and punished for it. ■ **Rap** is a style of pop music which involves talking rhythmically rather than singing. A person who performs rap is called a **rapper.**

rapacious (rapacity) If you call someone **rapacious** or talk about their **rapacity,** you mean they are extremely greedy for something, especially money.

rape (raping, raped; rapist) Rape is the crime of forcing sexual intercourse upon someone against their will. When this is done to someone, you say they have been **raped** or there has been a **rape.** A **rapist** is someone who has committed a rape. ■ **Rape** or **oilseed rape** is a plant with bright yellow flowers, grown on farms to provide oil and fodder.

rapid (rapidly, rapidity) If something is **rapid,** it moves or happens quickly. *...the rapid increase in population.* You can talk about the **rapidity** with which something happens. ■ **Rapids** are parts of a river where it is rocky and the water is very fast-moving.

rapid eye movement See **REM.**

rapier (*pron:* **ray**-pyer) A **rapier** is a thin pointed sword.

rapist See **rape.**

rapper See **rap.**

rapport (*pron:* rap-**pore**) If you have a **rapport** with someone, you get on well and feel you understand each other.

rapporteur (*pron:* ra-pore-**tur**) A **rapporteur** is a person appointed by an investigating committee to prepare reports for the organization it belongs to.

rapprochement (*pron:* ra-**prosh**-mong) If there is a **rapprochement** between two countries, the relationship between their governments becomes friendly, after a period when it had been hostile.

rapt is used to describe a person who is fascinated by something and is concentrating all their attention on it. *A rapt expression had come over her face.*

rapture is an intense feeling of delight.

rapturous (rapturously) A **rapturous** response to something shows great joy and enthusiasm. *...rapturous applause.*

rare If something is **rare,** it is very uncommon. ■ **Rare** meat is only slightly cooked.

rarebit See **Welsh rarebit.**

rarefied (*pron:* **rare**-if-ide) is used to describe things which seem far removed from everyday life. *...the rarified world of haute couture.*

rarely If something **rarely** happens, it hardly ever happens.

raring If you say someone is **raring to go,** you mean they are excited and eager to start doing something.

rarity (rarities) You can call something a **rarity** or talk about its **rarity** when it is very uncommon.

rascal If you call a man or child a **rascal,** you mean they are mischievious, rude, or dishonest.

rash (rashes, rashly, rashness) You say someone is being **rash** when they do or say something without thinking properly about the consequences might be. ■ If you have a **rash,** an area of your body is covered in small red spots, as a result of illness or allergy. ■ When a lot of the same kind of things happen in a short time, you can say there is a **rash** of them. *...a rash of revelations about the rich and famous.*

rasher A slice of bacon is called a **rasher.**

rasp If something **rasps,** it makes a low dry harsh sound. A **rasp** is a sound like this.

raspberry (raspberries) Raspberries are soft red fruit made up of a mass of small red balls. ■ If you **blow a raspberry,** you make a sound by putting your tongue out and blowing, in order to insult someone.

Rasta is short for 'Rastafarian'.

Rastafarian – Rastafarians are people who follow a religious faith which originated in Jamaica. Rastafarian men usually wear their hair in long dreadlocks.

rat – Rats are long-tailed animals which look like large mice. ■ The **rat race** is the everyday struggle of daily life in a city, especially when this involves trying to succeed in a job in the business world.

ratchet (ratcheting, ratcheted) A **ratchet** is a wheel or bar with sloping teeth which is only able to move in one direction because a piece of metal prevents the teeth from moving backwards. ■ If the level of something **ratchets up** or **ratchets down,** something causes it to rise or fall. When this cause is removed, the thing does not return to its previous level but stays where it is.

rate (rating, rated) The **rate** at which something is happening is the speed or frequency with which it is happening. *Tropical forests are disappearing at the rate of between 40 and 50 million acres a year.* ■ The **rate** of something is its level expressed as a percentage. *...an unemployment rate of over 10%.* See also **exchange rate.** ■ In Britain until 1990, **rates** were local taxes paid by people who owned buildings or paid rent on unfurnished buildings. ■ When you talk about the way someone **rates** a person or thing, you mean their opinion or assessment of them. ...*the highly-rated Brazilian international.* ■ You say **at any rate** when you want to add to or amend what you have just said. *Western democracy has bested, or at any rate outlasted, its rival system.*

rather means 'to some extent'. *I think it's rather sad.* ■ When you are speaking positively about something, **rather** means 'to quite a large extent'. *Prospects do sound rather good.* ■ You use **rather than** to say something is one thing and not something else. *The scandal was greeted with hilarity rather than indignation.* ■ If you **would rather** do one thing than another, you would prefer to do the first thing. *I'd rather be skiing.*

ratify (**ratifies, ratifying, ratified; ratification**) When a government or organization **ratifies** an agreement or proposal, it formally approves and adopts it.

rating A **rating** of something is a score or assessment of how good or popular it is. ■ The **ratings** are the statistics published each week which show how popular each TV programme is. ■ **Ratings** are the sailors in national navies who are not officers or who have no rank.

ratio (**ratios**) A **ratio** is a measurement of the relationship between two numbers which shows how many times greater one is than the other. For example, if there are 6 girls and 2 boys in a room, the ratio of girls to boys is 3 to 1.

ration (**rationing, rationed**) If something is **rationed**, each person is only allowed a limited amount of it, because it is scarce. The amount each person gets is called their **ration.** ■ **Rations** are amounts of food supplied each day to someone like a soldier or a member of an expedition.

rational (**rationally, rationality**) **Rational** behaviour is based on reason rather than emotion. *He was not thinking clearly and rationally at the time.* Basing behaviour on reason is called **rationality.**

rationale (*pron:* rash-a-**nahl**) The **rationale** for a decision is the reason or motive which leads to it being taken.

rationalise See **rationalize.**

rationalism (**rationalist**) **Rationalism** is the belief that reason should be valued above emotion or religious belief. A **rationalist** is someone who believes this.

rationalize (*or* **rationalise**) (**rationalizing, rationalized; rationalization**) If you **rationalize** actions or attitudes which are difficult to accept, you think of reasons to justify or explain them. *Mr Kesri said he was not trying to rationalize or justify the violence.* ■ If a company or other organization is **rationalized,** it is made more efficient, usually by getting rid of staff who are not essential. A change like this is called a **rationalization.**

rattan (*pron:* ra-**tan**) is the tough thin stems of various climbing palms, used to make wickerwork.

rattle (**rattling, rattled**) When something **rattles** or is **rattled,** it makes a rapid series of short knocking sounds, for example because it is being shaken or

is hitting against something hard. This sound is called a **rattle.** ■ A **rattle** is a baby's toy. It consists of a container with loose bits inside which make a noise when the container is shaken. ■ If something **rattles** you, it gives you a shock or makes you feel nervous and uneasy. ■ If you **rattle** something **off,** you do or say it quickly and without much effort. ■ An exciting and enjoyable book is sometimes called a **rattling** good read.

rattlesnake The **rattlesnake** is a poisonous American snake with a series of horny segments on the end of its tail which it can rattle.

raucous A **raucous** sound is loud, harsh, and rather unpleasant.

raunchy If you describe a film, a person, or the way someone is dressed as **raunchy,** you mean they are sexually exciting or sexually explicit.

ravage (**ravaging, ravaged**) If people or places are **ravaged,** they are severely harmed or damaged. ...*the recession-ravaged east coast.* ■ The **ravages** of something like war, pollution, or time are its damaging effects.

rave (**raving, raved; raver**) If you **rave** about something, you speak or write about it excitedly and enthusiastically. ■ A **rave** review is a very enthusiastic one. ■ If someone **raves,** they talk loudly about something without making much sense, because they are very angry or worked up. You can call what they say their **ravings.** ■ A **rave** is a party held at a place such as a club, at which very loud dance music is played. People who go to these parties are called **ravers.**

raven The **raven** is a large black bird.

ravening is used to describe animals which are fierce and hungry. ...*ravening wolves.*

ravenous If you are **ravenous,** you are very hungry. ■ If you are **ravenous** for something, you want or need it badly. ...*his school's ravenous demands for cash.*

raver See **rave.**

ravine (*pron:* rav-**veen**) A **ravine** is a deep narrow steep-sided valley, especially one formed by a river.

ravioli (*pron:* rav-ee-**oh**-lee) is small squares of pasta with a filling of meat, cheese, or vegetables.

ravish (**ravishes, ravishing, ravished; ravishingly**) If you say a place has been **ravished** by war, famine, or disease, you mean it has been severely harmed by it. ■ If you say a person or thing is **ravishing** you mean they are extremely beautiful. ■ If a woman is **ravished** by a man, she is raped by him.

raw food is uncooked. ■ **Raw** is used to describe things which are in their natural state and have not yet been treated or processed. ...*raw sewage.* ...*raw data.* ■ **Raw** emotions are natural, basic, and uncontrolled. ■ If something is achieved by **raw** power, it is achieved by power alone, rather than by skill. ■ You can call people **raw** when they are untrained and inexperienced. ...*raw recruits.* ■ If you say someone has had a **raw deal,** you mean they have been treated unfairly. ■ **raw nerve:** see **nerve.**

raw material – **Raw materials** are the natural substances used to make things, for example in an industrial process. ■ **Raw materials** are the basic things you need for something. *The raw material of an outstanding international team is available.*

ray A **ray** is a beam of light or heat. *...the sun's rays.*
■ If something provides a **ray of hope**, it suggests that a bad situation may eventually improve.

rayon is a smooth fabric made from synthetic fibres.

raze (razing, razed) If a building or town is **razed** or **razed to the ground,** it is completely destroyed.

razor A **razor** is a tool for shaving.

razor blade A **razor blade** is a small, sharp, flat piece of metal which you fix into a razor for shaving.

razor wire is strong wire with sharp-edged pieces of metal on it.

razzmatazz (or razzamatazz) is a noisy and showy display. *...the colour and razzmatazz of a US election.*

RC stands for 'Roman Catholic'.

RE stands for 'Religious Education'.

re is used, especially in business letters, to say what something applies to. *There have been several complaints lodged against him re the lax discipline on A Wing.*

re- at the beginning of a word indicates that something is being done again. *A warrant for his re-arrest has been issued... The pupil cannot be readmitted to school.*

reach (reaches, reaching, reached) When you **reach** a place, you arrive there. ■ If you **reach** for something, you stretch out your arm so you can get it. ■ If you **reach** someone who is in a different place, you manage to contact them. ■ If something **reaches** a certain point or level, it gets to that point or level. *Profit margins reached 20%.* ■ If people **reach** a decision, agreement, or result, they succeed in achieving it. ■ If you are **within reach** of a place, it is close enough for you to get to it. ■ The upper **reaches** of something are its upper parts or highest levels. *...the upper reaches of government.* Similarly, you can talk about the lower **reaches** or further **reaches** of something.

react If you **react** to something in a particular way, you feel or behave in that way because of it. *France and Italy reacted angrily to the decision.* ■ If you **react** against the way other people do things, you deliberately do things in a different way. ■ When substances **react,** they change chemically when they come into contact with each other, and new substances are formed.

reactant A **reactant** is any substance taking part in a chemical reaction.

reaction Your **reaction** to something is what you feel, say, or do as a result of it. ■ If there is a **reaction** against something, it becomes unpopular. ■ Your **reactions** are your ability to move quickly in response to something. *Table tennis requires faster reactions than almost any other sport.* ■ A chemical **reaction** takes place when substances change chemically as a result of coming into contact with each other. ■ A **reaction** is an unintended harmful or unpleasant effect which something like a drug can have on your body.

reactionary (reactionaries) You call someone a **reactionary** when they are stubbornly opposed to political or social change. You can also call their behaviour **reactionary.**

reactivate (reactivating, reactivated) If something is **reactivated,** it is started up again.

reactive A **reactive** chemical is one which tends to react with other chemicals. ■ If you call a person's behaviour **reactive,** you mean they behave in response to what happens, rather than deciding in advance what to do.

reactor See **nuclear.**

read (reading, read *pron:* **red)** When you **read,** you look at a piece of writing and understand the words or say them aloud. ■ When people talk about the way a piece of writing **reads,** they are talking about its style or the impression it gives. *Most of the book reads like office gossip... Falcone's memoirs are a compelling read.* ■ If you can **read** someone's moods or mind, you can judge what they are feeling or thinking. ■ The way you **read** a situation is the way you interpret it. *He said it would be unwise to read too much into next week's expected fall in inflation.* ■ If you **take** something **as read,** you assume it is true or right, and do not feel it needs to be discussed or proved. ■ If you can **read** music, you know which note each symbol represents. ■ When you **read** a meter or gauge, you look at the figure or measurement on it. You can also say a measuring device **reads** a particular amount. ■ If you **read** a subject at university, you study it.

readable If you describe a book or article as highly **readable,** you mean it is interesting and easily understandable.

reader The **readers** of a newspaper or magazine are the people who read it regularly. *...Guardian readers.* ■ People who read books regularly can be called **readers.** *...an avid reader.* ■ If you talk about **the reader** of a book, you mean anyone who happens to read it. ■ At a British university, a **reader** is a senior lecturer just below the rank of professor.

readership The **readership** of a magazine, newspaper, or book is all the people who read it.

readily If you do something **readily,** you do it willingly. ■ **Readily** is used to say something is easily obtained or easily understood. *Food is readily available.*

readiness If you do something **in readiness** for something happening, you do it to be prepared for it. *Security has been tightened in readiness for a general strike tomorrow.* ■ Your **readiness** to do something is your willingness to do it. *Albania has declared its readiness to accept the Helsinki agreements.*

reading room A **reading room** is a quiet room in a library or museum where you can read and study.

readjust (readjustment) If you **readjust** your attitude or approach to something, you alter it to make it more effective or appropriate.

ready (readier, readiest; readies, readying, readied) If you are **ready,** you are prepared for something. ■ You say someone is **ready** to do something when they are willing to do it. ■ If something is **ready,** it has reached the stage where it can be used. If you **ready** something, you get it ready for use. ■ If there is a **ready supply** of something, people can get it quickly and easily. ■ If you have **ready access** to something, you can get to it or use it whenever you need to. **Ready money** or **ready cash** is money immediately available for spending. ■ **Ready-made** is used to describe something which can be used immediately. *All the parts are delivered ready-made to the site... Neither Moscow nor Washington had a ready-made solution to achieve a settlement.* **Ready-** is used in a similar way with words like 'mixed' and 'cooked'. *...ready-prepared meals.*

reaffirm (reaffirmation) If you **reaffirm** something, you state it again clearly and firmly.

reafforestation is the same as reforestation.

reagent (*pron:* ree-**age**-ent) Any substance used in a chemical reaction can be called a **reagent,** especially when the reaction is used to produce or analyze other substances.

real You use **real** when you are talking about the thing that counts most in a situation. *The real question is whether to take military action.* ■ You use **real** when you are saying what something actually is, as distinct from what it appears to be. *The firm's real aim may be to grab Hong Kong's commercial-television market.* ■ If something is **real,** it actually exists and is not imagined, invented, or theoretical. ■ You say something is **real** when it is genuine rather than artificial or an imitation. *...a real diamond bracelet.* ■ **Real** is used for emphasis when describing something. *It's a real thrill.* ■ **Real** is used to say the effect of inflation has been deducted from an amount. *The duty on whisky has now fallen by 23% in real terms since 1980.*

real ale is traditionally brewed beer which is stored in a barrel and pumped from it without the use of carbon dioxide.

real estate In the US, property in the form of land and buildings is called **real estate.**

realign (realignment) When people **realign** their ideas, policies, or plans, they alter them to take account of new circumstances. ■ If a country's currency is **realigned,** changes are made to the upper and lower exchange-rate levels between which it is supposed to be kept.

realisable See realizable.

realise See realize.

realistic (realistically; realism, realist) If you are **realistic** about a situation, you recognize and accept its true nature, and try to deal with it practically. This is called showing **realism.** Someone who regularly behaves like this can be called a **realist.** ■ If a goal is **realistic,** you can reasonably expect to achieve it. ■ A **realistic** painting, novel, or film represents people and things in a way that is like real life. *...'Goodfellas', Martin Scorsese's realistic portrayal of the New York Mafia.* A **realist** painter, writer, or director tries to do this. **Realism** is representing people and things in a realistic way in art. ■ If an imitation of something is **realistic,** it looks like the real thing.

reality (realities) **Reality** is the real nature of things. ■ If something you have imagined or wanted to happen becomes a **reality,** it actually hap-

pens. ■ **In reality** is used to say what is actually true, in contrast with what is supposed to be true or what seems to be true. *He came across as streetwise, but in reality he was not.*

realizable (*or* **realisable**) If assets are **realizable,** they can be sold or turned into cash quickly and easily. ■ If your aims or goals are **realizable,** you can reasonably expect to achieve them.

realize (*or* **realise**) **(realizing, realized; realization)** If you **realize** something, you know it or become aware of it. When people become aware of something, you can say there is a **realization** of it. ■ If your hopes or fears are **realized,** they come true. ■ If a business **realizes** its assets, it turns them into cash by selling them. When this happens, you can say a certain amount of cash is **realized** from the sale.

reallocate (reallocating, reallocated; reallocation) If something is **reallocated,** it is given to different people from those who had it before, or from those who were originally meant to have it.

really People use **really** to emphasize what they are saying. *It was really good.* ■ You use **really** when you are talking about the facts of a situation, in contrast to what people may mistakenly believe. *The investigation will determine what really happened.*

realm Any area of activity, interest, or thought can be called a **realm.** *...the economic realm.* ■ A **realm** is a kingdom.

realpolitik (*pron:* ray-**arl**-pol-i-**teek**) In politics, **realpolitik** means dealing with issues in a practical realistic way, especially by recognizing who is powerful and who is not powerful, rather than trying to do what is morally right.

real time If something is done in **real time,** there is no noticeable delay between the action and its effect or consequences. ■ **Real-time** is used to describe computer systems or programs which process and respond to information as soon as it is received.

realtor In the US, estate agents are sometimes called **realtors.**

real world When people talk about the **real world,** they are talking about what actually exists and the true nature of things, as distinct from what someone imagines things to be like or wants them to be like.

reams If you talk about **reams** of something, especially paper or writing, you mean very large amounts of it. *...reams of data.*

reap (reaping, reaped) When people **reap** a crop like corn, they cut and gather it. ■ If you get a benefit from something you have done, you can say you **reap** the benefit.

reaper A **reaper** is a person or machine that cuts and gathers crops.

rear (rearing, reared) The **rear** of something like a building or vehicle is its back part. A **rear** window or door is at the back of a building or vehicle. ■ If you are **bringing up the rear,** you are at the back of a moving line of people or vehicles. ■ When people **rear** children or animals, they bring them up until they are able to look after themselves. ■ If a horse **rears** or **rears up,** it raises the front part of its body, so that its front legs are high in the air and it is standing on its hind legs. ■ If something unpleasant **rears its head,** it happens or appears.

rearguard You say someone is fighting a **rearguard action** when they are trying to stop something they disapprove of from happening and they have little chance of success.

rearrange (rearranging, rearranged; rearrangement) If you **rearrange** something, you organize or arrange it differently.

rear-view A **rear-view** mirror is a mirror inside a car which lets you see the traffic behind you.

reason (reasoning, reasoned) The **reason** for something is the fact or situation which explains why it happens or exists. *The reason for the killings is still unclear.* ■ If you say you **have reason to** believe or feel something, you mean there are facts or circumstances which justify what you believe or feel. ■ **Reason** is the ability to think logically and sensibly. **Reasoned** is used to describe things which involve the use of logical thought. *...his carefully reasoned arguments.* **Reasoning** is the process of reaching conclusions by considering things logically. ■ If you **reason** with someone, you try to convince them of something using logical arguments. Similarly, if you get someone to **listen to reason,** you persuade them to listen to sensible arguments and be influenced by them. ■ If you **reason** that something is true, you decide it must be true after thinking about all the facts. ■ A person's reasons for doing something can be called their **reasoning.** ■ If you can do anything **within reason,** you can do anything you like so long as it is sensible and it is not too extreme.

reasonable (reasonably, reasonableness) If you say what someone decides or does is **reasonable,** you mean it is fair and sensible. *...a perfectly reasonable decision.* ■ You say a person is **reasonable** when they talk sensibly. ■ If the price of something is **reasonable,** it is not at all expensive. ■ A **reasonable** amount of something is fairly large. *The discriminating viewer should be able to find a reasonable number of watchable programmes.* ■ **Reasonably** is used to say something is true to a fair extent. *It worked reasonably well.*

reassert (reassertion) When people **reassert** themselves or **reassert** their authority or control, they make it clear they are still in charge, by issuing strict orders and making sure they are carried out. ■ If you **reassert** a claim or demand, you make it again, firmly and forcefully. *General Kadijevic reasserted that the army had not acted illegally.* ■ If an idea or custom **reasserts** itself, it becomes significant or dominant again. *Tribalism seems to be reasserting itself.*

reassess (reassesses, reassessing, reassessment) If you **reassess** something or make a **reassessment** of it, you reconsider it carefully.

reassign If people are **reassigned** to new jobs, they are given them in place of their old ones.

reassure (reassuring, reassured; reassurance, reassuringly) If you **reassure** someone or provide them with **reassurance,** you say things to make

them less worried. *The numbers involved seem to be reassuringly low.*

reawaken (reawakening, reawakened) If feelings or principles are **reawakened,** they come into existence again. *...the reawakening of democracy after many years of war.*

rebarbative If you describe something as **rebarbative,** you mean it is extremely unattractive and repellent. *...one of this century's most rebarbative historical realities.*

rebate If you get a **rebate,** some of the money you have paid for something is returned to you.

rebel (rebelling, rebelled; rebellion) Rebels are people who are fighting against their own country's army, in order to change the political system. You say people like these are **rebelling** (*pron:* re-**bel**-ing). You call their actions a **rebellion.** ■ You call someone a **rebel** or say they are **rebelling** when they refuse to conform to other people's ideas about normal acceptable behaviour.

rebellious (rebelliousness) You call a group of people **rebellious** when they are involved in a rebellion, or are likely to start one. *...the increasingly rebellious republics.* ■ You call people **rebellious** when they reject the values and behaviour of people around them. *She has a strong rebellious streak.*

reborn (rebirth) If you say something has been **reborn** or talk about its **rebirth,** you mean it has appeared again after being absent, or has changed into something better. *...Spain's rebirth as a modern state after the long years of backwardness.*

rebound If something **rebounds** from a solid surface, it bounces back after hitting it. ■ If an action someone takes **rebounds** on them, it has unexpected unpleasant effects for them.

rebuff If you are **rebuffed** when you propose something or ask for something, your proposal or request is turned down. You then say you have received a **rebuff.**

rebuild (rebuilding, rebuilt) If people **rebuild** a town or building, they build it again after it has been damaged. ■ When people **rebuild** something like an institution or an aspect of their lives, they take action to restore it to its previous condition. *The Prime Minister will not easily rebuild his power and authority.*

rebuke (rebuking, rebuked) If you **rebuke** someone or give them a **rebuke,** you speak sternly to them, because they have done something you disapprove of.

rebut (rebutting, rebutted; rebuttal) If someone **rebuts** a charge made against them, they give reasons why it is untrue. You call what they say a **rebuttal.**

recalcitrant (recalcitrance) If you call someone **recalcitrant** or talk about their **recalcitrance,** you mean they stubbornly refuse to conform or obey orders.

recall If you **recall** something, you remember it. ■ If you are **recalled** to a place, you are ordered to return there. ■ If a player is **recalled** to a team, he or she is included in the team again after being left out for a while. ■ If something is lost or harmed beyond **recall,** it is no longer possible to recreate it.

recant If someone **recants,** they publicly declare they have rejected beliefs they used to hold.

recap People say **'To recap...'** when they are about to go over the main points of something like a discussion again.

recapitulate (**recapitulating, recapitulated; recapitulation**) If something is **recapitulated,** it is repeated, either in full or in a summarized form.

recapture (**recapturing, recaptured**) When an army **recaptures** territory which it had lost, it captures it back again. ■ When prisoners are **recaptured,** they are captured again after escaping. ■ If you **recapture** the ability to do something, you are able to do it again.

recast (**recasting, recast** not *'recasted'*) If something like a system or policy is **recast,** it is organized in a different way. *The Labour Party has recast many of its ideas.* ■ If a play or film is **recast,** parts in it are given to different actors from those originally chosen.

recede (**receding, receded**) If an object is **receding,** it is moving away from you into the distance. ■ If something like a storm or dispute **recedes,** it becomes less and gradually dies away. ■ If a man's hair or hairline is **receding,** he is losing his hair at the front of his head, above his forehead.

receipt A **receipt** is a piece of paper which confirms that money or goods have been received. ■ If you have received something, you can talk about your **receipt** of it. ■ The money taken in a place like a shop or theatre is often called the **receipts.**

receive (**receiving, received**) When someone gives or sends you something, you say you **receive** it. ■ **Receiving** stolen goods is the crime of buying or accepting them, knowing they have been stolen. ■ When you **receive** a visitor or guest, you greet them. ■ If you say something is **received** in a particular way, you mean people react to it in that way. *The idea has been received coolly by the British Prime Minister.* ■ If you are on the **receiving end** of something unpleasant, it is directed at you. *He has been on the receiving end of abuse from business associates.* ■ The **received** opinion about something is the one which is generally accepted as correct. *The received wisdom has it that the main culprit is ABC.*

Received Pronunciation or **RP** is a way of pronouncing English which is often considered to be the standard English accent. This accent is most common in the south-east of England.

receiver (**receivership**) A telephone's **receiver** is the part you hold to your ear and speak into. ■ The **receiver** of a radio or TV set is the part which picks up incoming signals. ■ A **receiver** is an official who is appointed to look after the affairs of a company that has been declared bankrupt. If a business is in **receivership,** it has been taken over by the receiver. You call businesses in this situation **receiverships.**

recent (**recently**) A **recent** event is one that took place only a short time ago. Similarly, you can talk about things happening **in recent times** or **in recent years.**

receptacle A **receptacle** is any object you put or keep things in.

reception The **reception** in a hotel, office, or doctor's surgery is the part of the building where people are received and their reservations, appointments, or enquiries are dealt with. ■ A **reception** is a formal party. ■ The **reception** someone or something gets is the way people react to them. *He was given a warm reception by spectators... MPs can hardly be surprised at the hostile reception their decision has met.* ■ You use **reception** to talk about the quality of a TV picture or the quality of the sound on your radio.

reception centre A **reception centre** is a place which provides temporary accommodation for people like refugees.

reception class In an infant school, the **reception class** is the first class children go into when they start school.

receptionist In a hotel, office, or doctor's surgery, the **receptionist** is the person whose job is to deal with people when they first arrive, answer the telephone, and arrange reservations or appointments.

reception room Estate agents often call the rooms in a house where people can sit, for example a living room or a dining room, **reception rooms.**

receptive If someone is **receptive** to new ideas, they are willing to consider them.

receptor – Receptors are nerve endings in the body which detect changes in conditions and cause the body to respond accordingly.

recess (**recesses**) A **recess** is a break between the sessions of work of an official body such as a committee or court. When a parliament has a break like this, you say it is **in recess.** ■ In a room, a **recess** is part of a wall built further back than the rest. ■ The **recesses** of a place are the remote or hidden parts of it. *...the darkest recesses of the jungle.*

recession (**recessionary**) A **recession** is a period when a country's economy is doing badly, for example because industry is producing less and unemployment is increasing. **Recessionary** means connected with recession.

recharge (**recharging, recharged; recharger**) If you **recharge** a battery, you put an electrical charge back into it by connecting it to a machine called a **recharger** which draws power from another source of electricity such as the mains. Similarly, you can **recharge** a device containing rechargeable batteries.

rechargeable batteries can be recharged and used again.

recherché (*pron:* rish-**air**-shay) If you call something like a book **recherché,** you mean it is exotic, strange, and likely to be appreciated or understood by only a few people.

recidivist (*pron:* ris-**sid**-iv-ist) (**recidivism**) A **recidivist** is someone who repeatedly commits crimes even though they are caught and punished for them. Behaviour like this is called **recidivism.**

recipe (*pron:* **res**-sip-ee) A **recipe** is a list of ingredients and a set of instructions telling you how to cook something. ■ If you say something is a **recipe** for success or disaster, you mean it is a sure way of achieving it. *This is hardly a recipe for a booming economy.*

recipient The **recipient** of something is the person who receives it.

reciprocal (*pron:* ris-**sip**-pro-kal) (**reciprocally**) A **reciprocal** action or agreement involves two people or groups doing the same thing to each other or helping each other in a similar way.

reciprocate (**reciprocating, reciprocated; reciprocation**) If your feelings or actions towards someone are **reciprocated,** the other person feels or behaves in the same way towards you.

reciprocity (*pron:* ress-i-**pross**-i-tee) If there is **reciprocity** between two people or groups, each does something for the other or behaves in the same way towards the other.

recital A **recital** is a performance of music or poetry, usually given by one person. ■ When someone repeats something which has been heard many times before, you can call this a **recital** of it.

recitative (*pron:* ress-it-at-**teev**) is speech-like singing which continues the story of an opera between songs.

recite (**reciting, recited; recitation**) If you **recite** a piece of writing, you read or say it aloud. What you say is called a **recitation.** ■ When someone is talking and they give a list of things, you can say they **recite** the list. *He could recite the names of all the ships in the Spanish Armada.*

reckless (**recklessly, recklessness**) If you call someone's behaviour **reckless,** you mean they foolishly do things without thinking about the dangers involved or the consequences of their actions.

reckon (**reckoning, reckoned**) If you **reckon** something is true, you think it is true. *I reckon I'll save about £80 a year.* ■ If you say someone **reckons** to do something, you mean they expect to do it. ■ If you **reckon on** something, you expect it and take it into consideration when making your plans. ■ If you say you had not **reckoned with** something or had **reckoned without** it, you mean you had not expected it and so were not prepared for it. ■ If you have to **reckon with** a difficult person or situation, you have to deal with them. ■ If you say someone is a **force to be reckoned with,** you mean they are formidable and difficult to deal with. ■ When an amount is **reckoned,** it is calculated or estimated. *Forbes magazine reckoned his personal wealth at $2.1 billion.* ■ Someone's **day of reckoning** or **moment of reckoning** is a time when they have to face the consequences of what they have done in the past.

reclaim (**reclaiming, reclaimed; reclamation**) If you **reclaim** some lost property of yours which has been found, you go to the place where it is being kept and get it back. ■ If you **reclaim** some money you have spent or some tax you have paid, you succeed in getting that amount paid back to you. ■ When people **reclaim** land, they make it suitable for purposes like farming or building, for example by draining it.

reclassify (**reclassifies, reclassifying, reclassified; reclassification**) If something is **reclassified,** it is officially given a different classification from the one it had before.

recline (**reclining, reclined**) If you **recline,** you relax in a position between sitting and lying with the upper part of your body supported at an angle. A **reclining** chair or seat has a back which can be adjusted so you can recline on it.

recluse (**reclusive**) A **recluse** is a person who lives alone and deliberately avoids other people. You say someone like this is **reclusive.**

recognisable See **recognizable.**

recognise See **recognize.**

recognition If there is **recognition** of something, people acknowledge that it exists or is true. ■ When someone receives **recognition** for something they have done, people acknowledge the significance of their achievements. *Mr Specter's strong record on human rights has not received the recognition it deserves.* ■ When something such as a country is granted **recognition,** it is officially accepted as legal or valid, or as existing in its own right.

recognizable (or **recognisable**) (**recognizably**) If something is **recognizable,** it can be recognized or identified as a certain type of thing. *...a stained but recognizably navy blue tie.*

recognize (or **recognise**) (**recognizing, recognized**) If you **recognize** someone or something, you realise that you know who or what they are. *I suddenly recognised the voice.* ■ If you **recognize** that something is true, you accept or acknowledge it. ■ **Recognized** organizations have received official approval for what they are doing.

recoil (**recoiling, recoiled**) If you **recoil** (*pron:* ri-**koil**) from something, you view it with fear or disgust, and do not want to be near it or associated with it. ■ **Recoil** (*pron:* **ree**-koil) is a sudden backward movement, especially of a gun when it is fired.

recollect (**recollection**) If you **recollect** something or have a **recollection** of it, you remember it.

recommend (**recommendation**) If you **recommend** something, you tell people it is enjoyable, useful, or good value. ■ If you **recommend** a course of action, you say it would be the best thing to do.

recompense (**recompensing, recompensed**) If you are **recompensed,** you get money or something else which makes up for some harm that has been done to you. You say the thing you get is a **recompense** for the harm that has been done.

reconcile (**reconciling, reconciled; reconciliation**) If you **reconcile** two beliefs, facts, or demands which seem to be opposed or completely different, you find a way in which they can both be true or both be fulfilled. *...someone who find's it hard to reconcile his dreams with hard facts.* ■ If you are **reconciled** with someone after a quarrel, you become friends or partners again. *Any hopes of a permanent reconciliation between the couple have been dashed.* ■ If you are **reconciled** to an unpleasant situation or have **reconciled** yourself to it, you accept that it cannot be changed or avoided and are prepared to make the best of it.

recondite (*pron:* **rek**-kon-dite) If you call a fact or area of knowledge **recondite,** you mean it is not at all well-known, or of interest only to experts.

recondition (**reconditioning, reconditioned**) If a machine is **reconditioned,** its worn or damaged parts are replaced or repaired.

reconnaissance (*pron:* rik-**kon**-iss-anss) is the process of obtaining military information about the size and positioning of an enemy army or the geographical features of an area using soldiers, planes, or satellites. ...*a reconnaissance mission.*

reconnoitre (*Am:* **reconnoiter**) (**reconnoitring, reconnoitred**) When people **reconnoitre** an area, they explore it to obtain information about its geographical features or the size and positioning of armies stationed there.

reconsider (**reconsidering, reconsidered; reconsideration**) If you **reconsider** a decision or opinion, you think about it and try to decide whether it should be changed.

reconstitute (**reconstituting, reconstituted**) If an organization is **reconstituted,** it begins to operate in a new way, with different principles or a different structure. ■ When things like dried foods or building materials are **reconstituted,** they are returned to their original form by adding water to them.

reconstruct (**reconstruction**) If you **reconstruct** something which has been badly damaged, destroyed, or taken apart, you rebuild it and get it going again. ■ If you **reconstruct** an event, you try to get a complete picture of it, by piecing together all the information available.

reconstructive surgery is the same as plastic surgery.

reconvene (**reconvening, reconvened**) If a parliament, court, or conference **reconvenes** or is **reconvened,** it meets again after a break.

record If you **record** (*pron:* ri-**kord**) information or keep a **record** (*pron:* **rek**-ord) of it, you write it down, film it, or enter it on a computer, so people can look it up in the future. ■ Your **record** is everything that is known about your achievements or past activities. ■ A **record** is a round flat piece of plastic on which sound, especially music, is recorded. ■ When music or other sounds are **recorded,** they are put on record or tape. A **recording** of something is a record or tape of it. ■ A **record** is the best result ever achieved in a sporting or other activity, for example the fastest time ever run in a race. ■ **Record** is used to describe something which is higher, lower, better, or worse than it has ever been before. *Water levels are at a record low.* ■ If someone speaks **off the record,** they do not intend what they say to be taken as official, or published with their name attached to it.

recorded delivery is a Post Office service which gives you an official record of a letter or parcel being posted and delivered.

recorder A **recorder** is a machine which records information, especially one which records sound or TV pictures, such as a tape recorder or video recorder. ■ In England and Wales, a **recorder** is someone who has been a barrister or solicitor for at least 10 years and has been appointed to sit as a part-time judge in a crown court. ■ The **recorder** is a hollow wooden or plastic musical instrument you

play by blowing down one end and covering a series of holes with your fingers.

record player A **record player** is a machine which plays records.

recount If you **recount** (*pron:* ri-**count**) a story, you tell it. ■ If there is a **recount** (*pron:* **ree**-count) in an election, the votes are counted again. This happens when the result is very close.

recoup (*pron:* ri-**koop**) (**recouping, recouped**) If you **recoup** a sum of money you have spent or lost, you get it back.

recourse If you have **recourse** to something, you use it to help you in a difficult situation. *Is it possible to challenge discrimination without recourse to the law?*

recover (**recovering, recovered**) When you **recover** from an illness or an unpleasant situation, you get better or you get over it. ...*a tragedy from which he never fully recovered.* ■ If you **recover** something which has been lost or stolen, you find it or get it back.

recoverable If debts, costs, or expenses are **recoverable,** you are entitled to claim your money back. *The money you have spent on the surveys is not recoverable.* ■ If natural resources are **recoverable,** it is possible and financially worthwhile to get them out of the ground.

recovery (**recoveries**) If a sick person makes a **recovery,** they get well again. ■ If something makes a **recovery** after a period of difficulty or weakness, it improves or becomes stronger again. ...*a fragile economic recovery.* ■ You talk about the **recovery** of something when you get it back after it has been lost or stolen.

recreate (*or* **re-create**) (**recreating, recreated**) If you **recreate** something, you make something similar happen or exist again. *It's not possible to recreate the conditions in the laboratory.*

recreation Recreation (*pron:* rek-kree-**ay**-shun) is the various activities people take part in for enjoyment, during their spare time. ■ A **recreation** (*pron:* ree-kree-**ay**-shun) of something from the past is a new version of it, made to look or operate like the original. ■ The **recreation** of something is the process of bringing it into existence again. *He urges the recreation of local councils.* For this meaning 'recreation' can be spelled 're-creation'.

recreational means to do with recreation. *His chief recreational interest was horticulture.*

recreation ground A **recreation ground** is a piece of public land where people can go to play sport and games.

recrimination You say there is **recrimination** when people or groups make angry accusations about each other. These accusations are called **recriminations.**

recruit (**recruiting, recruited; recruitment, recruiter**) When people are **recruited** for an organization, they are selected for it and persuaded to join it. People or organizations that recruit people are sometimes called **recruiters.** ...*the Association of Graduate Recruiters.* ■ **Recruits** are people who have recently joined an organization.

rectal See **rectum.**

rectangle (**rectangular**) A **rectangle** is any four-sided shape in which all the angles are right angles, especially one where two sides are longer than the other two. **Rectangular** means shaped like a rectangle.

rectify (**rectifies, rectifying, rectified; rectification**) If you **rectify** something which is unacceptable, you put it right.

rectitude is moral correctness and honesty of character.

rector A **rector** is a Church of England priest who is in charge of a parish. ■ In some universities, a **rector** is a high-ranking official.

rectory (**rectories**) A **rectory** is a house in which a rector and his family live.

rectum (**rectal**) A person's **rectum** is the last part of the tube down which waste material passes from their body. **Rectal** is used to talk about things which involve the rectum. ...*rectal examinations*.

recumbent If you are **recumbent**, you are lying down.

recuperate (**recuperating, recuperated; recuperation**) When you **recuperate**, you recover your health or strength after an illness, an injury, or an exhausting experience.

recur (**recurring, recurred; recurrence, recurrent**) If something **recurs** or there is a **recurrence** of it, it happens again. ■ You use **recurring** or **recurrent** to describe things which keep happening over and over again. ...*a recurring nightmare... He suffered from recurrent bouts of psychotic illness*.

recycle (**recycling, recycled; recyclable**) If you **recycle** things which have already been used, you process them so they can be used again. ...*recycled materials*. If something is **recyclable**, it can be recycled.

red (**redder, reddest**) **Red** is the colour of blood. ■ **Red** hair is between red and brown in colour. ■ If you say someone's face is **red**, you mean it is redder than usual, because they are embarrassed, angry, or out of breath. ■ If you say there are **red faces**, you mean people are very embarrassed about something. ■ People with left-wing ideas are sometimes called **reds** by people who disapprove of them. ■ If you **see red**, you become very angry. ■ If you are **in the red**, your bank account is overdrawn.

red alert If an organization is on **red alert**, it is ready to deal with an emergency.

red-blooded People sometimes call a man **red-blooded** when he has what people think of as typical male characteristics, for example strength and courage.

redbrick British universities built in industrial cities in the Victorian and Edwardian periods are sometimes called **redbrick** universities.

red carpet The **red carpet** is a strip of red carpet laid out for an honoured visitor to walk on.

Red Crescent The **Red Crescent** is an organization in Muslim countries with the same functions as the Red Cross.

Red Cross The **Red Cross** is an international organization which helps people who are suffering because of war, famine, or natural disaster.

redcurrant – **Redcurrants** are small red edible berries which grow in bunches on bushes.

redden (**reddening, reddened**) If someone's face **reddens**, it turns pink or red, for example because they are hot or embarrassed.

reddish If something is **reddish**, it is slightly red.

redecorate (**redecorating, redecorated; redecoration**) If you **redecorate** a room or a building, you put new paint or wallpaper on it.

redeem (**redeeming, redeemed**) If you **redeem** yourself, you do something which gives people a good opinion of you again after you have behaved badly. ■ If one thing **redeems** another which is of poor quality, it helps make up for the bad things about it. *I could not find a single redeeming feature in this book*. ■ If you **redeem** a loan, you finish paying back the money you owe.

redeemable If something is **redeemable**, it can be exchanged for a certain sum of money or for goods worth a certain sum. ■ If a company issues shares which are **redeemable**, it has the right to buy them back.

redeemer In Christianity, the **Redeemer** is Jesus Christ.

redefine (**redefining, redefined; redefinition**) If you **redefine** something, you change it or make people consider it in a new way. *He has redefined the concept of a public museum*. A change like this is called a **redefinition**.

redemption (**redemptive**) The **redemption** of a loan is the repayment of the money which is owed. ■ **Redemption** is freedom from the consequences of sin and evil, which Christians believe was made possible by Christ's death. **Redemptive** means connected with this idea. ...*the redemptive power of love*. ■ If you say something is **beyond redemption**, you mean it is so bad that nothing can put it right.

Red Ensign The **Red Ensign** is the flag of the British Merchant Navy. It is red with the Union Jack in the top left corner.

redeploy (**redeployment**) If military forces or equipment are **redeployed**, they are moved to different positions where they will be more useful. Similarly, if the people who work for an organization are **redeployed**, they are moved to different jobs.

redesign If something is **redesigned**, plans are drawn up to rebuild or change it with the intention of improving it.

redevelop (**redeveloping, redeveloped; redevelopment**) When an area is **redeveloped**, existing buildings and roads are removed and new ones are built in their place.

red-handed If someone is caught **red-handed**, they are caught in the act of doing something wrong.

redhead (**red-headed**) A **redhead** is a person whose hair colour is between red and brown. You say someone like this is **red-headed**.

red herring If you think a subject someone has raised is irrelevant and distracting, you can call it a **red herring**.

red-hot If metal is **red hot**, it is so hot it is glowing red. Similarly, you can talk about **red hot** coals or cinders. ■ Food which is very hot can be called **red**

hot. *...red-hot curry.* ■ **Red-hot** is used to emphasize the strength of someone's enthusiasm or commitment. *...red hot lovers.*

Red Indian See **American Indian.**

redirect (redirection) If something like traffic is **redirected,** it is sent in a different direction. ■ If you **redirect** something you receive in the post, you send it on somewhere else, because it is addressed to someone who no longer lives in your house.

rediscover (rediscovering, rediscovered) If you **rediscover** someone or something that has been lost or forgotten, you find them again. *Weller has rediscovered his old enthusiasm.*

redistribute (redistributing, redistributed; redistribution, redistributive) If money or property is **redistributed,** it is shared out differently. **Redistributive** is used to talk about methods for achieving this. *...redistributive taxation.*

red-letter day A **red-letter day** is a day you will always remember because something good happened to you then.

red light A **red light** is a traffic signal which indicates that traffic must stop. ■ The **red light** district of a city is the part where prostitutes operate.

red meat When people talk about **red meat,** they mean meat like lamb and beef which is dark brown in colour after it has been cooked.

redneck When Americans talk about **rednecks,** they mean men in country areas who are uneducated and narrow-minded.

redolent is used to say (a) that something reminds you strongly of something else. *...a stark, ugly building, redolent of Soviet architecture.* (b) that a place or thing smells strongly of something. *The room is redolent of sweat and massage oil.*

redouble (redoubling, redoubled) If you **redouble** your efforts, you try much harder to achieve something.

redoubt A **redoubt** is a temporary defence work built inside a fortification as a last defensive position. ■ You can call something like an organization, a situation, or a set of ideas a **redoubt** when it represents all that is left of something which was once widespread. *...the Home Office, for long the redoubt of passionately pro-Enoch Powell elements.*

redoubtable If you call someone **redoubtable,** you mean they are bold and have a strong character, and people tend to respect or fear them.

redound If something you do **redounds** to your advantage, it has an advantageous effect for you.

redraw (redrawing, redrew, have redrawn) If the borders or boundaries of a country or region are **redrawn,** they are changed so the country or region covers a slightly different area. ■ If things like plans or rules are **redrawn,** they are altered to take account of changing circumstances.

redress (redresses, redressing, redressed) If you **redress** something such as a wrong or a grievance, you do something to put it right. **Redress** is compensation for a wrong done to someone. *He attempted to seek redress through the German courts.*

red shift is the lengthening of the wavelengths of light given off by galaxies, which is thought to

show they are moving away from the Earth. This supports the theory that the universe is expanding.

redskin In the past, Native Americans in North America were sometimes called **redskins.**

red tape When people talk about **red tape,** they mean official rules and procedures which waste time when you want to get something done.

reduce (reducing, reduced; reduction) If something is **reduced** or there is a **reduction** in it, it is made smaller or there is less of it. ■ In a shop, **reduced** goods are for sale at a reduced price. ■ If people or things are **reduced** to an unpleasant condition or state, they have reached that condition or state. *She was reduced to begging on the streets.*

reductio ad absurdum The **reductio ad absurdum** of something like a principle is the absurd result you get if you take it to its extreme.

reduction See **reduce.**

redundant (redundancy, redundancies) If you are made **redundant,** you lose your job, because your employer can no longer afford to pay you, or because the work you have been doing is no longer necessary. **Redundancy** is losing your job like this. When several people are dismissed in this way, you say there are **redundancies.** ■ If something is **redundant,** it is no longer needed, because it is not serving any useful purpose or has been replaced by something else. ■ If something you do is **redundant,** it is pointless, because it cannot achieve anything.

redwood – **Redwoods** are extremely tall trees which grow in forests in California and Oregon.

reed – **Reeds** are tall grasslike plants which grow in shallow water or marshy ground. ■ A **reed** is a small piece of cane inserted into the mouthpiece of a woodwind instrument like a clarinet or oboe. The reed vibrates when you blow through it and makes a sound.

reedbed – **Reedbeds** are areas of shallow water or marshy ground where reeds grow.

re-educate When an authoritarian government **re-educates** people, it tries to force them to adopt new attitudes and beliefs.

reef A **reef** is a narrow line of sand, rocks, or coral, the top of which is just above or just below the sea's surface.

reefer A **reefer** is (a) a home-made cigarette in which marijuana is mixed with tobacco. (b) a thick double-breasted jacket or short coat.

reef knot A **reef knot** is a type of double knot for tying two pieces of rope or string firmly together.

reek (reeking, reeked) If someone or something **reeks,** they have a strong unpleasant smell you cannot escape. A **reek** is a smell like this. *...the reek of floor polish.* ■ You can criticize someone's behaviour by saying it **reeks** of something unpleasant. *The clamour to draw a veil over the minister's extramarital activities reeks of hypocrisy.*

reel (reeling, reeled) A **reel** is a cylindrical object designed to have something like film, fishing line, or cotton thread wound around it. ■ If you **reel off** information, you repeat it from memory quickly and easily. ■ If someone is **reeling,** they are moving around unsteadily as if they are about to fall.

...reeling drunks. ■ If you are **reeling** from an unpleasant experience, you are in a state of shock and are confused or upset. ■ A **reel** is a fast traditional Scottish dance.

reel-to-reel magnetic tape goes from one reel of a tape recorder or computer to another and is not enclosed in a cassette.

re-enact (**re-enactment**) If people **re-enact** an incident, they act out what happened.

re-entry When people return to something like a country, an organization, or a field of activity after being away from it for a while, you can talk about their **re-entry** into it. *The military men are contemplating a re-entry into politics.* ■ **Re-entry** is the moment when a spacecraft comes back into the Earth's atmosphere after being in space.

ref In a football or boxing match, the referee is often called the **ref.**

refashion (**refashioning, refashioned**) If you **refashion** something, you change it significantly to take account of changing circumstances or to suit your own requirements.

refectory (**refectories**) In a university or a monastery, the **refectory** is the dining hall.

refectory table A **refectory table** is a long narrow dining table supported on two trestles.

refer (**referring, referred**) If you **refer** to something, you mention it or talk about it. ■ If you **refer** to people or things by a particular name, that is what you call them. *...a group of men referred to as 'the technocrats'.* ■ **Refer** is used to say what something relates to. *The figures in the survey refer only to the published prices.* ■ If you **refer** to a source of information such as a book, you look at it to find something out. ■ If a person or problem is **referred** to another person or to an organization, that person or organization is asked to deal with them.

referee (**refereeing, refereed**) A **referee** is an official who controls something like a football match or a boxing match. You say this person **referees** the match. ■ A **referee** is someone who gives you a reference, for example when you are applying for a job.

reference If you make a **reference** to someone or something, you mention them. *Yesterday's statement made no reference to the present ceasefire.* ■ **With reference to** is used to say what something relates to. *Sir, with reference to the article on buying goods from America (Weekend Money, August 8) may I urge caution?* ■ **Reference** books are books, such as encyclopedias, which you consult when you need information. ■ A **reference** or **reference number** is a series of letters or numbers which identifies something. ■ A **reference** is a letter written by someone who knows you which describes your character and abilities. Employers usually ask for references if you apply for a job.

referendum (*plural:* **referendums** *or* **referenda**) A **referendum** is a vote in which all the people in a country are asked whether they agree or disagree with a proposal or policy.

referral is sending someone to a person who is authorized or better qualified to deal with them. A

referral is an occasion when this is done. *He talks of unnecessary referrals to hospital consultants.*

refill If you **refill** something, you fill it again after it has been emptied.

refinance (**refinancing, refinanced**) If a person or organization **refinances** a debt, they create a new debt by borrowing money to pay the old one.

refine (**refining, refined; refinement, refiner**) When a substance is **refined,** it is made pure by having other substances removed from it. A **refiner** is a firm or organization which refines a substance like oil or sugar in order to sell it. ■ If something like an idea or process is **refined,** slight alterations are made to it, to make it more effective or efficient. These alterations or improvements are called **refinements.** ■ If you call something **refined** or talk about its **refinement,** you mean it shows elegance and good taste. *...a refined, civilized play.* ■ **Refined** is used to describe people who have good taste and good manners.

refinery (**refineries**) A **refinery** is a factory where a substance like oil or sugar is refined.

refit (**refitting, refitted**) When a ship, train, or building is **refitted** or given a **refit,** it is made ready for further use, for example by repairs being done to it.

reflate (**reflating, reflated; reflation, reflationary**) If a government **reflates** the economy, it increases the amount of money available for spending, for example by cutting interest rates, to stimulate demand for goods and create more jobs. *...a US-style reflation strategy.*

reflect (**reflection**) If something **reflects** an attitude or desire, it shows people have it. *Concern about the economic situation was reflected in the government's budget.* You can say something is a **reflection** of an attitude or desire. ■ If something **reflects** badly on someone, it gives a bad impression of them. *The library is unique and its break-up would be a sad reflection on the value we place on our heritage.* ■ When light or heat is **reflected** off a surface, it bounces back from it rather than passing through it. This phenomenon is called **reflection.** ■ When something is **reflected** in a mirror or water, you can see its image there. The image is called a **reflection.** ■ When you **reflect,** you think carefully about something. If you change your mind about something **on reflection,** you change your mind after thinking about it carefully. ■ People's comments or writings on a subject are sometimes called their **reflections.**

reflective If a material or surface is **reflective,** light or heat bounces off it rather than being absorbed by it or passing through it. ■ If you are **reflective,** you are thinking deeply about something. *...a sombre and reflective mood.*

reflector A **reflector** is a small piece of specially patterned glass or plastic which glows when light shines on it. ■ A **reflector** is a type of telescope which contains a concave mirror.

reflex (**reflexes**) A **reflex** is a body movement which happens automatically in response to something else, and is not controlled by your conscious mind, for example blinking. ■ If someone has quick **re-**

flexes, they are able to react quickly when something unexpected happens. ■ If someone responds to something in an automatic way out of habit, you can call this a **reflex** or a **reflex action.** ■ A **reflex** angle is any angle between 180 degrees and 360 degrees. See also **acute, obtuse.**

reflexive If something you do is **reflexive,** you do it immediately and without thinking about it, as a habit or as a reaction. *...that reflexive urge for concealment.*

reflexive pronoun A **reflexive pronoun** is a pronoun which refers back to the subject of the sentence. For example, in the sentence 'She washed herself', 'herself' is a reflexive pronoun.

reflexology is the practice of massaging the feet in the belief that this can help with medical problems.

refloat (**refloating, refloated; reflotation**) If a company is **refloated,** shares in it are offered for sale to the public again after a period when it has been controlled by a small number of private owners. ■ If a ship is **refloated,** it is made to float again after it has run aground.

reforestation is planting trees on areas of open land where there had been woodland in the past.

reform (**reformer, reformist**) **Reform** is used to talk about significant changes and improvements being made in the way an organization is run. *...radical economic reforms.* When a system or organization is being changed, you can say it is being **reformed.** A person who tries to bring about reforms is called a **reformer;** you call their behaviour and ideas **reformist.** ■ If someone **reforms,** they stop doing something socially unacceptable and start to live a better life. *...a reformed drug trafficker.*

Reformation (*pron:* ref-for-**may**-shun) The **Reformation** was the movement to reform the Catholic Church begun by Martin Luther in the sixteenth century. It led to the Protestant Church being formed.

reformer (**reformist**) See **reform.**

refract (**refraction**) When rays of light are **refracted,** their direction is changed as a result of leaving one substance and entering another, for example when they move from air to water. This process is called **refraction.**

refractory (**refractories**) You say someone is **refractory** when they are stubborn or unmanageable. ■ **Refractories** are materials like fireclay and alumina which can withstand high temperatures and are used to line things like furnaces.

refrain (**refraining, refrained**) If you **refrain** from doing something, you deliberately do not do it. ■ A **refrain** is a short simple part of a song which is repeated after each verse. ■ When someone keeps saying the same thing, you can call what they say a **refrain.**

refresh (**refreshes, refreshing, refreshed; refreshingly**) If something **refreshes** you when you have become tired, hot, or thirsty, it cools you or makes you more energetic again. ■ You can call something **refreshing** when it is pleasantly different from what you are used to. *He was refreshingly honest.* ■ If something **refreshes** your memory, it reminds you of things you had forgotten.

refresher course A **refresher course** is a training course intended to improve people's knowledge or skills and bring them up to date with new developments.

refreshment – **Refreshments** are drinks and snacks. ■ Food and drink is sometimes called **refreshment.** *They took refreshment at an ancient pub.*

refrigerate (**refrigerating, refrigerated; refrigeration**) A **refrigerated** building or vehicle is one whose inside is kept at a low temperature to preserve food. ■ When food or drink is **refrigerated,** it is kept cool in a refrigerated building or a refrigerator. This process is called **refrigeration.**

refrigerator See **fridge.**

refuel (**refuelling, refuelled**) (*Am:* refueling, refueled) When an aircraft or other vehicle **refuels** or is **refuelled,** it is filled with more fuel.

refuge If you take **refuge,** you go to a place where you can get protection, for example from physical attack. A place like this is called a **refuge.** ■ If you take **refuge** in an argument or type of behaviour, you use it to defend or protect yourself from unpleasantness. *Mr Aznar has repeatedly taken refuge in claims that the Socialists are hiding the true figures.* ■ If you call a place the **last refuge** of an attitude, you mean it is the only place where it still exists, although it used to be very common. *The golf club and the Garrick now seem to be the last refuges of the male chauvinist.*

refugee – **Refugees** are people who have been forced to leave their homes or their countries and live elsewhere.

refund A **refund** (*pron:* **ree**-fund) is a sum of money which is returned to you, for example because you have returned goods to a shop. When this happens, you say your money is **refunded** (*pron:* re**fund**-id).

refundable A **refundable** deposit or charge will be paid back in certain circumstances.

refurbish (**refurbishes, refurbishing, refurbished; refurbishment**) If something like a building is **refurbished,** it is cleaned and redecorated and new equipment or furnishings are installed. *...the refurbishment of many splendid dockside buildings.* ■ If people try to **refurbish** the image of an organization or regime, they try to make it respected or popular again.

refuse (**refusing, refused; refusal**) If you **refuse** to do something, you say firmly that you will not do it. *...the government's refusal to negotiate.* ■ If someone **refuses** you something, they do not give it to you, or do not allow you to have it. ■ If you **refuse** something which is offered to you, you do not accept it. ■ If you have **first refusal** on something, it is offered to you before it is offered to anyone else. ■ **Refuse** (*pron:* **ref**-yoos) is rubbish or waste.

refute (**refuting, refuted; refutation**) If you **refute** an allegation or theory, you prove it is wrong or untrue. ■ If you say you **refute** something you are accused of, you mean you strongly deny it. Similarly, if you say you **refute** a suggestion, you mean you reject it completely. Some people think these uses of 'refute' are wrong.

regain (**regaining, regained**) If you **regain** something you have lost, you get it back. *The Peronists have regained control of the western province of San Juan.*

regal (**regally**) If you describe something as **regal,** you mean it is typical of a king or queen, or suitable for one. *He inclined his head regally.*

regale (**regaling, regaled**) If someone **regales** you with stories or jokes, they keep telling you them, one after another.

regalia The **regalia** of someone like a monarch is their traditional clothing and objects they wear or carry on formal occasions. *...an officious-looking man in full military regalia.*

regally See **regal.**

regard If you **regard** someone or something in a certain way, that is how you think of them or feel about them. *Sir Ralph was regarded with suspicion in the City.* ■ If you have **regard** for someone, you respect and admire them. ■ You use **regarding, in regard to, with regard to,** and **as regards** to show what you are referring to. *The verdict regarding the arms charges is expected at 1130 GMT... The department is reviewing its policy with regard to immunisation.* ■ If you send someone your **regards,** you are expressing friendly greetings to them.

regardless If something happens **regardless** of something else, it is not affected or influenced by it. *Humanitarian missions should include everyone regardless of nationality or creed.* ■ If you say someone carries on **regardless,** you mean they carry on doing something even though circumstances make it difficult to do so.

regatta A **regatta** is a sporting event at which sailing or rowing races are held.

Regency The **Regency** was the period of British history between 1811 and 1820, when the Prince Regent acted as king, because of his father's madness. **Regency** is used to describe the art, architecture, and furniture popular during this period. *...a grand old Regency hotel.*

regenerate (*pron:* ree-**jen**-er-ate) (**regenerating, regenerated; regeneration**) If something like an area or an industry is **regenerated,** it is developed and improved after a period of decline. ■ If living things or parts of living things **regenerate,** they grow back again after they have been lost or damaged. *...forest regeneration.*

regenerative powers cause something to heal or become active again after it has declined or been damaged. *...the regenerative power of nature.*

regent A **regent** is a person who rules a country when the king or queen is unable to rule, for example because they are too young or too ill.

reggae (*pron:* **regg**-ay) is a type of music which originated in Jamaica. It has a steady four-beat rhythm and a strong bass line.

regicide is the crime of killing a king or queen.

regime (*pron:* ray-**zheem;** *the 'zh' sounds like 's' in 'pleasure'*) The rulers of a country are sometimes called a **regime,** especially when they are not democratically elected and run the country in a harsh restrictive way. *...General Pinochet's military regime.* ■ A **regime** is a strict set of rules and requirements.

regimen A **regimen** is a strict programme or procedure, especially one involving medical treatment, diet, or exercise.

regiment (**regimental**) A **regiment** is a large group of soldiers commanded by a colonel. **Regimental** means belonging to or connected with a regiment. ■ A large group of people can be described as a **regiment.**

regimented (**regimentation**) If something is **regimented,** everything about it is strictly controlled. You call this control **regimentation.** *...Pyongyang, one of the most regimented cities in the world.*

region A **region** is a large area distinguished from others by geographical features or the type of people living there. *...the Gulf region. ...the Muslim region of western China.* ■ The parts of a country which are away from its capital are sometimes called the **regions.** *48 staff have been moved from London to the regions.* ■ Some areas of the body are called **regions.** *...the lumbar region.* ■ You use **in the region of** when you are giving an approximate figure. *...an annual running cost in the region of £25m.*

regional (**regionally**) **Regional** means to do with geographical regions. *...regional issues.*

regionalism (**regionalist**) **Regionalism** is a strong feeling of pride or loyalty which people have for the region they live in, often including a desire to govern themselves. **Regionalist** is used to describe people like these and their organizations and activities.

register (**registering, registered**) A **register** is an official record in the form of a list. *...registers of births, deaths and marriages.* See also **electoral register.** ■ If you **register** for something, you put your name down for it. ■ If something is **registered,** it is accepted officially and placed on a register. *Britain has more than ten thousand registered fishing vessels.* ■ A **registered** letter or parcel is sent by a special postal service, for which you pay extra money to insure it in case it is lost. ■ If an instrument **registers** a measurement, it shows it. *The earthquake registered 7.5 on the Richter scale.* ■ If you **register** your feelings of disapproval about something, you tell people about them, or do something which makes them clear. ■ If a piece of information does not **register** with you, you fail to take it in.

register office A **register office** is a place where births, marriages, and deaths are officially recorded, and where people can get married without a religious ceremony.

registrar A **registrar** is a person whose job is to keep official records, especially of births, marriages, and deaths. ■ At a university, a **registrar** is a senior administrative official.

registration The **registration** of something like a person's name or the details of an event is its inclusion on an official record. *...a national dog registration scheme.* ■ The **registration number** or **registration** of a road vehicle is the sequence of letters and numbers displayed on plates at the front and back. The plates are called **registration plates** or **number plates.**

registry (registries) A **registry** is a collection of official records or a place where records like these are kept.

registry office A **registry office** is the same as a register office.

regress (regresses, regressing, regressed; regression, regressive) When people **regress,** they return to an earlier, less advanced stage of development. When this happens, you call their behaviour **regressive.** ...the teacher's regression to small-boy fury and helplessness. ■ In a **regressive** taxation system, the rate of taxation becomes lower as the amount to be taxed increases.

regret (regretting, regretted) If you **regret** something you have done or feel **regret** about it, you wish you had not done it. ■ **Regret** is a feeling of sadness and disappointment that something has happened. Lillee said he had no regrets about retiring. ■ People say **I regret...** when they are apologizing for something, or breaking bad news. We regret no personal replies can be given.

regretful (regretfully) **Regretful** is used to describe someone's behaviour when it shows they are sad and disappointed. Mr Griffin gave a regretful smile. ■ People sometimes use **regretful** and **regretfully** to say something is unfortunate and undesirable. He added that regretfully the extremist wing had made no peace offer. Some people think this use is incorrect and that you should say 'regrettable' and 'regrettably'.

regrettable (regrettably) If you describe something as **regrettable,** you mean that it is unfortunate and undesirable.

regroup (regrouping, regrouped) When soldiers **regroup,** they form an organized group again, ready to continue fighting. ■ When an organization comes to an end, you can say its members **regroup** to form a new organization.

regular (regularly, regularity) **Regular** is used to describe things which happen repeatedly with the same time gap between each occasion. The European Commission will assemble for its regular weekly meeting on Wednesday. ■ **Regular** is used to describe things which happen often. These tests are regularly used in selecting people for jobs. You can also say something happens with **regularity.** ■ **Regular** is used to say a person often does something. He was a regular attender at opera first nights in London. ■ People who often do something, for example drink in a certain pub, are called the **regulars.** ■ **Regular** is used to describe professional soldiers who are a permanent part of an official national army. ■ **Regular** is used, especially in the US, to say something is the standard size. ...a large or regular soft drink of your choice. ■ **Regular** is used to describe something which has a symmetrical or orderly appearance. ...a bookcase with regularly spaced shelves. This characteristic is called **regularity.**

regularize (or **regularise**) (regularizing, regularized) If something is **regularized,** it becomes legal and official by being made to conform to certain rules and requirements. ■ If something like an area of business is **regularized,** a single set of rules and standards are created to govern it. The first necessity is to regularize accounting practices.

regulate (regulating, regulated; regulation) If something is **regulated,** it is controlled by a set of rules called **regulations.** ■ If you **regulate** the amount of something, you control it, for example by means of a mechanical device.

regulator A **regulator** is (a) a person or organization that controls the activities of companies and other organizations, usually by means of rules. (b) a device which automatically controls something, for example pressure or temperature.

regulatory organizations, powers, and measures are intended to control the activities of companies and other organizations, usually by means of rules.

regurgitate (pron: rig-**gur**-jit-tate) (regurgitating, regurgitated) If someone **regurgitates** information, they repeat it without thinking about it or understanding it properly. ■ If a person or animal **regurgitates** food, they bring it back up from their stomach.

rehabilitate (rehabilitating, rehabilitated; rehabilitation) When people are **rehabilitated,** they gradually return to living normal lives as part of the community, for example after they have been in prison, addicted to drugs, or ill. ■ You say someone who has been in disgrace is **rehabilitated** when people no longer condemn them but begin to accept them or think well of them. You can also say someone's reputation is **rehabilitated.** ■ If something like a building or area of land is **rehabilitated,** it is improved so it can be used again.

rehash (rehashes, rehashing, rehashed) If you **rehash** old ideas, you use them again, often rearranging them to try to make them appear new. You call something produced like this a **rehash.**

rehearse (rehearsing, rehearsed; rehearsal) When people like actors, dancers, and musicians **rehearse,** they practise for a public performance. Each occasion when they practise is called a **rehearsal.** See also **dress rehearsal.** ■ You can say people **rehearse** things when they practise them, to make sure they get them right before doing them properly. She had rehearsed her speech over and over. ■ You can say something is a **rehearsal** for a later event when it is similar to it, but is less important or on a smaller scale.

rehydrate (rehydrating, rehydrated; rehydration) When someone who is suffering from lack of water is **rehydrated,** they are given liquid to drink, or liquid is put back into their body through a tube.

reign When a king or queen **reigns,** they rule a country. The period when they are king or queen is called their **reign.** ■ The period when someone is in charge of an organization is sometimes humorously called their **reign.** ■ The **reign** of a sporting champion is the period when they are champion. The **reigning** champion of a sport is the person who is champion at the moment. ■ If you say confusion **reigns,** you mean everyone is very confused about what is happening. You can talk about other things **reigning** in a similar way. *All around him, chaos reigned.*

reimburse (**reimbursing, reimbursed; reimbursement**) If you are **reimbursed** for money you have spent or lost, you are paid back.

rein (**reining, reined**) **Reins** are the thin leather straps attached to a horse's bridle which are used to control the horse. ■ If you talk about someone holding the **reins** or holding the **reins of power,** you mean they are in control of a country or organization. ■ If someone is given **free rein** or **full rein,** they are allowed to do something without any controls or restrictions being imposed on them. ■ If you **rein** something **in** or **rein** it **back,** you reduce it or get it back under strict control.

reincarnated (**reincarnation**) Hindus, Buddhists, and followers of some other religions believe that people are **reincarnated,** that is, they are born again after their death in the body of another person or living thing. Being born again like this is called **reincarnation;** you say someone is the **reincarnation** of a person or animal. ■ If something like an organization is **reincarnated,** it is recreated in a different form or with a different name.

reindeer (*plural:* **reindeer**) The **reindeer** is a type of large deer with branched antlers. Reindeer live in northern areas of Europe, Asia, and North America. In North America, they are called **caribou.**

reinforce (**reinforcing, reinforced; reinforcement**) If an army or a group of police is **reinforced,** it is made stronger by increasing its size or providing it with more weapons. **Reinforcements** are soldiers or police sent to join an army or group of police to strengthen it. ■ If a place is **reinforced,** it is made stronger and better able to withstand an attack, by sending in more soldiers or weapons. ■ If someone's power is **reinforced,** they are made more powerful. ■ If something **reinforces** an idea or a belief, it provides more evidence or support for it. Similarly, if something **reinforces** a feeling, it makes it stronger. ■ A **reinforced** material has been made stronger or harder, by putting another material into it. For example, reinforced concrete has steel bars or mesh inside it.

reinstate (**reinstating, reinstated; reinstatement**) If someone is **reinstated,** they are given their position back. ■ If something like a law or a system is **reinstated,** it is brought back again. *The US Supreme Court reinstated the death penalty in 1976.*

reinterpret (**reinterpreting, reinterpreted; reinterpretation**) If you **reinterpret** something, you interpret it in a new way. The new interpretation is called a **reinterpretation.**

reinvent (**reinvention**) If something is **reinvented,** it is reorganized in such a way that it seems like something fresh and new.

reinvest (**reinvestment**) When a company **reinvests,** it spends its profits on improving itself in some way. This is called **reinvestment.**

reissue (**reissuing, reissued**) If something like a book or record is **reissued,** it is published or produced again when it has not been available for some time. The new version is called a **reissue.**

reiterate (*pron:* ree-**it**-er-ate) (**reiterating, reiterated; reiteration**) If you **reiterate** something which has already been said, you repeat it.

reject (**rejection**) If you **reject** something like a proposal, a request, or an offer, you do not accept it or do not agree to it. ■ If you **reject** something like a belief or a set of values, you do not accept it. ■ If you are **rejected** by someone, they show they do not want to have anything to do with you. ■ If you are **rejected** for a job or a place on a course, you are not accepted for it. ■ If someone's body **rejects** something like a new heart after a transplant, their own immune system starts attacking and destroying it. ■ A **reject** (*pron:* **ree**-ject) is a product which is sold cheaply or not sold at all, because it does not meet the standards required by the manufacturer.

rejectionist A **rejectionist** is someone who is strongly opposed to a change which is being proposed to a system.

rejig (**rejigging, rejigged**) If you **rejig** something, you alter it or reorganize it crudely or clumsily.

rejoice (**rejoicing, rejoiced**) If you **rejoice,** you are extremely pleased about something. ■ **Rejoicing** is behaviour in which people show their delight, usually in a noisy way. *...a day of national rejoicing.* ■ If you say someone or something **rejoices** in a certain name, you are drawing attention to how unusual or amusing their name is. *...a knife grinder who rejoices in the name of Mr Sharples.*

rejoinder A **rejoinder** is a quick, witty, or critical reply to what someone has just said.

rejuvenate (*pron:* ree-**joov**-en-ate) (**rejuvenating, rejuvenated; rejuvenation**) If something **rejuvenates** you, it makes you feel young and energetic again. ■ If something **rejuvenates** an organization or activity, it makes it more lively or successful.

rekindle (**rekindling, rekindled**) If things like feelings or problems are **rekindled,** something starts them up again.

relapse (**relapsing, relapsed**) If a sick person suffers a **relapse,** their health suddenly gets worse after it has been improving. ■ If someone or something **relapses,** they go back to behaving undesirably. You call this a **relapse.**

relate (**relating, related**) If something **relates** to a subject, it concerns that subject. *...the laws relating to inheritance.* ■ If things are **related** or one is **related** to the other, there is a connection between them. *...drug-related crimes.* ■ People who are **related** belong to the same family. ■ You say things like languages are **related** when they have developed from the same language. ■ If you can **relate** to someone or something, you have an understanding of them which helps you deal with them or makes you sympathetic to them. ■ If you **relate** a story, you tell it.

relation — **Relations** between people, groups, or countries are the contacts between them and the way they feel and behave towards each other. *Boston experimented with closer relations between schools and local business.* ■ The **relation** of one thing to another is the connection between them. *...the relation of fiction to life.* ■ Your **relations** are the members of your family. ■ **In relation to** is used to say what something concerns. *He has yet to face trial in relation to eight other charges.* ■ **In relation to** is used to compare two things. For example, if you say something is large **in relation to** something else, you mean the first thing is large when compared to the second.

relationship The **relationship** between two people or groups is the way they feel and behave towards each other. *His country's relationship with France is now very cordial.* ■ A **relationship** is a close romantic friendship between two people. ■ If there is a **relationship** between two things, they are connected in some way.

relative (relatively) Your **relatives** are the members of your family. ■ If one type of animal is a **relative** of another, both types evolved from the same ancestor. ■ You use **relative** and **relatively** to indicate that the accuracy of your description is based on a comparison with other things. *Land Rover markets a range of relatively highly-priced vehicles.* ■ The **relative** advantages and disadvantages of two things are their advantages and disadvantages compared to each other. *...the relative costs of gas and coal.* ■ If you say something is **relative**, you mean it needs to be judged in relation to other things. *Failure, like success, is relative.* ■ **Relative to** means (a) 'in comparison with'. *Academic salaries have fallen, relative to those in other professions.* (b) 'in proportion to'. *A formula now restricts weight relative to bat length.*

relativism is the view that there are no absolute standards of right and wrong and that there is only what an individual or society thinks is right or wrong.

relativity The theory of **relativity** is Einstein's theory concerning space, time, motion, mass, and gravitation.

relaunch (relaunches, relaunching, relaunched) If something like a product or a political campaign is **relaunched,** it is promoted in a new way in an attempt to increase its popularity.

relax (relaxes, relaxing, relaxed; relaxation) If you **relax,** you become calm, rather than worried or tense. When you are in this state, you say you are **relaxed.** If something is **relaxing,** it makes you feel like this. ■ If a discussion or meeting is **relaxed,** it is calm, unhurried, and informal. You can also say it takes place in a **relaxed** atmosphere. ■ You say you **relax** when you spend time in a pleasant way. **Relaxation** is spending time like this. ■ If rules or controls are **relaxed,** they are made less strict or severe. *A further relaxation of fiscal policy would risk overstimulating the economy.* ■ If someone who is in control of a country or organization **relaxes their grip,** they no longer keep it under such tight control.

relay A **relay** or **relay race** is a race between a number of teams of, for example, runners. Each member of the team runs one section of the race. There are usually four sections. ■ When radio or TV signals or programmes are **relayed,** they are transmitted, or received and re-transmitted. A transmission like this is called a **relay. Relay satellites** and **relay** stations are used in transmissions like these. ■ If you **relay** information, you pass it on to other people.

release (releasing, released) If a prisoner or captive animal is **released,** they are set free. You call this their **release.** ■ If you **release** something you are holding, you let go of it. ■ When energy or a substance is **released** from something, it escapes from it. ■ When information or documents are **released,** they are made available to the public or the press. ■ When something like a new record or film is **released** or **goes on release,** it is made available for the public to buy or see. New records and films are sometimes called **releases.** ■ If you are **released** from something like a duty, you no longer have to perform it.

relegate (relegating, relegated; relegation) If a team is **relegated,** it is moved to a lower division in a league. ■ If someone or something is **relegated** to a less important position or role, they are moved to that position or role.

relent If you **relent,** you give in over something you had previously opposed or insisted on. *Unless the unions relent on wage rises, productivity will slump.*

relentless (relentlessly, relentlessness) You say someone's behaviour is **relentless** when they keep doing something and refuse to stop or give in. ■ If something is **relentless,** it shows no sign of stopping or slowing down. *...a relentless downpour.*

relevant (relevance) If something is **relevant** to what is being discussed, it has some real bearing on it. You talk about the **relevance** of something like this. ■ You say something is **relevant** when it has some real importance or significance for people. *Anti-Communist songs have lost their relevance and popularity.* ■ The **relevant** person or thing in a particular situation is the appropriate one. *...a strong protest to the relevant authorities.*

reliable (reliably, reliability) If you say someone or something is **reliable,** you mean they can be depended on to work well or behave in the way you want. This characteristic is called **reliability.** ■ **Reliable** information is highly likely to be correct, because you can trust the source it comes from.

reliant (reliance) If you are **reliant** on someone or something, you cannot do without them. You can talk about your **reliance** on someone or something.

relic If you call something a **relic** of an earlier period, you mean they belonged to that period and have survived into the present. *The division between amateur and professional is a relic of England's Victorian class structure.* ■ **Relics** are things made or used a long time ago and kept for their historical importance. ■ A **relic** is an object kept in a church or chapel which people believe is connected with a saint and is therefore holy.

relief is a feeling of gladness and release from worry, because something unpleasant has not happened or has stopped happening, or a problem has been solved. *It's a relief to get out of the office.* ■ If something provides **relief** from pain, it eases it. ■ **Relief** is food, clothing, or shelter provided for poor or hungry people. ■ **Relief** is used to describe people who step in to do a job when the person who normally does it is not available. *No relief drivers were available.* ■ If one thing **throws** another **into relief,** it emphasizes it and exposes its characteristics. *...private affluence thrown into relief by public squalor.* ■ A **relief** is a sculpture carved so that it stands out of a vertical surface. See also **bas-relief.**

relieve (relieving, relieved) If you are **relieved,** you feel glad and released from worry, because something unpleasant has not happened or has stopped happening, or a problem has been solved. ■ If something **relieves** a pain, it eases it or stops it. *...pain-relieving drugs.* ■ If someone is **relieved** of their post or duties, they are discharged or sacked. ■ If you **relieve** someone, you take over from them and continue doing what they were doing, so they can leave. *At seven o'clock the night nurse came in to relieve her.* ■ If an army **relieves** a town or other place which has been besieged, it frees it. ■ When people or animals **relieve** themselves, they urinate or defecate.

religion is belief in a god or gods, and the activities connected with this belief, such as prayer or worship. A **religion** is a particular set of beliefs and activities of this kind.

religiosity If you talk about someone's **religiosity,** you are talking about what you see as their extreme and perhaps insincere religious beliefs and practices.

religious (religiously) Religious means connected with religion. *...a religious service.* ■ If someone is **religious,** they have a strong belief in a god or gods. ■ If you do something **religiously,** you do it conscientiously and regularly.

relinquish (relinquishes, relinquishing, relinquished; relinquishment) If you **relinquish** something, you give it up.

reliquary (*pron:* **rel**-lik-wer-ee) **(reliquaries)** A **reliquary** is a container in which a religious relic is kept.

relish (relishes, relishing, relished) If you **relish** something, you get a lot of enjoyment from it. You can talk about someone's **relish** for something. *He has lost his relish for the sport.* ■ If you **relish** the prospect or idea of something, you look forward to it eagerly. ■ **Relish** is a sauce or pickle you add to food after it has been served, to give it more flavour.

relive (reliving, relived) If you **relive** something from your past, you imagine you are going through it again, or you have a similar experience which reminds you of it.

relocate (relocating, relocated; relocation) If people or businesses **relocate** or are **relocated,** they move to a different place.

reluctant (reluctantly, reluctance) If you are **reluctant** to do something or do it **reluctantly,** you are unwilling to do it or unhappy about doing it. *Senior officers have made no secret of their reluctance to use force.*

rely (relies, relying, relied) If you **rely on** someone or something, you need and depend on them. ■ If

you say someone or something can be **relied on,** you mean they can be depended on to work well or behave in the way you want.

REM or **rapid eye movement** is a darting movement of the eyes beneath closed lids, which occurs when you are dreaming.

remade See **remake.**

remain (remaining, remained) If someone or something **remains** in a certain state, condition, or place they stay like that or stay there. *Residential property costs remain high.* ■ You say something **remains** when it still exists. *It's hoped that the remaining obstacles will be resolved within a few weeks.* ■ If something **remains** to be done, it has not yet been done. ■ You use expressions like **the fact remains** and **the question remains** to emphasize that an important point or problem still exists. ■ The **remains** of something are what is left of it after most of it has been destroyed or removed. *...dismantling the remains of apartheid.* ■ The **remains** of a person, animal, or thing are the parts that are left after they have died or been unused for some time.

remainder (remaindering, remaindered) The **remainder** of something like a period of time is the part which is still to come. ■ The **remainder** of something like a task is the part which has still to be dealt with. ■ The **remainder** of something is the part which is left after some of it has been taken away. ■ If a book is **remaindered,** it is sold at a reduced price because it has not been selling well.

remake (remaking, remade) If an old film is **remade,** a new film is made with a similar story and often with the same title as the old film. The new film is called a **remake.** ■ If something is **remade,** it is changed into a different form. *She ordered a vintage St Laurent evening dress to be remade for her.*

remand If someone who is accused of a crime is **remanded on bail,** they are freed and ordered to come back for trial at a later date. You say this person is **on remand.** If someone is **remanded in custody,** they have to stay in prison or a remand centre until their trial. A person like this is called a **remand prisoner.**

remand centre A **remand centre** is an institution where young people who are accused of crimes are sent until a decision about their punishment or trial has been made.

remark If you **remark** on something or make a **remark** about it, you say something about it, often in a casual way.

remarkable (remarkably) If you say someone or something is **remarkable,** you mean they are impressive or extraordinary.

remarry (remarries, remarrying, remarried; remarriage) If someone **remarries** after divorce or the death of their spouse, they marry someone else. You call this their **remarriage.**

remaster (remastering, remastered) If an item of recorded music is **remastered,** a new and better master copy is made, from which new copies can then be produced.

rematch (rematches) In sport, especially boxing, a **rematch** is a second match between the same two competitors.

remedial action is intended to correct something which has been unsuccessful or has gone wrong. ...*tough remedial measures.*

remedy (remedies, remedying, remedied) A **remedy** is a successful way of dealing with a problem. *The shortage can be remedied only by action on the part of developers.* ■ A **remedy** is something intended to cure illness or stop pain.

remember (remembering, remembered) If you **remember** people or things from your past, your mind still has an impression of them and you are able to think about them. ■ If you **remember** to do something you intended to do, you think of it and do it at the right time. ■ When people **remember** a person or an event, they hold a ceremony in honour of them.

remembrance If something is done in **remembrance** of people who have died, it is done to show respect for them.

Remembrance Day is the Sunday nearest to November 11th when people in Britain honour the memory of people killed in recent wars, especially the two World Wars.

remind If someone **reminds** you about something, they get you to remember it, by bringing your attention to it. ■ If you are **reminded** of a fact, something makes you aware of it again. *There was now a chill in the evening that reminded him that he was fifteen hundred feet above sea-level.* ■ If someone or something **reminds** you of another person or thing, they are similar to them and make you think of them. *The landscape reminded him of Kenya.*

reminder If something is a **reminder** of another thing, it makes you think about it. *The government decided to leave the building in ruins as a reminder of the follies of war.* ■ A **reminder** is a letter sent to remind you to do something you have forgotten.

reminisce (pron: rem-in-**iss**) **(reminiscing, reminisced; reminiscence)** If you **reminisce**, you remember things which have happened to you in the past, usually with pleasure. ...*his 80th birthday collection of reminiscences.*

reminiscent If something is **reminiscent** of a certain thing, it reminds you of it. ...*a spectacular operation reminiscent of a spy film.*

remiss If you say someone has been **remiss,** you mean they have not done something they ought to have done.

remission If a prisoner gets **remission,** their prison sentence is reduced, because they have behaved well in prison. ■ If a person with a serious illness is in **remission,** their symptoms are less severe for a time.

remit (remitting, remitted) The **remit** (pron: **ree**-mit) of a person or organization is the group of things they are authorized to deal with. *Traditionally, defence matters have been outside the Community's remit.* ■ If you **remit** (pron: ri-**mit**) money to someone, you send it to them as payment for something.

remittance A **remittance** is a sum of money sent to someone.

remix (remixes, remixing, remixed) When a pop record is **remixed,** the sound is altered to make it more suitable for dancing. The new version is called a **remix.**

remnant The **remnants** of something are small parts of it left over when the main part has disappeared or been destroyed.

remodel (remodelling, remodelled) (Am: **remodeling, remodeled)** If a building or room is **remodelled,** it is redesigned and its shape is altered. ■ If an organization is **remodelled,** its structure and the way it operates are changed significantly.

remonstrate (remonstrating, remonstrated) If you **remonstrate** with someone, you protest to them about something they have done or are doing.

remorse is a strong feeling of regret and guilt.

remorseless (remorselessly) You call someone's behaviour **remorseless** when they keep on doing something without showing any pity for the people harmed by it. ■ You say something undesirable is **remorseless** when it goes on happening. ...*the remorseless rise in budget deficits.*

remote (remoteness) Remote places are far away from large centres of population and are often difficult to get to. ■ If something is **remote** from what people want or need, it has little or no connection with it. *Teenagers are forced to study subjects that seem remote from their daily lives.* ■ If political leaders are **remote** from what is happening in their country, they are cut off from it and unaware of it. ■ If you call someone **remote,** you mean they do not get closely involved with other people. ■ If you say there is only a **remote** possibility that something will happen, you are emphasizing that there is very little chance of it happening. ■ See also **remotely.**

remote control (remote-controlled) Remote control is the control of something like a machine or vehicle from a distance, for example by radio signals. The device used to transmit the signals is called a **remote control.** ...*the TV remote-control.* A **remote-controlled** machine is controlled in this way.

remotely is used to emphasize that something is not true or not the case. *Nobody was remotely interested.* ■ If something is **remotely** situated, it is a long way from other things.

remould (Am: **remold**) If something is **remoulded** (pron: ree-**mold**-id), it is changed and reorganized completely. *The post-war constitution had the aim of remoulding Japanese society into a peaceful democracy.* ■ A **remould** (pron: **ree**-mold) is an old tyre with a new tread moulded on it so it can be used again.

removable If something is **removable,** it can be removed easily. ...*a removable sticker.*

removal When someone or something is removed, you can talk about their **removal.** ...*the removal of an appendix.* ■ A **removal company** transports furniture from one building to another when people move house. The vehicles the company uses to transport the furniture are called **removal vans.**

remove (removing, removed) When you remove something, you take it off, take it out, or take it away. *He removed his hat... Remove the loaf from the oven.* ■ If someone is **removed** from their position, for example, as head of an organization, they lose that position, usually against their will. ■ If you say one thing is **far removed** from another thing, you mean it is very different from it or has no connection with it. *The racing cars of today are far removed from the sporting vehicles of the past.*

remover A **remover** is a substance used to remove things like make-up or stains. *...paint remover.*

remunerate (*pron:* rim-**yoo**-ner-ate) (**remunerating, remunerated; remuneration**) If you are **remunerated** for doing something, you are paid for it. The money you receive is called **remuneration.**

remunerative (*pron:* rim-**yoo**-ner-at-ive) If something is **remunerative,** it is well-paid or profitable. *...a highly remunerative investment.*

renaissance (*pron:* ren-**nay**-sonss) The **Renaissance** was the period in Europe during the 14th, 15th, and 16th centuries when there was a great revival of interest in art, literature, and learning. ■ If something experiences a **renaissance,** it becomes popular or successful again. ■ If you call someone a **renaissance woman** or a **renaissance man,** you mean they have interests and skills in many subjects, especially in both the arts and the sciences.

renal (*pron:* **ree**-nal) means involving the kidneys. *...renal failure.*

rename (**renaming, renamed**) If something is **renamed,** it is given a new name.

render (**rendering, rendered**) **Render** is used to say someone's or something's condition, state, or significance is changed or weakened. For example, if something is **rendered** harmless, it is made harmless. ■ A **rendering** of a song or a piece of music is a performance of it. ■ If you **render** assistance to someone, you help them. ■ When people talk about **services rendered,** they mean services which have already been performed. ■ When a wall is **rendered,** it is covered with a layer of plaster or cement to protect it. This layer is called **rendering.**

rendezvous (*pron:* **ron**-day-voo) If you have a **rendezvous** with someone, you meet them by arrangement at a certain time and place. The place where you meet can also be called a **rendezvous.**

rendition A **rendition** of a play, poem, or piece of music is a performance of it.

renegade A **renegade** is a person who abandons his or her former group, and joins or forms a different or opposing one.

renege (*pron:* rin-**nayg**) (**reneging, reneged**) If someone **reneges** on a promise or agreement, they break it.

renegotiate (**renegotiating, renegotiated; renegotiation**) If something like a treaty or a contract is **renegotiated,** a new agreement with new terms and conditions is drawn up.

renew (**renewal**) If you **renew** something, you begin it again. When something is begun again, you can talk about its **renewal.** ■ If something like a licence or contract is **renewed,** the period for which it is valid is extended. ■ **Urban renewal** is the replacing of old buildings in towns and cities with new housing and facilities and the encouragement of investment there.

renewable A **renewable** source of energy is one which does not run out. Renewable resources are sometimes called **renewables.** ■ If a contract is **renewable,** it can be extended when it reaches the end of the period it is valid for.

renewal See **renew.**

rennet is a substance from the stomachs of cows which causes milk to become thick and sour and is used in making cheese.

renounce (**renouncing, renounced; renunciation**) If you **renounce** a belief, claim, or intention, you say you are giving it up, usually in a formal public announcement. An announcement like this is called a **renunciation.**

renovate (**renovating, renovated; renovation**) If you **renovate** a building, you repair it to get it back into good condition. The repairs you do are called **renovations.**

renown If someone gains **renown,** they become famous, as a result of their achievements. *...architects of international renown.*

renowned If someone is **renowned** for something, they are well-known for it.

rent If you **rent** something, you regularly pay its owner for the use of it. The money you pay is called **rent.** ■ If someone **rents out** property, they allow people to use it in exchange for rent.

rental is used to talk about things to do with renting out goods or property. *...car rental fees.* ■ **Rental** is money you pay regularly to the owner of something like an office, a car, or a television you are using. *Annual rental is $46,000.*

rent boy Young male prostitutes are sometimes called **rent boys.**

rent strike When people take part in a **rent strike,** they refuse to pay their rent as a form of protest.

renunciation See **renounce.**

reoffend If someone who has been in prison **reoffends,** they commit more crimes after they have been released.

reopen (**reopening, reopened**) If something like a shop or a restaurant **reopens** or is **reopened,** it opens again after it has been closed for some time. ■ If a border or a route is **reopened,** people are allowed to cross it or go along it again after a period when it has been closed. ■ If someone **reopens** something like a discussion or a legal case, they start it again after it has stopped or been closed. ■ You say wounds are **reopened** when old arguments or disagreements start again after it seemed they were over.

reorder (**reordering, reordered**) If you **reorder** things, you arrange them in a different order. A change like this is called a **reordering.**

reorganize (*or* **reorganise**) (**reorganizing, reorganized; reorganization**) If you **reorganize** something, you organize it differently. A change like this is called a **reorganization.**

reorient (**reorientation**) If you **reorient** something, you alter it to fit in with changing circumstances or objectives.

rep A **rep** is (a) a person whose job is to sell a company's products or services, usually by travelling round and visiting other companies and organizations. (b) a person who acts as a representative for a group of people, usually a group of colleagues. ■ In the theatre, **rep** is short for 'repertory'.

repackage (**repackaging, repackaged**) If someone or something is **repackaged**, they are presented in a different way or given a new image.

repaid See **repay.**

repair (**repairing, repaired**) If you **repair** something which is damaged or carry out **repairs** to it, you mend it. ■ If something like a building is in **good repair,** it is in good condition.

reparation If you make **reparation** for a wrong you have done to someone, you do something to make up for it, such as giving them money. ■ **Reparations** are sums of money paid after a war by a defeated nation for the damage and suffering caused.

repartee (*pron:* rep-part-**tee**) is an exchange of witty remarks between two people or groups.

repast A **repast** is a meal.

repatriate (**repatriating, repatriated; repatriation**) If someone is **repatriated,** they are sent back to their own country.

repay (**repaying, repaid; repayment**) If you **repay** money, you give it back to the person you borrowed it from. **Repayment** is giving money back; if you give it back in instalments, each one is called a **repayment.** ■ If you **repay** a favour, you do something in return for it.

repayable If a loan is **repayable** over a certain period, it must be paid back during that period.

repeal (**repealing, repealed**) If a law is **repealed,** it is abolished. You call this the **repeal** of the law.

repeat (**repeating, repeated; repeatedly**) If you **repeat** something, you say, write, or do it again. ■ If there is a **repeat performance** of something, especially something undesirable, it happens again. ■ If a TV or radio programme is **repeated,** it is broadcast again. You call this additional broadcast a **repeat.**

repeater A **repeater** is a device which amplifies or improves incoming electrical signals and retransmits them.

repel (**repelling, repelled**) When soldiers or police **repel** an attack or invasion, they succeed in driving back the people who are attacking or invading. ■ If something such as a chemical **repels** insects or other creatures, it keeps them away. ■ If something **repels** you, you find it horrible and disgusting.

repellent A **repellent** is a substance used to keep insects or other creatures away. ...*mosquito repellent.* ■ If you find something **repellent,** you find it horrible and disgusting.

repent (**repentant, repentance**) If someone **repents,** they show they are sorry for bad things they have done. When someone behaves like this, you say they are **repentant** or talk about their **repentance.**

repercussions If something has **repercussions,** other things happen as a result of it, especially undesirable things.

repertoire (*pron:* rep-et-twar) An actor's or musician's **repertoire** is all the parts or pieces of music they have learned and can perform. ■ Plays or pieces of music of a particular kind can be called a **repertoire.** ...*her goal to perform the entire Liszt piano repertoire.* ■ Someone's **repertoire** is all the things of a particular kind they are capable of making or doing.

repertory (**repertories**) A **repertory** company is a group of actors who perform plays for short runs of a few weeks. The plays are often performed in **repertory theatres.** When an actor is a member of a repertory company, you say they are **in repertory.** ■ An actor's or musician's **repertory** is all the parts or pieces of music they have learned and are able to perform. ■ Plays or pieces of music of a particular kind can be called a **repertory.** ...*a composer central to the UK operatic repertory.*

repetition If there is a **repetition** of something which has happened before, it happens again. *They fear a repetition of wartime atrocities which left few families intact.* ■ If there is **repetition** in something like a book or speech, the same things are written or said more than once.

repetitious means the same as 'repetitive'.

repetitive If something is **repetitive,** it involves doing the same things again and again or the same things happening again and again, and therefore tends to be boring.

repetitive strain injury People who suffer from **repetitive strain injury** or **RSI** have pains in their muscles or joints caused by performing the same movements over and over again every day, usually as part of their job.

rephrase (**rephrasing, rephrased**) If you **rephrase** something you have said, you say it again using different words.

replace (**replacing, replaced; replacement**) If you **replace** something with something else, you get rid of the first thing and use the second thing instead. When something takes the place of something else, you say it is a **replacement** for it. ■ If you **replace** something, you put it back where it was before.

replay On TV, a **replay** (*pron:* ree-play) is the same as an action replay. ■ If you **replay** (*pron:* ree-**play**) something you have recorded on tape or film, you play it back. ■ If there is a **replay** of something which happened in the past, something happens which is very similar in some way. *He is committed to avoiding a replay of the Vietnam War.* ■ In sport, when competitors **replay** a match, they play it again. The second match is called a **replay.**

replenish (**replenishes, replenishing, replenished; replenishment**) If you **replenish** something which has run out, you get in fresh stocks.

replete If something is **replete** with things, it is full of them. *The play is replete with Glasgow humour and local references.*

replica A **replica** of something is an exact copy of it.

replicate (**replicating, replicated; replication**) When organisms or molecules **replicate,** they multiply by creating exact copies of themselves. ■ If you **replicate** someone's work, you do the same work yourself in exactly the same way.

reply (**replies, replying, replied**) If you **reply** to something someone has said or written, you say or write something back to them. You can say something is said or written **in reply to** something else. ■ You say someone **replies** in a certain way when they do something in response to something someone else has done. *The army replied with a mortar attack.*

repo (*pron:* **ree**-po) is short for 'repossession'.

report If you **report** something which has happened, you tell people about it. *I reported the theft to the police.* ■ A **report** is an account of something which has happened, especially in a newspaper or on a news programme. ■ If you say there are **reports** of something, you mean people say it has happened, but you cannot be sure about it. *There are reports of heavy fighting around Gabiro military barracks.* ■ **Reporting** is the presenting of news in newspapers and on TV and radio. ■ If you **report** on something you have been asked to look into or **report back** on it, you tell people what you have found out about it. A **report** is an official document issued by a person or group of people in which they say what they have found out about a subject. ■ A school **report** is a written account of a pupil's progress at school, sent to their parents at the end of each term. In the US, school reports are called 'report cards'. ■ If you **report** a person, you tell people in authority about something wrong the person has done. ■ If you **report** to a place, you go there to start work or to be told what to do. You can also **report** to a person.

reportage (*pron:* **rep**-pore-tahzh; *the 'zh' sounds like 's' in 'pleasure'*) **Reportage** is the reporting of current events by the media.

reportedly If you say something is **reportedly** true, you mean people have said it, but you cannot be sure about it.

reported speech is a way of repeating things people have said. When reported speech is written down, quotation marks are not used. 'He said he wanted to wait' is an example of reported speech.

reporter A **reporter** is someone who writes news articles or broadcasts news reports.

repose is a state in which you are resting and feeling calm.

reposition (**repositioning, repositioned**) If you **reposition** something, you change its position.

repository (**repositories**) A **repository** is a place where something is kept safely. ■ If you call a place a **repository** of something useful or valuable, you mean a great deal of it is kept there. *...Punch magazine, long the repository of good writing.*

repossess (**repossesses, repossessing, repossessed; repossession**) If your house or car is **repossessed,** the people who supplied it or lent you the money for it take it back.

repot (**repotting, repotted**) If you **repot** a plant, you take it out of its pot and plant it in a larger one.

reprehensible If you say someone's behaviour is **reprehensible,** you mean it is very bad and morally wrong.

represent If someone **represents** an organization or another person, they act on their behalf. *...the Law Society, the body which represents solicitors in Eng-* land and Wales. ■ If you **represent** your country in a competition, you take part on its behalf. ■ If a group is well **represented** in an event, a lot of its members are taking part. ■ If you say something **represents** something such as a change or victory, you mean that it is a change or victory. *The small print in the new bill represents a victory for religious leaders.* ■ If someone or something is **represented** as a certain type of person or thing, people are led to believe they are that thing. ■ If you say something **represents** a particular thing for people, you mean they see it as standing for that thing.

representation If a group or person has **representation** in court, in parliament, or on a committee, they have someone there who will speak, vote, or make decisions on their behalf. ■ A picture or description of someone or something can be called a **representation** of them. ■ If you make **representations** to a government or other official group, you make a formal complaint or request to them.

representational art is intended to show people and things exactly as they look in reality. ■ If an organization has a **representational** role, it acts on behalf of a group of people.

representative A **representative** is (a) a person who has been chosen to act or make decisions on behalf of another person or a group. (b) someone whose job is to sell a company's products or services, usually by travelling round and visiting other companies and organizations. ■ If a person or thing is a good example of their type, you can say they are **representative** of it. *Shancarrig is representative of a thousand small-town communities.* ■ If a sample is **representative,** it is large and broad enough to provide useful information about the larger group it is taken from.

repress (**represses, repressing, repressed; repression**) If you **repress** a feeling, you make a deliberate effort not to show it or give way to it. ■ **Repressed** people do not allow themselves to have natural feelings and desires. *...repressed homosexual fantasies.* ■ You say people are **repressed** when their freedom is restricted and their activities are controlled by force. *...reports of continuing repression.*

repressive (**repressively**) A **repressive** government is one which uses force to control people and restrict their freedom.

reprieve (**reprieving, reprieved**) If someone who has been sentenced in a court is **reprieved** or given a **reprieve,** their punishment is officially postponed or cancelled. ■ A **reprieve** is a delay before an unpleasant situation. *Public opinion forced a reprieve for the London to Fort William sleeper services.*

reprimand If someone is **reprimanded** by someone in authority or given a **reprimand,** they are told off for something they have done.

reprint If a book or article is **reprinted,** additional copies are printed. A **reprint** is an occasion when a book is reprinted. *The book has already sold 30,000 copies and is in its fourth reprint.* The additional copies of the book are called **reprints.**

reprisal – Reprisals are violent or unpleasant actions against people or countries that have caused harm. *Precautions have been taken to prevent reprisal attacks.*

reprise (*pron:* ri-**preez**) (**reprising, reprised**) If an actor **reprises** a role, he or she plays the same character or a similar character to one they have played before. *Hoskins is rather wasted in what amounts to a reprise of his Roger Rabbit part.* ■ In music, if there is a **reprise,** an earlier track or section of music is repeated.

reproach (**reproaches, reproaching, reproached**) If you **reproach** someone or express **reproach,** you indicate that you are disappointed, upset, or angry because they have done something wrong. *Unhappy at the decision, Morris gave Jack Bond a look of reproach.* ■ If you say someone or something is a **reproach** to other people or things, you mean their high standards show up the low standards of the others. *The grandeur of the 18th and 19th century is a standing reproach to the shoddiness of the 20th.*

reproachful (**reproachfully**) If someone's behaviour is **reproachful,** they show you they are disappointed because you have done something wrong.

reprobate (*pron:* **rep**-roh-bate) A man who behaves in an immoral way is sometimes called a **reprobate.**

reprocess (**reprocesses, reprocessing, reprocessed**) When materials such as toxic waste are **reprocessed,** they are treated to make them safe or ready to be used again. *...the Sellafield nuclear reprocessing plant.*

reproduce (**reproducing, reproduced; reproduction, reproductive**) If you **reproduce** something, you make a copy or copies of it. A **reproduction** is a copy of something like a painting or an antique. *...reproduction furniture.* ■ If you **reproduce** an achievement, you repeat it. *Milan were unable to reproduce the tremendous football which swept aside Steaua Bucharest.* ■ When living things **reproduce,** they produce more of their own species. This process is called **reproduction. Reproductive** means to do with reproduction. *...reproductive organs.*

reproof is telling someone you disapprove of something they have done. *The father utters no word of reproof.*

reprove (**reproving, reproved**) If you **reprove** someone, you tell them off.

reptile (**reptilian**) **Reptiles** are cold-blooded, scaly-skinned creatures which lay eggs. Lizards, snakes, crocodiles, and tortoises are all reptiles. **Reptilian** (*pron:* rep-**till**-ian) means to do with reptiles.

republic (**republican, republicanism**) A **republic** is a country which does not have a monarch and which has a government chosen to represent the people. *...nations that had adopted the republican form of government.* People who favour such a system are called **republicans;** their beliefs are called **republicanism.** ■ In Northern Ireland, a **Republican** is someone who believes Northern Ireland should be part of the Republic of Ireland. Support for this point of view is called **Republicanism.** ■ In

the US, a **Republican** is a person who belongs to or supports the Republican Party.

repudiate (*pron:* rip-**pew**-dee-ate) (**repudiating, repudiated; repudiation**) If you **repudiate** someone or something, you show you strongly disagree with them and do not want to be connected with them.

repugnant (**repugnance**) If you find something **repugnant,** you think it is horrible and disgusting. You can talk about your **repugnance** for something like this.

repulse (**repulsing, repulsed**) When soldiers **repulse** an enemy that is attacking them, they successfully defend themselves and drive the enemy back.

repulsive (**repulsion**) If you find something **repulsive,** you find it horrible and disgusting. You call the feeling it gives you **repulsion.**

reputable (*pron:* rep-yoo-tab-bl) A **reputable** person or company is known to be reliable and trustworthy.

reputation Your **reputation** is the opinion people have of you. If you have a good reputation, people have a high opinion of you. *The trial has severely damaged her reputation.* ■ If you have a **reputation** for something, you are well-known for it.

repute A person or organization **of repute** is highly thought of. *...an engineer of international repute.* ■ A person's **repute** is their reputation, especially when it is a good one. *Under his stewardship, the UN's repute has risen immeasurably.*

reputed (**reputedly**) If you say something is **reputed** to be true, you mean people say it is true but you cannot be certain about it.

request If you **request** something or make a **request** for it, you ask for it.

requiem (*pron:* rek-wee-em) A **requiem** or **requiem mass** is a Catholic church service held in memory of someone who has recently died. ■ A **requiem** is a piece of music for singers and musicians which can be performed either as part of a requiem mass or in a concert.

require (**requiring, required**) If something is **required,** it is needed. *The injury is expected to require surgery.* ■ If you are **required** to do something, for example by law, you have to do it. *New EU regulations require companies to replace ancient equipment.*

requirement A **requirement** is something like a quality you must have or a standard you must reach before you are allowed to do something. *The selection procedures include a minimum height requirement.* ■ Your **requirements** are your needs.

requisite (*pron:* rek-wizz-it) is used to describe things which are needed for a certain purpose. *Neither bloc has the requisite two-thirds support.* Something which is needed like this can be called a **requisite.**

requisition (**requisitioning, requisitioned**) If something like a car or a building is **requisitioned,** it is taken from its owners by the authorities to use for their own purposes.

requite (**requiting, requited**) If someone's love is **requited,** the person they love responds and loves them back.

reredos (*usual pron:* **rear**-doss) (**reredoses**) A **reredos** is a decorated wood or stone screen or partition wall behind the altar in a church.

reroute (*or* **re-route**) (**rerouting, rerouted**) If vehicles are **rerouted**, they are sent along a different route, because the usual one cannot be used.

rerun (*or* **re-run**) (**rerunning, reran, have rerun**) If something like an election is **rerun**, it is held again, for example because the correct procedures were not followed. *A rerun of the contest is almost certain.* ∎ If a TV series is **rerun**, it is put on again. *Bill Cosby will earn millions from reruns of the show.* ∎ If you say something is a **rerun** of something which happened previously, you mean it is very similar to it. *It was the world's second worst air disaster, a horrific re-run of the runway collision in 1977.*

reschedule (**rescheduling, rescheduled**) If an event is **rescheduled**, arrangements are made for it to take place at a different time. ∎ If a debt is **rescheduled**, the country or bank which lent the money agrees that it can be paid back over a longer period.

rescind (*pron:* ris-**sind**) If a law, agreement, or decision is **rescinded**, it is withdrawn and no longer applies.

rescue (**rescuing, rescued; rescuer**) If you **rescue** someone or come to their **rescue**, you get them out of a dangerous or difficult situation. Someone who rescues someone else can be called their **rescuer**.

research (**researches, researching, researched; researcher**) If you **research** a subject, you study it and try to discover facts about it. Work like this is called **research**. A person who does research is called a **researcher**.

resemble (**resembling, resembled; resemblance**) If something **resembles** something else or bears a **resemblance** to it, it is similar to it.

resent (**resentment; resentful, resentfully**) If you **resent** something, you feel bitter and annoyed about it. This feeling is called **resentment**. If you are **resentful**, you feel like this. *He looked at me resentfully.*

reservation If you have **reservations** about a proposal, you have serious doubts about it. ∎ If you make a **reservation**, you arrange for something like a table in a restaurant or a room in a hotel to be kept for you.

reserve (**reserving, reserved**) If something is **reserved** for certain people, it is kept for them and cannot be used by anyone else. Similarly, you can say something is **reserved** for a particular purpose. *...airspace reserved for military use.* ∎ A **reserve** is an extra supply of something kept in case it is needed. You say you keep something like this **in reserve**. ∎ **Reserve** soldiers or police are people who only act as soldiers or police if they are needed in an emergency. ∎ In sport, a **reserve** is an extra person who is kept ready to take the place of a team member who cannot play. ∎ If you call someone **reserved**, you mean they keep their feelings well hidden. You talk about the **reserve** of someone like this. ∎ **reserve judgment:** see **judgment**.

reserve price When something is sold by auction, the **reserve price** is the lowest price the owner will accept for it.

reservist – **Reservists** are reserve soldiers or police.

reservoir A **reservoir** is a place where liquid is stored, especially an artificial lake used to supply an area with water.

reset (**resetting, reset** *not* '*resetted*') When a doctor **resets** a broken bone, he or she puts it back in its correct position. ∎ If you **reset** a machine or device, you adjust it so it is ready to work again or ready to do something different.

resettle (**resettling, resettled**) If people like refugees are **resettled** by a government or other organization, they are found somewhere else to live. This process is called **resettlement.**

reshape (**reshaping, reshaped**) If something is **reshaped,** it is altered or adapted to fit changing circumstances.

reshuffle (**reshuffling, reshuffled**) If a government or the management of a company is **reshuffled,** people's jobs or responsibilities are changed around, usually with some people losing their jobs in the process. This is called a **reshuffle.**

reside (*pron:* riz-**zide**) (**residing, resided**) If someone **resides** somewhere, they are living there at present. ∎ **Reside** is used to say what it is that gives something a particular quality. *Komsomol's power has for decades resided in its role as a pillar of the establishment.*

residence Your **residence** is the place where you live. ∎ If you obtain **residence** in a country, you are officially allowed to live there. ∎ If you **take up residence** somewhere, you start living there. If you are **in residence** somewhere, you are living there. ∎ An artist or writer **in residence** teaches or works in an institution like a university.

residency (**residencies**) If you obtain **residency** in a country, you are officially allowed to live there. ∎ When a person or organization is based at a place, you can talk about their **residency** there. *...the official inauguration of the London Philharmonic's residency at the South Bank.*

resident The **residents** of a place are the people who live there. ∎ **Resident** is used to describe (a) people who live in the place where they work. *...the resident caretaker.* (b) people who are employed by a company for their special knowledge or skill. *...the company's resident choreographer.*

residential is used (a) to describe buildings and areas where people live, as distinct from places used for some other purpose such as business or industry. *...a smart residential district.* (b) to describe places where people can live and be looked after by the staff. *...residential homes.*

residue (**residual**) A **residue** is a small amount of something which is left over after most of it has gone. You call an amount like this a **residual** amount. *A small residual staff will be retained.*

resign (**resignation**) If someone **resigns** from a position, they formally announce that they are leaving it. This announcement is called their **resignation.** ∎ If you have **resigned** yourself to an unpleasant fact or situation, you have accepted it because you believe you cannot change it.

resilient (resilience) If you say someone is **resilient** or talk about their **resilience,** you mean they have the ability to recover quickly from unpleasant experiences. ■ If an object or substance is **resilient,** it is strong and does not damage easily.

resin (*pron:* rezz-in) is (a) a sticky substance produced by some trees. (b) a similar substance produced industrially and used to make plastics.

resist (resistance; resister) If someone **resists** something, they fight against it or refuse to accept it. When this happens, you talk about their **resistance** to it. People who refuse to accept or take part in something are sometimes called **resisters.** ...*war resisters.* ■ When soldiers **resist** an attack, they fight back. ■ When people talk about the **Resistance,** they mean one of various groups which fought against the Nazi occupation of their countries during the Second World War. ■ If an object or substance **resists** something harmful or damaging, it is not affected by it. *Aircraft engineers use the alloy because of its high strength and resistance to wear.* ■ **Resistance** is any force which slows down a moving object or vehicle. ■ In physics and electrical engineering, **resistance** is the ability of a substance or an electrical circuit to obstruct the flow of an electrical current through it.

resistant If something is **resistant** to something else, it is unlikely to be harmed or damaged by it. ■ If people are **resistant** to something, they are opposed to it and want to prevent it.

resister See resist.

resistor A **resistor** is a device which obstructs the flow of electric current within a circuit.

resit (resitting, resat) If someone **resits** an examination, they take it again, usually because they failed the first time. This additional examination is called a **resit.**

resolute (resolutely) If someone is **resolute,** they are determined not to change their mind about something.

resolution A **resolution** is a formal decision taken at a meeting by means of a vote. ■ **Resolution** is determination not to give in or change your mind. ■ If you make a **resolution** to do something, you promise yourself you will do it. ■ When a problem or a disagreement is sorted out, you can talk about its **resolution.** *China has consistently stressed it wants to see a peaceful resolution to the crisis.*

resolve (resolving, resolved) If a problem or a disagreement is **resolved,** it is sorted out. ■ If you **resolve** to do something, you make a firm decision to do it. ■ If you are **resolved** to do something, you are determined to do it. You can talk about people's **resolve** to do something. *He said sanctions would not weaken the resolve of the Lithuanian people.*

resonate (resonating, resonated; resonant, resonance) If something **resonates,** it vibrates and produces a deep strong sound. ■ A **resonant** sound is loud and echoing. You talk about the **resonance** of a sound like this. ■ **Resonant** is used to describe things which have a special meaning for people or are particularly important to them, often because

they remind them of something else. You can say things like these **resonate** or have a particular **resonance.** *The band's very name is full of resonance for anyone with even the vaguest knowledge of America's past.*

resort If you **resort** to doing something humiliating or morally wrong, you do it in order to survive, or because you can see no other way of achieving what you want. *Some people have resorted to begging for food.* ■ If you do something as a **last resort,** you do it when you have tried every other way of solving a problem, and this seems to be the only way left. ■ A **resort** is a place where many people spend their holidays.

resound (*pron:* riz-**zownd**) **(resoundingly)** If something **resounds,** it makes a loud echoing noise. You say a place **resounds** when it is full of noises like this. *The square resounded with cries.* ■ **Resounding** is used to describe a result which is powerful and definite. ...*a resounding victory.*

resource (resourcing, resourced) The **resources** of a country, organization, or person are the things available for their use, for example money, materials, and staff. The provision of resources, especially money, is called **resourcing.** If an organization does not have enough resources, you can say it is **under-resourced.**

resourceful (resourcefulness) **Resourceful** people are good at finding ways of dealing with problems.

respect If you **respect** someone or something or have **respect** for them, you have a high opinion of them. ■ If you **respect** the law, you do not break it. Similarly, if you **respect** people's wishes, rights, or beliefs, you do not interfere with them or go against them. ■ If you **pay your respects** to someone, you speak to them or call on them out of politeness. ■ If you **pay your respects** or **your last respects** to someone who has died, you express your respect or affection for them, for example by going to their funeral. ■ You use phrases like **with respect to** and **in respect of** to indicate what you are referring to. *We share a common purpose with respect to the problems in the Gulf... The children are not unintelligent – in fact, they seem quite normal in this respect.*

respectable (respectably, respectability) You say a person or organization is **respectable** when they live or operate in a way which most people approve of. *Her appointment will boost the industry's respectability.* ■ **Respectable** is used to describe things which are adequate or acceptable. *He batted respectably.*

respecter If you say something harmful is **no respecter** of distinctions between people, you mean it takes no account of these things, but affects everyone equally. *Pollution is no respecter of international borders.*

respectful (respectfully) If you are **respectful,** you show respect for someone.

respective means relating separately to each of the people or things you have just mentioned. *The two prime ministers hold little executive power in their respective countries.*

respectively means in the order you have just mentioned. *My father and mother, Liberal and Conservative, respectively, were thinking of voting Labour.*

respiration is the process by which living things take in the oxygen they need to create energy, and send out carbon dioxide. Humans and other mammals achieve this by breathing.

respirator A **respirator** is a machine which helps you to breathe when you are ill or have been injured. It is also called a 'ventilator'. ■ A **respirator** is a device you wear over your mouth and nose to breathe when you are surrounded by smoke or poisonous gas.

respiratory means connected with respiration. *...respiratory infections.*

respite (*pron:* **ress**-pit *or* **ress**-pite) A **respite** is a short period of rest or escape from something unpleasant.

resplendent If you talk about people or things being **resplendent**, you mean their appearance is bright, impressive, and expensive-looking.

respond (**response**) When you **respond** or give a **response** to something someone has said or done, you react by saying or doing something yourself. *America says it has received a positive response from Syria to its proposals.* You can also say something is done **in response** to something else. ■ If a patient **responds** to treatment, the treatment works and they get better.

respondent The **respondents** to a survey are the people who answer the questions. ■ In court, a **respondent** is someone who defends a lawsuit, especially a divorce suit.

response See **respond.**

responsibility (**responsibilities**) If you have **responsibility** for someone or something, or they are your **responsibility**, it is your job or duty to deal with them and to take decisions relating to them. *The government has a responsibility to help the poor.* ■ If someone is given **responsibility,** they are given the right or opportunity to make important decisions or to take action without asking permission. ■ If you claim or accept **responsibility** for something which has happened, you say you caused it.

responsible (**responsibly**) If you are **responsible** for something, it is your job or duty to deal with it and make decisions relating to it. *...the cabinet minister responsible for environmental matters.* ■ If you are **responsible** to a person or group, they have authority over you and you have to report to them about what you do. ■ If you are **responsible** for something happening, it happens as a result of what you have done. *Alison was 95 per cent responsible for our success.* ■ If you are **held responsible** for something bad which has happened, you are blamed for it. ■ **Responsible** behaviour is sensible and does not create problems for other people. ■ **Responsible** jobs involve making important decisions or carrying out important tasks.

responsive (**responsiveness**) If you are **responsive** to something, you are quick to react to it and show interest or concern about it.

rest – The **rest** of something is the other parts of it. *...the rest of your life.* ■ If you **rest** or have a **rest,** you do not do anything active for a time. ■ If you **rest** something somewhere, you put it on top of something else. *The ship rested on the sea-bed.* ■ A **rest** is an object used to support a part of your body, for example a headrest. ■ If responsibility for something **rests** with you, you are responsible for it. ■ If you **put** or **set** someone's **mind at rest,** you tell them something which stops them worrying. ■ If you **lay** something like a fear or a rumour **to rest,** you succeed in showing that it is unfounded. ■ The place where a dead person is buried is sometimes called their **resting place.**

restate (**restating, restated; restatement**) If you **restate** something, you say it again, usually in a different way, to emphasize it or make it clear. You call this a **restatement** of what you first said.

restaurant A **restaurant** is a place where you have a meal which you pay for.

restaurant car The part of a train where you sit down to have a meal is sometimes called the **restaurant car.**

restaurateur (*pron:* rest-er-a-**tur**) A **restaurateur** is a person who owns and manages a restaurant.

restful If something makes you calm and relaxed, you can say it is **restful.**

rest home A **rest home** is an institution where old people are cared for.

restitution If you demand **restitution** for something which has been taken away from you, you demand to have it back or to be compensated. *The victims are demanding full restitution.*

restive If people are **restive,** they are impatient and dissatisfied.

restless (**restlessly, restlessness**) If you are **restless,** you are bored and dissatisfied, and want to leave or do something else. ■ You say someone is **restless** when they find it difficult to keep still.

restock If you **restock** a shop, fridge, or shelf, you fill it with goods to replace the ones that have been sold or used.

restoration See **restore.**

restorative (*pron:* rest-**or**-a-tiv) If something is **restorative** or a **restorative,** it makes you feel livelier, stronger, or more cheerful after you have been feeling tired, weak, or miserable. *...the restorative powers of evening primrose oil.*

restore (**restoring, restored; restoration, restorer**) If something is **restored,** it is brought back into existence or returned to its previous condition. *...the restoration of the death penalty... Britain and Argentina restored diplomatic relations.* ■ When someone **restores** something like a painting, they repair and clean it, so it looks like new. A person who restores things as their job is called a **restorer.** ■ If something which was lost or stolen is **restored** to its owner, it is returned to them. ■ The **Restoration** period was the period following the crowning of Charles II in 1660 after a time when there had been no King or Queen. **Restoration** is used to talk about the drama, architecture, and furniture of this period. *...Restoration plays.*

restrain (**restraining, restrained**) If you **restrain** someone, you stop them doing what they intend to do or want to do, often by using physical strength. ■ If you **restrain** yourself from doing something, you stop yourself doing it. *He could not restrain himself from applauding.* ■ If you **restrain** something which is likely to get out of hand, you keep firm control over it. ...*a government dedicated to restraining expenditure.* ■ If you behave in a **restrained** way, you do not show any strong feelings.

restraint – **Restraints** are straps which prevent a person moving from a bed or chair. ■ Laws or rules which prevent people doing something can be called **restraints.** *Mr Birch said legal restraints made it impossible for the story to be fully reported.* ■ **Restraint** is calm, controlled, and unemotional behaviour.

restrict If you **restrict** something, you put a limit on it to prevent it becoming too great. *The Government has opted to restrict the number of days trawlers can fish.* ■ If people are unable to move or behave as they want, you can say their movements or behaviour are **restricted.** *The legislation will restrict press freedom.* ■ If something is **restricted** to a certain place or activity, it only exists in that place or activity. *Such difficulties are not restricted to desk-top publishing.* ■ If something is **restricted,** there is only a limited amount of it. ...*restricted space.*

restriction A **restriction** is something, especially a rule, which limits what you can do or limits the amount or size of something. ...*noise restrictions.*

restrictive If something is **restrictive,** it limits what people can do.

rest room In the US, the toilets in a public place like a restaurant or theatre are called the **rest room.**

restructure (**restructuring, restructured**) If a system or organization is **restructured,** the way it is organized is changed, and often some employees are laid off, to try to make it more efficient.

result If something **results** from something else or is a **result** of it, it happens because of it. ■ If something **results in** something else, it causes it. *Two of the boats capsized, resulting in the loss of ten lives.* ■ The number you get when you do a calculation is called a **result.** ■ A **result** is the outcome of something like a contest or an experiment. ...*the results of a detailed survey.* ■ When you take an exam, your **results** are the marks or grades you get. ■ In football, getting a **result** means winning a match, rather than just drawing.

resultant is used to say something is caused by the thing you have just mentioned. ...*recent travel company failures and the resultant losses to clients.*

resume (**resuming, resumed**) If you **resume** something, you start doing it again. ■ If you **resume** your place or position, you take it again. *I resumed my seat.*

résumé (*pron:* **rez**-yoo-may) A **résumé** is a short account of something which has happened or of something someone has said or written.

resumption If there is a **resumption** of something, it begins again. ...*a petition opposing Norway's resumption of commercial whaling.*

resurface (**resurfacing, resurfaced**) If something like an idea or problem **resurfaces,** it becomes important or prominent again. *The disease was said to have resurfaced in three countries.* ■ If someone who has not been seen or heard about for a long time **resurfaces,** they suddenly reappear or return to the public eye. ■ If something which has been underwater **resurfaces,** it comes back to the surface again. ■ When something like a road is **resurfaced,** it is given a new surface.

resurgence (**resurgent**) If there is a **resurgence** of something, it starts to grow in strength or popularity after a period of decline. You can say something like this is **resurgent.** ...*Serbia's resurgent nationalism.*

resurrect (**resurrection**) If something is **resurrected,** it is brought back into existence when it seemed to have finished or disappeared forever. ■ When people talk about a dead person being **resurrected,** they are talking about a miraculous event in which the person is supposedly brought back to life. ■ When Christians talk about the **Resurrection,** they mean the event when Jesus Christ is supposed to have come back to life on the third day after his execution.

resuscitate (*pron:* ris-**suss**-it-tate) (**resuscitating, resuscitated; resuscitation**) If you **resuscitate** someone, you get their heart and breathing to start again after they have stopped. ■ If you **resuscitate** something, you make it become active or successful again. *Wood attempted to resuscitate her husband's career.*

retail (**retailing, retailed**) **Retail** is the business of selling goods to the public, usually in fairly small quantities. **Retail** goods are sold in ordinary shops direct to the public. ...*retail jewellery.* ■ If you say something **retails** at a particular price, you mean that is how much it usually costs in the shops.

retailer A **retailer** is a person or business that sells goods to the public.

retail price index In Britain, the **retail price index** or **RPI** is a monthly list of prices of typical goods and services. It shows how much the cost of living and inflation change from one month to the next.

retain (**retaining, retained**) If you **retain** something, you keep it. ■ If someone **retains** a lawyer, they pay the lawyer a fee to make sure he or she will represent them if their case comes before court.

retainer If you pay someone a **retainer,** you pay them a fee to make sure they will be available to work for you if you need them. ■ A servant who has been with one family for a long time is sometimes called a **retainer.**

retake (**retaking, retook, have retaken**) If a military force **retakes** a place which it has lost to the enemy, it captures it again. ■ In film-making, if there is a **retake** of a scene, the scene is filmed again because it needs to be changed or improved. ■ If you **retake** an exam, you take it again.

retaliate (**retaliating, retaliated; retaliation**) If you **retaliate** or do something **in retaliation** when someone has harmed or upset you, you do something similar to them in return.

retaliatory means done in retaliation. ...*a retalia-tory strike.*

retard (**retardation**) If something **retards** the development or progress of something, it slows it down. ■ Someone who is **retarded** is much less advanced mentally than most people of their age. This condition is called mental **retardation.**

retch (**retches, retching, retched**) If you **retch,** you vomit or your stomach muscles move as if you are vomiting.

retd is short for 'retired'. It is written after someone's name to show they have retired from the army, navy, or air force.

retell (**retelling, retold**) If a story is **retold,** it is told again, often differently.

retention When something is kept somewhere, you can talk about its **retention.** *The case challenges M15's indefinite retention of files.*

retentive If you have a **retentive** memory, you are good at remembering things.

rethink (**rethinking, rethought**) If you **rethink** something like a plan or policy, you look closely at it to consider what changes could be made. This is called having a **rethink.**

reticent (**reticence**) If someone is **reticent** about something or shows **reticence,** they are unwilling to talk about it.

retina (**retinal**) The **retina** is the light-sensitive membrane at the back of the eye. It receives images and sends them to the brain. **Retinal** means to do with the retina.

retinue An important person's **retinue** is the group of servants, friends, or assistants who go with them and look after their needs.

retire (**retiring, retired; retirement**) When older people **retire,** they leave their job and usually stop working altogether. Similarly, when sports players **retire,** they stop playing competitively. ■ A person's **retirement** is the period in their life after they have retired from their work. ■ When a sports player **retires** from a race or a match, they stop taking part, usually because of injury. ■ When you **retire,** you go to bed. ■ If you **retire** to another room or place, you go there. ■ **Retiring** people do not like being the centre of attention. *She was a shy and retiring person off-stage.*

retiree Retired people are sometimes called **retirees.**

retold See **retell.**

retook See **retake.**

retool (**retooling, retooled**) If a factory **retools,** its machinery or equipment is changed so it can perform new tasks.

retort If someone **retorts,** they reply quickly and angrily. A **retort** is a reply like this.

retouch (**retouches, retouching, retouched**) If a photograph is **retouched,** it is altered or improved by painting over parts of it.

retrace (**retracing, retraced**) If you **retrace** your steps, you go back along the same route to where you started. ■ If you **retrace** another person's route, you follow the same route yourself.

retract If you **retract** something you have said or written, you say that you did not mean it. Taking

something back like this is called a **retraction.** ■ If part of something is **retracted,** it is pulled back into the main part. *The aircraft's wheels were retracted.*

retractable If a part of something is **retractable,** it can be pulled inwards or backwards. ...*a 20,000-seat arena with a retractable roof.*

retrain (**retraining, retrained**) If you **retrain,** you learn new skills, usually so you will be able to start a fresh career.

retread A **retread** is an old tyre which has been given a new outer surface.

retreat (**retreating, retreated**) If you **retreat,** you move away from someone or something. *He retreated from the public eye... The British 8th Army was in full retreat.* ■ If you **beat a retreat,** you leave a place quickly or end your involvement in something, to avoid an unpleasant situation. ■ If you **retreat** into something, you occupy yourself with it, rather than face up to other things. *People responded by retreating into their private lives.* ■ A **retreat** is a quiet secluded place where people go, for example to rest or to concentrate on their religion.

retrench (**retrenches, retrenching, retrenched; retrenchment**) If an organization **retrenches,** it reduces its costs. *There is a need for industrial retrenchment and restructuring.*

retrial See **retry.**

retribution is punishment. *He warned of very severe retribution if Baghdad resorted to chemical weapons.*

retried See **retry.**

retrieve (**retrieving, retrieved; retrieval**) If you **retrieve** something, you get it back. *The intensity of the fighting has prevented the retrieval of bodies from the battle zone.* ■ When you **retrieve** information stored on computer files, you print it out or bring it up on the screen.

retriever – **Retrievers** are large dogs traditionally used by people who go hunting to bring back birds and animals they have shot.

retro clothes, music, and objects are based on styles of the past. ...*retro-rock acts.*

retroactive (**retroactively**) **Retroactive** laws and decisions take effect from an earlier date than when they are officially approved.

retrograde When something has been improving, a **retrograde** action puts it back to the way it was before. *The Prime Minister described transferring education to central government funding as a retrograde step.*

retrogressive If you call an action or idea **retrogressive,** you mean it returns to old ideas and does not take advantage of recent progress.

retrospect The way things seem **in retrospect** is the way they seem some time afterwards, when you may have a better understanding of them. *In retrospect, though, it's clear that the leadership was right to be worried.*

retrospective (**retrospectively**) A **retrospective** is an exhibition of work done by an artist or film director over many years. ■ **Retrospective** laws and decisions take effect from an earlier date than when they are approved. ■ **Retrospective** feelings concern things which happened some time ago.

Retrospectively, it seems as if they probably were negligent.

retry (**retries, retrying, retried; retrial**) If someone is **retried** or given a **retrial,** they are tried again for the same offence, either because the jury at the first trial could not reach a decision or because the first trial was not carried out properly.

retsina (*pron:* ret-**see**-na) is a Greek wine flavoured with resin.

return If you **return** to a place, you go back there. When you go back to a place, this is called your **return.** ■ If you **return** something, you give it back or put it back. ■ If a feeling or situation **returns,** it comes back or happens again. *The pain returned.* ■ If you **return** to something you were doing before, you start doing it again. *He seems to be returning to his old ways.* Similarly, you can say you **return** to a previous condition or **return** to something you have said before. ■ When a judge or jury **returns** a verdict, they announce it. ■ A **return** or **return ticket** is a ticket for a journey to a place then back again. ■ The **return** on an investment is the profit from it. ■ A tax **return** is an official form on which you declare your income. ■ **Returns** are the results of votes in various places as part of an election or ballot. ■ If you do something **in return** for a favour, you do it to repay the favour.

returnee People who return to the country where they were born after living abroad are sometimes called **returnees.**

returning officer The **returning officer** is the official responsible for supervising an election in a town or district.

reunify (**reunifies, reunifying, reunified; reunification**) If a country is **reunified,** it becomes one country again, after being split into two or more separately controlled parts. *The reunification of East and West Beirut.*

reunion A **reunion** is a party or meeting for people who have not seen each other for a long time. *...a joyful reunion with his mother.*

reunite (**reuniting, reunited**) If close friends or family members are **reunited,** they meet each other again after being separated for some time. ■ If a divided organization or country is **reunited,** it becomes one united organization or country again. *...a reunited Germany.*

reusable If something is **reusable,** it can be used more than once. *...a fully reusable spacecraft.*

reuse (*or* re-use) (**reusing, reused**) When you **reuse** something, you use it again instead of getting rid of it. You call talk about the **reuse** (*pron:* ree-**yooss**) of something. *...the reuse of rubbish.*

rev (**revving, revved**) Engine speed is measured in **revs.** Revs are revolutions per minute. ■ If you **rev** a car engine, you increase its speed by pressing the accelerator. ■ **Rev** in front of someone's name stands for 'Reverend'. *...the Rev George Glover.*

revalue (**revaluing, revalued; revaluation**) If a country's currency is **revalued,** its value is increased so it can buy more foreign currency than before. ■ If a business **revalues** some of its property, it increases its value as shown in the accounts.

revamp If you **revamp** something or give it a **revamp,** you make changes to it to improve it, modernize it, or give it a fresh image. *...Poland's revamped local government system.*

revanchist When people call a government **revanchist,** they mean its foreign policy is based on a desire for revenge or a wish to recover lost territories.

reveal (**revealing, revealed; revealingly**) If you **reveal** something, you make people aware of it. *He prefers not to reveal the exact terms of the deal.* ■ If you say something like a book is **revealing,** you mean it provides interesting new information, not always intentionally. ■ If you **reveal** something which has been out of sight, you uncover it so people can see it. *A grey carpet was removed to reveal the original pine floor.* ■ You can call someone's clothes **revealing** when they allow more of their body to be seen than is usual.

revel (**revelling, revelled**) (*Am:* **reveling, reveled**) If you **revel in** a situation or experience, you enjoy it very much. ■ **Revels** are noisy and often drunken celebrations.

revelation (**revelatory**) When people are made aware of important facts, you talk about the **revelation** of these facts or say there are **revelations.** *...recent revelations that Iran may be trying to develop nuclear weapons.* ■ If something you experience is unexpectedly good or reveals unexpected qualities, you can call it a **revelation** or describe it as **revelatory.** *The Allegri Quartet gave a revelatory performance.*

reveller (*Am:* **reveler**) **Revellers** are people enjoying themselves in a noisy drunken way.

revelry (**revelries**) **Revelry** is noisy and often drunken enjoyment. *...Trafalgar Square, a traditional scene of New Year festivity.*

revenge (**revenging, revenged**) If you **revenge** yourself or get your **revenge,** you harm someone because they have harmed you. You can also say something is done **in revenge.**

revenue is money received by a company, organization, or government as a result of such things as sales, subscriptions, or taxes. *...television advertising revenue.* See also **Inland Revenue.**

reverb is a shaking or echoing effect added to a sound by an electronic device.

reverberate (**reverberating, reverberated; reverberation**) When a loud sound **reverberates** in a place, it echoes there. ■ You can say events or ideas **reverberate** when they have a powerful and long-lasting effect. You call these effects **reverberations.** *...the reverberations of last month's mass deportation are far from over.*

revere (**revering, revered**) If you **revere** someone or something, you respect them greatly.

reverence (**reverent, reverently**) If people show great respect for someone or something, you can talk about their **reverence** for the person or thing, or describe their behaviour as **reverent.**

Reverend is a title used before the name of an officially appointed religious leader. *...the Reverend Lou Sheldon.*

reverent See **reverence.**

reverential (**reverentially**) You call people's behaviour **reverential** when they show great respect, admiration, and awe for someone or something.

reverie A **reverie** is a pleasant daydream.

reverse (**reversing, reversed; reversal**) When something like a decision, policy, or trend is **reversed,** it is changed to its opposite. You call this its **reversal.** ...*last September's reversal of economic policy.* ■ If the positions or roles of two things are **reversed,** they are changed so each has the position or role the other had. ■ If things are arranged in **reverse order,** the last goes first, the next-to-last second, and so on. ■ **The reverse** is used to say something is the opposite to what has just been described. *The changes in international finance have not made the crisis any less likely. In some ways, quite the reverse.* ■ When a vehicle **reverses** or is **reversed,** it is driven backwards. If it is **in reverse,** it is in the gear used to drive it backwards. This gear is called the **reverse** gear. ■ You can call the other side, or the less important side, of a flat object the **reverse** or **reverse** side. ■ If you **reverse the charges** when you make a phone call, the person you are phoning pays for the call.

reversible If a process is **reversible,** its effects can be reversed so the original situation is restored. ■ **Reversible** clothing can be worn inside out. ...*a reversible waistcoat.*

revert (**reversion**) If someone or something **reverts** to their previous behaviour or form, they change back to it. ■ In law, if land, property, rights, or money **reverts** to someone, it becomes theirs again after someone else has had it for a time.

review When people **review** a situation or system or carry out a **review** of it, they study it carefully, to decide whether it should be changed or improved. ■ A **review** is a report, for example in a newspaper or on TV, in which someone gives their opinion of something like a new book or film. When someone gives a report like this on something, you say they **review** it. A person who does this regularly is called a **reviewer.**

reviewable If something is **reviewable,** it will be reconsidered, usually after a certain period, and changed if necessary. ...*a rent of £15 per sq ft reviewable after five years.*

reviewer See **review.**

revile (**reviling, reviled**) If someone or something is **reviled,** people hate them intensely or show hatred of them.

revise (**revising, revised; revision**) If you **revise** something, you alter it to improve it or make it more suitable or accurate. A **revision** is an alteration like this. ■ When you **revise** or do **revision** for an exam, you prepare for it by going over what you have already studied, to improve your understanding and refresh your memory.

revisionism (**revisionist**) **Revisionism** is the challenging of traditionally accepted political or historical beliefs. People who challenge beliefs in this way are called **revisionists;** you say they have **revisionist** ideas.

revitalize (*or* **revitalise**) (**revitalizing, revitalized; revitalization**) If someone or something is **revital-**

ized, they are made active, successful, and healthy again.

revival See **revive.**

revivalism (**revivalist**) Religious **revivalism** is activity aimed at producing conversion to a religion on a large scale, especially at mass meetings. A **revivalist** is someone involved in this kind of activity.

revive (**reviving, revived; revival**) If something is **revived,** it becomes active, popular, or successful again. When this happens, you talk about its **revival.** ■ When something like a play is **revived,** a new production of it is staged. This is called a **revival.** ■ If someone is **revived,** they are brought back to consciousness after they have fainted or stopped breathing.

revivify (**revivifies, revivifying, revivified**) If something is **revivified,** it becomes active and successful again.

revoke (**revoking, revoked; revocation**) If something like a declaration, law, or licence is **revoked,** it is officially cancelled. When this happens, you talk about its **revocation.**

revolt When people **revolt,** they rise up against the rulers of their country and try to overthrow them by force. When this happens, you can say there is a **revolt.** ■ You can call any rejection of authority a **revolt.** *The Prime Minister is facing a revolt by some of his mps.* ■ If you are **revolted** by something or find it **revolting,** you find it horrible and disgusting.

revolution If there is a **revolution** in a country, a large group of its people rises up and changes the country's political system by force. ■ You can call any great change a **revolution,** especially a change for the better. ...*a new device that's caused a revolution in infra-red astronomy.*

revolutionary (**revolutionaries**) **Revolutionary** organizations are involved in trying to bring about a political revolution. People belonging to these organizations are called **revolutionaries.** ■ If something like an idea or a development causes great changes, especially changes for the better, you can describe it as **revolutionary.**

revolutionize (*or* **revolutionise**) (**revolutionizing, revolutionized**) If something is **revolutionized,** it is dramatically changed, usually for the better, as a result of a new discovery or invention.

revolve (**revolving, revolved**) When something **revolves,** it turns round and round. ...*a revolving stage.* ■ If one object **revolves around** another, it moves in a circle around it. ■ If you say a book or conversation **revolves around** a particular thing, you mean that thing is its main focus. *The debate revolves around specific accounting techniques.*

revolver A **revolver** is a type of hand gun.

revolving door A **revolving door** consists of four glass doors which turn together around a vertical post.

revue A **revue** is a theatrical show with songs, dances, and jokes about recent events.

revulsion is a feeling of disgust or strong disapproval.

reward If someone **rewards** you or gives you a **reward,** they give you something in recognition of your hard work or good behaviour. ■ A **reward** is a sum of money offered to anyone who can give information about lost or stolen property or about someone wanted by the police. ■ If something is **rewarding,** it brings satisfaction or other benefits.

rewind (**rewinding, rewound**) When you **rewind** a tape, you make it go backwards so it can be replayed.

rewire (**rewiring, rewired**) If something like a building or an electrical appliance is **rewired,** a new system of electrical wiring is put into it.

reword If something like a speech or part of a law is **reworded,** it is written again in a different way, usually to avoid some problem arising from the way it was originally written.

rework If you **rework** something like an idea or a piece of writing, you reorganize it and make changes to improve it or bring it up to date. The new version is called a **reworking.**

rewound See **rewind.**

rewrite (**rewriting, rewrote, have rewritten**) If someone **rewrites** something, they write it again to try to improve it. *The Americans want us to rewrite the Common Agriculture Policy.* ■ In the film industry, a **rewrite** (*pron:* **ree**-rite) involves writing parts of a script again to try to improve it. ■ If you accuse someone of **rewriting** history, you mean they have selected and presented historical events to suit their own purposes rather than to reflect the truth.

rhapsodize (*or* **rhapsodise**) (**rhapsodizing, rhapsodized; rhapsodic**) If you **rhapsodize** about something, you express great delight or enthusiasm about it. ...*a rhapsodic love poem.*

rhapsody (**rhapsodies**) A **rhapsody** is a piece of music which has an irregular form and is full of feeling. ...*George Gershwin's Rhapsody In Blue.*

rhea (*pron:* **ree**-a) The **rhea** is a flightless South American bird which looks like a small ostrich.

rhesus The **rhesus** or **rhesus monkey** is a short-tailed monkey from Southern Asia, often used in medical research. ■ The **rhesus factor** is an antigen often present in blood. Blood containing this factor is called **rhesus positive** and blood without it is called **rhesus negative.**

rhetoric (*pron:* **ret**-o-rik) is fine-sounding speech or writing which is meant to convince and impress people. *Some suggest the party's attachment to socialism is no more than empty rhetoric.*

rhetorical (*pron:* rit-**tor**-ik-kal) (**rhetorically**) **Rhetorical** language is intended to seem grand and impressive. ■ A **rhetorical question** is used for effect and does not require an answer. You say a question like this is asked **rhetorically.**

rheumatic diseases are caused by rheumatism.

rheumatic fever is a serious disease which causes fever, a sore throat, and swelling and pain in the joints.

rheumatism (*pron:* **room**-at-izm) is an illness which makes the joints or muscles stiff and painful.

rheumatoid arthritis is a long-lasting disease which causes the joints, for example the wrists or knees, to swell up and become painful.

rheumatology (**rheumatologist**) **Rheumatology** is the branch of medicine concerned with diseases of the joints and muscles. A specialist in rheumatology is called a **rheumatologist.**

rheumy If someone has **rheumy** eyes, their eyes are moist and watery, usually because they are very ill or old.

rhinestone – **Rhinestones** are shiny glass jewels made to look like diamonds.

rhinitis If you suffer from **rhinitis** or **allergic rhinitis,** you have a constantly sore and runny nose.

rhino (**rhinos**) A **rhino** is the same as a rhinoceros.

rhinoceros (**rhinoceroses**) The **rhinoceros** is a large plant-eating African or Asian animal with thick grey skin and either one or two horns on its nose.

rhizome (*pron:* **rye**-zome) A **rhizome** is a thick underground stem, whose buds develop into new plants. Mint and Irises develop from rhizomes.

rhodium (*pron:* **rode**-ee-um) is a rare hard silvery-white metal similar to platinum. It does not corrode easily, and is used in alloys.

rhododendron The **rhododendron** is an evergreen bush with bell-shaped flowers.

rhombus (*plural:* **rhombuses** *or* **rhombi**) A **rhombus** is a shape with four equal sides and no right angles, for example a diamond shape.

rhubarb is a plant with long red stems which can be cooked with sugar to make jam and puddings.

rhyme (**rhyming, rhymed**) If one word **rhymes** with another, they sound very similar, except that they begin with a different sound. *June rhymes with moon.* ■ **Rhyme** is the use of rhyming words as a technique in poetry. ■ If you say something was done **without rhyme or reason,** you mean there seems to be no sensible reason why it was done.

rhyming slang is a form of language in which you do not use the normal word for something, but say a word or phrase which rhymes with it instead. For example, in rhyming slang, 'apples and pears' means 'stairs'.

rhythm is a regular pattern of sounds or movements. ...*a disturbance of the heart's rhythm.* ■ A **rhythm** is a regular pattern of changes, for example changes in the seasons.

rhythm and blues is a style of popular music developed in the 1940s from blues music, but using electrically amplified instruments.

rhythmic (**rhythmical, rhythmically**) A **rhythmic** movement or sound is repeated at regular intervals, forming a regular pattern or beat.

rhythm method The **rhythm method** is a form of contraception in which a couple try to prevent pregnancy by having sex only at times during the woman's monthly cycle when she is unlikely to become pregnant.

rhythm section The **rhythm section** of a band is the group of musicians whose main job is to supply the rhythm. It usually consists of keyboards, bass, and drums.

rib (**ribbing, ribbed**) The **ribs** are the 24 bones which curve round from the spine to form the **rib cage** in the human chest. The rib cage protects the lungs and other organs. ■ A **rib** of beef, pork, or veal is a piece of meat which has been cut to include one or more ribs. ■ You can call a series of long thin supports **ribs.** ...*the ribs of an umbrella.*

■ A **ribbed** surface, material, or garment has a raised pattern of parallel lines on it. ...*cotton-ribbed sweaters.* ■ If you **rib** someone, you tease them in a friendly way.

ribald (*pron:* **rib**-ald) You call songs, jokes, and remarks **ribald** when they mention sex in a humorous, rather rude way. ...*the Gallic tradition of ribald humour.*

ribbon A **ribbon** is a thin strip of colourful cloth used for tying things together or as a decoration. ■ A typewriter **ribbon** is a long narrow strip of cloth containing a special ink for printing letters.

riboflavin (*pron:* rye-boe-**flay**-vin) is a vitamin found mainly in milk, cheese, eggs, and liver.

rice is the edible grains of a tall grass, also called **rice,** which is grown mainly in warm countries on wet ground.

rice paper is very thin paper made from a tree grown in the Far East. Cakes can be baked on rice paper and it can also be eaten.

rice pudding is a dessert made by baking rice in milk and sugar.

rich (**richly, richness**) A **rich** person has a lot of money or valuable possessions. Rich people are sometimes called **the rich.** ■ **Rich** countries have a strong economy and produce a lot of wealth. Many of their inhabitants have a high standard of living. ■ If a place is **rich** in something, it contains a lot of it. ...*a swampland rich in wildlife.* ...*Mongolia's rich coal deposits.* ■ **Rich** food contains a lot of sweet or fatty ingredients. ■ You can call colours, smells, or sounds **rich** when they are pleasantly deep or strong. ...*his rich baritone voice.* ■ You can describe something as **rich** when it covers or contains a wide and interesting variety of different things. ...*richly varied countryside.* ...*the richness of human experience.* ■ You use **richly** to say something is lavish or extravagant ...*the richly decorated silver pot.*

riches are valuable possessions or large amounts of money. *I would like to conserve the riches of our culture.*

Richter Scale The **Richter Scale** is a scale used to measure how severe an earthquake is.

rickets is a condition people, especially children, get when their food does not contain enough Vitamin D. It makes children's bones remain soft, causing deformities.

rickety If something is **rickety,** it is not very strong and seems about to collapse, because it is old or badly made. ...*a rickety wooden table.*

rickshaw In Asia, a **rickshaw** is a small two-wheeled carriage, usually pulled by a person and used as a sort of taxi.

ricochet (*pron:* **rik**-osh-ay) (**ricocheting, ricocheted**) When a fast-moving object like a bullet **ricochets,** it hits a surface and bounces away from it.

rid (**ridding, rid** *not* '**ridded**') If you **get rid of** someone or something you do not want or **rid** yourself of them, you remove them or do something so you no longer have them. *They want to get rid of the monarchy.* ■ When you are no longer troubled by someone or something, you can say you are **rid** of them.

riddance You say **good riddance** to show you are glad someone or something has gone.

ridden See **ride.**

riddle A **riddle** is a puzzle or joke in which you ask a question which seems to be nonsense but which has a clever or amusing answer. ■ You can call something a **riddle** when people have been trying to understand or explain it but have so far failed to do so. *The book will solve the riddle of why he quit the presidential race.*

riddled You can say someone or something is **riddled** with damaging or undesirable things when they contain a lot of them. *Four people were found riddled with bullets.... The report is riddled with inaccuracies.*

ride (**riding, rode, have ridden**) If you **ride** something like a horse or a bicycle, you sit on it and control it as it moves along. ■ If you **ride** in or on a vehicle, you travel in it. ■ A **ride** is a journey on a horse or bicycle, or in a vehicle. ■ If one thing is **riding on** another, its success is dependent on the other thing. *I have £100 riding on the result.* ■ If a garment **rides up,** it moves upwards, out of its proper position. ■ If you say someone is **riding high,** you mean they are doing very well. ■ When people talk about the sort of **ride** someone gets, they mean the extent to which people criticize them and make things difficult for them. *He gets an easy ride from fans and refs.* ■ If someone **rides out** a crisis, they manage to get through it without suffering serious harm. ■ If you say someone has been **taken for a ride,** you mean they have been deceived or cheated.

rider A person riding a horse, bicycle, or motorcycle is called its **rider.**

ridge A **ridge** is a long strip of land which is higher than the land on each side of it. ■ A **ridge** is a raised line on a flat surface.

ridicule (**ridiculing, ridiculed**) If people **ridicule** someone or something, they make fun of them in an unkind way. When someone is treated like this, you can say they are made an object of **ridicule** or are held up to **ridicule.**

ridiculous (**ridiculously**) If you say something is **ridiculous,** you mean it is very silly.

rife When something is extremely common, you can say it is **rife.** *Corruption is rife... Dhaka is rife with rumours.*

riff In jazz and rock music, a **riff** is a short repeated tune or sequence of chords.

riffle (**riffling, riffled**) If you **riffle** through papers or the pages of a book, you turn them quickly and have a look at them without reading everything.

riff-raff If someone calls a group of people **riff-raff,** they are showing their disapproval of them, because they think they are not respectable or of low social standing.

rifle (**rifling, rifled**) A **rifle** is a gun with a long barrel, which can be fired accurately over a long range. ■ If you **rifle** through something, you make a quick search through it. *Thieves had rifled through his suitcase.*

rifle range A **rifle range** is a place where people practise rifle shooting.

rift A **rift** is a large crack in the ground. ■ A **rift** between people or countries is a serious quarrel.

rift valley A **rift valley** is a valley with steep sides and a flat bottom, formed when the land between two faults sinks.

rig (rigging, rigged) If someone **rigs** something like an election or a game, they dishonestly arrange it to get the result they want or to give someone an unfair advantage. ■ If you **rig up** a device or structure, you make it and fix it in place using any available materials. *He managed to rig up a makeshift radio.* ■ You can use **rig** to refer to a set of special or unusual clothes and any extras which go with them. *He was decked out in full highland rig with dirk, pistols and powder horn.* ■ The ropes which support a ship's masts and sails are called the **rigging.** ■ See also **oil rig.**

rigger A **rigger** is (a) a person skilled at using things like pulleys, lifting gear, and cranes. (b) a person who works on oil-rigs.

rigging See **rig.**

right (rightly, rightness) If you say something is **right,** you mean it is correct. ■ The **right** choice, action, or decision is the best one. ■ When people talk about **right and wrong,** they are distinguishing between morally correct and morally incorrect behaviour. *...the rightness of their cause.* ■ People or places that are fashionable or socially correct are sometimes called the **right** people or things. *Through his father he had met all the right people.* ■ If you **right** something which is wrong or has got into a bad state, you correct it or get it back to the way it should be. ■ If you turn to the **right,** you turn quarter of a circle in a clockwise direction. ■ The **right** are people who support capitalism and conservatism. ■ **Right** is used to emphasize things. *The lamp-post was right in front of a hospital.* ■ Your **rights** are the things you are morally entitled to do or have. *...a bill of rights.* ■ If someone is a successful or respected person **in their own right,** they are so because of their own efforts and talents rather than those of the people they are closely connected with.

right angle A **right angle** is an angle of 90°. If two things are **at right angles** they form an angle of 90° where they touch or cross each other.

righteous (righteously, righteousness) Righteous behaviour is morally good. *What matters in waging a war is not righteousness but victory.* ■ If someone feels **righteous** anger at something, they are angry because they think it is unfair or unjust.

rightful (rightfully) The **rightful** owner of something is the person who should have it, because it belongs to them. If someone or something returns to their **rightful** position, they take the position they are morally or legally entitled to. *South Africa was poised to take its rightful place in the international community.*

right-hand The **right-hand** side of something is the side towards the right. ■ Someone's **right-hand man** or **right-hand woman** is the person who is most useful to them in their work.

right-handed (right-hander) Right-handed people use their right hand rather than their left for things

like writing. In sport, people like these are called **right-handers.**

rightist People who have capitalist and conservative ideas and opinions are sometimes called **rightists.**

right-of-centre people or organizations have political views closer to conservatism and capitalism than to socialism.

right of way (rights of way) A **right of way** is a public path across private land. ■ When a car or other vehicle has **right of way** at a junction or roundabout, traffic approaching from other directions must stop for it.

rightward (or rightwards) When a politician or party becomes more right-wing, you can talk about a **rightward** change in their views, or say they have moved **rightwards.**

right-wing (right-winger) Right-wing people have capitalist and conservative ideas and opinions. People like these are sometimes called **right-wingers.** You can say these people are on the **right wing** of a party.

rigid (rigidly, rigidity) If something is **rigid,** it is stiff and does not bend or stretch easily. You talk about the **rigidity** of something like this. ■ If a law or system is **rigid,** it cannot be changed or departed from. *...the rigidity of the British class system.*

rigmarole You can call a complicated procedure a **rigmarole.**

rigor See **rigour.**

rigor mortis is stiffness in the joints and muscles of a body soon after death.

rigorous (rigorously) Rigorous is used to describe procedures which are carried out thoroughly.

rigour (Am: rigor) If something is done with **rigour,** it is carried out strictly and thoroughly. *...traditional scientific rigour.* ■ When something makes life difficult and unpleasant, you can talk about its **rigours.** *...birds escaping the rigours of a northern European winter.*

rile (riling, riled) If someone or something **riles** you, they make you angry.

rim (rimmed) The **rim** of something like a cup or a glass is its top edge. ■ The **rim** of a wheel is its outside edge. The outside edge of an area can also be called its **rim.** *...the ex-republics around Russia's rim.* ■ If something is **rimmed** with a substance or colour, it has that substance or colour around its border. *...black-rimmed spectacles.*

rind The **rind** of a fruit such as a lemon or orange is its thick outer skin. ■ The **rind** of cheese or bacon is the hard outer part.

ring (ringing, rang, have rung) When you **ring** someone, **ring** them **up,** or **give** them **a ring,** you phone them. When a telephone **rings,** it makes a sound which lets you know someone is phoning you. ■ When a bell **rings** or you **ring** it, it makes a metallic sound. This sound is called a **ring.** ■ If something **rings out,** it can be heard loudly and clearly. *Shots rang out.* ■ You can use **ring** to say something like a statement or an argument has a certain quality. *Much of what Mr Kryuchkov had to say had a familiar ring to it... Every phrase rang true.* ■ A **ring** is a small circle of metal such as gold you wear on your finger. ■ Some things shaped like circles are called **rings.** ...*a single electric cooking ring.* ■ If people or things are arranged in a circle, you can say they form a **ring.** You can also say something is **ringed** by people or things. *Kabul is ringed by mountains.* ■ An organized group of people involved in an illegal activity is sometimes called a **ring.** ...*a spy ring.* ■ A **ring** is an enclosed space with seats around it where, for example, a boxing match or circus performance takes place.

ring binder A **ring binder** is a hard cover with metal rings inside, used to hold loose papers.

ringer If you say one person is **a dead ringer** for another, you mean they look exactly alike.

ringleader The **ringleaders** in a disturbance or illegal activity are the people who start it or cause most of the trouble.

ringlet – **Ringlets** are long curls of hair.

ringmaster The **ringmaster** in a circus is the person who introduces the acts.

ring road A **ring road** is a road which goes all the way round the edge of a town, so traffic can avoid the centre.

ringside The **ringside** is the area immediately around the edge of a circus ring, boxing ring, or show jumping ring. ■ If you are close to something and can follow exactly what is going on, you can say you have a **ringside seat.**

ringworm is a skin disease caused by a fungus. It produces itchy red patches on a person's or animal's skin, especially on their scalp or trunk.

rink A **rink** is a large area for ice-skating or roller-skating.

rinse (**rinsing, rinsed**) When you **rinse** something or give it a **rinse,** you wash it without using soap. You also say you **rinse** something when you dip it in water or run water over it to remove soap from it. ■ If you **rinse** your mouth, you wash it with a mouthful of water or an antiseptic mouthwash. ■ A hair **rinse** is a hair dye which fades after you have washed your hair a number of times.

riot (**rioting, rioted; rioter**) When crowds of people **riot** or **run riot,** they behave violently in a public place, for example by fighting, throwing stones, or damaging buildings and vehicles. An outbreak of behaviour like this is called a **riot;** the people taking part are called **rioters.** ■ A **riot** of something means a lot of different kinds of it mingled together in a striking way. ...*a riot of colour.* ■ If something **runs riot,** it gets out of control. *My imagination ran riot.* ■ If someone **reads the riot act,** they give people a stern warning.

rioter See **riot.**

riot gear is the special clothing and equipment worn and carried by police when they are trying to control violent crowds.

riotous When people are rioting, you can describe them as **riotous.** ■ You can describe a party or someone's behaviour as **riotous** when it is noisy, lively, and rather uncontrolled.

riot shield – **Riot shields** are see-through shields used by police officers to control crowds and protect themselves from attack.

RIP is written on gravestones and expresses the hope that the person buried there may rest in peace. 'RIP' is short for the Latin expression 'requiescat in pace'.

rip (**ripping, ripped**) If you **rip** something, you tear it. A **rip** is a tear. ■ **Rip** is used to describe the violent effects of something like a wind or an explosion. *The first explosion ripped open one of the gas tanks.* ■ If you **let rip,** you do something forcefully and without restraint. ■ If someone **rips** you **off,** they cheat you, for example by charging you too much for something. An unfair deal like this is called a **rip-off.**

ripcord The cord used to open a parachute is called the **ripcord.**

ripe (**ripeness**) **Ripe** fruit or grain is fully grown and ready to be harvested or eaten. *Test the figs for ripeness.* ■ If someone lives to be very old, you can say they reach a **ripe old age.** ■ If you say something is **ripe** for a change of some kind, you mean it is ready for it. ...*offices ripe for conversion.* ■ If you say **the time is ripe** for something, you mean a suitable time has arrived for doing it.

ripen (**ripening, ripened**) When fruit or grain **ripens,** it becomes ripe.

riposte (*pron:* rip-**posst**) (**riposting, riposted**) A **riposte** is a quick reply, especially a clever, witty, or angry one. When someone **ripostes,** they give a reply like this.

ripple (**rippling, rippled**) **Ripples** are little waves on the surface of water caused by something like the wind. When water **ripples,** waves like these appear on its surface. ■ When something such as an emotion passes through a group of people, you can say it **ripples** through them, or talk about a **ripple** of emotion. *When it was Jackson's turn, you could sense a ripple of anticipation.* ■ If a man has **rippling** muscles, he has extremely well developed muscles.

rip-roaring A **rip-roaring** film or story is full of action and excitement.

rise (**rising, rose, have risen**) If something **rises,** it moves upwards. ■ When the sun or moon **rises,** it appears above the horizon. ■ When you **rise,** (a) you stand up. (b) you get out of bed. *He rose at 6.30.* ■ If land **rises,** it slopes upwards. ■ If something **rises,** it increases. ...*a rise in interest rates.* ■ If sound **rises,** it becomes louder or higher. ■ When people **rise** or **rise up,** they start fighting against their rulers. A rebellion like this is called a **rising.** ■ If you **rise above** something, you do not let it affect you. *Serena has risen above her troubles.* ■ If one thing **gives rise to** another, it causes it.

riser Early **risers** are people who get up early. ■ The flat vertical part of a step or stair is called a **riser.**

risible (*pron:* riz-**zib**-bl) (**risibly**) If you think something is ridiculous and does not deserve to be taken seriously, you can describe it as **risible.**

rising damp If a building has **rising damp,** moisture which has entered the brickwork from the ground has moved upwards above floor level, causing damage to the walls.

risk If there is a **risk** of something undesirable, there is a possibility it will happen. *If economic re-*

form doesn't succeed, there is a risk of a return to dictatorship. ■ If you **risk** something undesirable or **run the risk** of it, you do something which might result in it. *...a brave reporter who had risked death to bring the story to the world.* ■ If something is a good **risk,** the chances of it going wrong are very small. ■ If you **risk** something or **put it at risk,** you do something which might result in it being damaged or lost. *He condemned the Home Office for putting the lives of his officers at risk.* ■ If you tell someone they do something **at their own risk,** you mean it will be their own responsibility if they are harmed or suffer a loss.

risky (**riskier, riskiest; riskily, riskiness**) If something you do is **risky,** there is a chance it will fail or have undesirable consequences.

risotto is an Italian dish of rice cooked in stock, sometimes with vegetables, meat, or seafood.

risqué (*pron:* risk-ay) A **risqué** joke or performance is one which might offend some people because of its sexual content.

rissole – **Rissoles** are pieces of chopped meat or vegetables pressed into a flat round shape and fried.

rite A **rite** is a traditional ceremony. *...initiation rites.* ■ A **rite of passage** is an event which seems to represent a change from one stage of your life to another, especially a change from childhood to adulthood. ■ See also **last rites.**

ritual (**ritually; ritualistic, ritualized** *or* **ritualised**) A **ritual** is a religious service or some other kind of ceremony which involves a series of actions performed in a fixed order. **Ritual** and **ritualistic** are used to describe activities performed as part of a ritual. *...ritual sacrifices.* ■ If something is always done in the same way, you can call it a **ritual.** *The Japanese go in for highly ritualised outings.*

ritzy (**ritzier, ritziest**) **Ritzy** is used to describe things which are fashionable, glamorous, and expensive. *...Washington's ritzier hotels.*

rival (**rivalling, rivalled; rivalry, rivalries**) (*Am:* rivaling, rivaled**) You call people **rivals** when they are competing against each other, or have similar aims but are hostile to each other. *...clashes between rival groups of students. ...a city torn by deep ethnic rivalries.* ■ If you say something **rivals** something else, you mean it is of a similar standard. ■ If you say something has no **rival,** you mean nothing else is as good.

riven If an organization is **riven** by conflict, its members are divided into groups opposed to each other. *...a nation riven by inter-clan hatreds.*

river A **river** is a large amount of fresh water flowing between banks towards the sea. ■ A long line of moving things or people can be called a **river.**

riverbank The edge of a river is sometimes called the **riverbank.**

riverboat A **riverboat** is a large boat which carries passengers along a river.

riverside The area of land next to a river is called the **riverside.**

rivet (*pron:* riv-vit) (**riveting, riveted; rivetingly**) **Rivets** are short metal pins with flat heads, used to fasten flat pieces of metal together. If pieces of metal are **riveted,** they are joined together using

rivets. ■ If you are **riveted** by something, you are fascinated by it and it holds your attention completely. *...a riveting book.*

rivulet A **rivulet** is a small stream.

RN after a person's name stands for 'Royal Navy'. *...Captain Neil Blair, RN.*

roach The **roach** (*usual plural:* **roach**) is a European freshwater fish. ■ In the US, a **roach** (*plural:* **roaches**) is a cockroach.

road A **road** is a long strip of hard material built across land for vehicles to travel along. ■ You can call a means of achieving something a **road** to it. *His priority is to put France's economy on the road to recovery.*

road block When the police or army set up a **road block,** they stop all traffic at a certain place on a road, and search the vehicles or question their occupants.

road hog If you think someone's driving is selfish and reckless, you can call them a **road hog.**

roadholding A car's **roadholding** is its ability to grip the road and not slide or skid when turning corners.

roadie – **Roadies** are people hired by rock musicians to transport, maintain, and erect equipment for their stage shows.

road rage is aggressive behaviour by a driver in response to the actions of another driver.

roadshow A **roadshow** is a travelling show organized by something like a radio station.

roadside The area next to a road is called the **roadside.** *...a roadside restaurant.*

roadster A **roadster** is a two-seater sports car with no roof.

road test A **road test** is a test of a vehicle on public roads to see if it is fit to be driven or to review its performance..

roadway The **roadway** is the part of a road used by traffic.

roadworks are repairs or improvements being carried out to a road.

roam (**roaming, roamed**) If you **roam** an area, you wander around it, not heading for anywhere in particular.

roar (**roaring, roared**) When a lion or other large animal **roars** or lets out a **roar,** it makes a loud threatening noise in its throat. ■ If a crowd **roars,** all the people shout together, producing a loud noise. ■ If someone **roars** with laughter, they laugh in a very noisy way. ■ If something **roars,** it makes a long loud noise. *...a roar of engines.* ■ If something is a **roaring** success, it is very successful indeed.

roast When you **roast** meat or other food, you cook it in an oven in a small amount of oil or fat. **Roast** is used to describe meat and vegetables cooked this way. *...roast potatoes.* ■ A **roast** is a large roasted piece of meat. ■ If someone is given a **roasting,** they are severely told off.

rob (**robbing, robbed; robbery, robberies; robber**) If you are **robbed,** money or valuables are stolen from you. *He was convicted of robbing a bank.* When this happens, you say there has been a **robbery.** A person who steals things like this is called a **rob-**

ber. ■ If someone is **robbed** of something they deserve or need, it is taken away from them. *Tenants could be robbed of their compensation rights.*

robber baron A person who makes a lot of money in business by acting in a dishonest way is sometimes called a **robber baron.**

robe A **robe** is a long loose piece of clothing which covers your whole body. ■ A **robe** is a bathrobe.

robin The **robin** is a small brown bird, often seen in gardens. Adult robins have orangey-red faces and breasts.

robot (**robotic, robotics**) A **robot** is a machine which is programmed to move and perform certain tasks automatically. **Robotic** is used to describe machines like these and the tasks they perform. *...robotic roving vehicles.* **Robotics** is the science of designing and building robots. ■ You call a person **robotic** when they move in a jerky way like a robot, or think in a logical unemotional way.

robust (**robustly**) A **robust** person is strong and healthy. ■ You say something like a machine or tool is **robust** when it is strong and durable. ■ If your speech or manner is **robust,** you express yourself in a forceful way. ■ **Robust** humour is rather coarse.

rock is the hard substance the Earth is made of. ■ A **rock** is a large piece of rock. ■ In the US, stones are also called **rocks.** ■ If something **rocks,** it moves slowly and regularly backwards and forwards or from side to side. ■ If people are **rocked** by an event or some information, they are shocked and upset by it. ■ **Rock** is loud music with a strong beat. ■ **Rock** is a sweet made in long hard sticks. ■ If you have a drink like whisky **on the rocks,** you have it with ice cubes in it. ■ If something like a marriage is **on the rocks,** it is in serious trouble and unlikely to last. ■ When things are as bad or as low as they are likely to get, you can say they are at **rock bottom.**

rockabilly is a type of pop music which combines aspects of rock and roll and hillbilly country music.

rock and roll (or **rock'n'roll**) is a type of pop music which developed in the late 1950s. It has a strong beat and simple repeated phrases.

rock cake A **rock cake** is a small fruit cake with a rough surface.

rocker People who perform or enjoy rock music are sometimes called **rockers.** ■ In the US, rocking chairs are called **rockers.**

rockery (**rockeries**) A **rockery** is a raised part of a garden, built of small rocks and soil, in which small plants are grown.

rocket (**rocketing, rocketed**) A **rocket** is (a) a gas-powered missile. (b) a firework which shoots high into the air. ■ A space **rocket** is a tube-shaped vehicle which is launched into space. ■ When something increases suddenly and rapidly, you can say it **rockets.** *Sales have rocketed.*

rocketry is the science of designing and launching rockets.

rockfall A **rockfall** is a mass of falling or fallen rocks.

rocking chair A **rocking chair** is a chair built on two curved pieces of wood so you can rock backwards and forwards when you sit in it.

rocking horse A **rocking horse** is a toy horse built on two curved pieces of wood so a child can sit on it and rock backwards and forwards.

rock pool A **rock pool** is a small pool left between rocks on the seashore when the tide goes out.

rock salt is layers of hard salt formed in the ground in places where the sea or some other salt water evaporated a long time ago.

rocky (**rockier, rockiest**) A **rocky** place is covered with rocks.

rococo (*pron:* rok-**koe**-koe) is a style of art and design which was popular in Europe in the eighteenth century. Its main features were complicated curly decoration and delicate colours.

rod A **rod** is a long thin metal or wooden bar.

rode See **ride.**

rodent – **Rodents** are small mammals such as rats, mice, and squirrels, which have sharp front teeth for gnawing.

rodeo (**rodeos**) A **rodeo** is a show in which cowboys demonstrate their skills in events such as riding wild horses and catching calves with ropes.

roe is fish eggs or sperm eaten as food.

roe deer The **roe deer** is a small deer with a brown coat and a stumpy tail. The male has short antlers.

rogue When someone behaves in a dishonest, immoral, or criminal way, people sometimes call them a **rogue.** A group of people like this can be called a **rogues' gallery.** ■ People call someone a **rogue** when they cannot help liking them, although they disapprove of their behaviour. ■ **Rogue** is used to describe people and things that behave differently from others of their kind, especially when this results in harm or damage. *...a rogue elephant.*

roguish If someone behaves in a mischievous but rather likeable way, you can describe their behaviour as **roguish.**

role Your **role** is your position and function in a given situation. *Mr Rabin was last in Egypt in 1989 in his role as defence minister.* Similarly, you can talk about the **role** of an organization, institution, or means of communication. *...the role of television in modern society.* ■ A **role** in a film, play, or opera is one of the characters in it. ■ **Role playing** is acting out the behaviour of people in a particular situation. ■ You say someone is a **role model** when their behaviour is admired by a group of people, especially young people, who try to behave in the same way.

roll If a round object **rolls,** it moves along, turning over and over. ■ You say a vehicle **rolls** somewhere when it moves at a slow steady pace. *Tanks rolled into the city.* ■ If drops of liquid **roll** down a surface, they run down it. *Tears rolled down her face.* ■ If you **roll** something into a tube shape or a ball, you form it into this shape by wrapping it several times around itself or turning it over again and again. ■ A **roll** of paper, plastic, cloth, or wire is a long piece wrapped many times around itself or around a tube. ■ If you **roll** a cigarette, you make one using a cigarette paper and some tobacco. ■ When you **roll** pastry, you spread it out into a flat shape using a rolling pin. ■ If you **roll up** your sleeves or trouser legs, you fold the ends back several times, exposing your forearms or calves. People also say they are **rolling up their sleeves** when they are preparing themselves for a demanding task. ■ If a machine is **rolling,** it is operating. ■ If you **roll** your eyes, you turn them upwards briefly, as a way of showing annoyance or disapproval. ■ If someone is repeatedly successful and this seems likely to continue, you can say they are **on a roll.** ■ If something like money is **rolling in,** it is being received in large amounts. ■ When people **roll up** somewhere, they arrive in large numbers, to see something interesting. ■ **Rolling** hills are gently sloping ones which extend a long way into the distance. ■ A **roll** is a small rounded individually baked piece of bread. ■ A **roll** is an official list of people's names.

roll-call If someone takes a **roll-call,** they check which members of a group are present by reading their names out.

roller A **roller** is a revolving cylinder in a machine or device. ■ **Rollers** are tubes which you can wind your hair around to make it curly.

Rollerblade – Rollerblades are similar to roller-skates except that the wheels are arranged in a single line from front to back. 'Rollerblade' is a trademark.

roller-coaster (*or* **rollercoaster**) A **roller-coaster** is a fairground ride which involves a train-like vehicle travelling up and down steep slopes, and sometimes doing loops, at high speed. ■ If you call an experience a **roller-coaster,** you mean it involves many dramatic changes in a short space of time. ...*a week of roller-coaster emotions.*

roller-skate – Roller-skates are shoes with four small wheels on the bottom, two at the front and two at the back. If you **roller-skate,** you move over a flat surface on roller-skates.

rollicking books and films are fast-moving, entertaining, and enjoyable.

rolling mill A **rolling mill** is a machine or factory which uses rollers to flatten metal into sheets or bars.

rolling news A **rolling news** network, service, or programme broadcasts news and news commentaries continuously.

rolling pin A **rolling pin** is a cylinder you roll over pastry to flatten it out.

rolling stock is railway engines, carriages, and wagons.

roll of honour A **roll of honour** is a list of the names of people who have achieved great success in some field, for example in a sport.

roll-on/roll-off A **roll-on/roll-off** ship is designed so cars and lorries can drive on at one end before the ship sails, then drive off at the other end after the voyage.

roll up A **roll up** is a cigarette you make yourself by wrapping a cigarette paper around a small amount of tobacco.

roly-poly people are fat and round.

ROM is the permanent part of a computer's memory in which the information stored there can be read but not changed. ROM is an abbreviation for 'read-only memory'.

Roman is used to describe things related to or connected with ancient Rome and its empire. ...*Roman ruins.* The **Romans** were citizens of ancient Rome. ■ **Roman** is used to describe things to do with present-day Rome. ...*a Roman hotel room.* A **Roman** is someone who lives in or comes from Rome.

Roman alphabet The **Roman alphabet** is the alphabet used for writing in most European languages, including English.

Roman Catholic means the same as 'Catholic'. A **Roman Catholic** is a Catholic.

Roman Catholicism is the same as Catholicism.

romance A **romance** is a love affair. ■ A novel about a love affair is called a **romance.** ■ You can talk about the **romance** of something when it is exciting and mysterious. ...*the romance of the desert.* ■ The **Romance** languages are languages like French, Spanish, and Italian, which developed from Latin.

Romanesque architecture is in the style which was common in western Europe from the 9th to the 12th centuries. It is characterized by rounded arches and thick pillars.

Roman numerals are the letters used by the ancient Romans to represent numbers. For example V means 5, VI means 6, X means 10, and IX means 9.

romantic (**romantically, romanticism**) If someone is **romantic,** they say and do things which make their partner feel special and loved. ■ **Romantic** means connected with sexual love. ...*romantically involved.* ■ A **romantic** play, film, or story deals with a love affair. ■ **Romantic** is used to describe things which are beautiful or exciting in a way which strongly affects your feelings. ...*a wild romantic landscape.* ■ You call someone a **romantic** or say they are **romantic** when you think they are idealistic or impractical. You can talk about their **romanticism.** ...*a romantic view of the past.* ■ The **Romantic** movement was an artistic movement in the 18th and 19th centuries which was concerned with the expression of the individual's feelings. The people involved in this movement are often called the **Romantics.** The movement is sometimes called **Romanticism.**

romanticize (*or* **romanticise**) (**romanticizing, romanticized**) If you **romanticize** something, you think or talk about it in an unrealistic way which makes it seem better than it really is.

Romany (**Romanies**) A **Romany** is a gypsy. ■ **Romany** is a language spoken by gypsies.

romp When children or animals **romp,** they play noisily and happily. ■ If people **romp** or have a **romp,** they have sex in a casual, care-free way, without any emotional commitment. ■ You can call something like a book, film, or play a **romp** when it is funny, light-hearted, and full of action. ■ You use **romp** in expressions like **romp** home or **romp** to victory, to say someone wins a race or competition easily. *Her horse romped home at 20-1.*

romper – Rompers are a one-piece garment for babies combining a top and trousers. They can also be called a **romper suit.**

rondo (**rondos**) A **rondo** is a piece of classical music in which the main tune is repeated several times.

roof (**roofs, roofed**) The **roof** of a building or vehicle is the covering on top of it. ■ **Roofed** is used to say a building has a roof, or to describe its roof. *...a roofed stadium. ...tin-roofed houses.* ■ The **roof** of your mouth or of a cave is its upper surface.

roofer A **roofer** is a person whose job is repairing roofs or putting new roofs on buildings.

roofing is (a) material used for making or covering roofs. (b) the work of repairing or constructing roofs.

roof rack A **roof rack** is a frame fixed on top of a car for carrying things.

rooftop The **rooftop** of a building is the outside part of its roof. ■ **Rooftop** is used to describe things on the roof of a building. *...a rooftop demonstration.* ■ If you **shout** something **from the rooftops,** you say it or announce it in a very public way.

rook The **rook** is a large black bird, a member of the crow family. ■ In chess, a **rook** is the same as a castle.

rookery (**rookeries**) A **rookery** is a place in a group of trees where many rooks have their nests.

rookie In the US, a **rookie** is an inexperienced new recruit, especially in the army or police force.

room (**-roomed**) A **room** is a separate section in a building, divided from other rooms by walls. ■ **-roomed** is used to say how many rooms a building has. ■ If there is **room** for something, there is enough space for it. *With room for 15 guests, here is a house to laze in.* ■ If there is **room** for a particular kind of activity or development, it is possible for it to be done or achieved. *There is still plenty of room for improvement.*

roomful When there are a lot of people or things in a room, you can say there is a **roomful** of them.

room-mate Your **room-mate** is someone you share a rented room with, for example when you are a student.

room service is a service in a hotel in which meals or drinks are brought to guests in their rooms.

roomy (**roomier, roomiest**) If a place is **roomy,** it is large and spacious.

roost When birds **roost** somewhere, they settle there for the night. The place is called their **roost.** ■ If bad or wrong things which someone has done in the past **have come home to roost,** or if their **chickens have come home to roost,** they are now suffering the unpleasant effects of these actions. *The financial scandals of the Eighties came home to roost on the Conservative benches.* ■ If you say someone **rules the roost,** you mean they are the most powerful person in a group.

rooster A **rooster** is the same as a cockerel.

root (**rooting, rooted**) The **roots** of a plant are the parts which grow underground. ■ If a plant **roots,** roots form on it and it starts to grow. ■ Plants which have large edible roots, such as carrots and potatoes, are called **root vegetables** or **root crops.** ■ If things **take root,** they start to grow or develop. ■ The **root** of a hair or tooth is the part beneath the skin. ■ Your **roots** are the place or culture you grew up in. ■ The **root** of something is its original cause or basis. ■ If you **root** someone or something **out,** you find them and force them out. ■ If you **root for** someone, you support and encourage them in a difficult or competitive situation.

root crop See **root.**

rootless (**rootlessness**) You say people are **rootless** when they have no permanent home or job, or are not settled in any community.

rope (**roping, roped**) A **rope** is a thick strong length of cord. If you **rope** one thing to another, you tie the two things together with a rope. ■ If an area is **roped off,** ropes are tied between posts around it, to stop people entering without permission. ■ In boxing, **the ropes** are the fence of ropes surrounding the ring. ■ If you are **learning the ropes,** you are learning how to do something. ■ If you are **roped in** to do something, you are persuaded to help with it.

rope ladder A **rope ladder** is a ladder made of two long ropes connected by short pieces of rope, wood, or metal.

ropey (**ropier, ropiest**) If you say something is **ropey,** you mean it is of poor quality.

ro-ro is a short way of referring to roll-on roll-off vehicle ferries.

rosary (**rosaries**) A **rosary** is a string of beads which Catholics use for counting prayers.

rose The **rose** is a large garden flower with many petals and often a pleasant smell. Roses grow on bushes with thorny stems. ■ **Rose** is a reddish-pink colour. ■ If you say someone is looking at a situation through **rose-tinted** or **rose-coloured spectacles,** you mean they believe it is better than it really is. ■ A **rose** is a device with very small holes in it which fits onto the end of a hose or the spout of a watering can, so the water comes out in a fine spray. ■ See also **rise.**

rosé (*pron:* roe-zay) wine is pale pink in colour.

rosemary is a herb with thin spiky greyish-green leaves.

rosette A **rosette** is a large circular badge made from coloured ribbons, worn to show support for a political party or sports team, or given as a prize in a competition.

rose window A **rose window** is a large round stained-glass window.

rosewood is a hard dark-coloured wood used for making furniture. Rosewood comes from various tropical trees.

roster A **roster** is a list of people who take it in turn to do a particular job.

rostrum A **rostrum** is a raised platform on which someone stands to speak to an audience or to conduct an orchestra.

rosy (**rosier, rosiest**) If something is **rosy,** it is reddish-pink. ■ If you say the situation looks **rosy,** you mean things look good for the future.

rot (**rotting, rotted**) When food, wood, or some other substance **rots,** it decays and falls apart. ■ When wood begins to rot, you say there is **rot** in it. ■ The **rot** is used to talk about a gradual worsening of something. *In many schools, the rot is beginning to set in. Standards are falling all the time.* ■ If someone is left to spend their life in an undesirable situation, for example in prison, you can say they are left to **rot.**

rota A **rota** is a list giving details of the order in which people take turns to do something.

rotarian A **rotarian** is a member of a Rotary Club.

rotary is used to describe things which turn with a circular movement or have parts which turn like this. *...the old rotary dial telephones. ...a turbo-charged rotary engine.*

Rotary Club A **Rotary Club** is a club for business and professional men in a town. Its members work together to raise money for the local community.

rotate (**rotating, rotated; rotation**) When something **rotates,** it turns with a circular movement. A movement like this is called a **rotation.** *...a rotating chair.* ■ When you **rotate** a group of things, you use each one of them in turn, beginning with the first again when you reach the end. *Once a month we met, and in rotation each one led the group.*

rote If you learn something **by rote,** you learn it by memorizing it, without trying to understand it. This way of learning things is called **rote-learning.**

rotor The **rotor** or **rotor blades** of a helicopter are the long strips of metal which rotate and lift it off the ground.

rotten If a substance like food or wood is **rotten,** it has decayed and is no longer usable. ■ If you say something is **rotten,** you mean it is bad or of poor quality. *The aboriginal people have had a rotten deal.*

rotter In the past, a person who behaved in an unkind or selfish way was sometimes called a **rotter.**

Rottweiler (*pron:* rot-vile-er) **Rottweilers** are large strong dogs with short black fur and tan face markings. They can be aggressive and are often used as guard dogs.

rotund (*pron:* roe-**tund**) A **rotund** person is round and fat.

rotunda A **rotunda** is a round building or room, especially one with a dome.

rouble (*pron:* roo-bl) The **rouble** is the unit of currency in Russia and some other republics of the former Soviet Union.

rouge (*pron:* roozh; *the 'z' sounds like 's' in 'pleasure'*) is a red cosmetic which women and actors sometimes put on their cheeks to give them more colour.

rough (**roughly, roughness**) If a surface is **rough,** it is not smooth or even. ■ On a golf course, the **rough** is the uneven ground with longer grass around the edges of the fairway. ■ **Rough** and **roughly** are used to say something is approximate. *They all follow roughly the same training programmes.* ■ **Rough** behaviour involves using too much force and not enough care or gentleness. *He was roughly handled.* ■ If someone is **roughed up,** they are beaten. ■ A **rough** area of a town or city is unpleasant and dangerous because there is a lot of violence or crime there. ■ When people sleep **rough,** they sleep out of doors, usually because they have no home. ■ If you have to **rough it,** you have to live without the possessions and comforts you are used to. ■ If you talk about the **rough and tumble** of something, you mean it is exciting because it in-

volves people competing hard against each other. *He is enjoying his return to political rough and tumble.*

roughage If food contains **roughage,** it contains fibre which helps your bowels work properly.

roughen (**roughening, roughened**) If something is **roughened,** it is made rough.

rough-hewn wood or stone has been cut into a shape but has not yet been smoothed or finished off.

roughneck Men who work on oil rigs or oil wells are sometimes called **roughnecks,** especially in the US. ■ People can be called **roughnecks** when they are not gentle or polite. *He is regarded as something of a political roughneck.*

roughshod If you say someone **rides roughshod over** another person, you mean they use their power and authority to selfishly get what they want.

roulette is a gambling game in which a ball is dropped onto a revolving wheel with numbered holes in it. The players bet on which hole the ball will be in when the wheel stops spinning.

round (**roundness**) If people or things are positioned **round** or **around** something, they surround it. *Four men sat round a table.* ■ If you **round** or go **round** an obstacle, you move in a curve to the other side. ■ If you go **round** to someone's house, you visit them. ■ If you turn **round,** you turn so you are facing the opposite direction. ■ If something is spinning or moving in circles, you say it is going **round.** ■ If something is passed **round,** it is passed from person to person in a group. ■ **All round** is used to say something applies to all parts of a situation or all the members of a group. *It ought to make life much easier all round.* ■ If someone changes their mind and begins to agree with you, you can say they have **come round.** ■ A **round** is a set of events such as a series of games which form one stage of a larger series. *After round three, two Americans share the lead. ...the latest round of negotiations.* ■ A **round trip** is a journey to a place and back again. ■ If you buy a **round** of drinks, you buy a drink for each member of the group you are with. ■ A **round** of ammunition is a bullet. ■ When people clap, you say there is a **round** of applause. ■ If something is **round,** it is shaped like a circle or ball. ■ If something is **rounded,** it is curved in shape, without any points or sharp edges. ■ If you say a book, article, or film gives a **rounded** picture, you mean it is fair and balanced. ■ A performance **in the round** is a performance of a play on a stage which is surrounded by the audience. ■ If you give an amount as a **round** number or **round** it up or down, you give it to the nearest multiple of 10, 100, or 1000, etc. *The money goes into the team pool, which this summer, in round figures, has now reached £78,000.* ■ If you **round off** an enjoyable or successful experience, you end it in a pleasing or satisfying way. ■ If someone **rounds on** you, they suddenly criticize you aggressively. ■ If people or animals are **rounded up,** they are gathered together.

roundabout A **roundabout** is a circular structure at a place where several roads meet. You drive round it until you come to the road you want. ■ In a playground, a **roundabout** is a revolving structure which children can push round and ride on. ■ A merry-go-round is sometimes called a **roundabout.** ■ If you go somewhere by a **roundabout** route, you go by a route which is not the shortest and quickest one. ■ If you do or say something in a **roundabout** way, you do it or say it in a long and indirect way.

rounders is a British ball game, similar to baseball, in which a player hits a ball and then runs round the edge of a square area. Rounders is usually played by children.

roundly If you say something **roundly,** you say it very forcefully.

round robin A **round robin** tournament is a sports competition in which each player or team plays every other player or team.

round table In a **round table** discussion, all the participants meet on equal terms.

round-the-clock See **clock.**

roundup On TV or radio, a **roundup** is a summary of the main items in the news.

rouse (**rousing, roused**) If someone **rouses** you, they wake you up. ■ You can say someone or something **rouses** people when they make them very emotional or excited. ...*a rousing speech... He used the civil rights legislation to rouse the fears of white voters.*

rout (**routing, routed**) If you **rout** your opponents, you defeat them completely. A defeat like this is called a **rout.**

route (**routing, routed**) A **route** is a way from one place to another. ■ A bus, air, or shipping route is a way between two places along which buses, planes, or ships travel regularly. ■ When people or vehicles are **routed** in a particular direction, they are made to travel in that direction. ■ You can call a way of achieving something a **route** to it. ■ See also **en route.**

routine (**routinely**) **Routine** or a **routine** is doing things regularly in a fixed order. ■ **Routine** activities are done regularly. ■ **Routine** things are standard and unexciting. ■ In entertainment, a **routine** is a sequence of things such as jokes or actions, forming part of a longer performance. ...*a dance routine.*

roving is used to describe people who travel around, rather than staying in one place. ...*Alan Wicker, the roving reporter.*

row If people **row** or have a **row,** (*pron: rhymes with 'cow'*) they quarrel or have a serious argument or disagreement. ■ If someone is making a **row,** they are making a loud unpleasant noise. ■ A **row** (*pron: rhymes with 'snow'*) of people or things is a number of them arranged in a line. ■ If something happens several times **in a row,** it happens that number of times, one after another. ■ When you **row** a boat, you move it through the water using oars. ■ **Rowing** is a sport in which people in special rowing boats race against each other.

rowan The **rowan** is a tree with red berries and small leaves. It is also called the 'mountain ash'.

rowdy (**rowdier, rowdiest; rowdies, rowdiness**) If people are **rowdy,** they are noisy and rough. People like these are sometimes called **rowdies;** their behaviour is called **rowdiness.**

rower A **rower** is someone who rows a boat, especially as a sport.

rowing boat A **rowing boat** is a small boat you move through the water using oars.

rowlock (*pron:* **rol-**lok) **Rowlocks** are the U-shaped pieces of metal on the sides of a rowing boat which hold the oars in position.

royal A **royal** person is a king, queen, or emperor, or a member of their family. **Royal** means connected with a king, queen, or emperor, or their family. ...*the royal wedding.* ■ **Royal** is used in the names of institutions or organizations which are officially appointed or supported by a member of a royal family.

royal blue is a deep blue colour.

royalist A **royalist** is someone who supports their country's royal family, or believes their country should have a king or queen.

royal jelly is a substance made by bees and fed to their larvae.

royally If you say something is done **royally,** you are emphasizing it is done grandly or impressively, or done to a great degree. *They got royally drunk.*

royalty (**royalties**) The members of royal families can be referred to as **royalty.** ■ **Royalties** are payments made to authors and musicians when their work is sold or performed. ■ Payments made to someone whose invention or property is used by a commercial company are called **royalties.**

RP See **Received Pronunciation.**

RPI See **retail price index.**

rpm is a measure of how many times per minute something goes round in a circle. It is usually used to indicate record playing speeds.

RSI See **repetitive strain injury.**

RSVP stands for 'répondez s'il vous plaît', which is French for 'please reply'. It is written at the bottom of invitations.

Rt Hon is a short way of writing 'Right Honourable' as part of the formal title of some members of the Privy Council and some judges. ...*the Rt Hon Gordon Brown, MP.*

rub (**rubbing, rubbed**) If you **rub** something or give it a **rub,** you move your hand or a cloth backwards and forwards on it, pressing it firmly. ■ If two things **rub** together, they move backwards and forwards, pressing against each other. ■ If you **rub out** something written, you remove it by rubbing it with a rubber or a cloth. ■ A **rubbing** is a picture you make by putting a piece of paper over a carved surface and rubbing crayon, charcoal, or chalk over it. ■ If someone keeps reminding you of something you would rather forget, you can say they are **rubbing it in.** ■ If two people **rub along,** they manage to live or work together in a fairly friendly way. ■ If someone's qualities or habits **rub off** on you, you develop some of them yourself after spending time with them.

rubber is a strong waterproof elastic substance made from the sap of a tropical tree or produced chemically. **Rubber** things are made from rubber. ■ A **rubber** is a small piece of rubber or other material used to rub out mistakes made while writing, drawing, or typing. ■ In the US, a **rubber** is a condom. ■ In bridge and some other games, a **rubber** is a series of games played between the same two people or teams.

rubber band A **rubber band** is the same as an elastic band.

rubber bullet A **rubber bullet** is a bullet made of hard rubber. Rubber bullets are intended to injure people rather than kill them, and are used by the authorities for crowd control.

rubber stamp A **rubber stamp** is a small device with something like a name or date on it. You press it onto an ink pad and then onto a document, to show the document has been officially dealt with. ■ When someone in authority **rubber-stamps** a decision, plan, or law, they agree to it.

rubbery If something is **rubbery,** it is soft and stretchy like rubber.

rubbish (rubbishes, rubbishing, rubbished) Rubbish is unwanted things or waste material. ■ If you think an idea or statement is foolish or wrong, you can say it is **rubbish.** ■ If you **rubbish** a person, their ideas, or their work, you say they are of little value.

rubble When a building is destroyed, the remaining bits of brick, stone, or other materials are called **rubble.**

rubella See **German measles.**

rubric (*pron:* roo-brik) A **rubric** is a set of rules or instructions, for example the rules at the beginning of an examination paper. ■ A **rubric** is a heading under which something is considered. *The other problem falls under the general rubric of nationalism.*

ruby (rubies) A **ruby** is a clear red jewel. ■ **Ruby** is a dark red colour.

ruby wedding A **ruby wedding** is a 40th wedding anniversary.

ruched (*pron:* rooshd) curtains or clothes are pleated or gathered to produce a frilled effect.

ruck A **ruck** is a situation where a group of people are fighting or struggling. ■ In rugby union, a **ruck** is a situation where a group of players are struggling for possession of the ball.

rucksack A **rucksack** is a bag with straps which go over your shoulders so you can carry things on your back.

ruction If someone or something causes **ructions,** they cause a lot of trouble.

rudder A **rudder** is a vertical wooden or metal blade at the back of a boat, used to steer the boat.

rudderless If you say an organization or country is **rudderless,** you mean it does not have a good leader to follow or a clear aim to pursue.

ruddy If someone's face is **ruddy,** it is a reddish colour.

rude (rudely, rudeness) When people are **rude,** they behave impolitely. *He pushed past her rudely.* ■ You say things are **rude** when they refer to sex or bodily functions in a way which is meant to amuse or titillate people. ■ If someone receives a **rude** shock, something unpleasant happens to them unexpectedly. ■ If you say someone is in **rude health,** you

mean they are strong and healthy. ■ **rude awakening:** see **awaken.**

rudimentary things are simple, basic, and undeveloped.

rudiments The **rudiments** of something are its simplest or most essential parts. *...the rudiments of a common defence policy.*

rue (ruing, rued) If you **rue** something you have done, you regret it. You can also say you **rue the day** you did it.

rueful (ruefully) If someone is **rueful,** they show regret or disappointment about something which has happened to them.

ruff A **ruff** was a starched finely-pleated white collar shaped like a wheel, worn in Europe in the 16th century. ■ A **ruff** is a thick band of feathers or fur round the neck of a bird or animal.

ruffian Men who behave in a bad-mannered or violent way are sometimes called **ruffians.**

ruffle (ruffling, ruffled) If something **ruffles** you, or **ruffles** your **feathers** it makes you angry or upset. ■ When a bird **ruffles** its feathers, it makes them stand out from its body because it is cleaning itself or is frightened. ■ When the wind **ruffles** something like grass, it makes it move gently with a wave-like motion. ■ **Ruffles** are small decorative frills, especially on clothes.

rug A **rug** is a piece of thick material you put on a floor. It is like a small carpet. ■ A **rug** is a small blanket.

rugby or **rugby football** is a type of football played by two teams using an oval ball which can be kicked or handled. There are two types of rugby: **Rugby League** is played by teams of thirteen players, **Rugby Union** by teams of fifteen players.

rugged (*pron:* rug-gid) **(ruggedness)** A **rugged** area of land is rocky, rough, and impressive. *...a rugged coastline.* ■ A **rugged** man is strong, tough, and rather handsome. ■ You say people are **rugged** when they are determined and resilient. *Rugged individualism forged America's frontier society.*

rugger is another word for rugby.

ruin (ruining, ruined) If you **ruin** something or bring about its **ruin,** you spoil, destroy, or severely damage it. *...a ruined church.* ■ The **ruins** of something are the parts which remain after the rest has been destroyed or severely damaged. *The Pope said he hoped a united Christian Europe could be built from the ruins of Communism.* ■ If someone is **ruined,** they lose all their money. *Thousands of small businesses now face ruin.*

ruinous (ruinously) If something is **ruinous,** it has a disastrous effect, especially financially or economically. *...a ruinously expensive court case.*

rule (ruling, ruled) Rules are instructions which tell you what is allowed and what is not. ■ If someone in authority **rules** on a matter or gives a **ruling,** they give an official decision. ■ The people who **rule** a country are the ones who run its affairs. ■ If workers **work to rule,** they protest about something by just doing the minimum required by their contracts. ■ If something is the **rule** or happens as **a rule,** it is the normal state of affairs. ■ If you **rule out** an idea or a course of action, you reject it. ■ If you **rule** a straight line, you draw it using something like a ruler. ■ **rule of thumb:** see **thumb.**

ruler A country's **rulers** are its government. A monarch or dictator is sometimes called a **ruler.** ■ A **ruler** is a long flat piece of wood, metal, or plastic with straight edges marked in centimetres or inches.

rum is a strong alcoholic drink made from sugar cane juice. ■ If you say something is **rum,** you mean it is rather odd. *It is a rum old industry, British pensions assurance.*

rumba The **rumba** is a ballroom dance from Cuba.

rumble (**rumbling, rumbled**) A **rumble** is a low continuous sound. *The thunder of heavy artillery rumbles round the mountains.* ■ If something like an argument or a dispute **rumbles on,** it goes on without any sign of a settlement. *There were rumblings of revolt from the left of the party.* ■ If someone is **rumbled,** the truth about them or their actions is discovered.

rumbustious A **rumbustious** person is energetic, cheerful, and noisy.

ruminant (*pron:* roo-min-ant) **Ruminants** are animals which chew the cud and have a stomach divided into four compartments. Deer, cattle, sheep, and goats are all ruminants.

ruminate (*pron:* roo-min-ate) (**ruminating, ruminated; rumination**) If you **ruminate** on something, you think about it slowly and carefully. Thoughts like these are called **ruminations.** ■ When animals like cattle **ruminate,** they bring food back from their stomach into their mouth and chew it again.

rummage (**rummaging, rummaged**) If you **rummage** through something, you search for something in it by moving things around in a careless or hurried way.

rummy is a card game in which players try to collect cards of the same value or cards in a sequence in the same suit.

rumour (*Am:* rumor) (**rumoured**) A **rumour** is a piece of information circulating among people which may or may not be true. *He is rumoured to have at least 53 yachts.*

rump An animal's **rump** is its rear end. ■ **Rump** or **rump steak** is meat cut from the rear part of a cow's back. ■ The **rump** of a group or organization is what is left when most of it has gone or been removed.

rumpled clothes or bedclothes are creased and disordered. If you say a person is **rumpled,** you mean their clothes and hair look like this.

rumpus (**rumpuses**) If someone or something causes a **rumpus,** they cause a lot of noise, fuss, and argument.

run (**running, ran, have run**) When you **run,** you make your way quickly on foot, leaving the ground during each stride. If you go for a **run,** you do this over a long distance, for training or exercise. ■ In games like cricket and baseball, a **run** is a score of one, made by players running between marked places on the pitch after hitting the ball. ■ If you **run** someone somewhere, you drive them there. ■ If trains or buses **run** from one place to another,

they regularly travel between them. You can also say a road or river **runs** somewhere. ■ In sports like skiing, a **run** is a course or route. ■ If you **run** a tap, you turn it on. ■ If the dye in a piece of clothing **runs,** the colour comes out in the wash. ■ If you **run** your hand **through** something, you move your hand through it. ■ If you **run** an experiment or computer program, you start it and let it continue. ■ The person who **runs** an organization is the person in charge. ■ If someone **runs** in an election, they stand as a candidate. ■ If something such as a show **runs** for a certain length of time, that is how long it continues before it is taken off. This length of time is called its **run.** ■ **Running** and **long-running** are used to describe things which continue or keep occurring over a period of time. *...running jokes. ...long-running investigations.* ■ You say feelings are **running high** when people are very angry or excited. ■ When a newspaper or magazine **runs** a story, it prints it. ■ You say an amount is **running** at a certain level when it is at that level. *Inflation is running at 10.6 per cent.* ■ A **run** of successes or failures is a series of them. ■ A **run** of a product is the amount a company or factory decides to produce at one time. *...a weekly print run of over four million copies.* ■ If there is a **run** on something, there is a sudden increase in demand for it. ■ If you talk about what will happen in the **long run,** you mean what will happen over a long period of time in the future. ■ If something **runs out,** there is none left. ■ When a legal document or agreement **runs out,** it expires. ■ If an organization is being **run down,** its activities are being deliberately reduced. ■ If the amount of something is **run down,** it is deliberately allowed to decrease. ■ If someone is **run down** or **run over,** they are knocked down by a vehicle. ■ If you **run** people or things **down,** you criticize them strongly. ■ If you **run through** a number of items of information, you read all of them quickly. Similarly, actors can **run through** a play or give it a **run-through.** ■ If a theme or feature **runs through** something like a book, it keeps occurring in it. *The theme of rootlessness runs through many of his poems.* ■ If someone **runs up** large debts, they accumulate them.

runabout A **runabout** is a small car used mainly for short journeys.

runaway A **runaway** is someone who leaves home without telling anyone or without permission. ■ **Runaway** is used to describe things which suddenly increase rapidly and cannot be controlled. *...runaway inflation.*

run-down If someone is **run-down,** they are tired or slightly ill, often because they are under a lot of stress or have been working too hard. ■ A **run-down** building or area is in very poor condition because it has not been properly maintained. *...its run-down council estates.*

rune – **Runes** are letters from an ancient alphabet which were carved in wood or stone by people in Northern Europe from the third century AD to the Middle Ages. They were believed to have magical properties.

rung See **ring**. ■ The **rungs** of a ladder are the wooden or metal bars which form the steps.

run-in If you have a **run-in** with someone, you have an argument or fight with them.

runner A **runner** is someone who runs for sport or pleasure. ■ A drug **runner** or gun **runner** is someone who illegally gets drugs or guns into a country. ■ **Runners** are long shoots which grow out from a plant's main stem, put down roots, and become new plants. ■ The **runners** on something like a sledge are thin strips of wood or metal underneath it which enable it to move smoothly.

runner bean – Runner beans are the long green edible pods of a climbing plant.

runner-up (runners-up) The **runner-up** is someone who finishes second in a competition.

running commentary If someone gives a **running commentary** on something that is happening, they continuously describe and comment on it as it happens.

running costs An organization's **running costs** are the amounts of money it spends on day-to-day requirements, rather than on things like expansion or development.

running mate In an American election campaign, a candidate's **running mate** is the person they have chosen to have the next-ranking political office if they win.

running order The **running order** of the items in a broadcast, concert, or show is the order in which they are to be presented.

runny If someone has a **runny** nose, mucus is dribbling out of it.

run-off A **run-off** is an extra vote or contest held to decide the winner of an election or competition when nobody has yet clearly won. ■ **Run-off** is rainwater which is not absorbed by the ground and forms a stream.

run-of-the-mill people or things are very ordinary, with no special or interesting features. ...*run-of-the-mill politicians.*

runt The **runt** is the smallest and weakest of a group of animals born to the same mother at the same time.

runway A **runway** is a long strip of ground with a hard surface for planes to land on and take off from.

rupee The **rupee** is the unit of currency in India, Pakistan, and some other countries.

rupture (rupturing, ruptured) If something **ruptures** or there is a **rupture** in it, it tears or bursts open. See also **hernia**. ■ If relations between people or groups are **ruptured** or there is a **rupture** in their relations, something happens which spoils them or puts an end to them.

rural means in or connected with the countryside. ...*rural communities.*

ruse A **ruse** is a clever trick or plan intended to deceive someone.

rush (rushes, rushing, rushed) If you **rush,** you go somewhere or do something as quickly as you can. *I rushed in five minutes late... She was rushed to hospital. ...the rush to privatise.* ■ If you are in a **rush,** you need to go somewhere or do something quickly.

■ If a place like a shop has a regular busy period, this period is often called the **rush.** ...*the Christmas rush.* ■ If you **rush** something, you do it in a hurry, often without enough care. ■ If you **rush** into something, you do it without taking time to think about it properly. ■ If something like air, water, or blood **rushes** or there is a **rush** of it, it moves rapidly. ■ If you experience a sudden powerful feeling, you can say you have a **rush** of it. *I felt a rush of pure joy.* ■ **Rushes** are plants with long thin stems which grow near water. ■ The **rushes** of a film are the parts which have been filmed but have not yet been edited.

rush hour The **rush hour** is a period during the day when roads and railways are particularly busy because most people are travelling to or from work.

rusk – Rusks are hard dry biscuits fed to babies.

russet is a reddish-brown colour.

Russian roulette When someone plays **Russian roulette,** they put a bullet in one of the chambers of a gun, spin the chambers, then fire the gun at their own head, not knowing whether it will go off or not.

rust is a reddish-brown coating formed on iron or steel when it is in continual contact with water or water vapour. When a metal **rusts,** rust forms on it. ■ **Rust** is a reddish-brown colour.

rust belt A **rust belt** is a part of a country which used to be a centre of industrial activity but is now suffering economically because its industries have declined.

rustic is used to describe things which are considered typical of the countryside. ...*rustic furniture.* ■ Unsophisticated country people used to be called **rustics.**

rustle (rustling, rustled; rustler) If something **rustles,** it makes soft whispering sounds as it moves. Sounds like these are called **rustlings.** ...*the tiny rustlings of mice.* ■ If you **rustle** something **up,** you make, prepare, or get hold of it quickly, with little time to plan or arrange it. ■ **Rustling** is stealing farm animals, especially cattle. People who do this are called **rustlers.**

rusty If a metal object is **rusty,** rust has formed on it. ■ If you are **rusty,** you are not as good at something as you used to be, because you are out of practice.

rut (rutting, rutted) If a road or track is **rutted** or has **ruts** in it, its surface has deep narrow grooves, made by the wheels of vehicles. ■ If you say someone or something is **stuck in a rut,** you mean they carry on in the same way without changing or adapting, and so are unable to progress. ■ The **rut** is the period of the year when some animals, especially deer, are sexually active, and males fight each other before mating with the females. During this period, you say the males are **rutting.**

ruthless (ruthlessly, ruthlessness) A **ruthless** person will do anything necessary to achieve what they want. *The demonstration was ruthlessly crushed by the authorities.*

rye is a cereal grown in colder countries. Its grains can be used to make flour, bread, and other foods.

S s

Sabbath The **Sabbath** is the day of the week which Jews and Christians devote to religious worship. Jews celebrate the Sabbath on Saturdays and Christians celebrate it on Sundays.

sabbatical When someone, especially a university lecturer, takes a **sabbatical,** they take time off from their normal work, to study or travel. They often receive their normal pay during this period.

sable The **sable** is a small weasel-like animal which lives in northern Europe and northern Asia. **Sable** is the very expensive brown fur of these animals.

sabotage (*pron:* **sab**-ot-ahzh; *the 'zh' sounds like 's' in 'pleasure'*) (**sabotaging, sabotaged; saboteur**) If someone **sabotages** something like a piece of machinery, they damage it for some political or military purpose. Damaging and destroying things like this is called **sabotage;** someone who does it is called a **saboteur.** ■ If someone **sabotages** something like negotiations or a policy, they prevent them from being successful.

sabre A **sabre** is (a) a heavy sword with a curved blade, formerly used by soldiers on horseback. (b) a light sword used in fencing.

sabre-rattling is an aggressive show of force by one country, intended to intimidate other countries.

sac A **sac** is a part inside a person's or an animal's body shaped like a balloon and containing something like air or fluid.

saccharine (*or* **saccharin**) (*both pron:* **sak**-er-rin) is a sweet chemical substance. It is used instead of sugar by people who want to lose weight. ■ If you call something **saccharine** (*pron:* **sak**-er-reen), you mean it is too sweet or sentimental.

sachet (*pron:* **sash**-ay) A **sachet** is a small sealed packet, containing a small quantity of something.

sack A **sack** is a large bag made of rough material, for carrying or storing things. ■ If you are **sacked** or given the **sack,** you are dismissed from your job. ■ If an army **sacks** a place, they destroy it and take away anything of value.

sackcloth is rough woven material used to make sacks. ■ When people talk about **sackcloth and ashes,** they are referring to someone's public display of regret or sorrow for something they have done.

sackload When something is normally delivered in sacks, you can talk about receiving **sackloads** of it, meaning a great deal of it.

sacrament (**sacramental**) A **sacrament** is an important Christian religious ceremony such as communion, baptism, or marriage. **Sacramental** means to do with the sacraments.

sacred (*pron:* **say**-krid) objects, places, or people are believed to be holy. **Sacred** is used to describe other things connected with religion or used in religious ceremonies. *...sacred music.* ■ **Sacred** is used to describe things which are considered to be too important to be changed or interfered with. *...the once sacred notions of socialism and anti-fascism.* ■ If you call something like a custom a **sacred cow,** you mean people regard it as something which cannot be criticized or questioned.

sacrifice (**sacrificing, sacrificed; sacrificial**) If you **sacrifice** something or someone that is important to you, you give them up for something worthwhile. You call this making a **sacrifice.** ■ In the past, if a person or animal was **sacrificed,** they were killed as an offering to a god or gods. This was called making a **sacrifice. Sacrificial** means to do with making sacrifices.

sacrilege (*pron:* **sak**-ril-ij) (**sacrilegious**) Sacrilege is disrespectful behaviour towards something holy or something people think should be respected. Behaviour like this can be called **sacrilegious.**

sacrosanct (*pron:* **sak**-roe-sangkt) is used to describe things which are considered so important or special that they must not be criticized or changed in any way. *The weekend rest days were considered sacrosanct by staff.*

sacrum The **sacrum** is the triangular bone at the bottom of the spine between the hip bones.

SAD or **Seasonal Affective Disorder** is a depressive condition which some people suffer from during the winter. It is thought to be caused by a lack of sunlight.

sad (**sadder, saddest; sadly, sadness**) If you are **sad,** you are unhappy, especially about something which has recently happened. ■ If you say something like a story is **sad,** you mean it makes you feel sad. ■ **Sad** and **sadly** are used to say something is regrettable. *It is sad that his knowledge of English is poor.*

sadden (**saddening, saddened**) If you are **saddened** by something, it makes you feel sad.

saddle (**saddling, saddled**) If you **saddle** a horse, you fasten a leather seat called a **saddle** on its back, so you can ride it. ■ If you talk about someone being **in the saddle,** you mean (a) they are riding a horse. (b) they are in control of something or in power. ■ The seat on a bicycle or motorbike is called a **saddle.** ■ A **saddle** is a large cut of meat, especially mutton, from the middle part of an animal's back. ■ If you are **saddled with** something unpleasant or difficult, you have to put up with it.

saddlebag A **saddlebag** is a bag attached to the saddle of a horse or bike.

sadism (**sadist; sadistic, sadistically**) Sadism is getting pleasure from inflicting physical or mental cruelty on someone. A **sadist** is someone who gets pleasure this way. **Sadistic** is used to describe people like this and their behaviour. *...sadistic beatings.*

sado-masochism (**sado-masochistic, sado-masochist**) Sado-masochism is sexual behaviour between two people in which one of them has a sadistic role and the other a masochistic one. **Sado-masochistic** means connected with sado-masochism. *...the classic sado-masochistic novel.* A

sado-masochist is someone who gets pleasure from inflicting suffering or receiving it or both.

sae (*pronounce each letter separately*) An **sae** is an envelope which you stamp and address to yourself. You send it to someone so they do not have any costs when they reply. 'sae' stands for 'stamped addressed envelope'.

safari A **safari** is an expedition for hunting or observing animals, especially in Africa.

safari park A **safari park** is a large enclosed area of land where wild animals live and move around freely. People pay to drive their cars through these parks to watch the animals.

safe (**safer, safest; safely**) If you are **safe,** you are unharmed or not in danger. ■ If it is **safe** to do something, you can do it without any risk. *We stayed away until we thought it was safe to come back.* A **safe** way of doing something is one which carries no risk. ■ If something is **safe,** it is not harmful or dangerous. ■ A **safe** is a strong metal cupboard with special locks for keeping money and valuables in.

safe conduct If someone is given **safe conduct,** enemy authorities guarantee they will not be harmed while travelling through their territory.

safe deposit boxes are containers, usually in a special room at a bank, in which people keep money and valuables.

safeguard If you **safeguard** something, you protect it from harm. Something which is introduced to give protection from harm can be called a **safeguard.**

safe house A **safe house** is a place where someone like a spy can hide and be protected from danger.

safekeeping If something is given to someone for **safekeeping,** it is handed over so it will be protected and kept safe from harm.

safe passage If someone is guaranteed **safe passage,** they are given a promise that they can pass from one place to another without any risk of harm.

safe seat A **safe seat** has been held by the same party with a large majority for a long time and is unlikely to be won by any other party.

safe sex is having sex in a responsible way, for example using a condom, to prevent the spread of sexually transmitted diseases, especially AIDS.

safety is being safe and secure, and protected from harm or danger. ■ If you are concerned about the **safety** of something like a nuclear installation, you are concerned about how dangerous it might be. ■ **Safety** measures and equipment are intended to make something less dangerous.

safety belt A **safety belt** is the same as a seat belt.

safety catch A **safety catch** is a device on a gun which is there to prevent the gun being fired accidentally.

safety net A **safety net** is a large net spread out as a precaution beneath a person trying to do a difficult stunt high up in the air. ■ A **safety net** is part of a system which is there to prevent serious harm being done if something goes wrong.

safety pin A **safety pin** is a bent metal pin, used to fasten things together. The point of the pin has a cover over it when closed, to stop it doing any harm.

safety valve A **safety valve** is a piece of equipment in something like a boiler which allows steam to escape when too much pressure has built up. ■ You call something a **safety valve** when it acts as a release for built-up emotions or energy without harming other people.

saffron is a yellowish-orange spice from a type of crocus. It is used to colour and flavour food. **Saffron** is a yellowish-orange colour.

sag (**sagging, sagged**) If part of a person's body **sags,** it looses its firmness, usually because of age. ■ If something like a bed **sags,** it dips in the middle. ■ If you say a person's reputation is **sagging,** you mean people do not think as highly of them as they used to. You can also say there is a **sag** in their reputation. ■ If something like a level **sags,** it goes down. *The paper's circulation had sagged to barely 15,000.*

saga (*pron: sah-*ga) A **saga** is a long story composed in medieval times in Norway and Iceland. ■ A **saga** is any long story, account, or sequence of events. *The saga of a hostile takeover that backfired took another turn yesterday.*

sagacious (*pron: sag-gay-*shuss) (**sagacity**) If you call someone **sagacious** or talk about their **sagacity,** you mean they behave in a wise and intelligent way.

sage (**sagely**) Sage is a strongly flavoured herb with long greyish-green leaves. ■ A **sage** is a person who is regarded as being wise. ■ **Sage** people are wise and knowledgeable.

sago (*pron: say-*go) The **sago** is a type of palm tree whose trunk produces an edible starch, also called **sago.** This starch is used for making puddings and for thickening sauces.

said See say.

sail (**sailing, sailed**) When a ship **sails** somewhere, it goes there. When a ship starts its journey, you can say it **sets sail.** ■ A **sailing** is a regular voyage made by a ship from one place to another. ■ A **sail** is a large piece of material fastened to a ship's mast, which catches the wind and makes the ship move. ■ A **sailing ship** is a ship with sails, especially one used to carry passengers and cargo in the past. A **sailing boat** is a smaller vessel with sails. ■ **Sailing** is the activity of going out in sailing boats, for sport or pleasure. ■ If you **sail through** a difficult situation, you get through it easily. ■ If you say something is **plain sailing,** you mean it is uncomplicated and easy to achieve. ■ The **sails** on a windmill are the flat parts which are turned by the wind.

sailboard A **sailboard** is a flat board with a sail attached, used for windsurfing.

sailing See sail.

sailor A **sailor** is a member of a ship's crew.

saint A **saint** is a dead person who has been officially recognized and honoured by the Christian Church because of their holy life. 'Saint' is often shortened to 'St'; 'Saints' is shortened to 'SS'. ■ People sometimes call someone a **saint** when their behaviour is unusually kind, patient, and unselfish.

sainthood When someone becomes a saint, you can say they achieve **sainthood.**

saintly people behave in a very good or holy way. **Saintly** is also used to describe things connected with people like these. ...*a saintly reputation.*

sake If something is done for someone's **sake**, it is done for their benefit. ■ **Sake** is used in several phrases which explain why something is done. *The Free Democrats are arguing for a coalition for the sake of stability.* ■ **Sake** (*pron:* **sah**-kee) is a Japanese alcoholic drink made from fermented rice.

salacious If you call something like a story, picture, or song **salacious,** you mean it is too concerned with sex.

salad A **salad** is a mixture of uncooked vegetables which are often eaten as an accompaniment to a meal. ■ See also **fruit salad.** ■ If you talk about someone's **salad days,** you mean the period in their life when they were young and inexperienced.

salamander The **salamander** is a lizard-like amphibian in many parts of Asia, Europe, and North America.

salami (*pron:* sal-**lah**-mee) is a type of spicy sausage.

salary (**salaries; salaried**) A **salary** is the money someone is paid for their job, usually monthly. A **salaried** person or job receives a salary.

sale When something is sold, you talk about its **sale.** ■ The **sales** of a product are the numbers that have been sold. ...*the drop in car sales.* ■ **Sales** is used to talk about the part of a company which deals with selling its products. ...*retail sales staff.* ■ A **sale** is (a) an occasion when a shop sells goods at lower than normal prices. (b) an auction. ■ **jumble sale:** see **jumble.**

saleable things can be sold easily or are suitable for being sold.

saleroom A **saleroom** is a place where things are sold by auction.

salesmanship is the skill of persuading people to buy things.

salient (*pron:* **say**-lee-ent) The **salient** features of something are its most prominent or striking ones.

saline (*pron:* **say**-line) (**salinity**) **Saline** things contain salt. ...*a saline drip.* **Salinity** (*pron:* sal-**lin**-it-ee) is used to talk about the amount of salt in something. ...*soil salinity.*

saliva (*pron:* sal-**lie**-va) (**salivary**) **Saliva** is the clear liquid produced in your mouth by glands called the **salivary** glands. Saliva helps in the swallowing and digesting of food.

salivate (**salivating, salivated**) When a person or animal **salivates,** they start to produce extra saliva, often as a result of seeing or smelling food. ■ You can say someone **salivates** at something when they get very excited at the thought of seeing or having it.

sallow If someone has **sallow** skin, their complexion is an unhealthy pale yellow colour.

sally (**sallies, sallying, sallied**) When someone sets out in an energetic way to do something, you can say they **sally forth** to do it. ■ A **sally** is a clever and amusing remark.

salmon (*usual plural:* **salmon**) **Salmon** are large silver-coloured fish with edible pink or reddish flesh called **salmon.**

salmonella is a kind of bacteria which can cause severe food poisoning.

salon A hairdresser's or beautician's **salon** is a place where they carry out their business. ■ In the past, a **salon** was (a) an elegant reception room. (b) a gathering of important or famous people in a fashionable household.

saloon A **saloon** is a car with a fixed roof and seats for four or more people. ■ In Britain, the **saloon** or **saloon bar** in a pub or hotel is a comfortable bar where the drinks are more expensive than in the other bars. ■ In the US, a **saloon** is a place where alcoholic drinks are sold and drunk.

salsa is (a) a type of Puerto Rican big-band dance music. (b) a spicy tomato-based sauce.

salt is a crystalline substance used to flavour or preserve food. **Salted** foods have added salt. ...*salted butter.* ■ If you say something should be **taken with a pinch of salt,** you mean it is probably not completely true. ■ People use **salt** with 'worth' to say something would not be acceptable to a competent person of a certain kind. *No photographer worth his salt would let a picture opportunity like that go by.* ■ **Salt** water is seawater. ■ In chemistry, a **salt** is a compound formed from an acid. ■ **Salts** are certain minerals used for medicinal purposes. ...*liver salts.* ■ If someone **salts away** money, they store it somewhere secretly for safekeeping.

salt cellar A **salt cellar** is a small container for salt.

salt flat A **salt flat** is a flat area covered with salt left behind when the salt water has completely evaporated.

salty things taste of salt or contain salt.

salubrious (*pron:* sal-**loo**-bree-uss) A **salubrious** place is pleasant or healthy. *He found himself in one of the city's less salubrious areas.*

salutary If you call an experience **salutary,** you mean it is good for you or you learn something from it, although it is unpleasant or difficult at the time.

salutation A **salutation** is a greeting.

salute (**saluting, saluted**) If you **salute** someone, you greet them, usually by raising the fingers of your right hand to the side of your forehead. A sign like this is called a **salute.** ■ On some ceremonial occasions, cannons or other large guns are fired into the air; this is called a **salute.** ■ If you **salute** a person or their achievements, you express your admiration for them.

salvage (**salvaging, salvaged**) If something is **salvaged** from a sunken ship or the wreckage of a plane or building, it is removed and used again. Items like this are called **salvage.** ■ If you **salvage** something from a disastrous situation, you manage to get something useful out of it.

salvation In Christianity, **salvation** is being saved from sin and punishment for your sins by belief in Jesus Christ. ■ When someone or something is rescued from a very serious situation, you can call this their **salvation.**

Salvation Army The **Salvation Army** is a Christian evangelical organization, structured like an army, which helps people in need.

salve (**salving, salved**) If you **salve your conscience** by doing something, you do it to feel less guilty. ■ A **salve** is a substance you put on your skin or lips to prevent soreness or dryness.

salvo (**salvoes**) When several guns are fired at the same time, for example as part of a ceremony, this is called a **salvo.**

Samaritan If someone generously helps you out when you are in difficulty, you can call them a **good Samaritan.** ■ The **Samaritans** is a voluntary organization which tries to help people who are suicidal or in despair, especially by talking to them on the phone.

samba The **samba** is a lively Brazilian dance.

same You use **the same** (a) to say two or more things are exactly alike. *He married a woman with the same name as his mother.* (b) to indicate that you are talking about only one person, thing, place, or time. *The same area was struck by a bigger earthquake in May.* (c) to indicate that you are talking about the person or thing you have just mentioned. *Now there are day tours from Morecambe to those same towns.* ■ **All the same** or **just the same** means in spite of what has just been said. *He speaks almost no English and may not want the job. All the same, he is the sort of man that is needed.*

sameness The **sameness** of something is its lack of variety.

samizdat In the former Soviet bloc, **samizdat** was a system in which banned literature was secretly printed and distributed.

samovar A **samovar** is a large decorated metal container used mainly in Russia for boiling water to make tea.

sample (**sampling, sampled**) A **sample** of a product or substance is a single item or a small amount of it, provided so you can see what it is like. ■ If you **sample** something, you try it to see what it is like. ■ A **sample** of something like blood is a small amount used for scientific analysis. ■ A **sample** of people or things is a number of them chosen from a larger group, so they can be used in tests to provide information about the whole group. ■ When a musician **samples** another musician's music, he or she uses parts of it in their own music. Each sampled part is called a **sample.**

sampler A **sampler** is a collection of samples of things, for example a tape or CD containing music by different artists. ■ A **sampler** is a piece of equipment that copies and remixes pieces of music which have already appeared on another artist's records. ■ A **sampler** was a piece of embroidery sewn by a young girl to show her skill at needlework.

samurai (*plural:* **samurai**) A **samurai** was a member of a powerful class of warriors in Japan from the 12th to the 19th century.

sanatorium (*plural:* **sanatoriums** *or* **sanatoria**) A **sanatorium** is an institution where people who are suffering from long-term illnesses are sent for medical treatment and rest.

sanctify (**sanctifies, sanctifying, sanctified**) If a priest **sanctifies** a person or thing, he blesses them to make them holy. ■ You can say something like an informal arrangement is **sanctified** when it is officially approved.

sanctimonious (**sanctimoniousness**) If you accuse someone of being **sanctimonious,** you mean they are making a great show of being more virtuous than other people.

sanction (**sanctioning, sanctioned**) If someone in authority **sanctions** something, they give it their official approval. *...a resolution sanctioning the use of force.* You can say something has the **sanction** of someone in authority. ■ **Sanctions** are measures taken by countries to restrict trade and official contact with a country which has broken international law. *...trade sanctions.* ■ A **sanction** is a tough course of action intended to make people obey the law or comply with accepted standards. *As an ultimate sanction, the umpires should have the power to send a player off the field.*

sanctity If you talk about the **sanctity** of a place, you mean it should be respected because it is holy. ■ You can talk about the **sanctity** of things you think should be respected. *...the sanctity of marriage. ...the sanctity of life.*

sanctuary (**sanctuaries**) A **sanctuary** is a place of safety where a person can be sure of protection. If you give someone **sanctuary,** you provide them with a place like this. ■ A wildlife **sanctuary** is a place where birds or animals are protected and can live freely.

sanctum The **sanctum** or **inner sanctum** of a religious building is a part which is regarded as especially holy. If you talk about the **inner sanctum** of some other building, you mean a part which is supposed to be very private and used by only a few people.

sand is a powdery substance consisting of tiny rock or mineral grains. ■ Large areas of sand are sometimes called **sands.** *...the desert sands.* ■ If you **sand** an object, you rub it with sandpaper.

sandal – **Sandals** are light open shoes with straps.

sandalwood is a sweet-smelling wood from the sandalwood tree. **Sandalwood** is also an oil extracted from sandalwood and used to make perfume.

sandbag (**sandbagged**) **Sandbags** are sacks filled with sand which are used to form barriers against floods or explosions. **Sandbagged** positions or places have had sandbags piled around them.

sandbank A **sandbank** is a raised area of sand just below the surface of the sea or a river which may be uncovered at low tide.

sandblast If you **sandblast** something like a building, you clean it with a high-pressure jet of sand or grit.

sandcastle A **sandcastle** is a heap of sand, shaped roughly like a castle, which children make when they are playing on the beach.

sandpaper is a piece of strong paper with a covering of sand on it which you rub over a surface to make it smooth or clean.

sandpit A **sandpit** is a shallow hole in the ground or a box filled with sand, for children to play in.

sandstone is a type of rock composed mainly of sand.

sandstorm A **sandstorm** is a strong wind in the desert which creates large moving clouds of sand.

sandwich (**sandwiches, sandwiching, sandwiched**) A **sandwich** is two slices of bread with a filling between them. ■ If something is **sandwiched** between two other things, it occupies a narrow space between them.

sandwich board A **sandwich board** consists of two connected boards with advertisements or other messages on them. Someone walks around wearing the boards to display the advertisements.

sandwich course A **sandwich course** is an educational course in which you alternate periods of study with periods working.

sandy is used to describe things which contain a lot of sand. ...*sandy soils.*

sane (**saner, sanest**) You say someone is **sane** when they are not mentally ill. ■ If you say something like a policy or idea is **sane,** you mean it is sensible and reasonable.

sang See **sing.**

sang-froid (*pron:* sahng-**frwah**) A person's **sang-froid,** is their ability to stay calm in a difficult situation.

sanguine (*pron:* **sang**-gwin) If you say someone is **sanguine** about something, you mean they are cheerful and confident.

sanitary means connected with hygiene and cleanliness. ...*appalling sanitary conditions.*

sanitary towel A **sanitary towel** is a pad of soft absorbent material worn by women to absorb blood during their periods.

sanitation is the practice of keeping places clean and hygienic, especially by providing a sewage system and clean water supply.

sanitize (*or* **sanitise**) (**sanitizing, sanitized**) If someone **sanitizes** an unpleasant activity or situation, they deal with it in a way which makes it more acceptable.

sanity Your **sanity** is your ability to think and act normally and reasonably. ■ If someone brings **sanity** to a situation, they begin to make it sensible and reasonable again after a long period of confusion and worry.

sank See **sink.**

Sanskrit is an ancient language of India.

sap (**sapping, sapped**) **Sap** is a liquid in trees and plants. It contains things like mineral salts and sugar. ■ If something **saps** your strength, it slowly weakens you. You can also talk about something **sapping** your confidence, energy, or enthusiasm.

sapling A **sapling** is a young tree.

sapper A **sapper** is a soldier of the lowest rank in the Royal Engineers. ■ A **sapper** is any soldier whose job is to dig trenches and prepare minefields.

sapphire A **sapphire** is a precious stone which is usually blue. ■ **Sapphire** is a bright blue colour.

sarcastic (**sarcastically, sarcasm**) You say someone is being **sarcastic** when they mock someone else in an unpleasant way, usually by saying something good about them when it is obvious that the opposite is true. Mocking someone like this is called **sarcasm.**

sarcoma is a form of cancer which affects tissues such as muscle and bone.

sarcophagus (*pron:* sar-**kof**-fag-uss) (*plural:* **sarcophagi** *or* **sarcophaguses**) A **sarcophagus** is a large coffin, often decorated and usually made of stone.

sardine – **Sardines** are any small sea fish belonging to the herring family, especially small pilchards.

sardonic (**sardonically**) If a speaker or writer is being **sardonic,** they are being mocking or scornful.

sari (*pron:* **sah**-ree) (**saris**) A **sari** is a traditional piece of clothing worn by Indian women. It consists of a long piece of thin material, which is wrapped around the body.

sarong (*pron:* sar-**rong**) A **sarong** is a traditional piece of clothing worn by men and women in places like Malaysia. It consists of a piece of material tied around the waist or under the armpits.

sartorial is used to talk about the style of someone's clothes. *Eton's last concession to sartorial modernity was to do away with top hats.*

SAS The **SAS** is a team of highly trained British soldiers who work on secret or very difficult military operations. SAS stands for 'Special Air Service'.

sash (**sashes**) A **sash** is a long piece of material which a person wears round their waist or over one shoulder, usually at formal ceremonies. ■ A **sash window** is a window consisting of two sliding frames placed one above the other.

sashay (**sashays, sashaying, sashayed**) If someone **sashays** somewhere, they walk there gracefully but in a rather noticeable way. *The models sashayed down the catwalk.*

Sassenach Scottish people sometimes call English people **Sassenachs.**

sassy When Americans call someone **sassy,** they mean they are cheeky and full of life.

sat See **sit.**

Satan (**Satanic, Satanism, Satanist**) **Satan** is the name given to the Devil in the Jewish, Christian, and Muslim religions. **Satanic** means connected with or influenced by the Devil. ...*satanic forces.* **Satanists** are people who worship the Devil. This practice is called **Satanism.**

satchel A **satchel** is a school bag.

sate (**sating, sated**) If someone's desire for something is **sated,** it is fully satisfied.

satellite A **satellite** is a man-made device sent into orbit to collect information or to form part of a communications system. ■ A planet's or star's **satellite** is a natural object which orbits it. ■ If you talk about a country's **satellites,** you mean other countries which it has control over. ■ **Satellite** is used to describe things which depend on something larger and more powerful. ...*satellite towns.*

satiate (*pron:* **say**-she-ate) (**satiating, satiated**) If something **satiates** someone's appetite or need, it satisfies it fully.

satin is a smooth shiny type of cloth, like thick silk.

satire (*satirical, satirist*) Satire is writing or entertainment which uses humour and exaggeration to ridicule something, especially something to do with present-day life. A **satire** is a book or play like this. ...*a satirical poem.* A person who uses satire in their writing is called a **satirist.**

satirize (*or* **satirise**) (**satirizing, satirized**) When a writer **satirizes** someone or something, he or she uses satire to criticize or mock them.

satisfaction is the feeling of pleasure or contentment you get when you have achieved something you wanted. ■ **Satisfaction** is being content with the standard of something you have bought or with a service which has been provided. ■ If you **get satisfaction** from someone, they give you an apology or make amends for some harm they have caused you.

satisfactory (**satisfactorily**) If you say something is **satisfactory,** you mean it is good enough for what is needed. If you say something is **highly satisfactory,** you mean you are very pleased with it.

satisfy (**satisfies, satisfying, satisfied**) If you **satisfy** someone, you make them happy or contented, by giving them what they want. ■ If you are **satisfied** with something, you find it acceptable. If you are **highly satisfied** with something, you are very pleased with it. ■ If something **satisfies** certain requirements, it fulfils them. ■ If someone or something **satisfies** you that something is true, they persuade you of it.

satisfying (**satisfyingly**) If something is **satisfying,** it gives you a feeling of pleasure, contentment, or fulfilment.

satsuma (*pron:* sat-**soo**-ma) A **satsuma** is a type of small seedless orange.

saturate (**saturating, saturated; saturation**) If someone or something **is saturated,** they are extremely wet. ■ If you say a place or system is **saturated** with something, you mean it is so full of it, it cannot take any more. When this happens, you say the place or system has reached **saturation point.** *British radio is saturated with news.* ■ **Saturated fats** are mainly animal fats such as butter and lard.

saturnine people are gloomy and unfriendly.

sauce A **sauce** is a liquid served with food to add to its flavour.

saucepan A **saucepan** is a deep cooking pot, usually made of metal and often with a long handle and lid.

saucer A **saucer** is a small round dish which you stand a cup on.

saucy (**saucier, sauciest; saucily**) Saucy is used to describe people and things that are rude or cheeky in an entertaining way.

sauerkraut (*pron:* **zow**-er-krowt) is sliced pickled cabbage.

sauna (*pron:* **saw**-na) If you have a **sauna,** you sit in a very hot room, called a sauna, and sweat until your skin and pores are clean.

saunter (**sauntering, sauntered**) If you **saunter** somewhere, you walk there in a slow casual way.

sausage A **sausage** is a mixture of finely minced meat, bread, and seasonings wrapped in a skin in a long thin shape. The contents are called **sausage**

meat. A **sausage roll** is a small amount of sausage meat wrapped in pastry.

sauté (*pron:* **so**-tay) (**sautés, sautéing, sautéed** *or* **sautéd**) If you **sauté** food, you fry it quickly in a little oil or butter.

savage (**savaging, savaged; savagely, savagery**) Savage behaviour is violent and cruel. Behaviour like this is also called **savagery.** ■ Fierce criticism of someone or something can be called **savage.** When someone criticizes someone else in a fierce way, you can say they **savage** them. ■ Actions which are likely to cause suffering can be called **savage.** ...*savage cuts in public spending.* ■ In the past, people thought to be primitive and uncivilized were often called **savages.** ■ A **savage** animal is dangerous, because it is likely to attack people or other animals. ■ If an animal like a dog **savages** someone, it attacks them and bites them, causing injury.

savannah (*or* **savanna**) A **savannah** is an open flat stretch of grassland, especially in Africa.

save (**saving, saved**) If you **save** someone or something, you prevent them from being harmed, or get them out of an unpleasant situation. ■ If something **saves** you from having to do something, it makes it unnecessary for you to do it. ■ If you do something to **save** money, time, space, or energy, you do it to avoid wasting it. ...*energy-saving equipment.* ■ If you **save** something, you keep it or set it aside for later use. ■ When a goalkeeper **saves** a shot or makes a **save,** he stops the ball going into the goal. ■ **Save** can be used when mentioning an exception to something. *The streets are completely empty save for the presence of the soldiers.* ■ **save face:** see **face.**

saver People who save money by putting it aside, especially in a bank or building society, are called **savers.**

saving A **saving** is a reduction in the cost of something, or in the amount of money, time, or energy spent or needed. *Commercial companies claim they could do the job for 2p an item – a saving of nearly £10m sterling a year.* A person's **savings** are the money they have saved. ■ If you talk about someone's or something's **saving grace,** you mean their one good quality, which prevents them being completely bad or worthless. ■ See also **save.**

saviour If you talk about someone or something being your **saviour,** you mean they have saved you from a difficult or dangerous situation. ■ In Christianity, the **Saviour** is Jesus Christ.

savoir-faire (*pron:* sav-wahr-**fair**) If you talk about someone's **savoir-faire,** you mean they have the confidence and ability to behave in the right way in any situation.

savour (Am: **savor**) (**savouring, savoured**) If you **savour** something, you take great pleasure and delight in it. *Savour the flavour of each mouthful.* ■ The special taste or smell of a kind of food or drink can be called its **savour.**

savoury (Am: **savory**) (**savouries**) Savoury food has a salty or meaty flavour, rather than a sweet one. ■ **Savouries** are small savoury titbits. ■ If you say something is not too **savoury,** you mean it is rather unpleasant or not very respectable.

savvy If you say someone has a certain kind of **savvy,** you mean they have practical knowledge or skill in that field. *The corporate-finance bankers lacked political savvy.* ■ **Savvy** is used to describe people who are shrewd or well-informed.

saw (**sawing, sawed, have sawn**) See **see.** ■ A **saw** is a long-bladed cutting tool with sharp teeth. If you **saw** through something, you cut through it with a saw. ■ A **saw** is a well-known short saying or proverb.

sawdust is the very fine pieces of wood produced as a waste product when wood is sawn.

sawmill A **sawmill** is a factory where wood is sawn into planks.

sawn See **saw.**

sawn-off A **sawn-off** shotgun has had its barrel sawn off to make it easier to handle and hide.

sax (**saxes**) A **sax** is the same as a saxophone.

saxophone (**saxophonist**) A **saxophone** is a curved metal wind instrument with keys and a single reed. It is often used in jazz and military bands.

say (**saying, said**) When you **say** something, you speak. ■ You can say a piece of writing **says** something when you are quoting from it or mentioning what is in it. *The Bible says we are sinners.* ■ If you **have a say** in something, your opinion influences decisions about it. ■ If something **says** something about a person, situation, or thing, it reveals something about them. *The way you present information says a lot about the way you do business.* ■ You can use **say** to introduce an example of something or to provide an estimate of something. *My opinion is that between, say, five and ten years from now, we will have a device which will operate in a very reliable fashion.* ■ If you say **there is a lot to be said for** something, you mean it is a good idea. ■ If something **goes without saying,** it is obvious.

saying A **saying** is something like a proverb which is often repeated and which is supposed to be a wise comment on some aspect of life.

say-so If something needs a certain person's **say-so,** it can only be done with their permission.

scab A **scab** is a hard dry crusty covering which forms on a wound. ■ People who continue to work during a strike are called **scabs** by the people who are on strike.

scabbard A **scabbard** is a holder for a sword or knife, especially one which hangs from a belt.

scabies (*pron:* **skay**-beez) is an infectious skin condition which causes severe itching. It is caused by mites.

scabrous (*pron:* **skay**-bruss) When people call something **scabrous,** they mean it is indecent.

scaffold (**scaffolding**) A **scaffold** or **scaffolding** is a temporary structure for supporting people and their materials while they are erecting, repairing, or decorating a building. The materials scaffolds are built from are also called **scaffolding.** ■ In the past, a **scaffold** was a raised platform on which people were executed.

scald If you **are scalded** or **scald** part of your body, you burn yourself with boiling liquid or steam. ■ If

you say something is **scalding** or **scalding hot,** you mean it is very hot.

scale (**scaling, scaled**) The **scale** of something is its size or extent. *AIDS in Africa is already frightening in its scale.* ■ If a company makes **economies of scale,** it produces things in larger numbers, so the average cost of each item is less. ■ **Scales** are a piece of equipment for weighing things. ■ A **scale** is a graded set of levels or figures. *...a new ten-point pay scale for teachers.* ■ In music, a **scale** is a sequence of notes played or sung in a rising or falling order. ■ The **scale** of a map, plan, or model is the length of any part of it compared with the length of the thing it represents. *...a map whose scale was set at one inch to 3.156 miles.* ■ A **scale** or **scaled-down** model is smaller than the original but has the same proportions. ■ If the amount of something is **scaled down** or **scaled back,** it is reduced. ■ A fish's or reptile's **scales** are the flat hard plates covering its body. ■ If you **scale** something like a wall or cliff, you climb it. ■ **Scale** is (a) a hard substance made from calcium which forms on the teeth. (b) a hard layer of a substance such as calcium which forms on the inside of kettles and hot water pipes. ■ **tip the scales:** see **tip.**

scallion A **scallion** is the same as a spring onion.

scallop — Scallops are edible shellfish with two fan-shaped shells.

scalloped objects are decorated with a series of small curves along the edges. *The quilt has pretty, scalloped edges and intricate quilting.*

scalp Your **scalp** is the skin on top of your head, which your hair is attached to. ■ If someone **is scalped,** their scalp is removed from their head, for example in an accident. ■ If you gain someone's **scalp,** you win a victory over them.

scalpel A **scalpel** is a knife with a short, thin, extremely sharp blade, used by surgeons in operations.

scaly animals are covered in scales. ■ If a person's skin is **scaly,** it is covered in stiff flaking patches.

scam A **scam** is an illegal or dishonest scheme for making money.

scamper (**scampering, scampered**) If a small animal **scampers** somewhere, it moves with small quick bouncing steps. ■ When people **scamper** somewhere, they make their way there as quickly as they can.

scampi is a dish of large prawns dipped in batter or crumbs and fried.

scan (**scanning, scanned**) If you **scan** written material, you glance through it quickly. ■ If a machine **scans** something, it examines it quickly, for example by moving X-rays over it. An examination of a person's body carried out in this way is called a **scan.** *...a brain scan.* ■ If a machine **scans** a picture or document, it passes a beam of light over it to produce a copy of it in a computer. ■ If you **scan** an area, you look towards all parts of it, because you are hoping to see something.

scandal (**scandalous, scandalously**) A **scandal** is something which happens, often involving money or sex, which people talk about a lot and which is thought to be shocking and immoral. You say something like this is **scandalous.** ■ **Scandal** is (a) scandals generally. (b) the spreading of stories about scandals. ■ You say something is **scandalous** or a **scandal** when you think it is very wrong or unfair.

scandalize (or **scandalise**) (**scandalizing, scandalized**) If you are **scandalized** by something, you are very shocked by it.

scandalous See **scandal.**

Scandinavia (**Scandinavian**) Scandinavia is usually taken to mean Norway, Sweden, and Denmark. Finland, Iceland, and the Faroe Islands are also sometimes considered to be part of Scandinavia. **Scandinavian** means in or from Scandinavia. ...*Scandinavian art.* People from Scandinavia are sometimes called **Scandinavians.**

scanner A **scanner** is (a) a machine used to examine people's bodies, for example by moving X-rays or ultra-sound waves over them. (b) an electronic device which can read things like bar-codes and transfer this information into a computer. (c) an aerial or similar device used to send out and receive radio or radar signals.

scant If, for instance, you pay **scant** attention to something, you pay very little attention to it. *Banks are paying scant regard to the commission's recommendations.*

scanty (**scantier, scantiest; scantily**) If you describe something as **scanty,** you mean there is very little of it. ■ **Scanty** clothing is sexually revealing. ...*scantily dressed women.*

scapegoat (**scapegoating**) If someone is made a **scapegoat,** they are blamed or punished for something which has gone wrong, although it may not have been their fault. **Scapegoating** is making someone a scapegoat.

scapula The **scapula** is the medical name for the shoulder blade.

scar (**scarring, scarred**) A **scar** is a mark left on your body as a result of a wound. If a part of your body is **scarred,** it has a mark or marks like this. ■ If something like a building or piece of land is **scarred,** its exterior or surface has been damaged as a result of war or industry, leaving ugly marks. ■ If a bad experience **scars** someone's mind or leaves a **scar,** it has a permanent adverse effect on it.

scarce (**scarcity, scarcities**) If something is **scarce,** there is very little of it. You can talk about the **scarcity** of something like this. ■ If you **make yourself scarce,** you leave a place quickly, usually to avoid a difficult or embarrassing situation.

scarcely is used to say someone or something is only just a certain thing. *He was scarcely a toddler at the time.* ■ If there is **scarcely any** of something, there is almost none of it. ■ If you say **scarcely** had one thing happened when something else happened, you mean the second thing happened immediately after the first.

scarcity See **scarce.**

scare (**scaring, scared**) If something **scares** you or gives you a **scare,** it frightens or worries you. If you are **scared** of someone or something, you are frightened of them. ■ If there is a **scare** about

something, many people are frightened or worried by it. ■ A **scare story** is something that is said or written to make people feel frightened and think that a situation is much more unpleasant or dangerous than it really is. ■ If you say someone is using **scare tactics,** you mean they are trying to frighten people, to get them to do something. ■ If you **scare off** a person or animal or **scare** them **away,** you frighten them away.

scarecrow A **scarecrow** is an object shaped like a human figure, made of things like straw and old clothes and placed in a field to scare birds away.

scaremongering (**scaremonger**) If you call someone a **scaremonger** or accuse them of **scaremongering,** you mean they are deliberately trying to frighten people by spreading worrying stories which may not be true.

scarf (**scarves**) A **scarf** is a piece of material which you wear around your neck, head, or shoulders.

scarlet is a bright red colour.

scarlet fever is an infectious disease which gives you a sore throat, a high temperature, and a red rash.

scary (**scarier, scariest; scarily**) If you say something is **scary,** you mean it is frightening. *As always in his books, vulnerability is scarily conveyed.*

scathing (**scathingly**) If you are **scathing** about something, you criticize it scornfully.

scatological (**scatology**) If you call a book or song **scatological** or talk about the **scatology** in it, you mean it is full of references to excrement.

scatter (**scattering, scattered**) If you **scatter** things around an area, you drop or throw them over the whole area. ■ If things or people are **scattered** over an area, they are spread sparsely around it. You can talk about a **scatter** or **scattering** of things or people. ■ If a group of people or animals **scatter,** they suddenly move off in different directions.

scatty If you call someone **scatty,** you mean they are absent-minded and unreliable.

scavenge (**scavenging, scavenged; scavenger**) When someone **scavenges** for something, especially food, they search through rubbish for it. A person who does this is called a **scavenger.** ■ If a bird or an animal **scavenges,** it obtains food by eating the flesh of dead creatures and other waste material. Birds and animals like these are called **scavengers.**

SCE stands for 'Scottish Certificate of Education'. This qualification covers the two Scottish public exams – the Standard Grades and the Higher Grades (or 'Highers').

scenario (*pron:* sin-**nar**-ee-oh) (**scenarios**) If you talk about a likely or possible **scenario,** you are talking about a sequence of events which might develop. *I tend to think the least likely scenario is a military takeover.* ■ The **scenario** of a film or play is a summary of the plot and a description of the characters.

scene A **scene** in a film, play, or book is one part of it, in which all the action happens in one place. ■ What you see when you look around you can be called a **scene.** ...*a scene of incredible beauty.* ■ The **scene** of an incident, especially an accident or a disaster, is the place where it happened. ■ If someone **makes a scene,** they embarrass people by losing their temper in public. ■ You can refer to an area of activity as a **scene** of a particular kind. *...the British political scene.* ■ If something is being done **behind the scenes,** it is happening without the general public being aware of it. ■ If someone or something **sets the scene** for a certain event, they create the conditions which make it likely to happen.

scenery The **scenery** is everything you see around you when you are outside, especially in the countryside. ■ In the theatre, the **scenery** is the backcloth and other things used to represent where the action is taking place.

scenic (**scenically**) **Scenic** is used to describe places and routes which have attractive views of the countryside. *...an arduous, but scenically rewarding, trip.*

scent (**-scented**) A **scent** is a pleasant smell. *...delicately-scented freesias.* ■ **Scent** is perfume. ■ A creature's **scent** is its smell, especially when it allows another creature to identify it. ■ If you are **on the scent** of something you are looking for, you are getting close to finding it. ■ If you **scent** something like an opportunity, you feel it is going to come your way soon.

scepter See **sceptre.**

sceptical (*Am:* **skeptical**) (**sceptically, sceptic, scepticism**) If you are **sceptical** about something, you have doubts about it. You call someone a **sceptic** when they have doubts about something which other people believe in.

sceptre (*Am:* **scepter**) (*both pron:* **sep**-ter) A **sceptre** is an ornamental rod which a monarch carries on some ceremonial occasions.

Schadenfreude (*pron:* **shah**-den-froid-eh) is delight in someone else's misfortune.

schedule (*pron:* **shed**-yool *or* **sked**-yool) (**scheduling, scheduled**) A **schedule** is a plan or timetable which lists the times at which things should happen or be done. ■ If something is **scheduled** to happen at a certain time, it is due to happen then. If it happens **on schedule,** it happens at the planned time. If it goes **according to schedule,** everything happens at the right time and in the right way. ■ A **schedule** is a written list of things such as prices or conditions. If something is **scheduled,** it is on a list of this type. *The main area has been scheduled as an ancient monument.*

schematic A **schematic** representation of something is a simplified description or illustration of it.

scheme (**scheming, schemed; schemer**) A **scheme** is a plan for achieving something. ■ A **scheme** is a large-scale plan produced by a government or other organization. *...company pension schemes.* ■ When people **scheme,** they make secret plans. *...scheming politicians.* You can call a person who schemes a lot a **schemer.** ■ See also **colour scheme.**

schilling The **schilling** is the unit of currency in Austria.

schism (*pron:* **skizz**-um *or* **sizz**-um) When a **schism** occurs, a group splits in two as a result of differences in beliefs.

schizophrenia (*pron:* skit-soe-**free**-nee-a) (**schizophrenic**) Schizophrenia is a serious mental disorder which makes people have delusions and lose touch with the world around them. You say someone who suffers from this disorder is **schizophrenic** or a **schizophrenic.** ■ You can say someone's behaviour is **schizophrenic** when their attitudes or intentions keep changing dramatically.

schlock If you call films, pop songs, or books **schlock,** you mean that they have no artistic or social value.

schmaltz (*pron:* **shmalts**) is excessive sentimentality.

schmooze (**schmoozing, schmoozed**) When people **schmooze,** they chat or gossip.

schnapps (*pron:* **shnaps**) is a strong alcoholic spirit from Germany.

scholar A **scholar** is (a) someone who studies a subject deeply and knows a lot about it. (b) a pupil or student who holds a scholarship.

scholarly A **scholarly** person enjoys studying and knows a lot about academic subjects. ■ A **scholarly** piece of writing is carefully researched, detailed, and displays a lot of knowledge.

scholarship If you win a **scholarship** to a school or university, you receive money or a free place to study there. ■ **Scholarship** is academic achievement or learning.

scholastic means to do with schools and schoolwork. *...scholastic examinations.*

school (**schooling, schooled**) A **school** is a place where children are educated. ■ In the US, education is sometimes called **schooling.** ■ University departments, colleges, and institutions for specialized subjects are sometimes called **schools.** *...business schools.* ■ If someone is **schooled** in something, they are taught it. *They have been well-schooled in the tricks of the trade.* ■ If you **school** a horse, you train it. ■ A **school** of artists, writers, or thinkers is a group of them with similar ideas or theories. ■ A **school of thought** is a set of opinions shared by a group of people. ■ If you say someone is one of the **old school,** you mean they have qualities or opinions which are no longer common. ■ When people talk about **the old school tie,** they mean the assistance, especially in business, which ex-pupils of the same public school sometimes give each other. ■ A **school** of whales, dolphins, or fish is a large group of them.

schoolboy A **schoolboy** is a boy who goes to school. ■ **Schoolboy** behaviour by adults is childish and immature.

schoolchild (**schoolchildren**) **Schoolchildren** are children who go to school.

schooldays Your **schooldays** are the period of your life when you are at school.

schoolfriend Your **schoolfriends** are the friends you have while you are at school.

schoolgirl A **schoolgirl** is a girl who goes to school.

schoolhouse In the US, Australia, and some other countries, a **schoolhouse** is a building used as a school, especially in a village.

schoolmaster A **schoolmaster** is a male schoolteacher, especially in an independent school.

schoolmate Your **schoolmates** are the other children at your school.

schoolmistress (**schoolmistresses**) A female schoolteacher used to be called a **schoolmistress.**

schoolroom A **schoolroom** is the same as a classroom.

school teacher (or **schoolteacher**) A **school teacher** is a person who teaches in a school.

schoolwork is the work a pupil does while at school or as homework.

schoolyard A **schoolyard** is a school playground.

schooner A **schooner** is a sailing ship or yacht with at least two masts. ■ A **schooner** is a large sherry glass.

sciatica (pron: sigh-**at**-tik-ka) is severe pain in the **sciatic nerve,** which is in your buttock and thigh.

science is the study of the nature and behaviour of everything in the universe using observation and experiments, and trying to arrange the results into a system of laws. A **science** is a particular branch of science, for example biology or physics. See also **life science, social science.** ■ Anything which is studied in a systematic way can be called a **science.** Property appraisal has always been the most inexact of sciences.

science fiction is stories, films, and other forms of entertainment which describe events taking place in the future or in other parts of the universe.

science park A **science park** is an area where several companies carry out scientific research and commercial development, often in co-operation with a nearby university.

scientific (**scientifically**) **Scientific** means to do with science. ...scientific research. ■ If you do something in a **scientific** way, you do it systematically, using experiments or observations.

scientist A **scientist** is a person who studies or does work in one of the sciences.

sci-fi (pron: **sie fie**) is short for 'science fiction'.

scimitar (pron: **sim**-mit-ar) A **scimitar** is a short curved oriental sword.

scintilla (pron: **sin**-til-a) A **scintilla** of something is a tiny amount of it.

scintillating (pron: **sin**-til-late-ing) is used to describe things which are lively, sparkling, and amusing.

scion (pron: **sigh**-on) A **scion** of a famous or aristocratic family is an heir, descendant, or young member of it.

scissors are a tool for cutting things, consisting of two blades hinged together.

sclerosis (**sclerotic**) **Sclerosis** is a disease in which the tissue in part of a person's body becomes abnormally hard or thick. See also **multiple sclerosis.** ■ If a system is **sclerotic** or suffering from **sclerosis,** it has seized up and is not making any headway.

scoff If you **scoff** at someone or something, you mock them or speak about them with contempt. ■ When someone **scoffs** food, they eat it greedily.

scold If you **scold** someone or give them a **scolding,** you tell them off.

scone (pron: **skon** or **skone**) **Scones** are small plain cakes made from flour and fat.

scoop (**scooping, scooped**) If you **scoop** something or **scoop** it **up,** you lift it up with a shovelling motion, using your hands or a tool of some kind. ■ A **scoop** is a device consisting of a handle and a hollow part for scooping up food such as ice-cream. ■ If you **scoop** a lot of something desirable or **scoop** it **up,** you obtain it, as a result of luck or skill. In the election of October 5th he scooped 54% of the votes. ■ A **scoop** is an exciting news story which a newspaper gets hold of and prints before other papers. When this happens, you say it **scoops** the other papers.

scoot (**scooting, scooted**) If you **scoot** somewhere, you go there quickly.

scooter A **scooter** is the same as a motor scooter. ■ A child's **scooter** is a simple small-wheeled cycle which the child stands on and pushes along with one foot.

scope If there is **scope** for a certain kind of behaviour, there is opportunity for it. There is some scope for a reduction in interest rates below present levels. ■ The **scope** of something is the range of things it deals with or includes. The scope of the survey makes it so authoritative.

scorch (**scorches, scorching, scorched**) If something hot **scorches** something else, it burns it slightly and damages it. ■ **Scorching** weather is extremely hot. ■ A **scorched earth policy** is the deliberate burning, destruction, and removal of everything in an area which could be useful to an enemy.

score (**scoring, scored; scorer**) If you **score** in a game, you get a goal, run, or point. The person who gets a goal in a football match is called the **scorer.** ■ The total numbers of goals, runs, or points obtained in a game is called the **score.** You can also talk about someone's **score** in a test or exam. ■ If someone **scores** or keeps the **score** in a game, they record the score obtained by the players. ■ If you **score** a success, you succeed at something. Labour has scored a propaganda point. ■ 20 of something is sometimes called a **score.** ■ The **score** of a film is the music used to accompany it. The written version of any piece of music is also called the **score.** ■ If you say someone **knows the score,** you mean they know all the facts about a situation. ■ If someone gets revenge for something done to them in the past, you can say they **settle a score.** ■ On this **score** means in relation to the thing just mentioned. Japan has responded well to international pressure to open its markets. European complaints on this score have largely ceased. ■ If you **score** a surface with a sharp object, you cut lines into it.

scoreboard The **scoreboard** is a large board which shows the current score in a match or competition.

scorecard A **scorecard** is a printed card which tells you who is playing or taking part in a match or race, and on which you can record the scores.

scoreline The **scoreline** is the score or final result of a match.

scorer See **score.**

scorn is a strong feeling of contempt for someone or something. When someone talks about someone or something with contempt, you can say they **scorn** them or **pour scorn** on them. ■ If you **scorn** something, you reject it because you do not consider it to be good enough.

scornful (**scornfully**) If you are **scornful** of someone or something, you show contempt for them.

scorpion The **scorpion** is a small tropical creature. It has a long tail which bends upwards and has a poisonous sting at its end.

Scot A **Scot** is someone who comes from Scotland. ■ **Scots** is used to talk about people and things in or from Scotland. ...*the Scots climate.* ■ **Scots** is the dialect of English spoken in Scotland.

scotch (**scotches, scotching, scotched**) **Scotch** is an old-fashioned word for 'Scottish'. ■ **Scotch** or **scotch whisky** is whisky made in Scotland. A **scotch** is a glass of scotch. ■ If you **scotch** something like a rumour or plan, you put an end to it.

Scotch egg A **Scotch egg** is a hard-boiled egg which has been covered with sausage meat and breadcrumbs and then fried in oil.

scot-free If you say someone has got off **scot-free**, you mean they have not been punished at all for something they have done.

Scotland Yard is the headquarters of the London Metropolitan Police Force. This police force is itself sometimes called **Scotland Yard** or **the Yard**, especially the department dealing with serious crime.

Scotsman (**Scotswoman**) A **Scotsman** or **Scotswoman** is a person who comes from Scotland.

Scottish (**Scottishness**) **Scottish** is used to talk about people and things in or from Scotland. ...*the Scottish west coast.* ■ The dialect of English spoken in Scotland is sometimes called **Scottish.**

scoundrel You call someone a **scoundrel** when they cheat and deceive people in an unscrupulous way.

scour (**scouring, scoured; scourer**) If you **scour** a place, you make a thorough search of it to try to find something. ■ If you **scour** something like a saucepan, you clean it with a rough pad called a **scourer.**

scourge (*rhymes with 'urge'*) If you call something a **scourge**, you mean it causes a lot of trouble or suffering. *Disease, drugs and crime are the scourges of daily life here.*

scout (**scouting, scouted**) A **Scout** or **Boy Scout** is a member of the Scout Association, which aims to develop the character and responsibility of older boys. ■ A **scout** is a person sent out to discover the position of an enemy army. ■ If you **scout** around for people or things of a certain kind, you try to find them. ■ A **scout** is a talent scout.

scowl If someone **scowls**, they frown, because they are angry or disapprove of something or someone. You call an expression like this a **scowl.**

scrabble (**scrabbling, scrabbled**) If you **scrabble** for something, you move your fingers and hands about, trying to find it or get hold of it. ■ You say people **scrabble** for something when they struggle to obtain it for themselves, often in an undignified way. ■ **Scrabble** is a word game played by putting letter tiles on a special board to make words. 'Scrabble' is a trademark.

scramble (**scrambling, scrambled; scrambler**) If you **scramble** somewhere, especially over rough ground, you move there with difficulty, often using your hands to help you. ■ If you **scramble** for something or are involved in a **scramble** for it, you are one of several people competing for it in an undignified way. ■ If you **scramble** a radio, telephone, or other transmitted message, you interfere with the signal using an electronic device called a **scrambler;** the message can then only be understood by someone with special equipment. ■ When fighter planes **scramble** or are **scrambled,** they take off immediately. ■ A **scramble** is a motorbike rally in which riders race across rough ground. This activity is called **scrambling.**

scrambled egg is a dish made of eggs beaten up with milk and then cooked for a short time in a little butter while stirring.

scrap (**scrapping, scrapped**) A **scrap** of something is a very small amount of it. ■ **Scraps** are pieces of unwanted food which are thrown away or given to animals. ■ If something is **scrapped,** it is got rid of or cancelled, because it is no longer needed. ■ **Scrap** or **scrap metal** is metal from old machinery or vehicles which is reprocessed so it can be used again. ■ If you say something is heading for the **scrap heap** or **scrapheap,** you mean it is no longer required, because it is no longer suitable or useful. ■ If people **scrap** or have a **scrap,** they have a quarrel or fight.

scrapbook A **scrapbook** is a book with blank pages in which people stick things such as pictures or newspaper cuttings.

scrape (**scraping, scraped**) If you **scrape** something from a surface or **scrape** it **off,** you remove it by rubbing something sharp against it. ■ If something **scrapes** against something else, it rubs against it, damaging it or making a harsh noise. ■ If you **scrape a living,** you make just enough money to survive. ■ If you **scrape** something **together,** you manage to arrange or complete it with difficulty. ■ If you **scrape through** in something like an exam, you just manage to pass. ■ If you are in a **scrape,** you are in a difficult situation which you have caused yourself.

scrapheap See **scrap.**

scrappy (**scrappier, scrappiest**) If you say something is **scrappy,** you mean it is uneven, untidy, and not well organized.

scrapyard A **scrapyard** is a place where scrap, especially from old vehicles, is collected and often reprocessed.

scratch (**scratches, scratching, scratched**) If you **scratch** something, you make a small mark or cut on it with a sharp object. The mark or cut is called a **scratch.** ■ If you **scratch** yourself, you scrape your fingernails over your skin because it is itching. ■ If you **scratch around** for something you need, you try hard to find it. ■ **Scratch** is used to describe things which are put together in a hurry. ...*a scratch supper.* ■ If you do something **from scratch,** you do it without using anything that has been done before. *It uses less energy to melt old glass than to make* *new glass from scratch.* ■ If you say something is **not up to scratch,** you mean it is not good enough.

scratchard A **scratchcard** is a ticket in a competition that has a surface you scratch off to see whether you have won anything.

scratchy If something sounds **scratchy,** it sounds like an old poorly-recorded record. ■ If you say someone is **scratchy,** you mean they are irritable.

scrawl If you **scrawl** something, you write it in a careless untidy way. Writing like this can be called a **scrawl.**

scrawny (scrawnier, scrawniest) A **scrawny** person is thin and bony.

scream (screaming, screamed) If someone **screams** or lets out a **scream,** they make a loud piercing sound. ■ If someone shouts something in a high-pitched voice, you can say they **scream** it. ■ When something like a machine makes a loud high-pitched noise, you can say it **screams.**

scree is a mass of loose stones on the side of a mountain or lying at its foot.

screech (screeches, screeching, screeched) If someone or something **screeches** or gives a **screech,** they make a loud high-pitched sound.

screen (screening, screened) The **screen** of a TV set or computer is the flat vertical surface on which you see the display or picture. ■ In a cinema, the **screen** is the surface on which films are shown. ■ **Screen** is used to talk about films or the film industry. *...a screen actress.* ■ When a programme or a film is **screened** or given a **screening,** it is shown on TV or at the cinema. ■ A **screen** is a movable vertical panel used to divide a room into smaller areas, or to hide something. ■ If you are **screened** from something harmful, something else is in the way and prevents it reaching you. ■ When people are **screened** for a medical condition, they are examined to make sure they do not have it. ■ When an organization **screens** people, they investigate them to make sure they are suitable for a particular position or task. ■ See also **small screen.**

screenplay The **screenplay** of a film is the script.

screen-printing is the same as silk-screen printing.

screenwriter (screenwriting) A **screenwriter** is a person who writes screenplays.

screw A **screw** is a small sharp piece of metal with a spiral groove, used to fix one thing firmly to another. If an object is **screwed** somewhere, it is fixed there by a screw. ■ If you **screw** something onto something else, you fix it there by twisting it round and round. ■ You can say someone has been **screwed** when someone else cheats them or takes advantage of them. ■ If you **screw** something **up,** you twist it or squeeze it so it no longer has its proper shape. *She screws up her face in concentration.* ■ If someone **screws** something **up,** they make it go badly wrong. ■ If you **screw up** the courage to do something, you force yourself to do it.

screwball comedy is zany and eccentric.

screwdriver A **screwdriver** is a tool for fixing screws into place.

scribble (scribbling, scribbled; scribbler) If you **scribble** something, you write it quickly and untidily. Something written like this can be called a

scribble. ■ Writers are sometimes called **scribblers** and their work is referred to as their **scribblings.**

scribe In the past, a **scribe** was a person who made copies of books or documents by hand. ■ Authors and journalists are sometimes called **scribes.**

scrimp If you **scrimp,** you spend as little money as possible.

script (scripted) The **script** for a film, play, or TV programme is the written version of it. If a writer **scripts** a film or TV programme, he or she writes the script. ■ A **scripted** speech or lecture has been written in advance. ■ **Script** is used to talk about different systems of writing. *...Latin script.*

scripture (scriptural) The sacred writings of a religion are called its **scriptures.** ■ When Christians talk about **Scripture** or the **Scriptures,** they mean the Bible. **Scriptural** means things connected with the Bible. *...scriptural arguments.*

scriptwriter A **scriptwriter** is a person who writes scripts for films, radio, or TV.

scroll A **scroll** is a long roll of paper, parchment, or other material with writing on it. ■ A **scroll** is a painted or carved decoration made to look like a scroll. ■ If you **scroll** through text on a computer screen, you move the text up or down to find the information you need.

Scrooge If you call someone a **Scrooge,** you mean they are very mean with their money.

scrotum A man's **scrotum** is the bag of skin which contains his testicles.

scrounge (scrounging, scrounged; scrounger) If you **scrounge** something, you ask people for it, rather than buying it or earning it. People who regularly scrounge things are called **scroungers.**

scrub (scrubbing, scrubbed) If you **scrub** something or give it a **scrub,** you rub it hard with water and a stiff brush to clean it. ■ If you **scrub** dirt off something, you remove it by rubbing hard. ■ If you **scrub** something you were thinking of doing, you cancel it. ■ **Scrub** is stunted trees and bushes in a very dry area. An area like this can be called **scrub** or **scrubland.**

scruff The **scruff** of an animal's neck is the loose skin at the back. ■ If you take something **by the scruff of its neck,** you deal with it directly and forcefully. *He took this club by the scruff of the neck and made them Championship winners.*

scruffy (scruffier, scruffiest) **Scruffy** people or things are untidy and dirty.

scrum In rugby, a **scrum** is a formation in which players from both sides form a tight group and push against each other with their heads down to try to get the ball. ■ Any tightly packed crowd of people can be called a **scrum.**

scrum-half (scrum-halves) In rugby, the **scrum-half** is the player who puts the ball into a scrum.

scrummage (scrummaging) A **scrummage** is the same as a scrum. Taking part in a scrum is called **scrummaging.**

scrumptious If you say food is **scrumptious,** you mean it is delicious.

scrunch (scrunches, scrunching, scrunched) If something **scrunches,** it makes a loud sound as it is crushed or as it crushes something else. *The sand* on the floor scrunched under our feet. ■ If you **scrunch** something or **scrunch** it up, you squeeze, bend, or crush it into a smaller shape.

scruple – **Scruples** are moral principles which make people unwilling to do something which seems wrong.

scrupulous (**scrupulously**) A **scrupulous** person takes great care to do what is fair, honest, and morally correct. ■ **Scrupulous** means thorough, exact, and careful about details. *The little house was scrupulously clean.*

scrutineer A **scrutineer** is an official who checks that something meets a required standard or rule.

scrutinize (*or* scrutinise) (**scrutinizing, scrutinized**) If you **scrutinize** something, you examine it very carefully.

scrutiny If something comes under **scrutiny,** it is being observed or examined very carefully.

scuba diving is swimming underwater using cylinders containing compressed air which are strapped to the swimmer's back and attached to a face mask. Scuba stands for 'self-contained underwater breathing apparatus'.

scud (**scudding, scudded**) If clouds **scud** along, they move quickly across the sky.

scuff If you **scuff** something, you mark the surface by scraping or rubbing it. *...scuffed brown shoes.* ■ If you **scuff** your feet, you drag them along the ground as you walk.

scuffle (**scuffling, scuffled**) A **scuffle** is a short, disorganized fight. When people fight like this you say they **scuffle.**

scull (**sculling**) A **scull** is a light rowing boat, which is moved through the water using two short oars, called **sculls.** Rowing in boats like these is called **sculling.**

scullery (**sculleries**) A **scullery** is a small room next to a kitchen where jobs such as washing up or vegetable preparation are done.

sculpt If you **sculpt** something, you carve it out of a material such as stone, marble, or wood.

sculptor (**sculptress, sculptresses**) A **sculptor** is a person who makes sculptures. You can refer to a female sculptor as a **sculptress,** although most prefer to be called 'sculptors'.

sculpture (**sculptured, sculptural**) A **sculpture** is a work of art created by carving or shaping stone, wood, clay, or some other material. **Sculptured** objects have been carved or shaped like this. **Sculpture** is the art of creating sculptures. **Sculptural** means relating to sculpture.

scum is a layer of an unpleasant-looking substance on the surface of a liquid. ■ If someone refers to people as **scum,** they are expressing their feelings of strong dislike and disgust for them.

scupper (**scuppering, scuppered**) If someone **scuppers** a plan or an attempt, they do something which completely ruins it.

scurrilous accusations or stories are untrue or unfair, and are likely to damage someone's reputation.

scurry (**scurries, scurrying, scurried**) If a person or small animal **scurries** somewhere, they run there very quickly.

scurvy is a disease caused by a lack of Vitamin C.

scuttle (**scuttling, scuttled**) If a person or animal **scuttles** somewhere, they run there with short quick steps. ■ When a ship is **scuttled,** it is deliberately sunk. ■ If a plan or proposal is **scuttled,** something prevents it continuing or succeeding.

scythe A **scythe** is a tool with a long handle and a long curved blade for cutting grass or grain.

SDLP The **SDLP** or **Social Democrat and Labour Party** is a political party formed in Northern Ireland in 1970. Its supporters are mainly Catholic. It aims to unite Ireland by peaceful and democratic means.

sea The **sea** is the area of salty water which covers most of the earth's surface. ■ A **sea** is a large area of salty water which is part of an ocean or is surrounded by land. *...the Irish Sea.* ■ You use **seas** when you are describing the sea at a particular time or in a particular area. *The seas were fairly rough.* ■ **At sea** means on or under the sea. **On the high seas** means on a part of the sea which is beyond the control of any country. ■ A **sea** of people or things is a large number of them. ■ A large area of something can be called a **sea.** ■ If you say someone is **at sea** or **all at sea,** you mean they are confused.

sea anemone A **sea anemone** is a sea animal which lives fixed to a rock. It has tentacles which trap food.

sea bird (*or* seabird) **Sea birds** are birds which live on or near the sea and get their food from it.

seaboard The **seaboard** of a country is the part which borders the sea.

seaborne actions or events take place on the sea in ships.

sea breeze A **sea breeze** is a light wind blowing from the sea.

sea-change A **sea-change** in someone's attitudes or behaviour is a complete change.

seafarer (**seafaring**) **Seafarers** are people who work on ships or who travel regularly on the sea. **Seafaring** means working or travelling like this.

seafood consists of various types of sea creatures which you can eat, especially shellfish.

seafront (*or* sea front) The **seafront** of a seaside town is the part next to the sea.

sea-going (*or* seagoing) boats and ships are designed for travelling on the sea.

seagull A **seagull** is the same as a gull.

seahorse The **seahorse** is a small fish with a head which looks like a horse's head.

seal (**sealing, sealed**) When a place is **sealed** or **sealed off,** all the entrances are blocked and nobody can get in or out. ■ If you **seal** something, you close or fasten it in some way, often to make it airtight or watertight. ■ A **seal** is (a) a substance or device for closing an opening tightly. (b) a substance or device fixed to the opening of something like a container or letter, which must be broken to get at the contents. ■ If you **seal** an envelope, you stick down the flap. ■ If you **seal** a victory or **put the seal** on it, you make it complete. *He sealed his 5-1 victory with a break of 104.* ■ If a person in authority **seals** an important document, they put an official mark on it called a **seal,** to show it is genuine. ■ When people in authority officially authorize something or show they approve of it, you can say they give it their **seal of approval**. ■ **Seals** are large mammals with flippers. They eat fish and live partly on land and partly in the sea.

sealant A **sealant** is a substance used to fill in or cover a gap of some kind, usually to make it waterproof.

sea level is the height of the sea's surface.

sea lion – Sea lions are large seals from the north Pacific.

sealskin is the skin or fur of a seal.

seam A **seam** is a straight line of stitching joining two pieces of material together. ■ A **seam** is a long narrow underground layer of a mineral such as coal. ■ When there is something useful which can continue to be exploited, you can say there is a **rich seam** of it. *...a rich seam of talent.*

seaman (seamen) A **seaman** is a sailor, especially one who is not an officer.

seamanship is the skill of being able to navigate, look after, and handle a vessel at sea.

seamless (seamlessly) A **seamless** piece of clothing has no seams. ■ You call the way something is done or presented **seamless** when you cannot see where the different parts join together. *Archive footage of the actual disaster was seamlessly woven into the film.*

seamstress (seamstresses) In the past, a **seamstress** was a woman whose job was sewing and making clothes.

seamy (seamier, seamiest) You say something is **seamy** when it involves things like crime, pornography, or violence.

séance (*or* seance) (*pron:* **say**-anss) A **séance** is an occasion when a group of people attempt to communicate with the dead, usually through a person called a medium.

seaplane A **seaplane** is a type of plane which is able to land and take off on water.

seaport A **seaport** is a town or city with docks or a large harbour.

sear (searing, seared; searingly) If you say someone has been **seared** by a bad experience, you mean it has had a lasting harmful effect on them. ■ **Searing** is used to describe intense heat, or other things which are very intense. *...searing determination.* ■ A **searing** piece of writing or speech uses forceful language and is very critical.

search (searches, searching, searched; searcher) If you **search** for someone or something or **go in search** of them, you try to find them. People who are looking for someone or something can be called **searchers.** If you **search** a place or make a **search** of it, you examine it in the hope of finding someone or something. ■ If someone in authority **searches** you, they examine your clothing for hidden objects. ■ **Searching** questions are likely to reveal important or interesting information, especially when people do not wish to reveal it.

search engine A **search engine** is a service on the Internet that helps you to find the information you want.

searchlight A **searchlight** is a light with a large powerful beam which can be turned to shine a long way in any direction.

search party A **search party** is a group of people taking part in an organized search for someone.

search warrant A **search warrant** is an official document which entitles the police to enter a building to search for things connected with criminal activities, for example stolen goods.

seascape A **seascape** is the scenery of the sea, or a painting of it.

seashell A **seashell** is the empty shell of a small sea creature.

seashore The **seashore** is sand, shingle, or rocks next to the sea.

seasick (seasickness) If someone in a boat is **seasick,** they feel nauseous because of the boat's movements, and may vomit.

seaside The **seaside** is parts of the land next to the sea, especially parts where people spend their holidays.

season (seasoning, seasoned) The **seasons** are spring, summer, autumn, and winter, the four periods into which the year is divided. ■ A **season** is a period of the year when a particular activity takes place. *...the tourist season.* ■ If shellfish, fruit, or vegetables are **in season,** it is the time of the year when they are naturally available. ■ If fish or game are **in season,** it is the time when you are officially allowed to hunt or catch them. ■ If you visit a resort **out of season,** you go outside the usual holiday period. ■ A **season** of films, plays, or concerts is a series of them with something in common. *...a Mozart season.* ■ If you **season** food, you add salt, pepper, or spices to it, to give it extra flavour. Things added to food like this are called **seasoning.** ■ See also **seasoned.**

seasonal (seasonally) Seasonal means connected with a particular season or time of the year. *Seasonal variations need to be taken into account.*

Seasonal Affective Disorder See **SAD.**

seasoned is used to describe people who have had a lot of experience of something. *Dayton was a seasoned traveller.*

season ticket A **season ticket** is a ticket which you can use as many times as you like over a certain period, for example a ticket to a football ground or one for use on public transport.

seat (seating, seated) A **seat** is an object made for people to sit on. ■ The part of a chair you sit on is called the **seat.** ■ If you are **seated** somewhere, you are sitting there. ■ If a building or vehicle **seats** a certain number of people, it has seats for that number. You can also say a building has **seating** for a certain number of people. ■ If someone wins a **seat** in parliament, they are elected as the MP for a particular constituency. Similarly, someone can have a **seat** on a council or committee. ■ The **seat** of an organization is the place where it has its base. ■ The **seat** of a pair of trousers is the part which covers your bottom.

seat belt A **seat belt** is a safety strap you fasten around your body in a vehicle or plane.

-seater is used to say how many people something like a vehicle or stadium can hold. ...*a new 105-seater twin-engined jet.*

sea urchin The **sea urchin** is a small sea animal with a round hard spiny shell.

sea wall A **sea wall** is a defence like an embankment built against the sea, for example to stop it eroding the land.

seaweed is any of various plants which grow in the sea.

seaworthy If a boat or ship is **seaworthy,** it is in a fit state to travel on the sea.

secateurs (pron: sek-at-**turz**) are a gardening tool like a pair of scissors with short powerful blades, used for cutting flowers and pruning.

secede (pron: siss-**seed**) (**seceding, seceded; secession**) If a region **secedes** from a country, it breaks away and becomes an independent country. Similarly, a group of people can **secede** from an organization.

secessionist (**secessionism**) People who want their region to secede from a country are called **secessionists;** their aims or policies are called **secessionism.**

secluded (**seclusion**) A **secluded** place is quiet, private, and undisturbed. You talk about the **seclusion** of a place like this. ■ If someone is **in seclusion,** they are living apart from other people.

second (**seconding, seconded; secondly, seconder**) A **second** is one of the sixty parts a minute is divided into. ■ The **second** item in a series is the one you count as number 2. ...*the second week in January.* ■ If you have **second thoughts** about a decision you have made, you begin to have doubts about it. ■ **Seconds** are goods sold cheaply because they are slightly imperfect. ■ If you **second** a proposal or motion in a meeting, you indicate formally that you support it. You are called the **seconder** of the proposal or motion. ■ A boxer's **seconds** are people who assist him before and after a match and in between rounds. ■ If you are **seconded** (pron: si-**kond**-id) somewhere, you are sent to work there temporarily. ■ **second nature:** see **nature. second wind:** see **wind.**

secondary (**secondarily**) **Secondary** is used to describe things which are less important than something else in a particular situation. *Women's work was always seen as secondary to that of men.* ■ **Secondary** education is for pupils from the age of 11 until they leave school. ■ **Secondary** is used to describe things which come after something else, or which result or develop from something which has already happened. *The secondary effects on the miners' health are considerable.*

secondary modern In the past, a **secondary modern** school was a school for pupils aged over 11 which concentrated on teaching more practical skills than grammar schools.

secondary school A **secondary school** is a school for pupils aged 11 to 18.

second-class If people are treated as **second-class** citizens, they are not given the same rights as other people. You can also say things provided for them are **second-class.** ...*a second-class education.*

■ If you travel **second-class,** you use standard accommodation rather than first-class. ■ If you send a letter **second class,** it costs less than first-class mail and may take longer to get to its destination.

second cousin Your **second cousins** are the children of your parents' cousins.

seconder See **second.**

second-guess If you try to **second-guess** something, you try to anticipate what someone will say or do or what will happen.

second-hand (or **secondhand**) A **second-hand** object has already been owned by someone else. ■ A **second-hand** shop sells second-hand goods. ■ If you experience something or find out about it **second-hand,** you experience it indirectly, as a result of hearing or reading about it.

second language Someone's **second language** is a language which is not their own language but which they use for certain purposes, for example for work or school.

secondment (pron: sik-**kond**-ment) If someone is on **secondment,** they have been sent somewhere temporarily to do a job.

second person If you make a statement in **the second person,** you make it about the person or people you are talking to, using 'you'.

second-rate If you call someone or something **second-rate,** you mean they are of poor quality or ability.

second string If you describe a person or thing as someone's **second string,** you mean that they are a substitute and only used if someone or something else is not available. ...*her second-string horse.*

secrecy is keeping things secret.

secret (**secretly**) If something is **secret** or a **secret,** only a few people know about it and they are careful not to tell anyone else. You can also say something is done **in secret.** ■ **Secret** is used to describe people who have opinions or take part in activities which they do not tell anyone else about. ...*a secret anarchist.* ■ The **secret** of achieving something is what you need to do to achieve it. *Staying one jump ahead of the pack is the secret of successful property-buying.* ■ A **secret** is a mystery which has never been explained.

secret agent A **secret agent** is a person employed to discover the secrets of governments or organizations.

secretarial See **secretary.**

secretariat A **secretariat** is a department responsible for the administration of an international organization.

secretary (**secretaries; secretarial**) A **secretary** is someone whose job is to type letters, answer phone calls, and carry out other office work. **Secretarial** means connected with this work and the people who do it. ...*secretarial staff.* ■ **Secretary** is used in the titles of government ministers and officials who are in charge of main government departments. ...*the United States Treasury Secretary.* ■ The **secretary** of a club or other organization is the person whose job is to keep records and write letters.

Secretary General (Secretaries General) The **Sec-retary General** of an international political organization is the person in charge of its administration.

Secretary of State (Secretaries of State) In Britain, a **Secretary of State** is a senior government minister who is usually also a cabinet minister. ■ In the US, the **Secretary of State** is the foreign minister.

secrete (secreting, secreted) If part of an animal or plant **secretes** a fluid, it produces it. *The sweat glands secrete water.* Producing fluids like this is called **secretion**; a **secretion** is a substance which has been secreted. ■ If you **secrete** something somewhere, you hide it there.

secretive (secretiveness) A **secretive** person tries to keep their feelings, intentions, or actions hidden from other people.

secret police In some non-democratic countries, the **secret police** is a police force which operates secretly against people opposed to the government.

secret service A country's **secret service** is a government department responsible for espionage and counter-espionage. ■ In the US, the **Secret Service** is a government agency responsible for protecting the President and certain other police activities.

sect A **sect** is a religious group which has broken away from a larger group and has its own beliefs and practices.

sectarian means connected with the differences between sects. In Northern Ireland, **sectarian** is used to talk about things based on the differences between the Protestant and Roman Catholic communities. *...sectarian killings.*

sectarianism is strong, often narrow-minded support for a sect or faction.

section A **section** of something is one of the parts it can be divided into or which it is formed from. *...a vast percussion section.* ■ A **section** of an official document is one of the parts it is divided into. ■ A **section** is a cross-section.

sectional interests are the interests of a particular group within a country or community.

sector (sectoral) A **sector** of something is a part of it, for example part of a country's economy. *...the service sector.* **Sectoral** means to do with a sector or sectors. *...sectoral strikes.* See also **private sector, public sector.** ■ A **sector** is one of the areas a place is divided into, often for military reasons. ■ A **sector** of a circle is one of the two parts you divide it into when you draw two straight lines from its centre to its edge.

secular is used to describe things which are not based on religion. *...a secular state.*

secularise See secularize.

secularism (secularist) **Secularism** is the belief that religion should not have any influence on such things as a country's political or educational system. A **secularist** is someone who believes this.

secularize (or secularise) (secularizing, secularized; secularization) If something is **secularized,** it is changed so that it no longer has any religious connection.

secure (securing, secured; securely) If you **secure** something, you obtain it. *They secured 80 seats in the first round.* ■ You say something is **secure** when it can be relied on to continue. *...secure jobs.* If you **secure** something, you make it secure. *Cheap labour alone will not secure Indonesia's economic future.* ■ If you feel **secure,** you feel safe because you have nothing to worry about. ■ When a place is **secured** or made **secure,** it is made safe so that it is very difficult to get in or out. *...a secure prison.* ■ If you **secure** one thing to another, you fix or fasten it firmly. You then say it is **secure.** ■ If you **secure** a loan, you promise to give something valuable to the lender if you are not able to repay it.

security (securities) **Security** is the measures and precautions taken to protect someone or something. *Strict security measures are in place.* ■ If you say someone or something is a **security risk,** you mean they may be a threat to the safety of a country or organization. ■ **Security** is a situation in which you feel safe and do not need to worry about the future. *...the security of a happy home life.* ■ A **security** is something valuable you promise to give someone if you fail to repay a loan. ■ **Securities** are shares, stocks, or bonds, or certificates showing that you own them. ■ See also **social security.**

Security Council The **Security Council** is a permanent body of the United Nations whose purpose is to maintain world peace. It is made up of five permanent and ten elected member countries.

sedan In the US, a saloon car is called a **sedan.**

sedan chair In the 17th and 18th centuries, a **sedan chair** was an enclosed chair for one person which was carried on poles by two men.

sedate (sedately; sedating, sedated; sedation, sedative) If you go somewhere at a **sedate** pace, you do not hurry. ■ A **sedate** person is calm, serene, and dignified. ■ If a person or animal is **sedated,** they are given a drug called a **sedative** to calm them or make them sleep. When someone has been given a sedative, you say they are under **sedation.**

sedentary A **sedentary** occupation or way of life involves a lot of sitting down and not much exercise.

sediment is small grains of solid material which settle at the bottom of a liquid.

sedimentary rocks are rocks such as sandstone and limestone which are formed when layers of mud, sand, or shells, which were once underwater, become compressed.

sedition (seditious) If someone is charged with **sedition,** they are charged with encouraging people to rebel against the government. The things they have written or said are described as **seditious.**

seduce (seducing, seduced; seduction, seducer; seductress, seductresses) If someone **seduces** another person, they persuade them to have sex with them. Seducing someone is called **seduction.** A person who does it is called a **seducer;** a woman who seduces someone can be called a **seductress.** ■ If you are **seduced** into doing something, someone persuades you to do it, by making it seem very attractive.

seductive (**seductively**) A **seductive** person is sexually attractive. You can also call someone's behaviour **seductive**. ■ You can say something like an idea or offer is **seductive** when it is tempting and attractive.

seductress See seduce.

see (**seeing, saw, have seen**) If you **see** something, you are looking at it or you notice it. ■ If you **see** someone, you visit them or meet them. ■ If you **see** someone **off,** you go with them to the place where they are catching a train, plane, or ship, and say goodbye to them there. ■ You can say you **see** something when you understand it or realize it exists. *I see what you mean... I saw there was a gap in the market.* ■ If you **see** a situation or someone's behaviour in a certain way, you have the opinion that it is really like that. *Others saw it as a betrayal.* ■ If you **see to** something, you deal with it. *While Frank saw to the luggage, Sara took Eleanor home.* ■ If you **see off** a challenge or threat, you successfully defeat the person who challenged or threatened you. ■ If you say you will **see if** you can do something, you mean you will try to do it. ■ If you **see to it** that something is done, you make sure it is done. ■ If you **see about** something, you try to arrange it or sort it out. *I went to the local employment bureau to see about a job.* ■ If you **see** something **through,** you make sure it is completed. ■ If you **see** if something is true, you try to find out about it. *The Highway Patrol routinely tests the exhausts of lorries to see if they are too smoky.* ■ If you say a period of time **sees** something happening, you mean it happens during that time. *The last year has seen a spate of neighbourhood watch schemes spring up.* ■ If you **see** something happening in the future, you expect it or predict it. ■ If you **see through** someone, you realize what their intentions are, even though they are trying to hide them. ■ **Seeing that** or **seeing as** is used to mention the reason for something. *Few people bother to put any effort into their work, seeing that it is so poorly rewarded.* ■ A bishop's **see** is the city where his cathedral or diocese is.

seed (**seeding, seeded**) A **seed** is the fertilized grain of a plant, from which a new plant can grow. *...a packet of cabbage seed.* ■ The **seeds** of something are its origins or beginnings. *The agreement to talk contains the seeds of a more serious problem still.* ■ In some sports tournaments, the best players or teams are **seeded,** which means they are ranked according to their playing ability to avoid them playing each other in the early stages of the competition. These players are called **seeds.**

seed-bed (*or* **seedbed**) If you say a situation is a **seed-bed** for something like a political movement, you mean it provides a good opportunity for it to develop.

seedling A **seedling** is a young plant grown from a seed.

seed money or **seed capital** is money provided for setting up some kind of enterprise.

seedy (**seediness**) A **seedy** place or person is shabby, untidy, and unpleasant.

seek (**seeking, sought**) If you **seek** something, you try to obtain it. *France is expected to seek support for its demands.* ■ If you are **seeking** to achieve something, you are trying to achieve it.

-seeker is added to words to describe people who are looking for something or trying to obtain something. *...sun-seekers. ...peace-seekers.*

seem If you say something **seems** to be the case, you mean you get the impression that it is the case. *Sanctions, it seemed, had failed... He seemed like a nice bloke.* ■ If you say you cannot **seem** to do something, you mean you have tried doing it without success.

seeming (**seemingly**) **Seeming** is used to say something appears to exist or be true. *...his seeming astonishment. ...a seemingly impossible task.*

seemly behaviour or dress is considered appropriate in the particular circumstances. *She felt it would not be seemly for her to attend the wedding.*

seen See see.

seep (**seeping, seeped**) If a liquid or gas **seeps** into or out of something, it slowly leaks in or out. ■ If news or information **seeps** out of a place, it comes out slowly, a bit at a time. ■ If someone's power or confidence **seeps** away, it slowly disappears.

seepage When a liquid or gas slowly leaks out of something, you can say there is a **seepage.** ■ When small quantities of something are gradually and secretly transferred from one place to another, you can say there is a **seepage** of those things.

seer People who make predictions about what will happen in the future are sometimes called **seers.**

see-saw (*or* **seesaw**) (**see-sawing, see-sawed**) A **seesaw** is a long board for children to play on with a seat at each end. It pivots on a fixed part in the middle. ■ If you talk about something **see-sawing** from one opposite state to another, you mean it keeps changing between the two states. *Over the last two months the crisis has see-sawed between hopes of peace and fears of war.*

seethe (**seething, seethed**) If someone is **seething** with anger, they are very angry indeed. ■ If a place is **seething** with people, there are a lot of them there moving around constantly.

see-through materials or objects are transparent.

segment (**segmentation**) A **segment** of something is a part which can be considered separately from the rest. *Three-to-five day cruises are the fastest-growing segment of the market.* If something is **segmented,** it is divided into segments. ■ A **segment** of a fruit like an orange is one of the sections it is easily divided into. ■ A **segment** of a circle is one of the two parts you divide it into when you draw a straight line across it, cutting the edge at two points.

segregate (**segregating, segregated; segregation, segregationist**) If people are **segregated,** they are kept apart. ■ **Segregated** is used to describe systems or places where people are kept apart because of their race. *...a segregated night club.* People who are in favour of segregation are called **segregationists.**

segue (*pron:* **seg**-way) (**segues, segueing, segued**) If one piece of music **segues** into another, it changes into the other or is followed by it without a break. This change is called a **segue.**

seismic (*pron:* **size**-mik) means to do with earthquakes. *...seismic activity.*

seismograph A **seismograph** is an instrument which registers and records the strength of earthquakes or large explosions.

seismology (**seismologist**) Seismology is the scientific study of earthquakes. A **seismologist** is a person who studies seismology.

seismometer A **seismometer** is an instrument similar to a seismograph.

seize (**seizing, seized; seizure**) If you **seize** someone or something, you take hold of them quickly and firmly. ■ You say someone is **seized** when they are captured or arrested. Similarly, illegal drugs or weapons can be **seized** by the police. You can talk about a **seizure** of drugs or weapons. ■ When people **seize** a place or **seize** control of it, they take control of it quickly and suddenly. *...the seizure of Kuwait.* ■ If you **seize** an opportunity, you quickly take advantage of it. ■ If you **seize on** something, you make use of it for your own purposes. *The international press also siezed on the story.* ■ If you are **seized** by an emotion, you feel it strongly. ■ If an engine **seizes up,** it stops working. Similarly, a system can **seize up.** ■ A **seizure** is a sudden violent attack of illness, especially a stroke or epileptic fit.

seldom If something **seldom** happens, it hardly ever happens.

select (**selection**) If you **select** a person or thing, you choose them. A **selection** of people or things is a group of them chosen from among others. *Paul McCartney played a selection of Beatles songs.* ■ A **select** group of people or things is a small one of special merit or quality. ■ A **select committee** is a small committee of MPs or lords set up to investigate a topic.

selective (**selectively, selectivity**) A **selective** process is one in which some people or things are carefully chosen in preference to others. *I am selective about what I eat. ...a move towards selectivity.*

selector The **selectors** are the people who choose the members of a sports team for a particular match.

self (**selves**) Your **self** is your basic personality or nature. *Lara has shown his true self in the past two matches.*

self- is used at the beginning of a word to describe something a person does to himself or herself. *...self-destructive behaviour such as suicide. ...self-help organizations.*

self-appointed If you call someone a **self-appointed** leader, you mean they have taken on their position of leader without anyone asking them to do it. You can also talk about someone doing a **self-appointed** task.

self-assertion (**self-assertive**) Self-assertion is putting forward your opinions or demanding your rights boldly and confidently.

self-assured (**self-assurance**) Self-assured people show confidence in their own abilities.

self-centred people think only about themselves and their own desires and needs.

self-confessed is used to describe someone who openly admits to being something, or to having done something. *...a self-confessed railway fanatic.*

self-confident (**self-confidence**) Self-confident people behave confidently because they feel sure of their own abilities.

self-conscious (**self-consciously, self-consciousness**) A **self-conscious** person is shy and easily embarrassed, and feels everyone is looking at them and judging them. ■ You can describe someone or something as **self-conscious** when they are strongly aware of who they are or what they are doing. *...the self-conscious artiness of his character.*

self-contained accommodation, for example a flat, has all its own facilities, including a bathroom and kitchen. ■ If you say something is **self-contained,** you mean it is complete and separate and needs no help from outside. *...a formidable self-contained fighting force.* ■ A **self-contained** person does not need the company of other people.

self-control If you exercise **self-control,** you control your emotions and keep calm, even though you are angry or afraid.

self-declared means the same as 'self-proclaimed'.

self-defeating If you say a plan or course of action is **self-defeating,** you mean it is bound to fail, because it would spoil its own chances of success.

self-defence (*Am:* **self-defense**) is using violence or special physical skills to protect yourself when attacked by another person. ■ If someone says or writes something **in self-defence,** they do it in response to criticism, to try to justify their actions.

self-denial If you practise **self-denial,** you do not allow yourself to have things you like or do things you enjoy.

self-deprecating (**self-deprecation**) Self-deprecating people make jokes about their own faults.

self-determination is people's right to choose whether their country should be independent or be part of another country.

self-discipline (**self-disciplined**) See **discipline.**

self-drive cars are cars which people hire to drive themselves, as opposed to cars hired with a driver.

self-effacing people are modest and do not draw attention to themselves or their achievements.

self-employed (**self-employment**) A **self-employed** person is their own boss and organizes their own work, pay, tax, and national insurance payments.

self-esteem If you have **self-esteem,** you have a good opinion of yourself and believe you deserve to be respected.

self-evident (**self-evidently**) If you say something is **self-evident,** you mean it is so obvious it does not need to be proved or explained.

self-explanatory If you say something is **self-explanatory,** you mean it is clear and easy to understand and does not require an explanation.

self-expression is expressing your personality and feelings through a creative activity such as painting.

self-financing If something is **self-financing,** it provides enough money to pay its own costs and needs no outside financial support.

self-governing (**self-government**) A **self-governing** area is administered by its own people, rather than by another country or central authority. *...the right to self-government.* Similarly, a **self-governing** organization is run by its own members.

self-important (**self-importance**) If you call someone **self-important,** you mean they have an exaggerated idea of their own importance. You can also say they are full of **self-importance.**

self-imposed If something someone does is **self-imposed,** it was their own idea to do it and it was not forced on them by someone else.

self-indulgent (**self-indulgently,** **self-indulgence**) If you are **self-indulgent,** you are too ready to let yourself do things you enjoy. This is called **self-indulgence.**

self-inflicted When people injure themselves deliberately, you say their injuries are **self-inflicted.**

self-interest (**self-interested**) **Self-interest** is showing concern only for what benefits you. You say people who behave like this are **self-interested.**

selfish (**selfishly, selfishness**) **Selfish** people are only concerned about their own needs, and do not consider other people.

selfless (**selflessly, selfishness**) A **selfless** person considers other people's needs rather than their own.

self-made people become successful and rich through their own efforts.

self-perpetuating If you say something is **self-perpetuating,** you mean it is organized or structured in such a way that it will continue indefinitely.

self-pity (**self-pitying**) **Self-pity** is feeling sorry for yourself.

self-portrait A **self-portrait** is a portrait of an artist painted by himself or herself. A person's written description of himself or herself can also be called a **self-portrait.**

self-possessed (**self-possession**) A **self-possessed** person is calm, confident, and in control of their emotions. You talk about the **self-possession** of someone like this.

self-preservation is making sure you are not harmed in a dangerous situation.

self-proclaimed is used to say someone has adopted a name or title without getting anyone else's agreement to it. *...the self-proclaimed provisional government.*

self-raising flour contains baking powder to make cakes rise.

self-regulation (**self-regulatory**) **Self-regulation** is making sure yourself that certain standards are met in what you do, rather than having someone else do it for you. A system which allows people to do this is called a **self-regulatory** system.

self-reliant (**self-reliance**) **Self-reliant** people and organizations are able to look after themselves. *...activities designed to develop youngsters' self-reliance.*

self-respect (**self-respecting**) **Self-respect** is a feeling of pride in your own abilities and worth. You say people who have this feeling are **self-respecting.**

self-restraint If you show **self-restraint,** you manage to control your feelings or desires.

self-righteous (**self-righteously,** **self-righteousness**) You call someone's behaviour **self-righteous** when they are much too confident that what they are doing is morally right.

self-rule is the same as self-government.

self-sacrifice is sacrificing yourself or something important to you, to help other people.

self-same means the same one or ones you have just mentioned. *In the USA and England, political parties are calling for a return to traditional methods, while in France the government wants to move away from these self-same traditions.*

self-satisfied (**self-satisfaction**) You call people **self-satisfied** when you think they are much too pleased with themselves and with what they have achieved.

self-seeking You say people are **self-seeking** when they are only interested in doing things which serve their own interests.

self-service restaurants, petrol stations, etc are ones where you serve yourself rather than being served by someone else.

self-serving people do a certain kind of work only because it serves their own interests.

self-styled names or descriptions are ones which people have chosen for themselves.

self-sufficient (**self-sufficiency**) A **self-sufficient** person does not need other people's help or company. Similarly, a **self-sufficient** country is not dependent on other countries. You can talk about the **self-sufficiency** of a person or country.

self-supporting You say people or organizations are **self-supporting** when they earn enough to support themselves financially.

self-willed If you say someone, especially a child, is **self-willed,** you mean they are obstinate and not prepared to listen to other people's advice.

sell (**selling, sold**) If you **sell** something, you give it to someone in exchange for money. ■ If a shop **sells** a certain product, it normally has it available for sale. If a shop has **sold out** of a product, it has sold all of its stock of that product. ■ If something **sells** at a certain price, it is for sale at that price. ■ If you say a certain thing **sells** a product, you mean it makes people buy it. You call something like this a **selling point.** ■ If you **sell yourself,** you present yourself in a way which gives people confidence in you and your abilities. ■ If you **sell** an idea to someone, you convince them it is worthwhile. ■ If you accuse someone of **selling out,** you mean they have betrayed their principles to gain some personal advantage. ■ **sell** someone **short:** see **short.** See also **hard sell, soft sell.**

sell-by The **sell-by** date printed on food packaging is the date it must be sold by to be sure it is fresh and safe to eat. ■ If you say something or someone is past their **sell-by** date, you mean they are old, or no longer interesting, important, or useful.

seller The **seller** of something is the person or company selling it. ■ If you say a product is a big **seller,** you mean a lot of it is sold. See also **best-seller.**

Sellotape is a thin transparent sticky tape sold in rolls. 'Sellotape' is a trademark.

selves See **self.**

semantic (**semantics**) **Semantic** means to do with the meaning of words. ...*a semantic error.* **Semantics** is the study of the meaning of words.

semaphore is a system of sending messages using two flags which are held in various positions representing different letters of the alphabet.

semblance If you achieve a **semblance** of something, you achieve something like it, although it may not be the real thing. *Can Europe maintain a semblance of unity?*

semen (*pron:* **see**-men) is the liquid containing sperm produced by the sex organs of men and male animals.

semester A **semester** is one of the two periods into which the academic year in some colleges and universities is divided.

semi (**semis**) A **semi** is a semi-detached house.

semi- is combined with other words to talk about someone or something being almost but not completely in a particular state. ...*semi-independent states... Brie should be sold in a semi-ripe state.*

semi-automatic A **semi-automatic** weapon reloads itself but has to have its trigger pulled each time to make it fire.

semibreve A **semibreve** is a musical note with the same time value as four crotchets.

semi-circle (*or* **semicircle**) (**semi-circular**) A **semi-circle** is half a circle or something with this shape. Things with this shape are described as **semi-circular.**

semi-colon A **semi-colon** is the mark ; used in writing to separate parts of a sentence or to indicate a pause.

semiconductor A **semiconductor** is a substance used in electronics whose ability to conduct electricity increases with greater heat.

semi-detached A **semi-detached** house is joined to another house on one side.

semi-final (**semi-finalist**) A **semi-final** is one of two matches or races in a competition to decide who will compete in the final. The people taking part in a semi-final are called **semi-finalists.**

seminal is used to describe things such as books, events, and experiences which have a great influence in a particular field. ...*a seminal figure in the history of rap music.*

seminar A **seminar** is a class at a university in which a tutor and a small group of students discuss a topic. ■ A **seminar** is a meeting where a group of people discuss a topic or problem.

seminary (**seminaries; seminarian**) A **seminary** is a college where priests or rabbis are trained. A student at a seminary is called a **seminarian.**

semiotics is the study of signs and symbols and their function and meaning in communication.

semi-precious stones are stones like agates and turquoises which are used in jewellery but are less valuable than precious stones like diamonds and rubies.

semiquaver A **semiquaver** is a musical note.

semi-skilled workers have some training and skills but not enough to do specialized work. The work they do can be described as **semi-skilled.**

semi-skimmed milk has had about half of its fat removed.

semi-staged A **semi-staged** production of a play or opera is one in which no costumes, scenery, or props are used.

semitone In Western music, a **semitone** is the smallest interval between two notes.

semolina is tiny particles of wheat used for making pasta and for making sweet puddings with milk.

Semtex is an odourless plastic explosive.

senate The **Senate** is one of the two law-making bodies in some countries, for example the US. ■ The governing body in some universities is called **senate** or **the senate.**

senator (**senatorial**) A **senator** is a member of a law-making senate. **Senatorial** means belonging to or relating to a Senate. ...*the State's conservative senatorial candidate.*

send (**sending, sent**) If you **send** something to someone, you have it delivered to them, for example by post. ■ If you **send for** something, you write and ask for it to be delivered to you. ■ If someone **sends for** you, they send a message asking you to come and see them. ■ If someone **sends** you somewhere, they tell you to go there. ■ If something **sends** you somewhere, it causes you to go there. *The charges are enough to send him to prison.* Similarly, if something **sends** you into a certain state, it puts you into that state. *This sent him positively wild.* ■ In football, if a player is **sent off,** he is made to leave the pitch, because he has seriously broken the rules. You call an incident like this a **sending-off.** ■ If a machine **sends out** sound or light, it transmits it. ■ If you **send** someone or something **up,** you make fun of them by imitating them. Anything which makes fun of something like this can be called a **send-up.**

sender The **sender** of a letter or other communication is the person who sent it.

sending-off See **send.**

send-off If someone who is going away is given a **send-off,** people gather to say goodbye to them.

send-up See **send.**

senile (**senility**) If old people become **senile,** they become confused and cannot look after themselves. Their condition is called **senility.**

senile dementia is an illness affecting old people in which the person's mind deteriorates.

senior If someone has a **senior** position in an organization or profession, they are of higher rank or greater importance than other people in it. You can call people at your workplace who have a more important job than you your **seniors**. ■ If someone is your **senior,** they are older than you.

senior citizen A **senior citizen** is a person old enough to receive an old-age pension.

seniority is being older than other people, or more experienced or higher in rank.

sensation is the ability to feel things physically. A **sensation** is a physical feeling. ■ The emotional effect of an experience can be called a **sensation.** ...*a sensation of despair.* ■ Someone or something that causes great interest and excitement can be called a **sensation.**

sensational (sensationally) If you say something is **sensational,** you mean it is remarkable and causes great interest and excitement. ■ If you call a news report **sensational,** you mean it presents facts in a way intended to produce strong feelings of shock or excitement. ■ If you are extremely impressed by something, you can say it is **sensational.**

sensationalise See **sensationalize.**

sensationalism (sensationalist) If you accuse someone of **sensationalism** or of being **sensationalist,** you mean they are presenting facts in a way which makes them seem more shocking than they really are.

sensationalize (or sensationalise) (sensationalizing, sensationalized) If someone, especially a journalist, **sensationalizes** a situation, they present the facts in a way which makes them seem more shocking than they really are.

sense (sensing, sensed) Your **senses** are your ability to see, smell, hear, touch, and taste. ■ A **sense** is a feeling. ...*a sense of urgency.* ■ If you **sense** something such as danger, you become aware of it, although you cannot see or hear anything. ■ A **sense** is a natural ability or talent. ...*their dress sense.* ■ If someone has a **sense** of duty or justice, they believe it is important. ■ **Sense** is the ability to think and behave sensibly. ■ If you say something like a proposal **makes sense,** you mean it seems sensible. ■ If you can **make sense** of something, you can understand it. ■ If you say someone has **come to their senses,** you mean they are acting sensibly again after behaving foolishly. ■ A **sense** of a word is one of its meanings. ■ **In a sense** is used to say something is partly true or is true from a certain point of view. *She has in a sense already been punished.* ■ **sense of humour:** see **humour.** See also **common sense.**

senseless (senselessness) If you describe something as **senseless,** you mean it serves no purpose. ■ If someone has been beaten **senseless,** they have been hit until they are unconscious.

sensibility (sensibilities) If something upsets people's **sensibilities,** it shocks or offends them. ■ **Sensibility** is the ability to experience and express deep feelings.

sensible (sensibly) A **sensible** person is able to make good decisions and judgments based on reason rather than emotion. A **sensible** action or decision is reasonable and well thought out. ■ **Sensible** shoes or clothes are practical rather than fashionable.

sensitise See **sensitize.**

sensitive (sensitively; sensitivity, sensitivities) If you are **sensitive** to other people's needs, problems, or feelings, you show awareness and understanding of them. ■ **Sensitive** people are easily offended or hurt by other people's behaviour. People's **sensitivities** are the things which are likely to upset them. ■ A **sensitive** issue needs to be handled carefully, because it is likely to cause disagreement or to upset people. ■ **Sensitivity** is delicacy of feeling or style. *The company danced with fine sensitivity.* ■ If something is **sensitive** to something else, it is easily affected by it. ...*light-sensitive plastic.* ...*gentle cosmetics for sensitive skin.* ■ A **sensitive** piece of equipment is capable of recording or measuring very small changes.

sensitize (or sensitise) (sensitizing, sensitized) If people are **sensitized** to a situation, they are made aware of it. ■ If someone or something is **sensitized** to a certain thing, they are made sensitive to it. *Many people become sensitised to pollen at the beginning of the season and then develop an allergy to it by the end of the year.*

sensor A **sensor** is an instrument which reacts to certain physical conditions and which can provide information. ...*a blood-pressure sensor.*

sensory is used to talk about things to do with the physical senses. ...*sensory loss.* ...*sensory pleasures.*

sensual (sensuality) **Sensual** things give pleasure to your physical senses rather than to your mind. You can talk about the **sensuality** of something like this. ...*sensual dance rhythms.* ■ A **sensual** person shows a fondness for physical pleasures, especially sexual ones. You can talk about the **sensuality** of someone like this.

sensuous (sensuously) You say something is **sensuous** when it is pleasing to the senses.

sent See **send.**

sentence (sentencing, sentenced) A **sentence** is the punishment a criminal receives after being found guilty in a court of law. You say the criminal is **sentenced** to a particular punishment. ■ A **sentence** is a group of words which, when written down, begin with a capital letter and end with a full stop, question mark, or exclamation mark.

sententious (sententiously) If you say someone is being **sententious,** you mean they are trying to make wise remarks but just sound pompous.

sentient (pron: sen-tee-ent) A **sentient** creature is capable of experiencing things through its senses.

sentiment If people have strong feelings about something, you can say there is **sentiment** of a particular kind. ...*anti-war sentiment.* ■ A person's **sentiments** are their opinions about something. ■ **Sentiment** is emotion such as tenderness, romance, or sadness expressed in speech or writing, often to an excessive or foolish extent.

sentimental (sentimentally, sentimentality; sentimentalist) You say a person is **sentimental** or call them a **sentimentalist** when they show exaggerated feelings of tenderness, affection, or sadness. You call a book, film, or song **sentimental** when it is too full of feelings of this sort. *The main weakness of his play is sentimentality.* ■ If something you own is of **sentimental** value, it is valuable to you because of its associations with someone or something in the past, rather than because it is useful or worth a lot of money. Similarly, you can talk about something being done for **sentimental** reasons.

sentimentalize (*or* **sentimentalise**) (**sentimentalizing, sentimentalized**) When people **sentimentalize** something, they think or talk about it in a sentimental way, overlooking its unattractive features.

sentinel is an old word for a sentry. Someone or something standing on their own like a sentry can be called a **sentinel.**

sentry (**sentries**) A **sentry** is a soldier who stands outside a place, guarding it.

sentry-box A **sentry-box** is a narrow shelter with an open front which can be used by a sentry on duty.

separate (**separating, separated; separately, separateness, separation**) If things or people **separate** or are **separated,** they move apart. ■ If one thing is **separate** from another, the two things are apart and not connected. ■ If something like an obstacle **separates** people, it keeps them apart. ■ If a married couple **separate,** they start to live apart. ■ If some feature **separates** one person or thing from another, it shows they are different. ■ **Separates** are individual items of women's clothing, such as skirts, which are not part of a matching outfit.

separatism (**separatist**) **Separatism** is a movement in which an ethnic or cultural group within a country tries to achieve independence. Supporters of a movement like this are called **separatists.**

sepia (*pron:* **see**-pee-er) is the reddish brown colour of old photographs.

septic If a wound is **septic,** it has become infected.

septicaemia (*pron:* sep-tis-**see**-mee-a) is blood poisoning.

septic tank A **septic tank** is a tank, usually underground, where sewage is broken down by bacteria.

septuagenarian (*pron:* sept-yoo-a-jin-**nair**-ee-an) A **septuagenarian** is a person in their seventies.

sepulchral (*pron:* sip-**pulk**-ral) things are gloomy and solemn.

sepulchre (*pron:* **sep**-pull-ker) A **sepulchre** is a tomb or vault where dead people are buried.

sequel The **sequel** to a book or film is another one which continues the story or has the same characters. ■ The **sequel** to an event is something else which happens after it or as a result of it.

sequence A **sequence** of things or events is a series of them coming one after the other. ■ If things happen or are arranged in a particular **sequence,** they happen or are arranged in that order. ■ A film **sequence** is a part of a film which shows a single set of events. ...*a chase sequence.*

sequential (**sequentially**) **Sequential** is used to talk about things happening in a definite order. *Anthologies are things to be browsed through at leisure, rather than read sequentially.*

sequester (**sequesters, sequestering, sequestered**) **Sequester** means the same as **sequestrate.** ■ If someone is **sequestered** somewhere, they are

isolated from other people. *This jury is expected to be sequestered for at least two months.*

sequestrate (**sequestrating, sequestrated; sequestration**) When property is **sequestrated,** it is taken away from its owner by court authority, either because its ownership is in question or because the owner owes money or has disobeyed the court.

sequin (**sequinned** *or* **sequined**) **Sequins** are small shiny discs sewn onto clothes as a decoration. **Sequinned** clothes are decorated with sequins. ...*a sequinned jacket.*

serenade (**serenading, serenaded**) A **serenade** is a piece of music in several movements, usually for a small orchestra. ■ If one person **serenades** another, they sing or play a piece of music for them. Traditionally a man did this outside the window of the woman he loved.

serendipity (**serendipitous**) **Serendipity** is a natural talent for making interesting or valuable discoveries by accident. You say a discovery made like this is **serendipitous.**

serene (**serenely, serenity**) If you call a place **serene** or talk about its **serenity,** you mean it is calm and peaceful. ■ A **serene** person is quiet and calm.

serf (**serfdom**) In medieval Europe, **serfs** were people who worked on their master's land and could not leave without his permission. **Serfdom** was the state of being a serf.

serge is a type of strong woollen cloth used to make coats, suits, and other clothes.

sergeant A **sergeant** is a middle-ranking NCO in the army and the RAF. ■ A police **sergeant** is a police officer between constable and inspector in rank.

sergeant major A **sergeant major** is a high-ranking NCO in the army.

serial A **serial** is a story which is broadcast or published in several parts, usually at regular times. ■ A **serial** killer is someone who has committed a series of murders. ■ A product's **serial number** is a special number which identifies it. Similarly, each member of the armed forces has a **serial number.**

serialize (*or* **serialise**) (**serializing, serialized; serialization**) If a book is **serialized,** it is broadcast or published in a number of parts, usually at regular times.

series A **series** of people, things, or occurrences is a number of them coming one after the other. ■ A TV or radio **series** is a set of related programmes with the same title, often with the same characters or about the same subject.

serious (**seriously, seriousness**) A **serious** problem or situation is very bad and causes concern. ...*the seriousness of his injuries.* ■ **Serious** matters are important and should be thought about carefully. ■ **Serious** music and literature requires thought and concentration and is not just for entertainment. ■ If you are **serious** about something, you mean what you say and are not joking. *He talked seriously of retiring.*

sermon A **sermon** is a talk on a religious or moral subject given during a religious service. ■ Any speech in which someone tells you how you ought to behave can be called a **sermon.**

serpent is an old word for a snake.

serpentine is used to describe things which have a curved winding shape like a snake. *...serpentine woodland pathways.*

SERPS stands for 'State Earnings-Related Pension Scheme'. SERPS is a government-run scheme which pays out pensions in addition to the normal state pension.

serrated A **serrated** edge has a row of V-shaped points along it.

serried things or people are closely packed together in a regular arrangement.

serum (*pron:* **seer**-um) A **serum** is a liquid which is injected into someone's blood to protect them against a poison or disease. ■ **Serum** is the watery, pale yellow part of blood.

servant A **servant** is someone employed to work in someone else's house, for example as a maid or cook. ■ If you want to emphasize that someone's job is to help a group of people, you can say they are the **servant** of those people. *...the idea that a police officer is the servant of the community.* You can also say someone is the **servant** of an ideal or a cause. *...a servant of peace.*

serve (**server**) If something **serves** as a particular thing, it has that use or function. *...a cinema serving as a makeshift opera house.* You can also say something **serves** a particular purpose. *Denials only serve to heighten speculation.* ■ If you **serve** a country, organization, or person, you do useful work for them. ■ If something **serves** a community, it provides people with something useful or necessary. *The temple was built to serve a mainly Thai immigrant community.* ■ If someone in a shop **serves** you, they provide you with what you want to buy. ■ If you **serve** food or **serve** it **up**, you put it on plates and present it to people. A **serving** of food is an amount given to one person at a meal. A **serving** dish or spoon is used for serving food. ■ If a legal document like a writ or summons is **served** on someone, it is officially delivered or presented to them. ■ If someone is **serving** a prison sentence, they are spending a period of time in jail as a punishment. ■ If it is your **serve** in tennis or badminton, it is your turn to start play by hitting the ball or shuttlecock towards your opponent's half of the court. When you do this, you say you **serve** or are the **server.**

service (**servicing, serviced**) A **service** is an organization or system which provides something for the public. *...the postal service.* ■ Some government organizations are called **services.** *...the diplomatic service.* ■ The **services** are the army, navy, and air force. ■ **Services** are activities like tourism, banking, and selling which contribute to a country's economy, but which are not directly concerned with producing or manufacturing goods. ■ If you **do** someone **a service,** you do something which helps or benefits them. ■ If you offer your **services,** you offer to help someone, usually by doing something you are good at. ■ If a vehicle or machine is **in service,** it is working or it can be used.

■ Motorway service stations are often called **services.** ■ If something **services** a group of people, it provides them with something they need. *Refuse collection can be designed and planned to service a specific area.* ■ When a machine or vehicle is **serviced** or given a **service,** it is examined, adjusted, and cleaned so it will work efficiently. ■ **Service** is being served in a shop or restaurant. ■ Your length of **service** with an organization is the period of time you have spent working for it. ■ A dinner or tea **service** is a complete set of crockery for dinner or tea. ■ A **service** is a religious ceremony. ■ If you **service** a debt, you pay interest and capital repayments on it. ■ In tennis and badminton, a person's **service** is the same as their serve.

serviceable If you describe something as **serviceable,** you mean it is good enough to be used and to perform its function adequately.

service charge A **service charge** is (a) an amount added to your restaurant bill for the services of your waiter or waitress. (b) a charge made for providing a service. *The flat owners pay a service charge to a management company... The bank levied service charges on accounts of this nature.*

service industry A **service industry** is one which provides services, such as transport or entertainment, rather than goods.

serviceman (**servicewoman**) A **serviceman** or **servicewoman** is a person in the armed forces.

service station A **service station** is a garage which carries out repairs and maintenance and often sells petrol and oil. ■ A motorway **service station** is a place beside a motorway where you can stop, and buy petrol and something to eat.

serviette A **serviette** is a square of cloth or paper used to protect your clothes or to wipe your mouth when you are eating.

servile (**servility**) You say someone is **servile** or talk about their **servility** when you think they are too eager to obey someone or to do things for them.

serving See serve.

servitude is the condition of being a slave or of being completely under the control of another person.

sesame (*pron:* **sess**-am-ee) seeds are the seeds of a tropical plant. They are used for their edible oil, and in cooking.

session A **session** is a meeting of a court, parliament, or official group. A period during which meetings like these are regularly held is also called a **session.** You can say the court or parliament is **in session.** ■ A **session** of an activity is a period when you do it. *...a training session.* ■ **Session** musicians play backing music in record studios.

set (**setting, set** *not* '**setted**') A **set** of people or things is a number of them that belong together or form a group. *...a boxed set of CDs. ...a member of her social set.* ■ **Set** is used to say something is put into a certain state. *The birds were to be set free in the woods.* ■ If you **set** something somewhere, you put it there carefully and deliberately. ■ If you **set** the table, you place the plates, cutlery, and glasses on it. ■ If something is **set** somewhere, that is where it is. *...a studio set back from the sea.* ■ If a teacher **sets** you a task, they require you to do it. You can also talk about books which must be read by students doing a particular course as **set** books. *The play is now a set text in many schools.* ■ **Set** is used to describe something which is fixed and cannot be varied. *The enquiry will also examine whether set procedures were followed.* ■ If something is **set** to happen, it seems likely to happen. ■ If you are **set on** a particular goal, you are determined to achieve it. ■ When glue, jelly, or cement **sets**, it becomes hard or firm. ■ When the sun **sets**, it goes down below the horizon. ■ If a story or poem is **set** to music, someone writes or arranges music to go with it. ■ If you **set** a device or piece of machinery, you adjust it so that it operates in a particular way. ■ If you **set** a standard, time, or level, you establish or decide what it is. ■ If a play, film, or story is **set** in a particular place or period, that is where or when the action happens. ■ The **set** for a play or a film scene is the scenery. ■ A television **set** is a television. ■ A **set** is one of the groups of six or more games which make up a tennis match. ■ If you **set about** doing something, you begin doing it in a purposeful way. ■ If something **sets** you **back** a certain amount, especially a large amount, that is how much it costs you. ■ If something **sets back** a project or scheme, it delays it. ■ If something unpleasant **sets in**, it starts and seems likely to continue. ■ When you **set off** or **set out**, you start a journey. ■ When one thing **sets off** another, it causes the other thing to begin. *The food price rises set off violent demonstrations.* ■ If someone **sets off** a bomb, they detonate it. ■ If you **set out** to do something, you start trying to do it. ■ If you **set** something **out,** you present it in an organized way. *He has written a letter to The Times setting out his views.* ■ If you **set up** somewhere, you start a business there. ■ If you **set** something **up,** you make the necessary preparations for it. ■ If you have been **set up,** someone has deliberately made it seem that you have done something wrong when you have not. ■ **set out** your **stall:** see **stall. set foot on:** see **foot. set your heart on:** see **heart. set great store by:** see **store. set fire to:** see **fire. set the stage for:** see **stage. set sail:** see **sail.** See also **setting.**

set-aside In the European Union, **set-aside** is a scheme in which a proportion of a farmer's land is deliberately left uncultivated, to reduce crop surpluses.

setback If you suffer a **setback** when you are trying to achieve something, something happens which delays your progress.

set-piece In a game like football, a **set-piece** is a move like a corner kick which has been carefully rehearsed and which usually occurs at the restart of play following an infringement of the rules. ■ In a novel or film, a **set-piece** is an episode or scene which seems complete in itself, and is often not an essential part of the story.

set square A **set square** is a flat piece of plastic or metal in the shape of a right-angled triangle which is used for drawing angles and lines.

sett A badger's **sett** is its burrow.

settee A **settee** is the same as a sofa.

setter A **setter** is a breed of gun dog.

-setter is added to words to describe people who set a standard or trend. *...fashion-setters.*

setting The **setting** for something is the surroundings in which it takes place. ■ A **setting** is one of the positions which the controls of a machine can be adjusted to. ■ See also **place setting.**

settle (settling, settled; settlement) If you **settle** in a place, you make it your permanent home. ■ If you **settle** yourself somewhere, you make yourself comfortable. ■ When someone **settles down,** they begin to lead an orderly routine life and behave in a responsible way, for example when they get married or start a permanent job. ■ If a situation **settles down,** it becomes calmer and more stable. ■ If something **settles** your nerves, it makes you calmer. ■ If you **settle** a bill, you pay it. ■ If you **settle for** something, you accept it although it may not be what you really want. ■ If you **settle on** something or someone, you choose them. ■ If something is **settled,** any details or problems are dealt with satisfactorily. ■ A **settlement** is an official agreement to end a conflict. ■ If something **settles** at a certain level, it stabilizes at that level after a period of going up and down. ■ If something **settles** somewhere, it lands there. *Two days later a blanket of snow settled.* ■ If a mood **settles** over a place, it strongly affects the people there. ■ A **settle** is a long wooden seat with sides and a high back.

settler – Settlers are people who go to live in a place where nobody has lived before, or which other people have been driven out of.

set-to If people have a **set-to,** they have an argument or fight.

set-top box A **set-top box** is a box that you plug into your television to convert digital signals into a form that you can watch on a standard set.

set-up A system or way of organizing things can be called a **set-up.** ■ If you describe a situation as a **set-up,** you mean people have planned it to deceive you or make others think you have done something wrong.

seven (seventh) Seven is the number 7. ■ **at sixes and sevens:** see **six.**

seventeen (seventeenth) Seventeen is the number 17.

seventy (seventieth, seventies) Seventy is the number 70. ■ The **seventies** was the period from 1970 to 1979. ■ If someone is in their **seventies,** they are aged 70 to 79.

sever (severing, severed; severance) If you **sever** a connection with someone, you end it. This is called the **severing** or **severance** of the connection. *Parliament ordered the immediate severing of all ties with Serbia.* ■ If something such as a part of someone's body is **severed,** it is cut off. ■ If one group of people is **severed** from another, they are separated completely and are unable to reach each other. ■ **Severance** is the process of getting rid of employees who are no longer needed.

several is used in an imprecise way to talk about a number of things or people, when the number is more than two but not large. *...several hundred pounds.* ■ **Several** is used to mean separate or different. *They were both as militant as ever in their several ways.*

severance See **sever.**

severe (severer, severest; severely, severity) If you say something is **severe** or talk about its **severity,** you are emphasizing how bad or serious it is. *...severe injuries.* ■ A **severe** punishment or criticism is strict or harsh.

sew (sewing, sewed, have sewn) If you **sew,** you join things together, usually pieces of cloth, using a needle and thread or a sewing machine. ■ If you have something **sewn up,** you have arranged things so you are certain of success.

sewage is water containing waste matter from homes and industries and also water from drains, all of which is carried away along sewers to be treated at a sewage works.

sewage works A **sewage works** or **sewage treatment works** is a place where sewage is treated so it can be disposed of safely.

sewer A **sewer** is a large channel, usually underground, which carries away sewage from homes, drains, and industries.

sewerage is the system of pipes and sewers used to take sewage away from homes, drains, and industries.

sewing machine A **sewing machine** is a machine which sews by means of a needle driven by an electric motor. Old-fashioned sewing machines were operated by pedals or by turning a handle.

sewn See **sew.**

sex (sexes) Sex is the physical activity by which people can produce children. ■ **Sex** is used to talk about various things to do with sex. *...a sex scandal.* ■ The **sex** of a person or other living thing is whether they are male or female.

sexagenarian (*pron:* sex-a-jin-**nair**-ee-an) A **sexagenarian** is a person in their sixties.

sex appeal If you say someone has **sex appeal,** you mean they are sexually attractive.

sex education is teaching children about sex and matters connected with it such as contraception and protection against disease.

sexiness See **sexy.**

sexism (sexist) Sexism is prejudice and discrimination against members of one sex, especially women. **Sexist** is used to describe people and things that show prejudice of this sort. *...a sexist joke.*

sex object If a woman is treated as a **sex object,** she is treated as though she is important only for her sexual attractiveness and not for other reasons such as her intelligence or skills.

sex shop A **sex shop** is a shop which sells things connected with sexual pleasure such as pornographic magazines and videos.

sex symbol A **sex symbol** is someone such as a film star who is very attractive.

sextant A **sextant** is an instrument for measuring angles, for example between the sun and the horizon, so that the position of a ship or plane can be calculated.

sextet A **sextet** is (a) a piece of music for six instruments or singers. (b) a group of six people who sing or play music together.

sexton In the past, a **sexton** was a person employed by the church authorities whose main job was to dig the graves in a churchyard.

sextuplet – Sextuplets are six children born to the same mother at the same time.

sexual (sexually) Sexual activities and feelings are connected with the act of sex or with desire for sex. ■ **Sexual** is used to talk about the biological process by which people, animals, and plants produce young. *...sexual reproduction.* ■ **Sexual** means connected with the differences between men and women. *...sexual equality.*

sexual harassment is repeated unwelcome sexual comments, looks, or touching, especially in the workplace.

sexual intercourse See **intercourse.**

sexuality A person's **sexuality** is their ability to experience sexual feelings. ■ You can refer to a person's **sexuality** when you are talking about whether they are heterosexual, homosexual, or bisexual.

sexually transmitted disease A **sexually transmitted disease** is a disease such as syphilis or AIDS which is mainly passed on through sexual contact. 'Sexually transmitted disease' is sometimes shortened to 'STD'.

sexy (sexier, sexiest; sexiness) If you say someone is **sexy,** you mean they are sexually attractive. ■ Things which excite people sexually can also be called **sexy.** *The clothes are classic but very sexy.* ■ Non-sexual things are sometimes described as **sexy** when people find them exciting and stimulating. *...the less sexy bits of the business such as distribution and licensing.*

shabby (shabbier, shabbiest; shabbily, shabbiness) Shabby things or places look old and in bad condition. You can say a person is **shabby** when their clothes are old and worn. ■ You can say someone's behaviour is **shabby** when they behave unfairly or dishonestly. *He has been treated shabbily by his party.*

shack A **shack** is a small makeshift dwelling built from things like pieces of wood and metal.

shackle (shackling, shackled) Shackles are two metal rings joined by a chain which are fastened around a person's wrists or ankles to prevent them from moving or escaping. You say the person is **shackled.** ■ You say someone is **shackled** when they are prevented by laws or other restrictions from doing something they want to. You can call these restrictions **shackles.** ■ If you are **shackled** to someone or something, you are closely linked with them in some way and cannot break free from them.

shade (shading, shaded) Shade is an area which is cooler and darker than other parts because the sun does not reach it. ■ If an area is **shaded** by something like a tree, it is protected by it from the heat or glare of the sun. ■ A **shade** is something which partly covers an electric light and prevents it shining too brightly in your eyes. ■ **Shades** are sunglasses. ■ In the US, **shades** are blinds. ■ If something **puts** something else **in the shade,** it is so impressive it makes the other thing seem unimportant. ■ A **shade** of a colour is one variation of it. For example, navy blue is a dark shade of blue. ■ The **shades** of something are its many slightly different forms. *...individuals representing all shades of opinion.* ■ A **shade** means a very small amount. *He started to sound a shade defensive.*

shadiness See **shady.**

shadow A **shadow** is a dark shape on a surface caused by something standing between a light and the surface. ■ The **shadows** are the dark parts of a place which the light does not reach. ■ If someone **shadows** you, they follow you very closely wherever you go. ■ If you **shadow** what someone else does, you do the same thing. ■ In Britain, the **shadow cabinet** consists of members of the main opposition party. There is a shadow cabinet member for each member of the official cabinet and they speak for their party on the same things as that person. *...the shadow Secretary of State for Wales.* ■ If something **casts a shadow** over something else, it prevents it being completely happy or successful. ■ If someone **lives in the shadow** of a famous person, they are known only because of their connection with that person, rather than because of their own achievements or talents. ■ If you say there is not a **shadow of a doubt** about something, you mean there is absolutely no doubt about it. ■ If you say someone is a **shadow of their former self,** you mean they are nothing like as lively or capable as they used to be.

shadow-boxing You say someone is **shadow-boxing** when they threaten to do something just to test people's reactions, rather than because they really mean to do it.

shadowy is used to describe people and activities that very little is known about. *...the shadowy world of spies.* ■ **Shadowy** places are dark and full of shadows. Things which can just be seen in places like these are also called **shadowy.**

shady (**shadier, shadiest; shadiness**) **Shady** activities are dishonest or illegal. You can also call the people involved in them **shady.** ■ **Shady** places are cool because there is a lot of shade there.

shaft A **shaft** is a vertical passageway in a building or mine for a lift to travel up and down. ■ The **shaft** of something like a spear is the straight part which you hold. ■ A **shaft** is a revolving rod which transfers motion or power from one part of a machine to another. *...the transmission shaft.* ■ A **shaft** of light is a narrow beam of light. ■ A **shaft** of humour or wit is a humorous or witty remark, especially one made as an attack on someone or something.

shaggy animals have a lot of long untidy hair or fur.

Shah In the past, the ruler of Iran was called the **Shah.**

shake (**shaking, shook, have shaken**) If something **shakes,** it moves quickly backwards and forwards or up and down. If you **shake** something or give it a **shake,** you make it move like this. ■ If someone is **shaking,** they are trembling uncontrollably because they are nervous, afraid, or ill. ■ If some-

thing **shakes** you, it shocks or upsets you. ■ If something **shakes** your beliefs, it makes you less certain about them. ■ If you **shake hands** with someone, you grasp their hand, for example as a greeting. ■ If you **shake your head,** you move it from side to side repeatedly, for example as a way of saying 'no'. ■ If you **shake off** something which is troubling you, you succeed in getting rid of it. ■ If someone **shakes up** an organization, system, or profession, they make major changes to it. The changes are called a **shake-up.** ■ If you say something is **no great shakes,** you mean it is not very good or effective.

shake-out If there is a **shake-out** of an organization or an industry, the workforce is reduced.

shake-up See **shake.**

shaky (**shakier, shakiest**) You say things are **shaky** when they seem unlikely to succeed or last. ■ If an object is **shaky,** it is unsteady and shakes about. ■ If a person is **shaky,** their body shakes or their hands shake, because they are nervous, ill, or very old.

shale is smooth soft rock which breaks easily into thin layers.

shall You use **shall** when you are talking or asking about something you are going to do, or something you and someone else are going to do. You also use **shall** when you are talking about something which is going to happen to you, or to you and someone else. *Soon we shall know the name of the novel that has won the Booker prize.* ■ **Shall** is used to say something must happen or be done, especially in official or legal documents. *The state shall regulate all domestic and foreign trade.*

shallot (*pron:* shal-**lot**) **Shallots** are vegetables similar to small onions. They are eaten cooked or pickled.

shallow (**shallows, shallowness**) **Shallow** is used to describe something which is not deep. ■ The parts of an area of water which are not very deep are sometimes called the **shallows.** ■ If you say someone is **shallow,** you mean they are not capable of thinking deeply about things.

sham If you say something is **sham** or a **sham,** you mean it is not what it is supposed to be. *The students believe the forthcoming elections will be a sham.*

shaman A **shaman** is a priest in some religions who is thought to be able to influence and control good and evil spirits.

shamble (**shambling, shambled**) If you say a place, organization, or event is a **shambles,** you mean it is in disorder or confusion. ■ A large slow clumsy person is sometimes described as **shambling.**

shambolic is used to describe things which are disorganized and chaotic. *...shambolic public services.*

shame (**shaming, shamed**) **Shame** is an uncomfortable feeling of regret and guilt you have when you have done something wrong or when someone close to you has. ■ If something **shames** you, it makes you feel ashamed. ■ If you **shame** someone **into** doing something, you get them to do it by making them feel ashamed that they have not done it already. ■ If you say something is a **shame,** you mean it is regrettable. *It would clearly be a great* shame if work like this were not carried out. ■ If you say something **shames** something else or **puts it to shame,** you mean it is so much better that it makes the other thing look unimpressive by comparison.

shamefaced If someone is **shamefaced,** they are ashamed or embarrassed about something they have said or done.

shameful (shamefully) If you say someone's behaviour is **shameful,** you mean they ought to be ashamed of it. *Getting into debt was considered a shameful failure.*

shameless (shamelessly) If you say someone's behaviour is **shameless,** you mean they do wrong or immoral things without feeling ashamed.

shampoo A **shampoo** is a liquid soap or detergent which you use to wash things, for example carpets or your hair.

shamrock is the name given to a number of similar plants which have three small leaves on each stem and grow in Ireland. The shamrock is the national emblem of Ireland.

shandy (shandies) Shandy is a drink made of beer or lager mixed with lemonade.

Shangri-La If you call a remote place a **Shangri-la,** you mean everything seems so wonderful there that it seems like paradise.

shanty (shanties) A **shanty** is a small rough dwelling made of pieces of flimsy material such as tin or wood. A place where many dwellings of this kind have been built is called a **shanty town.** ■ A **shanty** is a song sailors used to sing at sea.

shape (shaping, shaped) The **shape** of something is its form or outline, for example whether it is round or square. *...a heart-shaped silver balloon.* ■ You can call a person, animal, or object a **shape** when you cannot see them clearly, because it is too dark or because they are too far away. ■ Things like circles, squares, and triangles can be called **shapes.** ■ If you **shape** a material, you form it into a particular shape. ■ The **shape** of something like an organization is the way it is organized or structured. *...the future shape of the nuclear industry.* ■ If you say something is **shaping up,** you mean it is developing the way you want it to. ■ If something is **shaped** by events or circumstances, it has a certain form because of them. *Munro's stories are shaped by life in rural Ontario.* ■ If you say a person is **in shape,** you mean they are healthy and fit. ■ You use **in the shape of** when you are saying precisely what you mean after describing something in a general way. *The Voyager has a European rival in the shape of the Renault Espace.*

shapeless If you say something is **shapeless,** you mean it does not have a definite shape, or its shape is unattractive.

shapely If you say someone or something is **shapely,** you mean they have an attractive shape.

shard A **shard** is a fragment of broken pottery or glass.

share (sharing, shared) If you **share** something with someone else, you both use it. ■ If something like an amount of money is **shared** between people, they each get some of it. The amount each person gets is called their **share.** *...the share-out of seats in*

the transitional government. ■ If people **share** tasks, duties, or responsibilities, they each do or take on some of them. You can also say each person does their **share.** ■ If people **share** a feeling, characteristic, or opinion, each of them has it. ■ If you **share** something like a piece of information, you tell someone else about it. ■ If two competitors **share** the lead, they have the same number of points and are ahead of everyone else. ■ A company's **shares** are the equal parts its capital stock is divided into.

shareholder (shareholding) People who own shares in a company are called its **shareholders.** You say each person has a **shareholding** in the company.

shareware – Shareware is computer software that you can try before you buy the legal right to use it.

shark – Sharks are powerful fish with long bodies and several rows of sharp teeth. ■ If you call a person a **shark,** you mean they try to swindle people out of money. ■ **loan shark:** see **loan.**

sharp (sharply, sharpness) A **sharp** object has a very thin edge or a pointed end and can cut or pierce things easily. You can also describe other things which are not able to cut or pierce as **sharp** when they have an edge or point. *...trousers with razor-sharp creases.* ■ A **sharp** change is sudden and significant. *Theft from farms has risen sharply this year.* ■ If you say someone is **sharp,** you mean they are clever and think quickly. ■ If you call something someone does **sharp practice,** you mean it is cunning and dishonest. ■ If you say something in a **sharp** way, you say it firmly and rather angrily. *Sharp words were exchanged between Spain and Cuba.* ■ A **sharp** action is abrupt and firm. *She braked sharply.* ■ A **sharp** outline or distinction is easy to see. ■ If you say someone, especially a man, is looking **sharp,** you mean he is dressed smartly and fashionably. ■ A **sharp** pain is sudden and very painful. ■ If something has a **sharp** taste, it tastes bitter. ■ **Sharp** is used after giving a time to mean precisely at that time. *They always kick you out at 2.30pm sharp.* ■ In music, **sharp** is used to talk about a note a semitone higher than another note. For example, F sharp is a semitone higher than F. 'Sharp' is usually written ♯. ■ If a note is played or sung **sharp,** it is slightly higher than it should be.

sharpen (sharpening, sharpened; sharpener) If you **sharpen** something like a knife or a pencil, you make its edge or point sharper. A **sharpener** is a device for sharpening something. ■ If you **sharpen** something or **sharpen** it **up,** you make it more effective. ■ If something **sharpens** a problem or feeling, it makes it more intense.

sharp-eyed If someone is **sharp-eyed,** they are quick to see or notice things.

sharpish If you do something **sharpish,** you do it quickly and without delay.

sharpshooter A **sharpshooter** is a person who can fire a gun very accurately.

shatter (shattering, shattered) If something **shatters,** it breaks into small pieces. ■ If a belief or hope is **shattered,** it is destroyed completely. ■ You can say the peace in a place is **shattered** when violence breaks out there. ■ If you are **shat-**

tered by something that happens, you are extremely shocked and upset by it. ■ You can say you are **shattered** when you are exhausted.

shave (**shaving, shaved**) When a man **shaves** or has a **shave,** he removes the hair from his face with a razor. People also remove hair from other parts of their body in this way. ■ If a price or rate is reduced by a very small amount, you can say it is **shaved** by that amount. ■ **Shavings** are very thin pieces of something cut from a larger piece. ...*wood shavings.*

shaven is used to describe a person's head when it has been shaved. ...*shaven-headed youths.* See also **clean-shaven.**

shaver A **shaver** is an electric device for shaving hair.

shawl A **shawl** is a large woollen cloth for wrapping around a person's shoulders or around a baby.

she You use **she** to talk about a woman or girl you have already mentioned. ■ **She** is sometimes used to talk about something such as a nation or a ship. *Hundreds of small boats clustered round the yacht as she sailed into Southampton docks.*

sheaf (**sheaves**) A **sheaf** of papers is a bundle of them. ■ A **sheaf** of corn is a bundle of ripe corn plants tied together.

shear (**shearing, sheared, have shorn** or **have sheared**) **Shears** are a garden tool like a large pair of scissors with long blades, used especially for trimming hedges. ■ When people **shear** animals, especially sheep, they cut off their wool. See also **shorn.**

sheath A **sheath** is a close-fitting covering for something like a sword or knife. ■ A **sheath** is a condom.

sheathe (**sheathing, sheathed**) You say something is **sheathed** in a covering of some sort when the covering fits closely to it. ■ If you **sheathe** a sword or knife, you put it back into its sheath.

sheaves See **sheaf.**

shed (**shedding, shed** not *'shedded'*) A **shed** is a small building for storing things such as garden tools. ■ If someone **sheds** their clothes, they take them off. ■ When snakes and some other creatures **shed** their skin, their skin drops off. ■ You use **shed** to talk about getting rid of something. *The firm was forced to shed 1,600 jobs... Harry caused Esther to shed a stone in weight.* ■ If someone **sheds light on** something, they increase people's understanding of it. ■ If someone **sheds blood,** they kill or wound someone else. ■ If you **shed tears,** you cry.

sheen If a surface has a **sheen,** it is smooth and shiny. ■ If something loses its **sheen,** it seems less impressive or admirable.

sheep (*plural:* **sheep**) **Sheep** are animals with thick woolly coats. ■ If you say people behave **like sheep,** you mean if one person does something, all the others do it.

sheepdog A **sheepdog** is any dog trained to control sheep, or any breed of dog originally used for this task.

sheepish (**sheepishly**) If someone looks **sheepish,** they look embarrassed because they have done or said something silly.

sheepskin A **sheepskin** is the wool-covered skin from a dead sheep. ...*a sheepskin coat.*

sheer is used to emphasize the completeness or extent of a quality. *He has reached the top through sheer force of personality... Obviously, my immediate reaction is sheer delight.* ■ A **sheer** cliff or drop is vertical or nearly vertical. ■ **Sheer** fabrics are very fine and therefore transparent.

sheet A **sheet** is a thin covering for a bed. ■ A **sheet** of something like paper, metal, glass, or wood is a flat thin piece cut in a regular shape. ■ An **ice sheet** is a thick layer of ice covering a large area. ■ If you say someone has a **clean sheet,** you mean they have a good record and have never done anything wrong or made a bad mistake.

sheeting is a material such as plastic, cloth, or metal, used as a covering.

sheet music is music printed on sheets of paper fastened without a hard cover.

sheikh (*or* **sheik**) (*usual pron:* **shake**) A **sheikh** is an Arab chief or ruler. ■ A **sheikh** is a Muslim religious leader.

shekel The **shekel** is the unit of currency in Israel.

shelf (**shelves**) A **shelf** is a ledge for keeping things on, typically made of wood, metal, or glass. Shelves are attached to a wall or are part of a piece of furniture. ■ If you buy something **off the shelf,** you get it ready-made, usually from existing stock. ■ A **shelf** is a natural ledge of ice or rock.

shelf-life The **shelf-life** of a product, especially food, is the length of time it is usable or can exist without deteriorating. ■ The **shelf-life** of a person or thing is how long they can be expected to last or be useful. *Even the biggest of the supermodels accepts that her shelf-life is limited.*

shell (**shelling**) A **shell** is an explosive device fired from a large gun over long distances. If a place is **shelled,** shells are fired at it. ■ The **shell** of an egg or nut is its hard outer casing. If you **shell** an egg or nut, you remove its shell. Similarly, if you **shell** peas, you remove them from their pods. ■ Some creatures have a hard protective covering called a **shell,** for example tortoises and snails. ■ If someone **comes out of their shell,** they are no longer quiet, shy, and reserved. ■ The **shell** of something like a building or car is its frame, around which the rest of it is built. ■ If you **shell out** for something, you pay a lot of money for it.

shellfire is the firing of shells during a battle or conflict.

shellfish (*plural:* **shellfish**) are sea creatures which have shells, for example mussels, oysters, and lobsters.

shell-shock (**shell-shocked**) Shell-shock is a mental illness affecting people who have had horrific experiences in battle and have been close to many explosions. You say people suffering from this illness are **shell-shocked.** ■ You say people are **shell-shocked** when they have had a bad experience or some bad news and are unable to think clearly because of it.

shell suit A **shell suit** is a casual suit similar to a tracksuit and made of thin nylon.

shelter (sheltering, sheltered) A **shelter** is a building or covered place providing protection from bad weather or danger. If something **shelters** you or provides **shelter,** it gives protection of this kind. ■ If you **shelter** somewhere, you go somewhere where you are protected from bad weather or danger. ■ A **sheltered** place is protected from bad weather. ■ If something is **sheltered** from something which could harm it, it is protected from it. ■ If someone has had a **sheltered** upbringing, they have been protected from harmful or upsetting experiences and therefore may be rather innocent and trusting. ■ **Sheltered** accommodation consists of small dwelling units supervised by a warden. It is designed for elderly people or for other people who want homes of their own but need help.

shelve (shelving, shelved) If a scheme or proposal is **shelved,** it is dropped or put to one side for a while. ■ **Shelves** is the plural of 'shelf'. ■ If you **shelve** objects, especially books, you put them on shelves. ■ **Shelving** is a set or system of shelves.

shenanigans You can use **shenanigans** to refer to behaviour which is dishonest or immoral but rather amusing. *...the 66-year-old millionaire's sexual shenanigans with a judge's wife.*

shepherd (shepherdess, shepherdesses) A **shepherd** is a person whose job is to look after a herd of sheep. In the past, a female shepherd was called a **shepherdess.** ■ If you **shepherd** a group of people somewhere, you guide them to make sure they reach the right place.

shepherd's pie is a dish consisting of minced meat, usually lamb, covered with a layer of mashed potato.

sherbet is a sweet edible powder with a fizzy taste.

sheriff In the US, a **sheriff** is a person elected to make sure the law is obeyed in a particular county. ■ In Scotland, a **sheriff** is a legal officer whose chief duty is to act as judge in a Sheriff Court. These courts deal with all but the most serious crimes and with most civil actions. ■ The **sheriff** of an English or Welsh county is a person appointed by the monarch to carry out ceremonial duties.

sherpa – **Sherpas** are a group of people who live on the slopes of the Himalayas in Nepal. They are well known for their abilities as mountain guides.

sherry (sherries) Sherry is a fortified white wine.

Shetland pony A **Shetland pony** is a very small strong pony with long shaggy hair.

shibboleth A **shibboleth** is a principle or practice, especially one which is thought of as old-fashioned and no longer appropriate.

shield A **shield** is a large piece of a strong material such as metal or plastic, carried for protection by someone likely to be involved in fighting. ■ If someone or something **shields** you, they protect you from harm or danger by being between you and the danger. Other things which provide protection of some kind are called **shields.** *Greenpeace intends to form a human shield to protect the whales.* ■ A **shield** is a sports trophy.

shift If you **shift** something somewhere, you move it there. If something **shifts,** it moves slightly. *...shifting sand dunes.* ■ A **shift** in a situation, policy, or someone's opinion is a change in it. *Attitudes to mental illness have shifted in recent years.* ■ When responsibility or blame is transferred to a different person, you can say it is **shifted** to them. ■ When a kind of work goes on continuously, people often work set periods called **shifts.** The people who work a particular shift are themselves called a **shift.** *Most of the morning shift at the shipyard stopped work.* ■ A **shift** is a sleeveless, waistless dress. ■ See also **red shift.**

shift key A **shift key** on a typewriter or computer keyboard is the button you press to make the next letter you type a capital.

shifty (shiftiness) Shifty is used to describe people who behave in a cunning and deceitful way.

shilling Before the change to decimal currency in 1971, the **shilling** was a British coin worth 5p. ■ The **shilling** is the unit of currency in some African countries.

shilly-shally (shilly-shallies, shilly-shallying, shilly-shallied) If you say someone is **shilly-shallying,** you mean they keep putting off making a decision about something.

shimmer (shimmering, shimmered) If something **shimmers,** it shines with a faint unsteady light, like the moon does when reflected in water.

shin (shinning, shinned) A person's **shin** is the front part of their leg between their knee and their ankle. The bone in this part of the leg is called the **shin bone** or **tibia.** ■ If you **shin up** a pole or tree, you climb it quickly by gripping it with your hands and legs.

shine (shining, shone) When something **shines,** it gives off or reflects a bright light. ■ If you **shine** a torch or searchlight on something, you direct its light there. ■ If you **shine** metal, you make it gleam by rubbing or polishing it. *...shining aluminium machines.* ■ If you put a **shine** on something, you improve the impression it makes. ■ If you **shine** at an activity or skill, you are particularly good at it. ■ If something like a feeling or a quality **shines** from someone, it is very obvious that they have it. ■ **Shining** is used to talk about behaviour and personal qualities which are outstandingly good. *...a shining reputation.*

shingle is small pieces of stone you find on the sea shore or the edge of a river.

shingles is a disease, mainly affecting elderly people, which causes a painful red rash, usually on just one side of the body.

Shinto is the traditional religion of Japan. Its followers worship many gods, who they believe live in places like rivers and mountains.

shiny (shinier, shiniest) Shiny things have a gleaming surface and reflect light.

ship (shipping, shipped) A **ship** is a large boat which carries passengers or cargo. ■ **Shipping** is used to talk about ships in general. *All shipping in the vicinity was directed to the scene.* ■ If things or people are **shipped** somewhere, they are transported there.

shipboard is used to talk about (a) objects used on a ship. *...shipboard winches.* (b) things which happen on a ship. *...shipboard romances.*

shipbuilding (shipbuilder) Shipbuilding is the activity or industry of building ships. A **shipbuilder** is a person or business that builds ships.

shipment A **shipment** of something is a large amount being transported somewhere by sea, land, or air. ■ When something is being transported somewhere, you call this the **shipment** of it.

shipowner A **shipowner** is a person who owns or has shares in a ship or ships.

shipping See **ship.**

shipshape If you say something is **shipshape**, you mean it is neat, tidy, and in good order.

shipwreck If there is a **shipwreck**, a ship is destroyed in an accident at sea. After the accident, what remains of the ship is also called a **shipwreck.** ■ If you have been **shipwrecked**, the ship you were sailing in has been destroyed but you have managed to survive.

shipwright A **shipwright** is a person who builds or repairs ships.

shipyard A **shipyard** is a place where ships are built or repaired.

shire is an old-fashioned word for a county. *...northern shires.* ■ The **shires** or **shire counties** are the counties in the central part of England which are mainly rural.

shire horse A **shire horse** is a large strong horse used for pulling loads.

shirk (shirker) If someone **shirks** something difficult or unpleasant that needs to be done, they avoid dealing with it. A person who behaves like this or who avoids work can be called a **shirker.**

shirt (-shirted) A **shirt** is a piece of clothing worn on the upper part of the body. **-shirted** is used to describe the kind of shirt someone is wearing. *...black-shirted militiamen.* ■ If you **lose your shirt**, you lose most or all of your money, for example as a result of a business venture. ■ **stuffed shirt:** see **stuff.**

shirt-sleeved (shirt sleeves) If a man is **shirt-sleeved** or **in shirtsleeves**, he is wearing a shirt but not a jacket, usually because it is hot.

shish kebab See **kebab.**

shit is a rude word for faeces. ■ Some people describe things or people as **shit** when they have a poor opinion of them.

shiver (shivering, shivered) If you **shiver**, you shake or tremble uncontrollably, because you are cold, frightened, or ill.

shoal A **shoal** of fish is a large group of them swimming together. ■ You can call a large number of things or people a **shoal.**

shock (shocking, shockingly) Shock is the feeling of distress you get when something unpleasant happens to you or when you get some bad news. **Shock** is used to describe things which give you this feeling. *...yesterday's shock announcement.* ■ If you are **shocked** by something, it gives you a feeling of horror, disgust, or dismay. *The film was considered shockingly violent.* ■ If someone is in **shock**, they are suffering from a serious physical condition in which their blood cannot circulate properly, for example because they have had a bad injury. ■ A **shock** is a slight movement in something like a

building when it is hit by something. *The padding should absorb any sudden shocks.* ■ A **shock** is an electric shock. ■ A **shock** of hair is a thick mass of it.

shock absorber A **shock absorber** is a device designed to reduce the effect of a force or shock, especially a device fitted to a vehicle in order to give it a smoother ride.

shocker A **shocker** is (a) a story or film which is meant to shock or frighten people. (b) a piece of news which shocks or upsets someone.

shock-horror headlines and stories are meant to shock people but are usually exaggerated.

shock wave A **shock wave** is a wave of intense pressure moving through air, earth, or water. Shock waves can be caused by earthquakes, explosions, or by supersonic planes. ■ You say a serious incident produces a **shock wave** when its effects are felt for some time afterwards.

shod See **shoe.**

shoddy (shoddier, shoddiest; shoddiness) Shoddy is used to describe things which have been done or made badly, or are of poor quality.

shoe (shod) Shoes are matching objects worn on your feet, usually over socks, tights, or stockings. Shoes usually cover most of your foot but end at your ankle. ■ You can describe what someone is wearing on their feet by saying they are **shod** in a particular way. *...workers shod in carpet slippers.*

shoehorn A **shoehorn** is a slightly curved piece of metal or plastic which you place at the back of your shoe and slide your heel down so you can put the shoe on more easily.

shoelace — Shoelaces are the long narrow cords used to fasten some kinds of shoes.

shoemaker A **shoemaker** is a person whose job is making and repairing shoes and boots.

shoestring If you do something **on a shoestring**, you do it with very little money.

shone See **shine.**

shoo If you **shoo** an animal somewhere, you make it go there by waving your arms or hands at it and shouting 'shoo' while you do it. ■ If you **shoo** people away when they are being a nuisance, you tell them to go somewhere else.

shook See **shake.**

shoot (shooting, shot) If someone **shoots** a person or animal, they fire a bullet or arrows at them, killing or injuring them. When there is a **shooting**, someone is killed or injured by being shot with a gun. ■ A **shoot** is an event at which people hunt birds or animals using guns. ■ If you **shoot** somewhere, you move there suddenly and quickly. ■ If you **shoot** someone a glance, you look at them briefly. ■ When a film is **shot**, it is filmed. ■ In sports like football and basketball, when someone **shoots**, they try to score by kicking, hitting, or throwing the ball towards goal. ■ A **shoot** is a plant which is just beginning to grow above the soil, or a new part growing from a plant or tree. ■ If something **shoots up**, it increases or grows very quickly.

shooting star A **shooting star** is the same as a meteor.

shoot-out A **shoot-out** is a fight in which people shoot at each other with guns.

shop (**shopping, shopped**) A **shop** is a building or part of a building where things are sold. ■ When you **go shopping,** you go to the shops to buy things. Your **shopping** is the things you buy when you go shopping. ■ A number of things a government or organization wants to obtain or achieve can be called a **shopping list.** ■ If you **shop around,** you go to different shops or businesses to compare prices and quality before buying something. ■ A **shop** is a part of a factory where a certain kind of work is carried out. ...*the machine shop.* ■ If you **set up shop,** you start a business. If a business or other organization **shuts up shop,** it closes, either at the end of the day or permanently. ■ See also **closed shop.**

shop assistant A **shop assistant** is a person who works in a shop selling things to customers.

shop floor The **shop floor** is used to refer to all the workers in a factory or the area where they work, especially as distinct from the management. *The pay of company directors and managers is well ahead of earnings on the shop floor.*

shop-front (*or* shopfront) A **shop-front** is the outside part of a shop which faces the street.

shopkeeper A **shopkeeper** is a person who owns a small shop.

shoplifting (**shoplifter**) **Shoplifting** is stealing things from shops while the shop is open for business. A person who does this is called a **shoplifter.**

shopper A **shopper** is a person who is shopping.

shopping See **shop.**

shopping centre A **shopping centre** is an area in a town where a lot of shops have been built close together.

shop-soiled goods are slightly dirty or damaged, and are sold cheaply.

shop steward A **shop steward** is a trade union member who has been elected to represent other members of the union.

shore (**shoring, shored**) The **shore** of a sea, lake, or wide river is the land along its edge. ■ You can use **shores** to refer to a country or continent. ...*returning to our native shores.* ■ If you **shore up** something which is weak or about to fail, you support it or strengthen it.

shoreline The **shoreline** is the place where the sea, a lake, or a wide river meets the land.

shorn If a person's or animal's hair is **shorn,** it is cut off close to their skin. ■ If you are **shorn of** something, it is taken away from you. ...*a team shorn of several stars.* ■ See also **shear.**

short is used to describe (a) things which do not last long. *He died on August 21 after a short illness.* (b) things which are small in length or distance. ...*a short journey.* (c) people or things that are of less than average height. ■ A **short** is a short film, often shown before the main film in a cinema. ■ If you are **short** of something, you do not have enough of it. ■ If something is **cut short,** it is forced to stop before it would normally end. ■ If you **sell** someone or something **short,** you make them appear to be worth less than they really are. ■ If you **stop**

short of an action, you come close to doing it, but do not actually do it. ■ If something **falls short** of a standard or level, it fails to reach it. You can also say it **comes up short.** ■ If you have a **short** temper, you get angry easily. ■ You say **in short** when you are summing up what you have just said. *He's relaxed, charming – in short, a regular guy.* ■ If a name is **short for** another name, it is a short version of it. ■ A **short** is a measure of a strong alcoholic drink like whisky. ■ **Shorts** are trousers with short legs.

shortage If there is a **shortage** of something, there is not enough of it.

shortbread is a kind of biscuit made from flour, sugar, and butter.

short-change If someone **short-changes** you, they do not give you enough change when you have bought something from them. ■ If you are **short-changed,** you are treated unfairly or dishonestly, often because you are given less of something than you deserve.

short-circuit (**short-circuiting, short-circuited**) If an electrical system or device **short-circuits,** a faulty connection or damaged wire causes electricity to travel along the wrong route, damaging the system or device. When this happens, you say there has been a **short-circuit.** ■ If you **short-circuit** a procedure, you find a quicker way of doing something which misses out some parts of the procedure.

shortcoming A person's or thing's **shortcomings** are their faults or weaknesses.

short cut A **short cut** is a quicker way of getting somewhere than the usual route. ■ A **short cut** is a quicker way of achieving something than the usual way.

shorten (**shortening, shortened**) If an event or the length of time something lasts is **shortened,** it is made to last for a shorter period. ■ If something like an object or route is **shortened,** it is reduced in length.

shortfall If there is a **shortfall** of something, there is not enough of it, or less than was expected.

shorthand is a quick way of writing which uses signs to represent words and syllables.

short-handed If a company or organization is **short-handed,** it does not have enough people to work on a particular job.

short-haul See **haul.**

shortlist (*or* short-list) If you are **shortlisted** or put on a **shortlist,** you are included in a small number of people being considered for a job or prize.

short-lived things do not last very long.

shortly If something is going to happen **shortly,** it is going to happen soon. If something happens **shortly** before or after something else, it happens just before it or just after it.

short-range things reach or cover only a short distance.

short-sighted (**short-sightedness**) If you are **short-sighted,** you cannot see distant things clearly. ■ A **short-sighted** decision does not take account of the way things may develop in the future. ...*the short-sightedness of the government's approach.*

short story A **short story** is a short piece of fiction.

short-tempered people get angry easily.

short-term problems or actions last for only a short time.

short-time If workers in a factory or business are put on **short-time,** they work less hours than a normal working week.

short wave is used to talk about the range of radio waves up to 100 metres which are used in broadcasting.

shot See **shoot.** ■ If you fire a **shot,** you fire a gun once. ■ If someone is a good **shot,** they can shoot accurately. ■ In sport, a **shot** is hitting or kicking the ball in an attempt to score. ■ A **shot** is a photograph or a single picture or uninterrupted sequence in a film. *...the opening shots.* ■ An injection of a drug is often called a **shot.** *...a shot of penicillin.* ■ If you say something is a **shot in the arm,** you mean it provides help and encouragement, and is likely to produce an improvement. ■ If you **have a shot** at something, you try to do it. ■ If you say a course of action is a **long shot,** you mean it is unlikely to succeed but is worth trying anyway. ■ The person who **calls the shots** is in a position to control what happens. ■ If you do something **like a shot,** you do it without delay. ■ If you want to **get shot of** something, you want to get rid of it. ■ If you say something is **shot through** with a particular quality or element, you mean it is full of it. ■ A **shot** of a strong alcoholic drink is a small measure of it. ■ See also **shot put.**

shotgun A **shotgun** is a gun designed for shooting birds and animals. It fires a lot of small metal balls at one time.

shot put (**shot putter**) In athletics, the **shot put** or **shot** is a field event in which contestants throw a heavy metal ball called the **shot** as far as possible. A **shot putter** is someone who competes in the shot put.

should If you think something **should** happen, you think it is right or a good idea. ■ You can say something **should** happen when you are expecting it to happen. *Germination should take 14-21 days.* ■ You say **'I should think...'** or **'I should imagine...'** when you are saying you think something is probably true. ■ You say **'I should like...'** when you are expressing a wish. ■ **Should** is used (a) when asking for advice, permission, or information. *Should I give him the benefit of the doubt?* (b) when giving advice. *I should press for a rematch, if I were you.* ■ **Should** is used when mentioning the effect something might have if it happened. *Should the lobbying succeed, then changes could occur over here as well.*

shoulder (**shouldering, shouldered**) Your **shoulders** are the parts of your body between your neck and the tops of your arms. ■ If you **shoulder** a heavy object, you carry it across your shoulder. ■ If you **shoulder** a responsibility, you accept it. ■ You can say someone is **looking over their shoulder** when they are worried by a possible challenge or threat. ■ If you **rub shoulders** with famous people, you meet them and talk to them. ■ If you talk about a group of people standing **shoulder to shoulder,** you mean they are supporting each oth-

er. ■ A **shoulder** is a joint of meat from the upper part of the front leg of an animal.

shoulder blade Your **shoulder blades** are the two large flat triangular bones in the upper part of your back. In biology, they are called the **scapulas** or **scapulae.**

shout (**shouting, shouted**) If you **shout,** you raise your voice when you speak, usually because you are angry or you want to be heard a long way away. ■ If you **shout** someone **down,** you prevent them from being heard by shouting at them. ■ A **shout** is a loud call or cry.

shove (**shoving, shoved**) If you **shove** someone or something or give them a **shove,** you push them hard. If you **shove** them somewhere, you push them there forcefully.

shovel (**shovelling, shovelled**) (*Am:* **shoveling, shoveled**) A **shovel** is a tool like a spade, for lifting and moving things like earth, coal, or snow. If you **shovel** something somewhere, you move it there using a shovel. ■ If you **shovel** something into a container, you push a lot of it in quickly.

show (**showing, showed, have shown**) If something **shows** that something is the case, it proves it or makes people aware of it. *The survey shows that children use the phone more than adults.* ■ If something **shows,** it is obvious or visible. *Faint glimmers of daylight were showing through the trees.* ■ If a person or thing **shows** a quality or characteristic, you can see they have it. *In the past he has shown reluctance to intercede.* ■ What a picture **shows** is what it represents. ■ If you **show** something to someone, you give it to them, take them to it, or point it out, so they can see it. ■ If you **show** someone how to do something, you demonstrate how to do it. ■ If you **show** someone to a room or a seat, you take them to it. ■ If you make a **show** of doing something, you do it in an obvious way because you want people to see you doing it. ■ If you do something **for show,** you do it just to make a good impression. ■ If someone **shows off,** they try to impress people. If they do it a lot, you can call them a **show-off.** ■ If you **show off** something you have and are proud of, you show it to a lot of people. ■ If something **shows** something else **off,** it emphasizes its good qualities or features. ■ A **show** is a form of light entertainment at the theatre or on TV. ■ When a film or TV programme is **shown,** it appears in a cinema or on TV. ■ A **show** is an exhibition of things, often involving things entered in a competition. *...the Chelsea Flower Show.* ■ If something like a collection of paintings is **shown** or **on show,** it appears in an exhibition or an art gallery. ■ If you **show up** somewhere, you arrive there. ■ If you **have** something **to show** for your efforts, you have achieved something definite as a result of them.

showbiz is another name for show business.

showbusiness (*or* **show business**) is the entertainment industry, including films, theatre, and television.

showcase (**showcasing, showcased**) A **showcase** is a situation or setting in which something is shown off to its best advantage. *Graduate Fashion Week has* become the most important showcase for young designers. When something is placed in a situation or setting like this, you can say it is **showcased.** ■ A **showcase** is a glass container used to display valuable or interesting things.

showdown A **showdown** is a big argument or conflict which is intended to settle a dispute once and for all.

shower (showering, showered) A **shower** is a device which sprays water on you so you can wash yourself. If you **shower** or have a **shower,** you wash yourself by standing under a shower. ■ A **shower** is a short period of rain or snow. ■ A lot of small objects falling can be called a **shower.** If you are **showered** with small objects, a lot of them fall on you. ■ If you **shower** someone with something, you give them a lot of it.

showery If the weather is **showery,** it keeps raining on and off.

showily See **showy.**

showing See **show.** ■ If you talk about someone's **showing,** you are talking about how well or badly they have done in a contest. *...their strong showing in the local elections.* ■ Each presentation of a film is called a **showing.**

show jumping (or **showjumping**) is a sport in which horses are ridden in competitions to demonstrate their skill in jumping over fences.

showman (showmen; showmanship) If you call a man a **showman** or talk about his **showmanship,** you mean he keeps trying to impress people by presenting things in a dramatic or entertaining way.

shown See **show.**

show-off See **show.**

showpiece You call something like a piece of music a **showpiece** when it can be used to show a performer's skill. ■ A **showpiece** is something which is meant to be admired, because it is supposed to be the best possible example of a certain type of thing. *Betws drift mine, opened in 1978 as a showpiece pit, is now reduced to 95 miners.*

showroom A **showroom** is a shop where goods such as cars, furniture, or electrical goods are displayed for sale.

show trial People describe a trial as a **show trial** if they believe that the trial is unfair and is held for political reasons rather than to establish the truth.

showy (showily) If you call something **showy,** you mean it is large or expensive-looking and meant to impress people.

shrank See **shrink.**

shrapnel is small pieces of metal scattered from exploding bombs and shells.

shred (shredding, shredded; shredder) If you **shred** something, you cut or tear it into very small pieces. A **shredder** is a machine which shreds things like paper. ■ A **shred** of a material is a small piece cut or torn from a larger piece. ■ If you say there is not a **shred** of something, you are emphasizing that there is none of it.

shrew The **shrew** is a small mouse-like animal with a long pointed nose. ■ A bad-tempered woman is sometimes called a **shrew.**

shrewd (shrewdly, shrewdness) A **shrewd** person is able to judge a situation quickly and use their judgement to their own advantage. You call an action **shrewd** when it shows this ability.

shriek (shrieking, shrieked) If someone **shrieks** or lets out a **shriek,** they give a loud scream, because they are in pain or suddenly frightened. You can also say people **shriek** with laughter.

shrift If someone or something is given **short shrift,** they are dealt with quickly and unsympathetically.

shrill (shrilly) A **shrill** sound is high-pitched, piercing, and unpleasant.

shrimp — **Shrimps** are small shellfish with a long tail and many legs.

shrine A **shrine** is a holy place of worship which is associated with a sacred person or object. ■ A **shrine** is a place which people visit and treat with respect because it is associated with a famous person or event.

shrink (shrinking, shrank, have shrunk) If something **shrinks,** it gets smaller. ■ If you **shrink away** from doing something, you are reluctant to do it because you find it unpleasant. ■ People sometimes call a psychiatrist a **shrink.**

shrinkage is a decrease in the size or amount of something.

shrivel (shrivelling, shrivelled) (Am: **shriveling, shriveled**) If something like a plant **shrivels** or **shrivels up,** it becomes dry and wrinkled. ■ You can say something **shrivels** when it gets smaller in size, amount, or influence.

shroud (shrouding, shrouded) If something is **shrouded** in secrecy or mystery, very little is known about it. ■ If a place is **shrouded** in darkness, cloud, or fog, it is hidden by it. ■ A **shroud** is the cloth a dead body is sometimes wrapped in before it is buried.

Shrove Tuesday is the day before the beginning of Lent. It is also known as Pancake Day because people traditionally make pancakes on this day.

shrub A **shrub** is a plant like a small tree with several woody stems instead of a trunk.

shrubbery (shrubberies) A **shrubbery** is an area where shrubs are grown. ■ **Shrubbery** is shrubs in general. *...clumps of exotic shrubbery.*

shrug (shrugging, shrugged) If you **shrug** your shoulders or give a **shrug,** you raise and lower your shoulders to show you do not know or care about something. ■ If you **shrug** something **off,** you treat it as trivial or unimportant.

shrunk See **shrink.**

shrunken If something is **shrunken,** it has become smaller.

shudder (shuddering, shuddered) If you **shudder** or give a **shudder,** you tremble with fear or disgust. ■ If a machine **shudders,** it shakes violently.

shuffle (shuffling, shuffled) If you **shuffle** somewhere, you walk there without lifting your feet properly. ■ If you **shuffle** about, you move about and fidget because you feel uncomfortable or embarrassed. ■ If you **shuffle** cards, you mix them up before a game. ■ If you **shuffle** things such as pieces of paper, you move them around or change their order.

shun (**shunning, shunned**) If you **shun** someone or something, you deliberately avoid them.

shunt When railway engines **shunt**, they push or pull carriages or wagons from one railway line to another. ■ If someone or something is **shunted** about, they are moved from one place to another.

shut (**shutting, shut**) If you **shut** something, you close it. ■ If a shop or other business **shuts**, it is no longer open for business. If it **shuts down**, work stops there permanently. When this happens, you say there is a **shutdown**. ■ If you **shut** yourself **away** or **shut** yourself **off**, you avoid going out and seeing other people, usually because you are depressed. ■ If people are **shut out** of a place, they are prevented from getting in. Similarly, you can talk about people being **shut out** of something like a competition. ■ If you **shut up**, you stop talking.

shutter (**shuttering, shuttered**) Shutters are wooden or metal covers fitted on the outside of a window. They can be closed to protect the window or shut out light. ■ The **shutter** in a camera is the part which opens to allow light through when a photograph is taken.

shuttle (**shuttling, shuttled**) A **shuttle** service is an air, bus, or train service which makes frequent journeys between two places. See also **space shuttle**. ■ If someone or something **shuttles** between places, they move frequently between them. ■ **Shuttle diplomacy** is the movement of diplomats between countries in order to mediate between leaders who refuse to talk directly to each other.

shuttlecock A **shuttlecock** is a cone-shaped object you hit over the net in a game of badminton.

shy (**shyly, shyness; shies, shying, shied**) A **shy** person is nervous and uncomfortable with other people. You can also say a wild animal is **shy** when it avoids people. ■ If you are **shy of** doing something, you do not want to do it, because you are afraid of the consequences. ■ If you **fight shy** of something, you try to avoid it. ■ If you **shy away** from something, you avoid becoming involved in it. ■ If a figure is **shy of** a particular amount, it does not quite reach it. ■ If a horse **shies**, it makes a sudden violent movement, because it is frightened.

shyster If you call someone like a lawyer or a politician a **shyster,** you mean they are dishonest and unscrupulous.

SI The **SI** system is an international system of metric units. There are seven basic SI units, including the metre, kilogram, second, and amp. SI is short for 'Système International d'Unités'.

Siamese twins are twins who are born joined to each other by part of their bodies.

sibilant – Sibilants are speech sounds like 's' or 'z' which produce a hissing effect. You can say someone's voice is **sibilant** when it contains a lot of these sounds.

sibling Your **siblings** are your brothers and sisters.

sic When you are reproducing a piece of writing, you write **sic** in brackets after a mistake to show it is the author's mistake, not your own.

sick (**sickness, sicknesses**) If you are **sick,** you have a disease or illness. A **sickness** is a disease or illness. The **sick** are people who are sick. ■ If you feel **sick,** you feel as if you are going to vomit. If you are **sick,** you vomit. ■ If you are **sick** of something, you are annoyed or bored by it and want it to stop. ■ A **sick** story or joke deals frivolously or tastelessly with death, cruelty, or suffering.

sick bay A **sick bay** is an area, for example on a ship, where people can be given medical care.

sick bed Your **sick bed** is the bed you are lying in while you are ill.

sick building syndrome is a name given to a collection of symptoms, including tiredness and depression, experienced by some people who work in air-conditioned and artificially-lit office buildings.

sicken (**sickening, sickened; sickeningly**) If something **sickens** you, it makes you feel disgusted and horrified.

sickle A **sickle** is a tool with a short handle and a curved blade, used for cutting long grass or grain crops.

sick leave If you are on **sick leave,** you are officially allowed to spend time away from work because of illness or injury.

sickle cell anaemia is a hereditary disease occurring mainly in black people, in which the red blood cells become sickle-shaped, causing jaundice, attacks of pain, and fever.

sickly (**sicklier, sickliest**) A **sickly** person is weak and often ill. ■ A **sickly** smell or taste is unpleasantly sweet and may make you feel slightly sick. ■ A **sickly** colour or light is unpleasantly pale or weak.

sickness benefit is money you can sometimes get from the government or an insurance company if you are unable to work because of illness.

sick pay is money you can sometimes get from your employer if you are ill and unable to work.

side (**siding, sided**) If something is at the **side** of a person or thing, it is in the position to the left or right of them. *I saw him standing at the side of the bed.* ■ The **sides** of something are its edges or outside surfaces. ■ The **sides** of something are its two halves. *The pursuing car was on the wrong side of the road.* ■ The two **sides** in a competition, argument, or battle are the two opposing groups. If you **side** with someone, you support them and oppose their enemies. ■ A particular **side** of something is an aspect of it. *...the darker side of our natures.* ■ If you get **on the wrong side of** someone, you do something to annoy them and make them dislike you. ■ If you say, for example, something is on the large **side,** you mean it is rather too large. ■ **Side** is used to describe things which are not the main or most important ones of their kind. *...a side road. ...a side issue.* ■ If you do some work **on the side,** you do it in addition to your main job.

sideboard A **sideboard** is a long low cupboard, in which plates and glasses are kept. ■ **Sideboards** are the same as sideburns.

sideburns If a man has **sideburns,** he has a strip of hair growing down the side of each cheek, in front of his ears.

sidecar A **sidecar** is a small structure attached to the side of a motorbike for carrying a passenger.

side effect The **side effects** of a drug are the unwanted and non-beneficial effects it has in addition to the intended ones. ■ The **side effects** of an action or situation are other things which happen in addition to its main consequences.

sidekick If you talk about a powerful person's **sidekicks,** you mean their assistants.

sideline (sidelining, sidelined) A **sideline** is an extra job you do in addition to your main one. ■ If you are **on the sidelines** when something is happening, you are not actively involved in it. ■ If you are **sidelined,** you are not included in what other people are doing, and are made to seem unimportant.

side-saddle If you ride a horse **side-saddle,** you sit with both your legs on one side.

sideshow The **sideshows** at a fairground are the stalls where you do things like shooting and throwing darts. ■ If you call an event or issue a **sideshow,** you mean it is less important than other things happening at the same time.

sidestep (sidestepping, sidestepped) If you **sidestep** a problem or question, you avoid dealing with it. ■ If you **sidestep** something like a punch, you avoid it by stepping sideways.

sideswipe If you take a **sideswipe** at something, you make an unexpected attack on it while discussing something else.

sidetrack If you are **sidetracked** by something, it makes you forget what you are supposed to be doing and start doing something else.

sidewalk is the usual American word for a pavement.

sideways If you move **sideways,** you have to your left or right.

siding A railway **siding** is a short stretch of track beside the main tracks where engines, trucks, or carriages can stand when they are not being used.

sidle (sidling, sidled) If someone **sidles** up to you, they come up to you cautiously, because they do not want to be noticed.

SIDS is the sudden death of a young baby in sleep, which doctors cannot account for. The letters stand for 'sudden infant death syndrome', also known as 'cot death'.

siege A **siege** is a military or police operation in which soldiers or police surround a place in order to force the people inside to surrender or come out. You can say the soldiers or police are **laying siege** to a place or it is **under siege.** ■ You can say someone or something is **under siege** when they are constantly being criticized or put under pressure. ■ If a person or organization has a **siege mentality,** they refuse to co-operate because they think other people are constantly trying to harm them.

sierra A **sierra** is a range of mountains with jagged peaks, especially in Spain or America.

siesta In hot countries, when people have a **siesta,** they have a short sleep in the afternoon.

sieve (sieving, sieved) A **sieve** is an implement consisting of a metal or plastic ring with a wire or plastic net underneath. You pass substances through the net when you want to sift or strain them. ■ If you **sieve** a liquid or powder, you put it through a sieve.

sift If you **sift** something such as evidence or **sift through** it, you examine it carefully, to separate what is important or useful from what is not. ■ If you **sift** a powdery substance such as flour or sand, you put it through a sieve to remove large lumps.

sigh If you **sigh** or let out a **sigh,** you let out a deep breath which is loud enough to be heard. ■ If you **sigh** something, you say it in a voice which expresses disappointment or sadness.

sight (sighting, sighted; -sighted) Sight is the ability to see. A **sighted** person is not blind. **-sighted** is added to some words to describe the extent to which someone can see. *...a near-sighted person.* ■ The **sight** of something is seeing it. *The sight of blood made him sick.* ■ If something is **in sight,** you can see it. ■ When something unusual is **sighted,** someone notices it. An occasion like this is called a **sighting.** ■ If you do something **on sight,** you do it as soon as you see someone. *Police were given the legal right to fire on sight at suspects.* ■ If you **lose sight of** an aim or objective, you become confused or distracted by other issues and forget the point of what you are doing. ■ If a result or decision is **in sight,** it is likely to happen soon. *His supporters claimed that a breakthrough was in sight.* ■ A **sight** is something you see. *It was an awe-inspiring sight.* ■ **Sights** are interesting places which tourists visit. ■ The **sights** of a gun are the part which helps you aim more accurately. ■ If you **set your sights on** something, you decide you want it, and try hard to get it. ■ If you say something is **a sight** better or **a sight** worse than something else, you mean it is very much better or very much worse.

sight-read Musicians who can **sight-read** can play or sing music from the printed sheet the first time they see it, without practising beforehand.

sightscreen In cricket, the **sightscreens** are the tall white wooden screens which are placed behind the bowler so that the batsman can see the ball clearly.

sightseeing (sightseer) If you go **sightseeing,** you travel around, looking at the interesting places tourists usually visit. People who do this are called **sightseers.**

sign (signing) If you **sign** a document, you write your signature on it. ■ If you **sign on,** you officially state you are unemployed so you can receive money from the government. ■ If you **sign for** something, you officially state you have received it by signing a form. ■ If a sports team makes a **signing,** a new player signs a contract to play for them. ■ If you **sign up** for something, you sign a form to say you will do a job or course of study. ■ A **sign** of something is evidence that it exists or is happening. *...signs of infection.* ■ A **sign** is a mark or shape with a particular meaning, for example in maths or music. *...an equals sign.* ■ If you make a **sign**, you move your hand or hands in a way which conveys a special meaning. **Signing** is the use of sign language to communicate with and between deaf people. ■ A **sign** is a piece of wood, metal, or plastic with words and sometimes a picture on it, giving information or instructions. ■ The **signs** of the zodiac are the twelve areas into which astrologers divide the heavens.

signal (**signalling, signalled; signally**) (*Am:* **signaling, signaled**) If an event or action **signals** something or is a **signal** of it, it suggests it exists or is going to happen. *Pundits were divided over whether the budget signalled a June election.* ■ If you **signal** something, you indicate it by means of a gesture. *The referee signalled that the fight was over.* ■ A **signal** is a series of sound or light waves which carry information. ■ A **signal** is a piece of equipment beside a railway which tells train drivers if it is safe to go on or not. ■ A **signal** success or failure is a particularly significant and noticeable one. *...the measures that have so signally failed since 1990.*

signal box A **signal box** is a building next to a railway which houses the switches and buttons controlling the signals and points.

signalman (**signalmen**) A **signalman** is a person whose job is to control the signals and points on a stretch of railway track.

signatory (*pron:* **sig**-na-tree) (**signatories**) The **signatories** of an official document are the people who have signed it.

signature Your **signature** is your name as you write it yourself, for example on a cheque.

signature tune The **signature tune** of a regular TV or radio programme is the tune played at the beginning or end of it.

signboard A **signboard** is a piece of wood with information written or printed on it.

signet ring A **signet ring** is a ring with a panel in the middle engraved with an initial or design.

significant (**significantly, significance**) If something is **significant**, it is important. *The legislation was of immense significance.* ■ A **significant** amount is a large amount.

signify (**signifies, signifying, signified**) If you talk about what something **signifies**, you are talking about what it means. *Their help signified a silent protest against the government.*

sign language is a way of communicating using gestures, used especially by people who are deaf or unable to speak.

signpost A **signpost** is a road sign showing where different roads go to and how far it is to the nearest towns and villages. Signposts are also placed on footpaths. ■ If a route is **signposted**, it has signposts beside the road or path showing the way. ■ If something **signposts** something else or is a **signpost** for it, it is a good indication of it. *The work signposts hope one day for a cure.*

Sikh (**Sikhism**) **Sikhism** is an Indian religion which separated from Hinduism in the 16th century and which teaches that there is only one God. Someone who practises this religion is called a **Sikh**.

silage (*pron:* **sile**-ij) is a crop such as grass which is harvested when it is green and then partially fermented in a silo to make fodder for animals.

silence (**silencing, silenced**) If there is **silence**, there is no noise at all. ■ If something or someone is **silenced**, they are prevented from making a noise or speaking. ■ If you say there is **silence** on an issue, you mean nothing is being said about it. ■ If someone **breaks their silence**, they speak out about something they had earlier refused to discuss.

silencer A **silencer** is a device on a vehicle exhaust, or on a gun, which makes it quieter.

silent (**silently**) If you are **silent**, you are not speaking or not making any noise. ■ A **silent** person does not talk much. ■ If you are **silent** about a particular matter, you are not saying anything about it. ■ You call an action **silent** when it takes place without any words being spoken. *...silent prayer.* ■ A **silent** film has no sound or speech.

silhouette (**silhouetted**) A **silhouette** is the outline of a dark shape against a bright light or a pale background. When you see a person or object like this, you say you see them **silhouetted** against the light or background; you also say you see them **in silhouette**.

silica is a mineral found in sand, quartz, and flint. It is used to make glass.

silicon is an element used to make parts of computers and other electronic equipment.

silicon chip A **silicon chip** is a tiny square of silicon with electronic components on it. Silicon chips are used as part of a circuit in computers and electronic equipment.

silicone is a tough artificial substance made from silicon. It is used in paints and non-stick surfaces and in cosmetic surgery.

silk is a substance produced by silkworms to make their cocoons. It is made into smooth fine cloth or sewing thread. The cloth and thread are also known as **silk**. ■ When a barrister **takes silk**, he or she becomes a Queen's Counsel or 'QC'. QCs are sometimes called **silks**.

silken things are smooth and soft. ■ **Silken** material is made of silk.

silk-screen (**silk-screening**) **Silk-screen** printing or **silk-screening** is a method of printing patterns onto paper or cloth by forcing ink through a patterned mesh, usually of silk.

silkworm — **Silkworms** are a type of caterpillar. They are reared to obtain silk from their cocoons.

silky things are smooth, soft, and shiny like silk.

sill A **sill** is a ledge at the bottom of a window.

silly (**sillier, silliest; silliness**) If you say someone is being **silly**, you mean they are behaving in a foolish or childish way. *She looked round to make sure there was no giggling or silliness.* ■ In Britain, the **silly season** is the period in the summer when Parliament and the law courts are not sitting, and the newspapers often run trivial stories because they have little serious news to report.

silo (**silos**) A **silo** is (a) a tall round metal tower on a farm in which silage is made or grain is stored. (b) a specially built place underground where missiles are kept ready to be launched.

silt is fine sand or mud carried along by a river. If a river, lake, or harbour **silts up,** it becomes blocked with silt which has settled at the bottom.

silver is a valuable greyish-white metal used for making jewellery and ornaments. ■ In a house, the **silver** is the things made of silver, such as cutlery or dishes. ■ **Silver** is coins such as 10p and 5p pieces, which look like silver. ■ **Silver** is the colour of silver. ■ The runner-up in a contest often gets a **silver** medal. ■ If you say there is a **silver lining,** you are talking about something positive that comes out of a sad or unpleasant situation. ■ The cinema is sometimes called the **silver screen.** ■ If you celebrate a **silver** jubilee or wedding, you are celebrating a 25th anniversary.

silver birch The **silver birch** is a tree with greyish-white bark.

silversmith A **silversmith** is a person whose job is making things out of silver.

silver-tongued If you call someone **silver-tongued,** you mean they are very persuasive.

silverware is cutlery and dishes made of silver or of a metal which looks like silver.

silvery is used to describe things which look like silver.

simian is used to talk about things to do with monkeys and apes. *...our simian ancestors.* ■ **Simian** is used to describe people whose features remind you of a monkey.

similar (similarity, similarities) If things are **similar** or there is a **similarity** between them, they are quite like each other. ■ **Similarities** are features things have in common. *The two books show remarkable similarities in their plots.*

similarly You use **similarly** to say things are alike. *...two similarly dressed girls.*

simile (*pron:* **sim**-ill-lee) A **simile** is a way of describing something by saying it is like something else.

simmer (simmering, simmered) When you **simmer** food, you cook it by keeping it just below boiling point. ■ If a violent situation or quarrel is **simmering,** it is not openly expressed, but is liable to break out at any time.

simper (simpering, simpered) If someone **simpers,** they smile in a silly self-conscious way.

simple (simpler, simplest; simplicity) If you say something is **simple** or talk about its **simplicity,** you mean it is easy to understand. ■ A **simple** task is easy to do. ■ **Simple** things are plain and not elaborate in style. ■ If you need a **simple majority** to win a vote, you only need to gain more than half of the votes, rather than any higher percentage.

simple interest is interest calculated only on the amount of money you originally invest, and not on any interest which is added to it later. See also **compound interest.**

simple-minded You say someone is **simple-minded** when they interpret things in a way which is too simple and do not understand how complicated things really are.

simpleton If you call someone a **simpleton,** you mean they are of very low intelligence.

simplicity See **simple.**

simplify (simplifies, simplifying, simplified; simplification) If you **simplify** something, you make it simpler. You can call a simpler version of something a **simplification.**

simplistic (simplistically) A **simplistic** view or interpretation makes something seem less complicated than it really is.

simply You use **simply** to emphasize that something has only one component, cause, or function. *I am simply a science reporter... Most of the damage that occurred was simply because of fallen trees.* ■ You use **simply** to emphasize what you are saying. *We simply must find a better way to do it.* ■ If you do something **simply,** you do it in an uncomplicated way, without adding any unnecessary elements. *The flat was painted very simply in white throughout.*

simulate (simulating, simulated; simulation) If you **simulate** something, you imitate it or produce an artificial version of it. *Training includes realistic simulation of casualty procedures.*

simulator A **simulator** is a device designed to reproduce actual conditions, for example to train pilots or test new cars.

simulcast If a programme is **simulcast,** it is broadcast on two or more TV channels at the same time, or on TV and radio at the same time. A **simulcast** is a programme broadcast in this way.

simultaneous (simultaneously) Simultaneous things happen or exist at the same time.

sin (sinning, sinned; sinner) In many religions, **sin** is breaking God's laws by doing something bad or immoral. Someone who behaves like this is called a **sinner.** The thing they do is called a **sin.** If someone **sins,** they commit a sin.

sin-bin In some team sports such as ice hockey and rugby league, the **sin-bin** is the place where players sit when they have been temporarily sent off.

since If something has been happening **since** a particular time, it has been happening from that time until now. ■ **Since** is used to say something happened at some point between a time in the past and the present. *He died in 1984 and has since been named as a key member in the so-called Oxford spy ring.* ■ **Since** is used to say something happened a certain length of time ago. *It is 250 years since the wolf became extinct in Britain.* ■ If something has **long since** ceased to happen, it has not happened for a very long time.

sincere (sincerely, sincerity) If someone is **sincere,** they genuinely mean the things they say. You talk about the **sincerity** of someone like this. ■ You write **Yours sincerely** followed by your signature at the end of a formal letter when you have addressed it to someone by their name. For example, if you begin a letter 'Dear Mr Smith' you end it 'Yours sincerely'.

sinecure (*pron:* **sign**-i-cure) If you call a job a **sinecure,** you mean it is well-paid but does not involve much work or responsibility.

sine die (*pron:* **sign**-ee **die**-ee) If something is postponed **sine die,** it is postponed indefinitely. Similarly in sport, a player can be suspended **sine die.**

sine qua non (*pron:* **sign**-ee kwa **non**) If something is a **sine qua non,** it is essential if you want to achieve something or take part in something.

sinew A **sinew** is a cord which connects a muscle to a bone.

sinewy A **sinewy** person is lean and muscular.

sinful When religious people talk about behaviour being **sinful,** they mean it is wicked or immoral.

sing (**singing, sang, have sung**) If you **sing,** you use your voice to produce a tune and sometimes the words that go with it. ■ When birds or insects **sing,** they make pleasant high-pitched sounds. ■ If you **sing** someone's **praises,** you praise them enthusiastically.

singe (**singeing, singed**) If something is **singed,** it is burned slightly so that it changes colour but does not catch fire.

singer A **singer** is someone who sings, especially as their job.

single (**singling, singled**) A **single** thing is just one thing and not more. ■ If you talk about each **single** thing, you mean each one taken individually. *Everyone believed it was the right way forward for Europe but not everyone liked every single point.* ■ If you are **single,** you are not married. You can also say a person is **single** when they do not have a boyfriend or girlfriend. **Singles** activities and organizations are aimed at people who are single and looking for a partner. *...a singles bar.* ■ **Singles** is a game between two players in tennis, badminton, and several other sports. ■ A **single** bed or room is intended for one person. ■ A **single** ticket is a one-way ticket. ■ A **single** is a recording of one or two short pieces of music on a small record, CD, or cassette. ■ If you **single** someone or something **out,** you pick them from a group for special treatment. ■ **single file:** see **file.**

single-breasted A **single-breasted** coat or jacket meets in the middle of the chest and has only one set of buttons.

single cream is thin cream with less fat than most other types.

single-decker A **single-decker** bus does not have an upstairs area.

single-handed (**single-handedly**) If you do something **single-handed** or **single-handedly,** you do it without help from anyone else.

single-minded If someone is **single-minded,** they have one aim and are determined to achieve it.

single sex schools, clubs, or other organizations accept people of only one sex.

singlet A **singlet** is a sleeveless T-shirt shaped like a vest.

singly If things happen **singly,** they happen one at a time.

sing-song A **sing-song** is an occasion when a group of people sing songs together for pleasure. ■ A **sing-song** voice rises and falls in pitch.

singular (**singularity**) If you call something **singular** or talk about its **singularity,** you mean it is unusual and remarkable. ■ A **singular** noun or pronoun is used to talk about just one person or thing.

singularly means to a remarkable or extraordinary degree. *The property market, in particular, is singularly depressed.*

sinister is used to describe people or things that seem evil or threatening.

sink (**sinking, sank, have sunk**) A **sink** is a basin with taps. ■ If something **sinks,** it moves slowly downwards, especially through water. ■ If a ship is **sunk,** it is attacked with weapons until it sinks. ■ If you **sink** something sharp into an object, you push it deep into the object. *He sank his teeth into an apple.* ■ If an amount **sinks,** it decreases. ■ If something **sinks** into an undesirable or less active state, it passes gradually into it. *The American economy sank into recession in 1990.* ■ If your **heart sinks,** you feel dismayed. ■ When a fact **sinks in,** you fully understand it or realize it.

sinner See **sin.**

Sino- is used to talk about something involving China and another country. *...the Sino-Russian border.*

sinuous is used to describe (a) things which are full of turns or curves. *It's a great drive, a sinuous meander through redwoods.* (b) people and animals that are supple and graceful.

sinus (**sinuses**) Your **sinuses** are the spaces in the bones around your nose.

sinusitis is a painful inflammation of the sinuses.

sip (**sipping, sipped**) If you **sip** a drink, you drink a small amount at a time. Each mouthful can be called a **sip.**

siphon (*or* **syphon**) (**siphoning, siphoned**) If someone **siphons** money or **siphons** it **off,** they use it for a purpose it was not intended for. ■ If you **siphon** a liquid or **siphon** it **off,** you draw it out of a container through a tube using atmospheric pressure.

sir A man is sometimes addressed as **sir.** ■ **Sir** is used in front of the name of a knight or baronet. *...Sir Charles Chadwyck-Healey.*

sire (**siring, sired**) A horse's **sire** is its father. You talk about a male horse **siring** a foal.

siren A **siren** is a warning device which makes a long loud wailing sound. ■ **Siren** is used to talk about ideas which are attractive and tempting, but which are likely to lead to disaster. You can talk about the **siren song** or **siren call** of ideas like these. ■ A woman is sometimes called a **siren** when she is attractive and dangerous to men.

sirloin A **sirloin** is a piece of beef cut from the lower part of the animal's back.

sisal (*pron:* **sigh**-sal) is a tropical plant which is cultivated so that the fibre from its leaves can be used to make rope.

sissy (*or* **cissy**) (**sissies**) When children call someone, especially a boy, a **sissy,** they mean he is cowardly and physically weak.

sister Your **sister** is a girl or woman who has the same parents as you. See also **half-sister.** ■ A **sister** is a member of a female religious community. ■ In a hospital, a **sister** is a female senior nurse who supervises a ward. ■ If you talk about a woman's **sisters,** you mean other women she has something in common with. *The score for American women managers is also strikingly lower than the 8% reached by their British sisters.* ■ **Sister** is used to describe something of the same kind as the thing you have just mentioned, when they are both owned or run by the same company. *...an upmarket sister newspaper to The Voice.*

sisterhood is affection and loyalty between women who have something in common, especially women who support feminism. ■ A **sisterhood** is a female religious community.

sister-in-law (**sisters-in-law**) Your **sister-in-law** is the sister of your wife or husband, or your brother's wife.

sisterly is used to describe the feelings sisters have for each other, and the ways they typically behave to each other. ■ **Sisterly** is used to describe feelings of affection and loyalty between women, especially women who support feminism.

sit (**sitting, sat**) When you are **sitting** somewhere, your body weight is resting on your buttocks rather than your feet. When you **sit,** you lower your body until you are sitting on something. ■ If you **sit tight** or **sit** something **out,** you wait for it to finish without taking any action. ■ If you **sit back** while something bad is happening, you do not do anything to stop it. ■ If you **sit** an examination, you take it. ■ If you **sit** on a committee, you are a member of it. ■ If you **sit in on** a meeting, you are present but do not take part. ■ When a parliament, law court, or other official body **sits,** it assembles officially to carry out its work. Each time it does this is called a **sitting.** ■ A **sitting tenant** is a person who rents a house or flat as their home and is often legally entitled to stay there if the owner sells the property. ■ If you say someone is **sitting on** something, you mean they are avoiding dealing with it. ■ **sitting pretty:** see **pretty.**

sitar The **sitar** is a type of Indian stringed musical instrument with a long neck.

sitcom A **sitcom** is a TV comedy series which shows a set of characters becoming involved in amusing situations which are similar to everyday life. 'Sitcom' is short for 'situation comedy'.

sit-down In a **sit-down** protest, the protesters refuse to move until they get what they are asking for. ■ A **sit-down** meal is served to people sitting down at tables.

site (**siting, sited**) A **site** is a piece of ground which is being used or will be used for a particular purpose. *...a building site... Disney were slow to put hotels on the Florida site.* ■ If something is **sited** in a particular place or position, it is put there or built there. *Member states will also decide on the siting of the central bank.* ■ The **site** of something which existed or happened in the past is the place where it was. ■ A **site** is a publication on the World Wide Web that contains information on a particular subject. It is short for 'website'

sit-in A **sit-in** is a protest in which people sit in a public place and refuse to move.

sitter A **sitter** is (a) someone who sits for an artist. (b) a baby-sitter.

sitting See **sit.**

sitting room A **sitting room** is a room in a house where people sit and relax.

situated is used to describe the location of a place, such as a building. *Hotels are discreetly situated on the West Coast.*

situation When you talk about the **situation,** you are talking generally about what is happening in a particular place at a particular time. *The UN withdrew its relief personnel because it judged the situation too dangerous. ...the current financial situation.* ■ Your **situation** is your circumstances and the things which are happening to you. *I do what many others would do in my situation.* ■ The **situation** of something like a building or town is the place where it is, for example its surroundings or its distance from other buildings or towns. *With moated castle and riverside situation, this is an excellent base for exploring the lower part of the Blavet valley.*

situation comedy See **sitcom.**

six (**sixth**) Six is the number 6. ■ If people are **at sixes and sevens,** they are in a state of confusion. ■ If you say someone has a **sixth sense,** you mean they know things, or seem to know them, without having any direct evidence of them. *His sixth sense in locating the fish was uncanny.*

six-pack A **six-pack** is a set of six cans or bottles of a drink, especially beer.

sixpence The **sixpence** was a small silver coin which was used in Britain until the 1970s. It was worth six old pence (2½p).

sixteen (**sixteenth**) Sixteen is the number 16.

sixth form (**sixth former**) In English, Welsh, and Northern Irish schools, the **sixth form** is the class pupils go into at sixteen to study for 'A'-levels. Pupils normally spend two years in this form. Sixth form pupils are called **sixth-formers.**

sixty (**sixties, sixtieth**) Sixty is the number 60. ■ The **sixties** was the period from 1960 to 1969. ■ If someone is in their **sixties,** they are aged 60 to 69.

sizable See **sizeable.**

size (**sizing, sized**) The **size** of something is how big or small it is. ■ The **size** of something is the fact that it is very large. *More details are emerging of the sheer size of the disaster.* ■ A **size** is one of a series of graded measurements for things like clothes and shoes. *...size 12 feet.* ■ If someone is **cut down to size,** they are made to realize that they are not as important or powerful as they thought they were. ■ If you **size** someone or something **up,** you look at them or think about them carefully, so you can decide how to deal with them.

sizeable (or **sizable**) If you say something is **sizeable,** you mean it is fairly large.

-sized (or **-size**) You add **-sized** or **-size** to a word to describe the size of something. *...small and medium-sized companies.*

sizzle (**sizzling, sizzled**) When food which is being fried or roasted **sizzles,** it makes a hissing sound. ■ **Sizzling** is sometimes used to describe things which are exciting. *...a sizzling effort by McMahon. ...her reputation for sizzling sexuality.*

skate (**skating, skated**) A **skate** is an ice-skate or roller-skate. If you **skate,** you move about on skates. ■ If you **skate over** a difficult subject, you avoid dealing with it fully. ■ The **skate** (*plural:* **skate**) is a flat sea fish.

skateboard (skateboarding, skateboarder) A **skateboard** is a narrow board on wheels which you can stand on and ride for pleasure. **Skateboarding** is riding on a skateboard; people who do it are called **skateboarders.**

skater A **skater** is someone who ice-skates or roller-skates.

skein (*pron:* **skane**) A **skein** is a loosely coiled length of thread, especially wool or embroidery cotton.

skeletal means to do with skeletons. ...*skeletal remains.* ■ If a person is **skeletal,** they are so thin you can see the shape of their bones through their skin.

skeleton Your **skeleton** is the framework of bones in your body. ■ The **skeleton** of a building or other structure is its basic framework. ■ The **skeleton** of a plan or scheme is its basic outline, to which details may be added later. ■ If an organization operates with a **skeleton** staff, it keeps going with the smallest possible number of staff. ■ If someone has a **skeleton in the closet,** they are keeping secret something scandalous or embarrassing in their past.

skeptical (skeptic, skepticism) See **sceptical.**

sketch (sketches, sketching, sketched) If you **sketch** something or make a **sketch** of it, you make a quick rough drawing of it. ■ If you **sketch** something or **sketch** it **out,** you give a brief description of it. ■ A **sketch** is a short funny piece of acting, usually part of a comedy show.

sketchbook A **sketchbook** is a book of blank pages for drawing on.

sketchpad A **sketchpad** is the same as a sketchbook.

sketchy (sketchily) Sketchy reports or accounts are brief and incomplete. You can also say your knowledge of something is **sketchy.**

skew If something is **skewed,** it is altered or distorted so people do not get an accurate picture of a situation. ■ If something **skews,** it turns aside sharply from the direction it should be going in.

skewer (skewering, skewered) A **skewer** is a long sharp metal pin for holding food together during cooking. ■ If you **skewer** something, you push a long thin pointed object through it.

ski (skiing, skied) Skis are long flat narrow objects which you fasten to boots so you can slide over snow. When people **ski,** they slide down slopes on skis. ■ **Ski** is used to talk about various things to do with skiing. ...*ski instructors.* ...*ski boots.*

skid (skidding, skidded) If a vehicle **skids** or goes into a **skid,** it slides sideways while moving, for example on a wet or icy road. ■ If you say something like a plan is **on the skids,** you mean it is going badly wrong and is about to fail.

skier A **skier** is someone who skis.

skiff A **skiff** is a small light boat.

skiffle A **skiffle** band plays music on guitars and instruments made from household objects.

ski jump A **ski jump** is a specially-built steep slope covered in snow. People ski down it and shoot into the air when they get to the end.

skilful (skilfully) (*Am:* **skillful, skillfully**) If you are **skilful** at something, you do it very well, often because you have had a lot of experience of it.

ski-lift A **ski-lift** is a machine for taking people to the top of a ski slope.

skill is the knowledge and ability which enables you to do something well. ■ A **skill** is a type of work or activity which requires special training and knowledge.

skilled If someone is **skilled,** they have the knowledge and ability to do something well. ...*a skilled fisherman.* ■ **Skilled** work can only be done by people who have been trained to do it.

skillet A **skillet** is a shallow cast-iron frying pan.

skillful See **skilful.**

skim (skimming, skimmed) If you **skim** something from the surface of a liquid, you remove it. ■ If something **skims** a surface, it moves over it quickly and lightly. ■ If you **skim through** a piece of writing, you read it quickly without looking at all the details. ■ If someone **skims off** money or some other resource, they take some of it for their own use.

skimmed milk is milk with the cream removed.

skimp If you **skimp** on something, you use less time, money, or material for it than you really need, so the result is not good enough.

skimpy (skimpier, skimpiest) Skimpy clothes do not cover much of your body. ...*a skimpy black miniskirt.*

skin (skinning, skinned) Your **skin** is the thin outer covering of your body. You use **-skinned** to describe someone's or something's skin. ...*fair-skinned people.* ■ An animal **skin** is skin removed from a dead animal, for example to make a coat or rug. If you **skin** a dead animal, you remove its skin. ■ The **skin** of a fruit or vegetable is its outer covering. If you **skin** a fruit or vegetable, you remove its skin. ■ If you say someone **gets under your skin,** you mean they irritate you.

skinflint You can call someone a **skinflint** when they are mean and hate spending money.

skinhead A **skinhead** is a young man whose hair is shaved or cut very short.

skinny A **skinny** person is unattractively thin.

skint If you are **skint,** you have no money.

skin-tight clothes fit very tightly.

skip (skipping, skipped) If you **skip** something you usually do or are supposed to do, you deliberately do not do it. ■ If you **skip** somewhere, you move along with a series of little jumps from one foot to the other. Lambs and other small animals can also **skip.** ■ When someone **skips,** they jump up and down over a rope which they or two other people are holding at each end and turning round and round. ■ A **skip** is a large open metal container used to hold and take away rubbish.

skipper (skippering, skippered) The **skipper** of a boat or ship is its captain. The captain of a sports team is also sometimes called the **skipper.** You can say someone **skippers** a boat or team.

skipping-rope A **skipping-rope** is a rope for skipping, usually with a handle at each end.

skirmish (skirmishes, skirmishing, skirmished) A **skirmish** is a short battle which is not part of a planned war strategy. If two armed groups **skirmish,** they have a short battle like this. ■ A **skirmish** is a brief fight or quarrel. *An ugly skirmish developed involving around 16 players.*

skirt A **skirt** is a piece of clothing worn by women and girls. It fastens at the waist and hangs down around the legs. ■ If you **skirt** something, you go round the edge of it. ■ If you **skirt** a problem or question, you avoid dealing with it.

skirting board A **skirting board** is a narrow length of wood which goes round the bottom edge of a wall in a room.

skit A **skit** is a short performance in which actors make fun of things like films or current events by imitating them.

skitter (skittering, skittered) If an animal **skitters** somewhere, it moves quickly and lightly.

skittish If you call someone **skittish,** you mean they do not concentrate on anything for long or take life seriously. ■ If an animal is **skittish,** it is nervous and easily frightened.

skittle – Skittles is a game in which players throw a ball at a group of nine wooden objects called **skittles.** The idea is to knock down as many as possible.

skive (skiving, skived) If you **skive,** you avoid working, especially by staying away from the place where you should be working.

skulduggery is behaviour in which someone acts dishonestly to achieve their aim.

skulk If someone **skulks** somewhere, they stay there quietly because they do not want to be seen.

skull Your **skull** is the bony part of your head which encloses your brain. ■ A **skull and crossbones** is a picture of a human skull above a pair of crossed bones, used to warn of danger.

skunk The **skunk** is a small black and white American animal which gives off an unpleasant smell when it is frightened.

sky (skies) The **sky** is the space around the earth, which appears white or pale blue in the daytime. ■ The air or space above a country or region is sometimes called its **skies.** *...fighters patrolling the skies over southern Iraq.*

sky-blue is a pale blue colour.

sky-diving is the sport of jumping out of an aircraft and falling freely through the air before opening your parachute.

sky-high If prices are **sky-high,** they have reached an exceptionally high level.

skylight A **skylight** is a window in a roof.

skyline The **skyline** is the outline of buildings, hills, or mountains seen against the sky.

skyscraper A **skyscraper** is a very tall building in a city.

skyward (skywards) If you look **skyward** or **skywards,** you look up towards the sky. ■ If you talk about prices going **skyward** or **skywards,** you mean they are going up very rapidly.

slab A **slab** of something such as meat, concrete, or ice is a thick flat piece of it.

slack (slackness) A **slack** period is one when there is not much activity. ■ If you say someone is **slacking,** you mean they are not working as hard as they should. *Many publishers have become far too slack.* ■ If a rope between two places is **slack,** it is hanging loosely. ■ If there is **slack** in a country's economy, it has resources which are not being fully employed. ■ If someone **takes up the slack** in an organization, they start making full use of all its resources or potential. ■ Casual trousers are sometimes called **slacks.**

slacken (slackening, slackened) If something **slackens** or **slackens off,** it becomes slower, less active, or less intense. *The protests show no sign of slackening.* ■ If you **slacken** your grip on something, you hold it less tightly.

slacker A **slacker** is someone who is lazy and does less work than they should.

slag (slagging, slagged) **Slag** is waste material such as rock left over from mining or waste products from blast furnaces. A **slag heap** is a hill made from large amounts of this material. ■ If you **slag** someone **off,** you criticize them in an unpleasant way.

slain See **slay.**

slake (slaking, slaked) If you **slake** your thirst, you drink something to take your thirst away.

slalom (*pron:* **slah**-lom) A **slalom** is a race, on skis or in canoes, in which competitors follow a twisting difficult course.

slam (slamming, slammed) If a door or window **slams,** it shuts noisily and with great force. ■ If you **slam** something somewhere, you put it there quickly and noisily. ■ If a reviewer **slams** something like a new play, he or she criticizes it severely.

slammer Prison is sometimes called the **slammer.**

slander (slandering, slandered; slanderous) If you **slander** someone or make **slanderous** comments about them, you say untrue things about them, with the intention of damaging their reputation. The things you say are called **slanders.** ■ **Slander** is the offence of making untrue spoken statements about someone with the intention of damaging their reputation.

slang (slangy) A **slang** word is an informal one which you would normally only use in conversation. **Slangy** speech or writing has a lot of slang in it. ■ When people have a **slanging match,** they quarrel and insult each other.

slant If information is **slanted,** it is presented in a way which is biased towards a particular opinion. ■ A **slant** on a subject is one way of looking at it or describing it. ■ If a surface is **slanting,** it is sloping rather than horizontal or vertical. If something is on a slanting surface, you can say it is **on a slant** or **at a slant.**

slap (slapping, slapped) If you **slap** someone or give them a **slap,** you hit them with the palm of your hand. ■ If you **slap** someone on the back, you hit them on their back in a friendly way. Hearty friendly behaviour is sometimes called **back-**

slapping. ■ If you **slap** something onto a surface, you put it down quickly, carelessly, and noisily. ■ If something like a tax is **slapped** on something, it is imposed suddenly and unexpectedly. ■ If you say something is **slap bang** in the middle of a place, you are emphasizing that that is where it is.

slapdash If something is done in a **slapdash** way, it is done carelessly without much thought or planning.

slapstick is a simple type of comedy in which actors or clowns behave in a silly, boisterous way.

slap-up meals are large enjoyable ones.

slash (slashes, slashing, slashed) If jobs or costs are **slashed,** they are reduced by a large amount. *Yale is contemplating slashing its academic staff by 11%.* ■ If you **slash** something with a knife, you make a long deep cut in it. ■ A **slash** is the symbol **/** which is used when giving alternatives. *A person can get married at the age of 16, that's two years before he/she can vote.*

slash and burn is a method of tropical farming which involves clearing land for cultivation by cutting down and burning the natural vegetation on it, farming there for a short time, and then starting again on new land.

slat (slatted) Slats are flat narrow pieces of wood, metal, or plastic in things such as Venetian blinds or cupboard doors. *...slatted window blinds.*

slate (slating, slated) Slate is a dark grey rock which can easily be split into thin layers. **Slates** are small flat pieces of slate used for covering roofs. ■ If you **wipe the slate clean** or **start with a clean slate,** you decide to forget previous failures, mistakes, or debts and make a fresh start. ■ If you **slate** someone or something, you criticize them severely. ■ If something is **slated** to happen, it is planned or expected to happen.

slaughter (slaughtering, slaughtered) If a large number of people are unjustly or cruelly killed, you can say they are **slaughtered** or describe their killing as **slaughter.** ■ When animals like cows are **slaughtered,** they are killed for their meat. You can talk about the **slaughter** of farm animals. ■ If you **slaughter** someone in a competition, you beat them easily and by a large margin.

slaughterhouse A **slaughterhouse** is a place where animals are killed for their meat.

Slav (pron: slahv) The **Slavs** are a group of mainly Eastern European peoples who speak similar languages. **Slav** means to do with Slavs and their countries. *...the first Slav Pope in history.*

slave (slaving, slaved; slavery) A **slave** is someone who is owned by someone else and has to work for them without pay. The practice of having slaves is called **slavery.** ■ The **slave trade** was the buying and selling of slaves, especially the transport of black Africans to the Americas from the 16th century to the early 1800s. ■ If work is done by **slave labour,** it is done using slaves or very badly-paid workers working long hours in very unpleasant conditions. ■ If you **slave** or **slave away** at something, you work very hard at it. ■ If you are a **slave** to something, you allow yourself to be strongly influenced or controlled by it.

slaver (slavering, slavered) If a person or animal **slavers,** saliva drips from their mouth.

slavery See **slave.**

slavish (pron: slave-ish) (slavishly) You use **slavish** to describe things which copy or imitate something exactly, without any attempt to be original. *...a slavish follower of fashion.*

slay (slaying, slew, have slain) If someone **slays** a person or animal, they kill them.

sleazy (sleazier, sleaziest; sleaze) If you call an activity **sleazy,** you mean it is dishonest or immoral. **Sleaze** is immoral activities, and the reporting of them in some newspapers.

sled A **sled** is the same as a sledge.

sledge A **sledge** is a vehicle on runners designed to travel over snow.

sledgehammer A **sledgehammer** is a large heavy hammer with a long handle.

sleek (sleeker, sleekest) A **sleek** person looks stylish and smart. ■ A **sleek** vehicle has a smooth graceful shape. ■ **Sleek** hair or fur is smooth and glossy.

sleep (sleeping, slept) Sleep is the natural state of rest in which your eyes are closed and you are inactive and unconscious. When you **sleep,** you are in this state. If you have a **sleep,** you sleep for a short time. ■ If you say a building or room **sleeps** a certain number of people, you mean it has beds for that number of people. ■ If you **sleep with** someone you have sex with them. When two people are doing this regularly, you say they are **sleeping together.** ■ If someone **sleeps around,** they have many different sexual partners. ■ If an animal is **put to sleep,** it is painlessly killed.

sleeper A **sleeper** is an overnight train with beds for passengers. These beds are in compartments, also called **sleepers.** ■ On a railway track, the **sleepers** are the large heavy beams, usually of wood or concrete, which support the rails. ■ You can use **sleeper** to describe the way someone sleeps. *I'm a very light sleeper.*

sleeping bag A **sleeping bag** is a large warm bag for sleeping in, especially when you are camping.

sleeping car A **sleeping car** is a railway carriage with beds for passengers to sleep in.

sleeping pill A **sleeping pill** or **sleeping tablet** is a pill you take to help you sleep.

sleeping sickness is a serious disease carried by certain types of insects in Africa, which eventually causes a deep coma.

sleepless (sleeplessness) If you have a **sleepless** night, you are unable to sleep, usually because you are worrying about something. If you suffer from **sleeplessness,** you are often unable to sleep.

sleepwalk If someone **sleepwalks,** they get up and walk around while they are still asleep.

sleepy (sleepier, sleepiest; sleepily, sleepiness) If you are **sleepy,** you feel tired and ready to go to sleep. When someone is in this state, you can talk about their **sleepiness** or say they do something **sleepily.** ■ A **sleepy** place is quiet and does not have much activity or excitement.

sleet is a mixture of falling snow and rain.

sleeve (**-sleeved**) The **sleeves** of a garment are the parts which cover your arms. You use **-sleeved** to describe the sleeves on a garment. ...*a short-sleeved shirt*. ■ If you have something **up your sleeve,** you have an idea or plan you have not told anyone about. ■ The **sleeve** of a gramophone record is the stiff envelope it is kept in. Some other kinds of protective coverings are also called **sleeves.**

sleigh (*pron:* **slay**) A **sleigh** is a vehicle which can slide over snow and is usually pulled by horses.

sleight (*pron:* **slite**) If something is done by **sleight of hand,** it is done using a skilful piece of deception.

slender A **slender** person is thin in an attractive way. ■ **Slender** is used to say something is quite small. *The United States held a slender lead.*

slept See **sleep.**

sleuth (**sleuthing**) A **sleuth** is a detective. The work a detective does is sometimes called **sleuthing.**

slew (**slewed**) See **slay.** ■ If a vehicle **slews,** it slides or skids to one side. ■ A **slew** of people or things is a lot of them.

slice (**slicing, sliced**) If you **slice** food, you cut it into thin pieces or wedges called **slices.** ■ A **slice** of something is a part of it. *Dealing costs would cancel out a large slice of the profit.* ■ If a certain amount is **sliced off** something, it is reduced by that amount. ■ If something **slices through** a substance, it cuts through it like a knife. ■ If you **slice** the ball in tennis, golf, or cricket, you hit its edge rather than its centre, so it travels at an angle.

slick (**slickly, slickness**) A **slick** is the same as an oil slick. ■ A **slick** person is impressive and persuasive, but may not be sincere. Similarly, you say something like a book or film is **slick** when it is well-made but lacks depth or sincerity. ■ You can call an action or performance **slick** when it appears quick and effortless. ■ If you **slick back** your hair, you smooth it close to your head and make it shiny using something like hair oil or gel.

slide (**sliding, slid**) When something **slides,** it moves smoothly over or against a surface. ■ A **slide** is a structure which has a steep slippery slope for children to slide down. ■ If there is a mud **slide** or a rock **slide,** a large amount of mud or rock comes loose and falls down a hill. ■ If something like the economy **slides** or goes into a **slide,** it gradually gets worse. ■ If a country **slides towards** a bad situation or **slides into** it, it gradually and inevitably gets closer to it. *The republic will slide into political anarchy.* ■ If you say someone **slides** somewhere, you mean they move smoothly and quietly. ■ A **slide** is a small piece of photographic film which can be projected onto a screen. ■ A **slide** is a piece of glass which you put a substance on to examine it under a microscope. ■ A **slide** is the same as a hair slide.

slide rule A **slide rule** is an instrument which was used for making calculations before people started using calculators.

sliding scale A **sliding scale** is a system for calculating something like taxes, in which the amounts paid vary as other things vary.

slight (**slightly**) If something is **slight,** it is quite small. ...*a slight increase.* ■ **Slightly** is used to say something has a quality to a small extent. *Their boat was slightly damaged.* ■ A **slight** person is small and slim. ■ If you call a book or play **slight,** you mean there is nothing in it of real interest or importance. ■ If someone **slights** you, they insult you by ignoring you or treating you as if you were unimportant. You call their behaviour a **slight.**

slim (**slimmer, slimmest; slimming, slimmed**) A **slim** person has an attractively thin body. ■ If you are **slimming,** you are trying to lose weight by dieting. People who do this are called **slimmers.** ■ A **slim** object is smaller or thinner than usual. *He published only three slim volumes of verse.* ■ If you **slim** something or **slim** it **down,** you reduce it. ■ If you say the chances of something happening are **slim,** you mean it is unlikely to happen.

slime is a thick slippery unpleasant substance, for example the substance that comes from a slug.

slimline objects are thinner than other objects of their kind. ...*a slimline storage heater.*

slimmer See **slim.**

slimy (**slimier, slimiest**) If something is **slimy,** it is covered in slime. ■ You can say a person is **slimy** when they flatter people and act as if they are friendly, but you find them very unpleasant and insincere.

sling (**slinging, slung**) If you **sling** something over your shoulder, you hang it there so you can carry it. ■ If something is **slung** between two points, it hangs loosely between them. ■ If you **sling** something somewhere, you throw it there carelessly. ■ A **sling** is (a) a device made of ropes or straps, for lifting and carrying heavy loads. (b) a piece of cloth hung round your neck to support a broken or injured arm. (c) a device for carrying a baby on your back or across the front of your body.

slingshot A **slingshot** is the same as a catapult.

slink (**slinking, slunk** *not* 'slinked') If you **slink** somewhere, you move there slowly and secretively.

slinky clothes fit closely to a woman's body in a sexually attractive way.

slip (**slipping, slipped**) If you **slip,** your feet start to slide and you lose your balance. You can also talk about objects **slipping** when they slide out of place or out of your hands. ■ If something **slips** to a lower level, it falls to that level. ■ If someone or something **slips** into a certain state, they gradually worsen until they are in that state. *The little boy was slipping into a coma.* ■ If you **slip** somewhere, you go there quickly and quietly. ■ If you **slip** something somewhere, you put it there quickly and secretively. ■ If you **slip up** or make a **slip,** you make a mistake. ■ If you **let** a secret **slip,** you accidentally tell someone about it. ■ If something **slips your mind,** you forget about it. ■ If you **slip into** clothes or **slip** them **on,** you put them on quickly and easily. ■ A **slip** is a small piece of paper, for example a receipt. ■ A **slip** is a petticoat. ■ **slip a disc:** see **disc.**

slip-on shoes have no laces and can be put on and taken off easily.

slippage is failure to maintain a steady level or to meet a deadline. ...*a substantial slippage in the value of sterling.*

slipper — **Slippers** are soft comfortable shoes for wearing indoors.

slippery (**slipperiness**) If something is **slippery**, it is smooth, wet, or greasy, and is difficult to keep hold of or walk on. ■ A **slippery** person is dishonest and cannot be trusted. ■ You can say something is **slippery** when it is hard to pin down or define. *Anti-Americanism is a slippery concept.*

slip road A **slip road** is a road used to drive on or off a motorway.

slipshod If you describe something as **slipshod**, you mean it has not been done carefully or thoroughly.

slipstream The **slipstream** of a fast-moving object like a car or plane is the flow of air directly behind it.

slipway A **slipway** is a large platform sloping down into water, from which boats are launched.

slit (**slitting, slit** *not 'slitted'*) If you **slit** something or make a **slit** in it, you make a long narrow cut in it. ■ A **slit** is a long narrow opening in something.

slither (**slithering, slithered**) If something **slithers**, it slides along in an uneven way.

sliver A **sliver** is a small thin piece of something.

Sloane Young people from London who have upper-class accents and wear expensive clothes are sometimes called **Sloanes** or **Sloane Rangers.**

slob (**slobbish**) If you call someone a **slob** or describe them as **slobbish**, you mean they are lazy, dirty, and untidy.

slobber (**slobbering, slobbered**) If someone **slobbers**, they let saliva fall from their mouth.

sloe — **Sloes** are small sour fruit which have a dark purple skin and are often used to flavour gin.

slog (**slogging, slogged**) If you say a piece of work is a **slog**, you mean it is difficult and needs a lot of effort. ■ If you **slog** at something, you work hard and steadily at it. ■ A **slog** is a long and difficult journey on foot. If you **slog** somewhere, you make your way there on foot. ■ If two people **slog it out,** they fight, compete, or argue over something.

slogan — **Slogans** are short easily-remembered phrases used in advertising and politics.

sloganeer (**sloganeering, sloganeered**) If you accuse someone of **sloganeering**, you mean they are using slogans rather than reasoned arguments to get people's support.

sloganize (*or* **sloganise**) (**sloganizing, sloganized**) **Sloganizing** is the same as sloganeering.

sloop A **sloop** is a small sailing boat with one mast.

slop (**slopping, slopped**) If you **slop** some liquid somewhere, you spill it messily over the edge of its container. ■ **Slop** or **slops** is a mixture of food waste and liquid which is fed to animals.

slope (**sloping, sloped**) A **slope** is a side of a hill or mountain. ■ A **slope** is a flat surface which is at an angle, so that one end is higher than the other. You say a surface like this **slopes.** The **slope** of something is the angle at which it slopes. ■ If you **slope off,** you leave quickly and quietly, often because you are trying to avoid something.

sloppy (**sloppily, sloppiness**) If you call a piece of work **sloppy,** you mean it has been carelessly done. ■ A **sloppy** substance is soft and almost liquid.

slosh (**sloshes, sloshing, sloshed**) If a liquid **sloshes**, it splashes or moves around messily. ■ When people walk noisily through water or mud, you can say they **slosh** through it.

slot (**slotting, slotted**) A **slot** is a narrow opening in a machine or container. ■ If something **slots** into something else, it fits into it exactly. ■ A **slot** is a place in a schedule or scheme, especially a place kept for a particular purpose. ■ If you **slot** someone or something into a schedule or scheme, you find a place for them in it.

sloth (*rhymes with 'both'*) is laziness. ■ The **sloth** is a slow-moving animal found mainly in Central and South America.

slothful If someone is **slothful,** they are lazy and unwilling to work.

slot machine A **slot machine** is a gambling machine, operated by putting coins into a slot.

slouch (**slouches, slouching, slouched**) If you **slouch**, you sit or walk with your shoulders and head drooping downwards. ■ If you say someone is **no slouch** at an activity, you mean they are skilful at it or know a lot about it.

slough If you **slough off** something you no longer need, you get rid of it. (*For this meaning, 'slough' rhymes with 'rough'.*) ■ If someone is in a **slough** of despair or self-pity, they are in a bad emotional state which they cannot get rid of. (*For this meaning, 'slough' rhymes with 'now'.*)

slovenly A **slovenly** person is untidy or careless.

slow (**slowly, slowness**) **Slow** is used to describe things which move or happen without much speed. ...*a slow train.* ■ If something **slows**, it moves or happens less quickly. ■ If someone **slows down,** they become less active, usually because they are getting old. ■ If you say someone is **slow,** you mean they are not very clever and take a long time to understand something. ■ If a clock is **slow,** it is showing a time earlier than the real time.

slowdown A **slowdown** in an activity is a reduction in it.

slow motion If a film is shown in **slow motion,** it is shown at a slower speed than normal.

slow-witted If you say someone is **slow-witted,** you mean they are not very clever.

sludge is a mixture of liquid and solids, for example sewage.

slug (**slugging, slugged**) The **slug** is a small slow-moving creature with a long slimy body. ■ If you take a **slug** of a drink, you take a large mouthful of it. ■ If two people **slug it out,** they fight each other.

sluggard A **sluggard** is a lazy person.

sluggish (**sluggishly, sluggishness**) You say something is **sluggish** when it is moving or operating slowly or lacks energy. *The continued sluggishness of the economy has worsened the property slump.*

sluice (**sluicing, sluiced**) A **sluice** is a man-made passage of flowing water. It has an opening called a **sluice gate** which can be used to control the flow. ■ If you **sluice** something, you wash it with a stream of water.

slum (**slumming, slummed**) A **slum** is an area of a city with bad housing conditions. ■ If someone says they are **slumming it,** they mean they are doing something more cheaply than usual, such as staying in a cheap hotel.

slumber (**slumbering, slumbered**) **Slumber** is sleep. If someone is **slumbering,** they are asleep.

slump If there is a **slump** in something such as demand or if it **slumps,** it falls suddenly and sharply. *Porsche sales have slumped badly.* ■ A **slump** is a period when a country's economy slows down, causing high unemployment and poverty. ■ If you **slump** somewhere, you sit down heavily, because you are very tired.

slung See **sling.**

slunk See **slink.**

slur (**slurring, slurred**) A **slur** is an insulting remark which could damage someone's reputation. ■ If someone **slurs** their speech, they do not pronounce their words clearly, often because they are ill or drunk.

slurp If someone **slurps** a liquid, they drink it noisily.

slurry is a watery mixture of something such as mud, cement, or manure.

slush (**slushy**) **Slush** is dirty snow which has begun to melt. You say snow like this is **slushy.** ■ A **slushy** story is romantic and sentimental.

slush fund A **slush fund** is money put aside to finance an illegal activity, especially in politics or business.

slut A woman is sometimes called a **slut** when people think her sexual behaviour is immoral.

sly (**slyly**) A **sly** look or remark shows you know something other people do not. ■ A **sly** person is clever at deceiving people. ■ If something is done **on the sly,** it is done secretively.

smack If you **smack** someone or give them a smack, you hit them sharply with the flat of your hand. ■ If one thing **smacks** of another, it suggests that thing is present or happening. *The announcement smacked of panic.* ■ If something is **smack** in a particular place, it is exactly in that place. ■ **Smack** is heroin.

small is used to describe things which are not as large in size, number, or amount as usual. *...a small group of architects. ...a small garden.* ■ A **small** child is a very young child. ■ **Small** is used to describe things which are not significant or great in degree. *It's now becoming clear that Vietnam is content to play a smaller role in Cambodia.* ■ If you refer to people as **small fry,** you mean they are unimportant.

small ad The **small ads** in a newspaper are the short advertisements usually selling people's personal property.

small arms are guns such as rifles and pistols, as opposed to artillery.

small change is coins of low value.

smallholding (**smallholder**) A **smallholding** is a piece of agricultural land run like a very small farm. A person who runs a smallholding is called a **smallholder.**

smallish means fairly small.

small-minded (**small-mindedness**) If you say someone is **small-minded** or talk about their **small-mindedness,** you mean they have a narrow range of interests and very fixed opinions.

smallpox was a serious infectious disease which caused a high fever and a rash that scarred the skin badly. Smallpox now appears to have been wiped out.

small screen The **small screen** is television.

small talk is polite conversation at social occasions, usually about fairly trivial things.

small-town You can refer to less populated cities in the USA and their slower pace of life as **small town** America. **Small-town** is also used to describe attitudes thought to be typical of people living in small towns.

smarmy If you call someone **smarmy,** you mean they are unpleasantly over-polite and flattering.

smart (**smartly**) A **smart** person is clean and well-dressed. ■ A **smart** place or event is connected with rich and fashionable people. ■ **Smart** means clever. ■ A **smart** movement or action is sharp and quick. *...a smartly taken goal.* ■ If a part of your body **smarts,** you feel a sharp stinging pain there. ■ If you are **smarting** from criticism, you are upset about it, because you feel it was unfair.

smart-alec (*or* **smart-aleck**) If you call someone a **smart-alec,** you mean they keep trying to appear cleverer than other people.

smart card A **smart card** looks like a credit card and can store and process computer data.

smarten (**smartening, smartened**) If you **smarten** something or **smarten** it **up,** you make it look neater and tidier.

smash (**smashes, smashing, smashed**) If you **smash** something, you hit it, throw it, or drop it so that it breaks into a lot of pieces. ■ If you **smash** something **up,** you deliberately destroy it by hitting it. ■ If you **smash** through a wall, gate, or door, you get through it by hitting and breaking it. ■ If one thing **smashes** into something else, it hits it with great force. ■ A car crash is sometimes called a **smash.** ■ If someone **smashes** an organization, they destroy it. ■ If a song, play, or film is a **smash** or a **smash hit,** it is very successful. ■ In tennis, a **smash** is a stroke in which a player hits the ball downwards very hard.

smash-and-grab In a **smash-and-grab** robbery, a thief smashes a shop window, seizes the goods which are on display, and runs off with them.

smashing If you call something **smashing,** you mean you admire it very much.

smattering A **smattering** of something is a small amount of it.

smear (**smearing, smeared**) A **smear** is an unpleasant and untrue rumour or accusation. If someone **smears** your reputation, they spread rumours or accusations about you. ■ If you **smear** a surface with a substance, you spread it over the surface. ■ If something **smears** a surface, it leaves a dirty or greasy mark called a **smear** on the surface. ■ A **smear** or a **smear test** is a medical test in which a few cells from a woman's cervix are removed and analysed to look for signs of cervical cancer.

smell (**smelling, smelled** or **smelt; -smelling**) If you **smell** something, you become aware of it through your nose. The quality you become aware of is called its **smell.** If something has a strong unpleasant smell, you say it **smells.** ■ **-smelling** is used to describe something's smell. ...*sweet-smelling shrubs.* ■ If you say you **smell** something like danger, you mean you feel it is present or likely to happen.

smelly (**smellier, smelliest**) If you call something **smelly,** you mean it has an unpleasant smell.

smelt (**smelter**) See **smell.** ■ When an ore is **smelted,** it is heated in a furnace called a **smelter** until it melts, so the metal can be extracted.

smidgeon (or **smidgen** or **smidgin**) A **smidgeon** of something is very small amount of it.

smile (**smiling, smiled; smilingly**) When you **smile,** the corners of your mouth curve outwards and slightly upwards, because you are pleased or amused. An expression like this is called a **smile.** ■ **Smile** is used to say someone is smiling when they say something. *Mr Kantor smilingly announced that America would go along with its original plan.*

smirk If someone **smirks,** they smile smugly. You call their expression a **smirk.**

smite (**smiting, smote, have smitten**) If you **smite** something, you hit it hard. ■ If you are **smitten** by something, you are very impressed with it and enthusiastic about it. ■ If you are **smitten** with another person, you are strongly attracted to them or in love with them.

smith A **smith** is the same as a blacksmith.

smithereens If something is smashed to **smithereens,** it is completely destroyed.

smithy (**smithies**) A **smithy** is a place where a blacksmith works.

smitten See **smite.**

smock A **smock** is (a) a loose garment, rather like a long blouse, worn especially by women. (b) a loose garment worn over other clothes to protect them.

smog (**smoggy**) **Smog** is a mixture of smoke and fog which occurs in some industrial cities. A **smoggy** city is badly affected by smog.

smoke (**smoking, smoked; smoker**) **Smoke** consists of gas and particles of solid material released into the air when something burns. If something is **smoking,** it is giving off smoke. ■ When someone **smokes** a cigarette, cigar, or pipe, they breathe in smoke from it, then blow it out again. If someone **smokes** or is a **smoker,** they do this regularly. ■ A **smoking** area is one where people are allowed to smoke. ■ When food is **smoked,** it is hung over burning wood so the smoke will preserve it and give it flavour.

smokeless fuel burns without producing any smoke.

smoker See **smoke.**

smokescreen If you call what someone does or says a **smokescreen,** you mean it is intended to hide the truth about their actions or intentions.

smokestack A **smokestack** is a tall chimney used to carry smoke away from a factory.

smoky You say a place is **smoky** when there is a lot of smoke there. ■ **Smoky** food tastes or smells of smoke.

smolder See **smoulder.**

smooch (**smooches, smooching, smooched; smoochy**) When people **smooch,** they kiss and hold each other closely, usually while dancing slowly. **Smoochy** songs and music are slow and suitable for this sort of dancing.

smooth (**smoothly; smoothie** or **smoothy**) A **smooth** surface or object has no roughness, lumps, or holes. ■ If you **smooth** something or **smooth** it **out,** you remove the creases or roughness from it and make it flat. ■ A **smooth** liquid or mixture has been mixed well and has no lumps in it. ■ A **smooth** movement or process is steady and even, with no sudden changes or breaks. ■ If something goes **smoothly,** it goes well and there are no problems. ■ If you **smooth over** a problem, you make it seem less serious. ■ If you call a man **smooth** or a **smoothie,** you mean he is confident and polite, but possibly not sincere. You say someone is **smooth-talking** when they are persuasive but you do not trust them.

smorgasbord is a type of Scandinavian buffet with a wide choice of savoury dishes.

smote See **smite.**

smother (**smothering, smothered**) If something is **smothered** in things, it is completely covered with them. ■ If you **smother** a fire, you cover it with something to put it out. ■ If someone **smothers** someone else, they kill them by covering their face to stop them breathing. ■ If an activity or process is **smothered,** it is prevented from continuing or developing.

smoulder (Am: **smolder**) (**smouldering, smouldered**) If something **smoulders,** it burns slowly, producing smoke but not flames. ■ If a feeling such as hatred **smoulders,** people keep it inside themselves and do not express it. ■ You can say someone **smoulders** when they are attractive and seem passionate and mysterious.

smudge (**smudging, smudged**) A **smudge** is a dirty mark. If you **smudge** something, you make it dirty or messy by touching it.

smudgy If something is **smudgy,** it is blurred and unclear. ...*smudgy photos.*

smug (**smugly, smugness**) You say someone is **smug** when they show too much pleasure at their own achievements or good fortune.

smuggle (**smuggling, smuggled; smuggler**) If you **smuggle** things or people into or out of a place, you get them in or out illegally or secretly. A person who smuggles goods into or out of a country is called a **smuggler.**

smut (**smutty**) You can call stories, films, or pictures **smut** when they deal crudely with sex or nudity. ...*a smutty sex film.* ■ **Smut** or **smuts** is dirt in the air, especially soot, which leaves dirty marks on things.

snack A **snack** is a quick light meal. ■ **Snacks** are small light things to eat like nuts or chocolate bars. If you **snack,** you eat things like these.

snack bar A **snack bar** is a place where you can buy light meals and drinks.

snaffle (snaffling, snaffled) If you **snaffle** something or **snaffle** it **up,** you quickly take it for yourself.

snag (snagging, snagged) A **snag** is a small problem or disadvantage. ■ If something like clothing or a rope **snags** on an object, it gets caught on it.

snail The **snail** is a small slow-moving creature with a slimy body and a spiral-shaped shell on its back.

snail mail is the ordinary postal system, as opposed to e-mail.

snake (snaking, snaked) **Snakes** are long thin scaly reptiles with no legs. ■ If something **snakes** in a particular direction, it goes along in a series of curves. *The path snaked on up the side of a volcano.*

snap (snapping, snapped) If an object **snaps,** it breaks suddenly with a sharp cracking sound. ■ If you **snap** your fingers, you make a clicking sound using your thumb and middle finger. ■ If a dog **snaps** at you, it shuts its jaws suddenly as if it was going to bite you. ■ If someone **snaps** at you, they speak to you in a sharp unfriendly way. ■ If your patience **snaps,** you suddenly lose your temper. ■ A **snap** decision or action is made suddenly, often without careful thought. ■ A **snap** is a photograph taken quickly and casually. If you **snap** someone or something, you take a photograph of them. ■ If you **snap** something **up,** you buy it quickly. ■ A **cold snap** is a sudden short period of cold and frosty weather.

snapdragon The **snapdragon** is a common garden plant with small colourful flowers which can be opened and shut like a mouth.

snappy (snappier, snappiest; snappily) If you call something like a show **snappy,** you mean it is lively and entertaining. ■ A **snappy** slogan is brief and to the point. ■ A **snappy** dresser wears smart stylish clothes. ■ If someone is **snappy,** they answer in a sharp unfriendly way when you speak to them.

snapshot A **snapshot** is a photograph taken quickly and casually. ■ If something gives you a good indication of what a situation is like at a particular time, you can call it a **snapshot** of the situation. *This poll offers a snapshot of public opinion.*

snare (snaring, snared) A **snare** is a trap used to catch birds or small animals. If a bird or animal is **snared,** it is caught in a snare. ■ If someone **snares** an opponent or enemy, they get them into a dangerous or difficult situation by deceiving them. ■ If someone **snares** something like a prize, they win it.

snarl When an animal **snarls,** it makes a fierce growling sound and shows its teeth. ■ If you **snarl** something, you say it fiercely and angrily. ■ If a process is **snarled up,** it is slowed down or brought to a standstill by something that is happening. You call a situation like this a **snarl-up.**

snatch (snatches, snatching, snatched) If you **snatch** something, you quickly take it from a person or place. ■ You say someone **snatches** something when they steal it. ■ If you **snatch** an opportunity, you quickly make use of it to do what you want. ■ If you **snatch** victory in a contest, you defeat your opponent narrowly at the last minute. ■ If you hear a **snatch** of a conversation or song, you hear a brief part of it.

snazzy (snazzier, snazziest) If you say something is **snazzy,** you mean it is stylish and attractive, sometimes in a rather showy way.

sneak (sneaking, sneaked) If you **sneak** somewhere, you go there quietly, trying not to be seen or heard. Similarly, if you **sneak** something somewhere, you put it there secretly. ■ If you **sneak** a look at something, you look at it when you think nobody is watching. ■ **Sneak** is used to describe things people do which they hope will not be noticed. *Earlier this year senators had sneaked through a pay rise for themselves.* ■ If you get a **sneak preview** of something like a film, you get to see it before its official opening. ■ A **sneaking** feeling is one which you cannot explain, and may be unwilling to admit to. *I have a sneaking suspicion that they are going to succeed.*

sneaker — **Sneakers** are light casual shoes, usually made of canvas, with rubber soles.

sneaky (sneakily) If you call an action **sneaky,** you mean it is done secretly, in the hope that people will not notice.

sneer (sneering, sneered) If someone **sneers** at something, they show by their remarks or the expression on their face that they think it is stupid or inferior. You call their expression a **sneer.**

sneeze (sneezing, sneezed) When you **sneeze,** you suddenly and involuntarily gasp in air then blow it hard down your nose. This is called a **sneeze.**

snicker (snickering, snickered) If someone **snickers,** they laugh quietly and disrespectfully.

snide If someone makes **snide** remarks, they criticize someone or something in a indirect sarcastic way.

sniff When you **sniff,** you breathe in air noisily through your nose, for example because you have a cold, or are trying not to cry. ■ If you **sniff** something, you smell it by breathing in through your nose. ■ If someone **sniffs** a substance like glue, they deliberately breathe in the substance or its fumes to get its effects as a drug. ■ You can use **sniff** to say someone says something in a superior or contemptuous way. *'You can't have peacekeepers if there's no peace to keep,' a British minister sniffed.* ■ If you **sniff** something **out,** you eventually find it after looking for it.

sniffer dog A **sniffer dog** is a dog trained to find drugs or explosives by sniffing their scent.

sniffle (sniffling, sniffled) If you **sniffle,** you sniff repeatedly, because you have a cold or have been crying.

sniffy (sniffier, sniffiest; sniffily) If someone is **sniffy,** they are scornful or contemptuous about something.

snigger (sniggering, sniggered) If you **snigger,** you laugh quietly and disrespectfully. A laugh like this is called a **snigger.**

snip (snipping, snipped) If you **snip** something or **snip** through it, you cut it with a pair of scissors. ■ If you say something which is for sale is a **snip,** you mean it is cheap and good value.

snipe (sniping, sniped; sniper) If someone **snipes** at you, they keep criticizing you. ■ **Sniping** is shooting at people from a hidden position. A person who does this is called a **sniper.** ■ The **snipe** is a bird with a long beak which normally lives in marshy areas.

snippet A **snippet** of news or information is a small piece of it.

snivel (**snivelling, snivelled**) (*Am:* **sniveling, sniveled**) If someone **snivels,** they keep crying or complaining in an irritating way.

snob (**snobbish, snobbishly, snobbishness, snobbery**) If you call someone a **snob,** you disapprove of them because they look down on others, because they think they have better taste than them or they regard them as lower class. You call their attitude **snobbishness** or **snobbery.**

snook If you **cock a snook** at someone in authority, you do something cheeky which they cannot punish you for, and which shows your contempt for them.

snooker is a game played by two people on a large table covered in smooth green cloth with six pockets at the edges. The players use long sticks called cues to hit a white ball so that it knocks coloured balls into the pockets.

snoop (**snooping, snooped; snooper**) You say someone is **snooping** or call them a **snooper** when they are secretly trying to find out things about a person's private or business affairs.

snooty (**snootier, snootiest; snootily, snootiness**) If you say someone is **snooty** or talk about their **snootiness,** you mean they behave as if they are superior to other people.

snooze (**snoozing, snoozed**) If you **snooze** or have a **snooze,** you have a short light sleep.

snore (**snoring, snored**) If someone **snores** when they are asleep, they make a loud noise when they breathe. This noise is called a **snore.**

snorkel (**snorkelling, snorkelled**) (*Am:* **snorkeling, snorkeled**) A **snorkel** is a tube through which a person swimming just under the surface of the water can breathe. If you **snorkel,** you swim underwater using a snorkel.

snort If you **snort** or let out a **snort,** you blow air out noisily through your nose. ■ If someone **snorts** a drug like cocaine, they breathe it in quickly through one nostril.

snout An animal's **snout** is its nose.

snow is the soft white bits of frozen water that sometimes float from the sky in cold weather. When snow falls, you say it is **snowing.** ■ If you are **snowed in,** you cannot go anywhere because of heavy snow. ■ If you are **snowed under,** you have a great deal of work to deal with, especially paperwork.

snowball A **snowball** is snow pressed into a ball. Children often throw snowballs at each other. ■ If a situation **snowballs,** it gets out of hand and rapidly becomes more serious.

snowboard (**snowboarding, snowboarder**) A **snowboard** is a narrow board like a skateboard without wheels, which some people use for travelling over snow instead of skis. Riding a snowboard is called **snowboarding;** a person doing it is called a **snowboarder.**

snowbound If a road is **snowbound,** it is blocked by snow. If a place is **snowbound,** you cannot get to it because of heavy snow.

snow-capped A **snow-capped** mountain is covered with snow at the top.

snowdrift A **snowdrift** is a deep pile of snow.

snowdrop The **snowdrop** is a small white flower which appears in early spring.

snowfall The **snowfall** in an area is the amount of snow which falls there over a certain period. ■ A **snowfall** is a shower of snow which settles on the ground and covers it.

snowflake A **snowflake** is one of the soft white bits of frozen water which float to the ground as snow.

snowline The **snowline** is the height on a mountain above which there is snow all year round.

snowman (**snowmen**) A **snowman** is a mass of snow pressed together to look roughly like a person.

snowplough (*Am:* **snowplow**) A **snowplough** is a vehicle used to clear snow.

snowstorm A **snowstorm** is a very heavy fall of snow, usually with a strong wind.

snow-white If something is **snow-white,** it is a pure white colour.

snowy A **snowy** place is covered in snow. ■ You say something is **snowy** when it is white like snow.

SNP The **SNP** is the Scottish National Party. It campaigns for Scottish independence from the United Kingdom.

snub (**snubbing, snubbed**) If someone **snubs** you, they insult you by ignoring you or being rude to you. You call what they say or do a **snub.**

snuff If you **snuff** a candle or **snuff** it **out,** you put it out, usually by covering it with something. ■ If someone in power **snuffs out** something like a rebellion, they put a stop to it quickly and forcefully. ■ A **snuff** movie is a film in which one of the actors is actually killed. ■ **Snuff** is powdered tobacco which people take by sniffing it up one nostril.

snuffle (**snuffling, snuffled**) If people or animals **snuffle,** they make sniffing noises.

snug (**snugly**) If you feel **snug** or you are in a **snug** place, you feel warm and comfortable, especially because you are protected from the weather. ■ If something like a piece of clothing is **snug,** it fits closely or tightly. ■ A **snug** or **snug bar** is a small room in a pub.

snuggle (**snuggling, snuggled**) If you **snuggle** somewhere, you settle yourself into a warm comfortable position there, especially by moving closer to another person.

so is used to refer back to what has just been mentioned. *'We'll go again, won't we?' 'I hope so,'* I said. ■ You use **so** when saying that something which is true of one person or thing is also true of another one. *I enjoyed it and so did the crowd.* ■ You use **so** when mentioning the result of something. *I had no money, so I couldn't play.* ■ You use **so** when mentioning the reason for doing something. *It can be wired in several ways so that thieves cannot easily learn how to override the system... The authorities had to act so as not to be seen showing weakness.* ■ You use **so** to emphasize the degree or extent of something. *Don't go so fast.* ■ You use **so** with words like 'much' and 'many' to indicate that there is a limit to something. *You can only go so far by car before you have to walk.* ■ You use **so many** when you are saying what a group of things reminds you of. *...those unblinking television cameras hanging over them like so many black spiders.* ■ You use **or so** when you are giving an approximate number. *If this continues, the red squirrel will be extinct in ten years or so.* ■ You use **and so on** or **and so forth** at the end of a list to show there are other items you could also mention. *Hospitals, universities, airports and so forth require a great deal of maintenance.*

soak (soaking, soaked) If you **soak** something, you put it into a liquid and leave it there for a period of time. ■ When a liquid **soaks** something, it makes it very wet. If someone or something is **soaked** or **soaking,** they are very wet. ■ If a liquid **soaks** through something, it passes through it. ■ If one thing **soaks up** another, it absorbs it. ■ If you **soak up** the sun, you sunbathe. ■ If you call someone an **old soak,** you think they drink too much.

soap (soaping, soaped) **Soap** is a substance used with water for washing. If you **soap** your body, you wash it with soap. ■ A **soap** or **soap opera** is a long-running TV drama serial about the daily lives of a group of people.

soapbox (soapboxes) A **soapbox** is a small temporary platform which a person stands on when making a speech outdoors to passers-by. ■ If you say someone is on their **soapbox,** you mean they are speaking or writing about something they feel passionate about.

soapy If something is **soapy,** it is full of soap or covered with soap.

soar (soaring, soared) If an amount **soars,** it grows very quickly. ■ If something **soars** into the air, it moves quickly upwards. ■ **Soaring** is used to describe very tall trees or buildings.

sob (sobbing, sobbed) When someone **sobs,** they cry in a noisy way, taking short gasping breaths. The noises they make are called **sobs.** ■ You call what someone tells you a **sob story** when you think they are telling you about it to get your sympathy.

sober (sobering, sobered; soberly) If someone is **sober,** they are not drunk. ■ When someone **sobers up,** they become sober after being drunk. ■ A **sober** person is serious and thoughtful. ■ You say things have a **sobering** effect when they make you take a more serious view of something. ■ **Sober** clothes are plain and dull.

sobriety is (a) serious and thoughtful behaviour. (b) the state of being sober rather than drunk.

sobriquet (pron: **so**-brik-ay) (or **soubriquet**) A **sobriquet** is the same as a nickname.

so-called is used (a) to show you think the following word or expression is incorrect or misleading. *I was ripped off by so-called friends.* (b) to show something is generally referred to by the name you are about to use. *...BSE, the so-called mad cow disease.*

soccer is the same as football.

sociable (sociability) **Sociable** people are friendly and enjoy talking to other people. You talk about the **sociability** of people like these.

social (socially) **Social** means to do with society or the way it is organized. *...social classes.* ■ The **social order** in a place is the way society is organized there. ■ **Social** means to do with activities which involve meeting other people. *...social events such as the summer Garden Party.* ■ **Social** animals live in groups and co-operate with other members of the group. *...social insects like bees and ants.*

social climber (social climbing) If you describe someone as a **social climber,** you mean they mix with people of a higher social class, hoping they will be accepted by them. Behaviour like this is called **social climbing.**

social engineering consists of attempts by a government to change the way people behave in order to produce the type of society it wants.

socialise See **socialize.**

socialism (socialist) **Socialism** is a set of left-wing political principles whose general aim is to create a system in which everyone has an equal opportunity to benefit from the country's wealth. Under socialism, the country's main industries are owned by the state. ■ **Socialist** is used to talk about things connected with or based on socialism. A **socialist** is a person who believes in socialism or is a member of a socialist party.

socialite A **socialite** is a person who goes to many fashionable upper-class social events.

socialize (or socialise) (socializing, socialized; socialization) If you **socialize,** you meet other people socially, for example at parties. ■ You say people are **socialized** when they learn to behave in a way which is acceptable in their society. This process is called **socialization.**

social life (social lives) Your **social life** consists of the time you spend with your friends and acquaintances, for example at parties or in their homes.

social science (social scientist) **Social science** is the scientific study of society. ■ The **social sciences** are the various branches of social science, for example sociology and politics.

social security is the system by which the government pays money regularly to people who have no income or only a very small income. The payments can also be called **social security.**

social services are the services and facilities provided by a local authority to help people who have social and financial problems.

social studies is a subject taught in some schools and colleges. It includes sociology, politics, and economics.

social work (social worker) **Social work** is work which involves helping and advising people with serious personal, family, or financial problems.

society (societies) **Society** is people in general, thought of as a large organized group. *...women's role in society.* You talk about the people in a country or region, or the people living in a certain period, as a particular kind of **society.** *...a multi-cultural society.* ■ A **society** is an organization for people who have the same interests or aims. ■ **Society** is the rich upper-class fashionable people in a place who meet on social occasions.

socio- is added to some words to say something has two aspects, one of them being a social aspect. *...socio-economic conditions.*

sociology (sociologist, sociological) Sociology is the study of human societies and of the relationships between groups in these societies. **Sociological** means things to do with sociology.

sociopath A **sociopath** is the same as a **psychopath.**

sock — Socks are pieces of clothing which cover the foot and ankle and are worn inside shoes. ■ If you tell someone to **pull their socks up,** you mean they should make an effort to do better.

socket A **socket** is a device on a wall or on a piece of electrical equipment which you put something like a plug or bulb into. ■ A **socket** is a hollow part or opening which another part fits into, for example in the body. *...eye sockets.*

sod A **sod** is a chunk of grass-covered earth, held together by the roots of the grass.

soda or **soda water** is fizzy water which people add to alcoholic drinks or fruit juice. ■ In the US, **soda** or **soda pop** is a sweet fizzy flavoured drink.

sodden If something is **sodden,** it is very wet.

sodium is a silvery-white chemical element which combines with other chemicals. Salt is a compound of sodium.

sodomy is anal sexual intercourse.

sofa A **sofa** is a long comfortable seat with a back and arms, for two or more people to sit on.

sofa-bed A **sofa-bed** is a sofa with a seat which folds out for use as a bed.

soft (softly, softness) If something is **soft,** it changes shape easily when you press it and is not hard or stiff. ■ **Soft** is used to say something is gentle or quiet. *...a soft tap on your bedroom door.* ■ You use **soft** to describe a course of action or a way of life which is easy and does not involve hard work. *We're not giving young offenders a soft option.* ■ If you are **soft** on someone or something, you do not deal with them as strictly as you should. ■ If you say someone is a **soft touch,** you mean they are easily persuaded to do things. ■ If you have a **soft spot** for someone or something, you are particularly fond of them. ■ **Soft** is sometimes used to describe things which are not considered as strong or harmful as other similar things. *...soft drugs.* ■ **Soft** water contains relatively small amounts of calcium and so lathers easily.

softball is a game similar to baseball, but played with a larger softer ball and a smaller bat. The ball used in this game is called a **softball.**

soft-core pornography is the same as soft porn.

soft drink — Soft drinks are cold drinks like lemonade or fruit juice, as distinct from alcoholic drinks.

soften (softening, softened) If something is **softened,** it becomes less hard, stiff, or firm. ■ If one thing **softens** the shock or the damaging effect of another, the first thing reduces the second. ■ If you **soften** towards someone or something, you become more sympathetic towards them. ■ If you **soften** someone **up,** you put them in a good mood before asking them to do something.

soft-focus If a photograph or film is in **soft-focus,** it has been made to look slightly blurred, to give a romantic effect.

soft furnishings are things like cushions and curtains.

soft-hearted people are kind and sympathetic.

softie See **softy.**

softly-softly A **softly-softly** approach to something is cautious and patient, avoiding direct force.

soft-pedal If you **soft-pedal** something, you reduce the amount of activity or pressure you have been using to get something done. *He refused to soft-pedal an investigation into the scandal.*

soft porn is pornography which shows or mentions sexual acts, but not in an explicit or violent way.

soft sell A **soft sell** is a method of selling or advertising which involves gentle persuasion rather than pressure.

soft-soap If you **soft-soap** someone, you flatter them to try to persuade them to do something.

soft target A **soft target** is one which can be easily attacked.

software Computer programs are often referred to as **software.**

softwood is wood such as pine, which can be sawn easily.

softy (or softie) (softies) If you call someone a **softy,** you mean they are emotional and can easily be made to feel sympathy for someone.

soggy If something is **soggy,** it is unpleasantly soft and wet.

soil (soiling, soiled) Soil is the top layer on the surface of the earth, which plants grow in. You can say an area has a particular **soil.** *...thin, dry sandy soils.* ■ If something is **soiled,** it becomes dirty and stained.

soiree (or soirée) (pron: swah-ray) A **soiree** is a social gathering in the evening.

sojourn (pron: soj-urn) A **sojourn** is a short stay in a place which is not your home.

solace (pron: sol-iss) If you find **solace** in something, you get comfort from it when you are sad.

solar means to do with the sun. *...solar radiation.* ■ **Solar** is used to describe things which use the sun's light and heat as a source of energy. *...solar powered fridges.*

solar cell A **solar cell** is a device which converts the sun's rays into electricity.

solar eclipse See **eclipse.**

solarium A **solarium** is a place where you can go to get a suntan using sun-lamps. ■ A **solarium** is a room which is mostly made of glass, to allow as much sun in as possible.

solar panel A **solar panel** is a device for generating electricity, made up of solar cells.

solar plexus (solar plexuses) The **solar plexus** is the area between the navel and the breastbone.

solar system A **solar system** consists of a sun and all the planets, comets, and asteroids which go round it. When people talk about **the solar system,** they usually mean the system the Earth belongs to.

solar wind – Solar winds are streams of ions and electrons which are constantly released by the sun and which travel at very high speeds.

sold See **sell.**

solder (soldering, soldered) If you **solder** two pieces of metal together, you join them by heating a piece of metal called **solder** between them, so that when it cools down it holds them together. A **soldering iron** is a tool used for soldering things together.

soldier (soldiering, soldiered) A **soldier** is a person who serves in an army. ■ If you **soldier on** with something, you keep working hard at it, although it is difficult.

soldiery is soldiers thought of as a group rather than as individuals. *...the local soldiery.*

sole (solely) The **sole** thing or person of a certain type is the only one. *...Dublin's sole remaining racecourse.* ■ **Sole** is used to describe something which is not shared with anyone or anything else. *...a museum devoted solely to his work.* ■ The **sole** of your foot is the underneath part which you stand on. ■ The **sole** of a shoe is the underneath part towards the front. ■ **Sole** are a kind of edible flat sea fish.

solecism (*pron:* **sol**-iss-izz-um) A **solecism** is an embarrassing mistake.

solemn (solemnly, solemnity) Solemn behaviour is serious, rather than humorous or cheerful. *With great solemnity we assented.* ■ A **solemn** promise or oath is made in a very formal and sincere way.

solemnize (*or* **solemnise**) **(solemnizing, solemnized; solemnization)** When a wedding ceremony is held in a place of worship, you say the marriage is **solemnized.**

solicit (soliciting, solicited) If you **solicit** something such as money from someone, you try to get them to give it to you. ■ When a prostitute **solicits,** she or he approaches someone and offers to have sex with them for money. The offence of publicly offering sex for money is called **soliciting.**

solicitor A **solicitor** is a lawyer who gives legal advice and prepares legal documents and cases.

Solicitor General In England, Scotland, and Wales, the **Solicitor General** is the second most important law officer.

solicitous (solicitude) If someone is **solicitous,** they show a lot of concern for someone such as a guest, and are anxious that everything should be all right for them. You call behaviour like this **solicitude.**

solid (solidly, solidity) A **solid** substance or object is firm and does not change shape easily. Solid substances can be called **solids.** ■ You say an object is **solid** when it is not hollow. ■ **Solid** is used to say an object is made of the same substance all the way through. For example, you say an object is **solid** gold. ■ A **solid** structure is strong and not likely to collapse or fall over. You can talk about the **solidity** of a structure like this. ■ **Solid** people are respectable and reliable. ■ **Solid** facts are specific and definite, rather than vague. ■ If support for someone is **solid,** everyone supports them and there is no opposition. *Public opinion in Egypt*

seems solidly behind the government's policy. ■ **Solid** is used to say something takes place throughout a period of time. *We had worked together for two solid years.*

solidarity If a group of people show **solidarity,** they show unity and agreement in their aims or actions.

solid fuel is any fuel which is not a liquid or a gas, for example coal.

solidify (solidifies, solidifying, solidified) When a liquid **solidifies,** it changes into a solid. ■ If something like a system or someone's opinion **solidifies,** it becomes firmer or more definite and is less likely to change.

solid-state electronic equipment is made using transistors, silicon chips, or other semi-conductors instead of valves or mechanical parts.

soliloquy (soliloquies) A **soliloquy** is a speech in a play in which a character speaks his or her thoughts aloud to the audience, rather than to another character.

solitary If there is a **solitary** thing of a particular kind, there is just one. *He left a solitary fingerprint.* ■ A **solitary** activity is one you do on your own. ■ A **solitary** person or animal spends a lot of time alone. ■ If a place is **solitary,** there are no people there.

solitary confinement If a prisoner is kept in **solitary confinement,** he or she is kept alone.

solitude is being on your own.

solo (solos; soloist) In an orchestral or choral work, an important part for an individual player or singer is called a **solo.** The person who plays it or sings it is called a **soloist.** ■ A **solo** is a piece of music played or sung by just one person or a performance given by just one person. You can also talk about someone doing something **solo.** *She lost her life when flying solo in 1937.*

solstice The **solstices** are the two times in the year when the sun is farthest away from the equator.

soluble A **soluble** substance will dissolve in a liquid. ■ If a problem is **soluble,** it can be solved.

solution A **solution** to a problem is a way of dealing with it. ■ The **solution** to a question or puzzle is the answer or explanation. ■ A **solution** is a liquid in which a solid substance or a gas has been dissolved.

solve (solving, solved) If you **solve** a problem or a puzzle, you find a solution to it.

solvent (solvency) If a person or an organization is **solvent,** they have enough money to pay all their debts. Being in this position is called **solvency.** ■ **Solvents** are liquids which dissolve other substances. ■ **Solvent abuse** is the illegal practice of inhaling the vapour from glue and other substances, to experience pleasant sensations.

sombre (*Am:* **somber**) **(sombrely)** If you say someone is **sombre,** you mean they are serious or pessimistic. ■ **Sombre** colours are dark and dull.

sombrero (sombreros) A **sombrero** is a Mexican hat with a very wide brim.

some is used to talk about an amount of something or a number of people or things. *I've managed to find some money.* ■ **Some of** is used to talk about a part of something, or part of a group of people or things. *Attempts have been made to release some of the captives.* ■ **Some** is used to say a distance or period of time is fairly large. *He is likely to remain an officer for some years to come.* ■ **Some** is used to show that something is vague or approximate. *Every day there's a column written by some economist or other saying let the dollar fall.* ■ **Some day** or **some-day** means at a date in the future which is unknown or has not yet been fixed. *Like the dinosaur, the human race could some day face extinction.*

somebody See **someone.**

someday See **some.**

somehow You use **somehow** to say you do not know how something was done or how it will be done. *We'll manage somehow.* ■ You use **somehow** to indicate that you do not know the reason for something. *The giants of the industry are somehow supposed to be different.*

someone (or **somebody**) is used to talk about a person without saying who. *Maybe somebody's listening.*

someplace In the US, **someplace** means somewhere. *He decided he would go someplace for a beer.*

somersault If you **somersault** or turn a **somersault,** you roll forward on the ground or in mid-air, so your body goes over your head. ■ You can say someone does a **somersault** when they completely reverse their opinions or policies.

something is used to talk about an action, event, object, or quality, without saying which one. *Something must be done... Every traveller looks for something different from a guidebook.* ■ If you say a person or thing is **something of** a particular thing, you mean they are that thing to a limited extent. *The portrait caused something of a scandal.* ■ If you say there is **something in** what someone says, you mean it is at least partly true.

sometime means at a time in the future which is undecided or unknown. *The drug will be launched in Europe sometime this year.* ■ **Sometime** is used to say someone had a particular job or role in the past. *...the portrait painter and sometime architect Paul Vauche.*

sometimes You use **sometimes** to say something happens on certain occasions or in certain cases rather than all the time or in every case. *Sometimes it doesn't work.*

somewhat means to some extent. *This year, things are somewhat better.*

somewhere is used to talk about a place without saying where. *A siren started up somewhere.* ■ You use **somewhere** when you are giving an approximate number, amount, or time. *There are somewhere around 42 million amateur golfers in America.* ■ If you say you are **getting somewhere,** you mean you are making progress.

somnolent If you feel **somnolent,** you are drowsy or sleepy. ■ If you describe a place as **somnolent,** you mean it is very peaceful, often to the point where it lacks vitality.

son Someone's **son** is their male child. ■ If you say a man is the **son** of a place, you mean that is where he comes from. *...New Orleans's most famous son, Louis Armstrong.*

sonar is a device on a ship which uses sound waves to measure the depth of the sea or to find the position of underwater objects.

sonata (*pron:* sonn-**nah**-ta) A **sonata** is a piece of classical music, usually written for a solo instrument or for a piano and one other instrument.

son et lumière (*pron:* **sonn** eh **loo**-mee-air) is an entertainment held at night in an old building such as a castle. A person describes the history of the place while different parts of the building are brightly lit and music is played.

song A **song** is a piece of music with words which are sung to the music. ■ A bird's **song** is the pleasant musical sounds it makes. ■ If you buy something **for a song,** you buy it for much less than its real value.

songbird A **songbird** is any bird which produces pleasant musical sounds.

sonic is used to talk about things to do with sound. *...sonic scanning.* ■ A **sonic boom** is the sudden loud noise heard at the moment when an aircraft exceeds the speed of sound.

son-in-law (**sons-in-law**) Someone's **son-in-law** is their daughter's husband.

sonnet A **sonnet** is a poem with 14 lines in which some lines rhyme with others according to a fixed pattern.

sonorous (**sonority, sonorities**) A **sonorous** sound is deep and rich. You talk about the **sonority** of a sound like this. ■ **Sonorous** words sound important and impressive.

soon (**sooner, soonest**) If something is going to happen **soon,** it will happen after a short time. If something happened **soon** after a particular time or event, it happened a short time after it. ■ If you say you **would sooner** do something, you mean you would prefer to do it.

soot (**sooty**) **Soot** is a black powder which rises in the smoke from a fire and collects on the insides of chimneys and other surfaces. A **sooty** place is covered in soot.

soothe (**soothing, soothed; soothingly**) If something like an ointment **soothes** pain, it makes it less severe. ■ If you **soothe** someone who is angry, worried, or upset, you make them feel calmer.

soothsayer A **soothsayer** is someone who claims to be able to predict the future.

sooty See **soot.**

sop A **sop** is something small or unimportant you offer to someone who is discontented to prevent them from getting angry or causing trouble. *Taxes on diesel are lower than on petrol - not for green reasons, but as a sop to drivers of commercial vehicles.*

sophisticated (**sophistication, sophisticate**) A **sophisticated** device, machine, or method is advanced and complex. ■ You describe people as **sophisticated** when they have become knowledgeable in a particular field and are able to deal with fairly complicated matters. *As users become more sophisticated, they are often happy to install the equipment themselves.* ■ A **sophisticated** person knows about culture, fashion, and other matters considered to be socially important. People like these are sometimes called **sophisticates.** You can also talk about their **sophistication.**

sophistry (*pron:* **soff**-iss-tree) (**sophistries**) **Sophistry** is using clever arguments which sound convincing but are actually false. Arguments like these are called **sophistries.**

sophomore In the US, a **sophomore** is a student in the second year of college or high school.

soporific If something is **soporific,** it makes you feel sleepy.

soppy If you say someone or something is **soppy,** you mean they are sentimental and silly.

soprano (**sopranos**) A **soprano** is a woman, girl, or boy with a high singing voice.

sorbet (*pron:* **sor**-bay) is a dessert made from semi-frozen syrup of sugar and water flavoured with liqueurs or fruit.

sorcery (**sorcerer; sorceress, sorceresses**) In stories, **sorcery** is performing magic using the power of evil spirits. A person who does this is called a **sorcerer.** A female sorcerer is sometimes called a **sorceress.**

sordid behaviour is dishonest or immoral. ■ You can say a place is **sordid** when it is dirty, unpleasant, and depressing.

sore (**sorely**) If part of your body is **sore,** it is causing you pain and discomfort, for example because of a wound or infection. ■ A **sore** is a painful place where the skin is infected. ■ If you are **sore** about something, you are angry and upset about it. ■ If you are **in sore need** of something, you need it very badly. ■ **Sore** is used to emphasize something. *His judgement and advice will be sorely missed by the board.*

sorghum is a tall cereal grass which looks similar to maize.

sorority (**sororities**) In the US, a **sorority** is a social society of women students.

sorrel is a leafy bitter-tasting herb used in salads and soups.

sorrow is a feeling of great sadness or regret. ■ **Sorrows** are events or situations which cause great sadness. *The region can blame man, rather than God, for its sorrows.*

sorrowful (**sorrowfully**) If someone is **sorrowful,** they are very sad. ■ **Sorrowful** things make you feel sad. *...a sorrowful tale.*

sorry (**sorrier, sorriest**) You say **sorry** when you are apologizing for something. ■ You say you are **sorry** when you are expressing regret about something. *He was sorry to see them go.* ■ If you feel **sorry** for someone who is in an unpleasant situation, you feel sympathy for them. ■ **Sorry** is used to describe people or things that are in a bad state. *The bicycle looked a sorry sight.*

sort A particular **sort** of thing is a particular type of that thing. ■ You use **of sorts** or **of a sort** to say something is a particular kind of thing, but not a very good example of it. *Guests can always get a meal of sorts in the hotel restaurant.* ■ You use **sort of** when you are giving a rough description of something. *I use the top floor as a sort of office-cum-apartment.* ■ If things are **sorted** or **sorted out,** they are arranged into groups according to some kind of system. *At the recycling plant the bags are automatical-*

ly sorted by colour. ■ If you **sort out** a problem, you deal with it and find a solution to it. ■ If you feel **out of sorts,** you are not your usual self, because you are discontented or unwell.

sortie A **sortie** is a brief military attack into enemy territory. ■ You can say someone makes a **sortie** when they make a brief trip away from their home or base, especially a trip to an unfamiliar place.

sorting office A **sorting office** is a place where letters and parcels are taken after posting and are sorted according to their delivery address.

SOS An **SOS** is a signal which indicates to other people that you are in danger and need help quickly.

sotto voce (*pron:* sot-toe **voe**-chay) If you say something **sotto voce,** you say it very quietly.

soubriquet See **sobriquet.**

souffle (*or* **soufflé**) (*pron:* **soo**-flay) A **souffle** is a light fluffy food made from whisked egg whites and other ingredients.

sought See **seek.**

sought-after If something is **sought-after,** it is in great demand, because it is rare or of very good quality.

souk (*pron:* **sook**) In Muslim countries, a **souk** is an open-air market.

soul A person's **soul** is the spiritual part of them which some people believe goes on existing after their body is dead. ■ Your **soul** is your mind, character, thoughts, and feelings. ■ **Soul** can be used to mean person. *He's a jolly soul... He moved through rooms of sleeping couples without ever waking a soul.* ■ **Soul** or **soul music** is a type of pop music performed mainly by black American musicians. It developed from gospel and blues music and often expresses deep emotions.

soul-destroying work is boring and depressing.

soulful music expresses deep emotions.

soulless If you call a place where people live or work **soulless,** you mean it is dull and depressing.

soulmate If you call someone your **soulmate,** you mean they are very close friends who share your views or interests.

soul-searching is long and careful examination of your thoughts, feelings, and motives, especially when you are trying to make a difficult decision.

sound (**soundings**) A **sound** is something you hear. **Sound** is everything that can be heard. *...babies who respond to sound and light in the womb.* ■ If something such as a bell **sounds,** it produces a noise. ■ You can give your impression of something you have heard about by talking about the way it **sounds.** *That sounds like a pretty good compromise.* ■ If something is **sound,** it is in good condition. ■ If a piece of advice is **sound,** it is reliable and sensible. ■ If you **sound off** about something, you express your opinions loudly and strongly to everyone without being asked. ■ If you use someone as a **sounding board,** you discuss your ideas with them to help you develop them. ■ **Soundings** are measurements of the depth of something like the sea, using sonar or a weighted line.

sound barrier The **sound barrier** is the sudden increase in the force of the air against an aircraft when it approaches the speed of sound.

soundbite A **soundbite** is a phrase or sentence usually taken from a politician's speech which is quoted in the media because it seems to sum up a situation or political view.

sound effect – Sound effects are sounds created artificially to make a play or film more realistic.

soundings See **sound.**

soundly If someone is **soundly** defeated, they are defeated thoroughly. ■ If you sleep **soundly,** you sleep deeply.

soundproof (**soundproofing, soundproofed**) If you **soundproof** a room or building, you line it with materials to stop noise getting into it or out of it. *The studio isn't soundproof.*

sound system A **sound system** is electrical equipment used for playing and amplifying music, for example at a disco or rock concert.

soundtrack The **soundtrack** of a film is its sound, including speech, music, and sound effects.

soup (**souping, souped**) **Soup** is savoury liquid food. ■ If a car is **souped up,** it is made more powerful. *...a souped up Morris Minor.*

soup kitchen A **soup kitchen** is a place which provides free food for poor and homeless people.

sour (**souring, soured; sourly, sourness**) **Sour** food has a sharp taste like the taste of a lemon. ■ **Sour** milk has an unpleasant taste because it is no longer fresh. ■ **Sour** people are bad-tempered and unfriendly. ■ If a relationship **sours** or turns or goes **sour,** it becomes less friendly. *The dispute has soured the atmosphere surrounding the summit.*

source The **source** of something is the person, place, or thing it comes from. *Botanic gardens are an invaluable source of plant material for scientists.* ■ A **source** is a person or book that provides you with information. *One senior source said yesterday: 'He still seems to be fighting the leadership campaign.'* ■ The **source** of a river is the place where it begins.

sour cream is cream used in cooking which has been artificially made sour.

south (**southern**) **South** is one of the four main points of the compass. ■ The **south** is the direction on your right when you look towards the place where the sun rises. If you go in that direction, you go **south;** a place in that direction is **south of** the place where you are now. ■ The **south** or **southern** part of a place is the part south of its centre. *...Belize's large southern neighbour, Guatemala.* ■ **South** winds blow from the south.

southbound traffic is heading towards the south.

south-east (*or* **southeast**) (**south-eastern**) The **south-east** is the direction halfway between south and east. ■ The **south-east** or **south-eastern** part of a place is the part south-east of its centre.

south-easterly A **south-easterly** wind blows from the south-east. ■ If you travel in a **south-easterly** direction, you travel towards the south-east.

south-eastern See **south-east.**

southerly winds blows from the south. ■ If you travel or face in a **southerly** direction, you travel or face towards the south. ■ The most **southerly** part of a place is the part furthest to the south. Similarly, the most **southerly** place of a group of places is the one furthest to the south.

southern See **south.**

southerner A **southerner** is a person who was born or lives in the southern part of a country or region.

southernmost The **southernmost** part of a place is the part furthest to the south.

southpaw A **southpaw** is a boxer who leads with his left hand.

southward (**southwards**) If you go **southward** or **southwards,** you go towards the south.

south-west (*or* **southwest**) (**south-western**) The **south-west** is the direction between south and west. ■ The **south-west** or **south-western** part of a place is the part south-west of its centre.

south-westerly A **south-westerly** wind blows from the south-west. ■ If you travel in a **south-westerly** direction, you travel towards the south-west.

south-western See **South-West.**

souvenir A **souvenir** is something you buy or keep to remind you of a holiday, place, or event. *...a souvenir of the Royal Wedding.*

sovereign A **sovereign** is a king, queen, or other royal ruler. ■ A **sovereign** state or country is independent and not under the authority of any other country. ■ The **sovereign** was an old British coin worth one pound.

sovereignty is the political power a country has to govern itself or to govern other territories.

Soviet is used to talk about things to do with the former Soviet Union and its people. *...the Soviet ambassador to Britain.* ■ The **Soviets** were the people of the former Soviet Union. ■ A **soviet** was an elected local, regional, or national council in the former Soviet Union.

sow (**sowing, sowed, have sown**) If you **sow** seeds, you plant them in the ground. ■ If someone **sows** confusion or panic, they cause it to develop. ■ A **sow** (*rhymes with 'now'*) is an adult female pig.

soya – Soya beans are protein-rich beans which are eaten as a vegetable or used to make flour, oil, or soy sauce. **Soya** flour, butter, etc is made from soya beans.

soy sauce is a dark brown salty liquid made from soya beans. It is used as a flavouring, especially in Chinese cooking.

sozzled If you say someone is **sozzled,** you mean they are drunk.

spa A **spa** is a place where water which is rich in minerals bubbles out of the ground. People sometimes drink the water or bathe in it to improve their health.

space (**spacing, spaced**) **Space** is the unoccupied parts of a place which are available to be used for a particular purpose. *Rapid growth means a big demand for office space.* ■ A **space** is a gap or an empty place in something. *Local papers sometimes appear with white spaces where stories should have been.* ■ The **space** you have to do something is the amount of freedom you have for it. *This leaves elected officials little space to make decisions.* ■ A **space** of time is a certain period of time. *All of the centre's fifty terminals were infected by a virus in the space of a week.* ■ **Space** is the area beyond the Earth's atmosphere which contains all the other planets and stars. ■ If you **space** things **out,** you arrange them so they have gaps between them. The **spacing** between a series of things or actions is the distance or amount of time between them.

space age The **space age** is the present period in history, in which travel in space has become possible. ■ **Space-age** is used to describe things which are very modern and high-tech. *...space-age yachts.*

spacecraft (*plural:* **spacecraft**) A **spacecraft** is a vehicle which can travel in space.

spaced-out If someone is **spaced-out,** they feel as if nothing around them is real, usually because they are on drugs.

spaceman (**spacemen**) A **spaceman** is the same as an astronaut.

space probe A **space probe** is a small unmanned computer-controlled spacecraft sent into space to transmit information back about space or other planets.

spaceship A **spaceship** is the same as a spacecraft.

space shuttle A **space shuttle** is a spacecraft designed to travel into space and back several times.

space station A **space station** is an object sent into orbit to be used as a base by astronauts.

space suit (*or* **spacesuit**) A **space suit** is a special protective suit worn by an astronaut.

spacing See **space.**

spacious (**spaciousness**) If a room or other place is **spacious,** it is large, with plenty of room.

spade A **spade** is a tool for digging. It has a broad flat metal blade and a long wooden handle. ■ **Spades** is one of the four suits in a pack of playing cards. All cards in this suit have the symbol ♠ on them.

spadework (*or* **spade work**) The **spadework** for a project or activity is the routine or uninteresting work which has to be done as a preparation.

spaghetti is a type of pasta formed into long thin strings. ■ A **spaghetti western** is a film about the Wild West made in Spain by an Italian director.

span (**spanning, spanned**) If something **spans** a period of time, it lasts for that time. *...a professional career spanning 11 years.* You can also talk about a **span** of time between two events. ■ Your attention **span** is the length of time you are able to concentrate on something or stay interested in it. ■ If something **spans** a range of things, it includes all of them. A **span** of things is a range of them. *...his broad span of interests.* ■ The **span** of something is the distance from one side to the other. *Adult albatrosses have a wing-span of more than 6 feet.* ■ If a bridge **spans** a river or valley, it stretches right across it. ■ See also **spick and span.**

spangle (**spangled**) **Spangles** are small pieces of metal or plastic which sparkle brightly and are used for decoration. If something is **spangled,** it is decorated with spangles. *...a spangled mini-dress.*

Spaniard A **Spaniard** is someone who comes from Spain.

spaniel – **Spaniels** are a type of dog with long drooping ears.

Spanish is used to talk about people and things in or from Spain. *...the Spanish authorities.* ■ The **Spanish** are the Spanish people. ■ **Spanish** is the main language spoken in Spain and most countries in South and Central America.

spank (**spanking**) If someone **spanks** a child or gives it a **spanking,** they hit it on the bottom with their hand, usually several times, as a punishment. ■ If you describe something as **spanking new,** you are emphasizing that it is very new. *...a spanking new Mercedes.*

spanner A **spanner** is a metal tool with a specially shaped end for loosening or tightening nuts.

spar (**sparring, sparred**) When boxers **spar** with each other, they fight less fiercely than usual, because they are in training. ■ If you **spar** with someone, you argue with them fairly light-heartedly. ■ The mast, boom, etc on a sailing ship are called **spars.**

spare (**sparing, spared; sparingly**) **Spare** objects or **spares** are things you keep handy in case they are needed to replace the ones in use at present. *...spare bulbs.* ■ **Spare** is used to describe things which are not being used at present and are therefore available. *He would like to be able to lease out spare space to independent businesses.* ■ If you can **spare** something, you can afford to part with it or make it available. *He doesn't have a lot of cash to spare.* ■ If you are **sparing** with something, you use it or give it away only in very small quantities. ■ Your **spare time** is time when you do not have to work and can do what you want. ■ If you are **spared** an unpleasant experience, it does not happen to you.

spare ribs are the ribs of a pig with most of the meat trimmed off.

spark A **spark** is a tiny bright piece of burning material which flies up from a fire. ■ A **spark** is a flash of light caused by electricity. ■ A **spark** of a feeling or a quality is a small but noticeable amount of it. *His phrasing lacked that vital spark of imagination.* ■ If something **sparks** something else or **sparks** it **off,** it starts it happening.

sparkle (**sparkling, sparkled**) If something **sparkles,** it shines with a lot of small points of flickering light. *...the sparkling sea.* ■ If someone **sparkles,** they are lively and witty. *...sparkling wit.* ■ **Sparkling** drinks are slightly fizzy.

sparkler A **sparkler** is a small firework you hold in your hand.

spark plug A **spark plug** is a device in the engine of a motor vehicle which produces an electric spark to ignite the fuel.

sparky people and things are lively and amusing.

sparrow The **sparrow** or **house sparrow** is a very common small bird with brown and grey feathers.

sparrowhawk The **sparrowhawk** is a hawk which preys on smaller birds.

sparse (**sparsely**) If something is **sparse,** there is very little of it and it is spread out over a large area or a long period of time. *Information from the region has been sparse. ...a sparsely inhabited region of Siberia.*

spartan A **spartan** way of life is very simple with no luxuries.

spasm A **spasm** is a sudden uncontrollable tightening of the muscles in a part of your body. ■ A

spasm of pain or painful emotion is a sudden short burst of it.

spasmodic (**spasmodically**) If something is **spasmodic,** it happens for short periods at irregular intervals.

spastic People with cerebral palsy used to be called **spastics.**

spat See **spit.** ■ A **spat** is a brief quarrel which is not very serious. ■ **Spats** are specially shaped pieces of cloth or leather which button down one side. They used to be worn by men over their ankles and part of their shoes.

spate A **spate** of bad things is a lot of them happening or appearing within a short time. ...*this spate of misfortunes.* ■ When a river is **in spate,** it contains a lot more water than usual and is flowing very fast.

spatial means relating to size, area, or position, rather than, for example, to time. ...*spatial information.* ■ A child's **spatial** ability is its ability to see and understand the relationships between shapes, spaces, and areas.

spatter (**spattering, spattered**) If a liquid **spatters** a surface, it covers the surface in small drops. ■ If a conversation or piece of writing is **spattered** with something, it is full of it. ...*sentences spattered with four-letter words.*

spatula A **spatula** is (a) a tool used in cooking with a handle and a flexible blunt blade. (b) a small, flat-bladed instrument used by doctors.

spawn If something **spawns** something else, it causes it to happen or be created. *The Dollar films spawned many imitators.* ■ When fish, frogs, and other amphibians **spawn,** they lay their eggs. The eggs are called **spawn.**

spay (**spays, spaying, spayed**) When a female animal is **spayed,** it has its ovaries removed so it cannot become pregnant.

speak (**speaking, spoke, have spoken**) When you **speak,** you say words. ■ If you **speak** a foreign language, you know it. ■ If you **speak for** a group of people, you represent them, or make their views or demands known. ■ If you **speak out** about something or **speak up** about it, you give your opinion about it publicly. ■ If you ask someone to **speak up,** you are asking them to speak louder. ■ If you say something **speaks volumes,** you mean it tells you a lot about something in an indirect way.

-speak is added to the name of a person, group, or organization to describe words they are fond of using, or words they use in a different way from anyone else. ...*his tendency to fall into football-speak.*

speaker In the parliament of many countries, the **Speaker** is the person in charge of the meetings of the parliament. ■ A **speaker** at a conference or meeting is someone who makes a speech. ■ A **speaker** of a language is someone who can speak it. *My parents were Gaelic speakers.* ■ Anyone who is speaking at a particular time can be called the **speaker.** *This must be as boring to the speaker as it is to the listener.* ■ A **speaker** is a loudspeaker.

spear (**spearing, speared**) A **spear** is a weapon consisting of a long pole with a sharp tip. ■ If you **spear** something, you push a pointed object such

as a fork into it. ■ An asparagus or broccoli **spear** is an individual stalk of it.

spearhead (**spearheading, spearheaded**) The person or group that **spearheads** a campaign or attack is the one that leads it. They can also be called its **spearhead.**

special If something is **special,** it is different from normal, and often better or more important. *It will be a special day for me.* ■ A **special** is something which is available only for a limited period or in limited numbers. *Bar meals include some specials, such as half a roast duckling in orange sauce.* ■ **Special** is used to describe a person or group that has been officially appointed to carry out a task. *The UN special envoy arrives in Johannesburg today.* ■ **Special** schools or other institutions are for people who have particular needs, for example people with physical handicaps or learning difficulties. You say people like these have **special needs.** ■ **Special** is used to describe something designed and made for a particular purpose. *To turn the water off outside your house you need a special key.* ■ In films and TV, **special effects** are unusual things you see on the screen or hear on the soundtrack which are achieved using special techniques.

Special Branch The **Special Branch** is the department of the British police force concerned with political security. It deals, for example, with terrorism and visits by foreign leaders.

special constable – **Special constables** are unpaid volunteers who assist the police in their spare time.

specialise See **specialize.**

specialism Someone's **specialism** is something they have studied or practised a lot and which they are an expert in.

specialist A **specialist** is someone who studies or practices a subject or skill and knows a lot about it. ■ A **specialist** company or organization deals in one type of product or area of work. ...*a specialist comic shop.* ■ A **specialist** is a doctor or surgeon who specializes in one area of medicine.

speciality (**specialities**) Someone's **speciality** is the kind of work they do best or the subject they know most about. *Wine-making was his speciality.* ■ If a product is the **speciality** of a place, it is made a lot there, usually to a high standard. *Green sage cheese is an old Derbyshire and Lancashire speciality.*

specialize (or **specialise**) (**specializing, specialized; specialization**) If you **specialize** in something, you concentrate most of your time and resources on it. *Many solicitors now specialize in business affairs.* ■ **Specialized** things have been developed for a particular purpose. *It can be reached only with the aid of specialised machinery.* Similarly, **specialized** people have been trained to do an unusual job.

specially is used to say something is done, made, or provided for a particular purpose. ...*replica Ferraris specially built for the project.* ■ **Specially** is used to mean 'especially'. *The finale, if not specially witty, was at least vivacious.*

specialty (**specialties**) A **specialty** is the same as a speciality.

species (*plural:* **species**) A **species** is a class of plants or animals whose members have the same main characteristics and are able to breed with each other.

specific You use **specific** to emphasize that you are talking about one particular thing or subject. *No specific organisation has been linked with the document.* ■ If something is **specific** to a particular thing, it relates to that thing and nothing else. *Many of the reasons for IBM's swift decline are specific to the computer industry.* ■ If a statement is **specific**, it is precise and exact. ■ The **specifics** of a subject are its details. *Well, of course I don't know the specifics of your problem.*

specifically is used to emphasize that something is being given special attention and considered separately from other things of the same kind. *We haven't specifically targeted school children.* ■ If you state something **specifically,** you state it precisely and clearly. *We specifically asked for sash windows.*

specification A **specification** is a clearly stated detail or requirement, for example about the features in the design of something. *The house has been built to the engineer's specifications.*

specific gravity The **specific gravity** of a substance is the ratio of the density of the substance to the density of water.

specify (**specifies, specifying, specified**) If you **specify** something, you state or describe it precisely. *The statement did not specify which countries would attend.*

specimen A **specimen** is a single plant or animal which is an example of a particular type and is examined by scientists. ■ A **specimen** is a small quantity of someone's blood or urine taken for analysis. ■ If you say someone or something is a fine **specimen** of a type of thing, you mean they are a fine example of it.

specious (*pron:* **spee**-shuss) (**speciously**) A **specious** argument or claim appears to be correct, but is in fact false.

speck A **speck** is a very small mark or shape. *An astronomer first spotted the asteroid as a fast-moving dark speck.* ■ A **speck** of a substance is a very small amount of it.

speckled If something is **speckled**, it is covered in a pattern of small marks or spots. *...speckled feathers.*

specs Someone's **specs** are their glasses.

spectacle (**spectacles**) Someone's **spectacles** are their glasses. ■ You can describe something you see happening as a **spectacle** of a particular kind. *...the bizarre spectacle that ensued when he got up on stage.* ■ You can call a grand impressive event or performance a **spectacle.**

spectacular (**spectacularly**) You say something is **spectacular** when it is very impressive to see or watch. ■ A **spectacular** is a grand impressive show or performance.

spectate (**spectating, spectated**) If someone is **spectating** at an event, they are watching rather than taking part.

spectator A **spectator** is someone who is watching something, especially a sporting event. ■ A **spec-** tator sport is one which many people enjoy watching.

spectral is used to describe (a) something to do with ghosts. (b) someone who looks like a ghost. ■ **Spectral** means to do with the wavelengths of different colours of light. *...spectral characteristics.*

spectre (*Am:* **specter**) A **spectre** is a ghost. ■ You can call something which seems likely to happen a **spectre** when you find it alarming. *...the spectre of higher taxes.*

spectrograph A **spectrograph** is an instrument for photographing a spectrum. The photograph it takes is also called a **spectrograph.**

spectrometer A **spectrometer** is a device which splits light into a spectrum.

spectrum (*plural:* **spectra** *or* **spectrums**) The **spectrum** is the range of different colours, arranged in order of their wavelengths, which is produced when light passes through something like a drop of water. ■ A **spectrum** of things is a complete range of them, especially when one end of the range is in complete contrast to the other. *Her reviews at the Edinburgh Festival had covered the spectrum from reverent awe to disgust.*

speculate (**speculating, speculated; speculation, speculator**) If you **speculate** about something, you make guesses about it. *Speculation about his fate is rife.* ■ When people **speculate** financially, they buy property, stocks, or shares in the hope of selling them quickly at a profit. People who do this are called **speculators.**

speculative (**speculatively**) **Speculative** statements are based on guesses rather than facts. ■ **Speculative** investments involve taking a risk in the hope of making a quick profit.

speculator See **speculate.**

sped See **speed.**

speech (**speeches**) Speech is the ability to speak, or the act of speaking. ■ A person's **speech** is their characteristic way of speaking. *...the crisp, clipped speech of most BBC newsreaders.* ■ A **speech** is (a) a formal talk given to an audience. (b) a series of lines from a play, spoken by an actor.

speechify (**speechifies, speechifying, speechified**) **Speechifying** is making speeches.

speechless If you say someone is **speechless,** you mean they are so shocked or angry they cannot speak.

speech therapy (**speech therapist**) Speech therapy is the treatment of people who have difficulties with speech and language. A **speech therapist** is someone whose job is to help people overcome these difficulties.

speed (**speeding, sped; speeded**) (*If you are talking about the past, you say, for example, 'The car sped off' but 'The government speeded up its reforms.'*) The **speed** of something is the rate at which it moves or travels. ■ **Speed** is fast movement. *...a boat designed with speed in mind.* ■ If you **speed** somewhere, you move or travel there quickly. ■ If a motorist is **speeding,** he or she is driving faster than the legal speed limit. ■ The **speed** of something is the rate at which it happens or is done. *...the speed of economic reform.* ■ If something **speeds up,** it moves, happens, or is done more quickly. ■ See also **amphetamine.**

speedboat A **speedboat** is a light fast boat with a powerful engine.

speed limit The **speed limit** on a stretch of road is the maximum speed at which you can legally drive along it.

speedometer (*pron:* speed-**dom**-it-er) A **speedometer** is an instrument in a vehicle which shows how fast it is going.

speed trap A **speed trap** is a stretch of road on which the police are checking whether vehicles are travelling faster than the speed limit.

speedway is the sport of racing lightweight motorcycles without brakes on special tracks.

speedy (speedier, speediest; speedily) A **speedy** action happens or is done very quickly. *She was speedily transferred to Preston Royal Infirmary.* ■ You say someone or something is **speedy** when they move very quickly.

speleology (speleologist) **Speleology** is the study of caves. An expert on this is called a **speleologist.**

spell (spelling, spelled *or* spelt) When you **spell** a word, you say or write the individual letters in their correct order. The **spelling** of a word is the correct order of the letters in it. ■ If someone can **spell,** they can say or write the letters of most words in their correct order. **Spelling** is the ability to do this. ■ If you say something **spells** trouble or danger, you mean it is likely to lead to it. ■ If you **spell** something **out,** you explain it in detail and as clearly as possible. ■ A **spell** of something is a short period of it. *...a spell of hot weather.* ■ A **spell** is a sequence of words used to perform magic. ■ If you are **under** someone's **spell,** you are so fascinated by them you are prepared to believe anything they say or do anything they ask.

spellbound (spellbinding) If you are **spellbound** by something or it is **spellbinding,** you are fascinated by it and cannot think of anything else while it is happening.

spellchecker The **spellchecker** on your computer is a system that highlights any word in a word-processed document that it does not recognize as being correctly spelt.

spelt See **spell.**

spend (spending, spent; spender) When you **spend** money, you use it to pay for things. ■ You can say how much money someone spends by describing them as, for example, a big **spender.** *...the high-spenders of the 1980s.* ■ If you **spend** a period of time in a place, you are in that place during that time. Similarly, you can **spend** time doing something. *He spent a year studying Japanese in Tokyo.* ■ See also **spent.**

spendthrift A **spendthrift** is someone who spends money wastefully.

spent See **spend.** ■ If something is **spent,** it has already been used and cannot be used again. *...spent fuel.* ■ If you say someone is a **spent force,** you mean they no longer have the power they once had.

sperm (*plural:* sperm *or* sperms) A **sperm** is a cell produced in the sex organs of a man or male animal, which can join a female's egg and fertilize it.

spermatozoon (*pron:* sper-mat-ta-**zoe**-on) (*plural:* spermatozoa) A **spermatozoon** is the same as a sperm.

sperm whale The **sperm whale** is a large whale with a cavity in its head containing a large amount of oil.

spew If something **spews** things or **spews** them **out,** they flow out of it in large quantities. *Leaking oil spewed from the tanker for two days.*

sphere A **sphere** is a perfectly round three-dimensional object like a ball. ■ When you talk about activities within a particular **sphere,** you mean activities of a particular kind. ■ An organization's **sphere of activity** is all the activities it is involved in. ■ A country's **sphere of influence** is the area of the world where it is the dominant power. ■ People of a certain social class are said to belong to a particular **sphere.** *...the lowest sphere of society.*

spherical objects are shaped like a sphere.

sphinx (sphinxes) The **Sphinx** is a huge stone statue with a lion's body and a human head, built by the ancient Egyptians. There are also other smaller sphinxes located around Egypt.

spice (spicing, spiced) **Spices** are the seeds, powdered roots, or bark of certain plants which are used in cooking to add flavour. ■ If you **spice** food or **spice** it **up,** you add spices to it. ■ If you **spice** something you do or say or **spice** it **up,** you do something extra to make it more lively or exciting. You can also say you add **spice** to it.

spick and span means very clean and tidy.

spicy (spicier, spiciest; spiciness) **Spicy** food is strongly flavoured with spices. *...the fragrant spiciness of Thai food.*

spider – **Spiders** are small eight-legged creatures. Most spiders feed on insects which they catch by building webs.

spidery handwriting is very thin and angular and is difficult to read.

spiel (*pron:* shpeel) Someone's **spiel** is a speech they make, usually one they have made many times before and often one in which they try to persuade you to do or buy something.

spigot A **spigot** is a valve which controls the flow of a liquid from one source to another. ■ In the US, a tap or faucet is often called a **spigot.**

spike (spiking, spiked) A **spike** is a long pointed piece of metal. ■ The **spikes** on sports shoes are the pointed pieces of metal attached to the soles. Shoes with spikes on them are called **spikes.** ■ Some plants have tall stems called **spikes** covered with flowers or buds. ■ If someone **spikes** your drink, they put alcohol or a drug in it. ■ If you **spike** someone's plans, you do something which stops them being carried out.

spiky objects have a sharp point or points. ■ **Spiky** people are bad-tempered and easily irritated.

spill (spilling, spilled *or* spilt) If a liquid **spills** or is **spilled,** it accidentally flows out of its container. Liquid spilled like this can be called a **spill.** *...an oil spill.* ■ If people or things **spill** out of a place, they come out in large numbers. ■ If something in one place or situation **spills over** into another, it begins to happen or have an effect in the other one. *The fighting spilled over into surrounding areas.* ■ If you **spill the beans,** you tell someone something which has been kept secret.

spillage You say there is a **spillage** when something such as oil escapes from a ship into the sea.

spin (**spinning, spun**) If something **spins** or is **spun,** it turns quickly round its central point. ■ If you put **spin** on a ball, you deliberately make it spin rapidly when you hit it, kick it, or throw it, so that it curves or bounces in a certain way. ■ If your head is **spinning,** you feel dizzy and confused. ■ When someone **spins,** they make thread by twisting together strands of a natural fibre such as wool or cotton using a device or machine. ■ If you **spin** something **out,** you make it last longer than it normally would. ■ If you talk about someone **spinning a story** or **spinning a yarn,** you mean they are telling a story which is not true or only partly true.

spina bifida is a condition of the spine which some people are born with. It can cause paralysis.

spinach is a vegetable with large dark green leaves.

spinal means to do with the spine. *...a spinal injury.*

spinal column The **spinal column** is the spine.

spinal cord The **spinal cord** is a rope-like structure of nerve tissue inside the spine which connects the brain to nerves in all parts of the body.

spindle A **spindle** is a rod in a machine, around which another part of the machine turns.

spindly things are long, thin, and weak-looking.

spin doctor A **spin doctor** is someone skilled in public relations who advises political parties on how to present their candidates and policies in the best possible way.

spin dryer (*or* **spin drier**) A **spin dryer** is a machine which partly dries wet clothes by spinning them round at high speed.

spine The **spine** is the row of bones down the middle of your back which supports your body and has your spinal cord inside it. ■ The **spine** of a book is the stiff narrow part the pages and covers are attached to. ■ **Spines** are long sharp points on an animal's body or on a plant.

spine-chilling If you say something is **spine-chilling,** you mean it is very frightening.

spineless If you say someone is **spineless,** you mean they are weak and cowardly.

spinnaker The **spinnaker** on a racing yacht is its large three-cornered sail.

spinner A **spinner** is a cricketer who makes the ball spin when he or she bowls so that it changes direction when it hits the ground.

spinney A **spinney** is a small wood.

spin-off A **spin-off** is something useful which happens as a result of trying to achieve something else. ■ Products you can buy which are based on a successful book, film, or TV programme are called **spin-offs.**

spinster In the past, an older woman who had never married was sometimes called a **spinster.**

spiny animals and plants are covered in spines.

spiral (**spiralling, spiralled**) (*usual Am:* **spiraling, spiraled**) A **spiral** is a curved shape which winds round and round, with each curve above or outside the previous one. ■ If something **spirals,** it moves up or down in a spiral curve. ■ If an amount or level **spirals,** it rises quickly and at an increasing rate. *...spiralling costs.*

spire The **spire** of a church or cathedral is a tall cone-shaped structure rising from a tower.

spirit (**spiriting, spirited**) When people talk about a person's **spirit,** they mean a part of them which is not physical and which involves their deepest thoughts and feelings. ■ When some people talk about a dead person's **spirit,** they mean a non-physical part of them which continues to exist after they die. ■ Some people believe in supernatural beings called **spirits.** ■ The **spirit** in which you do something is the attitude you show when you do it. *...an agreement made in a spirit of trust and goodwill.* The **spirit** of a law or agreement is the way it was intended to be interpreted or applied. See also **letter.** ■ You use **spirits** when you are saying how you feel. *Faldo was in good spirits.* ■ If someone shows **spirit,** they are energetic, courageous, and self-confident. *Australia held off a spirited challenge from Holland to win 3-2.* ■ **Spirits** are strong alcoholic drinks such as whisky or gin. ■ If you **spirit** someone or something into or out of a place, you get them in or out quickly and secretly.

spirit level A **spirit level** is a device for testing a surface to see if it is horizontal. It consists of a piece of wood or metal containing a tube of liquid with a bubble of air in it.

spiritual (**spiritually**) Spiritual means connected with (a) people's deepest thoughts and feelings, rather than their bodies or physical surroundings. (b) people's religious beliefs. *...spiritual fulfilment.*

spiritualism (**spiritualist**) Spiritualism is the belief that dead people can communicate with the living. Someone who believes this is called a **spiritualist.**

spirituality If you talk about a person's **spirituality,** you mean their dedication to God and to spiritual things.

spit (**spitting, spat**) If someone **spits,** they make a small amount of saliva shoot out of their mouth into the air. A person can also **spit out** food or drink. ■ If you say someone is the **spitting image** of someone else, you mean they look just like them. ■ A **spit** is rod which is pushed through a piece of meat so the meat can be turned over an open fire and roasted. ■ A **spit** is a long flat narrow piece of land sticking out into the sea.

spite You use **in spite of** when you are mentioning something which might have prevented something happening, but which did not in fact prevent it. *In spite of overwhelming odds, they succeeded in conquering the world champions.* ■ If someone does something out of **spite,** they do it deliberately to annoy someone else, because they feel jealous or resentful. You can also say they do it **to spite** the other person.

spiteful If someone is **spiteful,** they deliberately try to annoy or upset people they dislike.

spittle is the watery liquid produced in your mouth.

spiv A **spiv** is someone who makes money, usually small amounts, in dishonest ways.

splash (**splashes, splashing, splashed**) When water **splashes** somewhere, it hits against something, sending up a lot of small drops. ■ A **splash** is the sound made when water hits something, or when something is dropped into water. ■ If you **splash** about in water, you move about in it, making a noise as you disturb it. ■ If you **splash** a liquid somewhere, you throw or spill it carelessly. ■ A **splash** of something like water is a small amount added to another drink. ■ A **splash** of bright colour is an area of it, which catches your attention. ■ If a newspaper or magazine **splashes** a story, it prints it in a noticeable way, usually on the front page. A story treated in this way is called a **splash.** ■ If you **splash out** on something, you buy it even though it costs a lot of money.

splashy is used to describe things which are intended to attract a lot of attention. *...a splashy new advertising campaign.*

splatter (**splattering, splattered**) If a surface is **splattered** with something like mud, the mud has been dropped or splashed on it leaving small amounts all over it.

splay If things **splay** out, their ends spread out away from each other. *He splayed his fingers across his face.*

spleen Your **spleen** is an organ near your stomach which controls the quality of your blood. ■ **Spleen** is violent and spiteful anger. *Griffiths vents her spleen on an array of topical issues.*

splendid (**splendidly**) If you say something is **splendid,** you mean it is extremely good or impressive. ■ A **splendid** building or work of art is very beautiful and impressive. *Here the battlements rise splendidly, a reminder of the town's place in history.*

splendour is great beauty and magnificence. The **splendours** of a place are its beautiful and magnificent features.

splenetic A **splenetic** person is bad-tempered and irritable.

splice (**splicing, spliced**) If you **splice** two pieces of rope, film, or tape together, you join them neatly at the ends so they make one continuous piece.

spliff A **spliff** is a marijuana cigarette.

splint A **splint** is a long piece of wood or some other stiff material which is fastened to a broken arm or leg to keep it straight and still.

splinter (**splintering, splintered**) A **splinter** is a thin sharp piece of wood, metal, or glass which has broken off from a larger piece. If something **splinters,** it breaks into splinters. ■ If a group or organization **splinters,** some of its members break away to form groups of their own, because they no longer agree with the main group's views. The new groups are called **splinter groups.**

split (**splitting, split** *not 'splitted'*) If something **splits,** it divides into two or more parts. ■ If material like wood **splits,** a long crack appears in it. The crack is called a **split.** ■ A **split** is a serious disagreement. *She tried to cause a split between me and one of my best friends.* ■ When a couple **split up,** they end their relationship or marriage. ■ If you say something happens in a **split second,** you mean it happens very quickly. ■ If you **split the difference,** you agree on a figure half way between

two numbers which have already been mentioned. ■ **split infinitive:** see **infinitive.**

splodge A **splodge** is a large uneven mark or stain, especially one caused by a liquid.

splurge (**splurging, splurged**) If you **splurge** or have a **splurge,** you spend a lot of money. ■ A **splurge** of something is a lot of it happening in a short time. *There was a splurge of last-minute fighting.*

splutter (**spluttering, spluttered**) If someone **splutters,** they have difficulty speaking clearly, because they are angry, embarrassed, or surprised. ■ If something like an engine **splutters,** it makes a series of short spitting noises.

spoil (**spoiling, spoiled** *or* **spoilt**) If something **spoils** an occasion or spoils something like a view, it makes it less enjoyable, attractive, or interesting. ■ If food is **spoilt,** it is unfit to eat. ■ If you **spoil** someone, especially a child, you give them everything they want. ■ If you are **spoiling for** something like a fight, you are eager for it to happen. ■ **Spoils** are the things people get as a result of winning a battle or doing something else successfully. *At the end of next year, the horses will be sold and the spoils, if any, divided.* ■ **Spoil** is waste material such as clay and rock removed from somewhere such as a mine.

spoilsport If you say someone is a **spoilsport,** you mean they behave in a way which ruins other people's pleasure.

spoke See **speak.** ■ The **spokes** of a wheel are the bars which connect the outer ring to the centre.

spoken See **speak.** ■ **Spoken** means produced by speaking. *Computers which recognise spoken commands are on the way.* ■ See also **well-spoken.**

spokesman (**spokesmen**) A **spokesman** is a male spokesperson.

spokesperson (**spokespersons** *or* **spokespeople**) The **spokesperson** for a group or organization is the person who speaks as its representative, especially to the media.

spokeswoman (**spokeswomen**) A **spokeswoman** is a female spokesperson.

sponge (**sponging, sponged; sponger**) A **sponge** is a squashy absorbent substance with holes in it, used for cleaning or washing your body. Sponges can be natural or synthetic. If you **sponge** something, you wipe it with a wet sponge. ■ A **sponge** is very light cake or pudding made from flour, eggs, sugar, and sometimes fat. ■ If someone **sponges off** you or **sponges on** you, they get money and other things from you without giving anything in return. A person who behaves like this is called a **sponger.**

spongy If something is **spongy,** it is soft and squashy.

sponsor (**sponsoring, sponsored; sponsorship**) If an organization **sponsors** something like an event or someone's training, they pay some or all of its costs, usually in return for publicity. An organization which sponsors something is called its **sponsor.** You talk about an organization's **sponsorship** of something. **Sponsorship** is also financial support given by a sponsor. *This year's Tests are expected to have attracted over £3m in sponsorship.* ■ If you

sponsor someone who is doing something to raise money for charity, you agree to give them a certain amount of money if they succeed in doing it. People who sponsor someone like this are called the person's **sponsors.** ■ If you **sponsor** a proposal, you officially put it forward and support it. ■ When an organization like the United Nations **sponsors** talks or negotiations, they arrange for them to take place and organize them. ...a UN-sponsored meeting.

spontaneous (spontaneously; spontaneity) You say something someone does is **spontaneous** when it happens because they feel like doing it, rather than because they planned it in advance. Spontaneous behaviour is called **spontaneity.** ■ **Spontaneous** is used to describe something which happens because of processes within something, rather than being caused by things outside it. ...spontaneous bleeding.

spoof A spoof is something like an article or TV programme which seems to be about a serious matter but is actually a joke.

spook (spooking, spooked) A **spook** is (a) a ghost. (b) a spy. ■ If something **spooks** you, it frightens you or makes you very nervous.

spooky If something is **spooky,** it is strange and frightening.

spool A **spool** is a round object which thread, film, or tape is wound onto.

spoon (spooning, spooned) A **spoon** is an object like a very small shallow bowl with a long handle, used for eating, stirring, or serving food. ■ If you **spoon** something somewhere, you put it there a small amount at a time, using a spoon.

spoonful (plural: **spoonfuls** or **spoonsful**) A **spoonful** of a substance is the amount one spoon can hold.

spoor The **spoor** of an animal is the visible trail it leaves as it moves along.

sporadic (sporadically) If something is **sporadic,** it happens at irregular intervals. Soldiers fired sporadically into the air.

spore – **Spores** are cells produced by non-flowering plants such as ferns, mosses, and fungi. They can develop into new plants.

sporran A **sporran** is a large purse, usually made of leather or fur, traditionally worn by Scotsmen on a belt round their waists when they are wearing a kilt.

sport (sporting) **Sport** is games like football and cricket and other competitive activities involving physical effort and skill. Each game or activity is called a **sport. Sporting** means to do with sport. ...sporting facilities. ■ If you **sport** something noticeable or unusual, you wear it. Richard sported a pink rose in his lapel. ■ If you have a **sporting chance** of achieving something, you have a reasonable chance.

sports car A **sports car** is a low fast car, usually with room for only two people.

sportsmanship is the behaviour and attitudes of someone who takes part in sport in a good-humoured way and does not take unfair advantage of their opponents.

sportswear is clothing worn for sports.

sporty people like playing sports.

spot (spotting, spotted) **Spots** are small round coloured areas on a surface. If something is **spotted,** it has a pattern of spots on it. ...a spotted handkerchief. ■ **Spots** on a person's skin are small lumps or marks, usually caused by a disease or infection. ■ A **spot** of something is a small amount of it. Add a spot of lemon juice. ■ A place is sometimes called a **spot.** It's a lovely spot for a picnic. ■ A **spot check** is a random inspection made without warning on one of a group of things. ■ If you are **put on the spot,** someone puts you in a situation where you are forced to make a difficult decision. ■ If you **spot** someone or something, you notice them. ■ A **spot** on a radio or TV show is a part which is regularly reserved for a particular performer or type of entertainment. ■ If something is **spot on,** it is exactly right or accurate.

spotless (spotlessly) If something is **spotless** or **spotlessly clean,** it is perfectly clean. ■ If someone's reputation is **spotless,** they are not known to have done anything bad or dishonest.

spotlight (spotlit) A **spotlight** is a powerful light which can be directed so that it lights up a small area. If something is **spotlit,** it is lit up brightly by one or more spotlights. ■ If something **spotlights** a situation or problem, it directs attention towards it.

spotty people have spots or pimples on their skin, especially their faces.

spouse Someone's **spouse** is their husband or wife.

spout (spouting, spouted) If you talk about someone **spouting** something, you mean they are saying things they have learned or been told, without really thinking about what they are saying. ■ When liquid or a flame **spouts** out of something, it comes out fast in a long stream. ■ A **spout** is a specially shaped opening or tube for pouring liquids out of a container.

sprain (spraining, sprained) If you **sprain** your ankle, knee, or wrist, you accidentally injure it by tearing the ligaments. An injury like this is called a **sprain.**

sprang See spring.

sprawl If you talk about something like a housing development **sprawling,** you mean it covers a large area. ...sprawling estates. ■ When people talk about **urban sprawl,** they mean places where a city or town has expanded out into the countryside in a seemingly uncontrolled way. ■ If you **sprawl** somewhere, you sit or lie with your arms and legs spread out carelessly.

spray (sprayer) **Spray** is a lot of small drops of water being splashed or forced into the air. ■ If you **spray** something with a liquid, you cover it with small drops of it, using something like a hose or an aerosol. ■ A **spray** or **sprayer** is a device for spraying water or some other liquid. ■ A **spray can** is a can containing liquid under pressure which can be forced out in a fine spray. ■ A **spray** is a liquid which you spray on something. ...nasal sprays. ■ A **spray** of flowers is a number of them on a single stem. ■ If gunmen **spray** something with bullets, they shoot a lot of bullets all over it very rapidly.

spread (**spreading, spread** not 'spreaded') If you **spread** something somewhere, you arrange it over a surface so all of it can be seen or used easily. ■ If you **spread** your arms or legs, you stretch them as far apart as they will go. ■ If you **spread** a substance on a surface, you put a thin layer of it on the surface. ■ A **spread** is a soft food which you spread on bread. ■ If something **spreads,** it moves outwards, reaching a wider area or more and more people. *The flames spread rapidly. ...the spread of political correctness.* ■ If people or things are **spread** over an area, they are far away from each other. ■ If people **spread out,** they move away from each other. ■ If something is **spread** over a period of time, it takes place over that period. *The course was spread over 3 months.* ■ A **spread** of ideas, interests, or other things is a range of them.

spreadeagled If someone is **spreadeagled,** they are lying with their arms and legs spread out.

spreadsheet A **spreadsheet** is a computer printout with columns of figures included. The program for creating this kind of printout can also be called a **spreadsheet.**

spree When someone does a lot of something in a short time, you can say they have been on a **spree** of a certain kind. *...a shopping spree.*

sprig A **sprig** of a plant, especially a herb, is a small piece of stem with leaves on it.

sprightly If you describe someone or something as **sprightly,** you mean they are lively and active.

spring (**springing, sprang, have sprung**) **Spring** is the season between winter and summer. ■ A **spring** is a coiled piece of wire which returns to its original shape after it has been pressed or pulled. ■ A **spring** is a place where water comes up naturally through the ground. ■ When a person or animal **springs,** they jump upwards or forwards suddenly. ■ **Spring** is used to say something happens very suddenly. *The experts immediately sprang into action.* ■ If something **springs up,** it suddenly appears or comes into existence. *...the many new soccer magazines that have sprung up.* ■ If one thing **springs from** another, it is the result of it. ■ If a boat or container **springs** a leak, it starts leaking.

springboard A **springboard** is a flexible board that you jump on before performing a dive or a gymnastic movement. ■ If you use something as a **springboard,** you use it to help you advance further in your aims.

springbok The **springbok** is a small southern African antelope.

spring chicken If you say someone is no **spring chicken,** you are emphasizing that they are no longer young.

spring-clean When you **spring-clean** a house, you clean everything in it thoroughly.

spring onion – Spring onions are small onions with long green leaves. They are often eaten raw in salads.

spring roll A **spring roll** is a Chinese food consisting of a deep-fried roll of thin pastry filled with vegetables and sometimes meat.

springy If something is **springy,** it returns quickly to its original shape after you press it.

sprinkle (**sprinkling, sprinkled; sprinkler**) If you **sprinkle** a liquid or powder over something, you scatter it. ■ A **sprinkler** is a device for sprinkling water, especially on lawns. ■ A **sprinkling** of something is a small amount of it. *Most high Swiss resorts have had at least a sprinkling of snow.*

sprint (**sprinter**) A **sprint** is a short fast race. A person who runs in sprints is called a **sprinter.** ■ If you **sprint** somewhere, you run there as fast as you can.

sprite A **sprite** is a type of fairy. ■ In computer graphics, a **sprite** is an object which can be moved round the computer screen.

spritzer A **spritzer** is a drink consisting of white wine and soda water.

sprout (**sprouting, sprouted**) When plants **sprout,** they produce new shoots or leaves. ■ If you talk about things **sprouting** somewhere, you mean a lot of them are appearing there rapidly. *Hair has recently begun sprouting from his nose and ears.* ■ **Sprouts** or **Brussels sprouts** are vegetables which look like very small cabbages.

spruce (**sprucing, spruced**) The **spruce** (usual plural: **spruce**) is an evergreen tree with needle-like leaves and cones, grown especially for making paper. ■ If someone is **spruce,** they look very smart. If you **spruce** yourself **up,** you make yourself look smarter.

sprung See **spring.**

spry If you say an old person is **spry,** you mean they are lively and active.

spud A **spud** is a potato.

spun See **spin.**

spunk (**spunky**) **Spunk** is courage. You say someone is **spunky** when they show a lot of courage.

spur (**spurring, spurred**) If something **spurs** you to do something or **spurs** you **on,** it encourages you to do it. You can also say it acts as a **spur.** ■ If you do something **on the spur of the moment,** you do it suddenly, without thinking about it beforehand. ■ **Spurs** are sharp metal points attached to the heels of a rider's boots which are used to urge a horse on. ■ If you **win** or **earn** your **spurs,** you earn a certain status by doing something successfully.

spurious (**spuriously**) If something is **spurious,** it is not genuine. *...a spurious academic qualification.* ■ A **spurious** argument or statement is based on faulty reasoning.

spurn If you **spurn** someone or something, you reject them. *He spurned the advice of management consultants. ...a spurned lover.*

spurt A **spurt** of activity is a sudden brief period of it. ■ If something **spurts** or **puts on a spurt,** it begins to happen much faster. ■ When a liquid or flame **spurts,** it shoots out quickly in a thin stream. You can refer to the stream of liquid as a **spurt.**

sputter (**sputtering, sputtered**) If something **sputters,** it keeps going, but in a very uneven way, as though it might stop at any moment. *...a sputtering economic recovery.*

spy (**spies, spying, spied**) A **spy** is a person whose job is to find out secret information about another country or organization. This activity is called **spying.** You say the person **spies for** their own country or organization. ■ If you **spy on** someone, you watch them secretly. ■ If you **spy** someone or something, you notice them. *They spied heavy objects being heaved onto lorries.*

sq is short for 'square' in measurements of area. For example, 'sq ft' is short for 'square feet'.

squabble (squabbling, squabbled) When people **squabble** or have a **squabble**, they quarrel, usually about something unimportant.

squad A **squad** is a group chosen to do a particular activity. *...a squad of commandos. ...the serious fraud squad.*

squaddie Soldiers of the lowest ranks are sometimes called **squaddies.**

squadron A **squadron** is a section of one of the armed forces, especially the air force.

squadron leader A **squadron leader** is a middle-ranking officer in the RAF.

squalid (squalor) You say a place is **squalid** when it is dirty and in bad condition. You talk about the **squalor** in a place like this. *Many were living in squalor on the streets.* ■ You can say activities are **squalid** when they are immoral.

squall A **squall** is a brief spell of heavy rain or snow with a strong wind.

squalor See **squalid.**

squander (squandering, squandered) If you **squander** something, you waste it. *...squandered opportunities.*

square (squaring, squared) A **square** is a shape with four sides of the same length and four corners which are all right angles. If something is **square,** it is shaped like this. ■ In a town or city, a **square** is a flat open space, surrounded by buildings. ■ **Square** is used in front of units of length to change them into units of area. *...square inches.* ■ **Square** is used to say how long each side of a square is. *...a piece of land measuring 50ft square.* ■ If you **square** a number, you multiply it by itself. The **square** of a number is the number obtained by multiplying that number by itself. For example, the square of 4 is 16. In maths, this is expressed as $4^2 = 16$. ■ If you **square** one thing with another, you find a way in which the two things can operate together or both be acceptable. *His tax pledges cannot be squared with his party's plans to boost public spending.* ■ If you **square** something with another person, you get their agreement on it. ■ If you **square up to** a problem, you get ready to deal with it. ■ If you say a person is **square,** you mean they are boring and unfashionable.

squarely If you face something **squarely,** you deal with it directly, and do not try to avoid it. *The management committee have faced the situation squarely.*

square root A **square root** of a number is another number which when multiplied by itself produces the first number. For example, the square roots of 16 are 4 and -4. In maths, this is expressed as $\sqrt{16} = 4$ or -4.

squash (squashes, squashing, squashed) If something is **squashed,** it is pressed or crushed forcefully, so that it becomes flat, loses its shape, or is damaged. ■ If someone **squashes** something which is causing them trouble, they put a stop to it, often using force. *The President and his security men will probably be successful in squashing the current wave of dissent.* ■ **Squash** is a game in which two players hit a small rubber ball against the walls of a court, using rackets. ■ A **squash** is a any vegetable belonging to the marrow family. ■ **Squash** is a drink made from fruit, sugar, and water.

squashy If something is **squashy,** it is soft and can be squashed easily.

squat (squatting, squatted; squatter) When people **squat** in a disused building or on unoccupied land, they live there illegally without paying rent. The people who live there are called **squatters.** When a building is used like this, it is called a **squat.** ■ If you **squat,** you crouch close to the ground, balancing on your feet with your legs bent. ■ A **squat** person or thing is unusually short and fat.

squawk When a bird **squawks** or lets out a **squawk,** it makes a loud harsh noise.

squeak (squeaking, squeaked) If someone or something **squeaks** or gives a **squeak,** they make a short high-pitched sound. ■ If someone succeeds in doing something by a narrow margin, you can say they **squeak** through. *Mr Isomura ought to squeak home, but it will be a close-run race.*

squeaky If something is **squeaky,** it makes squeaking noises.

squeaky-clean If you say someone like a politician is **squeaky-clean,** you mean they are very honest and moral.

squeal (squealing, squealed) If someone or something **squeals** or lets out a **squeal,** they make a long high-pitched sound.

squeamish (squeamishness) If someone is **squeamish** about something, they are reluctant to do it, watch it, or have it done to them. *Some people are squeamish about having needles inserted into their veins.*

squeeze (squeezing, squeezed) If you **squeeze** something or give it a **squeeze,** you press it firmly from two sides. ■ If you **squeeze** somewhere, you just manage to get through or into a small space. If getting into something is a **squeeze,** it is just possible to fit into it. ■ If you **squeeze** something out of someone, you get it by force or persuasion. *The bigger clubs would like to use this power to squeeze more money out of television.* ■ If a government **squeezes** the economy, it cuts back on public spending and makes it difficult to borrow money, because it is trying to fight inflation. *The CBI also says the squeeze is slowing down inflation.* ■ If you **squeeze** something into a small amount of time, you manage to fit it in. ■ If someone is **squeezed out** of something, they are prevented from being involved in it. *Private producers are being squeezed out of the credit markets.*

squelch (squelches, squelching, squelched) If something **squelches,** it makes a wet sucking sound.

squib A **squib** is a small firework which makes a loud bang. ■ If you say an event was a **damp squib,** you mean it did not live up to expectations.

squid (usual plural: squid) The **squid** is an edible sea creature with a soft body and ten tentacles.

squidgy If something is **squidgy,** it is very soft and squashy.

squiggle A **squiggle** is a line which twists and curves irregularly.

squint If you **squint** at something, you look at it with your eyes partly closed, to try to see it better. ■ A **squint** is a medical condition in which a person's eyes look in different directions.

squire The **squire** of an English village was the man who owned most of the land in and around it.

squirm If you **squirm,** you wriggle, because you are nervous or uncomfortable.

squirrel (squirrelling, squirrelled) (*Am:* **squirreling, squirreled)** Squirrels are small furry animals with long bushy tails. Most species live in trees. ■ If you **squirrel** things away, you collect them together and keep them in a safe place.

squirt If you **squirt** a liquid somewhere, it comes out of a narrow opening in a thin fast stream. The amount which comes out is called a **squirt.**

St is short for 'Street'. ■ See also **saint.**

stab (stabbing, stabbed) If someone **stabs** another person, they push a knife into their body. A **stabbing** is an incident in which someone is stabbed. ■ If you say someone has **stabbed you in the back,** you mean they have done something harmful to you when you thought you could trust them. ■ If you **stab** something, you poke it sharply with your finger or with a pointed object you are holding. ■ If you make a **stab** at something, you try to do it. *Several tennis stars have had a stab at acting.* ■ A **stab** of something such as pain or fear is a sudden feeling of it. *He felt a stab of jealousy.*

stabilise See **stabilize.**

stabiliser See **stabilizer.**

stability See **stable.**

stabilize (*or* **stabilise) (stabilizing, stabilized; stabilization)** If something **stabilizes,** it becomes stable.

stabilizer (*or* **stabiliser)** A **stabilizer** is a device which helps a plane, ship, or racing car remain stable.

stable (stabler, stablest; stability) If something is **stable,** it is not likely to change or come to an end suddenly. *...a stable marriage.* You can describe someone who is seriously ill as **stable** when their condition has stopped getting worse. ■ If an object is **stable,** it is not likely to move or fall over. ■ A **stable** or **stables** is (a) a building where horses are kept. (b) an organization which breeds and trains racehorses. ■ When horses are **stabled,** they are put into a stable. *The animals had been fed and stabled.*

stablemate If racehorses are **stablemates,** they come from the same stables. ■ If two organizations, especially newspapers, are **stablemates,** they are owned by the same person or company.

staccato (*pron:* stak-**ah**-toe) If a piece of music is played or sung **staccato,** the individual notes are played or sung very briefly with gaps in between them. ■ A **staccato** noise consists of a series of short sharp separate sounds. *...a staccato laugh.*

stack A **stack** of things is a neat pile of them. If you **stack** things, you arrange them in neat piles. ■ If a

place or surface is **stacked** with objects, it is filled with piles of them. ■ A **stack** of something is a very large amount of it. *They have stacks of cash.* ■ If you say **the odds** or **the cards** are **stacked against** someone, you mean they are unlikely to succeed in what they are doing because the conditions are not favourable.

stadium (*plural:* **stadiums** *or* **stadia)** A **stadium** is a large sports ground with tiers of seats all round it.

staff (staffing) The **staff** of an organization are the people who work for it. You can say an organization is **staffed** by particular people. *...a National Criminal Intelligence Service, staffed by Scotland Yard officers.* ■ The **staffing** in a place is the number of people employed to work there. *Staffing and investment are being cut.* ■ A **staff** is a strong stick or pole.

staffer A **staffer** is a member of staff of an organization, especially in a government organization or in journalism.

staffing See **staff.**

staff nurse A **staff nurse** is a hospital nurse whose rank is immediately below that of a sister or charge nurse.

staff room At a school or college, the **staff room** is a room where teachers can go to work or relax when they are not teaching.

stag A **stag** is an adult male deer. ■ All-male parties and social evenings are sometimes called **stag nights** or **stag parties.** A man often has a stag night just before he gets married.

stage (staging, staged) A **stage** is one part of a process or activity, or a particular point during it. *The legal action was the last stage of the campaign... At one stage, not only his wife but two of his four children were in the business.* ■ In a theatre, the **stage** is the raised platform where the actors or entertainers perform. The **stage** is also used to talk about acting in the theatre and the production of plays there. *Roy is leaving after six years on the popular ITV soap to return to the stage.* ■ If someone **stages** a play or event, they organize it and present or take part in it. ■ If you **set the stage** for something, you make preparations for it to happen. ■ You can refer to a particular area of activity as a particular **stage.** *The Party occupied the centre of the political stage.*

stage-coach (*or* **stagecoach)** A **stage-coach** was a large horse-drawn carriage which carried passengers and mail.

stage door The **stage door** of a theatre is the entrance used by the performers and theatre employees.

stage fright is the feeling of fear or nervousness some people have just before they appear in front of an audience.

stage hand In a theatre, the **stage hands** are the people whose job is to move the scenery and equipment on the stage.

stage-manage If an event is **stage-managed,** it is carefully organized and controlled, rather than happening spontaneously.

stage manager In a theatre, the **stage manager** is the person responsible to the director for the scenery and the lights, and for making sure nothing goes wrong during a performance.

stagger (**staggering, staggered; staggeringly**) If someone **staggers,** they walk very unsteadily, for example because they are ill or drunk. ■ If something **staggers** you, you are very surprised or shocked by it. You say something like this is **staggering.** ...*staggeringly expensive hotels.* ■ When things like people's hours of work are **staggered,** they are arranged so they do not all happen at the same time.

staging post A **staging post** is a place where people or things stop on their way somewhere.

stagnant If something like a business or economy is **stagnant,** there is very little activity or growth in it. ■ **Stagnant** water is not flowing, and therefore is often dirty and smelly.

stagnate (**stagnating, stagnated; stagnation**) If something **stagnates,** it does not change or develop. ...*Serbia's continuing economic stagnation.*

staid people are serious, dull, and rather old-fashioned.

stain (**staining, stained**) If a substance **stains** something, it leaves marks called **stains** which are difficult to remove.

stained glass is pieces of coloured glass fixed together by lead strips to make decorative windows or other objects.

stainless steel is a type of metal made from steel and chromium which does not rust.

stair – **Stairs** are a set of steps, usually inside a building.

staircase A **staircase** is a set of stairs inside a building.

stairway A **stairway** is a set of stairs inside or outside a building.

stairwell A **stairwell** is part of a building which contains a staircase.

stake (**staking, staked**) If something important is **at stake,** you are in danger of losing it as a result of something which is happening. *The credibility of both organisations is at stake.* ■ If you **stake** something you value on achieving a result, you risk losing it if you do not achieve that result. *Sotheby's staked its reputation on the Sevso sale.* ■ The **stakes** involved in a risky action are the things which can be gained or lost. ■ If you have a stake in something such as a business, you own part of it and so its success is important to you. ■ If you **stake a claim** to something, you claim a right to it. ■ When police officers **stake out** a building, they watch it secretly for evidence of criminal activity. ■ A **stake** is a wooden post with a pointed end.

stakeholder The **stakeholders** in an enterprise are all the people who have an interest in its success, for example shareholders, creditors, and employees.

stalactite A **stalactite** is a piece of rock like a large icicle hanging from the roof of a cave. It is formed over many years by the constant dripping of water containing lime.

stalagmite A **stalagmite** is a candle-shaped piece of rock which sticks up from the floor of a cave. It is

formed over many years by water containing lime dripping onto the same spot.

stale If something like food is **stale,** it is old or no longer fresh. ■ If you say something like an attitude or idea is **stale,** you mean it is old and dull.

stalemate If a situation reaches **stalemate,** it reaches a position where neither side can win and where no further progress seems possible. ■ In chess, **stalemate** is a position in which a player cannot make any move which is permitted by the rules, so the game ends in a draw.

stalk The **stalk** of a leaf, flower, or fruit is the thin part which joins it to the plant or tree. ■ If you **stalk** a person or animal, you follow them quietly and secretly, so you can kill, capture, or observe them. ■ If someone **stalks** somewhere, they walk in a stiff way, because they are proud or angry. *She stalked into the editor's office and threatened to resign.*

stalking horse ∧ **stalking horse** is something which is used to disguise someone's real intentions. In a political leadership contest, a stalking horse is someone who stands against a leader although they are not expected to win, to see how strong the opposition is.

stall If a process **stalls,** it stops but may start again later. ...*the peace process stalled.* ■ If you **stall,** you try to avoid doing something until later. ■ If a vehicle **stalls,** its engine stops suddenly. ■ The **stalls** in a theatre or concert hall are the seats on the ground floor directly in front of the stage. ■ A **stall** is a large table where people set out goods for sale or give information. ■ If someone **sets out their stall,** they do something publicly which shows their intentions.

stallholder A **stallholder** is a person who sells goods on a market stall.

stallion A **stallion** is an adult male horse.

stalwart (*pron:* **stawl**-wart) You say someone is a **stalwart** when they are loyal and reliable. ...*the stalwart fidelity of the islanders.*

stamen The **stamens** of a flower are the small delicate stalks which grow inside the blossom and produce pollen.

stamina is the physical or mental energy needed to do an activity for a long time.

stammer (**stammering, stammered**) If someone **stammers,** they speak with difficulty, hesitating and repeating words or sounds. You say someone like this has a **stammer.**

stamp A **stamp** or **postage stamp** is a small piece of gummed paper which you stick on an envelope or parcel to show you have paid the correct fee before posting it. ■ A **stamp** is a small block with words or a design on it. You press it onto an inky pad and then onto a document or object, to make the words or design appear there; what appears is also called a **stamp.** You say you have **stamped** the document or object. ■ If someone **puts their stamp** on something, they affect it in a way which makes it obvious they were involved in it. ■ If you **stamp** your foot, you bring it down hard. ■ If someone **stamps on** an activity they think is undesirable, they stop it happening or spreading. *The Treasury yesterday stamped on speculation about an* early cut in bank base lending rates. ■ If someone **stamps** something **out,** they put an end to it. *...on the spot fines to stamp the problem out.*

stamp duty is a tax which has to be paid on certain legal documents, especially when buying property.

stampede (**stampeding, stampeded**) When a group of people or animals **stampede,** they run together in a wild uncontrolled way. This is called a **stampede.** *Many pilgrims are reported to have died in a stampede in a crowded tunnel.* ■ If someone **stampedes** you into doing something, they rush you into it without giving you time to think about it properly.

stamping ground Someone's **stamping ground** is a place where they spent a lot of time in the past or did something they were famous for. *He is returning to his old stamping ground as the new deputy governor of the Bank of England.*

stance Your **stance** on a particular matter is your attitude to it. *Is Moscow hardening its stance on arms control issues?* ■ Your **stance** is the way you are standing. *The detective shifted her stance from one foot to another.*

stanchion A **stanchion** is a pole or bar which stands upright and is used as a support.

stand (**standing, stood**) When you **stand** or **stand up,** you move so your body is upright and your legs are straight. ■ If you **stand** something somewhere, you put it there in an upright position. *He stood the bottle on the bench.* ■ If something like a building **stands** somewhere, it is situated there. ■ You use **stand** when describing the state or condition of something. *The house stood empty for five years.* ■ If you **stand up** to someone or something, you defend yourself against their attacks or demands. ■ If you will not **stand for** something, you will not allow it to happen or continue. ■ If you take a **stand** on an issue, you state your position and stick to it. ■ If you **stand up** for a person or thing that is being criticized or threatened, you defend them. ■ If you **stand by** someone who is in trouble, you continue to give them support. ■ If someone or something can **stand** a situation or a test or **stand up** to rough treatment, they are good enough or strong enough to cope with it. *New trees are far less able to stand up to the ravages of cyclones.* ■ If evidence **stands up,** it proves to be true or satisfactory. ■ If you **stand in** for someone, you take their place while they are ill or away. Someone who does this is called a **stand-in.** ■ If you **stand** in an election, you are a candidate in it. ■ If someone **stands down** from an important position, they resign. ■ If something **stands out,** it can be easily noticed or is clearly better or more important than other similar things. *A restaurant of this calibre would stand out anywhere.* ■ If a group of letters **stand for** a name, they are a shortened version of it. *WPP stands for Wire and Plastic Products.* ■ If you are **standing by,** you are prepared and ready to provide help or take action. See also **standby.** ■ If you **stand by** and let something bad happen, you do nothing to stop it. ■ If you **stand by** an earlier decision or agreement, you do not change it. ■ If you cannot **stand** someone or something, you dislike them intensely. ■ If you

stand to lose something, you are in a position where you might lose it. ■ If something like a decision or offer still **stands,** it is still effective or valid. ■ When someone **stands trial,** they are tried in a court of law. ■ If someone does not turn up for a date, you can say they **stand** the other person **up.** ■ A **stand** is a small stall or shop at an exhibition or in the street. ■ A **stand** is a large structure constructed so that spectators can get a good view of an event. ■ The **stand** is the place in a court of law where the witness sits or stands when he or she is giving evidence. ■ See also **standing.**

standard A **standard** is a level of quality or achievement. *...the standard of service on Britain's railways.* A **standard** is also something which is used to judge the quality of something else. *Other firms are setting common standards to make it easier to do business together.* ■ **Standards** are moral principles which govern people's behaviour. *...protests by some clergy against what they describe as falling moral standards.* ■ See also **double standards.** ■ Your **standard of living** is the level of comfort and wealth you have. ■ The **standard** version of a product is the normal one. ■ A **standard** work on a subject is one which is widely known and often recommended.

standard-bearer The **standard-bearer** of a group is a person who acts as their leader or public representative.

standardize (*or* **standardise**) (**standardizing, standardized; standardization**) When things are **standardized,** they are made the same, or made to have the same features. *The committee wants to see a standardization of speed limits throughout the Community.*

standard lamp A **standard lamp** is a tall lamp which stands on the floor in a living room.

standby (*or* **stand-by**) If someone or something is **on standby,** they are ready to be used when needed. *Its crew were rescued by a standby vessel.* ■ Something which you keep ready for use can be called a **standby.** *Pasta and rice are two cheap, filling student standbys.* ■ **Standby** tickets are cheap tickets which sometimes become available just before something like a play starts.

stand-in See **stand.**

standing Someone's **standing** is their status, reputation, or popularity. *Mr Bush's standing in the opinion polls has deteriorated.* ■ **Standing** is used to describe things which exist all the time, rather than being formed or made when necessary. *...a standing commission on human rights.* ■ If you say something is of a certain number of years' **standing,** you mean it has existed for that number of years. *...a party boss of 18 years' standing.* See also **long-standing.**

standing order A **standing order** is an instruction to your bank to pay someone a fixed amount at regular intervals. ■ A **standing order** is a rule or order which is permanently in force.

standing stone A **standing stone** is a very large upright stone thought to have been erected in ancient times.

stand-off In a **stand-off,** two opposing groups each refuse to make a move until the other one does something.

stand-offish You say someone is being **stand-offish** when they behave in a formal and unfriendly way.

standpipe A **standpipe** is a vertical water pipe in a public place for use in emergencies.

standpoint If you look at something from a particular **standpoint**, you look at it from that point of view. *The argument was always questionable from an economist's standpoint.*

standstill If movement or an activity comes to a **standstill**, it stops completely. *The march brought lunchtime traffic to a standstill.*

stand-up comedy is a form of entertainment in which a comedian stands up alone in front of an audience and tells jokes. Someone who does this is called a **stand-up** comedian.

stank See **stink.**

stanza A **stanza** is a verse of a poem.

staple (**stapling, stapled; stapler**) A **staple** food or **staple** is a food which forms a basic part of someone's everyday diet. ■ **Staples** are small pieces of bent wire used to hold sheets of paper together. They are pushed through the paper using a special device called a **stapler.** If you **staple** something, you fix it in place using staples.

star (**starring, starred; stardom**) Famous actors, musicians, and sportspeople are often called **stars.** Being a star is called **stardom.** *...the pressures of stardom.* ■ If an actor or actress **stars** in a film or play, or a film or play **stars** that person, he or she has one of the main parts in it. ■ A **star** is (a) a large ball of burning gas in space that appears as a small point of light in the sky at night. (b) a shape with four, five, or more points sticking out of it in a regular pattern. ■ **Stars** are star-shaped marks printed against the name of something such as a hotel or a restaurant to indicate its quality. *...a three-star hotel.*

starboard The **starboard** side of a ship is the right side when you are facing the front.

starch (**starches; starched**) **Starch** is a carbohydrate in foods like bread, potatoes, and rice. ■ **Starch** is a substance used for stiffening cloth. **Starched** clothes have been treated with starch.

starchy foods contain a lot of starch.

stardom See **star.**

stare (**staring, stared**) If you **stare** at something, you look at it for a long time. A **stare** is a long fixed look. ■ If you say that someone is **staring** something unpleasant **in the face,** you mean that thing seems likely to happen to them. *The defeat leaves West Ham staring relegation in the face.* ■ If you say the answer to a problem is **staring** someone **in the face,** you mean it is so obvious they should have noticed it.

starfish (*plural:* **starfish**) are flat star-shaped sea creatures with five arms.

stark (**starkly**) A **stark** statement is unpleasantly clear and simple. *He gave a stark warning about the dangers of complacency.* ■ A **stark** choice is one between two unpleasant alternatives. If two things are in **stark** contrast, they are very different from each other in a way that is very obvious. *The college's conclusions contrast starkly with assertions last*

week by Eric Caines. ■ If someone is **stark** naked, they are completely naked. ■ **Stark** is used to describe things which have a very bare and plain appearance. *...stark white walls and blue woodwork.*

starlet A **starlet** is a young actress who is expected to become a film star in the future.

starling – **Starlings** are common European birds with greenish-black feathers.

starry A **starry** night is a very clear one, when you can see many stars. ■ A **starry** film or show has many famous people in it. You can also say it has a **starry** cast.

starry-eyed If someone is **starry-eyed,** they are so optimistic or idealistic they do not see things as they really are.

Stars and Stripes The **Stars and Stripes** is the American national flag.

star-studded shows or films have a lot of famous people in them.

start If you **start** doing something, you begin to do it. If something **starts,** it begins. ■ The **start** of something is the point or time at which it begins. ■ If you **start** a car or **start** it **up,** you get its engine running. ■ If something **starts** at a certain price, that is the cheapest price at which it is available. *Prices start at £550 per person.* ■ If you **start** or if something gives you a **start,** your body jerks because you are surprised or frightened. ■ **in fits and starts:** see **fit.**

starter A **starter** is a small amount of food served as the first course of a meal. ■ The **starter** in a car is the device which starts the engine. ■ The **starters** in a race are the people or animals who begin it, as distinct from the ones that finish. ■ The **starter** of a race is the person who starts it, usually by firing a gun or waving a flag. ■ You say **for starters** to indicate that there are other things of a particular kind, apart from the ones you are mentioning. *These prizes are just for starters.*

startle (**startling, startled; startlingly**) If something **startles** you, it surprises you and slightly frightens or worries you. You say something like this is **startling.**

starve (**starving, starved; starvation**) If people or animals are **starving,** they are suffering from lack of food and are likely to die. **Starvation** is death or extreme suffering caused by lack of food. ■ If people are **starved** into doing something, they are deprived of food to make them do it. ■ If you say you are **starving,** you mean you are very hungry. ■ If people or organizations are **starved** of something they need, they are suffering because they are being deprived of it. *Schools are being starved of funds.*

stash (**stashes, stashing, stashed**) If you **stash** something valuable somewhere, you store it there to keep it safe. You call something hidden like this a **stash.**

stasis is a state in which something remains the same, and does not change or develop. *...tension between order and chaos, between growth and stasis.*

state (**stating, stated**) Countries are sometimes called **states.** *All member states supported the idea except Britain.* ■ Some countries are divided into areas called **states,** each with a degree of self-government. ■ The government is sometimes called **the state**. *Every child has the right to a place in a state school.* ■ A **state** occasion is a formal one involving the head of a country. *...a state banquet.* ■ If the dead body of an important person **lies in state,** it is publicly displayed for a few days before it is buried. ■ If you **state** something, you say or write it in a definite and formal way. *The King has publicly stated that he is ready to serve his country in any capacity.* ■ Someone's or something's **state** is the condition they are in. *The property market in Tokyo was in a worse state than London's.* ■ If you are in **a state,** you are upset and nervous.

state- is added to words to describe something owned or controlled by the government. *...state-owned industries.*

State Department The **State Department** is the US government department which deals with foreign affairs.

statehood When a territory achieves **statehood,** it becomes an independent state.

stateless If someone is **stateless,** they are not a citizen of any country.

stately things are dignified and impressive.

stately home A **stately home** is a large old house belonging to an aristocratic family, especially one open to the public.

statement A **statement** is an official or formal announcement which has been specially prepared for a particular occasion or situation. *...a government statement.* ■ Anything you say in a definite way can be called a **statement.** ■ If you make a **statement** to the police, you officially give your version of events after a crime or accident. ■ Something a person does can be called a **statement** when it clearly shows their feelings about something. *...a heavy gold bracelet, which Charles presented to Amanda as a statement of intent.* ■ A bank or building society **statement** is a printed document showing all the money put into and taken out of an account.

state of affairs A situation which you have just described can be called a **state of affairs.** *How did this extraordinary state of affairs come about?*

state of mind (states of mind) Your **state of mind** is your mood at a particular time, especially as this shows in the way you behave.

state-of-the-art is used to describe things which make use of the most up-to-date methods, materials, or ideas. *...state-of-the-art manufacturing techniques.*

stateroom (or **state room**) The **staterooms** in a palace or other building are large splendid rooms used on formal occasions. ■ Luxurious cabins in liners and other ships are sometimes called **staterooms.**

Stateside means in, from, or to the United States. *...a Stateside holiday.*

statesman (statesmen; statesmanlike, statesmanship) A **statesman** is an experienced and respected senior politician. When politicians behave in a way which inspires respect, you can call their behaviour **statesmanlike,** or talk about their **statesmanship.** See also **elder statesman.**

statewide (or **state-wide**) In the US, if something is **statewide,** it covers the whole of a state. *...a statewide campaign.*

static If something remains **static,** it does not move or change. *The earnings of the middle classes had remained static.* ■ **Static** or **static electricity** is electricity created by friction, which builds up in things like metal objects. ■ **Static** on the radio or TV is atmospheric interference which causes loud crackling noises or makes the picture break up.

station (stationing, stationed) A **station** is a place on a railway line where trains stop to pick up and set down passengers. ■ A bus or coach **station** is a place where a large number of buses or coaches start their journey. ■ If you talk about a TV or radio **station,** you mean a TV or radio company and the programmes it broadcasts. ■ If soldiers or officials are **stationed** somewhere, they are sent there to do a job or to work for a period of time.

stationary If something is **stationary,** it is not moving.

stationer A **stationer** is a person or firm that sells paper, envelopes, and writing equipment. A shop where these things are sold is called a **stationer** or **stationer's.**

stationery is paper, envelopes, and writing equipment.

station master A **station master** is the person in charge of a railway station.

station wagon In the US, Australia, and New Zealand, an estate car is usually called a **station wagon.**

statistic (statistical, statistically) **Statistics** are facts which are expressed in numbers and which are obtained by gathering and analysing information. The branch of mathematics concerned with this type of analysis is also called **statistics.** ■ **Statistical** means relating to the use of statistics. *...statistical information.*

statistician A **statistician** is a person who studies statistics or who works using statistics.

statuary The **statuary** in a place is the statues and other sculptures there.

statue A **statue** is a large stone or metal sculpture of a person or animal.

statuesque (*pron:* stat-yoo-**esk**) A **statuesque** woman is big and tall and has good posture.

statuette A **statuette** is a very small statue.

stature Someone's **stature** is their reputation and importance. *Who can deny his stature as the world's greatest cellist?* ■ Someone's **stature** is their height and general size. *It's more than his physical stature that makes him remarkable.*

status Your **status** is your position or importance in society. *They called for a review of the status of women.* ■ A **status symbol** is something people like to own because it gives the impression they are important or rich. ■ The **status** of something is its position or importance compared to other similar things. *...the quality and status of technology.* ■ **Status** of a particular kind is an official classification giving people certain rights or advantages. *...diplomatic status.*

status quo When a place or organization has been run in the same way for a long time, you can refer to the established way of doing things as the **status quo.** *They fear that it will upset the status quo.* If someone restores the **status quo,** they return things to the way they were before something changed them.

statute A **statute** is a law passed by Parliament and formally written down. If a law is on the **statute book,** it is currently in force. ■ The **statutes** of an organization are its formal written rules.

statutory is used to describe things which are required by law. *...his statutory duty.*

staunch (**staunchly; staunches, staunching, staunched**) If you are a **staunch** supporter or opponent of someone or something, you support or oppose them firmly. ■ If you **staunch** the flow of something, you stop it or slow it down. *Increases in customs duties staunched the flow of imported cars.*

stave (**staving, staved**) If you **stave off** something unpleasant, you delay it or stop it happening. *...staving off defeat.* ■ **Staves** are strips of wood, like the strips wooden barrels are made of. ■ In music, a **stave** is the five parallel lines the notes are written on.

stay If you **stay** in a place or position or you **stay put,** you do not move. ■ If you **stay** somewhere, you spend time there as a visitor. *...an overnight stay in Helsinki.* If you **stay on,** you remain there longer than you intended. ■ If someone or something **stays** in a certain state or condition, they continue to be in it. *The office stayed open until midnight.* ■ If you have **staying power,** you have the ability to keep doing a task until it is finished. ■ If you are granted a **stay of execution,** you are allowed to delay obeying a ruling which a court has passed on you.

STD See **sexually transmitted disease.**

stead If you say something will **stand you in good stead,** you mean it will be useful to you in the future. ■ If you do something in someone else's **stead,** you do it instead of them.

steadfast (**steadfastly, steadfastness**) If someone is **steadfast,** they hold on firmly to their beliefs or principles and refuse to alter them.

steady (**steadier, steadiest; steadies, steadying, steadied; steadily, steadiness**) **Steady** is used to describe things which happen at the same pace, without any interruptions or sudden changes. *The rain came down steadily.* ■ If someone has a **steady** job, they have a regular job which is likely to last for a long time. ■ If you keep an object **steady** or **steady** it, you stop it moving about. ■ If you **steady** yourself, you control and calm yourself. ■ **Steady** is used to describe things which are calm and controlled. *...a slow, steady voice.* ■ A **steady** person is sensible and reliable.

steak A **steak** is a thick slice of meat or fish which is usually grilled or fried. When people talk about **steak** or a **steak,** they usually mean a beef steak. Various other cuts of beef are also called **steak,** for example braising steak and stewing steak.

steal (**stealing, stole, have stolen**) If someone **steals** something which does not belong to them, they take it without intending to return it. ■ If you **steal** somewhere, you move there quietly and se-

cretly. ■ If you **steal** something like the attention of an audience, you draw it towards yourself and away from someone else. *Another old-timer stole the limelight at Wimbledon yesterday.* ■ **steal a march:** see **march. steal someone's thunder:** see **thunder.**

stealth (**stealthy, stealthily**) If something is done by **stealth,** it is done quietly and secretly, in the hope that nobody will notice. ■ **Stealthy** actions or movements are quiet and not intended to be heard or noticed. *He was moving stealthily, doing his best not to disturb the household.* ■ **Stealth bombers** are types of military aircraft which use advanced technology to avoid enemy radar and infra-red detecting devices.

steam (**steaming, steamed**) **Steam** is the hot mist formed when water boils or when hot moist air meets cooler air. When a window is covered in steam, you say it is **steamed up.** ■ If something **steams,** it gives off steam. ■ If you **steam** food, you cook it in steam. ■ **Steam** vehicles and machines are powered by steam. When a ship **steams** somewhere, it moves along by steam or some other form of power. ■ **Steam** is used in phrases to talk about the amount of energy or enthusiasm someone or something has. *I decided to paint the bathroom ceiling but ran out of steam halfway through... Just as the presidential campaign was picking up steam, riots exploded in Los Angeles.* ■ If something **takes the steam out of** a situation, it calms it down. *The withdrawal of threatened trade sanctions took the steam out of the negotiations.*

steamboat – **Steamboats** were steam-powered boats which travelled mainly on rivers and lakes.

steam engine A **steam engine** is any engine which uses steam to operate machinery.

steamer A **steamer** is a ship powered by steam. ■ A **steamer** is a container with small holes in the bottom in which you steam food.

steam iron A **steam iron** is an electric iron that produces steam to make ironing out creases easier.

steamroller (**steamrollered**) A **steamroller** is a vehicle with heavy rollers at the front and back used for flattening the surface of new roads. ■ If you are **steamrollered** into doing something, you are made to do it against your will.

steamship In the past, **steamships** were large ocean-going ships powered by steam.

steamy A **steamy** place is hot and humid. ■ **Steamy** is used to describe erotic films or novels. *...steamy sex scenes.*

steed The horse someone is riding can be called their **steed.**

steel (**steeling, steeled; steely**) **Steel** is a strong metal made from iron and small quantities of other elements such as nickel. ■ **Steel** and **steely** are used to describe firm determined behaviour. *...nerves of steel. ...his steely determination.* ■ If you **steel** yourself, you prepare to do something difficult or unpleasant. ■ **Steely** is used to describe things which are a cold greyish colour. *...the steely grey North Sea.*

steel band A **steel band** is a group of musicians who play special drums traditionally made from metal oil barrels. Steel bands originated in the West Indies.

steel wool is a mass of fine steel threads, used for scouring things.

steelwork is the parts of a structure which are made from steel.

steelworks (steelworker) A **steelworks** is a factory where steel is made. A person who works in a steelworks is called a **steelworker.**

steep (steeper, steepest; steeply, steepness; steeping, steeped) A **steep** slope rises sharply. ■ **Steep** is used to describe a sudden large change in the amount or rate of something. *...a steep rise in interest rates.* ■ If you **steep** something in a liquid, you leave it to soak in it. ■ If people are **steeped** in something such as tradition, they are strongly influenced by it.

steeple A **steeple** is a tall pointed structure on top of a church tower.

steeplechase (steeplechaser) A **steeplechase** is a long horse race in which the horses have to jump over obstacles like fences and ditches. Horses specially trained to run in these races are called **steeplechasers.** ■ A **steeplechase** is a long race on an athletics track in which the competitors jump over hurdles and a water jump. Athletes who take part in steeplechases are called **steeplechasers.**

steeplejack A **steeplejack** is someone whose job is to maintain or repair steeples or factory chimneys.

steer (steering, steered) When you **steer** a vehicle, you control it so it goes in the direction you want. The **steering** in a vehicle is the mechanical parts which make it possible to steer. ■ If you **steer** someone towards a certain type of behaviour, you guide or persuade them in that direction. *These methods were much more likely to steer offenders away from crime.* ■ If you **steer** a certain course, you take a particular line of action. *He has proved himself very adept at steering a middle course between opposing views before.* ■ If you **steer clear** of someone or something, you manage to avoid them. ■ A **steering committee** or **group** is a group of people who manage the early stages of a project, setting out guidelines and overseeing progress. ■ A **steer** is a castrated bull.

steering wheel A vehicle's **steering wheel** is the wheel the driver uses to steer it.

stellar means to do with the stars. *...stellar explosions.*

stem (stemming, stemmed) If you **stem** something undesirable which is continuing, spreading, or increasing, you put a stop to it. *The international relief effort may have stemmed the worst of the starvation.* ■ If something like a condition or problem **stems** from a certain thing, that is what originally caused it. *The president's anger may stem from personal feelings.* ■ The **stem** of a plant is the thin central part which the leaves and flowers grow out of. ■ The **stem** of a glass is the thin part connecting the bowl to the base. ■ The **stem** of a pipe is the long hollow part which smoke is sucked through.

stench (stenches) A **stench** is a strong unpleasant smell.

stencil (stencilled) (*Am*: **stenciled**) A **stencil** is a piece of card, metal, or plastic with a design, letters, or other symbols cut out of it. You rest the stencil on a surface and use paint, pencil, or ink to reproduce the cut-out areas. **Stencilled** designs have been reproduced in this way.

stenography (stenographer) Stenography is writing in shorthand by hand or machine, especially taking verbatim notes of proceedings in court or at a meeting. A person who does this is called a **stenographer. Stenographer** is also the usual American word for a shorthand-typist.

stentorian A **stentorian** voice is extremely loud and strong.

step (stepping, stepped) A **step** is a movement which involves lifting the foot and putting it down again in a different place. ■ If you **step** somewhere, you walk in that direction. If you **step** on something, you tread on it. ■ A **step** is a raised flat surface, often one of a series, which you use to walk up or down to a different level. ■ A **step** is one of a series of actions or stages towards achieving something. *The meetings are a first step towards ending fifteen years of civil war.* ■ If someone **steps down** or **steps aside** from an important position, they resign. ■ If you **step in** to help someone, you intervene to help them. ■ If you **step up** an activity, you increase it. *The company has plans to step up production this year.* ■ If people march **in step,** their feet move forward at exactly the same time. ■ If people are **in step** with each other, they have similar ideas, opinions, or aims.

stepbrother Your **stepbrother** is the son of your stepfather or stepmother.

stepchild (stepchildren) Someone's **stepchildren** are their stepsons or stepdaughters.

stepdaughter Your **stepdaughter** is a daughter your husband or wife had by an earlier marriage.

stepfather Your **stepfather** is a man who has married your mother, but is not your natural father.

stepladder A **stepladder** is a ladder consisting of two parts hinged at the top so that it stands on its own when opened out.

stepmother Your **stepmother** is a woman who has married your father, but is not your natural mother.

steppe (*pron*: **step**) **Steppes** are large areas of land with grass but no trees, especially in Ukraine and Russia.

stepping stone – **Stepping stones** are a line of stones which you walk along to cross a shallow stream or river. ■ A **stepping stone** is something which enables you to make progress towards something else. *Many students now see university as a stepping stone to a good job.*

stepsister Your **stepsister** is the daughter of your stepfather or stepmother.

stepson Your **stepson** is a son your husband or wife had by an earlier marriage.

stereo (stereos; stereophonic) Stereo or **stereophonic** is used to describe a sound system or recording in which the sound is played through two speakers, with different sounds coming out of each speaker. *...stereo televisions. ...stereophonic broad-*

casts. ■ A **stereo** is a piece of stereophonic equipment for playing records, tapes, or CDs.

stereoscopic is used to describe things which involve two images of the same object being seen from slightly different angles, creating a three-dimensional effect. ...*stereoscopic images.*

stereotype (**stereotyping, stereotyped; stereotypical**) A **stereotype** of a kind of person or thing is what people commonly think of when they think of that person or thing. You can talk about someone or something being **stereotyped** in a certain way. ...*racial stereotyping.* **Stereotypical** is used to describe people or things that are like their stereotypes. ...*a stereotypical teenager.*

sterile (**sterility**) **Sterile** means completely free from germs. ...*sterile dressings.* ■ **Sterile** people and animals are unable to produce babies. This condition is called **sterility.** ■ If you call something **sterile** or talk about its **sterility,** you mean it is unproductive or unimaginative. ...*the sterile debates of the past.*

sterilize (*or* **sterilise**) (**sterilizing, sterilized; sterilization**) If something is **sterilized,** it is made free from germs. ...*a sterilised needle.* ■ If a person or animal is **sterilized,** they have an operation which makes it impossible for them to produce babies. Having this operation is called **sterilization.**

sterling is the money system of the United Kingdom. ■ **pound sterling: see pound.** ■ **Sterling silver** is an alloy containing not less than 92.5% silver. ■ **Sterling** is used to say someone has an excellent character. ...*a man of sterling reputation.* ■ If you say someone has done a **sterling** job, you mean they have done something worthwhile and have done it very well. *The Royal Family does a lot of sterling work for charity.*

stern (**sternly, sternness**) **Stern** behaviour is strict and severe. *I was told sternly to let her finish.* ■ **Stern** is used to describe things which are very difficult. *Racing around Britain is one of the sterner yachting challenges.* ■ If you say someone is **made of sterner stuff,** you mean they are tougher or more determined than they appear at first. ■ The **stern** of a boat is the back part.

sternum The **sternum** is the long flat vertical bone in the middle of the chest, often called the breastbone. The collar bones and the first seven pairs of ribs are attached to it.

steroid – **Steroids** are organic compounds which occur naturally in the body, for example as hormones, and can also be made artificially. They are sometimes prescribed by a doctor as a medical drug. See also **anabolic steroid.**

stet In a draft copy of a piece of writing, **stet** is written alongside something which has been deleted, to say it should be included after all.

stethoscope The **stethoscope** is a medical instrument consisting of two earpieces connected to a hollow tube with a disc at the end. It is used to listen to a patient's heart or breathing.

stetson A **stetson** is a tall broad-brimmed hat, traditionally worn by cowboys.

stevedore A **stevedore** is a dock worker who loads and unloads cargoes.

stew If you **stew** meat, vegetables, or fruit, you simmer them slowly in a liquid. ■ A **stew** is meat and vegetables simmered slowly in stock.

steward A **steward** is (a) a man who works on a ship or plane looking after passengers and serving meals. (b) an official who helps to organize and supervise a race, march, or other public event. ■ Someone who has the responsibility of looking after another person's property or land is sometimes called a **steward.** ■ See also **shop steward.**

stewardess (**stewardesses**) A **stewardess** is a woman who works on a ship or plane looking after passengers and serving meals.

stewardship is the responsibility of looking after something on someone else's behalf.

stick (**sticking, stuck**) A **stick** is a thin straight piece of wood. ■ A **stick** of something is a long thin piece of it. ...*a stick of celery.* ■ If you **stick** something somewhere, you put it there casually. ■ If you **stick** a pointed object into something, you push it in. ■ If you **stick** one thing to another, you fix them together using glue or sticky tape. ■ When things **stick together,** they become difficult to separate. ■ If you **stick around,** you stay where you are. ■ If something that can move **sticks,** it becomes fixed. ■ A **sticking point** in negotiations is an issue on which people cannot agree, and which may delay or stop the talks. ■ If you are **stuck** in a place or an unpleasant situation, you cannot get away from it. ■ If you are **stuck with** something you do not want, you cannot get rid of it. ■ If you are **stuck** you cannot continue with something because you do not know how to do the next stage. ■ If you **stick** to something, you keep to it and do not change to something else. *Some of the patients stuck to the diet rigorously.* ■ If you **stick up** for a person or principle, you support or defend them. ■ If you **stick by** someone, you continue to help and support them, especially when they are in difficulty. Similarly, you can talk about people **sticking together.** ■ If something **sticks out** or **sticks up,** it extends beyond or above something else. *The rocks stick up out of the sea.* ■ If something **sticks out,** it is very noticeable. ■ **carrot and stick: see carrot.**

sticker A **sticker** is a small piece of paper or plastic with writing or a picture on it. It has adhesive on the back so you can stick it onto a surface.

sticking plaster is material which you can stick over a cut or sore to protect it.

stick insect – **Stick insects** have long thin bodies and legs and look like sticks.

stick-in-the-mud is used to describe people with little imagination or enthusiasm for new ideas.

stickler If someone is a **stickler** for a certain type of behaviour, they insist on people behaving that way. *They were sticklers for tidiness.*

sticky (**stickier, stickiest; stickiness**) A **sticky** substance sticks to a surface when it comes into contact with it and makes it feel **sticky.** ■ **Sticky** paper or tape has glue on one side so you can stick it to something. ■ **Sticky** weather is unpleasantly hot and humid. ■ A **sticky** situation is difficult or embarrassing. ■ If you say someone **came to a sticky**

stiff (**stiffly, stiffness**) Stiff things are firm and rigid. ■ If you feel **stiff,** your muscles or joints ache when you move. ■ **Stiff** behaviour is formal and not relaxed. ■ **stiff upper lip:** see **lip.** ■ **Stiff** is used to describe things which are difficult or severe. *...stiffer penalties for drug criminals.* ■ A **stiff** drink is a strong alcoholic drink, such as whisky. ■ A **stiff** breeze blows strongly.

stiffen (**stiffening, stiffened**) If your joints or muscles **stiffen,** they become difficult to move. ■ You say someone **stiffens** when they suddenly stop moving and their muscles become tense. ■ If ideas or attitudes **stiffen,** they become fixed, or they change in a way which makes them tougher and less sympathetic. You can talk about a **stiffening** of ideas or attitudes. ■ If fabric or material is **stiffened,** it is made firmer so it does not bend easily.

stiff-necked people are proud and stubborn.

stifle (**stifling, stifled**) If something is **stifled,** it is prevented from happening or continuing. *...stifled laughter.* ■ If you feel **stifled,** you feel as if you cannot breathe properly. *...the hall's stifling heat.*

stigma If something has a **stigma** attached to it, people think it is unacceptable or disgraceful. *Today, there's much less stigma attached to cosmetic surgery.*

stigmata are marks which appear on a person's body and are like the wounds made on Christ when he was crucified.

stigmatize (*or* **stigmatise**) (**stigmatizing, stigmatized; stigmatization**) If someone or something is **stigmatized,** they are regarded as unacceptable or shameful. *Unjust laws and social stigmatization were hampering AIDS prevention efforts.*

stile A **stile** is a step or steps on either side of a fence or wall to enable people to get across from one side to the other.

stiletto (**stilettos**) A **stiletto** is a small dagger with a narrow blade. ■ **Stiletto shoes** or **stilettos** are women's shoes with high narrow heels.

still (**stillness**) You use **still** to say that a situation which existed previously has continued and exists now. *The fighting is still going on.* ■ You use **still** to say something is better, larger, etc than something else which is itself very good, large, etc. *Worse still was the threat of nuclear pollution.* ■ **Still** is used to say something is the case in spite of other things. *It wasn't a perfect disguise, but still, I did escape.* ■ If you stay **still,** you remain in the same position without moving. Similarly, you use **still** to say there is no movement or activity in a place. *...the stillness of the surrounding forest.* ■ A **still** is a photograph taken from a cinema film or video, often used for publicity purposes. ■ A **still** is an apparatus for distilling alcoholic drinks.

stillborn (**stillbirth**) A **stillborn** baby is born dead. The birth of a dead baby is called a **stillbirth.**

still life A **still life** is a painting or drawing of an arrangement of objects like flowers or fruit.

stilt – **Stilts** are two long vertical poles with supports for the feet. Performers who walk around on stilts to entertain people are called **stilt-walkers.** ■ In some parts of the world, buildings are supported on long wooden or metal poles called **stilts.**

stilted conversation or behaviour is very formal and seems awkward and unnatural.

stimulant – Stimulants are medicines and other substances such as caffeine which make the body work faster, increasing the heart rate.

stimulate (**stimulating, stimulated; stimulation**) If something **stimulates** you, it encourages you to think and develop ideas. *...stimulating conversation.* ■ If something is **stimulated,** it is made to grow or develop. *Interest in the book had been stimulated by press publicity.* ■ If something **stimulates** a process in the body, it encourages it to operate. *Drinking stimulates the production of enzymes in the liver.*

stimulus (*plural:* **stimuli**) A **stimulus** is something that encourages activity in people or things. *The country's economic troubles are providing the latest stimulus for unrest... To be a mother and still to have the stimulus of work would be superb.* ■ A **stimulus** is something which produces a response in an organism or part of the body.

sting (**stinging, stung**) If a creature or plant **stings** you or gives you a **sting,** it pricks your skin, leaving some poison behind which causes a sharp pain. The part it uses to sting you with is called its **sting.** ■ You say things **sting** when they give you a sharp tingling pain in part of your body. *The teargas in the air was stinging their eyes.* ■ If you are **stung** by someone's remarks, you are upset by them. ■ If something like a statement has **a sting in the tail,** it has a surprisingly unpleasant ending. *He warned that the Budget came with a sting in its tail – future tax increases.* ■ If you have had to pay an unreasonably large amount of money for something, you can say you have been **stung.** ■ A **sting** is a clever secret plan, for example a plan by undercover police to catch criminals.

stingy (*pron:* stin-jee) (**stinginess**) If you say someone is **stingy,** you mean they give or spend only small amounts of money, when they could easily afford more.

stink (**stinking, stank, have stunk**) If something **stinks,** it has a very unpleasant smell. A smell like this is called a **stink.** ■ If you say a situation or someone's behaviour **stinks,** you mean it is disgraceful. *Even in an election year, such hypocrisy stinks. ...the stink of dishonesty.* ■ If you create a **stink** about something, you make a lot of fuss about it, so people have to take notice.

stint A **stint** is a period of time spent doing a certain job or activity. *...his second stint as the theatre's director.* ■ If someone **does not stint** on something, they do not hesitate to use or provide a lot of it. *The average British businessman doesn't stint on wining and dining.*

stipend (*pron:* sty-pend) (**stipendiary**) A **stipend** is a fixed or regular allowance or salary, especially one paid to a clergyman or magistrate. ■ **Stipendiary** is used to describe a person who receives a stipend. *...a stipendiary magistrate.*

stippled things have the appearance of being covered with small dots or flecks. *...an expanse of sand, already stippled by the feet of thousands of sandpipers.*

stipulate (**stipulating, stipulated; stipulation**) If something is **stipulated** or is a **stipulation,** a person or rule states that it must be done. *A chess clock is used to ensure that each player completes the stipulated number of moves in the allotted time.*

stir (**stirring, stirred**) When you **stir** a liquid, you move it around with something like a spoon. ■ When something **stirs,** it moves slightly. *The boy stirred in his sleep.* ■ If something **stirs** you, it arouses strong feelings in you. *...a stirring speech in defence of family values.* If something **stirs** you into doing something, it makes you do it. *The protesters had been stirred into action.* ■ If someone **stirs up** trouble, they cause it by arousing strong feelings in people. ■ If an event causes a **stir,** it causes great excitement or anger.

stir-fry If you **stir-fry** food, you fry small pieces of it very quickly over a high heat, stirring at the same time.

stirrup – Stirrups are the two metal loops attached by leather straps to a horse's saddle and used to support the rider's feet.

stitch (**stitches, stitching, stitched**) If you **stitch** material, you use a needle and thread to join the pieces together or to create a design. Each resulting piece of thread is called a **stitch.** ■ In knitting and crochet, you make a **stitch** by passing a loop of yarn round a knitting needle or crochet hook. ■ If a complicated deal is **stitched up,** it is agreed. ■ If someone has been **stitched up,** they have been tricked or set up to take the blame for something. ■ A **stitch** is a sharp pain under your ribs, usually caused by running or laughing a lot. ■ If someone is **in stitches,** they cannot stop laughing.

stoat – Stoats are small long-bodied predatory mammals with brown fur on top and white below, and a black tip to their tail. See also **ermine.**

stock – Stocks are investments, usually in a government, on which a fixed amount of interest is paid. In the US, shares in a company are called **stocks.** ■ If a shop **stocks** certain goods, it normally has a supply of them for sale. A shop's **stock** is all the goods it has for sale. ■ If you **stock** something like a cupboard, you fill it with foodstuffs. If you **stock up,** you buy a large supply of things. ■ A **stock** of things is a supply of them. *...a large stock of weapons.* ■ **Stock** is a liquid made by simmering meat, bones, or vegetables in water. It is used as a basis for soups and sauces. ■ A person's or animal's particular **stock** is the type of people or animals they are descended from. *They were of German stock.* ■ A **stock** expression is one which is commonly used. *'Mind your own business' is her stock response to questions about their relationship.* ■ If you **take stock** of a situation, you stop and think about it before deciding what to do next. ■ The **stock** of a gun like a rifle is the part you hold against your shoulder. ■ If someone stands **stock still,** they stand without any part of their body moving. ■ See also **laughing stock.**

stockade A **stockade** is a wall of high wooden posts built round an area to keep out enemies or wild animals.

stockbroker (**stockbroking**) A **stockbroker** is a person whose job is to buy and sell stocks and shares for other people. The work a stockbroker does is called **stockbroking.**

stock car A **stock car** is an old car which has been strengthened and altered for a type of racing in which the cars often collide.

stock exchange A **stock exchange** is a place where people buy and sell stocks and shares.

stockholder In the US, a **stockholder** is a shareholder.

stocking (**stockinged**) **Stockings** are two pieces of clothing which fit closely over a person's feet and legs and are often held up by suspenders. ■ If someone is in their **stockinged feet,** they are wearing socks, tights, or stockings, but no shoes.

stock-in-trade A person's **stock-in-trade** is a usual part of their behaviour or work. *Although television became his stock-in-trade, he has published seven novels.*

stockist A **stockist** of a certain type of goods sells those goods in their shop. *...your local health food stockist.*

stock market The organization and business involved in buying and selling stocks and shares is called the **stock market.** A **stock market** is also a stock exchange.

stockpile (**stockpiling, stockpiled**) If people **stockpile** things, they store large quantities for future use. A **stockpile** is a large store of something.

stockroom In a place like a shop or factory, the **stockroom** is a room where a stock of goods is kept.

stocktaking is (a) counting and checking all the goods in a shop or warehouse. (b) thinking about the present situation and considering what to do in the future. *Ambassadors to the General Agreement on Tariffs and Trade met for a stocktaking session yesterday.*

stocky people are fairly short, but look strong and solid.

stockyard A **stockyard** is a large yard with pens or buildings, where farm animals are herded together or sold in an auction.

stodgy food is solid and makes you feel too full. ■ You say things are **stodgy** when they are dull and uninteresting. *...the firm's stodgy image.*

stoic (*pron:* stow-ik) (**stoical, stoically, stoicism**) If someone behaves in a **stoic** or **stoical** way, they accept difficulties and suffering without complaining or getting upset. *...stoical courage.* When someone behaves like this, you can call them a **stoic** or talk about their **stoicism** (*pron:* stow-iss-izz-um).

stoke (**stoking, stoked**) If you **stoke** a fire or **stoke** it **up,** you add fuel so it burns more fiercely. ■ If something **stokes** certain feelings, it makes people feel them more intensely. *He has sent in his proposal in the hope of stoking up interest for the idea.*

stole See **steal.** ■ A **stole** is a long scarf which a woman wears over her shoulders when she is in evening dress.

stolen See **steal.**

stolid (**stolidly**) **Stolid** people are unimaginative and do not easily get excited or show much interest in things. *He sat stolidly, drinking his coffee.*

stomach The **stomach** is the organ inside the body where food is digested. ■ The front part of a person's body, below the waist, is often called their **stomach.** ■ If you say you cannot **stomach** something, you mean you dislike it strongly and cannot accept it. You can also say something is hard to **stomach.**

stomp If someone **stomps** around, they tread or stamp heavily.

stone (**stoning, stoned**) **Stone** is a hard solid substance found in the ground and often used for building. A **stone** is a small piece of stone. ■ If people **stone** someone or something, they throw stones at them. ■ If you say a place is **a stone's throw** away, you mean it is not far away. ■ If you **kill two birds with one stone,** you achieve two things by a single action. ■ If you **leave no stone unturned,** you try everything you can think of to achieve what you want. ■ Jewels are sometimes called **stones.** ■ The **stone** in a fruit like a peach or plum is the large seed in the middle. ■ Weight is often expressed in **stones.** A stone is 14 pounds (about 6.35 kilograms). The plural of 'stone' is either 'stone' or 'stones'. *She weighed 14 stone.* ■ If someone is **stoned,** they are under the influence of drugs.

Stone Age The **Stone Age** was the period of human history in which stone tools were used, before metal ones were invented. It started about 2.5 million years ago, and continued in Europe until about 2000 BC.

stonewall You say someone **stonewalls** when they deliberately delay or prevent progress in something like a discussion or argument.

stoneware is a kind of hard pottery fired at a very high temperature.

stonework is objects or parts of a building which are made out of stone.

stony ground is rough and contains a lot of stones or rocks. ■ If someone's behaviour or expression is **stony,** it shows no friendliness or sympathy.

stood See **stand.**

stooge If you call someone a **stooge,** you mean they are being used by someone else to carry out unpleasant or dishonest tasks.

stool A **stool** is a seat without a back or arms, for one person. ■ If you say something **falls between two stools,** you mean it does not fit neatly into either of two categories. ■ A **stool** is also a piece of faeces.

stoop (**stooping, stooped**) If someone **stoops** or has a **stoop,** they walk or stand with their shoulders bent forwards. ■ If someone **stoops,** they bend forwards and down, for example to pick something up. ■ If you talk about someone **stooping** to do something, you mean they are lowering their standards by doing it. *His Lordship does not stoop to giving interviews.*

stop (**stopping, stopped**) If you **stop** doing something, you no longer do it. ■ If an activity or process **stops,** it comes to an end. *Bidding stopped at £74,000.* ■ If you **stop** something, you prevent it happening or continuing. *Police have tried to stop them carrying such weapons.* ■ If something like a machine **stops,** its parts are no longer moving. ■ If people or things going somewhere **stop,** they no longer move. You can also say people **stop off** or **stop over** or make a **stop.** *He stopped and let her catch up with him... His first stop is Spain.* ■ If someone **pulls out all the stops,** they do everything possible to make something happen or be successful. ■ If you say someone will **stop at nothing,** you mean they are prepared to do anything to achieve what they want, even if it is morally wrong.

stopcock A **stopcock** is a tap which controls the flow of liquid through a pipe.

stopgap A **stopgap** is something which serves a purpose for a short time, but is replaced as soon as possible.

stopover A **stopover** is a short stay somewhere during a journey.

stoppage When there is a **stoppage,** people stop working because of a disagreement with their employers. ■ If there is a **stoppage** in a game like football, play is held up briefly, for example because a player is injured. **Stoppage time** is time added on at the end of the match to make up for stoppages. ■ **Stoppages** are deductions made from pay, for example income tax or National Insurance contributions.

stopper A **stopper** is a piece of glass, plastic, or cork which fits into the top of a bottle or jar to seal it.

stop press The **stop press** is the latest news inserted into a special section of a newspaper after the rest has been printed.

stopwatch (**stopwatches**) A **stopwatch** is a type of watch used for timing things like sporting events. It can be started or stopped by pressing a button.

storage of materials or other things is keeping them in a special place until they are needed. **Storage** is also space where things can be stored. See also **cold storage.** ■ **Storage** is storing data in a computer.

storage heater A **storage heater** is an electric heater which stores heat generated by off-peak electricity overnight and then gives out heat gradually during the day.

store (**storing, stored**) When you **store** things, you keep them somewhere until you need them. ■ A **store** of something is a supply kept for future use. ■ A **store** is a place where things are kept until they are needed. *...a grain store.* ■ A shop can be called a **store.** ■ When you **store** information, you keep it in something like a file or on a computer. ■ The things **in store** for someone are the things which are going to happen to them. ■ If you **set great store** by something, you think it is extremely important.

storecard A **storecard** is the same as a charge card.

storehouse A **storehouse** of things or ideas is a large collection of them. *...a vast storehouse of natural resources.*

storekeeper A **storekeeper** is a person who owns or manages a shop.

storeroom A **storeroom** is a room where things are kept until they are needed.

storey (**storeys**) (*Am:* **story, stories**) The **storeys** of a building are its floors or levels.

stork – **Storks** are large wading birds with long legs and long bills.

storm (**stormy**) When there is a **storm**, there is heavy rain, a strong wind, and often thunder and lightning. You say weather like this is **stormy**. ■ An outburst of angry or excited behaviour can be called a **storm**. *His comments provoked a storm of protest... There had been twenty four hours of stormy debate.* ■ If someone **storms** somewhere, they go there suddenly and angrily. *She stormed off through the crowd.* ■ If people **storm** a place, they suddenly attack it. ■ If you say someone has **taken** a place **by storm,** you mean they have made a strong favourable impression there.

stormtrooper (*or* **storm-trooper**) **Stormtroopers** were members of a force of soldiers in Nazi Germany who were specially trained to be violent and ruthless. ■ People who use bullying tactics sometimes get called **stormtroopers.**

story (**stories**) A **story** is a description of imaginary people and events written or told to entertain people. ■ The **story** of something which has actually happened is an account of it. Similarly, a person's **story** is an account of their life, or of some particularly dramatic part of it. ■ In newspapers, a **story** is a report of something which has happened. ■ See also **storey.**

storybook A **storybook** is a book of stories for small children. ■ **Storybook** is used to describe real-life situations which seem like something in a fairy story. *...a storybook romance.*

storyline The **storyline** of a film, TV serial, or book is the plot.

storyteller (**storytelling**) A **storyteller** is a person who tells or writes stories. **Storytelling** is telling or writing stories.

stoup (*pron:* **stoop**) A **stoup** is a small stone basin for holy water in a church.

stout (**stoutly**) A **stout** person is quite fat. ■ **Stout** objects are thick and strong. *...a stout pair of shoes.* ■ **Stout** resistance to something is strong and determined. ■ **Stout** is a strong dark beer.

stove A **stove** is (a) a cooker, especially the top part of a cooker. (b) an enclosed device which burns fuel to heat a room.

stow (**stowaway**) If you **stow** something, you put it into a space or container until it is needed. ■ If a person **stows away** on a plane or ship, they hide on board in order to make their journey secretly or without paying the fare. You call someone who does this a **stowaway.**

straddle (**straddling, straddled**) If someone **straddles** something, they sit or stand with one leg on either side of it. ■ If an area **straddles** something like a boundary or a river, it is on both sides of it. *...an Indian reserve which straddles the border between the two countries.*

strafe (**strafing, strafed**) If an area is **strafed,** it is attacked by gunfire or bombs from low-flying enemy aircraft, or by enemy artillery.

straggle (**straggling, straggled; straggler**) When people or vehicles are **straggling,** they are moving along slowly in irregular and disorganized groups. *...straggling convoys of buses and vans. ...a straggle of refugees.* ■ Small numbers of people or vehicles following a larger group can be called **stragglers.**

straggly is used to describe things which grow or spread out untidily. *...a straggly beard.*

straight is used to describe things which continue in the same direction without curving or bending. *...a straight line. ...looking straight ahead.* ■ If you go **straight** to a place, you go there immediately and directly. ■ **Straight** is used to say something happens immediately after something else. *He joined the company straight from the Army.* ■ **Straight** is used to say a number of things of the same kind happen one after the other. *Newcastle's defeat on Saturday ended a run of 11 straight wins.* ■ A **straight** fight or choice involves only two people or things. ■ If someone is **straight** with you or gives you a **straight** answer, they are honest and truthful. ■ If you get things **straight,** you sort out a confused situation. ■ If you keep a **straight** face, you manage not to laugh. ■ You call people **straight** when you think they conform to normal social conventions. ■ If a criminal **goes straight,** he or she gives up being involved in crime. ■ When people talk about the **straight** theatre, they mean serious plays as distinct from comedies or musicals.

straighten (**straightening, straightened**) If you **straighten** something, you make it straight. ■ You say you **straighten** something when you arrange or adjust it so it is in its proper position or is neat and tidy. *He straightened his tie.* ■ If you **straighten** or **straighten up,** you make your body straight and upright, after you have been bending or stooping. ■ If you **straighten out** a confused situation, you deal with it and put it in order.

straightforward (**straightforwardly**) If something is **straightforward,** it is clear and simple without any special complications or difficulties. ■ A **straightforward** person is honest and frank.

strain (**straining, strained**) If there is **strain** on an object, it is being pushed, pulled, or stretched tightly, and may bend or break. ■ If there is **strain** on a system or if it is being **strained,** it is unable to cope with the demands being made on it, and may fail or collapse. *...an economy already strained to its very limits.* Similarly, you can talk about **strain** being put on a person. *...the strains of living on the street.* ■ If you say someone looks **strained,** you mean they look worried and nervous. ■ If you **strain** a muscle or some other part of your body, you injure it by using it suddenly and violently, or using it too much. An injury like this is called a **strain.** See also **repetitive strain injury.** ■ If you **strain** to do something, you make a great effort to do it. ■ When you **strain** food, you separate the liquid from the solid parts, usually by pouring it into a strainer. ■ A **strain** of a plant or some other living thing is a variety or type of it. ■ If you hear the **strains** of a piece of music, you hear it being played.

strainer A **strainer** is a small sieve used for separating liquids from solids.

strait You can refer to a narrow strip of sea which joins two large areas of sea as a **strait** or the **straits**. ■ If someone or something is in **dire straits,** they are in a very serious situation.

straitened If someone is living in **straitened** circumstances, they do not have as much money as they used to, and find it difficult to manage.

straitjacket A **straitjacket** is a type of jacket with extra long sleeves which are used to tie the arms of a violent person round their body. ■ Anything which restricts growth or freedom can be called a **straitjacket.**

strait-laced people have very strict and severe ideas about morality.

strand (**stranding, stranded**) A **strand** of something like thread or hair is a single piece of it. ■ A **strand** of an idea or a situation is one aspect of it. ...*a growing strand of nationalist opinion.* ■ If you are **stranded,** you are prevented from leaving a place, for example because of bad weather.

strange (**stranger, strangest; strangely, strangeness**) **Strange** is used to describe things which are unusual or unexpected. ■ A **strange** place is somewhere you have never been before. A **strange** person is someone you have never met before.

stranger A **stranger** is someone you have not met before. ■ If you are a **stranger** to a place or a situation, you have not been there or experienced it before.

strangle (**strangling, strangled; strangulation, strangler**) If a person is **strangled,** someone squeezes their throat until they are dead. Killing someone like this is called **strangulation;** a criminal who kills like this can be called a **strangler.** ■ You talk about things being **strangled** when something prevents their development and they are unable to survive. *The policy is strangling the economy.* ■ A **strangled** laugh or cry is muffled and unclear.

stranglehold If someone has a **stranglehold** on something, they have firm control of it.

strap (**strapping, strapped**) A **strap** is a narrow piece of leather or cloth used to fasten or hold things together. ■ If you **strap** something in position, you fasten it there with a strap. ■ **Strapping** is adhesive bandage used to provide support. ■ A **strapping** person is tall, strong, and healthy-looking. ■ If someone is **strapped for cash,** they do not have much money.

strapless A **strapless** dress or bra leaves the shoulders bare, with no straps over them.

strata See **stratum.**

stratagem A **stratagem** is a plan or tactic.

strategic (*pron:* strat-**tee**-jik) (**strategically**) **Strategic** means to do with the distribution and positioning of armies and weapons for military advantage. ...*a strategically important town.* ■ **Strategic** weapons are long-range weapons, especially nuclear ones, targeted to destroy an enemy's industry, economy, or military bases. ■ **Strategic** is used to talk about things intended or planned to

achieve something or gain an advantage. *I took up a strategic position near the exit.*

strategy (**strategies; strategist**) A **strategy** is a plan for achieving something. ...*marketing strategies.* ■ **Strategy** is the skill of planning the best way to achieve something, especially in war.

stratified (**stratification**) **Stratified** means divided into different layers or levels. ...*the stratification of American society.*

stratosphere The **stratosphere** is the layer of the earth's atmosphere which is between 10 and 50 kilometres above the earth.

stratum (*plural:* **strata**) The **strata** in the earth's surface are the different layers of rock. ■ The different social levels or classes in society can be called **strata.**

straw is the dried stalks of cereal crops. ■ A **straw** is a thin tube of paper or plastic which you use to suck a drink into your mouth. ■ If someone is **clutching at straws,** they are trying desperate or unusual methods to achieve something, because all other attempts have failed. ■ If something is **the last straw,** it is the latest in a series of bad things and makes you feel you cannot stand any more. ■ If you have **drawn the short straw,** you have been chosen from a number of people to do a job which nobody wants to do. ■ If you say an incident or piece of news is a **straw in the wind,** you mean it gives an indication of what might happen in the future.

strawberry (**strawberries**) **Strawberries** are small soft red fruit, eaten as a dessert or made into jam.

straw poll A **straw poll** is the unofficial questioning of a group of people to find out their opinion about something.

stray If someone **strays** somewhere, they wander away from where they are supposed to be. You can also say someone **strays** from what they usually do. ■ A **stray** or a **stray** animal is an animal which has wandered away from its owner's home. ■ If your thoughts **stray,** you lose concentration and start thinking about something different. ■ **Stray** is used to describe something which is separated from other similar things. ...*a stray bullet.*

streak (**streaking, streaked; streaky, streaker**) A **streak** is a long mark or stripe which contrasts with its surroundings because it is a different colour. When something has marks like this, you can say it is **streaked** or **streaky.** ■ You can refer to an aspect of someone's character as a certain **streak.** ...*a ruthless streak.* ■ If someone or something **streaks** somewhere, they move there extremely quickly. ■ If a person **streaks,** they run quickly through a public place without any clothes on. Someone who does this is called a **streaker.** ■ A **lucky** or **winning streak** is a series of successes, especially in sport or in gambling.

stream (**streaming, streamed**) A **stream** is a small river. ■ A steady flow of something or a series of events can be called a **stream.** ...*a stream of hot air.* ...*a continuous stream of phone calls.* ■ If you say something is **streaming,** you mean it is flowing in large quantities. If you have a **streaming** cold, your nose keeps running and your eyes water. ■ If people or things **stream** somewhere, they move there quickly in large numbers. ■ If a person's hair is **streaming** in the wind, it is blowing about freely. ■ If there is **streaming** in a school, pupils of the same age are put into groups according to their ability. A group like this is called a **stream.**

streamer A **streamer** is a long narrow strip of coloured paper used for decoration.

streamline (**streamlining, streamlined**) If something is **streamlined,** it has a smooth shape and can move easily through air or water. The smooth shape of something like this can be called its **streamlining.** ■ If an organization or a process is **streamlined,** it is altered to make it more efficient.

street A **street** is a road in a town or village, usually with buildings along it. ■ You can use **street** or **streets** when talking about activities that happen outdoors in a town rather than inside a building. *...street traders.* ■ If someone is **streets ahead** of you, they are much better at something than you are. ■ If something is **right up your street,** you are very interested in it or know a lot about it. ■ If you talk about **the man in the street,** you mean ordinary people in general. *The income tax cuts were not enough to impress the man in the street.*

streetcar is the usual American word for a tram.

street cred If someone says you have **street cred** or **street credibility,** they mean ordinary young people would approve of you and consider you to be part of their culture, usually because you share their sense of fashion or their views.

street value The **street value** of a drug is the price paid for it when it is sold illegally to drug users.

streetwalker A **streetwalker** is a prostitute.

streetwise If someone is **streetwise,** they know how to cope with rough people or dangerous situations, especially in big cities.

strength Your **strength** is your physical energy and power. ■ The **strength** of an object or material is its ability to stand up to rough treatment. ■ The **strength** of a relationship is its degree of success or closeness. ■ **Strength** can refer to the degree of someone's confidence or courage. ■ Good qualities or features can be called **strengths.** ■ You can refer to power or influence as **strength.** *...the political and economic strength of a unified Germany.* ■ The **strength** of a feeling or opinion is the degree to which it is felt or supported. ■ When there are large numbers of people in a place, you can say they are there **in strength.** ■ The **strength** of a group of people is the total number of people in it. *The regiment's strength is 650 men.* ■ If you do something **on the strength** of a fact or situation, this provides a basis or reason for your action. *She was convicted on the strength of forensic evidence.*

strengthen (**strengthening, strengthened**) If an object or material is **strengthened,** it is made stronger and better able to withstand rough treatment or heavy weights. ■ If something **strengthens** your body, it makes you stronger and fitter. *Regular exercise will strengthen joints and muscles.* ■ If something **strengthens** your beliefs, it makes them stronger. Similarly, something can **strengthen** an argument for doing something. *The net effect of the*

reforms would be to strengthen the case for certain rail investment schemes. ■ If something is **strengthened,** it is given more power, influence, or support, to make it more likely to succeed. *The President's visit is intended to strengthen ties between the two countries.* ■ If a currency **strengthens,** its value increases in relation to other currencies.

strenuous (**strenuously**) A **strenuous** action or activity involves a lot of effort or energy. *...strenuous physical labour.*

streptococcus (*plural:* **streptococci**) (**streptococcal**) Streptococci (*pron:* strep-toe-**kok**-eye) are a group of bacteria responsible for infections called **streptococcal** infections. Scarlet fever and sore throats are caused by infections like these.

stress (**stresses, stressing, stressed**) Stress is worry and nervous tension. If someone is **stressed,** they are anxious or worried. ■ **Stress** is strong physical pressure or strain on an object. *This exercise puts too much stress on the lower back.* ■ If you **stress** something, you emphasize its importance. *The report stresses the need to reduce military spending.* ■ If you put **stress** on a certain aspect of something, you concentrate on it. *The company is putting more stress on design and style to win competitive advantage.* ■ If you **stress** a word or part of a word when you are speaking, you emphasize it, making it slightly louder or longer than other words. This emphasis is called **stress.**

stressful situations cause a lot of anxiety and worry.

stretch (**stretches, stretching, stretched**) When something soft or elastic is **stretched,** it is pulled to make it longer or bigger. ■ **Stretch** fabric is soft and elastic and stretches easily without losing its original shape. ■ When you **stretch,** you hold your arms or legs out as far as you can and tighten your muscles, often just after waking up. A **stretch** is a movement like this. ■ If you **stretch out** part of your body, you hold it out straight. ■ If you **stretch** yourself **out,** you lie in a comfortable position with your legs and body in a straight line. ■ If something **stretches** over a period of time, it lasts that long. *...an unbroken home league record that had stretched back over 17 months.* ■ A period of time can be called a **stretch.** *...his five-year stretch as commissioner.* ■ If something **stretches** over a certain distance, it extends that far. *...a traffic jam that stretched for several miles.* ■ A **stretch** of land or water is a large area of it. *...a one mile stretch of beach.* ■ If someone's money or resources are **stretched,** they have hardly enough for their needs. ■ If your resources can **stretch** to something, you can just afford to do it. *If your pocket can stretch to it, do get some good advice.* ■ If a job or task **stretches** you, it satisfies you because you use all your energy and skill to complete it.

stretcher (**stretchered**) A **stretcher** is a long piece of material with a pole along each side used for carrying an injured person. When someone is carried off a sports field because of an injury, you say they are **stretchered off.** The people who carry a stretcher are called **stretcher-bearers.**

stretchy material stretches easily and returns to its normal shape when you let it go.

strew (**strewing, strewed, have strewn; -strewn**) If an area is **strewn** with things, a lot of them are scattered untidily across it. *The walkways into the underground are strewn with litter. ...rubbish-strewn streets.*

striated (*pron:* **strie**-ay-tid) (**striation**) If something is **striated**, it is marked with narrow bands of colour or with ridges or grooves. These marks or ridges are called **striations**. *...striated ridges of solid rock.*

stricken (**-stricken**) If someone or something is **stricken** by something unpleasant, they are badly affected by it. You add **-stricken** to a word to show that something has caused a bad effect on someone or something. *...drought-stricken areas.*

strict (**strictly, strictness**) A **strict** person controls other people very firmly. *The prison regime will be much stricter... She resented her parents' strictness.* ■ **Strict** is used to talk about rules and principles being firmly enforced or obeyed. *Security restrictions were being strictly enforced. ...a strict vegetarian.* ■ **Strict** can be used to mean 'precise' or 'exact'. *...in strict alphabetical order.* ■ **Strictly** can be used to emphasize that someone or something is of a particular kind, rather than something else. *The parade had originally been planned as a strictly military affair.* ■ If something is **strictly** for a particular thing or person, it is intended only for them. *...supplies intended strictly for medical purposes.* ■ The **strict** sense of a word is its precise meaning. *It's not quite peace in the strictest sense of the word, rather the absence of war.* ■ You say **strictly speaking** to correct a statement or add more precise information. *We cannot, strictly speaking, cure diabetes but we have some very effective treatments for treating the consequences.*

stricture When someone criticizes something severely, you can call what they say their **strictures**. *The campaign is justifying every stricture he has ever voiced about referendums.* ■ **Strictures** are limits or restrictions imposed on someone or something. *We whined and complained under our parents' strictures.*

stride (**striding, strode**) If you **stride** somewhere, you walk quickly with long steps. Each step you take when you walk or run can be called a **stride**. ■ **Stride** is used in expressions such as **get into your stride** or **make strides** to talk about someone's rate of progress towards achieving something. *Our struggle for freedom has made great strides.* ■ If you **take** something **in your stride,** you deal with it calmly and easily.

strident (*pron:* **stry**-dent) (**stridently, stridency**) You call someone's behaviour **strident** when they keep criticizing something in a noticeable or persistent way. ■ **Strident** sounds are loud and harsh. You talk about the **stridency** of sounds like these.

strife is trouble and fighting.

strike (**striking, struck; striker, strikingly**) If there is a **strike,** workers stop working as a protest. You also say people **strike** or **go on strike;** people taking part in a strike are called **strikers.** See also **hunger strike.** ■ If you **strike** a person or thing, you hit them. ■ In football, a **striker** is a player whose main function is to score goals. ■ If something like an illness or disaster **strikes,** it happens suddenly. ■ If someone is **struck** dumb or blind, they are suddenly unable to speak or see. ■ When a military force **strikes,** it attacks suddenly. The attack is called a **strike.** ■ If an idea **strikes** you, you suddenly have it. ■ If something **strikes fear** into someone, it makes them very frightened. ■ If something **strikes** you in a certain way, it gives you that impression. *He never struck me as much of a rebel.* ■ If someone or something is **striking,** they are very attractive or noticeable. ■ If you are **struck** by something, you are impressed by it. *What struck me was the enormous commitment of the students.* ■ When a clock **strikes,** its bells chime to show what the time is. ■ If you **strike** a deal with someone, you come to an agreement with them. ■ If you **strike** a match, you light it by scraping it against something. ■ If you are **within striking distance** of something, you are very near to reaching it or achieving it. ■ If someone **strikes** oil or gold, they discover it in the ground by mining or drilling. ■ If you **strike it lucky,** you have good luck. ■ If you **strike a balance,** you reach a compromise between two extremes. ■ If a doctor or lawyer is **struck off,** their name is removed from the professional register and they are not allowed to carry on in their profession, because they have done something wrong. ■ If you **strike up** a conversation or friendship with someone, you begin it. ■ **strike a chord:** see **chord.**

strike-breaker (**strike-breaking**) A **strike-breaker** is a person who continues to work during a strike, or is brought in to do the work of someone who is on strike. Working during a strike like this is called **strike-breaking.**

string (**stringing, strung**) **String** is thin cord made of twisted threads. ■ If something is **strung** somewhere, it is suspended between two or more points. *...a hammock strung between two coconut palms.* ■ If things are **strung** somewhere or **strung out** somewhere, they are spread out in a long line. *...the summer houses strung along the coast.* ■ A **string** of events or things is a series of them. *...a string of attacks.* ■ If you **string** a number of things together, you get them to follow each other in an unbroken sequence. *United began to string passes together effectively.* ■ The **strings** on a musical instrument are the tightly-stretched lengths of wire or nylon which vibrate to produce notes. In an orchestra, the **strings** are the stringed instruments. ■ If you say someone has **another string to their bow,** you mean they have another idea, job, or ability which they can use if the first one is not successful. ■ **Second string** is used to describe people or things that are not the best of their kind but are kept in reserve in case the best ones are not available. *...her second-string horse.* ■ When someone **pulls strings,** they use their influence to achieve something. ■ If someone **strings** you **along,** they deceive you over a period of time by encouraging you to think they share your views or feelings. ■ If someone is **strung out** on drugs, they are addicted to them. You also say a drug addict is **strung out** when he or she is suffering because of lack of drugs.

string beans are the same as runner beans.

stringent (*pron:* **strin**-jent) (**stringently; stringency**) Stringent laws or rules are very severe or are strictly enforced. You can talk about the **stringency** of laws or rules like these. ■ **Stringency** is spending very little money, or having very little to spend. *...a period of great stringency in public expenditure.*

stringer A **stringer** is a journalist employed part-time to report on a certain area.

string quartet A **string quartet** is a group of four musicians who play together. Their instruments are two violins, a viola, and a cello. A piece of music written for this combination is also called a **string quartet.**

stringy food is tough and difficult to chew.

strip (**stripping, stripped**) A **strip** of something is a long narrow piece of it. *...strips of brown paper.* ■ If someone **strips,** they take off all their clothes. If they are **stripped,** their clothes are taken off by someone else, often to search for illegal items. See also **strip-search.** ■ If someone is **stripped** of something like their property or power, it is taken away from them. ■ If you **strip** a place, you remove everything from it. You can also say you **strip** it of certain things. *They are rapidly stripping the forest of its mahogany trees.* ■ If you **strip** paint or varnish from a surface, you remove it. ■ If you **strip** a piece of equipment or strip it **down,** you take it to pieces to clean or repair it. ■ **Stripped-down** is used to describe something which is very basic or has only the bare essentials. *...a stripped-down theatre company.* ■ A **strip cartoon** is a series of drawings which tell a story, with the words spoken by the characters printed in each drawing. ■ In sport, especially football, a player's **strip** is the kit they wear to play a match.

strip club A **strip club** is a club where striptease is performed.

stripe (**striped, stripy**) Stripes are long thin lines, usually of different colours. You use **striped** or **stripy** to describe something which has stripes on it. *...red and black striped ribbon. ...a stripy T-shirt.*

strip lighting is a type of electric lighting which uses long tubes rather than light bulbs.

stripling You call someone a **stripling** to emphasize how young they are.

stripper A **stripper** is a person who performs striptease.

strip-search If a person is **strip-searched** or given a **strip-search,** someone such as a police officer makes them take off all their clothes and searches their body, usually to see if they are carrying drugs or weapons.

striptease is a form of entertainment in which a performer takes off their clothes slowly and in a sexy way to music.

strive (**striving, strove** or **strived, have striven** or **have strived**) If you **strive** for something, you try hard to achieve it.

strobe A **strobe** or **strobe light** is a bright light which flashes on and off very quickly.

strode See **stride.**

stroke (**stroking, stroked**) If you **stroke** something, you move your hand slowly and gently over it. ■ The **strokes** of a brush are the movements or marks you make when you use it. ■ If someone has a **stroke,** they suffer a blockage or rupture in a blood vessel in their brain, causing loss of consciousness and often resulting in brain damage or paralysis. ■ In rowing, a **stroke** is a single pull of the oar. ■ In swimming, a **stroke** is a single movement of the arms and legs. Different styles of swimming are also called **strokes.** *...back stroke.* ■ In sports like tennis and golf, a **stroke** is one hit of the ball, or a particular way of hitting it. *He won the US Golf Open by two strokes. ...forehand strokes.* ■ If you say, for example, that something happens **on the stroke of** seven, you mean it happens at exactly seven o'clock. ■ If something is achieved **at a stroke,** it is achieved suddenly and completely by a single action. *At a stroke the prime minister had upset her three principal colleagues.* ■ A **stroke** of luck is a piece of good luck. ■ A sudden brilliant idea can be called a **stroke** of genius.

stroll If you **stroll** somewhere, you walk there in a slow relaxed way. A **stroll** is a slow pleasant walk.

strong (**strongly**) Strong people or animals have powerful muscles. ■ If someone has a **strong** personality, they are not easily influenced by other people. ■ Your **strong** points are your good qualities or skills. ■ A **strong** competitor is likely to do well or win. ■ If someone has a **strong** belief in something, they believe in it very firmly, and are not likely to change their mind. *...his strongly-held views.* ■ Swearing or obscene language is sometimes called **strong** language. ■ **Strong** is used to describe things which are forceful or distinct. *...a strong wind. ...a strong smell. ...a strongly worded letter of protest.* ■ **Strong** objects are not easily damaged. ■ A **strong** relationship is close and likely to last. ■ A **strong** economy or currency is successful and stable. ■ If there is a **strong** case for something, there are very good reasons for it. ■ A **strong** drink or drug contains a lot of the substance which makes it effective. ■ You can use **strong** to talk about the number of people in a group. *...a ten-thousand strong crowd.* ■ **strong suit:** see **suit.**

strong-arm You say people use **strong-arm** tactics when they use threats or force to get what they want.

stronghold A **stronghold** is a place which is held and defended by an army or other military force. ■ If you say a place is a **stronghold** of a type of attitude or belief, you mean a lot of people there share it.

strong-minded people have firm opinions or attitudes and are not easily influenced.

strong room A **strong room** is a reinforced fireproof room in a bank with a special security door, where money and valuable documents are kept.

strong-willed people are very determined to get their own way.

strontium is a soft silvery-white metal used in making fireworks.

stroppy If you say someone is **stroppy,** you mean they are bad-tempered and difficult.

strove See **strive.**

struck See **strike.**

structural (structurally) Structural means to do with the structure of buildings. ...*severe structural damage.* ■ Structural means to do with the structure of a system or organization. ...*structural changes to the welfare system.*

structuralism (structuralist) Structuralism is an academic theory which suggests you can study subjects like literature, language, or society as if they were made up of structures, each structure consisting of smaller components which have meaning in relation to the whole. A person who studies subjects in this way is called a **structuralist.**

structure (structuring, structured) The **structure** of something like a building is the way it is constructed. The building itself can be called a **structure.** ■ The **structure** of something like a system is the way it is organized. ■ If you **structure** something, you arrange it in an organized system. ...*a new way of structuring the work force.*

struggle (struggling, struggled) If you **struggle** to do something, you try hard to do it, even though it is difficult. ■ When it is difficult to do something, you can say it is a **struggle** to do it. *England face a hard struggle to save the Fourth Test against the West Indies.* ■ You use **struggling** to talk about a person or organization trying hard to do something but not having much success. ...*the struggling Third Division club.* ■ If you talk about the **struggle** for something, you mean the efforts people make to achieve it. ...*the non-violent struggle for freedom and democracy.* Similarly, you can talk about a **struggle** against something. ...*the struggle against apartheid.* ■ If someone **struggles** when they are being held, they try hard to get free. ■ If two people **struggle,** they fight each other. A fight can be called a **struggle.**

strum (strumming, strummed) If you **strum** a guitar, you play chords on it.

strung See **string.**

strut (strutting, strutted) If someone **struts,** they walk proudly with their head high and their chest out. ■ You say someone **struts their stuff** when they demonstrate their talents or abilities. *The pick of 200 youth theatre companies strutted their stuff at the National Theatre.* ■ A **strut** is a piece of wood, metal, or concrete used in the framework of a building to strengthen it or to support other parts within the building.

strychnine (*pron:* **strik**-neen) is a strong poison which can cause convulsions and death.

stub (stubbing, stubbed) The **stub** of a pencil or cigarette is the short piece left when the rest has been used. ■ The **stub** of a cheque or ticket is the small part you keep as a record of what you have paid. ■ When someone **stubs out** a cigarette, they put it out by pressing it against something hard. ■ If you **stub** your toe, you hurt it by accidentally kicking something hard.

stubble (stubbly) Stubble is short coarse hair which grows after shaving, especially on a man's face. *He had long unkempt hair and a stubbly chin.*

stubborn (stubbornly, stubbornness) Stubborn people are very determined to do what they want and are not easily put off. *His bravery can only be matched by his stubbornness.* ■ Stubborn stains or problems are very difficult to deal with. *Interest rates have remained stubbornly high.*

stubby things are short and thick. ...*stubby fingers.*

stucco (stuccoed) Stucco is a type of plaster used for covering outside walls or decorating ceilings. ...*stuccoed villas.*

stuck See **stick.**

stuck-up people are proud and conceited.

stud (studded) Studs are pieces of metal attached to and sticking out of a surface. ■ You can say a surface is **studded** with objects when there are a lot of them scattered over it. ...*diamond-studded high-heeled shoes.* ...*rich dark soil studded with large boulders.* ■ A **stud** is (a) a small earring attached so it lies flat against the ear. (b) a similar ornament attached to the side of the nose. ■ **Studs** are the small objects attached to the soles of outdoor sporting footwear to give a better grip. ■ Male animals, especially horses, which are kept for **stud** are kept for breeding purposes; the place where they are kept is called a **stud** or a **stud farm.**

student A **student** is a person studying at a university or college. ■ Older school pupils are sometimes called **students.** ■ You say someone is a **student** of something when they take a great interest in it. ...*a keen student of opinion polls.*

studentship A studentship is the same as a scholarship.

studied See **study.**

studio (studios) A **studio** is a room where TV or radio programmes, films, or records are made. You can also call film-making or recording companies **studios.** ■ A **studio** is a place where an artist, photographer, or designer works. ■ A **studio** is a room used for practice or rehearsals by dancers or actors. ■ A **studio** or **studio flat** is a small flat, usually with one room for living and sleeping, and a kitchen and bathroom.

studious (studiously) A **studious** person spends a lot of their time reading and studying. ■ If someone **studiously** avoids doing something, they are careful not to do it. *Any discussion of contentious issues was studiously avoided.*

study (studies, studying, studied) If you **study** a subject, you spend time learning about it. ...*the study of technology at A level.* ...*the right environment for quiet study.* ■ A **study** is a piece of research on a subject. ...*well-publicised studies on the decline of spelling.* ■ If someone **studies** something, they look at it carefully. ...*travellers studying maps.* ■ A **studied** action has been carefully planned. *Previous governments maintained a studied neutrality in most industrial disputes.* ■ A **study** by an artist or photographer is a drawing or photograph done in preparation for other work. ■ In music, a **study** is a piece of music for a single instrument written to show off the

stuff

643   **style**

player's technical skill. ■ A **study** is a room for reading, writing, and studying.

stuff You call actions, objects, or other things **stuff** when you are talking about them in a general way. *I do a lot of dangerous stuff in my show... The Red Cross has been shipping stuff in for months.* ■ If you **stuff** something somewhere, you push it there roughly. ■ If a place or container is **stuffed** with things, it is full of them. ■ If you **stuff** food, you put other food inside it before cooking it. ■ **Stuffing** is a mixture of chopped and seasoned ingredients put inside a piece of meat or poultry before cooking. ■ If a dead animal is **stuffed**, it is filled with special material so it can be preserved and displayed. ■ If you call someone a **stuffed shirt**, you mean they are extremely formal, old-fashioned, and pompous.

stuffy people are formal, old-fashioned, and dull. ■ If a place is **stuffy**, it is unpleasantly warm and there is not enough fresh air.

stultify (**stultifies, stultifying, stultified**) If something **stultifies** a person or an organization, it destroys their natural interest or prevents their development. *...the sort of corporate mentality that stultifies imagination and daring. ...Spain's campaign to emancipate itself from the stultifying years of Franco's rule.*

stumble (**stumbling, stumbled**) If you **stumble** when you are walking or running, you trip and fall or almost fall. ■ If you **stumble** when you are speaking, you hesitate or make a mistake. ■ If you make a lot of mistakes when you are doing something, you can say you **stumble** through it. ■ If you **stumble across** something or **stumble on** it, you discover it accidentally. *Scientists in the USA have accidentally stumbled across what may be the key to finding a cure for muscle and heart diseases.*

stumbling block A **stumbling block** is a problem which gets in the way and prevents you achieving something.

stump A **stump** is the lowest part of something, which remains when the rest has been broken off or removed. *...a tree stump.* ■ In cricket, the **stumps** are the three upright wooden sticks which, together with the bails, form the wicket. When a batsman is **stumped**, the wicketkeeper gets him or her out by knocking the bails off. ■ If a question or problem **stumps** you, you cannot think of a solution to it. ■ If you **stump up** an amount of money, you produce it to pay for something. *Buyers have to stump up deposits of at least 5%.* ■ If a politician is **on the stump**, he or she is campaigning for an election.

stumpy things are short and thick. *...the mole's stumpy tail.*

stun (**stunning, stunned; stunningly**) If you are **stunned** by something, you are very shocked by it. *The election result was a stunning blow to the regime.* ■ If you say someone or something is **stunning**, you mean they are extremely beautiful or impressive. *...stunning views.* ■ If a blow on the head **stuns** you, it knocks you out, or makes you confused and unsteady. ■ A **stun** grenade or gun is designed to knock someone out, rather than kill them or injure them seriously.

stung See **sting.**

stunk See **stink.**

stunning (**stunningly**) See **stun.**

stunt A **stunt** is something someone does to get publicity. *The view seems to be that his visit is a propaganda stunt.* ■ A **stunt** is a skilful and dangerous action performed to entertain people or as part of a film. Film stunts are usually performed by **stunt men** or **stunt women**, whose job is to stand in for leading actors so they do not get injured. ■ If something is **stunted**, it is prevented from growing or developing as it should. *Their imaginations are being stunted.*

stupefy (**stupefies, stupefying, stupefied; stupefaction**) If you say someone is **stupefied** or in a state of **stupefaction**, you mean they are so tired or bored they cannot think properly. If you find something very boring, you can call it **stupefying**. ■ You can say someone is **stupefied** when they are very surprised or shocked by something.

stupendous (**stupendously**) If something is extremely large or impressive, you can say it is **stupendous**. *...a stupendous meal.*

stupid (**stupidly; stupidity, stupidities**) If you call an idea or action **stupid**, you mean it is not at all sensible. If you call a person **stupid**, you mean they lack intelligence or keep doing silly things. You can also talk about their **stupidity** or refer to their stupid actions as **stupidities.** *I'd hate to see two innocent children suffer for my stupidities.*

stupor If you say someone is in a **stupor**, you mean they are almost unconscious, for example because they are drunk.

sturdy (**sturdier, sturdiest; sturdily, sturdiness**) A **sturdy** person is strong and healthy. ■ **Sturdy** objects are strongly made and not easily damaged. *...sturdy stone cottages.*

sturgeon (*pron:* stur-jon) The **sturgeon** is a large edible fish. Its eggs are called caviar when they have been prepared as food.

stutter (**stuttering, stuttered**) If someone **stutters** or has a **stutter**, they find it difficult to say the first sound of a word and hesitate or repeat it two or three times. ■ If something like a machine or a system **stutters**, it proceeds in a hesitant way. *...his stuttering economic reforms.*

sty (**sties**) A **sty** is the same as a pigsty. ■ See also **stye.**

stye A **stye** or **sty** is a painful red swelling on your eyelid.

style (**styling, styled, -style**) The **style** of something is the general way it is done or presented. *The biography is written in a straightforward yet lively style.* ■ Your **style** of doing something is your way of doing it. *...Liverpool's style of play.* ■ The **style** of a product is its distinctive design. ■ You add **-style** to a word to say someone or something is of a particular type. *...an old-style liberal.* ■ The **style** of something like a painting or piece of music is the special features which are typical of a particular artistic movement. *...architecture in the classical style.* ■ **Style** is fashionable good taste. If you say someone or something has **style,** you mean they are smart, fashionable, or elegant in a distinctive way.

■ If you do something **in style** or **in fine style,** you do it in a grand way. ■ If you **style** yourself a particular title, you call yourself by that title. *Ridley now styles himself Baron Ridley of Liddesdale.* See also **self-styled.**

stylised (**stylisation**) See **stylized.**

stylish (**stylishly, stylishness**) A **stylish** person or object is smart and fashionable. *The three bedrooms are all stylishly decorated. ...modern Italian stylishness.* ■ If you describe someone's performance as **stylish,** you mean it is efficient and impressive. *That was the most stylish performance I've seen from United this season.*

stylist A **stylist** is (a) a hairdresser. (b) someone like a designer who creates a certain image or effect. *...a fashion stylist.* ■ If you call a writer a **stylist,** you mean he or she writes in an attractive and elegant way.

stylistic (**stylistically**) **Stylistic** is used to talk about the methods, techniques, and principles involved in creating a great painting, a piece of writing, or music. *...her stylistic influence on other poets was wholly beneficial.*

stylized (or **stylised**) (**stylization**) **Stylized** means made or presented according to a certain fixed style, rather than realistically or naturally. *...a monochrome photograph of a stylized male torso.*

stylus (*usual plural:* **styluses**) The **stylus** on a record player is the needle-like device attached to the cartridge which picks up the sound signals on the records.

stymie (**stymieing, stymied**) If you are **stymied** by someone or something, you are prevented from doing the thing you want to do.

styptic is a substance used to stop bleeding. A **styptic pencil** contains this substance in the form of a small stick, for dabbing on shaving cuts.

suave (*pron:* **swahv**) (**suavely, suavity**) A **suave** person is smooth and sophisticated. *He is yet to convince party sceptics that there is depth behind his suavity.*

sub A **sub** is a submarine. ■ **Subs** are the fixed amounts of money which members of a club or society regularly pay into its funds.

sub- is used (a) to form words which describe something as being underneath something else. *...sub-sea vehicles.* (b) to form words which show that a job or rank is lower than another job or rank. *...a sub-lieutenant.* ■ **Sub-** is used to talk about something being below a certain level or point on a scale. *...sub-zero temperatures.* ■ **Sub-** is used to form words which describe something as being part of a larger thing. *...a sub-committee of the UN Commission on Human Rights.* ■ Some words beginning with **sub-** can be spelled with or without a hyphen. For example, 'sub-contract' can be spelled 'subcontract'. See entries at **subcontinent, subcontract, sub-standard, sub-tropical.**

sub-aqua means to do with underwater diving or sport using an aqualung. *...sub-aqua gear.*

sub-atomic A **sub-atomic** particle is one which is part of an atom.

subconscious (**subconsciously**) If something is in a person's **subconscious,** it is in their mind and can influence their behaviour, although they are unaware of it. *I've tried not to allow the crisis to affect me but I suppose subconsciously it has.*

subcontinent (or **sub-continent**) When people talk about the **Indian subcontinent,** they mean the whole of the area which includes India, Pakistan, Bangladesh, and Sri Lanka.

subcontract (or **sub-contract**) (**subcontractor**) If a firm which has the contract to do a job **subcontracts** some of the work to another firm, it pays the other firm to do it. The second firm is called the **subcontractor.** An arrangement or agreement like this is called a **subcontract.**

subculture A **subculture** is the ideas, art, and way of life of a particular group within a larger society.

subcutaneous (*pron:* sub-cute-**ayn**-ee-uss) means located or applied immediately beneath the skin. *...subcutaneous fat.*

subdivide (**subdividing, subdivided; subdivision**) If an area is **subdivided,** it is split up into smaller areas. The smaller areas are called **subdivisions.**

subdue (**subduing, subdued**) If soldiers or the police **subdue** a group of people, they defeat them or bring them under control using force. ■ If someone's behaviour is **subdued,** he or she is unusually quiet, because they are sad or worried. When a lot of people behave like this, you can say the atmosphere is **subdued.** ■ If things like lights or sounds are **subdued,** they are soft and muted, rather than bright or loud.

sub-editor A **sub-editor** is a person whose job is to check and correct articles in newspapers or magazines before they are published.

sub-human If someone is treated as **sub-human,** they are treated in a cruel or uncaring way, as if they were not really a human being.

subject (**subjection**) The **subject** of something such as a book or film is what it is about. ■ The **subject** of something like a photograph or a documentary is the main person or thing in it. ■ A **subject** is an area of study, for example maths. ■ The **subjects** of a king or queen are the people they rule. ■ **Subject** people or countries are controlled by the government of another country. ■ If an activity is **subject** to a law or rule, it has to obey that law or rule. *Newspaper mergers are subject to the Fair Trading Act 1973.* ■ If you are **subject** to something unpleasant, you are affected by it. *Sarajevo's residents were subject to a constant barrage of firepower.* ■ If someone **subjects** (*pron:* sub-**jects**) you to something unpleasant, they make you experience it. *He was subjected to continual racist taunts.* ■ If someone **subjects** someone to their control, they completely control them. *He was subjected to her will. ...the subjection of Britain to the Romans.*

subjective (**subjectively, subjectivity**) If you say someone is being **subjective,** you mean they are allowing their personal feelings to influence what they say or write; you can also talk about their **subjectivity.** *I reacted not as an ordinary member of an audience but very subjectively as an appalled and outraged mother.* See also **objective.**

sub judice (*pron:* sub joo-diss-ee) If something is **sub judice,** the media are not allowed to comment on it because it is the subject of a trial which is currently taking place.

subjugate (*pron:* **sub**-joo-gate) (**subjugating, subjugated; subjugation**) If someone **subjugates** a group of people, they take complete control of them, usually by defeating them in a war. *...brutal subjugation of native tribes.* ■ If someone's wishes are **subjugated** to someone or something else, they are treated as less important. *We must all subjugate ourselves to the rules of democracy.*

sub-let (**sub-letting, sub-let** *not* '*sub-letted*') If you **sub-let** a building or part of a building which you are renting, you rent it to someone else.

sublimate (**sublimating, sublimated; sublimation**) If you **sublimate** a strong desire or feeling, you express it in a different way, often a way which is more socially acceptable.

sublime (**sublimely**) If you say something is **sublime**, you mean it is so wonderful or beautiful that it affects you emotionally. *...some of the most sublime scenery on earth.*

subliminal (**subliminally**) **Subliminal** images or messages influence your mind without you being aware of it. *...subliminal advertising.*

sub-machine gun A **sub-machine gun** is a portable machine gun with a short barrel.

submarine A **submarine** is a ship which can travel either on or beneath the surface of the sea.

submerge (**submerging, submerged**) When something like a submarine **submerges**, it goes beneath the surface of the sea. ■ If something is **submerged,** it is completely covered by water. ■ If you are **submerged** by something that happens, you are overwhelmed by it. *His main thrust is reported to be preventing Tibetan culture becoming submerged by the influx of Chinese.* ■ If you **submerge** yourself in an activity, you give all your time and attention to it. *She submerged herself in academic work.*

submersible equipment is designed for use under water. A **submersible** is a small submarine designed to operate at depths which a diver cannot reach.

submission See **submit.**

submissive (**submissively**) If someone is **submissive,** they are quiet and obedient.

submit (**submitting, submitted; submission**) If you **submit** to something, you accept it because you are not powerful enough to resist it. You can talk about your **submission** to something. ■ If you **submit** a proposal or application to someone, you send it to them so they can decide what action to take.

subordinate (**subordinating, subordinated; subordination**) A person's **subordinate** is someone in a less important position than them. ■ If one thing or person is **subordinate** to another, they are considered to be less important. If you **subordinate** one thing to another, you treat it as less important. *...the subordination of economic goals to political ones... The movement questioned whether work was the answer to women's subordination.*

suborn If someone is **suborned,** they are bribed or incited to do something wrong.

subpoena (*pron:* sub-**pee**-na) (**subpoenaing, subpoenaed**) A **subpoena** is a legal document ordering a person to attend a court to give evidence or testimony. If someone is **subpoenaed,** they are issued with a subpoena. If evidence is **subpoenaed,** it must be produced in a court of law.

sub-post office A **sub-post office** is a small branch post office, often run as part of a shop.

sub-Saharan is used to refer to African countries south of the Sahara desert where people are mainly of African rather than Arab origin.

subscribe (**subscribing, subscribed; subscriber**) If you **subscribe** to a particular belief or opinion, you hold it. ■ If you **subscribe** to a magazine or newspaper or are one of its **subscribers,** you pay to receive it regularly. You can also **subscribe** to a service. ■ If you **subscribe** to a charity or campaign or are one of its **subscribers,** you send it money regularly. ■ If you **subscribe** for shares in a company, you apply to buy them.

subscription A **subscription** is an amount of money you pay regularly in order to belong to an organization, to help a charity or campaign, or to receive copies of a magazine or newspaper.

sub-section of a document is one of the smaller parts which its main parts are divided into. *...Section 19, Sub-section 11.*

subsequent (**subsequently**) You use **subsequent** to describe something which happens or comes into being later than something else.

subservient (**subservience**) If someone is **subservient,** they do whatever someone else wants them to. When someone behaves like this, you talk about their **subservience.** ■ If you treat one thing as **subservient** to another, you treat it as less important than the other thing. *The game has become increasingly subservient to the demands of sponsorship.*

subside (**subsiding, subsided; subsidence**) If water **subsides,** it sinks to a lower level. ■ If the ground **subsides,** parts of it sink. When this happens, you say there is **subsidence.** ■ You talk about things **subsiding** when they become less intense. *It took six hours before the pain subsided.*

subsidiarity In the EU, **subsidiarity** is the principle of allowing individual member states to make decisions on issues which specifically affect them, rather than leaving those decisions to the European Commission.

subsidiary (**subsidiaries**) A **subsidiary** or **subsidiary** company is a company which is part of a larger company. ■ **Subsidiary** is used to describe something which is less important than another thing it is connected with. *In addition to the principal crops, the tenants produced subsidiary crops which belonged entirely to them.*

subsidize (*or* **subsidise**) (**subsidizing, subsidized; subsidization**) If a government or other authority **subsidizes** something, they pay part of its cost. *...subsidized housing. ...the subsidization of Japanese agriculture.*

subsidy (**subsidies**) A **subsidy** is money paid by a government or other authority to help an industry or business, or to pay for a public service.

subsist If people **subsist**, they are just able to obtain the food or money they need in order to stay alive.

subsistence If someone lives at **subsistence** level, their income is barely enough to support them. ■ **Subsistence** farms produce just enough food to support the people who live there, with no surplus left to sell.

subsoil The **subsoil** is a layer of infertile soil lying between the surface soil and the rock beneath.

subsonic speeds are very fast, but not as fast as the speed of sound. **Subsonic** aircraft fly at these speeds. See also **supersonic.**

sub-species (*plural:* **sub-species**) A **sub-species** of a plant or animal is a group within the species which has characteristics distinguishing it from other members of the species.

substance Any solid, powder, liquid, or paste can be called a **substance.** ■ You can refer to the actions of drug users who take a lot of chemically manufactured drugs for social rather than medicinal reasons as **substance abuse.** ■ If you say there is **substance** to what someone says, you mean they are saying something meaningful and important. *There seems some substance to the opposition's grievance.* ■ The **substance** of what someone says is the main point they are making. ■ A person **of substance** is someone with a lot of money, power, and influence.

sub-standard (*or* **substandard**) A **sub-standard** product or service is unacceptable because it is below a required standard.

substantial (**substantially**) A **substantial** amount or change is a very large one. ■ **Substantial** is used to describe things which are large and very solid or strong. *...substantial Victorian houses.*

substantiate (**substantiating, substantiated; substantiation**) If you **substantiate** a statement or story, you provide evidence to prove it is true.

substantive is used to describe things which have real importance or significance. *...substantive progress.*

sub-station A **sub-station** is a place where high voltage electricity from power plants is converted to lower voltage electricity for homes or factories.

substitute (**substituting, substituted; substitution**) If you **substitute** one thing for another, you use it instead of the other thing or put it in the other thing's place. *...the substitution of machinery for human labour.* ■ A **substitute** is something you have or use instead of something else. *This oil could be used as a substitute for diesel.* ■ If you say one thing is no **substitute** for another, you are emphasising that it is unsatisfactory because it lacks the qualities of the other thing. *Trial and error is no substitute for thinking and planning.* ■ In team games, a **substitute** is a player who comes on to replace another player during a match. When this happens, you say the team makes a **substitution.**

substructure The **substructure** of a large structure like a bridge is its foundations or framework. You can also refer to the basis or framework of something like a large organization as its **substructure.**

subsume (**subsuming, subsumed**) If one thing is **subsumed** into another, it becomes a part of it and is no longer a separate thing.

subterfuge is a trick or dishonest way of getting what you want.

subterranean is used to talk about things under the ground. *...a subterranean labyrinth of rivers and caverns.*

subtext The **subtext** of a piece of writing or a film is its underlying subject or message. *There was always an erotic subtext to the Dracula films.*

subtitle (**subtitling, subtitled**) The **subtitle** of something like a book or film is a second title, which is often longer and explains more than the main title. *Ken Hom's recent book, Fragrant Harbour Taste, is subtitled 'The New Chinese Cooking of Hong Kong'.* ■ **Subtitles** are (a) the printed translation displayed at the bottom of the screen when a foreign film is shown. (b) a printed display at the bottom of a TV screen, shown for people with hearing difficulties.

subtle (*pron:* **sut**-tl) (**subtly; subtlety, subtleties**) **Subtle** is used to describe something which is not immediately obvious or noticeable. *...subtle changes in the earth's environment.* Very small details and differences like these can be called **subtleties.** *...the subtleties of human nature.* ■ **Subtlety** is the ability to notice and recognize things which are not obvious, especially small differences between things. ■ You say a person is **subtle** or talk about their **subtlety** when they use clever indirect methods to achieve something. ■ **Subtle** can be used to describe things which are delicate or understated. *...subtle oriental flavours.*

subtract (**subtraction**) If you **subtract** one number from another, you take the first one away from the second. For example, if you subtract 3 from 5, you get 2. Subtracting numbers is called **subtraction.**

sub-tropical (*or* **subtropical**) is used to describe the parts of the world between the tropical and temperate regions, which have no cold season. *...sub-tropical Florida. ...a steamy, subtropical island.*

suburb (**suburban, suburbanite**) The **suburbs** of a town or city are the residential areas outside its centre. **Suburban** is used to talk about things to do with suburbs; you can call people who live in suburbs **suburbanites.**

suburbia A city's suburbs are sometimes called **suburbia.** *...leafy suburbia.*

subvention A **subvention** is a grant or subsidy from a government or other authority.

subversive (**subversion**) **Subversive** activities are aimed at weakening or destroying a political system or government. Activities like these are called **subversion;** the people taking part in them are sometimes called **subversives.**

subvert If someone **subverts** something, they undermine it or make it fail. *Democrats accused the President of subverting America's foreign policy for political ends.*

subway A **subway** is a passage for pedestrians underneath a busy road. ■ In the US, a **subway** is an underground railway.

succeed If you **succeed** in doing something, you manage to do it. ■ If something **succeeds**, it has the result you want. ■ You can say someone **succeeds** when they do well in their life. ■ If you **succeed** another person, you take over their job when they leave. ■ If one thing **succeeds** another, it comes after it.

success (**successes**) Success is achieving something you have been trying to achieve. If something is a **success**, it achieves what it was intended to achieve. ■ If you are a **success** at something like your job, you do it very well.

successful (**successfully**) If you are **successful**, you achieve what you have set out to do. If something is **successful**, it achieves what it was intended to achieve. *Bone-marrow cells could be successfully transplanted.* ■ You say a person is **successful** when they do well in their life.

succession A **succession** of people or things is a number of them coming one after the other. *The country was ruled by a succession of military leaders.* ■ If something happens, for example, for a number of weeks **in succession**, it happens each week for that number of weeks. ■ **Succession** is being in line to take over or actually taking over an important job or position. *She is fourth in line of succession to the throne.*

successive (**successively**) Successive is used to talk about people or things coming one after another. *During his 34 years with the company he served under ten successive chairmen... They lived successively in Oxford, Ludlow and Cambridge.*

successor Someone's **successor** is the person who takes over their job when they leave. ■ The **successor** to something is the thing which replaces it.

succinct (*pron:* suk-**sinkt**) (**succinctly**) If something like a statement is **succinct**, it is expressed clearly and in very few words.

succour (*Am:* succor) (*pron:* suk-kur) If you give **succour** to someone, you give them help or support.

succulent food is juicy and delicious.

succumb If you **succumb** to persuasion or temptation, you give in to it. ■ If you **succumb** to an illness, you are badly affected or you die from it.

such You use **such** to talk about things of the kind you have just mentioned. *His members are voting on a strike. British Coal warned miners that such action would result in the loss of redundancy payments.* ■ You use **such as** when you are giving an example of something. *...early Italian painters such as Giotto.* ■ You use **such** to emphasize your description of something. *It's all been such fun.* ■ You use **such and such** to talk about a particular thing of a certain kind, without saying which one. *He can find 25 reasons why such and such a proposal is rubbish.* ■ You say **such as it is** to show you think something is not very good or not very significant. *Her cash, such as it was, was to go to me.*

suchlike means other things like the ones just mentioned. *...mince, barbecue kebabs and suchlike.*

suck If you **suck** something, you hold it in your mouth and pull at it with the muscles in your cheeks and tongue, for example to get liquid out of it. ■ If something is **sucked** somewhere, it is drawn there by a powerful force. *About 170 birds a year are sucked into aircraft engines.* ■ If you are **sucked** into a bad situation, you are unable to stop yourself becoming involved in it. ■ You can say a person is **sucking up** to someone in authority when they try to please them by flattering them or doing things for them.

sucker If you call someone a **sucker**, you mean they are easily tricked or cheated. ■ If you say you are a **sucker** for something, you mean you enjoy it very much and find it difficult to resist. *I'm a sucker for anything sung in French.* ■ A **sucker** is a rubber device which can attach itself to a surface by suction. ■ Some animals and insects have pads called **suckers** on their bodies which they use to cling to a surface.

suckle (**suckling, suckled**) When a mother **suckles** her baby, she feeds it with milk from her breast. You also say the baby **suckles**.

sucrose (*pron:* **syoo**-kroze) is sugar in crystalline form extracted from sugar cane or sugar beet.

suction is the force involved when a substance is drawn or sucked from one place to another. ■ **Suction** is the process by which two surfaces stick together when the air between them is removed.

sudden (**suddenly, suddenness**) You use **sudden** to describe things which happen quickly and unexpectedly. *...a sudden rise in house prices.*

sudden-death In sport, a **sudden-death** play-off is an extra game between two competitors who have finished with an equal score. In the play-off, the first competitor to take the lead is the winner.

sudden infant death syndrome See **SIDS**.

suds are the bubbles produced when soap is mixed with water.

sue (**suing, sued**) If you **sue** someone, you start a legal case against them, usually to claim money from them because they have harmed you in some way. ■ If someone **sues for** something, they formally ask for it. *He may hope to fight for a while, then stop and sue for peace.*

suede (*pron:* **swade**) is thin soft leather with a velvet-like surface.

suet is hard animal fat used in cooking.

suffer (**suffering, suffered; sufferer**) If you **suffer** pain, you feel it in your body or your mind. ■ If you **suffer** from an illness or from something such as stress or oppression, you are badly affected by it. ■ You say something **suffers** when it is badly affected by neglect or an unfavourable situation. *Sales to industry suffered because of recession.*

sufferance If you let someone do something **on sufferance**, you let them do it although you would rather they did not.

suffice (**sufficing, sufficed**) If something will **suffice**, it is enough for a particular purpose.

sufficient (**sufficiently; sufficiency**) Sufficient is used to say there is enough of something. *The facilities are not sufficient to meet demand... Analysts have questioned the sufficiency of the funding.*

suffix (**suffixes**) A **suffix** is a group of letters added at the end of a word to make a new word. For example, the suffix '-ist' can be added to 'sex' to form the word 'sexist'.

suffocate (suffocating, suffocates; suffocation) If someone **suffocates,** they die because they have too little air to breathe. ■ You can say you are **suffocating** when you feel as if you cannot breathe properly, for example in a hot and crowded room. **Suffocating** is used to describe situations like this. *During the summer the heat was suffocating.* ■ You say people are **suffocated** when they are prevented from developing properly. *Suffocated by male prejudice, the women have no opportunity to fulfill their potential.*

suffrage is the right to vote in the election of a government or national leader.

suffragette A **suffragette** was a woman involved in the campaign to get women the right to vote.

suffuse (suffusing, suffused) If something is **suffused** with light or colour, the light or colour is spread over it or through it. Similarly, you can talk about an experience or piece of writing being **suffused** with a certain feeling. *The book is suffused with great sadness.*

sugar (sugaring, sugared) Sugar is a sweet substance, often in the form of white crystals. If you **sugar** a drink, you add sugar to it.

sugar beet is a plant with a large white parsnip-shaped root from which sugar is obtained.

sugar cane is a tall tropical plant with thick stems. Sugar is obtained from its sap.

sugar daddy A young woman's **sugar daddy** is an older man who gives her money and presents, in return for her companionship or sexual favours.

sugar lump A **sugar lump** is a small cube of sugar, for putting in tea or coffee.

sugary food and drinks contain a lot of sugar. ■ **Sugary** is used to describe things which are excessively sentimental. *...sugary images of women as happy housewives.*

suggest If you **suggest** a plan or idea to someone, you mention it as a possibility for them to consider. ■ If something **suggests** something is true or will happen, it makes you think it is true or will happen. *Opinion polls are suggesting a close race.*

suggestible A **suggestible** person is easily influenced by what other people say.

suggestion A **suggestion** is a plan or idea mentioned as a possibility for someone to consider. ■ If there is a **suggestion** of something, there is a slight indication or faint sign of it. *There was no suggestion of yellowness in the blooms.*

suggestive (suggestively, suggestiveness) If one thing is **suggestive** of another, it makes you think of it. *The clink of ice in tall glasses is suggestive of hot sunny days.* ■ **Suggestive** remarks or gestures are meant to suggest something sexually indecent.

suicide (suicidal, suicidally) People who commit **suicide** deliberately kill themselves. If people are **suicidal,** they want to kill themselves. ■ **Suicidal** behaviour is so dangerous it is likely to result in death. ■ You say someone's behaviour is **suicide** or **suicidal** when they do something which is likely to ruin their future prospects. *...political suicide.*

sui generis (*pron:* **soo**-ee **jen**-e-ris) If you describe a person or thing as **sui generis,** you mean they are unique and cannot be judged by comparing them with another person or thing.

suit (suiting, suited) A **suit** is a jacket and matching trousers or skirt. ■ Clothing worn for a particular purpose is called a **suit.** *...a space suit.* ■ If a situation or course of action **suits** you, it is appropriate for your purpose. ■ If a piece of clothing or a colour **suits** you, it looks good on you. ■ If you do something to **suit** yourself, you do it for your own benefit, without considering other people ■ A **suit** is a legal action taken by one person against another. ■ A **suit** is one of the four types of playing cards. ■ You say someone **follows suit,** when they do the same as someone else has just done. *Some companies have cut their dividends, and BP is expected to follow suit.* ■ Your **strong suit** is the thing you are best at.

suitable (suitably, suitability) If someone or something is **suitable** for a certain purpose or occasion, they are right or acceptable for it.

suitcase A **suitcase** is a portable case for carrying your clothes when you are travelling.

suite (*pron:* **sweet**) A **suite** is (a) a set of rooms, for example in a hotel. (b) a set of matching furniture or bathroom fittings. (c) a piece of music, made up of several short pieces. ■ See also **en suite.**

suitor In the past, a man who was courting a woman and hoped to marry her was called her **suitor.** ■ A person or organization hoping to take over a company can be called a **suitor.**

sulfate See **sulphate.**

sulfur See **sulphur.**

sulk (sulky, sulkily) If someone **sulks** or goes into a **sulk,** they are silent or bad-tempered for a while, because they are annoyed. When someone behaves like this, you say they are being **sulky.**

sullen (sullenly) A **sullen** person is bad-tempered and does not speak much.

sully (sullies, sullying, sullied) If someone **sullies** something, they spoil it or make it dirty.

sulphate (*Am:* **sulfate**) A **sulphate** is a chemical compound formed when sulphuric acid reacts with a metal.

sulphur (*Am:* **sulfur**) is a chemical element which exists on its own in a yellow crystalline form which has an unpleasant smell when burnt. It is also found in various other compounds.

sulphur dioxide is a colourless poisonous gas with a strong unpleasant smell.

sulphuric acid is a colourless oily highly corrosive acid.

sulphurous (*Am:* **sulfurous**) is used to describe things which contain sulphur or one of its compounds, especially things which have a strong unpleasant smell.

sultan (sultanate) In some Muslim countries, the ruler is called a **sultan.** A country ruled by a sultan is called a **sultanate.**

sultana – **Sultanas** are dried grapes.

sultanate See **sultan.**

sultry weather is unpleasantly hot and humid. ■ If a man or especially a woman is described as **sul-**

try, they are attractive In a way which suggests hidden passion.

sum (summing, summed) A **sum** of money is an amount of it. ■ A **sum** is a simple calculation in arithmetic. ■ The **sum** of something, is the whole of it. *Has it added much to the sum of human happiness?* ■ If you say something is **more than the sum of** its **parts,** you mean it is better than you would expect from its individual parts, because the way they combine adds a different quality. ■ If you **sum** something **up,** you briefly describe its essential character. You call the speech a judge makes to a jury at the end of a trial, reminding them of the trial's main points, his or her **summing up.** ■ See also **lump sum.**

summarize (*or* **summarise) (summarizing, summarized)** If you **summarize** something, you give a brief description of its main points.

summary (summaries; summarily) A **summary** is a short account of something, giving the main points but not the details. ■ A **summary** action is carried out without delay and without careful consideration. *...summary executions.*

summation A **summation** is the same as a summing-up. See **sum.** ■ If something you have produced is a **summation** of all your earlier work or experiences, it is the result of everything you have learned from them.

summer is the season between spring and autumn when the weather is usually warm.

summerhouse A **summerhouse** is a small building in a garden where you can sit in the shade.

summer school A **summer school** is an educational course on a particular subject which is run during the summer.

summer time See **BST.**

summery is used to describe things which are suitable for summer or typical of summer.

summing-up See **sum.**

summit (summitry, summiteer) A **summit** is a meeting between the leaders of different countries. **Summitry** is conducting negotiations by meetings of this kind. The leaders taking part can be called **summiteers.** ■ The **summit** of a mountain is its top.

summon (summoning, summoned) If you are **summoned** somewhere, you are ordered to go there. ■ If someone **summons** a meeting, they tell people to come to it. ■ If you **summon up** a quality such as strength or courage, you make a great effort to be strong or brave. ■ If something **summons up** a vague memory, it brings it back.

summons (summonses, summonsed) A **summons** is an official order to appear in court. You say someone is **summonsed** to appear in court. ■ A **summons** is an order to go and see someone. *I received a summons to the Palace.*

sumo is a traditional Japanese style of wrestling.

sump The **sump** is the place under an engine which holds the engine oil.

sumptuous (sumptuously, sumptuousness) Sumptuous things are splendid or luxurious and obviously expensive. *...a sumptuous buffet.*

sun (sunning, sunned) The **sun** is the star which the planet Earth revolves around. You can refer to heat and light which reach us from the sun as the **sun.** *He sat in the sun reading books.* ■ If you are **sunning** yourself, you are sitting or lying in the sun.

sunbathe (sunbathing, sunbathed; sunbather) When people **sunbathe,** they lie in the sun to get a tan. A person who does this is called a **sunbather.**

sunbeam — Sunbeams are rays of light from the sun.

sunbed A **sunbed** is (a) a sun lounger. (b) a bed-like structure with sun lamps above it which people lie on to get a tan.

sunblock is the same as sunscreen.

sunburn (sunburnt *or* **sunburned)** If you have **sunburn** or are **sunburnt,** your skin is red and sore because you have spent too much time in the sun. ■ You say someone is **sunburnt** when their skin has become permanently brown because they have spent a long period of their life in the sun.

sun cream is the same as sunscreen.

sundae A **sundae** is a glass of ice cream with cream, nuts, a sweet sauce, and fruit on top.

Sunday school is a special class held on Sundays for children to learn about Christianity.

sundeck On a passenger ship, a **sundeck** is an open upper deck.

sundial A **sundial** is a device for telling the time. It has a pointer which casts a shadow on a flat base on which the hours of the day are marked.

sundown is an American word for sunset.

sun-drenched places have a lot of hot sunny weather. *...a sun-drenched beach.*

sundry things are of many different kinds. *...sundry stolen goods.* ■ **All and sundry** means 'everyone'.

sunflower — Sunflowers are tall plants with very large yellow flowers. The seeds are edible and are also used to make cooking oil.

sung See **sing.**

sunglasses are spectacles with dark lenses to protect your eyes from bright sunlight.

sunk See **sink.**

sunken is used (a) to describe things which have sunk to the bottom of the sea, a lake, or a river. *...a sunken wreck.* (b) to describe things built below the level of the surrounding area. *...a sunken bath.* ■ If part of a person's face is **sunken,** it seems to sink or curve inwards and makes them look thin and unwell. *...sunken cheeks.*

sun-kissed means the same as 'sun-drenched'.

sun lamp (*or* **sunlamp)** A **sun lamp** is a lamp which produces ultraviolet rays, and which people use to make their skin look tanned.

sunlight (sunlit) Sunlight is the light which reaches the Earth from the sun. If something is **sunlit,** it is brightly lit by the sun.

sun lounge A **sun lounge** is a room with walls made mostly of glass so that a lot of sunlight gets in.

sun lounger A **sun lounger** is a type of bed for sunbathing on.

sunny (sunnier, sunniest) When it is **sunny,** the sun is shining. ■ A **sunny** place is brightly lit by the sun.

sunrise is the time when the sun first appears above the horizon. A **sunrise** is the colours and light you see in the sky when this is happening.

sunroof A **sunroof** is a part of the roof of a car which you can open to let air in.

sunscreen is a cream which helps stop you getting burned by the sun, by blocking out ultraviolet rays.

sunset is the time when the sun goes down below the horizon. A **sunset** is the colours and light you see in the sky when this is happening.

sunshade A **sunshade** is a type of umbrella for protecting yourself from strong sunlight.

sunshine is the light and heat which comes from the sun.

sunspot – **Sunspots** are dark patches which appear temporarily on the sun's surface. They have a strong magnetic field.

sunstroke is an illness caused by spending too much time in very hot sunshine.

suntan (**suntanned**) If you have a **suntan** or are **suntanned,** the sun has turned your skin darker than usual. **Suntan** lotions and oils protect your skin from the sun and help you develop a suntan.

sup (**supping, supped**) If you **sup** something, you drink it.

super People say something is **super** when they are very pleased or excited by it. *What a super idea!*

super- is used (a) to form words which describe something as having a quality to an unusually large degree. *...a tiny super-rich state.* (b) to form words which describe things as being bigger, more powerful, or more important than other things of their kind. *...super-computers.*

superabundance If there is a **superabundance** of something, there is a very large amount of it, often more than is wanted or needed.

superannuated is used to describe people who no longer do the work they have done in the past, because they are too old for it. *...superannuated DJs.*

superannuation is money people pay regularly into a special fund so they will get a regular pension when they retire.

superb (**superbly**) If you say someone or something is **superb,** you mean they are very good indeed. *...superbly engineered cars.*

superbug A **superbug** is a tiny organism that causes infection and is too strong to be killed by antibiotics.

supercharged (**supercharger**) A **supercharged** engine has a device called a **supercharger** which increases the engine's power by forcing extra air in.

supercilious people are scornful of other people and think they are superior to them.

superconductor A **superconductor** is a substance which has almost no electrical resistance at temperatures close to absolute zero. Superconductors are used in making powerful electromagnets.

superficial (**superficially, superficiality**) If you describe something as **superficial** or talk about its **superficiality,** you mean it deals with only the most obvious or easily understood aspects of a subject. ■ **Superficial** people do not care very deeply about anything serious or important. ■ **Superficial** is used to describe the first impres-

sion something gives, especially when this does not reflect what it is really like. *...the superficial appearance of calm.* ■ A **superficial** wound is not deep or severe.

superfluous (*pron:* soo-**per**-flew-uss) If something is **superfluous,** it is unnecessary or no longer needed.

supergrass (**supergrasses**) A **supergrass** is a criminal who informs on serious crimes to the police.

superhero (**superheroes**) A **superhero** is a comic strip character with superhuman abilities or magic powers who fights against evil.

superhighway In the US, a **superhighway** is a long-distance motorway which vehicles can travel along at high speeds. ■ The **information superhighway** is the name given to the worldwide communications network which will enable people to send and receive information by computer anywhere in the world, and to have access to a range of services via their TV sets.

superhuman is used to talk about a quality or ability someone has which is greater than that of ordinary people. *...superhuman strength.*

superimpose (**superimposing, superimposed**) If one image is **superimposed** on another, the first one appears on top of the second.

superintend If you **superintend** an activity or the people doing it, you make sure it is carried out properly.

superintendent In the police force, a **superintendent** is an officer above the rank of inspector, but lower in rank than a chief superintendent. ■ A **superintendent** is someone who is officially responsible for an activity or department.

superior (**superiority**) **Superior** things are of higher quality than other things of their kind. You talk about the **superiority** of things like these. ■ If one army is **superior** to another, it is more powerful. *...their overwhelming military superiority.* ■ If someone is **superior** to you in an organization, they have a higher position than you. You call someone like this your **superior.** ■ A **superior** person behaves in a way which shows that they believe they are better than other people. *...feelings of superiority.*

superlative (*pron:* soo-**per**-lat-iv) (**superlatively**) **Superlative** is used to describe things which are of the highest quality. *...a superlative performance.* ■ **Superlatives** are words which are used to say that a person or thing has more of a quality than anyone or anything else. For example, 'biggest', 'smallest', and 'most remarkable' are superlatives.

superman (**supermen**) If you call a man a **superman,** you mean he has extraordinary physical or mental powers.

supermarket A **supermarket** is a large shop selling many kinds of food and household goods.

supermodel – **Supermodels** are highly-paid famous fashion models.

supernatural is used to describe things like ghosts which some people believe exist and which cannot be explained by normal scientific laws. *...supernatural powers.* Things like these are referred to as **the supernatural.**

supernova (*plural:* **supernovae** *or* **supernovas**) A **supernova** is a star which explodes and for a few days becomes much brighter than the sun.

superpower A **superpower** is a very powerful and influential country.

supersede (**superseding, superseded**) If one thing **supersedes** another, it replaces it, usually because it is better or more efficient.

supersonic aircraft can travel faster than the speed of sound.

superstar (**superstardom**) Very famous entertainers or sports players are sometimes called **superstars**. **Superstardom** is being a superstar.

superstition (**superstitious**) **Superstition** is belief in magic or in powers which bring good or bad luck. Beliefs like these are called **superstitions**. You say someone who has these beliefs is **superstitious**.

superstore A **superstore** is a very large supermarket.

superstructure The **superstructure** of a ship is the part above the main deck.

supervise (**supervising, supervised; supervision**) If you **supervise** an activity or the people doing it, you make sure it is done properly. ■ If you do something **under supervision**, someone supervises you while you are doing it. A **supervisor** is someone who supervises activities or people, especially an employee who supervises workers or a tutor who supervises students.

supervisory means to do with supervising activities or people. ...*a supervisory position.*

supine (*pron:* **soo**-pine) If you are **supine**, you are lying flat on your back. See also **prone**. ■ **Supine** is used to describe people who let things happen and do not try to influence them, because they are too lazy or afraid. ...*a largely supine press.*

supper is a meal eaten in the early part of the evening or just before going to bed.

supplant If one person or thing **supplants** another, they take their place.

supple (**suppleness**) A **supple** person moves and bends easily and gracefully. ■ If an object or material is **supple,** it is flexible and bends easily without cracking or breaking.

supplement (**supplementary**) If you **supplement** something, you add something else to it. The thing you add is called a **supplement.** *Lower-grade civil servants supplement their wages with other work.* ...*vitamin C supplements.* **Supplementary** things are added to other things. ...*a supplementary budget.* ■ A **supplement** is an extra amount of money you pay to get special facilities or services, for example when you are travelling or staying at a hotel. ■ A newspaper or magazine **supplement** is a separate part which comes with a newspaper or magazine, often covering a particular range of subjects. See also **colour supplement.**

supplemental means the same as 'supplementary'. ...*supplemental legislation.*

supplementary See **supplement.**

supplication (**supplicant**) **Supplication** is humbly asking or pleading for something. A person who does this is called a **supplicant.**

supply (**supplies, supplying, supplied; supplier**) If you **supply** someone with something, you provide them with it, by giving or selling it to them. A **supply** of something is an amount which is being supplied. A **supplier** is a person, company, or country that supplies something. ■ **Supply** is the amount of a commodity which can be made available for people to buy. ...*as the demand for silver begins to exceed supply.* ■ **Supplies** are food, equipment, and other things needed by a group of people over a period of time, for example people going on an expedition.

supply teacher A **supply teacher** is a teacher who stands in for other teachers at different schools when they are absent.

support (**supporting**) If you **support** someone, you agree with their aims and want them to succeed. *Support for the Christian Democrats slumped.* ■ If you **support** someone or give them **support,** you provide them with money or other things they need. *The reservists will give medical support to the British forces.* ■ If you give **support** to someone who is having a difficult time, you are kind to them and help them. ■ If you **support** a sports team, you go regularly to their games and cheer them on. ■ In a play or film, the **supporting** actors are those in minor roles. ■ If something **supports** an object, it is underneath it and holding it up. Something which does this is called a **support.** ■ If you **support** yourself, you prevent yourself from falling by holding onto something or leaning against it. ■ If a fact **supports** a statement or theory, it helps to show it is correct.

supporter A **supporter** is someone who supports something, for example a political party or a sports team. ...*a Leeds United supporter.*

supportive If you are **supportive,** you are kind and helpful to someone at a difficult time. ■ If you are **supportive** of someone or their aims, you show your support for them. *The team has been very supportive of my decision.*

suppose (**supposing, supposed; supposedly**) If you **suppose** something is true, you think it is true. *It is a fallacy to suppose that a single currency implies political union.* ■ If something is **supposed** to be true, people generally think it is true. *There are supposed to be large amounts of oil underneath the Gobi Desert.* ■ **Supposed** is used to show doubt about a way of describing someone or something, or about the truth of something. *Fewer and fewer of his supposed allies stick up for him in public.* ...*supposedly accidental deaths.* ■ If something is **supposed** to be done, it ought to be done, according to a rule or plan. *They've given us notice to quit – we're supposed to be out by 22nd March... The first shipment is supposed to be ready on Friday.* If you say something **was supposed** to happen, you mean it was planned or intended to happen, but did not in fact happen. ...*a new truck factory which was supposed to have been built near Berlin.* ■ You use **suppose** when you are considering a possible situation or action and trying to think what effects it would have. *Suppose I'd paid in cash? It would have been their word against mine.*

supposition is taking certain things to be true, often without any firm evidence. *Much of the report was based on supposition or inaccuracy.* A **supposition** is something which is taken to be true. *There's a popular supposition that we're publicly funded, but the bulk of our money comes from competitive contracts.*

suppository (**suppositories**) A **suppository** is a solid medicine inserted into the rectum or vagina, where it melts.

suppress (**suppresses, suppressed; suppression, suppressor**) If people in authority **suppress** an activity, they stop it continuing. ■ If information is **suppressed**, people are deliberately prevented from hearing about it. ■ If you **suppress** your feelings, you do not express them. ■ If something like a drug **suppresses** a disease, it stops it developing.

suppurate (**suppurating, suppurated**) When a wound **suppurates**, it produces pus.

supranational (*or* **supra-national**) (**supranationalism**) **Supranational** is used to describe things which cross national borders and involve more than one country. *...supranational institutions.* **Supranationalism** is the setting up of systems and organizations which involve more than one country.

supremacist A **supremacist** is someone who believes that a particular group of people should be more powerful and have more influence than other groups. *...white supremacists.*

supremacy If one group of people has **supremacy** over another, they are more powerful and can therefore control or defeat them.

supreme is used in a title to show that a person or group is at the highest level of an organization. *...NATO's Supreme Allied Commander in Europe. ...the Supreme Court.* ■ **Supreme** means the greatest possible. *He showed supreme confidence.*

supremely means 'extremely'. *...his supremely happy marriage.*

supremo (**supremos**) A **supremo** is someone who has overall charge of something. *...China's economic supremo.*

surcharge (**surcharging, surcharged**) A **surcharge** is an extra amount of money paid in addition to the usual payment for something. *...an import surcharge.* If you are **surcharged**, you have to pay a surcharge.

sure (**surer, surest; sureness**) If you are **sure** about something, you are certain about it. ■ If someone is **sure** of themselves, they have a great deal of self-confidence. ■ If something is **sure** to happen, it will definitely happen. ■ If you **make sure** something is done, you check it or take action to see that it is done. ■ **Sure** is used to say something is reliable or accurate. *Swollen lymph glands are a sure sign of infection.* ■ **Sure** is used to talk about someone's ability to judge situations well and do things without making mistakes. *...his sure touch. ...the sureness and composure of Chelsea's performance.*

sure-fire is used to describe things which are certain to succeed. *...a sure-fire hit.*

sure-footed people or animals can move easily over uneven ground without falling. Similarly, you can say someone is **sure-footed** when they handle a difficult situation well without making mistakes.

surely You use **surely** to emphasize that something is certainly true, and often to express surprise that anyone could think differently. *Surely such weighty matters merit a higher level of debate?* ■ If something is happening **slowly but surely,** it is only happening gradually but seems likely to continue.

surety (**sureties**) A **surety** is something valuable, especially money, given as a guarantee that you or someone else will do a particular thing.

surf (**surfing, surfer**) **Surf** is the white foam formed by waves as they break near the shore. ■ When someone **surfs** or goes **surfing,** they ride on big waves in the sea on a special board called a **surfboard;** people who surf are called **surfers.** ■ If you **surf** the Internet, you go from website to website reading the information.

surface (**surfacing, surfaced**) The **surface** of an area of land or water is its top part. ■ When something like a submarine **surfaces,** it comes up to the surface of the water. ■ **Surface** is used to talk about methods of transport which involve travel across land or sea, rather than by air. *...surface mail.* ■ A **surface** is a flat area, for example the top of a table. ■ The **surface** or **surfaces** of a solid object are its outside parts. ■ If information **surfaces** or **comes to the surface,** it becomes known. If feelings **surface** or **come to the surface,** people start to show them.

surface-to-air missiles are fired from the land or sea at aircraft or other missiles.

surface-to-surface missiles are fired from the land or sea at targets on the ground or at sea.

surfboard See **surf.**

surfeit (*pron:* **sur-**fit) If there is a **surfeit** of something, there is too much of it.

surfing (**surfer**) See **surf.**

surge (**surging, surged**) A **surge** is a sudden large increase in something. You say something **surges** when it increases like this. ■ A **surge** is a sudden powerful movement of something. If something moves like this you say it **surges.** *The crowd surged forward.* ■ If a feeling or emotion **surges** in you or you feel a **surge** of it, you feel it suddenly and powerfully. *...a surge of optimism.*

surgeon A **surgeon** is a doctor who is specially trained to perform surgery.

surgery (**surgeries**) **Surgery** is medical treatment which involves cutting open a person's body to repair or remove a diseased or damaged part. ■ A **surgery** is the room or building where a doctor or dentist works. ■ A doctor's **surgery** is the time each day when he or she sees patients at the surgery. Similarly, an MP's **surgery** is a regular time when constituents can visit him or her to discuss their problems. ■ cosmetic surgery: see **cosmetic.** See also **plastic surgery.**

surgical (**surgically**) **Surgical** means to do with surgery. ■ If you describe a military action as a **surgical** strike, you mean that it was aimed very precisely at a special military target.

surgical spirit is a liquid made from methylated spirit and other chemicals, used to clean and sterilize wounds or surgical instruments.

surly (**surliness**) If you say someone is **surly** or talk about their **surliness,** you mean they are rude and bad-tempered.

surmise (**surmising, surmised**) If you **surmise** that something is true, you guess it must be true because of other things you know.

surmount If you **surmount** a difficulty, you deal with it successfully. ■ If one thing is **surmounted** by another, the second thing is on top of the first. ...*a slim square tower surmounted by a cross.*

surname Your **surname** is the name you share with other members of your family.

surpass (**surpasses, surpassing, surpassed**) If one person or thing **surpasses** another, the first is better than the second, or has more of a particular quality. *He was determined to surpass the achievements of his older brothers.* ■ If something **surpasses** expectations, it is better than it was expected to be.

surplice A **surplice** is a loose white knee-length garment worn over a cassock by priests and choir members in some churches.

surplus (**surpluses**) If there is a **surplus** of something, there is more than is needed. **Surplus** is used to describe something which is extra or is more than is needed. ■ If a country has a trade **surplus,** it exports more than it imports. ■ If a government has a budget **surplus,** it has spent less than it has received in revenues.

surprise (**surprising, surprised; surprisingly**) A **surprise** is an unexpected event, fact, or piece of news. ■ **Surprise** is used to describe unexpected things. ...*a surprise victory.* ■ **Surprise** is the feeling you have when something unexpected happens. *The Foreign Office has expressed surprise at these allegations.* You say something like this **surprises** you. ■ If something is **surprising,** it is unexpected or unusual and makes you feel surprised. *Picture quality is surprisingly good considering the tiny screen.* ■ If you **surprise** someone, you do something they were not expecting. ■ If something **takes you by surprise,** it was unexpected and you were not prepared for it.

surreal If you describe something as **surreal,** you mean the elements in it are combined in a strange and dreamlike way that you would not normally expect.

surrealism (**surrealist**) **Surrealism** is a style in art and literature in which ideas, images, or objects are combined in a strange dreamlike way. **Surrealist** means to do with surrealism. ...*surrealist cinema.* A **surrealist** is an artist or writer whose work is based on the ideas of surrealism.

surrealistic means the same as 'surreal'.

surrender (**surrendering, surrendered**) When people **surrender,** they stop fighting and accept that the other side has won. Doing this is called **surrender.** ■ If you **surrender** something to someone, you give it up to them. ...*a complete surrender of weapons.* ■ If you **surrender** to a temptation or feeling, you allow it to gain control over you.

surrender value The **surrender value** of a life insurance policy is the money you receive if you decide you no longer wish to continue with the policy.

surreptitious (**surreptitiously**) A **surreptitious** action is done secretly.

surrogate (**surrogacy**) **Surrogate** is used to describe someone or something that acts as a substitute for someone or something else. You call someone or something like this a **surrogate.** ■ A **surrogate mother** is a woman who has agreed to conceive and give birth to a baby for another woman who is unable to have children of her own. **Surrogacy** is conceiving and giving birth like this.

surround (**surrounding, surroundings**) If someone or something is **surrounded** by something, that thing is situated all around them. *The small churchyard was surrounded by a rusted wrought-iron fence.* ■ If soldiers or police **surround** a person or place, they spread out so they are in positions all the way round them. ■ If you **surround** yourself with particular people or things, you make sure you have a lot of them near you all the time. ■ **Surrounding** is used to describe the area round a place. ...*Leicester Square and the surrounding streets.* The area and environment around a place or person is called their **surroundings.** ...*his home surroundings.*

surtax is an additional tax on incomes higher than the level at which ordinary tax is paid. ...*imposing a surtax on millionaires.*

surtitles are brief translations of the text of an opera which are projected above the stage when the opera is being sung in a foreign language.

surveillance (*pron:* sur-**vay**-lanss) If someone is under **surveillance,** their activities are being closely watched, for example by the police.

survey A **survey** is an investigation in which a group of people are asked about their opinions or behaviour. ■ If an area of land is **surveyed,** it is measured or photographed from the air so a map can be made of it. Doing this is called **surveying.** ...*the surveying profession.* ■ If someone **surveys** a building, they examine it carefully for any structural problems, especially when someone is planning to buy it. An examination like this is called a **survey.** ■ If you **survey** something, you look carefully at the whole of it.

surveyor A **surveyor** is someone whose job is to survey land or buildings.

survive (**surviving, survived; survival**) If someone **survives** in a dangerous or difficult situation, they do not die. Staying alive in situations like these is called **survival.** ■ If you **survive** someone, you continue to live after they have died. *She is survived by two daughters.* ■ If something **survives,** it continues to exist. You can talk about its **survival.**

survivor A **survivor** of a disaster is someone involved in it who is still alive at the end of it. ■ If you say someone is a **survivor,** you mean they seem able to carry on with their way of life in spite of difficulties.

susceptible (**susceptibility, susceptibilities**) If someone is **susceptible** to something, they are very likely to be influenced or affected by it. *He is susceptible to flattery.* You can also describe someone as **susceptible** when they are easily influenced. ■ If you are **susceptible** to a disease or injury, you are likely to suffer from it. ■ A person's

susceptibilities are their feelings which can be easily hurt. *Their patriotic susceptibilities are being exploited for partisan purposes.*

sushi (*pron:* **soo**-shee) is a Japanese dish of rice with sweet vinegar, often served with raw fish.

suspect If you **suspect** that something is true, you have a feeling it is true. ■ If you **suspect** someone of doing something dishonest or unpleasant, you think they probably did it. ■ A person who is thought to be guilty of a crime is called a **suspect.** ■ If something is **suspect,** it cannot be trusted or cannot be regarded as genuine.

suspend (**suspension**) If something is **suspended** from a high place, it is hanging from it. ■ If an event or activity is **suspended,** it is stopped for a while. When this happens, you talk about its **suspension.** ■ If someone is **suspended,** they are prevented from holding a particular job for a period of time, usually as a punishment. ■ If a criminal receives a **suspended** sentence, they are given a prison sentence which they do not serve unless they commit another crime within a specified period. ■ If small bits of a substance are **suspended** in a liquid, they are floating in it without dissolving. A **suspension** is a liquid mixture containing bits of an undissolved substance. ■ A vehicle's **suspension** is the springs and shock absorbers which support its body and enable it to give a smooth ride.

suspenders are fastenings for holding up stockings. They hang down from a belt called a **suspender belt.** ■ In the US, braces for holding up trousers are called **suspenders.**

suspense is excitement or anxiety caused by not knowing what is going to happen next.

suspension See suspend.

suspension bridge A **suspension bridge** is a bridge supported from above by cables attached to towers.

suspicious (**suspiciously, suspicion**) If you are **suspicious** of someone, you feel they cannot be trusted. This feeling is called **suspicion.** ■ If you describe something as **suspicious,** you mean it makes you think something is wrong. *...suspiciously large sums of money.* ■ **Suspicion** is a belief or feeling that someone has committed a crime or done something wrong. ■ If you have a **suspicion** that something is true, you think it may be true.

suss (**susses, sussing, sussed**) If you **suss** someone **out,** you discover what their true character is. ■ If you **suss** something **out,** you discover how it works or how to do it.

sustain (**sustaining, sustained**) If you **sustain** something you have achieved, you manage to hold on to it or keep it going. *...economies that are capable of sustained growth.* ■ If something **sustains** someone, it keeps them alive. Similarly, if something **sustains** a system or organization, it keeps it going. ■ If something **sustains** you through a difficult time, it stops you becoming depressed or giving up what you are doing. ■ If you **sustain** something like a defeat, loss, or injury, it happens to you.

sustainable (**sustainably, sustainability**) If a plan or system is **sustainable,** it can be kept going. *...a sustainable ceasefire.* ■ **Sustainable** methods of farming ensure that natural resources remain available at a steady level and that no serious harm is done to the environment.

sustenance is food and drink. ■ If something gives you **sustenance,** it gives you help, strength, or encouragement when you are having difficulties. *The writers and artists she entertained drew real sustenance from her interest and support.*

suture (*pron:* **soo**-cher) **Sutures** are stitches used to sew up a wound.

svelte A **svelte** person is slim and elegant.

Svengali If you say someone is a **Svengali,** you mean they seem to have a sinister ability to control or influence others.

swab A **swab** is a small piece of cotton wool, sometimes on a short stick, used to clean a wound or to take a sample. A sample taken like this is also called a **swab.**

swaddle (*pron:* **swod**-dl) (**swaddling, swaddled**) If a baby is **swaddled,** it is wrapped tightly in strips of cloth to keep it warm or prevent it from moving.

swag is stolen property.

swagger (**swaggering, swaggered**) If you **swagger,** or walk with a **swagger,** you walk proudly, holding your body upright and swinging your hips.

swallow If you **swallow** something, you make it go from your mouth down into your stomach. ■ If you **swallow,** you make a movement in your throat as if you were swallowing something, because you are nervous or frightened. ■ If someone **swallows** a story or statement, they believe it completely. ■ If one thing is **swallowed up** by another, it becomes part of it and no longer has a separate identity of its own. ■ If something **swallows up** money or resources, it uses them up at an unacceptable rate. ■ The **swallow** is a bird with long pointed wings and a forked tail.

swam See swim.

swamp (**swampy**) A **swamp** is an area of permanently waterlogged land. **Swampy** land consists mainly of swamps. ■ If an area is **swamped,** it is filled with water, because there has been heavy rain or a flood. ■ If you are **swamped** by things, there are more of them than you can cope with. *...action that will save our cities from being swamped by cars.*

swan (**swanning, swanned**) **Swans** are large water birds which are usually white. ■ You say someone **swans** around when they move around in a leisurely, confident, and carefree way.

swanky (**swankier, swankiest**) **Swanky** is used to describe things which are smart and fashionable. *...swanky sports facilities.*

swansong ■ Someone's **swansong** is the last time they do something they are famous for.

swap (*or* **swop**) (**swapping, swapped**) If you **swap** something, you give it in exchange for something else. An arrangement like this is called a **swap.** ■ You say you **swap** something when you replace it with something else. *He is swapping his job for a rather less exacting one.* ■ If you **swap** stories or information with someone, you tell each other stories or give each other information.

swarm When bees or other insects **swarm**, they move or fly in a large group. A group of insects like this is called a **swarm**. You can also say people **swarm** somewhere or a place is **swarming** with them.

swarthy A **swarthy** person has a dark complexion.

swashbuckling (**swashbuckler**) **Swashbuckling** is used to describe characters in historical stories and films who get involved in sword fights and other daring adventures. People in real life who remind you of these characters can also be described as **swashbuckling**; you can also call them **swashbucklers**.

swastika The **swastika** is an ancient symbol which looks like a cross with the arms bent at right angles. It was adopted as the emblem of Nazi Germany.

swat (**swatting, swatted**) If you **swat** an insect, you hit it with something. ■ If you **swat aside** an opponent, you deal with them quickly and easily.

swathe (**swathed**) A **swathe** of land is a long strip of it. *...a swathe of red-gold sand.* ■ A **swathe** of something is a large part of it. *Mexico has also privatized swathes of its economy.* ■ If something **cuts a swathe** through something else, it destroys or changes a large part of it. *The recession is cutting a swathe through America's managerial and professional elite.* ■ A **swathe** is strip of cloth, especially one for wrapping around someone or something. If you are **swathed** in something, you are wrapped in it. *I had my head swathed in bandages.*

sway When people or things **sway**, they lean or swing from side to side. ■ If you are **swayed** by something you hear or read, you are influenced by it. ■ If you are **under the sway** of someone or something, they have a lot of influence over you. ■ If a person or thing **holds sway**, they have more power or influence than anyone or anything else.

swear (**swearing, swore, have sworn**) If someone **swears**, they use words considered to be rude or blasphemous. Words like these are called **swear words**. ■ If you **swear** to do something, you formally promise to do it, sometimes by taking an oath. ■ When someone is **sworn in**, they solemnly promise to fulfil the duties of a new job or position. ■ If you **swear** something is true, you say very firmly that it is true.

sweat (**sweating, sweated**) **Sweat** is the salty colourless liquid produced by glands under your skin when you are hot or afraid. When you **sweat**, sweat comes out through your skin. If something makes this happen, you say it **brings you out in a sweat**. ■ If you **sweat it out**, you wait anxiously for a situation to improve or be resolved, because you cannot do anything about it.

sweater A **sweater** is a woollen garment which covers the upper part of your body, your arms and sometimes your neck.

sweatshirt A **sweatshirt** is a garment made of thick cotton which covers the upper part of your body and your arms.

sweatshop You call a factory or workshop a **sweatshop** when the people there work long hours in poor conditions for low pay.

sweaty A **sweaty** place or activity makes you sweat. ■ If your body or clothing is **sweaty**, it is covered or soaked with sweat.

swede – **Swedes** are large round root vegetables with yellow flesh and a brownish-purple skin. ■ A **Swede** is someone who comes from Sweden.

Swedish is used to talk about people and things in or from Sweden. *...Swedish farmers.* ■ **Swedish** is the main language spoken in Sweden.

sweep (**sweeping, swept** *not 'sweeped'*) If you **sweep** the floor or **sweep up,** you use a broom to gather up dust or rubbish. ■ If you **sweep** something off a surface, you push it off with a smooth movement of your arm. ■ If something is **swept** somewhere by the wind or by moving water, it is carried along by it. ■ If someone or something **sweeps** somewhere, they move along quickly and forcefully. *Periodically, convoys of cars sweep down the road to the city.* ■ If land **sweeps** somewhere, it stretches out in a long wide curved shape. *...lawns that sweep down to the sea.* ■ If ideas, beliefs, or emotions **sweep** a place, they spread quickly there. *Panic swept the city.* You can also talk about people being **swept along** by an idea, belief, or emotion. ■ If something is **swept away**, it is removed completely. *The law will also sweep away the 20% limit on foreign investment.* ■ **Sweeping** changes are wide-ranging and dramatic. ■ If someone makes a **clean sweep** in a competition, they win everything. ■ A **sweeping** statement is a general one made without considering all the facts properly. ■ If the police make a **sweep** of an area, they search it. ■ A **sweep** is the same as a chimney sweep. ■ **sweep the board:** see **board.**

sweeper A **road sweeper** is someone employed to sweep roads. ■ In football, a **sweeper** is a defender who does not have a fixed position.

sweepstake A **sweepstake** is a method of gambling in which each person is given, for example, the name of a horse in a race and pays a small amount of money. The person who has the winning horse's name wins all the money.

sweet (**sweeter, sweetest; sweetly, sweetness**) **Sweet** food and drink contains a lot of sugar, or tastes as if it does. ■ **Sweets** are things such as toffees, chocolates, and mints. ■ A **sweet** is a dessert. ■ You say someone has a **sweet tooth** when they like sweet foods. ■ You say something is **sweet** when you find it pleasant. *...a sweet and wistful tone. ...sweetly scented flowers.* ■ You can call someone's behaviour **sweet** when they are pleasant and kind.

sweet-and-sour sauce includes sweet substances like sugar and fruit, and also sharp ones like vinegar. It is served with savoury food.

sweetbread – **Sweetbreads** are meat obtained from the pancreas or thymus gland of a calf or lamb.

sweetcorn is the yellow seeds of the maize plant, which are eaten as a vegetable.

sweeten (**sweetening, sweetened; sweetener**) If you **sweeten** food or drink, you add sugar or some other sweet substance to it. ■ A **sweetener** is a sweet artificial substance used instead of sugar. ■ If someone **sweetens** an offer or business deal, they make it more attractive by offering something extra. Something which makes an offer or deal more attractive is called a **sweetener.**

sweetheart Someone's **sweetheart** is their boyfriend or girlfriend.

sweetie A **sweetie** is a sweet.

sweet pea – Sweet peas are climbing plants with delicate light-coloured fragrant flowers.

sweet potato – Sweet potatoes are large root vegetables with pink skins.

sweet-talk If you **sweet-talk** someone into doing something, you persuade them to do it by flattering them.

sweet william is a garden plant with round clusters of scented flowers.

swell (**swelling, swelled, have swollen** or **have swelled**) If something **swells**, it becomes larger and rounder than normal. When this happens, you say it is **swollen.** ■ A **swelling** is a raised curved patch on the body which appears as a result of an injury or infection. ■ If a river is **swollen,** there is much more water in it than usual, because of heavy rain. ■ If a number or amount **swells,** it increases. *The population of the capital has swollen to half-a-million.* ■ If a sound **swells,** it suddenly gets louder. ■ The **swell** of the sea is the regular up-and-down movement of the waves.

swelter (**sweltering, sweltered**) If you are **sweltering,** you are very uncomfortable because the weather is extremely hot. If the weather is **sweltering,** it is extremely hot.

swept See **sweep.**

swerve (**swerving, swerved**) If you **swerve,** you suddenly change direction, usually to avoid colliding with someone or something. A movement like this is called a **swerve.**

swift (**swiftly, swiftness**) A **swift** process or event happens very quickly. *...her swift rise to fame.* ■ If you are **swift** to do something, you do it quickly in response to something else. *The President reacted swiftly.* ■ If an animal is **swift,** it moves very quickly. ■ **Swifts** are small fast-flying birds with crescent-shaped wings.

swig (**swigging, swigged**) If you **swig** a drink, you drink it quickly and in large mouthfuls. If you **take a swig** at a drink, you drink one large mouthful and swallow it quickly.

swill If you **swill** an alcoholic drink, you drink a lot of it. *...beer-swilling men.* ■ If you **swill** something, you clean it by pouring water over it. ■ **Swill** is a liquid mixture containing waste food, which is fed to pigs.

swim (**swimming, swam, have swum**) When people or animals **swim,** they move through water using their body. ■ If you go **swimming** or go for a **swim,** you spend some time swimming for pleasure. ■ If you say your head or something around you is **swimming,** you mean you feel dizzy. *...the room swam.*

swimmer A **swimmer** is someone who swims regularly or takes part in swimming races.

swimming baths A **swimming baths** is a public swimming pool.

swimming costume A **swimming costume** is a tight-fitting piece of clothing a woman wears when she goes swimming.

swimmingly If something goes **swimmingly,** it goes very well.

swimming pool A **swimming pool** is a large hole which has been tiled and filled with water so that people can swim in it.

swimming trunks are shorts a man wears when he goes swimming.

swimsuit A **swimsuit** is the same as a swimming costume.

swindle (**swindling, swindled; swindler**) If someone **swindles** you, they trick you to get money or something valuable from you. You call a trick like this a **swindle.** Someone who tricks people in this way is called a **swindler.**

swine (*plural:* **swine**) If you call someone a **swine,** you mean they are cruel or very selfish. ■ **Swine** is an old word for a pig.

swing (**swinging, swung**) If something **swings,** it moves repeatedly backwards and forwards or from side to side, from a fixed point. A movement like this is called a **swing.** *...a swing of the hips.* ■ A **swing** is a seat hanging from a frame or branch, which moves backwards and forwards. ■ **Swings and roundabouts** is used to talk about a situation in which there are both gains and losses. ■ If someone or something **swings** in particular direction, they turn suddenly in that direction. *I swung around furiously.* ■ If you take a **swing** at someone, you try to hit them. ■ If people's opinions or attitudes **swing** in a particular direction, they change significantly. A change like this is called a **swing.** *...the recent swing in American public opinion against military action.* ■ If there is a **swing** in an amount or number, it suddenly increases or decreases. *...interest-rate swings.* ■ If something is **in full swing,** it is operating fully and is no longer in its early stages. ■ **Swing** was a style of big band dance music popular in the 1930s and 1940s.

swing door A **swing door** swings on a hinge so that it can open either towards you or away from you.

swingeing (*pron:* **swin**-jing) is used to describe things which are very severe. *...swingeing budget cuts.*

swipe (**swiping, swiped**) If you **swipe** at something, you try to hit it. ■ If you take a **swipe** at someone or something, you strongly criticize them. ■ If someone **swipes** something, they steal it. ■ If you **swipe** something like a credit card through a machine, you pass it through a slot in the machine. Some cards which can be used like this are called **swipe cards.**

swirl (**swirling**) If something **swirls,** it moves round and round. A movement like this can be called a **swirl.** *...swirling rain.* A **swirl** is also something shaped like a curl or spiral.

swish (**swishes, swishing, swished**) If something **swishes,** it moves quickly through the air, making a soft sound. *The cow swished her tail.* ■ **Swish** things are smart and fashionable. *...a swish restaurant.*

Swiss means in or from Switzerland. *...Swiss cheese.* ■ The **Swiss** are the Swiss people.

swiss roll A **swiss roll** is a flat oblong sponge cake spread with jam or cream and then rolled up.

switch (switches, switching, switched) A **switch** is a small control which you use to operate an electrical device. If you **switch on** a light or other electrical device, you make it work by pressing a switch. Similarly, you can **switch off** a light or other device. ■ If you **switch off,** you stop thinking about something. ■ If you **switch** to something different, you change to it from what you were doing or using before. A change like this is called a **switch.** *You're going to see a switch towards more recyclable plastics.* ■ If you **switch** two things, you replace one with the other. *The ballot boxes have been switched.*

switchback A **switchback** is something such as a mountain road, which rises and falls sharply many times or has many sharp bends.

switchblade A **switchblade** is the same as a flick knife.

switchboard The **switchboard** in an organization is a place where all the phone calls are received.

swivel (swivelling, swivelled) (Am: swiveling, swiveled) If something **swivels,** it turns around a central point so it is facing in a different direction. ■ If you **swivel** in a particular direction, you suddenly turn in that direction.

swollen See **swell.**

swoon (swooning, swooned) If someone **swoons** or goes into a **swoon,** they almost faint as a result of a strong emotion or shock.

swoop (swooping, swooped) When a bird or plane **swoops,** it suddenly moves downwards in a smooth curve. ■ If police **swoop** on a place, they move towards it suddenly and quickly to arrest someone. An action like this is called a **swoop.** ■ If you achieve something **in one fell swoop,** you do it on a single occasion or by a single action.

swop (swopping, swopped) See **swap.**

sword A **sword** is a weapon with a handle and a long blade. ■ If you **cross swords** with someone, you have a disagreement with them.

swordfish (usual plural: swordfish) The **swordfish** is a large sea fish with a very long upper jaw.

swore (sworn) See **swear.**

swot (swotting, swotted) If you **swot,** you study very hard, especially when preparing for an exam. ■ If you call someone a **swot,** you mean they study very hard and are not interested in other things. ■ If you **swot up** on a subject, you read as much about it as you can.

swum See **swim.**

swung See **swing.**

sybarite (pron: sib-bar-ite) (sybaritic) A **sybarite** is someone who likes to lead a life of luxury. **Sybaritic** is used to describe people like this and the things they enjoy.

sycamore The **sycamore** is a tree with large five-pointed leaves. Its seed cases have two wings and spin as they fall.

sycophantic (pron: sik-o-fan-tic) (sycophant, sycophancy) You say people are **sycophantic** or **sycophants** when they flatter an important person, to

gain some advantage for themselves. You describe behaviour like this as **sycophancy.**

syllable A **syllable** is a part of a word which contains a single vowel sound, and is pronounced as a unit. For example, 'book' has one syllable and 'reading' has two.

syllabus (syllabuses) The subjects studied for a course or exam are called the **syllabus.**

sylvan means to do with trees and woods. *...in this sylvan setting.*

symbiosis (symbiotic) Symbiosis is a relationship between two different organisms which benefits both. **Symbiotic** is used to describe relationships like this. ■ You can say a relationship between two people or organizations is **symbiotic** when it is beneficial to both of them. *...the party's symbiotic relationship with the ANC.*

symbol A **symbol** is something, for example a shape or design, which is chosen to represent something else. *The new symbol of the Italian Communist Party is to be a sturdy oak tree.* ■ A **symbol** is something which is seen by people as representing a particular thing. *According to native American legend, rainbows are a symbol of union.* ■ A **symbol** is a number, letter, or shape used, for example, in maths to represent an item in a calculation. ■ **status symbol:** see **status.** ■ See also **sex symbol.**

symbolic (symbolically; symbolism, symbolist) A **symbolic** action has a special meaning for a group of people. It often has little practical effect but represents an important feeling held by the group. *In a symbolic gesture, the parliament passed a declaration praising the 1956 uprising.* You can talk about the **symbolism** of an action like this. ■ **Symbolic** is used to talk about things to do with symbols or involving symbols. **Symbolism** is the use of symbols.

symbolize (or symbolise) (symbolizing, symbolized) If a person or thing **symbolizes** something else, they are regarded as a symbol of it.

symmetrical (symmetry, symmetries) If something is **symmetrical,** it has two halves which are the same except that one half is the mirror image of the other. You talk about the **symmetry** of something like this.

sympathetic (sympathetically) See **sympathy.**

sympathize (or sympathise) (sympathizing, sympathized; sympathizer) If you **sympathize** with someone who has had a misfortune, you show you feel sorry for them. ■ If you **sympathize** with someone's feelings, you understand them and are not critical of them. ■ If you **sympathize** with a proposal, action, or cause, you approve of it and are willing to support it. People who support an organization or cause are called its **sympathizers.** *...Communist party sympathizers.*

sympathy (sympathies; sympathetic, sympathetically) If you show **sympathy** for someone who has had a misfortune or are **sympathetic** to them, you show you feel sorry for them and understand their feelings. ■ If you describe someone as **sympathetic,** you mean you like them and approve of the way they behave. *He was a sympathetic character.* ■ If you have **sympathy** with a proposal, action, or cause or are **sympathetic** to it, you agree with it. ...*a priest with left-wing sympathies.*

symphony (**symphonies; symphonic; symphonic**) A **symphony** is a large-scale piece of music for an orchestra, usually in four movements. **Symphonic** means to do with or similar to a symphony. ...*a symphonic composer.*

symphony orchestra A **symphony orchestra** is a large orchestra.

symposium (*plural:* **symposia** *or* **symposiums**) A **symposium** is a conference in which experts or scholars discuss a particular subject.

symptom (**symptomatic**) A **symptom** is something wrong with you which is a sign of an illness. ■ If you say something is a **symptom** of a bad situation or is **symptomatic** of it, you mean it shows it exists. *The dispute is symptomatic of wider tensions.*

synagogue A **synagogue** is a building where Jewish people meet to worship or to study their religion.

synapse (*pron:* **sigh**-naps) (**synaptic**) A **synapse** is the point where a nerve impulse is relayed from one nerve cell to another. **Synaptic** means to do with synapses. ...*synaptic processes.*

sync (*or* **synch**) (*pron:* **sink**) If two things are **out of sync,** they are not synchronized with each other.

synchromesh In a gearbox, **synchromesh** is a system which allows a smooth gear change by making the gears spin at the same speed before engaging them.

synchronicity See **synchronous.**

synchronize (*or* **synchronise**) (**synchronizing, synchronized; synchronization**) If things are **synchronized,** they are made to happen in the same way and at the same time.

synchronous (*pron:* **sink**-kro-nuss) (**synchronicity**) If two things are **synchronous,** they happen in the same way and at the same time. You talk about the **synchronicity** of things like these.

syncopated (**syncopation**) If a piece of music is **syncopated,** the weak beats are stressed instead of the strong ones. You talk about the **syncopation** or **syncopations** of music like this.

syndicate (**syndicating, syndicated; syndication**) A **syndicate** is an association of people or organizations formed to carry out a business project together. ■ When a group or an organization **syndicates** something, it produces it or agrees to it through a syndicate. ...*syndicated loans.* ■ If articles, cartoons, or programmes are **syndicated,** they are sold to several different newspapers or TV companies who then publish or broadcast them.

syndrome A **syndrome** is a medical condition which produces a particular set of symptoms. ...*irritable bowel syndrome.* ■ A pattern of behaviour which keeps occurring over and over again with different people is sometimes called a **syndrome.** ...*the 'it won't affect me' syndrome.*

synergy (*pron:* **sin**-er-gee) (**synergies**) Synergy is the successful result of two firms or other organizations working together. An instance of this is called a **synergy.**

synod A **synod** is a special council of members of a Church, which meets regularly to discuss religious issues.

synonym (**synonymous**) If two words are **synonyms** or they are **synonymous,** they have the same meaning or a very similar meaning. ■ If two things are closely associated, you can say one is **synonymous** with the other. ...*the 1980s, a decade that has become synonymous with greed and corporate excess.*

synopsis (*plural:* **synopses**) A **synopsis** of a book, play, or film is a summary of the plot.

syntax (**syntaxes**) The **syntax** of a language is the way its words are put together to form sentences.

synth A **synth** is the same as a synthesizer.

synthesis (**syntheses**) A **synthesis** of different ideas or styles is a combination of them. ■ The **synthesis** of a substance is its production from other substances by means of a chemical or biological reaction.

synthesize (*or* **synthesise**) (**synthesizing, synthesized**) When a substance is **synthesized,** it is produced from other substances by a chemical or biological reaction.

synthesizer A **synthesizer** is an electronic machine which produces speech, music, or other sounds by using its computer to combine sounds which have already been recorded and stored.

synthetic (**synthetically**) **Synthetic** products are made from man-made substances rather than natural ones.

syphilis is a type of venereal disease.

syphon See **siphon.**

syringe (**syringing, syringed**) A **syringe** is a small tube with a plunger and a fine hollow needle used for injecting or extracting liquids.

syrup is a thick sweet liquid made with sugar, water, and sometimes fruit juice. ■ Various other thick sweet liquids containing sugar are also called **syrup.** ...*maple syrup.* ...*cough syrup.*

syrupy A **syrupy** liquid is sweet or thick like syrup. ■ **Syrupy** is used to describe things which are irritatingly sentimental. ...*a syrupy tale.*

system A **system** is a way of organizing or doing something which involves following a fixed plan or set of rules. ...*the system of proportional representation.* ...*a system of bartering.* ■ The network of roads, railways, or canals in a place can be called a **system.** Similarly, a transport network can be called a **system.** *Most bus systems in Britain are now privately owned.* ■ A set of equipment, or the parts which work together to carry out a process, can be called a **system.** ...*the central heating system.* ■ A **system** in your body is a set of organs or other parts which together perform a particular function. ...*the digestive system.* The functioning of a person's body as a whole can be called their **system.** ...*the level of barbiturates found in her system.*

systematic (**systematically**) You say something is **systematic** when it operates like a fully organized system. ...*the discovery of a massive and systematic fraud.*

systematize (*or* **systematise**) (**systematizing, systematized**) If you **systematize** things, you arrange them in a well-organized pattern or system.

systemic (*pron:* siss-**team**-ik) If something is **systemic,** it affects the whole of an organization or system, rather than just one part of it. *The economy* *is locked in a systemic crisis.* ■ **Systemic** chemicals or drugs are absorbed into the whole of an organism such as a plant or person, rather than being applied to one area.

systems analyst A **systems analyst** is someone who designs computer systems to suit the individual needs of an organization.

T t

TA See **Territorial Army.**

tab A **tab** is a small piece of cloth or paper attached to something, especially one used for identification. ■ **Tab** is a US word for a restaurant bill or a bill for goods or services. ■ If you **keep tabs** on someone, you make sure you always know where they are and what they are doing. ■ A **tab** is a tablet of a drug which is sold illegally. *...a tab of Ecstasy.*

Tabasco is a hot spicy sauce made from peppers. 'Tabasco' is a trademark.

tabby (**tabbies**) A **tabby** is a cat whose fur has dark stripes.

tabernacle Certain Christian churches call their place of worship a **tabernacle.** ■ In a Roman Catholic church, the **tabernacle** is a box containing the communion bread and wine.

table (**tabling, tabled**) A **table** is a piece of furniture you place things on or sit at. It has a flat top supported by one or more legs. ■ A **table** is a set of facts or figures arranged in columns. ■ If a proposal is **tabled** or put **on the table,** it is formally put forward for discussion. ■ If you **turn the tables** on someone, you reverse the situation so they have the problems they were causing you.

tableau (*pron:* **tab**-loh) (*plural:* **tableaux** *or* **tableaus**) A **tableau** is a scene from history or legend represented either by people standing on a stage wearing costumes or by a painting, sculpture, or photograph.

tablespoon A **tablespoon** is a large spoon for serving food.

tablet A **tablet** is a large pill of compressed powdered medicine. ■ You call a flat piece of stone with words cut into it a **tablet.**

table tennis is a game played on a special table by two or four people, using small bats to hit a small hollow plastic ball backwards and forwards across a net.

tableware consists of things like plates and cutlery which are put on the table at meals.

tabloid A **tabloid** is a newspaper with small pages, short news stories, and a lot of photographs. See also **broadsheet.**

taboo If there is a **taboo** on a subject or activity or it is **taboo,** there is a religious or social custom to avoid that subject or activity, because people find it embarrassing or offensive.

tabulate (**tabulating, tabulated; tabulation**) If you **tabulate** information, you arrange it in columns.

tachograph (*pron:* **tak**-o-graf) A **tachograph** is a device put in vehicles such as lorries and coaches to record things like the vehicle's speed and the distance it has travelled.

tacit (*pron:* **tass**-it) (**tacitly**) Tacit is used to say something is implied without being openly stated. *He gave tacit support to terrorists.*

taciturn (*pron:* **tass**-it-turn) (**taciturnity**) If you say someone is **taciturn,** or refer to their **taciturnity,** you mean they do not talk much.

tack A **tack** is a short nail with a broad flat head. If you **tack** something somewhere, you nail it there with tacks. ■ If you **tack** a piece of fabric, you sew it with long loose stitches before putting in permanent stitches. ■ You say one thing is **tacked on** to another thing when you think the other thing has been hurriedly added as an afterthought. ■ When a sailing boat is **tacking,** it is sailing towards a particular point in a series of zig-zags rather than in a straight line. ■ If you change **tack,** you try a different method for dealing with a situation.

tackle (**tackling, tackled**) If you **tackle** a problem, you make a determined attempt to deal with it. ■ If you **tackle** someone in a game like football, you try to take the ball off them. In rugby, if you **tackle** someone or make a **tackle,** you grab them around the legs and try to bring them down. ■ If you **tackle** someone on a matter, you talk to them about it, usually to get them to deal with it. ■ **Tackle** is equipment for sporting activities, especially fishing.

tacky (**tackier, tackiest; tackiness**) If you say something is **tacky,** you mean it is vulgar and of poor quality. ■ If something like paint is **tacky,** it is slightly sticky to touch.

tact (**tactful, tactfully**) If you behave with **tact** or are **tactful,** you are careful to avoid upsetting people.

tactic Your **tactics** are the strategies you use to get what you want.

tactical is used to describe actions and behaviour intended to help someone achieve a particular aim. *His speech was a tactical move, calculated to get the moderates on his side.* ■ **Tactical voting** is voting for a party or candidate not because you support them, but because you hope to prevent someone else from winning. ■ **Tactical** weapons or forces are those used on the orders of a military commander during a battle.

tactician If someone is a good **tactician,** they are good at planning the best way to achieve what they want.

tactile experiences or sensations involve the sense of touch. *...tactile stimulation.* ■ **Tactile** is used to describe things which are pleasant or distinctive to touch. ...*a texture as rich and tactile as leather.* ■ A **tactile** person likes touching and being touched by other people.

tactless If someone is **tactless,** their behaviour is likely to upset people.

tad – A **tad** means to a small extent or degree. *It was a tad confusing.*

tadpole – **Tadpoles** are small water creatures which grow into frogs or toads.

taffeta is a stiff shiny material made of silk or a man-made fibre, used mainly for making women's clothes.

tag (tagging, tagged) A **tag** is a label. If you **tag** something, you attach an identifying label to it. ■ An **electronic tag** is a device which is firmly attached to someone or something and sets off an alarm if that person moves away or that thing is removed. ■ A **tag** is a nickname or description given to someone or something. You can say a person or thing is **tagged** with a certain name or description. *The party is scared of being tagged federalist.* ■ The **tag line** is the phrase at the end of a joke or advertisement which is meant to be memorable or amusing. ■ If someone **tags along** with you when you go somewhere, they go with you because they want to, rather than because you have asked them to.

tagliatelle (*pron:* tal-lee-a-**tel**-lee) is pasta made in narrow strips.

tail (tailing, tailed) The **tail** of an animal, bird, or fish is the part which grows out of the rear end of its body. ■ You can use **tail** to refer to the end or back of something, especially something long and thin. *...the tail of a comet.* ■ If a man is wearing **tails,** he is wearing a formal evening jacket called a **tail coat,** which has two long pieces hanging down at the back. ■ If someone **tails** you, he or she secretly follows you, to find out where you go and what you do. ■ If a coin comes down **tails** when you toss it, the side facing upwards does not have a picture of a person's head. ■ If something **tails off,** it gradually decreases. ■ If you say someone **turns tail,** you mean they turn and run away.

tailback A **tailback** is a long queue of traffic.

tailgate (tailgating) A **tailgate** is a door at the back of a truck or car, which is hinged at the bottom so it opens downwards. **Tailgating** is the activity of driving too close to the vehicle in front.

tail light The **tail lights** on a vehicle are the two red lights at the back.

tailor (tailoring, tailored) A **tailor** is a person who makes outer garments like jackets and trousers. The work of a tailor is called **tailoring.** ■ **Tailored** clothes are designed to fit close to the body. ■ If something is **tailored** to particular requirements, it is specially designed or adjusted to fit those requirements.

tailor-made If something is **tailor-made** for a particular purpose, it has been specially designed for that purpose or is perfectly suitable for it.

tailplane The **tailplane** of an aeroplane is the part at the rear, consisting of the rudder and the stabilizers.

tailspin A **tailspin** is an uncontrolled spinning dive by a plane, in which the tail spins in a wider circle than the nose. ■ If you say something **goes into a tailspin,** you mean it begins a sudden and alarmingly rapid decline. *Share prices around the world went into a tailspin.*

tailwind A **tailwind** is a wind blowing in the direction you are travelling.

taint If water is **tainted,** impurities have got into it, and it may be dangerous to drink. ■ You say a person is **tainted** when they are associated with something bad and this harms their reputation. *He wanted to exclude from his new government any politicians tainted by scandal... The taint of the bad old strike-happy days still hangs over British industry.*

take (taking, took, have taken) Take is used to say what action or activity is being done. *He took a bath... I had to take a test.* ■ If you **take** a point of view, you have that point of view. *The Community ministers clearly take the view that more urgent action is necessary.* ■ The way you **take** a piece of news is the way you react to it. *New Yorkers took the news personally, and with great sadness.* ■ If you are **taken aback,** you are surprised or shocked by something. ■ If you cannot **take** something, you cannot endure it or tolerate it. ■ If something **takes** a certain amount of time, or a particular quality or ability, it requires it. ■ If you **take** something, you hold it or move it somewhere with your hand. *The constable took her arm... The gag was taken from his mouth.* ■ If you **take** something somewhere, you carry it there. ■ If you **take** someone somewhere, you drive them or lead them there. ■ If you **take** something which is offered to you, you accept it. ■ If you **take** responsibility or blame for something, you accept it. ■ If you **take** pills, you swallow them. ■ If someone **takes** your temperature or pulse, they measure it. ■ If someone **takes** something of yours, they steal it, or remove it without your permission. ■ If an army **takes** a place, it captures it. ■ If someone **takes office** or **takes power,** they start being in control of a government or organization. ■ If you **take** a road or a particular form of transport, you use it to travel somewhere. ■ If you **take down** what someone is saying, you write it down. ■ If you **take in** information, you understand it. ■ If someone is **taken in,** they are deceived. ■ When an aircraft **takes off,** it leaves the ground. The moment when it leaves the ground is called **take-off.** ■ If an employer **takes** you **on,** they give you a job. ■ If you **take** someone **on,** you fight them or compete against them. ■ If something **takes on** a new character or meaning, it begins to have it. *The anniversary has taken on a special significance.* ■ If you **take up** a job or hobby, you start doing it. ■ If you **take over** someone's job, you start doing it in their place. ■ If you **take to** doing something, you start doing it fairly often. *He took to criticising his ministers.* ■ If something **takes off,** it suddenly becomes successful. *She dropped out of art school when her modelling career took off.* ■ If you **take to** someone or something, you like them immediately. ■ You use **take** to introduce an example you want people to consider. *The city, however, is very far from quiet.*

Take, for example, the Trocadero fountains by the Eiffel Tower. ■ In filming, a **take** is a short piece of action filmed without stopping the camera.

takeaway A **takeaway** is a shop or restaurant which sells hot cooked food to be eaten elsewhere. A meal bought at a place like this is also called a **takeaway.**

take-home drinks are ones you buy to drink at home, rather than drinks bought in a pub or restaurant. *Guinness has captured a significant chunk of the take-home market.* ■ Your **take-home pay** is your pay after things like tax and pension contributions have been deducted.

taken See **take.**

take-off See **take.**

takeover A **takeover** occurs when someone buys enough shares in a company to gain control of it. ■ When someone takes control of a country by force, this can be called a **takeover.**

taker If there are few **takers** for an offer, hardly anyone is willing to accept it. ■ **Taker** is used to describe people who take things of various kinds. *...drug takers.*

takings A shop's **takings** is the money it receives from selling goods.

talcum powder or **talc** is a soft perfumed powder which people put on their bodies after a bath or shower.

tale A **tale** is a story, especially one which involves adventure.

talent (**talented**) **Talent** is natural ability to do something well. A **talented** person has this ability.

talent scout A **talent scout** is someone whose job is to find new people who have talent, for example as footballers, models, or actors, and offer them work.

talisman A **talisman** is an object someone carries around with them because they believe it has magic powers to protect them or bring them luck. ■ Anything people expect to bring them success or good luck can be called a **talisman.** *With four goals already he is the talisman of the team.*

talk When you **talk,** you communicate using speech. ■ If people **talk** something **over,** they discuss it fully and honestly. ■ **Talks** are formal discussions, especially between two parties in a dispute. *...the Arab-Israeli peace talks.* ■ A **talk** is a speech or lecture. ■ If someone **talks down** to you, they talk in a way which shows they think they are cleverer or more important than you. ■ If you **talk** something **down,** you try to make people think it is less significant than it really is. Similarly, you can **talk** something **up.** ■ If you **talk** someone **into** doing something, you persuade them to do it. Similarly, you can **talk** someone **out of** doing something.

talkative If someone is **talkative,** they talk a lot.

talker is used to describe the way someone talks. *...an animated talker.*

talkie When cinema films with sound as well as pictures first came in, they were called **talkies.**

talking book A **talking book** is the same as an audio book.

talking shop If you say a conference or committee is no more than a **talking shop,** you mean a lot of discussion takes place there but nothing useful is achieved.

talk show A **talk show** is the same as a chat show.

tall If someone or something is **tall,** their height is above average. ■ **Tall** is used in questions and statements about height. *How tall are you?... She was over six feet tall.* ■ If a task is a **tall order,** it will be very difficult. ■ If you call what someone says a **tall story,** you mean it is difficult to believe, because it seems so exaggerated or unlikely.

tallow is a hard animal fat used for making things like candles and soap.

tally (**tallies, tallying, tallied**) A **tally** is a total which keeps increasing. *Hick held three stunning catches to bring his tally to 31 for the season.* ■ If two accounts of an event **tally,** they are the same, and so are probably both correct. Similarly, you can say two sets of figures **tally.**

Talmud (**Talmudic**) The **Talmud** is the written collection of ancient Jewish laws. **Talmudic** means to do with the Talmud. *...the Talmudic tradition.*

talon A bird of prey's **talons** are its sharp hooked claws.

tamarind The **tamarind** is a tropical tree. It has pod-like fruit called **tamarinds,** which are used in chutneys and curries.

tambourine The **tambourine** is a musical instrument which you shake or hit with your hand. It consists of a skin on a circular frame with pieces of metal around the edge which clash together.

tame (**tamer, tamest; taming, tamed; tamely**) If someone **tames** a wild animal, they train it to be obedient and not to be afraid of people. You then say the animal is **tame.** A person who trains lions is called a lion **tamer.** ■ When people do what they are told without questioning it, you can call their behaviour **tame.** ■ If you **tame** people or things that are dangerous or likely to cause trouble, you bring them under control. *Belgium has been fairly successful at taming Flemish nationalism.* ■ If you call something **tame,** you mean it is not in any way exciting or shocking. *Last night's episode of 'Casualty' proved to be a tame, rather restrained affair.*

tam-o'-shanter A **tam-o'-shanter** is a woollen hat with a bobble on top.

Tampax (*plural:* **Tampax**) A **Tampax** is a tampon. 'Tampax' is a trademark.

tamper (**tampering, tampered**) If someone **tampers** with something, they interfere or meddle with it.

tampon A **tampon** is a firm, specially shaped piece of cotton wool which a woman places inside her vagina to absorb the blood during her period.

tan (**tanning, tanned**) If you **tan** or get a **tan,** your skin becomes darker as result of being exposed to the sun. ■ **Tan** is a pale brown colour.

tandem A **tandem** is a bicycle for two people to ride, with two saddles and two sets of pedals, one behind the other. ■ If two people or groups work **in tandem,** they work together. Similarly, you can say two things happen **in tandem.** *The shares have fallen in tandem with the oil price for the past year.*

tandoori is an Indian method of cooking meat in a clay oven.

tang A **tang** is a strong sharp taste or smell. *...a salty tang. ...the tang of fish.* ■ If something has some quality which you are strongly aware of, you can say it has a particular **tang.** *Set in a small town in the north of England, its language and its details have the tang of authenticity.*

tangent In geometry, a **tangent** is a straight line which touches a curve at one point but does not cross it. ■ If someone **goes off at a tangent**, they start talking about something not directly connected with what they were talking about before.

tangential (tangentially) If there is a **tangential** relationship between two things, they are only slightly or indirectly connected.

tangerine – Tangerines are a type of small sweet orange with a loose skin. ■ **Tangerine** is a reddish-orange colour.

tangible (tangibly) If something is **tangible,** it can be seen to exist or be happening. *He must make the reforms work in such a way as to improve people's lives tangibly.*

tangle (tangling, tangled) If something like hair is **tangled** or in a **tangle,** it is twisted together untidily. ■ A **tangled** story is extremely complicated. ■ If you are **tangled** in something like rope or **tangled up** in it, it has become twisted round your body so you are caught or trapped in it. ■ If you are involved in a complicated and difficult situation, you can say you are **tangled** or **tangled up** in it. You can call a situation like this a **tangle.** *...the complex tangle of claims and counter-claims.* ■ If you **tangle with** someone, you get involved in a fight or dispute with them.

tango (tangos) The **tango** is a South American dance for two people. When people **tango,** they dance the tango.

tangy If food is **tangy,** it has a strong sharp taste.

tank A **tank** is a large container for liquid or gas. ■ A **tank** is an armour-plated military vehicle which has caterpillar tracks instead of wheels and is equipped with guns or rockets.

tankard A **tankard** is a large metal beer mug.

tanker A **tanker** is a ship, lorry, or rail vehicle used for transporting large quantities of gas or liquid.

tankful A **tankful** of liquid or gas is the amount you can get in a tank.

tanned See **tan.**

tannery (tanneries) A **tannery** is a factory where animal skins are made into leather.

tannin is a yellow or brown chemical which occurs in the bark and leaves of many trees and plants, such as tea.

Tannoy A **Tannoy** is a system of loudspeakers used to make public announcements.

tantalize (or tantalise) (tantalizing, tantalized; tantalizingly) If something **tantalizes** you, it gives you an exciting feeling of anticipation without actually giving you what you want. *...a tantalizing glimpse of leg... The prospect of agreement is tantalizingly close.*

tantamount If something is **tantamount** to a certain thing, it has the same effects or implications, and can be regarded as that thing. *Mr Shapi said the raid was tantamount to a declaration of war.*

tantrum A **tantrum** is a noisy childish outburst of bad temper.

Taoiseach (*pron:* **tee**-shak) The **Taoiseach** is the prime minister of the Republic of Ireland.

Taoism (*pron:* **tow**-iz-zum) is a Chinese religious philosophy according to which people should live a simple honest life and not seek to interfere with the natural course of events.

tap (tapping, tapped) A **tap** is a device you turn to control the flow of liquid or gas from a pipe or container. ■ If you **tap** something, **tap on** it, or give it a **tap,** you hit it lightly. ■ If you **tap** your fingers, you repeatedly hit them against a surface like a table. Similarly, you can **tap** your feet on the floor, especially in time to music. ■ If your phone is **tapped,** a device is connected to it, so someone can secretly listen to your calls. ■ If someone **taps** a tree, especially a rubber tree, they get sap out of it by making a cut in its trunk. ■ If you **tap** a resource or situation, you make use of it. *The opposition parties could succeed by tapping this anti-government feeling.*

tap dance When people **tap dance,** they do a rapid dance wearing special shoes with metal on the heels and toes which make clicking noises as their feet hit the floor.

tape (taping, taped) Tape is a narrow plastic strip covered with a magnetic substance, used to record sounds, pictures, and computer information. ■ A **tape** is a cassette or spool with magnetic tape wound round it. ■ If you **tape** something, you record it on a tape. *...a taped interview.* ■ **Tape** or **sticky tape** is thin strips of plastic coated with adhesive, used to stick things together. If you **tape** one thing to another, you attach it using tape like this. *...a sign taped to the wall.*

tape deck A **tape deck** is a machine for playing or recording tapes on.

tape measure A **tape measure** is a strip of plastic, cloth, or thin flexible metal marked off in centimetres or inches, and used for measuring things.

taper (tapering, tapered) If something **tapers,** it gradually becomes narrower at one end. *...tapered trousers.* ■ If something **tapers off**, it gradually decreases. ■ A **taper** is a fast-burning strip of material, used for lighting fires.

tape recorder A **tape recorder** is machine for playing or recording tapes on.

tapestry (tapestries) A **tapestry** is a piece of heavy cloth with a picture or pattern woven into it.

tapeworm – Tapeworms are parasitic worms which live in the intestines of some animals, including humans.

tapioca (*pron:* tap-ee-**oh**-ka) is a starchy substance like tiny beads, obtained from dried cassava root and used in puddings.

tapir (*pron:* **tape**-er) **Tapirs** are large pig-like mammals in South and Central America and south-east Asia. They have long snouts and short legs.

tapper See **tap.**

tar (tarred) Tar is a thick black sticky substance obtained by distilling coal or wood. If something is **tarred,** it is coated in tar. ■ **Tar** is one of the poisonous substances in tobacco. ■ If you talk about someone being **tarred with the same brush** as someone else, you mean they are considered to have the same faults.

taramasalata (*pron:* tar-ram-as-sal-**lah**-ta) is a pinkish Greek food made from smoked cod roe.

tarantula (*pron:* ta-**rant**-yoo-la) **Tarantulas** are large hairy tropical spiders.

tardy (**tardiness**) If someone is **tardy** in doing something, they are not doing it quickly enough. *...Washington's tardy response.*

target (**targeting, targeted**) A **target** is an object you fire bullets or arrows at when you are practising shooting or archery. ■ In war, any place or object which a shell, bomb, or missile is aimed at can be called a **target.** You can also say a place or object is **targeted.** *The government had rejected claims that there were civilian casualties, saying the rebel bases were targeted very carefully.* ■ If someone is threatened or criticized, you can say they are the **target** of threats or criticism. *He was the target of abuse from the fans last season.* ■ Your **target** is the thing you are trying to achieve. *The prime minister set a target of 3.5% economic growth.* If you are **on target,** you are making good progress and are likely to achieve the thing you want. ■ If you **target** a particular group of people, you try to appeal to them or help them. *...products targeted at children.*

tariff A **tariff** is (a) a tax on imported goods. (b) a scale of charges. *...electricity tariffs.*

Tarmac is a material for making road surfaces, consisting of crushed stones mixed with tar. 'Tarmac' is a trademark. ■ You can refer to any area with a Tarmac surface as the **tarmac,** especially a runway at an airport.

tarn A **tarn** is a small mountain lake.

tarnish (**tarnishes, tarnishing, tarnished**) If a metal **tarnishes,** it becomes stained and loses its brightness. ■ If something **tarnishes** someone's reputation, it spoils it. *We are all aware of the undesirable minority who tarnish sport's image.*

tarot (*pron:* **tarr**-oh) The **tarot** is a set of special cards, used for fortune-telling.

tarpaulin A **tarpaulin** is a sheet of heavy waterproof material used as a protective cover.

tarragon is a herb with narrow green leaves.

tarred See **tar.**

tarry (**tarries, tarrying, tarried**) If you **tarry** somewhere, you stay longer than you intended.

tarsal (**tarsus**) The **tarsals** are the bones forming the ankle, heel, and upper foot. Together they are called the **tarsus.**

tart (**tartly, tarty**) A **tart** is a shallow pastry case with a sweet filling. ■ A **tart** remark is sharp and rather cruel. *'I'm sorry' -- 'That will be a new experience,' she said tartly.* ■ Prostitutes are sometimes called **tarts.** ■ Some people call women **tarts** or describe them as **tarty** when they dress or behave provocatively. ■ If you say something has been **tarted up,** you mean someone has tried to improve its appearance, but in a cheap and vulgar way.

tartan is woollen cloth with a pattern of woven stripes of different widths and colours crossing

each other at right angles. Each Scottish clan has its own design of tartan.

tartar is a hard yellowish substance which forms on teeth. ■ See also **tartare sauce.**

tartare sauce (*or* **tartar sauce**) is a thick sauce made of chopped onions, capers, and mayonnaise, usually eaten with fish.

tarty See **tart.**

task (**tasked**) A **task** is a job or piece of work. If someone is given an important job or responsibility, you can say they are **tasked** with it. *...international institutions tasked with keeping the peace.* ■ A **task force** is a group of people assembled to carry out a particular task, especially a section of an army, navy, or air force sent to carry out a military operation.

taskmaster If you say someone is a hard **taskmaster,** you mean they make the people under them work very hard.

tassel (**tasselled**) (*Am:* **tasseled**) A **tassel** is a bunch of loose threads or cords bound at one end, used for decoration. If something is **tasselled,** it is decorated with a tassel or tassels. *...tasselled loafers.*

taste (**tasting, tasted**) Your sense of **taste** is your ability to recognize the flavour of things with your tongue. ■ The **taste** of something is its flavour. If you **taste** something, you become aware of its flavour. If it **tastes** of a particular thing, it has that flavour. *...juicy white pulp that tastes of peach.* ■ If you **taste** food, for example when you are cooking, you put a small amount in your mouth to see what it tastes like. Similarly, you can **taste** a wine to judge its quality or see if you like it. ■ If you have a short experience of something, especially for the first time, you can say you have a **taste** of it. *His first taste of fame came after an appearance on 'Opportunity Knocks'.* ■ If you develop a **taste** for something, you get to like it. ■ A person's **tastes** are the types of thing they enjoy or like to have around them. *Our tastes are remarkably similar.* If you say that someone has **good taste,** you approve of their choices. ■ If you say something is in bad **taste,** you mean it does not conform to what is proper or decent, and is offensive. **Good taste** is conforming to what is proper and decent.

taste bud Your **taste buds** are the clusters of cells on the surface of your tongue which enable you to taste food and drink.

tasteful (**tastefully**) If you say something is **tasteful,** you mean it is attractive and elegant and shows good taste.

tasteless (**tastelessly, tastelessness**) If you say something is **tasteless,** you mean it is vulgar, unattractive, and shows poor taste. *...tasteless decorations.* ■ If you say a joke or remark is **tasteless,** you mean it is offensive. ■ **Tasteless** food has very little flavour.

taster A **taster** is someone whose job is tasting wines, teas, or other things to test their quality. ■ A **taster** is a small sample of something which gives an indication of what it is like. *I fear this is only a taster of what will happen when more services are privatised.*

tasty (**tastier, tastiest**) Tasty food has a strong pleasant flavour. **Tasty** is usually used to describe savoury rather than sweet food.

tat is used to talk about things which are tasteless, worthless, or of poor quality. *...shops selling an astounding variety of tat.*

tattered (**tatters**) Tattered paper or clothing is badly torn. ■ If a system, organization, or plan is **tattered** or **in tatters**, it is in a very bad state.

tattoo (**tattooist**) If someone is **tattooed**, they have designs drawn on their skin by a process which involves pricking little holes and filling them with coloured dye. These designs are called **tattoos**. A person who tattoos people is called a **tattooist**. ■ A military **tattoo** is a public display of parades, exercises, and music by the armed forces.

tatty If something is **tatty,** it is shabby and untidy.

taught See **teach.**

taunt If someone **taunts** you, they mock you about your weaknesses or misfortunes, to upset or annoy you. The things they say are called **taunts.**

taut (**tautly**) If something is **taut,** it is stretched very tight. *He pulled the rope taut.* ■ If you call something like a film **taut,** you mean it is concentrated and controlled, with no unnecessary details. ■ If a situation is **taut,** it is full of tension.

tautology (**tautologies; tautological**) Tautology is the use of different words to say the same thing twice in the same statement. For example, calling something a 'new novelty' would be a tautology. You say a statement like this is **tautological.**

tavern is an old word for a pub.

tawdry (**tawdriness**) Tawdry things are cheap, vulgar, and of poor quality. ■ If you say someone's actions are **tawdry,** you mean they are shameful and unpleasant.

tawny If something is **tawny,** it is yellowish-brown.

tax (**taxes, taxing, taxed**) Tax is money people have to pay to the government. It is used to pay for things like defence and education. ■ If a sum of money is **taxed,** the person who receives it must pay a proportion of it as tax. When goods are **taxed,** a proportion of their price must be paid to the government. If a person or company is **taxed,** they have to pay a proportion of their income or profits to the government. ■ **Tax evasion** is breaking the law by deliberately not paying any tax or not paying enough tax. **Tax avoidance** is finding ways of paying as little tax as possible without breaking the law. ■ A **tax haven** is a country where taxes are so low that wealthy people choose to live or register companies there, to save money on tax. Wealthy people who live in places like these are called **tax exiles.** ■ If something **taxes** you, it requires a lot of physical or mental effort. *...his taxing four-day schedule.*

taxable If something is **taxable,** you have to pay tax on it.

taxation is the system by which a government collects money from people to spend on things like defence, education, and health care. **Taxation** is also the amount of money collected. *They will have to increase local taxation.*

tax-deductible See **deductible.**

tax disc A tax disc is a circular piece of paper displayed on a motor vehicle, to show the owner has paid the annual road tax.

taxi (*plural:* **taxis**) (**taxies, taxiing, taxied**) A taxi is a car whose driver is paid by people to take them where they want to go. ■ When an aircraft **taxies,** it moves slowly along the runway, for example to get into position for take-off.

taxicab is an old name for a taxi.

taxidermy (**taxidermist**) Taxidermy is the craft of stuffing dead animals and birds so they can be displayed. A **taxidermist** is an expert at this.

taxing See **tax.**

taxi rank A taxi rank is a place where taxis wait for passengers.

taxman (**taxmen**) When people talk about the **taxman,** they mean the government department responsible for collecting taxes, the Inland Revenue.

taxonomy (**taxonomist**) Taxonomy is the naming of plants and animals and their classification into groups according to their similarities and differences. A **taxonomist** is a person who studies or specializes in taxonomy.

taxpayer – Taxpayers are people who pay a proportion of their income to the government as tax.

tax return See **return.**

tax year A tax year is a twelve-month period used by the government as a basis for calculating taxes and organizing its own finances and accounts. In Britain, the tax year begins on April 6th.

TB See **tuberculosis.**

tea is a drink made by pouring boiling water over the chopped dried leaves of a plant called the tea bush. The dried leaves are also called **tea.** Other drinks made by pouring hot water on dried leaves are also called **tea,** for example mint tea and camomile tea. ■ **Tea** is a meal. For some, it is a light afternoon meal consisting of things like sandwiches and cakes; for others, it is the main meal of the day, eaten in the early evening.

tea bag – Tea bags are small perforated paper bags with tea leaves in them.

tea caddy (**tea caddies**) A tea caddy is a small tin for storing tea.

teacake – Teacakes are round flat sweet rolls, usually containing raisins. You eat them toasted and spread with butter.

teach (**teaches, teaching, taught**) If you **teach** someone something, you explain it to them, to help them learn about it or learn how to do it. ■ If you **teach** a subject, you help students learn it. ■ If you have been **taught** to think or behave in a certain way, you have been brought up to believe that is the correct way to think or behave. ■ The **teachings** of a religious faith or political doctrine are the ideas and principles upheld and taught by its followers.

teacher A teacher is someone who teaches, especially at a school.

tea chest A tea chest is a large wooden box in which tea is packed when it is exported. People sometimes use tea chests to pack things in, for example when moving house.

teacloth A teacloth is a cloth for drying dishes.

tea cosy (**tea cosies**) A **tea cosy** is a soft cover you put over a teapot to keep the tea hot.

teacup A **teacup** is a cup you drink tea from.

teak is a hard wood often used to make high quality furniture.

teal (*plural:* **teal**) **Teal** are a kind of small wild duck.

tea leaf – **Tea leaves** are the small pieces of dried leaves left in a teapot or cup after you have drunk the tea.

team (**teaming, teamed**) A **team** is a group of people who play against another group in a sport or game. ∎ You can call any group of people who work together a **team.** ...*the management team.* ∎ **Team spirit** is a feeling of pride, loyalty, and companionship which helps people work well together. ∎ If you **team up** with someone, you join with them to work together for a particular purpose.

teamster In the US and Canada, lorry drivers are sometimes called **teamsters.**

teamwork is the ability of a group of people to work together effectively.

teapot A **teapot** is a container with a lid, handle, and spout, used for making and serving tea.

tear (*rhymes with 'peer'*) **Tears** are the drops of liquid which come out of your eyes when you cry. If someone is **in tears,** they are crying.

tear (*rhymes with 'hair'*) (**tearing, tore, have torn, -torn**) If you **tear** something like cloth or paper, you pull it so it starts to come apart or a long narrow hole appears in it. The hole is called a **tear.** If you **tear up** a piece of paper, you destroy it by pulling it into small pieces. ∎ If you **tear** clothes **off,** you take them off quickly and roughly. ∎ If people **tear** something **down,** they quickly dismantle or destroy it. ∎ **Tear** is used to describe the violent effects of something. *The blast tore away a granite block at the base.* ∎ **-torn** can be added to other words to describe places suffering the effects of fighting or conflict. ...*the war-torn capital.* ∎ If you say people are **torn,** you mean they cannot make up their minds about something, or they have desires or responsibilities which conflict. *Today's career woman is torn between family and work.* ∎ If you are **tear** somewhere, you rush or race there. *Two nurses came tearing after me.*

tearaway A **tearaway** is a badly-behaved young person.

teardrop A **teardrop** is a single tear.

tearful (**tearfully**) If someone is **tearful,** they are crying, or are on the verge of crying.

tear gas is a gas which makes the eyes sting and fill with tears. It is sometimes used by the police or army to control crowds.

tear-jerker (**tear-jerking**) If you call a play, film, or book a **tear-jerker** or describe it as **tear-jerking,** you mean it is very sad and sentimental.

tea room A **tea room** is a small restaurant or cafe where tea, coffee, cakes, and light meals are served.

tease (**teasing, teased**) If someone **teases** you, they say or do things to embarrass or upset you, because it amuses them. ∎ You say someone is **teasing** when they deliberately upset someone else by offering them something and then delaying or withdrawing the offer. ...*keeping us in teasing suspense.* ∎ If you **tease out** information, you discover it by persistent investigation.

teaser A **teaser** is a difficult problem or puzzle.

tea service A **tea service** or **tea set** is a set of cups, saucers, and plates with a milk jug, sugar bowl, and teapot.

teaspoon A **teaspoon** is a small spoon, often used to stir sugar in tea or coffee.

teat A female animal's **teats** are the pointed parts on her body which her babies suck to get milk. ∎ A **teat** is a piece of rubber shaped like a teat and fitted to a baby's feeding bottle.

technical (**technically**) **Technical** means involving the sorts of machines, processes, and materials used in industry, transport, and communications. *Production has been troubled by technical problems.* ∎ **Technical** is used to talk about the practical skills and methods used to do an activity such as an art, craft, or sport. ...*my technical skills as a writer.* ...*technically brilliant golfers.* ∎ **Technical** language involves using special words to describe the details of a specialized activity. *The technical term for sunburn is erythema.* ∎ If something is **technically** true, it is true according to a strict interpretation of the facts or rules, but may not be important or appropriate in a particular situation. *They are still technically in a state of war.*

technicality (**technicalities**) The **technicalities** of a process or subject are its practical details, especially those which only experts are likely to know about or understand. ∎ A **technicality** is a point based on a strict interpretation of a law or set of rules. *The earlier verdict was overturned on a legal technicality.*

technician A **technician** is someone whose job involves skilled practical work.

Technicolor is a system of colour photography used in making cinema films. 'Technicolor' is a trademark.

technique A **technique** is a way of doing something. ...*a manufacturing technique.* ∎ **Technique** is skill or ability developed through training and practice. *He went off to the Amsterdam Academy to improve his technique.*

techno is a form of dance music which has a repetitive thumping rhythm and usually no lyrics.

techno- is used to create words which describe things involving technology, especially high technology. ...*techno-parks full of computer companies.*

technocracy (**technocracies; technocrat, technocratic**) A **technocracy** is a system of government or management in which the important decisions are made by scientists, engineers, and other technical experts. A system like this can be called **technocratic;** the people in charge are called **technocrats.**

technology (**technologies; technological, technologist**) **Technology** is the application of scientific knowledge for practical purposes in industry, farming, medicine, or business. **Technological** means to do with technology. ...*this century's technological advances.* ∎ Advanced scientific equipment is often called **technology.** *Big firms can afford* to buy new technology. ■ A particular area of activity which requires scientific methods and knowledge is called a **technology**. ...*energy-saving new technologies*.

technophile (*pron*: **tek**-no-file) A **technophile** is someone who is very enthusiastic about technology and the changes it brings about.

technophobe (*pron*: **tek**-no-fobe) A **technophobe** is someone who is scared of the changes brought about by technology. Their fear is called **technophobia**.

tectonic – **Tectonics** or **plate tectonics** is the study of the earth's crust based on the theory that it is divided into large pieces called 'plates', which are drifting extremely slowly on the molten rock beneath. **Tectonic** means to do with this theory. ...*the tectonic history of continents*.

teddy (**teddies**) A **teddy** or **teddy bear** is a soft toy which looks like a friendly bear.

Teddy boy – **Teddy boys** were young men of the 1950s who wore long jackets, tight 'drainpipe' trousers, and soft thick-soled shoes, and were associated with early rock and roll music.

tedious (**tediously, tedium**) If something is **tedious,** it is boring, because it is repetitive or lasts for a long time. You can talk about the **tedium** of something like this.

tee (**teeing, teed**) In golf, a **tee** is a small piece of plastic used to support the ball on for the first shot of each hole. When a golfer plays this shot, you say he or she **tees off.** The flat area of ground at the start of each hole is also called a **tee.**

teem (**teeming, teemed**) If a place is **teeming** with people or animals, there are very many of them moving around. ...*a teeming city*.

teen See **teens.**

teenager (**teenaged, teenage**) Teenagers are young people aged 13 to 19. **Teenaged** describes young people of this age. ...*teenaged schoolchildren*. **Teenage** is used to describe things to do with teenagers. ...*teenage fashion*.

teens (**teen**) A person's **teens** are the years of their life when they are a teenager. ...*a girl in her late teens*. **Teen** means involving or associated with teenagers. ...*a teen idol*.

teeny means the same as 'tiny'.

teepee See **tepee.**

tee-shirt A **tee-shirt** is the same as a T-shirt.

teeter (**teetering, teetered**) If someone is **teetering,** they are wobbling or moving about unsteadily. ■ If something is **teetering** on the edge of disaster, it is very close to it. *The corporation was teetering on the edge of collapse.*

teeth See **tooth.**

teething If a baby is **teething,** its teeth are starting to appear. This can cause pain and make the baby irritable. ■ If a project experiences a few problems at its start, you can say it has **teething problems.**

teetotal (**teetotaller**) (*Am*: **teetotaler**) If someone is **teetotal** or a **teetotaller,** they never drink alcohol.

TEFL is teaching English to people whose first language is not English. TEFL stands for 'teaching English as a foreign language'.

Teflon is a type of plastic used to coat non-stick pans. 'Teflon' is a trademark.

telecom is short for 'telecommunications'.

telecommunications is the science and technology of sending and receiving signals and messages over long distances using methods such as radio, television, telephone, or fax.

telegenic If someone is **telegenic,** they look good on TV.

telegram A **telegram** is a message sent by telegraph and then printed and delivered.

telegraph (**telegraphic**) Telegraph is a system of sending messages over long distances by electrical or radio signals. **Telegraphic** is used to describe things involving this system. If you **telegraph** someone, you send them a message by telegraph.

telegraph pole – Telegraph poles are tall poles used to hold up telephone wires.

telemetry (*pron:* til-**lem**-i-tree) is the use of automatic equipment to transmit the readings of measuring instruments over a long distance by radio to a receiving station.

telepathy (**telepathic**) Telepathy is direct mind-to-mind communication without using words or visual signals, which some people believe to be possible. **Telepathic** is used to describe communication like this. ...*telepathic messages*.

telephone (**telephoning, telephoned**) The **telephone** is an electrical system you use to talk to someone in another place by dialling a number on a piece of equipment and speaking into it. The piece of equipment is called a **telephone.** When you **telephone** someone, you dial their number and speak to them by telephone.

telephone box A **telephone box** is a small shelter in the street with a public telephone in it.

telephone directory A **telephone directory** is a book containing an alphabetical list of names, addresses, and telephone numbers of the people in an area.

telephone exchange A **telephone exchange** is a building where telephone calls are connected.

telephone number Your **telephone number** is the number people dial when they telephone you.

telephonist (*pron:* tel-**lef**-o-nist) A **telephonist** is someone who works in a telephone exchange, or whose job is to answer the telephone.

telephony (*pron:* tel-**lef**-o-nee) is telephone communication, either by wires or radio signals.

telephoto A **telephoto** lens is a lens you attach to a camera and adjust to make distant things appear larger and clearer.

teleprinter A **teleprinter** is a telegraphic printer which prints out messages it receives from machines in other places, and can also be used to transmit messages.

telescope (**telescoping, telescoped**) A **telescope** is an instrument, usually long and tube-shaped, for looking at distant objects. Lenses in the telescope make the objects seem larger and nearer. ■ If something is **telescoped,** it is made to last for a shorter period, by leaving some parts out.

telescopic instruments make things seem larger and nearer. ■ A **telescopic** device has sections which slide into each other so its length can be adjusted.

teletext is a system of broadcasting pages of written information, for example news, weather, and sports reports, on TV.

telethon A **telethon** is a very long TV programme which is broadcast live to raise funds for charity.

televangelist – **Televangelists** are evangelists, chiefly in the US, who preach on TV, often on their own cable networks.

televise (**televising, televised**) If something is **televised**, it is shown on TV.

television or **TV** is the system of sending pictures and sounds by electrical signals over a distance so people can receive them in their homes. The device you receive them on is called a **television** or a **television set.**

televisual means to do with television. ...*a moment of televisual history.*

telework (**teleworker**) People who **telework** work from home and are connected to their office by a computer link and a telephone or fax. People like these are called **teleworkers.**

telex (**telexes, telexing, telexed**) **Telex** is an international system by which written messages are transmitted using electricity or radio signals and printed out by a machine at their destination. If you **telex** someone or send them a **telex**, you send them a message using this system.

tell (**telling, told; tellingly**) If someone **tells** you something, they speak or write to you, giving you information. ■ If something **tells** you something, you can draw conclusions from it. *The results tell us that it's a very effective treatment.* ■ If something is **telling**, it reveals the truth about a situation. *His list is tellingly short.* ■ If you can **tell** what is happening or what is true, you are able to make correct judgments about it. ■ If you cannot **tell** people or things **apart**, you cannot see the difference between them. ■ If you **tell** someone to do something, you order, instruct, or advise them to do it. ■ If you **tell** someone **off**, you speak crossly to them about something wrong they have done. ■ If you **tell** a story, you repeat it to someone. ■ If an unpleasant or tiring experience begins to **tell**, it begins to have a serious effect on you.

teller You can call someone who tells stories a **story-teller.** ■ A **teller** is a cashier, especially in a bank. ■ A **teller** is someone appointed to count votes, for example at an election or in parliament.

telly (**tellies**) **Telly** is television. A **telly** is a television set.

temerity (*pron:* tim-**merr**-it-tee) If someone does something impudent or disrespectful, you can say they have the **temerity** to do it. *He had the temerity to flatly refuse a Government edict.*

temp A **temp** is a secretary employed by an agency to work for short periods for different organizations.

temper (**tempering, tempered**) If you say someone has a **temper** or a **bad temper**, you mean they become angry easily. You can also say they are **quick-tempered.** When someone becomes angry on a particular occasion, you say they **lose** their

temper. ■ If you talk about the **temper** of a group of people, you mean their general mood or attitude to something. *The public temper is for stiff penalties, not tender care.* ■ When newly-made steel or a steel tool is **tempered**, it is re-heated at a lower temperature, to make it less hard and brittle. ■ If something is **tempered** by something else, it is softened or made less extreme. *Admiration of him is tempered by a sense that he is too aloof.*

temperament (**temperamentally**) Your **temperament** is your basic nature and outlook, which shows in the way you respond to various things that happen. You use **temperamentally** when you are talking about someone's temperament. *He was temperamentally unsuited to be president.*

temperamental people are emotional and subject to sudden mood changes. ■ If you say a machine is **temperamental**, you mean it is unreliable.

temperance is not drinking alcohol. ■ **Temperance** is very self-controlled behaviour.

temperate If a place is **temperate** or has a **temperate** climate, it never gets very hot or very cold there. **Temperate** plants grow best in temperate climates.

temperature The **temperature** is how hot or cold it is, usually expressed in degrees Celsius or Fahrenheit. ■ Your **temperature** is the temperature of your body. If you **have a temperature,** your temperature is higher than normal, because you are ill. If someone **takes your temperature,** they use a thermometer to measure your temperature. ■ If you talk about the **temperature** of a situation, you mean the level of excitement or emotion involved. *The political temperature in election year has gone up.*

tempest A **tempest** is a violent storm. ■ You can call an angry outburst a **tempest.** ...*a tempest of criticism.*

tempestuous If you call an event or relationship **tempestuous,** you mean the people involved keep having arguments.

template A **template** is a thin board or plate cut into a special shape or pattern, used as a guide for cutting materials like metal or fabric. ■ A **template** is a model or example which people try to follow.

temple In some religions, a building of worship is called a **temple.** ■ A **person's** temples are the flat parts on each side of their forehead.

tempo (*plural:* **tempos** or **tempi**) The **tempo** of a piece of music is the speed at which it is played. ■ The **tempo** of a situation is the speed at which things are taking place. ...*the tempo of change.*

temporal things are not concerned with religion or spirituality. ...*the need for the clergy not to become pre-occupied with temporal matters.* ■ The **temporal** parts of the brain are the parts near the temples. ...*a small but important area of the temporal lobe.*

temporary (**temporarily**) If something is **temporary,** it is not permanent or only lasts a short time. ...*a temporary ban on mining in the Antarctic.*

temporize (*or* **temporise**) (**temporizing, temporized**) If someone is **temporizing,** they are doing or saying unimportant things, to delay making a decision or giving an opinion.

tempt (temptation) If you **tempt** someone, you try to persuade them to do something by offering or promising them something. *Banks and building societies are using competitions to tempt customers to open savings accounts.* ■ If you are **tempted** by something, you feel you want to do it or have it, although it may not be a good idea. You say something like this is **tempting.** The desire to have it or do it is called **temptation.** *Most people seem to be resisting the temptation to spend lots of money.* ■ You say someone is **tempting fate** if you feel that by talking as if things will go right they are encouraging them to go wrong. *Things are at an early stage so I don't want to tempt fate by saying too much.*

temptress (temptresses) A **temptress** is a woman who sets out to allure or seduce men.

ten (tenth) Ten is the number 10.

tenable If you say something like an opinion is **tenable,** you mean it is reasonable and can be defended against criticism. *The claim is really not tenable.*

tenacious (tenaciously, tenacity) A **tenacious** person is very determined and does not give up easily. You talk about the **tenacity** of someone like this. *His tenacity saw him through 11 gruelling games.*

tenancy (tenancies) A **tenancy** is an arrangement in which someone pays rent to use another person's land or buildings.

tenant (tenanted) A **tenant** is a person who pays rent for the place they live in, or for other land or buildings they use. ■ If a pub is **tenanted,** the landlord or landlady rents it from the owner.

tench (*plural:* **tench**) The **tench** is a dark-green thick-bodied freshwater fish.

tend If something **tends** to happen, it usually or often happens. *...lighter cars tend to be noisy.* ■ If you **tend** a person or thing you look after them carefully. *...tending the garden.*

tendency (tendencies) If you have a **tendency** to do something, you often do it. You can say there is a **tendency** for something to happen. *...suicidal tendencies. ...the government's tendency towards secrecy in recent years.*

tendentious If you call what someone says **tendentious,** you mean it deliberately presents information or other people's views in a biased way.

tender (tenderly, tenderness; tendering, tendered) If someone is **tender,** they behave in a gentle caring way. ■ If someone is at a **tender** age, they are young and inexperienced. ■ If food is **tender,** it is soft and easy to cut or chew. ■ If a part of your body is **tender,** it hurts when you touch it. ■ When someone **tenders** for a contract, they make a formal offer to supply goods or services. This offer is called a **tender.** ■ If work is **tendered** or put **out to tender,** private companies or individuals are invited to make offers to do it. ■ If you **tender** your resignation, you formally resign. ■ **legal tender:** see **legal.**

tendon A **tendon** is a strong cord of tissue which joins a muscle to a bone.

tendril — **Tendrils** are thin curling stems which some plants put out to attach themselves to walls or other plants.

tenement A **tenement** is a large old building divided into several flats.

tenet (*pron:* **ten**-nit) The **tenets** of a theory or belief are the principles it is based on. *...the basic tenets of Marxism.*

tenner A **tenner** is ten pounds or a ten-pound note.

tennis is a game played on a rectangular court by two or four players. They use rackets to hit a ball backwards and forwards across a net.

tenon See **mortice.**

tenor A **tenor** is a man with a fairly high singing voice. ■ Several musical instruments have **tenor** as part of their name. They are often in the middle of a range of instruments of a particular type. *...a tenor saxophone.*

tenpin bowling is an indoor game in which you try to knock down ten bottle-shaped objects called **tenpins** by rolling a heavy ball at them.

tense (tensing, tensed; tensely) If you are **tense,** you are nervous and cannot relax. You say a situation is **tense** when the people involved feel like this. *...tense negotiations.* ■ If you **tense** your muscles, you tighten and stiffen them. ■ The **tense** of a verb is its form, which shows whether you are talking about the past, present, or future. For example, the past tense of 'run' is 'ran'.

tensile The **tensile** strength of a material is a measurement of its strength, and is the maximum stress it can stand without breaking when it is stretched.

tension is a feeling of stress or fear, especially before something difficult, dangerous, or important happens. *The incident follows a weekend of tension and uncertainty in the Republic.* ■ You can talk about the **tension** between two things which have conflicting requirements. *...the growing tension between price and quality.* ■ The **tension** in a rope or wire is how tightly it is stretched.

tent (tented) A **tent** is a canvas or nylon shelter held up by poles and ropes, which people sleep in when camping. A **tented** area has a tent or tents in it.

tentacle The **tentacles** of a creature like an octopus are the long thin flexible parts it uses to feel with and to hold things. ■ When people talk about the **tentacles** of a group or organization, they are talking about the extent of its power or influence. *The Mafia is spreading its tentacles into the industrialised north.*

tentative (tentatively) If something you do is **tentative,** you act hesitantly because you are nervous or uncertain. *I tentatively suggested that we ought to start again.* ■ **Tentative** arrangements are at an experimental or preparatory stage. *The Chancellor announced that tentative agreement had been reached.*

tented See **tent.**

tenterhooks If you are **on tenterhooks,** you are waiting to see what is going to happen and are nervous and excited about it.

tenuous (tenuously) If something such as a connection, some evidence for something, or someone's position is **tenuous,** it is very weak or uncertain.

tenure is the legal right to rent land or a building for a period of time. ■ **Tenure** is the period during which someone holds an important job. ...*his brief and unremarkable tenure as prime minister.* ■ If you have **tenure** in your job, you can hold it until you retire.

tepee (*or* **teepee**) (*pron:* **tee**-pee) A **tepee** is a tall pointed tent, usually made from animal skins, the traditional dwelling of many Native Americans.

tepid If a liquid is **tepid**, it is slightly warm, and rather unpleasant as a result. ...*a cup of tepid orange juice.* ■ If something is **tepid**, it lacks enthusiasm or liveliness. *He drew only tepid applause.* ...*tepid political debates.*

tercentenary (**tercentenaries**) A **tercentenary** is a year when you celebrate something which happened exactly 300 years earlier.

term A **term** is a word with a specific meaning. ...*pyrexia, the medical term for high body temperature.* ■ If something is **termed** a particular thing, that is what people call it. ...*the pollution of space by what has been popularly termed 'space junk'.* ■ A **term** is one of the periods an academic year is divided into. ■ A **term** is a fixed period of time. *His term of office lasts one year.* ■ The **terms** of an agreement are the conditions which all parties must abide by. ■ You use **terms** to say which aspect of something you are talking about. *What this means in terms of human misery and hardship can neither be imagined nor described.* ■ If you **come to terms with** something difficult or unpleasant, you learn to accept it. ■ If people are **on good terms,** they are friendly with each other.

terminal (**terminally**) A **terminal** illness or disease causes death, often slowly, and is incurable. ■ A **terminal** is a place where vehicles, passengers, or goods begin or end a journey. ...*the ferry terminal.* See also **air terminal.** ■ A computer **terminal** is a piece of equipment consisting of a keyboard and a screen which is used for entering information into a computer or getting information from it.

terminate (**terminating, terminated; termination**) If something is **terminated,** it is ended completely. *He terminated the contract.* ■ If a train or bus **terminates** at a place, it ends its journey there.

terminology (**terminologies**) The **terminology** of a subject is the set of specialized words and phrases used in connection with it.

terminus (**terminuses**) A **terminus** is a place where trains or buses begin or end their journeys.

termite – **Termites** are small white insects which live in large colonies and feed on wood.

tern – **Terns** are a group of seabirds with long pointed bills, long wings, and forked tails.

terrace (**terracing, terraced**) A **terrace** is a row of similar houses joined together by their side walls. A house in a row like this is called a **terraced** house. ■ A **terrace** is a flat area of stone or grass next to a building, where people can sit. ■ If a hillside is **terraced**, it is built up into a series of flat areas of ground like steps where crops can be grown. These flat areas are called **terraces.** ■ The **terraces** at a football ground are the wide flat steps where some spectators stand.

terracotta is a brownish-red clay which has been baked but not glazed and is used for making things like flower pots.

terra firma is used to talk about the ground when you are contrasting it with the sea or the air, especially because it seems safer. *At last Bailey had his feet on terra firma.*

terrain The **terrain** in an area is the type of land there. ...*hilly terrain.*

terrapin – **Terrapins** are a type of small turtle.

terrestrial means to do with the planet Earth. ■ **Terrestrial** TV or radio signals are sent over the earth's surface from a transmitter on land, rather than by satellite. ■ A **terrestrial** animal lives on land or on the ground rather than in the sea, in trees, or in the air.

terrible (**terribly**) ■ If you say something is **terrible,** you mean it is very bad, very unpleasant, or of very poor quality. ■ If you say you feel **terrible,** you mean (a) you feel ill. (b) you feel embarrassed or guilty about a bad situation you have caused. ■ Some people use **terribly** to emphasize certain words. *These tests are terribly important.*

terrier A **terrier** is a small breed of dog. There are many different types of terrier.

terrific (**terrifically**) If you say something is **terrific,** you mean you are very pleased with it or you like it a lot. ■ You can use **terrific** to say something is very great in amount, degree, or intensity. *The force of the explosion must have been terrific.*

terrify (**terrifies, terrifying, terrified; terrifyingly**) If someone or something **terrifies** you, they make you feel very frightened.

terrine (*pron:* **terr**-een) A **terrine** is a mixture of blended meat, vegetables, or fish, similar to pâté.

territorial means to do with ownership of land or water. ...*a territorial dispute.*

Territorial Army The **Territorial Army** or **TA** is a British armed force whose members are not professional soldiers but train as soldiers in their spare time.

territory (**territories**) **Territory** is land controlled by a country or ruler. ...*an oilfield on Russian territory.* ■ An animal's **territory** is the area it regards as its own and defends, especially from other animals of the same species. ■ **Territory** is a particular type of land. ...*Amazon rainforest territory.* ■ You can use **territory** when talking about an area of knowledge or experience. *The case plunged both the defence and prosecution into largely uncharted legal territory.*

terror is great fear. A **terror** is something which makes you very frightened. ...*the terrors of a difficult birth.* ■ **Terror** is violence or the threat of violence, especially when it is used for political purposes. ...*the IRA terror campaign in mainland Britain.*

terrorise See **terrorize.**

terrorism (**terrorist**) **Terrorism** is the use of violence to achieve political aims. A **terrorist** is someone who commits violent acts for political reasons. **Terrorist** means involving terrorism. ...*a wave of terrorist attacks.*

terrorize (*or* **terrorise**) (**terrorizing, terrorized**) If someone **terrorizes** you, they keep you in a constant state of fear by using or threatening violence.

terse (**tersely**) A **terse** statement or comment is brief and says no more than is necessary.

tertiary means third in order, third in importance, or at a third stage of development. ■ **Tertiary** education is education at university or college level.

Terylene is a light strong man-made cloth used especially for making clothes. 'Terylene' is a trademark.

TESSA A TESSA was a type of bank or building society savings account which paid tax-free interest provided you left your money in it for five years. TESSA stands for 'Tax-Exempt Special Savings Account'.

test When you **test** something, you try it to see what it is, what condition it is in, or how well it works. A **test** is a deliberate action or experiment to find out whether something works or how well it works. ■ If you **test** someone, you ask them questions to see how much they know about something. ■ A **test** is a set of questions or tasks given to someone to find out what they know or can do. ■ **Testing** problems or situations are very difficult to deal with.

testable If a theory is **testable**, it can be tested to see if it works or is true.

testament If one thing is a **testament** to another thing, the first thing is a proof of or tribute to the second. *The empty city centre shops stand testament to the recession.* ■ See also **Old Testament, New Testament.**

testator (**testatrix**) You call someone who makes a will a **testator.** A female testator can be called a **testatrix.**

test case A **test case** is a legal case which becomes an example for deciding other similar cases.

testes A man's **testes** are the same as his testicles.

testicle (**testicular**) A man's **testicles** are the two sex glands between his legs which produce sperm. **Testicular** is used to describe things relating to the testicles. *...testicular cancer.*

testify (**testifies, testifying, testified**) When someone **testifies**, they make a formal statement in a court of law. ■ If one thing **testifies** to another, it shows it exists. *Scorched earth and piles of rubble testified to the brutality of the war.*

testimonial A **testimonial** is a statement from someone in authority saying how good something or someone is. ■ A **testimonial** or **testimonial match** is a sports match specially arranged so that part of the profits can be given to a particular player.

testimony (**testimonies**) Someone's **testimony** is a statement they make in court. ■ If one thing is a **testimony** to another, it shows clearly that the second thing has a particular quality. *The fact that we've reached the final is a testimony to the character of everyone here.*

testing See **test.**

testosterone (*pron:* tess-**toss**-ter-rone) is a hormone produced mainly in the testicles and thought to be responsible for producing the male sexual instinct and other male characteristics.

test pilot A **test pilot** is a pilot who flies aircraft of a new design to test their performance.

test tube A **test tube** is a small glass container used in chemical experiments. ■ A **test tube baby** is a baby born as a result of an egg being fertilized outside a woman's body and then replaced in her womb.

testy (**testily**) If someone is **testy,** they are impatient and bad-tempered.

tetanus is a serious disease which is caused by germs getting into a wound. It causes muscle spasms and convulsions.

tetchy (**tetchily**) A **tetchy** person is irritable and gets angry suddenly for no obvious reason.

tête-à-tête (*pron:* tet ah tet) A **tête-à-tête** is a private meeting between two people.

tether (**tethering, tethered**) A **tether** is a rope or chain used to tie an animal to a post or fence so it can only move within a small area. If you **tether** an animal, you tie it up like this. ■ If you are **at the end of your tether,** you feel you cannot put up with an unpleasant situation any longer.

tetralogy (*pron:* tet-**ral**-o-jee) (**tetralogies**) A **tetralogy** is a series of four related works, for example four novels involving the same characters.

Teutonic is used to describe behaviour thought to be typical of German people. *...Teutonic thoroughness.*

text The **text** of a book is the main written part, rather than the pictures or index. ■ The **text** of a speech, broadcast, or recording is the written version of it. ■ **Text** is any written material. *...printed text.* ■ A **text** is a book or other piece of writing, especially one used for academic study. *His plays are set texts in universities.*

textbook A **textbook** is a book about a particular subject, for use by students or schoolchildren. ■ If you say something is a **textbook** example of a certain thing, you are emphasizing that it is a clear example of that thing.

textile – **Textiles** are cloths or fabrics, especially woven ones.

textual means to do with written texts, especially literary texts. *...textual analysis of Shakespeare's plays.*

texture The **texture** of something is the way it feels when you touch it, for example how rough or smooth it is. ■ You can call the structure of something its **texture**. *The cake has a crumbly texture.* ■ The **texture** of something like a piece of music or a film is the impression it makes on you as a result of the way its different elements are combined. *...the texture of the orchestral sound.*

textured A **textured** surface is not smooth but has a particular feel, for example rough or fluffy.

Thalidomide is a type of tranquilizer which was withdrawn from use after it was discovered that if taken by pregnant women it could cause foetuses to develop deformed limbs. 'Thalidomide' is a trademark.

than You use **than** (a) when you are comparing two things. *She was 12 years older than me.* (b) to emphasize how large or small something is, by comparing it to a particular figure or level. *Some top independent schools cost more than £10,000 a year.*

thank When you **thank** someone or express your **thanks** to them, you tell or show them how grateful you are for something, usually by saying **thanks** or **thank you.** ■ If you say something happens **thanks to** a certain thing, you mean it happens because of that thing.

thankful (**thankfully**) If you are **thankful** for something, you are happy and relieved about it.

thankless A **thankless** task involves a lot of hard work and is not appreciated by other people.

Thanksgiving or **Thanksgiving Day** is a public holiday in the autumn in the US and Canada. ■ A **thanksgiving** service is a special religious service held to thank God for something good.

thankyou If you refer to something as a **thankyou,** you mean it is intended to show thanks for something. *The gift is a thankyou for our help.*

that person or thing means the one you have just mentioned. *That evidence was not disputed.* **That** is also used on its own to refer to something you have just been talking about. *That is a view beginning to take hold in government ranks.* ■ **That** is used after words such as 'suggest' to introduce what someone said, thought, or felt. *He explained that the Scottish climate was ideal for wild mushrooms to flourish... I suggested that I take her to dine at the nearby Hilton Hotel.* ■ You use **that** to say which thing or things you are talking about. *...the gate that opened onto the lake.* ■ If you say, for example, something is **not that** good, you mean it is not really very good. *It isn't that difficult a job.*

thatch (**thatches, thatching, thatched; thatcher**) If someone **thatches** a house, they make a roof for it with straw or reeds. The straw or reeds they use are called **thatch. A thatcher** is a person whose job is to thatch roofs.

Thatcherism is the name given to the policies and aims of the British government when Margaret Thatcher was Prime Minister (1979 - 1990), in particular privatization, monetarism, self-help, and the reduction of state intervention.

Thatcherite is used to talk about people, especially politicians, who believe in the principles of Thatcherism. *...a Thatcherite ex-minister.*

thaw When ice or snow **thaws,** it melts. A **thaw** is a period of warmer weather when this happens. ■ When you **thaw** frozen food, you take it out of the freezer so it can reach room temperature ready for use. ■ If someone who has been unfriendly **thaws,** they start to be more friendly. Similarly, you can say an unfriendly relationship **thaws** or talk about a **thaw** in it. *...a thaw in US-Cuban relations.*

the is called the 'definite article'. You use it when it is clear which person or thing you are talking about. *...heat the oil. ...the Secretary of State.* ■ You use **the** in front of words referring to a species of animal, people's nationality, or people's social situation. *...animals such as the gazelle... He had been disloyal to Breton fishermen by siding with the English. ...training for the unemployed.* ■ You use **the** in front of the plural form of a surname to talk about a couple or family. *...The Lynches.*

theatre (*Am:* **theater**) A **theatre** is a building with a stage on which plays and other entertainments are performed. ■ **Theatre** is used to talk about the performing of plays and the people involved in their performance. *...some of the best-loved names in theatre.* ■ In the US, cinemas are often called **theaters** or **movie theaters.** ■ In a hospital, an operating theatre is often called a **theatre.** ■ A **theatre** of war is the area or region where it is happening.

theatregoer (*Am:* **theatergoer**) A **theatregoer** is someone who regularly goes to the theatre.

theatrical (**theatrically, theatricality**) **Theatrical** means to do with the theatre. *He began his theatrical career in Cardiff.* ■ **Amateur theatricals** is the performing of plays by amateur actors. ■ **Theatrical** behaviour is exaggerated, unnatural, and done for effect. You talk about the **theatricality** of behaviour like this.

thee is an old-fashioned word for 'you'.

theft is the crime of stealing.

their (**theirs**) You use **their** or **theirs** when you are talking about something belonging to or connected with people or things that have just been mentioned. *It's not fair to come round to someone's house and drink all their coffee.* ■ You use **their** when you are talking formally about two or more royal or titled people. *...their Royal Highnesses.*

them You use **them** to talk about people or things that have already been mentioned. *Two bowls of Unimix are given to each child every day and this provides them with 900 calories.*

thematic (**thematically**) If something is organized in a **thematic** way, it is divided up according to subjects or topics. *...thematic exhibitions.*

theme The **theme** of a discussion or lecture is its main subject. ■ A **theme** in an artist's or writer's work is an idea which is developed or repeated in it. ■ The **theme** of something like a concert is a common link between the different items in it. *The theme of this year's Royal Show is Global Partnership.* ■ In a piece of classical music, a **theme** is a short simple tune which is often repeated or developed. ■ A **theme** or **theme tune** is (a) a piece of music played at the beginning and end of a TV or radio programme. (b) a piece of music played several times during a film or musical, which has become very well-known. *...the theme from Dr Zhivago.*

theme park A **theme park** is a large outdoor area with fairground rides, amusement arcades, and other forms of entertainment, all of which have a common theme.

themselves You use **themselves** (a) to say that something which is done by two or more people affects those people. *Women are more likely than men to delude themselves about their drinking.* (b) to emphasize that your statement really does apply to the people you are talking about. *The biggest costs are often met by the groups themselves.*

then You use **then** to talk about a time in the past or future. *She had, by then, married and divorced a pharmacist.* ■ You use **then** to say one thing happens or comes after another. *Like his father, he became a teacher and then headmaster of a secondary school.* ■ You use **then** to introduce a summary or conclusion to what you have just said, or to end a conversation. *There is, then, no general pattern of decline in the fortunes of Green parties.* ■ You use **then** at the beginning of a sentence or after 'and' or 'but' to introduce an extra piece of information. *Then there is the little matter of electricity.* ■ **now and then:** see **now.**

thence is an old-fashioned word meaning 'from there'. *The mosaics found their way to Munich, and thence to Geneva.*

theocracy (theocratic) A **theocracy** or **theocratic** state is a society ruled by priests.

theodolite A **theodolite** is an instrument used in surveying for measuring angles.

theology (theologian; theological, theologically) **Theology** is the study of religion and ideas about God. A **theologian** is someone who studies these things. **Theological** means to do with religion. *Theologically Gladden was in the vanguard of liberalism.*

theorem A **theorem** is a mathematical statement which can be logically proved to be correct.

theoretical (theoretically) **Theoretical** is used (a) to talk about the ideas and abstract principles of a subject, rather than its practical aspects. ...*his theoretical knowledge of physics.* (b) to talk about scientists whose work involves theories and ideas, rather than experiments or research. ...*theoretical physicists.* ■ A **theoretical** situation is supposed to exist, but in reality may not do so. *Theoretically, Britons are able to work anywhere in the EU.*

theoretician A **theoretician** is the same as a theorist.

theorise See **theorize.**

theorist A **theorist** is someone who produces a theory to explain something.

theorize (or theorise) (theorizing, theorized) If you **theorize** about something, you develop ideas about it to try and explain it.

theory (theories) A **theory** is an idea or set of ideas intended to explain something. ■ The principles or ideas on which a practice or skill is based are called its **theory.** ...*two lectures on the theory and practice of central banking.* ■ You use **in theory** to say that although something is supposed to happen or be true, in reality it may not happen or be true. *In theory, the temperature of a planet is highest near ground level.*

therapeutic If something is **therapeutic,** it helps you to feel happier and more relaxed. ■ **Therapeutic** medical treatment is given to treat a disease or improve a person's health, using drugs or other methods.

therapy (therapies; therapist) **Therapy** is the medical treatment of any disease or abnormal condition. A **therapist** is a person skilled in a particular type of therapy. ...*a speech therapist.*

there You use **there** with words like 'is', 'are', 'was', or 'were' to say something does or does not exist. *He said there was no quick solution to the war.* ■ You use **there** (a) to talk about a place which has already been mentioned. *My school didn't have a drama club until I went there.* (b) to indicate a place you are pointing to or looking at. *Look! Over there!* ■ You use **there** to talk about a point someone has made

in a conversation. *He is right there, you know.* ■ You use **there** to talk about a stage in an activity or a process. *Its strategy is simply to pick the ending it likes best and work back from there.*

thereabouts You say **or thereabouts** after a number or date to show it is approximate. *They will hatch out in 17 days or thereabouts.*

thereafter means after the date or event you have just mentioned. *Reyes left school at 18 and married shortly thereafter.*

thereby means as a result of the thing you have just mentioned. *This increases our costs of manufacture, thereby making us less competitive.*

therefore You use **therefore** when you are mentioning the logical result of what you have just said. *He was out of a job and therefore immediately available.*

therein means in the place you have just mentioned, or in the book or document you have just mentioned. ■ You use **therein** when you are talking about the cause of a situation. *This argument goes down well with party activists – and therein lies the Democratic dilemma.*

thereof means of the thing just mentioned. ...*accounting practices and the abuse thereof.*

thereupon means straight after an event and as a result of it. *Growth had plunged in the second quarter of 1985. The government thereupon introduced a number of emergency measures.*

therm Heat is sometimes expressed in **therms.** A therm is about 105.5 million joules.

thermal means to do with heat. ...*the thermal efficiency of timber-frame homes.* ■ **Thermal** clothing is specially designed to keep you warm. ...*thermal vests.*

thermodynamics is the branch of physics concerned with the relationship between heat and other forms of energy.

thermometer A **thermometer** is an instrument for measuring temperature.

thermonuclear A **thermonuclear** weapon or device is detonated by the high temperatures generated by nuclear fission.

thermoplastic materials are made of a plastic which becomes soft when it is heated and hardens again when it cools.

Thermos (Thermoses) A **Thermos** or **Thermos flask** is a container used to keep hot or cold drinks at a constant temperature. 'Thermos' is a trademark.

thermostat A **thermostat** is a device which automatically keeps the temperature of something at a particular level.

thesaurus (thesauruses) A **thesaurus** is a reference book in which words with similar meanings are grouped together.

these is used to talk about people or things you have just mentioned. *These magnets are the largest part of the project's cost... There are many more where these came from.* ■ **These** is used when identifying people or things. *These are my children.*

thesis (plural: theses) A **thesis** is an idea or theory expressed as a statement and discussed in a logical way. *His thesis is that all economic systems are not alike.* ■ A **thesis** is a long piece of writing based on your own ideas and research, completed as part of a higher university degree.

thespian means to do with drama and the theatre. Actors are sometimes called **thespians.**

they You use **they** to talk about people or things that have already been mentioned. *15th-century sailors knew exactly how fast they were moving.* ■ You use **they** to talk about people in general, or a group of people whose identity is not actually stated. *It is, they say, the housing of the future.*

thick (**thickly, thickness**) If an object is **thick,** its opposite sides or surfaces are quite far apart. *...a thick stone wall.* ■ You use **thick** when giving the distance between the opposite sides or surfaces of something. *The metal is only an eighth of an inch thick.* ■ A **thick** liquid does not flow easily. ■ **Thick** smoke or fog is difficult to see through. ■ **Thick** is used to describe things growing or grouped closely together in large quantities. *...thick undergrowth.* ■ If you are **in the thick of** an activity or situation, you are very involved in it. ■ If you say someone is **thick,** you mean they are stupid. ■ If you say someone has a **thick skin** or is **thick-skinned,** you mean they are not easily hurt by what people say to them.

thicken (**thickening, thickened**) If something **thickens,** it becomes more closely packed. *The clouds thickened.* ■ When a liquid **thickens,** it becomes stiffer and flows less easily. ■ If you say **the plot thickens,** you mean the situation you are talking about is getting more and more complicated and mysterious.

thicket A **thicket** is a small group of trees or bushes growing closely together. ■ A **thicket** of people or things is a dense group of them. *The linesman's view was obscured by a thicket of players.*

thief (**thieves; thieving**) A **thief** is a person who steals something. **Thieving** is stealing things.

thigh A person's **thighs** are the top parts of their legs between their knees and their hips.

thimble A **thimble** is a small object which protects the end of your finger when you are sewing.

thin (**thinner, thinnest; thinly, thinness; thinning, thinned**) If an object is **thin,** its opposite sides or surfaces are closer together than usual. *...a thin strip of land.* ■ A **thin** person or animal has very little fat on their body. ■ **Thin** liquids flow very easily. ■ If someone's hair is **thinning,** they are beginning to go bald. ■ If your patience or temper is **wearing thin,** you are becoming impatient or angry. ■ If you **thin** something or **thin** it **out,** you make it less densely packed by removing certain items. *Heavy crops on fruit trees should be thinned out in June.*

thine is an old-fashioned or dialect word for 'your' or 'yours' when you are talking to one person. *Trust in the Lord with all thine heart.*

thing You use **thing** instead of a more precise word. *Everybody thinks they know at least one thing about red wine.* ■ A **thing** is a physical object. *He came into my father's house and started to smash things up.* ■ If you **have a thing** about someone or something, you are especially attracted to them or have very strong

feelings about them. *I guess I've always had a thing for cowboys.*

think (**thinking, thought**) If you **think** about something, you consider it. *The judge said he had thought about the case over the weekend.* ■ What you **think** about something is your opinion of it. *I think it's a lot of nonsense.* ■ If you **think** of something, you remember it or it comes to your mind. *This is not an entirely new idea: the Scots thought of it first.* ■ See also **thought.**

thinker You call someone a **thinker** when they spend a lot of time thinking deeply about important issues and produce new ideas which influence other people. *...two of the most brilliant and influential thinkers of the twentieth century.*

think-tank A **think-tank** is a group of experts appointed by an organization, especially a government, to consider various problems and work out possible solutions to them.

thinner See **thin.** ■ **Thinner** is a liquid like turpentine, which you add to paint or varnish to make it less thick and easier to use.

thin-skinned people are easily hurt by what other people say about them.

third (**thirdly**) The **third** item in a series is the one counted as number 3. ■ A **third** or **one third** is the fraction $\frac{1}{3}$. ■ You say **third** or **thirdly** when you are mentioning the third in a series of points or items. *He will attack him first as a tax-and-spend liberal, secondly on his record as governor of Arkansas, and thirdly on the character issue.*

third class is used to describe people or things considered to have low status or importance. *They don't want to be treated as third class citizens.*

third party A **third party** is a person who is not directly involved in a business agreement or legal case, but is affected by it or is asked to take part in a minor way. ■ If you have **third party** insurance and you cause an accident, your insurance company will pay money only to other people who are hurt or whose property is damaged and not to you.

third person If you make a statement in the **third person,** you make it about another person or thing, and not directly about yourself or about the person you are talking to, using 'he', 'she', 'it', or a name or noun.

third-rate If you describe something as **third-rate,** you mean it is of a very low quality or standard.

Third World The poorer countries of Africa, Asia, and South America are sometimes called the **Third World.**

thirst is not having enough to drink. *...dying of thirst.* ■ A **thirst** for something is a strong desire for it. If you **thirst for** something, you want it very much.

thirsty (**thirstily**) If you are **thirsty,** you feel the need to drink something.

thirteen (**thirteenth**) **Thirteen** is the number 13.

thirty (**thirtieth, thirties**) **Thirty** is the number 30. ■ The **thirties** was the period from 1930 to 1939. ■ If someone is in their **thirties,** they are aged 30 to 39.

this person or thing means the one you have just mentioned. *We are satisfied that this woman is taking* good care of the baby. **This** is also used on its own to refer to something you have just been talking about. *This was to be his debut as a director.* ■ You use **this** to talk about the place you are in at the moment. *Everyone eats out every night in this town.* ■ You use **this** to talk about the current week, month, etc. You also use **this** to talk about the morning, afternoon, etc of the current day. *About 100 students gathered outside this morning.* ■ You use **this** to talk about the next occurrence in the future of a particular day, month, or season. *The grand prix season ends this Sunday.* ■ **This and that** means a variety of things. *We chat about this and that.*

thistle The **thistle** is a wild plant with prickly leaves and purple flowers.

thither is an old word meaning 'to that place'. ■ **hither and thither:** see **hither.**

thong A **thong** is a long thin strip of leather, rubber, or plastic.

thorax (**thoraxes; thoracic**) In a human or animal, the **thorax** is the part of the body enclosing the ribs. **Thoracic** is used to talk about things to do with the thorax. *...the thoracic muscles.* ■ An insect's **thorax** is the central part of its body between its head and its abdomen, which its legs and wings are attached to.

thorn – **Thorns** are the sharp points on some plants and trees.

thorny (**thornier, thorniest**) A **thorny** plant or tree is covered in thorns. ■ A **thorny** question or issue is difficult to deal with.

thorough (**thoroughly, thoroughness**) **Thorough** is used to describe things which are done very carefully and methodically so that nothing is overlooked. *...a through investigation.* ■ If someone is **thorough**, they do things in a careful and methodical way. ■ You can use **thorough** to emphasize the great extent or degree of something. *...a thorough shambles. ...thoroughly contented.*

thoroughbred A **thoroughbred** is an animal, especially a racehorse, whose parents are both of the same high quality breed.

thoroughfare A **thoroughfare** is a main road in a town or city.

thoroughgoing is used to say someone or something has all the qualities of a particular type of person or thing. *...a thoroughgoing conservative.* ■ If you describe a piece of work as **thoroughgoing,** ·you mean it has been carefully and thoroughly put together. *...a thoroughgoing programme of constitutional reform.*

those is used to talk about people or things you have just mentioned. *Most of those houses are for sale... Those are the things which really matter.* ■ **Those** is used when you are saying which group of people you are talking about. *...those of us who knew her well.*

thou is an old-fashioned or dialect word for 'you' when you are talking to one person.

though You use **though** when you are mentioning something which contrasts with the rest of what you are saying. *It didn't turn out to be a difficult job, though it took me two hours.* ■ **Though** means 'in spite of what has just been said'. *Nobody, though,*

could begrudge the Sussex girl her victory.* ■ **as though:** see **as.**

thought See **think.** ■ **Thought** is the activity of thinking. ■ A **thought** is an idea in your mind. ■ Your **thoughts** on a subject are your opinions on it. ■ If a plan is well **thought out,** it has been prepared carefully. If it is badly **thought out,** it has not been prepared carefully. ■ **school of thought:** see **school. second thoughts:** see **second.**

thoughtful (**thoughtfully, thoughtfulness**) If you are **thoughtful,** you are quiet and serious, because you are thinking about something. ■ You say someone is **thoughtful** when they are kind and considerate to other people. ■ If you describe something like a book, film, or speech as **thoughtful,** you mean it is serious and well thought out. *...a thoughtful and scholarly book.*

thoughtless (**thoughtlessly, thoughtlessness**) If you do something in a **thoughtless** way, you do it without thinking. *It is possible that she just thoughtlessly stepped out onto the road.* ■ You say people are **thoughtless** when they forget or ignore what other people want, need, or feel.

thought-provoking If something like a novel, play, or film is **thought-provoking,** it makes you think deeply about the subject it deals with.

thousand A **thousand** is the number 1,000. ■ **Thousands** of things means a very large number of them.

thousandth The **thousandth** item in a series is the one counted as number 1,000. ■ A **thousandth** is the fraction $\frac{1}{1000}$.

thrall If you are in **thrall** to someone or something, you are completely in their power or under their influence. *He is not in thrall to the media.*

thrash (**thrashes, thrashing, thrashed**) If you **thrash** someone in a game or give them a **thrashing,** you defeat them by a large margin. ■ When people **thrash out** something like a policy, they discuss it until they reach an agreement. ■ If people or animals **thrash about,** they twist and turn quickly and violently.

thread (**threading, threaded**) **Thread** is a long thin piece of cotton, silk, nylon, or wool. ■ If you **thread** something like thread or ribbon through a hole or a space, you pass it through. ■ The **thread** on something like a screw is the thin raised spiral line around it. ■ If you **thread** your way through a group of people or things, you pass through the narrow gaps between them. ■ The **thread** of an argument or story is the idea or theme which connects the different parts.

threadbare If things like clothes are **threadbare,** they are old and have become thin and nearly worn out. ■ If you say something like an argument or plan is **threadbare,** you mean it no longer has much force or effect, and people are not convinced by it.

threat If someone makes a **threat,** they say they will harm you if you do not do what they want. ■ If someone or something is a **threat** to a person or thing, they may harm them. *Fishermen are incensed by this apparent threat to their livelihoods.* ■ If there is a **threat** of something unpleasant, it is likely or possible that it will happen. *The threat of nuclear war has diminished.*

threaten (**threatening, threatened**) If someone **threatens** to do something harmful, they say they will do it unless they get what they want. ■ You say something **threatens** people or things when it is likely to harm them or cause them problems. *The English countryside is threatened by a huge increase in traffic... The fighting is threatening to turn into full-scale war.*

threatening (**threateningly**) If someone's behaviour is **threatening,** they say they will harm you unless you do what they want. *A number of other newspapers have since received threatening calls.* ■ You say other things are **threatening** when they seem likely to cause harm. *The United States and big business were portrayed as threateningly rich and powerful.*

three is the number 3.

three-dimensional A **three-dimensional** shape is a shape like a cube or cylinder which can be measured in three different directions. ■ A **three-dimensional** image or picture gives the impression of being solid rather than flat.

threefold If a number or amount is increased **threefold,** it becomes three times as big. ■ If things such as the reasons for doing something are **threefold,** there are three of them. *The central lessons that the armed forces learned from Vietnam were threefold.*

three-line whip In Parliament, if a party imposes a **three-line whip,** it instructs its MPs to attend a debate and vote in a particular way.

three-quarters of something is half of it plus a quarter of it.

three Rs When talking about children's education, the **three Rs** are the basic skills of reading, writing, and arithmetic.

threesome A **threesome** is a group of three people.

threnody (**threnodies**) A **threnody** is a lament for the dead.

thresh (**threshes, threshing, threshed**) When people **thresh** corn, wheat, or rice, they beat it to separate out the grains.

threshold A **threshold** is an amount, level, or limit at which something begins to happen or take effect. *Every applicant will have to meet a minimum quality threshold.* ■ If you are **on the threshold** of something exciting or new, you are about to experience it. ■ The **threshold** of a building or room is the floor in the doorway, or the doorway itself.

threw See **throw.**

thrice is an old-fashioned or dialect word for 'three times'.

thrifty (**thrift**) If someone is **thrifty,** they save money and do not waste things. You talk about the **thrift** of someone like this. ■ In the US, certain types of banks are called **thrifts.**

thrill If something **thrills** you or gives you a **thrill,** it gives you a feeling of excitement and pleasure. You can also say something like this is **thrilling.** ■ If you are **thrilled** about something, you are pleased and excited about it.

thriller A **thriller** is a book, film, or play which tells an exciting story about dangerous, frightening, or mysterious events.

thrive (**thriving, thrived** or **throve**) When people or things **thrive,** they are healthy, happy, or successful.

throat A person's **throat** is (a) the back of their mouth and the top part of the tubes which go down into their stomach and lungs. (b) the front part of a their neck.

throaty If someone's voice or laugh is **throaty,** it sounds low and rather rough.

throb (**throbbing, throbbed**) If a part of your body **throbs,** you feel a series of strong painful beats there. *My head was throbbing.* ■ You say something **throbs** when it vibrates and makes a loud rhythmical noise. *You can hear the vehicle throb into action.*

throes If you are **in the throes of** something difficult, you are deeply involved in it. *Poland is in the throes of a painful economic reform.*

thrombosis (*plural:* **thromboses**) A **thrombosis** is a serious condition caused by a clot of blood blocking a blood vessel. See also **coronary.**

throne A **throne** is a special chair used by royalty on important formal occasions. ■ **The throne** is often used to talk about the position of being a monarch. *The Queen took the throne in 1952.*

throng A **throng** is a large crowd of people. If people **throng** somewhere, they go there in large numbers.

throttle (**throttling, throttled**) If someone **throttles** another person, they strangle them. ■ If someone **throttles** something like a process, they severely restrict it or destroy it. *...attempts to throttle the criminal supply of drugs.* ■ The **throttle** of a motor vehicle is the device which controls the engine's speed by regulating the flow of fuel entering it.

through If something moves **through** an opening or hole, it passes from one side to the other. ■ If you cut **through** something solid, you make a cut from one side to the other. ■ If you move **through** a place or area, you travel across it or within it. ■ If you see something **through** a window, you are on one side of the window and the thing you see is on the other side. Similarly, you can hear something **through** a wall or feel something **through** a layer of material. ■ If something happens **through** a period of time, it happens from the beginning to the end. ■ If you go **through** an experience, it happens to you. ■ If you say you are **through** with someone or something, you mean you are determined not to have any more to do with them. ■ If something happens **through** something else, it happens because of it. *The Sandinistas were deposed, not through force, but through the ballot box.* ■ If you do something **through** another person, they act on your behalf. ■ **Through and through** means completely and to the greatest extent possible. *The system was rotten through and through.*

throughout If something happens **throughout** an event or period of time, it happens during all of it. ■ If something happens or exists **throughout** a place or area, it happens or exists in every part.

throughput The **throughput** of an organization or system is the amount of things it does or deals with in a particular period of time. *Steel throughput rarely met the target figures because of labour disputes.*

throve See **thrive.**

throw (**throwing, threw, have thrown**) If you **throw** an object, you move your hand quickly and let go of the object so it moves through the air. An action like this is called a **throw.** ■ If you are **thrown** somewhere, for example in a collision, you are propelled there forcefully. ■ If you **throw** your hands or arms in a certain direction, you move them there quickly. *She threw her arms around Maria.* ■ If you **throw** yourself into an activity, you take part in it actively and enthusiastically. ■ If something **throws** you into a situation or state, especially an unpleasant one, it causes you to be in it. *The court ruling threw the government into a panic.* ■ If something like a remark or action **throws** you, it confuses or bewilders you, because it is unexpected. ■ If someone **throws** a tantrum, they have one. ■ If you **throw** a party, you organize it. ■ If you **throw** a switch, you turn it on or off. ■ If you **throw away** something you do not want or **throw** it **out,** you get rid of it, for example by putting it in a bin. ■ If you **throw away** an opportunity, you waste it. Similarly, you can **throw away** money on something worthless. ■ If a person who is selling you something **throws in** something else, they give you the extra thing free. *A glass of wine is thrown in with the ticket price.* ■ If you **throw off** something which is restricting you, you free yourself from it. *The Socialists hope they can throw off the burden of their communist past.* ■ If someone is **thrown out** of a place, they are forced to leave. ■ If you **throw up,** you vomit. ■ If people **throw up** a building or some other structure, they build it hurriedly.

throwaway A **throwaway** remark is made casually, but is meant to pass on information or to have a particular effect.

throwback If you say someone or something is a **throwback** to an earlier time, you mean they are like something which existed then.

thrown See **throw.**

thrush (**thrushes**) The **thrush** is a small brown songbird. ■ **Thrush** is a fungal disease of the mouth or vagina.

thrust (**thrusting, thrust** not *'thrusted'*) If you **thrust** something somewhere, you push or move it there quickly and forcefully. A **thrust** is a sudden forceful movement. ■ **Thrust** is the power or force needed to make a plane, rocket, or other vehicle move. ■ The **thrust** of something like an argument or activity is its main focus. *The thrust of his speech was that it was imperative to stick to the timetable already agreed for economic union.* ■ When people talk about the **cut and thrust** of an area of activity, especially politics, they mean the arguing and the competitiveness of it. ■ If you **thrust** something **upon** someone, you force them to have it, whether they want it or not.

thud (**thudding, thudded**) A **thud** is a dull sound, usually made by a solid object hitting something

soft. If something **thuds** against something else, it hits it making a noise like this.

thug (**thuggish, thuggery**) A **thug** is a rough violent man, especially a criminal. You say someone like this is **thuggish;** you call their behaviour **thuggery.**

thumb Your **thumb** is the jointed part which is like a finger but shorter and nearer your wrist. ■ If you are **under** someone's **thumb,** you are under their control. ■ A **rule of thumb** is a simple rule or principle you can follow when you have to make a decision. *The general rule of thumb is the smaller the chilli, the hotter it is.* ■ If you **thumb through** a book or magazine, you turn the pages quickly. ■ See also **well-thumbed.**

thumbnail Your **thumbnail** is the nail on your thumb. ■ A **thumbnail** sketch is very brief.

thumbs-down If you give something like a plan, idea, or suggestion the **thumbs-down,** you indicate that you do not approve of it.

thumbs-up A **thumbs-up** is a sign you make with your hand to show you agree with someone or are happy with an idea or situation. ■ If you give something like a plan, idea, or suggestion the **thumbs-up,** you indicate you approve of it or are willing to accept it.

thumb tack In the US, drawing pins are called **thumb tacks.**

thump If you **thump** something or give it a **thump,** you hit it with your fist. ■ If your heart **thumps,** it beats very strongly and quickly. ■ If something **thumps** against something else, it hits it making a loud dull sound. A **thump** is a loud dull sound. *He landed with a thump.*

thumping (**thumpingly**) A **thumping** amount is very large. *...a thumping Labour majority.* ■ If something is **thumpingly** obvious, it is very obvious.

thunder (**thundering, thundered**) **Thunder** is the loud noise you hear in the sky after a flash of lightning. ■ If something **thunders,** it makes a loud deep continuous noise. You talk about the **thunder** of something like this. *...the thunder of horses' hooves.* ■ If someone **thunders** something, they say it very loudly and forcefully. *'Arrant nonsense!' thundered the Commissioner.* ■ If you **steal** someone's **thunder,** you attract attention instead of them, often by saying or doing something they had intended to say or do.

thunderbolt A **thunderbolt** is a flash of lightning accompanied by thunder.

thunderclap A **thunderclap** is a short loud bang you hear just after a flash of lightning.

thunderous A **thunderous** noise is very loud and deep. *...thunderous applause.*

thunderstorm A **thunderstorm** is a storm in which there is thunder and lightning.

thunderstruck If you are **thunderstruck,** you are very surprised or shocked.

thundery If the weather is **thundery,** there is a lot of thunder, or there are heavy clouds which suggest there will be thunder soon.

thus You say **thus** when you are mentioning the consequences of an action or of something that happens. *Excessive litigation has inflated insurance premiums and thus the cost of goods and services.*

■ You say **thus** when you have described, or are about to describe, how something happened. *Thus was one of the crucial partnerships in the modern cinema formed.*

thwart If you **thwart** someone or **thwart** their plans, you prevent them from doing or getting what they want.

thy is an old-fashioned or dialect word for 'your'. *Love thy neighbour as thyself.*

thyme is a low-growing plant with scented leaves which are used in cooking.

thyroid Your **thyroid** or **thyroid gland** is a gland in your neck which produces hormones to control the way your body grows and functions.

thyself is an old-fashioned or dialect word for 'yourself'. *Know thyself and thou shalt know God.*

tiara A **tiara** is a small semi-circular crown, worn by a woman on formal occasions.

tibia The **tibia** is the inner and thicker of the two bones of the human leg below the knee, between the kneecap and the ankle. The tibia is often called the 'shinbone'.

tic If someone has a **tic,** a part of their face or body keeps twitching.

tick A **tick** is a written mark in the shape of a V with the right side extended upwards, used to show something is correct or has been dealt with. If you **tick** something or **tick** it **off,** you put a mark like this beside it. ■ When a clock or watch **ticks,** it makes a regular series of short sounds as it works. You call these sounds its **tick** or **ticking.** ■ If you say the seconds, minutes, or hours are **ticking away** or **ticking by,** you are emphasizing that time is passing. ■ If you talk about what makes someone **tick,** you are talking about why they behave or think the way they do. ■ If you **tick** someone **off** or give them a **ticking-off,** you speak to them crossly because they have done something wrong. ■ If an engine is **ticking over,** it is running at a low speed. ■ If a system or process is **ticking over,** it is working or operating at a low rate. *...a bill to provide temporary funds to keep services ticking over.* ■ **Ticks** are small flea-like creatures which live on the bodies of people and animals and suck their blood.

ticker-tape is long narrow strips of paper on which information such as stock exchange prices is printed.

ticket A **ticket** is an official piece of card or paper which shows you have paid for a journey or for entry to a place of entertainment. ■ When a motorist gets a **ticket,** they are given an official piece of paper stating they have committed a driving or parking offence. ■ In an American election, a party's **ticket** is its list of candidates. *His presence on the Democratic ticket has done more than anything else to please organised labour.* ■ If you say something is **just the ticket,** you mean it is just what is wanted. ■ See also **season ticket.**

ticking-off See **tick.**

tickle (**tickling, tickled**) When you **tickle** someone, you move your fingers lightly over a part of their body, to make them laugh. ■ If something **tickles,** it causes an irritating feeling by lightly touching part of your body. ■ If something like a remark or

situation **tickles** you, it amuses you. ■ If you are **tickled pink,** you are delighted by something.

ticklish If someone is **ticklish,** it is easy to make them laugh by tickling them. ■ A **ticklish** problem or situation is awkward and needs to be dealt with carefully.

tidal means to do with the movement of tides. *The tidal current gradually decreases in the shallows.*

tidal wave A **tidal wave** is a very large wave, often caused by an earthquake, that flows onto the land and destroys things.

tiddler A **tiddler** is a very small fish of any kind. ■ People or things which are very small or insignificant compared to others of the same kind can be called **tiddlers.** *...political tiddlers.*

tiddlywinks is a game in which players try to get small plastic counters into a cup by pressing their edges to make them jump up.

tide (**tiding, tided**) The **tide** is the regular change in the level of the sea on the shore, caused by the gravitational pull of the sun and moon. When it is at its highest level, you say the tide is in or it is **high tide.** When it is at its lowest level, you say the tide is out or it is **low tide.** ■ The **tide of opinion** is what the majority of people think about an issue. *There are signs that the tide of opinion is turning.* ■ A **tide** of something is an amount which is getting larger. *...a rising tide of violence.* ■ If you say something will **tide you over,** you mean it will help you to survive until something else becomes available. *The money was needed to tide Nicaragua over until US aid had been approved by Congress.*

tidily (**tidiness**) See **tidy.**

tidings are news. *They hope that next year will bring better tidings.*

tidy (**tidies, tidying, tidied; tidier, tidiest; tidily, tidiness**) You say something is **tidy** when it is neat and arranged in an orderly way. When you **tidy** a place, you make it like this. When you **tidy** things **away,** you put them where they belong. ■ A **tidy** person keeps things neat and arranged in an orderly way. *I used to be far more obsessive about tidiness.* ■ A **tidy** amount of money is a fairly large amount. *The business made a tidy profit.*

tie (**ties, tying, tied**) If you **tie** one thing to another, you fasten it using something like string or rope. ■ If you **tie** something like a piece of string round something, you put the string round it and fasten the ends with a knot or bow. ■ If you **tie** someone or something or **tie** them **up,** you fasten string or rope round them to secure them. *He tied her hands behind her back. ...a box tied up with ribbon.* ■ When you **tie** your shoelaces, you fasten the ends together with a knot or bow. ■ When an army is **tied down,** an opposing force keeps it in one place for a while. ■ You say something is **tied up** when it is used in such a way that it is not available for other people or other purposes. *More and more old people will also have capital tied up in a house.* ■ If you are **tied up,** you are very busy and are not available to do something. ■ A **tied** pub is owned by a brewery and has to sell the brewery's beer. ■ A **tied** cottage is owned by an employer, especially a farmer, and rented to a worker while they work for that employer. ■ **Ties** are close links between people, organizations, or countries. *...family ties.* ■ If an idea or fact **ties in with** something else, it fits in with it or agrees with it. *There will be videos and illustrated talks to tie in with exhibitions on the subject.* ■ In sport, a **tie** is a match played as part of a competition. The losers of the match are eliminated and the winners continue into the next round. *...an exciting Cup tie between First Division sides.* ■ If you **tie** with someone in a competition or a game or if the result is a **tie,** you finish with the same number of points. ■ A **tie** is a long narrow piece of cloth worn under someone's shirt collar and tied in a knot at the front.

tie-break A **tie-break** is an extra game played in a tennis match when the score in a set is 6-6. The player who wins the tie-break wins the set.

tie-breaker In tennis, a **tie-breaker** is the same as a tie-break. ■ A **tie-breaker** is an extra question or round which decides the winner of a competition or game when two or more people have the same score at the end.

tie-dye When a garment is **tie-dyed,** parts of it are tied in knots before it is immersed in a dye. The knotted parts soak up less dye than the rest.

tie-in A **tie-in** is a product like a toy or book which is connected in some way to a new film or TV show and is put on sale when the film or show is first shown.

tie-pin A **tie-pin** is an ornamental pin used to pin a person's tie to their shirt.

tier (**-tiered**) A **tier** is a row or layer which has other rows or layers above it or below it. *Spectators sat watching from tiers of seats.* You use **-tiered** to say how many tiers something has. *...a three-tiered silver chandelier.* ■ A **tier** in a system is one of the levels at which it operates. *...the existing two-tier structure of county and district councils.*

tie-up You say there is a **tie-up** between two organizations when they join together for a particular purpose. *The bill would block tie-ups between foreign banks and big American securities houses.*

tiff A **tiff** is a small unimportant quarrel.

tiger — **Tigers** are large carnivorous animals belonging to the cat family. They come from Asia and usually have an orange coat with black stripes.

tigerish behaviour is very fierce. *...the tigerish tackling of an inspired Britain team.*

tight (**tightly, tightness**) **Tight** clothes fit closely. ■ If you hold something **tight,** you hold it very firmly. If something is held **tight,** it is firmly secured and difficult to move. ■ If something like skin, cloth, or string is **tight,** it is stretched so it is smooth or straight. ■ A **tight** bend in a road is a place where it changes direction very suddenly. ■ You use **tight** to describe things which are closely packed together in a small space. *Many animals travel in tightly packed lorries.* ■ A **tight** schedule or budget allows very little time or money to do something. *Money is tight for students.* ■ You say your chest or stomach feels **tight** when it feels painful, because you are ill or anxious. ■ **Tight** controls or rules are very strict. ■ A **tight** situation is difficult or dangerous. ■ A **tight** contest is one

in which no competitor has a clear advantage, so it is difficult to say who will win. ■ **sit tight:** see **sit.**

tighten (**tightening, tightened**) If you **tighten** your hold on something, you hold it more firmly. ■ If you **tighten** something like a rope, chain, or strap, you stretch it or pull it until it is straight, or until it grips something firmly. ■ If you **tighten up** a fastening, you move it so it is more firmly in place or holds something more firmly. ■ When things like rules or conditions are **tightened,** they are made stricter. *They have tightened security along the border. ...new legislation to tighten up immigration law.*

tight-fisted You say someone is **tight-fisted** when they hate spending their money.

tight-lipped If someone is **tight-lipped,** they are unwilling to give any information about something. *The authorities are tight-lipped about the attack.* ■ You say someone is **tight-lipped** when they have their lips pressed together, because they are angry.

tightrope A **tightrope** is a tightly-stretched rope fixed high above the ground on which an acrobat balances and performs tricks.

tights are a piece of clothing, usually made of thin stretchy material like nylon, which fit closely over a person's feet, legs, and body up to their waist.

tigress (**tigresses**) A **tigress** is a female tiger.

tike See **tyke.**

tilde (*pron:* **til**-duh) The **tilde** is a symbol written over 'n' in Spanish (ñ) to show it is pronounced like the 'ni' in 'onion'.

tile (**tiling, tiled**) **Tiles** are flat regularly-shaped pieces of material such as baked clay, carpet, or cork, used to cover a surface. When a surface is **tiled,** it is covered with tiles.

till means the same as 'until'. *I didn't meet Doris till many years later.* ■ A **till** is a drawer or box where money is kept in a shop, usually as part of a cash register. ■ When people **till** the land, they prepare it for planting and growing crops.

tiller The **tiller** of a boat is a handle fixed to the rudder. It is used to turn the rudder and steer the boat.

tilt If something **tilts,** it changes position so one end or side is higher than the other. You then say it has a **tilt.** ■ If someone or something **tilts** towards a particular opinion, they change slightly so they become more in agreement with that opinion or position. You can say there is a **tilt** towards something. *He considered the new government to be too heavily tilted towards leftists... The chairman criticised the plan for its tilt towards higher taxes.* ■ If something is moving or happening **at full tilt,** it is moving or happening with as much speed, energy, or force as possible. *Firms have kept production lines running at full tilt.* ■ You can call an attempt to achieve something a **tilt** at it. *...a tilt at the world title.* ■ If you say someone is **tilting at windmills,** you mean they are fighting imaginary enemies.

tilth is soil with a fine crumbly surface.

timber (**timbered**) **Timber** is wood used for things like building houses or making furniture. ■ The **timbers** of a house or ship are the large pieces of wood forming part of its basic structure. ■ A **tim-**

bered building has a wooden frame or wooden beams showing on the outside.

timbre (*pron:* **tam**-bra) The **timbre** of a sound is a special quality which it has. *His voice retained its marvellous nasal timbre.*

time (**timing, timed**) **Time** is what we measure in hours, days, and years. ■ **Time** is used to say how long something lasts or how long someone takes to do something. *The argument will go on for a long time.* ■ If you **time** something, you measure how long it takes or lasts. ■ If an event or action is **timed** for a certain time, it is planned to happen then. *The advertisements were timed to coincide with the end of the Proms.* ■ **Time** is used to talk about a particular occasion or period during the day or in history. *This time it's different... We'd like to know what time people will be arriving... We have been producing wine in England since Roman times.* ■ **Time** is used to talk about punctuality. *I catch the 6.55, which usually arrives on time.* ■ **Time** is used to say how soon something will happen. *John will probably retire in ten years' time.* ■ If you say something will happen **in time**, you mean it will happen eventually. ■ If you say it is **time** for something to be done or to happen, you mean it ought to be done or happen now. ■ If you say you **have no time for** someone or something, you mean you do not approve of them or cannot be bothered with them. ■ In music, **time** is used to talk about the number of beats in each bar, which gives a piece its rhythm. ■ If you say someone is **doing time**, you mean they are in prison. ■ You use **times** when you are multiplying one number by another. *Exports are growing four times as fast as imports.* ■ You say **at the same time** when you are mentioning something which contrasts with what you have just said. *...somewhere not too far from home, but at the same time remote.*

time bomb A **time bomb** is a bomb which is set to go off at a particular time. ■ Something which is likely to have a devastating effect in the future can be called a **time bomb**. *This proposal is a political time bomb that could cost the government the next election.*

time capsule See **capsule**.

time-consuming If something is **time-consuming**, it takes up a great deal of time.

time frame The **time frame** for something is the period of time during which it is expected to happen or develop. *The spokesman added that no time frame for the release of the refugees had been fixed.*

time-honoured A **time-honoured** way of doing something has been used for a long time.

timekeeping (*or* **time-keeping**) If you talk about someone's **timekeeping**, you mean how good they are at being punctual or working the correct number of hours. You also use **timekeeping** to talk about the punctuality of something like a transport service. ■ **Timekeeping** is the process or activity of timing an event or series of events.

time lag The **time lag** between two events is the interval of time between them.

timeless (**timelessness**) If you say something is **timeless**, you mean it is so good or beautiful that it cannot be affected by the passing of time or changes in fashion. *...the timeless appeal of her designs.*

time limit If you set a **time limit** for something, you say it must be done before a certain time.

timely (**timeliness**) If something is **timely**, it happens at just the right time. *The recent outbreaks of cholera are a timely reminder that this disease is still a serious health hazard.*

timepiece is an old-fashioned word for a clock or watch.

timer A **timer** is a device which measures time, especially one which is part of a machine and makes it start or stop at a specific time.

time scale The **time scale** for something is the period of time during which it is expected to happen or develop.

time-server If you say someone is a **time-server**, you mean they make very little effort in their job and are just passing the time until they retire or leave.

timeshare A **timeshare** is holiday accommodation in which several people buy a share. Each person then has the right to use the accommodation for a certain amount of time each year.

time signature The **time signature** of a piece of music consists of two numbers written at the beginning that show the number of beats in each bar.

time switch A **time switch** is a device which makes a machine start or stop working at specific times.

timetable (**timetabling, timetabled**) A **timetable** is a schedule of the times when events or tasks are due to take place or be done. If you **timetable** something, you prepare a timetable for it. ■ A **timetable** is a list of the times when trains, boats, buses, or planes arrive and depart.

time trial A **time trial** is a race, especially a cycle race, in which each competitor goes separately over a specified course in as fast a time as possible.

time warp If you say someone is in a **time warp**, you mean they are living or behaving in a way which would have been acceptable many years ago, but now seems strange or inappropriate. *She said the judges were stuck in a mediaeval time warp where women must submit to men.*

time-worn is used to describe things which are old or have been used a lot over a long period of time.

time zone A **time zone** is one of the areas the world is divided into, where the time is a certain number of hours behind or ahead of GMT.

timid (**timidly, timidity**) A **timid** person or animal is shy and easily frightened. ■ You say someone's behaviour is **timid** or talk about their **timidity** when they are not very bold or adventurous.

timing Someone's **timing** is their skill in judging the right moment at which to do something. ■ The **timing** of an event is the time when it happens or is planned to happen. ■ A **timing device** is a mechanism attached to a bomb or missile to make it explode at a particular time.

timorous people are very frightened and nervous.

timpani (*pron:* **tim**-pan-ee) (**timpanist**) **Timpani** are large drums shaped like half a globe with the flat part uppermost.

tin (**tinned**) **Tin** is a soft silvery-white metal. ■ A **tin** is a metal container which is filled with food and sealed to preserve the food. You say food preserved like this is **tinned.** ■ Various types of metal containers, with or without lids, are called **tins.** *...a biscuit tin. ...a roasting tin.*

tincture (*pron:* **tingt**-chur) A **tincture** is an extract of a medicinal substance mixed with alcohol.

tinder is small pieces of something like dry wood or grass which burn easily and can be used for lighting a fire. If something is **tinder dry,** it is very dry and likely to catch fire easily.

tinderbox (**tinderboxes**) In the past, a **tinderbox** was a small metal box used to hold tinder and keep it dry. ■ If you say something is a **tinderbox,** you mean it is very dry and could catch fire and burn easily. ■ You say a place is a **tinderbox** when trouble or conflict could break out there very easily. *The region was once the tinderbox of Europe.*

tine The **tines** of a fork or a rake are its prongs.

tinge (**tinged**) A **tinge** of something like a feeling or a colour is a small amount of it. You can say one thing is **tinged** with another. *...a tinge of regret. ...pink-tinged granite rocks.*

tingle (**tingling, tingled**) If part of your body **tingles,** you feel a slight prickling feeling there. You call this feeling a **tingle.** ■ If you **tingle** with excitement or fear, you are very excited or frightened. This feeling can be called a **tingle.**

tinker (**tinkering, tinkered**) **Tinkers** are people who travel from place to place mending metal pots and pans or doing other small repair jobs. ■ If you **tinker** with something, you make small adjustments to it, in an attempt to repair or improve it. *The government is tinkering with tax concessions.*

tinkle (**tinkling, tinkled**) If something **tinkles,** it makes a sound like a small bell ringing. This sound is called a **tinkle.** *...the tinkle of teaspoons on china.*

tinned See **tin.**

tinnitus (*pron:* tin-**nie**-tuss) is a ringing, booming, or hissing sensation in the ear.

tinny If a sound is **tinny,** it has an unpleasant high-pitched quality. ■ If you describe something such as a car as **tinny,** you mean it is made of thin metal and is of poor quality.

Tin Pan Alley The popular music business is sometimes called **Tin Pan Alley.**

tinpot People use **tinpot** to talk about countries and governments they regard as inferior and unimportant.

tinsel consists of small strips of shiny paper attached to long pieces of thread. People use tinsel as a decoration at Christmas.

Tinseltown is a humorous name for Hollywood.

tint (**tinted**) A **tint** is a small amount of a colour. ■ If you **tint** your hair or use a **tint** on it, you dye it a slightly different colour. ■ **Tinted** things have a small amount of colour or dye in them.

tiny (**tinier, tiniest**) **Tiny** people or things are extremely small.

tip (**tipping, tipped**) The **tip** of something long and narrow is the end of it. *...the tips of their fingers.* ■ If an object is **tipped** with a certain colour or material, it has that colour or material at one end of it. *...a piece of wood tipped with metal.* ■ If you say a word is **on the tip of your tongue,** you mean you cannot think of it just at that moment but feel sure you do actually know it. ■ If you **tip** an object, you move it so it is no longer flat or upright. ■ If you **tip** something somewhere, you pour it or dump it there. ■ A **tip** is a place where rubbish is dumped. ■ If something **tips** into a certain state or situation, a small change or development puts it into that state or situation. *The economy tipped into recession.* ■ You say something **tips the balance** in a situation or **tips the scales** in someone's favour when it gives them a slight advantage. ■ A **tip** is a useful piece of advice or information. ■ If someone is **tipped** for success, people in the know say they are likely to be successful. ■ If you are **tipped off** or given a **tip-off** about something, you are given some information or a warning, often privately or secretly. ■ If you **tip** someone like a waiter or give them a **tip,** you give them money to show your appreciation of the service they have provided.

tip-off See **tip.**

tipple (**tippler**) A person's **tipple** is the alcoholic drink they usually drink. Someone who drinks alcohol regularly can be called a **tippler.**

tipster A **tipster** is a person who sells tips to people who bet on horses or greyhounds or speculate on the stock market.

tipsy If you are **tipsy,** you are slightly drunk.

tiptoe (**tiptoeing, tiptoed**) If you walk or stand on **tiptoe,** you walk or stand on your toes. ■ If you **tiptoe** somewhere, you walk there very quietly on your toes.

tip-top If you say something is **tip-top,** you mean it is as good as it could possibly be. *He is certainly in tip-top condition.*

tirade (*pron:* tie-**rade**) A **tirade** is a long angry speech, criticizing someone or something.

tire (**tiring, tired; tiredness**) If something **tires** you, it makes you use a lot of energy so you want to rest or sleep. *It had been a long and tiring day.* If something **tires** you **out,** it makes you exhausted. ■ If you are **tired,** you feel the need to rest or sleep. ■ If you **tire** of something, you become bored with it. *More Britons appear to be tiring of poolside package holidays to Spain.* ■ You use **tired** to describe something which is no longer very interesting because people have seen or heard it many times before. *...the same tired old cliches.* ■ See also **tyre.**

tireless (**tirelessly**) If you say someone is **tireless,** you mean they have a lot of energy and never seem to need a rest. *She campaigned tirelessly for his release.*

tiresome If someone or something is **tiresome,** they make you feel irritated or bored.

tissue Animal or plant **tissue** consists of similar cells grouped together and usually performing a particular function. *...brain tissue.* ■ **Tissue paper** is thin paper used for wrapping breakable objects. ■ A **tissue** is a small piece of soft paper used as a handkerchief.

tit — Tits are a common type of small bird. There are several species of tits, including blue tits, coal tits, and great tits.

titan (*pron:* **tie**-tan) (**titanic**) If you describe someone as a **titan** of a particular field, you mean that they are very important or successful in that field. *...the titans of industry.* ■ You use **titanic** to describe things which are very great or powerful. *...the titanic struggle which led to his first Senate victory.*

titanium (*usual pron:* ti-**tane**-i-um) is a strong, light, silvery metal used to make alloys.

titbit A **titbit** is (a) a small tasty piece of food. (b) a small piece of news or gossip.

tit-for-tat actions are harsh measures you take against someone in response to something similar they have done to you. *...tit-for-tat killings.*

tithe A **tithe** was a fixed part, originally one tenth, of a person's income or agricultural produce, paid as a tax to the church.

titillate (**titillating, titillated; titillation**) If something **titillates** someone, it pleases and excites them, especially in a sexual way. *They are there purely for purposes of titillation.*

title (**titled**) The **title** of a book, play, or piece of music is its name. You can say it is **titled** in a certain way. *...an album titled 'As Time Goes By'.* ■ Books, magazines, and videos are sometimes called **titles.** *A further eight titles are due to be launched by the end of the year.* ■ When an actor or singer plays the **title role,** he or she plays the part of the character with the same name as the play, film, or opera. *...her performance in the title role of The Marie Lloyd Story.* ■ The **title track** of an album is the song or piece of music with the same name as the album. ■ A person's **title** is a word which describes their rank, status, or job. ■ A **titled** person has a title like 'Princess', 'Lord', 'Lady', or 'Sir' which shows their high social rank. ■ In a sports competition, a **title** is the position of champion. *She won the Olympic title.* ■ The **title** to property or land is its legal ownership. *Your solicitor must have checked the title deeds.*

titter (**tittering, tittered**) If someone **titters** or gives a **titter,** they laugh quietly, either in a disrespectful way or because they are nervous.

tittle-tattle is gossip.

titular (*pron:* **tit**-yoo-lar) A **titular** position has a name which makes it seem important, although the person has no real power. *...the titular head of state.*

tizzy If someone is in a **tizzy,** they are excited, worried, or nervous, often over something which is unimportant.

TM is a short way of writing (a) 'trademark'. (b) 'transcendental meditation'.

TNT is a type of powerful explosive. TNT stands for 'trinitrotoluene'.

to If you go **to** a place, you go towards it. *Adam went to the station to meet Sheila.* You can also talk about going **to** an event. ■ You use **to** when talking about something's position, or where two or more things are joined or the direction they lead towards. *Atlanta was only an hour's drive to the north. ...a vessel tied to the docks... An external staircase leads to a downstairs room.* ■ You use **to** when saying who or what an action or feeling is directed towards. *He*

gave the money to the cook. ...the problem of cruelty to children. ■ You use **to** when saying what someone or something becomes. *The area has been converted to farmland.* ■ You use **to** when saying who holds a particular opinion. *To me this seems unlikely.* ■ You use **to** when mentioning the final thing in a range of things. *The colleges have anything from 100 to 2000 students.* ■ You use **to** when stating a time which is less then thirty minutes before an hour. *...ten minutes to 8.* ■ You use **to** when talking about ratios and rates. *The car gives a regular 40 miles to the gallon.* ■ **To** is used in the structures called 'infinitives'. For example, you use **to** when talking about intention. *...emergency programmes set up to save animals.*

toad – **Toads** are amphibians which look like frogs, but have drier skin and live more on land than in water.

toadstool – **Toadstools** are various types of poisonous mushrooms.

toady (**toadies; toadying**) A **toady** is someone who flatters important or powerful people in the hope of getting some advantage from them. Behaviour like this is called **toadying.**

toast (**toaster**) When you **toast** a slice of bread, you cook it at a high temperature under a grill or in an appliance called a **toaster,** so it becomes brown and crisp. Bread cooked like this is called **toast.** ■ If you **toast** someone or drink a **toast** to them, you drink a glass of wine or some other drink in their honour. ■ If you say someone is the **toast** of a place or organization, you mean they are very popular and greatly admired there, because they have done something especially well.

toastmaster A **toastmaster** is a person who leads the toasts and introduces the speakers at a formal reception or dinner.

tobacco is the dried leaves of a plant called the **tobacco** plant, which people smoke.

tobacconist A **tobacconist** or **tobacconist's** is a shop selling tobacco, cigarettes, and cigars. The person who runs it is sometimes called a **tobacconist.**

toboggan (**tobogganing, tobogganed**) When you **toboggan,** you slide downhill over snow on a type of sledge called a **toboggan.**

today is (a) the day on which you are writing or speaking. (b) the present period of history. *Business is the most powerful force in society today.*

toddle (**toddling, toddled**) When a small child **toddles,** it walks unsteadily with short quick steps.

toddler A **toddler** is a young child aged between about one and three.

toe (**toeing, toed**) A person's **toes** are the five jointed parts at the end of each of their feet. ■ If you **toe the line,** you behave in the way people in authority expect you to.

toehold If you have a **toehold** in a situation, you have managed to gain an uncertain position or a small amount of power in it, which you hope will eventually lead to something better. *Mitsubishi was anxious to get a toehold in the European market.*

toenail A person's **toenails** are the hard areas at the end of their toes.

toff Rich or upper-class people are sometimes called **toffs.**

toffee is a sticky chewy sweet made by boiling sugar and butter together with water.

toffee-nosed If you say someone is **toffee-nosed,** you mean they are snobbish.

tofu (pron: **toe**-foo) is a soft food made from soyabean curd.

tog (**togged**) A person's **togs** are their clothes. You say someone is **togged up** when they are wearing clothes designed for a particular purpose. ...*togged up in wetsuits.* ■ The **tog rating** of a quilt is an official measurement of how warm it is.

toga (pron: **toe**-ga) A **toga** was a long loose robe worn by ancient Romans.

together ■ If people do something **together,** they do it in company with each other. ■ If people are **together** on an issue, they have the same attitude about it. ■ When things or people are close **together,** they are very near to each other. ■ If things are joined **together,** they are joined to each other. ■ If two things happen **together,** they happen at the same time. ■ You can describe someone as **together** when you admire their confidence and ability to organize their life.

togetherness is a feeling of closeness and friendship.

togged See **tog.**

toggle A **toggle** is a bar-shaped button.

toil (**toiling, toiled; toiler**) You say people **toil** when they work very hard doing an unpleasant or difficult task. Work like this is called **toil.** ■ The **toilers** in an organization are the people who do the hard routine work.

toilet A **toilet** is a large bowl, connected by a pipe to the sewers, which you use for getting rid of urine or faeces from your body. A small room containing a toilet is also called a **toilet.**

toilet paper is thin soft paper you use to clean yourself after you have been to the toilet.

toiletries are things like soap, toothpaste, and deodorant which people use to clean or perfume themselves with.

toilet roll A **toilet roll** is a long strip of toilet paper wound round a cardboard tube.

toilet water is a lightly scented and inexpensive perfume.

to-ing and fro-ing See **fro.**

token (**tokenism**) A **token** is a piece of paper or card worth a certain amount of money, which can be exchanged for goods in a shop. ■ **Tokens** are flat round pieces of metal or plastic which are sometimes used instead of money. ■ If you give someone a present or do something for them as a **token** of your positive feelings, you give it or do it as a way of expressing those feelings. ■ **Token** actions are unimportant in themselves but are meant to show particular intentions or feelings. *Coal miners in Poland have staged a two-hour token stoppage.* ■ **Token** is used to describe someone who is chosen for a position just to show that a particular group is being represented. Choosing someone for this reason is called **tokenism.** *Is his promotion evidence of the minorities' advance, or mere tokenism?*

■ You use **by the same token** to say that if one thing is true, logically something else ought to be true too.

told See **tell.**

tolerable (**tolerably**) If you say something is **tolerable,** you mean it is acceptable or bearable but not pleasant or good.

tolerance (**tolerant, tolerantly**) **Tolerance** is allowing other people to say and do what they like, even if you do not agree with them or approve of what they say or do. A **tolerant** person shows tolerance to others. ■ **Tolerance** is putting up with something undesirable. *Today's tolerance of unemployment would have astonished people in the 1960s.* ■ If animals, plants, or people are **tolerant** to something or have **tolerance** to it, they have been exposed to it so often that it no longer has much effect on them. ...*crops resistant to disease or tolerant of weedkillers.* ■ **Tolerance** is an amount of variation permitted in certain measurements, to allow for such things as slight changes in materials affected by heat or cold.

tolerate (**tolerating, tolerated; toleration**) If you **tolerate** things you do not agree with or approve of, you allow them to exist or happen. ■ If you can **tolerate** something unsatisfactory or unpleasant, you can put up with it. *It's a question of how much more upheaval the populace can tolerate.*

toll The death **toll** in something like an accident or a war is the number of people killed. ■ You talk about something **taking its toll** when it causes serious loss or damage. *The recession has taken its toll on a lot of the bank's clients.* ■ A **toll** is a fee you have to pay when driving over certain roads or bridges. ■ When a bell is **tolled,** it is rung slowly and repeatedly.

tom See **tomcat.**

tomahawk A **tomahawk** is a small lightweight axe used by North American Indians.

tomato (**tomatoes**) **Tomatoes** are small round red fruit with soft juicy flesh.

tomb A **tomb** is a vault or chamber in which a dead body is placed. ■ Graves are sometimes called **tombs.**

tombola is a lottery in which tickets are drawn from a revolving drum.

tomboy Young girls who behave or dress in a boyish way are sometimes called **tomboys.**

tombstone A **tombstone** is the same as a gravestone.

tomcat A **tomcat** or **tom** is a male cat.

tome A **tome** is a large heavy book.

tomfoolery is childish, playful behaviour.

tomorrow is the day after today. ■ You can refer to the future as **tomorrow.** *Tomorrow's cars may be cleaner and more economical.*

tom-tom — **Tom-toms** are drums, originally from Africa and Asia, usually played with the hands.

ton (**-tonner**) Weight is sometimes expressed in **tons.** In Britain, a ton is 2,240 pounds (about 1,016 kilograms); in the US, it is 2,000 pounds (about 907 kilograms). See also **tonne.** ■ **-tonner** is used to describe a boat or lorry weighing a certain number of tons. ...*a two-tonner.* ■ If you have **tons** of something, you have a lot of it.

tonal is used (a) to talk about the quality or pitch of music or other sounds. *Her agility and tonal purity were impressive.* (b) to talk about shades and tones of colours. ...*a black and white print with a full tonal range.*

tone (**toning, toned**) The **tone** of a musical instrument or of someone's voice is the kind of sound it has. ...*talking in quiet, deferential tones.* ■ If you talk about someone's **tone,** you mean the manner they adopt when they are dealing with someone. *They are adopting a conciliatory tone towards intellectuals.* Similarly, you can talk about the **tone** of a speech or piece of writing. ■ If you **tone down** something you have written or said, you make it less forceful, severe, or offensive. *Sex scenes have been toned down in the television version of Lady Chatterley's Lover.* ■ In music, a **tone** is an interval between two notes, equal to two semitones. ■ A **tone** is a lighter, darker, or brighter shade of the same colour. *Carol painted the walls in two tones of blue.* ■ If one thing **tones** with another, the two things create a pleasing effect together because they are similar in colour. ■ If something **tones** your muscles, it makes them firm and strong. **Tone** is used to talk about the quality of a person's muscles. ...*poor muscle tone.*

toneless A **toneless** voice is dull and does not express any feeling.

tongs are a tool made of two long narrow pieces of metal or wood joined at one end. You press the pieces together to grip an object and pick it up.

tongue Your **tongue** is the soft movable part inside your mouth which you use for tasting, licking, and speaking. ■ If you say someone has a sharp **tongue,** you mean they say unpleasant or critical things. ■ If you **hold** your **tongue,** you do not say anything. Similarly, if you **bite** your **tongue,** you keep quiet about something although you really want to speak about it. ■ A **slip of the tongue** is a small mistake you make when you are speaking. ■ Languages are sometimes called **tongues.** ...*the Gaelic tongue.* ■ **mother tongue:** see **mother.** ■ **Tongue** is the cooked tongue of an ox.

tongue-in-cheek A **tongue-in-cheek** remark is made as a joke.

tongue-tied If you are **tongue-tied,** you cannot speak because you are shy or nervous.

tongue-twister A **tongue-twister** is an expression or group of words which is very difficult to say, especially if you try to say it quickly a number of times. An example is 'red lorry, yellow lorry'.

tonic or **tonic water** is a colourless fizzy drink with a slightly bitter flavour which is often mixed with alcoholic drinks. ■ A **tonic** is a medicine which makes you feel stronger, healthier, and less tired. ■ Anything which makes you feel stronger or more cheerful can be called a **tonic.** *His dry humour was a stimulating tonic.*

tonight is the evening or night which will come at the end of today.

tonnage (*pron:* tun-nij) The **tonnage** of a merchant ship is its capacity, or the weight of cargo it can

carry. ■ **Tonnage** is the total amount of tons that something weighs, or the total amount of something measured in tons. ...*the tonnage of fish taken from the North Sea.*

tonne (*pron:* tun) Large weights are often expressed in **tonnes.** A tonne is 1,000 kilograms (about 2,204.6 pounds). Tonnes are sometimes called 'metric tons'.

tonsil Your **tonsils** are the two small soft lumps in your throat at the back of your mouth.

tonsillectomy (**tonsillectomies**) A **tonsillectomy** is a surgical operation to remove a person's tonsils.

tonsillitis is a painful swelling of the tonsils caused by an infection.

tonsure (*pron:* ton-sher) A **tonsure** is a shaved area on the top of a man's head, leaving hair around the sides. Some monks have their heads shaved like this.

too means 'also' or 'as well'. *Taking special supplements may help too.* ■ **Too** is used to say an amount, distance, etc is greater than is desirable, necessary, or acceptable. *Too many people are out of work.* ■ You use **too** after words like 'not' to make what you are saying sound less forceful or more polite or cautious. *They are not too happy with the result.*

took See **take.**

tool A **tool** is any device or simple piece of equipment, for example a hammer or a knife, which you hold in your hand and use for a particular kind of work. See also **machine tool.** ■ Anything used for a particular purpose can be called a **tool.** ...*the effectiveness of computers as an educational tool.* ■ If you say someone or something is a person's **tool,** you mean they are controlled by them and used by them to do unpleasant or dishonest things. ...*a legal system that was the willing tool of the old regime.*

tool kit A **tool kit** is a set of tools kept together.

toot (**tooting, tooted**) If you **toot** a car horn, you get it to make a short loud sound. You can talk about the **toot** of a horn or say the horn itself **toots.**

tooth (**teeth**) A person's or animal's **teeth** are the hard white objects in their mouth used for biting and chewing. ■ The **teeth** of a comb, saw, zip, or cog are the hard parts which stick out in a row on its surface. ■ If you say an official body has **teeth,** you mean it is powerful and able to enforce its decisions. *The new council will be unconstitutional and without teeth.* ■ If you **get your teeth into** something, you get very involved in it and put a lot of energy and concentration into it.

toothache is a pain in a tooth or teeth.

toothbrush (**toothbrushes**) A **toothbrush** is a small brush for cleaning your teeth.

toothless If someone is **toothless,** they have no teeth. ■ If you say an organization is **toothless,** you mean it has no real power.

toothpaste is a thick paste you put on a toothbrush and use to clean your teeth.

toothpick A **toothpick** is a small pointed stick for removing food from between your teeth.

toothy If someone has a **toothy** smile, they show a lot of their teeth when they smile.

tootle (**tootling, tootled**) If you **tootle** somewhere, you go without hurrying. ■ If you **tootle** on an instrument like a flute, you play it.

top (**topping, topped; -topped**) The **top** of something is its highest part, point, or surface. **-topped** is used to describe the top of something. ...*a glass-topped coffee-table.* ■ If something is **on top** of something else, it is on its highest part. You can also say the first thing is **topped** by the second. ...*a huge dome topped by a copper cross.* ■ The **top** of something like a jar is its lid. ■ The **top** thing of a number of things is the highest one. ...*the top floor.* ■ A **top** is a piece of clothing worn on the upper part of the body. ■ The **top** people of a certain kind are the most important or successful ones. ...*one of Britain's top businessmen.* ■ If something **tops** an amount, it is greater than that amount. *Pre-tax profits in 1991 topped £3 million.* ■ You can say someone or something **tops** a league or table when they have the highest position in it. *It topped the UK charts for four weeks.* ■ If you **top** a remark or action, you follow it with an even better or more impressive one. ■ If you **top up** a partially empty container or give it a **top-up**, you fill it again. ■ On **top of** means 'in addition to'. *The Ombudsman's report comes on top of a spate of other bad news for the industry.* ■ If you are **on top of** a situation, you are in control of it and can cope easily. ■ If something gets **on top of** you, it depresses you because you cannot cope with it. ■ If you say something is **over the top,** you mean it is too extreme. ■ A **top** is a toy which can be made to spin on the floor.

topaz is a yellowish-coloured gemstone.

top-class is used (a) to describe people who achieve the highest standards in what they do. ...*top class athletes.* (b) to describe things of the highest quality. ...*a top-class hotel.*

top hat A **top hat** is a tall hat with a narrow brim, worn by men on formal occasions.

top-heavy If something is **top-heavy,** it is larger or heavier at the top than at the bottom, and this makes it unstable.

topiary (*pron:* **toe**-pee-ar-ee) is cutting bushes and hedges into ornamental shapes.

topic A **topic** is a subject which is discussed or written about. *The weather is a constant topic of conversation in Britain.*

topical (**topicality**) If something is **topical,** it is connected with events which are happening at the time when you are speaking or writing. *The film has a poignant topicality in Britain.*

topless If a woman is **topless,** she is not wearing anything to cover her breasts.

top-level discussions or activities involve the most important or successful people in a particular organization or sport. ...*a top-level meeting of American generals.*

topmost The **topmost** thing in a group of things is the highest one. ...*the topmost shelf.*

top-notch If you describe someone or something as **top-notch,** you mean they are of the highest standard or quality. ...*top-notch candidates.*

top-of-the-range or **top-of-the-line** things are the most expensive and highly developed ones of their kind.

topography (**topographical**) Topography is the study and description of the physical features of places, for example the hills, valleys, and rivers. ■ The **topography** of a place is its physical features. ...*a topographical description.*

topping is food like cream or cheese which is put on top of other food to decorate it or add to its flavour.

topple (**toppling, topples**) If something **topples,** it becomes unsteady and falls over. ■ If a government or leader is **toppled,** something happens which makes them lose power.

top-ranking is used to describe the most important or successful people in a country, organization, or activity. ...*a top-ranking Russian official.*

top secret is an official classification for military or government matters which must be kept absolutely secret.

topsoil is the layer of soil nearest the surface of the ground.

topsy-turvy is used to describe things which are in a state of confusion or disorder. ...*a topsy-turvy house.*

top-up See **top.**

tor A **tor** is a bare rocky hill.

Torah In the Jewish religion, the **Torah** is (a) the first five books of the Old Testament, and the scroll on which they are written, which is used in synagogue services. (b) the whole body of traditional Jewish teaching.

torch (**torches, torching, torched**) A **torch** is a small portable battery-powered lamp. ■ A **torch** is (a) a long stick with burning material at one end. (b) a device which produces a hot flame for tasks like welding and cutting metal. ...*acetylene torches.* ■ If a building is **torched,** someone sets fire to it deliberately. ■ If you say someone **carries the torch** for a belief, you mean they take over from someone else in making sure that it continues and develops. *She continued to carry the torch of the democratic movement.* ■ If you say someone **carries a torch** for another person, you mean they are in love with them, although their love may not be returned.

torchlight is the light produced by a torch or torches.

tore See **tear.**

toreador (*pron:* **tor**-ee-a-dor) A **toreador** is a bullfighter.

torment (**tormentor**) Torment (*pron:* **tor**-ment) is extreme pain or unhappiness. *He could find no words to express his torment.* ■ If someone or something **torments** (*pron:* tor-**ments**) you, they cause you extreme pain or unhappiness. You can call a person your **tormentor** if they deliberately make you suffer.

torn See **tear.**

tornado (**tornadoes** *or* **tornados**) A **tornado** is a violent storm with strong winds whirling round a funnel-shaped cloud.

torpedo (torpedoes, torpedoing, torpedoed) A **torpedo** is a tube-shaped underwater missile. When a ship is **torpedoed**, it is hit by a torpedo, and usually sunk. ■ If someone **torpedoes** a plan, they deliberately prevent it succeeding.

torpid (torpor) If someone is **torpid** or in a **torpor**, they are mentally or physically inactive, because they are lazy or sleepy. ■ You call a place or system **torpid** when everything is very slow-moving. ...the torpid state of local government.

torque (pron: **talk**) In engineering, **torque** is a force which causes something to rotate around a central point.

torrent (torrential) A **torrent** is a fast-flowing stream or river. ■ When it rains very heavily, you can talk about the rain falling in **torrents**. You describe rain like this as **torrential**. ■ A **torrent** of something like abuse is a lot of it directed continuously at someone.

torrid weather is very hot and dry. ■ A **torrid** situation involves strong passions and emotions. ...a torrid love affair.

torso (torsos) Your **torso** is the main part of your body, excluding your head, neck, arms, and legs.

tort In law, a **tort** is a civil wrong or injury for which damages may be claimed by an individual, as distinct from a criminal act which is prosecuted by the state.

tortilla (pron: tor-**tee**-a) A **tortilla** is a thin Mexican corn pancake.

tortoise The **tortoise** is a slow-moving reptile with a hard protective shell over its body.

tortoiseshell is the hard brown and yellow shell of a type of sea turtle. In the past, it was often polished and used to make jewellery and ornaments. Nowadays, objects described as **tortoiseshell** are usually made of a similar-looking synthetic material.

tortuous A **tortuous** route is full of bends and twists. ■ A **tortuous** process is long and complicated.

torture (torturing, tortured; torturer) If someone **tortures** another person, they deliberately cause them great pain. Making someone suffer like this is called **torture**; a person who tortures someone else is called a **torturer**. ■ You can call any mental or physical suffering **torture**. Waiting for the result was torture. ■ You can say something **tortures** you when it causes you mental suffering. I haven't tortured myself with their problems.

Tory (Tories; Toryism) A **Tory** is a member or supporter of the Conservative Party in Great Britain or Canada. Tory principles and beliefs are called **Toryism**.

tosh If you say something someone says or writes is **tosh**, you mean it is rubbish.

toss (tosses, tossing, tossed) If you **toss** something somewhere, you throw it there carelessly. ■ If something is **tossed**, it is moved or jerked around from side to side or up and down. ■ If you **toss** a coin, you decide something by throwing a coin up in the air and guessing which side will be facing upwards when it lands. You can say something is decided by the **toss** of a coin. See also **toss-up**. ■ If

someone **tosses and turns** when they are in bed, they move their body around restlessly, because they cannot sleep. ■ When someone **tosses** their head, they move it suddenly backwards, especially when they are angry or annoyed. Similarly, when someone **tosses** their hair, they flick it back by a movement of the head. You can say someone does something with a **toss** of their head or their hair.

toss-up If you call a situation a **toss-up,** you mean that either of two outcomes is equally likely.

tot (totting, totted) A **tot** is a very young child. ■ A **tot** of whisky, rum, or brandy is a small amount of it. ■ If you **tot up** numbers, you add them up.

total (totalling, totalled; totally) (Am: totaling, totaled) The **total** number of things of a particular kind is how many there are altogether. Similarly, the **total** cost of something is how much it costs altogether. You can say something **totals** a certain number, cost, weight, etc. Car sales for January totalled 153,682. ■ When you **total** a set of numbers or objects, you add them all together. The result you get is called the **total**. ■ **Total** means complete. ...a total ban on mining in Antarctica... Industry is a totally different matter.

totalitarian (pron: toe-tal-it-**tair**-ee-an) (totalitarianism) In a **totalitarian** system, one political party controls everything and does not allow other parties to exist. This system is called **totalitarianism**.

totality The **totality** of something is the whole of it. That is the totality of the story.

tote (toting, toted) The **tote** is an automated system of betting money on horses or greyhounds at a racetrack. 'Tote' is short for 'totalisator'. ■ If someone **totes** something, especially a gun, they carry it or have it on them. ...gun-toting rebels.

totem A **totem** is an object or person regarded as a symbol by a particular group of people, who treat them with great respect. ...the cultural totems of Western civilisation. ■ A **totem pole** is a tall wooden pole made by American Indians, with symbols and images carved or painted on it.

totter (tottering, tottered) When someone **totters**, they walk unsteadily. ■ If you say something like a system is **tottering**, you mean it is weak and unstable. ...an already tottering economy.

toucan (pron: **too**-kan) The **toucan** is a large fruit-eating tropical bird with brightly coloured plumage and a very large beak.

touch (touches, touching, touched) If you **touch** something, you put your fingers or hand on it. ■ Your sense of **touch** is your ability to tell how something feels when you touch it. ■ When things **touch**, their surfaces are in contact with each other. ■ If you are **touched** by something, you are emotionally affected by it. ...a touching story of violence redeemed by love. ■ You can say something **touches** something else when it has an effect on it. The reform programme was an extensive one, touching every area of economic and industrial life. ■ If you get **in touch** with someone, you contact them. ■ If you are **in touch** with a subject, you have all the latest information about it. If you are **out of touch** with it, your knowledge is out-of-date. ■ When an aircraft **touches down,** it lands. The landing of an aircraft is called **touchdown.** ■ If one thing **touches off** another thing, it makes the other thing happen or begin. *A US veto could touch off a violent reaction.* ■ If you **touch on** a subject, you mention it briefly. ■ In games like football, if the ball goes **into touch,** it goes over a line called the **touchline** which marks the edge of the pitch. ■ If someone will not **touch** something, they will not get involved with it. Similarly, you can say someone will not **touch** a certain kind of food or drink. ■ If something is **touch and go,** it is uncertain whether it will happen or succeed. ■ A **touch** is a detail added to improve or complete something. *He is putting the final touches to his plans.* ■ If you talk about a person's **touch,** you mean their skill at dealing with something. *He'd been losing his touch as a publisher.* ■ If a firm shows **the personal touch,** they treat you in a thoughtful and considerate way. ■ A **touch** of something is a very small amount of it. *...a touch of sadness. ...a touch of indigestion.* ■ **A touch** means 'slightly' or 'rather'. *This seems a touch over-confident.*

touchdown See **touch.**

touching See **touch.**

touchline See **touch.**

touch paper The **touch paper** on a firework is a small slow-burning piece of dark blue paper on one end, which you light to set off the firework.

touchstone A **touchstone** is a standard by which something is judged.

touchy (**touchier, touchiest**) If someone is **touchy,** they are easily upset or offended. ■ A **touchy** subject needs to be dealt with carefully because it might upset or offend people.

tough (**toughness**) **Tough** policies or actions are very strict and firm. *...the government's tough line on pay.* ■ A **tough** person is strong and independent and can put up with a lot of pain or hardship. ■ A **tough** substance is strong and difficult to break or tear. ■ A **tough** problem or task is difficult to deal with.

toughen (**toughening, toughened**) If something is **toughened,** it is made stronger so it will not break easily. *...toughened glass.* ■ If policies or actions are **toughened,** they are made stricter and firmer. *...the toughening of sentences in the courts.* ■ If an experience **toughens** you, it makes you stronger and more independent.

toupee (*pron:* **too**-pay) A **toupee** is a small wig worn by a man to cover a bald patch.

tour (**touring, toured**) When important people, sports teams, or performers **tour** an area, they go on an organized trip, stopping at various places to meet people, play, or perform. A trip like this is called a **tour.** You can also say people are **on tour.** ■ A **tour** is a short trip round something like a city or a famous building. ■ A **tour** is a holiday in which you visit a number of places in an area. When you have a holiday like this, you say you **tour** the area. *...holidaymakers touring Europe.*

tour de force (*pron:* toor de **forss**) A **tour de force** is a brilliant and impressive display of someone's skill or ability.

tourism (**tourist**) **Tourism** is the industry which provides services like hotels, sightseeing trips, and

leisure facilities for people on holiday. **Tourist** is used to talk about things to do with this industry. *...tourist attractions.* ■ A **tourist** is a person visiting a place for pleasure and interest. ■ When a sports team are on tour, they are sometimes called the **tourists.**

tournament A **tournament** is a sports competition in which the winner of each match goes on to the next round until one competitor or team is the overall winner.

tourniquet (*pron:* toor-nik-kay) A **tourniquet** is a strip of cloth tied tightly round an injured arm or leg to stop it bleeding.

tour operator A **tour operator** is a company which organizes holidays and sells them, usually through a travel agent.

tousled hair is tangled and untidy.

tout (**touting, touted**) If someone **touts** for business or custom, they offer their services in a very direct way. *...an advertising agency touting for clients.* ■ If someone **touts** something, they try to sell it or persuade people it is a good thing. *When Valium was launched as a tranquilliser in the 1960s, it was touted as a wonder drug.* ■ A **tout** is a person who unofficially sells tickets outside a sports ground or theatre, charging more than the official price.

tow If one vehicle **tows** another or gives it a **tow,** the first pulls the second behind it. ■ When a ship is being towed, you say it is **in tow** or **under tow.** ■ If you have to take someone around with you when you go somewhere, you can say you have them **in tow.**

towards (*or* **toward**) If you move, look, or point **towards** someone or something, you move, look, or point in their direction. ■ If you have a particular attitude **towards** someone or something, you feel like that about them. *Her feelings towards him were almost maternal.* ■ If you give money **towards** something, you help pay for it. ■ **Towards** a time or place means near to it. *...towards the end of October. ...a seat towards the back of the stalls.*

towel A **towel** is a piece of absorbent cloth for drying yourself. ■ If you **towel** yourself dry, you dry yourself with a towel. ■ If you **throw in the towel,** you stop trying to do something because you realize you cannot succeed.

towelling (*Am:* **toweling**) **Towelling** is thick soft cloth used for making things such as towels and bathrobes.

tower (**towering, towered**) A **tower** is a tall narrow building, often forming part of a larger building. ■ If someone or something **towers** over other people or things, they are much taller than them.

tower block A **tower block** is a tall building divided into flats or offices.

town A **town** is an area where a lot of people live close together. It is generally larger than a village and smaller than a city. ■ You can refer to a certain town or city simply as **town.** *...the best view in town.* ■ **Town** is the central part of a town or city where most of the shops and offices are. *We arranged to meet in town.* ■ If you go **on the town** for a night, you go into the centre of a town or city in the evening and enjoy yourself at places like nightclubs or pubs. ■ You say someone **goes to town** when they do something extremely thoroughly, or with a lot of enthusiasm or expense. *She had rather gone to town on her bridal outfit.*

town crier A **town crier** was a man who walked through the streets of a town shouting out news and official announcements.

town hall The **town hall** is a large building in a town or city owned and used by the council, often as its headquarters.

town house A **town house** is a tall narrow house in a town, usually in a row of similar houses. ■ The **town house** of a wealthy person is the house they own in a town or city, rather than the one they own in the country.

townie Country people sometimes call people who come from large towns and cities **townies.**

town planning is the planning, design, and development of things like new buildings, roads, and parks in towns and cities.

townscape A **townscape** is everything you can see when you look across an area of a town or city.

township In South Africa, a **township** is an urban area where mainly black or coloured people live.

towpath A **towpath** is a path which is alongside a canal or river.

toxaemia (*Am:* **toxemia**) (*pron:* tox-**seem**-ya) is (a) blood poisoning. (b) a disease causing seriously high blood pressure in pregnancy.

toxic (**toxicity**) A **toxic** substance is poisonous. *...toxic waste.* You can say how poisonous a substance is by saying it is of high or low **toxicity.**

toxicology (**toxicologist**) **Toxicology** is the study of poisons. A **toxicologist** is a person who is an expert in this field.

toxin A **toxin** is a poisonous substance produced by bacteria, which is harmful to people or other living things. Some poisonous substances produced by animals and plants are also called **toxins.**

toxoplasmosis is an infection spread by eating undercooked meat or by handling domestic cats and dogs. It is dangerous if caught by a pregnant woman, possibly causing serious damage to her unborn child.

toy A **toy** is an object for children to play with. ■ If you **toy** with an idea, you consider it casually without making any firm decisions about it. ■ If you **toy** with an object, you fiddle with it.

toy boy You can refer humorously to an older woman's lover as a **toy boy** when he is much younger than she is.

trace (**tracing, traced**) If you **trace** someone or something, you succeed in finding them. *The police traced him through bank records.* ■ If someone or something disappears **without trace,** or there is **no trace** of them, there is no sign of where they have gone. ■ A **trace** is a very small amount or hint of something. *He caught a trace of an Australian accent.* ■ If you **trace** the development of something, you find out or describe how it developed. *Many companies can trace their history back centuries.* ■ If you **trace** a drawing, you copy it by covering it with a piece of transparent paper called **tracing paper**

and drawing over the lines underneath. Copies made in this way are called **tracings.**

traceable is used to describe people or things that can be traced. *His residence is not so easily traceable.* ■ If it can be shown that something was caused by a particular thing, you can say it is **traceable** to that thing. *The numerous diseases suffered there are all traceable to malnutrition.*

trace element – Trace elements are chemical elements which are necessary for normal animal and plant growth but are needed only in very small amounts.

tracer – Tracers or tracer bullets are bullets which can be seen in flight because they contain a substance which burns brightly.

tracery is a decorative pattern of interlacing lines or bars, for example in the stonework towards the top of a stained glass window.

trachea (*pron:* trak-**kee**-a) Your **trachea** is your windpipe.

tracheotomy (*pron:* trak-ee-**ot**-a-mee) A **tracheotomy** is a surgical operation to cut into the trachea.

tracing paper See trace.

track A **track** is a narrow road or path. ■ The rails which trains travel on are called **tracks** or the **track.** ■ A **track** is an oval-shaped piece of ground which athletes, horses, dogs, or cars race around. In athletics, the **track** events are the races on the running track. ■ **Tracks** are marks left on the ground by a person or animal. If you **track** a person or animal, you follow their tracks. ■ If you **track** someone **down,** you search for them until you find them. ■ If you **keep track** of a situation or person, you follow closely what is happening to them. ■ If you say someone is **on track,** you mean they are following the right course of action to succeed in what they are doing. ■ A **track** is one of the songs or pieces of music on a record, tape, or CD.

tracker A **tracker** is a person or animal that finds other people or animals by following footprints and other signs that show where they have been. *...tracker dogs.*

tracker dog – Tracker dogs are dogs trained to search for people.

tracking shot In film-making, a **tracking shot** is a camera shot in which the camera follows a certain person as they move around, or moves along a certain route to give the impression of travelling along it.

tracking station A **tracking station** is a building from which the movement of things like spacecraft and satellites can be followed by means of radar or radio.

track record The **track record** of a person or company is their previous success or failure in what they do. *...an obscure company with a poor track record.*

tracksuit A **tracksuit** is a warm loose-fitting top and trousers, designed to be worn when taking exercise.

tract A **tract** of land is a large area of it. ■ A **tract** is a system of organs or tubes with a particular function in a person's or animal's body. *...the digestive* *tract.* ■ A **tract** is a pamphlet expressing a strong religious, moral, or political opinion.

tractable people or problems are easily controlled or dealt with.

traction is pulling something using a particular type of power. *...steam traction.* ■ A vehicle's **traction** is the grip its wheels have on the ground. ■ **Traction** is a form of medical treatment for an injured limb which involves a steady pull on the limb for long periods of time using a system of weights and pulleys. *Her legs were in traction for two weeks.*

traction engine A **traction engine** is a large heavy steam-powered vehicle used in the past for pulling heavy loads.

tractor A **tractor** is a farm vehicle with large rear wheels used for pulling machinery or trailers.

trad is traditional jazz.

trade (**trading, traded**) **Trade** is the activity of buying, selling, or exchanging goods or services. When firms or countries **trade,** they buy, sell, or exchange things. ■ If a country has a **trade gap,** the value of its imports is greater than the value of its exports. ■ When people **trade** ideas, compliments, or insults, they exchange them. ■ A person's **trade** is the kind of work they do, especially when it requires special training in practical skills. ■ If you **trade in** an old car or appliance, you give it to a dealer when you buy a new one so you get a reduction on the price. A deal like this is called a **trade-in.** ■ If you **trade off** one thing against another, you exchange all or part of one thing for another, as part of a negotiation or compromise. A situation in which gaining something means losing something else is called a **trade-off.** *...the trade-off between quality and affordability.* ■ If someone **trades on** something, they make use of it for their own advantage, often unfairly.

trade fair A **trade fair** is an exhibition where manufacturers show products they want to sell to other firms, rather than to members of the public.

trade-in See **trade.**

trademark A **trademark** is a name or symbol which a company uses on its products and which cannot legally be used by anyone else. ■ A feature which is associated with a certain person or thing can be called their **trademark.** *...her trademark pearl earrings.*

trade name A **trade name** is a name a manufacturer gives to a product or to a range of products.

trade-off See **trade.**

trader A **trader** is (a) a person or company that trades in goods or services. (b) a person who buys and sells stocks and shares.

tradesman (**tradesmen**) A **tradesman** is a person who sells goods or services, especially someone who owns their own small business or is skilled in a certain trade.

trade union (**trade unionism, trade unionist**) A **trade union** is an organization of workers which represents the interests of its members. **Trade unionism** is the system, practices, and ideology of trade unions; a **trade unionist** is an active member of a trade union.

trading estate A **trading estate** is the same as an industrial estate.

tradition A **tradition** is a custom or belief which a group of people have had for a long time. **Tradition** is all the customs of a country or group. ■ You can say a certain kind of behaviour is a **tradition** when it has existed in a place for a long time. *Farms there have a tradition of providing inexpensive meals and accommodation for tourists.*

traditional (**traditionally**) **Traditional** beliefs or customs have existed for a long time. ■ A country's or organization's **traditional** allies or enemies are other countries or organizations which have often been its allies or enemies in the past. ■ A **traditional** organization or institution is one in which older methods are used rather than modern ones.

traditionalist is used to describe people who support the established customs and beliefs of their society or group, and do not want them changed. You call people like this **traditionalists.**

traduce (**traducing, traduced**) If someone **traduces** you, they deliberately say things about you which are untrue and unpleasant.

traffic (**traffics, trafficking, trafficked; trafficker**) The vehicles moving along a road are called the **traffic.** Aircraft, ships, and trains following regular routes are also called **traffic.** *...cross-Channel traffic.* ■ **Traffic** is the transporting of people or goods from one place to another. *The ferries can cope with the traffic of both goods and passengers.* ■ If someone **traffics** in drugs or other goods, they buy and sell them illegally. A person who does this is called a **trafficker.** Illegal trade in something is called **traffic** in it.

traffic jam You say there is a **traffic jam** when vehicles cannot move or can only move very slowly because there are so many of them.

traffic lights are the set of red, amber, and green lights at a road junction which control the traffic flow.

traffic warden A **traffic warden** is a person whose job is to make sure cars are parked legally. Traffic wardens also help the police to direct traffic.

tragedy (**tragedies**) You can call a sad and terrible event a **tragedy.** ■ **Tragedy** is a type of literature, especially drama, which is serious and sad and usually ends with the death of the main character. A **tragedy** is a play like this.

tragic (**tragically**) You say something is **tragic** when it is very sad because it involves death, suffering, or disaster. ■ **Tragic** is used to talk about tragedy as a form of literature. *...Shakespeare's greatest tragic hero.*

tragicomedy (**tragicomedies; tragicomic**) A **tragicomedy** is a film or play which is both tragic and funny. **Tragicomic** is used to describe films, plays, and real-life situations which are like this.

trail (**trailing, trailed**) A **trail** is a rough path across open country or through forests. ■ A **trail** is a route along certain paths or roads, often one planned and marked out for a particular purpose. *Dublin is a good city for walking, with heritage trails well signposted.* ■ A **trail** is a series of marks or other signs left by someone or something as they move along. ■ If you **trail** someone or something, you follow them secretly. ■ You can say someone is on a certain **trail** when they take part in a series of events with the intention of achieving a particular aim. *We'll be back on the Championship trail this weekend.* ■ You say something **trails** when it hangs down loosely behind you as you move along. ...*a trailing velveteen skirt.* ■ If a speaker's voice **trails away** or **trails off,** it gradually becomes quieter or more hesitant until it stops completely. ■ If you say someone is **trailing** in a contest, you mean they are a long way behind their opponents. *His party had been trailing in recent opinion polls.* ■ If you are **on the trail of** a person or thing, you are trying hard to find them or find out about them. *The police were hot on his trail.*

trailblazer A pioneer in a certain field of activity is sometimes called a **trailblazer.**

trailer A **trailer** is a small vehicle which can be pulled behind a car or van. ■ A **trailer** is the long rear section of an articulated lorry, in which goods are carried. ■ Caravans are sometimes called **trailers.** ■ A **trailer** for a film or TV programme is a series of short extracts from it, shown to advertise it.

train (**training, trained**) A **train** is a number of connected carriages or trucks pulled by a railway engine. ■ You can call a long moving line of people or animals a **train.** ...*a train of camels.* ■ A connected series of things can be called a **train.** *The train of unsettling events continued.* ■ If something is **in train,** it is happening or being done. ■ The **train** on a formal dress or robe is a long part at the back which trails on the ground. ■ If you **train** for a certain job, you learn how to do it. ■ If you **train** for a sporting activity, you prepare for it by doing exercises. ■ If you **train** an animal or bird, you teach it to obey commands or perform tricks. ■ If a gun or a camera is **trained** on you, it is kept pointing at you.

trainee (**traineeship**) A **trainee** is someone being taught how to do a job. A **traineeship** is a job for a trainee in an organization. The period of time someone spends as a trainee is also called a **traineeship.**

trainer A **trainer** is a person who trains people or animals to do things. ■ **Trainer** aircraft are used for training pilots. ■ **Trainers** are sports shoes for running or jogging.

train spotter A **train spotter** is a person whose hobby is collecting the numbers of railway engines.

traipse (**traipsing, traipsed**) If you **traipse** somewhere, you walk there slowly and wearily.

trait (*pron:* **trate** *or* **tray**) A **trait** is a tendency in someone's behaviour. ...*personality traits.*

traitor (**traitorous**) A **traitor** is someone who betrays their country or the group they belong to. A person like this is sometimes called **traitorous.**

trajectory (*pron:* traj-**jek**-tor-ee) (**trajectories**) The **trajectory** of an object moving through the air is the curving path it follows. ■ The way in which something is changing can be called its **trajectory,**

especially when it is steadily improving or declining. ...*the trajectory of the British economy.*

tram A **tram** is a vehicle like a bus which travels through streets on rails called **tramlines.** Trams are powered by electricity, usually from an overhead wire.

tramcar A **tramcar** is the same as a tram.

tramp A **tramp** is a person with no permanent home or job who travels from place to place and gets money by begging or doing occasional work. ■ If you **tramp** somewhere, you walk with regular heavy footsteps. ■ If you go for a **tramp,** you go for a long walk.

trample (**trampling, trampled**) If people or animals **trample** on something, they tread all over it and damage or destroy it. ■ If a government treats people in a cruel or unjust way, you can say it **tramples** on their rights or liberties.

trampoline (**trampolining**) A **trampoline** is a gymnastic apparatus made of a large piece of strong cloth held taut by springs in a large frame. The sport of doing acrobatic jumps and somersaults on it is called **trampolining.**

trance A **trance** is a mental state in which someone appears to be asleep, but can see and hear things and respond to commands. ■ You can say someone is in a **trance** when they are in a stunned or dazed state.

tranche A **tranche** of something is a piece, section, or part of it. *They risk losing the next tranche of funding.*

tranquil (**tranquillity**) (*Am:* **tranquility**) A **tranquil** person is calm and relaxed. ■ A **tranquil** place is calm and peaceful.

tranquillize (*or* **tranquillise**) (**tranquillizing, tranquillized; tranquillizer**) (*Am:* **tranquilize,** *etc*) If a person or animal is **tranquillized,** they are given a drug called a **tranquillizer** to make them calm, sleepy, or unconscious.

trans- is used to form words which describe things going or extending from one side of a place to another. ...*the trans-Siberian railway.*

transact (**transaction**) When you **transact** a payment or some business, you carry it out or negotiate it. A **transaction** is a piece of business like this. *Keep careful records of all financial transactions.*

transatlantic describes things involving countries or regions on both sides of the Atlantic. ...*transatlantic flights.* ■ **Transatlantic** is sometimes used to mean 'American'. *His films were too slow and talkative for transatlantic tastes.*

transcend (**transcendence, transcendent**) If one thing **transcends** another, it goes beyond it or is superior to it. You talk about the **transcendence** of something like this or say it is **transcendent.** *The best fiction transcends genre.* ...*the transcendence of God.* ...*an all-powerful, transcendent deity.*

transcendental things are beyond normal human experience or understanding.

transcendental meditation is a form of meditation in which you mentally relax by silently repeating a special word or sound.

transcontinental means extending across a continent. ...*a transcontinental railway.*

transcribe (transcribing, transcribed; transcript, transcription) If you **transcribe** something that is spoken or written, you write it or copy it down in full. Writing or copying something down is called **transcription;** what you write is called a **transcript** or a **transcription.** *...a transcript of a telephone conversation.* ■ If someone **transcribes** a piece of music, they arrange it for different instruments. An arrangement like this is called a **transcription.**

transept The **transepts** of a church are the parts which project north and south of the main building, giving it the shape of a cross.

transfer (transferring, transferred) If someone or something is **transferred** from one place to another, they are moved there. Similarly, someone can be **transferred** to a different part of the same organization. A move like this is called a **transfer.** *The authority offered him a transfer to community nursing.* ■ If a sports player is **transferred,** he or she is sold to another team. ■ If something is **transferred** from one group or organization to another, it is taken from the first one and given to the second one. *...the transfer of power from the minority to the majority.* ■ A **transfer** is a piece of paper with a design on one side, which can be ironed or pressed onto cloth, paper, or china.

transferable If something is **transferable,** it can be passed to another person or organization and used by them. *Membership cards are not transferable.*

transference is sometimes used instead of 'transfer' to talk about the transferring of something to a different person, place, or group. *...a transference of power with the minimum of bloodshed.*

transfigure (transfiguring, transfigured; transfiguration) If someone or something is **transfigured,** their appearance is completely changed. A change like this is called a **transfiguration.**

transfix (transfixes, transfixing, transfixed) If you are **transfixed** by something, you are so impressed, fascinated, or frightened by it that you cannot move.

transform (transformation) If something is **transformed,** it is changed completely. *My life has been transformed.* A change like this is called a **transformation.**

transformer A **transformer** is a piece of electrical equipment which changes the voltage of a current.

transfuse (transfusing, transfused; transfusion) When blood is **transfused,** it is fed into someone's circulation system by means of a drip. This is called a blood **transfusion.**

transgenic plants and animals have been genetically altered so that they contain one or more genes from another species. *...transgenic tomato plants.*

transgress (transgresses, transgressing, transgressed; transgression, transgressor) If someone **transgresses** a rule or law, they break it. This is called a **transgression** of the rule or law; the person who breaks it is called a **transgressor.**

transient (transience) If something is **transient,** it does not last very long. *...the transience of fame.* ■ **Transients** are people who only stay in a place for a short time.

transistor A **transistor** is a tiny electronic device used to control the flow of electric current in, for example, a TV. ■ A **transistor** or **transistor radio** is a small portable radio containing transistors.

transit is the carrying of goods or people by vehicle from one place to another. If goods or people are **in transit,** they are being taken from one place to another. ■ A **transit** area or building is a place where people wait or goods are kept between different stages of a journey.

transition A **transition** is a change from one state to another. *...South Africa's transition to democracy.*

transitional A **transitional** period is one in which something is changing from one state to another. **Transitional** means happening or existing during a transitional period. *...a transitional government.*

transitory things last for only a short time.

translate (translating, translated; translation) If you **translate** something spoken or written, you say or write it in another language. A **translation** is a piece of speech or writing translated into another language. ■ If one thing is **translated** into another, the first is changed or converted into the second. *Your decision must be translated into specific, concrete actions.*

translator A **translator** is a person whose job is to translate speech or writing from one language into another.

transliterated (transliteration) If words or letters are **transliterated,** they are written in the corresponding letters of a different alphabet. Something written in this way is called a **transliteration.**

translucent If something is **translucent,** light passes through it, so that it seems to glow.

transmit (transmitting, transmitted; transmission) If something is **transmitted** from one person or thing to another, it is passed on to them. ■ When a radio or TV programme is **transmitted,** it is broadcast. You talk about the **transmission** of the programme. A **transmission** is a broadcast. ■ When electronic messages are **transmitted,** they are sent from one place to another, by cable, radio waves, or satellite. A message or signal sent like this is called a **transmission.** ■ The **transmission** on a car or other vehicle is the system of gears and shafts by which the power from the engine reaches and turns the wheels.

transmitter A **transmitter** is a piece of equipment used for sending TV or radio signals.

transmogrify (transmogrifies, transmogrifying, transmogrified) If someone or something is **transmogrified,** they are completely changed.

transmute (transmuting, transmuted; transmutation) If a substance is **transmuted** into something different, it is converted into it. *Alchemists never succeeded at transmuting base metals into gold.*

transnational is used to describe things which involve more than one country. *...transnational companies.*

transparent (transparently; transparency, transparencies) If something is **transparent,** you can see through it. You talk about the **transparency** of something like this. ■ If a feature, quality, or action is **transparent,** it is obvious or easily recognized. ...*his transparent sincerity.* ...*a transparent ploy to delay the transfer of power.* ■ A **transparency** is a small piece of photographic film mounted in a frame, viewed using a projector.

transpire (**transpiring, transpired**) When it transpires that something is the case, people discover that it is the case. *It transpired that his death was caused by lung cancer.* ■ When something transpires, it happens. *Nothing is known as yet about what transpired at the meeting.*

transplant (**transplantation**) When surgeons transplant an organ such as a heart, they use it to replace a patient's diseased organ. Tissue can also be **transplanted.** Transplanting organs or tissue is called **transplantation;** an operation in which this is done is called a **transplant.** ■ When someone or something is **transplanted,** they are moved to a different place.

transponder A **transponder** is an electronic device which receives and transmits a radio or radar signal, usually in response to a particular signal.

transport (**transportation**) When goods or people are **transported** from one place to another, they are moved there. **Transport** or **transportation** is the moving of goods or people from one place to another. ■ Vehicles which people travel in are referred to as **transport.** *Have you got your own transport?*

transportable things can be easily moved from place to place.

transporter A **transporter** is a large vehicle, used to transport large groups of people, or things such as cars.

transpose (**transposing, transposed; transposition**) If you **transpose** something from one place or situation to another, you move it there. ■ If you **transpose** two things, you get them the wrong way round, or you deliberately swap them round. *Three quarters of the spelling mistakes involved the transposition of letters.*

transputer A **transputer** is a type of fast powerful microchip.

transsexual A **transsexual** is a person who has decided to live as a person of the opposite sex, and changed their appearance in order to do this. Transsexuals sometimes have an operation to change their sex.

transubstantiation is the doctrine that the bread and wine consecrated in Holy Communion change into the body and blood of Christ.

transverse is used to describe something which is at right angles to something else.

transvestite (**transvestism**) A **transvestite** is a man who likes to dress in women's clothing.

trap (**trapping, trapped**) A **trap** is a device for catching an animal. If you **trap** an animal, you catch it in a trap. ■ A **trap** is a trick intended to catch or deceive someone. ■ If you **trap** someone into saying or doing something, you get them to say or do it although they did not want to. ■ If you are **trapped,** something is blocking your way or holding you down. ■ If you are **trapped** in an unpleasant situation, you cannot easily change it.

You can call a situation like this a **trap.** ■ A **trap** is a light horse-drawn carriage with two wheels.

trapdoor A **trapdoor** is a small horizontal door in a floor or ceiling, or on a stage.

trapeze A **trapeze** is a horizontal bar hanging from two ropes, on which acrobats and gymnasts perform.

trapper A **trapper** is a person who traps animals, especially for their fur.

trappings The **trappings** of a particular rank, position, or state, are the clothes or equipment which go with it. *The warlords of Somalia cling to the trappings of office.*

trash (**trashy; trashes, trashing, trashed**) In the US, rubbish is called **trash.** ■ If you call a book or film **trash** or describe it as **trashy,** you mean it is of very poor quality. ■ If someone **trashes** a person or their ideas, they ridicule them. ■ If someone **trashes** a place or a vehicle, they wreck it.

trattoria A **trattoria** is an Italian restaurant.

trauma (*pron:* **traw**-ma) (**traumatic**) A **trauma** is an extremely upsetting experience. You say an experience like this is **traumatic.** ■ In medicine, a wound or injury is called a **trauma.**

traumatize (*or* **traumatise**) (**traumatizing, traumatized**) If someone is **traumatized** by an event or situation, they are extremely upset by it.

travail You can refer to unpleasant hard work or difficult problems as **travail.** *The British economy, despite all its present travails, is a lot stronger than it was.*

travel (**travelling, travelled**) (*Am:* **traveling, traveled**) When you **travel,** you go from one place to another. ■ **Travel** is the activity of travelling. ■ Someone's **travels** are the journeys they make to places a long way from their home. ■ When something from one place reaches or becomes known in another place, you can say it **travels** to the other place. *News soon travels.* ■ If something **travels** at a particular speed, it moves at that speed.

travel agency (**travel agent**) A **travel agency** or **travel agent** is a business which makes arrangements for people's holidays and journeys. A **travel agent** is also a person who works in a travel agency.

travelcard A **travelcard** is a pass which enables you to travel on buses or trains without having to buy a ticket.

traveller (*Am:* **traveler**) A **traveller** is a person going from one place to another. ...*travellers on the London Underground.* ■ A **traveller** is also (a) someone who travels a lot, usually for pleasure. (b) someone who travels from place to place, often living in a van or other vehicle.

traveller's cheque (*Am:* **traveler's check**) Traveller's **cheques** are special cheques you can exchange for foreign currency when you are abroad.

travelogue (*Am:* **travelog**) A **travelogue** is a book, film, or talk about travel to a place, or about a person's travels.

traverse (**traversing, traversed**) If you **traverse** something, you cross it.

travesty (**travesties**) If you call something a **travesty,** you mean it is not what it is supposed to be, but a very poor imitation of it. ...*a travesty of justice.*

trawl When fishermen **trawl,** they fish by dragging a large bag-like net along the seabed. This net is called a **trawl** or a **trawl net.** ∎ If you **trawl** for things or people of a certain kind, you search among a large number of them, to find the best or most suitable ones. A search like this is called a **trawl.** *The trawl for investors will continue.*

trawler A **trawler** is a fishing boat from which fish are caught using a trawl.

tray A **tray** is a flat object with raised edges, used to carry things, especially food or drinks.

treacherous (treacherously) A **treacherous** person is likely to betray you. ∎ You say things are **treacherous** when they are unreliable and dangerous. *Rain made the ground treacherously slippery.*

treachery is betraying someone.

treacle is a thick sweet sticky liquid obtained as a by-product when sugar is refined.

treacly If something is **treacly,** it is thick and sticky like treacle.

tread (treading, trod, have trodden) If you **tread** on something, you step on it, or press your foot on it. *He trod on the accelerator.* ∎ If you **tread** something into the ground or into a carpet, you step on it and crush it in. ∎ Someone's **tread** is the sound their feet make when they walk. ∎ If you **tread** carefully, you behave cautiously. ∎ If you **tread water,** you stay afloat in an upright position by moving your legs slightly in the water. ∎ You can say someone is **treading water** when they are just doing the same things but not progressing. *The organisation's latest survey of its members revealed that 55 per cent were just about treading water.* ∎ The **tread** of a tyre or shoe is the pattern of ridges on it which stops it slipping. ∎ The flat part of a stair is called the **tread.**

treadle (*pron:* **tred**-dl) A **treadle** is a lever on something like a sewing machine, which you work with your foot to turn a wheel in the machine.

treadmill In the past, a **treadmill** was a large wheel, turned by people or animals walking on or inside it. ∎ A **treadmill** is an exercise machine with a moving belt which you run on. ∎ Any task which you must keep doing, even though it is unpleasant or tiring, can be called a **treadmill.**

treason (treasonable) Treason or **high treason** is the crime of betraying your country, for example by helping its enemies. You say activities of this kind are **treasonable.**

treasure (treasuring, treasured) Treasure is a collection of gold, silver, or jewels, especially one which has been hidden. ∎ **Treasures** are objects of great value, especially works of art. ∎ If you **treasure** something you have, you regard it as very valuable. *I treasure our friendship.*

treasurer The **treasurer** of an organization is the person in charge of its finances.

treasure trove is money or valuable objects which have been found and whose ownership is not known. ∎ If you call a place a **treasure trove,** you mean a lot of valuable things can be found there.

treasury (treasuries) In Britain and some other countries, the **Treasury** is the government department responsible for the country's finances. ∎ If you talk about a country's **treasury,** you mean the money it has available to spend. *Africa's wars are long-lasting conflicts which drain the money from already limited treasuries.*

treat (treating, treated) If you **treat** someone in a particular way, you behave in that way towards them. *He treated her badly.* ∎ If you **treat** something as a particular thing, you behave as if it was that thing. *I treated it as a joke.* ∎ When doctors **treat** patients, they give them medical care. You can also talk about a doctor **treating** an illness. ∎ When something like wood is **treated,** a substance is put on it to protect it or give it certain properties. *The woodwork is treated with preservative.* ∎ If you **treat** someone or give them a **treat,** you buy or arrange something special for them which they will enjoy.

treatable If an illness is **treatable,** it can be treated effectively. *Cerebral malaria is treatable if diagnosed in time.*

treatise (*pron:* **treat**-izz) A **treatise** is a long formal piece of writing on a particular subject. *...a treatise on accounting methods.*

treatment is medical attention given to a sick or injured person or animal. *They are being taken to American military hospitals for treatment.* ∎ A **treatment** is a way of treating an illness. *Deprenyl is sometimes used as a treatment for Parkinson's disease.* ∎ Your **treatment** of a person or thing is the way you behave towards them or deal with them. *His treatment of her was callous and cruel.*

treaty (treaties) A **treaty** is a written agreement between countries.

treble (trebling, trebled) If something **trebles,** it becomes three times as big. You then say it is **treble** the number, size, or amount it was before. *Some owners are charging treble the normal price.* ∎ A **treble** is a boy singer, especially in a choir.

tree – Trees are large plants with hard trunks, leaves, and usually branches.

treeless A **treeless** area has no trees.

treeline The **treeline** in a mountainous area is the height above which trees do not grow.

tree-lined streets have trees on both sides of them.

tree surgeon (tree surgery) A **tree surgeon** is a person who repairs damaged trees. This kind of work is called **tree surgery.**

trefoil (*pron:* **tref**-foil) is clover and other similar plants whose leaves divide into three smaller leaves.

trek (trekking, trekked; trekker) If you **trek** somewhere, you make a long and difficult journey, especially on foot. A journey like this can be called a **trek.** *Some of the refugees had trekked 200 miles to the frontier.* People who do this for pleasure are called **trekkers.** See also **pony trekking.**

trellis (trellises) A **trellis** is a frame made of bars crossing each other, which supports climbing plants.

tremble (trembling, trembled) If you **tremble,** you shake slightly, because you are frightened. ∎ If a building or other object **trembles,** it shakes slightly.

tremendous (**tremendously**) Tremendous is used to say an amount is very large or a feeling very intense. *It's been a tremendous boost to everybody.* ■ You can say something is **tremendous** if you think it is very good or impressive. *...a tremendous performance.*

tremor A **tremor** is (a) a shaking of your body or voice which you cannot control. (b) a small earthquake.

tremulous (**tremulously**) If your voice is **tremulous,** it shakes slightly.

trench (**trenches**) A **trench** is a long narrow channel dug into the ground.

trenchant (**trenchantly**) Trenchant opinions are forceful and to the point. *...trenchant public criticism of the cutbacks in education.*

trend A **trend** is a general change in a particular direction in something like people's behaviour or attitudes. *...the upward trend in consumer spending.*

trend-setter (**trend-setting**) A **trend-setter** is a person or thing that starts a new fashion or trend. **Trend-setting** is used to describe people and things like this. *...Madonna's trend-setting wardrobe.*

trendy (**trendier, trendiest; trendily, trendiness; trendies**) Trendy people or things are extremely fashionable. ■ People who try to keep up with the latest fashions in clothes and ideas are sometimes called **trendies.**

trepidation is fear or anxiety.

trespass (**trespasses, trespassing, trespassed; trespasser**) If you **trespass** on someone's land or property, you go onto it without permission. People who do this are called **trespassers;** they are said to commit a **trespass.**

tress (**tresses**) A woman's **tresses** are her long flowing locks of hair.

trestle – Trestles are a pair of wooden or metal structures which you stand on the floor and put a long board on, to form a table.

trews are close-fitting trousers.

triad A **triad** is a group of three similar things. *...the triad of mother, father, and child.* ■ A **Triad** is a secret Chinese criminal organization.

trial A **trial** is a legal process in which a judge and jury listen to evidence and the jury decides whether an accused person is guilty of a crime. ■ A **trial** is an experiment in which something is tested. ■ A **trial run** is a test to see if something works properly. ■ If you do something by **trial and error,** you try different ways of doing it, until you find the best one. ■ If you are given a **trial** for a job or a place in a team, you are tested to see if you are suitable for that job or good enough to join that team. ■ Trials are a sporting competition which tests a competitor's skill and ability. *...one-day horse trials.* ■ If you talk about someone's **trials,** you mean the unpleasant things they experience. *...the trials of adolescence.*

triangle A **triangle** is a shape with three straight sides. ■ The **triangle** is a percussion instrument consisting of a thin steel bar bent in the shape of a triangle. ■ **eternal triangle: see eternal.**

triangular means shaped like a triangle. ■ A **triangular** relationship involves three people or three groups of people. *...a triangular love affair.*

tribal (**tribally**) Tribal is used to talk about things to do with a tribe or tribes. *...tribal conflicts.*

tribalism (**tribalistic**) Tribalism is a feeling of loyalty towards a tribe felt by its members, often involving hostility towards other tribes. You can also talk about similar loyalties felt by different social and ethnic groups within a society as **tribalism,** or describe these feelings as **tribalistic.**

tribe A **tribe** is a group of people of the same race who speak the same language, have the same customs, and live together in a community, often ruled by a chief. ■ You can use **tribe** to talk about a group of people who are all doing the same thing. *...tribes of bicyclists.*

tribulation A person's **tribulations** are their troubles.

tribunal A **tribunal** is a special court or committee, appointed to pass judgment on a particular matter.

tributary (**tributaries**) A **tributary** of a river is a smaller river which flows into it.

tribute A **tribute** is something you say or do to show your admiration or respect for someone. ■ If one thing is a **tribute** to another, the first came about as a result of the second and shows how good it is. *His election was a tribute to his fearless impartiality.*

trice If you do something **in a trice,** you do it very quickly.

triceps (plural: **triceps**) Your **triceps** is the long muscle at the back of your upper arm.

trick (**trickery**) If someone **tricks** you or plays a **trick** on you, they deceive you. Tricking people is called **trickery.** *...salesmen's trickery.* ■ Something natural which misleads you can be called a **trick.** *...a trick of the light.* ■ A **trick** is a clever or skilful action done to entertain people. *...magic tricks.* ■ Trick devices and methods are designed to create misleading effects, to amuse and entertain people. *...trick photography.* ■ A clever or effective way of doing something can be called a **trick.** *The trick is to plan ahead for such emergencies.* ■ The cards played or won in a round of cards are called a **trick.**

trickle (**trickling, trickled**) When a liquid **trickles** somewhere, it flows in a thin stream. A **trickle** of liquid is a thin stream of it. *...a trickle of blood.* ■ If people or things **trickle** somewhere, they go there gradually in small groups or numbers. You talk about a **trickle** of people or things going somewhere. *The results trickled in. ...a trickle of customers.*

trick or treat is a custom, originally American, in which children in fancy dress go round to people's doors on Halloween and say 'Trick or treat.' If you do not give them a small gift, they play a practical joke on you.

trickster A **trickster** is a person who cheats or deceives people.

tricky (**trickier, trickiest**) If something is **tricky,** it is difficult and requires careful attention.

tricolour (Am: **tricolor**) (pron: **trick**-kol-lor) A **tricolour** is a flag which is made up of three stripes of different colours.

tricycle A **tricycle** is a vehicle similar to a bicycle but with two wheels at the back and one at the front. 'Tricycle' is sometimes shortened to 'trike'.

trident A **trident** is a three-pronged spear.

triennial is used to describe something which happens once every three years.

trier You say someone is a **trier** when they try very hard to do something.

trifle (**trifling**) ■ A **trifle** is a pudding made of sponge cake covered in layers of fruit, jelly, custard, and cream. ■ A **trifle** means 'slightly' or 'rather'. *He looked a trifle overwhelmed.* ■ You can call something of little importance or worth a **trifle** or describe it as **trifling**. *...a trifling matter.*

trigger (**triggering**, **triggered**) The **trigger** of a gun is the small lever you pull to fire it. ■ If something **triggers** an event or **triggers** it **off**, it makes it happen. *The announcement triggered a brief rise in share prices.* The immediate cause of an event is sometimes called its **trigger.** *The trigger was the killing by the security forces of 13 Kurdish separatists.*

trigger-happy people are too ready to use violence and weapons, especially guns.

trigonometry is the branch of mathematics concerned with calculating the angles of triangles, or the lengths of their sides.

trike See **tricycle.**

trilateral talks or negotiations involve three groups.

trilby (**trilbies**) A **trilby** is a man's hat made of felt with a narrow brim and a dent along the top from front to back.

trill A **trill** is two musical notes repeated one after the other several times, very quickly. ■ When a bird **trills,** it sings with short high-pitched repeated notes.

trillion (**trillionth**) A **trillion** is the number 1,000,000,000,000.

trilogy (**trilogies**) A **trilogy** is a series of three books, films, or plays with the same characters or subject.

trim (**trimming, trimmed**) If something is **trim,** it is pleasantly neat and tidy. *...the trim garden.* ■ **Trim** means slim. *...her trim figure.* ■ If a person or thing is **in trim,** they are in good physical condition. ■ If you **trim** something or give it a **trim,** you cut off small amounts of it, to make it look neater. *His hair needed a trim.* ■ If something is **trimmed,** it is reduced. *Student grants will be trimmed by 10%.* ■ The **trim** or **trimming** on something such as a piece of clothing is a decoration along its edges which is in a different colour or material. *...coats with fake-fur trim.* You can say something is **trimmed** with a particular material. *...crimson gowns trimmed with ermine.* ■ **Trimmings** are extra things added to accompany food when it is served. *...turkey and all the trimmings.*

trimaran (pron: **trime**-a-ran) A **trimaran** is a fast sailing boat similar to a catamaran, but with three hulls instead of two.

trimmer A **trimmer** is an electric tool for trimming grass or hedges.

trimmings See **trim.**

trinity In the Christian religion, the **Trinity** is the union of Father, Son, and Holy Spirit in one God. ■ A **trinity** is any group of three people or things, especially a powerful group. *...Germany's trinity of chemical giants.*

trinket – **Trinkets** are cheap ornaments or pieces of jewellery.

trio (**trios**) A **trio** is a group of three people or things, especially a group of three musicians. *...a jazz trio.*

trip (**tripping, tripped**) A **trip** is a journey. ■ If you **trip** or **trip up,** you catch your foot on something and fall. If you **trip** someone else or **trip** them **up,** you make this happen to them, usually by sticking your own foot out in front of them. ■ You can say you **trip up** when you make a mistake. If you **trip** someone else **up,** you get them to make a mistake. ■ You say someone is **tripping** or on a **trip** when they are experiencing the effects of an hallucinogenic drug such as LSD.

tripartite is used to describe something which has three parts or involves three groups of people. *...tripartite talks.*

tripe is the white stomach lining of a cow or ox, which people cook and eat. ■ If you call what someone says **tripe,** you mean it is nonsense.

triple (**tripling, tripled**) **Triple** means consisting of three parts or things. *...a triple somersault.* ■ If something **triples,** it becomes three times as big. You then say it is **triple** the number, size, or amount it was before.

triple jump The **triple jump** is an athletics event similar to the long jump but consisting of a connected series of three jumps. The first is a hop, the second a step, and in the third the competitor is allowed to land on both feet.

triplet – **Triplets** are three children born at the same time to the same mother.

triplicate If something has been produced **in triplicate,** there are three copies of it.

tripod A **tripod** is a stand with three legs, used to support something like a camera.

tripper A **tripper** is a person on a trip or holiday. *...day-trippers.*

triptych (pron: **trip**-tick) A **triptych** is a painting or carving on three panels fixed or hinged side by side.

tripwire (or **trip wire**) A **tripwire** is a wire stretched just above the ground, which triggers a trap or explosion if someone touches it.

trite (**tritely**) If a phrase or idea is **trite,** it is dull and unoriginal.

triumph A **triumph** is a great success or achievement. ■ **Triumph** is a feeling of great satisfaction when you win or achieve something. ■ If you **triumph,** you win a victory, or succeed in overcoming something.

triumphal means done or made to celebrate a victory or great success. *...a triumphal arch.*

triumphalism (**triumphalist**) You can call victory celebrations **triumphalism** or describe them as

triumphalist when you find them overdone and distasteful.

triumphant (**triumphantly**) If you are **triumphant**, you feel very happy because you have won a victory, or achieved something.

triumvirate (*pron:* try-**um**-vir-rit) You can call a group of three powerful people a **triumvirate**. ...*the Young Turk triumvirate of Enver Pasha, Jamal Pasha, and Talat Bey.*

trivia You can call things of little value or importance **trivia**.

trivial (**triviality, trivialities**) If you say something is **trivial** or talk about its **triviality,** you mean it is not important. ■ **Trivialities** are things which are of little importance.

trivialize (*or* **trivialise**) (**trivializing, trivialized; trivialization**) If someone is **trivializing** something, they are making it seem less important than it is. *His family complained that the show was a trivialization of his life.*

trod (**trodden**) See **tread.**

troglodyte A **troglodyte** is someone who lives in a cave.

troika You can refer to a group of three powerful people or countries as a **troika**. ■ A **troika** is a Russian sledge drawn by three horses.

troll (*usual pron:* **trole**) In Scandinavian mythology, **trolls** are unpleasant creatures which live in caves and under bridges.

trolley A **trolley** is a small cart on wheels, used to carry things such as shopping. ■ A hospital **trolley** is a table on wheels for moving patients around. ■ A **trolley** is a small table on wheels for carrying food and drinks. ■ In the US, trams are called **trolleys.**

trolley bus A **trolley bus** is a bus powered by electricity from an overhead wire.

trombone (**trombonist**) The **trombone** is a brass instrument with a U-shaped slide.

troop (**trooping, trooped**) **Troops** are soldiers. ■ A **troop** is a group of soldiers in a cavalry or armoured regiment. ■ When soldiers **troop the colour,** they take part in a ceremony to parade their regimental flag. ■ A **troop** of people or animals is a large group of them. ■ If people **troop** somewhere, they go there in a group. *We trooped back to the house.*

trooper A **trooper** is an ordinary soldier in the cavalry or in an armoured regiment. ■ In the US, a state **trooper** is a member of a state police force.

trophy (**trophies**) A **trophy** is something like a cup, given as a prize to the winner of a competition. ■ A **trophy** is something you keep to remember a success or victory. *They can keep the horn as a trophy.*

tropic (**tropical**) The **tropics** are hot parts of the earth, lying between two lines of latitude, the Tropic of Cancer, $23\frac{1}{2}^{\circ}$ north of the equator, and the Tropic of Capricorn, $23\frac{1}{2}^{\circ}$ south of the equator. **Tropical** is used to describe things to do with the tropics. ...*tropical diseases.*

trot (**trotting, trotted**) When a horse **trots**, it moves fairly fast, lifting one front foot together with the opposite back foot at each step. This pace is called a **trot**. ■ If a person **trots** or moves at a **trot,** they move fairly fast. ■ If things happen on **the trot,** they happen one after the other. *She lost five games on the trot.* ■ If you say someone **trots out** something like an old idea, you mean they repeat it. *He went on and on, trotting out exactly the same tedious arguments.*

trotter A pig's **trotters** are its feet, which can be cooked and eaten. ■ A **trotter** is a horse trained to trot fast and pull a carriage in races.

troubadour (*pron:* **troo**-bad-oor) In medieval times, a **troubadour** was a man who sang love songs which he had composed himself.

trouble (**troubling, troubled**) If something causes you **trouble**, it causes problems. You can call the problems **troubles.** ■ If you are **in trouble,** you are in a situation where you may be punished because you have done something wrong. ■ If there is **trouble,** people are quarrelling or fighting. ■ If you **take the trouble** to do something, you do it, although it requires time and effort. ■ If something **troubles** you, it makes you worried or anxious. ■ If you **trouble** someone for something, you disturb them in order to ask them for it.

troublemaker (**troublemaking**) If you call someone a **troublemaker** or accuse them of **troublemaking,** you mean they are responsible for causing trouble.

troubleshooter A **troubleshooter** is a person employed by an organization to sort out a problem.

troublesome people keep causing trouble. ■ You can call a painful injury **troublesome.** ...*a troublesome wrist injury.*

trough A **trough** is a long narrow container for animals to drink or feed from. ■ At sea, a **trough** is a low point between two waves. ■ In weather forecasting, a **trough** is a long narrow area of low pressure.

trounce (**trouncing, trounced**) In sport, if someone is **trounced,** they are thoroughly beaten.

troupe (*pron:* **troop**) (**trouper**) A **troupe** is a group of performers who work together. ...*a dance troupe.* ■ You can call an actor or other performer a **trouper** when they have a lot of experience and can cope with difficult situations.

trousers (**trousered**) **Trousers** are a piece of clothing worn over the body from the waist down and covering each leg separately. **Trousered** is used to say someone is wearing trousers, or to describe the kind of trousers they are wearing. *He slapped his leather-trousered thigh.*

trouser suit A **trouser suit** is a woman's suit of jacket and trousers.

trousseau (*pron:* **troo**-so) (*plural:* **trousseaus** *or* **trousseaux**) A bride's **trousseau** is the clothes and linen she collects for her marriage.

trout (*plural:* **trout**) **Trout** are spotted freshwater fish which are often caught and eaten.

trove See **treasure trove.**

trowel A **trowel** is (a) a small garden tool with a curved pointed blade. (b) a small tool with a flat diamond-shaped blade, for spreading mortar or cement.

troy weight is a system of weight for weighing precious metals and gemstones. In troy weight, 1 pound equals 12 ounces.

truant (**truancy**) When children **truant** or **play truant,** they stay away from school without permission. This is called **truancy;** the children who do it are called **truants.**

truce A **truce** is an agreement between two sides to stop fighting for a short time.

truck A **truck** is a lorry. If something is **trucked** somewhere, it is transported by truck. ■ A **truck** is a wagon for carrying goods on a railway. ■ If you have **no truck** with someone or something, you have nothing to do with them.

trucker A **trucker** is a person whose job is driving a truck.

truculent (*pron:* **truck**-yew-lent) (**truculently, truculence**) If someone is **truculent,** they are bad-tempered and aggressive. *Part of him wanted to apologize, but his stubborn truculence wouldn't allow it.*

trudge (**trudging, trudged**) If you **trudge** somewhere, you walk there with slow heavy steps. A long walk can be called a **trudge.**

true (**truer, truest**) If something is **true,** it is based on facts. ■ **True** is used to mean 'genuine'. *...a first step on the road to true equality.* ■ If you are **true** to something, you are faithful to it. *He was true to his word.* ■ If you are **true** to yourself, you stick to your principles. ■ If a dream, wish, or prediction **comes true,** it actually happens.

true-blue A **true-blue** person is completely loyal.

truffle A **truffle** is a soft round chocolate, sometimes flavoured with rum. ■ A **truffle** is a round mushroom-like fungus which grows underground, and is considered very good to eat.

truism A **truism** is a statement which is believed to be true and which is repeated so often it is no longer original. *It is a truism that charming people often have something to hide.*

truly means completely and genuinely. *...one of the few truly amateur sports.* ■ **Truly** is used to add emphasis. *Truly, I've never enjoyed myself more... It was truly awful.* ■ You can refer to yourself as **yours truly.** *...insomniacs like yours truly.* ■ Some people write **Yours truly** before their signature at the end of a formal letter.

trump In a game of cards, **trumps** is the suit with the highest value. A **trump** is a card belonging to this suit. ■ Your **trump card** is the most powerful thing you can use or do to gain an advantage. *He sees his foreign policy experience as a possible trump card in the election.* ■ If you **trump** something someone has said or done, you beat them by saying or doing something better. ■ If a person or thing **comes** or **turns up trumps** they do unexpectedly well at something.

trumped-up is used to describe accusations which are made up and not true. *...trumped-up charges of treason.*

trumpet (**trumpeter; trumpeting, trumpeted**) The **trumpet** is a brass wind instrument with three valves. ■ If you **trumpet** something, you announce it to everyone. ■ If you say someone is **blowing their own trumpet,** you mean they are boasting.

truncate (**truncating, truncated**) If something is **truncated,** it is shortened. *...a truncated version of its annual report.*

truncheon A **truncheon** is a short thick stick, used by the police as a weapon.

trundle (**trundling, trundled**) If a vehicle **trundles** somewhere, it moves there slowly. ■ If you **trundle** something like a wheelbarrow somewhere, you push it along slowly.

trunk The **trunk** of a tree is the large main stem which the branches grow from. ■ Your **trunk** is the main part of your body, excluding your head, neck, arms, and legs. ■ An elephant's **trunk** is its long nose. ■ A **trunk** is a large strong case or box with a hinged lid, used for storing things. ■ In the US, the boot of a car is called the **trunk.** ■ Swimming **trunks** are a man's swimming costume, similar to briefs.

trunk call A **trunk call** is a long-distance telephone call.

trunk road A **trunk road** is a main road, especially one suitable for heavy vehicles.

truss (**trusses, trussing, trussed**) A **truss** is a device worn to support a hernia. ■ A **truss** is a steel framework, used to support something like a roof or a bridge. ■ A **truss** is a cluster of flowers or fruit. ■ If you **truss** a bird, you prepare it for cooking by tying its legs and wings. ■ If a person is **trussed** or **trussed up,** they are tied up so they cannot move.

trust (**trusting, trustingly**) If you **trust** someone, you believe they are honest and sincere, and will not try to harm you. *...children's trust in adults.* ■ A person who trusts everyone is called **trusting.** *He'd offered to help, and she'd trustingly gone with him.* ■ **Trust** is responsibility for things which are secret or important. *...details on anyone employed in a position of trust.* ■ If you **trust** someone to do something, you have confidence in their ability to do it. ■ If you **trust** someone with something precious, you allow them to look after or deal with it. *I'd trust him with my life.* ■ If you **take** something **on trust,** you believe it without checking it. ■ A **trust** or **trust fund** is a financial arrangement in which a group of people or an organization looks after and invests money for someone else. You say the money is held **in trust.** See also **unit trust.** ■ In the US, a **trust** is a group of companies which illegally join together to control the market for their product.

trustee (**trusteeship**) A **trustee** is a person who is legally in control of money or property which is being looked after for someone else. The position of trustee is called a **trusteeship.**

trustworthy (**trustworthiness**) A **trustworthy** person is honest and reliable. *...trustworthy advice.*

trusty (**trusties**) A **trusty** person or thing can be relied on. *...my trusty camera.*

truth The **truth** is the facts about something, rather than things which are made up. ■ If you talk about the **truth** of something, you mean the fact that it is true. *I am absolutely certain of the truth of every one of the allegations.* ■ If you say there is **truth** in a statement, you mean it is true, or partly true. ■ A **truth** is an idea or principle which is generally accepted to be true.

truthful (**truthfully, truthfulness**) A **truthful** person or remark is honest and tells the truth.

try (**tries, trying, tried**) If you **try** to do something, you attempt to do it. An attempt to do something is called a **try**. ■ If you **try** something or **try** it **out,** you use it or do it to find out how useful, effective, or enjoyable it is. You can also say you give it a **try** or a **try-out.** See also **well-tried.** ■ If you find someone or something **trying** or they **try your patience,** they make you angry or frustrated. ■ If you say someone is **trying it on,** you mean they are doing something they should not do, to see if they can get away with it. ■ When a person is **tried,** they appear in court, and a jury or magistrate decides if they are guilty, after hearing the evidence. ■ When a rugby player scores a **try,** he puts the ball on the ground behind the opposing team's goal-line.

try-out See **try.**

tryst (*usual pron:* **trist**) A **tryst** is a secret meeting between lovers.

tsar (*or* **czar, tzar**) The **tsar** (*pron:* **zahr**) was the emperor of Russia in former times.

tsarist (*or* **czarist, tzarist**) is used to talk about things to do with Russia before 1917, when it was ruled by a tsar. ...*the tsarist empire.*

tsetse (*pron:* **tset**-see) (*plural:* **tsetse**) **Tsetse** or **tsetse flies** are African flies which feed on the blood of people or animals. Their bite can cause sleeping sickness in humans.

T-shirt A **T-shirt** is a short-sleeved shirt with no collar or buttons.

tub A **tub** is a container. ...*a tub of margarine.* ...*flower tubs.* ■ People sometimes call a bath a **tub.**

tuba The **tuba** is a large brass wind instrument which can produce some very low notes.

tubby A **tubby** person is rather fat.

tube A **tube** is a long hollow cylinder, especially one which air or a liquid passes through. ■ A **tube** is a narrow flexible container with a cap at one end, for holding a substance such as toothpaste. ■ The London Underground is often called the **Tube.**

tuber A **tuber** is the swollen and fleshy root of a plant such as a potato.

tubercular means suffering from or caused by tuberculosis. ...*a tubercular cough.*

tuberculosis or **TB** is an infectious disease which affects the lungs.

tubing is a tube or tubes. ...*rubber tubing.*

tubular If something is **tubular,** it is shaped like a tube. ...*tubular steel columns.*

tuck A **tuck** is a fold stitched in a garment. ■ If you **tuck** something somewhere, you put it there, to keep it safe. ■ If you **tuck** money **away,** you save it. ...*a worker who has some savings tucked away in the bank.* ■ If something is **tucked away,** it is in a place where it cannot easily be found. ...*a club tucked away in the back streets of the city.* ■ If you **tuck in** something such as a shirt, you put the loose ends inside your trousers or skirt. ■ If you **tuck into** food, you eat it with a lot of pleasure.

Tudor The **Tudor** period was from 1485 to 1603 when the Tudor family reigned in Britain. **Tudor** is used to describe people and things from that period.

tuft (**tufted**) A **tuft** of something like hair or grass is a bunch of it growing closely together. You say something which grows in tufts is **tufted.** ...*tufted grass.*

tug (**tugging, tugged**) If you **tug** something or give it a **tug,** you give it a quick hard pull. *I felt a tug at my sleeve.* ■ A **tug** or **tugboat** is a small powerful boat used to pull large ships.

tugboat See **tug.**

tug-of-love is used to describe a situation in which the parents of a child are divorced, and the parent without custody tries to get the child, for example by kidnapping it.

tug-of-war A **tug-of-war** is a contest in which two teams test their strength by pulling against each other on opposite ends of a rope. ■ You can call any situation in which people are trying hard to get an advantage over each other a **tug-of-war.** ...*a diplomatic tug-of-war between China and Taiwan.*

tuition is the teaching of a subject, especially to one person or a small group.

tulip – **Tulips** are brightly coloured cup-shaped spring flowers with long stems.

tulle (*pron:* **tewl**) is a fine net-like material made of silk or nylon, used to make dresses and veils.

tumble (**tumbling, tumbled**) If you **tumble** or take a **tumble,** you fall. ■ If prices **tumble,** they fall rapidly. ■ If water **tumbles,** it flows quickly over an uneven surface.

tumbledown A **tumbledown** building is in very bad condition, and is partly falling down.

tumble dryer (*or* tumble drier) A **tumble dryer** is a machine in which washing is dried inside a rotating drum, heated by hot air.

tumbler A **tumbler** is a drinking glass with straight sides. ■ A **tumbler** is an acrobat who performs on the ground.

tumbril A **tumbril** is a farm cart. **Tumbrils** were used during the French Revolution to transport prisoners to the guillotine.

tummy (**tummies**) People sometimes call their stomach their **tummy.**

tumour (*Am:* tumor) A **tumour** is a mass of diseased or abnormal cells growing in a person's or animal's body.

tumult (*pron:* **tew**-mult) A **tumult** is a lot of noise caused by a crowd of people. *He sat listening to the evening tumult of the bazaar outside.* ■ A **tumult** is a state of great confusion or excitement. ...*the recent tumult in global financial markets.*

tumultuous reactions are very noisy, because people are happy or enthusiastic. ...*tumultuous applause.* ■ A **tumultuous** time is one when a lot of exciting and confusing things are happening. ...*the tumultuous years between 1965 and 1974.*

tumulus (*pron:* **tew**-mew-luss) (*plural:* **tumuli**) A **tumulus** is an ancient burial mound.

tuna (*plural:* tuna) **Tuna** or **tuna fish** are large edible sea fish.

tundra is a flat treeless Arctic region where the ground below the top layer of soil is always frozen.

tune (**tuning, tuned**) A **tune** is a series of musical notes arranged in a pleasing way. ■ If you sing or play a piece of music **in tune,** you produce exactly the right notes. ■ If you **tune** an instrument, such as a guitar, you adjust it so it produces the right notes. When musicians **tune** or **tune up,** they adjust their instruments so that they are in tune with each other. ■ If you **tune** an engine, you adjust it so that it works as it is supposed to. ■ If you **tune** or **tune in** to a TV or radio programme, you adjust the controls to receive it. You can also say a TV or radio is **tuned** to a particular station. ...*a short-wave radio, tuned to the BBC World Service.* ■ If you are **in tune with** a group of people, you are in agreement or sympathy with them. ■ **To the tune of** a sum of money means amounting to that sum. ...*losses to the tune of almost $1 billion.*

tuneful (**tunefulness**) A **tuneful** piece of music is full of good tunes.

tuneless music has no tunes in it. **Tuneless** singing is out of tune.

tuner A **tuner** is a piece of equipment you adjust to receive TV or radio signals. ■ A piano **tuner** is a person whose job is tuning pianos.

tungsten is a greyish-white metal used to make light bulb filaments and to harden steel.

tunic In ancient Greece and Rome, a **tunic** was a loose-fitting sleeveless garment worn by men and women. ■ A **tunic** or **tunic top** is a woman's loose-fitting blouse or jumper. ■ A **tunic** is a close-fitting jacket worn as part of a uniform.

tuning fork A **tuning fork** is a two-pronged steel fork used when tuning an instrument like a piano. When you strike it, it produces a note of a fixed pitch.

tunnel (**tunnelling, tunnelled**) (*Am:* **tunneling, tunneled**) A **tunnel** is a long underground passage, especially one for vehicles to travel through. When people **tunnel** somewhere, they dig a tunnel there.

tunnel vision is a condition in which you are unable to see things which are not straight in front of you. ■ If you say someone has **tunnel vision,** you mean they have a narrow point of view, caused by concentrating on just one aspect of something.

tunny (*plural:* **tunnies** *or* **tunny**) is an old name for tuna.

tuppence is two old pence.

Tupperware is a range of plastic containers for storing food. 'Tupperware' is a trademark.

turban (**turbaned** *or* **turbanned**) A **turban** is a head covering worn by Sikh men, and some Muslim and Hindu men, consisting of a long piece of cloth wound round and round the head. If a man is **turbaned,** he is wearing a turban.

turbine A **turbine** is a machine or engine driven by water, wind, gas, or steam turning the blades of a wheel.

turbo (**turbos**) See **turbocharger.**

turbocharger (*or* **turbo-charger**) (**turbocharged**) A **turbocharger** or **turbo** is a turbine-driven fan which increases an engine's power by blowing the fuel vapour into it at a higher pressure than usual. A **turbocharged** engine or vehicle is fitted with a tur-

bocharger. Engines and vehicles like these are often just called **turbos.**

turbofan A **turbofan** or **turbofan** engine is an aircraft engine which sucks air in at the front and forces it out at the back, to increase the thrust.

turbo-prop (*or* **turboprop**) A **turbo-prop** or **turbo-prop** aircraft has propellers driven by gas turbine engines called **turbo-prop** engines.

turbot (*plural:* **turbot**) are large flat edible sea-fish.

turbulent (**turbulence**) A **turbulent** period is one when there is a lot of change and confusion. *There could still be turbulent times ahead.* You talk about the **turbulence** of a period like this. ...*the turbulence of the past week.* ■ **Turbulent** air or water contains strong currents which change direction suddenly. You talk about **turbulence** in air or water. *His plane encountered severe turbulence.*

turd A **turd** is a lump of faeces.

tureen (*pron:* tyu-**reen**) A **tureen** is a large covered dish for serving soup or vegetables.

turf is short thick even grass. ■ Your **turf** is your territory. *Both sides are jealously guarding their turf.* ■ If you **turf** someone **out,** you force them to leave a place.

turgid (*pron:* **tur**-jid) A **turgid** speech or piece of writing is long and boring.

Turk A **Turk** is someone who comes from Turkey.

turkey A **turkey** is a large bird bred for its meat. **Turkey** is the meat of a turkey. ■ People say a film or play is a **turkey** when it is an artistic or financial failure. ...*a box office turkey.* ■ You call a contest a **turkey shoot** when it is very one-sided. ■ See also **cold turkey.**

Turkish means in or from Turkey. ...*a Turkish businessman.* ■ **Turkish** is the main language spoken in Turkey.

Turkish bath A **Turkish bath** is (a) a health treatment which involves sitting in a hot dry room, then a steamy room, then having a wash, massage, and cold shower. (b) a place where you can have a Turkish bath.

Turkish delight is a jelly-like sweet coated in icing sugar.

turmeric is a mild yellow spice which is used in Indian cooking.

turmoil is a state of anxiety, confusion, and disorder. *The country was in turmoil.*

turn If you **turn,** you move so you are facing or moving in a different direction. A movement like this is called a **turn.** ■ A **turning** is a road leading away from another road. A **turn-off** is a road leading away from a major road or a motorway. ...*the M20 turn-off.* ■ If you **turn** something, you move or rotate it so it faces in a different direction. *He turned the chair around... She turned the page.* ■ If you **turn** a device **on** or **off,** you switch it on or off. If you **turn out** a light, you switch it off. ■ If you **turn down** a device like a TV, radio, or heater, you reduce the amount of sound or heat coming out of it. Similarly, you can **turn up** any of these things. ■ If you **turn** to something, you start becoming involved with it. *More young people are turning to crime.* ■ If you **turn** your attention to something, you start thinking about it. ■ If you **turn** to someone, you go to them for help. ■ If you do someone a **good turn,** you do something to help them. ■ When something **turns** into something else, it changes into it. *The water turns to steam.* ■ A **turn** is a change in the way something is happening or being done. *...a remarkable turn of events.* ■ When a group of people **take turns** to do something or do it **in turn,** they do it one after the other in a fixed order. If it is someone's **turn** to do it, they are the next person in the group to do it. ■ The **turn** of the century is the very last part of one century and the beginning of the next one. Similarly, you can talk about the **turn** of the year. ■ If you are **turned on** by someone or something, you are sexually aroused by them. You can say something which has this effect is a **turn-on.** Similarly, you can say you are **turned off** by something or that something is a **turn-off.** ■ If someone **turns on** you, they suddenly attack you, or start criticizing you. ■ If you **turn down** a request or offer, you refuse or reject it. ■ If you **turn** someone **away,** you refuse to let them enter a place. ■ If you are **turned out** of a place, you are forced to leave. ■ You say someone **turns up** when they arrive somewhere. ■ If something **turns up,** it is discovered somewhere. ■ If people **turn out** for an event or activity, they go and watch it or take part in it. See also **turnout.** ■ If you **turn in,** you go to bed. ■ If you **turn** someone **in,** you give them up to the police or authorities. ■ You can describe what happens in a situation by saying **turn out** in a particular way. *Everything turned out well.*

turnaround (turnabout) A **turnaround** or **turnabout** is a change in a politician's or government's attitude or policy. *He praised Brazil's turnaround in attitudes towards conservation of the Amazon rainforests.* ■ A **turnaround** or **turnround** is a sudden change in a situation, either for better or for worse. *...the turnround in South Africa's economic fortunes.*

turncoat You say someone is a **turncoat** when they leave your group or organization and join an opposing one.

turning point A **turning point** is a time when an important change takes place in something. *This was to be a turning point in his career.*

turnip – **Turnips** are round root vegetables with white or yellow skins.

turn-off See **turn.**

turn-on See **turn.**

turnout The **turnout** at an event is the number of people who go to it. ■ The **turnout** in an election is the number of people who vote.

turnover The **turnover** of people in an organization is the rate at which people leave and are replaced. ■ The **turnover** of a business is the value of goods or services sold over a particular period.

turnround See **turnaround.**

turnstile A **turnstile** is a revolving mechanical barrier, allowing only one person at a time to pass through it.

turntable A **turntable** is a revolving circular platform, especially the flat round part of a record player which you put a record on.

turn-up The **turn-ups** on a pair of trousers are the ends of the trouser legs folded upwards on the outside.

turpentine or **turps** is a strong-smelling colourless liquid used to clean paint off brushes.

turpitude is depraved behaviour.

turps See **turpentine.**

turquoise A **turquoise** is an opaque greenish-blue gemstone.

turret (turreted) A **turret** is a small tower on top of a building or wall. If a structure has turrets, you say it is **turreted.** ■ A **turret** is a revolving structure on a tank or warship, on which a gun is mounted.

turtle – **Turtles** are tortoise-like reptiles, which live mainly in water.

turtleneck A **turtleneck** sweater has a high, round, close-fitting neck.

tusk The **tusks** of an elephant, wild boar, or walrus are its two very long pointed teeth.

tussle (tussling, tussled) If people **tussle,** they grab hold of and struggle with each other. A struggle like this is called a **tussle.** ■ If you **tussle** with a difficult problem, you try hard to solve it.

tussock A **tussock** is a thick clump of grass.

tut (tutting, tutted) If you **tut** or **tut-tut,** you make a clicking sound with your tongue.

tutelage (*pron: tew-till-lij*) is guidance or instruction.

tutor (tutoring, tutored) A **tutor** is a teacher at a college or university. ■ A **tutor** is someone who gives private lessons to one pupil or a small group of pupils. ■ If someone **tutors** a person or subject, they teach that person or subject. *I tutored in economics.*

tutorial In a university or college, a **tutorial** is a regular meeting between a tutor and one or several students, to discuss a subject being studied.

tutti frutti ice cream contains small pieces of mixed candied fruit. **Tutti-frutti** flavoured foods or drinks taste like a mixture of fruits.

tutu (*pron: too-too*) A **tutu** is a short stiff skirt made of many layers of material, worn by a female ballet dancer.

tuxedo (tuxedos) In the US, a dinner jacket is called a **tuxedo.**

TV See **television.**

twaddle If you call what someone says **twaddle,** you mean it is nonsense.

twain is an old word meaning 'two'.

twang A **twang** is a sound like a wire being pulled then released. If you **twang** something, you pull it and release it to make a sound like this. ■ A **twang** is a nasal quality in someone's voice.

tweak (tweaking, tweaked) If you **tweak** something or give it a **tweak,** you hold it between your finger and thumb and twist or pull it. ■ If you **tweak** something like a plan or give it a **tweak,** you make a slight adjustment to it.

twee If you say something is **twee,** you mean it is supposed to be pretty but you find it sentimental and in bad taste.

tweed is a type of thick woollen cloth used to make clothes. You can refer to tweed clothes as **tweeds.**

tweedy clothes are made of tweed or look like tweed. ■ If you describe someone as **tweedy,** you mean they have an upper-class appearance and look as if they live in the country.

tweet (tweeting, tweeted) A **tweet** is a short, high-pitched sound made by a small bird. You say the bird **tweets** when it makes this sound.

tweezers are a small tool for pulling out hairs or picking up small objects.

twelve (twelfth) Twelve is the number 12.

twenty (twentieth, twenties) Twenty is the number 20. ■ The **twenties** was the period from 1920 to 1929. ■ If someone is in their **twenties,** they are aged 20 to 29.

twice means two times.

twiddle (twiddling, twiddled) If you **twiddle** something or **twiddle** with it, you twist or turn it with your fingers.

twig (twigging, twigged) A **twig** is a very small branch of a tree or bush. ■ If you **twig** something, you realize or understand it.

twilight is the period just before night when it is not completely dark. The dim light at this time can also be called **twilight.** ■ The **twilight** of something is the final stages of it.

twill is cloth woven in a way which produces diagonal lines or ridges across it.

twin (twinning, twinned) Twins are two children born at the same time to the same mother. ■ You can use **twin** to describe a pair of things. *The room had twin beds.* ■ When a place or organization in one country is **twinned** with a place or organization in another country, a special relationship is formally established between them. **Twin** towns or cities are twinned with each other.

twine (twining, twined) Twine is strong smooth string. ■ If you **twine** one thing round another, you twist or coil it round. *...twining a strand of hair around her finger.*

twinge A **twinge** is a sudden sharp feeling of pain or of an emotion.

twinkle (twinkling, twinkled) If something **twinkles,** it shines brightly with a small flickering light. A light like this is called a **twinkle.** ■ If your eyes **twinkle** or there is a **twinkle** in them, your face expresses amusement or delight. ■ If something happens **in the twinkling of an eye,** it happens instantly.

twinset (or twin-set) A **twinset** is a woman's matching jumper and cardigan.

twin-tub A **twin-tub** is a washing machine which has one section for washing and another for spin-drying.

twirl If you **twirl** something or it **twirls,** it turns round several times with a smooth, fairly fast movement. *He twirled his bat.* ■ If you **twirl** when you are dancing, you spin round.

twist If you **twist** something or give it a **twist,** you turn one end of it, while holding the other end. ■ If you **twist** part of your body, you turn it while keeping the rest of your body still. *He twisted his head to the right.* ■ If you **twist** your ankle or knee, you injure it by turning it sharply in an unusual way. ■ If a road or river **twists** or there is a **twist** in it, it

bends sharply. ■ If you say a person's mind or behaviour is **twisted,** you mean it is unpleasant and unnatural. ■ If someone **twists** what you say, they distort the meaning. ■ A **twist** is an unexpected development in a story.

twisty A **twisty** road or river has many sharp bends.

twit (twitting, twitted) You can call a silly person a **twit.**

twitch (twitches, twitching, twitched) If someone **twitches,** they make little jerky movements which they cannot control. You say they have a **twitch.** ■ If you **twitch** something, you make it move slightly with a jerky motion. *He twitched his shoulders.*

twitcher Enthusiastic bird spotters are sometimes called **twitchers.**

twitchy (twitchiness) If someone is **twitchy,** they are anxious or nervous.

twitter (twittering, twittered) When birds **twitter,** they make short high-pitched noises. ■ You can say people **twitter** when they speak in excited high-pitched voices.

two is the number 2.

two-bit People use **two-bit** to describe someone or something they think is of little importance. *...some two-bit artist.*

two-dimensional A **two-dimensional** shape is a shape like a square or circle which can be measured in two directions only, as distinct from a three-dimensional shape like a cube or cylinder. ■ If you describe fictional characters as **two-dimensional,** you mean they are too simple and not realistic enough to be taken seriously.

two-edged If something is **two-edged,** it has two opposite sides or aspects. *...a two-edged argument.* ■ If you call something a **two-edged sword,** you mean it has disadvantages as well as advantages.

two-faced If you say someone is **two-faced,** you mean they are deceitful or insincere.

twofold If something is **twofold,** it has two parts. *The answer is twofold.* ■ If there is a **twofold** increase in something, it doubles in size.

twosome A **twosome** is two people, especially a couple.

two-stroke engines deliver power in one up-and-down movement of a piston, rather than two.

two-way means moving or working in two opposite directions. *...two-way traffic. ...a two-way radio.*

tycoon A **tycoon** is a rich powerful businessman.

tyke (or tike) You can call a mischievous child a **tyke.**

type (typing, typed) A **type** of something is one kind of it. *...suitable for all skin types.* ■ You can describe a person as a particular **type.** *...intellectual types.* ■ If you **type,** you press keys to write something on a typewriter, word processor, or computer. ■ If you **type up** handwritten material, you produce a typed copy of it. ■ **Type** is used to talk about the size or style of printing used in a book or newspaper. *The type is larger and there is more colour.*

typecast (typecasting) If an actor or actress is **typecast,** they keep being given the same kind of roles to play.

typeface The **typeface** in a book or newspaper is the style of printing in it.

typescript A **typescript** is a typed copy of a piece of writing.

typeset (**typesetting, typeset** *not 'typesetted'*; **typesetter**) When a piece of writing is **typeset**, it is arranged on the page so that it is ready for printing. A person or machine that does this job is called a **typesetter**.

typewriter A **typewriter** is a machine with keys, which you press to produce print on a piece of paper.

typewritten If something is **typewritten**, it has been typed on a typewriter or word processor.

typhoid is a serious infectious disease spread by contaminated food or water.

typhoon A **typhoon** is a violent tropical storm in the China Seas or western Pacific.

typhus is an infectious disease spread by lice, fleas, or mites.

typical (**typically**) Typical is used to say something shows the usual characteristics of a person or thing. *...a typical summer day... This is a typically brave and selfless decision by the Prime Minister.* ■ **Typically** is used to say what normally happens in particular circumstances. *Typically, the cause of death will be entered in the medical records as 'cardiac arrest'.*

typify (**typifies, typifying, typified**) If someone or something **typifies** a certain thing, they are a typical example of it. *He typified a certain kind of British comedy.*

typist A **typist** is a person whose job is typing.

typographical means to do with the way printed material is arranged or presented. *...a typographical error.*

typography (**typographer**) Typography is the arranging and preparing of written material, ready for printing. A **typographer** is a person who does this kind of work.

tyrannical A **tyrannical** ruler is cruel and unjust.

tyrannize (*or* **tyrannise**) (**tyrannizing, tyrannized**) If someone **tyrannizes** you, they treat you cruelly and unjustly.

tyranny (**tyrannies**) Tyranny is cruel unjust rule by a person or government. A cruel unjust government can be called a **tyranny.** ■ You can talk about the **tyranny** of something when it makes severe demands on people in their work or daily life. *...the tyranny of daily commuting.*

tyrant A **tyrant** is a person, especially a ruler, who treats the people they have authority over cruelly and unjustly.

tyre (*Am:* **tire**) A **tyre** is a thick rubber ring fitted round the wheel of a vehicle.

tyro (**tyros**) A **tyro** is someone who is just beginning to learn something. *...a tyro journalist.*

tzar See **tsar.**

tzarist See **tsarist.**

U u

ubiquitous (*pron:* yew-**bik**-wit-uss) (**ubiquity**) You say things of a certain kind are **ubiquitous** or talk about their **ubiquity** when you seem to see them everywhere.

U-boat – **U-boats** were German submarines used in the two World Wars.

udder A cow's **udders** are the parts of its body which hang down between its back legs and produce milk.

UFO – **UFOs** are strange objects seen in the sky which some people think are alien spacecraft. UFO stands for 'unidentified flying object'.

ugly (**uglier, ugliest; ugliness**) Ugly people and things are unattractive to look at. ■ You call a situation **ugly** when it involves unpleasantness and violence.

UHT milk has been treated at a very high temperature so it will keep for a long time in a sealed container. UHT stands for 'ultra heat treated'.

UK See **United Kingdom.**

ulcer An **ulcer** is a painful open sore on the skin or inside the body.

ulna The **ulna** is the inner and longer of the two bones in the human forearm. See also **radius.**

ulterior If you say someone has an **ulterior** motive for doing something, you mean they have a hidden reason for it.

ultimate The **ultimate** aim of a series of actions is what they are finally intended to achieve. The **ultimate** result of a series of events is what finally happens as a result of them. ■ **Ultimate** is used to describe the greatest thing of a particular kind. *Are the Olympic Games still the ultimate test of sporting endeavour?*

ultimately is used to say something happens after a long series of events or after a long time. *Agreement was ultimately reached.* ■ You use **ultimately** when mentioning the most important factor in a situation. *Future computing ultimately depends on hardware.*

ultimatum An **ultimatum** is a warning that unless someone does a certain thing, serious action will be taken against them.

ultra- is added to words to talk about an extreme form of something. *...ultra-small computers.*

ultramarine is a bright blue colour.

ultrasonic (**ultrasound**) Ultrasonic sounds have very high frequencies which human beings cannot hear. Ultrasonic sound waves are sometimes called **ultrasound.**

ultraviolet light or radiation is invisible to humans and can harm the skin. It is produced, for example, by the sun or by special lamps.

umbilical cord (*pron:* um-**bill**-ik-al) The **umbilical cord** is the tube connecting an unborn baby to its mother, through which it gets oxygen and food.

umbrage If someone takes **umbrage** at something you say or do, they feel upset, annoyed, or hurt by it.

umbrella An **umbrella** is a device used to protect yourself from rain or hot sun. It consists of a stick with a folding frame covered in cloth. ■ Any arrangement which provides protection for people can be called an **umbrella**. *New work can be tried out under the protective umbrella of subsidy.* ■ An **umbrella** organization exists to co-ordinate the work of all organizations of a certain type. *...the umbrella body for the province's charities.*

umlaut (*pron:* **um**-lout) The **umlaut** is a two-dot symbol sometimes written over 'a', 'o', or 'u' in German and over certain letters in some other languages. It indicates a change in the pronunciation of the letter. For example the German word 'über' has an umlaut over the 'u'.

umpire (**umpiring, umpired**) The **umpire** in a game such as cricket or tennis is the person who supervises the match. You say this person **umpires** the match.

umpteen (**umpteenth**) **Umpteen** things means a very large number of them. *He has produced umpteen books.* ■ If you say something happens for the **umpteenth** time, you mean it happens yet again, when it has happened many times before.

UN See **United Nations.**

un- is used in front of other words to form words which have the opposite meaning. *'It was a very aggressive, unfriendly animal,' said a police spokesman. ...unknown, untried, and untested ideas.* ■ You can add **un-** to words which refer to a process or action to talk about the reverse of that process or action. *He unwrapped his presents.*

unabashed If someone is **unabashed** about what they say, do, or feel, they are not at all ashamed or embarrassed by it.

unabated If something unpleasant or undesirable continues **unabated,** it goes on just as much as ever.

unable If you are **unable** to do something, you cannot do it, for example because you do not have the skill or because something is preventing you.

unacceptable (**unacceptably**) If you say something is **unacceptable,** you mean you disapprove of it and feel it should not happen.

unaccompanied If you are **unaccompanied,** you have nobody with you. ■ **Unaccompanied** luggage or goods are being sent or transported separately from their owner. ■ An **unaccompanied** voice or instrument sings or plays alone, without other instruments playing at the same time.

unaccountable (**unaccountably**) If you say something is **unaccountable,** you mean there does not seem to be any explanation for it. ■ **Unaccountable** people or organizations do not have to explain or justify their actions to anyone else.

unaccounted If people or things are **unaccounted** for, it is not known where they are or what has happened to them.

unaccustomed If you are **unaccustomed** to something, you are not used to it. ■ If someone behaves in an **unaccustomed** way, they do not behave as they usually would.

unacknowledged If something is **unacknowledged,** people ignore it or are not aware of it. *...Russell's hitherto unacknowledged gift for alternative comedy.*

unadorned If you describe something as **unadorned,** you mean it is simple and plain, rather than having extra things added to it to make it more attractive. *...unadorned stone buildings.*

unadulterated is used to say something is pure and has not had its quality reduced by having things added to it. *...unadulterated honey.* ■ **Unadulterated** is used to emphasize how bad something is. *...ninety minutes of pure unadulterated rubbish.*

unaffected If something is **unaffected** by something else, it is not affected by it.

unaided If you do something **unaided,** you do it without help from anyone else.

unalloyed feelings are not spoiled or reduced by being mixed with other feelings. *The business world has greeted the interest rate cut with unalloyed relief.*

unalterable things cannot be changed.

unaltered If something is **unaltered,** it has not been changed.

unambiguous (**unambiguously**) An **unambiguous** statement has only one possible meaning.

unambitious An **unambitious** person is not particularly interested in becoming successful or rich. ■ You say something like a plan is **unambitious** when it is not at all risky or adventurous.

unanimous (*pron:* yew-**nan**-im-uss) (**unanimously, unanimity**) If a group of people are **unanimous** or there is **unanimity** (*pron:* yew-nan-**nim**-it-ee) among them, they all agree about something.

unannounced If you arrive somewhere **unannounced,** you do not tell anyone you are coming.

unanswerable An **unanswerable** question is one nobody can answer. ■ If an argument is **unanswerable,** it is so obviously correct that nobody could disagree with it.

unanswered questions or letters have not been answered.

unappealing If you find a person or thing **unappealing,** you find them unattractive or undesirable.

unappetizing (*or* **unappetising**) food does not look like it will be very nice.

unapproachable people are unfriendly and difficult to talk to.

unarguable (**unarguably**) If you say something is **unarguable,** you mean there can be no doubt about it. *This is unarguably wonderful music.*

unarmed people are not carrying weapons.

unashamed (**unashamedly**) **Unashamed** is used to say someone does something openly when other people might find it shocking or unacceptable. *We unashamedly wooed the media.*

unasked An **unasked** question is one nobody has asked, although it may be in many people's minds.

■ If you do something **unasked,** you do it without being asked to.

unassailable If someone or something is **unassailable,** they cannot be challenged or defeated. *Australia have an unassailable 3-1 lead over New Zealand.*

unassuming people are modest and quiet.

unattached If someone is **unattached,** they are not married nor in a steady relationship.

unattended When people or things are left **unattended,** they are not being watched or looked after.

unattractive people or things are unpleasant to look at. ■ If you describe something as **unattractive,** you mean people do not like it and do not want to be involved with it.

unauthorized (*or* **unauthorised**) actions are done without official permission. An **unauthorized** person does not have official permission to do something.

unavailable When things are **unavailable,** you cannot obtain them. When a person is **unavailable,** you cannot meet them or talk to them.

unavailing An **unavailing** attempt to do something does not succeed.

unavoidable (**unavoidably**) If something is **unavoidable,** it cannot be avoided or prevented.

unaware If you are **unaware** of something, you do not know about it.

unawares If something catches you **unawares,** it happens when you are not expecting it.

unbalance (**unbalancing, unbalanced**) If you say someone is **unbalanced,** you mean they seem disturbed or slightly mad. ■ An **unbalanced** account of something is an unfair one because it emphasizes some things and ignores others. ■ If something **unbalances** a relationship or a system, it disturbs or upsets it. ■ If you **unbalance** something, you make it unsteady so it becomes likely to tip over. *...unbalancing the ladder.*

unbearable (**unbearably**) You say something is **unbearable** when you find it so unpleasant or upsetting that you cannot tolerate it.

unbeatable If someone is in an **unbeatable** position in a competition, they are certain to win. ■ If you say something is **unbeatable,** you mean it is the best thing of its kind. *As a farm dog, the border collie is unbeatable.*

unbeaten In sport, if someone is **unbeaten** in a certain number of games or matches or has had an **unbeaten** run, they have not been defeated. ■ An **unbeaten** record is one which nobody has ever beaten.

unbecoming A person's behaviour is described as **unbecoming** when it is thought to be shocking and inappropriate.

unbeknown (*or* **unbeknownst**) If something happens **unbeknown** to you, you do not know anything about it.

unbelievable (**unbelievably**) Unbelievable is used to say something is extremely large, or extremely good or bad. ■ If you say a story or report is **unbelievable,** you mean it is so unlikely you cannot believe it.

unbeliever An **unbeliever** is someone who does not believe in a particular religion or who has no religious beliefs.

unbelieving is used to describe someone who does not believe something they have just been told. *He stared at me, dazed and unbelieving.*

unbending You say someone is **unbending** when they have very strict beliefs or attitudes which they refuse to change.

unbiased If you describe someone or something as **unbiased,** you mean they are fair and do not show prejudice or favouritism.

unborn An **unborn** child has not yet been born.

unbounded If you say something is **unbounded,** you mean there is no limit to it.

unbridled behaviour and feelings are not controlled. *...unbridled passion.*

unbroken is used to say something goes on throughout a period of time without stopping.

unburden (**unburdening, unburdened**) If you **unburden** yourself, you tell someone about something you have been secretly worried about. ■ If you are **unburdened** by problems, you do not have any problems.

unbutton (**unbuttoning, unbuttoned**) When you **unbutton** something, you unfasten the buttons on it.

uncalled-for You say a remark or criticism is **uncalled-for** when you think it is unkind or unfair.

uncanny (**uncannily**) If something is **uncanny,** it is strange and hard to explain.

uncaring If someone is **uncaring,** they do not care about other people's suffering.

unceasing (**unceasingly**) If something is **unceasing,** it goes on without stopping.

uncensored films and publications are released without any parts having been removed by an official censor.

unceremoniously If something is done **unceremoniously,** it is done suddenly and rudely, without dignity. *He was dragged to the front entrance, and unceremoniously dumped outside.*

uncertain (**uncertainly**) If you are **uncertain,** you are not sure what to do or think. ■ If something is **uncertain,** it is doubtful or unknown. ■ If you tell someone something **in no uncertain terms,** you say it firmly and clearly so there is no doubt about what you mean.

uncertainty (**uncertainties**) Uncertainty is a state of doubt about the future or what is the right thing to do. *...the uncertainties of his future.*

unchallenged If something goes **unchallenged,** people accept it without questioning it or opposing it.

unchanged If something remains **unchanged,** it stays the same.

uncharacteristic (**uncharacteristically**) If you call someone's behaviour **uncharacteristic,** you mean it is not the way they normally behave.

uncharitable If you say someone is being **uncharitable,** you mean they are being unkind or unfair to someone.

uncharted If you describe a situation, experience, or activity as **uncharted,** you mean it is new or unfamiliar. ■ **Uncharted** areas of land or sea are not shown on any maps.

unchecked If you say something undesirable is left **unchecked,** you mean nothing is done to prevent it continuing or increasing.

uncivil behaviour is rude and impolite.

uncivilized (*or* **uncivilised**) If you call someone's behaviour **uncivilized,** you mean it is very rude or very cruel.

unclaimed If something is **unclaimed,** nobody has claimed it or said it belongs to them.

uncle Your **uncle** is the brother of your mother or father, or the husband of your aunt.

unclean things are dirty and likely to cause disease. ■ If you describe someone or something as **unclean,** you mean they are spiritually or morally bad.

unclear If something is **unclear,** it is confusing and not obvious.

Uncle Sam Some people, especially Americans, refer to the United States as **Uncle Sam.**

unclothed If someone is **unclothed,** they are not wearing any clothes.

uncomfortable (**uncomfortably**) If you are **uncomfortable,** you are unable to relax and feel slight pain or discomfort. You can describe something which causes slight feelings of pain or discomfort as **uncomfortable.** ...*uncomfortable chairs.* ■ If a situation makes you **uncomfortable,** it makes you slightly worried or embarrassed.

uncommitted If someone is **uncommitted,** they are unwilling to show support for a particular idea or course of action.

uncommon (**uncommonly**) **Uncommon** things do not happen often or are not often seen. ■ If you describe a quality or ability as **uncommon,** you mean it is unusually great in degree or amount. *At the age of 13, Mary Whitehouse was uncommonly good at tennis.*

uncommunicative people are unwilling to talk to other people.

uncomplaining people do not complain when they have to do difficult or unpleasant things.

uncomplicated things are simple and straightforward.

uncomprehending is used to describe people who do not understand what is happening or why. *Nick frowned, uncomprehending.*

uncompromising (**uncompromisingly**) If someone is **uncompromising,** they are determined not to change their opinions or aims. ...*uncompromisingly modern music.*

unconcealed You say people's feelings, beliefs, or wishes are **unconcealed** when they do not try to hide them.

unconcerned (**unconcern**) If someone is **unconcerned** about something which is happening, they are not interested in it, or not worried by it. You say someone like this behaves with **unconcern.** ...*another demonstration of the terrorists' increasing unconcern about civilian casualties.*

unconditional (**unconditionally**) If you make an **unconditional** demand, you say something should

be done without any conditions being attached to it.

unconfirmed If a report is **unconfirmed,** it has not yet been established whether it is true or not.

unconnected If something is **unconnected** with something else, it has no connection with it.

unconscionable (*pron:* un-**con**-shun-ab-l) (**unconscionably**) If something is **unconscionable,** it cannot be justified. ...*unconscionable delays.*

unconscious (**unconsciously, unconsciousness**) If someone is **unconscious,** they are in a sleep-like state called **unconsciousness** in which they are unable to notice or react to things, for example because they have fainted or have had a blow to the head. ■ If you are **unconscious** of something, you are unaware of it. ■ Your **unconscious** feelings and attitudes are ones you are unaware of but which show in the way you behave. The part of your mind where these feelings and attitudes exist is called the **unconscious.**

unconstitutional (**unconstitutionally**) If something is **unconstitutional,** it goes against the constitution of a country or organization.

uncontrollable (**uncontrollably**) If something such as a feeling is **uncontrollable,** there is nothing you can do to stop it. *He wept uncontrollably.*

uncontrolled If something, especially a kind of behaviour, is **uncontrolled,** no attempt is made to stop or restrain it. ...*uncontrolled anger.*

uncooked food has not yet been cooked.

uncooperative You say someone is being **uncooperative** when they do not try to help you with what you want.

uncoordinated If something a group of people do is **uncoordinated,** it is badly organized and their different tasks do not fit in with each other. ■ **Uncoordinated** people do not have good control over the way they move, and their movements are clumsy.

uncork When you **uncork** a bottle, you open it by pulling out the cork.

uncounted is used to say a number of people or things is very large. ...*uncounted billions of dollars.*

uncouth people have bad manners and behave in a rude unpleasant way.

uncover (**uncovering, uncovered**) If you **uncover** a secret, you find out about it. ■ If you **uncover** an object, you take off its cover.

unctuous You say someone is **unctuous** when they pretend to be full of kindness, interest, or praise, but are obviously insincere.

uncut precious stones have not yet been cut into a regular shape and polished. ■ An **uncut** version of a film or play has not been shortened or censored.

undaunted If you are **undaunted** by a setback, you are not put off by it.

undecided If you are **undecided** about something, you have not yet made your mind up about it.

undeclared An **undeclared** war has never officially been declared. ■ An **undeclared** election candidate has not officially announced their decision to stand for election. ■ **Undeclared** sums of money have not been acknowledged to exist and have therefore not been taxed or officially approved.

undemanding things are not difficult to do, enjoy, or understand. *...undemanding jobs.* ■ If someone is **undemanding,** they do not expect you to do a lot for them.

undemocratic You say a government is **undemocratic** when it has not been elected in a free and fair election. ■ You say a decision is **undemocratic** when it is made unfairly by one person or a small group, rather than by all the people involved.

undeniable (**undeniably**) **Undeniable** is used to say something obviously exists or is obviously a particular thing. *...her undeniable intelligence.*

under If something is **under** something else, it is below or beneath it. ■ **Under** is used to talk about the circumstances in which people live, or in which something is done. *The poll was held under tight security conditions.* ■ If something happens **under** a person or organization, it happens while they are in power or have control. *Relations improved dramatically under President Bush.* ■ **Under** is used to talk about what is or is not allowed by a law or rule. *We believe an offence was committed under EU regulations.* ■ If someone works or studies **under** a person, that person is their boss or teacher. ■ **Under** is used to say something is less than an amount, rate, or level. *Johnson had run under 10.4sec only once.* ■ If a book is written **under** an invented name, that name appears on it as the name of the author.

under- is used to form words which say there is not enough of something, or that something has not been done as much or as well as is needed. *Mr Cook said that he agreed the NHS was underfunded.*

underarm is used to talk about people's armpits. *...underarm odour.* ■ If you throw or hit a ball **underarm,** you swing your arm upwards, keeping it below the level of your shoulder.

undercarriage An aircraft's **undercarriage** is its wheels and landing gear.

underclass An **underclass** is a group of people in a country who are much poorer than everyone else and who have little chance of improving their life.

underclothes Your **underclothes** are the clothes you wear next to your skin and under your other clothes, for example a vest, bra, or pants.

undercoat is a type of paint you use before putting on the top layer of paint.

undercover work is carried out secretly by the police to obtain information.

undercurrent If there is an **undercurrent** of a feeling, people do not express it openly, but show it in the way they behave.

undercut (**undercutting, undercut** not '*undercutted*') If a company **undercuts** another one or **undercuts** its prices, it charges less than the other company for a product or service. ■ If something **undercuts** your attempts to do something, it stops you succeeding.

underdeveloped countries and regions do not have modern industries or proper social organization and usually have a low standard of living.

underdog In a competitive situation, if you call a person, team, or organization the **underdog,** you mean they are the one least likely to win or be successful.

underemployed If someone is **underemployed,** they do not have enough work to do.

underestimate (**underestimating, underestimated**) If you **underestimate** something, you fail to realise how large, difficult, or complicated it is. ■ An **underestimate** is an estimate about how big something is which is wrong because it is too low. ■ If you **underestimate** a person or **underestimate** their capabilities, you fail to realize what they are capable of.

underfed You say people are **underfed** when they are unhealthy because they have not had enough to eat.

underfoot You use **underfoot** to talk about something you are walking or standing on. *It was still wet underfoot.* ■ If you trample something **underfoot,** you destroy or damage it by treading on it.

undergo (**undergoes, undergoing, underwent, undergone**) If you **undergo** something unpleasant, it happens to you or is done to you.

undergraduate An **undergraduate** is a university student who is studying for his or her first degree.

underground things are below the surface of the ground. ■ In London and Glasgow, the **Underground** is a railway system in which electric trains travel underground in tunnels. ■ **Underground** organizations operate secretly against the government in countries where no opposition is allowed. If someone **goes underground,** they carry on what they are doing in secret, to avoid arrest.

undergrowth is bushes and other plants growing close together under trees.

underhand If someone's behaviour is **underhand,** they secretly do things in an unfair or dishonest way.

underlay is a thick material you put on the floor before laying a carpet. ■ See also **underlie.**

underlie (**underlying, underlay, underlain**) You say one thing **underlies** another when it is the main cause or basis of the other thing. *The principle of individual dignity and freedom underlies all democratic theory. ...the underlying causes of the riots.*

underline (**underlining, underlined**) If one thing **underlines** another, it shows how serious or significant the other thing is. *Mr Clarke claimed the results underline the need to restore traditional teaching methods.* ■ If you **underline** a word or sentence, you draw a line under it, to draw attention to it.

underling If you talk about a person's **underlings,** you mean people with lower status who take orders from them.

underlying See **underlie.**

undermanned (**undermanning**) If an organization is **undermanned,** it does not have as many people working for it as it needs.

undermine (**undermining, undermined**) If someone **undermines** a person or **undermines** their position, they make it difficult for them to stay in power or continue with their work. Similarly, someone can **undermine** a system or **undermine** someone's efforts to do something.

underneath If one thing is **underneath** another, it is directly below the other thing, or covered by it. ■ **Underneath** is used to talk about feelings or qualities people have which they do not normally show. *Underneath her public personality was a tremendous generosity of heart.*

undernourished people are weak and unhealthy because they have not been eating enough.

underpaid If someone is **underpaid,** they are not paid enough for the work they do.

underpants are an item of male underwear with holes for the legs and an elasticated waist.

underpass (underpasses) An **underpass** is a place where a road or footpath goes underneath a railway or another road.

underpin (underpinning, underpinned) If one thing **underpins** another, it supports or strengthens the other thing. *...the reforms that have helped to underpin democracy.*

underplay If you **underplay** something, you make it seem less important than it really is.

underprivileged people have less money and opportunities than other people.

underrated If a person or thing is **underrated,** people do not realize how good they are.

underscore (underscoring, underscored) **Underscore** means the same as 'underline'.

undersea things are below the surface of the sea. *...undersea cables.*

underside The **underside** of something is the part which normally faces or touches the ground. ■ The **underside** of an activity or job is its unpleasant side, which you do not normally hear about.

understaffed If an organization is **understaffed,** it does not have as many people working for it as it needs.

understand (understanding, understood) If you **understand** a situation, you know why or how it happens, or what might happen as a result of it. ■ If you **understand** a person, you know how they feel and why they behave the way they do. ■ If you **understand** someone or **understand** what they say, you know what they are trying to tell you. ■ If you **understand** a language, you know what people are saying when they speak it. ■ If you say you **understand** that something has happened or is true, you mean you have been told it. ■ If you **understand** something a certain way, that is how you interpret it. *His turning to drinking could be understood as a fear of competing with his father.* ■ See also **understanding.**

understandable (understandably) You say someone's behaviour or feelings are **understandable** when they are what you would expect from someone in their situation.

understanding If there is **understanding** between people, they get on well together and trust each other. ■ An **understanding** person is kind and forgiving. ■ An **understanding** is an informal agreement. *We had an understanding that we'd talk in the summer.* ■ If you have an **understanding** of something, you know how it works or what it means. ■ Your **understanding** of a situation is the way you interpret it.

understate (understating, understated) If you **understate** something, you make it out to be smaller, less important, or less serious than it really is. ■ If something is **understated,** it is not made too obvious, and is more effective because of this. *Laura's style is all about sophisticated simplicity and understated elegance.*

understatement If you call what someone says an **understatement,** you mean it fails to describe how big something is, or how serious or important it is.

understood See **understand.**

understudy (understudies) An actor's **understudy** is a person who has learned their part in a play and can stand in for them, for example if they are ill.

undertake (undertaking, undertook, have undertaken) If you **undertake** a task, you start doing it and accept responsibility for it. You can call the task an **undertaking.** *It was an ambitious undertaking.* ■ If you give an **undertaking** to do something, you formally promise to do it.

undertaker An **undertaker** is a person whose job is to prepare bodies for burial and arrange funerals.

undertaking See **undertake.**

undertone If you say something has certain **undertones,** you mean it suggests ideas or attitudes which are not directly expressed.

undertook See **undertake.**

undertow An **undertow** is a strong current of water moving below the surface current and in a different direction to it.

undervalue (undervaluing, undervalued) If someone **undervalues** something, they say it is worth less money than it really is. ■ You say a person or thing is **undervalued** when people do not realize how important or good they are.

underwater is used to describe things which exist or happen below the surface of the sea, a river, or a lake. *...underwater currents.*

underway If an activity is **underway,** it has already started. If an activity gets **underway,** it starts.

underwear is the same as underclothes.

underwent See **undergo.**

underworld When people talk about the **underworld,** they mean criminals and their activities.

underwrite (underwriting, underwrote, have underwritten; underwriter) When an insurance company or other organization **underwrites** something like a business, it agrees, in return for a fee, to provide money if there are any losses or special expenses. An organization which does this is called an **underwriter.** ■ An **underwriter** is a person employed by an insurance company to work out the appropriate insurance charge for particular risks, such as a ship being lost at sea.

undeserved If you say something is **undeserved,** you mean the person who has it does not deserve it.

undesirable If you say something is **undesirable,** you mean it would be better if it did not happen or exist, because it is likely to have harmful effects. ■ People are sometimes called **undesirables** when it is thought they might cause trouble and the authorities are keen to get rid of them.

undetected If something is **undetected,** nobody notices it or finds out about it.

undeveloped If you say something is **undeveloped,** you mean it has not been used, improved, or increased as much as it could be. ■ An **undeveloped** country or region is the same as an underdeveloped one.

undid See **undo.**

undies Underwear is sometimes called **undies.**

undignified You say someone's behaviour is **undignified** when they do silly or embarrassing things which make people lose respect for them.

undiluted feelings or qualities are very strong and are not mixed with other feelings or qualities. ...*a smile of undiluted pleasure.* ■ An **undiluted** liquid is concentrated and has not been mixed with water to make it weaker.

undisciplined If you say someone's behaviour is **undisciplined,** you mean they behave badly, without much self-control.

undiscovered things have not yet been found or detected.

undisguised feelings or wishes are shown openly and not hidden.

undismayed If you are **undismayed** by something which goes wrong, you are not worried or upset by it.

undisputed If something is **undisputed,** everyone accepts that it exists or is true.

undistinguished things are not particularly good or interesting. *His short and undistinguished career as an art student came to an end.*

undisturbed If you say something has remained **undisturbed,** you mean it has not been moved or changed in any way. ■ If you do something **undisturbed,** you do it without anybody interfering with you or trying to stop you.

undivided If you give something your **undivided** attention, you concentrate on it fully.

undo (**undoes, undoing, undid, have undone**) If something **undoes** someone's achievements, it cancels them out. ■ If something was someone's **undoing,** it was the reason why they failed. ■ If you **undo** something that is tied, fastened, or held together, you unfasten it or release it.

undocumented events have not been recorded by anyone. ■ **Undocumented** is used to describe people who live and work in a country without official permission.

undoing (**undone**) See **undo.**

undoubted (**undoubtedly**) **Undoubted** is used to describe things which definitely exist or are definitely true. ...*his undoubted abilities.*

undreamed of (*or* **undreamt of**) is used to say something is much better, much worse, or much more unusual than anyone thought possible. ...*undreamt-of wealth.*

undress (**undresses, undressing, undressed**) When you **undress,** you take off most or all of your clothes.

undue means more than is reasonable or acceptable. *A hung parliament would mean minor parties having undue influence.*

undulate (**undulating, undulated**) If something **undulates,** it consists of gentle curves or slopes. ...*undulating countryside.*

unduly is used to talk about things being done or felt more than is necessary. *I don't think people should get unduly worried.*

undying is used to say something will last for ever. ...*the undying loyalty of Elvis's fans.*

unearned income is money obtained from things like investments and property rather than from working.

unearth If you **unearth** something hidden or secret, you discover it. *An amateur archeologist has unearthed a hoard of ancient British silver coins.*

unearthly things are strange and unnatural. ...*an unearthly silence.* ■ If you do something at an **unearthly** hour, you do it very early in the morning or very late at night.

uneasy (**uneasily, unease, uneasiness**) If you are **uneasy,** you feel something is wrong and are worried or tense about it. This feeling is called **unease** or **uneasiness.** *He shifted uneasily in his chair.* ■ **Uneasy** is used to describe situations which seem likely to come to an end and are not at all stable or definite. *There is currently an uneasy truce between the two factions.*

uneconomic (**uneconomical, uneconomically**) If something like a business is **uneconomic** or **uneconomical,** it wastes money or is not earning enough to be worth carrying on with. ...*an uneconomically large coal industry.*

unemotional people do not experience strong feelings, or do not show them.

unemployable If someone is **unemployable,** they are not likely to get a job, because of the way they behave or because they do not have any skills or qualifications.

unemployed If someone is **unemployed,** they want a job but cannot get one. People in this situation are often called **the unemployed.**

unemployment If there is **unemployment** in a place, many people who want jobs cannot get them.

unending If you say something is **unending,** you mean it carries on for a very long time and seems as though it will never stop. ...*a seemingly unending series of scandals.*

unenviable If someone is in an **unenviable** situation, they are in a difficult or unpleasant situation nobody would like to be in.

unequal (**unequally**) If something like a system is **unequal,** it is unfair because it treats different people differently. ...*the unequal treatment of women in state policy and legislation.* ■ **Unequal** things are different in size or amount. *This system was ruled to be unconstitutional, because rich and poor counties spent such unequal amounts of money on education.*

unequalled is used to say something is bigger, better, or more extreme than anything else of its kind. ...*remote alpine valleys of unequalled beauty.*

unequivocal (*pron:* un-i-**kwiv**-o-cal) (**unequivocally**) If something you say or do is **unequivocal,** it is clear and definite and can only have one meaning or purpose. *He was unwilling to commit himself unequivocally.*

unerring (*pron:* un-**er**-ing) (**unerringly**) If someone has an **unerring** ability to do something, they always manage to do it. ...*his unerring good judgement.*

UNESCO (*pron:* yew-**ness**-co) is part of the United Nations, set up to encourage education, science, and the arts world-wide. UNESCO stands for 'United Nations Educational, Scientific and Cultural Organization'.

uneven (**unevenly**) An **uneven** surface is not smooth or flat. ■ **Uneven** is used to describe things which are not completely the same in all their parts. ...*unevenly cooked loaves.*

unexceptionable If you say something is **unexceptionable**, you mean nobody is likely to disagree with it, object to it, or criticize it.

unexceptional things are not particularly good or bad, and not unusual in any way.

unexciting If something is **unexciting**, it contains no surprises and is rather boring.

unexpected (**unexpectedly**) **Unexpected** things surprise you because you did not think they would happen.

unfailing (**unfailingly**) **Unfailing** is used to describe a quality or ability which someone seems to have on all occasions. ...*John's unfailing sense of humour.*

unfair (**unfairly, unfairness**) If something is **unfair**, it is not right or just, because it treats some people differently from others.

unfathomable things are very difficult to understand or explain. ...*an unfathomable mystery.*

unfeeling If someone is **unfeeling**, they are not sympathetic to people who are suffering or unhappy.

unfettered is used to say someone is not limited in what they are allowed to do. ...*unfettered competition.*

unfinished things have not yet been completed.

unflagging (**unflaggingly**) **Unflagging** is used to say someone's positive feelings about something never change, or their ability to do something never gets any less. ...*his unflagging optimism.*

unflappable If someone is **unflappable**, they are always calm and never panic or get angry or upset.

unfocused (*or* **unfocussed**) If someone is **unfocused** in what they do, think, or want, they do not seem to be very clear about it, or do not seem to have a definite aim. ■ If someone's eyes are **unfocused**, they are open but not really looking at anything.

unfold When something like a situation **unfolds**, it develops in a certain way. ...*the events unfolding in Norway.* ■ If you **unfold** something which has been folded up, you open it out.

unforeseen things cannot be predicted.

unforgettable (**unforgettably**) If you say something is **unforgettable**, you mean you are not likely to forget it, because it is very good, very bad, or very unusual.

unforgivable (**unforgivably**) If you call someone's behaviour **unforgivable**, you mean it is so bad it can never be justified or accepted.

unforgiving You say people are **unforgiving** when they are unwilling to forgive someone for a wrong they have done. ■ You say something is **unforgiv**-ing when it is harsh and many people would be defeated by it. ...*unforgiving, sweltering conditions.*

unformed things are at an early stage of development and are not yet fully formed. ...*an unformed foetus.* ...*unformed ideas.*

unfortunate (**unfortunately**) If someone is **unfortunate**, they are unlucky and do not deserve something unpleasant which has happened to them. ■ If you say something is **unfortunate**, you mean it is a pity it happened.

unfounded If you say a statement is **unfounded**, you mean it is unreasonable because there is no evidence to back it up. Similarly, you can say people's fears are **unfounded**.

unfriendly If someone is **unfriendly**, they are not pleasant or welcoming. You can also talk about a place or system being **unfriendly**.

unfruitful An **unfruitful** attempt at something is unsuccessful.

unfulfilled If something like a hope or promise is **unfulfilled**, the thing that was hoped for or promised does not happen.

unfurl If you **unfurl** something like a flag, you unroll it or open it out.

unfurnished If you rent a house **unfurnished**, you have to provide your own furniture.

ungainly people move awkwardly or clumsily.

ungodly You can say something happens at an **ungodly** hour when it happens very early in the morning when most people are still in bed. ■ Some people use **ungodly** to describe language or behaviour which they think is sinful or blasphemous.

ungovernable If you say a country or region is **ungovernable**, you mean it cannot be controlled or administered effectively. You can call other things which cannot be controlled **ungovernable**. ...*ungovernable hatred.*

ungracious (**ungraciously**) You say someone is **ungracious** when they are not polite or friendly, especially to someone who is trying to help them.

ungrateful If you describe someone as **ungrateful**, you are criticizing them for not showing thanks or for being unkind to someone who has been good to them.

unguarded If someone makes an **unguarded** comment, they carelessly say something they did not want other people to know. You can also say someone says something **in an unguarded moment**. ■ If something is **unguarded**, nobody is protecting it or looking after it.

unhampered If you do something **unhampered**, you do it without being restricted or interfered with.

unhappy (**unhappier, unhappiest; unhappily, unhappiness**) If you are **unhappy**, you are sad or depressed. ■ An **unhappy** time for someone is one when things go badly for them. ■ If you are **unhappy** about something, you are not at all pleased about it. ■ An **unhappy** situation is unsatisfactory and needs to be put right. ■ You say **unhappily** when you are mentioning something which you think is regrettable. *It was a match that unhappily had to be decided by the Appeals Committee.*

unharmed If a person or thing is **unharmed** after an accident or violent incident, they are not harmed or damaged in any way.

unhealthy (**unhealthily**) Unhealthy conditions are likely to cause illness or bad health. ■ **Unhealthy** people are often ill. ■ An **unhealthy** economy or company is financially weak and unsuccessful. ■ You say something is **unhealthy** when you do not consider it to be normal and think it may be psychologically harmful. ...an unhealthy fear of sex.

unheard If a noise **goes unheard**, nobody hears it or takes any notice. ■ You use **unheard of** to describe situations which never happen, or have never happened before. They received orders on a previously unheard-of scale.

unheeded If something **goes unheeded**, it is ignored.

unhelpful (**unhelpfully**) If someone's comments or actions are **unhelpful**, they do not help to solve a difficulty, and may make it worse. ■ If something like a manual is **unhelpful**, it does not tell you what you want to know.

unheralded things happen unexpectedly and without any warning. ...an unheralded visit. ■ **Unheralded** can be used to describe someone who is suddenly successful when nobody has heard of them before. LeMond was fifth behind an unheralded Pole, Zenus Jaskula.

unhesitatingly If you do something **unhesitatingly**, you do it without hesitating, because you are sure it is the right thing to do.

unhinge (**unhinged**) If something **unhinges** you, it destroys your confidence and upsets your ability to do something well. ■ If you say someone is **unhinged**, you mean they are slightly mad.

unholy When two or more people or groups get together for a purpose you do not approve of, you can call them an **unholy alliance**. ■ A serious quarrel is sometimes called an **unholy row**.

unhook (**unhooking**, **unhooked**) If you **unhook** something which is fastened with a hook, you unfasten it.

unhurried is used to say something is done in a slow relaxed manner. He writes in a rich, unhurried style.

unhurt If a person is **unhurt** in an accident or violent incident, they are not injured at all.

unhygienic conditions are dirty and likely to spread disease.

unicorn In stories and legends, a **unicorn** is a white horse with a single horn growing out of its forehead.

unidentifiable If someone or something is **unidentifiable**, it is not possible to say exactly who or what they are.

unidentified is used to describe people whose identity is not known. ...unidentified attackers.

unified (**unification**) See **unify**.

uniform (**uniformed**; **uniformly**, **uniformity**) A **uniform** is a set of clothes which identifies a person as belonging to a particular organization. A **uniformed** person is wearing a uniform. ■ If something is **uniform**, it does not vary, but is even and regular throughout. Progress has not been uniform.

You talk about the **uniformity** of something like this.

unify (**unifies**, **unifying**, **unified**; **unification**) A **unified** country has been created by two or more countries joining together. ■ If something **unifies** people, it gets them to join together. ■ If countries or groups do something in a **unified** way, they do it together. Colonel Gaddafi called for a unified Arab oil policy.

unilateral (**unilaterally**) A **unilateral** action or decision is made by only one of the organizations or countries in a group, without the others consenting to it or agreeing to do the same thing.

unilateralism (**unilateralist**) Unilateralism is the belief that a country should get rid of its nuclear weapons without waiting for other countries to do the same. A person who believes this is called a **unilateralist**.

unimaginable (**unimaginably**) If you say something is **unimaginable**, you mean nobody can imagine it happening, or imagine what it is like. Conditions in prisons there are unimaginably bad.

unimaginative You say something like a plan is **unimaginative** when it is not very original or adventurous. You can also say a person is **unimaginative**.

unimpeachable If someone's behaviour or character is **unimpeachable**, nobody could find fault with it.

unimportant If something is **unimportant**, it has very little significance or importance.

unimpressed If you are **unimpressed** by something, you do not think it is particularly good or interesting.

unimpressive If you say someone or something is **unimpressive**, you mean they are very ordinary, without any special or exciting qualities.

uninformed You say people are **uninformed** when they do not know much about a subject. You can also call their remarks or decisions **uninformed**.

uninhabitable places are impossible to live in, for example because they are dangerous or unhealthy.

uninhabited places do not have anyone living in them.

uninhibited (**uninhibitedly**) Uninhibited people behave freely and naturally, and tend not to worry what other people think of their behaviour.

uninitiated People who know very little about a subject are sometimes called **the uninitiated**.

uninspired If you say something is **uninspired**, you mean it is dull and unimaginative.

uninspiring If you say something is **uninspiring**, you mean it is not interesting or exciting in any way.

unintelligible If a remark or piece of writing is **unintelligible**, nobody can understand it.

unintended If something that happens is **unintended**, it was not planned.

uninterested If you are **uninterested** in something, you do not find it interesting and do not want to know any more about it.

uninvited is used to describe things people do or say without being asked. He had been answering an uninvited question from a reporter. You can call someone who arrives somewhere without being asked to come an **uninvited** guest or visitor.

union A **union** is the same as a trade union. ■ The **union** of two or more things is the process of joining them together to become one. *We want political union in Europe.* You call the result of things joining together a **union.** *...a union of free republics.*

unionised See **unionized.**

unionism (unionist) Unionism is the same as trade unionism. A **unionist** is a trade unionist. ■ **Unionism** is the belief that Northern Ireland should remain part of the United Kingdom. **Unionists** are people who have this belief.

unionized (*or* **unionised**) A **unionized** workforce is one in which most of the workers are members of a union.

Union Jack The **Union Jack** is the national flag of the United Kingdom.

unique (*pron:* yew-**neek**) (**uniquely, uniqueness**) A **unique** person or thing is the only one of their kind. ■ If something is **unique** to a person or thing, they are the only person or thing that has it. *They have discovered a fragment of DNA which is unique to humans.* Similarly, you can say something is **unique** to a place or culture. *Having your baby sleep in a different room is almost unique to western society.*

unisex things can be used by either women or men. *...a unisex hair salon.*

unison If a group of people do something **in unison,** they all do it together at the same time.

unit If you think of something as a **unit,** you think of it as a single thing, complete and separate from other things. *The entire family did not move here as a unit.* ■ A **unit** is a small machine which has a particular function, often part of a larger machine. *...a digital display unit.* ■ A **unit** is a part of a large organization, or a group of people who do a specialized job. *...a specialist burns unit.* ■ A **unit** of measurement is a standard length, amount, weight, etc. For example, the metre is a unit of length.

Unitarian – **Unitarians** are a group of Christians who believe God is one being and reject the idea of the Holy Trinity.

unitary A **unitary** country or organization is one formed by two or more countries or organizations joining together because their aims and intentions are the same.

unite (**uniting, united; unity**) When people **unite,** they get together and act as a single group. ■ If people are **united** about something or there is **unity** among them, they agree about it and act together. ■ If two or more countries **unite,** they join together to form a single country. A **united** country is one which has been formed in this way. *...a united Germany.*

United Kingdom The **United Kingdom** is England, Scotland, Wales, and Northern Ireland. 'United Kingdom' is often shortened to 'UK'.

United Nations – **The United Nations** or **UN** is an international organization which tries to encourage peace, co-operation, and friendship between countries.

unit trust A **unit trust** is an organization which invests money in many different types of business

and which offers units for sale to the public, each of which entitles the holder to a share in any profits.

unity See **unite.**

universal (**universally**) If something is **universal,** it involves all the people in a group, or everyone in the world. *Condemnation of his actions was universal.*

universality If you talk about the **universality** of something, you mean it applies to all people, and not just the people of one place or culture.

universe The **universe** is the whole of space and all the stars, planets, and other forms of matter and energy in it.

university (**universities**) A **university** is an educational institution where students study for degrees and research is carried out.

unjust (**unjustly**) If you say something like a law is **unjust,** you mean it is wrong, because it treats people unfairly.

unjustified (**unjustifiable, unjustifiably**) If you say someone's comments or actions are **unjustified** or **unjustifiable,** you mean they are not deserved by the person they were aimed against.

unkempt You say someone is **unkempt** when they look scruffy and untidy. ■ An **unkempt** garden or similar place is very untidy, because it has been neglected.

unkind (**unkindly, unkindness**) You call a person **unkind** when they do or say unpleasant things to someone, or say unpleasant things about them.

unknowable If you say something is **unknowable,** you mean it is impossible to know much about it.

unknowing (**unknowingly**) You describe someone as **unknowing** when they are not aware of something important connected with what they are doing. *Some humans may unknowingly already have contracted the disease.*

unknown If something is **unknown,** people do not know, for example, what it is or how great it is. *An unknown number of rebels have been killed.* You can call something like this an **unknown.** *One of the significant unknowns is the general level of quality of the enemy forces.* ■ **The unknown** is used to talk generally about places or things people do not know about or understand. *...the fear of the unknown.* ■ If someone is **unknown** to you, you do not know their name, or do not know anything about them. ■ **Unknown** is used to describe people who are not well-known or famous. *Many of the artists are young and still unknown. ...a political unknown.* ■ If a type of situation is **unknown,** it never happens. *It's almost unknown for women to die during sporting exercise.*

unlawful (**unlawfully**) **Unlawful** things are against the law.

unleaded petrol has less lead in it than normal petrol.

unleash (**unleashes, unleashing, unleashed**) If something powerful is **unleashed,** it starts suddenly and has an immediate effect. *A 'no' vote on Sunday would unleash financial turmoil.*

unleavened bread is made without yeast or any other substance which would make it rise.

unless is used to introduce the only circumstances under which something will happen. *They never closed down unless there was an emergency.*

unlicensed If something is **unlicensed**, no licence has been issued for it. *...unlicensed handguns.* **Unlicensed** is also used to describe people who do something without a licence. *...Wimbledon tickets sold by unlicensed operators.*

unlike You use **unlike** when you are mentioning a difference between people, things, or situations. *Unlike India, Burma had no intellectual elite.*

unlikely (**unlikeliest**) If you say something is **unlikely** to happen or **unlikely** to be true, you mean it will probably not happen or is probably not true. ■ **Unlikely** is used to describe a strange or unexpected thing or occurrence, or a person who achieves something you would not expect them to achieve. *He was the unlikeliest British winner of the lot.*

unlimited If something is **unlimited**, there is no end to it, or people can have as much of it as they want. *...a month's unlimited train travel.*

unlit places are dark because there are no lights on. ■ An **unlit** fire or cigarette has not yet been lit.

unloved people are not loved by anyone. *He felt unloved by his mother.*

unlovely If something is **unlovely**, it is not pleasant or attractive.

unloving If someone is **unloving**, they do not show love to other people, especially to their partner or members of their family.

unmade beds have not been made.

unmanageable If something is **unmanageable**, people are unable to control it or cope with it. ■ **Unmanageable** children are naughty and difficult to control.

unmanned spacecraft or other vehicles do not have anyone in them. ■ **Unmanned** places do not have anyone working in them or in charge of them.

unmarked ■ If something is **unmarked**, it shows no signs of damage or injury. ◊ You say something is **unmarked** when there is nothing on it to identify it. *...an unmarked grave.* ■ An **unmarked** player in a football or rugby match has nobody from the other side standing near them to stop them getting the ball. ■ If an anniversary goes **unmarked**, nobody does anything to celebrate it.

unmarried An **unmarried** person is not married.

unmask If you **unmask** someone, you show who they really are, or what they are really like.

unmatched is used to say something is the best or most successful thing of its kind. *...an unmatched view of Windermere.*

unmentionable things are too unpleasant or embarrassing to talk about.

unmerciful (**unmercifully**) **Unmerciful** is used to describe something unpleasant which keeps being done to someone. *He would pester me unmercifully.*

unmistakeable (*or* **unmistakable**) (**unmistakeably**) If something is **unmistakeable**, there can be no doubt about what it is or what it means. *...the accent was unmistakeably Welsh.*

unmitigated means 'total' or 'absolute'. *...an unmitigated disaster.*

unmolested If someone does something **unmolested**, they are allowed to do it without being stopped or interfered with.

unmoved If someone is **unmoved** by something, it does not affect the way they behave, think, or feel. ■ If something such as the value of shares is **unmoved**, it stays at the same level.

unnamed people are mentioned in a statement or report without their names being given.

unnatural (**unnaturally**) If you say something is **unnatural**, you mean you do not approve of it, because it does not fit in with your idea of how things normally are or ought to be. *...a somewhat unnatural state of affairs.* ■ If you say there is an **unnatural** calm or silence, you mean things are very calm or silent and you find this strange or worrying. *The water seemed unnaturally still.* ■ If someone does something in an **unnatural** way, their way of doing it seems artificial and unconvincing.

unnecessary (**unnecessarily**) If something is **unnecessary**, there is no need for it to happen or be done.

unnerve (**unnerving**, **unnerved**; **unnervingly**) If something **unnerves** you, it alarms and worries you. You say something like this is **unnerving**.

unnoticed If something happens **unnoticed**, nobody notices it or realizes it is happening.

unobtrusive (**unobtrusively**) If someone or something is **unobtrusive**, they are not too obvious or do not attract too much attention. *They know how to trail cars unobtrusively.*

unoccupied places do not have anyone in them.

unopened packages or containers have not yet been opened.

unopposed If someone is **unopposed** in an election, nobody stands against them. ■ If an application or proposal is **unopposed**, nobody objects to it.

unorthodox beliefs or ways of doing things are different from the usual or accepted ones.

unpaid If someone is **unpaid**, they are not paid for their work. ■ If you take **unpaid** leave, you do not get paid while you are away from work. ■ If a bill is **unpaid**, the money that is owed has not been paid.

unpalatable truths are unpleasant and difficult to accept. ■ **Unpalatable** food is unpleasant to eat.

unparalleled is used to describe things which are bigger, better, or worse than anything else of their kind, or anything there has been before. *It comes at a time of unparalleled shortages of bread and flour.*

unpardonable If someone's behaviour is **unpardonable**, it is wrong or rude and cannot be excused.

unpick If you **unpick** something which someone else has done or organized, you change it completely.

unplanned events happen by accident. ■ You say something is **unplanned** when it is allowed to happen without being properly organized. *...unplanned development.*

unpleasant (**unpleasantly**, **unpleasantness**) If something is **unpleasant**, it upsets people or they react to it in some other unfavourable way. *...an unpleasantly strong odour.* ■ If a person is **unpleas-**

ant, they are unfriendly or rude. ■ If there is **unpleasantness** between people, they disagree, argue, or fight with each other.

unprecedented (**unprecedentedly**) If something is **unprecedented,** there has never been anything like it before. ...*the unprecedented number of large business failures.*

unprepared If you are **unprepared** for something, you are not ready for it.

unprepossessing If you say a person or thing is **unprepossessing,** you mean they do not look very attractive or impressive.

unpretentious people do not try to impress other people with their importance, intelligence, or wealth. Similarly, you say things are **unpretentious** when they have not been designed to impress people.

unprincipled If you call a person or their behaviour **unprincipled,** you mean they have no moral principles and do not care whether what they do is right or wrong.

unprintable If you say a remark is **unprintable,** you mean it cannot be repeated because it is very rude.

unproductive If something is **unproductive,** it does not produce anything useful. Similarly, an **unproductive** action does not have any useful results. *It would have been unproductive to send him to prison.*

unprofessional (**unprofessionally**) If you say someone's behaviour is **unprofessional,** you mean it is not the kind of behaviour expected of someone in their profession.

unprotected people or things are not protected from something that could harm them. ■ **Unprotected** sex is sex without a condom.

unprovoked You say an attack is **unprovoked** when someone attacks a person who has not harmed them in any way.

unqualified An **unqualified** person does not have the right qualifications for the job they are doing, or does not have any qualifications at all. ■ **Unqualified** feelings are not limited in any way. *Hadlee has won unqualified admiration for his achievements.* Similarly, something can be an **unqualified** success.

unquestionable (**unquestionably**) If something is **unquestionable,** there can be no doubt it exists or is true. ...*a man of unquestionable integrity.*

unquestioned If something is **unquestioned,** everyone accepts that it exists or is true. *The need for reform is unquestioned.* **Unquestioned** is used to say someone or something is accepted as a particular thing. ...*their unquestioned leader.*

unquestioning If someone has an **unquestioning** belief in something, they believe in it completely and never consider that it might be wrong. Similarly, someone can give a person or cause their **unquestioning** support.

unravel (**unravelling, unravelled**) (*Am:* **unraveling, unraveled**) If you **unravel** something woven or knitted, you take it apart, separating the material into strands or threads. ■ If you **unravel** a problem or mystery, you work out the answer or find out the truth about it.

unread You say a piece of writing is **unread** when the person it is intended for does not read it, or when nobody reads it.

unreal (**unreality**) If you say an experience is **unreal,** you mean it is so strange you find it difficult to believe it is really happening.

unrealistic (**unrealistically**) You say something is **unrealistic** when it shows a failure to recognize the truth about a situation. For example, if someone's hopes are **unrealistic,** there is little chance of them being fulfilled.

unreasonable (**unreasonably**) If someone is being **unreasonable,** they are behaving unfairly or illogically and are difficult to deal with because of this.

unrecognizable (*or* **unrecognisable**) If someone or something is **unrecognizable,** they have changed so much they cannot be recognized as the person or thing they were before.

unrecognized (*or* **unrecognised**) If a well-known person goes somewhere **unrecognized,** nobody recognizes them. ■ You can say certain things are **unrecognized** when people are not aware of them. *Marital conflicts may be the cause of much unrecognized suffering.* ■ If your achievements are **unrecognized,** they have not been properly acknowledged or appreciated by other people. ■ **Unrecognized** organizations are not officially approved.

unreconstructed If you say something like a policy is **unreconstructed,** you mean it has not changed at all, in spite of new ideas and circumstances. You can also use **unreconstructed** to describe a person whose attitudes have not changed. ...*an unreconstructed hardliner.*

unrefined substances have not been processed and are still in their natural state.

unrelated things are not connected with each other.

unrelenting is used to describe unpleasant things which carry on without stopping or becoming less intense. ...*unrelenting violence.* ■ **Unrelenting** is used to describe someone's behaviour when they carry on doing something in a very determined way. ...*her unrelenting efforts to secure his release.*

unrelieved is used to describe something unpleasant which goes on without stopping, or which has no good features at all. *The picture is one of unrelieved pessimism.*

unremarked If something goes **unremarked,** nobody pays any particular attention to it.

unremitting (**unremittingly**) **Unremitting** is used to describe something which continues without stopping or becoming less intense. ...*unremitting hostility.*

unrepresentative If you say a group is **unrepresentative,** you mean their ideas and beliefs are not typical of the people in the place they come from.

unrequited If someone's feelings or wishes are **unrequited,** they are not fulfilled or satisfied. ...*unrequited love.* ...*his unrequited ambitions.*

unreserved (**unreservedly**) **Unreserved** is used to describe feelings which are not limited in any way. *Democrats greeted the confusion with unreserved glee.*

unresolved An **unresolved** problem has not yet been solved or dealt with satisfactorily.

unresponsive If you are **unresponsive** to someone's suggestions, you do not change the way you work or behave because of them.

unrest If there is **unrest,** people are angry and dissatisfied and cause trouble.

unrestrained behaviour is not controlled or limited in any way.

unrestricted If you have an **unrestricted** view of something, there is nothing in your way and you can see all of it.

unrewarding If something you do is **unrewarding,** you get very little enjoyment or satisfaction out of it.

unrivalled If something is **unrivalled,** it is better than anything else of its kind.

unroll If you **unroll** something which has been rolled up, you open it out.

unruffled If someone is **unruffled** in a difficult situation, they stay calm.

unruly If people are **unruly,** they behave badly and are difficult to control.

unsafe If something is **unsafe,** it is likely to cause death, illness, or injury. ■ **Unsafe** is used to describe criminal convictions which are judged to be invalid because they were made on inadequate or false evidence.

unsaid If something is left **unsaid,** it is not said, although you might have expected it to be said.

unsaleable (*Am:* **unsalable**) If something is **unsaleable,** nobody wants to buy it.

unsatisfied If you are **unsatisfied,** you are disappointed because you have not got what you want. ■ If a need is **unsatisfied,** it is not being provided for.

unsaturated fats include most margarines. **Unsaturated** oils include most vegetable oils, for example olive oil and sunflower oil.

unsavoury (*Am:* **unsavory**) You call activities **unsavoury** when you disapprove of them because you think they are morally wrong.

unscathed If you are **unscathed** after being involved in something like an accident, you have not been injured or harmed by it.

unscheduled (*pron:* un-**shed**-yoold *or* un-**sked**-yoold) If something is **unscheduled,** it was not planned in advance.

unscrew If you **unscrew** something like a lid, you remove it by turning it. ■ If you **unscrew** something like a sign or a mirror which is fastened to something by screws, you remove it by taking out the screws.

unscripted If something like a speech is **unscripted,** it has not been composed or written down in advance. An **unscripted** action has not been planned in advance.

unscrupulous (**unscrupulously**) **Unscrupulous** people will do anything to get what they want, even if it is illegal or harms other people.

unseasonable (**unseasonably**) **Unseasonable** weather is unusual for the time of the year.

unseat (**unseating, unseated**) If someone is **unseated,** they are removed from power, usually by being beaten in an election. ■ If a horse you are riding **unseats** you, it throws you to the ground.

unseeded competitors in a sporting event, especially tennis, are not thought to have a good enough record to be given a special position in the draw.

unseemly behaviour is not appropriate for a particular place or occasion, because it is not polite or dignified.

unseen is used to describe people or things that you cannot see or have not seen.

unselfish (**unselfishly, unselfishness**) **Unselfish** people consider other people's needs rather than their own.

unsettle (**unsettling, unsettled**) If something **unsettles** people, it makes them feel restless, dissatisfied, or worried. You say people in this state are **unsettled.** ■ An **unsettled** situation is one where nothing is certain and things are liable to change. You can also call the weather **unsettled** when it changes unpredictably. ■ An **unsettled** problem has not been resolved.

unshakeable (*or* **unshakable**) (**unshakeably**) If you have an **unshakeable** belief in something, nothing can make you change your mind about it.

unshaken If your beliefs are **unshaken** by something that happens, they are not changed by it.

unshaven If a man is **unshaven,** he has not shaved recently.

unsightly If something is **unsightly,** it looks ugly. ...*an unsightly scar.*

unskilled work does not require any special training.

unsociable people dislike meeting or talking to other people.

unsocial If you work **unsocial** hours, you work at times when few other people are working, for example at night or at weekends.

unsolicited is used to describe things people are given which they did not ask for and which may be unwanted.

unsolved problems and mysteries have not yet been solved.

unsound If a conclusion or method is **unsound,** it is based on ideas which are wrong. ■ If someone or something is **unsound,** they are unreliable. ■ If you say something is **unsound** in some way, you mean it is damaging in that way or to the thing mentioned. ...*environmentally unsound.*

unspeakable (**unspeakably**) If you describe something as **unspeakable,** you are emphasizing that it is extremely unpleasant. ...*an act of unspeakable cruelty.*

unspecified You say something is **unspecified** when you are not told exactly what it is.

unspoilt (*or* **unspoiled**) If you describe a place as **unspoilt,** you mean it has not been changed and is still beautiful.

unspoken thoughts, wishes, and feelings exist but are not talked about. If there is an **unspoken** agreement or understanding between people, their behaviour shows they agree about something or share the same understanding of it, even though they may never speak about it.

unsporting If you say someone's behaviour is **unsporting,** you mean they use unacceptable methods to give them an unfair advantage over their opponents.

unstable If a situation is **unstable,** it is likely to change suddenly and create difficulty or danger. ■ If a person is **unstable,** their emotions and behaviour change suddenly and often, because their mind is disturbed. ■ **Unstable** objects are likely to move or fall.

unstated If something is **unstated,** it is not spoken or written down. *He left unstated many of the questions this conference might eventually tackle.*

unsteady (**unsteadily**) If you are **unsteady,** you have difficulty in controlling the movement of your legs or hands. ■ If something like an arrangement is **unsteady,** it is kept going with difficulty and may not last.

unstinting help is given generously and is not limited.

unstoppable If something is **unstoppable,** nobody can stop it happening or continuing.

unstructured If something like a meeting or activity is **unstructured,** it is not organized in a detailed way. ■ **Unstructured** clothing is loose and comfortable rather than tailored.

unstuck If someone or something comes **unstuck,** they fail. ■ If an object comes **unstuck,** it comes apart from the thing it is attached to.

unsubstantiated An **unsubstantiated** story, claim, or accusation has not been proved to be true.

unsuited If someone or something is **unsuited** to a particular job, situation, or place, they are not appropriate for it.

unsullied If something is **unsullied,** it has not been contaminated. *She possessed an innocence unsullied by contact with the world.*

unsung You use **unsung** to describe someone who is not appreciated or praised for their good work.

unsupported If a statement or theory is **unsupported,** there is nothing to show it is definitely true or right. ■ If someone is **unsupported** in something they are trying to do, nobody is helping them. ■ If someone or something is **unsupported,** they are not being held up by someone or something else.

unsurpassed is used to say something is better than anything else of its kind.

unsuspected is used to describe something which nobody had previously guessed was there. *...a previously unsuspected link between radon gas and cancer.*

unsuspecting people do not realize what is happening or what is going to happen. *The stolen cars were sold to unsuspecting buyers.*

unswerving (**unswervingly**) **Unswerving** beliefs and attitudes are strong and do not weaken or change.

unsympathetic If someone is **unsympathetic,** they are not kind, helpful, or understanding.

untangle (**untangling, untangled**) If you **untangle** rope that is twisted or knotted, you straighten it out and undo the knots in it. ■ If you **untangle** a complicated situation, you sort it out.

untapped is used to describe things which have not yet been used or developed. *...untapped deposits of gold.*

untenable If an argument, theory or position is **untenable,** it cannot be successfully defended.

untested things have not been tried out, so people do not know how good or effective they are.

unthinkable If you say something is **unthinkable,** you mean it cannot be considered or imagined as a possibility. *Nuclear weapons make war absolutely unthinkable.* **The unthinkable** is something which is unthinkable. *...the night when the unthinkable happened, and the two halves of Berlin were reunited.*

unthinking If someone behaves in an **unthinking** way, they do not consider the effects of their behaviour.

untidy (**untidily**) If something is **untidy,** it is not neat or well-arranged. ■ An **untidy** person leaves things in an untidy state.

untie (**untying, untied**) If you **untie** something, you undo the rope or string tied round it or fastening it.

until is used to say when a situation comes to an end. *The resignation was kept secret until a successor had been found.*

untimely You say something is **untimely** when it happens at a particularly bad time. ■ When someone dies before they reach old age, people say their death is **untimely.**

unto is sometimes used instead of 'to' in old-fashioned English. *I will do unto others what they did to me.*

untold is used to say an amount is very large, although it is not known exactly how large. *...untold wealth.*

untouchable Members of the lowest Hindu caste are sometimes called **untouchables.** ■ You can say someone such as a sports player is **untouchable** when they are far better than anyone else at what they do. ■ You can say someone is **untouchable** when they cannot be affected or punished in any way. *No one is untouchable in this investigation.*

untouched If a person or place is **untouched** by something, they have not been affected or harmed by it. *It is difficult to find any corner of Bosnia untouched by the war.* ■ If food is left **untouched,** none of it is eaten.

untoward (*pron:* un-to-**ward**) is used to talk about things which are out of the ordinary and usually cause trouble. *After a controlled explosion, the bag was found to contain nothing untoward.*

untrained people have not been taught the skills they need to do their job. ■ You use **untrained** with words like 'eye' and 'ear' to describe how something seems to someone who is not an expert. *And what does the untrained nose make of L'Egoiste?*

untrammelled (*Am:* **untrammeled**) If you are **untrammelled** by something, you are not affected or restricted by it.

untreated If an illness or injury is **untreated,** it has not received any medical treatment. ■ **Untreated** is used to talk about dirty or harmful things which have not been made clean or safe. *...untreated effluent.* ■ **Untreated** materials are in their natural or original state, often before being prepared for use. *...untreated timber.*

untried things have not yet been tested or tried out.

untroubled If you are **untroubled** by something, you are not affected or worried by it. *At this time he was untroubled by the burdens of office.*

untrustworthy If someone or something is **untrustworthy,** they cannot be trusted.

untruth If you say a statement is an **untruth,** you mean it is a lie.

untutored If someone is **untutored** in an activity, they have not been formally trained to do it.

unused If something is **unused,** it is not being used or has never been used. ■ If you are **unused** to something, you are not familiar with it, or have not experienced it before.

unusual If someone or something is **unusual,** there are not many other people or things like them.

unusually is used to say something is bigger, smaller, etc than usual. *...unusually heavy rain.* ■ You say **unusually** when mentioning an unusual occurrence. *The board was, unusually, prepared to divulge the size of its cash pile.*

unveil (**unveiling, unveiled**) When someone **unveils** a plan or proposal, they give details of it for the first time. ■ When someone **unveils** something like a statue, they uncover it in a special ceremony, and the public see it for the first time.

unwanted things are not desired or wanted, either by a particular person or by people in general.

unwarranted If something is **unwarranted,** it is not deserved or needed. *...unwarranted criticism.*

unwary people are not cautious enough and are likely to be hurt or tricked.

unwavering feelings and attitudes are strong and firm and do not change or weaken. *...a man of unwavering integrity.*

unwell If someone is **unwell,** they are ill.

unwieldy If an object is **unwieldy,** it is difficult to move or carry, because it is so big or heavy. ■ You say an organization or system is **unwieldy** when it does not work well because it is too large or complicated.

unwind (**unwinding, unwound**) When you **unwind,** you relax and rest, especially after doing something tiring or stressful. ■ If you **unwind** something which is wrapped round itself or round something else, you untangle it and straighten it out.

unwise If you say it would be **unwise** to do something, you mean it would not be a good idea.

unwitting (**unwittingly**) **Unwitting** is used to describe people who have become involved in something without understanding what is really happening. *He may have been an unwitting courier for the bombers.*

unwonted (*pron:* un-**woan**-tid) is used to describe things which do not happen often. *...an unwonted act of generosity.*

unworthy If someone is **unworthy** of something, they do not deserve to have it. ■ If you say someone's behaviour is **unworthy** of someone in their position, you mean they should behave better. *His accusations are unworthy of a British Prime Minister.*

unwound See **unwind.**

unwrap (**unwrapping, unwrapped**) If you **unwrap** something, you take off its covering.

unwritten rules and agreements have not been officially written down but are understood and accepted by everyone.

up (**upping, upped**) **Up** is used to talk about movement towards a higher place. *We climbed up the mountain.* ■ **Up** is used to talk about movement towards the north. *Why did you come up to Edinburgh?* ■ If you go **up** a river, you go along in it the opposite direction to its flow. ■ If you are **up,** you are awake and out of bed. ■ If an amount goes **up,** it increases. You can also say an amount is **upped.** *The US upped its offer of subsidy cuts from 70% to 75%.* ■ You use **up to** to say how large something can be or what level it has reached. *Up to 70 hotels face closure.* ■ If a period of time is **up,** it has ended. ■ If a computer is **up,** it is working. ■ If something is **up,** something is wrong. *My family rang the coastguard to find out what was up.* ■ If someone is **up to** something, they are secretly doing something they should not be doing. ■ If it is **up to** someone to do something, it is their responsibility. ■ If you are **up against** something, you have a difficult situation to deal with. ■ If you are not **up to** something, you are not well enough or competent enough to deal with it. ■ If you have your **ups and downs,** both good and bad things happen to you.

up-and-coming people are likely to be successful in the future. *...an up-and-coming actor.*

upbeat You say someone is **upbeat** when they are cheerful and optimistic.

upbraid (**upbraiding, upbraided**) If you **upbraid** someone, you tell them off.

upbringing Your **upbringing** is the way your parents treat you and the things they teach you to care about and believe in. *He had a strict Calvinist upbringing.*

upcoming things are about to happen soon.

update (**updating, updated**) If you **update** something like a system, you make it more modern. ■ An **update** is a report which gives the latest information on something.

upend If something like a box is **upended,** it is turned upside down.

upgrade (**upgrading, upgraded**) If you **upgrade** something, you improve it or give it more importance.

upheaval is major change.

upheld See **uphold.**

uphill If you go **uphill,** you go up a slope. ■ If you say someone has an **uphill** task, you mean they have a difficult task ahead, requiring a lot of effort and determination.

uphold (**upholding, upheld; upholder**) If someone **upholds** a system or principle, they support it and try to make it work. *...a staunch upholder of free trade.* ■ If someone in authority **upholds** a decision, they officially decide it is correct and should stand.

upholstered (**upholstery, upholsterer**) **Upholstered** chairs and sofas have a soft covering which makes them comfortable to sit on. This covering is called **upholstery**. An **upholsterer** is someone who covers chairs and sofas.

upkeep The **upkeep** of something like a building is the continual process of keeping it in a good condition. ■ The **upkeep** of a family is the process of providing for its needs.

uplands (**upland**) **Uplands** are areas of high land. **Upland** means situated in areas like these. ...*upland farms.*

uplift If something **uplifts** you or gives you **uplift**, it makes you happier and helps you do something more successfully. ■ If people's faces or arms are **uplifted**, they are pointing them upwards or holding them up.

upmarket is used to describe products and places intended to appeal to well-off, sophisticated people. ...*upmarket hotels.*

upon means 'on'. ...*sitting upon a low chair.* ■ If something is **upon** you, it is just about to happen to you. *With summer upon us, our thoughts naturally turn to picnics.* ■ **Upon** is used to talk about several things occurring straight after each other. ...*volunteers carrying out series upon series of exercises.*

upper is used to talk about (a) the top part of something. ...*the upper atmosphere.* (b) the higher ones of a series of things. *Nurses waved from upper windows.* ■ When a parliament consists of two parts meeting separately, one of them is usually called the **upper house** or **upper chamber**. In Britain, the **upper house** is the House of Lords. ■ If you have the **upper hand** in a situation, you are likely to get your own way. ■ The **upper** of a shoe is the top part which is attached to the sole and the heel.

upper case letters are capitals.

upper class (**upper classes**) People of high social status are sometimes called the **upper classes**. **Upper-class** means connected with the upper classes. ...*upper-class speech.*

upper crust Upper class people are sometimes called the **upper crust**.

uppercut In boxing, an **uppercut** is a hard upward blow to an opponent's chin.

upper lip Your **upper lip** is the part of your face between your mouth and your nose.

uppermost If something is **uppermost** in your mind, it is the main thing you are thinking about.

uppity If you call someone **uppity**, you mean they are behaving as if they are more important than they really are.

upright If you are sitting or standing **upright**, you are sitting or standing with your back straight, rather than bending or lying down. ■ You can call someone **upright** when they are very respectable. ...*an upright citizen.*

uprising If there is an **uprising** in a country, people start fighting against their own rulers there.

uproar If there is **uproar**, there is a lot of shouting and noise, because people are angry about something.

uproarious (**uproariously**) **Uproarious** laughter is very loud. You can say someone laughs **uproariously**. ■ You can say something like a film is **uproarious** when it is very funny.

uproot (**uprooting, uprooted**) If something like a tree is **uprooted**, it is torn out of the ground. ■ If you are **uprooted** from a place where you have lived for a long time, you have to leave it.

upset (**upsetting, upset** *not 'upsetted'*) If an experience **upsets** you or makes you **upset**, it makes you troubled and unhappy. ■ If something **upsets** a plan or system, it makes it go wrong. ■ If one competitor **upsets** another who is supposed to be superior to them, they beat them. A win like this is called an **upset**. ■ A stomach **upset** is a mild illness affecting a person's stomach, usually caused by something they have eaten.

upshot The **upshot** of a series of events is the final result.

upside The **upside** of something is the good things about it, as distinct from the bad ones.

upside down If something is **upside down**, it has been turned over so the top is underneath the rest. ■ If you turn a place **upside down**, you move everything around and make it untidy, because you are looking for something. ■ If an organization or system is turned **upside down**, it is changed completely.

upstage (**upstaging, upstaged**) If you **upstage** someone, you behave in a way which takes everyone's attention away from them and onto yourself.

upstairs If something is **upstairs**, it is on one of the upper floors of a building, or on a higher floor than you.

upstanding people are very respectable.

upstart If you call someone an **upstart**, you mean they are behaving as if they are important, and are not showing respect for people who have been doing something longer than they have.

upstream If you go **upstream**, you go along a river in the opposite direction to its flow.

upsurge If there is an **upsurge** in something, it suddenly increases by a large amount.

upswing If there is an **upswing** in something, it suddenly increases or improves.

uptake The **uptake** of something is the amount which is used. *The uptake of funds slowed compared with last year.*

uptight If someone is **uptight**, they are very tense, because they are worried or annoyed about something.

up-to-date If something is **up-to-date**, it is the newest thing of its kind. ■ If you keep **up-to-date** with something, you make sure you always have the latest information about it.

up-to-the-minute information is the latest information available.

uptown is sometimes used to talk about the parts of a city away from its centre. ...*uptown New York.*

upturn If there is an **upturn** in something, it increases or improves.

upturned If something is **upturned**, (a) it is facing upwards. *He sat crosslegged, his palms upturned.* (b) it is upside down. *He slid off the road as he tried to avoid the upturned Toyota.*

upward (**upwards**) If you move or look **upward** or **upwards**, you move or look towards a higher place.

■ If an amount moves **upward** or **upwards,** it increases. ■ **Upwards** of a certain number means more than that number.

upwardly mobile People are sometimes referred to as **upwardly mobile** when they are becoming richer and improving their social status.

upwards See **upward.**

upwind If you move **upwind,** you move directly into the wind. If you are **upwind,** the wind is blowing away from you.

uranium is a radioactive metal used in nuclear weapons and to produce nuclear energy.

urban means to do with towns and cities. *...the pressures of urban living.*

urbane (**urbanity**) If you describe someone as **urbane** or talk about their **urbanity,** you mean they have very good manners and seem relaxed in social situations.

urbanization (*or* **urbanisation**) (**urbanized**) **Urbanization** is a process in which more towns are built in country areas. When this happens to a place, you say it becomes **urbanized. Urbanized** people are accustomed to living in towns.

urchin Children are sometimes called **urchins** when they look dirty and are poorly dressed.

Urdu (*pron:* oor-doo) is the official language of Pakistan. It is also spoken by many people in India.

urethra (*pron:* yew-**reeth**-ra) A person's **urethra** is the tube which takes urine from their bladder out of their body. A man's sperm also passes down his urethra.

urge (**urging, urged**) An **urge** is a strong desire to do something. ■ If you **urge** someone to do something, you try hard to persuade them to do it. ■ If you **urge** someone **on,** you encourage them.

urgent (**urgently, urgency**) If something is **urgent,** it needs to be dealt with as soon as possible. You talk about the **urgency** of something like this. ■ If someone speaks in an **urgent** way, they show in the way they speak that they are anxious or excited.

urinal A **urinal** is a bowl or trough in a public lavatory for men to urinate in.

urinary means relating to urine and the parts of the body it flows through. *...a urinary infection.*

urinate (**urinating, urinated**) When someone **urinates,** they pass urine out of their body.

urine is the waste liquid people get rid of from their body when they go to the toilet.

urn – **Urns** are containers used to hold the ashes of people who have been cremated. ■ A tea or coffee **urn** is a metal container used for making a large amount of tea or coffee and keeping it warm.

US The **US** or **USA** is the United States of America.

us is used to talk about a group of people which includes the person who is speaking or writing. *They're the extremists, not us.*

USA See **US.**

usable things are in a good enough condition to be used.

usage is used (a) to talk about the ways words are used. *Many of the words may not even be in modern usage.* (b) to talk about the way other things are used, or the extent to which they are used. *The issue*

of global warming and energy usage is not going to go away.

use (**using, used**) If you **use** something or make **use** of it, you do something with it, to do a job or achieve something. You can also talk about something's particular use. *The drug is safe for widespread use... Iraq denies that the cargo had any military use.* ■ If something is **in use,** it is being used regularly. ■ If you **use up** a supply of something, you consume it until it is finished. ■ If you find a **use** for something, you find a purpose for it. ■ If something is **of use** to someone, it is useful to them. ■ If you have the **use** of something, you have permission or the ability to use it. ■ If you buy a **used** car, you buy one which has already had at least one owner. ■ If you say you are being **used,** you mean someone is getting you to do something that will benefit them, without caring about your feelings at all. ■ If you say **it's no use** doing something, you mean it will not achieve anything. ■ If something **used to** be true or **used to** be done, it was true or was done regularly in the past. ■ If you are **used to** something, you have experienced it and know what it is like.

useful (**usefully, usefulness**) If something is **useful,** it can be used to do a task or to achieve something. *...useful information.*

useless (**uselessly, uselessness**) If something is **useless,** it is no good for what you want, or cannot be used for anything at all. Similarly, if something you do is **useless,** it does not help to achieve anything beneficial. *She knew it was useless to protest.* ■ If you say someone is **useless** at something, you mean they are no good at it.

user The **users** of something are the people who use it.

user-friendly things are easy to understand or use.

usher (**ushering, ushered**) If someone **ushers** you somewhere, they go with you, to make sure you get there. ■ An **usher** is someone who shows people where to go or sit, for example at a wedding or a concert. ■ If a person or event **ushers in** an important change, they help make it happen. *...a collapse in world trade that would usher in an era of turmoil.*

usherette – **Usherettes** are women who show people where to sit in a cinema or theatre and sometimes sell refreshments.

USSR The **USSR** was the former Soviet Union. USSR stood for 'Union of Soviet Socialist Republics', which was the country's official name.

usual (**usually**) **Usual** and **usually** are used to talk about what normally happens in a certain situation. *It is usual to tip waiters and porters... Our father read aloud to us, usually after supper.*

usurp (*pron:* yewz-**zurp**) (**usurpation, usurper**) If you **usurp** someone's position or role, you take it over for yourself, without having any authority to do so. This is called a **usurpation** of their position or role. Someone who behaves like this is called a **usurper.**

usury (*pron:* **yewz**-yoor-ee) is an old word for lending people money, especially at high interest rates.

utensil – **Utensils** are the tools and other things you use for making or preparing something.

uterus (*pron:* **yew**-ter-russ) (**uterine**) A woman's **uterus** is her womb. **Uterine** (*pron:* **yew**-ter-rine) means to do with the womb. *...the uterine lining.*

utilise See **utilize.**

utilitarian things are designed to be useful and practical rather than attractive.

utilitarianism is the idea that all actions should be aimed at producing the greatest happiness for the greatest number of people.

utility (**utilities**) **Utility** is used to talk about how useful something is. *He inwardly questioned the utility of his work.* ■ **Utilities** are services such as water or electricity which are provided for the public to use.

utilize (*or* **utilise**) (**utilizing, utilized; utilization**) If you **utilize** something, you use it.

utmost If you do your **utmost** to achieve something, you do the best you can to achieve it. ■ **The utmost** in front of a word means 'the greatest'. *...a*

matter of the utmost importance.

utopia (**utopian**) A **utopia** is someone's idea of a perfect social system in which everyone is happy and all their needs are met. **Utopian** is used to describe ideas and systems like this. *...a utopian society.*

utter (**uttering, uttered; utterly**) If you **utter** words, you say them. You can also **utter** other sounds, such as a grunt. ■ **Utter** and **utterly** are used to emphasize certain words. *...utter confusion... This is utterly ridiculous.*

utterance An **utterance** is something a person says.

U-turn When a politician or government does a **U-turn,** they abandon a policy and start doing its opposite. ■ When a vehicle performs a **U-turn,** it turns through a half-circle and goes off in the direction it has just come from.

UV is short for 'ultraviolet'.

V v

v is used in writing to say two people or teams are competing against each other. 'v' is short for 'versus'.

vacancy (**vacancies**) A **vacancy** is a job or position which has not been filled. ■ If there are **vacancies** at a hotel, rooms are available for people to stay in.

vacant (**vacantly**) If something is **vacant,** it is not being used. *...vacant office space.* ■ If a job or position is **vacant,** it has not yet been filled. ■ If someone looks **vacant,** they do not seem to understand what is being said to them, or they show no sign of emotion or thought.

vacate (**vacating, vacated**) If you **vacate** a place or a job, you leave it and make it available for other people.

vacation A **vacation** is the period between academic terms or semesters at a university or college. ■ If you take a **vacation,** you have a holiday.

vaccinate (**vaccinating, vaccinated; vaccination**) When people or animals are **vaccinated** against a disease or have a **vaccination,** they are given a vaccine to stop them getting the disease.

vaccine A **vaccine** is a substance containing the bacteria or viruses which normally cause a disease. When given to patients, the vaccine makes their bodies produce antibodies to fight the disease, so they are protected against the disease itself.

vacillate (*pron:* **vass**-ill-late) (**vacillating, vacillated; vacillation**) If you **vacillate,** you keep changing your mind.

vacuous (**vacuity**) If you call someone or something **vacuous** or talk about their **vacuity,** you mean they do not express any intelligent ideas. *...vacuous slogans... His vacuity was a handicap in these debates.*

vacuum (**vacuuming, vacuumed**) A **vacuum** is a space containing no air, gases, or other matter. ■ If you say someone or something has created a

vacuum, you mean their absence has created a space which needs to be filled by another person or thing. ■ If you **vacuum** a carpet, you clean it using a vacuum cleaner.

vacuum cleaner A **vacuum cleaner** is an electric machine which cleans by sucking up dust and dirt.

vacuum flask A **vacuum flask** is a container used to keep drinks hot or cold. It has two thin silvery glass walls with a vacuum between them.

vacuum-packed food has been preserved by being packed in a container or packet from which most of the air has been removed.

vagabond A **vagabond** is a person who moves from place to place and does not have a fixed home or job.

vagaries (*pron:* **vaig**-a-reez) The **vagaries** of something are the unpredictable changes in it. *...the vagaries of the weather.*

vagina (*pron:* vaj-**jine**-a) (**vaginal**) A woman's **vagina** is the passage connecting her outer sex organs to her womb. **Vaginal** is used to talk about things involving the vagina.

vagrant (*pron:* **vaig**-rant) (**vagrancy**) A **vagrant** is a person who moves from place to place and has no home or job, and so has to beg or steal to live. This way of life is called **vagrancy.**

vague (**vaguer, vaguest; vaguely, vagueness**) If something is **vague,** it is not clear, distinct, or definite. *...the vagueness of the government's funding plans.* ■ If you are **vague** about something, you deliberately do not tell people much about it. *Mr Landsbergis was vague about how long fuel supplies could hold out.*

vain (**vainer, vainest; vainly**) A **vain** action or attempt is unsuccessful. *He returned to the scene in a vain search for his son's body.* You can also say an action or attempt is **in vain.** ■ A **vain** hope is unlikely to come true. ■ If you say someone is **vain,**

you mean they think too much of their own beauty, intelligence, or other good points.

vainglorious A **vainglorious** person is boastful and likes to show off.

valance (*pron:* val-lenss) A **valance** is a decorative frill which hangs around the edge of the bed.

vale A **vale** is the same as a valley.

valediction (*pron:* val-lid-**dik**-shun) (**valedictory**) A **valediction** is something you say or do as a way of saying farewell. **Valedictory** means said or done as a farewell. ...*his valedictory speech.*

valet (**valeting, valeted**) A **valet** (*pron:* **val**-lay or **val**-lit) is a wealthy man's personal manservant, who does things like look after his clothes. ■ If you have your car **valeted** (*pron:* **val**-it-id), the interior is thoroughly cleaned.

valiant (**valiantly**) You call someone's behaviour **valiant** when they are brave and determined, despite being in a situation where they are likely to fail.

valid (**validly, validity**) If something is **valid**, it is based on sound reasoning. You talk about the **validity** of something like this. *Her article casts doubt on the validity of this interpretation.* ■ If a ticket or document is **valid**, it can be used and will be accepted by people in authority.

validate (**validating, validated; validation**) If you **validate** something, you prove it is correct, or make it legitimate. *Auditors play a critical role in validating the information supplied to shareholders.*

Valium is a form of the drug diazepam, a tranquilizer usually prescribed for the relief of tension and anxiety. 'Valium' is a trademark.

valley A **valley** is an area of land between two lines of hills or mountains, often with a river running through it.

valour (*Am:* **valor**) is great bravery, especially in battle.

valuable If something is **valuable**, it is worth a lot of money. ■ **Valuables** are small valuable items people wear or carry around. ■ You say things are **valuable** when they are very useful. *The experience was very valuable.*

value (**valuing, valued; valuation**) The **value** of something is how much it is worth. ■ When experts **value** something, they judge how much it is worth. This is called making a **valuation**. ■ If something is **good value**, it is worth the money you pay for it. ■ The **value** of something is its importance or usefulness. *They appreciate the value of higher education.* ■ If you **value** someone or something, you think they are important and you appreciate them. *He values his new-found privacy.* ■ People's **values** are their moral principles. ■ The **face value** of something like a stamp is its value according to the price on it. ■ If you **take** something **at face value,** you accept its obvious meaning, rather than considering that it might be misleading.

value-added tax See **VAT.**

value judgment A **value judgment** is an opinion based on moral principles rather than facts which can be checked or proved.

valueless If something is **valueless**, it is not worth any money, or is not useful in any way.

valuer A **valuer** is a person whose job is to decide how much things are worth.

valve A **valve** is a device attached to a pipe or tube to control the flow of gas or liquid passing through. ■ In your body, **valves** are small flaplike structures in the heart and veins. They control the flow of blood and stop it going in the wrong direction.

vamp A **vamp** is a woman, especially a character in a film, who uses her feminine charms to entice and exploit men.

vampire In horror stories, **vampires** are dead people who come out of their graves at night and suck the blood of living people.

vampire bat – **Vampire bats** are tropical American bats which feed on the blood of live animals.

van A **van** is a small goods vehicle with an enclosed box-shaped body.

vandalize (*or* **vandalise**) (**vandalizing, vandalized; vandalism, vandal**) If someone **vandalizes** something, they deliberately damage it, for no special reason. This is called **vandalism;** the people who do it are called **vandals.**

vane A **vane** or **weather vane** is a metal object on top of a building which rotates to indicate which way the wind is blowing.

vanguard The **vanguard** of an army moving into battle is the group at the front. ■ If you say people are in the **vanguard** of a new development, you mean they are involved in its most advanced part.

vanilla is a food flavouring made from the dried pods of a tropical plant.

vanish (**vanishes, vanishing, vanished**) If something **vanishes,** it disappears suddenly or ceases to exist.

vanity (**vanities**) **Vanity** is excessive pride in your looks or abilities. Someone's **vanities** are the things they are excessively proud of.

vanquish (**vanquishes, vanquishing, vanquished**) If someone is **vanquished** in a battle or competition, they are defeated.

vantage point A **vantage point** is a place where you can get a good view of something.

vapid (*rhymes with 'rapid'*) If something is **vapid**, it is dull and uninteresting, because it contains nothing stimulating or challenging.

vapor See **vapour.**

vaporize (*or* **vaporise**) (**vaporizing, vaporized**) If a liquid or solid **vaporizes,** it changes into vapour or gas.

vapour (*Am:* **vapor**) is a mass of tiny drops of water or other liquid in the air.

vapour trail A **vapour trail** is a white trail of water vapour left in the sky by a high-flying plane.

variable (**variability**) If something is **variable**, it is liable to change. You can talk about the **variability** of something like this. ■ The factors which can change in a situation are called **variables.** ■ **Variable** is used to talk about things which you can alter or adjust yourself. ...*variable-speed turntables.* ■ You say something is **variable** when it is not always of good quality. *The cooking is variable.* ■ In maths, a **variable** is a symbol used to represent any number. In the equation $2(x + y) = 2x + 2y$, x and y are variables.

variance If something is **at variance** with something else, the two things seem to contradict each other.

variant If one thing is a **variant** of another, it is the same type of thing, but different in various small ways. ...*one of the variants of tennis that was played two or three hundred years ago.*

variation If there is **variation** in something, it exists in slightly different forms. Each form can be called a **variation.** ■ If there is **variation** in a level or amount, it does not stay the same. ■ If something is a **variation** on something else, it is the same thing but changed in some way. ...*a variation on an old Scots recipe.*

varicose veins are swollen painful veins, especially in the legs.

varied See **vary.**

variegated leaves or plants have different coloured markings on them.

variety (**varieties**) If something has **variety**, it consists of different things, and is therefore more interesting than it would be otherwise. ■ A **variety** of things is a number of different ones. *They are being released for a variety of reasons.* ■ A **variety** of something is a particular kind or type. ...*the many varieties of tomato.* ■ **Variety** is a type of entertainment which includes many different kinds of acts in the same show.

various is used to say there are several different things of the type mentioned. ...*jugs and bowls in various sizes.*

variously is used when mentioning the different ways in which something has been described, defined, or interpreted. ...*the disease known variously as ME, Chronic Fatigue Syndrome, or Yuppie Flu.*

varnish (**varnishes, varnishing, varnished**) Varnish is an oily liquid which you paint onto wood, where it dries and hardens to give a clear shiny protective coating. When you **varnish** wood, you put varnish on it.

varsity is another word for university.

vary (**varies, varying, varied**) If things **vary,** they are not all the same. ■ If something is **varied,** it consists of a lot of different things. ...*a varied diet.* ■ If you **vary** something you do, you keep changing the way you do it.

vascular means to do with the tubes or ducts which carry blood in animals and sap in plants. ...*vascular problems.*

vase A **vase** is a jar used for holding cut flowers or as an ornament.

vasectomy (**vasectomies**) A **vasectomy** is a surgical operation to cut the two ducts which carry sperm to a man's penis.

Vaseline is a clear greasy substance obtained from petroleum. It is used in ointments and as a lubricant. 'Vaseline' is a trademark.

vast (**vastly, vastness**) If something is **vast,** it is extremely large. ■ **Vastly** means 'very much' or 'very'. *Conditions have vastly improved.* ...*vastly enjoyable movies.*

VAT or **value-added tax** is a tax in Britain and many other European countries. It is added to the price of many goods and services, then paid to the government by the seller.

vat A **vat** is a large barrel or other container for holding liquids.

Vatican The **Vatican** is a tiny separate state within the city of Rome. In it are St Peter's Church and the Vatican Palace where the Pope lives. **The Vatican** is sometimes used to talk about the Pope and his officials. *The Vatican has remained reluctant to set a date for the visit.*

vaudeville (*pron:* **vaw**-de-vil) is a type of theatrical entertainment involving songs, jokes, and acts of skill.

vault A **vault** is a secure room where money and other valuable things can be kept safely. ■ A **vault** is a burial chamber, especially one underneath a church or cemetery. ■ A **vault** is an arched structure which forms a roof or ceiling. You say a roof or ceiling like this is **vaulted.** ■ In gymnastics, the **vault** is an event in which gymnasts jump over an apparatus called a **vaulting horse,** placing their hand or hands on top of it to support them. ■ If you **vault** over something, you jump over it using your hands or a pole to support you. See also **pole vault.**

vaunted You use **vaunted** or **much-vaunted** to describe things which are praised or admired a lot, especially when you think the praise or admiration is not justified. *For all his vaunted sex appeal, he looks his age.*

VCR A **VCR** is the same as a video recorder. VCR stands for 'video cassette recorder'.

VD is the same as venereal disease.

VDU A **VDU** is a device with a screen which is used to display information from a computer. VDU stands for 'visual display unit'.

veal is meat from a calf.

vector In maths, a **vector** is a variable quantity, such as a force, which has magnitude and direction. ■ In biology and medicine, a **vector** is a disease-carrying animal or plant.

veer (**veering, veered**) If a person or thing is moving quickly and suddenly changes direction, you can say they **veer** in the new direction. *The plane veered to the right.* ■ If someone starts behaving in a different or more extreme way, you can talk about them **veering** into a certain kind of behaviour. ...*fears that a stronger Germany might veer towards neutrality.* ■ If something **veers** towards a certain quality, it comes quite close to having that quality. *Some of the pieces of furniture veer towards the ridiculous.*

veg is short for 'vegetables'.

vegan (*pron:* **vee**-gan) A **vegan** is a person who does not eat meat or fish or any other animal products such as milk, butter, or cheese.

vegetable – Vegetables are edible plants and roots like cabbages, potatoes, and onions. ■ **Vegetable** matter comes from plants.

vegetarian (**vegetarianism**) A **vegetarian** is a person who does not eat meat or fish. **Vegetarian**

food does not contain meat or fish. The practice of not eating meat or fish is called **vegetarianism.**

vegetation is plant life in general.

vehement (*pron:* **vee**-i-ment) (**vehemently, vehemence**) If someone is **vehement** about something, they have strong feelings or opinions about it and express them forcefully and passionately. You can talk about the **vehemence** of someone like this.

vehicle A **vehicle** is a means of transport, especially one with wheels. ■ You can say something is a **vehicle** for something else when it is used to achieve it. *...a band that was not afraid to use music as a vehicle for making a political statement.*

vehicular means to do with vehicles. *...vehicular pollution.*

veil (**veiling, veiled**) If a woman is **veiled** or wearing a **veil,** she is wearing a piece of thin soft cloth over her head or face. ■ When people talk about **the veil,** they mean the traditional form of dress in some religions, especially Islam, which involves women covering all their body except their eyes whenever they go out. ■ If there is a **veil** of secrecy or silence over a subject, no information is being made available about it. ■ A **veiled** comment is expressed in a disguised form rather than directly and openly. *He made only a veiled reference to concerns over human rights.*

vein (**veined**) Your **veins** are tubes which carry blood back to your heart after it has been pumped out to the other parts of your body. ■ The **veins** of a leaf are the thin lines which run through it. ■ A mineral **vein** is a thin layer of the mineral which has formed in a mass of rock. ■ **Veined** is used to describe things which have veins in them, or a pattern which looks like veins. *...beautifully veined marble. ...a blue-veined cheese.* ■ If you talk about a **vein** of something being present somewhere, you mean it exists there. *Funar has tapped a rich vein of support at the margins of Romanian society.* ■ You can describe the style or mood of something by saying it is done in a particular **vein.** *The entire piece continued in the same comic vein.*

Velcro is a material consisting of two strips of nylon fabric which press together to form a strong bond. It is used to open and close parts of clothes and bags. 'Velcro' is a trademark.

veld (*or* **veldt**) (*both pron:* **velt**) A **veld** is a high area of flat open grassland in southern Africa.

vellum is fine parchment made from the skin of young sheep, goats, or cows. **Vellum** is also a name given to heavy fine-quality writing paper which looks like real vellum.

velocity (**velocities**) The **velocity** of a moving object is its speed in a particular direction.

velour (*pron:* vel-**loor**) is a cloth similar to velvet but thicker and cheaper.

velvet is a closely-woven material usually made of silk, nylon, or cotton, with a soft furry surface of short cut threads on one side.

velveteen is a cotton material similar to thin velvet.

velvety is used to describe things which make you think of velvet, because they have an attractive smooth quality. *...a velvety wine. ...her rich, dark velvety voice.*

venal (*pron:* **vee**-nal) (**venality**) If you call someone **venal** or talk about their **venality,** you mean they are corrupt and willing to take bribes.

vendetta If someone pursues a **vendetta** against you, they have a grudge against you and do everything they can to harm or upset you.

vending machine A **vending machine** is a machine from which you can buy things like coffee or sweets by putting money in a slot and pressing a button.

vendor A **vendor** is a person who sells things like newspapers or hamburgers in the street from a cart or stall. ■ The **vendor** of something such as a house is the person who owns it and is selling it.

veneer is a thin layer of wood, or plastic made to look like wood, used to improve the appearance of furniture. ■ If someone behaves in a way which hides their true feelings or intentions, you can call their behaviour a **veneer.**

venerable If you call someone **venerable,** you mean they are entitled to respect because they are old and wise.

venerate (**venerating, venerated; veneration**) If someone or something is **venerated,** they are greatly respected.

venereal disease (*pron:* ven-**ear**-ee-al) **Venereal diseases** are a group of diseases, including syphilis and gonorrhoea, which are passed on through sexual intercourse.

Venetian blind A **Venetian blind** is a window blind made of thin horizontal strips which can be adjusted to let in more or less light.

vengeance is revenge, usually in the form of violence. ■ You use **with a vengeance** to emphasize the extent to which something happens. *Finally, his luck changed with a vengeance.*

vengeful If someone is **vengeful,** they are eager for revenge.

venison is meat from a deer.

venom (**venomous**) The **venom** of a creature like a snake, scorpion, or spider is the poison it injects with its bite or sting. You say a creature like this is **venomous.** ■ When someone criticizes someone else angrily and bitterly, you can talk about the **venom** of their attack or describe it as **venomous.**

vent A **vent** is an opening designed to allow gases, fumes, or liquid to escape. ■ A **vent** is the shaft of a volcano. ■ When people **vent** strong feelings, especially anger, they express them forcefully. ■ A **vent** is a vertical slit at the back or both sides of a jacket.

ventilate (**ventilating, ventilated; ventilation**) If a room or building is **ventilated,** fresh air is allowed to get in.

ventilator A **ventilator** is a machine which helps you breathe when you cannot breathe naturally, for example because you have been injured. It is also called a 'respirator'. ■ A **ventilator** is a device in a room or building which lets fresh air in and stale air out.

ventricle (**ventricular**) The **ventricles** are the two chambers of the heart which pump blood into the arteries. **Ventricular** means to do with the ventri-

ventriloquist 722 very

cles. ...*the left ventricular muscle.* ■ The cavities of the brain are called **ventricles.**

ventriloquist (ventriloquism) A **ventriloquist** is an entertainer who holds a dummy and speaks without noticeable lip movements, so the words seem to be spoken by the dummy. This skill is called **ventriloquism.**

venture (venturing, ventured) A **venture** is a project or activity, especially one which is new, exciting, and risky. ...*one of the most successful ventures in space astronomy.* ■ If you **venture** into an activity, you do something which involves the risk of failure because it is new and different. *He enjoyed little success when he ventured into business.* ■ If you **venture** somewhere, you go there. *Few foreign nationals are said to be venturing outside their homes.*

venture capital (venture capitalist, venture capitalism) **Venture capital** is money lent to start up a new business, especially a risky one, in the hope of securing a high return. A person who lends money for this purpose is called a **venture capitalist;** lending money like this is called **venture capitalism.**

venue The **venue** for an event is the place where it will happen.

veracity If you talk about someone's **veracity,** you are talking about whether they are telling the truth or not. *She disputed Ms Perdue's veracity.* ■ If you talk about the **veracity** of an actor's performance, you mean it is true to life.

veranda (or verandah) A **veranda** is a roofed platform along the outside of a house.

verb A **verb** is a word such as 'run', 'sing', or 'feel' which is used to say what someone or something does, or what happens to them.

verbal (verbally) **Verbal** means involving words rather than actions. *The West must back up its verbal support with substantial economic aid.* ■ If something is **verbal,** it is spoken rather than written. ...*a verbal agreement.*

verbatim (pron: ver-bait-im) If you repeat something **verbatim,** you use exactly the same words.

verbiage is using too many words and making things over-complicated and unclear.

verbose (pron: verb-bohss) If someone is **verbose,** they use more words than are necessary, and are therefore tedious or annoying.

verdant places are covered with grass, trees, or other green plants.

verdict The **verdict** of a jury is the decision it reaches. ■ A **verdict** is a decision or opinion, especially one reached after careful consideration. *Arthur Cox offered a succinct verdict on yesterday's match.*

verge (verging, verged) A **verge** is a narrow strip of ground by the side of a road, usually with grass or flowers growing on it. ■ If you are **on the verge** of something, you are about to do it or it is about to happen to you. *He was on the verge of bankruptcy.* ■ If something is almost the same as something else, you can say it **verges on** it. *The congregation greeted him with admiration verging on awe.*

verger The caretaker of a Church of England church is called the **verger.**

verifiable If something is **verifiable,** it can be proved to be true or correct.

verify (verifies, verifying, verified; verification) If you **verify** something, you check that it is true or correct. ...*the verification of arms treaties.*

verisimilitude If a story or film seems realistic and convincing, you can talk about its **verisimilitude.**

veritable You use **veritable** when you are exaggerating in order to emphasize a feature of something. *The lake is a veritable ark of rare and threatened wildlife.*

verity (verities) **Verities** are general truths or principles.

vermilion is a bright red colour.

vermin are animals, such as rats, which people regard as pests.

vermouth (pron: ver-muth or ver-mooth) is an alcoholic drink made from wine flavoured with herbs.

vernacular (pron: ver-nak-yew-lar) The **vernacular** in a region is the language or dialect spoken by the ordinary people there.

verruca (pron: ver-roo-ka) A **verruca** is a type of wart on the sole of the foot.

versatile (versatility) If you say someone is **versatile** or talk about their **versatility,** you mean they have many different skills. ■ If something like a device is **versatile,** it can be used to do a variety of different jobs.

verse is writing arranged in lines which have a rhythm and often rhyme. You can also refer to poetry itself as **verse.** ■ A **verse** is one of the parts a poem, song, or chapter of the Bible or Koran is divided into.

versed If you are **versed** or **well-versed** in something, you know a lot about it.

version A **version** of something is one form of it. ...*a screen version of Virginia Woolf's 'Orlando'.* ■ Someone's **version** of an event is their description of what happened.

versus is used to say two people or groups are competing against each other. ...*the Leeds versus Liverpool match.*

vertebra (plural: vertebrae) The **vertebrae** are the bones which form the spinal column.

vertebrate A **vertebrate** is a creature with a backbone, for example a fish, bird, or mammal.

vertical (vertically) If something is **vertical,** it stands or points straight up from a flat surface. ■ **Vertical** is used to talk about movement straight up into the air, or straight down. ...*a vertical take-off plane.*

vertiginous You say something is **vertiginous** when it is sheer or high up and makes you feel dizzy.

vertigo is a dizzy feeling some people get when they look down from a high place. ■ **Vertigo** is the medical name for any severe dizziness.

verve If something is done with **verve,** it is done with energy and enthusiasm.

very is used to emphasize the words that come after it *Stephen was very brave... I was to go to the very top floor.*

vessel A **vessel** is a ship or large boat. ■ A **vessel** is a container, usually for liquid. ■ See also **blood vessel.**

vest A **vest** is a piece of underwear worn on the top half of the body. ■ In the US, a waistcoat is called a **vest.**

vested If something is **vested** in someone, it is given to them as a right or responsibility. ...*a constitutional monarchy with sovereignty vested in the people.* ■ If someone has a **vested interest** in something, they have a strong personal interest in it, because their own money, reputation, or position is at risk.

vestibule A **vestibule** is an enclosed area between the outside door of a building and the inner door.

vestige (*pron:* vest-ij) (**vestigial**) The **vestiges** of something are the parts left over when most of it has gone. *The last vestiges of Communism have been destroyed.* **Vestigial** (*pron:* vest-**tij**-ee-al) is used to describe the remaining parts of something. ...*the vestigial functions of the Crown.*

vestments are the robes worn by clergy during church ceremonies.

vestry (**vestries**) In a church, the **vestry** is the room used by the priest as an office and as a place to store vestments and change into them.

vet (**vetting, vetted**) A **vet** is a person qualified to treat sick or injured animals. 'Vet' is short for 'veterinary surgeon'. Vets are also sometimes called **veterinarians.** ■ A **vet** is a war veteran. ■ When people or things are **vetted,** they are carefully checked to make sure they are acceptable. ...*the vetting of job applicants.*

vetch is a type of flowering climbing plant.

veteran A **veteran** is someone who has served in their country's armed forces during a war. ...*a Falklands veteran.* ■ **Veteran** is used to describe someone who has been doing their job for a long time. ...*a veteran columnist on the San Francisco Chronicle.* ■ A **veteran** car is a very old one, reckoned as either one constructed before 1919 or before 1905. See also **vintage.**

veterinarian See **vet.**

veterinary means to do with the treatment of sick or injured animals. ...*veterinary medicine.*

veterinary surgeon See **vet.**

veto (**vetoes, vetoing, vetoed**) If a member of a voting group has a **veto,** they have the right to stop a decision being put into action, even if all the other members are in favour. If they exercise this right, you say they **veto** the decision.

vex (**vexes, vexing, vexed**) If something **vexes** you, it annoys or troubles you. ■ A **vexed** question or issue is very difficult and causes people a lot of trouble.

VHF is a range of radio frequencies which produce good sound quality. VHF stands for 'very high frequency'.

via If you go to one place **via** another, you pass through that place on your way to your destination. ■ If you do something **via** someone or something else, you make use of them. *The show will be broadcast via satellite from the Continent... The obvious way to establish consent is via a referendum.*

viable (**viability**) If an idea or product is **viable,** it would probably work and be profitable. ...*the shaky financial viability of the nuclear industry.*

viaduct A **viaduct** is a high bridge carrying a road or railway across a valley, usually supported by a series of arches.

Viagra is a drug that helps a man achieve and maintain an erection. It is used to treat impotence. 'Viagra' is a trademark.

vial A **vial** is the same as a phial.

vibe When people talk about the **vibes** they get from a person or place, they mean the kind of feelings they arouse.

vibrant (*pron:* **vibe**-rant) (**vibrantly, vibrancy**) If you describe someone as **vibrant** or talk about their **vibrancy,** you mean they are full of life, energy, and enthusiasm. ■ **Vibrant** colours are very bright and attractive.

vibraphone The **vibraphone** is an electronic musical instrument similar to a xylophone but with metal bars.

vibrate (**vibrating, vibrated; vibration**) When something **vibrates** or is **vibrated,** it makes rapidly repeated shaking movements called **vibrations.**

vibrato (*pron:* vib-**brah**-toe) is a rapidly repeated slight variation in the pitch of a musical note.

vibrator A **vibrator** is an electric device which vibrates, used in massage to relieve pain or to give sexual pleasure.

vicar A **vicar** is a priest in the Church of England.

vicarage A **vicarage** is a house a vicar lives in.

vicarious (*pron:* vick-**air**-ee-uss) (**vicariously**) A **vicarious** experience or feeling is one you get by watching, listening to, or reading about people doing something, rather than doing it yourself.

vice — Vices are faults or weaknesses in someone's character. ■ **Vice** refers to criminal activities, especially those connected with pornography and prostitution. ■ A **vice** (*Am:* **vise**) is a tool used to hold an object tightly while you work on it. ■ **Vice** is used before a rank or title to indicate someone who is next in importance to the person who holds the rank or title mentioned. ...*vice-president.*

vice-chancellor In a university, the **vice-chancellor** is the head of academic and administrative matters.

viceroy In the past, a **viceroy** was the man who ruled a colony on behalf of his king or queen.

vice versa (*pron:* vie-suh **ver**-sa *or* vice **ver**-sa) is used to indicate that the reverse of what you are saying also applies. For example, 'Women may bring their husbands, and vice versa' means men may also bring their wives.

vicinity (*pron:* viss-**in**-it-ee) If something is **in the vicinity** of a place, it is in the nearby area.

vicious (**viciously, viciousness**) A **vicious** person is violent and cruel. ...*a vicious attack by a gang of youths.* ■ A **vicious** remark is cruel and spiteful.

vicious circle A **vicious circle** is a situation in which one problem causes another one, which in turn tends to make the first one worse, and so on.

vicissitudes (*pron:* viss-**iss**-it-yewds) are the changes in circumstances, especially the difficult ones, which happen to someone or something at different times during their life or development.

victim A **victim** is someone who has been hurt or killed by someone or something. ■ If you **fall victim** to something or someone, you suffer because of them. *In the early 1960s, Blyton fell victim to Alzheimer's disease.*

victimize (*or* **victimise**) (**victimizing, victimized; victimization**) If someone is **victimized,** they are deliberately treated unfairly or picked on. ...*the victimization of ethnic groups.*

victor The **victor** in a contest or battle is the person who wins.

Victoria Cross The **Victoria Cross** is the highest award for gallantry in the face of the enemy awarded to British and Commonwealth armed forces.

Victorian The **Victorian** period was from 1837 to 1901, the reign of Queen Victoria. **Victorian** people and things are from that time. People who lived during that period are called **Victorians.**

Victoriana Interesting or valuable objects made during the Victorian period can be referred to as **Victoriana.**

victorious You use **victorious** to describe someone who has won a victory.

victory (**victories**) A **victory** is a success in a battle or contest.

vide (*pron:* **vie**-dee) is used in a piece of writing to indicate where further information or proof of a statement can be seen. *Some men improve in looks and style with age. Vide Howard Keel, the actor.*

video (**videos**) **Video** is the recording and showing of events and films, using a video recorder or camera, videotapes and a TV set. ■ A **video** is a video recorder. ■ A **video** is a film or TV programme recorded on videotape for people to watch on a TV set. ■ If you **video** something, you record it on videotape, using a video recorder or camera.

video camera A **video camera** is a camera which records sound and pictures on videotape.

video cassette A **video cassette** is a cassette containing videotape.

video cassette recorder See **video recorder.**

video conferencing is a system which enables people in various distant places to have a meeting by seeing and hearing each other on a screen.

video game – **Video games** are games created by a computer program, in which you manipulate images on a screen using an electronic control.

video nasty (**video nasties**) A **video nasty** is an extremely violent or horrific film on video.

video recorder A **video recorder** or **video cassette recorder** is a machine you attach to a TV set and use to record or playback programmes or films on a video cassette.

videotape (*or* **video-tape**) is magnetic tape used to record pictures or films so they can be played back on a TV set. A **videotape** is a video cassette or a piece of film recorded on videotape. If you **videotape** something, you record it on videotape.

vie (**vies, vying, vied**) If people **vie** for something, they compete for it.

view Your **views** are your personal opinions. ■ If you **view** something in a particular way, you think

of it in that way. *BBC Scotland was widely viewed as something of a backwater.* ■ The **view** from a place is everything you can see from it. If you have a **view** of something, you can see it. ■ If you **view** something, you watch it or look at it. ■ If something is **on view,** it is exhibited in public. ■ If your actions are directed towards achieving an aim, you can say you have that aim **in view.** ■ If you do something **with a view to** doing something else, you do it hoping or expecting to do that thing. ...*to acquire some skills with a view to finding jobs.* ■ You use **in view of** when mentioning the reason for an opinion or action. *Strangely, in view of all that was going on, Ann didn't look too upset.*

viewer People who watch TV are called **viewers.** ■ Anyone who watches or looks at something can be called a **viewer.** *Hirst's sculpture confronts the viewer with death and beauty.* ■ A **viewer** is a device for looking at transparent slides.

viewfinder The **viewfinder** on a camera is a small square of glass which you look through to see what you are going to photograph.

viewpoint Your **viewpoint** is your attitude towards something. ■ A **viewpoint** is a place from which you can get a good view of something.

vigil A **vigil** is a long period, especially at night, when people remain quietly in a place, for example to pray or to make a political protest.

vigilant (**vigilance**) If you are **vigilant,** you are careful and alert to danger or trouble.

vigilante (*pron:* vij-ill-**ant**-ee) **Vigilantes** are people who unofficially organize themselves into a group to protect their community and catch and punish criminals.

vignette (*pron:* vin-**yet**) A **vignette** is a short description, an illustration, or piece of acting, which expresses very clearly and neatly the typical characteristics of the thing it represents.

vigor See **vigour.**

vigorous (**vigorously**) **Vigorous** exercise uses a lot of energy. ■ A **vigorous** person is healthy and full of energy and enthusiasm. ■ **Vigorous** is used to describe things people do or say with a lot of energy and enthusiasm.

vigour (*Am:* **vigor**) is energy and enthusiasm.

Viking The **Vikings** were seagoing explorers from Scandinavia who landed in many parts of western Europe from the 8th to the 11th centuries. They sometimes attacked villages but often settled in places they reached.

vile (**vilely, vileness**) If you describe something as **vile,** you mean it is very unpleasant or disgusting.

vilify (**vilifies, vilifying, vilified; vilification**) If someone is **vilified,** people say or write unpleasant things about them.

villa A **villa** is a fairly large house, especially one used for holidays in a Mediterranean country.

village A **village** is a number of houses built close together in a country area, usually with a church, a shop, and a pub.

villager – **Villagers** are people who live in a village.

villain (**villainous**) The **villain** in a novel, film, or play is the main bad character. A bad character in fiction is often described as **villainous.** ■ Criminals or other people who deliberately harm other people are sometimes called **villains.** ■ You can call someone **the villain** or **the villain of the piece** when they are seen as the cause of all the trouble in a situation.

villainy is dishonest or criminal behaviour.

vim is energy and vigour.

vinaigrette is a salad dressing made from oil and vinegar with seasonings.

vindicate (vindicating, vindicated; vindication) If someone is **vindicated,** their ideas or actions are proved to be correct or worthwhile. You can also say something is a **vindication** of someone's ideas or actions. *He called the success a vindication of his party's free-market economic policy.*

vindictive (vindictiveness) If someone is **vindictive,** they are motivated by a desire to hurt others.

vine A **vine** is a climbing or trailing plant, especially one which produces grapes.

vinegar (vinegary) Vinegar is a sharp tasting liquid, usually made from fermented wine, cider, or malt. **Vinegary** food or drink tastes of vinegar.

vineyard (*pron:* **vinn**-yard) A **vineyard** is a piece of land planted with vines.

vintage wine is good quality wine which has been improved by being stored for several years. A wine's **vintage** is the year and place in which it was made. ■ A **vintage** car is an old one, usually reckoned to be one constructed between 1919 and 1930. See also **veteran.** ■ **Vintage** is used to describe things which are old but admired. *...vintage British comedy.* ■ You can use **vintage** to describe entertainment or sport which is the best of its kind. *This was vintage cricket, immensely skilful and exciting.*

vintner A **vintner** is someone who buys and sells wines.

vinyl is a strong plastic used for making things like floor coverings and records. ■ **Vinyl** is sometimes used to mean records rather than CDs or other forms of recorded music. *...albums previously only available on vinyl.*

viol (*pron:* **vie**-ol) **Viols** are a group of musical instruments with six strings, played using a curved bow. Viols were popular in the 16th and 17th centuries.

viola (*pron:* vee-**oh**-la) The **viola** is a musical instrument similar to a violin but slightly larger and with a lower range of notes.

violate (violating, violated; violation, violator) If someone **violates** an agreement or law, they break it. *The takeover amounted to a violation of banking laws. ...human rights violators.* ■ If an army, ship, or aircraft **violates** another country's territory, it enters it without permission. ■ If a woman is **violated,** she is raped.

violent (violently, violence) You say someone's behaviour is **violent** when they try to hurt, injure, or kill other people using weapons or physical force. Behaviour like this is called **violence.** ■ You say something like a film is **violent** when it contains a lot of violence. ■ **Violent** is used to say something happens with great force. *The cabins vi-*brated violently. ■ You use **violent** to describe things which are felt or expressed powerfully. *Jonathan violently disagreed with him.*

violet – Violets are small bluish-purple or white flowers which bloom in spring. ■ **Violet** is a bluish-purple colour.

violin (violinist) The **violin** is a wooden musical instrument with four strings. You play it by holding it under your chin and moving a bow across the strings.

VIP A **VIP** is someone who is given better treatment than ordinary people because he or she is famous or important. VIP stands for 'very important person'.

viper – Vipers are a group of poisonous snakes from Europe, Africa, and Asia.

viral (*pron:* **vie**-ral) means caused by or connected with viruses. *...viral meningitis.*

virgin (virginity) A **virgin** is someone, especially a woman or girl, who has never had sex. When someone **loses their virginity,** they have sex for the first time. ■ **Virgin** is sometimes used to describe things which are new or have never been used or spoiled. *...the last of the world's virgin forests.*

virginal If you describe someone as **virginal,** you mean they look young and innocent, as if they have had no experience of sex.

virginity See **virgin.**

virile (virility) If you describe a man as **virile** or talk about his **virility,** you mean he has characteristics which a man is traditionally supposed to have, especially energy and sex drive. ■ You can use **virile** to describe things which are healthy and active. *...a virile economy.*

virology (virologist) Virology is the branch of medicine concerned with the study of viruses.

virtual (virtually) Virtual is used to say something is so close to being a particular thing that for most purposes it can be regarded as that thing. *Industrial disputes have brought traffic to a virtual standstill... I am virtually bankrupt.*

virtual reality is the use of computers to generate an environment which people can interact with and which has the appearance of reality to them.

virtue is thinking and doing what is right and avoiding what is wrong. ■ A **virtue** is a good quality or way of behaving. *...the traditional American virtues of sportsmanship and modesty.* ■ You can call the benefits of something its **virtues.** ■ You use **by virtue of** to explain why something happens or is true. *You could make yourself indispensable by virtue of your specialist knowledge.*

virtuoso (*plural:* **virtuosi** or **virtuosos**) **(virtuosity, virtuosic)** You can call an exceptionally skilled musician, singer, or dancer a **virtuoso.** You can also talk about their **virtuosity.** ■ A **virtuoso** performance or **virtuosic** performance shows exceptional skill.

virtuous (virtuously) Virtuous behaviour is moral and correct. ■ **Virtuous** is sometimes used to criticize someone for being pleased with their own good behaviour. *They virtuously insist that they are opening markets for everyone, not just America.*

virulent (*pron:* **vir**-yew-lent) (**virulently, virulence**) Virulent feelings or actions are extremely bitter and hostile. ■ A **virulent** disease spreads quickly and is extremely harmful.

virus (**viruses**) **Viruses** are living things which are smaller than bacteria and can only reproduce themselves within the cells of animals or plants. Many viruses cause infectious diseases. ■ Computer **viruses** are programs which introduce themselves into a system, altering or destroying the information stored on the system.

visa A **visa** is a document issued to you, or a special stamp on your passport, which you need to enter or leave certain countries.

visage (*pron:* **viz**-zij) Someone's **visage** is their face.

vis-à-vis (*pron:* veez-ah-**vee**) is used to indicate what you are referring to or what you are comparing something with. *Moldova's position vis-à-vis the union treaty is unclear... The Socialists emerged from the elections stronger vis-à-vis their coalition partners.*

viscera are the organs inside the body, such as the heart, liver, and stomach.

visceral (*pron:* **viss**-er-al) emotions are based on powerful gut feelings rather than reason. *...sheer visceral hatred.*

viscosity The **viscosity** of a liquid is how thick and sticky it is.

viscount (*pron:* **vie**-count) A **viscount** is a nobleman ranking below an earl and above a baron.

viscountess (**viscountesses**) A **viscountess** is the wife of a viscount, or a woman who holds the title in her own right.

viscous liquids are thick and sticky.

vise See **vice.**

visibility (**visibilities**) The **visibility** in a place is how well or how far you can see in particular weather conditions. ■ The **visibility** of something is the extent to which people are aware of it. *...the visibility of gay-rights issues.*

visible (**visibly**) If something is **visible**, it can be seen.

vision is the ability to see. ■ **field of vision:** see **field.** ■ If someone says they have had a **vision**, they mean they have had a mysterious experience in which they saw something such as God or an angel. ■ A **vision** of something is a mental picture of it. *I had visions of him starving to death.* ■ Someone's **vision** of something in the future is their idea of how it will be or should be. *The Prime Minister has set out his vision of Britain's new role in Europe.* ■ If you say someone has **vision,** you mean they are good at foreseeing what will happen in the future and at making plans which are likely to succeed.

visionary (**visionaries**) A **visionary** is someone who is believed to have mysterious spiritual experiences during which things are revealed to them, for example by means of messages from God. ■ You say someone is a **visionary** when they have great and imaginative ideas or plans. You can also call their ideas or plans **visionary.**

visit (**visiting, visited**) If you **visit** someone or pay them a **visit,** you go to see them and spend some time with them. ■ If you **visit** a place, you go there.

visitation A **visitation** is an experience or vision thought to involve communication with God, an angel, or some other mysterious force.

visitor A **visitor** is someone who is visiting a person or place.

visor A **visor** is a piece of clear or tinted plastic, especially one attached to a helmet, used to protect someone's eyes or face.

vista A **vista** is a view.

visual (**visually**) **Visual** is used to talk about sight and things you can see. *...visual information. ...a visually stunning show.* ■ **Visuals** are things like photographs, slides, diagrams, and film, used to illustrate or explain something.

visual aid – **Visual aids** are things like films, models, maps, or slides, shown to help people understand or remember information, especially during a talk or lecture.

visual display unit See **VDU.**

visualize (*or* **visualise**) (**visualizing, visualized**) If you **visualize** something, you form a mental picture of it.

vital (**vitally, vitality**) If you say something is **vital**, you mean it is absolutely essential. *It is vitally important that any hearing loss is detected early.* ■ If you call a person **vital** or talk about their **vitality,** you mean they are energetic and full of life. You can also call organizations and activities **vital.** *The first objective is to restore and enhance the city's economic vitality.*

vitamin – **Vitamins** are substances found in small quantities in certain foods. They are essential for growth and good health.

vitiate (*pron:* **vish**-ee-ate) (**vitiating, vitiated**) If something is **vitiated,** it is made less effective.

vitriolic (**vitriol**) A **vitriolic** speech or piece of writing is extremely bitter and angry. Speech or writing like this can also be called **vitriol.**

vituperation (*pron:* vite-tyew-per-**ray**-shun) (**vituperative**) **Vituperation** is bitter spiteful abuse. A **vituperative** attack on someone is bitter and spiteful.

vivacious (**vivacity**) If you say someone is **vivacious** or talk about their **vivacity,** you mean they are energetic and full of life.

vivid (**vividly, vividness**) **Vivid** colours are very bright or brilliant. ■ You say things like memories and descriptions are **vivid** when they are powerful, clear, and detailed. *I vividly remember the 1974 premiere of the play.*

vivisection is using live animals in scientific experiments.

vixen A **vixen** is an adult female fox.

viz You use **viz** in writing to say exactly what you mean, when you have just mentioned something in a general way. *I had only one object, viz. to beat the Germans.*

V-neck A **V-neck** is a V-shaped neckline on a piece of clothing.

vocabulary (**vocabularies**) Your **vocabulary** is all the words you know. ■ The **vocabulary** of a language is all the words in it. ■ The **vocabulary** of a subject is the words typically used when discussing it. *...the vocabulary of environmentalism.*

vocal (**vocally**) **Vocal** is used to talk about things involving the voice, especially singing. ...*the vocal talents of Jocelyn Brown.* ■ The singing in a pop song can be called the **vocals.** ■ You say someone is **vocal** when they speak loudly and forcefully about something. ...*a vocal minority of MPs.*

vocal cords Your **vocal cords** are the parts in your throat which enable you to speak. They vibrate and produce sound when air is passed through them.

vocalist A **vocalist** is a singer with a band.

vocation If you have a **vocation,** you have a strong feeling that you are especially suitable to do a particular job or to fill a particular role in life. You can call your job a **vocation** if you feel like this about it.

vocational (**vocationally**) **Vocational** training is specialized training for particular jobs, rather than more general education.

vociferous (*pron:* voh-**sif**-er-uss) (**vociferously**) If someone is **vociferous,** they express their views loudly and forcefully.

vodka is a strong clear alcoholic drink distilled from grain or potatoes.

vogue If something is **in vogue** or there is a **vogue** for it, it is popular and fashionable.

voguish means fashionable.

voice (**voicing, voiced**) When someone speaks or sings, you hear their **voice.** ■ If you **voice** an opinion or emotion or **give voice** to it, you say what you think or feel. ■ If you have a **voice** in something, you have the right to express an opinion and to influence any decisions which are made. *Parents will have some voice in drawing up school districts.* ■ If a person or organization provides a **voice** for a group of people, they speak or campaign on their behalf. *John Marsh was the recognised voice of British management.* ■ If you say a group of people **speak with one voice,** you mean they show unity and agreement in what they say. ■ If someone **finds their voice,** they find a way of getting their feelings, opinions, or ideas across effectively.

voice mail is an electronic system that transfers and stores your telephone messages so you can deal with them when it is convenient.

voice-over A **voice-over** is a commentary heard as part of a film or TV programme but spoken by someone who is not actually seen.

void A **void** is a large empty space.

volatile (**volatility**) A **volatile** situation could suddenly change at any moment, especially for the worse. You talk about the **volatility** of a situation like this. ■ A **volatile** person is temperamental and easily angered. ■ **Volatile** liquids and solids change into a gas at fairly low temperatures.

vol-au-vent (*pron:* **voll**-oh-von) A **vol-au-vent** is a small light pastry case with a savoury filling.

volcano (**volcanoes; volcanic**) A **volcano** is an opening in the earth's crust from which hot molten rock, steam, and gas sometimes burst out. The rock and ash often form a mountain around the opening; this mountain is also called a **volcano.** **Volcanic** means to do with volcanoes. ...*volcanic ash.* ...*volcanic activity.* ■ You can describe something as **volcanic** when it is powerful, exciting, or uncontrollable. ...*a volcanic outburst of rage.*

vole – **Voles** are small animals similar to mice but with a shorter tail.

volition If you do something **of your own volition,** you do it because you have chosen to, rather than because you have been forced to or told to.

volley A **volley** of gunfire is a lot of shots fired at the same time. Similarly, you can talk about a **volley** of stones or other missiles. You can also say someone is subjected to a **volley** of insults. ■ In games like tennis and football, a **volley** is a shot in which the player hits or kicks the ball before it has touched the ground. When this happens, you say the player **volleys** the ball.

volleyball is a game in which two teams hit a ball backwards and forwards over a high net with their hands or arms.

volt The force of an electric current is expressed in **volts.**

voltage The **voltage** of an electric current is its force in volts. ■ People sometimes use **voltage** when describing how powerful or exciting something is. *The game was high voltage stuff.*

volte-face (*pron:* volt-**fass**) If a government performs a **volte-face,** it completely changes its policy on something.

voluble (**volubly**) If someone is **voluble,** they have a lot to say, and they say it with energy and enthusiasm.

volume The **volume** of something is the amount there is of it. ...*the growing volume of traffic on country roads.* ■ The **volume** of an object is the amount of space it contains or occupies. ■ The **volume** of a sound, especially the sound from a TV, radio, or stereo, is how loud it is. ■ A **volume** is a book, especially a collection of poems, stories, or articles. *He published his first volume of poetry while still a teenager.* ■ A **volume** is one book or video in a series. ■ If something **speaks volumes,** it tells you a lot about someone or something. *The episode speaks volumes about the current state of the country.*

voluminous If something is **voluminous,** it is large and bulky. ...*voluminous skirts.* ...*a voluminous quantity of research notes.*

voluntary (**voluntarily**) **Voluntary** is used to describe things you do because. you choose to do them, rather than because you have to. ...*voluntary redundancy.* ■ **Voluntary work** is unpaid work which people do to help a good cause such as a charity. The organizations these people work for are called **voluntary organizations.**

volunteer (**volunteering, volunteered**) If someone **volunteers** to do something, they offer to do it. You call someone who does this a **volunteer.** ■ A **volunteer** is someone who does unpaid work, especially for a charity or some other good cause. ■ A **volunteer** is someone who chooses to join the armed forces, especially during wartime, as opposed to someone who is forced to join by law. ■ If you **volunteer** information, you tell someone something without being asked.

voluptuous A woman is sometimes described as **voluptuous** when she has attractively large breasts and hips.

vomit (**vomiting, vomited**) If you **vomit,** partly-digested food comes back up from your stomach and out through your mouth. The partly-digested food is called **vomit.**

voodoo is a form of religion involving witchcraft, practised by some people in the West Indies, especially Haiti.

voracious (**voraciously**) **Voracious** is used to say someone is eager to have a lot of something. *Shearing is a voracious reader. ...the band's voracious appetite for fun.*

vortex (*plural:* **vortexes** *or* **vortices**) A **vortex** is a mass of wind, water, or gas spinning round so fast that it pulls objects into its empty centre. ■ If someone is becoming trapped in a nasty situation, you can call the situation a **vortex.** *He drifts into a self-destructive vortex of alcoholic binges and blackouts.*

vote (**voting, voted**) A **vote** is an occasion when a group of people make a decision by each one indicating his or her choice. The choice most people support is then accepted by the group. When you **vote** or cast your **vote,** you indicate your choice, usually by raising your hand or making a mark on a piece of paper. The **vote** is the total number of votes cast. *The Social Liberals looked like getting less than 20 per cent of the vote.* The result of the voting is called a **vote** of a particular kind. *He believes a 'yes' vote might cause prices to go up.* ■ If people have a legal right to vote in an election, you say they have **the vote.** *The Swiss confederation granted women the vote in 1971.*

vote of thanks (**votes of thanks**) A **vote of thanks** is an official speech in which the speaker formally thanks a person for doing something.

voter – **Voters** are people who have the right to vote in an election.

vouch (**vouches, vouching, vouched**) If you say you can **vouch for** someone, you mean you can guarantee their good behaviour. ■ If you say you can **vouch for** something, you mean you have evidence from your own experience that it is true, correct, or reliable.

voucher A **voucher** is a piece of paper which can be used instead of money to pay for something.

vouchsafe (**vouchsafing, vouchsafed**) If something such as a secret is **vouchsafed** to you, you are told about it.

vow If you **vow** to do something or make a **vow** to do it, you make a solemn promise or decision to do it. *She has not broken her vow of silence... He vowed never to play cricket again.*

vowel A **vowel** is a sound such as the ones represented in writing by the letters 'a', 'e', 'i', 'o', and 'u', which you pronounce by letting the air flow freely through your mouth. See also **consonant.**

vox pop A **vox pop** is an inquiry carried out in the street by a TV or radio reporter who asks ordinary people's opinions on a matter of public interest.

voyage (**voyaging, voyaged; voyager**) A **voyage** is a long journey by ship or spacecraft. If someone is **voyaging** somewhere, they are making a journey like this. *...a replica of the ship that brought the voyagers to Massachusetts in 1620.*

voyeur (**voyeurism, voyeuristic**) A **voyeur** is a person who gets pleasure from watching other people's private or sexual activities. Watching people like this is called **voyeurism.** *...voyeuristic televised dating games.*

vs is sometimes used in writing to say two people or teams are competing against each other. 'vs' is short for 'versus'. *Arsenal vs Liverpool.*

V-sign In Britain, a **V-sign** is a rude gesture made by sticking up your first two fingers in a V shape, with the palm of your hand facing you. ■ A **V-sign** is a sign meaning 'victory' made by sticking up your first two fingers in a V shape, with the palm of your hand facing away from you.

VSO is a British organization which sends skilled people to developing countries to work on projects helping the local community. VSO stands for 'Voluntary Service Overseas'.

vulgar (**vulgarity, vulgarian**) If you describe something as **vulgar** or talk about its **vulgarity,** you mean it is lacking in taste or artistic quality. ■ **Vulgar** pictures, gestures, or remarks refer to sex or bodily functions in a rude and distasteful way. ■ People are sometimes described as **vulgar** or called **vulgarians** when they are thought to be rude or lacking in taste.

vulgarize (*or* **vulgarise**) (**vulgarizing, vulgarized; vulgarization**) If something is **vulgarized,** it is made vulgar. *He preached against the vulgarization of sex.*

vulnerable (**vulnerably, vulnerability**) If someone or something is **vulnerable,** they are weak and badly protected, and are open to attack, criticism, or misfortune. ■ You can say someone is **vulnerable** if they are easily influenced or led astray, because they are lacking in wisdom or experience.

vulture – **Vultures** are large birds which eat the flesh of dead or dying animals. ■ If you call a person a **vulture,** you mean they are eager to take advantage of other people's misfortune. *The vultures of the press have been circling for some time.*

vulva (*plural:* **vulvas** *or* **vulvae**) A woman's **vulva** is the outer part of her sexual organs.

vying See **vie.**

W w

wacko (*or* **whacko**) If you say someone is **wacko** or a **wacko,** you mean they are eccentric in a very strange way.

wacky (*or* **whacky**) If you say someone or something is **wacky,** you mean they are eccentric or unusual in a pleasant or funny way.

wad A **wad** of banknotes is a thick bundle of them. ■ A **wad** of something soft is a compressed ball of it. *...a wad of chewing-gum.*

wadding is soft material used as stuffing or padding.

waddle (**waddling, waddled**) If a creature like a penguin **waddles** somewhere, it walks with short steps, swaying slightly from side to side. Similarly, you can talk about a very fat person **waddling.**

wade (**wading, waded**) If you **wade** through water, you walk through it slowly and with difficulty. ■ If you **wade into** a difficult situation, you become involved in it before fully thinking through all the consequences. ■ If you **wade through** a lot of papers, you spend a lot of time reading them.

wader — **Waders** are long-legged birds which hunt for food in shallow water. ■ **Waders** are thigh length waterproof rubber boots.

wadi (*pron:* wod-dee) A **wadi** is a narrow valley in a desert area which is dry except in the rainy season.

wafer A **wafer** is (a) a thin crisp biscuit, often eaten with ice cream. (b) a thin round piece of a special kind of bread eaten as part of the service of Holy Communion.

waffle (*pron:* woff-l) (**waffling, waffled; waffler**) If you say someone is **waffling,** you mean they are talking or writing in a vague way, without saying anything important. You call what they say or write **waffle.** If someone often talks or writes like this, you can call them a **waffler.** ■ **Waffles** are thick crisp oblong pancakes with squares marked on them.

waft (*pron:* woft) If a smell or sound **wafts** through the air, it drifts gently through it.

wag (**wagging, wagged**) When a dog **wags** its tail, it waves it vigorously from side to side, because it is pleased or excited. ■ If you **wag your finger** at someone, you point your finger at them and repeatedly move it up and down. ■ If you say **tongues are wagging,** you mean people are gossiping about something, often spitefully. ■ A witty person can be called a **wag.**

wage (**waging, waged**) A person's **wages** or **wage** is the money they get for the work they do, especially weekly for a manual job. ■ **living wage:** see **living.** ■ If a person, group, or country **wages** a campaign or war, they start it and continue it over a period of time. *Our movement is committed to wage war on poverty.*

wage packet A person's **wage packet** is their wages.

wager (**wagering, wagered**) A **wager** is a bet. If you **wager** money on the outcome of something, you

bet money on it. ■ If you say that you will **wager** that something is the case, you are confident that it is the case.

waggle (**waggling, waggled**) If you **waggle** your fingers or toes, you move them backwards and forwards.

wagon (*or* **waggon**) A **wagon** is a strong four-wheeled vehicle for carrying heavy loads, pulled by a horse or tractor. ■ Railway **wagons** are vehicles pulled by a railway engine and used for carrying freight. ■ If someone is **on the wagon,** they have given up drinking alcohol.

wagtail — **Wagtails** are small birds with long tails which flick up and down.

waif A child or young person is sometimes called a **waif** when they are very thin and look as if they are hungry and uncared for.

wail (**wailing, wailed**) If someone **wails,** they make a loud continuous high-pitched sound, usually because they are in great distress. You can also say a bagpipe or siren **wails.** Any of these sounds can be called a **wail.** *...the wail of sirens.*

waist (**-waisted**) Your **waist** is the middle part of your body above your hips. ■ The **waist** of a piece of clothing is the part which fits around your waist. **-waisted** is used to describe the waist of a piece of clothing. *...a high-waisted skirt.*

waistband A **waistband** is a narrow piece of material sewn round the waist of a pair of trousers, skirt, or other garment to strengthen it.

waistcoat A **waistcoat** is a sleeveless garment which buttons up the front, usually worn under a jacket.

waistline If you talk about a person's **waistline,** you mean the size of their waist.

wait (**waiting, waited**) If you have to **wait** for something you want or need, you do not get it immediately. You can also say you have a **wait** for something. *A-level students continued the long wait for their results.* ■ If you **wait,** you spend some time in a place, usually doing very little, until something happens. ■ If something is **waiting** for you, it is ready for you to use or to take some action on. *There will be a great stack of letters waiting for them when they return.* ■ If you say something **can wait,** you mean it is not urgent and can be dealt with later. ■ If you **wait on** people in a restaurant, it is your job to serve them. ■ If you **wait on** someone **hand and foot,** you do everything for them.

waiter (**waitress, waitresses**) A **waiter** is a man whose job is to serve food and drink to people at their table in a restaurant. A woman who does this job is called a **waitress.**

waive (**waiving, waived**) If someone **waives** something they are entitled to have or do, they give up their right to have it or do it. *Four of the directors waived their fees.* ■ If someone **waives** a rule, they do not enforce it. A **waiver** is an official statement saying that a rule does not have to be enforced in a particular case.

wake (**waking, woke, have woken**) When you **wake,** or someone or something **wakes** you, you become conscious again after being asleep. ■ **Waking** is used to talk about the times when a person is awake. ...*his waking hours.* ■ If you **wake up to** a situation, you become aware of it. *British firms are waking up to their environmental responsibilities.* ■ The **wake** of a ship is the trail of waves it leaves behind. ■ If something is left **in the wake** of something else, it is left as a result of it. *The Arctic conditions are now sweeping south, leaving a trail of damage in their wake.* Similarly, if something follows **in the wake of** something else, it happens after it and usually as a result of it. *In the wake of the doctors' strike last November, hundreds of people were arrested.* ■ A **wake** is a gathering of people who have collected together to mourn someone's death.

waken (**wakening, wakened**) If you **waken** or are **wakened,** you wake up.

walk When you **walk,** you move forward, putting one foot after the other in front of you. ■ If you go for a **walk,** you walk a certain distance for pleasure or exercise. ■ A **walk** is a route or path which people walk along for pleasure. ...*the most spectacular coastal walk in the British Isles.* ■ If you **walk** someone somewhere, you escort them there. ■ If you **walk** your dog, you take it for a walk. ■ If someone **walks out** of a meeting, event, or situation, they leave it suddenly, often to show their disapproval of something. You can say workers **walk out** or stage a **walkout** when they go on strike. ■ If someone **walks over** another person, they treat them very badly. ■ You say someone **walks over** another person when they easily defeat them in a contest or argument. ■ If someone **walks away with** something like a prize, they obtain it easily. ■ If you **walk into** a job, you get it very easily.

walkabout When a politician or member of a royal family goes on a **walkabout,** they go among the crowds in a public place and talk to people.

walker A **walker** is a person who walks for pleasure or as a sport.

walkie-talkie A **walkie-talkie** is a small portable radio for talking to someone at a distance and receiving their replies.

walking stick A **walking stick** is a long wooden stick which a person uses to lean on while walking.

Walkman (**Walkmans**) A **Walkman** is a small portable cassette player, often with a radio, which you carry around and listen to through headphones. 'Walkman' is a trademark.

walk of life (**walks of life**) Your **walk of life** is your position in society and the kind of job you have.

walk-on A **walk-on** part in a play is a very small one, often involving just one brief appearance on the stage.

walkout (*or* **walk-out**) See **walk.**

walkover If you say a contest is a **walkover,** you mean it is won very easily.

walkway A **walkway** is a footbridge over a road, or a raised footpath by the side of one.

wall (**walled**) The **walls** of a building or room are its vertical sides. ■ A **wall** is a long narrow vertical structure, made of stone or brick, surrounding or dividing an area of land. A **walled** area is surrounded by a wall. ■ A high dense mass of something can be called a **wall.** *Survivors spoke of a wall of water up to twenty feet high smashing through the town.* ■ The **wall** of something hollow is its outer covering. ...*muscle fibres that line the walls of arteries.* ■ If you have your **back to the wall,** you are in a very difficult situation. ■ If you say **the writing is on the wall** for someone, you mean they are not likely to survive in their job or position. ■ If people see **the writing on the wall,** they are aware of a danger to themselves, and take some action to avoid it. ■ If a business **goes to the wall,** it is in such serious financial difficulties that it has to close down.

wallaby (**wallabies**) A **wallaby** is an animal similar to a kangaroo, but smaller.

wallet A **wallet** is a small flat folding case used for carrying banknotes, credit cards, etc.

wallflower – **Wallflowers** are garden plants with sweet-smelling yellow, red, orange, or purple flowers. ■ Shy people who do not like to attract attention to themselves are sometimes called **wallflowers.**

wallop (**walloping, walloped**) If someone **wallops** you, they hit you hard with something like a stick.

wallow If you **wallow** in something, you spend too much time thinking about it and taking pleasure in it. *Britain is currently wallowing in nostalgia.*

wallpaper is thick plain or patterned paper which people paste onto the walls of their rooms.

Wall Street is a street in New York where the Stock Exchange and the important banks are. **Wall Street** is often used to talk about the financial activities in Wall Street and the people who work there. *Wall Street is becoming gloomy about global economic prospects.*

wall-to-wall carpeting completely covers the floor of a room. ■ **Wall-to-wall** entertainment is available at all times on TV or radio. ...*wall-to-wall football.*

wally (**wallies**) You call someone a **wally** when they do something silly.

walnut The **walnut** is a tree which produces edible nuts, also called **walnuts.** The nuts have a wrinkled appearance and a hard light-brown shell.

walrus (**walruses**) The **walrus** is a sea mammal like a large seal with a tough skin, coarse whiskers, and two tusks.

waltz (**waltzes, waltzing, waltzed**) The **waltz** is a dance performed by couples. It has a rhythm of three beats in each bar. When people **waltz,** they perform this dance.

wan (**wanly**) If someone looks **wan,** they look pale and tired.

wand A **wand** is a thin rod which a magician pretends to use when he or she performs tricks.

wander (**wandering, wandered; wanderer**) If you **wander** somewhere, you go there in a casual unhurried way. ■ **Wandering** people travel around rather than staying in one place. People like these are called **wanderers.** ■ A person's **wanderings** are the journeys they make when they travel around. ■ If your mind or attention **wanders,** you start thinking about something else rather than the thing you are supposed to be thinking about.

wanderlust is a strong urge to travel.

wane (waning, waned) If something is **waning** or on **the wane,** it is decreasing or getting weaker. *But his interest soon waned... The government had been expressing confidence that certain types of crime were on the wane.* ■ When the moon **wanes,** a smaller area of brightness can be seen each day as it changes in its cycle from full moon to new moon. See also **wax.**

wangle (wangling, wangled) If someone **wangles** something, they manage to get it by cleverness or persuasion.

wannabe (or wannabee) (both pron: wan-a-bee) A **wannabe** is someone who wants to be a particular kind of person. For example, a Madonna wannabe is someone who wants to be like Madonna.

want If you **want** something, you feel a desire for it or a need to have it. ■ A **want** of something is a lack of it. *This shows a want of commitment on the part of the new minister.* If you say something is **wanting** in a certain thing, you mean it does not have it. *...a performance seriously wanting in imagination, energy and tension.* ■ If someone is **wanted,** the police are looking for them, because they have committed a crime. *...a wanted man.*

wanton is used to describe bad or cruel things which are done for no reason at all. *...wanton destruction.*

war (warring) A **war** is a period of armed conflict between two or more countries. **War** is used to talk about things connected with a war. *...the war effort. ...a war zone.* ■ **Warring** countries or groups are fighting against each other. ■ Certain kinds of conflict can be called **war.** *...the class war.* Commercial competition can be called a **war.** *...a price war.*

warble (warbling, warbled) If someone **warbles** a tune, they sing it.

warbler – Warblers are small songbirds.

war crime (war criminal) War crimes are acts such as the ill-treatment of prisoners which are committed during a war, in violation of the accepted rules of war.

war cry A **war cry** was a cry uttered by a soldier during a charge against the enemy. ■ Someone's **war cry** is a slogan they use to try to get people to support them. *'Affordable housing' remains the war-cry of every local politician.*

ward A hospital **ward** is a large room with beds for patients. ■ If you **ward off** a blow, you prevent it reaching the part of your body it was aimed at. ■ If you **ward off** something unpleasant, you prevent it reaching or harming you. *...urgent measures to ward off the threat of starvation.* ■ A **ward** is one of the districts a city or town is divided into for administration purposes. Each ward is represented by a councillor. ■ A **ward** or **ward of court** is a person, usually a child, officially put in the care of a court of law or a guardian because they need protection.

warden A **warden** is an official whose job is to make sure certain laws or regulations are obeyed. *Game*

wardens were appointed to enforce hunting laws.* ■ The person in charge of a building or institution is sometimes called the **warden.** *...a youth hostel warden.* ■ In the US, the person in charge of a prison is called the **warden.**

warder Prison officers used to be called **warders.**

wardrobe A **wardrobe** is a tall large wooden cabinet for keeping clothes in. ■ Your **wardrobe** is the clothes you own.

wardrobe mistress The **wardrobe mistress** is a woman in charge of the costumes in a theatre company.

ware Someone's **wares** are the goods or services they sell. ■ **Ware** is used to talk about products made of a certain material or made for a certain purpose. *...crystal ware. ...sanitary ware.*

warehouse A **warehouse** is a very large building where goods or materials are stored.

warehouse club A **warehouse club** is a large cash-and-carry store which sells goods at reduced prices to people who pay an annual subscription.

warfare is carrying on a war with another country. ■ Fighting between groups is sometimes called **warfare.** *...gang warfare between rival Mafia clans.*

warhead A **warhead** is the front end of a missile, where the explosive is carried.

warhorse An old soldier or politician is sometimes called a **warhorse** when they are still active and aggressive. ■ A play or piece of music which is often performed can be called a **warhorse.** *...an outstanding young pianist who kicked some new life into an old warhorse.*

warlike is used to describe hostile and aggressive talk and actions.

warlock A **warlock** is a male witch.

warlord A **warlord** is a military leader of a country or part of a country, especially one who is not answerable to anyone else.

warm (warmly; warming) If something is **warm,** its temperature is fairly high, but not high enough to be hot. If you are **warm,** you feel comfortable because you are not cold or hot. ■ **Warm** clothes and blankets keep you from getting cold. ■ If something **warms** or **warms up,** it gets hotter. ■ When an athlete **warms up,** they exercise gently to prepare themselves for their event. A preparation like this is called a **warm-up.** ■ If people's behaviour is **warm,** they are friendly and welcoming. *The visiting team have been warmly welcomed by the crowds.* ■ If relations between people **warm,** they improve and become more friendly. ■ If you **warm to** a person or thing, you begin to like them. ■ **Warming** is used to describe things which give you a feeling of pleasure. *...the warming effect of comradeship.* ■ **Warm** colours have red or yellow in them rather than blue or green, and make you feel comfortable and relaxed.

warm-blooded A **warm-blooded** creature, for example a mammal, is one whose body temperature is kept at a constant warm level, regardless of the surrounding temperature. See also **cold-blooded.**

warm-hearted people are friendly, kind, and affectionate.

warmonger (**warmongering**) If you accuse someone of being a **warmonger,** you mean they are trying to start a war. You can also say they are **warmongering.**

warmth is friendliness or welcoming behaviour. *They were surprised by the warmth and hospitality they met with.* ■ **Warmth** is moderate heat.

warm-up See **warm.**

warn (**warning**) If you **warn** someone about something harmful, you tell them about it. You can also say you give them a **warning.** ■ If you **warn** someone not to do something, you advise them not to do it for their own safety. ■ **Warning** is used to describe things which are said or done to warn people. *Police fired warning shots.* ■ If you **warn** someone **off,** you tell them not to go somewhere.

warp If something **warps** someone's mind or character, it damages or corrupts it. *Their lives have been warped by war.* ■ If wood **warps,** it becomes distorted, often because of the effect of heat or water. ■ The **warp** in a piece of woven material is the threads which are stretched taut along the loom. See also **weft.** ■ See also **time warp.**

warpath If you say someone is **on the warpath,** you mean they are preparing for a fight or argument.

warplane A **warplane** is any plane designed for use in warfare.

warrant A **warrant** is an official document signed by a judge or magistrate which allows the police to perform a certain action, for example to arrest someone. ■ **death warrant:** see **death.** ■ If you say something **warrants** a certain thing, you mean it justifies it or makes it necessary. *The allegations are serious enough to warrant an investigation.*

warrant officer A **warrant officer** is an NCO of the highest rank in the army and the RAF.

warranty (**warranties**) A **warranty** is a written guarantee which enables you to get a product repaired or replaced free of charge within a certain period of time.

warren A **warren** is an underground system of holes connected by tunnels, where rabbits live. ■ You can call a place a **warren** when there are a lot of rooms or buildings with connecting passages where it would be easy to get lost.

warring See **war.**

warrior In the past, a **warrior** was a brave soldier or an experienced fighter.

warship A **warship** is any ship designed for use in warfare.

wart A **wart** is a small hard growth on someone's skin. ■ If you describe someone or something **warts and all,** you mention their bad points as well as their good ones. *...a warts-and-all look at Edinburgh.*

warthog – **Warthogs** are large African wild pigs with tusks.

wartime is used to talk about a period of war, especially the Second World War. *She seldom spoke of her wartime life.*

wary (**warier, wariest; warily, wariness**) If you are **wary** of something, you are nervous or cautious about it, because you think it may be dangerous or cause you problems. *He stepped ashore warily.*

was See **be.**

wash (**washes, washing, washed**) If you **wash** or have a **wash,** you clean yourself using soap and water. Similarly, you can **wash** clothes or other things. You call the clothes being washed the **wash** or the **washing.** ■ If you **wash up** or do the **washing-up,** you wash the crockery, pans, etc. ■ If something is **washed** somewhere, it is carried there by water. ■ If a sporting event is **washed out,** it is called off because of heavy rain. ■ You call the waves produced by a ship as it moves through the water the **wash.** ■ If you say an argument or excuse will **not wash,** you mean it is not convincing. ■ A **wash** of colour is a thin covering or layer of it.

washable clothes or materials can be washed without suffering damage.

washbasin A **washbasin** is a large basin, usually with hot and cold taps, which you can fill with water so you can have a wash.

washed-out colours are very pale. ■ If you feel **washed-out,** you feel very tired, because of illness or overwork.

washer A **washer** is a thin flat ring of metal, rubber, or plastic. Washers are used as a seal in something like a tap, or to make a tight connection with a nut and bolt.

washer-dryer (*or* **washer-drier**) A **washer-dryer** is an automatic machine which is both a washing machine and a tumble dryer.

washing See **wash.**

washing line A **washing line** is a cord stretched between two posts, on which you hang out washing to dry.

washing machine A **washing machine** is a machine for washing clothes, towels, etc.

washing-up See **wash.**

washroom A **washroom** is a room with toilets and washing facilities.

wasp – **Wasps** are insects which can sting. The most common kinds have yellow-and-black striped bodies.

waspish If you call someone **waspish,** you mean they have a sharp, critical sense of humour.

wastage If there is **wastage** of something valuable or useful, some of it is not used, or it is used wrongly or inefficiently. ■ See also **natural wastage.**

waste (**wasting, wasted**) If you **waste** time, money, or another resource, you use too much of it on something which is unnecessary or unimportant. You say the unnecessary or unimportant thing is a **waste** of time or money. ■ If you **waste** an opportunity, you do not take advantage of it. ■ **Waste** is material which has been used and is no longer wanted or which is left over from an industrial process. *...waste paper. ...nuclear waste.* ■ If something **goes to waste,** it remains unused or goes bad and has to be thrown away. ■ If something is **laid waste,** it is completely destroyed. ■ If someone is **wasting away,** they are slowly getting thinner and weaker. A **wasting** disease is one which has this effect. ■ **Waste** land is land which is not used or looked after, and is covered by wild plants and often rubbish. ■ **Wastes** are large barren and empty areas of land. *...the wastes of Mongolia.* ■ If you say something is **wasted** on someone, you mean they are too unsophisticated to appreciate it. *Fine brandy is wasted on you.*

wasteful (**wastefully, wastefulness**) A **wasteful** action uses money or other resources carelessly or inefficiently. *...companies that use energy wastefully.*

wasteland A **wasteland** is an area of land which is infertile or desolate and unused.

wasting See **waste.**

watch (**watches, watching, watched**) A **watch** is a device, usually worn on your wrist, which tells the time. ■ If you **watch** something, you look at it for some time and pay attention to what is happening. ■ If you **watch** a situation, you pay attention to it. *I'll watch her progress with interest.* ■ If you tell someone to **watch out,** you are warning them of something dangerous which is happening or which could happen. ■ If you **watch out** for something, you pay attention because it might be interesting or useful. ■ If you **watch over** someone or something, you make sure no harm comes to them. ■ If someone like a soldier is **on watch,** he or she is guarding a place. Each period of guard duty is called a **watch.**

watchable You can describe a TV programme or film as **watchable** when it is enjoyable to watch. You can also describe an actor's performance as **watchable.**

watchdog A **watchdog** is a person or committee whose job is to make sure that certain organizations do not act irresponsibly or illegally.

watcher can be used to form a word which refers to someone with a particular interest in certain people or things, and who studies them closely. *...a music-industry watcher.*

watchful (**watchfulness**) If someone is **watchful,** they notice everything that is happening.

watchman (**watchmen**) A **watchman** is a person whose job is to guard buildings or property.

watchtower A **watchtower** is a tall tower from which a guard has a good view of the area he or she is guarding.

watchword Someone's **watchword** is a word or phrase which sums up their attitude or what they are trying to achieve.

water (**watering, watered**) **Water** is the clear colourless liquid which is necessary for the survival of all plants and animals. ■ When you **water** plants, you pour water onto the soil around them, to help them grow. ■ You can use **waters** to refer to large areas of water, particularly the territorial area of sea around a country's coast. *The French have been fishing in British waters for centuries.* ■ If your eyes are **watering,** you have tears in them. ■ If your mouth is **watering,** it is producing extra saliva, because you can smell or see some appetizing food. See also **mouth-watering.** ■ If you **water** a liquid **down,** you add water to it to make it weaker. ■ If something like a plan or scheme is **watered down,** it is made less forceful or controversial.

waterbed A **waterbed** is a bed with a waterproof mattress filled with water.

water-borne diseases are passed on through infected water.

water buffalo — Water buffalo are large buffalo from the swampy regions of south Asia.

water cannon A **water cannon** is a machine which shoots out a powerful jet of water. It is used by the police to break up crowds.

water chestnut A **water chestnut** is the thick bottom part of the stem of a plant which grows in China. It is frequently used in Chinese cooking.

watercolour (*Am:* **watercolor**) (**watercolourist**) **Watercolours** are paints for painting pictures, which are diluted with water or put on the paper using a wet brush. A **watercolour** is a picture painted with watercolours.

watercourse A **watercourse** is the channel a river or stream flows along.

watercress is a small plant which grows in freshwater streams and pools. Its hot-tasting leaves are eaten raw in salads.

waterfall A **waterfall** is a stream of water flowing over the edge of a steep cliff and falling to the ground or water below.

waterfowl (*plural:* **waterfowl**) **Waterfowl** are birds which swim in water, especially ducks, geese, and swans.

waterfront A **waterfront** is a street or strip of land next to a harbour or the sea.

waterhole A **waterhole** is a pond or pool in a desert or other dry area where animals can find water to drink.

watering can A **watering can** is a container with a long spout, used to water plants.

watering hole You can refer to a pub or bar where people go to meet their friends as a **watering hole.**

waterlily (**waterlilies**) **Waterlilies** are plants with large flat leaves and attractive flowers which float on the surface of a lake or river.

waterline When a ship is afloat, the **waterline** is the part of its hull which is level with the surface of the water.

waterlogged ground is so wet it cannot absorb any more water, so a layer of water remains on the surface.

water main A **water main** is a large underground pipe which supplies water to houses or other buildings.

watermark A **watermark** is a design put into paper when it is made, which you can only see if you hold the paper up to the light. Bank notes have a watermark, to make them harder to forge.

watermelon — Watermelons are large round fruit with green skin, juicy pink flesh, and black seeds.

watermill A **watermill** is a mill powered by a water wheel.

water polo is a game played in a swimming pool by two teams of seven players who try to score by throwing a ball into their opponent's goal.

waterproof (**waterproofing, waterproofed**) If something is **waterproof,** water cannot pass through it. If you **waterproof** something, you make it waterproof. ■ Waterproof clothing can be called **waterproofs.**

water rates are charges made for the use of water from the public water supply.

watershed A **watershed** is an important event or period which acts as a turning point or marks the beginning of a new way of life. *The 1987 INF treaty was considered a watershed in arms control.* ■ The **watershed** is the point in time after which programmes containing material considered to be unsuitable for young children can be broadcast on TV. This is usually from 9pm. ■ A **watershed** is an area of high ground, such as a ridge, which divides two river systems, so they flow in different directions.

waterside is used to describe things which are situated or take place beside a stretch of water such as a lake or river.

water-ski (water-skiing) When someone **water-skis**, they ski on water while being pulled along by a boat. This activity is called **water-skiing.**

water-soluble If something is **water-soluble**, it dissolves in water.

water supply The **water supply** in an area is the water which is collected and passed through pipes to buildings.

water table The **water table** is the level under the ground below which rock is saturated with water.

watertight If a container is **watertight**, it does not let water in. ■ A **watertight** case, argument, or agreement is one which has been so carefully put together that nobody will be able to find a fault in it.

water tower A **water tower** is a large tank of water mounted on a tower so water can be supplied at a steady pressure to surrounding buildings.

waterway A **waterway** is a canal, river, or narrow channel of sea along which ships or boats travel.

water wheel A **water wheel** is a large wheel which is turned by water flowing through it and is used to provide power to drive machinery.

waterworks A **waterworks** is a place where water is stored and purified before being distributed to the public.

watery is used to describe something which contains, resembles, or consists of water. *...watery fluid in the eyeball.* ■ If food or drink is **watery**, it contains a lot of water. ■ You can say something is **watery** when it is pale or weak. *...a dim, watery smile.*

watt (*pron: wott*) Electrical power is measured in **watts**. One watt is equal to one joule per second.

wattage The **wattage** of a piece of electrical equipment is the amount of electrical power, expressed in watts, which it uses or generates.

wattle (*pron: wott-tl*) is a frame of branches woven together with thin twigs and used for making fences and walls.

wave (**waving, waved**) When you **wave,** you raise your hand in greeting and move it from side to side. You can also **wave** your hand, for instance, to say you do not want something, or you can direct someone somewhere by **waving** them there. ■ If you **wave** something, you hold it up and move it from side to side. ■ When something like a flag **waves**, it moves in the wind. ■ If you **wave aside** an idea or comment, you show you do not think it is worth serious consideration. ■ **Waves** are raised masses of water on the surface of the sea or a lake, caused by wind or tide. ■ A **wave** is the form in which some types of energy travel, for example light, sound, or radio signals. See also **shock wave.** ■ A **wave** of emotion is a powerful burst of it passing quickly among a group of people. ■ A **wave** of activity is a sudden increase in it. *...a fresh wave of violence.* ■ A **wave** of people is a large group of them moving somewhere. *...a fresh wave of refugees.* ■ If your hair has **waves**, it curves slightly instead of being straight.

waveband A **waveband** is a group of radio waves of similar frequency used for radio transmission.

wavelength A **wavelength** is the distance between the same point on consecutive cycles of a wave of energy such as light or sound. ■ A **wavelength** is the size of radio wave which a particular radio station uses to broadcast its programmes. ■ If two people are **on the same wavelength,** they share the same attitudes and get on well together.

waver (**wavering, wavered; waverer**) If you **waver,** you are uncertain and indecisive about something. People who cannot make up their minds about something are called **waverers.** ■ If something **wavers**, it shakes, moves, or changes very slightly. *His voice wavered.*

wavy (**wavier, waviest**) Wavy hair is not straight or curly, but curves slightly. ■ A **wavy** line has a series of regular curves along it.

wax (**waxes, waxing, waxed**) Wax is a solid, slightly shiny substance made of fat or oil and used to make candles and polish. ■ If you **wax** a surface, you spread a type of wax on it, to polish it. ■ If you have your legs **waxed,** you have the hair removed from your legs by having wax put on them and then pulled off quickly. ■ Wax is the sticky yellow substance found in your ears. ■ When the moon **waxes,** a larger area of brightness can be seen each night as it changes in its cycle from new moon to full moon. See also **wane.** ■ If something **waxes and wanes,** it increases and then decreases over a period of time. *Enthusiasm for croquet has waxed and waned over the years.* ■ **wax lyrical:** see **lyrical.**

waxen A **waxen** face is pale and unhealthy looking.

waxwork A **waxwork** is a model of a famous person, made out of wax. A **waxworks** (*plural:* **waxworks**) is a place where waxworks are on display.

way A **way** of doing something is a method by which it can be done. *Freezing isn't a bad way of preserving food.* ■ The **way** something is done is the manner in which it is done. *She smiled in a friendly way.* ■ The **way** you feel about something is your attitude to it or your opinion about it. ■ You use **way** to say something is true to a certain extent. *It's quite comforting in a way.* ■ You use **way** when talking about one of various possible decisions, positions, or directions. *If I were you, I wouldn't reveal which way you voted. ...a man wearing a baseball cap the wrong way round... A man coming the other way was shot dead.* ■ The **way** to a place is the route you take to get there. *...the quickest way to the bank.* If you **make your way** somewhere, you walk or travel there. ■ If you **lose your way,** you get lost. ■ If someone or something is **in the way,** they are blocking your path or stopping you doing something properly. ■ If one person or thing **makes way** for another, the first is replaced by the second. *At 37, he had to make way for younger people... She had no intention of abolishing the pound sterling to make way for a single currency.* ■ If something is **under way,** it has started. ■ You use **way** to talk about a person's or thing's progress. *Snead is the leader at the half-way stage... I am now out of hospital and well on the way to recovery... A long term solution is still some way off.* ■ If you **go out of your way** to do something, you make a special effort to do it. ■ **Way** is used when talking about distances. *Guntur is quite a way from the coast.* ■ You use **way** to emphasize that something is a great distance away, or very much below or above a certain level. *These exam results are way above average.* ■ If something is split a number of **ways,** it is divided into a number of parts or quantities, usually fairly equal in size. *There is a three-way split on the Conservative back benches over Europe.* ■ The **ways** of a person or group are their customs or usual behaviour. ■ If you have a **way** with people or things of a particular type, you are skilful at dealing with them. *He has a way with crowds.* ■ If someone or something **has a way of** doing a particular thing, they tend to do it. *Wars have a way of throwing up exceptional men and women.* ■ If you **get your own way,** you get what you want. ■ You say **by the way** when you are adding an extra piece of information. *It is, by the way, the largest show of Miró's sculpture ever staged.* ■ You use **in the way of** to say what kind of thing you are talking about. *Small companies are unlikely to offer much in the way of child-care facilities.*

waylay (waylaying, waylaid) If you are **waylaid** when you are on your way somewhere, you are stopped by someone.

way of life (ways of life) The **way of life** of a group of people is their typical behaviour and habits. ■ If you say a particular activity is **a way of life** for someone, you mean it has become a very important and regular feature of their life. *Smuggling is a way of life along this coastline.*

wayside things are by the side of a road. ■ If a person or plan **falls by the wayside,** they fail or stop before they complete what they set out to do. *Amateurs fall by the wayside when the going gets tough.*

wayward people are difficult to control and likely to change suddenly.

WC A **WC** is a toilet. WC stands for 'water closet'.

we is used to talk about a group of people which includes the person who is speaking or writing.

weak (weakly; weakness, weaknesses) If someone is **weak,** they do not have much strength, energy, or power. ■ A **weak** person is easily influenced by others. ■ If something like a blow or kick is **weak,** it is not powerful. ■ If something is **weak,** it is likely to break easily. ■ A **weak** argument is unconvincing and will not stand up to criticism. *...a weak excuse.* ■ A **weak** economy or currency is unsuccessful and unstable. ■ Your **weaknesses** or **weak points** are your faults or the things you are not very

good at. *I was weak in maths.* ■ If you have a **weakness** for something, you like it very much and find it hard to resist. ■ You say a drink like tea is **weak** when it contains very little tea in proportion to the amount of water in it.

weaken (weakening, weakened) If something **weakens,** it becomes less strong or powerful. *There will be no weakening in Western solidarity.* ■ If a person **weakens,** they become less able to resist something. ■ If a currency **weakens,** its value decreases in relation to other currencies.

weak-kneed If you call someone **weak-kneed,** you mean they lack courage and determination.

weakling A man or boy who is physically weak is sometimes called a **weakling.** ■ A person who gives in easily to other people can be called a **weakling.**

weal A **weal** is a swelling on someone's skin caused by a blow, often from something like a cane.

wealth is possessing money or other valuable things. ■ If you talk about a rich person's **wealth,** you mean the total value of everything they own. ■ If someone or something has a **wealth** of good features or qualities, they have a lot of them. *...a wealth of experience.*

wealthy (wealthier, wealthiest) A **wealthy** person has a lot of money or valuable possessions. Wealthy people are sometimes called **the wealthy.** ■ A **wealthy** area has a lot of rich people living in it. ■ A **wealthy** country has a large amount of financial and other resources, and its people have a high standard of living.

wean (weaning, weaned) When you **wean** a baby, you gradually start giving it solid food. ■ If you **wean** someone **off** something, you help them gradually give it up, often by replacing it with something else. *People can be weaned off cigarettes with nicotine chewing gum.*

weapon A **weapon** is an object like a gun, knife, or missile, used to kill or hurt people. ■ You can call something a **weapon** when you can use it to protect yourself or get what you want in a difficult situation. *Phone tapping is acknowledged as an effective weapon against serious crime.*

weaponry If you talk about a country's or group's **weaponry,** you mean all the weapons they have available to them.

wear (wearing, wore, have worn) When you **wear** things such as clothes or make-up, you have them on your body or face. ■ **Wear** is used to describe clothes suitable for particular occasions or activities. *...evening wear.* ■ If something **wears,** it gradually becomes thinner or weaker as a result of being used. You say something like this becomes **worn.** The damage is called **wear.** *...a large, well-upholstered armchair which showed signs of wear.* ■ If something is resistant to wear, you can say it **wears** well. ■ **Wear and tear** is the damage and gradual deterioration caused to something by normal use. ■ If something is **worn down,** it becomes flatter or smoother as a result of constantly rubbing against something else. ■ If something **wears out,** it becomes too old, weak, or damaged to be used any more. ■ If someone **wears** you **down,**

they gradually weaken your resistance to something. ■ If you find something **wearing**, it tires or irritates you. ■ If you say someone looks **worn**, you mean they look old and tired. ■ If something **wears you out**, it exhausts you. ■ If a feeling **wears off**, it gradually disappears. ■ You can talk about time **wearing on** when it seems to pass very slowly. *As Thursday morning wore on, the hotel foyer began to resemble a bazaar.*

wearable clothes are comfortable and practical.

wearer A **wearer** of something is a person who wears it. *...contact-lens wearers.*

wearisome If you call something **wearisome**, you mean it is tiring, boring, or frustrating.

weary (**wearier, weariest; wearily, weariness; wearies, wearying, wearied**) If you are **weary**, you are very tired. ■ If people are **weary** of something, they have had enough of it and wish it would end. You can also say people are **wearied** by something.

weasel — **Weasels** are small wild animals with long slender bodies, tails, short legs, and reddish-brown fur. They hunt creatures like mice and rabbits. ■ If you talk about people, especially politicians, using **weasel words**, you mean they are deliberately expressing themselves in an unclear way, to hide the truth about something or to avoid committing themselves.

weather (**weathering, weathered**) The **weather** is the day-to-day atmospheric conditions in a place, for example whether it is cloudy or hot. ■ If rock is **weathered**, it is worn down or broken up as a result of being exposed to things like hot sun, rain, or frost. ■ If you **weather** a difficult time or **weather a storm,** you get through it and are able to continue normally after it. ■ If you say someone is making **heavy weather** of a task, you mean they are handling it in an inefficient manner and making it seem more difficult than it really is.

weathercock A **weathercock** is a flat cockerel-shaped metal plate fixed to the roof of a tall building where it rotates and shows which way the wind is blowing.

weather forecast (**weather forecaster**) A **weather forecast** is details of what the weather will be like in the near future. Someone who studies the weather and predicts what it will be like is called a **weather forecaster.**

weatherproof (**weatherproofing, weatherproofed**) If something like a roof is **weatherproof**, it keeps out the wind and rain. If you **weatherproof** something, you make it weatherproof.

weather station A **weather station** is one of a network of observation posts where weather data is recorded.

weather vane See **vane.**

weave (**weaving, wove** or **weaved, have woven** or **have weaved**) When people **weave** cloth or a carpet, they make it by crossing threads over and under each other using a machine called a loom. ■ The **weave** of a cloth or carpet is the way the threads are arranged. ■ If someone **weaves** something like a basket, they make it by crossing long plant stems or fibres over and under each other. ■ If you **weave your way** somewhere, you move between and around things in order to get there. ■ If one thing is **woven** into another, it is added to it or combined with it, often in a complicated or creative way. *...the ability of electronics to weave together images, sound and information.*

weaver — **Weavers** are people who weave cloth or carpets.

web A **web** is a thin net made by a spider from a sticky substance which it produces in its body. ■ You can call a complicated pattern of connections or relationships a **web.** *He was at the centre of a web of 30 banks and advisers.* ■ The **Web** is the same as the **World-Wide Web.**

webbed Birds and animals with **webbed** feet have pieces of skin between their toes which make swimming easier.

webbing is strong material woven in strips and used to make things like straps.

website A **website** is a publication on the World Wide Web that contains information on a particular subject.

wed (**wedding, wed** or **wedded**) When two people **wed,** they get married. ■ If you are **wedded** to something like an idea, you are totally committed to it and unwilling to give it up.

wedding A **wedding** is a marriage ceremony and the party or special meal that follows it.

wedding ring A **wedding ring** is a plain ring you wear to show you are married.

wedge (**wedging, wedged**) If you **wedge** something, you keep it firmly in position by pushing something between it and the surface next to it, or by leaning something against it. *The door is wedged open by the pot plant.* ■ A **wedge** is an object with one pointed edge and one thick one, which you use for wedging things like doors open, or for splitting stone, slate, or wood. ■ A **wedge** is a piece of something that has a thick triangular shape. *...a wedge of cheese.* ■ If something is **wedged** somewhere, it is pushed there so it fits tightly. ■ A **wedge** is a type of golf club. ■ If something **drives a wedge** between people, it causes ill feeling between them and damages an otherwise good relationship. ■ If you call something **the thin end of the wedge**, you mean that although it may not seem significant in itself, it could lead to something extremely damaging or harmful.

wedlock is the state of being married.

wee means 'little'. *We've all been a wee bit hasty.*

weed (**weeding, weeded**) A **weed** is a wild plant growing where it is not wanted. If you **weed** an area of ground, you remove the weeds from it. ■ **Weed** is a flowerless plant which grows in water and usually forms a thick floating mass. There are many kinds of weed. ■ Tobacco and marijuana are sometimes called **weed.** ■ If you **weed out** unwanted people or things, you identify them and get rid of them.

weeder A **weeder** is a tool for removing weeds.

weedy If you call a person **weedy**, you mean they are thin and weak.

week A **week** is a period of seven days, especially one starting on a Sunday or Monday. ■ Your working **week** is the hours you spend at work each week. *Anthony works a six-day week.* ■ The **week** means the part of the week other than the weekend. *...looking after the children during the week.*

weekday A **weekday** is any day except Saturday and Sunday.

weekend The **weekend** is Saturday and Sunday.

weekender A **weekender** is someone who lives in a place only at weekends, especially a place they use as a second home in the country.

weekly (**weeklies**) **Weekly** is used to describe something which happens every week. *...a weekly column in The Guardian... Premiums can be paid weekly.* ■ A **weekly** is a newspaper or magazine which is published once a week.

weep (**weeping, wept; weepy, weepies**) If someone **weeps**, they cry. If they are **weepy**, they are sad and likely to cry at any moment. ■ Sad stories and music are sometimes called **weepies**, or described as **weepy**.

weevil – Weevils are small beetles which feed on grain and seeds and destroy crops.

weft The **weft** of a piece of woven material is the threads which are passed sideways in and out of the threads held in the loom. See also **warp.**

weigh If you **weigh** a person or object, you measure how heavy they are. You say an object or person **weighs** a certain amount. ■ If you **weigh** something **out,** you get a certain amount of it together, weighing it to make sure the amount is correct. ■ If you **weigh** the facts about a situation or **weigh** them **up,** you consider them carefully before making a decision. ■ If you **weigh** someone or something **up,** you consider them carefully and form an opinion about them. ■ If you are carrying something very heavy, especially on your back, you can say you are **weighed down** by it. ■ If you are **weighed down** by a difficulty or it is **weighing** on you, it is upsetting you or causing you great problems. ■ If you **weigh in** in a debate or competition, you join in enthusiastically. ■ **weigh anchor:** see **anchor.**

weigh-in The **weigh-in** before a boxing match or a horse race is a procedure in which the boxers or jockeys are weighed to check their weight.

weight (**weighting**) The **weight** of a person or thing is how heavy they are. ■ **Weights** are metal objects which weigh a known amount. They are used with scales to weigh things. People also lift weights as a form of exercise, to improve muscle performance. ■ You can call a heavy object a **weight,** especially when you have to lift it. ■ If you **weight** something or **weight** it **down,** you make it heavier, often to stop it moving. ■ A system which is **weighted** in favour of a person or group is organized to give them an advantage. ■ A **weighting** is a value given to something according to how important or significant it is. ■ The **weight** you give to something is the degree of importance you attach to it. *A Consumer Protection Commission would give more weight to environmental considerations.* ■ If you **pull your weight,** you work as hard as the other people working with you. ■ If you say someone is **throwing their weight about,** you mean they are using their strength or influence in a bullying way.

weightless (**weightlessness**) If something is **weightless,** it weighs nothing or seems to weigh nothing. You say people and objects are **weightless** when they are in space and the earth's gravity does not affect them, so they float around.

weight training is physical exercise which involves lifting weights to improve muscle performance.

weighty (**weightier, weightiest**) A **weighty** issue or debate is very serious or important. ■ You can call a heavy object **weighty.**

weir A **weir** is a low dam built across a river to control or direct the flow of water.

weird (**weirdly, weirdness**) If you say something is **weird,** you mean it is very odd and unusual. *...weirdly wonderful sculptures.* ■ If you say a person is **weird,** you mean they behave strangely. Similarly, you can say that a place is **weird**.

weirdo (*pron:* **weer**-doh) (**weirdos** *or* **weirdoes**) If you call someone a **weirdo,** you mean they behave strangely.

welcome (**welcoming, welcomed**) If you **welcome** someone or give them a **welcome,** you greet them in a friendly way when they arrive at the place where you are. ■ If you **make** someone **welcome** when they arrive in a new place, you make sure they have what they want and show you are pleased to see them. ■ If someone is **welcome** in a place, they can go there and people will be pleased to see them. ■ If you tell someone they are **welcome** to do something, you mean they can do it if they want to and you will be pleased if they do. ■ If you **welcome** something new, you approve of it and support it. You say something like this is **welcome.**

weld (**welder**) If you **weld** two pieces of metal together, you join them together using heat, pressure, or electricity. The join you make is called a **weld.** A **welder** is a person whose job is welding. ■ If you **weld** people into a group, you form them into a united organization.

welfare If you talk about a person's **welfare,** you mean their health and their ability to lead a contented life. You can also talk about the **welfare** of animals. *...the existing laws affecting animal welfare.* ■ **Welfare** is used to talk about services provided to help with people's living conditions and financial problems. *...welfare agencies.* ■ In the US, **welfare** is money paid by the government to people who are very poor.

welfare state A country's **welfare state** is the system in which its government uses money from taxes to provide things like health care, benefits, and pensions.

well If you do something **well,** you do it to a high standard. *He spoke English well.* ■ **Well** means 'thoroughly' or 'to a great extent'. *The process is not well understood.* ■ If something goes **well,** it happens in a successful or satisfactory way. ■ If you think or speak **well** of someone, you think or say good things about them. ■ If something **may well** happen, there is a good chance it will happen. ■ **As well as** means 'in addition to'. ■ **As well** means 'too' or 'also'. ■ If you say you **might as well** do something, you mean it would make no difference to the end result if you did it. ■ If you are **well**, you are in good health. ■ A **well** is a hole in the ground from which a supply of water is extracted. ■ If tears **well** or **well up**, they appear in someone's eyes. ■ If a feeling **wells** or **wells up** inside you, you start to feel it.

well-appointed A **well-appointed** room or building is equipped or furnished to a high standard.

well-balanced See **balance.**

well-behaved See **behave.**

well-being Your **well-being** is your health and happiness.

well-bred Upper-class people are sometimes described as **well-bred.**

well-built A **well-built** man is strong and muscular.

well-connected If someone is **well-connected,** they have important or influential relatives or friends.

well-dressed A **well-dressed** person is wearing smart or elegant clothes.

well-earned See **earn.**

well-educated See **educate.**

well-established If something is **well-established,** it has existed for a long time and is successful.

well-fed If someone is **well-fed,** they get plenty of good food.

well-founded See **found.**

well-groomed See **groom.**

well-grounded See **ground.**

well-heeled If someone is **well-heeled,** they are wealthy.

well-informed If someone is **well-informed,** they know a lot about a subject or situation.

wellington – **Wellingtons** are long rubber boots you wear to keep your feet dry.

well-intentioned means the same as 'well-meaning'.

well-known If a fact is **well-known,** a lot of people know it. ■ A **well-known** person or thing is known about by a lot of people, and so is famous or familiar.

well-mannered See **manner.**

well-meaning (**well-meant**) You say someone is **well-meaning** when they try to be kind or helpful but things do not work out the way they intend. You can also say what they do is **well-meaning** or **well-meant.**

well-nigh See **nigh.**

well-off If someone is **well-off,** they are wealthy.

well-preserved If something old is **well-preserved,** it does not show many signs of its age.

well-read A **well-read** person has read a lot of books and learned a lot from them.

well-received If something is **well-received,** people react favourably to it.

well-spoken A **well-spoken** person speaks in a polite correct way and with an accent considered socially acceptable.

well-thought-of If someone is **well-thought-of,** they are admired and respected, and have a good reputation.

well-thumbed A **well-thumbed** book or magazine is creased and marked because it has been read so often.

well-timed A **well-timed** action or comment is done or made at the most appropriate or suitable time.

well-to-do means the same as 'well-off'.

well-tried If something is **well-tried,** it has been used or done many times before and is known to work well or to be successful.

well-versed See **versed.**

well-wisher A **well-wisher** is someone who expresses their good wishes or support for a person or cause. *Gifts from well-wishers arrive daily.*

well-worn A **well-worn** expression or remark has been used so often it has lost much of its meaning or impact. ■ A **well-worn** object or piece of clothing has been used so much that it looks old and untidy.

welly (**wellies**) **Wellies** are the same as wellingtons.

Welsh is used to talk about people and things in or from Wales. *...a small Welsh town.* ■ **Welsh** is a language spoken by many people in Wales.

Welshman (**Welshwoman**) A **Welshman** is a man who comes from Wales.

Welsh rarebit or **Welsh rabbit** is melted seasoned cheese on hot buttered toast.

welt A **welt** is a mark on someone's skin, usually caused by a blow from a whip or stick. ■ A **welt** is a strengthened seam or edge sewn onto a garment. ■ The **welt** of a shoe is the leather strip between the sole and the upper part.

welter A **welter** of things is a large number of them jumbled together.

wench (**wenches**) **Wench** is an old word for a woman or girl, especially a servant.

wend If you **wend** your way somewhere, you go there slowly.

went See **go.**

wept See **weep.**

were See **be.**

werewolf (**werewolves**) In ancient folklore, a **werewolf** was a person who sometimes changed into a wolf.

west (**western**) **West** is one of the four main points of the compass. ■ The **west** is the direction where the sun sets. If you go in that direction, you go **west**; a place in that direction is **west of** the place where you are now. ■ The **west** or **western** part of a place is the part west of its centre. *...the West Midlands.* ■ **West** winds blow from the west. ■ The **West** is used to talk about the US, Canada, and Western and Southern Europe. *He wants the West to recognize his country.* ■ A **western** is a film or book about life in the west of America in the 19th century. ■ See also **Wild West.** ■ If you say that something has **gone west,** you mean it has been destroyed or is lost for good.

westbound traffic is heading towards the west.

westerly winds blow from the west. ■ If you travel or face in a **westerly** direction, you travel or face towards the west. ■ The most **westerly** part of a place is the part furthest to the west. Similarly, the most **westerly** place of a group of places is the one furthest to the west

western See **west.**

westerner A **westerner** is a person who was born in or lives in (a) the western part of a country or region. (b) the US, Canada, or Western or Southern Europe.

westernized (or **westernised**) (**westernization**) A **westernized** place or person has adopted the ideas and behaviour typical of Western Europe or North America, rather than retain their traditional identity. ...*fundamentalists unhappy with the Westernization of Afghan culture.*

westernmost The **westernmost** part of a place is the part furthest to the west.

Westminster is the area in London where the Houses of Parliament are. **Westminster** is also used to talk about parliament itself.

westward (**westwards**) If you go **westward** or **westwards,** you go towards the west.

wet (**wetter, wettest; wetness; wetting, wet** or **wetted**) If a something is **wet,** it is covered in or soaked with a liquid. ■ If something like paint, ink, or cement is **wet,** it is not yet dry or solid. ■ If you **wet** something, you pour or sprinkle liquid on it. ■ If the weather is **wet,** it is raining. ■ If people **wet** themselves or their bed, they urinate in their clothes or bed because they cannot control their bladder. ■ **Wet fish** is fresh fish, rather than salted or dried fish. ■ If you say someone is **wet,** you mean they are weak and lack confidence, energy, or enthusiasm. ■ A **Wet** is a Conservative politician who supports moderate political positions.

wet nurse In the past, a **wet nurse** was a woman who was paid to breast-feed another woman's baby.

wet suit (or **wetsuit**) A **wet suit** is a close-fitting rubber suit worn by people like divers to keep them warm in the water.

whack If you **whack** someone or something or give them a **whack,** you hit them hard. ■ A **whack** of something is a share of it. ...*a fair tax system which makes the super rich pay their whack.*

whacky See **wacky.**

whale (**whaling, whaler**) **Whales** are the largest sea mammals. Hunting whales is called **whaling.** It is done in special ships called **whalers;** the people who work on these ships are also called **whalers.**

whalebone is a hard substance taken from the mouth of a whale. It was used in the past for stiffening cloth, especially in corsets.

whammy See **double whammy.**

wharf (**wharves**) A **wharf** is a platform built by a river or the sea, where ships can be tied up for loading and unloading.

what You use **what** in various ways to refer to, or ask questions about, a specific thing. *I didn't know what to do... What are you going to do next?* ■ You use **what** with 'for' to ask about the purpose of something. *Just what is a car for?* ■ You say **what about...** when you are drawing someone's attention to something. *It does seem as if the climate is changing, but what about carbon dioxide levels?* ■ You say **what if...** when you are asking about the con-

sequences of something. *What if the train breaks down?* ■ You say **what** instead of 'the thing that', 'the amount that', etc. *Their assets are now worth less than what fund managers paid for them.* ■ You can say **what** instead of 'whatever'. *He can do what he wants.* ■ You use **what** to express your opinion of something. *What a pity!*

whatever You use **whatever** to talk about anything or everything of a particular kind. *Western nations will continue to scramble for whatever crude oil is available.* ■ You use **whatever** to talk about something you cannot be specific about. *She is the opposite of a pacifist, whatever that is.* ■ You use **whatever** or **whatsoever** with words like 'no' or 'nothing', for emphasis. ...*medical information which the patient has no right whatever to see.* ■ You say **whatever** instead of 'what' when you are asking about something in an emphatic way. *Whatever happened to her?*

whatnot You say **and whatnot** after a list to show there are other things you have not mentioned. *Rabbits can soon damage your crops and your sugar beet and whatnot.*

whatsoever See **whatever.**

wheat is a cereal grown for its grain, which is used to make flour. ■ **separate the wheat from the chaff:** see **chaff.**

wheatgerm is the vitamin-rich middle part of a grain of wheat.

wheatmeal is a brown flour made from wheat grains, including some of the husks.

wheedle (**wheedling, wheedled**) If someone **wheedles** you into doing something, they cleverly persuade or flatter you to do it. You can also say someone **wheedles** you out of something or **wheedles** their way somewhere. ■ If you **wheedle** something out of someone, you persuade them to give it to you.

wheel (**wheeling, wheeled; -wheel, -wheeled**) A **wheel** is a circular object, which turns on a rod in its centre. Wheels are fixed underneath vehicles so they can move along. **-wheeled** is used to say how many wheels a vehicle has. ...*a four-wheeled buggy.* ■ **-wheel** is used to say how a car is powered. For example, in a **front-wheel** drive car, the engine's power goes to the front wheels. See also **four-wheel drive.** ■ The **wheel** of a car or ship is its steering equipment. ■ If you **wheel** something like a bike or cart, you push it along. Similarly, you can **wheel** an object in a cart, or **wheel** a person in a wheelchair. ■ You say birds **wheel** when they fly round in large circles. ...*wheeling cormorants.* ■ **Wheeling and dealing** is using a variety of methods to get what you want, some of which are dishonest or illegal. A politician or businessman who behaves like this is called a **wheeler-dealer.**

wheelbarrow A **wheelbarrow** is a small cart with handles and one wheel, used for moving small loads on a building site or in a garden.

wheelbase The **wheelbase** of a vehicle is the distance between its front and back axles.

wheelchair A **wheelchair** is a chair on wheels which sick or disabled people use to move about in.

wheel clamp (**wheel clamping**) A **wheel clamp** is an immobilizing device fitted to one wheel of an illegally parked vehicle. Fitting a wheel clamp to a vehicle is called **wheel clamping.**

wheeler-dealer See **wheel.**

wheelhouse The **wheelhouse** on a boat is a small room or shelter above the level of the deck, where the wheel for steering is located.

wheelspin is what happens when a vehicle's wheels turn round but cannot get a grip on the road surface.

wheeze (**wheezing, wheezed**) If you **wheeze,** you breathe with difficulty, making a hissing or whistling sound.

whelk – **Whelks** are edible snail-like shellfish.

whelp A **whelp** is the young offspring of an animal, especially a dog or wolf.

when You use **when** to ask about the time of something, or to mention the time at which something happens. *When did you come back from Zambia?... His mother had died when he was a baby.* ■ You use **when** to state the reason for an opinion or question. *How can you enjoy conducting when it is such a responsibility?* ■ You use **when** to mean 'although'. *He was attempting to give the impression that there had been no change of policy, when in fact there had been.*

whence is an old word for 'from where'.

whenever You use **whenever** to say something always happens in certain circumstances. *The park is closed whenever filming is in progress.* ■ You use **whenever** to talk about an unknown time. *The general election, whenever it comes, looks like being very close.*

where You use **where** to ask about the location or destination of something, or about the place it comes from. *Where do you live?... He asked her where she wanted to go.* ■ You use **where** when you are talking about a situation, or a stage in something. *Asthma is increasing to a point where there will be three asthmatic children in every primary school class.* ■ **Where** is sometimes used to mean 'whereas'. *Sometimes a teacher will be listened to, where a parent might not.*

whereabouts A person's or thing's **whereabouts** is the place where they are. *There has been no word of his whereabouts.* ■ You use **whereabouts** to ask precisely where someone or something is. *Whereabouts in Liverpool are you from?*

whereas You say **whereas** when you are mentioning two contrasting facts. *The Ferrari did not fail, whereas my Lotus did.*

whereby means 'by which' when you are saying how something is achieved or made possible. *...a gradual retirement whereby a person works progressively fewer hours or days per week.*

wherefore See **why.**

wherein means 'in which'. *...a programme wherein children raise seedlings in the schools.*

whereupon is used to say something happened immediately after something else. *His enemies rejected his message, whereupon he tried again, offering to call off his war preparations in exchange for an amnesty for his supporters.*

wherever You use **wherever** to say something always happens or is always true in any place or situation. *Demonstrators howl abuse at the prime min-*

ister wherever he goes. ■ You use **wherever** to say someone can do something in any place they want to. *All citizens who met the legal requirements were free to travel abroad and settle wherever they chose.* ■ You use **wherever** to show you do not know where a place or person is. *They have been sent back to Germany or Belgium or wherever they came from.*

wherewithal is the money or resources needed to do something. *Japan has the financial wherewithal to provide much-needed assistance to Cambodia.*

whet (**whetting, whetted**) If something **whets** your appetite for something, it increases your desire for it. ■ If you **whet** a blade, you sharpen it.

whether You use **whether** when you are mentioning two or more alternatives. *He was unsure whether the others had been shot or arrested... He could not decide whether he wanted to move north.*

whetstone A **whetstone** is a stone for sharpening blades.

whey (*pron:* **way**) is the watery liquid which is separated from the curds in sour milk when cheese is made.

which You use **which** to ask questions when there are two or more possible answers or alternatives. *Which cake would you like?* **Which** is used in various other ways to talk about a choice between possible answers and alternatives. *...differences in the government over which way to proceed.* ■ You use **which** when you are adding an extra piece of information. *The bill, which has government support, is likely to become law.* ■ You use **which** to refer back to what you have just said. *The scan was clear, which is good news.*

whichever You use **whichever** to say something is unaffected by which of a number of possible things happens or is chosen. *The benefits from immunisation, whichever vaccine is used, are overwhelming.* ■ You use **whichever** to talk about the most appropriate one of a number of possibilities. *The recipe can be varied to use whichever vegetables take your fancy.*

whiff A **whiff** of something is a faint smell, sign, or trace of it. *...the familiar whiff of garlic.*

while (**whiling, whiled; whilst**) If something happens **while** or **whilst** something else is happening, it happens throughout the time the second thing is happening, or at some point during it. ■ A **while** is a period of time. *...something I've not done in a long while.* ■ If something happens **all the while**, it happens all the time, or throughout the time something else is happening. ■ **While** and **whilst** are used to mean 'whereas' or 'although'. *Whilst academic excellence is admirable, it is useless without maturity.* ■ If you **while away** the time in a particular way, you spend it that way because you are waiting for something or because you have nothing to do. ■ **worth your while:** see **worth.**

whilst See **while.**

whim A **whim** is a sudden desire to do or have something.

whimper (**whimpering, whimpered**) When children or animals **whimper,** they make little low unhappy sounds. You call these sounds **whimpers.** ■ If something ends with a **whimper,** it ends in a quiet unnoticed way.

whimsical (**whimsically, whimsy**) If something like a piece of writing is **whimsical,** it is amusing in a quaint or playful way, and is not trying to make a serious point. Playful humour of this kind is called **whimsy.**

whine (**whining, whined**) If something **whines,** it makes a long high-pitched noise. A noise like this is called a **whine.** ■ If someone **whines** about something, they complain about it in an annoying way.

whinge (**whingeing, whinged; whinger**) If someone **whinges** about something, they complain about it in an irritating way. People who behave like this are called **whingers.**

whinny (**whinnies, whinnying, whinnied**) When a horse **whinnies,** it neighs softly.

whip (**whipping, whipped**) A **whip** is a piece of leather or rope attached to a handle and used for hitting people or animals. If someone **whips** a person or animal, they hit them with a whip. ■ If you have the **whip hand** over someone, you have power over them or an advantage over them. ■ If you get a **fair crack of the whip,** you are allowed a reasonable opportunity to do something. ■ If you **whip** cream or eggs, you beat them quickly to make them thick and frothy. ■ If something **whips** somewhere, it moves there very quickly. ■ If you **whip** something **out,** you take it out quickly and suddenly. If you **whip off** your clothes, you quickly take them off. ■ If someone **whips up** a strong emotion, they deliberately make people feel it. *...a campaign designed to whip up terror ahead of the elections.* ■ In parliament, a **whip** is a member of a political party who is responsible for making sure members are there to vote on important issues.

whiplash (**whiplashes**) A **whiplash** is a blow with a whip. ■ A **whiplash injury** is a neck injury caused by someone's head suddenly jerking backwards and forwards.

whippet – **Whippets** are thin dogs which look like small greyhounds.

whipping boy When someone is made the **whipping boy,** they are blamed for something which has gone wrong, although it may not be their fault.

whipping cream is cream which becomes stiff when it is whipped.

whip-round If a group of people have a **whip-round,** money is collected from each person to buy something.

whir See **whirr.**

whirl If something **whirls** or if you **whirl** it round, it turns round quickly. ■ You can call a lot of intense activity a **whirl** of activity. *...the hectic whirl of interviews.* ■ If you **give** something **a whirl,** you try it.

whirlpool A **whirlpool** is a small area in a river or the sea where the water moves quickly round and round, so that objects which are floating near it are pulled into its centre. ■ A **whirlpool bath** is the same as a Jacuzzi.

whirlwind A **whirlwind** is a moving column of air which spins round and round very rapidly. ■ A situation in which there is a lot of frantic activity can be called a **whirlwind.** *...a whirlwind of deals.* ■ A **whirlwind** event happens much more quickly than usual. *...a whirlwind romance.*

whirr (or **whir**) (**whirring, whirred**) If something **whirrs,** it makes a low buzzing sound. A noise like this is called a **whirr.**

whisk If you **whisk** someone or something somewhere, you take them there quickly. ■ If you **whisk** eggs or cream, you stir air into them quickly with a device called a **whisk.**

whisker (**whiskered, whiskery**) The **whiskers** of an animal like a cat or mouse are the long stiff hairs growing near its mouth. ■ You can call the hair on a man's face, especially on his cheeks, his **whiskers.** If a man has hair like this, you can say he is **whiskered** or **whiskery.** ■ A **whisker** is a very small amount. *He escaped serious injury by a whisker.*

whiskey is the usual Irish and American spelling of 'whisky'.

whisky (**whiskies**) **Whisky** is a strong alcoholic drink made from barley or rye.

whisper (**whispering, whispered**) If you **whisper** something or say it in a **whisper,** you say it very quietly, using only your breath and not your voice. ■ You say people **whisper** when they talk about something secretly among themselves. A **whisper** is a rumour. *Ministers began to whisper that he would be sacked.* A **whispering campaign** is a deliberate attempt to discredit someone by spreading rumours about them. ■ You say trees **whisper** when they make a low quiet sound as the wind passes through their branches.

whist is a card game in which two people play against two other people. A **whist drive** is a social event where whist is played by several people.

whistle (**whistling, whistled**) If you **whistle** or let out a **whistle,** you form a small 'o' with your lips and force your breath out, making a high-pitched sound. By adjusting your lips, you can **whistle** a tune. ■ You say you **whistle** when you make a high shrill sound by forcing your breath out between your teeth and two fingers. A sound like this is called a **whistle.** ■ A **whistle** is a small metal tube you blow in to produce a whistling sound. ■ If you **blow the whistle** on someone, you tell someone in authority about something illegal or secret they are doing. A person who does this is called a **whistle-blower.** ■ If something **whistles,** it makes a loud high sound. *...a whistling kettle.*

whistle-stop If a politician makes a **whistle-stop** tour, he or she travels around calling briefly at several places as part of a political campaign.

whit A **whit** is a very small amount. **Whit** is often used with 'not' to emphasize that something is not the case at all. *My strategy hasn't changed one whit.* ■ **Whit** is the same as Whitsun.

white (**whiter, whiteness**) **White** is the colour of snow or milk. *...the whiteness of her teeth.* ■ A **white** person belongs to a race of people with pale skins. ■ **White** coffee or tea has milk or cream in it. ■ **White** wine is a pale yellowish colour. ■ **White** meat is meat like chicken which is pale in colour after it has been cooked. ■ The **white** of an egg is the transparent liquid surrounding the yolk, which turns white when cooked. ■ A **white lie** is a harmless one, told to avoid hurting someone's feelings. ■ **white elephant:** see **elephant. white knuckle:** see **knuckle.**

whitebait are very small young herrings or sprats, usually eaten fried.

white-collar workers work in offices rather than doing manual work. See also **blue-collar.**

white goods are large domestic appliances like fridges and cookers.

Whitehall is a street in an area of London where there are many government offices. **Whitehall** is often used to talk about the Civil Service, or about the Government itself.

white-hot If something is **white-hot,** it is extremely hot.

White House The **White House** is the official home of the US President. You can use the **White House** to refer to the President and his staff.

white light is the technical term for ordinary daylight, which contains all the wavelengths of the spectrum.

whiten (**whitening, whitened**) If something **whitens,** it becomes whiter or paler.

white noise is a sound with an equal amount of power at all its frequencies, for example the sound a radio makes when it is not tuned in.

white paper A **white paper** is an official government report, giving the government's policy on a particular matter.

white spirit is a colourless liquid made from petrol and used, for example, to thin paint or to clean paintbrushes.

whitewash (**whitewashes, whitewashing, whitewashed**) Whitewash is a mixture of water and lime or chalk, used for painting walls white. A **whitewashed** wall has been painted with whitewash. ■ If you say that people **whitewash** something, you are accusing them of hiding the unpleasant facts or truth about it, to make it acceptable. You call this a **whitewash.** *He dismissed the government's inquiry into those events as a whitewash.* ■ In sport, if a team or player suffers a **whitewash,** they are beaten without managing to get any points.

white water is a stretch of fast-flowing water with a broken foamy surface, for example rapids. **Whitewater** sports take place in or on water like this.

white wedding A **white wedding** is a wedding where the bride wears white and the ceremony takes place in a church.

whither is an old-fashioned word meaning 'to which place'.

whiting (*plural:* **whiting**) Whiting are a kind of sea fish related to cod.

Whitsun is the seventh Sunday after Easter, and the week following it.

whittle (**whittling, whittled**) If something is **whittled down** or **whittled away,** it is slowly made smaller or less effective. ■ If you **whittle** wood, you carve it into a particular shape, using a small knife.

whizz (*or* **whiz**) (**whizzes, whizzing, whizzed**) If someone or something **whizzes** somewhere, they move there very quickly. ■ If you are a **whizz** at something, you are very good at it.

whizz-kid (*or* **whiz-kid** *or* **whizzkid**) A **whizz-kid** is someone who is outstandingly successful in their career at an early age.

WHO See **World Health Organization.**

who You use **who** to ask about someone's name or identity. *Who is to blame for all this?* You use **who** in various other ways to talk about someone's identity. *We know who he is.* ■ You use **who** to say which person or people you are talking about, or to give more information about them. *She is waiting to join her family who have emigrated to Canada.*

whodunit (*or* **whodunnit**) A **whodunit** is a book, film, or play about a murder, in which the identity of the murderer is not revealed until the end.

whoever You use **whoever** to talk about any person or every person of a particular kind. *He can talk to whoever he wants.* ■ You use **whoever** to talk about someone whose identity is not known. *Whoever did this will sooner or later be caught.* ■ You use **whoever** to show that the identity of the person who does something will not affect a situation. *Whoever takes over the leadership will have little room for manoeuvre.*

whole (**wholeness**) The **whole** of something is all of it. ■ A **whole** is a single thing which contains several different parts. *The group's various businesses do not yet form a coherent whole.* You talk about the **wholeness** of something when all its parts or elements seem to belong together. *...the wholeness of human experience.* ■ **Whole** is used to mean 'in one piece'. *Onions can be roasted whole.* ■ You use **as a whole** to emphasize you are talking about all of something. *He described the move as a victory for the people of South Africa as a whole.* ■ You say **on the whole** to show that what you are saying is true in general, but not in every detail. *We know that women are on the whole having their children much later.*

wholefood – **Wholefoods** are foods which have been refined as little as possible, do not contain additives, and are eaten in their natural state.

wholehearted (*or* **whole-hearted**) (**wholeheartedly**) If you support something or agree to something in a **wholehearted** way, you do it enthusiastically and completely.

wholemeal flour or bread is made from the complete grains of the wheat plant, including the husks.

whole number A **whole number** is a number such as 7 or 24, rather than a fraction.

wholesale (**wholesaling, wholesaler**) Wholesale is the activity of buying goods cheaply in large quantities and selling them again, especially to shops. This activity is called **wholesaling;** someone who does it is called a **wholesaler.** ■ **Wholesale** is used to talk about something undesirable which is done or happens to an excessive extent. *...a wholesale collapse among small independent travel companies.*

wholesome (**wholesomeness**) If you describe something as **wholesome,** you mean it is likely to have a good influence on people's behaviour or mental state, especially because it does not involve anything sexually immoral. ■ **Wholesome** food is good for you.

wholly means 'completely'.

whom You use **whom** to ask about someone's name or identity. *Whom do we blame?* ■ You use **whom** to say which person or people you are talking about, or to give more information about them. *...a baby sister whom they all adored.*

whomever (*or* **whomsoever**) is used to talk about any person or every person of a particular kind. *They have the right to appoint whomever they choose.*

whoop (**whooping, whooped**) If you **whoop** or let out a **whoop**, you shout loudly in a happy or excited way.

whooping cough is a serious infectious disease which makes people cough and produce a loud noise when they breathe in.

whoosh (**whooshes, whooshing, whooshed**) If something **whooshes** somewhere, it moves there quickly with a sound of rushing wind. You call a noise like this a **whoosh.**

whopping (**whopper**) If you say something is **whopping** or a **whopper**, you mean it is unusually large. ■ A **whopper** is a lie.

whore (*pron:* **hore**) A **whore** is a prostitute.

whorehouse A **whorehouse** is a brothel.

who's is short for 'who is' or 'who has'.

whose You use **whose** to say something belongs or relates to the person or thing you have just mentioned. *...a scientist whose judgment is well respected.* You also use **whose** to ask who something belongs or relates to. *Whose fault is it?* You use **whose** in various other ways to talk about something belonging or relating to someone. *It's not known on whose initiative this meeting was called.*

whosoever means the same as 'whoever'.

why You use **why** to ask about the reason for something. *I asked him why he wrote the book.* You use **why** in various other ways to talk about the reason for something. *That is why unemployment is still high.* ■ You say **why not...** when you are making a suggestion. *Why not phase out export subsidies?* ■ The **whys and wherefores** are the reasons why certain things happen or are done. *The booklet helps to explain the whys and wherefores of will-making.*

wick The **wick** of a candle is the piece of string down the middle, which burns when it is lit. ■ The **wick** of a paraffin lamp or cigarette lighter is the part which supplies the fuel to the flame.

wicked (**wickedly, wickedness**) You use **wicked** to describe someone or something that is very bad in a way which is deliberately harmful to people. ■ If you describe someone or something as **wicked**, you mean they are mischievous in an amusing or attractive way. *...a wicked sense of humour.*

wicker or **wickerwork** objects are made from interwoven twigs or cane.

wicket In cricket, the **wicket** is one of the two sets of stumps and bails which the ball is bowled at. The area between the wickets is also called the **wicket.**

wicketkeeper In cricket, the **wicketkeeper** is the fielder who stands behind the wicket.

wide (**wider, widest; widely, -wide**) If something is **wide**, it measures a large distance from one side to the other. ■ **Wide** is used when mentioning the width of something. *The tunnel is twenty metres wide.* ■ If you open or spread something **wide,** you open or spread it as far as it will go. ■ A **wide** range of people or things is more extensive than usual. ■ **Wide** is used to describe something which is available to many people, or felt or known about by many people. *His work is now widely available in translation. ...widely-held fears... The case has attracted wide publicity.* ■ **-wide** is added to words to describe things which happen or exist throughout the whole of an area. *...a nation-wide strike.* ■ The **wider** aspects of a situation are the more general ones. *...the wider implications of her decision.* ■ If something like a shot goes **wide,** it misses the desired point.

wide-angle A **wide-angle** lens is a camera lens which allows you to photograph a wider view than a normal lens.

wide-eyed If someone is **wide-eyed,** their eyes are wider open than usual. ■ If you describe someone as **wide-eyed,** you mean they seem innocent and inexperienced.

widen (**widening, widened**) If something **widens,** (a) it gets wider. (b) it becomes greater in range, size, or variety, or affects a larger number of people or things. *The scope of the investigation continues to widen.*

wide-ranging If something is **wide-ranging,** it includes or deals with a great variety of different things. *...wide-ranging economic and agricultural reforms.*

widescreen is a type of film projection in which the picture is much wider than usual in proportion to its height.

widespread If something is **widespread,** it exists or happens over a large area or to a very great extent.

widget A **widget** is a plastic disc in a can of beer used to make the beer taste like draught beer. 'Widget' is a trademark. ■ You can refer to any small device as a **widget** when you do not know exactly what it is or how it works.

widow (**widower, widowed**) A **widow** is a woman whose husband has died and who has not remarried. A **widower** is a man whose wife has died and who has not remarried. A **widowed** person is someone whose husband or wife has died.

widowhood is the state of being a widow or the period of time when a woman is a widow.

width The **width** of something is the distance from one side of it to the other.

wield If someone **wields** power or influence, they have it and are able to use it. ■ If you **wield** a weapon or tool, you carry it or use it.

wife (**wives; wifely**) A man's **wife** is the woman he is married to. **Wifely** is used to describe things supposed to be typical of a good wife. *...wifely devotion.*

wig A **wig** is a false head of hair worn to cover someone's own hair or to hide baldness.

wiggle (**wiggling, wiggled**) If you **wiggle** something, you make it move around with small quick movements. Movements like these are called **wiggles.**

wigwam A **wigwam** is a cone-shaped tent traditionally made by Native American peoples, and consisting of bark or skins stretched over an arched framework of poles lashed together.

wild (**wildly, wildness**) **Wild** animals and birds live in natural surroundings and are not kept as pets or as farm animals. You say animals and birds like these live **in the wild. ■ Wild** plants grow naturally and are not specially grown as crops. **■ Wild** land is natural and uncultivated. **■** Remote areas, far away from towns, are sometimes called **the wilds. ■ Wild** is used to describe the weather or the sea when it is very stormy. ...*a wild October night.* **■ Wild** behaviour is excited and uncontrolled. *The crowd went wild with anger... He swung his boot wildly at the ball.* **■** If you say a comment is **wild,** you mean it is not based on reliable information or sound reasoning. *Rumours about payments are wildly exaggerated.* **■** If things vary **wildly,** they are very different from each other.

wild card In a sports contest, a **wild card** is a player or team allowed to take part although they have not qualified for it in the usual way. **■** If you refer to someone or something as a **wild card** in a particular situation, you mean they cause uncertainty because they are unpredictable.

wildcat The **wildcat** is a type of cat which lives in mountains and forests and looks like a larger version of the domestic cat. **■** A **wildcat** strike happens suddenly and without the official approval of the union. ...*unlawful wildcat action.*

wildebeest (*plural:* **wildebeest**) (*pron:* **wil**-di-beest) A **wildebeest** is the same as a gnu.

wilderness (**wildernesses**) A **wilderness** is an area of uncultivated natural land. **■** If a politician spends some time **in the wilderness,** he or she is not in an influential position in politics for that time.

wildfire If something spreads like **wildfire,** it spreads very quickly.

wildfowl are birds like wild duck, pheasants, and quails which are hunted and shot.

wild-goose chase If you are on a **wild-goose chase,** you waste a lot of time searching for something which you have little chance of finding because you have been given misleading information.

wildlife Wild animals and plants are sometimes called **wildlife.**

Wild West The **Wild West** is used to refer to the western part of the US during the time when it was first settled by Europeans.

wiles are the clever tricks which people use to persuade other people to do something.

wilful (*Am:* **willful**) (**wilfully, wilfulness**) **Wilful** is used to describe bad or harmful actions which are done deliberately. *The Front has wilfully perverted democracy.* **■** A **wilful** person is obstinate and determined to get what they want.

will (**-willed**) In spoken and informal written English, the form **won't** is often used in negative statements. **■** If you say something **will** happen, you mean it is going to happen. **■** If you say you **will** do something, you mean you intend to do it. **■** You use **will** to say you are willing to do something, or to ask someone if they are willing to do something. *We will accept personal or company cheques... Will you marry me?* **■** The **will** to do something is the determination to do it. **-willed** is used to describe the extent of someone's determination. *He's a strong-willed chap.* **■** If something is the **will** of a person or group, they want it to happen. *I have to bow to the will of the people.* **■** If you can do something **at will,** you can do it whenever you want to. **■** If you do something **with a will,** you do it with a lot of enthusiasm and energy. **■** If you **will** something to happen, you try to make it happen using mental effort. *I was amazed to find myself willing him to win.* **■** A **will** is a legal document saying what you want to happen to your money and property when you die.

willing (**willingly, willingness**) If someone is **willing** to do something or does something **willingly** (a) they do not mind doing it or have no objection to doing it. (b) they do it eagerly and enthusiastically, rather than because they are made to.

willow The **willow** is a tree with long thin branches and narrow leaves which often grows near water. Its wood is used for making baskets and cricket bats.

willowy people are tall and thin.

willpower (*or* **will-power**) is very strong determination to do something.

willy-nilly If someone does something **willy-nilly,** they do it in a careless and haphazard way. *Clerks bundled papers into files willy-nilly.* **■** If something happens to you **willy-nilly,** it happens whether you like it or not.

wilt If a plant **wilts,** it gradually bends downwards and becomes weak, because it needs more water or is dying. **■** If you **wilt,** you become weak and tired or lose confidence.

wily (**wilier, wiliest**) **Wily** people are clever and cunning.

wimp (**wimpish, wimpishness**) If you call someone a **wimp,** you mean they are feeble and timid.

wimple A **wimple** is a cloth wrapped round a woman's head so that only her face is showing. Wimples were worn in medieval times and are still worn by some nuns.

win (**winning, won**) If you **win** a fight, game, or argument, you defeat your opponent. **■ win the day:** see **day. ■** A **win** is a victory in a game or competition. **■** If you **win out** in a contest, you are the one who eventually wins. Similarly, you can say something like a course of action **wins out** when it is eventually chosen in preference to others. **■** If you **win** something like a medal or a prize, you are presented with it, because you are one of the most successful people in a competition or in some other activity. ...*an award-winning novelist.* You can also say an achievement **wins** you a medal or a prize. *His side's flying start won him the Manager of the Month award.* **■** If you **win** praise for something you do, people praise you for it. **■** If you **win** something you want, you succeed in getting it. *The scheme failed to win the trust of local farmers.* **■** If you **win** someone **over** or **win** them **round,** you persuade them to support you or agree with you.

wince (**wincing, winced**) If you **wince** or give a **wince,** the muscles in your face tighten suddenly, for instance because you are in pain.

winch (**winches, winching, winched**) A **winch** is a machine for lifting heavy objects. It consists of a cylinder which a rope or chain is wound around. If you **winch** an object or person somewhere, you lift them using a winch.

wind A **wind** is a current of air moving across the earth's surface. ■ If you **get wind** of something, you get to hear about it. ■ If you are **winded** by something like a punch, air is suddenly knocked out of your lungs and you have difficulty breathing. ■ If you get a **second wind,** you find more energy to continue doing something after being tired or out of breath. ■ **Wind** instruments are instruments you play using your breath, for example the flute.

wind (*pron:* rhymes with 'mind') (**winding, wound**) ■ If a road or river **winds** somewhere, it goes in that direction with many bends or turns along the way. Similarly, you can talk about a line of people **winding** somewhere. *...the procession of floats winding its way through the crowded streets.* ■ When you **wind** something round something else, you wrap it round it several times. ■ If you **wind up** a mechanical device like a clock, you turn a knob or key several times to make it operate. ■ If you **wind down** a car window, you open it by turning a handle. If you **wind** it **up,** you close it. ■ When a business is **wound up,** it stops trading and is closed down. ■ If an activity is **wound down,** the amount of work done is gradually reduced until it stops completely. ■ If you **wind up** in a certain place or situation, you end up in it, often unexpectedly. ■ If you are **wound up** about something, you are tense or excited about it. ■ If you **wind** someone **up,** you deliberately annoy or tease them. ■ If you **wind down,** you relax after a period of stress or exertion.

windbreak A **windbreak** is a barrier such as a line of trees or a fence which gives protection against the wind.

windcheater A **windcheater** is a warm jacket, usually with a close-fitting knitted neck, cuffs, and waistband. 'Windcheater' is a trademark.

windfall A **windfall** is a large sum of money you receive unexpectedly. ■ **Windfall** profits are unexpectedly large.

wind farm A **wind farm** is a large group of wind-driven generators for supplying electricity.

windlass (**windlasses**) A **windlass** is the same as a winch.

windmill A **windmill** is machine for grinding grain or pumping water. It is driven by vanes or sails turned by the wind. ■ **tilt at windmills:** see **tilt.**

window A **window** is a space filled with glass in a wall or roof or in the side of a vehicle. ■ If you go **window shopping,** you spend time looking at goods in shop windows without intending to buy anything. ■ In computing, a **window** is an area of the VDU display which can be manipulated separately from the rest of the area.

window box A **window box** is a long narrow container on a window sill for growing plants in.

window-dressing (**window-dresser**) **Window-dressing** is arranging goods attractively in a shop window. Someone who does this as their job is called a **window-dresser.** ■ If you say an action is **window-dressing,** you mean it is done to create a good impression and to hide the real situation.

window pane A **window pane** is a piece of glass in a window.

windowsill A **windowsill** is a ledge along the bottom of a window.

windpipe Your **windpipe** or **trachea** is the tube which carries air into your lungs when you breathe.

windscreen The **windscreen** of a vehicle is the window at the front which the driver looks through.

windscreen wiper – Windscreen wipers are electrically operated blades with rubber edges which wipe rain from a windscreen.

windshield is the usual American word for a windscreen.

windsock A **windsock** is a cone of material with the end cut off. It is flown from a mast, to show the local wind direction.

windsurfing (**windsurfer**) **Windsurfing** is the sport of moving along the surface of the sea or a lake standing on a sailboard. Someone who does this is called a **windsurfer.**

windswept places are exposed to high winds.

wind tunnel A **wind tunnel** is a passage designed so air can be made to flow through it at controlled speeds. Wind tunnels are used to test equipment and machinery, especially cars and planes.

windward The **windward** side of something is the side facing the wind.

windy If it is **windy,** the wind is blowing strongly.

wine (**wining, wined**) **Wine** is an alcoholic drink which is usually made from grapes fermented with water and sugar, but which can also be made using other fruit or vegetables. *...damson wine.*

wine bar A **wine bar** is a place where you can buy and drink wine, and usually also obtain food.

winery (**wineries**) A **winery** is a place where wine is made.

wing (**-winged**) A bird's or insect's **wings** are the parts it uses for flying. ■ A plane's **wings** are the long flat parts at each side which support it in the air. ■ **-winged** is used to describe a bird's or plane's wings. *...the bat-winged American B2 Stealth bomber.* ■ **Winged** things have wings. *...winged insects.* ■ If something **wings** somewhere or **wings its way** there, it flies there, or goes there quickly as if it was flying. ■ If you **spread your wings,** you start doing new activities or expand your activities into new areas. ■ If someone **clips your wings,** they restrict your freedom. ■ A **wing** of a building is a smaller part which sticks out from the main part or which has been added at a later date. ■ The **wings** of a stage are the parts at the sides which are hidden from the audience by curtains or scenery. ■ If someone is waiting **in the wings,** they are ready to take action if necessary. ■ A **wing** of an organization is a group within it which has a particular function or particular beliefs. *...the party's more liberal wing.* See also **left-wing, right-wing.** ■ The

wings of a car are the parts around and above the wheels.

wing commander A **wing commander** is a middle-ranking officer in the RAF.

winger In sports like football and hockey, a **winger** is an attacking player who plays mainly on the far left or far right of the pitch.

wingspan The **wingspan** of a bird, insect, or plane is the distance from the end of one wing to the end of the other.

wink If you **wink** or give someone a **wink,** you close one eye briefly, usually as a signal that something is a joke or a secret. ■ If a light **winks,** it shines in short flashes.

winkle (winkling, winkled) Winkles are small edible sea snails. ■ If you **winkle** information **out** of someone, you get it from them when they do not want to give it to you. ■ If you **winkle** someone **out** of a place they do not want to leave, you make them leave it.

winner The **winner** of a prize or competition is the person who wins it. ■ If you say someone or something is a **winner,** you mean they are popular and successful. ■ The **winners** in a situation are the people who have benefited from it. *He said there has never been any doubt that accountants are the real winners in a recession.* ■ In football, the goal which wins the match can be called the **winner.**

winning See **win.** ■ You call money you win your **winnings.** ■ **Winning** is used to describe actions and qualities which are charming and attractive. *...a winning smile.*

winnow When people **winnow** grain, they separate the chaff from the rest of it. ■ If you **winnow out** part of a group of things or people, you separate the part that is not useful or relevant from the part that is. *The committee will need to winnow out the nonsense and produce more practical proposals.*

wino (pron: wine-oh**) (winos)** Some people call homeless alcoholics **winos.**

winsome (winsomely) Winsome is used to describe people who are attractive and charming.

winter (wintering, wintered) Winter is the season between autumn and spring when the weather is usually cold. ■ If you **winter** somewhere, you spend the winter there.

winter sports are sports which take place on ice or snow, for example skating or skiing.

wintry If something is **wintry,** it has features typical of winter. ■ If someone's expression or behaviour is **wintry,** they seem cold and unfriendly.

wipe (wiping, wiped) If you **wipe** something, you rub its surface lightly, to remove dirt or liquid. You can also say you **wipe** the dirt or liquid from the surface. ■ If you **wipe** a magnetic tape or a computer disk, you remove the pictures, sounds, or information stored on it. ■ You can say someone or something is **wiped out** when they are completely destroyed. ■ If an amount is **wiped off** the value of something, its value is reduced by that amount.

wire (wiring, wired) Wire is metal in the form of a long thin flexible thread which can be used to make or fasten things, or to conduct an electric current. ■ If you **wire** something **up,** you connect it to the electricity supply. ■ The **wiring** in a building or electrical appliance is the system of wires which supplies electricity to it. ■ In the US, a **wire** is a telegram. If you **wire** someone, you send them a telegram.

wireless (wirelesses) Wireless is an old word for radio. A **wireless** or **wireless set** is a radio.

wire service In the US, a **wire service** is the same as a news agency.

wiretapping (wiretap) Wiretapping is spying on someone by making a connection to their telephone line to listen to their conversations secretly.

wire wool consists of very thin pieces of wire twisted together and used to clean metal objects, especially kitchen utensils.

wiring See **wire.**

wiry A **wiry** person is thin but has strong muscles.

wisdom is the ability to use experience or knowledge to make sensible decisions or judgments. ■ **Wisdom** is the store of knowledge which a society or culture has collected over a long period of time. ■ If you talk about the **wisdom** of an action or decision, you are talking about how sensible it is. *It was a tactic of dubious wisdom.* ■ You can use **wisdom** to refer to ideas which are accepted by a large number of people. *Health education wisdom in the UK differs from that of the United States.*

wisdom tooth Your **wisdom teeth** are the four teeth at the back of your mouth, which usually grow much later than the rest.

wise (wiser, wisest; wisely) Wise people are able to use their experience and knowledge to make sensible decisions and judgments. ■ If a decision or action is **wise,** it shows good sense. ■ If you **get wise** to something, you find out about it.

-wise is added to another word to indicate what aspect of something you are talking about. *Careerwise, this illness couldn't have come at a worse time.*

wisecrack (wisecracking) A **wisecrack** is a clever remark which is intended to be amusing, but is often rather unkind. A **wisecracking** person keeps making remarks like this.

wish (wishes, wishing, wished) A **wish** is a desire for something. ■ If you **wish** to do something, you want to do it. ■ If you **wish** for something or make a **wish** for it, you express the desire for it silently to yourself. ■ If you **wish** something were true, you would like it to be true, although you know it is impossible or unlikely. ■ If you **wish** someone something such as luck or happiness, you express the hope they will be lucky or happy. You can also offer someone your good **wishes. If you send your best wishes** to someone, you express your hope that they will be happy and successful.

wishful If you say a hope or desire is **wishful thinking,** you mean it is unlikely to be fulfilled.

wishy-washy If you say someone is **wishy-washy,** you mean their ideas are vague and unclear.

wisp (wispy) A **wisp** of hair is a thin untidy strand of it. **Wispy** hair grows in strands like this. ■ A **wisp** of something like smoke or fog is a long thin streak of it.

wisteria is a climbing garden plant with clusters of mauve or white flowers.

wistful (**wistfully, wistfulness**) If you are **wistful,** you are sadly thinking about something which you want but cannot have.

wit is the ability to use words or ideas in a clever and amusing way. A **wit** is someone who has this ability. ■ If you talk about a person's **wits,** you mean their ability to think quickly in a difficult situation. ■ If you **have** your **wits about** you, you are alert and ready to act in a difficult situation. ■ If you are **at your wits' end,** you have so many problems you do not know what to do next.

witch (**witches**) A **witch** is a woman who is believed to have magic powers.

witchcraft is the use of magic powers by witches, especially evil powers.

witch-doctor A **witch-doctor** is a man in some societies, especially in Africa, who is thought to have magic powers which he can use to heal or harm people.

witch hazel is a winter-flowering garden shrub. Its leaves and bark can be used to make a liquid, also called **witch hazel,** which is put onto sore or bruised skin to heal it.

witch-hunt A **witch-hunt** is a campaign to find and punish people who hold unpopular or unusual views, while claiming that the campaign aims to protect the interests of the public.

with is used to talk about people or things being together. *She is currently staying with her father.* ■ **With** is used to talk about an arrangement, relationship, or dispute between people. *...Egypt's peace treaty with Israel.* ■ **With** means using or having. *Doctors are treating him with the drug AZT. ...red-haired, with bright hazel eyes.* ■ **With** is used to describe how someone does something or how they feel. *My mum started crying with joy.* ■ **With** is used to introduce a factor which affects something. *With all the night school courses available, there is no excuse for not getting some sort of training.*

withdraw (**withdrawing, withdrew, have withdrawn; withdrawal**) If you **withdraw** something, you remove it or take it away. When something is removed, you call this a **withdrawal.** *The plan also calls for the withdrawal of troops.* ■ If you **withdraw** money from a bank account, you take it out so you can spend it or use it. The money you take out is called a **withdrawal.** ■ If you **withdraw** from an activity, you stop taking part in it. ■ If you **withdraw** to a quieter room, you go there. ■ If you **withdraw** a remark or statement, you formally say it no longer represents your views and you want it to be disregarded. ■ A **withdrawn** person is quiet and shy. ■ **Withdrawal symptoms** are the unpleasant physical and mental effects drug addicts experience when they stop taking drugs.

wither (**withering, withered**) If something **withers** or **withers away,** it becomes weaker until it no longer exists or is no longer effective. *If things go badly, support could wither.* ■ If a plant **withers,** it shrinks, dries up, and dies. ■ If you describe a person or part of their body as **withered,** you mean their skin is very wrinkled and dry, and looks old. *...a withered old man.* ■ A **withering** look or remark is intended to make the person it is directed at feel ashamed or stupid.

withhold (**withholding, withheld**) If you **withhold** something from someone, you do not let them have it.

within If something is **within** a place, it is inside it. Similarly, you say something is **within** a border or boundary. *...a village south of Cambridge but just within the city boundary.* ■ If something is **within** a certain distance of something, it is inside that distance. ■ If something happens **within** a certain length of time, it happens inside that length of time. *An announcement is expected within two weeks.* ■ If something happens **within** a society, organization, or system, it happens inside it, or to something which is part of it. *There are calls for a cabinet reshuffle from within his own party.* ■ If something is **within** certain limits or restrictions, it does not go beyond them. *The deal was constructed within the confines of American law.*

without If you are **without** something, you do not have it. ■ **do without:** see **do.** ■ If you do something **without** someone else, you do not have them with you when you do it, or you do not have their help. ■ If you do something **without** doing something else, you do not do the second thing when you do the first one. *We had begun to drift apart, almost without realising it.* ■ If you do something **without** a particular feeling, you do not have that feeling when you do it. *Women must be able to walk the streets without fear.*

withstand (**withstanding, withstood**) If you **withstand** something that happens to you, you survive it or do not give in to it. *Mr Gates has stubbornly withstood intense pressure for him to resign.* ■ If a material or plant can **withstand** certain extreme conditions, it is not harmed by them. *...a plastic which will withstand a nuclear explosion.*

witless If you call something like a film or show **witless,** you mean it is very silly.

witness (**witnesses, witnessing, witnessed**) If you **witness** something or **are witness to** it, you see it happen. Someone who has seen something happen can be called a **witness.** ■ A **witness** is someone who appears in court or at an inquiry to say what they know about a crime or other matter. ■ A **witness** is someone who signs their name under your signature to confirm that the signature is really yours. You say this person **witnesses** your signature. ■ If something **bears witness** to something else, it shows it existed or happened.

witness box In a court, the **witness box** or **witness stand** is the place where people stand or sit while they give evidence.

witter (**wittering, wittered**) If you say someone is **wittering,** you mean they are saying a lot of silly or unimportant things.

witticism A **witticism** is a witty remark.

wittingly If you do something **wittingly,** you are fully aware of what you are doing and what its consequences may be.

witty (**wittier, wittiest; wittily**) A **witty** person, remark, or piece of writing is amusing in a clever way.

wives See **wife.**

wizard In legends and fairy stories, a **wizard** is a man with magical powers. ■ You can call someone a **wizard** when they are very good at something. ...*a keyboard wizard.*

wizardry You can call a very clever piece of work **wizardry,** especially when you do not understand how it is done. ...*computer wizardry.*

wizened people are old and have wrinkled skin.

woad was a blue vegetable dye used by the ancient Britons to paint their bodies.

wobble (**wobbling, wobbled; wobbly**) If something **wobbles** or is **wobbly,** it makes small unsteady movements from side to side.

wodge A **wodge** of something is a large amount or large piece of it.

woe is great unhappiness or sorrow. You can call someone's problems or misfortunes their **woes.**
■ **woe betide:** see **betide.**

woebegone If someone looks or feels **woebegone,** they look or feel very sad.

woeful (**woefully**) If someone is **woeful,** they are very sad. You can say a story is **woeful** when it describes sad events. ■ You say something is **woeful** when it is very bad. ...*the woeful performance by England's cricketers at Lord's.*

wok A **wok** is a large bowl-shaped pan for frying Chinese-style food.

woke (**woken**) See **wake.**

wolf (**wolves**) The **wolf** is a wild animal which looks like a large dog. ■ If someone **cries wolf,** they say there is a problem when there is not, with the result that people do not believe them when there really is one. ■ If you **wolf down** food, you eat it quickly and greedily.

wolfhound The **wolfhound** is a type of very large dog.

wolf-whistle A **wolf-whistle** is a whistling sound usually made by a man to show he thinks a woman is attractive.

wolves See **wolf.**

woman (**women**) A **woman** is an adult female human being. ■ You can talk about women in general as **woman.** ...*the image of woman as either virgin or whore.*

womanhood is women in general. The **womanhood** of a country or community are its women.
■ **Womanhood** is the state of being a woman rather than a girl, or the period of a woman's adult life. ...*young girls approaching womanhood.*

womanizer (or **womaniser**) (**womanizing**) If a man is a **womanizer,** he likes to flirt with women and often has short sexual relationships with them. This kind of behaviour is called **womanizing.**

womankind is women in general.

womb (*pron:* **woom**) A woman's **womb** is the organ inside her body where a baby grows during pregnancy.

wombat The **wombat** is a furry Australian plant-eating animal with short legs and a pouch for carrying its young.

women See **woman.**

womenfolk The **womenfolk** of a community are its women.

women's movement The **women's movement** is a social and political movement which aims to achieve equality for women.

womenswear is women's clothing.

won See **win.**

wonder (**wondering, wondered**) If you **wonder** about something, you think about it and try to guess or understand more about it. *He must be wondering what he has done wrong.* ■ If you **wonder** at something, you are amazed by it. **Wonder** is a feeling of amazement. ...*shaking their heads in wonder.*
■ If you say something is a **wonder,** you mean it is very surprising. *It's a wonder no one was killed.* ■ **No wonder, little wonder,** and **small wonder** are used to say something is not at all surprising. *Small wonder that first-time buyers are now returning: buying a home has rarely been cheaper.* ■ A **wonder** is something remarkable which people admire. ...*the wonders of modern technology.* ■ If something **works wonders,** it produces amazing results.

wonderful (**wonderfully**) If you describe someone or something as **wonderful,** you think they are extremely good. *It's wonderful to see you... The weather was wonderfully warm.*

wonderland You can call a place a **wonderland** when it seems very beautiful or exciting. ...*a wonderland of amusement parks.*

wonderment is a feeling of amazement and admiration.

wondrous (**wondrously**) If you describe something as **wondrous,** you mean it is amazing and impressive.

wonky If something is **wonky,** it is likely to wobble or not work properly, because it is unsteady or not firmly in place.

wont (*rhymes with 'don't'*) If someone is **wont** to do something, they do it often. *Tolstoy was wont to consider his life a failure.* When someone has a habit or custom of doing something, you say they do it **as is their wont.**

woo (**woos, wooing, wooed**) If someone **woos** you, they try to get you to support or help them. *Republicans are concentrating on wooing suburban voters.*
■ When a man **woos** a woman, he spends time with her trying to win her love.

wood is the material which forms the trunks and branches of trees. ■ A **wood** is a large area of trees growing close together. ■ If you say someone is **not out of the woods** yet, you mean they are still involved in a difficult situation. ■ If you **can't see the wood for the trees,** you are so involved with the details of a situation or activity that you cannot see or understand its general purpose or important features.

woodcock (*plural:* **woodcock**) The **woodcock** is a small brown bird with a long beak.

woodcut A **woodcut** is a print made from an engraved design cut into a block of wood.

wooded A **wooded** area is covered in trees.

wooden A **wooden** object is made of wood. ■ If you say an actor is **wooden,** you mean his or her performance is dull and unconvincing.

wooden spoon A **wooden spoon** is a spoon made from wood, used in cooking. ■ You say the person or team that finishes last in a competition gets **the wooden spoon.**

woodland is land covered with trees.

woodlouse (*plural:* **woodlice**) The **woodlouse** is a very small grey oval creature with scales, found in damp places.

woodpecker The **woodpecker** is a bird with a long sharp beak which it uses to drill holes into trees to find insects.

wood pulp is wood which has been crushed to a pulp so it can be used to make paper.

woodwind instruments are musical instruments such as flutes, oboes, clarinets, and bassoons.

woodwork refers to the doors, skirting boards, or window frames of a building which are made of wood. ■ If you talk about people **crawling out of the woodwork,** you are criticizing them for suddenly appearing in public or revealing their opinions when previously they did not make themselves known. ■ **Woodwork** is the skill or craft of making things out of wood.

woodworm are the larvae of certain type of beetle which make holes in wood when feeding on it. You also call the damage they do **woodworm.**

woody plants have very hard stems. ■ A **woody** area is covered in trees.

woof is used to represent the sound of a dog's bark.

wool is the hair of sheep, goats, and some other animals. The yarn spun from it is also called **wool.** It is knitted or woven and used to make clothes, blankets, and carpets.

woollen clothes are made from wool.

woolly (**woollies**) A **woolly** garment is made from wool or looks like wool. ■ A **woolly** is a woollen garment, especially a jumper. ■ If you say people or their ideas are **woolly** or **woolly-minded,** you mean they are vague or confused.

woozy If you are **woozy,** you feel weak and unsteady and cannot think clearly.

word A **word** is one of the units a piece of speech or writing is divided into. ■ If you have **a word** with someone, you have a short conversation with them. ■ If you get **word** of something happening, you hear news of it. ■ Your **word** is a promise you make to someone. *I give you my word.* ■ If a statement is **worded** in a particular way, it is expressed in that way. *...a politely worded response... Diplomats have been working into the night on the final wording of the treaty.* ■ If you say someone has said something, but **not in so many words,** you mean they expressed that sentiment but said it more politely or discreetly. ■ If someone has the **last word,** they make the final decision about what is to be done. ■ If you say something is the **last word** in something such as luxury, you mean it is the most luxurious thing of its kind.

word-blindness is another name for dyslexia.

wordless is used to describe events which take place without any words being spoken.

word-perfect If you are **word-perfect,** you are able to repeat from memory the exact words of something you have learned.

word processor (**word processing**) A **word processor** is a small computer which is used as a type-writer to produce letters and documents. This kind of work is called **word processing.**

wordy If you say a piece of writing is **wordy,** you mean there are too many words in it, especially long ones.

wore See **wear.**

work If you **work,** you have a paid job. ■ If you have **work** or are **in work,** you have a job, rather than being unemployed. ■ **Work** is the tasks that have to be done. ■ **Work** is something produced as a result of people's work or as a result of research. *...a skilful piece of work.* ■ A writer's **works** are the books, poems, or plays he or she has written. Similarly, you can talk about an artist's or composer's **works.** ■ If a machine **works,** it operates properly. ■ If an idea, method, or system **works,** it is successful. Similarly, if a drug or medicine **works,** it produces the desired effect. ■ You say something is **at work** when it is influencing people's behaviour. *There is a kind of inverted snobbery at work here.* ■ The way a situation **works out** is what happens in the end. ■ If the cost of something **works out** at a particular amount, it comes to that amount. ■ If you **work out** the solution to a problem, you solve it. ■ If you **work on** an assumption, you make decisions based on it. ■ If you **work** yourself **into** a state, you gradually get into that state. *I worked myself into a frenzy.* ■ If you are **worked up,** you are upset or angry about something. ■ If you **work up** something such as enthusiasm or an appetite, you gradually develop it. ■ If you **work off** a feeling such as anger, you get rid of it by doing something energetic. ■ If you **work out,** you do exercises. You can call an exercise session a **workout.** ■ A factory is often called a **works.** *...a cement works.* ■ **Works** are activities like large scale building or digging. *Civil engineering works caused a traffic jam.* ■ See also **worker, working.**

workable If something like a plan is **workable,** it can be put into operation.

workaday things are ordinary and not especially interesting or unusual.

workaholic A **workaholic** is someone who finds it difficult to stop working.

workbench (**workbenches**) A **workbench** is a heavy wooden table which you make or repair things on.

worker The **workers** in an industry or business are the ordinary employees, as distinct from the employers or managers. ■ **Worker** is used (a) to say what kind of work someone does. *...a railway worker.* (b) to say how well or badly someone works. *...a hard worker.*

workforce The **workforce** is the total number of workers in a particular industry, company, region, or country.

workhorse You call someone a **workhorse** when they do a large amount of dull or routine work. Similarly, a much-used machine or vehicle can be called a **workhorse.** *...the 737, the workhorse of most short-haul airlines.*

workhouse A **workhouse** was a place where very poor homeless people worked in return for food and shelter.

working people have jobs which they are paid to do. ■ Your **working life** is the period of your life when you have a job, or are available to do a job. ■ **Working** is used (a) to talk about the period people spend working each day or week. *Recently, the company announced it will reduce working hours.* (b) to talk about the conditions people work in. *...a strike in support of better working conditions.* ■ A **working** meal is one arranged so people can discuss work matters informally. ■ If you have a **working** knowledge of something like a foreign language, you have a reasonable knowledge of it. ■ A **working** relationship is a good relationship you have with someone at work, or with someone you have to meet and deal with regularly. ■ If a government has a **working** majority in parliament, its majority is large enough for it to be able to carry out most of the measures it wants to. ■ The **workings** of a piece of equipment, an organization, or a system are the ways in which it operates. *...his contempt for the workings of government.*

working capital A company's **working capital** is the money it has available for use immediately, rather than money invested in property or equipment.

working class (working classes) The **working class** or **working classes** are the people in a society who do not own much property and whose work involves physical and practical skills, rather than intellectual ones.

working party A **working party** is a group of people set up to look into a matter and to produce a report about what should be done.

workload Your **workload** is the amount of work you have to do.

workman (workmen) A **workman** is a man whose job involves working with his hands, for example a plumber.

workmanlike is used to describe something which is done skilfully and efficiently, but not in a particularly imaginative way. *...a workmanlike performance.*

workmanship If you talk about the **workmanship** of something, you mean the skill with which it has been made or done.

workmate Your **workmates** are people you work with.

work of art (works of art) A **work of art** is a painting, drawing, or sculpture of high quality. ■ High-quality novels, plays, and pieces of music can be called **works of art.** ■ You can say anything is a **work of art** when it is made or done with unusual skill. *Michael's riding over the final three fences was a work of art.*

workout See **work.**

workplace Your **workplace** is the place where you work.

workshop A **workshop** is a room or building containing tools or machinery for making or repairing things. ■ A **workshop** is a period of discussion or practical work on a subject, in which a group of people learn about the subject by sharing their knowledge or experience. *...one-day workshops on vital business skills.*

work-shy If someone is **work-shy,** they are lazy and do not want to work.

workstation A **workstation** is a computer, including a keyboard and VDU, connected to a network of other computers, printers, and faxes.

work surface (or worksurface) A **work surface** is a flat surface over a low cupboard or kitchen appliance which you can prepare food on.

world The **world** is the planet we live on. Other planets are sometimes called **worlds.** *We haven't yet come across life from other worlds.* ■ **The world** is used to talk about people throughout the world, especially people who have power. *The world has chosen not to intervene to help the Kurds.* ■ **World** can be used to talk about groups of countries. *...the Arab world. ...the western world.* ■ **World** can be used to talk about periods in history. *...the Graeco-Roman world. ...the modern world.* ■ **World** can be used to talk about groups of living things. *...the animal world. ...the insect world.* ■ **World** can be used to talk about an area of activity. *...the world of high finance.* ■ A person's **world** is their way of life, the things they are involved in, and their relationships with other people. *Anthony Howard knew Crossman and his world intimately.* ■ If you call someone a **man of the world** or a **woman of the world,** you mean they are experienced and knowledgeable about life, and are not easily shocked by things like immorality and dishonesty.

world-class A **world-class** sports player or musician is one of the best in the world.

world-famous If someone or something is **world-famous,** people know about them all over the world.

World Health Organization The **World Health Organization** or **WHO** is the part of the United Nations concerned with improving health standards and services throughout the world.

worldly is used to talk about the ordinary things of life, especially things like possessions, rather than spiritual things. *I'd brought all my worldly goods with me.* ■ A **worldly** person is concerned with practical things, such as making money, rather than spiritual things.

worldly-wise If someone is **worldly-wise,** they are experienced and knowledgeable about life, and are not easily shocked or impressed by anything.

world war A **world war** is a war involving countries from many parts of the world.

world-weary (world-weariness) A **world-weary** person no longer feels excited or enthusiastic about anything. You talk about the **world-weariness** of someone like this.

worldwide means throughout the world. *...the worldwide recession of 1982.*

World-Wide Web — The World-Wide Web is a system which links documents and pictures into an information database that is stored in computers in many different parts of the world. World-Wide Web is often abbreviated to 'WWW' or 'Web'.

worm — Worms or **earthworms** are small, boneless, legless animals which live in the soil. ■ If an animal or person has **worms,** tiny worm-like creatures are living as parasites in their intestines. ■ When a normally timid person stands up to someone who has been bullying them, you can say the **worm has turned.** ■ If you call a situation a **can of worms,** you mean it is complicated, difficult, or unpleasant, and might be better left alone. ■ If someone **worms their way** into a position of power or influence, they get there using patience and cunning.

worm-eaten If something is **worm-eaten,** it has been damaged by insects eating holes in it.

wormwood is a bitter-tasting plant used to make alcoholic drinks.

worn See **wear.**

worn-out things are too old or damaged to be used any more. ■ If you are **worn-out,** you are very tired and feel no enthusiasm for anything.

worried See **worry.**

worrier Someone who worries a lot is called a **worrier.**

worrisome If you say something is **worrisome,** you mean people should be worried about it.

worry (**worries, worrying, worried; worrier**) If you **worry** or are **worried,** you keep thinking about a problem or about something unpleasant which might happen; the feeling you have is called **worry.** *Break-ins are a major source of worry to homeowners.* ■ If something **worries** you or is **worrying,** it makes you feel fearful or uneasy. Things which make you feel like this are called **worries.**

worse If something is **worse** than something else, it is more unpleasant or undesirable or of poorer quality. *Shortages are worse than ever.* ■ If a situation changes **for the worse,** it gets worse. ■ If someone who is ill gets **worse,** they become more ill. ■ If you are **worse off** as a result of something, you are in a worse situation than you were before. ■ If someone is **the worse for** drink, they are drunk. ■ If someone is **the worse** for an unpleasant experience, they are badly affected by it.

worsen (**worsening, worsened**) If something **worsens,** it becomes more difficult, unpleasant, or unacceptable.

worship (**worshipping, worshipped; worshipper**) (*Am:* worshiping, *etc*) When people **worship,** they show their love and respect for a god or goddess, for example by saying prayers. Their behaviour is called **worship.** People who are worshipping, for example in a church or mosque, are called **worshippers.** ■ If you **worship** a person, you love and admire them very much. ■ Certain people in positions of authority can be addressed as **Your Worship,** for example mayors or magistrates.

worst – The **worst** is used to refer to the most unpleasant, most undesirable, or poorest quality one or ones of several things. *...the worst railway line in Britain.* ■ If you say something is true or possible **at worst,** you mean it is true or possible when you consider a situation in the most pessimistic way. *At worst, Stemp could face a short ban from the game.* ■ If you talk about what would happen **if the worst comes to the worst,** you are talking about things developing in the most unfavourable way possible.

worst-case The **worst-case** situation or scenario is the most unfavourable one of a number of possible outcomes to a situation.

worsted (*pron:* **wuss**-tid) is a type of woollen cloth used to make jackets, trousers, and skirts.

worth If something is **worth** a certain amount of money, it can be sold for that amount. *...a house worth £60,000.* ■ **Worth** is used to describe an amount of something in terms of how much it costs. *We lost over $10,000 worth of equipment.* ■ **Worth** is used to say how long something will last. For example, a week's **worth** of food will last a week. ■ A person's **worth** is their value, usefulness, or importance. *Gish was an astute businesswoman who knew her worth.* ■ If you say something you have achieved was **worth** the trouble, you mean then the results are good enough to justify the trouble you have taken. Similarly, you can say something is **worth** the money you have paid for it. *The prices are high but worth it for cooking of quite exceptional quality.* ■ If it is **worth your while** to do something, it is to your advantage to do it. ■ If you do something **for all you are worth** or **for all it is worth,** you do it as much as possible and for as long as you can get any benefit from it. ■ You say **for what it's worth** when you are not sure that what you are saying is particularly valuable or helpful. *For what it's worth, I think the pictures are very good.*

worthless If something is **worthless,** it is of no real use or value.

worthwhile If you say something is **worthwhile,** you mean it is useful or helpful, and worth the time, money, or effort spent on it.

worthy (**worthiness; worthies**) If you say someone or something is **worthy** of respect, support, or admiration, you mean they deserve it because of their qualities or abilities. A **worthy** person or thing deserves respect, support, or admiration. ■ The important people in a place or organization are sometimes humorously called **worthies.**

would You use **would** to say what someone thought was going to happen. *We had assumed that it would be a big helicopter.* ■ You use **would** to say what did happen in the past. *We would talk a lot. I would suggest ideas, and many of them got into the film.* ■ You use **would** to say someone is willing to do something. *Scotland Yard would give no further details of the enquiries.* ■ You use **would** to talk about the effect of a possible situation. *Should he lose, it would take the edge off his Olympic achievement.* ■ If you say someone **would** do something, especially something bad or foolish, you mean it is typical of them. *Of course, they would say that, wouldn't they?* ■ You use **would** to ask a question politely. *Would you like a cup of tea?*

would-be is used to talk about what someone wants to become. For example, if you are a **would-be** artist, you want to become an artist.

wound (**wounded**) A **wound** is an injury to part of your body, especially a cut or hole caused by a weapon or sharp instrument. If someone has an injury like this, especially a fairly serious one, you say they are **wounded.** ■ If someone **wounds** you, they injure you using a gun, knife, or other sharp weapon. ■ If you are **wounded** by what someone says or does, you are hurt and upset by it. ■ See also **wind.**

wove (**woven**) See **weave**.

wow If something **wows** people, it thrills or impresses them.

WPC is used in front of the name of a female police officer of the lowest rank. It stands for 'woman police constable'.

wpm stands for 'words per minute'. It is used to talk about how fast someone can type or take shorthand. ...*a typing speed of 50wpm.*

wracked See **rack**.

wraith A **wraith** is a ghost.

wrangle (**wrangling, wrangled**) When people **wrangle,** they argue about something noisily or angrily. An argument like this is called a **wrangle.**

wrap (**wrapping, wrapped**) If you **wrap** an object or **wrap** it **up,** you fold paper or cloth tightly round it to cover it completely. You also say you **wrap** the paper or cloth round the object. ■ If you **wrap** your arms or fingers around something, you put them tightly around it. ■ If you **wrap up,** you put warm clothes on. ■ If you are **wrapped up** in something, you are giving it a lot of attention. ■ If you **wrap up** something like a job or an agreement, you complete it in a satisfactory way. ■ If something like a plan is **kept under wraps,** it is kept secret until a suitable time for making it public.

wrapper A **wrapper** is a piece of foil, plastic, or paper used to cover or protect something. ...*bubble-gum wrappers.*

wrapping is paper or plastic for covering or protecting something.

wrath (*pron: roth*) is anger.

wreak (**wreaking, wreaked** or **wrought**) If something **wreaks** changes, it causes them. ...*the changes wrought by German unification.* Similarly, if something **wreaks** havoc or damage, it causes it.

wreath A **wreath** is a circle of flowers and leaves put on a grave or memorial as a sign of remembrance for the dead.

wreathe (**wreathing, wreathed**) If something is **wreathed** in something else, it is surrounded by it. ...*a huge white monolith, wreathed in barbed wire.* ■ If someone is **wreathed in smiles,** they are smiling a lot.

wreck If something like a building is **wrecked,** it is very badly damaged. ■ If a ship is **wrecked,** it sinks in a storm or as a result of damage, or is driven onto rocks where it breaks up. The remains of the ship are called a **wreck.** ■ The remains of a badly damaged plane, car, or other vehicle can be called a **wreck.** ■ If you call a person a **wreck,** you mean they are in a very poor state mentally and physically. ■ If something **wrecks** an organization or system, it destroys it completely. *Incompetence and corruption wrecked the fragile economy.*

wreckage The **wreckage** of a car, plane, or building is what remains of it after it has been badly damaged or destroyed.

wrecker A **wrecker** is someone who destroys or spoils something.

wren A **wren** is a very small brown songbird. ■ Members of the former WRNS were often called **Wrens.**

wrench (**wrenches, wrenching, wrenched; -wrenching**) If you **wrench** something away from a place, you pull or twist it away violently. ■ If you **wrench** a limb or one of your joints, you twist and injure it. ■ If leaving someone or something is a **wrench,** it is difficult and you feel very sad about it. You can say something is **wrenching** when it makes you feel sad. ...*page after page of wrenching pictures of the Yugoslav civil war.* ■ You add **-wrenching** to words to add emphasis. For example, **gut-wrenching** scenes or activities bring on strong feelings of nausea, and **heart-wrenching** stories make you feel very sad. ■ A **wrench** is an adjustable metal spanner.

wrest If you **wrest** something from someone who is holding it, you take it away from them forcefully. ■ If you **wrest** power or control from someone, you succeed in taking it from them.

wrestle (**wrestling, wrestled; wrestler**) If you **wrestle** with someone, you fight them by forcing them into painful positions or throwing them to the ground, rather than by hitting them. People who do this as a sport are called **wrestlers;** the sport is called **wrestling.** ■ If you **wrestle** with a problem, you try to resolve it.

wretch (**wretches**) People sometimes call a wicked or unfortunate person a **wretch.**

wretched (**wretchedly, wretchedness**) You describe someone as **wretched** when you feel sorry for them, because they have suffered unpleasant experiences or are in an unpleasant situation. *The country's 37 million people are wretchedly poor.* You can also call someone's situation **wretched.** ...*the wretchedness of most people's lives.* ■ You can call a person **wretched** when you dislike them or are angry with them. *That wretched man she was going to marry has broken off the engagement.*

wriggle (**wriggling, wriggled**) If you **wriggle** a part of your body, you twist and turn it with quick movements. ■ If you **wriggle out of** something you do not want to do, you manage to avoid doing it.

wring (**wringing, wrung** not '*wringed*') If you **wring** a wet cloth or **wring it out,** you squeeze the water out of it by twisting it tightly. ■ When someone **wrings** a bird's neck, they kill it by twisting its neck. ■ If you **wring** something **out of** someone, you get them to give it to you when they do not want to. ■ If you say someone is **wringing their hands,** you mean they are complaining bitterly about something.

wringer If someone is put **through the wringer,** they have to undergo a difficult stressful experience.

wrinkle (**wrinkling, wrinkled**) Wrinkles are lines which appear on your face as you get older. When someone's face has lines like these, you say their skin is **wrinkled.** ■ If you **wrinkle** your nose or forehead, you tighten the muscles so that the skin folds. ■ If something **wrinkles,** little folds or lines appear in it.

wrinkly (**wrinklies**) If something is **wrinkly,** it has uneven folds or lines in it. ■ A **wrinkly** person has wrinkles as a result of getting older. Old people are sometimes humorously called **wrinklies.**

wrist Your **wrist** is the part of your arm between your hand and your forearm.

wristwatch (wristwatches) A **wristwatch** is a watch with a strap which you wear round your wrist.

writ A **writ** is a legal document ordering a person to do or not to do something. ■ If you say something is another thing **writ large,** you mean it is a more exaggerated or more obvious version of the same thing. *The nation is often described by Lady Thatcher as a household writ large... The legacy of their past incompetence is writ large on their balance sheets.*

write (writing, wrote, have written) When you **write** something, you use a pen or pencil to produce words or numbers on a surface. ■ If you **write** something **down,** you make a written record of it on paper. ■ If you **write up** notes, you re-write them in a neat and complete form. ■ If you **write out** a list, you write all the items on a piece of paper. ■ If you **write** something like a book or piece of music, you create it on paper. ■ If you **write** to someone, you write a letter and send it to them. ■ If you **write** something like a cheque, you put all the necessary information on it and sign it. ■ The **written word** is written or printed language in contrast to speech. ■ If you **write off** an amount of money you have lost or call it a **write-off,** you accept that you will never get it back. ■ If you **write off** a vehicle, you crash it so badly that it is not worth repairing. You call the vehicle itself a **write-off.** ■ If someone has been **written off,** people have decided they are unimportant or cannot succeed at something. *Eighteen months ago he had been written off as a failure.* ■ See also **writing.**

writer A **writer** is someone who writes stories, books, or articles as their job. ■ The **writer** of a piece of writing is the person who wrote it.

write-up A **write-up** is an article in a newspaper or magazine in which a reviewer gives their opinion of something like a play or a restaurant.

writhe (writhing, writhed) If someone **writhes,** they twist and turn their body violently, usually because they are in great pain.

writing Anything written or printed can be called **writing.** ■ A person's handwriting is often called their **writing.** ■ If you talk about the **writing** in a piece of written work, you mean the author's style. *The writing is very flat.* ■ An author's **writings** are all the things they have written.

writing desk A **writing desk** is a piece of furniture with drawers and a surface you can rest your paper on while writing.

written See **write.**

WRNS The **WRNS** was the women's branch of the Royal Navy. It was disbanded in November 1993, the women becoming regular members of the Royal Navy. WRNS stood for 'Women's Royal Naval Service'.

wrong (wrongly) You use **wrong** to say there is something unsatisfactory about a person, situation, or thing. *There was something wrong with the way the government made decisions... Pain is the body's way of telling us something is wrong.* ■ If something like a measurement or answer is **wrong,** it is incorrect. ■ If you are **wrong** about something, what you say or think is not correct. ■ If you choose the **wrong** thing or person, you make a mistake and do not choose the thing or person you really want or need. *Buying the wrong type of software can often turn out to be a costly error.* ■ If something **goes wrong,** it stops working or being successful. ■ If you say an action is **wrong,** you mean it is bad or immoral. ■ If someone **wrongs** you, they treat you unfairly or unjustly. A **wrong** is an unjust action or situation. ■ **right and wrong:** see **right.**

wrongdoer A **wrongdoer** is someone who does something illegal or immoral.

wrongdoing is illegal or immoral behaviour.

wrong-foot (wrong-footing, wrong-footed) If you **wrong-foot** your opponent in a game like tennis, you throw them off-balance by playing your shot in an unexpected way. ■ If something **wrong-foots** someone, it catches them by surprise and puts them in a difficult position.

wrongful (wrongfully) Wrongful actions are immoral, illegal, or unfair. *She claims she was wrongfully dismissed.*

wrong-headed If you call an action or decision **wrong-headed,** you mean it is mistaken and based on bad judgment.

wrote See **write.**

wrought metal has been made into a particular shape, usually a decorative one. *...wrought gold.* ■ **Wrought iron** is a pure type of iron often formed into decorative shapes and used to make things like gates and railings. ■ See also **wreak.**

wrung See **wring.**

wry (wryly) If someone has a **wry** expression, their face shows they find a bad or difficult situation slightly amusing. ■ A **wry** remark or piece of writing deals with a bad or difficult situation in an amusing or ironic way.

WTO The **WTO** is an international organization with rules that try to promote free and fair trade among countries. WTO stands for 'World Trade Organization'.

WWW See **World Wide Web.**

X x

x In mathematical calculations, **x** is used to represent a number whose value is unknown. ■ You can use **x** or **X** to refer to a number or amount when the exact number or amount is not known or is not important. *They don't need x thousands of pounds.* ■ **X** is used to represent the name of an unknown or secret person or place. *...Dr.X.*

X chromosome An **X chromosome** is one of an identical pair of chromosomes found in a woman's cells, or one of a non-identical pair found in a man's cells. X chromosomes are associated with female characteristics. See also **Y chromosome.**

xenophobia (*pron:* zen-oh-**fobe**-ee-a) (**xenophobic**) **Xenophobia** is strong and unreasonable fear and dislike of people from other countries. If someone is **xenophobic,** they show strong dislike or fear of people from other countries.

Xmas is a short way of writing 'Christmas'.

X-rated If you describe a film, play, or book as **X-rated,** you mean it involves a lot of sex or violence.

X-ray (X-raying, X-rayed) X-rays are a type of radiation which can pass through most solid materials. X-rays are commonly used to examine the bones or organs inside your body and at airports to see inside people's luggage. ■ An **X-ray** is a picture made by sending X-rays through something, usually someone's body. If someone or something is **X-rayed,** an X-ray picture is taken of them.

xylophone (*pron:* **zile**-oh-fone) The **xylophone** is a musical instrument consisting of wooden bars of different lengths which you play by hitting the bars with special hammers.

Y y

yacht (yachting) A **yacht** is a large boat with sails or a motor, used for racing or for pleasure trips. **Yachting** is the activity or sport of going out in a yacht.

yachtsman (yachtswoman) A **yachtsman** is a man who sails a yacht.

yak The **yak** is a type of long-haired long-horned ox found mainly in the mountains of Tibet.

yam – **Yams** are tropical root vegetables, similar to potatoes. ■ Certain kinds of sweet potatoes are called **yams.**

yank If you **yank** someone or something somewhere, you pull them there suddenly and forcefully. ■ People from the US are sometimes called **Yanks.**

Yankee People from the US are sometimes called **Yankees.** ■ In the US, people from the southern states sometimes refer to people from the northern states as **Yankees.**

yap (yapping, yapped) Yap is used to represent the sound of a small dog barking.

yard A **yard** is a flat area of concrete or stone next to a building, often with a wall around it. ■ In the US, a garden is often called the **yard.** ■ A **yard** is a large area where a particular type of work is done. *...a ship repair yard.* ■ Length can be expressed in **yards.** A yard is 91.44 centimetres. 'Yards' can be written 'yds'.

Yardie A **Yardie** is a member of a secret criminal organization, based in Jamaica, which is especially associated with drug dealing.

yardstick If you use someone or something as a **yardstick,** you use them as a standard for comparison when judging other people or things.

yarmulke (*pron:* yar-mull-ka) A **yarmulke** is a skullcap worn by male orthodox Jews at all times, and by other male Jews during prayer.

yarn is thread used for knitting or making cloth. ■ A **yarn** is a story, especially one involving adventure or fantastic events.

yashmak A **yashmak** is a veil some Muslim women wear to cover their faces in public.

yawn When you **yawn,** you open your mouth wide and breathe in more air than usual, because you are tired or bored. ■ A **yawning** gap is large and wide.

Y chromosome A **Y chromosome** is a single chromosome which exists together with a single X chromosome in a man's cells. The Y chromosome is associated with male characteristics. See also **X chromosome.**

yd (yds) See **yard.**

ye is an old-fashioned word for 'you' when you are talking to more than one person. *Abandon hope all ye who enter here.* ■ **Ye** is sometimes used to imitate the old written form of the word 'the'. *...Ye Olde King's Head.*

year A **year** or **calendar year** is a period of 365 or 366 days, beginning on the first day of January and ending on the last day of December. See also **financial year, tax year.** ■ A school **year** is the period of time in each 12 months when schools are open and students are studying there. ■ A **year** is any period of twelve months. ■ You use **-year-old**

to say how old someone or something is. *...her 12-year-old sister.* ■ You can say **a man of his years** or **a woman of her years** to talk about that person's age in relation to what you are discussing. *He was moving with surprising speed for a man of his years.*

yearbook A **yearbook** is a reference book published once a year containing updated information on a particular subject.

year-end is used to talk about a situation at the end of a year, especially a financial year. *...year-end profits.*

yearling A **yearling** is an animal between one and two years old.

yearly A **yearly** event happens once a year. ■ You use **yearly** to describe something such as an amount which relates to a period of one year. *Demand is growing at a yearly rate of 50%... Course fees will be paid yearly.*

yearn (yearning) If you **yearn** for something or have a **yearning** for it, you want it very much.

year-round is used to say something happens during all seasons of the year.

yeast is a kind of fungus which is used to make bread rise, and in making alcohol drinks such as beer.

yell If you **yell** or let out a **yell,** you shout loudly, because you are excited, angry, or in pain.

yellow is the colour of lemons or egg yolks. When something **yellows,** it turns yellow, often because it is old.

yellow fever is a serious infectious disease transmitted by mosquitoes in tropical countries.

yelp If a person or animal **yelps** or lets out a **yelp,** they let out a short loud cry, usually of excitement or pain.

yen The **yen** is the unit of currency in Japan. ■ If you have a **yen** to do something, you have a strong desire to do it.

yeoman (yeomen; yeomanry) In the past, a **yeoman** was a man who was free and not a servant, and who cultivated his own land. Yeomen were referred to collectively as the **yeomanry.**

yes is used to give a positive answer to a question, to accept an offer, or to give permission for something.

yes-man (yes-men) If you call a man a **yes-man,** you mean he always agrees with people who have authority over him, in order to win favour.

yesterday is the day before today. ■ You can refer to the past, especially the recent past, as **yesterday.** *He admitted that sometimes it was a bit difficult to consider as good friends the enemies of yesterday.*

yesteryear is used to talk about a time in the past when things were different from the way they are now. *The hippies of yesteryear are now mostly in their mid-forties.*

yet If something has not happened **yet,** it has not happened up to the present time. ■ If something cannot be done **yet,** it must wait until later. ■ **Yet** is used to say there is still a possibility something will happen. *A negotiated settlement might yet be possible.* ■ **Yet** is used to say how much longer something is expected to continue. *The forecasters say the bad weather will continue for some days yet.* ■ **Yet** can

be used for emphasis. *They fall in love, making Ross's life yet more complicated.* ■ **Yet** can be used to introduce a fact which seems surprising. *How long ago it all seems, yet it was only in the spring.*

yeti The **yeti** or **Abominable Snowman** is a large hairy ape-like animal which some people believe exists in the Himalayas.

yew – Yews or **yew trees** are coniferous trees with flattened needle-like leaves and cup-like red waxy cones which look like berries.

Yiddish is a language developed mainly from German, and spoken by many Jewish people of European origin.

yield When something **yields** an amount of something such as food or money, it produces that amount. You call the amount produced the **yield.** *The pits were no longer yielding enough coal to make mining profitable.* ■ If something like an investigation **yields** results, it produces them. ■ If you **yield** to someone or something, you stop resisting them. ■ If you **yield** something to someone, you give it to them. *There is little prospect that he will yield up the wanted men.* ■ If something **yields,** it breaks or gives way.

yob (yobbish) If you call a man or boy a **yob,** you disapprove of their noisy, bad-mannered, and sometimes threatening behaviour. You say behaviour like this is **yobbish.**

yodel (yodelling, yodelled; yodeller) (*Am:* **yodeling**) When someone **yodels,** they sing normal notes with high quick notes in between.

yoga is a Hindu philosophy in which physical exercise and meditation are used to help people become calmer and achieve spiritual fulfilment.

yoghurt (*or* **yogurt**) is a thick liquid food made from milk curdled by bacteria. It is often sweetened or flavoured with fruit.

yogi A **yogi** is a person who has spent many years practising or teaching yoga.

yogurt See **yoghurt.**

yoke (yoking, yoked) A **yoke** is a long piece of wood tied across the necks of animals such as oxen to harness them together when they are pulling a plough or other implement. ■ If two things are kept closely linked, you can say they are **yoked** together. *Hong Kong's dollar has been yoked to America's at the rate of 7.8 to 1 since 1983.* ■ When people are under the **yoke** of something, they are being oppressed by it. *People are still suffering under the yoke of slavery.*

yokel Country people are sometimes called **yokels,** especially by city people who see them as uneducated and simple.

yolk The **yolk** of an egg is the yellow part in the middle.

Yom Kippur or the **Day of Atonement** is the most sacred Jewish holy day, regarded as a day for fasting and prayers of repentance.

yon is an old-fashioned or dialect word for 'that' or 'those'. *Whit has yon bunch o' wasters ever did fur the workin' class?*

yonder is an old-fashioned word meaning 'over there'. *Look yonder, just beyond the wooden post there.*

yore You use **of yore** when you are talking about something which existed a long time ago. *...in days of yore.*

you A speaker or writer uses **you** (a) to refer to the person or people they are speaking to. *Have you just moved in?* (b) to refer to people in general. *Renting gives you flexibility.*

young A **young** person, animal, or plant has not lived for very long and is not yet mature. Young people are often called **the young.** ■ If you talk about a person's **young** days or **younger** days, you mean the time when they were young. ■ An animal's **young** are its offspring.

youngster A **youngster** is a child or young person.

your You use **your** (a) to talk about something belonging to or connected with the person or people you are speaking to. *Don't forget your coat.* (b) to talk about something relating to people in general. *Pain-killers are very useful in small amounts to bring your temperature down.* ■ You use **your** with words like 'typical' and 'average' to say something is a standard example of its type. *He is your typical South Londoner.* ■ **Your** is used when addressing people with certain titles. *...Your Majesty.*

yours You use **yours** when you are talking about something belonging to or connected with the person you are speaking to. *The choice is yours.*

yourself (yourselves) You use **yourself** (a) when the action you are describing is done by the person you are speaking to and affects only them. *You've cut yourself.* (b) when talking about people in general. *You can lose yourself among giant bamboo thickets.* ■ **Yourself** can be used to emphasize 'you'. *Who will look after you when you yourself are old?* ■ If you are **by yourself,** you are alone.

youth Your **youth** is the stage of your life before you are a fully mature adult. **Youth** is being at this stage, and therefore lacking experience. *...the impetuosity of youth.* ■ Teenage men are sometimes called **youths.** ■ The **youth** of a place or time are the young people considered as a whole. *...the youth of today.*

youthful (youthfulness) If you describe someone as **youthful,** you think they look or behave as if they are younger than they really are. *His relative youthfulness clearly appealed.* **Youthful** behaviour is typical of young people. *...youthful exuberance.*

youth hostel A **youth hostel** is a place where young people can stay cheaply when they are travelling.

yuan (*pron:* joo-**an**) (*plural:* **yuan**) The **yuan** is the unit of currency in the People's Republic of China.

yucca – **Yuccas** are tropical plants, with spiky leaves on thick woody stems and large white flowers.

Yuletide is another name for Christmas.

yuppie You can call a young person in a professional job with a high income who enjoys a fashionable and expensive lifestyle a **yuppie.** Yuppie is short for 'young upwardly-mobile professional'.

Z z

zany (zanier, zaniest; zaniness) If you call someone or something **zany,** you mean they are strange or eccentric in an amusing way. *...a zany comedy. ...his zaniest project yet.*

zap (zapping, zapped) If someone **zaps** a person or thing, they shoot them or fire something at them, usually a laser or some other electronic device.

zeal is great enthusiasm, especially in connection with work, religion, or politics. *...religious zeal.*

zealot (*pron:* zel-lot) (**zealotry**) A **zealot** is a single-minded fanatical supporter of a religion or political cause. You talk about the **zealotry** of someone like this.

zealous (*pron:* zel-luss) (**zealously**) If someone is **zealous,** they are fanatically enthusiastic about something. *...a zealous Communist.*

zebra The **zebra** is a type of African wild horse with black and white stripes.

zebra crossing A **zebra crossing** is a place marked with black and white stripes, where vehicles must stop to let people cross the road.

Zeitgeist (*pron:* zite-guyst) The **Zeitgeist** is the general spirit of a place or group of people during a particular time, as represented by their ideas and beliefs. *Swept along by the Zeitgeist of the 1980s, Berry ended up well out of his depth.*

Zen or **Zen Buddhism** is a Japanese form of Buddhism which concentrates on enlightenment through meditation.

zenith The **zenith** of something is the time when it is most successful or powerful. *His career is now at its zenith.*

zephyr A **zephyr** is a gentle wind.

zeppelin – **Zeppelins** were German airships used for passenger transport between 1910 and 1937 and for bombing during the First World War.

zero (*plural:* **zeros** or **zeroes**) (**zeroing, zeroed**) **Zero** is the number 0. ■ **Zero** is 0°C, freezing point on the centigrade scale. See also **absolute zero.** ■ You can use **zero** to say that something is at its lowest possible amount or level. *...zero gravity.* ■ If you **zero in on** a target, you focus or aim at it, or move towards it. You can also **zero in on** something such as a problem or ambition.

zest (zestful) Zest is keen enthusiasm and enjoyment. Something which shows enthusiasm and enjoyment like this can be called **zestful.** *...a zestful approach to life.* ■ The **zest** of a lemon, orange, or lime is its peel when it is grated and used to give flavour to things like cakes or drinks.

zigzag (*or* **zig-zag**) (**zigzagging, zigzagged**) A **zigzag** is a line with a series of angles in it, like a continuous series of 'W's. You say a line like this **zigzags.** *...zigzagging red and blue lines.* ■ If someone or something **zigzags,** they move in a zigzag course.

zillion is used to emphasize that there is a very large number of people or things.

zimmer A **zimmer** or **zimmer frame** is a portable metal frame for old or ill people to lean on when they are walking.

zinc is a bluish-white metal used in several alloys, and to coat other metals to stop them rusting.

zing is a quality in something that makes it lively or interesting. *His batting has lost its zing.*

Zionism (**Zionist**) **Zionism** is a movement which was originally concerned with establishing a political and religious state in Palestine for Jewish people, and is now concerned with the development of Israel. A **Zionist** is someone who supports Zionism.

zip (**zipping, zipped**) A **zip** is a fastening device consisting of two rows of teeth which separate or fasten together as you pull a small tag along them. If you **zip** something or **zip** it **up,** you fasten it using its zip. ■ **Zip** is used to say something happens or is done very quickly. *She zips through her repertoire.* ■ **Zip** is excitement, energy, and liveliness.

zip code In the US, postcodes are called **zip codes.**

zipper In the US, zips are called **zippers.**

zither The **zither** is a musical instrument consisting of two sets of strings stretched over a flat box, which you pluck to produce musical notes.

zloty (*plural:* **zloty** *or* **zlotys**) The **zloty** is the unit of currency in Poland.

zodiac The **zodiac** is a diagram used by astrologers to represent the positions of the planets and the stars. It is divided into 12 sections, each with a name and symbol, for example Cancer the crab.

zombie In horror stories, a **zombie** is a dead body which has been brought back to life. ■ If you describe someone as a **zombie,** you mean they show no awareness of things going on around them, or any sign that they are thinking at all.

zonal is used to talk about people or things connected with a particular zone. *...zonal commissioners.*

zone (**zoning, zoned**) A **zone** is an area with special features and often distinct boundaries. *...a U.S. plane patrolling the no-fly zone in the north.* See also **time zone.** ■ If an area is **zoned,** it is set aside for a particular purpose. The process of doing this is called **zoning.**

zoo A **zoo** is a park where live animals are kept in cages and enclosures so people can look at them.

zoology (**zoological, zoologist**) **Zoology** is the scientific study of animals. **Zoological** is used to talk about things to do with this subject. *...zoological research.* A **zoologist** is an expert in zoology.

zoom (**zooming, zoomed**) If you **zoom** somewhere, you go there very quickly. ■ A **zoom** or **zoom lens** is a lens you attach to a camera, allowing you to make the image larger or smaller while keeping it in focus. ■ If a camera **zooms** in on something, it gives a close-up of it.

zucchini (*plural:* **zucchini**) In the US, courgettes are called **zucchini.**